PRINCIPLES OF STATUTORY INTERPRETATION

Including the General Clauses Act, 1897 with Notes

First Edition	1966
Second Edition	1975
Third Edition	1983
Fourth Edition	1988
Fifth Edition	1992
Sixth Edition	1996
Seventh Edition	1999
Eighth Edition	2001
Ninth Edition	2004
Tenth Edition	2006
Eleventh Edition	2008
Twelfth Edition	2010
Thirteenth Edition	2012
Reprint (Oct.)	2012
Fourteenth Edition	2016
Reprint	2016
Reprint	2018
Reprint	2018
Reprint	2019
Reprint	2019
Reprint	2019
Reprint	2019
Reprint	**2019**
Reprint	2020
Reprint	2021
Reprint	2021
Reprint	**2022**

PRINCIPLES OF STATUTORY INTERPRETATION

Including the General Clauses Act, 1897 with Notes

JUSTICE G P SINGH

M.Sc., LL.B., LL.D. (Hon.)
Chief Justice, High Court of Madhya Pradesh, 1978-1984;
Chairman, Madhya Pradesh Law Commission, 1990-1992;
Lokayukt, Madhya Pradesh, 1992-1997.

14TH EDITION

Revised by

Justice A K Patnaik
Former Judge, Supreme Court of India

LexisNexis

This book is a publication of **LexisNexis**
(A Division of Reed Elsevier India Pvt Ltd)
14th floor, Building No 10, Tower–B, DLF Cyber City, Phase-II,
Gurgaon–122002, Haryana, India.
Tel: + 91 124 4774444 Fax: + 91 124 4774100
Website: www.lexisnexis.co.in / E-mail: help.in@lexisnexis.com

RELX India Pvt Ltd – owner of the LexisNexis brand – acquired all the publishing rights in this publication from O.P. Wadhwa, K.K. Wadhwa, V.K. Wadhwa and S.K. Wadhwa in 2008. O.P. Wadhwa, K.K. Wadhwa, V.K. Wadhwa and S.K. Wadhwa built the renowned firm Wadhwa & Co Nagpur which was founded by their father the late Sri Chetan Das Wadhwa and their mother the late Smt. Ram Pyari Wadhwa.

Justice G P Singh, *Principles of Statutory Interpretation*, 14th Edition, 2016.

ISBN: 978-93-5143-965-3

Printed at : Sai Printo Pack Pvt Ltd, A-102/4 Okhla Industrial Area, Phase-II, New Delhi-110020.

Printed and bound in India.

About the Author—Justice G P Singh

G.P. Singh, our father, was born in a small village in the Rewa District of Madhya Pradesh. His father was a Magistrate, which assignment he finally gave up and took to the legal profession. Later, his father shifted to Rewa town and lived in a house with better facilities and amenities. Our father got his education from the Banaras Hindu University, from where he did his M.Sc. in Chemistry and also his Bachelor of Laws. Incidentally, the day he completed his law degree, he also lost his father who had been suffering from tuberculosis, which was a terminal disease at that time. Being the eldest child, the responsibility of looking after the large joint family fell on his young shoulders. According to his younger brother (our uncle), he and all the family members passed through very difficult days, but he held his nerves and stood his ground with exemplary courage and determination. It was perhaps these challenging times which were responsible for bringing out the best in him as the years unfolded. True to the local culture and tradition, we respectfully addressed him as "Dau". Later, he was to become the "Dau Ji" of all those who were close to him, and it was in this way that everyone preferred to address him with affection.

He took to the legal profession in the Rewa district, where his father had become very respected and popular. He also undertook the job of Private Secretary to the then Maharaja of Rewa to make both ends meet, but later gave up this job offered to him by the Maharaja because he was not paid the emoluments he was promised. While he devoted more time to the legal profession, he also looked around for a suitable job, which he never got due to lack of opportunity. Having received some success in the legal profession, he was encouraged to devote his full time to it. Slowly he began to like the subject of law, and took to teaching law in the local T.R.S. College as part time work. This, according to him, gave him a better understanding of law. Once he started teaching, he was hardly left with any time for his family, as he had to burn the midnight oil to support his large family.

On the family front he was admirably supported by our mother, Bharti Devi. Born to an orthodox family in a small village of District Sultanpur, Uttar Pradesh, her world revolved around him and the family, and stood firmly by his side, both in good and bad times, like a pillar of strength. She considered it her dharma to carry out all that he wished for and desired, with the greatest of pleasure and responsibility. Her contribution and influence in shaping his success, and the success of all of us, has been immense, and cannot be measured in any way. Even our uncles considered her like their own mother.

Driven by necessity, the encouragement he received by his initial success, and the personal satisfaction he derived by teaching law, he evinced a greater interest in law and became totally immersed in, and a slave to, the legal profession. With sheer hard work he soon established himself in the legal profession, and the days of trials and tribulations soon became a thing of the past.

He was a voracious reader and had great admiration for the leaders of the freedom movement. He looked upon Rabindranath Tagore, Mahatma Gandhi, Pandit Madan Mohan Malviya, C. Rajagopalachari, Dr. Rajendra Prasad, Dr. Sarvepalli Radhakrishnan, Jawahar Lal Nehru and Sardar Patel, to name a few, as people of great learning, impeccable character, and integrity. He often wondered why India, post independence, became bereft of their character and vision, and was unable to produce leaders of their caliber and stature.

With the reorganization of states in India, on the advice of seniors and elders in the family, he shifted to Jabalpur, where he began the second phase of his struggle. At Jabalpur, he got the opportunity to work on a higher plane, with more established persons in the profession, and in a more competitive atmosphere. At that time he drew inspiration from, amongst those on the Bench, Justice Mohammad M. Hidayatullah and Justice P.V. Dixit, and amongst those at the bar, from Mr. Adhikari, who was also the first Advocate General of Madhya Pradesh, Mr. A.P. Sen, Sardar Rajendra Singh and S.D. Sanghi, to name a few. With his experience, knowledge and hard work, he soon established himself in Jabalpur and, perhaps because he was choosy in accepting briefs, he did not have a roaring practice, but was satisfied with whatever the profession had to offer him. His fondness for the subject made him interested in academics, and the availability of a good library at the Jabalpur Bench of the Madhya Pradesh High Court provided him with just the opportunity and atmosphere he was looking for. Slowly and steadily, he built up his own library, and began to devote in the library whatever time he could spare from his profession.

He had shifted to Jabalpur in 1957, and in 1966 he surprised everyone by his own very coveted contribution to the legal profession in the form of a book titled "Principles of Statutory Interpretation", which was later recognized as a locus classicus even by the giants in the legal profession. He admitted that this was the happiest moment of his life. His joy knew no bounds and, to describe his joy, he said that he felt as if a child had been born into the family. He wrote every word by hand because that was his habit of doing any serious work. Thereafter, he brought out several editions and revised this book several times, and each time he felt the same joy and happiness.

His hard work at the bar was rewarded when he was elevated to the Bench as a Judge of the Madhya Pradesh High Court in 1967. He later went on to become the Chief Justice of the Madhya Pradesh High Court and served in this capacity for more than five years. While he was Chief Justice of the Madhya Pradesh High Court, he got two opportunities to serve as Acting Governor of Madhya Pradesh for a few months. After his retirement in January, 1984, he lived almost a secluded life in his ancestral village in Rewa, but there also he continued to revise his book and kept himself updated on the developments in the legal field. After almost five years of his retirement, he was made Chairman of the State Law Commission, and served in this position for almost two and a half years. Thereafter, he was made the Lokayukta of Madhya Pradesh, where again he served for five years. After he retired as Lokayukta, he preferred to stay at his farm in Rewa but, owing to medical reasons, he opted to stay in Jabalpur instead, and visited his farm house in Rewa off and on for a much needed change

During our interactions with him after his retirement, he would frequently journey down the memory lane and share his joy at being a Judge. He felt joyous because he never felt any kind of pressure during his entire tenure except that of imparting as much justice as possible to the thousands of litigants who came to Court as speedily as possible. He would, however say that nothing gave him as much pleasure as writing a book and making an original contribution to the legal field in his own way. He also told us that his first love was writing on Constitutional Law and Jurisprudence, but he soon realized that there were already many valuable contributions in this area. He therefore decided to contribute to an area which was least traversed and actually required some contribution, and hence wrote his book on "Principles of Statutory Interpretation". Next to follow was the pleasure of having been able to support his family after the early demise of his father. He derived immense pleasure and satisfaction from having successfully supported his brothers, sisters and all other members of the family who looked to him for support in that hour of crisis.

However, despite all his achievements, the highest point of satisfaction in his life came when he was almost ninety years of age and "Butterworths", the publishers of his book, approached him for consent to publish a book containing some of his selected judgments. He declined to give his consent for almost three to four years, but finally gave his consent in 2011. The reasons for declining and then giving his consent are best told in his own words in the Preface to the first edition of the book containing his selected judgments.

He was just as well versed in the scriptures, which he regarded as a way of life, as he was in law. He drew inspiration from the teachings in the Ramayana, the Mahabharata and the Geeta to develop his moral fibre, to which he held on with all his might throughout his life. Our scriptures teach us that every individual has a dual existence - one is the physical body, which is decadent, as is everything else in nature, and the other is the soul, which resides in the physical body, but is eternal, unseen and unaffected under any situation, and survives even after the death of the body when its time is completed. So also it was with him. Age was taking its toll on him and he had to leave his physical self, which we were lucky that he was able to retain till beyond ninety. During the last two years of his life, he used to say that he achieved and did everything that he wanted to, and now his desire was to leave this world as he was finding it very difficult to cope with age and the problems associated with longevity. His loss is immeasurable and irreparable to the family, his friends, his admirers and, above all, the legal fraternity. His spirit, however, lives on in every page of his book, in the libraries, the Courts of law, the Universities and judicial academies. We miss him all the time.

Today is a proud moment for us. Our thanks to Justice A.K. Patnaik for toiling hard and using his lifelong study, knowledge and experience in revising this book, carrying forward our father's legacy, and ensuring that he continues to live in all our hearts and minds.

His sons,

Ajeya

Ajit

Preface to the Fourteenth Edition

The book Principles of Statutory Interpretation, authored by Justice G.P. Singh, is an authoritative work and is often quoted in judgements of the High Courts and the Supreme Court of India in support of propositions relating to interpretation of provisions of statutes. After the 13th Edition of the book was published in 2012, Justice G.P. Singh left for his heavenly abode on 5th October, 2013, after taking a commitment from me that I will continue revising his book from time to time. I have tried my humble best to live up to my commitment given to a great legal luminary on the subject of statutory interpretation in preparing the revised 14th Edition of the book.

While working on the 14th Edition of this book, I have retained the portion of the 13th Edition as authored by Justice G.P. Singh. I have only updated the book on the basis of decisions of the Supreme Court of India reported in 2012 to March, 2015, and have incorporated new propositions of law laid down by the Supreme Court, examples of application of old propositions in new decisions of the Supreme Court, as well as decisions of the Supreme Court which have altered the position of law after the 13th Edition of the book was prepared.

While preparing the 14th Edition, I found that there are distinct new trends in Supreme Court decisions. There is a shift from the earlier tradition of literal interpretation of statutes to a purposive interpretation, keeping in mind the object of the concerned statute. Further, the Supreme Court is now less inclined to sustain death sentences for the offence of murder under section 302 of the Indian Penal Code, 1860. Moreover, the Supreme Court is also hesitant to interfere with arbitral awards which have been upheld by High Courts, thus encouraging settlement of disputes through arbitration. In some cases, however, the Supreme Court has encroached upon policy decisions even in economic matters which, till very recently, were considered to be within the domain of the executive. We have to wait and see whether these new trends in the decisions of the Supreme Court continue in the years to come.

I could not have prepared the 14th Edition of this book without the assistance of Miss Bhabna Das, a young bright lawyer, and Mr. Vimal Kumar, my efficient Private Secretary, who have put in a lot of effort in ensuring that the revised 14th Edition of this book goes to the press in time.

New Delhi

Justice A K Patnaik

Former Judge, Supreme Court of India

Preface to the Thirteenth Edition

In preparing the 13th edition, the book has again been thoroughly revised. The General Clauses Act with updated notes is retained in the Appendix.

In the wake of global menace of terrorism, the Government of the United Kingdom issued orders under section 1 of the United Nations Act, 1946, the Terrorism (United Nations Measures) Order, 2006 and the Al Qaida and Taliban (United Nations Measures) Order, 2006. The first order applied the test of reasonable grounds for suspecting that the person may be involved in terrorism related activities, whereas the second order prohibited judicial review of the listing of a person as a designated person to whom the order applied. The UK Supreme Court held both the orders *ultra vires* section 1 of 1946 Act, for it could not be assumed that the parliament intended that the basic rights of a citizen or a person could be taken away on mere reasonable suspicion or that judicial review could be taken away to challenge the right of a person as a designated person[1]. It has also been held that even a person suspected of terrorism related activity is entitled to a fair hearing.[2]

The case of *Electric Corporation of India v. Commissioner of Income Tax* was referred to the Constitution Bench which has recently been decided[3]. It has been held that parliament is empowered to make laws with respect to aspects or causes that occur, arise or exist, or may be expected to do so, within the territory of India only and does not empower to legislate for any territory other than the territory of India or any part of it.

The Collegium system of appointment of the Judges of the High Court and the Supreme Court has come up for strong criticism. A Bench of 2 judges has formulated certain pertinent questions against the collegium system and has referred the matter to the Chief Justice of India for appropriate orders[4]. Similarly, the practice of issuing general directions and guidelines and also of declaring them in some cases to have force of law under Article 141 has also been criticized. It would also have been apt to refer this question for consideration to a larger bench whether the Supreme Court in exercise of powers under Article 141 of the Constitution of India can make laws[5].

The judicial review of policy decisions of the executive government, by the Supreme Court has also been strongly criticized[6]. The State Legislature to get around the Supreme Court order has enacted an Act, The Chhattisgarh Auxillary Armed Police Force Act, which provides that notwithstanding anything contained in any judgment, order or decree of any court, each person working as special officer, will have right to remain at the post[7].

In construing the words 'relationship in the nature of marriage' as used in section 2(f) of the Domestic Violence Act, 2005 it was held that if the aforesaid words are read simply 'live in relationship', the court would be legislating which is not permissible[8]. In holding that transfer of non performing assets between the Banks,

1. P. 506 (*page of 13th edition*).
2. P. 505 (*page of 13th edition*).
3. P. 621 (*page of 13th edition*).
4. P. 275-276 (*pages of 13th edition*).
5. P. 284 (*page of 13th edition*).
6. P. 446 (*page of 13th edition*).
7. The Indian Express 10th September 2011
8. P. 77 (*page of 13th edition*).

now is a legitimate banking activity, the Supreme Court has held that while interpreting Banking Regulation Act, 1949 one needs to keep in mind not only the frame work of the Banking law as it stood in 1949, but also the growth and new concepts that have emerged in the course of time[9].

While dealing with case of reservation of panchayats in scheduled areas, it was held by the Supreme Court that it is a fit case that warrants exceptional treatment with regard to reservations and the rationale of ceiling of 50% has no application. Reservations of at least half of the seats in panchayats in favour of STs and cent percent reservations of Chairpersons of Panchayats in favour of STs is not invalid[10].

I would like to acknowledge with gratitude the co-operation and assistance rendered to me by my friend Justice Alok Aradhe, Judge, M.P. High Court in revising this edition of the book. Without his assistance the editing of a new edition would not have been possible for me who is nearing the age of ninety and is suffering from many age related problems.

I hope the 13th edition, of this book will be useful to the readers and they will like it.

Jabalpur

December 2011 G P SINGH

9. P. 325 (*page of 13th edition*).
10. P. 261(*page of 13th edition*).

Preface to the Twelfth Edition

In preparing the 12th edition, the book has again been thoroughly revised. The General Clauses Act with updated notes is retained in the Appendix.

Having regard to the global menace of terrorism which in all democracies has to be met consistent with human rights two new subheadings have been added in Chapter 5 as 8(a3) 'Terrorism and Human Rights in U.K.' and 8(a4) 'Terrorism and Human Rights in U.S.A.' to notice recent cases decided by the House of Lords and the Supreme Court of U.S.A. In India the Prevention of Terrorism Act 2002 (POTA) was repealed by the Prevention of Terrorism (Repeal) Act 2004 without reenacting any law in its place. Even all pending prosecutions under the repealed Act were not allowed to continue. They were required to be examined by a Review Committee constituted under the Repealing Act and cases in which the Review Committee did not find any prima facie case were to terminate without compliance with section 321 of the Code of Criminal Procedure which requires an application by the public prosecutor and permission of the court for withdrawal of a pending prosecution. This provision in the repealing Act was held to be valid.[1] After repeal of POTA in 2004, there was no counter terrorism legislation in India even to implement resolution No. 1373 and other resolutions of the Security Council of the United Nations. This lacuna was realised by the Government after terrorist attack in Mumbai on 26/11 and the Unlawful Activities (Prevention) Amendment Bill 2008 and the National Investigation Agency Bill 2008 were introduced in Parliament which were unanimously passed and received the Presidential Assent on 31.12.2008 and are now part of the law of India as Act No. 35 of 2008 and Act No. 34 of 2008.

During the trial of a terrorist the safety of witnesses is often of prime importance as there may be a real risk to their life. The restrictions directed by the court to maintain anonymity of a witness with the object of protecting him may sometimes be such that the defendant does not get a fair trial. Statutory provisions have been made both in U.K. and India for directing anonymity of a witness. But protective measures for non-disclosure of identity of witnesses have to be fair to the accused also so that they do not infringe his right to a fair trial.[2]

Respect for human rights does not militate against the view that subject to rehabilitation of misguided youths who abjure violence, the states facing the menace of terrorism should have the requisite determination to flush out terrorists and to eliminate those who do not surrender and are not arrested to face trial according to law. Recent events in Sri Lanka support this view.

There is no general principle in commonwealth countries including India that unlawfully obtained evidence is not admissible. But the investigatory technique of providing an opportunity to the accused may in a particular case be so seriously improper as to bring the administration of justice in disrepute by amounting to 'a state created crime' and the court may stay the proceedings and release the accused.[3]

There is a principle recognized in America and Australia that it is impermissible for other branches of government to impose on judges a task amounting to grossly unjudicial chore in an attempt to borrow the judiciary's reputation for impartiality. But in India a survey of

---

1. p . 696 (*page of 12th edition*).
2. p . 905 (*page of 12th edition*).
3. p. 909 (*page of 12th edition*).

PILs in the High Courts may show that the judiciary itself is too willing to take up grossly unjudicial chores even though the courts are unable to cope up with the mounting arrears of real judicial work.[4]

A two judge Bench of the Supreme Court has held that the *Wednesbury* principles of judicial review have now been completely replaced by the principle of proportionality. The case in which these observations were made related to appropriateness of punishment imposed against an employee. It was a case in which applying any test the result would have been the same. Further, in many earlier cases it was held that proportionality principles are not applicable in judging the appropriateness of punishment imposed in disciplinary proceedings and *Wednesbury* principles apply. Even in cases where fundamental rights/ human rights are affected, in hand with proportionality principles is a concept of 'latitude' which requires the court to show appropriate degree of deference to the public authority's judgment.[5]

Although there is complete freedom of speech in Parliament and no member can be made liable for anything said in either House of Parliament, a minister's speech can be used in judicial review to explain the conduct occurring outside Parliament to show that it was an improper exercise of power.[6]

It has been clarified that when an industrial worker challenges an order on the ground of violation of the Constitution or gross violation of natural justice he is not restricted to the remedies under the industrial law and he can bring a civil suit to challenge the order.[7]

It could be expected that a Constitution Bench or a larger Bench of the Supreme Court will examine the constitutional validity of the power exercised by the court to supplement the existing law by its directions and if declared valid will lay down the range and guidelines for its exercise as also the scope if any left to the legislature to modify these directions. The decision of these matters by a larger Bench is now all the more necessary for some judges of the Supreme Court have expressed the view that there is no such power and that this is also the effect of the seven judge Bench judgment in *P. Ramchandra Rao.*[8] This highly controversial power must be distinguished from the power to add to the law by creative interpretation of a broad concept in the Constitution as in *D. K. Basu* or the power to reform the common law to meet the present day needs of the community as in *M. C. Mehta.*[9] The reference to a Constitution Bench on such a matter came sooner than expected. On November 11, 2009 a division Bench has referred to a Constitution Bench the question of validity of directions issued by another division Bench in September 2006 for implementation of Lingdoh Committee report containing guidelines for conduct of elections to students unions in colleges and universities.[10]

"The ability to balance the freedom of citizens to hold protests and processions with the amount of regulation necessary to preserve order and protect the rights of others is one of the distinguishing features of a developed democracy."[11] In England the balance is achieved by sections 11 and 12 of the Public Order Act, 1986 and by the decision of the House of Lords

---

4. p. 28 (*page of 12th edition*).
5. pp. 442, 444, 445 (*pages of 12th edition*).
6. p. 450 (*page of 12th edition*).
7. p. 760 (*page of 12th edition*).
8. p. 292 (*page of 12th edition*).
9. p. 294 (*page of 12th edition*).
10. The Times of India November 12, 2009 (New Delhi)
11. *Kay v. Metropolitan Police Commissioner* (2009) 2 All ER, 935 (H.L.) para 55 (Lord Carswell).

in *Austin v. Metropoliton Police Commissioner* [12] that the measures of crowd control adopted by the police resulting in detention of a crowd assembled on a public highway to prevent breach of peace and risk of injury to persons or property did not offend Article 5(1) of the European Convention for the Protection of Human Rights, which guarantees everyone right to liberty and security of person, so long as the measures adopted are taken in good faith, are proportionate and are enforced for no longer than is reasonably necessary. In India the balance is achieved by the guidelines issued by the Supreme Court in *Destruction of Public and Private Properties in Re* v. *State of Andhra Pradesh*[13] which can be read as adapting the common law to meet the present day needs, a principle earlier recognised in *M.C. Mehta*.

The Supreme Court in a case decided by a two judge Bench has held valid an explanation added by an amendment by the Andhra Pradesh Legislature in the Act imposing profession tax that 'every branch of a firm, company, corporation or other corporate body, any society club or association shall be deemed to be a person.' The court has failed to notice that this would be in effect indirectly evading the ban imposed by Article 276(2) of the maximum amount of profession tax per 'person' which could not have been done directly. There are also observations that the definition of 'person' contained in section 3(42) of the General Clauses Act cannot automatically apply for construction of the word 'person' in Article 276(2). There is no contrary context in section 276(2) to make the definition in section 3(42) inapplicable as required by Article 367 of the Constitution. If a State Legislature can enact any artificial definition of 'person' different from the one in the General Clauses Act, the ban of maximum limit of tax imposed by Article 276(2) will become wholly nugatory[14].

The criticism and disquiet "even within the judiciary" regarding the collegium method of appointment of judges to the Supreme Court has been noticed by Justice J. S. Verma who was the main architect of the first collegium judgment of 1993. He has suggested that needed modifications may be made in the present procedure "to ensure that neither the judiciary nor the executive can claim a veto in the matter and both work together to recommend the most suitable person for appointment after an effective consultation between them."[15] This means that the judiciary and the executive must both agree upon the suitability of a person before his name is recommended for appointment. But the modification in the procedure to bring about this result can be done only by the Supreme Court on reconsideration of the present system by another judicial verdict of which there does not appear to be any possibility in near future. The proper thing may be to replace the Collegium system altogether by amending the Constitution to provide for National Judicial Commission as recommended by the Constitution Review Committee headed by former Chief Justice of India M. N. Venkatchaliah. But that also may not be that easy as the procedure required for such an amendment will need a strong political consensus. The Supreme Court can however administratively bring about some transparency in the appointments by disclosing what considerations determine the merit for appointment, the names considered and the reasons why senior judges were overlooked. Such a disclosure will remove the impression that sometimes members of the collegium, for reasons of their own, exercise a power of veto to keep out a deserving judge from elevation. Openness in the matter of judicial appointments to the highest court is becoming in vogue in many countries. Advertisements were issued even in the United Kingdom inviting applications for appointment as Lords of Appeal in

12. (2009) 3 All ER 455 para 37 (p. 471) (HL)
13. p. 294 (*page of 12th edition*).
14. p. 815 (*page of 12th edition*).
15. 'Paradigms of Judicial Independence', B.P. Sinha Memorial Lecture 2008 delivered on 29th November 2008 at Patna by Justice J.S. Verma, Former Chief Justice of India.

Ordinary/Justice of the Supreme Court to be selected by a selection commission constituted under the Constitution Reform Act 2005.[16] The removal of lid of secrecy by the collegium judges will give respectability to their recommendations and will bring about the desired accountability in the system which is lacking at present.

On 2nd July, 2009, the Delhi High Court read down Section 377 of the Penal Code to make it inapplicable to homosexual sex between consenting adults in private as in the opinion of the court the prohibition of the same offends the fundamental rights in Articles 14, 15 and 21 of the Constitution. This view is in line with the law as it now exists in America, European Union, United Kingdom and most of the commonwealth countries.

Reference must also be made to an important decision of the Supreme Court, *Suchita Srivastava* v. *Chandigarh Administration,*[17] reported after the book had gone to the press where the question arose relating to the termination of pregnancy of a mentally retarded orphan woman who was living in a government run welfare institution. The woman had become pregnant as a result of an alleged rape. In holding that the pregnancy could not be terminated even by an order of the court without the consent of the woman, which she had declined, under the Medical Termination of Pregnancy Act, 1971 Balakrishnan CJI in delivering the judgment of the court observed as follows:

> "There is no doubt that a woman's right to make reproductive choices is also a dimension of "personal liberty" as understood under Article 21 of the Constitution of India. It is important to recognize that reproductive choices can be exercised to procreate as well as to abstain from procreating. The crucial consideration is that a woman's right to privacy, dignity and bodily integrity should be respected. This means that there should be no restriction whatsoever on the exercise of reproductive choices such as a woman's right to refuse participation in sexual activity or alternatively the insistence on use of contraceptive methods. Furthermore, women are also free to choose birth control methods such as undergoing sterilisation procedures. Taken to their logical conclusion, reproductive rights include a woman's entitlement to carry a pregnancy to its full term, to give birth and to subsequently raise children. However, in the case of pregnant women there is also a "compelling State interest" in protecting the life of the prospective child. Therefore, the termination of a pregnancy is only permitted when the conditions specified in the applicable statute have been fulfilled. Hence, the provisions of the MTP Act, 1971 can also be viewed as reasonable restrictions that have been placed on the exercise of reproductive choices."

A debate is going on whether it would be possible to replace or at least to supplement the current common law rules of statutory interpretation, sometimes referred as *Maxwellian* rules, by *Mimamsa* rules of interpretation. Justice Markandey Katju, who has edited the second edition of Kishorilal Sarkar's book on *Mimamsa* Rules of Interpretation, which was first published in 1909, is a great admirer of these rules.[18] Justice Katju has also referred to

16. (2009) 83 ALJ 7. The Supreme Court of the United Kingdom, which replaces the judicial wing of the House of Lords, was inaugurated on 1st October 2009. **See further** Judicial Activism: Authority, Principle, and Policy in the Judicial Method—The Hamlyn Lectures by Justice Michael Kirby pp. 71, 72 (2003). Openness in America in appointments to the Supreme Court of U.S.A. is unique. A recent example is the speech delivered by President Obama on May 26, 2009 while nominating federal appellate Judge Sonia Sotomayor to the Supreme Court.

17. (2009) 9 SCC 1.

18. (1993) 1 SCC (J) 16.

them in some of his judgments[19]. Justice B. N. Shrikrishna, however, in an article *Maxwell* v. *Mimamsa*[20] has expressed the view that any hasty application of the *Mimamsa* principles in statutory interpretation will result in "immense chaos" for their application at present "appears to be beset with formidable difficulties" which he has listed as follows:

> "First, the correct application of the *mimamsa* principle would require precise knowledge of Sanskrit language, particularly the principles and rules of its grammar. It would also require precise appreciation of the schematic representation of the *sutra* text. Commentators like Shabara, Kumarilbhatta and others repeatedly refer to Pannini's rules of grammar as to nominal case terminations, adjectival derivatives and compound words, all of which have great significance in Sanskrit. Any attempt to understand the *mimamsasutras* without a good working knowledge of Sanskrit language would be counterproductive.
>
> Secondly, several of the terms used in the system of *mimamsa* have acquired conventional meanings by usage over millennia, just like the technical terms used in the language of law. These conventional meanings may often differ from the lexical meanings. Unless there is familiarity with the technical meanings of terms used in the system, their usage would become indiscriminate, resulting in chaos.
>
> Thirdly, adeptness in the use of English language in jurisprudential parlance has been achieved over centuries as a result of debates in courts of law both in England and in India. Generations of lawyers have imbibed it and internalised it. While it may not be impossible effectively to substitute it by an indigenous system based on the *mimamsa* principles, it can only be attempted after at least two generations of lawyers are equally well trained in the discipline of *mimamsa*. This can only come about if *mimamsa* discipline along with the requisite study of Sanskrit language, together with its grammar and a basic knowledge of the principles of *nyaya*, are taught to the law students. In the absence of such academic training, to expect the lawyers or the judges to understand the fine-tuned technical arguments of *mimamsa* would be impracticable, if not impossible.

Jabalpur
16th November 2009

G P SINGH

---

19. *Ispat Industries Ltd. v. Commissioner of Customs*, (2006) 12 SCC 584; *Gujrat Urja Vikas Nigam Ltd. v. Essar Power Ltd.*, (2008) 4 SCC 755; *Surjit Singh v. Mahanagar Telephone Nigam Ltd.*, AIR (2008) SC 2226.

20. (2004) 6 SCC (J) 48.

Preface to the Eleventh Edition

In preparing the 11th edition the book has again been thoroughly revised. The General Clauses Act with updated notes, as in the earlier editions, continues to be a part of the book.

A two judge Bench of the Supreme Court recently said that departure from the literal rule should be done in very rare cases and there should be judicial restraint in this connection. The court also quoted with apparent approval the observations of Lord Cranworth made in a case in 1852 that if we depart from the literal meaning of the words used 'we launch into a sea of difficulties which it is not easy to fathom'.[1] The decision of the case in which the above observations were made by the Supreme Court cannot be faulted but the observations now over emphasize the role of literal construction. The modern approach to construction is that context is considered first and not after ambiguity is discovered and that meaning is given to the words which best fits in the context.[2] The context here means not only the statute read as a whole but also previous state of the law other statutes in *pari materia*, the general scope of the statute and the mischief that it was intended to remedy.[3] The widening of the idea of context does not now permit any rigid distinction between literal and purposive approaches to construction.[4]

The basic structure doctrine has been reaffirmed by a nine judge Bench which holds that laws inserted in the ninth schedule after 24-4-1973, when *Kesavananda* was decided, are open to challenge on the ground that they are violative of the basic structure doctrine. The basic structure doctrine has essentially been developed from the German Constitution and in particular from the writings of Professor Dieter Conrad of Germany.[5]

India like many other countries has been facing the menace of terrorism. The Supreme Court of India while noticing that 'terrorism has become a global threat' and that 'it was our international obligation also to pass necessary laws to fight terrorism' has cautioned that 'terrorism often thrives where human rights are violated. The lack of hope of justice provides breeding grounds for terrorism. In all cases, the fight against terrorism must be respectful to the human rights.' This is the general opinion in all democracies.[6] Courts in America and England have even exercised extraterritorial jurisdiction to prevent violation of Human Rights by military authorities in detention camps.[6A]

In *State of Gujarat v. Mirzapur Moti Kureshi Kassab Jamat,*[7] a Bench of seven judges by majority of six against one upheld a Gujarat Legislation imposing a total ban on the slaughter of progeny of cow and overruled an earlier Constitution Bench decision which permitted slaughter of bullocks when they ceased to be serviceable. The court differing from the earlier Constitution Bench decision gave an expansive interpretation to the words 'other

---

1. p. 88 (*page of 11th edition*).
2. pp. 38 (*page of 11th edition*).
3. p. 34 (*page of 11th edition*).
4. p. 32 (*page of 11th edition*).
5. pp. 268, 269 (*pages of 11th edition*).
6. p. 854 to 856 (*pages of 11th edition*).
According to a report in the Times of India of August 28, 2007 India loses more lives to terror than any other country in the world except Peru. Still after scrapping of TADA and POTA, India has no comprehensive counter terrorism legislation to implement resolution no. 1373 reports the counter Terrorism Committee of the U.N. Security Council: Hindustan Times September 12, 2007
6A. pp. 470, 471 (*pages of 11th edition*).
7. p. 260 to 262 (*pages of 11th edition*).

milch and draught cattle' as used in Article 48 to include even cattle which had become incapacitated for milch or draught purposes. The court also strongly relied upon the fundamental duty in Article 51A(g) which enjoins as a duty of every citizen to have compassion for living creatures. The court held that the State is all citizens placed together and the fundamental duty in Article 51A(g) is collectively speaking the duty of the State. It is submitted that the expansive interpretation given to Article 48 and reliance on Article 51A(g) for banning slaughter of unserviceable bullocks is far fetched. If it be correct the State may even be duty bound to legislate banning not only slaughter of bullocks but also of buffaloes, goats and sheep and killing of all living creatures compelling all those engaged in the businesses of production and sale of meat to close their businesses and forcing Indian citizens to become total vegetarians.

Of late the judiciary has been accused of 'overreach'. No one disputes that the Supreme Court has the final say regarding interpretation of the Constitution and can strike down legislative and executive acts which are not consistent with the Constitution. But it is finality of the decisions of the Supreme Court which makes it supreme. It is 'supreme but not infallible'. This is the title of the book which was issued on the occasion of the Golden Jubilee Celebrations of the court and correctly represents the legal position. Opinions will certainly differ on the question whether there has been any 'overreach'. In my submission 'overreach' occurs when by 'not infallible' judgments the Court encroaches upon the powers of the Executive or the Legislature. One important instance of this nature is the much debated interpretation given by the Court to Articles 124, 217 and 222 of the Constitution which has completely taken away the power of the Executive in the matter of appointment and transfer of judges which was *prima facie* vested in the Executive.[8] Another instance of 'overreach' in my submission is the assumption of power by the Court to supplement the existing law not by creative interpretation but by its directions which are patently legislative in nature and which are to remain in force until the Legislature or the Executive incorporates them in the existing law by making new Act or delegated legislation. Directions are also sometimes issued which directly require the Executive to introduce new legislation or to make delegated legislation under the existing law. All this clearly offends the doctrine of separation of powers which is one of the basic structures of the Constitution.[9]

The utility of PIL for securing justice to socially and economically deprived persons and protecting human rights of indigent, disadvantaged and exploited segments of Indian humanity cannot be denied. But that does not justify the large inflow of PIL cases in the High Courts clogging the disposal of old pending cases. As rightly said by Soli J. Sorabjee a former Attorney General: 'PIL is not a pill for every ill. Every matter of public interest cannot be the basis of a PIL, e.g. increase in the price of onions, or revision of air-fares or the dilapidated condition of railway stations or the problem of trains running in time. Judicial pendulum in PIL has swung erratically. Some orders and directions are beyond the judicial sphere and do more credit to the heart than to the head. It is doubtful whether the judiciary can direct the administration to construct roads and erect buildings, to secure lands in a particular locality for accommodating certain persons, to appoint managers at a remuneration fixed by the court or to give ad-hoc directions for huge monetary payments. Such orders have serious fiscal and budgetary implications and are more in the realm of the legislature

8. p. 266, 267 (*pages of 11th edition*).

9. pp. 274 to 282 (*pages of 11th edition*).
The conflict between judicial restraint and judicial activism in dealing with such issues came in the forefront in the differing opinions of two learned judges in *State of U. P. v. Jeet S. Bisht,* (2007) 6 SCC 586, though both the judges agreed that instead of directing the Central and State Governments to fix adequate salaries and allowances of the Consumer Fora they be only requested to consider to do so.

and the executive.' Sorabjee concludes: 'With a firm judicial jockey in the saddle and a responsible bar PIL can be prevented from becoming an unruly horse and be utilized for protection and promotion of human rights of the people.'[10]

In spite of various methods employed to control the pendency of cases, e.g. regular holding of Lok Adalats, transfer of judicial work to tribunals and forums, mediation centres, plea bargaining, arbitration, the arrears of cases in courts remain substantially unaffected. Even high profile cases of public men often monitored by superior courts and sensitive criminal cases, which need to be decided as early as possible remain pending for years and are not disposed of within a reasonable time. Apart from any question of jurisdiction, considerations of priority and propriety require that the courts instead of taking up the work of other organs of the State or statutory bodies should concentrate more on disposal of old pending cases. Counting independent judiciary as one of our many blessings, in comparison to our neighbours, Khushwant Singh recently wrote: 'We have an independent judiciary though it moves at a sluggish pace, at least it moves. And people have still faith in it.'[11] The duty of all those involved in the functioning of our judiciary is to make a concerted effort to improve this image.

After publication of the 10th edition, I had decided not to take up the editing of any further edition. But it is difficult to resist the persistent persuasion of my publishers, Wadhwa and Company, Nagpur. This only shows that it is easy to think of 'renunciation' or recite the 'Song of the Sanyasin' but difficult to practice it or may be the time has not yet come for me to say the 'task is done'.[12] So here is the 11th edition also edited by me. I hope, the readers will not be disappointed.

Jabalpur
9th November 2007 — G P SINGH
(Deepawali)

10. Judiciary and Human Rights.
11. Hindustan Times, July 29, 2007.
12. See Preface to the 10th edition footnotes 13 and 14.

Preface to the Tenth Edition

In preparing the 10th edition the book has been thoroughly revised. The General Clauses Act with updated notes continues to be a part of the book.

The question whether a company can at all be prosecuted and punished for an offence which is punishable with imprisonment and fine gave rise to a sharp divergence of opinion while construing penal provisions in Taxation and Fiscal statutes and has now been settled by a Constitution Bench by a majority of 3 against 2 in favour of the view that the company can be prosecuted but punished only with fine.[1] The difference on this issue between majority and minority opinions illustrates that the rules of construction "hunt in pairs."[2] The court cannot fill a *casus omissus* but it cannot readily infer a *casus omissus* which frustrates the purpose of the Act; penal and taxation Acts are strictly construed according to the natural and ordinary meaning of the words used but they are not islands of literal construction untouched by the tide of purposive construction. A Judge can build his conclusions on that rule which he finds most suited in the particular case and when judges constituting the Bench adopt different rules, difference of opinion often becomes inevitable. Or is it true as has sometimes been said that judges often reach their conclusions first by their instinctive sense and reliance on rules comes later for giving reasons in support of those conclusions?[3] And how is the majority decision reached in a multi member court. Is it exclusively based on the reasoned arguments contained in the majority opinions? Apparently so. There is nothing to suggest to the contrary so far as the Supreme Court of India is concerned. But as regards the Supreme Court of the United States it has been said: "In the contest for votes, it would appear that in addition to reasoned arguments justices have used personal flattery and emotional appeals, and have even traded votes."[4]

A three judge Bench has now ruled that public law wrongs which can be redressed by public law remedies under Articles 32 and 226 by award of compensation are limited to violation of Article 21 of the Constitution and violation by the State of any other provision of the Constitution or any provision of a statute will not qualify as a public law wrong redressable by a public law remedy.[5]

A Constitution Bench appears to settle the law that the doctrine of pith and substance with permissible incidental encroachment in the rival field can give rise to repugnancy between a Central Act and a State Act even outside the concurrent list and in such a case it is the Central Act which always prevails.[6]

In an attempt to reform the election law by general directions under Article 142 in providing for precensorship of election advertisements of political parties for being telecast on electronic media, the court, it appears, has again rendered a controversial decision.[7] It is submitted that a Constitution Bench or a larger Bench may soon lay down the scope and a regulatory regime for exercise of the power assumed by the court to supplement the existing law by its general directions and the freedom, if any, left to the Legislature for replacing the directions so issued by suitable legislation. This will bring about reasonable certainty and predictability in this branch of our law and prevent adhocism which is destructive of the Rule of Law to which we are committed.[8]

---

1. pp. 865 to 867 (*pages of 10th Edition*).
2. Paton, Jurisprudence (Third Edition) p. 218.
3. p. 31(*page of 10th Edition*), text and notes 33 and 34.
4. Harry H. Wellington, Interpreting the Constitution: The Supreme Court and The Process of Adjudication (1990) (First Indian Reprint 2005, Universal Law Publishing Co.) p. 81
5. p. 256 (*page of 10th Edition*).
6. p. 534 (*page of 10th Edition*).
7. p. 269 (*page of 10th Edition*).
8. pp. 270 to 272 (*pages of 10th Edition*).

In view of the decision in *Union of India v. Azadi Bachao Andolan* that the views of CHINNAPPA REDDY, J. in *Mc Dowell* were not shared by the other four judges constituting the Bench, the applicability of the *Ramsay* principle in India to tax evasion schemes becomes doubtful and it is submitted that the question requires re-examination by a larger Bench.[9] There seems to be no sound reason why the *Ramsay* principle as further explained in later decisions in England should not be applied in India to counter tax evasion.

In the context of human rights two recent decisions of the English Courts require special mention. In *A.V. Secretary of State for the Home Department*[10] the House of Lords held that section 23 of the Anti Terrorism Crime and Security Act, 2001 which permitted indefinite detention of foreign nationals suspected to be terrorists without trial on the ground of threat to national security was incompatible with right to liberty in Article 5 and non-discrimination provision in Article 14 of the European Convention. And, in *James v. Ministry of Interior of Saudi Arabia*[11] the Court of Appeal held that the officials of a foreign State, a party to the Torture Convention, where acts of torture were committed by them could not be allowed state immunity in an action for damages brought by the victims against them and the State in England and the State alone was entitled to claim immunity.

The assumption of the power by the Supreme Court in the matter of appointments to itself and the High Courts has never been free from controversy.[12] Power of appointment, promotion, transfer and directing an inhouse enquiry in respect of High Court judges, exercised by the Supreme Court, has virtually reduced the High Courts to Subordinate Courts. The Supreme Court wields enormous judicial and administrative powers and is said to be the most powerful court in the world. Is not the public entitled to know the considerations which lead to elevation of a High Court judge to the Supreme Court? Some transparency in this respect is essential. Will the Right to Information Act 2005 supply this want?

The year 2005 was declared to be the year of excellence for the judiciary by the Chief Justice of India. This led to a welcome drive to speed up disposals in the High Courts and Subordinate Courts. In Madhya Pradesh, High Court Judges and Advocates even sacrificed a week of their summer vacation and normal hearing of cases continued in that week. Lok Adalats were regularly organized in the High Courts and Subordinate Courts for disposal of cases by compromise or settlement. All this was commendable and received general appreciation. But in the effort to maximize disposals two precautions are necessary. First that care has to be taken that principles of fair hearing and quality of justice are in no case sacrificed and secondly that in bringing about compromise or settlement in Lok Adalats care has to be taken that judicial persuasion does not degenerate into judicial coercion.

Age related problems are now seriously affecting my working capacity. The time has now come for me to practice renunciation. Commenting upon a verse in *Ishopanishad* Dr. S. RADHAKRISHNAN said: "Find your enjoyment in renunciation."[13] I add to this the following line from a poem composed by Swamy Vivekanand: "Heed then no more how body lives or goes. Its task is done."[14]

The 10th edition is likely to be the last edition of this book through me. I hope the readers will like it.

JABALPUR — G P SINGH

1st November, 2005

(Deepawali)

---

9. p. 783 (*page of 10th Edition*).
10. p. 449 (*page of 10th Edition*).
11. p. 594 (*page of 10th Edition*).
12. Text and note 12, p. 259 (*page of 10th Edition*).
13. From Foreword by Dr. S. Radhakrishnan to Dr. Satyavrata's *Ekadashopanishad.*
14. 'Song of the Sanyasin' quoted from the Cultural Heritage of India (Vol. IV The Religions) 2nd edition 1956, Reprint 1965, p. 704 published by The Ramkrishna Mission Institute of Culture Calcutta.

Preface to the Ninth Edition

In preparing the ninth edition the book has been rearranged and rewritten at many places. In particular the topics relating to judicial review of administrative action and judicial review of delegated legislation have been suitably rearranged and enlarged.

The well known case of *Shah Bano* decided by a Constitution Bench led to the enactment of the Muslim Women (Protection of Rights on Divorce) Act, 1986. In the words of a two judge bench of the Supreme Court "the Parliament enacted the Act to undo the effect of" *Shah Bano.* But surprisingly later another Constitution Bench in *Daniel Latifi* came to the conclusion that Parliament has done nothing of that kind and the Act "actually and in reality codifies what was stated in *Shah Banos's* case". Both these decisions reflect the Court's desire to ameliorate the plight of Muslim women. As was stated in *Shah Bano* "the role of reformer has to be assumed by the courts because it is beyond the endurance of sensitive minds to allow injustice to be suffered when it is so palpable."[1] The same point of view was extra judicially expressed by justice Young of Australia: "Our society is so structured that if judges do not on appropriate occasions grasp the mettle, no one will".[2]

The Human Rights Act, 1998 (U.K.) which gives effect to the European Convention on Human Rights and Fundamental Freedoms, was enforced from 2nd October, 2000. As expected the Act gave rise to a flow of H.R. cases in courts and tribunals of all kinds and all levels. In the words of Lord Hope "new problems are being revealed every week, if not every day".[3] The Act brought about a change in statutory interpretation in England because of the duty laid on the courts to construe legislation compatible with Convention rights "so far as it is possible to do so."[4] The Act also led to recognition of 'proportionality' as a new ground of judicial review which provides a stricter test of reasonableness as compared to *Wednesbury* unreasonableness. The presumption of compatibility as now applied in England is similar to the presumption of constitutionality as applied in India. It has also been said that the Indian courts have been applying the principle of proportionality ever since 1950 without specifically naming it.[5] The Supreme Court recently referred to Article 6(1) of the European Convention which provides for right to a fair trial by an independent and impartial tribunal and deduced the same right from Article 14 of the Constitution.[6]

Social issues relating to transexuals and same sex partners have been engaging the attention of the courts in the Western world. The European Court of Human Rights held that in the twenty-first century the right of transexuals to personal development and to physical and moral security in the full sense enjoyed by others in society could not be regarded as a matter of controversy requiring lapse of time to cast clearer light on the issues involved. The Court directed the Government of the United Kingdom to implement appropriate measures in due course to secure the applicant's (a post operative male to female transexual) and other

---

1. See pages 22, 23 (*pages of 9th edition*).
2. See page 23, note 2 (*page of 9th edition*).
3. See page 415 (*page of 9th edition*).
4. See pages 413, 414 (*pages of 9th edition*).
5. See page 380 (*page of 9th edition*).
6. *Dwarka Prasad Agarwala v. B.D. Agarwal,* (2003) 6 SCC 230 pp. 245, 246. Article 14 of the International Covenant on Civil and Political Rights, 1966 (p. 631) which forms part of the definition of Human Rights in the Protection of Human Rights Act, 1993 is similarly worded as Article 6(1) of the European Convention (p. 414) (*page of 9th edition*)..

transexuals' right to respect for private life and right to marry.[7] After enforcement of the Human Rights Act, the Court of Appeal in England, to avoid discrimination on the ground of sexual orientation, held that same sex partners living together can be treated as husband and wife under a statute which in terms applied only to different sex partners as earlier held by the House of Lords.[8] The Supreme Court of the United States recently by a majority of 6 against 3 (the Chief Justice joined in the dissent) declared a Texas statute forbidding two persons of the same sex to engage in certain intimate sexual conduct, unconstitutional and overruled its earlier decision of 1986.[9] The decisions represent the modern trend in the Western world on these and related issues. Our Supreme Court may also have to decide some day same or similar issues. Will it leave these social and moral issues to be resolved by Parliament on assessment of community standards and demands or will it extend the right to life and personal liberty and the right to equality to solve them the way they have been solved in the Western world? The answer is difficult to predict.[10]

The question as to how far new technological advances can be accommodated within the existing laws by their interpretation has been considered in many cases. A recent important Indian case in this context is one which holds that evidence recorded in India with the help of video conferencing of a witness in America is evidence taken in presence of the accused under section 273 of the Criminal Procedure Code, 1973.[11]

A seven judge bench of the Supreme Court decided that the Court cannot prescribe periods of limitation for termination of criminal cases and overruled a number of earlier cases. The decision shows that there are certain areas where the court cannot enter on the plea that there is a gap left by the Legislature.[12]

Two cases decided by three judge benches held that a voter at an election has a right to information to know from the candidate himself his antecedents. The second case also deals with an additional important issue as to what is the Legislature's role if the Court issues directions on matters on which the existing legislation is silent. Both these cases related to important constitutional issues and the decisions would have gained more respectability had the cases been decided by Constitution Benches especially when in the second case there was no complete unanimity amongst the judges and one of them regretted that the first case was not decided by a Constitution Bench.[13]

A recent important international event was the inauguration of the International Criminal Court at the Hague on March 11, 2003 under the Statute of Rome which was adopted in 1998 and came into force on July 1, 2002. It is yet to be seen how far the Court will be effective to curb international crimes.[14]

The States are reluctant to raise the present strength of judges from 10.5 judges per million population to 50 judges per million population as recommended by the Law Commission. The implementation of this recommendation of the Law Commission is absolutely necessary for enabling the judiciary to dispose of cases within a reasonable time. Financial constraints

7. See pages 231, 232 (*pages of 9th edition*).
8. See page 231 (*page of 9th edition*).
9. *Lawrence v. Texas* decided on June 26, 2003 overruling *Bowers v. Hardwick*, (1986) 478 U.S. 186.
10. Section 377 Penal Code was challenged in the Delhi High Court but the petition was dismissed on the ground of want of *locus standi*. A petition raising the same question is now pending in the Supreme Court.
11. See page 233 (*page of 9th edition*).
12. See pages 251, 252 (*pages of 9th edition*).
13. See page 251 (*page of 9th edition*).
14. See page 548 (*page of 9th edition*).

cannot be cited as excuses for non-implementation of such a recommendation for right to disposal of cases without unnecessary delay is a fundamental right spelled out of Articles 14 and 21 of the Constitution as also from fair hearing provision in Article 14 of the International Covenant on Civil and Political Rights, 1966. As observed by the European Court of Human Rights the State cannot blame unacceptable delays "on a general want of prosecutors or judges or court houses or on *chronic underfunding of the legal system*."[15] Mounting arrears of cases in the High Courts are a matter of grave concern.[16] There is some criticism that courts pay more attention to PIL cases[17] which generally relate to functions assigned to the Executive but receive wide media coverage. It is also said that when the High Courts are unable to dispose of their normal work why should they take up the work of other organs of the State. The criticism may not be justified but there can be no doubt that first priority must be given to the disposal of old pending cases and the judiciary must "guard against the danger of judicial populism."[18]

After editing the eighth edition in 2001, I thought now the work is done and I will not be asked to edit the next edition. But the publishers have thought otherwise. They believe probably in what HOLMES said that "the work never is done while the power to work remains" and that I have still some power to work. I hope that the ninth edition will not disappoint the readers and they will find it as useful as were the earlier editions.

JABALPUR
8th November, 2003

G P SINGH

15. See page 238 note 46 (*page of 9th Edition*).
16. See Yatindra Singh (now a Judge of the Allahabad High Court), A LAWYER'S WORLD, (2nd Edition) pp. 143 to 145.
17. In addition to the guidelines laid down by the Supreme Court for entertaining PIL petitions in *Balco* (2002) 2 SCC 333 pp. 376, 377, and repeated in *Guruvayoor,* (2003) 7 SCC 546, pp. 572, 573, is it not possible to evolve a rule of practice that petitions, in particular PIL petitions, complaining of violations of Human Rights as defined in section 2(d) of the Protection of Human Rights Act, 1993 will not be generally entertained in the High Court unless the petitioner has first approached the State Human Rights Commission?
18. See page 25 note 11 (*page of 9th Edition*).

Preface to the Eighth Edition

In preparing the eighth edition the book has been revised and at places rearranged and rewritten with extensive additions. The General Clauses Act with updated notes continues to be a part of the book.

There can be no doubt that the interpretative function of judges is imbued with creativity but only in the sense that whenever the court decides a real question of interpretation the decision adds to the law especially in cases where application of the statute could not have been comprehended by the legislature or where the statute refers to broad concepts as in a constitution. But there is a limit to creativity, known in the current fashion as judicial activism, for there exists a dividing line between legitimate interpretation and usurpation of legislative function. The line is crossed when judges, who assume office to 'uphold the constitution and the laws', "in the guise of interpretation provide their own preferred amendments to statutes". The same point was recently stressed by the Chief Justice of Australia, Hon. Murray Gleeson. Speaking in the context of 'creativity' the Chief Justice said : "Judges whose authority comes from will of the people and who exercise authority upon trust that they will administer justice according to law, have no right to subvert the law because they disagree with a particular rule. No judge has a choice between implementing the law and disobeying it."[1]

With the widening of the idea of context to include the previous state of the law and the mischief to which the statute is directed together with the importance being given to the rule that literal meaning has also to be derived by reading the statute as a whole in its context, it is now being realized that there is no rigid distinction between literal and purposive approaches to construction.[2]

In view of the enlargement of fundamental rights by liberal interpretation, especially Article 21, which applies also to foreigners present in India, the doctrine that violation of fundamental rights is a public law wrong of strict liability redresssable in damages may need some control mechanism to limit the cases where damages may be allowed otherwise the blame for every misfortune would be laid on the Government for claiming damages in public law.[3]

Similar to the principle of constitutionality applied in India,the courts in England have developed the principle of legality which means that unless there is a clear provision to the contrary, long standing principles of constitutional law and administrative law are presumed not to have been affected. A question of 'compatibility' under the Human Rights Act, 1998 now enforced in England is also likely to be dealt with in like manner.[4]

The trend of making reference to international law and conventions in interpreting statutes continues and international conventions have quite often been construed by courts.[5] In this context, the doctrine of legitimate expecatation has been expanded in some decisions to cover expecatation from a convention which though ratified is yet to be enforced by legislation. But it has also been held that a provision in a convention, which has been enacted into law but is yet to come into force under a notification of the executive

1. Pages 22, 23; (2000) 74 ALJ 494, (*pages of 8th edition*).
2. Page 26, (*page of 8th edition*).
3. Pages 224, 225, (*pages of 8th edition*).
4. Pages 377, 378, (*pages of 8th edition*).
5. Pages 486-497, (*pages of 8th edition*).

Government, cannot give rise to legitimate expectation.[6]

The case of *Pinochet* decided by the House of Lords drew global attention to the international crime of Torture. The case is also important for the reason that it shows that a decision of the highest court can also be reviewed and set aside on the ground of bias of one of the judges who first heard the case.[7]

The *Ramsay* principle which enables scrutiny of tax saving schemes has been held to be inapplicable when the statute deals with a legal concept as distinguished from a commercial concept.[8]

Offences by companies have gained prominence. This subject and the rules of attribution applicable in this context have been separately dealt with.[9]

Two earlier decisions of the Supreme Court which held that a notification required to be published in the official Gazette comes into operation not on the date mentioned in the Gazette but on the date when the Gazette is made available for sale or circulation, have been overruled. The prevailing view is that the date of the Gazette (provided it is not antedated) will be the date of publication of the notification and itscoming into force[10].

For the first time in Australia there was recently a 'Courts Consulting the Community Conference' in South Australia in which representatives of the courts and the community participated. The expectations and suggestions of the community emerging in the conference are to be considered and implemented by the Council of the Courts Administrative Authority, a statutory body.[11] One wonders as to what would be the expectations and suggestions of the community if such a conference were to be organized in India. My own guess is that the community expects much better service from courts and its suggestions would be that appropriate steps be taken without any delay for the following : (1) To dispose off old pending cases in the High Courts and Subordinate Courts and to ensure that cases instituted at all levels are decided within a reasonable time; (2) to make the judicial officers and clerical staff in Subordinate Courts and the Registries of the High Courts effectively answerable under the Prevention of Corruption Act without affecting judicial independence; (3) to ensure acceptance of and fidelity to the 'values of judicial life' restated by judges themselves; and (4) to inform the community of the responses of the judiciary in these matters and the steps, if any, taken for implementing the suggestions.

Let me hope that the present edition of the book edited by me in my 80th year will be as useful to the readers as were the earlier editions. If that happens, I will feel satisfied that I am really living in the sense that I am still functional. I am here reminded of what Justice Holmes said in reply to felicitations on his 90th birthday : "*To live is to function. That is all there is in living.*" He then quoted a line from a Latin poet : "*Death plucks my ears and says, Live—I am coming.*"

JABALPUR — G P SINGH

7-7-2001

---

6. Page 490, (*page of 8th edition*).
7. Pages 502-507, (*pages of 8th edition*).
8. Page 667, (*page of 8th edition*).
9. Page 736, (*page of 8th edition*).
10. Page 801, (*page of 8th edition*).
11. (2001) 75 ALJ 2.

Preface to the Seventh Edition

In preparing the seventh edition the book has again undergone a complete revision. The notes on the General Clauses Act contained in the Appendix have also been revised.

The prevailing mood towards globalisation in matters of common interest has given rise to the practice of paying more attention to international agreements and conventions and international law in interpretation of statutes. Inspiration has also been drawn from decisions taken in International Conference of Judges.[1]

The question as to when a statute conferring power enables recourse to a private law remedy for damages in a case of omission to exercise the power has recently been considered by courts both in England and India. The Supreme Court in this context relied upon the controversial doctrine of 'General Reliance', applied in some Australian cases but which now stands rejected by the High Court of Australia.[2]

Normally there is no place for natural justice in making conditional legislation. But exception to this rule has been found in a case where conditional legislation was used to deprive workmen of the benefits which they were receiving.[3]

Difference of opinion on the question of *quasi* repeal by desuetude between two coordinate benches of three judges of the Supreme Court remains unresolved,[4] conflicting views of the Supreme Court in cases decided by co-equal benches, when the later case does not notice the earlier case and the two views cannot be reconciled, create confusion and a clear direction is needed on the question, on which the High Courts have differed, whether they can follow either of the cases which appears to them more sound or they are bound to follow the later case.[5]

Judicial creativity in widening the ambit of fundamental rights especially Article 21 continues. This article has been interpreted to give protection to all those aspects of life which go to make a man's life meaningful, complete and worth living with dignity and thus embracing his tradition, culture, heritage, health and privacy. One may wonder as to what remains outside Article 21 except right to end one's life which too was earlier conceded by a two Judge Bench but that view was later overruled by a five Judge Bench also impliedly showing the necessity of adhering to the discipline of Article 145(3).[6] It is also hoped that the fundamental rights will not be extended to protect any conduct generally

---

1. Pages 440 to 455 (*7th Edition*).
2. Pages 544 to 546 (*7th Edition*).
3. Pages 712, 713 (*7th Edition*).
4. Pages 503, 504 (*7th Edition*).
5. The only guidance that one gets on this point is that a co-equal bench "could not overrule" the earlier case and the later case, therefore, could not be "so read to have that effect"; *Indian Oil Corporation Ltd. v. Municipal Corporation,* AIR 1995 SC 1480 p. 1482 (para 8). This may support the view that the High Courts can follow either of the cases. The later decision may be held to be *per incurricum* and the earlier decision may be followed: *Babu Parasu Kaikadi v. Babu,* (2004) 1 SCC 681 pp. 689, 690 : AIR 2004 SC 754 p. 759.
6. Page 207 (*7th Edition*).

regarded as immoral in contemporary Indian society, especially when it is non-natural, leaving the State free to forbid, regulate or leave it untouched on assessment of community standards and demands.[7]

The words of a constitution, it has been said, are "empty vessels" into which a judge "can pour nearly anything he will".[8] This precept appeared to have been applied too liberally in many applications of Article 142(1). But the recent unanimous constitution bench decision delivered by Dr. Anand, J. (now CJI) in V.C. Mishra's case is expected to properly regulate the use of this provision as it holds that in its anxiety to render complete justice it is not permissible for the Court to travel beyond the cause or matter pending before it, or to ignore or supplant substantive statutory provisions, or to take over the role of other statutory bodies and organs of the State empowered to perform the same task.[9]

The Supreme Court continues to show extensive judicial creativity in interpreting the Articles relating to appointment and transfer of judges. The 1993 nine Judge Bench judgement giving a new meaning to these Articles has further been explained, elaborated and modified by another nine Judge Bench on a Presidential reference made under Article 143.[10]

In its drive against corruption, the Supreme Court had to innovate new tools, notable amongst them being the doctrine of "continuing mandamus" to activate the CBI and to oversee investigations against persons in high places.[11] But the drive against corruption in public life gets a bit impeded by the majority judgement in JMM bribery case[12] which gives a very wide meaning to Article 105(2) leading to an anomalous result that Members of Parliament who accept bribe for voting are liable to prosecution if they do not vote but become immune from prosecution after they cast their votes in Parliament. Further, little has been done in this context for the judiciary. Brennan, C.J. of the High Court of Australia in his address at the 30th Australian Legal Convention in Melbourne on 19th September, 1997, said: "In the years I have been privileged to be a Judge, I have not known a corrupt Judge; none has sought to do anything except justice according to law as he or she honestly saw it, none would yield to improper pressure that might impermissibly tilt the scales of justice".[13] Can the Chief Justice of India or the Chief Justice of any High Court in India make a statement of the nature made by the Chief Justice of Australia? Indeed, a former Chief Justice of India, soon after his retirement, is reported to have candidly said: "There is no point in saying that there is no corruption in the judiciary. No one is going to say it, much less accept it".[14] And, the reference here to the judiciary was inclusive of High Courts. No doubt the statement causes concern but still it is generally felt that corruption in High Courts, if at all, is minimal and the 'inhouse procedure', which is in a developing stage, has worked in many cases to

---

7. Soli J. Sorabjee tells us 'out of Court' (The Times of India, Nov. 23, 1998) that the consitutional court of South Africa in "refreshing contrast" to the United States Supreme Court has held that homosexuality is included in the right of privacy, the right to dignity and the right to equal protection. The State may or may not be justified in forbidding homosexual behaviour between consenting adults in private but the idea of elevating it to a constitutional right may not appear "refreshing" to many in India.

8. L. Hand 'Sources of Tolerance' quoted in 52 Harvard Law Review p. 470.

9. Pages 211 to 214 (*7th Edition*).

10. Page 209 (*7th Edition*).

11. *Union of India v. Sushil Kumar Modi*, AIR 1997 SC 1672 p. 1675; *Vineet Narain v. Union of India*, AIR 1998 SC 889 p. 901 (para 14).

12. P.V. Narsimha Rao v. State, AIR 1998 SC 2120.

13. (1997) 71 ALJ 809, 810; (1998) 72 ALJ 45.

14. The Indian Express, Jan. 23, 1998.

successfully tackle it.[15] The reported 'restatement of values of judicial life' by judges themselves and fidelity to those values will go a long way to remove aberrations, if any, found in the conduct of judges of superior courts.[16] What appears to be urgently needed is to "cleanse"[17] the Subordinate Courts by devising a machinery to make judicial officers effectively accountable under the Prevention of Corruption Act. One hardly hears of any prosecution under the P.C. Act of a judicial officer or even of a clerk employed in a court, not because corruption in courts is negligible, but because the normal police is ineffective against courts. The administrative vigilance exercised by the High Courts is now not enough to "cleanse" the courts. So it may be worthwhile to consider whether the problem can be tackled by having a Special Police Establishment, constituted by a new legislation, under the superintendence of each High Court with exclusive power to investigate cases of corruption involving judicial officers and clerical staff in Subordinate Courts and the High Court Registry. Such a measure will be in harmony with Articles 235 and 229, will reasonably ensure prosecution of corrupt officers and, at the same time, avoid any dilution of judicial independence and harassment of honest officers, as happened in the Nadiad[18] and Bareilly[19] Magistrates' cases. Further, the effective accountability of judicial officers under the P.C. Act to be brought about by this measure, will be enforcing equality and the rule of law which formed the basis for restructuring the CBI and allied agencies in *Vineet Narain*.

It is hoped that the new edition will prove as useful to all concerned as its predecessors.

JABALPUR

3-1-1999 GP SINGH

---

15. Fali S. Nariman in his article 'Caesar's Wife; A Judge should be above suspicion' (The Times of India, Nov. 97) gives some instances where the inhouse procedure gave positive results.
See further Soli J. Sorabjee; 3 Law and Justice (1996) 'Presidents page' IX; 'Dilatory Judges', The Times of India Feb. 27, 1998 (complaints are generally of lack of work culture e.g. unpunctuality, unwillingness to hear cases, laxity in delivering judgements). Justice Michael Kirby of the High Court of Australia while in India in 1997 got the following impression: "So far the upper judiciary has escaped—Not a few who might know told me that the problem of corruption in the courts of India was not with the judges, but with court officials controlling the priority of hearings in the crush of burgeoning cases": 'Our Region—The challenge for Law and Justice' (1998) 72 ALJ 197 p. 201.

16. Rakesh Bhatnagar, 'Restoring People's confidence in Judiciary', The Times of India, July 14, 1998.

17. Punchhi, CJI, while inaugurating a State Judicial Officers' Conference is reported to have said: "The judiciary at the lower rung needs to be cleansed and corrected." The Times of India, March 17, 1998.

18. *Delhi Judicial Service Association v. State of Gujarat*, AIR 1991 SC 2176.

19. The Times of India, March 8, 1994. See further *U.P. Judicial Officers Association v. Union of India*, J.T. 2002 (8) SC 133.

GENERAL CONTENTS

CONTENTS

CHAPTER 1

BASIC PRINCIPLES

CHAPTER 2

GUIDING RULES

CHAPTER 4

EXTERNAL AIDS TO CONSTRUCTION

CHAPTER 5

SUBSIDIARY RULES

CHAPTER 6
OPERATION OF STATUTES

CHAPTER 7

EXPIRY AND REPEAL OF STATUTES

CHAPTER 8

STATUTES AFFECTING THE CROWN OR THE STATE

CHAPTER 9

STATUTES AFFECTING JURISDICTION OF COURTS

CHAPTER 10

CONSTRUCTION OF TAXING STATUTES AND EVASION OF STATUTES

CHAPTER 11

REMEDIAL AND PENAL STATUTES

CHAPTER 12

DELEGATED LEGISLATION

APPENDIX

THE GENERAL CLAUSES ACT, 1897
(Act No. X of 1897)

Table of Cases

A

PAGE

PAGE

PAGE

PAGE

PAGE

B

PAGE

PAGE

PAGE

PAGE

PAGE

PAGE

PAGE

PAGE

C

PAGE

PAGE

PAGE

PAGE

PAGE

PAGE

PAGE

PAGE

PAGE

PAGE

D

PAGE

PAGE

PAGE

PAGE

PAGE

PAGE

PAGE

PAGE

PAGE

PAGE

PAGE

PAGE

PAGE

PAGE

H

PAGE

PAGE

PAGE

PAGE

PAGE

PAGE

PAGE

PAGE

PAGE

PAGE

PAGE

PAGE

PAGE

PAGE

PAGE

PAGE

PAGE

L

PAGE

PAGE

PAGE

M

PAGE

PAGE

PAGE

PAGE

PAGE

PAGE

PAGE

PAGE

PAGE

PAGE

PAGE

N

PAGE

PAGE

PAGE

PAGE

O

PAGE

PAGE

PAGE

PAGE

Q

PAGE

R

PAGE

PAGE

PAGE

PAGE

PAGE

PAGE

PAGE

PAGE

PAGE

PAGE

PAGE

PAGE

PAGE

PAGE

PAGE

PAGE

PAGE

PAGE

PAGE

PAGE

PAGE

PAGE

PAGE

PAGE

PAGE

PAGE

PAGE

PAGE

PAGE

PAGE

PAGE

PAGE

PAGE

PAGE

PAGE

PAGE

PAGE

PAGE

PAGE

PAGE

V

PAGE

PAGE

W

PAGE

PAGE

Table of Statutes

A

C

D

E

F

G

I

J

L

M

O

S

CHAPTER 1

BASIC PRINCIPLES

SYNOPSIS

1. MEANING OF INTERPRETATION OR CONSTRUCTION

Enacted laws, specially the modern Acts and Rules, are drafted by legal experts and it could be expected that the language used will leave little room for interpretation or construction. But the experience of all those, who have to bear and share the task of application of the law, has been different.[1] It is quite often that we find courts and lawyers busy in unfolding the meaning of ambiguous words and expressions and resolving inconsistencies.[2] The age old process of application of the enacted

1. "It is general judicial experience that in matters of law involving questions of construing statutory or constitutional provisions, two views are often reasonably possible and when judicial approach has to make a choice between the two reasonably possible views, the process of decision making is often very difficult and delicate.": (*Keshav Mills Co. Ltd. v. CIT,* AIR 1965 SC 1636, p. 1644 : 1965 (2) SCR 908 : (1965) 56 ITR 365).
2. In some cases the Draftsman has been severely criticised. Regarding section 22(2)(b) of the Limitation Act, 1939, (UK) it was said that the section was so obscure that "the Draftsman must have been of unsound mind": [*Kirby v. Leather,* (1965) 2 All ER 441, p. 445 (CA) (DANCKWERTS, LJ)]. **Referring** to section 45 of the General Rate Act, 1967, LORD WILBERFORCE said: "The section is a labyrinth, a minefield of obscurity" [*Vandyk v. Oliver (Valuation Officer)*, (1976) 1 All ER 466, p. 470 (HL)]. In dealing with section 23-A of the Income-tax Act, 1922, the Supreme Court observed: "The Act contains many mind twisting formulae but section 23-A along with some other sections takes the place of pride amongst them" : [*CIT, Gujarat v. Distributors (Baroda) (Pvt.) Ltd.,* AIR 1972 SC 288, p. 291 : 1972 (1) SCR 726 : (1972) 4 SCC 353]. For other cases **see** note 31, pp. 33, *infra* and ALLEN, Law in the Making, 7th Edition, pp. 484-86.

law has led to formulation of certain rules of interpretation or construction. Interpretation of a legal provision and its application to a set of facts are two different exercises requiring different approaches. While interpretation of a legal provision is always independent of the facts of any given case, the application of a statutory provision would always depend on the exact facts of a given case.[3]

"By interpretation or construction is meant", says SALMOND: "the process by which the courts seek to ascertain the meaning of the Legislature through the medium of authoritative forms in which it is expressed".[4] It has been said that there is a distinction between the two expressions.[5] As explained by COOLEY: "Interpretation differs from construction in sense that the former is the art of finding out the true sense of any form of words; that is, the sense which their author is intended to convey; and of enabling others to derive from them the same idea which the author intended to convey. Construction, on the other hand, is the drawing of conclusions, respecting subjects that lie beyond the direct expression of the text from elements known from and given in the text; conclusions which are in spirit though not within the letter of the law."[6] This distinction, however, "has been largely relegated to the realm of academic discussion",[7] and has been criticised as 'erroneous'.[8] Even conceding that there may be some abstract distinction between the two, it cannot be doubted, as was observed by WHITE, J. that "in common usage interpretation and construction are usually

---

3. *Sudevanand v. State, through CBI*, (2012) 3 SCC 387, pp. 397, 398.

4. SALMOND, Jurisprudence, 11th Edition, p. 152. In the words of GRAY: 'The process by which a judge (or indeed any person, lawyer or layman, who has occasion to search for the meaning of a statute) constructs from the words of a statute-book a meaning which he either believes to be that of the Legislature, or which he proposes to attribute to it, is called by us 'Interpretation'and by the Germans 'Auslegung'.' The Nature and Sources of the Law, 2nd Edition, p. 176. According to CROSS: 'Interpretation is the process by which the courts determine the meaning of a statutory provision for the purpose of applying it to the situation before them:' Statutory Interpretation, 3rd Edition, p. 34.

5. *In re*, Sea Customs Act, AIR 1963 SC 1760, p. 1794 (HIDAYATULLAH, J.) : 1964 (3) SCR 787.

6. COOLEY,Constitutional Limitations, Vol. I, p. 97; **referred** in *In re Sea Customs Act*, AIR 1963 SC 1760, p. 1794 : (1964) 3 SCR 787. **See further** *Corpus Juris Secondum*, Vol. 82, p. 529; CRAWFORD,Statutory Construction, pp. 240-41; *D.R. Venkatachalam v. Dy. Transport Commissioner,* AIR 1977 SC 842, p. 849 : (1977) 2 SCC 273 : (1977) 2 SCR 392; *The Commissioner of Wealth Tax v. Hashmatunnisa Begum,* AIR 1989 SC 1024, p. 1029 : 1989 Supp (2) SCC 43 : (1989) 176 ITR 98.

7. CRAWFORD,Statutory Construction, p. 241.

8. SUTHERLAND,Statutory Construction, Vol. 2, 3rd Edition, Article 4504, p. 319.

understood as having the same significance".[9] It may be added that the present work has followed this common usage and the two expressions, hereinafter, have been used as synonymous.

2. INTENTION OF THE LEGISLATURE

A statute is an edict of the Legislature[10] and the conventional way of interpreting or construing a statute is to seek the 'intention' of its maker. A statute is to be construed according 'to the intent of those that make it'[11] and 'the duty of judicature is to act upon the true intention of the Legislature—the *mens or sententia legis*'.[12] The expression 'intention of the Legislature' is a shorthand reference to the meaning of the words used by the Legislature objectively determined with the guidance furnished by the accepted principles of interpretation.[13] If a statutory provision is open to more than one interpretation the court has to choose that interpretation which represents the true intention of the Legislature,[14] in other words the

9. *United States v. F.W. Keitel,* 211 US 370, p. 386: 53 Law Ed 230, p. 240. 'Although there is some distinction between them, they are so hard to disentangle that they cannot afford a suitable basis for discussion.' DIAS, Jurisprudence, 2nd Edition, p. 105.

10. *Vishnu Pratap Sugar Works (Private) Ltd. v. Chief Inspector of Stamp, U.P.,* AIR 1968 SC 102, p. 104 : 1967 (3) SCR 920; *Institute of Chartered Accountants of India v. Price Waterhouse,* AIR 1998 SC 74, p. 90 : (1997) 6 SCC 312 : (1997) 90 Com Cases 113; *Padmasundara Rao v. State of T.N.,* AIR 2002 SC 1334, p. 1346 : (2002) 3 SCC 533 : (2002) 255 ITR 147.

11. *RMD Chamarbaugwala v. Union of India,* AIR 1957 SC 628, p 631 : 1957 SCR 930; *Chief Justice, Andhra Pradesh v. LVA Dikshitulu,* AIR 1979 SC 193, p. 205 : (1979) 2 SCC 37; *Prithi Pal Singh v. Union of India,* AIR 1982 SC 1413, p. 1419 : (1982) 3 SCC 140; *Girdharilal and Sons v. Balbirnath Mathur,* (1986) 2 SCC 237, p. 242 : AIR 1986 SC 1099; *Maunsell v. Olins,* (1975) 1 All ER 16, p. 19 (HL); *Stock v. Frank Jones (Tipton) Ltd.,* (1978) 1 All ER 948, p. 951 (HL); *Competition Commission of India v. Steel Authority of India Limited,* (2010) 10 SCC 744 para 52 : (2010) 10 JT 26.

12. SALMOND, Jurisprudence, 11th Edition, p. 152. 'The object of interpreting a statute is to ascertain the intention of the Legislature enacting it:' *South Asia Industries (Pvt.) Ltd. v. S. Sarup Singh,* AIR 1966 SC 346, p. 348 : 1965 (3) SCR 829. **See further** *S. Narayanaswami v. G. Panneerselvam,* AIR 1972 SC 2284, p. 2285 : (1972) 3 SCC 717; *Kartar Singh v. State of Punjab,* JT (1994) 2 SC 423, p. 463 : 1994 (3) SCC 569 : 1994 Cr LJ 3139 (SC); *Institute of Chartered Accountants of India v. Price Waterhouse,* AIR 1998 SC 74, p. 90 : (1997) 6 SCC 312; *J.P. Bansal v. State of Rajasthan,* 2003 AIR SCW 1848, p. 1854 : (2003) 5 SCC 134 : AIR 2003 SC 1405.

13. **See** *R v. Secretary of State for the Environment exparte Spath Holme,* (2001) 1 All ER 195, p. 216 (HL). **See further** text and notes 46, 47 and 48, pp. 11-12 *infra.*

14. *Venkataswami Naidu, R. v. Narasram Naraindas,* AIR 1966 SC 361, p. 363 : 1966 (1) SCR 110; *District Mining Officer v. Tata Iron and Steel Co.,* AIR 2001 SC 3134, p. 3152 : (2001) 7 SCC 358; *Bhatia International v. Bulk Trading SA,* AIR 2002 SC 1432, p. 1437 : (2002) 4 SCC 105, **prospectively overruled** in *Bharat Aluminium Company v. Kaiser Aluminium Technical Services Inc.,* (2012) 9 SCC 552.

'legal meaning'[15] or 'true meaning'[16] of the statutory provision. The task is often not an easy one and the difficulties arise because of various reasons. To mention a few of them: Words in any language are not scientific symbols having any precise or definite meaning, and language is but an imperfect medium to convey one's thought, much less of a large assembly consisting of persons of various shades of opinion. It is impossible even for the most imaginative Legislature to forestall exhaustive situations and circumstances that may emerge after enacting a statute where its application may be called for. The function of the courts is only to expound and not to legislate. The numerous rules of interpretation or construction formulated by courts are expressed differently by different judges and support may be found in these formulations for apparently contradictory propositions.

The problem of interpretation is a problem of meaning of words and their effectiveness as a medium of expression to communicate a particular thought. A word is used to refer to some object or situation in the real world and this object or situation has been assigned a technical name referent. 'Words and phrases are symbols that stimulate mental references to referents.'[17] But words of any language are capable of referring to different referents in different contexts and times.[18] Moreover, there is always the difficulty of borderline cases falling within or outside the connotation of a word. Language, therefore, is likely to be misunderstood. In ordinary conversation or correspondence it is generally open for the parties to obtain clarification if the 'referent' is imperfectly communicated. The position is, however, different in the interpretation of statute law. A statute as enacted cannot be explained by the individual opinions of the legislators, not even by a resolution of the entire Legislature. After the enacting process is over, the Legislature becomes *functus officio* so far as that particular statute is concerned, so that it cannot itself interpret it. The Legislature can no doubt amend or repeal any previous statute or can declare its meaning but all this can be done only by a fresh statute after going through the normal process

---

15. BENNION, Statutory Interpretation, 5th Edition p. 24; *Dinesh Chandra Jamanadas Gandhi v. State of Gujarat,* AIR 1989 SC 1011, p. 1017 : (1989) 1 SCC 420.

16. *Black Clawson International Ltd. v. Papierwerke Waldhof Aschaffenburg AG,* (1975) 1 All ER 810, p. 814 (HL) (LORD REID); *R. v. Hinks,* (2000) 4 All ER 833, p. 839 (HL).

17. G. WILLIAMS, 'Language and the Law', 61 Law Quarterly Review, p. 73. **See further** pp. 94, 95 *infra* for meaning of 'word'.

18. "Each word is but a symbol which may stand for one or a number of objects": *Deputy Chief Controller of Imports and Exports v. K.T. Kosalram,* AIR 1971 SC 1283, p. 1289 : (1970) 3 SCC 82. "Words and phrases take colour and character from the context and the times and speak differently in different contexts and times" *Municipal Corporation, Delhi v. Mohd. Yasin,* (1983) 3 SCC 229, p. 231 : AIR 1983 SC 617.

of law making.[19] There are no doubt references that in good old days it was permissible for the judges to go to the Legislature and enquire what they meant, where the language of an Act was ambiguous or contradictory but happily enough the practice is dead and bygone and there is no hope of its revival.[20] The courts have, therefore, to look essentially to the words of the statute to discern the 'referent' aiding their effort as much as possible by the context. Apart from controversies as to the limits of the context outside the statute, there is a difficulty arising out of 'fringe' meaning of words. There may be certain objects or situations which may without any controversy fall within the content of a word, but there may be many others on or near the borderline in respect of which it may be a matter of doubt and serious argument whether they are within or outside the connotation of the word. It is, therefore, said that words, in addition to a hard central core of meaning have a "penumbra, a dim fringe";[21] and cases falling within or near to this fringe are apt to give rise to a sharp difference of opinion. No one will dispute that the structure in which the High Court of Madhya Pradesh is located is a 'building' but it may be a matter of surprise to find that an open platform having no wall or roof is a building[22] whereas a brick kiln (a pit dug in the ground with bricks by its side) is not

---

19. See Chapter 4, under title 4(c) 'Assistance of later statutes', text and notes 48 to 52, pp. 346; *J.P. Bansal v. State of Rajasthan,* 2003 AIR SCW 1848, p. 1854 : AIR 2003 SC 1405 : (2003) 5 SCC 134; *State of Jharkhand v. Govind Singh,* AIR 2005 SC 204, p. 297.

20. *Spencer v. State (Supreme Court of Indiana),* (1853) 5 Ind. 41 (PERKINS, J.), condensed in REID MACDONALD AND FORDHAM , Cases and Other Materials on Legislation , 2nd Edition, pp. 978, 980, 981. **See further** DIAS Jurisprudence, 2nd Edition, p. 110, footnote 2. A Legislature cannot be asked to sit to resolve the difficulties: *Girdharilal and Sons v. Balbirnath Mathur,* (1986) 2 SCC 237, p. 242 : AIR 1986 SC 1099. After Parliament has enacted the Act "only the Court may say what Parliament meant to say… None-else": *Sanjeev Coke Manufacturing Company v. Bharat Coking Coal Ltd.,* AIR 1983 SC 239 : (1983) 1 SCC 147; *Doypack Systems Pvt. Ltd. v. Union of India,* AIR 1988 SC 782, p. 796 : (1988) 2 SCC 299; *P.V. Narsimha Rao v. State,* JT 1998 (3) SC 318, p. 373 : AIR 1998 SC 2120 : 1998 (4) SCC 626; *Union of India v. Elphinstone Spinning & Weaving Co. Ltd.,* JT 2001 (1) SC 536, p. 583 : AIR 2001 SC 724, p. 734 : (2001) 4 SCC 139. But this does not mean that Parliament cannot subject to constitutional restrictions enact statute specific or general rules of interpretation. The Central General Clauses Act and the corresponding State Acts contain general rules of interpretation and their validity has never been in doubt. **See further** on this point NICHOLAS QUINN ROSENKRANZ, Federal Rules of Interpretation, (2002) 115 Harvard Law Review, 2086.

21. *Commissioner v. Ickelheimar,* 132 F. (2d) 660, p. 662: **referred** in 60 Harvard Law Review 370, p. 376. For full quotation **see** text and note 87, p. 22.

22. *State of Bombay v. Venkat Rao Krishna Rao, Gujar,* AIR 1966 SC 991 : 1963 (1) SCR 428. **See further** *International Airport Authority Employees Union v. International Airports Authority of India,* AIR 2001 SC 276 : (2001) 1 SCC 205 (Parking areas of the airports held to be 'building').

a building.[23] Again, the assumption that a massive building like one hous-ing the High Court is a 'structure' may itself be debated. Indeed, it was seriously though unsuccessfully argued in the House of Lords that a large substantial permanent two storey building was not a structure.[24] Further, a question may arise which may be answered differently in different contexts whether 'building' includes land over which the superstructure stands or whether it is confined to the superstructure.[25] To take another example the question, whether a railway workman who was engaged in cleaning and oiling a permanent way, was engaged in repairing it, was answered in the negative by a margin of three to two in the House of Lords.[26] The core of such problems is indicated by LORD JOWITT, L.C. in the following words: "The question is essentially one of degree and that it is impossible to fix any definite point at which 'maintenance' ends and 'repair' begins".[27] To the same effect are the words of LORD CRANWORTH, L.C.:

---

23. *State of Bihar v. S.K. Roy*, AIR 1966 SC 1995 : 1966 Supp SCR 259.

24. *Almond v. Birmingham Royal Institution for the Blind*, (1967) 2 All ER 317 (HL) For meaning of 'structure' **see** *Indian City Properties Ltd. v. Municipal Commissioner of Greater Bombay,* (2005) 6 SCC 417, p. 422 (para 19) : AIR 2005 SC 3802. See *Purushottam Das Bangur & Ors. v. Dayanand Gupta*, (2012) 10 SCC 409, pp. 417- 418, for a discussion on what would constitute a "permanent structure" under section 108(p) of the Transfer of Property Act, 1882.

25. *Corporation of the City of Victoria v. Bishop of Vancouver Island*, (1921) 2 AC 384 (PC) : AIR 1921 PC 240; *D.G. Ghouse & Co. v. State of Kerala*, AIR 1980 SC 271, p. 277 : (1980) 2 SCC 410. **Contrast**: *CIT, Punjab v. Alps Theatre*, AIR 1967 SC 1437 : (1967) 3 SCR 181. For meaning of 'building' and 'structure' in the context of property tax **see** *Municipal Corporation of Greater Bombay v. Indian Oil Corporation*, AIR 1991 SC 686 : 1991 Supp (2) SCC 18 (Petroleum storage tanks held to be structures). In the context of depreciation allowable in respect of a building for income-tax purposes; it has been held that 'building' will include roads and drains laid within factory premises: *CIT v. Gwalior Rayon Silk Manufacturing Co. Ltd.*, AIR 1992 SC 1782 : (1992) 3 SCC 326 : (1992) 196 ITR 149. Building may include a roofless structure: *Ashok Kapil v. Sona Ullah*, 1996 (7) Scale 339, p. 342: 1996 (6) SCC 342. For meaning of 'building' **see further** *B. Kandaswamy v. Gomathi Ammal*, AIR 2001 SC 1931, p. 1937 : (2001) 4 SCC 394; *Jai Narain Parasrampuria v. Pushpa Devi Saraf,* (2006) 7 SCC 756, paras 70 and 72 : (2006) 8 Scale 477.

26. *London and North Eastern Rly. Co. v. Berriman*, (1945) 1 All ER 255 (HL).

27. *Ibid*, p. 258 (HL); (LORD JOWITT, L.C.). But 'maintenance' may mean more than 'servicing' and may include 'repair': *Hamilton v. National Coal Board*, (1960) 1 All ER 76 (HL) and similarly 'repair' may include 'maintenance': *State of U.P. v. Devidayal Singh,* AIR 2000 SC 961, pp. 965, 966 : (2000) 3 SCC 5. For difference between 'preservation' or 'repair' and 'restoration', **see** *Robins v. Secretary of State for the Environment*, (1989) 1 All ER 878 (HL); *Ballimal Naval Kishore v. Commissioner of Income Tax*, AIR 1997 SC 851, p. 852 : 1997 (2) SCC 296. *Raichurmathan Prabhakar v. Rawatmal Dugar*, (2004) 4 SCC 766, p. 778 : AIR 2004 SC 3976 (The expression 'addition, improvement or alteration' will include demolition and reconstruction); *Commissioner of Income Tax v. Sarvana Spg. Mills (P)*

[Footnote No. 27 Contd.]

"There is no possibility of mistaking midnight for noon; but at what precise moment twilight becomes darkness is hard to determine."[28] Faced with such problems the courts although conscious of a dividing line, do not attempt to draw it for reasons of practical impossibility and decide the particular case in hand as falling within or outside the purview of the relevant words of the statute, after laying down a working line or more appropriately some general working principles.[29] But in doing so the courts should avoid laying down so-called tests to be applied in every case for the danger in prescribing and designating tests is that it may divert attention from the language used in the statutory provision and encourage an approach not intended by the Legislature.[30]

Legislation in a modern State is actuated with some policy to curb some public evil or to effectuate some public benefit.[31] The legislation is

---

[Footnote No. 27 Contd.]

Ltd., (2007) 7 SCC 298 (meaning of 'current repairs' under section 31(i) of the Income-tax Act, 1961. It will not cover 'replacement' or bringing a new asset into existence). **See further** *K. Ramnathan v. State of Tamil Nadu*, (1985) 2 SCC 116, p. 131 : AIR 1985 SC 660; where in the same tune A.P. SEN, J. said: "The question essentially is one of degree and it is impossible to fix any definite point where 'regulation' ends and 'prohibition' begins." But in the same case it was held that 'regulation' may in some context include 'Prohibition'. **See also** *Jiyajeerao Cotton Mills Ltd. v. The Madhya Pradesh Electricity Board*, AIR 1989 SC 788, p. 807 : 1989 Supp (2) SCC 52. (The word 'regulation' has different shades of meaning depending on the context). For meaning of 'regulation' **see further** pages 1088 to 1091, *infra*.

28. *Jane Straford Boyse v. John T. Rossborough*, (1857) 6 HLC 2, p. 45 : 10 ER 1192 (HL).

29. *State of Bombay v. Hospital Mazdoor Sabha*, AIR 1960 SC 610, pp. 615, 616 : 1960 (2) SCR 866 (Industry); *Inder Lal v. Lal Singh*, AIR 1962 SC 1156, pp. 1159, 1160 : 1962 Supp (3) SCR 117 (Public Character); *Ranjit D. Udeshi v. State of Maharashtra*, AIR 1965 SC 881, pp. 886 (para 9), 887 (para 16) : 1965 (1) SCR 65 (Obscene); *J & F Stone Lighting and Radio Ltd. v. Haygarth*, (1966) 3 All ER 539, pp. 546, 550 (HL). Though in many cases it may be difficult to draw a line of demarcation, it is easy to discern on which side of the borderline a particular case falls : *Collector of Central Excise v. Ballarpur Industries Ltd.*, AIR 1990 SC 196, p. 201 : (1989) 4 SCC 566 (Goods used as raw-material). **See** the following observations of SIR WILFRID GREENE, M.R. in *IRC v. British Salmson AE Ltd.*, (1938) 3 All ER 283, p. 289 (CA) (Capital or revenue): "There have been many cases which fall upon the borderline. Indeed, in many cases it is almost true to say that the spin of a coin would decide the matter almost as satisfactorily as would an attempt to find reasons." **Referring** to these observations LORD UPJOHN remarked: "Somewhat cynical but true" : *Regent Oil Co. Ltd. v. Strick*, (1965) 3 All ER 174, p. 199 (HL). The dividing line or the frontier zone may shift with the change of time : *Commissioner of Customs & Excise v. Beecham Foods Ltd.*, (1972) 1 All ER 498, p. 506 (HL).

30. *Muray v. Foyle Meats Ltd.*, (1999) 3 All ER 769, p. 773 (HL).

31. "Legislation has an aim, it seeks to obviate some mischief, to supply an inadequacy, to effect a change of policy, to formulate a plan of government. That aim, that

[Footnote No. 31 Contd.]

primarily directed to the problems before the Legislature based on infor-mation derived from past and present experience. It may also be designed by use of general words to cover similar problems arising in future.[32] But from the very nature of things, it is impossible to anticipate fully the var-ied situations arising in future in which the application of the legislation in hand may be called for, and, words chosen to communicate such indefinite 'referents' are bound to be, in many cases lacking in clarity and precision and thus giving rise to controversial questions of construction.[33] This anal-ysis later met the approval of the Supreme Court.[34]

In all real controversies of construction if it were open to consult the Legislature as to its intention, the answer of most of the legislators in all probability will be: 'such a problem never occurred to us, solve it as best

[Footnote No. 31 Contd.]

policy is not drawn, like nitrogen, out of the air, it is evidenced in the language of the statute, as read in the light of other external manifestations of purpose." [FRANKFURTER, Some Reflections on the Reading of Statutes (ESSAYS' on *Juris-prudence from the Columbia Law Review*) quoted by JAGANNATHA RAO J. in *Unit-ed Bank of India, Calcutta v. Abhijit Tea Co. Pvt. Ltd.*, AIR 2000 SC 2957, p. 2962 : (2000) 7 SCC 357]. **See further** the following observations of LORD BINGHAM in *R (on the application of Quintavalle) v. Secretary of State for Health*, (2003) 2 All ER 113, p. 118 (HL): "Every statute other than a pure consolidating statute is, after all, enacted to make some change, or address some problem, or remove some blemish or effect some improvement in the national life. The court's task, within the per-missible bounds of interpretation, is to give effect to Parliament's purpose. So the controversial provisions should be read in the context of the statute as a whole and the statute as a whole should be read in the historical context of the situation which led to its enactment."

32. "Those who seek to replace the common law by a statutory Code always have to choose between certainty and flexibility. Are they or are they not to include in the Code some provision enabling the provisions of the Code to be extended to meet new situation?": *American Cyamid Co. v. Upjohn Co.*, (1970) 3 All ER 785, p. 789 (HL) (LORD REID).

33. Statutes designed to curb tax evasion may be cited as examples. For criticism of the generality usually found in these statutes, **see** *Commissioner of Customs & Excise v. Top Ten Promotions Ltd.*, (1969) 3 All ER 39, pp. 93, 95 (HL).

"No draftsman can envisage all the circumstances which may possibly arise. From time to time, therefore, events occur which are within the plain words of the statute yet are outside its evident purpose or *vice versa*. This is the battle ground on which are fought the battles between the literal constructionists and the purposive constructionists." [LORD MILLETT, Construing Statutes (1999) 20 Statute Law Re-view 107, p. 109].

34. *Union of India v. Elphinstone Spinning and Weaving Co. Ltd.*, JT 2001 (1) SC 536, p. 557 : AIR 2001 SC 724, p. 736 (para 10) : (2001) 4 SCC 139 : (2001) 105 Comp Cases 309 (Constitution Bench); *District Mining Officer v. Tata Iron and Steel Co.*, AIR 2001 SC 3134, p. 3152 : (2001) 7 SCC 358; *Ameer Trading Corporation Ltd. v. Shapoorji Data Processing Ltd.*, AIR 2004 SC 355, p. 360 : (2004) 1 SCC 702; *Reema Agarwal v. Anupam*, (2004) 3 SCC 199, pp. 211, 212 : AIR 2004 SC 1418; *National Insurance Co. Ltd. v. Laxmi Narain Dhut*, (2007) 3 SCC 700, p. 718 : AIR 2007 SC 1563.

as you can, consistent with the words used, and the purpose indicated by as in the statute'.[35] The legislative intent in such cases is a fiction representing the attitude of judges in arriving at a solution by striking a balance between the letter and spirit of the statute without acknowledging that they have in any way supplemented the statute.[36] That the duty of judges is to expound and not to legislate is a fundamental rule, but this is now and has ever been merely an 'aspiration'. There is a marginal area in which the courts 'mould or creatively interpret legislation' and they are thus 'finishers, refiners and polishers of legislation which comes to them in a state requiring varying degrees of further processing'.[37] In deciding that 'repair' does not include cleaning and oiling;[38] that there is notional extension of employment in the phrase 'accident arising out of and in the course of employment;[39] that the word 'accident' in the same phrase includes murder;[40]

---

35. In the words of ROSCOE POUND: 'Where the legislature has had an intent and has sought to express it there is seldom a question of interpretation. The difficulties arise in the myriad cases in respect to which the law-maker had no intention because he had never thought of them. Indeed perhaps he could never have thought of them.' ROSCOE POUND, The Spirit of the Common Law (Beacon Paperback) p. 174. In 'An Introduction to the Philosophy of Law' (Yale Paper bound) p. 50, ROSCOE POUND expressed his agreement and quoted similar views of GRAY: 'The fact is that the difficulties of so-called interpretation arise when the Legislature has had no meaning at all; when the question which is raised on the statute never occurred to it; when what the judges have to do is not to determine what the Legislature did mean on a point which was present to its mind, but to guess what it would have intended on a point not present in its mind, if the point had been present.' GRAY, The Nature and Sources of the Law, 2nd Edition, p. 171. The 'guess' 'must be informed by the wording of the Act and arrived at in accordance with the recognised guides to legislative intention.' BENNION, Statutory Interpretation, 5th edition, p. 481.

36. Said to be 'the proper criteria' in *Union of India v. Elphinstone Spinning and Weaving Co. Ltd., supra,* p. 563 (JT) : p. 739 (AIR).

37. *Corocraft Ltd. v. Pan American Airways Inc.*, (1968) 3 WLR 714, p. 732 : (1970) 33 Modern Law Review 197; *State of Haryana v. Sampuran Singh*, AIR 1975 SC 1952, p. 1957 : (1975) 2 SCC 810; *Carew and Company Ltd. v. Union of India*, AIR 1975 SC 2260, p. 2274 : (1975) 2 SCC 791 : (1976) 1 SCR 626; *Union of India v. Elphinstone Spinning and Weaving Co. Ltd. supra,* p. 563 (JT) : p. 739 (AIR). The Judicial art of interpretation and appraisal is imbued with creativity and realism. (*D.R. Venkatachalam v. Dy. Transport Commissioner*, AIR 1977 SC 842, p. 857 : 1977 (2) SCC 273.) **See further** *Bhatia International v. Bulk Tradings S.A.*, AIR 2002 SC 1432, pp. 1437, 1438 : (2002) 4 SCC 105, **prospectively overruled** in *Bharat Aluminium Company v. Kaiser Aluminium Technical Services Inc.*, (2012) 9 SCC 552. 'Since interpretation always implies a degree of discretion and choice, hence of creativity, a degree which is especially high in certain areas such as constitutional adjudication dealing with social and diffuse rights.' MAURO CAPPELLETTI, The Judicial Process in Comparative Perspective, p. 54.

38. *London & North Eastern Rly. Co. v. Berriman*, (1946) 1 All ER 255 (HL).

39. *BEST Undertaking v. Agnes (Mrs.)*, AIR 1964 SC 193 : 1964 (3) SCR 930.

40. *Nisbet v. Rayne and Burn*, (1910) 2 KB 689 (CA); *Board of Management of Trim Joint District School v. Kelly*, (1914) AC 667 (HL). For meaning of 'accident' in

[Footnote No. 40 Contd.]

that telephone is 'telegraph' within the meaning of that word in Acts of 1863 and 1869 when telephone was not invented,[41] and in all alike cases of which examples can be multiplied, the courts have in effect added a definition clause either to include or exclude something which was not *prima facie* included or excluded in the words used by the Legislature. There are indeed opinions where the fiction of intention is lifted and judges are seen acknowledging that they are filling in the gaps,[42] or that they have, by construction 'added'[43] certain words not contained in the enactment, or that

---

[Footnote No. 40 Contd.]

the same context **see further** *Chief Adjudication Officer v. Faulds,* (2000) 2 All ER 961, pp. 964-69, 977-79 (HL). The Supreme Court has also held that, in the phrase 'accident arising out of the use of motor vehicle' as used in section 163A of the Motor Vehicles Act, 1988 the word 'accident' will include murder: *Rita Devi v. New India Assurance Co. Ltd.,* AIR 2000 SC 1930 : (2000) 5 SCC 113 : (2000) 1 LLJ 1656.

41. *Attorney-General v. Edison Telephone Co.*, (1880) 6 QBD 244, **referred** in *Senior Electric Inspector v. Laxminarayan Chopra*, AIR 1962 SC 159 : 1962 (3) SCR 146.

42. "We sit here to find out the intention of Parliament and of Ministers and carry it out, and we do this better by filling in the gaps and making sense of the enactment than by opening it up to destructive analysis." (PER DENNING, LJ in *Magor and St. Mellons Rural District Council v. Newport Corporation*, (1950) 1 All ER 1226, p. 1236). These observations were however, **disapproved** in appeal by the House of Lords. **See** (1951) 1 All ER 839 (HL). But they have been **approved** by the Supreme Court: *Bangalore Water Supply v. A. Rajappa*, AIR 1978 SC 548, pp. 522, 561 : (1978) 2 SCC 213. **See further** Chapter 2, text and notes 40 to 55, pp. 77 to 79.

LORD DUE PARCQ was also of the view that in some cases it becomes necessary for courts "to fill in such gaps as Parliament may choose to leave in its enactments": *Cutler v. Wandsworth Stadium Ltd.*, (1949) 1 All ER 544, p. 550 (HL).

"The necessary generality in the wordings of many statutes, and ineptness of drafting in others frequently compels the court, as best as they can, to fill in the gaps, an activity which no matter how one may label it, is in part legislative. Thus the courts in their way, as administrators in their way perform the task of supplementing statutes. In the case of courts we call it 'interpretation' or 'filling in the gaps'; in the case of administrators we call it 'delegation' or authority to supply the details." Per JUDGE FRANK in *Guiseppi v. Walling*, 144F (2d) 608, pp. 620, 622 (CCA 2d, 1944), **referred** in 60 Harvard Law Review 370, p. 372. **See further** *Directorate of Enforcement v. Deepak Mahajan*, JT 1994 (1) SC 281, p. 301 : AIR 1994 SC 1775, p. 1785 : (1994) 3 SCC 440 : (1994) 70 ELT 12.

"Judges do and must legislate, but they do so only interstitially; they are confined from molar to molecular motion": HOLMES, J. in *Southern Pacific Co. v. Jensen,* (1916) 244 US 205, p. 221.

'Obscurity of statute—may leave the law unsettled, and cast a duty upon courts to declare it retrospectively in the exercise of a power frankly legislative in function. They (Judges) have the right to legislate within gaps, but often there are no gaps.' CARDOZO, The Nature of the Judicial Process, pp. 128, 129.

See further *United Bank of India, Calcutta v. Abhijit Tea Co. Pvt. Ltd.,* AIR 2000 SC 2957, p. 2963 : (2000) 7 SCC 357.

43. 'Long catena of decisions (under section 181, Indian Limitation Act, 1908) may well be said to have, as it were, added the words 'under the Code' in the first column of that Article': *Sha Mulchand and Co. Ltd. v. Jawaher Mills Ltd.*, AIR 1953

[Footnote No. 43 Contd.]

the conclusion reached by them is as if a like definition clause existed in the statute itself.[44] Some judges proclaim that they perform creative functions even in interpretation.[45] But such an attitude may lead less disciplined amongst them to conclusions which have a strong legislative flavour.[46] So it is wise to adhere to the traditional expression and to call every process of construction a search for 'intention' express or implied in the statute, since the metaphor 'by setting a goal to which the judge aspires'[47]

[Footnote No. 43 Contd.]
SC 98, p. 104; *Bombay Gas Co. Ltd. v. Gopal Bhiva*, AIR 1964 SC 752, p. 758 : (1964) 3 SCR 709 : (1963) 2 LLJ 608; *Prativa Bose (Smt.) v. Rupendra Deb*, AIR 1965 SC 540, p. 543 : 1964 (4) SCR 69. Same view has been taken of the corresponding section 137 in the Limitation Act 1963: *Ajaib Singh v. Sirhind Co-operative Marketing-cum-Processing Service Society Ltd.*, AIR 1999 SC 1351, pp. 1353-54 : (1999) 6 SCC 82 : (1999) 1 LLJ 1260. Interpreting section 304A of the Indian Penal Code,1860 it was held that though the word 'gross' does not occur there 'the expression 'rash or negligent act' as occurring in section 304A has to be read as qualified by the word 'grossly':' *Jacob Mathew v. State of Punjab,* (2005) 6 SCC 1, p. 33 (para 48-6).

44. After reaching the conclusion that 'property' in the Hindu Women's Right to Property Act, 1937, meant property other than agricultural lands for Governor's provinces and all property for Chief Commissioner's Provinces, VARADACHARIAR, J. observed: "If the enactment had contained a definition clause stating that 'property' in the Act meant all property in respect of which the Legislature was competent to legislate, the result would have been the same." (*Umayal Achi v. Laksmi Achi*, AIR 1945 FC 25, p. 31 : 7 FCR 1).

45. *Captain Ramesh Chandra Kaushal v. Veena Kaushal*, AIR 1978 SC 1807, p. 1811 : (1978) 4 SCC 70 : 1979 Cri LJ 3.

46. *CIT v. B.N. Bhattacharjee*, AIR 1979 SC 1725, p. 1735 : (1979) 4 SCC 121 : (1979) 118 ITR 461. (The word 'assessee' in section 245M(7) of the Income-tax Act, 1961 was construed to mean all parties affected by assessment including the Department.) **See further** text and notes 92-96 and 1-7, pp. 23 to 26 *infra*.

47. ARCHIBOLD COX, Judge Learned Hand and the Interpretation,of Statutes, 60 Harvard Law Review 370, p. 372. PROF. REED DICKERSON says that the concept of legislative intent is indispensable for the postulation of some actual, though not directly knowable, legislative intent underlines the very idea of a legislative process; and even if there were no actual legislative intent, judicial deference to the constitutional separation of powers would require the courts to act as if there were, because the concept is necessary to put courts in an appropriately deferential frame of mind. (REED DICKERSON, The Interpretation and Application of Statutes, pp. 78-79). According to PROF. CROSS the expression 'Intention of Parliament' is not so much a description as a linguistic convenience (CROSS, Statutory Interpretation, 3rd Edition, p. 28). BENNION says that 'legislative intention is not a myth or fiction, but a reality founded in the very nature of legislation' (BENNION, 'Statutory Interpretation, 5th Edition, p. 472). In disagreeing with the objection that collective bodies of persons, such as legislatures do not possess a mind and are, therefore, not capable of having intentions and thus the existence of legislative intention is a myth which cannot play a role in judicial interpretation, STEFAN VOGENAUER argues: 'This radical objection is surprising. After all, lawyers, judges and legal scholars alike have been referring to the 'intention of Parliament' for centuries in all legal systems. These statements are so well-established in the relevant linguistic

[Footnote No. 47 Contd.]

has a tendency while present in his mind to reduce judicial law making to its necessary minimum.[48]

The intention of the Legislature thus assimilates two aspects: In one aspect it carries the concept of 'meaning', *i.e.,* what the words mean and in another aspect, it conveys the concept of 'purpose and object' or the 'reason and spirit' pervading through the statute. The process of construction, therefore, combines both literal and purposive approaches. In other words the legislative intention, *i.e.*, the true or legal meaning of an enactment is derived by considering the meaning of the words used in the enactment in the light of any discernible purpose or object which comprehends the mis-

---

[Footnote No. 47 Contd.]

community that we may well assume a linguistic convention admitting a conceptual link between 'intention' and 'legislation':' 'What is the proper role of Legislative Intention in Judicial Interpretation' (1997) 18 Statute Law Review 235. According to BRIAN BIX: 'The term (legislative intent) might best be seen not as naming a thing, but as a shorthand for the process (and the result) of interpretation. Legislative intent in England and America atleast appears to stand for whatever aspect of legislative texts or the legislative record is used to clarify or settle the meaning and application of legislation': 'Questions in Legal Interpretation', 'Law and Interpretation' (Essays in Legal Philosophy) edited by ANDREI MARMOR, p. 146. LORD MILLETT uses the expression "the legislative intent" or "the intention of the legislation" in preference to the expression "the intention of the legislature": 'Construing Statutes' (1999) 20 Statute Law Review 107, p. 110.

48. There is a school of thought that the traditional methodology of interpreting a statute with reference to 'intention of the Legislature' should now, be replaced by a new methodology of 'attribution of purpose'. The following extract from an article in (1970) 33 Modern Law Review, pp. 199, 200 by HARRY BLOOM, explains the new idea: 'In time however, somebody will have to tackle the basic question how long can we sustain the fiction that when the Legislature prescribes for a problem, it provides a complete set of answers; and that the court, when confronted with a difficult statute merely uses the techniques of construction to wring an innate meaning out of the words. PROFESSOR HART AND SACHS of Harvard University have expressed ideas on this which seem to be highly attractive. They argue that interpretation should not be regarded as a search for the purpose of the Legislature or even for the purpose of the statute, but as one of 'attribution of purpose'. The court, by asking 'what purpose do we attribute to the statute?' allows an inquiry into how best the statute can be interpreted and applied, or related to other legislation. What this means is explained by PROFESSOR ROBERT E. KEETON, also of Harvard, in the book 'Venturing to do justice': 'I do not understand HART AND SACKS to imply that the purpose to be attributed to the statute need be one that was or even could have been consciously formulated at the time the statute was enacted. I understand them to choose this formulation for the very reason that they wish to free the court from the handicaps of dealing with the fiction that the statute contains within it an answer to every question that might arise in its application'.' This theory known as the 'Legal Process Theory' is discussed by WILLIAM N. ESKRIDGE, JR., in Chapter V of 'Dynamic Statutory Interpretation' (First Indian Reprint, 2000) and is said to be 'the first systematically developed American theory of Dynamic Statutory Interpretation' (p. 143).

chief and its remedy to which the enactment is directed.[49] This formulation later received the approval of the Supreme Court and was called the 'cardinal principle of construction'.[50] In both Constitutional and statutory interpretation, the Court is supposed to exercise discretion in determining the proper relationship between the subjective and objective purposes of the law and help the law achieve its purpose.[51]

In all ordinary cases and primarily the language employed is the determinative factor of legislative intention.[52] "The first and primary rule of construction", said GAJENDRAGADKAR, J. "is that the intention of the

---

49. **See** *State of Himachal Pradesh v. Kailash Chand Mahajan*, AIR 1992 SC 1277, p. 1300 : 1992 Supp (2) SCC 351 : 1992 Lab IC 1371. (The purpose or object of an enactment relates to the mischief to which the enactment is directed and its remedy, legislative intention relates to the legal meaning of the enactment).
50. *Union of India v. Elphinstone Spinning and Weaving Co. Ltd.*, JT 2001 (1) SC 536, p. 563 : AIR 2001 SC 724, p. 740 : (2001) 4 SCC 139 (Constitution Bench); *District Mining Officer v. Tata Iron and Steel Co.*, AIR 2001 SC 3134, p. 3152 : (2001) 7 SCC 358; *Ameer Trading Corporation Ltd. v. Shapoorj Data Processing Ltd.*, AIR 2004 SC 355, p. 360 : (2004) 1 SCC 702; *Ruma Aggarwal v. Anupam*, (2004) 3 SCC 199, pp. 211, 212 : AIR 2004 SC 1418; *National Insurance Co. Ltd. v. Laxmi Narain Dhut,* (2007) 3 SCC 700, p. 718 : AIR 2007 SC 1563; **See further** *Competition Commission of India v. Steel Authority of India Limited*, (2010) 10 SCC 744 para 58 : (2010) 10 JT 26.
51. *Badshah v. Urmila Badshah Godse*, (2014) 1 SCC 188 pp. 195 - 198. In this case, the Supreme Court has held that the Legislature, while enacting section 125 of the CrPC, always intended to give the relief of maintenance to a woman who became the 'wife' of a person under circumstances where he had suppressed the factum of his subsisting first marriage from her, even though she may not be his 'legally wedded wife'.
52. *New Piece Goods Bazar Co. Ltd. v. CIT, Bombay*, AIR 1950 SC 165, p 168 : 1950 SCR 553; *Ramkrishan v. State of Delhi*, AIR 1956 SC 476, p. 478 : 1956 SCR 182; *Kanailal Sur v. Paramnidhi Sadhukhan*, AIR 1957 SC 907, p. 910 : 1958 SCR 360; *Ramkrishna Ram Nath v. Janpad Sabha*, AIR 1962 SC 1073, p. 1079 : 1962 Supp (3) SCR 70; *Controller of Estate Duty v. Kantilal Tikamlal*, AIR 1976 SC 1935, p. 1939 : 1977 SCC (Tax) 90. ("Law to a large extent, lives in the language even if it expands with the spirit of the statute"); *Union of India v. Sankalchand Himmatlal Sheth*, AIR 1977 SC 2328, p. 2337 : (1977) 4 SCC 193; *Chief Justice of Andhra Pradesh v. LVA Dikshitulu*, AIR 1979 SC 193, p. 205 : (1979) 2 SCC 340; *Om Prakash Gupta v. Digvijendrapal Gupta*, AIR 1982 SC 1230, p. 1233 : (1982) 2 SCC 61; *Babaji Kondaji Garod v. Nasik Merchants Co-operative Bank Ltd.*, (1984) 2 SCC 50, p. 59 : AIR 1984 SC 192; *Doypack Systems Pvt. Ltd. v. Union of India*, AIR 1988 SC 782, p. 801 : 1988 (2) SCC 299; *Member Secretary, Andhra Pradesh State Board for Prevention and Control of Water Pollution v. Andhra Pradesh Rayons Ltd.*, AIR 1989 SC 611, p. 615 : 1989 (1) SCC 44; *Keshavji Ravji and Co. v. Commissioner of Income Tax*, AIR 1991 SC 1806, p. 1812 : (1990) 2 SCC 231; *Bola v. B.D. Sardana*, AIR 1997 SC 3127, pp. 3208, 3209 : (1997) 8 SCC 522; *Unique Butyle Tube Industries (P.) Ltd. v. U.P. Financial Corporation*, (2003) 2 SCC 455, p. 462. **See further** *Nasiruddin v. Sita Ram Agarwal*, (2003) 2 SCC 577, p. 589 : AIR 2003 SC 1543.

Legislature must be found in the words used by the Legislature itself."[53] The question is not what may be supposed to have been intended but what has been said.[54] "I do not care what their intention was," said Mr. JUSTICE HOLMES in a letter: "I only want to know what the words mean."[55] LORD BROUGHAM has more emphatically stated the importance of the text of the statute in the following words: "If the Legislature did intend that which it has not expressed clearly; much more, if the Legislature intended something very different; if the Legislature intended pretty nearly the opposite of what is said, it is not for judges to invent something which they do not meet within the words of the text (aiding their construction of the text always, of course, by the context)."[56] These and like opinions lay stress on one aspect of intention, *i.e.*, what the words mean; and undoubtedly to the extent the 'referent' is clearly indicated and the words have a 'plain' meaning, the courts are not to busy themselves with 'supposed intention'[57] or with 'the policy underlying the statute'.[58]

However, words used by the Legislature do not always bear a plain meaning. Moreover, judges quite often differ on the issue whether certain words are plain and even when there is an agreement that the words are plain, difference of opinion may result on the question as to what the plain

---

53. *Kannailal Sur v. Paramnidhi Sadhukhan, supra*; *Padmasundara Rao v. State of T.N.*, AIR 2002 SC 1334, p. 1340 : (2002) 3 SCC 533; *Unique Butyle Tube Industries (P.) Ltd. v. U.P. Financial Corporation, supra.* **See further** *Gem Granites v. Commissioner of Income tax*, (2005) 1 SCC 289, p. 296 (What one may believe or think to be the intention of Parliament cannot prevail if the language of the statute does not support that view).

54. *Brophy v. AG of Manitoba*, (1895) AC 202, p. 216 (PC), **referred** to in *Henrietta Muir Edwards v. AG of Canada*, AIR 1930 PC 120, p. 126; *Wazirchand Mahajan v. Union of India*, AIR 1967 SC 990, p. 992 : 1967 (1) SCR 303; *Padmasundara Rao v. State of T.N. supra; Unique Butyle Tube Industries (P.) Ltd. v. U.P. Financial Corporation, supra.* **See further** *Black Clawson International Ltd. v. Papier-Werke Waldh of Aschaffanburg*, (1975) 1 All ER 810, p. 814 (HL) (LORD REID); *Docker's Labour Club v. Race Relations Board*, (1974) 3 All ER 592, p. 600 (HL) (LORD SIMON); *Reference under section 48A of the Criminal Appeal (Northern Ireland) Act, 1968*, (1976) 2 All ER 937, p. 957 (HL).

55. REID MACDONALD AND FORDHAM, 'Cases and other Materials on Legislation' by, 2nd Edition, p. 1005. In *Northern Securities Co. v. United States*, 193 US 197, p. 400 JUSTICE HOLMES said: "Their (Judges) function is merely academic to begin with—to read English intelligently".

56. *Robert Wigram Crawford v. Richard Spooner*, 4 MIA 179, p. 187 (PC).

57. *Pakala Narayanswami v. Emperor*, AIR 1939 PC 47, p. 51 : 66 IA 66; *Bola v. B.D. Sardana*, AIR 1997 SC 3127, pp. 3208, 3209 : (1997) 8 SCC 522.

58. *S. Gurmej Singh v. Sardar Pratap Singh Kairon*, AIR 1960 SC 122, p. 128 : 1960 (1) SCR 909; *Bola v. Sardana, supra.*

meaning is.[59] In case of doubt, therefore, it is always safe to have an eye on the object and purpose of the statute, or reason and spirit behind it.[60] "I say that we must look to what the purpose is", was said by LORD CAIRNS:[61] and it was observed by SIR JOHN NICHOLL that 'the key to the opening of every law is the reason and the spirit of the law'.[62] This aspect of 'purpose' is the very foundation of the rule in *Heydon's case* reported by LORD COKE as far back as 1584.[63] Statutes "should be construed not as theorems of Euclid", said JUDGE LEARNED HAND, "but with some imagination of the purposes which lie behind them."[64] "Each word, phrase or

---

59. See text and notes 64 to 68 page 62, **see further** *Newbury District Council v. Secretary of State for the Environment*, (1980) 1 All ER 731 : 1981 AC : (1980) 2 WLR 379 (HL). In this case all the members of the Divisional Court (LORD WIDGERY, C.J. and DAVIES AND GOFF, JJ.), and all the members of the Court of Appeal (LORD DENNING, MR, LAWTON AND BROWNE, L. JJ.) agreed that the use of hangars by the Home Office for storing fire pumps or synthetic rubber was not use as a "repository". LORD DENNING said that no one conversant with English language would dream of calling the hangars a "repository" and LAWTON, LJ observed that no literate person would say that the use of the hangars by the Home Office was use as a "repository". The House of Lords, however, held that to describe the above use of hangars as "repository" was a perfectly correct use of English language.

60. See *Utkal Contractors and Joinery Pvt. Ltd. v. State of Orissa*, (1987) 3 SCC 279, p. 288 : AIR 1987 SC 1454 ("A statute is best understood if we know the reason for it"; per CHINAPPA REDDY, J.); *Oriental Insurance Co. Ltd. v. Hansrajbhai v. Kodala,* AIR 2001 SC 1832, p. 1839 : (2001) 5 SCC 175 : (2001) 105 Comp Case 743.

61. *Arthur Hill v. East and West India Dock Co.*, (1884) 9 AC 448, p. 455 (HL).

62. *Brett v. Brett*, (1826) 3 Add 210 : 162 ER 456, p. 458; **referred** to in *Attorney-General v. HRH Prince Ernest Augustus of Hanover*, (1957) 1 All ER 49, p. 57 (HL). In *Charan Lal Sahu v. Union of India*, AIR 1990 SC 1480, p. 1536 : (1990) 1 SCC 613, the majority inferred an obligation on the part of the Central Government to give interim relief to Bhopal gas victims being the major inarticulate premise, and inconsonance with the 'spirit' of the Bhopal Gas Leak Disaster (Processing of Claims) Act, 1985. In *Sarla Mudgal (Smt.) v. Union of India*, AIR 1995 SC 1531, pp. 1536 (para 18), 1537 (para 22) : (1995) 3 SCC 635 it was held that a second marriage after conversion to Islam of a Hindu who was already married though not 'strictly a void marriage under' the Hindu Marriage Act, 1955 was yet void being 'against the spirit of the statute'. In *All India judges' Association v. Union of India*, AIR 1993 SC 2493, p. 2503 : 1993 (4) SCC 288, the Supreme Court found a role for the judiciary from 'the spirit of the Constitution' for formulating service conditions of judicial officers.

63. See Chapter 2, title 3(b) 'Rule in *Heydon's* case' p. 137, *infra*.

64. *Lehigh Valley Coal Co. v. Yensavage*, 218 Fed 547, pp. 552, 553 : 235 US 705 (1915); **referred** to in 60 Harvard Law Review 370, pp. 377, 378; *Union of India v. Filip Tiago De Gama of Vedem Vasco De Gama*, AIR 1990 SC 981, p. 985 : 1990 (1) SCC 277. **See further** *V.O. Tractoroexport, Mascow v. Tarapore & Co.*, AIR 1971 SC 1, p. 20 : (1969) 3 SCC 562; *Atma Ram Mittal v. Ishwar Singh Punia*, AIR 1988 SC 2031, p. 2034 : 1988 (4) SCC 284; *Anwar Hasan Khan v. Mohammad Shafi,* AIR 2001 SC 2984, p. 2986 : (2001) 8 SCC 540; *Padmasundara Rao v. State*

[Footnote No. 64 Contd.]

sentence" observed MUKHERJEA J. "is to be construed in the light of general purpose of the Act itself".[65] In the words of K. IYER, J. the interpretative effort "must be illumined by the goal though guided by the word".[66] For ascertaining the purpose of a statute, one is not restricted to the internal aid furnished by the statute itself,[67] although the text of the statute taken as a whole is the most important material for ascertaining both the aspects of 'intention'. Without intending to lay down a precise and exhaustive list of external aids, LORD SOMERVELL has stated: "The mischief against which the statute is directed and, perhaps though to an undefined extent the surrounding circumstances can be considered. Other statutes in *pari materia* and the state of the law at the time are admissible."[68] These external aids are also brought in by widening the concept of 'context' "as including not only other enacting provisions of the same statute, but its preamble, the existing state of the law, other statutes in *pari materia*, and the

---

[Footnote No. 64 Contd.]

of T.N., AIR 2002 SC 1334, p. 1340 : (2001) 8 SCC 540; *Unique Butyle Tube Industries (P.) Ltd. v. U.P. Financial Corporation*, (2003) 2 SCC 455, p. 462 : AIR 2003 SC 2103, p. 2107.

65. *Poppatlal Shah v. State of Madras*, AIR 1953 SC 274, p. 276 : 1953 SCR 677. **See further** *Aswinikumar Ghose v. Arabinda Bose*, AIR 1952 SC 369, p. 382 : 1953 SCR 1; *Darshan Singh Balwant Singh v. State of Punjab*, AIR 1953 SC 83, p. 86 : 1953 SCR 319; *Workmen of Dimakuchi Tea Estate v. Management of Dimakuchi Tea Estate*, AIR 1958 SC 353, p. 356 : 1958 SCR 1156; *State of U.P. v. C. Tobit*, AIR 1958 SC 414, p. 416 : 1958 SCR 1275; *R.L. Arora v. State of U.P.*, AIR 1964 SC 1230, pp. 1237, 1238, 1239; *Kanwar Singh v. Delhi Administration*, AIR 1965 SC 871 : 1965 (1) SCR 7; *Deputy Custodian v. Official Receiver*, AIR 1965 SC 951, pp. 956, 957 : 1965 (1) SCR 220; *Sheikh Gulfan v. Sanat Kumar*, AIR 1965 SC 1839, p. 1845 : 1965 (3) SCR 364; *Carew and Company Ltd. v. Union of India*, AIR 1975 SC 2260, p. 2269 : (1975) 2 SCC 791 (The law is a pragmatic instrument of social order and an interpretative effort must be imbued with the statutory purpose); *Chitan J. Vasvani v. State of West Bengal*, AIR 1975 SC 2473, p. 2476 : (1975) 2 SCC 829 (context-purpose teleological approach); *Bar Council of Maharashtra v. M.V. Dubholkar*, AIR 1975 SC 2092, p. 2103 : (1975) 2 SCC 702; *Girdharilal & Sons v. Balbir Nath Mathur*, (1986) 2 SCC 237, p. 245 : AIR 1986 (SC) 1499 ('A construction that would promote the purpose or object of an Act, even if not expressed, is to be preferred.' Section 15AA of Australian Interpretation Act, 1901, as amended in 1981); *Atma Ram Mittal v. Ishwar Singh Punia*, AIR 1988 SC 2031, p. 2034 : 1988 (4) SCC 284; *U.P. Bhoodan Yagna Samiti v. Brajkishore*, AIR 1988 SC 2239, p. 2244 : 1988 (4) SCC 274 (background and purpose of the statute to be kept in view).

66. *Kanta Goel (Smt.) v. B.D. Pathak*, AIR 1977 SC 1599, p. 1661 : 1977 (2) SCC 814. **Also see** *State Bank of Travancore v. Mohd. M. Khan*, AIR 1981 SC 1744, p. 1749 (para 18) :(1981) 4 SCC 82.

67. *Henrietta Muir Edwards v. AG of Canada*, AIR 1930 PC 120, pp. 121, 122. For internal aids **see** Chapter 3. For external aids, **see** Chapter 4.

68. *Attorney-General v. HRH Prince Ernest Augustus*, (1957) 1 All ER 49, p. 61 (HL); referred to in *Premchand Jain v. R.K. Chhabra*, (1984) 2 SCC 302, p. 307 : AIR 1984 SC 981 : 1984 Cri LJ 668; *District Mining Officer v. Tata Iron & Steel Co.*, AIR 2001 SC 3134, p. 3152 : (2001) 7 SCC 358.

mischief which the statute was intended to remedy."[69] In the words of CHINAPPA REDDY, J.: "Interpretation must depend on the text and the context. They are the bases of interpretation. One may well say if the text is the texture, context is what gives colour. Neither can be ignored. Both are important. That interpretation is best which makes the textual interpretation match the contextual. A statute is best interpreted when we know why it was enacted."[70]

The principle, as stated by MR. JUSTICE HOLMES, is to the following effect: "You construe a particular clause or expression by construing the whole instrument and any dominant purposes that it may express. In fact, intention is a residuary clause intended to gather up whatever other aids there may be to interpretation besides the particular words and the dictionary".[71]

According to BLACKSTONE the most fair and rational method for interpreting a statute is by exploring the intention of the Legislature through the most natural and probable signs which are 'either the words, the context, the subject-matter, the effects and consequence, or the spirit and reason of the law'.[72]

The meaning of the expression 'intention of the Legislature' is explained in another form by LORD WATSON in an oft-quoted passage where he called it a 'slippery phrase' and said: "In a court of law or equity, what

---

69. *Attorney-General v. HRH Prince Ernest Augustus*, (1957) 1 All ER 49, p. 53 (HL) (VISCOUNT SIMONDS); **See further** *London Borough of Ealing v. Race Relation Board*, (1972) 1 All ER 105, p. 114 (HL); *Utkal Contractors and Joinery Pvt. Ltd. v. State of Orissa*, (1987) 3 SCC 279, pp. 289, 290 : AIR 1987 SC 1454; *District Mining Officer v. Tata Iron & Steel Co. Supra*.

70. *Reserve Bank of India v. Pearless General Finance and Investment Co.*, (1987) 1 SCC 424, p. 450 : AIR 1987 SC 1023. **See further** *Utkal Contractors and Joinery Pvt. Ltd. v. State of Orissa, supra*, pp. 288, 289; *Kehar Singh v. State*, AIR 1988 SC 1883, pp. 1931, 1932 : 1988 (3) SCC 609; *R.S. Raghunath v. State of Karnataka*, AIR 1992 SC 81, p. 89; *S. Gopal Reddy v. State of Andhra Pradesh*, AIR 1996 SC 2184, p. 2188 : 1996 (4) SCC 596; *J.K. Industries v. Chief Inspector of Factories*, 1996 (7) Scale 247, p. 260: 1996 (6) SCC 665 : 1997 SCC (L&S) 1; *Associated Timber Industries v. Central Bank of India*, AIR 2000 SC 2689, p. 2693 : (2000) 7 SCC 93; *District Mining Officer v. Tata Iron & Steel Co. supra; Gujarat High Court v. Gujarat Kisan Mazdoor Panchayat*, AIR 2003 SC 1201, p. 1213 : (2003) 4 SCC 712; *Iridium India Telecom Ltd. v. Motorola Inc.*, (2005) 2 SCC 145, p. 159; *MCD v. Qimat Rai Gupta*, (2007) 7 SCC 309, para 21; *Central Bank of India v. State of Kerala*, (2009) 4 SCC 94 para 101 : (2009) 3 JT 216; *Special Land Acquisition Officer v. Karigowda*, (2010) 5 SCC 708 para 30 : AIR 2010 SC 2322; *V.N. Shrikhande (Dr.) v. Anita Sena Fernandes*, (2011) 1 SCC 53 para 22 : AIR 2011 SC 212.

71. REID MACDONALD AND FORDHAM, Cases and other Materials on Legislation, , 2nd Edition, p. 1005; *Special Land Acquisition Officer v. Karigowda*, (2010) 5 SCC 708 para 31 : AIR 2010 SC 2322.

72. BLACKSTONE, Commentaries on the Laws of England, Vol. 1, p. 59; **referred** to in *Atmaram Mittal v. Iswar Singh Punia*, AIR 1988 SC 2031, p. 2034 : (1998) 4 SCC 284; *A.P. Board for Water Pollution Control v. Andhra Pradesh Rayon's Ltd.*, AIR 1989 SC 611, p. 615 : (1989) 1 SCC 44; *Collector of Central Excise v. Parle Exports*, AIR 1989 SC 644, p. 652 : (1989) 1 SCC 345; *State of U.P. v. Radheyshyam*, AIR 1989 SC 682, p. 690 : 1989 (1) SCC 591; *District Mining Officer v. Tata Iron & Steel Co.*, AIR 2001 SC 3134, p. 3152 : (2001) 7 SCC 358.

the Legislature intended to be done or not to be done can only be legitimately ascertained from that which it has chosen to enact, either in express words or by reasonable and necessary implication".[73] But the whole of what is enacted 'by necessary implication' can hardly be determined without keeping in mind the purpose or object of the statute.[74] This formulation therefore does not in effect reject the concept of 'purpose' but contains the same within the import of the phrase 'necessary implication'.

Section 129D(1) of the Customs Act, 1962, provides that the Committee of Chief Commissioners of Customs may by order direct the Commissioner to apply to the Appellate Tribunal for determination of such points arising out of the decision or order of the Commissioner or the Adjudicating Authority, as may be specified by the Committee of Chief Commissioners of Customs in its Order. Section 129D(4) of the Act provides that where an application is made by the Commissioner to the Appellate Tribunal in pursuance of an Order under Section 129D(1), such application shall be heard by the Tribunal as if it were an appeal made against the decision or order of the Adjudicating Authority, and the provisions regarding appeals under Section 129A to the Tribunal, in so far as they are applicable, would be applicable to such application. The Supreme Court held that the provisions of section 129A(5), empowering the Tribunal to condone the delay and admit an appeal filed beyond the prescribed period, would also apply, as the Court must give effect to the purpose and object of Section 129D(4).[74a]

A bare mechanical interpretation of the words and application of a legislative intent devoid of concept of purpose will reduce most of the remedial and beneficent legislation to futility.[75] As stated by IYER, J. "to be literal in

---

73. *Aron Soloman v. A. Soloman & Co. Ltd.*, (1897) AC 22, p. 38 (HL); **referred** to in *Lord Howard de Walden v. IRC*, (1948) 2 All ER 825, p. 830 (HL); *Commonwealth of Australia v. Bank of New South Wales*, (1949) 2 All ER 755, p. 769 (PC); *R.L. Arora v. State of Uttar Pradesh*, AIR 1964 SC 1230, p. 1244 : (1964) 6 SCR 784; *Shahdara (Delhi) Saharanpur Light Railway Co. Ltd. v. Workers Union*, AIR 1969 SC 513, p. 519 : 1969 (2) SCR 131; *Hansraj Gordhandas v. H.H. Dave*, AIR 1970 SC 755, p. 759 : (1969) 2 SCR 253; *Shri Umed v. Raj Singh*, AIR 1975 SC 43, pp. 63, 64 : (1975) 1 SCC 76; *Commissioner of Sales Tax, U.P. v. Super Cotton Bowl Refilling Works*, AIR 1989 SC 922, p. 930 : (1989) 1 SCC 643; *State of Madhya Pradesh v. G.S. Dall and Flour Mills*, AIR 1991 SC 772, p. 785 : 1992 Supp (1) SCC 150; *Harbhajan Singh v. Press Council of India*, AIR 2002 SC 1351, p. 1356 : (2002) 3 SCC 722 : (2002) 96 DLT 691.

74. For example **see** *State of Punjab v. Okara Grain Buyers Syndicate Ltd.*, AIR 1964 SC 669 : 1964 (5) SCR 387. The question in this case was whether the State was bound 'by necessary implication' by Displaced Persons (Debts Adjustment) Act, 1951 and the court held that the State was bound, for a contrary result would have frustrated the beneficent purpose of the Act.

74a. *Thakkar Shipping Private Limited v. Commissioner of Customs (General)*, (2012) 12 SCC 189, p. 195 : 2012 (10) SCALE 600.

75. *Organo Chemical Industries v. Union of India*, AIR 1979 SC 1803, p. 1817 : (1979) 4 SCC 573; *Directorate of Enforcement v. Deepak Mahajan*, JT 1994 (1) SC 281, p. 302 : AIR 1994 SC 1775, p. 1785 : (1994) 3 SCC 440.

meaning is to see the skin and miss the soul. The judicial key to construction is the composite perception of the *deha* and the *dehi* of the provision."[76] Even in construing enactments such as those prescribing a period of limitation for initiation of proceedings where the purpose is only to intimate the people that after lapse of a certain time from a certain event a proceeding will not be entertained and where a strict grammatical construction is normally the only safe guide,[77] a literal and mechanical construction may have to be disregarded if it conflicts with some essential requirement of fair play and natural justice which the Legislature never intended to throw overboard.[78] Similarly, in a taxing statute provisions enacted to prevent tax

---

76. *Chairman, Board of Mining Examination and Chief Inspector of Mines v. Ramjee*, AIR 1977 SC 965, p. 968 : 1977 SCC (L&S) 226. **See further** *Directorate of Enforcement v. Deepak Mahajan, supra*, p. 1785 of AIR.

77. *Nagendranath Dey v. Sureshchandra Dey*, AIR 1932 PC 165, p.168; *Siraj-ul-Haq Khan v. Sunni Central Board*, AIR 1959 SC 198, p. 205 : 1959 SCR 1287; *Shakuntala S. Tiwari v. Hemchand*, (1987) 3 SCC 211, pp. 218, 220 : AIR 1987 SC 1823; *R. Rudraiah v. State of Karnataka*, AIR 1998 SC 1070, p. 1075 : 1998 (3) SCC 23; *Antonysami v. Arulanangam*, AIR 2001 SC 2967, p. 2972 : (2001) 9 SCC 658; *Hamid Joharan v. Abdulsalam*, AIR 2001 SC 3404, p. 3409 : (2001) 7 SCC 573; *State of A.P. v. Marki Venkaiah,* (2003) 7 SCC 280, p. 283 : AIR 2003 SC 2949. No implied saving can be read for persons under disability: **See** *Mahummud Bahadoor Khan v. Collector of Bareilly*, (1873) 1 IA 167, p. 176. The courts have no power to extend the period of limitation on equitable grounds: *P.K. Ramchandran v. State of Kerala*, AIR 1998 SC 2276, p. 2277 : 1997 (7) SCC 556. **See further** *Padmasundara Rao v. State of T.N.*, AIR 2002 SC 1334 : (2002) 3 SCC 533 (Proviso to section 6(1) of the Land Acquisition Act, 1894 as amended by Act 68 of 1984 providing period of limitation from the date of notification under section 4 for issuance of section 6 notification construed literally).

78. *State of Punjab v. Qaisar Jehan Begum*, AIR 1963 SC 1604, p. 1606 : 1964 (1) SCR 971; *Harish Chandra Raj Singh (Raja) v. Deputy Land Acquisition Officer*, AIR 1961 SC 1500, pp. 1504, 1505 : 1962 (1) SCR 676; *Madanlal v. State of U.P.*, AIR 1975 SC 2085 : (1975) 2 SCC 779; *Assistant Transport Commissioner, Lucknow v. Nandsingh*, AIR 1980 SC 15 : 1979 (4) SCC 19; *Dara Singh v. State*, AIR 1981 SC 427, p. 430 : (1980) 4 SCC 586; *Precision Steel and Engineering Works v. Prem Deva*, AIR 1982 SC 1518, p. 1519 : (1982) 3 SCC 270. **See further** *Anandilal v. Ram Narain*, (1984) 3 SCC 561, p. 567 : AIR 1984 SC 1383. (It is permissible to adopt a beneficent construction of a rule of limitation if alternative constructions are possible). The object and purpose of a limitation provision has also its impact on its construction: Compare *Harish Chandra Raj Singh's* case *(supra)*, a case under section 18 of the Land Acquisition Act, 1894 with *Kaliyappan v. State of Kerala*, AIR 1989 SC 239 : 1989 (1) SCC 113 a case under section 11A of the same Act. Under section 18 which provides for a reference within a certain period from the date of award at the instance of the owner, the date of award is construed to mean the date of communication of award to him. But under section 11A which requires making of award within two years of the declaration under section 6, the award is construed to be made when it is signed. For construction of the date of making of declaration under section 6 and requirement of publication in gazette **see** *Krishi Utpadan Mandi Samiti v. Makrand Singh*, 1995 (2) SCC 497 : 1995 (1) JT 487; *Eugenio Misquita v. State of Goa*, AIR 1997 SC 3939 : (1997) 8 SCC 47; *S.H. Rangappa v. State of Karnataka,* AIR 2001 SC 3868; *Sriniwas Ramdas Khatod v. State of Maharashtra,* AIR 2002 SC 187 : (2002) 1 SCC 689 : (2002) 1 KLT 140; *Kunwar Pal Singh v. State of*

[Footnote No. 78 Contd.]

evasion are given a liberal construction to effectuate the purpose of suppressing tax evasion although provisions imposing a charge are construed strictly, there being no *a priori* liability to pay a tax, and the purpose of a charging section being only to levy a charge on persons and activities brought within its clear terms.[79] However, the Supreme Court has held that it would be more inclined to give an interpretation to the provisions in Section 36 of the Income Tax Act, 1961 which would serve the legislative object and intent, rather than to subvert the same. Accordingly, deductions permissible under Section 36(1)(vii) should not be negated by reading into this provision the limitations of Section 36(1)(vii-a), on the reasoning that it will form a check against double deduction.[79a] For the same reason, in a legislation relating to defence services, 'the considerations of the security of the state and enforcement of high degree of discipline additionally intervene

---

[Footnote No. 78 Contd.]

U.P., (2007) 5 SCC 85 : AIR 2007 SC 1675 [Date of publication of the declaration under section 6 of Land Acquisition Act, 1894 for counting the period of two years for making the award under section 11-A is the last of the dates of publications required under section 6(2)]. Similarly, date of order with reference to the person or authority making the order is the date when it is signed, but with reference to party affected for going up in appeal or revision,date of order is the date of express or implied communication of the order to the party: *Collector of Central Excise v. M.M. Rubber & Co.,* AIR 1991 SC 2141 : 1992 S (1) SCC 471; *MCD v. Qimat Rai Gupta,* (2007) 7 SCC 309, para 21. 'The date of the order' under section 48AA of the Advocates Act, 1961 for filing review within sixty days is the date of the communication or knowledge of the order: *D. Saibaba v. Bar Council of India,* AIR 2003 SC 2502, p. 2505 : (2003) 6 SCC 186. Limitation of three years for revision to prevent fraud would start running from the date of discovery of the fraud: *State of Maharashtra v. Rattanlal,* AIR 1993 SC 1733 : (1993) 3 SCC 326. Limitation for suit for damages in tort against the state starts when there is refusal to pay the damages: *Jay Laxmi Salt Works (P) Ltd. v. State of Gujarat,* JT 1994 (3) SC 492, pp. 506, 507: 1994 (3) SCC 8. Principle of section 10 Limitation Act, 1963 which applies to original suits applied to extend limitation for appeal on grounds of public policy: *Varadraja Perumal Temple v. K. Ramchandra*, 1995 (6) Scale 25 : 1995 Supp (4) SCC 87. Provision requiring publication in official gazette *and* in such other manner as may be directed and prescribing period of limitation from 'such publication' construed to mean that period of limitation will start from the date of publication in official gazette and not from the other mode of publication which may be earlier in time: *Mohd. Abubakkar Siddique v. Mustafa-Shahidul Islam,* AIR 2000 SC 731, p. 732 : (2000) 2 SCC 62; *Raipur Development Authority v. Anupam Sahkari Griha Nirman Samiti,* JT 2000 (4) SC 60, pp. 70, 71 : (2000) 4 SCC 357. Provisions like section 14 of the Limitation Act, 1963 for condonation of delay and extention of limitation are liberally construed: *Union of India v. West Coast Paper Mills Ltd.*, (2004) 3 SCC 458, p. 464 (para 14) : AIR 2004 SC 3079. But *suo motu* power of revision to be exercised 'at any time' even in furtherance of social justice cannot be exercised after unreasonable delay: *Situ Sahu v. State of Jharkhand*, (2004) 8 SCC 340. A provision for limitation has to be specifically enacted and cannot be inferred by courts : *Collector of Central Excise v. Raghuvar (India) Ltd.,* AIR 2000 SC 2027, p. 2033 : (2000) 5 SCC 299.

79. See Chapter 10, title 1(d) 'Qualifications of the Rule of Strict Construction' text and notes 44 to 47 at p. 901.

79a. *Catholic Syrian Bank Limited v. Commissioner of Income Tax, Thrissur*, (2012) 3 SCC 784, p. 797 : AIR 2012 SC 1538 : 2012 (2) SCALE 573.

and have to be assigned weightage while dealing with any expression needing to be defined or any provision needing to be interpreted'.[80]

The Courts are warned that they are not entitled to usurp legislative function under the disguise of interpretation[81] and that they must avoid the danger of an *a priori* determination of the meaning of a provision based on their own preconceived notions of ideological structure or scheme into which the provision to be interpreted is somehow fitted.[82] Caution is all the more necessary in dealing with a legislation enacted to give effect to policies that are subject of bitter public and parliamentary controversy, for in controversial matters there is room for differences of opinion as to what is expedient, what is just and what is morally justifiable; it is the Parliament's opinion in these matters that is paramount.[83] This only means that Judges cannot interpret statutes in the light of their views as to policy; but they can adopt a purposive interpretation if they can find in the statute read as a whole or in the material to which they are permitted by law to refer as aids to interpretation an expression of Parliament's purpose or policy.[84] So there is no usurpation of function or danger when the purpose or object of a statute is derived from legitimate sources[85] and the words are given an interpretation which they can reasonably bear to effectuate that purpose or object. The correct interpretation is one that best harmonises the words with the object of the statute. "A right construction of the Act," said LORD PORTER, "can only be attained if its whole scope and object together with an analysis of its wording and the circumstances in which it is enacted are taken into consideration".[86] Judicial legislation, if any, in adopting such a course should not go beyond the inevitable minimum. It is well to remember what

---

80. *Union of India v. Harjeet Singh Sandhu,* AIR 2001 SC 1772, pp. 1780, 1781 : (2001) 5 SCC 593.

81. *Magor and St. Mellons Rural District Council v. New Port Corporation*, (1951) 2 All ER 839 (HL).

82. *D. A. Venkatachalam v. Dy. Transport Commissioner*, AIR 1977 SC 842, pp. 853, 854 : (1977) 2 SCC 273; *Union of India v. Elphinstone Spinning and Weaving Co. Ltd.*, JT 2001 (1) SC 536, p. 563 : AIR 2001 SC 724, p. 740 : (2001) 4 SCC 139; *District Mining Officer v. Tata Iron & Steel Co.*, AIR 2001 SC 3134, p. 3153 : (2001) 7 SCC 358; *Padmasundara Rao v. State of T.N.*, AIR 2002 SC 1334, p. 1340 : (2002) 3 SCC 533; *Harbhajan Singh v. Press Council of India*, AIR 2002 SC 1351, pp. 1355, 1356 : (2002) 3 SCC 722; *Unique Butyle Tube Industries (P) Ltd. v. U.P. Financial Corporation*, (2003) 2 SCC 455, p. 462 : AIR 2003 SC 2103, p. 2107; *Maulvi Hussain Haji Abraham Umerji v. State of Gujarat*, (2004) 6 SCC 672, p. 681 : AIR 2004 SC 3946.

83. *Duport Steels Ltd. v. Sirs*, (1980) 1 All ER 529, p. 541: (1980) 1 WLR 142 (HL); *Union of India v. Elphinstone Spinning and Weaving Co. Ltd., supra.*

84. *Shah v. Barnet London Borough Council*, (1983) 1 All ER 226, p. 238 : (1983) 2 AC 309 : (1983) 2 WLR 16 (HL); **referred** to in *S. Sundaram Pillai v. Pattabiraman*, (1985) 1 SCC 591, p. 627: AIR 1985 SC 582.

85. **See** text and notes 65 to 68, p. 16, *supra*.

86. *Bhagwan Baksh Singh (Raja) v. Secretary of State*, AIR 1940 PC 82, p. 86; **referred** to in *Prem Chand Jain v. R.K. Chabbra*, (1984) 2 SCC 302, p. 307 : AIR 1984 SC 981. For example, see majority and minority opinions in *R.L. Arora v. State of U.P.*, AIR 1964 SC 1230 : (1964) 6 SCR 784.

JUDGE LEARNED HAND said: "Compunctions about judicial legislation are right enough as long as we have any genuine doubt as to the breadth of the Legislature's intent, and no doubt, the most single factor in ascertaining its intent is the word it employs. But the colloquial words of a statute have not the fixed and artificial content of scientific symbols; they have a *penumbra, a dim fringe, a connotation*, for they express an attitude or will, into which our duty is to penetrate and which we must enforce when we can ascertain it, regardless of imprecision in its expression".[87] The application of a given legislation to new and unforeseen needs and situations broadly falling within the statutory provision is within the interpretative jurisdiction of courts. This is not legislation in strict sense but in application and is within the court's province.[88] In deriving an implied obligation on the part of the Government to give interim relief to the victims as the major inarticulate premise from the spirit of the Bhopal Gas Leak Disaster (Processing of Claims) Act, 1985, the scheme of the Act and the language of sections 9 and 10, SABYASACHI MUKHARJI, C.J.I, observed: "This approach to the interpretation of the Act can legitimately be called the 'constructive intuition' which, in our opinion is a permissible mode of viewing the Acts of Parliament."[89] The learned Chief Justice explained that the freedom to search for 'the spirit of the Act' or the quantity of mischief at which it is aimed opens up the possibility of liberal interpretation 'that delicate and important branch of judicial power, the concession of which is dangerous, the denial ruinous'.[90] The learned Chief Justice then said: "Given this freedom it is a rare opportunity though never to be misused and challenge for the judges to adopt and give meaning to the Act, articulate and inarticulate, and thus translate the intention of the Parliament and fulfil the object of the Act."[91]

87. *Commissioner v. Ickelheimer*, 132 F (2d) 660, p. 662, **referred** to in 60 Harvard Law Review 370, p. 376. The same learned judge in another case said : "Statutes always have some purpose or object to accomplish, whose sympathetic and imaginative discovery is the surest guide to their meaning:" *Cabell v. Markham,* (1945) 148 F (2nd) 737, p. 739 **also referred** at p. 386, text and note 63, *ante*.

88. *V. C. Rangadurai v. D. Gopalan*, AIR 1979 SC 281, p. 284 : (1979) 1 SCC 308. **See further** *Mohan Lal v. Jai Bhagwan*, AIR 1988 SC 1034, p. 1037 : 1988 (2) SCC 474. (The meaning of expressions must be found in the felt necessities of time); *Gurdial Batra v. Raj Kumar Jain,* AIR 1989 SC 1841, p. 1842 : 1989 (3) SCC 441. **See also** Chapter 4 title 3, pp. 275 to 329. This is called an updating approach; CROSS, Statutory Interpretation, 3rd Edition, p. 51.

89. *Charan Lal Sahu v. Union of India*, AIR 1990 SC 1480, p. 1536 : (1990) 1 SCC 613.

90. *Ibid*. Here the Chief Justice was referring to BENTHAM'S classification and views on interpretation. According to BENTHAM, interpretation is strict when you derive a meaning which you suppose the legislator really entertained and it is liberal when you arrive at a meaning which you suppose he failed to entertain by inadvertence but would have entertained had the case which calls for interpretation been present to his view. **See** BENTHAM, of Laws in General, pp. 162, 241 **quoted** in CROSS, Statutory Interpretation, 3rd Edition, pp. 35, 36. The words 'strict' and 'liberal' are frequently used, not in the sense used by BENTHAM, but to mean merely narrow and broad.

91. *Charan Lal Sahu v. Union of India, supra*, p. 1536.

This does not, however, mean that judges should go on proclaiming that they are playing the role of a law maker for an exhibition of judicial valour is likely to make the less disciplined amongst them forget the line between adjudication and legislation as the only sure safeguard against crossing the line is 'an alert recognition of the necessity not to cross it and instinctive, as well as trained reluctance to do so'.[92] Further, the perorations and sermons of judicial activism are likely to lead to confusion in the public mind and shake their confidence in the rule of law. As stated by LORD RADCLIFFE: "Judges will serve the public interest better if they keep quiet about their legislative function. No doubt they will discreetly contribute to changes in the law, because they cannot do otherwise even if they would. But the Judge who shows his hand, who advertises what he is about may indeed show that he is a strong spirit, unfettered by the past; but I doubt very much whether he is not doing more harm to the general confidence in the law as a constant, safe in the hands of the Judges, than he is doing good to the laws credit as a set of rules nicely attuned to the sentiment of the day".[93] The Judges have no doubt a genuine creative role but as warned by LORD SCARMAN "the Constitution's separation of powers, or more accurately functions, must be observed if judicial independence is not to be put at risk. For if people and Parliament come to think that the judicial power is to be confined by nothing other than the judge's sense of what is right (or, as SELDON put it by the length of the Chancellor's foot), confidence in the judicial system will be replaced by fear of it becoming uncertain and arbitrary in its application. Society will then be ready for

---

92. FRANKFURTER, Some reflections on the reading of statutes, Essays on Jurisprudence from the Columbia Law Review, p. 51; *Institute of Chartered Accountants of India v. Price Waterhouse*, AIR 1998 SC 74, p. 90 : (1997) 6 SCC 312 (6th Edition of this book, p. 15 is **referred**); *J.P. Bansal v. State of Rajasthan,* 2003 AIR SCW 1848, p. 1854 : AIR 2003 SC 1405 : (2003) 5 SCC 134; *State of Jharkhand v. Govind Singh*, AIR 2005 SC 294, p. 297; *Vemareddy Kumarswamy Reddy v. State of M.P.*, (2006) 2 SCC 670 para 15 : AIR 2006 SC 3517. **See further** *Stock v. Frank Jones (Tipton) Ltd.*, (1978) 1 All EC 948, p. 953 (HL). (The judge must bear in mind the limitations of judicial function). In his work, 'The Judicial Process In Comparative Perspective' PROF. MAURO CAPPELLETTI, who has strong bias for judicial law making (p. 56) says (p. 8): 'Words do often have a meaning so commonly accepted that even the most activist and dynamic judge would find it hard to ignore'. Further, the learned professor after pointing out certain limitations and weaknesses of judicial law making has the following words of caution (p. 39): 'A good judge is one who is aware of the above limits and weaknesses and sensitive to those many circumstances which might advise restraint in some periods, areas and cases and boldness in others'.

93. LORD RADCLIFFE, The Lawyer and his Times, **quoted** by Justice TULZAPURKAR in *Manohar Nathusao Samarth v. Marotrao*, AIR 1979 SC 1084, p. 1085 : 1979 (4) SCC 93.

Parliament to cut the power of judges. Their power to do justice will become more restricted by law than it needs be, or is today".[94]

In a case which related to the question whether workmen have a right to be heard in the winding up petition of a Company under the Companies Act, 1956, VENKATARAMAIAH, J. unsuccessfully exhorted his brethren to keep up the discipline and to avoid making inroads in the legitimate domain of the Legislature by a majority of one.[95] In a later case which related to interpretation of clause 3(b) of section 127 of the Code of Criminal Procedure, 1973 which makes the provision for maintenance to a wife inapplicable to a divorced woman when she has received 'the whole of the sum which, under any customary or personal law applicable to the parties was payable on such divorce', the Supreme Court in its zeal to ameliorate the condition of Muslim women held that deferred dower is not a sum payable 'on divorce' on the reasoning that it is an amount payable as a mark of respect for the wife although holding that divorce is a convenient or identifiable point of time at which the amount is payable.[96] The speech of the Minister for Home Affairs piloting the Bill in the Rajya Sabha, to which the court was referred, clearly showed that the clause 3(b) was inserted with a view not to change the Muslim Personal Law. The fine distinction drawn by the court that deferred dower though payable at the time of divorce is not payable on divorce is casuistical. The decision led to a great controversy and was followed by legislation, namely the Muslim Women (Protection of Rights on Divorce) Act, 1986, *prima facie* to nullify the decision. In the words of a two-Judge Bench of the Supreme Court "the Parliament enacted the Act to undo the effect of the Constitution Bench

---

94. *Duport Steels Ltd. v. Sirs*, (1980) 1 All ER 529, p. 551 (HL) : (1980) 1 WLR 142 : 124 SJ 133. In the same case LORD DIPLOCK said (p. 542): "It endangers continued public confidence in the political impartiality of the judiciary, which is essential to the continuance of the rule of law, if judges, under the guise of interpretation, provide their own preferred amendments to statutes which experience of their operation has shown to have had consequences that members of the court before whom the matter comes consider to be injurious to public interest." The passage from LORD SCARMAN'S speech quoted in the text was also **referred** to by AHMADI, J., in his dissenting Judgment in *Supreme Court Advocates on Record Association v. Union of India*, AIR 1994 SC 268, p. 367 : 1993 (4) SCC 441. The passage from Lord Diplock's speech quoted above was **referred** to by SHAGIR AHMAD J. in his dissenting judgment in *Institute of Chartered Accountants of India v. Price Waterhouse*, AIR 1998 SC 74, p. 90 : 1997 (6) SCC 312; and by ARIJIT PASAYAT J., in *J.P. Bansal v. State of Rajasthan,* 2003 AIR SCW 1848, p. 1855 : AIR 2003 SC 1405 : (2003) 5 SCC 134; *State of Jharkhand v. Govind Singh*, AIR 2005 SC 294, p. 297.

95. *National Textile Workers Union v. P.R. Ramkrishnan*, AIR 1983 SC 75, pp. 101, 103 : (1983) 1 SCC 228 : (1983) 1 LLJ 45.

96. *Mohd. Ahmed Khan v. Shah Bano Begum*, (1985) 2 SCC 556, pp. 569 to 571 : AIR 1985 SC 945.

decision in *Mohd. Ahmed Khan v. Shah Bano Begum,* (note 5, *infra*) because the said decision was strongly opposed by a section of the Muslim community".[1] But surprisingly later another Constitution Bench decision of the Supreme Court in *Daniel Latifi v. Union of India,*[2] came to the conclusion that Parliament did nothing of that kind and the Act instead of nullifying the decision in Shah Bano "actually and in reality codifies what was stated in *Shah Bano's* case."[3] In this case interpreting section 3(a) of the Act which provides that a divorced woman shall be entitled to 'a reasonable and fair provision and maintenance to be made and paid to her within the period of iddat by her former husband', the court held that the obligation of the former husband of making reasonable provision and paying maintenance to the divorced wife is not limited to the period of iddat, that the words 'within the iddat period' only indicate the time by which an arrangement for payment of provision and maintenance should be concluded and that the Act would exclude from liability for post iddat period maintenance to a man who has already discharged his obligations of both 'reasonable and fair provision' and 'maintenance' by paying these amounts in a lump sum within the iddat period for the post iddat period also.[4] It is the plight of the Muslim divorced women and not so much the words of the Acts which motivated the court in both the Constitution Bench decisions to reach its conclusions. As frankly observed in Shah Bano's case 'the role of the reformer has to be assumed by the courts because, it is beyond the endurance of sensitive minds to allow injustice to be suffered when it is so palpable.'[5] While dealing with sections 7 and 8 of Chota Nagpur Tenancy Act, 1908 which limits the succession of lands held by tenants of scheduled tribes to male descendants and excludes females, K. RAMASWAMI, J., was of the view that the expression 'male descendants' should be construed to include female descendants and the provisions of the Hindu Succession Act, 1956 and the Indian Succession Act, 1925 should be extended judicially to

---

1. *Secretary, Tamil Nadu Wakf Board v. Syed Fatima Nachi*, AIR 1996 SC 2423 (para 5) : 1996 (4) SCC 616. The Act does not affect the right of muslim children to get maintenance under section 127 CrPC; *Noor Sabha Khatoon v. Mohd. Quasim*, AIR 1997 SC 3280 : 1997 (5) Scale 248 : (1997) 6 SCC 233.

2. AIR 2001 SC 3958 : (2001) 7 SCC 740.

3. *Ibid* p. 3971.

4. *Ibid* p. 3969, 3973.

5. *Mohd. Ahmad Khan v. Shah Bano Begum,* (1985) 2 SCC 556, p. 573 : AIR 1985 SC 945. **See further** *Shamim Ara v. State of U.P.*, (2002) 7 SCC 518 : AIR 2002 SC 3551 where the court has proceeded to reform the Muslim law by curtailing the right of the husband to divorce the wife by talaq. Commenting on an article 'The rise of Hero judges' by John Gava of Adelaide University in (2001) 24 VNSW LJ 747 Justice P.W. YOUNG of Australia says : "There are clearly some good points made by Gava. There is also something to be said against his views. One such point is that our society is so structured that if judges do not on appropriate occasions grasp the mettle, no one will:" (2002) 76 ALJ 4.

apply to scheduled tribes to ameliorate the condition of females. But this ultraactivist view was not accepted by the majority (KULDIP SINGH AND PUNCHHI, JJ.) who advised self restraint and cautious approach in making Judge- made amendments though it may appear to be conservative.[6] In the words of CARDOZO, 'the judge is not to innovate at pleasure. He is not a knight-errant roaming at will in pursuit of his own ideal of beauty or of goodness.'[7]

The Courts cannot interpret a statute the way they have developed the common law 'which in a constitutional sense means judicially developed equity'.[8] In abrogating or modifying a rule of the common law the courts

---

6. *Madhu Kishwar v. State of Bihar*, AIR 1996 SC 1864, pp. 1879, 1881 : 1996 (5) SCC 125.

7. CARDOZO, The Nature of the Judicial Process, p. 141; *Idul Hasan v. Rajendra Kumar Jain*, AIR 1990 SC 678, p. 681 : 1989 (4) SCC 550.

8. *McLoughlin v. O'Brian*, (1982) 2 All ER 298, p. 310 : (1983) 1 AC 410 : (1982) 2 WLR 982 (HL). Under the English Common Law money paid under a mistake of law could not earlier be recovered back. The House of Lords by majority modified this rule by holding that levies and taxes paid to a local authority under *ultra vires* regulations can be recovered as of right. The majority was conscious that however compelling the principle of justice 'it would never be sufficient to persuade Government to promote its legislative recognition by Parliament; caution otherwise known as the Treasury, would never allow this to happen': *Woolwich Building Society v. Inland Revenue Commissioners (No. 2)*, (1992) 3 All ER 737, pp. 760, 761 763 : 1993 AC 70 : (1992) 3 WLR 366 (HL). Further, the original common law mistake of law rule was later completely abrogated by holding that 'English law should *now* recognise that there is a general right to recover money paid under a mistake whether of fact or law:' *Kleinwort Benson Ltd. v. Lincoln City Council*, (1998) 4 All ER 513, p. 553 (HL). This general right of restitution of money paid under a mistake of law also applies when money is paid under a mistake of law to the Revenue and the period of limitation starts from the date of discovery of mistake : *Deutsche Morgan Grenfell Group plc v. Inland Revenue Commissioners*, (2007) 1 All ER 449 (HL). The immunity enjoyed under the common law by barristers and advocates from being sued for professional negligence was also abrogated on the ground that changes in public policy no longer justified the continuance of the immunity : *Arthur J.S. Hall & Co. v. Simons*, (2000) 3 All ER 673 (HL). The rule in common law was that a court has no power in the absence of agreement to award interest as compensation for the late payment of a debt or damages: *London, Chatham and Dover Railway Co. v. South Eastern Railway Co.* (1893) AC 429 (HL). This rule was **overruled** in *Sempra Metals Ltd. v. Inland Revenue Commissioners*, (2007) 4 All ER 657 (HL). Lord Nicolls in this case (para 94) said: "The House should now hold that in principle it is always open to a claimant to plead and prove his actual interest losses caused by late payment of a debt." In Australia the common law, which for 200 years did not recognise any 'native title', *i.e.*, title of the aboriginal people of the land in their occupation, was altered by the High Court : *Mabo v. Queensland (No. 2)*, (1992) 175 CLR 1. But the High Court of Australia still sticks to the view that the Advocates cannot be sued for professional negligence in the conduct of a trial: *D'orta-Ekenaike v. Victoria Legal Aid*, (2005) HCA 12 (KIRBY J. dissenting). The decision was criticised in the media : (2005) 79 ALJ 201.

exercise 'the same power of creation that built up the common law through its exercise by judges of the past'.[9] The courts can exercise no such power in respect of statutes. Therefore, in their task of interpreting and applying a statute, judges have to be conscious that in the end the statute is the master and not the servant of the judgment[10] and that 'no judge has a choice between implementing the law and disobeying it.'[11]

---

9. CARDOZO, The Growth of the Law (Indian Economy Reprint 2002), p. 137.

10. DEVLIN, The Judge, p. 14. **See further** LORD STEYN: "The function of the courts is simply to construe and apply statutes. A judge's task is to interpret and not to interpolate. There is a Rubicon which judges may not cross : principles of institutional integrity forbid it. That is of course not a prescription for literal interpretation". Deferance : a Tangled Story, (2005) Public Law 347.

N. B. The Supreme Court of India is endowed with a residuary judicial power under Article 142 of the Constitution of passing such decree or making such order as is necessary for doing complete justice in a cause or matter pending before it. This power is not held by any other court not even by the High Courts [*State of Punjab v. Surinder Kumar*, AIR 1992 SC 1593 : (1992) 1 SCC 489 : (1992) 73 Com Cases 490]. The creative role that the Supreme Court has assumed under Article 142 of the Constitution is much wider than a court's creative role in interpreting statutes and is plainly legislative in nature. In *K. Veeraswamy v. Union of India*, (1991) 3 SCC 655, p. 708 : 1991 (3) JT 198 : 1991 SCC (Cri) 734, the Supreme Court by a majority of 3 against 2 issued directions to the Union of India that before registering FIR as also before sanctioning prosecution under the Prevention of Corruption Act against a sitting judge of a High Court or Supreme Court, Chief Justice of India should be consulted. In doing so the majority judges were conscious that such a requirement could not be spelled from the Act or the Constitution but they said that the Court's role was not merely of 'interstitial' law maker but also of 'a problem solver in the nebulous areas'. Similarly, in *P. V. Narsimha Rao v. State*, JT 1998 (3) SC 318 : AIR 1998 SC 2120, p. 2165 the Supreme Court has held that though technically sitting MPs can be prosecuted under the Prevention of Corruption Act, 1988 without obtaining any sanction for prosecution, the prosecuting agency shall obtain the permission of the Chairman, Rajya Sabha/Speaker, Lok Sabha before filing the chargesheet in court against a member of Parliament. On the same lines is the decision in *U.P. Judicial Officers Association v. Union of India*, JT 2002 (8) SC 133, p. 134, which directs that no FIR should be registered without permission of the Chief Justice of the concerned High Court against a judicial officer relating to allegations of having committed an offence in discharge or purported discharge of his official duties. Even normally the police may not in every case register a FIR on receipt of information of a cognizable offence and may hold a preliminary inquiry before registering FIR to check some credibility of the information: *Shashikant v. Central Bureau of Investigation*, AIR 2007 SC 351, para 21 : (2007) 1 SCC 630. Endowed with the power under Article 142, the Supreme Court claims to be a 'law maker' and a 'problem solver' in nebulous areas but only by supplementing the existing law and not by 'supplanting' it: *Supreme Court Bar Association v. Union of India*, AIR 1998 SC 1895, pp. 1908, 1909 : (1998) 4 SCC 409. **See further** pp. 309 to 322, *post* for Article 142.

11. GLEESON C.J. of the High Court of Australia in a speech made to the Australian Bar Association Conference in New york, (2000) 74 ALJ 494 (Aust) **see further** text and note 15, p. 29.

Judges have more freedom in interpreting a Constitution[12] but this freedom also has to be contained within permissible limits[13] for 'the Constitution does not give unlimited powers to anyone including the judges

---

12. **See** p. 285, *post*.
13. Even as regards interpretation of the Constitution some feel that the American Supreme Court and also our Supreme Court have gone much beyond the permissible limits. WILLIAM J. QUIRK in his article 'Judicial Dictatorship' writes: "The court, at will, takes great chunks of public business away from public control. The public at some point, will have to regain control of its business. 'The judiciary', said Hand 'will then cease to be independent' and 'its independence will be well lost'. The people after all, are the only ones who can keep liberty in the country": M.P. CHRONICLE, June 1, 1994. For criticism of our Supreme Court, **see** T.R. ANDHYARUJINA 'Judicial Activism and Constitutional Democracy in India'. **See further** NANI PALKHIVALA (Sunday Times, December 3, 1995): 'Not a day passes when front pages of Newspapers do not scream about a 'landmark' judgment of the Supreme Court which virtually involves usurping the function of the executive'. SOLI J. SORABJEE (Sunday Times, December 10, 1995): "True, the judicial pendulum has swung erratically on occasions. Some orders and directions passed by the Court are apparently beyond the judicial sphere and do more credit to the heart than the head. Undoubtedly, there can be no general amorphous judicial supervision of Government. The judiciary may overstep its limits and at times fail to guard against the danger of judicial populism". PROF. S.P. SATHE in his book Judicial Activism in India (2002) concludes (p. 251) : 'The court has clearly transcended the limits of the judicial function and has undertaken functions that really belonged to either the Legislature or the Executive. Its decisions clearly violated the limits that the doctrine of separation of powers had imposed on it.' In the context of PIL Prof. Sathe observes: 'They (the Courts) have entertained matters they ought not to have entertained and they have been guilty of populism as well as adventurism.' Prof. Sathe also quotes the caution administered by Dr. ANAND C.J.I.: "care has to be taken to see that PIL essentially remains public interest litigation and does not become either political interest litigation, or personal interest litigation or publicity interest litigation or used for persecution" (p. 308). The Supreme Court has reiterated this caution in subsequent cases : *Ashok Kumar Pandey v. State of West Bengal*, AIR 2004 SC 280, p. 283 : (2004) 3 SCC 349; *Dattaraj Nathuji Thaware v. State of Maharashtra*, (2005) 1 SCC 590, p. 595. For **further criticism** of PIL, see V.K.S. Chaudhary, The Ivory Tower, (2002), pp. 203 to 211. On the question as to who can file PIL. **See** *Kusam Lata v. Union of India,* (2006) 6 SCC 180 : AIR 2006 SC 2643; *Villianur Iyarkkai Padukappu Maiyam v. Union of India,* (2009) 7 SCC 561 para 114 : (2009) 8 JT 339. There is a principle recognized in America and Australia that 'it is impermissible for other branches of government to impose on judges a task amounting to a grossly unjudicial chore in an attempt to borrow the judiciary's reputation for impartiality': *Mistreta v. United States,* (1989) 488 US 361 p. 407; *Gypsy Jokers Motorcycle Club Inc. v. Commissioner of Police,* (2008) 82 ALJR 454 pp. 469, 470 (para 69). But in India a survey of PILs in the High Courts may show that the judiciary itself is too willing to take up 'grossly unjudicial chores' even though the courts are unable to cope up with the mounting arrears of real judicial work. In *State of Uttaranchal v. Balwant Singh Chanfal*, (2010) 3 SCC 402 para 181 : AIR 2010 SC 2550 detailed guidelines laid down for entertainment of Public Interest Litigations. For procedure to be adopted when a sole petitioner filing a PIL dies and none applies for being substituted in his place : **See** *Pragati Mahila Mandal Nanded v. Municipal Corporation, Nanded*, (2011) 3 SCC 464 : AIR 2011 SC 1512.

of all levels'[14] and it is necessary for protecting judicial independence that judges remain 'circumspect and self disciplined in the discharge of their judicial functions.'[15] As observed by the Chief Justice of Australia, "Judges have no right to subvert the law" in the name of creativity "because they disagree with a particular rule."[16] The abuse of power by the Government in areas which are not satisfactorily redressable by judicial review should not form the articulate or inarticulate reason for depriving the Government of a power conferred on it by the Constitution or a statute by a strained construction or overactivism.[17] Such abuses have to be left to be taken care of by public criticism and ultimately by the people.

The numerous decisions which the Courts have delivered and continue to deliver dealing with questions of exposition of enacted laws are the principal source for ascertaining the rules of interpretation or construction. The formulations of the rules even in leading decisions are not quite uniform as most often even a generalised statement in a case gets coloured by an emphasis on the problem in that case. Indeed the courts are, at times, seen lamenting over the growth of the rules and apparent conflict in them because of confusion and error of judgment that is likely to result in blind adherence to them. VISCOUNT SIMONDS said: 'Since a large and ever increasing amount of time of the courts has, during the last three hundred

---

14. *State of Rajasthan v. Prakashchand*, JT 1997 (9) SC 492, p. 529 (para 68) : 1998 (1) SCC 1 : AIR 1998 SC 1344.

15. *Ibid*, p. 516 (para 38). DR ANAND CJI in his inaugural address at the Golden jubilee celebrations of the Rajasthan High Court on August 29, 1999 at Jodhpur cautioned: "No civilised system can permit judicial authoritarianism and, therefore, the judges at all levels are expected to be circumspect and self disciplined in the discharge of their judicial functions." **See further** *M.P. Oil Extraction v. State of Madhya Pradesh,* AIR 1998 SC 145, p. 157 : (1997) 7 SCC 592: ("The power of judicial review of the executive and legislative action must be kept within the bounds of constitutional schemes so that there may not be any occasion to entertain misgivings about the role of judiciary in overstepping its limits by unwarranted judicial activism being very often talked of in these days." J.N. RAY J.); *Union of India v. Deoki Nandan Aggarwal*, AIR 1992 SC 96, p. 101 : 1992 supp. (1) SCC 323 ("To invoke judicial activism to set at naught legislative judgment is subversive of the constitutional harmony and comity of instrumentalities". V. RAMASWAMY, J.).

16. GLEESON C.J. of the High Court of Australia in a speech made to the Australian Bar Association Conference in Newyork, (2000) 74 ALJ 494 (Aust.) **See further** CARDOZO, The Nature of the Judicial Process p. 129: 'Judges have, of course, the *power*, though *not the right,* to ignore the mandate of a statute, and render judgment in despite of it. They have *the power*, though not *the right,* to travel beyond the walls of the interstices, the bounds set to judicial innovation by precedent and custom. None the less, by that abuse of power, they violate the law.'

17. The complete dilution of the power of the Executive in the matter of appointment and transfer of judges and the taking away of the power of superintendence of the Central Government over the C.B.I. may be cited as examples. **See** on these matters pp. 299, 300 301 and 311, *post*.

years, been spent in the interpretation and expositions of statutes, it is natural enough that in a matter so complex, the guiding principles should be stated in different language and with such varying emphasis on different aspects of the problem that support of high authority may be found for general and apparently irreconcilable propositions. I shall endeavour not to add to their number'.[18] In the same case LORD SOMERVELL, before citing a well-known formulation by SIR JOHN NICHOLL, observed: "It is, I hope, not disrespectful to regret that the subject was not left where SIR JOHN NICHOLL left in 1826".[19] LORD EVERSHED in his foreword to the 11th Edition of MAXWELL said: "It is my hope that out of the vast body of judicial decisions on the interpretation of statutes, there will, in the end, emerge rules few in number but well understood generally applicable or applicable to particular or defined classes of legislation, which may supersede and render obsolete other *dicta* derived from a different age and a different philosophy".[20]

The rules of interpretation are not rules of law and are not to be applied like the rules enacted by the Legislature in an Interpretation Act.[21] They serve as guides and such of them which serve no useful purpose now can be rejected by courts and new rules can be evolved in their place.[22] By boldly rejecting outmoded rules, by substituting, if necessary, new rules in their place[23] and by avoiding unnecessary generalisation[24] the superior courts can help in the task of rationalisation of the rules. In applying the rules it must be kept in view that as the rules are not binding in the ordinary sense like a legislation, 'they are our servants and not masters. They are aids to construction, presumptions or pointers. Not infrequently one rule points in one direction, another in a different direction. In each case we must look at all relevant circumstances and decide as a matter of judgment what weight to attach to any particular rule'.[25]

---

18. *Attorney-General v. HRH Prince Ernest Augustus*, (1957) 1 All ER 49, pp. 53, 54 (HL).

19. *Ibid*, p. 61. For full quotation of SIR JOHN NICHOLL'S *dicta* **see** text and note 62, at p. 39.

20. MAXWELL, Interpretation of Statutes, 11th Edition, Foreword, p. 6.

21. *Superintendent and Remembrancer of Legal Affairs v. Corporation of Calcutta*, AIR 1967 SC 997, pp. 1003, 1007 : 1967 (2) SCR 170 : 1967 Cri LJ 950. In this case the old rule that a Statute does not bind the State unless it is expressly named or brought in by necessary implication, was rejected and a new rule was formulated that a general Act applies to citizens as well as to State unless the Act expressly or by necessary implication excepts the State from its operation.

22. *Ibid*.

23. *Ibid*.

24. For example **see** the general observations of SHETTY J., in *Kehar Singh v. State*, AIR 1988 SC 1883, p. 1945 : 1988 (3) SCC 609 regarding the golden rule. **See** comments on it in note 31, p. 94.

25. *Maunsel v. Olins*, (1975) 2 All ER 16, p. 18 : (1974) 1 WLR 830 (HL) (LORD REID). According to LORD SIMON there are primary and secondary canons of

[Footnote No. 25 Contd.]

One need not blame the courts alone for creating some confusion in this branch of our law. Although a perfect draftsman exists only in theory not in practice,[26] some amount of responsibility must also be shared by the parliamentary draftsman.[27] The utility of the rules of interpretation is

---

[Footnote No. 25 Contd.]

construction. The primary rule of construction is to consider the plain meaning. If there is no plain meaning mischief rule is the most important rule amongst the secondary canons of construction. There is no hierarchy amongst the secondary canons and which rule will have paramountcy is likely to depend on all the circumstances of the particular case (*ibid*, p. 29). The above passage from LORD REID'S speech has been **quoted** with **approval** in *Utkal Contractors and Joinery Pvt. Ltd. v. State of Orissa*, (1987) 3 SCC 279, p. 290 : AIR 1987 SC 1454 and *Keshavji Ravji and Co. v. Commissioner of Income-tax*, AIR 1991 SC 1806, p. 1813 : 1990 (2) SCC 231 : (1990) 183 ITR 1. As **explained** by VEKATACHALIAH, J., in *Nyadar Singh v. Union of India*, AIR 1988 SC 1979, p. 1984 : 1988 (4) SCC 170: "The meaning to be given to a particular statutory language depends on the evaluation of a number of interpretative-criteria.—The general presumption is that these criteria do not detract or stand apart from, but are to be harmonised with, the well accepted legal principles. In a difficult case, the number of relevant interpretative-criteria may be so high that the task of the court in assessing their effect is, correspondingly difficult." **See further** BENNION, Statutory Interpretation 5th Edition pp. 511-515; **See also** *Central Bureau of Investigation v. Keshub Mahindra*, (2011) 6 SCC 216 (para 11) (No Judgement can be read in a manner so as to nullify the express provisions of an Act or the Code).

26. *Municipal Corporation of Hyderabad v. P.N. Murthy,* (1987) 1 SCC 568, p. 572 : AIR 1987 SC 92 : (1987) 167 ITR 204.

27. It is not uncommon to find enactments reminding one of the old British jingle: "I am the parliamentary draftsman. I compose the country's laws. And of half of the litigation, I am undoubtedly the cause": *Palace Administrative Board v. RVB Thampuran*, AIR 1980 SC 1187, p. 1195 : 1980 Supp SCC 234; *Institute of Chartered Accountats of India v. Price Waterhouse*, AIR 1998 SC 74, p. 90 : 1997 (6) SCC 312; *J.P. Bansal v. State of Rajasthan,* 2003 AIR SCW 1848, p. 1854 : AIR 2003 SC 1405 : (2003) 5 SCC 134; *State of Jharkhand v. Govind Singh*, AIR 2005 SC 294, p. 297. H. RAO in 'Unfathomable Mysteries of Legal Language' (Sunday Chronicle, 14-7-1996) quotes THOMAS JEFFERSON that statutes 'from their verbosity, their endless tautologies, their involutions of case within case, and parenthesis within parenthesis, and their multiplied efforts at certainty, by saids and aforesaids, by ors and ands, to make them more plain, are really rendered more perplexed and incomprehensible, not only to common readers, but to the lawyers themselves.' The Draftsman must abandon obsolescent vocabulary and style of expression and must use simple and plainer language: *Aluminium Corporation of India v. Union of India*, AIR 1975 SC 2279, pp. 2283, 2284 : (1975) 2 SCC 472; *Chitan J. Vaswani v. State of West Bengal*, AIR 1975 SC 2473, p. 2475 : (1975) 2 SCC 829. "A good legislation is that the text of which is plain, simple, unambiguous, precise and there is no repetition of words or usage of superfluous language:" *In the matter of Special Reference 1 of 2002 (Gujarat Assembly Election Matters)* (2002) 8 SCC 237, p. 279 (KHARE, J). There is a recent trend in some commonwealth countries for drafting and rewriting statutes in plain language or in otherwords user friendly terms which means that the statutes produced are designed to be readable and easy to use by the relevant audiences to whom they are addressed: RUTH SULLIVAN, Some

[Footnote No. 27 Contd.]

based on the theory that the Legislature in formulating its legislation keeps the rules in view so that it may not be misunderstood by the courts. "There is an inevitable interaction", said LORD DU PARCQ, "between the methods

---

[Footnote No. 27 Contd.]

Implications of Plain Language Drafting, (2001) 22 Statute Law Review 175; PETER BUCK AND RICHARD CASTLE 'Modern legal Drafting, Cambridge University Press, 2001; EDWIN JANNER, Clear Simple and Precise Legislative Drafting : Australian Guidelines, 25 (2004) Statute Law Review 223. The shift towards use of plain language for drafting statutes is not without controversy. The critics of the use of plain language say that 'the language of our legislation cannot be reduced to baby talk for consumption of the masses' and the attainment of precision and accuracy for enshrining policy, stating rights and obligations and regulating future events gives rise to the need for use of difficult language which is familiar to the lawyers but not to the layman: BRIAN HUNT, Plain Language Drafting : Is it Really the Answer, (2002) 23 Statute Law Review, 24, pp. 44, 45. **See further** (2003) 24 Statute Law Review 112 for another article by BRIAN HUNT to show "why plain language is not entirely suitable in legislative drafting". The debate about Plain Language drafting continues **see**: JEFREY BARNES, The Continuing Debate About 'Plain Language': A Law Reform conundrum, (2006) 27 Statute Law Review 83. M DOUGLAS BELLIS, Deputy Legislative Counsel, U.S. House of Representatives in his article Drafting in the U.S. Congress in (2001) 22 Statute Law Review 43, 44 tries to discover some universal drafting norms, which briefly stated are as follows: A good draft contains a clear expression of intent, uses a consistent terminology throughout, avoids passive voice and aspirational statements meaning thereby statement of hopes and opinions rather than commands. The terms used are either authoritatively defined in the draft or by judicial interpretation. Sentences are short. Simple words commonly used in ordinary speech are preferred. Convoluted subdivision is avoided and so is repetition. Parliamentary Counsel, DANIEL GREENBERG, in his article 'Nature of Legislative Intention and its Implications for Legislative Drafting' (2006) 27 Statute Law Review 1 at p. 26 concludes: 'The concept of the legislative intent is neither as straightforward as it might appear at the first glance nor as elusive as one might fear on closer examination. As traditionally understood by the courts, it is a concept that is capable of being discovered by reference to objective criteria. Its nature and the nature of those criteria, requires to be borne in mind by the draftsman in order to ensure that his draft will be given the meaning that he intends. In particular, the nature of the objective search for legislative intent requires the draftsman to determine the nature of primary target audience and the facilities likely to be available to them in applying and construing the legislation.' Can an action for damages lie for legislative negligence has recently been debated. Legislative negligence, in this context, means 'such an obvious in attention to the consequences of the wording of legislation that, if such workmanship had been perpetrated by a lawyer drafting a lease, will, trust deed, or any other legal document, it would have amounted to professional negligence.' It is argued that 'Legislative negligence is a cause of action arising out of the damage which has been caused by the failure of a government department or legislative draftsman to attend to the obvious adverse consequences of the legislation which the department is promoting'. LESLIE BLAKE, JOHN POINTING AND TIM SINNAMON, Over Regulation and Suing the State for Negligent Legislation (2007) 28 Statute Law Review 218 pp. 220, 221.

of parliamentary drafting and the principles of judicial interpretation".[28] However, the rules enunciated by courts are not binding on the Legislature and if the Legislature does not follow them, the court's duty is not to misinterpret the law. As observed by LORD DU PARCQ as Lord Justice: "the courts have not, and certainly do not, claim the right to say to Parliament or to its draftsman: observe the rules which we lay down or, though your meaning may be perfectly clear, we will teach you a lesson by interpreting your language in a sense which you obviously did not intend".[29] Whenever the draftsman departs from the rules, and it is certainly not a rare occurrence, the courts are led to the necessity of modifying the general rules or of engrafting exceptions to them, the result being that in many cases there ceases to be any general rule or at any rate any general intelligible rule. Further, 'fashions in parliamentary draftsmanship and attitude of the Legislature towards innovations in established law are not unchanging'.[30] Such changes have their interaction on the relative importance to be attached to the competing canons of construction. 'A trend away from purely literal towards the purposive construction of statutory provisions'[31] is a pointer in that direction.

With the widening of the idea of context and importance being given to the rule that the statute has to be read as a whole in its context[32] it is nowadays misleading to draw a rigid distinction between literal and purposive approaches. The difference between purposive and literal constructions is in truth one of degree only.[33] The real distinction lies in the balance to be struck in the particular case between literal meaning of the words on the one hand and the context and purpose of the measure in which they appear on the other. When there is a potential clash, the conventional English approach has been to give decisive weight to the literal meaning but this tradition is now

---

28. *Cutler v. Wandsworth Stadium Ltd.*, (1949) 1 All ER 544, p. 550 (HL). The canons of construction form 'that common code of juristic communication by which the draftman signals legislative intention'; they are also 'salutory in helping to ensure that legislators are not left in doubt what they are taking responsibility for': *London Borough of Ealing v. Race Relations Board*, (1972) 1 All ER 105, p. 114 (HL) (LORD SIMON OF GLAISDALE).

29. *No-Nail Cases Proprietary Ltd. v. No-Nail Boxes Ltd.*, (1944) 1 All ER 528, pp. 529, 530 (CA).

30. *Carter v. Bradbeer*, (1975) 3 All ER 158, p. 161 (HL) (LORD DIPLOCK).

31. *Ibid* **See further** *Fothergill v. Monarch Airlines*, (1980) 2 All ER 696, p. 705 : (1981) AC 251 : (1980) 2 WLR 209 (HL) (LORD DIPLOCK).

32. See p. 35 text and notes 39, 40.

33. *Oliver Ashworth (Holdings) Ltd. v. Bellard (Kent) Ltd.*, (1999) 2 All ER 791, p. 805 (LAWS L.J.) (C.A.). BENNION in his work on Statutory Interpretation (5th edition, pp. 951, 952) divides purposive construction into (i) purposive and literal construction and (ii) purposive and strained construction. **See further** *Tanna & Modi v. CIT Mumbai,* (2007) 7 SCC 434, para 22.

weakening in favour of the purposive approach[34] for the pendulum has swung towards purposive methods of constructions.[35]

A handbook compiling the rules attempts to present the guiding principles explaining as far as possible the apparent conflict in them and illustrating their application with reference to decided cases. But such a handbook only presents a set of tools and gives some general guidance for their use. Any book, for example, will tell that the text of a statute should not be sacrificed by lofty references to purpose or spirit which are not discernible, but when the purpose or object of a statute is clear it should not be defeated by a mechanical construction even if there is some ineptness in language. But these rules and similarly all other rules by themselves yield no solution.[36] An intelligent application of the rules and the solution in each real difficulty depends upon the individual skill of a Judge. The judges of the superior courts who form a dissenting minority on a question of construction of a statute are not ignorant of the rules of construction; the difference of opinion results mainly because of the spirit in which each judge applies the rules and how-far he can go to make the words promote the object and policy which the statute was designed to achieve.[37] By combining

---

34. *Oliver Ashworth (Holdings) Ltd. v. Bellard (Kent) Ltd., supra*, p. 805. **Also see** observations of LORD REID quoted in note 37, p. 34, 35.

According to LORD MILLETT: "We are all purposive constructionists now": 'Construing Statutes', (1999) 2 Statute Law Review 107, p. 108. A study under taken into the interpretative resources and tools used by the New Zealand Court of Appeal in 1976, 1986 and 1996 shows that the use of purposive approach to interpretation was relatively popular (ranging from 40 to 50 per cent) in all the three years: JAMES ALLAN, Statutory Interpretation and the Courts (1999) 18 New Zealand University Law Review 440, p. 441. **See further** JOHN F. MANING, What Divides Textualists from Purposivists, (2006) 106 Columbia Law Review 70 [The article begins with the words 'Recent scholarship has questioned whether there remains a meaningful distinction between textualism and purposivism' (p. 70), but in the end it concludes 'that textualism continues to represent a superior account of legislative supremacy despite the need for a more nuanced form of justification'. (p. 111)]

35. *R (On the application of Quintavalle) v. Secretary of State for Health,* (2003) 2 All ER 113, p. 123 (H.L.) (LORD STEYN).

36. Application of the same rule of construction by different judges may result in different conclusions. For example, see the application of the rule of harmonious construction in resolving the conflict between fundamental rights and Art. 194(3) of the Constitution in majority and minority opinions in *M.S.M. Sharma v. Shri Krishna Sinha*, AIR 1959 SC 395 : 1959 Supp (1) SCR 806 : (1959) 2 MLJ (SC) 125; and *In re*, *Article 143, Constitution of India*, AIR 1965 SC 745 : 1965 (1) SCR 413. In *Carter v. Bradbeer*, (1975) 3 All ER 158, pp. 161, 162 (HL), LORD DIPLOCK in his minority judgment remarked that when the difference of opinion is confined to the effect of applying undisputed canons of construction and does not extend to the nature of relative weight of the canons to be applied, no useful purpose is served by a detailed minority opinion of the highest tribunal.

37. **See** the following observation of LORD REID in *Jones v. Secretary of State*, (1972) 1 All ER 145 (HL); "In very many cases it cannot be said positively that one

[Footnote No. 37 Contd.]

knowledge, wisdom and experience great judges develop the instinct of finding out that solution which harmonizes the words with the policy or object behind them. JUDGE LEARNED HAND tells us that JUSTICE CORDOZO said: "A judge must think of himself as an artist, who although he must know the handbooks, should never trust to them for his guidance; in the end he must rely upon his almost instinctive sense of where the line lay between the word and the purpose which lay behind it."[38] What was that which made it possible for CORDOZO to reach a conclusion, "just that compromise between the letter and the spirit" is further told by HAND: "it was wisdom, and like most wisdom, his ran beyond the reasons which he gave for it."[39] And the same is true of all handbooks and all great judges.

3. STATUTE MUST BE READ AS A WHOLE IN ITS CONTEXT

When the question arises as to the meaning of a certain provision in a statute, it is not only legitimate but proper to read that provision in its context. The context here means, the statute as a whole, the previous state of the law, other statutes in *pari materia*, the general scope of the statute and the mischief that it was intended to remedy.[40] This statement of the rule was later fully adopted by the Supreme Court.[41]

[Footnote No. 37 Contd.]
construction is right and the other wrong. Much may depend on one's approach. If more attention is paid to meticulous examination of the language used in the statute the result may be different from that reached by paying more attention to the apparent object of the statute so as to adopt that meaning of the words under consideration which best accords with it."

38. MR. JUSTICE CORDOZO BY LEARNED HAND, 52 Harvard Law Review, pp. 361-63.

39. *Ibid.* In *State of Maharashtra v. Jagannath Achyut Karandikar*, AIR 1989 SC 1133, p. 1136 : 1989 Supp (1) SCC 393 : (1989) LLJ 441; SHETTY J. said: "We do not have to reflect upon the rules of interpretation. Since they are well settled. They are now like the habits of driving which have become ingrained. They come to our assistance by instinct." PROF. JAMES ALLAN remarks that 'the public rationalisation in a written judgement of how a decision has been reached may differ from the process by which the judge in fact came to decide a case.' : 'Statutory Interpretation And the Courts' (1999) 18 New Zealand University Law Review, 440. As observed by JUSTICE KIRBY OF AUSTRALIA "Interpretation is often, at base, an intuitive process, involving judgement", and "so judges may have difficulty in explaining exactly why they chose one interpretation over another": 'Towards a Grand Theory of Interpretation: The Case of Statutes and Contracts' (2003) 24 Statute Law Review 95, p. 110.

40. **See** text and notes 60 to 66, pp. 39, 40. **See further** *R. S. Raghunath v. State of Karnataka*, AIR 1992 SC 81, p. 89 : 1992 (1) SCC 335; *Powdrill v. Watson*, (1995) 2 All ER 65, p. 79 (HL); *R. v. Secretary of State for the Home Department, exparte Daly*, (2001) 3 All ER 433, p. 447 (HL) ("In law context is everything" Lord Steyn).

41. *Union of India v. Elphinstone Spinning and Weaving Co. Ltd.*, 2001 (1) JT SC 536, p. 563 : AIR 2001 SC 724, p. 740 : (2001) 4 SCC 139 (Constitution Bench). **See**

[Footnote No. 41 Contd.]

It is a rule now firmly established[42] that the intention of the Legislature must be found by reading the statute as a whole. The rule is referred to as an 'elementary rule' by VISCOUNT SIMONDS;[43] a "compelling rule" by LORD SOMERVELL OF HARROW;[44] and a "settled rule" by B.K. MUKHERJEE, J.[45] "I agree", said LORD HALSBURY, "that you must look at the whole instrument inasmuch as there may be inaccuracy and inconsistency; you must, if you can, ascertain what is the meaning of the instrument taken as a whole in order to give effect, if it be possible to do so, to the intention of the framer of it".[46] And said LORD DAVEY: "Every clause of a statute should be construed with reference to the context and other clauses of the Act, so as, as far as possible, to make a consistent enactment of the whole statute or series of statutes relating to the subject-matter."[47] It is spoken of construction '*ex visceribus actus*'.[48] "It is the most natural and genuine

[Footnote No. 41 Contd.]

further *Central Bank of India v. State of Kerala,* (2009) 4 SCC 94 para 98 : (2009) 3 JT 216.

42. *Philips India Ltd. v. Labour Court,* (1985) 3 SCC 103, p. 112 : AIR 1985 SC 1034 : (1985) 3 SCC 103; *Osmania University Teachers Association v. State of A.P.*, AIR 1987 SC 2034, p. 2042 : (1987) 4 SCC 671; *Captain Subhash Kumar v. The Principal Officer, Mercantile Marine Deptt.*, AIR 1991 SC 1632, p. 1638 : 1991 (2) SCC 449 : 1991 Cri LJ 2000. **See further** *Mohan Kumar Singhania v. Union of India*, AIR 1992 SC 1, p. 29 : 1992 Supp (1) SCC 594 [4th Edition of this book (p. 18) is **quoted**]; *Lalit Mohan Pandy v. Pooran Singh*, (2004) 6 SCC 626, p. 642; *Karnataka State Financial Corporation v. N. Narsimahaiah*, (2008) 5 SCC 176 para 29 : AIR 2008 SC 1797; *Subramanian Swamy v. Election Commission of India,* AIR 2009 SC 110 para 19 : (2008) 14 SCC 318.

43. *AG v. HRH Prince Ernest Augustus*, (1957) 1 All ER 49, p. 55 (HL).

44. *Ibid*, p. 61.

45. *Poppatlal Shah v. State of Madras*, AIR 1953 SC 274, p. 276 : 1953 SCR 677 : 1953 Cri LJ 1105.

46. *Charles Robert Leader v. Georage F. Diffey*, (1888) 13 AC 294, p. 301.

47. *Canada Sugar Refining Co. v. R*, (1898) AC 735, p. 742; **referred** to in *M. Pentiah v. Veeramallappa Muddala*, AIR 1961 SC 1 107, p. 1111 : (1961) 2 SCR 295; *Gamman India Ltd. v. Union of India*, AIR 1974 SC 960, p. 964 : (1974) 1 SCC 596; *Mysore State Road Transport Corporation v. Mirza Khasim Ali Beg*, AIR 1977 SC 747, p. 752 : (1977) SCC (L&S) 282 : (1977) 2 SCC 457; *Vaddeboyina Tulsamma v. Vaddeboyina Sesha Reddi*, AIR 1977 SC 1944, p. 1948 : (1977) 3 SCC 99; *Punjab Beverages Pvt. Ltd. v. Suresh Chand*, AIR 1978 SC 995, p. 998 : 1978 (2) SCC 667; *Commissioner of Income-tax v. National Taj Traders*, AIR 1980 SC 485, p. 489 : (1980) 1 SCC 370; *Sultana Begum v. Prem Chand Jain*, AIR 1997 SC 1006, pp. 1009, 1010 : 1997 (1) SCC 373; *Kailash Chandra v. Mukundi Lal,* AIR 2002 SC 829, p. 833 : (2002) 2 SCC 678, *Padmasundara Rao v. State of T.N.,* AIR 2000 SC 1334, p. 1340 : (2002) 3 SCC 533; *Godawat Pan Masala Products I.P. Ltd. v. Union of India*, (2004) 7 SCC 68, p. 88.

48. *Newspapers Ltd. v. Industrial Tribunal, U.P.*, AIR 1957 SC 532, p. 536 : 1957 SCR 754; *Superintendent and Remembrancer, West Bengal v. Abani Maity*, AIR 1979 SC 1029, p. 1032 : (1979) 4 SCC 85; *Mohan Kumar Singhania v. Union of India,* AIR 1992 SC 1, p. 20 : 1992 Supp (1) SCC 594; *Sultana Begum v. Prem Chand Jain, supra*; *Balaram Kumawat v. Union of India*, (2003) 7 SCC 628, p. 634 : AIR 2003 SC 3268.

exposition of a statute", laid down by LORD COKE "to construe one part of a statute by another part of the same statute, for that best expresseth the meaning of the makers".[49] To ascertain the meaning of a clause in a statute the court must look at the whole statute, at what precedes and at what succeeds and not merely at the clause itself,[50] and, "the method of construing statutes that I prefer", said LORD GREENE, M.R. "is to read the statute as a whole and ask oneself the question: "In this state, in this context, relating to this subject-matter, what is the true meaning of that word'?"[51] As stated by SINHA, C.J.I.: "The court must ascertain the intention of the Legislature by directing its attention not merely to the clauses to be construed but to the entire statute; it must compare the clause with the other parts of the law, and the setting in which the clause to be interpreted occurs."[52]

The rule is of general application as even the plainest terms may be controlled by the context,[53] and "it is conceivable," as LORD WATSON said, "that the Legislature whilst enacting one clause in plain terms, might introduce into the same statute other enactments which to some extent qualify or neutralise its effect".[54] The same word may mean one thing in one

---

49. 1 Inst 381 (b); *Punjab Beverages Pvt. Ltd. v. Suresh Chand*, AIR 1978 SC 995, p. 1000 : 1978 (2) SCC 144 : (1978) 2 LLJ 1; *Philips India Ltd. v. Labour Court*, (1985) 3 SCC 103, p. 112 : AIR 1985 SC 1034.

50. *Queen v. Eduljee Byramjee*, (1846) 3 MIA 468, p. 483 (PC) (DR. LUSHINGTON); *National Insurance Co. Ltd. v. Anjana Shyam*, (2007) 7 SCC 445, para 17 : AIR 2007 SC 2870.

51. *Re, Bidie (deceased)*, (1948) 2 All ER 995, p. 998 (CA); **See further** *Jagir Singh v. State of Bihar*, AIR 1976 SC 997, p. 1001 : 1976 SCC (Tax) 204 : (1976) 2 SCC 942; *Keshavananda Bharati v. State of Kerala*, AIR 1973 SC 1461, pp. 1497, 1577 : (1973) 4 SCC 225; *State of West Bengal v. Pranab Ranjan Roy*, 1998 (2) Scale 251, p. 255: AIR 1998 SC 1887, p. 1890 : (1998) 2 SCC 209.

52. *State of W.B. v. Union of India*, AIR 1963 SC 1241, p. 1265 : 1964 (1) SCR 371; referred to in *State of Punjab v. Okara Grain Buyers Syndicate Ltd.*, AIR 1964 SC 669, p. 679 : 1964 (5) SCR 387; *R.S. Raghunath v. State of Karnataka*, AIR 1992 SC 81, p. 89 : (1992) 1 SCC 335; *More Modern Co-operative Transport Society Ltd. v. Financial Commissioner*, AIR 2002 SC 2513, p. 2518 : (2002) 6 SCC 269; *Maniklal Majumdar v. Gauranga Chandra Dey*, (2005) 2 SCC 400, p. 407 : AIR 2005 SC 1090; *Prakash Kumar v. State of Gujarat*, (2005) 2 SCC 409 para 30 : AIR 2005 SC 1075; *Steel Authority of India Ltd. v. S.U.T.N.I. Sangam*, (2009) 16 SCC 1 para 67 : AIR 2010 SC 112; *Pallawi Resources Limited v. Protos Engineering Co. Private Limited*, (2010) 5 SCC 196 para 17 : AIR 2010 SC 1969.

53. *Bentley v. Rotherham*, (1876) 4 Ch D 588, p. 592 (JESSEL, MR); *More Modern Co-operative Transport Society Ltd. v. Financial Commissioner, supra*.

54. *Administrator-General of Bengal v. Premlal Mullick*, (1895) ILR 22 Cal 788, p. 797 (PC) : 22 IA 107, pp. 115, 116 **relied upon** in *Harbhajan Singh v. State of Himachal Pradesh*, C.A. No. 5767 of 2002 decided by Supreme Court on 23-11-2010 para 13. LORD WATSON'S view is to be preferred against the observations of the House of Lords in *Warburtan v. Loveland*, (1832) 2 D & Cl. 480, p. 500 that 'no rule of construction can require that when the words of one part of a statute convey a clear meaning it shall be necessary to introduce another part of a statute for the

[Footnote No. 54 Contd.]

context and another in a different context.[55] For this reason the same word used in different sections[56] of a statute or even when used at different places in the same clause or section[57] of a statute may bear different meanings. The conclusion that the language used by the Legislature is plain or ambiguous can only be truly arrived at by studying the statute as a whole.[58] How far and to what extent each component part of the statute influences the meaning of the other part would be different in each given case. But the effect of the application of the rule to a particular case, should not be confounded with the legitimacy of applying it.

In an appeal before the House of Lords,[59] where the question was of the true import of a statute, the Attorney-General wanted to call in aid the Preamble in support of the meaning which he contended should be given to the enacting part, but in doing so was met by the argument on behalf of the respondent that where the enacting part of a statute is clear and unambiguous, it cannot be controlled by the Preamble which cannot be read. The House of Lords rejected the objection to the reading of the Preamble, although, ultimately it came to the conclusion that the enacting part was clear and unambiguous. VISCOUNT SIMONDS (LORD TUCKER agreeing) in

---

[Footnote No. 54 Contd.]

purpose of controlling or diminishing the efficacy of the first part.' Moreover, these observations have no application in the interpretation of related provisions: *K.S. Paripoornan v. State of Kerala*, JT 1994 (6) SC 182, p. 217 : AIR 1995 SC 1012, p. 1037 : (1994) 5 SCC 593 : (1994) 2 KLT 763.

55. *D.N. Banerji v. P. R. Mukherjee*, AIR 1953 SC 58, p. 61 : 1953 SCR 302; *N. Subramania Iyer v. Official Receiver*, AIR 1958 SC 1, p. 10 : 1958 SCR 257; *Bangalore Water Supply and Sewerage Board v. A. Rajappa*, AIR 1978 SC 548, p. 564 : (1978) 2 SCC 213; *Gramophone Company of India Ltd. v. Birendra Bahadur Pandey*, (1984) 2 SCC 534, p. 553 : AIR 1984 SC 667; *Banaras Hindu University v. Indra Pratap Singh (Dr.)*, AIR 1992 SC 780, p. 784 : 1992 Supp (2) SCC 2.

56. *Forbes v. Attorney-General of Manitoba*, (1937) 1 All ER 249, pp. 255, 256 (PC) (use of word 'employer' in different sections); *Anand Nivas (P) Ltd. v. Anandji Kalyanji*, AIR 1965 SC 414, p. 424 : (1964) 4 SCR 892 (use of word 'tenant' in different sections and clauses); *Chief Justice, Andhra Pradesh v. LVA Dikshitulu*, AIR 1979 SC 193, p. 208 : 1979 SCC (L&S) 99 : (1979) 2 SCC 34. (The expression 'civil services of a State' was construed not to include High Court staff and subordinate judiciary in Article 371-D, though the same expression includes them in Article 311).

57. *Ramnarayan Mor v. State of Maharashtra*, AIR 1964 SC 949, p. 953 : 1964 (5) SCR 1064 : (1964) 2 Cri LJ 44 (use of word 'evidence' at three places in clause (6) of section 207-A, Code of Criminal Procedure,1898); *Indian Iron and Steel Co. Ltd. v. Biswanath Sonar*, AIR 1967 SC 77; pp. 79, 80 : 1966 Supp SCR 15 (use of word 'term' at two places in section 7(3) of the Bengal Non-Agricultural Tenancy Act, 1949); *K. Ramanathan v. State of T.N.*, (1985) 2 SCC 116, p. 129 : AIR 1985 SC 660 (use of word 'regulating' in section 3(1) and (2) of the Essential Commodities Act, 1955).

58. **See** text and note 58, p. 61.

59. *AG v. HRH Prince Ernest Augustus*, (1957) 1 All ER 49 (HL).

that connection said: 'I conceive it to be my right and duty to examine every word of a statute in its context, and I use context in its widest sense as including not only other enacting provisions of the same statute, but its preamble, the existing state of the law, other statutes in *pari materia*, and the mischief which I can, by those and other legitimate means, discern that the statute was intended to remedy.'[60] LORD SOMERVELL put the matter thus: "A question of construction arises when one side submits that a particular provision of an Act covers the facts of the case and the other submits that it does not or it may be agreed it applies, but the difference arises to its application. It is unreal to proceed as if the court looked first at the provision in dispute without knowing whether it was contained in a Finance Act or a Public Health Act. The title and general scope of the Act constitute the background of the contest. When the Court comes to the Act itself, bearing in mind any relevant extraneous matters, there is, in my opinion one compelling rule. The whole, or any part, of the Act may be referred to and relied on."[61] He then went on to quote with approval the following observations of SIR JOHN NICHOLL: 'The key to the opening of every law is the reason and the spirit of the law—it is the *animus imponentis*, the intention of the law-maker, expressed in the law itself, taken as a whole. Hence to arrive at the true meaning of any particular phrase in a statute, that particular phrase is not to be viewed detached from the context—meaning by this as well the title and the preamble as the purview or enacting part of the statute.'[62] LORD NORMAND was also of the same opinion.[63]

As rightly pointed out by the High Court of Australia, 'the modern approach to statutory interpretation (a) insists that the context be considered in the first instance, not merely at some later stage when ambiguity might be thought to arise, and (b) uses context in its widest sense to include such things as the existing state of the law and the mischief which, by legitimate means—one may discern the statute was intended to

---

60. *AG v. HRH Prince Ernest Augustus*, (1957) 1 All ER 49, p. 53 (HL); *Director of Public Prosecutions v. Schildkamp*, (1969) 3 All ER 1640, p. 1652 (HL); *Union of India v. Sankalchand*, AIR 1977 SC 2328, pp. 2358, 2372: 1977 SCC (L&S) 435 : (1977) 4 SCC 193.

61. *AG v. HRH Prince Ernest Augustus*, (1957) 1 All ER 49, p. 61 (HL).

62. *AG v. HRH Prince Ernest Augustus*, (1957) 1 All ER 49, p. 61 (HL) (**quotation** from *Brett v. Brett*, (1826) 3 Add 210, p. 216 : 162 ER 456, p. 458, SIR JOHN NICHOLL, MR). In *CET v. Darshan Surendra Parekh*, AIR 1968 SC 1125, p. 1229 : 1968 (2) SCR 589 : (1968) 69 ITR 683, SHAH, J. stated the rule in similar words. **See further** *In re, Presidential Election, 1974*, AIR 1974 SC 1682, p. 1686 : (1974) 2 SCC 33; *Union of India v. Sankalchand*, AIR 1977 SC 2328, p. 2372: 1977 SCC (L&S) 435: (1977) 4 SCC 193; *K. Balkrishna Rao v. Haji Abdulla Sait*, AIR 1980 SC 214, p. 221 : (1980) 1 SCC 321.

63. *AG v. HRH Prince Ernest Augustus*, (1957) 1 All ER 49, p. 57 (HL).

remedy.'[64] LORD STEYN expressed the same view as follows: "The starting point is that language in all legal texts conveys meaning according to the circumstances in which it was used. It follows that context must always be identified and considered before the process of construction or during it. It is therefore wrong to say that the court may only resort to evidence of the contextual scene when an ambiguity has arisen."[65] LORD BINGHAM in a later case said: 'The controversial provision should be read in the context of statute as a whole, and the statute as a whole should be read in the historical context of the situation which led to its enactment'.[66] And more recently LORD HOPE as Deputy President of the U. K. Supreme Court said: "It is an elementary principle, that the words of a statute should be construed in the context of the scheme of the statute as a whole."[67] But a word of caution is here necessary. Consideration of context is to assist the court in its 'fundamental duty' 'to give meaning to the legislative command according to the terms in which it has been expressed and not to deflect it from this duty which ultimately is always a text based activity'.[68]

The modern concept of context may in cases, when the language is borrowed from earlier legislation and judicial decisions, encompass the entire historical background of the statutory provision. In interpreting the words 'as of right' in section 22(1) of the Commons Registration Act, 1965, LORD HOFFMAN said: "The language is plainly derived from judicial pronouncements and earlier legislation on acquisition of rights by prescription. To *put the words in their context* it is therefore necessary to say something about the historical background."[69] LORD HOFFMAN then proceeded to refer to the development of the English Law of prescription *viz.*, all relevant statutes beginning from the Statute of Merton, 1235 (20 Henry 3, and 4), the common law rule that the user had to be *necvi, necclam, nec*

---

64. *CIC Insurance Ltd. v. Bankstown Football Club Ltd.* (1997) 187 CLR 384, p. 408 (Aust) referred in *Newcastle City Council v. GTO General Ltd.* (1998) 72 ALJR, p. 112 (Aust); *Australian Finance Direct Ltd. v. Director of Consumer Affairs,* (2007) 82 ALJR 20 p. 213; *K. Generation Pty. Ltd. v. Liquor Licensing Court,* (2009) 83 ALJR 327 para 52 (French C. J.). **See further** *Gurudevdatta VKSSS Maryadit v. State of Maharashtra,* AIR 2001 SC 1980, pp. 1990-1991 : (2001) 4 SCC 534 (Extracts from the Australian cases are quoted with apparent approval).

65. *R (on the application of Westminister City Council) v. National Asylum Support Service,* (2002) 4 All ER 654, p. 655 (HL). Referred in *Central Bank of India v. State of Kerala,* (2009) 4 SCC 94 para 102 with apparent **approval**.

66. *R (on the application of Quintavalle) v. Secretary of State for Health,* (2003) 2 All ER 113 (8) (HL); *R. v. Z.,* (2005) 3 All ER 95 (17) (HL).

67. *R (B A Nigeria) v. Secretary of State,* (2010) 2 All ER 95 (U. K. Supreme Court) para 27.

68. *Northern Territory v. Collins,* (2008) 83 ALJR 1 para 16 (SUMMOW ACJ and KIRBY J).

69. *R. v. Oxford, Shire County Council,* (1999) 3 All ER 385, p. 390 (a, b) (HL).

precario (not by force, nor by stealth, nor the licence of the owner) and the relevant decisions. He then held that the user which was apparently 'as of right' did not cease to be so merely because many of the users were subjectively indifferent, whether a right existed or did not exist for to hold otherwise would be inconsistent with the principles of prescription with an unbroken line of descent, from the common law rule and the Acts of 1832 and 1932, in English Law.[70]

In a case[71] relating to the Restrictive Trade Practices Act, 1956, the question before the House of Lords was whether Restrictive Practices Court has jurisdiction to entertain a reference in regard to an agreement which has been terminated before the reference is begun. Sections 20 and 21 looked at without regard to other sections of the Act are apt to lead to the conclusion that the jurisdiction is limited to subsisting agreements; but this view was not accepted by the House of Lords having regard to the Act read as a whole. LORD EVERSHED observed: "But in truth it is not, as I conceive, legitimate to read section 20 and section 21, bereft of their context—more particularly without having first read the first nineteen sections of the Act. There is, indeed, solid and respectable authority for the rule that you should 'begin at the beginning and go on till you come to the end; then stop'; and in my opinion the rule is—I conceive—peculiarly proper when construing an Act of Parliament and seeking to discover from the Act the Parliamentary intention."[72]

Similarly, while interpreting section 8 of the Punjab Tenancy Act, 1887, contextually, the Supreme Court has held that the phrase 'any person' should generally be given the widest possible import unless the statutory provisions suggest that the Legislature itself has intended to give a restricted meaning to the phrase. Section 8 of the Act provides that nothing shall preclude 'any person' from establishing a right of occupancy on any ground other than the grounds specified in the foregoing sections of the Chapter. Section 5 of the Act recognises the right of occupancy of 'tenants'. Section 10 of the Act states that no one of several 'joint owners' of

---

70. *Ibid.*, p. 396.

71. *Associated Newspapers Ltd. v. Registrar of Restrictive Trading Agreements*, (1964) 1 All ER 55 (HL).

72. *Associated Newspapers Ltd. v. Registrar of Restrictive Trading Agreements*, (1964) 1 All ER 55, pp. 58, 59 (HL). **Similarly** in *Director of Public Prosecutions v. Schildkamp*, (1969) 3 All ER 1640 (HL) Section 332(3) of the Companies Act, 1948 (corresponding to section 75(3) of the Companies Act, 1928) was construed to create an offence of fraudulent trading capable of prosecution only after the commencement of a winding up, although the sub-section read by itself was not so limited. The conclusion as to this limitation was reached mainly on the ground that the whole fascicule of sections in which section 323 appeared dealt with liquidation.

land shall acquire a right of occupancy therein in the absence of a custom to the contrary. The Court held, reading section 8 in the context of sections 5 and 10, and giving effect to the purpose of the Act, that the expression 'any person' will mean a 'tenant', and not a 'joint owner' of a land or a hissedar.[73]

Rule 7 of the Delhi Higher Judicial Service Rules, 1970 provides for recruitment by promotion and by direct recruitment. There is a proviso to the rule which says '*Provided* that not more than one-third of the substantive posts in the service shall be held by direct recruits.' By itself the language of the proviso is consistent with the view that it imposes a ceiling and does not provide for a quota. But this view was not accepted in face of Rule 8 which lays down that seniority of direct recruits *vis-a-vis* promotees shall be determined in the order of rotation of vacancies based on the quotas of vacancies reserved for both categories by Rule 7. It was held that having regard to Rule 8 the true intendment of the proviso to Rule 7 is that one-third of the substantive posts must be reserved for direct recruits. In that context CHANDRACHUD, C.J.I observed: "One must have regard to the scheme of the fasciculus of the relevant rules or sections in order to determine the true meaning of any one or more of them. An isolated consideration of a provision leads to the risk of some other interrelated provision becoming otiose or devoid of meaning."[74] Each word used in the enactment must be allowed to play its role, howsoever significant or insignificant the same may be in achieving the legislative intent and promoting legislative object. Therefore, the expression 'subject to the provisions of section 31' in section 30 of the Armed Forces Tribunal Act, 2007, was held by the Court to not be ornamental or inconsequential, but to mean that the right of appeal in section 30 can be exercised only in the manner and to the extent provided for in section 31, to which the said right is made subject.[75]

In construing the word 'sale' in the Madras General Sales Tax Act, 1939, before its amendment in 1947, the Supreme Court[76] held that the definition of 'sale' as it then stood laid stress on the element of transfer of property and that the mere fact that the contract for sale was entered into within the province of Madras did not make the transaction, which was completed in another province, a sale taxable within the meaning of the

---

73. *Tara Chand & Ors. v. Gram Panchayat, Jhupa Khurd & Ors.*, (2012) 13 SCC 269, pp. 275, 278 to 281.

74. *O.P. Singla v. Union of India*, (1984) 4 SCC 450, p. 461 : 1984 AIR (SC) 1595 : 1984 SCC (L&S) 657. **Referred** in *Kailash Chand v. Mukundi Lal*, AIR 2002 SC 829, p. 833 : (2002) 2 SCC 678.

75. *Union of India and Others v. Brigadier P.S. Gill*, (2012) 4 SCC 463, pp. 468, 469.

76. *Poppatlal Shah v. State of Madras*, AIR 1953 SC 274 : 1953 SCR 677.

Act. The Supreme Court in arriving at that conclusion referred to the title, preamble, definition and other enacting provisions of the statute as also to the subsequent amendments made in the statute. B.K. MUKHERJEA, J. speaking for the court stated: "It is a settled rule of construction that to ascertain the legislative intent, all the constituent parts of a statute are to be taken together and each word, phrase or sentence is to be considered in the light of the general purpose of the Act itself".[77] The same learned Judge, speaking again for the court, on an earlier occasion stated the rule thus: "Words and phrases occurring in a statute are to be taken not in an isolated or detached manner dissociated from the context, but are to be read together and construed in the light of the purpose and object of the Act itself."[78] To the same effect are the observations of S.K. DAS, J: "The meanings of words and expressions used in an Act must take their colour from the context in which they appear."[79] Applying the same principle in another case he again stated: "When the context makes the meaning of a word quite clear, it becomes unnecessary to search for and select a particular meaning out of the diverse meanings a word is capable of, according to lexicographers."[80]

In interpreting section 150 of the Representation of the People Act, 1951, which requires that on the happening of a casual vacancy 'the Election Commission shall, by a notification in the Official Gazette call upon the Assembly constituency concerned to elect a person for the purpose of filling the vacancy', the Supreme Court pointed out that the section cannot be read in isolation without reference to Part III of the Act which prescribes the machinery for calling in question the election of a returned candidate. It was held that on a reading of all these provisions, together the duty of the Election Commission to hold a bye-election, on resignation of a

---

77. *Poppatlal Shah v. State of Madras*, AIR 1953 SC 274, p. 276 : 1953 SCR 677. **See further** *Aswini Kumar Ghose v. Arabinda Bose*, AIR 1952 SC 369, p. 382 : 1953 SCR 1. 'But the value of such previous interpretation as a guide to construction will vary with the circumstances.' Even if the phrase earlier interpreted remains unchanged but if the system in which it is made to work is different it will be a factor to which full weight must be given: *R (B A Nigeria) v. Secretary of State*, (2010) 2 All ER 95 (U. K. Supreme Court) para 27.

78. *Darshan Singh Balwant Singh v. State of Punjab*, AIR 1953 SC 83, p. 86 : 1953 SCR 319.

79. *Ram Narain v. State of U.P.*, AIR 1957 SC 18, p. 23 : 1956 SCR 664. **See further** *Kehar Singh v. State*, AIR 1988 SC 1883, p. 1932 : 1988 (3) SCC 609 (The words and sections like men do not have their full significance when standing alone. Like men they are better understood by the company they keep); *CIT v. Venkateshwara Hatcheries*, AIR 1999 SC 1225, p. 1228 : (1999) 3 SCC 632 : (1999) 237 ITR 174.

80. *Mango Singh v. Election Tribunal*, AIR 1957 SC 871, pp. 874, 875 : 1958 SCR 418. **See further** *Deputy Chief Controller of Imports & Exports, Delhi v. K.T. Kosalram*, AIR 1971 SC 1283, p. 1289 : (1970) 3 SCC 82 : (1971) 2 SCR 507.

member imposed by section 150 need not be discharged forthwith if the election of that member has been called in question by an election petition in which the petitioner has also claimed a relief that he should be deemed to be duly elected; and that the Election Commission can await the final adjudication of the election petition for if the petitioner succeeds in getting the declaration that he has been duly elected, there would be no necessity of holding any bye-election.[81] The legal position still remains the same, even after insertion in 1951 of section 151A in the Representation of People Act, which fixes a period of six months for filling any vacancy referred in sections 147, 149, 150 and 151, and the Election Commission can await the adjudication of the election petition in respect of a vacancy if in that petition the petitioner has also claimed the relief of being declared elected.[82]

Similarly, it was held that section 82(b) of the Representation of People Act, 1951, on a plain reading, seems to require that all candidates against whom allegations of commission of corrupt practice are made in the petition must be made parties to the election petition but the provision must be interpreted in the context and scheme of the Act. When interpreted in the context of sections 80, 81, 83, 84 and 100 of the Act, it is seen that the provision requires that the returned candidate, his election agent or any other person committing a corrupt practice with the consent of either the returned candidate or his election agent or any other agent committing a corrupt practice falling within the scope of section 100(1)(d)(ii) of the Act, are to be made parties to the election petition.[83]

Section 202 of the Hyderabad Municipal Corporation Act, 1955 exempts 'buildings and lands vesting in the Corporation' from property tax and section 204 provides that property tax shall be leviable primarily from the occupier if he holds the premises directly from the Corporation. The question before the Court was whether Corporation property in possession of allottees under hire purchase agreements was exempt from tax. The Court held reading both the sections together that such property was not exempt and the exemption was limited to those cases where property vested in the Corporation both in title and possession as otherwise section 204 would become inoperative.[84]

---

81. *D. Sanjeevayya v. Election Tribunal, Andhra Pradesh*, AIR 1967 SC 1211, p. 1213 : 1967 (2) SCR 489.

82. *Election Commission of India v. Telangana Rashtra Samiti*, (2011) 1 SCC 370 : (2010) 13 SCALE 129.

83. *Ajay Maken v. Adesh Kumar Gupta & Anr.*, (2013) 3 SCC 489, pp. 499, 500, 507.

84. *Municipal Corporation of Hyderabad v. P. N. Murthy*, (1987) 1 SCC 568, p. 572 : AIR 1987 SC 92.

Similarly, the Supreme Court held that from a conjoint reading of sections 7, 10 and 16 of the Prevention of Food Adulteration Act, 1954, it will appear that the Act is intended to prohibit and penalise the sale of any adulterated article of food, and hence the term 'store' will take colour from the context and the collocation in which it occurs in sections 7 and 16 of the Act. Therefore, 'storage' of an adulterated article other than for sale would not fall within the purview of section 16 of the Act.[85]

Based on the settled canon of interpretation of statutes that the statute should be construed in its entirety, and a sub-section or a section therein should not be read and construed in isolation, the Supreme Court has held that all the provisions of the Sick Industrial Companies (Special Provisions) Act, 1985, have to be read conjointly. Every word and expression used by the Legislature has to be given its proper and effective meaning, as the Legislature uses no expression without purpose or meaning. Hence, the Supreme Court held that sections 22, 22A, 26 and 32 have to be read and construed jointly and, so construed, the common thread of legislative intent appears to be to treat this law as a special law and to ensure its effective implementation with utmost expeditiousness.[86]

Interpreting sections 10-A and 11, together with sections 10B and 33 of the Indian Medical Council Act, 1956, and Regulation 3(1) of the Medical Council of India Opening of a New or Higher Course of Study or Training (including Post graduate Course of Study or Training) and Increase of Admission Capacity in Any Course of Study or Training (including a Post graduate Course of Study of Training) Regulations, 2000, the Court held that the High Court was not right in coming to the conclusion that once permission was granted for establishment of the medical college, it would amount to grant of recognition, and that thereafter the medical college was free to increase the number of seats without the permission of either the Medical Council of India or the Central Government.[87]

Reading the plain and simple language of sections 2(j), 3, 18, 19 and 20 of the Right to Information Act, 2005, the Supreme Court held that the functions of the Information Commissions are limited to ensuring that a person who has sought information from a public authority is not denied such information except in accordance with the provisions of the Act, and they do not decide disputes between two or more parties concerning their legal rights other than their right to get information in possession of a public

---

85. *Rupak Kumar v. State of Bihar*, (2014) 4 SCC 277. p. 281.
86. *Raheja Universal Limited v. NRC Ltd. & Ors.*, (2012) 4 SCC 148, pp. 172 to 180.
87. *Medical Council of India v. Rama Medical College Hospital and Research Centre, Kanpur, & Anr.*, (2012) 8 SCC 80, pp. 103 to 105.

authority. This function is not a judicial function, but an administrative function conferred by the Act. The Court further held that, for this reason, in sections 12(5) and 15(5) of the Act, the Parliament has not provided for appointment of persons with judicial experience and acumen.

The principle that the statute must be read as a whole is equally applicable to different parts of the same section. The section must be construed as a whole whether or not one of the parts is a saving clause or a proviso.[88] SUBBARAO, J. calls it "an elementary rule that construction of a section is to be made of all the parts together,"[89] and that "it is not permissible to omit any part of it; the whole section should be read together".[90] The Supreme Court held that the expression 'transships' occurring under section 23 of the Narcotic Drugs and Psychotropic Substances Act, 1985, must necessarily be understood in the context of the scheme of the section, and the preceding expressions 'imports into India' and 'exports from India', to mean only transshipment for the purpose of either import into India or export out of India.[91]

Section 154(1) of the UP Zamindari Abolition and Land Reforms Act, 1950, provides that, save as provided in sub-section (2), no bhumidhar shall have the right to transfer, by sale or gift, any land other than tea gardens to 'any person' where the transferee shall, as a result of such sale or gift, become entitled to land which, together with land, if any, held by his family, will in aggregate exceed 5.0586 hectares (12.50 acres) in Uttar Pradesh. The Supreme Court held that the expression 'any person' in section 154(1) does not cover an artificial person such as a charitable trust, but will be restricted only to a natural person, because the expression is followed in the sentence by the words 'his family'. Having regard to the text of section 154(1) and also to the scheme of that provision, there was no doubt that the expression 'any person' refers to a natural person and not to an artificial person.[92]

---

88. *Jennings v. Kelly*, (1939) 4 All ER 464, pp. 470, 476, 477 (HL); *Tahsildar Singh v. State of U.P.*, AIR 1959 SC 1012, p. 1022 : 1959 Supp (2) SCR 875. **See further** Chapter 3, title 9(h) 'Broad General Rule of Construction', p. 232.

89. *Gurmej Singh S. v. Sardar Pratap Singh Kairon*, AIR 1960 SC 122, p. 124 : (1960) 1 SCR 909. **See further** *Balasinor Nagrik Co-operative Bank Ltd. v. Bababhai Shankerlal Pandya*, (1987) 1 SCC 606, p. 608 : AIR 1987 SC 849; *Kalawati Bai v. Soiryabai*, AIR 1991 SC 1581, p. 1586 : (1991) 3 SCC 410; *Mohan Kumar Singhania v. Union of India*, AIR 1992 SC 1, p. 20 : 1992 Supp (1) SCC 594 : 1992 SCC (L&S) 455.

90. *State of Bihar v. Hiralal Kejriwal*, AIR 1960 SC 47, p. 50 : 1960 (1) SCR 726 : 1960 Cri LJ 150.

91. *Union of India v. Sheo Shambhu Giri*, (2014) 12 SCC 692, p. 694.

92. *State of Uttarakhand & Ors. v. Guru Ram Das Educational Trust Society*, (2012) 11 SCC 648.

Sub-sections in a section must be read as parts of an integral whole and as being interdependent, "each portion throwing light, if need be, on the rest".[93]

Section 13(a)(ii) of the Punjab Rent Restriction Act, 1949, enables a landlord to obtain possession in the case of rented land if '(a) he requires it for his own use; (b) he is not occupying in the urban area for the purpose of his business any other such rented land; and (c) he has not vacated such rented land without sufficient cause after the commencement of the Act in the urban area concerned'. The High Court of Punjab held that the words 'for his own use' in clause (a) permitted the landlord to claim eviction for his own use whatever may be the nature of the use. In reversing the High Court the Supreme Court held that all the three clauses were to be read together and clause (a) was restricted to business use as is clauses (b) and (c). It was pointed out that if this restricted meaning is not given to the words 'for his own use' in clause (a) the latter two clauses would become inapplicable.[94]

LORD BLANESBURG, in an appeal from Bombay, criticising the judgment of the Chief Justice, said: "He has not availed himself, as an aid to construction of the light thrown upon each of its expressions by the presence within it of others. Further in his construction of the words he has, they think, hardly had sufficient regard to the setting in which they are found.'[95] In this case, the question involved was of construction of section 30 of the Sea Customs Act, 1878, which in clause (a) defines 'real value' as meaning 'wholesale cash price, less trade discount for which the goods of like kind and quantity are sold, or are capable of being sold'. The High Court held that the expression 'wholesale price' as here used meant a price paid on a sale of substantial quantity of goods rather than a price in contrast with retail price. The Privy Council[96] reversing the High Court held that 'wholesale price' was used in contradistinction with retail price as was indicated by the association of that expression in the said clause with words 'trade discount'.

---

93. *Jennings v. Kelly*, (1939) 4 All ER 464, p. 477 (HL) (LORD WRIGHT); *Madanlal Fakirchand v. Shree Changdeo Sugar Mills Ltd.*, AIR 1962 SC 1543, p. 1551 : 1962 Supp (3) SCR 973 (GAJENDRAGADKAR, J).

94. *Attar Singh v. Inder Kumar*, AIR 1967 SC 773 : 1967 (2) SCR 50.

95. *Vacuum Oil Co. v. Secretary of State*, AIR 1932 PC 168, p. 171. For meaning of 'wholesale cash price', **see** *A.K. Roy v. Voltas Ltd.*, AIR 1973 SC 225 : 1973 (3) SCC 503 and *Union of India v. Bombay Tyre International Ltd.*, (1984) 1 SCC 467 : AIR 1984 SC 420 : (1984) 2 SCC 102. For meaning of 'trade discount' **see** *Kirloskar Brothers Ltd. v. Union of India*, AIR 1992 SC 1324 : (1992) 2 SCC 658 : (1992) 39 ECC 1.

96. *Ibid.*

While holding that an appeal from an order of the Court granting or refusing bail to the High Court under section 21(1) of the National Investigation Agency Act, 2008, has to be heard by a bench of two judges of the High Court, as provided in section 21(2) of the Act, the Supreme Court observed that a section has to be read in its entirety, and its sub-sections are to be read in relation to each other, and not disjunctively, and that a few sub-sections of a section cannot be separated from other sub-sections and read to convey something altogether different from the theme underlying the entire section.[1]

As already stated, the rule that the statute has to be read as a whole and that words should be studied in their context is of general application but since 'you must have a context even more plain'[2] to control plain words, the practical utility of the rule is more visible in construction of general words and in resolving inconsistencies by recourse to harmonious construction.[3]

4. STATUTE TO BE CONSTRUED TO MAKE IT EFFECTIVE AND WORKABLE

The courts strongly lean against a construction which reduces the statute to a futility.[4] A statute or any enacting provision therein must be so construed as to make it effective and operative 'on the principle expressed in the maxim: *ut res magis valeat quam pereat*".[5] It is an application of this principle that courts while pronouncing upon the constitutionality of a statute start with a presumption in favour of constitutionality and prefer a construction which keeps the statute within the competence of the Legislature.[6] The importance of the principle can be judged from the fact that

1. *State of Andhra Pradesh v. Mohd. Hussain*, (2014) 1 SCC 258, p. 266.
2. *Bentley v. Rotherham*, (1876) 4 Ch D 588, p. 592 (JESSEL, MR.).
3. **See** Chapter 2, title 4(b) 'Inconsistency and Repugnancy to be Avoided; Harmonious Construction', and Chapter 5, title 8 'Construction of General Words'.
4. *M. Pentiah v. Veeramallappa Muddala*, AIR 1961 SC 1107, p. 1111 : 1961 (2) SCR 295; *Tinsukhia Electric Supply Co. Ltd. v. State of Assam*, AIR 1990 SC 123, p. 152 : (1989) 3 SCC 709.
5. *CIT v. S. Teja Singh*, AIR 1959 SC 352, p. 356 : (1959) 35 ITR 408. **See further** *Management of Advance Insurance Co. Ltd. v. Gurudasmal*, AIR 1970 SC 1126, p. 1132 : (1970) 1 SCC 633; *Municipal Council, Madurai v. Narayanan*, AIR 1975 SC 2193, p. 2197 : (1975) 2 SCC 497 : 1975 SCC (Tax) 386; *Commissioner of Income-tax v. Hindustan Bulk Carriers,* (2003) 3 SCC 57, p. 73; *D. Saiba v. Bar Council of India*, AIR 2003 SC 2502, p. 2507 (p. 36 of 8th edition of this book is **referred**); *Balaram Kumawat v. Union of India*, (2003) 7 SCC 628, p. 636 : AIR 2003 SC 3268; *Saurabh Chaudri v. Union of India*, AIR 2004 SC 361, p. 373 : (2003) 11 SCC 146; *Nand Kishore Ganesh Joshi v. Commr. Municipal Corporation Kalyan*, AIR 2005 SC 34, p. 37 (para 19).
6. **See** Chapter 6, title 3 'Operation Controlled on Considerations of Constitutionality; Presumption against Exceeding Constitutional Powers'. **See further** *Corporation of Calcutta v. Liberty Cinema*, AIR 1965 SC 1107, pp. 1113, 1114 : 1965 (2) SCR 477.

there is hardly any reported decision, where a statute may have been declared void for sheer vagueness, although theoretically it may be possible to reach such a conclusion in case of 'absolute intractability of the language used,'[7] or when 'it is impossible to resolve the ambiguity,'[8] *i.e.*, when the language is absolutely meaningless.[9] As laid down by FARWELL, J. "unless the words were so absolutely senseless that I could do nothing at all with them, I should be bound to find some meaning, and not to declare them void for uncertainty".[10] LORD DENNING approving FARWELL, J., stated the principle thus: "But when a statute has some meaning even though it is obscure, or several meanings, even though it is little to choose between them, the courts have to say what meaning the statute is to bear, rather than reject it as a nullity".[11] And it was said by LORD DUNEDIN: "It is our duty to make what we can of statutes, knowing that they are meant to be operative, and not inept, and nothing short of impossibility should in my judgment allow a judge to declare a statute unworkable".[12] The principle was reiterated by him in a later case where he observed: "A statute is designed to be workable, and the interpretation thereof by a court should be to secure that object, unless crucial omission or clear direction makes that end unattainable".[13] The courts will therefore reject that construction which will defeat the plain intention of the Legislature even though there

---

7. *Salmon v. Duncombe*, (1886) 11 AC 627, p. 634 (PC); *M. Pentiah v. Veeramallappa Muddala, supra*, pp. 1111 (para 10), 1115 (para 28).
8. *Fawcett Properties v. Buckingham County Council*, (1960) 3 All ER 503, p. 507 (HL) (LORD COHEN). A law which affects fundamental rights and is so vague that the persons applying it are in a boundless sea of uncertainty, may be declared unconstitutional and void: *K.A. Abbas v. Union of India*, AIR 1971 SC 481, p. 496 : 1970 (2) SCC 780. It is the basic principle of legal jurisprudence that an enactment is void for vagueness if its prohibitions are not clearly defined: *Kartar Singh v. State of Punjab*, JT 1994 (2) SC 423, p. 466: 1994 (3) SCC 569 : 1994 Cri LJ 3139. But a law may not be declared void for mere vagueness; *Municipal Committee, Amritsar v. State of Punjab*, AIR 1969 SC 1100, p. 1103 : (1969) 1 SCC 475.
9. *Tinsukhia Electric Supply Co. Ltd. v. State of Assam*, AIR 1990 SC 123, p. 152 : (1989) 3 SCC 709.
10. *Manchester Ship Canal Co. v. Manchester Racecourse Co.*, (1904) 2 Ch 352, pp. 360, 361; *Tinsukhia Electric Supply Co. Ltd. v. State of Assam, supra*.
11. *Fawcett Properties v. Buckingham County Council*, (1960) 3 All ER 503, p. 516 (HL); *Tinsukhia Electric Supply Co. Ltd. v. State of Assam, supra*.
12. *Murray v. IRC*, (1918) AC 541, p. 553; **referred** to in *Pye v. Minister for Land for NSW*, (1954) 3 All ER 514, p. 524 (PC). **See further** *Tinsukhia Electric Supply Co. Ltd. v. State of Assam, supra*.
13. *Whitney v. IRC*, (1926) AC 37, p. 52; **referred** to in *CIT v. S. Teja Singh*, AIR 1959 SC 352, p. 356 : 1959 Supp (1) SCR 394; *Gursahai v. CIT*, AIR 1963 SC 1062, p. 1065 : (1963) 3 SCR 893; *Sodhi Transport Co. v. State of U.P.*, (1986) 2 SCC 486, p. 492 : AIR 1986 SC 1099; *Tinsukhia Electric Supply Co. Ltd. v. State of Assam, supra*. **See further** *Shyam Kishori Devi v. Patna Municipal Corporation*, AIR 1966 SC 1678, p. 1682 : 1966 (3) SCR 466; *Commissioner of Income-tax v. Hindustan Bulk Carriers*, (2003) SCC 57, p. 73 : AIR 2003 SC 3942.

may be some inexactitude in the language used.[14] "If the choice is between two interpretations", stated VISCOUNT SIMON, L.C. "the narrower of which would fail to achieve the manifest purpose of the legislation, we should avoid a construction which would reduce the legislation to futility, and should rather accept the bolder construction, based on the view that Parliament would legislate only for the purpose of bringing about an effective result".[15] The courts may complain that the enactment is 'mind twisting' or an 'enigma' yet they do not readily concede that no meaning can be given to it,[16] and in their comity with the Legislature, they strive hard to give meaningful life to legislative enactments and avoid cadaveric consequences.[17] "It is not an adequate discharge of duty", said HOLMES J., "for courts to say: we see what you are driving at, but you have not said it, therefore we shall go on as before."[18] So the courts are at least now, when purposive construction is gaining momentum, very reluctant to hold that Parliament has achieved nothing by the language it used when it is tolerably plain what it wished to achieve.[19]

An example of the working of the rule is furnished in the construction of section 18-A(9) of the Indian Income-tax Act, 1922, by the Supreme Court.[20] The contention there, was that when action of imposing penalty

---

14. *Salmon v. Duncombe*, (1886) 11 AC 627, p. 634 (PC); *Curtis v. Stovin*, (1889) 22 QBD 513; *CIT v. S. Teja Singh, supra*, p. 356; *M. Pentiah v. Veeramallappa Muddala*, AIR 1961 SC 1107, p. 1111 : (1961) 2 SCR 295; *Deputy Custodian v. Official Receiver*, AIR 1965 SC 951, pp. 956, 957 : 1965 (1) SCR 220; *Commissioner of Income-tax v. Hindusthan Bulk Carriers, supra*, pp. 73, 74 (SCC).

15. *Nokes v. Doncaster Amalgamated Collieries*, (1940) 3 All ER 549, p. 554 (HL); **referred** to in *Pye v. Minister for Lands for NSW*, (1954) 3 All ER 514, p. 524 (PC); *M. Pentiah v. Veeramallappa Muddala, supra*, pp. 1110, 1111 : (1961) 2 SCR 295; *Union of India v. Sankalchand*, AIR 1977 SC 2328, p. 2381 : (1977) 4 SCC 193 : 1977 SCC (L&S) 435; *Superintendent and Remembrancer of Legal Affairs v. Abani Maity*, AIR 1979 SC 1029, p. 1033 : (1979) 4 SCC 85 : 1979 SCC (Cri) 902; *Mohan Kumar Singhania v. Union of India*, AIR 1992 SC 1, p. 19 : 1992 Supp (1) SCC 594; *Commissioner of Income-tax v. Hindustan Bulk Carriers, supra*, p. 74 (SCC). **See further** *Balram Kumawat v. Union of India*, (2003) 7 SCC 628, pp. 636, 637 : AIR 2003 SC 3268, pp. 3273, 3274; *M.T. Khan v. Govt. of A.P.*, (2004) 2 SCC 267, p. 272; *Bhakra Beas Management Board v. Krishna Kumar Vij*, (2010) 8 SCC 701 para 33 : AIR 2010 SC 3342.

16. *CIT v. Distributor (Baroda) (Pvt.) Ltd.*, AIR 1972 SC 288, p. 291 : 1972 (4) SCC 353.

17. *Krishna Chandra Gangopadhyaya v. Union of India*, AIR 1975 SC 1389, p. 1393 : (1975) 2 SCC 302.

18. *Johnson v. United States*, 163 F. 30, 32: 18 L.R.A. (NS) 1194. **See further** comments of LORD DIPLOCK in f.n. 57 p. 347.

19. *BBC Enterprises v. Hi-Tech Xtravision Ltd.*, (1990) 2 All ER 118, pp. 122, 123 : (1990) 2 WLR : 1990 Ch 609 (CA). **See further,** *Balram Kumawat v. Union of India, supra*, p. 637 (SCC) : p. 3274 (AIR); *M.T. Khan v. Govt. of A.P., supra*, p. 272. For purposive construction, **see** title 3(b), Chapter 2.

20. *CIT v. S. Teja Singh*, AIR 1959 SC 352 : 1959 Supp (1) SCR 394.

was sought to be taken under section 28 for failure to comply with section 18-A(3), the conditions as to notice under section 22(1) or 22(2) must be satisfied. The Supreme Court negatived this contention and supported its conclusion by pointing out that the construction suggested will make section 18-A(9)(b) wholly nugatory. GAJENDRAGADKAR, J. said: "If we accede to this contention we must hold that though the Legislature enacted section 18-A(9)(b) with the very object of bringing the failure to send estimates under section 18-A(3) within the operation of section 28, it signally failed to achieve its object. A construction which leads to such a result must, if that is possible, be avoided, on the principle expressed in the maxim *ut res magis valeat quam pereat*."[21] Another such example can be seen in the context of section 7(1) of the Indian Medicine Central Council Act, 1970, which provides that the President, Vice President or member of the Central Council shall continue until his successor shall have been duly elected or nominated. The Supreme Court, while repelling a challenge to the provision made under Arts. 14 and 16 of the Constitution, observed that the provision was made by Parliament to take care of situations when election to the post of President, Vice-President or member is delayed for various reasons and upheld the provisions of section 7(1) of the Act applying the principle that a statute is to be construed so as to make it effective and operative as expressed in the principle *ut res valeat potius quam pereat*.[22]

The Income-tax Act, 1961, which repeals the predecessor Act of 1922 provides in section 297(2)(j) that notwithstanding the repeal 'any sum payable by way of income-tax, super-tax, interest, penalty or otherwise under the repealed Act may be recovered under this Act, but without prejudice to any action already taken for the recovery of such sum under the repealed Act'. In spite of this provision the Mysore High Court held that the group of sections 220 to 234 of the 1961 Act which deal with collection and recovery of tax could not be applied for recovery of tax assessed under the old Act. Reversing the High Court the Supreme Court observed that the effect of the judgment of the High Court was to nullify section 297(2)(j) and to declare it to be of no consequence and that an interpretation leading to such a startling result should be avoided as it is opposed to all sound canons of construction. The Court held that the procedure of the new Act for recovery of tax will apply *mutatis mutandis* for recovery of tax assessed under the repealed Act.[23]

---

21. *Ibid.*, p. 356 (AIR).
22. *K.B. Nagpur, M.D. (Ayurvedic) v. Union of India*, (2012) 4 SCC 483, p. 490.
23. *ITO, Mangalore v. M. Damodar Bhat*, AIR 1969 SC 408, p. 412 : 1969 (2) SCR 29 : (1969) 71 ITR 806.

A further example of the application of the rule may be noticed in a case relating to the Hyderabad District Municipalities Act, 1956.[24] The Act repealed an earlier Act on the same subject and by section 320 continued the committees functioning under the repealed Act till the first meeting of the committee constituted under the new Act. By section 16(1) the Act provided: 'Every general election requisite for the purpose of this Act shall be held by the Collector in the manner prescribed within three months before the expiry of the term of office of the members of the committee as specified under section 34'. The term of three years specified under section 34 was inapplicable to a committee continued under section 320 for such a committee was to continue till the first meeting of the committee constituted under the Act. The argument on the language of section 16, therefore, was 'that the Collector's power to hold a general election is confined to section 16(1) and, as in the case of the members of the committee deemed to have been constituted under the Act the second limb of the section cannot apply and as the Collector's power is limited by the second limb of the section, the Collector has no power to hold the first general election under the Act'.[25] Countering this argument SUBBARAO, J. said: "If this interpretation be accepted, the Act would become a dead letter and the obvious intention of the Legislature would be defeated. Such a construction cannot be accepted except in cases of absolute intractability of the language used. While the Legislature repealed the earlier Act with an express intention to constitute new committees on broad based democratic principles, by this interpretation the committee under the old Act perpetuates itself indefinitely".[26] Section 16(1) was therefore held inapplicable to the first election after the Act came into force and was construed as confined to subsequent elections.

Another example of the rule is furnished in the construction of section 12 of the Limitation Act, 1963. There was a difference of opinion under the old Limitation Act whether time taken by the office in drawing up a decree or order before the making of application for copy of the decree or order could be included in the time requisite for obtaining the copy and thus excluded in computing the period of limitation for appeal, revision etc. The Law Commission recommended that this period should not be excluded in computing limitation. With the object of giving effect to this recommendation, an Explanation is provided in section 12 which reads: 'In computing under this section the time requisite for obtaining a copy of

---

24. *M. Pentiah v. Veeramallappa Muddala*, AIR 1961 SC 1107 : 1961 (2) SCR 295.
25. *Ibid.*, p. 1111 (AIR).
26. *M. Pentiah v. Veeramallappa Muddala*, AIR 1961 SC 1107, p. 1111 : 1961 (2) SCR 295.

decree or an order, any time taken by the court to prepare the decree or order before an application for a copy thereof is made shall not be excluded'. The Bombay and Orissa High Courts in construing the Explanation held that the words 'shall not be excluded' meant that the time covered by the Explanation would be included in computing the time requisite for obtaining the copy and thus excluded from computing the period of limitation. The result so reached was exactly opposite to the purpose for which the Explanation was added. The Supreme Court,[27] therefore, overruled the above view of the Bombay and Orissa High Courts and held that the words 'shall not be excluded' in the Explanation meant that the time covered by the Explanation shall not be excluded in computing the period of limitation and not that it shall not be excluded in computing the time requisite for obtaining a copy. The court, after referring to the recommendations of the Law Commission and the Objects and Reasons of the Bill, observed that it was happy that by its conclusion it was effectuating the object for which the Explanation was added.

The doctrine of purposive interpretation may be taken recourse to for the purpose of giving full effect to the statutory provisions, and the Courts must state what meaning the statute should bear rather than rendering the statute a nullity. A statute must be construed in such a manner as to make it workable. In light thereof, while interpreting section 3(1) of the Gujarat Lokayukta Act, 1986, which provides that the Governor shall appoint the Lokayukta 'after consultation with Chief Justice of the High Court', the Supreme Court held that the opinion of the Chief Justice has to be given primacy and can be overlooked only for cogent reasons.[28]

Applying the same principle the Supreme Court has rejected constructions advanced in respect of validation Acts which if accepted would have led to the conclusion that the Legislature failed to achieve the object of validating prior executive acts which it avowedly had as expressed in the preamble and also apparent from other provisions of the Acts in question.[29] A validating Act may even make ineffective judgments and orders

---

27. *Udayan Chinubhai v. R.C. Bali*, AIR 1977 SC 2319, p. 2327 : (1977) 4 SCC 309.

28. *State of Gujarat & Anr. v. Justice R.A. Mehta (Retd.) & Ors.*, (2013) 3 SCC 1, pp. 47, 48, 51.

29. *Krishnachandra Gangopadhyaya v. Union of India*, AIR 1975 SC 1389, p. 1393 : (1975) 2 SCC 302; *J.K. Jute Mills Co. Ltd. v. State of U.P.*, AIR 1961 SC 1534, p. 1538 : (1962) 2 SCR 1; *Hiralal Ratanlal v. STO*, AIR 1973 SC 1034, p. 1040 : 1973 SCC (Tax) 307; *West Ramnad Electric Distribution Co. Ltd. v. State of Madras*, AIR 1962 SC 1753, pp. 1758, 1759 : 1963 (2) SCR 747; *R.L. Arora v. State of U.P.*, AIR 1964 SC 1230, p. 1239 : 1964 (6) SCR 784. **See further** *Ramkissen Sinha v. Divisional Forest Officer*, AIR 1965 SC 625, pp. 627, 628 (para 6) : 1965 (1) SCR 1; *Hindustan Gum and Chemicals Ltd. v. State of Haryana*, (1985) 4 SCC 124, p. 131: AIR 1985 SC 1683. **See also** *Western Transport Pty. v. Kropp*, (1964) 3 All ER 722, p. 730 (PC).

of competent courts provided that it, by retrospective legislation, removes the cause of invalidity or the basis which had led to those judgments.[30] Yet by careless drafting the Legislature may sometimes wholly[31] or partially[32] fail to achieve the object of validation. For example, a validating Act cannot be valid and effective if it simply deems a legal consequence without amending the law from which the said legal consequence could follow. Thus if a certain area was not validly included in a municipality, a validating Act which simply declares it to be included would be ineffective unless the law is amended retrospectively curing the defect in the inclusion of the area.[33] Similarly a validation Act which effects validation by declaring non-existent facts as existing may also be ineffective if the declaration violates the Constitution.[34] A validating Act will also be ineffective to the extent it even otherwise violates the Constitution.[35]

---

30. *Bhubaneshwar Singh v. Union of India*, JT 1994 (5) SC 83, p. 88 : 1994 (6) SCC 77; *Comorin Match Industries (Pvt.) Ltd. v. State*, AIR 1996 SC 1916, p. 1924 : (1996) 4 SCC 281; *Indian Aluminium Co. v. State of Kerala*, AIR 1996 SC 1431, p. 1446 : (1996) 7 SCC 637; *K. Shankaran Nair v. Devki Amma Malathy Amma*, 1996 (7) Scale 292, pp. 298, 299 : 1996 (11) SCC 428; *Meerut Development Authority v. Satbir Singh*, AIR 1997 SC 1467, p. 1473 : (1996) 11 SCC 462; *State of Tamil Nadu v. Arooran Sugars Ltd.*, AIR 1997 SC 1815, pp. 1824, 1825; *S. S. Bola v. B. D. Sardana*, AIR 1997 SC 3127, pp. 3209 to 3216; *Indira Sawhney v. Union of India,* AIR 2000 SC 498, p. 509 : (2000) 1 SCC 168; *District Mining Officer v. Tata Iron and Steel Co.,* AIR 2001 SC 3134 : (2001) 7 SCC 358; *Satnam Overseas (Export v. State of Haryana,* (2003) 1 SCC 561, pp. 587, 588; *Easland Combines, Coimbatore v. Collector of Central Excise,* (2003) 3 SCC 410, pp. 420, 422 : AIR 2003 SC 843; *Bakhtawar Trust v. M.D. Narayanan,* AIR 2003 SC 2236, p. 2241 : (2003) 5 SCC 298; *ITW Signode India Ltd. v. Commr. of Central Excise*, (2004) 3 SCC 48, pp. 66 to 71; *Virendra Singh Hooda v. State of Haryana*, AIR 2005 SC 137, p. 154 (Effect of writs can also be taken away). *State of Bihar v. Bihar Pensioner's Samaj,* (2006) 5 SCC 65 : AIR 2006 SC 2100.

31. *B. Shama Rao v. Union Territory of Pondicherry*, AIR 1967 SC 1480, pp. 1488 1489 : 1967 (2) SCR 650 (instead of re-enacting a new Act with suitable changes the earlier void law was amended); *Janpada Sabha, Chhindwara v. Central Provinces Syndicate Ltd.*, (1970) 1 SCC 509 : AIR 1971 SC 57, p. 61 (retrospectively amending the Act without setting out the amendments); *D. Cawasji and Co. v. State of Mysore*, (1984) (Supp) SCC 490 : AIR 1984 SC 1780, (defect not cured and amount collected sought to be retained by retrospectively enhancing the rate of tax); *State of Haryana v. Karnal Co-op. Farmers Society Limited*, AIR 1994 SC 1, p. 12 : (1993) 2 SCC 363; *Government of Andhra Pradesh v. G.V.K. Girls High School,* AIR 2000 SC 26 51, p. 2658 : (2000) 8 SCC 370 (defect not cured).

32. *Jawaharmal v. State of Rajasthan*, AIR 1966 SC 764, pp. 770, 771 : 1966 (1) SCR 890 (mistake in mentioning period); *Wijesuriya v. Amit*, (1965) 3 All ER 701 (PC).

33. *Delhi Cloth and General Mills Co. Ltd. v. State of Rajasthan*, AIR 1996 SC 2930, p. 2935 : 1996 (2) SCC 449. **See further** *Sadchidananda Misra v. State of Orissa*, (2004) 8 SCC 599, p. 608 : (2004) 7 JT 602.

34. *Indira Sawhney v. Union of India,* AIR 2000 SC 498, pp. 512, 514 : (2000) 1 SCC 168.

35. *Virendra Singh Hooda v. State of Haryana*, AIR 2005 SC 137, p. 159.

The same principle is applied in construing machinery sections of a taxing statute so as to make that machinery workable.[36]

5. IF MEANING IS PLAIN, EFFECT MUST BE GIVEN TO IT IRRESPECTIVE OF CONSEQUENCES

When the words of a statute are clear, plain or unambiguous, *i.e.,* they are reasonably susceptible to only one meaning, the courts are bound to give effect to that meaning irrespective of consequences.[37] The rule stated by TINDAL, C.J. in *Sussex Peerage* case is in the following form: "If the words of the statute are in themselves precise and unambiguous, then no more can be necessary than to expound those words in their natural and ordinary sense. The words themselves do alone in such cases best declare the intent of the lawgiver".[38] The rule is also stated in another form:

---

36. *CIT v. Mahaliram Ramjidas*, AIR 1940 PC 124, pp. 126, 127; *Gursahai v. CIT*, AIR 1963 SC 1062, p. 1065 : 1963 (3) SCR 893 : (1963) 48 ITR (SC) 1.

37. *Nelson Motis v. Union of India*, AIR 1992 SC 1981, p. 1984 : (1992) 4 SCC 711; *Gurudevdata VKSSS Maryadit v. State of Maharashtra,* AIR 2001 SC 1980, p. 1991 : (2001) 4 SCC 534; *State of Jharkhand v. Govind Singh*, AIR 2005 SC 294, p. 296; *Nathi Devi v. Radha Devi Gupta*, AIR 2005 SC 648, p. 659 : (2005) 2 SCC 271, p. 277.

38. *Sussex Peerage case*, (1844) 11 Cl & F 85, p. 143. **See further** *Commissioners for Special Purposes of the Income-tax v. John Frederick Pamsel*, (1891) AC 531, p. 542 (HL); *Vacher & Sons v. London Society of Compositors*, (1913) AC 107: 82 LJKB 232 : 107 LT 722 (HL); *Pakala Narayanswami v. Emperor*, AIR 1939 PC 47, p. 51; *Corporation of City of Nagpur v. Its Employees*, AIR 1960 SC 675, p. 679 : 1960 (2) SCR 942; *Sri Ram Daya Ram v. State of Maharashtra*, AIR 1961 SC 674, p. 678 : 1961 (2) SCR 890; *Collector of Customs v. Digvijaysinhji Spinning & Weaving Mills Ltd.*, AIR 1961 SC 1549, p. 1551 : 1962 (1) SCR 896; *Philip John Plasket Thomas v. CIT*, AIR 1964 SC 587, p. 592 : 1964 (2) SCR 480; *R.L. Arora v. State of U.P.*, AIR 1964 SC 1230, p. 1244 : (1964) 6 SCR 784; *Anandji Haridas & Co. Pvt. Ltd. v. Engineering Mazdoor Sangh*, AIR 1975 SC 946, p. 949 : 1975 SCC (L&S) 165 : (1975) 3 SCC 862; *Govindlal Chagganlal Patel v. Agriculture Produce Market Committee*, AIR 1976 SC 263, p. 267 : (1975) 2 SCC 482; *Union of India v. Sankalchand*, AIR 1977 SC 2328, p. 2374 : (1977) 4 SCC 193 : 1977 SCC (Lab) 435; *Chief Justice, Andhra Pradesh v. L.V.A. Dikshitulu*, AIR 1979 SC 193, p. 205 : (1979) 2 SCC 34 : 1979 SCC (Lab) 99; *Shivram Anand Shiroor v. Radhabai Shantaram Kowshik (Mrs.)*, (1984) 1 SCC 588, p. 592 : AIR 1984 SC 786; *Ajay Pradhan (Dr.) v. State of Madhya Pradesh*, AIR 1988 SC 1875, p. 1878 : (1988) 4 SCC 514; *State of Kerala v. Dr. S.G. Savothama Prabhu,* JT (1999) 2 SC 41, p. 44 : 1999 AIR SC 1195 : (1999) 2 SCC 622; *State of Maharashtra v. Nandet Prabhani Operators Sangh,* AIR 2000 SC 725, p. 727 : (2000) 2 SCC 69; *State of West Bengal v. Scene Screen (Pvt.) Ltd.,* AIR 2000 SC 3089, p. 3094 : (2000) 7 SCC 686; *Commissioner of Agricultural Income-tax, Kerala v. Plantation Corporation of Kerala Ltd.,* AIR 2000 SC 3714, pp. 3717, 3718; *Steel Authority of India Ltd. v. National Union Water Front Workers,* AIR 2001 SC 3527, p. 3539 : (2001) 7 SCC 1; *Gurudevdatta VKSSS Maryadit v. State of Maharashtra, supra*; *Ombalika*

[Footnote No. 38 Contd.]

'When a language is plain and unambiguous and admits of only one meaning no question of construction of a statute arises, for the Act speaks for itself'.[39] The results of the construction are then not a matter for the court,[40] even though they may be strange or surprising,[41] unreasonable or unjust or oppressive.[42] "Again and again", said VISCOUNT SIMONDS, L.C., "this Board has insisted that in construing enacted words we are not concerned with the policy involved or with the results, injurious or otherwise, which may follow from giving effect to the language used".[43] As said by

[Footnote No. 38 Contd.]

Das v. Hulisa Shaw, AIR 2002 SC 1685, p. 1690; *Union of India v. Hansoli Devi*, AIR 2002 SC 3240, p. 3245; *Illachi Devi v. Jain Society, Protection of Orphans India*, (2003) 8 SCC 413, p. 426 : AIR 2003 SC 3397; *M.T. Khan v. Govt. of A.P.*, (2004) 2 SCC 267, p. 272 : AIR 2004 SC 2934; *State of Orissa v. Joginder Patjoshi*, AIR 2004 SC 1039, p. 1042 : (2004) 9 SCC 278; *Tamil Nadu State Electricity Board v. Central Electricity Regulatory Commission*, AIR 2007 SC 1711 (paras 18 and 19) : (2007) 6 Scale 26; *Promoters & Builders Ass. of Pune v. Pune Municipal Corpn.*, (2007) 6 SCC 143, para 11 : AIR 2007 SC 1956; *T.N. State Electricity Board v. Central Electricity Regulatory Commission*, (2007) 7 SCC 636, paras 20 to 22; *Ansal Properties and Industries Limited v. State of Haryana*, (2009) 3 SCC 553 para 40 : (2009) 4 JT 174; *Lalu Prasad Yadav v. State of Bihar*, (2010) 5 SCC 1 p.12 para 23 : AIR 2010 SC 1561.

39. *State of Uttar Pradesh v. Vijay Anand Maharaj*, AIR 1963 SC 946, p. 950 : (1963) 1 SCR 1 (SUBBA-RAO, J); **See further** *Thakur Amar Singhji v. State of Rajasthan*, AIR 1955 SC 504, p. 526 : (1955) 2 SCR 303; *Croxford v. Universal Insurance Co. Ltd.*, (1936) 1 All ER 151, p. 166 (CA); *Om Prakash Gupta v. Dig Vijendrapal Gupta*, AIR 1982 SC 1230, p. 1233 : (1982) 2 SCC 61; *Jitendra Tyagi v. Delhi Administration*, AIR 1990 SC 487, p. 492 : (1989) 4 SCC 653; *Nelson Motis v. Union of India*, AIR 1992 SC 1981, p. 1984 : (1992) 4 SCC 711; *Oswal Agro Mills Ltd. v. Collector of Central Excise*, AIR 1993 SC 2288, p. 2291 : 1993 Supp (3) SCC 716; *Council of Homoepathic System of Medicine, Punjab v. Suchintan*, AIR 1994 SC 1761, p. 1769 : (1993) Supp (3) SCC 99; *State of Orissa v. Joginder Patjoshi, supra*.

40. *A.W. Meads v. Emperor*, AIR 1945 FC 21, p. 23 : 75 IA 185; *Pakala Narayanaswami v. Emperor*, AIR 1939 PC 47, pp. 51, 52; *Emperor v. Benoari Lal Sarma*, AIR 1945 PC 48, p. 53; *CIT, Agri. v. Keshab Chandra Mandal*, AIR 1950 SC 265, p. 270 : 1950 SCR 435; *Johnson v. Moreton*, (1978) 3 All ER 37, p. 41 (HL); *Tamil Nadu State Electricity Board v. Central Electricity Regulatory Commission*, AIR 2007 SC 1711 (para 20) : (2007) 6 Scale 26.

41. *London Brick Co. Ltd. v. Robinson*, (1943) 1 All ER 23, p. 26 (HL); *Smith v. East Elloe RDC*, (1956) 1 All ER 855, p. 863 (HL).

42. *IRC v. Hinchy*, (1960) 1 All ER 505, pp. 508, 512 (HL); *Mahalaxmi Mills Ltd., Bhaunagar v. CIT, Bombay*, AIR 1967 SC 266, p. 269 (para 7) : (1964) 5 SCR 216; *Nasiruddin v. State Transport Appellate Tribunal*, AIR 1976 SC 331, p. 338 : (1975) 2 SCC 671; *Duport Streets Ltd. v. Sirs*, (1980) 1 All ER 529, p. 541 (HL); *Precision Steel and Engineering Works v. Premdeva*, AIR 1982 SC 1518, p. 1526 : (1982) 3 SCC 270; *Nasiruddin v. Sita Ram Agarwal,* (2003) 2 SCC 577, p. 588 : AIR 2003 SC 1593.

43. *Emperor v. Benoarilal Sarma*, AIR 1945 PC 48, p. 53. **See further** *Ajay Pradhan (Dr.) v. State of Madhya Pradesh*, AIR 1988 SC 1875, p. 1878 : 1988 (4) SCC 514;

[Footnote No. 43 Contd.]

GAJENDRAGADKAR, J.: "If the words used are capable of one construction only then it would not be open to the courts to adopt any other hypothetical construction on the ground that such construction is more consistent with the alleged object and policy of the Act".[44]

In deciding that a return of income signed by an illiterate person by the pen of his son (Bakalam) was not a valid return of income for purposes of the Bengal Agricultural Income-tax Act (II of 1946) which required that a return of income shall be verified and the declaration shall be signed in the case of an individual by the individual himself, S.R. DAS, J. observed: "Hardship or inconvenience cannot alter the meaning of the language employed by the Legislature if such meaning is clear on the face of the statute".[45] And in holding that the words 'any person' in section 162 of the Code of Criminal Procedure, 1898 included any person who may thereafter be an accused, LORD ATKIN speaking for the Privy Council said: "When the meaning of the words is plain, it is not the duty of courts to busy themselves with supposed intentions".[46] LORD ATKIN proceeded to add: "It, therefore, appears inadmissible to consider the advantages or disadvantages of applying the plain meaning whether in the interests of the prosecution or accused." Similarly, in construing section 123(7) of the Representation of the People Act, 1951, as it then stood, and in holding that persons employed by the father and paid by him who assisted the son in his election, were in relation to the son mere volunteers and not employed by him, the Supreme Court rejected the argument that such a construction would give candidates with rich friends or relations an unfair advantage over a poor rival and would, therefore, be against the spirit of the election law. S.R. DAS, J. observed: "The spirit of the law may well be an elusive

---

[Footnote No. 43 Contd.]

State of Maharashtra v. Nandet Prabhani Operators Sangh, AIR 2000 SC 725, p. 727 : (2000) 2 SCC 69; *Easland Combines Coimbatore v. CCE,* AIR 2003 SC 843, p. 850 : (2003) 3 SCC 410, p. 421; *Raghunath Rai Bareja v. Punjab National Bank,* (2007) 2 SCC 230, (paras 43, 44) : (2007) 1 JT 542 (9th Edition) pp. 45 to 49 of this book is **referred**).

44. *Kanailal Sur v. Paramnidhi Sadhu Khan*, AIR 1957 SC 907, p. 910 : 1958 SCR 360. **See further** *Rananjaya Singh v. Baijnath Singh*, AIR 1954 SC 749, p. 752 : 1955 (1) SCR 671; *Senior Superintendent, RMS, Cochin v. K.B. Gopinath*, AIR 1972 SC 1487, p. 1488 : (1973) 3 SCC 867; *State of Maharashtra v. Nandet Prabhani Operators Sangh, supra,* p. 727; *Union of India v. Hansoli Devi,* AIR 2002 SC 3240, pp. 3245, 3246 : (2002) 7 SCC 273; *Nathi Devi v. Radha Devi Gupta*, AIR 2005 SC 648, p. 652 : (2005) 2 SCC 291, p. 277.

45. *CIT, Agri. v. Keshab Chandra Mandal*, AIR 1950 SC 265, p. 270 : 1950 SCR 435.

46. *Pakala Narayanaswami v. Emperor*, AIR 1939 PC 47, pp. 51, 52. **See further** *State of Haryana v. Bhajanlal*, AIR 1992 SC 604, p. 617 : 1992 Supp (1) SCC 335 : 1992 Cri LJ 527.

and unsafe guide and the supposed spirit can certainly not be given effect to in opposition to the plain language of the sections of the Act".[47]

The rule applies to fiscal and penal statutes as well. Said LORD CAIRNS: "If the person sought to be taxed comes within the letter of the law he must be taxed, however great the hardship may appear to the judicial mind to be".[48] And in construing the word 'Butter' in the Prevention of Food Adulteration Rules, 1955, the Supreme Court gave effect to the plain meaning and held that the word included butter prepared from curd; rejecting the contention based on the rule of strict construction and on the rule that that construction should be adopted which is more favourable to the subject, SUBBARAO, J. said: "But these rules do not in any way affect the fundamental principle of interpretation, namely, that the primary test is—the language employed in the Act and when the words are clear and plain the court is bound to accept the expressed intention of the Legislature".[49] Similarly, the Supreme Court gave effect to the plain meaning of section 5(3) of the Prevention of Corruption Act, 1947 which lays down a rule of evidence, enabling the Court to raise a presumption of guilt in certain circumstances—'the rule which is a complete departure from the established principle of criminal jurisprudence that the burden always lies on the prosecution to prove all the ingredients of the offence charged and the burden never shifts on the accused to disprove the charge framed against him;'[50] and similar view has been taken on section 4(1) of the same Act.[51]

---

47. *Rananjaya Singh v. Baijnath Singh*, AIR 1954 SC 749, p. 752 : (1955) (1) SCR 671. **Referred** in *Dibya Singh Malana v. State of Orissa*, AIR 1989 SC 1737, pp. 1740, 1741 : 1989 Supp (2) SCC 312.

48. *Partington v. Attorney-General*, (1869) LR 4 HL 100, p. 122; referred to in *IRC v. Duke of Westminster*, (1936) AC 1, p. 24 (HL); *Bank of Chettinad Ltd. v. CIT*, AIR 1940 PC 183, p. 185; *A.V. Fernandez v. State of Kerala*, AIR 1957 SC 657 : 1957 SCR 837. **See further** Chapter 10, title 1(d) 'Qualifications of the Rule of Strict Construction'.

49. *M.V. Joshi v. M. U. Shimpi*, AIR 1961 SC 1494, p. 1498 : 1961 (3) SCR 986 : 64 Bom LR 158.

For example—Sentence of 'imprisonment for life' means a sentence for whole of the remaining period of the convicted person's natural life; *Gopal Vinayak Godse v. State of Maharashtra*, AIR 1961 SC 600, p. 603 : 1961 (3) SCR 440; *Mohd. Munna v. Union of India,* (2005) 7 SCC 417, pp. 426, 427; *R. v. Assa Singh*, (1965) 1 All ER 938, p. 940; *R. v. Church*, (1965) 2 All ER 72, p. 77. **See further** Chapter 11, title 3 'Strict Construction of Penal Statutes'.

50. *C.S.D. Swami v. State*, AIR 1960 SC 7, pp. 9, 10 : 1960 (1) SCR 461; **See further** *Sajjan Singh v. State of Punjab*, AIR 1964 SC 464, p. 468 : 1964 (4) SCR 630. Section 5(3) later became section 5(1)(e) and corresponds to section 13(1)(e) of the Prevention of Corruption Act, 1988.

51. *Dhanwantrai Balwantrai v. State of Maharashtra*, AIR 1964 SC 575 : 1963 Supp (1) SCR 485; *CI Emden v. State of U.P.*, AIR 1960 SC 548 : (1960) 2 SCR 592;

[Footnote No. 51 Contd.]

The court applied the plain meaning rule in construing sections 223 and 236 of the Indian Succession Act, 1925 which contain a prohibition for grant of Probate or Letters of Administration 'to any association of individuals unless it is a company' and held that Probate or Letters of Administration cannot be granted to a society registered under the Societies Registration Act as a society even after registration does not become distinct from its members and does not become a legal person like a company. The Court observed that 'the prohibitions laid down by sections 223 and 236 of the Act are categorical and comprehensive and leave no scope for creative interpretation.'[52]

Mere hardship cannot be a ground for not giving effective and grammatical meaning to every word of the provisions of a statute if the language used therein is unequivocal. Accordingly, the Supreme Court held that even if the designation of land in the final development plan lapses under section 20(2) of the Gujarat Town Planning and Urban Development Act, 1976, for non-acquisition of the land within a period of 10 years, the land can again be reserved in a town planning scheme as provided under section 40 of the Act, and be acquired again.[53]

6. APPRAISAL OF THE PRINCIPLE OF PLAIN MEANING

It may look somewhat paradoxical that plain meaning rule is not plain and requires some explanation. The rule, that plain words require no construction, starts with the premise that the words are plain, which is itself a conclusion reached after construing the words. It is not possible to decide whether certain words are plain or ambiguous unless they are studied in their context and construed.[54] The rule, therefore, in reality means that after

---

[Footnote No. 51 Contd.]

State of Madras v. A. Vaidyanatha Iyer, AIR 1958 SC 61 : 1958 SCR 580. Section 4 of the PC Act, 1947 corresponds to section 20 of the PC Act, 1988.

See also *V. D. Jhingan v. State of U.P.*, AIR 1966 SC 1762 : (1966) 3 SCR 736; *R. v. Carr Briant*, (1943) 2 All ER 156; the onus laid on the accused is not as onerous as is normally required from the prosecution to establish the charge beyond reasonable doubt and the accused may discharge the onus by proving preponderance of probability of his defence.

52. *Illachi Devi v. Jain Society Protection of Orphans India*, (2003) 8 SCC 413, p. 429 : AIR 2003 SC 3397.

53. *Ahmedabad Municipal Corporation & Anr. v. Ahmedabad Green Belt Khedut Mandal & Ors.*, (2014) 7 SCC 357, pp. 381, 382.

54. *D. Saibaba v. Bar Council of India*, AIR 2003 SC 2502, 2507 : (2003) 6 SCC 186 : (2003) 2 KLT 669. (This proposition is **approvingly referred** from p. 45 of 8th edition of this book). **See further** *Ibrahimpatnam Taluk Vyavasaya Coolie Sangham v. K. Suresh Reddy*, (2003) 7 SCC 667, pp. 677, 678; *Special Land Acquisition Officer v. Karigowda*, (2010) 5 SCC 708 para 35 : AIR 2010 SC 2322.

you have construed the words and have come to the conclusion that they can bear only one meaning, your duty is to give effect to that meaning.

The true import of the rule is well brought out in an American case where JUDGE PEARSON after reaching his conclusion as to the meaning of the statutory language said: "That seems to me a plain clear meaning of the statutory language in its context. Of course, in so concluding I have necessarily construed or interpreted the language. It would obviously be impossible to decide that language is 'plain' (more accurately that a particular meaning seems plain) without first construing it. This involves far more than picking out dictionary definitions of words or expressions used. Consideration of the context and setting is indispensable properly to ascertain a meaning. In saying that a verbal expression is plain or unambiguous, we mean little more than that we are convinced that virtually anyone competent to understand it and desiring fairly and impartially to ascertain its significance would attribute to the expression in its context a meaning such as the one we derive, rather than any other; and would consider any different meaning by comparison, strained, or far-fetched, or unusual or unlikely."[55]

For a proper application of the rule to a given statute, it is necessary, therefore, to determine first whether the language used is plain or ambiguous. As pointed out by LORD BUCKMASTER, "by 'any ambiguity' is meant a phrase fairly and equally open to diverse meanings".[56] "A provision is not ambiguous", says LORD REID, "merely because it contains a word which in different contexts is capable of different meanings". LORD REID, proceeds to add: "It would be hard to find anywhere a sentence of any length which does not contain such a word. A provision is, in my judgment, ambiguous only if it contains a word or phrase which in that particular context is capable of having more than one meaning".[57] To decide,

---

55. *Hutton v. Phillips*, 45 Del 156, 70A, 2nd 15; RIED MACDONALD and FORDHAM, Cases and other Materials on Legislation , 2nd Edition, pp. 1013, 1014; *Union of India v. Sankalachand*, AIR 1977 SC 2328, p. 2374 : (1977) 4 SCC 193 : 1977 SCC (L&S) 435; *Manohar Nathrao Samarth v. Marotrao*, AIR 1979 SC 1084, p. 1089 : 1979 (4) SCC 93; *Life Insurance Corporation v. D. J. Bahadur*, AIR 1980 SC 2181, p. 2191 : 1981 (1) SCR 1083; *Special Land Acquisition Officer v. Karigowda*, (2010) 5 SCC 708 para 36 : AIR 2010 SC 2322.

56. *Ormond Investment Co. v. Betts*, (1928) AC 143, p. 156 (HL); **referred** to in *Kirkness v. John Hudson & Co.*, (1955) 2 All ER 345, p. 350 (HL) (VISCOUNT SIMONDS). **See further:** *Imperial Chemical Industries Plc v. Colmel (Inspector of Taxes)*, (2000) 1 All ER 129, p. 133 (HL) ('An ambiguity is a word or phrase fairly open to diverse meanings, the classic example being 'twelve O'clock' which, save for users of the 24 hour clock, could equally mean midday or midnight.')

57. *Kirkness v. John Hudson & Co., supra*, p. 366. **See further** *Union of India v. Hansoli devi*, AIR 2002 SC 3240, p. 3246 : (2001) 4 SCC 404; *State of Orissa v. Joginder Patjoshi*, AIR 2004 SC 1039, p. 1042 : (2004) 9 SCC 278.

therefore, whether certain words are clear and unambiguous, they must be studied in their context. VISCOUNT SIMONDS, (LORD TUCKER agreeing) calls it an elementary rule: 'No one should profess to understand any part of a statute or of any other document before he has read the whole of it. Until he has done so, he is not entitled to say that it, or any part of it, is clear and unambiguous'.[58] Unambiguous means 'unambiguous in context'.[59] So ambiguity need not necessarily be a grammatical ambiguity, but one of appropriateness of the meaning in a particular context.[60] Context in this connection is used in a wide sense as including not only other enacting provisions of the same statute, but its preamble, the existing state of the law, other statutes in *pari materia* and the mischief which by those and other legitimate means can be discerned that the statute was intended to remedy.[61]

Normally a statutory provision consists of a general description of some factual situation and the legal consequences ensuing from it. Whether the general description is wide or narrow, it will have some limits. The question before a court of law in dealing with a statute is whether the factual situation proved before it falls within the general description given in the statute. A real difficulty in determining the right answer can be said to arise from an 'ambiguity' in the statute. It is in this sense that the words 'ambiguity' and 'ambiguous' are widely used in judgments.[62] Although the words of the statutory provision as a matter of language may be clear enough, ambiguity may arise as to the scope or subject matter of their intended reference, *e.g.*, scope of the power or right conferred.[63]

Difference of judicial opinion as to the true meaning of certain words need not necessarily lead to the conclusion that those words are ambiguous. Instances are not wanting where eminent judges agreed that the meaning was plain but they differed on the question as to what that meaning was. In construing section 1 of the Merchant Shipping (International Labour Convention) Act, 1925, all the speeches delivered in the House of Lords were in agreement that the meaning of the section was plain, but

---

58. *Attorney-General v. HRH Prince Ernest Augustus of Hanover*, (1957) 1 All ER 49, p. 55 (HL); *Union of India v. Sankalchand*, AIR 1977 SC 2328, p. 2336 : (1977) 4 SCC 193 : 1977 SCC (L&S) 435.

59. *Attorney-General v. HRH Prince Ernest Augustus of Hanover, supra*, p. 62 (LORD SOMERVELL OF HARROW).

60. *Nyadar Singh v. Union of India*, AIR 1988 SC 1979, p. 1984 : 1988 (4) SCC 170.

61. **See** text and Notes 59 to 69, pp. 38-40.

62. *Inland Revenue Commissioner v. Joiner*, (1975) 3 All ER 1050, pp. 1058, 1059 : (1975) 1 WLR 1701 : 50 TC 449 (HL) (LORD DIPLOCK).

63. *A Oliver Ashworth (Holdings) Pvt. Ltd. v. Ballard (Kent) Ltd.*, (1999) 2 All ER 791, pp. 807, 808 (C.A.) (Laws LJ).

LORD BLANESBURG differed from the majority on the issue as to what that meaning was.[64] Similarly, opinions of judges of equal weight and authority may differ on the question whether a particular language is ambiguous or not.[65] In construing the words 'is sold' as they occur in section 17(1)(a) of the Income-tax Act, 1945, the majority in the House of Lords took the view that these words were plain and did not include the case of compulsory acquisition of property on payment of compensation. LORD MORTON, however, was of opinion that the words were readily capable of more than one interpretation and in the context covered the case of compulsory acquisition.[66] As to how the approach should be made by each individual Judge is brought out in the speech of VISCOUNT SIMONDS where he said: "Each one of us has the task of deciding what the relevant words mean. In coming to that decision, he will necessarily give great weight to the opinion of others, but if, at the end of the day, he forms his own clear judgment and does not think that the words are 'fairly and equally open to diverse meanings' he is not entitled to say that there is an ambiguity".[67] Even when the meaning is obscure, judges may not be prepared to accept that the language is ambiguous. In his dissenting opinion in *Ellerman's* case, LORD BLANESBURG speaking of section 1 of the Act in question said: "I do not suggest that section 1 bears its meaning, as I have interpreted it, upon its sleeve. It yields up to its secret only to the patient enquirer; its truth lies at the bottom of the well. It is obscure; it remains oblique, but it is not in the result ambiguous".[68]

Use of syllepsis in a section does not make it ambiguous. 'It is not an ambiguity if a term 'T' means 'X' in relation to 'a' and 'Y' in relation to 'b'. It is only an ambiguity if 'T' means either 'X' or 'Y' in relation to 'a' or 'b'.'[69]

---

64. *Ellerman Lines Ltd. v. Murray*, 1931 AC 126 : (1930) All ER Rep 503 (HL).

65. *R.L. Arora v. State of U.P.*, AIR 1964 SC 1230 : 1964 (6) SCR 787. According to the majority opinion in this case, cl. (aa) of section 40(1), Land Acquisition Act, 1894 was capable of bearing two constructions whereas according to the **dissenting** opinion of AYYANGER, J, the clause could bear only one meaning).

66. *Kirkness v. John Hudson & Co. Ltd.*, (1955) 2 All ER 345 (HL).

67. *Kirkness v. John Hudson & Co. Ltd.*, (1955) 2 All ER 345, p. 351 (HL).

See for similar observations : *Director of Public Prosecutions v. Ottewell*, (1968) 3 All ER 153, p. 157 (HL) (LORD REID); *Farrel v. Alexander*, (1976) 3 All ER 721, p. 744 (HL) (LORD EDMUND DAVIES). But "a sense of modesty and respect for the ability of his fellow judges who think otherwise may make a judge hesitate before deciding that the words are not equally capable of bearing the meaning which they prefer and he does not": *Inland Revenue Commissioner v. Joiner*, (1975) 3 All ER 1050, p. 1063 : (1975) 1 WLR 1701 (HL) (LORD DIPLOCK).

68. *Ellerman Lines Ltd. v. Murray*, (1930) All ER Rep 503, p. 511 (HL).

69. *Customs and Excise Commissioners v. Thorn Electrical Industries Ltd.*, (1975) 3 All ER 881, p. 884 (HL). For example in the sentence—she went home in a sedan chair and a flood of tears,—'in' is not ambiguous.

Warning has sometimes been given that ambiguity should not be assumed where there is none.[70] In a case[71] relating to the construction of the words 'a submission made in pursuance of an agreement' as they occur in section 3 of the Foreign Awards (Recognition and Enforcement) Act, 1961, the Supreme Court by a majority of two against one held that the word 'submission' meant actual submission or completed reference and not merely an agreement to refer or an arbitral clause. The majority adopted this meaning on the view that the words were plain. They refused to give an extended meaning to the word 'submission' although the restricted meaning adopted by them failed to achieve the object of the Act which was to give effect to the convention on the recognition and enforcement of foreign arbitral awards which was set forth in a Schedule to the Act. In so holding, they differed from an English case[72] where a wider construction was adopted of the word 'submission' in a similar enactment. GROVER, J., speaking for the majority said: "We are aware of no rule of interpretation by which rank ambiguity can be first introduced by giving certain expressions a particular meaning and then an attempt can be made to emerge out of semantic confusion and obscurity by having resort to presumed intention of the Legislature to give effect to international obligations."[73] RAMASWAMY, J. in his dissenting opinion, did not find the language that plain and construed the word 'submission' in a wide sense as including an agreement to submit to arbitration. The case illustrates how sharp divergence of opinion may result on the question whether certain words are plain or ambiguous.

Apparently clear and simple language at times in its analysis is so ambiguous as to present great difficulty in construction.[74] Regarding Article 105(2) of the Constitution which provides that 'no member of

---

70. *Powell v. Kempton Park Racecourse Co.*, (1899) AC 143, p. 185 (HL); *Mahadeolal Kanodia v. Administrator General of West Bengal*, AIR 1960 SC 936, p. 940 : 1960 (3) SCR 578; *CIT v. Indian Bank Ltd., Madras*, AIR 1965 SC 1473, p. 1474 (para 8) : 1965 (1) SCR 833; *Patangrao Kadam v. Brithviraj Sayajirao Yadav,* AIR 2001 SC 1121, p. 1126 (para 13); *Duports Steels Ltd. v. Sirs*, (1980) 1 All ER 529, p. 541 : (1980) 1 WLR 142 : 124 SJ 133 (HL); *Inland Revenue Commissioners v. Rossminster Ltd.*, (1980) 1 All ER 80, p. 90 (HL).

71. *V.O. Tractoroexport v. Tarapore & Co.*, AIR 1971 SC 1, p. 9 : (1969) 3 SCC 562.

72. *T B & S Batchelor & Co. Ltd. v. Owners of S.S. Merak*, (1964) 3 All ER 638, p. 649; **upheld** in appeal (1965) 1 All ER 230 (CA).

73. *V.O. Tractoroexport v. Tarapore & Co.*, AIR 1971 SC 1, p. 9 : (1969) 3 SCC 562. For construction of statutes enacted to give effect to international conventions; **see** title 5(b2) Chapter 6 and see p. 705 where this case is referred.

74. 'It is often found that the more common place a word is, the more difficult it is to arrive at its exact meaning—and for a very good reason, since it is the commonplaces which are used most vaguely and with the least attention to precise significance': ALLEN,Law in the Making, 7th Edition, p. 489. "The simpler and more common the word or expression, the more meanings and shades of meaning it has": SHAH, J, in *Madhava Rao Scindia v. Union of India*, AIR 1971 SC 530, p. 577 : (1971) 1 SCC 85. **See further** observations of LORD UPJONH in *Commissioner of Customs v. Top Ten Promotions Ltd.*, (1969) 3 All ER 39, p. 90 (HL).

Parliament shall be liable to any proceeding in respect of anything said or any vote given by him in Parliament', the Supreme Court in *Tej Kiran Jain v. N. Sanjeeva Reddy*[75] said: 'The Article means what it says in language *which could not be plainer*'. But look at the sharp divergence of opinion that it later created in *P. V. Narsimha Rao v. State.*[76] Though all the five judges agreed that a member of Parliament who receives bribe for voting but does not vote can be prosecuted for the offence of bribery under the Prevention of Corruption Act, 1988, it was held by a majority of three against two that a member who voted in Parliament after receipt of bribe cannot be prosecuted as his prosecution would be a proceeding in respect of a vote given by him and barred by Article 105(2). The words 'Suit for land' occurring in clause 12 of the Letters Patent of Calcutta, Madras and Bombay High Courts have given rise to great divergence of judicial opinion and 'the numerous cases in the books on the construction of that clause reveal what a prodigious amount of judicial time has been expended on endless debate as to its meaning'.[77] The Court of the Judicial Commissioner of the Central Provinces in two Full Bench decisions held that certain decrees passed under that clause by the Bombay High Court following its own Full Bench view were in excess of jurisdiction and absolute nullities. That led to the passing of the Decrees and Orders Validating Act, 1936.[78] Even in the Federal Court where the matter came up before five eminent judges of our country, there was no unanimity and the questicn whether the suit out of which that appeal arose was a 'suit for land' remained undecided.[79] Another example is the word 'Court' itself which should *prima facie* appear to the courts quite simple and clear but has given rise to an 'endless oscillation between two views—each verging on a fringe of obscurity and vagueness'.[80]

---

75. (1971) 1 SCR 612 : (1970) 2 SCC 272 : AIR 1970 SC 1573.

76. JT 1998 (3) SC 318 : AIR 1998 SC 2120. **See further** *R v. Chaytor*, (2011) 1 All ER 805 (U.K.S.C.) (Prosecution of M.Ps. for making false claims for attending Parliament does not amount to breach of privilege as making expenses claims are not proceedings in Parliament and within exclusive cognizance of Parliament).

77. *Moolji Jaitha & Co. v. Khandesh Spinning and Weaving Mills Co. Ltd.*, AIR 1950 FC 83, p. 101 : 1949 FCR 849.

78. **See** Statement of Objects and Reasons, AIR Manual, 5th Edition, Vol. 20, p. 603.

79. *Moolji Jaitha & Co. v. Khandesh Spinning and Weaving Mills*, AIR 1950 FC 83, p. 101 : 1949 FCR 849. In *Adcon Electronics Pvt. Ltd. v. Daulat,* AIR 2001 SC 3712 : (2001) 7 SCC 698 a two- Judge Bench of the Supreme Court noticed the divergence of opinion in the Federal Court but preferred the opinion of MAHAJAN, J., in holding that a suit for specific performance of a contract of sale without claiming relief for possession is not a 'suit for land'.

80. *Baliram Waman Hiray (Dr.) v. Mr. Justice B. Lentin*, AIR 1988 SC 2267, p. 2280 : 1988 Supp (2) SCR 942 : (1988) 4 SCC 419. The word 'court' must be read in the context and in a certain context it can comprehend court of civil jurisdiction and other courts or tribunals exercising curial or judicial powers. Company Law Board was held to be a court in the context of section 9A of Special Court (Trial of

[Footnote No. 80 Contd.]

Language which on its construction results in absurdity, inconsistency, hardship or strange consequences is not readily accepted as unambiguous. 'Judges are not always prepared', says Maxwell, 'to concede as plain language which involves absurdity and inconsistency.[81] It is true as noticed earlier that when the language is fairly and reasonably open to only one meaning, hardship or inconvenience or surprising results are no considerations for refusing to give effect to that meaning. But such cases are rare for absurd and unreasonable results are not intended by the Legislature and the language used is seldom so plain or inflexible that the courts are not able to avoid them.'[82]

[Footnote No. 80 Contd.]

offences relating to Transactions in Securities) Act, 1992: *Canara Bank v. Nuclear Power Corporation of India Ltd.*, 1995 (2) Scale 162: 1995 Supp (3) SCC 381 : (1995) 84 Com Case 70; Deputy Commissioner (Appeals) functioning under Section 41 of the Tamil Nadu Shops and Establishment Act, 1947 held to be a 'court': *P. Sarathy v. State Bank of India,* AIR 2000 SC 2023 : (2000) 5 SCC 355; Compensation officer appointed under the Bihar Land Reforms Act, 1950 held not to be a 'court' for section 195(1)(b) CrPC, 1973: *Keshab Narayan Banerjee v. State of Bihar,* AIR 2000 SC 485 : (2000) 1 SCC 607; *Manoharlal v. Vinesh Anand,* AIR 2001 SC 1820 : (2001) 3 SCC 401 (Arbitrator is not a court in section 195 CrPC, 1973); *K. Shamrao v. Assistant Charity Commissioner,* (2003) 3 SCC 563 : 2003 Cri LJ 1575 (Assistant Charity Commissioner appointed under section 5 of the Bombay Public Trusts Act, 1950 is a 'court' for the purposes of the Contempt of Courts Act, 1971); *Prakash H. Jain v. Marie Fernandes*, (2003) 8 SCC 431, pp. 437, 438 : AIR 2003 SC 4591 (Competent Authority functioning under chapter VIII of the Maharashtra Rent Control Act, 1999 is not a court); *Manuverma (Dr.) v. State of U.P.*, (2005) 1 SCC 73, p. 82 (Chief Justice transferring a case which was being heard at Lucknow Bench to Allahabad after noticing and hearing the parties acts as a judicial authority with all the attributes of a court and his order is atleast quasi judicial amenable to correction in appeal under Article 136 of the constitution). *Greater Bombay Co-op. Bank Ltd. v. United Yarn Tex (P.) Ltd.,* (2007) 6 SCC 236 (para 76) : AIR 2007 SC 1584 : (2007) 5 JT 201 (Registrar or an officer designated as arbitrator under Cooperative Societies Act, is not a court in the context of section 31 of the Recovery of Debts Due to Banks and Financial Institutions Act, 1993). *State of Madhya Pradesh v. Anshuman Shukla,* (2008) 7 SCC 487 : AIR 2008 SC 2454. Is the tribunal constituted under M.P. Madhyastham Adhikaran Adhiniyam 1983 a court-matter referred to a larger Bench; *Jagadguru Annadamishwar Maha Swamy v. G.C. Allipur,* (2009) 4 SCC 625 para 12 : (2009) 5 JT 414 (Director of Pre-University Education is not a court for purposes of Contempt of Courts Act, 1971). *Nahar Industrial Enterprises Limited v. Hongkong and Shanghai Banking Corporation,* (2009) 8 SCC 646 paras 67, 68, 92 : (2009) 10 JT 199 (Debt Recovery Tribunal constituted under Recovery of Debts Due to Banks and Financial Institutions Act, 1993 are not civil court or court subordinate to High Court and the High Court has no jurisdiction to transfer a suit filed in the Civil Court to the tribunal under sections 22 to 25 and section 151 of the Code of Civil Procedure, 1908). On the question as to when a court can be said to be constituted. **See** *Supreme Court Legal Aid Committee (Representing Undertrial Prisoners) v. Union of India,* JT 1994 (6) SC 544, pp. 556, 557: 1995 (4) SCC 695 : 1995 SCC (Cri) 822.

81. MAXWELL, Interpretation of Statutes, 11th Edition, p. 6.

82. "If the words of an Act are so inflexible that they are incapable in any context of having any but one meaning, then the court must apply that meaning, no matter

[Footnote No. 82 Contd.]

Sometimes it is said that 'though a construction according to plain language should ordinarily be accepted, such a construction should not be adopted where it leads to anomalies, injustices and absurdities'.[83] This and similar statements[84] are not accurate statements of the rule and all that they really mean is that *prima facie* plain language may not be plain.[85] As already seen, plain meaning rule applies at the stage when the words have been construed in their context and the conclusion is reached that they are susceptible to only one meaning.[86] In that event the meaning so derived is to be given effect to irrespective of consequences for no alternative construction is really open. This, of course, is subject to the qualification in India that the statute is constitutional and unreasonableness, and that the injustice or absurdity is not of the nature and gravity which makes the statute offend the Constitution.[87]

[Footnote No. 82 Contd.]

how unreasonable the result—.But such cases are rare because the English Language is a flexible instrument". LORD REID in *Zenith Investment (Torquay) Ltd. v. Kammins Ballrooms Co. Ltd.*, (1970) 2 All ER 871, p. 874 (HL). 'A statutes true meaning' according to Prof. Allan, 'is as much the product of legal and moral judgment as of rules of semantics and syntax; and its authority is grounded in the reasons that best explain and qualify the text enacted.—The doctrine of legislative supremacy gives the last word to Parliament, then, only in a purely formal sense; even 'the last word' must be interpreted in accordance with those precepts of rule of law that distinguish constitutionalism from dictatorship and populism'. ALLAN, Legislative Supremacy and Legislative Intention : Interpretation, Meaning and Authority, (2004) 63 Cambridge Law Journal 685, p. 708. **See further** Chapter 2, Title 4 'Regard to consequences'.

83. *Girdharilal and Sons v. Balbir Nath Mathur*, (1986) 2 SCC 237, p. 246: AIR 1986 SC 1099; *Union of India v. Hansoli Devi,* AIR 2002 SC 3240 p. 3246 : (2002) 7 SCC 273.

84. 'Statutory enactment must ordinarily be construed according to its plain meaning and no words shall be added, altered or modified unless it is plainly necessary to do so to prevent a provision from being unintelligible, absurd, unreasonable, unworkable or totally irreconcilable with the test of the statute': *Bhavnagar University v. Palitana Sugar Mill (P.) Ltd.*, (2003) 2 SCC 111, p. 121 : AIR 2003 SC 511, p. 517 : (2003) 2 Cuj LR 1154. **See further** the following statement of the rule in *Jagdish Ch. Patnaik v. State of Orissa*, 1998 (2) Scale 662, p. 668 : (1998) 4 SCC 456 : 1998 SCC (L&S) 1156; which too it is submitted, suffers from the same defect: "When the language in the statute is unambiguous and on a plain grammatical meaning being given to the words in the statute, the end result is neither arbitrary, irrational or contrary to the object of the statute, then it is the duty of the court to give effect to the words used in the statute."

85. *Girdharilal and Sons v. Balbirnath Mathur, supra*, p. 242 of SCC.

86. Pp. 59 to 62, *supra*.

87. Unreasonableness may attract Article 14; (*Ajay Hasia v. Khalid Mujib*, AIR 1981 SC 487 : (1981) 1 SCC 722) and clauses 2 to 6 of Article 19 of the Constitution. For example, **see** *Bhagwanti v. Union of India*, AIR 1989 SC 2088 : (1989) 4 SCC 397; *State of Kerala v. Travancore Chemicals and Manufacturing Co.*, JT 1998 (7) SC 558 : (1998) 8 SCC 188 : AIR 1999 SC 230.

CHAPTER 2

GUIDING RULES

SYNOPSIS

1. LANGUAGE OF THE STATUTE SHOULD BE READ AS IT IS

The intention of the Legislature is primarily to be gathered from the language used, which means that attention should be paid to what has been said as also to what has not been said.[1] As a consequence a construction which requires for its support addition or substitution of words or which results in rejection of words as meaningless has to be avoided.[2] This rule like all other rules is subject to exceptions. The rule stated above has been quoted with approval by the Supreme Court.[3]

(a) Avoiding addition or substitution of words

As stated by the Privy Council: "We cannot aid the Legislature's defective phrasing of an Act, we cannot add or mend and, by construction make up deficiencies which are left there".[4] "It is contrary to all rules of construction

---

1. *Gwalior Rayon Silk Mfg. (Wvg.) Co. Ltd. v. Custodian of Vested Forests*, AIR 1990 SC 1747, p. 1752 : 1990 (2) JT 130 : 1990 Supp SCC 785; *Mohammad Alikhan v. Commissioner of Wealth Tax*, AIR 1997 SC 1165, p. 1167 : 1997 (3) SCC 511; *Institute of Chartered Accountants of India v. Price Waterhouse*, AIR 1998 SC 74, p. 90 : (1997) 6 SCC 312; *Dental Council of India v. Hari Prakash*, AIR 2001 SC 3303, p. 3308 : (2001) 8 SCC 61; *J.P. Bansal v. State of Rajasthan*, 2003 AIR SCW 1848, p. 1855 : (2003) 5 SCC 134 : AIR 2003 SC 1405; *Dental Council of India v. Hari Prakash*, (2001) 8 SCC 61, p. 69 : AIR 2001 SC 3303; *Illachi Devi v. Jain Society Protection of Orphans*, (2003) 8 SCC 413, p. 426; *State of Jharkhand v. Govind Singh*, AIR 2005 SC 294, p. 296; *Commissioner of Income Tax, Kerala v. Tata Agencies*, (2007) 6 SCC 429, paras 57 and 60; *Nagar Palika Nigam v. Krishi Upaj Mandi Samiti*, AIR 2009 SC 187 para 8 : (2008) 12 SCC 364.
2. *Shyam Kishori Devi v. Patna Municipal Corporation*, AIR 1966 SC 1678, p. 1682 : 1966 (3) SCR 466 (the words of a statute never should, in interpretation, be added to or subtracted from without almost a necessity); *Management, Shahdara (Delhi) Saharanpur Light Rly. Co. Ltd. v. S.S. Rly. Workers Union*, AIR 1969 SC 513, p. 518 : (1969) 2 SCR 131; *S. Narayanaswami v. G. Panneerselvam*, AIR 1972 SC 2284, p. 2289 : (1972) 3 SCC 717; *Union of India v. Sankalchand*, AIR 1977 SC 2328, p. 2337 : (1977) 4 SCC 193; *A.R. Antuley v. Ramdas Srinivas Nayak*, (1984) 2 SCC 500, pp. 518, 519 : AIR 1984 SC 718; *Mohammad Alikhan v. Commissioner of Wealth Tax, supra*; *Institute of Chartered Accountants of India v. Price Waterhouse, supra*; *State of Maharashtra v. Nanded Parbhani Operator Sangh*, AIR 2000 SC 725, p. 727 : (2000) 2 SCC 69; *Grasim Industries Ltd. v. Collector of Customs*, AIR 2002 SC 1706, p. 1709 : (2002) 4 SCC 297; *J.P. Bansal v. State of Rajasthan, supra*; *State of Jharkhand v. Govind Singh, supra*.
3. *Harbhajan Singh v. Press Council of India*, AIR 2002 SC 1351, p. 1354 : (2002) 3 SCC 722 (8th Edition p. 54 of this book is **quoted**); *Sakshi v. Union of India*, (2004) 5 SCC 518, p. 537 : AIR 2004 SC 3566, p. 3590 (9th Edition, p. 58 of this book is **referred**).
4. *Crawford v. Spooner*, (1846) 6 Moore PC 1, pp. 8, 9 : 4 MIA 179, p. 187 (PC); **referred** to in *Lord Howard de Walden v. IRC*, (1948) 2 All ER 825, p. 830 (HL); *Nalinakhya Bysack v. Shyamsunder Halder*, AIR 1953 SC 148, p. 152 : 1953 SCR 533; *State of Madhya Pradesh v. G.S. Dall and Flour Mills*, AIR 1991 SC 772, p. 785 : 1992 Supp (1) SCC 150; *Grasim Industries Ltd. v. Collector of Customs, supra*, p. 1709. **See further** *Union of India v. Deoki Nandan Aggarwal*, AIR 1992 SC 96, p. 101 : 1992 Supp (1) SCC 323; *State of Gujarat v. Dilipbhai Nathjibhai Patel*, JT 1998 (2) SC 253, p. 255: 1998 (2) Scale 145, p. 147 : (1998) 3 SCC 234. **See further** *Competition Commission of India v. Steel Authority of India Limited*, (2010) 10 SCC 744 para 53 : (2010) 10 JT 26.

to read words into an Act unless it is absolutely necessary to do so."[5] Similarly it is wrong and dangerous to proceed by substituting some other words for words of the statute.[6] Speaking briefly the court cannot reframe the legislation for the very good reason that it has no power to legislate.[7]

In holding that section 96(2) of the Motor Vehicles Act, 1939, is exhaustive of defences open to an insurer, the Supreme Court refused to add word 'also' after the words 'on any of the following grounds' and observed: "This, the rules of interpretation, do not permit us to do unless the section as it stands is meaningless or of doubtful meaning."[8]

While interpreting section 621-A(1) of the Companies Act, 1956, the Supreme Court held that the Court must avoid rejection or addition of words and resort to that only in exceptional circumstances to achieve the purpose of the Act or to give a purposeful meaning to the section. Section 621-A

---

5. *Renula Bose (Smt.) v. Rai Manmathnath Bose*, AIR 1945 PC 108, p. 110 : 72 IA 156; *Stock v. Frank Jones (Tiptan) Ltd.*, (1978) 1 All ER 948, p. 951 (HL); *Grunwick Processing Laboratories Ltd. v. Advisory Conciliation and Arbitration Service*, (1978) 1 All ER 338, p. 368 : (1978) AC 655 (HL); *Assessing Authority-Cum-Excise and Taxation Officer v. East India Cotton Mfg. Co. Ltd.*, AIR 1981 SC 1610, p. 1615 : (1981) 3 SCC 531; *Director General, Telecommunication v. T.N. Peethambaram*, (1986) 4 SCC 348, p. 349 : AIR 1987 SC 162 : 1986 SCC (L&S) 780; *Nagar Palika Nigam v. Krishi Upaj Mandi Samiti*, AIR 2009 SC 187 para 8 : (2008) 12 SCC 364.
6. *Pinner v. Everett*, (1969) 3 All ER 257, p. 259 (HL); *Brutus v. Cozens*, (1972) 2 All ER 1297, pp. 1299, 1303, 1304 (HL) ("We have been warned time and again not to substitute other words for the words of a statute. And there is very good reason for that. Few words have exact synonyms. The overtones are almost always different." This is especially true in case of an ordinary English word of common use for "the easiest word, whatever it may be, can never be translated into one more easy"); *Seramco Ltd. Superannuation Fund Trustees v. Income-tax Commissioner*, (1976) 2 All ER 28, p. 35 : 1977 AC 287 (PC) (In case of an ordinary word there should be no attempt to substitute or paraphrase of general application. Attention should be confined to what is necessary for deciding the particular case); *Murray v. Foyle Meats Ltd.*, (1999) 3 All ER 769, p. 773 (HL) (The temptation of substituting other expressions for the words of the statute by way of explaining what it is thought the legislature is endeavouring to say is to be discouraged); *Re Gilligan*, (2000) 1 All ER 113, p. 122 (HL); *Northern Securities Co. v. U.S.*, 193 U.S. 197, p. 400 per HOLMES J. (much trouble is made by substituting other phrases assumed to be equivalent, which then are reasoned from as if they were in the Act); *Sakshi v. Union of India*, (2004) 5 SCC 518, p. 537 : AIR 2004 SC 3566, p. 3570 (9th Edn., p. 59 of this book is **referred**), *Maulvi Hussain Haji Abraham Umarji v. State of Gujarat*, (2004) 6 SCC 672, p. 680; *Commissioner of Income Tax, Kerala v. Tata Agencies*, (2007) 6 SCC 429, para 61.
7. *State of Kerala v. Mathai Verghese*, (1986) 4 SCC 746, p. 749 : AIR 1987 SC 33; *Union of India v. Deoki Nandan Aggarwal*, AIR 1992 SC 96, p. 101 : 1992 Supp (1) SCC 323; *J.P. Bansal v. State of Rajasthan*, 2003 AIR SCW 1848, p. 1855 : (2003) 5 SCC 134 : AIR 2003 SC 1405; *State of Jharkhand v. Govind Singh*, AIR 2005 SC 294, p. 297.
8. *British India General Insurance Co. Ltd. v. Captain Itbar Singh*, AIR 1959 SC 1331, pp. 1334, 1335 : 1960 (1) SCR 168.

provides for compounding, by the Company Law Board, of any offence punishable under the Act, not being an offence punishable with imprisonment only, or with imprisonment and also with fine, either before or after the institution of any prosecution. It was held that the Company Law Board has the power to compound such offences without the permission of the Court. Since the Legislature, in its wisdom, has not put the rider of prior permission in the section, addition of the words 'with the prior permission of the court' to the provision is not permissible.[9]

Section 2(2) of the Arbitration and Conciliation Act, 1996, which is in Part I of the Act, provides that 'This Part shall apply where the place of arbitration is in India'. In *Bharat Aluminium Company v. Kaiser Aluminium Technical Services Inc.*,[10] a Constitution Bench of the Supreme Court rejected the contention that Part I of the Act was also applicable to arbitrations seated in foreign countries on the ground that in such a case certain words would have to be added to section 2(2), which would then have to provide that 'this part shall apply where the place of arbitration is in India and to arbitrations having its place out of India'. This would amount to a drastic and unwarranted rewriting or alteration of the language of section 2(2), and it is not permissible for the Court to reconstruct a statutory provision. In this case, the Constitution Bench prospectively overruled the decision of a three Judge Bench of the Supreme Court in *Bhatia International v. Bulk Trading SA*,[11] which had held that provisions of Part I would apply to international commercial arbitrations held outside India unless the parties, by agreement, express or implied, exclude all or any of its provisions.

Similarly, in construing Article 31-A(i)(a) of the Constitution and in holding that the 'extinguishment or modification' of any right in any estate is a distinct concept from the 'acquisition by the State of any estate or of any rights therein', the Supreme Court rejected the argument that the extinguishment or modification of any such rights should only be in the process of the acquisition by the State of any estate or any rights therein, as it necessitated reading the words 'in the process of such acquisition', which are not there, after the words 'extinguishment or modification of any such rights'.[12]

And, in construing section 14(f) of the U.P. Town Areas Act, 1914, which reads 'A tax on persons assessed according to their circumstances

---

9. *VLS Finance Limited v. Union of India*, (2013) 6 SCC 278, pp. 284, 285.

10. *Bharat Aluminium Company v. Kaiser Aluminium Technical Services Inc.*, (2012) 9 SCC 552, pp. 600, 601.

11. *Bhatia International v. Bulk Trading SA*, (2002) 4 SCC 105.

12. *Sri Ram Ramnarain v. State of Bombay*, AIR 1959 SC 459, p. 470 : 1959 Supp (1) SCR 489.

and property not exceeding such rate and subject to such limitations and restrictions as may be prescribed', the Supreme Court refused to read residence within the town area as a necessary part of the condition for imposition of the said tax.[13] S.K. DAS, J. said, "To do so will be to read in clause (f) words which do not occur there".[14]

Further in interpreting section 6(a) and section 43 of the Transfer of Property Act, 1882, the Supreme Court refused to read a further exception in section 43 excluding its operation in cases of transfer of *spes successionis*. VENKATARAMA AIYER, J. quoted with approval the observations of LORD LOREBURN, L.C., "We are not entitled to read words into an Act of Parliament unless clear reason for it is to be found within the four corners of the Act itself".[15]

Again in dealing with section 42(1) of the Motor Vehicles Act, 1939, which enacts that 'No owner of a transport vehicle shall use or permit the use of the vehicle in any public place save in accordance with the conditions of a permit granted or countersigned', it was held that the section did not make it necessary that the owner of the vehicle himself should obtain the permit and that there was no justification for reading the words 'to him' after the words 'permit granted'.[16]

On the same principle the House of Lords refused to read the word 'satisfied' in section 4 of the Matrimonial Causes Act, 1950 to mean 'satisfied beyond reasonable doubt'.[17]

The Supreme Court, refusing to read more into section 141 of the Negotiable Instruments Act, 1881, than what has been mandated thereunder, held that as per section 141 of the Act, the Directors who are in charge of and responsible to the Company 'for the conduct of the business of the company', and not the particular business for which the cheque was issued, fall within the mischief of section 138 of the Act. It would therefore

---

13. *Ramnarain v. State of U.P.*, AIR 1957 SC 18 : 1956 SCR 664.

14. *Ibid*, p. 23.

15. *Jumma Masjid v. Kodimaniandra*, AIR 1962 SC 847, p. 850 : 1962 Supp (2) SCR 554 [LORD LOREBURN, L.C's. observations in *Vickers Sons and Maxim Ltd. v. Evans*, (1910) AC 444, p. 445 (HL)].

16. *K.M. Viswanatha Pillai v. K.M. Sanmughan Pillai*, AIR 1969 SC 493, p. 495 : (1969) 1 SCC 188.

17. *Blyth v. Blyth*, (1966) 1 All ER 524 (HL). **Followed** in *N.G. Dastane (Dr.) v. S. Dastane (Mrs.)*, AIR 1975 SC 1534 : (1975) 2 SCC 326 while construing the word 'satisfied' in the Hindu Marriage Act, 1955. **See further** *Re, H (minors)* (sexual abuse: standard of proof), (1996) 1 All ER 1, p. 7 (HL) ['Satisfied' is a neutral word "with a wide range of meanings covering the criminal burden of proof (satisfied to be sure) through the civil burden of proof (satisfied on a balance of probabilities) to a synonym for 'conclude' or 'determine'."].

not be necessary to allege and prove that the Directors have any specific role in respect of the transaction leading to the issuance of the cheque.[18]

Sections 12(5) and 15(5) of the Right to Information Act, 2005, while providing that the Chief Information Commissioner and Information Commissioners shall be persons of eminence in public life, with wide knowledge and experience in law, science and technology, social science, management, journalism, mass media or administration and governance, do not further prescribe any basic qualification which such persons must have in the respective fields in which they work. As a result, the Court cannot read into the provisions of sections 12(5) and 15(5) of the Act the words that such persons must have a basic degree in their respective fields.[19]

In construing the expression 'establishment under the Central Government' the Supreme Court refused to substitute word 'of' for 'under' and held that an establishment not owned by the Central Government would fall within the expression if there is deep and pervasive control of the Central Government over the establishment.[20] In construing Part I of the first Schedule to the High Court Judges (Conditions of Service) Act, 1954, the Supreme Court strongly disapproved the view of the Allahabad High Court which had substituted the words 'more than five years' for the words 'not less than seven years' in para 2 of the Schedule.[21]

(b) *Casus omissus*

It is an application of the same principle that a matter which should have been, but has not been provided for in a statute cannot be supplied by courts, as to do so will be legislation and not construction.[22] But there is

---

18. *A.K. Singhania v. Gujarat State Fertilizer Co. Ltd. & Anr.*, (2013) 16 SCC 630, p. 638.

19. *Union of India v. Namit Sharma*, (2013) 10 SCC 359, p. 384.

20. *C.V. Raman v. Management of Bank of India*, AIR 1988 SC 1369, p. 1377 : (1988) 3 SCC 105 : (1998) 1 KLT 759.

21. *Union of India v. Deoki Nandan Aggarwala*, AIR 1992 SC 96 : 1992 Supp (1) SCC 323.

22. *Hansraj Gupta v. Dehra Dun Mussoorie Electric Tramway Co. Ltd.*, AIR 1933 PC 63, p. 65; *Kamalranjan Roy v. Secretary of State*, AIR 1938 PC 281, p. 283; *Hiradevi v. District Board, Shahjahanpur*, AIR 1952 SC 362, p. 365 : 1952 SCR 1122; *Nalinakhya Bysack v. Shyamsunder*, AIR 1953 SC 148, p. 152 : 1953 SCR 533; *Lord Howard de Walden v. IRC*, (1948) 2 All ER 825, p. 830 (HL); *Magor & St. Mellons Rural District Council v. Newport Corporation*, (1951) 2 All ER 839, pp. 841, 846, 850 (HL); *S. Narayanaswami v. G. Panneerselvam*, AIR 1972 SC 2284, p. 2289 (para 10) : (1972) 3 SCC 717; *Dhoom Singh v. Prakash Chandra Sethi*, AIR 1975 SC 1012, p. 1016 : (1975) 1 SCC 597; *Commissioner of Sales Tax, Uttar Pradesh v. Parson Tools and Plants, Kanpur*, AIR 1975 SC 1039, p. 1043 : 1975 SCC (Tax) 185 : (1975) 4 SCC 22; *Commissioner of Sales Tax v. Mangal Sen Shyamlal*, AIR 1975 SC 1106, p. 1110 : 1975 SCC (Tax) 201 : (1975) 4 SCC 35; *Tarulata Syam*

[Footnote No. 22 Contd.]

no presumption that a *casus omissus* exists and language permitting the court should avoid creating a *casus omissus* where there is none.[23]

While interpreting section 11-A of the Land Acquisition Act, 1894, the Supreme Court held that there is no apparent omission therein to justify application of the doctrine of casus omissus and, by that route, to rewrite section 11-A by providing for exclusion of time taken for obtaining a copy of the order, which exclusion is not provided for in the said section.[24]

Section 71 of the U.P. District Boards Act, 1922, provided that a Board may dismiss its secretary by special resolution which in certain cases required sanction of Local Government, and section 90 conferred a power to suspend the secretary 'pending inquiry into his conduct or pending the orders of any authority whose sanction is necessary for his dismissal'. By U.P. Act 1 of 1933, section 71 was amended and the amended section provided that a resolution of dismissal was not to take effect till the expiry of the period of appeal or till the decision of appeal if it was so presented. No corresponding amendment was, however, made in section 90 and it was held by the Supreme Court that a suspension resolved under section 90 to be operative till the appeal against dismissal was decided, was *ultra vires* the powers of the Board.[25] BHAGWATI, J. speaking for the court said : "It was unfortunate that when the Legislature came to amend the old section 71 of the Act it forgot to amend section 90 in conformity with the amendment of section 71. But this lacuna cannot be supplied by any such liberal construction as the High Court sought to put upon. No doubt it is the duty of the Court to try and harmonise the various provisions of an Act passed by the Legislature. But it is certainly not the

---

[Footnote No. 22 Contd.]

Smt. v. Commissioner of Income-tax, West Bengal, AIR 1977 SC 1802, p. 1811 : (1977) 3 SCC 305; *Johnson v. Moreton*, (1978) 3 All ER 37, p. 41 (HL); *Baliram Waman Hiray (Dr.) v. Mr. Justice B. Lentin*, AIR 1988 SC 2267, p. 2283 : (1988) 4 SCC 419; *Maruti Wire Industries Pvt. Ltd. v. STO 1st Circle Mattancherry,* AIR 2001 SC 1413, p. 1415; *Padmasundara Rao v. State of T.N.,* AIR 2002 SC 1334, p. 1340; *Unique Butyle Tube Industries (P) Ltd. v. U.P. Financial Corporation,* (2003) 2 SCC 455, p. 462; *Unique Butyle Tube Industries Pvt. Ltd. v. U.P. Financial Corporation,* AIR 2003 SC 2103, p. 2107 : (2003) 2 SCC 455 : 2003 All LJ 427 (Legislative *casus omissus* cannot be supplied by judi cial interpretative process); *Union of India v. Ravikumar,* (2003) 6 SCC 516, pp. 525, 526 : AIR 2003 SC 2917; *P.T. Rajan v. J.P.M. Sahir*, (2003) 8 SCC 498, p. 516 : (2003) 11 SCC 405; *Asst. Commissioner Assessment II Bangalore v. Velliappa Textiles Ltd.*, AIR 2004 SC 86, p. 91 : (2004) 9 JT 136; *Sri Rama Saha v. State of West Bengal*, AIR 2004 SC 5080, p. 5087 (para 20) : (2004) 9 JT 136; *State of Jharkhand v. Govind Singh*, AIR 2005 SCC 294, pp. 298, 299; *Karnataka State Financial Corporation v. N. Narsimahaiah,* (2008) 5 SCC 176 para 36 : AIR 2008 SC 1797.

23. **See** text and note 57, p. 79, *infra*.
24. *Singareni Collieries Co. Ltd. v. Vemuganti Ramakrishan Rao & Ors.*, (2013) 8 SCC 789, p. 802.
25. *Hiradevi v. District Board, Shahjahanpur*, AIR 1952 SC 362 : 1952 SCR 1122.

duty of the court to stretch the word used by the Legislature to fill in gaps or omissions in the provisions of an Act".[26]

Similarly, section 18(1) of the West Bengal Premises Rent Control (Temporary Provisions) Act, 1950, which gave power to court to rescind or vary 'any decree for recovery of possession' was held not to cover a power to rescind or vary an order for possession passed under section 43 of the Presidency Small Cause Courts Act, 1882.[27] S.R. DAS, J. for the Court observed: "Even when there is *casus omissus*, it is, as said by LORD RUSSELL OF KILLOWEN, for others than the Courts to remedy the defect".[28]

Section 24(2) of the Right to Fair Compensation and Transparency in Land Acquisition, Rehabilitation and Resettlement Act, 2013, provides that where an award under section 11 of the Land Acquisition Act, 1894, has been made five years or more prior to the commencement of the 2013 Act, but physical possession of the land has not been taken or the compensation has not been paid, the land acquisition proceedings under the 1894 Act shall be deemed to have lapsed. The Supreme Court held that the Legislature has consciously omitted to extend the period of five years indicated in section 24(2) of the Act, even if the acquisition proceedings were delayed on account of an order of stay or injunction granted by a Court of law or for any other reason, and this omission cannot be supplied by a Court of law.[29]

Section 52(3) and 68 of the Forest Act, 1927 as amended in Bihar provide for Confiscation of Vehicle used in a forest offence and do not provide for release of the vehicle on payment of fine. The vehicle could be released only when the offence is compounded and compensation money and full value of the vehicle is paid. It was, therefore, not possible to read a power to levy a fine in lieu of confiscation and release the vehicle.[30]

A similar example is furnished by an English Statute, the Agricultural Holdings Act, 1948. The Act in section 23, which applied to a tenancy from year to year, provided that notice to quit shall be invalid if it purported to terminate the tenancy before the expiration of twelve months from the end of the then current year of tenancy. Section 2(1) applied the same

26. *Ibid.*, p. 365.
27. *Nalinakhya Bysack v. Shyamsunder*, AIR 1953 SC 148 : 1953 SCR 930.
28. *Nalinakhya Bysack v. Shyamsunder, supra*, p. 152 **quoting** *Hansraj Gupta v. Dehra Dun Mussoorie Electric Tramway Co. Ltd.*, AIR 1933 PC 63, p. 65 : 60 IA 13 (LORD RUSSELL OF KILLOWEN).
29. *Sree Balaji Nagar Residential Association v. State of Tamil Nadu & Ors.*, (2015) 3 SCC 353, pp. 359 to 362, **followed** in *Rajiv Chowdhrie v. Union of India*, (2015) 3 SCC 541.
30. *State of Jharkhand v. Govind Singh*, AIR 2005 SC 294, p. 296.

provision to cases where land was let for an interest less than a tenancy from year to year and by section 3(1) provision was made that a tenancy for a term of two years or more was to continue after expiration of the term as a tenancy from year to year. These provisions of the Act, decided in the Court of Appeal, did not cover the case of a tenancy for eighteen months which terminated on expiry of the term without a quit notice.[31] The Act so interpreted, applied to tenancies for two or over two years, from year to year and under one year, but not to those between one and two years. There was no apparent reason why they should not have been included by the Legislature. DEVLIN, L.J. pointing out that this was apparently *casus omissus*, observed: "The court will always allow the intention of a statute to override the defects of wording but the court's ability to do so is limited by recognised canons of interpretation. The Court may, for example, prefer an alternative construction which is less well fitted to the words but better fitted to the intention of the Act. But here, there is no alternative construction; it is simply a case of something being overlooked. We cannot legislate for *casus omissus*. I may be sure in this case that I know exactly what Parliament would do if it perceived a gap. But, if this rule were to be relaxed, sooner or later the court would be saying what Parliament meant and might get it wrong and thus usurp the law-making function".[32]

An omission by the Legislature to amend a related provision presents great difficulties of construction. This is illustrated by three cases namely *Basavanatappa v. Gangadhar Naryana Dharwadkar*,[33] *P.K. Unni v. Nirmala Industries*,[34] and *Dadi Jagannadham v. Jammulu Ramulu*.[35] All these cases relate to the construction of Rule 89 of Order 21 of the Code of Civil Procedure after the amendment of Article 127 of the Limitation Act, 1963 by Act 104 of 1976. Rule 89 of Order 21 provides that if any person, claiming an interest in the property sold in execution of a decree, applies to have the execution sale set aside and deposits within thirty days from the date of the sale, five percent of the purchase money for payment to the purchaser and the amount payable to the decreeholder for recovery of which the sale was held, 'the court shall make an order setting aside the sale'. The period of limitation for applying under Rule 89 for setting aside the sale was also thirty days under Article 127 of the Limitation Act, 1963 before its amendment by Act 104 of 1976 by which this period of limitation was enlarged from thirty days to sixty days. Parliament,

---

31. *Gladstone v. Bower*, (1960) 3 All ER 353 (CA).
32. *Ibid.*, p. 358.
33. (1986) 4 SCC 273 : AIR 1987 SC 53 : (1986) 162 ITR 373.
34. AIR 1990 SC 933 : (1990) 2 SCC 378 : (1990) 1 KLT 903.
35. AIR 2001 SC 2699 : (2001) 7 SCC 71.

however, omitted to make corresponding amendment in Rule 89 of Order 21 to enlarge the period for making the deposit from thirty days to sixty days. The object and reasons of the Bill which became Act 104 of 1976 showed that the period was enlarged from thirty days to sixty days as the period of thirty days was considered to be too short for making the deposit often causing hardship. Having regard to this object a two judge bench of the Supreme Court in *Dharwadkar* held that not only the period of limitation for making an application for setting aside the sale was extended from thirty to sixty days but the period for making the deposit under Rule 89 was also impliedly extended from thirty days to sixty days. But this view was not accepted by a three judge bench in *Nirmala Industries* on the reasoning that the omission to amend Rule 89 by Parliament could not be supplied by the court. Later a five judge bench in *Ramulu* overruled *Nirmala Industries*. Although accepting that the court cannot make up deficiencies left by the legislature, it was observed that the court must try to harmonize the conflicting provisions. On this reasoning it was held that Rule 89 does not provide any limitation and it really directs that the court will have no discretion and will have to set aside the sale if the deposit is made within thirty days and that it does not prevent deposit being made later. Thus in view of this decision if an application for setting aside the sale is made within sixty days and deposit is also made within sixty days though beyond thirty days, the court will have a discretion to set aside the sale.

Another illustration of the difficulty faced in construction when a related provision is not amended is section 25 of the Code of Civil Procedure as substituted by the Amendment Act of 1976. Section 25 confers power on the Supreme Court to transfer any suit appeal or other proceeding from a High Court or Civil Court in one state to a High Court or Civil Court in another state. The amending Act did not delete or omit section 23(3) of the Code which provides that where several Courts having jurisdiction are subordinate to different High Courts, the application for transfer shall be made to the High Court within the local limits of whose jurisdiction the High Court in which the suit is brought is situate. Because of continuance of section 23, it was held by Bombay,[36] Andhra Pradesh[37] and Madhya Pradesh[38] High Courts that it was still open for a party to apply to the High Court for transfer of a proceeding pending in a Court Subordinate to it to a Court in another state and it was left to the choice of the party whether he should apply for transfer in the Supreme

36. *Priyavari Mehta v. Priyanath Mehta,* AIR 1980 Bom 337.
37. *Mamta Gupta v. Mukund Kumar Gupta,* AIR 2000 AP 394.
38. *Lakshmi Nagdev v. Jitendra Kumar Nagdev*, (2004) 4 MPLJ 310.

Court or in the High Court. This view was overruled by the Supreme Court in *Durgesh Sharma v. Jayshree*[39] which holds that section 23 must be read subject to section 25 and even if the High Courts had the power to transfer a case from one state to another state that must be taken to have been withdrawn from 1-1-1977 when the amendment Act 1976 came into force. The view so taken makes section 23(3) wholly nugatory and if this was the intention the amending Act ought to have deleted section 23(3) which it failed to do and it was this failure which led to the difference between the views taken by the High Courts and the Supreme Court.

Before leaving the topic a reference is necessary to certain observations of DENNING, L.J. which have been cited with approval by the Supreme Court.[40] DENNING, L.J. said: "When a defect appears a judge cannot simply fold his hands and blame the draftsman. He must set to work on the constructive task of finding the intention of Parliament and then he must supplement the written words so as to give 'force and life' to the intention of the Legislature. A judge should ask himself the question how, if the makers of the Act had themselves come across this ruck in the texture of it, they would have straightened it out? He must then do as they would have done. A judge must not alter the material of which the Act is woven, but he can and should iron out the creases".[41] In a subsequent case he restated the same thing in a new form: "We sit here to find out the intention of Parliament and of ministers and carry it out, and we do this better by filling in the gaps and making sense of the enactment than by opening it up to destructive analysis".[42] Both these observations of DENNING, L.J. came up

---

39. (2008) 9 SCC 648 para 55 : AIR 2009 SC 285.

40. *M. Pentiah v. Muddala Veeramallapa*, AIR 1961 SC 1107, p. 115 : (1961) 2 SCR 295; *State of Bihar v. Asis kumar Mukerjee*, AIR 1975 SC 192, p. 196 : (1975) 3 SCC 602 : (1975) 1 LLJ 198; *Union of India v. Sankalchand*, AIR 1977 SC 2328, p. 2337 : 1977 (4) SCC 193; *Bangalore Water Supply v. A. Rajappa*, AIR 1978 SC 548, pp. 552, 561 : 1978 (2) SCC 213; *State of Karnataka v. Hansa Corporation*, AIR 1981 SC 463, pp. 469, 470 : (1980) 4 SCC 697; *Hameedia Hardware Stores v. B. Mohan Lal Sowcar*, AIR 1988 SC 1060, pp. 1067, 1068 : 1988 (2) SCC 513; *Pushpa Devi v. Milkhiram*, AIR 1990 SC 808, p. 813; *N.K. Jain v. C.K. Shah*, AIR 1991 SC 1289, p. 1301 : 1991 (2) SCC 495; *Directorate of Enforcement v. Deepak Mahajan*, 1994 JT (1) SC 281, p. 301 : AIR 1994 SC 1775, pp. 1784, 1785; *S. Gopal Reddy v. State of Andhra Pradesh*, AIR 1996 SC 2184, p. 2188 : 1996 (5) Scale 78, p. 85; *State of Bihar v. Bihar Distillery Ltd.*, AIR 1997 SC 1511, p. 1520 : (1997) 2 SCC 453; *NEPC Micon Ltd. v. Magma Leasing Ltd.*, AIR 1999 SC 1952, p. 1957 : (1999) 4 SCC 253; *Gujarat Composite Ltd. v. Ranip Nagarpalika*, JT 1999 (9) SC 62, p. 66 : (1999) 8 SCC 675; *Reema Aggarwal v. Anupam*, (2003) 3 SCC 199, p. 213.

41. *Seaford Court Estates Ltd. v. Asher*, (1949) 2 All ER 155, p. 164 (CA).

42. *Magor & St. Mellons Rural District Council v. Newport Corporation*, (1950) 2 All ER 1226, p. 1236 (CA). LORD DENNING in a **dissenting** judgment reiterated

[Footnote No. 42 Contd.]

for severe criticism at the hands of the House of Lords and were plainly disapproved.[43] "It appears to me", said LORD SIMONDS, "to be a naked usurpation of the legislative function under the thin disguise of interpretation".[44] LORD MORTON (with whom LORD GODDARD entirely agreed) observed: "These heroics are out of place"[45] and pointed out LORD TUCKER: "Your Lordships would be acting in a legislative rather than a judicial capacity if the view put forward by DENNING, L.J., were to prevail".[46] It does not seem, however, reasonable to infer that LORD DENNING was intending to lay down a rule permitting usurpation of legislative function by courts and it is more proper to infer that he was emphasising in somewhat unconventional manner that when object or policy of a statute can be ascertained, imprecision in its language should not be readily allowed in the way of adopting a reasonable construction which avoids absurdities and incongruities and carries out the object or policy.[47] LORD DENNING's approach allows a gap to be filled in somewhat more freely.[48] Thus the difference, if at all, is regarding the extent of the limited creative role which the judges can play.[49] In other words, the difference is as to how much one can infer by necessary implication to fill in a *prima facie* gap.[50]

[Footnote No. 42 Contd.]

his liberal views; he said: "How should we construe an Act of Parliament? I have said before and I repeat it now, that we should so construe an Act of Parliament as to effectuate the intention of makers of it and not to defeat it. If they have by mistake overlooked something, we should do our best to smooth it out. We should construe it so as to avoid absurdities and incongruities and to produce a consistent and just result."; *Lucy v. W.T. Henleys Telegraph Works Co. Ltd.*, (1969) 3 All ER 456, p. 462 (CA). LORD DENNING later reaffirmed his views in the following words : "Faced with glaring injustice, the judges are, it is said, impotent incapable and sterile. Not so with us in this court—. Whenever the strict interpretation of a statute gives rise to an absurd and unjust situation, the judges can and should use their good sense to remedy it by reading words in, if neccessary, so as to do what Parliament would have done had they had the situation in mind." *Nothman v. London Borough of Barnet*, (1978) 1 All ER 1243, p. 1246 : (1978) 1 WLR 220 (CA). In the House of Lords, LORD RUSSELL was critical of these "Sweeping comments": **see** (1979) 1 All ER 142, p. 151 (HL).]

43. *Magor & St. Mellons R.D.C. v. Newport Corporation*, (1951) 2 All ER 839 (HL).

44. *Ibid.*, p. 841. LORD SIMONDS' **disapproval** of DENNING approach was cited with **approval** in *Punjab Land and Development Corporation v. Presiding Officer, Labour Court*, 1990 (3) SCR 111, pp. 153, 154 : (1990) 3 SCC 682 and **noticed** in *O.S. Singh v. Union of India*, 1995 (6) Scale 8 : 1996 (7) SCC 37 : 1996 SCC (L&S) 373.

45. *Ibid.*, p. 846.

46. *Ibid.*, p. 850.

47. **See** title 1(d) Departure from the Rule, title (3) Regard to Subject and Object, and title (4) Regard to Consequences, *infra*.

48. DENNING, The Closing Chapter, pp. 101 to 118.

49. The current tendency among English judges would appear to incline away from the Denning approach : CROSS, Statutory Interpretation, 3rd Edition, p. 47.

50. The two views on *casus omissus* are discussed in *O.S. Singh v. Union of India*, 1995 (6) Scale 8, pp. 16, 17 : 1996 (7) SCC 37 : 1996 SCC (L&S) 373.

The Supreme Court in *Bangalore Water Supply v. A. Rajappa*[51] approved the rule of construction stated by DENNING, L.J. while dealing with the definition of 'Industry' in the Industrial Disputes Act, 1947. The definition is so general and ambiguous that BEG, C.J.I., said that the situation called for "some judicial heroics to cope with the difficulties raised".[52] K. IYER, J., who delivered the leading majority judgment in *A. Rajappa* referred with approbation[53] the passage extracted above from the judgment of DENNING, L.J. in *Seaford Court Estates Ltd. v. Asher.*[54] But in the same continuation he also cited a passage from the speech of LORD SIMONDS in the case of *Magor & St. Mellons R.D.C. v. Newport Corporation*[55] as if it also formed a part of the judgment of DENNING, L.J. This passage reads : "The duty of the court is to interpret the words that the Legislature has used. Those words may be ambiguous, but, even if they are, the power and duty of the court to travel outside them on a voyage of discovery are strictly limited".[56] As earlier noticed LORD SIMONDS and other Law Lords in *Magor & St. Mellon's* case were highly critical of the views of DENNING, L.J. However, as submitted above, the criticism is more because of the unconventional manner in which the rule of construction was stated by him.[57]

In this connection it is pertinent to remember that although a court cannot supply a real *casus omissus* it is equally clear that it should not so interpret a statute as to create a *casus omissus* when there is really none.[58] Section 35(2) of the Foreign Exchange Regulation Act, 1973 and section 104(2) of the Customs Act, 1962, which are identically worded, provide

---

51. AIR 1978 SC 548 : 1978 (2) SCC 213. **See further** *CIT v. B.N. Bhattacharjee*, (1979) 4 SCC 121, p. 136 : AIR 1979 SC 1725; *Bhagmal v. Ch. Parbhu Ram*, (1985) 1 SCC 61, pp. 87, 88 : AIR 1985 SC 150; *State of Tamil Nadu v. Kodaikanal Motor Union*, (1986) 3 SCC 91, p. 100 : AIR 1986 SC 1173.

52. *Ibid.*, p. 552 (BEG, C.J.I., noticed the **disapproval** of the House of Lords and **referred** to the passages from the speeches of Law Lords which are quoted above; **See** text and notes 43 to 45, p. 78, *supra*).

53. AIR 1978 SC 548, p. 561 : 1978 (2) SCC 213.

54. **See** text and note 40, p. 77, *supra*.

55. (1951) 2 All ER 839.

56. *Magor & St. Mellons R.D.C. v. Newport Corporation*, (1951) 2 All ER 839, p. 841.

57. This paragraph in the book was **quoted** by SINHA, J., from 5th Edition of this book in *Gujarat High Court v. Gujarat Kishan Mazdoor Panchayat*, AIR 2003 SC 1201, p. 1214 : (2003) 4 SCC 712 : (2003) 2 LLN 328.

58. *Karnataka State v. Union of India*, AIR 1978 SC 68, p. 107 : (1977) 4 SCC 608; *CIT v. National Taj Traders*, AIR 1980 SC 485, p. 489 : (1980) 1 SCC 370; *M.G. Wagh v. Jay Engineering Works Ltd.*, (1987) 1 SCC 542, p. 546 : AIR 1987 SC 670; *Unique Butyle Tube Industries Pvt. Ltd. v. U.P. Financial Corporation*, AIR 2003 SC 2103, p. 2108 : (2003) 2 SCC 455 : 2003 All LJ 427; *Union of India v. Ranjit Kumar*, (2003) 6 SCC 516, pp. 525, 526 : AIR 2003 SC 2917; *Ramesh Mehta v. Sanwal Chand Singhavi*, (2004) 5 SCC 409, p. 423 (para 12) : AIR 2004 SC 2258. **See further** Chapter 10, text and notes 11 to 16, pp. 927, 928.

that every person arrested by any authorised officer of the Enforcement or Customs, as the case may be, if not released on bail by the officer arresting him 'shall, without unnecessary delay, be taken to a magistrate'. These Acts do not contain any provision empowering the magistrate to authorise further detention. The corresponding provision in the Code of Criminal Procedure,1973 is section 167(1). Section 167(2) empowers the magistrate to authorise detention of 'an accused person'. In holding that section 167(2) of the Code was applicable to authorise detention of a person produced before a magistrate under section 35(2) of the Foreign Exchange Regulation Act or section 104(2) of the Customs Act, 1962, the Supreme Court observed that otherwise the mandatory direction to take the person arrested, when not released on bail to a magistrate under these Special Acts "will become purposeless and meaningless and to say that the courts even in the event of refusal of bail have no choice but to set the person arrested at liberty by folding their hands as a helpless spectator in the face of what is termed as 'legislative *casus omissus*' or legal flaw or lacuna, it will become utterly illogical and absurd."[59] The Andhra Pradesh Building (Lease Rent and Eviction) Control Act, 1960 classifies buildings into two categories: I. residential, II. non-residential. There is no separate category of a building which has both residential and non-residential portions and is let out under a composite lease. But to avoid the lacuna that the landlord of such a building is left remedyless, it has been held that such a building is to be categorised either a residential or a non-residential building having regard to its nature, accommodation dominant purpose of the lease, primary use of the building and other relevant circumstances.[60]

It has been recognised by the Supreme Court[61] that if a matter, provision for which may have been desirable, has not been really provided for by the Legislature, the omission cannot be called a defect of the nature which can be cured or supplied by recourse to the mode of construction advocated by DENNING, L.J., in the case of *Seaford Court Estate Ltd.*[62] As observed by a Constitution Bench "a *casus omissus* cannot be supplied by the court except in the case of clear necessity and when reason for it is found in the four corners of the statute itself but at the same time a *casus omissus* should not be readily inferred."[63]

---

59. *Directorate of Enforcement v. Deepak Mahajan*, JT 1994 (1) SC 281, p. 325 : AIR 1994 SC 1775, p. 1803 : (1994) 3 SCC 440.

60. *Boddu Narayanamma v. Sri Venkatarama Aluminium Co.*, JT 1999 (7) SC 364 : (1999) 7 SCC 589.

61. *Petron Engineering Construction (Pvt.) Ltd. v. Central Board of Direct Taxes*, AIR 1989 SC 501, pp. 508, 509 : 1989 Supp (2) SCC 7 : (1989) 175 ITR 523.

62. **See** text and note 40, p. 77.

63. *Padmasundara Rao v. State of T.N.*, AIR 2002 SC 1334, p. 1340 : (2002) 3 SCC 533. **See further** *Unique Butyle Tube Industries (P.) Ltd. v. U.P. Financial Corporation*, (2003) 2

[Footnote No. 63 Contd.]

(c) Avoiding rejection of words

As on the one hand, it is not permissible to add words or to fill in a gap or lacuna, on the other hand effort should be made to give meaning to each and every word used by the Legislature. "It is not a sound principle of construction", said PATANJALI SHASTRY, C.J.I., "to brush aside words in a statute as being inapposite surplusage, if they can have appropriate application in circumstances conceivably within the contemplation of the statute".[64] And as pointed out by JAGANNATHDAS, J., "It is incumbent on the court to avoid a construction, if reasonably permissible on the language, which would render a part of the statute devoid of any meaning or application".[65] "In the interpretation of statutes", observed DAS GUPTA, J., "the courts always presume that the Legislature inserted every part thereof for a purpose and the legislative intention is that every part of the statute should have effect".[66] The Legislature is deemed not to waste its words or to say anything in vain[67] and a construction which attributes redundancy to the Legislature will not be accepted except for compelling reasons.[68]

[Footnote No. 63 Contd.]

SCC 455, pp. 462, 463 : 2003 All LJ 427 : AIR 2003 SC 2103; *Shiv Shakti Co-op. Housing Society Nagpur v. Swaraj Developers,* AIR 2003 SC 2434, pp. 2440, 2441 : (2003) 6 SCC 659; *State of Orissa v. Joginder Patjoshi*, AIR 2004 SC 1039, p. 1041 : (2004) 9 SCC 278; *State of Jharkhand v. Govind Singh*, AIR 2005 SC 294, p. 298; *Sangeeta Singh v. Union of India,* (2005) 7 SCC 484, pp. 489, 490 (Rule applied for construction of advertisement for grant of dealership and distribution of petrol pumps); *Union of India v. Shardindu,* (2007) 6 SCC 276 (paras 24, 25) : (2007) 7 JT 439 : (2007) 7 Scale 575.

64. *Aswini Kumar Ghose v. Arabinda Bose*, AIR 1952 SC 369, p. 377 : 1953 SCR 1; **see further** *Union of India v. Hansoli Devi,* AIR 2002 SC 3240, p. 3246 : (2002) 7 SCC 273; *State of Orissa v. Joginder Patjoshi*, AIR 2004 SC 1039, p. 1142 : (2004) 9 SCC 278.

65. *Rao Shiv Bahadur Singh v. State of U.P.*, AIR 1953 SC 394, p. 397 : 1953 SCR 1188.

66. *J.K. Cotton Spinning & Weaving Mills Co. Ltd. v. State of U.P.*, AIR 1961 SC 1170, p.1174 : (1962) 1 SCJ 417 : (1961) 1 LLJ 540; *Shri Mohammad Alikhan v. Commissioner of Wealth Tax*, AIR 1997 SC 1165, p. 1167 : (1997) 3 SCC 511; *Dilawar Balu Kurane v. State of Maharashtra,* AIR 2002 SC 564, p. 566 : (2002) 2 SCC 135; *Ramphal Kundu v. Kamal Sharma*, AIR 2004 SC 1039, p. 1042 : (2004) 9 SCC 278.

67. *Quebec Railway, Light, Heat & Power Co. v. Vandry*, AIR 1920 PC 181, p. 186 : 1920 AC 662; **see further** *Union of India v. Hansoli Devi, supra.*

68. *Ghanshyamdas v. Regional Asstt. Commr., Sales Tax*, AIR 1964 SC 766, p. 772 : 1964 (4) SCR 436. **See further** *CIT v. Kanpur Coal Syndicate*, AIR 1965 SC 325, p. 327 : 1964 (8) SCR 85; *State of Rajasthan v. Leela Jain*, AIR 1965 SC 1296, p. 1299 : (1965) 1 SCR 276; *Bhanu Pratap Singh (Raja) v. Asstt. Custodian, E.P., Bahraich*, AIR 1966 SC 245, p. 247 : (1966) 1 SCR 304; *CIT v. Moon Mills*, AIR 1966 SC 870, p. 873 : 1974 (3) SCC 554; *D.R. Jerry v. Union of India*, AIR 1974 SC 130, p. 133 : 1974 (3) SCC 554; *Shri Balaganeshan Metals v. Shanmugham Chetty*, (1987) 2 SCC 707, p. 713 : AIR 1987 SC 1668; *State of Uttar Pradesh v. Radhey Shyam*, AIR 1989 SC 682, pp. 689, 690 : 1989 (1) SCC 591; *State of Maharashtra v. Santosh Shankar Acharya,* (2000) 7 SCC 463, p. 469 : AIR 2000 SC 2504; *Borosil Glass Works Ltd.*

[Footnote No. 68 Contd.]

The application of this rule can be illustrated by a decision of the House of Lords[69] relating to the Gaming Act of 1845. The statute in section 18 provides: 'All contracts or agreements—by way of gaming or wagering, shall be null and void, and no suit shall be brought or maintained in any court of law and equity for recovering any sum of money or valuable thing alleged to be won upon any wager'.[70] The defendant in *Hill v. William* as a result of betting with the plaintiffs lost a certain sum and in consideration of the plaintiffs refraining from following up the procedure with TATTERSALL'S Committee which would have led to the defendant being then and there posted as a defaulter, promised to pay the said sum in instalments to the plaintiffs. On the defendant failing to pay, the plaintiffs brought the suit for recovery of the sum basing their claim on this fresh agreement as distinct from the betting transaction. The House of Lords overruling the Court of Appeal held that although the agreement contained a new promise for good consideration, which did not fall within the first limb of section 18, nevertheless, it was a promise to pay money 'won upon a wager' and was not enforceable under the second limb of section 18.[71] Countering the argument that the second limb of section 18 beginning with 'and no suit shall be filed' was only a procedural counterpart of the first and was applicable only to suits brought on wagering contracts declared by first limb to be void, VISCOUNT SIMON observed: "Though a parliamentary enactment (like parliamentary eloquence) is capable of saying the same thing twice over without adding anything to what has already been said once, this repetition in the case of any Act of Parliament is not to be assumed. When the Legislature enacts a particular phrase in a statute the presumption is that it is saying something which has not been said immediately before. The rule that a meaning should, if possible, be given to every word in the statute implies that, unless there is good reason to the contrary, the words add something which would not be there if the words were left out".[72]

Applying the rule of interpretation that every word used by the Legislature in a statutory provision should be given its due meaning, the Supreme

---

[Footnote No. 68 Contd.]

Employees Union v. D.D. Bambode, AIR 2001 SC 378, p. 380 : (2001) 1 SCC 350; *Union of India v. Hansoli Devi,* AIR 2002 SC 3240, p. 3246 : (2002) 7 SCC 273; *Nathi Devi v. Radha Devi,* (2005) 2 SCC 271, p. 277 : AIR 2005 SC 648, p. 652; *Promoters & Builders Ass. of Pune v. Pune Municipal Corpn.,* (2007) 6 SCC 143 (para 11) : AIR 2007 SC 1956; *Visitor AMU v. K. S. Misra,* (2007) 8 SCC 593 para 13 (9th Edition of this book is **referred**) : (2007) 11 JT 549.

69. *Hill v. Williams Hill (Park Lane) Ltd.*, (1949) 2 All ER 452 (HL); **referred to** in *Gherulal Parakh v. Mahadeodas Maiya*, AIR 1959 SC 781, pp. 789, 790, 791 : 1959 Supp (2) SCR 406.

70. **Cf**. section 30, Indian Contract Act, 1872.

71. *Hill v. Williams Hill (Park Lane) Ltd., supra.*

72. *Hill v. Williams Hill (Park Lane) Ltd., supra*, p. 461; **referred** to in *Umed v. Rajsingh*, AIR 1975 SC 43, p. 63 : (1975) 1 SCC 76.

Court held that the expression 'one of the parties or any person claiming through or under him' in section 45 of the Arbitration and Conciliation Act, 1996, is wider than the word 'party' in section 8 of the Act, and therefore not only a party to the arbitration agreement, but also any person claiming through or under a party to the arbitration agreement, can move the Court under section 45 to refer the disputes raised before it to arbitration.[73]

Similarly, in construing section 6(4) of the Bombay Land Requisition Act, 1948, which provides that 'the State Government may requisition the premises for the purpose of a State or any other public purpose', the Supreme Court rejected the argument that the words 'any other public purpose' are restricted to a public purpose which is also a purpose of the State and held: "If the words 'any other public purpose' in the statute in question have been used only to mean a State purpose, they would become mere surplusage; Court should lean against such a construction as far as possible".[74]

On the same principle it was held that the words 'but excluding other village officers' were not mere surplusage but carved out an exclusion from the genus of 'revenue officers' in section 123(7)(f) of the Representation of the People Act, 1951, which before amendment in 1958 read thus; "revenue officers including village accountants, such as, *Patwaris*, *Lekhpala*, *Talatis*, *Karnams* and the like but excluding other village officers".[75]

In construing section 14(1)(d) and (f) of the U.P. Town Areas Act, 1914, the Supreme Court held that taxes under these two items, *i.e.*, a tax on trade, calling and profession, and a tax on circumstances and property are in some respects overlapping otherwise the proviso to cl.(f)—'Provided that such person is not already assessed under clauses (a) to (e)'—will become meaningless.[76]

In holding that the words 'relationship in the nature of marriage' as used in section 2(f) of the Protection of Women from Domestic Violence Act, 2005 mean a relationship akin to a common law marriage and not every live-in relationship.[77] By reading 'relationship in the nature of marriage' to mean simply live-in relationship, the court would be legislating in the garb of marriage which is not permissible.[78]

---

73. *Chloro Controls India Pvt. Ltd. v. Severn Trent Water Purification Inc. & Ors.*, (2013) 1 SCC 641, pp. 691, 692.

74. *State of Bombay v. Ali Gulshan*, AIR 1955 SC 810, p. 816 : (1955) 2 SCR 867 : 58 Bom LR 490.

75. *S. Gurmej Singh v. S. Pratap Singh Kairon*, AIR 1960 SC 122, p. 125 : 1960 (1) SCR 909.

76. *Ramnarain v. State of U.P.*, AIR 1957 SC 18, p. 21 : 1956 SCR 664.

77. *D. Velusamy v. D. Patachaiamal*, (2010) 10 SCC 469 : AIR 2011 SC 479.

78. *Ibid* para 32.

And in interpreting the proviso in section 19 of the Hindu Adoption and Maintenance Act, 1956, which provides for maintenance to a Hindu wife 'from the estate of her husband or her father or mother', it was held that the provision conferred a personal right against the father or mother and the words 'the estate of' before the words 'her husband' are not to be read before the words 'her father or mother' for the right to maintenance of a widowed daughter from the estate of her parents specifically covered by section 21(vi) read with section 22(2) would become otiose.[79]

(d) Departure from the rule

In discharging its interpretative function, the court can correct obvious drafting errors and so in suitable cases "the court will add words, or omit words or substitute words".[80] But "before interpreting a statute in this way the Court must be abundantly sure of three matters: (1) the intended purpose of the statute or provision in question, (2) that by inadvertence the draftsman and Parliament failed to give effect to that purpose in the provision in question; and (3) the substance of the provision Parliament would have made, although not necessarily the precise words Parliament would have used, had the error in the Bill been noticed."[81] Sometimes even when these conditions are satisfied, the court may find itself inhibited from interpreting the statutory provision in accordance with underlying intention of Parliament, *e.g.* when the alteration in language is too far reaching or too big or when the subject matter calls for strict interpretation such as a penal provision.[82]

(i) *Addition of words when permissible.*—As already noticed it is not allowable to read words in a statute which are not there, but "where the alternative lies between either supplying by implication words which appear to have been accidentally omitted, or adopting a construction which deprives certain existing words of all meaning, it is permissible to supply the words".[83] A departure from the rule of literal construction may be legitimate so as to avoid any part of the statute becoming meaningless.[84] Words may

---

79. *Balwant Kaur v. Chanan Singh,* AIR 2000 SC 1908, p. 1914 : (2000) 6 SCC 310.

80. *Inco Europe Ltd. v. First Choice Distribution (a firm),* (2000) 2 All ER 109, p. 115 (HL).

81. *Ibid.*

82. *Ibid.*

83. CRAIES Statute Law, 7th Edition, p. 109. **See further** *Surjit Singh Kalra v. Union of India*, (1991) 2 SCC 87 (para 19); *H.C. Suman v. Rehabilitation Ministry Employees Co-operative House Building Society Ltd.*, AIR 1991 SC 2160, pp. 2167, 2168 : (1991) 4 SCC 485; *M.J. Exports Ltd. v. CEGAT*, AIR 1992 SC 2014, p. 2024 : 1992 (3) JT 398 : 1993 Supp (1) SCC 169; *Gujarat Urja Vikas Ltd. v. Essar Power Ltd.*, (2008) 4 SCC 755 paras 54 to 57 : AIR 2008 SC 1921.

84. *Siraj-ul-Haq v. Sunni Central Board of Waqf, U.P.*, AIR 1959 SC 198 : 1959 SCR 1287.

also be read to give effect to the intention of the Legislature which is apparent from the Act read as a whole.[85] Application of the mischief rule or purposive construction may also enable reading of words by implication when there is no doubt about the purpose which the Parliament intended to achieve.[86] But before any words are read to repair an omission in the Act, it should be possible to state with certainty that these or similar words would have been inserted by the draftsman and approved by Parliament had their attention been drawn to the omission before the Bill passed into law.[87]

In construing section 5(2) of the U.P. Muslims Waqfs Act, 1936, which provides, '*Mutwalli* of a *Waqf* or any person interested in a *Waqf*' or a Central Board may bring a suit in a Civil Court of competent jurisdiction for a declaration that any transaction held by the Commissioner of *Waqfs* to be a *Waqf* is not a *Waqf*, the Supreme Court interpreted the words 'any person interested in a *Waqf*' as meaning 'any person interested in what is held to be a *Waqf*'.[88] GAJENDRAGADKAR, J. speaking for the court observed: "It is well settled that in construing the provisions of a statute courts should be slow to adopt a construction which tends to make any part of the statute meaningless or ineffective",[89] and "where literal meaning of the words used in a statutory provision would manifestly defeat its object by making a part of it meaningless and ineffective, it is legitimate and even necessary to adopt the rule of liberal construction so as to give meaning to all parts of the provision and to make the whole of it effective and operative".[90]

Similarly the words "any debt due *before* the commencement of this Act to any banking company" as occurring in section 4(1) of the Kerala Agriculturists Debt Relief Act, 1970, were construed by the Supreme Court to

---

85. *Hameedia Hardware Stores v. B. Mohan Lal Sowcar*, AIR 1988 SC 1060, p. 1067 : 1988 (2) SCC 513; *H.C. Suman v. Rehabilitation Ministry Employees Co-operative House Building Society Ltd., supra.*

86. *Pickstone v. Freemans Plc.*, (1988) 2 All ER 803, pp. 813, 817 : 1989 AC 66 : (1988) 3 WLR 265 (HL); *Lister v. Forth Drydock and Engineering Co. Ltd.*, (1989) 1 All ER 1134 : (1990) 1 AC 546 (HL).

87. *Jones v. Wrotham Park Settled Estates*, (1979) 1 All ER 286, p. 289 (HL) (LORD DIPLOCK); *Inco Europe Ltd. v. First Choice Distribution (a firm) supra.* Academic opinion has been expressed that these cases have diluted or obliterated the *Casus Omissus* Rule: Benedict Coxon 'Open to Interpretation'; V. Niranjan 'Was the Death of the *Casus Omissus* Rule Undignified': 30 (2009) Statute Law Review 1 and 73. **See further** *Union of India v. Hansoli Devi,* AIR 2002 SC 3240, p. 3246 : (2002) 7 SCC 273.

88. *Siraj-ul-Haq v. Sunni Central Board of Waqf, U.P.*, AIR 1959 SC 198 : 1959 SCR 1287.

89. *Ibid.*, p. 204 (AIR) (paras 16 and 17).

90. *Siraj-ul-Haq v. Sunni Central Board, U.P.*, AIR 1959 SC 198 : 1959 SCR 1287.

mean "any debt due *at or before* the commencement of this Act".[91] CHANDRACHUD, C.J.I., delivering the judgment of the court said: "We would have normally hesitated to fashion the clause by so restructuring it but we see no escape from that course since that is the only rational manner by which we can give meaning and content to it, so as to further the object of the Act".[92]

In entry 70 Schedule I of the Gujarat Gram and Nagar Panchayats Taxes and Fees Rules 1964, one of the items mentioned is 'Grog Minerals'. As there is no such mineral as Grog Mineral whereas Grog and Minerals are known to the technical world as expression 'Grog Minerals' was read to mean 'Grog and Minerals' instead of rejecting it as meaningless.[93]

On the same principle, it was pointed out that the words 'any party to an arbitration agreement' occurring in section 33 of the Arbitration Act, 1940, must be taken to mean a person 'who is alleged to be' a party to an arbitration agreement[94] and the words "where any penalty is imposed" in Rule 14(1) of the Railway Servants (Discipline and Appeal) Rules, 1968, were construed to mean where any "penalty is imposable".[95]

Similarly the words 'be reckoned' which were inadvertently omitted in section 46(7)(iv) of the Indian Income-tax Act, 1922, were supplied by construction otherwise the provision would have become meaningless.[96]

Clauses (ii) and (iii) of section 10(3)(a) of the Tamil Nadu Buildings (Lease and Rent Control) Act, 1960 provide the grounds on which the landlord can obtain an order directing the tenant to put him in possession in respect of a non-residential building but clause (ii) alone contains the words 'if the landlord required it for his own use or for the use of any member of his family' making the requirement as a precondition for obtaining possession. But as the intention of the Legislature was not in doubt from the context and the Act read as a whole the words mentioned above were also read in clause (iii).[97]

---

91. *State Bank of Travancore v. Mohammad*, AIR 1981 SC 1744, p. 1750 : (1981) 4 SCC 82.

92. *Ibid.*

93. *Gujarat Composite Ltd. v. Ranip Nagarpalika,* JT 1999 (9) SC 62, p. 65 : AIR 2000 SC 135, p. 137 : (1999) 8 SCC 675.

94. *Chaturbhuj Mohanlal v. Bhicam Chand*, 53 Cal WN 410; *Mathu Kutty v. Varee Kutty*, AIR 1950 Mad 64; *Lalchand v. Basanta Mal Devi Dayal (M/s.)*, 49 Pun LR 246; **approved** in *Siraj-ul-Haq v. Sunni Central Board of Wakf*, AIR 1959 SC 198, p. 204 (para 17) : 1959 SCR 1287.

95. *Divisional Personnel Officer, Southern Railway v. T.R. Challappan*, AIR 1975 SC 2216 : (1976) 3 SCC 190 : 1976 SCC (L&S) 398.

96. *Champa Kumari Singhi v. Member, Board of Revenue, West Bengal*, AIR 1970 SC 1108, p. 1111 : (1970) 1 SCC 404.

97. *Hameedia Hardware Stores v. B. Mohan Lal Sowcar*, AIR 1988 SC 1060, p. 1067 : (1988) 2 SCC 513.

Section 17 of the Consumer Protection Act, 1986 constitutes a State Commission for each State but there is no provision in the Act limiting their territorial jurisdiction. But as the intention of Parliament could not have been that dispute arising in one State could be taken cognizance of by the State Commission of another State, applying a purposive construction, limitations of territorial jurisdiction on the lines provided in section 11 with reference to District Forums with suitable modifications were read into section 17.[1]

The Council of European Communities directed that the transfer of an undertaking, business or part of a business shall not in itself constitute grounds for dismissal of the employees by the transferor or the transferee. Regulations were made in the United Kingdom under the European Communities Act, 1972 to give effect to the aforesaid directive. The relevant regulations in terms gave protection to a 'person employed immediately before the transfer'. In a case before the House of Lords[2] the transferor dismissed the employees at 3.30 p.m. with immediate effect whereas the transfer was effected at 4.30 p.m. on the same date. It was contended that as the employees were dismissed before the transfer in point of time, they were not persons employed immediately before the transfer and were not protected by the regulations. Negativing this contention, the House of Lords held[3] that the legislative history made it clear that the regulations were made to give effect to the directive of the Council of European Communities and applying a purposive construction; the words a person 'employed immediately before the transfer' should be interpreted and read as including 'a person who would have been so employed if he had not been unfairly dismissed before the transfer for a reason connected with the transfer'.

When a choice has to be made out of two constructions, both of which require reading of some additional words, the court will naturally prefer that which is more in consonance with reason or justice.[4] In construing section 423(i)(a) of the Code of Criminal Procedure, 1898, which reads: 'In an appeal from an order of acquittal, reverse such order and find him guilty and pass sentence on him according to law', the question was 'find the accused person guilty of what?' Two constructions were suggested, one that the sub-section authorises to find the accused person guilty 'of such offence as has been charged and of which he has been acquitted' and the

---

1. *Union Bank of India v. Seppo Rally,* AIR 1999 SC 62, p. 66 : (1999) 8 SCC 357 : (1999) 35 CLA 203.
2. *Lister v. Forth Dry Dock and Engineering Co. Ltd.*, (1989) 1 All ER 1134 : (1990) 1 AC 546 : (1989) 2 WLR 634 (HL).
3. *Ibid*, pp. 1139, 1153.
4. *Ramaswamy Nadar v. State of Madras*, AIR 1958 SC 56, p. 58 : 1958 SCR 739 : 1958 Cri LJ 228.

other that the sub-section authorises to find him guilty 'of the offence disclosed'. The Supreme Court adopted the latter construction which was more in consonance with reason or justice.[5]

It may also be permissible to read words such as, 'subject to' or 'notwithstanding anything', in order to reconcile two apparently inconsistent provisions.[6] "The omission to make such cross references as may be required to reconcile two textually inconsistent provisions is a common defect of draftsmanship".[7] In such cases, therefore, the cross references may be read by implication to remove the inconsistency.[8]

(ii) *Rejection of words when permissible*.—At times the intention of the Legislature is clear but the unskilfulness of the draftsman in introducing certain words in the statute results in apparent ineffectiveness of the language. Since courts strongly lean against reducing a statute to a futility, it is permissible in such cases to reject the surplus words to make the statute effective and workable.[9]

An example of the application of this principle is furnished by a Privy Council decision[10] in an appeal from Natal. The Colonial Ordinance there in question provided: "Any natural born subject of Great Britain and Ireland resident within this district may exercise all and singular the rights which such natural born subject could or might exercise according to the laws and customs of England in regard to the disposal by last will or testament of property, both real and personal, situated in the district, to all intents and purposes 'as if such natural born subject resided in England". The intention of the Legislature was plain from the title and preamble that the Ordinance was passed to enable the British subjects resident in Natal, where Roman Dutch law was being administered, to make bequests according to English law. The difficulty in giving effect to this intention was created by the last nine words. The Supreme Court of Natal held that although the object of the statute was clear, the language used was entirely ineffective in that a resident in the colony could only make a bequest 'as if he resided in England', and the law of England referred him back to Roman Dutch law of Natal as the *lex situs or lex domicilii*. The Privy Council reversing this judgment held that as the broad intention of the Legislature was not in doubt, the last nine words could be rejected as immaterial to

---

5. *Ibid.*, p. 58.

6. *Food Controller v. Cork*, (1923) AC 647 : (1923) All ER Rep 463, p. 471 (HL); *Ramkissendas Dhanuka v. Satyacharan Lal*, AIR 1950 PC 81, p. 83; **Cf.** *Raj Krishna Bose v. Vinod Kanungo*, AIR 1954 SC 202, p. 203 (para 11) : 1954 SCR 913.

7. *Ramkissendas Dhanuka v. Satyacharan Lal, supra*, p. 81.

8. **See** footnote 6, p. 88, *supra*.

9. *Salmon v. Duncombe*, (1886) 11 AC 627 (PC) : 55 LJPC 69. **See further** *Union of India v. Hansoli Devi*, AIR 2002 SC 3240, p. 3246 : (2002) 7 SCC 273.

10. *Salmon v. Duncombe supra.*

make the statute effective.[11] It is "a very serious matter", stated LORD HOBHOUSE, "to hold that when the main object of the statute is clear it shall be reduced to a nullity by the draftsman's unskilfulness or ignorance of law".[12] And he proceeded to add: "It may be necessary for a court of justice to come to such a conclusion, but their Lordships hold that nothing can justify it except necessity or the absolute intractability of the language used".[13]

The above mentioned Privy Council decision[14] was followed by the House of Lords[15] in construing para 3A of schedule 3 to the Local Government (Miscellaneous Provisions) Act, 1982. It is an offence under the schedule to use premises as sex encounter establishment without a licence. Para 1 of schedule 3 prevents the grant of a licence for any sex establishment which would otherwise amount to public indecency offence. The appellant before the House of Lords was prosecuted for using the relevant premises without a licence as sex encounter establishment as described in para 3A(c). Para 3A defines sex encounter establishment. Clauses (a), (b) and (c) of para 3A refer to live performance, services or entertainment for sexual stimulation of customers. But each of these clauses uses the phrase 'which is not unlawful'. Because of the use of these words it was contended by the appellant that the prosecution must prove affirmatively that the activities at the premises were not so indecent in character as to amount to an offence at common law. This contention was negatived and the words 'which is not unlawful' as used in clauses (a), (b) and (c) were rejected as surplusage. It was pointed out that by use of the said words the draftsman and the promoters of the legislation wished to emphasise that the grant of licences for sex encounter establishment was not intended to give legal authority for activities which would otherwise amount to public indecency offence; but for this purpose the words were wholly *otiose* because para 1 clearly prevented the grant of a licence having any such effect. The literal reading of the words as contended by the appellant would have frustrated substantially the purpose of the enactment and would have led to the absurdity of supposing that the intention of the legislation was to subject to licensing control only those establishments conducted in the least offensive way and to leave those which pander more outrageously to the taste of voyeur immune from any control or legal restraint. The House of Lords,

---

11. *Ibid.*
12. *Ibid.*
13. *Ibid.*
14. *Salmon v. Duncombe*, (1886) 11 AC 627 (PC) : 55 LJ PC 69.
15. *McMonagle v. Westminster City Council*, (1990) 1 All ER 993 : (1990) 2 AC 716 : (1990) 2 WLR 823 (HL).

therefore, held that the words 'which is not unlawful' should be treated as surplusage and as having been introduced by incompetent draftsmanship.[16]

(iii) *Treating words or provisions as superfluous.*—The Legislature sometimes uses superfluous words or provision or even tautologic expressions because of ignorance of law or as a matter of abundant caution. "It is not so very uncommon in Act of Parliament", said LORD MACNAGHTEN, "to find special exemptions which are already covered by a general exemption".[17] "Such specific exemptions," stated LORD HERSCHELL in the same case, "are often introduced *ex majori cautela* to quiet the fears of those whose interests are engaged or sympathies aroused in favour of some particular institution, and who are apprehensive that it may not be held to fall within a general exemption".[18] And to the similar effect, are the observations of LORD REID: "It is not uncommon to find the Legislature inserting superfluous provision under the influence of what may be abundant caution".[19] Such superfluous provisions cannot lay the foundation for an argument resting on the maxim, '*expressio unius est exclusio alterious*'[20] and the maxim is inapplicable in such cases. However, insertion of

---

16. *Ibid*, pp. 997, 998. **See further** *R. v. R.*, (1991) 4 All ER 481, p. 489 : (1992) 1 AC 599 : (1991) 3 WLR 767 (HL) (Word 'un-lawful' in s. 1(2) of Sexual Offences (Amendment) Act, 1976, held surplusage); *Labour Contact Co-operative Society Palikur v. Director & Mines of Geology Hyderabad*, AIR 1993 SC 147, p. 150 : (1993) Supp (2) SCC 316 (word 'within' in Rule 12(4) A.P. Minor Mineral Concession Rules, 1966 ignored on the ground that it was inappropriate and was used incautiously by the draftsman).

17. *Commissioner for Special Purposes of Income-tax v. John Frederick Pemsel*, (1891-94) All ER Rep. 28, p. 59 : (1891) AC 531 (HL).

18. *Ibid*, p. 51.

19. *I.R. Commissioners v. Dowdall O'Mahoney & Co.*, (1952) 1 All ER 531, p. 537 : 1952 AC 401 (HL); *Gokaraju Rangaraju v. State of Andhra Pradesh*, AIR 1981 SC 1473, p. 1479 : (1981) 3 SCC 132; *Walker (Inspector of Taxes) v. Centaur Clothes Group Ltd.*, (2000) 2 All ER 589, p. 595 (HL). (It is not uncommon for Parliament to say expressly what the courts would have inferred anyway). **See further** *Hakim Ali v. Board of Revenue*, AIR 1991 SC 972, p. 972 : 1991 Supp (1) SCC 565. [This book (4th Edition, p. 51) is **referred**]; *State of Uttar Pradesh v. Union of India*, AIR 2003 SC 1147, pp. 1154, 1155 : (2003) 3 SCC 239 : (2003) 130 STC 1.

20. The maxim means that express mention of one or more persons or things of a particular class may be regarded as by implication excluding all others of that class. "It is doubtful whether the maxim does any more than draw attention to a fairly obvious linguistic point, *viz.*, that in many contexts the mention of some matters warrants an inference that other cognate matters were intentionally excluded:" (CROSS, STATUTORY INTERPRETATION, 3rd Edition p. 140). The maxim will not apply when the '*expressio*' is superfluous added by way of abundant caution or misunderstanding of the law or similar causes. It will also not apply when the provisions of the Act show that the exclusion could not have been intended. So, the maxim has been called "a valuable servant but a dangerous master": *Colquhoun v. Brooks*, (1889) 21 QBD 52; *CCE v. National Tobacco Co. of India Ltd.*, AIR 1972 SC 2563, p. 2573 : (1972) 2 SCC

[Footnote No. 20 Contd.]

any superfluous provision always gives rise to difficulty of construction[21] as courts start with a presumption that every portion of a statute has some purpose and its presence was necessary to effectuate that purpose.[22] It is only when other provisions of an Act give out that a provision in the Act owes its origin to a confusion of ideas or to a misunderstanding of the law or to abundant caution, the court reaches the conclusion that that provision is superfluous.[23]

2. THE RULE OF LITERAL CONSTRUCTION

(a) Natural and grammatical meaning

The words of a statute are first understood in their natural, ordinary or popular sense and phrases and sentences are construed according to their grammatical meaning, unless that leads to some absurdity or unless there is something in the context, or in the object of the statute to suggest the contrary.[24] "The true way", according to LORD BROUGHAM is, "to take the

---

[Footnote No. 20 Contd.]

560; *D.R. Venkatachalam v. Dy. Transport Commissioner*, AIR 1977 SC 842, p. 849 : (1977) 2 SCC 273; *Karnataka State v. Union of India*, AIR 1978 SC 68, p. 107 : (1977) 4 SCC 608; *Mary Angel v. State of Tamil Nadu*, AIR 1999 SC 2245, p. 2252 : 1999 (5) SCC 209.

21. **See** *Shri Gopal Jalan & Co. v. Calcutta Stock Exchange Association*, AIR 1964 SC 250, pp. 253, 254 : 1964 (3) SCR 698. **See further** Chapter 3 : Title 9 'Proviso': (e) 'At times added to allay fears' at p. 226; *Madanlal Fakir Chand Dudhediya v. Shree Changdeo Sugar Mills Ltd.*, AIR 1962 SC 1543 : 1962 Supp (3) SCR 973; *Curtis v. Maloney*, (1950) 2 All ER 982 (CA).

22. *J.K. Cotton Spinning & Weaving Mills v. State of U.P.*, AIR 1961 SC 1170, p. 1174 : 1962 (1) SCJ 417 : (1961) 3 SCR 185. **See** Title 1(c) 'Avoiding Rejection of Words', *supra*.

23. **See** cases in note. 21, p. 91, *supra*.

24. *Crawford v. Spooner*, (1846) 4 MIA 179, p. 181 : 6 MOO PC 1 (PC); *Grey v. Pearson*, (1857) 6 HLC 61, p. 106 : 10 ER 1216, p. 1234 (HL); *River Wear Commrs. v. Adamson*, (1877) 2 AC 743 : (1874-80) All ER Rep. 1, p. 12 (HL); *Attorney-General v. Milne*, (1914) AC 765 : (1914-15) All ER Rep 1061, p. 1053 (HL); *Corporation of the City of Victoria v. Bishop of Vancouver Island*, AIR 1921 PC 240, p. 242; *Nagendra Nath Dey v. Suresh Chandra Dey*, AIR 1932 PC 165, p. 167; *Pakala Narayana Swami v. Emperor*, AIR 1939 PC 47, pp. 51, 52; *Nokes v. Doncaster Amalgamated Collieries Ltd.*, (1940) AC 1014 : (1940) 3 All ER 549, p. 553 (HL); *Jugalkishore Saraf v. Raw Cotton Co. Ltd.*, AIR 1955 SC 376, p. 381 : (1955) 1 SCR 1369; *S.A. Venkataraman v. State*, AIR 1958 SC 107, p. 109 : 1958 SCR 1040; *Siraj-ul-Haq v. Sunni Central Board of Waqf*, AIR 1959 SC 198, p. 205 : 1959 SCR 1287; *Shri Ram Daya Ram v. State of Maharashtra*, AIR 1961 SC 674, p. 678 : (1961) 2 SCR 890; *Madanlal Fakir Chand Dudhediya v. Shri Changdeo Sugar Mills Ltd.*, AIR 1962 SC 1543, p. 1551 : 1962 Supp (3) SCR 973; *State of Uttar Pradesh v.*

[Footnote No. 24 Contd.]

words as the Legislature have given them, and to take the meaning which the words given naturally imply, unless where the construction of those words is, either by the preamble or by the context of the words in question, controlled or altered";[25] and in the words of VISCOUNT HALDANE, L.C., if the language used "has a natural meaning we cannot depart from that meaning unless, reading the statute as a whole, the context directs us to do so".[26] In an oft-quoted passage, LORD WENSLEYDALE stated the rule thus : "In construing wills and indeed statutes and all written instruments, the grammatical and ordinary sense of the word is adhered to, unless that would lead to some absurdity, or some repugnance or inconsistency with the rest of the instrument in which case the grammatical and ordinary sense of the words may be modified, so as to avoid that absurdity, and inconsistency, but no further".[27] And stated LORD ATKINSON: "In the

---

[Footnote No. 24 Contd.]

Vijay Anand Maharaj, AIR 1963 SC 946, p. 950 : (1963) 1 SCR 1; *Manmohan Das Shah v. Bishun Das*, AIR 1967 SC 643 : (1967) 1 SCR 836; *Electrical Manufacturing Co. Ltd. v. D.D. Bhargava*, AIR 1968 SC 247, pp. 249, 250 : (1968) 1 SCR 394; *Management, Shahdara (Delhi) Saharanpur Light Railway Co. Ltd. v. Workers Union*, AIR 1969 SC 513, p. 518 : (1969) 2 SCR 131; *Glaxo Laboratories (I) Ltd. v. Presiding Officer, Labour Court, Meerut*, (1984) 1 SCC 1, p. 9 : AIR 1984 SC 505; *Oega Tellis v. Bombay Municipal Corporation*, (1985) 3 SCC 545, p. 581 : AIR 1986 SC 180; *Doypack Systems Pvt. Ltd. v. Union of India*, AIR 1988 SC 782, p. 801 : (1988) 2 SCC 299; *Oswal Agro Mills Ltd. v. Collector of Central Excise*, AIR 1993 SC 2288, p. 2292 : 1993 (3) JT 260; *Mohammad Ali Khan v. Commissioner of Wealth Tax*, JT 1997 (3) SC 250, p. 253: AIR 1997 SC 1165, p. 1167; *Gurudevadatta VKSSS Maryadit v. State of Maharashtra*, AIR 2001 SC 1980, p. 1991; *Colgate Palmolive (India) Ltd. v. M.R.T.P. Commission*, AIR 2003 SC 317, p. 320 : (2003) 1 SCC 129; *M.P. Khan v. Govt. of A.P.*, (2004) 2 SCC 267, p. 272 : AIR 2004 SC 2934; *State of Himachal Pradesh v. Pawan Kumar*, AIR 2005 SC 2265, p. 2269 : (2005) 4 SCC 350 (9th Edn., p. 78 of this book is **referred**); *State of Rajasthan v. Babu Ram*, (2007) 6 SCC 55, p. 57 : AIR 2007 SC 2018; *State of Haryana v. Suresh*, AIR 2007 SC 2245, para 12 (9th edition p. 78 of this book is referred).

25. *Crawford v. Spooner*, (1846) 4 MIA 179, p. 181 : 6 Moo PC 1 (PC).

26. *Attorney General v. Milne*, (1914-15) All ER Rep 1061, p. 1063 : 1914 AC 765 (HL).

27. *Grey v. Pearson*, (1857) 6 HLC 61, p. 106 : 10 ER 1216, p. 1234 (HL); **referred** to in *Walton, Ex parte, Re, Levy*, (1881) 50 LJ Ch 657, p. 659 (JESSEL, M.R.); *Caledonia Rly. v. North British Rly.*, (1881) 6 AC 114, p. 131 (HL) (LORD BLACKBURN); *Vacher & Sons v. London Society of Compositors*, (1913) AC 107 : (1911-13) All ER Rep 241, p. 246 (HL) (LORD MACNAGHTEN); *Corporation of the City of Victoria v. Bishop of Vancouver Island*, AIR 1921 PC 240, p. 242 (LORD ATKINSON); *Pakala Narayana Swami v. Emperor*, AIR 1939 PC 47, p. 51 (LORD ATKINSON); *Keshavananda Bharati v. State of Kerala*, AIR 1973 SC 1461, p. 1538 : (1973) 4 SCC 225; *Nandini Satpathy v. P.L. Dani*, AIR 1978 SC 1025, p. 1039 : (1978) 2 SCC 424; *Chandavarkar Sita Ratna Rao v. Ashalata S. Guram*, (1986) 4 SCC 447, p. 476 : AIR 1987 SC 117; *Union of India v. Rajivkumar*, (2003) 6 SCC 516, p. 526 :

[Footnote No. 27 Contd.]

construction of statutes, their words must be interpreted in their ordinary grammatical sense unless there be something in the context, or in the object of the statute in which they occur or in the circumstances in which they are used, to show that they were used in a special sense different from their ordinary grammatical sense".[28] VISCOUNT SIMON, L.C., said: "The golden rule is that the words of a statute must *prima facie* be given their ordinary meaning".[29] Natural and ordinary meaning of words should not be departed from "unless it can be shown that the legal context in which the words are used requires a different meaning". Such a meaning cannot be departed from by the judges "in the light of their own views as to policy" although they can "adopt a purposive interpretation if they can find in the statute read as a whole or in material to which they are permitted by law to refer as aids to interpretation an expression of Parliament's purpose or policy".[30] For a modern statement of the rule one may refer to the speech of LORD SIMON OF GLAISDALE in a case where he said : "Parliament is *prima facie* to be credited with meaning what is said in an Act of Parliament. The drafting of statutes, so important to a people who hope to live under the rule of law, will never be satisfactory unless courts seek whenever possible to apply 'the golden rule' of construction, that is to read the statutory language, grammatically and terminologically, in the ordinary and primary sense which it bears in its context, without omission or addition. Of course, Parliament is to be credited with good sense; so that when such an approach produces injustice, absurdity, contradiction or stultification of statutory objective the language may be modified sufficiently to

---

[Footnote No. 27 Contd.]

AIR 2003 SC 2917. LORD WENSLEYDALE himself in *Abbot v. Middleton* [(1858) 28 LJ Ch 110, p. 114 (HL)], pointed out that the rule was in substance laid down by MR. JUSTICE BURTON in *Warburton v. Loveland* [(1828) 1 Hud & Brooke 623], was described as "a rule of common sense as strong as can be" by LORD ELLENBOROUGH in *Doe v. Jessep* [(1810) 12 East 288, p. 292], was stated to be "a cardinal rule" by LORD CRANWORTH in *Grundy v. Pinnigar*, (1852) 1 De GM & G 502 : (1852) 21 LJ Ch 404, p. 406 and "the golden rule", by JERVIS, C.J. in *Mattison v. Hart*, (1854) 14 CB 357 : (1854) 23 LJCP 108, p. 114. In *Becke v. Smith*, (1836) 150 ER 724, p. 726, also PARKE, B (before he became LORD WENSLEYDALE) **referred** to the rule laid down by BURTON, J., in *Warburton v. Loveland, supra*, and called it a "very useful rule in the construction of a statute".

28. *Corporation of the City of Victoria v. Bishop of Vancouver Island*, AIR 1921 PC 240, p. 242.

29. *Nokes v. Doncaster Amalgamated Collieries Ltd.*, (1940) AC 1014 : (1940) 3 All ER 549, p. 553 (HL); *Chandavarkar Sita Ratna Rao v. Ashalata S. Guram*, (1986) 4 SCC 447, p. 476 : AIR 1987 SC 117; *B. Permanand v. Mohan Koikal*, (2011) 4 SCC 266 (para 24) : AIR 2011 SC 1925.

30. *Shah v. Barnet London Borough Council*, (1983) 1 All ER 226, pp. 235, 238 (HL).

avoid such disadvantage, though no further".[31] The rules stated above[32] have been quoted with approval by the Supreme Court.[33]

In the case[34] from which the last mentioned quotation is taken, the question related to section 14(1) of the Immigration Act, 1971, which provides that 'a person who has a limited leave under this Act to enter or remain in the United Kingdom may appeal to an adjudicator against any variation of the leave or against any refusal to vary it'. The words 'a person who has a limited leave' were construed not to include a person "who has had" such limited leave and it was held that the section applied only to a person who at the time he lodged his appeal was lawfully in the United Kingdom that is in whose case leave had not expired at the time of lodgment of appeal.

In dealing with order 21, rule 16 of the Code of Civil Procedure, 1908, the Supreme Court applied the rule of literal construction and held that the said provision contemplates actual transfer of a decree by an assignment in writing after the decree is passed. S.R. DAS, J., referring to the rule under discussion said: "The cardinal rule of construction of statutes is to read the statutes literally, that is, by giving to the words their ordinary, natural and

---

31. *Suthendran v. Immigration Appeal Tribunal*, (1976) 3 All ER 611, p. 616 : (1976) 3 WLR 725 (HL). **See further** *Farrel v. Alexander*, (1976) 2 All ER 721, p. 736 : (1977) AC 59 (HL); ***Reference** under section 48A of the Criminal Appeal Northern Ireland Act, 1968* (1976) 2 All ER 937, p. 957 (HL); *Stock v. Frank Jones (Tipton) Ltd.*, (1978) 1 All ER 948, p. 952 : (1978) 1 WLR 231 (HL); *Applin v. Race Relations Board*, (1974) 2 All ER 73, p. 91 (HL); (The golden rule "always potent is particularly so if there are forensic situations which Parliament seemingly either did not envisage or preferred not to deal with rather leaving them to the courts".). In *Kehar Singh v. State*, AIR 1988 SC 1883, p. 1945 : 1988 (3) SCC 609, JAGANNATH SHETTY J. observed: "During the last several years the golden rule has been given a go-bye" (para 228). What he here meant by the golden rule is stated by him earlier as "the grammatical or literal meaning unmindful of consequences" (para 227). The golden rule as stated in the text of which LORD SIMON'S formulation is a modern example, is not unmindful of consequences and the observations of JAGANNATH SHETTY, J., have no application to it. The confusion arises because the literal rule even without qualification as to consequences is sometimes spoken of as the golden rule. [**See** CROSS, "Statutory Interpretation", 3rd Edition, p. 16 (footnote)]. According to CROSS, the rule permitting departure from the literal rule by recourse to the consequences of applying the natural or ordinary meaning is commonly called the golden rule to distinguish it from the literal and mischief rules. (CROSS, pp. 15, 16 *supra*). For 'golden rule of construction' **see** also: *Maulvi Hussein Haji Abraham Umarji v. State of Gujarat,* (2004) 6 SCC 672, (para 23) : AIR 2004 SC 3946; *Lalu Prasad v. State of Bihar,* (2007) 1 SCC 49, (para 8) : (2007) 1 JT 183.

32. **See** text and notes 30 and 31 *supra*.

33. *Harbhajan Singh v. Press Council of India,* AIR 2002 SC 1351, p. 1354 : (2002) 3 SCC 722 (8th Edition of this book p. 74 is **referred**); *Guru Jambheshwar University v. Dharam Pal,* (2007) 2 SCC 265, (para 16) : AIR 2007 SC 1040 [9th Edition (pp. 78, 79) of this book is **referred**].

34. *Suthendran v. Immigration Appeal Tribunal, supra.*

grammatical meaning. If, however, such a reading leads to absurdity and the words are susceptible of another meaning, the Court may adopt the same. But if no such alternative construction is possible, the court must adopt the ordinary rule of literal interpretation. In the present case the literal construction leads to no apparent absurdity and therefore, there can be no compelling reason for departing from that golden rule of construction".[35]

Section 35 of the Indian Stamp Act, 1899 provides that 'no instrument chargeable with duty shall be admitted in evidence *for any purpose*—unless such instrument is duly stamped'. Construing this section the Privy Council said that there was no reason why the words 'for any purpose' "should not be given their natural meaning and effect" and cover even a collateral purpose and that an unstamped partition deed cannot be used to corroborate the oral evidence for the purposes of determining even the factum of partition as distinct from its terms.[36]

In construing section 3 which laid down the grounds on which a *theka* tenant could be ejected and section 5(1) which prescribed that 'a landlord wishing to eject a *theka* tenant on one or more of the grounds specified in section 3 shall apply to the controller,' the Supreme Court held that these provisions of the Calcutta *Theka* Tenancy Act, 1949, did not apply to those cases where a decree had already been obtained. Rejecting the argument based on the mischief rule in *Heydon's* case, GAJENDRAGADKAR, J., observed: "The words used in the material provisions of the statute must be interpreted in their plain grammatical meaning and it is only when such words are capable of two constructions that the question of giving effect to the policy or object of the Act can legitimately arise".[37] Similarly, section 28 of the same Act which was omitted by Amending Act 6 of 1953 was held to be inapplicable even to pending proceedings on a grammatical construction of the Amending Act. DAS GUPTA, J., referring to the rules of construction said: "The intention of the Legislature has always to be gathered by words used by it, giving to the words their plain, normal, grammatical meaning";[38] and proceeding further he said: "If the strict grammatical interpretation gives rise to an absurdity or inconsistency such interpretation should be discarded and an interpretation, which will give effect to the

---

35. *Jugalkishore Saraf v. Raw Cotton Co. Ltd.*, AIR 1955 SC 376, p. 381 : 1955 (1) SCR 1369.

36. *Ram Rattan v. Parma Nand*, AIR 1946 PC 51 p. 53 **followed** in *Avinash Kumar Chauhan v. Vijay Krishna Mishra*, (2009) 2 SCC 532 para 26 : (2009) 1 JT 656 : AIR 2009 SC 1489.

37. *Kanai Lal Sur v. Paramnidhi Sadhukhan*, AIR 1957 SC 907 : 1958 SCR 360.

38. *Mahadeolal Kanodia v. Administrator General of West Bengal*, AIR 1960 SC 936, p. 939 : 1960 (3) SCR 499.

purpose of the Legislature. That could be done, if necessary even by modification of the language used".[39]

In interpreting section 6 of the Prevention of Corruption Act, 1947, the Supreme Court held that sanction is not necessary for taking cognizance of the offences referred to in that section if the accused has ceased to be a public servant on the date when the Court is called upon to take cognizance of the offences. The Court rejected the construction that the words 'who is employed—and is not removable' as they occur in clauses (a) and (b) of section (1) mean 'who was employed—and was not removable', as also the construction that the words 'competent to remove him from office' in clause (c) mean 'would have been competent to remove him from his office'. IMAM, J., pointed out: "In construing the provisions of a statute it is essential for a court to give effect to the natural meaning of the words used therein, if those words are clear enough".[40]

And in speaking of construction of the Indian Limitation Act, 1908, SIR DINSHAH MULLA stated: "The strict grammatical meaning of the words is, their Lordships think, the only safe guide".[41] This principle has been reaffirmed by the Supreme Court.[42]

In construing section 6(a) of the Payment of Bonus Act, 1965, the Supreme Court observed that the words "depreciation admissible in accordance with the provisions of sub-section (1) of section 32 of the Income-tax Act" have to be given their natural meaning and these words could not be read as "depreciation allowed by the Income-tax Officer in making

---

39. *Ibid.* **Referred** to in *Union of India v. Filip Tiago De Gamma of Vedum Vasco De Gama*, AIR 1990 SC 981, p. 983 : 1990 (1) SCC 277 : 1990 Mh CJ 724.

40. *S.A. Venkataraman v. State*, AIR 1958 SC 107, p. 109 : 1958 SCR 1040. **Confirmed** by Constitution Bench in *R.S. Nayak v. A.R. Antulay,* (1984) 2 SCC 183 : AIR 1984 SC 684. Same view taken of Section 19 of the Prevention of Corruption Act, 1988 : *Prakash Singh Badal v. State of Punjab,* (2007) 1 SCC 1 : AIR 2007 SC 1274; *Lalu Prasad v. State of Bihar,* (2007) 1 SCC 49 : (2007) 1 JT 183. For requirement of valid sanction **see** *State of Maharashtra v. Ishwar Pirajikalpatri,* (1996) 1 SCC 542 : AIR 1996 SC 722; *State of Madhya Pradesh v. Harishankar Bhagwan Prasad Tripathi,* (2010) 8 SCC 655 paras 11, 12 and 16 : (2010) 9 JT 82.

41. *Nagendra Nath Dey v. Suresh Chandra Dey*, AIR 1932 PC 165, p. 167. **See further** *General Accident Fire & Life Assurance Corporation v. Janmahomed Abdul Rahim*, AIR 1941 PC 6, p. 9.

42. *Siraj-ul-Haq v. Sunni Central Board of Waqf*, AIR 1959 SC 198, p. 205 : 1959 SCR 1287; *Boota Mal v. Union of India*, AIR 1962 SC 1716, pp. 1718, 1719 : (1963) 1 SCR 70; *Municipal Board, Pushkar v. State Transport Authority, Rajasthan*, AIR 1965 SC 458, pp. 464, 465, (Paras 22 and 23) : 1963 Supp (2) SCR 373. **But see** *State of Punjab v. Qaisar Jehan Begum*, AIR 1963 SC 1604, p. 1606 : 1964 (1) SCR 971. **See also** Chapter 1, Title 2 "Intention of the Legislature", text and notes 77, 78, p. 19.

assessment on the employer". It was, therefore, held that it was for the Industrial Tribunal to determine what was the depreciation admissible in accordance with section 32 of the Income-tax Act and the Tribunal could not just accept the amount allowed by the Income-tax Officer as depreciation under that section. It was further held that the finding of the Income-tax Officer was not even admissible before the Tribunal for purposes of the Bonus Act.[43]

By section 11 of the Assisted Schools and Training College (Supplementary Provisions) Act, 1960 (Ceylon), the Minister of Education is empowered if he is satisfied that an unaided school "is being administered in contravention of any of the provisions of the Act etc." to declare that such a school shall cease to be an unaided school and that the Director of Education shall be its manager. In holding that the Minister can only take action if the school at the time of making of the order is being carried on in contravention of the Act and not merely on the ground that a breach of the Act was committed in the past, the Privy Council (LORD PEARCE) pointed out : "The present tense is clear. It would have been easy to say 'has been administered' or 'in the administration of the school any breach of any of the provisions of the Act has been committed', if such was the intention, but for reasons which commonsense may easily supply, it was enacted that the Minister should concern himself with the present conduct of the school not the past, when making the order".[44] Similarly, Article 233(2) of the Constitution of India, provides that a person shall only be eligible to be appointed as a District Judge if he has been, for not less than seven years, an advocate or pleader, and is recommended by the High Court for appointment. A three Judge Bench of the Supreme Court held that it is clear from the expression 'has been' that the present perfect continuous tense is used for a position which began sometime in the past and is still continuing, and that therefore such person must, with the requisite period, still be continuing as an advocate on the date of his application.[45]

Sections 3(2)(a) and (b) of the Karnataka Lokayukta Act, 1984, provide that the Lokayukta and Upa-Lokayukta, respectively, 'shall be appointed on the advice rendered by the Chief Minister in consultation with the Chief Justice of the High Court of Karnataka, the Chairman, Karnataka

---

43. *Workmen of National and Grindlays Bank Ltd. v. National and Grindlays Bank Ltd.*, AIR 1976 SC 611, p. 618 : (1976) 1 SCC 925 : (1976) 1 LLJ 463.

44. *Maradana Mosque v. Badi-ud-din Mohmud*, (1966) 1 All ER 545, p. 551 (PC). **See further** *F.S. Gandhi v. Commissioner of Wealth Tax*, AIR 1991 SC 1866, p. 1869 : 1990 (3) SCC 624 : (1990) 84 CTR 35 (The word 'is' normally referring to the present often has a future meaning and may also have a past significance.)

45. *Deepak Aggarwal v. Keshav Kaushik & Ors.*, (2013) 5 SCC 277, p. 331.

Legislative Council, the Speaker, Karnataka Legislative Assembly, the Leader of Opposition in the Karnataka Legislative Council and the Leader of the Opposition in the Karnataka Legislative Assembly'. Sections 3(2)(a) and (b), when read literally and contextually, were held to admit no doubt that the Governor of the State can appoint a Lokayukta or Upa-Lokayukta only on the advice tendered by the Chief Minister, and that the Chief Justice of the High Court is only one of the consultees whose views have no primacy. Hence, the Governor, as per the statute, can appoint only on the advice tendered by the Chief Minister, and not on the opinion expressed by the Chief Justice or any of the other consultees.[46]

Sub-section (7) of section 6 of the Press Council Act, 1978 provides: 'A retiring member shall be eligible for renomination for not more than one term.' The Supreme Court applied the literal and grammatical meaning of these words and held that the provision applied to a member "just retiring" and not to a retired member and that a retired member who had held office for two terms sometime in the past is not debarred from being nominated again.[47] In holding so LAHOTI, J., observed: "Legislature chooses appropriate words to express what it intends, and therefore, must be attributed with such intention as is conveyed by the words employed so long as this does not result in absurdity or anomaly or unless material—intrinsic or external—is available to permit a departure from the rule."[48]

While interpreting section 41(1) of the Presidency Small Cause Courts Act, 1882 (as amended by the Maharashtra Act 19 of 1976), the Supreme Court observed that 'the golden rule is that the words of a statute must prima facie be given their ordinary meaning when the language or phraseology employed by the legislature is precise and plain'. Since section 41(1) does not specifically exclude a gratuitous licensee or make a distinction between a licensee with material consideration or without material consideration, the expression 'licensee' in section 41(1) was held to also include a 'gratuitous licensee'.[49]

An illustration of the above principle is also found in *Bharat Aluminium Company v. Kaiser Aluminium Technical Services Inc.*,[50] where a Constitution Bench of the Supreme Court was called upon to decide whether Part I

---

46. *Justice Chandrashekaraiah (Retd.) v. Janekere C. Krishna & Ors.*, (2013) 3 SCC 117, p. 159.

47. *Harbhan Singh v. Press Council of India,* AIR 2002 SC 1351 : (2002) 3 SCC 722.

48. *Ibid.*, p. 1353.

49. *Prabhudas Damodar Kotecha v. Manhabala Jeram Damodar & Anr.*, (2013) 15 SCC 358, pp. 371, 372.

50. *Bharat Aluminium Company v. Kaiser Aluminium Technical Services Inc.*, (2012) 9 SCC 552.

of the Arbitration and Conciliation Act, 1996 applies to arbitrations taking place outside India (also referred to earlier in the Chapter). Section 2(2) of the Act, which is in Part I of the Act, provides that, 'This Part shall apply where the place of arbitration is in India', and not that the Part shall 'only' apply where the place of arbitration is in India. It was held that the absence of the word 'only' from section 2(2) could not be construed so as to make Part I of the Act applicable to arbitrations taking place outside India, as the plain reading of section 2(2) makes it clear that Part I is limited in its application to arbitrations which take place in India. In this case, the Constitution Bench prospectively overruled the decision of a three Judge Bench of the Supreme Court in *Bhatia International v. Bulk Trading SA*,[51] which had held that provisions of Part I would apply to international commercial arbitrations held outside India unless the parties, by agreement, express or implied, exclude all or any of its provisions. The principle that the words of a statute must be understood in their natural, ordinary or popular sense, and construed according to their grammatical meaning unless such construction leads to some absurdity or unless there is something in the object of the statute to the contrary, was also applied by the Court in the interpretation of section 244A of the Income-tax Act, 1961, which is titled 'Interest on refunds'.[52]

According to a two judge bench of the Supreme Court departure from the literal rule should be done only in very rare cases and ordinarily there should be judicial restraint in this connection.[53]

"To adhere as closely as possible to the literal meaning of the words used", is, as stated by LORD CRANWORTH (when Lord Justice) a "cardinal rule," from which if we depart, "we launch into a sea of difficulties which it is not easy to fathom".[54] This statement over-emphasises the role of literal interpretation, but it is interesting to notice that earlier some of the leading controversies were resolved in favour of literal construction. The law that a minor's agreement is void was settled by the Privy Council on a literal construction of section 11 and other related provisions of the Indian

---

51. *Bhatia International v. Bulk Trading SA*, (2002) 4 SCC 105.

52. *Union of India v. Tata Chemicals Ltd.*, (2014) 6 SCC 335, pp. 344 to 350.

53. *Raghunath Rai Bareja v. Punjab National Bank*, (2007) 2 SCC 230 (para 43) : (2007) 1 JT 542. *B. Permanand v. Mohan Koikal*, (2011) 4 SCC 266 (para 13) : AIR 2011 SC 1925.

54. *Grundy v. Pinniger*, (1852) 1 De GM & G 502 : (1852) 21 LJ Ch 405, p. 406; **quoted** by LORD WENSLEYDALE in *Abbot v. Middleton*, (1858) 28 LJ Ch 110, p. 114 (HL). Also **approvingly quoted** in *Raghunath Rai Bareja v. Punjab National Bank*, (2007) 2 SCC 230 (para 42) : (2007) 1 JT 542.

Contract Act, 1872,[55] and so also the question whether money paid under mistake of law can be recovered back under section 72 of the same Act was resolved by giving to the word 'mistake', in that section, its ordinary meaning as including even a mistake of law.[56] Again, the difference of opinion between the Bombay High Court and other High Courts on the construction of section 80 of the Code of Civil Procedure, 1908 as to the necessity of notice under that section in a suit for injunction was settled by the Privy Council in approving the view, which was taken by reading the section in its literal sense, that a notice was necessary.[57] Further, the controversy whether a variation made by the appellate decree of the High Court in favour of an intending appellant to the Supreme Court is a decree of affirmance within Article 133(1) of the Constitution was resolved by the Supreme Court by "reading the clause as a whole and giving the material words their plain grammatical meaning". It was held that if the High Court varies the decree under appeal, the appellate decree is not a decree of affirmance and it is immaterial whether the variation is in favour of the intending appellant or against him.[58] Similarly, the divergence of opinion as to the starting point of limitation under Article 31 of the Indian Limitation Act, 1908 which arose on the construction of the words 'when the goods ought to have been delivered', was settled by the Supreme Court by adopting "their strict grammatical meaning". The view taken by some of the High Courts that time begins to run from the date of refusal by the railway to deliver the goods was overruled.[59] A strict literal interpretation was also given to section 34(3) of the Arbitration and Conciliation Act, 1996, which provides that an application for setting aside an arbitral award may not be made after three months have elapsed from the date on which the party making that application had received the arbitral award. The Supreme Court held that the word 'party' in this provision means a person who is party to

---

55. *Mohori Bibee v. Dharmodas Ghose*, ILR 30 Cal 539, pp. 547, 548 : 30 IA 114 (PC). As a minor's agreement is void, he cannot become promoter of a company and he cannot be proceeded against under the Securities and Exchange Board of India Act, 1992 : *Ritesh Agarwal v. Securities and Exchange Board of India,* (2008) 8 SCC 205 paras 22 and 29 : (2008) 7 JT 289.

56. *Sales Tax Officer, Benaras v. Kanhaiyalal Mukundlal Saraf*, AIR 1959 SC 135, p. 139 : 1959 SCR 1350. The view taken in this case has been modified to this extent that refund of tax paid under a mistake cannot be allowed if the plaintiff had passed on the burden to others: *Mafatlal Industries Ltd. v. Union of India*, JT 1996 (11) SC 283 : 1997 (5) SCC 536. For period of limitation in such suits **see** *Union of India v. West Coast Paper Mills Ltd.*, (2004) 2 SCC 747 : AIR 2004 SC 1596.

57. *Bhagchand Dagdusa Gujrati v. Secretary of State for India*, AIR 1927 PC 176, p. 185. **See further** *Sawai Singhai Nirmalchand v. Union of India*, AIR 1966 SC 1068 : 1966 (1) SCR 986.

58. *Tirumalachetti Rajaram v. Tirumalachetti Radhakrishnayya Chetty*, AIR 1961 SC 1795, pp. 1797, 1798 : 1962 (2) SCR 452.

59. *Boota Mal v. Union of India*, AIR 1962 SC 1716 : 1963 (1) SCR 70.

the arbitration agreement as indicated in section 2(1)(h) of the Act, and would not include an advocate, who is an agent of the party.[60]

A departure from the rule of literal construction outside the recognised limits in the guise of liberal or strict construction leads to unwarranted expansion or restriction of the meaning of words and gives rise to serious errors. In construing M.P. Abolition of Proprietary Rights Act, 1950, which in clause '(g)' of section 2 defines 'Home-farm' as meaning 'land recorded as *Sir* and *Khudkast* in the name of a proprietor in the annual papers for the year 1948-49', the Nagpur High Court held that this definition should be construed liberally and that land, though not recorded as *Khudkast* of the proprietor in the annual papers of 1948-49 but which ought to have been recorded as such, was within this definition. This decision was overruled by the Supreme Court by interpreting the said definition section in its natural and ordinary meaning and consequently holding that the basis for treating a particular land as home-farm under the Act "was the record and not the fact of actual cultivation". It was pointed out: "There is no ambiguity about the definition of 'home-farm' and so the question of strict or liberal construction does not arise".[61] Similarly, the words 'khas possession' occurring in sections 2(k) and 6 of the Bihar Land Reforms Act, 1950, were construed by the Patna High Court as embracing even a mere right to possess; and this view was overruled by the Supreme Court again showing the importance of literal construction.[62] And, in

60. *Benarsi Krishna Committee & Ors. v. Karmyogi Shelters Pvt. Ltd.*, (2012) 9 SCC 496, pp. 501, 502.

61. *Haji S.K. Subhan v. Madhorao*, AIR 1962 SC 1230, pp. 1236, 1238 : 1962 Supp (1) SCR 123. **See further** *Amba Prasad v. Mahboob Ali Shah*, AIR 1965 SC 54, pp. 58, 59 : 1964 (7) SCR 800; *Udai v. Director of Consolidation*, AIR 1990 SC 471 : 1991 (1) SCC 588. [Cases, under section 20, U.P. Zamindari Abolition Act (1 of 1951)]. But entries in the revenue record can be challenged on the ground that they were fraudulently or surreptitiously made: *Sonawati v. Shri Ram*, AIR 1968 SC 466, p. 468 : 1968 (1) SCR 617; *Vishwa Vijai v. Fakhrul Hussain*, AIR 1976 SC 1485, p. 1488 : (1976) 3 SCC 642; *Wali Mohammad v. Ram Surat*, AIR 1989 SC 2296 : 1989 Supp (1) SCR 211 : (1989) 4 SCC 574. In *Gorabai (Smt.) v. Ummed Singh*, (2004) 5 SCC 130 : AIR 2004 SC 2594 arising out of the Madhya Bharat Zamindari Abolition Act, 1951 Khudkast land 'so recorded in the annual village papers before the date of vesting' was liberally construed and it was held that land need not be so recorded immediately before the date of vesting.

62. *Suraj Ahir v. Prithinath Singh*, AIR 1963 SC 454, p. 458 : 1963 (3) SCR 290; **affirmed** in review—AIR 1963 SC 1041; *Ram Ran Bijai Singh v. Behari Singh*, AIR 1965 SC 524, p. 529 : (1964) 3 SCR 363; *Gurucharan Singh v. Kamala Singh*, AIR 1977 SC 5 : (1977) 2 SCC 152; *Ramesh Bijoy v. Pashupati Rai*, AIR 1979 SC 1769 : 1979 (4) SCC 27; *Baleshwar Tiwari v. Sheo Jatan Tiwary*, AIR 1997 SC 2089 : (1997) 5 SCC 112. **But** *Khas* possession of one co-sharer will be *Khas* possession of all the co-sharers: *Basudevanand v. Harihar*, AIR 1974 SC 1991 : (1974) 2 SCC 514. Similarly "has cultivated" cannot be construed as implying mere intention to cultivate: *P. Venkataswami v. D.S. Ramreddi*, AIR 1976 SC 1066 : 1976 (3) SCC 665 (**overruling** Andhra Pradesh High Court).

interpreting section 26(2) of the C.P. and Berar Sales Tax Act, 1947, which reads 'no prosecution or suit shall be instituted against any person in respect of anything done or intended to be done under this Act unless the suit or prosecution has been instituted within three months from the date of the Act complained of', the view of the Madhya Pradesh High Court was that the words 'any person' are restricted to Government servants. This departure from literal construction was also overruled by the Supreme Court.[63] Again "judicial activism in the reverse gear", by restricting the wide words 'any currency note or banknote' used in section 489A of the India Penal Code of 1860 to Indian Currency notes and bank notes, shown by the Kerala High Court was overruled by the Supreme Court holding that the words were large enough in amplitude to cover currency notes and bank notes of all countries.[64] Further in construing Article 171 of the Constitution and holding that a person elected from graduates constituency need not himself be a graduate as the words of the article do not in terms so provide, the Supreme Court overruled the contrary opinion of the Madras High Court and stressed the importance of the literal construction.[65]

(b) Explanation of the rule

In the statement of the rule "the epithets 'natural', 'ordinary', 'literal', 'grammatical' and 'popular' are employed almost interchangeably",[66] to convey the same idea. The word 'primary' is also used in the same sense.[67] When it is said that words are to be understood first in their natural, ordinary or popular sense, what is meant is that the words must be ascribed that natural, ordinary or popular meaning which they have in relation to the subject-matter with reference to which and the context in which they have been used in the statute. BRETT, M.R. called it a "cardinal rule" that "Whenever you have to construe a statute or document you do not construe it according to the mere ordinary general meaning of the words, but according to the ordinary meaning of the words as applied to the subject-

---

63. *Sitaram v. State of M.P.*, AIR 1962 SC 1146 : 1962 Supp (3) SCR 21. **See further** *Public Prosecutor, Madras v. R. Raju*, AIR 1972 SC 2504 : 1972 (2) SCC 410.
N.B.—But the words 'any person' may be used in a limited sense, for example, **see** *ITO, Sitapur v. Murlidhar Bhagwandas*, AIR 1965 SC 342, p. 349 : 1964 (6) SCR 411, (para 10). For different meanings of the word 'person' **see** Chapter 5, text and notes 4 to 9, pp. 537, 538.

64. *State of Kerala v. Mathai Verghese*, (1986) 4 SCC 746 : AIR 1987 SC 33 : 1987 Cri LJ 308.

65. *S. Narayanswami v. G. Panneerselvam*, AIR 1972 SC 2284, p. 2285 : 1972 (3) SCC 717.

66. CRAIES : Statute Law, 7th Edition, p. 65.

67. *Ibid.*

matter with regard to which they are used".[68] "No word", says PROFESSOR H.A. SMITH "has an absolute meaning, for no words can be defined in *vacuo*, or without reference to some context".[69] According to SUTHERLAND there is a "basic fallacy" in saying "that words have meaning in and of themselves",[70] and "reference to the abstract meaning of words", states CRAIES, "if there be any such thing, is of little value in interpreting statutes".[71] In the words of JUSTICE HOLMES: "A word is not a crystal transparent and unchanged; it is the skin of a living thought and may vary greatly in colour and content according to the circumstances and the time in which it is used."[72] Shorn of the context, the words by themselves are "slippery customers".[73] Therefore, in determining the meaning of any

---

68. *Lion Insurance Association v. Tucker*, (1883-84) 12 QBD 176, p. 186. **See further** *Re, Bidie (deceased), Bidie v. General Accident, Fire and Life Assurance Corporation Ltd.*, (1948) 2 All ER 995, p. 998 (LORD GREENE, M.R.); *Captain Subhash Kumar v. Principal Officer, Mercantile Marine Deptt.*, AIR 1991 SC 1632, p. 1638: 1991 (2) SCC 449.

69. 'Interpretation in English and Continental Law', Journal of Comparative Legislation, Nov. 1927, **quoted** in ALLEN: "Law in the Making", 5th Edition, p. 482; *Union of India v. Sankalchand*, AIR 1977 SC 2328, p. 2373 : (1977) 4 SCC 193 : 1977 SCC (L&S) 435.

70. SUTHERLAND : Statutory Construction, 3rd Edition, Vol. II, p. 316.

71. CRAIES : Statute Law, 7th Edition, p. 66. **See further** *R. v Brown*, (1996) 1 All ER 545, p. 560 : 1996 AC 543: (1996) 2 WLR 203 (HL): "The unit of communication by means of language is the sentence and not the parts of which it is composed. The significance of individual words is affected by other words and the syntax of whole;" (LORD HOFFMAN). In the felicitious language of judge LEARNED HAND, "the meaning of a sentence may be more than that of the separate words, as a melody is more than the notes, and no degree of particularity can ever obviate recourse to the setting in which all appear and which all collectively create"; **quoted** in *K.P. Verghese v. Income-tax Officer, Ernakulam,* (1981) 4 SCC 173, p. 180 : AIR 1981 SC 1922.

72. *Towne v. Eisner*, (1917) 245 U.S. 418, at p. 425; *Keshavananda Bharati v. State of Kerala*, AIR 1973 SC 1461, p. 1497 : (1973) 4 SCC 225, p. 316; *Union of India v. Filip Tiago De Gama of Vedem Vasco De Gama*, AIR 1990 SC 981, p. 985 : 1990 (1) SCC 277. According to CORBIN, the description given by Holmes that a word is "skin of a living thought" is not accurate for according to him a word is "merely a skin ready to be filled with the thought of its user, to be blown across space until, it can spill its contents into the mind of a receiver": ARTHUR L. CORBIN in his Foreword to the Growth of the Law by Benzamin N. Cardozo, Indian Economy Reprint, 2002, p. xiii.

73. *Nyadar Singh v. Union of India*, AIR 1988 SC 1979, p. 1984 : 1988 (4) SCC 170. To find out the exact connotation of a word in a statute, we must look to the context in which it is used; *Maharaj Singh v. State of U.P.*, AIR 1976 SC 2602, p. 2607 : 1977 (1) SCC 155; *Thiru Manickam & Co. v. State of Tamil Nadu*, AIR 1977 SC 518, p. 521 : 1977 SCC (Tax) 165 : (1977) 1 SCC 199; *Union of India v. Sankalchand*, AIR 1977 SC 2328, p. 2358 : (1977) 4 SCC 193 : 1977 SCC (L&S) 435; *State of Kerala v. Ranganatha Reddy*, AIR 1978 SC 209, p. 233 : 1978 (1) SCC 1; *Prithi Pal Singh v. Union of India*, AIR 1982 SC 1413, p. 1419 : (1982) 3 SCC 140; *Municipal Corporation of Greater Bombay v. Bharat Petroleum Corporation Ltd.*, AIR 2002 SC 1638, p. 1643 : (2002) 4 SCC 609.

word or phrase in a statute the first question to be asked is—"What is the natural or ordinary meaning of that word or phrase in its context in the statute? It is only when that meaning leads to some result which cannot reasonably be supposed to have been the intention of the Legislature, that it is proper to look for some other possible meaning of the word or phrase".[74] The context, as already seen, in the construction of statutes, means the statute as a whole, the previous state of the law, other statutes in *pari materia*, the general scope of the statute and the mischief that it was intended to remedy.[75] The above discussion relating to the meaning of a word or phrase in the construction of a statute has been approvingly quoted by the Supreme Court in a number of cases."[76] The said discussion was also quoted by the Supreme Court in *Kotak Mahindra Bank v. Hindustan National Gass & Industries*,[77] wherein it was called upon to interpret the term 'wilful default' in the RBI Master Circular on Wilful Defaulters. Though the definition of the term in the Master Circular used the word 'lender', the Court held that words in a statute or a document are to be interpreted in the context or subject-matter in which they are used and not according to their literal meaning. Therefore, the Court read the Master Circular as a whole, looked at the provisions of the Reserve Bank of India Act , 1934, and the Banking Regulation Act, 1949, under which the RBI has powers to issue circulars and instructions to banks, and also looked at the purpose for which the Master Circular was issued and the mischief that it intends to remedy, which is to disseminate credit information pertaining to wilful defaulters amongst banks and financial institutions so that no further bank finance is made available to such defaulters. In the above context, the

---

74. *Pinner v. Everett*, (1969) 3 All ER 257, p. 258 (HL) (LORD REID). **See further** *Maunsell v. Olins*, (1975) 1 All ER 16, p. 26 : (1975) AC 373 (HL) : "Statutory language, like all language, is capable of an almost infinite gradation of 'register'—*i.e.,* it will be used at the semantic level appropriate to the subject-matter and to the audience addressed (the man in the street, lawyers, merchants etc.). It is the duty of a court of construction to tune in to such register and so to interpret the statutory language as to give to it the primary meaning which is appropriate in that register. In other words statutory language must always be given presumptively the most natural and ordinary meaning which is appropriate in the circumstances." (LORD SIMON)

75. **See** text and notes 40 (p. 35) and 60 to 64 (pp. 39-40).

76. *Special Reference No. 1 of 2002 D/28-10-2002 (Under Article 143(1) of the Constitution* AIR 2003 SC 87, p. 138 : (2003) 8 SCC 237). The above discussion was again **quoted** with **approval** by Naolekar J. in *ICICI Bank v. Municipal Corporation of Greater Bombay,* (2005) 6 SCC 404, p. 414 : AIR 2005 SC 3315 which related to the meaning of 'advertisement' in section 328 of the Bombay Municipal Corporation Act 1888 and which was held to be one denoting the business activity of the displayer. Again **quoted** in *Central Bank of India v. State of Kerala,* (2009) 4 SCC 94 para 99 : (2009) 3 JT 216; *V.N. Shrikhande (Dr.) v. Anita Sena Fernandes*, (2011) 1 SCC 53 para 21 : AIR 2011 SC 212.

77. *Kotak Mahindra Bank Ltd. v. Hindustan National Glass & Industries Ltd. & Ors.*, (2013) 7 SCC 369, pp. 391 to 399.

word 'lender' was held to mean 'bank', and hence the Circular was held to not only cover default by a unit in meeting its payment obligations to a lender, but also default by a unit which in meeting its payment obligations to a bank under facilities such as a bank guarantee.

It is often said that a word, apart from having a natural, ordinary or popular meaning (including other synonyms *i.e.* literal, grammatical and primary), may have a secondary meaning which is less common *e.g.* technical or scientific meaning. But once it is accepted that natural, ordinary or popular meaning of a word, in the process of interpreting a statute, is derived from its context, the distinction drawn between different meanings loses much of its relevance.[78] In construing the word 'coal' in a Sales Tax Act, the Supreme Court ruled in favour of the popular meaning by applying the test: "What would be the meaning which persons dealing with coal and consumers purchasing it as fuel would give to that word".[79] On this test coal was held to include charcoal and not restricted to coal obtained as a mineral. In contrast, it was said that in the Colliery Control Order, the word 'coal' will be understood in its technical or scientific sense and will be interpreted as a mineral product and will, therefore, not include charcoal. In the words of the court: "The Colliery Control Order deals with collieries and obviously, therefore, the term coal there is used as a mineral product".[80] It can quite legitimately be said that the natural, ordinary or popular meaning of the term 'coal' would be coal used as fuel in the context of a Sales Tax Act, and coal as a mineral product in the context of the Colliery Control Order. In a another case[81] the question before the Supreme Court related to the construction of the word 'marble' as used in Entry 62, Appendix 2, Part B of the Import and Export Policy (April 1988-March 1991). Chapter 25 of Schedule 1, Appendix 1-B of the ITC schedule mentions mineral products which can be imported under the open General Licence. One of the items in Schedule 1 is item 25 which reads : 'Marble, travertine, ecaussinne and other calcareous monumental or building stone of an apparent specific gravity of 2.5 or more'. Appendix 2, Part B of the Imports and Exports Policy, where the word 'marble' alone

---

78. CROSS, Statutory Interpretation, 3rd Edition, p. 82, where the author **quotes** DREDGER: "The secondary meaning is the literal meaning in the context.—Except where a mistake is corrected or a meaning is given to senseless words, there is nosuch thing as a literal meaning as distinguished from some other meaning." DREDGER, Statutes : The Mischievous Golden Rule (1981) 59 Can Bar Rev. 781.

79. *Commissioner of Sales Tax, M.P., Indore v. Jaswant Singh Charan Singh*, AIR 1967 SC 1454, p. 1457 : 1967 (2) SCR 720.

80. *Ibid.*

81. *Akbar Badruddin Jiwani v. Collector of Customs, Bombay*, AIR 1990 SC 1579 : 1990 (2) SCC 203 : (1990) 27 ECC 69.

figures in Entry 62, enumerates the restricted items. In a generic sense 'marble' includes any calcareous rock which is sufficiently hard and coherent to take a good polish and which can be cut into desired sizes free of cracks. But technically *i.e.* in petrological or geological sense 'marble' is distinguished from other calcareous rocks by the fact that it is a metamorphic rock formed from re-crystallisation of limestones and has a visibly crystallined nature. Having regard to the context, specially the fact that in Entry 25 of ITC schedule other calcareous rocks were mentioned along with marble whereas in Entry 62 of Import and Export Policy marble alone was mentioned, the Supreme Court concluded: "The only *natural meaning* that follows from this is that Entry 62 is confined only to marble as it is understood in a petrological or geological sense."[82] Thus here the technical or scientific meaning was accepted as the natural meaning in the context.

However, it has been held that in interpretation of fiscal statutes, the entries must not, *prima facie*, be construed in their technical or scientific sense, but must be understood in their ordinary sense. Therefore the expression 'foodstuff' in Entry 56 of a notification issued under the U.P. Sales Tax Act, 1948, was held to mean food of some kind *i.e.*, anything of nutritive value which is consumed for growth or sustaining one's life, and hence would not include 'food colours' and 'food essences', which cannot be consumed as such.[83] It has also been held that Courts must interpret words as used or understood in the 'popular sense' if they are not defined under the Act or the Rules framed thereunder. As per Craies on Statute Law, 6th edition, 'popular sense' means 'that sense which people conversant with the subject matter, with which the statute is dealing, would attribute to it'.[84] In a case before the Supreme Court, the question was as to the meaning of the word 'vegetables' as it occurred in the C.P. and Berar Sales Tax Act, 1947 as amended by Act 16 of 1948, whether it included betel leaves or not. Although the word in natural history and according to dictionary meaning is comprehensive enough to include betel leaves, the Supreme Court held that "being a word of everyday use it must be construed in its popular sense, meaning that sense which people conversant with the subject-matter with which the statute is dealing would attribute to it" and so the word was construed to denote those classes of vegetable

82. *Akbar Badruddin Jiwani v. Collector of Customs*, AIR 1990 SC 1579, p. 1595 : 1990 (2) SCC 203 : (1990) 27 ECC 69.

83. *Gulati & Co. v. CST, Uttar Pradesh, Lucknow*, (2014) 14 SCC 286, p. 291.

84. *Commissioner of Central Excise, Mumbai v. Fiat India Pvt. Ltd. & Anr.*, (2012) 9 SCC 332, p. 351.

matter which are grown in kitchen gardens.[85] It was, therefore, held that betel leaves[86] and sugarcane[87] were excluded from its purview.

Popular sense of a word, as explained above is normally preferred as against scientific meaning in construing entries of goods in a fiscal statute.[88] Consumers' understanding of the expressions used in legislation relating to them is also an input in judicial construction.[89] So in construing entries of goods in Excise, Customs, Octroi or Sales Tax Acts resort should normally be had not to the scientific or technical meaning but to their popular meaning *viz.* the meaning attached to the expressions by those dealing in them.[90] Applying the test of popular meaning it was held while construing the Uttar Pradesh Sales Tax Act, 1948 that tooth powder

---

85. *Ramavatar Budhaiprasad v. Assistant Sales Tax Officer*, AIR 1961 SC 1325, p. 1326 : 1962 (1) SCR 279; **followed** in *Rambux Chaturbhuj v. State of Rajasthan*, AIR 1963 SC 351 : 1961 (12) STC 330.

86. *Ibid.*

87. *Motipur Zamindari Co. v. State of Bihar*, AIR 1962 SC 660 : 1962 Supp (1) SCR 498. Sugarcane is not 'vegetable product' and sugar mill is not 'Processing of vegetable products industry': *Saraswati Sugar Mills v. Haryana State Board*, AIR 1992 SC 224 : 1992 (1) SCC 418. Chillies and Lemons have been held to be vegetables; *Mongulu Sahu Ramahari Sahu v. Sales Tax Officer, Ganjam*, AIR 1974 SC 390 : 1972 (4) SCC 423. Green ginger has been held to be vegetables; *State of West Bengal v. Washi Ahmed*, AIR 1977 SC 1638 : 1977 SCC (Tax) 278 : (1977) 2 SCC 246. Coconut has been held to be neither 'fresh fruit' nor 'vegetables', *P.A. Thillai Chidambara Nadar v. Addl. Appellate Assistant Commissioner*, (1985) 4 SCC 30 : AIR 1985 SC 1678. Watery Coconut is neither green fruit nor dried fruit; *Shri Bharuch Coconut Trading Co. v. Municipal Corporation of the City of Ahmedabad*, AIR 1991 SC 494 : 1992 Supp (1) SCC 298.

88. *CCE v. Krishna Carbon Paper Co.*, AIR 1988 SC 2223, pp. 2228, 2229 : 1989 (1) SCC 150. Applying popular sense it was held in the context of U.P. Sales Tax Act,1948 that 'toffee' is a 'sweetmeat': *Pappu Sweets and Biscuits v. C.T.T.*, (1998) 1 SC 228; but 'Bubblegum is not sweetmeat': *Commissioner of Trade Tax v. Associated Distributors Ltd.*, (2008) 7 SCC 409 paras 8, 9 : (2008) 8 Scale 466.

89. *Trimbuk Kothul v. State of Maharashtra*, AIR 1977 SC 435, p. 440 : 1977 (1) SCC 300.

90. *United Offset Process Pvt. Ltd. v. Asstt. Collector of Customs*, AIR 1989 SC 622, p. 624 : 1989 Supp (1) SCC 131; *Union of India v. Garware Nylons Ltd.*, AIR 1996 SC 3509, p. 3512 : 1996 (6) Scale 667, p. 672 : (1996) 10 SCC 413 (Sixth Edition of this book, p. 67 is **referred**); *Municipal Corporation for the City of Thane v. Asmaco Plastic Industries*, 1998 (4) Scale 196, p. 199 : JT 1998 (5) SC 1, p. 15 : AIR 1998 SC 2440 : (1999) 1 SCC 372; *Alpine Industries v. Collector of Central Excise New Delhi*, (2003) 3 SCC 111, p. 114 (para 5) : AIR 2003 SC 935; *Naturalle Health Products (P.) Ltd. v. Collector of Central Excise*, AIR 2004 SC 669, p. 681 (para 41) : (2004) 9 SCC 136) (Ayurvedic medicine). For test to determine whether an article is 'medicament' (medicinal preparation) or cosmetic, **see** *Puma Ayurvedic Herbal (P) Ltd. v. Commissioner Central Excise*, (2006) 3 SCC 266 : AIR 2006 SC 1561 and cases referred to therein. For test to determine whether an article is 'cosmetic' or 'drug' **see** *Ponds India Limited v. Commissioner of Trade Tax Lucknow*, (2008) 8 SCC 369 : (2008) 9 Scale 277 and cases referred to therein.

is a 'toilet requisite"[1] and powerloom cloth is not 'cloth manufactured by the mills'.[2] The popular meaning in the context of a Sales Tax Act is that meaning which is popular in commercial circles for the Act essentially, in its working, is concerned with dealers who are commercial men.[3] Rice and paddy were, therefore, held to be different commodities for purposes of the Punjab Sales Tax Act, 1969.[4] Applying the same test, the word 'tex-

---

1. *Sarin Chemical Laboratory v. Commissioner of Sales Tax, U.P.*, AIR 1971 SC 65 : 1970 (2) SCC 403. **See further** *State of Gujarat v. Prakash Trading Co., Ahmedabad*, AIR 1973 SC 960 : 1972 (2) SCC 689.

2. *Sales Tax Commissioner, U.P. v. Ladha Singh Mal Singh*, AIR 1971 SC 2221 : 1971 (2) SCC 407. **See further** *Commissioner of Sales Tax, U.P. v. S.N. Bros., Kanpur*, AIR 1973 SC 78, p. 80 : 1973 SCC (Tax) 254 ("Dyes and colours" will not include "food colours" and "Scents and perfumes" will not include "syrup essences"). *Avadh Sugar Mills Ltd. v. Sales Tax Officer, Sitapur*, AIR 1973 SC 2440 : 1973 SCC (Tax) 569 ("Oil seeds" will include groundnut); *State of Uttar Pradesh v. Kores (India) Ltd.*, AIR 1977 SC 132 : 1977 SCC (Tax) 40 : (1976) 4 SCC 477. (Carbon paper is not covered in the expression "paper other than hand paper" and typewriter ribbon is not included in "typewriters and parts thereof"); *Commissioner of Sales Tax, U.P. v. Macneill and Barry Ltd., Kanpur*, (1986) 1 SCC 23 : AIR 1986 SC 386 (Ammonia paper and Ferropaper are not covered in the expression 'paper other than hand made paper'); *State of Uttar Pradesh v. Indian Hume Pipe Co. Ltd.*, AIR 1977 SC 1132 : 1977 SCC (Tax) 335. (Sanitary fitting does not cover "RCC or Hume pipes which are extremely heavy for use in lavatories, urinals or bathrooms etc."); *Deputy Commissioner of Sales Tax v. G.S. Pai & Co.*, AIR 1980 SC 611 : 1980 (1) SCC 142. ("Bullion Specie" does not include ornaments or articles of gold); *P.S.T. Data System Ltd. v. Collector Central Excise*, AIR 1997 SC 785 : (1997) ? SCC 78 (Software *e.g.* floppies, discs etc. sold alongwith computer not covered in tariff item 'computers all sorts'); *Associated Cement Companies Ltd. v. Commissioner of Customs,* AIR 2001 SC 862 : (2001) 4 SCC 593 (Drawings designs relating to machinery or industrial technology are 'goods' under section 2(22)(e) of the Customs Act, 1962 and chargeable to duty under Chapter 49 of the Customs Tariff Act, 1975).

3. *Ganesh Trading Co. v. State of Haryana*, AIR 1974 SC 1362, p. 1363 : 1974 SCC (Tax) 100 : (1974) 3 SCC 620 **affirmed** in *Baburam Jagdish Kumar & Co. v. State of Punjab,* (1979) 3 SCC 616 : AIR 1979 SC 1475; *Satnam Overseas (Export) v. State of Haryana,* (2003) 1 SCC 561, pp. 583, 584 : AIR 2003 SC 66. **See further** *Mukesh Kumar Aggarwal & Co. v. State of M.P.*, AIR 1988 SC 563, p. 564 : 1988 Supp SCC 232 ("The common commercial" sense of the words and not "their scientific or technical sense" is to be adopted for our merchants are not supposed to be "naturalists, geologists or botanists"); *State of Goa v. Leukoplast (India) Ltd.*, AIR 1997 SC 1875, pp. 1877, 1878 : 1997 (4) SCC 82 (The question whether certain articles could in ordinary commercial sense be treated as 'drugs and medicines' in a Central Sales Tax Act, 1956 is a question of fact to be agitated before the authorities under the Act); *Union of India v. Garware Nylons Ltd.,* AIR 1996 SC 3509, p. 3512 : 1996 (6) Scale 667, p. 672 : (1996) 10 SCC 413 (Sixth Edition of this book, p. 67 is **referred**).

4. *Ganesh Trading Co., Karnal v. State of Haryana, supra.* Flour, maida and suji derived from wheat are not 'wheat': *Rajasthan Roller Flour Mills Association v. State of Rajasthan*, AIR 1994 SC 64 : 1994 Supp (1) SCC 413. Seeds prepared after applying insecticides and other chemicals to foodgrains are not 'agricultural produce';

[Footnote No. 4 Contd.]

tiles' was construed to cover cotton/woollen dryer felts.[5] Construing in the popular sense the words 'Livestock, that is to say all domestic animals such as oxen, bulls, cows buffaloes, goats, sheep, horses etc.', as they occur in the Andhra Pradesh General Sales Tax Rules, 1957, it was held that 'chicks' will not be covered by these words although in literal sense 'animal' refers to any and every 'animate' object as distinct from inanimate object.[6] Another principle in considering entries in a schedule of a Sales Tax Act is that resort to residuary entry should be taken as a last resort. If the article in question answers the description in a specific entry which is also the commercial meaning or trade meaning it is the specific entry that should be applied more so when the rate of tax under the residuary entry is higher than the tax under the specific entry for when two views are possible one which favours the assessee should be adopted as also when the authorities had adopted that meaning in earlier years. These principles were applied and 'yeast' was held to be a 'chemical' falling under a specific entry reading 'chemicals of all kinds.'[7]

Popular meaning has also been applied in the context of the Central Excises and Salt Act, 1944 for holding that exemption from tax granted in respect of 'condensed milk' by a notification did not cover condensed skimmed milk.[8] The same test was applied in holding that toilet soap was

---

[Footnote No. 4 Contd.]
State of Rajasthan v. Rajasthan Input Dealers Association, AIR 1996 SC 2179 : (1996) 5 SCC 479. **Followed** in *Krishi Utpadan Mandi Samiti v. Pilibhit Pantnagar Beej Ltd.*, (2004) 1 SCC 391 : (2003) 9 JT 548 **but** distinguished in *Seedsman Association v. Principal Secretary Govt. of A.P.*, AIR 2004 SC 1690 : (2004) 9 SCC 56 (In this case there was no allegation that seeds became unfit for human consumption).

5. *Porritts and Spencer (Asia) Ltd. v. State of Haryana*, AIR 1979 SC 300 : (1979) 1 SCC 82 : 1979 SCC (Tax) 38. But only those varieties of felt constitute 'Cloth' which are pliable and capable of being wrapped folded or wound around, *Filterco v. Commissioner of Sales Tax*, (1986) 2 SCC 103 : AIR 1986 SC 626. Carpets are covered by 'textiles'; *Ess Dee Carpet Enterprises v. Union of India*, AIR 1990 SC 455 : (1990) 1 SCC 461. The terms 'yarn' and fibre in the definition of 'textiles' in the Textiles Committee Act, 1963 to be understood in the popular commercial sense as prevalent in the textile industry; *Sir Silk Ltd. v. Textiles Committee*, AIR 1989 SC 317, p. 328 : 1989 Supp (1) SCC 168.

6. *Royal Hatcheries Pvt. Ltd. v. State of Andhra Pradesh*, AIR 1994 SC 666 : 1993 (6) JT 248. *Compare and Contrast ITC Ltd. v. Person in charge Agricultural Market Committee Kakinada*, (2004) 2 SCC 794, pp. 798, 799 : AIR 2004 SC 1794 [Construction of definition of Livestock in the A.P. (Agricultural Produce and Livestock) Markets Act, 1966; 'Fish', 'Prawn' held to be 'animal' within the definition of Livestock.] **See further** text and note 72, p. 204.

7. *Mauri Yeast India Private Ltd. v. State of Uttar Pradesh*, (2008) 5 SCC 680 paras 34, 45, 46, 47, 53 : (2008) 6 Scale 241.

8. *Healthways Dairy Products Co. Regd., Gauhati v. Union of India*, AIR 1976 SC 2221, p. 2222 : 1976 (2) SCC 887. Same test applied in construing exemption granted in respect of 'all kinds of food products and food preparations' and in

[Footnote No. 8 Contd.]

'Household' soap and not soap of 'other sorts' in Schedule I of the Central Excises and Salt Act, 1944.[9] In that context it was observed: "if anybody goes to market and asks for toilet soap he must ask only for household bathing purpose and not for industrial or other sorts. Even the people dealing with it would supply it for household purpose."[10] Ordinary meaning was also used in holding that the expression 'Printed Books' in an exemption notification did not cover printed loose sheets of drawing designs, etc. put up in a folder.[11] But if a tariff schedule prescribes its own rules of interpretation those rules must necessarily be first followed.[12]

[Footnote No. 8 Contd.]

olding that the exemption did not cover non-alcoholic beverage bases like Gold Spot base, Limca base or Thumps up base; *Collector of Central Excise v. Parle Exports Ltd.*, AIR 1989 SC 644 : 1989 (1) SCC 345. Similarly exemption granted for 'Broadcasting television receiver' was interpreted not to cover 'Projection television receiver Set' for the two are entirely different products in the mind of consumers: *Collector of Central Excise v. Fusebase Eltoto Ltd.*, AIR 1994 SC 1289, p. 1291 : 1993 (4) JT 280 : 1993 Supp (3) SCC 385. For other cases under the Central Excises Act, 1944 and Indian Tariff Act, 1934, **see** text and notes 40 to 45, pp. 117 to 121 and notes 54 to 60, p. 123. For a case under the Companies (Profits) Surtax Act, 1964 **see** *CIT, Bombay v. NS Fibres*, AIR 1981 SC 1524 : (1981) 3 SCC 152.

9. *Oswal Agro Mills Ltd. v. Collector of Central Excise*, AIR 1993 SC 2288 : 1993 (3) JT 260 : 1993 Supp (3) SCC 716 : (1993) 66 ELT 37.

10. *Ibid*, p. 2295.

11. *Commissioner of Customs v. Parasrampuria,* AIR 2001 SC 3501, p. 3506 : (2001) 9 SCC 74 : (2001) 133 ELT 9.

12. *Fenner (India) Ltd. v. Collector of Central Excise*, 1995 (2) Scale 508, p. 510 : 1995 Supp (2) SCC 678. **See further** *Collector of Central Excise, Hyderabad v. Bakelite Hylam Ltd.*, AIR 1997 SC 1988, p. 1991 : 1997 (3) JT 639 : (1997) 10 SCC 350. (The Central Excise Tariff Act, 1986 is based on the Harmonised System of Nomenclature (HSN) and the internationally accepted nomenclature has been adopted to reduce disputes on account of tariff classification. Accordingly HSN is a safe guide for ascertaining the true meaning of any expression in the Act. Further the Act lays down specific Rules of Interpretation and contains Notes which govern the Interpretation of various entries in it); *Union of India v. Pesticides Manufacturing & Formulators Association of India,* (2002) 8 SCC 410, p. 419 : AIR 2003 SC 1 (HSN nomenclature of insecticides used); *Forbes Gokak Ltd. v. Collector of Central Excise Aurangabad,* (2003) 6 SCC 128 (construction in confirmity with HSN explanatory notes and Rules for interpretation of schedule). *Commissioner of Central Excise Nagpur v. Simplex Mills Co. Ltd.*, (2005) 3 SCC 51, p. 56 (Rules for interpretation of the Schedule applied); *DCL Polyester Ltd. Nagpur v. Collector of Central Excise Customs, Nagpur*, (2005) 3 SCC 455, p. 466 (para 22) (Rules of Interpretation applied); *O.K. Play (India) Ltd. v. Commissioner Central Excise Delhi*, (2005) 2 SCC 460 (HSN and explanatory notes thereto provide a safe guide); *Muller and Phipps (India) Ltd. v. Collector of Central Excise*, (2004) 4 SCC 787, p. 797 (when HSN meaning not to be followed). *Camlin Limited v. Commissioner of Central Excise*, (2008) 9 SCC 82 paras 16 and 24 : (2008) 10 JT 49 (It is settled law that when the entries in HSN and the tarrif are not aligned, reliance cannot be placed upon HSN); *Bakelite Hylam Ltd. v. Collector of Central Excise, Hyderabad*, JT 1998 (5) SC 77,

[Footnote No. 12 Contd.]

The popular meaning test was applied in holding that the word 'houses' in the Bombay Village Panchayats Act, 1933, which empowers a *Panchayat* to levy a tax upon owners or occupiers of 'houses and land', meant all buildings including factory buildings.[13]

In deciding that the word 'Poultry' in the Fertilisers and Feeding Stuffs Act, 1926 which provides for statutory warranty on the sale of an article 'for use as food for cattle or poultry' does not include pheasants, the Court of Appeal held that 'poultry' being a common English word should be construed in its ordinary sense, *i.e.*, that sense which an ordinary educated Englishman would attach to that word.[14] It was pointed out that the fact that according to scientific evidence pheasants and domestic hens are ancestrally of the same species as the jungle fowl or the fact that an American Dictionary of 1961 gives a meaning of 'poultry' as including pheasants, or the fact that hand reared or artificially reared pheasants are often fed food sold under the description 'poultry food' and thus need the protection of the Act, are irrelevant considerations for departing from the ordinary sense of the word.[15]

Section 2(f) of the Kerala Forest Act, 1961 defines forest produce to include the following whether found in or brought from a forest or not that is to say: 'timber, charcoal, wood-oil'. The question in a case[16] before the Supreme Court was whether sandal wood oil is 'wood-oil' as used in the above definition of forest produce. Sandal wood oil is produced at a

---

[Footnote No. 12 Contd.]

pp. 80, 81 : AIR 1998 SC 2556, p. 2558 (If the tariff item contains its own definition that has to be followed in preference to popular meaning); *Sprint R.P.G. India Ltd. v. Commissioner of Customs,* AIR 2000 SC 749, p. 753 : (2000) 2 SCC 486 : (2002) 116 ELT 6 (Rules of Interpretation contained in First Schedule to the Customs Tariff Act applied in holding that imported computer software loaded on hard disk drive is taxable under heading 85.24, as 'computer software' and not as 'hard disk' simpliciter under heading 84.71); *Commissioner of Customs Excise Pondicherry v. ACER India Ltd.*, (2004) 8 SCC 173, pp. 188, 193 : (2004) 7 JT 248 (Computer and Software are different marketable commodities. Rule 1 of General rules of Interpretation contained in the schedule applied).

13. *Tata Engineering and Locomotive Co. Ltd. v. Gram Panchayat, Pimpri Waghere,* AIR 1976 SC 2463, pp. 2466, 2468 : 1976 SCC (Tax) 457 : (1976) 4 SCC 177.

14. *Hardwick Game Farm v. Suffolk etc. Association Ltd.*, (1966) 1 All ER 309, pp. 323, 324, 334 (CA); **affirmed** in appeal on this point (1968) 2 All ER 444 (HL). **See further** *Earl of Normanton v. Giles*, (1980) 1 All ER 106 : (1980) 1 WLR 28 (HL). (Pheasants reared for sport are not 'livestock' and rearing of pheasants is not agriculture.)

15. *Hardwick Game Farm v. Suffolk etc. Association Ltd.*, (1966) 1 All ER 309, pp. 323, 324, 334 (CA).

16. *Forest Range Officer v. Khushboo Enterprises*, AIR 1994 SC 120, p. 124 : 1993 (3) JT 222 : 1993 Supp (3) SCC 627.

factory level by mechanised process utilising the heart wood and roots of sandal wood trees removed from forest as a raw material. The argument before the Supreme Court by referring to technical dictionaries was that wood oil is a natural produce of the forest derived as an exudation from living trees in the forest belonging to the family of Dipterocarpus trees and it will not include sandal wood oil which is a bye-product from sandal wood by industrial process. The above argument was not accepted. It was pointed out that the object of the Act was to conserve forest wealth and there was no indication in the Act to exclude what was ordinarily and in common parlance spoken of as wood oil. On this reasoning it was held that sandal wood oil was wood oil within the definition of forest produce.

In holding that '*supari*' or 'betel nut' though derived and prepared out of the usufruct of the Areca-palm tree, is not for that reason 'Fruit product' within Rule 29(f) of the Prevention of Food Adulteration Rules, 1955, the Supreme Court referred to the rule that it is not the technical or scientific sense but the sense as understood in common parlance that generally matters in construing statutes.[17]

The principle that in statutes directed to commercial men, words having definite commercial sense must be understood in that sense as that would be "the natural and proper sense" in that context[18] has been applied in the construction of Income-tax Acts. It was, therefore, held that the words 'profits and gains', when used in an Income-tax Act should be understood in a sense which no commercial man would misunderstand.[19] Applying the same principle the expression 'borrowed money' or 'capital borrowed' when used in an Income tax Act has to be understood in its ordinary commercial usage implying a transaction of loan with relationship of borrower and lender.[20] Similarly the word 'investments' in section 23A of the Income-tax Act, 1922 was construed in the ordinary popular sense of the word as used by businessmen and it was held that it is not limited to investments in shares, debentures, stocks etc. but also covers investments in house property or other income yielding property.[21] In determining the commercial sense of an

---

17. *Dinesh Chandra Jamanadas Gandhi v. State of Gujarat*, AIR 1989 SC 1011, p. 1017 : 1989 (1) SCC 420.

18. *CIT (Central), Calcutta v. Moon Mills Ltd.*, AIR 1966 SC 870, p. 872 (para 4) : 1966 (2) SCR 393. **See further** under title (d) 'Technical words in Technical Sense', *infra*.

19. *Ibid*; *Challapalli Sugar Ltd. v. Commissioner of Income-tax, A.P.*, AIR 1975 SC 97, pp. 99, 100 : 1975 SCC (Tax) 65 : (1975) 3 SCC 572.

20. *Inland Revenue Commissioners v. Rowntree and Co. Ltd.*, (1948) 1 All ER 482 (CA); *Commissioner of Income-tax v. Bazpur Co-operative Sugar Factory Ltd.*, AIR 1989 SC 1866, p. 1870 : 1989 (2) JT 562.

21. *Nawab Estates (P) Ltd. v. Commissioner of Income-tax, West Bengal*, AIR 1977 SC 153, pp. 156, 157 : 1977 (1) SCC 7.

expression in a statute directed to commercial men but not containing any definition of that expression, it may be relevant to refer to the normal rules of accountancy prevailing in commerce and industry.[22]

"In legislations pertaining to the world of business and commerce the dictionary to refer to is the dictionary of the inhabitants of that world" observed THAKKER, J. in holding that the word '*khandsari*' in section 2(a) of the U.P. Krishi Utpadan Mandi Adhiniyam, 1964 embraced *Khandsari* sugar manufactured in factories by open pan process.[23]

The justification of the rule that the words are to be understood in their natural, ordinary or popular sense is well expressed by JUSTICE FRANKFURTER: "After all legislation when not expressed in technical terms is addressed to common run of men and is therefore to be understood according to sense of the thing, as the ordinary man has a right to rely on ordinary words addressed."[24] In determining, therefore, whether a particular import is included within the ordinary meaning of a given word, one may have regard to the answer which everyone conversant with the word and the subject-matter of statute and to whom the legislation is addressed, will give if the problem were put to him.[25] In holding that a railway workman who was oiling an apparatus was not engaged in 'repairing' the same, LORD SIMONDS observed: "Had one of these workmen after oiling the apparatus been asked whether he had been repairing it, he would surely have answered, 'No'. And that is the answer which I must give unless the

---

22. *Challapalli Sugars Ltd. v. Commissioner of Income-tax, A.P., supra* (meaning of 'actual cost'); *Surana Steels Pvt. Ltd. v. Dy. Commissioner of Income-tax,* AIR 1999 SC 1455, p. 1459 : (1999) 4 SCC 306 (meaning of 'loss'); *Collector of Central Excise Pune v. Dai Ichi Karkaria Ltd.,* JT 1999 (5) SC 595, pp. 606, 607 : AIR 1999 SC 3234, p. 3241 (meaning of 'cost') : (1999) 7 SCC 448; *Commissioner Central Excise, Pune v. Cadbury India Ltd.,* (2006) 7 SCC 228 (para 12) : AIR 2006 SC 2838 (meaning of 'cost').

23. *Rathi Khandsari Udyog v. State of Uttar Pradesh,* (1985) 2 SCC 485, p. 506 : AIR 1985 SC 679 : 1985 All LJ 226.

24. *Wilma E. Addison v. Holly Hill Fruit Products,* 322 US 607, p. 618 : 88 Law Ed 1488, p. 1496. **See further** *Union of India v. Garware Nylons Ltd.,* AIR 1996 SC 3509, p. 3512 : 1996 (6) Scale 667, p. 672 (passages from Sixth Edition, p. 70 of this book are **referred**).

25. *Commr. of Sales Tax, M.P., Indore v. Jaswant Singh Charan Singh,* AIR 1967 SC 1454, p. 1457 : 1967 (2) SCR 720. **See further** text and notes 79 and 80, p. 105. *Union of India v. Garware Nylons Ltd.,* AIR 1996 SC 3509, p. 3512 : 1996 (6) Scale 667, p. 672 : (1996) 10 SCC 413 (passages from Sixth Edition, p. 70 of this book are **referred**). *Maheshwari Fish Seed Farm v. T.N. Electricity Board,* (2004) 4 SCC 705, p. 710 : AIR 2004 SC 2341 (9th Edition, p. 95 of this book is **referred.** 'Agriculture' for purposes of T.N. Revision of Tariff Rates on Supply of Electrical Energy Act, 1978 will not include aquaculture/pisciculture).

context compels me to something else than the ordinary meaning".[26] Similarly, in emphasising that the ordinary meaning of 'sale' does not include compulsory acquisition of property on payment of compensation, VISCOUNT SIMONDS said: "So far as the ordinary use of language is concerned it is difficult to avoid being dogmatic, but, for my part, I can only echo what SINGLETON, L.J., said 'what would any one accustomed to the use of words 'sale' or 'sold' answer? It seems to me that everyone must say the tax-payers did not sell'. I am content to march in step with everyone and say the tax-payers did not sell".[27]

The same method was adopted by LORD DIPLOCK in construing the words 'he makes any unwarranted demand with menaces' as they occur in section 21 of the Theft Act, 1968. The question in the case[28] was whether the act of posting a letter containing a demand with menaces fell within the section irrespective of whether the letter was or was not delivered to the addressee. LORD DIPLOCK observed that the words should be construed by ascribing to them their ordinary meaning which should be ascertained by answering the question: "Would a man say in ordinary conversation 'I have made a demand' when he had written a letter and posted it to the person to whom the demand was addressed? or would he not use those words until the letter has been received and read by the addressee?" LORD DIPLOCK then answered the question thus: "My answer to the question is that it would be normal for him to say 'I have made a demand' as soon as he had posted the letter, for he would have done all that was in his power to make the demand".[29] And this method was also applied in determining the commercial sense of 'cost' in the context of the MODVAT scheme and as used in section 4(1)(b) of the Central Excises and Salt Act 1944 (read with Rule 6 of the Valuation Rules), a statute directed to commercial men. The Court (BHARUCHA, J.) observed: "A man of commerce would in our view look at the matter thus 'I paid Rs. 100 to the seller of the raw material as the price thereof. The seller of the raw material had paid Rs. 10 as the excise duty thereon. Consequent upon purchasing the raw material by virtue of the MODVAT scheme, I have been entitled to the credit of Rs. 10 with the excise authorities and can utilise this credit when I pay excise duty on my finished product. The real *cost* of the raw material to me is therefore

---

26. *London & North Eastern Rly. Co. v. Berriman*, (1946) 1 All ER 255, p. 271 : 1946 AC 278 (HL).

27. *Kirkness v. John Hudson & Co. Ltd.*, (1955) 2 All ER 345, p. 348 (HL).

28. *Treacy v. Director of Public Prosecutions*, (1971) 2 WLR 112, p. 128 : (1971) 1 All ER 110 : 1971 AC 536 (HL). For further illustration of the application of this method **see** *Thomas v. Frayer*, (1970) 2 All ER 1, p. 5 (CA) (letters 'g' and 'h').

29. *Treacy v. Director of Public Prosecutions*, (1971) 2 WLR 112, p. 128 : 1971 AC 537 (HL).

Rs. 90. In reckoning the *cost* of the final product I would include Rs. 90 on this account.' This in real terms is the cost of the raw material and it is this, in our view, which should be included in computing the cost of the excisable product."[30]

Apart from context,[31] the consequences flowing from rival constructions have an important bearing in the selection of the true meaning.[32]

(c) Exact meaning preferred to loose meaning

There is a presumption that words are used in an Act of Parliament correctly and exactly and not loosely and inexactly.[33] In ascribing to the word 'contiguous' its exact meaning, *i.e.*, 'touching' in preference to its loose meaning, *i.e.*, 'neighbouring', LORD HEWART, C.J., stated: "It ought to be the rule, and we are glad to think that it is the rule, that words are used in an Act of Parliament correctly and exactly and not loosely and inexactly. Upon those who assert that the rule has been broken, the burden of establishing their proposition lies heavily, and they can discharge it only by pointing to something in the context which goes to show that the loose and inexact meaning must be preferred".[34] This principle was approved and followed by the Privy Council where the question was as to the true meaning of the word 'adjoining'. It was pointed out that the exact meaning of the word was 'conterminous' as distinguished from its loose meaning of 'near' or 'neighbouring'; the former meaning was, therefore, preferred.[35] In selecting, therefore, the ordinary meaning of a word one should prefer the exact meaning unless the context clearly directs otherwise.

---

30. *Collector of Central Excise Pune v. Dai Ichi Karkaria Ltd.*, JT 1999 (5) SC 595, p. 607 : AIR 1999 SC 3234, pp. 3241, 3242 : (1999) 7 SCC 448. For MODVAT and CENVAT schemes, **see further** *Vikram Cement v. Commissioner Central Excise, Indore*, (2006) 2 SCC 351 : (2006) 1 JT 385.

31. **See** Chapter 1, title 3 'Statute must be Read as a whole in its context'.

32. **See** title 4 'Regard to Consequences', *infra*.

33. *Prithipal Singh v. Union of India*, AIR 1982 SC 1413, p. 1419 : (1982) 3 SCC 140; *A.P. Board for Pollution Control v. Andhra Pradesh Rayons Ltd.*, AIR 1989 SC 611, p. 615 : (1989) 1 SCC 44.

34. *Spillers Ltd. v. Caradix Assessment Committee & Pritchard*, (1931) 2 KB 21 : (1931) All ER Rep 524, pp. 528, 529. **Distinguished** in *Attorney-General's Reference (No. 1 of 1988)*, (1989) 2 All ER 1 (HL).

35. *Mayor, Councillors and Burgesses v. Taranaki Electric Power Board*, AIR 1933 PC 216. **See further** *Buckinghamshire County Council v. Trigg*, (1963) 1 All ER 403, p. 406 (words 'adjoins', 'fronts' or 'abuts' envisage actual contact). **Cf.** *Mayor, etc. of the City of Wellington v. Mayor, etc. of Lower Hutt*, (1904) AC 773, p. 775 (PC) (word 'adjacent' includes place close to or near and not only places adjoining). **Also see**, *Hukma v. State of Rajasthan*, AIR 1965 SC 476, p. 479 : 1964 (4) SCR 708 (the words 'areas adjoining the Land Customs Frontier' do not mean only a few miles touching the frontier but may include an entire district or even an entire State adjoining the frontier).

But in applying the rule the secondary meaning, *i.e.*, the less common meaning of a word should not be confounded with its loose meaning. Preference for secondary meaning of a word when the purpose of the statute in which it is used points to that meaning is permissible and adoption of that course does not offend the rule that preference should not be given to loose meaning. For example, the word 'obtain' in its primary sense requires some request or effort to acquire or get something, but in its secondary sense it means to acquire or get without any qualification, and if in a statute, having regard to the mischief aimed at, this secondary meaning of the word is preferred, it cannot be said that preference has been given to loose meaning.[36]

(d) Technical words in technical sense

(i) *Special meaning in trade, business, etc.*—As a necessary consequence of the principle that words are understood in their ordinary or natural meaning in relation to the subject-matter, in legislation relating to a particular trade, business, profession, art or science, words having a special meaning in that context are understood in that sense. Such a special meaning is called the technical meaning to distinguish it from the more common meaning that the word may have.[37] LORD JOWITT, L.C., has stated the rule as follows: "It is, I think, legitimate in construing a statute relating to a particular industry to give to the words used a special technical meaning if it can be established that at the date of the passing of the statute such special meaning was well understood and accepted by those conversant with the industry".[38] As pointed by LORD ESHER, M.R.: "If the Act is one passed with reference to a particular trade, business or transaction and words are used which everybody conversant with that trade, business or transaction knows and understands to have a particular meaning in it, then the words are to be construed as having that particular meaning".[39] The same rule applies in construing the words in a taxing statute which describes the goods that are liable to taxation. The Supreme Court "has consistently taken the view that, in determining the meaning or connotation of words and expressions describing an article in a tariff Schedule, one principle which is fairly well settled is that those words and expressions

---

36. *Attorney-General's Reference (No. 1 of 1988)*, (1989) 2 All ER 1 (HL).

37. **See** *Union of India v. Garware Nylons Ltd.*, AIR 1996 SC 3509, p. 3512 : 1996 (10) SCC 413 (passages from Sixth Edition, pp. 72, 73 of this book are referred).

38. *London & North Eastern Rly. Co. v. Berriman*, (1946) 1 All ER 255, p. 257 : 1946 AC 278 (HL). **See also** *AG v. Emily Moore*, AIR 1938 PC 238, p. 241.

39. *Unwin v. Hanson*, (1891) 2 QB 115 (CA), p. 119; **referred** to in *London & North Eastern Rly. Co. v. Berriman, supra*, pp. 266, 268; *Indian Cable Company Ltd. v. Collector of Central Excise*, AIR 1995 SC 64, pp. 67, 68 : JT 1994 (6) SC 243, p. 250 : (1994) 6 SCC 610; *Union of India v. Garware Nylons Ltd.*, AIR 1996 SC 3509, pp. 3511, 3512 : (1996) 10 SCC 413; *Chemical and Fibres of India v. Union of India*, AIR 1997 SC 558; p. 561 : 1997 (2) SCC 664.

should be construed in the sense in which they are understood in the trade by the dealer and the consumer. The reason is that it is they who are concerned with it, and, it is the sense in which they understand it which constitutes the definitive index of legislative intention".[40] In other words "the true test for classification was the test of commercial identity and not the functional test. It needs to be ascertained as to how the goods in question are referred to in the market by those who deal with them, be it for the purposes of selling, purchasing or otherwise."[41] Similar test is applied for

---

40. *Indian Aluminium Cables Ltd. v. Union of India*, (1985) 3 SCC 284, p. 290 : AIR 1985 SC 1201. **See further** *Delhi Cloth and General Mills Ltd. v. State of Rajasthan*, (1980) 4 SCC 71, pp. 75, 76 : AIR 1980 SC 1552; *Asian Paints India Ltd v. Collector of Central Excise*, AIR 1988 SC 1087, p. 1089 : 1988 (2) SCC 470; *Collector of Customs v. Swastik Woollen (P.) Ltd.*, AIR 1988 SC 2176, p. 2179; *State of U.P. v. Renusagar Power Co.*, AIR 1988 SC 1737, p. 1746 : 1988 (4) SCC 59; *Collector of Customs v. S.K. Mohan & Co.*, AIR 1989 SC 2250, pp. 2253, 2254 : 1989 Supp (2) SCC 337 ; *Madanlal Manoharlal v. State of Haryana*, AIR 1990 SC 556, p. 558; *Chemical and Fibres of India v. Union of India*, AIR 1997 SC 558, pp. 561, 564 (Polymides of textile grade are not plastic material nor synthetic resin in the textile trade); *Union of India v. Garware Nylons Ltd.*, AIR 1996 SC 3509, p. 3512 : 1996 (10) SCC 413 (passages from Sixth Edition of this book, pp. 72, 73 are **referred**); *Union of India v. V. M. Salgaoncar and Bros. (P) Ltd.*, AIR 1998 SC 1367, p. 1370 : 1998 (4) SCC 263 (Trans-shippers are 'ocean-going vessels' as understood in maritime enterprises); *Real Optical Co. v. Appellate Collector of Customs,* JT 2001 (3) SC 125, p. 127 (Rough optical glass Blanks are not 'other glass, glassware'); *Cemento Corporation Ltd. v. Collector Central Excise,* (2002) 8 SCC 139, p. 145 : AIR 2002 SC 3680, p. 3684 (meaning of 'cement' as known in the trade and not dictionary meaning used. 'Lympo' used as a substitute for cement was not held to be 'cement'); *Kedia Agglomerated Marbles Ltd. v. Collector of Central Excise,* (2003) 2 SCC 494, p. 500 : AIR 2003 SC 938 (meaning assigned by those trading in and using the product, meaning of 'mosaictiles'); *Alpine Industries v. Collector of Central Excise,* (2003) 3 SCC 111, p. 115 : AIR 2003 SC 935 (Commercial Parlance); *Collector of Customs v. Agfa Ltd.*, (1997) 71 ALJR 123, p. 128 (High Court of Australia) (When construing revenue statutes that utilise trade or technical terms, the law generally favours interpretation of the terms as they are understood in the trade to which the statute applies).

41. *G.S. Auto International Ltd. v. Collector of Central Excise Chandigarh,* AIR 2003 SC 986, p. 989 : (2003) 2 SCC 371, p. 378 : (2003) 152 ELT 3 (nuts, bolts, etc. found to be parts of automobiles classifiable as such). **See further** *Union of India v. Garware Nylons Ltd.,* 1996 (6) Scale 667, pp. 671, 672 : AIR 1996 SC 3509, pp. 3512, 3513 (on evidence produced 'Nylon twine' was held to be included in 'Nylon yarn'); *Purewal Associates Ltd. v. Collector of Central Excise,* 1996 (7) Scale 378, pp. 381, 382 : 1996 (10) SCC 752 (on affidavit evidence of people in the trade, the articles which were components of watches known as Lid screw, Barrel axle screw, Bridge screw and Dial key screw were held to fall under the general tariff item 68 and not under item 52 (of the Central Excise Tariff) relating to 'Bolts, nuts and screws'); *National Mineral Development Corporation Ltd. v. State of M.P.*, (2004) 6 SCC 281, p. 295 : AIR 2004 SC 2456, p. 2464 (The principles stated above were **referred** with approval from 9th Edition, pp. 97 to 99 of this book in finding

[Footnote No. 41 Contd.]

determining when manufacture takes place or in other words whether an article after subjecting it to processing becomes a different article or remains the same.[42] Same test is applied for deciding whether an article has

---

[Footnote No. 41 Contd.]

out the meaning of 'slimes' produced in iron ore processing); *Kumar Motors, Bareilly v. Commissioner of Sales Tax, U.P.*, (2007) 4 SCC 140 (para 15) : (2007) 3 JT 193 (A commodity is identified by ordinary commercial parlance); *Kesarwani Zarda Bhandar v. State of Uttar Pradesh,* (2008) 8 SCC 305 para 18 : AIR 2008 SC 2733 (Zafrani Zarda being a manufactured tobacco would not answer the description of processed tobacco. The common parlance test applied); *Godrej Industries Ltd. v. D. G. Ahire Assistant Collector of Central Excise,* (2008) 8 SCC 600 para 49 : (2008) 7 JT 628 (Liquid hair dye is not 'hair lotion' having regard to its chemical composition and also common parlance test).

42. *Atul Glass Industries (P) Ltd. v. Collector of Central Excise*, (1986) 3 SCC 480 : AIR 1986 SC 1730 ('Glass mirrors' is a different article from 'glass and glass ware'); *Trutuf Safety Glass Industries v. CST,* (2007) 7 SCC 242 : (2007) 9 JT 622 (In this case, the entry was 'Glass and glassware in all forms'. Automobile Safety toughened glass was held to fall in this entry. *Atul* case distinguished); *Sterling Foods v. State of Karnataka*, (1986) 3 SCC 469 : AIR 1986 SC 1809 (Shrimps, prawns and lobsters do not become different article after the process of cutting their heads and tails, peeling, deveining, cleaning, freezing and packing); *Deputy Commissioner of Sales Tax v. Shiphy International Alleppey*, AIR 1988 SC 992 : 1998 Supp SCC 458 (Fresh frog legs do not become a different commodity after they are washed and frozen); *Aditya Mills Ltd. v. Union of India*, AIR 1988 SC 2237, p. 2239 : 1988 (4) SCC 274 (when two plies of Polyester yarn and one ply of Rayon Filament yarn are doubled together, the resultant yarn known as PPRF yarn is a separate and distinct item for taxation); *Ujagar Prints v. Union of India*, AIR 1989 SC 516, p. 526 : 1989 (3) SCC 488 (Gray fabric after bleaching, Dyeing, Printing, Sizing shrink proofing, etc. becomes a different commodity); *Collector of Central Excise v. Eastend Paper Industries*, AIR 1990 SC 1893, pp. 1895, 1896 : (1989) 4 SCC 244 (manufacture includes all incidental or ancillary processes for making the goods marketable); *Narne Tulaman Manufacturers Pvt. Ltd., Hyderabad v. Collector of Central Excise, Hyderabad*, AIR 1989 SC 79 : 1989 (1) SCC 172 (Assembling of components may amount to manufacture if the product obtained from the work of assembling is a new product known in the market); *Delhi Cold Storage Pvt. Ltd. v. Commr. of Income-tax*, AIR 1991 SC 2125 : 1991 (4) SCC 239 (meaning of processing); *B.P. Oil Mills Ltd. v. Sales Tax Tribunal,* JT 1998 (6) SC 210, p. 212 : AIR 1998 SC 3055 : (1998) 6 SCC 577 (meaning of 'processing'); *Collector of Central Excise v. Rajasthan State Chemical Works*, AIR 1991 SC 2222 : 1991 (4) SCC 473 (Difference between 'manufacture' and 'Processing'); *Saraswati Sugar Mills v. Haryana State Board*, AIR 1992 SC 224, p. 229 : 1992 (1) SCC 418 (Difference between 'processing' and 'manufacture'); *Commissioner of Income Tax, Kerala v. Tara Agencies,* (2007) 6 SCC 429 (Difference between 'manufacture' and 'produced') paras 12, 19, 20, 37 : (2007) 9 JT 65; *Commissioner of Central Excise v. Indian Aluminium Co. Ltd.,* (2006) 8 SCC 314 (paras 17, 19, 20) : (2006) 9 JT 266 : (2006) 10 Scale 34 (meaning of manufacture. 'Dross' obtained in the manufacture of Aluminium sheets from Aluminium Oxide is not a manufactured commodity liable to excise duty); *Commissioner of Central Excise v. Tarpaulin International*, (2010) 9 SCC 103 paras 15, 17, 19, 20 and 25 : (2010) 8 JT 38 (Process of sticking and fixing eyelets in Tarpaulin does not amount to manufacture as the process does not bring

[Footnote No. 42 Contd.]

[Footnote No. 42 Contd.]

about a new product); *Commissioner of Income-tax, Haryana v. Krishna Copper Steel Rolling Mills*, AIR 1992 SC 422, p. 430 : 1992 Supp (1) SCC 732 (The raw material may assume 'semi-finished' or 'finished' forms at different stages of processing before manufacture results. The case deals with articles manufactured from iron and steel); *Commissioner of Sales Tax v. Bharat Petroleum Corporation*, AIR 1992 SC 959 : 1992 (2) SCC 579 (Production of by-product may also amount to manufacture); *TVL K.A.K. Anwar & Co. v. State of Tamil Nadu*, JT 1997 (9) SC 384: AIR 1998 SC 518 (Tanning of raw hides and skins results in manufacture); *Edward Keventer Pvt. Ltd. v. Bihar State Agricultural Marketing Board,* AIR 2000 SC 1796 : (2000) 6 SCC 264 (Beverages 'Frooti' and 'Appy' are different commercial commodities from 'Mango' and 'Apple' from which they are manufactured); *Aspinwall & Co. v. Commissioner of Income-tax, Ernakulam,* AIR 2001 SC 3708 : (2001) 7 SCC 525 (conversion of raw berries into coffee beans is manufacture); *BPL India Ltd. v. Commissioner of Central Excise,* AIR 2002 SC 2104, pp. 2106, 2107 : (2002) 5 SCC 167 (Assembling of VTR and colour monitors from components by use of fasteners is manufacture); *State of Andhra Pradesh v. Modern Protein Ltd.*, JT (1994) 3 SC 431 : 1994 Supp (2) SCC 496 (Deoiled ground nut cake after being granuled by grinding is turned into 'ground nut protein flour' which is a different commercial commodity and a separate taxable entity); *The Gramophone Co. of India v. The Collector of Customs,* JT 1999 (9) SC 275, p. 280 : 1997 (11) SCC 557 (mass production of prerecorded cassettes from blank cassettes is manufacture); *Kores India Ltd. Chennai v. Commissioner of Central Excise Chennai*, (2005) 1 SCC 385 (meaning of 'manufacture'. Cutting of duty paid typewriter/telex ribbons in jumbo rolls into standard predetermined lengths results in manufacture); *O.K. Play (India) Ltd. v. Commissioner of Central Excise*, (2005) 2 SCC 555 : AIR 2005 SC 1031 (meaning of 'manufacture' conversion of low density polyethylene and high density polyethylene granules into moulding powder for using the same as inputs to manufacture plastic water storage tanks and toys, amounts to 'manufacture'); *Prabhat Sound Studios v. Additional Collector of Central Excise*, JT 1997 (10) SC 392 : (1997) 10 SCC 543 (Recording of sound on blank tapes does not result in manufacture); *Union of India v. J.G. Glass Industries Ltd.*, AIR 1998 SC 839, pp. 844, 845 : 1998 (2) SCC 32 (Printing on glass bottles does not amount to manufacture); *Commissioner of Income-tax, Orissa v. N.C. Budhraja and Company*, AIR 1993 SC 2529 : 1994 Supp (1) SCC 280 (Construction of a dam or a bridge or a building as a whole does not amount to manufacture or production of an article); *Commissioner of Income-tax v. Venkateshwara Hatcheries P. Ltd.,* AIR 1999 SC 1225, p. 1231 : (1999) 3 SCC 632 (Hatching of chicks in a hatchery does not amount to production of articles or things); *Hyderabad Industries Ltd. v. Union of India,* (1995) 5 SCC 338 : JT (1999) 5 SC 594 (separation of asbestos fibre from the rock in which it is embedded by manual and mechanical means does not result in manufacture); *Rajasthan State Electricity Board v. Associated Stone Industries,* JT 2000 (6) SC 522, p. 529 : (2000) 6 SCC 141 : AIR 2000 SC 2382 (Excavation of stones does not result in manufacture); *Rajasthan State Electricity Board v. Associated State Industries,* AIR 2000 SC 2382 : (2000) 6 SCC 141 (Energy consumed for pumping out water from mines cannot be said to be energy consumed in manufacture, processing or repair of goods); *Indian Hotels Co. Ltd. v. The Income-tax Officer,* AIR 2000 SC 2645, p. 2650 : (2000) 7 SCC 39 (In the context of hotel business preparation of foodstuffs by cooking or by other process does not result in manufacture); *CST v. Lal Kunwa Crusher (P.) Ltd.,* (2000) 3 SCC 525 : AIR 2000 SC 1161 (Crushing of stone boulders into

[Footnote No. 42 Contd.]

[Footnote No. 42 Contd.]

stone chips, gittis and stonebalast does not result in manufacture); *India Cable Company Ltd. v. Collector Central Excise*, JT 1994 (6) SC 243, pp. 250, 251 : AIR 1995 SC 64 (Meaning of manufacture, marketability essential for levy of excise duty); *Tega India Ltd. v. Commissioner of Central Excise Calcutta*, (2004) 2 SCC 727 : AIR 2004 SC 2785 (Meaning of 'manufacture'-Rubberising and painting of pipes does not alter them into a new commodity so as to amount to manufacture); *Shyam Oil Cake Ltd. v. Collector of Central Excise*, (2005) 1 SCC 264 : AIR 2005 SC 1192 (Process of refining vegetable oil does not result in manufacture); *Metalex (I) P. Ltd. v. Commissioner of Central Excise*, (2005) 1 SCC 271 : AIR 2004 SC 4889 (Laminating / lacquering / metalling of film does not result in manufacture); *Aman Marble Industries (P.) Ltd. v. Collector of Central Excise*, (2005) 1 SCC 279 (cutting of marble blocks into slabs does not result in manufacture); *Hindustan Poles Corporation v. Commissioner of Central Excise,* (2006) 4 SCC 85 (para 40) : (2006) 4 JT 185. (The activity of merely joining of three pipes of different dimensions to obtain a desired length cannot result in manufacture). *Crane Betel Nut Powder Wroks v. Commissioner of Customs & Central Excise,* (2007) 4 SCC 155 : (2007) 4 JT 485 (Crushing of betel nuts and processing them with spices, sweetening agent and oil to obtain supari powder did not amount to manufacture). For imposition of excise duty there should be manufacture and the article manufactured should be marketable. It is then only that the article comes in the category of 'goods' for imposition of excise duty and this will be the position also in cases of captive consumption of the article: *Moti Laminates Pvt. Ltd. v. Collector, Central Excise*, 1995 (1) Scale 713 : 1995 (3) SCC 23; *Union of India v. Delhi Cloth and General Mills*, AIR 1997 SC 2429 : (1997) 5 SCC 767; *Mittal Engineering Works Pvt. Ltd. v. Collector of Central Excise*, 1996 (8) Scale 452 : 1997 (1) SCC 203 : (1997) 106 STC 201; *Union of India v. Delhi Cloth and General Mills Co. Ltd.*, JT 1997 (5) SC 474 : 1997 (92) ELT 315 (SC); *Collector of Central Excise Baroda v. United Phosphorous Ltd.*, JT 2000 (4) SC 323 : (2000) 4 SCC 18; *Cadila Laboratories Pvt. Ltd. v. C.C.E.,* AIR 2003 SC 1700, p. 1703 : (2003) 4 SCC 12. (It is for the Department to show that the intermediate product is marketable before it could be separately taxed to excise duty). *Commissioner of Central Excise v. Mahavir Aluminium Ltd.,* (2007) 5 SCC 260 : (2007) 7 JT 72 (When the intermediate product is a new commercial commodity and is marketable, it will be subjected to Excise duty). *Union of India v. Ahmedabad Electricity Co. Ltd.*, AIR 2004 SC 11, p. 20 : (2003) 11 SCC 129 (mention of an item in the schedule to the Central Excise Tariff Act, 1986 does not by itself make it exigible to Excise tax unless the article is manufactured produced as provided in section 3 of the Central Excise Act, 1944. Use of coal in furnaces of boilers as fuel for producing steam used in factory in manufacturing of articles and resulting in some unburnt coal called 'cinder' cannot be said to be manufactured or produced and made liable to Excise duty); But the definition of 'manufacture' in section 2(f) of the Central Excises and Salt Act, 1944 is not confined to its natural meaning and is an expansive definition: *Collector of Central Excise v. S.D. Fine Chemicals*, 1995 (2) Scale 550 : 1995 Supp (2) SCC 336. Similarly the definition of 'manufacture' in MP General Sales Tax Act includes processing which does not result in production of new article: *Ashirwad Ispat Udyog v. State Level Committee,* JT 1998 (7) SC 558, p. 591 : AIR 1999 SC 111 : (1998) 8 SCC 85. Similar is the position in the definition of manufacture in U.P. Trade Tax Act, 1948, which too is an expansive definition : *Sonebhadra Fuels v. Commissioner of Trade Tax U.P.,* (2006) 7 SCC 322 : (2006) 7 JT 73; *Kumar Motors Bareilly v. Commissioner of Sales Tax U.P.,* (2007) 4 SCC 140 para 17 : (2007) 3 JT 193. If the processes result in erection of immovable property, it will not

[Footnote No. 42 Contd.]

been consumed or used in a local area in the context of levy of octroi tax.[43] The question to be asked in such cases is: "How is the product identified by the class or section of people dealing with or using the product?[44] There is also a distinction between 'production' and 'manufacture.' Production has a wider connotation than manufacture. Production may bring about new goods, which may or may not amount to manufacture. For example ship-breaking results in production of articles but it does not amount to manufacture.[45] If a word has acquired a particular meaning in the trade or commercial circles that meaning becomes the popular meaning in the context and should normally be accepted.[46]

The power, therefore, given to a Surveyor under section 65 of the English Highways Act, 1835 to 'lop' trees growing near a highway was construed as conferring the power to cut off the branches but not to 'top', *i.e.*, to cut off the top of the tree.[47] Illustrating the principle, said LORD ESHER : "The 'waist' or the 'skin' are well-known terms applied to a ship and nobody would think of their meaning the waist or skin of a person when they

---

[**Footnote No. 42 Contd.**]
amount to manufacture of goods liable to excise duty : *Triveni Engineering and Industries Ltd. v. Commissioner of Central Excise*, AIR 2000 SC 2896, p. 2901 : (2000) 7 SCC 29; *T.T.G. Industries Ltd. Madras v. Collector of Central Excise Raipur*, (2004) 4 SCC 751 : AIR 2004 SC 3422. [**See further** on this point, pp. 1146-1147].

43. *HMM Limited v. Administrative Bangalore City Corporation*, AIR 1990 SC 47 : (1989) 4 SCC 640 ('Horlicks' milk powder brought in large bulk containers large steel drums and packed in unit containers glass bottles within octroi limits and then exported was not held to be 'consumed' or 'used'.); *Mafatlal Industries Ltd. v. Nadiad Nagar Palika*, AIR 2000 SC 1223, p. 1225 : (2000) 3 SCC 1 (cloth pieces of 100 metres length brought within octroi limits and cut into smaller pieces and then exported, not held to be consumed or used.)

44. *Atul Glass Industries (P) Ltd. v. Collector of Central Excise, supra*, p. 485. **See further** *Plasmac Machine Manufacturing Co. Pvt. Ltd. v. Collector of Central Excise*, AIR 1991 SC 999, pp. 1002, 1003 : 1990 (4) JT 549; *Union of India v. Parle Products Pvt. Ltd.*, AIR 1994 SC 106, p. 108 : 1994 Supp (3) SCC 662 (Evidence may have to be produced for showing that the article resulting after processing is commercially different from the article subjected to processing and 'manufacture' has taken place); *Collector of Central Excise v. Steel Strips Ltd.*, 1995 (3) Scale 106 : AIR 1995 SC 1483 (Technical evidence to the effect that certain processing led to manufacture and production of a new marketable commodity including authoritative publications should be introduced by the Department before the adjudicating authority).

45. *Vijay Ship-breaking Corporation v. C.I.T.*, (2010) 10 SCC 39.

46. *Dunlop India Ltd. & Madras Rubber Factory Ltd. v. Union of India*, AIR 1977 SC 597, p. 605 : (1976) 2 SCC 241. (V.P. latex which is synthetic rubber falls within item 39 'Rubber Raw' of the first schedule to the Indian Tariff Act, 1934); *Union of India v. Gujarat Woollen Felt Mills*, AIR 1977 SC 1548 : 1977 SCC (Tax) 399. ('Woollen fabrics' in schedule 1, entry 21, Central Excises and Salt Act, 1944 does not include non-woven felts manufactured from woollen fibres by machine pressing and used for filteration in heavy industries). **See further** text and notes 54 to 58, p. 123.

47. *Unwin v. Hanson*, (1891) 2 QB 115 : 60 LJ QB 531 (CA).

are used in an Act of Parliament dealing with ships".[48] Similarly, construing the word 'practice' in Supreme Court Advocates (Practice in High Court) Act, 1951, PATANJALI SHASTRI, C.J. said: "The practice of law in this country generally involves the exercise of both the functions of acting and pleading on behalf of a litigant party; accordingly when the Legislature confers upon an advocate 'the right to practice' in a court, it is legitimate to understand that expression as authorising him to appear and plead as well as to act on behalf of suitors in that Court".[49]

In applying the rule, however, its limitations must be kept in view. The special meaning contended for a particular word must have been understood as such by all those conversant with the trade, business or industry concerned, that is, by the class as a whole and not by a portion only, *viz.*, the management of the industry. Further, this general understanding and acceptance of a special meaning must have been in vogue at the time of the passing of the Act using the particular word for which that meaning is contended.[50] Because of these limitations of the rule, the House of Lords did not accept the contention that the phrase 'Permanent way' or 'Permanent way man' has a special meaning in the Railway Industry.[51] Evidence to show that a word has acquired a special meaning in the business or industry concerned is admissible.[52] It has been suggested that in dealing with economic and technological laws the court should have the benefit of expert advice in the shape of assessor evidence.[53] Further the opinion expressed by the relevant Government Department which is expected to have expert knowledge in the matter may be relied upon. So a non-statutory notification of the Ministry of Finance declaring *Dhania, Jeera, Postak* and *Methi* to be oil-seeds under section 14, item VI of the Central Sales Tax Act, 1956, was relied upon for holding that these articles are included in the expression 'oil-seeds'.[54]

In dealing with a question of Excise duty on 'refined oil', it was held that purification of raw oil in the process of manufacture of *Vanaspati*

---

48. *Ibid*, p. 119.

49. *Aswinikumar Ghose v. Arabinda Bose*, AIR 1952 SC 369, p. 373 : 1953 SCR 1; **See further** *In re, Lily Isabel Thomas*, AIR 1964 SC 855, p. 857 : 1964 (6) SCR 229.

50. *London & North Eastern Rly. Co. v. Berriman*, (1946) 1 All ER 255, p. 257 : 1946 AC 278 (HL).

51. *Ibid.*

52. *Ibid*, pp. 257, 260, 262, 266, 269; *Union of India v. Delhi Cloth & General Mills Co. Ltd.*, AIR 1963 SC 791 : 1963 Supp (1) SCR 586; *South Bihar Sugar Mills v. Union of India*, AIR 1968 SC 922 : 1968 (3) SCR 21. **See further** *Attorney-General v. Emily Moore*, AIR 1938 PC 238, p. 241 and cases in note 44, p. 121.

53. *Carew and Company Ltd. v. Union of India*, AIR 1975 SC 2260, pp. 2271, 2272 : (1975) 2 SCC 791.

54. *State of Orissa v. Dinabandhu Sahu and Sons*, AIR 1976 SC 1561 : 1977 SCC (Tax) 57 : (1976) 4 SCC 431. **See further** text and notes 46 to 52, pp. 382-384.

where deodorization is not done after hydrogenation does not at any stage transform the oil into refined oil as known to the consumers and commercial community because in commercial world oil is always deodorised before hydrogenation it is marketed as refined oil.[55] In reaching this conclusion the Supreme Court considered the evidence of manufacturers of refined oil and the specification of refined oil by the Indian Standards Institution. In similar context it was held that kiln gas produced by burning limestone and coke in a lime kiln and used in the manufacture of sugar by carbonisation process and of soda ash by solvay ammonia soda process is not 'carbondioxide' as known to the trade.[56] These cases were distinguished in a later case where it was held that uncut circles manufactured by rolling billets of copper alloys were liable to Excise duty as 'circles of any form'. It was pointed out that no evidence had been led to show that in commercial community uncut circles are not known as circles.[57] Similarly, commercial sense will not have much relevance in the context of goods which are not marketable, and in such cases, what will have to be seen, in the context of a tariff schedule, is whether the broad description of the article in question fits in with the expression used in the tariff.[58] For this reason 'properzi rods' were held to fall within the description of 'wire rods' in entry 27(a)(ii) of the first schedule to the Central Excises and Salt Act, 1944.[59] If the Legislature has itself adopted a technical term in a tariff schedule, then that entry has to be understood in the technical sense and an article falling within the ambit of the technical term cannot be relegated to the residuary entry.[60] On this reasoning the entry of 'Cellulose Ether' in the Central Excise Tariff Act, 1986 was held to include an article manufactured under the name 'Sodium Carboxymethye Cellulose' which was tested and found to be Cellulose Ether.[61]

In construing item 8 in the Schedule to the Minimum Wages Act, 1948, which reads 'Employment in stone breaking or stone crushing', it has been pointed out that the activity of stone breaking or stone crushing in commercial world means that activity by which common rock is reduced to fragments by mechanical means—such fragments being marketed and

55. *Union of India v. Delhi Cloth & General Mills Co. Ltd.*, AIR 1963 SC 791 : 1963 Supp (1) SCR 586.
56. *South Bihar Sugar Mills v. Union of India*, AIR 1968 SC 922 : 1968 (3) SCR 21.
57. *Union of India v. Ramlal Mansukhrai,* AIR 1971 SC 2333, p. 2335 : 1970 (2) SCC 472.
58. *Indian Aluminium Cables Ltd. v. Union of India*, (1985) 3 SCC 284, p. 291 : AIR 1985 SC 1201.
59. *Ibid.*
60. *Reliance Cellulose Products Ltd., Hyderabad v. CCE*, AIR 1997 SC 3414, p. 3419 : 1997 (5) JT 742 : (1997) 6 SCC 464.
61. *Ibid*, p. 3420 (AIR).

used for profit.[62] On this reasoning the incidental activity of breaking stones to get at manganese in a manganese mine has not been held to be stone breaking or stone crushing.[63] Similarly the removal of thick layers of limestone by breaking for reaching the thin layers which are cut into flooring stones and are marketed as such has also not been held to be stone breaking or stone crushing operation in commercial sense.[64]

The context may show that a word having a special meaning in commercial world has not been used in that sense. The word 'hank' in commercial world is understood to mean a coil of yarn of 840 yards in length but in certain notifications issued under the Central Excise Rules, 1944, it was construed in its ordinary sense to mean a coil of yarn not of any particular length.[65] The court interpreting tariff entries may have to consider both, trade meaning and dictionary meaning and adopt that meaning which is suited in the context.[66] Applying this method cigarette packets were held to be 'boxes' and not 'other packing containers' while interpreting tariff item 17(4) of the Central Excise and Salt Act 1944 which refers to 'boxes, cartons, bags and other packing containers'.[67]

(ii) *Legal sense of words.*—On the same principle when words acquire a technical meaning because of their consistent use by the Legislature in a particular sense or because of their authoritative construction by superior courts, they are understood in that sense when used in a similar context in subsequent legislation.[68] This is also sometimes referred to as the legal

---

62. *Labour Inspector, Central v. Chittapur Stone Quarrying Co. (Pvt.) Ltd.*, AIR 1972 SC 1177 : (1972) 3 SCC 605.

63. *Madhya Pradesh Mineral Industry Association, Nagpur v. Regional Labour Commissioner (Central), Jabalpur*, AIR 1960 SC 1068 : 1960 (3) SCR 476. **See further** *Mineral and Metals Trading Corpn. v. Union of India*, AIR 1972 SC 2551 : 1972 (2) SCC 620 and *Indian Hard Metals (P) Ltd. v. Union of India*, AIR 1979 SC 397 : (1979) 4 SCC 155, for meaning of 'Wolfram Ore' in commercial sense.

64. *Labour Inspector, Central v. Chittapur Stone Quarrying Co. (Pvt). Ltd., supra.*

65. *Cannanore Spinning & Weaving Mills Ltd. v. Collector of Customs & Central Excise, Cochin*, AIR 1970 SC 1950 : 1969 (3) SCC 112.

66. *CCE v. ITC Ltd.*, (2003) 3 SCC 379, p. 390 : AIR 2003 SC 1484 : (2003) 152 ELT 241.

67. *Ibid.*

68. *Her Highness Ruckmaboye v. Lulloobhoy Motichand*, (1851-52) 5 MIA 234, pp. 250, 260 (PC) (meaning of beyond the seas); *Commissioner for Special Purposes of Income-tax v. John Frederick Pemsel*, (1891-94) All ER Rep 28, p. 54 (HL) (meaning of 'charitable institution'); *State of Madras v. Gannon Dunkerly & Co.*, AIR 1958 SC 560, p. 573 : 1959 SCR 379 (meaning of 'Sale of goods'); *Diamond Sugar Mills v. State of U.P.*, AIR 1961 SC 652 : 1961 (3) SCR 242 (meaning of 'Local Area'); *Gordhandas Hargovindas v. Municipal Commissioner, Ahmedabad*, AIR 1963 SC 1742, p. 1749 : 1964 (2) SCR 608 (meaning of 'Rate'); *Diwan Brothers v. Central Bank*, AIR 1976 SC 1503, p. 1515 : (1976) 3 SCC 800 (Decree should be

[Footnote No. 68 Contd.]

sense of such words.[69] When a word has acquired a special connotation in law, dictionaries cease to be helpful in interpreting that word.[70] The context may, however, show that the Legislature intended to use the word in its literal sense and not in its legal sense.[71]

In construing the words 'beyond the seas' and in holding that the said words have acquired a technical meaning and are synonymous in legal import with the words 'out of the realm' or 'out of territories'. SIR JOHN JERVIS speaking for the Judicial Committee of Privy Council said: "These words 'beyond the seas' are of extensive application in the law, many ancient rights being saved by the common law to persons 'beyond the seas'. It is, therefore, of considerable importance to ascertain what has been deemed to be the legal import and meaning of them, because, if it shall appear that they have long been used, in a sense which may not improperly be called technical, and have been judicially construed to have a certain meaning, and have been adopted by the Legislature in that sense long prior to the statute, the rule of construction of statutes will require that the words in the Statute should be construed according to the sense in which they had been so previously used, although that sense may vary from the strict literal meaning of them".[72]

As stated by LORD MACNAGHTEN: "In construing Acts of Parliament, it is a general rule, that words must be taken in their legal sense unless the contrary intention appears".[73] The words 'charitable institution' have thus

---

[Footnote No. 68 Contd.]

understood as defined in CPC) *Shah v. Barnet London Borough Council*, (1983) 1 All ER 226, pp. 233, 234 (HL) (meaning of ordinarily resident in United Kingdom); *Thampanoor Ravi v. Charupara Ravi*, JT 1999 (7) SC 231, pp. 244, 245 : AIR 1999 SC 3309, p. 3316 : (1999) 8 SCC 74 (The expression 'undischarged insolvent' has acquired a technical meaning in law). Meaning well accepted in law is to be preferred to natural meaning: **See** *Duckering v. Gollan*, (1965) 2 All ER 115, p. 120 (HL) (Letter G).

69. *Commissioner for Special Purposes of Income-tax v. John Frederick Pemsel, supra*, p. 54; *State of Madras v. Gannon Dunkerley & Co. supra*, p. 573; *Thampanoor Ravi v. Charupara Ravi, supra*.

70. *State of Punjab v. Inder Singh*, JT 1997 (8) SC 466, p. 479 : AIR 1998 SC 7 : (1997) 8 SCC 372. (The word 'deputation' has a different connotation in service law and dictionary meaning is of no help); *Thampanoor Ravi v. Charupara Ravi, supra*.

71. **See** text and notes 87 to 89, p. 129.

72. *H.H. Ruckmaboye v. Lulloobhoy Motichand*, (1851-52) 5 MIA 234, p. 250 : 8 Moo PC 4 (PC). **Referred** in *Keshavji Ravji and Co. v. Commissioner of Income tax*, AIR 1991 SC 1806, p. 1813 : (1990) 2 SCC 231.

73. *Commissioner for Special Purposes of Income-tax v. John Frederick Pemsel*, (1891-94) All ER Rep 28, p. 54 : (1891) AC 531 (HL); **referred** to in *Chesterman v. Federal Commissioner of Taxation*, (1926) AC 128, p. 131 (PC); *Laurence Arthur Adamson v. Melbourne & Metropolitan Board of Works*, AIR 1929 PC 181, p. 182.

a technical meaning and it has been held that 'Lost Dogs Home' is such an institution.[74]

Similarly, the words, 'Judgment' and 'Final Order' have acquired a technical meaning. 'Judgment' means "the declaration or final determination of the rights of the parties in the matter brought before the court" and 'Final Order' means "an order which finally determines the rights of the parties and brings the case to end".[75] These words were given the same meaning by the Privy Council in construing section 109 of the Code of Civil Procedure, 1908;[76] by the Federal Court in construing section 205 of the Government of India Act of 1935;[77] and by the Supreme Court in construing Articles 133 and 134 of the Constitution.[78] A decision arrived at in the consultative jurisdiction of the High Court was therefore held not to be a judgment or final order within the meaning of clause 39 of the Letters Patent (Bombay), or clause 31 of the Letters Patent (Patna).[79]

In construing the expression 'taxes on sale of goods' as they occur in entry 48, List II, Government of India Act, 1935, the Supreme Court

---

74. *Laurence Arthur Adamson v. Malbourne & Metropolitan Board of Works, supra.*
N.B.—The definition of 'Charitable purpose' under the Indian Income-tax Legislation is not identical with definition of 'Charity' formulated in *Pemsel's* case, *supra*; **see** *CIT v. Andhra Chamber of Commerce, Madras*, AIR 1965 SC 1281, p. 1287 : 1965 (1) SCR 565; *Lokshikshan Trust v. CIT, Mysore*, AIR 1976 SC 10; *Indian Chamber of Commerce v. CIT, West Bengal*, AIR 1976 SC 348 : 1976 SCC (Tax) 41 : (1976) 1 SCC 324. **See further** *Municipal Corporation Delhi v. Children Book Trust*, AIR 1992 SC 1456 : 1992 (3) SCC 390 (Society running school when entitled to exemption from tax under the Delhi Municipal Corporation Act,1957).

75. *S. Kuppuswami Rao v. King*, AIR 1949 FC 1, pp. 3, 4. For meaning of 'final order' **see also** *Haron Bin Mohd. Zaid v. Central Securities (Holdings) Ltd.*, (1982) 2 All ER 481 (PC).

76. *Ramchand Manjimal v. Goverdhandas etc.*, AIR 1920 PC 86 : 47 IA 124.

77. *S. Kuppuswami Rao v. King, supra*, pp. 3, 4.

78. *Sardar Syedna Taher Saifuddin v. State of Bombay*, AIR 1958 SC 253, p. 255 : 1958 SCR 1010; *Jethanand & Sons v. State of U.P.*, AIR 1961 SC 794, p. 795 : 1961 (3) SCR 754; *State of U.P. v. Sujan Singh, (Col.)*, AIR 1964 SC 1897, p. 1901 : 1964 (7) SCR 734. **See further** *Petlad Turkey Red Dye Works Co. Ltd. v. Commissioner of Income-tax, Bombay*, AIR 1963 SC 1484, pp. 1486, 1487; *Samarendra Nath Sinha v. Krishna Kumar Nag*, AIR 1967 SC 1440, p. 1442 : 1967 (2) SCR 18. For meaning of 'judgment' in Letters Patents **see also** *Employer in Relation to Management of Central Mine Panning and Design Institute Ltd. v. Union of India,* AIR 2001 SC 883 : (2001) 2 SCC 588.

79. *Tata Iron & Steel Co. v. Chief Revenue Authority of Bombay*, AIR 1923 PC 148; *Delhi Cloth & General Mills Co. Ltd. v. CIT, Delhi*, AIR 1927 PC 242; *Premchand Satramdas v. State of Bihar*, AIR 1951 SC 14 : 1950 SCR 799; *Petlad Turkey Red Dye Works Co. Ltd. v. Commissioner of Income-tax*, AIR 1963 SC 1484, pp. 1486, 1487 : 1963 Supp (1) SCR 871; *Thomas (Arthur) v. Queen*, (1979) 2 All ER 142, p. 149 (PC); For meaning of *Letters Patent* **see** *P.V. Hemalatha v. Kattamkandi Puthiya Maliackal Saheeda,* AIR 2002 SC 2445, p. 2457 : (2002) 5 SCC 548.

rejected the argument that supply of materials under a building contract amounts to sale and held that the words 'sale of goods' have been used in the entry in the legal sense which comprises of two essentials (i) agreement to sell movable for a price and (ii) property passing therein pursuant to that agreement. VENKATARAMA AIYER, J., explaining the principle of construction observed: "The ratio of the rule of interpretation that words of legal import occurring in a statute should be construed in their legal sense is that those words have, in law, acquired a definite and precise sense and that, accordingly, the legislative must be taken to have intended that they should be understood in that sense. In interpreting an expression used in a legal sense, therefore, we have only to ascertain the precise connotation which it possesses in law".[80] The rule stated above was applied in construing the expression 'undischarged insolvent' in Article 191(1)(c) of the Constitution.[81] It was held that the said expression has acquired a legal sense in the law of insolvency meaning a person adjudged insolvent by the Insolvency court and not discharged by the Court under the Insolvency Act, and it is this meaning which is to be applied to that expression in

80. *State of Madras v. Gannon Dunkerly & Co.*, AIR 1958 SC 560, p. 573 : 1959 SCR 379. **See further** *Esso Petroleum Ltd. v. Commissioner of Customs and Excise*, (1976) 1 All ER 117, p. 133 (HL); *Everest Copiers v. State of Tamil Nadu*, 1996 (5) Scale 533 : AIR 1996 SC 2662 (making of photocopies is a contract of work and labour and not sale of goods); *Hindusthan Shipyard Ltd. v. State of Andhra Pradesh*, JT 2000 (8) SC 29 : AIR 2000 SC 2411 : (2000) 6 SCC 579 (manufacture and supply of ships held to be 'sale' and not 'works contract'); *State of A.P. v. Kone Elevators India Ltd.*, (2005) 3 SCC 389 (supply of lift by the manufacturer who brought it in a knocked down condition and installed it at the site kept ready by the customer was held to be sale and not 'works contract').

Note.—The Constitution 46th Amendment Act, 1982 added clause (29A), in Article 366 to widen the meaning of 'tax on sale or purchase of goods' and now sales tax can be levied on the value of building material used in execution of a works contract even in a single and indivisible contract (*Builders Association of India v. Union of India*, AIR 1989 SC 1371 : (1989) 2 SCC 645; *Builders Association of India v. State of Karnataka*, AIR 1993 SC 991) : (1993) 1 SCC 409; *State of U.P. v. PNC Construction Co. Ltd.*, (2007) 7 SCC 320 (paras 22 and 26), or on the supply of food and drinks by Hoteliers and Restaurant holders (*K. Damodaraswamy Naidu and Bros. v. State of Tamil Nadu*, AIR 1999 SC 3909 : (2000) 1 SCC 521) or on the transfer of right to use any goods (*20th Century Finance Corporation v. State of Maharashtra*, JT 2000 (7) SC 177 : AIR 2000 SC 2436 : (2000) 6 SCC 12; *State of U.P. v. Union of India*, (2003) 3 SCC 239 : AIR 2003 SC 1147), or on the sale of Electricity (*State of A.P. v. National Thermal Power Corporation of India*, AIR 2002 SC 1895 : (2002) 5 SCC 203) or on the supply of telephone connection (*State of Uttar Pradesh v. Union of India*, AIR 2003 SC 1147 : (2003) 3 SCC 239). Sales under the compulsion of a statute are also exigible to sales tax; *Food Corporation of India v. State of Kerala*, AIR 1997 SC 1252 : (1997) 3 SCC 410.

81. *Thampanoor Ravi v. Charupara Ravi*, JT 1999 (7) SC 231, pp. 244, 245 : AIR 1999 SC 3309, p. 3316 : (1999) 8 SCC 74.

Article 191(1)(c) and not the general sense of a person who is in impecunious circumstances unable to repay his debts.[82]

Similarly in dealing with section 73 of the Bombay Municipal Boroughs Act, 1925 which authorises a municipality to impose 'a rate on buildings or lands', the Supreme Court held that the word 'rate' should be construed in a technical sense because it had acquired a special meaning to connote a tax imposed by local authorities on the annual value which is arrived at by one of three modes namely: (i) actual rent fetched, (ii) where it is not let, rent based on hypothetical tenancy and (iii) where either of these two modes is not available by valuation based on capital value.[83] It was further held that the rate could not be imposed at a percentage of capital value though it could be imposed on a percentage of annual value derived from capital value.[84] For the same reason a rate on land and buildings cannot be levied on a flat rate method according to floor area[85] or on machinery situated on the building.[86]

And in construing item 2 of Schedule III to the Payment of Bonus Act, 1965, it was observed that the words 'working funds' when used in the context of a banking company must be understood in the technical sense which they have acquired in that context. Reference in this connection was made to Sen Award of 1949 and Sastri Award of 1953. The words 'working funds' were therefore, construed to mean 'paid-up capital, reserves and average of the deposits for 52 weeks of each year for which weekly returns of deposits are submitted to the Reserve Bank of India'.[87]

But the intention of the Legislature may not be to use a word or expression having a legal meaning in that sense and to use it in its natural or literal sense. Section 32 of the Race Relations Act, 1976 (U.K.) provides that acts of racial discrimination done by a person 'in the course of his employment' shall be treated as done by his employer as well as by him, whether or not it was done with the employer's knowledge or approval. The words 'in the course of employment' have a technical or legal meaning in the tort law relating to vicarious responsibility. But that meaning of the words in section 32 would have severely restricted its operation and largely frustrated the object of the Act to prevent racial discrimination.

---

82. *Ibid.*

83. *Gordhandas Hargovindas v. Municipal Commissioner, Ahmedabad*, AIR 1963 SC 1742, p. 1749 : 1964 (2) SCR 608; **followed** in *Godhara Borough Municipality, Godhara v. Godhara Electricity Co. Ltd.*, AIR 1968 SC 1504 : 1968 (3) SCR 481.

84. *Ibid.*

85. *New Manak Chowk Spg. and Wvg. Mills Co. Ltd. v. Municipal Corporation of the City of Ahmedabad,* AIR 1967 SC 1801 : (1967) 2 SCR 679.

86. *Ibid; Krishna Mohan (P.) Ltd. v. Municipal Corporation of Delhi,* (2003) 7 SCC 151 : AIR 2003 SC 2935.

87. *Workmen of National and Grindlays Bank Ltd. v. National and Grindlays Bank Ltd.*, AIR 1976 SC 611, p. 621 : (1976) 1 SCC 925.

Therefore in interpreting section 32 the words in question were given their natural everyday meaning.[88] Similarly the word 'consideration' which has a technical meaning in contract law was construed to be used not in that sense but in a broad sense in Section 25(a) of the Greater London Council (General Powers) Act, 1978.[89] The section defines 'use as temporary sleeping accommodation' to mean also 'use for a consideration and arising by reason of the employment of the occupant'. The purpose of the legislation was plainly to enable the planning authority to control short term transitory occupation by employees and their families visiting London. This purpose would have been frustrated if planning authority was required to consider in each case whether the occupation was linked to some contractual obligation of the person using the flat so as to be 'consideration' for it in the contractual sense. It was, therefore, held that the word 'consideration' was not used in that sense but in a broad sense and it was sufficient that the flat was used 'by the reason of' or 'on account of' the existence of employment relationship.[90]

3. REGARD TO SUBJECT AND OBJECT

(a) General

As stated earlier[91] and as approved by the Supreme Court: "The words of a statute, when there is doubt about their meaning, are to be understood in the sense in which they best harmonise with the subject of the enactment and the object which the Legislature has in view. Their meaning is found not so much in a strict grammatical or etymological propriety of language, nor even in its popular use, as in the subject or in the occasion on which they are used, and the object to be attained".[92] The courts have

---

88. *Jones v. Tower Boot Co. Ltd.*, (1997) 2 All ER 406 : (1997) 1 RLR 168 (CA).

89. *R. v. Kensington and Chelsea Royal London Borough Council,* (1999) 3 All ER 929 (HL).

90. *Ibid,* pp. 931, 934.

91. **See** Chapter 1, title 2 'Intention of the Legislature', text and notes 59 to 71, pp. 15 to 17.

92. *Workmen of Dimakuchi Tea Estate v. Management of Dimakuchi Tea Estate*, AIR 1958 SC 353, p. 356 : 1958 SCR 1156; *State of U.P. v. C. Tobit*, AIR 1958 SC 414, p. 416 : 1958 SCR 1275; *Santasingh v. State of Punjab*, AIR 1976 SC 2386, p. 2389: 1976 SCC (Cri) 546 : (1976) 4 SCC 190; *Mukesh K. Tripathi v. Senior Divisional Manager*, (2004) 8 SCC 387, p. 401 : AIR 2004 SC 4179.

N.B.—This passage in the Supreme Court Cases is taken from MAXWELL on Statutes, 11th Edition, p. 51, 12th Edition, p. 76 which is based on the dictum of ABBOT, C.J. in *R. v. Hall*, (1822) 107 ER 47, p. 51, and which was cited with **approval** by LORD ROMILLY in *Lion*, (1869) 16 ER 688, p. 691 (PC). Similar language is used in Broom's Legal Maxims, pp. 466, 467 which is **referred** to in *Ashok Singh v. Assistant Controller of Estate Duty*, AIR 1992 SC 1756, p. 1761 : 1992 (3) SCC 169 : (1992) 196 ITR 160.

declined "to be bound by the letter, when it frustrates the patent purposes of the statute".[93] In the words of SHAH, J., "It is a recognised rule of interpretation of statutes that expressions used therein should ordinarily be understood in a sense in which they best harmonise with the object of the statute, and which effectuate the object of the Legislature".[94] Therefore, when two interpretations are feasible the court will prefer that which advances the remedy and suppresses the mischief as the Legislature envisioned.[95] The Court should adopt an object oriented approach keeping in mind the principle that legislative futility is to be ruled out so long as interpretative possibility permits.[96] The object oriented approach, however, cannot be carried to the extent of doing violence to the plain lauguage used by rewriting the section or substituting words in place of the actual words used by the Legislature.[97]

---

93. *Cabell v. Markham*, 148 F 2d 737 (2d Cir 1945), (Judge Learned HAND).

94. *New India Sugar Mills Ltd. v. Commissioner of Sales Tax, Bihar*, AIR 1963 SC 1207, p. 1213 : 1963 Supp (2) SCR 459; **see further** *Kanwar Singh v. Delhi Administration*, AIR 1965 SC 871 : (1965) 1 SCR 7; *Deputy Custodian, v. Official Receiver*, AIR 1965 SC 951, pp. 956, 957: 1965 (1) SCR 220; *Motor Owners Insurance Co. Ltd. v. J.K. Modi*, AIR 1981 SC 2059, p. 2065 : (1981) 4 SCC 660; *Ambica Quarry Works v. State of Gujarat*, (1987) 1 SCC 213, p. 221 : AIR 1987 SC 1073; *Kameshwar Singh Srivastava v. IV. Addl. District Judge, Lucknow*, AIR 1987 SC 138, p. 141 : 1987 (1) SCR 224; *Municipal Corporation of Greater Bombay v. Indian Oil Corporation*, AIR 1991 SC 686, p. 689 : 1991 Supp (2) SC 18; *N.K. Jain v. C.K. Shah*, AIR 1991 SC 1289, pp. 1304, 1305 : 1991 (2) SCC 495; *K. Veeraswamy v. Union of India*, (1991) 3 SCC 655, p. 702 : 1991 (3) JT 198; *Land Acquisition Officer and Mandal Revenue Officer v. Narsaiah*, JT 2001 (3) SC 157, p. 161 : (2001) 3 SCR 530 : AIR 2001 SC 1177.

95. *Carew & Company v. Union of India*, AIR 1975 SC 2260, p. 2270 : (1975) 2 SCC 791; *State of Haryana v. Sampuran Singh*, AIR 1975 SC 1952, pp. 1955, 1957 : (1975) 2 SCC 810. [In *Sampuran Singh's* case, the court **reiterated** what it had said in *Amarsingh's* case AIR 1974 SC 994, p. 996 : (1974) 2 SCC 70 that if the constitutionally envisioned socio-economic revolution is not to be a paper tiger, agrarian laws have to be meaningfully enacted, interpreted and executed and the court is not the anti hero in the drama of limping land reform]. *Glaxo Laboratories (I) Ltd. v. Presiding Officer, Labour Court, Meerut*, (1984) 1 SCC 1, p. 9 : AIR 1984 SC 505; *Reserve Bank of India v. Peerless General Finance and Investment Co. Ltd.*, 1996 (1) Scale 13 at p. 15: AIR 1996 SC 646, p. 655 (Para 22) : (1996) (1) SCC 642; *A-One Granites v. State of U.P.*, AIR 2001 SC 1203, p. 1209; *The Mor Modern Co-operative Transport Society Ltd. v. Financial Commissioner and Secretary to Govt. of Haryana*, AIR 2002 SC 2513, p. 2518 : (2002) 6 SCC 269; *Bipinchandra Parshottamdas Patel v. State of Gujarat*, (2003) 4 SCC 642, pp. 657, 658 : AIR 2003 SC 2256.

96. *Busching Schmitz Private Ltd. v. P.T. Menghani*, AIR 1977 SC 1569, pp. 1575, 1576 : 1977 (2) SCC 835; *S.P. Jain v. Krishan Mohan Gupta*, (1987) 1 SCC 191, p. 201 : AIR 1987 SC 222. **See further** *Nath Devi v. Radha Devi*, (2005) 2 SCC 271, p. 277.

97. *CIT v. Budhraja and Company*, AIR 1993 SC 2529, p. 2535 : 1994 Supp (1) SCC 280 : (1993) 204 ITR 412.

Having regard to the object of the U.P. Bhoodan Yagna Act, 1953 to implement the *Bhoodan* movement, which aimed at distribution of land to landless labourers who were versed in agriculture and who had no other means of subsistence, it was held that the expression 'landless persons' in section 14, which made provision for grant of land to landless persons, was limited to landless labourers as described above and did not include a landless businessman residing in a city.[1]

Similarly, in section 2(k) of the Industrial Disputes Act, 1947 which reads, "'Industrial dispute' means any dispute or difference between employers and employees or between employers and workmen, or between workmen and workmen which is connected with the employment or non-employment or the terms of employment or with the conditions of labour, of any person," the expression 'any person' was construed, having regard to the scheme and object of the Act, to be subject to two crucial limitations: "(1) The dispute must be a real dispute between the parties to the dispute so as to be capable of settlement or adjudication by one party to the dispute giving necessary relief to the other, and (2) the person regarding whom the dispute is raised must be one in whose employment, non-employment, terms of employment, or conditions of labour the parties to the dispute have a direct or substantial interest.[2]

This principle was also used in the interpretation of section 17(1-A) of the Employees' Provident Funds and Miscellaneous Provisions Act, 1952, which provides that where an exemption has been granted to an establishment under section 17(1)(a) of the Act, the provisions of sections 6, 7-A, 8 and 14-B shall, 'so far as may be', apply to the employer of the exempted establishment. Section 14-B of the Act provides for recovery of damages from an employer who defaults in the payment of any contribution under the Act. The Supreme Court held that the Act is a social welfare and remedial legislation, and if there is any doubt, the same should be resolved in favour of the class of persons for whose benefit the statute is enacted. Hence, a purposive approach which will promote the purposes of the Act was adopted for construing section 17(1-A) of the Act, and it was accordingly held that in case of default by the employer of an exempted establishment in making its contribution to the provident fund, section 14-B of the Act will be applicable.[3]

---

1. *U.P. Bhoodan Yagna Samiti v. Braj Kishore*, AIR 1988 SC 2239 : 1988 (4) SCC 274.
2. *Workmen of Dimakuchi Tea Estate v. Management of Dimakuchi Tea Estate*, AIR 1958 SC 353, p. 364 : 1958 SCR 1156. **See further** *Workmen v. Dharampal Premchand (Saugandhi)*, (1965) 3 SCR 394 : AIR 1966 SC 182; *J.H. Jadhav v. Forbes Gokak Ltd.*, (2005) 3 SCC 202, p. 205 : AIR 2005 SC 998.
3. *Regional Provident Fund Commissioner v. Hooghly Mills Company Ltd. & Ors.*, (2012) 2 SCC 489, pp. 499 to 506.

Similarly, applying the rule of purposive interpretation, the catering department of a club, which prepares and serves/supplies food to members of a club was held to be an an 'eating house' under section 3(ff) the Mumbai Municipal Corporation Act, 1888, as even though the primary activity of the club was to provide sporting facilities, the supply of food was an integral part of such activity.[4]

In interpreting section 235(2) of the Code of Criminal Procedure, 1973, which provides that "if the accused is convicted, the Judge shall hear the accused on the question of sentence and then pass sentence on him according to law", the Supreme Court held that the section was mandatory and that it was not confined to hearing oral submissions, but was also intended to give an opportunity to the prosecution and the accused to place before the court facts and material relating to various factors bearing on the question of sentence, and if they are contested by either side, then to produce evidence for the purpose of establishing the same. This conclusion was reached having regard to the object of Parliament in enacting section 235(2) to bring the law in conformity with the modern trends in penology and sentencing procedure.[5]

While interpreting section 319, CrPC, its plain language and object, which is that the real culprit should not go unpunished, was relied on by a Constitution Bench of the Supreme Court to hold that the Court can exercise its power to summon a person other than the accused under this provision. The Court further held that even though a person may not be named in the FIR or in the charge-sheet, or though named in the FIR, has not been named in the main part of the charge-sheet, but in Column 2 thereof, and against whom cognizance has not been taken, such person can also be summoned under section 319, CrPC. However, a person who has been discharged cannot be summoned directly under this provision without taking recourse to sections 300(5) and 398 of the CrPC.[6]

In dealing with section 19 of the Delhi Rent Control Act, 1958 which obliges the landlord to occupy the premises from which he evicts a tenant on the ground of his *bona fide* need under section 14 and prohibits him to re-let it, the Supreme Court held that the section was applicable to premises of which possession is obtained by the landlord under section 14A on the ground that he is required to vacate the premises allotted to him by the

---

4. *Brihanmumbai Mahanagarpalika & Anr. v. Willingdon Sports Club & Ors.*, (2013) 16 SCC 260, p. 274.

5. *Santa Singh v. State of Punjab*, AIR 1976 SC 2386 : 1976 SCC (Cri) 546. **See further** *Ram Deo Chauhan v State of Assam,* AIR 2001 SC 2231, p. 2235 : (2001) 5 SCC 714.

6. *Hardeep Singh v. State of Punjab & Ors.*, (2014) 3 SCC 92.

Government. This result was reached having regard to the object of sections 19 and 14A and to avoid any obvious lacuna.[7] The Supreme Court has observed that the object of rent law is to balance the competing claims of the landlord, on the one hand, to recover possession of the building let out to the tenant, and of the tenant, on the other hand, to be protected against arbitrary increase of rent or arbitrary eviction when there is acute shortage of accommodation, and that though it is for the Legislature to resolve such competing claims in terms of statutory provisions, the object of the Act has to be kept in view by the Court. It was accordingly held that mere use of the present tense in section 12(3) of the UP Urban Buildings (Regulation of Letting, Rent and Eviction) Act, 1972, is not intended to limit the applicability of the provision to acquisition of accommodation by the tenant after the Act becomes applicable, but also covers a situation where the tenant has acquired alternative accommodation before the Act became applicable.[8]

Section 23 of the Representation of the People Act, 1951 permits 'inclusion of the names in the electoral roll till the last date for making nominations' for an election in the concerned constituency. Section 33(1) of the Representation of the People Act, 1951 specifies that the nomination paper shall be presented 'between the hours of 11 O'clock in the forenoon and 3 O'clock in the afternoon'. Reading these provisions together in the light of the object behind them, the Supreme Court construed the words 'last date' in section 23 of the 1951 Act as follows: "If the purpose of the provision were to illumine its sense, if the literality of the text is to be invigorated by a sense of rationality, if conscionable commonsense were an attribute of statutory construction, there can hardly be any doubt that the expression 'last date for making nominations' must mean the last hour of the last date during which presentation of nomination papers is permitted under section 33 of the 1951 Act".[9]

Section 40(1) of the Gujarat Municipalities Act, 1963 empowers the authorised officer to suspend a President or Vice-President 'who has been detained in a prison during trial under the provision of any law for the time being in force'. Having regard to the object of the Act to enable smooth functioning of the municipality and to keep shady characters away the words in section 40(1) were not given a restricted meaning to limit the

---

7. *Busching Schmitz Private Ltd. v. P.T. Menghani*, AIR 1977 SC 1569, p. 1577 : 1977 (2) SCC 835.

8. *Siddharth Viyas v. Ravi Nath Misra & Ors.*, (2015) 2 SCC 701, pp. 704, 705, 709, 710.

9. *Narendra Madivalapa Kheni v. Manikrao Patil*, AIR 1977 SC 2171, p. 2180 : (1977) 4 SCC 16.

detention in prison after charge is framed and were given a wider meaning to permit suspension even when detention in prison was during investigation by police.[10]

Under section 8(3) of the Representation of the People Act, 1951 'a person convicted of any offence and sentenced to imprisonment for not less than two years' is disqualified for being chosen as and for being a member of the Legislature of a State. Having regard to the object that the provision was meant to prevent persons with criminal background from entering the legislature, the expression 'a person convicted of any offence' was construed as 'all offences of which a person has been charged and held guilty at one trial' and the expression 'sentenced to imprisonment for not less than 2 years' was required to be calculated by taking the total term of imprisonment for which the person has been sentenced. Thus a person who is sentenced for two offences in one trial but is not sentenced for any of the offences to a sentence of more than 2 years will still be disqualified if the total sentence of imprisonment for the two offences to run consecutively exceeds 2 years.[11] For the same reason section 8(4) of the Act, which suspends the disqualification, when a person is a member of the Legislature at the time when he is sentenced, for a period of three months and till the disposal of his appeal or revision if it is filed within that period, has been held not to apply after the person ceases to be a member of the Legislature or the House is dissolved.[12]

Section 8 of the Police and Criminal Evidence Act, 1984 empowers a Justice of the Peace to issue a warrant authorising a police constable to enter and search premises for material likely to be of evidential value in relation to a serious arrestable offence and to seize and retain such material. Items subject to legal privilege are expressly excluded from the ambit of material which may be the subject-matter of such a warrant. The expression 'items subject to legal privilege' is defined in section 10(1) of the Police and Criminal Evidence Act, 1984 in short to mean communications between a professional legal adviser and his client when in possession of a person who is entitled to possession. Section 10(2) of the Police and Criminal Evidence Act, 1984, however, provides that "items held with the intention of furthering a criminal purpose are not subject to legal privilege". The question before the House of Lords,[13] which gave rise to a sharp divergence of opinion, was as to whose intention the expression 'with the

10. *Bipinchandra Parshottamdas Patel v. State of Gujarat,* (2003) 4 SCC 642 : AIR 2003 SC 2256 : (2003) 4 SCC 642.

11. *K. Prabhakaran v. P. Jayarajan*, (2005) 1 SCC 754, p. 783 : AIR 2005 SC 688.

12. *Ibid.*, pp. 781, 782.

13. *Francis & Francis (a firm) v. Central Criminal Court*, (1988) 3 All ER 775 (HL).

intention of furthering a criminal purpose' contained in section 10(2) referred to. Did it refer to the intention of any person including the holder? The communications protected as items of legal privilege are generally in possession of solicitors who rarely have the intention of furthering a criminal purpose. The purpose of the Act was to give the police the power with the authorisation of a judicial authority to search for and seize material likely to be of evidential value. Therefore, if the intention of furthering a criminal purpose in section 10(2) referred only to the intention of the holder that would do little to assist in achieving the purpose of the Act. Whereas if the intention referred to therein embraced the intention of any person that would promote the purpose of the Act and would prevent the legal privilege being used to protect the perpetrators of serious crimes. On these considerations essentially, the majority[14] in the House of Lords held that the intention referred to in section 10(2) embraced the intention of any person including the holder. The minority,[15] on the other hand, adopted the ordinary grammatical meaning and were of the view that the words "items held with the intention of furthering a criminal purpose" as occurring in section 10(2) of the Police and Criminal Evidence Act, 1984 referred only to the intention of the holder.

Section 20-A(3) of the Ancient Monuments and Archaeological Sites and Remains Act, 1958, provides that in a case where the Central Government or the Director General, as the case may be, is satisfied that -

(a) it is necessary or expedient for carrying out such public work or any other project essential to the public; or

(b) such other work or project, in its opinion, shall not have any substantial adverse impact on the preservation, safety, security of, or access to, the monument or its immediate surrounding,

it or he may, notwithstanding anything contained in sub-section (2), in exceptional cases, and having regard to the public interest, by order and for reasons to be recorded in writing, permit such public work or project essential to the public or other constructions, to be carried out in a prohibited area.

The Supreme Court held that the expression 'such other work or project' in section 20-A(3)(b) has to be interpreted keeping in view the mandate of Article 49 of the Constitution and the objects sought to be achieved by enacting the 1958 Act *i.e.,* preservation of ancient and historical monuments, archaeological sites and remains of national importance. 'Public interest'

---

14. *Ibid.* (LORD BRANDON, LORD GRIFFITH and LORD GOFF).
15. *Ibid.* (LORD BRIDGE and LORD OLIVER).

must be the core factor to be considered by the Central Government or the Director General before allowing any construction and in no case construction should be allowed if the same adversely affects the ancient and historical monuments or archaeological sites.[16]

The Court, while interpreting Rule 100(2) of the Central Motor Vehicles Rules, 1989, which provides that the glass of the windscreen and rear window of every motor vehicle shall be such, and shall be maintained in such a condition, that the visual transmission of light is not less than 70%, and on side windows, not less than 50%, and shall conform to Indian Standards [IS: 2553 – Part 2 – 1992], held that the use of black films of any density on the windscreen and windows of a motor vehicle is impermissible. By relying on the objects and reasons of the Act the Court reasoned that the legislative intent attached due significance to 'public safety', and an interpretation which would serve this legislative intent and the object of framing such Rules should be adopted.[17]

The Supreme Court rejected the contention that section 126 of the Electricity Act, 2003, which deals with assessment with respect to unauthorized usage of electricity, has to be given strict and textual construction, and preferred an effective and purposive interpretation. Explanation (b) to the section defines the term 'unauthorised use of electricity' and uses the word 'means'. The Supreme Court held that it cannot be stated as an absolute proposition of law that usage of the term 'means' in a provision would inevitably render that provision exhaustive and limited. The purpose of section 126 is to put an implied restriction on unauthorised consumption of electricity. In light thereof, the phrase 'unauthorised use of electricity' cannot be restricted to the stated causes under Explanation (b), but has to be given a wider meaning so as to cover cases of violation of the terms and conditions of supply, the Regulations and the provisions of the 2003 Act governing such supply.[18]

In the context of the Customs Act, 1962, the Supreme Court held that the provisions of section 129A(5), empowering the Tribunal to condone the delay and admit an appeal filed beyond the prescribed period, would also apply to an application under section 129D(4) of the Act, as the Court must give effect to the purpose and object of the section. Section 129D(4) of the Act provides that where an application is made by the Commissioner

---

16. *Archaeological Survey of India v. Narender Anand & Ors.*, (2012) 2 SCC 562, pp. 581, 582.

17. *Avishek Goenka v. Union of India and Another,* (2012) 5 SCC 321, pp. 328, 329, 331.

18. *Executive Engineer, Southern Electricity Supply Co. of Orissa Ltd. & Anr. v. Sri Seetaram Rice Mill,* (2012) 2 SCC 108, pp. 120, 121, 133, 134.

to the Appellate Tribunal in pursuance of an order under Section 129D(1), such application shall be heard by the Tribunal as if it were an appeal made against the decision or order of the Adjudicating Authority, and the provisions regarding appeals under Section 129A shall, insofar as they are applicable, apply to such an application.[19]

The same expression used in two different enactments in similar context may have different meanings having regard to the object of each enactment. This is illustrated by the construction of the expression 'interlocutory order' in section 397(2) of the Code of Criminal Procedure, 1973, and section 11 of the Special Courts Act, 1979. In the former it is understood in a strict sense but in the latter, in a wide sense having regard to the object of speedy trial.[20]

It has already been seen that even ordinarily the meaning of a word is not to be taken in abstract but regard must be had to the setting in which the word occurs as also to the subject-matter and object of the enactment. However, in case of doubt these factors gain great prominence in selecting the true meaning out of the rival interpretations which may be reasonably open.

(b) Rule in *Heydon's* case; purposive construction: mischief rule

When the material words are capable of bearing two or more constructions the most firmly established rule for construction of such words "of all statutes in general (be they penal or beneficial, restrictive or enlarging of the common law)" is the rule laid down in *Heydon's* case[21] which has now attained the status of a 'classic'.[22] The rule which is also known as 'purposive construction' or 'mischief rule',[23] enables consideration of four matters in construing an Act: (i) What was the law before the making of the Act, (ii) What was the mischief or defect for which the law did not provide, (iii) What is the remedy that the Act has provided, and (iv) What is the reason of the remedy. The rule then directs that the courts must adopt that construction which "shall suppress the mischief and advance the remedy". The rule was explained in the *Bengal Immunity Co. v. State of Bihar*[24] by S.R. DAS, C.J.I. as follows,

---

19. *Thakker Shipping Pvt. Ltd. v. Commissioner of Customs (General)*, (2012) 12 SCC 189, pp. 194 to 196.

20. *V.C. Shukla v. State*, AIR 1980 SC 962 : 1980 SCC (Cri) 695 : 1980 Supp SCC 92.

21. (1584) 3 Co. Rep. 7a, p. 7b : 76 ER 637.

22. *Kanailal Sur v. Paramnidhi Sadhukhan*, AIR 1957 SC 907, p. 910 : 1958 SCR 360.

23. *Anderton v. Ryan*, (1985) 2 All ER 355, p. 359 (HL). The Law Commission (U.K.) in 1969 **disapproved** of the term 'mischief' being archaic and preferred a 'purposive' approach to construction : CROSS: "Statutory Interpretation", 3rd Edition, pp. 17, 18.

24. AIR 1955 SC 661, p. 674 : 1955 (2) SCR 603, **see further** *CIT, Patiala v. Shahzada Nand & Sons*, AIR 1966 SC 1342, p. 1347 : 1966 (3) SCR 379; *Sanghvi Jeevraj*

[Footnote No. 24 Contd.]

"It is a sound rule of construction of a statute firmly established in England as far back as 1584 when *Heydon's* case[25] was decided that for the sure and true interpretation of all Statutes in general (be they penal or beneficial, restrictive or enlarging of the common law) four things are to be discerned and considered:

1st — What was the common law before the making of the Act,

2nd — What was the mischief and defect for which the common law did not provide,

3rd — What remedy the Parliament hath resolved and appointed to cure the disease of the commonwealth, and

4th — The true reason of the remedy;

and then the office of all the judges is always to make such construction as shall suppress the mischief, and advance the remedy, and to suppress subtle inventions and evasions for continuance of the mischief, and *pro privato commodo*, and to add force and life to the cure and remedy, according to the true intent of the makers of the Act, *pro bono publico*."[26]

[Footnote No. 24 Contd.]

Ghewar Chand v. Madras Chillies, Grains & Kirana Merchants Workers Union, AIR 1969 SC 530, p. 533 : 1969 (1) SCR 366; *Union of India v. Sankalchand*, AIR 1977 SC 2328, p. 2358 : (1977) 4 SCC 193; *K.P. Verghese v. I.T. Officer*, AIR 1981 SC 1922, p. 1929 : (1981) 4 SCC 173; *Raipur Development Authority v. Anupam Sahkari Griha Nirman Samiti*, JT 2000 (4) SC 60, pp. 70, 71 : (2000) 4 SCC 357; *Steel Authority of India Ltd. v. National Union Water Front Workers*, AIR 2001 SC 3527, p. 3552 : (2001) 7 SCC 1; *Zile Singh v. State of Haryana*, AIR 2004 SC 5100, p. 5105 : (2004) 8 SCC 1.

25. *Heydon's* case, (1584) 3 Co. Rep. 7a, p. 7b : 76 ER 637.

26. *Bengal Immunity Co. v. State of Bihar*, AIR 1955 SC 661, p. 674 : 1955 (2) SCR 603. **See further** *CIT, Patiala v. Shahzada Nand & Sons*, AIR 1966 SC 1342, p. 1347 : 1966 (3) SCR 379; *Sanghvi Jeevraj Ghewar Chand v. Madras Chillies, Grains & Kirana Merchants Workers Union*, AIR 1969 SC 530, p. 533 : 1969 (1) SCR 366; *Swantraj v. State of Maharashtra*, AIR 1974 SC 517, p. 520 : 1974 SCC (Cri) 930 : (1975) 3 SCC 322; *Applin v. Race Relations Board*, (1974) 2 All ER 73, p. 89 (HL); *Rani Choudhury v. Surajit Singh Choudhury*, AIR 1982 SC 1397, p. 1399 : (1982) 2 SCC 596; *Babaji Kondaji Garad v. Nasik Merchants Co-operative Bank Ltd.*, (1984) 2 SCC 50, p. 59 : AIR 1984 SC 192; *Baliram Waman Hiray (Dr.) v. Mr. Justice B. Lentin*, AIR 1988 SC 2267, p. 2281 : 1988 (4) SCC 419; *PEK Kalliani Amma (Smt.) v. K. Devi*, 1996 (4) Scale 131, pp. 148, 149: AIR 1996 SC 1963, p. 1975; *Pawan Kumar v. State of Haryana*, JT 1998 (1) SC 565, p. 571: AIR 1998 SC 958, p. 963 : (1998) 3 SCC 309; *Ameer Trading Corporation Ltd. v. Shapoorji Data Processing Ltd.*, AIR 2004 SC 355, p. 359 : (2004) 1 SCC 702. *National Insurance Co. Ltd. v. Baljit Kaur*, (2004) 2 SCC 1, pp. 6, 7 : AIR 2004 SC 1340.

In Re, Mayfair Property Co.,[27] LINDLEY, M.R. in 1898 found the rule "as necessary now as it was when LORD COKE reported *Heydon's* case".[28]

In *Eastman Photographic Materials Co. v. Comptroller General of Patents, Designs and Trade Marks*,[29] EARL OF HALSBURY **re-affirmed** the rule as follows: "My lords, it appears to me that to construe the Statute in question, it is not only legitimate but highly convenient to refer both to the former Act and to the ascertained evils to which the former Act had given rise, and to the later Act which provides the remedy. These three being compared, I cannot doubt the conclusion."[30]

In the above mentioned formulations of the rule, as pointed out by LORD REID, "the word mischief is traditional". He expanded it to include "the facts presumed to be known to Parliament when the Bill which became the Act in question was before it" and "the unsatisfactory state of affairs" disclosed by these facts "which Parliament can properly be supposed to have intended to remedy by the Act".[31] The rule is more briefly stated by LORD ROSKILL, "Statutes should be given what has become known as a purposive construction, that is to say that the courts should identify the 'mischief' which existed before passing of the statute and then if more than one construction is possible, favour that which will eliminate the mischief so identified".[32] In the words of LORD GRIFFITH, "The courts now adopt a purposive approach which seeks to give effect to the true purpose of legislation and are prepared to look at much extraneous material that bears on the background against which the legislation was enacted."[33] When two competing Acts construed to further the purposes behind them produce a conflict, the court may resolve the conflict by taking into consideration as to which Act represents "the superior purpose" in addition to other relevant factors.[34] In applying a purposive construction a word of caution is necessary that the text of the statute is not to be sacrificed and the court cannot

---

27. (1898) 2 Ch 28, p. 35; **see further** *Thomson v. Lord Clanmorris*, (1900) 1 Ch D 718, p. 725 (LINDLEY, M.R.).

28. *Supra*.

29. (1898) AC 571, p. 576.

30. *Ibid*, **referred** to in *Bengal Immunity Co. v. State of Bihar*, AIR 1955 SC 661, p. 674 : 1955 (2) SCR 603.

31. *Black-Clawson International Ltd. v. Papierwerke Waldhof Aschaffenburg*, (1975) 1 All ER 810, p. 814 : (1975) 2 WLR 512 : 1975 AC 591 (HL); *Goodyear India Ltd. v. State of Haryana*, AIR 1990 SC 781, p. 789 : (1990) 2 SCC 71.

32. *Anderton v. Ryan*, (1985) 2 All ER 355, p. 359 : (1985) AC 567 : (1985) 2 WLR 968 (HL).

33. *Pepper v. Hart*, (1993) 1 All ER 42, p. 50 (HL). **See further** *Lalit Mohan Pandey v. Pooran Singh*, (2004) 6 SCC 626, pp. 642, 643.

34. *Allahabad Bank v. Canara Bank*, JT 2000 (4) SC 411, p. 432 (para 34) : (2000) 4 SCC 406 : AIR 2000 SC 1535.

rewrite the statute on the assumption that whatever furthers the purpose of the Act must have been sanctioned.[35] Therefore, the court cannot add to the means enacted by the legislature for achieving the object of the Act.[36] As expressed by the Supreme Court of United States, "No legislation pursues its purposes at all costs. Deciding what competing values will or will not be sacrificed to the achievement of a particular objective is the very essence of legislative choice—and it frustrates rather than effectuates legislative intent simplistically to assume that whatever furthers the statute's primary objective must be the law".[37]

In the context of purposive construction SINHA J. recommends: "To interpret a statute in a reasonable manner the court must place itself in the chair of a reasonable legislator/author. So done the rules of purposive construction have to be resorted to which would require the construction of the Act in such a manner as to see that the object of the Act is fulfilled."[38] He then quotes a passage from Barak from his work on Purposive Construction which refers to two elements of objectivity in the process of construction as introduced by HART and SACHS: "first the interpreter should assume that the legislature is composed of reasonable people seeking to achieve reasonable goals in a reasonable manner; and second the interpreter should accept the non-rebuttable presumption that members of the legislative body sought to fulfill their constitutional duties in good faith. This formulation allows the interpreter to inquire not into the subjective intent of the author, but rather the intent the author would have had, had he or she acted reasonably."[39]

The Supreme Court in *Bengal Immunity Co.'s* case[40] applied the rule in construction of Article 286 of the Constitution. After referring to the state

---

35. *Shri Ram Saha v. State*, AIR 2004 SC 5080, p. 5089 (para 18) : (2004) 9 JT 136 (Requirement of permission of collector for felling trees from non-forest private plantation cannot be imported if not enacted to prevent pilferage of forest). **See further** text and note 63, p. 145, *infra*.

36. *Director of Public Prosecutions v. Bhagwan*, (1970) 3 All ER 97 (HL). This case is **discussed** at page 929, *infra*.

37. *Rodriguez v. United States*, (1987) 480 US 522, pp. 525, 526. Also **quoted** by KIRBY J. in *Attorney General (WA) v. Marquet*, (2003) 78 ALJR 105, p. 130.

38. *New India Assurance Co. Ltd. v. Nusli Neville Wadia*, (2008) 3 SCC 279 para 51 : AIR 2008 SC 876.

39. *Ibid para* 52. For views of HART and SACHS **see further** note 48 p. 12 *ante*. **See further** *Krishna Kumar Birla v. Rajendra Singh Lodha*, (2008) 4 SCC 300 p. 340; (2008) 4 JT 82; *UCO Bank v. Rajinderlal Capoor*, (2008) 5 SCC 257 para 27 : AIR 2008 SC 1831; *Union of India v. Ranbaxy Laboratories Ltd.*, (2008) 7 SCC 502 para 31 : AIR 2008 SC 2286; *D. Purushotama Reddy v. K. Sateesh*, (2008) 8 SCC 505 para 36 : AIR 2008 SC 3202; *Mahalakshmi Sugar Mills Co. Ltd. v. Union of India*, AIR 2009 SC 792 para 64 : (2008) 6 JT 177.

40. *Bengal Immunity Co. v. State of Bihar*, AIR 1955 SC 661 : 1955 (2) SCR 603.

of law prevailing in the provinces prior to the Constitution as also to the chaos and confusion that was brought about in inter-State trade and commerce by indiscriminate exercise of taxing powers by the different provincial Legislatures founded on the theory of territorial nexus S.R. DAS, C.J.I., proceeded to say, "It was to cure this mischief of multiple taxation and to preserve the free flow of inter-State trade or commerce in the Union of India regarded as one economic unit without any provincial barrier that the constitution-makers adopted Article 286 in the Constitution".[41] The rule was again applied by the Supreme Court in similar context while construing the changes brought about by the Constitution 46th Amendment Act, 1982.[42]

An illustration of the application of the rule is also furnished in the construction of section 2(d) of the Prize Competitions Act, 1955. This section defines 'Prize Competition' as meaning "any competition in which prizes are offered for the solution of any puzzle based upon the building up arrangement, combination or permutation of letters, words or figures". The question was whether in view of this definition, the Act applies to competitions which involve substantial skill and are not in the nature of gambling. The Supreme Court, after referring to the previous state of the law, to the mischief that continued under that law and to the resolutions of various States under Article 252(1) authorising Parliament to pass the Act stated, "Having regard to the history of the legislation, the declared object thereof and the wording of the statute, we are of opinion that the competitions which are sought to be controlled and regulated by the Act are only those competitions in which success does not depend on any substantial degree of skill".[43]

A further example finds mention in the construction of section 16(3) of the Indian Income-tax Act, 1922. The sub-section reads: "In computing the total income of any individual for the purpose of assessment, there shall be included (a) so much of the income of a wife or minor child of such individual as arises indirectly or directly—". The question before the Supreme Court was whether word 'individual' occurring in the aforesaid sub-section meant only a male or also included a female. After finding that the said word in the setting was ambiguous, BHAGWATI, J., observed: "In order to resolve this ambiguity, therefore, we must of necessity have resort to the state of the law before the enactment of the provisions, the mischief and the defect for which the law did not provide; the remedy which the Legislature resolved and appointed to cure the defect; and the true reason of the

---

41. *Ibid*, p. 675.
42. *Goodyear India Ltd. v. State of Haryana*, AIR 1990 SC 781 : 1990 (2) SCC 71.
43. *RMD Chamarbaugwalla v. Union of India*, AIR 1957 SC 628, p. 632 : 1957 SCR 930; (**See also** page 631 of AIR wherein *Heydon's* case is referred).

remedy."[44] After referring to these factors, BHAGWATI, J., proceeded to point out: "It is clear that the evil which was sought to be remedied was the one resulting from the wide-spread practice of husbands entering into nominal partnerships with their wives and fathers admitting their minor children to the benefits of the partnerships of which they were members. This evil was sought to be remedied by the enactment of section 16(3) in the Act. If this background of the enactment of section 16(3) is borne in mind there is no room for any doubt that howsoever that mischief was sought to be remedied by amending the Act, the only intention of the Legislature in doing so was to include the income derived by the wife or minor child, in computation of the total income of the male assessee, the husband or the father, as the case may be, for the purpose of assessment."[45] The words 'any individual' were, therefore, construed as restricted to males.[46]

A more recent example is provided in the construction of section 195(3) of the Code of Criminal Procedure, 1973 which reads: "In clause (b), of sub-section (1) the term court means a Civil, Revenue or Criminal Court and includes a Tribunal constituted by or under a Central, Provincial or State Act if declared by that Act to be a Court for the purposes of this section." The Supreme Court pointed out that this section was enacted to implement the recommendations of the 41st report of the Law Commission which had referred to the unsatisfactory state of the law due to conflict of opinion between different High Courts as to the meaning of the word 'Court' in section 195 of the earlier Code and had recommended that a tribunal might be regarded as a court only if declared by the Act constituting it to be a court for purposes of section 195.[47] On this view it was held that a Commission of Inquiry constituted under the Commissions of Inquiry Act, 1952 was not a court for purposes of section 195 of the Code of Criminal Procedure, 1973 as it was not declared to be so under the Act.[48] More recently purposive construction was applied in interpreting an exception and it was observed that "if exception has been added to remedy the mischief or defect, it should be so construed that it remedies the

---

44. *CIT v. Sodra Devi*, AIR 1957 SC 832, pp. 837, 838 : 1958 SCR 1; (**see also** page 835 of AIR Report wherein *Heydon's* case is **referred**). **See further** *CIT v. Shri Om Prakash,* JT 1999 (5) SC 104 : AIR 1999 SC 2534 : (1999) 6 SCC 349 (construction of section 64(1) of the Income-tax Act, 1961 which holds that 'individual' does not include karta of a joint Hindu family).

45. *CIT v. Sodra Devi, supra*, p. 839 : 1957 SCR 930. For another example of application of the rule in *Heydon's* case, **see** *Mahijibhai v. Manibhai*, AIR 1965 SC 1477, p. 1482 : 1965 (2) SCR 436.

46. *Ibid.*

47. *Baliram Waman Hiray (Dr.) v. Mr. Justice B. Lentin*, AIR 1988 SC 2267, p. 2280 : 1988 (4) SCC 419.

48. *Baliram Waman Hiray (Dr.) v. Mr. Justice B. Lentin*, AIR 1988 SC 2267, p. 2283 : (1988) 4 SCC 419.

mischief and not in a manner which frustrates the very purpose." In this case the expression 'in the port areas' used in an exception to a notification issued by the MOEF was construed to mean "in or through the port areas" to advance the purpose for which it was added.[49]

Purposive construction has very often been employed in construction of laws passed to implement international agreements or conventions and regulations made to give effect to the directions of the Council of European Communities.[50]

Purposive construction has also been applied to penal statutes to avoid a lacuna and to suppress the mischief and advance the remedy.[51] An interpretation which promotes the object sought to be achieved by the legislation, should be adopted in preference to an interpretation which defeats such object. Applying this rule to section 138 of the Negotiable Instruments Act, 1881, the Supreme Court has held that a prosecution based on a second or successive default in payment of a cheque amount should not be impermissible only because prosecution based on the first default, followed by a statutory notice and a failure to pay, had not been launched. The Court further observed that the entire purpose of section 138 is to compel the drawers to honour their commitments made in course of their business or other affairs, and that there is no reason why a person who has issued a cheque which is dishonoured, and who fails to make payment despite statutory notice served upon him, should be immune to prosecution simply because the holder of the cheque has not rushed to the Court.[52]

The Supreme Court in *Sodra Devi's* case[53] expressed the view that the rule in *Heydon's* case[54] is applicable only when the words in question are ambiguous and are reasonably capable of more than one meaning. In that case BHAGWATI, J., criticising the mode of approach of the High Court, stated: "The High Court plunged headlong into a discussion of the reason which motivated the Legislature into enacting section 16(3) of the Indian Income-tax Act, 1922, and took into consideration the recommendations made in the Income-tax Enquiry Report, 1936 and also the Statement of Objects and Reasons for the enactment of the same, without considering in the first instance whether there was any ambiguity in the word, 'individual'

---

49. *M. Nizamuddin v. Chemplast Sanmar Ltd.*, (2010) 4 SCC 240 paras 38, 39 : AIR 2010 SC 1765.
50. **See** text and notes 20 (p. 244) and 72-73 (p. 694).
51. **See** text and notes 71, 72, p. 967, Chapter 11.
52. *MSR Leathers v. S. Palaniappan & Anr.*, (2013) 1 SCC 177, pp. 194 to 196.
53. AIR 1957 SC 832, p. 835 : 1958 SCR 1.
54. *Supra*.

as used therein." It was pointed out that the rule in *Heydon's* case[55] is applicable only when language is ambiguous and the said rule in that case was only applied after first finding that the words 'any individual' in the setting are ambiguous.[56] Similarly, in another case[57] GAJENDRAGADKAR, J., stated that the recourse to object and policy of the Act or consideration of the mischief and defect which the Act purports to remedy is only permissible when the language is capable of two constructions. But it has already been seen that for deciding whether the language used by the Legislature is plain or ambiguous it has to be studied in its context,[58] and 'context' embraces previous state of the law and the mischief which the statute was intended to remedy.[59] Therefore, it is not really correct to say that the rule in *Heydon's* case[60] is *not* applicable when the language is not ambiguous. The *correct principle* is that after the words have been construed in their context and it is found that the language is capable of bearing only one construction, the rule in *Heydon's* case ceases to be controlling and gives way to the plain meaning rule.[61]

The Supreme Court in *P.E.K. Kalliani Amma (Smt.) v. K. Devi*[62] referred extensively to the rule in *Heydon's* case and to the opinions of BHAGWATI and GAJENDRAGADKAR Judges and of LORD SIMON but did not resolve the difference in them. The court said: "Be that as it may, we are not invoking the Rule but we have nevertheless to keep in mind the principles contained therein." It is submitted that keeping in mind the principles of the Rule without first coming to the conclusion that the statutory provision in question was ambiguous is a tacit approval of the *correct principle* stated above.

But the rule cannot be used to "the length of applying unnatural meanings to familiar words or of so stretching the language that its former shape is transformed into something which is not only significantly

---

55. *P.E.K. Kalliani Amma (Smt.) v. K. Devi,* (1584) 3 Co Rep 7a : 76 ER 637.

56. *CIT, M.P. & Bhopal v. Sodra Devi*, AIR 1957 SC 832, p. 835 : 1958 SCR 1.

57. *Kanailal Sur v. Paramnidhi Sadhukhan*, AIR 1957 SC 907, pp. 910, 911 : 1958 SCR 360.

58. **See** Chapter 1, title 6, p. 59.

59. **See** Chapter 1, text and note 40, p. 35; and text and notes pp. 60-63, p. 39.

60. *Supra.*

61. LORD SIMON explains this aspect by saying that the rule in *Heydon's* case is available at two stages; firstly, before ascertaining the plain and primary meaning of the statute and secondly, at the stage when the court reaches the conclusion that there is no such plain meaning: *Maunsell v. Olins*, (1975) 1 All ER 16, p. 29 : (1974) 1 WLR 830 : (1974) 2 All ER 250 (HL).

62. 1996 (4) Scale 131, p. 149 : AIR 1996 SC 1963, p. 1975 : (1996) 4 SCC 76.

different but has a name of its own" especially when "the language has no evident ambiguity or uncertainty about it.[63]

It has also been said that the application of the rule in *Heydon's* case should not be taken to extremes; that if there were many problems before the enactment of the statute it does not follow that in an effort to solve some of them the Parliament intended to solve all; and that loyalty to the rule does not require the adoption of a construction which leads manifestly to absurd results. These propositions stated by LORD ROSKILL in *Anderton v. Ryan*[64] are unexceptional but their misapplication may lead to a narrow construction defeating the object of the statute as actually happened in that case which was overruled within a year in *R. v. Shivpuri.*[65] Further, if the statutory language in its primary or ordinary meaning in the context has a wider effect, it cannot be artificially confined to remedy the single identified mischief which is conceived to have occasioned the statutory provision for once a mischief has been drawn to the attention of the parliamentary draftsman he would have considered whether any concomitant mischiefs should be dealt with as a necessary corollary.[66]

4. REGARD TO CONSEQUENCES

If the language used is capable of bearing more than one construction, in selecting the true meaning regard must be had to the consequences resulting from adopting the alternative constructions. A construction that results in hardship, serious inconvenience, injustice, absurdity or anomaly or which leads to inconsistency or uncertainty and friction in the system which the statute purports to regulate has to be rejected and preference should be given to that construction which avoids such results.[67] This rule

---

63. *Cutter v. Eagle Star Insurance Co. Ltd.,* (1998) 4 All ER 417, p. 425 (HL) ('Road' not construed to include 'carpark').

64. (1985) 2 All ER 355, p. 363 : (1985) 2 WLR 986 : (1985) AC 567 (HL).

65. (1986) 2 All ER 334 : (1987) AC 1 : (1986) 2 WLR 988 (HL).

66. *Maunsell v. Olins,* (1975) 1 All ER 16, p. 27 : (1987) AC 1 : (1986) 2 WLR 988 (HL); *R. v. Secretary of State for the Environment ex parte Spath Holme,* (2001) All ER 195, pp. 205, 210 (J) (HL).

67. **See** titles 4(a): 'Hardship, Inconvenience, Injustice, Absurdity and Anomaly to be avoided'; and 4(b) 'Inconsistency and Repugnancy to be avoided; Harmonious Construction', *infra*. The real role that is played by consideration of consequences in the process of construction is correctly appreciated by MAX RADIN: "It is true that the consideration of consequences of a decision has at all times been a controlling factor in the judicial process. Those courts who declare vigorously that they are completely indifferent to the consequences of what they decide and would decide as they do though the heaven fell, merely mean that they do not believe that the consequences will be seriously harmful. If they meant what they said, and acted on it, they would

[Footnote No. 67 Contd.]

has no application when the words are susceptible to only one meaning and no alternative construction is reasonably open.[68]

(a) Hardship, inconvenience, injustice, absurdity and anomaly to be avoided

In selecting out of different interpretations "the court will adopt that which is just, reasonable and sensible rather than that which is none of those things"[69] as it may be presumed "that the Legislature should have used the word in that interpretation which least offends our sense of justice".[70] If the grammatical construction leads to some absurdity or some

---

[Footnote No. 67 Contd.]

be taking a long step towards the destruction of our judicial system" (33 Calif. L. Rev. 219, p. 228) **referred** in *Brij Gopal v. State of M.P.*, (1978) MPLJ 70, p. 75 (G.P. SINGH J.). **See further** *D. Saibaba v. Bar Council of India,* AIR 2003 SC 2502, p. 2507 : (2003) 6 SCC 186; and *Modern School v. Union of India*, AIR 2004 SC 2236, pp. 2256, 2257 : (2004) 5 SCC 583 where the rule as stated above has been **quoted** with approval from earlier editions of this book.

68. **See** Chapter 1, title 5 'If meaning is plain, effect must be given to it irrespective of consequences'.

69. *Holmes v. Bradfield Rural District Council*, (1949) 1 All ER 381, p. 384 (KBD) (FINNEMORE, J.); *Nasiruddin v. State Transport Appellate Tribunal*, AIR 1976 SC 331, p. 338 : (1975) 2 SCC 671; *State of MP v. Narmada Bachoo Andolan,* (2011) 7 SCC 639 (Para 76) (The aforesaid rule has been **quoted with approval** by the Supreme Court).

70. *Simms v. Registrar of Probates*, (1900) AC 323, p. 335 (PC) (LORD HOBHOUSE). **See further** *Cramas Properties Ltd. v. Cannaught Fur Trimmings Ltd.*, (1965) 2 All ER 382 (HL), p. 385 (LORD REID), p. 387 (LORD GUEST) (A reasonable construction is to be preferred to an irrational construction leading to uncertainty); *Trent River Authority v. National Coal Board*, (1970) 1 All ER 558, p. 563 (HL) (LORD WILBERFORE) ("When the statutory words are capable of two meanings preference should be given to that meaning which produces the more reasonable and just result."); *Madhav Rao Jivajirao v. Union of India*, AIR 1971 SC 530, p. 576 : 1971 (1) SCC 85, p. 162 (SHAH, J.) ("The court will interpret a statute, as far as possible, agreeable to justice and reason and that in case of two or more interpretations, one which is more reasonable and just will be adopted, for there is always a presumption against the law-maker intending injustice and unreason"); *Union of India v. B.S. Agarwal*, AIR 1998 SC 1537, p. 1546 : (1997) 8 SCC 89 (court to lean in favour of such interpretation which conforms to justice and fair play and prevents potentiality to injustice); *Debenhams Plc. v. Westminster City Council*, (1987) 1 All ER 51, p. 55 : (1987) AC 396 : (1986) 3 WLR 1063 ((HL) (That meaning which produces an unrea sonable result is to be rejected in favour of that which does not); *Paradise Printers v. Union Territory of Chandigarh*, AIR 1988 SC 354, p. 358 : 1988 (1) SCC 440 (when there is a choice of meanings, there is a presumption that one which produces an unjust or inconvenient result was not intended); *Union of India v. North Telumer Colliery*, AIR 1989 SC 1728, p. 1732 : (1989) 2 SCC 342 (construction which leads to 'unjust benefit' to be avoided'); *Sachida Nand Singh v. State of Bhiar*, AIR 1998 SC 1121, p. 1123 : 1998 (2) SCC 493 (natural meaning leading to mischievous

[Footnote No. 70 Contd.]

repugnance or inconsistency with the rest of the instrument, it may be departed from so as to avoid that absurdity, and inconsistency.[71] Similarly, a construction giving rise to anomalies should be avoided.[72] As approved by VENKATARAMA AIYAR, J., "Where the language of a statute, in its ordinary meaning and grammatical construction, leads to a manifest contradiction of the apparent purpose of the enactment, or to some inconvenience or absurdity, hardship or injustice, presumably not intended, a construction may be put upon it which modifies the meaning of the words, and even the structure of the sentence."[73]

[Footnote No. 70 Contd.]

consequences to be avoided when alternative construction is open); *Bhatia International v. Bulk Trading S.A.*, AIR 2002 SC 1432, p. 1438 : (2002) 4 SCC 105 (**prospectively overruled** in *Bharat Aluminium Company v. Kaiser Aluminium Technical Services Inc.*, (2012) 9 SCC 552); *Rakesh Wadhwa v. Jagadamba Industrial Corporation,* AIR 2002 SC 2004, p. 2014 : (2002) 5 SCC 440 (8th Edition p. 113 of this book is **referred**); *Unique Butyle Tube Industries P. Ltd. v. U.P. Financial Corporation,* (2003) 2 SCC 455, p. 463 : 2003 All LJ 427; *D. Saibaba v. Bar Council of India,* AIR 2003 SC 2502, p. 2507 (8th edition of this book p. 113 is **referred**); *Ibrahimpatnam Taluk Vyavasaya Coolie Sangham v. K. Suresh Reddy,* (2003) 7 SCC 667, p. 678 : (2003) 7 SCC 667 : AIR 2003 SC 3592; *Lalit Mohan Pandey v. Pooran Singh*, (2004) 6 SCC 626, pp. 643, 644 : AIR 2004 SC 2303.

71. *Grey v. Pearson*, (1857) 6 HLC 61, p. 106: 10 ER 1216, p. 1234 (HL); **See further** title 2(a) 'Natural and Grammatical Meaning', text and notes 24 (pp. 91-92), 27 (pp. 92-93).
Also see *Shamrao v. District Magistrate, Thana*, AIR 1952 SC 324, p. 327 : 1952 SCR 683. "The object of the construction of a statute being to ascertain the will of the Legislature, it may be presumed that neither injustice nor absurdity was intended. If, therefore literal interpretation would produce such a result, and the language admits of an interpretation which would avoid it, then such an interpretation may be adopted": *Owen Thomas Mangin v. IRC*, (1971) 2 WLR 39, p. 42 (PC) (LORD DONOVAN): (1971) 1 All ER 179, p. 182 **referred** in *Imperial Chemicals Industries v. Colmer*, (1996) 2 All ER 23, p. 32; *Mahmadhusen Abdulrahim Kalota Shaikh v. Union of India,* (2009) 2 SCC 1 para 101 : (2008) 13 Scale 398.

72. *Veluswami Thevar v. G. Raja Nainar*, AIR 1959 SC 422, pp. 427, 428: 1959 Supp (1) SCR 404. *K. Prabhakaran v. P. Jayarajan*, (2005) 1 SCC 754, p. 773 (para 33).

73. *Tirath Singh v. Bachittar Singh*, AIR 1955 SC 830, p. 833 : 1955 (2) SCR 457 (passage from MAXWELL, Interpretation of Statutes, 11th Edition, p. 221 **approved**); *State of M.P. v. Azad Bharat Finance Co.*, AIR 1967 SC 276, p. 278 : 1966 Supp SCR 473; *Union of India v. Sankalchand*, AIR 1977 SC 2328, pp. 2337, 2358, 2373 : (1977) 4 SCC 193 : 1977 SCC (Lab) 435; *CIT v. National Taj Traders*, AIR 1980 SC 485, p. 490 : (1980) 1 SCC 370; *K.P. Verghese v. I.T. Officer*, AIR 1981 SC 1922, p. 1928 : (1981) 4 SCC 173; *Bhag Mal v. Ch. Parbhu Ram*, (1985) 1 SCC 61, p. 88 : AIR 1985 SC 150; *State of Tamil Nadu v. Kodaikanal Motor Union*, (1986) 3 SCC 91, p. 100 : AIR 1986 SC 1173; *Commissioner of Income-tax v. J.H. Gotla Yadgiri*, (1985) 4 SCC 343, p. 359 : AIR 1985 SC 1698; *C.W.S. (India) Ltd. v. Commissioner of Income-tax*, JT 1994 (3) SC 116, p. 121: 1994 Supp (2) SCC 296; *R. Rudraiah v. State of Karnataka*, JT 1998 (1) SC 435, pp. 443, 444: AIR 1998 SC 1070, p.1075 : (1998) 3 SCC 23; *Molar Mal v. Kay Iron Works (P.) Ltd.*, AIR 2000 SC 1261, p. 1266

[Footnote No. 73 Contd.]

Nowadays when laws are made by the representatives of the people, it is proper to assume that law-makers enact laws which the society considers as honest, fair and reasonable and thus justice and reason constitute the great general legislative intent in every piece of legislation. In the absence, therefore, of some other indication that harsh or ridiculous effect was actually intended by the Legislature, it cannot be readily accepted that it represents the legislative intent.[74] The word 'held' in section 9 of the Uttar Pradesh Zamindari Abolition and Land Reforms Act, 1950 was, on this principle, construed as meaning 'lawfully held' as a contrary construction would have conferred title on trespassers and would have deprived real owners of the benefit of the provision.[75]

In a case already noticed[76] the Supreme Court was concerned with the construction of section 99 of the Representation of the People Act, 1951 (as it stood prior to amendment by Act 27 of 1957) which authorises the

---

[Footnote No. 73 Contd.]
: (2000) 4 SCC 285; *Padmasundara Rao v. State of T.N.,* AIR 2002 SC 1334, pp. 1340, 1341 : (2002) 3 SCC 533; *Modern School v. Union of India*, AIR 2004 SC 2236, p. 2257 : (2004) 9 SCC 741. (This entire para **quoted with approval** by SINHA, J. from 9th Edition., pp. 121, 122 of this book).

74. *Budhan Singh v. Nabi Bux*, AIR 1970 SC 1880, p. 1883 : 1969 (2) SCC 481, *State of Uttar Pradesh v. Sarjudevi*, AIR 1977 SC 2196, p. 2200 : 1977 (4) SCC 2; *Bharat Petroleum Corporation Ltd. v. Maddula Ratnavalli,* (2007) 6 SCC 81 para 22 : (2007) 6 JT 264 (Parliament is presumed to have enacted a reasonable statute); *New India Assurance Co. Ltd. v. Nusli Neville Wadia*, (2008) 3 SCC 279 para 53 : AIR 2008 SC 876.

75. *Ibid*. 'Hold' may cover a case of ownership without possession as also lawful possession without ownership: *State of Andhra Pradesh v. Mohd. Ashrafuddin*, AIR 1982 SC 913 : (1982) 2 SCC 1. For other cases where the word 'Lawfully' was similarly read, **see** *Adlam v. Law Society*, (1968) 1 All ER 17; *In re*, *Abdul Manan*, (1971) 1 WLR 859, p. 861 (CA). Money 'payable' or money 'due' may mean money, legally recoverable and not barred by limitation: *New Delhi Municipal Committee v. Kaluram*, AIR 1976 SC 1637, p. 1639 : (1976) 3 SCC 407; 'amounts due' has also the same meaning, *State of Kerala v. V.R. Kallianikutty,* JT 1999 (2) SC 541 : AIR 1999 SC 1305 : (1999) 3 SCC 657 and 'occupation' may mean 'lawful occupation', *K.M. Mathew v. Hamsa Haji*, (1987) 3 SCC 326, p. 330 : 1987 AIR (SC) 1326; *Modern Industries v. Steel Authority of India Ltd.*, (2010) 5 SCC 44 para 42 : AIR 2010 SC 1625 (word 'due' has a variety of meanings and in different context it may have different meaning). **Also see** paras 28 to 36. **But** in the context of rent control legislation requiring the tenant to deposit 'entire amount of rent due' or 'the arrears of rent' to save eviction these expressions have been construed to include even that part of arrears which have become barred by limitation: *Rakesh Wadhwan v. Jagadamba Industrial Corporation,* AIR 2002 SC 2004, p. 2010 : (2002) 5 SCC 440. The word 'lawfully' cannot also be generally read in a provision which refers to domicile or habitual residence for a person may acquire a domicile of choice at a place or may be habitually resident at a place though his residence at that place was unlawful: *Mark v. Mark,* (2005) 3 All ER 912 (paras 33, 36, 49) (HL).

76. **See** first case in footnote 73, *supra.*

Election Tribunal at the conclusion of the trial to name all persons who have been guilty of corrupt practice. The power, however, is subject to a proviso which prior to its amendment read, 'provided that no person shall be named in the order unless—(a) he has been given notice to appear before the Tribunal and to show cause why he should not be so named; and (b) if he appears in pursuance of the notice, he has been given opportunity of cross-examining any witness who has already been examined and of calling evidence in his defence and of being heard'. The contention before the Supreme Court was that even parties to the election petition were entitled to the benefit of the proviso as the words 'no person shall be named' interpreted in literal sense included such persons. The Supreme Court, rejecting this contention pointed out: "If the contention is to be accepted, then the result will be that even though there was a full trial of the charges set out in the petition, if the tribunal is disposed to hold them proved it has first to give notice of the finding which it proposes to give, to the parties and to hold a fresh trial of the very matters that had been already tried. That is an extraordinary result for which it is difficult to discover any reason or justification".[77]

Principles of sincerity, substantial justice and fairness were applied in interpreting section 2 of the Hindu Widows' Remarriage Act, 1856 and the Madras Hindu (Bigamy Prevention) Act, 1949. Section 2 of the former Act provides that all rights and interest which a Hindu widow had in her husband's property 'shall upon her remarriage cease and determine'. The Madras Act prohibited a bigamous marriage, therefore, marriage of a Hindu widow with a person whose first wife was living could not be held to be a valid marriage. Still it was held that such a marriage amounted to 'remarriage' within section 2 of the 1856 Hindu Widows' Remarriage Act and the widow ceased to hold any rights in the property held by her deceased husband.[78] The question of 'remarriage' was also held to be concluded by a prior decision on principles of *res judicata* and the final outcome may have been just and equitable in the special facts of the case. But the view that an invalid or void marriage could amount to 'remarriage' under section 2 of the 1856 Act is open to objection. It is submitted that apart from other reasons the Act made the widow lose her rights in the property left by her deceased husband for the reason that the widow on remarriage got rights in the property of her new husband and this could be possible only if the remarriage was valid. So if the widow was made to lose her rights in the property of her deceased husband as a result of invalid remarriage she would be wholly unprotected even for her maintenance and the view taken

77. *Thirath Singh v. Bachittar Singh*, AIR 1955 SC 830, p. 833 : 1955 (2) SCR 457.
78. *Velamuri Venkata Sivaprasad v. Kothuri Venkateswarlu,* JT 1999 (9) SC 249 : AIR 2000 SC 434 : (2000) 2 SCC 139.

will not be in furtherance of either gender equality or fairness to which reference was made by the court in its judgment.

Section 13(2)(i) of the East Punjab Urban Rent Restriction Act, 1949 provides for eviction of a tenant who has not paid or tendered the rent due. There is a proviso to that section which reads: 'Provided that if the tenant on the first hearing of the application for ejectment after due service' pays or tenders the arrears of rent and interest at 6% per annum on such arrears together with cost of application assessed by the controller, the tenant shall be deemed to have duly paid or tendered the rent'. The proviso does not in terms provide that if there be a genuine dispute regarding the arrears due, the controller will provisionally determine the arrears and give time to the tenant to deposit the same to save eviction. But such a provision was read by implication to avoid hardship and injustice to the tenant in case of a genuine dispute of arrears of rent. The court reached this conclusion by holding that the qualifying expression 'assessed by the controller' in the proviso qualified also 'the arrears of rent' and not merely 'cost of application'.[79]

The issue of whether, if Part I of the Arbitration and Conciliation Act, 1996, is limited to arbitrations which take place in India, the same would leave parties remediless, came up for consideration before a Constitution Bench of the Supreme Court in *Bharat Aluminium Co v. Kaiser Aluminium Technical Services*.[80] Sub-section (2) of section 2 of Part I of the Arbitration and Conciliation Act, 1996 states: "This part shall apply where the place of arbitration is in India." The High Courts of Orissa, Bombay, Madras, Delhi and Calcutta took the view that Part I of the Act does not apply where the place of arbitration is not in India. This view of the High Courts was overruled by a three Judge Bench of the Supreme Court in *Bhatia International v. Bulk Trading S.A.*, on the ground that it would lead to anomalous consequences and will leave a party remedyless for obtaining any interim relief in international commercial arbitrations which take place out of India though the properties and assets are in India. As section 2 does not provide that Part I will not apply where the place of arbitration is not in India the Court held: "Part I would apply to all arbitrations and to all proceedings relating thereto. Where such arbitration is held in India the provisions of Part I would compulsorily apply and parties are free to deviate only to the extent permitted by the derogable provisions of Part I. In cases of international commercial arbitrations held out of India

---

79. *Rakesh Wadhawan v. Jagadamba Industrial Corporation,* AIR 2002 SC 2004, p. 2012 : (2002) 5 SCC 440.

80. *Bharat Aluminium Co. v. Kaiser Aluminium Technical Services Inc.*, (2012) 9 SCC 552.

provisions of Part I would apply unless the parties by agreement express or implied exclude all or any of its provisions."[81] However, this decision was prospectively overruled by the Constitution Bench of the Supreme Court in *Bharat Aluminium Co v. Kaiser Aluminium Technical Services*, wherein the Court opined that the approach adopted in *Bhatia International* to remove the perceived hardship is not permissible under law. Merely because the remedy may be more onerous from the viewpoint of one party, that is not the same as a party being left without a remedy, and if there is a gap or lacuna in the law, it would be for the Parliament to rectify the same.[82] Subsequently, the Arbitration and Conciliation (Amendment) Ordinance, 2015, was promulgated by the President on 23rd October, 2015. This Ordinance extends the remedy under section 9 to all arbitrations by amending section 2(2) of the Act to provide that, subject to an agreement to the contrary, section 9 of the Act would also apply to international commercial arbitrations, even if the place of arbitration is outside India.

In construing section 66(1) of the Central Provinces and Berar Municipalities Act, 1922 which authorised imposition of 'a terminal tax on goods or animals imported into or exported from the limits of a municipality', the question before the Supreme Court was whether the said clause empowered the municipality to levy a tax on goods in transit. The High Court had adopted the derivative meaning of words import and export, *i.e.*, to bring in and to carry away and had therefore held that the municipality had the power to levy terminal tax on goods in transit. The Supreme Court in reversing the decision of the High Court pointed out that the words import and export in their ordinary commercial sense do not refer to goods in transit; and in selecting the commercial sense of the words in preference to derivative sense, KAPUR, J., observed, "The effect of the construction of 'import' or 'export' in the manner insisted upon by the respondent (municipal committee) would make railborne goods passing through a railway station within the limits of a municipality liable to the imposition of the tax on their arrival at the railway station or departure therefrom or both which would not only lead to inconvenience but confusion, and would also result in inordinate delays and unbearable burden on trade both *inter*-State and *intra*-State. It is hardly likely that, that was the intention of the

---

81. *Bhatia International v. Bulk Trading SA*, AIR 2002 SC 1432 para 32 : (2002) 4 SCC 105. **Followed** in *Venture Global Engineering v. Satyam Computer Services Ltd.*, (2008) 4 SCC 190 : AIR 2008 SC 1061. For criticism of this case **see** O. P. Malhotra and Indra Malhotra. 'The Law and Practice of Arbitration and Conciliation' pp. 190 to 194.

82. *Bharat Aluminium Co. v. Kaiser Aluminium Technical Services Inc.*, (2012) 9 SCC 552, pp. 638, 639, 640.

Legislature. Such an interpretation would lead to absurdity which has according to rules of interpretation, to be avoided".[83]

On the presumption that a statute is intended to be just and reasonable, it is not construed to take away private rights of property without compensation unless the intention to do so is expressed in clear and unambiguous terms.[84] On the same principle expropriatory legislation is strictly construed[85] and a regulatory Act relating to regulation of user of land is not construed prohibiting transfer which does not affect its user.[86] Similarly the presumption is that in the absence of an express provision to the contrary Parliament does not intend to authorise tortious conduct, for example to take away the common law right to keep one's home free from an intruder even if he is a public officer.[87] So the Court does not countenance the expropriation by a public authority without clear statutory sanction of money or property belonging to an individual even if it is suspected to be proceeds of illegal drug dealing.[88] And, on the same principle, it is presumed that the law does not compel the doing of impossibilities. Therefore, a statutory provision laying down a duty is construed as not applying

---

83. *Central India Spinning, Weaving and Manufacturing Co. Ltd., Empress Mills, Nagpur v. Municipal Committee, Wardha*, AIR 1958 SC 341, p. 346 : 1958 SCR 1102. **But** in section 53 of the Copyright Act, 1957 the word 'import' has been construed to include importation for transit across the country. *Gramophone Co. of India Ltd. v. Birendra Bahadur Pandey*, (1984) 2 SCC 534, p. 555 : AIR 1984 SC 667.

84. *Minister of Housing & Local Government v. Hartnell*, (1965) 1 All ER 490 (HL); *Hughes v. Doncaster Metropolitan Borough Council*, (1991) 1 All ER 295, p. 303 : (1991) 1 AC 382 : (1991) 2 WLR 16 (HL); *R. v. Secretary of State for the Environment ex parte Spath Holme Ltd.*, (2001) 1 All ER 196, p. 203 (HL). **But** this principle will not apply to welfare legislations like Zamindari Abolition Acts or Ceiling Acts; For example **see** *Raja Satyendra Narain Singh v. State of Bihar*, (1987) 3 SCC 319, p. 325: AIR 1987 SC 1390; *State of M.P. v. Board of Revenue*, 1983 MPLJ 148, p. 156 (G.P. SINGH C.J.). The principle will also not apply to a nationalisation Act passed to give effect to Article 39(b) and (c) of the Constitution; *Doypack Systems Pvt. Ltd. v. Union of India*, AIR 1988 SC 782, pp. 803, 804 : 1988 (2) SCC 299.

85. *DLF Qutab Enclave Complex Educational Charitable Trust v. State of Haryana*, 2003 AIR SCW 1046, p. 1056 (para 36) : (2003) 5 SCC 622, pp. 634, 635; *State of Maharashtra v. B.E. Billimoria*, (2003) 7 SCC 336, p. 347 : AIR 2003 SC 4368; *Bharat Petroleum Corporation Ltd. v. Maddula Ratnavalli*, (2007) 6 SCC 81 (para 29) : (2007) 6 Scale 353 : (2007) 6 JT 264; *Chairman Indore Vikas Pradhikaran v. Pure Industrial Coke & Chemicals Ltd.*, (2007) 8 SCC 705 para 57, 58 : AIR 2008 SC 2458; *Devender Singh v. State of Punjab*, AIR 2008 SC 201 (para 41) : (2008) 1 SCC 278.

86. *DLF Qutab Enclave Complex Educational Charitable Trust v. State of Haryana*, *(supra)* (para 35). For meaning of regulation **see** pp. 1040-1043.

87. *Morris v. Beardmore*, (1980) 2 All ER 753, p. 757 : (1981) AC 446 (HL).

88. *Webb v. Chief Constable of Merseyside Police*, (2000) 1 All ER 200 (CA).

to a case where performance is impossible.[89] Similarly, a *prima facie* absolute statutory obligation may be construed subject to an implied limitation that its performance can be refused on grounds of public policy *e.g.* when the performance may give rise to a real risk of a serious crime.[90] And codes of procedure regulating proceedings in courts are to be construed as to render justice wherever reasonably possible,[91] to avoid injustice from a mistake of the court[92] and even to enable recalling of an order obtained by

---

89. *Cochin State Power & Light Corporation Ltd. v. State of Kerala*, AIR 1965 SC 1688, p. 1691 : (1965) 3 SCR 187; *Burns v. Bidder*, (1966) 3 All ER 29. *In re, Presidential Election*, 1974, AIR 1974 SC 1682, p. 1686 : (1974) 2 SCC 33 ; *Superintendent of Taxes v. Onkarmal Nathumal Trust*, AIR 1975 SC 2065, pp. 2069, 2074, 2077 : (1976) 1 SCC 766; *Rajkumar Dey v. Tarapada Dey*, (1987) 4 SCC 388, pp. 402, 403 : AIR 1987 SC 2195; *B.P. Khemka Pvt. Ltd. v. Birendra Kumar Bhowmik*, AIR 1987 SC 1010, p. 1013 : (1987) 2 SCC 407; *Vatan Mal v. Kailash Nath*, AIR 1989 SC 1534, pp. 1538, 1539 : (1989) 3 SCC 79; *Ashok Singh v. Assistant Controller of Estate Duty*, AIR 1992 SC 1756, p. 1761 : 1992 (3) SCC 169; *Vinod Krishna Kaul v. Union of India*, 1995 (6) Scale 570, p. 571 : (1996) 1 SCC 41; *Special Reference No. 1 of 2002 (*under Article 143(1) of the Constitution*)* AIR 2003 SC 87, p. 140 : (2002) 8 SCC 237, p. 322. *Kishansingh Tomar v. Municipal Corporation, city of Ahmedabad,* AIR 2007 SC 269 (Const. Bench) (paras 17 to 20) : (2006) 8 SCC 352. (Period for holding elections to Municipal Corporation fixed by Article 243-U of the Constitution is mandatory and electoral rolls should be revised within a reasonable time before holding election. But if it is not possible to revise the electoral rolls before the period fixed for holding elections, the election must be held on old electoral rolls. In this case, the case of Special Reference No. 1 of 2002: AIR 2003 SC 87, which is also a Constitution Bench decision regarding elections to a legislative assembly under Article 174(1) of the Constitution and where similar view was taken was **followed**). **But see** *Pilloo Dhunji Shaw v. Municipal Corporation, City of Poona*, AIR 1970 SC 1201, pp. 1203, 1204 : 1970 (1) SCC 213.

90. *R. v. Registrar General, ex parte, Smith*, (1990) 2 All ER 170 : (1991) 2 QB 393 : (1991) 2 WLR 782 (QBD). **See** further for meaning of 'Public Policy' *India Financial Association of Seventh Day Adventists v. M.A. Unneerikutty*, (2006) 6 SCC 351 (para 17) : (2006) 6 JT 351 ("The term 'Public Policy' has an entirely different and more extensive meaning from the policy of the law. Winfield defined it as a principle of judicial legislation or interpretation founded on the current needs of the community. Judges as trusted interpreters of law, have to interpret it. While doing so, precedents will also guide them to a substantial extent.")

91. *Saiyad Mohammad Bakar El-Edroos v. Abdulhabib Hasan Arab*, AIR 1998 SC 1624, p. 1627 : 1998 (4) SCC 343; *Shreenath v. Rajesh*, AIR 1998 SC 1827, p. 1828 : (1998) 4 SCC 543; *New India Assurance Co. Ltd. v. R. Srinivasan*, AIR 2000 SC 941, p. 493 : (2000) 3 SCC 242.

92. *A.R. Antulay v. R.S. Nayak*, AIR 1988 SC 1531, p. 1561 : (1988) 2 SCC 602; *Chinnammal v. Arumugham*, AIR 1990 SC 1828, p. 1833 : 1990 (1) SCC 513. **See further** the maxim *Actus Curiae neminem gravabit*, (which means that an act of the court shall prejudice none) and the following cases : *South Eastern Coalfields Ltd. v. State of M.P.*, (2003) 8 SCC 648 : AIR 2003 SC 4482; *Karnataka Rare Earth v. Senior Geological Department of Mines and Geology*, (2004) 2 SCC 783, pp. 790, 791 : AIR 2004 SC 2915.

fraud.[93] On the principle that codes of procedure are not construed to frustrate justice, the maximum period of detention in police custody of an accused prescribed by section 167(2) of the Code of Criminal Procedure was held to apply to offences committed in one transaction, but not in respect of an offence committed in a different transaction, for a contrary construction would frustrate the investigation of such a different offence by denying police custody normally available for investigation.[94]

The Railway Claims Tribunal Act, 1987 excludes the jurisdiction of all courts to entertain claims against a railway administration and vests the same in the Claims Tribunal constituted under the Act. The Act confers certain powers of civil courts exercisable under the Code of Civil Procedure on the Tribunal but there is no specific mention of the power under Order 33 of the Code of Civil Procedure to entertain claims of indigent persons. Still the Supreme Court ruled that the Tribunal must be held to have the implied power of invoking the provisions of Order 33 of the Code.[95] A contrary conclusion would have resulted in gross injustice to persons unable to pay the required fee as they would have been left without a remedy of either approaching the civil court because of bar of jurisdiction or of moving to the Tribunal because of inapplicability of Order 33.[96]

In the context of Order 22 of the Code of Civil Procedure, 1908 and abatement of entire appeal, when the legal representatives of one of the appellants who died during pendency of appeal are not brought on record in time, a Constitution Bench of the Supreme Court observed, "Laws of procedure are meant to regulate effectively, assist and aid the object of doing substantial and real justice and not to foreclose even an adjudication on the merits of substantial rights of citizens under personal property and other laws. Procedure has always been viewed as the handmaid of justice and not meant to hamper the cause of justice.—Technical objections which tend to be stumbling blocks to defeat and delay substantial and effective justice should be strictly viewed for being discouraged except when mandate of the law inevitably necessitates it."[97]

---

93. *United India Insurance Co. Ltd. v. Rajendra Singh*, AIR 2000 SC 1165 : (2000) 3 SCC 581.

94. *Central Bureau of Investigation v. Anupam J. Kulkarni*, AIR 1992 SC 1768, p. 1779 : (1992) 3 SCC 141.

95. *A.A. Hajee Muniuddin v. Indian Railways*, AIR 1993 SC 361, p. 364 : 1992 (4) SCC 736.

96. *Ibid.*

97. *Sardar Amrjit Singh Kalra v. Pramod Gupta*, (2003) 3 SCC 272 (paras 26 and 31) : AIR 2003 SC 2588.

Consideration of hardship, injustice or absurdity as avoiding a particular construction is a rule which must be applied with great care. "The argument *ab inconvenienti*", said LORD MOULTON, "is one which requires to be used with great caution".[1] Explaining why great caution is necessary LORD MOULTON further observed, "There is a danger that it may degenerate into a mere judicial criticism of the propriety of the Acts of Legislature. We have to interpret statutes according to the language used therein, and though occasionally the respective consequences of two rival interpretations may guide us in our choice in between them, it can only be where, taking the Act as a whole and viewing it in connection with existing state of the law at the time of the passing of the Act, we can satisfy ourselves that the words cannot have been used in the sense to which the argument points".[2] According to BRETT, L.J., the inconvenience necessitating a departure from the ordinary sense of the words should not only be great but should also be what he calls an "absurd inconvenience".[3] Moreover, individual cases of hardship or injustice have no bearing for rejecting the natural construction,[4] and it is only when the natural construction leads to some general hardship or injustice and some other construction is reasonably open that the natural construction may be departed from. It is often found that laws enacted for the general advantage do result in individual hardship; for example laws of Limitation, Registration, Attestation although enacted for the public benefit, may work injustice in particular cases but that is hardly any reason to depart from the normal rule to relieve the supposed hardship or injustice in such cases.[5] "It is the duty of

---

1. *Vacher & Sons v. London Society of Compositors*, (1913) AC 107 : (1911-13) All ER Rep 241, p. 252 (HL).
2. *Vacher & Sons v. London Society of Compositors*, (1913) AC 107 : (1911-13) All ER Rep 241, pp. 252, 253 (HL).
3. *R. v. Townbridge Overseers*, (1884)13 QBD 339, p. 342. **See** *Nasiruddin v. State Transport Appellate Tribunal*, AIR 1976 SC 331, p. 338 : (1975) 2 SCC 671.
4. *Young & Co. v. Leamington Spa Corporation*, (1883) 8 AC 517, p. 527 (HL); *In re, Hindu Women's Rights to Property Act*, AIR 1941 PC 72, p. 77; *Dominion of India v. Shrinbai*, AIR 1954 SC 596, p. 600 : (1955) 1 SCR 206; *Lord Advocate v. De Rosa*, (1974) 2 All ER 849, p. 863 (HL); *Orissa Warehousing Corporation v. Commissioner of Income-tax,* JT 1999 (2) SC 527, p. 540 : AIR 1999 SC 1388 : (1999) 4 SCC 197. The same principle applies in adjudicating upon the constitutionality of a law on the ground of unreasonableness: "A law has to be adjudged for its constitutionality by the generality of cases it covers, not by the freaks and exceptions it martyrs;" *R.S. Joshi v. Ajit Mills Ltd.*, (1977) 4 SCC 98, p. 106 : AIR 1977 SC 2279; *Maharashtra State Board of Secondary and Higher Secondary Education v. Paritosh Bhupesh kumar Sheth*, (1984) 4 SCC 27, p. 50 : AIR 1984 SC 1543; *Shiv Shakti Co-op. Housing Society v. Swaraj Developers,* AIR 2003 SC 2434, pp. 2441, 2442 : (2003) 6 SCC 659.
5. For a case of hardship from Limitation Act, **see** *Lucy v. Henleys Telegraph Works*, (1969) 3 All ER 456, p. 465 (CA). Normally the strict grammatical construction of a

[Footnote No. 5 Contd.]

all courts of justice", said LORD CAMPBELL, "to take care for the general good of the community, that hard cases do not make bad law".[6] 'Absurdity' according to WILLES, J., should be understood "in the same sense as repugnance that is to say something which would be so absurd with reference to the other words of the statute as to amount to a repugnance".[7] "Absurdity", said LORD GREENE, M.R., "like public policy, is a very unruly horse".[8] He proceeded to add: "There is one rule, I think which is clear that, although the absurdity or the non-absurdity of one conclusion as compared with another may be and very often is, of assistance to the court in choosing between two possible meanings of ambiguous words, it is a doctrine which must be applied with great care, remembering that judges may be fallible in this question of an absurdity and in any event it must not be applied so as to result in twisting language into a meaning which it cannot bear. It is a doctrine which must not be used to re-write the language in a way different from that in which it was originally framed".[9] The alternative construction contended for must be such which does not put an undue strain on the words used;[10] and does not require recasting of the Act or any part of it. It must be possible to spell the meaning contended for out of the words actually used.[11]

[Footnote No. 5 Contd.]

limitation provision is the only safe guide: *R. Rudraiah v. State of Karnataka*, JT 1998 (1) SC 435, pp. 443, 444: AIR 1998 SC 1070, p. 1075 : (1998) 3 SCC 23. **See further** text and notes 77, 78, p. 19, *ante*.

6. *East India Company v. Odichurn Paul*, 7 Moo (PC) 85: (1849) 5 MIA 43, p. 69 (PC); *Joseph v. Joseph*, (1966) 3 All ER 486, p. 492 (CA); *Lord Advocate v. De Rosa*, (1974) 2 All ER 849, p. 863 (HL); *State Bank of India v. N. Sundara Money*, AIR 1976 SC 1111, p. 1115 : 1976 SCC (L&S) 132 : (1976) 1 SCC 822; *Mohan Kumar Singhania v. Union of India*, AIR 1992 SC 1, p. 26 : 1992 Supp (1) SCC 594; *Orissa Warehousing Corporation v. Commissioner of Income-tax,* JT 1999 (2) SC 527, p. 540 : AIR 1999 SC 1388 : (1999) 4 SCC 197. LORD DENNING was critical of this maxim; **see** *In re, Vandervell's Trust (No. 2)*, (1974) Ch 269, p. 322. **But** HOLMES, J., in *Northern Securities Co. v. U.S.*, 193 U.S. 197, p. 400 said : "Great cases like hard cases make bad law:" **Referred** in *Indira Nehru Gandhi (Smt.) v. Raj Narain*, AIR 1975 SC 2299, p. 2370 : 1975 Supp SCC 1. Both maxims "Hard cases make bad law" and "Great cases like hard cases make bad law" **referred** by Ravindran, J. in *Vinod Seth v. Devinder Bajaj*, (2010) 8 SCC 1 para 36 : (2010) 8 JT 66.
7. *Christopherson v. Lotinga*, (1864) 33 LJ CP 121, p. 123.
8. *Grundt v. Great Boulder Proprietary Gold Mines Ltd.*, (1948) 1 All ER 21, p. 29 (CA).
9. *Grundt v. Great Boulder Proprietary Gold Mines Ltd.*, (1948) 1 All ER 21, pp. 29, 30 (CA). **See further** *State of Rajasthan v. Leela Jain*, AIR 1965 SC 1296, p. 1301 (Para 16) : (1965) 1 SCR 276: *Keshavananda Bharati v. State of Kerala*, AIR 1973 SC 1461, pp. 1539, 1540 : (1973) 4 SCC 225.
10. *Kanailal Sur v. Paramnidhi Sadhukhan*, AIR 1957 SC 907, p. 911 : 1958 SCR 360.
11. *Shamrao V. Parulekar v. District Magistrate, Thane*, AIR 1952 SC 324, p. 327 : 1952 SCR 683.

No doubt in cases of ambiguity that construction which better serves the ends of fairness and justice will be accepted, but otherwise it is for the Legislature in forming its policy to consider these elements.[12] If no alternative construction is open, the court cannot ignore a statutory provision "to relieve what it considers a distress resulting from its operation; a statute has to be given effect to whether the court likes it or not".[13] The function of the court is to find out what is legal and not what is right.[14] It is presumed that a legislative body intends which is the necessary effect of its enactments; the object, the purpose and the intention of the enactment is the same; it need not be expressed in any recital or preamble; and it is not competent for any court judicially to ascribe any part of the legal operation of the statute to inadvertence.[15]

The Courts should as far as possible avoid a construction which results in anomalies.[16] In a case arising under the Representation of the People Act, 1951, the Supreme Court held that if the Returning Officer had rejected a nomination paper of a candidate on one disqualification, it was open for the Election Tribunal to find the rejection proper on some other ground of disqualification which may not have been raised before the Returning Officer. It was pointed out that if this construction is not placed on section 100(1)(c) Representation of the People Act, 1951 the result will be anomalous in that if the decision under section 36(6) of the Returning Officer on the objection on which he rejected the nomination paper is held to be bad, the Tribunal will have no option but to set aside the election under section 100(1)(c) even though the candidate was disqualified and his nomination paper was rightly rejected. In holding so VENKATARAMA AIYAR, J. observed, "It is no doubt true that if on its true construction, a statute leads to anomalous results, the Courts have no option but to give effect to it and leave it to the Legislature to amend and alter the law. But when on a construction of a statute, two views are possible, one which results in an anomaly and the other not, it is our duty to

---

12. *IRC v. Mutual Investment Co.*, (1966) 3 All ER 265, p. 268 (PC).

13. *Martin Burn Ltd. v. Calcutta Corporation*, AIR 1966 SC 524, p. 535 : (1966) 1 SCR 493.

14. *Chandavarkar Sita Ratna Rao v. Ashalata S. Guram*, (1986) 4 SCC 447, p. 476 : AIR 1987 SC 117.

15. *Kariapper v. Wijesinha*, (1967) 3 All ER 485, p. 494 : 1968 AC 717 (PC).

16. *N.T. Veluswami Thevar v. G. Raja Nainar*, AIR 1959 SC 422, pp. 427, 428 : 1959 Supp (1) SCR 623; *Indo China Steam Navigation Co. Ltd. v. Jasjit Singh*, AIR 1964 SC 1140, p. 1149 : (1964) 6 SCR 594 (para 23); *Banarsi Devi v. ITO*, AIR 1964 SC 1742, p. 1746 (para 11) : 1964 (7) SCR 539; *Lalji Haridas v. State of Maharashtra*, AIR 1964 SC 1154, pp. 1159, 1160 (para 16) : 1964 (6) SCR 700 : 66 Bom LR 460; *Deputy Custodian v. Official Receiver*, AIR 1965 SC 951, p. 955 (para 9) : 1965 (1) SCR 220; *Mahijibhai v. Manibhai*, AIR 1965 SC 1477, p. 1485 (para 29) : 1965 (2) SCR 436.

adopt the latter and not the former, seeking consolation in the thought that the law bristles with anomalies."[17]

Rule 11(VI) of the Central Services (Classification, Appeal and Control) Rules, 1965 empowers the imposition of the penalty of "reduction to a lower time-scale of pay, grade, post or service". In construing this rule the Supreme Court held that a person initially recruited to a higher time-scale, grade or post or service cannot be reduced to a post in a lower time-scale, grade or service or to a lower post. Though the language of the rule is *prima facie* wide, a restricted construction was placed to avoid the anomaly which a wider construction would have produced for a person directly recruited to a higher post may not have the requisite qualification or skills for the lower post and his reduction to a lower post may affect the recruitment policy itself.[18]

In construing section 446(1) of the Companies Act, 1956, which provides that when a winding up order has been made or the official liquidator has been appointed no suit or legal proceedings shall be commenced or continued against the company except with the leave of the court, the Supreme Court held that assessment proceedings under the Income-tax Act do not fall within the section. This conclusion was reached on the ground that only such proceedings fall under section 446(1) which could appropriately be dealt with by the winding up court under section 446(2) and "it would lead to anomalous consequences if the winding up court were to be held empowered to transfer the assessment proceeding to itself and assess the company to income-tax".[19]

But when a statute deals with a subject-matter which is productive of many difficulties, not all of which can be perceived and provided against in advance, anomalies cannot be treated as a satisfactory guide in matters of construction, and the courts can do no more than look at the language used and give it a fair and reasonable construction.[20] Similarly, when none of the alternative constructions can steer clear of the anomalies, the question cannot be resolved by a balancing of the anomalies[21] and grammatical construction of the provision in question is the only safe guide.[22] It must also be remembered that a court would only be justified in departing from

17. *N.T.Veluswami Thevar v. G. Raja Nainar*, AIR 1959 SC 422, pp. 427, 428 : 1959 Supp (1) SCR 623.
18. *Nyadar Singh v. Union of India*, AIR 1988 SC 1979, pp. 1985, 1986 : 1988 (4) SCC 170.
19. *S.V. Kondeakar v. V.M. Deshpande*, AIR 1972 SC 878, p. 886 : 1972 (1) SCC 438 : (1972) 83 ITR 685.
20. *Duckering v. Gollan*, (1965) 2 All ER 115, p. 120 (HL).
21. *Dawson v. Inland Revenue Commissioner*, (1989) 2 All ER 289, p. 292 : (1990) 1 AC 1 (HL).
22. *Bhagwandas v. Parasnath*, AIR 1970 SC 971, p. 976 : 1969 (2) SCR 297.

the plain word of the statute when it is satisfied that (1) there is clear and gross balance of anomaly, (2) Parliament, the legislative promoters and the draftsman could not have envisaged such anomaly and could not have been prepared to accept it in the interest of a supervening legislative objective, (3) the anomaly can be obviated without detriment to such a legislative objective, and (4) the language of the statute is susceptible of the modification required to obviate the anomaly.[23] Therefore, the court cannot decline to give effect to clear and unambiguous language to avoid an anomaly even if it was the result of an omission on the part of the draftsman which went undetected during passage of the Bill through Parliament.[24]

(b) Inconsistency and repugnancy to be avoided; harmonious construction

It has already been seen that a statute must be read as a whole and one provision of the Act should be construed with reference to other provisions in the same Act so as to make a consistent enactment of the whole statute.[25] Such a construction has the merit of avoiding any inconsistency or repugnancy either within a section or between a section and other parts of the statute. It is the duty of the courts to avoid "a head on clash"[26] between two sections of the same Act and, "whenever it is possible to do so, to construe provisions which appear to conflict so that they harmonise".[27] Accordingly, the provisions of the Maharashtra Regional and Town Planning Act, 1966, were read together by the Supreme Court after noting the purpose of the Act. The Act was held not to envisage a situation of conflict, and therefore, the edges were required to be ironed out to read those provisions of the Act which were slightly incongruous, so that all of them are read in consonance with the object of the Act, which is to bring about orderly and planned development.[28] It should not be lightly assumed that "Parliament

---

23. *Stock v. Frank Jones (Tipton) Ltd.*, (1978) 1 All ER 948, p. 954 : (1978) 1 WLR 231 (HL) (LORD SIMON) **quoted with approval** in *Afcons Infrastructure Ltd. v. Cherian Varkey Construction Co. (Pvt. Ltd.)*, (2010) 8 SCC 24 para 21.6 : (2010) 7 JT 616.

24. *Regina v. Secretary of State for Foreign and Commonwealth Affairs*, (1991) 3 WLR 146 : (1991) 2 AC 439 : (1991) 3 All ER 353 (HL).

25. **See** Chapter 1, title 3, 'Statute must be read as a whole in its context' p. 35.

26. *Raj Krushna v. Binod Kanungo*, AIR 1954 SC 202, p. 203 : 1954 SCR 913; *Sultana Begum v. Premchand Jain,* AIR 1997 SC 1006, pp. 1009, 1010 : 1997 (1) SCC 373; *Kailash Chandra v. Mukundi Lal,* AIR 2002 SC 829, p. 834 : (2002) 2 SCC 678; *CIT v. Hindustan Bulk Carriers,* (2003) 3 SCC 57, p. 74 : AIR 2003 SC 3942.

27. *Ibid.* **See further** *University of Allahabad v. Amritchand Tripathi*, AIR 1987 SC 57, p. 60 : 1986 (4) SCC 176; *Krishna Kumar v. State of Rajasthan*, AIR 1992 SC 1789, pp. 1793, 1794 : 1991 (4) SCC 258; *Sultana Begum v. Premchand Jain, supra; Commissioner of Income-tax v. Hindustan Bulk Carriers, supra*; *Afjal Imam v. State of Bihar*, (Paras 55, 56 and 60).

28. *Manohar Joshi v. State of Maharashtra and Others*, (2012) 3 SCC 619, p. 676.

had given with one hand what it took away with the other".[29] The provisions of one section of a statute cannot be used to defeat those of another "unless it is impossible to effect reconciliation between them".[30] The same rule applies in regard to sub-sections of a section. In the words of GAJENDRAGADKAR, J., "The sub-sections must be read as parts of an integral whole and as being interdependent; an attempt should be made in construing them to reconcile them if it is reasonably possible to do so, and to avoid repugnancy".[31] As stated by VENKATARAMA AIYAR, J., "The rule of construction is well settled that when there are in an enactment two provisions which cannot be reconciled with each other, they should be so interpreted that, if possible, effect should be given to both. This is what is known as the rule of harmonious construction".[32] That, effect should be given to both, is the very essence of the rule. Thus a construction that reduces one of the provisions to a "useless lumber"[33] or "dead letter"[34] is not

---

29. *Dormer v. Newcastle-on-Tyne Corpn.*, (1940) 2 All ER 521, p. 527 (CA) (GODDARD, L.J.). **See further** *Tahsildar Singh v. State of U.P.*, AIR 1959 SC 1012, p. 1022 : 1959 Supp (2) SCR 875; *K.M. Nanawati v. State of Bombay*, AIR 1961 SC 112, p. 137 : (1961) 1 SCR 497; *Krishna Kumar v. State of Rajasthan, supra; Central Bank of India v. Ravindra*, AIR 2001 SC 3095, p. 3114 : (2002) 1 SCC 367 (7th Edition p. 113 of this book is **referred**); *Commissioner of Income-tax v. Hindustan Bulk Carriers, supra*; *Godawat Pan Masala Products India P. Ltd. v. Union of India*, (2004) 7 SCC 68, p. 88 : AIR 2004 SC 4057 [Power of Central Government to make rules under section 22(1-A)(f) of the Prevention of Food Adulteration Act, 1954 to prohibit manufacture and sale of such articles, which are injurious to health, shows that the State Government has no such power and the power conferred by section 7(iv) on the Food (Health) Authority to prohibit sale 'for the time being' is to meet an exigency for a short term.]

30. *Mohammad Sher Khan v. Raja Seth Swami Dayal*, AIR 1922 PC 17, p. 19. **See further** *Sanjeevayya D. v. Election Tribunal, Andhra Pradesh*, AIR 1967 SC 1211, p. 1213 (para 4) : 1967 (2) SCR 489; *Krishna Kumar v. State of Rajasthan, supra*; *Sultana Begum v. Premchand Jain, supra; Commissioner of Income-tax v. Hindustan Bulk Carriers, supra.*

31. *Madanlal Fakirchand Dudhediya v. Shree Changdeo Sugar Mills Ltd.*, AIR 1962 SC 1543, p. 1551 : (1962) 2 SCR 36; **see further** *Tahsildar Singh v. State of U.P., supra*, p. 1022. **See** Chapter 1, title 3 'Statute must be read as a whole' in its context, text and notes 88, p. 46; and Chapter 3, title 9(h) 'The Broad General Rule of Construction', text and notes 25 to 31, pp. 233-234.

32. *Venkataramana Devaru v. State of Mysore*, AIR 1958 SC 255, p. 268 : 1958 SCR 895; *Krishna Kumar v. State of Rajasthan*, AIR 1992 SC 1789, p. 1794 : 1991 (3) SCR 500 : (1991) 4 SCC 258; *Sultana Begum v. Premchand Jain*, AIR 1997 SC 1006, pp. 1009, 1010 : 1997 (1) SCC 373. **See further,** *British Airways Plc v. Union of India,* AIR 2002 SC 391, p. 393 : (2002) 2 SCC 95.

33. *Calcutta Gas Co. (Proprietary) Ltd. v. State of W.B.*, AIR 1962 SC 1044, p. 1051 : 1962 Supp (3) SCR 1; *Sultana Begum v. Premchand Jain, supra; CIT v. Hindustan Bulk Carriers,* (2003) 3 SCC 57, p. 74 : (2003) 159 ITR 449.

34. *J.K. Cotton Spinning & Weaving Mills v. State of U.P.*, AIR 1961 SC 1170, p. 1174 : 1962 (1) SCJ 417 : (1961) 3 SCR 185; *Sultana Begum v. Premchand Jain, supra; Anwar Hasan Khan v. Mohammad Shaji,* AIR 2001 SC 2984, p. 2986 : (2001) 8 SCC 540; *Commissioner of Income-tax v. Hindustan Bulk Carriers, supra.*

harmonious construction. To harmonise is not to destroy.[35] A familiar approach in all such cases is to find out which of the two apparently conflicting provisions is more general and which is more specific and to construe the more general one as to exclude the more specific.[36] The question as to the relative nature of the provisions general or special has to be determined with reference to the area and extent of their application either generally or specially in particular situations.[37] The principle is expressed in the maxims *Generalia specialibus non derogant*,[38] and *Generalibus specialia derogant*.[39] If a special provision is made on a certain matter, that matter is excluded from the general provision.[40] Apart from resolving conflict between two provisions in the Act, the principle can also be used for resolving a conflict between a provision in the Act and a rule made under the Act.[41] Further, these principles have also been applied in resolving a conflict between two different Acts[42] and two provisions in the Constitution

---

35. *J.K.Cotton Spinning & Weaving Mills v. State of U.P.*, AIR 1961 SC 1170, p. 1174 : 1962 (1) SCJ 417 : (1961) 3 SCR 185; *Chief Inspector of Mines v. Karam Chand Thaper*, AIR 1961 SC 838, p. 843 (para 13) : 1962 (1) SCR 9; *Sultana Begum v. Premchand Jain, supra*.
36. *South India Corporation (P) Ltd. v. Secretary, Board of Revenue, Trivandrum*, AIR 1964 SC 207, p. 215 : 1964 (4) SCR 280; *Weverly Jute Mills Co. Ltd. v. Raymon & Co. (India) (Pvt.) Ltd.*, AIR 1963 SC 90, p. 95 : (1963) 3 SCR 209; *J.K. Cotton Spinning & Weaving Mills v. State of U.P.*, AIR 1961 SC 1170, p. 1194 : 1962 (1) SCJ 417 : (1961) 3 SCR 185; *Paradip Port Trust v. Their Workmen*, AIR 1977 SC 36, p. 44 : 1977 SCC (L&S) 253; *U.P. State Electricity Board v. Harishanker*, AIR 1979 SC 65 : (1978) 4 SCC 16 : 1978 SCC (Lab) 481; *Life Insurance Corporation of India v. D.J. Bahadur*, AIR 1980 SC 2181, pp. 2202, 2208; *State of U.P. v. Renusagar Power Co.*, AIR 1988 SC 1737, p. 1751 : 1988 (4) SCC 59; *State of Rajasthan v. Gopikishan, supra*, p. 1756. **See further** *Life Insurance Corporation of India v. S.V. Oak*, AIR 1965 SC 975, p. 980 : 1965 (1) SCR 403 (Compulsive provision will control a discretionary provision).
37. *Collector of Central Excise Jaipur v. Raghuvar (India) Ltd.*, JT 2000 (7) SC 99, p. 111 : (2000) 5 SCC 299 : AIR 2000 SC 2027.
38. General things do not derogate from special things. OSBORN'S Law Dictionary.
39. Special things derogate from general things. OSBORN'S Law Dictionary.
40. *Venkateshwar Rao v. Govt. of Andhra Pradesh*, AIR 1966 SC 828 : 1966 (2) SCR 172; *CIT, Patiala v. Shahzada Nand & Sons*, AIR 1966 SC 1342, p. 1347 : (1966) 3 SCR 379; *State of Gujarat v. Patel Ramajibhai Danabhai*, AIR 1979 SC 1098, p. 1103 : 1979 (3) SCC 347; *State of Bihar v. Yogendra Singh*, AIR 1982 SC 882, p. 886 : (1982) 1 SCC 664; *Maharashtra State Board of Secondary and Higher Secondary Education v. Paritosh Bhupesh Kumar Sheth*, (1984) 4 SCC 27, p. 47 : AIR 1984 SC 1543; *State of Rajasthan v. Gopikishan, supra*, p. 1756.
41. *Collector of Central Excise, Jaipur v. Raghuvar India Ltd., supra*, (section 11A of the Central Excise Act,1944 and Rule 57-I of the Central Excise Rules,1944).
42. **See** text and notes 83-97, pp. 410-414, Chapter 7, title 5(b) and 5(c), pp. 741 to 752. For example, **see** *Jogendra Lal Saha v. State of Bihar*, AIR 1991 SC 1148, p. 1149 : 1991 Supp (2) SCC 654; (Sections 82 and 83 of the Forest Act, 1927 are special provisions which prevail over the provisions in the Sale of Goods Act, 1930);

[Footnote No. 42 Contd.]

added by two different Constitution Amendment Acts.[43] and in the construction of statutory rules[44] and statutory orders.[45] But the principle, that a special provision on a matter excludes the application of a general provision on that matter, has not been applied when the two provisions deal with remedies, for validity of plural remedies cannot be doubted.[46] Even if the two remedies happen to be inconsistent, they continue for the person concerned to choose from, until he elects one of them.[47]

For instance, section 32 of the Securities and Exchange Board of India Act, 1992, provides that the provisions of the Act shall be in addition to

---

[Footnote No. 42 Contd.]

Jasbir Singh v. Vipin Kumar Jaggi, AIR 2001 SC 2734, p. 2743 : (2001) 8 SCC 289 (Section 64 of NDPS Act, 1985 will prevail over section 307 CrPC, 1973 as it is a special provision in a Special Act which is also later); *P.V. Hemalatha v. Kattamkandi Puthiya Maliackal Saheeda,* AIR 2002 SC 2445, p. 2457 : (2002) 5 SCC 548 : (2002) 1 KLJ 665 (conflict between section 23 of the Travancore Cochin High Court Act and section 98(3) Civil Procedure Code, 1908 resolved by holding the latter to be special law. Reference is made to pp. 113, 114 of 7th Edition of this book). *Talchar Municipality v. Talcher Regulated Market Committee*, (2004) 6 SCC 178 : AIR 2004 SC 3954 (Section 4(4) of the Orissa Agricultural Produce Markets Act, 1956 was held to prevail over section 295 of the Orissa Municipalities Act, 1950 as the former was a special provision and also started with a *non-obstante* clause); *Iridium India Telecom Ltd. v. Motorola Inc*, (2005) 2 SCC 145, pp. 163, 164 (Letters Patent and rules made under it constitute special law for the High Court concerned and are not displaced by the general provisions of the Civil Procedure Code, 1908.); *Gujrat Urea Vikas Nigam Ltd. v. Essar Power Ltd.,* (2008) 4 SCC 755 paras 25 and 28 : AIR 2008 SC 1921 (Section 86(1)(f) of the Electricity Act, 2003 is a special provision and will prevail over section 11 of the Arbitration and Conciliation Act, 1996). *Sesa Sterlite Ltd. v. Orissa Electricity Regulatory Commission & Ors.*, (2014) 8 SCC 444, pp. 463 to 468 (The proviso to section 14(b) of the Electricity Act, 2003, provides that the developer of an SEZ notified under section 4(1) of the Special Economic Zones Act, 2005, shall be deemed to be a licensee for the purposes of this clause. By this proviso the developer of an SEZ only gets an exemption from specifically applying for licence under section 14 of the Electricity Act, but in order to avail further benefits under the Electricity Act it must have a distribution system and consumers to whom it supplies electricity as required under the said Act).

43. *Ashoka Kumar Thakur v. Union of India*, (2008) 6 SCC 1 para 126 : (2008) 5 JT 1 [Conflict between Articles 15(4) and 15(5) of the Constitution added respectively by the Constitution (First Amendment) Act 1951 and Constitution (Ninety Third Amendment) Act, 2005].

44. *A.N. Sehgal v. Raje Ram Sheoram*, AIR 1991 SC 1406, p. 1413 : 1991 (2) JT 123 : 1992 Supp (1) SCC 304; *State of Rajasthan v. Gopikishan*, AIR 1992 SC 1754, p. 1756 : 1993 Supp (1) SCC 522; *Jagdish Singh v. Lt. Governor, Delhi*, AIR 1997 SC 2239, p. 2242 : 1997 (4) SCC 435.

45. *J.K. Cotton Spinning & Weaving Mills Ltd. v. State of U. P.*, AIR 1961 SC 1170 : 1962 (1) SCJ 417 : (1961) 3 SCR 185.

46. *Bihar State Co-operative Marketing Union Ltd. v. Uma Shankar Saran*, AIR 1993 SC 1222, p. 1224 : 1992 (4) SCC 196.

47. *Ibid.*

and not in derogation of the provisions of any other law. The Supreme Court held that the SEBI Act is a special Act dealing with a specific subject, which has to be read in harmony with the provisions of the Companies Act, 1956, and that both the Acts will have to work in tandem in the interest of the investors, especially when public money is raised by issue of securities from the people at large.[48]

The Supreme Court applied the rule in resolving a conflict between Articles 25(2)(b) and 26(b) of the Constitution and it was held that the right of every religious denomination or any section thereof to manage its own affairs in matter of religion [Article 26(b)] is subject to a law made by a State providing for social welfare and reform or throwing open of Hindu religious institutions of a public character to all classes and sections of Hindus [Article 25(2)(b)].[49]

Same rule was applied to resolve the conflict between Articles 19(1)(a) and 194(3) of the Constitution and it was held that the right of freedom of speech guaranteed under Art. 19(1)(a) is to be read as subject to powers, privileges and immunities of a House of the Legislature which are those of the House of Commons of the United Kingdom as declared by latter part of Article 194(3).[50] It is, however, interesting to notice that in *Special Reference No. 1 of 1964*,[51] it was decided that Article 194(3) is subordinate to Articles 21, 32, 211 and 226. This conclusion was also reached by recourse to the rule of harmonious construction.

By invoking the same rule the Supreme Court held that the apparently absolute power of the Governor under Article 161 of the Constitution to grant pardon or to suspend a sentence passed on an accused person is not available during the period the matter becomes *sub judice* before the Supreme Court as otherwise it will conflict with the judicial power of that court provided under Article 142 of the Constitution.[52] A similar result was reached in interpreting sections 401 and 426 of the Code of Criminal Procedure, 1898.[53]

Applying the same rule it has been held that the general provision under Article 372 of the Constitution regarding continuance of existing laws is subject to Article 277 of the Constitution which is a special provision

---

48. *Sahara India Real Estate Corporation Ltd. & Ors. v. SEBI & Anr.*, (2013) 1 SCC 1, pp. 57, 60.

49. *Venkataramana Devaru v. State of Mysore*, AIR 1958 SC 255 : 1958 SCR 895.

50. *M.S.M. Sharma v. Krishna Sinha*, AIR 1959 SC 395, p. 410 : 1959 Supp (1) SCR 806.

51. AIR 1965 SC 745, p. 761 (para 36) : 1965 (1) SCR 413.

52. *K.M. Nanawati v. State of Bombay*, AIR 1961 SC 112, pp. 122, 123, 124 : 1961 (1) SCR 497.

53. *Ibid.*, p. 121.

relating to taxes, duties, cesses or fees lawfully levied at the commencement of the Constitution.[54]

The principle of harmonious construction has very often been applied in construction of apparently conflicting legislative entries in Schedule VII of the Government of India Act, 1935 and the Constitution.[55]

An important question as to the power of courts to decide a question of privilege concerning documents relating to affairs of State was answered by the Supreme Court by harmonising sections 123 and 162 of the Indian Evidence Act, 1872.[56] The affidavit of the head of the department or the minister is not conclusive that a particular document relates to affairs of State. The opinion of the Head of the Department or the Minister is open to judicial review and if necessary the court can inspect the document. In deciding upon the question of privilege the court has to balance the public interest which demands the withholding of the document against the public interest in the administration of justice that the courts should have fullest possible access to all relevant materials[57] and in the citizen's right of information under Article 19(1)(a) of the Constitution.[58]

An interesting question relating to a conflict between two equally mandatory provisions, *viz*., sections 17(1) and 18(1) of the Industrial Disputes Act, 1947, is a good illustration of the importance of the principle that every effort should be made to give effect to all the provisions of an Act by

---

54. *South India Corporation (P) Ltd. v. Secy., Board of Revenue, Trivandrum*, AIR 1964 SC 207, p. 215 : 1964 (4) SCR 280.

55. *In re, C.P. & Berar Motor Spirit & Lubricants Taxation Act*, AIR 1939 FC 1, p. 5; *G.G. In Council v. Province of Madras*, AIR 1945 PC 98, pp. 100, 101; *Calcutta Gas (Proprietary) Ltd. v. State of W.B.*, AIR 1962 SC 1044, p. 1050 : 1962 Supp (3) SCR 1; *Waverly Jute Mills Co. Ltd. v. Raymon & Co. (India) (Pvt.) Ltd.*, AIR 1963 SC 90, p. 95 : 1963 (3) SCR 209.

56. *State of Uttar Pradesh v. Raj Narain*, AIR 1975 SC 865 : (1975) 4 SCC 478; *S.P. Gupta v. President of India*, AIR 1982 SC 149 : 1981 Supp SCC 87. **See further** *Doypack Systems Pvt. Ltd. v. Union of India*, AIR 1988 SC 782, pp. 797, 798 : (1988) 2 SCC 299; *R.K. Jain v. Union of India*, AIR 1993 SC 1769, pp. 1774, 1788, 1795-97 : 1993 (4) SCC 119.

57. *Ibid*. The law is the same in America and England; **see** *Nixon v. U.S.A.*, (1975) 418 U.S. 683; *Conway v. Rimmer*, (1968) 1 All ER 874 (HL); *Burmah Oil Co. Ltd. v. Bank of England*, (1979) 3 All ER 700 : 1980 AC 1090 : (1979) 3 WLR 722 (HL) (This case makes a distinction between a 'class' objection and a 'contents' objection; **see** pp. 732, 733 All ER). On the question as to when will the court direct production of the document for its inspection to decide the objection of privilege **see** *Air Canada v. Secretary of State for Trade*, (1983) 1 All ER 910 : (1983) 2 AC 394 : (1983) 2 WLR 494 (HL).

58. *Peoples Union for Civil Liberties v. Union of India*, AIR 2004 SC 1442 : (2004) 2 SCC 476 (Govt. order of non-disclosure of the report of the Atomic Energy Regulatory Board Privilege held justified).

harmonising any apparent conflict between two or more of its provisions. Section 17(1) of the Act requires the Government to publish every award of a Labour Tribunal within thirty days of its receipt and by sub-section (2) of section 17 the award on its publication becomes final. Section 18(1) of the Act provides that a settlement between employer and workmen shall be binding on the parties to the agreement. In a case where a settlement was arrived at after receipt of the award of a Labour Tribunal by the Government but before its publication, the question was whether the Government was still required by section 17(1) to publish the award. In construing these two equally mandatory provisions, the Supreme Court held that the only way to resolve the conflict was to hold that by the settlement, which becomes effective from the date of signing, the industrial dispute comes to an end and the award becomes infructuous and the Government cannot publish it.[59]

Another example of application of the rule is found in the construction of section 100(4) and section 217(2)(e) of the Motor Vehicles Act, 1988. Section 217(2)(e) requires that all pending Nationalisation Schemes under the repealed Act should be finalised in accordance with section 100 of the new Act. Section 100(4) provides that schemes not finalised within one year from the date of publication of the proposal shall lapse. There was no such limitation under the repealed Act and schemes remained pending for years after the proposal was published. To give effect to both sections 100(4) and 217(2)(e) it was held that in cases of schemes pending under the repealed Act the period of one year will be counted from the commencement of the new Act and not from the publication of the proposal.[60]

A further example may be found in the interpretation of section 6 of the Madhya Pradesh Motor Vehicles Taxation Act, 1947 which prohibits a local Authority to impose "a tax toll or licence fee in respect of a motor vehicle". Section 3(1) of the Taxation Act authorises imposition of a tax on "motor vehicles used or kept for use" at the specified rates. Section 127(1)(iii) of the Madhya Pradesh Municipalities Act, 1961 authorises imposition of tax on "vehicles-entering the limits of the municipality". On a comparison of the two Acts the Supreme Court held that on harmonious

---

59. *Sirsilk Ltd. v. Govt. of Andhra Pradesh*, AIR 1964 SC 160, pp. 162, 163 : 1964 (2) SCR 448.
N.B.—For further illustration **see** *Life Insurance Corporation of India v. S. V. Oak*, AIR 1965 SC 975, p. 980 : 1965 (1) SCR 403 (sections 9 and 28 of the Life Insurance Corporation Act 1958); *Sadanandan Bhadran v. Madhavan Sunil Kumar,* AIR 1998 SC 3043, p. 3047 : 1998 (6) SCC 514 (sections 138 and 142 of the Negotiable Instruments Act, 1881).

60. *Krishna Kumar v. State of Rajasthan*, AIR 1992 SC 1789 : 1991 (4) SCC 258.

construction of the two Acts the prohibition in section 6 of the Taxatio Act related to a tax on vehicles used or kept for use which could be levie under section 3(1) and not the entry tax which could be imposed by a mu nicipality under section 127(1)(iii) of the Act.[61]

The rule of harmonious construction was also applied in construing an resolving the conflict between sections 276B and 278B of the Income-ta Act, 1961.[62] Section 276B lays down that if a person fails to pay to th credit of the Central Government the tax deducted at source, he shall b punished with rigorous imprisonment for a term which shall not be les than three months and shall also be liable to fine. Section 278B expressl and also as supported from the recommendation in the Law Comissio report makes a company and its officers liable for the offences under th Act. The mandatory sentence of imprisonment prescribed by section 276I obviously could not be applied to a company. The question, therefore arose whether a company could at all be prosecuted under section 276B Resolving the conflict by harmonious construction, it was held that th company would be liable for the offence but it will be liable to be punishe only by imposition of fine. By adopting the rule of harmonious constructio the mandatory sentence of imprisonment in section 276B was interpreted t mean that it will be imposed where it is possible to impose it.[63] Sectio 129(6) of the Customs Act, 1962, which prohibits the President, Vice Presi dent and any other Member of the Appellate Tribunal from appearing, act ing or pleading before the Appellate Tribunal on ceasing to hold office, an section 146-A(2)(c) of the Act, which refers to appearance by a legal practi tioner who is entitled to practice in accordance with law, were therefore rea conjunctively and harmoniously to hold that the President, Vice-President c any Member, on ceasing to hold office, cannot appear before the Appellat Tribunal.[64]

As already seen the principle of harmonious construction is also appli cable in construction of provisions of subordinate legislation.[65] For exam ple the principle was applied in resolving a conflict between clause 5(a and clause 23 of the Government Order, 1948, passed under the Uttar Pra desh Industrial Disputes Act, 1947. It was held that the special provisio made in clause 23 relating to discharge or dismissal of workmen pendin

---

61. *Cantonment Board, Mhow v. M.P. State Road Transport Corporation*, AIR 1997 S 2013, p. 2019 : 1997 (4) JT 561 : (1997) 9 SCC 450.
62. *M. V. Javali v. Mahajan Borewell & Co.*, JT 1997 (8) SC 386 : (1997) 8 SCC 72 AIR 1997 SC 3964.
63. *M.V. Javali v. Mahajan Borewell & Co.*, JT 1997 (8) SC 386, pp. 391, 392 : 1997 (8 SCC 72.
64. *N.K. Bajpai v. Union of India & Anr.*, (2012) 4 SCC 653, p. 683.
65. **See** text and notes 44 and 45, p. 162 *supra*.

an inquiry or appeal was outside the more general provisions of clause 5(a) which related to all industrial disputes in general.[66]

This rule was also applied in interpreting different exemption entries under the Sales Tax New Incentive Scheme for Industries, 1985, notified in the State of Rajasthan. The Court held that the rule of statutory construction that the specific governs the general is not an absolute rule but is merely a strong indication of statutory meaning that can be overcome by textual indications that point in the other direction. However, this rule is particularly applicable where the Legislature has enacted a comprehensive scheme and has deliberately targeted specific problems with specific solutions. A subject-specific provision relating to a specific, defined and descriptable subject is regarded as an exception to, and would prevail over, a general provision relating to a broad subject. Accordingly, an assessee, which fulfilled the criteria of a large scale cement industry, was held to be entitled to the specific exemption of 25% for new cement units under Item 1-E of the Scheme, and not to general exemption of 75% for prestigious units under Item 4 of the Scheme.[67]

(c) When Reconciliation not possible

If two sections of an Act cannot be reconciled, as there may be absolute contradictions, it is often said that the last must prevail.[68] But this should be accepted only in the last resort. As observed by LORD EVERSHED, M.R., "It is no doubt true that if two sections of an Act of Parliament are in truth irreconcilable, then *prima facie* the later will be preferred. But these are arguments of the last resort. The first duty of the court must be, if the result is fairly possible, to give effect to the whole expression of the parliamentary intention".[69] In a case in which two provisos were somewhat repugnant to each other, LORD MACMILLAN said: "If proviso 2 is repugnant in any way to proviso 1, it must prevail for it stands last in the enactment and so to quote LORD TENTERDEN, C.J., 'speaks the last intention of the makers'. The last word is with the respondent and must prevail".[70] But the rule that the later section should always be preferred in case it is irreconcilable with a prior section, seems somewhat doubtful and illogical for as JERVIES, C.J., observed during the course of arguments in a case: "How can we say that one provision is repealed by the other when both received

---

66. *J.K. Cotton Spinning & Weaving Mills Ltd. v. State of U.P.*, AIR 1961 SC 1170 : 1962 (1) SCJ 417 : (1961) 3 SCR 185.

67. *CTO v. Binani Cements Ltd. & Anr.*, (2014) 8 SCC 319, pp. 338, 339.

68. *Wood v. Riley*, (1867) LR 3 CP 26, p. 27; *K.M. Nanavati v. State of Bombay*, AIR 1961 SC 112, p. 137 : 1961 (1) SCR 497.

69. *Eastbourne Corpn. v. Fortes Ltd.*, (1959) 2 All ER 102, p. 107 (CA).

70. *King v. Dominion Engineering Co. Ltd.*, AIR 1947 PC 94, p. 95.

the Royal assent at the same time"?[71] In case of conflict between two sections of the same Act a more logical approach is indicated by LORD HERSCHELL, L.C., "You have to try and reconcile them as best as you may. If you cannot, you have to determine which is the leading provision, and which the subordinate provision and which must give way to the other".[72] After quoting these words of LORD HERSCHELL L.C., the High Court of Australia observed: "only by determining the hierarchy of the provisions will it be possible in many cases to give each provision the meaning which best gives effect to its purpose and language maintaining the unity of the statutory scheme."[73] In case of a conflict between two sections of a statute which cannot be reconciled, the Court must determine which the leading provision is, and which the subordinate provision is, and which must give way to the other. Hence, the Supreme Court held that section 47 of the Persons with Disabilities (Equal Opportunities, Protection of Rights and Full Participation) Act, 1995, was the 'leading provision', being a positive provision, and that section 73 was the 'subordinate provision', being a machinery provision, and accordingly section 73 must give way to section 47.[74]

(d) Avoiding uncertainty and friction in the system which the statute purports to regulate

This principle has been stated by LORD SHAW in the following words: "Where words of a statute are clear, they must, of course, be followed but in their Lordships' opinion, where alternative constructions are equally open that alternative is to be chosen which will be consistent with the smooth working of the system which the statute purports to be regulating; and that alternative is to be rejected which will introduce uncertainty, friction or confusion into the working of the system".[75]

The above principle was accepted and the observations of LORD SHAW were quoted from Maxwell by SUBBARAO, J., in construing section 193 of the Sea Customs Act, 1878 and in coming to the conclusion that the Chief

---

71. *Castrige v. Page*, (1853) 138 ER 1278, p. 1279.

72. *Institute of Patent Agents v. Lockwood*, (1894) AC 347, p. 360 : 63 LJ PC 75 (HL); **quoted** in another connection in *Chief Inspector of Mines v. Karam Chand Thapar*, AIR 1961 SC 838, p. 844 : (1962) 1 SCR 9. **See further** *Laxmi Devi v. Mukund Kanwar*, AIR 1965 SC 834, p. 838 (Para 16) : 1965 (1) SCR 726, where section 2(d) of the Transfer of Property Act, 1882 was held to prevail over section 5 of the same Act.

73. *Project Blue Sky Inc. v. Australian Broadcasting Authority*, (1998) 72 ALJR 841, p. 855 (Aust.).

74. *Union of India v. Dileep Kumar Singh*, (2015) 4 SCC 421, pp. 428 to 429.

75. *Shannon Realties Ltd. v. St. Michel (Ville De)*, (1924) AC 185, pp. 192, 193 (PC); *Central Bank of India v. Ravindra,* AIR 2001 SC 3095, p. 3114 : (2002) 1 SCC 367 (Reference is made to 7th Edition p. 119 of this book).

Customs Authority was not an 'Officer of Customs'.[76] Same principle was applied in construing section 2(c) of the Suppression of Immoral Traffic in Women and Girls Act, 1956, which defines a Magistrate to mean 'a District Magistrate, a Sub-Divisional Magistrate of the First Class specially empowered by the State Government—'.[77] It was held that the empowering does not require the process of selection or discrimination as regards an individual on whom the special power is conferred and the adverb 'specially' refers to the special purpose of empowerment. One of the reasons given was that a contrary conclusion would impede the efficacy of the provision and introduce inconvenience, friction, confusion and artificiality in the working of the provision.

Similar principle was applied by the Supreme Court in construing the fundamental right under Article 22(1) and (2) of the Constitution; and it was held that the said Article applies to give protection against such arrests as are effected otherwise than under a warrant issued by a court on the allegation or accusation that the arrested person has committed some criminal or *quasi*-criminal act and that the physical restraint put upon an abducted person in process of recovering and taking into custody and delivery of the person to the custody of an officer-in-charge of the nearest camp under section 4 of Abducted Persons (Recovery and Restoration) Act, 1949, is not arrest and detention within the meaning of Article 22(1) and (2). In holding so S.R. DAS, J., observed: "If two constructions are possible then the court must adopt that which will ensure smooth and harmonious working of the Constitution and eschew the other which will lead to absurdity or give rise to practical inconvenience or make well-established provision of existing law nugatory".[78]

And in construing Article 371-D of the Constitution, the Supreme Court held that the words 'civil service of the State' as used therein did not include the High Court staff and the subordinate judiciary, although the same words used in Article 311 include these categories. The narrower construction of these words in Article 371-D was adopted on the ground that a wider construction would encroach upon the principle of independence of judiciary enshrined in Articles 229 and 235 of the Constitution and the narrower construction ensures smooth working of the Constitution and harmony amongst its various provisions. The court observed: "Where two

---

76. *Collector of Customs v. Digvijaya Singhji Spinning & Weaving Mills Ltd.*, AIR 1961 SC 1549, pp. 1551, 1553 : 1962 (1) SCR 896.

77. *State of Gujarat v. Chaturbhuj Maganlal*, AIR 1976 SC 1697, p. 1700 : 1976 SCC (Cri) 359 : (1976) 3 SCC 54.

78. *State of Punjab v. Ajaib Singh*, AIR 1953 SC 10, p. 14 : 1953 SCR 254; *Chandra Mohan v. State of U.P.*, AIR 1966 SC 1987, p. 1993 : 1967 (1) SCR 77.

alternative constructions are possible, the court must choose the one which will be in accord with the other parts of the statute and ensure its smooth, harmonious working and eschew the other which leads to absurdity, confusion or friction, contradiction and conflict between its various provisions, or undermines or tends to defeat or destroy the basic scheme and purpose of the enactment".[79]

79. *Chief Justice of Andhra Pradesh v. L.V.A. Dikshitulu*, AIR 1979 SC 193, p. 205 : (1979) 2 SCC 34.

CHAPTER 3

INTERNAL AIDS TO CONSTRUCTION

SYNOPSIS

1. LONG TITLE

It is now settled that Long Title of an Act is a part of the Act and is admissible as an aid to its construction.[1] The Long Title which often pre-

---

1. *R. v. Secretary of State for Foreign and Commonwealth Affairs*, (1994) 1 All ER 457, p. 465 : 1994 QB 552 : (1994) 2 WLR 115 (QBD). (The days are long since past when courts declined to regard the Long Title as an aid to construction).

cedes the Preamble must be distinguished with the Short Title; the former, if being taken along with the Preamble or even in its absence, is a good guide regarding the object, scope or purpose of the Act,[2] whereas the latter being only an abbreviation for purposes of reference is not a useful aid to construction.[3]

Referring to the Trade Disputes Act, 1906 (6 Edw. 7, c. 47), LORD MOULTON said: "The title of an Act is undoubtedly part of the Act itself, and it is legitimate to use it for the purpose of interpreting the Act as a whole, and ascertaining its scope. This is not the case with the Short Title, which in this case is 'the Trade Disputes Act, 1906'. This is a title given to the Act solely for the purpose of facility of reference. If I may use the phrase, it is a statutory nickname to obviate the necessity of always referring to the Act under its full and descriptive title. The full title of the Act is: 'An Act to provide for the regulation of Trade Unions and Trade Disputes'. The title as it stands is not only intelligible, but describes admirably the purposes of the Act".[4]

While dealing with the Supreme Court Advocates (Practice in High Courts) Act, 1951 which bears a full title, 'An Act to authorise Advocates of the Supreme Court to practise as of right in any High Court', S.R. DAS, J., observed: "One cannot but be impressed at once with the wording of the full title of the Act. Although there are observations in earlier English cases that the title is not a part of the statute and is, therefore, to be excluded from consideration while construing the statutes, it is now settled law that the title of a statute is an important part of the Act and may be referred to for the purpose of ascertaining its general scope and of throwing

---

2. *Fielding v. Morley Corpn.*, (1899) 1 Ch 1, pp. 3, 4, (LINDLEY, M.R.) **affd.** *sub-nom Fielden v. Morley Corpn.*, (1900) AC 133 (HL); *Vacher & Sons Ltd. v. London Society of Compositors*, (1913) AC 107 : (1911-13) All ER Rep 241, pp. 244, 252 (HL); *Aswinikumar Ghose v. Arabinda Bose*, AIR 1952 SC 369, p. 388 : 1953 SCR 1; *Poppatlal Shah v. State of Madras*, AIR 1953 SC 274, p. 276 : 1953 SCR 677; *Kedar Nath Bajoria v. State of West Bengal*, AIR 1953 SC 404, pp. 406, 407 : 1954 SCR 30; *Bishwambhar Singh v. State of Orissa*, AIR 1954 SC 139, p. 144 : 1954 SCR 842; *In re, Kerala Education Bill, 1957*, AIR 1958 SC 956, p. 974 : 1959 SCR 995.
3. *Vacher & Sons v. London Society of Compositors*, (1911-13) All ER Rep 241 : 1913 AC 107 (HL); *National Telephone Co. Ltd. v. Postmaster General*, (1913) AC 546, p. 560 (HL); *Re, Boaler*, (1915) 1 KB 21, pp. 27, 35 (CA). **But see** *Middle-sex Justices v. R*, (1884) 9 AC 757, p. 772 (HL). **See** *Union of India v. Elphinstone Spinning & Weaving Co. Ltd.*, JT 2001 (1) SC 536, pp. 563, 564 : AIR 2001 SC 724, p. 740 : (2001) 4 SCC 139, p. 140 (In 1st column last 7 lines p. 740 of AIR at one place it is observed: "the Preamble being only an abbreviation for purposes of reference is not a useful aid to construction." Here by clerical mistake 'Short Title' is referred to as 'Preamble'.)
4. *Vacher & Sons v. London Society of Compositors, supra*, p. 252.

light on its construction, although it cannot override the clear meaning of the enactment."[5]

The title of the Madras General Sales Tax Act, 1939 was utilised to indicate that the object of the Act is to impose taxes on sales that take place within the province.[6]

The title and the Preamble were used as indicative of underlying purpose and policy of the West Bengal Criminal Law Amendment (Special Courts) Act, 1949 and for upholding the classification of offences triable by special courts under special procedure.[7]

The words 'free' and 'compulsory' in the Long Title of the Right of Children to Free and Compulsory Education Act, 2009, were relied on by the Supreme Court to hold that the Act has been enacted by the Parliament to give effect to the right of the child to education as enshrined under Articles 21 and 21-A of the Constitution.[8]

Wide discretion conferred on the Government under a statute and challenged as arbitrary, has been upheld on the ground that the discretion so conferred can be exercised only in furtherance of the object and policy of the Act as given out by the Long Title and Preamble and is thus not unfettered or unguided.[9]

The title although part of the Act is in itself not an enacting provision and though useful in case of ambiguity of the enacting provisions, is ineffective to control their clear meaning.[10] As stated by DONOVAN, J.: "The Long Title is a legitimate aid to the construction. When Parliament proclaims what the purpose of an Act is, it would be wrong to leave that out of account when construing the Act in particular, when construing some doubtful or ambiguous expression. In many cases the Long Title may supply the key to the meaning. The principle, as I understand it, is that where something is doubtful or ambiguous, the Long Title may be looked to resolve the doubt or ambiguity, but in the absence of doubt or ambiguity, the

---

5. *Aswinikumar Ghose v. Arabinda Bose*, AIR 1952 SC 369, p. 388 : 1953 SCR 1.
6. *Poppatlal Shah v. State of Madras*, AIR 1953 SC 274 : 1953 SCR 677.
7. *Kedar Nath Bajoria v. State of Bengal*, AIR 1953 SC 404 : 1954 SCR 30.
8. *Society for Unaided Private Schools of Rajasthan v. Union of India & Anr.*, (2012) 6 SCC 1, p. 28.
9. *Bishwambhar Singh v. State of Orissa*, AIR 1954 SC 139 : 1954 SCR 842; *In re, Kerala Education Bill*, AIR 1958 SC 956 : 1959 SCR 995.
10. *R. v. Bates and Russell*, (1952) 2 All ER 842, p. 844; *Re, Wykes' Will Trusts, Riddington v. Spencer*, (1961) 1 All ER 470, p. 475; *Ward v. Holman*, (1964) 2 All ER 729, p. 731; *Manoharlal v. State of Punjab*, AIR 1961 SC 418, p. 419 : (1961) 2 SCR 343; *R. v. Galvin*, (1987) 2 All ER 851, p. 855 (CA).

passage under construction must be taken to mean what it says, so that if its meaning be clear, that meaning is not to be narrowed or restricted by reference to the Long Title."[11] To the same effect are the observations of AYYANGER, J.: "The Long Title of the Act—on which learned counsel placed considerable reliance as a guide for the determination of the scope of the Act and the policy underlying the legislation, no doubt, indicates the main purposes of the enactment but cannot, obviously, control the express operative provisions of the Act."[12]

2. PREAMBLE[13]

The Preamble of a statute like the Long Title is a part of the Act and is an admissible aid to construction. Although not an enacting part, the Preamble is expected to express the scope, object and purpose of the Act more comprehensively than the Long Title. It may recite the ground and cause of making the statute, the evils sought to be remedied[14] or the doubts which may be intended to be settled. In the words of SIR JOHN NICHOLL: "It is to the Preamble more specially that we are to look for the reason or spirit of every statute, rehearsing this, as it ordinarily does, the evils sought to be remedied, or the doubts purported to be removed by the statute, and so evidencing, in the best and most satisfactory manner, the object or intention of the Legislature in making or passing the statute itself."[15] As enunciated by TINDAL, C.J., in delivering the opinion of the judges who advised the House of Lords in *Sussex Peerage* case[16]: "If any doubt arise from the terms employed by the Legislature, it has always been held a safe means of collecting the intention to call in aid the ground and cause of

11. *R. v. Bates and Russell*, (1952) 2 All ER 842, p. 844.
12. *Manoharlal v. State of Punjab*, AIR 1961 SC 418, p. 419 : 1961 (2) SCR 343.
13. It was pointed out by justice M. Hidayatullah in Constitutional Law of India, Vol. 1, p. 39 (published by the Bar Council of India, Trust, 1984) that the importance of Preamble to statutes was expressed by Plato 2000 years back (Plato: 'The Laws'—Penguin classics, p. 185) who said that Preamble to enacted laws were essential and added in explanation: "The 'dictatorial prescription'...... is the law pure and simple; and the part that comes before it, which is essentially 'persuasive'...... has an additional function analogous to that of a preamble in a speech. It seems obvious to me that the reason why the legislator gave the entire persuasive address was to make the persons to whom he promulgated his law accept his orders—the law—in a more cooperative frame of mind and with a correspondingly greater readiness to learn. That is why, as I see it, the element ought properly to be termed not the 'text' of the law, but the preamble."
14. For example **see** *Secretary, Regional Transport Authority v. D.P. Sharma*, AIR 1989 SC 509, p. 511 : 1988 (4) JT 666 : 1989 Supp (1) SCC 407 (Preamble of the Karnataka Contract Carriages Acquisition Act, 1974).
15. *Brett v. Brett*, (1826) 162 ER 456, pp. 458, 459.
16. (1844) 11 Cl & F 85, p. 143.

making the statute, and to have recourse to the Preamble, which according to CHIEF JUSTICE DYER[17] is a 'key to open the minds of the makers of the Act, and the mischiefs which they intended to redress'."[18] The subject has been explained lucidly in a decision of the House of Lords.[19] The decision establishes the following propositions: the Preamble being a part of the statute can be read along with other portions of the Act to find out the meaning of words in the enacting provisions as also to decide whether they are clear or ambiguous;[20] the Preamble in itself is not an enacting provision and is not of the same weight as an aid to construction of a section of the Act as are other relevant enacting words to be found elsewhere in the Act;[21] the utility of Preamble diminishes on a conclusion as to clarity of enacting provisions.[22] The Supreme Court approvingly quoted these propositions.[23]

Referring to the question as to how far the enacting provisions are controlled or restricted by the Preamble, LORD SIMONDS (LORD TUCKER agreeing) said: "But where it is in the Preamble that the reason for restriction is to be found, the difficulty is far greater. For, as has so often been said, Parliament may well intend the remedy to extend beyond the immediate mischief. The single fact, therefore, that enacting words are more general than the Preamble would suggest is not enough. Something more is needed—. To say then that you may not call in aid the Preamble in order to create an ambiguity in effect means very little—.[24] I would suggest that it (the rule) is better stated by saying that the context of the Preamble is not to influence the meaning otherwise ascribable to the enacting part unless there is a compelling reason for it. And I do not propose to define that expression except negatively by saying—that it is not to be found merely in the fact that the enacting words go further than the Preamble has

---

17. **See** *Stowel v. Lord Zouch*, (1569) 1 Plowd 353, p. 369 : 75 ER 536.
18. *Sussex Peerage case*, (1844) 11 Cl & Fin 85 : 8 ER 1034 (HL), **referred to** in *Commissioners for Special Purposes of Income-tax v. John Frederick Pemsel*, (1891-94) All ER Rep 28, p. 36 : 1891 AC 531 (HL) (LORD HALSBURY, L.C.); *Bhola Prasad v. Emperor*, AIR 1942 FC 17, p. 21 (GWYER, C.J.); **see further** *A. Thangal Kunju Musaliar v. M. Venkatachala Potti*, AIR 1956 SC 246, p. 264 : (1955) 2 SCR 1196 (BHAGWATI, J.); *Arnit Das v. State of Bihar*, JT 2000 (6) SC 320, p. 333 : AIR 2000 SC 2264, p. 2271 : (2000) 5 SCC 488.
19. *A.G. v. HRH Prince Ernest Augustus*, (1957) 1 All ER 49 : 1957 AC 436 (HL).
20. *Ibid*, pp. 55, 57, 61.
21. *Ibid*, pp. 55, 57, 62.
22. *Ibid*, pp. 54, 58, 60, 62.
23. *Union of India v. Elphinstone Spinning & Weaving Co. Ltd.*, JT 2001 (1) SC 536, p. 564 : AIR 2001 SC 724, p. 740 : (2001) 4 SCC 139 (Constitution bench).
24. LORD SIMONDS is here referring to the rule laid down by LORD DAVEY in *Powell v. Kemption Park Race-course Co. Ltd.*, (1899) AC 143, to the effect: "You must not create or imagine an ambiguity in order to bring in the aid of preamble".

indicated. Still less can the Preamble affect the meaning of enacting words when its own meaning is in doubt."[25] LORD NORMAND on the same matter observed: "There may be no exact correspondence between Preamble and enactment, and the enactment may go beyond, or it may fall short of, the indications that may be gathered from the preamble. Again the Preamble cannot be of much, or any, assistance in construing provisions which embody qualifications or exceptions from the operation of the general purpose of the Act. It is only when it conveys a clear and definite meaning in comparison with relatively obscure or indefinite enacting words that the Preamble may legitimately prevail."[26] LORD SOMERVELL stated the principle thus: "Preambles differ in their scope and, consequently, in the weight, if any, which they may have on one side or the other of a dispute. There can be no rule. If, in an Act the Preamble is a general or brief statement of the main purpose, it may well be of little, if any, value. The Act may, as has been said, go on beyond, or, in some respects fall short of, the purpose so briefly stated. Most Acts contain exceptions to their main purpose, on the meaning of which such a Preamble would presumably, throw no light. On the other hand, some general and most local Acts have their limits set out in some detail. I will not hazard an example but there may well be cases in which a section, read with the Preamble, may have a meaning different from that which it would have if there were no Preamble. Court will, of course, bear in mind that a Preamble is not an enacting provision, but I think it must have such weight as it can support in all contests as to construction."[27] LORD MORTON on the same point laid down that if the Preamble is ambiguous it cannot, in any way, control the enacting part. He proceeded to observe: "In fact, if the Preamble were clear one way and the enacting part were equally clear the other way, there can be no doubt that the latter must prevail".[28]

The principle has also been enunciated by the Supreme Court, where MUDHOLKAR, J., speaking for the court observed: "It is one of the cardinal principles of construction that where the language of an Act is clear, the Preamble must be disregarded though, where the object or meaning of an enactment is not clear, the Preamble may be resorted to explain it. Again, where very general language is used in an enactment which, it is clear must be intended to have a limited application, the Preamble may be used to indicate to what particular instances, the enactment is intended to apply.

---

25. *A.G. v. HRH Prince Ernest Augustus of Hanover*, (1957) 1 All ER 49, pp. 54, 55 : 1957 AC 436 (HL).
26. *Ibid*, pp. 57, 58.
27. *Ibid*, p. 62.
28. *A.G. v. HRH Prince Ernest Augustus of Hanover*, (1957) 1 All ER 49, p. 60 : 1957 AC 436 (HL).

We cannot, therefore, start with the Preamble for construing the provisions of an Act, though we could be justified in resorting to it, nay, we will be required to do so, if we find that the language used by the Parliament is ambiguous or is too general though in point of fact the Parliament intended that it should have a limited application."[29] It is the statutory provision which will have to be read and analysed for the purpose of understanding the scope and purpose for which the legislation was intended, and the brief statement contained in the Preamble will be of very little value.[30] These observations, it is submitted, must be read subject to the rule that the Act including the Preamble must be read as a whole to decide whether any part of the enacting provision is clear or ambiguous.[31]

"If, however, having read the Act as a whole, including the Preamble, the enacting words clearly negate the construction which it is sought to support by the Preamble, that is an end of it."[32]

The Rajasthan (Protection of Tenants) Ordinance, 1949 contained a Preamble which ran as follows: 'Whereas with a view to putting a check on the growing tendency of landlords to eject or dispossess tenants from their holdings and in the wider national interest of increasing the production of foodgrains, it is expedient to make provisions for the protection of tenants in Rajasthan from ejectment or dispossession from their holdings.' The

---

29. *Burakar Coal Co. Ltd. v. Union of India*, AIR 1961 SC 954, pp. 956, 957 : 1962 (1) SCR 44. **See further** *State of Rajasthan v. Leela Jain*, AIR 1965 SC 1296, p. 1299 : 1965 (1) SCR 276. ("The Preamble may, no doubt, be used to solve any ambiguity or to fix the meaning of words which may have more than one meaning, but it can, however, not be used to eliminate as redundant or unintended, the operative provisions of a statute.") *Venkataswami R. Naidu v. Narasram Naraindas*, AIR 1966 SC 361, p. 363 : 1966 (1) SCR 110; *Tribhuvan Parkash Nayyar v. Union of India*, AIR 1970 SC 540, p. 543 : 1969 (3) SCC 99; *Y.A. Mamarde v. Authority under the Minimum Wages Act*, AIR 1972 SC 1721, p. 1726 : (1972) 2 SCC 108; *A.C. Sharma v. Delhi Administration*, AIR 1973 SC 913, p. 917 : 1973 SCC (Cri) 608; *Rashtriya Mill Mazdoor Sangh v. National Textile Corporation*, 1995 (6) Scale 609, p. 617 : AIR 1997 SC 710, p. 713; *Munishwar Pandey v. Ramjeet Tiwari*, 1996 (8) Scale 736, p. 750 : AIR 1997 SC 1571, p. 1583; *Arnit Das v. State of Bihar*, JT 2000 (6) SC 320, p. 333 : AIR 2000 SC 2264, p. 2271 : (2000) 5 SCC 488; *Union of India v. Elphinstone Weaving and Spinning Co. Ltd.*, JT 2001 (1) SC 536, p. 564 : AIR 2001 SC 724, p. 740 : (2001) 4 SCC 139.

30. *Maharishi Mahesh Yogi Vedic Vishwavidalaya v. State of M.P.*, (2013) 15 SCC 677, p. 716.

31. *A.G. v. HRH Prince Ernest Augustus of Hanover*, (1957) 1 All ER 49 : 1957 AC 436 (HL) text and note 20 *supra*. **See further** Chatper 1, title 3 "Statute must be read as a whole in its context". **Also see** Chapter 1, title 6 "Appraisal of the Principle of plain meaning".

32. *A.G. v. HRH Prince Ernest Augustus of Hanover, supra*, p. 62 (LORD SOMERVELL). This case was **discussed** in *Oliver Ashworth (Holdings) Ltd. v. Ballard (Kent) Ltd.*, (1999) 2 All ER 791, pp. 805, 806 (CA).

Ordinance by section 3 was to remain in force for two years unless the period was further extended by the *Rajpramukh*. Section 4 of the Ordinance provided that during the continuance of the Ordinance no tenant could be ejected or dispossessed and by section 15 power was conferred upon the Government to exempt any person or class of persons from the operation of the Ordinance. It was contended before the Supreme Court that the power conferred upon the *Rajpramukh* to extend the life of the Act amounted to delegation of legislative function and was bad and further the power of granting exemption conferred by section 15 was unfettered and uncanalised and therefore repugnant to Article 14 of the Constitution. In rejecting the first contention the Supreme Court pointed out that the Preamble of the Ordinance clearly recited the state of facts necessitating the enactment of the law; and the power to extend the life of the Act conferred on the *Rajpramukh* was dependent on his satisfaction as to those state of facts continuing to exist on expiry of the original period of the Act. It was, therefore, a case of conditional legislation and not a case of delegated legislation.[33] Dealing with the second contention regarding section 15, it observed: "It is true that the section does not itself indicate the grounds on which exemption can be granted, but the Preamble to the Ordinance sets out with sufficient clearness 'the policy of the Legislature'; and as that governs section 15 of the Ordinance, the decision of the Government thereunder cannot be said to be unguided."[34] Thus, discretionary power conferred in wide terms and challenged as unfettered and unguided was upheld by recourse to the Preamble and by holding that the discretion so conferred was restricted in that, it could be used only in furtherance of the object and policy of the Act as disclosed in the Preamble.[35]

Similarly, section 23(1) of the Urban Land (Ceiling and Regulation) Act, 1976 which permits the allotment of any land vesting in the Government to any person for any purpose relating to, or in connection with any industry or for providing residential accommodation of such type as may be approved by the State Government to the employees of any industry was given a restrictive construction having regard to the Act's Preamble and section 23(4). The Preamble shows that the Act was passed with the object of preventing concentration of urban land in the hands of a few persons and with a view to bringing about an equitable distribution of land in

33. *Sardar Inder Singh v. State of Rajasthan*, AIR 1957 SC 510, p. 516 : 1957 SCR 605.
34. *Ibid*, pp. 516, 517.
35. *Ibid*; *Bhatnagar & Co. Ltd. v. Union of India*, AIR 1957 SC 478, pp. 485, 486 : 1957 SCR 701. **See further** *Bishwambhar Singh v. State of Orissa*, AIR 1954 SC 139, p. 144 : 1954 SCR 842; *In re, Kerala Education Bill*, AIR 1958 SC 956, p. 974 : 1959 SCR 995. (These cases relate to use of Long Title and Preamble and are **noticed** in title 1 'Long Title' text and note 9, p. 173).

urban agglomerations to subserve the common good. Section 23(4) provides that subject to the provisions of section 23(1) all vacant land shall be disposed of by the State Government to subserve the common good. Although section 23(4) was 'subject to' section 23(1), yet it was held that disposal of land under section 23(1) can only be for the common good and not otherwise. A contrary construction would have made section 23(1) unconstitutional as was held by the minority. The majority, however, gave it a restricted interpretation observing: "The Preamble to the Act ought to resolve interpretational doubts arising out of the defective drafting of section 23."[36]

The Bihar Annual Finance Act, 1950 amended the definition of 'dealer' in the Bihar Sales Tax Act, 1947. It was contended before the Supreme Court[37] that having regard to the Preamble, change in definition of 'dealer' was applicable only for the financial year beginning from April 1, 1950 and was not applicable for subsequent years. The Preamble of the Finance Act to which recourse was taken for this contention ran as follows: 'Whereas it is expedient to amend the Bihar Sales Tax Act, 1947 to lay down rates of sales tax payable under the Bihar Sales Tax Act, 1947, for the financial year beginning on the 1st day of April, 1950 and to make further provisions in connection with the finance of the State of Bihar'. In rejecting the contention so put forward, KAPUR, J., observed: "The Preamble cannot limit or change the meaning of the plain words of section 2(c) of the Act which apply to the appellant and therefore the amended section is applicable to the present case. It is erroneous approach to the question to say that because of the words 'for the financial year beginning on the first day of April, 1950' in the particular context in the Preamble, the definition of the word 'dealer' was amended only for one year. Nothing has been shown indicating that section 2(i) of Bihar Finance Act intended to effect a temporary amendment in the previous definition of the word 'dealer' in clause (c) of section 2 of the Act."[38]

Use of the word 'may' in section 5 of the Hindu Marriage Act which provides: 'A marriage may be solemnized between any two Hindus....' has been construed to be mandatory in the sense that both parties to the marriage must be Hindus as defined in section 2 of the Act. It was, therefore, held that a marriage between a Christian male and a Hindu female solemnized under the Hindu Marriage Act was void. This result was reached

---

36. *Maharao Sahab Shri Bhimsinghji v. Union of India*, AIR 1981 SC 234, p. 237 : (1981) 1 SCC 166.

37. *Motipur Zamindary Company (Private) Ltd. v. State of Bihar*, AIR 1962 SC 660, p. 662 : 1962 Supp (1) SCR 498.

38. *Ibid.*, p. 662.

also having regard to the Preamble of the Act which reads: 'An Act to amend and codify the law relating to *marriage among Hindus.*'[39]

The Coal Bearing Areas (Acquisition and Development) Act, 1957 in section 4(1) provides: 'whenever it appears to the Central Government that coal is likely to be obtained from land in any locality, it may, by notification in the Official Gazette, give notice of its intention to prospect for coal therein.' On issue of such a notification in respect of any land, any prospecting licence or mining lease granted to any person ceases to have effect and provision is made for acquisition of land so notified as also for payment of compensation etc. The Act contains a Preamble which runs as follows: 'An Act to establish, in the economic interest of India, greater public control over the coal mining industry and its development by providing for the acquisition by the State of unworked land containing or likely to contain coal deposits or of right in or over such land, for the extinguishment or modification of such rights accruing by virtue of any agreement, lease, licence or otherwise, and for matters connected therewith.' The argument before the Supreme Court was that the Act applied only to virgin lands and not to those lands which are being worked or were worked in the past. Support for this contention was taken from the words 'unworked land' in the Preamble. Rejecting the contention on the ground that the language of the enacting provisions was clear and therefore not controlled by the Preamble, the Supreme Court pointed out: "On the plain language of sub-section (1) of section 4, the Central Government has been empowered to issue a notification with reference to its intention of prospecting any land in a locality and not only such land as is virgin."[40] This case was followed in holding that reference to 'mismanagement' in the Preamble of the Textile Undertakings (Taking over of Management) Act, 1983 could not restrict the operation of the Act to only those mills of the companies mentioned in the Schedule whose financial condition was deplorable only on account of mismanagement but not otherwise.[41]

By section 5 of the Displaced Persons (Claims) Supplementary Act, 1954, power is conferred on the Chief Settlement Commissioner to revise any verified claim. The expression 'verified claim' is defined in section 2(f) to mean any claim registered under the Displaced Persons (Claim) Act, 1950 in respect of which a final order has been passed under that Act. The Supplementary Act contains a Preamble which recites that it was enacted

---

39. *Gullipilli Sowria Raj v. Bandaru Pavani*, (2009) 1 SCC 714 para 16 : AIR 2009 SC 1058.

40. *Burrakur Coal Co. v. Union of India*, AIR 1961 SC 954, p. 957 : 1962 (1) SCR 44.

41. *Union of India v. Elphinstone Spinning & Weaving Co. Ltd.*, AIR 2001 SC 724, p. 741 : (2001) 4 SCC 139.

to provide for the disposal of certain proceedings pending under the 1950 Act and for matters connected therewith. It was argued on the basis of the Preamble that the power of revision under the Supplementary Act was limited to pending proceedings and a verified claim which had become final after revision by the Chief Claims Commissioner under the 1950 Act, could not be reopened and revised by the Chief Settlement Commissioner under the Supplementary Act. This contention was negated having regard to the clear words of section 5 read with the definition of verified claim in section 2(f) and it was observed: "A Preamble is a key to open the mind of the Legislature, but it cannot be used to control or qualify precise and unambiguous language of the enactment."[42]

A Preamble retrospectively inserted into an earlier Act is not of much assistance for gathering the intention of the original Act. The point was stressed by GWYER, C.J., in the following words: "But we doubt very much whether a Preamble retrospectively inserted in 1940 in an Act passed 25 years before can be looked at by the court for the purpose of discovering what the true intention of the Legislature was at the earlier date. A Legislature can always enact that the law is, and shall be deemed always to have been such and such, but that is wholly different thing from imputing to dead and gone Legislators a particular intention merely because their successors at the present day think that they might or ought to have had it."[43]

Similarly, it seems the repeal of a Preamble simpliciter will not affect the construction of the statute.[44]

3. PREAMBLE OF THE CONSTITUTION[45]

The drafting committee of the Constituent Assembly formulated the Preamble in the light of the Objective Resolution but restricted it "to define the essential features of the new State and its basic socio-political objective".[46] The draft of the Preamble was considered by the Assembly last after considering other parts of the Draft Constitution—"to see that it was

---

42. *Tribhuvan Parkash Nayyar v. Union of India*, AIR 1970 SC 540, p. 543 : 1969 (3) SCC 99.

43. *Bhola Prasad v. Emperor*, AIR 1942 FC 17, p. 21 : 1942 FLR 17 : 43 Cri LJ 481. (The case **refers** to a Preamble inserted by the Bihar Excise (Amendment) Act, 1940 in the Bihar & Orissa Excise Act, 1915).

44. CRAIES : Statute Law, 7th Edn., p. 206.

45. For **further** study **see**: 'Preamble' contributed by justice G.P. Singh in 'Constitutional Law of India', Vol. 1, pp. 13 to 44 published by the Bar Council of India Trust under the Chief Editorship of Justice M. Hidayatullah, (1984); and 'Preamble' by Justice R.C. Lahoti, Anundoram Borooah Law Lecture, Published by Eastern Book Company, Lucknow (2004).

46. SHIVA RAO, The Framing of India's Constitution, A Study, p. 128.

in conformity with the Constitution"[47] and a motion was adopted by the Assembly that "the Preamble stands part of the Constitution".[48] The Preamble of the Constitution like the Preamble of any statute furnishes the key to open the mind of the makers of the Constitution more so because the Constituent Assembly took great pains in formulating it so that it may reflect the essential features and basic objectives of the Constitution. The Preamble is a part of the Constitution. The Constitution, including the Preamble, must be read as a whole and in case of doubt interpreted consistent with its basic structure to promote the great objectives stated in the Preamble.[49] But the Preamble can neither be regarded as the source of any substantive power nor as a source of any prohibition or limitation.[50] The Preamble of a Constitution Amendment Act can be used to understand the object of the amendment.[51]

The majority judgments in *Keshavananda* and *Minerva Mills* strongly relied upon the Preamble in reaching the conclusion that the power of amendment conferred by Article 368 was limited and did not enable Parliament to alter the basic structure or framework of the Constitution.[52]

By section 2 of the Constitution (42nd Amendment) Act, 1976, two amendments were made in the Preamble. *First* for the words 'Sovereign Democratic Republic' the words 'Sovereign Socialist Secular Democratic Republic' were substituted and, *secondly*, for the words 'Unity of India', the words 'Unity and Integrity of the Nation' were substituted. These amendments were held to be valid in *Minerva Mills*.[53] The addition of the

---

47. *Ibid.*, p. 130.

48. Constituent Assembly Debates, Vol. X, pp. 429-56.

49. *Kesavananda v. State of Kerala*, AIR 1973 SC 1461 : (1973) 4 SCC 225; *Minerva Mills Ltd. v. Union of India*, AIR 1980 SC 1789 : 1980 (3) SCC 625. **See further** *Behram Khurshid Pesikaka v. State of Bombay*, AIR 1955 SC 123, p. 146 : 1955 (1) SCR 613; *In re, Kerala Education Bill*, 1957, AIR 1958 SC 956, p. 965 : 1959 SCR 995; *Basheshar Nath v. Income-tax Commissioner*, AIR 1959 SC 149, pp. 158, 160 : 1959 Supp (1) SCR 528. These cases are **noticed** by SHELAT and GROVER, JJ. in *Kesavananda, supra,* at p. 1579. The contrary opinion expressed *in the reference on the Agreement relating to Berubari Union and Exchange of Enclaves*, AIR 1960 SC 845, p. 856 : (1960) 3 SCR 250 was **overruled** in *Kesavananda, supra*. **See further** *Ashoka Kumar Thakur v. Union of India,* (2008) 6 SCC 1 para 212 : (2008) 5 JT 1 (It has been said in many decisions that when a constitutional provision is interpreted, the cardinal rule is to look to the Preamble to the Constitution as the guiding star and directive principles of state policy as the book of interpretation).

50. *Indira Nehru Gandhi (Smt.) v. Raj Narain*, AIR 1975 SC 2299 (para 666) : 1975 Supp SCC 1; *Raghunathrao Ganpatrao v. Union of India*, AIR 1993 SC 1267 : 1994 Supp (1) SCC 191, pp. 1307, 1308 : 1993 (1) JT 374.

51. *Raghunathrao Ganpatrao v. Union of India, supra*, p. 1308.

52. *Kesavananda v. State of Kerala*, AIR 1973 SC 1461 : (1973) 4 SCC 225; *Minerva Mills Ltd. v. Union of India*, AIR 1980 SC 1789, pp. 1798, 1806 : 1980 (3) SCC 625.

53. *Minerva Mills Ltd. v. Union of India*, AIR 1980 SC 1789, pp. 1798-99 : 1980 (3) SCC 625.

word 'Socialist' enabled the Courts to lean more in favour of nationalisation[54] and economic equality.[55] It was also used for rejection of a classification based on notions of feudalistic society *e.g.* Kinship.[56]

4. HEADINGS

The view is now settled that the Headings or Titles prefixed to sections or group of sections can be referred to in construing an Act of the Legislature.[57] But conflicting opinions have been expressed on the question as to what weight should be attached to the headings. ; *A 'Heading'*, according to one view, "is to be regarded as giving the key to the interpretation of the clauses ranged under it, unless the wording is inconsistent with such interpretation;"[58] and so the headings might be treated "as Preambles to the provisions following them".[59] But according to the other view resort to 'the heading' can only be taken when the enacting words are ambiguous. So LORD GODDARD, C.J., expressed himself as follows: "While, however, the court is entitled to look at the headings in an Act of Parliament to resolve any doubt they may have as to ambiguous words, the law is clear that those headings cannot be used to give a different effect to clear words in the section where there cannot be any doubt as to the ordinary meaning of the words."[60] Similarly, it was said by PATANJALI SHASTRI, J.: "Nor can the title of a Chapter be legitimately used to restrict the plain terms of an enactment."[61]

---

54. *Excel Wear v. Union of India*, AIR 1979 SC 25, p. 36 : (1978) 4 SCC 224 : 1978 SCC (L&S) 509; *Sanjeev Coke Manufacturing Company v. Bharat Coking Coal Ltd.*, AIR 1983 SC 239, p. 251 : (1983) 1 SCC 147.

55. *D.S. Nakara v. Union of India*, AIR 1983 SC 130, p. 139 : (1983) 1 SCC 305; *Kerala Hotel and Restaurant Association v. State of Kerala*, AIR 1990 SC 913, p. 916 : (1990) 2 SCC 502; *Dharwad Distt. P.W.D. Literate Daily Wages Employees Association v. State of Karnataka*, AIR 1990 SC 883, pp. 887, 888 : 1990 (2) SCC 396.

56. *Atam Prakash v. State of Haryana*, (1986) 2 SCC 249 : AIR 1986 SC 859.

57. *Hammer Smith & City Ry. v. Brand*, (1869) LR 4 HLC 171; *Ingils v. Robertson*, (1898) AC 616, pp. 624, 629 (HL); *Toronto Corporation v. Toronto Ry.*, (1907) AC 315, p. 324 (PC); *Martins v. Fowler*, (1926) AC 746, p. 750 (PC); *Qualter Hall & Co. Ltd. v. Board of Trade*, (1961) 3 All ER 389, pp. 392, 394 (CA); *Bhinka v. Charan Singh*, AIR 1959 SC 960, p. 966 : 1959 Supp (2) SCR 798; *Director of Public Prosecutions v. Schildkamp*, (1969) 3 All ER 1640 (HL).

58. *Toronto Corporation v. Toronto Ry. Co.*, (1907) AC 315, p. 324 (PC) (LORD COLLINS); **referred** to in *Re, Ralph George Cariton*, (1945) 1 All ER 559, p. 562; *Qualter Hall & Co. v. Board of Trade, supra*, p. 392.

59. *Martins v. Fowler, supra* p. 750; **referred** to in *Qualter Hall & Co. v. Board of Trade, supra*, p. 392.

60. *R. v. Surrey (North Eastern, Area) Assessment Committee*, (1947) 2 All ER 276, pp. 278, 279.

61. *CIT v. Ahmedbhai Umarbhai*, AIR 1950 SC 134, p. 141 : 1950 SCR 335.

The Supreme Court has expressed itself as follows: "It is well-settled that the headings prefixed to sections or entries (of a Tariff Schedule) cannot control the plain words of the provision; they cannot also be referred to for the purpose of construing the provision when the words used in the provision are clear and unambiguous; nor can they be used for cutting down the plain meaning of the words in the provision. Only in the case of ambiguity or doubt the heading or sub-heading may be referred to as an aid in construing the provision but even in such a case it could not be used for cutting down the wide application of the clear words used in the provision."[62]

After referring to the conflicting opinions[63] relating to the use of headings or titles prefixed to sections or group of sections, LAHOTI, J., expressed himself as follows: "It is permissible to assign the heading or title of a section, a limited role to play in the construction of statutes. They may be taken as very broad and general indicators of the nature of the subject-matter dealt with thereunder. The heading or title may also be taken as a condensed name assigned to indicate collectively the characteristics of the subject matter dealt with by the enactment underneath; though the name would always be brief having its own limitations. In case of conflict between the plain language of the provision and the meaning of the heading or title, the heading or title would not control the meaning which is clearly and plainly discernible from the language of the provision thereunder."[64]

An example of this is to be found in the interpretation of section 33 of the Persons with Disabilities (Equal Opportunities, Protection of Rights and Full Participation) Act, 1995, which is titled 'Reservation of posts', and provides that 'every appropriate Government shall appoint in every establishment such percentage of vacancies not less than three percent for persons or class of persons with disability…'. It was contended that the reservation for persons with disabilities is post-based, and not vacancy-based, relying on the heading of section 33. However, the Supreme Court held that it is clear from the simple and unambiguous language of section 33 that the computation of reservation has to be against the total number of vacancies in the establishment, and not against the 'identified posts', as the heading of a section will not play a crucial role when the language of the section is clear and unambiguous.[65]

---

62. *Frick India Ltd. v. Union of India*, AIR 1990 SC 689, p. 693 : (1990) 1 SCC 400. **Applied in** *Forage & Co. v. Municipal Corporation of Greater Bombay,* JT 1999 (9) SC 57, p. 61 : AIR 2000 SC 378, p. 380 : (1999) 8 SCC 577.

63. *Raichurmatham Prabhakar Rawatmal Dugar*, (2004) 4 SCC 766, p. 775 : AIR 2004 SC 3625, p. 3631 (9th Edn., pp. 153-155 of this book is **referred**).

64. *Ibid.*, p. 775 (SCC) : p. 3631 (AIR). **See further** *Karnataka Power Transmission Corporation v. Ashok Iron Works Pvt. Ltd.,* (2009) 3 SCC 240 para 26 : (2009) 2 JT 447.

65. *Union of India & Anr. v. National Federation of the Blind & Ors.*, (2013) 10 SCC 772, pp. 792 to 798.

The conflicting views on the utility of Headings were referred to and are reflected in the speeches delivered in the House of Lords while construing section 332(3) of the Companies Act, 1948.[66] Headings like side notes and punctuation are inserted by the draftsman and it is seldom that any attention is paid to them in the Legislature. According to the strict view, therefore, they should be disregarded. But, as stated by LORD REID: "It may be more realistic to accept the Act as printed as being the product of the whole legislative process, and to give due weight to everything found in the printed Act. I say more realistic because in very many cases the provision before the court was never even mentioned in debate in either House, and it may be that its wording was never closely scrutinised by any member of either House. In such a case it is not very meaningful to say that the words of the Act represent the intention of Parliament but that punctuation, cross-headings and sidenotes do not—. I would not object to taking all these matters into account provided that we realise that they cannot have equal weight with the words of the Act—. A cross-heading ought to indicate the scope of the sections which follow it but there is always a possibility that the scope of one of these sections may have been widened by amendment."[67]

LORD UPJOHN, in the same case, after referring to the conflict in authorities observed: "In this somewhat conflicting state of authorities what role do cross-headings play? In my opinion, it is wrong to confine their role to the resolution of ambiguities in the body of the Act. When the court construing the Act is reading it through to understand it, it must read the cross-headings as well as the body of the Act and that will always be a useful pointer as to the intention of Parliament in enacting the immediately following sections. Whether the cross-heading is no more than a pointer or label or is helpful in assisting to construe or even in some cases to control the meaning or ambit of those sections must necessarily depend on the circumstances of each case and I do not think it is possible to lay down any rules."[68] On the other hand LORD HODSON said: "The construction of the relevant section ought not to be governed ultimately by consideration of cross-headings, even though some attention may be paid to them—. I am impressed by the consideration that they are not part of the enacted words in a piece of legislation but are added by the officers of the House of Parliament before they reach the form embodied in the King's Printer's copy. I would not therefore give them a controlling effect."[69] Similarly, VISCOUNT DILHORNE observed: "While I would not suggest that, when one is

---

66. *Director of Public Prosecutions v. Schildkamp*, (1969) 3 All ER 1640 : 1971 AC 1 (HL).
67. *Director of Public Prosecutions v. Schildkamp*, (1969) 3 All ER 1640, p. 1641 : (1970) 2 WLR 279 (HL).
68. *Ibid.*, p. 1656.
69. *Ibid.*, pp. 1643, 1644.

considering an Act of Parliament, one is not entitled to look at the title given to a part of the Act and to cross headings, the weight to be attached to them is, in my opinion, very slight and less than that which should be given to a preamble—. In my view the title given to a part of an Act and the cross-heading to a modern Act which are inserted by the draftsman and not subject to amendment by the members of either House, are no more than guides to the contents of the part or sections which follow. They are not meant to control the operation of the enacting words and it would be wrong to permit them to do so."[70]

In the case of *Schildkamp*, LORD UPJOHN with whom LORD REID agreed, used the headings of the Part and Sub-Part and the cross-headings under which section 323(2) of the Companies Act, 1948 occurred to restrict the prosecution for the offence created by the said section when company went into liquidation and prosecution was held to be not tenable while it was a going concern.[71] In an earlier case,[72] cross-heading was used by LORD REID and LORD HODSON to limit the natural meaning of the word 'property' in section 56(1) of the Law of Property Act, 1925.

Under section 180 of the Uttar Pradesh Tenancy Act, 1939 a remedy was provided for ejectment of a person who was retaining possession of land 'otherwise than in accordance with the provisions of the law for the time being in force'. The question before the Supreme Court[73] was whether a person having no title but retaining possession by virtue of an order passed under section 145 of the Code of Criminal Procedure could be ejected under the aforesaid provision. In reaching the conclusion that such a person could be ejected, the Supreme Court construed the words 'possession in accordance with the law for the time being in force' as meaning possession with title. Support, for arriving at this conclusion, was taken from the heading of the section which reads 'Ejectment of person occupying land without title'. SUBBARAO, J., quoted with approval the following passage from MAX-WELL:[74] "The heading prefixed to sections or sets of sections in some modern statutes are regarded as Preambles to those sections. They cannot control the plain words of the statute but they may explain ambiguous words."[75]

The heading of section 36(2) of the Protection of Human Rights Act, 1994—'Matters not subject to jurisdiction of commission'—was used in

---

70. *Ibid.*, p. 1650.

71. *Director of Public Prosecutions v. Schildkamp*, (1969) 3 All ER 1640, pp. 1655, 1656, 1657 : 1971 AC 1 : (1970) 2 WLR 279.

72. *Beswick v. Beswick*, (1967) 2 All ER 1197, pp. 1204, 1207 : (1967) 3 WLR 932 (HL).

73. *Bhinka v. Charan Singh*, AIR 1959 SC 960 : 1959 Supp (2) SCR 798.

74. MAXWELL on Statutes, 11th Edition, pp. 48, 49.

75. *Bhinka v. Charan Singh*, AIR 1959 SC 960, p. 966 : 1959 Supp (2) SCR 798.

support of the conclusion that the period of one year prescribed in that section was not merely a procedural provision but took away the jurisdiction of the commission to enquire into a matter after expiry of that period.[76] The court observed that: "It is a settled rule of interpretation that the section heading or marginal note can be relied upon to clear any doubt or ambiguity in the interpretation of the provision and to discern the legislative intent."[77] This was a case of 'heading' not merely of a marginal note which is not a heading. But as already seen the headings do not have any controlling effect when other relevant considerations and the language leave no doubt as to the meaning of the statutory provision. For example, the heading of Chapter XXXVI of the Code of Criminal Procedure, 1973 which reads 'Limitations for taking cognizance of certain offences', was not held to be controlling and it was held that a cumulative reading of various provisions in the said chapter clearly indicated that the limitation prescribed therein was only for the filing of the complaint or initiation of the prosecution and not for taking cognizance.[78] Similarly, the heading 'Insurance of Motor Vehicles against Third- Party Risks' given to Chapter XI of the Motor Vehicles Act, 1988, was relied on by the Supreme Court to hold that the intention of the Legislature is to make third-party insurance compulsory in order to protect persons from the risk attendant upon the user of motor vehicles on the road, and to ensure that the victims of accidents would be able to get compensation for the death or injuries suffered. The Legislature has therefore made it obligatory that no motor vehicle shall be used unless a third-party insurance is in force.[79]

If the language of a section is plain and clear then the heading used in the section strengthens that meaning. Accordingly, relying on the heading of section 29(1) of the Foreign Exchange Regulation Act, 1973, which reads 'Restrictions on establishment of place of business in India', as well as the plain language of the provision, the Supreme Court held that there is a specific bar on foreign companies and foreign nationals mentioned in section 29(1)(a) from establishing or carrying on any business in India or opening any branch in India without obtaining permission of the RBI, and any act done in breach thereof will be illegal. However, these restrictions are not applicable to an Indian Company.[80]

---

76. *N.C. Dhondial v. Union of India*, AIR 2004 SC 1272 : (2004) 2 SCC 579.
77. *Ibid.*, p. 1278 (AIR) : p. 587 (SCC).
78. *Bharat Damodar Kale v. State of A.P.*, AIR 2003 SC 4560, p. 4563 : (2003) 8 SCC 559. **See further** *Iqbal Singh Marwah v. Meenakshi Marwah*, AIR 2005 SC 2119, p. 2125 : (2005) 4 SCC 370. (Heading of Chapter XXVI Cr.P.C., 1973 relied upon for construing section 195).
79. *S. Iyyapan v. United India Insurance Co. Ltd. & Anr.*, (2013) 7 SCC 62, p. 76.
80. *Union of India v. ABN Amro Bank & Ors.*, (2013) 16 SCC 490, pp. 517, 518.

The headings contained in Schedule VII of the Companies Act, 1948 were used by the Court of Appeal for purposes of construction of paras in the Schedule to which they were prefixed.[81] The Supreme Court relied on the heading of section 163A of the Motor Vehicles Act, 1988, which reads 'Special provisions as to payment of compensation on structured formula basis', and the section itself, as well as the scheme provided therein, to hold that since a pre-structured formula is to be used to evaluate the compensation, the liability thereunder may be huge, and hence the section cannot be based on the principle of no-fault liability.[82] Similarly, relying on the heading of section 37 of the SARFAESI Act, 2002, which reads 'Application of other laws not barred', the Supreme Court held that application of the SARFAESI Act will be in addition to, and not in derogation of, the provisions of the Recovery of Debts Due to Banks and Financial Institutions Act, 1993.[83]

5. MARGINAL NOTES

Although opinion is not uniform the weight of authority is in favour of the view that the marginal note appended to a section cannot be used for construing the section.[84] LORD MACNAGHTEN emphatically stated: "It is well-settled that marginal notes to the sections of an Act of Parliament cannot be referred to for the purpose of construing the Act. The contrary opinion originated in a mistake, and has been exploded long ago. There seems to be no reason for giving the marginal notes in an Indian statute

---

81. *Qualter Hall & Co. v. Board of Trade*, (1961) 3 All ER 389, pp. 392, 393, 394 (CA).

82. *National Insurance Co. Ltd. v. Sinitha & Ors.*, (2012) 2 SCC 356, p. 378.

83. *Mathew Varghese v. M. Amritha Kumar & Ors.*, (2014) 5 SCC 610, pp. 640, 641.

84. HALSBURY : Laws of England, Vol. 36 (3rd Edition), p. 373. In two cases, marginal notes were used by Court of Appeal as an aid to construction: **See** *Stephens v. Cuck-field Rural District Council*, (1960) 2 All ER 716, p. 720 (CA); and *Re, Cohen (a Bankrupt)*, (1961) 1 All ER 646, p. 656 (CA). But in *Chandler v. Director of Public Prosecutions*, (1962) 3 All ER 142, pp. 145, 146 : (1962) 2 WLR 694 : 1964 AC 763 (HL), LORD REID expressed the view that marginal notes cannot be used as an aid to construction. In *Director of Public Prosecution v. Schildkamp*, (1969) 3 All ER 1640, p. 1641 : 1971 AC 1 : (1970) 2 WLR 279 (HL), LORD REID again stated that "a side-note is a poor guide to the scope of a section for it can do no more than indicate the main subject with which the section deals". In the same case LORD UPJOHN said (p. 1657): "A side-note is a very brief precis of the section and therefore forms a most unsure guide to the construction of the enacting section, but it is as much a part of the Bill as a cross-heading and I can conceive of cases where very rarely it might throw some light on the intentions of Parliament just as a punctuation mark." And LORD DILHORNE (p. 1650) **also** agreed with this view. **See further** *Karnatak Rare Earth v. Senior Geologist Department of Mines and Geology*, (2004) 2 SCC 783, p. 793 (para 14) : AIR 2004 SC 2915, p. 2920, where reference is made to 8th Edn., p. 147 of this book and to LORD REID AND LORD UPJOHN'S, opinions.

any greater authority than the marginal notes in an English Act of Parliament."[85] PATANJALI SHASTRI, J., after referring to the above case with approval observed: "Marginal notes in an Indian statute, as in an Act of Parliament, cannot be referred to for the purpose of construing the statute."[86] At any rate, there can be no justification for restricting the section by the marginal note,[87] and the marginal note cannot certainly control the meaning of the body of the section if the language employed therein is clear.[88]

The appellate committee of the House of Lords, consisting of five Law Lords, in a joint opinion noticed that according to the change in practice starting in 2001, the side notes now appear as headings and although headings and side notes are not debated in Parliament and are, therefore, unamendable they cannot be entirely ignored. Their Lordships said: "The question then is whether headings and sidenotes, although unamendable, can be considered in construing a provision in an Act of Parliament. Account must, of course, be taken of the fact that these components were included in the Bill not for debate but for ease of reference. This indicates that less weight can be attached to them than to the parts of the Act that are open for consideration and debate in Parliament. But it is another matter to be required by a rule of law to disregard them altogether. One cannot ignore the fact that the headings and sidenotes are included on the face of the Bill throughout its passage through the Legislature. They are there for guidance. They provide the context for an examination of those parts of the Bill that are open for debate. Subject, of course, to the fact that they are unamendable, they ought to be open to consideration as part of the enactment when it reaches the statute book."[89]

Some Indian cases also show that reference to marginal notes may be permissible in exceptional cases for construing a section in a statute.[90]

---

85. *Balraj Kunwar v. Jagatpal Singh*, ILR 26 All 393, p. 406 : 31 IA 132 : 1 All LJ 384 (PC).

86. *C.I.T. v. Ahmedbhai Umarbhai & Co.*, AIR 1950 SC 134, p. 141 : 1950 SCR 335; *Board of Muslim Waqfs, Rajasthan v. Radhakishan*, AIR 1979 SC 289, pp. 295, 296 : (1979) 2 SCC 468; *Kalawati Bai v. Soiryabai*, AIR 1991 SC 1581, p. 1586 : (1991) 3 SCC 410; *Guntaiah v. Hambamma*, (2005) 6 SCC 228, pp. 233, 234 (para 11) : AIR 2005 SC 4013. **But see** *Uttam Das Chela Sunderdas v. Shiromani Gurdwara Prabandhak Committee*, 1996 (4) Scale 608, pp. 613, 614 : AIR 1996 SC 2133, p. 2137 : (1996) 5 SCC 71 (para 16), where **contrary** view is expressed. But it appears that the court in this case was dealing with 'Heading' and not 'Marginal note' and no final opinion was expressed.

87. *Emperor v. Sadashiv*, AIR 1947 PC 82, p. 84 : 74 IA 89 : 48 Cri LJ 791.

88. *Nalinakhya Bysack v. Shyam Sundar Haddar*, AIR 1953 SC 148, p. 150 : 1953 SCR 533; *Western India Theatres Ltd. v. Municipal Corporation, Poona*, AIR 1959 SC 586, p. 589 : 1959 Supp (2) SCR 71; *Nandini Satpathy v. P.C. Dani*, AIR 1978 SC 1025, p. 1039 : 1978 (2) SCC 424.

89. *R v. Montila*, (2005) 1 All ER 113, p. 124 (HL).

90. *Deewan Singh v. Rajendra Pd. Ardevi*, (2007) 10 SCC 528 : AIR 2007 SC 767; *Sarabjit Rick Singh v. Union of India*, (2008) 2 SCC 417 para 54 : (2007) 14 Scale 449.

Marginal notes appended to Articles of the Constitution have been held to constitute part of the Constitution as passed by the Constituent Assembly and therefore they have been made use of in construing the Articles, *e.g.* Article 286, as furnishing *'prima facie'*, 'some clue as to the meaning and purpose of the Article'.[91]

A note appended to a statutory provision or subordinate legislation is merely explanatory in nature and does not dilute the rigour of the main provision.[92] Notes under the rules cannot control the rules but they can provide an aid for interpretation of those rules. Further, a note which is made contemporaneously with the rules is part of the rule, and is not inconsistent with the rule, but makes explicit what is implicit in the rule.[93]

6. PUNCTUATION

In England, before 1850, there was no punctuation in the manuscript copy of any Act which received the Royal assent, therefore, the Courts cannot have any regard to punctuation for construing the older Acts. Even as regards more modern Acts, it is very doubtful if punctuation can be looked at for purposes of construction.[94] The opinion on Indian statutes is not very much different. Dealing with Regulation VIII of 1819, LORD HOBHOUSE stated: "It is an error to rely on punctuation in construing Acts of the Legislature."[95] Again, while construing Article 48 of the Indian Limitation Act, 1908 which reads 'for specific moveable property lost or acquired by theft, or dishonest misappropriation or conversion, or for compensation for wrongfully taking or detaining the same', LORD WARRINGTON rejected the contention that the word 'dishonest' qualified

---

91. *Bengal Immunity Co. Ltd. v. State of Bihar*, AIR 1955 SC 661, p. 676 : (1955) 2 SCR 603. For another example **see** *Golaknath v. State of Punjab*, AIR 1967 SC 1643,
p. 1658 : 1967 (2) SCR 762, where marginal note to Article 368 was referred.

92. *V.B. Prasad v. Manager P.M.D.U.P. School,* AIR 2007 SC 2053 (para 11) : (2007) 5 JT 378; *Punjab Electricity Board v. Zora Singh,* (2005) 6 SCC 776 (paras 23, 24) : AIR 2006 SC 182.

93. *Prem Parkash Pahwa v. United Commercial Bank & Anr.*, (2012) 1 SCC 123, p. 129.

94. *IRC v. Hinchy*, (1960) 1 All ER 505, p. 510 : 1960 AC 748 (HL) (LORD REID). In *Director of Public Prosecutions v. Schildkamp*, (1969) 3 All ER 1640, p. 1641 : 1971 AC 1 : (1970) 2 WLR 279 (HL), LORD REID said: "Punctuation can be of some assistance in construction". In *Hanlon v. Law Secretary*, (1980) 2 All ER 199, p. 221 : (1981) AC 124 : (1980) 2 WLR 756 (HL). LORD LOWRY observed: "I consider that not to take account of punctuation disregards the reality that literate people such as parliamentary draftsman, punctuate when they write, if not identically at least with grammatical principles. Why should not other literate people such as judges look at the punctuations in order to interpret the meaning of the legislation as accepted by Parliament?"

95. *Maharani of Burdwan v. Krishna Kamini Dasi*, ILR 14 Cal 365, p. 372 (PC).

not only 'misappropriation' but also 'conversion' bringing only dishonest conversion within the Article, and observed: "The truth is that, if the article is read without the commas inserted in the print, as a court of law is bound to do, the meaning is reasonably clear."[1] B.K. MUKHERJEA, J., in *Aswini Kumar Ghose v. Arabinda Bose*,[2] expressed himself as follows: "Punctuation is after all a minor element in the construction of a statute, and very little attention is paid to it by English Courts.... It seems, however, that in the vellum copies printed since 1850, there are some cases of punctuation, and when they occur they can be looked upon as a sort of *contemporanea expositio*.... When a statute is carefully punctuated and there is doubt about its meaning, a weight should undoubtedly be given to punctuation—. I need not deny that punctuation may have its uses in some cases, but it cannot certainly be regarded as a controlling element and cannot be allowed to control the plain meaning of a text." In *Gopalan's* case,[3] KANIA, C.J.I., in construing Article 22(7)(a) of the Constitution, referred to the punctuation and derived assistance from it in reaching his conclusion that Parliament was not obliged to prescribe both the circumstances under which, and the class or classes of cases, in which a person may be detained for a period longer than three months, without obtaining the opinion of Advisory Board and that Parliament on a true construction of the clause could prescribe either or both.[4] The use of the word 'which' twice, read with the comma put after each 'which' was relied upon as indicative of this construction.[5] This view was later overruled in the case of *Sambhu Nath Sarkar v. State of W.B.*[6] But it would appear, at any rate, with respect to modern statutes that if the statute in question is found to be carefully punctuated, punctuation though a minor element, may be resorted to for purposes of construction.[7] An illustration of the aid derived from punctuation may be furnished from the case of *Mohd. Shabbir v. State of Maharashtra,*[8] where section 27 of the Drugs and Cosmetics Act, 1940 came up for construction. By this section whoever 'manufactures for sale, sells, stocks or exhibits for sale or distributes' a drug without a licence, is liable for punishment. In holding that mere stocking is not an offence within the section, the Supreme Court pointed out the presence of comma after 'manufactures for sale'

---

1. *Lewis Pugh Evans Pugh v. Ashutosh Sen*, AIR 1929 PC 69, p. 71 : 56 IA 93.
2. AIR 1952 SC 369, p. 383 : 1953 SCR 1.
3. *A. K. Gopalan v. State of Madras*, AIR 1950 SC 27, p. 45 : 1950 SCR 88.
4. A.K. Gopalan v. State of Madras, supra.
5. *Ibid*, **see further** *S. Krishnan v. State of Madras*, AIR 1951 SC 301, p. 304 : 1951 SCR 621.
6. AIR 1973 SC 1425 : 1973 SCC (Cri) 618 : (1973) 1 SCC 856.
7. **See** text and note 2, *supra*.
8. AIR 1979 SC 564, p. 565 : (1979) 1 SCC 568 : 1979 SCC (Cri) 356.

and 'sells' and absence of any comma after 'stocks'. It was, therefore, held that only stocking for sale could amount to offence and not mere stocking. For another example of the use of punctuation, reference may be made to *M.K. Salpekar (Dr.) v. Sunil Kumar Shamsunder Chaudhari*,[9] where the court construed clause 13(3)(v) of the Central Provinces and Berar Letting of Houses and Rent Control Order. This provision permits ejectment of a tenant on the ground that "the tenant has secured alternative accommodation, or has left the area for a continuous period of four months and does not reasonably need the house". In holding that the requirement that the tenant 'does not reasonably need the house' has no application when he 'has secured alternative accommodation' the court referred and relied upon the punctuation comma after the words 'alternative accommodation'. However, if a statute is revised and re-enacted but the section under construction in the revised statute is brought in identical terms as in the old statute except as to variation of some punctuation, that in itself will not be indicative of any intention on the part of the Legislature to change the law as understood under the old section.[10]

7. ILLUSTRATIONS

Illustrations appended to a section form part of the statute and although forming no part of the section, are of relevance and value in the construction of the text of the section and they should not be readily rejected as repugnant to the section.[11] But Illustrations cannot have the effect of modifying the language of the section and they cannot either curtail or expand the ambit of the section which alone forms the enactment.[12]

---

9. AIR 1988 SC 1841 : 1988 (4) SCC 21. **See further** *Sama Alana Abdulla v. State of Gujarat*, 1995 (6) Scale 407, pp. 409, 410 : AIR 1996 SC 569, p. 571. (Construing the words "any secret official code or password, or any sketch, plan, model etc.", it was held that the presence of comma after password showed that the adjective 'secret' only qualified the expression "official code or password").

10. *Pope Appliance Corporation v. Spanish River Pulp & Paper Mills Ltd.*, AIR 1929 PC 38, p. 45.

11. *Mahomed Shydol Ariffin v. Yeah Oai Gark*, 43 IA 256, p. 263 : (1916) 2 AC 575, p. 581 : AIR 1916 PC 247 (PC); *Muralidhar Chatterjee v. International Film Co.*, AIR 1943 PC 34, p. 38 : 70 IA 35; *Sopher v. Administrator General of Bengal*, AIR 1944 PC 67, p. 69; *Jumma Masjid v. Kodimaniandra Deviah*, AIR 1962 SC 847, p. 851 : 1962 Supp (2) SCR 554. **But see** *Mahesh Chandra Sharma v. Raj Kumari Sharma (Smt.)*, AIR 1996 SC 869, p. 877 : (1996) 8 SCC 128, where it is said that "illustrations to the section are parts of the section and help to elucidate the principle of the section".

12. *Bengal Nagpur Railway Co. Ltd. v. Ruttanji Ramji*, AIR 1938 PC 67, p. 70 : 65 IA 66; *Aniruddha Mitra v. Administrator General of Bengal*, AIR 1949 PC 244, p. 250; *Shambhu Nath Mehra v. State of Ajmer*, AIR 1956 SC 404, p. 406 : 1956 SCR 199; *Lalit Mohan Pandey v. Pooran Singh*, AIR 2004 SC 2303, p. 2315 : (2004) 6 SCC 626, p. 645.

In *Ariffin's* case,[13] the question involved was as to the admissibility of a diary maintained by a deceased father containing the dates of births, deaths and marriages in his family in proof of age of his son under section 32(5) of the Straits Settlement Ordinance, 1893 which is in similar terms as section 32(5) of the Indian Evidence Act, 1872.[14] There is an Illustration (b) appended to the section which runs: 'The question is, what is the date of the birth of *A*? A letter from *A*'s deceased father—announcing the birth of *A* on a given day, is a relevant fact'. The Privy Council held the diary to be admissible on the footing that a statement as to date of birth relates to the commencement of one's relationship by blood and therefore relates to the existence of such relationship as that referred to in section 32(5). Support for this view was taken from the Illustration. LORD SHAW in delivering the opinion observed: "It is the duty of a court of law to accept, if that can be done, the Illustrations given as being both of relevance and value in the construction of the text. The Illustrations should in no case be rejected because they do not square with ideas possibly derived from another system of jurisprudence as to the law with which they or the sections deal. And it would require a very special case to warrant their rejection on the ground of their assumed repugnancy to the section themselves. It would be the very last resort of construction to make this assumption. The great usefulness of the Illustrations which have, although not part of the sections, been expressly furnished by the Legislature as helpful in the working and application of the statute, should not be thus impaired."[15]

Illustrations appended to sections 39, 64, 65 and 75 of the Indian Contract Act were used by the Privy Council[16] in construing these sections and in deciding that a contract which may be 'put an end to' under section 39 is 'voidable' under section 64; the resulting position being that when a party puts an end to a contract under section 39 on the other party refusing or disabling himself from performing his promise in entirety, the party rescinding the contract becomes liable to restore the benefit received under the contract to the person from whom it was received (*vide* section 64), although he (the party rescinding) is entitled to compensation for any

13. *Mahomed Syedol Ariffin v. Yeah Oai Gark, supra.*

14. Section 32 : "Statements, written or verbal of relevant facts made by a person who is dead..... are themselves relevant facts in the following cases:

* * * * * * * * *

(5) When the statement relates to the existence of any relationship by blood, marriage or adoption between persons as to whose relationship by blood, marriage or adoption the person making the statement had special means of knowledge, and when the statement was made before the question in dispute was raised."

15. *Mohomed Shydol Ariffin v. Yeah Oai Gark*, 43 IA 256, p. 263 : AIR 1916 PC 242 : referred to in *Jumma Masjid v. Kodimaniandra Deviah*, AIR 1962 SC 847, p. 851 : 1962 Supp (2) SCR 554.

16. *Muralidhar Chatterjee v. International Film Co.*, AIR 1943 PC 34 : 70 IA 35.

damage which he has sustained through the non-fulfilment of the contract (*vide* section 75). In reaching this conclusion SIR GEORGE RANKIN said: "The presence of Illustration (c) to section 65 cannot be made consistent with any other view. The effect of section 39 is explained by the example there given of a singer who wilfully absents himself from the theatre. The same example serves also under section 65 as Illustration (c) and under section 75—. Nor can the Illustration be ignored or brushed aside because it is not part of the body of the section."[17]

Similarly in interpreting section 113 of the Indian Succession Act, 1925 and in deciding that 'later' bequest to be valid must comprise of all the testator's remaining interest, if the legatee to the later bequest is not in existence at the time of the testator's death, and that a conferment of a life estate under such a bequest is not valid, the Privy Council took the aid of Illustrations appended to that section. VISCOUNT MAUGHAM pointed out: "Illustrations 2 and 3 would seem to show—What is not clear from the language of the section—that however complete may be the disposition of the Will, gift after the prior bequest may not be a life interest to an unborn person for that would be a bequest to a person not in existence at the time of testator's death of something less than the remaining interest of the testator."[18]

The Supreme Court took the aid of Illustration appended to section 43, Transfer of Property Act, 1882 for the conclusion that the said provision applies to transfers of *spes successionis* and enables the transferee to claim the property, provided other conditions of the section are satisfied. VENKATARAMA AIYAR, J., quoted the judgment in *Ariffins'* case[19] and observed: "It is not to be readily assumed that an Illustration to a section is repugnant to it and rejected."[20]

Attention must also be made of Illustration (b) to section 114, Indian Evidence Act, which reads: 'The court may presume that an accomplice is unworthy of credit unless he is corroborated in material particulars'. The impact of this Illustration on the construction of section 133 of the Evidence Act—'An accomplice shall be a competent witness against an accused person; and a conviction is not illegal merely because it proceeds upon the uncorroborated testimony of an accomplice'—is too well-known. The rule evolved on the basis of the Illustration is that "it is almost always unsafe", to convict an accused on the uncorroborated testimony of

---

17. *Ibid.*, p. 38.
18. *Sopher v. Administrator General of Bengal*, AIR 1944 PC 67, p. 69.
19. 43 IA 256, p. 263 : AIR 1916 PC 242.
20. *Jumma Masjid v. Kodimaniandra Deviah*, AIR 1962 SC 847, p. 851 : 1962 Supp (2) SCR 554.

an accomplice,[21] and that the corroboration required to sustain a conviction must be independent and must relate to the participation of the accused in the offence.[22] The Supreme Court has never felt any difficulty in setting aside a conviction based on uncorroborated or insufficiently corroborated testimony of an accomplice.[23] Thus the rule of law enacted in the later part of section 133 has, from practical point of view, been reduced to a dead letter on the basis of a rule of practice developed under a mere Illustration and that too appended to a different section. Such a result, which is exceptional from the point of view of principles of construction, is the outcome of the anxiety of courts to safeguard the liberty of the subject and to make sure that a conviction is not obtained merely on tainted evidence.

The utility of Illustration in interpreting the section cannot, however, detract the prime importance of the language of the section which is the enacting provision. Illustrations, therefore, cannot, as already noticed,[24] have the effect of controlling the real content of the section and must give way in case of repugnance with the text of the section.

In holding that section 73 of the Indian Contract Act, 1872 does not permit the award of interest as damages for mere detention of a debt, the Privy Council rejected the argument that Illustration (u) to that section can be used for arriving at a contrary result. SIR SHADILAL observed: "Nor can an Illustration have the effect of modifying the language of the section which alone forms the enactment."[25]

Similarly, in deciding that section 115 of the Indian Succession Act, 1925 is sufficiently wide and is not limited in its application to members of a class who are in existence at the date of testator's death, SIR MADHAVAN NAIR with reference to Illustrations appended to that section pointed out: "The words of the section are not ambiguous. It is well-settled that just as Illustrations should not be read as extending the meaning of a section, they should also not be

---

21. *Bhiva v. State of Maharashtra*, AIR 1963 SC 599, p. 601 : 1963 (3) SCR 830.

22. *Ibid.*, p. 600; *Jnanendra Nath Ghose v. State of W.B.*, AIR 1959 SC 1199, p. 1202 : 1960 (1) SCR 126; *Gajendranath Dwari v. State of Orissa*, 1965 SCN 246; *Mohd. Hussain Umer Kochra v. K.S. Dalip Singhji*, AIR 1970 SC 45 : 1969 (3) SCC 429; *Balwant Kaur v. Union Territory of Chandigarh*, AIR 1988 SC 139, p. 142 : (1988) 1 SCC 1; *Shanker v. State of Tamil Nadu*, JT 1994 (3) SC 54 : 1994 (4) SCC 478 : 1994 Cri LJ 3071; *K. Hashim v. State of T.N.*, (2005) 1 SCC 237, pp. 248 to 251.

23. *Sarwan Singh Rattan Singh v. State of Punjab*, AIR 1957 SC 637 : 1957 SCR 953; *R.R. Chari v. State of U.P.*, AIR 1962 SC 1573 : 1963 (1) SCR 121; *Bhiva v. State of Maharashtra, supra*; *Saravanabhavan and Govindaswami v. State of Madras*, AIR 1966 SC 1273 : 1966 Cr LJ 949; *Balwant Kaur v. Union Territory of Chandigarh, supra*.

24. **See** text and note 12, p. 192.

25. *Bengal & Nagpur Railway v. Ruttanji Ramji*, AIR 1938 PC 67, p. 70 : 65 IA 66; **referred** to in *Union of India v. Rallia Ram*, AIR 1963 SC 1685, pp. 1694, 1695 : 1964 (3) SCR 164.

read as restricting its operation especially so when the effect would be to curtail a right which the plain words of the section would confer."[26]

In a case before the Supreme Court which involved the interpretation of section 106 of the Indian Evidence Act, 1872, the Court held that the said provision was not intended to relieve the prosecution of the burden of proof and was designed to meet certain exceptional cases and had no application to those cases where the information was as much within the knowledge of the prosecution as of the accused. Referring to the Illustration to section 106, BOSE, J., observed: "We recognise that an Illustration does not exhaust the full content of the section which it illustrates but it can neither curtail nor expand its ambit."[27]

8. DEFINITION SECTIONS OR INTERPRETATION CLAUSES

In spite of severe criticism as to utility of definitions section or interpretation clauses[28], it is common to find in a statute 'Definitions' of certain words and expressions used elsewhere in the body of the statute. The object of such a definition is to avoid the necessity of frequent repetitions in describing all the subject-matter to which the word or expression so defined is intended to apply.[29] For instance, the Supreme Court held that when the word 'securities' has been defined under the Securities Contracts (Regulation) Act, 1956, its meaning would not vary when the same word is used at more than one place in the same statute, as otherwise it will defeat the very object of the definitive section.[30]

A definitions section may borrow definitions from an earlier Act and the definitions so borrowed may not necessarily be in the definitions section but may be in some other provision of the earlier Act.[31] A definition borrowed by incorporation or reference may be sometimes found in the rules made under

---

26. *Aniruddha v. Administrator General of Bengal*, AIR 1949 PC 244, p. 250.

27. *Shambhu Nath Mehra v. State of Ajmer*, AIR 1956 SC 404, p. 406 : 1956 SCR 199.

28. *Knightsbridge Estates Trust Ltd. v. Byrne*, (1940) AC 613: (1940) 2 All ER 401, p. 407 (HL); *H.H. Prince Azam Jha Bahadur v. Expenditure Tax Officer, Hyderabad*, AIR 1972 SC 2319, p. 2324 : 1971 (3) SCC 621. The following guidelines in Canada as to when to use definitions in Acts appear to be fairly universal: "Definitions should be used sparingly and only for the following purposes: (a) to establish that a term is not being used in a usual meaning or is being used in one of the several meanings; (b) to avoid excessive repetition; (c) to allow the use of an abbreviation; (d) to signal the use of unusual or novel term." **Quoted** from Bilika H. Simamba, 'The Placing and Other Handling of Definitions', (2006) 27 Statute Law Review 73, pp. 75, 76.

29. *Nahalchand Laloochand Private Ltd. v. Pancholi Co-operative Housing Society Ltd.*, (2010) 9 SCC 536 para 31 : AIR 2010 SC 3607 (12th edition of the book is **referred**).

30. *Bhagwati Developers Pvt. Ltd. v. Peerless General Finance Investment Co. Ltd. & Anr.*, (2013) 9 SCC 584, p. 597.

31. *Life Ins. Corporation of India v. Crown Life Insurance Co.*, AIR 1965 SC 1985, p. 1986 : 1965 (3) SCR 474.

the referred statute. For example, Article 366(1) of the Constitution defines 'agricultural income' to mean 'agricultural income as defined for the purpose of enactments relating to Indian Income-tax'. In construing this definition the Supreme Court has consistently taken the view that its meaning has to be considered not merely by looking to the Income-tax Act, 1922 or the Income-tax Act, 1961 but also with reference to the Rules made under these Acts for computation of income when the same is derived in part from agriculture and in part from business and so only 60% of the income on sale of tea grown and manufactured by an assessee as provided in the Rules can be held to be agricultural income which the States can tax.[32] But in the absence of incorporation or reference it is hazardous to interpret a word in accordance with its definition in another statute[33] and more so when such statute is not dealing with any cognate subject[34] or the statutes are not in *pari materia.*[35] On this principle the meaning given to the word 'industry' in the Industrial Disputes Act was not used for construing that word in an exemption notification under section 25 of the Customs Act, 1962;[36] and the definition of 'currency note' in the Indian Paper Currency Act, 1822 was not applied for interpreting that expression in section 489A of the Penal Code.[37]

While it has been the practice of the legislative bodies, following British Parliamentary practice, to define certain words employed in any given statute for a proper appreciation of the understanding of the scheme and purport of the Act, in the event a statute does not contain the definition of a particular expression employed in it, it becomes the duty of the Courts to expound the meaning of the undefined expressions in accordance with the well-established rules of statutory interpretation.[38]

(a) Restrictive and extensive definitions

The Legislature has power to define a word even artificially.[39] So the definition of a word in the definitions section may either be restrictive

---

32. *Tata Tea Ltd. v. State of Bombay*, AIR 1988 SC 1435 : 1988 Supp SCC 316. **See further** *Commissioner of Income Tax v. Williamson Financial Services,* (2008) 2 SCC 202 : (2007) 13 JT 581.

33. *Maheshwari Fish Seed Farm v. T.N. Electricity Board,* (2004) 4 SCC 705, p. 713 (9th Edn., p. 163 of this book is **referred**); *Agricultural Produce Market Committee v. Commissioner of Income Tax,* (2008) 9 SCC 434 para 40 : (2008) 10 JT 17.

34. **See** cases in footnotes 35 and 36, *infra.*

35. *Jagatram Ahuja v. Commr. of Gift-tax,* AIR 2000 SC 3195, p. 3201 : (2000) 8 SCC 249.

36. *MSCO Pvt. Ltd. v. Union of India*, (1985) 1 SCC 51, p. 54 : AIR 1985 SC 76.

37. *State of Kerala v. Mathai Vergese*, (1986) 4 SCC 746, p. 753 : AIR 1987 SC 33.

38. *Keshavlal Khemchand and Sons Pvt. Ltd. & Ors. v. Union of India & Ors.*, (2015) 4 SCC 770, p. 796.

39. *Kishanlal v. State of Rajasthan*, AIR 1990 SC 2269, p. 2270 : 1990 Supp SCC 742; *CIT v. Sundaram Spinning Mills,* AIR 2000 SC 490, p. 491 : (2000) 1 SCC 466; *Feroze N. Dotivala v. P.M. Wadhwani,* (2003) 1 SCC 433, p. 442.

of its ordinary meaning or it may be extensive of the same. When a word is defined to 'mean' such and such, the definition is *prima facie* restrictive and exhaustive.[40] For instance, section 2(f) of the Protection of Women from Domestic Violence Act, 2005, defines 'domestic relationship' to mean a relationship between two persons who live or have, at any point of time, lived together in a shared household, when they are related by consanguinity, marriage or through a relationship in the nature of marriage, adoption or are family members living together as a joint family. The Supreme Court held that the definition clause mentions only five categories of relationships, and is exhaustive since the expression 'means' has been used.[41] Whereas, where the word defined is declared to 'include' such and such, the definition is *prima facie* extensive.[42] When by an amending Act, the word 'includes' was substituted for the word 'means' in a definitions section, it was held that the intention was to make it more extensive.[43] Further, a definition may be in the form of 'means and includes', where again the definition is

---

40. *Vanguard Fire & General Insurance Co. Ltd., Madras v. Fraser & Ross*, AIR 1960 SC 971, p. 975 : (1960) 3 SCR 857; *Inland Revenue Commissioner v. Joiner*, (1975) 3 All ER 1050, pp. 1060, 1061 (HL); *Kasilingam v. P.S.G. College of Technology*, 1995 (2) Scale 387, p. 394 : AIR 1995 SC 1395, p. 1400 : 1995 Supp (2) SCC 348; *Feroze N. Dotivala v. P.M. Wadhwani, supra; Commissioner of Trade Tax U.P. v. Kajaria Ceramics Ltd.,* AIR 2005 SC 2968 (paras 65, 66); *Commercial Taxation Officer, Udaipur v. Rajasthan Tax Chem. Ltd.,* (2007) 3 SCC 124 (para 22) : (2007) 2 SLT 13 : (2007) 2 Scale 120.

41. *Indra Sarma v. V.K.V. Sarma*, (2013) 15 SCC 755, p. 778.

42. *Dilworth v. Commissioner of Stamps*, (1899) AC 99, p. 105 (PC); *Reynolds v. John*, (1956) 1 All ER 306, p. 309; *State of Bombay v. Hospital Mazdoor Sabha*, AIR 1960 SC 610, p. 614; *Ardeshir H. Bhiwandiwala v. State of Bombay*, AIR 1962 SC 29, p. 30; *Sant Ram v. Labh Singh*, AIR 1965 SC 314, p. 316; *CIT, AP v. Taj Mahal Hotel, Secunderabad*, AIR 1972 SC 168, p. 170 : 1971 (3) SCC 550; *Inland Revenue Commissioner v. Joiner, supra*; *Doypack Systems Pvt. Ltd. v. Union of India*, AIR 1988 SC 782, p. 803 : 1988 (2) SCC 299; *Kishan Lal v. State of Rajasthan*, AIR 1990 SC 2269, p. 2270 : 1990 (1) JT 550 : 1990 Supp SCC 742; *Municipal Corporation of Greater Bombay v. Indian Oil Corporation*, AIR 1991 SC 686, p. 689 : 1991 Supp SCC 18; *Regional Director Employees' State Insurance Corporation v. High Land Coffee Works of PFX Saldanha & Sons*, AIR 1992 SC 129, p. 131 : 1991 (3) SCC 617; *Kasilingam v. P.S.G. College of Technology*, 1995 (2) Scale 387, p. 394 : AIR 1995 SC 1395, p. 1400 : 1995 Supp (2) SCC 348; *Feroze N. Dotivala v. P.M. Wadhwani, supra*; *Associated Indian Mechanical (P.) Ltd. v. W.B. Small Industries Development Corpn. Ltd.,* (2007) 3 SCC 607 (para 13) : AIR 2007 SC 788; *Ramanlal Bhailal Patel v. State of Gujrat,* (2008) 5 SCC 449 para 23 : AIR 2008 SC 1246; *Karnataka Power Transmission Corporation v. Ashok Iron Works Pvt. Ltd.,* (2009) 3 SCC 240 paras 15 to 17 : (2009) 2 JT 447.

43. *Gollaleshwar Dev v. Gangavwa Kom Shantayya Math*, (1985) 4 SCC 393, p. 401 : AIR 1986 SC 231.

exhaustive;[44] on the other hand, if a word is defined 'to apply to and include', the definition is understood as extensive.[45] These meanings of the expressions 'means', 'includes' and 'means and includes' have been reiterated in *Delhi Development Authority v. Bhola Nath Sharma.*[46] The use of word 'any', *e.g.* any building also connotes extension for 'any' is a word of very wide meaning and *prima facie* the use of it excludes limitation.[47]

A definition which defines a word to mean *A* and to include *B* and *C* cannot in its application be construed to exclude *A* and to include only *B* and *C*. The definition of 'owner' in the Bihar Taxation on Passengers and Goods (Carried by Public Service Motor Vehicles) Act, 1961 means the owner and includes bailee of a public carrier vehicle or any manager acting on behalf of the owner. It was held that the definition could not be applied to exclude the actual owner and to free him from liability.[48] Further, the natural meaning of the 'means' part of the definition is not narrowed down by the 'includes' part.[49] Thus the definition of 'sale price' in section 2(d) of the West Bengal Sales Tax Act, 1954 to mean 'money consideration for the sale' and to include 'any sum charged for containers etc.' was construed to include freight and delivery charges paid by the seller as being within the ordinary meaning of the words 'money consideration for the sale' though not mentioned in the inclusive part of the definition.[50]

Referring to the definition of 'charitable bequest' in a New Zealand statute, the Privy Council pointed out: "It is not said in terms that charitable bequest shall mean one or other of the things which are enumerated, but that it shall include them. The word 'include' is very generally used in interpretation clauses in order to enlarge the meaning of words or phrases occurring in the body of the statute; and when it is so used those words or phrases must be construed as comprehending, not only such things, as they signify according

---

44. *Dilworth v. Commissioner of Stamps, supra*, p. 105; *Jagir Singh v. State of Bihar*, AIR 1976 SC 997, pp. 999, 1001 : 1976 SCC (Tax) 204 : (1976) 2 SCC 942; *Kasilingam v. P.S.G. College of Technology, supra*; *Bharat Coop. Bank (Mumbai) Ltd. v. Coop. Bank Employees Union*, (2007) 4 SCC 685 (para 23) : (2007) 4 JT 573 : (2007) 2 LLJ 825 : AIR 2007 SC 2320; *Paul Enterprises v. Rajib Chatterjee and Company*, (2009) 3 SCC 709 para 28 : (2009) 1 JT 632.

45. *Nutter v. Accrington Local Board*, (1879) 4 QBD 375, pp. 384, 385 (CA).

46. (2011) 2 SCC 54 paras 25 to 28 : AIR 2011 SC 428.

47. *Associated Indian Mechanical (P.) Ltd. v. W.B. Small Industries Development Corpn. Ltd.*, (2007) 3 SCC 607 (para 13) : AIR 2007 SC 788.

48. *Jagir Singh v. State of Bihar*, AIR 1976 SC 997, pp. 999, 1001 : 1976 SCC (Tax) 204 : (1976) 2 SCC 942.

49. *Black Diamond Beverages v. Commercial Tax Officer*, JT 1997 (8) 128, pp. 132, 133 : AIR 1997 SC 3550, p. 3532 : (1998) 1 SCC 458.

50. *Ibid.*

to their natural import, but also those things which the interpretation clause declares that they shall include. But the word 'include' is susceptible of another construction, which may become imperative, if the context of the Act is sufficient to show that it was not merely employed for the purpose of adding to the natural significance of the words or expressions used. It may be equivalent to 'mean and include' and in that case it may afford an exhaustive explanation of the meaning which for the purposes of the Act must invariably be attached to those words or expressions."[51] Thus the word 'include' may in certain contexts be a word of limitation.[52]

In section 201(1) of the Licensing Act, 1964, 'bar' is defined to include a place which is exclusively or mainly used for the sale and consumption of intoxicating liquor. Referring to this definition the House of Lords held that the use of the word 'include' showed that the definition did not exclude what would ordinarily and in common parlance be spoken of as a bar, and therefore counters used for serving liquor were held to be 'bar' within section 75(5) of the Act.[53]

The inclusive definition of 'district judge' in Article 236(a) of the Constitution has been very widely construed to include hierarchy of specialised Civil Courts *viz.*, Labour Courts and Industrial Courts which are not expressly included in the definition.[54] But the this case of *Labour Law Practitioners' Association*[54] has been distinguished in *R.D. Joshi v. High Court of Bombay.*[55] It has been held that on fulfilling the criteria in Article 233(2) of the Constitution alone, can a candidate be appointed to a judicial office in accordance with the procedure stated in Article 233(1). Article 236(a) clearly

---

51. *Dilworth v. Commissioner of Stamps*, (1899) AC 99, pp. 105, 106 : 79 LT 473 : 15 TLR 61 (PC). **See further** *Municipal Council, Raipur v. State of M.P.*, AIR 1970 SC 1923, p. 1925 : 1969 (2) SCC 582; *Jenkins v. Cohen & Co.*, (1971) 1 WLR, pp. 1285, 1286 (CA); *South Gujarat Roofing Tiles Manufacturers Association v. State of Gujarat*, AIR 1977 SC 90, p. 93 : 1977 SCC (L&S) 15; *Dadaji v. Sukhdeobabu*, AIR 1980 SC 150, p. 153 : 1980 (1) SCC 621; *Reserve Bank of India v. Pearless General Finance and Investment Co. Ltd.*, (1987) 1 SCC 424, p. 449 : AIR 1987 SC 1023; *Hemens (Valuation Officer) v. Whitsbury Farm and Stud Ltd.*, (1988) 1 All ER 72, pp. 77, 78 : (1988) AC 601 (HL); *Mahalakshmi Oil Mills v. State of Andhra Pradesh*, AIR 1989 SC 335, p. 339 : (1989) 1 SCC 164; *N.D.P. Namboodaripad v. Union of India,* (2007) 4 SCC 502 (para 19) : AIR 2007 SC 1782; *Hamdard (Wakf) Laboratories v. Dy. Labour Commissioner,* (2007) 5 SCC 281 (para 33) : (2007) 6 Scale 423 : (2007) 6 JT 329 (10th edition, pp. 173 and 175 of this book are **referred**).

52. *Godfray Phillips India Ltd. v. State of U.P.*, (2005) 2 SCC 515, pp. 548, 550 (paras 74 and 84). **See further** *Ponds India Ltd. v. Commissioner of Trade Tax Lucknow,* (2008) 8 SCC 369 para 30 : (2008) 9 JT 94; *Karnataka Power Transmission Corporation v. Ashok Iron Works Pvt. Ltd.,* (2009) 3 SCC 240 paras 15 to 17 : AIR 2009 SC 1905 : (2009) 2 JT 447.

53. *Carter v. Bradbeer*, (1975) 3 All ER 158, pp. 164, 168 (HL).

54. *State of Maharashtra v. Labour Law Practitioners' Association*, AIR 1998 SC 1233, p. 1237 : 1998 (2) SCC 688.

55. (2011) 1 SCC 252 paras 37 and 39 : AIR 2011 SC 848.

shows that the expression 'district judge' includes different kinds of judges but not Family Court judges who are not members of 'judicial service' as defined in Article 236(b). The inclusive definition of 'lease' under Section 2 (16)(c) of the Stamp Act, 1899 has been widely construed to cover a transaction for the purpose of Stamp Act which may not amount to a lease under section 105 of the Transfer of Property Act, 1882.[56] Para 2(a) of the Drugs (Prices Control) Order, 1995, defines 'bulk drug' to mean any pharmaceutical, chemical, biological or plant product, including its salts, esters, stereoisomers and derivatives, conforming to pharmacopoeial or other standards specified in the Second Schedule to the Drugs and Cosmetics Act, 1940. The Supreme Court held that the usage of the word 'includes' implies that the definition of bulk drug in para 2(a) is very wide and it not only applies to 'base drugs' but also to its salts, esters, stereoisomers and derivatives.[57]

Referring to the definition of the word 'street' in an English Statute, COTTON, L.J., said: "It does not say that the word street shall be confined to any highway not being a turnpike road, but that it shall 'apply to and include any highway not being a turnpike road' etc. That is enlarging, not restricting the meaning of 'street'."[58] In dealing with the definition of 'Industry' in the Industrial Disputes Act, 1947, GAJENDRAGADKAR, J., observed: "It is obvious that the words used in an inclusive definition denote extension and cannot be treated as restricted in any sense. Where we are dealing with an inclusive definition, it would be inappropriate to put a restrictive interpretation upon terms of wider denotation."[59] In holding that sanitary and pipe line fittings in a building which is run as a hotel fall within the word 'plant' in section 10(2)(vi-b) of the Income-tax Act, 1922, for grant of depreciation allowance, GROVER, J., referred to the definition of 'plant' in section 10(5)[60] of the Act and observed: "The very fact that even books have been included shows that the meaning intended to be given to 'plant' is wide. The word 'includes' is often used in interpretation clauses in order to enlarge the meaning of the words or phrases occurring in the body of the statute. When it is so used these words and phrases must be construed as comprehending not only such things as they signify according to their nature and import but also those things which the interpre-

---

56. *State of Uttarakhand v. Harpal Singh Rawat*, (2011) 4 SCC 575 (para 8) : AIR 2011 SC 1506.
57. *Union of India & Anr. v. Swiss Garnier Life Sciences & Ors.*, (2013) 8 SCC 615, p. 631.
58. *Nutter v. Accrington Local Board*, (1879) 4 QBD 375, pp. 384, 385(CA).
59. *State of Bombay v. Hospital Mazdoor Sabha*, AIR 1960 SC 610, p. 614 : 1960 (2) SCR 866.
60. Definition of Plant in section 10(5) of Income-tax Act, 1922 is as under: " 'Plant' includes vehicles, books, scientific apparatus and surgical equipment purchased for the purpose of the business, profession or vocation."

tation clause declares that they shall include."[61] The words 'including the power to punish for contempt of itself' in Article 129 of the Constitution which declares the Supreme Court to be a court of record, were held not to limit the inherent power of the Supreme Court as a court of record to punish for contempt of itself as also of subordinate courts.[62] The word 'income', which is of broadest connotation, is not restricted by the several clauses in section 2(24) of the Income-tax Act, 1961 and even a receipt not falling in any of the clauses may yet constitute income for to say otherwise would mean reading the several clauses as exhaustive.[63] It was, therefore, held that prize money received by a participant in a motor rally was 'income' and taxable even if did not fall in any of the clauses in section 2(24).[64] Section 2(1)(o) of the Consumer Protection Act, 1986 which is an inclusive definition of 'service' was held to include 'housing construction' even before this service was included expressly by amendment in 1993.[65] Section 2(1)(m) of the same Act which contains an inclusive definition of 'person' has been held to include a 'company' although it is not specifically named therein.[66] The definition of 'tax arrears' in the Kar Vivad Samadhan Scheme, 1998, is an inclusive definition, and hence it was held that instances where a demand in a notice or show-cause notice has been issued under the indirect tax enactment on or before 31.03.1998, but has not been complied with, will also be treated as tax arrears by legal fiction.[67] Similarly,

---

61. *CIT, A.P. v. Taj Mahal Hotel, Secunderabad*, AIR 1972 SC 168, p. 170 : (1971) 3 SCC 550. But a building used for the business of hotel or cinema is not a 'plant' for there is a specific provision for granting depreciation allowance for a building; *CIT Trivandrum v. Anand Theatres,* JT 2000 (6) SC 407, pp. 434, 435 : AIR 2000 SC 2356, p. 2374 : (2000) 5 SCC 393; *Scientific Engineering House Pvt. Ltd. v. Commissioner of Income-tax*, AIR 1986 SC 338 : (1986) 1 SCC 11 (Technical Knowhow in the shape of drawings, designs, plans, processing data, etc. held to be plant). **See further** *Narmada Bachao Andolan v. Union of India*, (2005) 4 SCC 32, p. 50. (It is now well settled that when the interpretation clause used an inclusive definition, it would be expansive in nature. 9th Edn., p. 166 of this book is **referred**.) *Commercial Taxation Officer, Udaipur v. Rajasthan Tax Chem. Ltd.*, (2007) 3 SCC 124 (para 22) : (2007) 2 SLT 13 : (2007) 2 Scale 120.

62. *Delhi Judicial Service Association v. State of Gujarat*, AIR 1991 SC 2176, p. 2190 : 1991 (4) SCC 406.

63. *Commissioner of Income-tax, Madras v. G.R. Karthikeyan*, AIR 1993 SC 1671, p. 1675 : 1993 Supp (3) SCC 222 : (1993) 201 ITR 866.

64. *Ibid.* Income as defined may also cover losses *i.e.* negative profit: *Commissioner of Income Tax I, Ahmedabad v. Gold Coin Health Food Pvt. Ltd.*, (2008) 9 SCC 622 paras 10 and 15 : (2008) 9 JT 312.

65. *Lucknow Development Authority v. M.K. Gupta*, AIR 1994 SC 787, p. 791 : 1994 (1) SCC 243.

66. *Karnataka Power Transmission Corporation v. Ashok Iron Works Pvt. Ltd.,*(2009) 3 SCC 240 para 21 : AIR 2009 SC 1905 : (2009) 2 JT 447.

67. *Union of India v. Nitdip Textile Processors Pvt. Ltd. & Anr.*, (2012) 1 SCC 226, p. 245.

section 2(1)(a) of the Border Security Force Act, 1968 defines 'active duty', in relation to a person subject to the Act, to mean any duty as a member of the Force during the period in which such person is attached to, or forms part of, a unit of the Force which is engaged in operations against an enemy, or which is operating at a picket or engaged on patrol or other guard duty along the borders of India, and 'includes' duty by such person during any period declared by the Central Government by notification in the Official Gazette as period of active duty. The Supreme Court held that the use of the expression 'includes' enlarges the meaning of the word 'active duty' and therefore, it shall not only mean the duty specified in the section, but also those duties declared by the Central Government by notification in the Official Gazette.[68]

But as stated earlier,[69] the word 'include' may in exceptional cases be construed as equivalent to 'mean and include'. Entry 22 added by the Gujarat Government to Part I of the Schedule to the Minimum Wages Act, 1948 furnished an illustration of such use. The Entry refers to 'Employment in Potteries Industries' and is followed by an *Explanation* which reads: 'For the purpose of this Entry potteries industry *includes* the manufacture of the following articles of pottery namely—(a) Crockery, (b) Sanitary appliances, (c) Refractories, (d) Jars, (e) Electrical accessories, (f) Hospital wares, (g) Textile accessories, (h) Toys, (i) Glazed tiles'. Construing the *Explanation* the Supreme Court held that the items included in it were plainly comprised in the expression 'potteries industry' which showed that the word 'includes' was not used to extend the normal meaning of this expression. For the same reason it was clear that the *Explanation* was not added to indicate by way of abundant caution that the items included in it were comprised in 'potteries industry'. The conclusion was reached that the word 'includes' was used in the *Explanation* in the sense of 'means' and the definition provided by the *Explanation* was exhaustive. It was, therefore, held that Mangalore pattern roofing tiles manufactories were not covered by Entry 22 as they were not included in the *Explanation*.[70] Similarly in construing the definition of 'prize chit' as contained in section 2(e) of the Prize Chits and Money Circulation Schemes (Banning) Act, 1978, the Supreme Court held that the inclusive definition was not intended to expand the meaning of 'prize chit' to cover all transactions or arrangements of the nature of prize chits by whatever name called and that a recurring deposit scheme without any

68. *State of Jammu & Kashmir v. Lakhwinder Kumar & Ors.*, (2013) 6 SCC 333, p. 339.
69. **See** text and note 51, p. 200, *supra*.
70. *South Gujarat Roofing Tile Manufacturers Association v. State of Gujarat*, AIR 1977 SC 90, pp. 93, 94 : 1977 SCC (L&S) 15. **See further** *Hindustan Aluminium Corporation v. State of U.P.*, AIR 1981 SC 1649 : 1981 (3) SCC 578; *Philips Medical Systems (Cleveland) v. Indian MRI Diagnostic and Research Ltd.*, (2008) 10 SCC 227 paras 18 and 19 : AIR 2009 SC 1052.

element of prize was not a prize chit as defined in the Act.[71] And in construing section 2(3) of the Rating Act, 1971 which defines 'livestock' to include any mammal or bird kept for the production of food or wool or for the purpose of its use in the farming of land, the word 'livestock' was not given the wide meaning (in contradiction to deadstock) to include any animal whatsoever and was held not to extend to thorough bred horses not kept for use in the farming of land.[72] In holding so LORD KEITH observed: "There can be no doubt that in some cases the language of an inclusive definition considered with the general context, can have the effect that the ordinary general meaning of a word or expression is to some extent cut down."[73] The word 'includes' in a particular context may only mean 'comprises' or 'consists of'.[74]

As earlier seen[75] a definition in the form 'mean and include' will be considered as exhaustive. In other words the definition will embrace only what is comprised within the ordinary meaning of the 'means' part together with what is mentioned in the 'includes' part of the definition.[76] As an example reference may be made to the definition of tobacco in Item 4 of the First Schedule to the Central Excises and Salt Act, 1944. It reads: 'Tobacco means any form of tobacco whether cured or uncured and whether manufactured or not and includes the leaf stalks and stems of the tobacco plant—'. Construing this definition the Supreme Court held that the definition is exhaustive and tobacco seeds, which are not mentioned in the inclusive part, do not fall within the definition.[77] Similarly, section 2(h) of the Right to Information Act, 2005, uses the expressions 'means' and 'includes' in the definition of 'public authority'. Hence, the Supreme Court held that the categories of public authorities mentioned in the definition would exhaust themselves.[78] Another example is seen in the interpretation of section 2(1)(e) of the Arbitration and Conciliation Act, 1996, which defines 'Court' to mean the Principal Civil Court of Original Jurisdiction in a district and to include the High Court in exercise of its ordinary original civil jurisdiction. The Supreme Court held that in no circumstances is the

---

71. *Reserve Bank of India v. Pearless General Finance and Investment Co. Ltd.*, (1987) 1 SCC 424 : AIR 1987 SC 1023.

72. *Hemens (Valuation Officer) v. Whitsbury Farm and Stud Ltd.*, (1988) 1 All ER 72 : (1988) 2 WLR 72 : 1988 AC 601 (HL).

73. *Ibid.*, p. 78. **See also** *Maheshwari Fish Seed Farm v. T.N. Electricity Board*, (2004) 4 SCC 705 ('Livestock' will not normally cover 'fish').

74. *N.D.P. Namboodripad v. Union of India,* (2007) 4 SCC 502 (para 10) : AIR 2007 SC 1782; *Hamdard (Wakf) Laboratories v. Dy. Labour Commr.,* (2007) 5 SCC 281 (para 34) : (2007) 6 Scale 423 : (2007) 6 JT 329 : AIR 2008 SC 968.

75. **See** text and note 42, p. 198.

76. **See** text and notes 49, 50, p. 199.

77. *Mahalakshmi Oil Mills v. State of Andhra Pradesh*, AIR 1989 SC 335, pp. 339, 340 : 1989 (1) SCC 164.

78. *Thalappalam Service Co-Op Bank Ltd. & Ors. v. State of Kerala & Ors.*, (2013) 16 SCC 82, p. 103.

Supreme Court a 'Court' under section 2(1)(e) of the Act since the expressions 'means' and 'includes' used in section 2(1)(e) make the definition of 'Court' exhaustive.[79]

A definitions section may also be worded in the form 'is deemed to include' which again is an inclusive or extensive definition and such a form is used to bring in by a legal fiction something within the word defined which according to its ordinary meaning is not included within it.[80]

A definition may be both inclusive and exclusive *i.e.* it may include certain things and exclude others.[81] Limited exclusion of a thing may suggest that other categories of that thing which are not excluded fall within apparently wide or inclusive definition.[82] But the exclusion clause may have to be given a liberal construction if the purpose behind it so requires.[83]

(b) Ambiguous definitions

Although it is normally presumed that the Legislature will be specially precise and careful in its choice of language in a definitions section, at times the language used in such a section itself requires interpretation.[84] As pointed out by SIR GEORGE RANKIN: "A phrase having been introduced and then defined the definition '*prima facie*' must entirely determine the application of the phrase; but the definition must itself be interpreted before it is applied, and interpreted, in case of doubt in a sense appropriate to the phrase defined and to the general purpose of the enactment."[85] If literal

---

79. *State of West Bengal & Ors. v. Associated Contractors*, (2015) 1 SCC 32, pp. 39, 40, 44.

80. **See** Chapter 5, title 5 "Legal Fiction", p. 416.

81. **See** section 2(vi) of the Payment of Wages Act, 1936 defining 'wages'. **Also see** *Purshottam H. Judye v. B. Potdar*, AIR 1966 SC 856, p. 858 : 1966 (2) SCR 353. **See** definition of 'dividend' in section 2(6-A)(c) Income-tax Act, 1922. **See further** *CIT, Gujarat v. Vadilal Lallubhai*, AIR 1973 SC 1016 : 1973 SCC (Tax) 1 : (1973) 3 SCC 17.

82. *Ibid*; *Narpatchand A. Bhandari v. Shantilal Moolshankar Jain*, AIR 1993 SC 1712, p. 1717 : (1993) 3 SCC 351. (Landlord defined in section 5(3) of the Bombay Rents Hotel and Lodging Houses Rents Control Act, 1947 to mean any person who is for the time being receiving or entitled to receive rent. *Explanation* to section 13(1)(g) stating that 'landlord' as used therein will not include a rent-farmer or rent collector or estate manager. Held a mortgagee in possession is not excluded.)

83. *Pioneer Rubber Plantation Nilambur v. State of Kerala*, AIR 1993 SC 192, p. 195 (para 12) : 1992 (4) SCC 175.

84. *Re, Wyke's Will Trust*, (1961) 1 All ER 470, p. 477; *Walker v. Leeds City Council*, (1976) 3 All ER 709, p. 713 : (1978) AC 403 : (1976) 3 WLR 736 (HL). For example the definition of "Industry" in the Industrial Disputes Act, 1947 is so ambiguous that it "had defied analysis." Instead of promoting precision and rounding of blurred edges, it has achieved the opposite: *Bangalore Water Supply and Sewerage Board v. A. Rajappa*, AIR 1978 SC 548, p. 561 : 1978 (2) SCC 213.

85. *ILM Cadija Umma v. S. Don Manis Appu*, AIR 1939 PC 63, p. 65.

reading of a '*prima facie*' *vide* definition leads to absurdity, a restricted meaning may have to be given to it to avoid the absurdity.[86] The definitions section may itself be ambiguous and may have to be interpreted in the light of the other provisions of the Act and having regard to the ordinary connotation of the word defined. A definition is not to be read in isolation. It must be read in the context of the phrase which it defines, realising that the function of a definition is to give precision and certainty to a word or phrase which would otherwise be vague and uncertain but not to contradict it or supplant it altogether.[87]

In deciding that the word 'retrenchment' as defined in section 2(oo)[88] of the Industrial Disputes Act, 1947 and also as ordinarily understood does not include discharge of the services of all workmen on a real and *bona fide* closure of whole business, or on the business or undertaking being taken over by another employer, S.K. DAS, J., observed: "What is being defined is 'retrenchment', and that is the context of the definition. It is true that an artificial definition may include a meaning different from or in excess of the ordinary acceptation of the word which is the subject of definition; but there must then be compelling words to show that such a meaning different from or in excess of the ordinary meaning is intended. Where within the frame-work of the ordinary acceptation of the word, every single requirement of the definition clause is fulfilled, it would be wrong to

---

86. *S.R. Batra v. Smt. Taruna Batra*, AIR 2007 SC 1118 (paras 21 to 26) : (2007) 3 SCC 169. (Definition of 'shared household' in section 2(s) of the Protection of Women from Domestic Violence Act, 2005 restricted to house belonging to or taken on rent by the husband or the house which belongs to a joint family of which the husband is a member where they lived.)

87. *Hotel and Catering etc. Board v. Automobile Proprietary Ltd.*, (1968) 3 All ER 399, p. 402 (CA) (a members' club is not engaged in an 'industry' or commerce); *Bangalore Water Supply and Sewerage Board v. A. Rajappa*, AIR 1978 SC 548, p. 561 : (1978) 2 SCC 213; *Vice Chancellor, L.N. Mithila University v. Dayanand Jha*, (1986) 3 SCC 7, p. 10 : AIR 1986 SC 1200; *Reserve Bank of India v. Pearless General Finance & Investment Co. Ltd.*, (1987) 1 SCC 424, p. 450 : AIR 1987 SC 1023. **See further** *State of Maharashtra v. Shiv Datt & Sons*, AIR 1992 SC 692, p. 695 : 1993 Supp (1) SCC 222 (wide definition of 'manufacture' in the Bombay Sales Tax Act should be interpreted in a practical and workable manner and not to be interpreted so widely as to render it practically meaningless); *Ichchapur Industrial Co-operative Society Ltd. v. Competent Authority, Oil and Natural Gas Commission*, 1996 (9) Scale 421, p. 427 : 1997 (2) SCC 42 (Having regard to the context, scheme and object of the Act 'mineral' as defined in the Mines Act, 1952, which definition is incorporated by reference in the Petroleum & Minerals Pipelines (Acquisition of Right of User in Land) Act, 1962, was held to include 'water'); *Mukesh K. Ambani v. Senior Divisional Manager*, (2004) 8 SCC 387, p. 400 : AIR 2004 SC 4179.

88. The definition runs "'Retrenchment' means the termination by the employer of the service of a workman for any reason whatsoever otherwise than as punishment inflicted by way of disciplinary action, but does not include".

take the definition as destroying the essential meaning of the word defined."[89] Proceeding further S.K. DAS, J., said: "There is another way of looking at the problem. Let us assume that the definition clause is so worded that the requirements laid down therein are fulfilled whether we give a restricted or a wider meaning. To that extent there is an ambiguity and definition clause is readily capable of more than one interpretation. What then is the position? We must see what light is thrown on the true view to be taken of the definition clause by other provisions of the Act or even by the aim and provisions of subsequent statutes amending the Act or dealing with the same subject-matter."[90] There are observations in this case that retrenchment involves only termination of surplus staff; but this limited meaning was not accepted in later cases and even automatic termination by expiry of period of employment or resulting from absence of the employee was held to fall within the definition of retrenchment.[91] This wide meaning of the words 'for any reason whatsoever', had been given to promote the object of the Act to enable the workmen to get retrenchment benefits. But by Act 49 of 1984, the definition of retrenchment was amended to exclude termination of the service as a result of the non-renewal of the contract of employment on its expiry or of such contract being terminated under a stipulation in that behalf contained therein. Termination of the service of a probationer in accordance with the terms of his employment, therefore, now does not amount to retrenchment.[92] Similarly termination of service of a seasonal worker after the work was over does not amount to retrenchment.[93]

Section 2(o) of the Monopolies and Restrictive Trade Practices Act, 1969 defined 'restrictive trade practice' to be a trade practice which has, or

---

89. *Hariprasad Shivshanker Shukla v. A.D. Divekar*, AIR 1957 SC 121, p. 127 : 1957 SCR 121.

90. *Ibid.*

91. *L. Robert D'Souza v. Executive Engineer, Southern Railway*, AIR 1982 SC 854, pp. 857, 858 : 1982 (1) SCC 645. A punitive discharge may also amount to retrenchment: *State Bank of India v. Workmen of State Bank of India*, AIR 1990 SC 2034 : 1991 (1) SCC 13. But voluntary retirement brought about by resignation does not amount to retrenchment. *J.K. Cotton Spg. & Wvg. Mills Company Ltd. v. State of U.P.*, AIR 1990 SC 1808 : 1990 (4) SCC 27.

92. *M. Venugopal v. Divisional Manager. LIC*, JT 1994 (1) SC 284, pp. 286, 287 : AIR 1994 SC 1343, p. 1346 : (1994) 2 SCC 323; *Life Insurance Corporation of India v. Raghvendra Sheshagiri Rao*, JT 1997 (8) SC 373 : (1997) 8 SCC 461.

93. *Anil Bapurao Karase v. Krishna Sahkari Sakhar Karkhana*, AIR 1997 SC 2698 : 1997 (10) SCC 599. **See further** *Haryana State FCCW Store Ltd. v. Ram Niwas*, AIR 2002 SC 2495 : (2002) 5 SCC 654. But the termination of employment of a daily wager engaged in a project on completion of the project will amount to retrenchment if the worker had not been told when employed that his employment will end on completion of the project. *S.M. Nilajkar v. Telecom District Manager Karnataka*, (2003) 4 SCC 27, p. 37 : 2003 SCC (L&S) 380.

may have, the effect of preventing, distorting or restricting competition in any manner. Dealing with this definition, the Supreme Court[1] observed that the decision whether a trade practice is restrictive or not has to be arrived at by applying the rule of reason and not on the doctrine that any restriction as to area or price will *per se* be a restrictive trade practice. Every trade agreement restrains or binds persons or places or prices but merely for that reason it cannot be held to be a restrictive trade practice. That is clearly not the intention of the definition although couched in wide words. The question to be determined in such cases is whether the restraint is such as regulates and thereby promotes competition or whether it is such as may suppress or even destroy competition.

In dealing with the definition of 'transfer of property' in the Gift-tax Act, 1958, it was pointed out that the words 'disposition', 'conveyance', 'assignment', 'settlement', 'delivery', and 'payment' were used in the definition as signifying different modes of transfer of property, and that the word 'transaction' occurring in it must also be construed to mean a transaction which is a transfer of property in someway. It was therefore held that a partition of Hindu Undivided Family did not fall within the definition. In construing the definition, HEGDE, J., observed: "An interpretation clause is not meant to prevent the word receiving its ordinary, popular and natural sense whenever that would be properly applicable but to enable the word as used in the Act when there is nothing in the context or the subject-matter to the contrary to be applied to some things to which it would not ordinarily be applicable."[2]

Even when the definition clause uses words of very wide denotation a line may have to be drawn so as to exclude categories obviously not intended to be included. In a case already noticed[3] which construed the definition of 'Industry', as contained in section 2(j) of the Industrial Disputes Act, 1947, the Supreme Court stated: "though section 2(j) uses words of very wide denotation, line would have to be drawn in a fair and just manner so as to exclude some callings, services or undertakings. If all the words used are given their widest meaning, all services and all callings would come within

---

1. *Tata Engineering and Locomotive Co. Ltd., Bombay v. Registrar of the Restrictive Trade Agreement*, AIR 1977 SC 973, p. 978 : (1977) 2 SCC 55. **Followed in** *Mahindra and Mahindra Ltd. v. Union of India,* (1979) 2 SCC 529 : AIR 1979 SC 798; *Rajasthan Housing Board v. Parvati Devi,* JT 2000 (6) SC 237 : 2000 (6) SCC 104 : AIR 2000 SC 1940; *Principal, Apeejay School v. M.R.T.P. Commission,* AIR 2001 SC 3858, p. 3860 : (2001) 8 SCC 702; *State of Uttar Pradesh v. Gir Prasad,* AIR 2004 SC 1756. **See further** *Peico Electronics & Electricals v. Union of India,* (2004) 3 SCC 658 : (2003) 9 JT 178.

2. *Commissioner of Gift-tax, Madras v. N.S. Getty Chettiar,* AIR 1971 SC 2410, p. 2413 : 1971 (2) SCC 741.

3. *State of Bombay v. Hospital Mazdoor Sabha,* AIR 1960 SC 610 : 1960 (2) SCR 866; **see** text and note 58, p. 201.

the purview of the definition; even service rendered by a servant purely in a personal or domestic matter or even in a casual way would fall within the definition. It is not and cannot be suggested that in its wide sweep, the word 'service' is intended to include service howsoever rendered in whatsoever capacity and for whatsoever reason."[4] After reviewing earlier cases and overruling a number of them,[5] the Supreme Court in a later case held that (i) where systematic activity, (ii) organised by co-operation between employer and employee, (iii) for the production and or distribution of goods and services calculated to satisfy human wants and wishes (not spiritual or religious but inclusive of material things or services geared to celestial bliss *e.g.*, making on a large scale prasad or food) is carried on *prima facie*, there is an 'industry' in that enterprise.[6] Absence of profit motive or gainful objective is irrelevant, the decisive test being the nature of the activity with special emphasis on employer-employee relations.[7]

---

4. *Ibid.*, pp. 614, 615.

5. The following cases were **overruled** : *Management of Safdarjung Hospital v. Kuldip Singh*, AIR 1970 SC 1407 : 1970 (1) SCC 735 (Hospital is not an industry); *National Union of Commercial Employees v. M.R. Mehar*, AIR 1962 SC 1080 : 1962 Supp (3) SCR 157 (Solicitor's firm is not an industry); *University of Delhi v. Ramnath*, AIR 1963 SC 1873 : 1964 (2) SCR 703 (work of education is not an industry); *Madras Gymkhana Club Employees Union v. Management*, AIR 1968 SC 554 : 1968 (1) SCR 742 (non-proprietary Member's Club is not an industry). But now **see** Act No. 46 of 1982 which amends the definition. The amendment has not yet been brought into force.

6. *Bangalore Water Supply and Sewerage Board v. A. Rajappa*, AIR 1978 SC 548, p. 595 : 1978 (2) SCC 213. For a criticism of this case **see** *Jain, Meaning of Industry*, (1986) 3 SCC (Journal) 1. The case has been **followed** in holding that Irrigation Department of Punjab is an Industry; *Des Raj v. State of Punjab*, AIR 1988 SC 1182 : 1988 (2) SCC 537; that Telecommunications Department of Central Government is an Industry: *General Manager Telecom v. S. Srinivasan Rao*, JT 1997 (9) SC 234 : AIR 1998 SC 656 : (1997) 8 SCC 767; and that All India Radio and Doordarshan are industries: *All India Radio v. Santosh Kumar*, AIR 1998 SC 941 : (1998) 3 SCC 237. A company engaged in real estate rendering various services to its tenants through its employees has been held to be an industry: *Karnani Properties Ltd. v. State of West Bengal*, AIR 1990 SC 2047 : 1990 (4) SCC 472. Research Laboratory functioning under the Department of Space of the Central Government and engaged in pure research work in space science (the knowledge acquired not meant for sale) held to be not an industry: *Physical Research Laboratoy v. K. G. Sharma*, JT 1997 (4) SC 527, p. 534 : AIR 1997 SC 1855, p. 1860 : (1997) 4 SCC 257. Agricultural Produce Market Committee constituted under Karnataka Agricultural Produce Marketing (Regulation) Act, 1966 and performing welfare activities is an industry as welfare activities are not sovereign functions of the State: *Agriculture Produce Market Committee v. Ashok Harikuni,* AIR 2000 SC 3116, pp. 3125, 3126 : (2000) 8 SCC 61. Law Department of the Govt. of Rajasthan is not an industry: *State of Rajasthan v. Ganeshilal,* (2008) 2 SCC 533.

7. *Ibid. Bangalore Water Supply and Sewerage Board case* has been criticised by a two judge bench with a recommendation for constituting a larger bench to reconsider

[Footnote No. 7 Contd.]

Wide words used in an interpretation clause may thus be given a limited meaning having regard to the context as a whole for a word in a statute whether it be in the body of the statute or in the interpretation clause is not to be construed without reference to the context in which it appears. However, it will not be correct to say that a wide word in an inclusive definition should be given a limited scope by reference merely to the ordinary meaning of the word defined.[8]

Sometimes the ambiguity in the definition arises because of its bad drafting and the court may have to recast it to bring out its clear meaning. An illustration of this kind is furnished by section 2(c) of the Prize Chits and Money Circulation Schemes (Banning) Act, 1978 which reads:

> 'money circulation scheme' means any scheme, by whatever named called, for the making of quick or easy money, or for the receipt of any money or valuable thing as the consideration for a promise to pay money, on any event or contingency relative or applicable to the enrolment of members into the scheme, whether or not such money or thing is derived from the entrance money of the members of such scheme or periodical subscription.'

Construing the definition the Court said[9] that it could never have been intended to ban every kind of scheme or activity for making quick money but only a scheme where the chance or opportunity of making quick or easy money depended upon an event or contingency relative or applicable to the enrolment of members into that scheme. This intention, the court said, will be clear if the definition without changing any word or comma is reshaped as follows:

> 'money circulation scheme' means any scheme, by whatever name called,
>
> (i) for the making of quick or easy money, or
>
> (ii) for the receipt of any money or valuable thing as the consideration for a promise to pay money,
>
> on any event or contingency relative or applicable to the enrolment of members into the scheme, whether or not such money or thing is

---

[Footnote No. 7 Contd.]

that decision: *Coir Board Ernakulam Cochin v. Indira Devai P.S.*, AIR 1998 SC 2801 : 1998 (3) SCC 259. The *Coir Board* case was placed before a three judge bench which held that the *Bangalore Water Supply* case was decided by a seven judge bench and does not need reconsideration: (2000) 1 SCC 224 : (1998) 6 Scale 288(2). A Constitution Bench has now recommended reconsideration of the *Bangalore Water Supply* case by a larger Bench; *State of U.P. v. Jaibir Singh*, (2005) 5 SCC 1.

8. *Hood-Barrs v. IRC*, (1946) 2 All ER 768, p. 774 : 176 LT 283 (HL).

9. *State of West Bengal v. Swapan Kumar Guha*, (1982) 1 SCC 561 pp. 568, 569 paras 5 to 7 : AIR 1982 SC 949. **See further** *Kuriachan Chacko v. State of Kerala*, (2008) 8 SCC 708 pp. 716, 717 paras 24, 25 : (2008) 7 JT 614.

derived from the entrance money of the members of such scheme or periodical subscription.'

(c) Definitions are subject to a contrary context

When a word has been defined in the interpretation clause, *prima facie* that definition governs whenever that word is used in the body of the statute.[10] As was observed by LORD DUNEDIN: "It is a novel and unheard of idea that an interpretation clause which might easily have been so expressed as to cover certain sections and not to cover others should be when expressed in general terms divided up by a sort of theory of *applicana singula singulis*, so as not to apply to sections where context suggests no difficulty of application."[11] And as stated by LORD LOWRY: "If Parliament in a statutory enactment defines its terms (whether by enlarging or by restricting the ordinary meaning of a word or expression), it must intend that, in the absence of a clear indication to the contrary, those terms as defined shall govern what is proposed, authorised or done under or by reference to that enactment."[12] But where the context makes the definition given in the interpretation clause inapplicable, a defined word when used in the body of the statute may have to be given a meaning different from that contained in the interpretation clause; all definitions given in an interpretation clause are therefore normally enacted subject to the qualification—'unless there is anything repugnant in the subject or context', or 'unless the context otherwise requires'.[13] For instance, para 2(t) of the General

---

10. *Indian Immigration Trust Board of Natal v. Govindaswamy*, AIR 1920 PC 114, p. 116; *Vanguard Fire and General Insurance Co. Ltd., Madras v. Fraser & Ross*, AIR 1960 SC 971, p. 975 : 1960 (3) SCR 857.

11. *Indian Immigration Trust Board of Natal v. Govindaswamy, supra*, p. 116.

12. *Wyre Forest District Council v. Secretary for State for the Environment*, (1990) 1 All ER 780, p. 785 : (1990) 2 AC 357 (HL).

13. *Knightsbridge Estates Trust Ltd. v. Byrne*, (1940) AC 613 : (1940) 2 All ER 401, p. 405 (HL); *Vanguard Fire & General Insurance Co. Ltd., Madras v. Fraser & Ross, supra*, p. 975; *Dhandhania Kedia & Co. v. CIT*, AIR 1959 SC 219, pp. 221, 222 : 1959 Supp (1) SCR 204; *Commissioner of Expenditure Tax v. Darshan Surendra Parekh*, AIR 1968 SC 1125, p. 1129 : 1968 (2) SCR 589; *Bennett Coleman & Co. (Pvt.) Ltd. v. Punya Priya Das Gupta*, AIR 1970 SC 426, pp. 432, 433 : (1969) 2 SCC 1; *State of M.P. v. Saith & Skelton (P.) Ltd.*, AIR 1972 SC 1507, p. 1511 : (1972) 1 SCC 702; *National Buildings Construction Corporation Ltd. v. Pritam Singh Gill*, AIR 1972 SC 1579, pp. 1584, 1585 : (1972) 2 SCC 1; *CIT, Gujarat v. Vadilal Lallubhai*, AIR 1973 SC 1016 : 1973 SCC (Tax) 1 : (1973) 3 SCC 17; *Jagir Singh v. State of Bihar*, AIR 1976 SC 997, p. 1001 : 1976 SCC (Tax) 204 : (1976) 2 SCC 942; *Shri Balganesan Metals v. Shanmugham Chetty*, (1987) 2 SCC 707, p. 713 : AIR 1987 SC 1668; *Pushpa Devi v. Milkhi Ram*, AIR 1990 SC 808, p. 812 : (1990) 2 SCC 134; *N.K. Jain v. C.K. Shah*, AIR 1991 SC 1289, pp. 1303-05 : (1991) 2 SCC 495; *Printers (Mysore) Ltd. v. Asst. Commercial Tax Officer*, JT 1994 (1) SC 692, pp. 702, 703: 1994 (2) SCC 434; *K.V. Muthu v. Angamuthu Ammal*, AIR

[Footnote No. 13 Contd.]

Insurance (Employees') Pension Scheme, 1995, defines the term 'retirement' to mean, *inter alia*, voluntary retirement in accordance with para 30 of the Scheme. The word 'means' used in statutory definitions generally implies that the definition is exhaustive, but this general rule of interpretation is not without an exception. An equally well-settled principle of interpretation is that the use of the word 'means' in a statutory definition is subject to the context in which the word is used. The Supreme Court, observing that, para 2 of the Pension Scheme, 1995, starts with the words 'In this Scheme, unless the context otherwise requires', held that there is nothing in the context of the Pension Scheme, 1995, which would exclude its beneficial provisions from application to employees who have opted for voluntary retirement under the General Insurance Employees' Special Voluntary Retirement Scheme, 2004, or *vice versa*. Accordingly, the term 'retirement', in the context of the two Schemes, includes retirement not only under para 30 of the Pension Scheme, 1995, but also those retiring under the Special Voluntary Retirement Scheme, 2004.[14]

Even in the absence of an express qualification to that effect, such a qualification is always implied.[15] However, it is incumbent on those who contend that the definition given in the interpretation clause does not apply to a particular section to show that the context in fact so requires.[16] An argument based on contrary context which will make the inclusive definition inapplicable to any provision in the Act cannot be accepted as it would

---

[Footnote No. 13 Contd.]

1997 SC 628, p. 631 : (1997) 2 SCC 53; *Special Officer and Competent Authority Urban Land Ceilings v. P.S. Rao,* AIR 2000 SC 843, p. 844 : (2000) 2 SCC 451; *State of Maharashtra v. Indian Medical Association,* AIR 2002 SC 302, p. 307 : (2002) 1 SCC 589; *Mukesh K. Tripathi v. Sr. Divisional Manager LDC*, AIR 2004 SC 4179, pp. 4186, 4187 : (2004) 8 SCC 387, p. 400; *National Insurance Co. Ltd. v. Deepa Devi,* (2008) 1 SCC 414 : AIR 2008 SC 735. [In a situation where the definition is not applicable in the context, common sense point of view may be adopted. Definition of owner in section 21(30) of the Motor Vehicles Act 1988 is inapplicable when a vehicle is under requisition by the Govt. and in such a situation Govt. should be treated as the owner and when an accident happens when the vehicle is under requisition, it is the Govt. which is liable and not the real owner and the insurer.] *Bharat Coking Coal Ltd. v. Annapurna Construction,* (2008) 6 SCC 732 para 8: AIR 2008 SC 2028; *Paul Enterprises v. Rajib Chatterjee and Company,* (2009) 3 SCC 709 : (2009) 1 JT 632.

14. *National Insurance Co. Ltd. & Anr. v. Kirpal Singh*, (2014) 5 SCC 189, pp. 195 to 198.

15. *Knightsbridge Estates Trust Ltd. v. Byrne*, (1940) AC 613 : (1940) 2 All ER 401, p. 405 (HL); *Printers (Mysore) Ltd. v. Asst. Commercial Tax Officer, supra; Indian City Properties Ltd. v. Municipal Commissioner of Greater Bombay,* (2005) 6 SCC 417, pp. 420, 421.

16. *Ibid.*

make the definition entirely useless.[17] Repugnancy of a definition arises only when the definition does not agree with the subject or context; any action not in conformity with the definition will not obviously make it repugnant to subject or context of the provision containing the term defined under which such action is purported to have been taken.[18] When the application of the definition to a term in a provision containing that term makes it unworkable and *otiose*, it can be said that the definition is not applicable to that provision because of contrary context.[19] Further, when after amendment of the Constitution and the Act a basic difference is brought about in the working of the Act but the definition section remains unamended, the change so brought about will be contrary context and the definition will not be applicable.[20]

In the words of WANCHOO, J.: "It is well- settled that all statutory definitions or abbreviations must be read subject to the qualification variously expressed in the definition clauses which created them and it may be that even where the definition is exhaustive inasmuch as the word defined is said to mean a certain thing, it is possible for the word to have a somewhat different meaning in different sections of the Act depending upon the subject or context. That is why all definitions in statutes generally begin with the qualifying words, similar to the words used in the present case, namely 'unless there is anything repugnant in the subject or context'. Therefore, in finding out the meaning of the word 'insurer' in various sections of the Act (Insurance Act, 1938) the meaning to be ordinarily given to it is that given in the definition clause. But this is not inflexible and there may be sections in the Act where the meaning may have to be departed from on account of the subject or context in which the word had been used and that will be giving effect to the opening sentence in the definitions section, namely 'unless there is anything repugnant in the subject or context'. In view of this qualification, the Court has not only to look at the words but also to look at the context, the collocation and the object of such words relating to such matter and interpret the meaning intended to be conveyed by the

---

17. *Chowgule and Co. Pvt. Ltd. v. Union of India*, (1987) 1 SCC 730, pp. 739, 740 : AIR 1986 SC 1176.

18. *State Bank of India v. Yogendra Kumar Srivastava*, (1987) 3 SCC 10, p. 21 : AIR 1987 SC 1399.

19. *Special Officer and Competent Authority Urban Land Ceilings Hyderabad v. P.S. Rao,* AIR 2000 SC 843, p. 844 : (2000) 2 SCC 451.

20. *Ramesh Mehta v. Sanwal Chand Singhvi*, (2004) 5 SCC 409, pp. 425, 428 : AIR 2004 SC 2258, pp. 2264, 2267 (After Constitution 74th Amendment Act which makes nominated members ineligible to vote at a meeting of a municipality the definition in section 3(36) of the Rajasthan Municipalities Act, 1959 which defines 'whole number' or 'total number' with reference to the members of the Board to mean 'total number of members holding office at the time' has to be understood in the context of a no confidence motion for removal of chairperson not to include nominated members.)

use of the words under the circumstances."[21] In this case[22] the question before the Supreme Court was as to construction of the word 'insurer' as used in sections 33(1) and 2D of the Insurance Act, 1938 which read as follows: Section 33(1): 'The Central Government may at any time by order in writing direct the Controller or any other person specified in the order to investigate the affairs of any insurer and to report to the Central Government on any investigation made by him;' Section 2D: 'Every insurer shall be subject to all the provisions of this Act in relation to any class of insurance business so long as his liabilities in India in respect of business of that class remain unsatisfied and not otherwise provided for'. The Act by section 2(9) defines an 'insurer' as a person carrying on the business of 'insurance', and the contention before the Supreme Court was that sections 33(1) and 2D did not apply to an insurer who had closed his business completely as the definition of the word insurer in section 2(9) postulates actual carrying on of the business. Rejecting the above contention the Court pointed out that in the context of sections 33(1) and 2D and "taking into account the policy of the Act and the purposes for which the control envisaged by the Act was imposed on insurers", the word 'insurer' in the said sections also refers to insurers who were carrying on the business of insurance but have closed it.[23]

Section 13(2)(i) of the East Punjab Urban Rent Restriction Act, 1949 permits a landlord to apply for eviction of a tenant on the ground of arrears of rent. A proviso enables the tenant to avoid eviction on this ground by paying the arrears on the first date of hearing with interest and cost. 'Tenant' is defined in section 2(h)(i) to mean a person by whom or on whose account rent is payable but does not include a person placed in occupation by the tenant without the consent in writing of the landlord. In construing these provisions the Supreme Court held that the context of the proviso to section 13(2)(i) made the definition of tenant inapplicable to it and a defendant who claimed to be a tenant but who was not admitted to be a tenant by the plaintiff landlord and who was alleged to have been inducted by the tenant without the plaintiff's consent could take the benefit of the proviso and make the deposit.[24]

Because of Article 367 of the Constitution, the General Clauses Act, 1897, 'unless the context otherwise requires', applies for construction of the Constitution. The definition of 'State' in section 3(58) of the General

---

21. *Vanguard Fire and General Insurance Co. Ltd., Madras v. Fraser & Ross*, AIR 1960 SC 971, pp. 974, 975 : 1960 (3) SCR 857; *Whirlpool Corporation v. Registrar of Trade Marks,* JT 1998 (7) SC 243, p. 252 : 1998 (8) SCC 1 : AIR 1999 SC 22.

22. *Vanguard Fire and General Insurance Co. Ltd., Madras v. Fraser & Ross, supra.*

23. *Vanguard Fire and General Insurance Co. Ltd., Madras v. Fraser & Ross*, AIR 1960 SC 971, pp. 974, 975, 976 : 1960 (3) SCR 857.

24. *Pushpa Devi (Smt.) v. Milkhi Ram*, AIR 1990 SC 808 : 1990 (2) SCC 134.

Clauses Act, 1897 includes 'Union Territories' and, therefore, the word 'State' in Article 3[25] and Entry 80[26] of the Union List in the Constitution includes Union Territories. But as the context otherwise requires the word 'State' in Article 246 does not include Union Territories.[27]

In construing the word 'court' in section 14(2) of the Arbitration Act, 1940 it was held that the word court as used therein meant a court which appointed the arbitrator and the definition in section 2(c) of the Act which defines 'court' as meaning a court which would entertain a suit on the subject-matter does not govern section 14(2) as the context made that definition inapplicable.[28]

Similarly in construing the word 'workman' in section 33C(2) of the Industrial Disputes Act, 1947, it was held that the word included a dismissed workman although in the definition of that word as given in section 2, a dismissed workman is included only for the purpose of industrial disputes under section 10.[29]

When a word is defined to bear a number of inclusive meanings, the sense in which the word is used in a particular provision must be ascertained from the context of the scheme of the Act, the language of the provision and the object intended to be served thereby.[30]

9. PROVISO

(a) Its real nature

The normal function of a proviso is to except something out of the enactment or to qualify something enacted therein which but for the proviso would be within the purview of the enactment.[31] As stated by LUSH, J.: "When one finds a proviso to a section the natural presumption is that, but

---

25. *Ram Kishore Sen v. Union of India*, AIR 1966 SC 644 : 1961 (1) SCR 643.
26. *Management of Advance Insurance Co. Ltd. v. Gurudasmal*, AIR 1970 SC 1126 : 1970 (1) SCC 633.
27. *T.M. Kanniyan v. ITO, Pondicherry*, AIR 1968 SC 637 : 1968 (2) SCR 103.
28. *State of M.P. v. Saith & Skelton (P) Ltd.*, AIR 1972 SC 1507 : (1972) 1 SCC 702.
29. *National Building Construction Corporation Ltd. v. Pritam Singh Gill*, AIR 1972 SC 1579 : 1972 (2) SCC 1.
30. *Anand Nivas (P.) Ltd. v. Anandji Kalyanji's Pedhi*, AIR 1965 SC 414, p. 424 (para 32) : 1964 (4) SCR 892.
31. *Kedarnath Jute Manufacturing Co. Ltd. v. Commercial Tax Officer*, AIR 1966 SC 12, p. 14 (para 8) : 1965 (3) SCR 626; *Ishvarilal Thakorelal Almaula v. Motibhai Nagjibhai*, AIR 1966 SC 459, p. 465 : 1966 (1) SCR 367; *Nizam's Religious Endowment Trust, Hyderabad v. CIT, A.P.*, AIR 1966 SC 1007, p. 1010 : (1966) 2 SCR 384; *Kush Sahgal v. M.C. Mitter*, AIR 2000 SC 1390, p. 1398 : (2000) 4 SCC 526; *Haryana State Cooperative Land Development Bank Ltd. v. Haryana State Cooperative Land Development Bank Employees Union*, (2004) 1 SCC 574, pp. 578, 579 : (2003) 10 JT 383; *Romesh Kumar Sharma v. Union of India*, (2006) 6 SCC 510 (para 12) : (2006) 7 JT 209 : (2006) 5 SLT 602; *Nagar Palika Nigam v. Krishi Upaj Mandi Samiti*, AIR 2009 SC 187 para 8 : (2008) 12 SCC 364.

for the proviso, the enacting part of the section would have included the subject-matter of the proviso."[32] In the words of LORD MACMILLAN: "The proper function of a proviso is to except and to deal with a case which would otherwise fall within the general language of the main enactment, and its effect is confined to that case."[33] The proviso may, as LORD MACNAGHTEN laid down, be "a qualification of the preceding enactment which is expressed in terms too general to be quite accurate".[34] The general rule has been stated by HIDAYATULLAH, J., in the following words: "As a general rule, a proviso is added to an enactment to qualify or create an exception to what is in the enactment, and ordinarily, a proviso is not interpreted as stating a general rule".[35] And in the words of KAPUR, J.: "The proper function of a proviso is that it qualifies the generality of the main enactment by providing an exception and taking out as it were, from the main enactment, a portion which, but for the proviso would fall within the main enactment".

An example of how a proviso is to be interpreted can be seen in the context of section 376(1) of the Indian Penal Code, 1860, before its amendment, which provided that in a case of rape, the minimum punishment is 7 years, but contained a proviso which stated that the Court may, for adequate and special reasons to be mentioned in the judgment, impose a sentence of imprisonment for a term less than 7 years. Relying on its earlier decisions, the Supreme Court held that a proviso is used to remove special

32. *Mullins v. Treasurer of Survey*, (1880) 5 QBD 170, p. 173; **referred to** in *Shah Bhojraj Kuverji Oil Mills and Ginning Factory v. Subhash Chandra Yograj Sinha*, AIR 1961 SC 1596, p. 1600; *Calcutta Tramways Co. Ltd. v. Corporation of Calcutta*, AIR 1965 SC 1728, p. 1730 : 1965 (3) SCR 354; *Maulvi Hussein Haji Abraham Umarji v. State of Gujarat*, (2004) 6 SCC 672, p. 679 : AIR 2004 SC 3946; *Haryana State Cooperative Land Development Bank Ltd. v. Haryana State Cooperative Land Development Bank Employees Union*, (2004) 1 SCC 574, pp. 578, 579 : (2003) 10 JT 383; *Romesh Kumar Sharma v. Union of India, Supra.*

33. *Madras & Southern Maharatta Rly. Co. Ltd. v. Bezwada Municipality*, AIR 1944 PC 71, p. 73 : 71 IA 113; **referred** to in *CIT, Mysore etc. v. Indo Mercantile Bank Ltd.*, AIR 1959 SC 713, p. 719 : 1959 Supp (2) SCR 256; *S. Sundaram Pillai v. P. Pattabiraman*, (1985) 1 SCC 591, p. 608 : AIR 1985 SC 582; *Haryana State Cooperative Land Development Bank Ltd. v. Haryana State Cooperative Land Development Bank Employees Union*, (2004) 1 SCC 574, pp. 578, 579 : (2003) 10 JT 383; *Romesh Kumar Sharma v. Union of India, Supra.*

34. *Local Govt. Board v. South Stoneham Union*, (1909) AC 57, p. 62 (HL).

35. *Shah Bhojraj Kuverji Oil Mills and Ginning Factory v. Subhash Chandra Yograj Sinha*, AIR 1961 SC 1596, p. 1690 : (1962) 2 SCR 159. **See further** *S. Sundaram Pillai v. Pattabiraman*, (1985) 1 SCC 591, p. 608: AIR 1985 SC 582; *Motiram Ghelabhai v. Jagannagar*, (1985) 2 SCC 279, p. 285 : AIR 1985 SC 709; *Haryana State Cooperative Land Development Bank Ltd. v. Haryana State Cooperative Land Development Bank Employees Union*, (2004) 1 SCC 574, pp. 578, 579 : (2003) 10 JT 383.

cases from the general enactment, and may change the very concept of the intendment of the enactment by insisting on certain mandatory conditions to be fulfilled in order to make the enactment workable. Hence the power under the proviso is not to be used indiscriminately, but the court, while exercising discretion thereunder, has to record "exceptional reasons" for resorting to the proviso.[36] Similarly, section 376(2)(g) of the IPC, prior to its amendment, provided for a minimum punishment of rigorous imprisonment for a term not less than ten years, *inter alia*, for the offence of gang rape. The proviso to section 376(2) stated that the Court may, for adequate and special reasons to be mentioned in the judgment, impose a sentence of imprisonment of either description for a term of less than ten years. The Supreme Court held that the proviso must be considered in relation to the main provision to which it stands as a proviso, particularly, in such penal provisions, and cautioned that the power under the proviso should not be used indiscriminately in a routine, casual and cavalier manner, for the reason that an exception clause requires strict interpretation.[37] It is pertinent to note, however, that section 376 of the IPC has now been amended *vide* the Criminal Law (Amendment) Act, 2013, and the above provisos find no mention in the provision as it stands today. Pursuant to the amendment, gang rape is now covered under section 376D of the IPC, which does not have a similar proviso.

Another instance of interpretation of a proviso is seen in the context of rule 3(iv) of the Border Security Force (Seniority, Promotion and Superannuation of Officers) Rules, 1978, which provides that the seniority of officers, subject to clauses (i), (ii) and (iii) of rule 3, shall be determined according to the date of their continuous appointment in that rank. The proviso to rule 3(iv) states that in case of direct entrants, the date of appointment shall be the date of the commencement of their training course at the BSF Academy. In this case, direct entrants to the post of Assistant Commandant had been split into two batches for training: batch 16, which commenced training on 01.02.1993, and batch 17, which commenced training on 02.07.1993. Meanwhile, a person was promoted to the rank of Assistant Commandant with effect from 15.03.1993. The issue before the Court was whether the promotee was senior to batch 17 of direct entrants. The Court held that the proviso will have application in a case where officers who have been selected pursuant to the same selection process are split into separate batches and, applying the proviso, held that the direct

36. *State of Rajasthan v. Vinod Kumar*, (2012) 6 SCC 770, pp. 776 to 781.
37. *Shimbhu & Anr. v. State of Haryana*, (2014) 13 SCC 318, pp. 324, 325, 328.

entrants who, though selected prior to the promotee, started their training after the promotee joined the said post, were junior to the promotee.[38]

Ordinarily it is foreign to the proper function of proviso to read it as providing something by way of an addendum or dealing with a subject which is foreign to the main enactment."[39] Further, a proviso is not normally construed as nullifying the enactment or as taking away completely a right conferred by the enactment.[40] As a consequence of the aforesaid function of a true proviso certain rules follow.

(b) Not construed as excluding or adding something by implication

Except as to cases dealt with by it, a proviso has no repercussion on the interpretation of the enacting portion of the section so as to exclude something by implication which is embraced by clear words in the enactment.[41] Further, as stated by LORD WATSON in an oft-quoted passage: "If the language of the enacting part of the statute does not contain the provisions which are said to occur in it, you cannot derive these provisions by implication from a proviso."[42] So when on a fair construction the principle provision is clear, a proviso cannot expand or limit it.[43]

---

38. *Rohitash Kumar & Ors. v. Om Prakash Sharma & Ors.*, (2013) 11 SCC 451, p. 462.

39. *CIT, Mysore etc. v. Indo Mercantile Bank Ltd.*, AIR 1959 SC 713, p. 717 : 1959 Supp (2) SCR 256. **See further** *Kedarnath Manufacturing Co. Ltd. v. Commercial Tax Officer*, AIR 1966 SC 12, p. 14 : 1965 (3) SCR 626; *T.M. Kanniyan v. ITO, Pondicherry*, AIR 1968 SC 637, p. 641 : 1968 (2) SCR 103; *Dibya Singh Malana v. State of Orissa*, AIR 1989 SC 1737, pp. 1739, 1740 : 1989 Supp (2) SCC 312; *J.K. Industries v. Chief Inspector of Factories*, 1996 (7) Scale 247, p. 261: 1996 (6) SCC 665.

40. **See** text and notes 2, 3, p. 230.

41. *Madras & Southern Maharatta Rly. Co. Ltd. v. Bezwada Municipality*, AIR 1944 PC 71, p. 73 : 71 IA 113; *CIT, Mysore etc. v. Indo Mercantile Bank Ltd.*, AIR 1959 SC 713, p. 718 : 1959 Supp (2) SCR 256.

42. *West Derby Union v. Metropolitan Life Assurance Co.*, (1897) AC 647, p. 652 (HL); **referred** to in *Jennings v. Kelly*, (1939) 4 All ER 464, p. 470 (HL); *G.G. in Council v. Municipal Council, Madura*, AIR 1949 PC 39, p. 42; *Balchandra Anantrao Rakvi v. Ramchandra Tukaram*, AIR 2002 SC 3994, p. 4002 : (2001) 8 SCC 616; *Haryana State Cooperative Land Development Bank Ltd. v. Haryana State Cooperative Land Development Bank Employees Union*, (2004) 1 SCC 574, pp. 578, 579 : (2003) 10 JT 384.

43. *Dwarka Prasad v. Dwarka Das Saraf*, AIR 1975 SC 1758, p. 1763 : (1976) 1 SCC 128. **See further** *A.N. Sehgal v. Rajeram Sheoram*, AIR 1991 SC 1406, p. 1414 : 1991 (2) SCR 198; *Tribhovandas Haribhai Tamboli v. Gujarat Revenue Tribunal*, AIR 1991 SC 1538, p. 1541 : (1991) 3 SCC 442; *Kerala State Housing Board v. Rampriya Hotels (P.) Ltd.*, JT 1994 (5) SC 113, p. 119: 1994 (5) SCC 672 : (1994) 2 KLT 529; *Maulvi Hussain Haji Abraham Umraji v. State of Gujarat*, (2004) 6 SCC 672, p. 679 : AIR 2004 SC 3946.

The Madras District Municipalities Act, 1920 empowered a municipality to levy property tax on all lands and buildings at such percentage of the annual value as may be fixed by the municipal council. The Act by section 82(2) defined annual value of lands and buildings in terms: 'shall be deemed to be the gross annual rent at which they may be reasonably expected to let from month to month or year to year—'. A proviso appended to section 82(2) provided that in case of certain classes of buildings the annual value of such premises was deemed to be 6 per cent of their capital value. Certain vacant lands belonging to a Railway Company were assessed to property tax by the Bezwada Municipality and the method adopted in order to arrive at the annual value was first to ascertain their capital value and to fix 6 per cent of the same as annual value. The tax was levied at a certain percentage of the annual value so calculated. The contention before the Privy Council was that the proviso appended to section 82(2) indicated that capital value as basis for ascertaining annual value could be used only in case of specified classes of buildings in the proviso and that resort to this method was by necessary implication prohibited in every other case. It was not disputed that but for the proviso, section 82(2) would have permitted resort to any of the recognised methods of arriving at the rent which a hypothetical tenant might reasonably be expected to pay for the lands in question, including the method of taking a percentage of capital value. Rejecting the contention LORD MACMILLAN observed: "The proviso does not say that the method of arriving at annual value by taking a percentage of capital value is to be utilised only in the case of the classes of buildings to which the proviso applies. It leaves the generality of the substantive enactment in the sub-section unqualified except insofar as concerns the particular subject to which the proviso relates. Where, as in the present case, the language of the main enactment is clear and unambiguous, a proviso can have no repercussion on the interpretation of the main enactment so as to exclude from it by implication what clearly falls within its express terms."[44]

By Article 240(1) of the Constitution, power is conferred on the President "to make Regulations for the peace, progress and good Government" of the Union territories. There is a proviso appended to Article 240(1) which directs that the President shall not make any regulation after the Constitution of a Legislature of a Union territory for that Union territory. It was contended on the basis of the proviso that the power of the President is co-extensive with the power of the Legislature which may be constituted for a Union territory and hence the President's power to make regulations

---

44. *Madras & Southern Maharatta Rly. Co. Ltd. v. Bezwada Municipality*, AIR 1944 PC 71, pp. 72, 73 : 71 IA 113; *Kerala State Housing Board v. Rampriya Hotels (P.) Ltd.*, JT 1994 (5) SC 113, p. 119 : 1994 (5) SCC 672 : (1994) 2 KLT 529.

is limited to subjects falling within the Concurrent and State List. This argument was negated on the reasoning that the enacting part of Article 240(1) in plain terms confers plenary powers of making regulations which are not curtailed by the proviso.[45]

Under section 11(1)(b) of the Railways Act, 1890, a railway administration is bound to make and maintain all necessary arches, tunnels, culverts, etc., 'of such dimensions as will, in the opinion of the Provincial Government, be sufficient at all times to convey water as freely from or to the lands lying near or affected by the railway as before the making of the railway, or as nearly so as may be'. By section 11(3)(b) the aforesaid duty is subject to a proviso that, 'a railway administration shall not, except on the requisition of the Provincial Government, be compelled to defray the cost of executing any further or additional accommodation works for the use of the owners or occupiers of the lands after the expiration of ten years from the date on which the railway passing through the lands was first opened for public traffic'. A railway having been opened in Madura in 1902, a culvert was constructed by the railway administration for conveying water of a water-channel. With the growth of the town the culvert was found insufficient and in 1938, the Provincial Government ordered the Railway to widen the channel under section 11(3)(b) at its own cost. In holding that such an order was invalid, LORD SIMONDS quoted the observations of LORD WATSON[46] and laid down that the proviso did not impose any new duty on the railway apart from that imposed by the enacting provision.[47] Interpreting the enacting provision and the proviso, LORD SIMONDS said: "The obligation imposed upon the Railway is to make and maintain a culvert which will in the opinion of the Provincial Government be sufficient at all times to convey water as freely from or to the lands lying near or affected by the railway as before the making of the Railway or as nearly so as may be. It is clear that the obligation under sub-section (1) is to be measured by the conditions existing at the time of the making of the railway. The *status quo* is to be preserved. It is the proviso in (b) [sub-section (3)(b)] that is immediately relevant and it must first be observed that it is in form negative. It does not purport to vest any new rights in any person or to impose any new duty upon the railway. It is by no means impossible to give meaning and effect to proviso without doing violence to its language and to the canon of construction to which reference has been made, for the 'further or additional accommodation works' mentioned in the subsection may be required not because those originally constructed have become insufficient owing to change of conditions; but because the adjoining landowner has miscalculated what the conditions originally existing would

45. *T.M. Kanniyan v. ITO, Pondicherry*, AIR 1968 SC 637, p. 641 : 1968 (2) SCR 103.
46. **See** text and note 42, p. 218.
47. *G.G. in Council v. Municipal Council, Madura*, AIR 1949 PC 39.

demand for the commodious use of his land, and is given an opportunity within a limited time for making a fresh demand. Nor would it be unreasonable in the circumstances which prevail in large parts of India that unlimited time should be given to the Government to require that the same standard should be established and maintained."[48]

(c) Construed in relation to the section or sections to which it is appended

The language of a proviso even if general is normally to be construed in relation to the subject-matter covered by the section to which the proviso is appended.[49] In other words normally a proviso does not travel beyond the provision to which it is a proviso.[50] "It is a cardinal rule of interpretation", observed BHAGWATI, J., "that a proviso to a particular provision of a statute only embraces the field which is covered by the main provision. It carves out an exception to the main provision to which it has been enacted as a proviso and to no other."[51] It was, therefore, held that the proviso appended to Article 286(2) of the Constitution authorising the President to lift the ban imposed by the said provision was not available to lift the ban imposed by Article 286(1).[52] As observed by DAS, C.J.I.: "It is a fundamental rule of construction that proviso must be considered in relation to the principal matter to which it stands as a proviso."[53] On this principle, it was held that a proviso enabling the Government to declare that it would

---

48. *G.G. in Council v. Municipal Council, Madura*, AIR 1949 PC 39, pp. 42, 43.

49. *Dwarka Prasad v. Dwarka Das Saraf*, AIR 1975 SC 1758, p. 1764 : (1976) 1 SCC 128.

50. *Mackinnon Mackenzie & Co. Ltd. v. Audrey D'Costa*, (1987) 2 SCC 469, p. 482 : AIR 1987 SC 1281.

51. *Ram Narain Sons Ltd. v. Assistant Commissioner of Sales Tax*, AIR 1955 SC 765, p. 769 : (1955) 2 SCR 483; **referred** to in *CIT, Mysore etc. v. Indo Mercantile Bank Ltd.*, AIR 1959 SC 713, p. 718 : 1959 Supp (2) SCR 256; *State of Punjab v. Kailashnath*, AIR 1989 SC 558, p. 553 : 1989 (1) SCC 321. **See further**, *A.N. Sehgal v. Rajeram Sheoran*, AIR 1991 SC 1406, p. 1414 : 1992 Supp (1) SCC 304 : 1991 (2) JT 123; *Tribhovandas Haribhai Tamboli v. Gujarat Revenue Tribunal*, AIR 1991 SC 1538, p. 1541 : 1991 (3) SCC 442; *Kerala State Housing Board v. Rampriya Hotels (P) Ltd.*, JT 1994 (5) SC 113, p. 119 : 1994 (5) SCC 672 : (1994) 2 KLT 529; *Haryana State Cooperative Land Development Bank Ltd. v. Haryana State Cooperative Land Development Bank Employees Union*, (2004) 1 SCC 574, pp. 578, 579 : (2003) 10 JT 383; *Nagar Palika Nigam v. Krishi Upaj Mandi Samiti*, AIR 2009 SC 187 para 8 : (2008) 12 SCC 364.

52. *Ram Narain Sons Ltd. v. Assistant Commissioner of Sales Tax, supra*, [construction of Article 286 as it stood prior to the Constitution (Sixth Amendment) Act, 1956].

53. *Abdul Jabbar Butt v. State of J & K*, AIR 1957 SC 281, p. 284 : 1957 SCR 51; **referred** to in *CIT, Mysore etc. v. Indo Mercantile Bank Ltd.*, AIR 1959 SC 713, p. 717 : 1959 Supp (2) SCR 256. **Cf.** similar language used by FLETCHER MOULTON, L.J. in *R. v. Dibdin*, 1910 P 57, p. 125; **referred** to in *Dormer v. Newcastle-on-Tyne Corporation*, (1940) 2 All ER 521, p. 524 : (1940) 2 KB 217 (CA).

not be in public interest to communicate the grounds of detention to a detenu, should be construed along with the enacting portion which required communication of grounds of detention 'as soon as may be' and therefore enjoining that the necessary declaration dispensing with this communication in public interest must also be made 'as soon as may be'.[54] On the same principle, proviso 1 to section 24(1) of the Indian Income-tax Act, 1922 was construed as limited in its application to set-off of profits and losses arising under different heads, a subject dealt with by section 24(1) and was held inapplicable to set-off of profits and losses arising under the same head, a subject dealt with under sections 7 to 12B.[55] Similarly the proviso and the *Explanation* appended to section 7 of the Hindu Adoption and Maintenance Act, 1956 were not permitted to be read in section 8 of the Act in support of the argument that when there are two widows adoption by one widow can be made only with the consent of her co-widow.[56] And on the same reasoning a proviso to rule 147 of the Rules framed under the Bihar and Orissa Excise Act, 1915 was held applicable merely to foreign liquor imported under bond as the main part of the rule was limited to such foreign liquor.[57] Another example is furnished by rule 2.2 of the Punjab Civil Service Rules which reserves to the Government the right to withhold or withdraw a pension or part of it or to order recovery from it if the pensioner is subsequently found guilty of grave misconduct or negligence during the period of his service in a departmental or judicial proceeding. There is a proviso to the rule which says: "No such judicial proceeding if not instituted while the officer was in service—shall be instituted in respect of a cause of action which arose or an event which took place more than four years before such institution." The Supreme Court held that the proviso had to be read as an exception to the main provision meaning that if the judicial proceeding is not instituted within the period mentioned in the proviso, the Government will not have the right to withhold or withdraw the pension and that the proviso does not provide a general embargo on the prosecution of the officer after the expiry of that period.[58]

The application of this rule presents difficulty when a proviso in a statute does not form part of a section but is itself enacted as a separate section. The drafting of a proviso in such a form makes it necessary to determine as to which section or sections the section containing the proviso is

---

54. *Abdul Jabbar Butt v. State of J. & K.*, AIR 1957 SC 281, p. 284 : 1957 SCR 51.
55. *CIT, Mysore etc. v. Indo Mercantile Bank, Ltd.*, AIR 1959 SC 713 : 1959 Supp (2) SCR 256.
56. *Vijayalakshmamma (Smt.) v. B.T. Shankar,* AIR 2001 SC 1424, p. 1435 : (2001) 4 SCC 558.
57. *Mohan Meakin Breweries Ltd. v. Commissioner of Excise, Bihar*, AIR 1970 SC 1171, p. 1173 : 1969 (2) SCR 457.
58. *State of Punjab v. Kailash Nath*, AIR 1989 SC 558 : 1989 (1) SCC 321.

enacted as exception or qualification. The Newcastle-on-Tyne Improvement Act, 1865, in section 65 furnishes an illustration of such a proviso. Section 65 which is worded as a proviso reads: '*Provided always* that nothing in this Act shall authorise the Corporation or any lessee of the Corporation to do or be party to any act or thing amounting to a nuisance.' On a scrutiny of the sections the Court of Appeal held that section 65 was a proviso to the group of sections dealing with Sewers and Sanitary arrangement, *i.e.*, sections 62 to 64 and not to section 22 which dealt with Streets.[59] The words in section 65 'nothing in this Act', were therefore on construction limited to the principal matter to which that section was a proviso, *i.e.*, to the exercise of power in relation to Sewers and Sanitary arrangements under sections 62 to 64, and section 65 was thus held as not applicable to section 22.[60] Another illustration of such a proviso is furnished by section 27 of the Indian Evidence Act, 1872 which has been construed as a proviso to sections 24 to 26 and not only to section 26.[61]

(d) Use as guide to construction of enactment

If the enacting portion of a section is not clear, a proviso appended to it may give an indication as to its true meaning. As stated by LORD HERSCHELL: "Of course a proviso may be used to guide you in the selection of one or other of two possible constructions of the words to be found in the enactment, and show when there is doubt about its scope, when it may reasonably admit of doubt as to having this scope or that, which is the proper view to take of it."[62] And LORD WATSON in the same case said: "I perfectly admit that there may be and are many cases in which the terms of an intelligible proviso may throw considerable light on the ambiguous import of the statutory words."[63] MUDHOLKAR, J., stated the rule thus: "There is no doubt that where the main provision is clear, its effect cannot be cut down by the proviso. But where it is not clear, the proviso, which cannot be

---

59. *Dormer v. Newcastle-on-Tyne Corporation*, (1940) 2 All ER 521 : (1940) 2 KB 217 (CA).

60. *Ibid.*

61. *State of U.P. v. Deoman Upadhyaya*, AIR 1960 SC 1125, p. 1145 : 1961 (1) SCR 14; *Ramkishan Mithanlal Sharma v. State of Bombay*, AIR 1955 SC 104, p. 115; *Aghnoo Nagesia v. State of Bihar*, AIR 1966 SC 119 : 1966 (1) SCR 134; *Delhi Administration v. Balkrishan*, AIR 1972 SC 3 : 1972 (4) SCC 659.

62. *West Derby Union v. Metropolitan Life Assurance Society*, (1897) AC 647, p. 655 : 66 LJ Ch 726 : 77 LT 284 (HL), **referred to** in *Jennings v. Kelly*, (1940) AC 206: (1939) 4 All ER 464, p. 470 (HL).

63. *West Derby Union v. Metropolitan Life Assurance Society, supra*, p. 652, **referred to** in *Hindustan Ideal Insurance Co. v. Life Insurance Corporation*, AIR 1963 SC 1083, p. 1087 : 1963 (2) SCR 56.

presumed to be a surplusage, can properly be looked into to ascertain the meaning and scope of the main provision."[64]

A striking illustration of the utility of a proviso in construing the main portion of the section is furnished by section 9(c)[65] of the Intoxicating Liquor Act (Northern Ireland), 1923. The question arising out of this section before the House of Lords[66] was as to the correct meaning of the words 'an increase of not less than 25 per cent of the population according to last census' as occurring in the enacting clause. The problem was thus posed: Must there be a 25 per cent increase in the population of the whole city or town, or will it suffice if there is a 25 per cent increase in the population of some ward or electoral division of the city or town? In answering that it was sufficient for the operation of the section, if there was an increase of 25 per cent in the population of some ward or electoral division, the House of Lords derived assistance from the language of the proviso. LORD MAUGHAM after quoting a passage from LORD HERSCHELL'S opinion in *West Derby Union's* case[67] observed: "That is precisely the method of construction which, in my view, is applicable to the present case—. It cannot I think, be disputed that, in construing a section of an Act of Parliament, it is constantly necessary to explain the meaning of words by an examination of purport and effect of other sections in the same Act. This principle is equally applicable in the case of different parts of a single section, and nonetheless so because the latter part is introduced by the words 'provided that' or like words."[68] LORD RUSSEL expressed himself thus: "Although a proviso may well be incapable of putting upon preceding words a construction which they cannot possibly bear, it may without doubt operate to explain which of the two or more possible meanings is

---

64. *Hindustan Ideal Insurance Co. Ltd. v. Life Insurance Corporation of India*, AIR 1963 SC 1083, p. 1087 : 1963 (2) SCR 56.

65. Section 9(c) : "Where owing to an increase of not less than 25 per cent of the population according to the last census, there is growth or extension of any city or town, and the licensing authority is satisfied after hearing any evidence tendered to it by any resident or owner of property in such city or town that the restrictions in this section on the granting of licences may be relaxed, the licensing authority may grant a licence to any applicant notwithstanding that the same would be otherwise forbidden by this section:

Provided that such licence shall be granted only for premises situated in the ward or district electoral division in which such increase of population has taken place, and in substitution for at least two existing licences held in respect of premises situate within the city or town (as the case may be) comprising such ward or district electoral division."

66. *Jennings v. Kelly*, (1939) 4 All ER 464 : 1940 AC 206 (HL); **Referred** to in *S. Sundaram Pillai v. Pattabiramam*, (1985) 1 SCC 591, pp. 608, 609 : AIR 1985 SC 582.

67. **See** text and note 63, *supra*.

68. *Jennings v. Kelly*, (1939) 4 All ER 464, p. 470 (HL).

the right one to attribute to them—. One must, however, read the whole clause before attempting to construe any portion of it, and a perusal of the proviso fixes the meaning of the words which precede it. It tells you where the increase of population has to take place—namely, in the ward or electoral division in which the premises proposed to be licensed are situate."[69] In the same case LORD WRIGHT laid down: "It is said that, where there is a proviso, the former part which is described as the enacting part, must be construed without reference to the proviso. No doubt, there may be cases in which first part is so clear or unambiguous as not to admit in regard to the matters which are there clear any reference to any other part of the section. The proviso may simply be an exception of what is clearly defined in the first part, or it may be some qualification not inconsistent with what is expressed in the first part. In the present case not only is the first part of the section deficient in express definition, but also the second part is complementary and necessary in order to ascertain the full intention of the Legislature."[70]

Since the natural presumption is that but for the proviso, the enacting part of the section would have included the subject-matter of the proviso,[71] the enacting part should be generally given such a construction which would make the exceptions carved out by the proviso necessary and a construction which would make the exceptions unnecessary and redundant should be avoided.[72] This is so because, "the legislative device of exclusion is adopted only to exclude a part from the whole, which but for the exclusion, continues to be a part of it" and words of exclusion are presumed to have some meaning and are not readily recognised as mere surplusage.[73]

The principle was applied by the Privy Council in overruling a decision of the Bombay High Court regarding the construction of section 4(b) of the Bombay Revenue Jurisdiction Act, 1876 to which are appended four

---

69. *Jennings v. Kelly*, (1939) 4 All ER 464, pp. 471, 472 : 1940 AC 206 (HL).

70. *Ibid.*, p. 477.

71. **See** text and notes 31 to 39, pp. 215-218.

72. *Govt. of the Province of Bombay v. Hormusji Manekji*, AIR 1947 PC 200, pp. 205, 206; *Durga Dutt Sharma v. Navaratna Pharmaceutical Laboratories*, AIR 1965 SC 980, p. 988 : 1965 (1) SCR 737; *Kedarnath Jute Manufacturing Co. Ltd. v. Commercial Tax Officer*, AIR 1966 SC 12, p. 14; *Kush Sahgal v. M.C. Mitter*, AIR 2000 SC 1390, p. 1398 : (2000) 4 SCC 526, (7th edition p. 163 of this book is **referred**).

73. *S. Gurmej Singh v. S. Pratap Singh Kairon*, AIR 1960 SC 122, p. 125 : 1960 (1) SCR 909. **See further** *Durga Dutt Sharma v. Navaratna Pharmaceutical Laboratories, supra*, p. 988; *Abboy Pada Saha v. Sudhir Kumar Mondal*, AIR 1967 SC 115 : 1966 Supp SCR 387; *Damodar Valley Corporation v. State of Bihar*, AIR 1976 SC 1956, p. 1960 : 1976 SCC (Tax) 389; *Indian Aluminium Co. Ltd. v. Asstt. Commissioner of Commercial Taxes*, AIR 2001 SC 795, p. 797 : (2001) 2 SCC 201 : (2001) 128 ELT 18.

exceptions by a proviso; LORD THANKERTON observed: "It is a familiar principle of statutory construction that where you find in the same section 'express exceptions' from the operative part of the section, it may be assumed, unless it otherwise appears from the language employed, that these exceptions were necessary, as otherwise the subject-matter of the exceptions would have come within the operative provisions of the section. There are four exceptions in the proviso to section 4 which are clearly general exceptions to the operative provisions of the section. If the construction adopted by CHANDRAVARKAR, J., in 21 Bombay 74, and adopted by the High Court in the present case be correct, these exceptions were unnecessary."[74]

The Supreme Court in construing rule 12 of the Life Insurance Corporation Rules, 1956 which prescribes a period of limitation within which a reference can be made, observed that the rule considered without the proviso may well be construed as applying to a reference made by the Corporation; but considering the rule along with the proviso, it was held that the rule was meant to govern a reference by someone else and not the the Corporation.[75]

Further the proviso appended to section 9 of the Coal Bearing Area (Acquisition and Development) Act, 1957 which reads '*provided* that, where the declaration relates to any land, or to any rights in or over land belonging to a State Government which has or have not been leased out, no such declaration shall be made except after previous consultation with the State Government', was held to have an important bearing on the construction of the Act that the Union has power to acquire the interest of a State in coal-bearing lands.[76]

(e) At times added to allay fears

The general rule in construing an enactment containing a proviso is to construe them together without making either of them redundant or otiose. Even if the enacting part is clear effort is to be made to give some meaning to the proviso and to justify its necessity. But a clause or a section worded as a proviso, may not be a true proviso and may have been placed by way of abundant caution. As was pointed out by LORD HERSCHELL: "I am satisfied that many instances might be given where provisos could be found in legislation that are meaningless because they have been put in to allay fears when those fears were absolutely unfounded and no proviso at all

74. *Govt. of the Province of Bombay v. Hormusji Manakji, supra*, pp. 205, 206.
75. *Hindustan Ideal Insurance Co. Ltd. v. Life Insurance Corporation of Inida*, AIR 1963 SC 1083, p. 1087 : 1963 (2) SCR 56.
76. *State of West Bengal v. Union of India*, AIR 1963 SC 1241, p. 1248 : 1964 (1) SCR 371.

was necessary to protect the persons at whose instance they were inserted."[77] In such cases the proviso has no effect whatsoever on the enactment and "cannot be relied on as controlling the operative words."[78] But such a construction if appears, will be reached only when the operative words of the enactment are abundantly clear.

The construction of section 76 of the Companies Act, 1956, illustrates the difficulty arising out of such provisos.[79] The argument before the Supreme Court was that the limit imposed by section 76(1)(ii) was inapplicable where the commission was claimed not out of capital but out of profits and reliance was placed on the words, 'capital moneys'[80] as they occurred in section 76(2) as giving the clue to the limitation imposed by section 76(1). The majority (GAJENDRAGADKAR and WANCHOO, JJ.) rejected the contention holding that section 76(1) was unambiguous and section 76(2) was "inserted to allay fears or to remove misapprehensions."[81] SARKAR, J. (dissenting) however, found section 76(1) not so clear and restricted its operation to payment of commission out of capital, having regard to the provision made in section 76(2).[82]

The difficulty in construction arising out of inept provisos introduced to 'remove any doubts' is further illustrated by section 15 of the Bankruptcy and Deeds of Arrangement Act, 1913. The Court of Appeal, not without some difficulty, held that the proviso to section 15 could not be read so as to contradict and render meaningless the operative words of the section giving protection to the execution purchaser and that the proviso was inserted to remove any doubts as to the rights of the true owner to sue the execution creditor for money he had received.[83]

---

77. *West Derby Union v. Metropolitan Life Assurance Society*, (1897) AC 647, p. 656 : 66 LJ Ch 726 : 77 LT 284 (HL). **See further** *Director of Public Prosecutions v. Good Child*, (1978) 2 All ER 161, p. 165 : (1978) 1 WLR 578 (HL).

78. *S.M.K.R. Meyappa Chetty v. S.N. Subramanian Chetty*, (1916) 43 IA 113, p. 122 : 35 IC 323, p. 326 (PC).

79. *Madanlal Fakirchand Dudhediya v. S. Changdeo Sugar Mills Ltd.*, AIR 1962 SC 1543 : 1962 Supp (3) SCR 973 (Construction of section 76, Companies Act, 1956, as it stood before Amending Act 65 of 1960).

80. By Amending Act 65 of 1960 the words 'any of its moneys' have been substituted for the words 'any of its capital moneys' to make it clear that the restriction imposed by section 76(1) operated irrespective of whether commission is paid out of profits or capital moneys. The majority decision in *Madanlal's* case (*supra*) is thus in accord with the intention of Parliament as disclosed by the amending Act.

81. *Madanlal Fakirchand Dudhediya v. S. Changdeo Sugar Mills Ltd, supra*, pp. 1551, 1552.

82. *Ibid.*, pp. 1556, 1557.

83. *Curtis v. Maloney*, (1950) 2 All ER 982, pp. 985, 986 (CA).

[Footnote No. 83 Contd.]

(f) At times a fresh enactment

The normal rule is that it is "a very dangerous and certainly unusual course to import legislation from a proviso wholesale into the body of the statute,"[84] as to do so will be to treat it "as if it were an independent enacting clause instead of being dependent on the main enactment."[85] To read a proviso as providing something by way of an addendum or as dealing with a subject not covered by the main enactment or as stating a general rule as distinguished from an exception or qualification is ordinarily foreign to the proper function of a proviso.[86] However, this is only true of a real proviso. The insertion of a proviso by the draftsman is not always strictly adhered to its legitimate use and at times a section worded as a proviso may wholly or partly be in substance a fresh enactment adding to and not merely excepting something out of or qualifying what goes before.[87] Referring to the

---

[Footnote No. 83 Contd.]

Section 15 of the Bankruptcy and Deeds of Arrangement Act, 1913, is **quoted** below:

"Where any goods in the possession of an execution debtor at the time of seizure by a sheriff, high bailiff, or other officer charged with the enforcement of a writ, warrant, or other process of execution, are sold by such sheriff, high bailiff, or other officer without any claim having been made to the same, the purchaser of the goods so sold, shall acquire a good title in the goods so sold, and no person shall be entitled to recover against the sheriff, high bailiff, or other officer, or any one lawfully acting under the authority of either of them, except as provided by the Bankruptcy Acts, 1883 and 1890, for any sale of such goods or for paying over the proceeds thereof, prior to the receipt of a claim to the said goods unless it is proved that the person from whom recovery is sought had notice, or might by making reasonable inquiry have ascertained that the goods were not the property of the execution debtor: Provided that nothing in this section contained shall affect the right of any claimant who may prove that at the time of sale he had a title to any goods so seized and sold to any remedy to which he may be entitled against any person other than such sheriff, high bailiff, or other officer as aforesaid."

84. *West Derby v. Metropolitan Life Assurance Co.*, (1897) AC 647, p. 653 : 66 LJ Ch 726 : 77 LT 284 (HL) (LORD WATSON); *S. Sundaram Pillai v. Pattabiraman*, (1985) 1 SCC 591, p. 608 : AIR 1985 SC 582.

85. *R. v. Dibdin*, (1910) P 57, p. 125 (FLETCHER MOULTON, L.J.).

86. *CIT, Mysore, etc. v. Indo Mercantile Bank Ltd.*, AIR 1959 SC 713, p. 717 : 1959 Supp (2) SCR 256; *Shah Bhojraj Kuverji Oil Mills v. Subhash Chandra Yograj Sinha*, AIR 1961 SC 1596, p. 1600; *Dwarka Prasad v. Dwarka Das Saraf*, AIR 1975 SC 1758, p. 1764 : (1976) 1 SCC 128.

87. *Rhondda Urban District Council v. Taff Vale Rly. Co.*, (1909) AC 253, p. 258 (LORD LOREBURN, L.C.); *Mohumud Bahadoor Khan v. Collector of Bareilly*, (1874) 1 IA 167, p. 175 (PC); *Shah Bhojraj Kuverji Oil Mills v. Subhash Chandra Yograj Sinha*, AIR 1961 SC 1596, p. 1600 : (1962) 2 SCR 159; *State of Orissa v. Debaki Debi*, AIR 1964 SC 1413, pp. 1417, 1418 : 1964 (3) SCR 253; *CIT, Kerala v. P. Krishna Warriar*, AIR 1965 SC 59, p. 63 : 1964 (8) SCR 36; *State of Rajasthan v. Leela Jain*, AIR 1965 SC 1296, p. 1300 : 1965 (1) SCR 276; *Commissioner of Commercial Taxes, Board of Revenue, Madras v. Ramkishan Shrikishan Jhaver*,

[Footnote No. 87 Contd.]

rule of limitation enacted in section 20 of the Forfeiture Act, 1859, which is introduced by way of a proviso, SIR MONTAGUE E. SMITH said: "Looking at the various parts of the Act and gathering the purpose and intention of the Legislature from the whole, this was a substantive enactment; and that although it appears under the form of a proviso, it was a limitation intended by the Legislature to apply to all suits brought by any person in respect of forfeited property."[88] Similarly, it has been held by the Supreme Court that the period of limitation contained in the proviso in sub-section (6) of section 12 of the Orissa Sales Tax Act, 1947, was an independent legislative provision and applied both to original assessments as well as to assessments made in appeal or revision.[89] Same view has been taken of proviso (b) to section 4(3)(i) of the Indian Income-tax Act, 1922.[90] In a Privy Council case,[91] the question related to the construction of section 102(2)(a) of the Stamp Duties Act of New South Wales. This section provided that for the purpose of death duty the estate of a deceased person shall be deemed to include and consist of 'all property which the deceased has disposed of by a settlement containing any trust in respect of that property to take effect after his death'. A proviso to the section said: '*Provided* that the property deemed to be included in the estate of the deceased shall be the property which at the time of his death is subject to such trust.' The Privy Council read the proviso as a substantive provision stating that the words "provided that" were inept and were merely used to mean "and" or "in which case". It was, therefore, held that the property falling within the proviso was not limited to that property which was initially the subject-matter of disposition by the deceased but also included property which was acquired with the aid of that property and which was subject to the trust at the time of the death of the deceased. As was pointed out by the Supreme Court of United States : "It is a common practice in legislative proceedings, on the consideration of bills, for parties desirous of securing amendments to them, to precede their proposed amendments with the term

---

[Footnote No. 87 Contd.]

AIR 1968 SC 59, p. 63 : 1968 (1) SCR 148; *CIT, U.P. v. Jagannath Mahadeo Prasad*, AIR 1969 SC 209, p. 211 : 1969 (1) SCR 537; *Hiralal Ratan Lal v. Sales Tax Officer III, Kanpur*, AIR 1973 SC 1034, p. 1039 : 1973 SCC (Tax) 307 : (1973) 1 SCC 216; *Commr. of Stamp Duties v. Atwill*, (1973) 1 All ER 576, p. 581 (PC); *Dattatraya Govind Mahajan v. State of Maharashtra*, AIR 1977 SC 915, p. 927; *S. Sundaram Pillai v. Pattabiraman*, (1985) 1 SCC 591, pp. 608, 610 : AIR 1985 SC 582; *Motiram Ghelabhai v. Jagannagar*, (1985) 2 SCC 279, pp. 285, 289 : AIR 1985 SC 709.

88. *Mohummud Bahadoor Khan v. Collector of Bareilly*, (1874) 1 IA 167, p. 175 (PC).

89. *State of Orissa v. Debaki Debi*, AIR 1964 SC 1413, pp. 1417, 1418 : 1964 (5) SCR 253.

90. *CIT, Kerala v. P. Krishna Warrier*, AIR 1965 SC 59, p. 63 : 1964 (8) SCR 36.

91. *Commr. of Stamp Duties v. Atwill*, (1973) 1 All ER 576 (PC).

'provided' so as to declare that, notwithstanding existing provisions, the one thus expressed is to prevail, thus having no greater significance than would be attached to the conjunctive 'but' or 'and' in the same place, and simply serving to separate or distinguish the different paragraphs or sentences."[1]

A proviso will not be normally construed as reducing the purview of enactment to a nullity,[2] or to take away a right clearly conferred by the enactment[3] but it has been held that if a proviso on its true construction "is directly repugnant to the purview, the proviso shall stand and be a repeal of the purview, as it speaks the last intention of the makers".[4] And, on similar logic, it has also been held that if out of two provisos the later is repugnant to the earlier one, the later prevails.[5]

(f1) Summary of purposes of a proviso

In *Sundaram Pillai v. Pattabiraman,*[6] Fazal Ali J., observed that by and large a proviso may serve the following four different purposes:

(1) qualifying or excepting certain provisions from the main enactment;

(2) it may entirely change the very concept of the intendment of the enactment by insisting on certain mandatory conditions to be fulfilled in order to make the enactment workable;

---

1. *Georgia Railroad & Banking Co. v. James M. Smith*, 128 U.S. 174, p. 181 : 32 Law Ed 377, p. 380. **See further** *D.M. McDonald v. United States of America*, 279 U.S 12, pp. 21, 22: 73 Law Ed 582, p. 585; *Commr. of Stamp Duties v. Atwill*, (1973) 1 All ER 576, p. 581 (PC). **See also** text and note 16, p. 232.
2. **See** Chapter 2, title 4(b) 'Inconsistency and Repugnancy to be avoided; Harmonious Construction', notes 27 to 39, pp. 159-161. (A proviso is normally in the nature of a qualification or exception and therefore it does not wholly nullify the enactment. "Exception cannot be allowed to swallow up the general rule") *Macbeth v. Ashley*, (1874) 2 Sc-and Div 352 (HL) **considered** in *Raghuthilakathirtha Sreepadangalavaru Swami (Sree) v. State of Mysore*, AIR 1966 SC 1172 : 1963 (2) SCR 226. **See further** *Director of Education (Secondary) v. Pushpendra Kumar,* AIR 1998 SC 2230, p. 2234 : (1998) 5 SCC 192 (A provision in the nature of an exception cannot be so construed as to subsume the main provision and thereby nullify the right conferred by the main provision).
3. *Madan Gopal v. VI Addl. District Judge*, AIR 1989 SC 155, p. 157 : (1988) 4 SCC 644.
4. *A.G. v. Chelsea Waterworks Co.*, 94 ER 716.
5. *King v. Dominion Engineering Co. Ltd.*, AIR 1947 PC 94, p. 95.
6. (1985) 1 SCC 591 (paras 43, 44) : AIR 1985 SC 582; *Swadeshi Match AB v. Securities and Exchange Board of India,* (2004) 11 SCC 641 (para 68) : AIR 2004 SC 4219; *Southern Petrochemical Industries Co. Ltd. v. Electricity Inspector & ETIO,* (2007) 5 SCC 447 (para 98) : AIR 2007 SC 1984.

(3) it may be so embedded in the Act itself as to become an integral part of the enactment, and thus acquire the tenor and colour of the substantive enactment itself; and

(4) it may be used merely to act as an optional addenda to the enactment with the sole object of explaining the real intendment of the statutory provision.

The above summary cannot, however, be taken as exhaustive and ultimately a proviso like any other enactment ought to be construed upon its terms.[7]

(g) Distinction between proviso, exception and saving clause

A distinction is said to exist between provisions worded as 'proviso', 'Exception' or 'Saving Clause'. 'Exception' is intended to restrain the enacting clause to particular cases; 'Proviso', is used to remove special cases from the general enactment and provide for them specially; and 'Saving Clause' is used to preserve from destruction of certain rights, remedies or privileges already existing.[8] 'Savings' means that it saves all the rights, the party previously had; it does not mean that it gives him any new rights. Saving clauses are introduced into Acts which repeal others to safeguard rights which, but for the savings, would be lost and these clauses are seldom used to construe the Act.[9] It has also been pointed out that a 'saving' repugnant to the enactment would be void for contrariety;[10] whereas as already seen a repugnant proviso is construed as repeal of the enactment.[11] A saving worded in the cloak of a proviso was, therefore, not used to determine whether a section in the enactment was on its own terms retrospective or not.[12] This case was followed in interpreting the saving clause (cl. 15) in the Export Control Order, 1988 to preserve only the right which existed prior to the issuance of the order and not to confer any new or

---

7. **See** title 9(h) Broad general rule of construction, p. 232.
8. HORACK : Cases and Materials on Legislation, 2nd Edition, p. 572.
9. *Arnold v. Mayor and Corporation of Gravesend*, 2 K. & J. 574 : (1856) 25 LJ Ch 776, (PAGE WOOD V.C.): *Fitzgerald v. Champneys*, (1861) 30 LJ Ch 777, p. 783 (PAGE WOOD V.C.); *Shah Bhojraj Kuverji Oil Mills v. Subhash Chandra Yograj Sinha*, AIR 1961 SC 1596, p. 1600 : (1962) 2 SCR 159; *Agricultural and Processed Food Products v. Union of India*, AIR 1996 SC 1947, p. 1952 : (1996) 4 SCC 297.
10. *Alton Wood* case; *Attorney-General v. Bushopp*, (1600) 1 Co Rep 40b, pp. 47a, 52b : 76 ER 89, pp. 107, 119. **See further** an interesting *Australian case, Kropp v. Cobb & Co. Ltd.*, (1964) Queensland Reports 167, pp. 168, 169; **referred to** in *Western Transport Pty. Ltd. v. Kropp*, (1964) 3 All ER 722, pp. 726, 727 (PC).
11. **See** text and notes 4-5, p. 230.
12. *Shah Bhojraj Kuverji Oil Mills v. Subhash Chandra Yograj Sinha*, *supra*, p. 1600.

additional right which did not then exist.[13] A further distinction that used to be pointed out for purposes of pleading was that it was for the party pleading the statute to negative the exceptions but that it was for the defendant to raise a defence under a proviso. This distinction cannot be said to exist in our country either in criminal[14] or in civil proceedings.[15]

(h) Broad general rule of construction

The better rule appears to be not to give undue weight to the aforesaid distinctions which are somewhat obscure, and to direct one's attention to the substance rather than to the form adopted by the Legislature. Dealing with the effect of the use of the term 'provided', the Supreme Court of United States pointed out: "But a proviso is not always limited in its effect to the part of the enactment with which it is immediately associated; it may apply generally to all cases within the meaning of the language used. Little, if any, significance is to be given to the use of the word 'provided'. In Acts of Congress, this word is employed for many purposes. Sometimes, it is used merely to safeguard against misinterpretation or to distinguish different paragraphs or sentences. For the proper construction of the provision in question, consideration need not be limited to the sub-division in which it is found; the general purpose of the section may be taken into account."[16] Referring to the proviso appended to section 3(1) of the Indian Press Act, 1910, LORD PHILLIMORE, differing from the construction placed on it by the majority of the Madras High Court, said: "It is well settled that there is no magic in the words of a proviso, and that the plain meaning must be given to the words of the Legislature."[17] Therefore, where the language used in a proviso is quite clear and no alternative view is possible, it is futile to go into the question whether the proviso operates as a substantive provision or only by way of an exception, and the plain meaning must be adopted.[18] Countering an argument against literal construction of the proviso in section 29 of the Patents and Designs Act, 1907-1939, based on the well-known principle that a proviso must be construed in relation to the principal matter to which it stands as a proviso, DU PARCQ, L.J., observed: "The object of the rule is to ensure that effect shall be given to the true intention of Parliament, and not to prevent the Court from giving effect to that intention. Still less is the rule designed for the purpose of

13. *Agricultural and Processed Food Products v. Union of India, supra.*
14. See section 105, Indian Evidence Act, 1872.
15. See Order 6, rule 6; and Order 8, rule 2, Code of Civil Procedure, 1908.
16. *D.M. Macdonald v. United States of America*, 279 US 12, pp. 21, 22 : 73 Law Ed 582, p. 585.
17. *Besant v. A.G. of Madras*, ILR 43 Mad 146, p. 155 (PC).
18. *CIT, U.P. v. Jagannath Mahadeo Prasad*, AIR 1969 SC 209 : 1969 (1) SCR 537.

defeating the intention of the Legislature."[19] Just as a proviso is expected to except or qualify something in the enacting part and presumed to be necessary,[20] so also a saving clause may, in a proper case, negate an argument which results in making it unnecessary.[21] And just as a proviso may be redundant having been added to allay fears,[22] so also a saving clause may often be added by way of abundant caution.[23] The thin distinction existing between an 'Exception', a 'Proviso' and a 'Saving Clause' and use of such forms having often been corrupted by Draftsmen, the more safe rule is stated in KENT'S *Commentaries on American Law* (12th Edition, Vol. 8, p. 463): "The true principle undoubtedly is, that the sound interpretation and meaning of the statute, on a view of the enacting clause and proviso, taken and construed together is to prevail."[24] The House of Lords has affirmed this principle;[25] VISCOUNT MAUGHAM observed that there can be no doubt that the view expressed in the above quotation is correct.[26] In the same case, LORD WRIGHT stated: "The proper course is to apply the broad general rule of construction which is that a section or enactment must be construed as a whole, each portion throwing light, if need be, on the rest. I do not think there is any other rule, even in the case of a proviso in the strict and narrowest sense."[27] These views have been accepted and applied also by the Privy Council[28] and our Supreme Court.[29] A sincere effort should be made to reconcile the different provisions in case of apparent conflict bearing in mind that Parliament will not at the same time

---

19. *No-Nail Cases Proprietary Ltd. v. No-Nail Boxes Ltd.*, (1944) 1 All ER 528, pp. 529, 530 (CA); **affirmed** in *Craddock v. Zevo Finance Co.*, (1946) 1 All ER 523 : (1946) 27 TC 267 (HL).

20. **See** text and notes 73, 74, pp. 225, 226.

21. *Punjab Province v. Daulat Singh*, AIR 1942 PC 38, p. 42.

22. **See** text and notes 77 to 83, pp. 227-228.

23. *Punjab Province v. Daulat Singh, supra* p. 42; *London Borough of Ealing v. Race Relations Board*, (1972) 1 All ER 105, p. 115 (HL).

24. **See** MAXWELL : Interpretation of Statutes, 11th Edition, p. 155.

25. *Jennings v. Kelly*, (1939) 4 All ER 464 (HL).

26. *Ibid.*, p. 470.

27. *Ibid.*, p. 477.

28. *Commr. of Stamp Duties v. Atwill*, (1973) 1 All ER 576, pp. 579, 580, 581 (PC).

29. *Tahsildar Singh v. State of U.P.*, AIR 1959 SC 1012, p. 1022 : 1959 Supp (2) SCR 875; *Madanlal Fakirchand Dudhediya v. S. Changdeo Sugar Mills Ltd.*, AIR 1962 SC 1543, p. 1551 : 1962 Supp (3) SCR 973; *CIT, Kerala v. P. Krishna Warriar*, AIR 1965 SC 59, p. 63 : (1964) 8 SCR 36; *Commissioner of Commercial Taxes, Board of Revenue, Madras v. Ramkishan Shrikishan Jhaver*, AIR 1968 SC 59, p. 64 : 1968 (1) SCR 148. *Hiralal Ratanlal v. Sales Tax Officer III, Kanpur*, AIR 1973 SC 1034, p. 1039 : 1973 SCC (Tax) 307 : (1973) 1 SCC 216; *Dwarka Prasad v. Dwarka Das Saraf*, AIR 1975 SC 1758, p. 1764 : (1976) 1 SCC 128; *Krishna Prasad Gupta v. Controller Printing and Stationery*, 1995 (6) Scale 89, pp. 93, 94. (Construction of saving clause in section 28 of the Administrative Tribunals Act, 1985).

give something by one hand and take back the same thing by another.[30] In case, however, of a real conflict, a question will arise as to which of the two conflicting provisions should prevail. The answer to such a question should not be so much made to depend on the form of the provisions or on their sequence in the statute as on their substance by determining which of them is the leading provision and which of them is subordinate one.[31]

The best that can be said for preferring a construction which favours the form has been said by PATANJALI SHASTRI, C.J.I., while dealing with an *'Explanation'* and the observations being general can aptly apply to a provision bearing any other form such as 'Proviso', 'Exception', or 'Saving Clause'. The learned Chief Justice said: "It may be that the description of a provision cannot be decisive of its true meaning or interpretation which must depend on the words used therein but, when two interpretations are sought to be put upon a provision, that which fits the description which the Legislature has chosen to apply to it, is, according to sound canons of constructions, to be adopted, provided of course, it is consistent with the language employed in preference to the one which attributes to the provision a different effect from what it should have according to its description by the Legislature."[32]

10. EXPLANATION

An *Explanation* is at times appended to a section to explain the meaning of words contained in the section.[33] It becomes a part and parcel of the enactment.[34] The meaning to be given to an *Explanation* must depend upon its terms, and "no theory of its purpose can be entertained unless it is to be inferred from the language used".[35] But if the language of the *Explanation* shows a purpose and a construction consistent with that purpose can be

---

30. **See** Chapter 2, title 4(b) 'Inconsistency and Repugnancy to be avoided; Harmonious Construction' text and notes 25 to 40, pp. 159 to 161.

31. **See** Chapter 2, title 4(c) 'When Reconciliation not possible', text and notes 72, 73, p. 168.

32. *State of Bombay v. United Motors (India) Ltd.*, AIR 1953 SC 252, p. 258 : 1953 SCR 1069. **See further** *Dattatraya Govind Mahajan v. State of Maharashtra*, AIR 1977 SC 915, p. 928 : 1977 (2) SCC 548; *S. Sundaram Pillai v. Pattabiraman*, (1985) 1 SCC 591, p. 612 : AIR 1985 SC 582; *Aphali Pharmaceuticals Ltd. v. State of Maharashtra*, AIR 1989 SC 2227, p. 2238 : 1989 (4) SCC 378.

33. *S. Sundaram Pillai v. Pattabhiraman*, (1985) 1 SCC 591, pp. 611, 613 : AIR 1985 SC 582; *Dipak Chandra Ruhidas v. Chandan Kumar Sarkar*, (2003) 7 SCC 66, p. 71 : AIR 2003 SC 3701.

34. *Bengal Immunity Co. Ltd. v. State of Bihar*, AIR 1955 SC 661, p. 733 : 1955 (2) SCR 603.

35. *Krishna Ayyangar v. Nattaperumal Pillai*, ILR 43 Mad 550, p. 564 (PC); *Dattatraya Govind Mahajan v. State of Maharashtra*, AIR 1977 SC 915, p. 928 : 1977 (2) SCC 548; *Aphali Pharmaceuticals Ltd. v. State of Maharashtra*, AIR 1989 SC 2227, p. 2238 : 1989 (4) SCC 378; *Keshavji Raoji and Co. v. Commissioner of Income-tax*, AIR 1991 SC 1806, p. 1818 : 1990 (2) SCC 231.

reasonably placed upon it, that construction will be preferred as against any other construction which does not fit in with the description or the avowed purpose.[36] In the *Bengal Immunity Co.'s* case[37] the *Explanation* appended to Article 286(1) of the Constitution was restricted to its avowed purpose of explaining an outside sale for purpose of clause (1) and was construed as not conferring any taxing power or as restricting the ban imposed by clause (2) of the same Article. However, an identical *Explanation* contained in a State legislation was construed differently and was held as conferring taxing power. The context and setting of the two enactments, it was pointed out, made the entire difference although the language was identical.[38] *Explanation VIII* to section 11 of the Code of Civil Procedure, inserted by amendment in 1976, has been construed to promote the object for which it was inserted *viz.*, that an issue once decided by a competent court should not be litigated over again even though the court deciding it was a court of 'limited jurisdiction' not competent to decide the subsequent suit. Consistent with this object the words 'a court of limited jurisdiction' were construed as wide enough to include a court whose jurisdiction is subject to pecuniary limitation.[39]

When the section deals with two categories of cases *e.g.*, residential and non-residential accommodations, an *Explanation* to the section which is limited in scope to one category, namely residential accommodations, cannot affect the scope of the section with reference to the second category, namely non-residential accommodations.[40] When a section contains a number of clauses and there is an *Explanation* at the end of the section, it should be seen as to which clause it applies and the clarification contained in it applied to that clause.[41] But when the *Explanation* added towards the end of the section opens, with the words 'for the purpose of this section' or 'nothing in this section' it will *prima facie* indicate that the *Explanation* applies to all the clauses in the section.[42]

---

36. **See** text and note 32, p. 234.
37. *Bengal Immunity Co. Ltd. v. State of Bihar*, AIR 1955 SC 661, p. 733 : 1955 (2) SCR 603.
38. *M.P.V. Sundararamier & Co. v. State of Andhra Pradesh*, AIR 1958 SC 468, pp. 479, 480 : 1958 SCR 1422; *Mohanlal Hargovinddas v. State of M.P.*, AIR 1967 SC 1022 : 1967 (2) SCR 88.
39. *Sulochana Amma v. Narayanan Nair*, AIR 1994 SC 152, p. 156 : (1994) 2 SCC 14. **See** for another illustration *Amir Ahmad v. Ram Niwas Agarwala*, AIR 1994 SC 1145, p. 1148 : (1994) 2 SCC 50.
40. *M.K. Salpekar (Dr.) v. Sunil Kumar Shamsunder Chaudhari*, AIR 1988 SC 1841, p. 1843 : 1988 (4) SCC 21.
41. *Patel Roadways Ltd. v. Prasad Trading Company*, AIR 1992 SC 1514, p. 1518 : 1991 (4) SCC 270 (*Explanation* to section 20, CPC).
42. *CIT v. Plantation Corporation of Kerala Ltd.*, AIR 2000 SC 3714, p. 3717 : (2001) 1 SCC 207 : (2001) 247 ITR 155.

An *Explanation* may be added to include something within or to exclude something from the ambit of the main enactment or the connotation of some words occurring in it.[43] Even a negative *Explanation* which excludes certain types of a category from the ambit of the enactment may have the effect of showing that the category leaving aside the excepted types is included within it.[44] An *Explanation,* normally, should be so read as to harmonise with and clear up any ambiguity in the main section and should not be so construed as to widen the ambit of the section.[45] It is also possible that an *Explanation* may have been added in a declaratory form to retrospectively clarify a doubtful point in law and to serve as a proviso to the main section[46] or *ex abundanti cautela* to allay groundless apprehensions.[47]

In *Sundaram Pillai v. Pattabiraman,*[48] FAZAL ALI, J., culled out from earlier cases, the following as objects of an *Explanation* to a statutory provision:

(a) to explain the meaning and intendment of the Act itself,

(b) where there is any obscurity or vagueness in the main enactment, to clarify the same so as to make it consistent with the dominant object which it seems to subserve.

(c) to provide an additional support to the dominant object of the Act in order to make it meaningful and purposeful,

(d) an *Explanation* cannot in any way interfere with or change the enactment or any part thereof but where some gap is left which is relevant for the purpose of the *Explanation,* in order to suppress the mischief and advance the object of the Act it can help or assist the

---

43. See *Explanations I* and *II* in Article 3 of the Constitution of India added by the Constitution Eighteenth Amendment Act, 1966. **See further** *Explanation 2* of section 2(15) of the Estate Duty Act, 1953 and the *Controller of Estate Duty v. Kantilal Trikamlal,* AIR 1976 SC 1935 : 1977 SCC (Tax) 90 : (1976) 4 SCC 643; *Keshavji Raoji and Co. v. Commissioner of Income-tax, supra.*

44. *ITO (First), Salem v. Short Brothers (P) Ltd.,* AIR 1967 SC 81, p. 83 : 1966 (3) SCR 84.

45. *Bihta Co-operative Development and Cane Marketing Union Ltd. v. Bank of Bihar,* AIR 1967 SC 389, p. 393; (1967) 1 SCR 848; *Oblum Electrical Industries Pvt. Ltd. v. Collector of Customs,* AIR 1997 SC 3467, p. 3471 : (1997) 7 SCC 581. But if on a true reading an *Explanation* widens the scope of the main section, effect must be given to it : **see** *Hiralal Ratan Lal v. Sales Tax Officer III, Kanpur,* AIR 1973 SC 1034, p. 1040 : 1973 SCC (Tax) 307 : (1973) 1 SCC 216; *Aphali Pharmaceuticals Ltd. v. State of Maharshtra,* AIR 1989 SC 2227, p. 2238 : 1989 (4) SCC 378; *Zakiya Begum v. Shahnaz Ali,* (2010) 9 SCC 280 para 19 : AIR 2010 SC 3385.

46. *Y.P. Chawla v. M.P. Tiwari,* AIR 1992 SC 1360, p. 1362 : 1992 (2) SCC 672.

47. *Abdul Latif Khan v. Abadi Begum (Mrs.),* AIR 1934 PC 188, p. 191 : 61 IA 322; *Keshavji Raoji and Co. v. Commissioner of Income-tax,* AIR 1991 SC 1806, p. 1818 : 1990 (2) SCC 231.

48. (1985) 1 SCC 591, p. 613 : AIR 1985 SC 582, **referred** in *M.P. Cement Manufacturer's Association v. State of M.P.,* (2004) 2 SCC 249, p. 261 : (2003) 10 Scale 547; *Swedish Match AB v. Securities & Exchange Board of India,* (2004) 11 SCC 641.

Court in interpreting the true purport and intendment of the enactment, and

(e) it cannot, however, take away a statutory right with which any person under a statute has been clothed or set at naught the working of an Act by becoming an hindrance in the interpretation of the same.

But it would be wrong to always construe an *Explanation* limited to the aforesaid objects. As earlier stated, the meaning to be given to an *Explanation* will really depend upon its terms and not on any theory of its purpose.[49]

11. SCHEDULES

Schedules appended to statutes form part of the statute.[50] They are added towards the end and their use is made to avoid encumbering the sections in the statute with matters of excessive detail. They often contain details and forms for working out the policy underlying the sections of the statute,[51] and at times they contain transitory provisions which remain in force till the main provisions of the statute are brought into operation.[52] Occasionally they contain such rules and forms which can be suitably amended according to local or changing conditions by process simpler than the normal one required for amending other parts of the statute.[53] The division of a statute into sections and Schedules is a mere matter of convenience and a Schedule therefore may contain substantive enactment[54] which may even go beyond the scope of a section to which the Schedule may appear to be connected by its heading. In such a case a clear positive provision in a Schedule may be held to prevail over the *prima facie* indication furnished by its heading and the purpose of the Schedule contained in the Act.[55] However, if the language is not so clear, the provision in the

---

49. See text and note 35, p. 234 and text and note 32, p. 234.

50. *A.G. v. Lamplough*, (1878) 3 Ex D 214, p. 229 : 38 LT 87 : 47 LJ QB 555 (BRETT, L.J.); *Ujagar Prints v. Union of India*, AIR 1989 SC 516, p. 531 : 1989 (3) SCC 488; *Aphali Pharmaceuticals v. State of Maharashtra*, AIR 1989 SC 2227, p. 2237 : 1989 (4) SCC 378.

51. See the Schedules appended to the Constitution of India, the Companies Act, 1956, the Limitation Act, 1963 and the Motor Vehicles Act, 1939.

52. See Ninth Schedule to the Government of India Act, 1935.

53. See 5th and 6th Schedules to the Constitution of India; First Schedule to the Code of Civil Procedure, 1908.

54. *A.G. v. Lamplough*, (1878) 3 Ex D 214, p. 229 : 38 LT 87 : 47 LJ QB 555 (BRETT, LJ); *Ujagar Prints v. Union of India*, AIR 1989 SC 516, pp. 531, 532 : 1989 (3) SCC 488; *Aphali Pharmaceuticals Ltd. v. State of Maharashtra*, AIR 1989 SC 2227, pp. 2237, 2238 : 1989 (4) SCC 378.

55. *IRC v. Gittus*, (1920) 1 KB 563, p. 576 (LORD STERNDALE, M.R.); *CIT, W.B. v. Calcutta National Bank Ltd.*, AIR 1959 SC 928, pp. 941, 942 : 1960 SCJ 980. **See further** *Ujagar Prints v. Union of India, supra*; *Aphali Pharmaceuticals Ltd. v. State of Maharashtra, supra*.

Schedule may be construed as confined to the purpose indicated by its heading and the section in the statute to which it appears connected.[56] In case of conflict between the body of the Act and the Schedule the former prevails.[57] Much importance ordinarily is not given to the forms in the Schedule,[58] as they are intended "to suit the generality of cases rather than all cases,"[59] and they give way to clear provision of enactment.[60] But in case of doubtful words in the enactment, a scheduled form may be utilised "for the purpose of throwing light" on their meaning.[61] At times, the prescribed form may contain some imperative requirement and may be mandatory, *e.g.*, a form of return of agricultural income, incorporated in Rules to the Bengal Agricultural Income-tax Act, 1944, which contained a footnote requiring that the declaration of the return of income 'shall be signed in the case of an individual by the individual himself' was construed as mandatory; and it was held that it was not a sufficient compliance that the return was signed by an illiterate person by the pen of his son.[62] Whether a particular requirement prescribed by a form is mandatory or directory may have to be decided in each case having regard to the purpose or object of the requirement and its inter-relation with other enacting provisions of the statute, and it is difficult to lay down any uniform rule.[63] Forms prescribed under rules become part of rules and, therefore, if the Act confers an

---

56. *Ibid.*

57. *Aphali Pharmaceuticals Ltd. v. State of Maharashtra*, AIR 1989 SC 2227, p. 2239 : 1989 (4) SCC 378.

58. **See** *Modi Spinning & Weaving Mills Co. Ltd. v. Commissioner of Sales Tax*, AIR 1965 SC 957 : 1965 (1) SCR 592 (Form of Certificate held impliedly modified by change in the Act and Rules). A form cannot control the Act or the Rules, *Life Insurance Corporation of India v. Escorts Ltd.*, (1986) 1 SCC 264, p. 319 : AIR 1986 SC 1370; *Jagdish Prasad v. State of Rajasthan*, (2011) 7 SCC 789 (para 26). Schedule of the Rules has to be in conformity with and is required to advance the object of primary statutory provision. A Schedule can not in any way wipe out the statutory provisions of the Act in effect and spirit.

59. *R. v. Bains*, (1840) 112 ER 792, p. 792 (LORD DENMAN, CJ).

60. **See** note 58, *supra*.

61. HALSBURY'S Laws of England, Vol. 44, pp. 536, 537 (4th edition). **See further** *Anar Devi v. Nathuram*, JT 1994 (4) SC 164, pp. 170, 171 : (1994) 4 SCC 250 (para 16). **See further** *CIT v. Ajanta Electricals*, 1995 (3) Scale 337 : 1995 AIR SCW 3378 : (1995) 4 SCC 182 : AIR 1995 SC 2172. (A Form prescribed by rules used for interpreting section 139(2) of the Income-tax Act, 1961).

62. *CIT (Agr.), W.B. v. Keshab Chandra Mandal*, AIR 1950 SC 265 : 1950 SCR 435.

63. **See** *Banarsi Das v. Cane Commissioner, U.P.*, AIR 1963 SC 1417, p. 1425 : 1963 Supp (2) SCR 760 and other cases **referred** to therein. **See further** *Virji Ram Sutaria v. Nathalal Premji Bhanvadia* AIR 1970 SC 765, pp. 767, 768 : 1969 (1) SCC 77; *Maharashtra State Road Transport Corporation v. Babu Goverdhan Regular Motor Service, Warora*, AIR 1970 SC 1926, pp. 1932, 1933 : 1969 (2) SCC 746; *Megna Mills Co. Ltd. v. Ashoka Marketing Ltd.*, AIR 1971 SC 166, p. 170 : 1970 (3) SCC 168; *Shere Punjab Silk Stores, Delhi v. CIT, Delhi*, AIR 1973 SC 2401, p. 2405 (para 4) : 1973 SCC (Tax) 437 : (1973) 4 SCC 206.

authority to prescribe by rules particulars of an application, the authority may be exercised by prescribing a form of application which indicates the particulars.[64] But a form prescribed under the Rules can never have any effect on the interpretation or operation of the parent statute.[65]

12. TRANSITIONAL PROVISION

At times a statute contains a transitional provision which enacts as to how the statute will operate on the facts and circumstances existing on the date it comes into operation.[66] However, "it is not possible to give a definitive description of what constitutes a transitional provision".[67] Therefore, the construction of such a provision must depend upon its own terms.[68] "One feature of a transitional provision is that its operation is expected to be temporary, in that it becomes spent when all the past circumstances with which it is designed to deal have been dealt with although it may be envisaged that that could take a considerable period of time while the primary legislation continues to deal indefinitely with the new circumstances which arise after its passage."[69] Section 30 of the Land Acquisition (Amendment) Act, 1984 is one such provision which enacts as to what extent the new provisions will apply to proceedings pending on the commencement of the Amending Act or in other words as to how far the new provisions which amended substantive provisions of the parent Act are retrospective.[70] The statute may, instead of itself enacting a provision as to how the new provisions in the statute will apply to existing facts and circumstances, leave this to be laid down by delegated legislation to be made under the statute.[71] A transitory provision may also be of the nature that it remains in force till the main provisions of the statute come into operation.[72]

---

64. *Maharashtra State Road Transport Corporation v. Babu Goverdhan Regular Motor Service, Warora*, AIR 1970 SC 1926, p. 1932 : 1969 (2) SCC 746.
65. *Commissioner of Income Tax v. Tulsyan NEC Ltd.*, (2011) 2 SCC 1 para 20 : (2010) 13 SCALE 460.
66. *Britnell v. Secretary of State for Social Security*, (1991) 2 All ER 726, p. 730 (HL).
67. *Ibid.*
68. *Milkfood Ltd. v. GMC Icecream (P.) Ltd.*, (2004) 7 SCC 288, p. 327 (**Reference** is made to 8th Edn., p. 188 of this book).
69. *Britnell v. Secretary of State for Social Security, supra.*
70. *K.S. Paripoornan v. State of Kerala*, JT 1994 (6) SC 182, p. 216 : AIR 1995 SC 1012, pp. 1035, 1036 : (1994) 5 SCC 593 : (1994) 2 KLT 763.
71. It was such a provision with which the House of Lords was concerned in the case of *Britnell v. Secretary of State for Social Security, supra.*
72. **See** Ninth Schedule to the Government of India Act, 1935.

CHAPTER 4

EXTERNAL AIDS TO CONSTRUCTION

SYNOPSIS

Apart from the statute itself there are many matters which may be taken into account for construing it especially when the statute is ambiguous. These matters are called external aids. They are discussed below. The Law Commission in its 183rd report recommended that the rules of admissibility of external aids can neither be codified nor be included in the General Clauses Act, 1897.

1. PARLIAMENTARY HISTORY

(a) English practice

(i) *Traditional view.*—According to the traditional English view "the 'intent of the Parliament which passed the Act', is not to be gathered from the parliamentary history of the statute".[1] A Bill in its original form,[2] or the amendments considered during its progress in the Legislature,[3] are not admissible aids to construction. The language of a minister of the Crown in proposing in Parliament a measure which eventually becomes law is inadmissible;[4] and the same rule applies to the reports of the debates and to the resolutions passed by either House of Parliament.[5] Recommendations contained in the report of a Royal Commission which may have led to the introduction of the measure in Parliament cannot be used as evidence for the purpose of showing the intention—that is the purpose or object of the Act.[6]

Since the Courts are entitled to consider such external or historical facts as may be necessary to understand the subject-matter to which the statute

---

1. *A.G. v. HRH Prince Ernest Augustus of Hanover*, (1957) 1 All ER 49, p. 61 : 1957 AC 436 (HL) (LORD SOMERVELL OF HARROW); *London Borough of Ealing v. Race Relations Board*, (1972) 1 All ER 105, p. 114 (HL) (LORD SIMON).
2. *Herron v. Rathmines & Rathgar Improvment Commrs.*, (1892) AC 498, p. 502 (HL).
3. *Viscountess Rhondda's Claim*, (1922) 2 AC 339, pp. 383, 390 (HL).
4. *Assam Railways & Trading Co. Ltd. v. IRC*, (1935) AC 445; (1934) All ER Rep 646, p. 655 (HL); (LORD WRIGHT); **referred** to in *Magor & St. Mellons R.D.C. v. Newport Corporation*, (1951) 2 All ER 839, p. 841 : 1952 AC 189 (HL), same rule applies to recommendations of a committee, **see** *Letang v. Cooper*, (1964) 2 All ER 929, p. 933 : (1965) 1 QB 232 (CA) (LORD DENNING, M.R.); *Central Asbestos Co. Ltd. v. Dodd*, (1972) 2 All ER 1135, pp. 1138, 1139 (HL) (LORD REID). In *Lucy v. W.T. Henleys Telegraph Works*, (1969) 3 All ER 456, pp. 465, 466 (CA). EDMUND DAVIES, L.J., referred to the report of "the committee on Limitation of Actions in cases of personal injury" of which he himself was the President and admitted that the unfortunate result reached by him on the construction of the Limitation Act, 1963, was not contemplated by the Committee or possibly by the sponsors of the Bill during its passage in Parliament, but he said that, that consideration was irrelevant as the law was to be found not in reports but in statutes.
5. *Hollinshead v. Hazleton*, (1914-15) All ER Rep 1117, p. 1121: (1916) 1 AC 428 (HL) (LORD ATKINSON). In *Beswick v. Beswick*, (1967) 2 All ER 1197, p. 1202 (HL) LORD REID said: "For purely practical reasons, we do not permit debates in either House to be cited; it would add greatly to the time and expense involved in preparing cases involving the construction of a statute if counsel were expected to read all the debates in Hansard, and it would often be impracticable for counsel to get it"; *Davis v. Johnson*, (1978) 1 All ER 1132 (HL), Hansard can never be relied on; **Reaffirmed** in *Hadmore Productions Ltd. v. Hamilton*, (1982) 1 All ER 1042, p. 1053 : (1983) 1 AC 191 (HL).
6. **See** note 4, *supra*.

relates,[7] or to have regard to the mischief which the statute is intended to remedy,[8] the exclusionary rule was relaxed to admit the reports of the commissions preceding a statutory measure as evidence of 'surrounding circumstances'[9] with reference to which the words in the statute are used. LORD HALSBURY, L.C., admitted the report of a Commission that had been set to inquire into the working of an earlier Act, which had been superseded by the Act construed by him, and observed: "No more accurate source of information as to what was the evil or defect which the Act of Parliament now under construction was intended to remedy could be imagined than the report of that Commission".[10] LORD ATKIN in delivering the opinion of the Privy Council in an appeal from Canada, referred to the report of a Royal Commission as "indicating the materials which the Government of the province (Ontario) had before them before promoting in the Legislature the statute" in question.[11] In an appeal from Ceylon, LORD OAKSEY observed: "It is in their Lordships' opinion the correct view, that judicial notice ought to be taken of such matters as the reports of parliamentary commissions, and of such other facts as must be assumed to have been within the contemplation of the Legislature when the Acts in question were passed".[12] Similarly, it is legitimate to look at the report of a committee leading to a legislation so as to see what was the mischief at which the Act was directed.[13] In dealing with the Law of Property Act, 1925, LORD UPJOHN considered the proceedings of the joint committee of both Houses on consolidation bills not for construing the Act but to see whether the weight of the presumption that a consolidation Act does not alter the existing law was weakened by anything that took place in those proceedings.[14] The House of Lords in *Black-Clawsan International Ltd. v. Papierwerke Waldhof-Aschaffenburg, A.G.*,[15] unanimously held that the report of a committee presented to parliament preceding the legislation could be seen for finding out the then state of the law and the mischief

---

7. LORD LANGDALE'S judgment of Privy Council in *Gorham's* case reported by EF MOORE, (1852) ED, p. 462; referred to in *R. v. West Riding of Yorkshire County Council*, (1906) 2 KB 676, p. 717 (FARWELL, L.J.) and **approved** in *Assam Railways v. IRC*, (1934) All ER Rep 646, p. 655 (HL).
8. **See** Chapter 2, title 3(b) "Rule in *Heydon's* case", p. 137.
9. *Assam Railways v. IRC*, (1934) All ER Rep 646, p. 655 (HL).
10. *Eastman Photographic Materials Co. v. Comptroller-General of Patents, Designs and Trade Marks*, (1898) AC 571, p. 576 : 67 LJ Ch 628 (HL). **Referred** to in *Assam Railways v. IRC*, (1934) All ER Rep 646, p. 655 (HL).
11. *Ladore v. Benett*, (1939) 3 All ER 98, p. 101 : 1939 AC 468 (PC).
12. *Govindan Pillai v. Punchi Banda Mudanayake*, (1955) 2 All ER 833, p. 837 (PC).
13. *Letang v. Cooper*, (1964) 2 All ER 929, p. 933 : (1965) 1 QB 232 (CA); *Comdel Commodities Ltd. v. Siporex Trade, S.A.*, (1990) 2 All ER 552, p. 557 (HL).
14. *Beswick v. Beswick*, (1967) 2 All ER 1197, p. 1223 : (1968) AC 58 (HL).
15. *Black-Clawsan International Ltd. v. Papierwerke Waldhof-Aschaffenburg, A.G.* (1975) 1 All ER 810 (HL).

required to be remedied. The majority[16] (LORD REID, LORD WILBERFORCE and LORD DIPLOCK), however, held that the report could not be looked at for finding out the intention of Parliament, *i.e.*, for a direct statement of what the proposed enactment meant even though the report set out a draft bill which was enacted without any alteration. The minority[17] (VISCOUNT DILHORNE and LORD SIMON) were of the view that when the draft bill was enacted without any alteration, it was Parliament's intention to do what the committee recommended and to achieve the object the committee had in mind, and therefore, the committee's observations on the draft bill would form the most valuable guide to the intention of Parliament. Following the majority view it has been held that while considering an Act passed to give effect to a scheme formulated at a commonwealth law ministers conference, the scheme could be looked at to see the mischief in need of a remedy and the steps proposed to effectuate the remedy[18] and a white paper preceding a legislation can be used for the same purpose.[19]

Regulations made under the European Communities Act, 1972 to give effect to the directives of the Council of European Communities have been construed consistent with the directives by taking recourse to the legislative history and by giving to the regulations a purposive construction and if necessary by reading or implying words which are not there.[20] In *Pickstone's* case[21] reference was made to proceedings in Parliament and to the speech of the minister as indicative of the intention of Parliament in approving the regulations which were made under the European Communities Act, 1972 to give effect to the ruling by the Court of Justice of the

---

16. *Ibid.*, pp. 814, 815 (LORD REID); p. 828 (LORD WILBERFORCE); p. 835 (LORD DIPLOCK). The objection to the reading the report as direct evidence of intention of Parliament is based partly on the constitutional function of courts to interpret the law. This function which is essential part of the rule of law—as distinct from the rule of the King (*i.e.* Executive) or the rule of Parliament, would suffer degradation if the courts were merely a reflecting mirror of what some other interpretation agency might say.

17. *Ibid*, p. 823 (VISCOUNT DILHORNE); p. 847 (LORD SIMON): "It is refusing to follow what is perhaps the most important clue to meaning. It is perversely neglecting the reality, while chasing shadows." The minority view has been followed in India by the Supreme Court: *R.S. Nayak v. A.R. Antulay*, (1984) 2 SCC 183, pp. 214, 215 : AIR 1984 SC 684.

18. *Government of Canada v. Aronson*, (1989) 2 All ER 1025, p. 1039 (HL). **See further** *Owens Bank Ltd. v. Bracco*, (1992) 2 All ER 193, p. 202 (1) : (1992) 2 AC 443 : (1992) 2 WLR 621 (HL) [Report of a committee used for removing any doubt as to the construction of section 9(2)(d) of the Administration of Justice Act, 1920].

19. *Attorney-General's Reference* (*No. 1 of 1988*), (1989) 2 All ER 1, p. 6 : (1989) 2 WLR 729 (HL).

20. *Pickstone v. Freemans Plc*, (1988) 2 All ER 803 (HL); *Lister v. Forth Dry Dock and Engineering Co. Ltd.*, (1989) 1 All ER 1134 : (1990) 1 AC 534 (HL).

21. (1988) 2 All ER 803, p. 814 (HL).

European Communities that the United Kingdom failed to fulfill obligations under the EEC treaty. This case thus made a clear departure from the traditional rule that Hansard can never be relied on.[22]

(ii) *Criticism of the traditional view.*—The distinction drawn between the refusal to admit the report of a committee or commission for purpose of finding out 'the intention of Parliament' and its relevance as evidence of 'surrounding circumstances' or as aid to understand the subject-matter to which the statute relates or as indicative of 'the evil or defect which the Act was intended to remedy', is somewhat obscure. It has been referred to as "casuistical".[23] But the English practice continued to make this distinction. In *R. v. Allen,*[24] the House of Lords had occasion to construe section 3(1) of the Theft Act, 1978 which insofar as relevant provides: "A person who knowing that payment on the spot for any goods supplied or services done is required or expected from him dishonestly makes off without having paid as required or expected and with intent to avoid payment of the amount due shall be guilty of an offence". The question before the House of Lords was whether 'intent to avoid payment' required by the section was intent to avoid payment permanently or merely an intent to avoid payment on the spot. The Act was passed in persuance of the Criminal Law Revision Committee's thirteenth report which indicated that the mischief intended to be remedied was to rope in those customers who made off "without having paid and intending never to pay". The report was accompanied by a draft bill, Cl. 3 of which was in terms identical to section 3 of the Act. The House of Lords held that the words 'intent to avoid payment' as used in the Act meant intent to avoid payment permanently. In holding so they observed that they used the Committee's report "for the purpose of defining the mischief to be dealt with by the section"[25] but that in accordance with the present practice they "did not use it as an aid to construction".[26] Many less disciplined will say that this is nothing but quibbling in words. If the key to opening of every law is the reason and the spirit of the law and if a statute is best interpreted when we know why it was enacted[27] then the steps taken for understanding or defining the object of or the mischief intended to be dealt with by the statute are themselves a part of the process for getting its meaning. When the court starts upon the task of interpreting a statute, it is unrealistic and impractical to

22. **See** text and note 5, p. 242.
23. ALLEN: Law in the Making, 7th Edition, p. 519.
24. (1985) 2 All ER 641 : 1985 AC 1029 (HL).
25. *Ibid.*, p. 644.
26. *Ibid.* For another example, **see** *Attorney-General's Reference (No. 1 of 1988)*, (1989) 2 All ER 1 : (1989) 2 WLR 729 (HL) (use of white paper for discerning the mischief but not for getting the meaning of the Act.)
27. **See** Chapter 1, pp. 14 to 18.

divide the exercise into different compartments, *viz.*, one leading to discerning the object or mischief and the other leading to discerning the true meaning of the statute. The exercise in its entirety is one process for discerning the true meaning of the Act or in other words the intention of the Legislature. In a later case *R. v. Burke,*[28] the House of Lords construed section 1(3)(a) of the Protection from Eviction Act, 1977. The section enacts: "If any person with intent to cause the residential occupier of any premises to give up the premises or any part thereof—does acts calculated to interfere with the peace or comfort of the residential occupier—he shall be guilty of an offence." The question before the House of Lords was whether the acts prohibited by the section must involve a civil wrong. The section was reenactment of a provision creating criminal offence of harassment in an Act of 1965 which was enacted in response to the report of the Committee on Housing in Greater London. The report revealed a shocking variety of abuses which could not be brought squarely within the purview either of crime or civil wrong. Having regard essentially to the social evil set out in the report, the House of Lords concluded that Parliament deliberately chose the language not to confine the acts of harassment prohibited by the Act to acts involving a civil wrong. The speech of LORD GRIFFITH which was agreed to by the other Law Lords does not expressly say whether the report of the Committee was used only to discern the mischief or also the intention of Parliament. It is more realistic to say that it was used for both.[29] Reports of Law Commissions preceding a legislation constitute important material for understanding the legislation and it has been acknowledged that a careful reading of such a report would have avoided an erroneous construction which was very soon overruled.[30] Another case showing the importance of Law Commission's report is *R v. G*[31] which overruled an earlier case of the House of Lords where due importance was not given to the Law Commission's report.

Complete exclusion of Hansard and speeches in Parliament was also not always adhered to. Relevant passages were sometimes quoted in textbooks and eminent judges referred to them in their judgments from the textbook.[32] As already seen, proceedings in Parliament and the speech of the minister were admitted for construing a regulation made under the European Communities Act, 1972.[33]

---

28. (1990) 2 All ER 385 (HL).
29. *Ibid.*, p. 389.
30. *R. v. Shivpuri*, (1986) 2 All ER 334, p. 343 (I) : 1987 AC 1 : (1986) 2 WLR 988 (HL).
31. (2003) 4 All ER 765, p. 784 (para 29), p. 788 (para 45) (HL).
32. *R. v. Local Commissioner for Administration*, (1979) 2 All ER 881, pp. 897, 898 : (1979) QB 287 : (1979) 2 WLR 1 (CA) (LORD DENNING).
33. **See** text and note 21, p. 244.

(iii) *Modern trend.*—The school of thought that limited but open use should be made of parliamentary history in construing statutes has been gaining ground.[34] Direct judicial approval of this trend by the House of Lords came in *Pepper v. Hart.*[35] In that case LORD BROWNE WILKINSON who delivered the leading speech which was agreed to by five other law Lords (LORD KEETH, LORD BRIDGE, LORD GRIFFITHS, LORD ACKNER and LORD OLIVER), laid down: "Reference to parliamentary material should be permitted as an aid to the construction of legislation which is ambiguous or obscure or the literal meaning of which leads to absurdity. Even in such cases references in court to parliamentary material should only be permitted where such material clearly discloses the mischief aimed at or the legislative intention lying behind the ambiguous or obscure words. In the case of statements made in Parliament, as at present advised, I cannot foresee that any statement other than the statement of the minister or other promoter of the Bill is likely to meet these criteria."[36] In reaching this conclusion LORD BROWNE WILKINSON reasoned that "the Court cannot attach a meaning to words which they cannot bear, but if the words are capable of bearing more than one meaning why should not Parliament's true intention be enforced."[37] It was pointed out that white papers and official reports could be looked at for finding the mischief and as a ministerial statement made in Parliament was an equally authoritative source of such information there was no reason why the courts be cut off from this source. Stressing the same point it was said: "Clear and unambiguous statements made by ministers in Parliament are as much the background to the enactment of legislation as white papers and parliamentary reports."[38] It was also observed that "the distinction between looking at reports to identify the mischief aimed at but not to find the intention of Parliament in enacting

---

34. *English Law Commission and Scottish Law Commission Recommendations*, (1970) 33 Modern Law Review 197, pp. 198, 199.

"The rule against references to legislative history is no longer so much a 'canon of construction'as 'a counsel of caution'. In other words, it is for courts to consider what weight to give to the materials that emerge from a scrutiny of legislative history rather than automatically to exclude such materials from all considerations as an aid to interpretation." MERRILLAT, 'The Sound Proof Room': A matter of Interpretation, (1967) 9 Journal of the Indian Law Institute, pp. 521, 529, 530.

"No body, so far as I know, has advocated that an unlimited and undefined mass of travaux preparatoires be cast upon the courts, but there are certain alternative sources of information which, it seems somewhat pedantic to withhold from the judicial purview." ALLEN, Law in the Making, 7th Edition, p. 527. **See further** title 1(a)(ii), '*Criticism of the traditional view*', Chapter 4.

35. (1993) 1 All ER 42 : 1993 AC 466 : (1992) 3 WLR 1032 (HL).

36. *Ibid.*, p. 64.

37. *Ibid.*, p. 64.

38. *Ibid.*, p. 65.

the legislation is highly artificial."[39] It was further observed: "Given the purposive approach to construction now adopted by courts in order to give effect to the true intention of the Legislature, the fine distinctions between looking for the mischief and looking for the intention in using words to provide the remedy are technical and inappropriate."[40] As regards the objection that parliamentary materials are not readily available it was pointed out that the experience in New Zealand and Australia (where the strict rule has been relaxed for some years) has not shown that the non-availability of materials has raised any practical problem.[41] There was also an objection that recourse to parliamentary material will be questioning the freedom of speech and debates in Parliament. Rejecting this objection, it was observed that "far from questioning the independence of Parliament and its debates, the courts would be giving effect to what is said and done there."[42]

The appeal in *Pepper's* case before the House of Lords was by tax-payers who were teachers in a school. Under a scheme of the school the members of the staff were entitled to have their children educated at the school on payment of only one-fifth of the normal fee chargeable from members of the public. "Cash equivalent of this benefit" was chargeable to income-tax under section 61(1) of the Finance Act, 1976. The concessionary fees more than covered the additional cost to the school of educating the tax-payers' children. By section 63(1) cash equivalent of the benefit meant "an amount equal to the cost of the benefit" and by section 63(2) cost of the benefit meant "the amount of any expense incurred in or in connection with its provision." The crucial question in the case was the true meaning of section 63(2), *i.e.*, whether the words "the amount of any expense incurred in or in connection with its provision" referred to the actual expense incurred by the school in providing the benefit or whether they referred to the hypothetical expense incurred by the school arrived at by the formula of dividing the total cost of running the school by the number of pupils attending it; or to put it more shortly did they refer to the additional cost or the average cost of the provision of the benefit. The tax-payers contended for acceptance of the former construction and the revenue for the latter. The tax-payers' case was that all the cost of running the school generally would have had to be incurred in any event and the small additional or marginal cost to the school caused by the presence of their children was fully covered by the concessional fees that they paid, so the "cash equivalent of the benefit" was nil as no extra expense was incurred in or in connection with its provision within the meaning of section 63(2).

39. *Ibid.*, p. 65.
40. *Ibid.*, p. 65.
41. *Ibid.*, p. 66.
42. *Ibid.*, p. 67.

The House of Lords found section 63(2) ambiguous. Reference was, therefore, made to the parliamentary history and statements made by the Financial Secretary to the Treasury during committee stage of the Bill which showed clearly that Parliament had passed the legislation with the intention that the concessionary benefits for teacher's children would be worked out on the additional or marginal cost to the employers and not on the average cost. The construction contended for by the taxpayers was on this basis upheld.

The rule permitting admissibility of parliamentary material to resolve an ambiguity in interpretation of a statute as laid down in *Pepper's* case was followed in quick succession as decisive of statutory ambiguity in *Warwickshire County Council v. Johnson*;[43] *Stubbings v. Webb*[44] and *Chief Adjudication Officer v. Foster*.[45] Adverting to this fact in *Foster's* case LORD BRIDGE observed: "The significance of this—is to illustrate how useful the relaxation of the former exclusionary rule may be in avoiding unnecessary litigation. Certainly in this case, if it had been possible to take account of the parliamentary material at the outset, it would have been clear that it refuted the appellant's contention and there would probably never have been any appeal to the Commissioner, let alone beyond him. I doubt if any of us who were party to the decision in *Pepper v. Hart* anticipated that within so short a time after it Hansard would be found to provide the answer in three other cases before the House. But this encourages the hope that as time passes, the effect of the new rule will be to prevent or to curtail much litigation relating to ambiguous statutory provisions which would otherwise be fought through the courts."[46]

A word of caution was later added by the House of Lords that the new rule should not be misused and that under this rule "the only materials which can properly be introduced are clear statements made by a minister or other promoters of the Bill directed to the very point in question in the

---

43. (1993) 1 All ER 299 (HL).

44. (1993) 1 All ER 322 : (1993) AC 498 (HL), this case has been **overruled** on other grounds in *A. v. Hoare,* (2008) 2 All ER 1.

45. (1993) 1 All ER 705 : 1993 AC 54 (HL).

46. *Ibid.*, p. 717. **See further** DAWN OLIVER, 'Statutory Interpretation and the Intention of Parliament 1 Law and Justice (Inaugural Journal of United Lawyers Association), p. 197; *Director of Public Prosecutions v. Bull*, (1994) 4 All ER 411, pp. 415, 416 (The Report which led to the enactment of the Street Offences Act, 1959 was relied upon for limiting the words 'common prostitute' to females. It was also noted that reference to debates on the authority of *Pepper v. Hart* would also have led to the same conclusion); *R v. Secretary of State for the Environment,* (2000) 1 All ER 884, pp. 899, 900 (CA) (Speeches admitted for construing the Landlord and Tenant Act, 1985). **See also** *Practice Note,* (1995) 1 All ER 234 (Party intending to refer to Hansard has to serve copies of the relevant extract on all other parties and the court together with a brief summary of the argument to be based upon such extract).

litigation."[47] It was again emphasised that the conditions mentioned in *Pepper v. Hart* must be strictly satisfied before reference can be made to speeches in Parliament for interpretation or in other words reference to Parliamentary speeches can be made only where the legislation is ambiguous, obscure or its literal meaning leads to an absurdity.[48] LORD NICHOLAS in that case said that Parliamentary material admitted as an external aid on the fulfilment of conditions laid down in *Pepper v. Hart* constitute "as part of the legislative background but they are no more than this"; they "cannot control the meaning" and their "weight will depend on all the circumstances."[49] Further, LORD BINGHAM and LORD HOPE in the same case observed that when ambiguity relates to the scope of a discretionary power a categorical assurance by the Minister that the power would not be used in a particular situation may alone be admissible.[50] LORD NICHOLAS reiterated his views as quoted above in a later case which related to question of compatibility.[51] LORD STEYN, extra judicially,[52] has been critical of *Pepper v. Hart.* According to him its application should be confined to its use against the executive when it appeared to be going back on an assurance given in Parliament, *i.e.,* to a type of estoppel.[49] Similar views were expressed by LORD HOPE in *Wilson v. First Council Trust Ltd.,*[53] However, LORD STEYN in delivering the leading speech in *Lesotho Highlands Development Authority v. Impregilo SPA*[54] made extensive reference to the speech of LORD WILBERFORCE during the second reading of the Bill in the House of Lords for interpreting the Arbitration Act, 1996. It is also doubtful if *Pepper v. Hart* can be used to extend the ambit of a criminal statute which is ambiguous for it is arguable that if a criminal statute is ambiguous the defendant should have the benefit of the ambiguity.[55]

---

47. *Melluish (Inspector of Taxes) v. BMI (No. 3) Ltd.*, (1995) 4 All ER 453, p. 468 : (1996) AC 454 : (1995) 3 WLR 630 (HL). **See further** *Secretary of State for Social Security v. Remilien*, (1998) 1 All ER 129, pp. 146, 147 (HL) (One of the conditions for admissibility is that the statement must be clear).

48. *R. v. Secretary of State for the Environment exparte Spath Holme,* (2001) 1 All ER 195 (HL). **See further** *R. (National Grid Gas plc) v. Environment Agency*, (2007) 3 All ER 877, p. 885(e) (H.L.) (*Pepper v. Hart* is no authority for recourse to Hansard in order to alter plain and unambiguous statutory language).

49. *Ibid.*, p. 218.

50. *Ibid.*, pp. 211, 212, 227.

51. *Wilson v. First County Trust Ltd.*, (2003) 4 All ER 97, pp. 116, 117.

52. *'Pepper v. Hart, A Re-examination'*, (2001) 2J OJ LS 59; **Referred** by LORD STEYN in *R (on the application of Westminister City Council) v. National Asylum Support Service,* (2002) 4 All ER 654, p. 657 (J) (HL). **See further,** LORD PHILLIPS, Keating Lecture (10-10-2001); *Aileen Kavanagh, 'Pepper v. Hart and Matters of Constitutional Principle'*, (2005) 121 LAW QUARTERLY, Review, p. 98.

53. *Supra.* p. 130 para 113 (H.L.).

54. (2005) 3 All ER 789 paras 18, 19 (H.L.)

55. *Thet v. Director of Public Prosecutions*, (2007) 2 All ER 425 (QBD) para 15 (LORD PHILLIPS CJ).

A minister's speech admissible under the rule laid down in *Pepper v. Hart* will not be ruled out of consideration on the ground that it is expressed to be based on the advice of the Attorney-General for ministers' act on advice and "it cannot make any difference whether or not the source of the advice is made explicit".[56]

Relevant publicly available contextual material, *e.g.*, reports of Law Commissions and Law Revision Committees, are readily admitted in aid of the construction of statutes; but the court cannot delve into the intention of individual members of the commission or committee and will not admit their communications as aid to construction.[57]

Explanatory notes issued by the departments concerned before a Bill is introduced in Parliament, though not forming part of the Bill, may also be admitted in so far as they cast light on the objective setting or contextual scene of the statute, and the mischief at which it is aimed.[58] A clear assurance by the executive to Parliament contained in explanatory notes that a power will or will not be used in certain circumstances may be used against the executive in proceedings where the executive places a contrary contention before the court.[59] Explanatory notes issued on the Act following its receipt of the Royal assent have also been similarly admitted as aid to construction.[60] A more flexible approach may be needed while construing a statute enacted to give effect to an international convention.[61]

(b) American practice

In contrast to the traditional English practice, under the American practice the old rule of exclusion of parliamentary history has been very much relaxed. Although it is generally accepted that "debates in Congress are

---

56. *R. v. Secretary of State for Foreign and Commonwealth Affairs*, (1994) 1 All ER 457, p. 466 : 1994 QB 552 : (1994) 2 WLR 115 (QBD).

57. *R v. Hinks,* (2000) 4 All ER 833, p. 839 (HL). **See further** *I v. Director of Public Prosecutions,* (2001) 2 All ER 583, p. 592 (HL) [Law Commission's report accepted in White Paper (Review of Public Order Law) preceding enactment of the Public Order Act 1986 used for interpreting the definition of 'affray' in section 3(1)].

58. *R (on the application of Westminister City Council) v. National Asylum Support Service,* (2002) 4 All ER 654, p. 657 (HL); *R (on the application of S) v. Chief Constable of South Yorkshire*, (2004) 4 All ER 193, p. 198 (HL). **See further** *R. v. Montila*, (2005) 1 All ER 113, p. 124 (para 35) (HL); *Serious Fraud Office v. King,* (2009) 2 All ER 223 (H.L.) para 33.

59. *R (on the application of West Minister City Council) v. National Asylum Support Service, supra.*

60. Attorney General's Reference (No. 5 of 2002) : (2004) 4 All ER 901, p. 913 (para 21) (HL).

61. *Three Rivers District Council v. Bank of England (No. 2)*, (1996) 2 All ER 363. **See further** title 5(b2) '*Acts passed to give effect to international treaties and conventions*', Chapter 6.

not appropriate or even reliable guides to the meaning of the language of an enactment",[62] it has been held that the said rule "is not violated by resorting to debates as a means of ascertaining the environment at the time of enactment of particular law, that is, the history of the period when it was adopted."[63] Further, it appears to have been well accepted that "the reports of a committee, including the bill as introduced, changes made in the frame of the bill in the course of its passage and the statement made by the committee chairman in charge of it, stand upon a different footing, and may be resorted to under proper qualifications".[64]

It is easy to find opponents and supporters of these views. Some critics even in America feel that recourse to legislative history "is a badly overdone practice of dubious help to true interpretation".[65] It has been characterised as "the custom of re-making statutes to fit their histories", and it has been pointed out that the practice "poses serious practical problems for a large part of legal profession". The formal Act "is no longer a safe basis on which a lawyer may advise his client" and he "must consult all of the committee reports on the bill, and all its antecedents, and all that its supporters and opponents said in debate, and then predict what part of the conflicting views will likely appeal to a majority of the court".[66] Further, it is pointed out that "the most unfortunate consequence of resort to legislative history is that it introduces the policy controversies that generated the Act into the deliberations of the Court".[67] Prof. Reed Dickerson after analysing the uses and abuses of legislative history concludes that "the more realistic approach to legislative history would be to end or severely limit its judicial use".[68] On the other hand, those who favour the liberal use of legislative materials for purposes of construction say that "the meaning of the words of a statute be resolved in the light of their setting in the legislative process rather than in the light of the intuition of the judge".[69]

---

62. *United States v. St. Paul, M. & M. Rly. Co.*, 62 Law Ed 1130, p. 1134, where reference is made to *United States v. Trans-Missouri Freight Association*, 41 Law Ed 1007, p. 1020.

63. *Standard Oil Co. of New Jersey v. United States*, 55 Law Ed 619, p. 641. **See further** *Federal Trade Commission v. Raladam Co.*, 75 Law Ed 1324 (Debates admissible to see the purpose of the Act and the evils sought to be remedied).

64. *United States v. St. Paul, M. & M. Rly. Co.*, 62 Law Ed 1130, p. 1134. **See further** *Duplex Printing Press Co. v. Emil J. Deering*, 65 Law Ed 349 : 254 US 443, p. 474; *Robert Page Wright v. Vinton Branch of Mountain Trust Bank*, 300 US 440, p. 463.

65. JACKSON, The Meaning of Statutes: What Congress says or what the court says, (1948) 34 ABAJ 535, collected in 'Cases and Materials on Legislation' by HORRACK, 2nd Edition, pp. 1029 and 1030.

66. *Ibid.*

67. *Ibid.*

68. REED DICKERSON, The Interpretation and Application of Statutes, p. 195.

69. Legislative Materials to aid Statutory Constructions, 50 Harvard Law Review, 822.

According to this view a liberal use of legislative material is one of the modern efforts "so that judicial law-making under the guise of interpretation may be reduced to its necessary minimum".[70]

It will appear that a wholesale exclusion of parliamentary history as also a wholesale inclusion thereof are both extremes equally open to objections, and the correct solution lies in finding out a middle course as now adopted by the House of Lords.[71]

(c) Indian view

The Supreme Court, speaking generally, to begin with, enunciated the rule of exclusion of Parliamentary history in the way it was traditionally enunciated by the English Courts, but on many an occasion, the court used this aid in resolving questions of construction. The court has now veered to the view that legislative history within circumspect limits may be consulted by courts in resolving ambiguities.[72] But the court still sometimes, like the English courts, makes a distinction between use of a material for finding the mischief dealt with by the Act and its use for finding the meaning of the Act.[73] As submitted earlier this distinction is unrealistic[74] and has now been abandoned by the House of Lords.[75]

Indeed, the basis for the rigid view had already been laid by the Privy Council. LORD WATSON, in delivering the opinion of the Judicial Committee, in an appeal which related to the Administrator General's Act, 1874, differing from the High Court, observed: "Their Lordships observe that the two learned Judges who constituted the majority in the Appellate Court, although they do not base their judgments upon them, refer to the proceedings of the Legislature which resulted in the passing of the Act of 1874 as legitimate aids to the construction of section 31. Their Lordships think it right to express their dissent from that proposition. The same reasons which exclude these considerations when the clauses of an Act of the

---

70. *Ibid.*

71. **See** title 1(a)(iii) 'Modern trend'.

72. *State of Mysore v. R.V. Bidop*, AIR 1973 SC 2555 : (1973) 2 SCC 547; *Fagu Shaw v. State of W.B.*, AIR 1974 SC 613, p. 628, 629 : (1974) 4 SCC (Cri) 316 : 1974 SCC 152; *Union of India v. Sankalchand*, AIR 1977 SC 2328, p. 2373 : (1977) 4 SCC 193 : 1977 SCC (Lab) 435; *R. S. Nayak v. A.R. Antulay*, (1984) 2 SCC 183, pp. 214, 215 : AIR 1984 SC 684; *B. Prabhakar Rao v. State of Andhra Pradesh*, AIR 1986 SC 210, p. 215 : 1985 Supp SCC 432; *Sub-Committee of Judicial Accountability v. Union of India*, AIR 1992 SC 320, p. 366 : (1991) 4 SCC 699.

73. For example **see** *Shashikant Laxman Kale v. Union of India*, AIR 1990 SC 2114, pp. 2119, 2120 : (1990) 4 SCC 366 : (1990) 4 SCC 366.

74. **See** pp. 216 to 217.

75. **See** text and notes 38, 39, p. 225.

British Legislature are under construction, are equally cogent in the case of an Indian statute."[76] So it was held that speeches made by the members of the Constituent Assembly in the course of the debates on the draft Constitution cannot be admitted as extrinsic aid to the construction of the Constitution,[77] and similarly the debates in Parliament on a Bill are not admissible for construction of the Act which is ultimately enacted.[78] The reason of the rule was explained by PATANJALI SHASTRI, J. in *Gopalan's* case,[79] which he subsequently affirmed as Chief Justice in delivering the opinion of the court in *State of Trav.-Co. v. Bombay Co. Ltd.*,[80] in the following words: "A speech made in the course of the debate on a bill could at best be indicative of the subjective intent of the speaker, but it could not reflect the inarticulate mental process lying behind the majority vote which carried the Bill. Nor is it reasonable to assume that the minds of all those legislators were in accord". "A statute", said SINHA, C.J.I., "is the expression of the collective intention of the Legislature as a whole and any statement made by an individual, albeit a minister, of the intention and object of the Act, cannot be used to cut down the generality of the words used in the statute".[81] FAZL ALI, J. however in *Chiranjitlal's* case[82] admitted parliamentary history including the speech of the minister introducing the bill as evidence of "the circumstances which necessitated" the passing of the Act, a course apparently approved in a later decision.[83] In *Gopalan's* case[84] KANIA, C.J.I., was of the view that the debates can be referred to, to show that the use of a particular word was up for consideration at all or not.The rigid view was slowly given up in subsequent cases. Reference to debates

---

76. *Administrator General of Bengal v. Premlal Mullick*, ILR 22 Cal 788, pp. 799, 800 (PC); **see further** *Krishna Ayyangar v. Nallaperumal Pillai*, ILR 43 Mad 550, pp. 564, 565 (PC).

77. *State of Trav.-Co. v. Bombay Co. Ltd.*, AIR 1952 SC 366, pp. 368, 369 : 1952 SCR 1112.

78. *Aswini Kumar Ghose v. Arabinda Bose*, AIR 1952 SC 369, p. 378 : 1953 SCR 1; *K.S. Paripoornan v. State of Kerala*, JT 1994 (6) SC 182, p. 220 : AIR 1995 SC 1012 : (1994) 5 SCC 593.

79. *A.K. Gopalan v. State of Madras*, AIR 1950 SC 27, p. 73 : 1950 SCR 88.

80. AIR 1952 SC 366, p. 369; also **see** *Gopalan's* case, *supra*.

81. *State of West Bengal v. Union of India*, AIR 1963 SC 1241, p. 1247 : 1964 (1) SCR 371.

82. *Chiranjit Lal Chowdhury v. Union of India*, AIR 1951 SC 41, pp. 45, 46 : 1950 SCR 869.

83. *A. Thangal Kunju Musaliar v. M. Venkatachalam Potti*, AIR 1956 SC 246, p. 265 : 1955 (2) SCR 1196. **See further** *State of Gujarat v. Shyamlal Mohanlal*, AIR 1965 SC 1251, p. 1255 : 1965 (2) Cr LJ 256 (PER SHAH, J., **dissenting**; use of speech in Legislature to ascertain the 'historical setting'); *Narendra Kumar Maheshwari v. Union of India*, AIR 1989 SC 2138, p. 2163 : 1989 (2) JT 338 (use of debates to ascertain the purpose of the Bill); *Karnataka Small Scale Industries Development Corporation Ltd. v. Commissioner of Income-Tax,* (2003) 7 SCC 224, p. 231 : (2002) 10 JT 41 (Reference to Finance Minister's Speech to ascertain the purpose of section 115-J of the Income-Tax Act, 1961).

84. AIR 1950 SC 27, p. 38 : 1950 SCR 88.

in the Constituent Assembly was made to support a narrow construction of Article 16(3) of the Constitution in *A.V.S. Narasimha Rao v. State of Andhra Pradesh,*[85] and in *Union of India v. Harbhajan Singh Dhillon,*[86] extensive references were made to speeches in the Constituent Assembly to support the construction that wealth-tax on net wealth including capital value of agricultural lands falls within the residuary power of Parliament. In *Indira Sawhney v. Union of India,*[87] while interpreting Article 16(4) of the Constitution the Supreme Court referred to Dr. Ambedkar's speech in the Constituent Assembly and observed: "That the debates in the Constituent Assembly can be relied upon as an aid to interpretation of a Constitition provision is borne out by a series of decisions of this court. Since the expression backward class of citizens' is not defined in the Constitution, reference to such debates is permissible to ascertain at any rate the context, background and objective behind them. Particularly where the court wants to ascertain the 'original intent' such reference may be unavoidable."[88] The court, however, earlier clarified that the debates or even the speech of Dr. Ambedkar could not be taken as conclusive or binding on the court.[89] While interpreting Article 28(1) of the Constitution, which prohibits 'religious instructions' in educational institutions maintained wholly out of state funds, reference was made to the debates in the constituent assembly which were said to be "illuminating and helpful" in

---

85. AIR 1970 SC 422, p. 425 : 1969 (1) SCC 839. **See further** *Ajit Singh v. The State of Punjab,* JT 1999 (7) SC 153, p. 172 : (1999) 7 SCC 209 : AIR 1999 SC 3471 where speech of Dr. Ambedkar was referred for supporting a narrow construction of Article 16(4) so that the affirmative discrimination does not lead to reverse discrimination and the reservation does not destroy the equality of opportunity rule in Article 16(1).

86. AIR 1972 SC 1061, pp. 1071 to 1074 : (1971) 2 SCC 779. **See further** *Fagu Shaw v. State of W.B.*, AIR 1974 SC 613, pp. 628, 629 : (1974) 4 SCC 152 (use of debates by BHAGWATI, J. for construing Article 22); *Builders Association of India v. Union of India*, AIR 1982 SC 1737, p. 1736 (Dr. Ambedkar's speech referred to in the context of Article 286 of the Constitution); *Sub-Committee of Judicial Accountability v. Union of India*, AIR 1992 SC 320, pp. 340, 342 : 1991 (4) SCC 699 (Use of Constituent Assembly Debates and speech of Sir Alladi Krishnaswami Ayyar for interpreting Article 124 of the Constitution); *Marri Chandra Shekhar Rao v. Dean Seth G.S. Medical College*, 1990 (3) SCC 13 (Use of Dr. Amedkar's speech for interpreting Articles 341 and 342 of the Constitution); *T.N. Seshan, Chief Election Commissioner v. Union of India*, 1995 (4) Scale 285 : 1995 (4) SCC 611 (speeches in Constituent Assembly used for interepreting Article 324); *Balaji Raghavan v. Union of India*, AIR 1996 SC 770, pp. 774 to 776 : (1996) 1 SCC 361 (Extensive use of committee discussion and report and debates in the Constituent Assembly in interpreting Article 18 of the Constitution.) *State of Maharashtra v. Milind,* AIR 2001 SC 303, p. 401 : (2001) 1 SCC 4 (Reference to the speech of Dr. Ambedkar in Constituent Assembly for construing Articles 341 and 342 of the Constitution).

87. AIR 1993 SC 477 : 1992 (6) JT 273 : 1992 Supp (3) SCC 217.

88. *Ibid.*, p. 551.

89. *Ibid.*

giving a restricted meaning to the expression 'religious instructions' and in holding that what the Article prohibits is "teaching of customs, ways of worship practices and rituals" and not study of different religions existing in India and outside India.[90] It is now a settled view that debates in the Constituent Assembly may be relied upon to interpret a provision in the Constitution.[91] Debates in the House on a Constitution Amendment Bill can also be referred to for the same purpose. Debates were thus used to hold that para 7 of the Tenth Schedule to the Constitution inserted by the Constitution (52nd Amendment) Act, 1985 was enacted with the object to bar the jurisdiction of the Supreme Court and High Courts under Articles 136, 226 and 227 of the Constitution and required ratification under the proviso to Article 368(2) of the Constitution and was ineffective.[92]

Parliamentary Debates were also relied on by the Supreme Court while interpreting provisions of the Patents Act, 1970. Section 2(1)(j) of the Patents Act, 1970, defines 'invention' to mean a new product or process involving an inventive step and capable of industrial application and section 2(ja) defines 'inventive step' to mean a feature of an invention that involves technical advance as compared to the existing knowledge or having economic significance or both and that makes the invention not obvious to a person skilled in the art. By an amendment to the Act effective from 1.1.2005, it was *inter alia* provided in section 3(d) of the Act that the mere discovery of a new form of a known substance which does not result in the enhancement of the known efficacy of that substance would not be an invention and also added an explanation to section 3(d). The Supreme Court referred to the Parliamentary Debates preceding the 2005 amendment and noted that the amendment to section 3(d) was the only provision cited by the Government to allay the fears of the Opposition concerning the abuses

---

90. *Aruna Roy v. Union of India,* AIR 2002 SC 3176, p. 3199 : (2002) 7 SCC 368. **See further** *DAV College v. State of Punjab*, (1971) 2 SCC 269 : AIR 1971 SC 1737 (To provide for academic study of life and teaching or the philosophy and culture of any great saint of India, Guru Nanak in this case, in relation to its impact on the Indian and World Civilization cannot be considered as making provision for religious instructions); *Santosh Kumar v. Secretary Ministry of Human Resources*, (1994) 6 SCC 599 (teaching of Sanskrit alone as an elective subject can in no way be regarded as against secularism); *P.M. Bhargava v. University Grants Commission*, AIR 2004 SC 3478 (Prescription of 'Jyotir Vigyan', *i.e.*, Astrology as a course of study does not have the effect of saffronising education and does not militate against the concept of secularism).

91. *S.R. Chaudhury v. State of Punjab,* AIR 2001 SC 2707, p. 2717 : (2001) 7 SCC 118 (Construction of Article 164); *Special Reference No. 1 of 2002 under Article 143(1) of Constitution*, AIR 2003 SC 87, p. 101 : (2002) 8 SCC 237, p. 265 (construction of Article 174); *TMA Pai Foundation v. State of Karnataka,* (2002) 8 SCC 481, p. 604 : AIR 2003 SC 255, pp. 415, 430 (Construction of Articles 29 and 30).

92. *Kihota Hollohon (Shri) v. Zachilhu (Ms.),* AIR 1993 SC 412, p. 437 : 1992 (1) JT 600.

to which a product patent in medicines may be vulnerable. Hence, it was held that the amendment to the provision was meant especially to deal with chemical substances, and particularly pharmaceutical products and that, in addition to the standards laid down in sections 2(1)(j) and (ja), the amended portion of section 3(d) clearly sets up a second tier of qualifying standards for chemical substances/ pharmaceutical products in order to leave the door open for true and genuine inventions but, at the same time, to check any attempt at repetitive patenting or extension of the patent term on spurious grounds.[93]

In *State of M.P. v. Dadabhoy's New Chirimiri Ponri Hill Colliery Co. (Pvt.) Ltd.*[94] reference was made to the speech of the Minister introducing the Bill to find out the object intended to be achieved and to support a narrow construction of section 30-A of the Mines and Minerals (Regulation and Development) Act, 1957 as amended in 1958. Further, in *Union of India v. Steel Stock Holders Syndicate*[95] reference was made to the speech of the Deputy Minister introducing the Bill and the objects and reasons for supporting the view that the object behind Act 39 of 1961 which amended the Railways Act, 1890 was to extend the liability of the Railway Administration and the provisions contained in the new sections 72 to 78 did not affect the liability of the Railway Administration to pay damages in accordance with the Contract Act for loss arising from money being locked up as a result of delay in transit of the goods. Again in *K.P. Verghese v. I.T. Officer*[96] the speech of the Finance Minister introducing the amendment to amend section 52 of the Income-tax Act, 1961 by adding sub-section (2) was admitted to find out the object behind the amendment. In another case VERMA J. in *R.Y. Prabhoo (Dr.) v. P.K. Kunte*[97] made extensive reference to the speech of the Law Minister in Parliament for construing the word 'his' in section 123(3) of the Representation of the People

93. *Novartis AG v. Union of India & Ors.*, (2013) 6 SCC 1, p. 158.

94. AIR 1972 SC 614 : (1972) 1 SCC 298.

95. AIR 1976 SC 879 : (1976) 3 SCC 108.

96. AIR 1981 SC 1922, p. 1930 : 1981 (4) SCC 173. For further examples where speech of the Minister introducing the Bill was relied upon, **see**—*Sole Trustee Loka Shikshana Trust v. Commissioner of Income Tax*, AIR 1976 SC 10, pp. 21-23 : 1976 SCC (Tax) 14 : (1976) 1 SCC 254; *Indian Chamber of Commerce v. CIT, West Bengal*, AIR 1976 SC 348, p. 351 : 1976 SCC (Tax) 41; *Diwan Brothers v. Central Bank*, AIR 1976 SC 1503, pp. 1507, 1508 : (1976) 3 SCC 800; *Amarnath v. State of Haryana*, AIR 1977 SC 2185, p. 2188 : (1977) 4 SCC 137; *Chern Taong Shong v. Commander S.D. Baijal*, AIR 1988 SC 603, p. 608 : (1988) 1 SCC 507; *Doypack Systems Pvt. Ltd. v. Union of India*, AIR 1988 SC 782, p. 797 : (1988) 2 SCC 299; *Narendra Kumar Maheshwari v. Union of India*, AIR 1989 SC 2138, pp. 2162-64 : 1990 Supp SCC 440; *Union of India v. Deepchand Pandey*, AIR 1993 SC 382 : (1992) 4 SCC 432 (use of minister's speech for construing Administrative Tribunals Act, 1985).

97. 1995 (7) Scale 1, pp. 10, 11.

Act, 1951. The speeches made by the Finance Minister while presenting the Budget of 1998-1999, and while replying to the debate on the amendments to the Finance (No. 2) Bill, 1998, were relied on by the Supreme Court to hold that the object and purpose of the Kar Vivad Samadhan Scheme, 1998, is to minimise litigation and realise the arrears of tax by way of settlement in an expeditious manner.[1]

The change brought about in England by the decision of the House of Lords in *Pepper v. Hart*[2] was noticed by the Supreme Court in *P. V. Narsimha Rao v. State*.[3] In that case, in holding that a member of Parliament was a public servant as defined in section 2(c)(viii) of the Prevention of Corruption Act, 1988, the court declined to admit the minister's speech in Parliament for finding the intention of Parliament in enacting the above provision under the rule of *Pepper v. Hart* (*supra*) as according to the court that provision was unambiguous and the minister's speech was also equivocal.[4] The court observed that according to the earlier decisions of the court, the statement of a minister who had moved the Bill can be looked at to ascertain the mischief sought to be remedied and object and purpose for which the legislation is enacted, but it is not taken into account for interpreting the provisions of the enactment.[5] The court, however, did not differ from the view taken in *Pepper's* case but only found the case to be inapplicable. It is submitted that the distinction between using a material for finding the mischief to be remedied and the object or purpose of a legislation and using it for finding the intention of Parliament is artificial and inappropriate as pointed out is *Pepper's* case[6] and the time has now come to abandon it in India also. *Pepper's* case and criticism of the distinction between using a material for finding the mischief to be remedied and the object or purpose of a legislation and using it for finding the intention of Parliament as also the submission made above to abandon the distinction in India also were noticed by the Supreme Court in *Surana Steels Ltd. v. Dy. Commissioner of Income-tax*.[7] In this case reference was made to the Finance Minister's speech in Parliament introducing the Bill to incorporate section 115-J in the Income-tax Act, 1961 as explaining "the rationale behind its introduction".[8] Reference to *Pepper's* case was also

1. *Union of India & Ors. v. Nitdip Textile Processors Pvt. Ltd.*, (2012) 1 SCC 226, p. 237.
2. (1993) 1 All ER 42 (HL). **See** title 1(a)(iii) 'Modern Trend'; pp. 247 to 251.
3. JT 1998 (3) SC 318: AIR 1998 SC 2120 : (1998) 4 SCC 626.
4. *Ibid.*, p. 373 (JT); p. 2158 (AIR).
5. *Ibid.*
6. **See** p. 247 and 248 text and notes 38, 39; **See further** title 1(a)(ii) 'Criticism of the traditional view', pp. 237 to 239.
7. AIR 1999 SC 1455, p. 1458 (para 7) : (1999) 4 SCC 306.
8. *Ibid.*

made in *Theyssen Stahlunia GMBH v. Steel Authority of India*,[9] and *Haldiram Bhujiawala v. Anand Kumar Deepak Kumar*.[10] In none of the cases in which *Pepper's* case was noticed so far by the Supreme Court there are observations dissenting from the view taken in that case. The views expressed by LORD STEYN and LORD HOPE in the context of *Pepper v. Hart* on the question of use of a parliamentary material as a sort of estoppel against Government[11] were referred and applied by SINHA, J. in *Mahalaxmi Sugar Mills Ltd. v. Union of India*.[12] Debates in Parliament were recently referred to in *Amar Singh v. Union of* India[13] while referring the matter to a Constitution Bench for reconsidering the case of *G. Vishwanathan v. T.N. Legislative* Assembly[14] in which it was held, in the context of para 2(1)(a) and Explanation (a) thereto in the Tenth Schedule to the Constitution, that a member expelled by a political party also stands in the same footing as a member who voluntarily gives up his membership of the political party from which he was elected.

The amendments considered during the progress of the Bill were also ruled out as inadmissible for purposes of construction of the Act. PATANJALI SHASTRI, C.J.I., speaking for majority of the court in *Ashwini Kumar's* case[15] observed: "It was urged that acceptance or rejection of amendments to a bill in the course of parliamentary proceedings forms part of the pre-enactment history of a statute and as such might throw valuable light on the intention of the Legislature when the language used in the statute admitted of more than one construction. We are unable to assent to this proposition. The reason why a particular amendment was proposed or accepted or rejected is often a matter of controversy, as it happened to be in this case; and without the speeches bearing upon the motion, it cannot be ascertained with any reasonable degree of certainty. And where the Legislature happens to be bicameral, the second chamber may or may not have known of such reason when it dealt with the measure".[16] This principle was again referred to by the Supreme Court and substantially modified in *Express Newspapers'* case.[17] BHAGWATI, J., speaking for the court observed that there is a consensus of opinion that the circumstances under which a particular word came to be deleted from the original Bill as introduced in the Parliament and the fact of such deletion when the

---

9. JT 1999 (8) SC 66, p. 105 : (1999) 9 SCC 334 : AIR 1999 SC 3923.
10. AIR 2000 SC 1287, p. 1291 : (2000) 3 SCC 250.
11. See notes 52 and 53 p. 250.
12. AIR 2009 SC 792 paras 67 to 73 : (2008) 6 Scale 275.
13. (2011) 1 SCC 210 para 11 : (2010) 12 JT 451.
14. (1996) 2 SCC 253 : AIR 1996 SCC 1060.
15. *Aswini Kumar Ghose v. Arabinda Bose*, AIR 1952 SC 369, pp. 378, 379 : 1953 SCR 1.
16. *Ibid.*, pp. 378, 379.
17. *Express Newspapers (Pvt.) Ltd. v. Union of India*, AIR 1958 SC 578 : 1959 SCR 12.

Act came to be passed in the final shape are not aids to the construction of the terms of the statute.[18] He, however, added a rider: "It is only when the terms of the statute are ambiguous or vague that resort may be had to them for the purpose of arriving at the true intention of the Legislature",[19] and although asserting that it was not necessary in that case to refer to the circumstance of deletion of the word 'minimum' from the bill, he proceeded in the next paragraph to consider that very circumstance and to hold that it had the effect of widening the enquiry before the wage-Board.[20] And in *Har Sharan Verma v. Tribhuvan Narain Singh*[21] while construing Article 164(4) of the Constitution that it did not require that a Minister should be a member of the Legislature at the time of his being chosen as such, the Supreme Court referred to an amendment which was rejected by the Constituent Assembly requiring that a Minister at the time of his being chosen should be a member of the Legislature.

As regards the Statement of Objects and Reasons appended to a Bill, PATANJALI SHASTRI, C.J.I., in *Ashwini Kumar's* case,[22] speaking for the majority of the court, emphatically ruled them out as an aid to the construction of a statute. To quote his words: "As regards the propriety of the reference to the Statement of Objects and Reasons, it must be remembered that it seeks only to explain what reasons induced the mover to introduce the Bill in the House and what objects he sought to achieve. But those objects and reasons may or may not correspond to the objective which the majority of members had in view when they passed it into law. The Bill may have undergone radical changes during its passage through the House or Houses, and there is no guarantee that the reasons which led to its introduction and the objects thereby sought to be achieved have remained the same throughout till the Bill emerges from the House as an Act of the Legislature, for they do not form part of the Bill and are not voted upon by members. We, therefore, consider that the Statement of Objects and

---

18. *Ibid.*, p. 622.

19. *Ibid.*

20. *Ibid.* **See further** *S.P. Watel v. State of U.P.*, AIR 1973 SC 1293, p. 1297 : (1973) 2 SCC 238. (In this case the change made by the Secretary of the Legislative Assembly in the Bill as originally passed by the Assembly and before it was sent up to the Legislative Council was noticed as an aid to interpretation of section 2(1)(d) of the U.P. Urban Area Zamindari, Abolition and Land Reforms Act, 1957.) *CIT, Ernakulam v. P.K. Noorjahan,* AIR 1999 SC 1600 : (1997) 11 SCC 198 ('May' substituted in place of 'shall' during the progress of the Bill in Parliament cannot be construed as 'shall') : (1997) 11 SCC 198 : AIR 1999 SC 1600.

21. AIR 1971 SC 1331, p. 1333 : (1971) 1 SCC 616. **See further** *S.P. Anand v. H.D. Deve Gowda*, AIR 1997 SC 272, p. 276 : (1996) 6 SCC 734 (Construction of Articles 74 and 76 involving the same point).

22. AIR 1952 SC 369, p. 378 : 1953 SCR 1.

Reasons appended to the Bill should be ruled out as an aid to the construction of the statute."[23] Similarly, S.K. DAS, J. reiterated the principle: "The Statement of Objects and Reasons is not admissible, however, for construing the section far less can it control the actual words used".[24] The rule was stated by SINHA, C.J.I., in the following words: "It is well settled that the Statement of Objects and Reasons accompanying a Bill, when introduced in Parliament, cannot be used to determine the true meaning and effect of the substantive provisions of the statute. They cannot be used except for the limited purpose of understanding the background and the antecedent state of affairs leading up to the legislation."[25] In the last mentioned case[26] a clear declaration in the Statement of Objects and Reasons that "the Central Government does not intend to acquire the proprietary rights vested in the States" was held to be ineffective to cut down the generality of the words used in the statute which was construed as conferring power upon the Union to acquire the rights of States in coal bearing lands. And while considering the validity of Tamil Nadu Act 2 of 1971, the Supreme Court did not accept the recital in the Objects and Reasons that there was need of opening the office of priesthood to any person irrespective of cast, creed and race and held that in view of section 28 of the Act, *Archakas* could be appointed in accordance with the usage of the institution and hence if usage of an institution required that *Archakas* could only be from a particular denomination that restriction continued in spite of recitals to the contrary in the Objects and Reasons.[27]

Similarly, in dealing with an Act which in 1954 amended section 89 of the Bombay Panchayat Act, 1933 and substituted the word 'building' in place of 'houses', the Supreme Court did not accept the recital in the

---

23. *Ibid.* **See further** *S.S. Bola v. B.D. Sardana*, AIR 1997 SC 3127, p. 3208 : 1997 (8) SCC 522.

24. *Central Bank of India v. Their Workmen*, AIR 1960 SC 12, p. 21 : 1960 (1) SCR 200. **See further** *S.S. Bola v. B.D. Sardana, supra; Gurudevdatta V. KSSS Maryadit v. State of Maharashtra,* AIR 2001 SC 1980, p. 1988 : (2001) 4 SCC 534.

25. *State of West Bengal v. Union of India*, AIR 1963 SC 1241, p. 1247 : 1964 (1) SCR 371, **see further** *Jailal v. Delhi Admininstration*, AIR 1962 SC 1781, p. 1787 : 1963 (2) SCR 864 (VENKATARAMA AIYAR, J.); *Ranjit Singh v. State of Punjab*, AIR 1965 SC 632, p. 637 : 1965 (1) SCR 82 (HIDAYATULLAH, J.); *P. Vajravelu Mudaliar v. Special Deputy Collector for Land Acquisition*, AIR 1965 SC 1017, p. 1021 : 1965 (1) SCR 614; *Narain Khamman v. Parduman Kumar Jain*, (1985) 1 SCC 1, p. 8 : AIR 1985 SC 4; *K.S. Paripoornan v. State of Kerala*, JT 1994 (6) SC 182, p. 219 : AIR 1995 SC 1012; *S.S. Bola v. B.D. Sardana*, AIR 1997 SC 3127, p. 3208; *Devadoss (dead) v. Veera Makali Amman Koil Athalur*, JT 1997 (10) SC 70, pp. 79, 80 : AIR 1998 SC 750, p. 756; *Subash Ramkumar Bind v. State of Maharashtra,* (2003) 1 SCC 506, p. 520 : AIR 2003 SC 269, p. 270.

26. *State of West Bengal v. Union of India, supra.*

27. *Srimad Perarulala Ethiraja Ramanuja Jeeyar Swami v. State of Tamil Nadu*, AIR 1972 SC 1586 : (1972) 2 SCC 11.

Statement of Objects and Reasons that the amendment was made for the reason that the *Panchayats* could not levy tax on buildings and held that the word 'houses' as originally used was comprehensive enough to include all buildings including factory buildings and that the amendment only made explicit what was implicit.[28] Further, in holding that section 3(1) of the Customs Tariff Act, 1975 was not a charging section providing for countervailing duty the Supreme Court did not take into account the recital in the Objects and Reasons which *prima facie* indicated to the contrary as there was no ambiguity in the wording of the section.[29]

Reference to the Statement of Objects and Reasons is permissible for understanding the background, the antecedent state of affairs, the surrounding circumstances in relation to the statute, and the evil which the statute was sought to remedy.[30] S.R. DAS, J. in *Subodh Gopal's* case,[31]

28. *Tata Engineering and Locomotive Co. Ltd. v. Gram Panchayat, Pimpri Waghere*, AIR 1976 SC 2463, p. 2468 : (1976) 4 SCC 177.

29. *Khandelwal Metal and Engineering Works*, (1985) 3 SCC 620, p. 628 : AIR 1985 SC 1211.

30. *Sanghvi Jeevraj Ghewar Chand v. Secretary, Madras Chillies, Grains and Kirana Merchants Workers Union*, AIR 1969 SC 530, p. 543 : 1969 (1) SCR 366; *Virji Ram Sutaria v. Nathalal Premji Bhanvadia*, AIR 1970 SC 765, p. 767 : (1969) 1 SCC 77; *Shiv Kirpal Singh v. V.V. Giri*, AIR 1970 SC 2097, p. 2113 : (1970) 2 SCC 567; *Danthuluri Ramaraju v. State of A.P.*, AIR 1972 SC 828, p. 829 : (1972) 1 SCC 421; *State of M.P. v. Dadabhoy's New Chirimiri Ponri Hill Colliery Co. (Pvt.) Ltd.*, AIR 1972 SC 614, p. 620 : (1972) 1 SCC 298; *A.C. Sharma v. Delhi Administration*, AIR 1973 SC 913, p. 917 : (1973) 1 SCC 726; *Workmen of Firestone Tyre & Rubber Co. of India (P) Ltd. v. Management*, AIR 1973 SC 1227, p. 1239 : (1973) 1 SCC 813; *Hiralal Ratan Lal v. Sales Tax Officer III, Kanpur*, AIR 1973 SC 1034, p. 1037 : (1973) 1 SCC 216; *Santa Singh v. State of Punjab*, AIR 1976 SC 2386, p. 2393 : (1976) SCC (Cri) 546; *Amarnath v. State of Haryana*, AIR 1977 SC 2185, p. 2188 : (1977) 4 SCC 137; *Udyan Chinubhai v. R.C. Bali*, AIR 1977 SC 2319, p. 2326 : (1977) 4 SCC 309; *Organo Chemical Industries v. Union of India*, AIR 1979 SC 1803, pp. 1816, 1817 : (1979) 4 SCC 573; *Winifred Ross (Mrs.) v. Ivy Fanseca (Mrs.)* , (1984) 1 SCC 288, pp. 291, 292 : AIR 1984 SC 458; *Narain Khamman v. Parduman Kumar Jain*, (1985) 1 SCC 1, p. 8 : AIR 1985 SC 4; *Secretary, Regional Transport Authority v. D.P. Sharma*, AIR 1989 SC 509, p. 511 : 1989 Supp (1) SCC 407; *Committee for Protection of Rights of ONGC Employees v. National Gas Commission*, AIR 1990 SC 1167, p. 1172 : (1990) 2 SCC 472; *Shashikant Laxman Kale v. Union of India*, AIR 1990 SC 2114, p. 2119 : (1990) 4 SCC 366; *State of Himachal Pradesh v. Kailash Chand Mahajan*, AIR 1992 SC 1277, p. 1300 : 1992 Supp (2) 351; *Rishya Shringa Jewellers Ltd. v. Stock Exchange, Bombay*, 1995 (6) Scale 177, p. 180 : AIR 1996 SC 480, pp. 482, 483; *Devadoss (dead) v. Veera Makali Amman Koil Athlur,* JT 1997 (10) SC 70, pp. 79, 80 : AIR 1998 SC 750, p. 756; *Gurudevdatta VKSSS Maryadit v. State of Maharashtra,* AIR 2001 SC 1980, p. 1989 : (2001) 4 SCC 534; *The Oriental Insurance Co. Ltd. v. Hansrajbhaivkodla,* AIR 2001 SC 1832, pp. 1838, 1839 : (2001) 5 SCC 175; *British Airway Plc. v. Union of India,* AIR 2002 SC 391, p. 393 : (2002) 2 SCC 95.

31. *State of West Bengal v. Subodh Gopal Bose*, AIR 1954 SC 92 : 1954 SCR 587.

after referring to *Aswini Kumar's* case[32] and stating that it is well-settled that the Statement of Objects and Reasons is not admissible as an aid to the construction of statute, proceeded to add: "I am not therefore referring to it for the purpose of construing any part of the Act or of ascertaining the meaning of any word used in the Act but I am referring to it only for the limited purpose of ascertaining the conditions prevailing at the time which actuated the sponsor of the Bill to introduce the same and the extent and urgency of the evil which he sought to remedy".[33] In this case, S.R. DAS, J. was in fact using the Objects and Reasons for judging the reasonableness of the restrictions imposed by the Act on the fundamental right guaranteed under Article 19(1)(f) of the Constitution. However, the passage quoted above from his opinion has not been restricted to that use alone. In construing the words 'any sale held without leave of the court of any of the properties' occurring in section 232(1) of the Companies Act, 1913 (as amended by Act 22 of 1936), BHAGWATI, J., relying upon the dictum of S.R. DAS, J., used the Objects and Reasons appended to the Bill which became the amending Act 22 of 1936 for restricting the words 'any sale held' to sales held through the intervention of the Court and not applying to a sale effected by a secured creditor outside the winding up and without the intervention of the court.[34] In another case,[35] BHAGWATI, J., while dealing with section 16(3) of the Indian Income-tax Act, 1922, as introduced by the amending Act IV of 1937, and in construing the words 'any individual' and 'such individual' occurring therein restricted their meaning to 'males' on a consideration that the Statement of Objects and Reasons appended to the Bill of the amending Act made it clear that the evil which was sought to be remedied was the one resulting from the widespread practice of husbands entering into nominal partnerships with their wives and fathers admitting their minor children to the benefits of the partnerships of which they were members and that the only intention of the Legislature was to include the income derived by the wife or a minor child, in the computation of the total income of the male assessee, the husband or the father, as the case may be. The Supreme Court referred to the Statement of Objects and Reasons appended to the Bill inserting Chapter VI A in the Legal Services Authorities Act, 1987, as well as the long title of the Chapter to hold that it provides for pre litigation conciliation and settlement procedure since disputes relating to public utility services deserve to be settled expeditiously. By bringing in the law, such litigation was sought to be nipped in the bud by first affording the parties an opportunity to

---

32. *Aswini Kumar v. Arabinda Bose*, AIR 1952 SC 369 : 1953 SCR 1.
33. *State of West Bengal v. Subodh Gopal Bose, supra.*
34. *M.R. Ranganathan v. Govt. of Madras*, AIR 1955 SC 604, p. 608 : 1955 (2) SCR 374.
35. *CIT, M.P. v. Sodra Devi*, AIR 1957 SC 832, p. 839 : 1958 SCR 1.

settle their dispute through the Permanent Lok Adalat before the dispute was brought before any court.[36] The Statement of Objects and Reasons was used for holding that the Orissa Forest Produce (Control of Trade) Act, 1981 did not apply to forest produce grown in Government forests and that the Act was restricted in its application to forest produce grown on private land.[37] The statement of Objects and Reasons appended to the Bill which became the Prevention of Corruption Act, 1988 was used for holding that "the legislative intent is manifest" that abettors of all offences under the Act be dealt with along with the public servant by the special judge appointed under the Act.[38] And the Statement of Object and Reasons appended to the Bill, which became the Prevention of Corruption Act, 1947, that the changes in the law were being made to ensure speedy trial of corruption cases, was used for holding that the requirement to furnish a list of defence witnesses (section 7-A of the 1947 Act corresponding to section 22 of the 1988 Act) before the accused is called upon to enter his defence enabled the court to shortlist the witnesses whose examination was unnecessary to prove the defence plea or whose names were added to delay the trial.[39] In construing the proviso to section 7(1) of the Provincial Small Cause Courts Act, 1887 as amended by Act 9 of 1935, the court relied upon the Statement of Objects and Reasons appended to the Bill for holding that the requirement of a 'previous application' for seeking indulgence of the court to give such security as the court may order in place of depositing the decretal amount at the time of making an application for setting aside an *ex-parte* decree was mandatory and an application for security made subsequent to the application for setting aside the *ex-parte* decree could not be entertained.[40] In *District Mining Officer v. Tata Iron & Steel Co.*,[41] the Statement of Objects and Reasons, which occurred as a prefatory note after preamble in the Act, was used to limit the validation by the Cess and Other Taxes on Minerals (Validation) Act, 1992 to cess and taxes already collected till 4th April, 1991. And in *New India Assurance Co. Ltd. v. Asha Rani*[42] the Statement of Objects and Reasons was used to support the conclusion that section 46 of the Motor Vehicles (Amendment) Act, 1994 is not clarificatory and retrospective. Relying on the Statement of Objects and Reasons to the Amendment Bill which

---

36. *Bar Council of India v. Union of India*, (2012) 8 SCC 243, pp. 254, 255.

37. *Utkal Contractors and Joinery Pvt. Ltd. v. State of Orissa*, (1987) 3 SCC 279, pp. 290, 291 : AIR 1987 SC 1454. **See further** *Chern Taong Shang v. Commander S.D. Baijal*, AIR 1988 SC 603, pp. 607, 608 : 1988 (1) SCC 507.

38. *P. Nallammal v. State,* AIR 1999 SC 2556, p. 2560 : (1999) 6 SCC 559.

39. *Arivazhagan v. State,* AIR 2000 SC 1198, pp. 1201, 1202 : (2000) 3 SCC 328.

40. *Kedarnath v. Mohan Lal Kesarwar,* AIR 2002 SC 582, p. 585 : (2002) 2 SCC 16.

41. AIR 2001 SC 3134 : (2001) 7 SCC 358.

42. (2003) 2 SCC 223, p. 232 : AIR 2003 SC 607.

inserted section 25FFA into the Industrial Disputes Act, 1947, the Supreme Court held that the requirement of serving a notice to the appropriate Government at least 60 days prior to the intended closure of the department/unit was mandatory and not directory, as the provision affords statutory protection to the workmen against arbitrary, unreasonable and unfair retrenchment.[43]

Summarising the use of the Statement of Objects and Reasons in the process of construction LAHOTI, J., said: "Reference to the Statement of Objects and Reasons is permissible for understanding the background, the antecedent state of affairs, the surrounding circumstances in relation to the statute and the evil which the statute sought to remedy. The weight of judicial authority leans in favour of the view that the Statement of Objects and Reasons cannot be utilized for the purpose of restricting and controlling the plain meaning of the language employed by the legislature in drafting a statute and excluding from its operation such transactions which it plainly covers."[44] In this case the court declined to restrict the words 'every person' in section 170B(1) of the Madhya Pradesh Land Revenue Code, 1959 to non-tribals by recourse to the object stated in the Statement of Objects and Reasons.

The Statement of Objects and Reasons appended to a Bill seeking the amendment of the Constitution has similarly been utilised for "the purpose of ascertaining the conditions prevailing at the time the Bill was introduced and the purpose for which the amendment was made".[45] It has already been noticed that in *Subodh Gopal's* case[46] S.R. DAS, J. purported to use the Statement of Objects and Reasons to the Bill for judging the reasonableness of the Act in the context of the fundamental right under Article 19(1) of the Constitution.[47] Similar use of the Statement of Objects and Reasons has been made for judging the reasonableness of a classification under an Act to see if it infringes the fundamental right guaranteed under Article 14 of the Constitution.[48]

---

43. *Mackinnon Mackenzie & Co. Ltd. v. Mackinnon Employees Union*, (2015) 4 SCC 544, pp. 561 to 567.

44. *Bhaiji v. Sub-divisional Officer Thandla*, (2003) 1 SCC 692, p. 700 (Pages 206 to 209 of 8th Edition of this book are referred). A *Manjula Bhashini v. Managing Director Andhra Pradesh Women's Cooperative Finance Corporation Ltd.*, (2009) 8 SCC 431 Paras 34, 40 : (2009) 9 JT 229.

45. *Kavalappara Kottarathil Kochuni v. States of Madras & Kerala*, AIR 1960 SC 1080, pp. 1086, 1087 : 1960 (3) SCR 887.

46. *State of West Bengal v. Subodh Gopal Bose*, AIR 1954 SC 92 : 1954 SCR 587.

47. **See** p. 240.

48. *A. Thangal Kunju Musaliar v. M. Venkatachalam Potti*, AIR 1956 SC 246, p. 265 : 1955 (2) SCR 1196; *Shashikant Laxman Kale v. Union of India*, AIR 1990 SC 2114 : 1990 (4) SCC 366.

The Statement of Objects and Reasons has however been held not admissible for determining whether a certain provision of the Act, which was *ultra vires* was or was not severable from other provisions of the Act.[49] A recital as to the source of the legislative power in the Statement of Objects and Reasons is not conclusive.[50] Further, when a provision is inserted after the Bill is introduced and is under consideration before Parliament, the statement of Objects and Reasons of the Bill cannot obviously throw any light on the circumstances in which the provision came to be inserted and enacted.[51]

In *Ajoy Kumar Bannerjee v. Union of India*,[52] while construing section 16 of the General Insurance Business (Nationalisation) Act, 1972 the Supreme Court, relied on the memorandum regarding delegated legislation submitted to Parliament to explain the object of clause 16 of the Bill which became section 16 of the Act. But in *Shashikant Laxman Kale v. Union of India*,[53] it has been held that an explanatory memorandum is usually not an accurate guide of the final Act. While interptreting explanation (baa) to section 80HHC of the Income-tax Act, 1961, the Supreme Court has held that it is not necessary to refer to the explanatory memorandum when the language of the provision was clear. The Court held that only 90% of receipts by way of brokerage, commission, interest, rent, charges or any other receipt of a similar nature included in such profits, computed under the head 'Profits and Gains of Business or Profession', could be deducted under explanation (baa), and not 90% of any of the aforesaid receipts which are allowed as expenses, and therefore not included in the profits of business of the assesse.[54] The High Court of Australia permits reference to explanatory memorandum to the Bill in order to ascertain the mischief which the statute was intended to remedy.[55]

---

49. *Jailal v. Delhi Administration*, AIR 1962 SC 1781, p. 1787 : 1963 (2) SCR 864.

50. *Kerala State Electricity Board v. Indian Aluminium Co.*, AIR 1976 SC 1031, p. 1040 : (1976) 1 SCC 466.

51. *K.S Paripoornan v. State of Kerala*, JT 1994 (6) SC 182, p. 220 : AIR 1995 SC 1012 : (1994) 5 SCC 593.

52. (1984) 3 SCC 127, pp. 146, 149 : AIR 1984 SC 1130.

53. AIR 1990 SC 2114, p. 2120 : 1990 (4) SCC 366.

54. *ACG Associated Capsules Private Limited v. CIT, Central-IV, Mumbai*, (2012) 3 SCC 321, p. 328.

55. *CIC Insurance Ltd. v. Bankstown Footballclub Ltd.* (1997) 187 CLR 384 (Aust), p. 408; *Newcastle City Council v. GIO General Ltd.* (1998) 72 ALJR 97 (Aust). **See further** *Gurudevdata VKSSS Maryadit v. State of Maharashtra*, AIR 2001 SC 1980, p. 1990 (extracts from these Australian cases including section 15 of the Australian Interpretation Act are quoted. For English law on this point **see** text and notes 57 to 60, p. 251, *supra*.

In *Hyderabad Industries Ltd. v. Union of India*,[56] notes on clauses were relied upon by a Constitution Bench for understanding the Legislative intent. The Finance Bill, 2002, introduced a proviso to section 113 of the Income-tax Act, 1961. By the said proviso, the tax chargeable in the case of block assessment of a search case under section 113 was to be increased by a surcharge, if any, levied by any Central Act and applicable in the assessment year relevant to the previous year in which the search is initiated under section 132 or the requisition is made under section 132A of the Act. A Constitution Bench of the Supreme Court noted that the "Notes on Clauses" appended to the Finance Bill, 2002, clearly states that the amendment would take effect from 1.6.2002, in contradiscinction to other amendments which were stated to be clarificatory or retrospective depicting the clear intention of the legislature. It was therefore held that the said amendment was not clarificatory or retrospective but was intended to operate prospectively. The Constitution Bench of the Supreme Court also overruled the decision of a 2 Judge Bench of the Supreme Court in *CIT v. Suresh N. Gupta*,[57] which had taken the view that the proviso to section 113 of the Act was clarificatory in nature, and therefore retrospective.[58]

Reports of Commissions or Inquiry Committees preceding the introduction of a Bill have also been referred to as evidence of historical facts or of surrounding circumstances or of mischief or evil intended to be remedied and at times for interpreting the Act. For example, reference was made to the Indian States Finance Enquiry Committee Reports (1948-49) in *Musaliar's* case,[59] to the Income-tax Enquiry Report (1936) in *Sodra Devi's* case,[60] to the Press Commission's Reports (1952-54) in *Express Newspapers'* case,[61] and to the report of a Committee appointed to bring about changes in Company Law resulting in the passing of amending Act No. 65 of 1960 in *Madanlal's* case.[62] And, reference to the report of the Expert Committee on Financial Provisions was made in *Union of India v. Harbhajan Singh Dhillon*.[63] The Supreme Court referred to the Report of the Committee on Banking Laws submitted in 1975, which suggested penalizing the issuance of cheques without sufficient funds, as well as the

---

56. (1995) 5 SCC 338 : 1995 AIR SCW 3367 (para 15).
57. (2008) 4 SCC 362.
58. *CIT (Central)-I, New Delhi v. Vatika Township Pvt. Ltd.*, (2015) 1 SCC 1, pp. 30, 31.
59. *A. Thangal Kunju Musaliar v. Venkatachalam Potti*, AIR 1956 SC 246, p. 256 : 1955 (2) SCR 1196.
60. *CIT, M.P. v. Sodra Devi*, AIR 1957 SC 832, p. 838 : 1958 SCR 1.
61. *Express Newspapers (Pvt.) Ltd. v. Union of India*, AIR 1958 SC 578, pp. 587, 589, 622, 623 : 1959 SCR 12.
62. *Madanlal Fakirchand Dudhediya v. S. Changdeo Sugar Mills Ltd.*, AIR 1962 SC 1543, p. 1553 : 1962 Supp (3) SCR 973.
63. AIR 1972 SC 1061, p. 1070 : 1971 (2) SCC 779.

Parliamentary debates preceding the amendment to the Negotiable Instruments Act, 1881, which introduced sections 138 to 142 therein, to hold that a civil liability was being converted to criminal liability by the deeming fiction of culpability, which severely curtailed defences to prosecution. The Supreme Court further held that civil law concepts such as 'cause of action' are alien to criminal law, and hence the words 'cause of action' in section 142 are apposite for taking cognizance but irrelevant for determining commission of the offence. Since section 177 of the CrPC states that every offence shall ordinarily be inquired into and tried by a court within whose local jurisdiction the offence was committed, and section 138 of the Negotiable Instruments Act defines the offence as being the dishonor/ return of cheques by the drawee bank, the complaint under section 138 must be instituted, and the trial must be conducted, where the drawee bank is located, and not where the statutory notice was issued or delivered or where the complainant chooses to present the cheque.[64] It is pertinent to note that after this decision, the President has promulgated the Negotiable Instruments (Amendment) Ordinance, 2015, and, after its lapse, the Negotiable Instruments (Amendment) Second Ordinance, 2015, which provide that the offence under section 138 shall be inquired into and tried only by the court within whose local jurisdiction the branch of the bank where the payee or holder in due course maintains his/her account is located, if the cheque is delivered for collection through an account.

It was however held in *CIT, A.P. v. Jayalakshmi Rice and Oil Mills Contractor Co.*,[65] that the report of the special committee which had been appointed by the Government of India to examine the provisions of the Bill which later became the Partnership Act cannot be admitted for interpreting the provisions of the Act. But in *CIT, Gujarat v. Vadilal Lallubhai*,[66] report of the Select Committee was referred to for finding out the mischief which was intended to be remedied by introduction of section 44-A in the Income-tax Act, 1922. And in *R.S. Nayak v. A.R. Antulay*[67] a

---

64. *Dashrath Rupsingh Rathod v. State of Maharashtra & Anr.*, (2014) 9 SCC 129, pp.150 to 155.

65. AIR 1971 SC 1015, p. 1016 (para 5) : 1971 (1) SCC 280.

66. AIR 1973 SC 1016 : 1973 SCC (Tax) 1. **See further** *Sole Trustee Loka Shikshan Trust v. Commissioner of Income-tax*, AIR 1976 SC 10, p. 23 : 1976 SCC (Tax) 14 (reference made to Select Committee's Report). *State of Punjab v. Balwant Singh*, AIR 1991 SC 2301, p. 2304 : 1992 Supp (3) SCC 108 (Report of Joint Committee of both houses of Parliament was **relied** upon for interpreting section 15(2) of the Hindu Succession Act, 1956).

67. (1984) 2 SCC 183, pp. 214, 215 : AIR 1984 SC 684. But departmental proposals and notings in the files by different officials before the cabinet took the final decision are neither internal nor external aids for construction of the Act; *Doypack Systems Pvt. Ltd. v. Union of India*, AIR 1988 SC 782, p. 796 : 1988 (2) SCC 299.

Constitution Bench of the Supreme Court differing from the view taken in *Jayalakshmi Rice and Oil Mills Contractor Co.'s* case held that report of the committee which preceded the enactment of a legislation, reports of Joint Parliamentary Committee and report of a commission set up for collecting information leading to the legislation are permissible external aids to construction of the Act. Following the view in *R.S. Nayak v. A.R. Antulay*,[68] the Supreme Court in *Haldiram Bhujiawala v. Anand Kumar Deepak Kumar*,[69] held that the view taken in *Jayalakshmi Rice and Oil Mills Co.'s* case is no longer good law and admitted the Report of the Special Committee which had not been admitted in that case for construing section 69(2) of the Indian Partnership Act, 1932. Further, in *Mithilesh Kumari v. Prem Bihari Khare*,[70] the Supreme Court observed that "where a particular enactment or amendment is the result of recommendation of the Law Commission of India, it may be permissible to refer to the relevant report." In that case the report of the Law Commission preceding the enactment of the Benami Transactions (Prohibition) Act, 1988 was referred to and relied upon in holding section 4 thereof to be retrospective. Reference to Law Commission's 41st report was made for interpreting section 209 of the Code of Criminal Procedure, 1973 and in reaching the conclusion that proceedings under that section are ministerial and do not

---

68. *Ibid.*

69. AIR 2000 SC 1287, p. 1291 : (2000) 3 SCC 250 (pp. 196, 197 of 7th edition of this book are referred). **See further,** *Allahabad Bank v. Canera Bank,* JT 2000 (4) SC 411, pp. 425, 432, 433 : (2000) 4 SCC 406 : AIR 2000 SC 1535 (Reports of committes preceeding the enactment of the Recovery of Debts Due to Banks and Financial Institutions Act, 1993 were referred.) *Shrimant Shamrao Suryavanshi v. Prahlad Bhairoba Suryavanshi,* AIR 2002 SC 731 : (2002) 3 SCC 676. (Report preceeding the legislation adding section 53A in the Transfer of Property Act,1882 was held admissible for its construction.) *Sarva Shramik Sangh v. Indian Smelting and Refining Co. Ltd.*, AIR 2004 SC 269, p. 277. (The report of the committee on Unfair Labour Practices preceding the enactment of the Maharashtra Recognition of Trade Unions and Prevention of Unfair Labour Practices Act, 1971 was used for the Act's construction.) *Expharsa v. Eupharma Laboratories*, (2004) 3 SCC 688, p. 693 : AIR 2004 SC 1682 (use of joint committee report for construction of section 62 of the Copyright Act, 1957). *Commissioner of Income Tax I, Ahmedabad v. Gold Coin Health Food Private Ltd.*, (2008) 9 SCC 622 para 12 : (2008) 9 JT 312 [Wanchoo Committee report which led to addition of Explanation 4(a) in Section 271(1)(c)(iii) of the Income-tax Act,1961 referred for its construction].

70. AIR 1989 SC 1247, p. 1252 : (1989) 2 SCC 95. **See further** *Waliram Waman Hiray (Dr.) v. Mr. Justice B. Lentin*, AIR 1988 SC 2267, p. 2280 : (1988) 4 SCC 419 (Law Commission's report was **referred** to for interpreting section 195(3) of the Code of Criminal Procedure, 1973); *Santa Singh v. State of Punjab,* AIR 1976 SC 2386, p. 2392 : 1976 SCC (Cri) 546 : (1976) 4 SCC 190 (reference made to Law Commission's Report); *Ravinder Kumar Sharma v. State of Assam,* AIR 1999 SC 3571, p. 3575 : (1999) 7 SCC 435. (Law Commission's Report relating to 1976 amendment in O. 41, R. 22, CPC **referred**.)

amount to an inquiry as defined in section 2(g) of the Code.[71] It was pointed out that the court in an earlier case[72] had taken a contrary view as it had then not been referred to the Law Commission's report. Section 468 (1) of the CrPC provides that no court shall take 'cognizance' of an offence of the category specified in sub-section (2) after the expiry of the period of limitation. The Supreme Court referred to the 42nd Report of the Law Commission and the Report of the Joint Parliamentary Committee to hold that the object of the limitation was to quicken prosecution and rid the system of cases displaying lethargy, inertia or indolence, and it was not intended to throw a diligent complainant out of court merely because the Magistrate has taken cognizance after the limitation period, which could be because of several reasons, systemic or otherwise. Accordingly, it was held that for the purposes of limitation under section 468(1), the relevant date is the date of filing complaint or institution of prosecution, and not the date on which the Magistrate takes cognizance.[73] The Supreme Court relied on the 154th Report of the Law Commission of India and the notes on Clause 37 of the Code of Criminal Procedure (Amendment) Bill, 1994, to hold that the appeal under section 378 of the CrPC, as amended by Act 25 of 2005, was provided to guard against reckless acquittals and arbitrary exercise of power.[74]

Reports of drafting committee and sub-committees of the Constituent Assembly, the draft Constitution and the changes made thereafter in giving the Constitution the final shape were referred in interpreting Para 5(2) of the 5th Schedule, but the inferences derived from this material in majority and minority judgments were different.[75]

White paper issued by the Government detailing the facts leading to enactment of a statute is also admissible for understanding the background when the court is called upon to interpret and decide the validity of the statute. Extensive reference was made by the Supreme Court to the white paper for understanding the background of the *Ram Janmabhumi Babri Masjid* dispute in deciding the reference made under Article 143 and the constitutionality of the Acquisition of Certain Areas at Ayodhya Act, 1993.[76]

---

71. *Rajkishore Prasad v. State of Bihar*, 1996 (4) Scale 87, pp. 89 to 91 : AIR 1996 SC 1931, pp. 1933, 1934.
72. *State of U.P. v. Lakshmi Brahman*, AIR 1983 SC 439, p. 445 : 1983 (2) SCC 372.
73. *Sarah Mathew v. Institute of Cardio Vascular Diseases & Ors.*, (2014) 2 SCC 62, pp. 89, 90, 95, 99.
74. *Subhash Chand v. State (Delhi Administration)*, (2013) 2 SCC 17, pp. 24, 28 to 29.
75. *Samatha v. State of Andhra Pradesh*, AIR 1997 SC 3297 : 1997 (8) SCC 191.
76. *M. Ismail Faruqqui (Dr.) v. Union of India*, JT 1994 (6) SC 632 : AIR 1995 SC 605.

It must further be remembered that the Supreme Court and the High Courts in India have often occasion to consider the reasonableness of a statutory measure in view of the fundamental rights in the Constitution, *viz.*, Articles 19 and 14 which cannot be bypassed by the Legislature. This duty opens up a much wider enquiry than that could be undergone under the British Constitution[77] and, therefore, the courts in India have reason to look much beyond the Act for finding the circumstances and the mischief or evil necessitating the statutory measure. In *Chiranjitlal's* case,[78] FAZL ALI, J., made extensive reference to parliamentary proceedings including the speech of the Minister to discern "the circumstances which necessitated" the enactment of the Sholapur Spinning and Weaving Company (Emergency Provisions) Act, 1950 and the information gained from this material was used to justify Parliament in treating the Sholapur Mill as a class by itself. This course adopted by FAZL ALI, J., was apparently approved in *Musaliar's* case.[79] In determining such issues even affidavit evidence of "the circumstances which prevailed at the time when the law had been passed and which necessitated the passing of that law", has been admitted.[80] In *Mohd. Hanif Quareshi v. State of Bihar*,[81] where the Supreme Court considered the constitutionality of various State Legislations banning slaughter of certain animals, references were made to religious books; Reports of Gosamvardhan Enquiry Committee of U.P. (1953); Report on the Marketing of Cattle in India; Report of Marketing of Hides in India; the First and Second Five-year Plans; Memorandum on Human Nutrition *vis-a-vis* Animal Nutrition in India by Nutrition Advisory Committee; Report of Cattle Preservation and Development Committee of the Government of India, 1948, etc., and it was stated that "in order to sustain the presumption of constitutionality the court may take into consideration matters of common knowledge; matters of common report; the history of the times; and may assume every state of facts which can be conceived existing at the time of legislation".[82] Reference may also be made to *Bhikusa Yamasa Kshatriya (P) Ltd. v. Union of India*,[83] where Reports of Royal Commission on Labour in India, 1929; and Labour Investigation

---

77. The enforcement of the Human Rights Act, 1998 and the introduction of the principle of proportionality in judicial review (see p. 392) may now make the difference.

78. *Chiranjit Lal Chowdhury v. Union of India*, AIR 1951 SC 41, p. 45 : 1950 SCR 869.

79. *A. Thangal Kunju Musaliar v. M. Venkatachalam Potti*, AIR 1956 SC 246, p. 265 : 1955 (2) SCR 1196.

80. *Ibid.*

81. AIR 1958 SC 731 : 1959 SCR 629.

82. *Ibid.*, p. 741. This case has been **overruled** on merits in *State of Gujarat v. Mirzapur Moti Qureshi Kassab Jamat,* (2005) 8 SCC 534 : AIR 2006 SC 212, which is discussed elsewhere in the context of fundamental duties. In this case differing from the earlier *Quareshi* case total ban on the slaughter of progeny of cow was upheld.

83. AIR 1963 SC 1591 : 1964 (1) SCR 860.

Committee, 1942 were taken into account to uphold the constitutionality of section 85 of the Factories Act, 1948. To take another example, in *Shriram Chits & Investments (P.) Ltd. v. Union of India*[84] reference was made to the report of the Banking Committee prepared in the year 1972, the report of the Study Group on Non-banking Financial Intermediaries constituted by the Banking Commission; Raj Committee report and the report of the Select Committee of Parliament in upholding the reasonableness and validity of the Chit Fund Act, 1982. It is evident that for purposes of construction proper, such a wide range of investigation will not be permitted even though the court is entitled to look into surrounding circumstances or historical facts for purposes of discerning the mischief or evil sought to be remedied.[85]

2. HISTORICAL FACTS AND SURROUNDING CIRCUMSTANCES

It has already been noticed that the court is entitled to take into account "such external or historical facts as may be necessary to understand the subject-matter of the statute" or to have regard to "the surrounding circumstances" which existed at the time of passing of the statute.[86] As stated by LORD HALSBURY: "The subject-matter with which the Legislature was dealing, and the facts existing at the time with respect to which the Legislature was legislating are legitimate topics to consider in ascertaining what was the object and purpose of the Legislature in passing the Act".[87] In the words of LORD ATKINSON: "In the construction of statutes it is, of course, at all times and under all circumstances permissible to have regard to the state of things existing at the time the statute was passed and to the evils, which, as appears from the provisions, it was designed to remedy".[88] The Supreme Court (S.K. DAS, J.) has referred with approval the following passage from an American decision: "We are not limited to the lifeless words of the statute and formalistic canons of construction in our search for the intent of Congress (Parliament in our case) and courts in construing

84. AIR 1993 SC 2063, pp. 2066, 2080 : 1993 Supp (4) SCC 226.

85. *Shashikant Laxman Kale v. Union of India*, AIR 1990 SC 2114, p. 2120 : (1990) 4 SCC 366 : (1990) 185 ITR 104.

86. **See** title 1 'Parliamentary History', pages 242-244 and 261-262, *supra*. **See further** *R.L. Arora v. State of U.P.*, AIR 1964 SC 1230, p. 1237 : (1964) 6 SCR 784; *Sanghvi Jeevraj v. Secretary, Madras Chillies, Grains and Kirana Merchants Workers Union*, AIR 1969 SC 530, p. 534 : (1969) 1 SCR 366.

87. *Herron v. Rathmines and Rathgar Improvement Commissioners*, (1892) AC 498, p. 502 (HL); referred to in *Herrietta Muir Edwards v. A-G of Canada*, AIR 1930 PC 120, p. 125.

88. *Keates v. Lewis Merthyr Consolidated Collieries Ltd.*, (1911) AC 641 : (1911-13) All ER 921, p. 922 (HL); referred to in *D.N. Banerjee v. P.R. Mukherjee*, AIR 1953 SC 58, p. 60 : 1953 SCR 302.

a statute, may with propriety refer to the history of the times when it was passed".[89] However, an argument based on history is not to be pushed too far as "the inferences to be drawn therefrom are exceedingly slight".[90] Like any other external aid, the inferences from historical facts and surrounding circumstances must give way to the clear language employed in the enactment itself. The rule of admissibility of this external aid in case of ambiguous enactments is of general application and a number of cases in this respect have already been discussed while dealing with the rule in *Heydon's* case,[91] and the admissibility of parliamentary History.[92]

The rule permits recourse to historical works, pictures, engravings and documents where it is important to ascertain ancient facts of a public nature;[93] and reference may be made to contemporary treatises which may have influenced the law-makers in using a particular phrase in the statute.[94] An interesting example is furnished in the use made of MILL'S Political Economy for interpreting the phrase 'direct taxation' in the British North America Act, 1867. To quote the words of VISCOUNT SIMON, L.C. "The guide to be followed is that provided by the distinction between direct and indirect taxes which is to be found in the treatise of JOHN STUART MILL. The question, of course, as LORD HERSCHELL said, is not what is the distinction drawn by writers on political economy but in what sense the words were employed in the British North America Act, 1867. MILL'S Political Economy was first published in 1848 and appeared in a popular edition in 1865. Its author became a member of Parliament in this latter year and commanded much attention in the British House of Commons. Having regard to his eminence as a political economist in the epoch when the Quebec Resolutions were being discussed and the 1867 Act was being framed, the use of MILL'S analysis and classification of taxes for the purpose of construing the expression now under review is fully justified."[95]

The policy followed in the working of an earlier Act can be presumed to be known to Parliament while legislating subsequently on a related subject

---

89. *Great Northern Rly. Co. v. United States of America*, (1942) 315 US 262, p. 273 : 86 Law Ed 836, p. 841, **referred to** in *Hariprasad Shivshankar Shukla v. A.D. Divelkar*, AIR 1957 SC 121, p. 131 : 1957 SCR 121.

90. *R. v. West Riding of Yorkshire County Council*, (1906) 2 KB 676, pp. 716, 717 (CA) (FARWELL, L.J.); referred to in *Henrietta Muir Edwards v. A.G. of Canada*, AIR 1930 PC 120, p. 125.

91. **See** Chapter 2, under title 3(b) "Rule in *Heydon's* case".

92. **See** text and note 86, *supra*.

93. *Read v. Bishop of Lincoln*, (1892) AC 644: (1891-94) All ER Rep 227, pp. 228, 229 (PC) (LORD HALSBURY, L.C.).

94. **See** text and note 95, p. 273.

95. *Atlantic Smoke Shops Ltd. v. Conlon*, (1943) 2 All ER 393, p. 397 (PC).

and will thus be admissible in construing the later Act.[1] Thus the policy followed by the local authorities in providing adequate accommodation for 'gipsies' (including those who are only seasonally nomadic) residing in or resorting to their area under section 6 of the Caravan Sites Act, 1968 was held admissible as a powerful pointer to the intention of the Legislature in excluding local authority sites 'providing accommodation for gipsies' from the definition of protected site in seciton 5(1) of the Mobile Homes Act, 1983.[2]

The function of the court being to find out the intention of the law makers, the court has to discover that particular meaning of a given word in an enactment which the law makers intended it to be given. In case of older statutes a knowledge of the historical facts relating to them helps in understanding the meaning of ambiguous words and expressions used in them. "For the purpose of appreciating the scope and object of an old statute and for explaining its language which may be susceptible of different meanings", observed MUKHERJEE, J., "It may be useful to remember the well-known historical facts that led to the enactment."[3] MUKHERJEE, J., proceeded to say: "It is a settled canon of construction that the interpreter should place himself, as far as possible, in the position of those whose words he is interpreting and the meaning of certain words and terms used in an ancient document or a statute can be properly explained only by reference to the circumstances existing at the time when the statute was enacted or the document was written."[4] The court in deciding that production bonus was not included in the definition of 'basic wages' in section 2(b) of the Employees' Provident Funds and Miscellaneous Provisions Act, 1952, which expressly excluded 'bonus', observed that the exclusion of bonus without any qualification must be referrable to every kind of bonus prevalent in the industrial field before 1952 and in that connection the court noticed the circumstance that production bonus was prevalent in industrial concerns long before 1952.[5] The Supreme Court has considered the background in which the Consumer Protection Act, 1986, was enacted as well as its salient features to hold that farmers/growers would fall within the wide definition of "consumer" in section 2(1)(d) of the Act, and would be entitled to claim compensatory relief for loss suffered on account of defective

---

1. *Greenwich London Borough Council v. Powell*, (1989) 1 All ER 65, p. 70 : (1989) AC 995 : (1989) 2 WLR 7 (HL).
2. *Ibid.*
3. *Auckland Jute Co. Ltd. v. Tulsi Chandra Goswami*, AIR 1949 FC 153, p. 169 : 1949 FCR 201.
4. *Ibid.* **See further** *Doypack Systems Pvt. Ltd. v. Union of India*, AIR 1988 SC 782, p. 797 : 1988 (2) SCC 299.
5. *Bridge & Roofs Co. Ltd. v. Union of India*, AIR 1963 SC 1474, p. 1478 : 1963 (3) SCR 978. For the nature of 'production bonus' see further *The Daily Pratap v. The Regional Provident Fund Commissioner*, AIR 1999 SC 2015, p. 2027 : (1998) 8 SCC 90.

seeds supplied to them, and that arbitration was not the only available remedy, but rather an optional remedy.[6] Historical evolution of a provision in the statute is also sometimes a useful guide to its construction.[7]

3. LATER SOCIAL, POLITICAL AND ECONOMIC DEVELOPMENTS AND SCIENTIFIC INVENTIONS

(a) General

It is possible that in some special cases a statute may have to be historically interpreted "as if one were interpreting it the day after it was passed." But generally statutes are of the "always speaking variety" and the court is free to apply the current meaning of the statute to present day conditions.[8] There are atleast two strands covered by this principle. The first is that courts must apply a statute to the world as it exists today. The second strand is that the statute must be interpreted in the light of the legal system as it exists today.[9] Reference to the circumstances existing at the time of the passing of the statute does not, therefore, mean that the language used, at any rate, in a modern statute, should be held to be inapplicable to social,

---

6. *National Seeds Corporation Limited v. M. Madhusudhan Reddy & Anr.*, (2012) 2 SCC 506.
7. **See** pp. 343-347, *infra.*
8. *R v. Ireland*, (1997) 4 All ER 225, p. 233 : (1997) 3 WLR 534 (HL) (LORD STEYN): "Bearing in mind that statutes are usually intended to operate for many years it would be most inconvenient if courts could never rely in difficult cases on the current meaning of statutes. Recognising the problem LORD THRING, the great victorian draftsman of the second half of the last century exhorted draftsmen to draft so that 'An Act of Parliament should be deemed to be always speaking'.—In cases where the problem arises it is a matter of interpretation whether a court must search for the historical or original meaning of a statute or whether it is free to apply the current meaning of the statute to present day conditions. Statutes dealing with a particular grievance or problem may sometimes require to be historically interpreted. But the drafting technique of LORD THRING and his successors has brought about the situation that statutes will generally be found to be of the 'always speaking' variety." (In this case psychiatric injury resulting from persistent silent telephone calls was held to amount to bodily harm and 'assault' within the ambit of sections 20 and 47 of the Offences Against the Person Act of 1861. **See also** for this case text and note 82, p. 968). For more information about LORD THRING **see** – 'Editorial; Henry Thring – A hundred years on' (2007) 28 Statute Law Review (No. 1) p. iii to v. **See further** *Fitzpatrick v. Sterling Housing Association Ltd.*, (1999) 4 All ER 705, p. 726 (HL); *State v. S.J. Choudhary,* AIR 1996 SC 1491 : 1996 (2) SCC 428; *State of Maharashtra v. Dr. Praful B. Dasai,* 2003 AIR SCW 1885, p. 1894 : AIR 2003 SC 2053 : (2003) 4 SCC 601; *Union of India v. Naveen Jindal*, (2004) 2 SCC 510, p. 538; *Rabindra Singh v. Financial Commissioner,* (2008) 7 SCC 663 para 16 : (2008) 8 Scale 242 [with the development of science and technology the ongoing statutes cannot be construed in such a manner so as to make the society backward and not forward.]; *Kashmir Singh v. Union of India,* (2008) 7 SCC 259 paras 55, 68 and 72 : (2008) 9 Scale 224.
9. *McCartan Turkington Breen (a firm) v. Times Newspapers Ltd.*, (2000) 4 All ER 913, p. 926 (HL) (LORD STEYN).

political and economic developments or to scientific inventions not known at the time of the passing of the statute. "Legislative standards are generally couched in the terms which have considerable breadth. Therefore, a statute may be interpreted to include circumstances or situations which were unknown or did not exist at the time of enactment of the statute."[10] The question again is as to what was the intention of the law makers: Did they intend, as originalists may argue, that the words of the statute be given the meaning they would have received immediately after the statute's enactment or did they intend, as dynamists may contend, that it would be proper for the court to adopt the current meaning of the words? The courts have now generally leaned in favour of dynamic construction.[11] But the doctrine has also its limitations. For example, it does not mean that the language of an old statute can be construed to embrace something conceptually different.[12]

The guidance on the question as to when an old statute can apply to new state of affairs not in contemplation when the statute was enacted was furnished by LORD WILBERFORCE in his dissenting speech in *Royal College of Nursing of the U.K. v. Dept. of Health and Social Security,*[13] which is now treated as authoritative.[14] LORD WILBERFORCE said: "In interpreting an Act

---

10. *Senior Electric Inspector v. Laxminarayan Chopra*, AIR 1962 SC 159, p. 162 : 1962 (3) SCR 146, **citing with approval** a passage from SUTHERLAND: Statutory Construction, Vol. 2, p. 508; *Vishnu Agencies (Pvt.) Ltd. v. Commercial Tax Officer*, AIR 1978 SC 449, p. 460 : (1978) 1 SCC 520; *J.K. Cotton Spinning & Weaving Mills Ltd. v. Union of India*, AIR 1988 SC 191, p. 204 : 1987 (4) JT 421 : 1987 Supp SCC 350; *Municipal Corporation of Greater Bombay v. Indian Oil Corporation,* AIR 1991 SC 686, p. 690 : 1990 (4) JT 533 : 1991 Supp (2) SCC 18. (Effort should be made to harmonise the law with changes in social, economic, political and technological fields.) *ICICI Bank Limited v. Official Liquidator of APS Star Industries Ltd.*, (2010) 10 SCC 1 para 43 : AIR 2011 SC 1521. In holding that transfer of debts (NPA *i.e.* Non-Productive Assets) now between banks is a legitimate banking activity, the Supreme Court held that while interpreting Banking Regulation Act, 1949 "one needs to keep in mind not only the framework of the banking law as it stood in 1949 but also the growth and new concepts that have emerged in the course of time." 11th edition of this book is referred.

11. **See** text and notes 8 to 10, *supra*. It has been suggested that when an interpretative problem is the result of vague language the court may invoke dynamic construction and where the interpretative problem arises as the result of an ambiguity the court should adopt originalist construction: *Randal N. Grahm, A Unified Theory of Statutory Interpretation,* (2002) 23 Statute Law Review 91, p. 134. But this suggestion seems to be too vague for being adopted in practice.

12. *Birmingham City Council v. Oakley,* (2001) 1 All ER 385, p. 396 (HL).

13. (1981) 1 All ER 545, pp. 564, 565 : (1982) AC 800 : (1981) 2 WLR 279 (HL).

14. *Fitzpatrick v. Sterling Housing Association Ltd.*, (1999) 4 All ER 705, pp. 710, 721, 739-740, 744 (HL); *R (on the application of Quintavalle) v. Secretary of State for Health,* (2003) 2 All ER 113, pp. 119, 125 (HL). But see *R (on the application of Quintavalle) v. Human Fertilisation and Embyology Authority*, (2005) 2 All ER 555, p. 564 (para 33) where LORD HOFFMAN said: "But like all guidance on construction, LORD WILBERFORCE'S remarks are more appropriate to some cases than others".

of Parliament it is proper, and indeed necessary, to have regard to the state of affairs existing, and known by Parliament to be existing, at the time. It is a fair presumption that Parliament's policy or intention is directed to that state of affairs. Leaving aside cases of omission by inadvertence, this being not such a case when a new state of affairs, or a fresh set of facts bearing on policy, comes into existence, the courts have to consider whether they fall within the parliamentary intention. *They may be held to do so, if they fall within the same genus of facts as those to which the expressed policy has been formulated. They may also be held to do so if there can be detected a clear purpose in the legislation which can only be fulfilled if the extension is made.* How liberally these principles may be applied must depend on the nature of the enactment, and the strictness or otherwise of the words in which it has been expressed. The courts should be less willing to extend expressed meanings if it is clear that the Act in question was designed to be restrictive or circumscribed in its operation rather than liberal or permissive. They will be much less willing to do so where the new subject matter is different in kind or dimension from that for which the legislation was passed. In any event there is one course which the courts cannot take under the law of this country: they cannot fill gaps; they cannot by asking the question, 'What would Parliament have done in this current case, not being one in contemplation, if the facts had been before it?' attempt themselves to supply the answer, if the answer is not to be found in the terms of the Act itself."[15]

As stated by LORD BRIDGE: "When a change in social conditions produces a novel situation, which was not in contemplation at the time when a statute is first enacted, there can be no *a priori* assumption that the enactment does not apply to the new circumstances. If the language of the enactment is wide enough to extend to those circumstances, there is no reason why it should not apply."[16] Thus, when in the changed circumstances the common law fiction that by marriage the wife must be deemed to have irrevocably consented to sexual intercourse in all circumstances has become anachronistic, the husband can be convicted of rape under the Sexual Offences (Amendment) Act, 1976, if he has sexual intercourse with his wife without her consent.[17]

---

15. Note 11, *supra*.

16. *Comdel Commodities Ltd. v. Siporex Trade, SA*, (1990) 2 All ER 552, p. 557 : (1991) 1 AC 148 : (1990) 3 WLR 1 (HL).

17. *R v. R (rape: marital exemption)*, (1991) 4 All ER 481 : (1992) 1 AC 599 : (1991) 3 WLR 767 (HL). A husband can be convicted for raping his wife after the decision in *R v. R*, for a rape committed before the decision. This conviction will not amount to retrospective penalty offending Article 7 of the European Convention on Civil and Political Rights : *R v. C*, (2004) 1 All ER 1 (CA). Change in social outlook has also resulted in the view that a man recklessly infecting a woman or his wife with HIV or

[Footnote No. 17 Contd.]

Changed social psyche and expectations are important factors to be considered in the upkeep of law.[18] Section 30 of the Punjab Excise Act, 1914 prohibited the employment of any man under the age of 25 years or any woman in any part of premises in which liquor or intoxicating drugs were consumed by the public. This law which may have been good having regard to the social conditions as they prevailed in the 20th Century, but having regard to the present social conditions and equality to sexes guaranteed under the Constitution, the same was declared invalid.[19]

The effect of change in social attitude bringing about a change in interpretation is also reflected in the construction of the word 'person'. In bad old days when the common law incapacitated women from exercising political rights, the word 'person' in section 27 of the Representation of the People (Scotland) Act, 1868 was held in 1909 not to include women thereby disentitling them to vote.[20] In contrast the word 'person' in section 24 of the British North America Act, 1867 was held by the Privy Council in 1929, overruling the Supreme Court of Canada, to include women as eligible to become members of the senate of Canada.[21] And, in the light of importance of the freedom of expression in the law as it now exists, qualified privilege granted to newspaper reports of any 'public meeting' by the Defamation Act (Northern Ireland), 1955 was construed to cover the report referring to contents of a press release distributed at a press conference but not read aloud and the press conference was held to be a 'public meeting'.[22]

Further, with the change in social attitude towards homosexuals, two persons of the same sex cohabiting and living together for a long time with mutual degree of interdependence have been held as constituting a 'family';[23] but till recently they were not regarded as husband and

---

[Footnote No. 17 Contd.]

any STD even during consensual intercourse, when the woman or the wife did not know that the man was suffering from a disease which could be transmitted by sexual intercourse, would be guilty of inflicting grievous bodily harm under section 20 of the Offences Against the Person Act, 1861 and *R v. Clarence*, (1889) 22 QBD 22 holding to the contrary is no longer authoritative: *R v. Dica*, (2004) 3 All ER 593, pp. 598, 608 (CA). For comments **see** MATTHEW WATT, 'Criminal Law and the Sexual Transmission of HIV', *R v. Dica'*, (2005) 68(1) Modern Law Review 121-34.

18. *Anuj Garg v. Hotel Association of India,* (2008) 3 SCC 1 para 9 : AIR 2008 SC 663; *Krishna Kumar Birla v. Rajendra Singh Lodha,* (2008) 4 SCC 300 para 105 : (2008) 4 JT 82.

19. *Anuj Garg v. Hotel Association of India (supra).*

20. *Nairn v. University of St Andrews,* (1909) AC 147 (HL).

21. *Henreitta Muir Edwards v. Attorney General of Canada,* AIR 1930 PC 120 : 1930 AC 124.

22. *McCartan Turkington Breen (a firm) v. Times Newspapers Ltd.*, (2000) 4 All ER 913, pp. 927, 928 (HL).

23. *Fitzpatrick v. Sterling Housing Association Ltd.*, (1999) 4 All ER 705 (HL).

wife,[24] though different sex partners living together without marriage were so regarded under a special provision.[25] Now after the enforcement of the Human Rights Act, 1998 in England from October 2000 for giving effect to the European Convention on Human Rights, Article 14 of which makes sexual orientation as an impermissible ground of discrimination, the same statute has been construed to regard even same sex partners living together as husband and wife to avoid incompatibility with human rights.[26] As cautioned by LORD SLYNN "when considering social issues in particular judges must not substitute their own views to fill gaps".[27] Thus, though there is considerable change in social attitudes towards transsexuals, the Court of Appeal in *Bellinger v. Bellinger*[28] held that a male-to-female transsexual who underwent irreversible surgery for gender reassignment could not in the absence of legislation of Parliament, be treated as 'female' for purposes of marriage under section 11(c) of the Matrimonial Causes Act, 1973 and her marriage with a male was held to be void. But in *Goowin v. U.K.*,[29] the European Court of Human Rights, expressed the view that in the twenty first century the right of transsexuals to personal development and to physical and moral security in the full sense enjoyed by others in society could not be regarded as a matter of controversy requiring the lapse of time to cast clearer light on the issues involved.[30] The court directed the Government of the United Kingdom to implement such measures in due course as it considered appropriate "to fulfill its obligations to secure the applicant's (a post operative male to female transsexual) and other transsexual's right to respect for private life and right to marry in compliance with the judgment."[31] Soon thereafter the Court of Appeal in *A v. Chief Constable of Yorkshire*[32] held that a post operative male to female transsexual was to be regarded as female for purposes of complaint of sex discrimination and the House of Lords in appeal in the case of *Bellinger v. Bellinger*[33] declared section 11(c) of the Matrimonial Causes

---

24. *Ibid.*
25. *Ibid.*
26. *Ghaidan v. Mendoza,* (2002) 4 All ER 1162 (CA); **Affirmed**, (2004) 3 All ER 411 (HL). See further p. 490. Before enforcement of the Human Rights Act, 1998 in U.K., discrimination on the ground of homosexuality was not held to be discrimination on the ground of sex under the Sex Discrimination Act, 1975 unless it could be proved that male and female homosexuals were treated differently: *MacDonald v. Advocate General of Scotland*, (2004) 1 All ER 339 (HL).
27. *Fitzpatrick v. Sterling Housing Association Ltd.,* (1999) 4 All ER 705, p. 710 (HL).
28. (2002) 1 All ER 311 (CA).
29. [2002] 2 FCR 577.
30. *Ibid.*, p. 602.
31. *Ibid.*, p. 608.
32. (2003) 1 All ER 255 (CA), pp. 265, 267.
33. (2003) 2 All ER 593 (HL).

Act, 1973 incompatible with the Convention rights. The House of Lords later in appeal confirmed the decision of the Court of Appeal in *A v. Chief Constable of Yorkshire*[34] on the ground that a transsexual had a right to be recognised his or her reassigned gender for the purposes of discrimination between men and women in the fields covered by the Equal Treatment Directive of the Community law and section 54(9) of the Police and Criminal Evidence Act, 1984 which requires that intimate searches must be carried out by a constable who 'shall be of the same sex as the person searched'.

On the same principles, general words are construed to include new inventions and technological advances not known at the time when the Act was passed. It has, accordingly, been held that telephone is 'telegraph' within the meaning of that word in the Telegraph Acts, 1863 and 1869 although telephone was not invented in 1869;[35] that a photographic copy is 'copy' under the Engraving Copyright Act, 1734;[36] and that an electric tram car is a stage carriage within the meaning of the Stage Carriage Act, 1832.[37] Similarly, 'broadcasting' has been held to be covered by the word 'telegraph' as used in the phrase 'Telegraph & other works and undertaking' in section 92(1)(a) of the British North America Act, 1867;[38] and radio broadcasting has been held to be included in the expression 'postal, telegraphic, telephonic and other like services' under section 51(5) of the Australian Constitution.[39] Following the same principle, it has been held by the Supreme Court that the definition of

---

34. (2004) 3 All ER 145 (HL).

35. *A.G. v. Edison Telephone Co. of London*, (1880) 6 QBD 244; **referred** to in *Senior Electric Inspector v. Laxminarayan Chopra*, AIR 1962 SC 159, p. 162 : (1962) 3 SCR 146, and *Vishnu Agencies (Pvt.) Ltd. v. Commercial Tax Officer*, AIR 1978 SC 449, p. 460 : (1978) 1 SCC 520.

36. *Gambart v. Ball*, (1863) 32 LJCP 166. **See further** *R v. Fellows*, (1997) 2 All ER 548 : 1997 Crim LR 524 (CA) (The definition of 'indecent photograph' set out in sections 1 and 7 of the Protection of Children Act, 1978, even before its amendment in 1994 was held to be wide enough to include 'data stored on a computer disc', a technology not anticipated in 1978 when the Act was passed). **See** for this case also text and note 83, p. 969.

37. *Chapman v. Kirke*, (1948) 2 All ER 556.

38. *In re, Regulation and Control of Radio Communications in Canada*, (1932) AC 304 (PC), referred to in *Senior Electric Inspector v. Laxminarayan Chopra, supra*; *State of Madras v. Gannon Dunkerley & Co.*, AIR 1958 SC 560, pp. 573, 574 : 1959 SCR 379; *Vishnu Agencies (Pvt.) Ltd. v. Commercial Tax Officer, supra.*

39. *R v. Brislan, Ex parte, Williams*, (1935) 54 CLR 262. **See further** *Telstra Corporation Ltd. v. Asian Performing Right Association*, (1997) 71 ALJR 1312, p. 1339. ("In certain circumstances, general language originally designed to apply to an earlier technology may apply to supervening technology." The new technology of music on hold, *i.e.*, music played when the telephone lines are engaged, by a telecommunications company was held to amount to 'diffusion service' and 'broadcast' within the Copyright Act, 1968).

'telegraph line' in the Indian Telegraph Act, 1885, which is included by reference in the Indian Electricity Act, 1910, is wide enough to take in electric lines used for the purpose of wireless telegraph;[40] the definition of 'cinematograph' contained in section 2(e) of the Cinematograph Act, 1952 and in Cinema Regulation Acts enacted by the States in 1952 will cover video cassette recorders/players (developed in 1970s) for representation of motion pictures on a television screen;[41] the word 'handwriting' in section 45 of the Evidence Act, 1872 will embrace typewriting although it was only in 1874 that the first practical typewriter was marketed;[42] a tape recorded statement of a speech is admissible provided the voice of the person alleged to be speaking is duly identified and possibilities of tampering are ruled out;[43] and evidence taken of a witness in America by video conferencing in India where the accused is being tried will satisfy the requirement of evidence taken in presence of the accused under section 273 of the Criminal Procedure Code enacted in 1973 when the technique of video conferencing had not developed;[44] and power to

---

40. *Senior Electric Inspector v. Laxminarayan Chopra, supra*. But **see** *Bhagwandas Goverdhandas Kedia v. Girdharilal Purshottamdas & Co.*, AIR 1966 SC 543 : 1966 (1) SCR 656, where a majority of the Supreme Court held that section 4 of the Indian Contract Act, 1872, which read with the Illustrations contains rules regarding acceptance of proposal by post and telegraph does not apply when acceptance is made by telephone although the language of the section is quite general. HIDAYATULLAH, J. took a contrary view and held that the language was wide enough to cover cases of new inventions. And it has been now held that unqualified acceptance of proposal by email satisfies the requirement of section 4: *Trimax International FZE Limited v. Vedanta Aluminium Ltd.*, (2010) 3 SCC 1 paras 50, 51 : (2010) 1 JT 474.

41. *Laxmi Video Theatres v. State of Haryana*, AIR 1993 SC 2328 : 1993 (3) SCC 715; *Shanker Video v. State of Maharashtra*, AIR 1993 SC 2111 : 1993 (3) SCC 696.

42. *State v. S.J. Choudhary*, 1996 (2) Scale 37, pp. 40, 41: AIR 1996 SC 1491, p. 1496 : (1996) 2 SCC 428 (para 16).

43. *Tukaram S. Dighole v. Manikrao Shivaji Kokate*, (2010) 4 SCC 329 paras 23, 36 : AIR 2010 SC 965.

44. *State of Maharashtra v. Dr. Praful B. Desai*, 2003 AIR SCW 1885 : (2003) 4 SCC 601 : AIR 2003 SC 2053. See further *Kalyan Chandra Sarkar v. Rajesh Ranjan alias Pappu Yadav*, (2005) 3 SCC 284, pp. 297, 298 (trial of accused by video conferencing when he cannot be safely brought to court from jail); *Polanski v. Conde Nast Publications Ltd.*, (2005) 1 All ER 945 (HL). (A non-resident claimant who has good reason for not coming to United Kingdom for fear of being extradited to USA can be allowed to give evidence by a video conference link.) *R (on the application of D) v. Camberwell Green Youth Court*, (2005) 1 All ER 999 (HL). (A child witness needing protection can be examined by a video conference link).

The question whether polygraph test (lie detection test) can be used in evidence against the accused during trial was left open in *Ram Singh v. Sonia*, (2007) 3 SCC 1 (para 29) : AIR 2007 SC 1218; *Central Electricity Regulatory Commission v. National Hydroelectric Power Corporation Ltd.*, (2010) 10 SCC 280 : (2010) 7 SCALE 485 (court notices can now be sent by email in commercial litigation).

alter meter in section 20 of the Electricity Act, 1910 will cover power to replace electromechanical meters by electronic meters which were not in vogue when the Act was enacted.[45] Similarly, the provision in section 14 of the Punjab General Sales Tax Act, 1948 authorising the officers to seize account books and return the same after putting their signature and seal was also held to apply when the account books were contained in a hard disk. It was pointed out that the provision could be complied with by seizing the hard disk. The officers could make out copies of the said hard disk or obtain a hard copy and fix their signature and official seal in physical form thereupon and furnish a copy thereof to the dealer.[46]

The Supreme Court adverted to the principles (as discussed in chapter 4 of this book[47]) as to when a statute can be applied to recent developments and new inventions or techniques while interpreting 'explanation' added in sections 53, 53A and 54 of the Criminal Procedure Code, 1973 relating to examination of accused. The explanation defines 'examination' to include "the examination of blood, blood stains, semen, swabs in case of sexual offence, sputum and sweat, hair samples and finger nail clippings by the use of modern and scientific techniques including DNA profiling and *such other tests* which the registered medical practitioner thinks necessary in a particular case." The Supreme Court declined to read the expression 'such other tests' to cover narco analysis technique; polygraph examination and Beep Test as testimony obtained after involuntary administration of these tests would amount to testimonial compulsion offending Article 20(3) and would also be restrictive of personal liberty of the accused under Article 21. Further other enumerated tests in the explanation are examination of bodily substances and the safe inference was that Parliament did not deliberately enumerate the impugned tests in the explanation.[48] When the new technological advances becoming known after the passing of the statute fall within the same genus covered by it and when its purpose would be defeated unless extension were made, the court may even be willing to strain the language a bit to cover the new advances. On these considerations section 1(1) of the Human Fertilisation and Embryology Act, 1990 which defines 'embryo' to mean 'a live human embryo where fertilisation is complete' was construed to cover even an embryo produced not by fertilisation but by Cell Nuclear Replacement (CNR), a method developed by scientists after 1990, by reading the definition of

45. *Suresh Jindal v. BSES Rajdhani Power Ltd.*, AIR 2008 SC 280 paras 43, 44 : (2008) 1 SCC 341.
46. *State of Punjab v. Amritsar Beverages Ltd.*, (2006) 7 SCC 607 : AIR 2006 SC 2820.
47. Now pp. 275 - 328 of the 12th edition.
48. *Selvi v. State of Karnataka*, (2010) 7 SCC 263, 264 paras 170 to 172 : AIR 2010 SC 1974.

embryo to mean 'a live human embryo where if it is produced by fertilization, fertilisation is complete'.[49]

Dealing with section 123 of the Indian Evidence Act, 1872, and the phrase 'Affairs of the State', GAJENDRAGADKAR, J. observed: "It may be that when the Act was passed, the concept of Governmental functions and their extent was limited; and so was the concept of the words 'affairs of the State' correspondingly limited; but as is often said, words are not static vehicles of ideas or concepts. As the content of the ideas or concepts conveyed by respective words expand, so does the content of the words keep pace with the said expanding content of the ideas or concepts and naturally tend to widen the field of public interest which the section wants to protect."[50] Similarly, while considering the word 'necessaries' in section 5 of the Admirality Courts Act, 1861, SINHA J. observed: "Global changes and outlook in trade and commerce could be a relevant factor.—What was not considered a necessity a century back may be held to be so now."[51]

In dealing with the word 'textiles' and in holding that cotton/woollen dry felts are textiles, the Supreme Court said that it must be remembered that the concept of textiles is not a static concept and it has, having regard to newly developing materials, methods, techniques and processes, a continually expanding content and new kinds of fabrics may be invented which may legitimately, without doing any violence to the language, be regarded as textiles.[52]

When a comparatively modern device and equipment was becoming in vogue at the time when the Act was enacted, there can be no difficulty in holding that general words used in the Act will cover such device and equipment. Thus 'notice in writing' required by section 138 of the Negotiable

---

49. *R (On the application of Quintavalle) v. Secretary of State for Health,* (2002) 2 All ER 625, pp. 633, 637 (CA) (LORD PHILLIPS) : **affirmed**, (2003) 2 All ER 113 (H.L.). **See further** *R (on the application of Quintavalle) v. Human Fertilisation and Embryology Authority (HFEA),* (2003) 3 All ER 257 (CA) (HFEA can grant a licence to permit tissue typing to test an embryo for tissue compatibility with a sibling affected by a particular disease to provide a source of stem cells for him, a technique not known when the Act was passed). **Affirmed**, (2005) 2 All ER 555 (HL).

50. *State of Punjab v. Sodhi Sukhdev Singh,* AIR 1961 SC 493, p. 502 : 1961 (2) SCR 371; **See further** observations of SUBBARAO, J. in this case at p. 527 (AIR).

51. *Liverpool and London SP&I Association v. M.V. Sea Success & Asso. Ltd.,* (2004) 9 SCC 512 (para 65) : (2003) Supp (5) SCR 851 : (2003) 9 JT 218 (claim for unpaid insurance premium of P&I club will fall under section 5 for under the present changed context getting the ship insured with P&I club will fall under the expression necessaries).

52. *Porritts and Spencer (Asia) Ltd. v. State of Haryana,* AIR 1979 SC 300, p. 303 : 1979 (1) SCC 82.

Instruments Act, 1881, which was inserted in 1968 when Facsimile (Fax) had become vogue was held to include notice transmitted by Fax.[53]

A domain name, the original role of which was only to provide an address for computers on the internet now after it is being used as a business identifier and provides information/services on the internet has been held to be a trade mark under section 2(zb) of the Trade Marks Act, 1999 and passing off action can be based on it.[54]

In yet another case relating to the Indian Penal Code, 1860, the Supreme Court pointed out that the Code should as far as its language permits, be construed with reference to modern needs not with reference to notions of criminal jurisdiction prevailing at the time when the Code was enacted.[55]

A distinction is said to exist in this respect between ancient statutes and statutes which are comparatively modern. The principle is thus explained by SUBBARAO, J.: "It is perhaps difficult to attribute to legislative body functioning in a static society that its intention was couched in terms of considerable breadth so as to take within its sweep the future developments comprehended by the phraseology used. It is more reasonable to confine its intention only to the circumstances obtaining at the time the law was made. But in modern progressive society it would be unreasonable to confine the intention of a Legislature to the meaning attributable to the word used at the time the law was made, for a modern Legislature making laws to govern society which is fast moving must be presumed to be aware of an enlarged meaning the same concept might attract with the march of time and with the revolutionary changes brought about in social, economic, political and scientific and other fields of human activity. Indeed, unless a contrary intention appears, an interpretation should be given to the words used to take in new facts and situation, if the words are capable of comprehending them."[56]

---

53. *SIL Import USA v. Exim Aides Silk Exporters,* AIR 1999 SC 1609, p. 1612 : (1999) 4 SCC 567.
54. *Satyam Infoway Ltd. v. Sifynet Solutions Pvt. Ltd.*, AIR 2004 SC 3540 : (2004) 6 SCC 145.
55. *Mobarik Ali Ahmad v. State of Bombay*, AIR 1957 SC 857, p. 871 : 1958 SCR 328. **Cf.** the following dicta of LORD JOWITT, L.C. in *Joyce v. Director of Public Prosecutions*, (1946) 1 All ER 186, p. 189 (HL). "It is not an extension of a penal law to apply its principle to circumstances unforeseen at the time of its enactment, as long as the case is fairly brought within its language."
56. *Senior Electric Inspector v. Laxminarayan Chopra*, AIR 1962 SC 159, p. 163 : 1962 (3) SCR 146. **See further** *Rajaram Jaiswal v. State of Bihar*, AIR 1964 SC 828, p. 836 : 1964 (2) SCR 752.

(b) Constitution Acts[57]

Insofar as a Constitution Act is concerned, there is greater reason in giving to its language a liberal construction so as to include within its ambit the future developments in various fields of human activity than in restricting the language to the state of things existing at the time of the passing of the Act.[58] A Constitution, unlike other Acts, is intended to provide an enduring instrument to serve through a long lapse of ages without frequent revision. It is not only designed to meet the needs of the day when it is enacted but also the needs of the altering conditions of the future. It contains a framework of Government, a mechanism for making laws and resolution of constitutional disputes; and in a federation distribution of legislative fields between the centre and the units. It very often refers to the ideals which it seeks to achieve and secures certain fundamental rights to the citizens. The fields of legislation, the ideals and the rights are expressed in general terms which are compressed sentences if not Chapters. "In the interpretation of a constitutional document 'words are but a framework of concepts and concepts may change more than words themselves'. The significance of the change of the concepts themselves is vital and the

---

57. For rules relating to construction of the Constitution, **see** generally: *Karnataka State v. Union of India*, AIR 1978 SC 68, pp. 107-15 : (1977) 4 SCC 608; *India Cement Ltd. v. State of Tamil Nadu*, AIR 1990 SC 85, pp. 90, 91 : (1990) 1 SCC 12; *Goodyear India Ltd. v. State of Haryana*, AIR 1990 SC 781, p. 791; *Federation of Hotel and Restaurant v. Union of India*, AIR 1990 SC 1637 : 1989 (3) SCC 634; *Elel Hotels and Investments Ltd. v. Union of India*, AIR 1990 SC 1664 : (1989) 3 SCC 698; *Synthetics and Chemicals Ltd. v. State of U.P.*, AIR 1990 SC 1927, pp. 1950, 1951; *Life Insurance Corporation of India v. Prof. Manubhai D. Shah*, AIR 1993 SC 171, pp. 176-179 : (1992) 3 SCC 637; *Kihota Hollohan (Shri) v. Zachilhu (Mr.)*, AIR 1993 SC 412, p. 428 : 1992 Supp (2) SCC 651 (Construction of 10th Schedule). SEERVAI, Constitutional Law of India, 4th Edition, Vol. 1, pp. 172-259. JUSTICE D.M. DHARMADHIKARI, 'The Principle of Constitutional Interpretation: Some Reflections', AIR 2004 Journal, pp. 65 to 76; FALI S. NARIMAN, 'Silences in Our Constitutional Law' (2006) SCC (J) 15 (The First DURGA DAS BASU Endowment Lecture.); RABINDER SINGH Q. C., 'Interpreting Bill of Rights' (2008) 29 Statute Law Review 82. **See further** *A.G. of Gambia v. Momodon*, (1984) AC 689, p. 700 (PC) (generous and purposive construction to be adopted); *Societe United Docks v. Govt. of Mauritius*, (1985) 1 All ER 864, p. 873 (PC); *Attorney- General of Trinidad and Tobago v. Waye Whiteman*, (1992) 2 All ER 924, p. 927 (PC) (broadly and purposively so as to give effect to its spirit); *Attorney-General of Hong Kong v. Lee Kwong Kut*, (1993) 3 All ER 939, p. 947 : 1993 AC 951 (PC). **See also** cases in note 62, pp. 261, 263.

58. *Union of India v. Naveen Jindal*, (2004) 2 SCC 510, p. 539 (para 39) : AIR 2004 SC 1559; *Pratap Singh v. State of Jharkhand*, (2005) 3 SCC 551, p. 580. ("Political social and economic development can throw light on the meaning of the Constitution"). **See further** on this point the dissenting opinion of SINHA J. in *State of Punjab v. Dewans Modern Breweries Ltd.*, (2004) 11 SCC 26, pp. 145-56 (paras 289 to 333) : (2003) 10 JT 485.

constitutional issues are not solved by a mere appeal to the meaning of the words without an acceptance of the line of their growth. It is aptly said that 'the intention of a constitution is rather to outline principles than to engrave details'."[59] No provision and indeed no word or expression of the Constitution exists in isolation. They are necessarily related to, transforming and in turn being transformed by, other provisions, words and phrases in the Constitution.[60] A Constitutional court, like our Supreme Court, is a nice balance of jurisdictions. It declares the law as contained in the Constitution but in doing so it rightly reflects that a Constitution is a living and organic thing which of all instruments has the greatest claim to be construed broadly and liberally[61] with an object oriented approach[62] and the

---

59. *R.C. Poudyal v. Union of India*, AIR 1993 SC 1804, p. 1850 : 1994 Supp (1) SCC 324; *Special Reference No. 1 of 2002 (under Article 143(1) of the Constitution)*, AIR 2003 SC 87, p. 138 : (2002) 8 SCC 237, p. 319; *Ashok Tanwar v. State of H.P.*, (2005) 2 SCC 104, p. 114 : AIR 2005 SC 614. Speaking in the context of fundamental rights REDDY, J. said: "Fundamental rights themselves have no fixed content, most of them are empty vessels into which each generation must pour its content in the light of its experience". *Peoples Union for Civil Liberties v. Union of India*, (2003) 4 SCC 399, p. 453 : AIR 2003 SC 2363.

60. *GVK Industries Ltd. v. ITO*, (2011) 4 SCC 36 (para 37) : (2011) 3 JT 356.

61. *Goodyear India Ltd. v. State of Haryana*, AIR 1990 SC 781, p. 791 : 1990 (2) SCC 71; *Synthetics Chemicals Ltd. v. State of U.P.*, AIR 1990 SC 1927, p. 1951 : 1990 (1) SCC 109; *Special Reference No. 1 of 2002 (under Article 143(1) of the Constitution)*, *supra*.

62. *S.R. Chaudhuri v. State of Punjab*, AIR 2001 SC 2707, pp. 2717, 2719 : (2001) 7 SCC 126. (Article 164(4) construed to further the principle of a representative and responsible government by holding that a person who is not a member of the legislature and does not get elected within six months of becoming a minister cannot be reappointed a minister during the same term of the legislature without getting elected as a member); *T.M.A. Pai Foundation v. State of Karnataka*, AIR 2003 SC 355, p. 415 : (2002) 8 SCC 481; This case overrules the view taken in *J.P. Unnikrishnan v. State of A.P.*, (1993) 1 SCC 645 : AIR 1993 JC 2178 that under Article 19(1)(g) there is no fundamental right to establish and administer educational institutions]; *Sobha Hymavathi Devi v. Sethi Gangadhar Swamy*, AIR 2005 SC 800 (Having regard to the object behind grant of reservation to scheduled castes and scheduled tribes in Articles 15(4), 16(4), 330 and 332 of the Constitution, the benefit of reservation cannot be allowed to a woman of a higher caste who claims by marriage to have acquired the status of a scheduled caste or scheduled tribe.) *M. Nagraj v. Union of India*, (2006) 8 SCC 212 (paras 122, 123) : AIR 2007 SC 71 (Even provisions for affirmative action in Articles 15(4), 15(5) and 16(4) are considered as restricted by the ceiling limit of 50 per cent, the concepts of creamy layer and the compelling reasons, namely, backwardness, inadequacy of representation and overall administrative efficiency); on the question of concept of creamy layers, **see further**, *Nair Service Society v. State of Kerala*, (2007) 4 SCC 1 : (2007) 4 Scale 106 : (2007) 3 SLT 730; *Indira Sawhney v. Union of India*, 1992 Supp (3) SCC 217 : AIR 1993 SC 477; *Ashok Kumar Thakur v. Union of India*, (2008) 6 SCC 1 pp. 501 to 512 : (2008) 5 JT 1 (creamy layer principle is applied to determine socially and educationally backward class. It has no application to Scheduled caste and Scheduled tribe); *Biharilal*

[Footnote No. 62 Contd.]

experience gained in its working.[63] The principle of broad and liberal construction does not, however, mean that limitations based on its scheme and basic structure cannot be read into its language when it becomes necessary to do so.[64] The judicial function of the court in interpreting the Constitution thus presents an "antinomy". It calls *both* for building upon a continuity of principles found in the instrument *and* for meeting the dominant needs and aspirations of the present.[65]

A court has more freedom in the interpretation of a Constitution than in the interpretation of other laws.[66] "The great generalities of the Constitution

---

[Footnote No. 62 Contd.]

Rada v. Anil Jain (Tinu), (2009) 4 SCC 1 para 40 (There is no separate category as 'general category'. Such an expression if employed will mean persons of all categories irrespective of their caste, class, community or tribe); *Union of India v. Rakesh Kumar,* (2010) 4 SCC 50 paras 44, 48, 49 : AIR 2010 SC 3244 (The case of Panchayats in *Scheduled Areas* is a fit case that warrants exceptional treatment with regard to reservations and the rationale of ceiling of 50% has no application. Reservation of at least half the seats in Panchayats to STs and cent percent reservation of chairpersons of Panchayat in favour STs is not invalid). **See further:** *K. Krishna Murthy v. Union of India,* (2010) 7 SCC 202 : (2010) 5 JT 601, for reservation generally in Local Self Government under Article 243-D and Article 243-T; *Union of India v. Ramesh Ram,* (2010) 7 SCC 234 : AIR 2010 SC 2691 (vacation of general seat by a reserved category candidate allowed to move in the reserved category where he has better prospects. The general seat vacated to go to a general category candidate in the waiting list).

63. *Aruna Roy v. Union of India,* AIR 2002 SC 3176, p. 3200 : (2002) 7 SCC 368.

64. *B.K. Kapur v. State of Tamil Nadu,* AIR 2001 SC 3435, pp. 3448, 3449 : (2001) 7 SCC 231. (Article 164(1) construed with limitations implied from Article 164(4) that a non-member cannot be appointed Chief Minister or Minister unless he is eligible on the date of appointment to contest the election to become a member inspite of the resolution of the majority party in the assembly to make him Chief Minister or Minister).

65. ARCHIBALD: COX, Court and the Constitution, pp. 70, 378. "It (the constitution) is rather to be likened to a floating dock which, while firmly attached to its moorings, and not therefore at the caprice of the waves, *yet rises and falls with the tide of the time and circumstances*". J.M. BECK, Constitution of the United States, Yesterday, Today and Tomorrow,' quoted in *Ajit Singh v. State of Punjab,* JT 1999 (7) SC 153, p. 165 : AIR 1999 SC 3471, p. 3479 : (1999) 7 SCC 209; *Special Reference No. 1 of 2002 (under Article 143(1) of the Constitution) supra.*

In the words of JUSTICE AHRON BARAK, President of the Supreme Court of Israel: "Purposive interpretation of the Constitution is based on the status of the judge as an interpreter of the constitution. A judge who interprets the constitution is a partner to the authors of the constitution. The authors establish the text, the judge determines its meanings. The authors formulate a will that they wish to realise; the judge locates this will within the larger picture of the constitution's role in modern life. He or she must strike a balance between the will of the authors of the constitution and the fundamental values of those living under it"; AHRON BARAK, 'A judge on Judging": The Role of a Supreme Court in a Democracy', 116 (2002-03) Harvard Law Review, pp. 73, 74.

66. HIDAYATULLAH, 'Judicial Methods', Miscellanea, p. 236.

have a content and a significance that vary from age to age"[67] and so the court is not bound to accept the meaning of a provision in a Constitution according to the original understanding of its makers.[68] The Constitution is

---

67. CARDOZO, The Nature of Judicial Process, p. 17.

68. BHAGWATI, 'Judicial Interpretation in Constitutional Law,' Dimensions of Law, p. 30; *Supreme Court Advocate-on-Record Association v. Union of India*, AIR 1994 SC 268, pp. 363, 397, 398; *Kapila Hingorani v. State of Bihar,* (2003) 6 SCC 1, p. 30 : (2003) 3 LLJ 31. In the context of the Australian Constitution, KIRBY J. said: "we are not bound to the imaginings of the men who, in the last decade of a past century, wrote the constitution. It is governmental charter of today's Australians:" *ABEBE v. Commonwealth*, (1999) 73 ALJR 584, pp. 624, 625 (Aust). KIRBY J. has expressed the view that 'originalist' approaches have been rejected in many decisions of the High Court of Australia : *Selim v. Lele,* (2009) 83 ALJR 271 para 93. The Supreme Court of the United Sates, in *Lawrence Et Al v. Texas*, (2003) 539 US 558 overruling its earlier decision of 1986, by a 6:3 vote held invalid laws banning homosexual sex as infringement of privacy and said the framers of the constitution "knew times can blind us to certain truths and later generations can see that laws once thought necessary and proper in fact serve only to oppress". JUDGE ROBERTS, the newly appointed Chief Justice of the Supreme Court of the United States during his confirmation hearing is reported to have said (The New York Times, September 26, 2005): "I think the framers, when they used broad language like 'liberty', like 'due process', like 'unreasonable' with respect to search and seizures, they were crafting a document that they intended to apply in a meaningful way down the ages"—and "how they apply to evolving societal conditions". As expressed by JUSTICE BRENNAN : "We current justices read the constitution in the only way we can: as the Twentieth Century Americans. We look to the history of the time of framing and to the intervening history of interpretation. But the ultimate question must be, what do the words of the text mean in our time"; WILLIAM J. BRENNAN JR., 'Construing the Constitution', 19 U.C. DAVIS L. REV. 2, 7 (1985) quoted in 116 (2002-03) Harvard Law Review by AHRON BARAK at p. 70. In the context of the Constitution of Barbados, LORD HOFFMAN speaking for the majority in *Boyce v. The Queen*, (2004) 3 WLR 786, p. 795 (PC), expressed the principles applicable in construing a constitution as follows:

"Parts of the Constitution, and in particular the fundamental rights provisions of Chapter III, are expressed in general and abstract terms which invite the participationof the judiciary in giving them sufficient flesh to answer concrete questions. The framers of the Constitution would have been aware that they were invoking concepts of liberty such as free speech, fair trials and freedom from cruel punishments which went back to the Enlightenment and beyond. And they would have been aware that sometimes the practical expression of these concepts—what limits on free speech are acceptable, what counts as a fair trial, what is a cruel punishment—had been different in the past and might again be different in future. But whether they entertained these thoughts or not, the terms in which these provisions of the Constitution are expressed necessarily co-opts future generations of judges to the enterprise of giving life to the abstract statements of fundamental rights. *The judges are the mediators between the high generalities of the constitutional text and the messy detail of their application to concrete problems. And the judges, in giving body and substance to fundamental rights, will naturally be guided by what are thought to be the requirements of a just society in their own time. In so doing, they are not performing a legislative function. They are not doing work of repair by bringing an obsolete text up to date.*

[Footnote No. 68 Contd.]

a living organic thing and must be applied to meet the current needs and requirements, and is not bound to be interpreted by reference to the original understanding of the constitutional economics as debated in Parliament. Accordingly, the Supreme Court held that the content and meaning of Article 149, which provides the duties and powers of the CAG, will vary from age to age and, given that spectrum is an important natural resource, CAG has the power to examine the accounts of telecom service providers under Article 149.[69]

It cannot, however, be said that the rule of literal construction or the golden rule of construction has no application to interpretation of the Constitution.[70] So when the language is plain and specific and the literal construction produces no difficulty to the constitutional scheme, the same has to be resorted to.[71] Similarly, where the Constitution has prescribed a method for doing a thing and has left no 'abeyance' or gap, if the court by a strained construction prescribes another method for doing that thing, the decision will become open to serious objection and criticism.[72]

The freedom and flexibility available to a court in dealing with a Constitution can be illustrated by taking a few examples.

Paragraph (2) of the 10th schedule to the Constitution which provides for disqualification of a member of a House 'if he has voluntarily given up his membership of such political party' from which he was elected has been widely construed to promote the object of curbing the menace of unprincipled defection and, therefore, to cover cases where the member has

---

[Footnote No. 68 Contd.]

On the contrary, they are applying the language of these provisions of the Constitution according to their true meaning. The text is a "living instrument" when the terms in which it is expressed, in their constitutional context, invite and require periodic re-examination of its application to contemporary life.

All this is trite constitutional doctrine. *But equally trite is the proposition that not all parts of a constitution allow themselves to be judicially adapted to changes in attitudes and society in the same way.* Some provisions of the Constitution are not expressed in general or abstract terms which invite judicial participation in giving them practical content. They are concrete and specific."

69. *Association of Unified Tele Services Providers & Ors. v. Union of India & Ors.*, (2014) 6 SCC 110, p. 138.

70. *M.T. Khan v. Govt. of A.P.*, (2004) 2 SCC 267, pp. 271, 272 : AIR 2004 SC 2934, p. 2937.

71. *Ibid* (Construction of Article 165. Only one Advocate General can be appointed); *Kuldip Nayar v. Union of India,* (2006) 7 SCC 1 (paras 201 to 204) : AIR 2006 SC 3127 (construction of the expression 'representative of the State' in Article 80 of the Constitution. The expression only means a person elected by the State legislature and does not necessarily require that the person elected to represent the State should be having domicile in that state.

72. **See text and notes,** 27 to 33, pp. 299 to 301.

impliedly given up the membership.[73] Similarly, the word 'aggression' in Article 355 has been given a wide meaning to include incessant flow of illegal immigrants from Bangladesh into Assam.[74]

Article 21 of the Constitution provides: "No person shall be deprived of his life or personal liberty except according to procedure established by law". It was understood originally to provide merely that no one can be deprived of life or liberty by executive action unsupported by law.[75] But later decisions have progressively deduced a whole lot of human rights from Article 21 which are not enumerated therein, *e.g.*, the right not to be hounded out by the police or CBI merely to find out whether the person has committed any offence or is living as a law abiding citizen;[76] the right to legal aid and speedy trial; the right to means of livelihood; the right to dignity and privacy; the right to health and pollution free environment; the right to education;[77] the right to 'opportunity'.[78] This enumeration

---

73. *Ravi S. Naik v. Union of India*, 1994 (Supp) 2 SCC 641 : AIR 1994 SC 1558 (A member going with leader of another political party to meet the Governor to show that that party had the requisite majority); *Dr. Manchandra Prasad Singh v. Chairman Bihar Legislative Council*, (2004) 8 SCC 747 : AIR 2005 SC 69 (A member of Bihar Legislative Council contesting Parliamentary election from the ticket of another political party); *Rajendra Singh Rana v. Swami Prasad Maurya,* (2007) 4 SCC 270 (paras 48, 49) : AIR 2007 SC 1305. (The act of giving a letter by some members requesting the Governor to call upon the leader of the other side to form a Government itself would amount to an act of voluntarily giving up the membership of the party on whose ticket the said members had got elected.)

74. *Sarbananda Sonowal v. Union of India*, (2005) 5 SCC 665 (paras 51 to 61); *Sarbananda Sonowal v. Union of India,* (2007) 1 SCC 174 : (2007) 1 SLT 648.

75. *A.K. Gopalan v. State of Madras*, AIR 1950 SC 27 : 1950 SCR 88.

76. *Common Cause a Registered Society v. Union of India,* AIR 1999 SC 2979, pp. 3024, 3025 : (1999) 6 SCC 667; *Secretary Minor Irrigation and Rural Engineering Service U.P. v. Sahngoo Ram Arya,* AIR 2002 SC 2225, p. 2227 : (2002) 5 SCC 521 : 2002 Cri LJ 2942.

77. *Unnikrishnan* (*J.P.*) *v. State of Andhra Pradesh*, AIR 1993 SC 2178, p. 2226 : 1993 (1) SCC 645 (**See also** the earlier cases mentioned therein), p. 2190 (mentions more rights and some additional cases). The decision in *Unnikrishnan* regarding interpretation of Articles 29 and 30 has been modified to some extent in *T.M.A. Pai Foundation v. State of Karnataka,* AIR 2003 SC 355 : (2002) 8 SCC 481. *TMA Foundation* case (11 Judge Bench case) further explained in *P.A. Inamdar v. State of Maharashtra,* (2005) 6 SCC 537 (7 Judge Bench) [State cannot appropriate quota for enforcement of its reservation policy in professional unaided (minority and non-minority) educational institutions. It would amount to nationalization of seats]. *Sindhi Education Society v. Govt. (NCT of Delhi)*, (2010) 8 SCC 49 paras 111, 112, 114 : (2010) 7 JT 98 (No reservation in selection of teachers of minority institutions can be directed by Government as it will violate Article 30 of the Constitution). On the question of right to privacy and therefrom right to freedom from unreasonable search and seizure derived from Article 21. **See** *Dist. Registrar and Collector Hyderabad v. Canara Bank*, AIR 2005 SC 136 : (2005) 1 SCC 496.

78. *Reliance Energy Ltd. v. Maharashtra State Road Development Corpn. Ltd.,* (2007) 8 SCC 1 para 36 : (2007) 11 JT 1.

is not exhaustive and more and more rights are being spelled out of Article 21. For example the right that a friend or relative of an arrested person be informed of the arrest and of the place of detention;[79] the right to a free, fair and impartial trial;[80] the right to bail[81] and even of discharge or acquittal[82] when the trial is delayed; the right of atleast one

---

79. *Joginder Kumar v. State of U.P.*, JT 1994 (3) SC 423, p. 430 : AIR 1994 SC 1349 : (1994) 4 SCC 260; **Followed** in *D.K. Basu v. State of West Bengal*, AIR 1997 SC 610 and additional safeguards laid down.

80. *K. Anbazhogan v. Superintendent of Police*, (2004) 3 SCC 767, p. 739 (para 30) : AIR 2004 SC 524; *Zahira Habibulla H. Sheikh v. State of Gujarat*, (2004) 4 SCC 158, p. 184 (para 36) : AIR 2004 SC 3114.

81. *Supreme Court Legal Aid Committee representing under trial prisoners v. Union of India*, JT 1994 (6) SC 544, p. 559 : 1994 (6) SCC 731; *Akhtari Bai v. State of M.P.*, AIR 2001 SC 1528 : (2001) 4 SCC 355; *Siddharam Satlingappa Mhetre v. State of Maharashtra*, (2011) 1 SCC 694 paras 109, 110 : AIR 2011 SC 312 (Liberalised use of anticipatory bail under section 438(1) of the Code of Criminal Procedure has also been recommended in the light of Article 21).

82. *P. Ramchandra v. State of Karnataka*, AIR 2002 SC 1856; *Compare Dyer (Procurator, Fiscal Linlithgow) v. Watson*, (2002) 4 All ER 1, p. 21 (PC). [Article 6(1) of the European Convention for the Protection of Human Rights and Fundamental Freedoms enforced in England by the Human Rights Act, 1998 contains a guarantee that criminal trial be over within 'a reasonable time'. The factors to be considered on the question of violation of this right as explained by the European Court of Human Rights are: complexity of the case, conduct of the accused and the manner in which the case has been dealt with by the administrative and judicial authorities. It is pertinent to note that in this context it has been observed that the *State cannot blame unaccountable delays "on a general want of prosecutors or judges or court houses or on chronic under funding of the legal system"*]; *Attorney General's Reference* (No. 1 of 2001), (2004) 1 All ER 1049 (HL). (On the question of the effect of breach of reasonable time requirement under Article 6(1) of the European Convention, it has been held that in very exceptional cases alone where it could be said for compelling reasons that it would be unfair to try the defendant or a fair hearing was not possible that a trial could be stayed or a conviction could be quashed. Normally when such a breach is established before the hearing is over, all efforts should be made to expedite the hearing to the greatest extent practicable and if the defendant is in custody to release him on bail. In cases where the breach is established after the hearing, the appropriate remedy may be a reduction in the penalty imposed if the defendant is convicted or payment of compensation where the defendant is acquitted). The counterpart of Article 6(1) of European Convention in the International Covenant on Civil and Political Rights, 1966 which is enforced in India by the Protection of Human Rights Act, 1993 is Article 14 which in clause 3(c) guarantees to an accused the right to be tried without undue delay. In *Vakil Prasad Singh v. State of Bihar,* (2009) 3 SCC 355 : AIR 2009 SC 1822 in a case under the Prevention of Corruption Act, 1947 where the bribe money (currency notes) was allegedly recovered and the appellant was caught red handed in 1981 but the challan was filed in 1998 when the appellant applied for quashing of proceedings under section 482 Cr.P.C., 1973 complaining of harassment and there was no reasonable explanation for the delay the Supreme Court held that right to speedy trial under Article 21 was violated and quashed the proceedings. In America the ordinary rule is that only the prosecution delays count

[Footnote No. 82 Contd.]

appeal against conviction with the right to apply for suspension of sen tence;[83] the right of a worker to medical aid;[84] the right of an employee tc receive subsistence allowance during suspension;[85] the right to residence and settlement to live with dignity;[86] the right to regulation of traffic in busy cities for ensuring public safety;[87] the right to hygiene, clear and safe environment, freedom from stray cattle and animals in urban areas;[88] the right of children to protection against exploitation,[89] the right of a woman for protection against sexual harassment at the place of work,[90] and the right to sustained development, *i.e.*, right to development coupled with protection of environment.[91] Briefly stated the protection under Article 21 is to all those aspects of life which go to make a man's life meaningful complete and worth living.[92] It will cover his tradition, culture, heritage and health.[93] The protection of Article 21 is not restricted to citizens but covers even a foreigner when he is in India.[94] One may wonder as to what

[Footnote No. 82 Contd.]

against the government and delays caused by the defendant or his lawyer, whether court appointed or not, did not violate the right to speedy trial: *Vermont v. Brillon,* No. 08-88 decided by the Supreme Court on March 9, 2009, The New York Times. March 10, 2009.

83. *Dadu v. State of Maharashtra,* AIR 2000 SC 3203, pp. 3209, 3210 : (2000) 8 SCC 437. **See further** *Dilip S. Dahanukar v. Kotak Mahindra Co. Ltd.,* (2007) 6 SCC 528, paras 12, 72 : (2007) 6 JT 204 (The appellant can be put to terms while suspending the sentence but no such term can be put as a condition precedent for entertaining the appeal which is a constitutional and statutory right).

84. *Consumer Education and Research Centre v. Union of India*, 1995 (1) Scale 354, p. 375 : AIR 1995 SC 922 : (1995) 3 SCC 42; *State of Punjab v. Mohinder Singh Chawla*, AIR 1997 SC 1225, p. 1227 : 1997 (2) SCC 83.

85. *Capt. M. Paul Anthony v. Bharat Gold Mines Ltd.*, AIR 1999 SC 1416, p. 1424 : (1999) 3 SCC 679.

86. *J.P. Ravidas v. Navyuvak Harijan Uthapan Multi Unit Industrial Co-operative Society*, 1996 (4) Scale 594, p.596: AIR 1996 SC 2151, p. 2152 : (1996) 9 SCC 300.

87. *M.C. Mehta v. Union of India*, AIR 1998 SC 186, p. 190 : 1997 (8) SCC 770.

88. *Milkmen Colony Vikas Samiti v. State of Rajasthan,* (2007) 2 SCC 413 (paras 22 to 24) : AIR 2007 SC 1046.

89. *Bandhua Mukti Morcha v. Union of India*, AIR 1997 SC 2218, p. 2222 : 1997 (10) SCC 549.

90. *Apparel Export Promotion Council v. A.K. Chopra,* AIR 1999 SC 625, p. 634 : (1999) 1 SCC 759.

91. *N.D. Jayal v. Union of India*, AIR 2004 SC 867, p. 878 (paras 23, 24) : (2004) 9 SCC 362; *M.C. Mehta v. Union of India*, AIR 2004 SC 4016, p. 4044 : (2004) 4 JT 181.

92. *Ashok (Dr.) v. Union of India*, AIR 1997 SC 2298, pp. 2304, 2305 : 1997 (5) SCC 10.

93. *Ibid. Kapila Hingorani v. State of Bihar,* (2003) 6 SCC 1, pp. 28, 29.

94. *National Human Rights Commission v. State of Arunachal Pradesh*, AIR 1996 SC 1234 : (1996) 1 SCC 742; *Chairman Railway Board v. Chandrima Das*, AIR 2000 SC 988, pp. 997, 998 : (2000) 2 SCC 465. **See further** *Sarbananda Sonowal v. Union of India*, (2005) 5 SCC 665 (paras 73 to 79) (The protection to illegal immigrants like Bangladeshis in Assam is of life and liberty only and not of just, fair and reasonable

[Footnote No. 94 Contd.]

remains outside Article 21 except right not to live a forced life which too was earlier conceded by a two Judge Bench[95] but later that view was overruled by a Constitution Bench.[96] In the Constitution Bench case of *Gian Kaur* it was also held that euthanasia and assisted suicide are not lawful in India and observed that euthanasia could be made lawful only by legislature. In *Aruna Ramchandra Shanbaug v. Union of India*[97] a two Judge Bench of the Supreme Court has held that passive euthanasia is permissible. In India where attempt to suicide and abetment to suicide are still offences it is difficult to lay down the scope of passive euthanasia and the learned Judges may have better referred the case to a Constitution Bench. Right to life does not also include a right to enjoy all the materialistic pleasures and to procreate as many children as possible, therefore, a provision disqualifying a person having more than two children from contesting a Panchayat or Municipal election has been held to be valid.[98] The right to life does not also at present include right to employment.[99] The human rights enumerated above were so derived from Article 21 mainly by reading the Directive Principles (more specifically Articles 39, 39A, 41, 42

[Footnote No. 94 Contd.]

procedure in the matter of their expulsion and the power of the Government of India for expelling an illegal immigrant is absolute) **affirmed in** (2007) 1 SCC 174 : (2006) 13 Scale 33 : (2007) 1 SLT 648. In contrast, when a foreigner who is lawfully in India can be expelled, as provided in Article 13 of the International Covenant on Civil and Political Rights to which India is a party, only pursuant to a decision reached by law of a competent court after he is given opportunity to state his reasons against expulsion except where compelling reasons of national security otherwise require: Sarbananda Sonowal, (2007) 1 SCC 174 : (2007) 1 SLT 648 : (2006) 13 Scale 33; Hasan Ali v. Union of India, (2006) 3 SCC 705 (para 8) : AIR 2006 SC 1714. Wages of seamen of a foreign ship which is confiscated will constitute an integral part of their right to life and can be recovered from the sale proceeds of the vessel: O Konavalov v. Commander Coast Guard Region, (2006) 4 SCC 620 (para 45) : (2006) 3 JT 567; Peoples Union For Civil Liberties v. Union of India, (2010) 5 SCC 423 : (2010) 1 SCALE 546 (Homeless and destitute persons have in winter right to night shelters, food and basic amenities).

95. *P. Rathinam Nagbhusan Patnaik v. Union of India*, AIR 1994 SC 1844 : 1994 (3) SCC 394.

96. *Gian Kaur (Smt.) v. State*, AIR 1996 SC 946 : 1996 (2) SCC 648. **See further** *NHS Trust v. M,* (2001) 2 All ER 801 (Withdrawal of nutrition and hydration on expert medical opinion, though hastening death, from insensate patients in permanent vegetative state does not infringe their right to life.). *R (on the application of Pretty) v. Director of Public Prosecutions,* (2002) 1 All ER 1 (HL). (Convention's rights enforced by the Human Rights Act, 1998 do not oblige the state to legalise assisted suicide).

97. (2011) 4 SCC 454 : AIR 2011 SC 1290. **See further** on euthanasia, Law of Torts, 26th edition edited by G. P. SINGH, p. 564.

98. *Javed v. State of Haryana,* AIR 2003 SC 3057, pp. 3067, 3068 : (2003) 8 SCC 369; *Zile Singh v. State of Haryana*, (2004) 8 SCC 1, p. 8 : AIR 2004 SC 5100.

99. *Secretary, State of Karnataka v. Umadevi,* (2006) 4 SCC 1 (para 51) : AIR 2006 SC 1806.

and 45) in or with Article 21 and thereby in effect making the Directiv Principles in Part IV enforceable, even though Article 37 provides tha these Principles shall not be enforced by any court,[1] and it is accepted tha these Principles by themselves do not confer any legislative power.[2] Th Supreme Court has, thus, by interpretation brought in the 'due process concept of the American Constitution which the Constitution makers de liberately avoided to incorporate.[3]

A guarantee of right to life has been construed broadly even in other ju risdictions[4] but not as broadly as in India. Too much reliance by the Su preme Court on Article 21 and its extensive extension by judicial extrapo lation has given rise to the criticism that all sorts of "goodness" so derivec

1. *Unnikrishnan (J.P.) v. Union of India, supra*; *Ashok (Dr.) v. Union of India, supra* **See further** *Rajeeva Mankotia v. Secretary to President of India*, AIR 1997 SC 276(: (1997) 10 SCC 441. (The Supreme Court directed protection and maintenance o Viceregal Lodge at Shimla and other national monuments and thereby enforced Arti cle 49 of the Directive Principles.) *State of Punjab v. Ram Lubhaya Bagga*, JT 199 (2) SC 136, p. 140 : AIR 1998 SC 1703 : (1998) 4 SCC 117 (Duty to improve public health in Article 47 relied for inferring right to health from Article 21); *A.I.I.M.S Students Union v. A.I.I.M.S.*, AIR 2001 SC 3262, pp. 3280, 3281 : (2002) 1 SCC 42 (Directive principles in Articles 41 and 47 were taken into account in striking dowr excessive institutional reservation at post graduate level in A.I.I.M.S.). **See further** JAYNA KOTHARI, 'Social Rights and the Constitution', (2004) 6 SCC (J) 31. (The ar ticle shows how 'social rights' that protect the basic necessities of life, *e.g.*, right tc food have been derived from Article 21 by recourse to Part IV of the constitution).
2. *Koluthara Exports Ltd. v. State of Kerala,* AIR 2002 SC 973, p. 977 : (2002) 2 SCC 459 : 2002 SCC (L&S) 304.
3. GRANVILLE AUSTIN, The Indian Constitution, Corner Stone of a Nation, pp. 101 to 106; BHAGWATI, Judicial Interpretation in Constitutional Law, Dimensions of Law, p. 30. "The true author of this interpretational innovation was JUSTICE V.M. TARKUNDE" of the Bombay High Court in a Judgment rendered in 1965 : Y.V. CHANDRACHUD, 'A Peep into the Past. A Gaze into the Future', Constitutionalism Human Rights and the Rule of Law, Essays in the honour of Soli J. Sorabjee, p. 9 (Universal Law Publishing Co.).
4. Article 2 of the European Convention for the Protection of Human Rights and Fundamental Freedoms, 1950 (set out in Sch. I to the (U.K.) Human Rights Act, 1998) provides: "Everyones right to life shall be protected by law." As summarised by LORD BINGHAM in *R (on the application of Middletown) v. West Somerset Coroner*, (2004) 2 All ER 465, p. 470 (HL) the European Court of Human Rights has repeatedly interpreted Article 2 as imposing on member states substantive obligations not to take life without justification and also to establish a framework of laws, precautions, procedures and means of enforcement which will to the greatest extent reasonably practicable protect life. Further, the European Court has also interpreted Article 2 as imposing on member states a procedural obligation to initiate an effective public investigation by an independent official body into any death occurring in circumstances in which it appears that one or other of the foregoing substantive obligations has been or may have been, violated and it appears that agents of the state are, or may be, in some way implicated. **See further** pp. 497-498 for the width of a coroner's inquest after the enforcement of the Human Rights Act, 1998; *R (on the application of Gentle) v. Prime Minister,* (2008) 3 All ER 1 (H.L.) paras 4 and 5.

as rights from Article 21 "are only euphoric—they simply cannot be enforced."[5] Another criticism of the way Article 21 has been interpreted is that if that were correct "the entire scheme of Part III could have been telescoped into only one provision namely Article 21."[6]

Fundamental Duties of citizens contained in Article 51A of Part IVA of the Constitution, which by themselves are not enforceable for "it may be necessary to enact suitable legislation wherever necessary to require obedience to obligations by the citizens",[7] have also been used alongwith Directive Principles for interpretation of the Constitution.[8] Article 48A added as a new Directive Principle and Article 51A providing Fundamental Duties, both added by the Constitution 42nd Amendment, read along with the Directive Principle in Article 48 were strongly relied upon in *State of Gujarat v. Mirzapur Moti Kureshi Kassab jamat*[9] by a Constitution Bench of seven judges while upholding by a majority of six to one the validity of the Gujarat Act 4 of 1994 which imposed a total ban on the slaughter of progeny of cow. This case overruled an earlier Constitution Bench decision in *Mohd. Hanif Quareshi v. State of Bihar*[10] and cases following it which permitted slaughter of bullocks when they ceased to be serviceable after the age of 16 years. Article 48 requires the State to take steps for 'prohibiting the slaughter of cows and calves and other milch and draught cattle.' The provision was interpreted in *Mohd. Hanif Quareshi* to be confined only for giving protection to cows and calves and those animals which are presently or potentially capable of yielding milk or of doing

---

5. FALI S NARIMAN, '*50 Years of the Supreme Court—a balance sheet of performance* (R.B. Datar Memorial Lecture), 'Lawyers Update' July-December, 1999. DR. ANAND C.J.I. also voiced "the danger of the judiciary creating a multiplicity of rights without possibility of adequate enforcement" (Inaugural speech delivered on August 29, 1999 at the Golden Jubilee Celebrations of the Rajasthan High Court).

6. 'Skinning a cat', JUSTICE B. N. SRIKRISHNA, (2005) 8 SCC J3, p. J12.

7. Recommendations of Justice Verma Committee quoted in *Rangnath Misra v. Union of India*, (2003) 7 SCC 133 : (2003) 3 JT 206; *Union of India v. Naveen Jindal*, (2004) 2 SCC 510, pp. 549, 550 : AIR 2004 SC 1559.

8. *Union of India v. Naveen Jindal, supra*, pp. 548 to 556 (SCC) [Right to fly National flag derived from Art. 19(1)(a) read with Art. 51A(a) and (c)], *Om Prakash v. State of U.P.*, (2004) 3 SCC 402, p. 414 : AIR 2004 SC 1896 [Reasonableness of ban of trade in non-vegetarion articles in Rishikesh, Haradwar and Muniki Reti supported under Art. 51A(e) and (f).]; *Hinsa Virodhak Sangh v. Mirzapur Moti Kureshi Jamat*, (2008) 5 SCC 33 : AIR 2008 SC 1892 (Resolution for closure of slaughter houses which were owned by the Ahmedabad Municipal Corporation during nine days of Jain festival of Paryushan held valid). **See further** *Intellectual Forum v. State of A.P.*, (2006) 3 SCC 549 : AIR 2006 SC 1350 (Articles 48A and 51A can be used to understand the scope of fundamental rights).

9. (2005) 8 SCC 534 : AIR 2006 SC 212.

10. AIR 1958 SC 731 : 1959 SCR 629. This case has been **overruled** on merits in *State of Gujarat v. Mirzapur Moti Qureshi Kassab Jamat,* (2005) 8 SCC 534 : AIR 2006 SC 212.

work as draught cattle but not to extend to cattle which at one time were milch or draught cattle but which had ceased to be such. This view was not accepted in *Kureshi Kassab Jamat* and the words 'milch and draught cattle' used in Article 48 were given expansive interpretation to include even cattle which had become permanently incapacitated for milch and draught purposes.[11] The court held that "the expression 'milch and draught cattle' is a description of a classification or species as distinct from cattle which by their nature are not milch or draught and the said words do not exclude milch or draught cattle which on account of age or disability cease to be functional for that purpose." This meaning the court reached in the context of the preceding words "cows or calves". It is submitted that the specific mention of 'cows' showed that the intention was to give special protection to cows irrespective of whether they were functional or not as milch cattle. If the intention was to give the same protection to all milch and draught cattle there would not have been any specific mention of 'cows' which on the interpretation which has found favour with the court becomes redundant. The wording then would have been 'milch and draught cattle and calves'. It was also reasoned that cow progeny excreta is scientifically recognized as a source of rich organic manure by the farmers which avoids the use of chemicals and inorganic manure and helps in improving the quality of health and environment within the meaning of Article 48A. This factor was not overlooked in *Mohd. Hanif Quareshi,* though Article 48A was then not in the Constitution. As observed by A.K. MATHUR, J. it was admitted that the output of urine and cow dung of aged bulls and bullocks was considerably reduced. The little benefit on this account has to be ignored having regard to the cost of maintenance of useless cattle which, as pointed out in *Mohd. Hanif Quareshi,* involves a severe drain on the nation's cattle feed, deprives the useful cattle of much needed nourishment and tends to deteriorate the breed. Further, Article 51A(g) of the Fundamental Duties which enjoins as a fundamental duty of every citizen "to have compassion for living creatures" was strongly relied upon in *Kureshi Kassab Jamat* for protecting the slaughter of aged bulls and bullocks and in upholding total ban on the slaughter of progeny of cow. It was reasoned that as the State is "all citizens placed together", the fundamental duty in Article 51A(g) is collectively speaking duty of the State. It was also held that in "testing the constitutional validity of any statutory provision or an executive act or for testing the reasonableness of any restriction cast by law in the exercise of fundamental right by way of regulation, control or prohibition, the Directive Principles of State Policy and Fundamental Duties as enshrined in

---

11. (2005) 8 SCC 534, p. 571 (para 68) : AIR 2006 SC 212.

Article 51A of the Constitution play a significant role."[12] It is submitted that reliance on the fundamental duty 'to have compassion for living creatures' for prohibiting slaughter of even such animals, which have ceased to be useful as milch or draught cattle, for production of meat is a bit far fetched. If this view be correct the State will be duty bound to pass legislation banning not only slaughter of bullocks but also of buffalos, goats and sheep and killing of all living creatures, compelling all those engaged in the businesses of production and sale of meat and edible flesh to close their businesses and forcing Indian citizens to become total vegetarians.[13] It has, however, been held that Articles 48 and 58A by themselves do not make a legislation which imposes a total prohibition on slaughter of bovine cattle and make their slaughter unconstitutional.[14] It is submitted that the dissenting judgment of A.K. MATHUR, J. in *Kureshi Kassab Jamat* is more convincing and *Mohd. Hanif Quareshi* ought not to have been overruled.

Decline of the doctrine of Sovereign Immunity which originated from the interpretation by a Constitution Bench[15] of Article 300 on the basis of its historical origin[16] and the evolution of the concept of public law wrongs and strict liability of the State for such wrongs[17] is also an example how interpretation of the Constitution is not static but progressive to absorb new ideas and meet new situations. As the law now stands, a violation of fundamental rights by the State, or its instrumentalities or their officers acting in the course of employment is a public law wrong to which the doctrine of sovereign immunity has no application and the State is liable to compensate the victim on the principle of strict liability.[18] (The cases of *Nilbati Behra* and *D.K. Basu*[18] related to violation of Fundamental Right under Article 21 however the observations made in, *Nilbati Behra* decided by a three Judge Bench, are general incense that violation of Fundamental Rights will be a public law wrong, redressable by award of compensation under Articles 226 and 32). But another three Judge Bench, however, in *Hindustan Papers Corporation v. Ananta Bhattacharjee*[19] has held that the public law remedy for

---

12. (2005) 8 SCC 534, p. 569 (para 58) : AIR 2006 SC 212.
13. Similar views have been expressed in Constitution of India by ARVIND P. DATAR, (2nd Edition) Vol. 1, pp. 614-15.
14. *Akhil Bharat Goseva Sangh v. State of A.P.*, (2006) 4 SCC 162, p. 204 (paras 99, 100) : (2006) 4 JT 482 : (2006) 4 SLT 255.
15. *Kasturilal Ralia Ram Jain v. State of U.P.*, AIR 1965 SC 1039 : (1965) 1 SCR 375.
16. *Peninsular and Oriental Steam Navigation Co. v. Secretary of State for India*, (1868-1869) 5 Bom HCR App 1, p. 1.
17. For a discussion as to how evolution has taken place, **see** RATANLAL AND DHIRAJLAL, *Law of Torts* (24th edition by G.P. SINGH), pp. 44 to 62.
18. *Nilbati Behra v. State of Orissa*, AIR 1993 SC 1960, pp. 1968, 1969 : (1993) 2 SCC 746; *D.K. Basu v. State of West Bengal*, AIR 1997 SC 610 : (1997) 1 SCC 416.
19. (2004) 6 SCC 213, p. 216 : (2004) 9 Scale 46.

compensation can be resorted to only when the fundamental right of a citizen under Article 21 is violated and not otherwise. The court further said that "it is not every violation of the provisions of the Constitution or a statute which would enable the court to direct grant of compensation." The Constitution Bench decision in *Kasturilal* though not yet overruled by another Constitution Bench has been bypassed, distinguished and criticised in so many later decisions that as observed by a three Judge Bench "much of its efficacy as a binding precedent has been eroded."[20] But with widening of the area of Fundamental Rights under Article 21 by liberal interpretation as discussed above[21] it may become difficult even to hold that any breach of any right under Article 21 will amount to a public law wrong and sound in damages otherwise the blame for every misfortune will be laid at the doorstep of the State. The law on the point is in a developing stage and the Supreme Court is yet to devise some control mechanism to limit the cases where damages can be allowed against the State on the basis of strict liability. It is submitted that the law in this area should be developed incrementally on the principles of analogy and fairness. If in a new situation not covered by an authority of the Supreme Court, a question of this nature arises it may be seen as to how far the new situation resembles to those situations where damages have been allowed and whether it would be fair just and reasonable to award damages against the State in public law. This is the method which is followed in tort law in deciding cases of negligence which are not covered by authority. A distinction may also have to be drawn between State's liability to pay damages in public law for violation of fundamental rights and its duty as a welfare state to provide relief to needy citizens. Whatever may be said about limiting the liability of other organs and instrumentalities of the State, the Supreme Court and High Courts are safe for as held by a Constitution Bench of the Supreme Court, superior courts of justice do not fall within the definition of State in Article 12 of the Constitution and, therefore, they cannot be accused of violation of fundamental rights and the public law remedies under Articles 32 and 226 are not available against their orders.[22] It is, however, interesting to note that in the case of *Maharaj v. Attorney General of Trinidad and Tobago,*[23] which was followed by the Supreme Court in *Nilbati Behra v. State of Orissa,*[24] and which evolved the doctrine of public law wrongs, the violation of human

---

20. *Common Cause a registered society v. Union of India*, AIR 1999 SC 2979, p. 3002 : (1999) 6 SCC 667.

21. **See** pp. 281-288.

22. *Rupa Ashok Hurra v. Ashok Hurra,* AIR 2002 SC 1771, pp. 1776, 1777 : (2002) 4 SCC 388.

23. (1978) 2 All ER 670, pp. 679, 680 : (1978) 2 WLR 902 (PC).

24. AIR 1993 SC 1960 : (1993) 2 SCC 746. For fuller discussion of these cases **see** RATANLAL AND DHIRAJLAL, Law of Torts, (24th Edition by G.P. Singh), pp. 50, 51.

ights was by a judge of the High Court acting in his judicial capacity and he State was held liable in damages. And, in *Omwati v. State of U.P.*,[25] when a person remained in jail for a few days because of bailable warrants issued by the High Court the orders for which were passed as a result of "total non-application of mind" the Supreme Court allowed Rs. 10,000 as token compensation payable by the State.

Another illustration of the same nature is the interpretation of the requirement of consultation with the Chief Justice of India in Articles 124, 217 and 222 of the Constitution.

A seven Judge Bench of the Supreme Court[26] by majority earlier held that the power of appointment and transfer of judges is an executive function and the opinion of the Chief Justice of India expressed in the process of consultation, though of great weight, has no primacy and is not binding on the President but the order of appointment or transfer is open to judicial review. Later a nine Judge Bench[27] by majority gave primacy to the opinion of the Chief Justice of India as symbolising the judiciary and virtually equated consultation to 'concurrence' even though a proposal for use of the word 'concurrence' was not accepted in the Constituent Assembly during the making of the Constitution.[28] The executive interference in the appointment and transfer of judges which was telling upon the independence of the judiciary[29] led to this change in the attitude of the court. VERMA, J., who delivered the leading majority judgment considered the question of construction "in the context of independence of the judiciary as a part of the basic structure of the Constitution, to secure the 'rule of law', essential for the preservation of the judicial system and the broad scheme of separation of powers adopted in the Constitution together with the directive principle of 'separation of judiciary from executive' even at the lowest strata."[30] According to the minority view, the majority

---

25. (2004) 4 SCC 425, p. 426 : 2004 (Supp 1) JT 603.

26. *S.P. Gupta v. President of India*, AIR 1982 SC 149 : 1981 Supp SCC 87.

27. *Supreme Court Advocates-on-Record Association v. Union of India*, AIR 1994 SC 268, p. 442 : 1993 (4) SCC 441.

28. *Ibid.*, p. 384.

29. But the chief justices were not wholly blameless, **see** G.P. Singh, 'My Days in the High Court' 1996 MPLJ 24, p. 29 where in the context of appointments to 'High Courts' it is said: "Experience shows that a person, whom the chief justices (Chief Justice of India and the Chief Justice of the High Court concerned) feel is not fit, is not appointed unless atleast one of them gives in. And there is no reason why any chief justice should give in unless in a weak moment he, consciously or unconsciously, allows himself to go astray on latent considerations of his own promotional or post-retirement benefits or similar advantages." (The article was written in 1986 but was published in 1996).

30. AIR 1994 SC 268, p. 421 : 1993 (4) SCC 441.

opinion amounted to rewriting the Constitution.[31] Further, the majority held that if the appointment or transfer was made on the recommendation of the Chief Justice of India it will not be open to judicial review. By another nine Judge Bench judgment,[32] the primacy in these matters of the Chief Justice of India acting in consultation with two senior most judges of the Supreme Court now stands transferred to a collegium consisting of the Chief Justice of India and four senior most judges of the Supreme Court in the matter of appointments to the Supreme Court and transfer of High Court judges and to a collegium consisting of the Chief Justice of India and two senior most judges of the Supreme Court in the matter of appointments to High Courts. Details of various consultative steps, which have to be undertaken before finalising the opinion of the collegium, have also been laid down. Appointments and transfers have also been made justiciable if necessary consultative steps, as indicated in the judgment, have not been taken. By these decisions, for all practical purposes, the power of appointment and transfer of judges, which was *prima facie* vested in the executive, was assumed by the judiciary and the executive was denuded of that power.[33] It is also to be noted that not only in *S.P. Gupta's*

---

31. *Ibid.*, pp. 383, 454 (AIR).

32. Special Reference No. 1 of 1998 under Article 143(1) of the Constitution, JT 1998 (7) SC 304 : AIR 1999 SC 1 : (1998) 7 SCC 739 : AIR 1999 SC 1. While appointing an Additional Judge as Permanent Judge the CJI need not consult the collegium. Rigorous execise done at the time of initial appointment is not required to be redone at the time of appointment as Permanent Judge: *Shanti Bhushan v. Union of India,* (2009) 1 SCC 657 : (2009) 1 SLT 29. The collegium principle spelled out from the provisions of Articles 217 and 222 from the requirement of consultation with the Chief Justice of the Supreme Court or the Chief Justice of a High Court cannot be applied to a statutory provision requiring consultation with the Chief Justice, e.g., consultation with the Chief Justice of the High Court required for appointment of President of the State Commission under section 16 of the Consumer Protection Act, 1986. [*Ashok Tanwar v. State of H.P.*, (2005) 2 SCC 104 : AIR 2005 SC 614 overruling *Ashish Handa v. Honble C.J. of Punj & Har. H.C.*, AIR 1996 SC 1308.] But initiation of the proposal for appointment of a retired judge or sitting judge as President of the Commission has still to be by the Chief Justice whose opinion will have primacy. [*State of Haryana v. National Consumer Awareness Group*, AIR 2005 SC 2356, pp. 2360, 2361]. It has also been held that consultation with the District Judge cannot be interpreted to mean consultation with a collegium consisting of District Judge, Addl. District Judges and C.J.M., overruling a contrary decision of the Allahabad High Court. [*State of U.P. v. Johrimal*, (2004) 4 SCC 714, pp. 737, 738 : (2004) 3 SLR 734].

33. These decisions have invited the criticism that "the judiciary has rewritten the Constitution for its self-serving ends", (S. SAHAY, 'Judicial Accountability: Issues') and that "judicial activism here amounted to judicial expansionism because the court expanded its own powers" (S.P. SATHE, Judicial Activism in India, p. 126). **See for further** Criticism: T.R. ANDHYARUJINA, 'Judicial Accountability: Indian Methods and Experience', Judges and Judicial Accountability, (First Indian Reprint by Universal, 2004), pp. 111 to 124; LORD COOKE OF THORNDON, 'Where Angels Fear to

[Footnote No. 33 Contd.]

case but in all earlier cases it had been held that the advice expressed in the process of consultation was not binding.[34] As observed by PROF. WADE: "From the language of Articles 124 and 217 the constitutional plan appears clearly. The initiative formally rests with the President, but he must carry on consultations. The last word rests with him also, so that he may reject chief justice's advice. The sanction then, as in so many cases of last resort rests with the public opinion. When it becomes known that the chief justice's advice has been rejected, the Government will be in political hot water."[35] The Supreme Court has also spelled out from these Articles an inhouse procedure for disciplining judges[36] of superior courts who could *prima facie* be dealt with only by impeachment under Articles 124(4) and 218. This innovation by judicial activism may, if applied to the Supreme Court, divide the judges weakening the authority of the court and in case applied to the seniormost judge put a sort of veto in the hands of the retiring Chief Justice of India in the matter of appointment of his successor for it is he who has to initiate the proposal of

---

[Footnote No. 33 Contd.]

Tread', Supreme But not Infallible Essays in the Honour of Supreme Court' (Oxford University Press, 2000), p. 97. In the words of JUSTICE KRISHNA IYER: "The nine Judges Bench wrested authority to appoint judges, from the top executive to themselves by stroke of adjudicatory self enthroanment". He also said that the in house process of appointment "has often been dilatory, arbitrary and smeared by favourites" [cited FROM C.S. VAIDYANATHAN, Appointment of Judges to the Higher Judiciary' Constitutionalism Human Rights and the Rule of Law (Essays in Honour of Soli J. Sorabjee) (Universal Law Publishing Co.), p. 196]. Similar criticism has been levelled by senior Advocate FALI S. NARIMAN in his Krishna Iyer Foundation lecture, 2005: Dainik Bhaskar, Jabalpur, 14-6-2005.

The working of the collegium model judicially enacted by the Supreme Court for appointment of judges has also not satisfied a parliamentary committee headed by a very senior leader of the congress party, Shri Pranab Mukerjee (now a senior minister) and the committee is reported to have said :"The situation is alarming collegium members are prone to field candidates of their choice. The give and take in the collegiate consultation has the potential of undermining merit." The Committee attributed delay in the justice delivery system due to "politics of the judiciary". The Constitution Review Committee (CRC) headed by formar Supreme Court Chief Justice, M.V. VENKATCHALIAH recommended constitution of National Judicial Commission (NJC) for appointment of judges: RAKESH BHATNAGAR, 'Is Judicial Panel need of the hour', The Times of India 25-5-2004.

34. **See** text and note 86, p. 414. **See further** *Shamsher Singh v. State of Punjab*, AIR 1994 SC 2192 : 1994 Supp (1) SCC 512; *Union of India v. Sankalchand*, AIR 1977 SC 2328 : 1977 (4) SCC 193.
35. Public Law in Britain and India (Nambiyar Lectures), p. 104.
36. *C. Ravichandran Iyer v. Justice M.B. Bhattacharjee*, 1995 (5) SCC 457 : 1995 (6) JT 339. For the nature of inhouse procedure **see** *Indira Jaising v. Registrar General Supreme Court of India,* (2003) 5 SCC 494 : (2003) 3 KLT 198 (Report of inquiry held under this procedure is confidential and the Supreme Court cannot be approached under Article 32 for its publication.)

appointing the seniormost judge considered fit to hold the office as his successor.[37]

The assumption of absolute powers by the Supreme Court in the matter of appointments to itself and the High Courts by highly controversial interpretation of Articles 124 and 217,[38] can be said to be one major 'overreach' by the Judiciary. It not only denuded the Executive of its powers in these matters but also reduced the importance of the roles of the Chief Justice of India and the Chief Justices of High Courts which now has to be shared with the collegium of judges. The power of appointment, transfer, promotion and of directing an inhouse enquiry in respect of High Court judges exercised by the Supreme Court has virtually made the High Courts administratively subordinate to the Supreme Court which was never intended by the Constitution. No system of appointment can probably ensure that all functionaries involved in it will always act objectively or that there will be no scope for any case of conscious or sub-conscious favouritism or that persons in the range of selection when not appointed will not have any cause for grievance.[39] It cannot also be said that the judges appointed under the new procedure are on merits generally superior to those appointed earlier. Why then tinker with the Constitution? It cannot, however, be expected that the Supreme Court will review the collegium decisions and restore the original procedure. The solution probably lies in the appointment of National Judicial Commission as recommended by the Constitution Review Committee,[40] which provides for the effective participation of both the executive and the judiciary in the matter of appointment of judges.

An effort to overrule the two collegium cases has now recently started in *Suraz India* Trust[41] in which a Bench of two judges (JUSTICE DEEPAK VERMA AND JUSTICE (DR.) B. S. CHAUHAN) with the assistance of amicus curiae. Shri A. K. Ganguly formulated the following ten questions of constitutional importance:

(1) Whether the aforesaid two verdicts, *viz.* the 7-Judge Bench and 9-Judge Bench decisions of this Court referred to above really amount to amending Article 124(2) of the Constitution?

---

37. **See** FALI S. NARIMAN, 'Caesar's wife: A judge should be above suspicion'. The Times of India, November, 1997.

38. **See** note 33, p. 300 *supra*.

39. JUSTICE S.S. SODHI, 'The Other Side of Justice', Chief Injustice, pp. 293 to 298 (Hay House India, 2007).

40. Venkatachaliah Committee Recommendations, (Chapter 7), ARVIND P. DATAR, Constitution of India, 2nd Edition, Vol. 3, p. 2368. **See further** note 33, p. 300.

41. *Suraz India Trust v. Union of India*, writ petition (civil) No. 204 of 2010 decided on 4th April 2011.

(2) Whether there is any 'Collegium' system for appointing Supreme Court or High Court Judges in the Constitution?

(3) Whether the Constitution can be amended by a judicial verdict or it can only be amended by Parliament in accordance with Article 368?

(4) Whether the Constitutional scheme was that the Supreme Court and High Court Judges can be appointed by mutual discussions and mutual consensus between the judiciary and the executive; or whether the judiciary can alone appoint Judges of the Supreme Court and High Courts?

(5) Whether the word 'consultation' in Article 224 means 'concurrence'?

(6) Whether by judicial interpretation words in the Constitution can be made redundant, as appears to have been done in the aforesaid two decisions which have made consultation with High Court Judges redundant while appointing a Supreme Court Judge despite the fact that it is permissible on the clear language of Article 124(2)?

(7) Whether the clear language of Article 124(2) can be altered by judicial verdicts and instead of allowing the President of India to consult such Judges of the Supreme Court as he deems necessary (including even junior Judges) only the Chief Justice of India and four senior most Judges of the Supreme Court can alone be consulted while appointing a Supreme Court Judge?

(8) Whether there was any convention that the President is bound by the advice of the Chief Justice of India, and whether any such convention (assuming there was one) can prevail over the clear language of Article 124(2)?

(9) Whether the opinion of the Chief Justice of India has any primacy in the aforesaid appointments?

(10) Whether the aforesaid two decisions should be overruled by a larger Bench?

Shri Vahanvati, the Attorney General who also appeared in the case, supported the contention that the collegium judgments required reconsideration. But he submitted whether a Bench of two Judges could refer the matter for reconsideration as the collegium cases were decided by larger Benches.

The matter was therefore ordered to be placed by the Hon'ble Judges before Hon'ble the Chief Justice for appropriate directions.[41a]

The Supreme Court is also quite sensitive in protecting the independence of and the High Courts control over the District and subordinate courts and has construed Articles 233, 234 and 235 with great emphasis on these aspects. The Supreme Court by a majority of three against two held invalid an Act passed by the Bihar Legislature in so far it fixed without reference to the High Court, reservations to the posts in the higher and subordinate judicial services of the State on the ground that the same violated the scheme of consultation with the High Court in the matter of appointment to these posts as envisaged in Articles 233 and 234 and its control under Article 235 and impinged upon the independence of the judiciary and efficiency of judicial administration, which according to the court, were within the exclusive jurisdiction of the High Court.[42] It has to be noticed that neither Article 16(4), which empowers the State to make provision for reservation of posts in favour of backward class of citizens not adequately represented in the services, nor Article 335, which makes the claims for reservation in services to be taken into account consistent with the maintenance of efficiency of administration, provides for any consultation with the High Court. Further, the Bihar Act was not challenged on the ground that the reservations made were excessive or that the backward classes for whom reservations were made were adequately represented in the judicial services.

Another example is found in the interpretation of Article 368 of the Constitution which confers power on Parliament to amend the Constitution and provides the procedure therefor. Apart from the procedural restrictions, there is apparently no limitation as to the scope of the amending power and in two earlier cases[43] the Supreme Court conceded full amending power to Parliament. But later events led to rethinking in the matter and it was finally held that written Constitution like ours has certain undefined essential elements of its basic structure which are sacrosant and

---

41a. *In Supreme Court Advocate on Record Association and Ors. v. U.O.I.*, 2015 (11) SCALE 1, Supreme Court in a majority of 4:1 rejected the 99th Constitutional Amendment and declared National Judicial Appointments Commission Act, 2015 as "unconstitutional and void" to hold that the collegium system would again become operative.

42. *State of Bihar v. Bal Mukund Sah,* AIR 2000 SC 1296 : JT 2000 (3) SC 221 : (2000) 4 SCC 640. **See further** *A.C. Thalwal v. High Court of Himachal Pradesh,* AIR 2000 SC 2732 : (2000) 7 SCC 1; *Gauhati High Court v. Kuladhar Thukan,* AIR 2002 SC 1589 : (2002) 4 SCC 524 : (2002) SCC (L&S) 555. (**See also** cases referred therein); *Chandra Singh v. State of Rajasthan,* AIR 2003 SC 2889, p. 2901 : (2003) 6 SCC 545. (The power of 'control' enables the High Court to assess the performance of a judicial officer at any time with a view to discipline the blacksheep or weed out the dead wood which cannot be circumscribed by any rule or order).

43. *Shankar Prasad Singh v. Union of India,* AIR 1951 SC 458 : 1952 SCR 89; *Sajjan Singh v. State of Rajasthan,* AIR 1965 SC 845 : (1965) 1 SCR 933.

cannot be amended.[44] The basic structure doctrine has essentially developed from the German Constitution.[45] Its origin in India can be traced to Professor Dieter Conrad of Germany from his lecture 'Implied Limitations of the Amending Power' delivered in 1965 to the Law Faculty of the Banaras Hindu University.[46] The learned Professor in the article 'Basic Structure of the Constitution and Constitutional Principles"[47] points out that KHANNA, J. in his judgment in *Kesavananda* had quoted verbatim a sentence from his earlier article which reads: "Any amending body organized within the statutory scheme, however verbally unlimited its power, cannot by its very structure change the fundamental pillars supporting its constitutional authority."[48] The doctrine of basic structure as a principle has now become an axiom and the power to amend the Constitution is subject to this axiom.[49] The following have so far been spelled out as the essential elements of the basic structure of our Constitution:[50] (1) Supermacy of the Constitution;

---

44. *Kesavananda v. State of Kerala*, AIR 1973 SC 1461 : (1973) 4 SCC 225 (case decided by 13 judges). For criticism **see**: RAJU RAMCHANDRAN, 'The Supreme Court and the Basic Structure Doctrine', Supreme But Not Infallible, Essays in the Honour of Supreme Court, (Oxford University Press, 2000), p. 107; JUSTICE KRISHNA IYER calls it "a judicial riddle, a hidden agenda of the robed bretheren", The Hindu, 28-6-2005, p. 10.

45. *M. Nagaraj v. Union of India,* (2006) 8 SCC 212 (para 22) : AIR 2007 SC 71. In this case amendments in Article 16, by Constitution (Seventy-Seventh Amendment Act, 1995) and Constitution (Eighty Fifth Amendment Act, 2001) providing for reservation in promotion with consequential, seniority in favour of Scheduled Castes and Scheduled Tribes, which in the services are not adequately represented, were held to be valid. But it was further held that before exercising the power the state ought to be satisfied about inadequacy of representation of Scheduled Caste and Scheduled Tribe consistent with the mandate of Article 335 without affecting general efficiency of service. When questioned the state must place the quantifiable data touching backwardness and inadequacy of representation before the court. **See further** *Suraj Bhan Meena v. State of Rajasthan*, (2011) 1 SCC 467 paras 61 to 64 : (2010) 13 JT 341.

46. A.P. DATAR, Constitution of India, (Second Edition) Vol. 2, p. 2022.

47. Law and Justice, An Anthology, (2003), edited by SOLI J. SORABJI, p. 186.

48. *Ibid.*, p. 190; AIR 1973 SC 1861.

See further an article by T.R. ANDHYARUJINA, 'Basic Structure of the Constitution revisited' (The Hindu, 21-5-2007) which shows how JUSTICE KHANNA'S judgment that "Parliament did not have the power to amend the basic structure or framework of the Constitution" became the majority view.

49. *I.R. Coelho v. State of T.N.*, (2007) 2 SCC 1 (paras 147, 148) : AIR 2007 SC 861 (nine Judge Bench).

50. *Kesavananda v. State of Kerala, supra*, pp. 1535 (SIKRI, C.J.), 1663 (SHELAT and GROVER, JJ.), 1628 (HEGDE and MUKERJEE, JJ.), 1753 (J. REDDY, J.), 1860, 1900 (KHANNA, J.); *Indira Nehru Gandhi (Smt.) v. Raj Narain*, AIR 1975 SC 2299, pp. 2355 (KHANNA, J.), 2383 (MATHEW, J.), 2468, 2469 (CHANDRACHUD, J.) 1975 Supp SCC 1; *Minerva Mills v. Union of India*, (1980) 3 SCC 625 : AIR 1980 SC 1789;

[Footnote No. 50 Contd.]

(2) Democratic form of Government; (3) Secular and federal character of the Constitution; (4) Unity and integrity of the country; (5) Demarcation of powers between the legislature, the executive and the judiciary; (6) Rule of law and judicial review; (7) Liberty of thought expression, belief faith and worship; (8) Equality of status and opportunity; (9) Mandate to build a welfare state; (10) Limitation on the amending power that it is not used to alter or damage the essential elements of the basic structure of the Constitution, and (11) Independence of the judiciary.[51] It was earlier held that the basic feature of judicial review is not violated if the High Courts are deprived to examine findings of tribunals of like status.[52] This view now stands overruled.[53] The prevailing view now is that the power of judicial review under Articles 32 and 136 of the Constitution constitute essential feature of the basic structure and the same applies to the power of High Courts under Articles 226 and 227 of the Constitution to review decisions of all courts and tribunals within their respective jurisdiction.[54] Indeed, it may not be possible to legislatively create tribunals of the same status as a High Court whose independence is safeguarded by various

---

[Footnote No. 50 Contd.]

Sampat Kumar v. Union of India, (1987) 1 SCC 124 : AIR 1987 SC 386; *P. Sambamurthy v. State of Andhra Pradesh*, (1987) 1 SCC 362 : AIR 1987 SC 663; *S.R. Bommai v. Union of India*, JT 1994 (2) SC 218 : AIR 1994 SC 1918 : (1994) 3 SCC 1; *State of Karnataka v. Dr. Pravin Bhai Togadia*, (2004) 4 SCC 684, p. 694 (Secularism) : AIR 2004 SC 2081; *Indira Sawhney v. Union of India,* AIR 2000 SC 498, p. 517 : (2000) 1 SCC 168 (Parliament and Legislatures cannot transgress the basic features of the Constitution, *e.g.*, the principle of equality of which Article 16(1) is a facet); *I.R. Coelho v. State of T.N.*, (2007) 2 SCC 1 (para 141) : AIR 2007 SC 861. (Basic structure contemplates those parts which contain the core values, *e.g.* Articles 15, 21, 14 and 19 which if allowed to be abrogated would change the nature of the Constitution); *Ashok Kumar Thakur v. Union of India*, (2008) 6 SCC 1 paras 118, 120 : (2008) 5 JT 1 [The larger principles of equality as stated in Articles 14, 15 and 16 may be understood as an element of the 'basic structure' of the Constitution and may not be subject to amendment, although these provisons intended to cofigure these rights in a particular way, may be changed within the constraints of the broader principle. If any constitutional amendment is made which moderately abridges or alters the equality principle or the principle under Article 19(1)g, it cannot be said that it violates the basic structure of the Constitution. The case uphold the validity of The Constitution (93rd Amendment Act, 2005)]; *Mahmadhusen Abdulrahim Kalota Shaikh v. Union of India,* (2009) 2 SCC 1 paras 70 to 78, 91, 92 : (2008) 8 SLT 531 (separation of powers; power of judicial review exercised by the High Courts and Supreme Court). 'Basic Structure Theory' is said to be one of the silences in the Constitution : FALI S. NARIMAN, 'The Silences in our Constitutional Law, (2006) SCC (J) 15 (J19 to J26)'.

51. *Supreme Court Advocates-on-Record Association v. Union of India,* AIR 1994 SC 268, p. 421 : (1993) 4 SCC 441, **see** p. 298 and 299 *ante.*

52. *S.P. Sampat Kumar v. Union of India*, (1987) 1 SCC 124 : AIR 1987 SC 386.

53. *L. Chandra Kumar v. Union of India*, AIR 1997 SC 1125 : (1997) 3 SCC 261.

54. *Ibid.*, p. 1150 (paras 78, 79) (AIR).

provisions of the Constitution.[55] Negatively it may be stated that right to property,[56] concept of rulership with privy purses and privileges,[57] and right to unprincipled[58] defection are not essential features of the basic structure. The Supreme Court in upholding the validity of Articles 16(4A) and 16(4B) inserted by Constitution Amendments held that in judging whether the principle of basic structure has been violated, the court has to apply the twin tests namely the 'width test' and the test of 'identity'.[59] The concepts constituting the basic character are from their very nature neither rigid nor static and have been interpreted to meet the needs of the changing times. For example, reservation of a seat in favour of the *Sanghas* of Budhist Lamaic religious monasteries, with a special electorate of its own in the State of Sikkim has been held as not violative of the basic structure of the secular character of the Constitution on the ground that historically the *Sangh* is not merely a religious institution but also a political and social institution[60] and similarly reservation on ethnic principle of 12 seats to Sikkimese of Bhutia Lepcha origin in the same State has been held in the special circumstances of the State to be not destructive of the basic features of equality and democracy.[61] A perfect arithmetical equality of value of votes is not a constitutionally mandated imperative of democracy[62] and to demand any uniform value of one's voting right through the process of

---

55. *Ibid*, p. 1149 (para 78). **See further** *Duryodhan Sahu v. Jitendra Kumar Sahu,* AIR 1999 SC 114 : (1998) 7 SCC 273 (Administrative Tribunals unlike High Courts cannot entertain public interest litigation). **See also** *T. Sudhakar Prasad v. Govt. of A.P.*, JT 2001 (3) SC 204 : (2001) 1 SCC 516 : (2001) 1 LLN 829, regarding ambit of jurisdiction of Administrative Tribunals including power to punish for contempt; *Union of India v. R. Gandhi,* (2007) 4 SCC 341 : (2007) 8 JT 653 (Validity of the Companies (Amendment) Act, 2002, which transfers all jurisdictions exercised by the High Courts in company matters to tribunals constituted under the Act, has been referred to a Constitution Bench).

56. *Raghunathrao Ganpatrao v. Union of India*, AIR 1993 SC 1267, p. 1288 : 1993 (1) JT 374; *Jitubhai Nijbhai Kachar (Shri) v. State*, JT 1994 (4) SC 473 : AIR 1995 SC 142 : 1995 Supp (1) SCC 596.

57. *Ibid.* Right to property is now considered to be not only a constitutional or statutory right but also a human right: *P.T. Munichikkanna Reddy v. Revamma,* (2007) 6 SCC 59 (paras 40 to 43) : AIR 2007 SC 1753. Reference in this context is made to Article 17 of the Universal Declaration of Human Rights, 1948, in para 42, **See futher** to the same effect: *Chairman, Indore Vikas Pradhikaran v. Pure Industrial Coke and Chemicals Ltd.,* (2007) 8 SCC 705 para 53 : AIR 2007 SC 2458; *Karnataka State Financial Corporation v. N. Narasimahaiah,* (2008) 5 SCC 176 para 40 : AIR 2008 SC 1797.

58. *Kihota Hollohan (Shri) v. Zachirha (Mr.)*, AIR 1993 SC 412 : 1992 Supp (2) SCC 651.

59. *M. Nagaraj v. Union of India,* (2006) 8 SCC 212 (para 102) : AIR 2007 SC 71 (Constitution Bench).

60. *R.C. Poudyal v. Union of India*, AIR 1993 SC 1804, p. 1853 : 1994 Supp (1) SCC 324.

61. *Ibid.*

62. *Ibid* para 120 (SCC).

delimitation, disregarding the statutory and constitutional dispensation based on historical reasons is not a justifiable right.[63] It has also been held that democratic concept is not violated by providing for removal of an elected representative by a smaller and different body than the one that elected him.[64] Similarly, it has been held that federal character of the Constitution is not violated by not making it obligatory that a person elected by a State legislature for the Council of State to represent the State should also be a resident of the State and democratic form of government is not violated by providing for open ballot in cases where secret ballot is not insisted in the Constitution.[65] Another example is the ruling that national territory can be ceded by amending the Constitution without offending the basic structure of the unity and integrity of the country.[66] To save certain laws from being declared void and to validate certain laws already declared void on the ground of violation of fundamental rights, Article 31B and Ninth Schedule, containing the list of such laws, were added in the Constitution by the Constitution (1st Amendment) Act, 1951. By subsequent Constitution Amendments more and more laws were inserted in the Ninth Schedule. The effect of the basic structure doctrine as propounded in *Kesavananda* decided on 24.4.1973 is that laws inserted in the Ninth Schedule after this date are open to challenge on the ground that they are violative of the basic structure doctrine.[67] When a law inserted in the Ninth Schedule by a Constitutional Amendment after 24.4.1993 is challenged as violative of the basic structure *e.g.* of equality, the question to be answered will be whether it violates egalitarian equality as an overarching principle and not merely ordinary principle of equality in Article 14.[68] The 'basic structure doctrine' as formulated by the Supreme Court or similar doctrine has also been imported in other constitutions.[69] For example,

63. *J. & K. National Panthersporty v. Union of India*, (2011) 1 SCC 228 para 22 : AIR 2011 SC 3.

64. *Mohanlal Tripathi v. District Magistrate, Rae Bareilly*, AIR 1993 SC 2042 : (1994) 4 SCC 80; *Ram Beti v. District Panchayat Rajadhikari*, JT 1997 (10) SC 235, p. 240 : AIR 1998 SC 1222, pp. 1224, 1225 : (1998) 1 SCC 680.

65. *Kuldip Nayar v. Union of India*, (2006) 7 SCC 1 : AIR 2006 SC 3127. It was also held in this case that the basic structure doctrine does not apply to ordinary legislation and applies only to constitutional amendments (paras 96, 106 and 107) (Constitution Bench).

66. *Reference by the President of India under Article 143(1) of the Constitution of India on the implementation of the Indo Pakistan Agreement relating to Berubari Union and exchange of enclaves*, AIR 1960 SC 845 : (1960) 3 SCR 250.

67. *I.R. Coelho v. State of T.N.*, (2007) 2 SCC 1 (para 151) : AIR 2007 SC 861 (case decided by a Bench of nine Judges).

68. *Glanrock Estate Private Ltd. v. State of Tamil Nadu*, (2010) SCC 96 paras 26 to 29, 38 : (2010) 9 JT 568.

69. DIETER CONRAD, 'Basic structure of the Constitution and constitutional principles', collected in Law and Justice, An Anthology, (2003), edited by SOLI J. SORABJEE, p. 186.

although the Australian Constitution does not specify any fundamental or human right of freedom of speech or communication, the High Court of Australia in *Lange v. Australian Broadcasting Corporation*[70] unanimously held that "freedom of communication in matters of government and politics is an indispensable incident of that system of representative government which the constitution creates"[71] and a law infringing this freedom of communication will be declared invalid.

As power of judicial review by the Supreme Court and High Courts is part of the basic structure they can in exercising this power in exceptional cases entrust investigation of a case to the CBI without the consent of State Government to uphold fundamental right under Article 21 of the Constitution.[72]

Mention must also be made of Article 142(1) of the Constitution[73] which empowers the Supreme Court to 'pass such decree or make such order as is necessary for doing complete justice in a cause or matter pending before it'. The nature of this power came up for consideration before a Constitution Bench in *Prem Chand Garg v. Union of India*[74] and it was held that the power though wide did not enable the court to "make an order plainly inconsistent with the express statutory provisions of substantive law, much less, inconsistent with any constitutional provision".[75] The court also gave instances of cases where this power could be exercised and it is to be noted that all instances given related to matters of procedure, *viz.*, addition of parties, admission of additional evidence, remand of a case and permission to raise a new point for the first time. After giving these instances the court observed that "in exercising these and similar other powers, this court would not be bound by the relevant provisions of procedure if it is satisfied that a departure from the said procedure is necessary to do complete justice between the parties."[76] The views expressed in *Prem Chand Garg's* case, as noted above, relating to the court's power under Article 142(1) were fully accepted in *A.R. Antulay v. R.S. Nayak*,[77] a

---

70. (1997) 189 CLR 520.

71. *Ibid.*, p. 559. **See further** *Coleman v. Power*, (2004) 78 ALJR 1166, p. 1201.

72. *State of West Bengal v. Committee for Protecting Human Rights*, (2010) 3 SCC 571 : AIR 2010 SC 1476.

73. Two cases decided by three Judge Benches hold that Article 142(1) forms part of the basic structure of the Constitution: *Delhi Judicial Service Association v. State of Gujarat*, AIR 1991 SC 2176, p. 2204 : (1991) 4 SCC 406; *Ashok Kumar Gupta v. State of U.P.*, 1997 (5) SCC 201, p. 252 : 1997 (4) JT 251.

74. AIR 1963 SC 996 : 1963 Supp (1) SCR 885.

75. *Ibid*, p. 1003.

76. *Ibid.*

77. AIR 1988 SC 1531 : 1989 Supp (2) SCC 223.

case decided by a Bench of seven Judges. The court in the majority judgment emphasised that "an order which the court could make in order to do complete justice between the parties, must not only be consistent with the fundamental rights guaranteed by the Constitution but it cannot even be inconsistent with the substantive provisions of the relevant statutory laws."[78] The two judges who dissented in *Antulay's* case did not disagree on the nature of the court's power under Article 142. Indeed one of them namely RANGANATHAN J. observed: "However wide and plenary the language of the Article (142), the directions given by the court should not be inconsistent with, repugnant to or in violation of the specific provisions of any statute."[79] The nature of the power under Article 142(1) was again considered by a Constitution Bench in *Union Carbide Corporation v. Union of India*[80] and it was laid down that "the proper way of expressing the idea is that in exercising powers under Article 142 and in assessing the needs of 'complete justice' of a cause or matter, the apex court will take note of the express prohibitions in any substantive statutory provision based on some fundamental principles of public policy and regulate the exercise of its power and discretion accordingly. The proposition does not relate to the powers of the court under Article 142, but only to what is or is not 'complete justice' of a cause or matter and in the ultimate analysis of the propriety of the exercise of the power. No question of lack of jurisdiction or nullity can arise."[81] Earlier the court observed that in both *Garg's* as well as *Antulay's* case, the point was one of violation of constitutional rights and the observations in them relating to the effect of inconsistency with statutory provisions were really unnecessary.[82] The impression created by the decision in *Union Carbide's* case was that the observations in *Garg* and *Antulay* cases, that Article 142 does not enable the court to make an order inconsistent with provisions of substantive law, were no longer good law. Indeed it was so held in the case of *Vinay Chandra Misra*,[83] a Senior Advocate and Chairman of the Bar Council, who was not only punished for contempt of court in proceedings under Article 129 by award of a suspended sentence of imprisonment but whose licence to practice was also suspended with the aid of Article 142, treating the conduct amounting

---

78. *Ibid*, p. 1550.
79. *Ibid*, p. 1595.
80. AIR 1992 SC 248 : 1991 (4) SCC 584.
81. *Ibid*, p. 279.
82. *Ibid*, p. 278.
83. *In re, Vinay Chandra Misra*, AIR 1995 SC 2348, p. 2370 : 1995 (2) SCC 584. Instead of suspending the licence to practice for professional misconduct, the court could have prevented the Advocate concerned from appearing in court till he had purged himself of the contempt : *Pravin K. Shah v. K.A. Mohd Ali*, AIR 2001 SC 3041 : (2001) 8 SCC 650.

to contempt as professional misconduct, in complete disregard of the provisions of the Advocates Act, 1961 which vests this power exclusively in the State Bar Councils and the Bar Council of India with only appellate jurisdiction in the Supreme Court. Aggrieved by the order of suspension of the licence to practice as an Advocate, the Supreme Court Bar Association filed a petition challenging the said order which was heard and decided by a Constitution Bench.[84] The court held that a practising Advocate could not be debarred from practising his profession in exercise of power under Article 129 read with Article 142. The court reviewed the earlier cases dealing with Article 142 and the following propositions can be culled out from this decision: (1) It is not correct to say that the law laid down in *Prem Chand Garg's* case is no longer a good law;[85] (2) The power under Article 142 can be exercised only in respect of the 'case, cause or matter' before the court. (The case before the court was only regarding contempt and not of professional misconduct, so the court could not pass any order regarding suspension from practice even though in a given case the conduct amounting to contempt may also amount to professional misconduct);[86] (3) The power under Article 142 is curative and cannot be construed authorising the court to ignore the substantive rights of a litigant; (4) The power cannot be used to supplant substantive law applicable to the case; (5) The power cannot be used to build a new edifice by ignoring express statutory provisions; (6) The power is not meant to be exercised when its exercise may come directly in conflict with express provisions of a statute dealing expressly with the subject;[87] (7) It is not permissible for the court to take over the role of the statutory bodies or other organs of the State and perform their functions.[88] The decisions in *Union Carbide*, *Misra* and some other cases had given rise

---

84. *Supreme Court Bar Association v. Union of India*, JT 1998 (3) SC 184 : AIR 1998 SC 1895 : (1998) 4 SCC 409; *Yomesh Bhai Pranshankar Bhatt v. State of Gujarat*, (2011) 6 SCC 312 (para 6). It was reiterated that power under Article 142 cannot be exercised contrary to any express provision of law. However the Supreme Court by an interim order dated 11-4-2011 has directed Union of India to engage Mr. U.U. Lalit as special public prosecutor for trial in 2G Spectrum case, which is contrary to statutory provision.

85. *Ibid*, p. 207 (JT); pp. 1912, 1913 (AIR).

86. *Ibid*, p. 199 (JT); pp. 1906, 1907 (AIR).

87. *Ibid*, p. 202 (JT); pp. 1908, 1909 (AIR).

88. *Ibid*, p. 216 (JT); p. 1919 (AIR). **See** other Constitution Bench decisions : *ESP Rajaram v. Union of India*, JT 2001 (1) SC 573, p. 580 : AIR 2001 SC 581, p. 585 : (2001) 2 SCC 186, (has reiterated that the power under Article 142 cannot be exercised to override any express provision or to build up a case for which there is no basis in law); *Secretary State of Karnataka v. Umadevi*, (2006) 4 SCC 1 (para 44) : AIR 2006 SC 1806 (Article 142 cannot be used to regularise or make permanent employees appointed on *ad hoc* basis without any prior selection). **See further** *Textile Labour Association v. Official Liquidator*, (2004) 9 SCC 741 (para 7) : AIR 2004 SC 2336; *Union of India v. Shardindu*, (2007) 6 SCC 276 (para 33) : (2007) 7 JT 439.

to the criticism that the Supreme Court has assumed absolute powers to do whatever it wished to do.[89] The decision of the Constitution Bench holding that *Misra's* suspension was bad in law and the propositions flowing from that decision, which have been set out above, go a long way in removing the cause of the above criticism.

What possibly now remains to be done is to regulate the practice of issuing general directions and guidelines and also of declaring them in some cases to have the force of law under Article 141 and enjoining by virtue of Article 144 all authorities civil and criminal to act in aid of the Supreme Court for implementation of the directions and guidelines. As an example, in *Vishaka v. State of Rajasthan,*[90] the Supreme Court in effect imported in the domestic law the provisions of the 'Convention on the Elimination of All Forms of Discrimination against Women', without any legislation by Parliament under Article 253 to that effect, and gave various directions to prevent sexual harassment of working women in work places. These directions are directed to remain in force until suitably replaced by legislation.[90a] In addition to provisions in the penal code for punishing offenders when the conduct complained of is a criminal offence, *e.g.*, outraging the modesty of a woman, there exist in Government and corporate bodies conduct and discipline rules under which an employee can be suitably punished for unbecoming conduct which, properly interpreted, will cover cases of accusations of sexual harassment of a co-employee. But these probably were thought to be insufficient by the court and judicial legislation in the shape of directions followed to improve the existing law. Another example of this nature is the decision in *Vineet Narain v. Union of India*[91] in which a three Judge Bench of the Supreme Court virtually took away the power of superintendence over the CBI vested in the Central Government under section 3 of the Delhi Special Police Establishment Act, 1946, *without holding it ultra vires*, and transferred it to the Central Vigilance Commission which was directed to be given a *statutory* status. Numerous directions were also given for constitution and functioning of the said Commission, Enforcement Directorate, Nodal Agency and Prosecuting Agency. Do not the directions of this nature, however desirable, have the tendency "to tilt the delicate constitutional balance"?[92] Propositions

---

89. INDIRA JAISING, 'Judiciary's Absolute Powers', Indian Express, September 12, 1996.

90. AIR 1997 SC 3011 : (1997) 6 SCC 241, (**see further** for this case text and note 56, p. 690) followed in *D. S. Grewal v. Vimmi Joshi*, (2009) 2 SCC 210 : (2009) 1 SLT 216.

90a. The Sexual Harassment of Women at Workplace (Prevention, Prohibition and Redressal) Act, 2013 is now in force since 9 December 2013.

91. AIR 1998 SC 889, pp. 917 to 920 : (1998) 1 SCC 226.
For a criticism of the case **see** SHUBHANKAR DAM, (2005) Public Law, 239.

92. **See** SOLI J. SORABJEE, President's page, 3 Law and Justice (1996), p. VIII: "There can be no doubt that the dangers of judicial populism, judicial adventurism and judicial authoritarianism, particularly by recourse to Article 142, have to be safeguarded lest

[Footnote No. 92 Contd.]

[Footnote No. 92 Contd.]

they tilt the delicate constitutional balance." **See further** directions regarding uniform civil code in *Sarla Mudgal (Smt.) v. Union of India*, AIR 1995 SC 1531, p. 1539 (paras 37, 38) : (1995) 3 SCC 635 and SOLI J. SORABJI 'Obiter Dicta on Uniform Civil Code', Indian Express, August 14, 1995. Later the Supreme Court had to clarify that there were no directions to enact a uniform civil code: *Lily Thomas v. Union of India,* AIR 2000 SC 1650 : (2000) 6 SCC 224. **See** also directions given in *Sampat Kumar v. Union of India*, AIR 1987 SC 386 : (1987) 1 SCC 124, regarding mode of appointment to Administrative tribunals which were reiterated in review petitions (1987 Supp SCC 734, 735 : 1988 Cr LR (SC) 299) but were held to be advisory and directory in *Sarwan Singh Lamba v. Union of India*, AIR 1995 SC 1739 : (1995) 4 SCC 584. In *Gaurav Jain v. Union of India*, AIR 1997 SC 3021 : (1997) 8 SCC 114 a learned judge claimed that a single member of a two judge bench of the court could issue directions under Article 142 for rehabilitation of prostitutes though the other judge expressly dissented for, according to him, that question was not in issue. This patently erroneous interpretation of Article 142 would have given rise to utter confusion but for the prompt action of the Supreme Court Bar Association in filing a review petition. As expected the review petition was allowed by a bench of three judges overruling the above view of Article 142 and setting aside the directions given: *Gaurav Jain and Supreme Court Bar Association v. Union of India*, JT 1998 (2) SC 700 : AIR 1998 SC 2849 : (1998) 4 SCC 270. In one case the Supreme Court exercised original criminal jurisdiction of convicting a petitioner for perjury by recourse to Article 142 which also was set aside in a writ petition clarifying that Article 142 could not confer any such jurisdiction: *M.S. Ahlawat v. State of Haryana,* AIR 2000 SC 168 : 2000 (1) SCC 278. *Ashok Hurra v. Rupa Bipin Zaveri*, AIR 1997 SC 1266 : (1997) 4 SCC 226 is another controversial decision by a two Judge Bench in which divorce was granted under section 13B of the Hindu Marriage Act, 1955 with the aid of Article 142 of the Constitution, although consent of the wife had been withdrawn before conclusion of proceedings in the trial court, on the condition of the husband paying to the wife Rs. 10 lakhs for her maintenance. Further, directions were given that all pending proceedings between the parties including one taken by the wife against the husband, who had remarried, for his prosecution for *bigamy* will stand terminated. The wife did not accept this decision and filed a petition under Article 32 challenging the said decision, which ultimately failed not on merits but on the ground that the remedy under Article 32 is not available against orders of the Supreme Court: *Rupa Ashok Hurra v. Ashok Hurra,* AIR 2002 SC 1771 : (2002) 4 SCC 388. Mention may also be made of *Commissioner of Police v. Registrar Delhi High Court,* (1996) 6 SCC 323 : AIR 1997 SC 95 which gives the impression that Article 142 confers a new jurisdiction to entertain a petition which may not be entertainable under any other provision of the Constitution. *R. Prakash* in AIR 1999 (J) 119, p. 120 effectively demonstrates that this view is erroneous. Normally the law declared by the Supreme Court operates from the beginning of the law itself: *Sarwan Kumar v. Madan Lal Aggarwal,* (2003) 4 SCC 147 : AIR 2003 SC 1475. But the power to do complete justice in Article 142 has been used as a source of the doctrine of prospective over ruling [*Somaiya Organics (India) Ltd. v. State of Uttar Pradesh,* AIR 2001 SC 1723, pp. 1734, 1735 : (2001) 5 SCC 519], for making its order applicable to similar other matters without hearing the persons affected in those cases [*E.S.P. Rajaram v. Union of India,* AIR 2001 SC 581 : (2001) 2 SCC 186 (Constitution Bench)]; for transferring a politically influential sitting MP in judicial custody as an undertrial prisoner from a Jail in Bihar to Tihar Jail, Delhi though there is no

[Footnote No. 92 Contd.]

Nos. 5 and 6 extracted above from the Constitution Bench decision in *Misra's* case have relevance in this context. Further, direction to give statutory status to an authority is in effect a direction to the legislature for enacting a law which cannot be granted. As held by a three Judge Bench in an earlier case where the point was directly in issue the court cannot even "indirectly require the executive to introduce a particular legislation or the legislature to pass it or assume to itself a supervisory role over the law making activities of the executive and the legislature."[93]

The court cannot even ask an executive authority to make subordinate legislation which it has been empowered to make under the delegated authority of the legislature.[94]

As an extension of *Vineet Narayan* in *Prakash Singh v. Union of India,*[95] the task of extensive police reform was undertaken by the Supreme Court to insulate police machinery from outside interference and detailed directions were issued to that end which indirectly require repeal of the Indian Police Act, 1861, and rules and regulations made thereunder and enactment of new Act and making of new rules. There can be no doubt that police reforms as recommended by various commissions/committees were overdue but the question is whether the court has the right to issue directions to bring about the reforms as recommended in

---

[Footnote No. 92 Contd.]

provision for transfer of an undertrial prisoner from one state to another in the Transfer of Prisoners Act, 1950 [*Kalyan Chandra Sarkar v. Rajesh Ranjan Alias Pappu Yadav*, (2005) 3 SCC 284, pp. 297, 298 : AIR 2005 SC 972]; and for directing the State Government to issue executive orders for recording/registering marriages to be operative until a suitable legislation is made [*Seema v. Ashwini Kumar*, (2005) 4 SCC 443 : (2005) 11 JT 97].

93. *State of Himachal Pradesh v. Parents of a Student of Medical College,* AIR 1985 SC 910 : 1985 (3) SCC 169, pp. 174, 175; **see further** *Asif Hameed v. State of Jammu and Kashmir,* AIR 1989 SC 1899, (paras 17, 18, 19 and 29) : 1989 Supp (2) SCC 364; *Suresh Seth v. Commissioner, Indore Municipal Corporation*, AIR 2006 SC 767 (para 5) : (2005) 13 SCC 287; *Municipal Committee Patiala v. Model Town Residents Association* decided on 1.8.2007 (**see** separate judgment of B. SUDARSHAN REDDY J.); *Balram Bali v. Union of India,* (2007) 6 SCC 805 : AIR 2007 SC 3074. For this reason the non-compliance of the direction in *Vineet Narain* to give CVC a statutory status could not entail contempt of the order of the Supreme Court: *Union of India v. Prakash Hinduja,* (2003) 6 SCC 195, pp. 216, 217 : AIR 2003 SC 2612.

94. *Supreme Court Employees Welfare Association v. Union of India,* AIR 1990 SC 334, p. 353 (para 51) : (1989) 4 SCC 187; *Union of India v. Prakash P. Hinduja, supra,* (para 29), p. 2626 (AIR); *Suresh Seth v. Commissioner Indore Municipal Corporation* (supra).

95. (2006) 8 SCC 1 : (2006) 12 JT 225. For comments **see** ADITHYA REDDY, 'Judicial Activism or Overreach', (2009) 6 SCC J29, J346, J36.

view of the doctrine of separation of powers which forms one of the basic features of the Constitution?[96]

The court in the final order passed in *Seema v. Ashwani Kumar,*[97] carried judicial activism and judicial legislation to new heights. The court noticed that though India was a signatory to the Convention on the Elimination of All Forms of Discrimination against Women (CEDAW) and had also ratified the Convention, it had done so with a reservation on the question of compulsory registration of marriages provided in Article 16(2) on the ground that: 'It is not practical in a vast country like India with its variety of customs, religions and level of literacy' to make registration of marriage compulsory. The court also noticed that though all States and Union Territories indicated their stand to the effect that registration of marriagesis highly desirable, except in four States namely Gujrat, Karnataka, Himachal Pradesh and Andhra Pradesh registration of marriages is not compulsory in any of the other States. The court, however, came to the conclusion that it would be "in the interest of society", if marriages are made compulsorily registrable. The court also expressed the view that under section 8 of the Hindu Marriage Act, 1955 which enables making of rules regarding registration of marriages, registration can be made

---

96. In a conference of Chief Ministers and Chief Justices held on 8-4-2007, the Prime Minister Shri Manmohan Singh cautioned: "The dividing line between judicial activism and judicial overreach is a thin one. All organs, including the judiciary must ensure that the dividing line between them is not breached. This makes for a harmonious functioning": (2007) 4 SCC (J) 12.

In an article 'Democracy and Judiciary' Shri Somnath Chatterjee, Speaker of the Lok Sabha, said: "The doctrine of judicial independence is not to enable the judiciary to function as a kind of 'Super Legislature' or 'Super Executive'. The supermacy of the judiciary is in its assigned sphere. The principle of separation of powers is not an optional feature to be selectively recognized by each organs of the State, but it is one of the basic features of our Constitution which has to pervade every aspect of administration in the country." (High Court of Madhya Pradesh Golden Jubilee 1956-2006—A Remembrance by Advocate General, pp. 7, 8).

See further editorial in Hindustan Times of September 26, 2006 to the following effect: "It is a little difficult to suppress a sense of disquiet over the Supreme Court's directions on police reforms—But perhaps a greater reform is needed to make our democratic system work the way it should—The courts are meant to interpret laws and rules and not make them."

In a national conference of bar leaders Soli J. Sorabjee, a former Attorney General, is said to have warned that "Judicial activism should not degenerate into judicial authoritarianism". In the same conference T.R. Andyarujna, a former Solicitor General is reported to have said: "If Parliament or the executive overreaches its sphere of activity, the judiciary points out that it is unconstitutional. Is it not then unconstitutional, if judiciary does the same to the legislature and the executive": The Hindu, March 26, 2007.

97. (2006) 2 SCC 578 : AIR 2006 SC 1158; *Mohammad Ahmad v. Atmaram Chouhan*, (2011) 7 SCC 755 (Para 21). Wish an object to minimize the litigation between landlord and tenant the Supreme Court has laid down the norms and guidelines.

compulsory by the State Government and a person in breach of such a rule will be liable to punishment with fine. The court also observed that registration of marriage, though not determinative factor regarding existence or validity of marriage, will raise a rebuttable presumption. The court then concluded: "Accordingly, we are of the view that marriages of all persons who are citizens of India belonging to various religions should be made compulsorily registrable in their respective States, where the marriage is solemnised." And finally the court directed the States and the Central Government to take the following steps:

"(i) The procedure for registration should be notified by respective States within three months from today. This can be done by amending the existing rules, if any, or by framing new rules. However, objections from members of the public shall be invited before bringing the said rules into force. In this connection, due publicity shall be given by the States and the matter shall be kept open for objections for a period of one month from the date of advertisement inviting objections. On the expiry of the said period, the States shall issue appropriate notification bringing the rules into force.

(ii) The officer appointed under the said rules of the States shall be duly authorised to register the marriages. The age, marital status (unmarried, divorcee) shall be clearly stated. The consequence of non-registration of marriages or for filing false declaration shall also be provided for in the said rules. Needless to add that the object of the said rules shall be to carry out the directions of this court.

(iii) As and when the Central Government enacts comprehensive statute, the same shall be placed before this court for scrutiny.

(iv) Learned counsel for various States and Union Territories shall ensure that the directions given herein are carried out immediately."[98]

It will be noticed that the court in this case did not itself issue direction for compulsory registration of marriages but directed the States and the Central Government to do so by making new rules or by amending existing rules. Now it is well-settled that the court cannot direct the Legislature to make a law and similarly the court cannot direct the Executive Government to make rules or delegated legislation. The court cannot even

98. *Ibid*, para 18. These directions were given on 24-2-2006 by the order which is reported (f.n. 90, p. 312). By another order passed on 23-7-2007 it was clarified that "the marriages are to be made compulsorily registrable in respect of persons who are citizens of India even if they belonged to various religions." Further, on 25-10-2007 the court again directed that "the States and Union Territories who have not acted in line with the directions given on 14-2-2006 shall forthwith do it and in no case later than three months from today." On July 9, 2008 time further extended to four months: **see** (2008) 7 SCC 517.

adopt a supervisory role over the legislative functions of the Legislature or of the Executive.[1]

The directions of the court can be carried out by the States only by making statutory rules for example under section 8 of the Hindu Marriage Act, 1955. And, in cases where there is no statute, a State will have to first enact a statute enabling it to make the rules desired by the Supreme Court. Directions, which have such a consequence, it is submitted, blatantly violate the doctrine of separation of powers. Moreover, the direction that "As and when the Central Government enacts a comprehensive statute, the same shall be placed before the court for scrutiny" is a naked assumption of supervisory role over the law-making powers of Parliament which larger Benches of the court had ruled beyond its jurisdiction.[2] In all cases, where the Supreme Court finds that it would be in the "interest of Society" to supplement the existing law with new law it should only advise and not direct the State Government or the Central Government as the case may be to enact a suitable law or make new rules. For example, in *Naveen Kohli v. Neelu Kohli,*[3] the Supreme Court was of the view that irretrievable breakdown of marriage should be made a ground for divorce under the Hindu Marriage Act, 1955, but the court very rightly said that it was for the Legislature to do so and the court only recommended the Union of India to seriously consider bringing an amendment to that effect in the Hindu Marriage Act, 1955 and no directions were issued to supplement the Act till the amendment was enacted.

The assumption by the court of the power to issue directions to supplement the existing law on the ground that the court steps in because of the failure of the Legislature or the Executive to do their duty has been a matter of criticism by other organs of the State.[4]

In *Union of India v. Association for Democratic Reforms*[5] (1st case), and *People's Union for Civil Liberties v. Union of India* (2nd case),[6] both

1. **See** cases in note 93 and 94, p. 314.
2. **See** cases in note 93, p. 314.
3. (2006) 4 SCC 558 (paras 66 and 91) : AIR 2006 SC 1675.
4. In a Lecture on Separation of Powers the Speaker is reported to have criticized "the tendency of justifying judicial activism on the ground that courts step in because of the supposed failure of the legislature or the executive to do their duty." Since courts themselves are unable to cope with arrears, Chatterjee asked theoreticaly, if any other organ of the State can "take upon itself the right to exercise judicial powers on the plea that judiciary has not adequately been able to do so?" (Times of India, April 29, 2007). **See further** footnote 96, p. 315.
5. AIR 2002 SC 2112 : (2002) 5 SCC 294.
6. (2003) 4 SCC 399 : AIR 2003 SC 2363. The question whether right to vote is a necessary concomitant of the voter's freedom of expression under Article 19(1)(a) of the Constitution has been referred to a larger Bench: *People's Union for Civil Liberties v. Union of India*, (2009) 3 SCC 200 para 41 : (2009) 3 JT 136(2).

decided by three Judge Benches, the Supreme Court held that although right to vote is not a fundamental right, a citizen after he becomes a voter exercises the fundamental right of freedom of speech and expression under Article 19(1)(a) of the Constitution by casting his vote and, further, for exercising this right effectively he gets the right under the same Article to have information about the antecedents of a candidate from the candidate himself. Right of information of a citizen from another citizen does not flow from Article 19 and no one is bound to disclose any information about himself unless he is required to do so by a statute or a statutory rule. The court in these cases conferred on a voter right of information from the candidate himself without the backing of any statute and gave a new dimension to Article 19. In the 1st case the court found that the Representation of the People Act, 1951 and the Rules made thereunder were silent in this respect and though the court could not direct amendment of the Act or the Rules, it could issue directions or orders on the subject on which the Act or Rules are silent "to fill the vacuum or void till the suitable law is enacted." The court on this reasoning directed the Election Commission to call for information from each candidate seeking election as necessary part of his nomination paper furnishing therein information on certain enumerated aspects in relation to himself which briefly stated relate to: (i) his record of involvement in criminal cases, (ii) his assets and liabilities including those of his spouse and dependents, and (iii) his educational qualifications. After these directions were implemented by the Election Commission the President promulgated the Representation of the People (Amendment) Ordinance 2002 which was repealed and replaced by an identically worded Act namely the Representation of the People (Third Amendment) Act, 2002. The Ordinance and the Act do not require a candidate to disclose (a) the cases in which he is acquitted or discharged, (b) his assets and liabilities (which he is required to disclose only after he gets elected) and (c) his educational qualifications. Further, section 33B provides that no candidate shall be liable to disclose or furnish any such information in respect of his election which is not required to be disclosed or furnished under the Act or the Rules made thereunder. The Ordinance and the Act thus did not fully adopt the directions issued in the 1st case. The 2nd case related to the validity of the Ordinance and the Act because of these deficiencies. The question in this case was as to what happens if the law enacted does not fully adopt the directions given by the court to fill the gap till a suitable law is enacted. Do such directions only reflect the perception and tentative thinking of the court at a point of time when the Legislature did not address itself to the question leaving the Legislature some discretion in the matter or are they to be taken as inflexible and immutable? The answer given by the majority in the 2nd case is that the directions become final and are not "protempore" and to the extent they are not covered by the new legislation they remain operative and the provisions of the new law which go against the directions will be *ultra vires.* Does not this answer amount to indirectly requiring the Legislature to pass a law covering the directions and assuming a supervisory role over the law making activities of the Legislature which was held to be impermissible in an earlier case.[7] Further, it is not correct to say that voters get no information about antecedents of a candidate unless it is disclosed by the candidate himself. It is common experience that all good points about a candidate are propogated by him or his supporters and all his bad points by the rival candidates during electioneering and a sensible voter—the little man—is never in dark about the merits or demerits of a candidate. If candidates with criminal background are getting elected[8] the reasons for their election are essentially different, one of them being the inability of the courts to decide their cases speedily, and not the ignorance amongst the voters of their antecedents. The questions involved in the two cases were constitutional questions of great importance and should have been decided by a constitution bench at any rate when there was no unanimity on certain basic points in the 2nd case[9] and one of the judges was of the view that the 1st case itself should have been referred to a Constitution Bench as required by Article 145(3).[10]

In its effort to reform the election law by judicial legislation, a three Judge Bench of the Supreme court delivered another controversial decision[11] restricting fundamental right of freedom of speech and imposing precensorship by election commission or its delegate of election advertisements to be issued by political parties, candidates or other persons for being telecast on electronic media by cable operators and television channels. The Cable Television Networks (Regulation) Act, 1995 does not

---

7. **See** note 93, p. 314.
8. Even an undertrial prisoner facing serious criminal charges whose bail applications were rejected by the Supreme Court got elected as member of Parliament: *Kalyan Chandra Sarkar v. Rajesh Ranjan alias Pappu Yadav,* (2005) 3 SCC 284 : (2005) 3 SCC 307.
9. (2003) 4 SCC 399, pp. 456, 457, 465.
10. *Ibid,* p. 457.
11. *Secretary Ministry of Information and Broad Casting v. Gemini TV (P.) Ltd.*, (2004) 5 SCC 714. For critism of the case **see** A.G. NOORANI, 'Matters of Policy: courts cannot use interpretation of the law above it. Tipping the balance' The Hindustan Times, 20-10-2004. On the question of precensorship and freedom of the media **see** SOLI J. SORABJEE, 'Constitution Courts, and Freedom of the Press and the Media', Supreme but not Infallible, Essays in the Honour of the Supreme Court' (Oxford University Press), pp. 334, 342 to 356. For English law providing for prohibition on political advertising by television or radio services see section 321 of the Communications Act, 2003 and *R* (*on the application of Animal Defenders International*) *v. Secretary of State for Culture, Media and Sport*, (2008) 3 All ER 193 (HL).

provide for pre-censorship. It was also "clarified" in the nature of a declaratory penal enactment, and thus, restricting the fundamental right of personal liberty, that section 126 of the Representation of the People Act, 1951, which provides for a criminal offence shall apply to such advertisements. This is a case where judicial legislation under Article 142 was used not for enforcing a fundamental right but for restricting the fundamental rights of freedom of speech and personal liberty which could be done only by legislative enactments.

An analysis of the cases, where the power of supplementing the existing law by directions of the court has been exercised (*e.g.*, cases relating to police reform,[12] registration of marriages[13] and election reform[14]) will show that the power was used not to fill a gap or lacuna but because the existing law was not to the liking of the court and needed to be reformed. The activism lay in not merely recommending reform of the law by the Legislature or the competent authority (in case of delegated legislation) but in supplementing and reforming it by directions of the court and making them operative till the legislature or the competent authority amended the law on those lines. The consitutional validity of this power is seriously in doubt. The assumption of the power of issuing directions to supplement the existing law is another major 'overreach' made by the judiciary.

A seven Judge Bench of the Supreme Court speaking with near unanimity through LAHOTI, J., in *P. Ramchandra Rao v. State of Karnataka,*[15] overruling a number of earlier cases, it is submitted, rightly held that the court cannot prescribe periods of limitation at the end of which the trial court would be obliged to discharge or acquit the accused for this will amount to legislation outside the law making power available to constitutional courts howsoever liberally one may interpret Articles 32, 21, 141 and 142 of the Constitution. The court observed: "The dividing line is fine but perceptible. Courts can declare the law, they can interpret the law, they can remove obvious lacunae and fill the gaps but they cannot entrench upon in the field of legislation properly meant for the Legislature."[16] LAHOTI C.J.I. has also extra-judicially cautioned the courts in "assumption of proactive role" and advised them "to practice self restraint while innovating new tools. The court may assume an activist role only for the public good and under circumstances when no other efficacious means is available under the legal fraternity. Judicial creativity even when it takes the form of

---

12. Cases in f.n. 92 and 95, pp. 312-314.
13. Case in f.n. 97, p. 315.
14. Cases in f.n. 5, 6 and 11, pp. 317 and 319.
15. AIR 2002 SC 1856, p. 1871 : (2002) 4 SCC 578.
16. *Ibid.*

judicial activism should not result in rewriting the Constitution or any legislative enactments"[17]

It is to be noticed that in *Ramchandra Rao,* the periods of limitation laid down in earlier cases for termination of criminal cases were not supported on the ground that the directions of the court in that respect had only filled a gap left by the legislature and were to be operative till a suitable law is enacted. The case, therefore, establishes that there may be certain gaps in the existing law which the court cannot cover even temporarily by issuing directions. The court in *Ramchandra Rao* also noticed the criticism by reputed authors to its assumption of this new form of judicial legislation to fill a gap in a legislation or to provide for matters not provided by any legislation. Other organs of the State have, as earlier seen,[18] also questioned the constitutional validity of this power on the ground that it offends the doctrine of separation of powers which is one of the basic features of the Constitution.

The guidance available so far in judicial decisions and extra-judicial writing/speeches of judges that this form of judicial activism can be used only "for the public good" when "no other method is available in the legal framework"[19] is too vague. There is also no indication regarding the nature of 'gap' or 'lacuna' to which this doctrine applies. It is obviously not one which can be covered by the known techniques of interpretation. Further, confusion is created by the ruling that directions issued under Article 142 may not be the *ratio decidendi* or law declared to be followed in later cases.[20] It is hoped that a Constitution Bench or a larger Bench will soon advert to this power to decide its constitutional validity and in case it is declared valid to laydown its range and guidelines for its exercise as also the scope, if any, left for the Legislature to enact a suitable law for replacing the orders and directions of the court that were issued for the reason that there was a gap or lacuna in the laws in force. This is necessary so that the law may become reasonably predictable in application, like cases may be decided in like manner and judicial activism may not degenerate into judicial adhocism as these are the ideals that we pursue because of our commitment to the Rule of Law. JUSTICE J.S. VERMA, a former Chief Justice of India, who was a great exponent of this form of judicial activism is

---

17. 'Judicial Activism Constitutional Obligation of the Courts', (B.M. Patnaik Memorial Lecture delivered at Cuttack on Jan. 22, 2005) AIR 2005 Journal 177, pp. 188, 189.

18. **See** footnotes 96, p. 315 and 4, p. 317.

19. J.S. VERMA (former Chief Justice of India) 'The New Universe of Human Rights' p. 69 (Universal Law Publishing Co., 2004).

20. *Indian Bank v. ABS Marine Products (P) Ltd.*, (2006) 5 SCC 72 (para 26) : AIR 2006 SC 1899.

critical of judicial adhocism which he apprehends can result in "judicial tyranny."[21] The need for referring these questions to a larger Bench as submitted is now all the more necessary as some judges in the Supreme Court appear to be clearly in favour of judicial restraint.[22] KATJU J. has clearly expressed the view that the court has no power to issue directions which are legislative in nature.[23] Reference to a Constitutional Bench came in the context of Lyngdoh Committee report which was accepted by an interim order of 22.9.2006 for regulating students elections in colleges and universities in *University of Kerala v. Council of Principals of Colleges*,[24] when the matter again came before another Division Bench of KATJU AND GANGULY, JJ.[25] Although learned judges differed in their views, they agreed to refer the following questions to a Constitution Bench:

(1) Whether the court by an interim order dated 22.9.2006 can validly direct implementation of the Lyngdoh Committee's Report?

(2) Whether the order dated 22.9.2006 really amounts to judicial legislation?

(3) Whether under our Constitution the judiciary can legislate, and if so, what is the permissible limit of judicial legislation? Will judicial legislation not violate the principle of separation of powers broadly envisaged by our Constitution?

(4) Whether the judiciary can legislate when in its opinion there is a pressing social problem of public interest or it can only make a recommendation to the legislature or the authority concerned in this connection?

(5) Whether Article 19(1)(c) and other fundamental rights are being violated when restrictions are being placed by the implementation of the Lyngdoh Committee Report without authority of law?

(6) What is the scope of Articles 141 and 142 of the Constitution? Do they permit the judiciary to legislate and/or perform functions of the executive wing of the State?

---

21. Note 19, p. 321, *supra*.

22. *Divl. Manager Aravali Golf Club v. Chander Hass*, (2008) 1 SCC 683 : (2008) 3 JT 221 (A.K. Mathur and Markandey Katju JJ).

23. *Common Cause (A Regd. Society) v. Union of India*, (2008) 5 SCC 511 paras 19, 20, 21 : AIR 2008 SC 2116.

24. Reported in (2006) 8 SCC 304.

25. *University of Kerala v. Council of Principals of Colleges*, (2010) 1 SCC 353 para 16 : AIR 2010 SC 2532.

On the question as what is the scope left for the Legislature to replace the directions of the court, it is to be noted that when judicial decision is based on the common law or on interpretation of a statute, subsequent legislation can always change the regulatory effect of the adjudication. It is only the interpretation of the Constitution by the court which remains immune from legislative intervention and can be replaced only by an amendment of the Constitution[26] or by the court itself overruling its prior decision. Why cannot these principles apply when the court does not interpret a provision in the Constitution or declare a law invalid but steps in on the plea that there is a gap or lacuna in the law and issues general directions to cover it? This is an area where the Legislature has primacy and the court moves in because of the supposed inaction of the Legislature[27] and its directions are legislative in nature. Such a situation bears no analogy to cases where the court declares a law invalid for certain defects and the Legislature has to abide by the decision of the court to remove the defects if it wants to replace the law declared invalid by new legislation. It is, therefore, submitted that, contrary to what was decided by the majority in *Peoples Union for Civil Liberties v. Union of India,*[28] (1) general directions of this nature, even if constitutionally valid should be issued, if at all, in rarest of rare cases, not just for the asking by a Bench consisting of at least three judges, (2) should be presumed to be of a temporary nature to remain effective until replaced by a law enacted by the competent Legislature,[29] and (3) in judging the validity of a law replacing the general

---

26. *M. Nagaraj v. Union of India,* (2006) 6 SCC 212 (para 102) : AIR 2007 SC 71 (A Constitution Amendment which does not offend the basic structure doctrine can alter Supreme Court's interpretation of a provision of the Constitution.)

27. While continuing the two committees one for regulating admission procedure and the other for regulating fee structure relating to professional unaided (minority and non-minority) educational institutions constituted under Article 142 in *Islamic Academy of Education v. State of Karnataka,* (2003) 6 SCC 697 : AIR 2003 SC 3724 (5 judge bench) by *P.A. Inamdar v. State of Maharashtra* (7 Judge Bbench) (2005) 6 SCC 537 (paras 148 and 155) : AIR 2005 SC 3226 as a temporary measure and as an inevitable passing phase until the Central Government or the State Governments are able to devise a suitable mechanism for the same purpose by suitable legislation or regulation, the court observed: "The judicial wing of the State is called upon to act when the two other wings, the legislative and the executive, do not act." (para 155)

28. Discussed at pp. 309-312.

29. The nature of this power as explained in *Vineet Narain v. Union of India,* (1998) 1 SCC 226, p. 264, para 49 : AIR 1998 SC 1 is : "There are ample powers conferred by Article 32 read with Article 142 to make orders which have the effect of law by virtue of Article 141 and there is mandate to all authorities to act in aid of the orders of this court as provided in Article 144 of the Constitution. In a catena of decisions of this court, this power has been recognized and exercised if need be, by issuing necessary directions to fill the vacuum till such time the legislature steps in to cover the gap or the executive discharges its role". The same view was expressed in *Prakash Singh Badal v. Union of India,* (2006) 8 SCC 1 (para 30) : (2006) 12 JT 225 : (2006) 7 SLT 198.

directions of the court, the court should pay more respect to the wisdom of the Legislature and should not declare the law invalid simply on the ground that it does not conform to the directions of the court. The Legislature may consider modifying or even superceding directions of this nature which are neither interpretative of the Constitution nor issued for enforcing a fundamental right. For instance, directions issued for registering all marriages,[30] even if issued with the consent of the Executive Government, just to facilitate production of evidence of marriage in matrimonial proceedings may be thought by Parliament to be unnecessary and impractical and, therefore, restricted to certain specified marriages as the consent of the Executive Government to support such directions cannot be equated with the consent of Parliament. For another example, take the general direction issued in *U.P. Judicial Officers' Association v. Union of India,*[31] that no FIR should be registered without permission of the Chief Justice of the concerned High Court against a judicial officer relating to allegations of having committed an offence in discharge or purported discharge of his official duties. Why cannot Parliament enact a prospective provision in the Criminal Procedure Code to the effect that permission of the Chief Justice of the concerned High Court will be needed only in case of allegations against District Judges and so far as other subordinate judicial officers are concerned permission of the District Judge concerned will suffice for registration of FIR? But in any case, in this respect the court may, *at least*, follow the principle of 'Democratic Dialogue'[32] as applied by the Canadian Supreme Court. On this principle when the Legislature replaces the directions of the court by an enacted law the court may uphold the law even if it does not fully conform to the directions of the court. And, this should be specially so when the directions of the court relate to matters of policy or matters in which it has no expertise.[33] As observed by LORD COOKE OF THORNDON: "Reciprocal influence is an ongoing process. Neither the Government nor Parliament nor the courts have a monopoly of wisdom."[34]

A distinction must be drawn between the power exercised by the court in creative interpretation of a provision in the Constitution and its assumption of the power to supplement the existing law by its directions under

---

30. *Seema v. Ashwini Kumar*, (2005) 4 SCC 443 : (2006) 2 SCC 578.

31. JT 2002 (8) SC 133, p. 134 : (2003) 96 FLR 409.

32. (2004) Public Law, pp. 43 to 45; *R. v. Mill,* (1999) 3 SCR 668 (Canada); (2005) Public Law, pp. 329, 330.

33. **See** DAWN OLIVER, Constitutional Reform in U.K. (The Courts and Theories of Democracy, Citizenship, and Good Governance) page 205 quoted in *Modern School v. Union of India*, AIR 2004 SC 2236 by SINHA, J. at p. 2255 : (2004) 5 SCC 583.

34. 'How Like an Angel', Constitutionalism Human Rights and the Rule of Law, p. 37 (Essays in the honour of Soli J. Sorabjee; Universal Law Publishing Co.)

Article 142. For example in *D. K. Basu v. State of W.B.,*[35] the court laid down 11 requirements to be followed in all cases of arrest and detention till legal provisions are made in that behalf.[36] But the court made it clear that these requirements flow from Articles 21 and 22 of the Constitution.[37] The court was also of the view, following *Nilbati Behra* and other cases, that public law remedy of award of compensation under Article 32 or 226 for violation of fundamental right under Article 21 is an appropriate and an effective remedy on the principle of strict liability and the victim need not be relegated to the remedies available in civil law.[38] Distinction must also be drawn between the power exercised by the court to supplement the existing statute law by directions under Article 142 and its power to reform the common law to meet the present day needs of the community. In exercising this power of reform of the common law the court exercises "the same power of creation that built up the common law through its exercise by the judges of the past."[39] For example, in *M.C. Mehta v. Union of India*[40] the court laid down a more stringent rule of strict liability than the rule in *Ryland v. Fletcher*, [(1868) LR3 HL330] which the court said did not now fully meet the needs of a modern industrial society when harm results to anyone in the operation of hazardous or inherently dangerous enterprise. But it seems these distinctions were not appreciated in the case of *Destruction of Public and Private Properties, In Re v. State of Andhra Pradesh.*[41] In which taking serious note of various instances of large-scale destruction of public and private properties in the name of agitations, bandhs, hartals and the like *suo motu* proceedings were taken by the Supreme Court and two committees, one headed by a retired judge of the Supreme Court JUSTICE K. K. THOMAS, and the other headed by senior advocate Mr. F. S. Nariman, were appointed to make recommendations.

The recommendations of the committees and the decision of the Supreme Court have to be understood in the light of the existing law regarding

---

35. AIR 1997 SC 610 : (1997) 1 SCC 416; Article 22 guarantees that a person arrested shall be entitled to consult and defended by a legal practitioner of his choice. Professional ethics requires that a lawyer cannot refuse a brief provided a client is willing to pay his fee and the lawyer is not otherwise engaged: *Siddharam Satlingappa Mhetre v. State of Maharashtra*, (2011) 1 SCC 694 paras 22, 23 and 24 : AIR 2011 SC 312.

36. *Ibid* para 36.

37. *Ibid* para 37.

38. *Ibid* para 55.

39. CARDOZO; The Growth of the Law (Indian Economy Reprint 2002 by Universal) p. 137. **See further** pp. 25-27 supra.

40. AIR 1987 SC 965 : (1986) 2 SCC 176.

41. (2009) 5 SCC 212 : (2009) 6 JT 1.

use of highways by the public and the liability of those causing damage to property in strikes, bandhs, etc. Under the common law public right of way exists over highways and this right includes the right to take out processions whether it be religious social or political so long as the rights of others and lawful orders and directions of the authorities regulating the traffic are not infringed.[42] This right covers the right to hold meetings at a suitable time and place on a public street.[43] Similar views have been expressed by the House of Lords which held: "the law to be that the public highway is a public place which the public may enjoy for any reasonable purpose, provided the activity in question does not amount to a public or private nuisance and does not obstruct the highway by unreasonably impeding the right of the public to pass and repass; within these qualifications there is a public right of peaceful assembly on the highway."[44] It is misuse of this common law right which gives rise to harmful agitations, bandhs, hartals leading to destruction of public and private properties and sometimes causing personal injury and even death. Civil remedies in such cases are award of damages for injury to person and property and for causing public and private nuisance. In case of destruction of public property criminal liability, in addition to offences in the Indian Penal Code, 1860 is also regulated by the Prevention of Damage to Public Property Act, 1984 (PDP Act).

The *Thomas* Committee recommended amendment of the PDP Act to make its provisions more stringent by raising rebuttable presumption and to make the leaders of the organisation also guilty of abetment. The *Nariman* Committee recommended, on the lines of *M. C. Mehta* case, to make the civil liability absolute, for award of exemplary damages and to provide for speedy remedies. Having considered the reports of both these committees the court issued guidelines which are contained in paras 12 and 15 of the report.[45]

The court did not issue any guideline for amending the PDP Act as recommended by the *Thomas* Committee. The guidelines only regulate the common law right of user of highways and public places to prevent its misuse by directing its control and preventive action and providing absolute liability and exemplary damages when misuse of the right results in

---

42. *Shaikh Piru Bux v. Kalandi Pati*, AIR 1970 SC 1885 : (1969) 2 SCR 563.

43. *Himat Lal K. Shah v. Police Commissioner*, AIR 1973 SC 87 : (1973) 1 SCC 227.

44. *Director of Public Prosecution v. Jones*, (1999) 2 All ER 259 p. 265 (H.L).

45. (2009) 5 SCC 212 pp. 224, 226 : (2009) 6 JT 1 : (2009) 5 Scale 638. As regards Bandh no one can give call for *Bandh* nor can the same be enforced: *Communist Party of India (M) v. Bharat Kumar* (1998) 1 SCC 201 : AIR 1998 SC 184; *All India Anna Dravida Munnetra Kazhagam v. Chief Secretary Government of Tamii Nadu*, (2009) 5 SCC 452 : (2007) 11 Scale 607.

personal injury or death and damage to public or private property. The court has also directed the appointment of a Claims Commissioner to assess damages and report to the High Court when only one state is involved and to the Supreme Court when more than one state is involved. The guidelines issued by the court in this case only amend the common law to meet the present day needs of the community on the same principle as applied in *M. C. Mehta* case which was also relied upon by the *Nariman* Committee. The court, however, in support of its judgment referred to a number of cases in which guidelines were issued under Article 142, which, it is submitted, was unnecessary.

The following extracts from the judgments of great judges illuminate the wide power which a constitutional court has in interpreting a constitution. But they should not be taken to convey that this power is without limitations for in a country governed by the rule of law no one, not even the highest court, has unlimited power.[46]

In dealing with the construction of section 92 of the Commonwealth of Australia Constitution Act, 1900, LORD WRIGHT observed: "It is true that a Constitution must not be construed in a narrow and pedantic sense. The words used are necessarily general and their full import and true meaning can often only be appreciated when considered as the years go on, in relation to the vicissitudes of fact which from time to time emerge. It is not that meaning of the word changes, but the changing circumstances illustrate and illuminate the full import of that meaning—Nor can any decisive help here be derived from evidence of extraneous facts existing at the date of the Act of 1900; such evidence may in some cases help to throw light on the intention of the framers of the statute, though that intention can in truth be ascertained only from the language used. It may be that in 1900 the framers of the Constitution were thinking of border tariffs and restrictions in the ordinary sense and desired to exclude the difficulties of that nature and to establish what was and still is called 'free trade' and to abolish the barrier of the State boundaries so as to make Australia one single country. Thus, they presumably did not anticipate those commercial and industrial difficulties which have in recent years led to marketing schemes and price control, or traffic regulations such as those for the co-ordination of rail and road services, to say nothing of new inventions such as aviation or wireless. The problems, however, of the Constitution can only be solved as they emerge by giving effect to the language used."[47]

---

46. **See** pp. 27-29, *ante*.
47. *James v. Commonwealth of Australia*, (1936) 2 All ER 1449, pp. 1464, 1465 (PC).

Similarly, in construing the expression 'Banking' in head 15 of section 91 of the British North America Act, 1867, VISCOUNT SIMON observed: "The question is not what was the extent and kind of business actually carried on by Banks in Canada in 1867, but what is the meaning of the term itself in the Act. To take what may seem a frivolous analogy if 'skating' was one of the matters to which the exclusive legislative authority of the Parliament of Canada extended, it would be nothing to the point to prove that only one style of skating was practised in Canada in 1867 and to argue that the exclusive power to legislate in respect of subsequently developed styles of skating was not expressly conferred on the Central Legislature. Other illustrations may be drawn from section 91 as it stands—take for example, head 5 'Postal Services'. In 1867 postal services in Canada were rendered by the help of land vehicles, but nobody could contend that the modern use of aeroplanes for carrying mail is, on that account, not within the phrase."[48]

One may also recall here the language of MR. JUSTIC HOLMES used with reference to the American Constitution: "When we are dealing with words that also are a constituent Act, like the Constitution of United States, we must realize that they have called into life a being, the development of which could not have been foreseen completely by the most gifted of its begetters. It was enough for them to realize or to hope that they had created an organism; it has taken a century and cost their successors much sweat and blood to prove that they created a nation. The case before us must be considered in the light of our whole experience and not merely in that of what was said a hundred years ago."[49]

And the words of BOSE, J., with reference to the Indian Constitution may here be referred: "They are not just dull lifeless words static and hidebound as in some mummified manuscript, but living flames intended to give life to a great nation and order its being, tongues of dynamic fire potent to mould the future as well as guide the present. The Constitution must, in my judgment, be left elastic enough to meet from time to time the altering conditions of a changing world with its shifting emphasis and differing needs."[50]

---

48. *A.G. of Alberta v. A.G. of Canada*, AIR 1948 PC 194, p. 198 : 1947 AC 503.

49. *State of Missouri v. Rly. P. Holland*, 252 U.S. 416, p. 433; 64 Law Ed 641, p. 648. **See further** *Kapila Hingorani v. State of Bihar*, (2003) 6 SCC 1, p. 23; *Saurabh Chaudri v. Union of India*, AIR 2004 SC 361, p. 374 : (2003) 11 SCC 146.

50. *State of West Bengal v. Anwarali Sarkar*, AIR 1952 SC 75, p. 103 : 1951 SCR 603. **See further** *Jagdish Saran v. Union of India*, (1980) 2 SCC 768 : AIR 1980 SC 820 (para 7) and *Saurabh Chaudri v. Union of India*, AIR 2004 SC 361, p. 374 : (2003) 11 SCC 146.

Reference may also be here usefully made to the attitude adopted by the Court of Justice of the European Communities in construing the European Economic Community Treaty and Community Legislation. The court applies teleological rather than historical methods of interpretation. It seeks to give effect to what it conceives to be the spirit rather than the letter. It views the Communities as living and expanding organisms and the interpretation of the provisions of the treaties as changing to meet their growth.[51]

4. REFERENCE TO OTHER STATUTES

(a) Statutes in *pari materia*

It has already been seen that a statute must be read as a whole as words are to be understood in their context.[52] Extension of this rule of context permits reference to other statutes in *pari materia*, *i.e.* statutes dealing with the same subject-matter or forming part of the same system. VISCOUNT SIMONDS in a passage already noticed conceived it to be a right and duty to construe every word of a statute in its context and he used the word context in its widest sense including "other statutes in *pari materia*".[53] As stated by LORD MANSFIELD: "Where there are different statutes in *pari materia* though made at different times, or even expired, and not referring to each other, they shall be taken and construed together, as one system and as explanatory of each other."[54] In a case, the Court of Appeal, while holding that smuggled gold coins constituted 'goods' within the meaning of Customs & Excise Act, 1952, referred to a whole series of Customs Acts starting in 1833, going on to 1876, 1893, 1932 and 1939 and observed that reading through them it was plain that in the Customs Acts 'goods' does include gold and silver coins and bullion for when they are to be excluded they are excluded expressly by the words of the Acts.[55]

The meaning of the phrase *pari materia* has been explained in an American case in the following words: "Statutes are in *pari materia* which

---

51. *R. v. Henn*, (1980) 2 All ER 166, p. 196 (HL).
52. **See** Chapter 1, title 3, "Statute must be read as a whole in its context".
53. *A.G. v. HRH Prince Ernest Augustus of Hanover*, (1957) 1 All ER 49, p. 53 : 1957 AC 436 (HL). **See further** text and note 60, p. 39.
54. *R. v. Loxdale*, (1758) 97 ER 394, p. 395. **See further** *J.K. Steel Ltd. v. Union of India*, AIR 1970 SC 1173, p. 1183 (para 29); *Board of Trustees of the Port of Bombay v. Sriyanesh Knitters,* AIR 1999 SC 2947, p. 2952 (para 12) : (1999) 7 SCC 359; *Oliver Ashworth (Holdings) Ltd. v. Ballard (Kent) Ltd.*, (1999) 2 All ER 791, p. 808 (CA); *Ahmedabad Pvt. Primary Teachers Association v. Administrative Officers*, AIR 2004 SC 1426, pp. 1429, 1430 : (2004) 1 SCC 755 (8th Edn., of this book, pp. 235, 239 **referred**).
55. *Allgemeine Gold-Und Silberscheideanstalt v. Customs & Excise Commissioners*, (1980) 2 All ER 138, p. 141 : 1980 QB 390 : (1980) 2 WLR 555 (CA).

relate to the same person or thing, or to the same class of persons or things. The word *par* must not be confounded with the word *simlis*. It is used in opposition to it—intimating not likeness merely but identity. It is a phrase applicable to public statutes or general laws made at different times and in reference to the same subject."[56] The Supreme Court upheld the validity of the Pondicherry Protection of Interests of Depositors in Financial Establishments Act, 2004, on the ground that the Supreme Cout had previously upheld the validity of *pari materia* enactments of the Tamil Nadu Protection of Interests of Depositors (in Financial Establishments) Act, 1977, and the Maharashtra Protection of Interests of Depositors (in Financial Establishments) Act, 1999, which were also beneficial legislations intended to protect the interests of small depositors.[57] However, when the two pieces of legislation are of differing scopes, it cannot be said that they are in *pari materia*.[58] Thus the Bombay Rents, Hotel and Lodging House Rates Control Act, 1947; and the Bombay Land Requisition Act, 1948, were held to be Acts not in *pari materia* as they do not relate to the same person or thing or to the same class of persons or things.[59]

It is settled law that words used in a particular statute cannot be used to interpret the same word in a different statute especially when the two statutes are not *pari materia*. The Supreme Court has accordingly held that the definitions of "shop" in the Maharashtra Shops and Establishments Act, 1948, and the Karnataka Shops and Commercial Establishments Act, 1961, cannot be used to interpret the word "shop" in the context of notifications issued under the Employees' State Insurance Act, 1948, because though all three Acts deal with labour and workmen, in essence and spirit they have a different scheme and application. Hence, preferring a purposive interpretation, Turf Clubs were held to be duly covered under the term "shop" for the purposes of the ESI Act and the notifications issued thereunder.[60]

However, it is not necessary that the entire subject-matter in the two statutes should be identical before any provision in one may be held to be

---

56. *United Society v. Eagle Bank*, (1829) 7 Connecticut 457, p. 470, as cited in CRAIES, Statute Law, p. 134 (7th Edition). **See further** *Shah & Co., Bombay v. State of Maharashtra*, AIR 1967 SC 1877, pp. 1883, 1884 : 1967 (3) SCR 466; *Sirsilk Ltd. v. Textiles Committee*, AIR 1989 SC 317, p. 330 : 1989 Supp (1) SCC 168.

57. *New Horizon Sugar Mills Limited v. Government of Pondicherry & Anr.*, (2012) 10 SCC 575, p. 598.

58. *State of Punjab v. Okara Grain Buyers Syndicate Ltd., Okara*, AIR 1964 SC 669, pp. 684, 685 : 1964 (5) SCR 387.

59. *Shah & Co., Bombay v. State of Maharashtra, supra*, p. 1884.

60. *Bangalore Turf Club Ltd. v. Regional Director, ESI Corporation*, (2014) 9 SCC 657, pp. 685 to 689.

in *pari materia* with some provision in the other.[61] Thus, section 4 of the Prevention of Corruption Act, 1947, which directs that on proof that the accused has accepted any gratification other than legal remuneration, it shall be presumed unless the contrary is established by the accused that the gratification was accepted as a bribe, has been held to be in *pari materia* with the subject-matter dealt with by the Indian Evidence Act, 1872; and the definition of the expression 'shall presume' in the Evidence Act has been utilised to construe the words 'it shall be presumed' in section 4 of the Prevention of Corruption Act, 1947.[62] Similarly, section 19 of the Assam Agricultural Income-tax Act, 1939, has been held to be in *pari materia* with section 22 of the Indian Income-tax Act, 1922, and decisions construing it have been used for construing the former.[63] Section 20(c) of the Code of Civil Procedure and Article 226(2) of the Constitution have been held to be in *pari materia* and decisions interpreting the former have been held to apply in interpreting the latter for deciding the place or places where 'the cause of action wholly or in part arises' for entertainment of a writ petition in the High Court for challenging the *vires* of a Central Act.[64] The Industries (Development and Regulation) Act, 1951 in so far as it deals with textiles industry has been held to be in *pari materia* with the Textiles Committee Act, 1963.[65] And, the Indian Tariff Act, 1934 and the Imports and Exports (Control) Act, 1947, have been held to throw light on the construction of each other as they form part of the Import Control Scheme of the Government.[66]

The rule that related provisions in different Acts but having bearing on the same subject have to be read together can be illustrated from the case of *Common Cause, A Registered Society v. Union of India*[67] which interpreted Explantion 1 to section 77(1) of the Representation of the People Act, 1951. The Explanation provides that 'any expenditure incurred or authorised in connection with the election of a candidate by a political party—shall not be deemed to be—expenditure in connection with the election incurred or aurhorised by the candidate'. In construing this provision, the court read sections 13A and 139(4B) of the Income-tax Act, 1961 which though

61. *R. v. Harrod, ex parte, Leads City Districts Council*, (1976) 1 All ER 273 (CA); Definition of 'pleasure fair' in section 75 of the Public Health Act, 1961, applied for construing para 4(2) of Sch. 6 to the Betting and Gaming Act, 1963.
62. *State of Madras v. A. Vaidyanath Ayer*, AIR 1958 SC 61, p. 65 : 1958 SCR 580.
63. *State of Assam v. Deva Prasad Barua*, AIR 1969 SC 831, p. 834 : 1969 (1) SCR 698.
64. *Kusum Ingots & Alloys Ltd. v. Union of India*, (2004) 6 SCC 254, p. 259 (para 9) : AIR 2004 SC 3411.
65. *Sirsilk Ltd. v. Textiles Committee*, AIR 1989 SC 317, p. 330 : 1989 Supp (1) SCC 168.
66. *Dy. Chief Controller of Imports and Exports, New Delhi v. K.T. Kosalram*, AIR 1971 SC 1283, p. 1289 : (1970) 3 SCC 82.
67. 1996 (3) Scale 258, p. 266 : AIR 1996 SC 3081, p. 3087.

exempting the income of political parties from house property, other sources or voluntary contributions require them to maintain audited accounts and to file income-tax return for each assessment year. The court held that if a political party is not maintaining audited and authentic accounts and is not filing return of income, it cannot justifiably plead that it has incurred or authorised any expenditure in connection with the election of a party candidate within the meaning of Explanation (1) to section 77(1) and that the said provision does not give protection to the expenditure which comes from an unknown or black source. In the same context the court noticed that the main income of a political party comes from contributions from companies which are permitted to make these contributions under the conditions laid down in section 293A of the Companies Act, 1956 and are required to disclose them in their profit and loss account. Another example of the same principle is the case of *State of Madhya Pradesh v. Swaroop Chand*[68] which relates to the construction of section 22 of the MP Van Upaj (Vyapar Viniyaman) Adhiniyam, 1969. The *Adhiniyam* applies to certain specified forest produce and provides for their seizure alongwith receptacle or vehicle used for transportation in contravention of the provisions of the Act and Rules. The *Adhiniyam* provides for release of receptacle or vehicle on payment of its value but not for confiscation in case the value is not paid. Section 22 further provides that nothing contained in the Indian Forest Act, 1927 shall apply to specified forest produce in matters for which provision is made in the *Adhiniyam*. The Supreme Court held that the provision for confiscation made in the Forest Act would apply to seizures made under the *Adhiniyam* as this was a matter for which no provision was made in it. It is submitted that another way of looking at the problem was that the Act and the *Adhiniyam* dealt with allied subjects forming part of the same system and had to be read as complimentary to each other. It was, therefore, rightly held that on matters not provided in the *Adhiniyam* but provided in the Act, the provisions of the Act could be applied to the specified forest produce. And in *Board of Trustees of the Port of Bombay v. Sriyanesh Knitters*,[69] the Supreme Court read the Major Port Trusts Act, 1963 (MPT Act) along with the Indian Contract Act, 1872 and held that in so far as the Board of Trustees functioned as wharfingers under sections 42 to 48 of the MPT Act, it was entitled to the right of general lien contained in section 171 of the Indian Contract Act, 1872 which was not provided for in the MPT Act but which was also not expressly or impliedly excluded by its provisions.

Acts dealing with various socio-economic plans have to be read in a complementary manner so that they do not create contradictions while operating

---

68. AIR 1997 SC 301 : 1996 (11) SCC 175.
69. AIR 1999 SC 2947, pp. 2952, 2953 : (1999) 7 SCC 359.

in the same field.[70] For example, a tenancy act which is enacted to ameliorate the condition of tenants and which confers exclusive jurisdiction on revenue courts to decide whether tenancy right was acquired by a person has to be read complimentary to a Ceiling Act which is passed with the object of so distributing the agricultural resources of the community as to subserve the common good and which confers jurisdiction on an authority functioning under that Act to decide whether a tenancy right was created *bona fide* or to defeat the provisions of the Act.[71] A determination by revenue courts under the tenancy Act about the existence of tenancy right does not exclude the jurisdiction of the ceiling authorities to go into the question whether the tenancy right was created to defeat the provisions of the Ceiling Act.[72]

The Supreme Court relied on the *pari materia* provision in section 28 of the Bombay Rents, Hotel and Lodging House Rates (Control) Act, 1947, and section 41 of the Presidency Small Cause Courts Act, 1882, as amended by Maharashtra Act 19 of 1976, to hold that both the provisions confer exclusive jurisdiction on Small Cause Courts with respect to suits or proceedings relating to recovery of possession of the premises, and that where the premises are not governed by the Bombay Rent Act, section 41 of the Presidency Small Cause Courts Act, would apply.[73]

Similarly, it has been held that the Maharashtra Recognition of Trade Unions and Prevention of Unfair Labour Practices Act, 1971 has to be read and construed along with the other Labour Laws then in force such as the Industrial Disputes Act, 1947 and the Contract Labour (Regulation and Abolition) Act, 1970.[74] It was held in this case that workmen claiming to be employed by a company ostensibly through a contractor alleging this to be a camouflage to conceal the real relationship cannot directly complain against the company under the Maharashtra Act and they have first to raise an industrial dispute to have their status as directly employed by the company determined under the Industrial Disputes Act.[75] On the same principle, the definition of employee in section 2(e) of the Payment of Gratuity Act, 1972 was construed in the light of the definition of employee in other labour legislations and authoritative pronouncements construing the definition of employee in them and it was held that teachers cannot be said to be employed in any skilled, semi-skilled, or unskilled manual, supervisory,

70. *Jugal Kishore v. State of Maharashtra*, AIR 1989 SC 159, p. 162 : 1989 Supp (1) 589.
71. *Ibid.*
72. *Ibid.*
73. *Prabhudas Damodar Kotecha & Ors. v. Mahabala Jeram Damodar & Anr.*, (2013) 15 SCC 358, p.373.
74. *Sarva Shramik Sangh v. Indian Smelting and Refining Co. Ltd.*, AIR 2004 SC 269, p. 277 : (2003) 10 SCC 455.
75. *Ibid.*

technical or clerical work and, therefore, they do not fall under the definition of employee.[76]

Section 126 of the Maharashtra Regional and Town Planning Act, 1966, provides for acquisition of land for public purposes specified in any plan or scheme under the Act. Section 127 provides that if proceedings for acquisition of any land reserved, allotted or designated for any purpose specified in any plan under the Act are not commenced under the Act or the Land Acquisition Act, 1894, within 10 years from the date on which a final regional plan or final development plan comes into force, the owner or any person interested in the land may serve notice on the appropriate authority to that effect, and if within 6 months from the date of service of such notice, the land is not acquired or 'no steps as aforesaid' are commenced for its acquisition, the reservation, allotment or designation shall be deemed to have lapsed. The Supreme Court held that the expression 'no steps as aforesaid' in section 127 of the 1966 Act has to be read in the context of the provisions of the Land Acquisition Act, 1894. Hence, steps for acquisition of land would really commence when the State Government takes active steps which leads to publication of the declaration under section 6 of the 1894 Act. Mere passing of a resolution by the Planning Authority or sending of a letter to the Collector or State Government cannot be treated as commencement of proceedings for the acquisition of land under the 1966 Act.[77]

The application of this rule of construction has the merit of avoiding any apparent contradiction between a series of statutes dealing with the same subject;[78] it allows the use of an earlier statute to throw light on the meaning of a phrase used in a later statute in the same context;[79] it permits the raising of a presumption, in the absence of any context indicating a contrary intention, that the same meaning attaches to the same words in a later statute as in an earlier statute if the words are used in similar connection in the two statutes;[80] and it enables the use of a later

---

76. *Ahmedabad Pvt. Primary Teachers Association v. Administrative Officer*, AIR 2004 SC 1426, p. 1431 : (2004) 1 SCC 755.

77. *Shrirampur Municipal Council v. Satyabhamabai Bhimaji Dawkher & Ors.*, (2013) 5 SCC 627, p. 650.

78. *R. v. Oastler & Mews*, 43 LJ 403 : (1880) 50 LJMC 4 : 42 Digest, p. 661 (BRETT, L.J.); *R. v. Townbridge Overseers*, (1884) 13 QBD 339, p. 342 (BRETT, M.R.); **See further** Chapter 7, title 5 'Implied repeal'.

79. **See** pp. 333-336.

80. *Lenhon v. Gobson & Howes Ltd.*, (1919) AC 709, pp. 711, 712 (PC) (LORD SHAW). **See further** title 4(b) 'Assistance of Earlier Statutes' *infra*. For Example **see** *In re, Lily Isabel Thomas*, AIR 1964 SC 855; [The words 'rule as to persons practicing be fore the court' as they occur in Article 145(1)(a) of the Constitution of India were understood in the same sense in which these words were used in section 241(1), of the Government of India Act, 1935].

statute as parliamentary exposition of the meaning of ambiguous expressions in an earlier statute.[81]

(b) Assistance of earlier statutes

As already noticed, use of same words in similar connection in a later statute gives rise to a presumption that they are intended to convey the same meaning as in the earlier statute.[82] On the same logic when words in an earlier statute have received an authoritative exposition by a superior court, use of same words in similar context in a later Act will give rise to a presumption that Parliament intends that the same interpretation should also be followed for construction of those words in the later statute.[83] The rule as stated by GRIFFITH, C.J. and approved by the Privy Council (LORD HALSBURY) is: "When a particular form of legislative enactment, which has received authoritative interpretation whether by judicial decision or by a long course of practice, is adopted in the framing of a later statute, it is a sound rule of construction to hold that the words so adopted were intended by the Legislature to bear the meaning which has been so put upon them."[84] The rule in the form stated by JAMES, L.J. and approved by LORD BUCKMASTER is as follows: "When once certain words in an Act of Parliament have received a judicial construction in one of the superior courts, and the Legislature has repeated them without alteration in a subsequent statute, I conceive that the Legislature must be taken to have used them according to the meaning which a court of competent jurisdiction

---

81. **See** title 4(c) 'Assistance of later Statutes', *infra*; *Ahmedabad Pvt. Primary Teachers Association v. Administrative Officer*, AIR 2004 SC 1426, p. 1430 : (2004) 1 SCC 755 (Passage from 8th Edn., of this book, p. 239 is referred).
82. **See** footnote 88, *supra*.
83. *Kathama Natchiar v. Dorasinga Tever*, (1875) 2 IA 169, p. 187 (PC); *Bugga v. Emperor*, (1920) 47 IA 128, pp. 138, 139 (PC); *Kalyandappa v. Chanbasappa*, AIR 1924 PC 137, p. 142; *P. Vajaravelu Mudaliar v. Special Deputy Collector for Land Acquisition, West Madras*, AIR 1965 SC 1017, p. 1023 : 1965 (1) SCR 614. **See further** text and notes 52, 53, 54, at p. 329 and 56, 66 at p. 330 and 331 *supra*; *F.S. Gandhi v. Commissioner of Wealth Tax*, AIR 1991 SC 1866, p. 1871 (para 16) : (1990) 3 SCC 627; *Hughes v. Doncaster Metropolitan Borough Council*, (1991) 1 All ER 295, p. 301 : (1991) 1 AC 382 : (1991) 2 WLR 16 (h and i) (HL); *A.V. Hoare*, (2008) All ER 1 (H.L.) para 15 : "There is a good deal of authority for having regard, in the construction of a statute, to the way in which a word or phrase has been construed by the courts in earlier statutes." (LORD HOFFMAN).
84. *Webb v. Outrim*, (1907) AC 81, p. 89 (PC); referred to in *Barras v. Aberdeen Steam Trawling and Fishing Co. Ltd.*, (1933) AC 402 : (1933) All ER Rep 52, pp. 55, 66, 68, 72 (HL); *Gallagher (Valuation Officer) v. Church of Jesus Christ of Latter-Day Saints*, (2008) 4 All ER 640 (H.L.) paras 10, 26, 47.

has given to them".[85] JAMES, L.J. himself reiterated the rule in slightly different words and according to LORD MACMILLAN in a better form, in a later case thus: "If an Act of Parliament uses the same language which was used in a former Act of Parliament referring to the same subject, and passed with the same purpose, and for the same object, the safe and well-known rule of construction is to assume that the Legislature when using well-known words upon which there have been well known decisions uses those words in the sense which the decisions have attached to them".[86] It will be seen that LORD BUCKMASTER treated the rule as one of 'absolute obligation' whereas LORD MACMILLAN treated the same 'as a canon of construction', *i.e.,* as a presumption in the circumstances where judicial interpretation was well settled and well recognised and even then he thought that the rule must yield to the fundamental rule that in construing statutes grammatical and ordinary sense of the words is to be adhered to, unless it leads to some absurdity, repugnance or inconsistency. The House of Lords[87] (LORD SCARMAN, LORD BRANDAN and LORD TEMPLEMAN) observed that the view of LORD MACMILLAN accords with modern principles and should be preferred to that of LORD BUCKMASTER. The rule obviously will have no application when the decisions on the earlier Act are not consistent;[88] or when they are in fact shown to be erroneous.[89] The rule has also no application to a purely consolidation Act which affords no opportunity to Parliament of reconsidering the previous Acts which are consolidated.[90] Again it is not to be presumed that Parliament in any subsequent Act dealing with a related but identical subject-matter has taken account of and adopted as correct all judicial pronouncements as to the meaning of ordinary English words appearing in a statutory instrument

---

85. *In re, Cathcart, Ex parte, Campbell*, (1870) 5 Ch App 703, p. 709; **approved** by LORD BUCKMASTER in *Barras v. Aberdeen Steam Trawling & Fishing Co. Ltd., supra*, p. 55 (All ER Rep). **See further** *Banarsi Devi v. ITO, District IV, Calcutta*, AIR 1964 SC 1742, p. 1745 : (1976) 3 SCC 800 and *Diwan Brothers v. Central Bank*, AIR 1976 SC 1503, p. 1515 : (1964) 7 SCR 539 : (1976) 3 SCC 800, where the rule as stated by LORD BUCKMASTER in *Barras'* case, *supra*, p. 55 (All ER Rep.) is **quoted**.

86. *Greaves v. Tofield*, (1880) 14 Ch 563, p. 571, referred to in *Barras v. Aberdeen Steam Trawling & Fishing Co., supra*, p. 72 (All ER Rep).

87. *R. v. Chard*, (1983) 3 All ER 637, p. 644 : (1984) AC 279 : (1983) 3 WLR 835 (HL). **See also** to the same effect *Commissioner of Income-tax v. Bansidhar*, (1986) 1 SCC 523, p. 538 : AIR 1986 SC 421.

88. *Robinson Bros. (Brewers) Ltd. v. Durham Country Assessment Committee*, (1938) 2 All ER 79, pp. 87, 88 (HL) (LORD MACMILLAN).

89. *Royal Crown Derby Porcelain Co. Ltd. v. Russel*, (1949) 1 All ER 749, p. 755 (DENNING, L.J.); *Dun v. Dun*, (1959) 2 All ER 134, p. 143 (PC); *Re, Yeovil Glove Co. Ltd.*, (1964) 2 All ER 849, pp. 859, 860 (CA); *Farrel v. Alexander*, (1976) 2 All ER 721 : (1977) AC 59 : (1976) 3 WLR 145 (HL), p. 727 (LORD WILLBERFORCE), pp. 740, 741 (LORD SIMON), p. 746 (LORD EDMUND DAVIES).

90. *Haigh v. Charles W. Ireland Ltd.*, (1973) 3 All ER 1113, pp. 1149, 1150 (HL).

made under an earlier Act.[91] Further, the presumption arising under the rule is not conclusive and will be weak when the interpretation of the former Act was given by only one of the High Courts and the matter was not taken to the highest court in appeal.[92] "The true view", said LORD DENNING: "is that the court will be slow to overrule a previous decision on the interpretation of a statute when it has long been acted on, and it will be more than usually slow to do so when Parliament has, since the decision, re-enacted the statute in the same terms, but if the decision is in fact shown to be erroneous, there is no rule of law which prevents it being overruled".[93] In the words of LORD SIMON: "To pre-empt a court of construction from performing independently its own constitutional duty of examining the validity of a previous interpretation, the intention of Parliament to endorse the previous judicial decision would have to be expressed or clearly implied. Mere repetition of language which has been the subject of previous judicial interpretation is entirely neutral in this respect—or at most implies merely the truism that the language has been the subject of interpretation for whatever (and it may be much or little) that is worth".[94] But the legislature may though rarely use words in a later statute "to discourage the courts from taking a fresh look at the statutory language" which has been borrowed from an earlier Act and to re-examine and depart from the principles settled by courts on a construction of the language used "whatever their logic or merit."[95]

In dealing with Articles 245(1) and 246 of the Constitution which are in *pari materia* with sections 99(1) and 100 of the Government of India Act, 1935, VENKATARAMA AIYAR, J., observed: "It is a well-settled rule of construction that when a statute is repealed and re-enacted and words in the repealed statute are reproduced in the new statute, they should be

---

91. *Ibid.*

92. *Diamond Sugar Mills Ltd. v. State of U.P.*, AIR 1961 SC 652, p. 658 : 1961 (3) SCR 242; *Kumara Nund v. Brijmohan Lal Sharma*, AIR 1967 SC 808, p. 812 : 1967 (2) SCR 127; *CIT v. Bansidhar*, (1986) 1 SCC 523, p. 538 : AIR 1986 SC 421.

93. *Royal Crown Derby Porcelain Co. Ltd. v. Russel*, (1949) 1 All ER 749, p. 755; referred to in *Dun v. Dun*, (1959) 2 All ER 134, p. 143 (PC).

94. *Farrel v. Alexander*, (1976) 2 All ER 721, pp. 740, 741 : 1977 AC 59 : (1976) 3 WLR 145 (HL). In *R. v. Sheppard*, (1980) 3 All ER 899 : (1981) AC 394 : (1980) 3 WLR 960 (HL) the House of Lords **overruled** a long standing decision on the meaning of the word 'wilfully' as it operated to the disadvantage of the accused.

95. *Wildfree Hotels Ltd. v. Harrow Land on Borough Council*, (2000) 3 All ER 289, pp. 293, 294 (HL). This case relates to construction of section 10 of the Compulsory Purchase Act, 1965 which corresponds to section 68 of the Lands Clauses Consolidation Act 1845. Section 10(2) of the 1965 Act reads: 'This section shall be construed as affording in all cases a right to compensation for injurious affection to land *which is the same as the right which section 68 of the Land Clauses Consolidation Act, 1845 has been construed as affording.*'.

interpreted in the sense which had been judicially put on them under the repealed Act, because the Legislature is presumed to be acquainted with the construction which the courts have put upon the words, and when they repeat the same words, they must be taken to have accepted the interpretation put on them by the court as correctly reflecting the legislative mind."[96] Thus the Supreme Court while construing the words 'the court by which the person is found guilty' as they occur in section 6(1) of the Probation of Offenders Act, 1958, referred to decisions construing similar words in section 562 of the Code of Criminal Procedure, 1898, an enactment in *pari materia* and held in the light of those decisions that the words in question were wide enough to include an appellate court.[97] Similarly, it has been held that section 17(b) of the Wealth-tax Act, 1957, is in *pari materia* with section 34(b) of the Income-tax Act, 1922, and in interpreting the former, decisions interpreting the latter can be relied upon.[98]

However, it is not a sound principle of construction to interpret expressions used in one Act with reference to their use in another Act, and decisions rendered with reference to construction of one Act cannot be applied with reference to the provisions of another Act, when the two Acts are not in *pari materia*.[99] There is also no presumption that the Legislature while repealing one statute and substituting another in different terms intends to make the minimum changes in the previous law that it is possible to reconcile with the actual wording of the new statute particularly where the

---

96. *Bengal Immunity Co. Ltd. v. State of Bihar*, AIR 1955 SC 661, p. 749 : 1955 (2) SCR 603. **See further** *Sakal Deep Sahai Srivastava v. Union of India*, AIR 1974 SC 338, pp. 341, 342 : (1974) 1 SCC 338 : 1974 SCC (L&S) 158.

97. *Ramji Missar v. State of Bihar*, AIR 1963 SC 1088, p. 1091 : 1963 Supp (2) SCR 745.

98. *Commissioner of Wealth Tax, W.B. v. Imperial Tabacco Co. of India Ltd.*, AIR 1967 SC 230 : 1966 Supp SCR 174.

99. *Nippon Yusen Kaisha v. Ramjiban Serowgee*, AIR 1938 PC 152, p. 158; *Ram Narian v. State of U.P.*, AIR 1957 SC 18, p. 23 : 1956 SCR 664; *Lila Vati Bai v. State of Bombay*, AIR 1957 SC 521, p. 527 : 1957 SCR 721; *Ahmedabad Manufacturing and Calico Printing Co. Ltd. v. S.G. Mehta*, AIR 1963 SC 1436, p. 1443 : 1963 Supp (2) SCR 92; *State of Maharashtra v. Mishrilal Tarachand*, AIR 1964 SC 457, p. 459 : (1964) 5 SCR 230; *State of Punjab v. Okara Grain Buyers Syndicate Ltd., Okara*, AIR 1964 SC 669, pp. 684, 685 : (1964) 5 SCR 387; *Board of Muslim Wakfs, Rajasthan v. Radha Kishan*, AIR 1979 SC 289, p. 295 : (1979) 2 SCC 468; *Mohanlal v. R. Kondiah*, AIR 1979 SC 1132, p. 1134 : 1979 (2) SCC 616; *Gwalior Rayon Silk Mfg. (Wvg.) Co. Ltd. v. Custodian of Vested Forests*, AIR 1990 SC 1747, p. 1751 : 1990 (2) JT 130 : 1990 Supp SCC 785. **See further** *Shri Kumar Padma Prasad v. Union of India*, AIR 1992 SC 1213, p. 1226 : 1992 (2) SCC 428 [Meaning of 'judicial office' with reference to section 7(3) of the Industrial Disputes Act, 1947 as construed in *Statesman (Private) Ltd. v. H.R. Deb*, AIR 1968 SC 1495, p. 1499 : (1968) 3 SCR 614 cannot be used for construing that expression in Article 217(2)(a) of the Constitution for the two are not in *pari materia*].

new statute is passed with a new object *e.g.* to give effect to a new international convention.[1] When the new legislation, although re-enacting many provisions from earlier statutes, contains a good deal of fresh material and deals with a subject on which social views have drastically changed, it may not be proper to rely on the earlier authorities for construing the new legislation.[2] Further, when there is no ambiguity in the statute, it may not be permissible to refer to, for purposes of its construction, any previous legislation or decisions rendered thereunder.[3] Decisions relating to constitutional validity of one statute, on the same principles are not taken as a safe guide for pronouncing on the validity of another statute which may not be in *pari materia*.[4]

Again, instructive though it may be, an effort to construe a legislation of one State with the help of legislations on the same subject of other States has not been commended because similarity or variation of language in the laws of different States is not necessarily indicative of a kindred or a changed intention, but earlier legislations of the same State on the same subject may be referred to as indicative of the practice of the particular State and for deriving whatever assistance may be possible.[5] A decision interpreting a Central Act has been used for interpreting corresponding provisions of a State Act holding that they were in *pari materia*.[6] Similarly, a decision interpreting a State Act has been used for interpreting corresponding provisions of a Central Act.[7] Before utilising decisions rendered under a Central Act or a State Act, for construing an Act of another State on the same subject, attention must be drawn to the variance in language. For example, a statutory tenant under the Bombay Rents, Hotel and Lodging House Rates Control Act, 1947 has no heritable or transferable interest whereas a statutory tenant under the corresponding Act of Madhya Pradesh has a heritable interest like a tenant because of

---

1. *Rio Tinto Zinc Corporation v. Westinghouse Electric Corporation*, (1978) 1 All ER 434, p. 461 : 1978 AC 547 : (1978) 2 WLR 81 (HL) (LORD DIPLOCK).
2. *Smith v. Braintree District Council*, (1989) 3 All ER 897, p. 907 (HL).
3. *State of Punjab v. Okara Grain Buyers Syndicate Ltd., Okara, supra*, p. 684; *Board of Muslim Wakfs, Rajasthan v. Radhakishan, supra*.
4. *Hari Khemu Gawali v. Dy. Commissioner of Police*, AIR 1956 SC 559, p. 568 : 1956 SCR 506.
5. *Nathia Agarwalla v. Jahanara Begum*, AIR 1967 SC 92, p. 94 : 1966 (3) SCR 926. **See further** *M.K. Salpekar (Dr.) v. Sunil Kumar Shamsunder Chaudhari*, AIR 1988 SC 1841, p. 1844 : 1988 (4) SCC 21; *Babu Ram Gopal (M/s.) v. Mathra Das*, AIR 1990 SC 879, p. 881 : 1990 (2) SCC 279.
6. *Desh Raj Gupta v. Industrial Tribunal IV, Lucknow*, AIR 1990 SC 2174, p. 2175 : (1991) 1 SCC 249. **See further** *Union of India v. Dhanwanti Devi*, 1996 (6) Scale 431 : 1996 (6) SCC 44.
7. *Agencia E. Sequeira v. Labour Commissioner*, JT 1997 (2) SC 171, p. 181 (para 20).

the special definition of tenant in the Madhya Pradesh Accomodation Control Act, 1961.[8]

The principle under discussion is not applicable when an enactment is not re-enacted but is left unamended by the Legislature.[9] However, in case of an ill-penned enactment if judicial decisions have consistently adopted one construction, inaction of the Legislature in not amending the enactment may lend support to the view that the construction so adopted is in accord with the intention of the Legislature.[10] Referring to section 7 of the Bihar Money-lenders (Regulation of Transaction) Act, 1939, and after indicating that the section was obscure and ill-drawn and that the Patna High Court had been placing a consistent construction upon the language of the section from the very next year of its enactment, CHANDRASHEKHAR AIYAR, J., observed: "If the interpretation does not carry out the intentions of the Act by reason of unhappy or ambiguous phrasing, it is for the Legislature to intervene. But so far from doing so, it has acquiesced, during all these years, in the construction, which the Patna High Court has been placing upon the section from the very next year after the enactment of the statute. Having regard to the great obscurity in the language employed in the relevant provisions and the inaction of the Legislature, it is, in our opinion, legitimate to infer that the view expressed by the Patna High Court is in accord with the intention of the Legislature."[11] It must in this connection be kept in view that "the approval of the Legislature of a particular construction put on the provision of an Act on account of its making no alteration in those provisions is presumed only when there had been a consistent series of cases putting a certain construction on certain provisions",[12] and which is acquiesced in for a sufficiently long time.[13] But when after a provision in an Act has been construed by the Supreme Court the Act is amended leaving the provision intact and without affecting the

---

8. *S.J. Pande v. P.K. Balkrishnan*, AIR 1993 SC 2132, p. 2134 : (1993) 3 SCC 297 **distinguishing** *Damadilal v. Parashram*, AIR 1976 SC 2229 : 1976 (4) SCC 855.

9. *Dun v. Dun*, (1959) 2 All ER 134, p. 143 (PC).

10. *Union of India v. G.M. Kokil*, 1984 (Supp.) SCC 196, p. 203 (para 12) : AIR 1984 SC 1022. **See further** *Darshan Singh v. Rampal Singh*, AIR 1991 SC 1654, p. 1664 : 1992 Supp (1) SCC 191 (The principle of *stare decisis* will also apply in such cases).

11. *Ram Nandan Prasad Narayan Singh v. Kapildeo Ramjee*, AIR 1951 SC 155, p. 157 : 1951 SCR 138. **See further** *Gajanan v. Seth Brindaban*, AIR 1970 SC 2007, p. 2015 : (1970) 2 SCC 360 (the inference is presumptive and not conclusive); *State of Karnataka v. G. Seenappa*, AIR 1992 SC 1531, p. 1532 : 1993 Supp (1) SCC 648.

12. *Purushottamdas Dalmia v. State of W.B.*, AIR 1961 SC 1589, p. 1595 : 1962 (2) SCR 101. **See further** *Roop Chand v. State of Punjab*, AIR 1963 SC 1503, p. 1507 : 1963 Supp (1) SCR 539.

13. *Empress Mills, Nagpur v. Municipal Committee, Wardha*, AIR 1958 SC 341, p. 346 : 1958 SCR 1102.

construction placed by the Supreme Court, it may be inferred that the decision of the Supreme Court correctly brings out the legislative intention.[14]

Apart from any question of acquiescence of the Legislature, a long standing decision adopting a particular construction which may have been acted upon by persons in the general conduct of affairs may not be departed from on the doctrine of *stare decisis*.[15] The principle of *stare decisis* is also applicable to judgments of the Supreme Court.[16] The judgment of a larger Bench is binding on a Division Bench.[17] The pronouncement by a Division Bench is binding on another Division Bench.[18] Law should be certain and parties should know where they stand. Therefore, consistent view taken by the High Court on the question of interpretation of a State Act, which held the field for a number of years would not be readily overruled by the Supreme Court even if a different view were possible.[19] Even in respect of interpretation of a Central Act the Supreme Court will lean in favour of the view which is predominant view of the majority of the High Court.[20]But there is nothing in law to prevent the Supreme Court in overruling along standing interpretation of a State Act if it is plainly wrong and is contrary to the object of the Statute.[21] Further, the doctrine does not prevent the Supreme Court from overruling the High Court's or its own decisions which are contrary to the Constitution as properly interpreted.[22]

---

14. *Indian Oxygen Ltd. v. Their Workmen*, AIR 1972 SC 471, p. 479 : (1972) 4 SCC 578.

15. *Mishri Lal v. Dhirendra Nath,* JT 1999 (2) SC 586, pp. 591 to 594 : AIR 1999 SC 2286, pp. 2289, 2290 : (1999) 4 SCC 11 (see also cases referred to therein); *Janba v. Gopikabai,* JT 2000 (4) SC 280, p. 290 : (2000) 4 SCC 1 : AIR 2000 SC 1771; *Saurashtra Cement and Chemical Industries v. Union of India,* AIR 2001 SC 8, p. 23; *Iridium India Telecom Ltd. v. Motorola Inc*, (2005) 2 SCC 145, p. 160 (paras 40, 41). **See further** *Darshan Singh v. Rampal Singh,* AIR 1991 SC 1654, p. 1664 : 1992 Supp (1) SCC 191; **see** text and note 7, p. 375.

16. *Shanker Raju v. Union of India*, (2011) 2 SCC 132 paras 10, 12, 13, 14, 15 : (2011) 1 JT 49.

17. *Ibid.*

18. *Safiya Bee v. Mohd. Vajarat Hussain*, (2011) 2 SCC 94 paras 28, 29, 30 : AIR 2011 SC 421. The principles stated in 12B, 12C equally apply to High Courts.

19. *Rohini Prasad v. Kasturchand,* AIR 2000 SC 1283, p. 1286 : (2000) 3 SCC 668; *Janba v. Gopikabai,* AIR 2000 SC 1771, p. 1777 : (2000) 4 SCC 1; *Pyarelal v. Mani Ram,* AIR 2000 SC 2802, p. 2806 (prospective overruling) : (2000) 7 SCC 175.

20. *Synco Industries Ltd. v. Assessing Officer Income Tax,* (2008) 4 SCC 22 para 26 : (2008) 4 SCR 919.

21. *Molar Mal v. Kay Iron Works (P.) Ltd.,* AIR 2000 SC 1261, p. 1267 : (2000) 4 SCC 285.

22. *State of Maharashtra v. Millind,* AIR 2001 SC 393, pp. 406, 407 : (2001) 1 SCC 4. The Supreme Court in *Central Board of Dawoodi Bohra Community v. State of Maharashtra,* (2005) 2 SCC 673 : AIR 2005 SC 752 pointed out 7 principles which should be kept in view in **overruling** an earlier binding precedent which were again **referred** and **applied** in *Tika Ram v. State of U.P.,* decided on September 9, 2009:

[Footnote No. 22 Contd.]

The law declared by a court has retrospective effect, if not otherwise stated to be so.[23] The Supreme Court may in rare cases resort to prospective overruling to avoid injustice in cases, where the earlier view had been acted upon.[24] The doctrine of prospective overruling ordinarily applies where a statute is declared *ultra vires* and not in a case where the decree or order is passed by a court/tribunal in respect whereof it had no jurisdiction.[25] The High Courts have no power of prospective overruling but they may without applying this doctrine grant limited relief in exercise of equity jurisdiction.[26]

Just as use of same language in a later statute as was used in an earlier one in *pari materia* is suggestive of the intention of the Legislature that the language so used in the later statute is used in the same sense as in the earlier one, change of language in a later statute in *pari materia* is suggestive that change of interpretation is intended.[27] As was observed by BRETT, J.: "Where two statutes dealing with the same subject-matter use different language, it is an acknowledged rule of construction that one may be looked at as a guide to the construction of the other. If one uses distinct language, imposing a penalty under certain circumstances and other does not, it is always an argument that the Legislature did not intend to impose a penalty in the later, for where they did so intend they plainly said so."[28] Similarly, it was stated by COCKBURN, C.J.: "When the Legislature, in legislating in *pari materia* and substituting certain provisions in that Act for those which existed in the earlier statute, has entirely changed the language of the enactment, it must be taken to have done so with some

---

[**Footnote No. 22 Contd.**]

Hitvada September 28, 2009 (unreported); *Raju Ramsing Vasave v. Mahesh Deorao Bhivapurkar*, (2008) 9 SCC 54 paras 18 to 21 : (2008) 9 JT 445 (Parliament alone can amend the Constitution (Scheduled Tribes) Order, 1950 and it is not even permissible for the court to say that a tribe, or sub-tribes part or group of any tribe or tribal community is synonymous to one mentioned in the order. The court can review any earlier wrong decision on this question).

23. *P.V. George v. State of Kerala*, (2007) 3 SCC 557 (para 29) : AIR 2007 SC 1034.

24. *Raymond Ltd. v. Madhya Pradesh Electricity Board*, AIR 2001 SC 238, p. 239; *Somaiya Organics (India) Ltd. v. State of Uttar Pradesh*, AIR 2001 SC 1723, pp. 1734, 1735 : (2001) 5 SCC 519; *Gangaram Moolchandani v. State of Rajasthan*, AIR 2001 SC 2616, pp. 2624, 2625 : (2001) 6 SCC 89; *P.V. George v. State of Kerala, supra*, para 14.

25. *Rajasthan State Road Transport Corporation v. Bal Mukund Bairawa*, (2009) 4 SCC 299 paras 50 to 52 : (2009) 2 JT 423.

26. *State of H.P. v. Nurpur Private Bus Operators*, AIR 1999 SC 3880 : (1999) 9 SCC 559. *P.V. George v. State of Kerala, supra*, para 14. See further ARVIND P. DATAR, 'Prospective overruling: Correct Doctrine Incorrect Application' (2008) 7 SCC J-41 to J-52.

27. *State of Madhya Pradesh v. G.S. Dall and Flour Mills*, AIR 1991 SC 772, p. 783 : 1992 Supp (1) SCC 150 [4th Edition of this book (pp. 167-168) is referred]; *Lalu Prasad Yadav v. State of Bihar*, (2010) 5 SCC 1 p. 15 para 39 : AIR 2010 SC 1561 [12th edition p. 310 of this book is referred]; *R (A) v. Croydon London B C*, (2010) 1 All ER 469 (U K SC) p. 478 para 16.

28. *Dickerson v. Fletcher*, (1873) LR 9 CP 1, pp. 7, 8.

intention and motive."[29] To the same effect are the observations of LORD MACMILLAN: "When an amending Act alters the language of the principal statute, the alteration must be taken to have been made deliberately."[30] The dropping of the word 'reduce' and substitution of the word 'modify' in its place was on this principle construed to give to the word 'modify' a wider connotation so as to include not only reduction but also other kinds of alteration including enhancement.[31] Similarly, when the New Zealand Dairy Board Act, 1953, section 11 of which gave the Dairy Board power to appoint committees and to delegate to a committee with the consent of the minister any of its powers and functions was repealed and replaced by the New Zealand Dairy Production and Marketing Board Act, 1961, section 13 of which gave the Board power to appoint committees to advise it, it was held that the change in language was not accidental and gave rise to the inference that the Parliament deliberately refrained from giving the Board power to delegate any of its powers and functions to a committee with the consent of the minister.[32] An argument that change in law by an amending Act was not intended will be readily negatived if adherence to the law as it was before the amendment would make the words added by the amending Act *otiose*.[33] It was thus held that after amendment of section 17(4) of the Land Acquisition Act, 1894 by the Amendment Act of 1984, a notification under section 6 of the Act cannot be issued simultaneously with the notification under section 4, even in cases of emergency to which section 17 is applied, for that will make the words 'after the publication of the notification under section 4(1)' as added in section 17(4) redundant.[34] Numerous illustrations can be found where the Legislature not happy with a particular construction placed upon an enactment has changed the same by an amending statute and that is specially true of tax and welfare legislations. The alteration of the law by the Legislature, however, does not give rise to any inference that the previous decisions were wrong or even that those who proposed the alteration were of that

---

29. *R. v. Price*, (1871) LR 6 QB 411, pp. 416, 417.

30. *D.R. Fraser & Co. Ltd. v. Minister of National Revenue*, AIR 1949 PC 120, p. 123.

31. *Western India Theatres Ltd. v. Municipal Corporation, Poona*, AIR 1959 SC 586, p. 589 : 1959 Supp (2) SCR 71. **See further** *State of U.P. v. Malik Zarid Khalid*, AIR 1988 SC 132, p. 138 : (1988) 1 SCC 145 (Amending Act substituting a provision using wider language cannot be given a narrow construction so as to hold it a mere re-enactment of the old provision); *State of Madhya Pradesh v. G.S. Dall and Flour Mills*, AIR 1991 SC 772, pp. 783, 784 : 1992 Supp (1) SCC 150.

32. *Jeffs v. New Zealand Dairy Production etc.*, (1966) 3 All ER 863, p. 870 : (1967) 1 AC 551 (PC).

33. *State of U.P. v. Radhey Shyam*, AIR 1989 SC 682, pp. 689, 690 : 1989 (1) SCC 591.

34. *Ibid.* **See further** *V.M. Salgaokar & Bros. Pvt. Ltd. v. Commissioner of Income-tax*, JT 2000 (4) SC 473, pp. 493, 494 : (2000) 5 SCC 373.

opinion.[35] But when judicial decisions have taken two different views of a statutory provision which is re-enacted with certain modifications, the change in language may be suggestive of acceptance of one view by the Legislature and a meaning consistent with that view should be placed on the provisions re-enacted.[36] When the Legislature makes suitable amendments to give effect to a prior judicial decision, it should be inferred that the decision correctly interpreted the law before the amendment.[37]

It is no doubt true that after a statute is amended, the statute thereafter is to be read and construed with reference to the new provisions and not with reference to provisions that originally existed.[38] Further, the wisdom of the warning given by LORD WATSON cannot be doubted that it is an "extremely hazardous proceeding to refer to provisions which have been absolutely repealed in order to ascertain what the Legislature meant to enact in their room and stead".[39] However, "when it is contended that the Legislature intended by any particular amendment to make substantial changes in the pre-existing law, it is impossible to arrive at a conclusion without considering what the law was previously to the particular enactment and to see whether the words used in the statute can be taken to effect the change that is suggested as intended",[40] and similarly, when the terms of the enactment in the new shape are sufficiently difficult and ambiguous, the consideration of its evolution in the statute book is justified as a proper and logical course.[41] It is an example of the application of this principle that the

---

35. *Bharat Ins. Co. Ltd. v. CIT, Punjab*, AIR 1934 PC 45, p. 49. But alteration immediately following a decision cannot be overlooked as of no import: *Union of India v. V.M. Salgaonkar and Bros. (P.) Ltd.*, AIR 1998 SC 1367, p. 1371 : 1998 (4) SCC 263.

36. *Felix v. Thomas*, (1966) 3 All ER 21, p. 27 (PC).

37. *Bhimaji Shankar v. Dundappa Vithappa*, AIR 1966 SC 166, p. 169 : 1966 (1) SCR 145.

38. *Venkata Subamma v. Ramayya*, AIR 1932 PC 92; *Shamrao V. Parulekar v. District Magistrate, Thana*, AIR 1952 SC 324, p. 326 : 1952 SCR 683; *Ramnarain v. Simla Banking & Industrial Co. Ltd.*, AIR 1956 SC 614, p. 621 : 1956 SCR 630; *Laxmi Devi v. Mukund Kanwar*, AIR 1965 SC 834, p. 837 (para 14) : 1965 (1) SCR 726; *Onkarlal Nandlal v. State of Rajasthan*, (1985) 4 SCC 404, p. 415 : AIR 1986 SC 2164; *Orient Paper Industries Ltd. v. State of Orissa*, AIR 1991 SC 672, p. 682 : 1991 Supp (1) SCC 81; *Yadiapati Venkateswarlu v. State of Andhra Pradesh*, AIR 1991 SC 704, p. 709 : 1992 Supp (1) SCC 74; *State of Maharashtra v. Vithalrao Ganpatro Warhade*, JT (1998) 7 SC 177, p. 187 : 1998 (5) Scale 603 : (1998) 8 SCC 284.

39. *Bradlaugh v. Clarke*, (1883) 8 AC 354, p. 380. **See further** *Mohanlal Tripathi v. District Magistrate, Rai Bareilly*, AIR 1993 SC 2042, p. 2049 : (1992) 4 SCC 80.

40. *Abdur Rahim v. Syed Abu Mahomed Barkat Ali Shah*, AIR 1928 PC 16, p. 18 : 55 IA 96.

41. *Tumahole Bereng v. King*, AIR 1949 PC 172, p. 176 : 50 Cri LJ 642; *ITO, Sitapur v. Muralidhar Bhagwandas*, AIR 1965 SC 342, p. 346 : 1964 (6) SCR 411; *ITO, I, Salem v. Short Brothers*, AIR 1967 SC 81, p. 84 : (1966) 3 SCR 84; *Pacific Motor etc. v. Motor Credits*, (1965) 2 All ER 105, p. 113 (PC) (Heredity of a section as useful guide); *Armah v. Government of Ghana*, (1966) 3 All ER 177, pp. 181, 203 (HL) (use of statutory antecedents of the Act); *Beswick v. Beswick*, (1967) 2 All ER 1197,

[Footnote No. 41 Contd.]

Supreme Court "on historical evolution of section 21 (Indian Penal Code, 1860), adopted as an external aid to construction" held that an M.L.A. was not and is not a public servant as defined in that section.[42] Legislative history of separate and distinct provisions giving benefit of total or partial exemption from income-tax to those who were engaged in running poultry business was taken into account in holding that the provisions which provided incentive to industrial undertakings engaged in the business of manufacturing or producing articles or things did not apply to those engaged in the business of hatcheries which in this context could neither be termed industrial undertaking nor engaged in the business of producing articles or things.[43] And in dealing with the expression 'injury to health' in section 79 of the Environmental Protection Act, 1990 used in the context of statutory nuisance the abatement of which can be directed by a local authority, the Court of Appeal traced its legislative history beginning from the Public Health Act, 1875 and referred to the decisions under the earlier Acts and came to the conclusion that it had been always understood in the sense of risk of disease or illness, and so it could not be interpreted in section 79 to include risk of physical injury from the state of residential premises.[44]

An amending Act is construed in a way which does not result in its misfiring or in denying its efficacy[45] but without straining its language or re-writing or adopting it to cover cases other than those to which it clearly applies.[46] Change in language is not, however, always indicative of a change in construction.[47] The alteration in language in or by a later statute may be the result of many other factors. For instance, words may be

---

[**Footnote No. 41 Contd.**]

p. 1202 (HL) (Antecedents of a section); *Owen Thomas Mangin v. IRC*, (1971) 2 WLR 39, p. 42 (PC); *General Electric Co. v. General Electric Co. Ltd.*, (1972) 2 All ER 507, p. 518 (Legislative history of the Trade Marks Act, 1938 over the previous 63 years and the state of the Common Law as it existed before the first Act to alter it was passed nearly 100 years ago were considered); *Mohanlal Tripathi v. District Magistrate, Rai Bareilly*, AIR 1993 SC 2042, p. 2049 : (1992) 4 SCC 80.

42. *R. S. Nayak v. A. R. Antuley*, (1984) 2 SCC 183, p. 223 : AIR 1984 SC 684.

43. *Commissioner of Income-tax Bangalore v. Venkateshwara Hatcheries (P.) Ltd.*, JT 1999 (2) SC 338, pp. 343, 344 : AIR 1999 SC 1225, pp. 1228, 1229.

44. *R v. Bristol City Council exparte Everett*, (1999) 2 All ER 193 (CA). **See** the following cases where similar method was applied by the House of Lords: *Cadogan Estates Ltd. v. McMohan*, (2000) 4 All ER 897 (HL) (construction of the word 'obligation' in the Rent Act 1979); *Birmingham City Council v. Oakley*, (2001) 1 All ER 385, pp. 392, 394, 395 (HL) (Construction of the expression 'prejudicial to health' in the Environmental Protection Act, 1990.

45. *Green Cab Service v. Whitfield*, (1965) 3 All ER 695, p. 700 (PC).

46. *Wijesuriya v. Amit*, (1965) 3 All ER 701, p. 703 (PC).

47. *Hadley v. Perks*, (1866) LR 1 QB 444, p. 457; *Lawless v. Sullivan*, (1881) 6 AC 373, p. 383 (PC); *Hopes v. Hopes*, (1948) 2 All ER 920, p. 925; *Redrow Homes Ltd. v. Bett Bros. Plc.*, (1998) 1 All ER 385, p. 390 (g, h) (HL).

omitted in a later statute when they were mere surplusage[48] and the natural and ordinary meaning of the existing words indicates no intention of alteration of meaning.[49] Similarly, addition of words may be to make clear a meaning which was already implied.[50] Further, the change in wording may be because the draftsman wanted to improve the style.[51] As aptly stated by LORD UTHWATT, no alteration in meaning by alteration in language can result "unless, (1) the requirements of the English language demand it, (2) those requirements permit it and sense of the section demands it".[52] It must also be remembered that for bringing about fundamental changes such as departure from the general system of the law or imposition of new burdens, a clear intention to that effect is necessary and the courts will not infer such fundamental changes unless the language used expresses a clear intention to the contrary.[53]

(c) Assistance of later statutes

It is within the authority of the Legislature to amend an earlier Act or to declare its meaning by enacting a new Act and the Legislature is even competent to so declare a meaning that the "declaration offended the plain language of the earlier Act".[54] In such cases, the later statute operates directly by its own force and not merely as an aid to construction of the earlier statute.[55] But a legislation proceeding upon an erroneous assumption

---

48. *Madanlal Fakirchand Dudhediya v. S. Changdeo Sugar Mills*, AIR 1962 SC 1543, p. 1553: 1962 Supp (3) SCR 973; *Bhanupratap Singh (Raja) v. Asstt. Custodian, Evacuee Property, Bahraich*, AIR 1966 SC 245, p. 248 : (1966) 1 SCR 304.

49. *Redrow Homes Ltd. v. Bett Bros. Plc., supra.*

50. *Chandrika Prasad Tripathi v. Shiv Prasad Chanpuria*, AIR 1959 SC 827, p. 830 : 1959 Supp (2) SCR 527; *Mohamed Quasim Larry v. Mohomed Samsuddin*, AIR 1964 SC 1699 : (1964) 7 SCR 419; *Kajari Lal Agarwala v. Union of India*, AIR 1966 SC 1538, p. 1541 : 1966 (3) SCR 141; *Bhagat Ram v. State of Punjab*, AIR 1967 SC 927 : 1967 (2) SCR 165.

51. *Hopes v. Hopes*, (1948) 2 All ER 920, p. 925. **Referred** in *State of U.P. v. Radhey Shyam*, AIR 1989 SC 682, p. 690 : 1989 (1) SCC 591.

52. *Lord Howard de Walden v. IRC*, (1948) 2 All ER 825, p. 830 (HL). **Referred** in *State of U.P. v. Radhey Shyam, supra.*

53. *M.K. Ranganathan v. Govt. of Madras*, AIR 1955 SC 604, p. 609 : 1955 (2) SCR 374; *Empress Mills, Nagpur v. Municipal Committee, Wardha*, AIR 1958 SC 341, p. 348 : 1958 SCR 1102; *Byram Pestonji Gariwala v. Union Bank of India*, AIR 1991 SC 2234, p. 2242 : 1992 (1) SCC 31 (Implied authority of counsel to compromise not altered by CPC Amendment Act, 1976). **See further** *Murugiah v. Jainuddeen*, (1954) 3 WLR 682, p. 687 (PC); *National Assistance Board v. Wilkinson*, (1952) 2 All ER 255, p. 259; *Minet v. Leman*, (1855) 20 Beav 269, p. 278 : 52 ER 606, p. 610; *Beswick v. Beswick*, (1967) 2 All ER 1197 (HL); *Central Bank of India v. State of Kerala*, (2009) 4 SCC 94 para 136 : (2009) 3 JT 216. **See also** Chapter 5, title 8(a1) Principle of legality.

54. *Ormond Investment Co. v. Betts*, (1928) AC 143 : (1928) All ER Rep 709, p. 715 (HL).

55. *Kirkness v. John Hudson & Co. Ltd.*, (1955) 2 All ER 345, p. 366 : 1955 AC 696 : (1955) 1 WLR 1135 (HL).

of the existing law without directly amending or declaring the law is ineffective to change the law. "The beliefs or assumptions of those who frame Acts of Parliament cannot make the law" and a mere erroneous assumption exhibited in a statute as to the state of the existing law is ineffective to express an "intention" to change the law.[56] If by such a statute the idea is to change the law, it will be said that "the Legislature has plainly missed fire."[57] As has been observed by S.K. DAS, J.: "Legislation founded on a mistaken or erroneous assumption has not the effect of making that the law which the Legislature had erroneously assumed to be so."[58] The court will disregard such a belief or assumption and also the provision inserted in that belief or assumption.[59] Even a legislation proceeding on the basis of a common law rule which then had the approval of the highest court may be ineffective to prevent the court in departing from its earlier decision and changing the law.[60] A later statute, therefore, is normally not used as an aid to construction of an earlier one.[61] These principles were referred to (from 5th Edition, pp. 186, 187 of this book) and approved in *P.V. Murali v. Andhra Pradesh*.[62] In this case, Explanation II added to section 2(22) of the Andhra Pradesh Charitable and Hindu Religious Institution and Endowments Act, 1987 was held to be ineffective as it proceeded on the wrong assumption of the legal position that even after grant of *pattas*

---

56. *IRC v. Dowdall O'Mahoney & Co.*, (1952) 1 All ER 531, p. 544 : 1952 AC 401 (HL); *Kirkness v. John Hudson & Co.*, *supra*, p. 352; *Birmingham City Corporation v. West Midland Baptist*, (1969) 3 All ER 172, pp. 179, 188, 190 (HL); *ITO II, Kanpur v. Mani Ram*, AIR 1969 SC 543, p. 548 : (1969) 1 SCR 724; Reference under section 48A of the Criminal Appeal (Northern Ireland) Act, 1968, (1976) 2 All ER 937, p. 951 (HL).

57. *IRC v. Ayrshire Assn. Ltd.*, (1946) 1 All ER 637, p. 641 : 27 TC 331 (HL). LORD DIPLOCK'S *extra-judicial* comment on this case is "If the court can identify the target of legislation their proper function is to see that it is hit; not merely to record that it has been missed" quoted in *R (Electoral Commission) v. Westminster Mag. Ct.*, (2011) 1 All ER 1 (UKSC) para 117.

58. *Hariprasad Shivshankar Shukla v. A.D. Divelkar*, AIR 1957 SC 121, p. 131 : 1957 SCR 121. **See further** *Nalinikant Ambalal Mody v. CIT, Bombay*, AIR 1967 SC 193, p. 203 : 1966 Supp SCR 295.

59. *Dharangdhara Chemical Works v. Dharangdhara Municipality*, (1985) 4 SCC 92, p. 101 : AIR 1985 SC 1729.

60. *Arthur J.S. Hall v. Simmons*, (2000) 3 All ER 673, p. 684 (HL) (The immunity of Barristers from being sued for professional negligence which had the approval of the House of Lords was extended to Solicitor Advocates by section 62 of the Courts and Legal Services Act, 1990. But this did not prevent the House of Lords in departing from its earlier decision and thereby making Barristers and Solicitor Advocates liable for professional negligence).

61. *Gopee Mohun Thakoor v. Rajah Radhakant*, (1834) 5 SWR 72, p. 75 (PC); *Mungniram Marwari v. Mohunt Gursahai Nund*, (1889) 16 IA 195, pp. 200, 201 : 17 Cal 347, p. 357 (PC); *Nalinikant Ambalal Mody v. CIT, Bombay, supra*, pp. 202, 203; *ITO II, Kanpur v. Mani Ram, supra*, p. 548; *Vaijnath v. Guramma*, AIR 1999 SC 555, p. 557.

62. 1996 (1) Scale 298, p. 304.

of land of a religious institution under the Andhra Pradesh Inams (Abolition and Conversion into Ryotwari) Act, 1956, the property so granted did not become the personal property of the grantees but continued to be a religious endowment. Further, a legislation declaring certain non-existent facts as existing and proceeding on that basis may also be held to be ineffective.[63]

But when an earlier Act is truly ambiguous a later Act may in certain circumstances serve as a parliamentary exposition of the former.[64] The rule of construction applicable in such cases can be best stated in the words of LORD STERNDALE: "I think, it is clearly established—that subsequent legislation on the same subject may be looked to in order to see what is the proper construction to be put upon an earlier Act where that earlier Act is ambiguous. I quite agree that subsequent legislation, if it proceeds upon an erroneous construction of previous legislation, cannot alter that previous legislation, but if there be any ambiguity in the earlier legislation then the subsequent legislation may fix the proper interpretation which is to be put upon the earlier."[65] Referring to this passage LORD BUCKMASTER said: "This is in his opinion an accurate expression of the law."[66] But as expressed in the passage of LORD STERNDALE[67] and as explained authoritatively by the House of Lords this rule of construction applies only when the earlier enactment is ambiguous, *i.e.*, "fairly and equally

---

63. *Indira Sawhney v. Union of India*, JT 1999 (9) SC 557, pp. 579, 582 : AIR 2000 SC 498.

64. *Ram Kishana Ram Nath v. Janpad Sabha*, AIR 1962 SC 1073, p. 1079 : 1962 Supp (3) SCR 70; *ITO, Kanpur v. Maniram*, AIR 1969 SC 543, p. 548 : (1969) 1 SCR 724; *Jogendranath Naskar v. Commissioner of Income-tax*, AIR 1969 SC 1089, p. 1094 : 1969 (1) SCC 555; *Sone Valley Portland Cement Co. Ltd. v. General Mining Syndicate Pvt. Ltd.*, AIR 1976 SC 2520, p. 2528 : (1976) 3 SCC 852; *Thiru Manickam & Co. v. State of Tamil Nadu*, AIR 1977 SC 518, pp. 522, 523 : 1977 SCC (Tax) 165; *U.P. Co-operative Cane Union Federation Ltd. v. Liladhar*, AIR 1981 SC 152, p. 158 : 1980 Supp SCC 437; *Ghanshyam Dass v. Dominion of India*, (1984) 3 SCC 46, p. 58 : AIR 1984 SC 1004.

65. *Cape Brandy Syndicate v. IRC*, (1921) 2 KB 403, p. 414 (CA); *Jogendranath Naskar v. Commissioner of Income-tax*, AIR 1969 SC 1089, p. 1094 : (1969) 1 SCC 555; *Pappu Sweets & Biscuits v. Commissioner of Trade Tax (U.P. LKW.)*, AIR 1998 SC 3247, p. 3252 : (1998) 7 SCC 228; *Gem Granites v. Commissioner of Income Tax*, (2005) 1 SCC 289, p. 296 : AIR 2005 SC 1455.

66. *Ormand Investment Co. v. Betts*, (1928) All ER Rep 709, p. 716 (HL) : (1928) AC 143, p. 156 (LORD BUCKMASTER). **Reaffirmed:** *Kirkness v. John Hudson & Co.*, (1955) 2 All ER 345, pp. 350, 351 : 1955 AC 696 (HL) (VISCOUNT SIMONDS); *A.G. v. HRH Prince Ernest Augustus of Hanover*, (1957) 1 All ER 49, p. 61 : 1957 AC 436; *State of Bihar v. S.K. Roy*, AIR 1966 SC 1995, p. 1998 : 1966 Supp SCR 259; *Nalinikant Ambalal Mody v. CIT, Bombay*, AIR 1967 SC 193, pp. 202, 203 : 1966 Supp SCR 295.

67. *Cape Brandy Syndicate v. IRC, supra.*

open to diverse meanings"[68] and the same rule applies even though the later Act contains a provision that it is to be read as one with the earlier Act.[69] It has further been said that it is clearly wrong to construe an unamended section of the earlier Act in the light of the amendment made by the later Act in other parts of the earlier Act unless the unamended section is ambiguous, *i.e.*, "fairly and equally open to diverse meanings".[70]

The Coal Mines Provident Fund and Bonus Schemes Act, 1948, before its amendment by Act 45 of 1965, defined Coal Mine as including all works, machinery, tramways and sidings, whether above or below ground, in or adjacent to or belonging to a coal mine. In interpreting this definition and in holding that the conjunction 'or' preceding the expression 'belonging to the coal mine' should be read as 'and' the court derived assistance from the definition of 'Coal Mine' as introducted by the amending Act 45 of 1965, so as to fix proper interpretation of the Act before its amendment. RAMASWAMI, J. said: "It is a well recognised principle that subsequent legislation may be looked at in order to see what is the proper interpretation to be put upon the earlier Act where the earlier Act is obscure or ambiguous or readily capable of more than one interpretation."[71]

In *Anand Bros. Pvt. Ltd. v. Union of India*,[72] the issue before the Supreme Court was whether a non-speaking award under the Arbitration Act, 1940, had been correctly set aside on the ground that the arbitrator had not recorded 'findings' as was required under the contract between the parties. Relying on its earlier decisions in *Ram Kishna Ram Nath v. Janpad Sabha*,[73] and *Ghanshyam Dass v. Dominion of India*,[74] the Supreme Court held that it is one of well-known canons of interpretation of statutes that when an earlier enactment is truly ambiguous in that it is open to diverse meanings, the later enactment may in certain circumstances serve as the parliamentary exposition of the former. Hence, the Court referred to the provisions of the Arbitration and Conciliation Act, 1996, which repealed the Arbitration Act, 1940, to hold that the obligation to record 'findings' must be understood not only in light of the law laid down by the Court but

---

68. *Ormond Investment Co. v. Betts, supra*, p. 156; *Kirkness v. John Hudson & Co., supra*, pp. 350, 351. **See further,** *Commissioner of Sales Tax v. Industrial Coal Enterprises*, AIR 1999 SC 1324, p. 1330 : 1999 (2) SCC 607.

69. *Kirkness v. John Hudson & Co., supra*, pp. 355, 359, 370.

70. *London Borough of Lewisham v. Lewisham Juvenile Court Justices*, (1979) 2 All ER 297, p. 299 (HL) (VISCOUNT DILHORNE). **See further** *Pearson v. Inland Revenue Commissioners*, (1980) 2 All ER 479, pp. 483, 484 : 1981 AC 753 : (1980) 2 WLR 872 (HL) (VISCOUNT DILHORNE).

71. *State of Bihar v. S.K. Roy*, AIR 1966 SC 1995, p. 1998 : 1996 Supp SCR 259.

72. *Anand Bros. Pvt. Ltd. v. Union of India & Ors.*, (2014) 9 SCC 212, pp. 218 to 220.

73. AIR 1962 SC 1073.

74. (1984) 3 SCC 46.

also the statutory prescription under the 1996 Act which now mandates recording of reasons by the arbitrator.

Section 8(1) of the West Bengal (Requisition and Acquisition) Act, 1948 provides for a reference to the court against the award of the Collector. Section 8(2) of the same Act as originally enacted provided that the provisions of the Land Acquisition Act, 1894 shall *mutatis mutandis* apply in respect of any reference made under section 8(1). In holding that the words 'in respect of any reference' include the step of making an application for reference and are not confined to the stage of proceedings after reference is made and that the period of limitation prescribed by section 18(2) of the Land Acquisition Act, 1894 applies to applications for reference made under section 8(2) of the West Bengal (Requisition) Act, 1948 the Supreme Court relied upon West Bengal Act, 8 of 1954 which amended section 8(2) by specifically providing that section 18(2) of the Land Acquisition Act, 1894 shall apply in respect of any reference made under section 8(1). It was pointed out that the amended provision retained the words "in respect of any reference" which supported the view that these words even in the unamended section included the stage of making of an application for reference under section 18(2) of the Land Acquisition Act, 1894. In the opinion of the Court the amendment was unnecessary and it only made specific what was already implicit in the section.[75] Section 4A of the Mines and Minerals (Regulation and Development) Act, 1957 did not, before amendment in 1986, specifically provide for notice to the lessee before directing premature termination of his lease. Even so it was held that notice was impliedly necessary and the amendment supported this construction.[76]

Section 15(b) of the Central Sales Tax Act, 1956 before amendment by Act No. 61 of 1972 did not specifically indicate as to whom the state sales tax paid on declared goods would be refunded in the event the goods are later sold in the course of inter-State trade or commerce. The amendment Act which was not retrospective enacted that refund of tax was to be made to the person making the sale in the course of inter-State trade or commerce. The amendment was used as an exposition by Parliament itself of its intent contained in the section before its amendment and it was held that it was the person making the sale in the course of inter-State trade and commerce who was entitled to refund even when the unamended section was in force.[77]

---

75. *Kajari Lal Agarwala v. Union of India*, AIR 1966 SC 1538, p. 1541 : 1966 (3) SCR 141.
76. *Assam Sillimanite Ltd. v. Union of India*, AIR 1990 SC 1417, p. 1422 : 1990 (3) SCC 182.
77. *Thiru Manickam and Co. v. State of Tamil Nadu*, AIR 1977 SC 518, p. 522 : 1977 SCC (Tax) 165 : (1977) 1 SCC 199.

In deciding that the word 'retrenchment' in section 2(oo) and section 25-F of the Industrial Disputes Act, 1947, has no application where the services of all workmen have been terminated by the employer on a real and *bona fide* closure of business or on the business or undertaking being taken over by another employer, the Supreme Court rejected the argument that section 25-FF inserted by the Industrial Disputes (Amendment) Act, (41 of 1956) which proceeded on the assumption that such termination may come within the expression 'retrenchment' is a parliamentary exposition of the meaning of the said expression.[78] It was pointed out that the said section 25-FF was inserted to supersede the effect of certain judicial decisions which according to the Supreme Court were erroneous and the intention in enacting that section was not to give a parliamentary exposition of the existing law.[79] In the same case, the Supreme Court referred to the Industrial Disputes (Amendment and Miscellaneous Provisions) Act (No. 36 of 1956) and after pointing out that the said Act clearly proceeded on a distinction between closure of business and retrenchment, used it as a parliamentary exposition of the meaning of 'retrenchment' in preference to the Amending Act 41 of 1958 which inserted section 25-FF.[80] However, it is interesting to see that the Parliament in its turn did not abide by this decision of the Supreme Court and enacted Act 18 of 1957 by which the then existing section 25-FF was replaced by new provisions in sections 25-FF and 25-FFF expressly providing for compensation to workmen in case of transfer and closing down of undertakings.[81]

Section 293(4) of Criminal Procedure Code, 1973 before its amendment used the expression 'Director' only. After amendment, the expressions 'Deputy Director' and 'Assistant Director' were expressly included with the expression 'Director'. The Supreme Court after referring to this change held that 'Joint Director' who was higher in rank to Deputy Director and Assistant Director must be deemed to be included in 'Director' otherwise he would also have been expressly included by the amendment and that this construction was also applicable to the word 'Director' before the section was amended.[82]

---

78. *Hariprasad Shivshankar Shukla v. A.D. Divelkar*, AIR 1957 SC 121, pp. 130, 131 : 1957 SCR 121.

79. *Hariprasad Shivshankar Shukla v. A.D. Divelkar*, AIR 1957 SC 121, pp. 130, 131 : 1957 SCR 121.

80. *Ibid.*

81. *Anakapalli Co-operative Agricultural & Industrial Society v. Workmen*, AIR 1963 SC 1489, pp. 1494, 1495 : 1963 Supp (1) SCR 730; *S.M. Nilajkar v. Telecom District Manager Karnataka,* (2003) 4 SCC 27, p. 39 : 2003 SCC (L&S) 380 : (2003) 3 Mah LJ 9. **See further** *Maruti Udyog Ltd. v. Ramlal*, (2005) 2 SCC 638, p. 652.

82. *Ammini v. State of Kerala*, AIR 1998 SC 260, p. 265 : 1998 (2) SCC 301.

(d) Incorporation of earlier Act into later; Reference of earlier Act into later

Incorporation of an earlier Act into a later Act is a legislative device adopted for the sake of convenience in order to avoid verbatim reproduction of the provisions of the earlier Act into the later.[83] When an earlier Act or certain of its provisions are incorporated by reference into a later Act, the provisions so incorporated become part and parcel of the later Act as if they had been "bodily transposed into it".[84] The effect of incorporation is admirably stated by LORD ESHER, M.R.: "If a subsequent Act brings into itself by reference some of the clauses of a former Act, the legal effect of that, as has often been held, is to write those sections into the new Act as if they had been actually written in it with the pen, or printed in it."[85] The result is to constitute the later Act along with the incorporated provisions of the earlier Act, an independent legislation which is not modified or repealed by a modification or repeal of the earlier Act.[86] As observed by BRETT, J.: "Where a statute is incorporated, by reference, into a second statute, the repeal of the first statute by a third does not affect the second."[87] To the same effect is the statement by SIR GEORGE LOWNDES: "It seems to be no less logical to hold that where certain provisions from an existing Act have been incorporated into subsequent Act, no addition to the former Act, which is not expressly made applicable to the subsequent Act, can be deemed to be incorporated in it, at all events if it is possible

---

83. *Mary Roy v. State of Kerala*, (1986) 2 SCC 209, p. 216 : AIR 1986 SC 1011; *Nagpur Improvement Trust v. Amrik Singh,* AIR 2002 SC 3499, p. 3512 : (2002) 7 SCC 657.

84. *Ramsarup v. Munshi*, AIR 1963 SC 553, p. 558 : 1963 (3) SCR 858; *Nagpur Improvement Trust v. Amrik Singh,* AIR 2002 SC 3499, p. 3512 : (2002) 7 SCC 657.

85. *Re, Wood's Estate, Ex parte, Works and Buildings Commrs.*, (1886) 31 Ch D 607, p. 615; *Ram Kripal Bhagat v. State of Bihar*, AIR 1970 SC 951, p. 957 : (1969) 3 SCC 471; *Bolani Ores Ltd. v. State of Orissa*, AIR 1975 SC 17, p. 29 : 1975 (2) SCR 138 : (1974) 2 SCC 777; *Mahindra and Mahindra Ltd. v. Union of India*, AIR 1979 SC 798, pp. 810, 811 : (1979) 2 SCC 529; *Onkarlal Nandlal v. State of Rajasthan*, (1985) 4 SCC 404, p. 415 : AIR 1986 SC 2146; *Surana Steels Pvt. Ltd. v. Dy. Commissioner of Income-tax,* AIR 1999 SC 1455, p. 1459 : (1999) 4 SCC 306 (p. 233 of 7th edition of this book is approvingly quoted).

86. *Narottamdas v. State of M.P.*, AIR 1964 SC 1667, p. 1670 : (1964) 7 SCR 820; *Bolani Ores Ltd. v. State of Orissa, supra; Mahindra and Mahindra Ltd. v. Union of India, supra; Nagpur Improvement Trust v. Amrik Singh, supra*; *Sneh Enterprises v. Commr. of Customs,* (2006) 7 SCC 714 (para 13) : (2006) 8 JT 587 : (2006) 7 SLT 615 (passage from 10th edition of this book is approvingly quoted).

87. *Clarke v. Bradlaugh*, (1881) 8 QBD 63, p. 69; referred to in *Ramsarup v. Munshi*, AIR 1963 SC 553, p. 558 : (1963) 3 SCR 858; *Collector of Customs, Madras v. Nathelal Sampathu Chetty*, AIR 1962 SC 316, p. 334 : (1962) 3 SCR 786. **See further** *Jethanand Betab v. State of Delhi*, AIR 1960 SC 89, pp. 91, 92 : (1960) 1 SCR 755; *Bolani Ores Ltd. v. State of Orissa, supra; Mahindra and Mahindra Ltd. v. Union of India, supra; Nagpur Improvement Trust v. Amrik Singh, supra.*

for the subsequent Act to function, effectually without the addition."[88] Ordinarily if an Act is incorporated in a later Act, the intention is to incorporate the earlier Act, with all the amendments made in it up to the date of incorporation.[89] The rule that the repeal or amendment of the Act which is incorporated by reference in a later Act is not applicable for purposes of the later Act is subject to qualifications and exceptions.[90] A distinction is in this context drawn between incorporation and mere reference of an earlier Act into a later Act.[91] Further, a distinction is also drawn when what is referred to is not an earlier Act or any provision from it but law on a subject in general.[92] There is, however, no controversy on the point that when any Act or rules are adopted in any later Act or rules, such adoption normally whether by incorporation or mere reference takes in all the amendments in the earlier Act or rules till the date of adoption.[93]

In the Calcutta Improvement Act, 1911 (Bengal Act 5 of 1911) the provisions of the Land Acquisition Act (Central Act 1 of 1894) with certain modifications were incorporated by reference for purposes of acquisitions under the Bengal Act. By Central Act 19 of 1921 the Land Acquisition Act was amended and provision was made in that Act for an appeal to the Privy Council. In these circumstances it was held by the Judicial Committee that this amendment had not the effect of modifying the incorporated provision of the Land Acquisition Act in the Bengal Act and that it did not confer a right of appeal in relation to an award of compensation under the Bengal Act.[94]

The Calcutta Municipal Act, 1923, which applied to the Corporation of Calcutta, empowered the Provincial Government by sections 540 and 541 to extend all or any provisions of the said Act, subject to such modifications or restriction as may be specified, to the Municipality of Howrah. The Provincial Government acting under the said provisions extended the Act in 1932 to the Municipality of Howrah and one of the sections so

---

88. *Secretary of State v. Hindustan Co-operative Insurance Society Ltd.*, AIR 1931 PC 149, p. 152. **Referred to** in *Chairman of the Municipal Commrs. of Howrah v. Shalimar Wood Products (Private) Ltd.*, AIR 1962 SC 1691, p. 1694 : 1963 (1) SCR 47; *Bolani Ores Ltd. v. State of Orissa*, AIR 1975 SC 17, p. 29 : 1974 (2) SCC 777; *Mahindra and Mahindra Ltd. v. Union of India*, AIR 1979 SC 798, pp. 810, 811 : (1979) 2 SCC 529.

89. *State of Maharashtra v. Madhavrao Damodar Patil*, AIR 1968 SC 1395, p. 1400 : 1968 (3) SCR 712.

90. **See** text and notes 7-41, pp. 358-366.

91. **See** text and notes 12-19, pp. 359-362.

92. **See** text and notes 8-11, pp. 358, 359.

93. *Rajasthan State Road Transport Corporation Jaipur v. Poonam Pahwa*, AIR 1997 SC 2951, p. 2957 : 1997 (6) SCC 100. **Also see** text and note 89, *supra*.

94. *Secretary of State v. Hindustan Co-operative Insurance Society Ltd.*, *supra*.

extended was section 386 with a modification that in place of the words 'Corporation of Calcutta' the word 'Commissioners' was substituted. By the West Bengal Fire Services Act, 1950, section 386 of the Calcutta Municipal Act, was repealed and a question arose whether this repeal affected the application of section 386 to the Municipality of Howrah to which it was extended with certain modification by the Provincial Government. In holding that the repeal was not effective in so far as the Municipality of Howrah was concerned, the Supreme Court observed that what was applied to Howrah Municipality was not section 386 but its modified form and thus a different section, and therefore, when the West Bengal Act of 1950 repealed only section 386, it had not the effect of repealing section 386 as modified and applied to the Municipality of Howrah.[95] This decision is open to one criticism: When by virtue of powers flowing from the Calcutta Municipal Act itself, its provisions were extended with modifications to Howrah Municipality, the extension and the modifications in relation to Howrah Municipality became part and parcel of the Calcutta Municipal Act, so that the modification of section 386 could be read as part of section 386 in its application to Howrah, and therefore, when the West Bengal Act of 1950, which extended to the whole of Bengal repealed section 386, the repeal was effective to wipe out section 386 not only in its original form applying to the Corporation of Calcutta but also, in its modified form applying to the Howrah Municipality. This was not a case of two different statutes where the later incorporates the provisions of the earlier and the reliance placed by the Supreme Court on the Privy Council decision in *Secy. of State v. Hindustan Co-operative Insurance Society*[96] was hardly in point.

The Punjab Pre-emption Act (Punjab Act 1 of 1913) defined 'Agricultural land' by reference to the definition of this expression contained in the Punjab Alienation of Land Act, 1900, which Act was repealed by the Adaptation of Laws (Third Amendment) Order, 1951, but the Supreme Court held that the repeal of the Punjab Alienation of Land Act, 1900 had no effect on the continued operation of the Punjab Pre-emption Act and the definition of 'Agricultural land' incorporated in it.[97] Section 2(c) as substituted in 1943 in the Bihar and Orissa Motor Vehicles Taxation Act, 1930 defines 'Motor Vehicle' to have the same meaning as in the Motor Vehicles Act, 1939. Construing section 2(c) of the Taxation Act it was held that the

---

95. *Chairman of the Municipal Commissioners of Howrah v. Shalimar Wood Products, (Private) Ltd.*, AIR 1962 SC 1691, p. 1694 : 1963 (1) SCR 47.

96. AIR 1931 PC 149. **See also** text and notes 88 (p. 353) and 94 (p. 353).

97. *Ramsarup v. Munshi*, AIR 1963 SC 553, p. 558 : 1963 (3) SCR 858. **See further** *Narottamdas v. State of M.P.*, AIR 1964 SC 1667, p. 1670 (para 6) : 1964 (7) SCR 820.

definition of 'Motor Vehicle' in the Motor Vehicles Act as existing in 1943 got incorporated in the Taxation Act and the amendment of the definition of 'Motor Vehicle' in the Motor Vehicles Act in 1956 was not applicable for purposes of the Taxation Act.[1]

Section 55 of the Monopolies and Restrictive Trade Practices Act, 1969 provides for an appeal to the Supreme Court against the orders of the Monopolies and Restrictive Trade Practices Commission on 'one or more of the grounds specified in section 100 of the Code of Civil Procedure, 1908.' Section 100 of the Code of Civil Procedure was substituted by a new section in 1976 which narrowed the grounds of appeal under that section. In construing section 55 of the Monopolies and Restrictive Trade Practices Act the Supreme Court held that section 100 of the Code as it existed in 1969 was incorporated in section 55 and the substitution of new section 100 in the Code abridging the grounds of appeal had no effect on the appeal under section 55.[2]

The Industrial Disputes Act, 1947 (I.D. Act) came into force from 1.4.1947. By the Amendment Act 54 of 1949, section 2(bb) was inserted in the I.D. Act defining 'banking company' to mean a banking company as defined in section 5 of the Banking Companies Act, 1949 having branches or other establishments in more than one State and to include certain enumerated banks. By the same Amendment Act the definition of 'appropriate government' was amended whereby in relation to any industrial dispute concerning a banking company the Central Government was declared to be the appropriate government. The definition of 'banking company' was then limited to companies registered under the Companies Act and did not include co-operative banks. However, by Act 23 of 1965 the provisions of the Banking Regulation Act were made applicable to co-operative banks. The question before the Supreme Court was whether after 1965 the definition of banking company in the I.D. Act should be read as inclusive of co-operative banks. It was held that the definition of banking company as inserted in the I.D. Act from Banking Companies Act was incorporated therein and any further amendments to include co-operative banks in the definition could not be read in the I.D. Act and the appropriate government for the co-operative banks was the State Government and not the Central Government.[3]

---

1. *Bolani Ores Ltd. v. State of Orissa*, AIR 1975 SC 17 : (1974) 2 SCC 777.
2. *Mahindra and Mahindra Ltd. v. Union of India*, AIR 1979 SC 798, p. 811 : (1979) 2 SCC 529.
3. *Bharat Coop. Bank (Mumbai) Ltd. v. Coop. Bank Employees Union*, (2007) 4 SCC 685 : (2007) 4 JT 573 : (2007) 2 LLJ 825 : AIR 2007 SC 2320.

In case of legislation by incorporation as the incorporated provisions become part and parcel of a fresh statute, the constitutional validity of such a statute including the provisions so incorporated is judged with reference to the powers of the Legislature enacting the fresh statute and not with reference to the powers of the Legislature enacting the original legislation. The two statutes remain different and distinct and each is to be judged with reference to its own source. This proposition, which is a necessary consequence of incorporation, is illustrated in the decisions of the Supreme Court[4] dealing with Sales Tax legislations in force in Part A States and extended to Part C States by the Part C States Laws Act, 1950. In case of Part A States, the State Legislature had power to tax a transaction of 'sale of goods', but it had no power to tax a transaction, not in reality a sale, by legislating an artificial definition of 'sale'. In case, however, of Part C States, Parliament's powers of legislation were uncontrolled by any legislative entry. A parliamentary legislation, therefore, could levy sales tax on any transaction by defining the same artificially as 'sale'. The Part C States Laws Act, 1950, a parliamentary statute, by section 2 conferred power on the Central Government to extend to Part C States laws in force in Part A States with or without modification. In exercise of this power, the Central Government extended to Part C States legislations in respect of sales tax in force in Part A States. But these legislations which were enacted by State Legislatures of Part A States, contained artificial definitions of 'sale' and later on were held to be partly invalid in their application to the respective Part A States in so far as 'sale' was artificially defined. A question, therefore, arose whether these legislations as extended to Part C States under Part C States Laws Act, 1950 suffered from the same infirmity in their application to Part C States? The Supreme Court answered the question in the negative and held that on issue of a notification by the Central Government under section 2 of the Part C States Laws Act extending to a Part C State a Sales Tax law in force in a Part A State "the provision of the law which is extended becomes incorporated by reference in the Act (Part C States Laws Act) itself, and therefore, a tax imposed thereunder is a tax imposed by Parliament and that Parliament's power of legislation in relation to Part C States being plenary and absolute, the law so extended in the application to Part C States concerned remains wholly valid".[5] The principles stated above were affirmed by a nine judge bench in

4. *Mithanlal v. State of Delhi*, AIR 1958 SC 682, pp. 885, 886 : 1959 SCR 445; *Bhaiyalal Shukla v. State of Madhya Pradesh*, AIR 1962 SC 981, p. 985 : 1962 Supp (2) SCR 257. **See further** *Vaijnath v. Guramma*, JT 1998 (8) SC 125, p. 127 : 1998 (6) Scale 248 : (1999) 1 SCC 272 : AIR 1999 SC 555.

5. *Ibid.*

New Delhi Municipal Committee v. State of Punjab[1] in which it was held that the Punjab Municipal Act extended to the Part C State of Delhi by a notification issued under the Part C State Laws Act, 1950 was a Parliamentary enactment and taxes levied under it amounted to union taxation. On the same principle a State Act which is void for want of legislative competence of the State Legislature can be incorporated in a later Central Act if Parliament has legislative competence over the subject-matter. In such a case the incorporated Act though void as a State Act becomes part and parcel of the incorporating Central Act and gains validity and effect as a Central Act.[2] On the same reasoning administrative rules which were extensively amended by rules made under Article 309 of the Constitution were held to have attained statutory status by implied incorporation in the rules made under Article 309.[3]

As a corollary of the above principle a limited construction adopted of the provisions of an Act by restricting general words to save it from becoming unconstitutional will not apply when the same Act is adopted by incorporation by another legislature having wider legislative competence on the subject. Thus, though the word 'property' in the Hindu Women's Right to Property Act, 1937 which was passed by the Central Legislature was construed not to include agricultural land as the Central Legislature had then no legislative competence to legislate on the subject of succession to agricultural lands;[4] but when the same Act was adopted by incorporation by the Hyderabad Legislature by the Hyderabad (Application of Central Acts) Act, 1952, the word 'property' was construed to include agricultural lands as the Hyderabad Legislature had legislative power to legislate in respect of agricultural lands.[5] An amending Act passed in 1954 which expressly applied the Hyderabad Act to agricultural lands was held to have no effect on the construction of the Act before its amendment as it proceeded upon its wrong construction.[6]

It must, however, be remembered that when a later Act extends the area of operation of an earlier Act by making suitable amendments in the earlier Act itself, there is "neither precedent nor warrant for the assumption"

---

1. AIR 1997 SC 2847, p. 2896 : (1997) 7 SCC 339.
2. *Krishnachandra Gangopadhyaya v. Union of India*, AIR 1975 SC 1389 : (1975) 2 SCC 302. For another case of the same nature, **see** *District Mining Officer v. Tata Iron & Steel Co.*, AIR 2001 SC 3134 : (2001) 7 SCC 358.
3. *Bachan Singh v. Union of India*, AIR 1973 SC 441, p. 443 : (1972) 3 SCC 489; *S.B. Patwardhana v. State of Maharashtra*, AIR 1977 SC 2051, p. 2067 : (1977) 3 SCC 399 : 1977 SCC (L&S) 391.
4. *In re Hindu Women's Right to Property Act*, AIR 1941 FC 72 : 1941 FCR 12. **See** for this case pages 652-653 *infra*.
5. *Vaijnath v. Guramma*, AIR 1999 SC 555 : (1999) 1 SCC 292.
6. *Ibid.*

that the earlier Act gets incorporated in the later, rather the amendments introduced by the later Act get incorporated in the earlier Act and any further amendment of the earlier Act is operative both in respect of its original area of operation as also in respect of its extended operation to new area brought about by the later Act.[7]

Again, a statute may instead of referring to a particular previous statute or to any specific provision therein refer to the law on the subject generally. In such cases, the reference is construed to mean that the law is as it reads therafter including amendments subsequent to the time of adoption.[8] This principle was applied in construing section 151 of the Madhya Pradesh Land Revenue Code, 1954 which provides that 'subject to his *personal law*, the interest of a tenure holder shall on his death pass by inheritance, survivorship or bequest, as the case may be'. It was held that this was a case where the statute incorporated by reference the law on the subject generally, and therefore, the expression 'personal law' will not be limited to the personal law as it stood when the Code was enacted in 1954 but will also embrace all subsequent statutes, *e.g.* the Hindu Succession Act, 1956, which, from time to time, have amended the personal law.[9] By Section 2(2) of the Colonial Court of Admirality Act, 1890, a British statute applicable to India, it was enacted that "the jurisdiction of a Colonial Court of Admirality shall be over the like places, persons, matters and things as the Admirality jurisdiction of the High Court in England whether existing by virtue of any statute or otherwise." The High Courts of Bombay, Madras and Calcutta were declared to be Colonial Courts of Admirality. At the time when the Colonial Courts of Admirality Act was enacted the High Court in England exercised jurisdiction under the Admirality Court Acts of 1840 and 1861. These Acts were later repealed and the Admirality jurisdiction of the High Court in England was extended by

7. *Rajputana Mining Agencies v. Union of India*, AIR 1961 SC 56 : 1961 (1) SCR 453.

8. SUTHERLAND: Statutory Construction, Vol. 2 (3rd Edition), p. 550 and Supplement (1956), p. 119; *Bajya v. Gopikabai (Smt.)*, AIR 1978 SC 793, p. 797 : (1978) 2 SCC 542.

9. *Bajya v. Gopikabai (Smt.)*, AIR 1978 SC 793, p. 797 : (1978) 2 SCC 542. **Compare** and **contrast** *Hira v. Kasturibai*, 1996 (6) Scale 699: 1996 (6) SCC 82 (A case under section 83 of the Madhya Bharat Land Revenue and Tenancy Act which makes no reference to personal law and, therefore, remained unaffected by the Hindu Succession Act, 1956). *Bajya's* case was followed in construing Article 366(1) of the Constitution which defines 'agricultural income' to mean 'agricultural income as defined for the purposes of the enactments relating to Indian income-tax'. It was held that here the reference was not to any particular income-tax Act and, therefore, the definition in Article 366(1) will mean agricultural income as it is defined at the relevant time in the statute then current relating to income-tax: *Singhai Rakesh Kumar v. Union of India,* AIR 2001 SC 390, p. 392 : (2001) 1 SCC 364.

subsequent enactments. The Privy Council[10] in interpreting section 2(2) of the Colonial Courts of Admirality Act, 1890 in an appeal from Canada held that the effect of that provision was to limit the jurisdiction of a Colonial Court of Admirality to the Admirality jurisdiction of the High Court in England as it existed at the passing of the Act and the subsequently extended Admirality jurisdiction of the High Court in England did not apply to a Colonial Court of Admirality. The above interpretation was also followed by the High Courts in India. But the Supreme Court of India[11] rightly did not accept that interpretation and held that what the Act of 1890 did was not to incorporate any English statute in Indian law but to equate the Admirality jurisdiction of the Indian High Courts over places, matters and things to that of the English High Court and as the Admirality jurisdiction of the English High Court expanded with the progress of legislation and with the repeal of the earlier statutes there was a corresponding growth and expansion of Admirality jurisdiction of the Indian High Courts. It will be seen that in section 2(2) of the 1890 Act there was no incorporation of any English statute but a reference to the Admirality jurisdiction of the High Court in England whether existing by virtue of any statute or otherwise or in other words to the English law of Admirality jurisdiction as exercised by the High Court of England. Therefore, there was no reason to infer that the Admirality jurisdiction of the Indian High Courts stood frozen and atrophied as on the date of the passing of the 1890 Act and subsequent expansion of that jurisdiction in England did not apply to India.

A distinction has also been drawn between a mere reference or citation of one statute into another and incorporation. In the former case a modification, repeal or re-enactment of the statute that is referred will also have effect for the statute in which it is referred; but in the latter case any change in the incorporated statute by way of amendment or repeal has no repercussion on the incorporating statute.[12] It is a question of construction

---

10. *Yuri Maru v. Waron*, 1927 AC 906 (PC).

11. *M.V. Elisabeth v. Harwan Investment and Trading Pvt. Ltd.*, AIR 1993 SC 1014 : 1993 Supp (2) SCC 433, pp. 1024, 1034 : 1992 (2) JT 65. **See further** *Epoch Enterrepots v. M.V. WonFu*, AIR 2003 SC 24, p. 27 : (2003) 1 SCC 305, p. 310.

12. *Collector of Customs, Madras v. Nathelal Sampathu Chetty*, AIR 1962 SC 316, p. 336 : 1962 (3) SCR 786 (In this case it was held that there was no incorporation of the Sea Customs Act, 1878 in section 23-A of the Foreign Exchange Regulation Act, 1947); *Ram Kripal Bhagat v. State of Bihar*, AIR 1970 SC 951, p. 955 : 1969 (3) SCC 471 (Section 19 of the Sea Customs Act, 1878, is not incorporated in section 3(2) of the Imports and Exports (Control) Act, 1947); *New Central Jute Mills Co. Ltd. v. Assistant Collector of Central Excise*, AIR 1971 SC 451, p. 457 : 1970 (2) SCC 820. (Section 12 of the Central Excises and Salt Act, 1944, does not incorporate the provisions of the Sea Customs Act, 1878, but only refers to them, and therefore, after its repeal, the provisions of Customs Act, 1962 can be read in their place);

[Footnote No. 12 Contd.]

whether a particular former statute is merely referred to or cited in a later statute or is wholly or partially incorporated therein.[13] "The distinction between incorporation by reference and adoption of provisions by mere reference or citation is not too easy to highlight. The distinction is one of difference in degree and is often blurred. The fact that no clear-cut guidelines or distinguishing features have been spelt out to ascertain whether it belongs to one or the other category makes the task of identification difficult. The semantics associated with interpretation play their role to a limited extent. Ultimately, it is a matter of probe into legislative intention and/or taking an insight into the working of the enactment if one or the other view is adopted. The doctrinaire approach to ascertain whether the legislation is by incorporation or reference is, on ultimate analysis, directed towards that end. The distinction often pales into insignificance with the exceptions enveloping the main rule."[14]

Section 69(d) of the Madhya Pradesh Gram, Nagar Tatha Gram Nivesh Adhiniyam, 1973, enacted that the Special Area Development Authority shall for the purpose of taxation have the powers which a Municipal Corporation or Council has as the case may be under the M.P. Municipal Corporation Act, 1956, or the M.P. Municipalities Act, 1961. This was held to be not a case of incorporation but of mere reference and hence additional power of taxation were conferred on the Municipal

---

[Footnote No. 12 Contd.]

Western Coal Fields Ltd. v. Spl. Area Development Authority, AIR 1982 SC 697, p. 703 : (1982) 1 SCC 125; *State of Kerala v. Attessee (AIT Corpn.)*, AIR 1989 SC 222, pp. 226, 228 : 1989 Supp (1) SCC 733; *Ujagar Prints v. Union of India*, AIR 1989 SC 516, pp. 540, 541 : (1989) 3 SCC 488; *Bhatinda Improvement Trust v. Balwant Singh*, AIR 1992 SC 2214, p. 2217 : (1991) 4 SCC 368 (Land Acquisition Act, 1894 is not incorporated in Punjab Town Improvement Act, 1922 but is only referred with certain amendments); *U.P. Avas Evam Vikas Parishad v. Jainul Islam*, JT 1998 (1) SC 231, p. 243: AIR 1998 SC 1028, p. 1035 : (1998) 2 SCC 467 (Distinction between mere reference and incorporation); *Nagpur Improvement Trust v. Vasantrao*, AIR 2002 SC 3499, pp. 3511, 3512 : (2002) 7 SCC 657; *Sneh Enterprises v. Commr. of Customs*, (2006) 7 SCC 714 (para 14) : (2006) 8 JT 587. In *Agarwal Trading Corporation v. Assistant Collector of Customs*, AIR 1972 SC 648, p. 653 : (1972) 1 SCC 553, there are observations that section 23-A of the Foreign Exchange Regulation Act, 1947 incorporates the provisions of the Sea Customs Act without noticing the contrary decision in *Collector of Customs, Madras v. Nathelal Sampathu Chetty*, AIR 1962 SC 316, p. 336 : 1962 (3) SCR 786; *P.C. Agarwala v. Payment of Wages Inspector MP*, (2005) 8 SCC 104, pp. 117, 118 : AIR 2006 SC 3576. **See further** section 8 of the General Clauses Act, 1897.

13. *Ibid*.

14. *Maharashtra State Road Transport Corporation v. State of Maharashtra*, 2003 AIR SCW 1388, p. 1394 : (2003) 4 SCC 200, p. 208 : AIR 2003 SC 1909; *Bharat Coop Bank (Mumbai) Ltd. v. Coop. Bank Employees Union*, (2007) 4 SCC 685 (para 21) : (2007) 4 JT 553 : (2007) 2 LLJ 825.

Corporations or Municipalities by amending the Corporation Act and the Municipalities Act became applicable to the Special Area Development Authority.[15] Section 23 of the Mysore Improvement Act, 1903 provided that the acquisition under the Act 'shall be regulated by the provisions, so far as they are applicable, of the Land Acquisition Act, 1894'. Section 23 of the Land Acquisition Act,1894 sets out the matters to be considered in determining compensation. One of the matters so set out is the market value of the land. Till 1923, the market value required to be taken into account was the value at the date of publication of the declaration under section 6. By Act 38 of 1923, section 23 of the Land Acquisition Act was amended and the market value became relatable to the date of the notification under section 4. In a case before the Supreme Court,[16] the question was whether section 23 of the Land Acquisition Act as amended in 1923 will apply to the acquisitions under the Mysore Act or whether such acquisition even after 1923 will be governed by section 23 of the Land Acquisition Act as it originally stood. In holding that the Land Acquisition Act as amended would apply, the Supreme Court held that a fair interpretation of section 23 of the Mysore Act, 1903 was that it applied whatever procedure may be for the time being in force regarding matters regulating compensation under the Land Acquisition Act. In reaching this conclusion the Court said that section 23 of the Land Acquisition Act, 1923 lays down the procedure for award of compensation and it has to be followed as it exists on the date of acquisition for no one has a vested right in a particular procedure. This reasoning is open to serious objection. Whether the market value, on the basis of which compensation is determined, should be related to the date of the notification under section 4 or to the date of the declaration under section 6 is not a mere matter of procedure. Right to compensation and the basis of its calculation are matters falling within the area of substantive rights. The Court also did not consider the effect of incorporation of the provisions of an Act into a later Act and the rule that an amendment of the incorporated Act does not affect the incorporating Act and the provisions incorporated therein. The conclusion reached by the court, can, however, be supported on the ground that the Land Acquisition Act was not incorporated in the Mysore Act, but was only referred to or cited in it, and therefore, any amendment made in the Land Acquisition Act was also applicable for acquisitions under the Mysore Act.[17] This reasoning finds

---

15. *Western Coal Fields Ltd. v. Special Area Development Authority*, AIR 1982 SC 697 : (1982) 1 SCC 125.

16. *Special Land Acquisition Officer, City Improvement Trust, Mysore v. P. Govindan*, AIR 1976 SC 2517 : (1976) 4 SCC 697.

17. **See** text and note 12, pp. 359-360.

support from a later case[18] relating to section 37(2) of the Foreign Exchange Regulation Act, 1973 which provides that 'the provisions of Cr.P.C. relating to searches shall so far as may be apply to searches under section 37(1)'. It was held that the expression 'so far as may be' meant that those provisions may be generally followed to the extent possible and so the argument that the provisions of Cr. P.C. were incorporated by pen and ink in section 37(1) could not be accepted as correct.[19]

Indeed, the question whether an earlier Act is referred to in a later Act or whether it is incorporated in the later Act is at times a difficult question of construction. Section 55(1) of the U.P. Avas Evam Vikas Parishad Adhiniyam, 1966 provides that "any land or any interest therein required by the Board for any of the purposes of this Act, may be acquired under the provisions of the Land Acquisition Act, 1894 as amended in its application to Uttar Pradesh, which for this purpose shall be subject to the modifications specified in the schedule to this Act". Section 6 of the Land Acquisition Act, 1894 was amended in 1967 by adding a proviso that no declaration in respect of any land covered by a notification under section 4 shall be made after expiry of three years from the date of the publication of the notification. The question before the Supreme Court in a number of appeals decided by a common judgment[20] related to the applicability of the proviso so added in section 6 to the acquisitions under the U.P. Avas Evam Vikas Parishad Adhiniyam 1966. The answer to this question depended upon true construction of section 55(1) of the U.P. Avas Adhiniyam whether it merely referred to the Land Acquisition Act, in which case the proviso would apply, or incorporated the same in which case the proviso would not apply. The learned Judges hearing the matter in the Supreme Court came to differing conclusions on the question of construction. K. RAMASWAMY J. held that the Land Acquisition Act with modifications specified in the schedule formed a complete code and was incorporated in the U.P. Act whereas SAHAI J. took the view that it was merely referred to in the U.P. Act. Both the Judges, however, agreed that the acquisition was not to be quashed and the compensation in equity should be awarded at the market rate prevailing at the time of section 6 notification. The difference of opinion on the question of construction thus remained unresolved in this case. The principle involved was culled out from earlier cases by SAHAI J. as follows: "The determination if a legislation was by way of incorporation or reference is more a matter of construction by the courts keeping in view the language employed by the Act, the purpose of

---

18. *Pratap Singh (Dr.) v. Director of Enforcement*, (1985) 3 SCC 72 : AIR 1985 SC 989.

19. *Ibid*, p. 80. **See** for a similar provision *Ujagar Prints v. Union of India*, AIR 1989 SC 516, p. 541 : (1989) 3 SCC 488.

20. *Gauri Shanker Gaur v. State of U.P.*, AIR 1994 SC 169 : 1994 (1) SCC 92.

referring or incorporating provision of an existing Act and the effect of it on the day-to-day working. Reason for it is the courts' prime duty to assume that any law made by the Legislature is enacted to serve public interest".[21] Later cases have, however, taken the view on the question of construction as taken by RAMASWAMY J.[22] which now stands approved by a three Judge Bench in *U.P. Avas Evam Vikas Parishad v. Jainul Islam*[23] subject to the right to get compensation under the Land Acquisition Act as amended in 1984 to avoid discrimination.[24] The question in *Jainul Islam's* case was whether the provisions of sections 23(1-A), 23(2) and 28 of the Land Acquisition Act, 1894 as amended in 1984, which entitled a person whose land was acquired to get higher compensation, were applicable to acquisitions under the U.P. Act. The court relying upon the privy council decision in *Secretary of State v. Hindustan Co-operative Insurance Society Ltd.,*[25] which related to analogous provisions of the Calcutta Improvement Trust Act, 1911 held agreeing with the view of RAMASWAMI, J., in *Gaurishankers* case,[26] that the provisions of the Land Acquisition Act were incorporated in the U.P. Act and were not merely referred to.[27] On this view the 1984 amendments in the Land Acquisition Act could not be directly applied as part of the U.P. Act. The court, however, held that to avoid discrimination between persons whose lands were acquired under the U.P. Act and the persons whose lands were acquired under the Land Acquisition Act, which may make section 55 of the U.P. Act offend Article 14 of the Constitution, as a matter of construction, section 55 must be so interpreted that while incorporating the provisions of the Land Acquisition Act the intention of the Legislature was that later amendments in the Land Acquisition Act relating to determination and payment of compensation would also be applicable to acquisitions under the U.P. Act. The decisions in *Jainul Islam's* case was followed in *Nagpur Improvement Trust v. Vasantrao,*[28] which related to similar questions arising also under the

---

21. *Ibid,* p. 188 (AIR). The judgment of K. RAMASWAMY J. in this case is **relied upon** in *State of Maharashtra v. Sant Joginder Singh*, 1995(2) Scale 121, p. 125: AIR 1995 SC 2181, p. 2184 : 1995 Supp (2) SCC 475 without referring to the judgment of SAHAI J.

22. *U.P. Avas Evam Vikas Parishad Lucknow v. Pushpa Lata Awasthi*, (1995) 3 SCC 573; *Ramesh Chandra Tiwari v. U. P. Awas Evam Vikas Parishad, Lucknow*, 1996 1997 AIR SCW 2312; *Satya Pal v. State of U. P.*, AIR 1997 SC 2235 : 1997 (9) SCC 117.

23. JT 1998 (1) SC 231, p. 245: AIR 1998 SC 1028, p. 1037 : (1998) 2 SCC 467.

24. *Ibid*, p. 1041 (AIR).

25. AIR 1931 PC 149.

26. **See** text and note 20, *supra*.

27. AIR 1998 SC 1028, p. 1041 : (1998) 2 SCC 467.

28. AIR 2002 SC 3499 : (2002) 7 SCC 7657. **Followed** in *Maharashtra State Road Transport Corporation v. State of Maharashtra,* 2003 AIR SCW 1388 : AIR 2003 SC 1909; *Savitri Cairae v. U.P. Avas Evam Vikas Parishad,* (2003) 6 SCC 255. But not applied to acquisi-

[Footnote No. 28 Contd.]

Nagpur Improvement Trust Act, 1936, and the Punjab Town Improvement Act, 1922 in addition to the U.P. Act. The result of these decisions[29] is that only beneficial provisions in the Land Acquisition Act brought in by amendment subsequent to its incorporation in the State Acts, but not other amendments, e.g., amendment of section 6 in the year 1967 which provides for a time limit of three years for taking action after a notification under section 4, would apply to acquisitions under the States Acts. Section 11A of the Land Acquisition Act, 1894 also introduced by amendment in 1984, which fixes a time limit of 2 years for making the award from the date of declaration under section 6, has also not been applied to the State Acts in view of the decision in *State of Maharashtra v. Sant Joginder Singh*.[30] But the correctness of the decision in *Sant Joginder Singh's* case on this point has been doubted and has been referred for decision to a larger Bench.[31] The reference has now been decided.[32] It has been finally held that the Maharashtra Regional Town Planning Act (MRTP Act) is a self-contained code, the provisions introduced in the Land Acquisition Act, 1894 by Central Act, 68 of 1984 limited to the extent of acquisition of land, payment of compensation and recourse to legal remedies provided under the said Act can be read into the acquisition controlled under Chapter VII of the MRTP Act but section 11A of the Land Acquisition Act cannot be applied to MRTP Act which provides a different time frame and consequences of default. Similar view has been taken in respect of acquisitions under the Bangalore Development Authority Act (BDA) and section 11A of the Land Acquisition Act,1894 has been held to be inapplicable.[33]

It has further been observed that the rule that the repeal or amendment of an Act which is incorporated in a later Act has no effect on the later Act or on the provisions incorporated therein, is subject to four exceptions: (a) where the later Act and the earlier Act are supplemental to each other, (b) where the two Acts are in *pari materia*, (c) where the amendment of the earlier Act if not imported in the later Act would render it wholly unwork-

[Footnote No. 28 Contd.]

tions under the Defence of India Act, 1971 : *Union of India v. Chajju Ram,* (2003) 5 SCC 568 : AIR 2003 SC 2339 or to acquisitions under the W.B. Land (Requisition and Acquisition) Act, 1948: *State of W.B. v. Kedarnath Rajgarhia Charit Trust Estate*, (2004) 12 SCC 425.

29. Cases in notes 25, 29 and 30. **See further** *Maharashtra State Road Transport Corporation v. State of Maharashtra* (case related to Maharashtra Regional Town Planning Act, 1966): (2003) 4 SCC 200 : AIR 2003 SC 1909.
30. (1995) 2 Scale 121 : AIR 1995 SC 2181.
31. *Girnar Traders v. State of Maharashtra*, (2004) 8 SCC 505 : (2004) 8 scale 764. Case later referred to a Constitution Bench (2007) 7 SCC 555 : AIR 2007 SC 3180.
32. *Girnar Traders v. State of Maharashtra*, (2011) 3 SCC 1 para 191 : (2011) 1 JT 469.
33. *Offshore Holdings Private Limited v. Bangalore Development Authority*, (2011) 3 SCC 139 para 125 : (2011) 1 JT 384.

able, and (d) where the amendment of the earlier Act, either expressly or by necessary intendment, also applies to the later Act.[34]

The Supreme Court laid down these exceptions while considering the question whether the amendment of section 21 of the Indian Penal Code by the Criminal Law (Amendment) Act, 1958 was also applicable for purposes of the Prevention of Corruption Act, 1947 which by section 2 incorporates the definition of 'Public Servant' as contained in section 21 of the Penal Code. It was held that the two Acts were supplemental to each other, and therefore, the amendment Act was applicable to amend the definition of 'Public Servant' incorporated in the Prevention of Corruption Act. The exceptions mentioned above to the general rule were reiterated while dealing with the construction of item 7 of the third Schedule to the Kerala Sales Tax Act, 1963.[35] Section 9 of the Act granted exemption from Sales Tax to the goods specified in the third Schedule. Item 7 of the Schedule exempted "cotton fabrics—as defined in item no. 19 of the first Schedule to the Central Excises and Salt Act, 1944." The definition of cotton fabrics in item 19 of the first Schedule to the Central Act was amended by the Finance Act, 1969 to include "fabrics impregnated or 'coated with preparations of cellulose derivatives or of other artificial plastic materials." The question before the Supreme Court was whether this amendment also applied for the Kerala Act. In answering that the amendment applied, the court held that the definition of cotton fabrics was really referred to and not incorporated in the Kerala Act. It was further held that even on the hypothesis[36] that the definition was incorporated, the amendment would apply for the aforesaid Kerala and Central Acts read further with the Central Sales Tax Act and the Additional Duties of Excise (Goods of Special Importance) Act, 1957 formed part of an integrated scheme to give special treatment to certain goods including cotton fabrics and the Acts were supplemental to each other and it would be unrealistic or impractical not to read the amendment for the purposes of the Kerala Act.[37] The exceptions stated in *M. V. Narsimhan's* case[38] were again affirmed in considering the question whether section 11A of the Land Acquisition Act, 1894, introduced in it later by amendment, applied to acquisitions under the Karnataka Acquisition of Land for House

34. *State of Madhya Pradesh v. M.V. Narsimhan*, AIR 1975 SC 1835, p. 1841: 1976 SCC (Cri) 589 : (1975) 2 SCC 377.
35. *State of Kerala v. Attesee (AIT Corpn.)*, AIR 1989 SC 222, p. 226 : 1989 Supp (1) SCC 733.
36. *Ibid*, p. 228.
37. *Ibid*, p. 230. The exceptions pointed out in *State of M.P. v. M. Narsimham*, were again referred to in *Ujagar Prints v. Union of India*, AIR 1989 SC 516, p. 541 : 1989 (3) SCC 488; *U.P. Avas Evam Vikas Parishad v. Jainul Islam*, AIR 1998 SC 1028, pp. 1035, 1036 : 1998 (2) SCC 467.
38. **See** text and note 34, *supra*.

Sites Act, 1972 section 5 of which reads: "The provisions of the Land Acquisition Act, 1894 as amended by the Land Aquisition (Karnataka Extension and Amendment) Act, 1961 shall, *mutatis mutandis* apply in respect of enquiry and award by the Deputy Commissioner, the reference to the court, the apportionment of amount and the payment in respect of Land Acquisition under this Act." Section 11A of the Central Act, introduced later, requires that the award be made within two years from the issue of the notification under section 6 and in case it is not so made the entire acquisition proceedings lapse. The Supreme Court held that section 11A of the Central Act applied to the acquisitions under the Karnataka Act for the exceptions pointed out in *Narsimhan's* case applied. Three reasons were given in support of this view. *Firstly*, that the Karnataka Act could not be treated as a self contained or complete code. *Secondly*, that the Karnataka Act and the Central Act are supplemental to each other for without the latter the former cannot function. And *thirdly,* that the two Acts are in *pari materia.*[39] But this case was distinguished and the case of *U.P. Avas Evam Vikas Parishad v. Jainul Islam,*[40] was followed in construing the Bangalore Development Authority Act, 1976 and in holding that the said Act was a self contained code and a special statute to which section 11A subsequently added in the Land Acquisition Act, 1894 did not apply.[41]

Even though only particular sections of an earlier Act are incorporated into later, in construing the incorporated sections it may be at times necessary and permissible to refer to other parts of the earlier statute which are not incorporated. As was stated by LORD BLACKBURN: "When a single section of an Act of Parliament is introduced into another Act, I think, it must be read in the sense it bore in the original Act from which it was taken, and that consequently it is perfectly legitimate to refer to all the rest of that Act in order to ascertain what the section meant, though those other sections are not incorporated in the new Act".[42] The above statement of the law and the extract from the speech of LORD BLACKBURN were approvingly quoted (from 7th edition p. 244 of this book) in *Surana Steels Pvt. Ltd. v. Dy. Commissioner of Income-tax.*[43] In this case, in interpreting cl. (iv) of the Explanation to section 115-J of the Income-tax Act, 1961 which incorporates only clause (b) of the first proviso to sub-section (1) of section 205 of the Companies Act, 1956, the incorporated provision was given the same

---

39. *Mariyappa v. State of Karnataka*, JT 1998 (1) SC 734, p. 748 : AIR 1998 SC 1334, p. 1343 : (1998) 3 SCC 276.
40. AIR 1998 SC 1028 : (1998) 2 SCC 467 discussed at pp. 332-333, *supra.*
41. *Munithimmaiah v. State of Karnataka,* AIR 2002 SC 1574, p. 1581 : (2002) 4 SCC 326.
42. *Portsmouth Corporation v. Smith*, (1885) 10 AC 364, p. 371 (HL).
43. AIR 1999 SC 1455, p. 1459 : 1999 (4) SCC 306.

meaning as in the Companies Act and the entire section 205 of that Act was referred to. The view taken by the High Court that for interpreting the incorporated provision there was no occasion to refer to the Companies Act at all was not accepted by the Supreme Court.[44] This does not mean that a provision in the nature of a proviso or exception in the earlier Act which is not brought in by incorporation can be read so as to limit the meaning of the provision incorporated, as reference to other provisions of the earlier Act is only permissible to get to the meaning of the provision incorporated. LORD BLACKBURN in continuation of the passage quoted above proceeded to point out: "I do not mean that if there was in the original Act a section not incorporated, which comes by way of a proviso or exception on that which was incorporated, that should be referred to; but all others, including the interpretation clause, if there be one, may be referred to".[45] Therefore, when only sub-section (2) of a section of an earlier Act was incorporated in a later Act, sub-section (1) which had a restrictive effect on the operation of sub-section (2) was not allowed to be read for purpose of construing sub-section (2) as incorporated in the later Act.[46] The later Act may often contain modifications or alteration of the incorporated provisions or the incorporation may be subject to other provisions in the later Act. It seems that in all cases when the later Act for its purpose indicates a clear intention of the scope and meaning of the provisions incorporated, reference to other sections of the earlier Act from which these provisions are brought in may be altogether unnecessary. At any rate, the clear intention of the incorporating Act cannot be defeated by resort to such provisions of the earlier Act which have not been incorporated. The Banking Regulation Act, 1949 (BR Act) defines 'banking company' in section 5(c), 'co-operative bank' in section 5(cci) and 'primary co-operative bank' in section 5(ccv). In the Recovery of Debts Due to Banks and Financial Institutions Act, 1993, (RDB Act) section 2(e) defines 'banking company' to have the same meaning as in section 5(c) of the BR Act. As the intention of the RDB Act was clear not to apply its provisions to co-operative banks, the meaning of 'banking company' in section 2(e) was limited to a banking company as defined in section 5(c) of the BR Act and its meaning was not extended to cover co-operative banks by referring to sections 5(cci) and 5(ccv) of the BR Act which are not incorporated in the definition of banking company in the RDB Act.[47]

---

44. *Ibid*, p. 1460. **See further** *Sneh Enterprises v. Commr. of Customs*, (2006) 7 SCC 714 (para 18) : (2006) 8 JT 587.

45. Case in note 41, *supra*.

46. *Onkarlal Nandlal v. State of Rajasthan*, (1985) 4 SCC 404, pp. 415, 416 : 1986 AIR SC 2146.

47. *Greater Bombay Coop. Bank Ltd. v. United Yarn Tex (P) Ltd.*, (2007) 6 SCC 236 : AIR 2007 SC 1584.

In the interpretation of an incorporated provision the court is sometimes left to formulate variations of details in the context of the incorporating Act. A good illustration of such a task is furnished by the Assam Land (Requisition and Acquisition) Act, 1948 which applied the provisions of Land Acquisition Act, 1894 *mutatis mutandis* for determination of compensation in respect of requisitions and acquisitions under the Assam Act. The Land Acquisition Act, 1894, does not prescribe any principle for compensation in the matter of requisition as it only deals with acquisition as distinguished from requisition. The Supreme Court held that for purposes of requisition under the Assam Act the provisions relating to compensation in the Land Acquisition Act should be read "with due alteration of details" and it was pointed out that in place of the word 'acquisition' the word 'requisition' can be read and similarly in place of the words 'market value of the land' the words 'market value of the interest in land of which the owner has been deprived' should be read.[48] On the same lines is the case[49] which dealt with section 27 of the Bangalore Improvement Act, 1945 which provides that the acquisition of land under this Act shall be regulated by the provisions of the Mysore Land Acquisition Act, 1897 'so far as they are applicable'. In construing these words the Supreme Court held that they make applicable all general provisions of the Land Acquisition Act and exclude only those provisions which become inapplicable because of some special procedure prescribed by the Improvement Act.

The merit of legislation by incorporation is "brevity"[50] which is largely counterbalanced by "difficulties and obscurities" which it is likely to create.[51] Critising this mode of legislation, MATHEW, J., said: "Sometimes whole Acts of Parliament, sometimes groups of clauses of Acts of Parliament, entirely or partially, sometimes portions of clauses are incorporated

---

48. *Paresh Chandra Chatterjee v. State of Assam*, AIR 1962 SC 167, pp. 170, 171 : (1962) 3 SCR 88. For meaning of the expression *mutatis mutandis*. **See further** *Ashok Service Centre v. State of Orissa*, 1983 (2) SCC 82 : AIR 1983 SC 394; *Mariyappa v. State of Karnataka*, JT 1998 (1) SC 734, p. 741 : AIR 1998 SC 1334 : 1998 (3) SCC 276; *Prahlad Sharma v. State of U.P.*, (2004) 4 SCC 113, p. 120 : AIR 2004 SC 2705.

49. *Land Acquisition Officer, City Improvement Trust Board, Bangalore v. H.N. Narayanaiah*, AIR 1976 SC 2403, p. 2412 : (1976) 4 SCC 9.

50. *Narottamdas v. State of M.P.*, AIR 1964 SC 1667, p. 1670 (para 6) : 1964 (7) SCR 820.

51. *Willingale v. Norris*, (1909) 1 KB 57, p. 66; referred to in *Phillips v. Parnaby*, (1934) 2 KB 299, p. 304. **See further** *R. v. Eaton*, (1881) 8 QBD 158, p. 160; *Livingstone v. Westminster Corporation*, (1904) 2 KB 109, p. 117; *Minister of Housing and Local Government v. Hartnell*, (1965) 1 All ER 490, p. 494 (HL); *Farid Ahmad Abdul Samad v. Municipal Corporation of the City of Ahmedabad*, AIR 1976 SC 2095, p. 2101 : 1976 (3) SCC 719, p. 726. (Beneficial laws have to be simple and self-contained. To introduce provisions of another Act referentially in vital matters creates avoidable difficulties and litigation highlighted by the case in hand).

into later Act, so that the interpreter has to keep under his eye, or, if he can, bear in his mind, large masses of bygone and not always consistent legislation in order to gather the meaning of recent legislation. There is very often the further provision that these earlier statutes are incorporated only so far as they are not inconsistent with the statute into which they are incorporated; so that you have first to ascertain the meaning of a statute by reference to other statute, and then to ascertain whether the earlier Acts qualify only or absolutely contradict the later ones, a task sometimes of great difficulty, always of great labour, a difficulty and labour generally speaking wholly unnecessary."[52] The House of Lords later deprecated "the regrettable modern tendencies to overdo legislation by reference and to attempt brevity at the expense of lucidity".[53] Similar criticisms have been repeated from time to time.[54]

(e) Codifying and consolidating statutes

(i) *Codifying statutes.*—The purpose of a codifying statute is to present an orderly and authoritative statement of the leading rules of law on a given subject, whether those rules are to be found in statute law or common law.[55] The indication that the Act is a Code will generally be found in the preamble, if any or in the long title.[56] It has been said that a codifying Act is presumed not to alter the law unless a contrary intention appears.[57] But the presumption will be of help only after the language of the statute is first construed according to normal canons of construction and is found to be of doubtful import.[58] The principles applicable to the construction of such a statute are well stated in an oft-quoted passage of LORD HERSCHELL: "I think the proper course is, in the first instance, to examine the language of the statute and to ask what is its natural meaning, uninfluenced by any considerations derived from the previous state of the law, and not to start with inquiring how the law previously stood, and then, assuming that it was probably intended to leave it unaltered, to see if the words of the enactment will bear an interpretation in conformity with this view. If a statute intended to embody in a Code a particular branch of the law is to be treated in

---

52. *Knill v. Towse*, (1890) 24 QBD 186, pp. 195, 196 (MATHEW, J., for the Court, LORD COLERIDGE, C.J., and himself).

53. *Minister of Housing and Local Govt. v. Hartnell, supra*, p. 494 (letters F, G).

54. LORD BRIGHTMAN, Drafting Quagmires, (2002) 23 Statute Law Review 1.

55. HALSBURY: Laws of England (4th Edition), Vol. 44, p. 489 (para 809). Codification "Systematizes Case-Law as well as Statutes"; PATON: Jurisprudence, 3rd Edition, p. 215.

56. *Board of Trustees of the Port of Bombay v. Sriyanesh Knitters,* AIR 1999 SC 2947, p. 2952 : (1999) 7 SCC 114.

57. *Ibid.*

58. **See text** and note 59, p. 370.

this fashion, it appears to me that its utility will be almost entirely destroyed and the very object with which it was enacted will be frustrated. The purpose of such a statute surely was that on any point specifically dealt with by it, the law should be ascertained by interpreting the language used, instead of, as before, by roaming over a vast number of authorities in order to discover what the law was, extracting it by a minute critical examination of the prior decisions—.I am of course, far from asserting that recourse may never be had to the previous state of the law for the purpose of aiding in the construction of provisions of the Code. If, for example, a provision be of doubtful import, such resort would be perfectly legitimate. Or, again if in a Code—words be found which have previously acquired a technical meaning, or been used in a sense other than their ordinary one—the same interpretation might well be put upon them in the Code. I give these as examples merely. They, of course, do not exhaust the category. What, however, I am venturing to insist upon is, that the first step taken should be to interpret the language of the statute, and that an appeal to earlier decisions can only be justified on some special ground."[59]

The essence of a codifying statute "is to be exhaustive on the matters in respect of which it declares the law and it is not the province of a Judge to disregard or go outside the letter of the enactment according to its true construction".[60] Thus, a question of *res judicata* in relation to a suit has to be decided solely on terms of section 11 of the Civil Procedure Code, 1908 and not on general principles of *res judicata*.[61] A matter concerning

---

59. *Bank of England v. Vagliano Brothers*, (1891) AC 107, pp. 144, 145 : 7 TLR 333 (HL); referred to in *Norendra Nath Sarcar v. Kamalbasini Dasi*, ILR 23 Cal 563, pp. 571, 572 (PC); *Ravulu Subbarao v. CIT, Madras*, AIR 1956 SC 604, p. 610 : 1956 SCR 199; *Sales Tax Officer, Banaras v. Kanhaiya Lal Mukund Lal Saraf*, AIR 1959 SC 135, pp. 139, 140 : 1959 SCR 1350; *Union of India v. Mohendra Supply Co.*, AIR 1962 SC 256, p. 260 : (1962) 3 SCR 497; *R. v. Fulling*, (1987) 2 All ER 65, p. 69 (CA).

60. *Gokul Mandar v. Pudmanund Singh*, ILR 29 Cal 707, p. 715 (PC); *Joseph Peter v. State of Goa, Daman and Diu*, AIR 1977 SC 1812, p. 1814 : 1977 SCC (Cri) 486 : (1977) 3 SCC 280. (A Code is self contained and complete and that marks the distinction between a Code and an ordinary enactment); *Pioneer Aggregates (U.K.) Ltd. v. Secretary of State for the Environment*, (1984) 2 All ER 358, p. 363 : 1985 AC 132 : (1984) 3 WLR 302 (HL) ("Where the code is silent or ambiguous resort to the principles of private law may be necessary so that the courts may resolve difficulties by application of common law or equitable principles. But such cases will be exceptional. And, if the statute law covers the situation it will be an impermissible exercise of the judicial function to go beyond the statutory provision by applying such principles merely because they may appear to achieve a fairer solution to the problem being considered.")

61. *L. Janakirama Iyer v. P.P.M. Nilkanto Iyer*, AIR 1962 SC 633, p. 641 : 1962 Supp (1) SCR 206. **See also** *Gulabchand v. State of Gujarat*, AIR 1965 SC 1153, p. 1163 : 1965 (2) SCR 547.

the admission and disposal of criminal appeals has to be dealt with in terms of Code of Criminal Procedure and not outside those provisions;[62] and a court has no power to grant exemption from the bar of limitation except in accordance with the provisions contained in the Indian Limitation Act.[63] Similarly, in construing the Hindu Succession Act, 1956, which is an Act to amend and codify the law relating to intestate succession among Hindus, it is not permissible to apply the principles of Hindu Law on matters covered by the Act; for example a son inheriting his father's separate property under section 8 of the Act takes it as his exclusive property and the property does not become coparcenary property with his sons.[64] But a codifying statute may be a Code only with respect to a particular branch of a subject in which case it will be permissible to look at other laws.[65] So it has been held that the Payment of Bonus Act, 1965 does not cover all categories of bonus and is restricted to the subject of profit bonus. The result is that the Act speaks as a complete Code on the subject of profit bonus and does not annihilate by implication other different and distinct kinds of bonus such as customary bonus.[66]

(ii) *Consolidating statutes.*—The purpose of a consolidating statute is to present the whole body of statutory law on a subject in complete form, repealing the former statute.[67] In case of purely consolidating statutes the presumption is that such a statute is not intended to alter the law,[68] but this *prima facie* view has to yield to plain words to the contrary.[69] Consistent with the initial presumption, that alteration of law is not intended, certain principles logically follow. It is thus relevant to refer to the previous state of the law[70] or to judicial decisions interpreting the repealed Acts for purposes of construction of corresponding provisions in the consolidating

---

62. *King Emperor v. Dahu Raut*, AIR 1935 PC 89.

63. *Macqbul Ahmed v. Onkar Pratap Narain Singh*, AIR 1935 PC 85.

64. *CWT v. Chander Sen*, (1986) 3 SCC 567, p. 577 : AIR 1986 SC 1753.

65. *Board of Trustees of the Port of Bombay v. Sriyanesh Knitters*, AIR 1999 SC 2947, p. 2952 : 1999 (7) SCC 114. **See further** the observations of House of Lords quoted in f.n. 60, *supra*.

66. *Mumbai Kamgar Sabha, Bombay v. Abdullbhai Faizullabhai*, AIR 1976 SC 1455 : 1976 (3) SCC 832.

67. HALSBURY: Laws of England, (4th Edition), Vol. 44, p. 489 (para 809).

68. *IRC v. Hinchy*, (1960) 1 All ER 505, p. 512 : 1960 AC 748 (HL); *Beswick v. Beswick*, (1967) 2 All ER 1197, pp. 1202, 1206, 1209, 1223 (HL); *Director of Public Prosecutions v. Schildkamp*, (1969) 3 All ER 1640, pp. 1641, 1642, 1645, 1647, 1652 : 1971 AC 1 (HL); *Maunsell v. Olins*, (1975) 1 All ER 16, pp. 17, 19, 20 (HL).

69. *Grey v. IRC*, (1959) 3 All ER 603, p. 606 (HL); *Beswick v. Beswick*, (1967) 2 All ER 1197, pp. 1202, 1206, 1209, 1223 (HL).

70. *IRC v. Hinchy*, (1960) 1 All ER 505 : 1960 AC 748 (HL); *Maunsell v. Olins*, (1975) 1 All ER 16 (HL).

Act.[71] Indeed the question of construction of a section in a consolidating Act may for this reason be really a question of construction of an earlier Act in which that section first appeared,[72] and it may be necessary to refer to the various Acts in the series as also to the common law existing at the time when the earliest Act was enacted.[73] Further, as provisions in a consolidating Act may have their origin in different legislations, in case of inconsistency between two such provisions, it may be legitimate to refer to the respective dates of their first enactment for resolving the inconsistency.[74] Similarly, the presumption that same word when used at different places in the same Act has the same meaning, has hardly any application to consolidating Act when once it is shown that the different provisions where the same word occurs had their origin in different legislations.[75] And, statutes not expressly repealed or modified will be assumed not to have been affected by a consolidating Act by mere use of some general words in certain of its provisions.[76] On the same principle any well established principle of general law will not be taken to be abrogated without clear words by a consolidation Act.[77]

A consolidating statute is often not a mere compilation of earlier enactments. "The very object of consolidation", said LORD WATSON, "is to collect the statutory law bearing upon a particular subject, and to bring it down to date, in order that it may form a useful Code applicable to the circumstances existing at the time when the consolidating Act is passed".[78] The process of consolidation involves co-ordination and simiplification of former enactments resulting in modernisation of language with a view to

---

71. *Mitchel v. Simpson*, (1890) 25 QBD 183, pp. 185, 186, 189, 190 (CA); *O'Toole v. Scott*, (1965) 2 All ER 240, pp. 246, 247 (PC).

72. *Director of Public Prosecutions v. Schildkamp*, (1969) 3 All ER 1640, pp. 1641, 1642, 1645, 1647, 1652 : 1971 AC 1 (HL). In this case the question related to the construction of section 332(3) of the Companies Act, 1948 which had its origin in section 75(3) of the Companies Act, 1928 and, therefore, the question was considered as if it were a question of construction of the 1928 Act and was answered in the light of the provisions of that Act.

73. *General Electric Co. v. General Electric Co. Ltd.*, (1972) 2 All ER 507, p. 518 (HL). In this case in construing certain provisions of the Trade Marks Act, 1938 all the previous Acts beginning from 1875 and the common law then existing were considered.

74. *Higgs & Hill Ltd. v. Stepney Borough Council*, (1914) 1 KB 505, p. 510.

75. *R. v. Butt*, (1960) 1 All ER 424, p. 427 (DC); *IRC v. Hinchy*, *supra*, p. 520.

76. *Irrawady Flotilla Co. v. Bugwandas*, (1891) ILR 18 Cal 620, pp. 627 to 629 (PC). It was held that the Indian Carriers Act, 1865, and liability of common carriers were not affected by sections 151 and 152 of the Indian Contract Act.

77. *Beswick v. Beswick*, (1967) 2 All ER 1197 : 1968 AC 58 (HL). The rule that a person who is not a party to a contract cannot sue on it, even if it purports to be made for his benefit, has not been abrogated by section 56 of the Law of Property Act, 1925.

78. *Administrator General of Bengal v. Premlal Mullick*, ILR 22 Cal 788, p. 798 (PC).

make it applicable to changed circumstances.[79] It is not permissible to construe a section in a consolidating Act in such cases with reference to circumstances existing at the time when it was first enacted in a former Act.[80] A consolidating Act may further be an amending Act. This additional purpose is usually indicated in the preamble or in the long title by use of the words 'An Act to consolidate and amend'. It is not a sound canon of construction to refer to the provisions in repealed statutes when the consolidating statute contains enactment dealing with the same subject in different terms.[81] Even when a section from an earlier Act is repeated in a consolidation Act in identical terms the framework in which it is placed may be different. Referring to such a situation LORD WRENBURY said: "I derive little, if any, assistance from the knowledge that, for instance, a particular section is in terms identical with a section which as the law previously stood was found in a framework different from that in which it is now found. To ascertain the present law it is necessary to consider such a section in the framework in which it now stands. In other words, I have to consider the statute law as it is."[82] For the purpose of construing a statute which is a consolidating as well as an amending Act, the proper course is to have a "reasonable interpretation of its provisions"[83] and to apply the normal rule of construction "so as to give each word the meaning proper to it in its context".[84] The rule enunciated by LORD HERSCHELL[85] with reference to codifying statutes can be usefully applied to a consolidating and Amending statute.[86] The Supreme Court has applied the said rule for construing the Indian Income-tax Act, 1922, which was an Act to consolidate and amend the law relating to income-tax and super-tax.[87] The rule has also been applied for construing the Indian Contract Act, 1872 which defines and amends certain parts of the law relating to contracts;[88] and for construing the Arbitration Act, 1940, which is an Act to consolidate and amend the law relating to arbitration.[89] It may here be mentioned that observation of CHITTY, J., that LORD HERSCHELL'S rule has no application to

---

79. *Williams v. Permanent Trustee Co. of New South Wales*, (1906) AC 248, p. 253 (PC).
80. *Administrator General of Bengal v. Premlal Mullick, supra*, p. 798.
81. *Sydney Municipal Council v. Bourke*, (1895) AC 433, pp. 438, 439 (PC).
82. *Food Controller v. Cork*, (1923) All ER Rep 463, p. 471 (HL).
83. *Ramdas Vithaldas Durbar v. Amerchand & Co.*, (1916) ILR 40 Bom 630, p. 636 (PC).
84. *Grey v. IRC*, (1959) 3 All ER 603, p. 607 (HL). **See further** *Thakur Amar Singhji v. State of Rajasthan*, AIR 1955 SC 504, p. 526 : (1955) 2 SCR 303.
85. **See** text and note 59, p. 370.
86. *Conservators of the River Thames v. Smeed, Dean & Co.*, (1897) 2 QB 334, p. 346 (CA); *MacConnell v. Prill (E) & Co. Ltd.*, (1916) 2 Ch 57, p. 63.
87. *Ravulu Subbarao v. CIT, Madras*, AIR 1956 SC 604, p. 660 : 1956 SCR 577.
88. *Sales Tax Officer, Banaras v. Kanhaiya Lal Mukund Lal Saraf*, AIR 1959 SC 135, pp. 139, 140 : 1959 SCR 1350.
89. *Union of India v. Mohendra Supply Co.*, AIR 1962 SC 256, p. 260 : 1962 (3) SCR 497.

any consolidating statute[90] is incorrect. The statute with which CHITTY, J. was concerned was a consolidating as well as amending statute and the distinction drawn by him has been rightly criticised as obscure.[91]

The distinction between consolidating statutes and other statutes for purposes of interpretation is being obliterated. Recent decisions have emphasised that a consolidation Act should be interpreted according to normal canons of construction and recourse to repealed enactments can be taken only to solve any ambiguity, for the process of consolidation would lose much of its point if, whenever a question as to construction of a consolidating Act arose, reference had to be made to the statutes which it has consolidated and repealed. The primary rule of construction of a consolidation Act is to examine the language used in the Act itself without any reference to the repealed statutes. It is only when the consolidation Act gives no guidance as to its proper interpretation that it is permissible to refer to the repealed enactments for guidance and it is never legitimate to have recourse to repealed enactments to make obscure or ambiguous that which is clear in the consolidation Act.[92] It is only when there is a real or substantial difficulty or ambiguity that the court is to attempt to resolve the difficulty or ambiguity by reference to the legislation which has been repealed and re-enacted in the consolidation Act.[93] This rule applies to all types of consolidation Acts which are now three: (1) Pure consolidation. *i.e.*, re-enactment, (2) Consolidation with correction and minor improvement, and (3) Consolidation with Law Commission amendments.[94] But when "the provisions of the Act itself invited reference to the earlier law and in some cases were unintelligible without them" recourse to the earlier law for construing the Act becomes inevitable.[95]

The above paragraph was quoted with approval by the Supreme Court in holding that "the distinction between consolidating statute and other

---

90. *Re, Budgett, Cooper v. Adams*, (1894) 2 Ch 557, pp. 561, 562.

91. MAXWELL on Statutes, 11th Edition, p. 24.

92. *Inland Revenue Commissioner v. Joiner*, (1975) 3 All ER 1050, pp. 1057, 1059, 1060 : (1975) 1 WLR 1701 (HL); *Metropolitan Police Commissioner v. Curran*, (1976) 1 All ER 162, p. 168 (HL).

93. *Maunsell v. Olins*, (1975) 1 All ER 16 (HL); *Farrel v. Alexander*, (1976) 2 All ER 721, pp. 725, 726, 733, 735, 746 : (1995) 2 WLR 570 (HL); *Sheldon v. RHM Outhwaite Ltd.*, (1995) 2 All ER 558, p. 567 (HL); *Lowsley v. Forbes,* (1998) 3 All ER 897, p. 899 (HL); *R. v. Secretary of State for the Environment, exparte Spath Holme,* (2001) 1 All ER 196, p. 208 (HL) (Reference to statutory predecessor may also be made if it be helpful to see the social and factual context in which it was first enacted).

94. *R. v. Heron*, (1982) 1 All ER 993, p. 999 (HL).

95. *Goods v. East Sussex County Council,* (2000) 3 All ER 603, pp. 606, 607 : (HL) (construction of the Highways Act, 1959 the long title of which was 'An Act to consolidate with amendments certain enactments relating to highways').

statutes is no longer valid. It is only in certain exceptional circumstances that the language used in the earlier Act can be resorted to."[1]

5. EFFECT OF USAGE AND PRACTICE; *CONTEMPORANEA EXPOSITIO*

Usage or practice developed under a statute is indicative of the meaning ascribed to its words by contemporary opinion and in case of an ancient statute is an admissible external aid to its construction.[2] Referring to Magna Carta, LORD COKE said: "This and the like were the forms of ancient Acts and *graunts*, and the ancient Act and *graunts* must be construed and taken as the law was holden at that time when they were made".[3] A uniform notorious practice continued under an old statute and inaction of the Legislature to amend the same are important factors to show that the practice so followed was based on correct understanding of the law. "*Communis opinio*", LORD ELLENBOROUGH said: "is evidence of what the law is".[4] "There would be no safety for property or liberty", said LORD CAMPBELL: "If it could be successfully contended that all lawyers and statesmen have been mistaken for centuries as to the true meaning of an old Act of Parliament".[5] When the practice receives judicial or legislative approval it gains additional weight and is to be more respected. As stated by MARTIN, B.: "In construing old statutes it has been usual to pay great regard to the construction put upon them by the judges who lived at or soon after the time when they were made, because they were best able to judge of the intention of the makers at the time".[6] The doctrine of *stare decisis* may also be applied when the law is settled in a State for over 100 years by considered view of the High Court of that State.[7] As to legislative approval to a departmental practice LORD MACHNAGHTEN said: "When you find legislation following a continuous practice repeating the very words on which that practice was founded, it may perhaps fairly be inferred that the Legislature in re-enacting the statute intended those words to be understood in their received meaning. And perhaps it might be

1. *Southern Petrochemical Industries Co. Ltd. v. Electricity Inspector & ETIO*, (2007) 5 SCC 447 (para 82) : AIR 2007 SC 1984.
2. *Optimus legum interpres est consuetudo; Contemporanea expositio est Optima et fortissima in lege.*
3. *Senior Electric Inspector v. Laxminarayan Chopra*, AIR 1962 SC 159, p. 162 : 1962 (3) SCR 146.
4. *Isherwood v. Oldknow*, (1815) 3 M & S 382, p. 396; **referred to** in *Bastin v. Davies*, (1950) 1 All ER 1095, p. 1098 (LORD GODDARD, C.J.).
5. *Gorham v. Exeter (BP)*, (1850) 15 QB 52, p. 74 : 117 ER 377, p. 385.
6. *Morgan v. Crawshay*, (1871) LR 5 HL 304, p. 315; **referred to** in *Governors of Campbell College, etc. v. Commr. of Valuation*, (1964) 2 All ER 705, p. 727 (HL).
7. *Ram Adhar Singh v. Bansi*, (1987) 2 SCC 482, p. 485 : AIR 1987 SC 987.

argued that the inference grows stronger with each successive re-enactment."[8]

Subject to use made of contemporary official statements and statutory instruments[9] the principle of *contemporanea expositio* is not applicable to a modern statute.[10] Even if the persons who dealt with the Act understood it in a particular manner, that does not prevent the court in giving to the Act its true construction.[11] The doctrine "is confined to the construction of ambiguous language used in very old statutes where indeed the language itself have had a rather different meaning in those days".[12] LORD WATSON stated the rule in the following words: "In my opinion such usage as has been termed *contemporanea expositio* is of no value in construing a British statute of the year 1858. When there are ambiguous statements in an Act passed one or two centuries ago it may be legitimate to refer to the construction put upon their expression throughout a long course of years by the unanimous consent of all parties interested as exercising what must presumably have been the intention of the Legislature at the remote period. But I feel bound to construe a recent statute according to its own terms."[13] The Supreme Court has refused to apply the principle of *contemporanea expositio* to the Telegraph Act, 1885[14] and the Evidence Act, 1872.[15] Further, an interpretation to a statute received from contemporary authority is not binding upon the Courts and may have to be disregarded if such interpretation is clearly wrong. Section 5 of the Mines and Minerals (Regulation and Development) Act, 1957, provides that the State

---

8. *Commr. for Special Purposes of Income-tax v. Pemsel*, (1891) AC 531, pp. 590, 591 (HL).

9. **See** text and notes 34, 35, pp. 379, 380.

10. *Clyde Navigation Trustees v. Laird*, (1883) 8 AC 658, p. 673 (HL); *Assheton Smith v. Owen*, (1906) 1 Ch 179, p. 213; *Goldsmiths' Co. v. Wyatt*, (1907) 1 KB 95, p. 107 (CA); *Senior Electric Inspector v. Laxminarayan Chopra*, AIR 1962 SC 159, pp. 162 163 : 1962 (3) SCR 146; *Raja Ram Jaiswal v. State of Bihar*, AIR 1964 SC 828, p. 836 : (1964) 2 SCR 528; *J.K. Cotton Spinning & Weaving Mills Ltd. v. Union of India*, AIR 1988 SC 191, p. 204 : 1987 (4) JT 421; *Doypack Systems Pvt. Ltd. v. Union of India*, AIR 1988 SC 782, p. 802 : 1988 (2) SCC 299 [Reference is made to 3rd Edition of this book (pages 238 and 239)]; *Bhuwalka Steel Industries Ltd. v. Bombay Iron and Steel Labour Board*, (2010) 2 SCC 273 para 79 : (2009) 15 JT 269. (This book is **referred**).

11. *Punjab Traders v. State of Punjab*, AIR 1990 SC 2300, p. 2304 : 1991 (1) SCC 86.

12. *Governors of Campbell College etc. v. Commr. of Valuation*, (1964) 1 All ER 705, p. 727 (HL) (LORD UPJOHN); *Doypack Systems Pvt. Ltd. v. Union of India, supra*, p. 802.

13. *Clyde Navigation Trustees v. Laird*, (1883) 8 AC 658, p. 673 (HL), referred to in *Goldsmiths' Co. v. Wyatt*, (1907) 1 KB 95, p. 107 (CA); *Doypack Systems Pvt. Ltd. v. Union of India, supra*, p. 802.

14. *Senior Electric Inspector v. Laxminarayan Chopra*, AIR 1962 SC 159, pp. 162, 163 : 1962 (3) SCR 146.

15. *Raja Ram Jaiswal v. State of Bihar*, AIR 1964 SC 828, p. 836 : 1964 (2) SCR 752.

Government shall not grant a reconnaissance permit, prospecting licence or mining lease except with the previous approval of the Central Government. The Supreme Court held that the process evolved by the Central Government for allocation of coal blocks for captive use, whereby applications were made directly to, and allocation letters issued directly by, the Central Government, leaving virtually no power with the State Government to objectively consider the application, has significantly and effectively reversed the scheme provided in the 1957 Act, and was hence contrary to law and not binding on the Court.[16] However, the principle was applied in construing the Bombay Municipal Corporation Act, 1888[17] and reliance in that connection was placed on the observations of LORD BLACKBURN in *Clyde Navigation Trustees v. Laird*,[18] apparently ignoring the observations of LORD WATSON which have been quoted above. The principle was also referred to in construing section 21 of the Indian Penal Code, 1860 and in holding that an M.L.A. is not a public servant as defined therein.[19] The Supreme Court also referred to the actual practice in the matter of appointment of judges of Supreme Court and High Courts in the context of interpreting Articles 74 and 124 of the Constitution and observed that the practice being in confirmity with the constitutional scheme should be accorded legal sanction by permissible constitutional interpretation.[20]

A question as to the application of the rule of *contemporanea expositio* arose in a case of the House of Lords.[21] The Governors of a fee-paying public school claimed that the school was exempted from rates being 'used for charitable purposes' within section 2 of the Valuation (Ireland) Amendment Act, 1854. It was accepted that if the test in *Pemsel's* case[22] applied, the school would be entitled to exemption, for educational purposes were in law charitable purposes. It was, however, contended that under a long-standing practice supported by *Alexandra College's* case[23] the exemption had been confined to those educational charities whose

---

16. *Manohar Lal Sharma v. Principal Secretary & Ors.*, (2014) 9 SCC 516, pp. 550 to 552.

17. *National & Grindlays Bank v. Municipal Corporation for Greater Bombay*, AIR 1969 SC 1048 : (1969) 1 SCC 541.

18. *Supra*, p. 718.

19. *R.S. Nayak v. A. R. Antuley*, (1984) 2 SCC 183, p. 216 : AIR 1984 SC 684.

20. *Supreme Court Advocates-on-Record Association v. Union of India*, AIR 1994 SC 268, p. 431 : 1993 (4) SCC 441 (para 479). **See further** *Naga Peoples Movement of Human Rights v. Union of India*, AIR 1998 SC 431, p. 460 : 1998 (2) SCC 109.

21. *Governors of Campbell College etc. v. Commr. of Valuation*, (1964) 2 All ER 705, p. 727 : (1964) 1 WLR 912 (HL).

22. (1891) AC 531 (HL).

23. (1914) 2 Ir R 447; *Sub-nom, O'Neill v. Commr. of Valuation*.

purposes were concerned with the education of the poor. The House of Lords held that the decision in *Alexandra College's* case[24] was unsupportable and the school was entitled to the exemption. VISCOUNT RADCLIFFE pointed out that the decision rendered in 1914 relating to the Act of 1854 was not *contemporanea expositio*.[25] LORD UPJOHN in the same case[26] said: "For my part, I am quite unable to apply that principle to a statute although it was passed a hundred years ago, whose language is plain and unambiguous and was not misconstrued until the decision in *Alexandra College's* case,[27] sixty years later".

Even a longstanding practice sanctioned by judicial decisions as also recognised in text books and in legislation may be overruled if there was no legal basis for it and if in the changed circumstances its continuance led to great hardship. So the House of Lords in 1969 overruled a century old practice of assessing compensation by reference to values prevailing at the date of notice to quit and held that the same should be assessed with reference to the values prevailing when possession is taken or when assessment is made.[28] And similarly, in 1980 the House of Lords overruled a longstanding judicial acceptance of the meaning of the word 'wilfully' as that had operated to the prejudice of the accused.[29]

But a uniform and consistent departmental practice arising out of construction placed upon an ambiguous statute by the highest executive officers at or near the time of its enactment and continuing for a long period of time is an admissible aid to the proper construction of the statute by the court and would not be disregarded except for cogent reasons. The controlling effect of this aid which is known as 'executive construction' would depend upon various factors such as the length of time for which it is followed, the nature of rights and property affected by it, the injustice resulting from its departure and the approval that it has received in judicial decisions or in legislation.[30]

---

24. *Ibid.*

25. *Governors of Campbell College etc. v. Commr. of Valuation*, (1964) 2 All ER 705, p. 717 (HL).

26. *Ibid*, p. 727.

27. Note 25, *supra.*

28. *Birmingham City Corporation v. West Midland Baptist*, (1969) 3 All ER 172 (HL).

29. *R. v. Sheppard*, (1980) 3 All ER 899, p. 906 : 1981 AC 394 : (1980) 3 WLR 960 (HL). **See further** *Hemens (Valuation Officer) v. Whitsbury Farm and Stud Ltd.*, (1987) 1 All ER 430, p. 438 : 1988 AC 601 (CA) (The courts will be duty bound to disturb even a long standing practice which originated in a misunderstanding of a judicial decision).

30. Corpus Juris Secundum, Vol. 82, pp. 761 to 774. In *Commissioner of Income-tax M.P. v. Anand Bahari Steel and Wire Products*, 1984 MPLJ 301, p. 307 (G.P. SINGH

[Footnote No. 30 Contd.]

Relying upon this principle, the Supreme Court in *Ajay Gandhi v. B. Singh*,[31] having regard to the fact that the President of the Income Tax Appellate Tribunal had been from its inception in 1941 exercising the power of transfer of the members of the Tribunal to the places where Benches of the Tribunal were functioning, held construing sections 251(1) and 255(5) of the Income-tax Act that the President under these provisions has the requisite power of transfer and posting of its members. The court observed: "For construction of a statute, it is trite that the actual practice may be taken into consideration."[32]

The Supreme Court has held that though there is no specific requirement under section 173(8) of the Code of Criminal Procedure, 1973, to conduct "further investigation" or file "supplementary report" with the leave of the Court, the investigating agencies have not only understood but also adopted it as a legal practice to seek permission of the courts to conduct "further investigation" and file "supplementary report", and will therefore have to be read into, and is a necessary implication of section 173(8). The doctrine of *contemporanea expositio* will fully come to the aid of such interpretation as matters which are understood and implemented for a long time and such practice that is supported by law should be accepted as part of the interpretative process.[33]

Contemporary official statements throwing light on the construction of a statute and statutory instruments made under it have been used as *contemporanea expositio* to interpret not only ancient but even recent statutes both in England[34] and India.[35]

[Footnote No. 30 Contd.]

C.J.) relying upon SUTHERLAND, Statutory Construction, 3rd Edn., pp. 520, 521, 523, 524 the same rule was stated as follows: "Where contemporaneous and practical interpretation has stood unchallenged for a considerable length of time, it is regarded as of great importance in arriving at the proper construction of a statute. Further such an interpretation gains greater weight when the statute as interpreted is re-enacted and is regarded presumptively the correct interpretation of the law. This rule is based upon the theory that the legislature is acquainted with the contemporaneous interpretation of a statute, especially when made by an administrative body or executive officers charged with the duty of administering or enforcing the law, and, therefore, impliedly adops the interpretation upon re-enactment."

31. (2004) 2 SCC 120, p. 127 : AIR 2004 SC 1391, p. 1394.

32. *Ibid.*

33. *Vinay Tyagi v. Irshad Ali & Ors.*, (2013) 5 SCC 762, p. 793.

34. CROSS: Statutory Interpretation, 3rd Edition, p. 148. **See further** *R. v. Wandsworth London Borough Council, Ex parte, Beckwith*, (1996) 1 All ER 129, p. 132 (J) : (1996) 1 WLR 60 (HL) (The opinion of the Department concerned expressed in a circular is entitled to respect but if it is wrong, it has to be ignored.)

35. **See further** *Indian Metals and Ferro Alloys Ltd. v. Collector of Central Excise*, AIR 1991 SC 1028, p. 1034 : 1991 Supp (1) SCC 125 (contemporaneous exposition by

[Footnote No. 35 Contd.]

The principles stated above relating to use of contemporaneous official statements as 'executive construction' were reiterated and approved in *S.B. Bhattacharjee v. S.D. Majumdar*[36] and *Chairman, Indore Vikas Pradhikaran v. Pure Industrial Coke and Chemicals Ltd.*[37]

The principles of *contemporanea expositio* and executive construction though relevant for solving a case of an ambiguity cannot be used for bringing about an implied repeal or *quasi* repeal.[38]

Although acquiescence even for a long period does not make a void rule valid, but when rules are made by the Government under earlier enactments on the basis of a particular construction of the enabling section which is followed by omission of all concerned to dispute that construction for a long time by challenging the validity of the rules and the enabling section is re-enacted without any material change, an inference arises that the construction on which the rules proceeded correctly represents the intention of Parliament and has its approval.[39] This principle was applied in construing the expression 'capital employed' in section 80J of the Income-tax Act, 1961 and in upholding the validity of Rule 19A of the Income-tax Rules, 1962 which requires exclusion of borrowed moneys including long-term borrowings from computation of 'capital employed'.

In a case[40] relating to the construction of a service rule which enabled section officers possessing a recognised Degree in Civil Engineering

---

[Footnote No. 35 Contd.]

administrative authorities is a very useful and relevant guide); *Keshavji Ravji and Co. v. Commissioner of Income Tax*, AIR 1991 SC 1806, p. 1817 : (1990) 2 SCC 231; *Raymand Synthetics Ltd. v. Union of India*, AIR 1992 SC 847, p. 859 : (1992) 2 SCC 255 (The contemporaneous Construction placed upon an ambiguous section by the administrators entrusted with the task of executing the statute is extremely significant); *P. Kasilingam v. P.S.G. College of Technology*, 1995(2) Scale 387, p. 397 : AIR 1995 SC 1395, p. 1400 : 1995 Supp (2) SCC 348 (Rules made under a statute can be used as *contemporanea ex-positio*); *Union of India v. Azadi Bachao Andolan*, AIR 2004 SC 1107, p. 1124 : 2003 Supp (2) JT 205; *Godawat Pan Masala Products I.P. Ltd. v. Union of India*, (2004) 7 SCC 68, p. 89; *State of Karnataka v. Balaji Computers*, (2007) 2 SCC 743 (paras 3864) : (2007) 1 JT 250 : (2007) 1 SLT 393. **See further** pp. 1108-1111, for use of rules for construction of a statute.

36. AIR 2007 SC 2102 (para 24) : (2007) 7 JT 381 (10th edition p. 319 of this book is **referred**).

37. (2007) 8 SCC 705 para 85 (10th edition pp. 319, 320 of this book are **referred**) : AIR 2008 SC 2458.

38. *Municipal Corporation for the City of Pune v. Bharat forge Col. Ltd.*, 1995 (2) Scale 245, p. 251 : AIR 1996 SC 2856, p. 2861 : (1993) 3 SCC 434.
For *quasi* repeal by desuetude **see** title 8, Chapter 7.

39. *Lohia Machines Ltd. v. Union of India*, (1985) 2 SCC 197, pp. 223 to 226 : AIR 1985 SC 421.

40. *N. Suresh Nathan v. Union of India*, AIR 1992 SC 564 : 1992 Supp (1) SCC 584.

or equivalent to claim eligibility for promotion if they had put in 'three years service in the grade' whereas six years' service was required to make a Diploma holder eligible for promotion, the question was as to the point of time from which the period of three years was to be counted in a case, where the section officer obtained the degree during service. The practice over a long period was to count the period of three years from the date the officer obtained the degree and this practice was relied upon in construing the rule. Indeed it was observed: "If the past practice is based on one of the possible constructions which can be made of the rules then upsetting the same now would not be appropriate."[41]

The Scheduled Districts Act, 1874 authorised the Local Government to appoint officers to administer civil and criminal justice and to regulate the procedure of officers so appointed. In negativing the contention that the authority conferred was merely to make administrative rules and not subordinate legislation pertaining to the procedure to be followed in deciding cases, the Supreme Court referred to the rules of 1872, 1874, 1906 and 1937 containing comprehensive rules of procedure and said: "It is clear that a succession of officers saw the necessity of rules controlling not only the administrative side but also the judicial side of administration of justice."[42] This practice was relied upon as throwing light on the construction of section 6 of the Act.[43] Similarly, in construing section 146(2) of the Bombay Municipal Corporation Act, 1888, which provides that property taxes 'shall be primarily leviable, if the premises are let, from the lessor', the Supreme Court relied upon the long practice followed by the Corporation of treating the land and building constructed upon it as a single unit and of charging the property tax upon the owner of the land and held that in case where the land was let for a period of less than a year and thus did not fall under sub-section (3) which made special provision for cases where the lease was for a year or more, the primary liability to pay property tax treating the land and building as one unit was on the owner of the land, although the building was constructed and was owned by the lessee.[44] And in construing the word 'houses' in section 89 of the Bombay Village Panchayats Act, 1933, the Supreme Court relied upon the rules made in 1934 which used the word 'building' in place of 'houses' as one of the aids for holding that the word 'houses' as used in the Act was not limited to dwelling houses but included all buildings whether

---

41. *Ibid*, p. 565.
42. *State of Nagaland v. Ratan Singh*, AIR 1967 SC 212, p. 222 : 1966 (3) SCR 830.
43. *Ibid.*
44. *National & Grindlays Bank v. Municipal Corporation, Greater Bombay*, AIR 1969 SC 1048, pp. 1052, 1053 : (1969) 1 SCC 541. **See also** text and note 17, p. 377.

used for residence or commercial purposes.[45] Documents issued by the Government simultaneously with the notification under section 16(1) of the Securities Contracts (Regulation) Act, 1956 were used as *contemporanea expositio* of the notification.[46] But instructions and directions issued by the Revenue Department for enforcement of taxing Acts have not been used as admissible aids.[47] However, circulars issued under statutory power by the Central Board of Revenue, the Central Board of Direct Taxes and the Central Board of Excise and Customs have been held to be admissible and even binding on the Revenue.[48] A Constitution Bench of

---

45. *Tata Engineering and Locomotive Co. Ltd. v. Gram Panchayat, Pimpri, Waghere*, AIR 1976 SC 2463, p. 2467 : 1976 SCC (Tax) 457 : (1976) 4 SCC 177. On the question of use of delegated legislation for construction of the Act, **See further** pp. 1126 to 1131.

46. *Desh Bandhu Gupta & Co. v. Delhi Stock Exchange Association Ltd.*, AIR 1979 SC 1049, p. 1054 : (1979) 4 SCC 565.

47. *CIT, Madras v. K. Srinivasan*, AIR 1953 SC 113, 118 : 1953 SCR 486; *J.K. Steel Ltd. v. Union of India*, AIR 1970 SC 1173, p. 1184 : (1969) 2 SCR 481. As an instance of use of Government circular for construing a service rule framed under the Constitution **see** *State of Mysore v. M.H. Bellary*, AIR 1965 SC 868, p. 871 (para 5) : 1964 (7) SCR 471.

48. *Navnitlal C. Jhaveri v. R.K. Sen*, AIR 1965 SC 1375 : (1965) 1 SCR 909; *Ellerman Lines Ltd. v. Commr. of Income-tax*, AIR 1972 SC 524 : (1972) 4 SCC 474; *K.P. Verghese v. Income-tax Officer*, AIR 1981 SC 1922, pp. 1932, 1933 : (1981) 4 SCC 173. *Keshavji Raoji & Co. v. Commr. of Income Tax*, (1990) 2 SCC 231 : 1991 AIR SCW 1845 : AIR 1991 SC 1806; *Wilh Wilhelmsen v. Commissioner of Income Tax*, 1996 (5) Scale 41, p. 50 : AIR 1996 SC 3364, p. 3369; *Ranadey Micronutrients v. Collector of Central Excise*, 1996 (6) Scale 702, pp. 706, 707 : AIR 1997 SC 69, pp. 72, 73; *J.B. Doda & Co. Pvt. Ltd. v. Central Board of Direct Taxes*, AIR 1997 SC 1543, pp. 1548, 1549 : (1997) 1 SCC 719; *Central Board of Direct Taxes v. Oberoi Hotels (India) Pvt. Ltd.*, AIR 1998 SC 1666, pp. 1675, 1676 : (1998) 4 SCC 552; *UCO Bank, Calcutta v. Commissioner of Income-tax, West Bengal*, AIR 1999 SC 2082, pp. 2085, 2089 : (1999) 4 SCC 599 (Circulars can seek to mitigate the rigour of a provision for the benefit of the assessee but cannot detract from the Act to the prejudice of the assessee); *Paper Products Ltd. v. Commissioner of Central Excise*, 1999 SC 3341 (Department cannot challenge the binding nature of the Circular); *Karnataka Small Scale Industries Development Corporation Ltd. v. Commissioner of Income-tax*, (2003) 7 SCC 224, p. 231 (circular issued by Central Board of Direct Taxes relied upon as contemporaneous exposition of section 115-J of the Income-tax Act, 1961); *Commissioner of Central Excise Calcutta v. Sharma Chemical Works*, AIR 2003 SC 2448, p. 2454 (para 13) : (2003) 5 SCC 60; *Simplex Castings Ltd. v. Commissioner of Customs, Vishakhapatnam*, (2003) 5 SCC 528, p. 538 : (2003) 155 ELT 5; *Tega India Ltd. v. Commissioner of Central Excise Calcutta*, (2004) 2 SCC 727, p. 738 : AIR 2004 SC 2785 (circulars issued by Central Board of Excise and Customs are binding); *Union of India v. Azadi Bachao Andolan*, AIR 2004 SC 1107, pp. 1125, 1126 (The circulars of CBDT under section 119 of the Income-tax Act pertain to proper administration of the Act and are valid); *Pahwa Chemicals (P.) Ltd. v. Commissioner of Central Excise, New Delhi*, (2005) 2 SCC 720, pp. 727, 728 (circulars by Central Board of Excise and Customs under section 37B of the Central Excise Act, 1944 cannot be contrary to the provisions of the Act

[Footnote No. 48 Contd.]

the Supreme Court relied on the understanding of the Central Board of Direct Taxes, as expressed in CBDT Circular No. 8 of 2002, dated 27.8.2002, titled "Finance Act, 2002 - Explanatory Notes on Provision Relating to Direct Taxes", to hold that the amendment which inserted the proviso to section 113 of the Income Tax Act, 1961, would be prospective and not restrospective in its application.[49] Decisions of the Government of India construing an exemption notification under the Central Excises and Salt Act, 1944 have been used as *contemporanea expositio.*[50] Clarifications issued at the earliest point of time by the Ministry of Commerce regarding the meaning of the expression 'hides and skins in dressed state' as used in section 14 of the Central Sales Tax Act, 1956

[Footnote No. 48 Contd.]

and take away the jurisdiction vested under the Act in a Central Excise officer); *Tanna & Modi v. C.I.T. Mumbai,* (2007) 7 SCC 434, para 18. But **see** *Hindustan Aeronautics Ltd. v. Commissioner of Income-tax,* AIR 2000 SC 2178, p. 2180 : (2000) 5 SCC 365 (circulars contrary to law laid down by the High Court or Supreme Court cannot be given effect to). In *Collector of Central Excise, Vadodra v. Dhiren Chemical Industries,* AIR 2002 SC 453, p. 455 a constitution bench of the Supreme Court while giving an interpretation of an exemption notification made it clear that if there are circulars which have been issued by the Board of Excise and Customs which place a different interpretation, that interpretation will be binding on the Revenue. The same view was reiterated by a three Judge Bench in *Commissioner Central Excise v. Dhiren Chemical Industries Ltd.*, (2002) 10 SCC 64 : (2002) 143 ELT 19. In *Commissioner of Customs Calcutta v. Indian Oil Corpn. Ltd.*, (2004) 3 SCC 488 : AIR 2004 SC 2799, the Constitution Bench decision in *Dhiren Chemical Industries Ltd., supra* was followed by a two Judge Bench but doubt was expressed by REDDY J. about the correctness of the decision hoping that some day another Constitution Bench will review the whole matter. In *P.R. Prabhakar v. Commr. of Income-tax Coimbatore,* (2006) 6 SCC 86 (paras 8 and 9) : (2006) 6 SLT 72 : (2006) 284 ITR 548 circular of CBDT, that a particular amendment was prospective, was held to be binding; *Assistant Commissioner of Income Tax v. Hotel Blue Moon,* (2010) 3 SCC 259 para 24 : (2010) 2 JT 136 (Clarification circular of CBDT is binding on the Department but not on the court). *State of Kerala v. Kurian Abraham (P) Ltd.,* (2008) 3 SCC 582 : (2008) 2 JT 350 [construction of section 3 (1-A) of Kerala General Sales Tax Act, 1963 which empowers the Board of Revenue to issue orders direction and instructions as it may deem fit 'for the proper administration of this Act']; *Padinjarekara Agencies Ltd. v. State of Kerala*, (2008) 3 SCC 597 : (2008) 2 JT 403 (circulars issued by the Board of Revenue not binding on assessee). The purpose of the provisions like section 11G(1) of the Income-tax Act and section 3(1-A) the Kerala General Sales Tax Act, 1963 as pointed out by KAPADIA, J. in *Kurian Ibrahim (P) Ltd.* (supra paras 23 and 25), is to avoid difficulties which businessmen may facr in matters of tax administration and to provide a just and fair administration in the matter of imposition and collection of tax. **See further** *CIT v. Anjum M.H. Gharwala,* AIR 2001 SC 3868, p. 3877 (Press release clarificatory note is not a circular and is not binding).

49. *CIT (Central)-I, New Delhi v. Vatika Township Pvt. Ltd.*, (2015) 1 SCC 1, pp. 30, 31.

50. *Collector of Central Excises, Guntur v. Andhra Sugar Ltd.*, AIR 1989 SC 625, p. 627 : 1989 Supp (1) SCC 144 : 1988 (4) ST 410.

was also used as *contemporanea expositio.*[51] It has been observed that such opinions should be accepted as true interpretation unless shown to be clearly wrong.[52] Drastic powers conferred on army authorities under sections 4 and 5 of the Armed Forces (Special Powers) Act, 1958 in respect of a 'disturbed area' have been construed in the light of instructions (Do's and Dont's) issued by the Central Government to prevent misuse or abuse of the powers and the instructions have been held to be binding.[53]

6. DICTIONARIES

When a word is not defined in the Act itself,[54] it is permissible to refer to dictionaries to find out the general sense in which that word is understood in common parlance.[55] Rule 8-A of the Supreme Court Rules, 1966, provides that when on the complaint of any person or 'otherwise', the Court is of the opinion that an Advocate–on-Record, has been guilty of misconduct or of conduct unbecoming of an Advocate-on-Record, the Court may make an order removing his name from the register of Advocates-on-Record. The Supreme Court relied on the fact that the term 'otherwise' was defined in the dictionary to mean "contrarily, different from that to which it relates", and held that the Supreme Court is competent to proceed against an Advocate-on-Record *suo motu* under Rule 8-A, without any complaint from any person, if *prima facie* it is of the opinion that he is guilty of misconduct or conduct unbecoming of an Advocate-on-Record.[56] In another case the Court referred to the dictionary meanings of the

---

51. *State of Tamil Nadu v. Mahi Traders*, AIR 1989 SC 1167, p. 1170 : 1989 (1) SCC 724.
52. *Ibid.* **See also** *State of Madhya Pradesh v. G.S. Dall and Flour Mills*, AIR 1991 SC 772, pp. 786, 787 : 1992 Supp (1) SCC 150 (Instructions cannot run contrary to statutory language).
53. *Naga People's Movement of Human Rights v. Union of India*, AIR 1998 SC 431, pp. 460, 461 : 1998 (2) SCC 109.
54. *Nagulapati Lakshmamma v. Mupparaju Subbaiah*, 1998 (2) Scale 705, p. 708 : (1998) 5 SCC 285.
55. *R. v. Peters*, (1886) 16 QBD 636, p. 641 (LORD COLERIDGE): *Marquis Camden v. IRC*, (1914) 1 KB 641, p. 647, (COZEN HARDY, M.R.); *CIT, West Bengal v. Benoy Kumar Sahas Roy*, AIR 1957 SC 768, p. 772 : 1958 SCR 101 (BHAGWATI, J.); *Bhogilal Chunilal Pandya v. State of Bombay*, AIR 1959 SC 356, p. 357 : 1959 Supp (1) SCR 310; *India Carbon Ltd. v. Superintendent of Taxes, Gauhati*, AIR 1972 SC 154, p. 156 : (1971) 3 SCC 612; *CIT, A.P. v. Taj Mahal Hotel, Secunderabad*, AIR 1972 SC 168, p. 171 : (1971) 3 SCC 550; *Commissioner of Wealth Tax, Andhra Pradesh v. Officer in Charge*, AIR 1977 SC 113, p. 117 : 1976 SCC (Tax) 411 : (1976) 3 SCC 864; *Bolani Ores Ltd. v. State of Orissa*, AIR 1975 SC 17, pp. 25, 26 : 1974) 2 SCC 777; *Mohinder Singh v. State of Haryana*, AIR 1989 SC 1367, p. 1368 : 1989 (3) SCC 93; *Star Paper Mills Ltd. v. Collector of Central Excise, Meerut*, AIR 1989 SC 2066 : 1989 (4) SCC 724, p. 2068; *New Delhi Municipal Committee v. Allied Motor Pvt. Ltd.*, 1995 (6) Scale 37, p. 40.
56. *In Re Rameshwar Prasad Goyal, Advocate*, (2014) 1 SCC 572, pp. 576, 577.

expressions "therapeutic" and "prophylactic", as these expressions were not defined under the tariff entry, to hold that povidone iodine cleansing solution and wokadine surgical scrub were 'medicaments' under Chapter 30 of the Central Excise Tariff Act, 1985, and not 'detergents'.[57] However, in selecting one out of the various meanings of a word, regard must always be had to the context as it is a fundamental rule that "the meanings of words and expressions used in an Act must take their colour from the context in which they appear".[58] Therefore, "when the context makes the meaning of a word quite clear, it becomes unnecessary to search for and select a particular meaning out of the diverse meanings a word is capable of, according to lexicographers".[59] Relying on the definition of the word 'transfer' in Black's Law Dictionary, the Supreme Court held that the expression 'transfer' can, depending on its context, mean transfer of ownership or transfer of possession. Since under Rule 38 of the Bombay Stock Exchange Rules, a member only 'deposits' securities, in this context, the expression 'securities shall be transferred to and held' in the names of the Trustees of the Exchange thereunder was held to mean only transfer of possession of the securities to the Trustees.[60] As stated by KRISHNA AIYAR, J.: "Dictionaries are not dictators of statutory construction where the benignant mood of a law, and more emphatically, the definition clause

---

57. *Commissioner of Central Excise v. Wockhardt Life Sciences Ltd.*, (2012) 5 SCC 585, pp. 594, 595, 597.

58. *Ram Narain v. State of U.P.*, AIR 1957 SC 18, p. 23 : 1956 SCR 664; *Mangoo Singh v. Election Tribunal, Bareilly*, AIR 1957 SC 871, p. 874 : 1958 SCR 418; *Gramophone Co. of India Ltd. v. Birendra Bahadur Pandey*, (1984) 2 SCC 534, p. 553 : AIR 1984 SC 667; *CIT v. J.H. Gotla Yadgiri*, (1985) 4 SCC 343, p. 359 : AIR 1985 SC 1698; *R.S. Nayak v. A.R. Antuley*, (1984) 2 SCC 183, pp. 226, 227 : AIR 1984 SC 684; *S. Samuel M.D. Harrison's Malayalam v. Union of India*, AIR 2004 SC 218, p. 223 : (2004) 1 SCC 256 (8th Edn., p. 279 of this book is **referred**) 'foodstuff' was held not to include 'tea'.

See further Chapter 1, title (3) 'Whole in its context' and Chapter 2, title 2(b) 'Explanation of the rule', and **see** *Kanwar Singh v. Delhi Administration*, AIR 1965 SC 871, p. 874, (para 10).

59. *Mangoo Singh v. Election Tribunal, Bareilly*, AIR 1957 SC 871, p. 875 : 1958 SCR 418; *Dy. Chief Controller of Imports & Exports v. K.T. Kosalram*, AIR 1971 SC 1283, p. 1289 : (1970) 3 SCC 82; *R.S. Nayak v. A.R. Antuley, supra; Commissioner of Income-tax, Bangalore v. Venkateshwara Hatcheries (P.) Ltd.*, JT 1999 (2) SC 338, p. 341 : AIR 1999 SC 1225, p. 1228 : (2001) 10 SCC 569; *C.I. Trivandrum v. Anand Theatres,* JT 2000 (6) SC 407, p. 436 : (2000) 5 SCC 393; *Tarachand Deosharma v. State of Punjab,* AIR 2001 SC 2524, p. 2529; *Karnataka State Road Transport Corporation v. Ashrafulla Khan,* AIR 2002 SC 629, p. 635 : (2002) 2 SCC 560; *Amarendra Pratap Singh v. Tej Bahadur Prajapati*, AIR 2004 SC 3782, pp. 3789, 3790 (8th Edn., pp. 279, 280 of this book referred), *P. Prabhakaran v. P. Jayarajan*, (2005) 1 SCC 754, p. 779 (ninth edition p. 302 of this book is **referred**).

60. *Bombay Stock Exchange v. V.S. Kandalgaonkar & Ors.*, (2015) 2 SCC 1, p. 22.

furnish a different denotation".[61] In the words of JEEVAN REDDY, J.: "A statute cannot always be construed with the dictionary in one hand and the statute in the other. Regard must also be had to the scheme, context and to the legislative history."[62] JUDGE LEARNED HAND cautioned "not to make a fortress out of the dictionary" but to pay more attention to "the sympathetic and imaginative discovery" of the purpose or object of the statute as a guide to its meaning.[63] A dictionary meaning cannot be adopted if it will make some existing words redundant or will require reading of some additional words.[64] Further, words and expressions at times have a 'technical' or a 'legal meaning' and in that case they are understood in that sense.[65] Again, judicial decisions expounding the meaning of words in construing statutes in *pari materia* will have more weight than the meaning furnished by dictionaries.[66]

7. USE OF FOREIGN DECISIONS

On a question of construction of Indian statutes sobered use of foreign decisions of countries following the same system of jurisprudence as ours and rendered on statutes in *pari materia* has been permitted by practice in Indian Courts.[67] The assistance of such decisions is subject to the qualification that prime importance is always to be given to the language of the relevant Indian Statute, the circumstances and the setting in which it is enacted and the Indian conditions where it is to be applied and that it is not to be forgotten that there is always an element of risk in taking ready and hasty assistance from such decisions.[68] In other words, "statutory

---

61. *State Bank of India v. N. Sundara Money,* AIR 1976 SC 1111, p. 1114 : 1976 SCC (L&S) 132 : (1976) 1 SCC 822; *R.S. Nayak v. A.R. Antuley, supra.*

62. *Commissioner of Income-tax Orissa v. N.C. Budhraja and Co.*, AIR 1993 SC 2529, p. 2540 : 1993 (5) JT 346 : 1994 Supp (1) SCC 280.

63. *Cabell v. Markham*, 148 F 2d 737, p. 739 (2nd cr cir 1945); *Union of India v. Harjeet Singh Sandhu,* AIR 2001 SC 1772, p. 1785 : (2001) 5 SCC 593 (7th Edition of this book pp. 258, 259 **referred**); *Tarachand Deosharma v. State of Punjab,* AIR 2001 SC 2524, pp. 2529, 2530 (7th edition of this book pp. 258, 259 **referred**. **See further** *K.P. Verghese v. Income-tax Officer, Ernakulam,* (1981) 4 SCC 173, p. 180 : AIR 1981 SC 1922; *DLF Universals Ltd. v. Appropriate Authority,* AIR 2000 SC 1985, p. 1992 : (2000) 5 SCC 552.

64. *Dental Council of India v. Hari Prakash,* AIR 2001 SC 3303, p. 3309 : 2001 AIR SCW 3353.

65. **See** Chapter 2, title 2(d) 'Technical words in Technical sense'.

66. Chapter 4, p. 241.

67. **See** for instance *Indian Molasses Co. (Private) Ltd. v. CIT, West Bengal*, AIR 1959 SC 1049 : 1959 Supp (2) SCR 964, *CIT, Kerala v. Malayalam Plantation Ltd., Quilon*, AIR 1964 SC 1722, p. 1727 (para 8); *Ranjit D. Udeshi v. State of Maharashtra*, AIR 1965 SC 881, p. 887 (para 14) : 1965 (1) SCR 65.

68. *Sales Tax Officer, Banaras v. Kanhaiya Lal Mukund Lal Saraf*, AIR 1959 SC 135, pp. 139, 140 : 1959 SCR 1350; *State of West Bengal v. B.K. Mondal and Sons*,

[Footnote No. 68 Contd.]

construction must be home-spun even if hospitable to alien thinking".[69] And when guidance is available from binding Indian decisions, reference to foreign decisions may become unnecessary.[70]

Reference to English decisions was a common practice in the pre-constitution period because of historical reasons. The practice was not given up in spite of severe warning and caution administered by the Privy Council.[71] It cannot, however, be doubted that knowledge of English law and precedents when the language of an Indian Act was not clear or express, has often been of valuable assistance. Speaking about the Indian Codes, SHRI M.C. SETALVAD has stated: "Where the language of the Code was clear and applicable no question of relying on English authority would arise. But very often the general rule in the Indian Code was based on an English principle and in such cases the Indian courts frequently sought the assistance of English decisions to support the conclusions they reached. They could not do otherwise for not only the general rules contained in the Codes but some of the illustrations given to clarify the general rules were based on English decisions.[72] In the context of the Criminal Procedure Code of Malaysia the Privy Council said: "It is quite clear that the law of Malaysia has to be taken from the Code and not from cases on the common law. But when, as here, the Code is embodying common law principles, decisions of the courts of England and other Commonwealth countries in which the common law has been expounded can be helpful in the understanding and application of the

---

[Footnote No. 68 Contd.]

AIR 1962 SC 779, pp. 785, 786 : 1962 Supp (1) SCR 876; *Madanlal Fakirchand Dudhediya v. S. Changdeo Sugar Mills Ltd.*, AIR 1962 SC 1543, p. 1549 (para 15) : 1962 Supp (3) SCR 973; *CIT, Madras v. Gajapathy Naidu*, AIR 1964 SC 1653, pp. 1655 (para 6), 1656, 1657 (para 9) : (1964) 7 SCR 767; *Sterling General Insurance Co. Ltd. v. Planters Airways Pvt. Ltd.*, AIR 1975 SC 415 : (1975) 1 SCC 603; *American Home Products Corporation v. Mac Laboratories Pvt. Ltd.*, (1986) 1 SCC 465, pp. 505, 506 : AIR 1986 SC 137; *Kilpest Pvt. Ltd. v. Shekhar Mehra*, 1996 (7) Scale 444, p. 447: 1996 (9) JT 152 : (1996) 10 SCC 696.

69. *Bangalore Water Supply and Sewerage Board v. A. Rajappa*, AIR 1978 SC 548, p. 559 : 1978 (2) SCC 213.

70. *General Electric Co. v. Renusagar Power Co.*, (1987) 4 SCC 137, p. 150 : 1987 (3) JT 277 : (1987) 4 SCC 137.

71. *Raghunath Prasad Sahu v. Sarjuprasad Sahu*, AIR 1924 PC 60, pp. 61, 62; *Ramanandi Kuer (Mt.) v. Kalawati Kuer (Mt.)*, AIR 1928 PC 2, p. 4 : 55 IA 18; *Hansraj v. Bejoy Lal Seal*, AIR 1930 PC 59, pp. 59, 60; *Lasa Din v. Gulab Kunwar (Mt.)*, AIR 1932 PC 207, p. 211; *Thiagaraja Bhagavather v. Emperor*, AIR 1947 PC 113, p. 116; *G-G-in-Council v. Municipal Council, Madura*, AIR 1949 PC 39, p. 43 (para 13). **See further** *Gajanan v. Seth Brindaban*, AIR 1970 SC 2007, p. 2012 : 1970 (2) SCC 360.

72. M.C. SETALVAD: "The Common Law in India", p. 61.

Code."[73] The suggested limited application of foreign decisions is undoubtedly useful in understanding an Indian statute which embodies a common law principle.

With the enforcement of the Government of India Act, 1935, decisions rendered in interpreting Australian and Canadian Constitutions began to be listened with respect but caution was again administered in applying them without proper qualifications.[74]

The same attitude of respect with caution has been followed by the Supreme Court after advent of the Constitution[75] which because of incorporation of fundamental rights, has given more access to American precedents. It cannot be denied that our courts have gained considerable assistance from foreign decisions in interpreting certain provisions of our Constitution.[76]

---

73. *Shaaban Bin Hussein v. Chang Fook Kam*, (1969) 3 All ER 1626, p. 1632 (PC). (This case deals with section 23 of the Code of Criminal Procedure of Malayasia which empowers any police officer to arrest any person against whom there exists a reasonable suspicion of his having been concerned in any seizable offence. The section corresponds to section 54 of the Indian Criminal Procedure Code and is helpful in interpreting the expression "reasonable suspicion"). **See further** *Luc Thiet Thuan v. R.*, (1996) 2 All ER 1033 : (1997) AC 131 : (1996) 3 WLR 45 (PC) (In this case for interpreting section 3 of the Hongkong Homicide Act, 1957, which provides for a defence of 'provocation' to a charge of murder, apart from English cases, cases of other commonwealth countries were also referred).

74. *In re, C.P. & Berar Sales of Motor Spirit & Lubricants Taxation Act*, AIR 1939 FC 1, p. 5 : 1939 FCR 18.

75. *A.K. Gopalan v. State of Madras*, AIR 1950 SC 27, p. 102 : 1950 SCR 88; *Charanjit Lal Chowdhury v. Union of India*, AIR 1951 SC 41, pp. 44, 57, 58 : 1950 SCR 869; *M.P.V. Sundararamier & Co. v. State of Andhra Pradesh*, AIR 1958 SC 468, p. 495 (para 58) : 1958 SCR 1422; *Atiabari Tea Co. Ltd. v. State of Assam*, AIR 1961 SC 232, p. 250 : 1961 (1) SCR 809; *Automobile Transport, Rajasthan Ltd. v. State of Rajasthan*, AIR 1962 SC 1406, p. 1415 : 1963 (1) SCR 491; *Tika Ramji v. State of U.P.*, AIR 1956 SC 676, pp. 698, 699 : 1956 SCR 393; *State of West Bengal v. Union of India*, AIR 1963 SC 1241, pp. 1258, 1259 : (1964) 1 SCR 371; *State Trading Corporation of India v. Commercial Tax Officer*, AIR 1963 SC 1811, p. 1820 : (1964) 4 SCR 99; *In the matter of Article 143 of the Constitution of India, Special Reference No. 1 of 1964*, AIR 1965 SC 745 : (1965) 1 SCR 413.

76. For example, **see** cases in note 88 above. For an example of the use of decisions of the American Supreme Court **see** *Union of India v. The Motion Pictures Associates*, JT 1999 (4) SC 520 : AIR 1999 SC 2334 : (1996) 6 SCC 150, where following *Neat R. Wooby v. George Maynard*, (1977) 430 US 705 and *Turner Broadcasting System Inc. v. Federal Communications*, (1997) 512 US 622, it was held that a statutory provision compelling speech as a 'must carry provision' is not violative of freedom of speech guaranteed under Article 19(1) if it furthers informed decision making which is the essence to the right to free speech and expression.

When an Indian Act is modelled on a prior English Act, decisions construing the provisions of the English Act are referred to as helpful guide for construing corresponding provisions of the Indian Act.[77] For example, the court referred to *M'Naghten's case*[78] for interpreting and applying the defence of insanity in section 84 of the Penal Code which is modelled on the English law.[79]

Apart from the link of English Common Law and Jurisprudence and similarity of political thought, the use of English language as authoritative text of Indian statutes[80] is another factor which obliges the Indian courts in taking recourse to foreign precedents of English speaking countries. Just to take an example, even in construing a common place word 'Vegetable' in a taxing statute, reference was made to a Canadian decision interpreting that word in a similar statute.[81]

How different conditions prevailing in India may give rise to non-acceptance by Indian courts of an interpretation given by English courts of same or similar words can be illustrated by the case of *M.V. Elisabeth v. Harwan Investment & Trading Pvt. Ltd.*[82] In this case the Supreme Court differing from English decisions interpreted the words 'damage caused by a ship' in section 443 of the Merchant Shipping Act, 1958 as not limited to physical damage done by a ship by reason of its coming into contact with something and to include damage to cargo carried in a ship. The important consideration for giving to the words a wide interpretation is that there is no other Act in India covering claims for damage to cargo carried in a ship but in England this subject is covered expressly by a different Act. Moreover, in certain areas the Supreme Court of India may strive to be more progressive. For example, a statutory tenant (a tenant whose tenancy has

---

77. *Assistant Collector of Customs, Calcutta v. Sitaram Agarwala*, AIR 1966 SC 955, p. 965 : 1966 (2) SCR 1; *Godhara Borough Municipality v. Godhara Electricity Co. Ltd.*, AIR 1968 SC 1504, p. 1508 : 1968 (3) SCR 481; *Nawn Estates (P.) Ltd. v. CIT, West Bengal*, AIR 1977 SC 153, p. 156 : 1977 SCC (Tax) 119 : (1977) 1 SCC 7. Nearly the same view has been taken in Australia: *Owners of the Motor Vessel 'IRAN AMANAT' v. KMP Coastal Oil PTE Ltd.*, (1999) 73 ALJR 559, p. 563 (para 20) (Aust).

78. (1843) 8 ER 718 : (1843-60) All ER Rep. 229 (HL).

79. *B Sudhakaran v. State of Kerala*, (2010) 10 SCC 582 para 32 : AIR 2011 SC 265.

80. **See** Article 348, Constitution of India. **See further** *Nityanand Sharma v. State of Bihar*, 1996 (1) Scale 743, p. 749 : AIR 1996 SC 2306, p. 2311 : (1996) 3 SCC 576; *Park Leather Industry (P.) Ltd. v. State of U.P.*, JT 2001 (2) SC 577, p. 588 (Hindi text can be used to explain an ambiguity in the authorised English text).

81. **See** *Ramavatar Budhaiprasad v. Assistant Sales Tax Officer, Akola*, AIR 1961 SC 1325, p. 1326 : (1962) 1 SCR 279, where reference is made to *Planters Nut Chocolate Co. Ltd. v. King*, (1952) 1 Dom LR 385, p. 389.

82. AIR 1993 SC 1014, p. 1038 : 1992 (2) JT 65 : 1993 Supp (2) SCC 433.

determined and who continues in possession because of statutory protection in Rent Acts) is not recognised under English law to hold a heritable interest unless it is conferred by statute but in India such a tenant has been recognised to hold a heritable interest unless there be a contrary provision in the statute.[83] As observed by BHAGWATI, J., the contrary view (English law) proceeds because of reluctance to reconcile "to the idea that the law is moving forward from contract to status."[84] Another example of the same nature is that the English common law rule, that the crown is not bound by statute unless named specifically or by necessary implication, is not applicable in India. The rule applied in India is that the State is bound by statute unless excluded specifically or by necessary implication.[85]

Further, in cases concerning an international convention "it is obviously desirable that decisions in different jurisdictions should, so far possible, be kept in line with each other". Therefore, in such cases foreign decisions are more readily used for guiding the court.[86]

---

83. *Gian Devi Anand v. Jeevan Kumar,* (1985) 2 SCC 683 : AIR 1985 SC 796; *Gantusa H. Baddi v. Meerabai G. Pai,* AIR 2000 SC 1724, p. 1728 : (2000) 4 SCC 586.

84. *Gian Devi Anand v. Jeevan Kumar, supra,* p. 687 (SCC). For a discussion as to how the law first moved from status to contract and has now again been moving from contract to status **see** FREIDMAN, *Legal Theory,* (5th ed.) pp. 215-220.

85. **See** Chapter 8.

86. *T. v. Secretary of State for the Home Department*, (1996) 2 All ER 865, p. 891 : (1996) AC 742 : (1996) 2 WLR 766 (HL). **See further** Chapter 6, title 5 (b2) 'Acts passed to give effect to international conventions'.

CHAPTER 5

SUBSIDIARY RULES

SYNOPSIS

1. SAME WORD SAME MEANING

When the Legislature uses same word in different parts of the same section or statute, there is a presumption that the word is used in the same sense throughout.[1] The presumption is, however, a weak one and is readily displaced by the context.[2] It has been said that the more correct statement of the rule is that "where the draftsman uses the same word or phrase in similar contexts, he must be presumed to intend it in each place to bear the same meaning."[3]

In construing the word 'statement' in section 157 of the Indian Evidence Act, 1872, the Supreme Court referred to the use of the same word in sections 17 to 21, 32, 39 and 145, and came to the conclusion that the word in all these sections meant 'something that is stated' and communication was not necessary in order that it may be a statement; and the same meaning was attributed to the word as occurring in section 157 of the Act. It was, therefore, held that notes prepared by a prosecution witness recording the conversation that took place between him and other witnesses, was a statement which could be used for corroboration under section 157.

---

1. *Bhogilal Chunnilal Pandya v. State of Bombay*, AIR 1959 SC 356, p. 357 : 1959 Supp (1) SCR 310; *K.N. Guruswamy v. State of Mysore*, AIR 1954 SC 592 : (1955) 1 SCR 305; *Raghubans Narain Singh v. Uttar Pradesh Government*, AIR 1967 SC 465, p. 469 : 1967 (1) SCR 423; *Mohd. Shafi v. VII Additional District and Sessions Judge, Allahabad*, AIR 1977 SC 836, p. 840 : 1977 (2) SCR 464 : (1977) 2 SCC 226; *Suresh Chand v. Gulam Chisti*, AIR 1990 SC 897, p. 907 : 1990 (1) SCC 593.
2. *Shamrao Vishnu Parulekar v. District Magistrate, Thana*, AIR 1957 SC 23, pp. 26, 27 : 1956 SCR 644; *Aswini Kumar Ghose v. Arabinda Bose*, AIR 1952 SC 369, p. 392 : 1953 SCR 1; *Payne (Inspector of Taxes) v. Barratt Developments (Luton) Ltd.*, (1985) 1 All ER 257, p. 260 (HL); *CIT v. Venkateshwara Hatcheries (P.) Ltd.*, JT 1999 (2) SC 338, pp. 345, 346 : AIR 1999 SC 1225, p. 1231 : (2001) 10 SCC 569.
3. *Farrell v. Alexander*, (1976) 2 All ER 721, p. 736 (HL); *Central Bank of India v. Ravindra,* AIR 2001 SC 3095, p. 3114 : (2002) 1 SCC 367 (7th Edition of this book p. 263 is referred); *Chairman Indore Vikas Pradhikaran v. Pure Industrial Coke and Chemicals Ltd.*, (2007) 8 SCC 705 para 70 : AIR 2007 SC 2458 (10th edition of this book is referred).

Observed WANCHOO, J.: "Words are generally used in the same sense throughout in a statute, unless there is something repugnant in the context."[4]

Another illustration of this principle is found in the interpretation of the word 'sum' in section 31(7) of the Arbitration and Conciliation Act, 1996. Section 31(7)(a) provides that where an award is made for the payment of money, the Arbitral Tribunal may include, in the 'sum' for which the award is made, interest from the date of cause of action to the date of the award. A three Judge Bench of the Supreme Court, by majority, held that the word 'sum' used in this provision has not been qualified by using the word 'principal' before it, and hence may include 'principal' and 'interest' or one of the two, and once the meaning of the word 'sum'is clear, the same meaning must be ascribed to the word in section 31(7)(b) of the Act, which provides that a 'sum' directed to be paid by an award shall, unless the award otherwise directs, carry interest at the rate of 18% per annum from the date of award to the date of payment. Therefore, it was held that the 'sum' directed to be paid by the award under section 31(7)(b) is inclusive of interest pendente lite, and that the Tribunal may direct interest to be paid on such 'sum' for the post-award period.[5]

In interpreting the words 'the grounds on which the order has been made' as they occur in section 3(3) and section 7(1) of the Preventive Detention Act, 1950, the Supreme Court held that the words do not bear the same meaning in these two provisions for communicating to the detenu, the grounds of detention under section 7(1), the authority can withhold facts which it considers against the public interest to disclose, [*vide* section 7(2)]; whereas in reporting to the State Government the grounds of detention under section 3(3), these facts are likely to figure more prominently. VENKATARAMA AYYAR, J., referring to the rule that the same meaning is implied by the use of the same expression in every part of an Act, stated: "The rule of construction contended for is well-settled but that is only one element in deciding what the true import of enactment is to ascertain which it is necessary to have regard to the purpose behind the particular provision and its setting in the scheme of the statute".[6]

As pointed out by LORD MACDERMOTT: "The presumption that the same word is used in the same sense throughout the same enactment acknowledges the virtues of an orderly and consistent use of language, but it must

4. *Bhogilal Chunnilal v. State of Bombay, supra*, p. 357.
5. *Hyder Consulting (UK) Limited v. Governor, State of Orissa*, (2015) 2 SCC 189, pp. 200 to 202.
6. *Shamrao Vishnu Parulekar v. District Magistrate, Thana*, AIR 1957 SC 23, pp. 26, 27 : 1956 SCR 644.

yield to the requirements of the context and it is, perhaps, at its weakest when the word in question is of the kind that readily draws its precise import, its range of meaning, from its immediate setting or the nature of the subject with regard to which it is employed."[7] And in dealing with the meaning of the word 'publish' in the Copyright Act, 1957, LORD SCARMAN observed: "When construing words and phrases in an Act dealing with a subject as complex and varied as Copyright, it is perilous in the absence of clear indication in the Act to assume that in respect of every element or aspect of the subject ordinary English words of many applications, are used consistently to express only one particular application."[8]

For instance, section 34(2)(b)(ii) of the Arbitration and Conciliation Act, 1996, provides that an arbitral award may be set aside if it is in conflict with the 'public policy of India', and section 48(2)(b) of the Act also provides that enforcement of a foreign award may be refused if it is contrary to the 'public policy of India'. Overruling an earlier decision of a two Judge Bench in *Phulchand Exports,*[9] a three Judge Bench of the Supreme Court held that the wider meaning given to the expression 'public policy of India' occurring in section 34(2)(b)(ii) in the decision of *Saw Pipes*,[10] is not applicable where an objection is raised to the enforcement of a foreign award under section 48(2)(b). The expression 'public policy of India' was therefore given a narrower meaning for the purposes of section 48(2)(b), consistent with the narrow interpretation given to the expression 'public policy' in section 7(1)(b)(ii) of the Foreign Awards Act, 1961.[11]

Even when the same word is used at different places in the same clause of the same section it may not bear the same meaning at each place having regard to the context of its use.[12] Section 117(1) of the Uttar Pradesh Zamindari Abolition and Land Reforms Act, 1950, authorises the State Government to declare that *hats*, *bazars* and *melas* which had vested in the State shall vest in the *Gaon Sabhas*. Interpreting this section, it was held

---

7. *Madras Electric Supply Corporation Ltd. v. Boarland, (Inspector of Taxes)*, (1955) 1 All ER 753, pp. 759, 760 (HL).

8. *Infabrics Ltd. v. Jaytex Ltd.*, (1981) 1 All ER 1067, p. 1066 : (1982) AC 1 : (1982) 1 WLR 646 (HL).

9. *Phulchand Exports Ltd. v. O.O.O. Patriot*, (2011) 10 SCC 300.

10. *Oil and Natural Gas Corporation Ltd. v. Saw Pipes Ltd.*, (2003) 5 SCC 705.

11. *Shri Lal Mahal Ltd. v. Progetto Grano SpA*, (2014) 2 SCC 433, pp. 448, 449.

12. *Ramnarayan Mor v. State of Maharashtra*, AIR 1964 SC 949, p. 953 : (1964) 5 SCR 1064. **See further** *Anand Nivas (P.) Ltd. v. Anandji Kalyanji's Pedhi*, AIR 1965 SC 414, p. 428 : (1964) 4 SCR 892. (Word 'tenant' in different sections and different clauses construed differently.) *Samatha v. State of Andhra Pradesh*, AIR 1997 SC 3297 : 1997 (8) SCC 191. (The word 'person' in clause (a) of Regulation 3(1) of the Andhra Pradesh Scheduled Area Land Transfer Regulation, 1959 was construed to include 'State' whereas the same word in, clauses (b) and (e) did not obviously include 'State'.)

by the Supreme Court that although the vesting in the State was absolute, the vesting in the *Sabha* was limited to possession and management subject to divestiture by Government.[13] The case illustrates that a word which is used more than once in the same sub-section of a section may connote and denote divergent things depending upon the context.

2. USE OF DIFFERENT WORDS

When in relation to the same subject-matter, different words are used in the same statute, there is a presumption that they are not used in the same sense.[14]

In construing the words 'distinct matters' occurring in section 5 of the Stamp Act, 1899, and in concluding that these words have not the same meaning as the words 'two or more of the descriptions in Schedule I' occurring in section 6, VENKATARAMA AIYAR, J., observed: "When two words of different import are used in a statute in two consecutive provisions, it would be difficult to maintain that they are used in the same sense."[15] Similarly, while construing the word 'gain' under section 3(ff) of the Bombay Municipal Corporation Act, 1888, which uses the words 'profit or gain', the Supreme Court relied on the dictionary meanings of the words to hold that the word 'gain' is not synonymous with the word 'profit' as it is not restricted to

---

13. *Maharaj Singh v. State of U.P.*, AIR 1976 SC 2602, p. 2608 : 1977 (1) SCC 155. The word 'vest' even when used once in a section may mean merely vesting of management in the context of one property and vesting of ownership in the context of another property; *M. Ismail (Dr.) v. Union of India*, JT 1994(6) SC 632, p. 673 : AIR 1995 SC 605, p. 636.

14. *Brighton Parish Guardians v. Strand Union Guardians*, (1891) 2 QB 156, p. 167 (CA); *Member, Board of Revenue v. Arthur Paul Benthall*, AIR 1956 SC 35, p. 38 : 1955 (2) SCR 842; *CIT v. East West Import & Export (P.) Ltd., Jaipur*, AIR 1989 SC 836, p. 838 : (1989) 1 SCC 760; *B.R. Enterprises v. State of U.P.*, AIR 1999 SC 1867, p. 1902 : (1999) 9 SCC 700 ('trade and business' in Article 298 have different meaning from 'trade and commerce' in Article 301); *Shri Ishal Alloy Steels Ltd. v. Jayaswalas Neco Ltd.*, JT 2001 (3) SC 114, p. 119 : (2001) 3 SCC 609 : AIR 2001 SC 1161 (The words 'a bank' and 'the bank' in section 138 N.I. Act, 1881 do not have the same meaning); *The Oriental Insurance Co. Ltd. v. Hansrajbhai v. Kodala,* AIR 2001 SC 1832, p. 1842 : (2001) 5 SCC 175; *Kailash Nath Agarwal v. Pradeshiya Indust and Inv. Corp. of U.P.*, 2003 AIR SCW 1358, p. 1365 : (2003) 4 SCC 305, p. 313. (The words 'proceeding' and 'suit' used in the same section construed differently); But in *Paramjeet Singh Pathak v. ICDS Ltd.*, (2006) 13 SCC 322 : AIR 2007 SC 168 different view was taken therefore in *Zenith Steel Tubes v. Sicom Ltd.*, (2008) 1 SCC 533 : AIR 2008 SC 451 case referred to a larger Bench; *D.L.F. Qutab Enclave Complex Educational Charitable Trust v. State of Haryana,* 2003 AIR SCW 1046, p. 1057 : AIR 2003 SC 1648 : (2003) 5 SCC 622 (The expressions 'at his own cost' and 'at its cost', used in one section given different meanings).

15. *Member, Board of Revenue v. Arthur Paul Benthall*, AIR 1956 SC 35, p. 38 : 1955 (2) SCR 842.

pecuniary or commercial profits, and that any advantage or benefit acquired or value addition made by some activities would amount to 'gain'.[16]

A further example of the application of the rule may be seen in an another decision of the Supreme Court where the phrase 'rendered illegal' occurring in section 42 of the Central Provinces and Berar Industrial Disputes and Settlement Act, 1947 was construed to bear a different meaning from the phrase 'held illegal' used in sections 43, 44 and 45 of the same statute.[17] On the same principle the words 'test' and 'analysis' used in Rule 40 of the Central Rules made under the Drugs Act, 1940, were given different meanings and the requirement of stating 'full protocol of the tests applied' was held to be not applicable to 'analysis'.[18] Similarly the expressions 'at the end of the previous year' and 'in the course of such previous year' occurring in the *Explanation* to section 23A of the Income-tax Act, 1922 were construed differently; the former expression meaning the last day of the previous year and the latter expression meaning throughout the previous year.[19]

But much weight to the presumption arising out of use of different words in different parts of a statute cannot be given when dealing with a long complicated statute,[20] for instance, a consolidating Act containing incongruous provisions lumped together.[21] Even otherwise, the rule is subordinate to context as a less careful draftsman may use different words to convey the same meaning.[22] A construction deriving support from differing phraseology in different sections of a statute may be negatived on considerations that it will lead to unreasonable or irrational results.[23]

For instance, the Supreme Court has held that the words 'of', 'from' and 'after', may, in a given case, mean really the same thing, and accordingly, the word 'of' occurring in sections 138(c) and 142(b) of the Negotiable Instruments Act, 1881, is not to be interpreted differently as against the word 'from' occurring in section 138(a) of the Act. Therefore, for the

---

16. *Brihanmumbai Mahanagarpalika & Anr. v. Willingdon Sports Club & Ors.*, (2013) 16 SCC 260, p. 275.

17. *Labour Commissioner, M.P. v. Burhanpur Tapti Mills Ltd.*, AIR 1964 SC 1687, pp. 1688, 1689 : 1964 (7) SCR 484.

18. *T.A. Krishnaswamy v. State of Madras*, AIR 1966 SC 1022 : 1966 (3) SCR 31.

19. *CIT, v. East West Import & Export (P.) Ltd., Jaipur*, AIR 1989 SC 836, p. 838 : 1989 (1) SCC 760.

20. *Qualter Hall & Co. v. Board of Trade*, (1961) 1 All ER 210, p. 215.

21. *IRC v. Hinchy*, (1960) 1 All ER 505, p. 511 : 1960 AC 748 (HL).

22. *Ramdas Vithaldas Durbar v. Amerchand & Co.*, (1916) ILR 40 Bom 630, p. 638 (PC); *Kanhayalal Vishindas Gidwani v. Arun Dattatraya Mehta*, AIR 2000 SC 3681, p. 3687 : (2001) 1 SCC 78.

23. *Cramas Properties Ltd. v. Connaught Fur Trimmings Ltd.*, (1965) 2 All ER 382, pp. 385, 387 (HL).

purposes of section 142(b) of the Act, which prescribes that the complaint is to be filed within 30 days 'of' the date on which the cause of action arises, the starting day on which the cause of action arises is also to be included while computing the period of 30 days.[24]

3. RULE OF LAST ANTECEDENT

As a corollary to the rule that phrases and sentences in a statute are interpreted according to the grammatical meaning,[25] relative and qualifying words, phrases and clauses are applied to the antecedent immediately preceding.[26] The rule is, however, subordinate to context and may be better stated by saying that a qualifying phrase ought to be referred to the next antecedent which will make sense with the context and to which the context appears properly to relate it.[27]

The rule was applied in construction of section 1 of the Indian Contract Act, 1872, which reads: 'Nothing herein contained shall affect the provisions of any statute, Act or Regulation, not hereby expressly repealed, nor any usage or custom of trade, nor any incident of any contract not inconsistent with the provisions of this Act'. Interpreting this section, LORD MACNAGHTEN observed: "The words 'not inconsistent with the provisions of this Act' are not to be connected with the clause 'nor any usage or custom of trade'. Both, the reason of the thing and grammatical construction of the sentence, if such a sentence is to be tried by any rules of grammar, seem to require that the application of those words should be confined to the subject which immediately precedes them."[28]

In a case relating to the interpretation of the proviso to section 1, subsection (2) of the Calcutta Thika (Amendment) Act, 1953, which reads, 'provided that the provisions of the Calcutta Thika Tenancy Act, 1949, as amended by this Act, shall subject to the provisions of section 9, also apply and be deemed to have been always applied to all suits, appeals and

---

24. *Econ Antri Ltd. v. Rom Industries Ltd. & Anr.*, (2014) 11 SCC 769, p. 789.

25. **See** Chapter 2, title 2(a) 'Natural and Grammatical Meaning', text.

26. *Mahadeolal Kanodia v. Administrator General of W.B.*, AIR 1960 SC 936, p. 939 : 1960 (3) SCR 590; *Aswini Kumar Ghose v. Arabinda Bose*, AIR 1952 SC 369, p. 376 : 1953 SCR 1; *G.G. in Council v. Shiromani Sugar Mills Ltd.*, AIR 1946 FC 16, p. 23 : (1946) 19 ITR 248; *Irrawaddy Flotilla Company v. Bugwandas*, (1891) ILR 18 Cal 620, p. 627 : 18 IA 121 (PC).

27. *Eastern Counties and London and Blackwall Railway Companies v. Marriage*, 31 LJ Ex 73 (HL), p. 88 (LORD WENSLEYDALE), p. 90 (LORD CHELMSFORD); *Regional Provident Fund Commr., Bombay v. Shree Krishna Metal Manufacturing Co., Bhandara*, AIR 1962 SC 1536, pp. 1540, 1541 : 1962 Supp (3) SCR 815.

28. *Irrawaddy Flotilla Company v. Bhagwandas, supra*, p. 627.

proceedings pending', the argument was that the words 'as amended by this Act' qualify the word 'provisions'. Countering the argument, DAS GUPTA, J. stated: "We are unable to see how it is possible, unless rules of grammar are totally disregarded to read the words 'as amended by this Act' to qualify the word 'provisions'. If ordinary grammatical rules are applied, there is no escape from the conclusion that the adjectival phrase 'as amended by this Act' qualifies the proximate substantive, *viz.*, the Calcutta Thika Tenancy Act, 1949."[29]

In another case where the question for construction involved was of section 2 of the Supreme Court Advocates (Practice in High Courts) Act 1951, which reads 'notwithstanding anything contained in the Indian Bar Councils Act, 1926, or in any other law regulating the conditions subject to which a person not entered in the roll of Advocates of a High Court may be permitted to practise in that High Court, every Advocate of the Supreme Court shall be entitled as of right to practice in any High Court whether or not he is an advocate of that High Court', PATANJALI SHASTRI, C.J. said: "Having regard to the words 'anything contained' and the preposition 'in' used after disjunctive 'or', the qualifying clause cannot reach back to the words 'Bar Council Act'." It was held that the adjectival clause 'regulating the conditions etc.', qualified the word 'law' and not the words 'Bar Council Act'.[30]

And, while construing the definition of 'premises' in the Bombay Land Requisition Act, 1948, which reads 'any building or part of a building let or intended to be let separately', it was held that the words 'let or intended to be let separately' did not qualify the word 'building' but only the words 'part of a building'.[31]

The principle was also applied by the Federal Court in interpreting section 226(1) of the Government of India Act, 1935, which reads: 'Until otherwise provided by Act of the appropriate Legislature, no High Court shall have any original jurisdiction in any matter concerning the revenue, or concerning any act ordered or done in the collection thereof according to the usage and practice of the country or the law for the time being in force'. It was held that the words 'according to usage and practice of the country or the law for the time being in force' qualified the words immediately preceding, *viz.* 'concerning any act ordered or done in the collection

29. *Mahadeolal Kanodia v. Administrator General of W.B.*, AIR 1960 SC 936, p. 939 : 1960 (3) SCR 578.

30. *Aswini Kumar Ghose v. Arbinda Bose*, AIR 1952 SC 369, p. 376 : 1953 SCR 1.

31. *Mongibai Hariram v. State of Maharashtra*, AIR 1966 SC 882 : 1966 (2) SCR 322.

thereof', and not the words 'original jurisdiction in any matter concerning the revenue'.[32]

In construing Item 72(3) of Schedule I to the Indian Tariff Act, 1934 which reads: 'Component parts of machinery as defined in Items No. 72, 72(1) and 72(2) and not otherwise specified' it was held that the qualifying words 'not otherwise specified' related to 'machinery' and not to 'component parts'.[33]

The jurisdiction of the Special Court in the Special Court (Trial of Offences relating to Transactions in Securities) Act, 1992 is limited to offences referred to in section 3(2) of the Act which in so far as relevant provides: 'Any offence relating to transactions in securities after 1st day of April 1991 and on and before 6th June 1992'. In interpreting section 3(2) it was held that the period specified qualified the word 'transactions' and not the word 'offence' and therefore the Special Court had jurisdiction if the transaction in securities took place within the specified period irrespective of the date of the offence.[34]

But as already stated, the rule is subordinate to context. This principle may be illustrated by a decision of the Supreme Court relating to the construction of section 1(3)(a) of the Employees' Provident Funds Act, 1952 which reads: 'Subject to the provisions contained in section 16, it (the Act) applies to every establishment which is a factory engaged in any industry specified in Schedule I and in which fifty[35] or more persons are employed'. The contention before the court was that the requirement that the workmen employed should be fifty or more governed the word 'industry' and not the word 'factory'; and in support of this it was urged that the pronoun 'which', must under the ordinary rules of grammar qualify the noun immediately preceding it and that took it to the word 'industry' rather than to the word 'factory'. This contention was rejected on the basis of the context; and it was held that the requirement as to the prescribed number qualified the word 'factory' and not the word 'industry'. In overruling the contention GAJENDRAGADKAR, J., observed: "If the context definitely suggests that the relevant rule of grammar is inapplicable then the requirement of the context must prevail over the rule of grammar."[36]

---

32. *G.G. in Council v. Shiromani Sugar Mills Ltd.*, AIR 1946 FC 16, p. 23 : (1946) 14 ITR 248.
33. *Siemens Engineering and Manufacturing Co. v. Union of India*, AIR 1976 SC 1785 : 1976 (2) SCC 981.
34. *Hiten P. Dalal v. Bratindranath Banerjee,* AIR 2001 SC 3897, pp. 3899, 3900 : (2001) 6 SCC 16.
35. "Fifty" substituted by "twenty" by Act 46 of 1960 (w.e.f. 31-12-1960).
36. *Regional Provident Fund Commr., Bombay v. Shree Krishna Metal Manufacturing Co., Bhandara,* AIR 1962 SC 1536, p. 1540 : 1962 Supp (3) SCR 815.

Reference may also be made to section 2(1)(d) of the Bombay Lotteries and Prize Competitions Control and Tax Act, 1948, which reads: 'prize competition includes: (1) Crossword Prize Competition, (2) Missing Word Prize Competition, (3) Picture Prize Competition, (4) Number Prize Competition, or (5) any other prize competition, for which solution is or is not prepared beforehand by the promoters or for which the solution is determined by lot or chance'. The qualifying clause in the 5th item beginning with 'for which the solution' was construed by the Supreme Court to apply to all the five items and it was observed: "There is grammatically no difficulty in reading the qualifying clause as lending colour to each of those items."[37]

Further, in interpreting Article 194(1) of the Constitution, which reads 'subject to the provisions of this Constitution and to the rules and standing orders regulating the procedure of the Legislature, there shall be freedom of speech in the Legislature of every State', the Supreme Court has held that the adjectival clause 'regulating the procedure of the Legislature' governs both the preceding clauses *viz*., 'the provisions of this Constitution' and 'the rules and standing orders'.[38]

Some more examples may here be noticed. In construing the words 'no tax shall be levied on any advertisement which is exhibited within any railway station or upon any wall or other property of railway except any portion of the surface of such wall or property fronting any street', the Supreme Court held that the words 'fronting any street', qualified the noun 'advertisement' and not the words 'wall or property'.[39] It is submitted that on a proper construction the words in question qualified the word 'surface' and not 'advertisement'. Section 4(2) of the East Punjab Rent Restriction Act, 1949 requires the Controller to fix basic rent of an accommodation after taking into consideration the 'prevailing rates of rent in the locality for the same or similar accommodation in similar circumstances during the twelve months prior to 1st January 1939'. In construing this section, it was held that the phrase 'in similar circumstances', qualified and governed both the expressions namely 'the same' and 'similar accommodation'.[40]

Section 259 of the Cantonments Act, 1924, prior to its amendment, read: 'Arrears of any tax, rent on land and buildings and any other money recoverable by a Board or a Military Estates Officer under this Act or the rules made thereunder may be recovered on application to a Magistrate

37. *State of Bombay v. R.M.D. Chamarbaugwala*, AIR 1957 SC 699, p. 708 : 1957 SCR 874.

38. *In the matter of: Under Article 143 of the Constitution of India*, AIR 1965 SC 745, p. 760 : 1965 (1) SCR 413 (GAJENDRAGADKAR, C.J.).

39. *Links Advertisers and Business Promoters v. Commr., Corporation of the City of Bangalore*, AIR 1977 SC 1646 : 1977 SCC (Tax) 431 : (1977) 3 SCC 204.

40. *Miran Devi v. Birbal Dass*, AIR 1977 SC 2191 : 1977 (3) SCC 496.

having jurisdiction in the Cantonment'. The qualifying words 'recoverable by a Board or a Military Estates Officer under this Act or the rules made thereunder' were construed to qualify not only the words 'any other money' but also the words 'arrears of any tax, rent on land and buildings.' As a result it was held that rent of land payable under a lease was not recoverable under the special procedure prescribed by section 259.[41]

Also, "where several words are followed by a general expression which is as much applicable to the first and other words as to the last, that expression is not limited to the last word, but applies to all. For instance, in 'horses, oxen, pigs and sheep, from whatever country they may come'— the later words would apply to horses as much as to sheep."[42]

4. *NON OBSTANTE* CLAUSE

A clause beginning with 'notwithstanding anything contained in this Act or in some particular provision in the Act or in some particular Act or in any law for the time being in force', is sometimes appended to a section in the beginning, with a view to give the enacting part of the section in case of conflict an overriding effect over the provision or Act mentioned in the *non obstante* clause.[43] It is equivalent to saying that in spite of the provision or Act mentioned in the *non obstante* clause, the enactment following it will have its full operation or that the provisions embraced in the *non obstante* clause will not be an impediment for the operation of the enactment.[44] Thus a *non obstante* clause may be used as a legislative device to modify the ambit of the provision or law mentioned in the *non obstante*

---

41. *Cantonment Board, Ambala v. Pyare Lal*, AIR 1966 SC 108 : (1965) 3 SCR 341, For further illustration, **see** *Board of Revenue, U.P. v. Rai Saheb Sidhnath Mehrotra*, AIR 1965 SC 1092 : 1965 (2) SCR 269. (Construction of *Explanation* 1 to section 24 of the Stamp Act, 1899. In the phrase 'sale of property subject to mortgage', the words 'subject to mortgage' were construed as qualifying 'sale' and not 'property'.)

42. *Great Western Rly. Co. v. Swindon and Cheltenham Extension Rly. Co.*, (1884) 9 AC 787, p. 808 (HL) (LORD BRAMVELL).

43. *Union of India v. G.M. Kokil*, 1984 (Supp) SCC 196 : AIR 1984 SC 1022; *Chandavarkar Sita Ratna Rao v. Ashalata S. Guram*, (1986) 4 SCC 447, pp. 477, 478 : AIR 1987 SC 117; *Narcotics Control Bureau v. Kishan Lal*, AIR 1991 SC 558, p. 561 : (1991) 1 SCC 705; *Orient Paper and Industries Ltd. v. State of Orissa*, AIR 1991 SC 672, p. 678 : 1991 Supp (1) SCC 81.

44. *South India Corporation (P) Ltd. v. Secy., Board of Revenue, Trivandrum*, AIR 1964 SC 207, p. 215; *Chandavarkar Sita Ratna Rao v. Ashalata S. Guram*, *supra*; *M. Venugopal v. Divisional Manager, Life Insurance Corporation*, JT 1994 (1) SC 281, p. 289 : AIR 1994 SC 1343, p. 1348; *P.E.K. Kalliani Amma (Smt.) v. K. Devi*, 1996 (4) Scale 131, p. 149 : AIR 1996 SC 1963, pp. 1975, 1976 : (1996) 4 SCC 76 (This book is referred); *Moreshwar Balkrishna Pandare v. Vithal Vyanku Chavan*, AIR 2001 SC 2211, p. 2213 (Para 7) : (2001) 5 SCC 551; *Iridium India Telecom Ltd. v. Motorola Inc*, (2005) 2 SCC 145, pp. 158, 159.

clause[45] or to override it in specified circumstances.[46] The phrase 'notwithstanding anything in' is used in contradistinction to the phrase 'subject to',[47] the latter conveying the idea of a provision yielding place to another provision or other provisions to which it is made subject.[48] A *non obstante* clause must also be distinguished from the phrase 'without prejudice'. A provision enacted 'without prejudice' to another provision has not the effect of affecting the operation of the other provision and any action taken under it must not be inconsistent with such other provision.[49] Notwith-

---

45. *Pannalal Bansilal Patil v. State of Andhra Pradesh*, 1996 (1) Scale 405, p. 415 : AIR 1996 SC 1023, p. 1032 : (1996) 2 SCC 498.

46. *T.R. Thandur v. Union of India*, AIR 1996 SC 1643, p. 1651 (para 8) : 1996 (3) SCC 690.

47. *Punjab Sikh Regular Motor Service, Moudhapara, Raipur v. Regional Transport Authority, Raipur*, AIR 1966 SC 1318 : 1966 (2) SCR 221 (when a provision 'A' is subject to a provision 'B' a case falling under provision 'B' is taken out of the provision 'A'). *Clark Ltd. v. IRC*, (1973) 2 All ER 513, p. 520 (The phrase 'subject to' is a simple provision which merely subjects the provisions of the subject-subsections to the provisions of the master-sub-sections. Where there is no clash, the phrase does nothing; if there is collision, the phrase shows what is to prevail. The phrase provides no warranty of universal collision); *Commissioner of Wealth Tax v. Trustees of HEH Nizam's Family*, AIR 1977 SC 2103 : 1977 SCC (Tax) 457 : (1977) 3 SCC 362 (Construction of sections 3 and 21 of the Wealth Tax Act, 1957—Section 3 is subject to other provisions of the Act; hence the case of a trustee which falls under section 21 is outside section 3); **See further** for construction of the expression 'subject to': *Onkarlal Nandlal v. State of Rajasthan*, (1985) 4 SCC 404, p. 414 : AIR 1986 SC 2146; *Printers (Mysore) Ltd. v. M.A. Rasheed*, (2004) 4 SCC 460, p. 467; *Union of India v. Azadi Bachao Andolan*, AIR 2004 SC 1107, pp. 1120 (para 21), 1122 (para 28); *Ashok Leyland v. State of Tamil Nadu*, AIR 2004 SC 2836, p. 2858. **See also** cases in note. 51.

48. *South India Corporation (P) Ltd. v. Secy., Board of Revenue, Trivandrum*, AIR 1964 SC 207, p. 215 : 1964 (4) SCR 280; *Kerala State Electricity Board v. Indian Aluminium Co.*, AIR 1976 SC 1031, p. 1036 : (1976) 1 SCC 466 (Construction of Article 246 of the Constitution which uses both the phrases 'Nothwithstanding anything in' and 'subject to'); *Chandavarkar Sita Ratna Rao v. Ashalata S. Guram*, (1986) 4 SCC 447, p. 478.

49. *ITO v. Gwalior Rayon Silk Manufacturing (Weaving) Co. Ltd.*, AIR 1976 SC 43, p. 47 : 1975 SCC (Tax) 457 : (1975) 2 SCC 721. (The clause beginning with 'without prejudice' is wrongly referred to as a *non obstante* clause.) **See further** *Andhra Pradesh State Financial Corporation v. Gar Re-Rolling Mills*, JT 1994(1) SC 586 : AIR 1994 SC 2151 : (1994) 2 SCC 647. (When one remedy is without prejudice to another remedy, the recourse to one remedy does not bar the taking of the other remedy after abandoning the one which is earlier resorted to. The case relates to sections 29 and 31 of the State Financial Corporation Act,1951.) *Standard Chartered Bank v. Director of Enforcement,* (2006) 4 SCC 278 (paras 21, 22) : AIR 2006 SC 1301 (Construction of section 56 of FERA, 1973 which commences with the words 'without prejudice'); *Institute of Chartered Accountants of India v. Vimal Kumar Surana,* (2011) 1 SCC 534 para 19 : (2010) 13 JT 356 (The use of expression 'without prejudice' in sections 24A, 25 and 26 in the Chartered Accountants Act, 1949 show that the offences defined in the Act do not bar the prosecution for offences under the Penal Code.).

standing clause must also be distinguished from the phrase 'save as otherwise provided' which is a "reflection of the words 'except' – or 'save' – as hereinafter excepted".[50] Ordinarily, there is a close approximation between the *non obstante* clause and the enacting part of the section and the *non obstante* clause may throw some light as to the scope and ambit of the enacting part in case of its ambiguity,[51] but when the enacting part is clear its scope cannot be cut down[52] or enlarged[53] by resort to *non obstante* clause. Further, the wide amplitude of a *non obstante* clause must be kept confined to the legislative policy and it can be given effect to, to the extent Parliament intended and not beyond the same.[54] Therefore, while interpreting a *non statute* clause the court is required to find out the extent to which the Legislature intended to give it an overriding effect.[55]

The expression 'notwithstanding anything in any other law' occuring in a section of an Act cannot be construed to take away the effect of any provision of the Act in which that section appears.[56] In other words 'any other law' will refer to any law other than the Act in which that section occurs.[57] In contrast the expression 'notwithstanding anything contained in this Act' may be construed to take away the effect of any provision of the Act in which the section occurs but it cannot take away the effect of any other law.[58] The expression 'notwithstanding anything to the contrary in any enactment' cannot take away the effect of any provision in a law which is not an enactment.[59]

A provision beginning with the words 'Notwithstanding anything in this Constitution' added in the Constitution by a Constitution Amendment Act

---

50. *Lalu Prasad Yadav v. State of Bihar,* (2010) 5 SCC 1 p. 13 para 29; AIR 2010 SC 1561.

51. *Aswini Kumar Ghose v. Arabinda Bose*, AIR 1952 SC 369, p. 390 : 1953 SCR 1; *Dominion of India v. Shrinbai A. Irani*, AIR 1954 SC 596, p. 599 : 1955 (1) SCR 206.

52. *Aswini Kumar Ghose v. Arabinda Bose, supra*, pp. 376, 377; *Dominion of India v. Shrinbai A. Irani, supra*, p. 600.

53. *R.S. Raghunath v. State of Karnataka*, AIR 1992 SC 81, p. 89 : 1992 (1) SCC 335.

54. *ICICI Bank Ltd. v. SIDCO Ltd.*, (2006) 10 SCC 452 : AIR 2006 SC 2088; *Ramdev Food Products (P.) Ltd. v. Arvindbhai Rambhai Patel,* (2006) 8 SCC 726 (para 66) : AIR 2006 SC 3304.

55. *Central Bank of India v. State of Kerala*, (2009) 4 SCC 94 para 102 : (2009) 3 JT 216.

56. *P. Virudhachalam v. Management of Lotus Mills*, AIR 1998 SC 554, pp. 561, 562 : 1998 (1) SCC 650.

57. *Ibid.*

58. *Satyanarayan Sharma v. State of Rajasthan,* AIR 2001 SC 2856, pp. 2860, 2861 : (2001) 8 SCC 607 ('Notwithstanding anything contained in this code' in section 482 Cr. P.C., 1973 cannot take away the effect of section 19 of the PC Act, 1988 which prevents grant of stay).

59. *Sharda Devi v. State of Bihar,* AIR 2002 SC 1357, p. 1360 : (2002) 3 SCC 705. (In section 54 of the Land Acquisition Act, 1894 the expression 'notwithstanding anything contained in any enactment' does not exclude a Letters Patent appeal as Letters Patent is not an enactment.)

cannot be construed as taking away the provision outside the limitations on the amending power and it has to be harmoniously construed consistent with the foundational principles and basic features of the Constitution.[60] But subject to this limitation existing laws continued under such a provision cannot be held void on the ground that they infringe anything in the Constitution including Article 13 for the *non obstante* clause will preclude any such attack.[61]

By Ordinance No. 19 of 1946 (promulgated under section 72 of the Government of India Act, 1935) section 3 of which provided; 'notwithstanding the expiration of the Defence of India Act, 1939, and the Rules made thereunder, all requisitioned lands shall continue to be subject to requisition until the expiry of this Ordinance,' all requisitions made under the Defence of India Rules were continued. It was however, contended before the Supreme Court that section 3 continued only such requisitions which would have come to an end because of the expiry of the Defence of India Act and the Rules and not those, which, by their own language as to the limitation of the period, expired *ipso facto* on the date of expiration of the Act and the Rules; and support for this contention was sought in the *non obstante* clause. Rejecting the contention BHAGWATI, J., observed: "The *non obstante* clause need not necessarily and always be co-extensive with the operative part so as to have the effect of cutting down the clear terms of an enactment. If the words of the enactment are clear and are capable of only one interpretation on a plain and grammatical construction of the words thereof a *non obstante* clause cannot cut down the construction and restrict the scope of its operation. In such cases the *non obstante* clause has to be read as clarifying the whole position and must be understood to have been incorporated in the enactment by the Legislature by way of abundant caution and not by way of limiting the ambit and scope of the operative part of the enactment."[62]

The proper approach when the enacting part is not ambiguous has been indicated by the Supreme Court in *Aswini Kumar's* case,[63] where the question arose as to the true construction of section 2 of the Supreme Court Advocates (Practice in High Courts) Act, 1951, which contained a *non obstante* clause in the following form: 'Notwithstanding anything contained in the Indian Bar Councils Act, 1926, or in any other law regulating the conditions subject to which a person not entered in the roll of Advocates of

---

60. *R.C. Pocdyal v. Union of India*, AIR 1993 SC 1804, p. 1845 : 1993 (2) JT 1 : 1994 Supp (1) SCC 324.

61. *State of Sikkim v. Surendra Prasad Sharma*, JT 1994 (3) SC 372 : AIR 1994 SC 2342 : (1994) 5 SCC 282.

62. *Dominion of India v. Shrinbai A. Irani*, AIR 1954 SC 596, pp. 599, 600 : 1955 (1) SCR 206.

63. *Aswini Kumar Ghosh v. Arabinda Bose*, AIR 1952 SC 369 : 1953 SCR 1.

a High Court may be permitted to practise in that High Court'. The Calcutta High Court in construing section 2 of the Act held that an advocate of the Supreme Court was not entitled to act on the original side of that High Court. This result was reached by limiting the enacting part of the section by the *non obstante* clause. In overruling the said decision of the High Court, PATANJALI SHASTRI, C.J., observed: "This is not, in our judgment, a correct approach to the construction of section 2. It should first be ascertained what the enacting part of the section provides on a fair construction of the words used according to their natural and ordinary meaning, and the *non obstante* clause is to be understood as operating to set aside as no longer valid anything contained in relevant existing laws which is inconsistent with the new enactment."[64] Proceeding further, the Chief Justice said: "The enacting part of the statute must, where it is clear, be taken to control the *non obstante* clause where both cannot be read harmoniously."[65]

The above mode of approach in construing a *non obstante* clause was followed in construing section 26 of the Travancore Cochin General Sales Tax Act (11 of 1125 M.E.). The section which was added by an amendment in 1951 provided that 'Notwithstanding anything contained in this Act—a tax on the sale or purchase of goods shall not be imposed under this Act', in cases within the categories specified under Article 286 of the Constitution. It was held that sales falling within the categories specified under Article 286 were taken out of the purview of the Act and the value thereof could not be included in the turnover of the dealer either for assessment or for levy of tax.[66]

Section 16 of the Hindu Marriage Act, 1955 which legitimatises children born of void marriages, opens with a *non obstante* clause 'notwithstanding that a marriage is null and void under section 11', but having regard to the language and beneficient purpose of the enacting clause it was held to be not restricted to marriages that were void under section 11 and children born of all void marriages were held to be legitimatised.[67]

---

64. *Ibid*, p. 376.

65. *Ibid*, p. 377. Thus the Notwithstanding Clause 'Notwithstanding *anything contained in the Code of Criminal Procedure*' in section 37 of the Narcotic Drugs and Psychotropic Substances Act, 1985 which severaly restricts grant of bail by the court was held not to cover the provision for automatic bail in proviso to section 167(2) of the Code : *Union of India v. Thamisharasi*, 1995 (3) Scale 72 : 1995 AIR SCW 2543 : (1995) 4 SCC 190.

66. *A.V. Fernandez v. State of Kerala*, AIR 1957 SC 657, pp. 662, 663 : 1957 SCR 837. **See further** *Waman Shrinivas Kini v. Ratilal Bhagwandas & Co.*, AIR 1959 SC 689, p. 692 : 1959 Supp (2) SCR 217.

67. *PEK Kalliani Amma v. K. Devi*, 1996 (4) Scale 131, pp 147, 148: AIR 1996 SC 1963, p. 1976 : (1996) 4 SCC 76.

A special enactment or Rule cannot be held to be overridden by a later general enactment or simply because the latter opens up with a *non obstante* clause. There should be a clear inconsistency between the two before giving an overriding effect to the *non obstante* clause.[68]

Even though the notwithstanding clause is very widely worded, its scope may be restricted by construction having regard to the intention of the Legislature gathered from the enacting clause or other related provisions in the Act. This may be particularly so when the notwithstanding clause "does not refer to any particular provision which it intends to override but refers to the provisions of the statute generally".[69] Thus the notwithstanding clause in section 21A of the Tamil Nadu Land Reforms (Fixation of Ceiling on Land) Act, 1961 which reads 'notwithstanding anything contained in section 22 or in any other provision of this Act and in any other law for the time being in force' was construed not to override the definition of '*stridhana* land' in section 3(42) even if the case fell within the enacting part of section 21A which validated a partition effected by a registered instrument between 15-2-1970 and 2-10-1970.[70] The partition in that case was executed on 24-9-1970 giving certain lands in favour of the mother in lieu of her right of maintainance. But as the definition of *stridhana* in secton 3(42) required that the female should have held the land on 2-10-1970 as owner, the land given to the mother in the said partition was held not to have become her *stridhana* land. Similarly, section 6 of the Government Savings Certificates Act, 1959 by which a nominee of the certificate on the death of the holder becomes entitled to the certificate and to be paid the sum due thereon 'notwithstanding anything contained in any law for the time being in force, or in any disposing testamentary or otherwise in respect of any saving certificate, does not make the nominee owner of the sum so received to the exclusion of the legal heirs as is clear from section 8 and other provisions of the Act, the object of permitting nomination being essentially to prevent delay in collection of the money due under the certificate after the death of the holder.[71]

When the section containing a *non-obstante* clause does not refer to any particular provision of an Act which it intends to override but refers to the provisions of the statute generally, it is not permissible to hold that it excludes the whole Act, and there requires to be a determination as to which provision answers the description and which does not. Accordingly, the

---

68. *R.S. Raghunath v. State of Karnatak*, AIR 1992 SC 81, p. 89 : 1992 (1) SCC 335.
69. *A.G. Varadarajulu v. State of Tamil Nadu*, AIR 1998 SC 1388, p. 1392 : 1998 (4) SCC 231.
70. *Ibid.*
71. *Vishin N. Khanchandani v. Vidya Lachmandas Khanchandani,* AIR 2000 SC 2747, p. 2753 : (2000) 6 SCC 724.

Supreme Court held that the *non-obstante* clause in section 142 of the Negotiable Instruments Act, 1881, which starts with the words 'Notwithstanding anything contained in the Code of Criminal Procedure', is restricted to exclude two things only from the Code: (a) exclusion of oral complaints, and (b) exclusion of cognizance on complaint by anybody other than the payee or the holder in due course.[72]

But the wide meaning of the *non obsante* clause and the enacting words following it cannot be curtailed when the use of wide language accords with the object of the Act. Thus section 2(ii) of the Forest (Conservation) Act, 1980 which provides that 'Notwithstanding anything contained in any other law for the time being in force in any State, no State Government or other authority shall make, except with the prior approval of the Central Government any order directing that any forest land or any portion thereof may be used for any non-forest purpose', was construed to prevent not only grant of mining lease in a forest but also renewal of a lease which was at the option of the lessee under the Mineral Concession Rules made under the Mines and Minerals (Regulation and Development) Act, 1957, without prior approval of the Central Government.[73] Similarly, the Supreme Court has held that the *non-obstante* clauses contained in various provisions of the Juvenile Justice (Care and Protection of Children) Act, 2000, particularly sections 6, 15, 16, 18, 19 and 20, unambiguously render the legislative intent behind the Act, which is that the same, being a special law, would have overriding effect on any other statute for the time being in force.[74]

After referring to the principles and some of the cases mentioned above and the historical circumstances in which the precursor of section 129[75] of the Code of Civil Procedure, 1908 was introduced, the Supreme Court declined to construe the *non-obstante* clause in that section in a limited sense and held that it was indicative of Parliament's intention to prevent the application of CPC in respect of Civil Proceedings on the original side of the

---

72. *Indra Kumar Patodia & Anr. v. Reliance Industries Limited & Ors.*, (2012) 13 SCC 1, p. 10.

73. *Rural Litigation and Entitlement Kendra v. State of U.P.*, AIR 1988 SC 2187, p. 2200, 2201 : 1989 Supp (1) SCC 504; *T.N. Godavarman v. Union of India,* AIR 2003 SC 724, p. 738, 739 : (2002) 10 SCC 606.

74. *Union of India & Ors. v. Ajeet Singh*, (2013) 4 SCC 186, pp. 195, 196.

75. Section 129 reads as under:

'129. *Power of High Courts to make rules as to their Original Civil Procedure*—Notwithstanding anything in this code, any High Court,….may make such rules not inconsistent with the letters Patent or order or other law establishing it to regulate its own procedure in the exercise of its original civil jurisdiction as it shall think fit and nothing herein contained shall affect the validity of any such rules in force at the commencement of this code.'

High Courts which are to be governed by the rules made by the High Court which will prevail over the rules contained in the CPC.[76]

The influence of a *non obstante* clause on a question of construction is illustrated by the ruling in *Municipal Corporation, Indore v. Ratnaprabha (Smt.).*[77] In this case the Supreme Court considered section 138(b) of the Madhya Pradesh Municipal Corporation Act, 1956 which enacts that 'the annual value of any building shall notwithstanding anything contained in any other law for the time being in force be deemed to be gross annual rent at which such building might reasonably at the time of assessment be expected to be let from year to year'. In view of the *non obstante* clause the Supreme Court held that the annual letting value determined under section 138(b) need not in every case be limited to the standard rent which might be fixed for the building under the Rent Control Act. The court distinguished its earlier cases[78] on the ground that in the enactments dealt with in those cases there was no *non obstante* clause as contained in section 138(b) of the Madhya Pradesh Municipal Corporation Act. The reasoning in those cases is that a landlord commits an offence if he collects rent above the standard rent determinable under the relevant Rent Control Act, and therefore, it can legitimately be said that a landlord cannot be expected to let a building for a rent higher than the standard rent. In one of these cases[79] the standard rent under the Rent Control Act had not been fixed but it was observed that the authorities concerned ought to take into account the principles applicable for determining standard rent in fixing the annual letting value. This reasoning could also be applied to section 138(b) of the

---

76. *Iridium India Telecom Ltd. v. Motorola Inc.*, (2005) 2 SCC 145, pp. 158-60 : AIR 2005 SC 514.

77. AIR 1977 SC 308. **Reaffirmed** in *Indian Oil Corporation Ltd. v. Municipal Corporation*, 1995(2) Scale 744 : AIR 1995 SC 1480; *Assistant General Manager v. Commr., Municipal Corporation*, 1995 (3) Scale 561 : 1995(4) SCC 696; *The Commissioner v. Grihayajamanula Samkhya,* AIR 2001 SC 2046, pp. 2052, 2053 : (2001) 5 SCC 561. **See further** *India Automobiles (1960) Ltd. v. Calcutta Municipal Corporation,* AIR 2002 SC 1089, pp. 1102, 1103 : (2002) 3 SCC 388.

78. *Corporation of Calcutta v. Padma Devi*, AIR 1962 SC 151 : (1962) 3 SCR 49; *Corporation of Calcutta v. Life Insurance Corporation*, AIR 1970 SC 1417 : 1970 (2) SCC 44; *Guntur Municipal Council v. Guntur Town Rate Payers' Association*, AIR 1971 SC 353 : 1970 (2) SCC 803; *New Delhi Municipal Committee v. M.N. Soni*, AIR 1977 SC 302 : 1977 (1) SCR 731 : 1976 (4) SCC 535.

79. *Guntur Municipal Council v. Guntur Town Rate Payers' Association*, AIR 1971 SC 353 : (1970) 2 SCC 803. **See further** *Diwan Daulat Rai Kapoor v. New Delhi Municipality*, AIR 1980 SC 541 : (1980) 1 SCC 685; *Balbir Singh (Dr.) v. M.C.D.*, (1985) 1 SCC 167 : AIR 1985 SC 339; *Morvi Municipality v. State of Gujarat,* AIR 1993 SC 1508, pp. 1511, 1512 : (1993) 2 SCC 520; *East India Commercial Co. Pvt. Ltd. v. Corporation of Calcutta*, AIR 1998 SC 1789, p. 1794 : 1998 (4) SCC 368; *Municipal Corporation of Greater Mumbai v. Kamala Mills Ltd.,* AIR 2003 SC 2998 : (2003) 6 SCC 315.

Madhya Pradesh Corporation Act, but it was observed that the significance of the *non obstante* clause was that in cases where standard rent was not determined under the Rent Control Act, the authorities under the Corporation Act were not obliged to adopt the principles contained in the Rent Control Act as the basis for determining the annual letting value.

The notwithstanding clause was also used in construing the enacting part of section 32A of the Narcotic Drugs and Psychotropic Substances Act, 1985 (NDPS Act). This section reads: 'Notwithstanding anything contained in the Code of Criminal Procedure, 1973 or any other law for the time being in force—no sentence awarded under this Act—shall be suspended or remitted or commuted.' Section 36 provides for appeals and revision to the High Court and says that it 'may exercise, so far as may be applicable, all the powers conferred by Chapters XXIX and XXX of the Code of Criminal Procedure, 1973. The question before the Supreme Court was whether the High Court could exercise its power of suspending the sentence under section 389 which occurs in Chapter XXIX of the CrPC, pending an appeal. Having regard to the width of the notwithstanding clause in section 36A, which refers to the entire CrPC and any other law for the time being in force, as also to the qualifying words 'so far as may be applicable' in section 36B, it was held that the High Court has no such power and cannot suspend the sentence awarded under the NDPS Act pending an appeal before it.[80]

Similarly, sub-sections (1) and (2) of section 59 of the Delhi Excise Act, 2009, provide that notwithstanding anything contained in any other law, where anything liable for confiscation under section 58 is seized or detained, the officer seizing and detaining such thing shall produce the same before the Deputy Commissioner who, if satisfied that the offence under the Act has been committed, may order confiscation of such property. Section 61 of the Act further provides that no Court shall, notwithstanding anything to the contrary contained in any other law for the time being in force, have jurisdiction to make any order with regard to such property seized or detained under the Act. The Supreme Court held that the Legislature has used a *non-obstante* clause in sections 59 and 61 of the Act as a legislative device to give effect to the enacting part of the sections in case of conflict. Therefore, neither the Magistrate nor the High Court have the power under sections 451, 452 and 457 of the CrPC to pass an order dealing

---

80. *Maktool Singh v. State of Punjab*, JT 1999 (2) SC 176, p. 179 : AIR 1999 SC 1131, p. 1133 : (1999) 3 SCC 321. Section 32A in so far as it completely debars the appellate court from the power to suspend the sentence awarded to a convict has been held to be unconstitutional: *Dadu v. State of Maharashtra*, AIR 2000 SC 3203 para 25 : (2000) 8 SCC 437.

with the interim custody of a vehicle, which has been seized in connection with an offence under the Excise Act, on security or its release.[81]

Another such example is section 621-A(1) of the Companies Act, 1956, which provides that notwithstanding anything contained in the Code of Criminal Procedure, 1973, any offence punishable under the Act, not being an offence punishable with imprisonment only, or with imprisonment and also with fine, may, either before or after the institution of any prosecution, be compounded by the Company Law Board. The Supreme Court held that a non obstante clause is used as a legislative device to give the enacting part of the section, in case of conflict, an overriding effect over the provisions of the statute mentioned in the non obstante clause. Though ordinarily the offence is compounded under the provisions of the CrPC and the power to accord permission is conferred on the court (excepting those offences for which permission is not required), however, in view of the non obstante clause, the power of composition can be exercised by the court or the Company Law Board.[82]

Sometimes one finds two or more enactments operating in the same field and each containing a *non obstante* clause stating that its provisions will have effect 'notwithstanding anything inconsistent therewith contained in any other law for the time being in force'. The conflict in such cases is resolved on consideration of purpose and policy underlying the enactments and the language used in them.[83] Another test that is applied is that the later enactment normally prevails over the earlier one.[84] It is also relevant to consider as to whether any of the two enactments can be described a special one; in that case the special one may prevail over the more general one notwithstanding that the general one is later in time.[85]

---

81. *State (NCT of Delhi) v. Narender*, (2014) 13 SCC 100, pp. 102 to 104.

82. *VLS Finance Limited v. Union of India*, (2013) 6 SCC 278, pp. 284, 285.

83. *Sarwan Singh v. Kasturilal*, AIR 1977 SC 265, pp. 274, 275 : (1977) 1 SCC 750; *Kumaon Motor Owner's Union v. State of Uttar Pradesh*, AIR 1966 SC 785 : (1966) 2 SCR 121; *Adarsha Krishi Sewa Sangh v. Government of M.P.*, 1980 MPLJ 810, pp. 816, 817; *Ashoka Marketing Ltd. v. Punjab National Bank*, AIR 1991 SC 855, pp. 878, 879 : 1990 (4) SCC 406.

84. *Ibid*; *A.P. State Financial Corporation v. Official Liquidator,* AIR 2000 SC 2642, p. 2644 : (2000) 7 SCC 291. This is specially so when the earlier enactment is a State Act and the later enactment a Central Act both referable to list III and operating in the same field: *G. Sridharamurti v. Hindustan Petroleum Corporation Ltd.*, 1995 (5) Scale 612 : (1995) 6 SCC 605.

85. *Sanwarmal Kajriwal v. Vishwa Co-operative Housing Society Ltd.*, AIR 1990 SC 1563, p. 1575 : 1990 (2) SCC 288.

These principles were reiterated by THAKKER, J., in *KSL and Industries Ltd. v. Arihant Threads Ltd.*[86] But if the *non obstante* clause in a later enactment is subject to and supplemental to an earlier enactment also containing a *non obstante* clause the earlier enactment may be interpreted to prevail over the later enactment.[87] This led to a difference of opinion between THAKKER, J., and KABIR, J., in the case of *KSL and Industries Ltd.* According to Thakker, J., the *non obstante* clause in section 34 of the Recovery of Debts Due to Banks and Financial Institutions (RDDB) Act, 1993 which was a later Act prevailed over Sick Industrial Companies (Special Provisions) Act, (SICA) 1985 which also contained a *non obstante* clause in section 32. But KABIR, J., held that section 34(2) in RDDB Act made it subject to SICA and was to be read in addition to and not in derogation of SICA therefore SICA would prevail over RDDB Act. Both the judges agreed to allow the appeal and to set aside the judgment of the High Court under appeal but in view of the difference of opinion on interpretation directed that the papers be placed before the Chief Justice. This reference was eventually decided by a three Judge Bench of the Supreme Court in 2015. To elaborate, section 34(1) of the RDDB Act provides that save as provided under sub-section (2), the provisions of the Act shall have effect notwithstanding anything inconsistent therewith contained in any other law for the time being in force or in any instrument having effect by virtue of any law other than the Act. Section 34(2) of the RDDB Act, however, states that the provisions of the Act or the Rules made thereunder shall be in addition to, and not in derogation of, the Acts mentioned therein. The three Judge Bench, affirming the view taken by KABIR, J., as stated above, held that when an Act provides that its provisions shall be in addition to and not in derogation of another law or laws, it means that the Legislature intends that such an enactment shall co-exist along with the other Acts. As SICA is one of the Acts mentioned in section 34(2) of the RDDB Act, it was held that the effect of section 34(2) of the RDDB Act is to preserve the powers of the authorities under SICA and save the proceedings under SICA from being overridden by the later RDDB Act.[88]

Section 19 of the Slum Areas (Improvement and Clearance) Act, 1956 as amended by Act 43 of 1964, provides that proceedings for eviction of tenants cannot be taken without permission of the competent Authority notwithstanding anything contained in any other law for the time being in force. Section 39 of the Act further provides that the provisions of the Act

---

86. *KSL and Industries Ltd. v. Arihant Threads Ltd.*, (2008) 9 SCC 763 paras 70 and 92 : (2008) 9 JT 381.

87. *Ibid;* paras 120 to 122.

88. *KSL & Industries Ltd. v. Arihant Threads Ltd. & Ors.*, (2015) 1 SCC 166, pp. 179, 180.

shall take effect notwithstanding anything inconsistent therewith contained in any other law. By Act 18 of 1976, the Delhi Rent Control Act, 1958 was amended and sections 14A, 25A, 25B and 25C were introduced in it. Section 14A confers a right on a landlord to recover immediately possession of any premises let out by him in case he is required to vacate any residential premises allotted to him by the Central Government or any local Authority. The conferral of the right is 'notwithstanding anything contained elsewhere in this Act or in any other law for the time being in force or in any contract (whether express or implied), custom or usage to the contrary'. Section 25B provides the special procedure for enforcement of the right conferred by section 14A. Section 25A makes the provisions in section 25B to have effect 'notwithstanding anything inconsistent therewith contained elsewhere in this Act or in any other law for the time being in force'. Section 54 of the Delhi Rent Act provides that nothing in this Act shall affect the provisions of the Slum Areas Act. After considering these provisions the Supreme Court[89] held that the right to immediate possession conferred by section 14A of the Delhi Rent Act was not controlled by the Slum Clearance Act and this right could be enforced in the manner provided in section 25B without obtaining the permission of the competent Authority under the Slum Clearance Act. In reaching this conclusion, the court considered the object and policy of the relevant provisions. The court also took into account the fact that sections 14A, 25A, 25B and 25C were introduced in the Delhi Rent Act by an Amending Act which was later in time to the Slum Clearance Act. As regards section 54 of the Delhi Rent Act, the court held that it was overridden by the notwithstanding clauses in sections 14A and 25A. Applying the same principles it was held that the provisions of the Public Premises (Eviction of Unauthorised Occupants) Act, 1971, were a special and later law as against the Delhi Rent Control Act, 1958, and so the Premises Act prevailed in case of a conflict over the Rent Control Act although both the Acts contained *non obstante* clauses.[90] A conflict between provisions of two special statutes namely the Financial Corporation Act, 1951 and the Sick Industries Companies (Special Provisions) Act, 1985, both containing *non obstante* clauses (section 46B of the 1951 Act and section 32 of the 1985 Act) was resolved by giving overriding effect to the 1985 Act on the ground that the 1985 Act being a subsequent enactment, the non-*obstante* clause therein would prevail over the *non-obstante* clause in the 1951 Act unless it is found that 1985 Act is a

---

89. *Sarwan Singh v. Kasturilal, supra.* **See further** *Ravi Dutt Sharma v. Ratan Lal Bhargava*, (1984) 2 SCC 75 : AIR 1984 SC 967.

90. *Jain Ink Manufacturing Company v. Life Insurance Corporation*, AIR 1981 SC 670 : (1980) 4 SCC 435. Upheld in *Ashoka Marketing Ltd. v. Punjab National Bank*, AIR 1991 SC 855, pp. 877-880 : (1990) 4 SCC 406 (Public Premises Act was held to prevail on considerations of object and policy).

general statute and the 1951 statute is a special one.[91] The aforesaid principles were also applied in resolving the conflict between section 28 of the Bombay Rents, Hotel and Lodging House Rates Control Act, 1947 and section 91 of the Maharashtra Co-operative Societies Act, 1960.[92] Section 28 of the Rent Act, which opens with the words 'Notwithstanding anything contained in any law', confers jurisdiction on the court of small causes Bombay to entertain and try suits for recovery of rent and possession between landlord and tenant. Section 91 of the Co-operative Societies Act which also opens with a similar *non obstante* clause, provides that any dispute touching the business of a society shall be referred to the Registrar if both the parties thereto are one or other of the following namely, a society, a present or past member, or a person claiming through a member. Construing the provisions of the two Acts, it has been held that even in respect of a tenant co-partnership type housing society whose business includes acquiring and letting out building to its members, a claim by the society to eject a deemed tenant who was let in by a member would be entertainable by the court of small causes under the Rent Act and not by the Registrar under the Co-operative Societies Act. It was pointed out that although the Co-operative Societies Act was the later Act, the Rent Act was a special law relating to protection and eviction of tenants and so must prevail over the provisions of the Co-operative Societies Act.[93]

A conflict between two special Acts which have both notwithstanding clauses can also be resolved by seeing which is more special than the other in addition to the consideration that the conflict arose because of a provision added later in the Act which is more special.[94] This is illustrated by

---

91. *Maharashtra Tubes Ltd. v. State Industrial and Investment Corporation of India,* JT 1993 (1) SC 310 : 1993 (2) SCC 144. **Followed** in *Allahabad Bank v. Canara Bank,* AIR 2000 SC 1535, p. 1549 : (2000) 4 SCC 406. **See further** *Solidaire India Ltd. v. Fairgrowth Financial Services Ltd.,* JT 2001 (2) SC 639, p. 642 : (2001) 3 SCC 71 : AIR 2001 SC 958 (conflict between *non obstante* clauses of two Special Acts, namely section 32 of the Sick Industrial Companies Act, 1985 and section 13 of the Special Court Act 1992, was resolved by holding that the 1992 Act being the later Act will prevail); *West Bengal Electricity Regulatory Commission v. C.E.S.C. Ltd.,* AIR 2002 SC 3588, p. 3606 : (2002) 8 SCC 715; *Maruti Udyog Ltd. v. Ramlal,* (2005) 2 SCC 638, p. 653 : AIR 2005 SC 851 [Maruti Limited (Acquisition and Transfer of Undertakings) Act, 1980, being a later Special Act was held to prevail over an earlier Special Act, namely, the Industrial Disputes Act, 1947]; *Tax Recovery Officer v. Custodian,* (2007) 7 SCC 461, para 14 (Special Courts Act 1992 will prevail over the Income Tax Act, 1961).

92. *Sanwarmal Kejriwal v. Vishwa Co-operative Housing Society Ltd.,* AIR 1990 SC 1563, p. 1575 : 1990 (2) SCC 288.

93. *Ibid.* **See further** *O.N. Bhatnagar v. Rukibai Narsindas (Smt.),* AIR 1982 SC 1097 : (1982) 2 SCC 244.

94. *Bank of India v. Ketan Parekh,* (2008) 8 SCC 148 paras 18 and 19 : AIR 2008 SC 2361.

the conflict between the Special Court (Trial of Offences Relating to Transactions in Securities) Act, 1992 (in Short, 'the 1992 Act') and the Recovery of Debts Due to Banks and Financial Institutions Act, 1993 (in Short, 'the 1993 Act'). The conflict arose because insertion of section 9A by Act 24 of 1994 from 25-1-1994 in the 1992 Act which confers civil jurisdiction on the Special Court relating to any property attached under Section 3(3) and provides for transfer to the Special Court every suit, claim or other legal proceeding pending before any court in respect of such property. It is also provided that no court other than the Special Court shall have jurisdiction, power or authority in relation to any such matter. Section 13 of the 1992 Act provides for overriding effect of the Act notwithstanding anything inconsistent therewith contained in any other law. The 1993 Act relates to constitution of tribunals for recovery of debts due to Banks and Financial Institutions. Section 14 provides for the Act to have overriding effect notwithstanding anything to the contrary contained in any other law. The conflict was as to whether the Special Court in the 1992 Act or the Tribunal in the 1993 Act will have jurisdiction over a matter which could be taken cognizance of by both. The 1992 Act and the 1993 Act are both special Acts but the 1992 Act was found to be more special as it was restricted in application to the transactions in securities after the 1st day of April 1991 and before 6-6-1992. Further the conflict arose because of insertion of section 9A in the 1992 Act by an amendment in 1994 and was thus later in time to the enactment of the 1993 Act. On these considerations the conflict was resolved in favour of the Special Court in the 1992 Act.[95]

If the Acts containing wide notwithstanding clauses covering 'any other law for the time being in force' *operate in different fields,* harmonious construction has to be applied and when in a given case the application of the earlier Act is attracted, the question of its giving way to the later Act would not arise.[96] On this basis it was held that where section 22 of the Sick Industrial Companies (Special Provisions) Act, 1985 which bars execution against any of the properties of the company without the consent of the Board for Industrial and Financial Reconstruction, applies an award made by the Industry Facilitation Council under section 6(2) of the Interest on Delayed Payments to Small Scale and Ancillary Industrial Undertakings Act, 1993 which is deemed to be made under the Arbitration and Conciliation Act, 1996, cannot be executed without the consent of the

95. *Ibid* paras 19 and 28.

96. *Jay Engineering Works Ltd. v. Industry Facilitation Council,* (2006) 8 SCC 677 (paras 24 and 31) : AIR 2006 SC 3252.

Board as required by section 22 of the 1985 Act.[97] Both section 22 of the 1985 Act and section 10 of the 1993 Act contain wide notwithstanding clauses but as both the Acts operate in different fields, harmonious construction was applied and operation of section 22 of the 1985 Act in the case could not be negatived by the notwithstanding clause in section 10 of the 1993 Act. In a case the Supreme Court in *Central Bank of India v. State of Kerala*[98] had to interpret *non obstante* clauses in two sets of laws namely section 34 of the Recovery of Debts Due to Bank and Financial Institutions Act, 1993 (the DRT Act) and section 35 of the Securitisation and Reconstruction of Financial Assets and Enforcement of Security Interest Act, 2002 (the Securitisaction Act) on the one hand and section 38C of the Bombay Sales Tax Act, 1959 and section 26B of the Kerala General Sales Tax Act on the other. Briefly stated the *non obstante* clauses in section 34 of the DRT Act and section 35 of the Securitisation Act which are similarly worded provide that provisions of these Acts 'shall have effect notwithstanding anything inconsistent therewith contained in any other law for the time being in force.' Section 26B of the Kerala General Sales Tax Act provides that 'notwithstanding anything to the contrary contained in any other law for the time being in force, any amount of tax penalty, interest and any other amount, if any, payable by a dealer or any another person under this Act shall be the first charge on the property of the dealer or such person.' Similar priority of first charge in respect of tax and other sums due under the Bombay Sales Tax Act is provided in section 38C of the Act. Neither the DRT Act nor the Securitisation Act contains any provision by which first charge is created in favour of banks, financial institutions or secured creditors *qua* the property of the borrower. Interpreting these provisions the Supreme Court held that the *non obstante* clauses in section 34 of the DRT Act and section 35 of the Securitisation Act gave overriding effect to these Acts only if there was anything inconsistent in any other law. In the absence of any first charge provisions in these Acts it could not be held that the first charge provisions in the Sales Tax Acts regarding sales tax dues etc. were overridden by these Acts. The two sets of laws operated in different fields and, therefore, it was rightly held that *non obstante* clauses and priority provisions in the Sales Tax Acts though prior in time prevailed and could not be negatived by the *non obstante* clauses in the DRT Act and the Securitisation Act though they were later in time.

---

97. *Ibid.*

98. *Central Bank of India v. State of Kerala,* (2009) 4 SCC 94 paras 95, 111, 116, 129 : (2009) 3 JT 216.

On the other hand, in the absence of a *non obstante* clause, the applicability of provisions of other statutes cannot be excluded. Section 22 of the Mines and Minerals (Development and Regulation) Act, 1957 ('MMDR Act'), provides that no Court shall take cognizance of any offence punishable under the Act or any Rules made thereunder except upon complaint in writing made by a person authorised in this behalf by the Central or State Government. The Supreme Court observed that the provision does not begin with a *non obstante* clause, and accordingly held that though in a case where mining activity is carried out in contravention of the MMDR Act, a complaint can be filed only by an authorised person as provided under section 22 of the MMDR Act, mere initiation of proceedings under the MMDR Act on the basis of such a complaint would not debar the police from taking action against persons for committing theft of sand and minerals under the provisions of the Indian Penal Code by exercising powers under the CrPC. Hence, the police can register a case, investigate the same and submit a report under section 173, CrPC, before a Magistrate for taking cognizance as provided under section 190(1)(d) of the CrPC.[1]

5. LEGAL FICTION

The Legislature is quite competent to create a legal fiction, in other words, to enact a deeming provision for the purpose of assuming existence of a fact which does not really exist[2] provided the declaration of non-existent facts as existing does not offend the constitution.[3] Although the word 'deemed' is usually used, a legal fiction may be enacted without using that word.[4] For instance, the words 'as if' can also be used to create a legal fiction.[5]

---

1. *State (NCT of Delhi) v. Sanjay*, (2014) 9 SCC 772, pp. 787 to 812.
2. *J.K. Cotton Spinning & Weaving Mills Ltd. v. Union of India*, AIR 1988 SC 191, p. 202 : 1987 Supp SCC 350.
3. *Indira Sawhney v. Union of India*, JT 1999 (9) SC 557, p. 582 : (2000) 1 SCC 168 : AIR 2000 SC 498 (statutory declaration by Kerala legislature of non-existence of 'creamy layer' which was unrelated to existing facts was held to be violative of Articles 14 and 16 of the Constitution).
4. *CIT v. Urmila Ramesh*, AIR 1998 SC 2640, pp. 2645, 2646 : 1998 (3) SCC 6. For meaning of the word 'deemed' **see** *Smt. Sudha Rani Garg v. Jagdish Kumar,* AIR 2004 SC 5120, pp. 5121, 5122 : (2004) 8 SCC 329; *Mundri Lal v. Sushila Rani,* (2007) 8 SCC 609 para 26 : (2007) 11 JT 266.
5. *Rajasthan State Industrial Development & Investment Corporation & Anr. v. Diamond & Gem Development Corporation Ltd. & Anr.*, (2013) 5 SCC 470, p. 484.

In interpreting a provision creating a legal fiction, the court is to ascertain for what purpose the fiction is created,[6] and after ascertaining this, the Court is to assume all those facts and consequences which are incidental or inevitable corollaries to the giving effect to the fiction.[7] But in so construing the fiction it is not to be extended beyond the purpose for which it is created,[8] or beyond the language of the section by which it is created.[9] It

---

6. *Ex Parte, Walton, In re, Levy*, (1881) 17 Ch D 746, p. 756, *State of Trav-Co. v. Shan mugha Vilas Cashewnut Factory, Quilon*, AIR 1953 SC 333, pp. 342, 343 : 1954 SCR 53; *State of Bombay v. Pandurang Vinayak*, AIR 1953 SC 244, p. 246 : 1953 SCR 733.

7. *East End Dwelling Co. Ltd. v. Finsbury Borough Council*, (1951) 2 All ER 587, p. 599 : 1952 AC 109 (HL); *State of Bombay v. Pandurang Vinayak, supra*, p. 246; *CIT, Delhi v. S. Teja Singh*, AIR 1959 SC 352, p. 355 : 1959 Supp (1) SCR 394; *Chief Inspector of Mines v. Karam Chand Thapar*, AIR 1961 SC 838, p. 845 : 1962 (1) SCR 9; *Corporation Bank v. Saraswati Abharansala*, (2009) 1 SCC 540 para 17 : (2008) 15 Scale 186.

8. *In re, Coal Economising Gas Company*, (1875) 1 Ch D 182, pp. 188, 189; *Hill v. East and West India Dock Co.*, (1884) 9 AC 448, p. 458 (HL); *Bengal Immunity Co. Ltd. v. State of Bihar*, AIR 1955 SC 661, p. 680 : (1955) 2 SCR 603; *CIT, Bombay v. Amarchand N. Shroff*, AIR 1963 SC 1448, p. 1452 : 1963 Supp (1) SCR 699; *Mandalasa Devi v. M. Ramnarain Private Ltd.*, AIR 1965 SC 1718, p. 1720 : (1965) 3 SCR 421; *M.K. Balakrishna Menon v. Asstt. Controller of Estate Duty, Ernakulam*, AIR 1971 SC 2392 : (1971) 2 SCC 909; *C.I.T., Gujarat v. Vadilal Lallubhai*, AIR 1973 SC 1016, p. 1019 : 1973 SCC (Tax) 1; *State of Maharashtra v. Narayanrao Sham Rao Deshmukh*, (1985) 2 SCC 321, p. 330 : AIR 1985 SC 716; *C.I.T., Kanpur v. Mother India Refrigeration Industries (P) Ltd.*, (1985) 4 SCC 1, p. 9 : AIR 1985 SC 1720; *Waliram Waman Hiray (Dr.) v. Mr. Justice B. Lentin*, AIR 1988 SC 2267, p. 2283 : (1988) 4 SCC 419; *Union of India v. Sampat Raj Dugar*, AIR 1992 SC 1417, p. 1421 : (1992) 2 SCC 66, *M. Venugopal v. Divisional Manager Life Insurance Corporation*, AIR 1994 SC 1343, p. 1347 : (1994) 2 SCC 323; *K. Prabhakaran v. P. Jayarajan*, (2005) 1 SCC 754, p. 775 (para 39) : AIR 2005 688; *Maruti Udyog Ltd. v. Ramlal*, (2005) 2 SCC 638, p. 652; *Raymond Ltd. v. State of Chhattisgarh*, (2007) 3 SCC 79 (paras 28, 29) : (2007) 3 JT 582; *R. Kalyani v. Janak C. Mehta*, (2009) 1 SCC 516 para 32 : (2008) 12 JT 279. **See further** *Complete Insulations (P) Ltd. v. New India Assurance Company Ltd.*, 1995 (6) Scale 629 : (1996) 1 SCC 221 (Legal fiction of deemed transfer of policy of insurance with transfer of vehicle under section 157 in Chapter XI, M.V. Act, 1988, though without any apparent limitation, is limited to third party risk which is the object behind Chapter XI of the Act); *UCO Bank v. Rajinder Lal Capoor*, AIR 2007 SC 2129, para 20 (Legal fiction must be construed having regard to the purpose of the statute); *UCO Bank v. Rajinderlal Capoor*, (2008) 5 SCC 257 para 24 : AIR 2008 SC 1831; *Rajkumar Khurana v. State of (NCT of Delhi)*, (2009) 6 SCC 72 paras 10 and 11 : (2009) 7 JT 351. [Legal fiction cannot be taken recourse to for any purpose other than one mentioned in the statute. A penal provision created by a legal fiction must receive strict construction (Construction of section 138 of the Negotiable Instruments Act, 1881)].

9. *C.I.T., Bombay City II v. Shakuntala*, AIR 1966 SC 719, p. 722 : (1962) 2 SCR 871; *Mancheri Puthusseri Ahmed v. Kuthiravattam Estate Receiver*, 1996 (6) Scale 452, pp. 458, 459 : AIR 1997 SC 208, p. 214 : (1996) 8 SCC 185; *State of Maharashtra v. Laljit Rajshishah*, AIR 2000 SC 937, p. 940 : (2000) 2 SCC 699. **See further** *Prakash Jain v. Marie Fernandas*, (2003) 8 SCC 431, p. 438 : AIR 2003

[Footnote No. 9 Contd.]

cannot also be extended by importing another fiction.[10] The principles stated above are 'well-settled'.[11] A legal fiction may also be interpreted narrowly to make the statute workable.[12] A legal fiction in terms enacted 'for purposes of this Act' will cover the entire Act[13] but is normally restricted to that Act and cannot be extended to cover another Act.[14] Legal fictions may not be created only by the Legislature and delegated legislation may also create such fictions.[15] But it must be remembered that what can be deemed to exist under a legal fiction are facts and not legal consequences which do not flow from the law as it stands.[16] A legal fiction created by the Legislature in an Act, it appears, cannot be widened by rules made under the Act.[17] Further, a legal fiction created in a State Act by borrowing a definition from a Central Act in the concurrent field will be restricted for purposes of the State Act and will not have the effect of widening the definition in the Central Act unless that definition is properly amended with due compliance with Article 254 of the Constitution.[18] Thus section 161 of the Maharashtra Co-operative Societies Act, 1961, by which officers under the Act are deemed to be public servants within the meaning of section 21 of the Indian Penal Code, 1860 was held to be ineffective to widen the definition of public servant in section 21 of the Penal Code for purposes of offences under the Penal Code or the Prevention of Corruption Act, 1947.[19]

As was observed by JAMES, L.J.: "When a statute enacts that something shall be deemed to have been done, which in fact and in truth was not

---

[Footnote No. 9 Contd.]

SC 3331 (competent authority under the Maharashtra Rent Control Act, 1999 deemed to be a civil court for purposes of sections 345 and 346 CrPC, 1973 cannot be deemed to be court for other purposes).

10. *C.I.T., (Central) Calcutta v. Moon Mills Ltd.*, AIR 1966 SC 870, p. 873 : 1966 (2) SCR 393 ('received' cannot be read as 'receivable'); *Mancheri Puthusseri Ahmed v. Kuthiravattam, supra.*

11. *State of West Bengal v. Sadam K. Bormal*, AIR 2004 SC 3666, p. 3673 : (2004) 6 SCC 59.

12. *Nandkishore Ganesh Joshi v. Commr. Municipal Corporation Kalyan*, AIR 2005 SC 34, p. 37 (para 19).

13. *Ashok Leyland Ltd. v. State of Tamil Nadu*, AIR 2004 SC 2836, p. 2857 (paras 84, 86) : (2004) 3 SCC 1.

14. *State of Karnataka v. K. Gopalkrishna Shenoy*, (1987) 3 SCC 655, p. 666 : AIR 1987 SC 861.

15. *Union of India v. Jalyan Udyog*, AIR 1994 SC 88, p. 98 : 1994 (1) SCC 318.

16. *Delhi Cloth and General Mills Co. Ltd. v. State of Rajasthan*, 1996 (1) Scale 332, pp. 336 to 338 : AIR 1996 SC 2930, pp. 2934, 2935 : (1996) 2 SCC 449. **See further** text and note 35, p. 423.

17. *Agricultural Market Committee v. Shalimar Chemical Works Ltd.*, AIR 1997 SC 2502, p. 2508 : (1997) 5 SCC 516. **See further** for this case, p. 1044.

18. *State of Maharashtra v. Laljit Rajshi Shah,* AIR 2000 SC 937, p. 940 : (2000) 2 SCC 699.

19. *Ibid.* For another similar case, **see** *Ramesh Balkrishnan Kulkarni v. State of Maharashtra,* AIR 1985 SC 1655 : (1985) 3 SCC 606.

done, the court is entitled and bound to ascertain for what purposes and between what person the statutory fiction is to be resorted to."[20] "When a legal fiction is created", stated S.R. DAS, J., "for what purpose, one is led to ask at once, is it so created?"[21]

After ascertaining the purpose, "full effect must be given to the statutory fiction and it should be carried to its logical conclusion"[22] and to that end "it would be proper and even necessary to assume all those facts on which alone the fiction can operate".[23] In an oft-quoted passage, LORD ASQUITH stated: "If you are bidden to treat an imaginary state of affairs as real, you must surely, unless prohibited from doing so, also imagine as real the consequence and incidents which, if the putative state of affairs had in fact existed, must inevitably have flowed from or accompanied it.... The statute says that you must imagine a certain state of affairs; it does not say that having done so, you must cause or permit your imagination to boggle when it comes to the inevitable corollaries of that state of affairs."[24] Thus if *A* is deemed to be *B*,

---

20. *Ex parte, Walton, In re, Levy*, (1881) 17 Ch D 746; p. 756; **referred** to in *Hill v. East and West India Dock Co.*, (1884) 9 AC 448, pp. 456, 458 (HL); *State of Trav-Co. v. Shanmugha Vilas Cashewnut Factory*, AIR 1953 SC 333, p. 343 : 1954 SCR 53.

21. *State of Trav-Co. v. Shanmugha Vilas Cashewnut Factory, supra*, p. 342.

22. *State of Bombay v. Pandurang Vinayak*, AIR 1953 SC 244, p. 246 : 1953 SCR 773; *American Home Products Corporation v. Mac Laboratories*, (1986) 1 SCC 465, p. 501 : AIR 1986 SC 137; *Union of India v. Jalyan Udyog, supra*, pp. 96, 97; *P.E.K. Kalliani Amma v. K. Devi*, AIR 1996 SC 1963, p. 1976 : (1996) 4 SCC 33; *Mundri Lal v. Sushila Rani*, (2007) 8 SCC 609 para 26 : (2007) 11 JT 266.

23. *C.I.T., Delhi v. S. Teja Singh*, AIR 1959 SC 352, p. 355 : 1959 Supp (1) SCR 394.

24. *East End Dwelling Co. Ltd. v. Finsbury Borough Council*, (1951) 2 All ER 587, p. 589 : 1952 AC 109 (HL); **referred** to in *State of Bombay v. Pandurang Vinayak, supra*, p. 246; *C.I.T., Delhi v. S. Teja Singh, supra*, p. 355; *Rajendraswami v. Commissioner of Hindu Religious and Charitable Endowments, Hyderabad*, AIR 1965 SC 502, p. 505 : 1964 (8) SCR 252, *Shatrunjit (Raja) v. Mohammad Azmat Azim Khan*, AIR 1971 SC 1474, p. 1476 : 1971 (2) SCC 200; *Daya Singh v. Dhan Kaur*, AIR 1974 SC 665, p. 668 : (1974) 1 SCC 700; *Boucher Pierre Andre v. Superintendent, Central Jail, Tihar*, AIR 1975 SC 164, p. 166 : (1975) 1 SCC 192 : (1975) SCC (Cri) 70; *Sundar Dass v. Ram Parkash*, AIR 1977 SC 1201, p. 1205 : (1977) 2 SCC 662; *Gurupad Khandappa Magdum v. Hirabai Khandappa*, AIR 1978 SC 1239, p. 1243 : (1978) 3 SCC 383; *State of Andhra Pradesh v. Vallabhapuram Ravi*, (1984) 4 SCC 410, p. 420 : AIR 1985 SC 870; *American Home Products Corporation v. Mac Laboratories*, (1986) 1 SCC 465, p. 501 : AIR 1986 SC 137; *S. Appukuttan v. Thundiyal Janaki Amma*, AIR 1988 SC 587, p. 592 : (1988) 2 SCC 372; *Maganlal v. Jaiswal Industries*, AIR 1989 SC 2113, p. 2122 : (1989) 4 SCC 344; *Orient Paper and Industries Ltd. v. State of Orissa*, AIR 1991 SC 672, p. 681 : 1991 Supp (1) SCC 81; *H.C. Suman v. Rehabilitation Ministry Employment Cooperative House Building Society Ltd.*, AIR 1991 SC 2160, p. 2169 : (1991) 4 SCC 485; *Voltas Limited, Bombay v. Union of India*, 1995(1) Scale 455, p. 460 : 1995 AIR SCW 2928 : 1995 Supp (2) SCC 498 : AIR 1995 SC 1881; *G. Vishwanathan v. Hon'ble*

[Footnote No. 24 Contd.]

compliance with *A* is in law compliance with *B* and contravention of *A* is in law contravention of *B*.[25]

Article 341(1) of the Constitution empowers the President to specify with respect to any State by notification 'the castes, races or tribes or parts of or groups within castes, races or tribes which shall for the purposes of this Constitution be deemed to be Scheduled Castes in relation to that State'. Article 341(2) provides that the notification so issued shall not be varied except by Parliament. In interpreting this provision, it has been held that because of the legal fiction resulting from the deeming provision, the conglomeration of castes in the Presidential Order shall be considered as representing a class as a whole and the state concerned has no authority by legislation or otherwise to further subdivide the castes in the notification so as to give more preference in the matter of reservation to a minuscule proportion thereof in preference to other members of the same class.[26]

In interpreting a fiction created by the Indian Income-tax Act, 1922, which by section 43 provided that under certain circumstances an agent shall for all the purposes of this Act, be deemed to be such agent of a non-resident person and which by section 42 further provided that such agent shall be deemed to be, for all the purposes of this Act, the assessee, the Privy Council held that such agent was an assessee for all the purposes of

---

[Footnote No. 24 Contd.]

Speaker, Tamil Nadu Legislative Assembly, 1996 (1) Scale 531, p. 537 : AIR 1996 SC 1060, p. 1064; *P.E.K. Kalliani Amma v. K. Devi*, AIR 1996 SC 1963, p. 1976 : (1996) 4 SCC 76; *State of Tamil Nadu v. Arooran Sugars Ltd.*, AIR 1997 SC 1815, p. 1822; *Bhavnagar University v. Palitana Sugar Mill (P.) Ltd.*, (2003) 2 SCC 111, p. 123 : AIR 2003 SC 511, p. 518; *Commissioner of Wealth Tax v. Trustees of H.E.H.*, (2003) 5 SCC 122, pp. 131, 132; *Dipak Chandra Rutidas v. Chandan Kumar Sarkar*, (2003) 7 SCC 66, p. 72 : AIR 2003 SC 3701; *Bhavnagar University v. Palitana Sugar Mills Pvt. Ltd.*, AIR 2003 SC 511; *Prafulla Kumar Das v. State of Orissa*, AIR 2003 SC 4506, p. 4517 : (2003) 9 JT 477; *Ashok Leyland Ltd. v. State of Tamil Nadu*, (2004) 3 SCC 1 : AIR 2004 SC 2836, p. 2855; *State of West Bengal v. Sadam K. Bormal*, AIR 2004 SC 3666, p. 3673 : (2004) 6 SCC 59; *Ciariant International Ltd. v. Securities & Exchange Board*, (2004) 8 SCC 524, p. 545 : AIR 2004 SC 4236; *Mohd. Akram Ansari v. Chief Election Officer*, (2008) 2 SCC 95 paras 6 and 7 : (2007) 14 Scale 30 : (2008) 1 SLT 25. **See further** *Mohammed Iqbal Madar Sheikh v. State of Maharashtra*, (1996) 1 SCC 722, p. 727 : JT 1996 (1) SC 114 : 1996 SCC (Cri) 202; *A.S. Glittre D/5 I/S Garonne Co. v. Commissioner of Income-tax*, AIR 1997 SC 2361, p. 2163 : 1997 (4) JT 445 : (1997) 9 SCC 546; *Manorey Alias Manohar v. Board of Revenue (U.P.)*, (2003) 5 SCC 521, pp. 526, 527 (deeming provision to be given full effect).

25. *Chief Inspector of Mines v. Karam Chand Thapar*, AIR 1961 SC 838, p. 845 : 1962 (1) SCR 9. (Contravention of regulations deemed to be made under the Act is contravention of regulation made under the Act). **Cf.** *Avtar Singh v. State of Punjab*, AIR 1965 SC 666 : 1965 (1) SCR 103. (Theft of electricity is an offence under the Electricity Act, 1910 and not under the Penal Code.).

26. *V. Chinnaiah v. State of Andhra Pradesh*, AIR 2005 SC 162, p. 174 (para 43) : (2005) 1 SCC 394.

the Act and hence chargeable to income-tax, assessee being defined by section 2(2) as the person by whom income-tax is payable.[27] VISCOUNT DUNEDIN in that connection observed : "Now when a person is 'deemed to be' something the only meaning possible is that whereas he is not in reality that something the Act of Parliament requires him to be treated as if he were."[28] Similarly, section 21 of the Indian Penal Code, 1860, defines 'public servant', and section 87 of the Rajasthan Municipalities Act, 1959, provides *inter-alia*, that every member of the Municipal Board shall be deemed to be a public servant within the meaning of section 21 of the IPC. The Supreme Court held that section 87 of the Rajasthan Act has created a legal fiction for the purpose of assuming that the members of the Municipal Board, who otherwise may not be public servants within the meaning of section 21 of the IPC, shall be assumed to be so in view of the legal fiction created.[29]

In *Pandurang's* case[30] the facts were that the Bombay Building (Control on Erection) Ordinance, 1948, although applicable to certain areas mentioned in the Schedule to it, was extended by a notification under section 1(4) to all the areas in the province in respect of buildings intended to be used for the purposes of cinemas. The Ordinance was repealed and replaced by Act 31 of 1948, which again extended to areas mentioned in the Schedule with power under section 1(3) conferred on the Provincial Government to extend its operation to other areas. The Act, however, by section 15(1) applied section 7 and section 25 of the Bombay General Clauses Act, 1904, to the Ordinance as if 'that Ordinance were an enactment'. Section 25 of the General Clauses Act provides for continuance of a notification issued under a repealed enactment which is to 'be deemed to have been issued under the provisions re-enacted'. The notification issued under the Ordinance applying the same to other areas was thus deemed to have been issued under the Act but the High Court of Bombay held that the notification extended the 'Ordinance' and although it was to be deemed to be made under the Act the word 'Act' could not be read instead of 'Ordinance' in the notification so as to extend the Act to those areas. The Supreme Court overruled the decision of the High Court and held that the purpose of the legal fiction created by section 15 and the corollary of declaring section 25 of the General Clauses Act applicable necessitated that wherever the word 'Ordinance' occurred in the notification that word was to be read as 'enactment'.[31]

---

27. *C.I.T., Bombay v. Bombay Corporation*, AIR 1930 PC 54.
28. *Ibid*, p. 56.
29. *Manish Trivedi v. State of Rajasthan*, (2014) 14 SCC 420, p. 426.
30. *State of Bombay v. Pandurang Vinayak*, AIR 1953 SC 244 : 1953 SCR 773.
31. *Ibid.*

In another case[32] dealing with the Indian Income-tax Act, 1922, which by section 18A(3) required any person not hitherto assessed to send in certain circumstances an estimate of his income to the I.T.O. for purposes of advance payment of tax and which by clause (9) provided that if during the course of regular assessment the I.T.O. was satisfied that such person had without reasonable cause failed to comply with clause (3) the assessee 'shall be deemed to have failed to furnish the return of his total income and the provisions of section 28, so far as may be, shall apply accordingly', the question was whether a penalty could be levied under section 28 which provided for the levy of penalty when a person without reasonable cause failed to furnish a return of his total income after notices under section 22(2) or section 34 had been issued to him. The Supreme Court answered the question in the affirmative and held that the failure to send the estimate under clause (3) of section 18A was by the fiction created by clause (9) of the same section deemed to be a failure to send a return and consequently "all those facts on which alone there could be failure to send the return must be deemed to exist and it must accordingly be taken that by reason of this fiction notices required to be given under section 22 must be deemed to have been given"; making section 28 applicable.[33]

Explanation 2 of section 2(15) of the Estate Duty Act, 1953 furnishes example of a legal fiction which extends the normal meaning of a word. The *Explanation* provides: 'The extinguishment at the expense of the deceased of a debt or other rights shall be deemed to have been a disposition made by the deceased in favour of the person for whose benefit the debt or right was extinguished and in relation to such a disposition the expression 'property' shall include the benefit conferred by the extinguishment of a debt or right'. In view of this explanation it has been held that when the deceased, who was a coparcener in a Hindu Joint Family, entered into a partition within two years before his death in which he received as his share an allotment substantially lower in value than he could have legally got, there was a disposition by the deceased of his interest in the family property in favour of other members of the family to the extent of the difference between the value of the deceased's share which he could have received and what was actually received by him and that the value of this

---

32. *C.I.T., Delhi v. S. Teja Singh*, AIR 1959 SC 352, p. 355 : 1959 Supp (1) SCR 394. For another illustration of legal fiction from the Income-tax Act, 1922, **see** *Rajputana Trading Co. Ltd. v. C.I.T., West Bengal*, AIR 1969 SC 572 : 1969 (1) SCR 1013.

33. *C.I.T., Delhi v. S. Teja Singh*, AIR 1959 SC 352, p. 355 : 1959 Supp (1) SCR 394.

interest was includible in the principal value of estate of the deceased liable to estate duty.[34]

In a case[35] arising out of the Ajmer Merwara Municipalities Regulation, 1925, which by section 93 provided for appeals against the levy of any tax and by sub-section (4) of section 222 provided that any money recoverable by the Committee under sub-section (1) of the same section 'shall be recovered as if it were a tax levied by the Committee', the question was whether an appeal could be filed under section 93 against the claim of money by the municipal committee under section 222(1). The Supreme Court held that such an appeal could be filed and observed: "If by the fiction introduced by section 222(4) the amount in question is to be deemed as if it were a tax, it is obvious that full effect must be given to this legal fiction; and in consequence, just as a result of the said fiction the recovery procedure prescribed by section 234 (for taxes) becomes available to the committee so would the right of making an appeal prescribed by section 93(1) be available to the appellant."[36]

Amended Section 33(1) of the Monopolies and Restrictive Trade Practices Act, 1969 declared that any agreement falling within clauses (a) to (l) shall be deemed to be an agreement relating to restrictive trade practices and shall be subject to registration. Construing this provision it was held that an agreement falling within any of the clauses (a) to (l) will be held to be an agreement relating to restrictive trade practice because of the legal fiction and it will be immaterial to consider whether it falls within the definition of restrictive trade practice in section 2(o).[37] No exception can be taken to this view. It was, however, further held that if a person gets an agreement registered it is not open to him to contend that the agreement does not relate to restrictive trade practice as it does not fall under any of the clauses (a) to (l) or within the definition in section 2(o).[38] It is submitted that this view is open to the objection that it is not the registration of an agreement which makes the legal fiction operate but the fact that the agreement falls under any of the clauses (a) to (l). Therefore, if a person by

---

34. *Controller of Estate Duty v. Kantilal Trikamlal*, AIR 1976 SC 1935 : 1977 SCC (Tax) 90 : (1976) 4 SCC 643; **Contrast** *Controller of Estate Duty v. Kancharla Kesavrao*, AIR 1973 SC 2484 : 1973 SCC (Tax) 549 : (1973) 2 SCC 384.

35. *Dargah Committee, Ajmer v. State of Rajasthan*, AIR 1962 SC 574, p. 577 : 1962 (2) SCR 265. For further illustrations of a legal fiction, **see** *Delhi Cloth and General Mills Co. Ltd. v. Their Workmen*, AIR 1972 SC 299, p. 305 : 1971 (2) SCC 695; *C.I.T., B. & O. v. Maharaj Kumar Kamal Singh*, AIR 1973 SC 1056, p. 1059 : 1973 SCC (Tax) 333 : (1973) 3 SCC 819; *State of Andhra Pradesh v. Vallabhapuram Ravi*, (1984) 4 SCC 410, p. 420 : AIR 1985 SC 870.

36. *Dargah Committee, Ajmer v. State of Rajasthan, supra*, p. 577.

37. *Voltas Limited, Bombay v. Union of India*, 1995 (1) Scale 455, p. 462: 1995 AIR SCW 2928 : 1995 Supp (2) SCC 498 : AIR 1995 SC 1881.

38. *Ibid*, p. 464

way of abundant caution gets an agreement registered to avoid possibility of prosecution it should be open to him to contend that the agreement does not fall under any of the clauses and is not a restrictive trade agreement when proceedings are taken before the commission under section 37.

But although full effect must be given to the legal fiction, as already noticed it should not be extended beyond the purpose for which it is created.[39] S.R. DAS, J., referred to this principle in his opinion in *State of Travancore-Cochin v. Shanmugha Vilas Cashewnut Factory*[40] and as acting Chief Justice re-affirmed the same in his leading judgment in *Bengal Immunity Co. Ltd. v. State of Bihar*.[41] In the latter case the learned Chief Justice stated that "legal fictions are created only for some definite purpose", and he proceeded to add that "a legal fiction is to be limited to the purpose for which it was created and should not be extended beyond that legitimate field".[42]

It was, therefore, held in modification to the view expressed in *United Motor's* case[43] that the *Explanation* to Article 286(1)(a) of the Constitution (as it stood before the Constitution Sixth Amendment Act) could not be extended to Article 286(2) either as an exception or as a proviso thereto so as to convert inter-State transactions into intra-State transactions *qua* the delivery State. The *Explanation* on its true construction was for the purpose of explaining an outside sale referred to in sub-clause (a) of Article 286(1) and the fiction created by it could not be extended beyond that purpose.[44]

Similarly, section 5(2) of the Prevention of Corruption Act, 1988 ('PC Act'), provides that a Special Judge may, with a view to obtain evidence, tender a pardon to a person concerned with an offence, which shall, for the purposes of sub-sections (1) to (5) of section 308 of the CrPC, be deemed to have been tendered under section 307 of the Code. The Supreme Court held that while interpreting a provision creating a legal fiction, the purposes

---

39. **See** text and note 8, p. 417.
40. *State of Travancore-Cochin v. Shanmugha Vilas Cashewnut Factory*, AIR 1953 SC 333, pp. 342, 343 : 1954 SCR 53.
41. *Bengal Immunity Co. Ltd. v. State of Bihar*, AIR 1955 SC 661, p. 680 : (1955) 2 SCR 603; **referred** to in *C.I.T., Bombay v. Amarchand N. Shroff*, AIR 1963 SC 1448, p. 1452 : 1963 Supp (1) SCR 699; *C.I.T., Gujarat v. Vadilal Lallubhai*, AIR 1973 SC 1016, p. 1019; 1973 SCC (Tax) 1 : (1973) 3 SCC 17; *C.I.T., Kanpur v. Mother India Refrigeration Industries (P.) Ltd.*, (1985) 4 SCC 1, p. 9 : AIR 1985 SC 1720; *Maganlal v. Jaiswal Industries*, AIR 1989 SC 2113, p. 2122 : 1989 (4) SCC 344.
42. *Bengal Immunity Co. Ltd. v. State of Bihar*, AIR 1955 SC 661 : 1955 (2) SCR 603.
43. *State of Bombay v. United Motors (India) Ltd.*, AIR 1953 SC 252 : 1953 SCR 1069.
44. *Bengal Immunity Co. Ltd. v. State of Bihar, supra.*

for which the fiction is created must be ascertained, and that the deeming provision in section 5(2) is for a limited purpose *i.e.* section 308 of the CrPC, which is manifest from the text of the provision itself. Section 308 has been enacted for a very different purpose, namely, for holding trial of a person for not complying with the conditions of pardon. Accordingly, the power of a Special Judge to grant pardon at any stage of investigation, inquiry or trial as per section 306 of the CrPC, was held to be unfettered by the deeming provision under section 5(2) of the PC Act, and the contention that the same could only be exercised at the stage of trial under section 307, CrPC, was rejected.[45]

This principle was also applied in the interpretation of section 9(1)(i) of the Income-tax Act, 1961, which provides that all income accruing or arising, whether directly or indirectly, *inter alia* through the transfer of a capital asset situated in India, shall be deemed to accrue or arise in India. The Supreme Court held that income accruing or arising to a non-resident outside India, on transfer of a capital asset situated in India, is fictionally deemed to accrue or arise in India, which income is liable to be taxed by reason of section 5(2)(b) of the Act. However, the legal fiction has a limited scope and cannot be expanded by giving a purposive interpretation to the same, particularly if the result of such interpretation is to transform the concept of chargeability. Therefore, it was held that section 9(1)(i) cannot, by a process of interpretation, be extended to cover indirect transfers of capital assets/property situated in India, as to do so would amount to changing the context and ambit of section 9(1)(i).[46]

In construing section 19(3) of the Bengal Public Demands Recovery Act, 1913, which provided that 'the Certificate holder shall be deemed to be the representative of the holder of the attached decree, and to be entitled to execute such attached decree in any manner lawful for the holder thereof,' the Privy Council pointed out that the legal fiction created thereby was for a limited purpose of enabling the certificate holder to execute the decree and to satisfy his own claim out of proceeds of such execution but he was not in the position of an assignee of the decree, so as to acquire all the rights of the original decree-holder in the decree.[47]

Mention may also be made of cases relating to interpretation of section 24B of the Income-tax Act, 1922. According to the scheme of the Act, the individual assessee had to be a living person and the assessment had to be in respect of the income of previous year. By section 24B, legal

---

45. *Bangaru Laxman v. State (Through CBI) & Anr.*, (2012) 1 SCC 500, pp. 506, 507.
46. *Vodafone International Holdings BV v. Union of India & Anr.*, (2012) 6 SCC 613, pp. 672, 673.
47. *Radhakissen Chamaria v. Durga Prasad Chamaria*, AIR 1940 PC 167, p. 170.

representatives were by fiction made assessees for the purposes of the income received in the previous year, during which the assessee died. It was held that the fiction could not be extended to bring within its ambit sums received by the legal representatives subsequent to the previous year.[48]

Similarly the fiction enacted in section 7(3) of the Hindu Succession Act, 1956 by the words 'as if the sthanam property had been divided per capita immediately before the death of sthanamdar among himself and all the members of his family' was held to be introduced for the purpose of determining the shares of the members of the family and heirs of the sthanamdar and not for limiting the devolution of the sthanam property to the extent of the share which on such hypothetical division was held by the sthanamdar. The opening words of the section made it clear that on the death of the sthanamdar, the entire sthanam property devolved on the members and heirs, and, therefore, the entire property was held liable to payment of estate duty on the death of sthanamdar.[49]

Another illustration of restriction of the effect of the fiction to its avowed object is furnished by the decision of the Supreme Court which construed section 9(2) of the Central Sales Tax Act, 1956 before its amendment by Act 103 of 1976. This section enabled the assessing authorities under the general sales tax law of the appropriate State to assess, reassess, collect and enforce payment of tax including any penalty payable by a dealer under the Central Sales Tax Act as if the tax or penalty payable by such a dealer under this Act (the Central Sales Tax Act) is a tax or penalty payable under the general Sales Tax Law of the State; and the section 'for this purpose' authorised the authorities to exercise all or any of the powers under the general Sales Tax Law of the State. It was held by the Supreme Court that the deeming provision contained in the section could not mean that the penalty imposed under the State Act would be deemed to be exigible under the Central Act and that the section did not authorise assessment or collection of any tax or penalty not imposed by the Central Act.[50]

---

48. *C.I.T., Bombay v. Amarchand N. Shorff*, AIR 1963 SC 1448, p. 1452 : 1963 Supp (1) SCR 699; *C.I.T., Bombay v. James Anderson*, AIR 1964 SC 1761 : 1964 (5) SCR 590. For another Income-tax case, **see** *C.I.T., Gujarat v. Vadilal Lallubhai*, AIR 1973 SC 1016, p. 1019 : 1973 SCC (Tax) 1 : (1973) 3 SCC 17.

49. *M.K. Balakrishna Menon v. Assistant Controller of Estate Duty, Ernakulam*, AIR 1971 SC 2392, p. 2395 : 1971 (2) SCC 909.

50. *Khemka and Co. (Agencies) Pvt. Ltd. v. State of Maharashtra*, AIR 1975 SC 1549 : 1975 (2) SCC 22. For construction of the section after amendment, **see** *Pannalal Kankariya & Sons v. Additional Assistant Commissioner of Sales Tax*, 1981 MPLJ 580. The case of *Khemka and Co. followed in Collector of Central Excise v. Orient Fabrics (P.) Ltd.*, (2004) 1 SCC 597 : (2003) 10 JT 282 and was **distinguished** in *Mahim Patram (P) Ltd. v. Union of India*, (2007) 3 SCC 668 (paras 36, 37) : (2007) 4 JT 50.

Again the fiction enacted in section 2A of the Industrial Disputes Act, 1947 by which a dispute relating to termination of services of an individual workman is deemed to be an industrial dispute has been given a restricted construction and it has been held that pendency of such a dispute before the Industrial Tribunal does not bring into effect the suspension of the workers' right to strike under section 23 of the Act.[51]

Another example where a fiction has not been extended beyond its purpose is furnished by the case[52] construing clause 5(3)(ii) of the Imports (Control) Order which provides: 'It shall be deemed to be a condition of every such licence (Import's licence) that the goods for the import of which a licence is granted shall be the property of the licensee at the time of import and thereafter upto the clearance through customs.' It was held that the fiction created by this clause was for the proper implementation of the Imports (Control) Order and the Imports and Exports (Control) Act, 1947 and to hold the licensee responsible for anything and everything that happens from the time of import till the goods are cleared through customs and that the fiction cannot be employed to attribute ownership of the imported goods to the importer in a case where he abandons them, that is, in a situation where he does not pay and receive the documents of title. In another case the fiction enacted in section 36 of the Arbitration and Conciliation Act, 1996 that the award shall be enforced under the Code of Civil Procedure, 1908 in the same manner as if it were a decree of the court was not extended to make an award a 'decree' for purposes of section 9(2) of the Presidency-towns Insolvency Act, 1909.[53] In another 2007 case, the fiction enacted in section 32 of the Stamp Act, 1899 that when a document is stamped in accordance with the order of the Collector passed under section 31 and contains a certificate of the Collector that it 'shall be deemed to be duly stamped' was not extended to negative the revisional power of the Board of Revenue, against the order of Collector under section 31, arising under section 56(4) as amended in Madhya Pradesh.[54]

Section 14 of the Customs Act, 1962 which provides for valuation of goods for assessment of customs duty enacts a fiction that the value shall be deemed to be the price at which such goods are ordinarily sold in international market 'at the time and place of importation'. As the import of

---

51. *Chemicals and Fibres of India Ltd. v. State of Maharashtra*, AIR 1975 SC 1660: (1975) 4 SCC 332 : 1975 SCC (L&S) 168.

52. *Union of India v. Sampat Raj Dugar*, AIR 1992 SC 1417, p. 1423 : 1992 (2) SCC 66.

53. *Paramjeet Singh Patheja v. ICDS Ltd.*, AIR 2007 SC 168 (para 60) : (2006) 10 JT 41 : (2006) 8 SLT 295.

54. *Raymond Ltd. v. State of Chhattisgarh*, (2007) 3 SCC 79 (paras 23, 24) : (2007) 3 SLT 483.

goods is completed when the goods reach the customs barrier and the bill of entry for home consumption is filed, it was held that the value will include the landing charges which have to be paid before the goods are cleared for home consumption and that by its inclusion the fiction is not extended beyond its purpose.[55]

Section 73 of the Mumbai Municipal Corporation Act, 1949 empowers the commissioner to execute contracts on behalf of the corporation but clause (c) of the section restricts the power in case of contracts which invoke an expenditure of more than a lakh with the requirement of 'previous approval' of the standing committee. Clause (c), further provides that 'the standing committee shall consider and dispose of the proposal made by the commissioner in that behalf within fifteen days from the date on which the item is first included in the agenda of any meeting of that committee and failing which the approval to such contract shall be deemed to have been given by the committee'. Construing this provision, it has been held that if the standing committee in its meeting requires the commissioner to place before the committee relevant materials for deciding whether or not to grant approval, the fiction will not operate otherwise the provision requiring approval will not be workable and the object of providing for approval will be defeated.[56]

The Legislature may sometimes create a chain of fictions by the same Act or by succeeding Acts.[57] If *A* is deemed to be *B*, and *B* is deemed to be *C*, the inevitable consequence may be that *A* is deemed to be *C*. By section 8 of the Abolition of Privy Council Jurisdiction Act, 1949, any order made by His Majesty in Council on an Indian Appeal was to have effect as if it were an order or decree made by the Federal Court and by Article 374(2) of the Constitution, judgments and orders of the Federal Court are to have the same effect as if they had been delivered or made by the Supreme Court. The legal effect of these two fictions is, that an order in an Indian Appeal made by the Privy Council before its jurisdiction was abolished, is to have effect as if it were an order made by the Supreme Court.[58]

The Administration of Evacuee Property Ordinance (Central Ordinance 12 of 1949), was repealed and replaced by Ordinance 27 of 1949 with a deeming provision that anything done or action taken under the repealed

---

55. *Garden Silk Mills Ltd. v. Union of India*, JT 1999 (7) SC 552 : AIR 2000 SC 33, p. 39 : (1999) 8 SCC 744.

56. *Nandkishore Ganesh Joshi v. Commissioner Municipal Corporation, Kalyan*, AIR 2005 SC 34, pp. 37, 38.

57. *State of West Bengal v. Sadam K. Bormal*, AIR 2004 SC 3666, p. 3673 : (2004) 6 SCC 59.

58. *Yellappagouda Shankargouda Patil v. Basangouda Shiddangouda Patil*, AIR 1960 SC 808, pp. 809, 810 : 1960 (3) SCR 221.

Ordinance was deemed to have been done or taken under the repealing Ordinance as if it were in force when the thing was done or action was taken.Ordinance 27 of 1949, was replaced and repealed by Act 31 of 1950, which also contained a similar deeming clause that anything done or action taken under Ordinance No. 27 of 1949 was to be deemed to have been done or taken under the Act as if it were in force when the thing was done or the action taken. As a result of these fictions it was held that an order passed by the Deputy Custodian under Ordinance 12 of 1949, was to be deemed to be an order made under Act 31 of 1950, and was thus revisable under section 27 of that Act.[59]

In 1955, the Central Government acting under section 3 of the Imports and Exports (Control) Act, 1947, issued Imports (Control) Order, 1955, which consolidated all orders in one place and repealed all previous orders on the subject. It provided that all licences issued under the repealed orders were to be deemed to be issued under the new order. It further provided for certain deemed conditions of every licence. It was held that the deemed conditions of a licence under the new order became also the conditions of a licence issued under the repealed orders but deemed to be issued under the new order.[60]

Outside the bounds of the legal fiction the difference between the reality and the fiction may still persist in the provisions of the same Act which creates the fiction and the difference may be ascertained by referring to the subject and context of those provisions.[61]

It must, also, be noticed that the word 'deemed' which is normally used to create a statutory fiction may also be used to put beyond doubt a meaning which may otherwise be uncertain or to give to the statutory language a comprehensive description that it includes what is obvious, what is uncertain and what is in ordinary sense impossible.[62]

The principle stated and discussed above relating to the interpretation and application of a statutory fiction has also been applied to a non-statutory legal fiction that acquittal in appeal takes effect retrospectively and wipes out the sentence awarded by the lower court. This retrospective

---

59. *Bishambhar Nath Kohli v. State of U.P.*, AIR 1966 SC 573 : 1966 (2) SCR 158.

60. *State of West Bengal v. Motilal Kanoria*, AIR 1966 SC 1586 : 1966 (3) SCR 933.

61. *M. Pentiah v. Muddala Veeramallappa*, AIR 1961 SC 1107, p. 1110 : (1961) 2 SCR 295. For this case, **see** Chapter 1, title 4 'Statute to be construed to make it effective and workable'.

62. *St. Aubyn (LM) v. A.G. (No. 2)*, (1951) 2 All ER 473, p. 498 : 1952 AC 15 (HL); **referred** to in *Hira H. Advani v. State of Maharashtra*, AIR 1971 SC 44, p. 54 : 1969 (2) SCC 662; *Waliram Waman Hiray (Dr.) v. Mr. Justice B. Lentin*, AIR 1988 SC 2267, p. 2282 : 1988 (4) SCC 419; *Premier Breweries v. State of Kerala*, JT 1997 (10) SC 226, p. 231 : (1998) 1 SCC 641 : (1998) 1 KLT 186.

operation of acquittal only means that the stigma attached to the conviction and the rigour of the sentence are completely obliterated but that does not mean that the fact of conviction and sentence is wiped out and if a person was disqualified for being chosen to fill the seat for which an election is held on the date of scrutiny of his nomination paper by the returning officer because of his conviction, he will become qualified if later on his conviction is set aside in appeal.[63]

6. MANDATORY AND DIRECTORY PROVISIONS

(a) General

The study of numerous cases on this topic does not lead to formulation of any universal rule except this that language alone most often is not decisive, and regard must be had to the context, subject-matter and object of the statutory provision in question, in determining whether the same is mandatory or directory. In an oft-quoted passage LORD CAMPBELL said: "No universal rule can be laid down as to whether mandatory enactments shall be considered directory only or obligatory with an implied nullification for disobedience. It is the duty of courts of justice to try to get at the real intention of the Legislature by carefully attending to the whole scope of the statute to be considered."[64] As approved by the Supreme Court:

---

63. *K. Prabhakaran v. P. Jayarajan*, (2005) 1 SCC 754, p. 772 : AIR 2005 SC 688 (Constitution Bench) overruling *Mannilal v. Parmai Lal*, (1970) 2 SCC 462 : AIR 1971 SC 2333 and *Vidyacharan Shukla v. Purshottam Lal Kaushik*, (1981) 2 SCC 84 : AIR 1981 SC 547.

64. *Liverpool Borough Bank v. Turner*, (1861) 30 LJ Ch 379, pp. 380, 381; **referred** to in *Howard v. Bodington*, (1877) 2 PD 203, p. 211 (LORD PENZANCE); *Vita Food Products Inc. v. Unus Shipping Co.*, (1939) 1 All ER 513, p. 523 (PC); *H.N. Rishbud v. State of Delhi*, AIR 1955 SC 196, p. 200 : (1955) 1 SCR 1150; *State of U.P. v. Baburam Upadhya*, AIR 1961 SC 751, p. 765 : (1961) 2 SCR 679; *Bhikraj Jaipuria v. Union of India*, AIR 1962 SC 113, p. 119 : (1962) 2 SCR 880; *Banarasi Das v. Cane Commissioner, U.P.*, AIR 1963 SC 1417, p. 1424 : 1963 Supp (2) SCR 760;*Kailash v. Nanhku*, (2005) 4 SCC 480, pp. 496, 497 (9th Edn. of this book, p. 338 is **referred**). **See further** *Raza Buland Sugar Co. Ltd., Rampur v. Municipal Board, Rampur*, AIR 1965 SC 895, p. 899 : (1965) 1 SCR 413; *Article 143 of the Constitution of India, In the matter of*, AIR 1965 SC 745, p. 769 : (1965) 1 SCR 970; *Montreal Street Rly. v. Normandin*, (1917) AC 170 : AIR 1917 PC 142, p. 144; *Hiralal Agrawal v. Rampadarath Singh*, AIR 1969 SC 244, p. 251 : (1969) 1 SCR 328; *Ramchandra v. Govind*, AIR 1975 SC 915, p. 917 : (1975) 1 SCC 559; *K.K. Srinivasan v. State of Karnataka*, (1987) 1 SCC 658, p. 675 : AIR 1987 SC 1059; *Rubber House v. Excellsior Needle Industries Pvt. Ltd.*, AIR 1989 SC 1160, p. 1165 : (1989) 2 SCC 413; *Chief Education Officer v. Quinn*, (1996) 3 All ER 72, p. 79 (HL); *Shashikant Singh v. Tarkeshwar Singh*, AIR 2002 SC 2031, p. 2034 : (2002) 5 SCC 738. In the matter of Special Reference No. 1 of 2002

[Footnote No. 64 Contd.]

"The question as to whether a statute is mandatory or directory depends upon the intent of the Legislature and not upon the language in which the intent is clothed. The meaning and intention of the Legislature must govern, and these are to be ascertained not only from the phraseology of the provision, but also by considering its nature, its design, and the consequences which would follow from construing it the one way or the other."[65] "For ascertaining the real intention of the Legislature", points out SUBBARAO, J., "the court may consider *inter alia*, the nature and design of the statute, and the consequences which would follow from construing it the one way or the other; the impact of other provisions whereby the necessity of complying with the provisions in question is avoided; the circumstances, namely, that the statute provides for a contingency of the non-compliance with the provisions; the fact that the non-compliance with the provisions is or is not visited by some penalty; the serious or the trivial consequences, that flow therefrom; and above all, whether the object of the legislation will be defeated or furthered."[66] If object of the enactment

---

[Footnote No. 64 Contd.]

[*Gujarat Assembly Election matter,* (2002) 8 SCC 237, p. 322; *Bhavnagar University v. Palitana Sugar Mill (P.) Ltd.*, (2003) 2 SCC 111, p. 126 : AIR 2003 SC 511, p. 520; *Chandrika Prasad Yadav v. State of Bihar*, AIR 2004 SC 2036, p. 2042 : (2004) 6 SCC 331].

65. Passage from CRAWFORD: Statutory Construction, p. 516; **approved** in *State of U.P. v. Manbodhan Lal Shrivastava*, AIR 1957 SC 912, p. 918 : 1958 SCR 533; *State of U.P. v. Baburam, Upadhya*, AIR 1961 SC 751, p. 765 : (1961) 2 SCR 679; *Article 143 of the Constitution of India, In the matter of, supra*, p. 769; *State of Mysore v. V.K. Kangan*, AIR 1975 SC 2190, p. 2192 : (1976) 2 SCC 895; *Govindlal Chhaganlal Patel v. Agriculture Produce Market Committee*, AIR 1976 SC 263, p. 267 : (1976) 1 SCC 369; *Ganesh Prasad Sah Kesari v. Lakshmi Narayan*, (1985) 3 SCC 53, pp. 59, 60 : AIR 1985 SC 964; *B.P. Khemka Pvt. Ltd. v. Birendra Kumar Bhowmik*, (1987) 2 SCC 407, p. 415 : AIR 1987 SC 1010; *Owners and Parties interested in M.V. "Vali Pero" v. Fernandes Lopez*, AIR 1989 SC 2206, p. 2213 : (1989) 4 SCC 671; *State of M.P. v. Pradeep Kumar,* (2000) 7 SCC 372, p. 377 : (2000) 10 JT 349; *Sarla Goel v. Krishanchand,* (2009) 7 SCC 658 pp. 668, 669 para 30 : (2009) 9 JT 21.

66. *State of U.P. v. Babu Ram Upadhya, supra*, p. 765, **See further** *Raza Buland Sugar Co. Ltd., Rampur v. Municipal Board, Rampur, supra*, p. 899 (para 7), where it is said that the "object of the statute is determining factor". *Narsimhiah (K.) v. H.C. Singri Gowda*, AIR 1966 SC 330, p. 332 : (1964) 7 SCR 618; *Remington Rand of India Ltd. v. Workmen*, AIR 1968 SC 224, p. 226 : (1968) 1 SCR 164; *Hiralal Agrawal v. Rampadarath Singh*, AIR 1969 SC 244, p. 252 : (1969) 1 SCR 328; *Virji Ram Sutaria v. Nathalal Premji Bhanvadia*, AIR 1970 SC 765, p. 768 : (1969) 1 SCC 77; *Municipal Corporation of Greater Bombay v. BEST Workers' Union*, AIR 1973 SC 883, p. 891 : 1973 SCC (L&S) 177; *Satya Narain v. Dhuja Ram*, AIR 1974 SC 1185, p. 1190 : (1974) 4 SCC 237; *In re, Presidential Election*, 1974, AIR 1974 SC 1682, p. 1686 : (1974) 2 SCC 33; *Ajit Singh v. State of Punjab*, AIR 1983 SC 494, p. 499 : (1983) 2 SCC 217; *Dalchand v. Municipal Corporation, Bhopal*, (1984) 2 SCC 486 : AIR 1983 SC 303; *Rubber House v. Excellsior Needle*

[Footnote No. 66 Contd.]

will be defeated by holding the same directory, it will be construed as mandatory,[67] whereas if by holding it mandatory serious general inconvenience will be created to innocent persons without very much furthering the object of enactment, the same will be construed as directory.[68] But all this does not mean that the language used is to be ignored but only that the *prima facie* inference of the intention of the Legislature arising from the words used may be displaced by considering the nature of the enactment, its design and the consequences flowing from alternative constructions. Thus, the use of the words 'as nearly as may be' in contrast to the words 'at least' will *prima facie* indicate a directory requirement,[69] negative words a mandatory requirement,[70] 'may' a directory requirement[71] and 'shall' a mandatory requirement.[72]

For instance, section 3(f)(7) of the Haryana Apartment Ownership Act, 1983, defines 'common areas and facilities' to mean *inter alia*, 'such community and commercial facilities as *may* be provided for in the declaration'. The Supreme Court held that the expression 'may' used in section 3(f)(7) clearly indicates that no duty is cast on the coloniser/ land owner to give an undivided interest in community and commercial facilities

[Footnote No. 66 Contd.]

Industries Pvt. Ltd., AIR 1989 SC 1160, pp. 1165, 1166 : (1989) 2 SCC 413; *Karnal Leather Karamchari Sanghatan v. Liberty Footwear Co.*, AIR 1990 SC 247, p. 254 : (1989) 4 SCC 448; *Mohan Singh v. International Air Port Authority*, 1996 (8) Scale 251, p. 260 : 1996 (10) JT 311 : (1997) 9 SCC 132.

67. *Bhikraj Jaipuria v. Union of India*, AIR 1962 SC 113, p. 119 : 1962 (2) SCR 880; *Raza Buland Sugar Co. Ltd., Rampur v. Municipal Board, Rampur*, AIR 1965 SC 895, p. 900 (para 9) : (1965) 1 SCR 970.
68. *Montreal Street Railway v. Normandin*, AIR 1917 PC 142, p. 144, **referred** to in *Bishwanath Khemka v. Emperor*, AIR 1945 FC 67, p. 68; *State of U.P. v. Manbodhan Lal Shrivastava*, AIR 1957 SC 912, p. 917 : 1958 SCR 533; *L. Hazari Mal Kuthiala v. I.T.O., Special Circle, Ambala Cantt*, AIR 1961 SC 200, p. 202 : 1961 (1) SCR 892; *State of U.P. v. Babu Ram Upadhya*, AIR 1961 SC 751, p. 765 : 1961 (2) SCR 679; *Banwarilal Agarwalla v. State of Bihar*, AIR 1961 SC 849, p. 853 : 1962 (1) SCR 33; *Raza Buland Sugar Co. Ltd., Rampur v. Municipal Board, Rampur*, AIR 1965 SC 895, p. 899 : 1965 (1) SCR 970; *Kailash v. Nanhku*, (2005) 4 SCC 480, p. 497 : AIR 2005 SC 2441 (passage from 9th Edn. of this book pp. 339, 340 is approved).
69. *Jaishankar Prasad v. State of Bihar*, AIR 1993 SC 1906, p. 1911 : 1993 (2) SCC 597 [construction of proviso to article 316(1) of the Constitution]; *Kailash v. Nanhku*, (2005) 4 SCC 480, p. 493 : AIR 2005 SC 2441 (Construction of section 87 of the Representation of the People Act 1951). The expressions 'as far as it can be made applicable' or 'as far as applicable' will also be *prima facie* construed as directory: *Tarlok Singh v. Municipal Corpn. of Amritsar*, (1986) 4 SCC 27 : AIR 1986 SC 1957; *Direct Recruit Class II Engg. Officers' Asson. v. State of Maharashtra*, (1990) 2 SCC 715 : AIR 1990 SC 1607.
70. **See** title 6(c) p. 446.
71. **See** title 6(k) p. 519.
72. **See** title 6(e) p. 449.

exclusively to apartment owners of any particular colony, since the same have to be enjoyed by other apartment owners of the entire complex.[73] On the other hand, section 154 of the CrPC, which deals with information in cognizable offences and registration of FIRs, uses the word 'shall'. Accordingly, a Constitution Bench of the Supreme Court held that section 154 postulates the mandatory registration of the FIR on receipt of information of a cognizable offence. However, if the information given does not disclose a cognizable offence, a preliminary inquiry may be ordered, and if the inquiry discloses commission of a cognizable offence, the FIR must be registered.[74]

If a provision is mandatory an act done in breach thereof will be invalid, but if it is directory the act will be valid although the non-compliance may give rise to some other penalty if provided by the statute.[75] An illustration of this can be seen in the context of section 154(2) of the Criminal Procedure Code, 1973, which provides that a copy of the information (FIR) recorded under section 154(1) 'shall' be given forthwith, free of cost, to the informant. The Supreme Court held that in order to declare a provision mandatory, the test to be applied is as to whether non-compliance with the provision could render the entire proceedings invalid, and depends on the intent of the Legislature, and that the language used was not determinative of this issue. Applying this test, the Court reached the inescapable conclusion that the section is merely directory and not mandatory, as it prescribes only a duty to give a copy of the FIR.[76]

It has often been said that a mandatory enactment must be obeyed or fulfilled exactly, but it is sufficient if a directory enactment be obeyed or fulfilled substantially.[77] The latter half of this proposition is, however, not

---

73. *DLF Ltd v. Manmohan Lowe & Ors.*, (2014) 12 SCC 231, p. 254.

74. *Lalita Kumari v. Government of Uttar Pradesh & Ors.*, (2014) 2 SCC 1, pp. 59, 60, 61.

75. *Drigraj Kuer (Rani) v. Amar Krishna Narain Singh (Raja)*, AIR 1960 SC 444, pp. 449, 451 : 1960 (2) SCR 431; *L. Hazari Mal Kuthiala v. I.T.O., Ambala Cantt.*, AIR 1961 SC 200, p. 202 : 1961 (1) SCR 892; *Banwarilal Agarwalla v. State of Bihar, supra*, p. 851; *Bhikraj Jaipuria v. Union of India*, AIR 1962 SC 113, p. 119 : 1962 (2) SCR 880; *Union of India v. Tulsiram Patel*, (1985) 3 SCC 398, p. 484 : AIR 1985 SC 1416; (Breach of a directory provision does not entail any invalidity.) *Rubber House v. Excellsior Industries Pvt. Ltd.*, AIR 1989 SC 1160, p. 1165 : (1989) 2 SCC 413; *Ram Deen Maurya v. State of U.P.*, (2009) 6 SCC 735 para 43 (11th edition of this book is **referred**).

76. *State v. N.S. Gnaneswaran*, (2013) 3 SCC 594, p. 603.

77. *Woodward v. Sarsons*, (1875) LR 10 CP 733, p. 746 : (1874-80) All ER Rep 262, p. 268; *Punjab Co-operative Bank Ltd. v. C.I.T., Lahore*, AIR 1940 PC 230, p. 233; *Pratap Singh v. Srikrishna Gupta*, AIR 1956 SC 140, p. 141 : 1955 (2) SCR 1029; *Banarasi Das v. Cane Commr. U.P.*, AIR 1963 SC 1417, p. 1424 : 1963 Supp (2) SCR 760; *Hiralal Agarwal v. Rampadarath Singh*, AIR 1969 SC 244, p. 253 : 1969 (1) SCR 328; *Ram Autar Singh Bhadoria v. Ram Gopal Singh*, AIR 1975 SC 2182, p. 2189 : (1976) 1 SCC 43; *Dove Investment (P.) Ltd. v. Gujarat Industrial Investment Corpn.*, (2006) 2 SCC 619 (para 47) : AIR 2006 SC 1454.

quite accurate as even a complete non-compliance of a directory provision has been held in many cases as not affecting the validity of the act done in breach thereof.[78] It has been suggested that directory requirements fall under two heads: (1) those which should be substantially complied with to make the act valid; (2) those which even if not at all complied with have no effect on the act.[79] The correct position appears to be that substantial compliance of an enactment is insisted, where mandatory and directory requirements are lumped together, for in such a case, if mandatory requirements are complied with, it will be proper to say that the enactment has been substantially complied with notwithstanding the non-compliance of directory requirements.[80] The point may be explained by taking an example of a set of service rules which provide that adverse remarks shall be communicated to the civil servant concerned ordinarily within seven months.[81] The object of communicating the adverse remarks is to give an

---

78. See for example *State of U.P. v. Manbodhan Lal Shrivastava*, AIR 1957 SC 912, p. 917 : 1958 SCR 533; *Drigraj Kuer (Rani) v. Amar Krishna Narain Singh (Raja)*, AIR 1960 SC 444, pp. 449, 451 : (1960) 2 SCR 431; *L. Hazari Mal Kuthiala v. I.T.O., Ambala Cantt.*, AIR 1961 SC 200, p. 202 : 1961 (1) SCR 892. **See also** cases in note 68, *supra*.

79. *London and Clydeside Estates Ltd. v. Aberdeen District Council*, (1979) 3 All ER 876, p. 882 (HL).

80. See HALSBURY'S Laws of England, 4th Edition, Volume 44, page 584 (f.n. 1). For example, **see** *Pope v. Clarke*, (1953) 2 All ER 704; *K. Kamaraja Nadar v. Kunju Thevar*, AIR 1958 SC 687, p. 697 (S. 117 R.P. Act) : 1959 SCR 583; *Chandrika Prasad Tripathi v. Shiv Prasad Chanpuria*, AIR 1959 SC 827, p. 831 : 1959 Supp (2) SCR 527; *Ch Subbarao v. Member, Election Tribunal, Hyderabad*, AIR 1964 SC 1027, p. 1031 (para 14), p. 1033 (para 25) (S. 81(3) R.P. Act) : (1964) 6 SCR 213; *Raza Buland Sugar Co. Ltd., Rampur v. Municipal Board, Rampur*, AIR 1965 SC 895, pp. 900, 901 (Section 94(3) U.P. Municipalities Act) : (1965) 1 SCR 970; *Virji Ram Sutaria v. Nathalal Premji Bhanvadia*, AIR 1970 SC 765, p. 767 (Article 173 Constitution) : (1969) 2 SCR 627; *M. Karunanidhi v. H.V. Handa*, AIR 1983 SC 558 : (1983) 2 SCC 473. **But see** *Hari Vishnu Kamath v. Ahmad Ishaque*, AIR 1955 SC 233, p. 245 (last 13 lines of para 26) : 1955 (1) SCR 1104; *Delhi Administration v. Chandan Shah*, AIR 1969 SC 1108 : 1969 1 SCC 787 (It was wrongly held that if a directory provision is not substantially complied with, the resultant act is invalid.)

81. *State of Haryana v. P.C. Wadhwa*, (1987) 2 SCC 602, pp. 611, 612 : AIR 1986 SC 1201. **But see** *Baikunth Nath Das v. Chief District Medical Officer Boripada*, AIR 1992 SC 1020 : 1992 (2) SCC 410 (Uncommunicated remarks can be taken into account in compulsorily retiring a civil servant). The case of *Baikunth Nath Das* **distinguished** in *Madan Mohan Choudhary v. State of Bihar*, JT 1998 (1) SC 459 : AIR 1999 SC 1018 : (1999) 3 SCC 396 : AIR 1999 SC 1018, where remarks were not made in normal course. It has now been held that all remarks whether adverse or good should be communicated to the employee within a reasonable time as this requirement flows from constitutional obligation of fairness, non-arbitrariness and natural justice : *Devi Dutt v. Union of India*, (2008) 8 SCC 725 : AIR 2008 SC 2513. **See further** for this case text and note 78 p. 496; *Pyare Mohan Lal v. State of Jharkhand*, (2010) 10 SCC 693 paras 21, 22, 28 : AIR 2010 SC 3753 (The entire service record including uncommunicated entries can be taken into account in deciding compulsory retirement).

opportunity to the civil servant to improve his performance to make up the deficiency noticed in his work and to give him an opportunity to represent against the remarks, in case he disputes them, to the reviewing authority. In the light of this object and having regard to the part adverse remarks play in the service career, the rules on a proper construction will require: (i) communication of the remarks to the civil servant concerned; (ii) communication within a reasonable time; and (iii) communication ordinarily within seven months. The first two requirements will be construed as mandatory and non-compliance of either of them will make the remarks as also any adverse action on their basis invalid. The third requirement will be treated as directory and its non-compliance alone will not make the remarks invalid if the first two requirements are satisfied. To take another example, section 117 of the Representation of the People Act, 1951 provides: 'At the time of presenting an election petition, the petitioner shall deposit in the High Court in accordance with the Rules of the High Court a sum of two thousand rupees as security for costs of the petition'. Construing this section it has been held that the requirement of making the deposit of two thousand rupees as security is mandatory and the same has to be made while presenting an election petition, but the mode of deposit as well as the person who could make the deposit is directory. Therefore, if the deposit of two thousand rupees as security for costs has been made at the time of presentation of the petition although not by the petitioner, it would be said that section 117 has been substantially complied with and there is no non-compliance with its provisions to bring about the petition's dismissal.[82] Section 149(1) of the Patna Municipal Corporation Act, 1951 requires that the Executive Officer shall sign the assessment list and 'shall give public notice by beat of drum and by displaying placards posted in conspicuous places'. Interpreting the section it was held that requirement of public notice was mandatory but the requirement of manner of publication was directory, therefore, public notice in the newspapers was substantial compliance though there was no publication by beat of drum or by posting placards.[83] Section 13(3) and 13(4) of the Medical Council Act, 1956 as amended by Act 34 of 2001 require every Indian Citizen, obtaining medical qualification from any institution outside India, to qualify in a screening test in India for being enrolled in a medical register in India, after 'such date as the Central Government may by notification specify in the Official Gazette'. The Central Government specified 15-3-2002 as the date for bringing into effect the Screening Test Regulations. But the date

82. *M.Y. Ghorpade v. Shivaji Rao M. Poal,* AIR 2002 SC 3105, pp. 3107, 3109 : (2002) 7 SCC 289.

83. *Rai Vimal Krishna v. State of Bihar,* (2003) 6 SCC 401, pp. 412 to 414 : AIR 2003 SC 2676.

and the Regulations were published in the Official Gazette by a notification of the Medical Council of India and not by a notification of the Central Government which was held to be substantial compliance obviously for the reason that requirement of specification of date by the Central Government was construed as mandatory and the requirement of the Central Government notifying it in the Official Gazette directory.[84] These examples illustrate the lumping of mandatory and directory requirements at one place and substantial compliance with them if mandatory part is complied with cven if the directory part is not complied with.

A directory provision may be distinguished from a discretionary power. The former gives no discretion and is intended to be obeyed, but a failure to obey it does not render a thing duly done in disobedience of it a nullity. The latter, *i.e.*, a discretionary power leaves the donee of the power free to use or not to use it at his discretion.[85]

The problem of interpretation is not always solved by labelling a requirement either mandatory or directory and it may become much more important to focus on the consequences of non-compliance.[86] For example, in interpreting the words 'could be tried together with the accused' in section 319(1) of the Criminal Procedure Code, 1973 which enables the arrest or summoning of a person not an accused in a pending trial, the Supreme Court did not stop merely by saying that the provision is directory and held that having regard to consequences, the provision could not be construed to mean 'must be tried' together with the accused for otherwise such a person will escape the trial for the offence if the trial of the accused is over before he is brought before the court.[87]

The general rule that non-compliance of mandatory requirements results in nullification of the act is subject at least to two exceptions. One exception is when performance of the requirement is impossible; performance is then excused.[88] Another exception is of waiver. If certain requirements or conditions are provided by a statute in the interest of a particular person, the requirements or conditions although mandatory may be waived by him

---

84. *Sanjeev Gupta v. Union of India*, (2005) 1 SCC 45, pp. 67, 68 (para 45).

85. *Drigraj Kuer (Rani) v. Amar Krishna Narain Singh (Raja)*, AIR 1960 SC 444, p. 449 : 1960 (2) SCR 431.

86. *Attorney General's Reference* (No. 3 of 1999), (2001) 1 All ER 577, p. 583 (e-f) (HL).

87. *Shashikant Singh v. Tarkeshwar Singh,* AIR 2002 SC 2031, p. 2035 : (2002) 1 SCC 583. It is submitted that 'could be tried together with the accused' is a requirement for taking action against a person who is not an accused in a pending trial and to that extent the condition is mandatory. But it does not mean that the person against whom action is taken under section 319(1) must be tried along with the accused already facing trial.

88. See text and note 89, p. 153.

if no public interests are involved, and in such a case the act done will be valid even if the requirement or condition has not been performed.[89] It was, therefore, held that the requirement of notice under section 80 of the Code of Civil Procedure although mandatory could be waived by the defendant as the provision was enacted merely for the protection of the defendant State or Authority.[90] On the same principle, compliance of section 35 of the Bengal Money-lenders Act, 1940 which requires certain matters to be specified in a sale proclamation for the benefit of the judgment-debtor, although mandatory, can be waived by him.[91] It must, however, be remembered that the principle of waiver applies when the requirements of the statute do not involve any question of public interests or public policy for when the conditions are prescribed for protection of the public or on grounds of public policy, the performance of the conditions cannot be waived.[92] But it is possible that when conditions are prescribed for the protection of the public the resultant act done in violation of the conditions though invalid against persons generally may be valid between particular persons. This can be

---

89. *Quilibet potest renuniare juri pro se introducto* (Every man is entitled to renounce a right introduced in his favour); *Wilson v. McIntosh*, (1894) AC 129, p. 133 : 63 LJ PC 49 (PC); *Dhirendra Nath Ghorai v. Sudhir Chandra Ghosh*, AIR 1964 SC 1300, p. 1304 : 1964 (6) SCR 1001; *Lachoo Mal v. Radhey Shyam*, AIR 1971 SC 2213 : 1971 (1) SCC 619; *Superintendent of Taxes, Dhubri v. Onkarmal Nathumal Trust*, AIR 1975 SC 2065 : (1976) 1 SCC 766; *Director of Inspection, I.T. v. Pooranmall & Sons*, AIR 1975 SC 67, pp. 71, 72 : 1975 SCC (Tax) 346 : (1975) 4 SCC 568; *PDM Reddy v. P.A. Rao*, AIR 1974 SC 2089, pp. 2091, 2092 : (1974) 2 SCC 725; *Brajendra Nath Bhargava v. Harsh Wardhan*, AIR 1988 SC 293, pp. 296, 297 : 1988 (1) SCC 454; *Indira Bai v. Nand Kishore*, AIR 1991 SC 1055, p. 1058; *Krishna Lal v. State of Jammu & Kashmir*, JT 1994(2) SC 619, pp. 624-26; *Kerala State Housing Board v. Rampriya Hotels (P) Ltd.*, JT 1994 (5) SC 113, p. 117 : (1994) 2 KLT 529; *Martin & Harris Limited v. VIth Addl. Distt. Judge*, AIR 1998 SC 492, pp 501 to 503 : 1998 (1) SCC 732; *Commissioner of Customs Mumbai v. Virgo Steels Bombay*, AIR 2002 SC 1745, p. 1761 : (2002) 4 SCC 316 (Notice under section 28 of the Customs Act, 1962); *Krishna Bahadur v. Purna Theatre*, (2004) 8 SCC 229, p. 233 : AIR 2004 SC 4282.

90. *ALAR Vellayan Chettiar v. Govt. of Madras*, AIR 1947 PC 197, p. 199; *Dhian Singh Sobha Singh v. Union of India*, AIR 1958 SC 274, p. 282 : 1958 SCR 781.

91. *Dhirendra Nath Ghorai v. Sudhir Chandra Ghosh*, AIR 1964 SC 1300, p. 1304 : 1964 (6) SCR 1001.

92. *Equitable Life Assurance Society of United States v. Reed*, (1914) AC 587, p. 595; *Edward Ramia Ltd., v. African Woods Ltd.*, (1960) 1 All ER 627, p. 630 (PC); *Johnson v. Moreton*, (1978) 3 All ER 37, p. 47 : (1980) AC 37 (HL), (A liberty or right conferred by a statute or law which involves public as well as a private interest cannot be waived); *Murlidhar v. State of U.P.*, AIR 1974 SC 1924, pp. 1928, 1929 : (1974) 2 SCC 472; *Shalimar Tar Products Ltd. v. H.C. Sharma*, AIR 1988 SC 145 : (1988) 1 SCC 70 (statutory requirement of consent in writing by landlord for enabling tenant to sublet is in public interest to avoid disputes as to consent and cannot be waived); *Rai Chand Jain v. Miss Chandra Kanta Khosla*, AIR 1991 SC 744, p. 754 : (1991) 1 SCC 422 (permission of the rent controller to convert residential building into non-residential is mandatory).

illustrated from a case from Kenya where the Privy Council held on a construction of an Ordinance that the non-compliance with the requirement of attestation prescribed by the Ordinance did not make the document invalid between parties thereto although it became invalid against other persons.[93] Similarly, if some requirement is prescribed for protection of the Government as in Article 299 of the Constitution which has not been observed in execution of a contract of lease, but if there is no other illegality in the transaction, the lease is not void against other persons even if not enforceable against the Government.[94]

While considering the non-compliance with a procedural requirement, it has to be kept in view that such a requirement is designed to facilitate justice and further its ends and therefore, if the consequence of non-compliance is not provided, the requirement may be held to be directory.[95] Thus the requirement in section 13(2) of the Consumer Protection Act, 1986 that the opposite party is to file its reply within thirty days or such extended period not exceeding fifteen days as may be granted by the District Forum has been held to be directory and the Forum cannot be said to be debarred from taking on record a reply filed beyond forty-five days.[96] Approving this case, similar view has been taken by a three-Judge Bench of Order VIII, rule 1 of the Code of Civil Procedure, 1908 which requires a defendant to present a written statement within thirty days from the date of service of summons or within such extended period granted by the court but which shall not be later than ninety days from the date of service of summons.[97] The rules of procedure are to be construed not to frustrate or obstruct the holding of enquiry under the substantive provision. The requirement of rule 6(6) of the Bihar Legislative Council Members (Disqualification on Ground of Defection) Rules, 1994 made under Tenth Schedule of the Constitution requiring a petition to the chairman to be signed and verified in the manner laid down in the Code of Civil Procedure, 1908 for the verification of pleadings was not held to be mandatory so as to make any non-compliance with it to frustrate enquiry by the chairman for

---

93. *National and Grindlays Bank v. Dharamshi etc.*, (1961) 2 All ER 626 (PC).
94. *Biharilal v. Bhuri Devi*, AIR 1997 SC 1879, p. 1885 : 1997 (2) SCC 279.
95. *Sangram Singh v. Election Tribunal, Kota,* AIR 1955 SC 425 : (1955) 2 SCR 1; *Topline Shoes Ltd. v. Corporation Bank,* AIR 2002 SC 2487, pp. 2490, 2491 : (2002) 6 SCC 33; *Kailash v. Nanhka,* (2005) 4 SCC 480, pp. 495, 496 : AIR 2005 SC 2441. *Mahadev Govind Gharge v. Special Land Acquisition Officer,* (2011) 6 SCC 321 (para 37).
96. *Topline Shoes Ltd. v. Corporation Bank, supra.*
97. *Kailash v. Nanhku, supra*, pp. 498, 500 (SCC). **See** to the same effect *Salem Advocate Bar Association T.N. v. Union of India,* (2005) 6 SCC 344, p. 364 (para 21) : AIR 2005 SC 3353; *R.N. Jadi & Brothers v. Subhashchandra,* (2007) 6 SCC 420, para 16 : AIR 2007 SC 2571.

there is no provision in the Tenth Schedule to the effect that until a petition which is signed and verified as required by CPC is presented to the chairman he will not have jurisdiction to give his decision on the question of defection of a member under the Schedule.[1]

In the context of procedural requirements and their non-compliance, the approach suggested by LORD WOOLF M.R. is to regard the question whether a requirement is directory or mandatory as only atmost a first step. The other questions to be considered in this context, according to LORD WOOLF are: "Is the statutory requirement fulfilled if there has been substantial compliance with the requirement and, if so, has their been substantial compliance in the case in issue even though there has not been strict compliance? (The substantial compliance question). Is the non-compliance capable of being waived, and if so, has it or can it and should it be waived in this particular case? (The discretionary question). If it is not capable of being waived or is not waived then what is the consequence of non-compliance? (The consequence question)."[2] In this case the question related to the non-compliance with rule 13(3) of the Asylum Appeal (Procedure) Rules, 1993 which requires that if the secretary of State seeks to challenge the decision of the Immigration Appeal Tribunal 'an application for leave shall be made by serving upon the Tribunal, the Form prescribed in the Schedule'. Rule 38 of the Rules provides that any irregularity resulting from failure to comply with the Rules shall not by itself render the proceedings void and if the appellate authority finds that any person may have been prejudiced, it may before reaching the decision take such steps as it thinks fit to cure the irregularity. In this case although the prescribed form was not used, the only procedural omission was the absence of a declaration of truth as required in the Form. It was held that though this omission was a substantial non-compliance, the irregularity was cured by rule 38 and the requirement to use the form was not to be regarded as a strict requirement.[3] It will be seen that the rules considered in this case by rule 38 conferred a power on the Appellate Authority to waive or cure any irregularity resulting from failure to comply with the Rules. It is submitted that in cases where no such power is conferred on the court, failure to comply with a procedural requirement, which is held to be mandatory, and is not capable of being waived by the party concerned or if capable of being waived by him, has not been waived, may be fatal. For example, a provision requiring the tenant in a proceeding for eviction under the Maharashtra Rent Control Act, 1999 to apply to the Competent Authority within

---

1. *Dr. Mahachandra Prasad Singh v. Chairman Bihar Legislative Council,* (2004) 8 SCC 719, pp. 761, 762 : AIR 2005 SC 69.

2. *R. v. Immigration Appeal Tribunal,* (1999) 3 All ER 231, pp. 238, 239 (CA).

3. *Ibid.*

30 days of the service of summons for leave to defend by an affidavit stating the grounds of defence and providing further that in default the statement filed by the landlord shall be deemed to be admitted and he would be entitled to obtain an order for eviction has been held to be mandatory. It was held that the Authority not being a court has no discretion to extend the time for filing defence by the tenant and it was bound to pass the order of eviction on the default of the tenant to apply within 30 days for leave to defend.[4] But as further stated by LORD WOOLF provisions intended to have that effect 'will be few and far between' and in majority of cases the court's task 'will be to seek to do what is just in all the circumstances' of the case.[5] Further, sometimes a question of prejudice may also have to be considered while considering the effect of non-compliance with a procedural requirement.[6]

In a case of *Seal v. Chief Constable of South Wales Police,*[7] the House of Lords construed section 139(2) of the Mental Health Act, 1983 which provided that 'no civil proceeding shall be brought against any person in any case in respect of any act purporting to be done in pursuance of the Act without the leave of the High Court'. The Act does not provide the consequence of omission to take the leave of the High Court. But having regard to the history of the provision it was held by the majority (Lord WOOLF AND BARONESS HALL dissenting) to be a mandatory requirement non-compliance of which rendered the proceedings a nullity. In this case a person was arrested by the police for causing breach of the peace and removed by the police to a place of safety under the Mental Health Act. Subsequently, he commenced proceedings against the Chief Constable alleging that there was no justification for his arrest and detention and claiming damages. On application of the Chief Constable the claim so laid was struck of for non-compliance of section 139(2) holding the proceeding to be a nullity which was confirmed in appeal by the court of appeal and the House of Lords.

In another case another procedural provision, section 2(1) of the Administration of Justice (Miscellaneous Provisions Act) 1933 came up for consideration before the House of Lords. The section in so far as relevant provides: 'Subject to the provisions of this section, a bill of indictment charging any person with an indictable offence may be preferred by any person

---

4. *Prakash Jain v. Marie Fernandes*, (2003) 8 SCC 431, p. 439 : AIR 2003 SC 4591.

5. *R. v. Immigration Appeal Tribunal, supra.* The approach of Lord Woolf **approved** by House of Lords in Attorney General's Reference (No. 3 of 1999) (2001) 1 All ER 577, p. 583 (HL). **See further** *R. v. Sekhon,* (2003) 3 All ER 508, p. 517 (CA) (LORD WOOLF, C.J.). **See also** text and note 86, p. 436.

6. **See** text and note 47, p. 511.

7. (2007) 4 All ER 177 (H.L.).

before a court in which the person charged may lawfully be indicted for that offence and where a bill of indictment has been so preferred the proper officer of the court shall, if he is satisfied that the requirements of the next following section have been complied with, sign the bill, and it shall thereupon become the indictment and be proceeded with accordingly.' In *R v. Clarke,*[8] which came up in appeal before the House of Lords, the bill of indictment was signed by the proper officer after the trial was almost over. The court having regard to the legislative history of the Act and earlier authorities held that the requirement of signing the bill of indictment by the proper officer of the court before the trial began was mandatory and in its absence the trial which ended in conviction was vitiated and quashed.

(b) When consequences provided by statute

When consequence of nullification on failure to comply with a prescribed requirement is provided by the statute itself, there can be no manner of doubt that such statutory requirement must be interpreted as mandatory.[9]

The provisions of Ceylon Ordinance No. 7 of 1840, which by clauses 2 and 21 provided certain formalities for transfers and contracts and further provided that no transfer or contract 'shall be of force or avail in law' unless it was made in conformity with those requirements, were held by the Privy Council to be mandatory.[10]

The periods prescribed in the Schedule to the Indian Limitation Act, 1908, for bringing a legal proceeding are mandatory as the consequence of the expiry of the period of limitation is provided by section 3 of the Act in that the court is enjoined to dismiss a legal proceeding instituted after expiry of the prescribed period.[11] Similar result will follow if the court or the forum is directed as in section 24A of the Consumer Protection Act, 1986[12] not to admit a complaint unless it is filed within the period prescribed. The question of limitation in such cases is a jurisdictional

---

8. (2008) 2 All ER 865 (H.L.).

9. **See** text and notes 3-13, *infra*. **See further** *Rajsekhar Gogoi v. State of Assam*, AIR 2001 SC 2313, p. 2315 : (2001) 6 SCC 46 (para 11).

10. *Pate v. Pate*, (1915) AC 1100 (PC); *John H. Arseculeratne v. JBM Perera*, AIR 1928 PC 273, p. 275.

11. *Maqbool Ahmad v. Onkar Pratap Narain Singh*, AIR 1935 PC 85, p. 88.

12. *HUDA v. B. K. Sood*, (2006) 1 SCC 164 : (2005) 9 JT 503; *State Bank of India v. B.S. Agricultural Industries (I)*, (2009) 5 SCC 121 paras 11, 12 : AIR 2009 SC 2210.

fact and has to be considered by the court or forum even if not raised by any party.[13]

The requirement as to registration of certain documents prescribed by section 17 of the Registration Act, 1908, or by any provision of the Transfer of Property Act, 1882, is mandatory since the consequence of non-registration is provided by section 49 of the Registration Act in that such documents if not registered do not affect the property comprised therein.[14]

Section 82 of the Representation of the People Act, 1951, which requires certain candidates to be joined as respondents to an election petition was held to be directory before amendment of the Act by Act 27 of 1956, as no consequence of non-joinder was till then provided by the Act.[15] But after introduction of section 90(3) by the Amending Act which requires the Election Tribunal to dismiss an election petition for non-compliance of section 82, the said provision has been held to be mandatory.[16]

---

13. *Gannmani Anasuya v. Parvatini Amarendra Chowdhary*, (2007) 10 SCC 296 : AIR 2007 SC 238; *State Bank of India v. B. S. Agricultural Industries (I) Supra* para 15.

14. *Secretary of State v. Kuchwar Lime & Stone Co. Ltd.*, AIR 1938 PC 20, p. 22.

15. *Jagan Nath v. Jaswant Singh*, AIR 1954 SC 210, p. 254 : 1954 SCR 892. **See further** for effect of non-compliance of section 119-A of Representation of the People Act, 1951; *Kumaranand v. Brij Mohan Lal*, AIR 1965 SC 628, pp. 630, 631 : (1965) 1 SCR 116.

16. *K. Kamaraja Nadar v. Kunju Thewar*, AIR 1958 SC 687, p. 696 : 1959 SCR 583. **But see** *Shivchand v. Ujagar Singh*, AIR 1978 SC 1583 : (1980) 2 SCC 197. (A candidate, who ought to be joined himself applying for being made a party under section 90(4), now section 86(4): held election petition cannot be dismissed.) **See further** the following cases which hold that the requirement of supplying true attested copies of election petition under section 81(3) is mandatory as the petition is liable to be dismissed for its non-compliance under section 86: *Satya Narain v. Dhuja Ram*, AIR 1974 SC 1185 : (1974) 4 SCC 237 (Copies not filed with election petition, petition will be dismissed); *Sarifuddin v. Abdul Gani*, AIR 1980 SC 303 : (1980) 1 SCC 403 (Copies to be valid must be signed by the election petitioner himself, otherwise petition would be dismissed); *M. Karunanidhi v. H.V. Handa*, AIR 1983 SC 558 : (1983) 2 SCC 473 (Copy of a photograph forming part of election petition not supplied, petition will be dismissed); *Rajendra Singh v. Usha Rani*, (1984) 3 SCC 339 : AIR 1984 SC 956 (one page missing in the election petition but present in its true copy; petition will be dismissed); *V.S. Sasidharan v. K. Karunakaran*, AIR 1990 SC 924 : (1989) 4 SCC 482 (copy of a video cassette forming part of election petition not supplied, petition will be dismissed); *Shipra (Dr. Smt.) v. Shantilal Khoiwal*, AIR 1996 SC 1691 : (1996) 5 SCC 181 (copy of affidavit in support of corrupt practice supplied not containing notarial endorsement of the verification and affirmation on oath by election petitioner is not a true copy; petition will be dismissed). *Shipra's* case has been confined to the factual situation in that case; so if the copy supplied is substantially a true copy, (e.g., when only the name and the address of the notary is missing from the copy) it will still be a true copy and the defect will not entail dismissal: *T.M. Jacob v. C. Poulose,* AIR 1999 SC 1359 : 1999 (4) SCC 274 (Constitution Bench); *T. Phunzathang v. Hangkhalian,* AIR 2001 SC 3924 : (2001) 8 SCC 358; *Ramprasad Sarma v.*

[Footnote No. 16 Contd.]

Section 33(5) of the same Act which requires a candidate who is an elector of different constituency to produce a certified copy of his relevant entry in the Electoral Roll at the time of scrutiny has been interpreted as mandatory as the consequence of such non-compliance is provided by section 36(2) of the same Act which empowers the Returning Officer to reject a nomination paper for non-compliance of section 33.[17] GAJENDRAGADKAR, J., delivering the judgment of Supreme Court in this case observed: "Whenever a statute requires a particular act to be done in a particular manner and also lays down that failure to comply with the said requirement leads to a specific consequence, it would be difficult to accept the argument that the failure to comply with the said requirement should lead to any other consequence."[18] On the other hand, in the absence of any provision making a breach of the proviso to section 83(1) of the Representation of the People Act, 1951, a valid ground for dismissal of an election petition at the threshold, the Supreme Court has held that the requirement of filing an affidavit in a given format thereunder cannot be exalted to the status of a statutory mandate by judicial interpretation.[19]

It is an application of the same principle that the provisions of Order XXI, rules 84 and 85 of the Code of Civil Procedure, 1908 requiring an auction-purchaser to deposit twenty-five per cent of the purchase money forthwith and the balance on the fifteenth day from the sale, have been held to be mandatory, as on failure, in making either of these deposits

---

[Footnote No. 16 Contd.]

Manikumar Subba, AIR 2003 SC 51 : (2003) 1 SCC 289; *Chandrakant Uttam Chodankar v. Dayanand Rayu Mandrakar*, (2005) 2 SCC 188; *G.V. Sreerama Reddy v. Returning Officer*, (2009) 8 SCC 736 para 14 : (2009) 10 JT 316 (Requirement of Section 81(1) of the Representation of the People Act, 1951 that an election petition may be presented by any candidate or any elector has been held to be mandatory and presentation of an election petition by a candidate's advocate was held to be not a proper compliance in view of Section 86(1) which provides for dismissal of an election petition for non-compliance of Section 81).

17. *Baru Ram v. Parsanni (Smt.)*, AIR 1959 SC 93, p. 96 : 1959 SCR 1403; *Birad Mal Singhvi v. Anand Purohit*, AIR 1988 SC 1796, p. 1800 : 1988 Supp SCC 658.

    N.B.—But out of many requirements lumped together non-compliance of which is enacted to lead to a particular consequence, it may be possible to hold that a substantial compliance is sufficient; **see** *K. Kamaraja Nadar v. Kunju Thewar, supra*, p. 697; *Subbarao (Ch.) v. Member, Election Tribunal, Hyderabad*, AIR 1964 SC 1027, p. 1031 (para 14), p. 1033 (para 25) : (1964) 6 SCR 213. **See further** text and note 72, pp. 397.

18. *Baru Ram v. Parsanni (Smt.), supra*; *Sarifuddin v. Abdul Gani*, AIR 1980 SC 303, p. 306 : (1980) 1 SCC 403.
19. *Ponnala Lakshmaiah v. Kommuri Pratap Reddy & Ors.*, (2012) 7 SCC 788, p. 803.

within the time prescribed, the property has to be re-sold as provided in Order XXI, rule 84 and rule 86.[20]

In a case relating to interpretation of section 47 of the Punjab Municipal Act, 1911, which in sub-sections (1) and (2) lays down certain formalities for contracts or transfers made by a municipal committee and by sub-section (3) provides that 'no contract or transfer of the description mentioned in this section executed otherwise than in conformity with the provisions of this section shall be binding on the committee', SINHA, C.J., observed that: "It is settled law that provisions of a statute in those peremptory terms could not but be construed as mandatory."[21]

In some cases the consequence provided for breach of an imperative duty may itself require construction in the light of other provisions of the Act. Thus section 64 of the Police and Criminal Evidence Act, 1984 prohibiting use of a sample, which should have been destroyed, as evidence or for investigation was construed not to affect admissibility of other evidence in court collected in an investigation which was prohibited provided it did not affect fairness of the trial under section 78 of the same Act.[22]

When the statute does not expressly provide for nullification as a consequence of the non-compliance of the statutory injunction but imposes expressly some other penalty, it is a question of construction in each given case whether the Legislature intended to lay down an absolute prohibition or merely to make the offending person liable for the penalty. A large number of cases involving such a question have arisen in relation to enforcement of agreements made in contravention of some statutory requirements and principles that emerge out of them have been admirably summed up in HALSBURY'S Laws of England which may be usefully quoted: "If the penalty is recurrent, that is to say, if it is imposed not merely once for all but as often as the act is done, this amounts to a prohibition. Where the object of the Legislature in imposing the penalty is merely the protection of the revenue, the statute will not be construed as prohibiting the act in respect of which the penalty is imposed; but where the penalty is imposed with the object of protecting the public though it may also be for protection of the revenue, the act must be taken to be prohibited, and no action can be maintained by the offending party on a contract which is

---

20. *Manilal Mohanlal Shah v. Sardar Sayed Ahmed Sayed Mahmad*, AIR 1954 SC 349 : 1955 (1) SCR 108; *Rao Mahmood Ahmed Khan v. Ranbir Singh*, 1995(1) Scale 842 : 1995 AIR SCW 1584 : 1995 Supp (4) SCC 275 : AIR 1995 SC 2195.

21. *H.S. Rikhy (Dr.) v. New Delhi Municipal Committee*, AIR 1962 SC 554, p. 559 : 1962 (3) SCR 604. **See further,** *M.I. Builders Pvt. Ltd. v. Radhey Shyam Sahu*, JT 1999 (5) SC 42, pp. 57, 89 : 1999(6) SCC 464 : AIR 1999 SC 2468 [section 132(4) of U.P. Nagar Palika Adhiniyam, 1959] : (1999) 6 SCC 464 : AIR 1999 SC 2468.

22. *Attorney General's Reference (No. 3 of 1999)*, (2001) 1 All ER 577, pp. 583, 584 (HL).

made in contravention of the statute."[23] If the statute, having regard to its object, purpose and scope is found to be directory, penalty may be incurred for non-compliance but the act or thing done is regarded as good.[24] Thus violation of certain confidential unpublished directions, issued by the Reserve Bank of India under section 36(1)(a) and 36(1)(b) of the Banking Companies Act, which were known to the Banks but not to others, prohibiting Banks from entering into certain transactions was held not to affect the validity of the transactions but only to make the Banks liable for penalty under section 46 of the Act.[25] Further, even in cases where the agreement is illegal, any property transferred to achieve the illegal purpose will vest in the transferee and the court will not assist the transferor in recovering the property but may assist the transferee in protecting the property if he has not to rely on the illegal agreement.[26]

Further a provision expressly nullifying an agreement *prima facie* absolutely may as a proper construction be creating merely a temporaneous or transient nullity.[27] Article 85(1) of the EC Treaty (enforced in U.K. by the European Communities Act, 1972) prohibits as incompatible all agreements which affect trade between member States and which have their object or effect the prevention, restriction or distortion of competition within the common market; and Article 85(2) declares that any agreements prohibited pursuant to this Article shall be automatically void. On a proper construction of Article 85 it has been held that agreements are prohibited when and while they are incompatible with competition in the common market and not otherwise and that nullity imposed by Article 85(2) has a temporaneous or transient effect.[28] So if as a result of a change of circumstances the prohibition no longer applies as between the parties to the agreement, then the agreement between them ceases to be void.[29]

---

23. HALSBURY'S Laws of England (3rd Edition) Vol. 8, p. 141; **See further** *Vita Food Products Inc. v. Unus Shipping Co.*, (1939) 1 All ER 513, p. 523 : 1939 AC 277 (PC); *Lachoo Mal v. Radhey Shyam*, AIR 1971 SC 2213 : (1971) 1 SCC 619; *Mannalal Khetan v. Kedarnath Khetan*, AIR 1977 SC 536, p. 539 : (1977) 2 SCC 120; *Phoenix General Insurance Co. of Grace, SA v. Administratia Asigurarilor de stat*, (1987) 2 All ER 152, pp. 171 to 176 : 1988 QB 216 (CA).

24. *Banarsidas v. Cane Commrs.*, AIR 1963 SC 1417, p. 1424, 1425 : 1963 Supp (2) SCR 760.

25. *BOI Finance Ltd. v. Custodian*, AIR 1997 SC 1952, p. 1962 : 1997 (4) JT 15 : (1997) 10 SCC 488.

26. *Surasaibalini Debi v. Phanindra Mohan Majumdar*, AIR 1965 SC 1364 : 1965 (1) SCR 861; *BOI Finance Ltd. v. Custodian, supra*.

27. *Passmore v. Morland, plc.*, (1999) 3 All ER 1005 (CA).

28. *Ibid*, p. 1023.

29. *Ibid*.

(c) Use of negative words

Another mode of showing a clear intention that the provision enacted is mandatory, is by clothing the command in a negative form. As stated by CRAWFORD: "Prohibitive or negative words can rarely, if ever, be directory. And this is so even though the statute provides no penalty for disobedience."[30] As observed by SUBBARAO, J.: "Negative words are clearly prohibitory and are ordinarily used as a legislative device to make a statute imperative."[31] Section 80[32] and section 87B[33] of the Code of Civil Procedure, 1908; section 77[34] of the Railways Act, 1890; section 15[35] of the Bombay Rent Act, 1947; section 213[36] of the Succession Act, 1925; section 5-A[37] of the Prevention of Corruption Act, 1947; section 7[38] of the Stamp Act, 1899; section 108 of the Companies Act, 1956;[39] section 20(1) of the Prevention of Food Adulteration Act, 1954;[40] section 55 of the Wild Life Protection Act, 1972;[41] the proviso to section 33(2)(b) of the Industrial Disputes Act, 1947 (as amended in 1956);[42] section 10A of Indian Medical Council Act, 1956 (as amended in

---

30. CRAWFORD: Statutory Construction, p. 523; *Haridwar Singh v. Bagun Sumbrui*, AIR1972 SC 1242, p. 1247 : 1973 (3) SCC 889; *Lachmi Narain v. Union of India*, AIR 1976 SC 714, p. 726; 1976 SCC (Tax) 213 : (1976) 2 SCC 953; *Mannalal Khetan v. Kedarnath Khetan, supra. Rangku Dutta v. State of Assam*, (2011) 6 SCC 358. (12th edition, page 404-405 of this book **referred**).

31. *M. Pentiah v. Muddala Veeramallappa*, AIR 1961 SC 1107, p. 1113 : 1961 (2) SCR 295; *Mannalal Khetan v. Kedarnath Khetan, supra.* **See further** *Nasiruddin v. Sita Ram Agarwal,* (2003) 2 SCC 577, p. 589 : AIR 2003 SC 1553.

32. *Bhagchand v. Secretary for State*, AIR 1927 PC 176; *S. N. Dutt v. Union of India*, AIR 1961 SC 1449 : 1962 (1) SCR 560.

33. *Gaekwar Baroda State Railway v. Hafiz Habib-ul-Haq*, AIR 1938 PC 165; *Mohanlal Jain v. Sawai Man Singhji*, AIR 1962 SC 73 : 1962 (1) SCR 702.

34. *G.G. in Council v. Masaddi Lal*, AIR 1961 SC 725 : (1961) 3 SCR 647; *Jetmull Bhojraj v. Darjeeling Himalayan Railway Co. Ltd.*, AIR 1962 SC 1879 : 1963 (2) SCR 832.

35. *Waman Shriniwas v. Ratilal Bhagwandas & Co.*, AIR 1959 SC 689 : 1959 Supp (2) SCR 217.

36. *Hem Nolini Judah v. Isolyne Sarojabashini Bose*, AIR 1962 SC 1471 : 1962 Supp (3) SCR 294.

37. *H.N. Rishbud v. State of Delhi*, AIR 1955 SC 196, p. 203 : (1955) 1 SCR 1150; *State of Madhya Pradesh v. Mubarak Ali*, AIR 1959 SC 707, p. 710 : 1959 Supp (2) SCR 201; *State of Uttar Pradesh v. Bhagwant Kishore*, AIR 1964 SC 221, p. 225 : 1964 (3) SCR 71.

38. *Suraj Mull Nagoremull v. Tritorn Ins. Co.*, AIR 1925 PC 83.

39. *Mannalal khetan v. Kedarnath Khetan*, AIR 1977 SC 536 : 1977 (2) SCC 424.

40. *A.K. Roy v. State of Punjab*, (1986) 4 SCC 326, p. 333 : AIR 1986 SC 2160.

41. *State of Bihar v. Murad Ali Khan*, AIR 1989 SC 1, p. 5 : 1988 (4) SCC 655.

42. *Jaipur Zila Sahakari Bhoomi Vikas Bank v. Ram Gopal Sharma,* AIR 2002 SC 643, p. 648 : (2002) 2 SCC 244 (Constitution Bench) **overruling** *Punjab Beverages Pvt. Ltd. v. Sureshchand,* AIR 1978 SC 995 : (1978) 2 SCC 144.

1993),[43] and similar other provisions have therefore, been construed as mandatory. A provision requiring 'not less than three months' notice' is also for the same reason mandatory.[44]

Section 7 of the Armed Forces (Jammu and Kashmir) Special Powers Act, 1990, provides that 'no' prosecution, suit or other legal proceeding shall be instituted, except with the previous sanction of the Central Government, against any person in respect of anything done or purported to be done in exercise of the powers conferred by the Act. The Supreme Court held that use of the word 'no' in section 7 of the Act denotes the mandatory requirement of obtaining prior sanction of the Central Government before institution of the prosecution, suit or legal proceedings.[45]

Similarly, section 20-A(1) of the Terrorist and Disruptive Activities (Prevention) Act, 1987, provides that notwithstanding anything in the Criminal Procedure Code, 'no' information about the commission of an offence under the Act shall be recorded by the police without the prior approval of the District Superintendent of Police. The Supreme Court held that the Legislature, by using a negative word in section 20-A(1), had made its intention clear. Negative words can rarely be held to be directory and, on the face of it, the requirement of prior approval by the District Superintendent of Police, on principle, cannot be said to be directory in nature.[46]

The Rajasthan Land Acquisition Act, 1953, was amended by the Rajasthan Land Acquisition (Amendment and Validation) Act, 1981. Section 5(2) of the 1981 Amendment Act provides that 'no declaration' under section 6 of the 1953 Act in respect of any land for the acquisition of which notice under section 4(5) of the 1953 Act has been given before the commencement of the 1981 Amendment Act, 'shall be made' after the expiry of two years from the commencement of the 1981 Amendment Act. The Supreme Court held that the words 'no declaration' and 'shall be made' make it clear that the two years' time prescribed for making a declaration under section 6 in respect of the notice issued under section 4(5) of the 1953 Act is mandatory and permits no departure.[47]

But the principle is not without exception. Section 256 of the Government of India Act, 1935, was construed by the Federal Court as directory

---

43. *K.S. Bhoir v. State of Maharashtra,* AIR 2002 SC 444, p. 448 : (2001) 10 SCC 264.
44. *Lachmi Narain v. Union of India,* AIR 1976 SC 714, p. 726 : (1976) SCC (Tax) 213 : (1976) 2 SCC 953.
45. *General Officer Commanding, Rashtriya Rifles v. CBI & Anr.*, (2012) 6 SCC 228, p. 260.
46. *Ashraf Khan & Anr. v. State of Gujarat,* (2012) 11 SCC 606, p. 617.
47. *Laxman Lal & Anr. v. State of Rajasthan & Ors.*, (2013) 3 SCC 764, pp. 777, 778.

though worded in the negative form.[48] Directions relating to solemnization of marriages though using negative words have been construed as directory in cases where the enactments in question did not provide for the consequence that the marriage in breach of those directions shall be invalid.[49] Considerations of general inconvenience, which would have resulted in holding these enactments mandatory, appear to have outweighed the effect of the negative words in reaching the conclusion that they were in their true meaning merely directory. An interesting example, where negative words have been held to be directory, is furnished in the construction of section 25F[50] of the Industrial Disputes Act, 1947, where compliance of clause (c) has been held to be directory;[51] although compliance of clauses (a) and (b) which are connected by the same negative words is understood as mandatory.[52] These cases[53] illustrate that the rule, that negative words are usually mandatory, is like any other rule subordinate to the context, and the object intended to be achieved by the particular requirement.

(d) Affirmative words may imply a negative

Affirmative words stand at a weaker footing than negative words for reading the provision as mandatory;[54] but affirmative words may also be so

---

48. *Biswanath Khemka v. Emperor*, AIR 1945 FC 67; *G.S. Lamba v. Union of India*, (1985) 2 SCC 604, pp. 627, 628 : AIR 1985 SC 1019 (Requirement to consult the P.S.C. in negative form; held directory).

49. *Catterall v. Sweetman*, (1845) 163 ER 1047, p. 1052; *Lila Gupta v. Laxmi Narain*, AIR 1978 SC 1351, pp. 1354, 1355 : (1978) 3 SCC 258.

50. **'S. 25-F**—No workman employed in any industry who has been in continuous service for not less than one year under an employer shall be retrenched by that employer until—

(a) the workman has been given one month's notice in writing indicating the reason for retrenchment and the period of notice has expired, or the workman has been paid in lieu of such notice, wages for the period of the notice;

....

(b) the workman has been paid, at the time of retrenchment, compensation which shall be equivalent of fifteen days' average pay for every completed year of service or any part thereof in excess of six months; and

(c) notice in the prescribed manner is served on the appropriate Government.'

51. *Bombay Union of Journalists v. State of Bombay*, AIR 1964 SC 1617 : 1964 (6) SCR 22; *Krishna Bahadur v. Purna Theatre*, (2004) 8 SCC 229, p. 234 : AIR 2004 SC 4282.

52. *Ibid.*

53. Cases in Notes 37-41, *supra.*

54. *U.K. Gas Plant Manufacturing Co. v. Emperor*, AIR 1947 PC 38, pp. 41, 42. For example, **see** section 89 of the Registration Act, 1908 which provides: 'a prosecution for any offence under this Act may be commenced by or with the permission of Inspector General'; Compare this provision with section 70 of the Stamp Act which reads: 'no prosecution in respect of any offence under this Act shall be instituted without the sanction of

[Footnote No. 54 Contd.]

limiting as to imply a negative. In an appeal from West Africa, the Privy Council approved of a passage from the judgment of the President of West African Court of Appeal (SIR HENLEY COUSSEY) in which referring to the relevant sections of the Ordinance in question, the President stated: "It is true that there are no negative words in the section referred to but the affirmative words are absolute, explicit, and peremptory; and when you find in an Ordinance only one particular mode of effecting the object, one train of formalities to be observed, the regulative provisions which the section prescribes, are essential and imperative."[55] The rule stated by VINER is to the same effect: "Every statute limiting anything to be in one form, although it be spoken in the affirmative, yet it includes in itself a negative."[56] As an example of an Indian statute of this description, the provisions of sections 54, 59, 107 and 123 of the Transfer of Property Act, 1882, prescribing modes of transfer by sale, mortgage, lease or gift may be mentioned. The formalities prescribed by these provisions for effecting a transfer of the nature mentioned in them are mandatory and the language used although affirmative clearly imports a negative.[57]

(e) Use of 'shall' or 'shall and may'; 'must' and 'should'

The use of word 'shall' raises a presumption that the particular provision is imperative.[58] For instance, rule 57(2) of Schedule II to the Income-tax Act, 1961, provides that the full amount of purchase money payable

---

[Footnote No. 54 Contd.]
the Collector'. Section 89 of the Registration Act has been held to be permissive and enabling but section 70 of the Stamp Act has been held to be prohibitory: *Dharamdeo Rai v. Ram Nagina Rai*, AIR 1972 SC 928 : 1972 (1) SCC 460.

55. *Edward Ramia Ltd. v. African Woods Ltd.*, (1960) 1 All ER 627, p. 630 (PC).

56. VINER'S Abr, Vol. 15 Tit Negative, A, pl 2, p. 540.

57. *Pir Bux v. Mohamed Tahar*, AIR 1934 PC 235, p. 237; *GHC Ariff v. Jadunath Majumdar*, AIR 1931 PC 79, p. 80; *Makhan Singh Tarsikka v. State of Punjab*, AIR 1952 SC 27 : 1952 CrLJ 321; *N. Varada Pillai v. Jeevarathnammal*, AIR 1919 PC 44, p. 46; *Lim Charlie v. Official Receiver*, AIR 1934 PC 67, p. 68. (The property belonging to a person can vest in the State or in some other body only by transfer in the mode prescribed by the Transfer of Property Act or under a statutory enactment providing for vesting.) *Noorulla Ghazanfarull v. Municipal Board, Aligarh*, 1995 (1) Scale 643, p. 649 : AIR 1995 SC 1058, pp. 1063, 1064 : 1995 Supp (2) SCC 667. **See further** *Syndicate Bank v. Prabha D. Naik*, AIR 2001 SC 1968, p. 1974 : (2001) 4 SCC 713 ("Affirmative Statute introductive of a new law do imply a negative").

58. *State of U.P. v. Manbodhan Lal Srivastava*, AIR 1957 SC 912, p. 917 : 1958 SCR 533; *State of U.P. v. Babu Ram Upadhya*, AIR 1961 SC 751, p. 765 : (1961) 2 SCR 679; *Sainik Motors v. State of Rajasthan*, AIR 1961 SC 1480, p. 1485 : (1962) 1 SCR 517; *Govindlal Chagganlal Patel v. Agriculture Produce Market Committee*, AIR 1976 SC 263, p. 267 : 1975 (2) SCC 482; quoted with **approval** in *Pesara Pushpamala Reddy v. G. Veera Swamy*, (2011) 4 SCC 306 (para 28) : (2011) 3 JT 210.

'shall' be paid by the purchaser to the Tax Recovery Officer on or before the fifteenth day from the date of sale of property. The Supreme Court relied on the word 'shall' as well as earlier decisions of the Court on *pari materia* provisions in Order XXI of the CPC, to hold that making of the deposit by the intending purchaser is mandatory.[59] Similarly, section 45 of the Arbitration and Conciliation Act, 1996, provides that a judicial authority, when seized of an action in a matter in respect of which the parties have made an agreement referred to in section 44, '*shall*, at the request of one of the parties or any person claiming through or under him, refer the parties to arbitration, unless it finds that the said agreement is null and void, inoperative or incapable of being performed'. The Supreme Court held that the language of section 45 of the Act suggests that unless the Court finds that an agreement is null and void, inoperative and incapable of being performed, it is obligatory upon the Court to make a reference to arbitration.[60]

However, this *prima facie* inference about the provision being imperative may be rebutted by other considerations such as object and scope of the enactment and the consequences flowing from such construction. There are numerous cases where the word 'shall' has, therefore, been construed as merely directory.[61] The word 'shall', observes HIDAYATULLAH, J.,

---

59. *C.N. Paramsivam & Anr. v. Sunrise Plaza & Ors.*, (2013) 9 SCC 460, pp. 472 to 474.

60. *Chloro Controls India Pvt. Ltd. v. Severn Trent Water Purification Inc. & Ors.*, (2013) 1 SCC 641, pp. 708, 718.

61. *Burjore and Bhawani Pershad v. Bhagana*, ILR 10 Cal 557, pp. 561, 562 : 11 IA 7 (PC); *Shew Bux Mohata v. Tulsimanjari Dasi*, AIR 1961 SC 1453, pp. 1454, 1455 : 1962 (1) SCR 643 (Order 45, Rule 7, CPC); *Bishwanath Khemka v. Emperor*, AIR 1945 FC 67 (Section 256, Government of India Act, 1935); *State of U.P. v. Manbodhan Lal Srivastava, supra* (Article 320(3)(c), Constitution); *Drigraj Kuer v. Amar Krishna Narayan Singh*, AIR 1960 SC 444 : 1960 (2) SCR 431 (Section 56, U.P. Court of Wards Act, 1912); *L. Hazari Mal Kuthiala v. ITO, Ambala Cantt.*, AIR 1961 SC 200 : 1961 (1) SCR 892 (Section 5(5), Patiala Income-tax Act, 2001); *Sainik Motors v. State of Rajasthan*, AIR 1961 SC 1480 (Rule 8 of Rajasthan Passenger and Goods Taxation Rules); *Banarsi Das v. Cane Commr., U.P.*, AIR 1963 SC 1417 : 1963 Supp (2) SCR 760 (Section 18(2) U.P. Sugar Factories Control Act, 1938); *K. Venkataramiah v. Seetharama Reddy*, AIR 1963 SC 1526 : (1964) 2 SCR 35, (Order 41, Rule 27, CPC); *Raza Buland Sugar Co. Ltd. v. Municipal Board, Rampur*, AIR 1965 SC 895 : (1965) 1 SCR 20 (Section 94(3), U.P. Municipalities Act, 1916); *K. Narasimhiah v. Singri Gowda*, AIR 1966 SC 330 : 1964 (7) SCR 618 (Section 27(3) of the Mysore Town Municipalities Act, 1951, requiring that three clear days' notice shall be given was construed having regard to the context and section 36 as directory); *State of M.P. v. Azad Bharat Finance Co.*, AIR 1967 SC 276 : 1966 Supp SCR 473 (Section 11 of the Opium Act, 1955 as amended in M.P. using language 'shall be confiscated' construed as permissive); *Krishna Kumar Mediratta v. Phulchand Agarwala*, AIR 1977 SC 984, pp. 986, 987 : (1977) 2 SCC 5. (Rule 9(2) of the Mineral Concession Rules, 1960); *Ganesh*

[Footnote No. 61 Contd.]

"is ordinarily mandatory but it is sometimes not so interpreted if the context or the intention otherwise demands",[62] and points out SUBBARAO, J.: "When a statute uses the word 'shall', *prima facie* it is mandatory, but the court may ascertain the real intention of the Legislature by carefully attending to the whole scope of the statute".[63] This principle was used in the interpretation of section 202 of the CrPC, which provides that the Magistrate 'shall', in a case where the accused is residing at a

---

[Footnote No. 61 Contd.]

Prasad Shah Kesari v. Lakshmi Narayan Gupta, (1985) 3 SCC 53 : AIR 1985 SC 964; (The words 'shall order' the defence to be struck off in section 11-A of the Bihar Buildings (Lease Rent and Eviction Control) Act, 1947 were construed as directory.) *Paradise Printers v. Union Territory of Chandigarh*, AIR 1988 SC 354, p. 358 : (1988) 1 SCC 440 (Rule 8(3) of the Rules made under the Capital of Punjab Act, 1952); *Ammal Chandra Dutt v. II Addl. Dist. Judge*, AIR 1989 SC 255 : (1989) 1 SCC 1 (construction of Rule 18(1) of the U.P. Urban Buildings Rules, 1972. Words 'shall accept the finding' in earlier proceedings under the repealed Act 'as conclusive' in proceedings under the new Act were construed as directory 'shall' was read as 'may'); *Rubber House v. Excellsior Needle Industries Pvt. Ltd.*, AIR 1989 SC 1160 : (1989) 1 SCC 413 (Rule 4(c) of Haryana Urban Rules, 1970); *Shibu Chandra Dhar v. Pasupati Nath Auddya*, AIR 2002 SC 1252 : (2002) 3 SCC 617 (word 'shall' in section 17(2B) of the W.B. Premises Tenancy Act, 1969 construed as 'may' having regard to other related provisions); *P.T. Rajan v. TPM Sahir*, (2003) 8 SCC 498, p. 516 : AIR 2003 SC 4603 (use of 'shall' in a procedural provision will be construed as directory if thereby no prejudice is caused); *U.P. State Electricity Board v. Shiv Mohan Singh*, (2004) 8 SCC 402 : AIR 2004 SC 5009 (section 4(4) of the Apprentice Act, 1961 requiring a contract of apprenticeship to be sent to apprenticeship advisor for registration is held to be directory and an apprentice under the Act, declared to be a trainee and not a workman under section 18, does not become a workman under the Industrial Disputes Act, 1947 even though his contract is not sent for registration and the definition of 'workman' under the ID Act includes an apprentice). **See also** *Indo China Steam Navigation Co. v. Jagjit Singh*, AIR 1964 SC 1140, p. 1151 : (1964) 6 SCR 594 ('shall be liable to confiscation' held mandatory by a constitution bench) **followed** in *State of Karnataka v. Sareen Kumar Shetty*, AIR 2002 SC 1248, p. 1251 : (2002) 3 SCC 426 ('shall be liable to confiscation' held mandatory) and *Chern Taong Shang v. Commander S.D. Baijal*, AIR 1988 SC 603 : 1988 (1) SCC 507 (words 'shall also be liable to confiscation' construed as mandatory). **Compare** *State of M.P. v. Azad Bharat Finance Co., supra*, where similar words were construed as permissive, but in this case the constitution bench decision in *Indo China Navigation Co.* case was not noticed.

62. *Sainik Motors v. State of Rajasthan*, AIR 1961 SC 1480, p. 1485 : 1962 (1) SCR 517.

63. *State of U.P. v. Babu Ram*, AIR 1961 SC 751, p. 765 : (1961) 2 SCR 679, *Govindlal Chagganlal Patel v. Agriculture Produce Market Committee*, AIR 1976 SC 263, p. 267 : 1975 (2) SCC 482; *Mohan Singh v. International Air Port Authority*, 1996 (8) Scale 251, p. 260 : 1996 (10) JT 311 : (1997) 9 SCC 132. **See further** *Basavraj R. Patil v. State of Karnataka*, AIR 2000 SC 3214, p. 3222 : (2006) 8 SCC 740 (A mandatory obligation on the court arising from the use of 'shall' may be diluted to prevent hardship in exceptional cases. Section 313(1)(b) CrPC 1973 construed to be obligatory requiring examination of accused in person, yet not preventing the court to dispense with his presence in appropriate cases.)

place beyond the area in which he exercises his jurisdiction, postpone the issue of process against the accused, and either inquire into the case himself or direct an investigation to be made by a police officer or by such other person as he thinks fit, for the purpose of deciding whether or not there is sufficient ground for proceeding. The Supreme Court held that the word 'shall' is ordinarily mandatory but sometimes, taking into account the context or the intention, it can be held to be directory. However, on looking at the intention of the Legislature, the Court found that the provision is aimed at preventing innocent persons from being harassed by unscrupulous persons making false complaints, and therefore the inquiry or investigation contemplated by the provision before issuing summons was held to be mandatory.[64]

If different provisions are connected with the same word 'shall', and if with respect to some of them the intention of the Legislature is clear that the word 'shall' in relation to them must be given an obligatory or a directory meaning, it may indicate that with respect to other provisions also, the same construction should be placed.[65] If the word 'shall' has been substituted for the word 'may' by an amendment, it will be a very strong indication that use of 'shall' makes the provision imperative.[66] Similar will be the position when the Bill as introduced used the word 'may' and the Parliament substituted the word 'shall' in its place while passing the Act.[67] The use of word 'may' at one place and 'shall' at another place in the same section may strengthen the inference that these words have been used in their primary sense and that 'shall' should be construed as mandatory.[68] When the expressions 'shall' and 'may' are defined in the Act (for example 'shall

64. *Vijay Dhanuka & Ors. v. Najima Mamtaj & Ors.*, (2014) 14 SCC 638.
65. *Hari Vishnu Kamath v. Ahmad Ishaque*, AIR 1955 SC 233, p. 245 : 1955 (1) SCR 1104; *Ram Autar Singh Bhadauria v. Ram Gopal Singh*, AIR 1975 SC 2182, p. 2189 : (1976) 1 SCC 43; *State of U.P. v. Manbodhan Lal Srivastava*, AIR 1957 SC 912, p. 917 : 1958 SCR 533. But this indication is not conclusive, **see** *Bombay Union of Journalists v. State of Bombay*, AIR 1964 SC 1617 (**discussed** in text and notes 40 and 41, p. 405); **see also** *Raza Buland Sugar Co. v. Municipal Board, Rampur*, AIR 1965 SC 895, p. 905 : 1965 (1) SCR 970 (MUDHOLKAR, J.); *Juthika Bhattacharya (Smt.) v. State of Madhya Pradesh*, AIR 1976 SC 2534, p. 2536 : 1976 SCC (Lab) 561.
66. *Jaywant S. Kulkarni v. Minochar Dosabhai Shroff*, AIR 1988 SC 1817, p. 1820 : (1988) 4 SCC 108 ('shall pass a decree' substituted for 'may pass a decree').
67. *Tamil Nadu Cauvery Neerppasana Vilaiporulgal Padhugappa Sangam v. Union of India*, AIR 1990 SC 1316, p. 1321 (section 4 of Inter-State Water Disputes Act, 1956).
68. *Chairman Canara Bank, Bangalore v. M.S. Jasra*, AIR 1992 SC 1341, p. 1346 : AIR 1992 SC 1100 [Section 45(5)(i) of the Banking Regulation Act, 1949] ; *Mahalaxmi Rice Mills v. State of U.P.*, AIR 1999 SC 147, p. 149 : (1998) 6 SCC 590.

resume' and 'may presume' in section 4 of the Evidence Act, 1872) the ex-ressions have to be given the meaning as defined.[69]

The words 'shall and may' are construed imperatively.[70] As pointed ut by LORD BROUGHAM: "If the words are it 'shall and may' be so and o done, by such and such officer and body then the word 'may' is held n all soundness of construction to confer, a power but the word 'shall' is eld to make that power, or the exercise of that power compulsory."[71] Similarly, the words 'shall and lawfully may', are in their ordinary im-ort obligatory.[72] The use of the word 'shall' with respect to one matter nd use of word 'may' with respect to another matter in the same section f a statute, will normally lead to the conclusion that the word 'shall' im-oses an obligation, whereas the word 'may' confers a discretionary ower.[73] But that by itself is not decisive and the court may having regard o the context and consequences come to the conclusion that the part us-ng 'shall' is directory.[74]

The use of the word 'must' in place of 'shall' will itself be sufficient to old the provision to be mandatory and it will not be necessary to pursue he enquiry any further.[75] The use of the word 'should' instead of 'must' nay not justify the inference that the provision is directory if the context shows otherwise.[76]

f) Considerations of general inconvenience in statutes imposing public duty; provisions as to time; provisions for consultation

Where a statute imposes a public duty and lays down the manner in which and the time within which the duty shall be performed, injustice or

---

69. *M. Narsinga Rao v. State of Andhra Pradesh,* AIR 2001 SC 318, p. 322 : (2001) 1 SCC 691 : 2001 CrLJ 515 (meaning of these expressions as defined in section 4 of the Evidence Act applied also for construction of section 20 of the PC Act, 1988).

70. *A.G. v. Lock,* (1744) 26 ER 897, 898; *Queen v. Allooparao,* (1847) 3 MIA 488, p. 492; *Davies v. Evans,* (1882) 9 QBD 238, p. 243.

71. *Queen v. Allooparao, supra,* p. 492.

72. *Chapman v. Milvain,* (1850) 19 LJ Ex 228 : (1850) 155 ER 27, p. 28 (PARKE B.).

73. *Labour Commr., M.P. v. Burhanpur Tapti Mill,* AIR 1964 SC 1687, p. 1689 : (1964) 7 SCR 484; *Jamatraj v. State of Maharashtra,* AIR 1968 SC 178, p. 181 : 1967 (3) SCR 415; *T.R. Sharma v. Prithipal Singh,* AIR 1976 SC 367, p. 370 : 1976 SCC (L&S) 1 : (1976) 1 SCC 226. For construction of word 'May' see title 6(k) "May; 'It shall be lawful'; 'shall have power'".

74. *Ganesh Prasad Shah Kesari v. Lakshmi Narayan Gupta,* (1985) 3 SCC 53, p. 59 : AIR 1985 SC 964.

75. *Lachmi Narain v. Union of India,* AIR 1976 SC 714, p. 726 : 1976 SCC (Tax) 213.

76. *Juthika Bhattacharya (Smt.) v. State of Madhya Pradesh,* AIR 1976 SC 2534, p. 2536 : 1976 SCC (L&S) 561 : (1976) 4 SCC 96.

inconvenience resulting from a rigid adherence to the statutory prescriptions may be a relevant factor in holding such prescriptions only directory.

In considering whether a statute is imperative, DENMAN, J., stated: "A balance may be struck between the inconvenience of sometimes rigidly adhering to, and the convenience of sometimes departing from its terms."[77] It was held that where a public officer is directed by a statute to perform a duty within a specified time the cases establish that provisions as to time are only directory.[78] Similarly, it has been held while construing section 17(1) of the Industrial Disputes Act, 1947, that it is obligatory on the Government to publish an award, but the provision, that it should be published within thirty days, is not mandatory and an award published beyond thirty days is not invalid.[79] A provision fixing a time, within which a public officer or authority has to act in performance of a duty, generally means that the statute considers it reasonable for the officer or authority to act within the said period. The expiry of the period without more confers no right unless the statute by a legal fiction or otherwise confers a right. Thus a provision in a Municipal Act that an application for layout should be disposed of within a particular time does not mean that the application must be deemed to have been granted after expiry of the said period unless there is a provision to that effect made in the Act.[80] Similarly a provision in a standing order that an application for leave of an employee of the Madhya Pradesh Electricity Board shall be considered and orders thereon passed by the manager or officer concerned within the period specified therein has been held to be directory and if the application is not disposed of within the said period it cannot be held that the application for leave must be deemed to have been allowed.[81] If performance of a public duty is required to be done within a specified time, which is also related to a right given to a person, the provision as to time will still be held as directory unless it is shown that the person on whom the related

77. *Caldow v. Pixuell*, (1876) 2 CPD 562, p. 567; *R. v. Urbanowski*, (1976) 1 All ER 697, p. 681 (CA).

78. *Ibid., P.T. Rajan v. TPM Sahir*, (2003) 8 SCC 498.

79. *Remington Rand of India v. Workmen*, AIR 1968 SC 224, p. 226 : 1968 (1) SCR 164. For further examples, **see** *Parkash Chand Maheshwari v. Zila Parishad, Muzaffarnagar*, AIR 1971 SC 1696, p. 1703 : (1972) 2 SCC 489; *Manzoor Khan v. State of U.P.*, AIR 1973 SC 2548, pp. 2550, 2551 : 1973 (2) SCC 227; *Dalchand v. Municipal Corporation, Bhopal*, (1984) 2 SCC 486 : AIR 1983 SC 303; *Karnal Leather Karmchari Sanghatan v. Liberty Footwear Co.*, AIR 1990 SC 247, p. 254 : 1989 (4) SCC 448; *Municipal Committee, Charkhi Dadri v. Ramji Lal Bagla*, 1995 (4) Scale 559 : (1995) 5 SCC 272.

80. *Chet Ram Vashist v. Municipal Corporation of Delhi*, AIR 1981 SC 653, p. 656 : (1980) 4 SCC 647.

81. *Madhya Pradesh State Electricity Board v. S. K. Yadav*, (2009) 2 SCC 50 paras 18 to 20 : (2009) 1 JT 406.

right is conferred is prejudiced because of the non-performance of the duty within the specified time. Thus time prescribed by rule 7(3) of the Food Adulteration Rules, which requires that the Public Analyst 'shall within a period of forty-five days' deliver to the Local (Health) Authority a report of the result of his analysis has been held to be directory unless the delay has prejudiced the right of the accused to have the samples of food analysed by the Central Food Laboratory for example when the samples become unfit for analysis because of the delay.[82] It may be relevant to see whether the requirement of time is addressed to a party or an officer, for in the former case it may be mandatory.[83] Further, if the statutory provision as to time is a condition for exercise of a statutory power as distinguished from a duty, the prescription as to time will be construed as mandatory.[84] But whether it be a case of statutory duty or statutory power, the statute may expressly or impliedly make the authority *functus officio* on expiry of the prescribed period.[85] Further though when a public authority is required to do a certain thing within a specified period, the same is ordinarily directory, it is equally well-settled that when consequence for inaction on the part of the statutory authority within the specified time is expressly provided, it must be held to be imperative.[86]

---

82. *T.V. Usman v. Food Inspector Tellicherry Municipality*, JT 1994(1) SC 260, p. 266 : AIR 1994 SC 1818 : (1994) 1 SCC 754 : 1994 SCC (Cri) 187. **See further** *Wang v. Commissioner of Inland Revenue*, (1995) 1 All ER 367, 377 (PC): "When a question like the present one arises—an alleged failure to comply with a time provision—it is simpler and better to avoid these two words 'mandatory' and 'directory' and to ask two questions. The first is whether the Legislature intended the person making the determination to comply with the time provision, whether a fixed time or a reasonable time. Secondly, if so, did the Legislature intend that a failure to comply with such a time provision would deprive the decision-maker of jurisdiction and render any decision which he purported to make null and void?"

83. *R. v. Urbanowski*, (1976) 1 All ER 697, p. 681 (CA); *Nasiruddin v. Sita Ram Agarwal*,(2003) 2 SCC 577, p. 589 : AIR 2003 SC 1543; *Balwant Singh v. Anand Kumar Sharma*, (2003) 3 SCC 433, p. 436; *Visitor v. K. S. Misra*, (2007) 8 SCC 593 (para 18) : (2007) 11 JT 549.

84. *Supdt. of Taxes v. Onkarmal National Trust*, AIR 1975 SC 2065 : (1976) 1 SCC 766 : 1976 SCC (Tax) 73. *Collector of Central Excise, Madras v. M.M. Rubber & Co.*, AIR 1991 SC 2141, pp. 2145, 2147 : 1992 Supp (1) SCC 471. **See further** title 6(h) 'statute conferring power', *infra*.

85. *Balasinor Nagrik Co-operative Bank Ltd. v. Babubhai Shankerlal Pandya*, (1987) 1 SCC 606 : AIR 1987 SC 849. For example, **see** *Municipal Corporation of Greater Bombay v. Hakimwadi (Dr.) Tenants Association*, AIR 1988 SC 233 : 1988 Supp SCC 55 : 1987 (4) JT 448.

86. *Bhavnagar University v. Palitana Sugar Mill (P.) Ltd.*, (2003) 2 SCC 111, pp. 125, 126 : AIR 2003 SC 511, p. 520 (construction of section 20(2) of the Gujarat Town Planning and Urban Development Act, 1976); *Balwant Singh v. Anand Kumar Sharma*, (2003) 3 SCC 433, p. 436 : AIR 2003 SC 1543.

But periods fixed for holding election to a Legislative Assembly and a Municipality by Article 174(1) and Article 243U of the Constitution have been held to be mandatory by Constitution Benches and elections have to be held in time even though revision of electoral rolls is not possible within that time.[87]

Consent of the wife before adoption by a male Hindu as required by proviso to section 7 of the Hindu Adoption and Maintenance Act, 1956 has been held to be mandatory; mere presence of the wife at the time of adoption has not been held to be sufficient to prove consent.[88]

The principle was stated by the Privy Council in the following words: "When the provisions of a statute relate to the performance of a public duty and the case is such that to hold null and void acts in neglect of this duty would work serious general inconvenience, or injustice to persons who have no control over those who are entrusted with the duty, and at the same time would not promote the main object of the Legislature, it has been the practice to hold such provisions to be directory only."[89] In that case the question involved was whether the omission to revise the jury lists, as directed by statute, had the effect of invalidating the verdict of jury, and their Lordships held that the irregularities in the due revision of the jury lists did not in itself avoid the verdict of the jury.[90] This principle was followed by the Federal Court in construing section 256 of the Government of India Act, 1935, requiring consultation between public authorities before the conferment of magisterial powers and it was held that the provision was directory.[91] Similarly, the provision in Article 320(3)(c) of the Constitution requiring that the Public Service Commission shall be consulted on all disciplinary matters affecting a Civil Servant, has been interpreted as directory and its non-compliance was held as not vitiating

---

87. Special Reference No. 1 of 2002 under Article 143(1) of the Constitution, AIR 2003 SC 87; *Kihansing Tomar v. Municipal Corporation of the City of Ahmedabad,* AIR 2007 SC 269 : (2006) 8 SCC 352. See in this respect also f.n. 71, p. 138.

88. *Ghisalal v. Dhapubai,* (2011) 2 SCC 298 para 25 : AIR 2011 SC 644.

89. *Montreal Street Railway v. Normandin,* (1917) AC 170; AIR 1917 PC 142, p. 144; **See further** *State of U.P. v. Manbodhan Lal Shrivastava*, AIR 1957 SC 912, p. 917 : 1958 SCR 533; *Banarasi Das v. Cane Commissioner, U.P.*, AIR 1963 SC 1417, p. 1424 : 1963 Supp (2) SCR 760; *Mohan Singh v. International Air Port Authority,* 1996 (8) Scale 251, p. 260: 1996 (10) JT 311 : (1997) 9 SCC 132; *Oriental Insurance Co. Ltd. v. Inderjit Kaur*, AIR 1998 SC 588, p. 590 : 1998 (1) SCC 371; *Bhavnagar University v. Palitana Sugar Mill (P.) Ltd.*, (2003) 2 SCC 111, p. 126 : AIR 2003 SC 511, p. 520.

90. *Montred Street Railway v. Normandin, supra.*

91. *Biswanath Khemka v. Emperor*, AIR 1945 FC 67.

he disciplinary action taken.[1] On the same principle the provision of section 5(5) of the Patiala Income-tax Act, 2001 requiring the Commissioner of Income-tax to consult the minister in charge before investing the Income-tax Officers with their functions was held to be directory.[2] HIDAYATULLAH, J., after referring to the previous cases observed: "The essence of the rule is that where consultation has to be made during the performance of a public duty and an omission to do so occurs, the action cannot be regarded as altogether void, and the direction for consultation may be treated as directory and its neglect, as of no consequence to the result.[3]

These cases[4] must, however, be distinguished from other decisions of the Supreme Court[5] where provisions as to consultation were held mandatory.

In *K.S. Srinivasan's* case,[6] requirement of consultation with the Public Service Commission imposed by rule 4(b) of the Central Civil Service (Temporary Service) Rules, 1949, before declaration as to *quasi-permanent* status of a Civil Servant under rule 3, was held to be mandatory

---

1. *State of U.P. v. Manbodhan Lal Shrivastava*, AIR 1957 SC 912 : 1958 SCR 533; *U.R. Bhatt v. Union of India*, AIR 1962 SC 1344 : (1962) 1 LLJ 656; *Union of India v. T.V. Patel*, (2007) 4 SCC 785 (para 25) : (2007) 6 SLT 40 : (2007) 6 Scale 9. (The provisions of Article 320(3)(c) are not mandatory. The absence of any consultation or any irregularity in consultation process or non-furnishing of a copy of the advice tendered by UPSC, if any, does not furnish a ground to the delinquent government servant to challenge the final order passed against him in a court of law). **See further** *State of Andhra Pradesh v. Rahimuddin Kamol (Dr.)*, AIR 1997 SC 947 : (1997) 10 SCC 570 (Rule requiring consultation with vigilance commission before removal from service, held directory); *G. S. Lamba v. Union of India*, (1985) 2 SCC 604, pp. 627, 628 : AIR 1985 SC 1019. (Requirement of consultation with P.S.C. for relaxing quota rule, held directory); *Chandra Joshi v. Union of India*, AIR 1991 SC 284, p. 294 : 1992 Supp (1) SCC 272; (Requirement to consult PSC for relaxing the U.P. Forest Service Rules, 1952 held mandatory); *R. Hariharan v. V.K. Balchandra Nair,* AIR 2000 SC 2933 : (2000) 7 SCC 399 (consultation with PSC under the Kerala Act, 1963 for appointment of Assistant Engineer held mandatory); *Hindustan Zinc Ltd. v. Andhra Pradesh State Electricity Board*, AIR 1991 SC 1473, pp. 1483, 1484 : 1991 (3) SCC 299. (Non-consultation with the consultative council under section 16 of the Electricity Supply Act 1948 does not invalidate revision of tariffs).
2. *L. Hazari Mal Kuthiala v. I.T.O., Ambala Cantt.*, AIR 1961 SC 200 : 1961 (1) SCR892.
3. *Ibid*, pp. 202, 203.
4. Cases **referred** to in footnotes 77 to 79, *supra*.
5. *Banwarilal Agarwalla v. State of Bihar*, AIR 1961 SC 849 : 1962 (1) SCR 33; *K.S. Srinivasan v. Union of India*, AIR 1958 SC 419 : 1958 SCR 1295; *Jyoti Prakash Mitter v. Chief Justice, Calcutta High Court*, AIR 1965 SC 961 : 1965 (2) SCR 53; *Chandra Mohan v. State of U.P.*, AIR 1966 SC 1987 : (1967) 1 SCR 77; *Haridwar Singh v. Bagun Sumbrui*, AIR 1972 SC 1242, p. 1247 : 1973 (3) SCC 889. **Also see** *Rollo v. Minister of Town and Country Planning*, (1948) 1 All ER 13 (CA); *Municipal Corporation of Greater Bombay v. New Standard Engg. Ltd.*, AIR 1991 SC 1362 : 1991 (1) SCC 611.
6. *K.S. Srinivasan v. Union of India*, AIR 1958 SC 419, p. 430 : 1958 SCR 1295.

on the ground that the Civil Servant "cannot claim the benefit of rule 3 and ignore, at the same time the conditions laid down in rule 4(b). In other words, he cannot claim the benefit of a part of the rules and refuse to be bound by the conditions of the other part".[7]

Having regarded the gravity of a dispute as to the age of a High Court Judge the provision for consultation with the Chief Justice of India in Article 217(3) of the Constitution has been held to be mandatory.[8] Similarly having regard to the object of securing independence of subordinate judiciary, provision for consultation with the High Court in the matter of appointment of District Judges as enacted in Article 233 of the Constitution, has been held to be mandatory. It was held in this case that appointments of candidates recommended by the High Court on the basis of a list prepared by a selection committee were invalid. It was said in that context that if *A* is empowered to appoint *B* in consultation with *C*, he will not be exercising the power in the manner prescribed if he appoints *B* in consultation with *C* and *D*.[9] In another case, it was said in the same context that consultation is not complete or effective before parties thereto make their respective points of view known to the other or others and discuss and examine the relative merits of their views. If one party makes a proposal and the other party has a counter proposal in his mind which is not communicated to the proposer, an order issued to give effect to the counter proposal cannot be said to have been made after consultation.[10] But if a meeting of all the persons required to be consulted is called in which all of them have opportunity to be present and deliberate, a decision taken in the meeting cannot be challenged on the ground that some of the persons required to be consulted were absent in the meeting.[11] It is, however, accepted that if *A*

---

7. *Ibid.* Even the word 'may' used to require consultation may, having regard to the context, be construed as mandatory: *Keshav Chandra Joshi v. Union of India,* AIR 1991 SC 284, p. 294 : 1992 Supp (1) SCC 272; *Dinkar Anna Patil v. State of Maharashtra,* JT 1998 (7) SC 513, p. 524 : 1998 (6) Scale 54 : 1959 (1) SCC 354.
8. *Jyoti Prakash Mitter v. Chief Justice, Calcutta High Court,* AIR 1965 SC 961, p. 966 (para 21) : 1965 (2) SCR 53.
9. *Chandra Mohan v. State of U.P.*, AIR 1966 SC 1987, p. 1990 : 1967 (1) SCR 77. For consultation under Article 234 **see** to the same effect, *State of Jammu and Kashmir v. A.R. Zakki,* AIR 1992 SC 1546, pp. 1550, 1551 : 1992 Supp (1) SCC 548.
10. *Chandramouleshwar Prasad v. Patna High Court,* AIR 1970 SC 370, p. 375 : 1969 (3) SCC 56; **referred** to in *Prakash Chand Maheshwari v. Zila Parishad, Muzaffarnagar,* AIR 1971 SC 1696, p. 1704 : (1971) 2 SCC 489. **See** to the same effect *State of Kerala v. A. Lakshmi Kutty (Smt.)*, (1986) 4 SCC 632, pp. 647 to 650 : 1987 AIR (SC) 331.
11. *High Court of Judicature of Rajasthan v. P.P. Singh,* AIR 2003 SC 1029, p. 1037 : (2003) 4 SCC 239 (para 28). (A decision on a matter on which all the judges of the High Court are to be consulted in a full court meeting will not be invalid because of absence of some judges if the quorum required for the meeting is complete).

s to act after consulting *B*, the advice of *B* is not binding on *A*.[12] The nature of consultation and the question of primacy of the opinion of the Chief Justice of India in the context of appointment of Judges of the Supreme Court and High Courts, and transfers of Judges of High Courts as required by Articles 124, 217 and 222 of the Constitution was reconsidered by the Supreme Court[13] and the following propositions were laid down: (1) The nature of consultation amongst the different constitutional functionaries is 'an integrated participatory consultative process' and all the functionaries must act collectively to reach an agreed decision; (2) In the event of conflicting opinions by the constitutional functionaries the opinion of the judiciary 'symbolised by the view of the Chief Justice of India' and formed in the manner indicated has primacy; (3) No appointment of any Judge to the Supreme Court or any High Court can be made unless it is in confirmity with the opinion of the Chief Justice of India; (4) The opinion of the Chief Justice of India has not mere primacy but is determinative in the matter of transfers of High Court Judges.[14]

In *Hardwar Singh v. Bagun Sumbrui*,[15] the Supreme Court construed a rule made under Article 166(3) of the Constitution which provided that no department shall without previous consultation with the Finance Department authorise any orders affecting the finances of the State. In holding

---

12. *Chandramouleshwar Prasad v. Patna High Court, supra; Mani Subrat Jain v. State of Haryana*, AIR 1977 SC 276 : 1977 SCC (L&S) 166 : (1977) 1 SCC 486. But in special context it may be binding; **see** text and notes 90, 91, *post*.

13. *Supreme Court Advocates on Record Association v. Union of India*, AIR 1994 SC 268 : (1993) 4 SCC 441.

14. *Ibid*, p. 442. The consultative steps and primacy of the Chief Justice of India's opinion have been further explained and modified in *Special Reference no. 1 of 1998 under Article 143(1) of the Constitution of India*, JT 1998 (7) SC 304 : AIR 1999 SC 1 **Discussed** at p. 265, *supra*.

15. *Hardwar Singh v. Bagun Sumbrui*, AIR 1972 SC 1242, p. 1247 : 1972 (3) SCR 629 : (1973) 3 SCC 889. **See further** *Narayana Sankaran Mooss v. State of Kerala*, AIR 1974 SC 175 : (1974) 1 SCC 68. (Requirement of consultation with the State Electricity Board prescribed by section 4 of the Electricity Act, 1910, for exercising the power of revoking a licence by the State Government has been held to be mandatory). *Naraindas Indurkhya v. State of M.P.*, AIR 1974 SC 1232 : (1974) 4 SCC 788 (Requirement of consultation with the Education Board under section 4(1) of M.P. Act 13 of 1973 for prescription of text-books by the State Government is mandatory). *Municipal Corporation of Greater Bombay v. New Standard Engineering Co. Ltd.*, AIR 1991 SC 1362 : 1991 (1) SCC 611 (Requirement of consultation with the corporation under section 154 for recognising a subsidised housing scheme to enable the buildings to qualify for concessional rateable value, held mandatory). *Harpal Singh Chauhan v. State of U.P.*, AIR 1993 SC 2436, p. 2441 : 1993 (3) SCC 552 (consultation with the 'District judge' under section 24 of the Code of Criminal Procedure, 1973 for preparing a panel of names for appointment of a public prosecutor for the district, held mandatory).

the rule mandatory the Court pointed out that it was in a negative form and related to exercise of a power rather than to performance of a public duty.

Section 3 of the Orissa Lokpal and Lokayuktas Act, 1995 provides for appointment of Lokpal for conducting investigations into actions which are taken by or with the general or special approval of the Chief Minister or a Minister or Secretary in a case where a grievance or allegation is made or could be made. Only a person who is or has been a judge of the Supreme Court or a High Court is qualified for appointment as Lokpal. The appointment is to be made by the Governor 'after consultation with the Chief Justice of Orissa and the Leader of the Opposition'. Construing this provision it was held that having regard to the nature of functions to be discharged by the Lokpal and the nature of his qualification, consultation with the Chief Justice was not only mandatory but his opinion had primacy whereas the opinion of the Leader of the Opposition was not binding and he had no power to recommend some one else for the appointment.[16]

When authority to be consulted is expected to take a decision on the proposal sent to it forthwith and it whiles away the time, the conduct may invite the doctrine of acceptance subsilentio.[17]

In interpreting section 16(1)a of the Consumer Protection Act, 1986 the word 'consultation' in the proviso requiring consultation with the Chief Justice has been similarly construed as mandatory.[18] It has further been held that eligibility of a High Court Judge for appointment as President of a State Commission must include his suitability.[19] Therefore, an additional High Court Judge whom the Supreme Court Collegium had found unfit to continue as a Judge cannot be recommended for appointment and appointment of such a person even if recommended by the Chief Justice will be invalid.[20]

It is difficult to lay down any precise general formula for finding whether a particular provision requiring consultation is mandatory or directory and whether the opinion expressed by the person consulted would be binding or not and as to what would be the manner and extent of consultation required by the provision except to state that the answers to these questions will depend upon the right construction of the Act having regard to its scheme and object. The Supreme Court, however, in *Indian Administrative*

---

16. *Justice K.P. Mohapatra v. Sri Ramchandra Nayak,* (2002) 8 SCC 1, p. 7 : AIR 2002 SC 3578, p. 3581.

17. *L M L Ltd. v. State of U.P.,* (2008) 3 SCC 128 para 43 : AIR 2008 SC 1032.

18. *N. Kannadasan v. Ajoy Khose,* (2009) 7 SCC 1 paras 90, 91 : AIR 2010 SC 235.

19. *Ibid* para 66.

20. *Ibid* paras 71, 74, 75, 76, 92, 102.

Service (SCS) Ass. U.P. v. Union of India,[21] has in this context culled out the following six propositions:

(1) Consultation is a process which requires meeting of minds between the parties involved in the process of consultation on the material facts and points involved to evolve a correct or at least satisfactory solution. There should be meeting of minds between the proposer and the persons to be consulted on the subject of consultation. There must be definite facts which constitute the foundation and source for final decision. The object of the consultation is to render consultation meaningful to serve the intended purpose. Prior consultation in that behalf is mandatory.

(2) When the offending action affects fundamental rights or to effectuate built-in insulation, as fair procedure, consultation is mandatory and non-consultation renders the action *ultra vires* or invalid or void.

(3) When the opinion or advice binds the proposer, consulation is mandatory and its infraction renders the action or order illegal.

(4) When the opinion or advice or view does not bind the person or authority, any action or decision taken contrary to the advice is not illegal, nor becomes void.

(5) When the object of the consultation is only to apprise of the proposed action and when the opinion or advice is not binding on the authorities or person and is not bound to be accepted, the prior consultation is only directory. The authority proposing to take action should make known the general scheme or outlines of the actions proposed to be taken be put to notice of the authority or the persons to be consulted; have the views or objections, take them into consideration, and thereafter, the authority or person would be entitled or has/have authority to pass appropriate orders or take decision thereon. In such circumstances it amounts to an action 'after consultation'.

(6) No hard-and-fast rule could be laid, no useful purpose would be served by formulating words or definitions nor would it be appropriate to lay down the manner in which consultation must take place. It is for the court to determine in each case in the light of its facts and circumstances whether the action is 'after consultation'; 'was in fact consultated' or was it a 'sufficient consultation'.[22]

---

21. 1993 Supp (1) SCC 730 : 1992 Supp JT 83 : 1993 SCC (L&S) 252.

22. *Ibid.,* para 26 also quoted in AIR 2002 SC 3578 at p. 3581. **See further** for this case p. 1046, *infra.*

(g) Formalities prescribed for making contracts or transfers

Formalities and requirements for making contracts or transfers have generally been held to be imperative. Provisions of the Constitution Acts[23] and Municipal Acts[24] providing the manner in which contracts and transfers shall be executed have been held to be mandatory. Similarly, the mode of making sale, mortgage, lease or gift prescribed by the Transfer of Property Act,[25] and the formalities prescribed for transfer of shares under the Company Law,[26] have been held to be imperative. The language in these cases is held mandatory either on the view that by holding it directory the very object of the provisions will be defeated or on the view that the same implies a negative prohibiting any mode of transfer other than permitted by the statute.

---

23. Section 175(3), Government of India Act, 1935; Article 299, Constitution of India; *Bhikraj Jaipuria v. Union of India*, AIR 1962 SC 113 : 1962 (2) SCR 880; *Karamshi Jethabhai Somayya v. State of Bombay*, AIR 1964 SC 1714 : (1964) 6 SCR 984 (Agreement is void). **See further** *Union of India v. Rallia Ram*, AIR 1963 SC 1685 : (1963) 3 SCR 164 (formal document is not necessary, correspondence resulting in acceptance note sufficient); *State of Bihar v. Karam Chand Thapar*, AIR 1962 SC 110 : 1962 (1) SCR 827 (authority to execute on behalf of Government need not be conferred by notification); *State of West Bengal v. B.K. Mondal & Sons*, AIR 1962 SC 779 : 1962 Supp (1) SCR 876. (Agreement invalid but relief under section 70, Contract Act, can be granted); *New Marine Coal Co., Bengal (Pvt.) Ltd. v. Union of India*, AIR 1964 SC 152 : (1964) 2 SCR 859; *State of Punjab v. Om Prakash Baldeo Krishan (M/s.)*, AIR 1988 SC 2149 : 1988 Supp SCC 722; *Sohanlal v. Union of India*, AIR 1991 SC 955, p. 956 : 1991 (1) SCC 438 (no decree for specific performance can be passed). **See also** text and note 86, p. 396; *State of Uttar Pradesh v. Combined Chemical Company,* (2011) 2 SCC 151 para 23 : (2011) 1 JT 179.

24. *Young & Co. v. Leamington Spa Corporation*, (1883) 8 AC 517 (HL); *H.S. Rikhy (Dr.) v. New Delhi Municipal Committee*, AIR 1962 SC 554 : 1962 (3) SCR 604; *Pilloo Dhunji Shaw Sidhwa v. Municipal Corporation, Poona*, AIR 1970 SC 1201 : (1970) 1 SCC 213 (relief under section 70, Contract Act, can be granted); *B.C. Mohindra v. Municipal Board, Saharanpur*, AIR 1970 SC 729 : (1969) 1 SCC 56 (formal document is not necessary); *M.I. Builders Pvt. Ltd. v. Radhey Shyam Sahu,* JT 1999 (5) SC 42, p. 89 : AIR 1999 SC 2468, pp. 2549, 2500, 2504 : (1999) 6 SCC 464; *Nandkishore Ganesh Joshi v. Commissioner Municipal Corporation Kalyan and Dombivalli*, AIR 2005 SC 34, p. 37 (prior approval of standing committee mandatory). **See further** *M. Pentiah v. Muddala Veeramallappa*, AIR 1961 SC 1107, 1113 (para 15) : 1961 (2) SCR 295.

25. **See** text and note 46, p. 410 under title 6(d) 'Affirmative words may imply a negative.

26. *Greene v. Greene*, (1949) 1 All ER 167; *Howrah Trading Co. Ltd. v. CIT (Central), Calcutta*, AIR 1959 SC 775 : 1959 Supp (2) SCR 448; *Mannalal Khetan v. Kedarnath Khetan*, AIR 1977 SC 536 : (1977) 2 SCC 424. **See further** *Dove Investments (P.) Ltd. v. Gujarat Industrial Investment Corpn.*, (2006) 2 SCC 619 (paras 11 and 12) : AIR 2006 SC 1454.

If an agreement is required to be 'in writing', it does not necessarily follow that the statute in addition to the formality of a writing also requires that both parties should sign the writing.[27] Thus an arbitration agreement although required by the Arbitration Act, 1940, to be in writing need not be signed by parties for making it valid.[28] If an agreement is required to be 'in a prescribed form' a literal compliance is not essential if the material terms and conditions are reduced into writing,[29] and if the form indicates the place where the parties have to sign, absence of signatures of the parties does not vitiate the agreement.[30] The requirement of form may be mandatory if the statute provides for the consequence of nullification of agreement unless made in accordance with the form.[31]

If the Act confers power on the State Government to exempt any land from a restriction or prohibition on transfer contained in the Act, exemption granted after the transfer will be ineffective if the Act automatically invalidates the transfer made in violation of the restriction or prohibition but if a declaration under the Act is a pre-requisite for such an invalidity the transfer will be effective if the exemption is granted before such a declaration.[32]

(h) Statutes conferring power; Express and Implied conditions; Judicial Review

(i) General

In a country governed by the rule of law no authority exercises any absolute discretion or power.[33] A statutory functionary must act in a manner laid down in the statute. Thus issuance of an oral order or direction is not contemplated under the administrative law and statutory functionaries are enjoined with duty to pass written orders.[34] Similarly they are to act within

---

27. *T.A. Ruf & Co. Ltd. v. Pauwels*, (1919) 1 KB 660, p. 670; *Banarasi Das v. Cane Commr., U.P.*, AIR 1963 SC 1417, pp. 1423, 1424 : 1963 Supp (2) SCR 760.
28. *Jugal Kishore Rameshwardas v. Goolbai Hormusji*, AIR 1955 SC 812 : (1955) 2 SCC 867; *Banarasi Das v. Cane Commr., U.P., supra*, p. 1425; *Union of India v. Rallia Ram*, AIR 1963 SC 1685, p. 1689 : 1964 (3) SCR 164.
29. *Radhakisson Gopikisson v. Balmukund Ramchandra*, AIR 1933 PC 55; *Banarasi Das v. Cane Commr., U.P., supra*.
30. *Banarasi Das v. Cane Commr., U.P., supra*.
31. *Thomas v. Kelly*, (1883) 13 AC 506; *Banarasi Das v. Cane Commr., U.P., supra*, p. 1421.
32. *Murudeshwara Ceramics Ltd. v. State of Karnataka,* AIR 2001 SC 3017 : (2002) 1 SCC 116.
33. **See** text and note 9, p. 441.
34. *State Inspector of Police, Vishakhapatnam v. Surya Sankaram Karri,* (2006) 7 SCC 172 : (2006) 8 JT 177.

four corners of the Act empowering them and not on the dictates of a minister or Chief Minister.[35] A power conferred by a statute often contains express conditions for its exercise and in the absence of or in addition to the express conditions there are also implied conditions for exercise of the power.[36] An express condition relating to the exercise of a statutory power may imply a prohibition. But this may not take away incidental powers flowing from the grant of power. An exercise of a statutory power in breach of express or implied conditions will be illegal if the condition breached is mandatory. An illegal exercise of power can be challenged by the public law remedy of judicial review[37] or by a private law remedy of civil suit.[38] The distinction between public law and private law in this respect is too thin and has been almost obliterated.[39]

(ii) Express conditions; Implied prohibition; Incidental powers

In statutes conferring a power to be exercised on certain conditions, the conditions prescribed are normally held to be mandatory;[40] and a power inconsistent with those conditions is impliedly negatived. So, if a corporation is authorised to do an act, *e.g.* to borrow at interest, subject to certain conditions, it must be deemed to have been prohibited to do the said act except in accordance with the provisions of the Act which confers the authority on it.[41] Even an affirmative Act prescribing the conditions for exercise of a power conferred by it, is construed as mandatory. The rule stated in BACON'S Abr.[42] is: "If an affirmative statute which is introductive of a new law directs a thing to be done in a certain way, that thing shall not, even if there be no negative words, be done in any other way." It is an application of the principle of implied prohibition that the Coal Mines Nationalisation Act, 1973 permitting transfer of assets vested in the government to a government company impliedly prohibits privatisation of the government company to which the assets are transferred.[43] The rule of implied prohibition is, however, subservient to the basic principle that the

35. *Pancham Chand v. State of H.P.*, (2008) 7 SCC 117 para 18 : AIR 2008 SC 1888.
36. For implied conditions **see** pp. 481 to 512, *post.*
37. Articles 32, 136, 226 and 227 of the Constitution, pp. 801-808, *post.*
38. **See** Chapter 9, *post.*
39. **See** cases in f.n. 3, p. 758 and 'Cases of Nullity', pp. 797-800, Chapter 9.
40. *Haridwar Singh v. Bagun Sumbrui*, AIR 1972 SC 1242, p. 1247 : 1973 (3) SCC 889.
41. *Wenlock (Baroness) v. River Dee Co.*, (1885) 10 AC 354 (HL); *A-G v. Fulham Corporation*, (1921) 1 Ch 440. **See further** *M. Pentiah v. Muddala Veeramallappa*, AIR 1961 SC 1107, pp. 1113, 1114.
42. Bacon's Abr Tit Statute G quoted from CRAIES: Statute Law, 6th Edition, pp. 264, 265.
43. *Centre for Public Interest Litigation v. Union of India,* (2003) 7 SCC 532, p. 541 : AIR 2003 SC 3277, p. 3284.

court must, as far as possible, adopt a construction which effectuates the legislative intent and purpose.[44] Further, the rule of implied prohibition does not negative the principle that an express grant of statutory power carries with it by necessary implication the authority to use all reasonable means to make such grant effective.[45] For example when an Act of Parliament gives a justice Jurisdiction over an offence, it impliedly gives him a power to make out a warrant and bring before him any person charged with that offence.[46] If information of a cognizable offence is lodged in a police station under section 154 of the Code of Criminal Procedure, it is for the officer-in-charge of the police station to investigate the offence and no direction can be issued by the Chief Minister or the Government directly or through the Collector to give special protection to the person against whom the report is made.[47] Similarly, power conferred on a Magistrate to grant maintenance to a wife, child and parents under section 125, Criminal Procedure Code, 1973 to prevent vagrancy implies a power to allow interim maintenance, for the person seeking maintenance may not have means to subsist until the final order is passed.[48] Indeed, it has been said to be well settled that a statutory tribunal which has been conferred the power to adjudicate a dispute has implied power to implement and execute its order.[49] On this basis

---

44. *Asstt. Collector of Central Excise, Calcutta v. National Tobacco Co. of India Ltd.*, AIR 1972 SC 2563, p. 2573 : 1972 (2) SCC 560; **See further** *D.R. Venkatachalam v. Dy. Transport Commissioner*, AIR 1977 SC 842, p. 849 : 1977 (2) SCC 273; *Jamaluddin Ahmad v. Abusaleh Najmuddin*, (2003) 4 SCC 257, p. 267 : AIR 2003 SC 1917 : (2003) 2 KLT 638, (8th Edition, pp. 333, 334 of this book referred).

45. *ITO, Cannanore v. M.K. Mohammad Kunhi*, AIR 1969 SC 430 : (1969) 2 SCR 65; *Asstt. Collector of Central Excise v. National Tobacco Co. of India Ltd., supra*, p. 2573; *Re*, O., (1991) 1 All ER 330, p. 334 (CA); *Union of India v. Paras Laminates*, AIR 1991 SC 696, p. 699 : 1990 (4) SCC 453; *Reserve Bank of India v. Peerless General Finance and Investment Company Ltd.*, 1996 (1) Scale 13, p. 25 : AIR 1996 SC 646, p. 656 : (1996) 1 SCC 642; *Chief Executive Officer & Vice Chairman Gujarat Maritime Board v. Haji Daud Haji Harun Abu*, 1996 (8) Scale 608, p. 613 : 1996 (11) SCC 23; *J.K. Synthetics Ltd. v. Collector of Central Excise*, AIR 1996 SC 3527, p. 3528 : 1996 (6) SCC 92; *State of Karnataka v. Vishwabharati House Building Co-op. Society*, (2003) 2 SCC 412, p. 432 : AIR 2003 SC 1043, pp. 1055, 1056; *Jamaluddin Ahmad v. Abusaleh Najmuddin, supra*, p. 267 (8th Edition of this book pp. 333, 334 **referred**); *Govt. of Maharashtra v. Deokar's Distillery*, AIR 2003 SC 1216, p. 1238 : (2003) 5 SCC 669.

46. *State of U.P. v. Poosu*, AIR 1976 SC 1750, p. 1752 : 1976 SCC (Cri) 368 : 1976 SCC (Tax) 402.

47. *State of Maharashtra v. Sarangdhar Singh Shivadas Singh*, (2011) 1 SCC 577, paras 30, 31 : (2010) 13 JT 456.

48. *Savitri v. Govind Singh Rawat*, (1985) 4 SCC 337, pp. 341, 342 : 1986 AIR SC 984; **see further** *Shail Kumari Devi v. Krishan Bhagwan Pathak*, (2008) 9 SCC 632 paras 22 to 24 : AIR 2008 SC 3006. [The Code of Criminal Procedure (Amendment) Act 2001 in express terms confers power to grant interim maintenance which was implicit before the amendment].

49. *State of Karnataka v. Vishwabharati House Building Co-op. Society*, (2003) 2 SCC 412, p. 431 : AIR 2003 SC 1043, p. 1055.

it was held that a District Forum under the Consumer Protection Act, 1986 has power to execute its orders and it is only in case of its inability to execute its order that it has to send the order for execution to the civil court under section 25 of the Act.[50] On the same principle, when a corporation is conferred a power it impliedly authorises everything which could be fairly and reasonably regarded incidental or consequential to the power conferred.[51] Thus power conferred on a local authority to issue licences for holding '*hats*' or fairs will imply an incidental power to fix days therefor[52] and power conferred on Cane Commissioner to compel cane growers to supply cane to sugar factories will imply an incidental power to ensure payment of price of cane by the factories to the cane growers.[53] But a power which is said to be incidental cannot be inferred from an express power unless the power sought to be inferred is absolutely essential and not merley convenient for exercise of the power expressly conferred.[54] For instance, from an express power to prescribe syllabi or courses of instruction in languages an implied power to prescribe text books cannot be inferred.[55] 'It is not sufficient' that a power to be impliedly derived 'be sensible or desirable'. The implication has to be that it is 'necessary in order to make the statutory power effective to achieve its purpose'.[56] So a statutory power to issue a warrant for removal of a person suffering from mental disorder does not imply a power to direct named professionals to accompany the constable at the time of execution of warrant.[57]

---

50. *Ibid.*

51. *V.T. Khanzode v. Reserve Bank of India*, (1982) 2 SCC 7 : AIR 1982 SC 917 ; *Khargram Panchayat Samiti v. State of West Bengal*, (1987) 3 SCC 82, pp. 87, 88 : 1987 (2) JT 266; *Hazell v. Hammersmith and Fulham London Borough Council*, (1991) 1 All ER 545, p. 554 : (1992) 2 AC 1 (HL); *Reserve Bank of India v. Peerless General Finance and Investment Company Ltd.*, *supra*. **See further** *Akumah v. Hackney London Borough Council*, (2005) 2 All ER 148, p. 158 (HL).

52. *Khargram Panchayat Samiti v. State of West Bengal, supra.*

53. *State of Madhya Pradesh v. Jaora Sugar Mills Ltd.*, 1996 (8) Scale 88, p. 93 : AIR 1997 SC 600, p. 603 : (1997) 9 SCC 207. **See further** *Subhash Bakshi v. West Bengal Medical Council,* AIR 2003 SC 1563, p. 1568 : (2003) 9 SCC 269 (right or power to treat patients will imply power to prescribe medicines and issue certificates).

54. *S.D.O., Faizabad v. Shambhu Narain Singh*, AIR 1970 SC 140, p. 142 : (1969) 1 SCC 825. **See further** *Credit Suisse v. Allerdale Borough Council*, (1996) 4 All ER 129, p. 149 : (1997) QB 306 (CA) (Implied powers do not provide escape route from statutory controls); *Credit Suisse v. Waltham Forest London Borough Council*, (1996) 4 All ER 176 : (1997) QB 362 (CA) (A detailed statutory code regulating a function may negative any implied additional power to carry out that function.).

55. *Naraindas Indurkhya v. State of M.P.*, AIR 1974 SC 1232, pp. 1242, 1243 : (1974) 4 SCC 788.

56. *Ward v. Metropolitan Police Commissioner,* (2005) 3 All ER 1013, p. 1022 (para 24) (HL) (Baroness Hale).

57. *Ibid.*

Power conferred on Chairman of the Life Insurance Corporation of India by Regulation 51(2) of the Staff Regulations to regulate by instructions pay, dearness allowance or other allowances and other matters 'connected therewith or incidental thereto' will not include power to regulate gratuity and provident fund which cannot be said to be matters connected with or incidental to pay and dearness allowance as these matters are generally regulated by the Acts enacted by Parliament.[58]

Power conferred on the State Financial Corporation under section 29 of the State Financial Corporation Act, 1951 to take action against any industrial concern in case of default does not imply a power to proceed against a surety of the industrial concern if some properties are mortgaged or hypothecated by it for which separate provision is made under section 31 of the Act.[59]

Power conferred on a delegate by delegated legislation has to be exercised consistent not only with the delegated legislation and the parent Act but also consistent with provisions of other Acts.[60]

The principles set out above were restated and applied by LAHOTI, J., in *Jamaluddin Ahmad v. Abusaleh Najmuddin.*[61] The question in the case was whether presentation of an election petition to the Stamp Reporter of the High Court of Assam in accordance with the Rules of the High Court was valid presentation. Section 80A of the Representation of the People Act, 1951 confers jurisdiction on the High Court for trial of election petition and section 86 provides for presentation of the petition to the High Court. Section 169 of the Act confers power on the Central Government to make Rules for carrying out the purpose of the Act. Neither the Act nor any Rule made by the Central Govenrment indicates the officer or authority of the High Court to whom the election petition is to be presented. In such a situation the court held that the High Court had implied power to devise the procedure on the incidental and ancillary matter relating to the ministerial act of receiving the petition in the High Court and it could either continue with the existing practice of receiving petitions and documents just in other civil jurisdictions or make other convenient and workable procedure for receiving election petitions. In this view of the matter the presentation of the petition to the Stamp Reporter of the High Court was held to be valid.

---

58. *Life Insurance Corporation of India v. Retired Officers Association,* (2008) 3 SCC 321 para 18 : AIR 2008 SC 1485.

59. *Karnataka State Financial Corporation v. Narsimahaiah,* (2008) 5 SCC 176 paras 20 to 29 : AIR 2008 SC 1797.

60. *Life Insurance Corporation of India v. Retired Officers Association, supra* para 23.

61. *Jamaluddin Ahmad v. Abusaleh Najmuddin,* (2003) 4 SCC 166.

In deciding that a confession must be recorded in the manner prescribed by section 164, the Code of Criminal Procedure, 1898, or not at all, LORD ROCHE stated the rule in these words: "Where a power is given to do a certain thing in a certain way the thing must be done in that way or not at all. Other methods of performance are necessarily forbidden."[62] LORD ROCHE observed that this is a 'well recognised rule' and that this doctrine has often been applied to courts.[63] He referred to *Taylor's* case[64] where it is pointed out that "where a statutory power is conferred for the first time upon a court, and the mode of exercising it is pointed out, it means that no other mode is to be adopted". There is stronger reason to apply this rule when a confession recorded by a police officer is made admissible and so a confession recorded by a Superintendent of Police under section 15 of the Terrorist and Disruptive Activities (Prevention) Act, 1987 was held to be inadmissible unless recorded in the manner provided by the Act and rule 15 of the Rules made under the Act.[65] A settlement agreement in a conciliation proceeding can be recorded and authenticated by the conciliator only in the manner provided in section 73 of the Arbitration and Conciliation Act, 1996 and a court cannot confirm a settlement agreement which is not so recorded.[66] The same rule has been applied to purely administrative power, *e.g.*, of disconnecting a telephone in the event of any

---

62. *Nazir Ahmad v. King Emperor*, AIR 1936 PC 253, p. 257; **referred** to in *State of Uttar Pradesh v. Singhara Singh*, AIR 1964 SC 358, p. 361 : 1964 (4) SCR 485; *Dhananjay Reddy v. State of Karnataka,* AIR 2001 SC 1512, pp. 1518, 1519 : (2001) 4 SCC 9 (Requirement of obtaining signature of the accused is mandatory). **See** *A.K. Roy v. State of Punjab*, (1986) 4 SCC 326, p. 333 : AIR 1986 SC 2160; *Mayurdhwaj Co-op Group Housing Society Ltd. v. P.O. Delhi Co-op.,* AIR 1998 SC 2401, p. 2415 : 1998 (6) SCC 314 (Expulsion of a member of a cooperative society); *Chandra Kishore Jha v. Mahabir Prasad,* JT 1999 (7) SC 256, p. 263 : AIR 1999 SC 3558, p. 3562 : (1999) 8 SCC 266; *Gujrat Urja Vikas Nigam Ltd. v. Essar Power Ltd.,* (2008) 4 SCC 755 para 25 : AIR 2008 SC 1921; *Ram Deen Maurya v. State of U.P.,* (2009) 6 SCC 735 para 41 : (2009) 6 JT 333.

63. *Ibid.*

64. *Taylor v. Taylor,* (1875) 1 Ch D 426, p. 431; **referred** to in *Nazir Ahmad's* case, *supra* and *Singhara Singh's* case, *supra*.

65. *Ayyub v. State of U.P.,* (2002) 3 SCC 510 : AIR 2002 SC 1192; *Bharatbhai alias Jimi Premchandbhan v. State of Gujarat,* (2002) 8 SCC 447, p. 446 : AIR 2002 SC 3620, p. 3633.

66. *Haresh Dayaram Thakur v. State of Maharashtra,* JT 2000 (6) SC 349, p. 358 : (2000) 6 SCC 179 : AIR 2000 SC 2281. **See further** *Commissioner of Income Tax Mumbai v. Anjum M.H. Ghaswala*, AIR 2001 SC 3868, p. 3875 (para 24) : (2002) 1 SCC 633 (Commissioner settlement cannot waive or reduce statutory interest which can be waived or reduced only in the manner provided in the Act); *Ramphal Kundu v. Kamal Sharma,* AIR 2004 SC 1657 : (2004) 2 SCC 759 (The question as to who has been set up as an official candidate of a political party has to be decided only in accordance with paras 13 and 13A of the Symbols Order and not by any extrinsic evidence); *Captain Sube Singh v. Lt. Governor of Delhi*, (2004) 6 SCC 440, p. 452 (para 29) : AIR 2004 SC 3821.

emergency which is drastic in nature and dispenses with the requirement of natural justice,[67] and the power of the Bar Council of India of taking urgent action by circulation of a resolution to its members[68] as also to the exercise of power and duty of a registering officer not to register a document relating to transfer of land in the Union Territory of Delhi which is under acquisition unless the transferor produces a permission in writing of the competent authority for such transfer.[69] A statutory condition that while passing an order a public authority should intimate by the order itself that the person concerned has a right of appeal against the order has been held to be mandatory.[70] Requirement under a Municipal Act that a councilor could resign by tendering notice in writing in his handwriting addressed to Collector and *signed before Collector* is mandatory and a resignation notice which is not signed before Collector is invalid; mere initiating correction in the notice before Collector is not enough compliance.[71] The principle does not, however, mean that the power, the mode of exercise of which is laid down by a statute, must be exercised and the authority on whom the power is conferred has no discretion not to exercise it, [72] unless the circumstances are such that the power gets coupled with a duty to exercise it.[73]

When the statute provides a method of suspending a High Court Judge pending investigation of charges against him for his removal, that method alone can be adopted for suspending him and the Chief Justice has no administrative power to so fix the court roster as to virtually deprive him from functioning as a Judge.[74]

---

67. *Hukumchand Shyamlal v. Union of India*, AIR 1976 SC 789, p. 794 : 1976 (2) SCC 128 (para 18).

68. *Babu Verghese v. Bar Council Kerala*, JT 1999 (2) SC 200, pp. 210, 211 : AIR 1999 SC 1281, p. 1288 : (1999) 3 SCC 422.

69. *Meera Sahani v. Lt. Governor of Delhi*, (2008) 9 SCC 177 paras 32 and 36 : (2008) 8 JT 284.

70. *London and Clydeside Estates Ltd. v. Aberdeen District Council*, (1979) 3 All ER 876 : (1980) 1 WLR 182 (HL).

71. *Sau. Laxmi Verma v. State of Maharashtra*, (2010) 5 SCC 329 : AIR 2010 SC 2653.

72. *Mayurdwaj Co-operative Group Housing Society Ltd. v. Presiding Officer, Delhi Co-operative Tribunal*, JT 1998 (4) SC 555, p. 563 : AIR 1998 SC 2410 : (1998) 6 SCC 39.

73. **See** pages 488-526, *post.*

74. *Rees v. Crane*, (1994) 1 All ER 833 (PC) (Case from Trinidad and Tobago). In India the Constitution does not provide for suspension of a Supreme Court judge or a High Court judge pending proceedings for his removal under Article 124(4) of the Constitution. The Supreme Court in *Sub-Committee of Judicial Accountability v. Union of India*, AIR 1992 SC 320, pp. 357, 358 : (1991) 4 SCC 699 has held that no direction can be issued to the judge restraining him from discharging judicial functions and the matter is left to the sense of propriety of the judge himself and the advice that he may receive in that matter from the Chief Justice; *Ram Deen Maurya v. State of U.P.*, (2009) 6 SCC 735 para 41 : (2009) 6 JT 333 : (2009) 6 Scale 189.

A power to be exercised after 'prior approval' of a named authority cannot be validly exercised without such approval. For example restriction placed on police by section 20A of the Terrorists and Disruptive Activities (Prevention) Act, 1987 not to take cognizance of any offence 'without the prior approval of the District Superintendent of Police' has been held to be mandatory.[75] When the requirement is only of 'approval' and not of 'prior approval' the action holds good; only if it is disapproved it loses its force.[76]

When a statute prescribes the condition of 'permission' of some authority for acquisition of some property, it does not necessarily mean 'prior permission' and permission *ex post facto* may validate the acquisition; such a construction may be readily drawn when the statute at other places uses the words 'prior permission' whereas in the section in question it uses the word 'permission' without any qualification.[77] But generally action taken without complying with the requirement of 'permission', will not become effective till permission is obtained.[78]

Similarly a power to be exercised on recommendation of a named authority cannot be exercised without the recommendation of that authority. Recommendation in this context means 'giving of a favourable report' for exercise of the power.[79] Likewise, the power of the Registrar to supersede

---

75. *Anirudhsinhji v. Karansinhji Jadeja*, AIR 1995 SC 2390 : 1995 (5) SCC 302; *Mohd. Yunus v. State of Gujarat*, JT 1997 (8) SC 485 : (1997) 8 SCC 459; *Kalpnath Rai v. State*, JT 1997 (9) SC 18, p 32 : (1997) 8 SCC 732 (prior oral approval may be good). **See further** *Nandkishore Ganesh Joshi v. Commr. Municipal Corporation Kalyan*, AIR 2005 SC 34, p. 37 (Requirements of prior approval of standing committee for execution of contract); *Oswal Agro Furnace Ltd. v. Oswal Agro Furnace Workers Union*, (2005) 3 SCC 224, pp. 229, 230 (Requirement of prior permission of appropriate government in sections 25N and 25O of the Industrial Disputes Act, 1947 for closure of industrial undertaking).

76. *High Court of Judicature for Rajasthan v. P.P. Singh,* (2003) 4 SCC 239, p. 255 : AIR 2003 SC 1029.

For difference between 'approval' and 'acceptance', **see** *Ashok Kumar Saher v. Union of India,* (2006) 6 SCC 704, p. 713 (para 18) : AIR 2006 SC 2879. The case points out: 'Approval' presupposes an existing order. Acceptance means communicated acceptance. In case of 'acceptance' an application of mind on the part of the competent authority is *sine qua non,* 'approval' of an order only envisages statutory entitlement.

77. *Life Insurance Corporation of India v. Escorts Ltd.*, (1986) 1 SCC 264, pp. 313, 314 : AIR 1986 SC 1370 (construction of section 29(1) of the Foreign Exchange Regulation Act, 1973). **See further** *Burn Standard Company Ltd. v. McDermott International Inc.*, AIR 1991 SC 1191, pp. 1200, 1201 : (1991) 2 SCR 67 : (1991) 2 SCC 669 (permission may be inferred though not communicated. Construction of the section 28(1) of the Foreign Exchange Regulation Act, 1973).

78. *High Court of Judicature for Rajasthan v. P.P. Singh,* (2003) 4 SCC 239, p. 255 : AIR 2003 SC 1029.

79. *V.M. Kurian v. State of Kerala,* AIR 2001 SC 1409, p. 1412 : (2001) 4 SCC 215.

the Board of Directors of a cooperative bank under section 53(1) of the M.P. Cooperative Societies Act, 1960, cannot be exercised without previous consultation with the Reserve Bank as per the second proviso thereto. Accordingly, the previous consultation with the Reserve Bank was held to be a condition precedent before the Registrar forms an opinion on whether to supersede the Board of Directors or not.[80]

A requirement to obtain the 'views' of the Government before certain action is taken is not a requirement to obtain 'approval' of the Government.[81]

If a power is conferred on a particular body or person to institute legal proceedings for enforcement of the Act which confers such power, legal proceeding can only be instituted in the manner prescribed by the Act and not otherwise. It was, therefore, held that a person not authorised under section 537 of the Calcutta Municipal Act, 1923, to institute legal proceedings could not file a complaint for initiating criminal prosecution for an offence under the Act.[82]

On the same principle it has been held that a person can challenge the election of the President of India only in accordance with the provisions of the Presidential and Vice-Presidential Elections Act, 1952 and a person who neither is nor can claim to be a candidate cannot challenge the election for, under section 14A(1) only a candidate or 20 or more electors joined together can present an election petition.[83] And, it has been held that when the Patna High Court Rules (Rule 6 of Chapter XXI-E) provided that an election petition be presented to the designated election Judge in the open court and if the Judge be not available to the Bench hearing civil applications and motions, no other mode of presentation could be valid.[84]

---

80. *State of Madhya Pradesh & Ors. v. Sanjay Nagayach & Ors.*, (2013) 7 SCC 25, p. 40.

81. *Jaya Gokul Education Trust v. Commissioner and Secretary of Government,* AIR 2000 SC 1614, p. 1620 : (2000) 5 SCC 231.

82. *Ballabhdas Agarwala v. J.C. Chakravarty*, AIR 1960 SC 576 : 1960 (2) SCR 739. (The principle laid down in *R. v. Cubbit*, (1889) 22 QBD 622 and *Nazir Ahmad v. King Emperor*, *supra*, was applied). **See further** *K.M. Kanavi v. State of Mysore*, AIR 1968 SC 1339 : 1968 (3) SCR 821 (a case under the Bombay Municipal Boroughs Act, 1925); *Municipal Corporation, Delhi v. Jagdish Lal*, AIR 1970 SC 7 (a case under the Delhi Municipal Corporation Act). For a similar case under a Panchayat Act; **see** *K. Brahma Suraiah v. Laxminarayana*, AIR 1970 SC 816 : (1969) 1 SCC 138. *M.R. Patil v. Member, Industrial Court*, AIR 1997 SC 1429 : (1997) 4 SCC 545 (A case under the Maharashtra Recognition of Trade Unions and Prevention of Unfair Labour Practices Act, 1971). *P.D. Lakhani v. State of Punjab*, (2008) 5 SCC 15 paras 15 and 17 (A complaint under section 195 CrPC, 1973 has to be filed by the public servent concerned or by one to whom he is subordinate).

83. *Charan Lal Sahu v. Neelam Sanjeeva Reddi*, AIR 1978 SC 499, p. 503 : (1978) 2 SCC 500.

84. *Chandra Kishore Jha v. Mahavir Prasad,* JT 1997 (7) SC 256, pp. 262, 263 : AIR 1999 SC 3558, p. 3562 : (1999) 8 SCC 266.

In statutes conferring power to deprive the liberty of citizens, the conditions prescribed for the exercise of the power, including implied conditions and procedural requirements, must be strictly followed. Numerous cases dealing with arrest and preventive detention emphasise this principle.[85]

---

85. *Kishori Mohan Bera v. State of West Bangal*, AIR 1972 SC 1749 : (1972) 3 SCC 845; *Shaik Hanif v. State of West Bengal*, AIR 1974 SC 679, p. 683 : (1974) 1 SCC 637 : 1974 SCC Cri 292; *Bhut Nath Mate v. State of West Bengal*, AIR 1974 SC 806, p. 810 : (1974) 1 SCC 645 : 1974 SCC (Cri) 300 ; *Icchudevi v. Union of India*, AIR 1980 SC 1983 : (1980) 4 SCC 531; *A.K. Roy v. Union of India*, (1982) 1 SCC 271 : AIR 1982 SC 710; *Harbanslal v. M.L. Wadhwani*, (1987) 1 SCC 151 : AIR 1987 SC 217; *Hemlal Bhandari v. State of Sikkim*, (1987) 2 SCC 9, p. 14 : AIR 1987 SC 762; *Abdul Latif Abdul Wahab Sheikh v. B.K. Jha*, (1987) 2 SCC 22, p. 27 : AIR 1987 SC 725; *State of Punjab v. Sukhpal Singh*, AIR 1990 SC 231, p. 245 : 1990 (1) SCC 35; *Sajan Abraham v. State of Kerala,* AIR 2001 SC 3190, p. 3193 : (2001) 6 SCC 692 (But the procedural requirements should not be construed so literally as to make their compliance impossible). *Karnail Singh v. State of Haryana,* (2009) 8 SCC 539 para 35 (*Sajan Abraham's* case which related to non-compliance of section 42 of NDPS Act reconsidered and it was held that while total non-compliance with the requirement is impermissible, delayed compliance with satisfactory explanation about the delay will be acceptable compliance). **See further** *State of N.C.T. Delhi v. Sanjiv alias Bittoo*, AIR 2005 SC 2080 (Judicial review of externment order under the Delhi Police Act, 1978). *State of Maharashtra v. Bhaurao Punjabrao Gawande,* (2008) 3 SCC 613 : AIR 2008 SC 1705 (judicial review in cases of preventive detention) *K.K. Saravana Babu v. State of Tamil Nadu,* (2008) 9 SCC 89 : (2008) 9 JT 243 (judicial review of detention order under T.N. Prevention of Dangerous Activities of Bootleggers, Drug Offenders, Forest Offenders, Goondas, Immoral Traffic Offenders, Sand Offenders, Slum Grabbers and Video Pirates Act, 1982).

N.B.—In *Liversidge v. Anderson*, (1941) 3 All ER 338 : 1942 AC 954 (HL) the House of Lords, in dealing with a wartime Regulation permitting making of detention order, by majority, interpreted the words 'if the Minister has reasonable cause to believe' to mean 'if the Minister thinks he has reasonable cause'. LORD ATKIN dissented. According to him, what was essential was 'existence of reasonable cause' and not merley that 'the minister thought that he had reasonable cause'. The majority judgment had never many champions even in England and was regarded as the House of Lords "contribution to the war effort" (ALLEN *Law and order*, 2nd edition, p. 293). In *Ridge v. Baldwin,* (1963) 2 All ER 66, p. 76 : 1946 AC 40 (HL), LORD REID called the majority judgment as "a very peculiar decision" and in *Inland Revenue Commissioner v. Rossminister Ltd.*, (1980) 1 All ER 80, p. 93 (HL) LORD DIPLOCK said: "the time has come to acknowledge openly that the majority of this House in *Liversidge v. Anderson* were expediently, and at that time, perhaps, excusably wrong and dissenting speech of LORD ATKIN was right. In the same case (*Liversidge v. Anderson, supra*) LORD ATKIN also said "that in English law every imprisonment is *prima facie* unlawful and that it is for the person directing the imprisonment to justify his act." Referring to this statement the House of Lords in *Re Guisto,* (2003) 2 All ER 647, p. 663 said that it "has lost none of its force which it had when it was delivered over 60 years ago" and that "the courts must be vigilant to ensure that the extradition procedures are strictly observed" for it is a fundamental point of principle that use of the procedures that exist for depriving a person of his

[Footnote No. 85 Contd.]

The requirement implied under section 50 of the Narcotic Drugs and Psychotropic Substances Act, 1985, that the authorised officer should inform the person to be searched of his right that if he so requires he would be produced before a Gazetted Officer or Magistrate for search being conducted before him, has been held to be obligatory vitiating the conviction for possession of a contraband drug alleged to be found on search without informing the accused of the aforesaid right.[86] In holding so, DR. ANAND CJI for a Constitution Bench observed: "After *Maneka Gandhi v. Union of India,*[87] it is no longer permissible to contend that the right to personal liberty can be curtailed even temporarily, by a procedure which is not 'reasonable, fair and just' and when a statute itself provides for a just procedure it must be honoured."[88] But the question whether violation of a

---

[Footnote No. 85 Contd.]

liberty must be carefully scrutinised". **See further** *Emperor v. Vimlabai Deshpande,* AIR 1946 PC 123, p. 126 : 73 IA 144 (Exercise of a power to arrest if a police officer 'reasonably suspects' when challenged in court will require proof to the satisfaction of the court that the suspicion of the police officer was reasonable); *Khwaja v. Secretary of State for the Home Department*, (1983) 1 All ER 765 (HL) (When an executive officer's power to make a decision which would restrict or take away a subject's liberty, was dependant on the existence of certain facts, the court was not limited merely to inquiring whether the executive officer had reasonable grounds for believing that those precedent facts existed when he acted. Instead, the court had to be satisfied on the civil standard of proof to a high degree of probability that those facts did in fact exist at the time the power was exercised); *Tan Te Lam v. Superintended of Tai A Chau Detention Centre*, (1996) 4 All ER 256 (PC) (Courts will be slow to hold that statutory provisions authorised administrative detention for unreasonable periods or in unreasonable circumstances); *O'Hara v. Chief Constable of the Royal Ulster Constabulary*, (1997) 1 All ER 129, pp. 138, 139 (HL) (Power to arrest on reasonable grounds for suspicion requires both subjective and objective tests; the former relates to existence of genuine suspicion and the latter to the reasonableness of the grounds of suspicion); *Joginder Kumar v. State of U.P.*, AIR 1994 SC 1349, p. 1353 : (1994) 4 SCC 260 (It is not enough that it is lawful for the police to arrest a person and there should be justification for exercise of the power of arrest); *M.C. Abraham v. State of Maharashtra,* (2003) 2 SCC 649, pp. 657, 658 : 2003 SCC (Cri) 628 (since the power to arrest under section 41 CrPC is discretionary, a police officer is not always bound to make an arrest and he has to make up his mind whether it is necessary to arrest the accused person before making the arrest). *D.K. Basu v. State of West Bengal*, AIR 1997 SC 610 : (1997) 1 SCC 416 (safeguards for the benefit of arrested person laid down).

86. *State of Punjab v. Baldev Singh,* JT 1999 (4) SC 595, p. 622 : AIR 1999 SC 2378, p. 2395.

87. *Maneka Gandhi v. Union of India,* (1978) 1 SCC 248 : AIR 1978 SC 597.

88. *Ibid,* p. 620 (JT) : p. 2393 (AIR). But this procedure applies for search of person and not of baggage: (*Kalema Tumba v. State of Maharashtra,* JT 1999 (8) SC 293 : (1999) 8 SCC 257) or of something carried in his hand (*State of Punjab v. Makhanchand*, (2004) 3 SCC 453, p. 456) or of some bag or brief case carried by him (*State of Himachal Pradesh v. Pawan Kumar*, AIR 2005 SC 2265, p. 2270). **See further** *Roy VD v. State of Kerala,* AIR 2001 SC 137, p. 141 : (2000) 8 SCC 590

[Footnote No. 88 Contd.]

procedural step will make the detention *ab initio* void or make only continued detention invalid would depend upon the facts of each case and the nature of step which is violated. For example, it has been held that if an order of detention is validly made under section 3(1) of the Conservation of Foreign Exchange and Prevention of Smuggling Act, 1974 [COFEPOSA] but the detenue is not intimated of his right to make representation to the Advisory Board which is an implied obligation when by a declaration under section 9(1) of the Act the period of detention without obtaining the opinion of the Advisory Board is extended, the detention will not become void from the very beginning but will become invalid from the date of declaration under section 9(1) when he ought to have been intimated of his right to make representation resulting in denial of his right under Article 22(5) of the Constitution.[89] Further, though the provisions of the Act affecting personal liberty are to be strictly complied, the court cannot distort the meaning of plain words and give them a strained construction. For example, the requirement in section 3(5) of the National Security Act, 1980 that when the order of detention is made or approved by the State Government, it shall within seven days report the fact to the Central Government' could not be construed to mean that the report itself should reach the Central Government within seven days.[90]

Right to property is a constitutional right under Article 300-A as also a human right and statutory provisions affecting private property and restricting its use by the owners must be construed strictly.[91] But the State in the exercise of its power of eminent domain can acquire private property for public purpose and in this context the expression public purpose has

---

[Footnote No. 88 Contd.]

(Arrest and search under sections 41 and 42 of the NDPS Act, 1985 by an officer who is not empowered or authorised is inherently illegal and cannot give rise to a valid prosecution and will vitiate the trial); *Prabha Shankar Dubey v. State of M.P.*, (2004) 2 SCC 56 : AIR 2004 SC 486 (There is no particular mode or manner in which the accused has to be told of his right under section 50 of the NDPS Act, 1985 and a substantial compliance may be sufficient); *Vijay Singh Chandubha Jadeja v. State of Gujarat,* (2011) 1 SCC 609 : AIR 2011 SC 77 (Constitution Bench) (Theory of substantial compliance of the safeguard in section 50 as held in some cases has been disapproved).

89. *Meena Jayendra Thakur v. Union of India,* JT 1999 (7) SC 336 : (1999) 8 SCC 679 : AIR 1999 SC 3517.

90. *State of Manipur v. Sansam Ongbi,* JT 1999 (8) SC 228, p. 230 : (1999) 8 SCC 250 : AIR 1999 SC 3862.

91. *P. T. Munichikkanna Reddy v. Revamoma,* (2007) 6 SCC 59 paras 40 to 43 : AIR 2007 SC 1753; *Chairman Indore Vikas Pradhikaran v. Pure Industrial Coke & Chemicals Ltd.*, (2007) 8 SCC 705 para 53 : AIR 2007 SC 2458; *Bhikubhai Vithlbhai Patel v. State of Gujrat,* (2008) 4 SCC 144 para 37 : AIR 2008 SC 1771. **See further** *R & R Fazzolari Pty. Ltd. v. Parramatta City Council,* (2009) 83 ALJR 557 para 40 to 44 (French C.J.).

been widely construed to cover even an integrated project to make a city a major business-cum-leisure tourism infrastructure centre of the State.[1] Conditions prescribed for exercise of a power affecting private property must be strictly followed.[2] So it has been held that the preliminary notification under section 4 of the Land Acquisition Act, 1894, must be published in the manner required by that section[3] containing particulars of the land proposed to be acquired,[4] and particulars of the public purpose for which it is needed,[5] provision made in section 5A for objecting to the proposed acquisition cannot be lightly dispensed with[6] and urgency provisions in section 17 of the Act cannot be readily invoked to forego the normal procedure.[7] Provision of rule 4 of the Land Acquisition Company Rules, 1963 made by the Central Government under section 55 of the Land Acquisition Act, 1894 providing for an enquiry and requirement of satisfaction of the appropriate Government on certain matters when the acquisition is for a Company has been held to be mandatory and the enquiry has to precede before a notification under section 4 of the Act is issued.[8] When the acquisition is for a local authority or a company, the local authority or company concerned can appear before the Collector and

---

1. *Sooraram Pratap Reddy v. District Collector Ranga Reddy District,* (2008) 9 SCC 552 paras 129 to 134 : (2008) 9 JT 622.
2. *Bhavnagar University v. Palitana Sugar Mills (P.) Ltd.,* (2003) 2 SCC 111, p. 121 : AIR 2003 SC 511, p. 517.
3. *Narinderjit Singh v. State of Uttar Pradesh,* AIR 1973 SC 552 : 1973 (1) SCC 157; *Collector, Allahabad v. Raja Ram Jaiswal,* (1985) 3 SCC 1, pp. 11, 12 : AIR 1985 SC 1622; *Nutakki Seshratanam v. Sub Collector Land Aquisition,* AIR 1992 SC 131, p. 132 : 1992 (1) SCC 114; *M.P. Housing Board v. Mohd. Shafi,* (1992) 2 SCC 168 para 8 : (1992) 3 JT 523; *Special Deputy Collector, Land Acquisition v. J. Sivaprakasam,* (2011) 1 SCC 330 paras 23, 24, 27 : AIR 2011 SC 922 (necessity of publication in two daily newspapers circulated in the locality by Amendment Act 68 of 1984). **See further** *State of Haryana v. Raghubar Dayal,* (1995) 1 SCC 133 : 1994 (4) Scale 1084; *Mandi Samiti v. Makrand Singh,* (1995) 2 SCC 497; *Mohan Singh v. International Air Port Authority,* 1996 (8) Scale 251 : 1996 (10) JT 311; *Syed Hasan Rasul v. Union of India,* AIR 1991 SC 711, pp. 714, 715 : 1991 (1) SCC 401 (Same principle applied in construing sections 11 and 44 Delhi Development Act, 1957).
4. *Gunwant Kaur v. Municipal Committee, Bhatinda,* AIR 1970 SC 802 : 1969 (3) SCC 769.
5. *Munshi Singh v. Union of India,* AIR 1973 SC 1150 : 1973 (2) SCC 337.
6. *Munshi Singh v. Union of India, supra*; *Union of India v. Mukesh Hans,* AIR 2004 SC 4307, p. 4315 : (2004) 8 SCC 14; *ESSCO Fabs Pvt. Ltd. v. State of Haryana,* (2009) 2 SCC 377 paras 39, 53 to 56, 60 : (2008) 12 JT 315.
7. *Union of India v. Krishna Lal Arneja,* (2004) 8 SCC 453 : AIR 2004 SC 3582; *ESSCO Fabs Pvt. Ltd. v. State of Haryana, (supra).*
8. *Devinder Singh v. State of Punjab,* AIR 2008 SC 261 paras 43 to 50 (case of Somvanti AIR 1963 SC 151 holding to the contrary was not followed) : (2008) 1 SCC 728 : AIR 2008 SC 261. For principles relating to acquisition for a company **see further** *Fomento Resorts and Hotels Ltd. v. Minguel Martins,* (2009) 3 SCC 571 : (2009) 1 JT 470.

adduce evidence for determination of compensation. For this reason notice to them is necessary. Want of notice and opportunity in proceedings for determination of compensation to them will be fatal to the award.[9] Power conferred on a State Government to divest proprietary rights by publication of a notification in Official Gazette and in 'at least two issues of two newspapers' was held to be not effectively exercised when the notification was published in Official Gazette but not in two issues of two newspapers.[10] And similarly, power conferred on a State Electricity Board under section 6 of the Electricity (Supply) Act, 1948, to purchase the undertaking of a licensee by giving a notice 'requiring the licensee to sell the undertaking' was held not to have been effectively exercised by serving a notice intimating that the Board has decided to 'exercise the option of purchasing the undertaking'.[11] Requirement of notice to a person interested, before a town planning scheme is finalised has also been held to be mandatory for the provision for notice ensures fair procedure under Articles 14 and 21 of the Constitution before a person is made to lose his property as a result of the scheme.[12] Similarly a provision that designation / reservation of certain land for a particular purpose in a town planning scheme will lapse if the land is not acquired within ten years and thereafter within six months after notice by the owner has been held to be mandatory and steps for acquisition for the designated purpose under the scheme taken subsequently will be ineffective.[13] Statutory power conferred on the Government in an Act to exempt classes of persons or areas from the provisions of the Act which render it 'expedient' so to do has to be interpreted in the context and object of the exemption provision and the circumstances of the case.[14]

A stage has now come when it is necessary to ensure that the land losers do not feel alienated but welcome the acquisition. In addition to compensation if the acquisition is for setting up any industry they may be provided equity in the industry or service and if it is for colonization they may also be provided with small plots. The Collector and Land Acquisition officer

---

9. *Delhi Development Authority v. Bhola Nath Sharma,* (2011) 2 SCC 54 para 42 : AIR 2011 SC 428.

10. *Giriwar Prasad Narain Singh v. Dukhu Lal Das,* AIR 1968 SC 90 : 1967 (3) SCR 759.

11. *Gujarat Electricity Board v. Girdharilal Motilal,* AIR 1969 SC 267 : (1969) 1 SCR 312.

12. *Jaswant Singh Mathura Singh v. Ahmedabad Municipal Corporation,* AIR 1991 SC 2130, pp. 2135, 2136 : 1992 Supp (1) SCC 5.

13. *Municipal Corporation of Greater Bombay v. Dr. Hakimwadi Tenants Association,* AIR 1988 SC 233 : 1988 Supp SCC 55; *Bhavnagar University v. Palitana Sugar Mills (P.) Ltd.,* (2003) 2 SCC 111 : AIR 2003 SC 511.

14. *Amarjit Singh v. State of Punjab,* (2010) 10 SCC 43 paras 31 to 36 : (2010) 11 JT 82.

must be helpers for their rehabilitation.[15] This does not however mean that alternative sites must be made a condition for every acquisition of land. Neither Article 300A of the Constitution nor the Land Acquisition Act make any measures for rehabilitation of the expropriated owners a condition precedent for compulsory acquisition of land. Acquisition made for a public purpose and in accordance with procedure established by law cannot be assailed on the ground that it violates the right to livelihood under Article 21 of those dependants on the land being acquired.[16]

A statutory power must be exercised only by the person on whom it is conferred unless the statute, by express words or necessary implication, permits delegation in which case it may also be exercised by the delegate, if delegation is made in terms of the statute.[17] For example, if a University Act confers the power to dismiss an officer on the executive council and to delegate that power on approval of the Chancellor, the Vice-Chancellor cannot exercise the power if delegation to him is made without obtaining the approval of the Chancellor and, further, the Vice-Chancellor's act of dismissing an officer without valid delegation cannot also be ratified by the Executive Council.[18]

And when a power is conferred to take action on being satisfied as to certain conditions 'for reasons to be recorded', action cannot be taken simply on being satisfied without recording the reasons of satisfaction even though the satisfaction required is only subjective and the exercise of the power administrative. In such a case mere recording of satisfaction as to the existence of those conditions is not enough but the reasons which led to that satisfaction must be recorded, otherwise the exercise of the power will be in excess of jurisdiction; the same result will follow if the reasons recorded are totally irrelevant and not germane to the content and the scope of the power conferred by the statute.[19] Power to take

---

15. *Bondu Ramaswamy v. Bangalore Development Authority*, (2010) 7 SCC 129 paras 153.2, 153.3 : (2010) 6 JT 57.

16. *Amarjit Singh v. State of Punjab*, (2010) 10 SCC 43 paras 48 to 51 : (2010) 11 JT 82.

17. **See** Chapter 12, title 7, Sub-Delegation.

18. *Marathwada University v. Sheshrao Balwantrao Chavan*, AIR 1989 SC 1582 : (1989) 3 SCC 132.

19. *Collector of Monghyr v. Keshav Prasad Goenka*, AIR 1962 SC 1694, pp. 1700, 1701 : 1963 (1) SCR 98; *Associated Electrical Industries (India) Private Ltd., Calcutta v. Its Workmen*, AIR 1967 SC 284 : (1961) 2 LLJ 122; *Chandradeo Singh v. Prakash Chandra Bose*, AIR 1963 SC 1430, p. 1435 (para 13) : 1964 (1) SCR 639; *K. Venkataramiah v. A. Seetharama Reddy*, AIR 1963 SC 1526, p. 1529 (para 13) : (1964) 2 SCR 35; *Ajawtha Industries v. Central Board of Direct Taxes*, AIR 1976 SC 437 : 1976 SCC (Tax) 127; *Union of India v. H.P. Chothia*, AIR 1978 SC 1214, p. 1216 : (1978) 2 SCC 586 : 1978 SCC (Lab) 356. *Rajmallaiah v. Anil*

[Footnote No. 19 Contd.]

action conferred on the Government after 'stating the grounds of its opinions' has similarly been construed; and it has been held that grounds of opinion, *i.e.*, the conclusions of facts on which the opinion is based must be stated otherwise the exercise of power will be invalid.[20] But if the statute does not require either the recording of satisfaction or the reasons therefor, an order made without recording the satisfaction as to fulfilment of the conditions on which the exercise of the power depends, does not make the order invalid. In such cases it is the fact of satisfaction of the authority which gives rise to jurisdiction and not the recording of the satisfaction. The difference only is this, that if the satisfaction has been recorded, a presumption will arise that the authority was really satisfied and the person who disputes the existence of such satisfaction will have to establish the non-existence thereof; whereas if the satisfaction has not been recorded and a person challenges the existence of satisfaction, the authority will have to establish that it was in fact satisfied before passing

---

[Footnote No. 19 Contd.]

Kishore, AIR 1980 SC 1502 : 1980 Supp SCC 81. The reasons recorded must show the application of mind to the material on record; *Union of India v. M.L. Capoor*, AIR 1974 SC 87, p. 88 : (1973) 2 SCC 836; *Great Portland Estates v. Westminster City Council*, (1984) 3 All ER 744, p. 752 : 1985 AC 661 : (1984) 3 WLR 1035 (HL). The necessity of giving reasons is a healthy check against abuse or misuse of power for if the reasons recorded are extraneous or irrelevant the order would be struck down; *Maneka Gandhi v. Union of India*, AIR 1978 SC 597, p. 619 : (1978) 1 SCC 248. The requirement of recording satisfaction with reasons may be implicit in a statute, *Hukamchand Shyamlal v. Union of India*, AIR 1976 SC 789, p. 793 : (1976) 2 SCC 128. But the requirement of recording reasons may in some context be held to be a curable irregularity not vitiating the order, *G. Marulasiddaiah (Dr.) v. T. G. Siddapparadhya (Dr.)*, AIR 1971 SC 2264, pp. 2267, 2268 : (1971) 1 SCC 568; *R. v. Liverpool City Council*, (1975) 1 All ER 379, p. 384 (QBD); *G. S. Lamba v. Union of India*, (1985) 2 SCC 604, p. 626 : AIR 1985 SC 1019. **See further** on the question of sufficiency of reasons in the context of statutory requirement to give reasons: *South Bucks District Council v. Porter*, (2004) 4 All ER 775, p. 786 (HL) (The reasons for a decision must be intelligible and they must be adequate. They must enable the reader to understand why the matter was decided as it was and what conclusions were reached on the principal important controversial issues, disclosing how any issue of law or fact was resolved. Reasons can be briefly stated, the degree of particularity required depending entirely on the nature of issues falling for decision).

20. *Narayan Das Indurkhya v. State of Madhya Pradesh*, AIR 1972 SC 2086, pp. 2088, 2089 : 1972 (3) SCC 676; *State of Uttar Pradesh v. Lalaisingh Yadav*, AIR 1977 SC 202, p. 204 : 1976 SCC (Cri) 556 : (1976) 4 SCC 213; *State of Maharashtra v. Sangharaj Damoder Rupawate,* (2010) 7 SCC 398 paras 43, 44 : (2010) 6 Scale 667 (Power under section 95 CrPC of forfeiture of book, newspaper, etc. is a drastic power… 'stating the grounds of opinion' would mean stating the conclusions of fact on which that opinion is based).

the order. This principle will apply whether the order in question is executive or in the nature of subordinate legislation.[21]

The requirement to 'record the grounds of his belief', before an excise officer conducts a search under section 54 of the Mysore Excise Act, has been held to be mandatory and its violation rendering invalid the entire search and the conviction based on it.[22] Similarly, the requirement of 'recording the grounds of his belief' under the proviso to section 42(1) of the Narcotic Drugs and Psycotropic Substances Act, 1985, when an authorised officer conducts a search between sunset and sunrise, has been held to be mandotory and failure thereof invalidating the search and vitiating the trial.[23]

Section 6(1) of the Smugglers and Foreign Exchange Manipulators (Forfeiture of Property) Act, 1976 empowers the Competent Authority to issue notice for forfeiture of property if he has reason to believe that the property could not have been acquired from known sources of income, earnings or assets. But the section requires that the reasons for such belief be recorded in writing. This condition has been held to be mandatory and a notice of forfeiture issued without recording the reasons would be invalid.[24]

The power of the Central Government under the Proviso to section 3(3) of the Unlawful Activities (Prevention) Act, 1967 to declare an association to be unlawful with immediate effect for reasons to be stated

---

21. *Swadeshi Cotton Mills Co. Ltd. v. State Industrial Tribunal*, AIR 1961 SC 1381, pp. 1386, 1387 : (1962) 1 SCR 422; *Capital Multi-Purpose Co-operative Societies, Bhopal v. State of M.P.*, AIR 1967 SC 1815, pp. 1819, 1820 : 1967 (3) SCR 329; *Narayan Govind Gavate v. State of Maharashtra*, AIR 1977 SC 183, p. 192 : 1977 SCC (Cri) 49 : (1977) 1 SCC 133. *State of Haryana v. Hari Ram Yadav*, JT 1994(1) SC 126, pp. 129, 130 : AIR 1994 SC 1262, p. 1265. Same rule has been applied for requirement of prior consultation; *Naraindas Indurkhya v. State of M.P.*, AIR 1974 SC 1232, p. 1244 : (1974) 4 SCC 788 : (1994) 2 SCC 617. But the authorities should as a matter of practice record the satisfaction and the reasons therefor in the order, *Liberty Oil Mills v. Union of India*, (1984) 3 SCC 465, p. 498 : AIR 1984 SC 1271. Short reasons showing application of mind to relevant facts will suffice; *State of U.P. v. Committee of Management of SKM Inter College*, 1995 (3) Scale 50 : 1995 AIR SCW 3030 : 1995 (5) JT 196 : 1995 Supp (2) SCC 535.

22. *K.L. Subhayya v. State of Karnataka*, AIR 1979 SC 711 : (1979) 2 SCC 115. **But see** *Bai Radha v. State of Gujarat*, (1969) 2 SCR 799 : (1969) 1 SCC 43 : AIR 1970 SC 1396, where a similar requirement has not been held to be mandatory.

23. *State of Punjab v. Balbir Singh*, JT 1994(2) SC 108 : AIR 1994 SC 1872 : (1994) 3 SCC 299. **See further** *Directorate of Revenue v. Mohammed Nisar Holia*, (2008) 2 SCC 370 para 17 : (2007) 13 JT 408 (search of a room in a hotel).

24. *P.P. Abdullah v. Competent Authority*, (2007) 2 SCC 510 (paras 6 and 7) : AIR 2007 SC 1057.

in writing cannot be said to be validly exercised unless the reasons are recorded and communicated to the affected party by incorporating the same in the notification or otherwise by a communication simultaneously issued.[25] It has been held that 'to state' has a wider connotation than the words 'to record' and contemplates information to the party affected.[26] The same thing will follow if the statutory provision casts an obligation to serve a copy of the order to be passed 'for reasons to be recorded in writing'; it will imply that the copy served must contain the reasons.[27]

Even in cases where the statute confers on the authority a power to be exercised by use of the expressions 'considers necessary', 'has reason to believe' or 'is of the opinion' as to existence or otherwise of certain matters without the requirement of recording any reasons for exercising the power which is subjective in nature, there must exist some relevant material on which the authority's belief or opinion is based otherwise the exercise of the power will be held to be illegal.[28] A power to make an order 'without assigning any cause' or 'without assigning any reasons' does not confer any power to act arbitrarily. It only means that reasons for making the order need not be communicated to the person affected by the order; but reasons must exist for making the order.[29] As every State action must satisfy the rule of non-arbitrariness, the duty to record reasons may be impliedly inferred.[30]

Another principle which may be noticed in the context of statutory powers is that a public authority cannot fetter the future exercise of the power by a private contract but when the contract itself is entered into in the exericse of the statutory power the position is different and the stipulations in the contract are binding and the authority cannot disregard them and exercise the statutory power uninhibited or unfettered by them.[31] The

---

25. *Mohammad Jafar v. Union of India*, JT 1994(2) SC 597 : 1994 Supp (2) SCC 1.

26. *Ibid*, p. 603.

27. *C.B. Gautam v. Union of India*, (1993) 1 SCC 78 : AIR 1994 SC 771 (Construction of section 269UD of the Income-tax Act, 1961).

28. *Bhikhubhai Vithlabhai Patel v. State of Gujarat*, (2008) 4 SCC 144 paras 24, 25, 27, 29, 30, 31, 32, 33 : AIR 2008 SC 1771.

29. *Kumari Shrilekha Vidyarthi v. State of U.P.*, AIR 1991 SC 537, p. 546 : 1991 (1) SCC 212.

30. *T.R. Thandur v. Union of India*, AIR 1996 SC 1643, p. 1562 : (1996) 3 SCC 690. **See further** text and notes 79 to 81, pp. 497-498.

31. *Indian Aluminium Company v. Kerala State Electricity Board*, AIR 1975 SC 1967, pp. 1975, 1976 : (1975) 2 SCC 414 (Construction of section 49 of the Electricity (Supply) Act, 1948). **See further** *R. v. Hammersmith and Fulham London Borough Council, Ex parte, Beddowes*, (1987) 1 All ER 369, pp. 379, 383 : 1987 QB 1050 : (1987) 2 WLR 263 (CA).

latter statement must however be read as qualified to this extent that if the statute confers authority to disregard a contract entered into in exercise of the statutory power in specified circumstances the authority will have the power to disregard the contract in those circumstances.[32] Further, when the contract entered into in exercise of the statutory power itself enables or contemplates its variation by further exercise of the statutory power, the future exercise of the statutory power by the public authority remains unfettered.[33]

Conferral of power, however, does not take away an existing power which is different from that power which is conferred and regulated by the statute;[34] and when a statute deals with two powers the conditions and restrictions as to one do not affect the other.[35]

When a power is to be exercised in accordance with the rules or subject to rules, the power may still be exercisable even though no rules have been made.[36]

(iii) Implied Conditions and Judicial Review

(a) Administrative and quasi judicial orders.—A statutory discretion or power, whether it be administrative or *quasi*-judicial, although conferred in wide terms is subject to certain implied conditions or limitations.[37] A violation of these conditions or limitations even though there be no violation of any express condition can give rise to judicial review. The implied limitations arise for Parliament is presumed not to legislate contrary to the

---

32. *Ibid.*

33. *Bishun Stone Lime Co. Ltd., Orissa; Textiles Mills Ltd. v. Orissa State Electricity Board,* AIR 1976 SC 127 : (1976) 2 SCC 167.

34. *Ukha Kolhe v. State of Maharashtra,* AIR 1963 SC 1531, pp. 1539, 1542 : (1964) 1 SCR 926; (*Nazir Ahmad v. King-Emperor,* AIR 1936 PC 253, **distinguished).**

35. *Prabhani Transport Co-operative Society Ltd. v. Regional Transport Authority,* AIR 1960 SC 801, p. 804 : (1960) 3 SCR 177 (**N.B.:** *Nazir Ahmed's* case, *supra,* **distinguished).**

36. See text and notes 70 to 75, pp. 1087-1088, *infra.*

37. "Law has reached its finest moments when it has freed man from unlimited discretion": *United States v. Wunderlish,* 342 U.S. 98; *Shiv Sagar Tiwari v. Union of India,* AIR 1997 SC 2725, p. 2726 : (1997) 1 SCC 444. "In a system based on the rule of law, unfettered governmental discretion is a contradiction in terms": WADE, *Administrative Law* (5th edn.) pp. 355, 356 quoted in *Town Hamlets London Borough Council v. Chitnik Developments Ltd.,* (1988) 1 All ER 961, p. 966 (HL); *Bharat Heavy Electricals Ltd. v. M. Chandrashekhar Reddy,* 2005 (2) SCC 481, p. 486 (para 14) (No authority, be it administrative or judicial has any power to exercise the discretion vested in it unless the same is based on justifiable grounds supported by acceptable materials and reasons thereof).

rule of law[38] which enforces "minimum standard of fairness both substantive and procedural"[39] so that the exercise of statutory discretion conforms to the "principles of good administration".[40]

The implied conditions or limitations are: The person on whom the power is conferred must exercise it in good faith for furtherance of the object of the statute; he must not proceed upon a misconstruction of the statute; he must take into account matters relevant for exercise of the power; he must not be influenced by irrelevant matters; he must not act unreasonably, *i.e.*, irrationally or perversely;[41] he must not fetter his discretion in

---

38. LORD BINGHAM summarised the principles of Rule of Law in a lecture delivered on 16th November 2006 which very briefly stated are as follows:*

(1) The law must be accessible and so far as possible, intelligible, clear and predictable.
(2) The question of legal right and liability should ordinarily be resolved by application of the law and not by the exercise of discretion.
(3) The laws of land should apply equally to all save to the extent that objective differences justify differentiation.
(4) The law must afford adequate protection of fundamental human rights.
(5) Means must be provided for resolving without prohibitive cost for inordinate delay, *bonafide* civil disputes which the parties themselves are unable to resolve.
(6) Ministers and public affairs at all levels must exercise the powers conferred on them reasonably, in good faith, for the purpose for which the powers were conferred and without exceeding the limits of such powers.
(7) Adjudicating procedures provided by the state should be fair.
(8) Compliance by the state with its obligations in international laws whether deriving from treaty or international custom and practice.

* The Rule of Law Perspectives from Around the Globe (Lexis Nexis) edited by Francis Neak pp. 245 to 256.

39. *Pierson v. Secretary of State for the Home Department,* (1997) 3 All ER 577, pp. 604, 607 (HL). **See further** text and note 92, p. 494.

40. Terminology used by D.J. GALLIGAN, quoted in (1999) 115 LQR 119. **See further** *M.I. Builders Pvt. Ltd. v. Radhey Shyam Sahu,* AIR 1999 SC 2468, pp. 2501, 2502 : (1999) 9 SCC 182 (Judicial review promotes 'good governance').

N.B. 1. For conflicting views concerning the foundation of judicial review in English Law **see**: PAUL CRAIG, '*Competing Models of Judicial Review*', (1999) Public Law 428; JEFFREY JOWELL, '*Of vires and Vacuums : The Constitutional Context of Judicial Review',* (1999) Public Law 448. For expansion of judicial review in England **see** JOHN LEWIS, '*Is the High Court the Guardian of Fundamental Constitutional Rights*', (1993) Public Law 59. For criticism of this article **see** J.A.G. GRIFFITH, '*The Brave New World of Sir John Lewis*', (2000) 63 Modern Law Review, 159.

N.B. 2. The real function of the court in judicial review is declaration and enforcement of law and not simply removal of administrative injustice as distinguished from legality: *Attorney General (NSW) v. Quin,* (1990) 170 CLR 1, pp. 35, 36; *Minister for Immigration and Multi-cultural Affairs v. Yusuf,* (2001) 75 ALJR 1105, p. 1118.

41. For administrative power **see** *Associated Provincial Picture Houses Ltd. v. Wednesbury Corp.*, (1947) 2 All ER 680 : (1948) 1 KB 223 (CA); *Padfield v. Minister of Agriculture, Fisheries and Food*, (1968) 1 All ER 694 : 1968 AC 997 (HL);

[Footnote No. 41 Contd.]

[Footnote No. 41 Contd.]

Secretary of State for Education and Science v. Metropolitan Borough of Tameside, (1976) 3 All ER 665 (CA), 679 (HL); *United Kingdom Association of Professional Engineers v. Advisory Conciliation and Arbitrary Service*, (1980) 1 All ER 612, p. 620 : 1981 AC 424 : (1980) 2 WLR 254 (HL); *Brombay London Borough Council v. Greater London Council*, (1982) 1 All ER 129 (CA), 153 (HL); *Holgate Mohammed v. Duke*, (1984) 1 All ER 1054, p. 1057 (HL) (Power to arrest on reasonable grounds can be questioned on these grounds); *C.C.S.U. v. Minister for Civil Services*, (1984) 3 All ER 935, pp. 950, 951 (HL). (Grounds of challenge are illegality, irrationality and procedural impropriety); *Puhlhofer v. Hillingdon London Borough Council*, (1986) 1 All ER 467, p. 474 (HL); *Westminster City Council v. Greater London Council*, (1986) 1 All ER 278, p. 295 (HL); *Singh v. Immigration Appeal Tribunal*, (1986) 2 All ER 721, p. 728 (HL); *Nottinghamshire County Council v. Secretary of State for the Environment*, (1986) 1 All ER 199 (HL) (grounds of challenge to an order requiring approval of House of Commons); *Hammersmith and Fulham London Borough Council v. Secretary of State for the Environment*, (1990) 3 All ER 589, pp. 636, 637 (HL) (order requiring approval of House of Common in matters of economic policy; ground of challenge of irrationality is very much narrowed down); *Tower Hamlets London Borough Council v. Chetnik Developments Ltd.*, (1988) 1 All ER 961, p. 966 (HL) (no unfettered discretion); *Brunyate v. Inner London Education Society*, (1989) 2 All ER 417 (HL) (Governors of a school who were to function independently of the authority appointing them could not be removed by the authority on the ground of non-compliance of its wishes though power of removal conferred in wide terms); *Lonrho Plc. v. Secretary of State for Trade and Industry*, (1989) 2 All ER 609 (HL) (Discretion conferred by section 437(3) of the Companies Act, 1985 to publish report of inspectors relating to affairs of a company to be exercised on *Wednesbury* principles); *Doody v. Secretary of State for the Home Department*, (1993) 3 All ER 92, p. 107 (HL); *R. v. Secretary of State for Home Department, Exparte Launder*, (1997) 3 ALL ER 961, p. 976 (HL) (judicial review in extradiction cases); *R. v. Lord Chancellor*, (1996) 4 All ER 751 (QBD), p. 759 (judicial review of Lord Chancellor's discretion in the matter of deployment of judges); *R. v. Chief Constable of Sussex,* (1999) 1 All ER 129 (HL) (Judicial review of the discretion exercised by the Chief Constable in deploying the police force to prevent obstruction to lawful movement of goods by demonstrators); *Parter v. Magill,* (2002) 1 All ER (HL) (A local Authority has to act in public interest and not for promoting the electoral prospect of a party represented on the council); *R (Electoral Comm.) v. Westminster Mag. Ct.*, (2011) 1 All ER 1 (U.K.S.C.) para 15 (Lord PHILLIPS PRESIDENT) (If the purpose for which discretion is intended to serve is clear, the discretion can only be validly exercised for reasons relevant for the achievement of that purpose).

R (on the application of Bancoult) v. Secretary of State for Foreign and Commonwealth Affairs, (2008) 4 All ER 1055 (H.L.) [The British Indian Ocean Territory (Constitution) Order, 2004 made by prerogative order in council in exercise of Her Majesty's constituent power to make 'laws for the peace order and good government' could not be challenged on the ground that it was not conducive to peace order and good government but it was still open to judicial review on ordinary principles of legality, rationality and procedural impropriety as laid down in *Council of Civil Service Union v. Minister for the Civil Service (supra).* The restriction in the constitution order that no person was entitled to enter or be present in the Territory except as authorised by or under this order or any other law for the

[Footnote No. 41 Contd.]

[Footnote No. 41 Contd.]

time being in force had to be weighed in the balance against the defence and diplomatic interests of the State and the decision to impose immigration control on the Territory could not be said to be unreasonable or abuse of power]. *Rohtas Industries Ltd. v. S.D. Agarwal*, AIR 1969 SC 707 : (1969) 1 SCC 325; *Khudiram Das v. State of West Bengal*, AIR 1975 SC 550, pp. 557, 558 : 1975 SCC (Cri) 435 : (1975) 2 SCC 81; *Hukumchand Shyamlal v. Union of India*, AIR 1976 SC 789, p. 794 : (1976) 2 SCC 128; *Narayan Govind Gavate v. State of Maharashtra*, AIR 1977 SC 183, p. 192 : 1977 SCC (Cri) 49 : (1977) 1 SCC 183; *Indian Express Newspapers v. Union of India*, (1985) 1 SCC 641, pp. 691, 692, 693 : AIR 1986 SC 515; *Express Newspapers v. Union of India*, (1986) 1 SCC 133, pp. 218 to 220 : AIR 1986 SC 872. *State of U.P. v. Maharaja Dharamander Prasad Singh*, AIR 1989 SC 997, p. 1009 : (1989) 2 SCC 305; *Neelima Misra v. Harinder Kaur Paintal (Dr.)*, AIR 1990 SC 1402, p. 1411 : (1990) 2 SCC 746. *State of Haryana v. Bhajanlal*, AIR 1992 SC 604, pp. 618-20 : 1992 Supp (1) SCC 335 (Statutory power to investigate cognizable offences is not immune from judicial review); *Sarojini Ramaswamy v. Union of India*, AIR 1992 SC 2219, pp. 2248-58 : (1992) 4 SCC 506 (Impeachment of a Judge by Parliament is open to judicial review); *Harpal Singh Chauhan v. State of U.P.*, AIR 1993 SC 2436, p. 2441 : 1993 (3) SCC 552 (It is settled that even the exercise of power vested in subjective terms is open to judicial review); *Mansukhlal Vithaldas Chauhan v. State of Gujarat*, AIR 1997 SC 3400 : 1997 (7) SCC 622 (judicial review in matters of grant of sanction to prosecute); *S.R. Bommai v. Union of India*, AIR 1994 SC 1918 : (1994) 1 SCC 754 (Limited judicial review of President's order under Article 356 **see** on this point, pp. 743-44, *infra*. *Sarojini Ramaswamy* and *Bommai* cases show that Parliament's approval does not confer immunity from judicial review); *Naga People's Movement of Human Rights v. Union of India*, AIR 1998 SC 431, p. 461 : (1998) 2 SCC 109 (*Bommai* principle applied to an order declaring an area disturbed area); *A.K. Kaul v. Union of India*, AIR 1995 SC 1403 : (1995) 4 SCC 731 [*Bommai* principle applied to an order of dismissal under Article 311(2) Proviso (c)]; *Peerless General Finance and Investment Co. Ltd v. Reserve Bank of India*, AIR 1992 SC 1033, p. 1051 : (1992) 2 SCC 343 (In matters of economic policy judicial review is restrained); *Special Reference No. 1 of 1998 under Article 143(1) of the Constitution of India* AIR 1999 SC 1 : (1998) 7 SCC 739 (judicial review in the matter of appointment and transfer of judges); *Secretary Indian Tea Association v. Ajit Kumar Bareit,* AIR 2000 SC 915 : (2000) 3 SCC 93. (Judicial review in the matter of orders of Government under section 10 of the Industrial Disputes Act, 1947). (2011) 6 SCC 597- (Para 21) [In policy matters pertaining to continuance / discontinuance of courses/subjects in technical education institutions the scope of judicial review is limited and the court would interfere only if policy runs contrary to constitutional mandate, **See also** *State of M.P. v. Narmada Bachoa Andolan,* (2011) 7 SCC 639 (Para 36 and 37)].

Air India Ltd. v. Cochin International Airport Ltd., AIR 2000 SC 801, p. 804 : (2000) 2 SCC 617 (judicial review in the matter of award of contracts) : (2000) 2 SCC 617; *Master Marine Services Pvt. Ltd. v. Metcalfe & Hodkinson Pvt. Ltd.*, AIR (2005) SC 2299 (judicial review in award of contract); *Directorate of Education v. Educomp Datamatics Ltd.*, AIR 2004 SC 1962 : (2004) 4 SCC 19 (Judicial review of terms of tender notice inviting tenders for grant of contract); *Association of Registration Plates v. Union of India,* (2005) 1 SCC 679 (Judicial review of tender notice for supply of high security registration plates requiring foreign collaboration and experience in the field); *Shimnit Utsch India Private Ltd. v. West Bengal*

[Footnote No. 41 Contd.]

[Footnote No. 41 Contd.]

Transport Infrastructure Development Corporation Limited, (2010) 6 SCC 303 : (2010) 5 JT 237 (judicial review of contract for supply of high security plates); *Reliance Energy Ltd. v. Maharashtra State Road Development Corpn. Ltd.*, (2007) 8 SCC 1 paras 38,36 : (2007) 11 JT 1. [When tenders are invited, the terms and conditions must indicate with legal certainty, norms and bechmarks. This 'legal certainty' is an important aspect of the rule of law. If there is vagueness or subjectivity in the said norms it must result in unequal and discriminatory treatment. It may violate doctrine of 'level playing field' which is an important concept while construing Article 19(1)g of the Constitution]; *Delhi Development Authority v. Joint Action Committee Allottee of SFS Flats,* (2008) 2 SCC 672 paras 67, 62 (When a contract emanates from a statute or is otherwise governed by its provisions, the superior court can exercise the power of judicial review).

Noida Enterpreneurs Association v. Noida, (2011) 6 SCC 508 (para 38 to 40) (The State or public authority which holds the property for the public, acts as a trustee and therefore has to act, fairly and reasonably. The action/order of State or its instrumentality would stand vitiated if it lacks bonafides, as it would be a case of colourable exercise of power.).

Humanity and another v. State of West Bengal, (2011) 6 SCC 125 (In the matter of grant of largesee, the Government has to act fairly and without any semblance of discrimination. Once the Government has initiated the process of advertisement, it can not jettision the same and make allotment to an allottee without any advertisement)

Orix Auto Finance (India) Ltd. v. Jagmander Singh, (2006) 2 SCC 598 : (2006) 1 KLT 814 : (2006) 127 DLT 278 (No judicial review of Hire Purchase agreement conferring right on Financier to take possession of the vehicle unless terms unconscionable and opposed to public policy); *Noble Resources Ltd. v. State of Orissa,* AIR 2007 SC 119 (paras 20 to 30) : (2006) 10 SCC 236 (judicial review in contractual matters); *State of Karnataka v. All India Manufacturers Organisation,* (2006) 4 SCC 683, pp. 706, 707 : AIR 2006 SC 1846 (Even in exercise of contractual rights the Government or the State as defined in Article 12 has to act reasonably and without arbitrariness); *Ramchandra Murarilal Bhattad v. State of Maharashta,* (2007) 3 SCC 588 (paras 55, 59) : AIR 2007 SC 401 (Rejection of all bids as a result of change in policy, no reasons for rejection of bids required to be assigned); *United India Insurance Company Ltd. v. Manubhai Dharmasinhbhai Gajera II,* (2008) CPJ 43 (SC) page 53 para 31 (Public Sector insurance companies are State under Article 12 and fairness or reasonableness on the part of these companies must appear in all their dealings including renewal of insurance policies); *Verghese K. Joseph v. Custodian,* (2011) 3 SCC 294 para 34. [Special Court (Trial of offences relating to Transactions in Securities) Act, 1992 cannot arbitrarily fix a cut-off date beyond which it will decline to certify tainted shares when the investor is a *bonafide* purchaser of shares of certified companies which for reasons beyond their control were held to be tainted]; *Haryana State Warehousing Corporation v. Jagat Ram,* (2011) 3 SCC 422 : (2011) 2 JT 398 (Judicial review in matters of promotion and the difference between 'seniority-cum-merit' and 'merit-cum-seniority').

Secunderabad Cantonment Board v. Mohammad Mohiuddin, AIR 2004 SC 784, pp. 792, 793 (the Role of principle of *res judicata* in public law is restricted); *P.M. Bhargava v. University Grants Commission*, (2004) 6 SCC 661 : AIR 2004 SC 3478 (Academic matters, e.g. curriculum/syllabi fall outside judicial review); *Essar Oil Ltd. v. Halar Utkarshsamiti*, (2004) 2 SCC 392, pp. 407, 409 : AIR 2004 SC

[Footnote No. 41 Contd.]

[Footnote No. 41 Contd.]

1834 (judicial review of order passed under section 29 of the Wild Life Prosecution Act, 1972 permitting laying of pipelines for carrying crude oil through the Marine National Park and Sanctuary); *State of U.P. v. Johrimal*, (2004) 4 SCC 714, pp 730, 731 : AIR 2004 SC 3800 (Scope of judicial review in the matter of appointment of public prosecutor and district counsel); *State of U.P. v. Rakesh Kumar Keshari*, (2011) 5 SCC 341 : AIR 2011 SC 1705. (Scope of Judicial Review in the matter of appointment to the post of public prosecutor is very restricted and is confined only to *Wednesbury* unreasonableness.) *Union of India v. S.B. Vohra*, (2004) 2 SCC 150 (judicial review in refusal by the Union of India or the State to accord approval to the salaries recommended by the Chief Justice for High Court staff); *Peoples Union for Civil Liberties v. Union of India*, AIR 2004 SC 1442 : (2004) 2 SCC 476 (judicial review of order regarding non-disclosure of report of Atomic Energy Regulatory Board); *M.P. Special Police Establishment v. State of M.P.*, (2004) 8 SCC 788, pp. 805, 806 (If refusal to grant sanction to prosecute is based on non-consideration of relevant facts and irrational, the Governor can grant sanction) *Badrinath v. Government of Tamil Nadu*, AIR 2000 SC 3243, pp. 3253, 3257 (Judicial Review in matters of promotion of civil servants); *Centre for Public Interest Litigation v. Union of India*, AIR 2001 SC 80, pp. 90, 91 (Judicial review in matters of award of Contract); *Ugar Sugar Works Ltd. v. Delhi Administration*, AIR 2001 SC 1447, p. 1458 : (2001) 3 SCC 635 (judicial review in matters of liquor policy); *Union of India v. Harjeet Singh Sandhu*, AIR 2001 SC 1772, p. 1788 (judicial review of orders under section 19 of the Army Act, 1950 read with Rule 14); *N.R. Nair v. Union of India*, AIR 2001 SC 2337 : (2001) 6 SCC 84 (judicial review in respect of orders under section 22 of the Prevention of Cruelty to Animals Act, 1960); *R.K. Garg v. Union of India*, (1981) 4 SCC 676, pp. 690, 691, 706 : AIR 1981 SC 2138 (judicial review in matters of economic policy; no interference unless legislative judgment appears to be palpably arbitrary); *Bhavesh D. Parish v. Union of India*, (2000) 5 SCC 471, p. 486 : AIR 2000 SC 2047 (Interference in economic legislation only when the view reflected in it is not possible at all; *Balco Employees Union v. Union of India*, AIR 2002 SC 350, p. 381 : (2002) 2 SCC 333 (Policy decisions in economic matters, *e.g.*, disinvestment in public sector undertaking are not ordinarily open to judicial review unless contrary to constitution or any statute); *Federation of Railway Officers Association v. Union of india*, (2003) 4 SCC 289, p. 299 : AIR 2003 SC 1843 (on matters affecting policy and requiring technical expertise judicial review is of limited scope); *Indian Railway Construction Co. Ltd. v. Ajay Kumar*, (2003) 4 SCC 579 : AIR 2003 SC 1843 (Judicial Review of an order dispensing enquiry under Article 311(2); *State Financial Corporation v. Jagadamba Oil Mills*, AIR 2002 SC 834 (Judicial review of the discretion of the corporation to make recovery from the debtor); *Rayalseema Paper Mills Ltd. v. Govt. of A.P.*, AIR 2002 SC 3699, p. 3704 : (2003) 1 SCC 341 (Judicial review in price fixation). *Mahalashmi Sugar Mills Co. Ltd. v. Union of India*, AIR 2009 SC 792 paras 45 and 46 : (2008) 5 SCR 793 Judicial review in price fixation). *Onkar Lal Bajaj v. Union of India*, AIR 2003 SC 252 (Judicial review against en masse cancellation of allotments of petrol pumps, LPG gas agencies and Kerosene agencies when controversy related to only 5 to 10% of the allotments, *i.e.*, nearly 413 allotments); *Mukund Swarup Misra v. Union of India*, (2007) 2 SCC 536 : (2007) 3 JT 200; (*Onkar Lal Bajaj* case explained); *Union of India v. Shivendra Bikram Singh*, AIR 2003 SC 2481, p. 2491 : (2003) 6 SCC 359 (judicial review in matters of Court Martial proceedings); *Union of India v. Ex Fl. U.G.S. Bajwa*, AIR 2004 SC 808 :

[Footnote No. 41 Contd.]

[Footnote No. 41 Contd.]

(2003) 9 SCC 630 (judicial review of court martial proceedings); *Binny Ltd. v. Sadasivan,* (2005) 6 SCC 657 (Principles of public policy/judicial review cannot be applied in the employment of workers by private bodies unless a public law element is involved and writ petition by workers is not maintainable); *Directorate of Film Festivals v. Gaurav Ashwin Jain,* (2007) 4 SCC 737 (paras 16, 22, 23) : AIR 2007 SC 290 (Scope of judicial review in policy matters. Illegality in one case does not entitle another peson to obtain a similar order on the ground of Article 14). *Dhampur Sugar (Kashipur) Ltd. v. State of Uttaranchal,* (2007) 8 SCC 418 para 63 : (2007) 11 JT 209 [Scope of judicial review in *Policy matters* relating to social, economic and commercial matters is very limited for there are generally no objective, justiciable or manageable standards to judge the issues and courts are ill equipped to deal with these matters.] **also see,** *Joint Action Committee of Airlines Pilot's Association of India (ALPAI) v. Director General of Civil Aviation,* (2011) 5 SCC 435 : (2011) 6 JT 24.

Karnataka Industries Areas Development Board and another v. Prakash Dal Mill, (2011) 6 SCC 714 (Para 21) (Scope of Judicial Review in the matter of Price Fixation), **See also** *APM Terminals B.V. v. Union of India,* (2011) 6 SCC 756 (Para 69) (Scope of judicial review in the matter of alteration of government policy). *Balchandra L. Jrkiholi v. B.S. Yeddyurappa,* (2011) 7 SCC 1 (Order of Speaker under para 2(1)(a) of Schedule X of Constitution of India is subject to judicial review).

Nandini Sundar v. State of Chhattisgarh (Para 73 to 75). [It was held that appointment of special police officers to perform any of the duties of regular officers in counter insurgency activities is violative of Article 14 and 21 of the Constitution of India]. In an article the judgment of the Supreme Court has been criticised on the ground that the rationale of judgment is ideology, not the constitution. When a court acquires an ideology, it decides to frame a policy. It dismantles the constitutional mandate of separation of powers and enters the domain of the legislative and the executive. The rational in this judgement has upset the constitutional balance 'Wasn't justice blind? Arun Jaitley- Senior Advocate Supreme Court and Member of Opposition in the Rajya Sabha.

For judicial review in the matter of Construction of big dams see : *Tehri Bandh Virodhi Sangarh Samiti v. State of U.P.*, (1990) 4 JT (SC) 519 : 1992(1) SCC 44; *Narmada Bachao Andolan v. Union of India,* AIR 2000 SC 3751; *N.D. Jayal v. Union of India,* AIR 2004 SC 867 : (2004) 9 SCC 362. For judicial review of development providing right to shelter in the context of conservation of natural resources **see** *Intellectual Forum Tirupathi v. State of A.P.*, (2006) 3 SCC 549 : AIR 2006 SC 1350. For town planning and environment protection in the case of release of land of sick industries for development and considerations in judicial review, **see** *Bombay Dyeing Mfg. Co. Ltd. v. Bombay Environmental Group,* (2006) 3 SCC 434 (para 197) : (2006) 2 SLT 65. For issue of *mandamus* to demolish unauthorised construction as not justified when Corporation has discretion to regularise or demolish it, **see** *Muni Servrat Swami Jain S.M.P. Sangh v. Arun Nathuram Gaikwad,* (2006) 8 SCC 590, p. 610 (para 53) : AIR 2007 SC 38. For grounds of judicial review and extent of deference to the authority's views exercising discretion, **see** *Rameshwar Prasad (vi) v. Union of India,* (2006) 2 SCC 1 (paras 240, 241) : AIR 2006 SC 980; *Jayarajbhai Jayantibhai Patel v. Anilbhai Nathubhai Patel,* (2006) 8 SCC 200 (paras 13 to 19). For judicial review in the matter of fixation of price of coal by Nationalised Companies or Government in the context of Article 39(b) of the Constitution, **see** *Ashoka Smokeless Coal India (P.) Ltd. v. Union of India,* (2007) 2 SCC 640 (paras 110 to 114) : (2007) 1 JT 125.

[Footnote No. 41 Contd.]

advance by adopting a rigid rule or policy,[42] and in matters affecting fundamental rights he must follow the principle of proportionality. Further, the

---

[Footnote No. 41 Contd.]

Examples of abuse of power: Power conferred for requisitioning property cannot be validly exercised for acquiring property in the garb of requisition, *H.D. Vora v. State of Maharashtra*, (1984) 2 SCC 337 : AIR 1984 SC 886; power of acquisition cannot be exercised for an ulterior purpose of preventing construction of a cinema house, *Collector, Allahabad v. Raja Ram Jaiswal*, (1985) 3 SCC 1, pp. 19-21 : AIR 1985 SC 1622 or for denying renewal of a lease, *State of U.P. v. Lalji Tandon*, (2004) 1 SCC 1, p. 12 : AIR 2004 SC 32, p. 38; and acquisition for public purpose cannot be made to provide houses for those who are already in possession of houses, *Srinivasa Co-op. House Building Society Limited v. Madan Gurumurthy Sastry*, JT 1994(4) SC 197, p. 205 : 1994 (4) SCC 675. Acquisition for the public purpose of setting up of a new town cannot be directly made under the Land Acquisition Act, 1894, ignoring the comprehensive and mandatory provisions of a town planning legislation, *e.g.*, the Punjab Regional and Town Planning and Development Act, 1995: *State of Punjab v. Sanjeet Singh*, (2007) 6 SCC 292.

For the nature of irrationality, perversity or unreasonableness in administrative law, **see** *R. v. Chief Constable of Sussex,* (1999) 1 All ER 129, p. 157 (HL) (The simple test of unreasonableness applied by House of Lords is whether the decision in question was one which a reasonable authority could reach or conversely whether the conduct complained of is one which no sensible authority acting with due appreciation of responsibilities would have decided to adopt.); *G.B. Mahajan v. Jalgaon Municipal Council*, AIR 1991 SC 1153, pp. 1163-66 : (1991) 3 SCC 91; *U.P. Finaicial Corporation v. Gem Cap (India) Pvt. Ltd.*, AIR 1993 SC 1435, p. 1439 : (1993) 2 SCC 299; *Union of India v. G. Ganyutham*, AIR 1997 SC 3387, p. 3391 : 1997 (7) SCC 463 (Briefly stated it means that the decision is so outrageous that no reasonable person could have arrived at); *State of NCT Delhi v. Sanjiv alias Bittoo*, (2005) 5 SCC 181 (Judicial Review in general; nature of 'unreasonableness' or 'irrationality': case concerning externment order); *M.I. Builders Ltd. v. Radhey Shyam Sahu,* AIR 1999 SC 2468, pp. 2500, 2501 : 1999 (6) SCC 464; *Kruger v. Commonwealth*, (1997) 71 ALJR 991, p. 997 (Reasonableness may depend upon the community standards of the time; BRENNAN C.J.).

For *quasi*-judicial power **see** *Anisminic Ltd. v. Foreign Compensation Commission*, (1969) 1 All ER 208 : (1969) 2 AC 147 (HL); *Page v. Hull University Visitor*, (1993) 1 All ER 97, pp. 107-109 (HL); *Union of India v. Tarachand Gupta and Brothers*, AIR 1971 SC 1558 : 1971 (1) SCC 486; *Liberty Oil Mills v. Union of India*, (1984) 3 SCC 465, p. 494 (para 26) : AIR 1984 SC 1271 and other cases in note 9, pp. 800-802; *Surya Dev Rai v. Ram Chander Rai*, (2008) 4 SCC paras 23 to 25.

42. *British Oxygen Co. Ltd. v. Minister of Technology*, (1970) 3 All ER 165, p. 170 (HL); *Shri Rama Sugar Industries v. State of A.P.*, AIR 1974 SC 1745, p. 1750 : (1974) 1 SCC 534; *Asbestos Cement Ltd. v. Union of India*, 1983 MPLJ 501, pp. 506, 507 (G.P. SINGH C.J.); *Finlay v. Secretary of State for Home Department,* (1984) 3 All ER 801, p. 829 (HL); *U.P. State Road Transport Corporation v. Mohd. Ismail,* AIR 1991 SC 1099 (para 12) : (1991) 3 SCC 239 : (1991) 2 LLJ 332. In *R. v. Secretary of State for the Home Department, ex parte, Venables*, (1997) 3 All ER 97, pp. 120, 121 (HL), LORD BROWNE WILKINSON explained the law on the point that the person on whom the power is conferred is not precluded "from developing and applying a policy as to the approach which he will adopt in the generality of cases.

[Footnote No. 42 Contd.]

word 'discretion', when applied to a court of justice, means discretion guided by law, and must not be arbitrary, vague and fanciful, but legal and regular.[43]

Having regard to the object of Central Vigilance Commission the person appointed as Central Vigilance Commissioner must be of unimpeachable constitutional and personal integrity and appointment of person against whom criminal case is pending and departmental proceedings are contemplated will be *nonest* and invalid.[44]

Besides express restrictions in a statute or the Constitution, there can be implied restrictions as well, and the statutory or the constitutional authority cannot, in breach of such implied restrictions, exercise its discretionary power. Accordingly, the Supreme Court has held that even though Article 316 of the Constitution does not specify the qualities of the Chairman of a Public Service Commission, the State Public Service Commission is expected to act with independence from the State Government and with fairness, besides competence and maturity acquired through knowledge and experience. Therefore, these qualities are implied relevant factors which have to be taken into account while determining the competency of the person to be appointed as the Chairman. If it is shown that these relevant factors have not been taken into account by the State Government while selecting the Chairman, the High Court can invoke its wide and extraordinary powers under Article 226 of the Constitution and quash such an appointment to ensure that the discretion of the State Government is exercised within the bounds of the Constitution.[45]

The principle of proportionality requires the court to apply a three stage test: (1) whether the objective sought to be achieved is relevant and sufficiently important to justify limiting the fundamental rights; (2) whether the means chosen to limit that right are rational fair and not arbitrary, and (3) whether the means used impair the right as minimally as reasonably possible.[46] The judgment on proportionality must always involve the striking of

---

[Footnote No. 42 Contd.]

But the position is different if the policy adopted is such as to preclude the person from departing from the policy or from taking into account circumstances which are relevant to the particular case in relation to which the discretion is being exercised. If such an inflexible and invariable policy is adopted, both the policy and the decision taken pursuant to it will be unlawful."

43. *Ashwin S. Mehta & Anr. v. Union of India & Ors.*, (2012) 1 SCC 83, p. 99.

44. *Centre for PIL v. Union of India,* (2011) 4 SCC 1 : AIR 2011 SC 1267.

45. *State of Punjab v. Salil Sabhlok & Ors.*, (2013) 5 SCC 1, pp. 35, 36, 37.

46. *De Fruitas v. Permanent Secretary of Ministry of Agriculture, Fisheries and Housing,*(1999) 1 AC 69, p. 80 (PC); *R. v. Shayler,* (2002) 2 All ER 477, pp. 498, 506 (HL); *R v. A,* (2001) 3 All ER 1, p. 15 (HL); *R. v. Secretary of State for the Home Department*

[Footnote No. 46 Contd.]

a fair balance between the rights of the individual and the interests of the community.[47] And when the question is of pressing social need and whether the measure adopted by the legislature is proportionate to the legitimate aim pursued, the court may have also to show due respect to the judgment of a democratically elected representatives.[48] So in hand with proportionality principles is a concept of 'latitude' which recognizes that the court does not become the primary decision maker on matters of policy, judgment and discretion so that public authorities are left with room to make legitimate choices. The 'latitude' denotes the appropriate degree of deference by court to public body.[49]

The Supreme Court has held that the proportionality principle which involves a stricter test of reasonableness was being applied in India by courts as a primary reviewing authority in judicial review of legislative and administrative action affecting fundamental rights ever since 1950 without specifically naming it.[50] By proportionality, it is meant that the question whether while regulating exercise of fundamental rights, the appropriate or least restrictive choice of measures has been made by the Legislature or the administrator so as to achieve the object of the legislation or the purpose of the administrative order as the case may be.[51] The court will act as a primary reviewing authority in relation to statutes or statutory rules or

---

[Footnote No. 46 Contd.]

ex parte Daly, (2001) 3 All ER 433, pp. 445 to 447 (HL) (Difference between *Wednesbury* unreasonableness and proportionality principle in the context of Human Rights); *Matthews v. Ministry of Defence,* (2003) 1 All ER 689, p. 723 (HL); *Tweed v. Parades Commission for Northern Ireland,* (2007) 2 All ER 273, pp. 288, 289 (HL); *R (Begum) v. Denbigh High School,* (2006) 2 All ER 487, para 30 (HL) (Proportionality must be judged objectively. The court must make a value judgment or evaluation by reference to the circumstances prevailing at the relevant time); *Miss Behavin Ltd. v. Belfast City Council,* (2007) 3 All ER 1007, para 24 (HL) (The evaluation of legislation is not limited to the adequacy of minister's exploration of the policy opinions or his explanation in Parliament or to the circumstances and social needs existing at that time but also to those existing at the time when its application is called for). **See further** IAN LEIGH 'Taking rights Proportionately: Judicial Review, the Human Rights Act and Strasburg' (2002) Public Law 265; FRANCESCA KLUG & CHAIRE O' BRIEN, 'The First Two Years of the Human Rights Act' (2002) Public Law 649, pp. 658 to 660.

47. *Huang v. Secretary of State for the Home Department,* (2007) 4 All ER 15 (H.L.) para 19 page 29; *R (JF) v. Secretary of State,* (2010) 2 All ER 707 (U K SC) para 7 (Lord Phillips President).

48. *R (On the application of the countryside Alliance v. Attorney General*, (2008) 2 All ER 95 (H.L.) para 45.

49. *Tweed v. Parades Commission for Northern Ireland,* (2007) 2 All ER 273 (H.L.) p. 290 (LORD CARSWELL **quoting** *Fordham*).

50. *Om Kumar v. Union of India,* AIR 2000 SC 3689, p. 3702 (para 54) : (2001) 2 SCC 386; *Terioat Estates (P.) Ltd. v. U.T. Chandigarh,* (2004) 2 SCC 136.

51. *Terioat Estates (P.) Ltd. v. U.T. Chandigarh, supra*, p. 145.

any order which has the force of a statute.[52] In cases where the challenge is of unreasonable classification under Articles 14 the principle of proportionality as applied to other fundamental rights will apply.[53]

The fundamental right of equality in Article 14 has also been so construed as to make the concept of reasonableness and non-arbitrariness pervade the entire constitutional scheme as a golden thread running through the whole of the fabric of the Constitution.[54] The rule of law inhibits arbitrary action and also makes it liable to be invalidated. Every action of the State or its instrumentalities should not only be fair, legitimate or above board but should be without any affection or aversion, should neither be suggestive of discrimination nor even given an impression of bias, favouritism and nepotism.[55] So the 'State' acting whether as a 'landlord' or 'tenant' is required to act *bonafide* and not arbitrarily and every executive action must be informed by reason.[56] A corporation which is a State within the meaning of Article 12 of the Constitution has to prove fairness and reasonableness on its part in initiating eviction proceedings against a person under the Public Premises (Eviction of Unauthorised Occupants) Act 1971[57] and a public sector insurance company which is a State under Article 12 cannot arbitrarily and unreasonably decline to renew mediclaim policy of a senior citizen.[58] Similarly even in cases where there is no legal right, *e.g.*, for an appointment to a post even after selection if the Government drops the idea, relief can[59] be granted if the decision taken is wholly

---

52. *Ibid*, p. 146 (para 50).

53. *Omkumar v. Union of India*, *supra*, p. 3704 (para 66).

54. *Ajay Hasia v. Khalid Mujib Sehravardi,* (1981) 1 SCC 722, p. 741 : AIR 1981 SC 487 (Constitution Bench). **See further** *E.P. Royappa v. State of T.N.*, (1974) 4 SCC 3 : AIR 1974 SC 555. For criticism see PROF. WADE, 'Public Law in Britain and India, pp. 41, 42.

55. *State of Orissa v. Mamata Mohanty*, (2011) 3 SCC 436 para 59 : (2011) 2 JT 164.

56. *Bharat Petroleum Corporation Ltd. v. Maddula Ratnavalli,* (2007) 6 SCC 81 (para 16) : (2007) 6 JT 264. ('If so desired by the Central Government' construed to involve 'objective criteria' – para 13). **See further** *Karnataka State Forest Industries Corporation v. State of Karnataka,* (2009) 1 SCC 150 para 38 : AIR 2009 SC 684 (Although a contract is not ordinarily enforced in writ jurisdiction by a superior court, when an action of the State is arbitrary or discriminatory and violative of Article 14, a writ petition would be maintainable; *M.D. H.S.I.D.C. v. Hari Om Enterprises*, AIR 2009 SC 218 paras 36, 37, 40 (cancellation of allotment of industrial plot by a State Corporation which is unfair and unreasonable and violative of Article 14 can be interfered with in writ jurisdiction).

57. *New India Assurance Company Ltd. v. Nusli Neville Wadia,* (2008) 3 SCC 279 para 21 : AIR 2008 SC 876.

58. *United India Insurance Co. Ltd. v. Manubhai Dharmasinhbhai Gajera*, (2008) 10 SCC 404 paras 34, 50, 69 : AIR 2009 SC 446.

59. *Director, SCTI for Medical Science Technology v. M. Pushkaran,* (2008) 1 SCC 448 : AIR 2008 SC 559 and other cases referred therein; *East Coast Railway v. Mahadev Appa Rao,* (2010) 7 SCC 678 para 17, 21, 22, 23 : AIR 2010 SC 2794..

unreasonable and arbitrary. A power cannot be exercised simply because the authority has power to do so and the action taken must be fair and reasonable.[60] Where the challenge is not of unreasonable classification but only of arbitrariness under Article 14, the proportionality principle will not apply and the test of *Wednesbury* unreasonableness will apply.[61] But the spirit of the doctrine may be applied in appropriate cases.[62] But as observed by DHARMADHIKARI, J.: "The concept of 'reasonableness' defies definition" and "the functional conceptual implication of 'reasonableness' is that it is another word used for public policy" and "the test of 'reasonableness' is nothing substantially different from 'social engineering' 'balancing of interests' or any of the other formulas which modern sociological theories suggest as an answer to the problem of judicial function."[63] For this reason, the Supreme Court has held that the discretionary jurisdiction conferred on criminal courts under provisions of the CrPC, to grant bail to the accused pending trial or in appeal against convictions, has to be exercised with great care and caution by balancing the valuable right of liberty of an individual against the interest of the society in general.[64]

THAKKAR, J., has said that 'proportionality' involves 'balancing test' and 'necessity test'. Whereas the former (balancing test) permits scrutiny

---

60. *Union of India v. Naman Singh Shekhawat*, (2008) 4 SCC 1 para 29 : (2008) 4 JT 150 (A departmental proceeding against an officer cannot be initiated after his acquittal just as a matter of course. The action taken must be *bona fide* and reasonable); *Jogendra Kumar v. State of U.P.*, AIR 1994 SC 1349 p. 1353 : (1994) 4 SCC 260 (No arrest can be made simply because there is power to do so and there should be justification for its exercise).

61. *Omkumar v. Union of India, supra*, p. 3704 (para 67). Proportionality principle is not applicable in judging the appropriateness of punishment imposed in disciplinary proceedings and the test of *Wednesbury* reasonableness applies: *Union of India v. G. Ganayutham supra; Regional Manager UPSRTC v. Hotilal,* (2003) 3 SCC 650; *Chairman and Managing Director United Commercial Bank v. P.C. Kakkar,* (2003) 4 SCC 364 : AIR 2003 SC 1571. See also *Balaram Kumawat v. Union of India,* (2003) 7 SCC 628, p. 642; *Canara Bank v. V.K. Awasthy,* (2005) 6 SCC 321 (paras 25 to 32); *Hombe Gowda Education Trust v. State of Karnataka,* (2006) 1 SCC 430 (para 20) : (2005) 10 JT 598 : (2006) 1 LLJ 1004; *Commissioner of Police v. Syed Hussain,* (2006) 3 SCC 173 (paras 11 and 12) : AIR 2006 SC 1246; *A. Sudhakar v. Postmaster General,* (2006) 4 SCC 348 (para 28) : (2006) 4 JT 68. **See** for criticism ASHISH CHUG, 'Is the Supreme Court Disproportionately Applying the Proportionality Principle', (2004) 8 SCC (J) 33. Proportionately principle has also been **referred** in moulding the relief under Article 142; *Sandip Subhash Parate v. State of Maharashtra,* (2006) 7 SCC 501 (para 14) : AIR 2006 SC 3102.

62. *Terioat Estates (P.) Ltd. v. U.T. Chandigarh,* (*supra*), pp. 147, 148. **See also** *Saurabh Chandra v. Union of India*, AIR 2004 SC 361, p. 373. (The strict scrutiny test or the intermediate scrutiny test as applied in USA not applied in India).

63. *Om Prakash v. State of U.P.*, (2004) 3 SCC 402, p. 414 : AIR 2004 SC 1896, p. 1903. (**Reliance** is placed on FRIEDMAN, 'Legal Theory' 4th Edn., pp. 83, 85).

64. *Sanjay Chandra v. Central Bureau of Investigation*, (2012) 1 SCC 40, p. 53.

of excessive onerous penalties or infringement of rights or interests and a manifest "imbalance of relevant considerations, the latter (necessity test) requires infringement of human rights to the least restrictive alternative."[65] A two-Judge Bench of the Supreme Court speaking through SINHA, J., has expressed the view that "*Wednesbury* principle of unreason- ableness has been replaced by the doctrine of proportionality."[66] SINHA, J., also approvingly quoted[67] the following observations of LORD CARSWELL from *Tweedy v. Parades Commission*[68]:

"The starting point is that there is an overlap between the traditional grounds of review and the approach of proportionality. Most cases would be decided in the same way whichever approach is adopted. But the intensity of review is somewhat greater under the proportionality approach. Making due allowance for important structural differences between various convention rights, which I do not propose to discuss, a few generalisations are perhaps permissible. I would mention three concrete differences without suggesting that my statement is exhaustive. *First,* the doctrine of proportionality may require the reviewing court to assess the balance which the decision maker has struck, not merely whether it is within the range of rational or reasonable decisions. *Secondly,* the proportionality test may go further than the traditional grounds of review in as much as it may require attention to be directed to the relative weight accorded to interests and considerations. *Thirdly,* even the heightened scrutiny test developed in *R v. Ministry of Defence, ex P Smith*,[69] is not necessarily appropriate to the protection of human rights."

Hazarilal's case, where the above view was expressed by SINHA, J., was a case of appropriateness of punishment and the punishment of dismissal imposed was whimsical and arbitrary and could not be supported even under the traditional grounds of review. In a number of cases the court had earlier ruled that in judging the appropriateness of punishment proportionality

---

65. *Coimbatore District Central Co-operative Bank v. Coimbatore District Central Cooperative Bank Employees Assn.*, (2007) 4 SCC 669 (para 19). Reliance is placed on De Smith, Judicial Review of Administrative Action (1995), pp. 601-05.

66. *State of M.P. v. Hazarilal*, (2008) 3 SCC 27 para 11. **See further** *Manishankar v. Union of India*, (2008) 3 SCC 484 para 17; *Jitendra Kumar v. State of Haryana*, (2008) 2 SCC 161 paras 62, 63 : (2007) 14 Scale 125.

67. *State of M.P. v. Hazarilal supara* para 13.

68. *Tweedy v. Parades Commission*[68] (2007) 2 All ER 273 (H.L.) para 35 (The quotation is really from LORD STEYN'S opinion in *R v. Secretary of State for the Home Deptt. ex p Daly*, (2001) 3 All ER 433 paras 27, 28 which were reproduced by LORD CARSWELL in *Tweed's* case and again in *Re, E (a child)*, (2009) 1 All ER 467 para 52, p. 489 (H.L.).

69. *R v. Ministry of Defence, ex P Smith*, (1996) 1 All ER 257 at 263, (1996) QB 517 at 554.

principle is not applicable and *Wednesbury* principle applies.[70] In *Chairman, All India Railway Recruitment Board v. K. Shyam Kumar*,[71] a Bench of ALTAF ALAM AND RADHAKRISHNAN, JJ., has rightly held that the view expressed by SINHA, J., that *Wednesbury* principle has been replaced by proportionality principle is not correct.

The order of any statutory authority or tribunal is also open to judicial review by a public law remedy or by a private law remedy of civil suit when it suffers from jurisdictional errors and is a nullity.[72] An administrative order made without power to make it is, on well known principles, a nullity.[73] Judicial review seeks to ensure that statutory duty of High Power Committee to recommend under proviso to section 4(1) of the Central Vigilance Commission Act, 2003 is performed keeping in mind the policy and purpose of the 2003 Act. The word 'recommendation' in proviso to section 4(1), stands for an informed decision to be taken by High Power Committee on the basis of consideration of relevant material keeping in the mind the purpose, object and policy of the Act.[74]

Another well-settled rule is that an executive authority must be rigorously held to the standards by which it professes its actions to be judged and it must scrupulously observe those standards on pain of invalidation of an act in violation of them even though those standards are generous beyond what may be ordinarily required.[75]

---

70. See cases in note 20 *supra*; *State of Meghalaya v. Meckon Singh*, (2008) 7 SCC 580 paras 13, 14 : (2008) 9 SCR 46 (no interference in punishment unless shocking to the conscience of the court); PREM KUMAR in a well reasoned article. 'Is Wednesbury on the Terminal Decline' (2008) SCCJ-113 convincingly argues that *Wednesbury* principles are still alive and applicable for judicial review where no constitutional/fundamental rights are involved.

71. *Chairman, All India Railway Recruitment Board v. K. Shyam Kumar,* (2010) 6 SCC 614 : (2010) 5 JT 382 paras 28, 34, 35.

72. See title 2(b), 'cases of nullity', chapter 9, *infra*; *R (A) v. Croydon London BC,* (2010) 1 All ER 469 (UK SC) p. 482 para 32 (Local authority's determination as to age of the person whether he is a child or not under the Children Act 1989 is determination on a question of jurisdictional fact and the scope of interference is not limited in such a case to *Wednesbury* principles).

73. *Secretary of State for Home Department v. JJ*, (2008) 1 All ER 613 (H.L.) para 27; *Mc Laughlin v. Cayman Islands*, (2007) 1 WLR 2839 (P.C.).

74. *Centre for PIL v. Union of India*, (2011) 4 SCC 1 (paras 42 and 43) : AIR 2011 SC 1267.

75. *Ramana Dayaram Shetty v. International Airport Authority of India*, (1979) 3 SCC 489 p. 503 (para 10) : AIR 1979 SC 1626; *B. Ramakichenin v. Union of India*, (2008) 1 SCC 362 para 22 : (2007) 12 SCR 120; *H. V. Nirmala v. Karnataka State Financial Corporation*, (2008) 7 SCC 639 para 14 : AIR 2008 SC 2440; *Union of India v. Rajpal Singh*, (2009) 1 SCC 216 para 26 : (2008) 12 JT 476.

Conferment of *quasi*-judicial power further implies that the person concerned must follow the rules of natural justice,[76] and must give reasons for making the order which he is empowered to make.[77]

---

76. *Ridge v. Baldwin*, (1963) 2 All ER 66 (HL); *Wiseman v. Borneman*, (1969) 3 All ER 275 : 1971 AC 297 (HL); *Maneka Gandhi v. Union of India*, AIR 1978 SC 597, pp. 626, 627 : (1978) 1 SCC 248; *Liberty Oil Mills v. Union of India*, (1984) 3 SCC 465, pp. 486-91; *Mangilal v. State of Madhya Pradesh*, AIR 2004 SC 1280, pp. 1283, 1284 : (2004) 2 SCC 447. But when a party loses the opportunity of having his case heard because of the fault of his legal advisors he may not be able to complain of denial of natural justice: *Al-Mehadawi v. Secretary of State for the Home Department*, (1989) 3 All ER 843 : (1990) 1AC 876 (HL); *Mohd. Yunus Khan v. State of Uttar Pradesh*, (2010) 10 SCC 539 paras 22 to 27 : (2010) 10 JT 341 (An enquiry officer who is also a witness and passes the order of punishment acts illegally and in breach of natural justice and the order is void. It cannot be cured in appeal).

N.B. *In State of Himachal Pradesh v. Raja Mahendra Pal*, AIR 1999 SC 1786, p. 1791 : (1999) 4 SCC 43 (para 8), it is observed by a two judge bench that the primary test of determining that an authority is *quasi*-judicial is whether the authority has *any express duty to act judicially* in arriving at the decision. This view is, it is submitted, not correct. It ignores *Ridge v. Baldwin supra*, which holds that the duty to act judicially may arise from the very nature of the function performed by the authority. *Ridge v. Baldwin* has been followed by the Supreme Court in later cases, **see** *Maneka Gandhi v. Union of India, supra*, pp. 286, 287 (SCC) which is a constitution bench decision. Another two judge bench of the Supreme Court in *Indian National Congress v. Institute of Social Welfare*, AIR 2002 SC 2158, p. 2167 : (2002) 5 SCC 685, though rightly upholding that the Election Commission while deciding to register a political party acts quasi judicially, ignores *Ridge v. Baldwin, supra*, and *Maneka Gandhi, supra*, and omits to notice that duty to act judicially may arise from the nature of the power itself.

77. *Bhagat Raja v. Union of India*, AIR 1967 SC 1606 : 1967 (3) SCR 302; *Siemens Engineering and Manufacturing Co. of India Ltd. v. Union of India*, AIR 1976 SC 1785, p. 1789 : 1976 (2) SCC 981; *Mahindra and Mahindra v. Union of India*, AIR 1979 SC 798, p. 823 : (1979) 2 SCC 529; *Sitaram v. State of Uttar Pradesh*, AIR 1979 SC 745, p. 753 : (1979) 2 SCC 656 : 1979 SCC (Cri) 576; *Organo Chemical Industries v. Union of India*, AIR 1979 SC 1803 : (1979) 4 SCC 573; *Rama Varma Bharathan Thampuran v. State of Kerala*, AIR 1979 SC 1918, p. 1922 : (1979) 4 SCC 326; *A.L. Kalra v. Project and Equipment Corporation of India Ltd.*, (1984) 3 SCC 316, pp. 336, 337 : AIR 1984 SC 1361; *Vasudeo Vishwanath Saraf v. New Education Institute*, (1986) 4 SCC 31, p. 37 : AIR 1985 SC 2105; *S.N. Mukherjee v. Union of India*, AIR 1990 SC 1984, pp. 1995-97 : (1990) 4 SCC 594 (Except in cases where the requirement has been dispensed with expressly or by necessary implication, an administrative authority exercising judicial or *quasi*-judicial functions is required to record the reasons for its decision. This requirement can be regarded as one of the principles of natural justice); *Roop Singh Negi v. Punjab National Bank*, (2009) 2 SCC 570 para 23 : (2009) 2 JT 176 (orders of disciplinary authority and appellate authority must be based on recorded reasons). Under English law, a *quasi*-judicial authority need not give reasons unless required to do so by statute. **See** *Rex. v. Northumberland Compensation Appeal Tribunal*, (1952) 1 All ER 122. There is, however, a definite shift in favour of the view that reasons should be given. **See** *R. v. Immigration Appeal Tribunal, Ex parte, Khan Mohamad*, (1983) 2 All ER 420, p. 423 (CA); *R. v. Civil Services Appeal Board, ex parte, Bruce*,

[Footnote No. 77 Contd.]

Purely administrative bodies are also bound to act justly and fairly which may bring in the requirement of natural justice,[78] as also the duty to give

---

[Footnote No. 77 Contd.]

(1989) 2 All ER 907, p. 911 (CA); *Flannery v. Halifax Estate Agencies Ltd.*, (2000) 1 All ER 373, pp. 377, 378 (CA) (The duty to give reasons "is function of due process and therefore of justice. Its rationale has two principle aspects. The first is that fairness surely requires that the parties—especially the losing party—should be left in no doubt why they have won or lost.—The second is that a requirement to give reasons concentrates the mind and if it is fulfilled the resulting decision is much more likely to be soundly based.") Reasons recorded should be proper, intelligible and adequate depending upon the circumstances of the case and their quality should be judged by looking to the substance rather than to the form: *Save Britains Heritage v. Number 1 Poultry Limited*, (1991) 2 All ER 10, pp. 22-27 : (1991) 1 WLR 153 (HL). But in special Acts like Border Security Force Act or Army Act all the principles of natural justice cannot be imported : *Union of India v. Amrik Singh*, AIR 1991 SC 564, p. 569 : 1991 (1) SCC 654; *Union of India v. J.S. Bros*, AIR 1993 SC 773, p. 776 : 1993 (1) SCC 176.

78. *In re, K. (H) (an infant)*, (1967) 1 All ER 226; *R. v. Gaming Board*, (1970) 2 All ER 528 (CA); *A.K. Kraipak v. Union of India*, AIR 1970 SC 150 : (1969) 2 SCC 262; *Maneka Gandhi v. Union of India*, AIR 1978 SC 597, pp. 627, 628 : (1978) 1 SCC 248; *Ashok Kumar, Yadav v. State of Haryana*, (1985) 4 SCC 417, pp. 440-442 : 1985 AIR SC 454; *Harbhajan Singh Dhalla v. Union of India*, (1986) 4 SCC 678, p. 688 : AIR 1987 SC 9; *K.L. Shephard v. Union of India*, (1987) 4 SCC 431, pp. 444 to 447 : AIR 1988 SC 686, pp. 693, 694; *H.L. Trehan v. Union of India*, AIR 1989 SC 568 : 1989 (1) SCC 764; *Modi Industries Ltd. v. State of Uttar Pradesh*, AIR 1994 SC 536, p. 542 : 1994 (1) SCC 282; *Scooters India Ltd. v. M. Mohammad Yakub*, AIR 2001 SC 227 : (2001) 1 SCC 61; *State Govt. Houseless Harijan Employees Associtation v. State of Karnataka*, AIR 2001 SC 437, p. 443 : (2001) 1 SCC 610 (Reasons given in the order cannot be supplemented by affidavit at the time of hearing in court). **But see** *Neelima Misra v. Harinder Kaur Paintal (Dr.)*, AIR 1990 SC 1402, p. 1411 : (1990) 2 SCC 746; *Baikuntha Nath Das v. Chief District Medical Officer*, AIR 1992 SC 1020, p. 1032 (para 33) : 1992 (2) SCC 299. (Natural justice not to be imported if order is to be passed on subjective satisfaction). *Dr. Rash Lal Yadav v. State of Bihar*, JT 1994 (7) SC 62 (Natural justice cannot be imported if pleasure doctrine is introduced by the Legislature and order is to be passed on subjective satisfaction); *Py Mullai Hlychho v. State of Mizoram*, (2005) 2 SC 92, p. 101 (Pleasure doctrine may negative natural justice); Desig*nated Authority, Anti Dumping Directorate, Ministry of Commerce v. Holdor Topspoe A/S*, AIR 2000 SC 2556, p. 2565 : (2000) 6 SCC 626 (order extending time for investigation does not require notice) : (2000) 6 SCC 626 : AIR 2000 SC 2556; *State of Kerala v. N. Avinasiapan*, (2004) 2 SCC 344, p. 346 (order of Commissioner Excise under section 67F of the Kerala Abkari Act in declining to admit an application for *suo motu* revision is not bad for the reason that notice to the applicant was not given and the order does not give reasons).

N.B. 1. The rule of *audi alterum partem* is not necessarily excluded by use of the formulae 'where it appears to—' or 'if it appears to the satisfaction of—' or 'if the—considers necessary' or 'if the—is satisfied'; *Duryappa v. Fernando*, (1967) 2 AC 337 : (1967) 2 All ER 152 (PC); *Indore Textiles Ltd. v. Union of India*, 1981 MPLJ 236, p. 240 (G.P. SINGH, C.J.).

2. The principle of fairness in administrative matters is **explained** in *Doody v. Secretary of State for the Home Department*, (1993) 3 All ER 92, p. 106 : (1994) 1 AC 531 (HL), by LORD MUSTILL as follows: "(1) Where an Act of Parliament

[Footnote No. 78 Contd.]

reasons.[79] The Supreme Court has strongly deprecated the practice of some courts in dismissing appeal or revision without giving reason.[80] In the context of an order directing the assessee to have his accounts audited by an accountant under section 142(2A) of the Income Tax Act, 1961, the question of applicability of principles of natural justice was again elaborately discussed and in holding that the principles of natural justice

---

[Footnote No. 78 Contd.]

confers an administrative power there is a presumption that it will be exercised in a manner which is fair in all the circumstances. (2) The standards of fairness are not immutable. They may change with the passage of time. (3) The principles of fairness are not to be applied by rote identically in every situation. What fairness demands is dependant on the context of the decision, and this is to be taken into account in all its aspects. (4) An essential feature of the context is the statute which creates the discretion, as regards both its language and the legal and administrative system within which the decision is taken. (5) Fairness will very often require that a person who may be adversely affected by the decision will have an opportunity to make representation on his own behalf either before the decision is taken with a view to producing a favourable result, or after it is taken, with a view to procuring its modification or both. (6) Since the person affected usually cannot make worthwhile representations without knowing what factors may weigh against his interests, fairness will very often require that he is informed of the gist of the case which he has to answer."

79. *Hochtief Gamman v. State of Orissa*, AIR 1975 SC 2226, p. 2234 : (1975) 2 SCC 649 : 1975 SCC (L&S) 362; *Manager, Govt. Branch Press v. D.B. Belliappa*, AIR 1979 SC 429, p. 434; *Congreve v. Home Office*, (1976) 1 All ER 697, p. 709 (CA); *Harbhajan Singh Dhalla v. Union of India, supra*; *Gurbachan Singh v. Union of India*, JT 1996 (1) SC 215 (reasons are required to be recorded when it affects public interest); *Consumer Action Group v. State of Tamil Nadu*, AIR 2000 SC 3060, p. 3070: (2000) 7 SCC 425 (Exercise of wide discretionary power to exempt from the provisions of a statute impliedly requires the recording of reasons in the order itself.).

Under English law there is no general duty while exercising a statutory discretion to give reasons; but failure to give reasons does not take away the power of judicial review and if all known facts point in a different direction that may lead to the conclusion that the authority had no rational reasons: *Lanrho Plc. v. Secretary of State for Trade and Industry*, (1989) 2 All ER 609, p. 620 (HL). More recent English cases show insistance on greater openness or transparency and duty to give reasons is inferred from implied requirement of fairness in exercise of the power in appropriate circumstances : *Doody v. Secretary for State for the Home Department*, (1993) 3 All ER 92, pp. 106, 107, 110 : (1994) 1 AC 531 (HL); *R. v. Higher Education Funding Council*, (1994) 1 All ER 651 : (1994) 1 WLR 242 (CA). **See** E.G. JACOBS, *'Public Law—The Impact of Europe'* 1999 Public Law 232, pp. 235, 236 (The impact of community law is making the duty to give reasons for an administrative order as a necessary requirement to enable effective judicial review). In India non-communication of reasons is not fatal to the order; but reasons must exist and the record disclosing them must be produced at the time of judicial review; *Union of India v. E.G. Nambudiri*, AIR 1991 SC 1216, pp. 1219, 1220 : 1991 (3) SCC 38. **See further** *Maya Devi v. Rajkumari Batra*, (2010) 9 SCC 486 paras 23 to 27 : (2010) 9 JT 602; *Kranti Associates (P) Ltd. v. Masood Ahmed Khan*, (2010) 9 SCC 496 para 47 : (2010) 9 JT 362 where principles relating to giving of reasons are summarised.

80. *Assistant Commissioner Commercial Tax Department v. Shukla & Brothers*, (2010) 4 SCC 785 : (2010) 4 JT 35 and cases **referred** to therein.

including giving of reasons were implied before exercise of the said power, SINHA , J., observed: "When by reason of an action on the part of a statutory authority civil or evil consequences ensue, principles of natural justice are required to be followed."[81] If the statutory provision or rule requires the statutory authority to afford personal hearing, personal hearing must be afforded.[82] When civil consequences ensue there is hardly any distinction between an administrative order and a quasi judicial order and the principles of natural justice must be followed before passing the order.[83] SINHA, J., further observed: "It is beyond any cavil that ordinarily unless excluded by operation of a statute, the superior courts while exercising power of judicial review shall proceed on the basis that assignment of reasons is imperative in character."[84] These views were reiterated by SINHA, J., in the context of an order of confiscation of goods and imposition of penalty under the Customs Act, 1962 following an enquiry where the documents collected during the enquiry were not disclosed to the petitioner.[85] The legality of an order of a statutory authority must be judged on the basis of the reasons assigned therefor in the order which cannot be supplemented by affidavit or otherwise.[86] Even a non-statutory private body which is not a state under Article 12 of the Constitution but which exercises public functions is bound to follow the principles of 'fairness' and 'good faith' and to act reasonably[87] and its orders are amendable to judicial review under Article 226 of the Constitution.[88] Although there is complete freedom of speech in Parliament and no member can be made liable for anything said in either House of Parliament, a minister's

---

81. *Rajesh Kumar v. Dy. C.I.T.*, (2007) 2 SCC 181 (para 26) : AIR 2007 SC 181; *Radhy Shyam v. State of U.P.*, (2011) 5 SCC 553 (paras 40 to 52) : (2011) 4 JT 524.

82. *Automotive Tyre Manufacturers Association v. Designated Authority*, (2011) 2 SCC 258 paras 83, 84 : (2011) 1 JT 282.

83. *Ibid* paras 48, 49; *Automotive Tyre Manufacturers Association v. Designated Authority* (*supra*) para 65.

84. *Ibid* (para 23). **See further** text and notes 28 to 31, p. 506.

85. *Kothari Filaments v. Commissioner of Customs*, (2009) 2 SCC 192 paras 15 to 17 : (2009) 1 JT 516 : (2009) 1 Scale 117 : (2009) 13 SCR 225.

86. *Mohinder Singh Gill v. Chief Election Commissioner,* (1978) 1 SCC 405 p. 417 para 8 : AIR 1978 SC 851; *R.S. Garg v. State of U.P.,* (2006) 6 SCC 430 (para 33) : AIR 2006 SC 2912; *Chandra Singh v. State of Rajasthan,* AIR 2003 SC 2889, p. 2900; *Pancham Chand v. State of Himachal Pradesh,* (2008) 7 SCC 117 para 24 : AIR 2008 SC 1888. **But see** *Mahavir Jute Mills v. Shibbanlal,* AIR 1975 SC 2057 : (1975) 2 SCC 818; *R.S. Dass v. Union of India,* AIR 1987 SC 593, pp. 603, 604 : 1987 Supp SCC 617; *National Institute of Mental Health & Neuro Sciences v. K. Kalyana Raman (Dr.),* AIR 1992 SC 1806, p. 1808 : 1992 Supp (2) SCC 481.

87. *Board of Control for Cricket in India v. Netaji Cricket Club*, (2005) 4 SCC 741 : AIR 2005 SC 592.

88. *Zee Telefilms Ltd. v. Union of India*, (2005) 4 SCC 649, p. 682 (paras 32, 33) : AIR 2005 SC 2677.

speech can[89] be used in judicial review without alleging any impropriety or any other questioning of his right in making the speech. In such cases the minister's speech is relied upon to explain the conduct occurring outside Parliament, and the policy and motivation leading to it. This is unobjectionable although the aim and effect is to show that such conduct involved the improper exercise of a power for 'an alien purpose or in a wholly unreasonable manner'.[90] But reasons not expressed especially by a court is not 'information' as defined in section 2(f) of the Right to Information Act and cannot be obtained under section 6 of the Act. For example a person cannot apply under the RTI Act to know from the court why a particular argument was not considered. The court speaks only through its judgments.[91]

Section 4(1)(d) of the enacted statute, the Right to Information Act, 2005, also requires every public authority in India to 'provide reasons for its administrative or *quasi*-judicial decisions to affected persons'.

A legitimate expectation as distinguished from a right of receiving some benefit (substantive legitimate expectation) or of being heard before an adverse order is passed (procedural legitimate expectation) may by itself furnish a ground for challenge to an order if it is passed without hearing the person having such legitimate expectation.[92] The word 'legitimate' in

---

89. *Toussaint v. Attorney General of Saint Vincent and the Grenadines*, (2008) 1 All ER 1 (P.C.) para 16.

90. *Ibid*, para 17, **see further** other cases mentioned in paras 16 and 17.

91. *Khanapuram Gandaiah v. Administrative Officer*, (2010) 2 SCC 1 para 10 : AIR 2010 SC 615.

92. *O'Reilly v. Mackman*, (1982) 3 All ER 1124, pp. 1126, 1127 : (1983) 2 AC 237 (HL); *Attorney-General of Honkong v. Ng. Yuen Shiu*, (1983) 2 All ER 346, p. 350 : (1983) 2 AC 629 (PC); *C.C.S.U. v. Minister of Civil Service*, (1984) 3 All ER 935, p. 949 (HL); *R. v. Secretary for State for the Home Department, ex parte, Fire Brigade Union*, (1995) 2 All ER 244, p. 254 (HL); *R (on the application of Bancoult) v. Secretary of State for Foreign and Commonwealth Affairs*, (2008) 4 All ER 1055 (H.L.) para 160 (A legitimate expectation can be based only upon a promise which is clear, unambiguous and devoid of relevant qualification. It is not essential that the applicant should have relied upon the promise to his detriment but it is a relevant consideration in deciding whether the adoption of a policy in conflict with the promise would be an abuse of power and such a change in policy may be justified in public interest; *R (on the application of BAPIO Action Ltd.) v. Secretary of State for the Home Department*, (2009) 1 All ER 93 (H.L.) paras 38, 58, 59; *State of Kerala v. K.G. Madhavan*, AIR 1989 SC 49, pp. 61, 63, 64 : (1988) 4 SCC 669. *Indian Aluminium Co. Ltd. v. Karnataka Electricity Board*, AIR 1992 SC 2169, p. 2182 : (1992) 2 SCC 580; *Navjyoti Co-op. Group Housing Society v. Union of India*, AIR 1993 SC 155, pp. 165, 166 : (1992) 4 SCC 477; *Union Territory of Chandigarh v. Dilbagh Singh*, AIR 1993 SC 796, p. 801 (para 11) : (1993) 1 SCC 1543; *Food Cor poration of India v. Kamdhenu Cattle Feed Industries*, AIR 1993 SC 1601, p. 1604 : (1993) 1 SCC 71; *Union of India v. Hindustan Development Corporation*, AIR 1994 SC 988, pp. 1019, 1020; *Gaziabad Development Authority*

[Footnote No. 92 Contd.]

that expression falls to be read as meaning 'reasonable'. Accordingly, 'legitimate expectations' in this context are capable of including expectations which go beyond enforceable legal rights, provided they have some reasonable basis.[93] But it is something beyond a desire or hope and is grounded on the rule of law as requiring regularity, predictability and certainty in the Government's dealing with the public.[94] According to a Constitution Bench decision of the Supreme Court the doctrine of legitimate expectation can be invoked if the decisions of the administrative authority affect the person by depriving him of some benefit or advantage which either (i) he had in the past been permitted by the decision maker to enjoy and which he can legitimately expect to be permitted to continue to do until there have been communicated to him some rational ground for withdrawing it on which he has been given an opportunity to comment; or (ii) he has received assurance from the decision maker that they will not be withdrawn without giving him first an opportunity of advancing reasons for

---

[Footnote No. 92 Contd.]

v. Delhi Auto & General Finance Pvt. Ltd., JT 1994 (3) SC 275, p. 279 : AIR 1994 SC 2263 : (1994) 4 SCC 42 (The doctrine merely ensures procedural fairness); *Ashoka Smokeless Coal India (P) Ltd. v. Union of India,* (2007) 2 SCC 640 (paras 183 to 187) : (2007) 1 JT 125. (The doctrine has been developed in the context of principles of natural justice). *National Building Construction Corporation v. S. P. Singh,* AIR 1998 SC 2776, pp. 2783 to 2785. (Claims based on 'Legitimate Expectation' have been held to require reliance on representations and resulting detriment to the claimant in the same way as claims based on promissory estoppel); *Dr. Chanchal Goyal v. State of Rajasthan,* (2003) 3 SCC 485, pp. 495 to 501 : (2003) SCC (L&S) 322 (clear statutory words override any expectation, however founded); *Hira Tikkoo v. Union Territory Chandigarh,* AIR 2004 SC 3648, p. 3655 : (2004) 6 SCC 765 (Relief on the basis of 'legitimate expectation' cannot be granted if it is likely to harm larger public interest)'; *Bannari Amman Sugars Ltd. v. Commercial Tax Officer,* (2005) 1 SCC 625, p. 633 : (2004) 10 JT 500 (overriding public interest will negative legitimate expectation).

See PHILIP SALES & KAREN STEYN, 'Legitimate Expectations in English Public Law : An Analysis', (2004) Public Law 564. The author concludes (p. 595) : "Underlying the whole area is the need for a fair balance to be struck between the private interests of individuals in having their expectations based upon statements made by public authorities protected and the general public interest in affording decision makers with discretionary powers flexibility in responding to particular situations". **See further** (2004) 63 Cambridge Law Journal, pp. 261 to 264 (comment on the case of *Stretch v. U.K.*, 38 EHCR 12, a decision of the European court of Human Rights which allows atleast damages even in case of unlawful representation). *Stretch v. U.K., supra,* also **discussed** in *Ashoka Smokeless Coal India (P) Ltd. v. Union of India,* (2007) 2 SCC 640 (para 184) : (2007) 1 JT 125.

93. *Attorney-General of Hongkong v. Ng. Yuen Shiu, supra,* p. 636 (AC); *Regina (Bibi) v. Newham London Borough Council,* (2002) 1 WLR 237, p. 239 (CA).

94. *Jitendra Kumar v. State of Haryana,* (2008) 2 SCC 161 para 58 : (2007) 14 Scale 125 : (2007) 13 SCR 98.

contending that they should not be withdrawn.[1] Stated briefly, when a statute confers power upon a public official to destroy defeat or prejudice a person's rights, interests or legitimate expectations, the rules of natural justice regulate the exercise of that power unless they are excluded by plain words or necessary intendment.[2] This principle applies also to cases where administrative action has its origin in common law or prerogative; but duty to hear may be negatived on grounds of national security or like causes.[3] The ultimate decision in denial of substantive legitimate expectation will also be open to judicial review on *Wednesbury* principles[4] even when it is reached as a result of a change in policy[5] although the Court has to be more circumspect while interfering in matters of policy which are essentially within the domain of the Executive.[6] Therefore judicial review of denial of a claim based on the expectation arising from a policy which is changed before final decision of the authority concerned cannot succeed unless it can be held that the change in policy is not in public interest and

---

1. *Secretary, State of Karnataka v. Umadevi*, (2006) 4 SCC 1 paras 46, 47, 48, 49 : AIR 2006 SC 1806 (temporary or contractual or casual workers not appointed on proper selection according to relevant rules cannot invoke the doctrine of legitimate expectation or Articles 14 and 16 for regularisation or confirmation even though they were continued for a number of years). **Followed** by a three-Judge Bench in *Official Liquidator v. Dayanand*, (2008) 10 SCC 1 : (2008) 11 JT 467 and observation made by a two judge Bench diluting Umadevi's case in *U. P. State Electricity Board v. Pooran Chandra Pandey*, (2007) 11 SCC 92 : (2007) 12 JT 179 held to be obiter. **See further** text and note 54 p. 944 for *Umadevi's* case.

   The doctrine of legitimate expectation cannot also be invoked to invalidate a policy decision in a scheme fixing a cut off date for giving the benefit of being considered for absorption to employees who put in a certain number of years service by that date for there is a clear distinction between legitimate expectation and an anticipation: *CSIR v. Ramesh Chandra Agarwal*, (2009) 3 SCC 35 paras 29 to 33, 39 : (2009) 1 JT 562.
2. *Annetts v. McCann*, (1991) 65 ALJR 167 (High Court of Australia); *Re Minister for Immigration Ex parte Miah*, (2001) 75 ALJR 889, p. 910 (High Court of Australia).
3. *C.C.S.U. v. The Minister for Civil Services*, (1984) 3 All ER 935, p. 952 (HL) (procedural propriety gives way to national security). A statute may also expressly or by necessary implication exclude the application of natural Justice: *Union of India v. Tulsiram Patel*, (1985) 3 SCC 398, pp. 478, 479 : AIR 1985 SC 1416; *Rash Lal Yadav (Dr.) v. State of Bihar*, JT 1994 (4) SC 228, p. 241 : 1994 (5) SCC 267 : 1994 SCC (L&S) 1063.
4. Grounds mentioned in text and note 13, pp. 442-447 are known as *Wednesbury* principles as their origin is traced to the case of *Associated Provincial Pictures House Ltd. v. Wednesbury Corporation*, which is the first case mentioned in note 13.
5. *Punjab Communications Ltd. v. Union of India*, AIR 1999 SC 1801, p. 1815 : (1999) 4 SCC 727; *Union of India v. International Trading Co.*, (2003) 5 SCC 437, p. 446 : AIR 2003 SC 3983; *Bannari Amman Sugars Ltd. v. Commercial Tax Officer*, (2005) 1 SCC 625, p. 635.
6. *M.P. Oil Extraction v. K.N. Oil Industries*, AIR 1998 SC 145, pp. 156, 157 (para 41) : 1997 (7) SCC 592.

amounts to an abuse of power.[7] In all legitimate expectation cases, whether substantive or procedural, three questions arise. The *first* question is to who has the public authority, whether by practice or promise, committed itself; the *second* is whether the authority has acted or proposes to act unlawfully in relation to its commitment; the *third* is what the court should do.[8] There is also authority for the view that the court can interfere on the general ground of unfairness, whether or not it takes the form of a breach of legitimate expectations or some other jurisprudential notion, where a change in a policy or practice occurs without adequate or clear advance notification to those likely to be affected.[9] However, the doctrine of legitimate expectation cannot be pressed in aid for taking support of an Act which is yet to be brought into force in future by a decision of the executive Government as that would be treating inoperative statutory provisions as having immediate effect.[10] But the doctrine of legitimate expectation has been applied in some cases for giving benefit of International Conventions which are yet to be incorporated into municipal law.[11]

Similar to the doctrine of substantive legitimate expectation is the doctrine of promissory estoppel.[12] If the Government or an authority or a person who is competent to act on its behalf makes a promise or representation to a person knowing or intending that it would be acted upon by the person and the person, in fact, acts upon the promise or representation and alters his position, the Government will be bound by the promise or representation which would be enforceable against it and it would not be open to the Government to wriggle out on the plea that there was no consideration for the promise or that there was no contract as required by Article 299 of the Constitution or that some statutory order or notification was required to give the representation a binding effect which was not done. The doctrine of promissory estoppel is an equitable doctrine, therefore, if there is an overriding public interest that the Government should not be

---

7. *Sethi Auto Service Station v. D.D.A.*, (2009) 1 SCC 180 para 33; *Jasbir Singh Chhabara v. State of Punjab,* (2010) 4 SCC 192 paras 47 and 48 : (2010) 2 JT 637 (In para 48 para 32 of the *Sethi Auto Service* case **referred** as laying down the correct principle for application of the doctrine).
8. *Regina (Bibi) v. Newham Borough Council,* (2002) 1 WLR 237 (para 19) (CA). **See further** JAIN 'Substantive Legitimate Expectations: Striking the Right Balance' (2005) 121 LQR 300.
9. *R.v. Ministry of Defence, exparte Walker,* (1999) 3 All ER 935, p. 945 (C.A.) and cases **referred** to therein; affd. (2000) 1 WLR 806 (HL).
10. *R. v. Director of Public Prosecutions,* (1999) 4 All ER 801, p. 833 (HL).
11. **See text** and notes 60-62, pp. 691-92.
12. *Motilal Padampat Sugar Mills Co. Ltd. v. State of U.P.*, (1979) 2 SCC 409 : AIR 1979 SC 621; *State of Punjab v. Nestle India Ltd.*, (2004) 6 SCC 465 : 2004 Supp (2) JT 283; *Ashoka Smokeless Coal India (P) Ltd. v. Union of India,* (2007) 2 SCC 640 (paras 173 to 182) : (2007) 1 JT 125.

held by the promise or representation, the doctrine will not apply. The doctrine will also have no application if the promise or representation is prohibited by law for example if the promise or representation is to grant exemption but the relevant statute does not enable the Government to do so. The doctrine is also not available against the Legislature. In *State of Punjab v. Nestle India Limited,*[13] where earlier cases were reviewed, there were representations at various stages to manufacturers of milk products in Punjab that the State Government had decided in principle to abolish purchase tax on milk with effect from 1-4-1996. The manufacturers acting on this assurance did not pay purchase tax in 1996-1997 and passed on the benefit to the milk producers by providing various concessions and facilities. The State Government had requisite power under section 6(2) and section 30 of the Punjab General Sales Tax Act (46 of 1948) to exempt milk from purchase tax by issuing proper notification, which was not done. In spite of it, the Government was held by its representation and the demands for purchase tax for the year 1996-97 were quashed in writ petition filed by the manufacturers of milk products. In *MRF Ltd. v. Asst. Commissioner (Assessment) Sales Tax,*[14] it was held that when a manufacturer expanded and diversified his industrial unit on the assurance of exemption of sales tax for seven years and a statutory notification to that effect was also issued, withdrawal of the exemption notification by another statutory notification before the expiry of seven years will not apply to those who became entitled to exemption for a fixed period on the basis of promissory estoppel and that to apply the notification to deprive them of the exemption would make it unreasonable and arbitrary. This case clarifies that the case of *Rom Industries Ltd. v. State of J&K, (supra* note 74) does not disturb the settled position in law that where a right for exemption of tax for a certain period had already accrued, withdrawal of the exemption during that period will not ordinarily affect the accrued right unless there be some overriding public interest to prevail over the plea of promissory estoppel.[15] The case also reiterates that the doctrine of promissory estoppel has been repeatedly applied to statutory notifications.[16] The doctrine of promissory estoppel, "it is now well settled", said SINHA, J., in a 2009 case "applies also in the realm of a statute."[17] The Government cannot deny the exemption promised in an arbitrary

---

13. *State of Punjab v. Nestle India Ltd., (supra).* **See further** *Rom Industries Ltd. v. State of J&K,* (2005) 7 SCC 348, (Grant of exemption by a statutory notification for a certain period. Withdrawal thereof before that period consequent to a judgment of the Supreme Court does not give rise to a claim on basis of promissory estoppel.)

14. (2006) 8 SCC 702 (paras 30 to 39) : (2006) 12 JT 244.

15. *Ibid* (para 34).

16. *Ibid* (paras 30 and 33).

17. *Badrikedar Paper Private Ltd. v. Uttar Pradesh Electricity Regulatory Commission,* (2009) 3 SCC 754 para 23 : AIR 2009 SC 1783: (2009) 1 Scale 137.

way by alleging lapse in policy or because of non-issue of exemption notification.[18] Even retrospective amendment of statutory rules for withdrawing exemption can be hit by promissory estoppel.[19] This case has recently been explained that it does not negative the principle that a statutory concession in tax can be withdrawn under section 21 of the General Clauses Act in public interest.[20] Another case on the point is *Bannari Amman Sugars Limited v. Commercial Tax Officer,*[21] where the principles stated above about the doctrine of legitimate expectation and promissory estoppel were reiterated. In this case on facts found by the High Court the petitioner industries were not held to be established on the assurance of grant of concession in purchase tax and therefore the High Court held that the Government could validly withdraw the exemption of purchase tax. The Supreme Court, however, remanded the case to the High Court as no specific plea negating promissory estoppel was properly taken in the return and the case was decided by the High Court on the basis of files produced before it by the Government.[22]

---

18. *State of Bihar v. Kalyanpur Cement Ltd.,* (2010) 3 SCC 275 paras 73 and 84 : (2010) 1 JT 225.

19. *Mahabir Vegetable Oils Ltd. v. State of Haryana,* (2006) 3 SCC 620 : (2006) 3 JT 544.

20. *State of Haryana v. Mahabir Vegetable Oils (P.) Ltd.,* (2011) 3 SCC 778 paras 26, 27, 28 : (2011) 2 SCALE 577.

21. (2005) 1 SCC 625, p. 633 (para 7) p. 638 (para 21) : (2004) 10 JT 500.

22. *Ibid.* The principles relating to promissory estoppel were reiterated in *A.P. Steel Re-rolling Mills Ltd. v. State of Kerala,* (2007) 2 SCC 725 (para 11), but on the facts found by the High Court the Supreme Court held that the plea was rightly negatived. These principles were again reiterated and applied in *Southern Petrochemical Industries Co. Ltd. v. Electricity Inspector,* (2007) 5 SCC 447 (paras 118 to 131) : AIR 2007 SC 1984. A case of promissory estoppel cannot be founded on a budgetary speech of a minister: *Pine Chemicals Ltd. v. Assessing Authority,* (1992) 2 SCC 683; *Union of India v. Ganesh Rice Mills,* (1998) 9 SCC 630; *State of Karnataka v. K.K. Mohandas,* (2007) 6 SCC 484 (paras 23, 24, 28) : AIR 2007 SC 2917; *Shree Sidhbali Steels Limited v. State of Uttar Pradesh,* (2011) 3 SCC 193 paras 36 and 43 : AIR 2011 SC 1175 (A statutory notification under a Central Act granting a concession can on a change in policy may be withdrawn in exercise of the power conferred by sections 14 and 15 of the General Clauses Act and withdrawal of concession may not offend the rule of promissory estoppel). (Pursuant to industrial policy of the *State of U.P.,* the U.P. State Electricity Board framed tariffs by notification in which 33% hill development rebate to new industrial units for five years was allowed. Thereafter the concession was reduced to 17%. This was held to be bad in case of new industrial units established on the faith of the earlier concession as there was no overriding public interest shown and the notification was modified by delegated legislation and not by an Act of the legislature); *State of Arunachal Pradesh v. Nezone Law House Assam,* (2008) 5 SCC 609 : AIR 2008 SC 2045 (Allegation that Law Minister promised to purchase 500 sets of Local Act & Rules if published by petitioner was not found to be true. There were some notings in the file which had to be processed and approved by other departments. Case of promissory estoppel was not

[Footnote No. 22 Contd.]

Even an investigating body like a Commission functioning under a Commissions of Inquiry Act though not bound by the technical rules of evidence, must follow the principles of natural justice in that it must base its findings on evidence that has some probative value and it must listen fairly to any relevant evidence conflicting with the finding and any rational argument against the finding that a person represented at the inquiry whose interests (including in that term career and reputation) may be adversely affected by it, may wish to place or would have so wished if he had been informed of the risk of the finding being made.[23] But when the proceedings of a Commission are purely inquisitoreal, the complainant is not seeking to enforce any private right and the finding is not likely to expose the complainant to any pains or penalties or prosecution, the commission is not bound to give an opportunity to the complainant to rebut the finding of the commission.[24]

The Competition Commission when it directs the Director General to make an enquiry under section 26(1) of the Competition Act after finding a *prima facie* case, it does not perform any adjudicatory function but exercises an inquisitorial function and at that stage no notice to the person against whom inquiry is directed is needed.[25]

The rule of *audi alteram partem* is not attracted during the investigation of a crime under the Code of Criminal Procedure (except when expressly provided) even when the investigating agency applies to the court for issuance of a letter of Rogatory to a court in a foreign country.[26] Speaking generally a person is not entitled to be heard in a preliminary enquiry or

---

[Footnote No. 22 Contd.]
accepted.); *Tamil Nadu Electricity Board v. Status Spinning Mills Ltd.*, (2008) 7 SCC 353 paras 50 and 52 : AIR 2008 SC 2838 (If the public interest so requires a statutory notification granting concession can be rescinded or modified and in view of the existence of public interest the doctrine of promissory estoppel will have no application).

23. *Mahon v. Air Newzealand Ltd.*, (1984) 3 All ER 201, p. 210 : (1984) AC 808 : (1984) 3 WLR 884 (PC). In India there is express provision to this effect in section 8B of the Commissions of Inquiry Act, 1952. In this context, **see** *Kiran Bedi and Jinder Singh v. Committee of Enquiry*, AIR 1989 SC 714 : (1989) 1 SCC 494; *State of Jammu and Kashmir v. Bakshi Gulam Mohammad*, AIR 1967 SC 122 : 1966 Supp SCR 401; *State of Bihar v. Lal Krishna Advani*, (2003) 8 SCC 361.

24. *Public Disclosure Commission v. Isaacs*, (1989) 1 All ER 137, pp. 141, 142 : (1988) 1 WLR 1043 (HL).

25. *Competition Commission v. Steel Authority of India Ltd.*, (2010) 10 SCC 744 paras 87, 91 : (2010) 10 JT 26.

26. *Union of India v. W.N. Chadha*, AIR 1993 SC 1082 : 1993 (1) SCC 154. **See further** *Adalat Prasad v. Rooplal Jindal*, (2004) 7 SCC 338 para 13 : AIR 2004 SC 4674 (In a complaint case the accused is not entitled to be heard in the preliminary enquiry preceding issue of process under section 204 CrPC); followed in *Bholu Ram v. State of Punjab*, (2008) 9 SCC 140 para 41 : (2008) 9 JT 504.

investigation when at a later stage he is to get full opportunity of defending himself before any final decision is taken against him, yet there was no universal rule to that effect.[27] This general rule was followed in holding that a person is not entitled to be heard at the stage of grant of sanction for prosecution as he will get full opportunity to defend himself during trial following sanction.[28] But when the preliminary enquiry is against a person holding a high office, the charges are serious and the finding in the preliminary enquiry is likely to damage the reputation, fairness will require that the person concerned is given opportunity in the prelimianry enquiry itself to reply to the charges.[29] Also when in a so-called preliminary enquiry a definitive finding is reached against a temporary or probationer public servant which is made the foundation for his termination, omission to follow the principles of natural justice will make the termination invalid.[30]

In India a liberal interpretation of Articles 14 and 21 of the Constitution readily brings in the requirements of natural justice to administrative actions against a person.[31] It has become an implied principle of the rule of law that any order having civil consequences should be passed only after following the principles of natural justice.[32] The requirement of giving a

---

27. *Rees v. Crane*, (1994) 1 All ER 833, pp. 848, 849 : (1994) 2 AC 173 : (1994) 2 WLR 476 (PC) (Preliminary enquiry before representation to the President for appointing a tribunal for removal of a High Court judge under section 107 of the Constitution of Trinidad and Tobago); *Radhey Shyam Gupta v. U.P. Agro Industries Corporation Ltd.,* AIR 1999 SC 609, p. 612 (para 15), where reference is made in this context to DE SMITH, 5th Ed., p. 491 : (1999) 2 SCC 21.

28. *Assistant Commissioner Assessment II Bangalore v. Vellappa Textiles Ltd.*, AIR 2004 SC 86, p. 98 : (2003) 11 SCC 405.

29. *Rees v. Crane, supra.*

30. *Radhey Shyam Gupta v. Agro Industries Corportion Ltd., supra,* p. 617 (AIR).

31. *Union of India v. Tulsiram Patel*, (1985) 3 SCC 398, p. 476 : AIR 1985 SC 1416; *Olga Tellis v. Bombay Municipal Corporation*, (1985) 3 SCC 545, pp. 577-84; *Charan Lal Sahu v. Union of India*, AIR 1990 SC 1480, pp. 1540, 1541 : 1990 (1) SCC 613; *Managing Director, ECIL v. B. Karunakar*, AIR 1994 SC 1074, p. 1103 : 1993 (4) SCC 727.

32. *Raghunath Thakur v. State of Bihar*, AIR 1989 SC 620, p. 621 : (1989) 1 SCC 229; *Baldeo Singh v. State of H.P.*, AIR 1987 SC 1239 : (1987) 2 SCC 510, p. 515; *State of Haryana v. Ramkishan*, AIR 1988 SC 1301, p. 1308 : (1988) 3 SCC 416; *Cantonment Board, Dinapore v. Taramani Devi*, AIR 1992 SC 61, p. 62 : (1992) Supp (2) SCC 501; *Southern Painters v. Fertilizers & Chemicals Travancore Ltd.*, AIR 1994 SC 1277, p. 1280 : 1994 Supp (2) SCC 699; *Tejshree Ghag v. Prakash Parashuram Patil,* AIR 2007 SC 2141, para 15 (Transfer of an employee to a post which is not an equivalent post affects his status and results in civil consequences and attracts principles of natural justice). But the principle has to be pragmatically applied to the given fact situation and not extended to ridiculous limits as a ritual to be applied at every stage; *State of Madhya Pradesh v. R.P. Sharma*, 1996 (5) Scale 814, pp. 817, 818 : AIR 1996 SC 2665, p. 2667 : (1996) 10 SCC 516; Further, when the power to take action is conferred on the direction of an expert executive

[Footnote No. 32 Contd.]

reasonable opportunity of being heard before an order is made by an administrative, *quasi*-judicial or judicial authority, particularly when the order entails adverse civil consequences, cannot be sacrificed at the altar of administrative exigency. While there can be exceptions to this rule, the question as to whether the principle has to be applied or not is to be considered bearing in mind the express language and the basic scheme of the provision conferring the power, the nature of the power conferred, the purpose for which the power is conferred and the final effect of the exercise of that power on the rights of the person affected.[33] Further, the State and every public authority or instrumentality of the State must act reasonably in public interest and fairly for these requirements have also been spelled out of Article 14 and the concept of rule of law.[34] Article 14 is said to be the constitutional guardian of principles of natural justice.[35] These considera-

---

[Footnote No. 32 Contd.]
like the Reserve Bank of India for superseding the Board of Directors of a Corporative Bank the implication of natural justice may not arise; *Reserve Bank of India v. M. Hanumaiah,* (2008) 1 SCC 770 : AIR 2008 SC 994.

33. *Ashwin S. Mehta & Anr. v. Union of India & Ors.*, (2012) 1 SCC 83, pp. 98, 99.

34. *Dwarka Marfatia & Sons v. Board of Trustees of the Port of Bombay*, AIR 1989 SC 1644, p. 1648 (para 25 and the cases **referred** to therein) : 1989 (3) SCC 293; *Mahabir Auto Stores v. Indian Oil Corporation*, AIR 1990 SC 1031, p. 1037 : (1990) 3 SCC 752 (also cases **referred** to therein). The principle negativing arbitrary state action has been extended to contractual rights; *Kumari Shrilekha Vidyarthi v. State of U.P.*, AIR 1991 SC 537, p. 557 : 1991 (1) SCC 212; *Verigamto Naveen v. Govt. of Andhra Pradesh,* AIR 2001 SC 3609, pp. 3614, 3615 : (2001) 8 SCC 344; *Jamsed Hormusji Wadia v. Board of Trustees Port of Mumbai*, (2004) 3 SCC 214, p. 236 : AIR 2004 SC 1815 : (2004) 3 SCC 214; *ABL International Ltd. v. Export Credit Gurantee Corporation of India Ltd.*, (2004) 3 SCC 553, p. 570 (para 23) : (2003) 10 JT 300; *Food Corporation of India v. Seil Ltd.*, (2008) 3 SCC 440 paras 21 to 24: AIR 2008 SC 1101. The Supreme Court has stressed that in the distribution of Government benefits such as allotment of plots, houses, petrol pumps, gas agencies, mineral leases, contracts, quotas and licences etc. the Government must evolve a transparent and objective criteria/procedure so that the choice among the members belonging to the same class or category is based on reason/fair play and non-arbitrariness; *Common Cause, A Registered Society v. Union of India*, 1996 (7) Scale 156, p. 173 : AIR 1996 SC 3538, p. 3550, on review JT 1999 (5) SC 237, pp. 258 to 260 (principle of judicial review upheld but award of damages to State against minister set aside); *Onkarlal Bajaj v. Union of India,* (2003) 2 SCC 673 : AIR 2003 SC 2562. **See further,** *Tata Cellular v. Union of India,* JT 1994 (4) SC 532 : (1994) 6 SCC 551 which advises judicial restraint in administrative matters. Article 14 does not also assume uniformity in erroneous actions or decisions. Guarantee of equality is a positive concept and cannot be enforced in a negative manner to perpetuate an illegality: *State of Kerala v. K. Prasad,* (2007) 7 SCC 140 (paras 13 and 14); *Larsen & Toubro Ltd. v. Union of India*, (2011) 5 SCC 430 : 2011 6 JT 1.

35. *Charan Lal Sahu v. Union of India*, AIR 1990 SC 1480, pp. 1540, 1541 : 1990 (1) SCC 613; *Krishan Lal v. State of Jammu & Kashmir*, JT 1994(2) SC 619, p. 626 : 1994(4) SCC 422 : 1994 SCC (L&S) 885.

tions provide wide scope for expansion of natural justice. For example, till recently it was understood that adverse remarks in the annual confidential reports alone are required to be communicated to a public servant, and his representation, if any, be considered before his case is examined for promotion.[36] But in *Dev Dutt. v. Union of India*[37] KATJU, J., developed a new principle of natural justice by holding that fairness and transparency in public administration requires that all entries (whether poor, fair, average, good or very good) in the annual confidential report of a public servant must be communicated to him within a reasonable period. He also held that the principles of non-arbitrariness in State action as envisaged by Article 14 of the Constitution requires such communication and this will override if there be any rules or orders to the contrary.[38] It was further held that the public servant concerned will have a right of representation which should be decided by an authority higher than the one who gave the entry before his case is considered for promotion.[39]

Disclosure of adverse material was also held to be an important aspect of natural justice in the context of section 10-A of the Dentists Act, 1948, which is titled 'permission for establishment of new dental college, new courses of study etc'. The proviso to section 10-A(4) states that no scheme shall be disapproved by the Central Government except after giving the person, authority or institution concerned a 'reasonable opportunity of being heard'. The Supreme Court held that section 10-A, despite its heading, also applies to cases of renewal of permission. Further, the expression 'reasonable opportunity of being heard' occurring in the proviso to section 10-A(4) means that the material that goes against the applicant, and is to be taken into consideration, is to be supplied to the applicant with an opportunity to make a representation.[40]

Unless the statute provides otherwise, the implication of natural justice will require absence of bias[41] in (to be determined on the objective

---

36. *Satya Narayan Shukla v. Union of India*, (2006) 9 SCC 69 : AIR 2006 SC 2511 **followed** in *M. Mishra v. Central Bank of India*, (2008) 9 SCC 120 : AIR 2009 SC 1114 where *Dev Dutt*'s case **discussed** below was not cited.

37. *Dev Dutt v. Union of India*, (2008) 8 SCC 725 para 36 : AIR 2008 SC 2513.

38. *Ibid*.

39. *Ibid* para 37.

40. *Swamy Devi Dayal Hospital & Dental College v. Union of India & Ors.*, (2014) 13 SCC 506, pp. 511 to 520.

41. *R. v. Gough,* (1993) 2 All ER 724, p. 737 (HL) (The test of bias as laid down in this case was real danager of bias' rather than 'real likelihood', "to ensure that the court is thinking in terms of possibility rather than probability"). Accepting the criticism against the test of bias in *R. v. Gough supra,* which was not followed in other common law jurisdictions, the House of Lords modified the said test in

[Footnote No. 41 Contd.]

[Footnote No. 41 Contd.]

Porter v. Magill, (2002) 1 All ER 465, p. 507 (HL) (The test as laid down in this case is: "The court must first ascertain all the circumstances which have a bearing on the suggestion that the judge was biased, it must then ask whether those circumstances would lead to a fair minded and informed observer to conclude that there was a real possibility that the tribunal was biased: The question is whether a fair minded and informed observer, having considered the facts would conclude that there was a real possibility that the tribunal was biased." The test as now formulated is objective and accords with the view taken in Strasbourg court and also in other common law jurisdictions). This test was **reaffirmed** in *Lawal v. Northern Spirit,* (2004) 1 All ER 187, pp. 192, 193 (HL) and *R. (on the application of Al-Hasan) v. Secretary of State for the Home Department,* (2005) 1 All ER 927, p. 940 (HL), as also in *Helow v. Secretary of State for the Home Department,* (2009) 2 All ER 1031 paras 2, 14, 39 (The fair minded and informed observer is not unduly sensitive or suspicious as KIRBY, J. observed in *Johnson v. Johnson,* (2000) 201 CLR 488 para 53. **See further** *Exp. Pinochit Ugarta (No. 2),* (1999) 1 All ER 577 (HL) (A judge is automatically disqualified from hearing a matter in which he has a pecuniary interest in the outcome as also when the decision would lead to promotion of a cause in which he is involved, together with one of the parties); *Locabail (UK) Ltd. v. Bayfield Properties Ltd.,* (2000) 1 All ER 65 (CA) (A joint judgment on 'Bias' by LORD BINGHAM C.J., LORD WOLF MR and SIR RICHARD VC: Parties may waive their right to object on the ground of 'bias' when there is no automatic disqualification and facts concerning 'bias' have been disclosed. Extra judicial writing by a judge on a question will not normally disqualify a judge for deciding that question except in extreme cases).

Helljay Investments Pvt. Ltd. v. Deputy Commissioner of Taxation, 74 ALJR 68 (The bare fact that a judicial officer has earlier expressed an opinion on a question of law in a case will seldom if ever warrant a conclusion of apprehension of bias); *Johnson v. Johnson,* (2000) 74 AL JR 1380, pp. 1382, 1386-91 (Test of apprehended bias in Australia); *Ebner v. Official Trusty in Bankruptcy,* 75 ALJR 277 (The test is one of possibility, real and not remote, not probability); *Re Refugee Review Tribunal, Ex parte H,* (2001) 75 ALJR 982, p. 990 (The test of apprehended bias is objective test of possibility as distinct from probability); *Concrete Pty Ltd. v. Parramatta Design and Developments Pty Ltd.,* (2006) 81 ALJR 352, p. 371 (para 110). (A judge is disqualified if a fair-minded by-observer might reasonably apprehend that the judge might not bring an impartial mind to the resolution of the question the judge is required to decide).

Kumaon Mandal Vikas Nigam Ltd. v. Girja Shanker Pant, AIR 2001 SC 24, p. 35 : (2001) 1 SCC 182 (Bias depends on facts of each case and allegation should be supported by positive evidence. Apprehension of bias is not sufficient, and facts should show real danger of bias or real likelihood of bias); *Union of India v. B.N. Jha,* AIR 2003 SC 1416, p. 1424 : (2003) 4 SCC 531, p. 544, (objective test of real likelihood of bias); *M.P. Special Police Establishment v. State of M.P.,* (2004) 8 SCC 788, pp. 800, 803 (real danger of bias on objective test). *Crawford Bayley & Co. v. Union of India,* (2006) 6 SCC 25 (paras 18, 19) : AIR 2006 SC 2544. (The doctrine 'no man can be a judge in his own cause' cannot be applied simply on the ground that an officer of a statutory corporation has been appointed Estate Officer under the Public Premises Eviction Act, 1971, who will take action to evict persons in unauthorized occupation of premises belonging to the corporation).

[Footnote No. 41 Contd.]

tests of real likelihood or possibility of bias) and pre-decisional hearing by the adjudicating authority; and any omission by the adjudicating authority to hear the person concerned is not cured by a prior hearing given to him by the investigating authority or by a post-decisional hearing given in appeal.[42] But if prior hearing will defeat the object of the exercise of statutory power, the matter being one of real urgency, a post-decisional hearing by the adjudicating authority may meet the requirements of natural justice.[43] Similarly when the service of notice has not

---

[Footnote No. 41 Contd.]

Election Commission of India v. Subramanian Swamy, AIR 1996 SC 1810, p. 1817 (para 15) : (1996) 4 SCC 104 (objection on the ground of bias is subject to the doctrine of necessity. Thus if there is no other person excepting A to decide the issue, the doctrine of necessity will make it imperative on him to decide the issue inspite of any allegation of bias); *State of West Bengal v. Shivananda Pathak,* AIR 1998 SC 2050 : (1998) 5 SCC 513 (Bias on the ground of judicial obstinacy); *Amar Nath Chowdhury v. Braithwaite & Co. Ltd.,* AIR 2002 SC 678 : (2002) 2 SCC 290 (Managing Director dismissing an employee cannot sit in the Board of Directors to hear the employee's appeal. Doctrine of necessity was inapplicable as the Board could have delegated its appellate power to a committee); Reference under Article 317(1) of the *Constitution of India, In Re,* (2009) 1 SCC 337 para 26 : (2008) 12 JT 424 (Doctrine of bias may not be applied to a constitutional authority like a Chairman of Public Service Commission who cannot be replaced requiring him to withdraw altogether from the selection process if a close relative of his is appearing for selection).

See SIR BLOOM-COOPER's Comment on 'Bias in Appeal', (2005) Public Law 225 in which he quotes at p. 227 a very illuminating judgment of JEROME FRANK J. (on behalf of himself, Learned HAND and SWAM JJ.) in *Rt J.P. Linhan Inc.,* (138 F 20, 650), a brief excerpt from which reads: "Democracy must, indeed, fail unless our courts try cases fairly, and there can be no fair trial before a judge lacking in impartiality and disinterestedness. If, however, 'bias' and 'partiality' be defined to mean the total absence of preconceptions in the mind of the judge, then no one has ever had a fair trial and no one ever will." FRANK J. in *Linaham supra* also quoted in *Samya Sett v. Shambhu Sarkar,* (2005) 6 SCC 767, p. 775 : AIR 2005 SC 3309.

42. *Institute of Chartered Accountants of India v. L.K. Ratna,* (1986) 4 SCC 537 : AIR 1987 SC 71; *K.L. Shephard v. Union of India,* AIR 1988 SC 686 : (1987) 4 SCC 431; *H.L. Trehan v. Union of India,* AIR 1989 SC 568 : (1989) 1 SCC 764.

43. *Maneka Gandhi v. Union of India,* AIR 1978 SC 597 : (1978) 1 SCC 248; *Liberty Oil Mills v. Union of India,* (1984) 3 SCC 465, pp. 486-91 : AIR 1984 SC 1271; *Charan Lal Sahu v. Union of India,* AIR 1990 SC 1480, pp. 1544, 1545 : (1990) 1 SCC 613; *Canara Bank v. V.K. Awasthy,* (2005) 6 SCC 321 (paras 5 and 6) : AIR 2005 SC 2090. **See further** *Luga Bay Shipping Corporation v. Board of Trustees of the Port of Cochin,* AIR 1997 SC 544, p. 550 : 1997 (1) SCC 631. (Urgency for repair of the port and to have the damages in hand for that purpose may enable making of Regulations to enable unilateral fixation and recovery of damages, subject to a right of suit, against a ship causing damage to the Port.). The court will be extremely reluctant to construe the statute to exclude predecisional hearing except in very exceptional circumstances: *Swadeshi Cotton Mills v. Union of India,* (1981) 1 SCC 664 para 44; *Bidhannagar (Salt Lake) Welfare Association v. Central Valuation Board,* AIR 2007 SC 2276 para 32 : (2007) 6 SCC 668.

been effected for reasons beyond the control of the adjudicating authority within the time allowed by law for making the order, a post-decisional hearing will meet the need to afford opportunity to the person affected.[44] This is how the principle of natural justice is reconciled with the considerations of public interest or administrative necessity.[45] It cannot also be said that an omission of or a defect in hearing at the original stage can never be cured by a full hearing afforded in appeal.[46] Further, situations may arise, although very rarely, where necessity of prompt action to eradicate a grave social evil may need complete suspension of the requirement of natural justice, even though it is not unlikely that some innocents may suffer.[47]

Briefly stated 'natural justice' means 'fairplay in action' and requirements of natural justice depend upon the facts of each case.[48] Therefore, in judging the validity of an order when the complaint is about non-compliance with the principles of natural justice, in cases where the attack is not on ground of bias, a distinction has to be drawn between cases of 'no notice' or 'no hearing' and cases of 'no fair hearing' or 'no adequate hearing'. If the defect is of the former category, it may automatically make the order invalid[49] but if the defeat is of the latter category, it will have to be further examined whether the defect has resulted in prejudice and failure of justice and it is only when such a conclusion is reached that the

---

44. *I.J. Rao, Asstt. Collector of Customs v. Bibhuti Bhushan Bagh*, AIR 1989 SC 1884 : 1989 (3) SCC 202.

45. *Ibid*, p. 1890. **Also see**, cases in footnote 39, *supra*.

46. *Calvin v. Carr*, (1980) AC 574 (PC); *Lloyd v. McMahon*, (1987) 1 All ER 1118, p. 1165 (HL); *Union Carbide Corporation v. Union of India*, AIR 1992 SC 248 : (1991) 4 SCC 584; *Canara Bank v. Debasis Das,* (2003) 4 SCC 557, p. 576 : AIR 2003 SC 2041, p. 2051 (The case also discusses in detail the concept of natural justice); *Canara Bank v. V.K. Awasthy*, AIR 2005 SC 2090 : (2005) 6 SCC 321 (Natural Justice in the context of dismissal from service). **See further** *Commissioner of Sales Tax v. Subhash & Co.,* (2003) 3 SCC 454 : AIR 2003 SC 1628 (The appellate authority may in suitable cases remit the case to the original authority. The case also discusses the meaning of 'notice' and refers to various dictionaries and cases).

47. For example **see** cases relating to cancellation of examination on report of mass copying: *Bihar School Examination Board v. Subhas Chandra,* AIR 1970 SC 1269 : (1970) 1 SCC 648; *Chairman J&K State Board of Education v. Feyaz Ahmad,* AIR 2000 SC 1039 : (2000) 3 SCC 59.

48. **See** for the nature of flexibility in this matter *State of Maharashtra v. Jalgaon Municipal Council,* AIR 2003 SC 1659, p. 1677 (para 32) : (2003) 9 SCC 731.

49. *Municipal Corporation Ludhiana v. Inderjeet Singh,* AIR 2009 SC 195 para 16 : (2008) 13 SCC 506 (Demolition of alleged unauthorized construction without serving notice as required by section 269 of Punjab Municipal Corporation Act, 1976, is highly arbitrary. Corporation directed to restore the demolished construction which was according to the order of sanction at its cost).

order may be declared invalid.[50] Even in cases of 'no notice' or 'no hearing', the superior courts may in exercise of their discretion decline to interfere by judicial review (under Article 32 or 226 as the case may be) where on admitted or undisputed facts the view taken by the impugned order is the only possible view and it would be futile to issue any writ to compel observance of natural justice.[51] This is called the useless formality theory.[52] For example, when the petitioner was appointed even though he was not qualified on the cut off date (last date for receipt of applications) and was ineligible to be considered for appointment, cancellation of his appointment without hearing him was not interfered with as it would have been a futile exercise.[53] Sympathy for the petitioner as he became qualified before

---

50. *State Bank of Patiala v. S.K. Sharma*, AIR 1996 SC 1669, pp. 1683, 1684 : 1996 (3) SCC 364; *P.D. Agrawal v. State Bank of India,* (2006) 8 SCC 776 (para 39) : AIR 2006 SC 2064; *Haryana Financial Corporation v. Kailash Chandra Ahuja,* (2008) 9 SCC 31 paras 44, 45 : (2008) 8 JT 70 (Departmental enquiry-Non-supply of inquiry report does not make the action taken invalid unless there is finding of prejudice). **See further** *Unon of India v. Mustafa & Najibai Trading Co.*, JT 1998 (5) SC 16, pp. 36, 37 : AIR 1998 SC 2526 : 1998 (6) SCC 79; *State of U.P. v. Harendra Arora,* AIR 2001 SC 2319 : (2001) 6 SCC 392 (non-furnishing of enquiry report under Rule 55A of the Civil Services (Classification Control and Appeal) Rules, 1930); *Oriental Insurance Co. Ltd. v. S. Balkrishnan,* AIR 2001 SC 2400 : (2003) 11 SCC 734 (non-supply of enquiry report); *Canara Bank v. Debasis Das,* (2003) 4 SC 557, p. 578 : AIR 2003 SC 2041; *State of Maharashtra v. Jalgaon Municipal Council, supra,* pp. 1678, 1679; *Commissioner of Income Tax Chandigarh v. Pearl Mech. Eng. and Foundry Works*, (2004) 4 SCC 597: AIR 2004 SC 2345. (In a proceeding for a acquisition of property under section 269 of the Income-tax Act, 1961, the acquisition does not become invalid if notice to the owner is issued before publication of the notice in the Official Gazette and not after it for it causes no prejudice); *Union of India v. Jesus Sales Corporation*, AIR 1996 SC 1509, p. 1512 : (1996) 4 SCC 69 (Hearing does not always mean personal hearing); *Ganesh Santa Ram Sirur v. State Bank of India*, AIR 2005 SC 314, pp. 323, 324. (Personal hearing not always necessary); *Transmission Corpn. of A.P. Ltd. v. Shri Rama Krishna Rice Mill,* (2006) 3 SCC 74 (para 9) : AIR 2006 SC 1445 (cross-examination of a person whose statement is relied upon not always necessary); *Punjab National Bank v. Manjeet Singh,* (2006) 8 SCC 647 (paras 17, 18) : AIR 2007 SC 262 (In case of an industrial dispute individual workers are not required to be heard. Hearing given to unions is sufficient); *H. V. Nirmala v. Karnataka State Financial Corporation*, (2008) 7 SCC 639 paras 10, 20 and 21 : AIR 2008 SC 2440 [Appointment of enquiry officer if not objected to during enquiry cannot be raised later if no prejudice caused].

51. *Aligarh Muslim University v. Mansoor Ali Khan,* AIR 2000 SC 2783, pp. 2787, 2788 : (2000) 7 SCC 529; *M.C. Mehta v. Union of India,* JT 1999 (5) SC 114 : AIR 1999 SC 2583; *S.L. Kapoor v. Jagmohan,* 1980 (4) SCC 379 : AIR 1981 SC 136; *Venkateshwara Rao v. Government of Andhra Pradesh,* 1966 (2) SCR 172 : AIR 1966 SC 828. **See further** note 26, p. 858.

52. *M.C. Mehta v. Union of India, supra,* (paras 22, 23) (AIR); *State of Manipur v. Y. Token Singh,* (2007) 5 SCC 65 (paras 22, 30) : (2007) 3 JT 606.

53. *Ashok Kumar Sarkar v. Union of India,* (2007) 4 SCC 54 (para 28) p. 66 : (2007) 6 JT 127.

the date of interview was held to be not a good ground even for interference under Article 142 of the Constitution.[54]

(b) Subordinate legislation.—A power conferred to make subordinate legislation must be exercised in conformity with the express and implied limitations contained in the empowering statute. It has been said that the limitations which apply to the exercise of administrative or *quasi*-judicial power conferred by a statute,[55] except the requirement of natural justice, also apply to the exercise of legislative power.[56] So the exercise of a legislative power derived from a statute can be assailed on the grounds that it is in conflict with the Constitution or the governing statute; that there has been non-consideration of essential facts; and that it is manifestly arbitrary.[57] A detailed discussion of various aspects of judicial review of delegated legislation occurs in Chapter 12.

(c) Ordinances and orders under the Constitution.—A power to make law by Ordinance under the Constitution must, however, be distinguished from a statutory power to make subordinate legislation. Unlike the exercise of a statutory power, an Ordinance made by the President under Article 123 or by the Governor under Article 213 of the Constitution cannot be questioned on the ground of non-application of mind or *mala fides* or on the ground that the prevailing circumstances did not warrant the issue of the Ordinance.[58] But the Ordinance making power cannot be used to circumvent the Legislature by repromulgating an Ordinance time and again, after the Legislature is prorogued, in a routine manner.[59] Interference by the court in that event is illustrative of the general principle that the function of construing the provisions of the Constitution and the laws and consequently the function of determining whether the act of a constitutional or statutory functionary falls within the limits of the power entrusted to it or is vitiated by an erroneous application of the ambit of the power are

---

54. *Ibid,* para 33 pages 68-70.

55. **See** text and note 13, p. 442.

56. *State of U.P. v. Renusagar Power Co.*, AIR 1988 SC 1737, p. 1763 : (1988) 4 SCC 59; *Shri Sitaram Sugar Co. Ltd. v. Union of India*, AIR 1990 SC 1277, p. 1297 : (1990) 3 SCC 223; *West Bengal Electricity Regulatory Commission v. C.E.S.C. Ltd.*, AIR 2002 SC 3588, p. 3600 : (2002) 8 SCC 715. **See further** *Boddington v. British Transport Police,* (1998) 2 All ER 203, pp. 218, 219 (HL).

57. *Ibid.* For judicial review of Act passed by Parliament or State Legislature, **see**pp. 591 - 601, *post.*

58. *T. Venkata Reddy v. State of A.P.*, (1985) 3 SCC 198, pp. 211, 212 : AIR 1985 SC 724; *K. Nagaraj v. State of Andhra Pradesh*, (1985) 1 SCC 523, pp. 548, 549 : AIR 1985 SC 551; *Gurudevdatta VKSS Maryadit v. State of Maharashtra,* AIR 2001 SC 1980, p. 1987 : (2001) 4 SCC 534.

59. *D.C. Wadhwa (Dr.) v. State of Bihar*, (1987) 1 SCC 378 : AIR 1987 SC 579. **See further** *Krishna Kumar Singh v. State of Bihar*, JT 1998 (4) SC 58 : 1998 (5) SCC 643.

matters falling within the jurisdiction of the court.[60] Thus though the exercise of power by the President in the matter of grant or refusal of pardon under Article 72 of the Constitution cannot be questioned on merits, it can be subjected to judicial review when it is vitiated by self denial on an erroneous assumption that he has no power to go into the merits after it has been judicially concluded by the highest court.[61] The order granting pardon under Article 72 or 161 is subject to judicial review on the ground that order has been passed without application of mind, or the same suffers from vice of *mala fide* or the order has been passed on extraneous or on wholly irrelevant consideration or that the order suffers from arbitrariness.[62] Similarly an order of remission of life sentence passed by the Governor under Article 161, when certain vital facts about the prisoner, who was an MLA, were not disclosed can be quashed by the High Court in judicial review under Article 226.[63] Considerations of religion, caste or political loyalty are irrelevant in exercising the power of remission. Therefore, remission granted of about seven years unexpired sentence under Article 161 essentially on the ground that the convict was a good congress worker was

---

60. *Kehar Singh v. Union of India*, AIR 1989 SC 653, p. 659 : 1989 (1) SCC 204.

61. *Ibid*; *Maru Ram v. Union of India,* (1981) 1 SCC 107 para 31 sub-para (8,9) : AIR 1980 SC 2147 (The power of remission by President or Governor is to be exercised on the advice of the appropriate Government which is binding. Scope of interference by court limited but interference will be made if it is exercised on 'wholly irrelevant, irrational, discriminatory or *mala fide*' considerations); *Maru Ram's* case is also **referred** in *C.A. Pious v. State of Kerala,* (2007) 8 SCC 31. **See further** *Reckley v. Minister of Public Safety and Immigration*, (1996) 1 All ER 562 (PC) (Exercise of prerogative of mercy under section 92 of the Constitution of Bahamas is not open to judicial review); *De Freitas v. Benny*, (1976) 1 AC 239, p. 247 (PC) (similar view under the constitution of Trinidad and Tobago. As pithily put by LORD DIPLOCK: "Mercy is not the subject of legal rights. It begins where legal rights end."). For criticism, **see** CHRISTOPHER GOLBER, "Reckley (No. 2) and the Prerogative of Mercy: Act of grace or constitutional safeguard", 1997 Modern Law Review 572.

62. *Epuru Sudhakar v. Govt. of A.P.*, (2006) 8 SCC 161 (para 34) : AIR 2006 SC 3385 and *Narayan Dutt v. State of Punjab*, (2011) 4 SCC 353 (para 28).

63. *Swaran Singh v. State of U.P.*, JT 1998 (2) SC 452 : AIR 1998 SC 2026 : (1998) 4 SCC 75. **See further** *State (Govt. of NCT) v. Preem Rai,* (2003) 7 SCC 121 : 2003 SCC (Cri) 1586 (court has no power to commute sentence under section 433(c) CrPC. Difference between commutation, Pardon, Remission, Amnesty. Articles 72 and 161 also considered). In *Ramdeo Chauhan alias Rajnath Chauhan* delivered on November 19, 2010 AFTAB ALAM and ASHOK KUMAR GANGULY, JJ. held that National Human Rights Commission can recommend to the Governor for remission of death sentence into life imprisonment and the order of remission passed by the Governor on the recommendation of council of ministers cannot be questioned on the ground that it gives no reasons: *Hitwada December 6, 2010.*

quashed by the Supreme Court.[64] The powers of President under Article 72 and of Governor under Article 161 are not restricted by sections 432, 433 and 433A of the Code of Criminal Procedure though the authority has to meet the requirements of the rule of law while exercising the ... power.[65] If the remission policy at the time of conviction of the accused is made liberal as compared to the policy prevalent at the time when his case is taken up for consideration the prisoner is to be given the benefit of the more liberal policy.[66] The Governor's order on pardon is open to judicial review if it has been passed on extraneous or wholly irrelevant considerations. He cannot also pronounce on the innocence of the accused.[67] The principle of limited judicial review has also been applied to exercise of powers in certain sensitive areas under the Constitution. Limited judicial review has been exercised for examining the validity of a proclamation issued by the President under Article 356 of the Constitution.[68] Similarly satisfaction of the President under clause (c) of second Proviso to Article 311(2) of the Constitution, that in the interest of the security of the State it is not expedient to hold an enquiry, is also open to limited judicial review on the ground of *mala fides* and also on the ground that it was based on wholly extraneous ground.[69] President's order removing a Governor under Article 156 is also open to limited judicial review.[70]

Welfare schemes passed by Parliament under Article 114 such as MPLAD are valid and do not require separate enactment to make them valid.[71]

Proceedings in Parliament cannot be called into question on the ground of irregularity of procedure and the House is not subject to the control of the courts in the administration of its internal proceedings.[72]

---

64. *Epuru Sudhakar v. Govt. of A.P.*, (2006) 8 SCC 161 (paras 56, 65) : AIR 2006 SC 3385.

65. *State of Haryana v. Jagdish*, (2010) 4 SCC 216 para 38 : AIR 2010 SC 1690.

66. Para 54.

67. *Narayan Dutt v. State of Punjab*, (2011) 4 SCC 353 paras 28, 29, 34 : AIR 2011 SC 1216.

68. **See** pages 794-796, *infra*.

69. *A.K. Kaul v. Union of India*, AIR 1995 SC 1403, p. 1415 : 1995 (4) SCC 73. **See further** *Indian Railway Construction Co. Ltd. v. Ajaykumar*, AIR 2003 SC 1843, pp. 1848 to 1850 : (2003) 4 SCC 579 (Principles of judicial review in a case where departmental enquiry was dispensed with under Article 311(2)).

70. *B.P. Singhal v. Union of India*, (2010) 6 SCC 331 : (2010) 5 JT 640.

71. *Bhim Singh v. Union of India*, (2010) 5 SCC 538 : (2010) 5 JT 166.

72. *Ramdas Athawale v. Union of India*, (2010) 4 SCC 1 paras 34, 39 : AIR 2010 SC 1310 [President's address is required only when the House is prorogued and not when the House is merely adjourned. (Articles 85, 87, 122). But when it is a case of illegality and not merely of irregularly judicial review is not excluded.].

Even power of Parliament/State Legislature to punish for its contempt[73] or to expel a member[74] for breach of its privilege is not final and conclusive and is subject to the power of judicial review under Articles 32, 136 and 226 of the Constitution. Even a finality clause in a Constitution Amendment Act does not deprive the superior courts of their power of judicial review which forms part of the basic structure of the Constitution.[75]

(i) Manner of expression of exercise of power

The power to make an order must also be distinguished from the manner of expressing an order which may have been prescribed with a view to give the prescribed manner of expression an evidentiary value. In such a case the non-compliance with the prescribed manner of expression does not invalidate the order if the same is proved otherwise to have been validly made. It is on this principle that section 40 of the 9th Schedule to the Government of India Act, 1935,[76] and Article 77,[77] and Article 166[78] of the Constitution have been held to be directory. If, while passing an order in exercise of a power, the source of the power is not quoted or a wrong provision is quoted, it will not invalidate the order, and the exercise of the

---

73. *M.S.M. Sharma v. Srikrishna Sinha,* AIR 1959 SC 395 : 1959 Supp (1) SCR 806; *In re Keshav Singh* (special Reference No. 1 of 1964) AIR 1965 SC 745.

74. *Raja Ram Pal v. Hon'ble Speaker, Lok Sabha,* (2007) 3 SCC 184 : (2007) 2 JT 1. **Followed** in *Amarinder Singh v. Special Committee Punjab Vidhan Sabha,* (2010) 6 SCC 113 paras 53, 54, 55, 59 : (2010) 4 JT 350.

75. **See** pages 863-870, *post.*

76. *J.K. Gas Plant Manufacturing Co. (Rampur) Ltd. v. Emperor*, AIR 1947 PC 38.

77. *Major E.G. Barsay v. State of Bombay*, AIR 1961 SC 1762, p. 1776 : 1962 (2) SCR 195.

78. *Dattatraya Moreshwar v. State of Bombay*, AIR 1952 SC 181 : 1952 SCR 612; *State of Bombay v. Purushottam Jog Naik*, AIR 1952 SC 317 : 1952 SCR 674; *Joseph John, P. v. State of Trav-Co.,* AIR 1955 SC 160 : (1955) 1 SCR 1011; *Ghaio Mall & Sons v. State of Delhi*, AIR 1959 SC 65 : 1959 SCR 1424; *State of Rajasthan v. Sripal Jain*, AIR 1963 SC 1323, p. 1326 : (1964) 2 SCR 722; *R. Chitralekha v. State of Mysore*, AIR 1964 SC 1823, p. 1829 : (1964) 6 SCR 238; *Bijoya Lakshmi Cotton Mills Ltd. v. State of W.B.*, AIR 1967 SC 1145 : 1967 (2) SCR 406; *State Govt. Houseless Harijan Employees Association v. State of Karnataka,* AIR 2001 SC 437, p. 447 : (2001) 1 SCC 610. *Crawford Bayley & Co. v. Union of India,* (2006) 6 SCC 25 (para 26) : AIR 2006 SC 2544 (Rules of Business issued under Articles 77 and 166 of the Constitution are not mandatory). But mere passing of a cabinet resolution is not enough till some action is taken in terms of Article 166 for issuance of a Government order: *J.P. Bansal v. State of Rajasthan,* 2003 AIR SCW 1848, p. 1853 : (2003) 5 SCC 134 : AIR 2003 SC 1405. **See further** *Central Bureau of Investigation v. Ravishankar Srivastava,* (2006) 7 SCC 188 : AIR 2006 SC 2872; *M. Balakrishna Reddy v. CBI,* (2008) 4 SCC 409 : AIR 2008 SC 1754 (case law on the question whether Article 166 is mandatory or directory, reviewed).

power will be referable to a jurisdiction which confers validity upon it.[79] The same principle applies when a subordinate legislation such as a bye-law which although within jurisdiction is expressed to be made under a wrong provision.[80] But the principle has no application when the provision to which the exercise of power is sought to be referred contains certain conditions which are not shown to have been satisfied.[81] So a penalty imposed under one provision cannot be supported under another provision when no notice under that provision was issued to the party on whom the penalty is imposed.[82] Further, the principle cannot be used to widen the effect of a notification issued expressly under one provision so as also to relate it under some other provision.[83] Thus an exemption of excise duty by a notification under rule 8(1) of the Central Excise Rules, 1944 cannot be construed to cover exemption from special duty of excise levied under the Finance Act, 1979.[84]

(j) Statute conferring private rights and benefits

When certain requirements are prescribed by a statute as preliminary to the acquisition of a right or benefit conferred by the statute, such prescriptions are mandatory for acquisition of the right or benefit. Thus, if it is desired to have a partnership firm registered under the Income-tax Act, the requirements of the Act and the Rules framed under it must be strictly

---

79. *Balakotiah v. Union of India*, AIR 1958 SC 232, p. 236 : 1958 SCR 1052; *L. Hazarimal Kuthiala v. I.T.O.*, AIR 1961 SC 200, p. 202 : (1961) 1 SCR 892; *Berar Swadeshi Vanaspati v. Municipal Committee, Shegaon*, AIR 1962 SC 420 : (1962) 1 SCR 596; *Gopal Narain v. State of U.P.*, AIR 1964 SC 370, p. 377 : (1964) 4 SCR 869; *Roshan Lal Gautham v. State of U.P.*, AIR 1965 SC 991, p. 994 : (1965) 1 SCR 841, *J.K. Steel Ltd. v. Union of India*, AIR 1970 SC 1173, p. 1188 : (1969) 2 SCR 481; *N.B. Sanjana v. Elphinstone Spinning & Weaving Mills Co. Ltd.*, AIR 1971 SC 2039, p. 2045 : (1971) 1 SCC 337; *P. Radhakrishna Naidu v. Government of Andhra Pradesh*, AIR 1977 SC 854, p. 858 : (1977) 1 SCC 561; *Municipal Corporation, Ahmedabad v. Benttiraben Manilal*, AIR 1983 SC 537, p. 539 : (1983) 2 SCC 422; *Union of India v. Tulsiram Patel*, (1985) 3 SCC 398, p. 501 : AIR 1985 SC 1416; *Union of India v. Khazan Singh*, AIR 1992 SC 1535 : 1993 Supp (1) SCC 583, pp. 585, 586; *State of Karnataka v. Krishnaji Srinivas Kulkarni*, (1994) 2 SCC 558, p. 563; *M.T. Khan v. State of A.P.*, (2004) 2 SCC 267, p. 273 : AIR 2004 SC 2934; *Union of India v. Azadi Bachao Andolan*, AIR 2004 SC 1107, p. 1125 (para 46) : 2003 Supp (1) 220.

80. *Afzal Ullah v. State of U.P.*, AIR 1964 SC 264, p. 268 : 1964 (4) SCR 991; *Hukumchand Mills Ltd. v. State of M.P.*, AIR 1964 SC 1329, p. 1332 : 1964 (6) SCR 857; *Peerless General Finance and Investment Co. Ltd. v. Reserve Bank of India*, AIR 1992 SC 1033, p. 1043 : 1992 (2) SCC 343; *Om Prakash v. State of U.P.*, (2004) 3 SCC 402, p. 409 : AIR 2004 SC 1896.

81. *Amritsar Improvement Trust v. Baldev Inder Singh*, AIR 1972 SC 182, p. 186 (paras 18 and 19) : 1972 (1) SCC 165.

82. *Commissioner of Sales Tax U.P., Lucknow v. Anoop Wines Khuldabad, Allahabad*, AIR 1988 SC 2042, p. 2044 : 1988 Supp SCC 731.

83. *Union of India v. Modi Rubber Ltd.*, (1986) 4 SCC 66, pp. 74-77 : AIR 1985 SC 1992.

84. *Ibid.*

complied with because, by securing registration under the Act, the partners of the firm obtain the benefit of lower rates of assessment, and no tax is directly charged on the income of the firm.[85] And a dealer claiming benefit of a statutory exemption or concession from payment of sales tax on the ground that sales were made to registered dealers or the Government must prove that the sales were to registered dealers or the Government by production of declaration forms as required by the statute; and he is not entitled to the exemption if declaration forms are not produced.[86] Similarly, if a person wants a stage carriage permit, it is necessary for him to make an application in the manner and within the time as prescribed by the Motor Vehicles Act, 1939.[87] If a statute confers a concession or privilege and prescribes a mode of acquiring it, the mode so prescribed must be adopted as even affirmative words in such cases are construed imperative.[88] The principle applies even to procedural statutes and if a notice is required to be served before instituting an action the provision as to notice is construed as mandatory.[89] And if a person wants to exercise his right of appeal he must prefer his appeal in accordance with the statute conferring the right and if the statute requires filing of a certified copy of decree or order appealed against along with the memo of appeal, he must do so otherwise the appeal will become incompetent.[90] Similarly, any requirement as to sanction before

---

85. *Parekh Wadilal v. C.I.T., Nagpur*, AIR 1967 SC 448, p. 449 (para 4) : (1967) 1 SCR 998; *Steel Bros. v. C.I.T.*, AIR 1958 SC 315 : (1958) 33 ITR 1; *SRM Service v. CIT, Hyderabad*, AIR 1973 SC 1445, p. 1448 : 1974 (3) SCC 116. **See also** *Progressive Financers v. Commissioner of Income-tax*, JT 1997 (2) SC 729 : AIR 1997 SC 1021 : (1997) 3 SCC 79.

86. *Kedar Nath Jute Mfg. Co. Ltd. v. Commercial Tax Officer*, AIR 1966 SC 12 : 1965 (3) SCR 626; *Sales Tax Commissioner v. Prabhudayal Premnarain*, AIR 1988 SC 1775 : 1988 Supp SCC 729; *State of Andhra Pradesh v. Hyderabad Asbestos Cement Production Ltd.*, JT 1994(3) SC 456 : AIR 1994 SC 2364 : (1994) 5 SCC 100; *Phool Chand Gupta v. State of Andhra Pradesh*, AIR 1997 SC 914 : 1997 (1) Scale 419 : (1997) 2 SCC 591; *India Agencies (Regd.) Bangalore v. Additional Commissioner of Commercial Taxes*, (2005) 2 SCC 129, p. 141. For a similar case of concessional rate of octroi, **see** *Indian Aluminium Company Ltd. v. Thane Municipal Corporation*, AIR 1992 SC 53, pp. 57, 58 : 1992 Supp (1) SCC 480.

87. *Shrinivasa Reddy v. State of Mysore*, AIR 1960 SC 350 : 1960 (2) SCR 130.

88. *Edwards Ramia Ltd. v. African Woods Ltd.*, (1960) 1 All ER 627, p. 630 (PC). **But see** *Krishna Kumar Mediratta v. Phulchand Agarwala*, AIR 1977 SC 984, pp. 986, 987 : (1977) 2 SCC 5. (In this it has been held that the requirement of deposit of fees along with the application for a prospecting licence under Rule 9(2) of the Mineral Concession Rules, 1960 is directory).

89. **See** cases in notes 24 to 26, p. 408 under title 6(c) 'Use of negative words'.

90. *Jagat Dhish Bhargava v. Jawahar Lal Bhargava*, AIR 1961 SC 832 : 1961 (2) SCR 918; *State of U.P. v. C. Tobit*, AIR 1958 SC 414 : 1958 SCR 1275. But the requirement of filing three copies of record for preferring a Letters' Patent Appeal under the Punjab High Court Rules has been held to be directory; *State of Punjab v. Shamlal Murari*, AIR 1976 SC 1177 : (1977) 1 SCC 719.

initiation of any criminal proceeding has been held to be mandatory.[91] But procedural provisions, which are merely technical and have no special object behind them may be held directory if substantive requirements have been fulfilled.[92]

(k) Enabling words, e.g., 'may', 'it shall be lawful', 'shall have power'. Power coupled with duty

Ordinarily, the words 'May' and 'It shall be lawful' are not words of compulsion. They are enabling words and they only confer capacity, power or authority and imply discretion.[93] "They are both used in a statute to indicate that something may be done which prior to it could not be done".[94] The use of words 'Shall have power' also connotes the same idea.[95]

For instance, the Supreme Court has held that the use of the word 'may' in the Explanation to section 162 of the CrPC makes it clear that it is not every omission or discrepancy that amounts to a material contradiction, and that the word 'may' introduces an element of discretion which has to be exercised by the court to decide whether it is a case of a contradiction, or a material contradiction, which renders the entire evidence of the witness untrustworthy and affects the case of the prosecution materially.[96] Similarly, the Supreme Court relied on the fact that section 14 of the Kerala Abkari Act, 1902, uses the expression 'the Commissioner may', 'with the approval of the Government', and that rule 4 of the Kerala Foreign Liquor (Compounding, Blending and Bottling) Rules, 1975, also uses the expressions 'the Commissioner may', 'if he is satisfied' after making such enquiries as 'he may consider necessary', and 'licence may be issued', to hold that all these expressions confer discretionary powers on the Commissioner as well as the State Government, and that the power is not coupled with duty.[97]

---

91. *Gour Chandra Rout v. Public Prosecutor*, AIR 1963 SC 1198 : 1963 Supp (2) SCR 447. For difference between requirement of a complaint in writing by a prescribed officer and sanction, **see** *Electrical Manufacturing Co. v. D.D. Bhargava*, AIR 1968 SC 247, pp. 249, 250 : 1968 (1) SCR 394.

92. *Mangalore Chemicals & Fertilisers Ltd. v. Deputy Commissioner of Commercial Taxes*, AIR 1992 SC 152, pp. 157, 158 : 1992 (3) JT 482 : 1992 Supp (1) SCC 21.

93. *Madanlal Fakrichand Dudhediya v. S. Changdeo Sugar Mills*, AIR 1962 SC 1543, p. 1557 : 1962 Supp (3) SCR 973; *Chinnamar Kathiam v. Ayyavoo*, AIR 1982 SC 137, p. 140 : 1982 (1) SCC 159.

94. *Ibid.*

95. *Commissioner of Police v. Gordhandas Bhauji*, AIR 1952 SC 16, p. 20 : 1952 SCR 135.

96. *Shyamal Ghosh v. State of West Bengal*, (2012) 7 SCC 646, p. 674.

97. *State of Kerala & Ors. v. Kandath Distilleries*, (2013) 6 SCC 573, p. 584.

The Legislature may also use other form of words to confer discretion. For example, the words 'nothing is this Article shall prevent the State from making any provision for the reservation' in favour of backward class of citizens as used in Article 16(4) of the Constitution have been held to be only enabling not imposing any constitutional duty nor conferring any fundamental right for reservation.[1]

Generally a power conferred on an authority by use of the word 'may' to rule on a particular matter does not confer an exclusive jurisdiction and take away the jurisdiction of some other authority to decide the same matter. Thus the power conferred by section 16 of the Arbitration and Conciliation Act, 1996 on the arbitral tribunal that it 'may rule' on any objection as to existence of an arbitration agreement does not exclude the jurisdiction of the Chief Justice of India or his designate to decide that question, if need be, in a petition under section 11 seeking appointment of arbitrator.[2]

When a capacity or power is given to a public authority, there may be circumstances which couple with the power a duty to exercise it,[3] or the manner in which it may only be exercised.[4] In other words the legal and factual context in which the power is to be exercised may combine the power with an obligation to exercise it even though it is conferred by use of the word 'May'.[5] As stated by COTTON, L.J.: "'May' can never mean must, so long as the English language retains its meaning; but it gives a power and then it may be a question, in what cases, when any authority or body has a power given it by the word 'may', it becomes its duty to exercise that power."[6] As observed by LORD CAIRNS: "There may be something in the nature of the thing empowered to be done, something in the object for which it is to be done, something in the conditions under which it is to

---

1. *Ajit Singh v. State of Punjab,* JT 1999 (9) SC 542, p. 543 : 1999 (7) Scale 395 : (1999) 7 SCC 209.

2. *Wellington Association v. Kirit Mehta,* AIR 2000 SC 1379, p. 1383 : (2000) 4 SCC 272.

3. *Alcock Ashdown and Company v. Chief Revenue Authority*, AIR 1923 PC 138, p. 144; *Chief Controlling Revenue Authority v. Maharashtra Sugar Mills Ltd.*, AIR 1950 SC 218, pp. 220, 221 : 1950 SCR 536; *Commissioner of Police v. Gordhandas, supra*, p. 21, *Bhaiya Punjalal v. Bhagwat Prasad*, AIR 1963 SC 120, p. 127 : (1963) 3 SCR 312; *Ramji Missar v. State of Bihar*, AIR 1963 SC 1088, p. 1092, 1093 : 1963 Supp (2) SCR 745; *State of U.P. v. Jogendra Singh*, AIR 1963 SC 1618, p.1620 : 1964 (2) SCR 197; *Sardar Govind Rao v. State of Madhya Pradesh*, AIR 1965 SC 1222 : 1964 SCN 269 : 1965 MPLJ 566, p. 570 (SC). **See further** *Leach v. The Queen,* (2007) 81 ALJR 598, p. 608 (para 38) (The word 'may' is sometimes used not to confer a discretion but a power to be exercised upon the satisfaction of the matters described in the provision).

4. *Societe De Traction v. Kamani Engineering Co. Ltd.*, AIR 1964 SC 558, p. 562 : 1964 (3) SCR 116.

5. *Official Liquidator v. Dharti Dhan*, AIR 1977 SC 740, p. 744 : (1977) 2 SCC 166.

6. *In re, Nichols v. Baker*, 59 LJ Ch 661, p. 663.

be done, something in the title of the person or persons for whose benefit the power is to be exercised, which may couple the power with a duty, and make it the duty of the person in whom the power is reposed to exercise that power when called upon to do so."[7] It was further pointed out by LORD CAIRNS: "Where a power is deposited with a public officer for the purpose of being used for the benefit of persons specifically pointed out with regard to whom a definition is supplied by the Legislature of the conditions upon which they are entitled to call for its exercise, that power ought to be exercised and the court will require it to be exercised."[8] LORD BLACKBURN stated in the same case: "The enabling words are construed as compulsory whenever the object of the power is to effectuate a legal right."[9] In the words of BEG, J.: "If the conditions in which the power is to be exercised in particular cases are also specified by a statute then, on the fulfilment of those conditions, the power conferred becomes annexed with a duty to exercise it in that manner."[10] Following these principles it was held by the Privy Council interpreting section 51 of the Income-tax Act, 1918, that in case there was a serious point of law to be considered there was a duty on the Chief Revenue Authority to state a case to the High Court.[11] This principle was also applied by the Supreme Court in interpreting section 57 of the Stamp Act, 1899, and it was held thai it imposes a duty on the Chief Controlling Revenue Authority to make a reference to the High Court when an important question of law arises for consideration.[12] And in construing rule 63 of the Central Provinces and Berar Motor Vehicles Rules, 1940 which reads 'the authority by which a permit is renewed, may likewise renew any counter-signature of the permit', the

---

7. *Julius v. Lord Bishop of Oxford*, (1874-80) All ER Rep 43, p. 47 : (1880) 5 AC 214 (HL). **See further** *State (Delhi Administration) v. I.K. Nangia*, AIR 1979 SC 1977, p. 1980 : (1980) 1 SCC 258; *Tara Prasad Singh v. Union of India*, AIR 1980 SC 1682, p. 1698 : (1980) 4 SCC 179; *Ambica Quarry Works v. State of Gujarat*, (1987) 1 SCC 213, p. 218 : AIR 1987 SC 1073; *Superintending Engineer, Public Health v. Kuldeep Singh*, AIR 1997 SC 2133, p. 2137 : (1997) 9 SCC 199.

8. *Ibid*, p. 49, **referred** to in *L. Hirday Narain v. I.T.O. Bareilly*, AIR 1971 SC 33, p. 36 : (1970) 2 SCC 355.

9. *Ibid*, p. 59; **referred** to in *Punjab Sikh Regular Motor Service, Raipur v. R.T.A., Raipur*, AIR 1966 SC 1318 : (1996) 2 SCR 221; *Hirday Narain v. I.T.O. Bareilly, supra*, p. 36; *Ambica Quarry Works v. State of Gujarat, supra*; *Sub Committee of Judicial Accountability v. Union of India*, AIR 1992 SC 320, p. 352 : 1991 (4) SCC 699.

10. *Official Liquidator v. Dharti Dhan*, AIR 1977 SC 740, p. 745 : (1977) 2 SCC 166.

11. *Alcock Ashdown & Company v. Chief Revenue Authority*, AIR 1923 PC 138. **See further** *Jaswant Rai v. Central Board of Direct Taxes and Revenue*, AIR 1998 SC 1891, p. 1894 : (1998) 5 SCC 77 (Power of Commissioner under section 273A of the Income-tax Act 1961 is coupled with a duty).

12. *Chief Controlling Reveune Authority v. Maharashtra Sugar Mills Ltd.*, AIR 1950 SC 218 : 1950 SCR 536; *Banarasidas Ahluwalia v. Chief Controlling Revenue Authority, Delhi*, AIR 1968 SC 497, p. 502 : 1968 (2) SCR 685.

Supreme Court held that 'may' in the context was obligatory: that is to say the exercise of power under this rule depends not upon the discretion of the authority but upon proof of the particular case requiring renewal of the counter-signature.[13] Further in dealing with section 35 of the Income-tax Act, 1922, which provided that the authorities 'may rectify any mistake apparent on the face of the record', the Court held that authorities were bound to exercise the power if conditions for its exercise were shown to exist by a person interested. In holding so, SHAH, J., observed: "Even if the words used in the statute are *prima facie* enabling, the Courts will readily infer a duty to exercise power which is invested in aid of enforcement of a right—public or private—of a citizen."[14] Similarly, a power to comply with natural justice before taking an adverse action against an employee conferred by *prima facie* enabling words will be construed as mandatory.[15] For instance, section 10(5) of the Urban Land (Ceiling and Regulation) Act, 1976, provides that the competent authority 'may', by notice in writing, order a person in possession of land vested in the Government to surrender possession of the same. However, the word 'may' has been understood as 'shall', and the requirement of giving notice was held to be mandatory on the ground that the Legislature could not have intended that a landholder be dispossessed of his property under section 10(6) of the Act for non-compliance of an order under section 10(5), without having received notice of the same.[16]

Another illustration is to be found in the interpretation of section 489 of the Bombay Municipal Corporation Act, 1888. Section 354(1) of the Act provides that the Commissioner may, by written notice, require the owner or occupier of any structure in a ruinous condition to pull down, secure or repair such structure and to prevent all cause of danger therefrom. Section 489 of the Act provides, *inter-alia*, that if an order is made by the Commissioner by written notice, and the order is not complied with, the Commissioner 'may' take such measures or cause such work to be executed as, in his opinion, is necessary for giving due effect to the order. The Supreme Court noted that the primary object of section 354 is to safeguard the public from the danger of being forced to live in such a structure in a ruinous condition. Hence, though a plain reading of section 489 gives an impression that it is only an enabling provision, keeping in view the purpose of its enactment and the setting in which it is placed, the Court held that the Commissioner is duty bound to ensure that the written notice given to the

---

13. *Punjab Sikh Regular Motor Service, Raipur v. R.T.A., Raipur*, AIR 1966 SC 1318 : 1966 (2) SCR 221.
14. *L. Hirday Narain v. I.T.O., Bareilly*, AIR 1971 SC 33, p. 36 : (1970) 2 SCC 355, p. 359.
15. *Wasim Beg v. State of Uttar Pradesh*, AIR 1998 SC 1291, p. 1296 : 1998 (3) SCC 321.
16. *State of Uttar Pradesh v. Hari Ram*, (2013) 4 SCC 280, p. 298.

owner or occupier under section 354(1) is implemented in letter and spirit. The Court further held that the duty cast on the Commissioner is in the nature of a public law obligation and, in an appropriate case, the Court can issue directions for its enforcement.[17]

A power conferred by the Environmental Protection Act, 1986 having regard to its object cannot be treated as power simpliciter, but it is a power coupled with a duty and so it is the duty of the State to make sure that the conditions or directions under the Act are fulfilled.[18]

A Government memorandum providing that in the event of the candidate who is appointed to a statutory post resigning within six months 'the reserved list may be operated' to fill the vacancy where it may not be possible to keep the post vacant till the completion of fresh recruitment, when read along with the relevant statutory provision that the vacancy 'shall be filled up by the Central Government as soon as practicable' was construed to confer a discretion coupled with a duty to appoint the person next in order of merit from the approved reserved list to the post becoming vacant.[19] Power conferred on the State Government to constitute an Advisory Committee under section 3 of the Uttar Pradesh Sheera Niyantran Adhiniyam, 1964 in terms 'may by notification, in the Gazette constitute' was held to be coupled with a duty and it was obligatory on the Government to constitute Advisory Committee.[20]

When permissive words are employed by the Legislature to confer a power on a Court to be exercised in the circumstances pointed out by the statute, it becomes the duty of the Court to exercise that power on proof of those circumstances. As pointed out by JERVIES, C.J.: "When a statute confers an authority to do a judicial act in a certain case, it is imperative on those so authorised to exercise the authority, when the case arises and its exercise is duly applied for by a party interested and having a right to make that application."[21] "The use of permissive words in such cases", said JAMES, L.J. "is the usual courtesy of Legislature in dealing with the judicature".[22] The words 'it shall be lawful' may be used for the purpose of conferring a new jurisdiction which was not lawful for the authority concerned to exercise till then and when a case for the exercise of that

---

17. *Makarand Dattatreya Sugavkar v. Municipal Corporation of Greater Mumbai & Ors.*, (2013) 9 SCC 136, p. 149.
18. *N.D. Jayal v. Union of India*, AIR 2004 SC 867, p. 878 (para 24) : (2004) 9 SCC 362.
19. *A.P. Aggarwal v. Govt. of National Capital Territory of Delhi*, AIR 2000 SC 206, p. 207 : (2000) 1 SCC 600.
20. *Dhampur Sugar Mills Ltd. v. State of U.P.*, (2007) 8 SCC 338 para 52 : AIR 2008 SC 48 para 45.
21. *MacDougall v. Paterson*, (1851) 11 Ch 755, p. 773 : 138 ER 672, p. 679.
22. *Re, Neath and Brecon Ry. Co.*, (1874) LR 9 Ch 263, p. 264.

jurisdiction is made out, it would be the duty of the said authority to grant the relief and not to refuse to exercise its authority merely at its discretion.[23] As observed by AYYANGER, J.: "Though the word 'may' might connote merely an enabling or a permissive power in the sense of the usual phrase 'it shall be lawful', it is also capable of being construed as referring to a compellable duty, particularly when it refers to a power conferred on a court or other judicial authority."[24] It has, therefore, been held that the words 'an order under this Act may be made by any court' as they occur in section 11 of the Probation of Offenders Act, 1958, imposed a duty to pass an order under the Act subject to conditions and limitations imposed by the Act and that a court had no unfettered discretion in refusing to pass an order when an occasion to pass the same arose within the four corners of the Act.[25] Similarly, the words 'the court may pass a decree for eviction', have been construed as not conferring a discretion for refusing to pass a decree where a landlord in a suit has proved the fulfilment of all conditions entitling him to possession, and the court in such cases is bound to pass a decree in his favour in spite of the use of the word 'may'.[26] Further, the words 'the Magistrate may take cognizance of any cognizable offence' in section 190(1)(b) of the Code of Criminal Procedure, 1973, have been construed to mean 'must take cognizance' leaving no discretion to the Magistrate.[27] And so, a rule requiring that 'the court may engage a counsel to defend the person' in a capital sentence case was held to cast an obligatory duty on the court to provide a counsel if the conditions of the rule were satisfied.[28] Similarly, though rule 2-A(i) of the High Court of Karnataka Rules, 1959, provides that the Court 'may' appoint any advocate from a panel to represent an accused in a criminal case if he *inter alia*, has insufficient means, the expression 'may' was interpreted as laying down a mandatory direction to the court to engage advocate for the accused if the conditions in the rule are satisfied.[29]

When an Act conferring the power does not mention the conditions or the circumstances in which the power is to be exercised it will be construed as discretionary and directory. On this principle section 442 of the Companies Act, 1956, which empowers that the court 'may stay or

---

23. *Shelly v. London County Council*, (1948) 2 All ER 898, p. 901 (HL).
24. *Ramji Missar v. State of Bihar*, AIR 1963 SC 1088, p. 1092 : 1963 Supp (2) SCR 745.
25. *Ibid*, p. 1093.
26. *Bhaiya Punjalal v. Bhagvat Prasad*, AIR 1963 SC 120, p. 127 : 1963 (3) SCR 312.
27. *Sub-Divisional Magistrate, Delhi v. Ram Kali (Mst.)*, AIR 1968 SC 1, p. 5. **See further** *Jamatraj Kewalji Govani v. State of Maharashtra*, AIR 1968 SC 178, p. 181 : (1967) 3 SCR 415.
28. *Bashira v. State of U.P.*, AIR 1968 SC 1313 : 1969 (1) SCR 32.
29. *Chaluvegowda & Ors. v. State*, (2012) 13 SCC 538, p. 544.

restrain' a proceeding against a company after the presentation of a winding up petition, has been construed to be discretionary and directory.[30] But even in cases where the conditions or circumstances are not expressly indicated by the Act, a duty may arise to exercise the power conferred if it could be shown that on facts of the case exercise of the power would alone carry out the object of the Act. This is so because judicial power has to be justly and properly exercised.[31]

The word 'may' may also be used in the sense of 'shall' or 'must' by the Legislature while conferring power on a high dignitary.[32] When the context shows that the power is coupled with an obligation, "the word 'may' which denotes discretion should be construed to mean a command".[33] The use of the word 'may' in such cases is "out of deference to the high status of the authority on whom the power and the obligation are intended to be conferred and imposed".[34] It was, therefore, held that the words 'the Government may, in respect of a gazetted Government servant on his own request, refer his case to the Tribunal,' in the context of Rule 4(2) of the U.P. Disciplinary Proceedings (Administrative Tribunal) Rules, 1947, conferred a power coupled with an obligation on the Governor to exercise the power when a request was made by a gazetted Government servant in that behalf and that the Governor had no discretion in the matter.[35] Rule 30 of the Rajasthan Minor Mineral Concession Rules, 1955, which is to the effect that 'a mining lease may be granted for a period of five years unless the applicant himself desires a shorter period', has been construed to confer no discretion on the Government to fix a period less than five years if the applicant did not desire a shorter period. A proviso to the rule dealing with renewal has been similarly construed.[36] Section 5(3) of the Central Provinces and Berar Revocation of Land Revenue Exemptions Act, 1948 provided that 'the State Government may make a grant of money or pension—for suitable maintenance of any family of a descendant from a former ruling Chief'. In construing this provision it was held that except in those cases where there were good grounds for not granting the pension, the Government was bound to make a grant to those who fulfilled the required condition and the word 'may' had to be read as 'must'. It was also held that the

30. *Official Liquidator v. Dharti Dhan*, AIR 1977 SC 740, p. 744 : (1977) 2 SCC 166.
31. *Ibid*, p. 745.
32. *State of U.P. v. Jogendra Singh*, AIR 1963 SC 1618, p. 1620 : 1964 (2) SCR 197.
33. *Ibid; Rangaswami, Textile Commissioner v. Sagar Textile Mills (P.) Ltd.*, AIR 1977 SC 1516, p. 1517 : (1977) 2 SCC 578.
34. *State of U.P. v. Jogendra Singh*, AIR 1963 SC 1618, p. 1620 : 1964 (2) SCR 197.
35. *Ibid.*
36. *State of Rajasthan v. Harishanker Rajendrapal*, AIR 1966 SC 296 : 1965 (3) SCR 402.

Act laid a duty to be performed in a judicial manner.[37] Clause 20 of the Cotton Textiles (Central) Order, 1948 authorised the Textiles Commissioner to issue directions to manufacturers regarding the classes or specifications of cloth or yarn and the maximum and the minimum quantities thereof which they shall or shall not produce 'during such periods as may be specified in the directions'. It was held that the power conferred to issue directions is coupled with the duty to specify the particular period for which the directions shall be operative and directions issued without specifying the period will be *ultra vires*.[38] But, 'may' will not be construed as mandatory if such a construction would defeat the purpose of the Act or would lead to unjust results.[39] Further, if the word 'may' was substituted in place of 'shall' during the Bill's progress in Parliament, it may not be possible to construe 'may' as 'shall'.[40]

The principle that the word 'may' is sometimes used in the sense of shall or must, while conferring power on a high dignitory out of deference to him, has also been applied when power is conferred on Parliament to enact a law. Interpreting Article 124(5) of the Constitution, which provides that Parliament may by law regulate the procedure for the presentation of an address and for the investigation and proof of the misbehaviour or incapacity of a Judge, it has been held, that it is an enabling provision for 'the procedure for presentation of an address' but it is a compulsive provision for providing the procedure 'for the investigation and proof of the misbehaviour or incapacity of a Judge'.[41]

(l) Words conveying discretion; as he deems fit; think necessary; consider necessary

Where a statute provides for the grounds on which a person is entitled to a certain relief and confers power on a Tribunal to pass orders 'as it deems fit', the exercise of the power to grant the relief is not dependent upon the discretion of the Tribunal.[42] In a case where the tenancy had terminated

---

37. *Sardar Govindrao v. State of M.P.*, AIR 1965 SC 1222 : 1965 (1) SCR 678, **distinguished** in *Sahodara Devi v. Govt. of India*, AIR 1971 SC 1599 : 1972 (3) SCC 156. (Case dealing with Rule 27 of the Cantonment Land Administration Rules, 1937).

38. *Rangaswami, Textile Commissioner v. Sagar Textile Mills (P) Ltd.*, AIR 1977 SC 1516 : (1977) 2 SCC 578.

39. *Chief Settlement Commissioner v. Ram Singh*, (1987) 1 SCC 612, p. 614 : AIR 1987 SC 1834.

40. *CIT v. P.K. Noorjahan*, AIR 1999 SC 1600, p. 1601 : (1997) 11 SCC 198.

41. *Sub Committee of Judicial Accountability v. Union of India*, AIR 1992 SC 320, p. 352 : 1991 (4) SCC 699.

42. *R. v. Boteler*, (1864) 33 LJMC 101, p. 103; **referred** to in *Raja Ram Mahadeo Paranjype v. Aba Maruti Mali*, AIR 1962 SC 753, p. 757 : 1962 Supp (1) SCR 739.

according to the provisions of the statute and the landlord had applied for an order for possession to the *Mamlatdar* who is required by the Act 'to pass order thereon as he deems fit', the Supreme Court held that the *Mamlatdar* had no discretion to refuse the relief on equitable considerations not covered by the statute. SARKAR, J., observed: "Section 29(3) of the Bombay Tenancy and Agricultural Lands Act, 1948 only confers power to make an order in terms of the statute, an order which would give effect to a right which the Act has elsewhere conferred. The words 'as he deems fit' do not bestow a power to make any order on consideration *de hors* the statute which the authorities consider best according to their notions of justice."[43] The wide discretion conferred by these words has to be exercised 'fairly and *bona fide*' keeping in view the purpose for which it is conferred.[44] Similarly, the words 'shall take such action thereon as it may think fit' do not give a discretion to take action outside the statute.[45] When a power is conferred on an appellate or revisional Tribunal in similar words, the appellate or the revisional Tribunal cannot pass any and every order but can only pass such orders which the subordinate authority could have passed in that particular case.[46]

The words 'think necessary' or 'consider necessary' have also been held to confer a discretion but not an unfettered discretion.[47]

---

43. *Raja Ram Mahadeo Paranjype v. Aba Maruti Mali, supra*, p. 758.

44. *Chariant International Ltd. v. Securities and Exchange Board of India*, (2004) 8 SCC 524, p. 539 : AIR 2004 SC 4236.

45. *Akshaibar Lal (Dr.) v. Vice-Chancellor, BHU*, AIR 1961 SC 619, p. 626 : 1961 (3) SCR 386.

46. *A. St. Arunachalam Pillia v. Southern Roadways Ltd.*, AIR 1960 SC 1191, p. 1194 : 1960 (3) SCR 764; *Abdul Mateen v. Ram Kailash Pandey*, AIR 1965 SC 64, p. 69 : (1963) 3 SCR 523 (Both these cases deal with section 64, Andhra Pradesh Motor Vehicles Act, 1939 which empowers the revising authority to 'pass such order in relation to the case as it deems fit'). **See further** *R. v. Minister of Transport*, (1933) All ER Rep 604, p. 608 (CA), (LORD RUSSEL), p. 610, (ROMER, L.J.), (consideration of power of Minister of Transport while dealing with an appeal under section 81, Road Traffic Act, 1930 (20 and 21 Geo. 5, c. 43) 'to make such order as he thinks fit'); *C.I.T. v. Kanpur Coal Syndicate*, AIR 1965 SC 325, p. 328 : (1964) 8 SCR 85 (construction of sections 33, 34, Income-tax Act, 1922); *Jagat Bahadur v. State of M.P.*, AIR 1966 SC 945 : (1966) 2 SCR 822 (in appeal against acquittal, the High Court can pass only such sentence which the trial Court could have passed); *Joginder Singh v. Dy. Custodian General of Evacuee Property*, AIR 1967 SC 145 : 1962 (2) SCR 738. **But see** *J.S. Jadhav v. Mustafa Hazi Mohammad*, AIR 1993 SC 1535 : (1993) 2 SCC 562, where without referring to the cases noted above, section 38 of the Advocates Act 1961 which uses similar words was very widely construed and a decree was passed which the original disciplinary authority could not have passed.

47. *George v. Devan County Council*, (1988) 3 All ER 1002, p. 1006 (HL).

Even where there is not much indication in the Act of the ground upon which discretion is to be exercised it does not mean that its exercise is dependent upon mere fancy of the Court or Tribunal or Authority concerned. It must be exercised in the words of LORD HALSBURY, "according to the rules of reason and justice, not according to private opinion; according to law and not humour; it is to be not arbitrary, vague and fanciful, but legal and regular".[48] As stated by ROBSON: "Within certain limits, the individual who exercises discretion is quite free but if he ventures outside those frontiers his power ends, if he takes into consideration matters 'fantastic and foreign to subject-matter', if he decides the matter, according 'to his will and private affections', then he is regarded as having failed to exercise any discretion at all."[49]

(m) 'Have regard to'

The words 'Have regard to' when occurring in a statute should be construed in relation to the context and the subject-matter.[50] Ordinarily, these words are understood as 'a guide and not a fetter'.[51] They only oblige the authority on whom the power is conferred 'to consider as relevant data material to which it must have regard'.[52] Therefore, when some statutory

---

48. *Sharpe v. Wakefield*, (1886-90) All ER Rep 651, p. 53 : 1891 AC 173 (HL); *Hindusthan Tin Works Pvt. Ltd. v. Employees of Hindusthan Tin Works Pvt. Ltd.*, AIR 1979 SC 75, p. 78 : (1979) 2 SCC 80; *Sant Raj v. O.P. Singla*, (1985) 2 SCC 349, p. 352 : AIR 1985 SC 617; *Uma Devi Nambiar v. T.C. Sidhan*, (2004) 2 SCC 321, p. 336 : AIR 2004 SC 1772, p. 1781; *National Insurance Co. Ltd. v. Keshav Bahadur*, (2004) 2 SCC 370, p. 375 : AIR 2004 SC 1581; *Union of India v. Kuldip Singh*, AIR 2004 SC 827, p. 832 : (2004) 2 SCC 590; *Nandkishore Ganesh Joshi v. Commr. Municipal Corporation, Kalyan*, AIR 2005 SC 34, p. 37 (para 16). In a Government of Laws there is nothing like unfettered discretion immune from judicial reviewability; *Khudiram v. State of W.B.*, AIR 1975 SC 550, p. 558 : (1975) 2 SCC 81; *Manager, Government Branch Press v. D.B. Belliappa*, AIR 1979 SC 429, p. 434 : (1979) 1 SCC 477; *In re, Special Courts Bill*, AIR 1979 SC 478, p. 519 : (1979) 1 SCC 380; *Kumari Shrilekha Vidyarthi v. State of U.P.*, AIR 1991 SC 537, p. 554 : 1990 Supp (1) SCR 625. **See further** text and note 37, p. 481.

49. ROBSON: 'Justice and Administrative Law', 3rd Edn., p. 407. **See** *D.S. Chellammal Anni (Smt.) v. Masanan Samban*, AIR 1965 SC 498, p. 502 (para 10) : 1964 (7) SCR 197; *Gudi Kanti Narsimhulu v. Public Prosecutor*, AIR 1978 SC 429, pp. 432, 433 : (1978) 1 SCC 577; *Babu Singh v. State of U.P.*, AIR 1978 SC 527, p. 529 : (1978) 1 SCC 579. **See** cases in note 13, p. 442.

50. *Ryots of Garabandho v. Zamindar of Parlakimedi*, AIR 1943 PC 164, p. 180; *Shri Sitaram Sugar Co. Ltd. v. Union of India*, AIR 1990 SC 1277, p. 1290 : 1990 (1) SCR 909.

51. *Perry v. Wright*, (1908) 1 KB 441, p. 458 (CA); *State of Karnataka v. Ranganath Reddy*, AIR 1978 SC 215, p. 227 : (1977) 4 SCC 471; *Shri Sitaram Sugar Co. Ltd. v. Union of India*, AIR 1990 SC 1277, pp. 1290, 1291 : (1990) 3 SCC 223.

52. *Saraswati Industrial Syndicate Ltd. v. Union of India*, AIR 1975 SC 460, p. 462 : (1974) 2 SCC 630; *State of U.P. v. Renusagar Power Co.*, AIR 1988 SC 1737 : (1988) 4 SCC 59; *Sitaram Sugar Co. Ltd. v. Union of India*, AIR 1990 SC 1277, p. 1291 : 1990 (3) SCC 223.

power is to be exercised 'having regard to' certain specified provisions, it only means that those matters must be taken into consideration. But the statutory authority is not strictly bound by such provisions even if any of such provisions is worded in a negative form, and an exercise of the power does not become invalid or in excess of jurisdiction if those provisions are not strictly followed.[53] A grievance that due regard was not paid to such provisions may not give rise to any justiciable dispute.[54] Section 6(1)(e) of the Karnataka Contract Carriages (Acquisition) Act, 1976, empowers the arbitrator to determine by his award the amount of compensation which appears to him to be just and reasonable. In making the award the arbitrator is required to 'have regard to' the circumstances of each case and the provisions of the Schedule which provide for principles for determination of the amount of compensation. In interpreting the section, the Supreme Court held that the arbitrator is not obliged to fix the amount of compensation as specified in the Schedule and that he has to fix the amount which appears to him to be just and reasonable on the totality of circumstances keeping primarily in mind the amount mentioned in the Schedule.[55] Section 3(4) of the Uttar Pradesh Electricity Duty Act, 1952 provides that 'the State Government may in public interest having regard to the prevailing charges for supply of energy in any area, the generating capacity of any plant, the need to promote industrial production generally or any specific class thereof and other relevant factors either fix different rates of electricity duty in relation to different classes of consumption of energy or allow any exemption from payment thereof.' In construing this section the Supreme Court held that the expression 'having regard to' did not mean that it was a mandatory duty to consider the factors mentioned in the section and all that the section required was that these factors should be borne in mind but they were subordinated to the need of public interest.[56] Similar view was taken of section 3C of the Essential Commodities Act, 1955 which provides for price fixation of levy sugar having regard to certain matters and it was held that the words 'having regard to' are not strictly

---

53. *Ryots of Garabandho v. Zamindar of Parlakimedi*, AIR 1943 PC 164, p. 180; *Mysore State Electricity Board v. Bangalore Woollen, Cotton & Silk Mills*, AIR 1963 SC 1128, p. 1136 : 1963 Supp (2) SCR 127; *Saraswati Industrial Syndicate Ltd. v. Union of India*, AIR 1975 SC 460, p. 462 : (1974) 2 SCC 630; *State of U.P. v. Renusagar Power Co.*, AIR 1988 SC 1737, p. 1762 : (1988) 4 SCC 59; *Shri Sitaram Sugar Co. Ltd. v. Union of India*, AIR 1990 SC 1277, p. 1290 : (1990) 3 SCC 223. **See further** *Karam Singh Sobti v. Pratap Chand*, AIR 1964 SC 1305, p. 1310 : (1964) 4 SCR 647; *May v. City of London Real Property*, (1982) 1 All ER 660, p. 670 (HL).

54. *Mysore State Electricity Board v. Bangalore Woollen, Cotton & Silk Mills*, AIR 1963 SC 1128, p. 1136 : 1963 Supp (2) SCR 127.

55. *State of Karnataka v. Rangnatha Reddy*, AIR 1978 SC 215, p. 227 : (1977) 4 SCC 471.

56. *State of U.P. v. Renusagar Power Co.*, AIR 1988 SC 1737, p. 1762 : 1988 (4) SCC 59.

mandatory but in essence directory and if the enumerated matters have been generally considered the court will not strictly scrutinize the extent to which these matters and other matters have been taken into account.[57] But as the words 'have regard to' have to be construed according to the context and subject-matter, they may in a particular context have a compelling or mandatory effect.[58] Further, the words 'having regard to' certain enumerated matters do not mean 'having regard only to' those matters and, therefore, consideration of other relevant matters is not excluded.[59] When a Court is enjoined to 'have regard to' certain provisions in the trial of a proceeding and no regard is paid to them, the trial will not be 'in accordance with law' and such an error will be liable to correction in appeal or revision.[60]

7. CONJUNCTIVE AND DISJUNCTIVE WORDS 'OR' AND 'AND'

The word 'or' is normally disjunctive and 'and' is normally conjunctive[61] but at times they are read as *vice versa* to give effect to the manifest intention of the Legislature as disclosed from the context.[62] As stated by SCRUTTON, L.J.: "You do sometimes read 'or' as 'and' in a statute. But you

---

57. *Sitaram Sugar Co. Ltd. v. Union of India*, AIR 1990 SC 1277, pp. 1291, 1292 : (1990) 3 SCC 223. **See further** *Shri Malaprabha Co-op. Sugar Factory Ltd. v. Union of India*, AIR 1994 SC 1311, p. 1322 : 1994 (1) SCC 648. **But see** *Mahalakshmi Sugar Mills Co. Ltd. v. Union of India*, AIR 2009 SC 792 para 46 : (2008) 6 JT 177 where it has been said: "Where a price is determined without applying the principles underlying the factors enumerated in section 3(3-C) of the Act the superior courts can issue requisite direction".

58. *Union of India v. Komalabai*, AIR 1968 SC 377, pp. 382, 383 : 1968 (1) SCR 463.

59. *CIT v. Gangadhar Banerjee & Co. (P) Ltd.*, AIR 1965 SC 1977 : (1965) 3 SCR 439; *Shri Sitaram Sugar Co. Ltd. v. Union of India*, AIR 1990 SC 1277, p. 1290 : 1990 (3) SCC 223.

60. *V.K. Verma v. Radhey Shyam*, AIR 1964 SC 1317, p. 1320 : 66 Punj LR 990. **See further** section 47(a), Motor Vehicles Act, 1939 which required transport authorities in considering applications for stage carriage permits to 'have regard to' the matters specified in that section; and **see** *K.M. Shanmugam v. S.R.V.S. (P) Ltd.*, AIR 1963 SC 1626 : (1964) 1 SCR 809; *Syed Yakoob v. K.S. Radhakrishan*, AIR 1964 SC 477 : (1964) 5 SCR 64; *Patiala Bus (Sirhind) Pvt. Ltd. v. State Transport Appellate Tribunal, Punjab*, AIR 1974 SC 1174 : (1974) 2 SCC 215.

61. *Hyderabad Asbestos Cement Product v. Union of India*, JT 1999 (9) SC 505, p. 510 : 2000 (1) SCC 426 : AIR 2000 SC 314 'or' in its natural sense denotes an 'alternative' and is not read as 'substitutive': *Shri Jeyaram Education Trust v. A.G. Syed-Mohideen*, (2010) 2 SCC 513 para 12 : AIR 2010 SC 671.

62. *Ishwar Singh Bindra v. State of U.P.*, AIR 1968 SC 1450, p. 1454 : (1969) 1 SCR 219; *Municipal Corporation of Delhi v. Tek Chand Bhatia*, AIR 1980 SC 360, p. 363 : (1980) 1 SCC 158; *R.S. Nayak v. A.R. Antulay*, (1984) 2 SCC 183, pp. 224, 225 : AIR 1984 SC 684; *M. Satyanarayana v. State of Karnataka*, (1986) 2 SCC 512, p. 515 : AIR 1986 SC 1162.

do not do it unless you are obliged because 'or' does not generally mean 'and' and 'and' does not generally mean 'or'.[63] And as pointed out by LORD HALSBURY the reading of 'or' as 'and' is not to be resorted to, "unless some other part of the same statute or the clear intention of it requires that to be done."[64] Where provision is clear and unambiguous the word 'or' cannot be read as 'and' by applying the principle of reading down.[65]

For instance, section 52(f) of the Army Act, 1950, provides that any person subject to the Act, who 'does any other thing with intent to defraud, *or* to cause wrongful gain to one person or wrongful loss to another person', commits an offence in respect of property. The Supreme Court held that the two parts of section 52(f) are disjunctive, which can be seen from the use of a comma and the word 'or' between the two parts of the clause, and that if the Legislature had intended both the parts to be read together, it would have used the word 'and'. Hence, it was held that it is possible to charge someone under section 52(f) only for acting with 'intent to defraud', and it is not necessary to refer to the second part of the clause *viz.* causing wrongful gain or wrongful loss, in the charge.[66]

However, if the literal reading of the words produces an unintelligible or absurd result 'and' may be read for 'or' and 'or' for 'and' even though the result of so modifying the words is less favourable to the subject provided that the intention of the Legislature is otherwise quite clear.[67] Conversely if reading of 'and' as 'or' produces grammatical distortion and makes no sense of the portion following 'and', 'or' cannot be read in place of 'and'.[68] The alternatives joined by 'or' need not always be mutually exclusive.[69]

It is also not unusual to find use of pairs of words as a composite class. An example of this nature is found in section 22(1) of the Common Regulation Act, 1965 which uses the expression 'sports and pastimes' as a

---

63. *Green v. Premier Glynrhonwy Slate Co.*, (1928) 1 KB 561, p. 568; *Nasiruddin v. State Transport Appellate Tribunal*, AIR 1976 SC 331, p. 338 : (1975) 2 SCC 671; *Municipal Corporation of Delhi v. Tek Chand Bhatia, supra*; *State (Delhi Administration) v. Puran Mal*, (1985) 2 SCC 589 : AIR 1985 SC 741.

64. *Mersey Docks and Harbour Board v. Henderson Bros.*, (1888) 13 AC 595, p. 603 : 58 LJ QB 152 (HL). **See further** *Puran Singh v. State of M.P.*, AIR 1965 SC 1583, p. 1584, (para 5) : (1965) 2 SCR 853; *Municipal Corporation of Delhi v. Tek Chand Bhatia, supra*; *Competition Commission v. Steel Authority of India Ltd.*, (2010) 10 SCC 744 para 44 : (2010) 10 JT 26.

65. *Union of India v. Ind-Swift Laboratories Ltd.*, (2011) 4 SCC 635 (para 18) : (2011) 2 JT 352.

66. *Union of India & Ors. v. Rabinder Singh*, (2012) 12 SCC 787, p. 795.

67. *A.G. v. Beauchamp*, (1920) 1 KB 650; *R. v. Oakes*, (1959) 2 All ER 92.

68. *Sahney Steel & Press Works Ltd., Hyderabad v. Commissioner of Income-tax, Andhra Pradesh*, JT (1997) 8 SC 173, p. 188 : 1997 (7) SCC 764.

69. *J. Jayalalitha v. Union of India*, AIR 1999 SC 1912, p. 1919 : (1999) 5 SCC 138.

composite class. In interpreting this expression LORD HOFFMAN said: "As a matter of language I think that 'sports and pastimes' is not two classes of activities but a single composite class which uses two words in order to avoid arguments over whether an activity is a sport or pastime. The law constantly uses pairs of words in this way. As long as the activity can properly be called a sport or a pastime, it falls within the composite class."[70]

In section 2(1)(d)(i) of the Bombay Lotteries and Prize Competition Control and Tax Act, 1948, (as amended by Act 30 of 1952) the Supreme Court read 'or' as 'and' to give effect to "the clear intention of the Legislature as expressed in the Act read as a whole".[71] The words 'owner or master' as they occur in section 1(2) of the Oil in Navigable Waters Act, 1955 were construed by the House of Lords to mean 'owner and master' making both of them guilty of the offence under that section as reading of 'or' as 'or' would have produced an absurd result of leaving it to the Executive to select either the owner or master for being prosecuted without the Act giving any guidance for the selection. Such a result would have also been against the constitutional practice.[72] Similarly in section 42(2) of the Income-tax Act, 1922 the result produced by reading 'or' as 'or' "could not have been intended" and the word 'or' was read in the context as meaning 'and'.[73] In section 11 of the Suits Valuation Act, 1887, clauses (a) and (b) of sub-section (1) although separated by the word 'or' have been read conjunctively as that is the obvious intention disclosed by sub-section (2).[74] The expression 'established or incorporated' used in sections 2(f), 22 and 23 of the University Grants Commission Act, 1956 was read as 'established and incorporated' having regard to the constitutional scheme and in order to ensure that the Act is able to achieve its objective and the UGC is able to perform its duties and responsibilities.[75] Speaking generally, a distinction may be made between positive and negative conditions prescribed by a statute for acquiring a right or benefit. Positive conditions separated by 'or' are

70. *R. v. Oxfordshire County Council,* (1999) 3 All ER 385, p. 396 (HL).

71. *State of Bombay v. RMD Chamarbaugwala,* AIR 1957 SC 699, p. 709 : 1957 SCR 1002.

72. *Federal Steam Navigation Co. Ltd. v. Department of Trade and Industry,* (1974) 2 All ER 97 (HL).

73. *Mazagaon Dock Ltd. v. CIT & EPT,* AIR 1958 SC 861 : 1959 SCR 848.

74. *Kiran Singh v. Chaman Paswan,* AIR 1954 SC 340, p. 345 : 1955 (1) SCR 117. **See further** *Tilkayat Shri Govindlalji v. State of Rajasthan,* AIR 1963 SC 1638, p. 1652 (para 39) : (1964) 1 SCR 561; *Gopinder Singh v. Forest Department of Himachal Pradesh,* AIR 1991 SC 433, pp. 434, 435 : 1990 Supp SCC 272 ('or' read as 'and' to avoid absurd result).

75. *Prof. Yashpal v. State of Chattisgarh,* AIR 2005 SC 2026 (para 40) : (2005) 5 SCC 420.

read in the alternative[76] but negative conditions connected by 'or' are construed as cumulative and 'or' is read as 'nor' or 'and'.[77]

Section 3 of the Prevention of Corruption Act, 1988 empowers the Government to appoint as many special judges as may be necessary for such area or areas *or* for such case or group of cases, as may be specified in the notification. Construing the italised 'or' it was held that it would mean that the Government has the power to do either or both the things, *i.e.,* the Government may, even for an area for which a special judge has been appointed, appoint a special judge for a case or group of cases.[78] The case illustrates that the alternatives joined by 'or' need not always be mutually exclusive.

In section 7 of the Official Secrets Act, 1920(UK), which reads: 'Any person who attempts to commit any offence under the principal Act or this Act, or solicits or incites or endeavours to persuade another person to commit an offence, or aids or abets *and* does any act preparatory to the commission of an offence', the word 'and' printed in italics was read as 'or' for by reading 'and' as 'and' the result produced was unintelligible and absurd and against the clear intention of the Legislature.[79] Section 3(b)(i) of the Drugs Act, 1940, (before its amendment in 1962) defined drug as follows: 'All medicines for internal or external use of human beings or animals and all substances intended to be used for or in the diagnosis, treatment, mitigation or prevention of disease in human beings or animals other than medicines *and* substances exclusively used or prepared for use in accordance with the Ayurvedic or Unani systems of medicine'. The italised, word 'and' in this definition was read disjunctively as the context showed that it was the clear intention of the Legislature.[80]

---

76. *Star Co. Ltd. v. Commr. of Income-tax,* AIR 1970 SC 1559 : (1970) 3 SCC 864.

77. *Patel Chunibhai Dajibha v. Narayanrao,* AIR 1965 SC 1457, p. 1465 : 1965 (2) SCR 328; *Punjab Produce & Trading Co. v. C.I.T., West Bengal,* AIR 1971 SC 2471, pp. 2473, 2474 : (1971) 2 SCC 540; *Brown & Co. v. Harrison,* (1927) All ER Rep 195, pp. 203, 204 (CA).

78. *J. Jayalalitha v. Union of India,* AIR 1999 SC 1912, p. 1919 : (1999) 5 SCC 138.

79. *R. v. Oakes,* (1959) 2 All ER 92.

80. *Ishwar Singh Bindra v. State of U.P.,* AIR 1968 SC 1450, p. 1454 : 1969 (1) SCR 219. For another example, **see** *Joint Director of Mines Safety v. Tandur and Nayandgi Stone Quarries (P) Ltd.,* (1987) 3 SCC 208, p. 211 : AIR 1986 SC 1253; *Samee Khan v. Bindu Khan,* AIR 1998 SC 2765, p. 2769 : (1998) 7 SCC 59 ('and may also' in Order 39 Rule 2A CPC construed as 'or may likewise'); *Gujrat Urja Vikas Nigam Ltd. v. Essar Power Ltd.,* (2008) 4 SCC 755 paras 26, 27 : AIR 2008 SC 1921 [The italicised 'and' in Section 86(1) of the Electricity Act, 2003 which reads 'adjudicate upon the disputes between the licencees and generating companies and refer any dispute for adjudication' was read as or for otherwise reading of and as and would have produced anomalous situations].

Another example is found in the interpretation of the Maharishi Mahesh Yogi Vedic Vishwavidyalaya Adhiniyam, 1955. The Preamble to the Act states that it is to provide for education 'and' prosecution of research in Vedic learnings and practices and to provide for matters connected therewith or incidental thereto. Section 4(i) of the Act provides that the object of the Adhiniyam is to provide for instruction in all branches of Vedic learning and practices 'and' the promotion and development of the study of Sanskrit 'and' to make provision for research and for the advancement and dissemination of knowledge. The Supreme Court held that, considering the context in which the expression 'and' has been used in the Preamble and section 4(i), it has to be read disjunctively, as giving a restrictive or narrow interpretation to the provision would go against the basic tenets of education and create a serious restraint on the University in imparting education. Therefore, merely because a specific reference has been made to prosecution of research in Vedic learnings, the imparting of education in the University cannot be restricted to that subject alone.[81]

However, if the conjunctive sense of the word 'and' also subserves the object of the provision there can be no doubt that 'and' cannot be construed as 'or'. Hence, the words 'arms and ammunition' in section 5 of the Terrorist and Disruptive Activities (Prevention) Act, 1987, were read conjunctively, to hold that only a person in possession of both, a firearm and the ammunition therefor, is punishable thereunder.[82] However, a Constitution Bench of the Supreme Court overruled the aforementioned decision on the ground that the object of the Act is to prohibit unauthorised possession of forbidden arms and ammunition, which would be easily frustrated by one person carrying a forbidden arm, and his accomplice carrying its ammunition, so that neither would be covered by section 5. In light thereof, it was held that the term 'and' in the expression 'arms and ammunition' in section 5 of the Act is to be read disjunctively, and not conjunctively.[83]

8. CONSTRUCTION OF GENERAL WORDS

(a) General

The normal rule is that general words in a statute must receive a general construction unless there is something in the Act itself such as the subject-matter with which the Act is dealing or the context in which the said words

---

81. *Maharishi Mahesh Yogi Vedic Vishwavidayala v. State of Madhya Pradesh & Ors.*, (2013) 15 SCC 677, pp. 710 to 720.

82. *Paras Ram v. State of Haryana*, AIR 1993 SC 1212, p. 1214 : 1992 (4) SCC 662.

83. *Sanjay Dutt v. State*, (1994) 5 SCC 410, pp. 437, 438, **followed in** *Balbir Singh v. State*, (1996) 11 SCC 139.

are used to show the intention of the Legislature that they must be given a restrictive meaning.[84] Their import to have wider effect cannot be cut down by arbitrary addition or retrenchment in language.[85] Since general words have ordinarily a general meaning, the first task in construing such words, as in construing any word, is to give the words their plain and ordinary meaning and then to see whether the context or some principle of construction requires that some qualified meaning should be placed on those words.[86]

Paragraph 16 of Schedule I (Part 4) of the Acquisition of Land (Authorisation Procedure) Act, 1946 which provides that a compulsory purchase order shall not be questioned 'in any legal proceeding whatsoever', was construed by the House of Lords as prohibiting any attack to the order including one on the ground that the order was made in bad faith.[87] LORD RADCLIFFE in that case said: "It is quite true, as is said, that these are merely general words; but then, unless there is some compelling reason to the contrary, I should be inclined to regard general words as the most apt to produce a corresponding general result."[88] VISCOUNT SIMONDS in the same case observed: "There is, in fact, no justification for the introduction of limiting words such as 'if made in good faith', and there is the less reason for doing so when those words would have the effect of depriving the express words 'in any legal proceedings whatsoever' of their full meaning and content."[89] Similarly, the Supreme Court while construing the words 'any connection whatever' refused to limit them to direct connections for the restricted construction would not have given full meaning to the words 'any' and 'whatever'.[90] On the same principle the words 'coal including coke in all its form' were construed to include petroleum coke. A restricted

---

84. *Beckford v. Wade*, (1805) 34 ER 34, p. 35 (PC); *Phillips v. Poland*, (1866) LR 1 CP 204, p. 207.

85. *Beckford v. Wade, supra*, p. 35; *Liverpool Justices*, (1883) 11 QBD 638, p. 649; *Smith v. East Elloe Rural District Council*, (1956) 1 All ER 855, p. 870 : 1956 AC 736 (HL); *Felix v. Thomas*, (1966) 3 All ER 21, p. 27 (PC).

86. *Gardiner v. Admiralty Commrs.*, (1964) 2 All ER 93, p. 97 (HL) (LORD UPJOHN); *A.G. for Ontario v. Mercer*, (1883) 8 AC 767, p. 778 : 58 LJ PC 54 : 60 LT 191 (PC). **See** for example *H.K. Choudhury v. Issardas*, AIR 1965 SC 1647, p. 1651 (paras 13 and 14) : 1965 (3) SCR 78; (words "claims to properties—in West Pakistan" were not construed to exclude claims in respect of agricultural lands). **Cf.** case in note 58, p. 603, of Chapter 6, where 'property' was construed to exclude 'agricultural lands'.

87. *Smith v. East Elloe Rural District Council*, (1956) 1 All ER 855 (HL).

88. *Ibid*, p. 870.

89. *Ibid*, p. 859. This case has not been accepted by the Supreme Court in India, **see** text and note 73, p. 793.

90. *V.D. Jhingan v. State of U.P.*, AIR 1966 SC 1762 : 1966 (3) SCR 736.

meaning that these words were limited to coke derived from coal would have given no weight to the generality of the words 'in all its form'.[91]

In a case relating to section 26 of the Factories Act, 1937 which enjoins occupiers of a factory to provide safe means of access to 'every place' at which any person has at any time to work, the House of Lords held that a point on a vessel, which was being repaired in a dockyard, where a workman had to work was within the words 'every place' as occurring in the section.[92] It was argued in this case that section 26 was to be found in fasciculus of sections dealing with a safety provision which were restricted to plant and premises of the factory, and therefore, the words 'every place' in section 26 should also be restricted to plant and premises of the factory thereby excluding any object which came for repairs in the factory. This argument was rejected and in that connection LORD GUEST observed: "There is no principle which would compel a Court to restrict general words to be found in one section by a limitation to be found in other surrounding sections dealing with different matters."[93] Similarly the expression 'every order' in section 7 of the Bombay Government Premises (Eviction) Act, 1956 which provides for an appeal against 'every order' of the competent authority was construed to confer a right of appeal to the Government if the order be against the Government and the expression was not held restricted to orders in favour of the Government appealable by the alleged unauthorised occupier.[94]

It is, however, quite often that the object or the subject-matter or the collocation or speaking briefly the context has the effect of restricting the normal wide meaning of general words, "for words and particularly general words cannot be read in isolation; their colour and content are derived from their context".[95] "It is a recognised principle of construction", observed KAPUR, J., "that general words and phrases, however wide and

---

91. *India Carbon Ltd. v. Superintendent of Taxes, Gauhati*, AIR 1972 SC 154 : (1971) 3 SCC 612. **See further** *State of Bihar v. Hydrocarbons Co. Ltd.*, JT 1994 (6) SC 118 : AIR 1995 SC 991 : 1994 Supp (3) SCC 621. [Calcined Petroleum Coke (CPC) manufactured out of Raw Petroleum Coke (RPC) is not taken out of the entry 'coke in all its forms' and the fact that CPC and RPC are different commodities is of little consequence.]

92. *Gardiner v. Admiralty Commrs.*, (1964) 2 All ER 93 (HL).

93. *Ibid*, p. 96.

94. *State of Maharashtra v. Marwanjee P. Desai*, AIR 2002 SC 456, p. 462 : (2002) 2 SCC 318.

95. *A.G. v. HRH Prince Ernest Augustus*, (1957) 1 All ER 49, p. 53 : 1957 AC 436 (HL); *Maunsel v. Olins*, (1975) 1 All ER 16, pp. 21, 22 (HL); *Union of India v. Sankalchand*, AIR 1977 SC 2328, p. 2341 : (1977) 4 SCC 193; *Utkal Contractors and Joinery Pvt. Ltd. v. State of Orissa*, (1987) 3 SCC 279, p. 290 : AIR 1987 SC 1454.

comprehensive they may be, in their literal sense must usually be construed as being limited to the actual object of the Act".[1] It may in the same context be said that it is a sound rule of construction to confine the general provisions of a statute to the statute itself.[2] It has already been seen that the application of the rule in *Heydon's* case[3] in construing ambiguous provisions of a statute may have the effect of limiting general words in such provisions to the evil or mischief which the statute was intended to remedy. Similarly, the application of the rule of harmonious construction has the effect of restricting general provisions to avoid conflict with specific provisions of the same statute.[4]

"One of the safest guides to the construction of sweeping general words which it is difficult to apply in their full literal sense", stated the Privy Council, "is to examine other words of like import in the same instrument and to see what limitations can be placed on them".[5] In section 14(1) of the Factories Act, 1937(UK) which provides that 'every dangerous part of any machinery, other than prime movers and transmission machinery, shall be securely fenced', the words 'any machinery' were construed by the House of Lords as meaning any machinery used in the factory for or ancillary to its manufacturing processes but not a machinery emerging as a product of the factory.[6] This result was reached having regard to the collocation or the architecture of the sections 12, 13 and 14.[7] Sections 12 and 13 which dealt with prime movers and transmission machinery were limited in their scope to the machinery forming part of the equipment of the factory and the exception contained in section 14(1) in respect of prime movers and transmission machinery left no doubt to the court that the scope of that section also was similarly limited.

The Caravan Sites and Control of Development Act, 1960 prohibits any occupier of land to cause or permit his land to be used as a caravan site except under a licence granted by his local authority. The Act by section 5

---

1. *Empress Mills, Nagpur v. Municipal Committee, Wardha*, AIR 1958 SC 341, p. 348. **See further** *Chertsey UDC v. Mixnam's Properties*, (1964) 2 All ER 627 : 1965 AC 735 (HL) (LORD REID **quoted** MAXWELL on Statute, 11th Edition, p. 79 for the same proposition). *Utkal Contractors and Joinery Pvt. Ltd. v. State of Orissa, supra*.
2. *Rabindra Chamaria v. Registrar of Companies*, AIR 1992 SC 398, p. 403 : 1992 Supp (2) SCC 10. (The words 'any proceeding' in section 633 of the Companies Act confined to proceedings arising in respect of duties prescribed by the Companies Act only).
3. **See** Chapter 2, title 3(b), 'Rule in *Heydon's* case'.
4. **See** Chapter 2, title 4(b), 'Inconsistency and repugnancy to be avoided; harmonious construction'.
5. *Blackwood v. R.*, (1882) 8 AC 82, p. 94 (PC). **See further** *Kerala State Housing Board v. Rampriya Hotels (P.) Ltd.*, JT 1994 (5) SC 113, p. 116 : (1994) 5 SCC 672.
6. *Parvin v. Morton Machine Co. Ltd.*, (1952) 1 All ER 670 (HL).
7. *Ibid*, pp. 671, 673.

empowers the local authority to impose to a site licence 'such conditions as the authority may think it necessary or desirable to impose on the occupier of land in the interests of persons dwelling thereon in caravans, or any other class of persons, or of the public at large'. The powers conferred by the aforesaid provisions on a local authority although in most general terms were construed by the House of Lords as not authorising the imposition of a condition which did not relate to the use of the site but which restricted the site owners' freedom of contract in other respects with caravan dwellers.[8] This result was reached mainly on the ground that if Parliament intended to bring about such a fundamental change as to authorise the local authorities to restrict freedom of contract between the site owner and caravan dwellers it would have done so in quite clear terms.[9]

The words 'representation in regard to testator's estate' were construed in a case as referring to probate or letters of administration with the will annexed thereby excluding the grant of letters of administration simpliciter on the ground that the Act in question was limited in its scope to testamentary dispositions.[10]

The word 'vest' has no fixed connotation meaning in all cases that the property is owned by the person in whom it vests. It may vest in title or in possession or in some other limited sense "as indicated in the context in which it may have been used in a particular piece of legislation."[11] The word 'vest'or 'vesting' has different meanings, and may or may not include transfer of possession, depending on the context in which it has been placed. The Supreme Court has held that the mere declaration of 'vesting' of vacant land declared in excess of ceiling under section 10(3) of the Urban Land (Ceiling and Regulation) Act, 1976, would not give the State Government *de facto* possession of such land, and hence is not saved under section 3 of the Urban Land (Ceiling and Regulation) Repeal Act, 1999, which repeals the 1976 Act.[12]

---

8. *Chertsey Urban District Council v. Mixnam's Properties*, (1964) 2 All ER 627 (HL).

9. *Ibid*, pp. 631, 632 (LORD REID), 639, 640 (LORD UPJOHN).

10. *Re, Bidie (deceased)*, (1948) 2 All ER 995 : 1949 Ch 121.

11. *Fruit and Vegetable Merchants Union v. Delhi Improvement Trust,* AIR 1957 SC 344 : 1957 SCR 1; *Municipal Corporation of Greater Bombay v. Hindustan Petroleum Corporation,* AIR 2001 SC 3630, p. 3632 : (2001) 8 SCC 143; *Bharat Cooking Coal Limited v. Karamchand Thapar & Bros. Pvt. Ltd.*, (2003) 1 SCC 6, pp. 8, 9; *Sulochana Chandrakant v. Pune Municipal Transport*, (2010) 8 SCC 467 para 13 : AIR 2010 SC 2962.

12. *State of Uttar Pradesh v. Hariram*, (2013) 4 SCC 280, pp.293 to 300. Section 3(1)(a) of the Repeal Act provides that the repeal of the principal Act shall not affect the vesting of any vacant land under sub-section (3) of section 10, possession of which has been taken over by the State Government or any person duly authorized by the State Government in this behalf or by the competent authority.

The word 'person' has at times been construed as meaning only males,[13] whereas at times it has been given its full effect to include both males and females,[14] as also a company or a corporation,[15] and in some cases even the Crown,[16] or the State.[17] In the context of section 50 of the NDPS Act, 1985 which provides certain safeguards for search of 'any person' the word 'person' has been construed to mean "a human being with appropriate coverings and clothings and also footwear" but not to include a bag or briefcase which the person may be carrying.[18] Similarly the word 'family', the primary meaning of which is children,[19] has a variable connotation according to its context.[20] Thus a single person living alone or a master and servant living together may be regarded as a family,[21] a son-in-law may be regarded as a member of the family of his mother-in-law and wife,[22] and a brother's son living with and helping his father's brother in his business may be regarded as a member of his family.[23] Though it has been held that two adults living together in platonic relationship do not constitute a family on the ground that 'family' does not mean 'household' and a broadly

---

13. *Nairn v. St. Andrews University*, (1909) AC 147; *Viscountess Rhondda's Claim*, (1922) 2 AC 339 (HL).

14. *Henrietta Muir Edwards v. A.G. of Canada*, AIR 1930 PC 120.

15. *Motipur Zamindari Co. Ltd. v. State of Bihar*, AIR 1953 SC 320 : 1953 SCR 720; *Union Bank of India v. Khader International Construction*, AIR 2001 SC 2277 : (2001) 5 SCC 22.

16. *Madras Electric Supply Corporation Ltd. v. Boarland*, (1955) 1 All ER 753 : (1955) 2 WLR 632 (HL).

17. *State of Punjab v. Okara Grain Buyers Syndicate Ltd., Okara*, AIR 1964 SC 669 : (1964 (5) SCR 387; *Samatha v. State of Andhra Pradesh*, AIR 1997 SC 3297 : (1997) 8 SCC 191.

18. *State of Himachal Pradesh v. Pawan Kumar*, AIR 2005 SC 2265, p. 2270 : (2005) 4 SCC 350.

19. *Deoki Nandan v. Murlidhar*, AIR 1957 SC 133, p. 139 (para 11) : 1956 SCR 756.

20. *Price v. Gould*, 143 LT 333, p. 334; *Brock v. Wollams*, (1949) 1 All ER 715, p. 717; *Jones v. Whitehill*, (1950) 1 All ER 71, p. 72; *Gammans v. Ekins*, (1950) 2 All ER 140, p. 141; *American Economic Laundry Ltd. v. Little*, (1950) 2 All ER 1186, p. 1188; *Longdon v. Horton*, (1951) 1 All ER 60, pp. 61, 62; *Perry v. Dembowski*, (1951) 2 All ER 50, pp. 51, 52; *Baldeo Sahai v. R.C. Bhasin*, AIR 1982 SC 1091 : (1982) 2 SCC 210; *K.V. Muthu v. Angamuthu Ammal*, AIR 1997 SC 628, pp. 631, 632 : (1997) 2 SCC 53.

21. *Corporation of Nagpur v. Nagpur Handloom Cloth Market Co. Ltd.*, AIR 1963 SC 1192, p. 1197 : 1963 Supp (2) SCR 796. **But see** *Krishna Prasad v. CIT, Bangalore*, AIR 1975 SC 498, p. 500 : (1975) 1 SCC 160, where in the context of the Income-tax Act it has been held that a single individual does not constitute a family.

22. *S.N. Sudalaimuthu Chettiar v. Palaniyandavan*, AIR 1966 SC 469, p. 470 : 1966 (1) SCR 450. **See further** *Khurode Chandra v. Sarda Prasad*, 7 Ind. Cas 436 (Cal) **approved** in *Srilekha Ghosh (Roy) v. Parthasarathi Ghosh*, AIR 2002 SC 2500, p. 2503 : (2002) 6 SCC 359.

23. *K.V. Muthu v. Angamuthu Ammal, supra.*

recognisable *de facto* familial nexus is necessary,[24] but with the change in society's attitude towards homosexual relationships, two persons living together in a stable and permanent homosexual relationship have been held in law to constitute a 'family'.[25]

The word 'violence' is a word very similar to family and is capable of bearing several meaning and applying to many different types of behaviour.[26]

Another general word of common use is 'business' which according to LORD DIPLOCK is an "etymological chameleon; it suits its meaning to the context in which it is found".[27] The same *simile* has been applied by Thomas J. to the expression 'failure of justice.'[28] A similar general word of common use is 'suitable' which has been described by LORD HOFFMAN to be "an empty vessel which is filled with meaning by context and background".[29]

General words also receive a restricted meaning because of principle of legality as also when used in association with other words by application of the rules of *noscitur a sociis* and *ejusdem generis*.

---

24. *Carega Properties, S.A. (formerly Joram Development Ltd.) v. Sharrat*, (1979) 2 All ER 1084 (HL).

25. *Fitzpatrick v. Sterling Housing Association Ltd.*, (1999) 4 All ER 705 (HL). **See further**, text and note 21, p. 253.

26. *Yemshaw v. Hounslow London Borough Council*, (2011) 1 All ER 912 (U.K.S.C.) paras 27 and 28.

27. *Town Investments Ltd. v. Department of Environment*, (1977) 1 All ER 813, p. 819 : (1978) AC 359 : (1977) 2 WLR 450 (HL). (Occupation of the premises as a tenant by the Crown for Government purposes was held to be 'business tenancy'); *Vishwanath Jhunjhunwala v. State of U.P.*, (2004) 4 SCC 437, p. 438 : AIR 2004 SC 2568, p. 2570 ('Business' as used in Sales Tax Acts). **See further** *State of Tamil Nadu v. Board of Trustees of the Port of Madras,* JT 1999 (2) SC 410, p. 416 : AIR 1999 SC 1647, p. 165 : (1999) 4 SCC 630. (If the main activity is not business the incidental activities will not constitute business) followed in *Commissioner of Sales Tax v. Sai Publication Fund,* AIR 2002 SC 1582; *B.R. Enterprises v. State of U.P.,* AIR 1999 SC 1867, p. 1902 : 1999 (9) SCC 700. ('Business' is wider than 'trade and commerce'). In the context of Section 9 (1) of the Income-tax Act, 1961 ' business' was held to include 'profession'[*Barendra Prasad Ray v. ITO*, (1981) 2 SCC 693 : AIR 1981 SC 1047], but in the context of Section 32 (iv) of the Act, it was held not to include 'profession' [*G.K. Choksi & Company v. Commissioner of Income Tax,* (2008) 1 SCC 246 : (2007) 13 JT 182].

28. *Shamnsaheb M. Multani v. State of Karnataka,* AIR 2001 SC 921, p. 925 : (2001) 2 SCC 577.

29. *R (on the application of Quintavalle v. Human Fertilisation and Embryology Authority*, (2005) 2 All ER 556, p. 564 (fg).

(a1) Principle of Legality

As statutes are not enacted in a vacuum, it is assumed that long standing principles of constitutional law and administrative law are not displaced by use of merely general words.[30] This is styled as the principle of legality.[31] In the words of SIR JOHN ROMILLY: "The general words of the Act are not to be so construed as to alter the previous policy of the law, unless no sense or meaning can be applied to those words consistently with the intention of preserving the previous policy untouched."[32] Since every new law involves some change the above statement of LORD ROMILLY must be applied with caution[33] and should be normally confined to cases where 'the abrogation of a long standing rule of law is in question'.[34] There are many presumptions which an interpreter is entitled to raise which are not readily displaced merely by use of general words, *e.g.*, an intention to bind the Crown[35] or an intention to exclude the supervisory jurisdiction of superior courts[36] will not be inferred merely by use of general words. It is an application of the same principle that unless there be clearest provision to the contrary, Parliament is presumed not to legislate contrary to rule of law which enforces 'minimum standard of fairness both substantive and procedural'.[37] Thus a statutory power though conferred in wide terms has certain implied limitations;[38] provisions excluding challenge to an order have

---

30. *Pierson v. Secretary of State for the Home Department*, (1997) 3 All ER 577, p. 604 (HL).

31. *Ibid*; *R. v. Secretary of State for the Home Department, ex parte Simms*, (1999) 3 All ER 400, p. 411 (LORD STEYN) pp. 412, 413 (LORD HOFFMAN) (HL); *B (a minor) v. Director of Public Prosecution*, (2000) 1 All ER 833 pp. 844, 845 (HL) (LORD STEYN) (**see further** for this case text and note 2, p. 929) : *R. v. Secretary of State for the Home Department*, (2001) 3 All ER 433, p. 440 (HL); *Ahmed v. H.M. Treasury*, (2010) 4 All ER 745 (UK SC) paras 61, 75, 76.

32. *Minet v. Leman*, (1855) 20 Beav 269, p. 278; 24 LJ Ch 545, pp. 547, 548, **referred** to in *Chertsey U.D.C. v. Mixnam's Properties*, (1964) 2 All ER 627, p. 631 : (1965) AC 735 (HL). **See further** *State of Gujarat v. Shyamlal Mohanlal*, AIR 1965 SC 1251, p. 1259 : (1965) 2 CrLJ 256 (alternation of common law not intended; section 94, Cr.P.C.); *Maunsell v. Olins*, (1975) 1 All ER 16, pp. 18, 28 (HL); *Re, O*, (1991) 1 All ER 330, p. 336(f) (CA); *R (on the application of Rottman) v. Commissioner of Police*, (2002) 2 All ER 865, p. 890 (HL) (Power of police to search premises in or on which a person is arrested on warrant not affected by the (UK) Extradition Act, 1989); *Malika Holdings PTY Ltd. v. Streton*, (2001) 75 ALJR 626, pp. 631, 648, 649; (1991) 65 Australian Law Journal (current topics) 375 (presumption is also against alteration of equitable principles).

33. *Rose v. Ford*, (1937) 3 All ER 359, p. 370 (HL) (LORD WRIGHT).

34. *Maunsell v. Olins*, (1975) 1 All ER 16, p. 28 : (1975) AC 373 (HL) (LORD SIMON).

35. **See** Chapter 8.

36. **See** Chapter 9, title 3, 'Exclusion of jurisdiction of Superior Courts'.

37. *Pierson v. Secretary of State for the Home Department*, (1997) 3 All ER 577, p. 607 (HL).

38. **See** pp. 440-448, *supra*.

no application when the order is a nullity[39] and a provision excluding an appeal against an order of a criminal court does not bar an appeal against an order which the court had no power to make.[40] For the same reason, unless the statute expressly or by necessary implication provides otherwise an administrative decision does not take effect before it is communicated to the person concerned.[41]

The principle of legality is well accepted in Australia. It has been described as an aspect of the rule of law 'known both to Parliament and the Courts, upon which statutory language will be interpreted'.[42]

The principle of legality requires that in the absence of express language or necessary implication to the contrary, the courts will presume that even the most general words were intended to be subject to the basic rights of the individual and in this way the courts of the United Kingdom, though acknowledging the sovereignty of Parliament apply principles of Constitutionality little different from those which exist in countries where the power of the Legislature is expressly limited by a constitutional document.[43] This principle applies also in the construction of delegated legislation.[44] In this case paras 37 and 37A of Standing Order 5A (made under section 47(1) of the Prisons Act, 1952) were construed not to take away the right of free speech of a prisoner through oral interviews to persuade a journalist to investigate the safety of his conviction and to publish the findings in an effort to gain access to justice.[45]

(a2) Principle of Legality and the Human Rights Act (U.K.)[46]

Even after the enactment of the Human Rights Act, 1998 (U.K.) which gives statutory recognition to the European Convention for the Protection of Human Rights and Fundamental Freedoms, the principle of legality will apply being expressly recognised by section 3 of the Act and gaining

---

39. **See** p. 797, *infra*.

40. *R v. Cain*, (1984) 2 All ER 737, p. 741 : (1985) AC 46 : (1984) 3 WLR 393 (HL); *Pierson v. Secretary of State for the Home Department*, *supra*, p. 605.

41. *R (on the application of Anufrijeva) v. Secretary of State for the Home Department*, (2003) 3 All ER 827, pp. 838, 839 (HL).

42. *K-Generation Pty. Ltd. v. Liquor Licensing Court*, (2009) 83 ALJR 327 para 47.

43. *R. v. Secretary of State for the Home Department, Ex parte Simms*, (1999) 3 All ER 400, p. 412 (HL).

44. *Ibid*, p. 413.

45. *Ibid.* The principle of constitutionality as applied in India is **discussed** in Chapter 6 title 3.

46. **See.** 'The Interpretation of U.K. Domestic Legislation in the Light of European Convention and Human Rights Jurisprudence' by Lady Justice Arden, (2004) 25 Statute Law Review 165. ALEC SAMUELS, 'Human Right Act, 1998 Section 3 : A New Dimension to Statutory Interpretation', (2008) 29 Statute Law Review 130.

further support from the obligation of a Minister in charge of a Bill to make a statement of compatibility as required by section 19. But in cases, where the legislative infringement of fundamental rights is so clearly expressed as not to yield to the principle of legality, the courts will be able to draw this to the attention of Parliament by making a declaration of incompatibility and it will be then for the sovereign Parliament to decide whether or not to remove the incompatibility.[47] Indeed, section 3 of the Act[48] has been construed to enact a much stronger presumption that normally arises under the principle of legality.

In *R. v. A,*[49] LORD STEYN whose views were shared by the majority said: "In accordance with the will of Parliament as reflected in section 3 it will be sometimes necessary to adopt an interpretation which linguistically may appear strained. The techniques to be used will not only involve the reading down of express language in a statute but also the implication of provisions. A declaration of incompatibility is a measure of last resort. It must be avoided unless it is plainly impossible to do so. If a clear limitation on Convention rights is stated in terms such an impossibility will arise."[50] In this case the question related whether section 41 of the Youth Justice and Criminal Evidence Act, 1999 (UK), which imposed wide restrictions on evidence and questioning about complainant's sexual history, could be given effect in a way that was compatible with the fair trial guarantee under Article 6 of the Convention. The House of Lords held that it was possible to read section 41 'as subject to the implied provision that evidence or questioning which is required to ensure a fair trial under Article 6 of the Convention should not be treated as inadmissible'.[51]

Section 11(5)(b)(ii) of the Coroners Act, 1988 required that a coroner's inquisition, signed by the jury should set out 'how, when and where' the deceased came by his death and rule 36(1) of the 1984 Rules provided that

---

47. *R. v. Secretary of State for the Home Department, Exparte Simms, supra,* pp. 412, 413. **See further** *R. v. Director of Public Prosecution,* (1999) 4 All ER 801, p. 831 (HL); *R (on the application of Morgan Grenfell & Co. Ltd.) v. Special Commissioner of Income-tax,* (2002) 3 All ER 1, pp. 5, 12, 13 (HL). For cases where interpretation was influenced by the Human Rights Act: **see** *R. v. Offen,* (2001) 2 All ER 154; *MacDonald v. Ministry of Defence,* (2001) 1 All ER 620, p. 629, 630; *Hans. v. Comr. of Customs & Excise,* (2001) 4 All ER 687 (CA); *Housing and Regeneration Community Association v. Donoghue,* (2001) 4 All ER 604, p. 624 (C.A. LORD WOOLF C.J.) (approach to be adopted in Acts passed before the Human Rights Act, 1998); *Cachia v. Faluyi,* (2002) 1 All ER 192, p. 197 (C.A.).

48. 'So far as it is possible to do so, primary legislation and subordinate legislation must be read and given effect in a way which is compatible with the convention rights.'

49. *R. v. A,* (2001) 3 All ER 1 (HL).

50. *Ibid,* p. 17.

51. *Ibid. Compare Indian Cases in* text and notes 10 and 13, pp. 915-916, *infra.*

the proceedings and evidence at an inquest were to be directed solely to ascertaining certain matters including 'how, when and where' the deceased came by his death. After enforcement of the Human Rights Act, 1998 the above provisions of the Coroners Act and the Rules had to be read compatible with the State's procedural obligation for protection of right to life to provide for effective public investigation, *i.e.,* to investigate death under Article 2 of the Convention ordinarily to culminate in an expression of the jury's conclusion on the disputed factual issues at the heart of the case, *i.e.*, relating to the events leading up to the death. With this object the word 'how' in section 11(5)(b)(ii) and rule 36(1)(b) was construed as meaning not simply 'by what means' but 'by what means and in what circumstances'.[52] But this broad interpretation will apply only when the death took place after coming into force of the Human Rights Act, *i.e.*, after 2nd October, 2000. For inquests in respect of deaths before this date the word 'how' will only mean by 'what means' even though the inquest has been started or is continuing after 2nd October, 2000 for the reason that the obligations created by the Human Rights Act are not retrospective.[53]

In *Ghaidan v. Mendoza*[54] the House of Lords had to consider after enforcement of the Human Rights Act, 1998 the interpretation of para 2 of Schedule I to the Rent Act, 1977 which reads:

2. (1) The surviving spouse (if any) of the original tenant, if residing in the dwelling-house immediately before the death of the original tenant, shall after the death be the statutory tenant if and so long as he or she occupies the dwelling-house as his or her residence.

(2) For the purposes of this paragraph, a person who was living with the original tenant as his or her wife or husband shall be treated as the spouse of the original tenant....

This provision was earlier interpreted by the House of Lords in *Fitzpatric v. Sterling Housing Corporation*[55] and it was held that Para 2(2) was limited to heterosexual couples living together as husband and wife without getting married but did not apply to homosexual couples living togethher. But in *Ghaidan v. Mandoza*[56] the provision was interpreted under section 3 of the Human Rights Act to avoid discrimination on the ground of

52. *R (on the application of Middleton) v. West Somerset Coroner*, (2004) 2 All ER 465, p. 485 (HL); *R (on the application of Sacket) v. West Yorkshire Coroner*, (2004) 2 All ER 487, p. 499 (HL).

53. *R (on the application of Hurst) v. London Northern District Coroner,* (2007) 2 All ER 1025 (HL).

54. *Ghaidan v. Mendoza*, (2004) 3 All ER 411 (HL).

55. *Fitzpatric v. Sterling Housing Corporation*, (1999) 4 All ER 705 (HL).

56. *Ghaidan v. Mandoza*, (2004) 3 All ER 411 (HL).

sexual orientation to include homosexual couples. This was done by interpreting the words 'as his or her wife or husband' in para 2(2) to mean '*as if they were his wife or husband*' so that 'spouse' included the survivor of a same sex partnership.[57] It was held that the court could read in words which change the meaning of the enacted legislation so as to make it convention compliant. LORD STEYN emphasised that "interpretation under section 3(1) is the prime remedial remedy and that resort to section 4 must always be an exceptional course. In practical effect there is a strong rebuttable presumption in favour of an interpretation consistent with convention rights."[58]

An example of a case where the House of Lords found it impossible to construe an English statue compatible with Article 6(1) of the Convention[59] is furnished by *R (on the Application of Anderson) v. Secretary of State for the Home Department.*[60] The question in this case related to the power of the Secretary of State under section 29 of the Crime (Sentences) Act, 1997 to fix the minimum term of imrisonment on the expiry of which alone the case of a prisoner sentenced to mandatory life imprisonment could be sent to the Parole Board for consideration whether he could be released earlier. It was held that the fixing of such a tariff was a sentencing exercise involving an assessment of the quantum of punishment that the convicted murderer should undergo and its entrustment to the Secretary of State who was not independent of the executive was incompatible with Article 6(1) of the Convention. The court found it impossible to construe section 29 compatible with Article 6(1) of the Convention under section 3(1) of the Human Rights Act, 1998 and declared its incompatibility. According to LORD STEYN section 3(1) is not available where the suggested interpretation is contrary to express statutory words or is by implication necessarily contradicted by the statute.[61]

---

57. *Ibid*, p. 429.

58. *Ibid.*

59. Article 6(1) 'In the determination of his civil rights and obligation or of any criminal charge against him, everyone is entitled to a fair and public hearing within a reasonable time by an independent and impartial tribunal established by law.'

60. *R (on the Application of Anderson) v. Secretary of State for the Home Department*, [2002] 4 All ER 1089 : (2002) 3 WLR 1800 (HL). **See further** *Government of the United States of America v. Montgomery (No. 2)*, (2004) 4 All ER 280 (HL). (Registration and enforcement of a confiscation order passed by a United States court against a person, who was now a citizen and resident of United Kingdom, on the basis of fugitive disentitlement doctrine as applied in the United States did not violate his rights under Article 6(1) of the convention. For fugitive disentitlement doctrine, **see** pp. 293, 294 of the Report).

61. *Ibid*, pp. 1113, 1114. **See further** *R. (on the application of Rusbridger) v. Attorney General*, (2003) 3 All ER 784, p. 790 (HL). For non-disclosure of information to defence on the ground of public interest immunity and right to a fair trial **see** *R v. H*, (2004) 1 All ER 1269 (HL).

Another example of incompatibility is *Bellinger v. Bellinger,*[62] where the House of Lords declined to hold that a post operative male to female transexual could be treated as 'female' for purposes of marriage under section 11(c) of the Matrimonial Causes Act, 1973 to remove incompatibility by construction under section 3 of the Human Rights Act, 1998 and declared that provision incompatible with convention rights under section 4 of the Act leaving the choice with Parliament to remove incompatibility by legislation. The issue in this case related to the change in fundamental concept of marriage which the court held could not be brought about by any process of interpretation and needed parliamentary legislation.

It has been said that sections 3 and 4 of the Act give the Act its unique character as a participatory human rights setting it apart from earlier Bill of Rights based on a judicial interpretative monopoly. Even when the Parliament accepts the courts interpretation of incompatibility, which will be done in most of the cases, it will be for Parliament to choose what to put in place of the incompatible statutory provision.[63]

As expected the coming into force of the Human Rights Act, 1998 from 2nd October, 2000[64] gave rise to a flow of H.R. cases in courts and tribunals of all kinds and all levels in the United Kingdom. Any earlier decision on the interpretation of an Act became open to reconsideration on the question of compatibility with Convention rights. LORD HOPE in *R. v. Kansal,* aptly remarked: "The development of our jurisprudence on the Human Rights Act, 1998, has only just begun. New problems are being revealed every week, if not every day."[65]

(a3) Terrorism and Human Rights in U.K.

A. v. Secretary of State for the Home Department[66] related to the compatibility of the Anti Terrorism Crime and Security Act, 2001 with the provisions

---

62. *Bellinger v. Bellinger,* (2003) 2 All ER 593 (HL).
The Parliament's response came by enacting the Gender Recognition Act, 2004 which confers legal rights prospectively on all transsexual persons who are able to demonstrate to a panel that they have, or have had, gender dysphosia and that they live permanently in their acquired gender : (2005) Public Law 331.

63. 120 (2004) Law Quarterly Review, pp. 197, 198.

64. The Act has not been construed to be retrospective and has not been applied even to pending proceedings: *Wainwright v. Home Office,* (2003) 3 All ER 943, p. 950 (CA).

65. *R. v. Kansal,* (2002) 1 All ER 257, p. 272 (HL).

66. *A. v. Secretary of State for the Home Department* (2004) UK HL 56 : (2005) 2 WLR 87 (HL) : (2005) 3 All ER 169 (HL). The response of Parliament was enactment of Prevention of Terrorism Act, 2005, which repealed sections 21-32 of the Anti-terrorism Crime and Security Act, 2001. The 2005 Act in place of these sections

[Footnote No. 66 Contd.]

of the convention. Nine suspected foreign terrorists were arrested and detained in England under the Act in the wake of September 11 Al-Quaeda attack in New York. The detainees were detained indefinitely because the Home Secretary believed that their presence in the UK was threat to national security. They could not be deported back to their home countries because there was a threat that they would be subject to torture in breach of Article 3 of the Convention. The provisions of the Act in particular section 23 permitting indefinite detention without trial of only foreigners were held by a majority of eight against one to be violative of right to liberty provision in Article 5 and non-discrimination provision in Article 14 of the Convention. Article 15 permits derogation from Article 5 provision 'in time of war or other public emergency threatening the life of the nation' but requires that measures taken 'must be strictly required by the exigencies of the situation'. On this aspect it was held that the measures adopted were not proportionate to the threat. Section 23 of the Act was, therefore, declared incompatible with the Convention rights. This is an important case for it upholds liberty and equality even in times of great danger to national security.

In *R (on the application of Al-Keini) v. Secretary of State,*[67] the House of Lords faced a new problem of extra territorial application of the Human Rights Act which on the face of it does not provide for extra territorial operation. By relying upon the Srasbourg Human Rights jurisprudence it was held that the Act will apply to a territory outside the United Kingdom, which because of military occupation is in effective control of the Government of the U.K. Therefore, a relative of an Iraqi civilian, who was taken to a detention unit in a British military base at Basra in Iraq and was said to have been so brutally beaten that he died of his injuries, was granted judicial review of an order of the Secretary of State declining to hold enquiry for deprivation of right to life under Article 2 of the Convention. But in five other cases, where Iraqi civilians were killed outside the military base by British armed forces judicial review was refused.

[Footnote No. 66 Contd.]
provides for 'control orders' which, in case they did not involve derogation from the right to liberty under Art. 5 of the European Convention, could be made against suspected terrorists with the permission of the court but if the order violated Article 5 it could be made only by the court. **See further**: PROF. JEFFREY JOWELL, 'The Road to Constitutionalism in the United Kingdom : Renewal and Reform; Constitutionalism Human Rights and the Rule of Law (Essays in the honour of Soli J. Sorabjee, Universal Law Publishing Co.); PROF. ADAM TOMKINS 'Analysis', 2005 Public Law 255; MARY ARDEN, Lady Justice of Appeal, 'Human Rights in the Age of Terrorism', (2005) 121 LQR 604-27. For legality of 'control-order' **see** text-and notes 26 to 28 *infra*.

67. *R (on the application of Al-Keini) v. Secretary of State,* (2007) 3 All ER 685.

And in *R (on the application of Gentle) v. Prime Minister*[68] the House of Lords held on the application of mothers of two soldiers of British army killed in Iraq that Article 2 of the Convention did not impose a substantive duty that the government of the United Kingdom before going to war should have exercised due diligence to ensure that it would be lawful to do so under international law and that in case of a soldier dying in a war there was no procedural duty to initiate an effective public and independent enquiry into whether due diligence had in fact been exercised for examining lawfulness of the war. The court also held that the legality of an invasion under international law had nothing to do with the State's obligation under Article 2(1) to protect servicemen and women within its jurisdiction.

The question of legality of continued detention of a person by the British troops as part of multinational force in Iraq acting under United Nations Security Council Resolutions came up before the House of Lords in *R (on the application of Al-Jedda) v. Secretary of State for defence.*[69] On 20th March 2003 coalition forces of the United States and United Kingdom invaded Iraq and the combat operations were declared to be complete on May 1, 2003. As from that date the United States and the United Kingdom became occupying powers which functioned under the relevant U. N. Security Council Resolutions. Resolution no. 1546 of the Security Council provides that 'the multinational force shall have the authority to take all necessary measures to contribute to the maintenance of security and stability in Iraq in accordance with the letters annexed to the Resolution.' One of the annexed letters authorised internment where this is necessary for imperative reasons of security.' The appellant, who was a citizen of both the United Kingdom and Iraq, was arrested in Baghdad on 10th October, 2004 and detained by British forces in a detention camp in Basra. The appellant applied for judicial review of his detention complaining that it violated Article 5(1) of the European Convention. He was arrested and detained as the British authorities believed that he was personally responsible for recruiting terrorists and was involved in weapons smuggling and explosive attacks and that his detention was necessary for imperative reasons of security in Iraq. The States including the United Kingdom which contributed to the multinational force in occupation of Iraq were bound by Articles 2 and 25 of the United Nations Charter to carry out the decisions of the Security Council. Further, as provided in Article 103 of the Charter in the event of a conflict between the obligations under the Charter and obligations under any other international agreement, the obligations under the Charter were to prevail. There was thus a clash between, on the one hand, a power or

68. *R (on the application of Gentle) v. Prime Minister*, (2008) 3 All ER 1 (H.L.).

69. *R (on the application of Al-Jedda) v. Secretary of State for defence*, (2008) 3 All ER 28 (H.L.).

duty to detain exercisable on the express authority of the resolution of the Security Council and, on the other, a fundamental human right which the United Kingdom had undertaken to secure to the appellant under Article 5 of the European Convention. The conflict was resolved by holding that the United Kingdom could lawfully, where it was necessary for imperative reasons of security, exercise the power to detain authorised by Security Council Resolutions but also ensuring that the detainee's rights under Article 5 are not infringed to any greater extent than was inherent in such detention. The appeal was accordingly dismissed.

In some cases the question of compatibility of 'control orders' made under the Prevention of Terrorism Act, 2005 with the Convention rights came up before the House of Lords. Section 2(1) of the Act defines a control order as meaning 'an order made against an individual that imposes obligations on him for purposes connected with protecting members of the public from a risk of terrorism.' Section 1(4) specifies the obligations which a control order 'may include in particular'. It is therefore not an exclusive list, though a detailed list, containing 16 potential obligations. Section 1(2) provides: 'The power to make a control order against an individual shall be exercisable—(a) except in the case of an order imposing obligations that are incompatible with the individual's right to liberty under Article 5 of the Human Rights Convention, by the Secretary of State, and (b) in the case of an order imposing obligations that are or include derogating obligations, by the Court on an application by the Secretary of the State.' Article 5 of the Convention in so far as material provides:

'Everyone has the right to liberty and security of person. No one shall be deprived of his liberty save in the following cases and in accordance with a procedure prescribed by law: (a) the lawful detention of a person after conviction by a competent court; (b) the lawful arrest or detention of a person for non-compliance with the lawful order of a court or in order to secure the fulfillment of any obligation prescribed by law; (c) the lawful arrest or detention of a person effected for the purpose of bringing him before the competent legal authority on reasonable suspicion of having committed an offence or when it is reasonably considered necessary to prevent his committing an offence or fleeing after having done so; (d) the detention of a minor by lawful order for the purpose of educational supervision or his lawful detention for the purpose of bringing him before the competent legal authority; (e) the lawful detention of persons for the prevention of the spreading of infectious diseases, of persons of unsound mind, alcoholics or drug addicts or vagrants; (f) the lawful arrest or detention of a person to prevent his effecting an unauthorized entry into the country or of a person against whom action is being taken with a view to deportation or extradition....'

A person who contravenes an obligation imposed on him by a contro order is guilty of an offence.

The Secretary of State made non-derogating control orders against si Iraqi or Iranian nationals which were challenged in *Secretary of State fo the Home Deptt. v. JJ.*[70] The obligations imposed by the control order were essentially identical and are set out in the judgment of the House o Lords challenging the legality of control orders as follows:

"Each respondent is required to remain within his 'residence' at al times, save for a period of six hours between 10 a.m. and 4 p.m. In th case of GG the specified residence is a one-bedroom flat provided by th local authority in which he lived before his detention. In the case of th other five respondents the specified residences are one-bedroom flats pro vided by the National Asylum Support Service. During the curfew perioc the respondents are confined in their small flats and are not even allowec into the common parts of the buildings in which these flats are situated Visitors must be authorised by the Home Office, to which name, address date of birth and photographic identity must be supplied. The residence are subject to spot searches by the police. During the six hours when they are permitted to leave their residences, the respondents are confined to re stricted urban areas, the largest of which is 72 square kilometers. These deliberately do not extend, save in the case of GG, to any area in which they lived before. Each area contains a mosque, a hospital, primary health care facilities, shops and entertainment and sporting facilities. The re spondents are prohibited from meeting anyone by pre-arrangement who has not been given the same Home Office clearance as a visitor to the resi dence. They were required to wear an electronic tag and to report to a monitoring company on first leaving their flat after a curfew period and on returning to it before a curfew period. They were forbidden to use or pos sess any communications equipment of any kind save for one fixed tele phone line in their flat maintained by the monitoring company. They could attend a mosque of their choice if it was in their permitted area and approved in advance by the Home Office. Some of them are not permit ted, because of their immigration status, to work; those who are permit ted have not done so in the six-hour period between 10 a.m. and 4 p.m They received benefits of £30-£35 per week, mostly in vouchers, but in *JJ*'s case £57.45. A request by JJ to study English at a college outside his area was refused."

The House of Lords following Strasburg Jurisprudence held that the prohibition in Article 5 on depriving a person of his liberty has a wide

---

70. *Secretary of State for the Home Deptt. v. JJ.*, (2008) 1 All ER 613 (H.L.).

meaning and not restricted to his detention in prison or its equivalent. Account should be taken of a whole range of factors such as the nature, duration, effects and manner of execution or implementation of the order in question. There may be no deprivation of liberty if a single feature of an individual's situation is taken on its own but the combination of measures considered together may have that effect. "The difference between deprivation of and restriction on liberty is nonetheless merely one of degree or intensity, and not one of nature and substance. There is no bright line separating the two."[71]

The House of Lords by majority concluded that the effect of the 18-hour curfew coupled with the effective exclusion of social visitors, meant that the controlled persons were in practice in solitary confinement for this lengthy period everyday for an indefinite duration with very little opportunity for contact with the outside world, with means insufficient to permit provision of significant facilities for self entertainment and with knowledge that their flats were liable to be entered and searched at any time. The area open to them during non-curfew hours was an unfamiliar area where they had no family, friends or contact. The requirement to obtain prior Home Office clearance of any social meeting outside the flat in practice isolated the controlled persons during the non-curfew hours also. The cumulative effect of the restriction was that the controlled persons were deprived of their liberty contrary to Article 5 of the Convention. The Secretary of State had no power to make these orders which were nullities and the defects in them could not be cured by amending the obligations imposed under them.

The control orders held invalid in the case of *JJ* may be compared with a control order issued against AF which came up for consideration before the House of Lords in *Secretary of State for the Home Department V.A.F.*[72] AF was a dual United Kingdom and Libyan national. By the control order in question:

"AF was required to remain in the flat where he was already living (not including any communal area) at all times save for a period of 10 hours between 8 a.m. and 6 p.m. He was thus subject to a 14-hour curfew. He was required to wear an electronic tag at all times. He was restricted during non-curfew hours to an area of about nine square miles bounded by a

---

71. *Ibid* p. 629.

72. *Secretary of State for the Home Department V.A.F.*, (2008) 1 All ER 657 (H.L.). For other examples of control orders and the difference between deprivation of liberty and restriction of liberty in the context of Article 5 of the Convention, **see** *Secretary of State for the Home Department v. A.P.*, (2010) 4 All ER 245 and *Secretary of State for the Home Department v. A.P. (no.2)*, (2010) 4 All ER 259.

number of identified main roads and bisected by one. He was to report to a monitoring company on first leaving his flat after a curfew period had ended and on his last return before the next curfew period began. His flat was liable to be searched by the police at any time. During curfew hours he was not allowed to permit any person to enter his flat except his father, official or professional visitors, children aged ten or under or persons agreed by the Home Office in advance on supplying the visitor's name, address, date of birth and photographic identification. He was not to communicate directly or indirectly at any time with a certain specified individual (and, later, several specified individuals). He was only permitted to attend one specified mosque. He was not permitted to have any communications, equipment of any kind. He was to surrender his passport. He was prohibited from visiting airports, sea ports or certain railway stations, and was subject to additional obligations pertaining to his financial arrangements."

The House of Lords in this case unanimously held that the effect of the control order was not to deprive AF of his liberty in breach of Article 5. It was a case of restriction of liberty and not of deprivation.

Later, AF and some others namely AN and AE succeeded before the House of Lords[73] by invoking Article 6(1) of the European Convention which insofar as relevant provides: 'In the determination of his civil rights and obligations every one is entitled to a fair hearing.' AF and other controllees were subject of non-derogating control orders made by the Secretary of State under section 2 of the Prevention of Terrorism Act, 2005 on the ground that there was reasonable ground for suspecting that they were or had been involved in terrorism related activity. At the supervisory hearing before the High Court required under section 3 of the Act the material used against them was not disclosed and the special advocates provided for them had represented their interests at closed hearings. The House of Lords unanimously held that a controlled person had to be given sufficient information about the allegations against him to enable him to give effective instructions in relation to those allegations and where the case against the controlled person was based solely or to a decisive degree on closed materials the requirements of fair trial would not be satisfied. The result was that the appeals were allowed and the case was remanded to the judge concerned for further consideration in accordance with the decision of the House.[14]

It has also been held that basic rights of a citizen or a person present in the United Kingdom including the right of judicial review cannot be taken

73. *Secretary of State for the Home Department v. AF (no.3)*, (2009) 2 All ER 643 (H.L.). **See further** for a discussion of this case 'Treating Terrorist Suspects Fairly' a lecture of Lord David Parmick Q.C. (2010) 9 SCC J. 17.

away merely on reasonable suspicion unless the Parliament expressly so provides and principle of legality applies even while implementing resolutions of the United Nations relating to terrorism. Section 1 of the United Nations Act 1946 (U.K.) provides that if the Security Council of the United Nations call upon His Majesty's Government to apply any measures to give effect to any decision of that council, His Majesty may by Order in Council make such provision as appears to him necessary or expedient for enabling those measures to be effectively applied. Certain security council resolutions required all states to trace without delay funds and other financial assets or economic resources of persons who commit terrorist acts or participate in or facilitate the commission of terrorist acts. Similar steps were required to be taken in respect of persons designated by the sanctions committee of the United Nations. For implementing these resolutions of the security council the Government of the United Kingdom issued orders in council namely Terrorism (United Nations Measures) Order 2006 (the TO) and the Al-Qaida and Taliban (United Nations Measures Orders 2006 (the AQA). The TO and AQO were issued under section 1 of United Nations Act 1946 and were delegated legislation. The TO applied the test of reasonable grounds for suspecting that the person may be (briefly stated) involved in terrorism related activities. The AQO prohibited judicial review of the listing of a person as a designated person to whom AQO applied. The UK Supreme Court[74] held that both TO and the AQA were *ultra vires* section (1) of the 1946 Act for it could not be assumed that the Parliament intended that basic rights of a citizen or a person could be taken away on mere reasonable suspicion or that judicial review could be taken away to challenge the right of a person as a designated person.

(a4) Terrorism and Human Rights in U.S.A[75]

The impact of Human Rights on continued detention of prisoners taken in Afghanistan was also felt in the United States. In *Rasul v. Bush* [(2004) 124 SC 2686][76] the United States Supreme Court departed from its earlier view that foreigners held outside United States territory did not have any right to file *Habeas Corpus* petition in United States' courts. In this case, in the military operations in Afghanistan to hunt down members of Al-Qaeda, the troops captured many foreigners who were taken to the United States military base in Guantanamo in Cuba outside United States. The lower courts dismissed their *Habeas Corpus* petition on the ground of

---

74. *Ahmed v. H.M. Treasury*, (2010) 4 All ER 745 (UK SC) para 61, 75, 76.

75. *Fiona de Londras 'Guantanamo Bay : Towards Legality?'*, (2008) 71 Modern Law Review 36-58.

76. The case is fully **discussed** by MANUEL JOSE and GARCIA MANESILLA in an article in (2006) 80 ALJ 232.

jurisdiction based on earlier precedents. But in appeal the Supreme Court held that United States' courts have jurisdiction to review the legality of detention of foreigners captured outside United States territory during hostilities in Afghanistan and held abroad in United States military custody in Guantanamo base. The earlier view was departed from on the following considerations: (i) The foreigners captured were not citizens of countries at war with the United States; (ii) the prisoners had denied being involved in hostilities against United States; (iii) they were never given access to a tribunal; and (iv) they had never been accused of any crime and were held in detention for more than two years in a territory over which the United States had exclusive jurisdiction.

Rasul v. Bush was a case of statutory *Habeas Corpus* by invoking 28 USC Section 2241. The petitioners were declared enemy combatants by the Combatants Status Review Tribunal (CSRT). After the decision of the Supreme Court that the statutory jurisdiction extended to Guantanamo, the cases were remanded to the District Court. The response of the Congress was that it passed the Detainee Treatment Act, 2005 (DTA) which amended 28 USC Section 2241 to provide that 'no court, justice or judge shall have jurisdiction to consider an application for *Habeas Corpus* filed by or on behalf of an alien detained at Guantanamo.' In *Hamden v. Rumsfeld*, (548 US 557) the Supreme Court held that this provision had no application to cases which were pending when the DTA was enacted. The response of the Congress, was enactment of the Military Commissions Act 2006 (MCA) section 7 of which further amended 28 USC Section 2241 to deny jurisdiction with respect to *Habeas* action by detained aliens determined to be enemy combatants as also to deny jurisdiction to any action against the United States relating to any aspect of the detention, transfer, treatment, trial or conditions of confinement since September 11, 2001. The Act also gave the D.C. Circuit exclusive jurisdiction under the DTA to review CSRT decisions. The provisions introduced by the MCA were to apply to all cases without exception pending or otherwise. The *Habeas Corpus* cases of petitioners which were pending in the District Court were dismissed in view of section 7 of the MCA.

In appeal to the Supreme Court in *Boumedine v. Bush*,[77] petitioners invoked the Suspension Clause in Article 1 of the Constitution and challenged the validity of section 7 of the MCA. Article 1 Section 9(2) of the Constitution referred as the Suspension Clause, provides: 'The privilege of the Writ of *Habeas Corpus* shall not be suspended unless when in cases of Rebellion or Invasion the public safety may require it.' The court by majority held: (1) The petitioners have the constitutional privilege of *Habeas*

---

77. *Boumedine v. Bush*, 128 SC 2229 (decided on 12.6.2008).

Corpus. They are not barred from seeking the writ or invoking the Suspension Clause because they have been designated as enemy combatants or because of their presence in Guantanamo. (2) The Suspension Clause had full effect in Guantanamo over which the Government had absolute and indefinite control in spite of the legal sovereignty vesting in Cuba. (3) The DTA's procedures for reviewing detainees' status as enemy combatants determined by CSRT are not an adequate and effective substitute for the *Habeas Corpus.* (4) Section 7 MCA does not meet the Suspension Clause's requirements and operates as an unconstitutional suspension of the writ. As a result the dismissal of the cases of the petitioners was set aside and the cases remanded.[78]

(b) *Noscitur a Sociis*

The rule of construction *noscitur a sociis* as explained by LORD MACMILLAN means: "The meaning of a word is to be judged by the company it keeps".[79] As stated by the Privy Council: "It is a legitimate rule of construction to construe words in an Act of Parliament with reference to words found in immediate connection with them".[80] It is a rule wider than the rule of *ejusdem generis*; rather the latter rule is only an application of the former. The rule has been lucidly explained by GAJENDRAGADKAR, J., in the following words: "This rule, according to MAXWELL,[81] means that when two or more words which are susceptible of analogous meaning are coupled together, they are understood to be used in their cognate sense. They take as it were their colour from each other, that is, the more general

---

78. The majority opinion has been very well received in India. **See** SOLI J. SORABJEE (A former Attorney General for India) "The US apex courts' decision on Guantanamo Bay detainees is a vindication of the rule of law', Hindustan Times June 20, 2008; V. Gangadhar, 'Apex Court in Politics' Hitvada June 20, 2008 (Jabalpur edition). But the criticism that the Chief Justice was a Bush appointee which may have prompted him for delivering the minority opinion may not be justified. The difference of opinion may be because of the difference in perception of the menace of terrorism. The 2009 decisions of the Supreme Court show that the President has no power to order the indefinite military detention of legal residents of the United States to combat terrorism: The New York Times March 7, 2009 'Justices Erase Ruling That Allowed Detention'.

79. Law and Other Things, p. 166; **referred** to in SALMOND, Jurisprudence, 11th Edition, p. 153. *Rohit Pulp and Paper Mills Ltd. v. Collector of Central Excise*, AIR 1991 SC 754, p. 761 : (1990) 3 SCC 447.

80. *Angus Robertson v. George Day*, (1879) 5 AC 63, p. 69 : 64 LJ PC 9 (PC); **referred** to in *M.K. Ranganathan v. Govt. of Madras*, AIR 1955 SC 604, p. 609 : 1955 (2) SCR 374; *Ahmedabad Pvt. Primary Teachers Association v. Administrative Officer*, AIR 2004 SC 1426, p. 1432 : (2004) 1 SCC 755 (8th Edn., p. 379 of this book is **referred**). *Rasila S. Mehta v. Custodian*, (2011) 6 SCC 220 (Para 73)

81. MAXWELL: Interpretation of Statutes, 11th Edition, p. 321.

is restricted to a sense analogous to a less general. The same rule is thus interpreted in Words and Phrases."[82] "Associated words take their meaning from one another under the doctrine of *noscitur a sociis*, the philosophy of which is that the meaning of the doubtful word may be ascertained by reference to the meaning of words associated with it; such doctrine is broader than the maxim *ejusdem generis*." In fact the latter maxim 'is only an illustration or specific application of the broader maxim *noscitur a sociis*'. It must be borne in mind that *noscitur a sociis*, is merely a rule of construction and it cannot prevail in cases where it is clear that the wider words have been deliberately used in order to make the scope of the defined word correspondingly wider. It is only where the intention of the Legislature in associating wider words with words of narrower significance is doubtful, or otherwise not clear that the present rule of construction can be usefully applied.[83] The rule was applied in construing the word 'luxuries' in Entry 62 of List II of the Constitution which is a term of wide denotation not free from ambiguity.[84] Further, the rule cannot be used to make one of the associated words wholly redundant.[85]

Some examples where this doctrine has been applied may now be mentioned.

In a private Act a water company was empowered 'to break up the soil and pavement of roads, highways, footways, commons, streets, lanes, alleys, passages and public places' provided they did not enter upon any private lands without the consent of the owner and it was contended by the company that this power enabled the company to break up the soil of a private field in which there was a public footway. This contention, however, failed and the court construed the word 'footways' from the company it

82. "Words and Phrases", Vol. XIV, p. 207.

83. *State of Bombay v. Hospital Mazdoor Sabha*, AIR 1960 SC 610, pp. 613, 614 : 1960 (2) SCR 866. **See further** *Bank of India v. Vijay Transport*, AIR 1988 SC 151 : 1988 Supp SCC 47 (The rule has no application when the meaning is not in doubt.); *Rohit Pulp and Paper Mills Ltd. v. Collector of Central Excise*, AIR 1991 SC 754, pp. 761, 762 : (1990) 3 SCC 447; *Kerala State Housing Board v. Rampriya Hotels (P) Ltd.*, JT 1994 (5) SC 113, p. 116 : 1994 (5) SCC 672; *Samatha v. State of Andhra Pradesh*, AIR 1997 SC 3297, p. 3336 : (1997) 8 SCC 191; *K. Bhigirathi G. Shenoy v. K.B. Ballakuraya,* JT 1999 (2) SC 563, p. 565 : AIR 1999 SC 2143, p. 2146; *Brindavan Bangle Stores v. Assistant Commissioner of Commercial Taxes,* AIR 2000 SC 601, p. 604 : (2000) 1 SCC 674 (Rule not to apply when meaning not in doubt) : (2000) 1 SCC 674; *CBI, AHD, Patna v. Braj Bhushan Prasad,* AIR 2001 SC 4014, p. 4020.

84. *Godfrey Phillips India Ltd. v. State of U.P.*, (2005) 2 SCC 515, pp. 550, 551 (paras 81, 83).

85. *Shriram Vinyl and Chemical Industries v. Commissioner of Customs,* AIR 2001 SC 1283, p. 1285 : (2001) 4 SCC 286 (In the expression 'initial setting up or for the assembly or manufacture', 'assembly' cannot be equated to 'manufacture' as it will make it redundant.

kept as meaning those paved footways in large towns which are too narrow to admit of horses and carriages.[86]

While dealing with a Purchase Tax Act, which used the expression 'manufactured beverages including fruit-juices and bottled waters and syrups etc.', it was held that the description 'fruit-juices' as occurring therein should be construed in the context of the preceding words and that orange-juice unsweetened and freshly pressed was not within the description.[87]

Section 4(1) which provides an exception to the offence under section 2 of the Obscene Publications Act, 1959, and which corresponds to exception (a)(i) to section 292(2) of the Penal Code enables the accused to prove that 'publication of the article in question is justified as being for the public good on the ground that it is in the interest of science, literature, art or learning or of other objects of general concern'. It was held by the House of Lords[88] that the general words 'other objects of general concern' operated in the same area which was covered by the words science, literature, art or learning and that these words did not fall in a totally different area of sexual behaviour and could not enable the accused to prove that the articles seized, which were hard pornography, had some psycotherapeutic value for various categories of persons *e.g.*, for persons of heterosexual taste and perverts to relieve their sexual tensions.

In construing the word 'declare' in the phrase 'to create, declare, assign, limit or extinguish' as it occurs in section 17 of the Indian Registration Act, 1908, the Privy Council held that though the word 'declare' was capable of bearing a wider meaning but in section 17, being in association with other words, its meaning was restricted to connote a definite change of legal relationship as distinct from a mere statement of facts. VISCOUNT DUNEDIN quoted with approval the observations of WEST, J., from a Bombay case which are to the following effect: "'Declare' is placed along with 'create', 'limit' or 'extinguish' a right, title or interest and these words imply a change of legal relation to the property by an expression of will embodied in the document.—I think this is equally the case with the word 'declare'. It implies a declaration of will, not a mere statement of fact."[89]

---

86. *Scales v. Pickering*, 130 ER 840; **referred** to in *Devendra M. Surti (Dr.) v. State of Gujarat*, AIR 1969 SC 63 : 1969 (1) SCR 235.

87. *Commrs. v. Savoy Hotel*, (1966) 2 All ER 299.

88. *Director of Public Prosecutions v. Jordon*, (1976) 3 All ER 775 : (1977) AC 699 : (1976) 3 WLR 887 (HL).

89. *Bageshwari Charan Singh v. Jagannath*, AIR 1932 PC 55, pp. 56, 57; where observations of WEST, J., in *Sakharam Krishnaji v. Madan Krishnaji*, ILR 5 Bom 232, p. 236, are quoted with **approval**.

Rule 31 of the Rajasthan Rules of Business, which required that 'proposals for dismissing, removing or compulsory retiring of an Officer', should be referred to the Governor, was construed, as not necessitating any such reference in cases of compulsory retirement not amounting to punishment. It was held that the phrase 'compulsory retirement' as it occurs in the rule in association with 'dismissal' and 'removal' must be taken to cover only cases of punishment and not normal cases of compulsory retirement such as those which result on attaining superannuation age or those which fall under rule 244 of the Civil Service Rules.[90]

In section 232 of the Indian Companies Act, 1913 which enacted that 'where any company is being wound up by or subject to the supervision of the court, any attachment, distress or execution put into force without leave of the court against the estate or effects or any sale held without leave of the court of any of the properties of the company after the commencement of the winding up shall be void', the words 'any sale held without leave of the court' were construed in the light of the associated words, 'any attachment, distress, or execution put into force' and thereby restricted to a sale held through the intervention of the court thus excluding a sale effected by a secured creditor outside the winding up and without intervention of the court.[91]

Similarly, in construing the word 'posting' as it occurs in Article 233(1) of the Constitution in association with words 'appointment' and 'promotion' the Supreme Court held that the word 'posting' took its colour from the associated words and meant "the assignment of an appointee or promotee to a position in the cadre" and not his transfer from one station to another.[92] And the word 'use' in Entry 52 of List II occurring sandwiched between 'consumption' and 'sale' was held to take colour from the associate words and in order to attract octroi duty, to connote use of a commodity "for an indefinite period in such a way that it came to rest finally and permanently within the municipal limits."[93]

Further, in dealing with the definition of commercial establishment in section 2(4) of the Bombay Shops and Establishments Act, 1948 which reads 'commercial establishment means an establishment which carries on

90. *State of Rajasthan v. Sripal Jain*, AIR 1963 SC 1323, p. 1325 : 1964 (1) SCR 742.
91. *M.K. Ranganathan v. Government of Madras*, AIR 1955 SC 604, p. 609 : 1955 (2) SCR 374.
92. *State of Assam v. Ranga Muhammad*, AIR 1967 SC 903, p. 906 : 1967 (1) SCR 454.
93. *Acqueous Victuals Pvt. Ltd. v. State of U.P.*, AIR 1998 SC 2278, p. 2285 : 1998 (5) SCC 474.

any business, trade or profession', the word 'profession' was construed with the associated words 'business' and 'trade' and it was held that a private dispensary of a doctor was not within the definition.[94]

Again, in construing Article 194(3) of the Constitution which refers to Powers, Privileges and Immunities of a House of the Legislature of a State, the Supreme Court said that the word 'Powers' must take its colour from words in immediate connection with it and that it should be construed to refer not to legislative powers but to powers of a House which are necessary for the conduct of its business.[95]

And, in interpreting Entry 15 of the Schedule to the U.P. Sales Tax Act, 1948 which reads 'old, discarded, unserviceable or obsolete machinery stores or vehicles including waste products', the expression 'old' was construed to refer to old machinery which had become non-functional or non-usable.[96] When some articles are gouped together in an entry in the schedules of Sales Tax and Excise statutes, each word in the entry draws colour from the other words therein on the principle of *noscitur a sociis*.[97] Thus in Entry 16 of Schedule A to the Punjab General Sales Tax Act, 1948 which reads 'cosmetics, perfumery and toilet goods, excluding tooth paste, tooth powder, kumkum and soap, the word 'perfumery' was construed to mean such articles as are used as cosmetics and toilet goods and are upon the person, and it was held that the word had no application to *dhoop* and *aggarbatti*.[98]

Section 80HHC, as inserted by the Finance Act, 1983 in the Income-tax Act, 1961 grants a deduction from total income of 50% of the profits earned in the business of export of goods or merchandise; but the section does not apply to (i) 'mineral oil and (ii) minerals and ores'. The word 'minerals' here was construed on the basis of this doctrine in association with 'mineral oils' and 'ores', the three words taken together as intended to encompass all that is extracted from earth, and on this view all minerals

---

94. *Devendra M. Surti (Dr.) v. State of Gujarat*, AIR 1969 SC 63, p. 67 : 1969 (1) SCR 235.

95. *State of Karnataka v. Union of India*, AIR 1978 SC 68, pp. 99, 100 : (1977) 4 SCC 608.

96. *Rainbow Steels Ltd. v. Commissioner of Sales Tax*, AIR 1981 SC 2101 : (1981) 2 SCC 141. For further example, **see** *Rohit Pulp and Paper Mills Ltd. v. Collector of Central Excise*, AIR 1991 SC 754 : (1990) 3 SCC 447.

97. *Pradeep Aggarbatti, Ludhiana v. State of Punjab*, AIR 1998 SC 171, p. 173 : (1997) 8 SCC 511.

98. *Ibid*. **See further** *G. Radhakrishna Murthy & Co. v. Commercial Tax Officer*, JT 1998 (4) SC 426 : (1997) 8 SCC 37 : (1997) 8 SCC 37 (*Agarbatti* not included in 'perfumes' under item 36 of Andhra Pradesh General Sales Tax Act).

extracted from the earth including 'granite' were held to be covered, in the word 'minerals'.[1]

The rule was applied[2] in the construction of the exemption clause in section 3(1) of the Maharashtra Rent Control Act, 1999 which excludes from the operation of the Rent Act entities enumerated therein namely banks, Public Sector Undertakings (PSUs), statutory corporations, foreign missions, international agencies, multinational companies and private limited companies and public limited companies having a paid up capital of Rs. 1,00,00,000/- or more. The question in the case was whether Government companies were also excluded being covered by the expression Public Sector Undertakings. The Court held that the expression Public Sector Undertakings will include Government companies as it took colour from preceding and succeeding expressions namely 'Banks', 'Corporations', 'foreign missions', 'MNCs' etc. and therefore is to be interpreted widely to include all entities having sufficient paying capacity and not needing protection of the Rent Act. This construction was consistent with the object of the Act and non-exclusion of Government companies would have made the Act open to objection of discrimination.

(c) Rule of *ejusdem generis*

When particular words pertaining to a class, category or genus are followed by general words, the general words are construed as limited to things of the same kind as those specified.[3] This rule which is known as the rule of *ejusdem generis* reflects an attempt "to reconcile incompatibility between the specific and general words in view of the other rules of interpretation that all words in a statute are given effect if possible, that a statute is to be construed as a whole and that no words in a statute are presumed to be superfluous".[4] The rule applies when "(1) the statute contains

1. *Stonecraft Enterprises v. Commissioner of Income-tax*, JT 1999 (2) SC 332, p. 334 : AIR 1999 SC 1638, p. 1640.
2. *Leelabai Gajanan Pansare v. Oriental Insurance Company Ltd.* (2008) 9 SCC 720 : AIR 2009 SC 523.
3. *Kavalappara Kottarathil Kochuni v. State of Madras*, AIR 1960, SC 1080, p. 1103 : 1960 (3) SCR 887; *Thakur Amarasinghji v. State of Rajasthan*, AIR 1955 SC 504, p. 523 : 1955 (2) SCR 303; *Brownsea Haven Properties v. Pools Corporation*, (1958) 1 All ER 205, pp. 213, 214 : 1958 Ch 574 (CA); *Siddeshwari Cotton Mill (P) Ltd. v. Union of India*, AIR 1989 SC 1019, p. 1023 : (1989) 2 SCC 458; *Housing Board of Haryana v. Haryana Housing Board Employees Union*, 1995 (6) Scale 139, p. 150 : AIR 1996 SC 434, p. 441 : (1996) 1 SCC 95; *State of Karnataka v. Kempaiah*, AIR 1998 SC 3047, p. 3050 : 1998 (6) SCC 103.
4. *Tribhuwan Prakash Nayyar v. Union of India*, AIR 1970 SC 540, p. 545 : (1969) 3 SCC 99; *Siddeshwari Cotton Mills (P) Ltd. v. Union of India, supra*; *Housing Board of Haryana v. Haryana Housing Board Employees Union, supra*; *Lokmat Newspapers Pvt. Ltd. v. Shankar Prasad*, JT 1999 (4) SC 546, p. 579 : AIR 1999 SC 2423, p. 2444 : 1999 (6) SCC 275.

an enumeration of specific words; (2) the subjects of enumeration constitute a class or category; (3) that class or category is not exhausted by the enumeration; (4) the general terms follow the enumeration; and (5) there is no indication of a different legislative intent".[5] If the subjects of enumeration belong to a broad based genus as also to a narrower genus, there is no principle that the general words should be confined to the narrower genus.[6]

FARWELL, L.J., in applying this rule, so as to limit the phrase 'in consequence of war, disturbance or any other cause' to causes of the same kind as the two named instances, stated: "when there is a clear category followed by words which are not clear, unambiguous general words, it would violate rule of construction to strike out and render unmeaning two words which were presumably inserted for the purpose of having some meaning".[7] Later in his judgment he said: "Now if the words in this case had been 'in consequence of war, disturbance or any other cause whatsoever, whether similar to those preceding or not', there would have been no room for the argument, because there would be no real category at all; it is universality, and not a category; it is whole range of causes, but, inasmuch as you have simply the words 'any other cause' which are ambiguous, then the rule does apply".[8]

The above passages from the judgment of FARWELL, L.J. were quoted by LORD EVERSHED, M.R. in construing the words, 'in all times of public processions, rejoicings or illuminations, and in any case when the streets are thronged or liable to be obstructed'. It was held that the general words 'in any case' etc. were intended to be confined to cases within the genus or category of which public processions, rejoicings and illuminations were specific instances and they were limited to particular or extraordinary occasions. It was pointed out that the absence of the word 'other' before the

---

5. *Amar Chandra v. Collector of Excise, Tripura*, AIR 1972 SC 1863, p. 1868 : (1972) 2 SCC 442; *Housing Board of Haryana v. Haryana Housing Board Employees Union, supra; Grasim Industries Ltd. v. Collector of Customs, Bombay*, AIR 2002 SC 1766, p. 1710 : (2002) 4 SCC 297. In *Nagrik Upbhogta Manch v. Union of India*, AIR 2002 SC 2405 : (2002) 5 SCC 466 in the expression 'charges rates, duties and taxes', the term 'charges' was "read *ejusdem generis* taking colour from the succeeding terms, rates, duties and taxes". It is submitted that here the general category preceded the enumeration of specific categories and so the rule of *ejusdem generis* was technically not applicable and the court in fact applied the more general rule— *Noscitur a sociis*—**discussed** at p. 499, *ante* and rightly limited the meaning of the term charges.

6. *Uttar Pradesh S.E. Board v. Harishanker*, AIR 1979 SC 65, p. 73 : (1978) 4 SCC 16; *Grasim Industries Ltd. v. Collector of Customs Bombay, supra.*

7. *Tillmans & Co. v. S.S. Knutsford Ltd.*, (1908) 2 KB 385, p. 403.

8. *Ibid*, p. 404. **See further,** *Grasim Industries v. Collector of Customs, Bombay, supra.*

word 'case' was immaterial although it commonly occurs before the general words following particular instances.[9]

By application of this rule the words 'any other goods' occurring in section 43 of the Customs (Consolidation) Act, 1876 (UK) which empowered His Majesty by order in Council to prohibit the importation of 'arms, ammunition, or gun powder or any other goods' were construed as referring to goods similar to 'arms, ammunition or gun powder'.[10]

The rule was applied in construing the words 'any other process' in section 2(f)(v) of the Central Excises and Salt Act, 1944 which defines 'manufacture' in relation to goods in Item no. 19-I of the Schedule to the Central Excise Tariff Act, 1985 to include 'bleaching mercerising, dyeing, printing, water-proofing, rubberising, shrink-proofing, organdie processing or any other process—.' The Supreme Court held that the processes enumerated contemplate processes which import change of a lasting character to the fabric by either the addition of some chemical into the fabric or otherwise and 'any other process' in the section must share one or other of these incidents which constitute manufacture in the extended sense.[11]

The principle of *ejusdem generis* was also applied in interpreting the words 'such circumstances' in Regulation 27(1)(d) of the SEBI (Substantial Acquisition of Shares and Takeovers) Regulations, 1997. Regulation 27(1) provides that no public offer, once made, shall be withdrawn except under the following circumstances: (a) …; (b) the statutory approval(s) required have been refused; (c) the sole acquirer, being a natural person, has died; (d) such circumstances as in the opinion of the Board merits withdrawal. Clauses (b) and (c) were held to refer to circumstances which pertain to a class, category or genus, with the common thread running through them being the impossibility of carrying out the public offer. Therefore, the words 'such circumstances' in clause (d) would also be restricted to situations which would make it impossible for the acquirer to perform the public offer, and SEBI was required to exercise its discretion accordingly.[12]

---

9. *Brownsea Haven Properties v. Poole Corporation*, (1958) 1 All ER 205, pp. 213, 214 : 1958 Ch 574 (CA).

10. *A.G. v. Brown*, (1920) 1 KB 773.

11. *Siddeshwari Cotton Mills (P) Ltd. v. Union of India*, AIR 1989 SC 1019, p. 1023 : 1989 (2) SCC 458 (The question was whether 'calendering' was 'any other process'. The case was remitted to the Tribunal). **See further** *Asst. Collector of Central Excise, Guntur v. Ramdeo Tobacco Company*, AIR 1991 SC 506 : 1991 (2) SCC 119 (In the expression 'suit, prosecution or other legal proceedings', the words 'other legal proceedings' construed *ejusdem generis* as restricted to proceedings in a court of law).

12. *Nirma Industries Ltd. & Anr. v. SEBI*, (2013) 8 SCC 20, pp. 48 to 50.

Section 32 of the Income-tax Act, 1961, deals with depreciation of assets. Explanation 3 to section 32(1) defines 'assets' to mean *inter alia*, intangible assets, being know-how, patents, copyrights, trademarks, licences, franchises 'or any other business or commercial rights of similar nature'. Applying the principle of *ejusdem generis*, the Supreme Court held that 'goodwill' will fall under the expression 'any other business or commercial right of a similar nature', and hence be an 'asset' in terms of Explanation 3(b) to section 32(1).[13]

On the same principles the Privy Council held that the words 'any other sufficient reason' occurring in rule 1 of Order 47, the Code of Civil Procedure, 1908, must be taken as meaning a reason sufficient on the grounds at least analogous to those specified immediately previously,[14] and similarly the phrase 'further and other relief' occurring in section 92(1)(h) of the Code was held by the Privy Council to mean relief of the same nature as specified in clauses (a) to (g) of the same section.[15] Another such illustration is found in the construction of regulation 2(1)(k) of the Noida (Preparation and Finalisation of Plan) Regulations, 1991, which defines 'residential use' to mean the use of any land or building or part thereof for human habitation and 'such other uses incidental to residential uses'. The Supreme Court refused to give a wide interpretation to the term 'residential use' and held that the expression 'such other uses incidental to residential uses' has to take its colour from the use of the building for human habitation. Accordingly, the latter part of the Regulation was read *ejusdem generis* with the earlier part to hold that banking, nursing homes or any other commercial activity was impermissible in a development area earmarked for 'residential use'.[16]

The words 'or otherwise invalid', in para 15 of Schedule II to the Code of Civil Procedure, 1908, before enactment of the Arbitration Act, 1940, were construed by the Privy Council as *ejusdem generis* to the specific grounds of invalidity mentioned in the said para,[17] but this decision has not been followed in interpreting section 30 of the Arbitration Act, 1940,

---

13. *Commissioner of Income Tax v. SMIFS Securities Ltd.*, (2012) 13 SCC 488, p. 490.

14. *Chhajju Ram v. Neki*, AIR 1922 PC 112 : 49 IA 144; *Bisheswar Pratap Sahi v. Parath Nath*, AIR 1934 PC 213. Cf. *Tribhuvan Parkash Nayyar v. Union of India*, AIR 1970 SC 540, p. 545 : (1969) 3 SCC 99 (Relates to construction of Rule 18 of the Displaced Persons Verification of Claims Rules, 1954).

15. *Abdul Rahim v. Syed Abu Mohamed Barkat Ali Shah*, AIR 1928 PC 16.

16. *R. K. Mittal & Ors. v. State of Uttar Pradesh & Ors.*, (2012) 2 SCC 232, pp. 248, 259.

17. *Chhabba Lal v. Kallu Lal*, AIR 1946 PC 72, **approving** opinion of IQBAL AHMAD J., in *Mariam v. Amina*, AIR 1937 All 65.

which is similarly worded.[18] It also appears that the words 'or otherwise' have not been usually construed *ejusdem generis*.[19] They are words of wide import but the context may limit their scope.[20] A good example of the words 'or otherwise' not being construed *ejusdem generis* is found in the interpretation of section 11(1)(a) of the Prevention of Cruelty to Animals Act, 1960, which states that if any person beats, kicks, overrides, overdrives, overloads, tortures 'or otherwise' treats any animal so as to subject it to unnecessary pain or suffering, he commits the offence of treating animals cruelly. The Supreme Court held that the words 'or otherwise' are not used as words of limitation and that the Legislature intended the expression to cover all situations where animals are subjected to unnecessary pain or suffering which may not fall within the meaning of the preceding clause. Hence, jalikattu, bullock cart races and other such events were held to fall within the ambit of section 11(1)(a) of the Act.[21]

The introduction of the words 'whatsoever' after the general words following particular instances of a genus does not exclude the application of *ejusdem generis* principle.[22] The Privy Council construed the words 'any other person or persons whatsoever' by this rule and restricted their meaning to officers of similar kind as specified before these general words.[23]

In cases where the particular words can belong to a broad based genus it is not open to confine them to a narrower genus so as to limit the meaning of the general words. This principle is illustrated by the construction of section 13B of the Industrial Employment (Standing Orders) Act, 1946, which reads: 'Nothing in this Act shall apply to an industrial establishment

---

18. *Union of India v. Om Prakash*, AIR 1976 SC 1745, p. 1749 : (1976) 4 SCC 32. (It is said that sections 32 and 33 make the difference.)

19. *Lila Wati Bai v. State of Bombay*, AIR 1957 SC 521, pp. 528, 529 : 1957 SCR 721; *Kavallappara Kottarathil Kochuni v. State of Madras*, AIR 1960 SC 1080, p. 1103 : 1960 (3) SCR 887; *National Association of Local Govt. Officers v. Bolton Corporation*, (1942) AC 166: (1942) 2 All ER 425, p. 428 (HL); *Skinner & Co. v. Shew & Co.*, (1893) 1 Ch 413 (CA). **But see** *Eton Rural District Council v. Thames Conservators*, (1950) 1 All ER 996, 997; *George De Costa v. Controller of Estate Duty*, AIR 1967 SC 849, p. 851 (para 6) : (1967) 1 SCR 1004; *United Bank of India v. Pijush Kanti Nandy*, (2009) 8 SCC 605 para 15 (As a general rule, 'otherwise' when following an enumeration should receive an *ejusdem generis* interpretation).

20. *S. Prakash Rao v. Commy. of Commercial Taxes*, AIR 1990 SC 997, p. 1003 : (1990) 2 SCC 259. **See further** *Western India Plywood Limited v. P. Ashokan*, AIR 1997 SC 3883, p. 3886 (para 11) : (1997) 7 SCC 638; *Assistant Commissioner v. Nandanam Construction Company*, JT 1999 (7) 265, p. 270 : (1999) 8 SCC 69.

21. *Animal Welfare Board of India v. A. Nagaraja & Ors.*, (2014) 7 SCC 547, pp. 583, 584.

22. *R. v. Cleworth*, (1864) 4 B & S 927, p. 932; **referred** to in *Tillmans & Co. v. S.S. Knutsford Ltd.*, (1908) 2 KB 385, p. 404; *Brownsea Haven Properties v. Poole Corporation*, (1958) 1 All ER 205, p. 213 : 1958 AC 574 (CA).

23. *Re, Samuel*, (1913) AC 514, p. 525 (PC); 19 IC 765, p. 768 (PC).

in so far the workmen employed therein are persons to whom the Fundamental and Supplementary Rules, Civil Services (Classification Control and Appeal) Rules, Civil Services (Temporary Service) Rules, Revised Leave Rules, Civil Service Regulations, Civilians in Defence Service (Classification, Control and Appeal) Rules or the Indian Railway Establishment Code *or any other rules or regulations* that may be notified in this behalf by the appropriate Government in the Official Gazette apply'. The rules specifically mentioned in the section have a narrower genus of being applicable to Government Servants only; they have also a broader genus of being statutory in character. In holding that 'any other rules or regulations' should refer to all statutory rules governing workmen, the Supreme Court held that the specification of rules should not be attributed to the narrower genus and that the broad based genus should be applied so as not to narrow the effect of the general words.[24]

Ejusdem generis rule was used for construing the words 'a particular social group' as occurring in the definition of 'refugee' in Article 1A(2) of the Convention and Protocol Relating to the Status of Refugees which is enforced in the United Kingdom by the Asylum and Immigration Appeals Act, 1993. 'Refugee' as defined therein is a person who 'owing to well founded fear of being persecuted for reasons of race, religion, nationality, membership of a particular social group or political opinion, is outside the country of his origin and is unable or, owing to such fear, is unwilling to avail himself of the protection of that country'. The House of Lords[25] in this context quoted with approval and applied the reasoning in the case of *Acosta Re Interim Decision,* 1986 decided by the United States Board of Immigration Appeals. In that case the Board observed: "The other grounds of persecution listed in association with 'membership in a particular social group' are 'race', 'religion', 'nationality' and 'political opinion'. Each of these grounds describes persecution aimed at an immutable characteristic: a characteristic that either is beyond the power of an individual to change or is so fundamental to individual identity or conscience that it ought not be required to be changed.—Thus, the other four grounds of persecution enumerated restrict refugee status to individuals who are either unable by their own actions, or as a matter of conscience should not be required, to avoid persecution. Applying the doctrine of *ejusdem generis,* we interpret the phrase 'persecution on account of membership in a particular social group' to mean persecution that is directed towards an individual who is a member of a group of persons all of whom share a common, immutable characteristic. The shared characteristic might be an innate one such as sex, colour or kinship ties

---

24. *Uttar Pradesh S.E. Board v. Hari Shanker,* AIR 1979 SC 65, p. 73 : (1978) 4 SCC 16.
25. *R. v. Immigration Appeal Tribunal,* (1999) 2 All ER 545 (HL).

or in some circumstances it might be a shared past experience such as former military leadership or land ownership."[26] It was, therefore held that women could constitute 'a particular social group' if they were discriminated against in a country in the matter of protection of human rights.

It is essential for application of the *ejusdem generis* rule that enumerated things before the general words must constitute a category or a genus or a family which admits of a number of species or members.[27] "It is requisite" said CHANDRASHEKHAR AIYAR, J., "that there must be a distinct genus, which must comprise more than one species;"[28] and "it is clearly laid down by decided cases", said SUBBARAO, J., "that the specific words must form a distinct genus or category".[29] If the specified things preceding general words belong to different categories, this principle of construction will not apply.[30] Further, mention of a single species does not constitute a genus.[31] Thus, in the phrase 'a salary or income' as it finds place in section 60(2) of the Presidency Insolvency Act, 1909 the word 'income' has not been construed *ejusdem generis* for the preceding word 'salary' signifies only one species and does not constitute a genus.[32] Similarly, the expression

26. *Ibid*, p. 553. This case is **further discussed** at pp. 647-651, *post*.
27. *State of Bombay v. Ali Gulshan*, AIR 1955 SC 810, p. 812 : 1955 (2) SCR 867; *Kavallappara Kottarathil Kochuni v. State of Madras*, AIR 1960 SC 1080, p. 1103 : 1960 (3) SCR 887; *Indramani Pyarelal Gupta (Dr.) v. W.R. Natu*, AIR 1963 SC 274, p. 281 : (1963) 1 SCR 721; *Jagdish Chandra Gupta v. Kajaria Traders (India) Ltd.*, AIR 1964 SC 1882, p. 1885 : 1964 (8) SCR 50; *Hamdard Dawakhana v. Union of India*, AIR 1965 SC 1167, p. 1172 : (1965) 2 SCR 192; *Raja Bhanu Pratap Singh v. Asstt. Custodian*, AIR 1966 SC 245, p. 246 : (1966) 1 SCR 304; *Tribhuvan Parkash Nayyar v. Union of India*, AIR 1970 SC 540, p. 545 : (1969) 3 SCC 99; *Jaga Ram v. State of Haryana*, AIR 1971 SC 1033 : (1971) 1 SCC 671; *Mangalore Electric Supply Co. Ltd. v. C.I.T., W.B.*, AIR 1978 SC 1272, p. 1275 : (1978) 3 SCC 248; *Siddeshwari Cotton Mills (P) Ltd. v. Union of India*, AIR 1989 SC 1019, p. 1023 : 1989 (1) SCR 214.
28. *State of Bombay v. Ali Gulshan*, AIR 1955 SC 810, p. 812 : 1955 (2) SCR 867.
29. *Kavalappara Kottarathil Kochuni v. State of Madras*, AIR 1960 SC 1080, p. 1103 : 1960 (3) SCR 887.
30. *National Association of Local Govt. Officers v. Bolton Corporation*, (1942) 2 All ER 425 (HL); *Hood Barrs v. IRC*, (1946) 2 All ER 768, p. 773 : 176 LT 283 (CA); *Indramani Pyarelal Gupta (Dr.) v. W.R. Natu*, AIR 1963 SC 274, pp. 280, 281 : 1963 (1) SCR 721; *Hamdard Dawakhana v. Union of India*, AIR 1965 SC 1167, p. 1172; *Raja Bhanu Pratap v. Assistant Custodian, E.P., Bahraich*, AIR 1966 SC 245, p. 246 : 1966 (1) SCR 304.
31. *United Town Electric Co. Ltd. v. A.G. for Newfoundland*, (1939) 1 All ER 423 (PC); **referred** to in *Mysore State Electricity Board v. Bangalore Woollen, Cotton & Silk Mills*, AIR 1963 SC 1128, p. 1138; *Jagdish Chandra Gupta v. Kajaria Traders (India) Ltd.*, AIR 1964 SC 1882, p. 1885; *Quazi v. Quazi*, (1979) 3 All ER 897, p. 902 (HL); *Siddeshwari Cotton Mills (P) Ltd. v. Union of India*, AIR 1989 SC 1019, p. 1023 : 1989 (1) SCC 420.
32. *P. Veerasamy v. Official Assignee High Court Madras,* JT 1999 (1) SC 8, p. 16 : AIR 1999 SC 661, p. 667 : (1999) 2 SCC 505.

'discharge or dismissal' in Item 1 of Schedule IV of Maharashtra (Recognition of Trade Unions and Prevention of Unfair Labour Practice) Act, 1971 has not been construed by the rule of *ejusdem generis* to limit the word 'discharge' to discharge as a matter of penalty on the reasoning that the wider word 'discharge' does not follow the more limited word 'dismissal' and neither of them is a genus nor species of the same very genus.[33]

In construing the definition of 'workmen' in the Industrial Courts Act, 1919 which reads: 'means any person who entered into or works under a contract with an employer whether the contract be by way of manual labour, clerical work or otherwise...'; VISCOUNT SIMON, L.C. said: "The use of words 'or otherwise' does not bring into play the *ejusdem generis* principle for 'manual labour' and 'clerical work' do not belong to a single limited genus."[34]

And, said LORD SIMONDS in another case: "Indeed if a collection of items is heterogeneous, it almost seems a conflict in words to say that they belong to the same genus."[35]

In interpreting section 20 of the United Town Electrical Company Act which reads: 'the company shall be liable for water rates on all lands and buildings owned by it in the aforesaid town, but otherwise the company shall be exempt from taxation', the Privy Council rejected the contention that the word 'taxation' should be construed *ejusdem generis* with 'water rate'; LORD THANKERTON said: "There is no room for the application of the principle of *ejusdem generis* in the absence of any mention of a genus, since the mention of a single species for example of water rates does not constitute a genus."[36]

In construing section 33 of the Barrow-in-Furness Corporation Extension Act, 1872 which provided: "No theatre or other place of public entertainment (other than such places of entertainment as are now subject to the provisions of the Barrow-in-Furness Corporation Act, 1868, section 164, and which last mentioned places are to continue subject to the provisions of that Act) shall be opened or used unless the same shall first have been licensed—"; ASQUITH, J., rejected the contention that 'other place of

33. *Lokmat Newspapers Pvt. Ltd. v. Shankar Prasad,* JT 1999 (4) SC 546, p. 579 : AIR 1999 SC 2423, p. 2444 : (1999) 6 SCC 275.
34. *National Association of Local Govt. Officers v. Bolton Corporation*, (1942) 2 All ER 425 (HL).
35. *Russel v. Scott*, (1948) 2 All ER 1, p. 4 (HL). **See further** *Housing Board of Haryana v. Haryana Housing Board Employees Union*, 1995 (6) Scale 139, p. 150 : AIR 1996 SC 434, p. 441 (para 51) : (1996) 1 SCC 95.
36. *United Town Electric Company Ltd. v. A.G. for Newfoundland*, (1939) 1 All ER 423 (PC).

public entertainment' should be read as subject to *ejusdem generis* rule and gave three reasons in support of his conclusion which may usefully be quoted: "(a) Words excepting a species from a genus are meaningless unless the species in question *prima facie* falls within the genus. 'All hats other than top hats' makes sense. 'All top hats other than bowler hats' does not. Equally little does 'All top hats and other articles except gloves', if other articles' are to be read as *ejusdem generis* with 'top hats'. Here the 'places' covered by section 164 of the 1868 Act—the places excepted—do not fall within the assumed genus 'theatre or other' similar 'place of public entertainment' although there may be an overlap between the two. (b) No case was cited to us in which a genus has been held to be constituted, not by the enumeration of a number of classes followed by the words 'or other', but by the mention of a single class (in this case 'theatre') followed by those words. (c) The tendency of more modern authorities is to attenuate the application of the *ejusdem generis* rule."[37]

Section 49(3) of the Electricity Supply Act, 1948 empowers the Electricity Board 'to fix different tariffs for the supply of electricity to any person—having regard to the geographical position of any area, the nature of the supply and purpose for which the supply is required and any other relevant factors.' In construing this section the Supreme Court declined to apply the rule of *ejusdem generis* for limiting the ambit of 'other relevant factors' on the ground that there was no genus of the relevant factors.[38] The enumerated factors *viz.,* geographical position of the area and the nature and purpose of the supply could not be related to any common genus to enable the application of the *ejusdem generis* rule.

In construing the words 'a claim of set-off or other proceeding to enforce a right arising from contract', occurring in section 69 of the Indian Partnership Act, 1932, the Supreme Court refused to limit the generality of 'other proceeding' and to apply the *ejusdem generis* rule as the preceding phrase 'a claim of set-off', did not constitute a genus or category.[39] In that case, HIDAYATULLAH, J., in explaining the principle that the rule cannot be applied unless there be "a genus constituted or a category disclosed", gave the following illustration: "In the expression 'books, pamphlets, newspapers and other documents', private letters may not be held included if

---

37. *Allen v. Emmerson*, (1944) 1 All ER 344, p. 347 : 1944 KB 362 (KBD).

38. *Jiyajirao Cotton Mills Ltd. v. Madhya Pradesh Electricity Board*, AIR 1989 SC 788, p. 809 : 1988 (4) JT 737 : 1989 Supp (2) SCC 52; *Adoni Cotton Mills v. A.P. State Electricity Board*, AIR 1976 SC 2414 : 1976 (4) SCC 68; *Bihar State Electricity Board v. Parmeshwar Kumar Agarwala*, AIR 1996 SC 2214, p. 2215 : 1996 (4) SCC 686.

39. *Jagdish Chandra Gupta v. Kajaria Traders (India) Ltd.*, AIR 1964 SC 1882, p. 1885 : 1964 (8) SCR 50.

'other documents' be interpreted *ejusdem generis* with what goes before. But in a provision which reads 'newspapers or other documents, likely to convey secrets to the enemy', the words 'other documents' would include document of any kind and would not take their colour from newspaper."[40]

Similarly, section 141 of the Indian Penal Code, 1860, defines 'unlawful assembly' to be an assembly of five or more persons, if the common object of the persons composing that assembly is *inter alia*, to commit any mischief or criminal trespass, 'or other offence'. The Supreme Court refused to apply the principle of *ejusdem generis* to the words 'other offence', and thereby restrict it only to minor offences such as mischief or criminal trespass. The words 'other offence' were therefore held to mean all other offences which are punishable under the IPC in light of the definition of 'offence' in section 40 of the IPC.[41]

If the preceding words do not constitute mere specifications of a genus but constitute description of a complete genus, the rule has no application. In a policy of insurance, the insurers were given an option to terminate the policy if they so desired 'by reason of such change or from any other cause whatever'; the words 'by reason of such change' in the context referred to any and every act done to the insured property whereby the risk of fire was increased; the Privy Council in these circumstances refused to construe the words 'or from any other cause whatever' by the rule of *ejusdem generis*. LORD WATSON said: "In the present case, there appears no room for its application. The antecedent clause does not contain a mere specification of particulars but the description of a complete genus". It was held that the insurers could terminate the policy at will.[42] Similarly, if the preceding words and the general words in question constitute description of two categories or genera or the general words in question in themselves constitute

40. *Ibid.* For further illustrations where the rule was not applied for want of a genus, **see** the following cases: *Hamdard Dawakhana v. Union of India*, AIR 1965 SC 1167, p. 1172 : (1965) 2 SCR 192 (section 2(d)(o) of the Fruits Products Order); *Raja Bhanu Pratap Singh v. Assistant Custodian,* AIR 1966 SC 245, p. 246 : (1965) 3 SCR 499 (section 10(2)(n) of the Administration of Evacuee Property Act, 1950); *Akarapu Katta Mallu v. Purna Chandra Rao*, AIR 1967 SC 1363 : (1967) 2 SCR 309 (section 562-A, CrPC, 1898); *Tribhuwan Parkash Nayyar v. Union of India*, AIR 1970 SC 540, p. 545 : (1969) 3 SCC 99. (Rule 18 of the Displaced Persons (Verification of Claims) Supplementary Rules, 1954); *Collector of Central Excise, Coimbatore v. Protein Products of India Ltd.*, AIR 1989 SC 627, p. 629 : 1989 Supp (1) SCC 729 (Exemption notification Dt/30-6-1979 under the Central Excises and Salt Act, 1944).

41. *Manga v. State of Uttarakhand*, (2013) 7 SCC 629, pp. 650, 651.

42. *Sun Fire Office v. Hart*, (1889) 14 AC 98, p. 104 (PC); **referred** to with **approval** in *Central Bank of India v. Hartford Fire Insurance Co.*, AIR 1965 SC 1288, p. 1291 : (1965) 35 Com Cases 378. **See further** *United Bank of India v. Pijush Kanti Nandy*, (2009) 8 SCC 605 para 28.

description of a distinct category, the rule will have no application. In construing the words 'for the purpose of a State or any other public purpose' in section 6(4)(a) of the Bombay Land Requisition Act, 1948, the Supreme Court declined to apply the rule of *ejusdem generis* for the construction of the words 'or any other public purpose' and pointed out by referring to the legislative entries in the lists that 'State purpose' and 'any other public purpose' were in themselves two distinct categories.[43]

The rule of *ejusdem generis* has to be applied with care and caution. It is not an inviolable rule of law, but it is only permissible inference in the absence of an indication to the contrary,[44] and where context and the object and mischief of the enactment do not require restricted meaning to be attached to words of general import, it becomes the duty of the courts to give those words their plain and ordinary meaning.[45] As stated by LORD SCARMAN: "If the legislative purpose of a statute is such that a statutory series should be read *ejusdem generis*, so be it, the rule is helpful. But, if it is not, the rule is more likely to defeat than to fulfil the purpose of the statute. The rule like many other rules of statutory interpretation, is a useful servant but a bad master."[46] So a narrow construction on the basis of *ejusdem generis* rule may have to give way to a broader construction to give effect to the intention of Parliament by adopting a purposive construction.[47] In interpreting section 1 of the Sunday Observance Act, 1780 (UK) which reads—'any house, room or other place which shall be opened or used for public entertainment on any part of Lords Day—shall be deemed a disorderly house', the Court of Queens Bench Division rejected the argument that the word 'place' should be construed *ejudem generis* with the preceding words 'house' and 'room'. It was held that looking to the mischief aimed at, the intention of Parliament in the use of the word 'place' was deliberate to give it a wider meaning than the words 'house' and

---

43. *State of Bombay v. Ali Gulshan*, AIR 1955 SC 810 : 1995 (2) SCR 867.

44. *Kavalappara Kottarathil Kochuni v. State of Madras*, AIR 1960 SC 1080, p. 1103 : 1960 (3) SCR 887; *Tribhuwan Parkash Nayyar v. Union of India*, AIR 1970 SC 540, p. 545 : (1969) 3 SCC 99 (the rule is neither final nor conclusive). *Mangalore Electric Supply. Co. Ltd. v. C.I.T., West Bengal*, AIR 1978 SC 1272, p. 1275 : (1978) 3 SCC 248; *Grasim Industries Ltd. v. Collector of Customs Bombay,* AIR 2002 SC 1706, p. 1710 : (2002) 4 SC 297.

45. *Lilawati Bai v. State of Bombay*, AIR 1957 SC 521, p. 529 : 1957 SCR 721; *Hamdard Dawakhana v. Union of India*, AIR 1965 SC 1167, p. 1172 : (1965) 2 SCR 192; *Grasim Industries Ltd. v. Collector of Customs Bombay, supra.*

46. *Quazi v. Quazi*, (1979) 3 All ER 897, p. 916 : 1980 AC 744 : (1979) 3 WLR 823 (HL).

47. **See** *Re, C (a minor)*, (1996) 4 All ER 871, p. 877 (a to e) (HL). **See further** *Maharashtra University of Health Science v. Satchikitsa Prasarak Mandal*, (2010) 3 SCC 786 para 38 : AIR 2010 SC 1325.

'room'.[48] This case may be compared with a decision of the House of Lords where the words 'other place' were construed *ejusdem generis* in the phrase 'house, office, room or other place'.[49] The conflicting results illustrate the principle that the rule of *ejusdem generis* like many other rules is merely a canon of construction which gives way to the clear intention of the Legislature. Quoting the above portions of this book to illustrate that the principle of *ejusdem generis* does not apply in every situation, the Supreme Court held that in a widely worded contractual clause, which states that no interest shall be payable by the employer on earnest money, security deposit or on 'any money due to the contractor by the employer', the words 'any money due' cannot be read *ejusdem generis* with 'earnest money' or 'security deposit', and hence the employer was not liable to pay interest on the amount due to the contractor under an arbitral award prior to the date of the award.[50]

It may also be noticed that the rule of *ejusdem generis* has, it appears, no inverse application. General words preceding the enumeration of specific instances are not governed by this rule and their import cannot be limited by any such principle.[51] At any rate, when the Legislature before

---

48. *Culley v. Harrison*, (1956) 2 All ER 254.

49. *Powell v. Kempton Park Racecourse*, (1899) AC 143 : 80 LT 538 (HL).

50. *BHEL v. Globe Hi-Fabs Ltd.*, (2015) 5 SCC 718.

51. *Re, Wellsted's Will Trusts*, (1949) 1 All ER 577, p. 587 (CA); *Canadian National Railways v. Canada Steamship Lines Ltd.*, (1945) AC 204, p. 211 (PC); *Thakur Amarsinghji v. State of Rajasthan*, AIR 1955 SC 504, p. 523 : (1955) 2 SCR 303, *Timblo Irmaos Ltd. Margao v. Jorge Anibal Motos Sequeira*, AIR 1977 SC 734, p. 739 : (1977) 3 SCC 474.

N.B.—'*Vide*' or '*Videlicet*' means 'to wit' or 'that is to say'. 'Etc.' or 'etcetera' does not mean '*et alia*', but means 'and all the rest'. A clause in a charter party was worded as follows: 'Should the vessel be detained by causes over which the charterers have no control, *viz.* quarantine, ice, hurricane, blockade, clearing of the steamer after the last cargo is taken over, etc. no demurrage is to be charged and lay days not to count'; Held, the initial general words were not limited to particular instances mentioned but referred to all causes over which the charterers had no control; **See** *Ambatielos v. Anton Jurgens Margarine Works*, (1922) All ER 543, pp. 546, 549 : 1923 AC 175 (HL). The meaning of expression 'that is to say' varies according to context. It may have the object of explaining, extending or limiting the meaning of a preceding clause; *State of Tamil Nadu v. Pyarelal Malhotra*, AIR 1976 SC 800, pp. 803, 804 : (1976) 1 SCC 834; and it may be construed as exhaustive : *Sait Rikhaji Furtarnal v. State of Andhra Pradesh*, AIR 1991 SC 354 : 1991 Supp (1) SCC 202; *Commissioner of Sales Tax v. Popular Trading Company*, JT 2000 (4) SC 253, p. 256 : AIR 2000 SC 1578 : (2000) 5 SCC 511 ('that is to say' is descriptive, enumerative and exhaustive); *Castrol India Ltd. v. Commissioner of Central Excise, Calcutta*, (2005) 3 SCC 30, pp. 36, 37 ('that is to say' are words of limitation used in descriptive, enumerative and exhaustive sense); *Mahindra Engineering & Chemical Products Ltd. v. Union of India*, AIR 1993 SC 406, (para 3) : (1992) 1 SCC 727 (Use of expressions 'namely', or 'that is to say' followed by

[Footnote No. 51 Contd.]

enumerating specific examples uses the words 'without prejudice to the generality of the foregoing provision' the preceding general provision cannot be restricted by applying the rule of *ejusdem generis*.[52]

A word of caution is here necessary. The fact that the *ejusdem generis* rule is not applicable does not necessarily mean that the *prima facie* wide meaning of the word 'other' or similar general words cannot be restricted if the language or the context and the policy of the Act demand a restricted construction.[53] In the expression 'defect of jurisdiction or other cause of a like nature' as they occur in section 14(1) of the Limitation Act, 1963 the generality of the words 'other cause' is cut down expressly by the words 'of a like nature', though the rule of *ejusdem generis* is strictly not applicable as mention of a single species 'defect of jurisdiction' does not constitute a genus.[54] Another example that may here be mentioned is section 129 of the Motor Vehicles Act, 1939 which empowers any police officer authorised in this behalf or other person authorised in this behalf by the State Government' to detain and seize vehicles used without certification of registration or permit. The words 'other person' in this section cannot be construed by the rule of *ejusdem generis* for mention of single species namely 'police officer' does not constitute a genus but having regard to the importance of the power to detain and seize vehicles it is proper to infer that the words 'other person' were restricted to the category of Government

---

[Footnote No. 51 Contd.]

description of goods is usually exhaustive unless there are strong indications to the contrary); *State of Karnataka v. Balaji Computers,* (2007) 2 SCC 743 (paras 17 to 29) : (2007) 1 JT 250 (meaning of words 'namely', 'that is to say'); *Sree Durga Distributors v. State of Karnataka,* (2007) 4 SCC 465 (para 5) : AIR 2007 SC 1751 ('namely' followed by description of goods held exhaustive). **See further** *Royal Hatcheries Pvt. Ltd. v. State of Andhra Pradesh*, AIR 1994 SC 666, p. 667 : 1994 Supp (1) SCC 429 (use of 'etc.' after enumeration following 'that is to say' will not make the enumeration exhaustive).

52. *Chertsey UDC v. Mixnam's Properties Ltd.*, (1964) 2 All ER 627, pp. 630, 631 : 1965 AC 735 (HL). **See further** *Emperor v. Sibnath Banerji*, AIR 1945 PC 156; *Afzal Ullah v. State of U.P.*, AIR 1964 SC 264, p. 268 : (1964) 4 SCR 991; *Shiv Kirpal Singh v. V.V. Giri*, AIR 1970 SC 2097, p. 2112 : (1970) 2 SCC 567.

53. *R. v. Clarke*, (1985) 2 All ER 777, p. 782 : 1985 AC 1037; *Quazi v. Quazi*, (1979) 3 All ER 897, p. 903 : (1980) 2 AC 744 (HL). **See** title 8(b), *Noscitur a Sociis*.

54. *Zafar Khan v. Board of Revenue*, (1984) (Supp) SCC 505, p. 516 : AIR 1985 SC 39 (The rule of *ejusdem generis* wrongly applied, but the decision is correct). But if the words 'and the like' are preceded by more than one species of a genus they would be construed *ejusdem generis*; *Express Hotels Pvt. Ltd. v. State of Gujarat*, AIR 1989 SC 1949, p. 1960 : (1989) 3 SCC 677. For construction of the words 'or the like' **see further** *Shree Chamundi Mopeds Ltd. v. Church of South India Trust Association*, AIR 1992 SC 1439, p. 1445 : 1992 (3) SCC 1 : 1992 (3) JT 98.

Officers.[55] In the same category falls the case interpreting the words 'before filing a written statement or taking any other steps in the proceedings' as they occur in section 34 of the Arbitration Act, 1940. In the context in which the expression 'any other steps' finds place it has been rightly construed to mean a step clearly and unambiguously manifesting an intention to waive the benefit of arbitration agreement, although the rule of *ejusdem generis* has no application for mention of a single species *viz.,* written statement does not constitute a genus.[56]

(d) Words of Rank

As an outcome of the rule of *ejusdem generis*, there is another rule that statutes which deal with persons or things of inferior rank are not extended to those of superior degree by introduction of general words and the general words following particular words will not cover anything of a class superior to those to which the particular words relate.[57] Thus, it has been held that a duty imposed on 'copper, brass, pewter, and tin and all other metals not enumerated' did not cover silver or gold, these being of a superior kind to the particular metals enumerated.[58]

(e) *Reddendo Singula Singulis*

The rule may be stated from an Irish case in the following words: "Where there are general words of description, following an enumeration of particular things such general words are to be construed distributively, *reddendo singula singulis*; and if the general words will apply to some things and not to others, the general words are to be applied to those things to which they will, and not to those to which they will not apply; that rule is beyond all controversy."[59] Thus, 'I devise and bequeath all my real and

---

55. *Ishwar Singh Bagga v. State of Rajasthan*, (1987) 1 SCC 101, p. 113 : AIR 1987 SC 628 (The rule of *ejusdem generis* wrongly applied but the decision is correct). **Distinguished** in *Rajkumar Gupta v. Lt. Governor, Delhi*, AIR 1997 SC 2680 : (1997) 1 SCC 556 (Interpreting section 34 of the Industrial Disputes Act, 1947, it was held that the Government may authorise a private person to file a complaint).

56. *Food Corpn. of India v. Yadav Engineer and Contractor*, (1983) 1 SCR 95, p. 106 : (1982) 2 SCC 499 : AIR 1982 SC 1302 **referred** to in *Rachappa Guruadappa v. Gurusidappa Nariamappa*, AIR 1989 SC 635, p. 637 : (1989) 1 SCC 345 (rule of *ejusdem generis* wrongly applied).

57. *Canterbury's (Archbishop)* case, (1596) 76 ER 519; *Copland v. Powell*, (1823) 130 ER 149.

58. *Casher v. Holmes*, (1831) 109 ER 1263 : 109 ECR 1263.

59. *M'Neill v. Crommelin*, (1858) 9 Ir CLR 61 : 62 Digest, p. 672. In *Koteswar Vittal Kamnath v. K. Rangappa Baliga & Co.*, AIR 1969 SC 504, p. 511 : (1969) 1 SCC 255, the Supreme Court **quoted** the rule from BLACKS Interpretation of Laws as follows: "When a sentence in a statute contains several antecedents and several consequences, they are to be read distributively, that is to say each phrase or expression is to be referred to its appropriate objects".

personal property to A' will be construed, *reddendo singula singulis* by applying 'devise' to 'real' property and 'bequeath' to 'personal' property,[60] and in the sentence: 'If any one shall draw or load any sword or gun' the word 'draw' is applied to 'sword' only and the word 'load' to 'gun' only, because it is impossible to load a sword or draw a gun.[61]

An example of the application of the rule is furnished in the construction of section 59(1) of the Local Government Act, 1933 which reads: 'A person shall be disqualified for being elected or being a member of a local authority if he has within five years before the day of election or since his election been convicted of any offence and ordered to be imprisoned for a period of not less than three months without the option of fine'. CLAUSON, J., construing the section said: "The section provides for two matters: *first* what is to be disqualification for election? and, *secondly* what is to be disqualification for being a member after election? and it provides for two disqualifications: *first,* conviction within five years before the day of election; and *secondly,* conviction since election. It is obvious that the second disqualification mentioned does not fit the first case mentioned, namely that of election, but does fit the second case, and the second case only. It is also obvious that the first disqualification mentioned fits the first case, and it does not seem at all apt to fit the second case." And, after referring to certain strange results, if the first disqualification, were applied to the second case, he proceeded on to say: "All difficulty can be avoided by applying the well-known method of construction commonly known as *reddendo singula singulis*; and applying the first disqualification mentioned to first case dealt with, and the second disqualification to the second case dealt with—". It was, therefore, held that a conviction prior to election although a disqualification for the election was not a disqualification for continuing to be a member and if the election was not challenged by election petition within the time limited therefor, the member did not vacate his seat.[62]

Another example of the application of the rule is found in the construction of the Proviso to Article 304 of the Constitution which reads: '*Provided* that no Bill or amendment for the purpose of clause (b) shall be introduced or moved in the Legislature of a State without the previous sanction of the President'. It was held by the Supreme Court that the word 'introduced' referred to 'Bill' and the word 'moved' to Amendment.[63]

---

60. OSBORNE, Concise Law Dictionary, 7th Edition, p. 281.

61. WHARTON, Law Lexicon, 14th Edition, p. 850.

62. *Bishop v. Deakin*, (1936) 1 All ER 255, p. 257. Cf. *Election Commission, India v. Saka Venkata Rao*, AIR 1953 SC 210, p. 215 : 1953 SCR 1144.

63. *Koteswar Vittal Kamath v. K. Rangappa Baliga & Co.*, AIR 1969 SC 504, p. 511 : (1969) 1 SCC 255.

CHAPTER 6

OPERATION OF STATUTES

SYNOPSIS

1. COMMENCEMENT

'Commencement', used with reference to an Act, means the day on which the Act comes into force.[1] Unless provided otherwise, a Central Act comes into operation on the day it receives the Presidential assent and is construed as coming into operation immediately on the expiration of the day preceding its commencement.[2] Thus, if a Central Act is assented to by the President on 26th January at 10.30 a.m., it would be construed to have come into operation on the midnight between 25th and 26th January.[3]

Under the various State General Clauses Acts a State Act comes into force on the day when the assent of the Governor or the President, as the case may be, is first published in the Official Gazette of the State.[4]

---

1. Section 3(13), General Clauses Act, 1897.

2. Section 5, General Clauses Act, 1897; *C.I.T., Punjab v. R.B. Jodha Mal Kuthiala*, AIR 1966 SC 1433 : (1966) 2 SCR 645. Section 5 of the General Clauses Act has no application when the Act provides that it will come into force on a date to be notified by the Central Government : *Common Cause v. Union of India*, (2003) 8 SCC 250, p. 262 : AIR 2003 SC 4493.

3. **See** *Tomlinson v. Bullock*, (1879) 4 QBD 230. **See also** *S.S. Gadgil v. Lal & Co.*, AIR 1965 SC 171, p. 175 : (1964) 8 SCR 72; *B.N. Agarwalla v. State of Orissa*, 1995 (6) Scale 54, p. 56 : (1995) 6 SCC 509.

4. Section 5, Assam Act 2 of 1915; Section 6, Bengal Act 1 of 1899; Section 5, Bombay Act 1 of 1904; Section 6, Bihar & Orissa Act 1 of 1917; Section 3, Madhya Pradesh Act 3 of 1958; Section 5, Madras Act 1 of 1891; Section 3, Orissa Act 1 of 1937; Section 3, Punjab Act 1 of 1898; Section 5, U.P. Act 1 of 1904; Section 3, Travancore-Cochin Act 8 of 1125 M.E.; Section 5, Rajasthan Act 8 of 1959; Section 5(1)(iii), Mysore Act 3 of 1899. **See** *Deputy Commercial Tax Officer, Madras v. Sha Sukraj Peeraji*, AIR 1968 SC 67, p. 70 : (1967) 3 SCR 661 (a case under the Madras General Clauses Act, 1891).

Quite often the commencement of an Act is postponed to some specified future date or to such date as the appropriate Government may, by notification in the Official Gazette, appoint.[5] Provision is also at times made for appointment of different dates for coming into force of different parts of the same Act. Care has to be taken to bring into force all related provisions together for delay in bringing into force a related provision may defeat the legislative intent during the intervening period.[6]

An Act cannot be said to commence or to be in force unless it is brought into operation by legislative enactment or by the exercise of authority by a delegate empowered to bring it into operation.[7] Power to bring into force an Act can be exercised by the delegate even though the Legislature may have ceased to be competent to enact the Act if it was within the competence of the Legislature at the time of its enactment.[8] When enforcement of a statute or a provision therein is left to the discretion of the Government without laying down any objective standards, no writ of *mandamus* can be issued to the Government to enforce the statute or the provision.[9] But if considerable time has elapsed since passing of the statute a writ can be issued directing the Government to consider the question whether the statute or the provision should be brought into force.[10] Further, although the court has power to stay the operation of a statute, this should be done only in exceptional cases.[11]

---

5. **See** *State of Bombay v. Salat Pragji*, AIR 1957 SC 517, p. 521 : 1957 SCR 745. **See further** *Orient Paper Industries Ltd. v. State of Orissa*, AIR 1991 SC 672, p. 682 : 1991 Supp (1) SCC 81 (Original Act brought into force by notification; Retrospective amendment from its inception not to be brought into force by fresh notification).
6. *J. Mitra & Company Private Ltd. v. Assistant Controller of Patents and Designs*, (2008) 10 SCC 369 paras 26 and 29 : AIR 2009 SC 405 [Delay in bringing into force amended sections 116 and 117(2) of the Patents Act, 1970].
7. *State of Orissa v. Chandrashekhar Singh*, AIR 1970 SC 398 : (1969) 2 SCC 334; *Union of India v. Sukumar Sen Gupta*, AIR 1990 SC 1692 : 1990 Supp SCC 545.
8. *Ishwar Das v. Union of India*, AIR 1972 SC 1193 : (1972) 1 SCC 646. *State of Assam v. K.B. Kurkalang*, AIR 1972 SC 223 : (1972) 1 SCC 148; *J. Mitra & Company Private Ltd. v. Assistant Controller of Patents & Designs (supra)* para 27.
9. *A.K. Roy v. Union of India*, AIR 1982 SC 710 : (1982) 1 SCC 271; *Altmesh Rein v. Union of India*, AIR 1988 SC 1768 : (1988) 4 SCC 54. **See further** *Attorney-General for India v. Amratlal Prajivandas*, JT 1994 (3) SC 583, p. 618 : AIR 1994 SC 2179 : (1994) 5 SCC 54; *Union of India v. Prakash Hinduja,* (2003) 6 SCC 195, p. 217 : AIR 2003 SC 2612; *Common Cause v. Union of India,* (2003) 8 SCC 250, p. 262 : AIR 2003 SC 4493.
10. *Altmesh Rein v. Union of India, supra.*
11. *Factortome Ltd. v. Secretary of State for Transport*, (1991) 1 All ER 70 (CJEC and HL); *Bhavesh D. Parish & Co. v. Union of India,* JT 2000 (6) SC 604, p. 622 : AIR 2000 SC 2047, p. 2057 : (2000) 5 SCC 471 (The presumption being that the law is constitutional, there should be normally no stay especially in a matter relating to economic reform). For effect of the vacation of stay order on the operation of the Act, **see** *Employees State Insurance Corp. v. All India ITDC Employees Union,* (2006) 4 SCC 257 : (2006) 4 JT 26 and cases **referred** therein (court cannot direct that the statute shall operate prospectively).

The House of Lords has also held that when certain provisions of a statute are to come into force on a day to be appointed by a minister by order made by statutory instrument, the courts could not compel the minister to bring those provisions into effect;[12] but the minister's discretion was not unfettered and he was required to keep the question whether those statutory provisions should be brought into force under review and it would be an abuse or excess of power for him to exercise a prerogative power inconsistent with that duty.[13] A provision in a statute cannot be made operative by applying the doctrine of legitimate expectation when the provision is yet to come into force on a notification issued by the executive Government.[14]

A provision in a Bill does not come into operation unless the enacting process is over and the resultant Act containing that provision is brought into operation. But an Act can provide that provisions of a Bill on a given subject will come into operation on their introduction in the Legislature. Thus, section 4 of the Provisional Collection of Taxes Act, 1931 provides that a declared provision (which refers to a provision relating to increase of a duty of Customs and Excise with a declaration that it is in public interest that the provision should have immediate effect) will have the force of law immediately on the expiry of the day on which the Bill containing the provision is introduced and it will cease to have the force of law when the provisions of the Act come into operation as an enactment.[15]

When an Act is preceded by an identically worded Ordinance and the Act contains a provision that 'all actions and orders under the Ordinance are deemed to have been under the Act', for all practical purposes the Act will be deemed to be in operation and effective from the date of the commencement of the Ordinance.[16]

An Act not applicable to an area or a state cannot be made to apply there by judicial fiat but if a provision in such an Act embodies a principle of justice, equity or good conscience the principle so embodied may be applied to a case arising from an area or state to which the Act does not extend, if the fact situation of the case so requires.[17]

---

12. *R. v. Secretary of State for the Home Department, ex parte, Fire Brigade Union*, (1995) 2 All ER 244, p. 252 : (1995) 2 AC 513 (HL).

13. *Ibid*, p. 253.

14. *R. v. Director of Public Prosecutions exparte Kebeline,* (1999) 4 All ER 801, p. 833 (HL). For doctrine of legitimate expectation, **see** pp. 499-503, *ante*.

15. *Pieco Electronics & Electricals Ltd. v. Collector of Central Excise*, JT 1997 (10) SC 368, pp. 369, 370 : 1997 (2) SCC 220 : (1996) 87 ELT 577.

16. *Fuerst Day Lawson Ltd. v. Jindal Exports Ltd.*, AIR 2001 SC 2293, pp. 2296, 2301, 2302 : (2001) 6 SCC 336.

17. *Panchugopal Barua v. Umesh Chandra Goswamy*, JT 1997 (2) SC 554, pp. 565, 566 : AIR 1997 SC 1041, pp. 1046, 1047 : (1997) 4 SCC 713.

Although, unless otherwise provided, a Central Act comes into operation on the day it receives the Presidential assent, the gap between the date of assent and the date of promulgation of the Act may, in cases affecting personal liberty, give rise to a defence of want of fair procedure.[18]

2. RETROSPECTIVE OPERATION

(a) General principles

(i) *Power to make retrospective laws.*—The Union Parliament and State Legislatures have plenary powers of legislation within the fields assigned to them and subject to certain constitutional and judicially recognised restrictions[19] can legislate prospectively as well as retrospectively.[20] Competence to make a law for a past period on a subject depends upon present competence to legislate on that subject.[21] By retrospective legislation, the Legislature may make a law which is operative for a limited period prior to the date of its coming into force and is not operative either on that date or in future.[22] The power to make retrospective legislation enables the Legislature to obliterate an amending Act completely and restore the law as it existed before the amending Act.[23] This power has also been often used for validating prior executive and legislative acts by retrospectively curing the defect which led to their invalidity and thus even making ineffective judgments of competent courts declaring the invalidity.[24] It is not necessary

---

18. *R (On the application of L) v. Secretary of State for the Home Department,* (2003) 1 All ER 1062, pp. 1067 (para 17), 1068 (para 24), 1069 (para 26) (CA). **See further** text and note 11, p. 998.

19. *State of Gujarat v. Raman Lal Keshav Lal Soni,* (1983) 2 SCR 287 : 1983 (2) SCC 33 : AIR 1984 SC 161; *State of Tamil Nadu v. Arooran Sugars Ltd.*, AIR 1997 SC 1815, pp. 1822, 1823 : (1997) 1 SCC 326; *National Agricultural Cooperative Marketing Federation of India Ltd. v. Union of India,* (2003) 5 SCC 23, p. 30 : AIR 2003 SC 1329 (Implied judicially recognised limitations for making retrospective legislation).

20. *United Provinces v. Atiqa Begum (Mt.)*, AIR 1941 FC 16, p. 26 : 194 FCR 110; *Piare Dusadh v. Emperor,* AIR 1944 FC 1, pp. 9, 10; *M.P.V. Sundararamier v. State of A.P.*, AIR 1958 SC 468, p. 486 : 1959 SCR 1422; *J.K. Jute Mills Co. Ltd. v. State of U.P.*, AIR 1961 SC 1534, p. 1540 : (1962) 2 SCR 1; *Rai Ramkrishna v. State of Bihar,* AIR 1963 SC 1667, p. 1673 : (1964) 1 SCR 897; *K.C. Arora v. State of Haryana,* (1984) 3 SCC 281, pp. 288, 289 : AIR 1984 SC 1; *Bhubaneshwar Singh v. Union of India,* JT 1994 (5) SC 83, p. 87 : (1994) 6 SCC 77; *Bakhtawar Trust v. Narayana,* AIR 2003 SC 2236, p. 2241; *Virendra Singh Hooda v. State of Haryana,* AIR 2005 SC 137, pp. 147, 152 (can take away vested rights). **See** also *Sabally v. A.G.*, (1964) 3 All ER 377 (CA); *Western Transport Pvt. Ltd. v. Kropp,* (1964) 3 All ER 722 (PC).

21. *A. Hajee Abdul Shukoor & Co. v. State of Madras,* AIR 1964 SC 1729, p. 1735 (para 33) : (1964) 8 SCR 217.

22. *District Mining Officer v. Tata Iron & Steel Co.,* AIR 2001 SC 3134, pp. 3140, 3155 : (2001) 7 SCC 358.

23. *State of Tamil Nadu v. Arooran Sugars Ltd.*, AIR 1997 SC 1815 : 1997 (1) SCC 326.

24. **See** text and notes 29 to 35, pp. 53, 54, *supra*.

that the invalidity must be cured by the same Legislature which had passed the earlier invalid Act. Thus, if a state Legislature passes an Act on a subject which falls outside its competence and within the competence of Parliament and is for that reason held invalid, Parliament can by passing a retrospective Act which incorporates the State Act cure the invalidity.[25]

(ii) *Statutes dealing with substantive rights.*—It is a cardinal principle of construction that every statute is *prima facie* prospective unless it is expressly or by necessary implication made to have retrospective operation.[26] There is a presumption of prospectivity articulated in the legal maxim '*nova constitutio futuris formam imponere debet non praeteritis*', *i.e.* 'a new law ought to regulate what is to follow, not the past', and this presumption operates unless shown to the contrary by express provision in the statute or is otherwise discernible by necessary implication.[27] But the rule in general is applicable where the object of the statute is to affect vested rights or to impose new burdens or to impair existing obligations. Unless there are words in the statute sufficient to show the intention of the Legislature to affect existing rights, it is "deemed to be prospective only - '*nova constitutio futuris formam imponere debet non praeteritis*'[28] [2 c. Int. 392]."[29] In the words of LORD BLANESBURG, "provisions which touch a right in

---

25. *P. Kannadasan v. State of Tamil Nadu*, AIR 1996 SC 2560 : 1996 (5) SCC 670.

26. *Keshvan v. State of Bombay*, AIR 1951 SC 128, p. 130 : 1951 SCR 228; *Janardan Reddy v. State*, AIR 1951 SC 124, p. 127 : 1950 SCR 940; *Mahadeolal Kanodia v. Administrator General of W.B.*, AIR 1960 SC 936, p. 939 : (1960) 3 SCR 578; *State of Bombay v. Vishnu Ramchandra*, AIR 1961 SC 307, p. 309 : (1961) 2 SCR 924; *Rafiquennessa (Mst.) v. Lal Bahadur Chetri*, AIR 1964 SC 1511, p. 1514 : (1964) 6 SCR 876; *Arjan Singh v. State of Punjab*, AIR 1970 SC 703, p. 705 : (1969) 2 SCR 347; *K.C. Arora v. State of Haryana*, (1984) 3 SCC 281, pp. 288, 289 : AIR 1984 SC 1; *Mithilesh Kumari v. Prem Bahadur Khare*, AIR 1989 SC 1247, pp. 1253,1254 : (1989) 2 SCC 95; *State of Madhya Pradesh v. Rameshwar Rathod*, AIR 1990 SC 1849 : 1990 (4) SCC 21; *Shyam Sunder v. Ram Kumar,* AIR 2001 SC 2472, pp. 2481, 2482 : (2001) 8 SCC 24 : *Zile Singh v. State of Haryana*, AIR 2004 SC 5100, p. 5103 : (2004) 8 SCC 1, p. 8, (9th Edn., p. 438 of this book is **referred**); *Gem Granites v. Cammr. of Income Tax*, (2005) 1 SCC 229, p. 296; *C. Gupta v. Glaxo-Smithkline Pharmaceuticals Ltd.*, (2007) 7 SCC 171 (Broadening of the definition of 'Workman' by amendment in the Industrial Disputes Act, 1947 is not retrospective to affect the dismissal of an employee who was not a workman on the date of his dismissal). *J.S. Yadav v. State of Uttar Pradesh and another,* (2011) 6 SCC 570 (para 24).

27. *Monnet Ispat & Energy Ltd. v. Union of India & Ors.*, (2012) 11 SCC 1, p. 90. Applying the presumption of prospectivity, the Supreme Court held that as there is no indication in section 17-A of the Mines and Minerals (Development and Regulation) Act, 1957, or in the Amending Act of 1987, which inserted section 17-A, that Parliament intended to undo the state of affairs prior to 1987 by virtue of the same. Therefore, the provision was effective from 1987 and had no retrospective operation.

28. 'A new law ought to regulate what is to follow, not the past'. OSBORN: Concise Law Dictionary, p. 224.

29. *Doolubdass Pettamberdass v. Ramloll Thackoorseydass*, (1850) 5 MIA 109, pp. 126, 127 (BARON PARKE MR); *K.C. Arora v. State of Haryana, supra*; *Zile Singh v. State of Haryana, supra*. **See further** *K.S. Paripoornan v. State of Kerala*, JT 1994 (6) SC 182, pp. 213, 214 : AIR 1995 SC 1012, p. 1034 : (1994) 5 SCC 593; *Shakti Tubes Ltd. v. State of Bihar,* (2009) 7 SCC 673 Para 24 : (2009) 9 JT 386.

existence at the passing of the statute are not to be applied retrospectively in the absence of express enactment or necessary intendment."[30] "Every statute, it has been said", observed LOPES, L.J., "which takes away or impairs vested rights acquired under existing laws, or creates a new obligation or imposes a new duty, or attaches a new disability in respect of transactions already past, must be presumed to be intended not to have a retrospective effect".[31]

If rights created in favour of any person, whether they are property rights or rights arising from a transaction in the nature of a contract or rights protected under a statute, are to be taken away by any legislation, then that legislation will have to say so specifically by giving its provisions a retrospective effect. This principle was applied by the Supreme Court to protect a 'deemed tenant' under section 15A of the Bombay Rent Act, 1947, from eviction as an 'unauthorised occupant' under the Public Premises (Eviction of Unauthorised Occupants) Act, 1971. The Supreme Court held that a 'deemed tenant' under the 1947 Act continued to be protected under its succeeding Act, being the Maharashtra Rent Control Act, 1999, in view of the definition of 'tenant' under section 7(15)(a)(ii) thereof, and he therefore cannot be said to be in 'unauthorised occupation' of the premises. His right as a 'deemed tenant' cannot be destroyed by giving retrospective effect to the provisions of the Public Premises Act since there is neither such express provision therein, nor is it warranted by any implication.[32]

As a logical corollary of the general rule, that retrospective operation is not taken to be intended unless that intention is manifested by express words or necessary implication, there is a subordinate rule to the effect that a statute or a section in it is not to be construed so as to have larger

---

30. *Delhi Cloth Mills & General Co. Ltd. v. CIT, Delhi*, AIR 1927 PC 242, p. 244; citing *Colonial Sugar Refining Co. v. Irving*, (1905) AC 369 (PC); *Jose De Costa v. Bascora Sadasiva Sinai Narcornim*, AIR 1975 SC 1843, p. 1849 : (1976) 2 SCC 917; *K.C. Arora v. State of Haryana, supra.*

31. *Re, Pulborough Parish School Board Election, Bourke v. Nutt*, (1894) 1 QB 725, p. 737. **See further** *Amireddi Raja Gopala Rao v. Amireddi Sitharamamma*, AIR 1965 SC 1970, p. 1973 : (1965) 3 SCC 122. (A construction that affects vested rights "should never be adopted if the words are open to another construction.") *Shri Vijayalakshmi Rice Mills v. State of Andhra Pradesh*, AIR 1976 SC 1471, p. 1473 : (1976) 3 SCC 37; *K. Kapen Chako v. Provident Investment Company (P) Ltd.*, AIR 1976 SC 2610, p. 2617 : (1977) 1 SCC 593; *Govinddas v. Income-tax Officer*, AIR 1977 SC 552, p. 558 : (1976) 1 SCC 906; *Punjab Tin Supply Co. v. Central Government*, (1984) 1 SCC 206, p. 219 : AIR 1984 SC 87; *Mithilesh Kumari v. Prem Bahadur Khare*, AIR 1989 SC 1247, pp. 1253, 1254 : 1989 (2) SCC 95; *Pearce v. Secretary of State for Defence*, (1988) 2 All ER 348, p. 372 (HL); *Yew Bon Tew v. Kenderancen Bas Mara*, (1982) 3 All ER 833, p. 836 : 1983 AC 553 : (1982) 2 WLR 1026 (PC); *Plewa v. Chief Adjudication Officer*, (1994) 3 All ER 323, p. 328 (HL); *R. Rajgopal Reddy v. Padminichandra*, 1995(1) Scale 692, pp. 702, 703 : 1995 AIR SCW 1422 : (1955) 2 SCC 630; *K. Gopinathan Nair v. State of Kerala*, AIR 1997 SC 1925, p. 1939 : 1997 (4) JT 369.

32. *Suhas H. Pophale v. Oriental Insurance Co. Ltd.*, (2014) 4 SCC 657, pp. 681 to 685.

retrospective operation than its language renders necessary.[33] In othe words close attention must be paid to the language of the statutory provi sion for determining the scope of the retrospectivity intended by Parlia ment.[34] But if the literal reading of the provision giving retrospectivity pro duces absurdities and anomalies, a case not *prima facie* within the word may be taken to be covered, if the purpose of the provision indicates that th intention was to cover it.[35] The inhibition against retrospective constructio is not a rigid rule and must vary *secundum materium.*[36] It has been said tha "the basis of the rule is no more than simple fairness which ought to be th basis of every legal rule."[37]

It is not necessary that an express provision be made to make a statut retrospective and the presumption against retrospectivity may be rebutte by necessary implication especially in a case where the new law is mad

---

33. *Reid v. Reid*, (1886) 31 Ch D 402, p. 408; *Lauri v. Renad*, (1892) 3 Ch 402, p 421; *Gardner & Co. v. Cone*, (1928) All ER Rep 458, p. 459; *United Provinces v Atiqa Begum (Mt.)*, AIR 1941 FC 16, p. 47; *S.S. Gadgil v. Lal & Co.*, AIR 196 SC 171, p. 177 : (1964) 8 SCR 72; *Mohd Idris v. Sat Narain*, AIR 1966 SC 1499 p. 1501 : (1966) 3 SCR 15; *Arjan Singh v. State of Punjab*, AIR 1970 SC 703, p 706 : (1969) 2 SCR 347; *Ahmedabad Manufacturing & Calico Printing Co. Ltd. v. S.G. Mehta*, AIR 1963 SC 1436, p. 1446 : 1963 Supp (2) SCR 92; *Sales Ta Officer, Ward II, Moradabad v. Oriental Coal Corporation Moradabad*, AIR 1988 SC 648, p. 653 : 1988 Supp SCC 308; *Bhagat Ram Sharma v. Union of India*, AIR 1988 SC 740, p. 746 : 1988 Supp SCC 30; *Union of India v. Raghubi Singh*, AIR 1989 SC 1933, p. 1948; *K.S. Paripoornan v. State of Kerala*, AIR 1992 SC 1488, p. 1494 : (1992) 1 SCC 684 **Affirmed** by Constitution Bench, JT 1994(6) SC 182, p. 219 : AIR 1995 SC 1012, p. 1038; *R. Rajgopal Reddy v. Padminichandra, supra*; *Dy. Collector v. S. Venkata Ramanaiah*, 1995 (5) Scale 521, 531, 532 : AIR 1996 SC 224, p. 232; *Shyam Sunder v. Ram Kumar*, AIR 2001 SC 2472, pp. 2481, 2482 : (2001) 8 SCC 24; *Co-operative Company Ltd. v. Commissioner of Trade Tax U.P.*, (2007) 4 SCC 480 (para 29) : (2007) 6 JT 49 : (2007) 5 SLT 400.

34. *Union of India v. Raghubir Singh*, AIR 1989 SC 1933, p. 1948 : 1989 (2) SCC 754; *K.S. Paripoornan v. State of Kerala, supra*. Principles relating to retrospectivity stated above were reiterated and **reference** was made to pages 474 and 475 of 10th edition o this book in *S.L. Srinivas Jute Twine Mills (P) Ltd. v. Union of India,* (2006) 2 SCC 740 (para 18) : (2006) 2 JT 397 : (2006) 2 LLJ 225; *MRF Ltd. v. Asst. Commissioner (Assessment) Sales Tax,* (2006) 8 SCC 702 (para 28) : (2006) 12 JT 244 and *Sangam Spinners v. Regional Provident Commissioner*, (2008) 1 SCC 391 para 18 : AIR 2008 SC 739. *Union of India v. Glaxo India Limited,* (2011) 6 SCC 668 (Para 40).

35. *Union of India v. Filip Tiago De Gama of Vedem Vasco De Gama*, AIR 1990 SC 981, p. 985 : (1990) 1 SCC 277.

36. *Barber v. Pigden*, (1937) 1 All ER, 126 : (1973) 1 KB 664 (CA) (SCOTT, L.J.); *Carson v. Carson*, (1964) 1 All ER 681, p. 687.

37. *L'Office Cherifien des Phosphates v. Yamashita-Shinnihon Steamship Co. Ltd.*, (1994) 1 All ER 20, p. 29(J) : (1994) 1 AC 486 (HL); *United States Government v. Montgomery,* (2001) 1 All ER 815, p. 825 (d) (HL) . The doctrine of fairness in the context of retrospectivity was also **referred** to by SINHA J. in *Vijay v. State of Maharashtra,* (2006) 6 SCC 289 : (2006) 7 JT 112. **See further** pp. 583-586, *post*, for these cases.

to cure an acknowledged evil for the benefit of the community as a whole.[38] Instead of express words the device of legal fiction may also be used to bring about retrospective operation by implication.[39]

The rule against retrospective construction is not applicable to a statute merely "because a part of the requisites for its action is drawn from a time antecedent to its passing".[40] If that were not so, every statute will be presumed to apply only to persons born and things come into existence after its operation and the rule may well result in virtual nullification of most of the statutes. An amending Act is, therefore, not retrospective merely because it applies also to those to whom pre-amended Act was applicable if the amended Act has operation from the date of its amendment and not from an anterior date.[41] But this does not mean that a statute which takes away or impairs any vested right acquired under existing laws or which creates a new obligation or imposes a new burden in respect of past transactions will not be treated as retrospective.[42] Thus, to apply an amending

---

38. *Mithilesh Kumari v. Prem Bihari Khare*, AIR 1989 SC 1247, p. 1254 : 1989 (2) SCC 95; *Zile Singh v. State of Haryana*, (2004) 8 SCC 1, p. 9 : AIR 2004 SC 32 (9th Edn., p. 440 of this book is **referred**). **See further** text and notes 40 to 54 (p. 542) and 59 to 63 (p. 561); *Shakti Tubes Ltd. v. State of Bihar*, (2009) 7 SCC 673 para 25 : (2009) 9 JT 386.

39. *Mohd. Akram Ansari v. Chief Election Officer*, (2008) 2 SCC 95 (paras 6 and 7) : (2007) 12 SCR 901.

40. *R. v. St. Mary White Chapels (Inhabitants)*, (1848) 12 QB 120, p. 127; *Master Ladies' Tailors' Organisation v. Ministry of Labour*, (1950) 2 All ER 525, p. 527; *Rao Shiv Bahadur Singh v. State of U.P.*, AIR 1953 SC 394, p. 398 : 1953 SCR 1188; *Union of India v. Madan Gopal*, AIR 1954 SC 158, p. 163 : 1954 SCR 541; *State of Bombay v. Vishnu Ramchandra*, AIR 1961 SC 307, p. 310 : (1961) 2 SCR 26; *Sajjan Singh v. State of Punjab*, AIR 1964 SC 464, p. 468 : (1964) 4 SCR 630; *Kapur Chand v. B.S. Grewal*, AIR 1965 SC 1491, p. 1493 : (1965) 2 SCR 36; *Sree Bank Ltd. v. Sarkar Dutt Roy & Co.*, AIR 1966 SC 1953, p. 1957 : 1965 (3) SCR 708; *T.K. Lakshmana v. State of Madras*, AIR 1968 SC 1489, p. 1494 : 1968 (3) SCR 542; *Customs and Excise Commissioners v. Thorn Electrical Industries Ltd.*, (1975) 1 All ER 439, p. 447 (QBD); *D.S. Nakara v. Union of India*, AIR 1983 SC 130, p. 143 : (1983) 1 SCC 305; *R.L. Marwaha v. Union of India*, (1987) 4 SCC 31, pp. 37, 38 : 1987 SCC (L&S) 350; *Dilip v. Mohd. Azizul Haq*, AIR 2000 SC 1976, p. 1980 : (2000) 3 SCC 607.

41. *Bishun Narain Misra v. State of U.P.*, AIR 1965 SC 1567 : 1965 (1) SCR 693; *Punjab University v. Subash Chander*, (1984) 3 SCC 603, pp. 611, 612 : AIR 1984 SC 1415. **See further** *Mohinder Kumar v. State of Haryana*, (1985) 4 SCC 221, p. 231 : AIR 1986 SC 244, (a validating Act); *Dena Bank v. Bhikhabhai Prabhudas Parekh & Co.*, AIR 2000 SC 3654, p. 3660 : (2000) 5 SCC 694 (The passage in the text from this book is quoted from 7th edition, p. 369).

42. *K.S. Paripoornan v. State of Kerala*, JT 1994 (6) SC 182, pp. 213, 214 : AIR 1995 SC 1012, pp. 1034, 1035.

Act, which creates a new obligation to pay additional compensation,[43] or which reduces the rate of compensation,[44] to pending proceedings for determination of compensation for acquisitions already made, will be to construe it retrospectively which cannot be done unless such a construction follows from express words or necessary implication. Similarly, a new law enhancing compensation payable in respect of an accident arising out of use of motor vehicle will not be applicable to accidents taking place before its enforcement and pending proceedings for assessment of compensation will not be affected by such a law unless by express words or necessary implication the new law is retrospective.[45] It makes no difference in application of these principles that the amendment is by substitution or otherwise.[46] The cases where the principle, that a statute is not retrospective simply because it takes into account past events, has been applied are discussed hereinafter under titles 2(g) and 2(h).

Another principle flowing from presumption against retrospectivity is that "one does not expect rights conferred by the statute to be destroyed by events which took place before it was passed."[47]

In certain cases, a distinction is drawn between an existing right and a vested right and it is said that the rule against retrospective construction is applied only to save vested rights and not existing rights.[48] This distinction, however, has not been maintained in other cases.[49] The word 'retrospective' has thus been used in different senses causing a certain amount

---

43. *Ibid.* **See further,** *Land Acquisition Officer-cum-DSWO A.P. v. B.V. Reddy,* AIR 2002 SC 1045 : (2002) 3 SCC 463 (section 25 of the Land Acquisition Act before amendment in 1984 restricting compensation to not more than claimed was a substantive provision. Amendment removing this bar cannot be construed to be retrospective even to apply to a pending appeal).

44. *Maharaja Chintamani Saran Nath Shahdeo v. State of Bihar,* JT 1999 (8) SC 45, p. 56 : AIR 1999 SC 3609, p. 3614 : (1999) 8 SCC 16.

45. *Padma Srinivasan v. Premier Insurance Co. Ltd.*, AIR 1982 SC 836; *Maitri Koley v. New India Assurance Co.*, (2003) 8 SCC 718 : (2003) 9 JT 159; *State of Punjab v. Bhajan Kaur*, AIR 2008 SC 2276 para 9 : (2008) 12 SCC 112 [Amendment increasing compensation for no fault liability in section 140 of the Motor Vehicles Act is not retrospective].

46. *Ibid.* For effect of 'substitution', **see** text and notes 87 to 89, pp. 734-735, *post.*

47. *Birmingham City Council v. Walker,* (2007) 3 All ER 445, p. 449 (para 11) (HL).

48. *West v. Gwynne*, (1911) 2 Ch 1, p. 11, 12; *Trimbak Damodhar Raipurkar v. Assaram Hiraman Patil*, AIR 1966 SC 1758, p. 1761. **See also** *Shri Bakul Oil Industries v. State of Gujarat*, (1987) 1 SCC 31, p. 37 : AIR 1987 SC 122 : (1987) 165 ITR 6.

49. *Duke of Devonshire v. Barrow Haematite Steel Co. Ltd.*, (1877) 2 QBD 286, p. 289; *Indramani (Dr.) v. W.R. Natu*, AIR 1963 SC 274, p. 286 : (1963) 1 SCR 173; *Govinddas v. Income-tax Officer*, AIR 1977 SC 552, p. 558 : (1976) 1 SCC 906; *Mohd. Rashid Ahmad v. State of U.P.*, AIR 1979 SC 592, p. 598 : (1979) 1 SCC 596.

of confusion.[50] The real issue in each case is as to the scope of particular enactment having regard to its language and the object discernible from the statute read as a whole.

(iii) *Statutes dealing with procedure.*—In contrast to statutes dealing with substantive rights, statutes dealing with merely matters of procedure are presumed to be retrospective unless such a construction is textually inadmissible.[51] As stated by LORD DENNING: "The rule that an Act of Parliament is not to be given retrospective effect applies only to statutes which affect vested rights. It does not apply to statutes which only alter the form of procedure or the admissibility of evidence, or the effect which the courts give to evidence".[52] If the new Act affects matters of procedure only, then, *prima facie*, "it applies to all actions pending as well as future".[53] In stating the principle that "a change in the law of procedure operates retrospectively and unlike the law relating to vested right is not only prospective",[54] the Supreme Court has quoted with approval the reason of the rule as expressed in MAXWELL:[55] "No person has a vested right in any course of procedure. He has only the right of prosecution or defence in the manner prescribed for the time being by or for the court in which the case is pending, and if, by an Act of Parliament the mode of procedure is altered, he has no other right than to proceed according to the altered mode".[56] Relying upon this principle it has been held that "if a court has jurisdiction to

---

50. *Gardner & Co. v. Cone*, (1928) All ER Rep 458, p. 461.

51. *Gardner v. Lucas*, (1878) 3 AC 582, p. 603 (HL); *Delhi Cloth & General Mills Co. Ltd. v. CIT, Delhi*, AIR 1927 PC 242, p. 244; *Jose De Costa v. Bascora Sadashiva Sinai Narcornim*, AIR 1975 SC 1843, p. 1849 : (1976) 2 SCC 917; *Gurbachan Singh v. Satpal Singh*, AIR 1990 SC 209, p. 219 : (1990) 1 SCC 445; *Hitendra Vishnu Thakur v. State of Maharashtra*, AIR 1994 SC 2623, p. 2641 (para 25(i) : (1994) 4 SCC 602.

52. *Blyth v. Blyth*, (1966) 1 All ER 524, p. 535 : 1966 AC 643 (HL).

53. *A.G. v. Vernazza*, (1960) 3 All ER 97, p. 100 : 1960 AC 965 : (1960) 3 WLR 466 (HL); *K. Eapin Chako v. Provident Fund Investment Company (P) Ltd.*, AIR 1976 SC 2610, p. 2617 : (1977) 1 SCC 583.

54. *Anant Gopal Sheorey v. State of Bombay*, AIR 1958 SC 915, p. 917 : 1959 SCR 919. **See further** *Union of India v. Sukumar Pyne*, AIR 1966 SC 1206 : 1966 (2) SCR 34; *Tikaram & Sons v. Commr. of Sales Tax, U.P.*, AIR 1968 SC 1286, p. 1292 : (1968) 3 SCR 512; *State of Madras v. Lateef Hamid & Co.*, AIR 1972 SC 1781, p. 1784 : (1971) 3 SCC 560; *Balumal Jamnadas Batra v. State of Maharashtra*, AIR 1975 SC 2083 : (1975) 4 SCC 645. (An enactment relating to burden of proof like section 123, Customs Act, 1962, would be a matter of procedure); *Rai Bahadur Seth Sriram Durgaprasad v. Director of Enforcement*, (1987) 3 SCC 27, pp. 33, 34 : AIR 1987 SC 1364. (Section 113A, Evidence Act, 1872 inserted in the Act by Act 46 of 1983 providing for presumption as to abetment of suicide by a married woman is a procedural provision and applies to trial of offences committed earlier to the insertion of the section); *Gurbachan Singh v. Satpal Singh*, AIR 1990 SC 209, p. 219 : (1990) 1 SCC 445.

55. MAXWELL: Interpretation of Statutes, 11th Edition, p. 216.

56. **See** cases in footnote 54, *supra*.

try the suit, when it comes for disposal, it cannot refuse to assume jurisdiction by reason of the fact that it had no jurisdiction to entertain it at the time when it was instituted."[57] It has been said that law relating to forum and limitation is procedural in nature whereas law relating to right of action and right of appeal even though remedial is substantive in nature; that a procedural statute should not generally speaking be applied retrospectively where the result would be to create new disabilities or obligations or to impose new duties in respect of transactions already accomplished; that a statute which not only changes the procedure but also creates new rights and obligations shall be construed to be prospective, unless otherwise provided either expressly or by necessary implication.[58]

A change of forum except in pending proceedings[59] is a matter of procedure and, therefore, if a new Act requires certain types of original proceedings to be instituted before a special tribunal constituted under the Act to the exclusion of civil courts, all proceedings of that type whether based on old or new causes of action will have to be instituted before the tribunal.[60] The non-executability of a decree passed by an Indian court against a foreigner at a place in foreign country is also a matter of procedure and the decree becomes executable if the place where it is being executed ceases to be a foreign country and becomes part of India and the Indian Code of Civil Procedure is extended to that place.[61] On the same principle it was held that an arbitration award made in a foreign State is enforceable in the United Kingdom as a convention award under section 3 of the Arbitration Act, 1975 if the foreign State is a party to the New York Convention when proceedings for enforcing the award are taken although it was not such a party at the time of making of the award.[62] It was pointed out that in so construing the section it was not given a retrospective operation as it merely affected the form of procedure of enforcement in that an award which, at the time it was made, was enforceable by action at common law

---

57. *Sudhir G. Angur v. M. Sanjeev,* (2006) 1 SCC 141 (para 1) : AIR 2006 SC 351.

58. *Hitendra Vishnu Thakur v. State of Maharashtra.* AIR 1994 SC 2623, p. 2641 (para 25) : (1994) 4 SCC 602; *Maharaja Chintamani Saran Nath Shahdeo v. State of Bihar,* JT 1999 (8) SC 45, p. 56 : AIR 1999 SC 3609, p. 3614 : (1999) 8 SCC 16; *Shyam Sunder v. Ram Kumar,* AIR 2001 SC 2472, p. 2482 : (2001) 8 SCC 24. For forum **see** text and notes 59-60 below; for limitation, **see** title 2(d); for appeal, **see** titles 2(j) and 2(k).

59. **See** text and notes 38 and 39, pp. 630-631.

60. *New India Insurance Co. Ltd. v. Shanti Misra (Smt.),* AIR 1976 SC 237 : (1975) 2 SCC 840.

61. *B. Narhari Shivram Shet Narvekar v. Pannalal Umediram,* AIR 1977 SC 164 : (1976) 3 SCC 203.

62. *Kuwait Minister of Public v. Sir Frederick Snow & Partners,* (1984) 1 All ER 733, p. 737 (HL).

became enforceable under the Act on the foreign State becoming a party to the convention subsequent to the date of the award.[63] Section 45B the Employees' State Insurance Act, 1948, which enables the Employees' State Insurance Corporation to recover arrears of contribution from the employers as arrears of land revenue, has been held to be procedural and applicable to arrears falling due before coming into force of the section on January 28, 1968.[64] The reason is that statutes providing for new remedies for enforcement of an existing right are treated as procedural and apply to future as well past causes of action.[65]

(iv) *Statements of the rule against retrospectivity.*—The classification of a statute as either substantive or procedural does not necessarily determine whether it may have a retrospective operation. For example, a statute of limitation is generally regarded as procedural but if its application to a past cause of action has the effect of reviving or extinguishing a right of suit such an operation cannot be said to be procedural.[66] It has also been seen that the rule against retrospective construction is not applicable merely because a part of the requisites for its action is drawn from a time antecedent to its passing.[67] For these reasons the rule against retrospectivity has also been stated avoiding the classification of statutes into substantive and procedural and avoiding use of words like existing or vested.

One such formulation by DIXON C.J. is as follows: "The general rule of the common law is that a statute changing the law ought not, unless the intention appears with reasonable certainty, to be understood as applying to facts or events that have already occurred in such a way as to confer or impose or otherwise affect rights or liabilities which the law had defined by reference to the past events. But given rights and liabilities fixed by reference to the past facts, matters or events, the law appointing or regulating the manner in which they are to be enforced or their enjoyment is to be secured by judicial remedy is not within the application of such a presumption".[68]

Another more simple statement of the rule was made in *Secretary of State for Social Security v. Tunnicliffe*[69] by STAUGHTON L.J. in the following

63. *Ibid.*
64. *Employees' State Insurance Corporation v. Dwarka Nath Bhargawa*, AIR 1997 SC 3518, p. 3519 : 1997 (7) SCC 131.
65. *Dilip v. Mohd. Azizul Haq.*, AIR 2000 SC 1976, pp. 1979, 1980 : (2000) 3 SCC 607.
66. **See** title 2(d), Statutes of limitation, pp. 596 to 599.
67. **See** text and note 40, p. 583.
68. *Maxwell v. Murphy*, (1957) 96 CLR 261, p. 267 **applied** in *Rodway v. Queen*, (1990) 64 ALJR 305, pp. 306, 307 (HC Australia).
69. (1991) 2 All ER 712 : (1992) 4 Admin LR 57 (CA).

words: "The true principle is that Parliament is presumed not to have intended to alter the law applicable to past events and transactions in a manner which is unfair to those concerned in them unless a contrary intention appears. It is not simply a question of classifying an enactment as retrospective or not retrospective. Rather it may well be a matter of degree—the greater the unfairness, the more it is to be expected that Parliament will make it clear if that is intended."[70] The above statement was approved by the House of Lords in *L'office Cherifien des Phosphates v. Yamashita Shinnihon Steamship Co. Ltd.*[71] It was observed that the question of fairness will have to be answered in respect of a particular statute by taking into account various factors, *viz.*, value of the rights which the statute affects; extent to which that value is diminished or extinguished by the suggested retrospective effect of the statute; unfairness of adversely affecting the rights; clarity of the language used by Parliament and the circumstances in which the legislation was created.[72] "All these factors must be weighed together to provide a direct answer to the question whether the consequences of reading the statute with the suggested degree of retrospectivity is so unfair that the words used by Parliament cannot have been intended to mean what they might appear to say."[73]

In *Yamashita's* case during the pendency of a claim in arbitration the Arbitration Act, 1980 was amended by inserting section 13A which empowered the arbitrators to dismiss a claim if there has been inordinate and inexcusable delay on the part of the claimant in pursuing the claim which makes fair resolution of the issues difficult or causes serious prejudice to the respondent. The question in the case was whether delay by the claimant in pursuing the claim before the date of enactment of section 13A could be taken into account in considering the question of dismissal under that section and this question was answered in the affirmative. But it does not follow that the rule as stated in the traditional form has been abandoned. Indeed, the judgment of the Court of Appeal in *Tunnicliffe's* case where the rule of fairness was stated and applied by STAUGHTON L.J. was overruled by the House of Lords in *Plewa v. Chief Adjudication Officer*.[74] In that case the question related to the construction of section 53 of the Social Security Act, 1986. This section enabled the Secretary of State to recover over-payment of pension from either the recipient or from third parties on whose misrepresentation or failure to disclose over-payment

---

70. *Ibid*, p. 714. **See further** the **dissenting** opinion of SAHAI J. in *K.S. Paripoornan v. State of Kerala*, JT 1994 (6) SC 182, pp. 227, 228 : AIR 1995 SC 1012, pp. 1044, 1045 : (1994) 5 SCC 593.

71. (1994) 1 All ER 20, p. 30 : (1994) 1 AC 486 (HL).

72. *Ibid.*

73. *Ibid.* **See further**, *Wilson v. First County Trust Ltd.*, (2003) 4 All ER 97, p. 155 (HL).

74. (1994) 3 All ER 323 : (1995) 1 AC 249 : (1994) 3 WLR 317 (HL).

was made. The provision creating an obligation on third parties for repayment was a new provision. Further, the section removed the defence of due care and diligence that was earlier available to the recipient. The section was held to be retrospective by the Court of Appeal by applying the test of fairness. But the House of Lords held that the section created a new obligation and the presumption against retrospectivity applied.[75] The section, therefore, did not apply to over-payments made before its enactment. Even applying the test of fairness it was not possible to say that it would not be unfair to apply the section to over-payments made before its operation.[76] The over-payments before the new Act came into operation were thus held to be recoverable only under the repealed Acts from the recipient being liabilities incurred before the repeal.[77]

The test of fairness was applied by the Court of Appeal in *Antonelli v. Secretary of State for Trade and Industry,*[78] in interpreting section 3(1)(a)(i) of the Estate Agents Act, 1979. This section authorises the Director General of Fair Trading to make an order prohibiting a person from doing any estate agency work when he considers him to be unfit to practice on the ground that 'he has been convicted of an offence involving fraud or other dishonesty or violence'. The question in the case was whether a conviction which occurred prior to the passing of the Act could enable the Director to make a disqualification order. In holding that the Director could act on a conviction which occurred prior to the Act the court found that the test of fairness was satisfied for the power was intended for the protection of the public and the Director had a wide discretion in considering whether the conviction made the person unfit to carry on estate agency work.[79]

The doctrine of fairness was referred to by the Supreme Court in *Vijay v. State of Maharashtra.*[80] In this case a new law which enacted that 'no person shall be a member of a Panchayat or continue as such who has been elected as a councilor of Zila Parishad or as a member of the Panchayat Samiti' was held to be retrospective and applicable to existing members of a Panchayat. In holding so S.B. SINHA, J. observed: "It is now well-settled that when a literal reading of the provision giving retrospective effect does not produce absurdity or anomaly, the same would not be construed only prospective. The negation is not a rigid rule and varies with the intention and purport of the legislation, but to apply it in such a case is a *doctrine of*

---

75. *Ibid*, p. 328.
76. *Ibid*, p. 329.
77. *Ibid.*
78. (1998) 1 All ER 997 (CA).
79. *Ibid*, p. 1006. **See further** title 2(g) statutes prescribing posterior disqualification on past conduct, pp. 607 to 610.
80. (2006) 6 SCC 289 : (2006) 7 JT 112.

fairness. When a new law is enacted for the benefit of the community as a whole, even in absence of a provision the statute may be held to be retrospective in nature."[81]

(v) *Language not always decisive.*—In deciding the question of applicability of a particular statute to past events, the language used is no doubt the most important factor to be taken into account;[82] but it cannot be stated as an inflexible rule that use of present tense or present perfect tense is decisive of the matter that the statute does not draw upon past events for its operation. Thus, the words 'a debtor commits an act of bankruptcy' were held to apply to acts of bankruptcy committed before the operation of the Act.[83] The words 'if a person has been convicted' were construed to include anterior convictions.[84] The words 'has made', 'has ceased', 'has failed' and 'has become', may denote events happening before or after coming into force of the statute and all that is necessary is that the event must have taken place at the time when action on that account is taken under the statute.[85] The words 'dying intestate' were interpreted by the Judicial Committee not as connoting the future tense but as a mere description of the status of the deceased person without any reference to the time of his death.[86] So, the words, 'held on lease', may be only descriptive of land and may apply to lands held on lease prior to or after the coming into force

---

81. *Ibid.*

82. For example, **see** *P. Ganeshwar Rao v. State of Andhra Pradesh*, AIR 1988 SC 2068, p. 2092 : 1988 Supp SCC 740 : (1988) 4 SLR 548 (Amendment in recruitment rules for 'vacancies arising' was held to be not applicable to pre-amendment vacancies. In the absence of the word 'arising' the amendment would have applied even to existing vacancies). *Vinay Kumar Shukal v. Lakhpat Ram*, AIR 1990 SC 2171 : (1990) 4 SCC 246; (The words 'as may be' generally denote a future event.)

83. *Ex parte, Pratt*, (1884) 12 QBD 334; **referred** to in *State of Bombay v. Vishnu Ram Chandra*, AIR 1961 SC 307, pp. 309, 310 : 1961 (2) SCR 26.

84. *State of Bombay v. Vishnu Ram Chandra*, AIR 1961 SC 307, p. 310. For full discussion of this case **see** text and notes 6 to 8, p. 609. **See also** *Boucher Pierre Andre v. Superintendent, Central jail, Tihar, New Delhi*, AIR 1975 SC 164, p. 166 : (1975) 1 SCC 192. For discussion of this case, **see** text and note 15, p. 610. **See further** *Sahebram v. Financial Commissioner*, AIR 1971 SC 198 : (1970) 1 SCC 524 (The words 'has been in continuous occupation for six years' construed). But the words 'has been' may be used in the sense of 'shall have been' denoting only events taking place after the coming into force of the Act; *In re, Athlumney, Ex parte, Wilson*, (1898) 2 QB 547 : (1895-9) All ER 329 **referred** to in *Workmen of Firestone Tyre & Rubber Co. v. Management*, AIR 1973 SC 1227, p. 1248 : (1973) 1 SCC 813; *Secretary, Regional Transport Authority v. D.P. Sharma*, AIR 1989 SC 509, pp. 513, 514 : 1989 Supp (1) SCC 407.

85. *T.K. Lakshmana v. State of Madras*, AIR 1968 SC 1489, p. 1494 : 1968 (3) SCR 542.

86. *Lala Dunichand v. Anarkali (Mt.)*, AIR 1946 PC 173.

of the Act.[87] The words, 'when a person dies', may include a person who died prior to the coming into force of the Act.[88] And the word 'is' though normally referring to the present often has a future meaning and may also have a past signification in the sense of 'has been'.[89]

The real issue in each case is as to the dominant intention of the Legislature to be gathered from the language used, the object indicated, the nature of rights affected, and the circumstances under which the statute is passed.

(b) Statutes regulating succession

Statutes enacted for regulating succession are not applicable to successions which had already opened, as otherwise the effect will be to divest the estate from persons in whom it had vested prior to coming into force of the new statute.[90] The material point of time, for applicability of a law altering the order of succession is the date when succession opens thereafter.

It was, therefore, held that the Hindu Law of Inheritance (Amendment) Act, 1929, applied to a case where the female heir died after the coming into force of the Act though the male to whom she had succeeded had died prior to its enforcement.[91] By so applying the Act, it was not given a retrospective operation as to deprive persons of rights already vested in them for under the Hindu Law a female heir, though a limited owner, fully represents the estate, and the reversioners, during her lifetime, have no interest in it.[92] The words 'dying intestate', as used in the Act, were construed to mean "in the case of intestacy of a Hindu male".[93]

Section 8 of the Hindu Succession Act, 1956, which enacts that the property of a male Hindu 'dying intestate shall devolve' according to the provisions of the Act, has been held to be inapplicable to a case where succession opened before the Act.[94] But it has been applied to the case of a female limited owner who died after the Act although the male to whom

---

87. *S.N. Kamble v. Sholapur Borough Municipality*, AIR 1966 SC 538, p. 543 : 1966 (1) SCR 618.
88. *J.N. Sharma v. H.H. Vijaykuverba*, AIR 1966 SC 1074 : 1966 (2) SCR 618.
89. *Anand Gajpati Raju v. P.V.G. Raju*, JT 2000 (4) SC 590, p. 593 : (2000) 4 SCC 539 : AIR 2000 SC 1886 (Construing the words 'judicial authority before which an action *is* brought in a matter which *is* the subject of an arbitration agreement' in section 8(1) of the Arbitration Act, 1996, it was held that an arbitration agreement need not be in existence when the action is brought and they will also cover a case where the arbitration agreement comes into existence after the action is brought.)
90. *Muhammad Abdus Samad v. Qurban Hussain*, ILR 26 All 119, pp. 129, 130 (PC).
91. *Lala Dunichand v. Anarkali (Mt.)*, AIR 1946 PC 173; *Fateh Bibi v. Charan Dass*, AIR 1970 SC 789 : (1970) 3 SCC 658.
92. *Ibid.*
93. *Ibid.*
94. *Eramma v. Veerupana*, AIR 1966 SC 1879 : 1966 (2) SCR 626.

she had succeeded had died prior to the Act.[1] As already seen,[2] succession in such a case opens again after the death of the limited owner and to find out as to who are the heirs who can succeed to the deceased male, the law in force at the time of the limited owner's death has to be seen.[3]

By section 14 of the Hindu Succession Act, 1956, it is enacted that 'any property possessed by a female Hindu, whether acquired before or after the commencement of this Act, shall be held by her as full owner thereof and not as a limited owner'. The section on its own terms is retrospective; the only qualification being that the Hindu female should be possessed of the estate at the time the Act came into force. Having regard to the object of the section to ameliorate the status of Hindu females, the word 'possessed' has been construed in a broad sense so as to mean "the state of owning or having in one's hand or power" and to include actual as well as constructive possession.[4] But the section has not been given a retrospective operation larger than its language permits. It has, therefore, been held that if the female Hindu had alienated the estate prior to the coming into force of the Act, neither she nor her alienee get the right of full ownership under the section.[5] But if the alienee reconveys the property to the Hindu female after commencement of the Act, she would become full owner for she would then be possessed of property acquired after the commencement of the Act which is also covered by section 14(1).[6] A widow losing her right to the property or right to maintenance, by virtue of which she was possessed of the property, by her remarriage before the Act does not get benefit of section 14(1).[7] But a Hindu widow succeeding after the coming into force of the Hindu Succession Act, 1956 takes the estate absolutely and not as a limited owner and her remarriage does not deprive her of the property vested in her under the Hindu Widows Remarriage Act even before its repeal by Act 24 of 1983.[8]

---

1. *Daya Singh v. Dhan Kuar*, AIR 1974 SC 665 : (1974) 1 SCC 700.
2. **See** cases, *supra*.
3. *Daya Singh v. Dhan Kuar*, AIR 1974 SC 665 : (1974) 1 SCC 696.
4. *Kotturuswami v. Veeravva*, AIR 1959 SC 577, pp. 581, 582 : 1959 Supp (1) SCR 968; *Munnalal v. Rajkumar*, AIR 1962 SC 1493, pp. 1499, 1500 : 1962 Supp (3) SCR 418.
5. *Kotturuswami v. Veeravva, supra*, p. 581; [**approving** *Lukai (Mt.) v. Niranjan*, AIR 1958 MP 160 (FB); and *Harak Singh v. Kailash Singh*, AIR 1958 Pat 581 (FB)]; *Munshi Singh v. Sohanbai (Smt.)*, AIR 1989 SC 1179 : (1989) 2 SCC 265. Even if the alience be a female, she does not get full rights of ownership; *Kalawati Bai v. Soiryabai*, AIR 1991 SC 1581 : (1991) 3 SCC 410; *Naresh Kumari v. Sakshi Lal*, AIR 1999 SC 928 : (1999) 2 SCC 656.
6. *Jagannathan Pillai v. Kunjithapadam Pillai*, (1987) 2 SCC 572 : AIR 1987 SC 1493.
7. *Velamuri Vekata Sivaprasad v. Kothuri Venkateshwarlu*, JT 1999 (9) SC 242 : (2000) 2 SCC 139 : AIR 2000 SC 434. For interpretation of section 14, **see further** text and notes 12 and 13, p. 956.
8. *Cherotte Sugathan v. Cherotte Bharathi*, (2008) 2 SCC 610 : AIR 2008 SC 1467.

The right of a concubine and an illegitimate son of a *Sudra Hindu* to claim maintenance for their life from the estate, which right vested on the death of the *Sudra* prior to the coming into force of the Hindu Adoptions and Maintenance Act, 1956, is not defeated by sections 21, 22 and 25 of the Act.[9]

And a new law requiring sanction of adoption as a condition for its validity was held not to apply to an adoption previously made.[10]

(c) Statutes regulating transfers and contracts

Statutes prescribing formalities for effecting transfers are not applicable to transfers made prior to their enforcement,[11] and similarly, statutes dispensing with formalities which were earlier necessary for making transfers have not the effect of validating transfers which were lacking in these formalities and which were made prior to such statutes.[12] A transfer made in contravention of a statutory prohibition is invalid and is not validated by repeal of the statute containing the prohibition.[13] And permission obtained to make a transfer, under a law which allows transfer on permission, is of no avail if the law is amended before the transfer, prohibiting transfer completely.[14]

The Transfer of Property Act, 1882, on its own terms (section 2) is not retrospective and does not affect any right or liability arising out of legal relation constituted before the Act came into force, or any relief in respect of any such right or liability. An oral mortgage created before this Act came into force and valid according to the then existing law has been held to be enforceable even after the Act came into force.[15] Even such provisions of the Act which mainly deal with matters of procedure, *e.g.*, section 67 which refers to a suit for foreclosure, cannot be availed of for reviving a right which had become extinct before coming into force of the Act.[16]

---

9. *Amireddi Raja Gopala Rao v. Amireddi Shitharamamma*, AIR 1965 SC 1970, p. 1973 : 1965 (3) SCR 122.
10. *Sobhag Singh v. Jai Singh*, AIR 1968 SC 1328, p. 1330 : 1968 (2) SCR 848.
11. *Thakoor Hurdeo Bux v. Thakoor Jowahir Singh*, (1879) 6 IA 161, p. 166; *Hassanji & Sons v. State of M.P.*, AIR 1965 SC 470, p. 472 (para 9) : 1963 Supp (3) SCR 235, (Mineral Concession Rules, 1949, are not retrospective); *Dy. Collector v. S. Venkata Ramanaiah*, 1995 (5) SCALE 521, pp. 531, 532 : (1995) 6 SCC 545.
12. *Mata Prasad v. Nageshwari Sahai*, AIR 1925 PC 272, p. 278.
13. *Ram Kristo v. Dhankisto*, AIR 1969 SC 204, p. 208 : 1969 (1) SCR 342.
14. *Guruputrappa Mallappa Harkune v. Tahsildar*, AIR 1992 SC 92 : 1993 Supp (1) SCC 496.
15. *Ahmad Raza v. Abid Husain*, ILR 48 All 494, p. 501 (PC).
16. *Shrinath Das v. Khetter Mohan Singh*, ILR 16 Cal 693, p. 701 (PC).

Leases executed prior to the Act are not governed by technical rules of forfeiture enacted in section 111(g).[17] But, it has been held that defence of part-performance enacted in section 53A of the Act (introduced by amending Act 20 of 1929) is available to a transferee even when the transfer was made prior to coming into force of the amending Act.[18] This case can be supported on the view that section 53A does not create any substantive right in the property in favour of the transferee, but merely creates a right of defence and is thus procedural in nature.

Validity of existing contracts is not affected by a posterior Act making contracts of that nature invalid. It was, therefore, held that Act No. 21 of 1848, 'an Act for avoiding wagers', which provided that all agreements by way of gaming and wagering shall be null and void and not enforceable, did not affect the validity or enforceability of wagering agreements made prior to the coming into force of the Act.[19] Similarly, a transfer which was valid when made is not invalidated by a subsequent prohibition.[20]

But there are, very often, posterior laws which seriously affect the performance of existing contracts and the commonest example is where a contract is frustrated by supervening impossibility brought by subsequent statutes or by governmental steps taken under them.[21] A statute, which in the words of COCKBURN, C.J., "engrafts an enactment upon existing contracts" has in effect a retrospective operation.[22] Bye-laws framed under the Forward Contracts (Regulation) Act, 1952, which deal with forward contracts in cotton and refer to 'every contract', and 'every on-call contract' 'in so far as cotton is uncalled for thereunder or in so far as the price has not been fixed thereunder', and which required such contracts to be closed out on a day not originally contracted for at a price fixed by law, were held to be retrospective and to affect existing executory contracts made prior to the date of operation of the bye-laws.[23]

---

17. *Namdeo Lokman v. Narbadabai*, AIR 1953 SC 228, p. 230 : 1953 SCR 1009. **See also** *Maharaja of Jeypore v. Rukmini Pattamahadevi*, ILR 42 Mad 589, pp. 597, 598 : AIR 1919 PC 1 : 46 IA 109 (PC).

18. *Maneklal Mansukhbhai v. H.J. Ginwalla & Sons*, AIR 1950 SC 1, p. 4 : 1950 SCR 75.

19. *Doolubdass Pettamberdass v. Ramloll Thackoorseydas*, (1850) 5 MIA 109, pp. 126, 127; *Moon v. Durden*, (1848) 2 Ex 22; *Herschell v. Porter*, (1923) 2 KB 193.

20. *State of Kerala v. Philomina*, AIR 1976 SC 2363, p. 2367 : 1976 (4) SCC 314.

21. **See** *Satyabrata v. Mugneeram Bangur & Co. (P.) Ltd.*, AIR 1954 SC 44 : 1954 SCR 310; *Mugneeram Bangur and Co. (P) Ltd. v. Gurbachan Singh*, AIR 1965 SC 1523 : (1965) 2 SCR 630; HALSBURY'S Laws of England, Vol. 8 (3rd Edition), p. 184.

22. *Duke of Devonshire v. Barrow Haematite Steel Co. Ltd.*, (1877) 2 QBD 286, p. 289; referred to in *Indramani (Dr.) v. W.R. Natu*, AIR 1963 SC 274, p. 286 : (1963) 1 SCR 721; **See further** *Gardner & Co. v. Cone*, (1928) All ER Rep 458, p. 461.

23. *Indramani (Dr.) v. W.R. Natu*, AIR 1963 SC 274, p. 286 : (1963) 1 SCR 721.

Section 4 of the Benami Transactions (Prohibition) Act, 1988, which provides that no suit to enforce 'any right in respect of any property held benami' 'shall lie' by or on behalf of a person claiming to be the real owner; and 'no defence based on any right in respect of any property held *Benami*' 'shall be allowed in any suit' by or on behalf of a person claiming to be the real owner, has been construed by the Supreme Court to apply even to *Benami* transactions entered before the commencement of the Act.[24] The section was applied to pending suits including those in which only appeals were pending.[25] Though upholding the interpretation of section 4 that it applies also to *Benami* transactions entered before the coming into force of the Act, the view earlier taken that it applies even to pending suits including appeals has been considerably modified.[26] It has now been held that the bar of section 4 will apply to claims by the real owner in suits filed after the commencement of section 4 of the Act and not in pending suits;[27] and to a defence by the real owner in all suits filed after section 4 of the Act came into force and also in such pending suits in which the stage for filing the defence is reached after section 4 of the Act came into force.[28] The various propositions following from the decisions on the Act have been culled out by M. JAGANNADHA RAO J in *Rebti Devi v. Ram Dutt*.[29]

A statute extending the term of existing leases was held to have effectively extended a lease when the landlord had issued a notice terminating the lease but the period of notice had not expired before coming into force of the statute. It was held that as the period of notice had not expired the landlord had no vested right to eject the tenant when the new law came into force.[30]

A new law which enacts that transfers made 'shall not be declared to be invalid' will not apply to transfers which were already declared to be invalid before the coming into force of the new law.[31]

---

24. *Mithilesh Kumari v. Prem Bihari Khare*, AIR 1989 SC 1247, pp. 1254, 1255 : 1989 (2) SCC 95.

25. *Ibid*. This case has been severely criticised and shown to be erroneous by SEERVAI; **see** Constitutional Law Of India, 4th Edition, Vol. 1, p. 233 (para 2.125). *Mithilesh Kumari's* case **followed** in *Om Prakash v. Jai Prakash*, AIR 1992 SC 885 : (1992) 2 SCC 42.

26. *R. Rajgopal Reddy v. Padminichadra Chandrasekharan*, 1995 (1) Scale 692 : 1995 AIR SCW 1422 : AIR 1996 SC 238.

27. *Ibid*, pp. 698, 699.

28. *Ibid*, p. 700.

29. JT 1997 (9) SC 179, pp. 182, 183 : AIR 1998 SC 310, pp. 312-14 : (1977) 11 SCC 714. **See further** *G. Mahalingappa v. G.M. Savitha*, (2005) 6 SCC 441, pp. 448, 449 : (2005) 7 JT 174; *Samittri Devi v. Sampuran Singh*, (2011) 3 SCC 556 paras 20 and 23 : AIR 2011 SC 773.

30. *Trimbak Damodhar Rajpurker v. Assaram Hiraman Patil*, AIR 1966 SC 1758 : 1962 Supp (1) SCR 700.

31. *Bai Achhuba v. Kalidas*, AIR 1967 SC 651 : 1964 (5) SCR 853.

In the context of a contract of carriage of goods it has been held that the liability of the railway administration would be governed by Act 39 of 1961 which amended the Railways Act, 1890 if the amending Act had come into force on the date when the breach of contract took place.[32]

But a statute altering existing contracts and retrospective in that sense need not necessarily be construed to be so retrospective as to affect a breach of contract or its consequence which had taken place before its operation.[33] And a new law which retrospectively reduces rate of interest under existing mortgages may not be construed, in the absence of clear words to the contrary, to affect accounts settled before its operation, and it may, thus, have effect to reduce only outstanding and future liability as regards interest.[34]

(d) Statutes of limitation

Statutes of limitation are regarded as procedural and the law of limitation which applies to a suit is the law in force at the date of the institution of the suit irrespective of the date of accrual of the cause of action.[35] The object of a statute of limitation is not to create any right but to prescribe periods within which legal proceedings may be instituted for enforcement of rights which exist under the substantive law.[36] But, after expiry of the period of limitation, the right of suit comes to an end. Therefore, if a particular right of action had become barred under an earlier Limitation Act, the right is not revived by a later Limitation Act even if it provides a larger

---

32. *Union of India v. Steel Stock Holders Syndicate*, AIR 1976 SC 879, p. 894 : (1976) 3 SCC 108.

33. *Gardner & Co. v. Cone*, (1928) All ER Rep 458.

34. *Bhrigunandan Prasad v. Appellate Officer*, AIR 1966 SC 1683, p. 1685 : 1966 Supp SCR 55.

35. *C. Beepathuma v. V. Shankaranarayana*, AIR 1965 SC 241, p. 245 : (1964) 5 SCR 836; *Shahidganj (Masjid) v. S.G.P. Committee*, AIR 1940 PC 116, p. 121 : (1940) Lah 393; *Sonilal v. Kanhaiyalal*, 19 IC 291, p. 294 (PC) (Suit instituted when Act XV of 1877 was in force; acknowledgment relied upon to extend limitation made when earlier Act was in force; held, Act XV of 1877 applied to the suit and acknowledgment to be effective to extend limitation must conform to section 19 of that Act). **See further** *Allah Rakhi (Mt.) v. Shah Mohammad*, AIR 1934 PC 77, p. 78 : 61 IA 50 (pending proceedings are not affected by a change in the law of limitation); *Ramprasad v. Vijay Kumar*, AIR 1967 SC 278, p. 283 (para 13) : 1966 Supp SCR 188.

36. *Hari Nath Chatterjee v. Mothur Mohun Goswamy*, ILR 21 Cal 8 (PC); *R.C. Jall v. Union of India*, AIR 1962 SC 1281, p. 1284 : 1962 Supp (3) SCR 436. (The statute of limitation assumes the existence of a cause of action and does not define or create one). **See further** *Bhimsen Gupta v. Bishwanath Prasad Gupta*, (2004) 4 SCC 95 : AIR 2004 SC 1770 (Expiry of limitation for a suit only bars the remedy, it does not extinguish the right; for example, arrears of rent for recovery of which limitation period has expired still remains 'lawfully payable' though not 'lawfully recoverable' and can sustain a suit for ejectment on the ground of arrears of rent).

period of limitation than that provided by the earlier Act.[37] On the same principle, if right to execute a decree or judgment gets barred under an earlier Act, the right is not revived by a later Act.[38] When the later Act provides a shorter period of limitation than that provided by the earlier Act, a right of suit, which is subsisting according to the earlier Act on the date when the later Act comes into operation, will not be taken to be extinguished.[39] If there is still time even on the basis of the later Act within which such a suit can be filed, the right has to be availed of within that period, and the benefit of the earlier Act is not available.[40] Condonation of delay in such cases in filing the suit or claim will be governed by the provisions of the later Act and not by the provisions of the earlier Act.[41] But if the shorter period provided in the later Act had already expired on the date of its enforcement, the suit can be filed within a reasonable time after the commencement of the later Act, otherwise the effect of the later Act would be to extinguish a subsisting right of suit, an inference which cannot be reached except from express enactment or necessary implication.[42] To avoid these complications when a later Limitation Act enacts shorter periods, it is usual to postpone its coming into effect for some reasonable time, or to make provision for a time gap within which the benefit of the earlier Act can be taken.[43] Statutes of Limitation are thus retrospective in so far as they apply to all legal proceedings brought after their operation for enforcing causes of action accrued earlier, but they are prospective in the sense that they neither have the effect of reviving a right of action which is

---

37. *Appasami Odayar v. Subromanya Odayar*, ILR 12 Mad 26, p. 33 (PC); *Mahesh Narain Munshi v. Taruck Nath Moitra*, ILR 20 Cal 487, p. 497 (PC); *M. Ramyya v. U. Lakshmayya*, AIR 1942 PC 54, p. 56. **See further** *S.S. Gadgil v. Lal & Co.*, AIR 1965 SC 171, pp. 175, (para 8) : (1964) 8 SCR 72; *Yew Bon Tew v. Kenderaan Bas Mara*, (1982) 3 All ER 833 (PC); *Arnold v. Central Electricity Generatings Board*, (1987) 3 All ER 694, pp. 696, 697 : (1988) AC 228 : (1987) 3 WLR 1009 (HL).

38. *Abdul Majid v. Jawahirlal*, ILR 36 All 350, p. 353 (PC); *Sachindra Nath v. Maharaj Bahadur*, AIR 1922 PC 187, pp. 190, 191 : 48 IA 335.

39. *New India Insurance Co. Ltd. v. Shanti Misra (Smt.)*, AIR 1976 SC 237, pp. 241, 242 : 1975 (2) SCC 840.

40. *Gopaldas v. Tribhowan*, AIR 1921 Bom 40; *Begum Sultan v. Salvi Begum*, AIR 1926 All 93; *Mohammad Saleh v. Chandra Kumar*, AIR 1930 Cal 34.

41. *Vinod Gurudas Raikar v. National Insurance Co. Ltd.*, AIR 1991 SC 2156 : (1991) 4 SCC 33.

42. *New India Insurance Co. Ltd v. Shanti Misra*, AIR 1976 SC 237 : (1975) 2 SCC 840; *Vinod Gurudas Raikar v. National Insurance Co. Ltd.*, AIR 1991 SC 2156, 2158 : (1991) 4 SCC 333; *Union of India v. Harnam Singh*, AIR 1993 SC 1367, p. 1373 : 1993 (2) SCC 162.

Contrary intention is manifested when the new Act does not come into force at once and its enforcement is postponed for a reasonable time; **see** *Queen v. Leads and Bradford Rly. Co.*, (1852) 18 QB 343; and *Towler v. Chatterton*, (1829) 133 ER 1280 : (1829) 6 Bing 253.

43. **See** section 30, Limitation Act, 1963 (Act 36 of 1963); and original section 30, Limitation Act, 1908 (Act 9 of 1908).

already barred on the date of their coming into operation, nor do they have the effect of extinguishing a right of action subsisting on that date.[44]

These principles were applied in the construction of section 107 of the Wakf Act, 1995 which provides that nothing contained in the Limitation Act, 1963 shall apply to any suit for possession of immovable property comprised in any wakf or for possession of any interest in such property. It was held that section 107 will have no application when the right of suit for possession in respect of wakf property had already become barred before coming into force of section 107 of the Wakf Act and right in the property had been extinguished by force of section 27 of the Limitation Act.[45] But a statute may, expressly or impliedly by retrospectively extending limitation, revive a barred claim. Section 45-O of the Banking Companies Act introduced by Amending Act 52 of 1953, enacts that in computing the period of limitation prescribed for a suit or application by a banking company which is being wound up, the period commencing from the date of the presentation of the petition for winding up of the banking company shall be excluded. The section further provides that its provision shall also apply to a banking company in respect of which a petition for the winding up has been presented before the commencement of the amending Act. Interpreting the section it was held that its provisions applied to suits or applications by a banking company in respect of causes of action about which suits could be instituted, or applications made on the date of presentation of the winding up petition, before the commencement of the amending Act, even though the specified period of limitation for such action had expired before the commencement of the Act. This construction was arrived at in the background that the amending Act was passed in the interests of the depositors, and it could be inferred that the largest extension of limitation, which the language used was capable of giving was intended.[46] Section 166(3) of the Motor Vehicles Act, 1988 provided a period of limitation of six months for filing a claim petition before the tribunal constituted under the Act with power to extend limitation on sufficient cause but not beyond twelve months from the occurrence of the accident. This provision, that is, section 166(3) was deleted by MV (Amendment) Act, 1994, which came into force on 14.11.1994. The result of the deletion is that after 14.11.1994 there is no period of limitation for a claim petition. The deletion of section 166(3) is not expressly made retrospective. But having

---

44. *Thirumalai Chemicals Ltd. v. Union of India,* (2011) 6 SCC 739 (Para 34) – [Observations made in page 541 of 12 Edition of this book had been **referred** with approval].

45. *T. Kaliamurthi v. Five Gori Thaikkal Wakf,* (2008) 9 SCC 306 paras 40, 41, 42, 50, 53 : AIR 2009 SC 840.

46. *Sree Bank Ltd. v. Sarkar Dutt Roy & Co.*, AIR 1966 SC 1953, pp. 1956, 1961 : 1965 (3) SCR 708 : (1965) 35 Comp Cas 881.

regard to its object, it has been applied to pending (at any stage) claims and claims in respect of accidents occurring prior to 14.11.1994 but not filed till then even though they had become barred under section 166(3).[47] The deletion, however, will not reopen a decision holding a claim barred under section 166(3) which had become final.[48]

(e) Fiscal statutes

Fiscal legislation imposing liability is generally governed by the normal presumption that it is not retrospective[49] and it is a cardinal principle of the tax law that the law to be applied is that in force in the assessment year unless otherwise provided expressly or by necessary implication.[50] The above rule applies to the charging section and other substantive provisions such as a provision imposing penalty[51] and does not apply to machinery or procedural provisions of a taxing Act which are generally retrospective and apply even to pending proceedings.[52] But a procedural provision, as far as possible, will not be so construed as to affect finality of tax assessment or to open up liability which had become barred.[53] Assessment creates a vested right and an assessee cannot be subjected to reassessment unless a provision to that effect inserted by amendment is either expressly

---

47. *Dhannalal v. D.P. Vijayvargiya*, 1996 (4) Scale 458, pp. 461, 462 : AIR 1996 SC 2155, pp. 2157, 2158 : (1996) 4 SCC 652.

48. *Ibid.*

49. HALSBURY'S Laws of England, (3rd Edition), Vol. 36, p. 425; **See also** *Union of India v. Madan Gopal*, AIR 1954 SC 158 : 1954 SCR 541 (Income-tax Legislation imposing tax on the basis of income of previous year is not really restrospective). It is submitted that in *D.G. Ghouse & Co. v. State of Kerala*, AIR 1980 SC 271, p. 277 : (1980) 2 SCC 410 it has not been correctly stated that a tax on buildings which operates from an anterior date is not retrospective. For excise duty, **see** *Collector of Central Excise, Ahmedabad v. Ashoka Mills Ltd.*, AIR 1990 SC 33, p. 39 : (1989) 4 SCC 81. (Rate of Excise duty is that which prevails on clearance of the goods and a subsequent change in rate of duty is not construed as retrospective to apply to goods already cleared.)

50. *Reliance Jute and Industries Ltd. v. Commissioner of Income-tax*, AIR 1980 SC 251, p. 252 : 1980 (1) SCC 139.

51. *Collector of Central Excise Ahmedabad v. Orient Fabrics Pvt. Ltd.*, AIR 2004 SC 953 : (2003) 3 SCC 636.

52. *Commissioner of Wealth Tax, Meerut v. Sharvan Kumar Swarup*, JT 1994 (6) SC 446, pp. 451 to 454 : (1994) 6 SCC 623 : (1994) 210 ITR 886 (Rule 1BB of the Wealth Tax Rules inserted from 1-4-1979 laying down method of valuation of a house used for residential purpose was applied to pending assessments of the years 1977-78 and 1978-79).

53. *Income-tax Officer v. S.K. Habibullah*, AIR 1962 SC 918 : 1962 Supp (2) SCR 716; *Delhi Cloth & General Mill Co. Ltd. v. C.I.T., Delhi*, AIR 1927 PC 242 : 54 IA 421. **See** *State of Tamil Nadu v. Star Tabacco Co.*, AIR 1973 SC 1387 : (1974) 3 SCC 319 (Power to open an assessment is not a matter of procedure).

or by necessary implication retrospective.[54] A provision which in terms is retrospective and has the effect of opening up liability which had become barred by lapse of time, will be subject to the rule of strict construction.[55] In the absence of a clear implication such a legislation will not be given a greater retrospectivity than is expressly mentioned; nor will it be construed to authorise the Income-tax Authorities to commence proceedings which, before the new Act came into force, had by the expiry of the period then provided become barred.[56] But unambiguous language must be given effect to, even if it results in reopening of assessments which had become final after expiry of the period earlier provided for reopening them.[57] There is no fixed formula for the expression of legislative intent to give retrospectivity to a taxation enactment.[58] Though the Legislature has enormous power to make retrospective taxing laws, yet when a retrospective Act is entirely arbitrary and irrational it may be declared invalid as offending Article 14 of the Constitution.[59] But the retrospective operation would have to be found to be unduly oppressive and confiscatory before it can be held to be so unreasonable as to violate constitutional norms of Articles 14 and 19 of the Constitution.[60]

On the principle that a new Act affecting, existing rights or creating new obligations, is presumed to be prospective only, section 171(6) of the Income-tax Act, 1961 has been held not to be applicable to assessment made on a Hindu undivided family for any assessment year prior to 1st April, 1962, when the Act came into force.[61] Section 171(6) creates joint and

---

54. *Controller of Estate Duty Gujarat-I v. M.A. Merchant*, AIR 1989 SC 1710, p. 1713 : 1989 Supp (1) SCC 499.

55. *Banarsi Debi v. ITO, District IV, Calcutta*, AIR 1964 SC 1742, p. 1744; *C.I.T., Bombay v. Onkarmal Meghraj*, AIR 1973 SC 2585, pp. 2589, 2590 : (1974) 3 SCC 349.

56. *S.S. Gadgil v. Lal & Co.*, AIR 1965 SC 171, p. 177 (para 13) : (1964) 8 SCR 72; *K.M. Sharma v. Income-tax Officer New Delhi,* AIR 2002 SC 1715, p. 1718 (para 13) : (2002) 4 SCC 339; *National Agricultural Co-operative Marketing Federation of India Ltd. v. Union of India,* AIR 2003 SC 1329, p. 1337 : (2003) 5 SCC 23 : (2003) 260 ITR 548. **But see** *Mysore Rolling Mills (P.) Ltd. v. Collector of Central Excise*, (1987) 1 SCC 695, p. 697 : AIR 1987 SC 1488.

57. *Commercial Tax Officer v. Biswanath Jhunjhunwala*, 1996 (6) SCALE 211, p. 216 : AIR 1997 SC 357, p. 360; *Addl. Commissioner v. Jyoti Traders,* JT 1998 (8) SC 60, pp. 70, 71 : 1998 (6) Scale 141 : (1999) 2 SCC 77 : AIR 1999 SC 526.

58. *National Agricultural Co-operative Marketing Federation of India Ltd. v. Union of India, supra,* p. 1334.

59. *Tata Motors Ltd. v. State of Maharashtra*, AIR 2004 SC 3618, pp. 3622, 3623 : (2004) 5 SCC 783.

60. *R.C. Tobacco (P.) Ltd. v. Union of India,* (2005) 7 SCC 725 (paras 20 to 22).

61. *Govinddas v. Income-tax Officer*, AIR 1977 SC 552, pp. 558, 559 : (1976) 1 SCC 906.

several liability of the members to pay the tax assessed on a Hindu undivided family if the Income-tax Officer after completion of the assessment finds that the family has already effected a partition whether total or partial. It was pointed out that as the liability created by section 171(6) was not limited to the extent of the joint family properties coming to the hands of a member and made him personally liable, it was a new liability and the section could not be construed to apply to assessments completed under the old Act.

The liability to pay income-tax is a perfected debt on the last day of the previous year[62] but as that liability is computed according to the law in force at the beginning of the assessment year, *i.e.*, the first day of April, any change in law affecting tax liability after that date though made during the currency of the assessment year, unless specifically made retrospective, does not apply to the assessment for that year.[63] On the same principle when a surcharge on Agricultural Income-tax was enforced from 1st September, 1957; it was held that it could not apply to the assessment year 1957-58 as it was not brought into force from the beginning of that year, *i.e.*, 1st April, 1957.[64] Similarly, revision of Schedule to the Kerala Plantation Tax Act, 1960 by the Kerala Finance Act, 1987 with effect from 1.7.1987 which revised the tariff categories as well as the tariff structure was held to be applicable only in the next financial year, *viz.* 1988-89 and not in the financial year 1987-88.[65]

A taxing Act cannot, however, be called retrospective if it taxes an event which is continuing and not complete when the Act comes into force. So, instalments of hire paid after the coming into force of the Finance Act, 1972 under a hire-purchase agreement made before the Act were subjected to the value added tax and it was held that the tax was not retrospective.[66] A default, which is a continuing default and not a default once for all, can be dealt with under the provisions of the new Act, if it continues when the new Act comes into force, although it commenced when the old Act was in

---

62. *Kesoram Industries & Cotton Mills Ltd. v. CWT (Central), Calcutta*, AIR 1966 SC 1370, p. 1379 : (1966) 2 SCR 688; *ITO, Mangalore v. M. Damodar Bhat*, AIR 1969 SC 408, p. 413 : 1969 (2) SCR 29. **See further** *CIT v. Shelly Products*, (2003) 5 SCC 461, p. 476 : AIR 2003 SC 2532 (case of advance text and tax deducted at source. Liability does not depend on assessment).

63. *C.I.T., Bombay v. Scindia Steam Navigation Co. Ltd.*, AIR 1961 SC 1633, p. 1646 : 1962 (1) SCR 788.

64. *Karimtharuvi Tea Estates Ltd. v. State of Kerala*, AIR 1966 SC 1385 : 1966 (3) SCR 93.

65. *State of Kerala v. Alex George*, (2005) 1 SCC 299 : AIR 2005 SC 1224.

66. *Customs and Excise Commissioners v. Thorn Electrical Industries Ltd.*, (1975) 1 All ER 439 (QBD).

force. A default in filing a return of income is a continuing default till the return is filed; such a default, though it commenced when the Income-tax Act, 1922 was in force, can yet be dealt with under the provisions of the Income-tax Act, 1961 if it continued after the commencement of the new Act.[67]

(f) Penal statutes

Penal statutes which create offences or which have the effect of increasing penalties for existing offences will only be prospective by reason of the constitutional restriction imposed by Article 20 of the Constitution.[68] Even otherwise they are construed prospective "because it manifestly shocks one's sense of justice that an act, legal at the time of doing it, should be made unlawful by some new enactment".[69] Therefore, if an Act

---

67. *Maya Rani Punj v. Commissioner of Income-tax, Delhi*, (1986) 1 SCC 445 : AIR 1986 SC 293.

68. *West Ramnad Electric Distribution Co. Ltd. v. State of Madras*, AIR 1962 SC 1753, pp. 1758, 1760 : 1963 (2) SCR 747; *State of Maharashtra v. K.K.S. Ramaswamy*, AIR 1977 SC 2091 : 1977 (3) SCC 525; *Soni Devrajbhai Babubhai v. State of Gujarat*, AIR 1991 SC 2173 : (1991) 4 SCC 298 (Section 304B of the Penal Code provides a new offence of Dowry death and is not retrospective); *Kalpnath Rai v. State*, AIR 1998 SC 201, p. 210 : (1997) 8 SCC 733 (All the ingredients of the offence must happen after the new offence comes into force: Case relating to section 3(5) of TADA).

Article 20 corresponds to Article 7(1) of the European Convention, the second limb of which provides :'Nor shall a heavier penalty be imposed than the one that was applicable at the time the criminal offence was committed'. It was held by the House of Lords that penalty 'applicable' referred to the maximum sentence for the offence and Article 7(1) was not violated when there was a change in the release regime between the date of the offence, which permitted unconditional release subject to good behaviour after serving a part of the sentence whereas the release regime when he was convicted permitted his release after the same period but under a licence which placed him under supervision and imposed certain restrictions on his freedom on failure of which he could be recalled to serve the remaining sentence: *R. (on the application of Uttley v. Secretary of State for Home Department*, (2004) 4 All ER 1 (HL).

69. *Midland Rly. Co. v. Pyre*, (1861) 142 ER 419, p. 424 (ERLE, C.J.); referred to in *State of Bombay v. Vishnu Ramchandra*, AIR 1961 SC 307, p. 309 : (1962) 2 SCR 26; **See further** *Waddington v. Miah*, (1974) 2 All ER 377, p. 379 (HL). (Restrospective Criminal Legislation is against Article 11(2) of the Declaration of Human Rights of the United Nations and Article 7 of the European Convention for the Protection of Human Rights and Fundamental Freedom); *R. v. Kirk*, (1985) 1 All ER 453 (EEC Court) (The principle that penal provisions may not have retroactive effect is one which is common to all the legal orders of the member States); *Re, Barretto*, (1994) 1 All ER 447, p. 453 (CA) (Any provision which increases the penalty particularly if coupled with an additional liability to imprisonment cannot be construed retrospective). The rule against retrospectivity of penal statutes may also apply to "any law that alters the legal rules of evidence, thus accepting less or different testimony than the law required at the time of the commission of the offence, in order to convict the offender": ALY MOKHTAR, 'Nullum Crimen, Nulla Poena Sine Lege, Aspects and Prospects' 26 (2005) Statute Law Review 41, p. 48.

creates a new offence it will bring into its fold only those offenders who commit all ingredients of the offence after the Act comes into operation.[70] The same principle has been applied while dealing with a law which affects the power of grant of pardon or remission. Section 433A of the Code of Criminal Procedure, 1973 which requires that where a sentence of imprisonment for life is imposed on conviction of a person for an offence for which death is one of the punishments, such person shall not be released from prison unless he had served at least fourteen years of imprisonment, has been held to be applicable to sentences imposed after the coming into force of the section and not to person convicted before its coming into force.[71] Similar principle has been applied to cases where an offence compoundable when committed was later made non-compoundable. Offence of voluntarily causing hurt by dangerous weapons punishable under section 324 of the Penal Code was compoundable with the permission of the court before 23.5.2006 when it was made non-compundable by the Code of Criminal Procedure (Amendment) Act, 2005. In construing this amendment it was held by the Supreme Court that an offence committed before 23.6.2006 could yet be compounded with the permission of the court and the accused acquitted.[72]

---

70. *R. v. Griffiths*, (1891) 2 QB 145, p. 148 (LORD COLERIDGE, C.J.); **But see** *Sajjan Singh v. State of Punjab*, AIR 1964 SC 464, p. 468 : 1964 (4) SCR 630; *Sajjan Singh* was followed in *State of Maharashtra v. Krishnarao Dudhappa Shinde*, (2009) 4 SCC 219 : (2009) 2 JT 216 (The case of *Krishnarao* relates to the offence of criminal misconduct in discharge of official duty by a public servant under section 5(1)(e) of the Prevention of Corruption Act, 1947 'if he or any person on his behalf is in possession or has, at any time during the period of his office, been in possession, for which the public servant cannot satisfactorily account, of pecuniary resources or property disproportionate to his known sources of income'. Clause (e) in section 5(1) was added by Act 40 of 1964. Formerly it was in the form of presumption as section 5(4).

It was held in *Krishnarao* **following** *Sajjan Singh* that income received and property acquired prior to the enactment of section 5(1)(e) can be taken into account for a prosecution for that offence which must necessarily be after that provision came into force. The reasoning is that this is not a new offence of criminal misconduct but only prescribes a new rule of evidence for proving criminal misconduct. *Sajjan Singh* was decided before amendment of the section in 1964 when possession of assets disproportionate to public servant's known sources of income was only in the shape of a rule of evidence providing a presumption of criminal misconduct. But after amendment of 1964 it became a substantive offence in the shape of section 5(1)(e) when *Krishnarao* was decided. This difference does not seem to have been noticed in deciding *Krishnarao*.)

71. *Maruram v. Union of India*, AIR 1980 SC 2147, pp. 2167, 2168 : (1981) 1 SCC 107; *State of Haryana v. Ram Diya*, AIR 1990 SC 1336, pp. 1338, 1339 : 1990 (2) SCC 701.

72. *Mohd. Abdul Sufan Laskar v. State of Assam*, (2008) 9 SCC 333 paras 16, 17 : (2008) 9 JT 252.

It is a settled principle of interpretation of criminal law that such provisions have to be strictly construed and cannot be given a retrospective effect unless the legislative intent and expression is clear beyond ambiguity. To illustrate, section 42(2) of the Narcotic Drugs and Psychotropic Substances Act, 1985, prior to its amendment, provided that where an officer takes down any information in writing under section 42(1) or records grounds for his belief under the proviso thereto, he shall 'forthwith' send a copy thereof to his immediate official superior. The word 'forthwith' was substituted for 'within seventy-two hours' by Act 9 of 2001 with effect from 02.10.2001, thereby bringing more certainty to the requirement. The Supreme Court observed that amendments to criminal law would not intend that there should be undue delay in disposal of criminal trials or that there should be a retrial just because the law has changed. In the present case, information regarding the alleged commission of an offence was received by the officer on 04.02.1994, and the trial had already been concluded on 04.07.1998, prior to the coming into force of the Amendment Act of 2001. Since the law, as it existed at the time of commission of the offence, would govern the rights and obligations of the parties, the unamended section 42(2) was held to apply in the said case.[73]

The prohibition of Article 20 of the Constitution to enact retrospective penal laws, however, has no application to a law which only mollifies the rigour of an existing penal law. Indeed, Article 15.1 of the International Covenant on Civil and Political Rights, 1966 which was ratified by India on 10.4.1979 and which is included in the definition of Human Rights in section 2(d) of the Protection of Human Rights Act, 1993, in addition to the safeguards contained in Article 20 of the Constitution, provides: 'If subsequent to the commission of the offence, provision is made by law for imposition of a lighter penalty, the offender shall benefit thereby'.[74] The question whether a penal law which mollifies the rigour of an existing penal law is retrospective and to what extent will depend upon the construction of the Act having regard to the well settled rules of construction.[75] In *Rattan Lal v. State of Punjab*,[76] the Probation of the Offenders Act, 1958 did not apply to the area where the offence was committed at the time of

---

73. *Sukhdev Singh v. State of Haryana*, (2013) 2 SCC 212, pp. 219 to 222.

74. The courts in India have not paid much attention to this provision. This provision as incorporated in the Hongkong Bill of Rights was construed by the Privy Council in *Chau Chihung v. R*, (1996) 1 All ER 914 (PC). It was held that when the new law in force at the time of trial had no exact counterpart in the former law in force when the offence was committed the question to be determined would by what range of sentences would have been open to the court to impose if the defendant had been convicted and sentenced under new law.

75. *Rattan Lal v. State of Punjab*, AIR 1965 SC 444, p. 446.

76. *Ibid.*

commission of the offence or even when the accused was convicted but it was extended to that area where his appeal was pending before the Sessions Judge yet the Supreme Court held that the benefit of the Act could be given to the accused. In *State v. Gian Singh*,[77] the accused was convicted for the offence under section 3(1) of the TADA Act, 1985 for commission of a terrorist act resulting in death of a person for which the only punishment was death sentence under section 3(2) of the Act. The TADA Act, 1985 expired by efflux of time on 22.5.1987 but the proceedings were continued by a saving clauses under the Act. The Act of 1985 was replaced by the TADA Act, 1987. In this Act in the corresponding section 3(2) the harshness of the sentence was diluted and the accused could be sentenced to death or life imprisonment. The question before the Supreme Court, where the appeal of the accused and the reference for confirmation of death sentence were pending, was whether the benefit of the dilution of the harshness of death sentence in section 3(2) of the 1987 Act could be given to the accused and his sentence of death could be replaced by sentence for life imprisonment. The Supreme Court in these circumstances gave the benefit of section 3(2) of the 1987 Act to the accused and sentenced him to life imprisonment. The Supreme Court gave two reasons for applying section 3(2) of the 1987 Act. The court first applied a general principle in the case which was stated as follows: "If any subsequent legislation would downgrade the offence, it would be a salutory principle for administration of criminal justice to suggest that the said legislative benevolence can be extended to the accused who awaits judicial verdict regarding sentence."[78] The second reason that the Supreme Court gave was that the continued operation of the 1985 Act after expiry under a saving clause for continuance of criminal proceedings in respect of offences committed when the Act was in force became inconsistent, in so far the sentence part of section 3(2) was concerned, with section 3(2) of the 1987 Act and could not be given effect to in view of section 25 of the 1987 Act which gave an overriding effect to the Act over any enactment in case of inconsistency.[79] However, the benefit of mollification of sentence by amendment cannot be allowed to pending appeals when the amending Act expressly provides that it shall have no effect to the pending appeals.[80]

But the benefit of mollification of ingredients of the substantive offence after conviction during pendency of appeal has not been allowed to the accused. Thus, a notification making a distinction between a small quantity

---

77. AIR 1999 SC 3450 : (1999) 9 SCC 312.
78. *Ibid*, p. 3455 (para 32).
79. *Ibid*, p. 3455 (para 34).
80. *Jawahar Singh v. State of GNCT of Delhi*, (2009) 6 SCC 490, p. 495 : AIR 2009 SC 2391.

and commercial quantity of brown sugar and thereby making possession of a small quantity of brown sugar not an offence under section 2 of the Norcotic Drugs and Psychotropic Substances Act, 1985 has not been applied in a case where the notification was issued after commission of the offence and also after the accused was sentenced.[81] Similarly, benefit of mollification of prescribed standard of mineral oil in relation to hard-boiled sugar confectionery by a notification which came into force during pendency of appeal against conviction was not allowed to the accused.[82]

It is open to the Legislature to make a provision in the law amending and mollifying existing penal law that the amending Act will apply in cases pending trial but will not apply to cases pending in appeal.[83] By section 4(1) of the Narcotics Drugs and Psychotropic Substances (Amendment) Act, 2001 which rationalised the sentencing structure by providing graded sentences linked to the quantity of Narcotic Drug, made the amended provisions applicable to cases pending before the court or under investigation but excluded the application of the Act to cases pending in appeal. This provision was held to be valid.[84]

The procedure prescribed for trial of offence in a new Act may be applied for trial of similar offences under a repealed Act. Thus, sanction for prosecution granted under the provisions of the new Act will be good for prosecution of an offence requiring sanction under the repealed Act, for sanction pertains to procedure.[85] But the question whether a law which does not affect the punishment but applies a procedure, which is prejudicial to the accused by curtailing his procedural right, can be retrospectively applied to offences taking place earlier and is not violative of Article 20 of the Constitution has been referred to a Constitution Bench.[86]

The enforcement of the Human Rights Act, 1998 in England from 2nd October, 2000, section 7 of which enables the victim of an unlawful act by

---

81. *P.P. Fathima v. State of Kerala*, (2003) 8 SCC 726 : (2003) 8 JT 527.

82. *Dayal Singh v. State of Rajasthan*, (2004) 5 SCC 721 : AIR 2004 SC 2608.

83. *Basheer alias N.P. Basheer v. State of Kerala*, (2004) 3 SCC 609 : AIR 2004 SC 2757.

84. *Ibid.* **See further**, *Pratap Singh v. State of Jharkhand*, (2005) 3 SCC 551, pp. 570 (para 32), p. 587-89 : AIR 2005 SC 2731 [Juvenile Justice (care and Protection of Children) Act, 2000, which repealed Juvenile Justice Act, 1986, in section 20 gives benefit of the new Act in pending cases to those who were juvenile under the new Act when the new Act came into force though they may have ceased to be juvenile under the old Act. This was held to be consistent with Article 20 of the Constitution].

85. *Kapur Chand v. State of Bombay*, AIR 1958 SC 993, pp. 997, 998 : 1959 SCR 250.

86. *Transmission Corporation of A.P. v. Ch. Prabhakar*, (2004) 5 SCC 551 : AIR 2004 SC 3368.

a public authority to rely on the Act in 'proceedings brought by or at the investigation of a public authority whenever the act in question took place' was held not to apply when the person complaining had been convicted before the enforcement of the Act, though his appeal was pending when the Act came into force.[87] But this decision was not unanimous and was later followed with considerable hesitation.[88]

In *Pyare Lal Sharma v. Managing Director, Jammu & Kashmir Industries Ltd.*,[89] regulation 16.14 of the Jammu & Kashmir Industries Employees Service Rules which was amended on April 20, 1983 came for consideration. The amendment added certain more grounds for termination of service of an employee and one of the grounds so added was: 'If he (the employee) remains on unauthorised absence'. In construing the Regulation the Supreme Court held that the period of unauthorised absence prior to the date of amendment could not be taken into consideration for terminating the services of an employee. In so construing the regulation the court observed: "It is the basic principle of natural justice that no one can be penalised on the ground of a conduct which was not penal on the day it was committed."[90] This case shows that the rule of construction against retroactivity of penal laws is not restricted to Acts providing for criminal offences but applies also to laws which provide for other penal consequences of a severe nature, *e.g.*, termination of service. Similarly, a statute or statutory regulation enabling imposition of restrictions on carrying on business guaranteed under Article 19(1)(g) of the Constitution, *e.g.*, by preventing access to capital market, will be treated as a penal provision and will be presumed to be prospective and will not apply to a case where the conduct inviting penal action was complete before its enforcement.[91]

(g) Statutes prescribing posterior disqualification on past conduct

But, "no man has such a vested right in his past crimes and their consequences as would entitle him to insist that in no future legislation shall any regard whatever be had to his previous history".[92] It was, therefore, held that if a statute increased penalty on second conviction of an offence, a conviction before commencement of the statute could be taken into account.[93]

---

87. *R v. Lambert,* (2001) 3 All ER 577 (HL).
88. *R v. Kansal (No. 2),* (2002) 1 All ER 257 (HL).
89. AIR 1989 SC 1854 : (1989) 3 SCC 448.
90. *Ibid,* p. 1860.
91. *Ritesh Agarwal v. Securities and Exchange Board of India*, (2008) 8 SCC 205 para 25 : (2008) 7 JT 289.
92. *R. v. Austin*, (1913) 1 KB 551, p. 556 (PHILLIMORE, J.); **referred** to in *State of Bombay v. Vishnu Ramchandra*, AIR 1961 SC 307, p. 310 : 1961 (2) SCR 26.
93. *R. v. Austin*, (1913) 1 KB 551, p. 556 (PHILLIMORE, J.).

Similarly, if the object of a statute is not to inflict punishment but to protect the public from the activities of undesirable persons who bear the stigma of a conviction or misconduct on their character, the conviction or misconduct of such a person before the operation of the statute may be relied upon.[1]

In *Queen v Vine*,[2] the question related to the construction of section 14 of 33 & 34 Vict. c. 29, which enacted that 'every person convicted of felony shall be for ever disqualified from selling spirits by retail'. It was held that the disqualification applied to every convicted felon irrespective of whether he was so convicted prior to or after the Act came into operation. In the course of his judgment, COCKBURN, C.J., observed: "Here the object of the enactment is not to punish offenders, but to protect the public against public houses in which spirits are retailed being kept by persons of doubtful characters—. On looking at the Act, the words used seem to import the intention to protect the public against persons convicted in the past as well as in future; the words are in effect equivalent to 'every convicted felon'."[3]

In *Re, A Solicitor's Clerk*,[4] the question related to disqualification regarding employment as a solicitor's clerk. By section 16(1) of the Solicitors Act, 1941, it was provided that where a solicitor's clerk has been convicted of certain offences including larceny in respect of any money or property which belonged to his employer or to a client of his, an application may be made on behalf of the Law Society to the disciplinary committee for an order that no solicitor shall employ the said person without the written permission of the Law Society. This provision was amended by the amending Act of 1956, which allowed the society to apply for an order where a clerk 'has been convicted' of larceny irrespective of whether the money or property belonged to his employer or one of his clients or to some one else. A clerk, who was convicted of larceny in 1953 of property which belonged neither to his employer nor to a client of his, was proceeded against under the amended section, and it was contended by him that the amending Act of 1956 was not retrospective so as to apply to convictions before its operation. In rejecting the contention LORD GODDARD, C.J., observed: "In my opinion, this Act is not in truth retrospective. It enables an order to be made disqualifying a person from acting as a solicitor's clerk in the future and what happened in

1. *Queen v. Vine*, (1875) 10 QB 195; *Re, A. Solicitor's Clerk*, (1957) 3 All ER 617 (DC); *State of Bombay v. Vishnu Ramchandra*, AIR 1961 SC 307 : (1961) 2 SCR 26; *Bashiruddin Ashraf v. B.S.S. Majlis*, AIR 1965 SC 1206, p. 1209 : 1965 (2) SCR 205.
2. (1875) 10 QB 195.
3. *Ibid.*
4. (1957) 3 All ER 617.

the past is the cause or reason for the making of the order; but the order has no retrospective effect. It would be retrospective if the Act provided that anything done before the Act came into force or before the order was made should be void or voidable, or if a penalty were inflicted for having acted in this or any other capacity before the Act came into force or before the order was made. This Act simply enables a disqualification to be imposed for the future which in no way affects anything done by the appellant in the past. Accordingly, in our opinion, the disciplinary committee had jurisdiction to make the order complained of."[5]

In *State of Bombay v. Vishnu Ramchandra*,[6] the question was whether a person convicted in 1949 of theft could be directed to remove himself outside a specified area under section 57 of the Bombay Police Act, 1951, which authorised removal of a person who 'has been convicted' of certain offences including theft. The contention raised was that the conviction being prior to the Act, no removal could be founded on such a conviction. In overruling the High Court, where the above contention had found favour, HIDAYATULLAH, J. for the Supreme Court stated: "Section 57 of the Bombay Police Act, 1951, does not create a new offence nor makes punishable that which was not an offence. It is designed to protect the public from the activities of undesirable persons who have been convicted of offences of a particular kind. The section only enables the authorities to take note of their convictions and to put them outside the area of their activities, so that the public may be protected against a repetition of such activities. An offender who has been punished may be restrained in his acts and conduct by some legislation, which takes note of his antecedents; but so long as the action taken against him is after the Act comes into force, the statute cannot be said to be applied retrospectively."[7] It was further observed that the words 'has been' described in the context past actions without regard to time.[8]

The last three cases[9] may be compared with the case of *Re, Pulborough Parish School Board Election, Bourke v. Nutt,*[10] where the Court of Appeal

---

5. *Ibid*, p. 619. **See further** *Antonelli v. Secretary of State for Trade and Industry*, (1998) 1 All ER 997 (CA) (discussed at pp. 687-688; *R. v. Field*, (2003) 3 All ER 769 (CA) (order disqualifying individual from working with children can be made in respect of offence committed before the statutory provision under which order is issued).

6. AIR 1961 SC 307 : 1961 (2) SCR 26.

7. *Ibid*, p. 310. **See further** *Bashiruddin v. B.S.S. Majlis*, AIR 1965 SC 1206, p. 1209 (para 10) : (1965) 2 SCR 205; *Sajjan Singh v. State of Punjab*, AIR 1964 SC 464, p. 468 : 1964 (4) SCR 630; *Kapurchand v. B.S. Grewal*, AIR 1965 SC 1491, p. 1493 : 1965 (2) SCR 36.

8. *Ibid*.

9. **See** cases **referred** to in notes 93-6, pp. 607-609.

10. (1894) 1 QB 725 : (1891-94) All ER 834 (CA).

(LORD ESHER, M.R. dissenting) held that the provisions of the Bankruptcy Act, 1883, which impose certain disqualifications 'where a debtor is adjudged bankrupt', did not apply to past adjudications by virtue of the presumption against retrospection. The comparison only illustrates that the word 'retrospective' is used in more senses than one causing a certain amount of confusion and that the real issue in each case is as to the scope of the particular enactment having regard to its language and the object discernible from the statute read as a whole.[11]

(h) Statutes conferring prospective benefit on antecedent facts: Remedial statutes

Just as the fact that a prospective disqualification under a statute results from anterior misconduct, is not always taken as sufficient to make the statute retrospective,[12] so also the fact that a prospective benefit under a statutory provision is in certain cases to be measured by or depends on antecedent facts does not necessarily make the provision retrospective.[13] Cases under these heads illustrate that the rule against retrospective construction is not always applicable to a statute merely "because a part of the requisites for its action is drawn from time antecedent to its passing".[14]

In *Boucher Pierre Andre v. Superintendent, Central Jail, Tihar, New Delhi.*[15] The Supreme Court held that the benefit to set off pre-conviction detention period against the term of imprisonment conferred by section 428 of the Criminal Procedure Code, 1974 'where an accused person, has, on conviction been sentenced to imprisonment for a term' is also available where the sentence was imposed before the commencement of the Code to reduce the unserved portion of the sentence and that in so construing the section it was not given any retrospective effect for it did not affect the sentence already undergone but affected only that part of the sentence which remained to be served in future. It was further held that words 'has been sentenced' were neutral and could take in the convictions prior to coming into force of the Code.

---

11. **See** text and notes 48-50, p. 584-585.
12. **See** under title 2(g) 'Statutes prescribing Posterior Disqualification on Past Conduct', *supra*.
13. *Master Ladies' Tailors' Organisation v. Ministry of Labour*, (1950) 2 All ER 525; *Sree Bank Ltd. v. Sarkar Dutt Roy & Co.*, AIR 1966 SC 1953, p. 1957 (para 9) : 1965 (3) SCR 708; *Ramji Purshottam v. Laxmanbhai Kurlawala*, (2004) 6 SCC 455, p. 463 : AIR 2004 SC 4010, p. 4015. (The text from 9th Edn., p. 462 of this book is **quoted**).
14. **See** text and note 40, p. 583 and text and notes 16, 17, p. 611, *infra*.
15. AIR 1975 SC 164 : (1975) 1 SCC 192.

In *R. v. Mary Whitechappel (St.) (Inhabitants)*,[16] the question related to the construction of section 2 of the Poor Removal Act, 1846, which provided that 'no woman residing in any parish with her husband at the time of his death shall be removed from such parish, for twelve calendar months next after his death, if she so long continues a widow'. In that case it was sought to remove a widow within twelve months from the date of the death of her husband who had died prior to the Act came into force; and it was argued that to apply the Act to such a case was to construe it retrospectively. In rejecting the contention, LORD DENMAN, C. J. observed: "It was said that the operation of the statute was confined to persons who had become widows after the Act was passed, and that the presumption against a retrospective statute being intended supported this construction; but we have shown before that the statute is in its direct operation prospective, as it relates to future removals only, and that it is not properly called a retrospective statute because a part of the requisites for its action is drawn from time antecedent to its passing".[17] In this case the words 'shall be removed' were thus found appropriate to cover all cases of future removals irrespective of whether the husband had died prior to the Act but they were not found wide enough to nullify completed removals prior to the Act, even if the widow was removed within twelve months of her husband's death.[18]

In *R. v. Birwistle, etc. Justices,*[19] which arose under the Married Woman (Maintenance in Case of Desertion) Act, 1886, the Act was held to apply, without express words, to desertions which took place prior to the Act. It was said: "It was intended to cure an existing evil and to afford to married women a remedy for desertion, whether such desertion took place before the passing of the Act or not".[20]

In *Lane v. Lane*,[21] section 4 of the Summary Jurisdiction (Married Women) Act, 1895, which entitled a married woman 'whose husband shall have been guilty of persistent cruelty to her' to apply for an order under the Act, was held to apply even to acts of cruelty committed before the passing of the Act.

---

16. (1848) 12 QB 120 : 116 ER 811.
17. *Ibid*, p. 127.
18. *Ibid.*
19. (1889) 58 LJMC 158: **referred** to in *State of Bombay v. Vishnu Ram Chandra*, AIR 1961 SC 307, p. 309 : 1961 (2) SCR 26.
20. *Ibid.*
21. (1896) P 133 : 65 LJP 63.

In *Weldon v. Winslow*,[22] construing a statutory provision to the effect—'a married woman shall be capable of suing and being sued either in contract or in tort, or otherwise, in all respects as if she were a *Femme sole* and her husband need not be joined with her as plaintiff or defendant or be made a party to any action or other legal proceeding brought by or taken against her and any damages or costs recovered by her in any such action or proceeding shall be her separate property,' it was held that a married woman was competent to file in her own name an action for tort although the cause of action arose before the statute came into operation.

But, although opinion was not uniform,[23] section 2(4) of the Hindu Women's Right to Separate Residence and Maintenance Act, 1946, which entitled a Hindu married woman to claim separate residence and maintenance from her husband 'if he marries again' was generally held to apply to cases where the husband married again after the date on which the Act came in to force.[24]

When rate of interest payable upon compensation for 'land acquired' by a municipal council was raised by an Act from four to six per cent, it was held by the Privy Council that benefit of increase in interest from the date of operation of the Act was available also in respect of land acquired before the Act and that such a construction of the Act did not give rise to any question of retrospective operation of the Act.[25] The decision may have been different if in the place of the word 'acquired' some such words as 'to be acquired' or 'hereafter acquired' might have been used in the Act.[26]

Protection from eviction conferred by an Act upon a tenant who 'has actually built' a permanent structure on the land of the tenancy was held to cover even such cases where the structure was built by the tenant before the coming into force of the Act.[27] A provision in a Rent Control and Eviction Act, which was added by an amendment and which enabled a tenant

---

22. (1884) 13 QBD 784. **See further** *Chebarao v. Chebarao*, (1987) 1 All ER 999 (CA); (Words 'has been dissolved or annulled' in section 12(1) of the Matrimonial and Family Proceedings Act, 1984 were construed to cover cases where marriage was dissolved or annulled prior to the Act).
23. MULLA : Hindu Law, (12th Edition), p. 707.
24. *Sukhribai (Mt.) v. Pohkalsingh*, AIR 1950 Nag 33, pp. 36, 37; (HIDAYATULLAH, J.).
25. *Municipal Council of Sydney v. Troy*, AIR 1928 PC 128, p. 130.
26. *Ibid*, **distinguished** in *K.S. Paripoornan v. State of Kerala*, JT 1994 (6) SC 182, p. 219 : AIR 1995 SC 1012 : (1994) 5 SCC 593, on the ground that there was a *non obstante* clause in the new Act which increased rate of interest.
27. *Rafiquennessa (Mst.) v. Lal Bahadur Chhetri*, AIR 1964 SC 1511, p. 1514 : 1964 (6) SCR 876.

to adjust water taxes and water charges paid by him towards rent due from him, was held to apply to pending suits which related to eviction on the ground of arrears of rent and the tenant was held entitled to adjust water taxes and charges paid by him although the arrears of rent due and water taxes and charges paid related to periods before coming into force of the amendment.[28]

A new law enhancing compensation in case of death by electric shock and saying that 'cases already closed shall not be reopened', was construed to apply to all cases which were not closed, *i.e.*, to all cases pending or yet to be instituted in respect of accidents taking place before the amendment.[29]

In *Barber v. Pigden*,[30] the question related to the Law Reform (Married Women and Tortfeasors) Act, 1935, which provided in section 3 that 'the husband of a married woman shall not, by reason only of his being her husband, be liable in respect of any tort committed by her, whether before or after the marriage'. Section 4 saved from the operation of the Act, legal proceedings already commenced. The question before the Court of Appeal was: whether the Act applied to a tort committed prior to the Act in respect of which proceedings had not commenced when the Act came into operation. In holding the Act applicable to such torts, SCOTT, LJ., pointed out that the purpose of the Act was to make a clean sweep of the old legal fiction that a woman on marriage became merged in the personality of her husband, and thus to confer on a married woman full human status; that the legal fictions so removed were in their origin inextricably mixed up with old procedural law; that a statute abolishing old legal fictions of this nature is akin to a procedural statute; and that only expressed exception pointed out in the Act was in respect of pending proceedings which implied that there is no room for any other exception.[31]

Remedial statutes, though favoured by courts are not for that reason retrospective to affect vested rights;[32] but since such statutes are to be

---

28. *Ramji Purshottam v. Laxman Bhai D. Kurlawala*, (2004) 6 SCC 455, p. 463 : AIR 2004 SC 4010.

29. *Shashikalabai v. State of Maharashtra*, AIR 1999 SC 706 : (1998) 5 SCC 332 (case of circular of Maharashtra State Electricity Board).

30. (1937) 1 All ER 115 : (1937) 1 KB 664 (PC).

31. *Ibid*, pp. 125, 126.

32. *Central Bank of India v. Their Workman*, AIR 1960 SC 12, p. 17 : 1960 (1) SCR 200.

construed liberally, the inhibition of the rule against retrospective construction may be applied with less insistence.[33]

In *Central Bank of India v. Their Workmen*,[34] the proviso introduced in section 10(b)(ii) of the Banking Companies Act, 1949, by the amending Act of 1956, though held to be remedial, was not applied for a period anterior to the date of operation of the amending Act. S. K. DAS, J. in that case observed: "A remedial Act is not necessarily retrospective; it may be either enlarging or restraining; and it takes effect prospectively, unless it has retrospective effect by express terms or necessary intendment".[35] So in *Kerala State Electricity Board v. Valsala*,[36] amendment of the Workmen's Compensation Act, 1923 by Act No. 30 of 1995 enhancing the amount of compensation and rate of interest in respect of death or permanent disablement resulting from an accident was held not to apply to accidents taking place before the amending Act came into force. But in *Rathi Menon v. Union of India*,[37] it has been held that compensation payable for an 'untoward incident' resulting in personal injury under the Railway Accident Compensation Rules, 1990 will be the revised amount, when increased by revision of the Rules after the accident but before the order was passed by the claims Tribunal.

In *Workmen of F.T. & R. Co. v. Management*,[38] the question related to the construction of section 11A of the Industrial Disputes Act, 1947, which was added by an amendment in 1971. The section was brought into force sometime after the amending Act was passed. The section empowers a labour court to interfere with the finding of misconduct and the punishment imposed on a workman in a domestic enquiry 'where an industrial dispute relating to the discharge or dismissal of a workman has been referred' to it. In holding that the section did not apply to pending references, the Supreme Court pointed out that the section abridged the rights of the employer, it was not brought into force immediately when the amending Act

---

33. Corpus Juris Secundum, Vol. 82, Art. 416, pp. 992, 993. For example, **see** *Rattan Lal v. State of Punjab*, AIR 1965 SC 444 : (1964) 7 SCR 676, for this case, **see** page 604, *supra,* where it is discussed; *Workmen of Firestone Tyre & Rubber Co. v. Management*, AIR 1973 SC 1227 : 1973 (1) SCC 813; *Bharat Singh v. Management of Tuberculosis Centre*, (1986) 2 SCC 614 : AIR 1986 SC 842. **See** cases in notes 14-22, 28-30, *supra* and in notes 39-46, *infra*. **Also see** title 2(a), Chapter 11 text and notes 68-72, p. 947.

34. AIR 1960 SC 12 : 1960 (1) SCR 200.

35. *Ibid*, p. 17.

36. JT 1999 (7) SC 292 : (1999) 8 SCC 254 : AIR 1998 SC 3502, **overruling** an earlier decision of 1996.

37. JT 2001 (3) SC 457 : AIR 2001 SC 1333 **followed** in *N. Parmeshwaran Pillai v. Union of India,* AIR 2002 SC 1834 : (2002) 4 SCC 306.

38. AIR 1973 SC 1227 : (1973) 1 SCC 813.

was passed, and in a proviso it referred to 'a proceeding under the section' which could take in only references made after coming into force of the section. It will be seen that the language 'has been referred' as used in the section could have been construed to include even pending references but other considerations prevailed to hold that pending references were not affected by the section. However, section 10 of the Industrial Disputes Act, 1947, which authorises the appropriate Government, where it is of opinion that an industrial dispute exists or is apprehended, to refer the dispute for adjudication under the Act has been construed to authorise reference of an industrial dispute which arose on facts existing before the coming into force of the Act. It has been held that all that the section requires is that the dispute must exist on the date of the reference and it is immaterial whether it arose earlier to the commencement of the Act.[39] On a similar reasoning section 2A of the Act, which enlarges the definition of Industrial Dispute by including certain individual disputes, has also been construed to authorise reference of a dispute which arose earlier to the addition of the section in the Act by amendment.[40] And the same approach is exhibited in the construction of section 17B of the same Act (added by an amendment) which enables a workman to receive full wages after an award of reinstatement during the pendency of a proceeding to challenge the award taken by the employer in a High Court or the Supreme Court. The section has been held to apply to an award made and a proceeding challenging the award taken before the section was inserted in the Act provided the proceeding was pending when the section came into force.[41]

Statutes providing new remedies for enforcement of existing rights will apply to future as well as past causes of action, the reason being that such statutes since they do not affect existing rights, are classified as procedural.[42] Thus, the introduction by a new law of certificate procedure for recovery of certain type of claims as it applies for recovery of land revenue, will be retrospective and will apply to all claims of that type whether arising before or after the introduction of the new law.[43] A new law providing

---

39. *Jahiruddin v. Model Mills, Nagpur*, AIR 1966 SC 907 : 1966 (2) SCR 660.

40. *Rustom and Hornsby (P) Ltd. v. T.B. Kadam*, AIR 1975 SC 2025 : (1976) 3 SCC 71.

41. *Bharat Singh v. Management of New Delhi Tuberculosis Centre*, (1986) 2 SCC 614 : AIR 1986 SC 842.

42. *Idas*, (1863) 167 ER 309, p. 302; *Abdul Karim v. Dy. Custodian General*, AIR 1964 SC 1256, p. 1258 : (1964) 6 SCR 837; *Jahiruddin v. Model Mills*, AIR 1966 SC 907 : 1966 (2) SCR 660.

43. *Abdul Karim v. Dy. Custodian General*, AIR 1964 SC 1256, p. 1258 : 1964 (6) SCR 837.

a new remedy to the Government to recover arrears of rent will be similarly treated.[44] An amendment Act which introduced a provision in a Sales-tax Act enabling recovery of tax assessed on a firm also from its partners was held to apply for recovery of tax assessed before the amendment by recovery proceedings taken after the amendment.[45] And a new law providing for alternative adjudication proceeding for punishment of certain offences will apply for adjudication of the offences committed prior to the coming into force of the law.[46]

(i) Declaratory statutes

The presumption against retrospective operation is not applicable to declaratory statutes. As stated in CRAIES and approved by the Supreme Court: "For modern purposes a declaratory Act may be defined as an Act to remove doubts existing as to the common law, or the meaning or effect of any statute. Such Acts are usually held to be retrospective. The usual reason for passing a declaratory Act is to set aside what Parliament deems to have been a judicial error, whether in the statement of the common law or in the interpretation of statutes. Usually, if not invariably, such an Act contains a preamble, and also the word 'declared' as well as the word 'enacted'."[47] But the use of the words 'it is declared' is not conclusive that the Act is declaratory for these words may, at times, be used to introduce new rules of law and the Act in the latter case will only be amending the law and will not necessarily be retrospective.[48] In determining, therefore, the nature of the Act, regard must be had to the substance rather than to the form.[49] If a new Act is 'to explain' an earlier Act, it would be without object unless construed retrospective.[50] An explanatory Act is generally passed to supply an obvious omission or to clear up doubts as to the meaning

---

44. *State of U.P. v. Anand Swarup*, AIR 1974 SC 125, p. 128 : 1974 SCC 421.

45. *Dena Bank v. Bhikabhai Prabhudas Parekh & Co.*, AIR 2000 SC 3654, pp. 3660, 3661 : (2000) 5 SCC 694 (The liability of the partners for paying the dues of the firm was an existing liability and the amendment only provided a new remedy for enforcing that liability. This is probably the basis of the decision).

46. *Union of India v. Sukumar Pyne*, AIR 1966 SC 1206 : 1966 (2) SCR 34; *Rai Bahadur Seth Shreeram Durgaprasad (M/s.) v. Director of Enforcement*, (1987) 3 SCC 27, pp. 33, 34 : AIR 1987 SC 1364. **See further** for retroactivity of procedural laws, pp. 515 to 519.

47. CRAIES: Statute Law, 7th Edition, p. 58, **approved** in *Central Bank of India v. Their Workmen*, AIR 1960 SC 12, p. 27 : (1960) 1 SCR 200. **See** *Jones v. Bennet*, (1890) 63 LT 705, p. 708 (LORD COLERIDGE, C.J.); *Madras Marine & Co. v. State of Madras*, (1986) 3 SCC 552, p. 563 : AIR 1986 SC 1760; *Satnam Overseas (Export) v. State of Haryana*, AIR 2003 SC 66, p. 84 : (2003) 1 SCC 561.

48. *Harding v. Queensland Stamp Commissioners*, (1898) AC 769, pp. 775, 776 (PC).

49. *Ibid.*

50. *R. v. Dursley (Inhabitants)*, (1832) 110 ER 168, p. 169.

of the previous Act.[51] It is well settled that if a statute is curative or merely declaratory of the previous law retrospective operation is generally intended.[52] The language 'shall be deemed always to have meant'[53] or 'shall be deemed never to have included'[54] is declaratory, and is in plain terms retrospective. In the absence of clear words indicating that the amending Act is declaratory, it would not be so construed when the pre-amended provision was clear and unambiguous.[55] An amending Act may be purely clarificatory to clear a meaning of a provision of the principal Act which was already implicit. A clarificatory amendment of this nature will have retrospective effect and, therefore, if the principal Act was existing law when the constitution came into force, the amending Act also will be part of the existing law.[56]

The above statement of the law relating to the nature and effect of a declaratory statute has been quoted with approval by the Supreme Court from earlier editions of this book in a number of cases.[57]

"In *Mithilesh Kumari v. Prem Bihari Khare*,[58] section 4 of the Benami Transactions (Prohibition) Act, 1988 was, it is submitted, wrongly held to

---

51. *Keshavlal Jethalal Shah v. Mohanlal*, AIR 1968 SC 1336, p. 1339 : (1968) 3 SCR 623. The question whether an 'explanation' added by an amending Act is really explanatory or not would depend on its construction. In *S.K. Govindan and Sons v. Commr. of Income-tax, Cochin,* AIR 2001 SC 254, p. 260 : (2001) 1 SCC 460 : (2001) 247 ITR 192, *Explanation 2* inserted in section 139(8) of the Income-tax Act, 1961 was held to be clarificatory. But in *Birla Cement Works v. The Central Board of Direct Taxes,* JT 2001 (3) SC 256, p. 262 : (2001) 9 SCC 35 : AIR 2001 SC 1080, it was held that mere addition of an 'explanation' by an amending Act in a taxing Act cannot, without more, be held to be clarificatory and retrospective. In *Commissioner of Income-tax Bhopal v. Shelly Products,* (2003) 5 SCC 461, pp. 477, 478 : AIR 2003 SC 2532 provisos (a) and (b) added in section 240 of the Income-tax Act, 1961 by amending Act which came into force on 1-4-1989 were held to be clarificatory and retrospective.

52. *Channan Singh v. Jai Kuar (Smt.)*, AIR 1970 SC 349, p. 351 : (1969) 2 SCC 429.

53. *CIT v. Straw Products*, AIR 1966 SC 1113 : 1966 (2) SCR 881.

54. *Union of India v. S. Muthyam Reddy,* JT 1999 (7) SC 596, p. 597 : 1999 (7) SCC 545 : AIR 1994 SC 3881.

55. *Sakuru v. Tanoji*, (1985) 3 SCC 590, p. 594 : AIR 1985 SC 1279.

56. *Punjab Traders v. State of Punjab*, AIR 1990 SC 2300, p. 2304 : 1991 (1) SCC 86.

57. *R. Rajgopal Reddy v. Padmini Chandrasekharan*, 1995 (1) Scale 692, p. 704 : AIR 1996 SC 238, p. 246 : (1995) 2 SCC 630; *Allied Motors (P.) Ltd. v. CIT*, AIR 1997 SC 1361, pp. 1366, 1367 : 1997 (3) SCC 472; *CIT v. Podar Cement Pvt. Ltd.*, AIR 1997 SC 2523, pp. 2537, 2538 : 1997 (5) SCC 482; *Shyam Sunder v. Ram Kumar,* AIR 2001 SC 2472, p. 2487 : (2001) 8 SCC 24; *Zile Singh v. State of Haryana,* (2004) 8 SCC 1, p. 9 : AIR 2004 SC 5100, pp. 5103, 5104; *Commissioner of Income Tax I, Ahmedabad v. Gold Coin Health Food Pvt. Ltd.,* (2008) 9 SCC 622 paras 19, 20 : (2009) 9 JT 312. **See further** *S.B. Bhattacharjee v. S.D. Majumdar,* AIR 2007 SC 2102 (paras 26 to 29) : (2007) 7 JT 381.

58. AIR 1989 SC 1247, p. 1255 : 1989 (2) SCC 95.

be an Act declaratory in nature for it was not passed to clear any doubt existing as to the common law or the meaning or effect of any statute. The conclusion, however, that section 4 applied also to past *benami* transactions may be supportable on the language used in the section." These observations and criticism of *Mithilesh Kumari's* case also received the approval in *R. Rajgopal Reddy v. Padmini Chandrasekharan,*[59] where the Supreme Court after quoting them (from 5th Edition pp. 315, 316) said: "No exception can be taken to the above observations".[60]

A proviso added from 1.4.1988 to section 43B inserted in the Income-tax Act, 1961 from 1.4.1984 came up for consideration in *Allied Motors (P.) Ltd. v. Commissioner of Income-tax*[61] and it was given retrospective effect from the inception of the section on the reasoning that the proviso was added to remedy unintended consequences and supply an obvious omission so that the section may be given a reasonable interpretation and that in fact the amendment to insert the proviso would not serve its object unless it is construed as retrospective. In *Commisioner of Income-tax, Bombay v. Podar Cement Pvt. Ltd.*,[62] the Supreme Court held that amendments introduced by the Finance Act, 1987 in so far they related to section 27(iii), (iiia) and (iiib) which redefined the expression 'owner of house property', in respect of which there was a sharp divergence of opinion amongst the High Courts, was clarificatory and declaratory in nature and consequently retrospective. Similarly, in *Brij Mohan Das Laxman Das v. Commissioner of Income-tax.*[63] Explanation 2 added to section 40 of the Income-tax Act, 1961 from 1.4.1985 on a question on which there was a divergence of opinion was held to be declaratory in nature and, therefore, retrospective. And in *Zile Singh v. State of Haryana,*[64] substitution of the word 'upto' for the word 'after' in the proviso to section 13A (added in 1994) in the Haryana Municipal Act, 1973 by the Haryana Municipal (Second Amendment) Act, 1994 was held to be correction of an obvious drafting error to bring about the text in conformity with the legislative

---

59. 1995 (1) Scale 692 : 1995 AIR SCW 1422 : AIR 1996 SC 238.
60. *Ibid*, p. 704 (Scale) : p. 246 (AIR).
61. AIR 1997 SC 1361, pp. 1366, 1367 : 1997 (3) SCC 472; *Similarly in Commissioner of Income Tax v. Suresh N. Gupta,* (2008) 4 SCC 362 paras 38 and 39 : AIR 2008 SC 572, proviso inserted in section 113 of the Income-tax Act with effect from 1-6-2002 was held to be clarificatory and retrospective. Again in *Commissioner of Income Tax v. Alom Extensions Ltd.*, (2010) 1 SCC 489 : (2009) 14 JT 441 deletion of a second proviso and consequent amendment in second proviso to section 43B of Income-tax Act, 1961 by the Finance Act, 2003 was held to be curative and retrospective.
62. AIR 1997 SC 2523, p. 2538 : (1997) 5 SCC 482.
63. AIR 1997 SC 1651, p. 1654 : 1997 (1) SCC 352; **Affirmed** in *Suwalal Anandlal Jain v. Commr. of Income-tax,* AIR 1997 SC 1279 : (1997) 4 SCC 89 and *Commissioner of Income-tax Bombay v. Kanji Shivji and Co.,* AIR 2000 SC 774 : (2000) 2 SCC 253. **See further** cases in note 42, *supra*.
64. (2004) 8 SCC 1 : AIR 2004 SC 5100.

intent and, therefore, retrospective. Even without the amendment of the proviso, the court in all probability would have read and interpreted the section as corrected by the amendment.[65]

(j) Statutes regulating appeals

An appeal is the "right of entering a superior court and invoking its aid and interposition to redress an error of the court below"[66] and "though

---

65. *Ibid*, p. 23 (SCC).

66. *A.G. v. H.J. Sillem*, (1864) 11 ER 1200, p. 1209 (HL) (LORD WESTBURY, L.C.); referred to in *Dayawanti v. Inderjit*, AIR 1966 SC 1423, p. 1427 : (1966) 3 SCR 275; *Sitaram v. State of Uttar Pradesh*, AIR 1979 SC 745, p. 756 : (1979) 3 SCC 656; *James Joseph v. State of Kerala*, (2010) 9 SCC 642 para 19(vi) : (2010) 9 JT 294 (where the statute does not place any limitations or restrictions to the scope and width of the appeal (whether first or second appeal), it shall be construed that the appeal provides a right of rehearing on law as well as facts); *Snehdeep Structures Private Limited v. Maharashtra Small Scale Industries Development Corporation Limited*, (2010) 3 SCC 34 para 65 (The term appeal in section 7 of Interest on Delayed Payments to Small Scale and Ancillary Industrial Undertakings Act, 1993 includes an application for setting aside the award under section 34 of the Arbitration and Conciliation Act, 1996 requiring deposit of the amount as required by section 7 of the Interest Act). **See** *Shanker Ramchandra Abhyanker v. Krishnaji*, AIR 1970 SC 1, p. 4 : (1969) 2 SCC 74 (Revision is exercise of appellate jurisdiction); *Nalakath Saimuddin v. Koorikadan Sulaiman*, AIR 2002 SC 2562, pp. 2566, 2567 : (2002) 6 SCC 1; *Rani Manprasad v. Gopichand*, AIR 1973 SC 566, p. 568 : (1973) 4 SCC 87, (Rights of appeal and revision are creatures of Statute); *Shiv Shakti Co-op. Housing Society, Nagpur v. Swaraj Developers*, AIR 2003 SC 2434, pp. 2439, 2443 : (2003) 6 SCC 659 (Difference between Appeal and Revision pointed out. Revision does not confer any substantive vested right and a curtailment of revisional power by an amending Act will also apply to pending revisions); *Gujrat Agro Industries Co. Ltd. v. The Municipal Corporation of the City of Ahmedabad*, AIR 1999 SC 1818 : (1999) 4 SCC 468 (The right appeal may be conferred subject to certain conditions); *Ramchandra Goverdhan Pandit v. Charity Commissioner*, (1987) 3 SCC 273, p. 278 : AIR 1987 SC 1598 (The word need not be expressly used to create a right of appeal); *Kashinath G. Jalmi (Dr.) v. Speaker*, AIR 1993 SC 1873, p. 1883 : (1993) 3 SCC 703 (Power to review is not an inherent power it should be conferred expressly or inferred by necessary implication). But **see** *Budhia Swain v. Gopinath*, AIR 1999 SC 2089, p. 2091 : (1999) 4 SCC 396 (A court or tribunal has inherent jurisdiction to recall an order in certain circumstances); *M.M. Thomas v. State of Kerala*, JT 2000 (1) SC 26 : AIR 2000 SC 540 : (2000) 1 SCC 666 (High Court being a court of record has plenary power to review its judgment when error is apparent). **See also** *Jagir Singh v. Ranbir Singh*, AIR 1979 SC 381, p. 384 : (1979) 1 SCC 560 (Judicial power of Superintendence of the High Court under Article 227 of the Constitution does not create any vested right even in a pending application for exercise of that power); *Ramchandra v. Dattatrya*, AIR 1986 MP 191, p. 194 (FB) (Revisional Jurisdiction under section 115 CPC does not confer a vested right). **See further** *Northern Plastics Ltd. v. Hindustan Photo Film Mfg. Co. Ltd.*, JT 1997 (3) SC 101, pp. 117 to 119 : 1997 (4) SCC 452 (The expression 'any person aggrieved' for purposes of entitlement of appeal is wider than the expression 'any party aggrieved', even so the person who claims the right to appeal must have suffered some legal injury); *Roopchand v. State of Punjab*, AIR 1963 SC

[Footnote No. 66 Contd.]

procedure does surround an appeal the central idea is a right".[67] The right of appeal has been recognised by judicial decisions as a right which vests in a suitor at the time of institution of original proceedings.[68] The right is a statutory right and it can be circumscribed by the conditions of the statute granting it.[69] It is not a natural or inherent right and cannot be assumed to exist unless provided by statute.[70] For example, section 53A of the Competition Act, which establishes Competition Appellate Tribunals, provides for appeals against orders passed by the Competition Commission against "any direction issued decision made or order passed by the Commission under sub-sections (2) and (6) of section 26" but not against any direction under sub-section (1) of section 26 to the Director General to investigate a case when it finds a *prima facie* case, no right of appeal can be impliedly

---

[Footnote No. 66 Contd.]

1503 : 1963 Supp (1) SCR 539 **followed** in *Behari Kunj Sahkari Awas Samiti v. State of U.P.*, AIR 1997 SC 3123, p. 3125 : (1997) 7 SCC 37 (A delegating to B its jurisdiction in certain matters. Orders of B in those matters are not appealable to or revisable by A under a general power of appeal or revision against orders of B). For doctrine of merger and appellate jurisdiction under Article 136 **see** *Kunhayammed v. State of Kerala,* AIR 2000 SC 2587 : (2000) 6 SCC 359, *Union of India v. West Coast Paper Mills Ltd.*, (2004) 2 SCC 747, pp. 755, 756 : AIR 2004 SC 1596; *Chandi Prasad v. Jagdish Prasad*, (2004) 8 SCC 724, pp. 731, 732; *State of Kerala v. Kondottyparambanmoosa*, (2008) 8 SCC 65 para 20 to 24 : (2008) 9 JT 289 (Doctrine of merger). For the nature of right to file cross objection see *Municipal Corporation of Delhi v. International Security and Intelligence Agency Ltd.*, (2004) 3 SCC 250. For use of appellate jurisdiction under Article 136 for rebuking the High Court and for expunging of disrespectful remarks made by the High Court against the Supreme Court in its judgment, **see** *Tirupati Balaji Developers Pvt. Ltd. v. State of Bihar*, (2004) 5 SCC 1 : AIR 2004 SC 2351. The appellate court has an inherent power to dismiss even a first appeal or statutory appeal summarily: *Bolin Chetia v. Jagdish Bhuyan,* (2005) 6 SCC 81 (para 16).

67. *Radhakrishan v. Shridhar*, AIR 1950 Nag 177, p. 184 (FB) (HIDAYATULLAH, J.); *Nahar Industrial Enterprises Limited v. Hongkong and Shanghai Banking Corporation,* (2009) 8 SCC 646 paras 126 and 127 : (2009) 10 JT 199.

68. *Colonial Sugar Refining Co. v. Irving*, (1905) AC 369 : 92 LT 733 : 21 TLR 513 (PC); *Hossein Kasam Dada (India) Ltd. v. State of M.P.*, AIR 1953 SC 221 : 1953 SCR 987; *Garikapati v. N. Subbiah Chaudhry*, AIR 1957 SC 540; *State of Bombay v. Supreme General Films Exchange*, AIR 1960 SC 980 : (1960) 3 SCR 640; *Kasibai v. Mahadu*, AIR 1965 SC 703, p. 705 : (1965) 2 MLJ (SC) 116; *Jose De Costa v. Bascora Sadasiva Sinai Narconim*, AIR 1975 SC 1843, p. 1849 : (1976) 2 SCC 917. **See further** *Lakshmi Narayan v. First Addl. District Judge*, AIR 1964 SC 489 : 1964 (1) SCR 362.

N.B.—Different considerations will apply to a change in law which enlarges rights of appeal. **See** title (k), 'Statutes affecting finality of orders', text and notes 10-14, p. 626-627.

69. *Government of Andhra Pradesh v. P. Laxmi Devi,* (2008) 4 SCC 720 paras 23 to 25 : (2008) 2 JT 639 : AIR 2008 SC 1640.

70. *Super Cassettes Industries Ltd. v. State of U.P.*, (2009) 10 SCC 531 para 232 : (2009) 13 JT 272; *Competition Commission of India v. Steel Authority of India Ltd.*, (2010) 10 SCC 744 para 48 : (2010) 10 JT 26.

inferred.[71] But any change in the law relating to appeals, after institution of original proceedings, which adversely touches this vested right is presumed not to be retrospective.[72]

The leading case on the point is the decision of the Privy Council in *Colonial Sugar Refining Company v. Irving*.[73] In that case an action was brought in the Supreme Court of Queensland in October, 1922. At that time the Order in Council of 1860 gave a right of appeal to His Majesty in Council from the judgment of the Supreme Court. The judgment in the case was delivered by the Supreme Court on September 4, 1903. About ten days before this judgment the Judiciary Act, 1903, came into force, the effect of which was that Her Majesty in Council ceased to be a Court of Appeal from decisions of the Supreme Court and the only appeal under this Act lay to the High Court of Australia. In spite of this Act an appeal was taken to the Privy Council against the judgment of the Supreme Court and the question, therefore, arose whether the Judiciary Act, 1903, was retrospective so as to take away the right of appeal to the Privy Council in an action brought before the coming into force of this Act. In sustaining the right of appeal, LORD MACNAGHTEN observed: "To deprive a suitor in a pending action of an appeal to a superior tribunal which belonged to him as of right, is a very different thing from regulating procedure. In principle, their Lordships see no difference between abolishing an appeal altogether and transferring the appeal to a new tribunal. In either case there is an interference with existing rights contrary to the well-known general principle that statutes are not to be held to act retrospectively unless a clear intention to that effect is manifested."[74]

The principle laid down by the Privy Council in the above case[75] has been accepted by the Supreme Court in *Garikapati v. Subbiah Choudhry*[76] where, on a review of earlier authorities, S.R. DAS, C.J. deduced the following five propositions: "(i) The legal pursuit of a remedy, suit, appeal and second appeal are really but steps in a series of proceedings all connected by an intrinsic unity and are to be regarded as one legal proceeding; (ii) the right of appeal is not a mere matter of procedure but is a substantive right; (iii) the institution of the suit carries with it the implication that all rights of appeal then in force are preserved to the parties thereto till the rest of the carrier of the suit; (iv) the right of appeal is a vested right and such a right to enter the superior court accrues to the litigant and exists as on and from the date the *lis* commences and although it may be actually

71. *Competition Commission of India v. Steel Authority of India*, (*supra*), para 45.
72. Cases in note 68.
73. (1905) AC 369 (PC).
74. *Ibid*, pp. 372, 373.
75. *Ibid*.
76. AIR 1957 SC 540 : 1975 SCR 488. **See** however, the forceful **dissent** of VENKATRAMA AIYAR, J.

exercised when the adverse judgment is pronounced, such right is to be governed by the law prevailing at the date of the institution of the suit or proceeding and not by the law that prevails at the date of its decision or at the date of filing of appeal; (v) this vested right of appeal can be taken away only by a subsequent enactment if it so provides expressly or by necessary intendment and not otherwise."[77] Construing Articles 133 and 135 of the Constitution in the light of the above principles, it was held in this case[78] that in suits filed in British India before the date of coming into force of the Constitution an appeal lay to the Supreme Court against a decision of the High Court rendered after that date, if the suit satisfied the requirement of valuation for appealing to the Privy Council or the Federal Court according to the law in force at the date of institution of the suit, although it did not satisfy the requirement of valuation as laid in Article 133 of the Constitution.

It must, further, be noticed that the same principle of construction applies whether the change in law abolishes altogether the right of appeal available at the date of initiation of original proceedings, or whether it merely hampers its exercise by imposing restrictions.[79] Indeed, in the *Colonial Sugar Refining Company's* case[80] the right of appeal was only transferred to another tribunal by the subsequent law which was construed as not affecting appeals arising from pending actions. It has, therefore, been held that an assessee's right of appeal against assessment of tax which vested in him on the date of filing of return, was not affected by a subsequent change in law which required as a condition to the exercise of right of appeal the making of deposit of the tax assessed.[81] On the same principle,

---

77. *Garikapati v. N. Subbiah Choudhry*, AIR 1957 SC 540, p. 553 : 1957 SCR 488.

78. *Ibid.*

79. *Kasibai v. Mahadu,* AIR 1965 SC 703, p. 705; *Ganpat Rai Hiralal v. Chamber of Commerce,* AIR 1952 SC 409, p. 410 (para 9) : 1953 SCR 752; *Hossein Kasam Dada (India) Ltd. v. State of M.P.*, AIR 1953 SC 221 : 1953 SCC 987; *State of Bombay v. Supreme General Films Exchange*, AIR 1960 SC 980 : (1960) 3 SCR 488. **See further** the **following** cases which were **approved** in *Garikapati v. N. Subbiah Choudhry*, AIR 1957 SC 540 : 1957 SCC 488: *Sadar Ali v. Dolimuddin*, AIR 1928 Cal 640 (FB); *In re, Vasudeo Samiar*, AIR 1929 Mad 381 : 52 Mad 361 (FB). (In these two cases the question related to the effect of change in law in Letters Patent restricting the right of appeal from judgment of a single Judge by putting condition of leave to be obtained from that Judge): *Nagendra Nath Bose v. Mon Mohan Singh*, AIR 1931 Cal 100 (Change in law imposing condition of deposit of decretal amount before exercise of right of appeal for setting aside an execution sale).

80. *Colonial Sugar Refining Co. v. Irving*, (1905) AC 369 : 92 LT 733 (PC).

81. *Hossein Kasam Dada (India) Ltd. v. State of M.P.*, AIR 1953 SC 221 : 1953 SCR 987; **referred** to with **approval** in *Collector of Customs & Excise, Cochin v. A.S. Bava*, AIR 1968 SC 13, p. 15 : (1968) 1 SCR 82. But a change in law in this respect before assessment proceedings are commenced will apply to assessment orders

[Footnote No. 81 Contd.]

it was decided that an amendment enhancing court-fees did not apply to a memorandum of appeal presented after coming into force of the amendment, if it related to a decree passed in a suit instituted prior to the coming into force of the amendment.[82] Similarly, a change in law restricting grounds of appeal will not apply to suits instituted earlier.[83] But a provision laying down a special procedure which is required to be gone through before a litigant is entitled to raise in appeal a material point left undecided by the lower court does not create any vested right and the procedure cannot be insisted upon in appeals from pending suits after the repeal of the provision.[84]

A right of appeal, however, cannot exist without the existence of a Court to which the appeal is to be taken; and "a litigant has no right to contend that a tribunal, before whom he should have taken an appeal when he instituted the suit, should not be abolished",[85] for the Legislature is fully competent "to enact a law of that kind".[86] It, therefore, follows that "if the court, to which an appeal lies, is altogether abolished without any forum substituted in its place for the disposal of pending matters or for the lodgment of appeals, the vested right perishes no doubt".[87] In other words, if the Legislature after the institution of a legal proceeding abolishes simpliciter the court to which the appeals would have lain according to the law then in force and provides for no court in substitution, it will be understood that the right of appeal inhering in a suitor at the date of institution of the legal proceeding is taken away by necessary implication. To obviate this consequence, when the Constitution repealed the Government of India Act, 1935, and thereby abolished the Federal Court of India and created instead the Supreme Court of India, provisions were made in Articles 135

[Footnote No. 81 Contd.]

made after the change although they are in respect of a period prior to the change; *Hardeodas Jagannath v. State of Assam*, AIR 1970 SC 724 : (1969) 1 SCC 372. Further when the right of appeal as originally granted is itself conditional requiring the deposit, *Hossein Kasam Dada's* case has no application; *Vijay Prakash and Jawahar v. Collector of Customs*, AIR 1988 SC 2010, p. 2012 : (1988) 4 SCC 402. *Hossein Kasam Daba's* case **followed** in interpreting the proviso to section 173 Motor Vehicles Act, 1988 which requires deposit of a certain portion of the amount awarded before right of appeal against the award is exercised: *Ramesh Singh v. Cinta Devi*, AIR 1996 SC 1560 : 1996 (3) SCC 142.

82. *State of Bombay v. Supreme General Films Exchange*, AIR 1960 SC 980 : 1960 (3) SCR 640.

83. *Kasibai v. Mahadu*, AIR 1965 SC 703 : (1965) 2 MLJ (SC) 116.

84. *Jose De Costa v. Bascora Sadasiva Sinai Narconim*, AIR 1975 SC 1843 : (1976) 2 SCC 917, p. 926 (Abolition of such a procedure in effect removes a restriction for an appeal and will be presumed to be retrospective; **see** text and notes 11 to 13, pp. 626-627).

85. *Ittyavira Mathai v. Varkey Varkey*, AIR 1964 SC 907, p. 914 : 1964 (1) SCR 495.

86. *Ibid.*

87. *Daji Saheb v. Shankar Rao*, AIR 1956 SC 29, p. 30 : 1955 (2) SCR 872. **Also see** *Jose De Costa v. Bascora Sadasiva Sinai Narconim*, AIR 1975 SC 1843 : (1976) 2 SCC 917.

and 374(2) of the Constitution to confer on the Supreme Court the jurisdiction and powers, with respect to any matter, which were exercisable by the Federal Court before the commencement of the Constitution.[88] Similarly, the Constitution by Article 374(4) abolished the authorities functioning as Privy Councils in Princely States which later on became Part B States and provision was made for transfer of all pending appeals and other proceedings before these authorities to the Supreme Court.[89] However, in respect of Privy Councils functioning in Princely States the conferral of jurisdiction on the Supreme Court was only in respect of proceedings pending before these authorities on the commencement of the Constitution. Therefore, the decision of a High Court in these States which was rendered before the Constitution and in respect of which no appeal or leave to appeal was pending before the State Privy Council was not made appealable to the Supreme Court even if such a decision could have been appealed to the State Privy Council had that authority continued.[90] Thus, in such cases there was a destruction of the right of appeal as a result of abolition of the Court of Appeal. But as already discussed the right of appeal is not affected if one set of courts are abolished and another set of courts of equal status are constituted; and provision is made for a change over of proceedings.[91] When a court, to which the appeals would have lain in accordance with the law in force at the time of institution of proceedings, is abolished by a subsequent law which also establishes a court of a like status, the question, as to how far the right of appeal vesting on the institution of proceedings is taken away, altered, modified or preserved, will have to be answered on a careful analysis of the subsequent law to

---

88. *Daji Saheb v. Shankar Rao*, AIR 1956 SC 29, p. 30 : 1955 (2) SCR 872 (Decree passed by the High Court of Bombay before the Constitution, held appealable to the Supreme Court according to the law in force before the coming into force of the Constitution); *Garikapati v. N. Subbiah Choudhry*, AIR 1957 SC 540, pp. 555, 556 : 1957 SCR 488 (Decree of High Court of Andhra Pradesh passed after the Constitution in a suit instituted prior to the Constitution, held appealable to the Supreme Court according to the law in force at the time of institution of suit). **See further** *Yellappagouda v. Basangouda*, AIR 1960 SC 808 : (1960) 3 SCR 221 (An order of the Privy Council passed before Abolition of Privy Council Jurisdiction Act, 1949 is deemed for purposes of enforceability a decision of the Federal Court; and a decision of the Federal Court given before the Constitution is deemed to be for that purpose a decision of the Supreme Court by Article 374(2) of the Constitution. The latter fiction, it was held, also brings in within its ambit a decision of the Privy Council deemed to be a decision of the Federal Court. It was further held that a petition for cancellation of such a decision of Privy Council, under section 10, Bombay Hereditary Offices Act was entertainable by the Supreme Court for such a petition could have been entertained by the Privy Council before abolition of its jurisdiction and later on by the Federal Court.)

89. *Garikapati v. N. Subbiah Choudhry, supra*, p. 556.

90. *Janardhan Reddy v. State*, AIR 1951 SC 124, p. 125 : 1950 SCR 940.

91. *Ganpat Rai Hiralal v. Chamber of Commerce*, AIR 1952 SC 409, p. 410 (para 9) : 1953 SCR 752.

find out as to what extent the new court has been endowed with the jurisdiction and power of the court abolished.[1]

It must also be noticed that the right of appeal that vests at the commencement of original proceeding is limited to the various stages of the same proceeding, *e.g.*, suit, appeal or second appeal; but is not available in respect of a later original proceeding even if the same is somewhat connected with the earlier one, *e.g.*, an application for amendment of a decree under section 152, Code of Civil Procedure, 1908.[2]

Further, though a right of appeal to a particular court is a vested right, no party has a vested right to have his appeal heard by a specified number of judges of that court and a change in law in that matter will be regarded merely as a change in procedure; and therefore retrospective.[3] Again, when existing civil courts are abolished and new civil courts are created by the new law, an appeal against a decision in a pending suit decided by the new civil court, to which it is transferred, will lie to the court which has power to hear appeals under the new law.[4] This is on the principle that when the repealing Act abolishes the existing courts and provides for new courts, the forum for pursuing the vested right of appeal must be as provided in the repealing Act.[5]

(k) Statutes affecting finality of orders

An order, which on the date it is made is final, gives rise to vested rights; and a subsequent change in law giving rise to new right of appeal or revision is presumed not to affect the finality of orders already made.[6] This principle was settled by the Privy Council in *Delhi Cloth & General Mills Ltd. v. C.I.T., Delhi.*[7] In this case certain orders were made in January,

---

1. The principle stated can be deduced from the following cases; *Ittyavira Mathai v. Varkey Varkey,* AIR 1964 SC 907, p. 914 : 1964 (1) SCR 495; *Garikapati v. N. Subbiah Choudhry,* AIR 1957 SC 540 : (1957) SCR 488; *Daji Saheb v. Shankar Rao*; AIR 1956 SC 29 : 1955 (2) SCR 872; *Ganpat Rai Hiralal v. Chamber of Commerce*, AIR 1952 SC 402; *Janardhan Reddy v. State*, AIR 1951 SC 124 ; 1950 SCR 940. **See further** *Hukumchand Mills v. State of M.P.*, AIR 1964 SC 1329, pp. 1332, 1333 (para 5).
2. *Ganpat Rai Hiralal v. Chamber of Commerce*, AIR 1952 SC 409, p. 410 (para 8) : 1953 SCR 752.
3. *Ittyavira Mathai v. Varkey Varkey,* AIR 1964 SC 907, p. 914 : (1964) 1 SCR 495; *P. Mohd. Meera Lebbai v. Thirumalaya Gounder Ramaswami*, AIR 1966 SC 430 : 1966 (1) SCR 574.
4. *Maria Cristina De Souza Sodder v. Amria Zurana Pereira Pinto*, AIR 1979 SC 1352 : (1979) 1 SCC 92.
5. *Ibid.* (But the wide observations that forum of appeal is always a matter of procedure are not correct, **see** text and notes 68-74, pp. 620-621).
6. *Dafedar Niranjan Singh v. Custodian, Evacuee Property*, AIR 1961 SC 1425 : 1962 (1) SCR 214; *Keshavlal Jethalal Shah v. Mohanlal*, AIR 1968 SC 1336 : 1968 (3) SCR 623.
7. AIR 1927 PC 242 : 54 IA 421.

1926, by the High Court at Lahore on reference to that court under section 66(2) of the Indian Income-tax Act, 1922. At that time there was no statutory provision for appeal to the Privy Council against such orders, and this was the position until the first April, 1926, when the Indian Income-tax (Amendment) Act, 1926, came into force which inserted section 66-A in the Income-tax Act, conferring a right of appeal to the Privy Council against orders of the High Court made under section 66. In a petition for special leave against the orders made in January, 1926, the Privy Council held that the finality of these orders, as they were passed prior to the commencement of the amending Act, was not affected as the Act did not clearly so provide; and, therefore, no appeal lay to the Privy Council.[8] LORD BLANESBURG in delivering the opinion of the Privy Council observed: "Provisions, which, if applied retrospectively, would deprive of their existing finality of orders, which, when the statute came into force, were final, are provisions which touch existing rights. Accordingly, if the section now in question is to apply to orders final at the date when it came into force, it must be clearly so provided."[9] On the same principle, conferral of a wider jurisdiction on the High Court to interfere in revision by an amending Act is not a mere matter of procedure but relates to substantive rights; and the wider jurisdiction cannot be invoked against an order made before the commencement of the Amending Act.[10]

But the right to finality does not vest or accrue until the making of the order; and, therefore, if a new right of appeal or revision is conferred before making of the order, although after institution of proceedings, the right of appeal or revision is available against all orders subsequently made.[11] It has, therefore, been held that an appeal will lie to the Supreme Court under Article 133 of the Constitution against a decree of a High Court in a Part B States (previously Princely States) made after the commencement of the Constitution in a previously instituted suit, even though when the suit was instituted, there existed no right of appeal to His Majesty in Council or the Federal Court.[12] The same principle can be said to have been applied when a Sales Tax Act was amended during the pendency of a revision, providing for a reference at the instance of Commissioner

---

8. *Ibid.*
9. *Ibid*, p. 244.
10. *Keshavlal Jethalal Shah v. Mohanlal*, AIR 1968 SC 1336, p. 1339 : 1968 (3) SCR 623.
11. *Indira Sohanlal v. Custodian of Evacuee Property*, AIR 1956 SC 77, p. 84 : (1955) 2 SCR 1117; *Moti Ram v. Suraj Bhan*, AIR 1960 SC 655, p. 657 : (1960) 2 SCR 896; *Rathbone v. Munn*, (1868) 18 LT 857 (BLACKBURN, J.).
12. *Nathoo Lal v. Durga Prasad*, AIR 1954 SC 355, p. 357 : 1955 (1) SCR 51; *Garikapati v. N. Subbiah Choudhry*, AIR 1957 SC 540, pp. 562, 563, 564 (paras 43, 46, 47) : 1957 SCR 488.

of Sales Tax. It was held that the Commissioner could apply for reference against the order made in the pending revision.[13]

Alteration in law relating to appeals when it reduces already existing rights of appeal is, as already seen, presumed to be prospective and will not affect pending proceedings;[14] but if such alteration increases rights of appeal, it will be presumed to be retrospective applying to orders subsequently made in pending proceedings, though it will not affect finality of orders already made.[15]

On the principle that finality of decided cases is not affected, it was held that extension of time limited for appeal from decisions in cases which had been adjudicated upon prior to the passing of the Mortgagees Legal Costs Act, 1895, and which were right at the time when they were pronounced, will not be allowed, notwithstanding that section 3 of that statute was retrospective in its operation, and applied to 'mortgages made and business transacted and acts done either before or after the commencement of' the Act.[16] And a final adjudication of invalidity of certain transfers was held to be not affected by a new law which enacted that the transfers 'shall not be declared to be invalid'.[17] Similarly, an order granting a stage-carriage permit was not held to be invalidated by a subsequent law which was retrospective and which provided for review of earlier orders until the order was actually reviewed in accordance with the provisions of the new law.[18]

But, if a new Act provides that the orders made under the old Act are deemed to be made under the new Act as if it were in force on the day when the orders were made, the orders though made under the old Act will become appealable or revisable under the new Act.[19] Similarly, a retrospective change in law may enable a court to review its earlier decision and to modify it even in the absence of an express conferral of such

---

13. *Tikaram & Sons v. Commr. of Sales Tax, U.P.*, AIR 1968 SC 1286, p. 1292 : 1968 (3) SCR 512.
14. **See** title 2(j) 'Statutes Regulating appeals', *supra*.
15. **See** text and cases in notes 11 to 13, pp. 626-627, *supra*.
16. *Eyre v. Wynn McKenzie*, (1896) 1 Ch 135 (CA).
17. *Bai Achhuba v. Kalidas*, AIR 1967 SC 651 : 1964 (5) SCR 853.
18. *Sharif Ahmad v. Regional Transport Authority, Meerut*, AIR 1978 SC 209, p. 214 : (1978) 1 SCC 1.
19. *Bishambhar Nath Kohli v. State of U.P.*, AIR 1966 SC 573, p. 579 : (1966) 2 SCR 158; *Mithoo Shahni v. Union of India*, AIR 1964 SC 1536, pp. 1539, 1540 : (1964) 7 SCR 103. **See further** *Special Military Estates Officer v. Munnivenkataramaiah*, AIR 1990 SC 499 : (1990) 2 SCC 168 [An award fixing annual compensation for requisition of land under the Defence of India Act, 1962 made before its expiry though final for the period the Defence of India Act was in force was held to be appealable under the Requisitioning and Acquisition of Immovable Property Act, 1952 for a period subsequent thereto as the requisition was deemed to be made under section 25 (substituted in 1968) of the Requisitioning Act.].

power.[20] And, a retrospective statute may by implication without using express words, invalidate an order previously made.[21] Thus, a decree passed by a Civil Court in a suit was invalidated when by a retrospective change in law the subject-matter of the suit was taken out of the jurisdiction of Civil Courts.[22] Conversely, a decree passed by a Small Cause Court and held to be inexecutable for want of jurisdiction may be validated and made executable by a retrospective legislation.[23]

(l) Pending proceedings

(i) *Alteration of substantive rights.*—A retrospective statute which affects rights in existence is not readily construed to affect adjudication of pending proceedings.[24] The courts insist that to have that result the language should be sufficiently clear,[25] although it need not be express.[26] Courts have undoubtedly leaned very strongly against applying a new Act to a pending action, when the language of the statute does not compel them to do so.[27] In the words of S.R. DAS, C.J.: The golden rule of construction is that, in the absence of anything in the enactment to show that it is to have retrospective operation, it cannot be so construed as to have the effect of altering the law applicable to a claim in litigation at the time when the Act was passed.[28]

---

20. *Shatrunjit v. Md. A. Azim Khan*, AIR 1971 SC 1474 : 1971 (2) SCC 200. **But see** *Gurdit Singh v. State of Punjab*, AIR 1974 SC 1791 : (1974) 2 SCC 260.

21. *Jyoti Prakash Mitter v. C.J., Calcutta*, AIR 1965 SC 961, p. 969 : 1965 (2) SCR 53.

22. *Sunder Dass v. Ram Parkash*, AIR 1977 SC 1201, p. 1205 : (1977) 2 SCC 662.

23. *Dulare Lodh v. Third Addl. Dist. Judge, Kanpur*, (1984) 3 SCC 99 : AIR 1984 SC 1260.

24. *United Provinces v. Atiqa Begum (Mt.)*, AIR 1941 FC 16, pp. 37, 47 : 1940 FCR 110.

25. *Venugopala v. Krishnaswami*, AIR 1943 FC 24, p. 27; *Moti Ram v. Suraj Bhan*, AIR 1960 SC 655, p. 658; *K.S. Paripoornan v. State of Kerala*, JT 1994 (6) SC 182, p. 219 : AIR 1995 SC 1012.

26. *Shyabuddinsab Mohidinsab Akki v. Gadag Betgeri Municipal Borough*, AIR 1955 SC 314, pp. 319, 320 : (1955) 1 SCR 1268; *K.C. Mukherjee v. Mt. Ramratan Kuer*, AIR 1936 PC 49 : 63 IA 47. **See further** text and notes 41-47, pp. 631-632; *K.S. Paripoornan v. State of Kerala, supra*, p. 214.

27. *United Provinces v. Mt. Atiqa Begum, supra*, p. 57 (SULAIMAN, J.); *K.S. Paripoornan v. State of Kerala, supra*, p. 214.

28. *Garikapati v. N. Subbiah Choudhry*, AIR 1957 SC 540, p. 553 (para 25) : 1957 SCC 488; referred to in *R. Rajgal Reddy v. Padmini Chandrasekharan*, 1995(1) Scale 692, p. 703 : AIR 1996 SC 238, p. 246; *Dy. Collector v. S. Venkata Ramanaiah*, 1995 (5) Scale 521, pp. 531, 532; *Maharaja Chintamani Saran Nath Shahdeo v. State of Bihar*, JT 1999 (8) SC 45, p. 54 : AIR 1999 SC 3609, p. 3613 : (1999) 8 SCC 16; *Shyam Sunder v. Ram Kumar*, AIR 2001 SC 2472, p. 2478 : (2001) 8 SCC 24; *State of Punjab v. Bhajan Kaur*, AIR 2008 SC 2276 para 18 : (2008) 12 SCC 112.

The above principle has also been applied to proceedings pending for selection of candidates for appointment to a post. In this case[29] proceedings for selection to the post of Principal were pending before the Director of Education under section 16F of the U.P. Intermediate Education Act, 1921 when the Act was amended taking away the power of the Director to make an appointment. It was held that the amending Act could not in the absence of express words or necessary implication be construed to take away the power of the Director in the pending proceedings for selection.[30] But steps taken under an existing law which take away the jurisdiction of an authority may affect a pending proceeding before it especially when the authority is a tribunal of limited jurisdiction. In such a case, the authority's power to deal with the matter must continue when the decision is rendered by it and if the authority's power is taken away before that stage is reached, it will cease to have jurisdiction even in a pending matter. For example, clause 16(3) of the Banking Ombudsman Scheme, 1995 made under the Banking Regulation Act provides that 'no complaint to the Banking Ombudsman shall lie unless—the complaint is not the subject matter for which any proceeding before any court, tribunal or arbitrator or other forum is pending'. In a case where during the pendency of a complaint before the Ombudsman, the Debts Recovery Tribunal was moved on the same subject matter, it was held, that the Ombudsman lost the jurisdiction to deal with the complaint.[31] The word 'lie' in clause 16(3) of the scheme was construed to mean that the Ombudsman must continue to have foundation in law to deal with the matter till the stage of decision and not merely when the complaint is filed.[32]

In *Smithies v. National Association of Operative Plasterers*[33] section 4 of the Trade Disputes Act, 1906 which enacted that 'an action for tort against a trade union shall not be entertained by any court' was held not to affect disposal of an action commenced before passing of the Act.

In *Beadling v. Goll,*[34] the Gaming Act, 1922, which had repealed a section of an earlier Gaming Act, was held not to terminate a pending action even though it had enacted that 'no action for the recovery of money under the said section shall be entertained by any court'.

---

29. *A.A. Cotton v. Director of Education*, AIR 1983 SC 1143 : (1983) 3 SCC 33.

30. *Ibid.* **See further** *P. Mahendran v. State of Karnataka*, AIR 1990 SC 405 : (1990) 1 SCC 411; *Gopal Krushna Rath v. M.A.A. Baig,* AIR 1999 SC 2093, p. 2094 : (1999) 1 SCC 544.

31. *Durga Hotel Complex v. Reserve Bank of India,* (2007) 5 SCC 120 (paras 13 and 14) : AIR 2007 SC 1467.

32. *Ibid.*

33. (1909) 1 KB 310, pp. 319, 320.

34. (1929) 38 TLR 128 (CA).

In *Chandrasingh v. Surjitlal,*[35] section 12(2) of the Bombay Rents, Hotel and Lodging House Rates Control Act, 1947, which enacted that 'no suit for recovery of possession shall be instituted' was held to be prospective not affecting a suit commenced earlier to the passing of the Act.

In *Provincial Government of Madras v. J.S. Basappa,*[36] section 18A of the Madras General Sales Tax Act, 1939, which was inserted by an amending Act of 1951, and which enacted that 'no suit or other proceeding shall be instituted in any court to set aside or modify any assessment made under this Act, was held not to apply to suit instituted before the amending Act came into force.

In *Venugopala v. Krishnaswami,*[37] section 46(2) of the Government of India Act, 1935, which enacted that Burma shall cease to be part of India, was construed not to affect the continuance of pending action in an Indian court which related to properties situated in Burma.

A new law bringing about a change in forum does not affect pending actions,[38] unless a provision is made in it for change over of proceedings or

---

35. AIR 1951 SC 199, p. 201 : 1951 SCR 221. Referred with apparent **approval** in *Motiram Ghelabhai v. Jagan Nagar*, (1985) 2 SCC 279, p. 282 : AIR 1985 SC 709. In *Vineet Kumar v. Mangal Sain Wadhera*, (1984) 3 SCC 352 : AIR 1984 SC 817, Section 20 of the U.P. Act, which uses similar language, was applied to a pending suit when a house which was exempt from the operation of the Act came within its operation after expiry of ten years during the pendency of the suit but this case was **dissented** from in *Nand Kishore Marwah v. Samundri Devi*, (1987) 4 SCC 382 : AIR 1987 SC 2284 and it was held that section 20 was inapplicable in such cases. *Nandkishore's* case was **followed** in *Atma Ram Mittal v. Ishwar Singh Punia*, AIR 1988 SC 2031 : 1988 (4) SCC 284 (which related to exemption under the Haryana Act and where also the period of exemption, *i.e.,* 10 years expired during the pendency of the suit); *Suresh Chand v. Gulam Chisti*, AIR 1990 SC 897 : (1990) 1 SCC 593; *Ramesh Chandra v. III Additional District Judge*, AIR 1992 SC 1106 : (1992) 1 SCC 751, and *Bholanath Varshney v. Mulk Raj Madan*, AIR 1994 SC 1664 (Cases under the U.P. Act); *Kishan v. Manoj Kumar*, JT 1998 (1) SC 633: AIR 1998 SC 999 : (1998) 2 SCC 710 (a case under the Haryana Act). **See also** *Shyam Charan v. Sheoji Bhai*, AIR 1977 SC 2270, p. 2272 : 1977 (4) SCC 393 (The M.P. Accommodation Control Act, 1961 does not apply to pending suits).

36. AIR 1964 SC 1873, p. 1876 : 1964 (5) SCR 517. **Approved** on this point in *State of Kerala v. Ramaswami Iyer & Sons*, AIR 1966 SC 1738 : 1966 (3) SCR 582.

37. AIR 1943 FC 24.

38. *Manujendra v. Purnendu Prasad*, AIR 1967 SC 1419, p. 1422 : 1964 (6) SCR 654; *Dewaji v. Ganpatlal*, AIR 1969 SC 560 : (1969) 1 SCR 573; *CIT v. Dhadi Sahu*, 1993 AIR SCW 3578 : 1994 Supp (1) SCC 257; *CIT v. R. Shardamma (Smt.)*, AIR 1996 SC 3199, p. 3200 : (1996) 8 SCC 388; *R. Kapilnath v. Krishna,* (2003) 1 SCC 444, p. 446 : AIR 2003 SC 565, p. 567 (8th edition p. 442 of this book is **referred** with approval).

there is some other clear indication that pending actions are affected.[39] Thus, if the new law which is enacted during the pendency of a suit in a Civil Court is worded in the form that 'no Civil Court shall have jurisdiction to settle, decide or deal with'certain questions which are committed to the jurisdiction of Revenue Courts and the pending suit relates to these questions, the jurisdiction of the Civil Court would be ousted.[40]

The principle, that pending proceedings are not affected, does not go beyond this that in every case language of the statute has to be examined to determine whether the Legislature clearly intended to bring within reach of the statute even pending proceedings.[41] It is, therefore, not essential that the Legislature, if it intends to apply a statute to pending proceedings, must enact an express provision to that effect.[42] A retrospective conferral of new rights or a retrospective restoration of rights which had earlier been taken away, will in general, affect pending proceedings.[43] It is the duty of Courts, whether trying original proceedings or hearing an appeal, to take notice of the change in law affecting pending actions and to give effect to the same.[44] Thus, if a taxing Act is retrospectively changed after reference,

---

39. *Mohd. Idris v. Sat Narain*, AIR 1966 SC 1499, p. 1501; *Commr. of Income Tax v. Dhadi Sahu*, 1993 AIR SCW 3578 : 1994 Supp (1) SCC 257; *CIT v. R. Shardamma (Smt.)*, AIR 1996 SC 3199, p. 3200 : 1996 (8) SCC 388; *R. Kapilnath v. Krishna, supra.*

40. *Inacio Martines v. Narayan Hari Naik*, AIR 1993 SC 1756 : 1993 (3) SCC 123; *Judith Fernandes (Mrs.) v. Conceicao Antonio Fernandes*, AIR 1996 SC 2821 : (1996) 10 SCC 401. **See further** *United Bank of India, Calcutta v. Abhijit Tea Co. Pvt. Ltd.*, AIR 2000 SC 2957 : (2000) 7 SCC 357 (construction of section 18 of the Recovery of Debts Due to Banks and Financial Institutions Act, 1993).

41. *Shyabuddinsab v. Municipality of Gadag Betgeri*, AIR 1955 SC 314, p. 320 : (1955) 1 SCR 1268; *Mohanlal Jain v. Sawai Man Singhji*, AIR 1962 SC 73, p. 76 : 1962 (1) SCR 702.

42. **See** cases in note 26, p. 628, *supra*. **See further** *King v. Southampton Income-tax Commrs., Ex parte, W.M. Singer*, (1916) 2 KB 249, p. 259; *K.C. Mukherjee v. Mt. Ramratan Kuer*, AIR 1936 PC 49 : 63 IA 47; *United Provinces v. Mt. Atiqa Begum*, AIR 1941 FC 16, p. 40; *Dayawati v. Inderjit*, AIR 1966 SC 1423 : 1966 (3) SCR 275. Omission of a *restriction* to file a suit for a partition of a dwelling house by a female heir contained in section 23 of the Hindu Succession Act, 1956 by the Hindu Succession (Amendment) Act, 2005 was held also to apply to a suit filed by a female heir before the amendment and pending at the time of amendment: *G. Sekar v. Geetha*, (2009) 6 SCC 99 : (2009) 5 JT 496.

43. *Ishverlal Thakorelal Almaula v. Motibhai Nagjibhai*, AIR 1966 SC 459, p. 466 (para 12) : (1966) 1 SCR 450.

44. *Quilter v. Mapleson,* (1882) 9 QBD 672, p. 676; *Stovin v. Fairbrass*, (1919) 88 LJKB 1004, p. 1010; *A.G. v. Vernazza*, (1960) 3 All ER 97, p. 101 : (1960) AC 965 : (1960) 3 WLR 466 (HL); *Lachmeshwar v. Keshav Lal*, AIR 1941 FC 5, pp. 12, 13, 14; *Kotturuswami v. Veeravva*, AIR 1959 SC 577, p. 579 : 1959 Supp (1) SCC 968; *Dayawati v. Inderjit*, AIR 1966 SC 1423; *Lakshmi Narayan Gun v. Niranjan Modak,* (1985) 1 SCC 270, p. 274 : AIR 1985 SC 111; *United Bank of India, Calcutta v. Abhijit Tea Co. Pvt. Ltd.*, AIR 2000 SC 2957, p. 2962 : (2000) 7 SCC 357 (7th edition p. 406 of this book is **referred**).

the High Court and Supreme Court must take notice of it.[45] For example, if a refund provision in a taxing Act is amended by incorporating the principle of 'unjust enrichment' by providing that no refund shall be made unless the applicant proves that the incidence of tax has not been passed on by him to any other person, the amendment will be taken notice of even when the matter is pending in appeal before the Supreme Court and refund will be disallowed if the applicant fails to establish that the tax burden has not been passed on by him to any other person[46]. Similarly, if a law providing for compensation for an acquisition is retrospectively altered the Collector in making an award and the courts in deciding a reference or appeal relating to compensation must give effect to the change in law.[47]

Proceedings pending for quantification of compensation in respect of acquisitions already made are not affected by a change in law which enhances or reduces the rate of compensation unless the new law expressly or impliedly provides otherwise.[48] Further, the new law may confer only limited retrospectivity. The principle of limited retrospectivity of an amending statute, which makes changes in substantive law, applicable to pending proceedings is illustrated by the Land Acquisition (Amendment) Act, 1984. Section 23(1) of the principal Act prescribes the matters which are required to be considered in determining compensation. Section 23(2) makes provision for award of 'solatium' in consideration of compulsory nature of acquisition. Prior to the amending Act the solatium required to be paid was 15% of the market value. Section 28 of the principal Act before amendment allowed interest at the rate of 6% on the amount awarded by court in excess of the sum awarded by the collection. The Bill amending the principal Act was introduced in the Lok Sabha on April 30, 1982. The amending Act came into force on September 24, 1984. The amending Act introduced section 23(1A) in the principal Act which allows additional compensation in the shape of interest at the rate of 12% from the date of the notification under section 4 upto the date of Collector's award or taking over possession whichever is earlier. The amending Act also enhanced the solatium payable under section 23(2) from 15% to 30% and rate of interest prescribed in section 28 from 6% to 9%. Section 30 of the amending Act which was headed as 'Transitional provisions' enacted in sub-section (1) that section 23(1A) as inserted in the principal Act shall apply and shall be deemed to have applied also to: (a) every proceeding for the acquisition of any land pending on April 30, 1982 in which no award has

---

45. *CIT v. Straw Products*, AIR 1966 SC 1113 : 1966 (2) SCR 881.

46. *Union of India v. ITC Limited*, AIR 1993 SC 2135, pp. 2141, 2145 : 1993 Supp (4) SCC 326.

47. *Union of India v. Filip Tiago De Gama of Vedem Vasco De Gama*, AIR 1990 SC 981, pp. 984, 985 : 1990 (1) SCC 277.

48. **See** text and notes 43 and 44, p. 584.

been made by the Collector before that date, and (b) every proceeding for the acquisition of any land commenced after April 30, 1982 whether or not an award has been made by the Collector before the date of commencement of the amending Act, *i.e.*, September 24, 1984. Sub-section (2) of section 30 enacted that section 23(2) and section 28 of the principal Act as amended shall apply and shall be deemed to have applied also to any award made by the Collector or court or to any order passed by the High Court or Supreme Court in appeal against such award under the provisions of the principal Act after April 30, 1982 and before the commencement of the amending Act, *i.e.*, September 24, 1984. Section 30 of the amending Act created a lot of controversy as to the extent of retrospectivity of section 23(1A) and section 23(2) as amended. It is, however, now settled by two Constitution Bench decisions that these provisions have to be read along with section 30 of the amending Act and cannot be given larger retrospectivity than allowed by section 30.[49] It was, therefore, held that entitlement to additional compensation allowed by section 23(1A) depends upon pendency of acquisition proceedings as on April 30, 1982 or commencement of acquisition proceedings after that date and if the Collector had made the award before that date then additional compensation cannot be awarded even if the reference arising out of the Collector's award or appeal against the court's award was pending when the amending Act came into force.[50] It was similarly held that entitlement to increased solatium by section 23(2) as amended depended upon section 30(2) of the amending Act and was available only when the award of the Collector or the court was made between April 30, 1982 and September 24, 1984 and the benefit of enhanced solatium will not apply to a pending appeal against the court's award if the above condition was not satisfied. It will, however, be seen that literal reading of section 30(2) of the amending Act limited the retrospectivity of the amendment in section 23(2) to awards made by the Collector or the court between the introduction of the Bill and coming into force of the Act. There was, however, no reason why if the amended provision applied to awards already made after the introduction of the Bill,

---

49. *Union of India v. Raghubir Singh*, AIR 1989 SC 1933 : 1989 (2) SCC 754; *K.S. Paripoornan v. State of Kerala*, JT 1994 (6) SC 182 : AIR 1995 SC 1012 : (1994) 5 SCC 593 **followed** in *Ghaziabad Development Authority v. Anoop Singh*, (2003) 2 SCC 484 : AIR 2003 SC 1004. **See further** *Union of India v. Swarn Singh*, AIR 1997 SC 462 : (1996) 5 SCC 501 (There is no inherent power to give the benefit of the amending Act to awards to which it does not apply and any order giving such a benefit is a nullity and can be challenged even in execution proceedings). *Prashad v. State of Maharashtra*, (2010) 10 SCC 458 : (2010) 10 JT 428 (Land owners who did not file any appeal in the High Court if entitled to benefit of section 23(1A) as amended can invoke the provisions of Order 41, Rule 33 of CPC to get the benefit in state's appeal challenging enhancement by the reference court) paras 17 to 22.

50. *K.S. Paripoornan v. State of Kerala*, *supra*, p. 209.

it should not apply to awards made after the commencement of the Act in pending matters.[51] It was, therefore, held that it was implicit in section 30(2) of the Amending Act that the benefit of section 23(2) as amended should also be given to awards made after commencement of the Act in pending proceedings.[52]

In *K.C. Mukherjee v. Mst. Ramratan Kuer*,[53] a landlord had sued for ejectment of the tenant and his transferee of a non-transferable occupancy holding on the ground that the transfer was made without the plaintiff's consent. When the matter was pending in appeal before the Privy Council, the Bihar Tenancy Amendment Act, 1934, came into force which enacted that every landlord shall be deemed to have given his consent to every transfer made before 1923. The transfer in question before the Privy Council was of 1916 and was held to be validated negativing plaintiff's right to recover possession although the amending Act contained no express provision applying the Act to pending proceedings.

In *Shyabuddinsab v. Municipality of Gadag Betgeri*,[54] where certain elections to the offices of President and Vice-President were called into question and while the matter was pending in appeal before the Supreme Court, the Municipal Act was amended by a retrospective Act and all elections to the offices of President and Vice-President were validated, it was held that the elections in question were also validated although the Act made no express reference to elections which were already in challenge in a court.

In *S.B.K. Oil Mills v. Subhash Chandra,*[55] section 12(1) of the Bombay Rents, Hotel and Lodging House Rates Control Act, 1947, which enacted that 'a landlord shall not be entitled to the recovery of possession', and section 12(3)(b) of the same Act which enacted that 'no decree for eviction shall be passed' were held to enact a rule of decision applicable to pending suits.[56] Similarly, in *Raffiquennesa v. Lal Bahadur Chhetri*,[57] section 5(1)

---

51. *Union of India v. Raghubir Singh, supra*, pp. 1948, 1949.

52. *Union of India v. Filip Tiago De Gama of Vedem Vasco De Gama*, AIR 1990 SC 981 : 1990 (1) SCC 277.

53. AIR 1936 PC 49 : 63 IA 47.

54. AIR 1955 SC 314 : 1955 (1) SCR 1268.

55. AIR 1961 SC 1596, p. 1601. **See further** on the same point *Lakshmi Narayan Gun v. Niranjan Modak,* (1985) 1 SCC 270, p. 274 : AIR 1985 SC 111. **But see** *Moti Ram v. Suraj Bhan*, AIR 1960 SC 655, p. 658 : (1960) 2 SCR 974 (Amendment during pendency of proceeding restricting ground of ejectment, held not retrospective). Compare cases in text and footnote 35, p. 630.

56. **See also** *Motiram Ghelabhai v. Jagan Nagar*, (1985) 2 SCC 279 : AIR 1985 SC 709 (But not to a pending appeal because of a special proviso in the nature of a saving).

57. AIR 1964 SC 1511, pp. 1514, 1515 : 1964 (6) SCR 876. **Also see** *Lakshmi Narayan Gun v. Niranjan Modak, supra.*

of the Assam Non-Agricultural Urban Tenancy Act, 1955, which enacted that a 'tenant shall not be ejected by the landlord from the tenancy except on the ground of non-payment of rent', was held to apply to pending proceedings for ejectment even at the appellate stage.[58] It was pointed out in this case that if the Legislature had intended that the protection afforded by the Act should operate prospectively, *i.e.*, only in respect of suits filed after the coming into force of the Act, it should have been easy to say so by providing that 'the tenant shall not be sued in ejectment' instead of providing that 'the tenant shall not be ejected'.[59] After referring to these cases the Supreme Court observed: "In some statutes the Legislature says that no suit shall be 'entertained' or 'instituted' in regard to a particular subject matter. It has been held by this court that such a law will not affect pending actions and the law is only prospective. But the position is different if the law states that after its commencement, no suit shall be 'disposed of' or 'no decree shall be passed' or 'no court shall exercise power or jurisdiction'. In this class of cases the Act applies even to pending proceedings—."[60] But, though the words 'shall not be ejected' are appropriate to cover pending suits, they may not be sufficient to bar execution of decrees already obtained unless the context gives a clear indication to the contrary.[61] It has also been held that the words 'no decree for eviction shall be passed in a suit or proceeding filed and pending against a tenant' though wide enough to cover a pending appeal,[62] are not wide enough to cover a leave petition under Article 136 of the Constitution or an appeal under that provision after leave is granted.[63] But the words 'a tenant shall not be evicted whether in execution of a decree or otherwise' have been held to cover even an appeal under Article 136 pending in the Supreme Court.[64]

---

58. *Ibid.*

59. *Ibid*, pp. 1514, 1515.

60. *United Bank of India, Calcutta v. Abhijit Teo Co. Pvt. Ltd.*, AIR 2000 SC 2957, p. 2962 : (2000) 7 SCC 357.

61. *Nathia Agarwalla v. Jahanara Begum*, AIR 1967 SC 92 : 1966 (3) SCR 926. **See further** *Kanailal Sur v. Paramnidhi Sadhu Khan*, AIR 1957 SC 907 : 1958 SCR 360; *M. Subbarao & Sons v. Yoshodamma*, AIR 2002 SC 3284 : (2002) 7 SCC 553 (An eviction decree which has became final before repeal of the Act though not yet executed is not affected by the new Act unless there be clear words to the contrary). **But see** *H. Shiva Rao v. Cecila Pereira*, (1987) 1 SCC 258, pp. 260, 261 : AIR 1987 SC 248 in which it was held that the words 'no order or decree for recovery of possession shall be made' barred even pending execution proceedings.

62. *Dilip v. Mohd. Azizul Haque*, AIR 2000 SC 1796, p. 1979 : (2000) 3 SCC 607.

63. *Laxman Marotrao Navakhare v. Keshavrao Eknathsa Tapar*, AIR 1993 SC 2596 : 1993 (2) SCC 270. For the nature of the power under Article 136, **see** *Teherakhatoon v. Salambin Mohammad*, JT 1999 (2) SC 452 : AIR 1999 SC 1104 : (1999) 2 SCC 635 and cases **referred** to therein.

64. *East India Corporation Ltd. v. Shree Manakshi Mills Ltd.*, AIR 1991 SC 1094 : 1991 (3) SCC 230.

The case *Qudrat Ullaeh v. Municipal Board Bareilly,*[65] will show that if a new Rent Control Act permits a pending suit to be amended to bring it in conformity with the provisions of the new Act, it is the new Act that will govern pending suits. But even in such a case the new Act will not apply where the rights of the parties had crystallised and the suit had been decreed by the trial court before the coming into force of the new Act which contained provisions to save accrued rights.[66]

In *Ramsarup v. Munshi,*[67] a suit for pre-emption was decreed by courts below and while an appeal from that decree was pending in the Supreme Court, the Punjab Legislature passed Act 10 of 1960, amending its earlier Act of 1913, and inserting in it a new section 31 to the effect that 'no court shall pass a decree in a suit for pre-emption whether instituted before or after the commencement' of the amending Act inconsistent with its provisions. It was held that the bar of the provision had to be taken note of by the Supreme Court, and it made no difference whether the appeal was from a decree dismissing the suit or decreeing the suit. The court in that case set aside the decree of pre-emption passed by courts below, which had been passed before the Act came into force and dismissed the suit in obedience to the new Act. To enable a plaintiff to succeed in a suit for pre-emption, the right of pre-emption must continue to exist till the passing of the decree but if the right is taken away by a change in law after passing of the decree in the trial court, it will not affect the decree which may have been challenged in appeal unless the change in law is retrospective and contains a provision analogous to section 31 referred to above.[68]

In *Mithilesh Kumari v. Prem Bihari Khare,*[69] a suit was filed by the real owner against the *benamidar* for declaration of his title in respect

---

65. AIR 1974 SC 396, p. 402 : (1974) 1 SCC 202.

66. *Idul Hasan v. Rajindra Kumar Jain,* AIR 1990 SC 678, p. 681 : 1989 (4) SCC 550.

67. AIR 1963 SC 553, pp. 562, 563 : (1963) 3 SCR 858. **Followed** in *Mula v. Godhu,* AIR 1971 SC 89, p. 91. **See further** *Amarjit Kaur v. Pritam Singh,* AIR 1974 SC 2068 : (1974) 2 SCC 363; *Sadhu Singh v. Dharundev,* AIR 1980 SC 1654 : (1981) 1 SCC 510. A new law applying to 'suits pending' will apply to all stages of the suit including appeals, at any rate to an appeal against a preliminary decree: *Dayawati v. Inderjit,* AIR 1966 SC 1423. A new law applying to 'a suit or proceeding' will not ordinarily apply to pending appeals: *Dewaji v. Ganpatlal,* AIR 1969 SC 560 : (1969) 1 SCR 573 especially appeals under Article 136 pending in Supreme Court, *Marotrao Navakhare v. Keshavrao Eknathsa Tapar,* AIR 1993 SC 2596, p. 2601 : 1993 (2) SCC 270.

68. *Shyam Sunder v. Ram Kumar,* AIR 2001 SC 2472 : (2001) 8 SCC 24.

69. AIR 1989 SC 1247 : 1989 (2) SCC 95. **See further** *Darshan Singh v. Rampal Singh,* AIR 1991 SC 1654 : 1990 (4) JT 561 : 1992 Supp (1) SCC 191 (Amending Act to the effect 'no person shall contest any alienation of immovable property' was held to apply to a suit pending in appeal).

of a house which was decreed. The decree was confirmed in appeal by the Additional District Judge and the High Court. The defendant appealed to the Supreme Court by special leave. During the pendency of the appeal in the Supreme Court the Benami Transaction (Prohibition) Act, 1988 came into force. Section 4(1) of this Act provides that no suit to enforce any right in respect of any property held *benami* 'shall lie' by or on behalf of a person claiming to be the real owner. The Supreme Court took notice of the Act and dismissed the suit. This case was followed in *Duvuru Jaya Mohan Reddy v. Alluru Naga Reddy*[70] which was also pending in the Supreme Court when the said Act came into force. In this case the suit was filed by the *benamidar* against the real owner and the auction purchaser and had been dismissed by the High Court. Section 4(2) of the Act provides that 'no defence based on any right in respect of any property held *benami* shall be allowed in any suit'. The Supreme Court took notice of the Act and allowed the appeal and decreed the suit. Both these cases are no longer good law on the point that pending suits and appeals were affected by section 4 of the Act as that view has now been substantially overruled in *R. Rajgopal Reddy v. Padmini Chandrasekharan.*[71]

In *Mohanlal v. Sawai Mansinghji,*[72] while the suit against the ruler of an Indian State was pending, section 87B was inserted in the Civil Procedure Code, 1908, by Amending Act II of 1951. This section applied to rulers of former Indian States, the provisions of section 86 which is to the effect: 'No ruler of a foreign State may be sued'. It was held by the Supreme Court that this provision applied also to pending suits for the word 'sued' embraced not only the institution but also continuance of previously instituted suit and the ban of the section operated for both.

In *Safali Ray Chowdhary v. A.K. Datta,*[73] a suit for ejectment by a tenant against a sub-tenant was pending under the West Bengal Premises Rent Control (Temporary Provisions) Act, 1950, when this Act was repealed and replaced by the West Bengal Tenancy Act, 1956. The new Act contained a saving clause that pending proceedings may be continued as if the repealed Act 'had been in force and had not been repealed'. The new Act also made provision for upgrading of a sub-tenant as tenant and for bringing him into direct relationship with the landlord. It was held that it was open even to a sub-tenant against whom a suit was pending when the new

---

70. AIR 1994 SC 1647, p. 1648 : 1994 Supp. (2) SCC 559.
71. 1995 (1) Scale 692: AIR 1996 SC 238 : (1995) 2 SCC 630. For this case **see** p. 595.
72. AIR 1962 SC 73, p. 76 : 1962 (1) SCR 702.
73. AIR 1976 SC 1810 : (1976) 3 SCC 602.

Act came into force to take the benefit of the new Act and to contend that the plaintiff tenant's right has come to an end.

In *Dahiben widow of Ranchhodji Jivanji v. Vasanji Kevalbhai,*[74] the question that was considered was regarding the applicability of the Bombay Tenancy and Agricultural Lands Act, 1948, which gave protection to the tenants against eviction to pending suits. Section 88(1) of the Act as originally enacted made the Act inapplicable to any area within the limits *inter alia* of the municipal borough of Surat and within a distance of two miles of the limit of borough. During the pendency of a suit relating to a land situate within the area excluded from the operation of the Act, section 88(1) was amended making the Act applicable to the area where the suit land was situated. It was held that the Act though it affected substantive rights, applied to the pending suit for it was a beneficial legislation and had to be given a liberal interpretation.

In *Mathew M. Thomas v. Commissioner of Income-tax,*[75] circular No. 455 dated 16.9.1986 issued by the Central Board of Direct Taxes which 'with a view to achieve early finalisation of proceedings under Chapter XXA of the Income-tax Act, 1961' (which had been deleted and made inapplicable in respect of properties transferred after September 30, 1986) directed that where acquisition proceedings have been initiated under section 269D the proceedings will be dropped if the apparent consideration was below Rs. 5 lakhs, was held to be a beneficient provision and was applied not only to original proceedings pending before the competent authority but also to proceedings pending in appeal before the Tribunal and the High Court in appeal.

(ii) *Alterations in matters of procedure.*—It has already been noticed[76] that for the reason that a litigant has no vested right in any matter of procedure, alterations in procedural law are generally held to be retrospective in the sense that they apply to future as well as to pending actions.

In *Attorney-General v. Vernazza,*[77] a provision enacted during the pendency of appeal preferred by a person who was declared a vexatious litigant, and authorising the court to order that any legal proceedings instituted by him in any court before the making of the order shall not be continued by him without leave of the High Court, was held to embrace proceedings instituted before commencement of the Act and also to authorise the

---

74. 1995(2) Scale 657 : AIR 1995 SC 1215 : 1995 Supp (2) SCC 295.
75. AIR 1999 SC 999 : (1999) 2 SCC 543.
76. **See** title 2(a)(iii) Statutes dealing with procedure, pp. 585-587.
77. (1960) 3 All ER 97 : 1960 AC 965 : (1960) 3 WLR 466 (HL).

Court of Appeal to make the order in terms thereof. It was pointed out that the Act was procedural for "no man, let alone a vexatious litigant, has a vested right to bring or continue proceedings which are an abuse of the process of the court".[78]

In *Craxford's (Ramsgate) Ltd. v. Williams and Steer Manufacturing Co. Ltd.*,[79] the question related to the effect of section 2 of the Law Reform (Enforcement of Contracts) Act, 1954, on pending proceedings. Section 2 of the Act of 1954, repealed 'section 4 of the Sale of Goods Act, 1893, in relation to any contract, whether made before or after the commencement of this Act'. The repealed section 4 of the Act of 1893, was to the effect that 'a contract for the sale of any goods of the value of £10 or upwards shall not be enforceable by action unless the buyer shall accept part of the goods so sold and actually receive the same or give something in earnest to bind the contract or in part payment, or unless some note or memorandum in writing of the contract be made and signed by the party to be charged or his agent in that behalf'. In an action filed on a contract, the defence rested under section 4 of the Act of 1893. During the trial, but before judgment, the 1954 Act came into operation giving rise to the question whether the defence under the repealed section 4 of the 1893 Act remained a valid plea. It was held that section 4 was only a procedural section fettering the power of court to grant a remedy unless the contract was established in a particular manner; and no one had any vested right under it; and that the fetter having been removed by repeal of the provision in respect of all contracts, the court could grant the remedy even in an action which was instituted earlier to the repeal.

In *Anant Gopal Sheorey v. State of Bombay*,[80] section 342A of the Code of Criminal Procedure, 1898, introduced by Amending Act 26 of 1954, which enacted that any accused person shall be a competent witness and may give evidence on oath in disproof of the charges, was held to be applicable to a prosecution which was pending at the time the amending Act came into force.

In *Blyth v. Blyth*,[81] section 1 of the Matrimonial Causes Act, 1963, which enables rebuttal by evidence of presumption of condonation arising from marital intercourse has been held to be procedural and applicable to a pending divorce proceeding irrespective of the date of events to which the evidence might be directed.

---

78. *Ibid*, p. 101.
79. (1954) 3 All ER 17.
80. AIR 1958 SC 915 : 1959 SCR 919.
81. (1966) 1 All ER 524 : 1966 AC 643 (HL).

But proceedings or trials completed before the change in law of procedure are not reopened for applying the new procedure.[82] In *Nani Gopal Mitra v. State of Bihar*,[83] the accused was convicted for criminal misconduct in the discharge of his official duty by recourse to presumption contained in section 5(3) of the Prevention of Corruption Act, 1947, which provision was repealed by Act 40 of 1964 when the appeal was pending. It was held that the repeal of section 5(3) after completion of trial did not affect the trial and the conviction could not be set aside in appeal on the ground that section 5(3) which was a procedural provision was repealed during pendency of appeal. Anti Corruption Law (Amendment) Act 16 of 1967 section 5(3) as it stood before its repeal was made applicable to all pending proceedings.[84]

3. OPERATION CONTROLLED ON CONSIDERATIONS OF CONSTITUTIONALITY: PRESUMPTION AGAINST EXCEEDING CONSTITUTIONAL POWERS

(a) Legislative Powers

In India legislative powers of Parliament and State Legislatures are conferred by Article 246 and distributed by Lists I, II and III in the seventh schedule of the Constitution. Parliament has exclusive power to make laws with respect to any of the matters in List I and State Legislatures have exclusive power to make laws with respect to matters in List II. Parliament and State Legislatures have both power to make laws with respect to matters in List III which is called the Concurrent List. Residuary power of legislation is vested in Parliament by virtue of Article 248 and Entry 97 in List I. The power of State Legislatures to make laws is subject to the power of Parliament to make laws with respect to matters in Lists I and III. While examining the legislative competence of Parliament to make a law all that is required to be seen is whether the subject matter falls in List II which Parliament cannot enter for in view of the residuary power vesting in Parliament other matters are not outside the legislative competence of Parliament.[85]

---

82. *Nani Gopal Mitra v. State of Bihar*, AIR 1970 SC 1636, p. 1639 : 1969 (2) SCR 411.
83. *Ibid.*
84. *G.P. Nayyar v. State*, AIR 1979 SC 602 : (1979) 2 SCC 593.
85. *Naga Peoples Movement of Human Rights v. Union of India*, AIR 1998 SC 431, p. 446 (para 20) : 1998 (2) SCC 1093 (also the cases **referred** to therein); *State of Karnataka v. Viswabarathi House Building Co-op. Society,* AIR 2003 SC 1043, p. 1052 : (2003) 2 SCC 412. **See further**, *Peoples Union for Civil Liberties v. Union of India*, AIR 2004 SC 456, p. 467 : (2004) 9 SCC 580 (As terrorism is much wider than Law and Order/Public Order, laws enacted for prevention of terrorism will fall within the residuary jurisdiction of Parliament).

Entries in the legislative lists are fields of legislation and receive widest construction unless their import is cut down by competing entries and other parts of the Constitution.[86] A matter mentioned in an entry is construed to cover all ancillary or subsidiary matters which can be reasonably be said to be comprehended in it.[87] For example, Entry 45 List I which reads 'Banking' has been construed to enable Parliament to provide for recovery of debts due to banks and to constitute for that purpose Banking Tribunals.[88] And a law for regulating recognition of educational institutions conducting courses of Bachelor of Education, enacted under Entry 66 of List I of Sch. VII, can provide that a qualification obtained in teacher education from any institution which is not recognised will not be treated as a valid qualification for appointment under the Central Government or a State Government or a University.[89] Further, power to enact a law on a particular topic includes the power to make provision in the law enacted to prevent its evasion.[90] But when wide construction of an entry leads to a conflict or overlapping with another entry in the same or different list, the rule of harmonious construction is applied so as to reconcile the conflict and to give effect to all of them.[91] Thus, the expression 'industries' in Entry 52 of List I has been construed in a limited sense to comprise only of manufacturing activities and not to include raw material and disposal of

---

86. *Balaji v. I.T. Officer*, AIR 1962 SC 123, p. 125 : 1962 (2) SCR 983; *Union of India v. H. S. Dhillon*, AIR 1972 SC 1061, p. 1070 : 1971 (2) SCC 779; *Union of India v. Shah Goberdhanlal Kabra Teachers' College*, (2002) 8 SCC, pp. 233, 234; *Welfare Association ARP Maharashtra v. Ranjit P. Gohil*, AIR 2003 SC 1266, p. 1278 : (2003) 9 SCC 358.

87. *State of Madras v. Gannon Dunkerley*, AIR 1958 SC 560, pp. 564, 565 : 1959 SCR 379; *Jagannath Baksh Singh v. State of U.P.*, AIR 1962 SC 1563, p. 1568 : (1963) 1 SCR 220; *Express Hotels Private Ltd. v. State of Gujarat*, AIR 1989 SC 1949, p. 1956 : (1989) 3 SCC 677; *E, P.N. Krishna Lal v. Government of Kerala*, 1995 AIR SCW 1325, p. 1332 : 1995 Supp (2) SCC 187; *Union of India v. Shah Goberdhanlal Kabra Teachers College, supra; Welfare Association ARP Maharashtra v. Ranjit P. Gohil, supra*, pp. 1278, 1279.

88. *Union of India v. Delhi High Court Bar Association*, AIR 2002 SC 1479 : (2002) 2 SCC 642. But 'Co-operative Banks' do not fall under Entry 45 List 1 and they are constituted under Entry 32 List II which relates to 'co-operative societies'. As a result the Recovery of Debts Due to Banks and Financial Institutions Act, 1993 enacted by Parliament has no application to co-operative banks: *Greater Bombay Co-op. Bank Ltd. v. United Yarn Tex (P.) Ltd.*, (2007) 6 SCC 236 para 98 : AIR 2007 SC 1584. **See** p. 367 also for this case.

89. *Union of India v. Shah Goberdhan L. Kabra Teachers' College*, (2002) 8 SCC 228 : AIR 2002 SC 3675.

90. *Indian Handicrafts Emporium v. Union of India*, AIR 2003 SC 3240, p. 3257 : (2003) 7 SCC 589.

91. *Cal. Gas (Prop.) Ltd. v. State of W. B.*, AIR 1962 SC 1044, p. 1050 : 1962 Supp (3) SCR 1 ; *Waverly Jute Mills v. Raymon & Co.*, AIR 1963 SC 90, p. 95 : 1963 (3) SCR 209; *Union of India v. Shah Goberdhanlal Kabra Teachers College, supra; Welfare Association ARP Maharashtra v. Ranjit P. Gohil, supra.*

final product.[1] This construction was adopted to avoid clash of Entry 52 List I with Entries 14, 27, 28 and 66 of List II and Entry 33 of List III.[2] Similarly, Entry 25 in the State List which reads "Gas and gas Works" has been held to be restricted to manufactured gas and not to cover natural gas which has been held to be covered by Entry 53 of List ,I *viz.*, 'Regulation and development of oil fields and mineral resources; petroleum and petroleum products.'[3] And on the same principle Entry 32 in List II relating to 'Incorporation-of-Universities' has been given a restricted construction because of Entry 66 in List I which relates to 'Co-ordination and determination of standards in institutions for higher education or research and scientific and technical institutions.'[4]

The question whether the Legislature has kept itself within the jurisdiction assigned to it or has encroached upon a forbidden field is determined by finding out the true nature and character or pith and substance of the legislation[5] which may be different from its consequential effects.[6] If the pith and substance of the legislation is covered by an entry within the permitted jurisdiction of the Legislature any incidental encroachment in the rival field is to be disregarded.[7] There is a presumption

---

1. *ITC Ltd. v. Agricultural Produce Market Committee,* AIR 2002 SC 852 : (2002) 9 SCC 232 (Constitution Bench).
2. *Ibid.*
3. *Special Reference No. 1 of 2001*, (2004) 4 SCC 489 : AIR 2004 SC 2647.
4. *Prof. Yashpal v. State of Chhattisgarh,* (2005) 5 SCC 420, p. 444.
5. *Subramanyan v. Muttuswami*, AIR 1941 FC 47, p. 51; *Assistant Commissioner of Urban Land Tax, Madras v. Buckingham and Carnatic Co. Ltd.*, AIR 1970 SC 169, p. 176 : 1969 (2) SCC 55; *Union of India v. Shah Goberdhanlal Kabra Teachers College,* (2002) 8 SCC 228, p. 234; *Welfare Association ARP Maharashtra v. Ranjit P. Gohil,* AIR 2003 SC 1266, pp. 1278, 1279 : (2003) 9 SCC 358; *Hindustan Liver Ltd. v. State of Maharashtra*, AIR 2004 SC 326, p. 339 : (2004) 9 SCC 438, *Bharat Hydro Power Corpn. v. State of Assam*, (2004) 2 SCC 553, p. 561 : AIR 2004 SC 3173; *E.V. Chinnaiah v. State of Andhra Pradesh*, AIR 2005 SC 162, p. 171, *Jamshed N. Guzdar v. State of Maharashtra*, (2005) 2 SCC 591, pp. 635 to 637. The expression 'pith and substance' was first used by LORD WATSON in *Union Colliery Co. of British Columbia v. Bryden*, (1899) AC 580, p. 599 [**see** in this context STREET, 'Doctrine of *Ultra Vires*' (1930), (Sweet and Maxwell), p. 455].
6. *A.G. of Sakatchewan v. A.G. of Canada*, AIR 1949 PC 190, p. 193; *Kannan Deval Hills Produce Co. Ltd. v. State of Kerala*, AIR 1972 SC 2301, p. 2307 : (1972) 2 SCC 218, p. 229 (para 28).
7. *Prafulla Kumar v. Bank of Commerce Khulna*, AIR 1947 PC 60, p. 65; *State of Bombay v. F.N. Balsara,* AIR 1951 SC 318, p. 322 (para 8) : 1951 SCR 682; *Chaturbhai v. Union of India*, AIR 1960 SC 424, p. 429 : (1960) 2 SCR 362; *Ishwari Khetan Sugar Mills (P) Ltd. v. State of Uttar Pradesh*, (1980) 4 SCC 136, p. 147: AIR 1980 SC 1955; *Federation of Hotel and Restaurant Association of India v. Union of India*, (1989) 3 SCC 634, pp. 652, 653 : AIR 1990 SC 1637; *Siel Ltd. v. Union of India*, AIR 1998 SC 3076, p. 3081 : 1998 (7) SCC 26; *Union of India v. Shah Goberdhanlal Kabra, Teachers College, supra*; *T.N. Kalyan Mandal Association v. Union of India*, (2004) 5 SCC 632, p. 652 : AIR 2004 SC 3757.

of constitutionality of statutes and hence, prior to determining whether there is any repugnancy between a Central Act and a State Act, it has to be determined whether both Acts relate to the same entry in List III, and whether there is a 'direct' and 'irreconciliable' conflict between the two, applying the doctrine of 'pith and substance'. This principle was applied by the Supreme Court to decide whether the Private Security Agencies (Regulation) Act, 2005, which is a Central Act, was in conflict with the Maharashtra Private Security Guards (Regulation of Employment and Welfare) Act, 1981, which is a State Act. The Court held that the subject matters of the two Acts are substantially different as the State Act is a labour legislation, which seeks to regulate the employment of private security guards employed in factories and establishments in Maharashtra, and is hence relatable to Entry 24 in List III, whereas the Central Act only regulates the business of private security agencies, which is relatable to the residuary Entry 97 in List I. Hence, both Acts were found to be valid as they occupied different fields, and the conflict in the operation of the two Acts was merely incidental.[8]

A law made by a State Legislature with respect to a matter in the concurrent list if repugnant to a law made by Parliament will be void to the extent of the repugnancy unless the state law has received the assent of the President in which case it will prevail in that state.[9] When a Central Act is enacted earlier, although brought into force later to the law enacted by the State which has received the assent of the President, the Central Act being earlier law will give way to the State law on matters covered by it.[10] The assent of the President which gives primacy to the state law has to be after due consideration. The primacy of the state law will, therefore, be restricted against the law enacted by Parliament which is mentioned in the proposal for seeking assent of the President to the state law and the primacy of the state law will not extend against any other law enacted by Parliament which is not mentioned in the proposal.[11] But the assent of the President to the State law does not prevent Parliament from, enacting later any law with respect to the same matter including a law adding,

---

8. *Security Association of India & Anr. v. Union of India & Ors.*, (2014) 12 SCC 65, pp. 87 to 91.
9. Article 254.
10. *Rishikesh v. Salma Begum (Smt.),* (1995) 4 SCC 718 : AIR 1995 SCW 2476; *M.P. Shikshak v. R.P.F. Commissioner,* AIR 1999 SC 443, pp. 446, 447 : (1999) 1 SCC 396; *Engineering Kamgar Union v. M/s. Electro Steel Castings Ltd.*, AIR 2004 SC 2401, pp. 2410, 2411 : (2004) 6 SCC 36.
11. *Kaiser-I-Hind Pvt. Ltd. v. National Textile Corporation,* AIR 2002 SC 3404 : (2002) 8 SCC 182; *Grand Kakatiya Sheraton Hotel and Towers Employees and Workers Union v. Srinivas Resorts Ltd.,* (2009) 5 SCC 342 para 81 : AIR 2009 SC 2337.

amending or repealing the State law.[12] Repugnancy may also arise outside the concurrent list for a State Legislature's power, even in respect of matters in the exclusive state list, is subject to Parliament's power to make laws in respect of matters in Lists I and III. Because of the doctrine of pith and substance which permits incidental encroachment in the rival field, it is possible that a law made by a State Legislature, which in pith and substance is a law in respect of a matter in List II, has made incidental encroachment on some matter in List I. Such an incidental encroachment will be valid if the field of encroachment is not covered but it will be void, to the extent of repugnancy, if the field be already covered or it will become void if the field be later covered by a law made by Parliament.[13] But what will happen when a Central Act which in pith and substance is a law in respect of a matter in List I, incidently encroaches upon a matter in List II and thereafter the State Legislature covers the field of encroachment by enacting a law which in pith and substance relates to a matter in List II? As the exclusive power of the State Legislature in respect of List II under Article 246(3) is subject to clauses (1) and (2) of the same Article which confer legislative power upon Parliament in respect of matters in Lists I and III and as the power of Parliament in respect of List I, under clause (1) is *notwithstanding anything in clauses (2) and (3),* the answer may be that the Central Act will still be effective and the State Act, to the extent of the encroachment by the Central Act, will be ineffective. The observations made by BALAKRISHNAN, J. who delivered the unanimous opinion of a Constitution Bench in *Special Reference (1) of 2001*[14] fully supports this answer. These observations are: "Although Parliament cannot legislate on any of the entries in the State list it may do so incidently while essentially dealing with the subject coming within the purview of the entry in the Union list. Conversely, the State Legislature also may incidently trench upon the subject covered in the Union List. Such incidental encroachment in either event need not make the legislation *ultra vires* the Constitution. The doctrine of pith and substance is sometimes invoked to find out the nature and content of the legislation. *However, when there is irreconcilable conflict between the two legislations the Central Legislation shall prevail.* However, every attempt would be made to reconcile the conflict."[15] These observations

12. Article 254.

13. *Madhya Pradesh State Road Transport Corporation v. Heeralal Chotelal,* 1980 MPLJ 8 (FB) pp. 17, 18 (G.P. SINGH C.J.); *ITC Ltd. v. Agricultural Produce Market Committee,* AIR 2002 SC 852, p. 921 : (2002) 9 SCC 232.

14. (2004) 4 SCC 489 : AIR 2004 SC 2647.

15. *Ibid,* pp. 499, 500. These observations have also been quoted with **approval** in *Jamshed N. Guzdar v. State of Maharashtra,* (2005) 2 SCC 591, p. 637 which is

[Footnote No. 15 Contd.]

will appear to settle the view that in cases where conflict arises between a Central Act and a State Act because of incidental encroachment on a subject in the rival exclusive list, it is the Central Act which will always prevail. But in *ITC Ltd. v. Agricultural Produce Market Committee,*[16] SMT. RUMA PAL, J. had held that in a case where the conflict is between a State Act and a Central Act, because of incidental encroachment of the Central Act on a subject in the State List, the State legislation being within the exclusive power of the State Legislature will be the dominant legislation and shall prevail over the Central Act in the field of encroachment. It has been held in some cases that the doctrine of covered field or occupied field can be applied only to matters in List III.[17] In *Central Bank of India v. State of Kerala*[18] there is a good deal of discussion on the question of repugnancy. In that case the question related to conflict between State Acts (Bombay Sales Tax Act, 1959 and Kerala General Sales Tax Act, 1963) on the one hand and Central Acts (Recovery of Debts Due to Banks and Financial Institutions Act, 1993 and Securitisation and Reconstruction of Financial Assests and Enforcement of Security Interest Act, 2002) on the other. The State Acts were enacted under Entry 54 List II and the Central Acts under Entry 45 in List I. The court also found no overlapping or conflict between the two sets of legislations.[19] Therefore, the question of repugnancy did not factually arise. It cannot, however, be said that repugnancy cannot arise outside the concurrent list or outside Article 254. As discussed earlier the Constitution Bench decision[20] delivered by BALAKRISHNAN, J. which has been again quoted by another Constitution Bench settled the law that the doctrine of pith and substance which permits incidental encroachment may result in repugnancy outside the concurrent list and in that event the central law shall prevail. These cases were not referred in the *Central Bank of India* case.

[Footnote No. 15 Contd.]

also a Constitution Bench decision. **See further** *Govt. of A.P. v. J.B. Educational Society*, (2005) 3 SCC 212, pp. 219, 220 (paras 9, 10, 11 and 12). *Zameer Ahmed Latifur Rehman Sheikh v. State of Maharashtra*, (2010) 5 SCC 246 p. 266 : AIR 2010 SC 2633 (The Maharashtra Control of Organized Crime Act, 1999 (MACOCA) creates a new crime of 'organized crime' and is valid and is not repugnant to the central Act. The Unlawful Activities Prevention Act (UAPA) as amended in 2008)

16. AIR 2002 SC 852, p. 921 : (2002) 9 SCC 232 (para 130).

17. *Hindustan Lever v. State of Maharashtra*, AIR 2004 SC 326, p. 339 (para 35) : (2004) 9 SCC 438 and cases **referred** to therein; *State of Bihar v. Shree Baidyanath Ayurvedic Bhavan (P.) Ltd.*, (2005) 2 SCC 762, p. 779 (para 25).

18. *Central Bank of India v. State of Kerala,* (2009) 4 SCC 94 : (2009) 3 JT 216 : (2009) 3 Scale 451.

19. *Ibid* paras 35, 36.

20. Cases in notes 30 and 31.

Repugnancy arises when the conflict between competing legislations cannot be reconciled and it is not possible to give effect to both. But before reaching the conclusion that there is repugnancy arising from conflict, effort should be made to remove the conflict by harmonious construction.[21] Repugnancy may also arise, even in the absence of direct conflict, when the superior legislation evinces an intention to cover the entire field leaving no room for the rival legislation to operate in that field.[22] For example, if the Central Act provides only for fixation of minimum price, there would be no repugnancy if the State Act provides for fixation of higher price.[23] In contrast, when regulation of tobacco products was entirely taken over under the Central Act 34 of 2003, it was held that the State Government had no power to prohibit 'Gutka' containing tobacco even for a limited period under the Prevention of Food Adulteration Act, 1954.[24] The effect of repugnancy is not repeal of the subordinate law by the superior law but only to eclipse it till the repugnancy persists. Therefore, when repugnancy caused by superior law is removed by

---

21. *Bar Council of India v. Board of Management of Dayanand College of Law,* (2007) 2 SCC 202 (paras 12 and 13) : AIR 2007 SC 1342.

22. *Deepchand v. State of U.P.*, AIR 1959 SC 648, p. 665 : 1959 Supp (2) SCR 8; *State of Orissa v. Tulloch & Co.*, AIR 1964 SC 1284, p. 1292 : 1964 (4) SCR 461; *M. Karunanidhi v. Union of India*, AIR 1979 SC 898, pp. 909, 910 : (1979) 3 SCC 431; *Kulwant Kaur v. Gurdial Singh,* AIR 2001 SC 1273; *Kanka Griha Nirman Sahakari Sangha v. Narayanamma Smt.*, AIR 2002 SC 3659, p. 3663 : (2003) 1 SCC 228, p. 235; *M.P. AIT Permit Owners Ass. v. State of M.P.*, (2004) 1 SCC 320 : AIR 2004 SC 981 (State Act enhancing penalty for an offence under the Central Act will give rise to repugnancy and the State Act would be void unless President's assent is obtained to the State Act); *Mehsana District Central Co-operative Bank Ltd. v. State of Gujarat*, (2004) 2 SCC 463, p. 467 : AIR 2004 SC 1576; *Govt. of A.P. v. J.B. Education Society*, (2005) 3 SCC 212, pp. 221, 222. If the entire field is not covered, repugnancy must exist in fact and must not be a mere possibility: *Ch. Tikaramji v. State of Uttar Pradesh,* AIR 1956 SC 676 : 1958 SCR 393; *Siel Ltd. v. Union of India,* AIR 1998 SC 3076, p. 3080 : (1998) 7 SCC 26; *Saurashtra Oil Mills Association v. State of Gujarat,* AIR 2002 SC 1130, p. 1136 : (2002) 3 SCC 202; *Punjab Dairy Development Board v. Cepham Milk Specialities Ltd.*, (2004) 8 SCC 621, p. 628 (para 12) : (2004) 7 JT 5; *Bharat Hydro Power Corpn. Ltd. v. State of Assam*, (2004) 2 SCC 553, pp. 564, 565, 569, 570 : AIR 2004 SC 3173 (Even if both competing legislations are enacted under the same entry in List III, there can be no repugnancy if both can be obeyed without any clash between them. **See further** *Northern Territory v. GPAO,* (1999) 73 ALJR 470, pp. 480, 481 (Paras 58 to 59); *Telstra Corporation Ltd. v. Worthing,* (1999) 73 ALJR 565, p. 571 (Paras 27 to 29). **Also see,** Chapter 7 title 5(a) 'Implied repeal' pp. 737 to 741.

23. *U.P Co-operative Cane Unions Federations v. West U.P. Sugar Mills Association*, (2004) 5 SCC 430, p. 449 (para 12) : AIR 2004 SC 3697 (case of *Tika Ramji v. State of Uttar Pradesh, supra*, **distinguished**).

24. *Godawat Pan Masala Products P. Ltd. v. Union of India*, (2004) 7 SCC 68 : AIR 2004 SC 4057.

its repeal or amendment the subordinate law will revive automatically without its re-enactment.[25]

It is said that a Legislature cannot assume a power by colourable legislation. This doctrine really means that the Legislature in passing a statute, though purporting to act within the limits of its powers, has in substance and in reality trangressed these powers. The question even in these cases is not of *bona fides* or *mala fides* but only of competence to enact the particular law.[26]

It is also sometimes said that Parliament can never do indirectly, what it cannot do directly. But this is not a correct statement of the principle. Whether or not Parliament can do something indirectly, which it cannot do directly, may depend upon why it cannot do directly. In law, as in life, there are many examples of things that can be done indirectly, although not directly. The true principle is that "it is not permissible to do indirectly what is prohibited directly."[27]

The doctrine of separation of powers does not prevent the Legislature from validating a law or executive order declared invalid by court by passing a suitable validating Act which effectively removes the cause of invalidity and thereby makes the judgment inoperative.[28] In any case a judgment declaring an Ordinance unconstitutional which is challenged in appeal but the appeal is dismissed as infructuous on the expiry of the Ordinance pending the appeal cannot stand as a final judgment which can affect the validity of a new Ordinance promulgated later.[29]

Even acting within its competence neither Parliament nor a State Legislature can violate any provision of the Constitution, *e.g.*, the fundamental rights. A law enacted by Parliament and State Legislatures is, therefore, open to judicial review on the grounds of lack of legislative competence and violation of other provisions of the Constitution.[30] Since Article 14

---

25. *Carter v. Egg and Egg Pulp Marketing Board,* (1942) 66 CLR 557, p. 573 (LATHAM C.J.) **approvingly quoted** in *Deepchand v. State of U.P.,* AIR 1959 SC 648, p. 658 : 1959 Supp (2) SCR 8.

26. *K.C.G. Narayan Deo v. State of Orissa,* AIR 1953 SC 375, pp. 379, 381 : 1954 SCR 1; *Naga Peoples Movement of Human Rights v. Union of India,* AIR 1998 SC 431, pp. 450, 451 : 1998 (2) SCC 109; *Welfare Association ARP Maharashtra v. Ranjit P. Gohil,* AIR 2003 SC 1266, pp. 1282, 1283; *State of Kerala v. Peoples Union of Civil Liberties,* (2009) 8 SCC 46 Paras 37, 39 and 40 : (2009) JT 579.

27. GLEESON C.J., in *Re Pacific Coal Pvt. Ltd., Ex Parte Construction, Forestry, Mining and Energy Union,* (2000) 74 ALJR 1034, p. 1040 **quoting** MASON C.J., GLAUDRON and MCHUGH JJ. in *Caltex Oil (Aust.) Pvt. Ltd. v. Best,* (1990) 170 CLR 516, p. 522.

28. *Dharm Dutt v. Union of India,* AIR 2004 SC 1295, pp. 1317 to 1320 : (2004) 1 SCC 712. **See further** text and note 29 to 35, pp. 53-54 and text and note 24, p. 579.

29. *Dharm Dutt v. Union of India, supra,* pp. 1319, 1320.

30. *Public Services Tribunal Bar Association v. State of U.P.,* (2003) 4 SCC 104, p. 120 (para 26) : AIR 2003 SC 1344; *Bakhtawar Trust v. M.D. Narayan,* AIR 2003 SC 2236, p. 2241; *Mahmadhusen Abdulrahim Kalota Shaikh v. Union of India,* (2009) 2 SCC 1 para 34(c) : (2008) 13 Scale 398 : (2008) 13 JT 207.

strikes at arbitrariness in state action whether of the Legislature or the Executive, a law enacted by Parliament or State Legislatures will also be open to judicial review on the ground of 'manifest' arbitrariness as it will make it offend the fundamental right under Article 14.[31] It has been said that no enactment can be struck down just by saying that it is arbitrary or unreasonable.[32] In deciding whether a provision is violative of a fundamental right the test to be applied is of its "direct and inevitable effect" on the fundamental right.[33] But motives of the Legislature are irrelevant for judicial review.[34]

Section 30 of the Punjab Excise Act, 1914 prohibited employment of 'any man under the age of 25 years' or 'any woman' in any part of such premises in which liquor or intoxicating drug is consumed by the public. Right to autonomy in employment or to be considered for employment was held to be a fundamental right and a facet of right to livelihood. It was further held that legislative interference to these rights by the impugned legislation even if valid when enacted could not now be justified in principle or held proportionate for protecting the interests of women or young men. Section 30 was consequently held to be constitutionally invalid.[35]

(b) Presumption of Constitutionality

As already discussed,[36] a statute is construed so as to make it effective and operative on the principle expressed in the maxim '*ut res magis valeat*

---

31. *Ajay Hasia v. Khalid Mujib,* (1981) 1 SCC 722, p. 741 : AIR 1981 SC 487. For examples, **see** *P. Tulsi Das v. Govt. of A.P.,* AIR 2003 SC 43, p. 50 : (2003) 1 SCC 364; *Mardia Chemical Ltd. v. Union of India*, AIR 2004 SC 2371, p. 2395 (para 64); *Punjab Dairy Development Board v. Chepham Milk Specialities Ltd.*, (2004) 8 SCC 621, p. 629 : (2004) 7 JT 5; *Satyawati Sharma v. Union of India*, (2008) 5 SCC 287 : AIR 2008 SC 3148 (A classification valid when enacted may become discriminatory with the passage of time); *Grand Kakatiya Sheraton Hotel and Towers Employees and Workers Union v. Srinivas Resorts Ltd.,* (2009) 5 SCC 342 para 77 : AIR 2009 SC 2337; *V. Subramaniam v. Raghuvandra Rao*, (2009) 5 SCC 608 : AIR 2009 SC 1858. **See further** text and notes 39 to 43, *infra*. In this context it is to be remembered that simply because the action taken under a statute is arbitrary which offends Article 14, the statute cannot be declared unconstitutional though the action would be open to correction in judicial review: *Government of Andhra Pradesh v. P. Laxmi Devi*, (2008) 4 SCC 720 para 30 : (2008) 2 JT 639 : AIR 2008 SC 1640.

32. *State of A.P. v. McDowell & Co.,* (1996) 3 SCC 709 : AIR 1996 SC 1627. The question has been referred to a larger Bench: *Subramanian Swamy v. Director of C.B.I.,* (2005) 2 SCC 317 : 2005 CrLJ 1413 : 2005 SCC (L&S) 241.

33. *Maneka Gandhi v. Union of India,* (1978) 1 SCC 248, p. 299 : AIR 1978 SC 597, p. 635.

34. *Bakhtawar Trust v. M.D. Narayan,* AIR 2003 SC 2236, p. 2244 : (2003) 5 SCC 298.

35. *Anuj Garg v. Hotel Association of India*, (2008) 3 SCC 1 paras 49, 50, 56 : AIR 2008 SC 663.

36. **See** Chapter 1, title 4 "Statute to be construed to make it effective and workable", p. 48.

quam pereat'. There is, therefore, a presumption that the Legislature does not exceed its jurisdiction, and the burden of establishing that the Act is not within the competence of the Legislature, or that it has transgressed other constitutional mandates, such as those relating to fundamental rights, is always on the person who challenges its *vires*.[37] "Unless it becomes clear beyond reasonable doubt that the legislation in question transgresses the limits laid down by the organic law of the Constitution it must be allowed to stand as the true expression of the national will".[38] The principle is, however, subject to the exception that once the citizen is able to establish that the impugned legislation has invaded his fundamental rights under Article 19(1)(g) of the Constitution, the State must justify that the law is saved under clause (6) of the same Article.[39] The exception stated above has been widened in later decisions by general observations to apply to other fundamental rights.[40] After approvingly referring to the above discussion relating to the presumption of constitutionality from 8th edition, pp. 453, 454 of this book LAHOTI, J., summed up the principles in which he said: "If a case of violation of a constitutional provision is made out

---

37. *Chiranjitlal Chowdhury v. Union of India*, AIR 1951 SC 41, p. 45 : 1950 SCR 869; *State of Bombay v. F.N. Balsara*, AIR 1951 SC 318, p. 326 : 1951 SCR 682; *Kanaiyalal v. Indumati*, AIR 1958 SC 444, p. 447 : 1958 SCR 1394; *Mohd Hanif Quareshi v. State of Bihar*, AIR 1958 SC 731, pp. 740, 744 : 1959 SCR 629; *In re, Kerala Education Bill*, AIR 1958 SC 956, p. 972 : 1959 SCR 995; *Motilal v. S.P. Sahi*, AIR 1959 SC 942, p. 947 : 1959 Supp (2) SCR 563; *Hamdard Dawakhana v. Union of India*, AIR 1960 SC 554, p. 569 : (1960) 2 SCR 671; *Waverley Jute Mills v. Raymon & Co.*, AIR 1963 SC 90, p. 96 : (1963) 3 SCR 209; *Sub Divl. Magistrate v. Ramkali*, AIR 1968 SC 1, p. 3 : (1968) 1 SCR 205; *State of Bihar v. Bihar Distillery Ltd.*, AIR 1997 SC 1511, p. 1519 : 1997 (2) SCC 453; *B.R. Enterprises v. State of U.P.*, AIR 1999 SC 1867, p. 1907 : (1999) 9 SCC 700; *Union of India v. Elphinstone Spinning & Weaving Co.*, JT 2001 (1) SC 536 : AIR 2001 SC 724, p. 733 : (2001) 4 SCC 139; *Mahmadhusen Abdulrahim Kalota Shaikh v. Union of India*, (2009) 2 SCC 1 para 34(b) : (2008) 13 Scale 398.

38. *Shell Company of Australia v. Federal Commissioner of Taxation*, (1931) AC 275, p. 298 (PC); **referred** to in *Suntharalingam v. Inspector of Police*, (1971) 3 WLR 896, p. 893 (PC); *Union of India v. Ephinstone Spinning & Weaving Co., supra* ; *Government of Andhra Pradesh v. P. Laxmi Devi*, (2008) 4 SCC 720 para 66 : AIR 2008 SC 1640 : (2008) 2 JT 639.

39. *Saghir Ahmad v. State of U.P.*, AIR 1954 SC 728, p. 738 : 1955 (1) SCR 707; *Khyerbari Tea Co. v. State of Assam*, AIR 1964 SC 925, pp. 938, 939 : 1964 (5) SCR 975.

40. In *Kantilal Babulal and Bros. v. H. C. Patel*, AIR 1968 SC 445, p. 449 (para 12) : (1968) 1 SCR 735, similar rule was **applied** in the context of Article 19(1)(f). And, in *Harichand Sarda v. Mizo District Council*, AIR 1967 SC 829, p. 832 : (1967) 1 SRC 1012; *Md. Faruk v. State of Bihar*, AIR 1970 SC 93, p. 96 : (1969) 1 SCC 853; *Vrajlal M. & Co. v. State of M.P.*, AIR 1970 SC 129, p. 135 : (1969) 2 SCC 248; *Sukhnandan Saran Dinesh Kumar v. Union of India*, AIR 1982 SC 902, p. 911 : (1982) 2 SCC 150, the observations are general though the cases relate to Article 19(1)(g). In *Union of India v. Elphinstone Spinning & Weaving Co., supra.*, also the observations are general but the case relates to Articles 14 and 19(1)(g).

then the State must justify that the law can still be protected under a saving provision."[41] Further, the state may also have to satisfy that the restrictions imposed on fundamental rights satisfy the test of proportionality which requires a stricter test of reasonableness.[42] Similarly, if a law is shown to invade the freedom of trade under Article 301, the onus shifts to the State to satisfy that the restrictions imposed are reasonable and in the public interest within the meaning of Article 304(b).[43] But in *State of Gujarat v. Mirzapur Moti Kureshi Kassab Jamat,*[44] which also related to Article 19(1)(g) a Bench of seven Judges laid down: (1) A restriction placed on any fundamental right which is aimed at securing directive principles and fundamental duties can be taken into account in judging the reasonableness of the restrictions;[45] (2) When the facts stated in the objects and reasons and the Preamble justify the enactment of the law a presumption of reasonableness of the restriction will arise;[46] (3) Restriction may even amount to prohibition but it must satisfy the test that a lesser alternative would have been inadequate.[47] The principles laid down by the Supreme Court of United States such as 'suspect legislation', 'strict scrutiny' and 'compelling state necessity' for judging the validity of affirmative action are not applicable in India for judging the validity of reservation made in favour of backward classes and Scheduled castes and Scheduled tribes as the law making reservations under Articles 15 or 16 is presumed to be valid.[48]

(c) Rule of Construction

The above principle in its application as a rule of construction is that if on one construction a given statute will become *ultra vires* the powers of the Legislature, whereas on another construction, which may be open, the statute remains effective and operative, the court will prefer the latter, on the ground that the Legislature is presumed not to have intended an excess

---

41. *Welfare Association A.R.P. Maharashtra v. Ranjit P. Gohil,* AIR 2003 SC 1266, p. 1278 : (2003) 9 SCC 1266. **See further** *Hindustan Lever v. State of Maharashtra,* AIR 2004 SC 326, p. 329 (para 34 : (2004) 9 SCC 438; *Dhram Dutt v. Union of India,* AIR 2004 SC 1295, p. 1313 (para 43) : (2004) 1 SCC 712.

42. See pp. 489-490.

43. *Khyerbari Tea Co. v. State of Assam,* AIR 1964 SC 925, p. 938 : 1964 (5) SCR 975. **See also** *Amrit Banaspati Co. Ltd. v. Union of India,* 1995 (1) Scale 809 : AIR 1995 SC 1340 : (1995) 3 SCC 335.

44. (2005) 8 SCC 534.

45. *Ibid,* para 58.

46. *Ibid,* para 71.

47. *Ibid,* para 75.

48. *Ashoka Kumar Thakur v. Union of India,* (2008) 6 SCC 1 p. 520 para 209 : (2008) 5 JT 1, *Saurabh Chaudri v. Union of India,* (2003) 11 SCC 146 p. 164 para 36 : AIR 2004 SC 361.

of its jurisdiction.[49] According to HOLMES, J., the rule requires that "the statute must be construed in such a way as not merely to save its constitutionality but so far as it is consistent with fair interpretation, not to raise grave doubts on that score."[50] This rule is general for all law-making bodies of limited powers and is equally applicable for construction of bye-laws.[51] But the rule applies only where two views are possible as to the meaning of the statutory language.[52] The principle of reading down is a

---

49. *Blackwood v. Reg*, (1882) 8 AC 81, p. 98 (PC); *Macleod v. A-G of New South Wales*, (1891) AC 455 : 62 LJ PC 44 : 68 LT 326 (PC); *United States v. Delware*, (1909) 213 US 366, pp. 407, 408; *In re, Hindu Women's Right to Property Act*, AIR 1941 FC 72, p. 75; *Express Newspapers Ltd. v. Union of India*, AIR 1958 SC 578, p. 623 : 1959 SCR 12; *State of Bihar v. Charusiladasi*, AIR 1959 SC 1002, p. 1010 : 1959 Supp (2) SCR 601; *Kedarnath v. State of Bihar*, AIR 1962 SC 955, p. 969 : 1959 Supp (2) SCR 769; *Anant Prasad v. State of Andhra Pradesh*, AIR 1963 SC 853, p. 859 : 1959 Supp (1) SCR 844; *Govindlalji v. State of Rajasthan*, AIR 1963 SC 1638, p. 1655 : (1964) 1 SCR 561; *New India Sugar Mills v. Commr. of Sales Tax*, AIR 1963 SC 1207, p. 1213 : 1963 Supp (2) SCR 459; *R.L. Arora v. State of Uttar Pradesh*, AIR 1964 SC 1230, p. 1238 : (1964) 6 SCR 784; *Life Insurance Corporation of India v. S.V. Oak*, AIR 1965 SC 975, p. 980 : (1965) 1 SCR 403; *Corporation of Calcutta v. Liberty Cinema*, AIR 1965 SC 1107, pp. 1113, 1114 : (1965) 2 SCR 477; *Venkataraman & Co. v. State of Madras*, AIR 1966 SC 1089, pp. 1104, 1105: (1966) 2 SCR 229; *Johrimal v. Director of C. & H., Punjab*, AIR 1967 SC 1568, p. 1574 : (1967) 3 SCR 286; *Shah & Co., Bombay v. State of Maharashtra*, AIR 1967 SC 1877, p. 1883 : (1967) 3 SCC 466; *Vrijlal M. & Co. v. State of M.P.*, AIR 1970 SC 129, p. 135 : (1969) 2 SCC 248 : (1967) 3 SCR 466; *T.S. Mankad v. State of Gujarat*, AIR 1970 SC 143, p. 146 : (1969) 2 SCC 120; *Jothi Timber Mart v. Calicut Municipality*, AIR 1970 SC 264, p. 266 : (1969) 2 SCC 348; *Rayala Corporation v. Director of Enforcement*, AIR 1970 SC 494, p. 499 : (1969) 2 SCC 412; *State of Kerala v. Krishnan Nayar*, AIR 1978 SC 747, p. 759 : (1978) 1 SCC 552; *Sita Ram v. State of U.P.*, AIR 1979 SC 745 : (1979) 2 SCC 656; *Winifred Ross v. Ivy Fonesca*, (1984) 1 SCC 288, pp. 292, 293, 295 : AIR 1984 SC 458; *Union of India v. Tulsiram Patel*, (1986) 3 SCC 398, p. 484 : AIR 1986 SC 1541; *Olga Tellis v. Bombay Municipal Corporation*, (1985) 3 SCC 545, p. 581 : AIR 1986 SC 180. *Anirudha Ramkrishna Karlekar v. Janakibai R. Bedekar*, AIR 1991 SC 503, p. 505 : (1991) 1 SCC 649; *Hotel Balaji v. State of Andhra Pradesh*, AIR 1993 SC 1048, p. 1078 : (1992) 6 JT 182 : 1993 Supp (4) SCC 536; *Githa Hariharan v. Reserve Bank of India*, JT 1999 (1) SC 524, p. 529 : 1999 AIR SC 1149; *B.R. Enterprises v. State of U.P.*, AIR 1999 SC 1867, pp. 1906, 1907 : (1999) 9 SCC 700; *Union of India v. Elphinstone Spinning and Weaving Co. Ltd.*, JT 2001 (1) SC 536, p. 553 : AIR 2001 SC 724, p. 733 : (2001) 4 SCC 139; *Daniel Latif v. Union of India*, AIR 2001 SC 3958, p. 3972 : (2001) 7 SCC 740; *Uttar Pradesh Power Corporation Ltd. v. Ayodhya Prasad Misra*, (2008) 10 SCC 139 para 41 : AIR 2009 SC 296; *M. Rathinaswami v. State of Tamil Nadu*, (2009) 5 SCC 625 paras 28 to 31 : (2009) 5 JT 556 (**Reference** is also made to this book).

50. *Northern Securities Company v. United States*, 193 US 197, p. 400 (The Mind and Faith of Justice Holmes, edited by MAXLERNER, p. 224).

51. *Colman v. Mills*, (1897) 1 QB 396, p. 396; *D'Emden v. Pedder*, (1904) CLR 91, pp. 119, 120; *In re, Hindu Women's Right to Property Act*, AIR 1941 FC 72, p. 75. **See further** Chapter 12, pp. 1078-79.

52. For limitations of the rule, **see** p. 660.

rule of harmonious construction. It is generally utilized to straighten the crudities or ironing out of creases to make a statute workable.[53]

While rejecting the contention that the Juvenile Justice (Care and Protection of Children) Act, 2000, needs to be read down to save it from the vice of unconstitutionality, RANJAN GOGOI, J., observed: "Reading down the provisions of a statute cannot be resorted to when the meaning thereof is plain and unambiguous and the legislative intent is clear. The fundamental principle of the "reading down" doctrine can be summarised as follows. Courts must read the legislation literally in the first instance. If on such reading and understanding the vice of unconstitutionality is attracted, the Courts must explore whether there has been unintended legislative omission. If such intendment can be reasonably implied without undertaking what, unmistakably, would be a legislative exercise, the Act may be read down to save it from unconstitutionality". Since there is no ambiguity, much less any uncertainty, in the language used to convey what the Legislature had intended in the Juvenile Justice Act, wherein all persons below the age of 18 are put in one class/ group and a separate scheme of investigation, trial and punishment for offences committed by them is provided, in light of the country's international commitments, the same was held to be wholly consistent with Article 14 of the Constitution. In the absence of any unconstitutionality, the Act was not required to be read down to exclude from its purview those juveniles who are intellectually, emotionally and mentally mature enough to understand the implications of their acts and who have committed serious crimes.[54]

General words may be construed, narrowly or widely, with reference to the powers of the Legislature and their meaning applied to those matters in respect of which the legislative competence exists.[55] Thus, if it is possible to read the statutory language as subject to an implied term which avoids conflict with constitutional limitations, the court should be very ready to make such an implication.[56]

The principle was examined in some detail by the Federal Court,[57] in considering the validity of the Hindu Women's Right to Property Act,

---

53. *Union of India v. Ind-swift Laboratories Ltd.*, (2011) 4 SCC 635 (para 18) : (2011) 2 JT 352.

54. *Subramanian Swamy & Ors. v. Raju & Anr.*, (2014) 8 SCC 390, pp. 419 to 422.

55. **See** cases in note 51, *supra.* **See further** *New Delhi Municipal Committee v. State of Pubjab*, AIR 1997 SC 2847, pp. 2901 to 2904 : (1997) 7 SCC 339.

56. *A.G. of Gambia v. Momodon Jobe*, (1984) AC 689, p. 702 (PC); *Hector v. Attorney-General of Antique and Barbuda*, (1990) 2 All ER 103, p. 107 : (1990) 2 AC 312 (PC).

57. *In re, Hindu Women's Right to Property Act, supra*, **reaffirmed** in *Umayal Singh Achi v. Lakshmi Achi*, AIR 1945 FC 28 : 1945 FC R 1.

1937. The Act, which was passed by the Council of State after commencement of Part III of the Government of India Act, 1935, when the subject of devolution of agricultural land had been committed exclusively to Provincial Legislatures, dealt in quite general terms with the 'Property' or 'separate property' of a Hindu dying intestate or his 'interest in joint family property'. A question, therefore, arose whether the Act was *ultra vires* of the powers of the Central Legislature. The Federal Court held the Act *intra vires* by construing the word 'Property' as meaning 'property other than agricultural land'; GWYER, C.J. observed: "If that word (property) necessarily and inevitably comprises all forms of property, including agricultural land, then clearly the Act went beyond the powers of the Legislature; but when a Legislature with limited and restricted powers makes use of a word of such wide and general import, the presumption must surely be that it is using it with reference to that kind of property with respect to which it is competent to legislate and to no other.[58] The learned Chief Justice further observed: "There is a general presumption that a Legislature does not intend to exceed its jurisdiction, and there is ample authority for the proposition that general words in a statute are to be construed with reference to the powers of the Legislature which enacts it."[59]

The rule was applied by the Supreme Court[60] in its construction of section 124A of the Indian Penal Code. The section which relates to offence of sedition makes a person punishable who 'by words, either spoken or written, or by signs, or by visible representations, or otherwise, brings or attempts to bring into hatred or contempt, or excites or attempts to excite disaffection towards the Government established by law'. The section, as construed by the Privy Council,[61] did not make it essential for an activity to come within its mischief that the same should involve intention or tendency to create disorder, or disturbance of law and order or incitement to violence. The Federal Court[62] had, however, taken a different view. In the Supreme Court when the question came up as to the constitutional validity of the section, the court, differing from the Privy Council, adopted the construction placed by the Federal Court and held that on a correct construction, the provisions of the section are limited in their application "to acts involving intention or tendency to create disorder or disturbance of

---

58. AIR 1941 FC 72, p. 75.
59. *Ibid.*
60. *Kedarnath v. State of Bihar*, AIR 1962 SC 955 : 1962 Supp (2) SCR 769.
61. *Bal Gangadhar Tilak v. Queen Empress*, ILR 22 Bom 528 (PC); *Annie Besant v. A-G of Madras*, AIR 1919 PC 31 : 46 IA 176; *Emperor v. Sadasiv Narain*, AIR 1947 PC 84. **See further** a decision in an appeal from West Africa relating to section 330, Criminal Code of Gold Coast Colony, *Wallace-Johnson v. R.*, (1940) 1 All ER 241 (PC).
62. *Niharendra Dutt v. Emperor*, AIR 1942 FC 22.

law and order or incitement to violence; and one of the reasons for adopting this construction was to avoid the result of unconstitutionality in view of Articles 19(1)(a) and 19(2) of the Constitution."[63] SINHA, C.J., in speaking for the court said: "It is well settled that if certain provisions of law, construed in one way, would make them consistent with the Constitution and another interpretation would render them unconstitutional, the court would lean in favour of the former construction."[64] The application of this rule in this case is, however, open to one objection. The basis of the rule being the assumed intention of the Legislature not to transgress the constitutional barriers, how can that intention be assumed when at the time the law was passed there were no such barriers; and the limitations as to legislative competence were brought in by a Constitution long after the enactment of the law? This criticism finds support from the decision of the Supreme Court in *Gulabbhai v. Union of India*,[65] but as held in this case, the principle of severability in application or separability in enforcement, if that be possible, may still be applied. However, in spite of the above criticism it seems now settled that a pre-constitution law can be read down by interpretation to avoid its being declared invalid as violating the Constitution. In *Sunil Batra v. Delhi Administration*,[66] the Supreme Court upheld the validity of section 30(2) of the Prisons Act, 1894, which provides for solitary confinement of a prisoner under sentence of death in a cell and section 56 of the same Act, which provides for the confinement of a prisoner in irons for his safe custody, by construing them narrowly so as to avoid their being declared invalid on the ground that they were violative of the rights guaranteed under Articles 14, 19 and 21 of the Constitution. And in *New India Sugar Mills v. Commissioner of Sales Tax*,[67] a wide definition of the word 'sale' in the Bihar Sales Tax Act, 1947, was restricted by construction to exclude transactions, in which property was transferred from one person to another without any previous contract of sale; a wider construction would have resulted in attributing to the Bihar Legislature an intention to legislate beyond its competence.

In section 6(a) of the Hindu Minority and Guardianship Act, 1956 which provides that the natural guardian of a minor's person or property

---

63. *Kedarnath v. State of Bihar*, AIR 1962 SC 955 : 1962 Supp (2) SCR 769.

64. *Ibid*, p. 969. *Compare R. (on the application of Rusbridger) v. Attorney General*, (2003) 3 All ER 784 (HL) (construction of section 3 of the Treason Felony Act, 1848 after enforcement of the Human Rights Act, 1998).

65. AIR 1967 SC 1110, p. 1117 (para 18) : (1967) 1 SCR 190. This criticism is also referred with approval in the minority judgment of AHMADI, C.J.I., for himself and three other judges in *New Delhi Municipal Committee v. State of Punjab*, AIR 1997 SC 2847, p. 2883 (para 113) : (1997) 7 SCC 339.

66. AIR 1978 SC 1675 : (1978) 4 SCC 494.

67. AIR 1963 SC 1207, p. 1213 : 1963 Supp (2) SCR 459.

will be 'the father and after him, the mother', the words 'after him' were construed not to mean 'only after the lifetime of the father' but to mean 'in the absence of' as the former construction would have made the section unconstitutional for violating constitutional provision against sex discrimination.[68]

Provisions in the municipal laws extended or enacted by Parliament for the territory of Delhi (*viz.* the Punjab Municipal Act, 1911 extended to Part C State of Delhi by a notification under the Part C State Laws Act, 1950; the Delhi Municipal Act, 1957, and the New Delhi Municipal Council Act, 1994) levying property tax on lands and buildings do neither contain any exception in respect of the property of a State, nor do they contain any specific provision that property of a State used or occupied for the purposes of any trade or business carried on by the Government of the State shall be liable to taxation. Article 289 of the Constitution makes the property of a State exempt from Union taxation but the exemption does not apply to any property used or occupied for the purposes of any trade or business carried on by the State. The above mentioned municipal laws governing the territory of Delhi being union laws were construed consistent with the legislative power of Parliament in Article 289 not to authorise levy of property tax on property of a State used for purpose of the Government but to authorise levy of tax on property of a State used for the purposes of trade or business.[69]

In *Election Commission of India v. St Mary's School*[70] the Supreme Court construed the wide power to requisition staff of certain authorities in section 150 of the Representation of the People Act, 1951 for election duties to exclude the *teaching staff* of educational institutions on working days as that would have come in conflict with the fundamental right to education and the state's duty to provide facilities for education.

In *Govindlalji v. State of Rajasthan,*[71] where a question arose as to the constitutional validity of the Rajasthan Nathdwara Temple Act (13 of 1959), the words 'affairs of the temple' occurring in section 16 of the said Act were construed as restricted to secular affairs as on a wider construction the section would have violated Articles 25 and 26 of the Constitution.

The Supreme Court[72] applied the same principle in construing section 40(1), cl. (aa) of the Land Acquisition Act, 1894, as amended by Act 31 of 1962, so as to confine its application to such 'building or work' which will

---

68. *Gita Hariharan v. Reserve Bank of India,* JT 1999 (1) SC 524, p. 529 : AIR 1999 SC 1149, p. 1152 : (1999) 2 SCC 228.
69. *New Delhi Municipal Committee v. State of Punjab,* AIR 1997 SC 2847, p. 2904 : (1997) 7 SCC 339.
70. (2008) 2 SCC 390 paras 28 and 33 : AIR 2008 SC 655.
71. AIR 1963 SC 1638, pp. 1655, 1664 : 1964 (1) SCR 561.
72. *R.L. Arora v. State of U.P.,* AIR 1964 SC 1230, p. 1238 : 1964 (6) SCR 784.

subserve the public purpose of the industry or work in which the company, for which acquisition is made, is engaged; a wider and a literal construction of the clause would have brought it in conflict with Article 31(2) of the Constitution and would have rendered it unconstitutional. In *Indian Oil Corporation v. Municipal Corporation,*[73] section 123 of the Punjab Municipal Corporation Act, 1976 which empowered the Corporation to levy octroi on articles and animals 'imported into the city' was read down to mean articles and animals 'imported into the municipal limits for purposes of consumption, use or sale' only as a wide construction would have made the provision unconstitutional being in excess of the power of the State Legislature conferred by Entry 52 of List II of Schedule VII of the Constitution.

Another illustration of restriction of general words by construction so as to avoid invalidity is furnished by a case[74] in which the question related to the construction of a service rule which was to the effect: 'A Government servant shall, unless for special reasons otherwise directed by Government, retire from service on his completing 55 years of age'. The words 'unless for special reasons otherwise directed by Government' which were quite general, were not construed to authorise the Government to retire a civil servant before attaining the age of 55 years as that construction would have brought the rule in conflict with Article 311 of the Constitution as interpreted in *Motiram Deka v. General Manager, N.E.F. Railways,*[75] for the rule did not provide for any period of service on completion of which the power to retire before the attainment of the age of superannuation could be exercised. The aforesaid general words were, therefore, confined as giving power to the Government to allow the civil servant to remain in service even beyond the age of 55 years for special reasons.[76] A proviso in a service rule, relating to the Government's right to withhold or withdraw pension if the pensioner was subsequently found guilty of grave misconduct or negligence in a judicial proceeding, laid down that no such judicial proceeding if not instituted within the period of service shall be instituted in respect of a cause of action which arose on an event which took place more than four years before such institution. Article 309 of the Constitution, under which the rule was made, empowers the Government to

---

73. AIR 1993 SC 844, p. 848 : (1993) 1 SCC 333.

74. *T.S. Mankad v. State of Gujarat*, AIR 1970 SC 143, p. 146 : (1969) 2 SCC 120.

75. AIR 1964 SC 600 : 1964 (5) SCR 683.

76. *T.S. Mankad v. State of Gujarat, supra*, p. 146. **See further** *N.C. Dalwadi v. State of Gujarat*, (1987) 3 SCC 611, p. 620 : AIR 1987 SC 1933 (A power to retire a government servant after the age of 55 and before the age of superannuation of 58 conferred in wide terms by a service rule was held to be exercisable only 'in public interest' and these words of restriction were read by implication in the rule for otherwise the rule would have contravened Article 311(2) of the Constitution). But **see** *Senior Supdt. of Post Office v. Izhar Hussain*, AIR 1989 SC 2262 : (1989) 4 SCC 318 (words of restriction 'in public interest' were not read and the rule was **declared invalid**. *Dalwadi's* case was **not cited**).

regulate conditions of service; it does not empower the Government to lay down periods of limitation for institution of civil or criminal proceedings against a government servant. In this background the proviso to the rule was read down to provide an exception to the Government's right to withhold or withdraw pension if proceedings are not instituted within the period mentioned in the proviso and not to create an embargo on the prosecution of the government servant after that period.[77]

A further illustration, where general words were read down to keep the legislation within permissible constitutional limits, is furnished in the construction of section 5 of the Lotteries (Regulation) Act, 1998 which reads: 'A State Government may, within the State prohibit the sale of tickets of a lottery organised conducted or promoted by every other State'. To avoid the vice of discrimination and excessive delegation, the section was construed to mean that a State can only ban lotteries of other States, when it decides as a policy to ban its own lotteries, or in other words, when it decides to make the State a lottery free zone.[78]

The principle under discussion applies also for construction of Constitution Amendment Acts. The Constitution (Forty-sixth Amendment) Act, which came into force on 2nd February, 1983, inserted clause 29A in Article 366 to widen the ambit of 'tax on sale or purchase of goods' by including in it a tax on the supply of food and drink. Before the amendment the States were not competent to levy sales tax on supply of food and drink by hoteliers and restaurant owners in exercise of their taxing power under Entry 54 in List II of the Constitution which enables them to levy taxes on sale or purchase of goods and their effort in that direction proved abortive.[79] Section 6 of the Constitution (Forty-sixth) Amendment Act, 1982 which was headed as 'validation and exemption' provided that for the purpose of every provision of the Constitution in which the expression 'tax on the sale or purchase of goods' occurs *and for the purposes of any law passed or made, or purporting to have been passed or made before the commencement of this Act in pursuance of any such provision, the said expression shall be deemed to include and shall be deemed always to have included* a tax on the supply of food or any drink. Relying on section 6 it was contended before the Supreme Court that the section validated the sales tax laws of the States with retrospective effect and that the States were entitled to levy the tax on the supply of food and drink *regardless of*

---

77. *State of Punjab v. Kailash Nath*, AIR 1989 SC 558 : 1989 (1) SCC 321.

78. *BR Enterprises v. State of U.P.*, AIR 1999 SC 1867, pp. 1910, 1911 : (1999) 9 SCC 700.

79. *State of Punjab v. Associated Hotels of India Ltd.*, 1972 (2) SCR 937 : (1972) 1 SCC 472 : AIR 1972 SC 1131; *Northern India Caterers (India) Ltd. v. Lt. Governor of Delhi*, 1978 (4) SCC 361 : 1980 (2) SCC 167.

the fact that there was no provision in the State Acts for such levy prior to 2nd February, 1983.[80] This argument was rejected on the ground that Parliament, when exercising the power to amend the Constitution under Article 366, has no power to amend State laws in respect of matters listed in List II and section 6 would be bad in law if it were construed to be an essay by Parliament exercising constituent powers to amend the Sales Tax Laws of the States. Section 6, therefore, was read as only giving retrospective operation to the expansion of the expression 'tax on the sale or purchase of goods' in Entry 54, List II to include a tax on the supply of food or drink and thus validating retrospectively State Sales Tax Acts *that had theretofore made provision for the levy of sales tax on the supply of food or drink.*[81]

Just as general words may be construed in a limited sense[82] to avoid the statute becoming unconstitutional, so also words may be construed in a wider sense[83] if a narrower construction renders the law unconstitutional and that result is avoided by giving the words a wider meaning. This principle can be deduced from the Supreme Court's decision in *Express Newspapers Ltd. v. Union of India.*[84] Section 9(1) of the Working Journalists (Condition of Service) and Miscellaneous Provisions Act, 1955, directs that in fixing rates of wages of working journalists, the Wage Board shall have regard to the cost of living, the prevalent rates of wages for comparable employments the circumstances relating to newspaper industry in different regions of the country and to any other circumstances which to the Board may seem relevant. One of the objections on behalf of the industry was that the Act imposes unreasonable restrictions on the freedom to carry on business amongst other on the ground that it was not made incumbent on the Board to consider the capacity of the industry to pay as an essential circumstance in fixing the rates of wages. The Supreme Court although observing that the criticism "would appear to be justified" negatived the contention by holding that 'the circumstances relating to newspaper industry in different regions of the country' which the Board was required to take into consideration should be read as including a consideration as to 'capacity of the Industry to pay'. In reaching this conclusion BHAGWATI, J. observed: "It is, however, well recognised that the courts would lean towards the constitutionality of an enactment and if it is possible to read this

---

80. *K. Damodarasamy Naidu and Bros. v. The State of Tamil Nadu,* JT 1999 (8) SC 309, p. 319 : AIR 1999 SC 3909, pp. 3915, 3916 : (2000) 1 SCC 521.

81. *Ibid.*

82. **See** text and notes 57 to 81, pp. 652 to 658.

83. *Express Newspapers Ltd. v. Union of India*, AIR 1958 SC 578 : 1959 SCR 12; *Corporation of Calcutta v. Liberty Cinema,* AIR 1965 SC 1107, p. 1114 : 1965 (2) SCR 477. ('Fee' construed as 'tax'); *State of Kerala v. M.K. Krishnan Nayar*, AIR 1978 SC 747, p. 759 : (1978) 1 SCC 552.

84. AIR 1958 SC 578 : 1959 SCR 12.

circumstance, as comprised within the category of circumstances relating to the newspaper industry in different regions of the country, the court should not strike down the provisions as in any manner whatever unreasonable and violative of the fundamental right of the petitioners".[85] In an extreme case[86] the Supreme Court, while upholding the validity of the Bhopal Gas Leak Disaster (Processing of Claims) Act, 1985 which confers exclusive power on the Central Government to make and prosecute all claims for compensation arising out of the Bhopal Gas Leak Disaster, inferred an implied obligation of the Government to give interim relief to the victims or their dependants for their sustenance and maintenance. This obligation was inferred, as according to the majority view, it was necessary to sustain the constitutionality of the Act which had deprived the claimants, who were poor persons, to sue for damages or to enter into compromise or settlement in respect of their claims.[87] This obligation was said to be implicit in the spirit of the Act and constituted 'the major inarticulate premise' upon which the Act proceeded.[88] It was further held that sections 9 and 10 of the Act, which empowered the Government to frame a scheme for registration and processing of claims, and creation of a fund for administration of the scheme and which contemplated payments to claimants before adjudication or settlement of the claims by the court, ought to be meaningfully construed to effectuate the implied obligation.[89]

When the powers of a Legislature undergo a change during the pendency of a legislative measure, the construction of general words is made with reference to the powers of the Legislature existing at the time when the process of law making is completed. This principle can be gathered from the decision of the Federal Court[90] relating to the validity of the Hindu Women's Right to Property Act, 1937. The Bill which became the Act had been passed by the Legislative Assembly before 1st April, 1937, and by the Council of State after that date, the said date being the date of commencement of the Government of India Act, 1935, which brought in the change in the legislative powers. At the time when the Bill was passed by the Assembly, the Legislature could have dealt with any kind of property including agricultural lands but at the time when it was passed by the Council of State and was assented to by the Governor General the powers as to agricultural lands had been vested in the Governors' provinces exclusively. The question, therefore, was whether in

---

85. *Ibid*, p. 623.
86. *Charan Lal Sahu v. Union of India*, AIR 1990 SC 1480 : 1990 (1) SCC 613.
87. *Ibid*, p. 1536.
88. *Ibid*.
89. *Ibid*.
90. *Umayal Singh Achi v. Lakshmi Achi*, AIR 1941 FC 28, p. 31. *In re, Hindu Women's Right to Property Act*, AIR 1941 FC 72, p. 75.

these circumstances the word 'property' could be construed as 'property other than agricultural lands' and the Federal Court construed it in that way and held the law to be *intra vires*.[91]

(d) Limitations of the Rule

In applying the rule of construction of confining the general words to the field of legislative competence, the limitations of this doctrine must also be kept in view. In the words of GWYER, C.J.: "If the restriction of the general words to purposes within the power of the Legislature would be to have an Act with nothing or next to nothing in it or an Act different in kind, and not merely in degree, from an Act in which the general words were given the wider meaning then it is plain that the Act as a whole must be held invalid, because in such circumstances it is impossible to assert with any confidence that the Legislature intended the general words which it has used to be construed only in the narrower sense. If the Act is to be upheld, it must remain even when a narrower meaning is given to the general words, an Act which is complete, intelligible and valid and which can be executed by itself.[92] So, the rule applies unless the restricted meaning of the words makes the legislation incomplete, unintelligible or unmeaning.[93] The rule will not apply when the offending words can reasonably have only one meaning, *e.g.*, when the restricted meaning makes them useless or redundant.[94] In the garb of reading down a provision it is not open to read words and expressions not found in the provision and to venture into a kind of judicial legislation.[95]

Regulation 9(b), made under the Delhi Road Transport Authority Act, 1950, conferring unrestricted power to terminate the services of a permanent or confirmed employee and expressed in unambiguous terms, was not read down to save it and was declared *ultra vires* offending Articles 14 and 21 of the Constitution.[96] It was held by the majority that when the provision in

---

91. *Umayal Singh Achi v. Lakshmi Achi*, AIR 1941 FC 28, p. 31.

92. *In re, Hindu Women's Right to Property*, Act, AIR 1941 FC 72, p. 77.

93. *Venkatraman & Co. v. State of Madras*, AIR 1966 SC 1089, p. 1105 : 1966 (2) SCR 229.

94. *State of Punjab v. Prem Sukhdas*, AIR 1977 SC 1640, p. 1642 : (1977) 2 SCC 774; *Commissioner of Wealth Tax v. Hasmatunnisa Begum*, AIR 1989 SC 1024, p. 1030 : 1989 Supp (2) SCC 43; *Hector v. Attorney-General of Antiqua and Barbuda*, (1990) 2 All ER 103, p. 107 : (1990) 2 WLR 606 : (1990) 2 SC 312 (PC); *M.P. Cement Manufacturer's Association v. State of M.P.*, (2004) 2 SCC 249, p. 260 : (2003) 10 Scale 547.

95. *Union of India v. Ind-swift Laboratories Ltd.*, (2011) 4 SCC 635 (para 19) : (2011) 2 JT 352.

96. *Delhi Transport Corpn. v. DTC Mazdoor Congress*, AIR 1991 SC 101 : 1991 Supp (1) SCC 600.

question is cast in a definite and unambiguous language or when the remaking of the provision will lead to its distortion or when extensive additions or alterations will be needed to save it, the rule will have no application and the court will have no option but to declare the provision *ultra vires.*[1] But sections 7 and 8 of the Chhota Nagpur Tenancy Act, 1908 which provide for succession of certain classes of tribal tenants to 'descendants in the male line' or 'heirs male in the line' and do not provide any right to any female were construed to protect the right of livelihood from the land of the dependant family females of the deceased male holder spelled out from Article 21 of the Constitution. On this basis it was held that "the exclusive right of male succession conceived of in sections 7 and 8 has to remain in suspended animation so long as the right of livelihood of female descendants of the last male holder remains valid and in vogue."[2]

In its effort to save laws from being declared invalid the court sometimes appears to exhibit judicial 'heroics'[3] in recasting them. Rule 7 of the Rules made by the Ahmedabad Municipal Corporation for admission to the Municipal Medical College defines 'A local student' as 'a student who has passed HSC/New SSC examination and the qualifying examination from any of the High Schools or Colleges situated within the Ahmedabad Municipal limits'. The rules reserve 15% of the seats for all India candidates and the rest of the seats are reserved for local students as defined in rule 7, the object being to provide medical education to the students of Ahmedabad. Rule 7 was, however, found to be *prima facie* discriminatory in two ways. First, that permanent resident students of Ahmedabad, who for fortuitous circumstances happened to acquire qualifications from institutions within the limits of the Ahmedabad Development Authority, but outside the municipal limits, were not eligible for admission. Secondly, the rule created an artificial distinction from amongst students who were residents of Ahmedabad city and those who may not be the residents of Ahmedabad city but who studied in educational institutions situated within the Ahmedabad Municipal Corporation limits.[4] To meet these lacunae in rule 7 and to avoid declaring it invalid for violating Article 14 of the Constitution, it was judicially recast as follows: "Local student means a student who has passed HSC/New SSC examination from any of the High Schools or Colleges situated within the Ahmedabad Municipal Corporation limits and includes a permanent resident student of Ahmedabad who

---

1. *Ibid.*
2. *Madhu Kishwar v. State of Bihar,* AIR 1996 SC 1864, p. 1884 : (1996) 5 SCC 230.
3. DENNING, approach called 'heroics' by House of Lords and BEG, C.J., **see** text and notes 44 and 51, pp. 78, 79.
4. *Ahmedabad Municipal Corporation v. Nilaybhai R. Thakore,* JT 1999 (8) SC 244, pp. 249, 250 : AIR 2000 SC 114, p. 117 : (1999) 8 SCC 139.

acquires the above qualifications from any of the High Schools or Colleges situated within Ahmedabad Urban Development Authority."[5] In another case[6] a rule of six lines (as printed in J.T.)[7] providing for cessation of membership of a society on non-payment of membership fee in advance by March for a year was "read down" and recast into a rule consisting of thirty three lines (as printed in J.T.)[8] to provide opportunity to the member to prove that the fee was payed in time or that there was sufficient cause for non-payment in time. This was done to avoid the rule being declared void for unreasonableness. Difference of opinion may arise on the question whether a particular provision should be read down or struck down. This is illustrated by the decision of the Constitution Bench in *20th Century Finance Corporation Ltd. v. State of Maharashtra*.[9] The case deals with various State Acts which levied sales tax on the transfer of any right to use any goods for any purpose for cash, deferred payment or other valuable consideration as permitted by Article 366 [29A(d)] of the Constitution. These Acts contained provisions that the transfer of the right to use goods shall be deemed to have taken place in the State imposing the tax if the goods are in that State at the time of their use irrespective of the place where the agreement for such transfer of the right was made. These deeming provisions fixing the situs of sale in every case merely on the presence of the goods at the time of their use offended the constitutional provisions which did not enable the states to tax outside sales, or the sales in the course of import or export, or interstate sales. The majority judges did not strike down these provisions and read them down not to apply to such sales[10] but judges in the minority struck them down on the ground that their presence was likely to result in confusion.[11]

(e) Severability

If the enactment cannot be saved by construing it consistent with its constitutionality, it may be seen whether it can be partly saved. When the Act is held to be in part inconsistent with the higher law in the Constitution, it can be partly saved if the test of severability is satisfied. The doctrine of severability was considered by the Supreme Court in *RMD Chamarbaugwala v. Union of India*,[12] where VENKATRAMA AIYYAR, J., speaking for the court observed that

---

5. *Ibid*, p. 252 (JT), p. 118 (AIR).
6. *Hyderabad Karnataka Education Society v. Registrar of Societies,* JT 1999 (9) SC 482 : AIR 2000 SC 301 : (2000) 1 SCC 566.
7. *Ibid*, rule 7A, p. 491 (JT), pp. 307, 308 (AIR).
8. *Ibid*, p. 499 (JT) : p. 312 (AIR).
9. JT 2000 (7) SC 177 : (2000) 6 SCC 12 : AIR 2000 SC 2436.
10. *Ibid*, p. 209.
11. *Ibid*, p. 234.
12. AIR 1957 SC 628 : 1957 SCR 930.

"when a statute is in part void, it will be enforced as against the rest, if that is severable from what is invalid".[13] The court also summarised the rules of construction for determining severability, essentially from American authorities, into the following seven propositions:

"1. In determining whether the valid parts of a statute are separable from the invalid parts thereof, it is the intention of the Legislature that is the determining factor. The test to be applied is whether the Legislature would have enacted the valid part if it had known that the rest of the statute was invalid. 2. If the valid and invalid provisions are so inextricably mixed up that they cannot be separated from one another, then the invalidity of a portion must result in the invalidity of the Act in its entirety. On the other hand, if they are so distinct and separate that after striking out what is invalid, what remains is in itself a complete code independent of the rest, then it will be upheld notwithstanding that the rest has become unenforceable. 3. Even when the provisions which are valid are distinct and separate from those which are invalid, if they all form part of a single scheme which is intended to be operative as a whole, then also the invalidity of a part will result in the failure of the whole. 4. Likewise, when the valid and invalid parts of a statute are independent and do not form part of a scheme but what is left after omitting the invalid portion is so thin and truncated as to be in substance different from what it was when it emerged out of the Legislature, then also it will be rejected in its entirety. 5. The separability of the valid and invalid provisions of a statute does not depend on whether the law is enacted in the same section or different section; it is not the form, but the substance of the matter that is material, and that has to be ascertained on an examination of the Act as a whole and of the setting of the relevant provision therein. 6. If after the invalid portion is expugned from the statute what remains cannot be enforced without making alterations and modifications therein, then the whole of it must be struck down as void, as otherwise it will amount to judicial legislation. 7. In determining the legislative intent on the question of separability, it will be legitimate to take into account the history of the legislation, its object, the title and the preamble to it."[14]

Applying these principles to the definition of 'prize competition' in section 2(d) of the Prize Competition Act, 1955 as meaning 'any competition' 'in which prizes are offered for the solution of any puzzle based upon the building up, arrangement, combination or permutation of letters, words or figures', the court held that even if the regulatory provisions of the Act were invalid in respect of competitions in which success depends to a substantial extent on skill, the Act will still apply to competitions of a

---

13. *Ibid,* p. 636.
14. *Ibid,* pp. 636, 637.

gambling character for the two types of competitions formed two distinct and separate categories and as one can be in no doubt that Parliament would have still enacted the law even if it had known that it would fail as regards competitions involving skill.[15] The test is not of textual severability but of substantial severability which permits even modification of the text in order to achieve severance but "this can be only done when the court is satisfied that it is affecting no change in the substantial purpose and effect of the impugned provision".[16]

4. OPERATION CONTROLLED ON CONSIDERATIONS OF TERRITORIAL NEXUS: PRESUMPTION AGAINST EXCEEDING TERRITORIAL POWERS

(a) Principle of territorial nexus

(i) *General.*—In case of Legislatures which may for convenience be called non-sovereign Legislatures like those of Colonies, Australian States or Canadian Provinces, it has been said that they are incompetent to legislate with extra-territorial effect.[17] This is only a convenient mode of stating that a law made by such a Legislature must bear a real territorial connection with the subject-matter with which it is dealing. Before the Statute of Westminster, 1931, the Dominion Parliaments were also subject to the same limitation. This principle or rule forbidding extra-territorial legislation has been characterised "as a doctrine of somewhat obscure extent".[18] The obscurity lies in defining by any exact formula the territorial nexus which will be sufficient for holding the legislation *intra vires*. "Any connection" which is "relevant" or "real" with the exercise of the power of the State concerned has been held to be sufficient[19] and at times stress has

---

15. *Ibid*, p. 637. **See further** for test of severability *Sawai Bhawani Singh v. State of Rajasthan*, 1996 (1) Scale 733, pp. 738, 739: 1996 (3) SCC 105.
16. *DPP v. Hutchinson*, (1990) 2 All ER 836, p. 845 (HL); *Commissioner of Police v. Davis*, (1993) 4 All ER 476, p. 487 : (1994) 1 AC 283 : (1993) 3 WLR 846 (PC).
17. *Macleod v. A.G. of New South Wales*, (1891) AC 455 : 60 LJ PC 55 (PC); *Bressard v. Smith*, (1925) AC 371 (PC); *London and South American Investment Trust v. British Tobacco Co. (Australia)*, (1927) 1 Ch 107; *Commissioner of Stamp Duties (NSW) v. Millar*, (1932) 48 CLR 618; *Provincial Treasurer of Alberta v. Kerr*, (1933) AC 710 (PC); *Johnson v. Commissioner of Stamp Duties*, (1956) 1 All ER 502, pp. 509, 510 (PC).
18. *British Coal Corporation v. R.*, (1935) AC 500 : (1935) All ER Rep 139, p. 146 (PC) (LORD SANKEY, L.C.).
19. *Broken Hill South Ltd. v. Commissioner of Taxation (NSW)*, (1937) 56 CLR 337, pp. 361, 375; **referred** to in *G-G in Council v. Raleigh Investment Co.*, AIR 1944 FC 51, p. 58; *A.H. Wadia v. C.I.T., Bombay*, AIR 1949 FC 18, pp. 24, 37; *Tata Iron and Steel Co. v. State of Bihar*, AIR 1958 SC 452, p. 459 : 1958 SCR 1355.

been mainly laid on the topic of legislation committed to the Legislature.[20] But it is also equally well established by high authority that "a connection which is too remote" or which is "completely irrelevant" will not be enough for holding the legislation *intra vires*.[21]

By the Customs Act of Canada (1927) the Dominion Legislature of Canada authorised seizure of vessels and cargo hovering in territorial waters of Canada within twelve marine miles from the coast. The Act was challenged as *ultra vires*, the powers of Dominion Parliament as it was designed to operate beyond the shores or beyond a marine league from the coast. In holding the Act *intra vires*, the Privy Council,[22] although accepting as the general principle that States can legislate effectively only for their own territories observed: "It is maintained that it (the Dominion Legislature) is debarred from introducing into such (customs) legislation any provision designed to operate beyond its shores or at any rate beyond a marine league from the coast. In their Lordships' opinion the Parliament of Canada is not under any such disability. Once it is found that a particular topic of legislation is among those upon which the Dominion Parliament may competently legislate—their Lordships think no reason to restrict the permitted scope of such legislation by any other consideration than is applicable to the Legislature of a fully sovereign State."[23]

Three cases noticed below[24] bring into bold relief the contrast between a connection which is real or relevant to support a legislation and a connection

---

20. *Croft v. Dunphy*, (1933) AC 156 (PC) : AIR 1933 PC 16, p. 18; **referred** to in *Wallace Brothers v. CIT, Bombay*, AIR 1948 PC 118, p. 120.

21. *Commr. of Stamp Duties (NSW) v. Millar*, (1932) 48 CLR 618, p. 642; *Johnson v. Commissioner of Stamp Duties*, (1956) 1 All ER 502, pp. 509, 510 (PC); *State of Bihar v. Charusiladasi*, AIR 1959 SC 1002, p. 1010 : 1959 Supp (2) SCR 601.

22. *Croft v. Dunphy*, (1933) AC 156 (PC) : AIR 1933 PC 16.

23. *Ibid*, p. 18, For a case of mandated territory, **see** *Naim Malvan v. A-G of Palestine*, AIR 1948 PC 186.

24. *Commissioner of Stamp Duties (NSW) v. Millar*, (1932) 48 CLR 618; *Broken Hill South Ltd. v. Commr. of Taxation (NSW)*, (1937) 56 CLR 337; *Johnson v. Commr. of Stamp Duties (NSW)*, (1956) 1 All ER 502 (PC).

N.B.—In 1986 the Parliaments of the United Kingdom and the Commonwealth of Australia passed the Australia Acts which provide: '2(1). It is hereby declared and enacted that the legislative powers of the Parliament of each State include full power to make laws for peace, order and good Government of that State that have extra-territorial operation. It has been held that section 2(1) merely codifies the nexus rule and does not bring about any change;' *Union Steamship Co. of Australia Ltd. v. King*, (1988) 62 ALJR 645. The law still is that legislation of a State Parliament "should be held valid if there is any real connection—even a remote or general connection—between the subject matter of the legislation and the State." This proposition does not deny that there may remain the question about what is meant in a particular case by "real connection": *Mobil Oil Australia Pty. Ltd. v. Victoria*, (2002) 76 ALJR 926, p. 936.

which is too remote or irrelevant for that purpose. In each of these cases, the competence of the Legislature to enact the law depended upon section 5 of the New South Wales Constitution Act which provides: 'The Legislature shall subject to the provisions of the Commonwealth of Australia Constitution Act have power to make laws for the peace, welfare and good Government of New South Wales in all cases whatsoever. The cases bring out the principle that legislation which has no relevant territorial connection with New South Wales falls outside the power conferred by this section.'

The first case[25] dealt with a provision of the Stamp Duties Act of New South Wales which imposed death duty on shares of any company, registered or incorporated within or without New South Wales, belonging to a deceased person; provided the company was carrying on business in New South Wales. The deceased in this case had died resident and domiciled outside New South Wales, and the company, in which he had shares, was incorporated out of, and had no share registered within that State. The shares, therefore, could not be regarded as situate in New South Wales and as the enactment was not confined to companies whose sole business was in that State, what was taxed was not the advantage to the deceased from the business of the company within that State, but the whole value of shares which might have been due in part or entirely to operations conducted outside the State. The High Court of Australia by a majority decision held the enactment to be beyond the competence of New South Wales, as the Legislature in taxing the shares out of the jurisdiction of the State had, to quote the judgment, adopted a connection which was too remote to entitle its enactments to the description a law 'for the peace, welfare and good Government of New South Wales';[26] or to state the matter in another way, although some connection between the shareholder and New South Wales could be discovered in the existence therein of part of the company's undertaking, the enactment went beyond legislating in respect of that connection.[27]

In the second case,[28] it was held by the High Court of Australia that the imposition of Income-tax on a foreign company in respect of interest on money secured by mortgage on property in New South Wales, was within the constitutional power of the State Legislature. On the question of necessity of territorial nexus LATHAM, C.J. said: "The circumstances in respect of which the law operates must be something which really appertains to

25. *Commr. of Stamp Duties (NSW) v. Millar*, (1932) 48 CLR 618.
26. *Ibid.*
27. *Ibid.*
28. *Broken Hill South Ltd. v. Commr. of Taxation (NSW)*, (1937) 56 CLR 337.

New South Wales."[29] In the same case, DIXON, J. observed: "But it is within the competence of the State Legislature to make any fact, circumstance, occurrence or thing in or connected with the territory the occasion of the imposition upon any person concerned therein of a liability to taxation or of any other liability."[30]

Both these decisions and the passages from them quoted above[31] were approved by the Privy Council in the third case which also arose from New South Wales.[32] The question in this case was as to the validity of death duties levied on the properties situate within and outside the State of New South Wales in which the deceased, who died domiciled within the State, had only a life interest by virtue of a will of a previous owner. The Privy Council affirming the decision of the New South Wales Supreme Court held that the Act in so far as it levied death duty on property situate within the State was valid and in so far as it levied the duty on property situate outside the State, in which the deceased had only a life estate, was invalid and that the fact of domicile of the deceased being in New South Wales was an insufficient nexus to support such a levy. So far as the duty levied on property situate within the State was concerned, LORD KEITH observed: "The presence of property within a State's jurisdiction has always been regarded as a cogent reason for recognising the right and power to tax that property. The property enjoys the protection of the State's Law and, in their Lordships' judgment, fiscal legislation taxing that property can be regarded as a law for peace, welfare and good Government of that State.[33] The decision further shows that in respect of property situate within the State, it is immaterial whether the holder of the life estate dies domiciled outside the State or the remaindermen are domiciled outside the State; and that the existence within the State of the property is sufficient nexus for exercising taxing power of the State." With regard to property situate outside the State, in rejecting the contention that the domicile of the holder of life estate was a sufficient nexus, LORD KEITH stated: "The case is not that of a deceased dying possessed of personal estate, or a case of a deceased who has given away property shortly before his death without valuable consideration. The deceased's only interest was a limited interest ceasing on her death, and it is not her estate that is brought into charge—. The domicile of a deceased within New South Wales at the date of his death is, in their Lordships' judgment, a quite insufficient ground by itself to make good the lack of any other connection with the State."[34]

---

29. *Ibid*, p. 358.
30. *Ibid*, p. 375.
31. **See** text and notes 24 to 29, *supra*.
32. *Johnson v. Commr. of Stamp Duties*, (1956) 1 All ER 502 (PC).
33. *Ibid*, p. 509.
34. *Ibid*, pp. 510, 511.

(ii) *Legislation under the Government of India Act, 1935*.—Under the Government of India Act, 1935, by section 99(1), the Federal Legislature was empowered to 'make laws for the whole or any part of British India' and Provincial Legislatures were empowered to 'make laws for the Province or any part thereof'. By section 99(2) certain matters were enumerated, and it was provided that no Federal law shall, on the ground that it would have extra-territorial operation, be deemed to be invalid in so far as it applied to those enumerated matters. Thus, both the Federal [except in respect of matters falling under section 99(2)] and the Provincial Legislatures were subject to the rule forbidding extra-territorial legislation in the sense that presence of a 'sufficient' or 'real' territorial connection with British India in respect of Federal laws and with the Province concerned in respect of Provincial laws, was necessary to bring a law within their legislative competence.

A leading judgment of the Privy Council relating to Income-tax law made by the Centre may here be noticed.[35] By an amendment in 1935, section 4A was introduced in the Indian Income-tax Act, 1922, which made a company resident in India for purposes of the Act, if its income arising in British India in the particular year exceeded its income arising outside British India in that year and as a result thereof a company, although incorporated outside British India and although managed exclusively from outside, became liable to be assessed to income-tax in British India on its entire income including that part of its income which arose outside British India. The validity of this provision was upheld by the Privy Council. LORD UTHWATT said: There is no rule of law that the territorial limits of a subordinate Legislature define the possible scope of its legislative enactments or mark the field open to its vision. The ambit of the powers possessed by subordinate Legislature depends upon the proper construction of the statute conferring those powers. No doubt the enabling statute has to be read against the background that only a defined territory has been committed to the charge of the Legislature. Concern by a subordinate Legislature with affairs or persons outside its own territory may, therefore, suggest a query whether the Legislature is in truth minding its own business. It does not compel the conclusion that it is not.[36] Proceeding further, LORD UTHWATT observed: "The resulting general conception as to the scope of Income-tax is that given a sufficient territorial connection

---

35. *Wallace Bros. v. CIT, Bombay,* AIR 1948 PC 118 : (1948) 161 ITR 240 (PC). **See further** *Trinidad Lake Asphalt Operating Co. Ltd. v. Trinidad & Tobago Income-tax Commrs.*, (1945) 1 All ER 9, pp. 10, 11 (PC).

36. *Wallace Bros. v. CIT, Bombay,* AIR 1948 PC 118, p. 120 (para 13) : (1948) 161 ITR 240 (PC).

between the person sought to be charged and the country seeking to tax him Income-tax may properly extend to that person in respect of his foreign income."[37] The Federal Court of India also applied the same test in judging the vires of Income-tax legislation.[38]

It may further be noticed that if sufficient territorial connection exists, the legislation will be valid and it will be entirely immaterial to see whether the liability imposed is proportionate or disproportionate to the territorial connection. "But it is of no importance upon the question of validity"; pointed out DIXON, J. in *Broken Hill's* case[39] "that the liability imposed is, or may be altogether disproportionate to the territorial connection". This principle was accepted by the Federal Court of India.[40] SPENS, C.J., after citing DIXON, J. observed: "If some connection exists, the Legislature is not compelled to measure the taxation by the degree of benefit received in particular cases by the tax-payer. This affects the policy and not the validity of legislation."[41]

By section 6 of the Independence Act, 1947, the Legislature of the Dominion of India was conferred full power to make laws for that Dominion including laws having extra-territorial operation. The position of the Provinces, however, still remained the same. In this respect, therefore, there arose a close similarity between the Dominion of India and other self-governing Dominions such as Canada and Australia. The result of section 6 of the India Independence Act was the same as that produced by section 3 of the Statute of Westminster, 1931. The laws made by the Dominion Legislature in India thereafter were not open to challenge for want of a territorial nexus or on the ground of any difficulty as to their effective enforcement. In an appeal arising from Canada, the Privy Council dealt with the effect of section 3 of the Statute of Westminster, and pointed out that "courts of the country must enforce the law with the machinery available to them; and they are not entitled to question the authority of the Dominion Legislature in making a law which is extra-territorial."[42] Their Lordships approved of a passage from the judgment of RAND, J. wherein he

---

37. *Ibid*, (para 17).

38. *G.G. in Council v. Raleigh Investment Co.*, AIR 1944 FC 51; *Wallace Brothers v. C.I.T., Bombay*, AIR 1945 FC 9; *A.H. Wadia v. C.I.T., Bombay*, AIR 1949 FC 18.

39. *Broken Hill South Ltd. v. Commr. of Taxation*, (1937) 56 CLR 337, p. 357.

40. *G.G. in Council v. Raleigh Investment Co. Ltd.*, AIR 1944 FC 51 : 1944 FCR 229.

41. *G.G. in Council v. Raliegh Investment Co. Ltd.*, AIR 1944 FC 51, p. 58 : 1944 FCR 229; *referred to in A.H. Wadia v. CIT, Bombay*, AIR 1949 FC 18, p. 24 (KANIA, C.J.I.).

42. *British Columbia Electric Railway Co. Ltd. v. King*, AIR 1946 PC 180. **See further** *British Coal Corporation v. R.*, (1935) AC 500: (1935) All ER Rep 139 (PC) and *A.G. for Ontario v. A.G. for Canada*, (1947) AC 127 : (1947) 1 All ER 137 (PC); in these two cases legislations abolishing appeals to Privy Council were **upheld**.

said: Within the State, however, it becomes an obligatory rule to be enforced whenever enforcement is feasible. The specific investment of extra-territorial power by section 3 of the Statute of 1931, was designed no doubt to remove the generally accepted limitation of colonial legislative jurisdiction, a limitation which the courts of the colony itself were bound to recognise,[43] and any such jurisdictional inadequacy no longer hampers the legislative freedom of the Dominion. Within its field there is now a legislative sovereignty.[44]

(iii) *Legislation under the Constitution of India.*—The Constitution, as regards the Union Parliament, makes it clear that 'No law made by Parliament shall be deemed to be invalid on the ground that it would have extra-territorial operation'.[45] No question, therefore, can possibly arise about any legislation by Parliament being questioned on the ground that it has extra-territorial operation. Even though the legislation may not be effectively enforceable because it may deal with objects or persons beyond the territories of the Republic, yet no court within the Republic can refuse enforcement of the legislation by Parliament on the ground that it is invalid for want of a territorial nexus. The position, thus, in this respect, is exactly the same as that of British Parliament or of Dominion Parliaments after the Statute of Westminster, 1931.[46]

The case of *Electric Corporation of India v. Commissioner of Income Tax* which was referred to the Constitution Bench has recently been decided.[47] The discussion above regarding the extra-territorial powers of Parliament must be read subject to the following proposition laid down by the Constitution Bench:

We now turn to answering the two questions that we set out with:

(1) Is Parliament constitutionally restricted from enacting legislation with respect to extra-territorial aspects or causes that do not have, nor expected to have any, direct or indirect, tangible or intangible impact(s) on or effect(s) in or consequences for:

---

43. *McLeod v. Att. Gen., New South Wales*, (1891) AC 455 : 60 LJ PC 55 : 65 LT 321 (PC).
44. *British Columbia Electric Rly. Co. Ltd. v. King*, AIR 1946 PC 180, p. 184.
45. Article 245 (2), Constitution of India. But some nexus with India may still be necessary. **See** the observations in *Electronics Corporation of India Ltd. v. Commissioner of Income Tax*, AIR 1989 SC 1707 : 1989 Supp (2) SCC 642, where the question of validity of section 9(1)(vii) of the Income-tax Act, 1961 was referred to a Constitutional Bench.
46. **See** text and notes 41 and 43, *supra*.
47. *GVK Industries Limited v. Income Tax Officer*, (2011) 4 SCC 36, paras 124 to 127 : (2011) 3 JT 356.

(a) the territory of India, or any part of India; or

(b) the interests of, welfare of, well-being of, or security of inhabitants of India, and Indians?

The answer to the above would be yes. However, Parliament may exercise its legislative powers with respect to extra-territorial aspects or causes-events, things, phenomena (howsoever commonplace they may be), resources, actions or transactions, and the like that occur, arise or exist or may be expected to do so, naturally or on account of some human agency, in the social, political, economic, cultural, biological, environmental or physical spheres outside the territory of India, and seek to control, modulate, mitigate or transform the effects of such extra-territorial aspects or causes, or in appropriate cases, eliminate or engender such extra-territorial aspects or causes, *only when* such extra-territorial aspects or causes have, or are expected to have, some impact on, or effect in, or consequences for: (a) the territory of India, or any part of India; or (b) the interests of, welfare of, well-being of, or security of inhabitants of India, and Indians.

It is important for us to state and hold here that the powers of legislation of Parliament with regard to all aspects or causes that are within the purview of its competence, including with respect to extra-territorial aspects or causes as delineated above, and as specified by the Constitution, or implied by its essential role in the constitutional scheme, ought not to be subjected to some a *priori* quantitative tests, such as "sufficiency" or "significance" or in any other manner requiring a predetermined degree of strength. All that would be required would be that the connection to India be real or expected to be real, and not illusory or fanciful.

Whether a particular law enacted by Parliament does show such a real connection, or expected real connection, between the extra-territorial aspect or cause and something in India or related to India and Indians, in terms of impact, effect or consequence, would be a mixed matter of facts and of law. Obviously, where Parliament itself posits a degree of such relationship, beyond the constitutional requirement that it be real and not fanciful, then the courts would have to enforce such a requirement in the operation of the law as a matter of that law itself, and not of the Constitution.

(2) Does Parliament have the powers to legislate "for" any territory, other than the territory of India or any part of it?

The answer to the above would be no. It is obvious that Parliament is empowered to make laws with respect to aspects or causes that occur, arise or exist, or may be expected to do so, within the territory of India, and also with respect to extra-territorial aspects or causes that have an impact on or nexus with India as explained above in the answer to Question 1 above. Such laws would fall within the meaning, purport and ambit of the grant of powers to Parliament to make laws "for the whole or any part of the territory of India", and they may not be invalidated on the ground that they may require extra-territorial operation. Any laws enacted by Parliament with respect to extra-territorial aspects or causes that have no impact on or nexus with India would be *ultra vires*, as answered in response to Question 1 above, and would be laws made "for" a foreign territory."

As regards the States in the Republic, the Constitution does not bring about any change from the position of the Provinces under the Government of India Act, 1935; and the power of State Legislatures 'to make laws for the whole or any part of the State'[48] leaves it open to scrutiny whether a particular law is really for the State enacting it. Since "the laws which a State is empowered to make must be for the purpose of that State,"[49] the laws enacted by State Legislatures "cannot in the absence of a territorial nexus have any extra-territorial operation."[50] The doctrine of territorial nexus has, therefore, been applied to State Acts under the Constitution. In the words of S.R. DAS, C.J.I.: "Sufficiency of the territorial connection involves a consideration of two elements, namely: (a) the connection must be real and not illusory; and (b) the liability sought to be imposed must be pertinent to that connection."[51] If the nexus is rational on a consideration of the aforesaid two elements, any further examination of the sufficiency of nexus cannot be a matter of adjudication before the court.[52]

The general principle regarding sales tax legislation of the States under Article 246(3) read with Entry 54 of List II Schedule VII of the Constitution was laid down by PATANJALI SHASTRI, C.J.I. in *State of Bombay v.*

---

48. Article 245(1) and Article 246(3), Constitution of India.

49. *State of Bombay v. United Motors (India) Ltd.*, AIR 1953 SC 252, p. 256 : 1053, 1069.

50. *State of Bombay v. R.M.D. Chamarbaugwala*, AIR 1957 SC 699, p. 711 : 1957 SCR 874. **See Further** *R.S.D.V. Finance Co. Pvt. Ltd. v. Shree Vallabh Glass Works*, AIR 1993 SC 2094, p. 2102 : 1993 (2) SCC 130.

51. *State of Bombay v. R.M.D. Chamarbaugwala*, AIR 1957 SC 699, p. 714 : 1957 SCR 874; **referred** to in *Tata Iron and Steel Co. v. Bihar State*, AIR 1958 SC 452, p. 461 : 1958 SCR 1355 ; *State of Bihar v. Charusiladasi*, AIR 1959 SC 1002, p. 1010 : 1959 Supp (2) SCR 601; *Shrikant Bhalchandra Karulkar v. State of Gujarat*, JT 1994 (5) SC 91, p. 94 : 1994 (5) SCC 459 (2). **See further** *State of A.P. v. National Thermal Power Corporation Ltd.*, AIR 2002 SC 1895, p. 1911 : (2002) 5 SCC 203.

52. *Khyerbari Tea Co. v. State of Assam*, AIR 1964 SC 925, p. 942 : 1964 (5) SCR 975.

United Motors (India) Ltd.[53] The Chief Justice said: "The Legislature of any State has under these provisions, the exclusive power to make laws 'for such State or any part thereof' with respect to taxes on the sale or purchase of goods other than newspaper. The expression 'for such State or any part thereof' cannot, in our view, be taken to import into Entry 54 the restriction that the sale or purchase referred to must take place within the territory of the State. All that it means is that the laws which a State is empowered to make must be for the purpose of that State." The Privy Council in *Wallace Brothers & Co. Ltd. v. C.I.T., Bombay*,[54] in dealing with the competency of the Indian Legislature to impose tax on the income arising abroad to a non-resident foreign company, pointed out that the constitutional validity of the relevant statutory provisions did not turn on the possession by Legislature of extra-territorial powers but on the existence of a sufficient territorial connection between the taxing State and what it sought to tax. In the case of sales tax, "it is not necessary that the sale or purchase should take place within the territorial limits of the State in the sense that all the ingredients of sale like the agreement to sell, the passing of title, delivery of the goods etc., should have a territorial connection with the State. Broadly speaking local activities of buying or selling carried on in the State in relation to local goods would be sufficient basis to sustain the taxing power of the State, provided of course, such activities ultimately resulted in a concluded sale or purchase to be taxed."[55] A further challenge to the application of the nexus theory to sales tax legislation was rejected by the Supreme Court in *Tata Iron and Steel Co. v. Bihar State*.[56] S.R. DAS, C.J.I. delivering the majority opinion, referred to the decisions of the Privy Council,[57] Federal Court[58] and High Court of Australia,[59] and approved of the principle of 'any connection' which is real being sufficient to sustain the legislation and also the principle that it was immaterial on the question of validity that the liability imposed is or may be altogether

---

53. AIR 1953 SC 252, p. 256 : 1953 SCR 1069.

54. AIR 1948 PC 118; **See** text and notes 36 to 37, *supra*.

55. *State of Bombay v. United Motors (India) Ltd.*, AIR 1953 SC 252, p. 256 : 1953 SCR 1069. **See also** *Poppatalal Shah v. State of Madras*, AIR 1953 SC 274 : 1953 SCR 677.

56. AIR 1958 SC 452, pp. 459 to 462 : 1958 SCR 1355. **Followed** in *Tikaram & Sons v. Commr. of Sales Tax*, AIR 1968 SC 1286 : 1968 (3) SCR 512.

57. *Wallace Brothers v. Commissioner of Income-tax, Bombay*, AIR 1948 PC 118. **See** text and notes 36 to 37, *supra*.

58. *G.G. in Council v. Raleigh Investment Co.*, AIR 1944 FC 51 : 1944 FCR 229; *A.H. Wadia v. Commissioner of Income tax, Bombay*, AIR 1949 FC 18 : 17 ITR 63.

59. *Trustees, Executors & Agency Co. Ltd. v. Federal Commissioner*, (1933) 49 CLR 220; *Wangmue Rangitikei Electric Power Board v. Australian Mutual Provident Society*, (1934) 50 CLR 581; *Broken Hill South Ltd. v. Commr. of Taxation (NSW)*, (1937) 56 CLR 337.

disproportionate to the territorial connection. It was further pointed out that although the tax was on a completed sale, one or more of the several ingredients constituting a sale could furnish the connection between the taxing State and the sale. Existence of goods within the State at the time of contract of sale and in case of a sale by producer or manufacturer, the production or manufacture of the goods in the State were held to be sufficient nexus to sustain the legislation impugned in that case.[60] The existence of 'any' territorial connection though generally sufficient for legislative competence of States is not sufficient for transgressing the ban for taxing sales in the course of import or export imposed by Article 286 as also for taxing interstate sales.[61]

Legislation pertaining to taxes on gambling under Entry 62 of List II was also sustained by the Supreme Court by adopting the nexus theory.[62] A company incorporated in the State of Mysore conducted and ran cross-words prize competition through agents and depots established in the State of Bombay and by circulating a newspaper in that State although the newspaper was printed and published outside the State of Bombay. Holding the tax levied by the State of Bombay valid, S.R. DAS, C.J.I., said: "The standing invitations, the filling up the forms and the payment of money, take place within the State which is seeking to tax only the amount received from the petitioners from the State of Bombay. The tax is on gambling although collected from the promoters. All these, we think, constitute sufficient territorial nexus which entitles the State of Bombay to impose a tax on the gambling that takes place within its boundaries and the law cannot be stuck down on the ground of extra-territoriality."[63]

A further illustration of application of nexus theory to taxing laws is found in imposition of taxes on goods carried by road or inland waterways, [Entry 56, List II]. Tea carried by producers in West Bengal, though the starting point and the point of destination were both in West Bengal, had to traverse for a very short distance of a mile and half on the inland waterways of the State of Assam, but this was held to give a rational nexus for the State of Assam to tax the goods.[64] In holding the tax valid, GAJENDRAGADKAR, J. observed: "Whether the goods are carried for a long

---

60. *Tata Iron & Steel Co. v. Bihar State*, AIR 1958 SC 452, pp. 459 to 462 : 1958 SCR 1355. **Followed** in *Tikaram & Sons v. Commissioner of Sales Tax*, AIR 1968 SC 1286 : 1968 (3) SCR 512.

61. *20th Century Finance Corporation Ltd. v. State of Maharashtra*, AIR 2000 SC 2436, pp. 2448, 2449 : (2000) 6 SCC 12; *State of A.P. v. National Thermal Power Corporation Ltd.*, AIR 2002 SC 1895, pp. 1911, 1912 : (2002) 5 SCC 203.

62. *State of Bombay v. R.M.D. Chamarbaugwala*, AIR 1957 SC 699 : 1957 SCR 874.

63. *Ibid*, p. 712.

64. *Khyerbari Tea Co. v. State of Assam*, AIR 1964 SC 925 : 1964 (5) SCR 975.

distance or a short distance cannot affect the legislative competence of the Legislature—." The nexus in question must be rational but it would be impossible to accede to the argument that sufficiency of nexus can be a matter for adjudication of the court. In the present case, undoubtedly tea has been carried over a part of inland waterways in Assam and that satisfies the test of nexus.[65]

The nexus theory was also applied by the Supreme Court in upholding the validity of the Bihar Hindu Religious Trust Act, 1951, which applies to all trusts in Bihar any property of which is in that State.[66] Negativing the argument that the Act could not apply to that property of the trust which was outside the State of Bihar, S.K. DAS, J. said: "It cannot be disputed that if the religious endowment is itself situated in Bihar and the trustees function there, the connection between the religious institution and the property appertaining thereto is real and not illusory.[67] It may, however, be noticed that this case shows that if the trust were situate outside a State, that State cannot seek to legislate in respect of administration of such trust simply on the nexus of existence of a portion of the trust property in that State." This view has been confirmed by a later decision of the Supreme Court,[68] and it has been held that a State cannot legislate for administration of a trust which is not situate within that State even though a portion of the trust property is situate within it.

Nexus theory was again applied in upholding the validity of section 6(3A) of the Gujarat Ceiling Act, 1960 enacted by the Gujarat Legislature.[69] This provision took into account land held in any other part of India for computation of permissible ceiling area of land in the State of Gujarat. The Act was held to be valid and it was held that mere consideration of some factors which exist outside the State would not make the law extra territorial.[70]

But legislation of one State essentially directed to properties will, it appears, have no application in respect of properties in another State. On this principle a law passed by the Madras Legislature that every *sthanam* shall be deemed and shall remain deemed always to have been properties

---

65. *Ibid*, p. 942.
66. *State of Bihar v. Charusiladasi (Smt.)*, AIR 1959 SC 1002 : 1959 Supp (2) SCR 601.
67. *Ibid*, pp. 1010, 1011.
68. *Anant Prasad v. State of Andhra Pradesh*, AIR 1963 SC 853, p. 859 : 1963 Supp (1) SCR 844.
69. *Shrikant Balchandra Karulkar v. State of Gujarat*, JT 1994 (5) SC 91 : 1994 (5) SCC 459 (2).
70. *Ibid*, p. 96.

belonging to *tarward* was held not to apply to *sthanam* properties in the quondam Cochin State, although they were held by the same *sthanee* who held other *sthanams* in the Madras State.[71] On the same principle the provisions of the Karnataka Contract Carriages (Acquisition) Act, 1976 was construed not to authorise acquisition of a vehicle kept and registered in or plying on an initial permit granted by another State. It was also held that the Act could not authorise acquisition of that portion of an inter-State permit which was for a route in another State and was effective by virtue of being countersigned in that State.[72] It has also been held that Entry 17 in the State List (water, that is to say, water supplies, irrigation and canals, drainage and embankments, water storage and water power—) does not authorise a state to pass legislation with respect to or affecting any aspect of the waters of an inter-state river beyond its territory.[73] On this view it was held that the Karnataka Cauvery Basin Irrigation Protection Ordinance promulgated by the State of Karnataka, which vested in the State Government an absolute power to appropriate any quantity of water from the Cauvery river and its tributaries, was unconstitutional being extraterritorial for the effect of the Ordinance was to affect the flow of the waters of the river Cauvery into the territory of Tamil Nadu and Pondicherry, the lower riparian states.[74]

The Gujarat Legislature acting under Entries 22 (Industrial and Labour Disputes), 24 (welfare of labour) and 20 (economic and social planning) of List III applied the Bombay Relief Undertakings (Special Provisions) Act, 1958 with certain amendments to the State of Gujarat, section 4(1)(IV), of this Act enacted that the State Government may by notification direct that 'any right, privilege, obligation or liability accrued or incurred before the undertaking was declared a relief undertaking and any remedy for the enforcement thereof shall be suspended and all proceedings relative thereto pending before any court, tribunal, officer or authority shall be stayed'. In construing this provision it was held that though the Gujarat Legislature could confer an immunity upon an undertaking declared to be a relief undertaking effective within the State of Gujarat, it could not extend the

---

71. *Kavalappara Kottarathil Kochuni v. State of Madras*, AIR 1960 SC 1080, p. 1085 : 1960 (3) SCR 887.

72. *State of Karnataka v. Rangnatha Reddi*, AIR 1978 SC 215, p. 231 : (1977) 4 SCC 471. Even under the international law a Sovereign State cannot by legislation change title to a property situate in a different State; thus, compulsory acquisition of property to be recognised must be limited to properties within the State: *Williams and Humbert Ltd. v. W.P. and Trade Marks (Jersey) Ltd.*, (1986) 1 All ER 129, p. 133 : 1986 AC 368 : (1986) 2 WLR 24 (HL).

73. *In the matter of Cauvery Water Disputes Tribunal*, AIR 1992 SC 522 : 1993 Supp (1) SCC 96 (2) : 1991 (4) JT 361.

74. *Ibid*, pp. 544, 550, 552.

immunity so as to suspend obligations and liabilities incurred outside the state and to stay suits and proceedings instituted in respect of those liabilities outside the State.[75]

A law of one State may in certain circumstances have to be recognised and given effect to by courts in another State; but that by itself will not make such law extra-territorial. This principle can be illustrated by reference to a decision of the Supreme Court, where execution by a transferee court in Bihar of an order made by a special Judge of Uttar Pradesh under the U.P. Encumbered Estates Act, 1934, which was deemed to be decree of a civil court under the provisions of the said Act, was held to be valid; and it was held that the transferee court in Bihar has to take notice of the U.P. law for determining whether what was transferred to it for execution is a decree or not under the Civil Procedure Code.[76]

(b) Rule of construction

It may thus be taken as settled that laws enacted by Legislatures having no extra-territorial powers of legislation like those of colonies, Australian States, Canadian Provinces,[77] and States in the Indian Republic[78] must for their validity satisfy the test of real territorial nexus. In its application as a rule of construction, the principle is that if on one construction the statute offends the rule forbidding extra-territorial legislation, and if, by another construction, which may be open, such a result is avoided, the latter construction will be preferred.[79] Indeed the principle is a corollary of the more general rule that a Legislature is presumed not to have exceeded its constitutional powers and a construction consistent with those powers is to be put upon the laws enacted by the Legislature.[80]

In a well-known case,[81] the Legislature of New South Wales had enacted a law to the effect: 'whosoever being married, marries another person

---

75. *R.S.D.V. Finance Co. Pvt. Ltd. v. Shree Vallabh Glass Works,* AIR 1993 SC 2094, p. 2102 : 1993 (2) SCC 130.

76. *S.K. Sahgal v. Kishore Kumar*, AIR 1959 SC 809 : 1959 Supp (2) SCR 364. But if because of a statute law of the state in which the transferee court is located, the execution of decrees against the judgment-debtor is suspended, the execution of the transferred decree will also remain suspended; *Binod Mills Co. Ltd. v. Suresh Chandra Mahavir Prasad Mantri*, (1987) 3 SCC 99 : AIR 1987 SC 1739.

77. **See** title 4(a)(i) 'General', *ante*.

78. **See** title 4(a)(iii) 'Legislation under the Constitution of India', *ante*.

79. **See** cases discussed in text and notes 81-92, pp. 677-680, *infra*.

80. **See** title 3, 'Operation Controlled on considerations of constitutionality'; Presumption against excess of constitutional powers; *supra*.

81. *Macleod v. Att. General, of New South Wales*, (1891) AC 455 : 60 LJPC 55 : 65 LT 321 (PC).

during the life of the former husband or wife, wheresoever such second marriage take place, shall be liable to penal servitude for seven years'. The appellant in that case had married within the colony and contracted a bigamous marriage in America. Having been convicted within the colony he went up in appeal to the Privy Council and contended that the Act on its true construction was limited to offences committed within the jurisdiction of the local Legislature as upon any other construction, the statute will be *ultra vires*. In accepting this contention, the Privy Council observed that if the statute was construed upon the bare words, any person married to any other person, who married a second time anywhere in the habitable globe, was amenable to the criminal jurisdiction of New South Wales, if he could be caught in that colony. But said LORD HALSBURY: "That seems to their Lordships to be an impossible construction of the statute: the colony can have no such jurisdiction, and their Lordships do not desire to attribute to the colonial Legislature an effort to enlarge their jurisdiction to such an extent as would be inconsistent with the powers committed to a colony."[82] Proceeding further LORD HALSBURY observed: "The more reasonable theory to adopt is that the language was used, subject to the well-known and well-considered limitation that they were only legislating for those who were actually within their jurisdiction and within the limits of the colony."[83]

In another case in which certain provisions of an Insurance Act passed by the Ontario Legislature were challenged as *ultra vires*, the Privy Council said: The terms of the statute as a whole, are in their Lordships' judgment, capable of receiving a meaning according to which its provisions, whether enabling or prohibitive, apply only to persons and acts within the territorial jurisdiction of the province. In their opinion it ought to be interpreted in consonance with the presumption which imputes to the Legislature an intention of limiting the direct operation of its enactments to such persons or acts.[84]

Similarly, in a statute of the State of Victoria the word 'mortgage' though defined in general terms wide enough to cover "any mortgage of any land anywhere in the world" was restricted by construction to Victorian mortgages, as to hold otherwise would have been to attribute to the Victorian Legislature an intention to legislate in regard to matters outside its territorial jurisdiction.[85]

---

82. *Ibid*, p. 457.

83. *Ibid*, p. 459, **Cf.** *Sussex Peerage* case, 8 ER 1034 (HL); and *Trial of Earl Russel*, (1901) AC 446.

84. *A.G. for Ontario v. Reciprocal Insurers*, (1924) AC 328, p. 345 (PC).

85. *Mount Albert Borough Council v. Australian Temperance & General Mutual Life Assurance Society Ltd.*, (1937) 4 All ER 206, pp. 216, 217 : 1938 AC 224 (PC).

A further illustration of the principle can be seen in another Privy Council decision[86] relating to the construction of the word 'employer' in the Manitoba Special Income-tax Act, 1933. In sections 4, 5 and 6 of the Act where the duties of deduction of Income-tax, of accounting, of making returns and of keeping records were imposed under penalties on 'every employer', the word 'employer' was held on construction not to apply to any employer outside the province, as such employers were not subject to the legislative jurisdiction of the province of Manitoba for imposing any such duty or penalty.[87] But the word 'employer' in section 7 of the same Act where a duty was imposed on an employee within the province to pay the tax on receiving wages without the tax being deducted by 'his employer', was construed as referring to every employer wherever or whoever he may be, the reason being that this section did not seek to impose any duty on employers and was not *ultra vires* of the Provincial Legislature even on a wider construction of the word 'employer'.[88]

The principle was applied by the Supreme Court in upholding the validity of the Bihar Hindu Religious Trusts Act, 1951.[89] The Act by section 3 provides: 'This Act shall apply to all religious trusts, whether created before or after the commencement of the Act any part of the property of which is situated in the State of Bihar'. The argument was that the Act applied to every religious trust whether within or outside the State if any part of the property of the trust was in the State of Bihar, and the Act was *ultra vires* as it affected trusts outside the State. Negativing this argument, the Supreme Court construed the Act consistent with the presumption of constitutionality, and held that the Act applied to trusts "which are situate in the State of Bihar and any part of the property of which is in that State" making these two conditions cumulative.[90] Similarly, the definition of public trust in section 2(4) of the Madhya Pradesh Public Trusts Act, 1951, has been confined by construction to public trusts situate in the State of Madhya Pradesh.[91] These cases were referred to in interpreting section 1(5) of the Employees State Insurance Act, 1948. Section 1(4) applies the Act in the first instance to all factories and by section 1(5) provision is made for extending the Act to any other establishment by a notification of the appropriate Government. By a notification, the Government of Andhra

---

86. *Forbes v. A.G. of Manitoba*, (1937) 1 All ER 249 (PC).
87. *Ibid*, pp. 255, 256.
88. *Ibid*, p. 256.
89. *State of Bihar v. Charusiladasi*, AIR 1959 SC 1002 : 1959 Supp (2) SCR 601.
90. *Ibid*, p. 1010. **See further,** *State of Bihar v. Bhabapritnanda Ojha,* AIR 1959 SC 1073 : 1959 Supp (2) SCR 624.
91. *Anant Prasad v. State of Andhra Pradesh*, AIR 1963 SC 853, p. 859 : 1963 Supp (1) SCR 844.

Pradesh, which was the appropriate Government, extended the Act to Road Motor Transport Establishments. It was held that such a notification applied the Act to the Transport Corporation of India which had its head office or principal establishment in Andhra Pradesh and to all its branches in that State as also to all its branches outside the State which had functional integrality with the activities of the main establishment and were directly under the control and supervision of the main establishment and that such an interpretation did not give the notification any extra-territorial operation.[92]

5. OTHER RELEVANT CONSIDERATIONS RELATING TO OPERATION

(a) Presumption that Legislation is territorial

Even when the legislative competence is not restricted on considerations of territorial nexus, it is presumed that statutes are not intended, in the absence of contrary language or clear implication, to operate on events taking place or persons outside the territories to which the statutes are expressed to apply.[93] Thus, there is a general principle applicable to Income-tax Acts that either the source from which the taxable income is derived should be within the territorial limits of the country imposing the tax or the person whose income is to be taxed should be resident there.[94]

Section 10 of the Carriage by Air Act, 1961, enacted to give effect to the Hague Convention, empowered making of delegated legislation by order in council to apply the provisions of the Act with adaptations and modifications as may be specified to carriage by air (to which the convention

92. *Transport Corporation of India v. Employees State Insurance Corpn.*, JT 1999 (9) SC 15, pp. 34, 35 : (2000) 1 SCC 332 : AIR 2000 SC 238.

93. *Jagir Kaur v. Jaswant Singh*, AIR 1963 SC 1521, p. 1525 : (1964) 2 SCR 73; *CIT, Kerala v. Malayalam Plantation*, AIR 1964 SC 1722, p. 1725 : (1964) 7 SCR 693. **See further** *A.G. of the Province of Alberta v. Huggard Assets Ltd.*, (1953) 2 All ER 951, pp. 956, 957 : 1953 AC 420 (PC); *CEB Draper v. Edward Turner*, (1964) 3 All ER 148, pp. 150, 152 : (1965) QB 424 (CA) (An Act of the United Kingdom Parliament unless it provides otherwise applies to the whole of United Kingdom and to nothing outside the United Kingdom. It was, therefore, held that the words 'On the sale' in section 2(2) of the Fertilisers and Feeding Stuffs Act, 1926 (16 & 17 G 5, c 45), did not apply to sale of goods which took place outside the United Kingdom). But, as held in *BBC Enterprises Ltd. v. Hi Tech Extravision Ltd.*, (1991) 3 WLR 1, p. 8 (HL), there is no presumption that the Act will not apply to conduct or events taking place within United Kingdom which have consequential effects outside United Kingdom. **See further** *R (on the application of Al-S Keini) v. Secretary of State*, (2007) 3 All ER 685 (HL) discussed at p. 546, *supra*.

94. *Dawson v. Inland Revenue Commissioners*, (1988) 3 All ER 753, p. 758 : (1989) 2 WLR 481 (CA).

did not apply) of such description as may be specified in the order. In conformity with the rule against giving extra-territorial effect to legislation, section 10 was construed as authorising legislation limited to carriage wholly within the United Kingdom or non-convention carriage involving a place of departure or destination or an agreed stopping place in the United Kingdom or other British territory; and as not authorising legislation in respect of a contract of carriage made and to be performed wholly within the territory of a single foreign State or between two foreign States.[1]

The Code of Criminal Procedure, 1898, extends to the whole of India, and therefore, the words 'last resided' in section 488(8) of the Code were construed to mean last resided in the territories of India.[2] Similarly, section 77 of the Estate Duty Act, 1953, which empowers a person, required to pay estate duty in respect of property of some other person, to sell such property to raise the amount of the duty has been construed as not authorising sale of property belonging to a person domiciled outside India.[3]

The Monopolies and Restrictive Trade Practices Act, 1969 extends to the whole of India except the State of Jammu and Kashmir. The Act has no extra-territorial operation. Therefore, the MRTP Commission cannot exercise jurisdiction in respect of goods outside India until they are imported into India. But the Act also recognises 'effect doctrine' and if any agreement executed outside India has the effect of eliminating competition or competitor of the sale of goods in India and the same is prejudicial to public interest the commission has jurisdiction to enquire into it.[4] In other words, if the agreement executed outside India has resulted in a restrictive trade practice in India, the commission will have jurisdiction.[5]

(b) Operation as to foreigners: Regard to principles of International Law in that respect

The presumption that a statute is not intended to apply to persons outside the territories of the State enacting it, is particularly strong in case of foreigners, for as to them the normal presumption is further strengthened

---

1. *Holmes v. Bangladesh Biman Corp.*, (1989) 1 All ER 852 : (1989) 2 WLR 858 (HL).
2. *Jagir Kaur v. Jaswant Singh*, AIR 1963 SC 1521, p. 1525 : 1964 (2) SCR 73.
3. *C.I.T., Kerala v. Malayalam Plantation*, AIR 1964 SC 1722, p. 1725 : 1964 (7) SCR 693. **See Further** *Gwalior Dugdh Sangh Sahakari Ltd. v. G.M. Govt. Milk Scheme Nagpur*, (2003) 7 SCC 529 (Provision for reference of dispute to Registrar under section 64 of the M.P. Co-operative Societies Act, 1960 does not apply to the dispute relating to a contract which was entered outside Madhya Pradesh).
4. *Haridas Exports v. All India Float Glass Mfrs. Association*, AIR 2002 SC 2728, pp. 2739, 2741 : (2002) 6 SCC 600.
5. *Man Roland Druckimachinen A.G. v. Multi Colour Offset Ltd.*, (2004) 7 SCC 447, p. 458.

by another presumption that the Legislature intends to respect the rules of International Law.[6] Without anything more Indian statutes are ineffective against foreign property and foreigners outside the jurisdiction.[7]

Dealing with a case under bankruptcy legislation, JAMES, L.J. stated: "the broad general universal principle that: English legislation, unless the contrary is expressly enacted or so plainly implied as to make it the duty of an English court to give effect to an English statute, is applicable only to English subjects or to foreigners who by coming into this country, whether for a long or a short time, have made themselves during that time subject to English jurisdiction. Every foreigner who comes into this country, for however a limited time, is, during his residences here within the allegiance of the Sovereign, entitled to the protection of the Sovereign and subject to all the laws of the Sovereign. But, if a foreigner remains abroad, if he has never come into this country at all, it seems—impossible to imagine that the English Legislature could have ever intended to make such a man subject to a particular English legislation."[8] But the rule so stated is merely a rule of construction for example: "British tax liability has never been exclusively limited to British subjects and foreigners resident within the jurisdiction."[9]

In the words of LORD SELBORNE, no territorial legislation can give jurisdiction which any foreign court ought to recognise against foreigners, who owe no allegiance or obedience to the Power which so legislates.[10] It was, therefore, held that a decree obtained *in absentem* against a non-resident foreigner in a personal action was an absolute nullity and will be so regarded by the courts of every nation except (when authorised by special local legislation) in the country of the forum by which it was pronounced.[11] The

---

6. *General Iron Screw Collier Co. v. Schuramanns*, 70 ER 712, p. 716 (PAGE WOOD V.C.); *Grant v. Anderson & Co.*, (1892) 1 QB 108, p. 112 (LORD COLERIDGE, C.J.); *Wallace v. A.G.; Jeeves v. Shadwell,* (1865) LR 1 Ch 1, p. 9 (LORD CRANWORTH, L.C.); *Philipson Stow v. IRC*, (1960) 3 All ER 814, p. 821 (HL).
7. *Brithis India Steam Navigation Co. Ltd. v. Shanmughavilas Cashew Industries*, (1990) 3 SCC 481; *World Tanker Carrier Corporation v. SNP Shipping Services Pvt. Ltd.*, JT 1998 (3) SC 468, p. 476 : AIR 1998 SC 2330 : 1998 (5) SCC 310.
8. *Ex parte Blain*, (1879) 12 Ch D 522, p. 526; **referred** to in *Cooke v. Vogeler (Charles A) Co.,* (1901) AC 102 : (1900-03) All ER Rep 660, pp. 663, 664, 666 (HL); *Re Dulles' Settlement Trust, Dulles v. Vidler*, (1950) 2 All ER 1013, p. 1014 : (1951) 1 Ch 842 (CA). *Holmes v. Bangladesh Biman Corp.*, (1989) 1 All ER 852, pp. 857, 872 : (1989) 2 WLR 481 (HL).
9. *Clark (Inspector of Taxes) v. Oceanic Contractors Inc.,* (1883) 1 All ER 133 (HL), p. 138; *Agassi v. Robinson (Inspector of Taxes),* (2006) 3 All ER 97 (HL), p. 104 (para 16).
10. *Sirdar Gurdial Singh v. Raja of Faridkot*, ILR 22 Cal 222, p. 238 (PC); *Moloji Narsingh Rao v. Shankar Saran*, AIR 1962 SC 1737, p. 1742 : 1963 (2) SCR 577.
11. *Ibid.*

Supreme Court has, however, held that such a decree is not a nullity if it is authorised by the law of the country where it is passed; and that it may be more appropriate to say that the decree is not executable in courts of other countries.[12] The non-executability of a decree of a foreign court, which is valid according to the law of the country where it is passed, is merely a matter of procedure and when the place where the decree is passed and the place where it is sought to be executed become subsequently part of the same country governed by the same procedural law there would be no impediment in the execution of the decree in accordance with that law.[13]

A foreign judgment obtained in a personal action to have extra-territorial validity must satisfy at least one of the following conditions: (i) The defendant was a subject of the foreign country; (ii) The defendant was resident in the foreign country at the time when the action was begun against him; (iii) The defendant was served with process while temporarily present in the foreign country for even a short period; (iv) The defendant in his character as plaintiff in the foreign action himself selected the forum where the judgment was given against him; (v) The defendant voluntarily appeared; (vi) The defendant had contracted to submit to the jurisdiction of the foreign court.[14] When a defendant voluntarily submitted to the jurisdiction in respect of a claim in the foreign proceedings, he could also be taken to have submitted to jurisdiction of the foreign court in respect of claims arising out of the same subject matter and to related claims.[15] The presence of a foreign defendant who appears under protest to contest jurisdiction cannot be considered as conferring jurisdication on the court to take action.[16] A foreign judgment in a personal action to be conclusive in India has to be on merits.[17] But where the subject-matter is a *res* so situated as to be within lawful control of the State, the courts of that State have generally jurisdiction to decide about it.[18] The courts of a country generally impose a threefold restriction upon the exercise of their jurisdiction: (1)

---

12. *Lalji Raja & Sons v. Hansraj Nathuram*, AIR 1971 SC 974, p. 977 : (1971) 1 SCC 721.

13. *Ibid, Narhari Shivram Shet Narvekar v. Pannalal Umediram*, AIR 1977 SC 164 : (1976) 3 SCC 203.

14. HALSBURY'S Laws of England, Vol. VII (3rd Edition), pp. 144, 145, (para 257); *Moloji Narsingh Rao v. Shankar Saran*, AIR 1962 SC 1737, p. 1741 : (1963) 2 SCR 577. For jurisdiction over a Stateless infant, **see** *Re, P (GE) (an infant)*, (1964) 3 All ER 977 (CA).

15. *Murthi v. Sivajoti*, (1999) 1 All ER 721 (CA).

16. *World Tanker Carrier Corporation v. SNP Shiping Services Pvt. Ltd.*, JT 1998 (3) SC 468, p. 482 : AIR 1998 SC 2330 : (1998) 5 SCC 310 (case of a limitation action under Part XA of the Merchant Shipping Act, 1958 filed in the Bombay High Court under its Admirality jurisdiction).

17. *International Woolen Mills v. Standard Wool (UK) Ltd.*, AIR 2001 SC 2134 : (2001) 2 SCC 642.

18. *Ingenohl v. Wing On & Co.*, AIR 1928 PC 83, p. 85.

Jurisdiction in *res* (binding not only the parties but the world at large) by a court over *res* outside the jurisdiction will not be exercised, because it will not be recognised by other courts; (2) The court will not deal directly or indirectly with title to immovable property outside the jurisdiction of the State from which it derives its authority; and (3) The court will not assist in the enforcement within its jurisdiction of foreign penal or revenue law.[19] It has, therefore, been held that a court in India has no jurisdiction to refer to arbitration a claim to immovable property situate in Burma.[20]

The courts in England will disregard a foreign law, on grounds of public policy, if it is against basic principles of justice and fairness applied in administration of justice by English courts, *e.g.*, against a fundamental principle of international law judged by contemporary standards.[21]

Under Article 16(1) of the Convention on Jurisdiction and the Enforcement of Judgments in Civil and Commercial Matters, 1968 (the Brussels Convention), enforced in the United Kingdom by the Civil Jurisdiction and Judgments Act, 1982, in proceedings which have as their object rights in rem in immovable property or tenancies of immovable property, the court of the State in which the property is situated have exclusive jurisdiction. Interpreting Article 16(1), it has been held by the Court of Justice of the European Communities that for the Article to apply the action must be based on a right *in rem* and not a right *in personam*, save in the case of an exception concerning tenancies.[22] It was, therefore, ruled that an action brought in England by a father against his son that a flat in France in the name of the son was held by him for the exclusive benefit of the father and the son was under a duty to execute documents necessary to convey ownership of the flat to the father, was not barred by Article 16(1).[23]

But regard to the International Law is possible only when the municipal law does not provide contrary to it. As stated by LORD ESHER, M.R.: "The question whether courts of a nation will or will not entertain jurisdiction of any dispute is to be determined exclusively by the nation itself, *i.e.* by its municipal law. If by express legislation the courts are directed to exercise jurisdiction, the courts must obey. If there is a proper inference to the same effect, the result is the same."[24] The Code of Civil Procedure, 1908, permits a personal action to be filed in a court within whose jurisdiction

---

19. *Vishwanathan v. Abdul Wajid*, AIR 1963 SC 1, p. 16 : 1963 (3) SCR 22.
20. *Nachiappa v. Subramaniam*, AIR 1960 SC 307 : 1960 (2) SCR 209.
21. *Kuwait Airways Corp. v. Iraqi Airways Co. (No. 3)*, (2002) 3 All ER 209, pp. 216 to 218 (HL).
22. *Webb v. Webb*, (1994) 3 All ER 911, p. 930 (CJEC).
23. *Ibid.*
24. *Compania de Mozambique v. British South Africa Co.*, (1892) 2 QBD 358, p. 394.

'the cause of action wholly or partly arises', and it has been held that a suit can be entertained by an Indian court against a non-resident foreigner if cause of action for the suit arises within the local limits of the Indian court.[25] The principles of International Law are administered by the municipal courts only at the sufferance of municipal law and they can be pressed in aid to limit the apparent generality of municipal legislation when it is ambiguous or when there is doubt as to its meaning[26] for it is highly unlikely that Parliament intends to require the courts to act contrary to International Law unless the clear language of the statute compels such a conclusion;[27] but when the language of municipal legislation is clear it cannot be restricted in operation by referring to the principles of International Law; and the courts are bound to give effect to the legislation of their State in spite of it being contrary to or inconsistent with any principle of International Law, and in spite of there being difficulties regarding the effective enforcement of their decrees or orders.[28]

As regards foreign states or sovereigns the modern trend is to apply the restrictive theory of immunity and to distinguish between acts *jure imperii* and acts *jure gestionis* and to restrict the immunity to the former.[29] In U.K. the matter is now governed by the State Immunity Act, 1978.[30] In India, as provided in section 86 of the Code of Civil Procedure, 1908 a foreign state cannot be sued except with the consent of the Central Government certified in writing by a Secretary to that Government. Consent to sue cannot be given unless it appears to the Central Government that the foreign state: (a) has instituted a suit in the court against the person desiring to sue it; or (b) by itself or another, trades within the local limits of the jurisdiction of

---

25. *Girdhar Damodar v. Kassigar Hiragar*, (1893) ILR 17 Bom 662, p. 666; **approved** in *Annamali Chetty v. Murugesa Chetty*, (1903) ILR 26 Mad 544, p. 552 (PC). **See further** *Vishwanathan v. Abdul Wajid*, AIR 1961 SC 1, p.16 (paras 18 and 20) : (1962) 1 SCR 929; *Lalji Raja & Sons v. Hansraj Nathuram*, AIR 1971 SC 974, p. 977 : (1971) 1 SCC 721.

26. A statute, if possible should be construed to promote the rights included in the Universal Declaration of Human Rights: *R. v. Secretary of State*, (1975) 3 All ER 497, p. 511 (CA).

27. *Alcan Ltd. v. Republic of Colombia*, (1984) 2 All ER 6, pp. 9, 10 (HL).

28. *Theophile v. Solicitor General*, (1950) 1 All ER 405, pp. 407, 408 (HL); *Collco Dealings Ltd. v. IRC*, (1961) 1 All ER 762 (HL), p. 765; *Gramophone Co. of India Ltd. v. Birendra Bahadur Pandey*, (1984) 2 SCC 534, pp. 540, 541 : AIR 1984 SC 667.

29. *Philipine Admiral (owners) v. Wallen Shipping (Hongkong) Ltd.*, (1976) 1 All ER 78 (PC); *Congreso Del Partido*, (1983) AC 244 (HL).

30. The immunity under the Act covers anything done in the exercise of 'sovereign authority'. Thus, acts in exercise of statutory authority are not protected; **see** *Kuwait Airways Corp. v. Iraqi Airways Co.*, (1995) 3 All ER 694 : (1995) 1 WLR 1147 : (1995) 2 Lloyd's 317 (HL).

the court; or (c) is in possession of immovable property situate within those limits and is to be sued with reference to such property or money charged thereon; or (d) has expressly or impliedly waived the privilege accorded to it. The immunity under section 86 also covers foreign corporations which are state owned and are like government departments.[31] Having regard to the modern trend of taking a restricted view of state immunity, the Supreme court has ruled that consent to sue should generally be granted if conditions of the section are satisfied.[32]

(b1) Regard to International agreements or conventions and International Law[33]

The power of entering into a treaty or international agreement or convention is a sovereign power of the State and this power in India is exercised by the President as a part of the Executive power of the Union under Article 73 of the Constitution and does not need the necessity of legislative backing for its exercise.[34] A change in the form of Government of a contracting State does not put an end to its treaties. Therefore, treaties entered into by the British Government prior to 15.8.1947 or 26.1.1950 on behalf of India are still subsisting and operative.[35] But the terms of a treaty or convention do not form part of the municipal law unless they are enforced directly by legislation enacted by Parliament under Article 253 and Entries 10 and 14 of List I of the Seventh Schedule or by delegated legislation made under it.[36] But rules of international law or even specific treaty obligations by themselves do not restrict the legislative power of Parliament. The well settled interpretation of an existing law is not affected by subsequent ratification of an international treaty on grounds of inconsistency

---

31. *Veb Deautfracht Seereederei Rostock (D.S.P. Lines) a Department of the German Democratic Republic v. New Central Jute Mills Co. Ltd.*, AIR 1994 SC 516 : 1994 (1) SCC 282.

32. *Harbhajan Singh Dhalla v. Union of India*, AIR 1987 SC 9 : 1986 (4) SCC 678; *Shanti Prasad Agarwalla v. Union of India*, AIR 1991 SC 814 : 1991 Supp (2) SCC 296.

33. JUSTICE S.B. SINHA, 'A Contextualised Look at the Application of the International Law : The Indian Approach', 2004 AIR Journal 33.

34. *Union of India v. Azadi Bachao Andolan*, AIR 2004 SC 1107, 1119 : 2003 Supp (2) SCC 205. (India - Mauritius Double Taxation Avoidance Agreement. Grant of specific exemption in terms of the Agreement by Parliament not necessary. Section 9 of the Income-tax Act, 1961 empowers the Central Government to issue a notification for implementation of the Agreement). **See further** *DTI (International Taxation) Mumbai v. Morgan Stanley & Co. Inc.*, (2007) 7 SCC 1 (Indo-US Double Taxation Avoidance Agreement. What constitutes service Permanent Establishment (PE) of a US company in India?)

35. *Suman Sood v. State of Rajasthan,* (2007) 5 SCC 634 (paras 22, 23) : (2007) 5 SLT 522 : (2007) 7 JT 101 : (2007) 9 JT 453. (The extradition treaty between India and United States of America entered in the year 1931 is still operative).

36. *Ibid.*, pp. 1121, 1122.

with it unless the Legislature modifies the law to bring it in accord with treaty obligations.[37] Therefore, if the terms of a statute are clear and unambiguous, they must be given effect to whether or not they carry out the State's treaty obligations, for the sovereign power of legislation extends to breaking treaties and any remedy for a breach of an international obligation lies in a forum other than the State's Municipal Courts.[38] If the terms of the legislation are not clear, however, and are reasonably capable of more than one meaning, the treaty itself becomes relevant, for there is a *prima facie* presumption that Parliament does not intend to act in breach of International Law, including therein specific treaty obligation; and if one of the meanings which can reasonably be ascribed to the legislation is consonant with the treaty obligations and another or others are not, the meaning which is consonant is to be preferred.[39] This is all the more relevant in India for Article 51(c) of the Constitution lays down as one of the directive principles of State Policy that "the State shall endeavour to foster respect for International Law and treaty obligations in the dealings of organised people with one another". This directive though not enforceable by courts can be kept in view in interpreting other parts of the Constitution and statutes made under it which are reasonably capable of more than one meaning.[40] Indeed, it has been said that "the courts are under an obligation to give due regard to international conventions and norms for construing domestic laws more so when there is no inconsistency between them and there is a void in domestic law."[41] The Proclamation on the Full Participation

---

37. *Sakshi v. Union of India*, (2004) 5 SCC 518, pp. 534 (para 15) : AIR 2004 SC 3566.

38. *Saloman v. Commr. of Customs and Excise*, (1966) 3 All ER 871, p. 875 (CA). **See further,** *R. v. Lyons*, (2002) 4 All ER 1029, p. 1040 (HL).

39. *Saloman v. Commr. of Customs and Excise*, (1966) 3 All ER 871, p. 875 (CA); *Kubic Dariusz v. Union of India*, AIR 1990 SC 605, p. 615 : (1990) 1 SCC 568; *Chairman Railway Board v. Chandrima Das*, AIR 2000 SC 988, p. 997 : (2000) 2 SCC 465. **See further** *Benin v. Whimster*, (1975) 3 All ER 706, p. 712 (CA); *R. v. Chief Immigration Officer, Heathrow Airport, Ex parte, Salamat Bibi*, (1976) 3 All ER 843, p. 847 (CA); *A.G. v. B.B.C.*, (1980) 3 All ER 161, p. 176 : (1980) 3 WLR 109 (HL); *R. v. Crown Court at Southwark*, (1989) 3 All ER 673, pp. 677, 678 (QBD); *Brind v. Secretary of State*, (1999) 1 All ER 720, pp. 722, 723 (HL); *R. v. Lyons*, (2002) 4 All ER 1029, p. 1040 (HL).

40. *Peoples Union for Civil Liberties v. Union of India*, AIR 1997 SC 568, p. 575 : 1997 (1) SCC 301 (Telephone tapping permitted by section 5(2) of the Indian Telegraph Act, 1885 was severely regulated by directions of the court having regard to right to privacy implicit in Article 21 and recognised by Article 17 of International Covenant on Civil and Political Rights, 1966 as also by Article 12 of Universal Declaration of Human Rights, 1948); *Nair Service Society v. State of Kerala*, (2007) 4 SCC 1 (para 33) : (2007) 3 SLT 730 : (2007) 6 JT 103. (Relevance of International law in interpreting domestic legislation "in a grey area cannot be lost sight of.")

41. *Apparel Export Promotion Council v. A.K. Chopra*, JT 1999 (1) SC 61, p. 74 : AIR 1999 SC 625, p. 634 : (1999) 1 SCC 579. **See further** *Githa Hariharan v. Reserve Bank of India*, JT 1999 (1) SC 524, p. 532 : 1999 AIR SC 1149 : (1999) 2 SCC 228.

and Equality of People with Disabilities in the Region, to which India is a signatory, which was adopted in 1992 at a meeting held in Beijing by the Economic and Social Commission for Asian and Pacific Region, was used for applying the Persons with Disabilities (Equal Opportunities Protection of Rights and Full Participation) Act, 1995 and in directing the Indian Airlines to grant to persons suffering from locomotor disability to the extent of 80% the same concession which the Airlines was giving to those suffering from blindness.[42] Article 13 of the Universal Declaration of Human Rights which declares that everyone has a right to freedom of opinion and expression 'regardless of frontiers' was referred to in holding that the right of freedom of speech and expression guaranteed by Article 19(1)(*a*) of the Constitution is not restricted to the territory of India.[43] And, Article 11 of the International Covenant on Civil and Political Rights, which provides that no one shall be imprisoned *merely* on the ground of inability to fulfil a contractual obligation has greatly influenced the court in giving a limited meaning to section 51 and order 21 Rule 37 of the Code of Civil Procedure.[44] Article 9(5) of the same covenant which says that "any one who has been the victim of unlawful arrest or detention shall have an enforceable right to compensation" has been referred to in support of the view that damages can be allowed under Articles 32 and 226 of the Constitution for violation of the Fundamental Right in Article 21.[45] Article 6(1) of the European Convention on Human Rights and Fundamental Freedoms, 1950 which provides for right to a fair trial by an independent and impartial tribunal was referred to for deducing the same right from Article 14 of the Constitution.[46] The International Convention on the Rights of Child accepted by India, which aims at protecting not merely the child's social and political rights but also extends protection to child's economic,

---

42. *Javed Abidi v. Union of India*, AIR 1999 SC 512, p. 514 : (1999) 1 SCC 467 **see further** pp. 928, 929, *post*, for use of international conventions for construing welfare legislations.

43. *Maneka Gandhi v. Union of India*, AIR 1978 SC 597, p. 637 : (1978) 1 SCC 248.

44. *Jolly George Verghese v. Bank of Cochin*, AIR 1980 SC 470 : 1980 (2) SCC 360.

45. *Nilabati Behra v. State of Orissa*, AIR 1993 SC 1960 : (1993) 2 SCC 746; *Peoples Union for Civil Liberties v. Union of India*, AIR 1997 SC 1203, pp. 1207, 1208 : (1997) 3 SCC 433. ("The provisions of the covenant, which elucidate and go to effectuate the Fundamental Rights guaranteed by our Constitution can certainly be relied upon by courts as facets of those Fundamental Rights and enforceable as such").

46. *Dwarka Prasad Agarwala v. B.D. Agarwala*, (2003) 6 SCC 230, pp. 245, 246 : AIR 2003 SC 2686 [The court may have more appropriately referred to Article 14 of the International Covenant on Civil and Political Rights, 1966 to which India is a party and which also forms part of the definition of Human Rights in section 2(d) read with section 2(f), of the Protection of Human Rights Act, 1993. Article 14 (**quoted** in N.B. 2, p. 759) is similarly worded as Article 6(1) of the European Convention which is quoted at note 59, p. 545].

social, cultural and humanitarian rights, was referred to while interpreting the Child Labour (Prohibition and Regulation) Act, 1986.[47] In a case where guidelines were issued to prevent sexual harassment of women and to enable gender equality in employment, the court referred to Articles 11, 24 and general recommendations 22, 23 and 24 in that respect of the Convention on the Elimination of All Forms of Discrimination against Women and observed: "Any International Convention not inconsistent with the Fundamental Rights and in harmony with its spirit must be read into these provisions (Articles 14, 15, 19 and 21 of the Constitution) to enlarge the meaning and content thereof, to promote the object of constitutional guarantee".[48] The aforesaid Convention on the Elimination of All Forms of Discrimination against Women which was ratified by India in June, 1993 was also relied upon in construing section 6 of the Hindu Minority and Guardianship Act, 1956 and in holding that mother's right of guardianship as a natural guardian of minor's person or property does not arise only after the lifetime of the father but can arise during his lifetime also.[49] Article 11 of the same convention was also relied upon in interpreting the Maternity Benefits Act, 1951 and it was also said that the principles contained in Article 11 have to be read into the contract of service between the Delhi Municipal Corporation and the women employees.[50] Article 1 of the Declaration on the Right to Development adopted by the World Conference on Human Rights and Article 18 of the International Covenant on Civil and Political Rights, 1966 were relied upon in support of the decision that section 118 of the Succession Act, 1925 which imposes restrictions on christians alone in the matter of making bequests for religious and charitable purposes is violative of Article 14 of the Constitution.[51] If States are parties to a convention which permits a foreigner when sentenced to imprisonment for a crime to be transferred to the State of which he is the citizen for serving out the sentence on humanitarian grounds, it may not be proper to detain him under a preventive detention law instead of prosecuting him for a criminal offence as that will deprive him of the beneficial provisions of the convention of being transferred to his home State.[52] But unless

---

47. *M.C. Mehta v. State of Tamil Nadu,* AIR 1997 SC 699, pp. 705, 706 : (1996) 6 SCC 756. **See further,** for this case text and note 25, p. 938, *post.*

48. *Vishaka v. State of Rajasthan,* AIR 1997 SC 3011, p. 3014 : 1997 (6) SCC 241.

49. *Githa Hariharan v. Reserve Bank of India,* AIR 1999 SC 1149 : JT 1999 (1) SC 524, p. 532 : (1999) 2 SCC 228.

50. *Municipal Corporation of Delhi v. Female Workers (Muster Roll),* AIR 2000 SC 1274, p. 1283 : (2000) 3 SCC 224; International treaties *vis-à-vis* the rights of women and cases discussed above were noticed again in *Anuj Garg v. Hotel Association of India,* (2008) 3 SCC 1 paras 10 to 16 : AIR 2008 SC 663.

51. *John Vallamattom v. Union of India,* (2003) 6 SCC 611, p. 624 : AIR 2003 SC 2902.

52. *Kubic Dariusz v. Union of India,* AIR 1990 SC 605, p. 615 : 1990 (1) SCC 568.

Parliament enacts a law to enforce the provisions of an International Convention or Treaty, the convention or the treaty does not become part of the country's domestic law and its provisions cannot be directly applied by the courts.[53] The common law as also section 78 of the Police and Criminal Evidence Act, 1984 of the United Kingdom permits relevant evidence to be admitted in a criminal trial even though it was improperly or unlawfully obtained unless the court rules it out on the ground of having an adverse effect on the fairness of the trial. Article 8 of the European Convention for the Protection of Human Rights and Fundamental Freedoms, 1950 to which U.K. is a party, briefly stated, provides for right to privacy. The House of Lords, before the convention was enforced as law in U.K., held that in spite of the convention, tape recorded conversation, obtained by installing electronic listening device in a private house without the knowledge of owner or occupier was admissible in the trial as the trial court in its discretion did not exclude it on the ground that it would have adverse effect on the fairness of the trial.[54] But if a convention incorporates principles derived from the common law of nations as embodying the felt necessities of the international trade they may be applied as common law of India even if the convention has not been adopted by legislation.[55]

The Supreme Court in some of its judgments[56] has referred to objectives of the judiciary formulated in the Beijing statement of Principles of the Independence of the Judiciary in Law Asia region which were accepted by the Chief Justices of the Asia and the Pacific at Beijing in 1995 and has also drawn some inspiration from them. These objectives are: "(a) to ensure that all persons are able to live securely under the Rule of law; (b) to promote within the proper limits of the judicial function, the observance and the attainment of human rights and to administer the law impartially among persons and between persons and the State". It is extremely doubtful if the judges can enlarge their jurisdiction by decisions taken and agreed to by them in an international conference of judges. Further, the objectives formulated at Beijing do not really go beyond what is contemplated by the oath which a judge in India takes at the time of entering upon

---

53. *M. v. H.*, (1988) 3 All ER 5, pp. 15, 16 (HL); *Maclaine Watson & Co. Ltd. v. Department of Trade and Industry*, (1989) 3 All ER 523 (HL).

54. *R. v. Khan (Sultan)*, (1996) 3 All ER 289 : (1997) AC 558 : (1996) 3 WLR 162 (HL). **See further** *R. v. P.*, (2001) 2 All ER 58 (HL) (similar view taken after the convention became law under the Human Rights Act, 1998).

55. *M.V. Elisabeth v. Harvan Investment & Trading Pvt. Ltd. Goa*, AIR 1993 SC 1014, p. 1036 : (1992) 2 JT 65 : 1993 Supp (2) SCC 433.

56. *Vishaka v. State of Rajasthan*, AIR 1997 SC 3011 : 1997 (6) SCC 241; *Vineet Narain v. Union of India*, JT 1997 (10) SC 247, p. 290 : AIR 1998 SC 889, p. 916 : (1998) 1 SCC 226.

his office to perform the duties of his office without fear or favour, affection or ill will and to uphold the Constitution and the laws.

In a judicial colloquim held at Bangalore in December, 1998 certain principles, 22 in number, known as 'Bangalore Principles'[57] were formulated. Principle No. 2 declares: 'It is the vital duty of judiciary to interpret and apply national constitutions and ordinary legislation in harmony with international human rights codes and customary international law, and to develop the common law in the light of the values and principles enshrined in international human rights law.' The comment relating to Beijing statement of Principles also applies to Bangalore Principles.

A survey of the Indian cases will show that International Law and International Conventions have been used not only for interpretation of statutes but also for interpretation of the Constitution[58] which has been facilitated because of Article 51(c) and incorporation of fundamental rights in the Constitution. In Australia although recourse to international law can be taken for interpretation of statutes, the High Court has so far not accepted the position that the international law or international conventions can be used for interpretation of the Australian Constitution.[59]

The High Court of Australia in *Minister of State for Immigration and Ethnic Affairs v. Teoh,* (1995) 183 CLR 273, appears to have taken the view that the entry into a treaty may give rise to a legitimate expectation that administrative decision makers will make decisions consistent with the treaties ratified by Australia. This view was resented by politicians and Bills were introduced to overturn it.[60] The Australian case and the criticism that it invited were noticed by the Supreme Court in *Punjab Communications Ltd. v. Union of India.*[61] In England also the benefit of Article 31 of the Convention on the Status of Refugees, which was not incorporated into English Law, was held to be available, in accordance with the developing doctrine of legitimate expectation, to prevent imposition of penalties on the refugees who present themselves without delay to the authorities and

---

57. ANTHONY LESTER, 'The Bangalore Principles', 'Constitutionalism, Human Rights and the Rule of Law (Essays in the honour of Soli J. Sorabjee),' p. 48 (Universal Law Publishing Co.).

58. **See** cases in notes 40 to 52, pp. 687 to 689.

59. *Polites v. The Commonwealth,* (1945) 70 CLR 60. **See further** *Al-Katale v. Godown,* (2004) 7 SALJR 1099, pp. 1112, 1128, for opposing views on this question by MC HUGH J. and KIRBY J. in his Grotius Lecture for the American Society of International Law (April, 2005) KIRBY J. has referred to this controversy.

60. *Stephen Bouwhuis, 'International Law by the Back Door'*, (1998) 72 ALJ 794.

61. AIR 1999 SC 1801, p. 1812 : (1999) 4 SCC 727.

show good cause for their illegal entry or presence.[62] But the benefit of a provision in a convention, which has been enacted into law, has not been allowed on the doctrine of legitimate expectation when the provision was yet to come into force as part of the law on a notification issued by the executive Government.[63]

Though the courts will strive when they can to interpret statutes as conforming with the obligations under the convention, they are nevertheless bound to give effect to statutes which are free from ambiguity in accordance with their terms even if those statutes may be in conflict with the convention.[64] Further, the rule that the Legislature does not intend to depart from inter-State agreements does not furnish any useful aid when the agreement is about taxation which, by its own terms, is subordinated to the approval of the respective Legislatures of the States concerned and persists only so long as its terms are maintained in force as law by those Legislatures.[65]

(b2) Acts passed to give effect to international treaties and conventions

The interpretation of international treaties and conventions is governed by Articles 31 and 32 of the Vienna Convention on the Law of Treaties of 1969. The convention in terms applies to the treaties concluded after it came into force but as Articles 31 and 32 do no more than codify already existing public international law[66] they have been referred even for interpreting treaties and conventions concluded earlier.[67] These Articles read as follows:[68]

Article 31: *General rule of Interpretation*

'1. A treaty shall be interpreted in good faith in accordance with the ordinary meaning to be given to the terms of the treaty in their context and in the light of its object and purpose.

2. The context for the purpose of the interpretation of a treaty shall comprise, in addition to the text, including its preamble and annexes: (a) any agreement relating to the treaty which was made between all the parties in

62. *R. v. UxBridge Magistrates' court exp Adimi,* (1999) 4 All ER 520 (QBD). For doctrine of legitimate expectation **see further** pp. 505-511, *ante.*
63. *R. v. Director of Public Prosecutions exparte Kebeline,* (1999) 4 All ER 801, pp. 811, 825, 833 (HL).
64. *M. v. H., supra.*
65. *Collco Dealings Ltd. v. IRC,* (1961) 1 All ER 762, p. 768 : (1981) AC 251 : (1980) 3 WLR 209 (HL); *Woodent v. IRC,* (1970) 2 All ER 801, p. 808 (PC).
66. *Fothergill v. Monarch Airlines,* (1980) 2 All ER 696, p. 707 (HL) (LORD DIPLOCK).
67. *Ibid.*
68. **See** *Sepet v. Secretary of State for the Home Department,* (2003) 3 All ER 304, pp. 309, 310 (HL).

connection with the conclusion of the treaty; (b) any instrument which was made by one or more parties in connection with the conclusion of the treaty and accepted by the other parties as an instrument related to the treaty.

3. There shall be taken into account together with the context: (a) any subsequent agreement between the parties regarding the interpretation of the treaty or the application of its provisions; (b) any subsequent practice in the application of the treaty which establishes the agreement of the parties regarding its interpretation; (c) any relevant rules of international law applicable in the relations between the parties.

4. A special meaning shall be given to a term if it is established that the parties so intended.'

Article 32: *Supplementary means of interpretation*

'Recourse may be had to supplementary means of interpretation, including the preparatory work of the treaty and the circumstances of its conclusion, in order to confirm the meaning resulting from the application of article 31, or to determine the meaning when the interpretation according to article 31: (a) leaves the meaning ambiguous or obscure; or (b) leads to a result which is manifestly absurd or unreasonable.'

When statutes are enacted to give effect to a treaty or convention, Articles 31 and 32 of the Vienna Convention become relevant also for interpretation of such statutes.[69] The rule stated by the House of Lords is that if there be any difference between the language of the statutory provision and that of the corresponding provision of the convention, the statutory language should be construed in the same sense as that of the convention if the words of the statute are reasonably capable of bearing that meaning.[70] "The court must search untramelled by notions of its national legal culture, for the true, autonomous and international meaning of the treaty. And, there can only be one true meaning."[71] It has further been held that the correct approach in

---

69. *R. v. Secretary of State for the Home Department exparte Adan,* (1999) 4 All ER 774, p. 785 (CA); *Applicant v. Minister for Immigration,* (1997) 71 ALJR 381, p. 383.

70. *Jade* (1976) 1 All ER 920, p. 924 (HL); *Quazi v. Quazi*, (1979) 3 All ER 897, p. 903 (HL); *Garland v. British Rail Engineering Ltd.*, (1982) 2 All ER 402, p. 415 : (1983) 2 AC 751 : (1982) 2 WLR 918 (HL); *Kuwait Minister of Public Works v. Sir Frederick Snow*, (1984) 1 All ER 733, p. 738 (HL); *Antonis Plemos*, (1985) 1 All ER 895, p. 703 (HL); *Marshall v. Southampton A.H.A.*, (1986) 2 All ER 584 (CJEC), p. 592 (AG). **But see** *Katikuro of Bunganda v. Attorney General*, (1960) 3 All ER 849, p. 855 (PC).

71. *R. (on the application of Mullen) v. Secretary of State for the Home Department*, (2004) 1 All ER 65, p. 84 (LORD STEYN) [construction of section 133 of the Criminal Justice Act, 1985 which gives effect to Article 14(6) of the International Covenant on Civil and Political Rights, 1966].

construing a United Kingdom statute which incorporates and gives effect to a European convention is to interpret the English text as set out in the statute in the normal manner appropriate for interpretation of an international convention, unconstrained by technical rules of English law or by legal precedent but on broad principles of general acceptation.[72]

The same method was adopted in construing the Carriage by Air Act, 1961 which was enacted to give effect to the Warsaw Convention. The Act sets out the convention in a schedule in two parts. Part I sets out the English text and Part II, the French text. In case of inconsistency, the Act says that the French text is to prevail. The House of Lords held that in dealing with such an Act, a purposive construction should be applied and reference could be made to the opinion of international jurists as also to *travaux preparatoires* of the convention in a limited sense.[73] The court also noticed that this practice was consistent with Articles 31 and 32 of the Vienna Convention on the Law of Treaties.[74] In considering claims by passengers of an international flight which were outside the Warsaw Convention and were based on common law for personal injury, the House of Lords held that the claims were not maintainable having regard to the objects and structure of the convention which was intended to be exclusive also of any resort to the rules of domestic law.[75] In the words of LORD HOPE: "The language used and the subject matter with which it deals demonstrate that what was sought to be achieved was a uniform international code, which could be applied by courts of all the High Contracting Parties without reference to the rules of their own domestic law."[76] A question arose in this case[77] whether mental injury such as stress and psychological damage

---

72. *James Buchanon & Co. Ltd. v. Babco Forwarding & Shipping (U.K.) Ltd.*, (1977) 3 All ER 1048 : (1978) AC 141 : (1977) 3 WLR 907 (HL); *Hollandia*, (1982) 3 All ER 1141, p. 1145 (HL). **See further** *C. v. C.*, (1989) 2 All ER 465 : (1989) 1 WLR 654 (CA); *Sepet v. Secretary of State for the Home Department,* (2003) 3 All ER 304,
pp. 309, 310 (HL).

73. *Fothergill v. Monarch Airlines*, (1980) 2 All ER 696 : (1981) AC 251 : (1980) 3 WLR 209 (HL); **see further** *Effort Shipping Co. Ltd. v. Linden Management SA*, (1998) 1 All ER 495, p. 509 (HL) (Travaux preparatories to be admissible should clearly and indisputably point to a definite legal intention); *Re H,* (2000) 2 All ER 1, p. 24 (HL) (Purposive construction); *Re Burke,* (2000) 3 All ER 481, p. 486 (HL) (Liberal construction according to its language, object and intent); *Horvath v. Secretary of State for the Home Department,* (2000) 3 All ER 577, p. 580 (HL) (Broad meaning in the light of the purposes and as far as possible uniformly by national courts of all covenanting states).

74. *Fothergill v. Monarch Airlines, supra,* p. 706, 707.

75. *Sidhu v. British Airway, plc.,* (1997) 1 All ER 193 : (1997) AC 430 : (1997) 2 WLR 26 (HL).

76. *Ibid,* p. 212.

77. *Ibid,* p. 201.

were bodily injury within Article 17 of the Convention[78] for which damages could be allowed but that question was not decided as the claims were outside the Convention because of lapse of time and other reasons. That question, however, arose for decision in a later case.[79] Consistent with the principle that the Convention should as far as possible be given a common construction in all jurisdictions and giving more importance to American decisions because of the United States being a large participant in carriage by air, the House of Lords held that when a mental injury or illness lacked a physical cause or origin it could not constitute a 'bodily injury' redressable under Article 17 but that expression did cover physical manifestations of a mental injury, *e.g.*, peptic ulcer and psychiatric disorders arising from injury to brain or nervous system which are as much part of the body as any other part.[80] The word 'accident' in Article 17 of the convention has also been construed in the light of the decision of the United States' Supreme Court in *Air Frans v. Saks*,[81] to comprise of two elements: "(1) There must be an event, (2) The event must be unusual, unexpected or untoward."[82] On this analysis it was held that the existence of permanent integral features of the aircraft such as cramped seating, alterations of air pressure, atmosphere and temperature or the subjecting of passengers to carriage in aircraft with those features were not capable of amounting to events that satisfied the first limb of the definition of an accident and the passengers suffering Deep Vein Thrombosis (DVT) because of these reasons were not entitled to damages.[83] Carriage of a person by helicopter[84] or by a tandem glider[85] or by a hot air baloon[86] would amount to carriage of passenger by aircraft.

The explanatory report published, along with the text of the Convention on the transfer of sentenced persons, by the committee by whom the Convention was drawn up was admitted as an aid to construction as part

---

78. *Article 17:* 'The carrier is liable for damage sustained in the event of death or wounding of a passenger or any *other bodily injury* suffered by a passenger if the accident which caused the damage so sustained took place on board the aircraft or in the course of any of the operations of embarking or disembarking'.

79. *Morris v. KLM Royal Dutch Airlines,* (2002) 2 All ER 565 (HL).

80. *Ibid* pp. 568, 569, 613, 622, 623. In this case the claimant was indecently assaulted by a fellow passenger while she was sleeping. She suffered mental injury but not physical injury and so was not found entitled to any damages.

81. (1985) 470 US 392.

82. *Re Deep Vein Thrombosis and Air Travel Group Litigation,* (2004) 1 All ER 445, p. 452, para 23 (CA). Same view has been taken by the High Court of Australia in *Povey v. Quantas Airways Ltd.,* (2005) 79 ALJR 1215.

83. *Ibid.*

84. *Fellows (or Herd) v. Clyde Helicopter Ltd.,* (1997) 1 All ER 775 (H.L.).

85. *Disley v. Levine,* (2002) 1 WLR 785 (C.A.).

86. *Laroche v. Spirit of Adventure (U.K.) Ltd.,* (2009) 2 All ER 175 (C.A.).

of *travaux preparatoires* to resolve any doubt as to the meaning of the Convention.[87]

But if the words used in the Convention and the Act have no internationally acceptable meaning, their meaning may be derived by recourse to the legislative history and the acceptable meaning according to the English law; and assistance may also be taken of the meaning of those words in the country in respect of which the application of the Act is called for in a particular case.[88]

Dealing with Asylum and Immigration Appeals Act, 1993 and Immigration Rules, 1994 which give effect to the Convention relating to the Status of Refugees, 1951 as amended by the 1967 Protocol, and in interpreting the expression 'non-political crime' as it appears in Article 1F of the Convention (which sets out circumstances, including commission of a serious non-political crime, which disentitles the asylum seeker to take the benefit of the convention), it was observed: "In a case concerning an international convention, it is obviously desirable that decisions in different jurisdictions should, so far possible, be kept in line with each other."[89] The House of Lords, therefore, referred not merely to the English authorities but also to the American, Canadian and other authorities and held that a crime of detonating a bomb at an airport by a member of a political organisation to overthrow the Government of Algeria was a serious non-political crime as it involved indiscriminate injury to innocent persons and such a person could not be given political asylum in the United Kingdom.[90] The asylum seeker for taking benefit of the same convention has to qualify as a 'refugee' which as defined in Article 1A(2) is a person who 'owing to well grounded fear of being persecuted for reasons of race, religion, nationality, *membership of a particular social group* or political opinion, is outside the country of his nationality and is unable or, owing to such fear, is unwilling to avail himself of the protection of that country. Two women from Pakistan, who had been driven out by their husbands from their homes and who were being falsely accused of adultery and immorality sought the benefit of the convention by claiming that they were members of 'a particular social group' for women as a class were

87. *Read v. Secretary of State for the Home Department*, (1988) 3 All ER 993, p. 999 (HL). **See further** *Ji Mac William Co. Inc. v. Mediterranian Shipping Co. SA The Rafaela SA,* (2003) 3 All ER 359, pp. 389 to 394 (use made of *travaux preparators* for interpreting Hague Rules given effect to in U.K. by the Carriage of Goods by Sea Act, 1971).

88. *Re, State of Norway's Applications (Nos. 1 and 2)*, (1989) 1 All ER 745 (HL).

89. *T. v. Secretary of State for the Home Department*, (1996) 2 All ER 865, p. 891 : (1996) AC 742 : (1996) 2 WLR 766 (HL).

90. *Ibid.*

discriminated against in Pakistan in matters of fundamental human rights and they would be unprotected by the State and face risk of criminal proceedings and severe punishment if forced to return to Pakistan. After referring to cases and practices from United States, Australia, Canada New Zealand and European countries, which are not uniform, and the broad objective of the convention reflected in its preamble, *viz.*, to counteract discrimination in enjoyment of fundamental rights, the House of Lords took a liberal view of the expression 'a particular social group' and held that women could themselves constitute a social group if they lived in a society such as Pakistan where they were discriminated against on the ground of sex in the matter of protection of human rights although Article 1A(2) does not specially refer to persecution for the reasons of sex along with race, religion, nationality and political opinion.[91] The court

---

91. *R v. Immigration Appeal Tribunal,* (1999) 2 All ER 545 (HL). For a somewhat similar Australian case **see** *Minister for Immigration and Multicultural Affairs v. Khawar,* (2002) 76 ALJR 667. **See further** *Horvath v. Secretary of State for the Home Department,* (2000) 3 All ER 577, p. 581 (HL) which holds that Article 1A(2) of the Convention extended protection to persons who feared persecution by non-state agents where the State was not complicit but was unable or unwilling to afford protection, a view not held in France and Germany but shared by majority of contracting States including United States and Canada. **See further** on the same point *R. v. Secretary of State for the Home Department exparte Adam.,* (2001) 1 All ER 593 (HL). For evidence to show likelihood of persecution for convention reason: **see** *R. v. Secretary of State for the Home Department, exp. Sivkumaran,* (1988) 1 All ER 193 : (1988) AC 958 : (1988) 3 SJ 22 (HL); *Karanakaran v. Secretary for the State for the Home Department,* (2000) 3 All ER 449 (CA); *Minister for Immigration and Multicultural Affairs v. Ibrahim,* (2000) 74 ALJR 1556 (Australia) (Fear of persecution due to civil unrest may not be enough); *Sepet v. Secretary of State for the Home Department* (2003) 3 All ER 304 (HL) (Fear of persecution on conscientious objection to military service not enough); *R. (on the application of Sivakumar) v. Secretary of State for the Home Department,* (2003) 2 All ER 1097 (HL) (case relating to a Tamil from Jafna who was tortured by army and police of Sri Lanka on the suspicion that he belonged to LTTE); *Applicants v. Minister for Immigration and multicultural affairs,* (2004) 78 ALJR 854 (meaning of 'particular social group'. Threat of forcible recruitment in Afghanistan by Taliban whether persecution of applicant and whether able bodied men in Afghanistan constituted particular social group); *Appellants S 395 and S 396/2002 v. Minister for Immigration and Multicultural Affairs*, (2003) HCA 71 (Australia) (persecution in Bangladesh on the ground that the refugee was homosexual); *NAGV and NAGW of 2002 v. Minister for Immigration and Multicultural and Indigenous Affairs*, (2005) 79 ALJR 609 (A 'refugee' lawfully in Australia may be entitled to a 'protection visa'); *K. v. Secretary of State,* (2007) 1 All ER 671 (HL) (membership of a family could constitute membership of a particular social group. Further, all indigenous females in Sierra Lone or all Sierra Leonian women would constitute a particular social group for purposes of Article 1A(2) of the Convention).

A person who fails in his effort to seek an asylum in a country in accordance with the Convention on the Status of Refugees, 1951 as amended by the 1967 Protocol, may possibly still resist his expulsion or deportation on the ground of apprehended

[Footnote No. 91 Contd.]

also applied the *ejusdem generis* rule in construing the expression 'a particular social group'.[92]

The decision in *R v. Uxbridge Magistrates' Court ex p Adimi*[93] exposed a serious lacuna in the English law as it had till then failed to give any immunity by legislation against criminal penalties in accordance with Article 31 of the Refugee Convention which in the said case was allowed on the basis of legitimate expectation.[94] Article 31 of the Convention reads as follows:

> '*Refugees unlawfully in the country of refuge*
>
> (1) The Contracting States shall not impose penalties, on account of their illegal entry or presence, on refugees who, coming directly from a territory where their life or freedom was threatened in the sense of article 1, enter or are present in their territory without authorization, provided they present themselves without delay to the authorities and show good cause for their illegal entry or presence.
>
> (2) The Contracting States shall not apply to the movements of such refugees restrictions other than those which are necessary and such restrictions shall only be applied until their status in the country is regularized or they obtain admission into another country. The Contracting States shall allow such refugees a reasonable period and all the necessary facilities to obtain admission into another country.'

The above lacuna was made good by section 31 of the Immigration and Asylum Act, 1999. But the defence under Article 31 of the Convention allowed by section 31 of the Act was limited to offences listed in sub-section 3 of section 31. In *R v. Asfaw*[95] the defendant refugee was an Ethiopian

---

[Footnote No. 91 Contd.]

violation of human rights under the International Covenant on Civil and Political Rights, 1966 or the corresponding European convention: *R. (on the application of Ullah) v. Special Adjudicator*, (2004) 3 All ER 785 (HL); *R. (on the application of Razgar) v. Secretary for the Home Department*, (2004) 3 All ER 821 (HL).

The courts have developed the principle of relocation which means that a person will not qualify as a refugee if, though suffering from well founded fear of persecution in one part of his country, he could be returned to another part of the country, the place of relocation, in which the circumstances are such that he would not have a well founded fear of being persecuted, provided that he should not be returned if it would be unduly harsh or unreasonable to expect him to relocate in that particular place: *Tanuzi v. Secretary of State for the Home Department,* (2006) 3 All ER 305 (HL) (paras 8, 63).

92. **See** pages 563, 566, *ante*.

93. (1999) 4 All E.R. 520 (Q.B.D.).

94. **See** note 62, p. 692, *supra*.

95. (2008) 3 All E.R. 775.

national who left Ethiopia with the help of an agent travelling by air on a false Ethiopian passport for claiming asylum in the United States. They arrived in the United Kingdom at the Heathrow airport where the defendant was left at the airport by the agent for an hour before giving her a false Italian passport and a ticket to Washington D.C. The defendant then checked in for a flight from Heathrow to Washington. The airline official recognized the passport as false and informed the police. The defendant was arrested and charged with two offences: (1) Using a false instrument, viz., a false Italian passport with intent contrary to section 3 of the Forgery and Counterfeiting Act, 1981 and (2) Attempting to obtain services by deception (the air transport services) by falsely representing that she was authorized to use the Italian passport contrary to section 1(1) of the Criminal Attempts Act, 1981. The defendant was acquitted for the first offence which was listed in section 31(3) of the Act but was convicted for the second offence which was not listed in section 31(3). The first question that arose before the House of Lords was whether protection under Article 31 was available to a refugee who was apprehended enroute in a country before reaching the country of his destination. Adopting a purposive construction consistent with its humanitarian purpose and in the light of the jurisprudence developed under Article 31 and its construction in *Adimi's* case, the House of Lords held that a transit passenger like the defendant was entitled to protection of that Article.[1] The second question in the case was whether if the defendant is charged with an offence not specified in section 31(3) of the Act can he still rely on the protection under Article 31 of the Convention. The House of Lords held that it was for Parliament to determine the extent to which international obligations were to be incorporated domestically and the determination having been made in unambiguous terms the courts could not add further offences in the list of those to which Parliament had said section 31 applied and there was in such a case no scope for a free standing defence or legitimate expectation for covering offences not listed in section 31(3).[2] The second offence for which the defendant was charged and convicted, as it was not covered by section 31(3), was however found to be indistinguishable on facts from the first offence for which he was acquitted. In the circumstances of the case it was held to be an abuse of the process of the Court to prosecute him for that offence and his conviction was quashed on this ground.

In construing the Child Abduction and Custody Act, 1985 which makes the Convention on the Civil Aspects of International Child Abduction, 1980, part of the law of England and sets it out in a schedule, the House of Lords held that the English law concepts of 'acquiescence', which are not

---

1. *Ibid,* paras 26, 54 to 59.
2. *Ibid,* paras 28, 29, 69.

to be found in the Convention or in the general law of all developed countries, have no application to the proper construction of the word 'acquiescence' occurring in Article 13 of the Convention.[3] The reasoning on which this conclusion was reached is that "an international convention, expressed in different languages and intended to apply to a wide range of differing legal systems, cannot be construed differently in different jurisdictions. The convention must have the same meaning and effect under the laws of all contracting States."[4]

The Convention is enforced in Australia by the Family Law (Child Abduction Convention) Regulations, 1986. In interpreting the Regulations the High Court of Australia said that International treaties should be interpreted uniformly by contracting states and unless the contrary intention appears, an expression used in the Regulations and the Convention must be given the same meaning.[5] The court in interpreting the meaning of the expression 'habitual residence' in Regulation 1A(2) referred to the Explanatory Report commenting on the Convention which said that the 'notion of habitual residence is a well established concept in the Hague Conference which regards it as a question of pure fact differing in that respect from domicile' and gave the same meaning to the expression in the Regulations.[6]

While interpreting the word 'counter claim' in Article 11 of the Convention on Jurisdiction and the Enforcement of Judgments in Civil and Commercial Matters, 1968 (the Brussels Convention) entered into between members states of the European Economic Community, which is enforced in England by the Civil Jurisdiction and Judgments Act, 1982 and forms Sch. 1 to the Act, the House of Lords did not straightaway accept the argument that the word in question was derived from the Belgian Judicial Code where 'counterclaim' was permitted only against original plaintiff and not against new parties observing that "the primary search must be for an objective and independent interpretation capable of accommodating the needs of a diversity of national legal systems"[7] although ultimately by

---

3. *Re, H (minor)*, (1997) 2 All ER 225 (HL).

4. *Ibid*, p. 234, **see further** *Re Ismail* (1998) 3 All ER 1007, p. 1011 (HL) (Extradition treaties and extradition statutes ought to be accorded a broad and generous construction so far as the text permits to facilitate extradition and not solely from the perspective of English criminal procedure.)

5. *L K v. Director General Department of Community Service*, (2009) 83 ALJR 525 para 36.

6. *Ibid* para 21.

7. *Jordan Grand Prix Ltd. v. Baltic Insurance Group,* (1999) 1 All ER 289, p. 294 (HL). In the context of IPR development in India, LAHOTI C.J.I. has extra-judicially commended this approach for interpreting treaties relating to IPR rights so as to protect our economy and commercial world: (2004) 8 SCC 5 (J).

contextual interpretation, it was held that counterclaim in Article 11 was restricted to counterclaim against original plaintiff and did not include counterclaim against new parties.[8]

The High Court of Australia holds that "if a statute transposes the text of a treaty or a provision of a treaty into the statute so as to enact it as part of domestic law, the *prima facie* legislative intention is that the transposed text should bear the same meaning in the domestic statute as it bears in the treaty."[9] Therefore, "the rules applicable to the interpretation of treaties must be applied to the transposed text and the rules generally applicable to the interpretation of domestic statutes give way".[10] Treaties, as earlier noticed, are interpreted according to Articles 31 and 32 of the Vienna Convention.[11] These Articles have been interpreted to require a holistic approach which means "a consideration of both the text and the object and purposes of the treaty to ascertain its true meaning."[12] In order to ascertain the object and purpose, apart from the text, assistance may be obtained from extrinsic sources. "The form in which a treaty is drafted, the subject to which it relates, the mischief that it addresses, the history of its negotiation and comparison with earlier or amending instruments relating to the same subject may warrant consideration in arriving at the true interpretation of its text."[13]

The need to eliminate bribery in international transactions led to the OECD (Organization for Economic Cooperation and Development) Convention on Combating Bribery of Foreign Public Officials which was adopted by 37 countries in November, 1997. Australia implemented the convention by the Criminal Code Amendment (Bribery of Foreign Public Officials) Act, 1999. The Act creates in section 70.4 a defence known as *facilitation payment* defence which reads: A person is not guilty of the offence of bribing a foreign public official 'if (a) the value of the benefit was of a minor nature and (b) the person's conduct was engaged in for the sole

---

8. *Ibid* p. 295. **See further** *Canada Trust Co. v. Stolzenberg,* (2000) 4 All ER 481 (HL) (construction of the word 'sued' in Articles 2 and 6 of the Lugano Convention enforced by the same Act as the Brussels Convention).

9. *Applicant v. Minister for Immigration*, (1997) 71 AL JR 381, p. 383.

10. *Ibid.*

11. *Ibid*, p. 395.

12. *Ibid*, p. 383.

13. *Ibid*, **see further** *Phonographic Performance Co. of Australia v. Federation of Australian Commercial Television Station* (1998) 72 ALJR 924, p. 930 (An international convention can be used to interpret a statute intended to give effect to the convention even if the statute is enacted before ratification of the convention); *Morrison v. Peacock,* (2002) 76 ALJR 545 [construction of the Marine Pollution Act, 1973 (NSW) which gave effect to the 1973 convention on the subject].

or dominant purpose of expediting or securing the performance of a routine government action of a minor nature and (c) as soon as practicable after the conduct occurred the person made a record of the conduct.' The American counterpart Foreign Corrupt Practices Act, 1977 which preceded the convention also contains exemptions for small payments by American Companies to secure the provision of routine governmental services abroad. These exemption clauses pose difficult questions but are yet to be authoritatively interpreted by courts.[14] The OECD Convention was enforced in the United Kingdom by sections 108 to 110 of the Anti Terrorism Crime and Security Act, 2001 and gave rise to a new problem. By these provisions it was made an offence triable in U. K. for a U. K. national or company to make a corrupt payment or pay a bribe to a public officer abroad. Section 1 of the Criminal Justice Act, 1987 constituted a Serious Fraud Office (SFO) and conferred on its Director the power to investigate any suspected offence which appeared to him involve serious or complex fraud. The Director was required to discharge his functions under the superintendence of the Attorney General but any decision he made as to investigation or prosecution was for him to make independently. The Director of SFO carried out investigation into allegations of bribery by a defence and aerospace company in relation to military aircraft contracts with Saudi Arabia. In 2006 a threat was made by Saudi representatives that if the investigations were continued Saudi Arabia would withdraw from the existing bilateral counter-terrorism cooperation arrangements with the United Kingdom, withdraw cooperation from the United Kingdom in relation to its strategic objectives in the Middle East and end the negotiations then in train for the procurement of certain aircraft. The Director and the Attorney General were advised by the ministers that if the investigations were continued those threats would be carried out and the consequences would be grave for the arms trade and for the safety of British citizens and service personnel. The Director was told by the British ambassador to Saudi Arabia that threats to national and international security were grave and that British lives on British streets were at risk. The Prime Minister requested the Attorney General to reconsider the public interest issues raised by the ongoing investigation in relation to national security. In December, 2006 the Director concluded that to continue the investigation risked real and imminent damage to the United Kingdom's national and International security and decided to discontinue the investigation considering the need to safeguard national and international security and to balance the need to maintain the rule of law against the wider public interest. In a challenge to the Director's decision by judicial review the House of

14. *Facilitation payments in international Business,* (2008) 82 ALJ 92, 99.

Lords[15] held that the right question was whether in deciding that the public interest in pursuing an important investigation into an alleged bribery was outweighed by the public interest in protecting the lives of British citizens and that on the facts the Director's decision to discontinue the investigation was one which he was lawfully entitled to make and involved no affront to the rule of law to which the principle of judicial review gave effect.

An international convention and the Act passed to give effect to it may also have to be construed consistent with Customary International Law. For example, Article 6 of the European Convention for the Protection of Human Rights and Fundamental Freedoms enforced in the United Kingdom by the Human Rights Act, 1998, which requires contracting States to maintain fair and public judicial processes and forbids them to deny any individual access to those processes for enforcement of civil rights, has been construed not to affect the limitation of jurisdiction on the ground of State immunity, which is a creature of customary international law and follows from the equality of sovereign States.[16]

The principles stated above have also been followed by the Supreme Court of India and statutes enacted for giving effect to international conventions are construed as far as possible consistent with the terms of the convention and assistance can also be taken from the relevant branch of the International Law for it is almost accepted that the rules of customary International Law which are not contrary to the municipal law are deemed to have been incorporated in the domestic law.[17] Thus, 'Sustainable Development' as a balancing concept between ecology and development, which has been accepted as a part of the customery International Law and the 'Precautionary Principle' and the 'Polluter Pays Principle' which are its essential features were used for construing the functions of the authority under section 3(3) of the Environment (Protection) Act, 1986 which was enacted to give effect to the decisions taken at the United Nations Conference on Human Environment at Stockholm.[18] The

---

15. *R (on the application of Corner House Research) v. Director Serious Fraud Office,* (2008) All ER 927 (H.L.).

16. *Holland v. Lampen Wolfe,* (2000) 3 All ER 833, p. 847 (HL).

17. *Vellore Citizens Welfare Forum v. Union of India*, AIR 1996 SC 2715, pp. 2720, 2722 : 1996 (5) SCC 647.

18. *Ibid*, p. 2726. These principles mentioned in Vellore judgment have been further explained in: *A.P. Pollution Control Board v. Prof. M.V. Nayudu (Retd.),* JT 1998 (1) SC 162, pp. 173-180 : AIR 1999 SC 812, pp. 819-23 : (1999) 2 SCC 718; *T.N. Godavarman Tirumalpad v. Union of India,* AIR 2003 SC 724, pp. 737, 738 : (2002) 10 SCC 606. **See further** for use of Stockholm convention for construction of the Environment (Protection) Act, 1986, *Essar Oil Ltd. v. Halar Utkarsh Samiti,* (2004) 2 SCC 392, pp. 400, 405, 406 (need to balance economic and social needs with environmental considerations); *Intellectual Forum Tirupathi v. State of A.P.*,

[Footnote No. 18 Contd.]

principle of sustainable development, which has now become a constitutional requirement, means that development which meets the needs of the present without compromising the ability of the future generations to meet their own needs.[19] The court, therefore, insists on laying down various conditions to that end before grant of permission for diversion of forest land to other purposes (*e.g.*, mining operation) one of them being deposit of Net Present Value (NPV) of the forest land sought for diversion to be utilized later for afforestation and other purposes.[20] Net Present Value (NPV) represents the net present value of the forest land diverted for non-forestry purposes.

In construing the expression 'public policy' in section 7(1)(b)(ii) of the Foreign Awards (Recognition and Enforcement) Act, 1961 which was enacted for giving effect to the New York Convention (1958) assistance was taken from terms of the convention and the meaning of 'public policy' as understood in the private International Law.[21] The expression 'public policy' was in this manner construed as restricted to fundamental policy of Indian law, interests of India and justice or morality. It was, therefore, held that mere contravention of Indian law did not attract any bar to the enforcement of foreign award.[22] The word 'commercial' in section 3 of the same Act was liberally construed to include contracts for consultancy services to promote speedy settlement of disputes arising in international trade and recourse was

---

[Footnote No. 18 Contd.]

(2006) 3 SCC 549 : AIR 2006 SC 1350 (need to balance development needs with conservation of natural resources – public water tanks in this case); *Bombay Dyeing and Mfg. Co. Ltd. v. Bombay Environmental Action Group*, (2006) 3 SCC 434 para 272 : AIR 2006 SC 1489; *Bihar Finance Service House Construction Coop. Society Ltd. v. Gantam Goswamy,* (2008) 5 SCC 339 paras 26 to 28 : AIR 2008 SC 1975. *Goan Real Estate and Construction Limited v. Union of India*, (2010) 5 SCC 388 : (2010) 3 JT 462 (Environmental Protection and Pollution Control in the context of construction in coastal areas).

19. *T.N. Godavarman Thirumulpad v. Union of India.* In the matter of *Vedanta Aluminium Ltd.*, (2008) 2 SCC 222 para 3 : (2007) 13 Scale 430.

20. *Ibid*, para 11 see further (2000) 1 SCC 1 : AIR 2000 SC 145 (under the same heading); (2008) 7 SCC 126 (Determination of NPV; principles relating thereto and rate fixed for three years). In the case of *Sterlite Industries India Ltd. (SIIL)* the court directed the floating of a company as a Special Purpose Vehicle (SPV) for the development of the area in which State of Orissa, Orissa Mining Corporation Ltd. (OMCL) and the company concerned *i.e.* SIIL which requires diversion of forest land for mining purposes will be shareholders and directed SIIL to deposit every year 5% of the annual profit before tax and Interest or Rs. 10 crores whichever is higher for the development of the area with the SPV: (2008) 2 SCC 222 : (2008) 9 SCC 711.

21. *Renusagar Power Co. Ltd. v. General Electric Co.*, AIR 1994 SC 860 : 1994 Supp. (1) SCC 644.

22. *Ibid. Venture Global Engineering v. Satyam Computer Services*, (2010) 8 SCC 660 paras 29, 32 to 35 : AIR 2010 SC 3371 (concept of public policy). **See further** *Smita Conductors Ltd. v. Euro Alloys Ltd.,* AIR 2001 SC 3726, p. 3734 : (2001) 7 SCC 728 (The expression 'agreement in writing' in section 2(a) construed in the light of Article II of the Convention to include an agreement arrived at by exchange of letters).

also taken to the meaning of the word 'commercial' in the Model Law prepared by the United Nations Commission on International Trade Law (UNCITRAL).[23] But, while interpreting the same Act, the Court by majority, it is submitted, took an unduly restricted view of the meaning of 'submission' in section 3 on the ground that there was no ambiguity[24] though fully realising that by taking this view the purpose and object of the convention will not be fully carried out[25] and that an English authority[26] had taken a contrary view on identical language in the corresponding English Act. Further, though in drafting the Arbitration and Conciliation Act, 1996 UNCITRAL Model Law and Rules were taken into account but as the two are not identically worded different meaning of a provision in the Act may have to be adopted from the corresponding provision in the Model Law. For example, it was held by a Constitution Bench that the power of the Chief Justice in the matter of appointment of arbitrators under section 11 is not a power exercisable by a court or tribunal and is not appealable under Article 136 of the Constitution though in the Model Law that power is exercised by a court.[27] But this view was later overruled by a larger Bench and it was held that the power of the Chief Justice was a judicial power.[28] The case also points out the issues which the Chief Justice may have to decide at that stage, for example, he has to decide whether the party approaching has approached the right High Court, whether there is an arbitration agreement, whether the person approaching is a party to the agreement and whether the claim is still a live issue and not dead.[29] Further, noting the similar phrase-

---

23. *R. M. Investment & Trading Co. Pvt. Ltd. v. Boeing & Co.*, AIR 1994 SC 1136 : (1994) 2 SCC 406. **See further** *Shah v. Presiding Officer*, AIR 1978 SC 12, p. 17 : (1977) 4 SCC 384 (Reference to Maternity Protection Convention for construing the Maternity Benefit Act, 1961); *Sundaram Finance Ltd. v. NEPC India Ltd.*, JT 1999 (1) SC 49, pp. 53-55 : AIR 1999 SC 565, pp. 569, 570 : (1999) 2 SCC 479 (use of UNCITRAL Model Law for interpreting section 9 of the Arbitration and Conciliation Act, 1996); *Dadu v. State of Maharashtra*, AIR 2000 SC 3203, pp. 3210, 3211 : (2000) 8 SCC 437 (United Nations Convention Against Illicit Traffic in Narcotic Drugs and Psychotropic Substances, 1988 considered in interpreting section 32A added in 1988 in NDPS Act, 1985).

24. *V. O. Tractoroexport Moscow v. Tarapore & Company*, 1969 (3) SCC 562 : AIR 1971 SC 1.

25. *Ibid*, p. 572 (SCC). For this case **see also** p. 63, *ante*.

26. *T.B. & S. Batchelor & Co. Ltd. v. Owner of S.S. Merak*, (1965) 1 All ER 230 (CA).

27. *Konkan Railway Corporation Ltd. v. Ram Construction P. Ltd.*, AIR 2002 SC 778, p. 786 : (2002) 2 SCC 388.

28. *SBP & Co. v. Patel Engineering Ltd.*, (2005) 8 SCC 618 : AIR 2006 SC 450. For criticism of this case, **see** O.P. MALHOTRA AND INDU MALHOTRA, 'The Law and Practice of Arbitration and Conciliation,' 2nd edition, p. 557.

29. *SBP & Co. v. Patel Engineering Ltd.*, *supra* para 39. **See further** *Shree Ram Mills Ltd. v. Utility Premises (P) Ltd.*, (2007) 4 SCC 599 (para 27), pp. 607, 608 : (2007) 4 JT 501. By para 46 of *SBP & Co.* case prior orders and proceedings have been saved and are still governed by *Konkan Railway* case: *Maharshi Dayanand University v. Anand Co-op. Society Ltd.*, (2007) 5 SCC 295 (para 12) : (2007) 5 SLT 99 : (2007) 6 JT 175.

ology used in section 11(9) of the Arbitration and Conciliation Act, 1996, and Article 11 of the UNCITRAL Model Law, the Supreme Court looked to the latter as a legitimate aid in appropriately interpreting the provisions of section 11 of the 1996 Act, and held that in order to ensure at least the appearance of neutrality, the presiding/ third arbitrator appointed by CJI under section 11 should be of a nationality other than that of the parties to the arbitration.[30]

A law enacted to implement an International Convention may make suitable changes to suit local conditions. Therefore, the Wild Life Protection Act, 1972 as amended in 1991 and 2003 enacted in furtherance of the Convention on International Trade in Endangered Species (CITES) of Wild Fauna and Flora imposing complete ban on trade in Ivory including imported African Ivory to protect Indian elephant cannot be faulted as unreasonable though limited trade has been allowed for certain African elephant population by changes made in CITES.[31]

Section 21 of the Extradition Act, 1962 (as amended in 1993) enacted to give effect to extradition treaties has to be construed consistent with the treaties and the principle of International Law known as the principle of 'speciality' which is to the effect that the State to which a person has been extradited cannot without the consent of the requisitioned State try a person extradited save for the offence for which he was extradited or any lesser offence disclosed by the facts proved for the purposes of securing his surrender or return; or the offence in respect of which the foreign state has given its consent.[32] While interpreting rule 14(d) of the Customs Tariff

30. *Reliance Industries Ltd. & Ors. v. Union of India*, (2014) 11 SCC 576, pp. 597 to 603.

31. *Indian Handicrafts Emporium v. Union of India*, AIR 2003 SC 3240, p. 3256 : (2003) 7 SCC 589.

32. *Daya Singh Lahotia v. Union of India*, AIR 2001 SC 1716, p. 1718 : (2001) 4 SCC 516; *Suman Sood v. State of Rajasthan*, (2007) 5 SCC 634 (paras 31 to 33) : (2007) 7 JT 101 : (2007) 5 SLT 522. **See further** the Australian case *Truong v. The Queen*, (2004) 78 ALJR 473 (The appellant was surrendered for trial in Australia by the United Kingdom for the offences of conspiracy to kidnap and conspiracy to murder and his trial and conviction for the offences of kidnapping and murder on the same facts was not held to be against the extradition treaty or principle of speciality). The principle of specialty as enacted in section 95(4) of the Extradition Act, 2003 (U.K.) provides that the person extradited can be tried, in the country to which he is extradited for the following offences: (a) the offence in respect of which he is extradited; (b) an extradition offence disclosed by the same facts as that offence other than one in respect of which a sentence of death could be imposed; (c) an extradition offence in respect of which the Secretary of State consents to the person being dealt with; (d) an offence in respect of which the person waives the right to be dealt with. **See** on this point *Welsh v. Secretary of State for the Home Department*, (2006) 3 All ER 204 (QBD). According to High Court of Australia

[Footnote No. 32 Contd.]

(Identification, Assessment, and Collection of Anti-Dumping Duty on Dumped Articles and for Determination of Injury) Rules, 1995, which provides that if the Designated Authority determines that the *volume* of the dumped imports actual or potential from a particular country accounts for less than 3% of the imports of the like product, he shall terminate the proceedings immediately, the court[33] relied upon Article 5.8 of the Agreement on Implementation of Article VI of GATT (General Agreement on Tariff and Trade), which is the basis for imposition of anti-dumping duty under section 9A of the Customs Act, and to which India is a party. The Customs Excise and Gold (Control) Appellate Tribunal (CEGAT) had held that the word 'volume' in the context of rule 14 meant value. In overruling this interpretation the court quoted Article 5.8 of the Agreement which makes it clear that the *de minimis* rule for termination of proceedings as far as the price is concerned is when the margin or the difference between the export price of the article and the normal value, is less than 2%, in other words, when the exporter is selling the goods in India at almost the same price that it does in its country. As far as the quantity is concerned, *de minimis* rule applies if the export accounts for less than 3% of the total imports of the like article in India which is treated as too trivial for the law and is ignored. It was, therefore, held that when rule 14(d) says that the investigation must be terminated if the *volume* of the dumped imports is less than 3% of the imports of the like product, it must mean that the quantity of dumped imports must account for less than 3% of the total imports.[34]

But when the language of the Indian Act is clear, its meaning cannot be affected by international declarations or United Nations' resolutions to which India is a party and has to be given effect to. It was so held in deciding

---

[Footnote No. 32 Contd.]

extradition, even of an Australian citizen, to a foreign country is removal by an executive act undertaken with legislative authority, it is not removal by judicial authority though it is subject to judicial review and no extradition treaty is essential for validity of a law providing for extradition of fugitive offenders: *Vasiljkovic v. Commonwealth,* (2005) 80 ALJR 1399. In U.K. extradition of a person to a country where he would be subjected to inhuman or degrading punishment offending Article 3 of the European Covention may be refused but a sentence of imprisonment for life without eligibility for parole and release only by order of the Governor does not fall in that category: *R (on the application of Wellington) v. Secretary of State for the Home Department*, (2009) 2 All ER 436 (H.L.). For procedure of enquiry and report under the Extradition Act, 1962 when a request is made by a treaty State to India for extradition of a person **see** *Rosiline George v. Union of India,* (1994) 2 SCC 80 : 1993 Supp (3) SCR 141; *Sarabjit Rick Singh v. Union of India*, (2008) 2 SCC 417 : (2007) 14 Scale 263.

33. *S & S Enterprise v. Designated Authority*, (2005) 3 SCC 337, p. 340 : AIR 2005 SC 1527.

34. *Ibid*, p. 341.

that a retired police officer 'having knowledge of, or practical experience in the matters relating to human rights' can be appointed a member of the National Human Rights Commission being qualified to be so appointed under section 3(2)(d) of the Protection of Human Rights Act, 1994 and his appointment cannot be challenged on the basis of Paris Principles regarding the protection of human rights, subsequently endorsed by the U.N. General Assembly.[35]

(c) Operation as to crimes

Apart from statute and international crimes,[36] the general principle of criminal jurisprudence is that the quality of an act depends on the law of the place where it is done.[37] It has been said that "all crime is local" and "the jurisdiction over the crime belongs to the country where the crime is committed".[38] A State exercises jurisdiction to punish all criminal acts against its laws done within its territories by its subjects or aliens, and jurisdiction may also be exercised by proper legislation to punish criminal acts of subjects wherever done. The power to legislate for subjects wherever they may be, is supported on the basis of allegiance of the subject to the sovereign.[39] But as regards foreigners "no proposition of law can be more incontestable or more universally admitted that, according to general law of nations, a foreigner, though criminally responsible to the law of nation not his own, for acts done by him while within the limits of its territory, cannot be made responsible to its law for acts done beyond such limits".[40] These principles have given rise to a rule of construction which, as explained by LORD SIMONDS, means: "A statute creating an offence and imposing a penalty for it, should be so construed as to apply only to those persons who by virtue of residence or, in some cases, citizenship or nationality, are regarded as subject to the jurisdiction of the State which has enacted the statute."[41] In other words there is a presumption that a statute creating a criminal offence does not, in the absence of clear and specific words to the contrary, make an act done by a foreigner outside the territorial

35. *People's Union for Civil Liberties v. Union of India*, AIR 2005 SC 2419, p. 2426.
36. For international crimes **see** title 5(d), p. 713.
37. *A.G. for Colony of Hongkong v. Kwok-a-Singh*, (1873) LR 5 PC 173, p. 199 (MELLISH, L.J.).
38. *Macleod v. A.G. of NSW*, (1891) AC 455, p. 458 : 60 LJPC 55 : 65 LT 321 (PC) (LORD HALSBURY); *Reg. v. Treacy*, (1971) 2 WLR 112, p. 116 (HL); *Kubic Dariusz v. Union of India*, AIR 1990 SC 605, p. 615. *Macleod's* case has been **distinguished** in *Nasiruddin Khan v. State of Bihar*, AIR 1973 SC 186 : (1973) 3 SCC 99.
39. *Sussex Peerage* case, (1844) 11 Cl & Fin 85, p. 146 (HL) (TINDAL, C.J.) : 8 ER 1034, p. 1058. **See further** *Trial of Earl Russel*, (1901) AC 446.
40. *Keyn*, (1876) 2 Ex D 63, p. 160 (COCKBURN, C.J.).
41. *Naim Malvan v. Director of Public Prosecutions*, AIR 1948 PC 186, p. 190.

jurisdiction of the State an offence triable in a criminal court of the State.[42] It also follows that the same principle will apply to a section in a statute conferring power to make delegated legislation.[43] In the absence of express words power to make delegated legislation making acts done by a foreigner outside the State a criminal offence triable by State Courts cannot be inferred.[44]

This rule of construction will, however, not apply if restriction of the general words to citizens and residents will "largely stultify the purpose and effect" of the statute.[45] Again there is no presumption that any reference in an Act of Parliament to the doing of any act is to be understood as excluding the doing of that act within the territories of another State, the presumption only is that an Act of British Parliament does not make anything done within the territories of another State an offence punishable by English courts.[46] In construing the Obscene Publications Act, 1959 which extends to England and Wales and which authorises seizure of obscene articles kept for publication for gain, it was held that even obscene articles meant for publication in foreign country when found in England could be seized and that this construction did not bring in any element of extra-territoriality.[47] Similarly, in construing section 4(1) of the Explosives Substances Act, 1883, which makes it an offence to make or possess explosive substances in such circumstances as to give rise to a reasonable suspicion that they were not made or possessed for a lawful object, it was held that the 'lawful object' specified therein is not confined to a purpose which takes place in the United Kingdom and the lawfulness of which is to be determined by the English law and the section will cover a person who made or possessed explosives for unlawful use in a foreign country.[48] Further, the general rule that a criminal statute of a State does not apply to

---

42. *Air India v. Wiggins*, (1980) 2 All ER 593 : (1980) 1 WLR 815 (HL).

N.B.—But foreigners who are permanently resident may by legislation be bracketed with citizens for extra-territorial offences in certain sensitive areas. For example, Australia has enacted Crimes (Child Sex Tourism) Amendment Act, 1994, which makes it an of- fence for Australian citizens or residents to engage in sexual intercourse or acts of indecency with minors outside the country; **see** (1997) 71 ALJ, 108 (International Focus). **see further** TIM MACINTOSH, 'Exploring the Boundaries: The Impact of the Child Sex Tourism Legislation', (2000) 74 ALJ 613. The validity of the legislation has been uphold: *XYZ v. Commonwealth,* (2006) 80 ALJR 1036 (The judgment points out that similar legislation has been enacted by 34 countries).

43. *Ibid.*

44. *Ibid.*

45. *Air India v. Wiggins*, (1980) 2 All ER 593 : (1980) 1 WLR 815 (HL).

46. *Lawson v. Fox*, (1974) 1 All ER 783, pp. 785, 786 (HL).

47. *Gold Star Publications v. Director of Public Prosecutions*, (1981) 2 All ER 257 : (1981) 1 WLR 732 (HL).

48. *R. v. Berry*, (1984) 3 All ER 1008 : (1985) AC 246 : (1984) 3 WLR 1274 (HL).

outside foreigners is subject to certain exceptions. If a foreigner, thoug outside the territories of a State, has continued to seek its protection h may become liable for punishment like any other subject of the State fo acts against the laws of the State, though done outside its territories. Thus an American citizen who left England, on a British passport describin himself a British subject, and who went to Germany and during the wa broadcast from that country propaganda against the British, was convicte of high treason in England.[49] It was held that the person concerned thoug a foreigner began to owe allegiance to the King by his presence in Englan and he continued this duty of allegiance even after he left England by ob taining a British passport describing himself a British subject; and that i was immaterial that he had obtained the passport by misrepresentation, o that he was not, in law, a British subject.[50] Again, in certain cases, act done outside the territories of a State may be regarded as acts done withi the State, although the person who did the act may be outside the territory For instance, a person who being abroad procures an innocent agent or us es the post office to commit a crime in England is deemed to commit a act in England. If a person, being outside England, initiated an offence part of the essential elements of which take effect in England, he is ame nable to English Jurisdiction. It appears that even though the person wh has initiated such an offence is a foreigner, he can be tried if he subse quently comes to England.[51] Similarly, a conspiracy entered into outsid for committing an unlawful act in England, can be tried there if it is whol ly or partly performed there.[52] In the case of what is a result crime in Eng lish law, the offence is committed in England and justiciable by an Englis court if any part of the proscribed result takes place in England.[53] Th same principle applies in case of an attempt to commit a result crime. I the intended consequences forming part of the crime would have take place in England had the crime been complete, the accused can b

---

49. *Joyce v. Director of Public Prosecutions*, (1946) 1 All ER 186 (HL).

N.B.—Principle applied for exercise of jurisdiction over an alien infant fo wardship jurisdiction, **see** *Re, P (GE) (an infant)*, (1964) 3 All ER 977 (CA).

50. *Joyce v. Director of Public Prosecutions*, (1946) 1 All ER 186 (HL).

51. HALSBURY'S Laws of England, Vol. 10 (3rd Edition), p. 316, **quoted** in *Mobari Ali Ahmad v. State of Bombay*, AIR 1957 SC 857, p. 868 : 1958 SCR 328; *Regin v. Baxter*, (1971) 2 WLR 1138, p. 1147 (CA). **See further** G. WILLIAMS: *Venu an the ambit of Criminal Law*, (1965) 81 Law Quarterly Review, pp. 276, 518. **Als see** *Reg v. Treacy*, (1971) 2 WLR 112, pp. 124, 127 (HL). The rules of internationa comity do not call for more than that each sovereign State should refrain from pun ishing persons for their conduct within the territory of another sovereign State whe that conduct has had no harmful consequences within the territory of the Stat which imposes the punishments. (LORD DIPLOCK)

52. *Director of Public Prosecution v. Doot*, (1973) 1 All ER 940 (HL).

53. *Secretary of State for Trade v. Markus*, (1975) 1 All ER 958, p. 966 (HL).

punished in England even though all the acts constituting the attempt took place in a foreign country.[54] But when a foreigner committing an offence in England and leaving United Kingdom is brought within the territorial jurisdiction of an English court by forcibly abducting him in violation of international law and in disregard of extradition procedure to which the police or other executive authorities in United Kingdom were a knowing party, the court will stay the prosecution as an abuse of the process of the court and release the prisoner.[55] In deciding the question of stay the court will also weigh two competing public interests: *one* that those engaged in grave offences should be tried, and *the other* that an impression should not be conveyed that the end justifies the means. Thus, more latitude is given to police and other law enforcement agencies to plan penetration of drug dealing organisations for bringing to trial those engaged in illicit drug trade.[56]

The Indian Penal Code, 1860, extends to the whole of India and enacts that 'every person shall be liable to punishment under this Code and not otherwise for every act or omission contrary to the provisions thereof, of which he shall be guilty within India; (section 2), By section 4, the Code has been given extra-territorial operation and 'the provisions of the Code apply also to any offence committed by: (1) any citizen of India in any place without and beyond India; (2) any person on any ship or aircraft registered in India wherever it may be.' A person, therefore, who commits an act contrary to the Code outside the territory of India (not in any ship or aircraft registered in India) will not be amenable to the Indian criminal jurisdiction and will not be liable to punishment under the Code, if, at the time of commission of the act, he was not a citizen of India even if he subsequently acquires the status of an Indian citizen.[57] But it is not essential in every case that a foreigner should be corporeally present within Indian territories at the time of the commission of the offence for making him liable

---

54. *Director of Public Prosecutions v. Stone House*, (1977) 2 All ER 909, p. 916 : (1978) AC 55 : (1977) 3 WLR 143 (HL); *R. v. Latif*, (1996) 1 All ER 353, p. 365 : (1996) 1 WLR 104 (HL). For offences committed by British subjects in a foreign ship to which they do not belong, **see** *R. v. Kelly*, (1981) 2 All ER 1098 (HL).

55. *Bennet v. Horsenferry Road Magistrate's Court*, (1993) 3 All ER 138 : (1994) 1 AC 42 (HL). Same view has been taken in New Zealand and South Africa : *Moevao v. Dept. of Labour*, (1980) 1 NZLR 464; *SV. Ebrahim*, 1991(2) SA 553. The U.S. Supreme Court by majority has taken a **contrary** view : *US v. Alvarez Machain*, (1992) 119 L. Ed 2d 441.

56. *R. v. Latif*, (1996) 1 All ER 353, pp. 359, 361 : (1996) 1 WLR 104 (HL); *Liangsiriprasert v. U. S. Government*, (1990) 2 All ER 866, p. 872 (HL).

57. *Central Bank of India Ltd. v. Ramnarain*, AIR 1955 SC 36 : 1955 (1) SCR 697. Followed in *Fatima Bibi Ahmed Patel v. State of Gujarat*, (2008) 6 SCC 789 : AIR 2008 SC 2392.

under the Code for an offence committed within India. Thus, if a foreigner initiates an offence from outside the territories of India, he can be punished for an offence committed within India if the essentials of the offence occur within India.[58] It was, therefore, held that a Pakistani national, who from Karachi made false and dishonest representations by letters, telegrams and trunkcalls to the complainant at Bombay, who, on the faith of these representations, paid money to the accused's agent at Bombay, could be prosecuted and punished for the offence of cheating under the Penal Code by the courts in India.[59] Further, a foreigner can be detained in India not only for facilitating his expulsion,[60] but also for preventing him from going to a foreign country, and from there to continue to indulge in activities prejudicial to the security and integrity of India.[61]

For inquiry into and trial of offences committed outside India but made amenable to Indian Jurisdiction by section 4 of the Penal Code a court of the place 'at which he may be found'[62] in India will have jurisdiction as provided in section 188 of the Code of Criminal Procedure but previous sanction of the Central Government is necessary. But such a permission may not be necessary when the overt acts outside India are committed in furtherance of a conspiracy hatched within India. A conspiracy to cheat the Punjab National Bank at Chandigarh between certain persons including a non-resident Indian based at Dubai was hatched at Chandigarh culminating in cheating the Bank at Chandigarh. On an objection that permission of the Central Government was necessary, it was held that conspiracy being a continuing offence all the offences resulting from the overt acts whether committed at Dubai or Chandigarh could be tried in India at Chandigarh without obtaining permission of the Central Government.[63]

---

58. *Mobarik Ali Ahmad v. State of Bombay*, AIR 1957 SC 857 : 1958 SCR 328. For cases of attempt to cheat, **see** *Reg v. Baxter*, (1971) 2 WLR 1138 (CA); *Director of Public Prosecutions v. Stone House*, (1977) 2 All ER 909 : (1978) AC 55 : (1977) 3 WLR 143 (HL).

59. *Mobarik Ali Ahmad v. State of Bombay, supra.*

60. *Hans Muller of Nuremberg v. Superintendent, Presidency Jail, Calcutta*, AIR 1955 SC 367 : (1955) 1 SCR 1284.

61. *Giani Bakshish Singh v. Government of India*, AIR 1973 SC 2667, p. 2671 : (1973) 2 SCC 688.

62. *Om Hemrajani v. State of U.P.*, (2005) 1 SCC 617 (word 'found' has been given very extensive interpretation. Any court before whom the accused appears or is produced will have jurisdiction).

63. *Ajay Agarwala v. Union of India*, AIR 1993 SC 1637, p. 1648 : (1993) 3 SCC 609. **Distinguished** in *Fatima Bibi Ahmed Patel v. State of Gujarat*, (2008) 6 SCC 789 : AIR 2008 SC 2392.

(d) International crimes

The international law recognises certain international crimes as crimes of universal jurisdiction. Such a crime comes under the jurisdiction of all States wherever it be committed and all States are entitled to apprehend and punish the offenders.[64] This jurisdiction applies traditionally to international crimes of piracy and war crimes.[65]

After the second world war and the Nuremberg trials in respect of Nazi atrocities, international law has recognised many other international crimes. This has been done by international treaties and conventions adopted into domestic law by legislation by the contracting States enabling them to try these crimes even in cases where such crimes were not committed by their nationals or within their geographical boundaries, thus giving rise to the principle of universality limited among the contracting States. Some examples of such legislation by the Indian Parliament are the Anti Apartheid (United Nations Convention) Act, 1981 which gives effect to the international convention on the suppression and punishment of the crime of Apartheid; the Anti-Hijacking Act, 1982, which gives effect to the convention for the suppression of unlawful seizure of aircraft known as the Hague Convention, 1970; and the Suppression of Unlawful Act against the Safety of Civil Aviation Act, 1982, which gives effect to the convention for the suppression of unlawful act against the safety of civil aviation known as the Montreal Convention, 1971.

Can courts of a country, which has ratified an International Convention creating an international crime but which has not implemented the convention by enacting a law, take cognizance of the international crime? Such a question arose before the Federal Court of Australia in relation to genocide which has not been made a crime by Australian legislation although Australia has ratified the 1948 Convention on the Prevention and Punishment of the Crime of Genocide. By majority, the Federal Court of Australia held that the crime was not cognizable by Australian courts.[66] In India, unlike in England, all offences are statutory and the common law in India does not by itself recognise any offence.[67] Therefore, the view taken by the Federal Court of Australia will apply with stronger reason for India.

Even in England the courts now cannot create new criminal law offences and statute is now the sole source of new crimes. Therefore, even if a convention or International Law recognizes a crime which has not been made a crime by legislation it would not be recognized as a crime punishable

---

64. S.K. KAPOOR, *International Law,* 12th Edition p. 210.

65. *Ibid,* p. 689.

66. *Nulyarimma v. Thompson,* (1999) FCA 1192 discussed by RYSARD PIOTROWICZ in International Focus, (2000) 74 ALJ 738.

67. SETALVAD, *The Common Law in India,* p. 139.

by courts in England. It was so held by the House of Lords in *R. v. Jones*[68] in the context of the International crime of 'aggression' which has been recognized in customary international law ever since 1945, but has not yet been assimilated in English domestic law by statute. On this reasoning the plea of protestors causing damage that they were acting for prevention of 'crime' of aggression by the United Kingdom on Iraq and had a valid defence under section 3 of the Criminal Law Act, 1967 was rejected.

One international crime considered by the House of Lords[69] is torture by a public official or a person acting in public capacity regulated by the Convention against Torture and Other Cruel and Inhuman or Degrading Treatment or Punishment, 1984 (the Torture Convention) and implemented in the United Kingdom by section 134(1) of the Criminal Justice Act, 1988. Senator Pinochet was Head of State of Chile between 1973 to March, 1990. During this period appalling acts of barbarism were committed in Chile and elsewhere allegedly in pursuance of a conspiracy to which Pinochet was a party at his instigation and with his knowledge. In 1998 when Pinochet came to the United Kingdom for medical treatment, judicial authorities in Spain sought to extradite him to stand trial in Spain on a large number of charges most of which occurred in Chile and had no connection with Spain. 110 or more States including Chile, Spain and the United Kingdom are parties to the Torture Convention.[70] The House of

---

68. (2006) 2 All ER 741 (HL).

69. *R v. Bow Street, Metropolitan Stipendary Magistrate, exparte Pinochet Ugarte*, (1999) 2 All ER 97 (HL).

N.B. 1.—Article 1 of the Torture Convention sets out internationally agreed definition of torture which as adopted in U.K. by section 134(2) of the Criminal Justice Act, 1988 reads: 'A public official or person acting in an official capacity, whatever his nationality, commits the offence of torture if in the United Kingdom or elsewhere he intentionally inflicts pain or suffering on another in the performance or purported performance of his official duties.' It is immaterial whether the pain or suffering is physical or mental.

N.B. 2.—Another international crime considered in the case, though not applied against Pinochet, was Hostage Taking which is governed by the International Convention against the Taking of Hostages, 1979 applied in U.K. by the Taking of Hostages Act, 1982. Section 1(1) of this Act defines the offence as under: 'A person, whatever his nationality, who, in the United Kingdom or elsewhere—(a) detains any other person (the hostage), and (b) in order to compel a State, international government organisation or person to do or to abstain from doing any act, threatens to kill, injure or continue to detain the hostage, commits an offence.'

N.B. 3.—India is a signatory to the Torture Convention but it has yet not been ratified and no law has been enacted for its implementation still it has significant persuasive value because it represents evolving international consensus on human rights norms: *Selvi v. State of Karnataka*, (2010) 7 SCC 263 para 236 : AIR 2010 SC 1974.

70. India signed the Convention in 1997.

Lords in disposing of the appeal in the extradition case held that Pinochet could be extradited to Spain in respect of acts of torture committed after the convention was enforced in U.K. by the Criminal Justice Act, 1988. It was also held that Pinochet had no immunity as former Head of State in respect of acts of torture committed after ratification of the convention by Spain, Chile and the United Kingdom.

Inspite of the decision of the House of Lords, Pinochet was not extradited to Spain by the Government of the United Kingdom and was allowed to return to Chile for reasons of health. But his misery did not end even thereafter, and he faced investigations in many cases in Chile also.[71] The case of Pinochet drew global attention to the international crime of Torture and to the fact that even a Head of State committing the offence can be made answerable for it. The case was also important for it was the first time that a decision of the House of Lords was reviewed and set aside and the case reheard on the ground that one of the Law Lords, who first heard the case, was automatically disqualified from hearing the case on the ground of bias as he had such links with one of the parties (Amnesty International) that the decision led to the promotion of a cause in which both were involved.[72]

As an extension of *Pinochet*, it was held by the Court of Appeal in *Jones v. Ministry of Interior of Saudi Arabia*[73] that in an action for damages for acts of torture committed in a foreign State, the State alone will have immunity but the officials responsible for torture will not have any immunity. In this case, the claimants who were British and Canadian nationals alleged that they were systematically tortured while they were imprisoned in Saudi Arabia. They claimed damages against the Kingdom of Saudi Arabia and the officials allegedly responsible for the torture. Saudi Arabia is also a party to the Torture Convention. The Court of Appeal held that the Kingdom of Saudi Arabia was entitled to State immunity under the State Immunity Act, 1978 but the officials who were responsible for the torture or even a former head of State could not be allowed State immunity whether under the Act or the international law after torture constituted an international crime under the Torture Convention.[74] The reasoning is that as the States were obliged to ensure under Article 14(1) of the Convention that victims obtained legal redress, the acts of torture could not be treated as the exercise of any function of the State to attract immunity in criminal or civil proceedings against

---

71. Pinochet died on Dec. 11, 2006. He left a dubious legacy. Hated for the cruelty of his regime, he received popularity with many Chileans possibly because of the success of his initial economic policies which turned Chile into the richest country in Latin America. Hindustan Times, December 13, 2006.

72. *R. v. Bow Street Metropolitan Stipendary Magistrate, exparte Pinochet Ugarte,* (1999) 1 All ER 577 (HL).

73. (2005) 2 WLR 808.

74. *Ibid*, pp. 862 to 864.

individuals.[75] But in appeal the House of Lords[76] reversed the decision of the Court of Appeal. It was held that though the Torture Convention had established a universal criminal jurisdiction it did not provide for universal civil jurisdiction and Article 14 of the Convention required a private right of action only for acts of torture committed in territory under the jurisdiction of the forum state. There was also no evidence nor any consensus of judicial or learned opinion that states had recognized or given effect to an international law obligation to exercise universal jurisdiction over claims arising from alleged breaches of peremptory norms of international law. Therefore, the immunity enacted by the State Immunity Act, 1978, both in favour of the State and Officials acting for the State remained unaffected.

An important development[77] in the context of international crimes is the establishment of a permanent International Criminal Court (ICC) by the Rome Statute which became effective on 1st July, 2002 after its ratification by sixty states. The court was inaugurated on March 11, 2003 after swearing in of 18 judges at the Hague. The ICC will exercise jurisdiction in respect of crime of genocide, crimes against humanity, war crimes and the crime of aggression. All these crimes except the crime of aggression are defined in the statute in Articles 6, 7 and 8. The crime of aggression is yet to be defined in accordance with Articles 121 and 123 of the statute. The ICC's jurisdiction is complimentary and it does not replace the national criminal justice systems. India and Pakistan are not parties to the Rome Statute. It is yet to be seen how effective the court will be. Questions have been raised relating to the court's independence because of the role of the Security Council in influencing its functioning.[78] Sudanese President Umar al-Bashir became the first head of State to be indicted by the ICC. The court issued an international arrest warrant against the Sudanese President on March 4, 2009 on charges of war crimes and crimes against humanity committed during the six year old civil war in Darfur, the main region of Western Sudan. But the indictment is facing serious obstacles and the "ICC's Sudanese adventure may well result in its exposure as a paper tiger."[79]

---

75. *Ibid*. For comments **see** (2005) 121 Law Quarterly Review, 353.

76. *Jones v. Ministry of Interior of the Kingdom of Saudi Arabia,* (2007) 1 All ER 103.

77. JUSTICE C STEYTLER, International Criminal Court, (2002) 76 ALJ 469; SOLI J. SORABJEE, International Criminal Court, The Times of India, March 17, 2003.

78. RAKESH BHATNAGAR : 'UNSC's role in ICC Charter Objectionable'. The Times of India, September 7, 2004; 'International Court needs to come out of UN control', The Times of India, November 30, 2004. **See further**, Report of the Berlin Conference (2004) of International Law Association relating to International Criminal Court. (The report discusses in detail Article 16 of the Rome Statute and the Security Council's resolutions pursuant to that Article as also Article 98 of the Rome Statute and the 'bilateral impunity agreements' made under it.)

79. The Hindu, March 6, 2009.

CHAPTER 7

EXPIRY AND REPEAL OF STATUTES

SYNOPSIS

1. PERPETUAL AND TEMPORARY STATUTES

A statute is either perpetual or temporary. It is perpetual when no time is fixed for its duration,[1] and such a statute remains in force until its repeal, which may be express or implied.[2] A perpetual statute is not

1. *Jotindranath v. Province of Bihar*, AIR 1949 FC 175, p. 178 : 1949 FCR 595; *District Mining Officer v. Tata Iron & Steel Co.*, AIR 2001 SC 3134, p. 3155 : (2001) 7 SCC 358.
2. **See** title 4 'Express Repeal' and 5 'Implied Repeal' in this Chapter.

perpetual in the sense that it cannot be repealed; it is perpetual in the sense that it is not abrogated by efflux of time or by non-user.[3] A statute is temporary when its duration is only for a specified time,[4] and such a statute expires on the expiry of the specified time unless it is repealed earlier. Simply because the purpose of a statute, as mentioned in its preamble, is temporary, the statute cannot be regarded as temporary when no fixed period is specified for its duration.[5] The Finance Acts which are annual Acts are not temporary Acts and they often contain provisions of a general character which are of a permanent operation.[6] A cessation of transitional legislative power has also no effect on the continuance of a perpetual Act enacted during the continuance of that power.[7] The duration of a temporary statute may be extended by a fresh statute or by exercise of a power conferred under the original statute.[8] When the life of a temporary Act is merely extended, it cannot be said that a new law has been enacted; but if the extension is accompanied by any substantial amendment, it would not be a case of mere extension. [9]It appears that after a temporary statute expires, it cannot be made effective by merely amending the same. The only apt manner of reviving the expired statute is by re-enacting a statute in similar terms or by enacting a statute expressly saying that the expired Act is herewith revived.[10]

---

3. *Hebbert v. Purchas*, (1871) LR 3 PC 605, p. 650 (PC), 'Neither contrary practice nor disuse can repeal the positive enactment of a statute' (LORD HATHERLEY, L.C.); *Metropolitan Police Commr. v. Hammond*, (1964) 2 All ER 772, p. 780 (HL), 'The mere passing of time does not warrant their being ignored' (LORD MORRIS); *State of Maharashtra v. Narayan*, AIR 1983 SC 46, p. 52 : (1982) 3 SCC 519. **But see** title 8 '*Quasi* repeal by desuetude'.
4. *Jotindranath v. Province of Bihar*, AIR 1949 FC 175 : 1949 FCR 545.
5. *Maganti v. State of Andhra Pradesh*, AIR 1970 SC 403, p. 404 : (1969) 2 SCC 96.
6. *Madurai District Central Co-operative Bank Ltd. v. Third Income-tax Officer, Madurai*, AIR 1975 SC 2016, p. 2021 : (1975) 2 SCC 454.
7. *State of Assam v. K.B. Kurkalang*, AIR 1972 SC 223 : (1972) 1 SCC 148. *Ishwardas v. Union of India*, AIR 1972 SC 1193 : (1972) 1 SCC 646.
8. *Inder Singh v. State of Rajasthan*, AIR 1957 SC 510 : 1957 SCR 605.
9. *Kaiser-I-Hind Pvt. Ltd. v. National Textiles Corporation,* AIR 2002 SC 3404, p. 3426 : (2002) 8 SCC 182.
10. *Jotindranath v. Province of Bihar*, AIR 1949 FC 175 : 1949 FCR 545.

    N.B.—This point has been **left open** in *Inder Singh's* case, *supra,* Note 8. It has been held that an Act void for want of constitutionality is a still born law and its defect cannot be cured by an amending Act: the proper course is to re-enact a new Act with retrospective effect and with suitable changes; *Shama Rao v. Union Territory, Pondicherry*, AIR 1967 SC 1480, pp. 1488, 1489. This proposition will hold good even though the Article of the Constitution which invalidated the enactment has itself been **repealed**: *Abukhan v. Union of India*, (1984) 1 SCC 88, p. 90: AIR 1983 SC 1301.

2. EFFECT OF EXPIRY OF TEMPORARY STATUTES

When a temporary Act expires, section 6 of the General Clauses Act, 1897,[11] which in terms is limited to repeals, has no application.[12] The effect of expiry, therefore, depends upon the construction of the Act itself. The leading authority on the point is the dicta of PARK, B, in *Steavenson v. Oliver*:[13] "The extent of the restrictions imposed and the duration of its provisions, are matters of construction."

(a) Legal proceedings under an expired statute

A question often arises in connection with legal proceedings in relation to matters connected with a temporary Act, whether they can be continued or initiated after the Act has expired. The answer to such a question is again dependent upon the construction of the Act as a whole.[14] The Legislature very often enacts in the temporary Act a saving provision similar in effect to section 6 of the General Clauses Act, 1897.[15] But in the absence of such a provision the normal rule is that proceedings taken against a person under a temporary statute *ipso facto* terminate as soon as the statute expires.[16] A person, therefore, cannot be prosecuted and convicted for an offence against the Act after its expiration in the absence of a saving provision; and if a prosecution has not ended before the date of expiry of the

---

11. Corresponding to section 38(2), Interpretation Act, 1899 (52 & 53 Vict. c 63).

12. *Wicks v. Director of Public Prosecutions*, (1947) 1 All ER 205, p. 206 : 1947 AC 362 (HL); *State of U.P. v. Jagmanderdas*, AIR 1954 SC 683, p. 684; *Gopichand v. Delhi Administration*, AIR 1959 SC 609, p. 615; *State of Orissa v. Bhupendra Kumar*, AIR 1962 SC 945, p. 953 : 1962 Supp (2) SCR 380.

13. (1841) 151 ER 1024, pp. 1026, 1027; **See further** *Spencer v. Hooten*, (1920) 37 TLR 280; *R. v. Ellis*, (1921) 125 LT 397; *R. v. Wicks*, (1946) 2 All ER 529, p. 531; *State of Orissa v. Bhupendra Kumar, supra*. The question relating to effect of expiry may give rise to sharp divergence of opinion; For example **see** *Krishna Kumar Singh v. State of Bihar*, JT 1998 (4) SC 58 : (1998) 5 SCC 643 (case **referred** to larger bench) : (2005) 13 SCC 375 (now **referred** to a seven-Judge Bench).

14. *R. v. Wicks*, (1946) 2 All ER 529, pp. 531, 532.

15. *Gopichand v. Delhi Administration*, AIR 1959 SC 609 : 1959 Supp (2) SCR 87; *State of Orissa v. Bhupendra Kumar*, AIR 1962 SC 945, p. 953 : 1962 Supp (2) SCR 380; *Wicks v. Director of Public Prosecutions*, (1947) 1 All ER 205, pp. 206, 207 : 1947 AC 362 (HL). For example **see** section 1(3) of TADA, 1985 and section 1(4) TADA, 1985, *State v. Gian Singh*, AIR 1999 SC 3450, p. 3454 and *Abdul Aziz v. State of West Bengal*, 1995 (5) Scale 169: AIR 1996 SC 3305. Because of section 1(4) bail cannot be granted even after expiry of TADA contrary to its provisions; *Mohammad Iqbal Madar Sheikh v. State of Maharashtra*, 1996 (1) Scale 123 : 1996 (1) SCC 722 : (1996) SCC (Cri) 202.

16. *S. Krishnan v. State of Madras*, AIR 1951 SC 301, p. 304 : 1951 SCR 621; *State of U.P. v. Jagmanderdas*, AIR 1954 SC 683, p. 685 : 1954 CriLJ 1736; *Gopichand v. Delhi Administration, supra*, p. 615; *State of Orissa v. Bhupendra Kumar, supra*, p. 953.

Act, it will automatically terminate as a result of the termination of the Act.[17] Contrary dicta, in this respect both by the CHIEF BARON LORD ABINGER and ALDERSON, B. in *Steavenson v. Oliver*[18] have not been accepted as correct.[19]

Certain State Acts imposed cess or other taxes on minerals which were declared void in different cases by the Supreme Court. Thereafter Parliament enacted the Cess and other Taxes on Minerals (Validation) Act, 1992 which included the said Acts in a Schedule. Section 2 of the Validation Act provides: "The laws specified in the Schedule to this Act shall be, and shall be deemed always to have been, as valid as if the provisions contained therein relating to cess or other taxes on minerals had been enacted by Parliament and such provisions *shall be deemed to remain in force upto the 4th day of April 1991*". The question before the Supreme Court in *District Mining Officer v. Tata Iron and Steel Co.*[20] was whether because of the Validation Act the States were entitled to retain only the cess and taxes already collected before 4th April, 1991 or whether they were also entitled to collect the cess and taxes due upto 4th April 1991 but not collected till that date. In holding that the Validation Act did not enable the States to collect the cess and taxes not collected till 4th April 1991, one of the reasons given by the Court was that the effect of section 2 was that the Acts invalidated became temporary statutes expiring on 4th April, 1991 and as there was no saving clause in the Validation Act and as section 6 of the General Clauses Act had no application to the expiry of a temporary statute. There could not be recovery and collection of cess and taxes which may have become due but were not collected till 4th April, 1991.[21]

The Defence of India Act, 1939, was enacted in exercise of the powers conferred on the Central Legislature under section 102 of the Government of India Act, 1935. Section 1(4) of the Defence of India Act provided that the Act, shall remain in force during the continuance of the war and for a period of six months thereafter. The war came to an end on 1st April, 1946, and the Act expired on 30th September,1946. By Ordinance No. XII of 1946, section 1(4) of the Defence of India Act, was amended on

---

17. *R. v. Wicks, supra*, pp. 531, 532; *State of U.P. v. Jagmanderdas, supra*; *State of Orissa v. Bhupendra Kumar, supra*, p. 953.

18. (1841) 15 ER 1024.

19. *Spencer v. Hooten*, (1920) 37 TLR, 280; *R. v. Ellis*, (1921) 125 IT, 397; *R. v. Wicks*, (1946) 2 All ER 529, pp. 531, 532.

20. AIR 2001 SC 3134 : (2001) 7 SCC 358.

21. P. 3155 **overruling** *P. Kannadasan v. State of T.N.*, AIR 1996 SC 2560 : (1996) 5 SCC 670; correctness doubted in *Assistant Director of Mines & Geology v. Deccan Cement Ltd.*, (2008) 3 SCC 451 : (2008) 2 Scale 6 and matter **referred** to larger bench.

30th March, 1946, and a saving clause similar in terms as section 6 of the General Clauses Act was added. By Act II of 1948, Ordinance No. XII of 1946 was repealed from 5th of January, 1948, and this repeal was subject to a saving clause preserving the effect or consequence of anything already done or suffered or any obligation or liability acquired or incurred or any remedy or proceeding in respect thereof. Sub-section (4) of section 102 of the Government of India Act, 1935, had provided that a law made by the Federal Legislature which it could not have made but for a Proclamation of Emergency shall cease to have effect on the expiration of a period of six months after the proclamation had ceased to operate, except with regard to things done or omitted to be done. The Government of India Act was repealed by Article 395 of the Constitution but without any saving clause and section 6 of the General Clauses Act has no application to this repeal. On 16th January, 1950, a prosecution was commenced against a person for infringing during the years 1943-45 the provisions of Non-ferrous Metals Control Order, 1942, an order made under the Defence of India Rules which were framed under the Defence of India Act. The proceedings were pending when the Constitution came into force and repealed the Government of India Act. A question, therefore, arose whether the prosecution could be continued or whether it automatically terminated. It was held that the saving clause added by Ordinance No. XII of 1946 to the Defence of India Act, ceased to be effective because of the repeal of the Ordinance by Act II of 1948, and the saving clause contained in this Act was of no avail as nothing was done under the repealed Ordinance in respect of which the saving clause could operate. It was further held that the saving contained in section 102 of the Government of India Act also became ineffective after its repeal by the Constitution. On this analysis, after 26th January, 1950, there existed no saving provision to continue the prosecution of an offender for an offence under the Defence of India Act which had expired on 30th September, 1946, and the Supreme Court applied the normal rule that the offender could not be prosecuted after expiry of the Act.[22] This decision of the Supreme Court[23] may be compared with an earlier case of the Federal Court[24] relating again to a prosecution for violation of an order (Iron and Steel Order, 1941) made under the Defence of India Act. In the Federal Court case,[25] the offence was committed in 1943, and the prosecution was started in February, 1946. The prosecution was still pending when the Defence of India Act expired on 30th September, 1946. One of the

---

22. *State of U.P. v. Jagmanderdas*, AIR 1954 SC 683 : 1954 CriLJ 1736. **See further** *Om Prakash v. State of Haryana*, AIR 1970 SC 654 : (1970) 3 SCC 107.
23. *Ibid.*
24. *J.K. Gas Plant Mfg. Co. v. Emperor*, AIR 1947 FC 38, pp. 46, 47 : 1947 FCR 141.
25. *Ibid.*

questions raised before the Federal Court, was whether the prosecution terminated after expiry of the Act. The matter came up before the Court at a time when both the savings, one inserted by Ordinance No. 12 of 1946, and the other contained in section 102(4) of the Government of India Act were in force and following a previous decision of the House of Lords in *Wicks v. Director of Public Prosecutions*,[26] the Federal Court held that the prosecution could be continued.[27]

In *Wicks'* case[28] the appellant Wicks was tried and convicted for violating in 1943-44 the Defence (General) Regulations, 1939, made under the Emergency Powers (Defence) Act, 1939. The trial took place in May, 1946, when the Emergency Powers (Defence) Act had come to an end because of its expiry in February, 1946. Section 11(1) of the Act (as amended) read: "Subject to the provisions of the section, this Act shall continue in force until the expiration of the period of six months beginning with the twenty-fourth day of August, 1945, and shall then expire". Section 11(3) provided: "The expiry of the Act shall not affect the operation thereof as respects things previously done or omitted to be done". The question in the case was whether these words in section 11(3) authorised the prosecution and conviction of the offender notwithstanding the expiration of the Act. The Court of Criminal Appeal accepted the principle that "but for the provisions in section 11(3) it could hardly be contended that a person could be convicted of an offence against the Act after its expiration."[29] As to the effect of section 11(3) it was contended that the sub-section operated only on matters past and completed while the Act was in force. Refuting this argument the court said: "While, no doubt it does cover completed acts or transactions, we think the language is wide enough to make provisions of the Act apply, or, in the language of the section, to operate, in respect of any act done before the expiration, even though not perfected or completed till afterwards."[30] And proceeding further, it was observed: "We are bound to construe the sub-section as meaning that the expiration of the Act is not to affect the liability or punishment incurred under the enactment or the prosecution of legal proceedings for the purpose of inflicting that punishment."[31] The same question was again agitated in the House of Lords. In affirming the decision of the Court of Criminal Appeal, VISCOUNT SIMON in the leading judgment observed: "It is clear that Parliament did not

---

26. (1947) 1 All ER 205 : 1947 AC 362 (HL), **affirming** *R. v. Wicks* (1946) 2 All ER 529 (CCA).
27. *J.K. Gas Plant Mfg. Co. v. Emperor, supra.*
28. *Supra*, note 26.
29. *R. v. Wicks*, (1946) 2 All ER 529, p. 532 (CCA).
30. *Ibid.*
31. *Ibid*, p. 533.

intend sub-section (3) to expire with the rest of the Act; and that its presence in the statute preserves the right to prosecute after the date of expiry."[32] The decision in this case has also been accepted in India.[33]

But in *Rayala Corporation v. Director of Enforcement*,[34] the case of *Wicks*[35] was distinguished. Rule 132A of the Defence of India Rules, 1962, which related to the prohibition of dealings in foreign exchange was by the Amendment Rules, 1965, 'omitted except as respects things done or omitted to be done under that rule'. The question before the Supreme Court in *Rayala Corporation* case[36] was whether a prosecution in respect of contravention of Rule 132A could be commenced after the Rule was omitted. The Supreme Court answered the question in the negative, holding that initiation of a new proceeding will not be a thing done or omitted to be done under the rule but a new act of initiating a proceeding after the rule had ceased to exist. *Wick's* case[37] was distinguished on the ground that the saving clause in that case was much wider and also saved the 'operation' of the expired Act 'as respects things previously done or omitted to be done'. It is submitted that the distinction drawn is unreal. The words 'omitted except as respects things done' *etc.*, themselves indicate that the rule was not omitted for things already done and continued in operation in respect thereof. This saving clause, it is submitted, was of the same scope and effect as the saving clause in *Wick's* case.[38]

Article 352 of the Constitution provides for proclamation of Emergency in case of war or external aggression or armed rebellion. Article 358 suspends the fundamental rights under Article 19 and Article 359 enables the President to suspend enforcement of other fundamental rights except Articles 20 and 21 during the period of Emergency. The result is that a law made during the Emergency even if violative of any fundamental right (except Articles 20 and 21) is not open to challenge on that ground. But such laws 'cease to have effect-except as respects things done or omitted

---

32. *Wicks v. Director of Public Prosecutions*, (1947) 1 All ER 205, p. 207 : (1947) AC 362 (HL).

33. *J.K. Gas Plant Mfg. Co. v. Emperor*, AIR 1947 FC 38, pp. 46, 47 : 1947 FCR 141; *Gopichand v. Delhi Administration*, AIR 1959 SC 609, p. 615 : 1959 Supp (2) SCR 87; *State of Orissa v. Bhupendra Kumar*, AIR 1962 SC 945, p. 953 : 1962 Supp (2) SCR 380; *Om Prakash v. State of Haryana*, AIR 1970 SC 654 : (1970) 3 SCC 107.

34. AIR 1970 SC 494, p. 504 : (1969) 2 SCC 412; **Followed** in *Lennart v. Director of Enforcement*, AIR 1970 SC 549, p. 553 : (1970) 1 SCC 152.

35. *Supra*, note 26.

36. *Rayala Corporation v. Director of Enforcement*, AIR 1970 SC 494 : (1969) 2 SCC 412.

37. *Supra*, note 26.

38. *Ibid.*

to be done' during their operation after the proclamation of Emergency is withdrawn. During the period of Emergency, when the fundamental right under Article 22 was suspended by an order of the President under Article 359, Parliament added section 12A in the Conservation of Foreign Exchange and Prevention of Smuggling Act, 1974 (COFEPOSA). This section which was to have effect only during the period of emergency enabled detention in violation of clauses (4) and (5) of Article 22. Detention orders passed under section 12A of COFEPOSA were withdrawn after the Emergency when the section itself expired. But such orders were made the foundation for taking action under the Smugglers and Foreign Exchange Manipulators (Forfeiture of Property) Act, 1976 (SAFEMA). In proceedings to challenge the notices under SAFEMA it was contended that the detention orders under section 12A of COFEPOSA were void being violative of fundamental right under Article 22 and could not be relied upon for SAFEMA. This contention was negatived on the ground that the detention orders under section 12A COFEPOSA were 'things done' under that section and could not be treated to be void after expiry of section 12A because of the saving clause 1A of Article 359 'as respects things done or omitted to be done' during the period section 12A was in operation.[39]

It has been held that an offence which is triable under the general law as a warrant case, and which became triable as a summons case under a temporary statute, could not be tried as a summons case after expiry of the statute, even though the trial had begun during the period when the statute was effective.[40] It has also been held that if offences under the expired Act could be tried only by special courts constituted under it, the offences could not be tried after the expiry of the Act if the special courts are abolished, although they could have been continued to function for trial of offences committed before the expiry of the Act.[41] But offences which are punishable under the ordinary laws but were being tried by special courts, being connected with the offences under the expired Act, could still be tried by ordinary courts without the necessity of a *de novo* trial.[42] An

39. *Attorney General for India v. Amratlal Prajivandas*, JT 1994(3) SC 583 : (1994) 5 SCC 54, pp. 603, 607, 608 : AIR 1994 SC 2179, pp. 2196, 2197. **See further** *Gangadevi v. Union of India*, 1996 (7) Scale 389 : 1996 (6) SCC 40; *Kesar Devi v. Union of India,* (2003) 7 SCC 427, p. 431 : AIR 2003 SC 4195 : 2003 SCC (Cri) 1652; *Fatima Mohd. Amin v. Union of India,* (2003) 7 SCC 436.

40. *Gopichand v. Delhi Administration*, AIR 1959 SC 609, p. 615 : 1959 Supp (2) SCR 87.

41. *Bhaskar v. State,* JT 1999 (7) SC 355, pp. 358-60 : AIR 1999 SC 3539, pp. 3541, 3542 : (1999) 9 SCC 551.

42. *Ibid.* **See further** *State of Tamil Nadu v. Paramasiva Pandian,* AIR 2001 SC 2972, p. 2976 : (2002) 1 SCC 15.

appeal under a temporary statute pending at the time of the expiry of the statute will in the absence of a saving clause automatically terminate.[43]

(b) Notifications, Orders, Rules, *etc.* made under temporary statute

When a temporary Act expires, the normal rule is that any appointment, notification, order, scheme, rule, form or bye-law made or issued under the Act will also come to an end with the expiry of the Act and will not be continued even if the provisions of the expired Act are re-enacted; the reason being that section 24 of the General Clauses Act, 1897, does not apply to such a situation.[44] Similarly, a person's detention under a temporary statute relating to preventive detention will automatically come to an end on the expiry of the statute.[45]

(c) Expiry does not make the statute dead for all purposes

But a temporary statute, even in the absence of a saving provision like section 6 of the General Clauses Act, is not dead for all purposes. As already stated the question is essentially one of construction of the Act.[46] The nature of the right and obligation resulting from the provisions of the temporary Act and their character, may have to be regarded in determining whether the said right or obligation is enduring or not.[47] Thus, a person who has been prosecuted and sentenced during the continuance of a temporary Act for violating its provisions cannot be released before he serves out his sentence, even if the temporary Act expires before the expiry of full period of the sentence.[48]

Under section 4 of VI Geo. 4, c. 133, every person who held a commission or warrant as surgeon or assistant surgeon became entitled to practice as an apothecary without having passed the usual examination. This statute was temporary and expired on 1st August, 1826. It was held that a person who had acquired a right to practice as an apothecary under the Act without passing the usual examination was not deprived of that right on expiration of the Act.[49]

---

43. *Spencer v. Hooten*, (1920) 37 TLR 280.

44. *Trust Mai Lachhmi Sialkoti Bradari v. Amritsar Improvement Trust*, AIR 1963 SC 976, p. 979 : (1963) 1 SCR 242 (Case under section 22 of the Punjab General Clauses Act) : 1963 (1) SCR 242.

45. *S. Krishnan v. State of Madras*, AIR 1951 SC 301, p. 304 : 1951 SCR 621.

46. **See** title 2, 'Effect of Expiry of Temporary Statute', text and note 13, p. 719.

47. *State of Orissa v. Bhupendra Kumar*, AIR 1962 SC 945, p. 953 : 1962 Supp (2) SCR 380.

48. *Ibid*, p. 954.

49. *Steavenson v. Oliver*, (1841) 151 ER 1024.

Certain elections to the Cuttack Municipality were held to be invalid by the High Court because of defective electoral rolls. The Governor of Orissa, however, in the exercise of his powers under Article 213 of the Constitution promulgated an Ordinance validating the electoral rolls as also the elections and declaring that any order of the court holding the electoral rolls and the elections invalid shall be deemed to be and always to have been of no legal effect. The Ordinance lapsed on April 1, 1959. It was contended thereafter that the invalidity of the election which had been cured by the Ordinance revived on its expiry. In overruling the contention GAJENDRAGADKAR, J. observed: "In our opinion having regard to the object of the Ordinance and to the rights created by the validating provisions, it would be difficult to accept the contention that as soon as the Ordinance expired, the validity of the elections came to an end and their invalidity was revived. The rights created by this Ordinance are in our opinion, very similar to the rights with which the court was dealing in the case of *Steavenson*;[50] and they must be held to endure and last even after the expiry of the Ordinance. The Ordinance has in terms provided that the order of the court declaring the elections to Cuttack Municipality to be invalid shall be deemed to be and always to have been of no legal effect whatever, and that the said elections are thereby validated. That being so, the said elections must be deemed to have been validly held under the Act and the life of the newly elected municipality would be governed by the relevant provisions of the Act, and would not come to an end as soon as the Ordinance expires."[51] This case was followed in holding that the posts of part-time village officers abolished by Ordinance No.1 of 1984 promulgated by the Governor of Andhra Pradesh did not revive on the expiry of the Ordinance.[52]

A decision of the Privy Council,[53] in an appeal from Ontario, also illustrates that a temporary Act, after its expiry is not to be treated for all purposes as if it had never been enacted. In that case the power of the Canadian Radio Broadcasting Commission to acquire existing private stations by lease was curtailed by a temporary Act, in that the power was expressly made subject to the approval of the Governor in Council. A lease obtained by the Commission during the currency of the temporary Act, was challenged after the expiry of the Act in a legal proceeding, on the ground that the lease was invalid being not in accordance with the approval of the

---

50. *Ibid.*

51. *State of Orissa v. Bhupendra Kumar*, AIR 1962 SC 945, p. 955 : 1962 Supp (2) SCR 380.

52. *T. Venkata Reddy v. State of Andhra Pradesh*, (1985) 3 SCC 198, pp. 213 to 215 : AIR 1985 SC 724.

53. *Gooderham & Worts v. C.B. Corporation*, AIR 1949 PC 90.

Governor in Council as required by the expired Act. This plea, though resisted on the ground that it could not be raised after expiry of the Act, was sustained by the Privy Council on the view that the temporary Act was not for all purposes to be treated as if it had never been enacted.[54]

(d) Repeal by a temporary statute

When a temporary statute effects a repeal of an existing statute, a question arises whether the repealed statute revives on the expiry of the repealing statute. Section 11(1) and section 38(2)(a) of the Interpretation Act, 1899, in terms are limited to cases of repeals of a repealing enactment and have no application to a case of expiry of a repealing Act. As regards the General Clauses Act, 1897, section 6(a), which corresponds to section 38(2)(a) of the Interpretation Act, is also in terms limited to repeals; and therefore has no application on expiry of a repealing statute.[55] But in section 7 of the General Clauses Act, which corresponds to section 11(1) of the Interpretation Act, the language is slightly different. However, having regard to the context and the setting of the section it appears also to be inapplicable to a case of expiry of a repealing statute. The answer, therefore, to the question, whether a statute which is repealed by a temporary statute revives on the expiry of the repealing statute, will depend upon the construction of the repealing statute. As regards the effect of the repealing of an earlier Act made by a temporary Act, observed GAJENDRAGADKAR, J. "the intention of the temporary Act in repealing the earlier Act will have to be considered, and no general or inflexible rule in that behalf can be laid down."[56] As was stated by ELLENBOROUGH, C.J.: "A law, though temporary in some of its provisions, may have a permanent operation in other respects. The statute 26 Geo. 3, c. 108 professes to repeal the statute 19 Geo. 2, c. 35, absolutely, though its own provisions, which it substituted in place of it, were to be only temporary."[57] Following these principles, it was

---

54. *Ibid*, pp. 93, 94.

55. **But see** *Om Prakash v. State of U.P.*, AIR 1957 SC 458, p. 463 : 1957 SCR 423, where a contrary opinion is expressed.
It is submitted that the view expressed in this case of section 6(a) is not correct. The opening words of section 6 which apply to all the clauses in section 6 are inapplicable to the case of expiry of a temporary statute and it seems impossible to give to them a different meaning for purposes of clause (a) alone. The said clause will, however, be attracted when a repealing temporary statute is itself repealed.

56. *State of Orissa v. Bhupendra Kumar*, AIR 1962 SC 945, p. 954 : 1962 Supp (2) SCR 380.

57. *Warren v. Windle*, (1803) 102 ER 576, p. 578 : 102 ER 576 (KB); **referred** to in *Bhupendra Kumar's case*, *supra*, note 56. **See further** the observation of **[Footnote No. 57 Contd.]**

held that the Jind State Civil Service Regulations, 1945 which were repealed by Pepsu Ordinance No. 16 of Samvat 2005 did not revive after six months when the Ordinance expired for the intention in repealing the Regulations was to repeal them absolutely.[58] Similarly Rule 49 of the U.P. Sugarcane (Regulation of Supply and Purchase) Rules substituted by the Amendment Rules 1992 (which were to have effect from 1-10-1991 to 30-9-1992) in place of the then existing rule 49 was held to repeal the existing rule absolutely which was not revived after the expiry of the substituted rule.[59]

If the repealing section in a temporary statute on construction, is held to expire with the expiry of the Act, the repeal will be construed only as a temporary repeal. Section 1 of Statute 46 Geo. 3 repealed the provisions of Statute 42 Geo. 3 and substituted some other provisions. Section 14 of the repealing Act provided that the Act shall continue in force till a certain period. It was held that 'the Act' referred to in section 14 included whole of the Act and incorporating section 1 with section 14, the repeal expired with the expiry of the Act reviving the operation of the earlier Act.[60]

In the Privy Council case already noticed,[61] there are observations to the effect that a repeal by a temporary Act is *prima facie* only a temporary repeal resulting in revival of the repealed provisions after the expiry of the repealing Act. Those observations may here be quoted: "The result is that on 31st March, 1936, the temporary legislation contained in the first Act of 1933 repealing provisions of the principal Act of 1932 and substituting other provisions came to an end not by the repeal of the temporary legislation but by the efflux of the prescribed time. No question, as to the revival of the temporary repealed provisions of the principal Act of 1932 by the repeal of repealing legislation, arises. The repeal, effected by the temporary legislation, was only a temporary repeal. When by the fiat of Parliament the temporary repeal expired, the original legislation automatically resumed its full force. No enactment of it was required."[62]

[Footnote No. 57 Contd.]

ELLENBOROUGH, C.J. in *R. v. Rogers*, (1809) 103 ER 891, p. 893; which are to the following effect: "It is a question of construction of every Act professing to repeal or interfere with the provisions of a former law, whether it operates as a total or a partial and temporary repeal". **See** further text and note 60, *infra.*

58. *State of Haryana v. Amarnath Bansal*, 1997 (1) Scale 343, pp. 351, 352 : AIR 1997 SC 718, pp. 725, 726 : (1997) 10 SCC 700.

59. *West U.P. Sugar Mills Association v. State of U.P.*, AIR 2002 SC 948 : (2002) 2 SCC 645.

60. *R. v. Rogers*, (1809) 103 ER 891, p. 893.

61. *Gooderham & Worts v. C.B. Corporation*, AIR 1949 PC 90. **See** text and notes 53 and 54, *supra.*

62. *Gooderham & Worts v. C.B. Corporation*, AIR 1949 PC 90, p. 94.

But when a permanent Ordinance imposing a cess on coal was repealed by a temporary Ordinance which specifically applied the provisions of section 6, General Clauses Act, it was held that the provisions of the repealed Ordinance, which were continued for enforcing the right acquired and obligations incurred before the repeal, did not expire with the expiry of the repealing Ordinance.[63] It seems to have been assumed in this case that the repeal, though brought about by a temporary Ordinance, was a permanent repeal.

3. POWER TO REPEAL IS CONSISTENT WITH POWER TO ENACT AND IS NOT CONTROLLED BY PREVIOUS LEGISLATION : REPEAL MAY BE EXPRESS OR IMPLIED

A power to make a law with respect to the topics committed to Parliament or State Legislatures carries with it a power to repeal a law on those topics. Subject to any Constitutional restriction, the general rule is that 'the power of a legislative body to repeal a law is co-extensive with its power to enact such a law,' and a Legislature which has no power to enact a law on a particular subject-matter has also no power to repeal the same.[64] A Legislature, however, has no power to bind itself or its successor as to the course of future legislation for to acknowledge such a power will mean that a Legislature can curtail its own or its successor's powers which are conferred by the Constitution and which cannot be restricted or taken away except by an amendment of the Constitution. It is an axiom of British Constitutional law that "Acts of Parliament derogatory from the subsequent Parliament bind not."[65] "Because the Legislature, being in truth the

---

63. *R.C. Jall v. Union of India*, AIR 1962 SC 1281, p. 1286 : 1962 Supp (3) SCR 436.

64. *Ramkrishna v. Janpad Sabha*, AIR 1962 SC 1073, p. 1080 : 1962 Supp (3) 70 **citing** *A.G. for Ontario v. A.G. for the Dominion* (1896) AC 348, p. 366 (PC); *Karstinyeri v. The Commonwealth* (1998) 72 ALJR 722, p. 729 (Aust); *Mahmadhusen Abdulrahim Kalota Shaikh v. Union of India*, (2009) 2 SCC 1 para 34 (d) : (2008) 13 Scale 398 (11th edition p. 633 of this book is **referred**).

65. 1 Bl Comm. 90. This proposition though sound in legal theory must give way to practical politics; for example, it is impossible to imagine that the British Parliament could have ever **repealed** section 4 of the statute of Westminster, 1931 [*Blackburn v. Attorney General*, (1971) 1 WLR 1037, p. 1040 (CA)] or can effectively **repeal** the corresponding section 1 of the Australia Act, 1986 (U.K.) which provides that no Act of U.K. Parliament shall extend or be deemed to extend to the commonwealth [*Sue v. Hill*, (1999) 73 ALJR 1016, p. 1029 (para 64)]. It is also a debatable question whether the British Parliament can lawfully abolish the House of Lords; **see** (1979) 95 LQR 36, 38. Even the validity of the Parliament Act, 1949 which amended the Parliament Act, 1911 and which only reduces the period of delay when the House of Lords does not approve a Bill, is a matter of controversy; **See also** SAMUELS,

[Footnote No. 65 Contd.]

[Footnote No. 65 Contd.]

'Is the Parliament Act, 1949 valid', (2003) 24 Statute Law Review 237. Search for a suitable building to accommodate the Supreme Court seems to be the cause of delay for implementing this reform: LORD DAVID HOPE, 'A Phoenix From the Ashes? Accommodating A New Supreme Court', (2005) 121 LQR 253-72. Implementation of the Constitution Reform Act, 2005 will abolish the judicial wing of the House of Lords and establish a new Supreme Court in its place which is likely to function from October 2009. Doubts about the validity of The Parliament Act, 1949 have been dispelled by the House of Lords. The Parliament Act, 1911 prescribed the circumstances when 'any public Bill' could be enacted without the consent of the House of Lords. This Act was enacted with the consent of the House of Lords. The Parliament Act, 1949 was enacted according to the procedure laid down in the Act of 1911 without the consent of the House of Lords. The Act of 1949 amended the 1911 Act by reducing the number of sessions in which a Bill had to pass the commons from three to two and reducing from two to one the number of years which had to elapse before the consent of the Lords could be dispensed with. The Hunting Act, 2004, which made it an offence to hunt a wild animal with a dog, was enacted according to the procedure laid down in the Act of 1949. On a challenge to both the Parliament Act, 1949 and the Hunting Act, 2004, both were held to be valid by the House of Lords: *R. (on the application of Jackson) v. Attorney General,* (2005) 4 All ER 1253 (HL). (The argument that the Parliament Act of 1911 was delegated legislation was rejected). For **criticism, see** ROBIN COOKE 'A Controversial Retreat', (2006) 122 LQR 224-31. Further, it is now accepted that the community law, *i.e.,* EEC. Treaty enforced by the European Communities Act, 1972 prevails over anything inconsistent in an English statute for section 2(4) of the Act provides that 'any enactment passed or to be passed' will take effect subject to community law; *R. v. Secretary of State for Transport, ex parte, Factortame Ltd.*, (1990) 2 AC 85; (No. 2) (1991) 1 AC 603. After **referring** to these decisions which dealt with a British statute of 1988' Prof. Wade comments: "The Parliament of 1972 has bound the Parliament of 1988. To that extent we have had a constitutional revolution": (1992) Public Law in Britain and India (Nambiyar Lectures) p. 8. There is a **contrary view** that the 1972 Act creates only a rule of construction requiring express words to the contrary for displacing the community law and that there is no constitutional revolution. **See** ALLAN 'Parliamentary Sovereignty: Law Politics and Revolution', (1997) 113 LQR 443. Wade's reply to this argument is that such express provision would be quite inconsistent with the continued membership of the community and so "while Britain remains in the community we are in a regime in which Parliament has bound its successors successfully, and which is nothing if not revolutionary:" (1996) 112 LQR 568, p. 571. Action taken under a United Kingdom legislation which is in conflict with community law may also give rise to state's liability to pay damages: *R. v. Secretary of State for Transport, ex parte, Factortame Ltd.,* (1999) 4 All ER 906 (HL). **See further** K.J. Keith (Judge of the Supreme Court of New Zealand), 'Sovereignty, at the beginning of the 21st Century: Fundamental or outmoded', (2004) 63 Cambridge Law Journal 581. The Hunting Act, 2004 was later challenged as violative of Human Rights enforced by the Human Right Act, 1998 and the EEC Treaty but this challenge also **failed**: *R (on the application of Countryside Alliance) v. Attorney General*, (2008) 2 All ER 95 (H.L.).

- The U.K. Supreme Court was inaugurated on 1st October 2009 when the judicial wing of the House of Lords shifted to its new headquarters. This completes the reform of separating the judicial and law making functions of the House of Lords.

[Footnote No. 65 Contd.]

sovereign power, is always of equal, always of absolute authority: it acknowledges no superior upon earth, which the prior Legislature must have been, if its Ordinances could bind a subsequent Parliament."[66] It follows as a logical result that provisions in a statute that it cannot be repealed expressly[67] or impliedly,[68] are of no legal effect. What Parliament has done Parliament can undo.[69]

The Acquisition of Land (Assessment of Compensation) Act, 1919, in section 7 laid down: "The provisions of the Act or Order by which the land is authorised to be acquired, or of any Act incorporated therewith, shall in relation to the matters dealt with in this Act, have effect subject to this Act, and so far as inconsistent with this Act those provisions shall cease to have or shall not have effect". The Housing Act, 1925, in codifying all the Housing Acts inserted certain provisions as to compensation inconsistent with the provisions in the Act of 1919. It was contended before the Court of Appeal that the effect of section 7 of the Act of 1919 was that inconsistent provisions in the Act of 1925 were to have no effect. In countering this argument MAUGHAM, L.J., observed: "It seems to me plain that the Legislature is unable, according to our Constitution, to bind itself as to the form of subsequent legislation—; it is impossible for Parliament to say that in a subsequent Act of Parliament dealing with this subject-matter there shall never be an implied repeal. If Parliament chooses, in a subsequent Act, to make it perfectly plain that the previous one is being to some extent repealed or abrogated, that must have effect, because it is the will of the Legislature."[70]

Similarly, if a general Act says that its provisions shall apply unless 'expressly excluded' by any special law, it does not mean that the exclusion must be by express words; and exclusion by necessary implication will be

---

[Footnote No. 65 Contd.]

Ten Law Lords then holding office became the first justices of the Twelve member Supreme Court and their senior member Lord Phillips of worth Matravers became the first President of the Supreme Court. Eleventh place was taken by Lord Clarke who was then Master of the Rolls. Lord Neuberger was appointed to replace Lord Clarke as Master of the Rolls and so he did not move to the new court.

66. *Ibid.*

67. *Duke of Argyll v. IRC* (1913) 109 LT 893, p. 895.

68. *Ellen Street Estate Ltd. v. Minister for Health*, (1934) 1 KB 590; (1934) All ER Rep 385, pp. 389, 390; *Vauxhall Estates Ltd. v. Liverpool Corporation*, (1932) 1 KB 733.

69. *Duke of Argyll v. IRC, supra.*

70. *Ellen Street Estates Ltd. v. Minister of Health*, (1934) All ER Rep 385, p. 390. **See further** *Thoburn v. Sunderland City Council*, (2002) 4 All ER 156, pp. 177, 180 (QBD); *Kumaon Motor Owners Union v. State of U.P.*, AIR 1966 SC 785 : (1966) 2 SCR 121, (Construction of section 68B of the Motor Vehicles Act, 1939 and section 43 of the Defence of India Act, 1962).

equally effective.[71] Section 29 of the Limitation Act, 1963, provides that sections 4 to 24 of the Act shall apply only in so far as they are not 'expressly excluded' by special or local law. In holding that section 5 of the Act does not apply to election petitions presented to the High Court under section 80A of the Representation of the People Act, 1951, as amended by Act 47 of 1966, the Supreme Court observed that "even in a case where the special law does not exclude the provisions of sections 4 to 24 of the Limitation Act, 1963 by an express reference, it would none the less be open to the court to examine whether and to what extent the nature of those provisions, or the nature of the subject-matter and scheme of the special law, exclude their operation".[72]

An Act, therefore, may be repealed by a later 'distinct and repealing enactment or an enactment inconsistent and irreconcilable therewith'.[73] In other words no repeal can be brought about 'unless there is an express repeal of an earlier Act by the later Act, or unless the two Acts cannot stand together'.[74] A repeal may thus be by express words of a later statute, or may be implied on considerations of inconsistency, or irreconcilability of the provisions of an earlier statute, with those of a later statute. A power 'to amend or repeal' will, therefore, imply a power to amend or repeal by implication, *i.e.*, by making inconsistent laws.[75] A repeal, express or implied, cannot be brought about by subordinate legislation, since a power to repeal cannot be delegated either by Union Parliament or by State

---

71. *Hukumdev v. Lalitnarain*, AIR 1974 SC 480, p. 490 : (1973) 2 SCC 133.

72. *Ibid.* For construction of section 29(2) of the Limitation Act, 1963, **see** *Mukri Gopalan v. Cheppilat Puthanpurayil Aboobacker*, 1995 (4) Scale 438 : 1995 AIR SCW 3389 : AIR 1995 SC 2272 : (1995) 4 SCC 5; *Union of India v. Popular Construction Co.,* AIR 2001 SC 4010, pp. 4012, 4013 : (2001) 8 SCC 470 (Special Act providing for extension for 3 days 'but not thereafter' construed to exclude section 5 of the Limitation Act); *Gopal Sardar v. Karuna Sardar*, (2004) 4 SCC 252, p. 265 (para 13) : AIR 2004 SC 3068. *L.S. Synthetics Ltd. v. Fairgrowth Financial Services,* AIR 2005 SC 1209 (paras 38, 39); *Consolidated Engineering Enterprises v. Principal Secretary (Irrigation Department)*, (2008) 7 SCC 169 : (2008) 6 Scale 748; *Commissioner of Customs and Excise v. Hongo India Pvt. Ltd.,* (2009) 5 SCC 791 para 34 to 37 : (2009) 7 JT 83 (High Court has no power to condone delay beyond period specified in section 35 H of the Central Excise Act); *Chhattisgarh State Electricity Board v. Central Electricity Regulatory Commission*, (2010) 5 SCC 23 paras 25, 26 : AIR 2010 SC 2061 (period of limitation for appeal to Supreme Court under section.125 of the Electricity Act cannot be extended beyond 120 days as provided in section.125 of the Electricity Act which is a Special Act).

73. *Ridsdale v. Clifton*, (1877) 36 LT 865, p. 879 (PC); **see further** *Kariapper v. Wijesinha*, (1967) 3 All ER 485, pp. 494, 495 (PC).

74. *Mathraprasad & Sons v. State of Punjab*, AIR 1962 SC 745, p. 748 : 1962 Supp (1) SCR 913.

75. *Kariapper v. Wijesinha*, (1967) 3 All ER 485, pp. 494, 495 : 1968 AC 717 (PC); *Standard Motors v. Kerala State*, AIR 1969 SC 273, p. 275 : (1969) 1 SCR 464.

Legislatures.[76] A minister's speech in Parliament announcing the Government's decision to abolish a cess levied under an Act of Parliament is entirely ineffective to abolish the ¢ess until the decision is embodied in another Act of Parliament repealing the earlier Act.[77]

The doctrine of implied repeal discussed above has undergone a change in the English law. It has now been judicially recognised that its application is limited to ordinary statutes and that it does not apply to Constitutional statutes meaning thereby statutes which condition the legal relationship between citizen and state of which the recent examples of Acts of British Parliament are the European Communities Act, 1972, the Human Rights Act, 1998, the Scotland Act, 1998 and the Government of Wales Act, 1998.[78] In India the Constitution of India can be amended only by a Constitution Amendment Act passed in accordance with Article 368 of the Constitution and which does not affect its basic structure.[79]

4. EXPRESS REPEAL

The use of any particular form of words is not necessary to bring about an express repeal.[80] All that is necessary is that the words used show an intention to abrogate the Act or provision in question. The usual form is to use the words 'is or are hereby repealed' and to mention the Acts sought to be repealed in the repealing section or to catalogue them in a Schedule. The use of words 'shall cease to have effect', is also not uncommon. When the object is to repeal only a portion of an Act words 'shall be omitted' are

---

76. *Article 143 of Constitution of India and Delhi Laws Act, etc., In the matter of,* AIR 1951 SC 332; *Rajnarayan v. Chairman, Patna Municipality,* AIR 1954 SC 569 : (1955) 1 SCR 290 (A power to modify in essential features any existing or future law cannot be delegated).

But see *Harishanker v. State of M.P.*, AIR 1954 SC 465 : (1955) 1 SCR 380 (when a law is merely overriden for certain purposes it is not a case of repeal and such a power can be delegated).

77. *B.K. Industries v. Union of India,* AIR 1993 SC 2123 : 1993 (2) JT 709 : 1993 Supp (3) SCC 621.

78. *Thobwon v. Sunderland City Council,* (2002) 4 All ER 156, pp. 184, 185 (Laws LJ) (QBD). LORD JUSTICE LAWS has further elaborated this point in an article 'Constitutional Guarantees' published in (2008) 29 Statute Law Review 1. According to him even common law constitutional guarantees such as no one shall be confined or imprisoned save by force of law or the right to access to Queen's Court cannot be abrogated by implication and will need crystal clear provisions for their abrogation. **See further** Principle of Legality pp. 486, 488.

79. See pp. 303-307, *supra.*

80. *R v. Longmead,* (1795) 2 Leach 694 : 168 ER 448 ('The Legislature when they intend to pass, to continue, or to repeal a law are not bound to use any precise form of words.')

normally used.[81] The legislative practice in India shows that 'omission' of a provision is treated as amendment[82] which signifies deletion of that provision and is not different from repeal.[83] It has been held that 'there is no real distinction between repeal and an amendment.'[84] It has also been held that 'where a provision of an Act is omitted by an Act and the said Act simultaneously re-enacts a new provision which substantially covers the field occupied by the *repealed provision* with certain modification, in that event such re-enactment is regarded having force continuously and the modification or changes are treated as amendment coming into force with effect from the date of enforcement of re-enacted provision.'[85]

When a Central Act has been adopted under Article 252 by a State by a resolution passed by the House or Houses of the Legislature of the State, the amendment or repeal of the Central Act by Parliament does not affect its continuance as a State Act unless the Central amending or repealing Act is also adopted under Article 252 by the State by a resolution of the House or Houses of the Legislature.[86]

Substitution of a provision results in repeal of the earlier provision and its replacement by the new provision.[87] Substitution thus combines repeal

---

81. **See** HALSBURY'S Laws of England, 4th Edition Vol. 44, p. 604 (f.n. 4). In *Rayala Corporation v. Director of Enforcement*, AIR 1970 SC 494, p. 503 (para 15) : (1969) 2 SCC 412, which was **followed** in *Kolhapur Canesugar Works Ltd. v. Union of India,* AIR 2000 SC 811, pp. 819, 820 : (2000) 2 SCC 536, and *Shiv Shakti Co-op. Housing Society Nagpur v. Swaraj Developers,* AIR 2003 SC 2434, p. 2443 : (2003) 6 SCC 659; there are observations that omission of a provision is different from repeal. It is submitted that this view is not correct and needs reconsideration on this point. **See further,** p. 755.

82. For example **see** sections 6(a), 13, 22(a), 52, 71, 72, 77 of the Finance Act, 1999 and section 6A of the General Clauses Act, 1897.

83. *Bhagat Ram Sharma v. Union of India,* AIR 1988 SC 740, p. 746 : (1988) Supp SCC 30.

84. *Ibid.* **See further** *Attorney General (WA) v. Margret,* (2003) 78 ALJR 105, p. 113 ('The central meaning of 'amend' is to alter the legal meaning of an Act or provision, short of entirely rescinding it, and the central meaning of 'repeal' is to rescind the Act or provision in question. The cases, however, reveal that the words can be used in ways in which there appears to be overlapping in their meanings. Thus, if a section is deleted it can be said that it has been repealed whilst the statute itself has been amended.' In this case the procedure prescribed for amending an Act was held to apply also for its repeal).

85. *CIT v. Venkateshwara Hatcheries,* AIR 1999 SC 1225, p. 1229 : 1999 (3) SCC 632.

86. *State of West Bengal v. Pronob Kr. Sur,* AIR 2003 SC 2313, p. 2319 : (2003) 9 SCC 490.

87. *State of Rajasthan v. Mangilal Pindwal,* AIR 1996 SC 2181, p. 2183 : 1996 (5) SCC 60. **See further** *West U.P. Sugar Mills Association v. State of U.P.,* AIR 2002 SC 948, p. 949 : (2002) 2 SCC 645; *Zile Singh v. State of Haryana,* (2004) 8 SCC 1,

[Footnote No. 87 Contd.]

and fresh enactment. Therefore, when a new provision is 'substituted' in place of or is made in supersession of an existing provision, the declaration of invalidity of the new provision on the ground of want of competence will also invalidate the repeal; but if the declaration of invalidity is on other grounds, *e.g.*, arbitrariness or violation of fundamental rights, the repeal, speaking generally will be effective although the new provision is declared invalid unless from the totality of circumstances and the context it is found that there was no intention to repeal in the event of the new provision being struck down.[88] In *Shambhu Dayal v. State of Uttar Pradesh,*[89] it was held that the amending Act 49 of 1964 which substituted new sections 8 and 9 in the Prevention of Food Adulteration Act, 1954 had not the effect of repealing the original sections 8 and 9 and therefore, the appointment of Food Inspector under the original section 9 continued. It is submitted that the decision though correct is based on wrong reasoning. The effect of the amending Act was to repeal the original sections 8 and 9 and to enact the new sections 8 and 9 in their place. But the appointment of Food Inspector under the old section continued to be valid as if made under the new provision in view of section 24 of the General Clauses Act, 1897. The question whether a substituted provision is prospective or retrospective will depend on its construction. When it is clarificatory or supplies an obvious omission it would be construed as retrospective.[90]

An amending Act which limits the area of operation of an existing Act by modifying the extent clause, results in partial repeal of the Act in respect of the area over which its operation is excluded.[91]

[Footnote No. 87 Contd.]

p. 12 : AIR 2004 SC 5100, p. 5106 (9th Edn., p. 565 of this book is **referred**); *Government of India v. India Tobacco Association,* (2005) 7 SCC 396 (para 25), p. 402 : AIR 2005 SC 3685 (9th edition, p. 565 of this book is **referred**.); *PTC India Ltd. v. Central Electricity Regulatory Commission*, (2010) 4 SCC 603 para 91 : AIR 2010 SC 1338. (11th edition of this book is **referred**).

88. *Indian Express Newspapers v. Union of India*, (1985) 1 SCC 641, pp. 708 to 710 : AIR 1986 SC 515. In this case the court **discussed** its earlier cases and placed them in two categories: (a) Where there was want of competence in enacting the new law; *Koteshwar v. K. Rangappa Baliga & Co.*, AIR 1969 SC 504 : (1969) 1 SCC 255; *Mulchand v. Rajkot Municipality*, AIR 1970 SC 685 : (1970) 3 SCC 884; *Mohd. Shaukat Hussain Khan v. State of A.P.*, AIR 1974 SC 1480 : (1974) 2 SCC 376; *State of Maharashtra v. Central Provinces Manganese Ore Co. Ltd.*, AIR 1977 SC 879 : (1977) 1 SCC 643; (b) where the law was struck down on other grounds, *B.N. Tiwari v. Union of India*, AIR 1965 SC 1430 : (1965) 2 SCR 421; *Firm Mehtab Majid & Co. v. State of Madras*, AIR 1963 SC 928 : 1963 Supp (2) SCR 435.

89. AIR 1979 SC 310 : 1979 (1) SCC 202.

90. *Government of India v. India Tobacco Association,* (2005) 7 SCC 396 (para 25), p. 402, 403 : AIR 2005 SC 3685.

91. *Ekambarappa v. EPTO*, AIR 1967 SC 1541, p. 1543 : 1967 (3) SCR 864.

The Legislature sometimes does not enumerate the Acts sought to be repealed, and only says that 'all provisions inconsistent with this Act' are hereby repealed. With respect to such a repealing provision, it has been said that it merely substitutes for the uncertainty of the general law an express provision of equal uncertainty;[1] and in determining whether a particular earlier provision is repealed by such a repealing provision on the ground of inconsistency with it, the same principles which are applicable in determining a question of implied repeal have to be applied.[2] Another equally uncertain formula is when the later Act provides that a particular earlier Act 'shall to the extent necessary to give effect to the provisions of this Act be deemed to have been repealed or modified.' Such a formula is used in section 13 of the Madras City Tenants Protection Act, 1922 to restrict the application of the Transfer of Property Act, 1882. The Supreme Court on analysing the provision of the Madras Act, especially section 9, held that determination of tenancy by forfeiture as envisaged by section 111(g) of the Transfer of Property Act must be deemed to have been repealed or modified for 'its applicability by itself will nullify and make section 9 inoperative.'[3] Thus here also the principles applicable in determining a question of implied repeal become relevant. In certain Acts passed in India which had the effect of extending to Part B and certain Part C States, numerous laws of the Union, the repealing section was expressed to repeal 'any law corresponding to any of the Acts or Ordinance extended'.[4] This device was adopted because Parliament was not in a position to know with any exactness the laws in force in those States which were formerly 'Indian States'. In interpreting these provisions the Supreme Court has observed that "where the Act repealed provides substantially for all matters contained in the Act effecting the repeal there is correspondence between the two Acts; and the earlier Act would thus stand repealed. It is not necessary that there should be complete identity between the repealing Act and the Act repealed in every respect".[5] There will, however, be no

---

1. *Garnett v. Bradley*, (1878) 3 AC 944, p. 965 : (1874-80) All ER 648 (HL).
2. For example, **see** *Nanakchandra v. Chandra Kishore*, AIR 1970 SC 446, p. 448 : (1969) 3 SCC 802. The question in this case was whether section 488 of the Code of Criminal Procedure, 1898, which provides for maintenance to children was inconsistent with section 20 of the Hindu Adoptions and Maintenance Act, 1956, and was repealed in its application to Hindus by section 4 of the Act.
3. *Palani Ammal v. Viswanath Chettian*, AIR 1998 SC 1309, p. 1320 : 1998 (3) SCC 654.
4. Part B States Laws Act (Act 3 of 1951), section 6; Part C States Laws Act (now called Union Territories Laws Act) (Act 30 of 1950), section 4.
5. *Abdul Kadir v. State of Kerala*, AIR 1962 SC 922, p. 925 : 1962 Supp (2) SCR 741; *Custodian of Evacuee Property v. Abdul Shakoor*, AIR 1961 SC 1087 : (1961) 3 SCC 855; *Harish Chandra v. State of M.P.*, AIR 1965 SC 932, p. 936 (para 12) :

[Footnote No. 5 Contd.]

'correspondence' and therefore no repeal, where the two Acts are substantially of differing scopes.[6] But if the Act extended covers the entire subject of the earlier Act and also deals with other subjects, the earlier Act will still be the corresponding Act and shall stand repealed.[7] It is also possible that there may be a partial correspondence resulting in partial repeal.[8]

5. IMPLIED REPEAL

(a) General

There is a presumption against a repeal by implication; and the reason of this rule is based on the theory that the Legislature while enacting a law has complete knowledge of the existing laws on the same subject-matter, and therefore, when it does not provide a repealing provision, it gives out an intention not to repeal the existing legislation.[9] When the new Act contains a repealing section mentioning the Acts which it expressly repeals, the presumption against implied repeal of other laws is further strengthened on the principle *expressio unius est exclusio alterius.*[10] Further, the

---

[Footnote No. 5 Contd.]

(1965) 1 SCR 323. **But see** *Kaushi Ram v. State*, AIR 1966 SC 805 : (1962) 2 SCR 942 (In this case it was held that a Rubkar of Patiala State imposing Royalty on manufacture of bricks was not repealed by extension of the Central Excises and Salt Act, 1944, on the reasoning that in this Act there is no negative provision exempting unscheduled articles from Excise Duty). For meaning of the Expression 'corresponding provision', **see** *Jagir Singh v. Ranbir Singh*, AIR 1979 SC 381, p. 386 : (1979) 1 SCC 560. For meaning of the word 'correspond' **see** *Re Gilligan,* (2000) 1 All ER 113, p. 122, 125 (HL).

6. *Anant Prasad v. State of A.P.*, AIR 1963 SC 853, pp. 859, 860 : (1963) Supp (1) SCR 844; *Indian & C.P. Works v. State of A.P.*, AIR 1966 SC 713 : (1966) 2 SCR 110.

7. *Mary Roy v. State of Kerala*, (1986) 2 SCC 209, pp. 214, 215 : AIR 1986 SC 1011.

8. *Hyderabad Chemical and Pharmaceutical Works Ltd. v. State of A.P.*, AIR 1964 SC 1870, pp. 1871, 1872 : 1964 (7) SCR 376.

9. *Municipal Council, Palai v. T.J. Joseph*, AIR 1963 SC 1561, p. 1564 : 1964 (2) SCR 87; *Tansukhrai v. Nilratan Prasad*, AIR 1966 SC 1780, p. 1782 : 1965 (2) SCR 6; *Northern India Caterers (P) Ltd. v. State of Punjab*, AIR 1967 SC 1581, p. 1585 : 1967 (3) SCR 399; *Delhi Municipality v. Shivshanker*, AIR 1971 SC 815 : (1971) 1 SCC 442, p. 445; *Ratanlal Adukia v. Union of India*, AIR 1990 SC 104, p. 110 : 1989 (3) SCC 537; *R.S. Raghunath v. State of Karnataka*, AIR 1992 SC 81, p. 90 : (1992) 1 SCC 335; *Union of India v. Venkatesan*, AIR 2002 SC 1890, p. 1895 : (2002) 5 SCC 285; *State of M.P. v. Kedia Leather and Liquor Ltd.*, (2003) 7 SCC 389, pp. 394, 395 : (2003) SCC (Cri) 1642 : AIR 2003 SC 3236. A repeal by implication will not be inferred merely from something contained in the preamble of the Act, *Maganti v. State of A.P.*, AIR 1970 SC 403, p. 405 : (1969) 2 SCC 96; *Shanta Talwar v. Union of India*, (2011) 5 SCC 287 (para 18) : AIR 2011 SC 1578.

10. *Garnett v. Bradley*, (1878) 3 AC 944, p. 965 : (1874-80) All ER 648 (HL), (LORD BLACKBURN); *Headland v. Coster*, (1905) 1 KB 219, p. 226 (CA); *Re, Chance*, (1936) Ch 266, p. 268. For applicability of this maxim in other cases **see** p. 90, *ante*.

presumption will be comparatively strong in case of virtually contemporaneous Acts.[11] The continuance of existing legislation, in the absence of an express provision of repeal, being presumed, the burden to show that there has been a repeal by implication lies on the party asserting the same.[12] The presumption is, however, rebutted and a repeal is inferred by necessary implication when the provisions of the later Act are so inconsistent with or repugnant to the provisions of the earlier Act 'that the two cannot stand together'.[13] But, if the two may be read together and some application may be made of the words in the earlier Act, a repeal will not be inferred.[14] Thus the Prevention of Food Adulteration Act, 1954 and Rules, 1955 made thereunder relating to vinegar were not held to be impliedly repealed by the Essential Commodities Act, 1955 and the Fruit order made thereunder although both contained regulatory provisions and laid down certain standards of quality and composition for vinegar for it was not possible to say that the two could not stand together.[15] In the words of the court: 'If the Adulteration Act or rules impose some restrictions on the manufacturer, dealer or seller of vinegar then they have to comply with them irrespective of the fact that the fruit order imposes lesser number of restrictions in respect of these matters. The former do not render compliance with the latter impossible, nor does compliance with the former necessarily and

---

11. *Unnoda Persaud Mookerjee v. Kristo Coomar Moitra*, (1872) 19 WR 5, p. 7 (PC) (The two Acts were passed within a space of three days).

12. *Lybbe v. Hart*, (1883) 29 Ch D 8, p. 15.

13. *Municipal Council, Palai v. T.J. Joseph*, AIR 1963 SC 1561, p. 1562 : (1964) 2 SCR 87; *Trust Mai Lachhmi Sialkoti Bradari v. Amritsar Improvement Trust*, AIR 1963 SC 976, p. 979; *Mathra Prasad and Sons v. State of Punjab*, AIR 1962 SC 745, p. 748 : 1962 Supp (1) SCR 913; *Kutner v. Phillips*, (1891) 2 QB 267, pp. 271, 272; *Flannagan v. Shaw*, (1920) 3 KB 96, p. 105 (CA); *Wallwork v. Fielding*, (1922) 2 KB 66, p. 94 (CA); *R. v. National Arbitration Tribunal, Ex parte, (Bolton) Corporation*, (1941) 2 KB 405, p. 415 (CA); *Woodent v. IRC*, (1970) 2 All ER 801, p. 807 (PC); *Suntharalingam v. Inspector of Police*, (1971) 3 WLR 896, p. 901 (PC). **See further** *Delhi Municipality v. Shivshanker*, AIR 1971 SC 815 : (1971) 1 SCC 442, p. 446; *Basti Sugar Mills v. State of U.P.*, AIR 1979 SC 262, p. 269 : (1979) 2 SCC 88; *M. Karunanidhi v. Union of India*, AIR 1979 SC 898, pp. 909, 910 : (1979) 3 SCC 431; *Dharangdhara Chemical Works v. Dharangdhara Municipality*, (1985) 4 SCC 92, pp. 98, 99 : AIR 1985 SC 1729; *Yogendra Pal Singh v. Union of India*, (1987) 1 SCC 624, p. 641: AIR 1987 SC 1015; *Ratanlal Adukia v. Union of India*, AIR 1990 SC 104, p. 110 : 1989 (3) SCC 537; *R.S. Raghunath v. State of Karnataka*, AIR 1992 SC 81, p. 90 : (1992) 1 SCC 335; *A.K. Sabhapathy (Dr.) v. State of Kerala*, AIR 1992 SC 1310, pp. 1313, 1314 : 1992 Supp (3) SCC 147; *Cantonment Board, Mhow v. M.P. State Road Transport Corporation*, AIR 1997 SC 2013, p. 2019 : 1997 (4) JT 561 : (1997) 1 SCC 450.

14. *A.G. v. Moore*, (1878) 3 Ex D 276, p. 281 (BRETT, L.J.); *Ratanlal Adukia v. Union of India, supra; R.S. Raghunath v. State of Karnataka, supra.*

15. *Delhi Municipality v. Shivshanker*, AIR 1971 SC 815 : (1971) 1 SCC 442.

automatically involve violation of the latter.'[16] The Supreme Court has indicated that the test applied for determining repugnancy under Article 254 of the Constitution, may be applied for solving a question of implied repeal and that it should be seen: "(1) Whether there is direct conflict between the two provisions; (2) Whether the Legislature intended to lay down an exhaustive Code in respect of the subject-matter replacing the earlier law; (3) Whether the two laws occupy the same field."[17] The doctrine of implied repeal is based on the theory that the Legislature, which is presumed to know the existing law, did not intend to create any confusion by retaining conflicting provisions and, therefore, when the court applies the doctrine, it does no more than give effect to the intention of the Legislature by examining the scope and the object of the two enactments and by a comparison of their provisions.[18] The matter in each case is one of construction and comparison of the two Acts. 'But in a conceivable case, the very existence of two provisions may by itself, and without more, lead to an inference of mutual irreconcilability if the later set of provisions is by itself a complete code with respect to the same matter. In such a case the actual detailed comparison of the two sets of provisions may not be necessary.'[19] In the words of a Constitution Bench of the Supreme Court, speaking through S.H. KAPADIA, C.J., "Repeal

---

16. *Ibid*, p. 451 of (1971)1 SCC. Similarly it has been held that section 33(1)(j) of the Monopolies and Restrictive Trade Practices Act, 1969 has not been affected by section 9A of the Customs Tariff Act, 1975 and the Anti Dumping Rules made thereunder for the two operate in different and distinct spheres and the question of implied repeal does not arise: *Haridas Exports v. All India Float Glass Mfrs. Association*, AIR 2002 SC 2728, p. 2743 : (2002) 6 SCC 600.

17. *Municipal Council, Palai v. T.J. Joseph*, AIR 1963 SC 1561, p. 1565 : (1964) 2 SCR 87. **See further** *Tansukh Rai v. Nilratan Prasad Sahu*, AIR 1966 SC 1780, p. (1965) 2 SCR 6. **Cf.** *Harish Chandra v. State of M.P.*, AIR 1965 SC 932, p. 937 (para 14) : (1965) 1 SCR 323. If the two laws 'operate in the same field' without collision they cannot be said to 'occupy the same field' and there will be no inconsistency and no implied repeal unless the later law intends to be an exhaustive code. Further, it is the point of time of making the law and not its commencement in deciding which is the prior law and which the later law for purposes of Article 254 of the Constitution, *Rishikesh* (*Pt.*) *v. Salma Begum*, 1995 (3) Scale 354 : 1995 AIR SCW 2476 : 1995(4) SCC 718 : 1995 All LJ 1336; *Dodha Rangarao v. Rambhupal Prasad*, (2004) 7 SCC 63, p. 93 (para 42). When conditions of any particular service, *e.g.*, fire services are regulated by a law made by the Legislature under Article 309, rules made by the Governor under the proviso to that article cannot operate in the field occupied by the legislative enactment and the rules made thereunder: *A.B. Krishna v. State of Karnataka*, JT 1998 (1) SC 613, p. 617 : AIR 1998 SC 1050 : 1998 (3) SCC 495.

18. *Municipal Council, Palai v. T.J. Joseph*, AIR 1963 SC 1561, p. 1564 : (1964) 2 SCR 87; *Delhi Municipality v. Shivshanker*, AIR 1971 SC 815 : (1971) 1 SCC 442, p. 446.

19. *Ratan Lal Adukia v. Union of India*, AIR 1990 SC 104, p. 110 : 1989 (3) SCC 537.

of an enactment is a matter of substance. It depends on the intention of the Legislature. If by reason of the subsequent enactment, the Legislature intended to abrogate or wipe off the former enactment, wholly or in part, then, it would be a case of pro tanto repeal." Applying this principle, the Chit Funds Act, 1982, which is a Central Act, was found to have repealed the Kerala Chitties Act, 1975, which is a State Act. The intention of the Parliament in enacting the Central Act was to cover the entire field relating to or with respect to chits and there were direct inconsistencies between the two Acts, and as a consequence of this repugnancy, the Kerala Chitties Act was held to have become void under Article 254(1) of the Constitution on the enactment of the Chit Funds Act.[20]

After referring to the principles set out in the preceding paragraph, the Supreme Court in *State of M.P. v. Kedia Leather and Liquor Ltd.*[21] came to the conclusion that section 133, Criminal Procedure Code, 1973 was not impliedly repealed by the Water (Prevention and Control of Pollution) Act, 1974[22]. The principles stated above were reiterated in *Kishorebhai Khamanchand Goyal v. State of Gujarat*,[23] where it was held that the Bombay Shops and Establishment Act, 1948 (State Act) was not overridden by the Motor Transport Workers Act, 1961 (Central Act) by reason of repugnancy. Implied repeal affects not only legislative enactments but statutory rules and even directions of the court pending legislation on the subject which are inconsistent with the provisions of the new Act.[24]

The general principle that there is a strong presumption against implied repeal recently came up for consideration before the High Court of Australia in *Shergold v. Tanner*.[25] In a joint judgment the court (GLEESON, C.J., MCHUGH, GUMMOW, KIRBY AND HAYNE JJ.) quoted with approval the following observations of GAUDRON J. in *Saraswati v. The Queen*:[26] "It is a basic rule of construction that in the absence of express words, an earlier statutory provision is not repealed, altered or derogated from by a later provision unless an intention to that effect is necessarily to be implied. There must be very strong grounds to support that implication, for there is a general presumption that the Legislature intended that both provisions

---

20. *State of Kerala & Ors. v. Mar Appraem Kuri Company Ltd.*, (2012) 7 SCC 106, p. 145.
21. (2003) 7 SCC 389, pp. 394, 395 : AIR 2003 SC 3236, pp. 3239, 3240.
22. *State of M.P. v. Kedia Leather and Liquor Ltd* (2003) 7 SCC 389, pp. 394, 395 : AIR 2003 SC 3236, pp. 3239, 3240.
23. AIR 2004 SC 1006, p. 1008 : (2003) 8 JT 399.
24. *Union of India v. C. Dinakar*, (2004) 6 SCC 118, p. 125 (para 14) : AIR 2004 SC 2498.
25. (2002) 76 ALJR 808, p. 814.
26. (1991) 172 CLR 1, p. 17.

should operate and that, to the extent that they would otherwise overlap, one should be read as subject to the other." The joint judgment in *Shergold*[27] also summarised the opinions expressed by KITTO. J in an earlier case of *Butler v. Attorney General,*[28] which is as follows: "the question as being whether the two items of legislation could stand or live together". In the same case FULLAGAR J. spoke of 'contrariety', TAYOLOR J. of 'direct conflict' and WINDEYER J. asked whether the two statutes were clearly and indisputably contradictory displaying such repugnancy that they could not be reconciled.[29]

If a prior law provides both for right and remedy and a later general law undoubtedly replaces the right, the remedy of the prior law must also be taken to have been impliedly repealed. On this reasoning the provisions of the Portugese Civil Code applicable in the State of Goa regulating contracts and remedies as also providing for limitation were taken to be impliedly repealed by extension of the Indian Contract Act, the Negotiable Instruments Act and the Indian Limitation Act to Goa.[30]

A recital in a later Act that it was not repealing an earlier Act will be of no avail if the later Act enacted a provision which was quite contrary to the earlier Act; and the earlier Act would stand repealed as effectively as if it had been expressly repealed.[31] A repeal by implication is just as effective as by express words.[32] Section 6 of the General Clauses Act applies also to implied repeals.[33]

(b) Prior particular law and later general law

As an application of the above principles a prior particular or special law is not readily held to be impliedly repealed by later general enactment.[34] The particular or special law deals only with a particular phase of

---

27. (2002) 76 ALJR 808, p. 814.
28. *Butler v. Attorney General* (1961) 106 CLR 268.
29. (2002) 76 ALJR 808, p. 814.
30. *Syndicate Bank v. Prabha D. Naik,* AIR 2001 SC 1968, pp. 1973 to 1975 : (2001) 4 SCC 713.
31. *Dobbs v. Grand Junction Waterworks Co.*, (1883) 9 AC 49, p. 58 (HL) (LORD BLACKBURN).
32. *Summers v. Holborn District Board of Works*, (1893) 1 QB 612, p. 617 (LORD COLERIDGE, C.J.).
33. *State of Orissa v. M.A. Tulloch & Co.,* AIR 1964 SC 1284, p. 1294 : 1964 (4) SCR 461.
34. *Unnoda Persaud Mookerjee v. Kristocoomar Moitra*, (1872) 19 WR 5, p. 7 (PC); *Barker v. Edgar*, (1898) AC 748, p. 754 (PC); *Nicolle v. Nicolle*, (1922) 1 AC 284, p. 290 : 126 LT 777 (PC); *Montreal Corporation v. Montreal Industrial Land Co.*, AIR 1932 PC 252, p. 254; *Municipal Council, Palai v. T.J. Joseph,* AIR 1963 SC 1561,

[Footnote No. 34 Contd.]

the subject covered by the general law and, therefore, a reconciliation is normally possible between a prior particular Act and a later general Act, and so the particular Act is construed as an exception or qualification of the general Act. To quote the words of LORD PHILIMORE: "It is a sound principle of all jurisprudence that a prior particular law is not easily to be held to be abrogated by a posterior law, expressed in general terms and by the apparent generality of its language applicable to and covering a number of cases, of which the particular law is but one. This, as a matter of jurisprudence, as understood in England, has been laid down in a great number of cases, whether the prior law be an express statute, or be the underlying common or customary law of the country. Where general words in a later Act are capable of reasonable and sensible application without extending them to subjects specially dealt with by earlier legislation, that earlier and special legislation is not to be held indirectly repealed, altered, or derogated from merely by force of such general words, without any indication of a particular intention to do so."[35] The principle has been accepted by the Supreme Court and has been expressed by MUDHOLKAR, J. as follows: "A general statute applies to all persons and localities within its jurisdiction and scope as distinguished from a special one which in its operation is confined to a particular locality and, therefore, where it is doubtful whether the special statute was intended to be repealed by the general statute the court should try to give effect to both the enactments as far as possible."[36] A law applicable to a locality or to a class of cases or individuals is a special law as distinguished from a general law which applies to

---

[Footnote No. 34 Contd.]

p. 1565 : (1964) 2 SCR 87; *Woodent v. IRC*, (1970) 2 All ER 801, p. 807 (PC); *Paradip Port Trust v. Their Workmen*, AIR 1977 SC 36, p. 44 : (1977) 2 SCC 337; *U.P. State Electricity Board v. Harishanker*, AIR 1979 SC 65, p. 72 : (1978) 4 SCC 16; *Ashoka Marketing Ltd. v. Punjab National Bank*, AIR 1991 SC 855, p. 877 : (1990) 4 SCC 406; *R.S. Raghunath v. State of Karnataka*, AIR 1992 SC 81, pp. 86, 87 : (1992) 1 SCC 335; *Cantonment Board, Mhow v. M.P. State Road Transport Corporation*, AIR 1997 SC 2013, p. 2018 : 1997 (4) JT 561 : (1997) 9 SCC 450; *Chandra Prakash Tiwari v. Shakuntala Shukla,* AIR 2002 SC 2322, pp. 2335-36 : (2002) 6 SCC 127.

N.B.—The principle is based on the maxim—*Generalia specialibus non derogant.*

35. *Nicolle v. Nicolle*, (1922) 1 AC 284, p. 290 (PC). **See further** *Pratap Singh v. Man Mohan Dey*, AIR 1966 SC 1931, p. 1934 : (1966) 3 SCR 663; *Krishna District Co-operative Marketing Society Ltd. v. N.V. Purnachandra Rao*, (1987) 4 SCC 99, p. 110 : AIR 1987 SC 1960; *A.B. Krishna v. State of Karnataka*, JT 1998 (1) SC 613, p. 617: AIR 1998 SC 1050, p. 1053 : (1998) 3 SCC 495; *Chandra Prakash Tiwari v. Shakuntala Shukla,* AIR 2002 SC 2322, p. 2328 : (2002) 6 SCC 127.

36. *Municipal Council, Palai v. T.J. Joseph*, AIR 1963 SC 1561, p. 1565 : 1964 (2) SCR 87; *R.S. Raghunath v. State of Karnataka*, AIR 1992 SC 81, pp. 86, 87 : 1992 (1) SCC 335.

the whole community.[37] A law which is essentially general in nature may contain special provisions on certain matters and in respect of these matters it would be classified as a special law.[38] If the general law by its own terms recognises the existence or continuance of special law on the subject, no question of inconsistency with or repeal of the special law can arise. Thus, section 5 of the Code of Criminal Procedure, 1973, recognises the continuance of special form of procedure under any law for the time being in force and hence it was held that the Haryana Childrens Act, 1974, which came into force on 1st March, 1974, was not repealed by the Code which came into force on 1st April, 1974.[39] But if the intention of the later general law is clear to repeal or modify a prior particular law, the general law will prevail over the particular law.[40]

The provisions of a Municipal Act which empowered a Municipal authority to provide for bus stands, were not held to be repealed by a subsequent Motor Vehicles Act, which empowered the Government or its delegate to do the same. The reasons for this conclusion were mainly twofold: (1) that the Municipal Act was a special law applying to Municipal areas, and the Motor Vehicles Act was a general law applying to all areas in general; and (2) that both the provisions were enabling ones and there could be no question of conflict till the authority in the later Act also provided for bus stands for the same areas for which bus stands had already been provided under the Municipal Act.[41]

On the same principle it was held that a provision in the Bengal Ghatwali Lands Act, 1859, enabling the Court of Wards to grant leases of Ghatwali Land in perpetuity for erection of dwelling houses and certain other purposes was not affected by the Court of Wards Act, 1870, which enacted that no lease in respect of land under the management of the Court of Wards shall except under the sanction of the Board of Revenue,

---

37. *Justiniano Augusto De Piedade Barrets v. Antonio Vincente Da Fonseca*, AIR 1979 SC 984, pp. 988, 989 : (1979) 3 SCC 47; *Kaushalya Rani v. Gopal Singh*, AIR 1964 SC 260, pp. 262, 263 : 1964 (4) SCR 982.

38. *Life Insurance Corporation v. D.J. Bahadur*, AIR 1980 SC 2181, p. 2200 : 1981 (1) SCC 315; *Ashoka Marketing Ltd. v. Punjab National Bank*, AIR 1991 SC 855, p. 877 : (1991) 4 SCC 406; *Allahabad Bank v. Canara Bank*, JT 2000 (4) SC 411, p. 434 : AIR 2000 SC 1535, p. 1548 : (2000) 4 SCC 406.

39. *Rohtas v. State of Haryana*, AIR 1979 SC 1839 : (1979) 4 SCC 229.

40. **See** text and notes 47 to 50, p. 745.

41. *Municipal Council, Palai v. T.J. Joseph*, AIR 1963 SC 1561, pp. 1565, 1566 : 1964 (2) SCR 87.

For another example, **see** *Union of India v. India Fisheries (Pvt.) Ltd.*, AIR 1966 SC 35 : (1965) 3 SCR 697. This case dealt with sections 228 and 229 of the Companies Act, 1913 and section 49E of the Income-tax Act, 1922. It was held that the provisions of the Companies Act were special provisions.

be given for a term exceeding 10 years nor beyond the expiration of the ward's minority.[42]

Similarly section 36(4) of the Industrial Disputes Act, 1947, which provides that a party cannot be represented by a legal practitioner before a Labour Court, Tribunal or National Tribunal except with the consent of the other parties and with the leave of the Labour Court, Tribunal or National Tribunal is not affected by section 30 of the Advocates Act, 1961 which provides that every advocate shall be entitled as of right to practise in all courts and before any tribunal.[43]

By applying the same principle it was held that the Industrial Employment (Standing Orders) Act, 1946 is a special Act dealing with the conditions of service of workmen in industrial establishments and, therefore, the standing orders made under the Act were not abrogated, by the regulations [except when notified under section 13(B)] relating to conditions of service made under the Electricity (Supply) Act, 1948, which is a special Act for development of Electricity but which contains a general provision for making regulations regarding the conditions of service of the employees of the Electricity Boards.[44]

And, similarly the Industrial Disputes Act, 1947 has been held to be a special statute in matters of settlement of Industrial Disputes and the bonus payable to workmen under a settlement cannot be affected by a regulation made under section 49 of the Life Insurance Corporation Act, 1956.[45]

Another example is that of the M.P. Krishi Upaj Mandi Adhiniyam, 1972, which, despite being a subsequent legislation, with one of its objectives being to regulate buying and selling of agricultural produce, including sugarcane, the general provisions contained therein were held to not prevail over the M.P. Sugarcane (Regulation of Supply and Purchase) Act, 1958, and the Sugarcane (Control) Order, 1966, which are special legislations exclusively dealing with issues relating to increase in the production of sugarcane, supply of sugarcane by cane- growers/ Cane Growers' Cooperative Societies to factories, and payment of the price of cane by the occupier of the factory. Therefore the Supreme Court held that the 1972 Act will not prevail over the 1958 Act and the 1966 Control Order, and hence transactions involving purchase of sugarcane by factories would not be governed by the provisions of the 1972 Act.[46]

---

42. *Pratap Singh v. Man Mohan Dey*, AIR 1966 SC 1931 : (1966) 3 SCR 663.
43. *Paradip Port Trust v. Their Workmen*, AIR 1977 SC 36, p. 44 : (1977) 2 SCC 337.
44. *U.P. State Electricity Board v. Hari Shankar*, AIR 1979 SC 65 : (1978) 4 SCC 16.
45. *Life Insurance Corporation v. D.T. Bahadur*, AIR 1980 SC 2181, pp. 2202, 2203 : (1981) 1 SCC 315.
46. *Krishi Upaj Mandi Samiti, Narsingpur v. Shiv Shakti Khansari Udyog & Ors.*, (2012) 9 SCC 368, pp. 394, 395 and 407.

Where, however, the intention to supersede the special law is clearly evinced the later general law will prevail over the prior particular law, for the principle that a prior special law is not presumed to be repealed is only a principle of construction, and there is no rule of law to prevent repeal of a special law by a later general statute.[47] So a later general law may abrogate a prior special law by express repeal or by making provisions which are inconsistent with it.[48] But a prior special law cannot be taken to be repealed merely by presence of a *non obstante* clause in the later general law; the *non obstante* clause can be given an overriding effect only when there is a clear inconsistency between the two laws.[49]

The principle that a prior particular or special law may be abrogated by a later general law if that intention be clearly evinced was applied in holding that note 3, added in 1992 to the Kerala State and Subordinate Services Rules, 1958 providing that the number of vacancies to be filled in from direct recruits and transferees should be decided by applying the fixed ratio or percentage to the cadre strength *whenever* a ratio or percentage is fixed for different method of recruitment *and not to the vacancies existing at that time*, will prevail over prior special provision in the Kerala Agricultural and Income-tax and Sales-tax Services Rules which contemplated that the percentage or ratio should be fixed by taking into account the successive substantive vacancies arising at a particular time. The italicised words of Note 3 made the intention clear to apply it to all services. The object and reasons for introducing Note 3 contained in the Explanatory memorandum also supported that conclusion.[50]

(c) Prior general law and later particular law

A prior general Act may be affected by a subsequent particular or special Act,[51] if the subject-matter of the particular Act prior to its enforcement was being governed by the general provisions of the earlier Act.[52] In

---

47. *Dalmia Dadri Cement Co. Ltd. v. CIT*, AIR 1958 SC 816, p. 822 : 1959 SCR 729; *Umaid Mills v. State of Rajasthan*, AIR 1963 SC 953, p. 960 : 1963 Supp (2) SCR 515.

48. *Ajay Kumar Bannerjee v. Union of India*, (1984) 3 SCC 126, pp. 153, 154 : AIR 1984 SC 1130; *S. Prakash v. K.M. Kurian*, AIR 1999 SC 2094, pp. 2097 to 2099 : (1999) 5 SCC 624.

49. *R.S. Raghunath v. State of Karnataka*, AIR 1992 SC 81, p. 89 : (1992) 1 SCC 335.

50. *S. Prakash v. K.M. Kurian*, AIR 1999 SC 2094, p. 2099 : (1999) 5 SCC 624.

51. For distinction between general Act and particular Act, **see** text and notes 35 to 38, pp. 742-743.

52. *Generalibus Specialia derogant.*

For examples, **see** *Damji v. LIC*, AIR 1966 SC 135 : (1965) 3 SCR 665 [Section 446 of the Companies Act (1 of 1956) is a general provision and sections 15 and 41 of the Life Insurance Corporation Act (31 of 1956) are special provisions, and

[Footnote No. 52 Contd.]

such a case the operation of the particular Act may have the effect of partially repealing the general Act,[53] or curtailing its operation,[54] or adding conditions to its operation for the particular cases.[55] The distinction may be important at times for determining the applicability of those provisions of the General Clauses Act, 1897, (Interpretation Act, 1889 of U.K. now Interpretation Act, 1978) which apply only in case of repeals.

By section 25 of the Private Street Works Act, 1892, it was provided that certain sections, including section 150, of the Public Health Act, 1875, were not to apply to any district in which the Act of 1892 may be adopted. After adoption of the 1892 Act to an area a question arose whether a prior notice issued under section 150 of the 1875 Act could continue to be effective. The answer depended upon the applicability of section 38(2) of the Interpretation Act, 1889, (corresponding to section 6 of the General Clauses Act, 1897), which applies only in case of repeals. The Court of Appeal held that the notice under section 150 of the earlier Act continued to be valid in respect of the area where the later Act was brought into force.[56] LINDLEY, L.J. observed: "I cannot help thinking that when section 150 by force of section 25 ceases to apply to this district as from August 1, 1897, that is a repeal of section 150 as from that day so far as regards this district".[57]

[Footnote No. 52 Contd.]

therefore, on matters falling within the latter, the Company Court has no jurisdiction even during the winding-up.] *Punjab State Electricity Board v. Bassi Cold Storage*, JT 1994(2) SC 682, pp. 686, 687 : AIR 1994 SC 2544 : 1994 Supp (2) SCC 124. [The general provisions of the Arbitration Act, 1899 (now of 1940) are affected by section 52 of the Indian Electricity Act, 1910, and only matters directed to be determined by arbitration between the consumer and the licensee under the Electricity Act can be **referred** for arbitration]; *Suresh Nanda v. Central Bureau of Investigation*, (2008) 3 SCC 674 paras 10 and 18 : AIR 2008 SC 1414 [Section 10 of the Passport Act, 1967 which provides for impounding of passport is a special provision and section 104 Cr.P.C. is a general provision relating to impounding of documents before the court. Therefore for impounding a passport resort should be taken to section 10 of the Passport Act and not to section 104 of Cr.P.C. This book is **referred** in para 18]. But operation of prior general law is not affected in respect of cases not falling within the later particular law; for example, **see** *Official Receiver v. Abdul Shakoor*, AIR 1965 SC 920, pp. 925, 926 : (1965) 1 SCR 254; [Section 114, Illustration (c), Evidence Act, 1872 and section 118, Negotiable Instrument Act, 1881].

53. *Mirfin v. Attwood*, (1869) LR 4 QB 333 (LUSH & HAYES, JJ.); *Heston & Isleworth Urban District Council v. Grout*, (1897) 2 Ch 306, p. 313 (CA) (LINDLEY, L.J.); *Municipal Board, Bareilly v. Bharat Oil Co.*, AIR 1990 SC 548 : (1990) 1 SCC 311.

54. *Re, Willaims, Jones v. Williams*, (1887) 36 Ch D 573, p. 577 (NORTH, J.); *Mirfin v. Attwood, supra*, p. 340 (HANNON, J.); *Harishanker Bagla v. State of M.P.*, AIR 1954 SC 465, p. 469 : (1955) 1 SCR 380.

55. *Mount v. Taylor,* (1868) LR 3 CP 645; *Mirfin v. Attwood, supra*, p. 340.

56. *Heston & Isleworth Urban District Council v. Grout*, (1897) 2 Ch 306 (CA).

57. *Ibid*, p. 313.

Section 80 of the Railways Act, 1890, substituted in 1961, provides for the forum where a suit for compensation for the loss of life of, or personal injury to, a passenger or for loss, destruction, damage, deterioration or non-delivery of animals or goods against a railway administration may be brought. It was held that the said section was a special provision and a self contained code and that it impliedly repealed in respect of suits covered by it the general provisions of section 20 of the Code of Civil Procedure, 1908.[58] It is submitted that the better view may be to hold it to be a case of by-passing of the general law on matters covered by the special law[59] or as observed by the Supreme Court in a later case[60] the principle applied was that 'a special subsequent legislation which is a code in itself excludes the general law on the subject.' Accordingly, the Supreme Court has held that in the case of the Railways, the transmission of electricity is governed by the provisions of a special enactment *i.e.* the Railways Act, 1989, and not by the enactments governing electricity *i.e.* the Electricity Act, 1910, and the Electricity Act, 2003. The Court held that the decision of the Northern Railways to stop drawing power from UPSEB on account of its excessive tariff, and to construct their own transmission lines to draw power from the plants of NTPC was held to be legal in light of section 11 of the Railways Act, which empowers a Railway Administration to make or construct electric supply lines and erect, operate, maintain or repair any electric traction equipment, power supply and distribution system in connection with the working of the railway.[61]

In *Municipal Board, Bareilly v. Bharat Oil Co.*,[62] the State Government had framed rules regulating the levy of octroi in general by all municipalities. Thereafter, rules were framed by the State Government for levy of octroi by the Bareilly municipality expressly providing that the new rules will apply in supersession of the existing rules. It was held that there was deemed repeal of the earlier rules in respect of Bareilly municipality.

By section 4 of the Bihar Finance Act (Act 5 of 1981), provision was made for levy of purchase tax on goods in general. Provision was also made for levy of purchase tax on sugarcane later by section 49 of the

---

58. *Ratan Lal Adukia v. Union of India*, AIR 1990 SC 104, pp. 108, 110, 111 : 1989 (3) SCC 537.

59. **See** text and note 67, p. 749.

60. *Shriram Mandir Sansthan v. Vatsalabai*, AIR 1999 SC 520, p. 524 : (1999) 1 SCC 657 : (Special law providing its own code for inheritance of tenancies will impliedly exclude the general law and tenancies not heritable under the special law will not be heritable under the general law).

61. *General Manager, Northern Railways v. Chairman, Uttar Pradesh State Electricity Board & Ors.*, (2012) 3 SCC 329.

62. AIR 1990 SC 548 : 1990 (1) SCC 311.

Bihar Sugarcane (Regulation of Supply and Purchase) Act (Act 37 of 1982) which was a special Act for the control of the activities of production, supply and regulation of sugarcane including the levy of purchase tax. In so far as the activity of levy of purchase tax on sugarcane was concerned both the Acts operated in the same field. As the Sugarcane Act was a special Act the rule that 'general provision should yield to special provision' was applied and it was held that purchase tax on sugarcane could be levied only under the sugarcane Act and not under the Finance Act.[63] On the same principle it was also held in another case that dealings in sugarcane were exclusively regulated by the Sugarcane Act and its provisions excluded the operation of the Bihar Agricultural Produce Markets Act, 1980 which was a general Act for regulating sale and purchase of all types of agricultural produce.[64]

Section 19(1) of the Prevention of Corruption Act, 1988, deals with previous sanction from the Central or State Government or other competent authority for prosecution of public servants under the Act, and section 190 of the Code of Criminal Procedure, 1973, deals with cognizance of offences by Magistrates. A.K. GANGULY, J., agreeing with G.S. SINGHVI, J., applying the principle of *generalia specialibus non derogant*, has held, relying on *Dilawar Singh v. Parvinder Singh*,[65] that since the Prevention of Corruption Act is a special statute enacted to consolidate and amend the law relating to prevention of corruption, section 19 of the Act will have an overriding effect over the general provisions contained in section 190 of the CrPC.[66]

By section 3 of the Essential Supplies (Temporary Powers) Act, 1946, the Central Government was given powers to issue orders regulating or prohibiting the production, supply and distribution of essential commodities and trade and commerce therein. By section 6 of the Act any order under section 3 was to have effect notwithstanding anything inconsistent therewith contained in any other enactment. The High Court of Madhya Pradesh took the view that by virtue of section 6, the orders issued under section 3, in so far as they were inconsistent with prior general law, repealed the same by implication in respect of the essential commodity dealt with by them. The Supreme Court differing from the High Court pointed out: "Section 6 does not either expressly or by implication repeal any of

---

63. *Gobind Sugar Mills Ltd. v. State of Bihar,* AIR 1999 SC 3097, p. 3100 : (1999) 7 SCC 76.

64. *Belsund Sugar Co. Ltd. v. The State of Bihar,* JT 1999 (5) SC 422, pp. 450, 451 : AIR 1999 SC 3125, p. 3146 : (1999) 9 SCC 620.

65. *Dilawar Singh v. Parvinder Singh,* (2005) 12 SCC 709.

66. *Subramanian Swamy v. Manmohan Singh & Anr.*, (2012) 3 SCC 64, pp. 99, 100.

the provisions of pre-existing laws; neither does it abrogate them. Those laws remain untouched and unaffected so far as the statute book is concerned. The repeal of a statute means as if the repealed statute was never on the statute book. It is wiped out from the statute book. The effect of section 6 certainly is not to repeal any one of those laws or abrogate them. Its object is simply to by-pass them where they are inconsistent with the provisions of the Essential Supplies (Temporary Powers) Act, 1946, or the orders made thereunder. In other words, the orders made under section 3 would be operative in regard to the essential commodity—wherever there is repugnancy with the existing laws and to that extent the existing laws with regard to those commodities will not operate. By-passing a certain law does not necessarily amount to repeal or abrogation of that law. That law remains unrepealed but during the continuance of the order made under section 3, it does not operate in that field for the time being. The ambit of its operation is thus limited without there being any repeal of any one of its provisions."[67] This case also decides that if the provisions of the later special statute or orders issued thereunder are supplementary to the provision of the prior general Act, no conflict arises, and there is no supersession of the general Act.[68]

By Act 27 of 1950, as amended by Act 1 of 1954, the Bihar Legislature added section 64A in the Motor Vehicles Act, 1939, which confers power on the State Government to revise an order passed by any authority or officer in any proceeding under Chapter IV of the Act. Parliament also by Central Act 100 of 1956, added section 64A in the Motor Vehicles Act which empowers the State Transport Authority to revise an order made by a Regional Transport Authority in a case in which no appeal lies. Construing the two sections, *viz.*, Bihar section 64A and Central section 64A, it was held by the Supreme Court,[69] that the Bihar section being more general and wider in application, was not impliedly repealed by the Central section which was more limited in application. It was pointed out that the power of revision under Bihar section 64A, even after the insertion of Central section 64A, would be available in case of appealable orders, after the appeal is decided by the appellate authority, and in case of non-appealable orders after the revision is decided under Central section 64A. Thus an implied repeal in this case was not inferred because the general provision of Bihar section 64A could be given effect to even after the enactment of Central section 64A as the effect of the Central section was merely to

67. *Harishanker Bagla v. State of M.P.*, AIR 1954 SC 465, p. 469 (para 12) : 1955 (1) SCR 380.
68. *Ibid*, p. 469 (para 11)
69. *Tansukh Rai v. Nilratan Prasad*, AIR 1966 SC 1780 : 1965 (2) SCR 6.

curtail the operation of the Bihar section to the extent and up to the stage the Central section provided for revisions.

A general Act's operation may be curtailed by a later Special Act even if the general Act contains a *non obstante* clause.[70] The curtailment of the general Act will be more readily inferred when the later Special Act also contains an overriding *non obstante* provision.[71] Section 446(1) of the Companies Act 1956 (Act 1 of 1956) provides that when the winding up order is passed or the official liquidator is appointed as a provisional liquidator, no suit or other legal proceeding shall be commenced, or if pending at the date of winding up order shall be proceeded with against the company except by leave of the court. Under section 446(2), the company court, *notwithstanding anything contained in any other law for the time being in force* is given jurisdiction to entertain any suit, proceeding or claim by or against the company and decide any question of priorities or any other question whatsoever, whether of law or fact, which may relate to or arise in the course of the winding up. The Life Insurance Corporation Act, 1956 (Act 31 of 1956) constituted a Tribunal and section 15 of the Act enabled the Life Insurance Corporation to file a case before the tribunal for recovery of various amounts from the erstwhile Life Insurance Companies in certain respects. Section 41 of the Life Insurance Corporation Act conferred exclusive jurisdiction on the tribunal in these matters. On examination of these Acts, it was held that the provisions conferring exclusive jurisdiction on the tribunal being provisions of the special Act, *i.e.*, the Life Insurance Corporation Act prevailed over the aforesaid provisions of the general Act, *viz.*, the Companies Act which is an Act relating to companies in general and, therefore, the tribunal had jurisdiction to entertain and proceed with a claim of the Life Insurance Corporation against a former insurer which had been ordered to be wound up by the company court.[72] This case was followed in giving to the provisions of the Recovery of Debts due to Banks and Financial Institutions Act 1993 (RDB Act) overriding effect over the provisions of the Companies Act, 1956. The RDB Act constitutes a tribunal and by sections 17 and 18 confers upon the tribunal *exclusive jurisdiction* to entertain and decide applications from the banks and financial institutions for recovery of debts (defined to mean any liability which is claimed as due). The Act also lays down the procedure for recovery of the debt as per the certificate issued by the tribunal. The provisions of the RDB Act, which is a special Act, were held to prevail

---

70. *Damji Valji Shah v. Life Insurance Corporation of India,* AIR 1966 SC 135 : (1965) 3 SCR 665.

71. *Allahabad Bank v. Canara Bank,* JT 2000 (4) SC 411 : AIR 2000 SC 1535 : (2000) 4 SCC 406.

72. Case in note 66, *supra*.

over sections 442, 446, 537 and other sections of the Companies Act which is a general Act, more so because section 34 of the RDB Act gives over-riding effect to that Act by providing that the provisions of this Act shall have effect notwithstanding anything inconsistent therewith contained in any other law for the time being in force.[73] A number of other cases where both the competing Acts contain *non obstante* clauses have already been discussed earlier in Chapter 5.[74]

The aforesaid principles were applied and followed in holding that the Sick Industrial Companies (Special Provisions) Act, 1985 (SICA) is a special Act and will prevail over the Companies Act, 1956, which is a general Act, wherever any inconsistency is seen in the provisions of the two Acts.[75] As a result when a reference has been made to the Board for Industrial and Financial Reconstruction [BIFR] constituted under SICA the jurisdiction of the company judge under the Companies Act on a question of winding up of a sick company will arise only when BIFR or the Appellate Authority for Industrial and Financial Reconstruction (AAIFR) constituted under SICA has exercised its jurisdiction under section 20 of SICA recommending winding up of the company upon arriving at a finding that there does not exist any chance of revival of the company.[76] Similarly, SICA, being a special law, was held to also prevail over the provisions of the Transfer of Property Act, 1882, which is a general law and operates in a very wide field.[77]

Similarly, the Supreme Court held that sections 65-A and 65-B of the Evidence Act, 1872, introduced by the amendments made to the Evidence Act by the Information Technology Act, 2000, are special provisions relating to proof of electronic records, and will prevail over the general law on secondary evidence under sections 63 and 65 of the Evidence Act because of the principle *generalia specialibus non derogant.*[78]

This principle was also used in the interpretation of section 89 of the Gujarat Tenancy and Agricultural Lands (Vidarbha Region and Kutch Area) Act, 1958, which bars transfers of agricultural lands to non-agriculturalists, save as provided in the Act, and section 89-A of the Act, which permits sale

---

73. Case in note 67, *supra.* **Followed** in *Unique Butyle Tube Industries P. Ltd. v. U.P. Financial Corporation,* (2003) 2 SCC 455, pp. 460, 46 : (2003) 113 Comp Cas 374 : AIR 2003 SC 2103.

74. Pp. 401-416.

75. *NGEF Ltd. v. Chandra Developers (P) Ltd.,* (2005) 8 SCC 219 : (2005) 7 Scale 715.

76. *Ibid.* para 39. **See further** *Tata Motors Ltd. v. Pharmaceutical Products of India Ltd.,* (2008) 7 SCC 619 para 24 : AIR 2008 SC 2805; *Raheja Universal Ltd. v. NRC Ltd.,* (2012) 4 SCC 148, pp. 180, 181.

77. *Raheja Universal Ltd. v. NRC Ltd.,* (2012) 4 SCC 148, pp. 181, 182.

78. *Anvar P.V. v. P.K. Basheer & Ors.,* (2014) 10 SCC 473, pp. 485, 486.

of such agricultural land for a *bona fide* industrial purpose, subject to certain conditions specified thereunder. The Supreme Court held that the Gujarat Tenancy Act is a welfare legislation enacted for the protection of agriculturists, and is a special statute, and hence the special provisions made in the said Act for sale of agricultural land will prevail over sections 7 and 10 of the Transfer of Property Act, 1882.[79]

(d) Affirmative enactments

One affirmative enactment is not easily taken as repealed by another later affirmative enactment.[80] The rule was stated in *Foster's* case[81] that: "This Act—is all in the affirmative, and therefore, shall not abrogate a precedent affirmative law before; and the said rule that *leges posteriores priores contrarias abrogant* was well agreed; but as to this purpose *contrarium est multiplex*: (1) in quality, scil, if one is an express and material negative and the last is an express and material affirmative, or if the first is affirmative, and the latter negative,[82] (2) In matter, although both are affirmative." *(Foster's* case *supra)*. Therefore, the contrariety between two affirmative enactments results only when they are irreconcilable in matter and when the new affirmative words are such as by their necessity import a contradiction of the earlier.[83] So, if the later affirmative enactment does not imply a negative it will not be construed as impliedly repealing an earlier affirmative enactment.[84]

A temporary Act, the Punjab Damaged Areas Act, 1947, expired on August 15, 1949. In the meantime the East Punjab Damaged Areas Act, 1949, was enacted covering the same subject-matter and came into force from April, 1949. This later Act did not contain any express provision repealing the earlier Act. In 1948, a notification had been issued under the earlier Act declaring a certain area a 'damaged area'. After the expiry of the earlier Act, a question arose whether the notification under it could be deemed to be a notification under the later Act by virtue of section 22 of the Punjab General Clauses Act which applies only in case of repeals. The argument

---

79. *Dipak Babaria & Anr. v. State of Gujarat & Ors.*, (2014) 3 SCC 502, p. 542.

80. *Trust Mai Lachhmi Sialkoti Bradari v. Amritsar Improvement Trust*, AIR 1963 SC 976, p. 979 : (1963) 1 SCR 242.

81. (1615) 77 ER 1222.

82. If the later Act is precise negative of whatever authority existed under an earlier Act, repeal shall be **inferred**; *Suntharalingam v. Inspector of Police*, (1971) 3 WLR 896, p. 901 (PC).

83. *Garnett v. Bradley*, (1878) 3 AC 944, p. 966 : (1874-80) All ER 648 (HL) (LORD BLACKBURN).

84. *Northern India Caterers (P) Ltd. v. State of Punjab*, AIR 1967 SC 1581, p. 1585 : (1967) 3 SCR 399.

was that by reason of the very existence of the enactments of 1947 and 1949 on the Statute Book in terms identical with each other, the earlier statute was impliedly repealed. Repelling the argument AYYANGER, J. observed: "Where two enactments are entirely affirmative and identical no question of inconsistency could arise. Where the operative terms of the two enactments are identical and the enactments so as to speak run parallel to each other, there would be no scope for the application of the doctrine of implied repeal."[85] Similarly, it has been held that the Punjab Public Premises and Land (Eviction and Rent Recovery) Act, 1959, which provided a speedier remedy for eviction of persons in unauthorised occupation of Government premises and lands, did not take away the right of the Government to file suits in the normal courts according to the Code of Civil Procedure, 1908, for eviction of such persons.[86] On the same principle conferral of similar powers under two enactments at different levels does not result in implied repeal of the prior enactment.[87] So it was held that power conferred by section 22B of the Electricity Act, 1910, which was introduced in 1959, to regulate supply of electricity for securing equitable distribution of energy did not take away a similar power conferred on the Board by section 49 of the Electricity (Supply) Act, 1948.[88] And, on the same principle it was held that where higher rate of price of an essential commodity was fixed by a notification issued by the Central Government under an order made under the Essential Commodities Act, 1955, the State Government was competent to issue an order under the Defence of India Rules, 1971 clarifying that the higher rate could not be charged in respect of the stock already existing since prior to the upward revision of the rate.[89] It was observed that there is no legal bar to creating two sources of power to achieve the same purpose and that there was no real inconsistency as the order of the State was supplementary to the notification issued by the Centre and as the obedience to the State's order did not

---

85. *Trust Mai Lachhmi Sialkoti Bradari v. Amritsar Improvement Trust*, AIR 1963 SC 976, p. 979 : (1963) 1 SCR 242. **Compare**–*Harischandra v. State of M.P.*, AIR 1965 SC 932, p. 937 : (1965) 1 SCR 82, (two Control Orders achieving the same object but not identical in their provisions held earlier Order stood repealed and replaced by the later Order).

86. *Northern India Caterers (P) Ltd. v. State of Punjab*, AIR 1967 SC 1581, p. 1585 : 1967 (3) SCR 399. However, the view taken in this case was that the special procedure was discriminatory and so the Act was void being in conflict with Article 14 of the Constitution. But this view has been later **overruled** in *Maganlal Chhagganlal v. Municipal Corporation of Greater Bombay*, (1975) 1 SCR 1 : AIR 1974 SC 2009.

87. **See** text and note 41, p. 743. **See further** *Ramchandra Mawalal v. State of U.P.*, (1984) (Supp) SCC 28, p. 57 : AIR 1987 SC 1837.

88. *Adoni Cotton Mills Ltd. v. Andhra Pradesh Electricity Board*, AIR 1976 SC 2414, p. 2421 : (1976) 4 SCC 68.

89. *Ramchandra Mawalal v. State of U.P.*, (1984) (Supp) SCC 28 : AIR 1987 SC 1837.

involve any disobedience to or contravention of the Centre's notification.[90] But if the earlier affirmative enactment conferring a power on *A* for benefit of *B* was intended to last until the same power was exercised by *B* under a later enactment, the assumption of that power by *B* will result in implied repeal of the earlier enactment. So rules made by the State Government under an Ordinance levying octroi for benefit of the municipality were deemed to be impliedly repealed when the municipality made rules and bylaws imposing octroi at an enhanced rate under the Municipalities Act.[91]

(e) Laws defining offences and penalties

If a later statute again describes an offence created by an earlier statute and imposes a different punishment, or varies the procedure, the earlier statute is repealed by implication.[92] "If a statute deals with a particular class of offences", said MARTIN, B, "and a subsequent Act is passed which deals with precisely the same offences, and a different punishment is imposed by the later Act, I think that, in effect, the Legislature has declared that the new Act shall be substituted for the earlier Act".[93] The principle, however, has no application where the offence described in the later Act is not the same as described in the earlier Act, *i.e.*, when the essential ingredients of the two offences are different.[94]

Section 26 of the General Clauses Act provides that where an act or omission constitutes an offence under two or more enactments, then the offender shall be liable to be punished under either or any of those enactments; but shall not be liable to be punished twice for the same offence. Article 20(2) of the Constitution directs that no person shall be prosecuted and punished for the same offence more than once. Both these provisions apply only when the two offences which form the subject of prosecution or prosecutions are the same, *i.e.*, the ingredients which constitute the two offences are the same. If the offence under the two enactments are distinct

---

90. *Ibid*, pp. 57, 59, 61.

91. *Dharangdhara Chemical Works v. Dharangdhara Municipality*, (1985) 4 SCC 92, pp. 99, 100 : AIR 1985 SC 1729.

92. *Mitchell v. Brown*, (1859) 120 ER 909, p. 912; *Smith v. Benabo*, (1937) 1 All ER 523, p. 526 : (1937) 1 KB 518; *Zaverbhai v. State of Bombay*, AIR 1954 SC 752 : (1955) 1 SCR 799; *T. Barai v. Henry Ah Hoe*, AIR 1983 SC 150, p. 158 : (1983) 1 SCC 177. The same principle was applied to levy of tax at an enhanced rate by a different authority under a later enactment; *Dharangdhara Chemical Works v. Dharangdhara Municipality*, (1985) 4 SCC 92, pp. 99, 100 : AIR 1985 SC 1729.

93. *R. v. Youle*, (1861) 158 ER 311, pp. 315, 316.

94. *Om Prakash v. State of U.P.*, AIR 1957 SC 458 : (1957) SCR 423; *M. Karunanidhi v. Union of India*, AIR 1979 SC 898, pp. 909, 910 : (1979) 3 SCC 431; *T. Barai v. Henry Ah Hoe*, AIR 1983 SC 150, p. 158 : 1983 (1) SCC 218.

and not identical, none of these provisions will apply.[95] The construction placed upon section 26 of the General Clauses Act that it applies only when the offences described in the two enactments are identical very much limits its operation, for in most cases where a subsequent enactment will describe an offence identical in terms with an earlier enactment, the earlier enactment will be deemed to be repealed on principles stated in the preceding paragraph. It is submitted that the emphasis in the opening words of section 26 is not upon the identity of offences but upon the identity of act or omission constituting the offence.[96]

6. CONSEQUENCES OF REPEAL

(a) General

Under the common law rule the consequences of repeal of a statute are very drastic. Except as to transactions past and closed, a statute after its repeal is as completely obliterated as if it had never been enacted. The

---

95. *State of Madhya Pradesh v. Veereshwar Rao*, AIR 1957 SC 592 : 1957 SCR 868; *State of Bombay v. S.L. Apte*, AIR 1961 SC 578 : 1961 (3) SCR 107; *Bishambharnath v. State of U.P.*, AIR 1966 SC 573, p. 578 : (1966) 2 SCR 158; *V.K. Agarwal v. Vasantraj Bhagwanji Bhatia*, AIR 1988 SC 1106, p. 1111 : (1988) 3 SCC 467; *State of Bihar v. Murad Ali Khan*, AIR 1989 SC 1, p. 8 : 1988 (4) SCC 655; *A.A. Mulla v. State of Maharashtra*, AIR 1997 SC 1441, p. 1445 : 1996 (11) SCC 606; *State of Rajasthan v. Hat Singh*, (2003) 2 SCC 152, pp. 158, 159 : AIR 2003 SC 701, pp. 704, 705; *Jitendra Panchal v. Intelligence Officer, Narcotics Control Bureau*, (2009) 3 SCC 57 para 42 : (2009) 2 SLT 124 : AIR 2009 SC 1938; *Monica Bedi v. State of Andhra Pradesh*, (2011) 1 SCC 284 : (2010) 11 SCALE 629 (Head Note A); *Institute of Chartered Accountants of India v. Vimal Kumar Surana*, (2011) 1 SCC 534 para 25 : (2010) 13 JT 356.

96. **See** the observations in *Delhi Municipality v. Shivshanker*, AIR 1971 SC 815, p. 822 : (1971) 1 SCC 442. **See also** section 403, Criminal Procedure Code, 1898 (now section 300, Criminal Procedure Code, 1973) which bars the retrial of a person not only for the same offence but also for any other offence based on the same facts; *Thakurram v. State of Bihar*, AIR 1966 SC 911, p. 912 : (1966) 2 SCR 740. **But see** *V.K. Agarwal v. Vasantraj Bhagwanji Bhatia, supra*. In American law in the context of double *jeopardy* guarantee, distinct statutory offences are treated as involving separate offences only if each provision requires proof of an additional fact which the other does not and so where the same evidence suffices to prove both crimes, they are the same for double *jeopardy* purposes: *State of Bihar v. Murad Ali Khan, supra*, p. 7. In *R v. J*, (2005) 1 All ER 1 (HL) the accused had sexual intercourse with a minor girl. He could be prosecuted for this act for the offences of rape and indecent assault which prescribed the same sentence. He was not prosecuted for rape and the period of limitation for prosecution expired. Thereafter, he was prosecuted for the offence of indecent assault as for this offence there was no period of limitation. In quashing the conviction and sentence, the House of Lords held that on a true construction the period of limitation prescribed by Parliament could not thus be circumvented.

effect is to destroy all inchoate rights and all causes of action that may have arisen under the repealed statute.[1] Therefore, leaving aside the cases where proceedings were commenced, prosecuted and brought to a finality before the repeal, no proceeding under the repealed statute can be commenced or continued after the repeal.[2] Another result of repeal under the common law rule is to revive the law in force at the commencement of the repealed statute. Thus if one statute is repealed by a second which in turn is repealed by a third, the effect is to revive the first statute unless a contrary intention is indicated in the third statute.[3] The confusion resulting from all these consequences gave rise to the practice of inserting saving clauses in repealing statutes, and later on, to obviate the necessity of inserting a saving clause in each and every repealing statute a general provision was made in section 38(2) of the Interpretation Act, 1889.[4] Similar provision is made in India in section 6 of the Central General Clauses Act, 1897 (Act X of 1897)[5] as also in corresponding State legislations.

As a result of the principle of obliteration associated with repeal,[6] the continuation of pending proceedings under a repealed statute depends upon either under the savings contained in the repealing Act or under section 6 of the General Clauses Act. The Parliament has therefore the power to lay down conditions for continuance of pending proceedings and to provide that in cases those conditions are not satisfied the proceedings will terminate. For example—the repealing Act may provide that all pending prosecutions under the repealed Act will be examined by a Review Committee and in cases *prima facie* case is not found by the Committee the proceedings will terminate even without the necessity of the Public Prosecutor applying to the court for withdrawal of the cases under section 321 of the Cr.P.C. In this context the Supreme Court in upholding the validity of section 2(3) of the Prevention of Terrorism (Repeal) Act, 2004 which repealed the Prevention of Terrorism Act, 2002 observed as follows:[7]

---

1. *Keshavan v. State of Bombay*, AIR 1951 SC 128, pp. 131, 132 : 1951 SCR 228 (FAZAL ALI, J.), 134 (MAHAJAN, J.); *State of Punjab v. Mohar Singh*, AIR 1955 SC 84, p. 87 (B.K. MUKHERJEA, J.) : (1955) 1 SCR 893; *Qudrat Ullah v. Bareilly Municipality*, AIR 1974 SC 396, p. 401 : (1974) 1 SCC 202; *State of Rajasthan v. Mangilal Pindwal*, AIR 1996 SC 2181, p. 2183 : 1996 (5) SCC 60.
2. *Keshavan v. State of Bombay, supra*; *Mohan Raj v. Dimbeshwari Saikia,* AIR 2007 SC 232 (para 23) : (2007) 2 SLT 212. This book, 10th edition p. 631 is **referred.**
3. *Ameer-un-Nissa-Begum v. Mehboob Begum*, AIR 1955 SC 352, p. 362.
4. **See** cases in footnote 1, p. 756, *supra*. Section 38(2) of the Interpretation Act, 1899 is now section 16(1) of the Interpretation Act, 1978.
5. *Ibid.*
6. See text and notes 1 and 2 p. 756, supra.
7. *Mahmadhusen Abdulrahim Kalota Shaikh v. Union of India,* (2009) 2 SCC 1 para 37 : (2008) 13 JT 207 (BALAKRISHNAN CJI for himself and RAVEENDRAN J.); paras 91, 92, 100 and 101 (BHANDARI J. **concurring**).

"When Parliament has the power to repeal a law outright without any savings and thereby put an end to all pending prosecution and proceedings forthwith (without any need to comply with section 321 of the Code), can it be said that it does not have the power to make a provision in the repealing Act for the pending proceeding to continue, but those proceedings to come to an end, when a duly constituted Review Committee with a sitting or retired judge of the High Court as Chairman, reviews the cases registered under the repealed Act and reaches the opinion that there is no *prima facie* case for proceeding against the accused? Surely, the wider and larger power includes the narrower and smaller power. It should be remembered that continuation of a proceedings in respect of any offence under an Act, after the repeal of such Act, is itself as a result of a deeming fiction. Natural consequence of repeal, as noticed above, is complete obliteration including pending proceedings. Continuation of a pending proceeding is possible only on account of the deeming fiction created by the savings clause in the repealing Act which provides for continuation of the proceedings as if the principal Act had not been repealed. Therefore, any provision in the repealing Act for saving a pending proceedings, with any further provision for termination of such pending proceedings, is a provision relating to 'winding-up' matters connected with the repealed Act. By no stretch of imagination can such a provision be termed as interference with judicial power, even assuming that such a provision in a live unrepealed statue may be considered as interference with judicial power. It is, therefore, unnecessary to examine whether section 2(3) of the repealing Act is an encroachment of judicial power, though such an examination was done with reference to the challenge to sections 60(4) to (7) of POTA."

An Act repealing an earlier Act may provide for abatement of all proceedings pending under the Act repealed except as otherwise provided in the repealing Act. The Urban Land (Ceiling and Regulation) Act, 1976 was repealed by the Urban Land (Ceiling and Regulation) Act of 1999 and all proceedings pending stood abated except where possession of the land had been taken by the State. In such cases the repeal did not benefit the original land owner.[8]

Since repeal of a law takes effect from the date of repeal and the law repealed remains in operation for the period before its repeal without assistance of any saving clause for transactions past and closed, it can be retrospectively amended to affect such transactions even after its repeal. Thus

---

8. *Sulochana Chandrakant Galande v. Pune Municipal Transport*, (2010) 8 SCC 467 para 36 : AIR 2010 SC 2962.

when Rule B made under Article 309 of the Constitution substitutes Rule A, which in effect means that A is repealed and B is enacted in its place, A can be amended retrospectively for the period during which it was in operation to validate transactions past and closed. In the case[9] from which the above principle is deduced, a rule permitted compulsory retirement of a Government servant by paying three months salary. This rule was later repealed by substituting another rule in its place. During the period the earlier rule was in operation, a Government servant was retired on payment of an amount as salary but which was found on calculation later to be a little short of three months salary making the retirement invalid. The rule was after its repeal retrospectively amended for the period it was in operation to enable the Government to retire a Government servant forthwith without paying him three months salary but entitling him to claim three months salary after retirement. This amendment was held to be valid and effective to validate the retirement of the Government servant concerned.

Section 6 of the General Clauses Act applies to all types of repeals. The section applies whether the repeal be express or implied,[10] entire or partial[11] or whether it be repeal simpliciter or repeal accompanied by fresh legislation.[12] The section also applies when a temporary statute is repealed before its expiry,[13] but it has no application when such a statute is not repealed but comes to an end by expiry.[14] The section on its own terms is limited to a repeal brought about by a Central Act or Regulation. A rule made under an Act is not a Central Act or regulation and if a rule be repealed by another rule, section 6 of the General Clauses Act will not be attracted. It has been so held in two Constitution Bench decisions.[15] The passing observation in these cases[16] that 'section 6 only applies to repeals and not to omissions' needs reconsideration for omission of a provision results in abrogation or obliteration of that provision in the same way as it happens in repeal. The stress in these cases was on the question that a

---

9. *State of Rajasthan v. Mangilal Pindwal*, AIR 1996 SC 2181, p. 2183 : 1996 (5) SCC 60.

10. *State of Orissa v. M.A. Tulloch & Co.*, AIR 1964 SC 1284, p. 1294 : 1964 (4) SCR 461.

11. *Ekambarappa v. EPTO*, AIR 1967 SC 1541, p. 1543 : 1967 (3) SCR 864.

12. *Indira Sohanlal v. Custodian of EP*, AIR 1956 SC 77, p. 83 : 1955 (2) SCR 1117; *State of Punjab v. Mohar Singh*, AIR 1955 SC 84, p. 88 : (1955) 1 SCR 893 (Unless the new legislation manifests a **contrary** intention); *Bansidhar v. State of Rajasthan*, AIR 1989 SC 1614, p. 1618 : 1989 (2) SCC 557; *Gajraj Singh v. State Transport Appellate Tribunal,* (1997) 1 SCC 650 (para 24) : AIR 1997 SC 412; *Southern Petro-chemical Industries Co. Ltd. v. Electricity Inspector and E.T.I.O.*, (2007) 5 SCC 447 (para 88) : AIR 2007 SC 1984.

13. *State of Punjab v. Mohar Singh, supra*, p. 87.

14. **See** title (2), "Effect of Expiry of Temporary Statutes", text and note 12, p. 719.

15. *Rayala Corporation v. Director of Enforcement*, AIR 1970 SC 494, p. 503 (para 15) : (1969) 2 SCC 412; *Kolhapur Cane Sugar Works Ltd. v. Union of India,* AIR 2000 SC 811, pp. 819, 820 : (2000) 2 SCC 536.

16. Cases in note 96 above.

'rule' not being a Central Act or Regulation, as defined in the General Clauses Act, omission or repeal of a 'rule' by another 'rule' does not attract section 6 of the Act and proceedings initiated under the omitted rule cannot continue unless the new rule contains a saving clause to that effect. The cases imply abrogation or obliteration of the omitted rule in the same way as would have happened in case of its repeal.[17] In *General Finance Co. v. Assistant Commissioner of Income-tax*,[18] the question before a three- Judge Bench of the Supreme Court was as to the effect of omission of section 276-DD of the Income-tax Act, 1961 from 1-4-1989 on a prosecution pending for its violation. Following the two Constitution Bench decisions discussed above, it was held that neither the prosecution could be continued nor could punishment be imposed for section 6 of the General Clauses Act was inapplicable to omissions. Although the court found the submission for referring the matter to a larger bench forceful, it did not accede to that request for it did not find the case an appropriate one for that purpose as the cases pending in relation to section 276-DD were few.

Though by Article 367 of the Constitution the General Clauses Act has been made applicable for interpretation of the Constitution, it has been held that section 6 is not applicable to the repeal brought about by the Constitution itself,[19] on the reasoning that the Constitution is not a Central Act or Regulation.[20] The judgment of the High Court in the last mentioned case,[21] which was approved by the Supreme Court shows that if a statute enacted by the British Parliament and applicable to India is repealed by a Central Act,[22] section 6 of the General Clauses Act will apply for the section applies to a repeal of 'any enactment'.[23] It has also been held that if a pre-Constitution law is repealed by the President under Article 372(2) of the Constitution, the repeal will attract the operation of section 6 of the General Clauses Act.[24] The principles of the section have also been applied when a State legislation is overridden for reasons of repugnancy by a later Union legislation.[25]

---

17. **See further** pp. 733, 735, *ante*.
18. AIR 2002 SC 3126 : (2002) 7 SCC 1.
19. Article 395 **repeals** Indian Independence Act, 1947 and Government of India Act, 1935, but laws made thereunder are continued under Art. 372.
20. *Jugmender Das v. State*, AIR 1951 All 703, p. 708; **affirmed** in *State v. Jugmender Das*, AIR 1954 SC 683, p. 686 : 1954 CriLJ 1736.
21. *Ibid.*
22. **See** British Statutes (Application to India) Repeal Act, 1960 (Act LVII of 1960).
23. **See** pp. 756-757, *supra*.
24. *Keshavan v. State of Bombay*, AIR 1951 SC 128, p. 129 : 1951 SCR 228.
25. *State of Orissa v. M.A. Tulloch & Co.*, AIR 1964 SC 1284 : (1964) 4 SCR 461; *Deep Chand v. State of U.P.*, AIR 1959 SC 648, pp. 668, 669; *Kanthimathy Plantation Pvt. Ltd. v. State of Kerala*, AIR 1990 SC 761, p. 763 : (1989) 4 SCC 650; *K.S. Paripoornan v. State of Kerala*, AIR 1992 SC 1488, p. 1495 : 1992 (1) SCC 684.

The meaning of repeal in the context of provisions like sections 6 and 7 of the General Clauses Act is well brought out in section 8A of the Acts Interpretation Act, 1901 of the Commonwealth of Australia in which sections 7 and 8 correspond to sections 6 and 7 of the Indian Act. Section 8A of the Australian Act provides: "A reference in section 7 or 8 to the repeal of an Act or of a part of an Act includes a reference to: (a) repeal effected by implication; (b) the abrogation or limitation of the effect of the Act or part; and (c) the exclusion of the application of the Act or part to any person, subject matter or circumstances."[26] It may be worthwhile to consider inclusion of a similar definition in the Indian Act.

(b) Revival

The common law rule of revival has been abrogated by sections 6(a) and 7 of the General Clauses Act, 1897.[27] The result, therefore, is that if one Act is repealed by a second which again is repealed by a third, the first Act is not revived unless the third Act makes an express provision to that effect.[28] As regards revival of enactments section 6(a) covers what is more emphatically declared by section 7, but the latter is limited in operation to enactments; whereas the former is wider in operation and will prevent the revival of many other matters, *e.g.* the revival of a void contract[29] or of common law.[30] When a provision is repealed by substitution of another provision in its place and the Act making the substitution is declared invalid, the question of revival of the original provision requires consideration of whether the Act has been declared invalid for want of legislative competence or on other grounds.[31]

(c) Saving of rights acquired

The effect of clauses (c) to (e) of section 6, General Clauses Act is, speaking briefly, to prevent the obliteration of a statute in spite of its repeal to keep intact rights acquired or accrued and liabilities incurred during its

---

26. **See** *Attorney General (QLD) v. Australian Industrial Relations Commission,* (2002) 76 ALJR 1502, 1514.
27. **Cf.** section 38(2) and section 11 of Interpretation Act, 1889 of U.K. now sections 15 and 16(1)(a) of the Interpretation Act, 1978.
28. *Ameer-un-Nissar Begum v. Mehboob Begum*, AIR 1955 SC 352, p. 362.
29. *Coutes v. Diment*, (1951) 1 All ER 890, pp. 895, 896.
30. CRAIES, Statutes Law, 7th Edition, page 355.
31. **See** text and note 88, p. 735, *supra.* **See further** *Property Owners' Association v. State of Maharashtra*, 1996 (4) Scale 225: 1996 (4) SCC 49, where the question, whether Article 31C as it stood before Constitution 42nd Amendment Act declared invalid in *Minerva Mills* and *Waman Rao* has revived, has been **referred** to a Constitution Bench. **See further** *Property Owners' Association v. State of Maharashtra,* AIR 2001 SC 1668 : (2001) 4 SCC 455. Where the matter has been **referred** to a bench of seven judges also on the question of interpretation of Article 39(b).

operation and permit continuance or institution of any legal proceedings or recourse to any remedy which may have been available before the repeal for enforcement of such rights and liabilities.[32] Thus, offences committed during the continuance of a statute can now be prosecuted and punished even after its repeal, a course which would not have been possible under the common law rule of complete obliteration of a repealed statute. It must. however, be noticed that 'any investigation, legal proceeding or remedy' saved by clause (e) is only in respect of any right and privilege 'acquired' or 'accrued' and any obligation, liability, penalty, forfeiture or punishment 'incurred' within the ambit of clauses (c) and (d) of section 6.[33] In respect of other matters though 'anything done' under the statute will not be invalidated after its repeal by virtue of clause (b) of section 6, but it will be rendered abortive if no right was acquired or had accrued and no liability had been incurred prior to repeal.[34] Further, the saving of rights and liabilities is in respect of those rights and liabilities which were acquired or incurred under a repealed statute and not under the general law which is

---

32. *Gajraj Singh v. State Transport Appellate Tribunal*, AIR 1997 SC 412, p. 421 : (1997) 1 SCC 650 (The text in this book from 6th Edition, p. 413 is quoted); *Gammon India Ltd. v. Special Chief Secretary,* (2006) 3 SCC 354 (para 68) : (2006) 2 JT 494 : (2006) 2 SLT 317 (same passage from 10th edition p. 635 of this book is quoted).

33. *Director of Public Works v. Ho Po Sang*, (1961) 2 All ER 721, p. 731 : (1963) 3 WLR 39 (PC).

34. *Director of Public Works v. Ho Po Sang*, (1961) 2 All ER 721, p. 732 : (1963) 3 WLR 39 (PC), **see** *Sonilal v. Kanhaiyalal*, (1913) 19 IC 291, p. 295 (PC); (An acknowledgment of liability which only extends limitation is not a 'thing done' within the meaning of section 6, General Clauses Act). A saving clause that preserves the operation of a repealed Act for 'things done or omitted to be done', even in the absence of other savings as contained in section 6 of the General Clauses Act, is liberally construed; *Ram Parshad v. State of Punjab*, AIR 1966 SC 1607, p. 1610 : (1966) 3 SCR 486. Such a saving clause has been interpreted to preserve the legal effects and consequences of the things done though these effects and consequences project into post-repeal period; *Universal Imports Agency v. Chief Controller*, AIR 1961 SC 41 : (1961) 1 SCR 305; *Hasan Nurani v. Assistant Charity Commissioner*, AIR 1967 SC 1742 : (1967) 1 SCR 110; *Dharangdhara Chemical Works v. Dharangdhara Municipality*, (1985) 4 SCC 92, p. 104 : AIR 1985 SC 1729. So the saving clause permits prosecution of a person subsequent to repeal for an offence committed during pre-repeal period; *Wicks v. Director of Public Prosecutions*, (1947) 1 All ER 205 (HL). It allows the continuity of regulations made under Article 357 even after the expiry of the period mentioned in that Article; *Ram Prashad v. State of Punjab*, AIR 1966 SC 1607 : (1966) 3 SCR 486. **But see** *M.S. Shivananda v. Karnataka State Road Transport Corporation*, AIR 1980 SC 77, p. 81 : (1980) 1 SCC 149, where the expression 'things done' was narrowly construed as not to include rights acquired. A saving clause preserving 'liability incurred' even in the absence of a specific saving preserving 'punishment incurred' will enable the punishment of the offender for a criminal offence; *Kapurchand v. State of Bombay*, AIR 1958 SC 993, p. 995 : 1959 SCR 250.

modified by a statute.[35] In respect of rights and liabilities acquired or incurred under the general law which is modified by a statute the inquiry should be as to how far the statute is retrospective.[36] And when a Code dealing with procedure is repealed and replaced by a new Code, the new Code would speaking generally apply for investigations or trials pending under the old Code for no person has a vested right in any matter of procedure,[37] unless the new Code by an express saving clause preserves the continuance of the old Code for pending investigations and trials.[38]

The distinction between what is, and what is not a right preserved by the provisions of section 6, General Clauses Act is often one of great fineness.[39] What is unaffected by the repeal of a statute is a right acquired or accrued under it and not a mere 'hope or expectation of', or liberty to apply for, acquiring a right.[40] A distinction is drawn between a legal proceeding for enforcing a right acquired or accrued and a legal proceeding for acquisition of a right. The former is saved whereas the latter is not. In construing identical provisions of section 10 of the Hong Kong Interpretation Ordinance, LORD MORRIS speaking for the Privy Council observed: "It may be, therefore, that under some repealed enactment, a right has been given, but that, in respect of it, some investigation or legal proceeding is necessary. The right is then unaffected and preserved. It will be preserved even if a process of quantification is necessary. But there is a manifest distinction between an investigation in respect of a right and an investigation which is to decide whether some right should be or should not be given. On a repeal the former is preserved by the Interpretation Act. The latter is not."[41] The LORD CHANCELLOR'S (LORD HERSCHELL'S)

35. *Rao Nihalkaran v. Ram Gopal*, AIR 1966 SC 1485, p. 1490 : 1966 (3) SCR 427.
36. **See** Chapter 6, title 2(a)(ii), p. 580.
37. **See** Chapter 6, title 2(a)(iii), p. 585.
38. *Natbar Parida v. State of Orissa*, AIR 1975 SC 1465, p. 1469 : (1975) 2 SCC 220. Section 484(2)(a) of the Code of Criminal Procedure (1974) preserves the provisions of 1898 Code for pending investigations and, therefore, an accused cannot claim his release under section 169 of the new Code in a pending investigation.
39. *Free Lanka Insurance Co. v. Ranasinghe*, (1964) 1 All ER 457, p. 462 : 1964 AC 541 (PC); *Bansidhar v. State of Rajasthan*, AIR 1989 SC 1614, p. 1621 : 1989 (2) SCC 557.
40. *Director of Public Works v. Ho Po Sang*, (1961) 2 All ER 721, p. 731 : (1963) 3 WLR 39 (PC); *Bansidhar v. State of Rajasthan, supra*; *Gajraj Singh v. State Transport Appellate Tribunal*, AIR 1997 SC 412, p. 426 : (1997) 1 SCC 650.
41. *Director of Public Works v. Ho Po Sang*, (1961) 2 All ER 721, p. 731 : (1963) 3 WLR 39 (PC). **Also referred** to in *Free Lanka Insurance Co. v. Ranasinghe*, (1964) 1 All ER 457, p. 462 : 1964 AC 541 (PC) [Interpretation of section 6(3). Ceylon Interpretation Ordinance, 1900]; *Isha Valimohamad v. Haji Gulam Mohamad*, AIR 1974 SC 2061, p. 2065 : (1974) 2 SCC 484; *M.S. Shivananda v. Karnataka State Road Transport Corporation*, AIR 1980 SC 77, p. 81 : (1980) 1 SCC 149; *Kanaya*

[Footnote No. 41 Contd.]

observations in an earlier Privy Council case, that "mere right to take advantage of an enactment without any act done by an individual towards availing himself of that right cannot properly be deemed a right accrued",[42] are not to be understood as supporting the view that if steps are taken under a statute for acquiring a right, the right accrues even if the steps taken do not reach the stage when the right is given,[43] nor do the said observations support the view that if no steps are taken for enforcement of a right come into existence, the right is not an accrued right.[44] As explained by SINHA, C.J. the observations of LORD HERSCHELL are only authority for the proposition that "the mere right, existing at the date of a repealing statute to take advantage of provisions of the statute repealed is not a right accrued".[45] Inchoate or contingent rights and liabilities, *i.e.*, rights and liabilities which have accrued but which are in the process of being enforced or are yet to be enforced are unaffected for clause (c) clearly contemplates that there will be situations when an investigation, legal proceeding or remedy may have to be continued or resorted to before the right or liability can be enforced.[46] Such a right or liability is not merely a 'hope' which is destroyed by the repeal.[47] It must also be noticed that the object of clause (c) is to preserve rights and privileges acquired and accrued on the one side, and the corresponding obligation or liability incurred on the other side, so that if no right had accrued under the repealed statute there is no question of any liability being preserved.[48] Further,

---

[Footnote No. 41 Contd.]

Ram v. Rajender Kumar, (1985) 1 SCC 436, p. 441 : AIR 1985 SC 371; *Bansidhar v. State of Rajasthan*, AIR 1989 SC 1614, p. 1623 : (1989) 2 SCC 557; *Vinod Gurudas Raikar v. National Insurance Co. Ltd.*, AIR 1991 SC 2156, p. 2159 : (1991) 4 SCC 333; *P.V. Mohammad Barmay Sons v. Director of Enforcement*, AIR 1993 SC 1188, p. 1192 : (1992) 4 JT 565; *Thyssen Stahlunion GMBH v. Steel Authority of India*, JT 1999 (8) 66, pp. 98, 108 : AIR 1999 SC 3923, p. 3942; *Ambalal Sarabhai Enterprises Ltd. v. Amrit Lal & Co.*, AIR 2001 SC 3580, p. 3589 : (2001) 8 SCC 397.

42. *Abbot v. Minister of Land*, (1895) AC 425, 431 : 72 LT 113 (PC).

43. *Director of Public Works v. Ho Po Sang*, (1961) 2 All ER 721, pp. 732, 733 (PC).

44. *Sakharam v. Manikchand*, AIR 1963 SC 354, pp. 356, 357. **See further** *Hungerford Investment Trust v. Haridas Mundhra*, AIR 1972 SC 1826, p. 1832 : (1972) 3 SCC 684; *Lalji Raja & Sons v. Hansraj Nathuram*, AIR 1971 SC 974, p. 979 : (1971) 1 SCC 721; *Zoharabi v. Arjuna*, AIR 1980 SC 101, p. 102 : (1980) 2 SCC 203; *Kanaya Ram v. Rajender Kumar*, (1985) 1 SCC 436, p. 441 : AIR 1985 SC 371; *Bansidhar v. State of Rajasthan*, AIR 1989 SC 1614, pp. 1621, 1622; *Thyssen Stahlunion GMBH v. Steel Authority of India*, JT 1999 (8) 66, p. 107, 108 : AIR 1999 SC 3923, pp. 3947, 3948 : (1999) 9 SCC 334.

45. *Sakharam v. Manikchand, supra*.

46. *Plewa v. Chief Adjudication Officer*, (1994) 3 All ER 323, p. 331 : (1995) 1 AC 249 : (1994) 3 WLR 317 (HL) (For this case see also text and note 74, p. 588).

47. *Aitken v. South Hams District Council*, (1994) 3 All ER 400, p. 405 : (1995) 1 AC 262 : (1994) 3 WLR 33 (HL).

48. *Ogden Industries Ltd. v. Lucas*, (1969) 1 All ER 121, p. 125 (PC).

although the application of section 6(1)(d) is confined to the criminal field, the words 'obligation or liability' in section 6(1)(c) are not restricted to a civil obligation or liability and these words also cover an obligation or liability enforceable under the criminal law.[49]

The question whether a right was acquired or a liability incurred under a statute before its repeal will in each case depend on the construction of the statute and the facts of the particular case. The central issue in considering this question in a controversial case will generally be whether the steps that remained to be taken under the repealed statute were steps necessary for acquiring a right or incurring a liability or whether they were steps required merely for enforcing a right or liability (at least contingent) that had come into existence.

Control of Pollution Act, 1974 empowered a local authority to serve a notice requiring abatement of a nuisance within a stated time and making a person served with the notice and contravening its provisions liable for a criminal offence. After service of a notice but before its expiry the Act was repealed. It was held that the effectiveness of the notice was continued under clause (b) and obligation to comply with it was preserved by clause (c) of section 16(1) of the Interpretation Act, 1978 [corresponding to clauses (b) and (c) of section 6 of the General Clauses Act] and that a person contravening the notice after repeal of the Act was liable to be punished for the offence under the repealed Act.[50] Here the obligation to comply with the notice enforceable by recourse to criminal law was held to be a real and continuing obligation which accrued on service of the notice.

Provisions contained in a Public Health Act, which entitled a local authority to give notice to the frontagers in a street to execute certain works within a certain period and empowered the local authority, in the event of default of the frontagers, to execute the works themselves and to recover the expenses from the frontagers, were construed as conferring a right on the local authority on default of the frontagers after notice, which would be preserved even if the enactment was repealed after default of the frontagers and before any work was done by the local authority.[51]

The right of a tenant of an agricultural holding to recover compensation under an Act from his landlord who served a notice to quit in view of an intended sale of the holding was held to have arisen on service of the

---

49. *Aitken v. South Hams District Council*, (1994) 3 All ER 400, p. 405 : (1995) 1 AC 262 : (1994) 3 WLR 33 (HL).
50. *Ibid.*
51. *Heston and Isleworth Urban District Council v. Grout*, (1897) 2 Ch 306.

notice by the landlord.[52] The Act also required the tenant to give notice of his intention to claim compensation within two months of the service of the notice by the landlord and to make his compensation claim within three months of quitting the holding. The tenant complied only with the first condition of service of notice of his intention to claim compensation before the Act was repealed, yet it was held that the tenant had acquired the right to receive compensation by the fact of his landlord having given a notice to quit in view of sale and the right was enforceable even after repeal of the Act. According to SCRUTTON, L.J., the steps required to be taken by the tenant were not for acquisition of the right but for its enforcement.[53] According to ATKIN, L.J., those steps related to *accrual* of the right which had been *acquired*.[54] The distinction drawn by ATKIN L.J., between acquisition and accrual of a right was referred to recently in *Chief Adjudication Officer v. Maguire*,[55] but the majority did not accept this distinction. This case related to the Special Hardship Allowance (SHA) payable as a disablement benefit, resulting from industrial injury, under the Social Security Act, 1975 which was replaced by the Reduced Farming Allowance (RFA) from 1st October 1986 by the Social Security Act, 1986 which repealed the 1975 Act. The claimant in this case suffered the industrial injury in April 1985 but he did not make a claim for SHA as required by the 1975 Act before its repeal. The question in the case was whether the claimant was entitled to SHA for the period between 1st April, 1985 and 1st October 1986. The Court of Appeal held that he was so entitled as he had an acquired right and what had remained was only enforcement of that right. SIMON BROWN L.J., who delivered the main judgment did not find any distinction between an 'acquired' or 'accrued' right. He pointed out that in certain of the saving legislations reference was made to only one of these expressions and the court is really concerned with only one question: has the claimant established that at the time of repeal he had a right?[56] CLARKE, L.J., agreed with this view and said that it was not desirable to introduce narrow distinctions between 'acquired' rights and 'accrued' rights.[57] WALLACE, L.J., however was inclined to agree with the distinction made by ATKIN, L.J.[58] It is submitted that as pointed out by SIMON BROWN, L.J., the two expressions are generally used in saving legislations to convey the same idea and are not mutually exclusive. Yet a possible distinction may be made between cases where some step, after the Act comes into force, is needed to be taken by the claimant for getting the right and

52. *Hamilton Gell v. White,* (1922) 2 KB 422 : 127 LT 728 (CA).
53. *Ibid,* p. 430.
54. *Ibid,* p. 431.
55. (1999) 2 All ER 859 (CA).
56. *Ibid,* p. 868.
57. *Ibid,* p. 871
58. *Ibid,* p. 870.

cases where the Act, without anything being further done by the claimant, confers the right. In the former class of cases, it would be a right acquired after the necessary step is taken whereas in the latter class of cases it would be a right accrued by mere force of the Act.

The right of an injured third party to recover damages against the insurers of a motor vehicle will be an accrued right on the happening of the accident resulting in the injury and will be enforceable against them even after repeal of the enactment creating the liability, even though the process of quantification is not complete before the repeal.[59]

The right of a tenant, who has the land for a certain number of years and who has personally cultivated the same for that period 'to be deemed to be a protected tenant' under the provisions of a statute has been held to be an accrued right which will survive the repeal of the statute.[60] Similarly, a right conferred by an Act that every lease shall be deemed to be for a period of ten years, is a right acquired and will be unaffected by repeal of the Act.[61] But the so-called right of a statutory tenant to protection against eviction under a Control of Eviction Act is mere advantage and not a right in the real sense and does not continue after repeal of the Act.[62] Similarly on the reasoning that the right of a tenant to get standard rent fixed and not to pay contractual rent in excess of standard rent under a Rent Control Act is only a protective right and not a vested right, it has been held that when during the pendency of an application for fixation of standard rent, the Act is amended and it ceases to apply to the premises in question, the application is rendered incompetent and has to be dismissed as infructuous.[63]

The right of a landlord to file a suit for ejectment under a Control of Eviction Act against a tenant without terminating the tenancy by a quit notice on the ground that the tenant had sublet the premises, conferred by an

59. *Free Lanka Insurance Co. v. Ranasinghe*, (1964) 1 All ER 457, p. 462 : 1964 AC 541 (PC).

60. *Sakharam v. Manikchand*, AIR 1963 SC 354 : 1962 (2) SCR 59.

61. *Hiralal v. Nagindas*, AIR 1966 SC 367 : 1964 (6) SCR 773. For other vested rights in the context of landlord and tenant, **see** *Ishverlal v. Motibhai*, AIR 1966 SC 459 : 1966 (1) SCR 367.

62. *Qudrat Ullah v. Bareilly Municipality*, AIR 1974 SC 396 : (1974) 1 SCC 202. The same result will follow if the Act ceases to apply to certain tenancies by an amendment made by the Legislature or by a notification issued by the Government in exercise of a power conferred by the Act: *D.C. Bhatia v. Union of India*, 1995 (1) SCC 104 : 1994 AIR SCW 5011; *Parripati Chandra Shekhar Rao v. Alapati Jalaiah*, 1995 (3) Scale 197 : AIR 1995 SC 1781 : (1995) 3 SCC 709. (Even pending proceedings will be affected); *Ambalal Sarabhai Enterprises Ltd. v. Amrit Lal & Co.*, AIR 2001 SC 3580 : (2001) 8 SCC 397 (pending proceeding will be affected).

63. *Vishwant Kumar v. Madanlal Sharma*, AIR 2004 SC 1887, pp. 1888, 1889 : (2004) 4 SCC 1.

Act, was held to be an accrued right which survived the repeal of the Act.[64] In cases where a suit or proceeding for eviction is pending when the Act ceases to apply, the landlord will have the option of either proceeding with the suit or proceeding or to withdraw it and file a fresh suit under the general law after giving quit notice.[65]

A right to purchase an electricity undertaking on expiration of its period of licence by giving two years prior notice conferred by original section 7 of the Electricity Act, 1910, was held to be a right accruing after notice of option, and therefore, unaffected by repeal of the section before expiry of the licence.[66]

Provision made by Rule 30 of the Displaced Persons (Compensation and Rehabilitation) Rules, 1955 that where the property is in the occupation of more persons than one, it shall be offered to the person whose gross compensation is the highest was construed to confer a substantive right and it was held that the repeal of the rule did not affect pending actions.[67]

The liability to take insurance policy for the full value of the factory or goods under the Emergency Risks (Factories) Act, 1962 and the Emergency Risks (Goods) Act, 1962 was absolute and could be enforced after the expiry of these Acts on revocation of proclamation of emergency issued in connection with the Chinese aggression even though the full value of the factory or goods was determined by the authorised officer under these Acts after their expiry.[68]

The right of the State to take over land of a landholder in excess of the ceiling area prescribed by a Ceiling Act with reference to an appointed date is an accrued right which survives the repeal of the Act before quantification of the surplus area.[69]

---

64. *Isha Valimohamad v. Haji Gulam Mohamad,* AIR 1974 SC 2061 : (1974) 2 SCC 484, pp. 490, 491 (This case also refers to the meaning of the word 'privilege' as used in section 6).

65. *Ambalal Sarabhai Enterprises Ltd. v. Amrit Lal & Co.,* AIR 2001 SC 3580 : (2001) 8 SCC 397.

66. *Gujarat Electricity Board v. Shantilal,* AIR 1969 SC 239 : 1969 (1) SCR 580.

67. *Joint Secretary to the Government of India v. Khilluram,* AIR 1975 SC 2275, p. 2277 : (1976) 1 SCC 88.

68. *Amadalavalasa Co-operative Agricultural & Industrial Society Ltd. v. Union of India,* AIR 1976 SC 958 : (1976) 2 SCC 934. [Section 6 of the General Clauses Act, 1897 was made applicable upon their expiry by section 1(3) of the Acts]; **followed** in *Andhra Pradesh State Electricity Board v. Union of India,* AIR 1988 SC 1020, p. 1024 : 1988 Supp SCC 371.

69. *Bansidhar v. State of Rajasthan,* AIR 1989 SC 1614, pp. 1622, 1623 : 1989 (2) SCC 557.

The right of an establishment to be exempt from the provisions of the Employees Provident Funds and Miscellaneous Provisions Act, 1952 during the infancy period of three years by virtue of section 16(1)(d) of the Act has been held to be a vested right which remained unaffected by omission of section 16(1)(d) by a later ordinance.[70]

The liability of a landholder not to cut trees in a forest declared to be a reserved forest under Chhota Udepur Forest Rules, 1934 was held to survive after repeal of the rules by application of the Forest Act, 1927 to Chhota Udepur under the Application of Laws Order, 1948.[71]

A marriage performed during the continuance of a prior marriage and void being in contravention of Madras Act XXII of 1933 was not validated on repeal of the Madras Act by the Kerala Act 30 of 1976.[72]

The option given to a grantee to make additional purchases of Crown land on fulfilment of certain conditions under the provisions of the statute, was held to be not an accrued right when the statute was repealed before the exercise of the option.[73]

A privilege to get an extension of a licence under an enactment is not an accrued right and no application can be filed after the repeal of the enactment for renewal of the licence.[74]

The right of a Crown lessee to obtain vacant possession from his tenants on grant of a rebuilding certificate by the Governor which he could grant at his absolute discretion has been held to be not an accrued right before the grant of the certificate, and therefore, when the statute making these provisions was repealed before the grant of the certificate, it was held that proceedings taken before the repeal for getting the certificate became abortive and could not be continued thereafter.[75]

The right of dependants to claim compensation on the death of a workman under a Workmen's Compensation Act accrues on workman's death

---

70. *S.L. Srinivasa Jute Twine Mills (P.) Ltd. v. Union of India,* (2006) 2 SCC 740 : (2006) 2 JT 397 : (2006) 2 LLJ 225.

71. *Salchbhai Mulla Mohamadali v. State of Gujarat*, AIR 1993 SC 335, p. 339 : 1992 (1) SCC 742.

72. *PEK Kalliani Amma v. K. Devi*, AIR 1996 SC 1963 : 1996 (4) SCC 76.

73. *Abbot v. Minister of Lands*, (1895) AC 425, 431 (PC).

74. *Reynolds v. A.G. for Nova Scotia*, (1896) AC 240 : 65 LJ PC 16 : 74 LT 108 (PC). **See further** *Gajraj Singh v. State Transport Appellate Tribunal*, AIR 1997 SC 412, p. 422 : (1997) 1 SCC 650 (The text in this book from 6th Edition, p. 418 is quoted).

75. *Director of Public Works v. Ho Po Sang*, (1961) 2 All ER 721 : (1961) 3 WLR 39 : 1961 AC 901 (PC). **See further** *Chairman Indore Vikas Pradhikaran v. Pure Industrial Coke and Chemical Ltd.*, (2007) 8 SCC 705 para 107 : AIR 2007 SC 2458.

and not at the time when the injury resulting in death is caused. Therefore, when the law is changed after injury but before death providing for enhanced compensation, it is not open to the employer to contend that he had incurred the liability when the injury was caused and was not liable to pay enhanced compensation. The right of dependants and the liability of the employer towards them arises at the same time, *i.e.*, at the happening of the death of the workman.[76]

The non-executability of a valid decree passed by a British Indian Court in 1949 under the Code of Civil Procedure, 1908, in Madhya Bharat, where another Civil Procedure Code was applicable, was held to be not an accrued right but a mere procedural advantage which came to an end after extension of the Code of 1908 to Madhya Bharat and repeal of the corresponding Code in force there.[77]

The right of a judgment-debtor against whom a decree for specific performance of sale of shares was passed, to apply for rescission of the decree under section 35 of the Specific Relief Act, 1877, on default of the decree-holder in payment of money, was held to be not an accrued right when no default had taken place before repeal of the Act by the Specific Relief Act, 1963.[78] Relief was, however, granted in the exercise of inherent powers on general principles.

The right or privilege to claim benefit of condonation of delay is not an accrued right under a repealed provision when the delay had not occurred before the repeal of the said provision.[79]

The right of pre-emption conferred by an Act is a remedial right or in other words a right to take advantage of an enactment for acquiring a right to land or other property and cannot be said to have been acquired or accrued until a decree is passed and does not survive if the Act is repealed before passing of the final decree.[80]

The right of a Government servant to be considered for promotion in accordance with existing rules is not a vested right and does not survive if the Government takes a policy decision not to fillup the vacancy pending

---

76. *Ogden Industries Ltd. v. Lucas*, (1969) 1 All ER 121 (PC).

77. *Lalji Raja & Sons v. Hansraj Nathuram*, AIR 1971 SC 974 : (1971) 1 SCC 721.

78. *Hungerford Investment Trust v. Haridas Mundhra*, AIR 1972 SC 1826, p. 1832 : (1972) 3 SCC 684.

79. *Vinod Gurudas Raikar v. National Insurance Co. Ltd.*, AIR 1991 SC 2156, p. 2160 : 1991 (4) SCC 333.

80. *Nirmala Devi v. Renuka*, AIR 1973 MP 120 **approved** in *Krishna Dass Agarwal v. Kanhaiyalal*, AIR 1996 SC 3464 : 1996 (9) SCC 488.

revision of the rules and the revised rules which repeal the existing rules do not make him eligible for promotion.[81]

Repeal of an Act providing for tenure appointment to a post has the effect of abolishing the post and terminating the tenure of the incumbent of the post whose right to continue on the post for his full term or to get compensation for loss of the remaining period is not preserved by section 6 of the General Clauses Act.[82] But if the Act deprives the incumbent even to seek any other employment in future, he would be entitled to compensation for the loss of the remaining period of his service.[83]

General savings of rights accrued, and liabilities incurred under a repealed Act by force of section 6, General Clauses Act, are subject to a contrary intention evinced by the repealing Act.[84] In case of a bare repeal, there is hardly any room for a contrary intention;[85] but when the repeal is accompanied by fresh legislation on the same subject, the provisions of the new Act will have to be looked into to determine whether and how far the new Act evinces a contrary intention affecting the operation of section 6, General Clauses Act.[86] 'The line of enquiry would be, not whether the new Act expressly keeps alive old rights and liabilities but whether it manifests

---

81. *Ramulu (Dr.) v. S. Suryaprakash Rao (Dr.)*, AIR 1997 SC 1803, p. 1808 : 1997 (3) SCC 59.

82. *Sri Justice S.K. Roy v. State of Orissa,* (2003) 4 SCC 21, pp. 24, 25 : AIR 2003 SC 924.

83. *Ibid.*

84. *Karam Singh v. Pratap Chand*, AIR 1964 SC 1305, p. 1309 (para 10) : (1964) 5 SCR 647; *Ishverlal v. Motibhai*, AIR 1966 SC 459, p. 466 : 1966 (1) SCR 367.

85. By a subsequent statute a penal section in an earlier statute ceased to have effect and was also repealed. It was held that even such a double repeal did not show a contrary intention and prevent prosecution for an offence committed before the repeal; *Commissioner of Police v. Simeon*, (1982) 2 All ER 813 : (1983) 1 AC 234 : (1982) 3 WLR 289 (HL).

86. *State of Punjab v. Mohar Singh*, AIR 1955 SC 84, p. 88 : (1955) 1 SCR 833; *Indira Sohanlal v. Custodian of E.P.*, AIR 1956 SC 77, p. 83 : (1955) 2 SCR 1117; *Brihan; Maharashtra Sugar Syndicate v. Janardan*, AIR 1960 SC 794, p. 795 : (1960) 3 SCR 85; *Mahadeolal v. Administrator General of WB*, AIR 1960 SC 936, pp. 938, 939 (para 7) : (1960) 3 SCR 578; *State of Kerala v. N. Sami Iyer*, AIR 1966 SC 1415, pp. 1417, 1418; *Jayantilal v. Union of India*, AIR 1971 SC 1193, p. 1196 : (1972) 4 SCC 174; *T. Barai v. Henry Ah Hoe*, AIR 1983 SC 150, p. 156 : (1983) 1 SCC 177; *Bansidhar v. State of Rajasthan*, AIR 1989 SC 1614, p. 1619 : (1989) 2 SCC 557; *Manphul Singh Sharma v. Ahmedi Begum*, JT 1994 (5) SC 49, p. 53 : (1994) 5 SCC 465; *D. Srinivasan v. The Commissioner,* AIR 2000 SC 1250, p. 1255 : (2000) 3 SCC 548. For construction of a Saving Clause which opens with the words 'Save as expressly provided in this Act', **see** *S.N. Kamble v. Sholapur Municipality*, AIR 1966 SC 538 : (1966) 1 SCR 618. For a saving clause which preserves old rights but applies new procedure, **see** *Ramchandra v. Tukaram*, AIR 1966 SC 557 : 1966 (1) SCR 594.

an intention to destroy them,'[87] for, unless such an intention is manifested by the new Act, the rights and liabilities under the repealed Act will continue to exist by force of section 6, General Clauses Act. It is the repealing Act and not the Act repealed which is to manifest the contrary intention so as to exclude the operation of section 6.[88] The silence of the repealing Act is consistent and not inconsistent with section 6 applying.[89] Another line of approach may be to see as to how far the new Act is retrospective in operation.[90] When, a saving clause in a new Act is comprehensively worded and is detailed, it may be possible to infer that it is exhaustive and expresses an intention not to call for the application of section 6, General Clauses Act.[91]

---

87. *State of Punjab v. Mohar Singh*, AIR 1955 SC 84, p. 88 : (1955) 1 SCR 893; *T.S. Baliah v. T.S. Rangachari*, AIR 1969 SC 701, p. 705 : (1969) 3 SCR 65; *Tiwari Kanhaiyalal v. Commissioner of Income-tax, Delhi*, AIR 1975 SC 902, p. 905 : (1975) 4 SCC 401; *State of Maharashtra v. Atmaram Sadashiv Dongarwar*, AIR 1978 SC 1635, p. 1641 : (1978) 4 SCC 170; *Mohd. Rashid Ahmal v. State*, AIR 1979 SC 592, p. 598 : (1979) 1 SCC 596; *M.S. Shivananda v. Karnataka State Road Transport Corporation*, AIR 1980 SC 77, pp. 80, 81 : (1980) 1 SCC 149; *T. Barai v. Henry Ah Hoe*, AIR 1983 SC 150, p. 156 : (1983) 1 SCC 177; *Commissioner of Income-tax, U.P. v. Shah Sadiq and Sons*, (1987) 3 SCC 516, p. 524 (para 14) : AIR 1987 SC 1217; *Bansidhar v. State of Rajasthan*, AIR 1989 SC 1614, p. 1619; *Manphul Singh Sharma v. Ahmedi Begum*, JT 1994 (5) SC 49, p. 53 : 1994 (5) SCC 465; *Mohanraj v. Dimbeshwari Saikia*, AIR 2007 SC 232 (para 24); *Gammon India Ltd. v. Special Chief Secretary*, (2006) 3 SCC 354 (paras 52, 53); *Southern Petrochemical Industries Co. Ltd. v. Electricity Inspector and ETIO*, (2007) 5 SCC 447 (para 84) : AIR 2007 SC 1984; *Sangam Spinners v. Regional Provident Fund Commissioner*, (2008) 1 SCC 391 para 13 : AIR 2008 SC 739 [Section 16 (1)d Employees Provident Funds and Miscellaneous Provisions Act, 1952 granting exemption to infant establishments for three years omitted with effect from 22-9-1997 but that will not affect the right to exemption for establishments commencing production before that date].

88. *Aitken v. South Hams District Council*, (1994) 3 All ER 400, p. 406 : (1995) 1 AC 264 : (1994) 3 WLR 333 (HL) (a case under section 16 of the Interpretation Act, 1978 which corresponds to section 6 of the General Clauses Act); *Gammon India Ltd. v. Special Chief Secretary, supra.*

89. *Ibid., Gammon India Ltd. v. Special Chief Secretary, supra.*

90. **See** Chapter 6, title 2 'Retrospective Operation'. **See further** *M.S. Shivananda v. Karnataka State Road Transport Corporation*, AIR 1980 SC 77, p. 81 : 1980 (1) SCC 149.

91. *Kalawati Devi v. CIT*, AIR 1968 SC 162, p. 168 : (1967) 3 SCR 833; *ITO, Mangalore v. Damodar*, AIR 1969 SC 408, p. 412 : (1969) 2 SCR 29; *Mahmadhusen Abdulrahim Kalota Shaikh v. Union of India*, (2009) 2 SCC 1 para 34 (f) : (2008) 13 Scale 398. **But see** *Tiwari Kanhaiyalal v. Commissioner of Income-tax*, AIR 1975 SC 902 : (1975) 4 SCC 401, which holds that the detailed savings contained in section 297, of the Income-tax Act, 1961 are not exhaustive. Recourse in this case was taken to section 6, General Clauses Act for holding that a person's liability for an offence under section 52 of the Income-tax Act, 1922 continued even after its repeal. In *Commissioner of Income-tax, U.P. v. Shah Sadiq and Sons*, (1987) 3 SCC 516, p. 524 : AIR 1986 SC 1217. Section 6 of the General Clauses Act was again applied to continue the right of set-off accrued under section 24(2) of the 1922 Act after its repeal by the 1961 Act.

But normally a saving provision is not exhaustive of the rights and obligations saved or of the rights that survive the repeal and so the rights and obligations not expressly saved by the saving clause survive by recourse to section 6 of the General Clauses Act.[92] A provision in the repealing Act (which also enacts a new law) that the provisions of the new law 'shall have effect notwithstanding anything inconsistent contained in any other law for the time being in force' does not show a contrary indication to displace the application of section 6 of the General Clauses Act for the repealed law deemed to be in force for enforcement of accrued rights and liabilities by virtue of that section is not a law 'for the time being in force'.[93]

Section 81 of the Foreign Exchange Regulation Act, 1973 repealed the corresponding Act of 1947 and provided that 'anything done—under the Act hereby repealed shall, in so far it is not inconsistent with the provisions of this Act, be deemed to have been done or taken under the corresponding provisions of this Act'. Interpreting this section, it was held that section 81(2) did not evince a contrary intention to exclude section 6 of the General Clauses Act and that section 81(2), empowers to effectuate the liabilities, penalties *etc.*, incurred during the period when the repealed Act was in force, as if they have been in existence and amenable to be pursued under the new Act or under the repealed Act by force of section 6 of the General Clauses Act.[94] It is submitted that the effect of a provision like section 81(2) would be to apply the remedial and procedural provisions of the new Act for enforcing the rights and liabilities accrued and incurred under the repealed Act and not the substantive provisions of the new Act. Acts done which incur a liability under the repealed Act, *e.g.* acts constituting a crime, are not 'anything done under the Act' but in violation thereof and cannot be deemed to have been done under the new Act by recourse to section 81.

---

92. *Bansidhar v. State of Rajasthan*, AIR 1989 SC 1614, p. 1621 : 1989 (2) SCC 557. **See further** *Tiwari Kanhaiyalal v. Commissioner of Income-tax, supra* and *Commissioner of Income-tax, U.P. v. Shah Sadiq and Sons, supra*. **See** for example *M. Subbarao and Sons v. Yashodamma*, AIR 2002 SC 3284, p. 3286 : (2002) 7 SCC 553 (Section 70 of the Karnataka Rent Act 1961 and section. 6 of the Karnataka General Clauses Act, 1899). **See also** an Australian case *Dosset v. TKJ Nominees Pty. Ltd.*, (2003) 78 ALJR 161.

93. *Bansidhar v. State of Rajasthan, supra*, pp. 1620, 1621.

94. *P.V. Mohammad Barmay Sons v. Director of Enforcement*, AIR 1993 SC 1188, p. 1192 : 1992 (4) JT 565 : 1993 Supp (2) SCC 724. **See further** *Central Bureau of Investigation v. Subodh Kumar Dutt*, AIR 1997 SC 869, p. 870 : (1997) 10 SCC 567 (Construction of section 30(2) of the Prevention of Corruption Act, 1988 which is similar to section 81(2) of FERA, 1973).

A tax exemption granted by a notification under an Act *permanently* may survive repeal of the Act even though there be no corresponding provision in the repealing Act under which it could continue.[1] Section 3 of the Tamil Nadu Electricity (Taxation on Consumption) Act, 1962 provided for levy of electricity tax on consumption of electricity. Section 13 empowered the Government to exempt by notification any specified class of persons from payment of electricity tax. By a notification issued in 1996 under Section 13, the Government exempted certain industries *permanently* from electricity tax on the *consumption* of self-generated electrical energy for captive generation. The 1962 Act was repealed by TamilNadu Tax on Consumption or Sale of Electricity Act, 2003. Section 3 of the 2003 Act imposed electricity tax on the *electricity sold or consumed.* Section 14 of the 2003 Act did not provide for grant of exemption of tax *on consumption of electricity* though it provided for exemption of tax *on electricity sold for consumption.* It was, therefore, not a corresponding provision under which the notification of exemption under the 1962 Act could be read and continued by reason of the saving clause in section 20(2) similar in terms to section 24 of the General Clauses Act. But it was held that the exemption granted under the 1962 Act from tax on consumption of electricity was a 'thing duly done' and the exemption 'a right or privilege acquired' respectively under clauses (b) and (c) of section 20(1), which corresponds to section 6 of the General Clauses Act except that it does not contain the words 'unless a different intention appears' which occur in section 6, and they survived the repeal of the 1962 Act. The right of exemption granted to the industries *permanently* by the notification, the court said, was a vested right, permanence meant unless altered by statute and the notification would continue to govern unless the same is repealed.[2] The court declined to read by implication the words 'unless a different intention appears' in section 20(1) and in the absence of these words found no conflict between sections 20(1) and 20(2).[3] As the industries had invested hugesums in establishing their factories on the faith of the exemption notification the doctrines of promissory estoppel[4] and legitimate expectation[5] were also used for continuing the exemption.

Inchoate acts done under an Act, before maturing into a right or liability cannot survive the repeal of the Act followed by fresh legislation containing a saving clause to preserve 'anything done *etc.*' under the repealed Act

---

1. *Southern Petrochemical Industries Co. Ltd. v. Electricity Inspector and ETIO,* (2007) 5 SCC 447 : AIR 2007 SC 1984.
2. *Ibid,* para 100.
3. *Ibid,* paras 92 to 96.
4. *Ibid,* para 131.
5. *Ibid,* para 132.

so as to continue under the corresponding provisions of the new Act 'in so far—not inconsistent with its provisions' if on comparison relevant provisions of the two Acts are found to be inconsistent.[6] Dealing with a similar provision in section 217(2)(a) of the Motor Vehicles Act, 1988 which repealed the Act of 1939 the Supreme Court in *Gajraj Singh v. State Transport Appellate Tribunal*[7] observed: "If analogous provision in the repealed Act does not find place in the Act (1988 Act) the rights acquired or accrued thereunder would not continue under the Act unless fresh rights are acquired under the Act."[8] It is submitted that these observations do not mean that the rights accrued or acquired under the repealed Act are annihilated. If there be no analogous provision in the repealing Act, the rights acquired under the repealed Act would continue under that Act by virtue of section 6 of the General Clauses Act unless the repealing Act shows a contrary intention to exclude the operation of section 6. The question in *Gajraj Singh's* case, in the context of which the above observations were made, was whether a stage carriage permit granted under the repealed Act could be held to be a permit granted under the repealing Act by virtue of section 217(2)(a) and the answer was rightly given in the negative as the provisions in the two Acts relating to grant of permit are materially different. Such a permit as further rightly held by the court is expressly continued to be effective under section 217(2)(b) for the period for which it would have been effective under the repealed Act.[9] Even if there would have been no express provision like section 217(2)(b) the permit would have continued to be effective for the same period by virtue of section 6 of the General Clauses Act, the application of which is saved by section 217(4). The reason is that the right acquired by grant of the permit was to ply the stage carriage covered by the permit for the full duration of the permit. This right was unaffected by repeal of the 1939 Act by operation of section 6(c) of the General Clauses Act.

The Motor Vehicles Act, 1939 in section 58(2) provided for preferential consideration of an application for renewal of a permit as against fresh applicants, other conditions being equal. There is no corresponding provision of this nature in the Motor Vehicles Act, 1988. This right of preferential

---

6. *Ahmedabad Urban Development Authority v. Manilal Gordhandas,* AIR 1996 SC 2804 : 1996 (11) SCC 482 (Plan of development submitted for approval of the Government under the Bombay Town Planning Act, 1954. **Pending approval**, the Bombay Act repealed by section 124 of the Gujarat Planning and Urban Development Act, 1976 containing a saving as mentioned in the text. The plan pending for approval at the time of repeal of the Bombay Act could not be approved under the new Act as the provisions of the two Acts were inconsistent).

7. AIR 1997 SC 412 : 1997 (1) SCC 650.

8. *Ibid*, p. 424.

9. *Ibid.*

consideration of a renewal application could accrue or arise only on making of an application for renewal. Therefore, if no application for renewal was pending when the 1939 Act was repealed, there could be no question of preferential right of renewal of a permit.[10] A permit holder whose permit granted under the 1939 Act expired after coming into force of the 1988 Act could not claim any preferential right of renewal and his remedy was to apply for a fresh permit under the new Act[11] except in cases of a permit of a named operator saved and continued under a nationalisation scheme as such schemes amount to law and are preserved by the repealing section 217(2)(a).[12] But in a case where an application for renewal was pending under section 58 of the 1939 Act when it was repealed by the 1988 Act, it would be treated to be an application for enforcement of an accrued right for preferential consideration for renewal and will be determined according to the provisions of the repealed Act.[13]

Punjab Ordinance No. 7 of 1948, made provision for the registration of land claims of the East Punjab refugees. Section 7 of the Ordinance made it an offence for any person to submit with regard to his claim under the Act, any information which was false. On 1st April, 1948, this Ordinance was repealed and Act 12 of 1948 was passed by the East Punjab Legislature re-enacting all the provisions of the repealed Ordinance. A claim was filed when the Ordinance was in force. The claim contained information which was false and constituted an offence under section 7. In a prosecution begun after repeal of the Ordinance, it was held that the repealing Act did not evince an intention to destroy the liability under the Ordinance and the offender could be prosecuted and punished on principles contained in section 6 of the General Clauses Act.[14]

It has been held that the Companies Act, 1956, which repealed the earlier Act of 1913, did not evince an intention to destroy the rights created under section 153C of the repealed Act and a proceeding pending at the time of repeal in respect thereof could be continued as if the new Act had not been passed.[15]

Central Ordinance No. 27 of 1949 was repealed and replaced by Central Act 31 of 1950. The Act in section 58 contained the following provision: 'The repeal by this Act of the Administration of Evacuee Property

---

10. *Ibid*, p. 426.
11. *Ibid*, p. 427.
12. *Ibid*, pp. 428, 429.
13. *Ibid*, p. 430; *Gurcharan Singh Baldev Singh v. Yeshwant Singh*, AIR 1992 SC 180, p. 183 : 1992 (1) SCC 428.
14. *State of Punjab v. Mohar Singh*, AIR 1955 SC 84 : 1955 (1) SCR 893.
15. *Brihan Maharashtra Syndicate v. Janardan*, AIR 1960 SC 794 : 1960 (3) SCR 85.

Ordinance, 1949 (27 of 1949) shall not affect the previous operation thereof, and subject thereto, any thing done or any action taken in the exercise of any power conferred by or under the Ordinance, shall be deemed to have been done or taken in the exercise of the powers conferred by or under this Act, as if this Act were in force on the day on which such thing was done or action was taken'. In construing this section the Supreme Court pointed out that the section provided for the operation of the previous law in the first part and in negative terms, as also for the operation of the new law in the other part and in positive terms; and thus, the section was self-contained and indicative of an intention to exclude the application of section 6, General Clauses Act.[16] The deeming provision in the second part of section 58 is "contrary to what is contemplated under section 6, General Clauses Act",[17] and it was held that the scheme underlying section 58 is that 'every matter to which the new Act applies has to be treated as arising, and to be dealt with, under the new law except in so far as certain consequences have already ensued or acts have been completed prior to the repeal, to which it is the old law that will apply'.[18] The above view of section 58 was approved by the Constitution Bench decision in *Bishambhernath Kohli v. State of Uttar Pradesh,*[19] where it was held that a revision against an order passed by the Deputy Custodian under the repealed ordinance could be entertained and decided by the Custodian General under the new Act. These cases[20] were followed in construing section 30(2) of the Prevention of Corruption Act, 1988 which repealed the earlier Act of 1947. The saving contained in section 30(2) of the 1988 Act reads: 'Notwithstanding such repeal but without prejudice to section 6 of the General Clauses Act, 1897 (10 of 1897) anything done or any action taken or purported to have been done or taken under or in pursuance of the Acts so repealed shall, in so far as it is not inconsistent with the provisions of this Act, be deemed to have been done or taken under or in pursuance of the corresponding provision of this Act.' Construing the saving contained in section 30(2), it was held[21] that a special judge, appointed under section 3 of the 1988 Act to try offences punishable under the said Act, could also take cognizance of an offence committed under the 1947 Act on a report filed before him after repeal of that Act for the legal fiction contained in the last part of section 30(2) expresses a different intention to that in section 6(e) of the General clauses Act which enables institution and continuation

---

16. *Indira Sohanlal v. Custodian of E.P.*, AIR 1956 SC 77 : 1955 (2) SCR 1117.
17. *Ibid.*
18. *Ibid*, p. 85.
19. AIR 1966 SC 573, p. 579 : 1966 (2) SCR 158.
20. Cases in notes 16 and 19, *supra.*
21. *Nar Bahadur Bhandari v. State of Sikkim,* AIR 1998 SC 2203, pp. 2205, 2206 : (1998) 5 SCC 39.

of legal proceedings under the repealed Act as if the repealing Act had not been passed. In another case[22] where also the offence was committed when the 1947 Act was in force but the conviction of the accused by the special judge was entered after repeal of the 1947 Act, it was held that the provisions relating to appeal and revisions in the 1988 Act would apply and in view of section 19(3)(a) of this Act no conviction could be set aside in appeal for want of sanction unless the Court was of the view that a failure of justice has been occasioned thereby.[23]

The Bombay Agricultural Debtors Act, 1939, was repealed and replaced by the Bombay Agricultural Debtors Relief Act, 1947. The repealing section in the new Act provided that the proceedings original and appellate pending under the repealed Act were to be continued and disposed of as if instituted under the new Act. It was held that the new Act applied both, the substantive as well as procedural provisions, to pending proceedings.[24]

Section 85(1) of the Arbitration and Conciliation Act, 1996 repeals three Acts namely the Arbitration (Protocol and Convention) Act, 1937, the Arbitration Act, 1940 and the Foreign Awards (Recognition and Enforcement) Act, 1961. Section 85(2)(a) enacts a saving clause which provides: 'Notwithstanding such repeal, the provisions of the said enactments shall apply in relation to arbitral proceedings which commenced before this Act came into force unless otherwise agreed by the parties but this Act shall apply in relation to arbitral proceedings which commenced on or after this Act came into force.' This Act came into force on January 25, 1996. In *Thyssen Stahlunion GMBH v. Steel Authority of India*,[25] the Supreme Court held that an award made after the new Act came into force in an arbitration proceeding commenced under the Arbitration Act, 1940 before the new Act came into force will be enforceable under the 1940 Act and not under the new Act. This conclusion was reached by widely construing the words 'in relation to arbitral proceedings' in the saving clause to cover

---

22. *Central Bureau of Investigation v. V.K. Sehgal*, JT 1999 (8) SC 170, pp. 176, 177 : (1999) 8 SCC 501.

23. *Ibid.*

24. *Rambhai v. Dayabhai*, AIR 1967 SC 162 : 1966 Supp SCR 146. For a saving clause that preserves rights and liabilities accrued and incurred but requires the legal proceedings to be instituted, continued or enforced under the corresponding provisions of the new Act, **see** *E.V. Mathal v. Sub-Judge, Kottayam*, AIR 1970 SC 337, p. 339 : (1969) 2 SCC 194. And, for a Saving Clause which preserves rights and liabilities accrued and incurred under the repealed Act but subject thereto requires anything done under the repealed Act to be deemed to have been done under the new Act. **See further** *STO, Jabalpur v. Hanuman Prasad*, (1967) MPLJ 138 (SC) : AIR 1967 SC 565 : (1967) 1 SCR 831 and *Commr. of Sales Tax, M.P. v. Amarnath Ajitkumar*, AIR 1972 SC 38 : 1972 (4) SCC 347.

25. JT 1999 (8) SC 66 : AIR 1999 SC 3923 : (1999) 9 SCC 334.

not only proceedings before the arbitrator but also proceedings pending or required to be taken before the court for enforcing the award. It was also held that in this view of the matter section 6 of the General Clauses Act was inapplicable in such cases.[26] But the court later held that the right to have the award (though made after the new Act came into force) enforced in accordance with the provisions of the 1940 Act was an accrued right and a contrary conclusion would produce unjust results as the provisions of the two Acts were materially different.[27] The court also held that the words 'unless otherwise agreed by the parties' in the saving clause would cover an agreement before the new Act came into force, therefore, in a case where the parties had agreed in the arbitration agreement for application of the 1940 Act or any statutory modification or re-enactment thereof, an award made in a pending arbitration proceeding after the new Act came into force would be enforceable in accordance with the provisions of the new Act.[28] But in respect of a foreign award made after the new Act came into force in a pending arbitration in a foreign country, the court held that the award could be enforced in India only under the new Act and not under the Foreign Awards (Recognition and Enforcement) Act, 1961. In this connection the court noticed that the 1961 Act did not contain any provision for regulating the arbitration proceedings and contained provisions only for enforcing the awards which were not materially different from the provisions of the new Act and the saving clause in section 85(2) could not be applied to such a case.[29] It is submitted that the more correct view of the saving clause would have been to hold that a foreign award made in a pending arbitration was enforceable under the 1961 Act and not under the new Act more so when, as the court noticed, the provisions of the two Acts were not very much different and this view would not have led to any unjust results. Such a construction apart from being consistent with the wide meaning given to the words 'in relation to arbitral proceedings' to include even proceedings for enforcement of the award, would have given due meaning to the word 'enactments' in the saving clause which in the context plainly includes all the three Acts repealed by section 85(1) of the new Act.

---

26. *Ibid,* pp. 103, 104 (JT) : pp. 3944, 3945 (AIR).
27. *Ibid,* pp. 107, 109, 110 (JT) pp. 3947, 3948 (AIR).
28. *Ibid,* p. 111 (JT) : 3949, 3950 (AIR). **Followed** in *Delhi Transport Corporation Ltd. v. Rose Advertising,* (2003) 6 SCC 36 : AIR 2003 SC 2523. **Distinguished** in *N.S. Nayak and Sons v. State of Goa,* (2003) 6 SCC 56. **See further** *Milkfood Ltd. v. GMC Ice Cream Ltd.*, (2004) 7 SCC 288, p. 315 : AIR 2004 SC 3145 (section 21 of the 1940 Act will determine whether arbitration proceeding had commenced before coming into force of the 1996 Act)
29. *Ibid,* pp. 113, 114 (JT) : 3951 (AIR). **Affirmed** in *Fuerst Day Lauson Ltd. v. Jindal Exports Ltd.,* AIR 2001 SC 2193 : (2001) 6 SCC 356.

With a view to give some protection to *Thika* tenants against eviction, the West Bengal Legislature enacted the Calcutta Thika Tenancy Act, 1949. Under this Act the eviction of *Thika* tenants was restricted to grounds specified in the Act and provision was made in section 28 for rescinding or varying previous decrees of ejectment which had not been executed. A *Thika* tenant against whom a decree for eviction had been made, applied under section 28, praying that the decree be rescinded or varied in terms of that section. The application, however, remained pending when Calcutta Thika Tenancy Amendment Act, 1953, came to be enacted. One of the amendments introduced by this Act was, that section 28 of the original Act was omitted. Further, the amending Act in section 1(2) enacted that the Act as amended shall apply and be deemed to have always applied to all pending proceedings. It was held that section 1(2) of the Amending Act showed a contrary intention for applicability of the general savings contained in section 8 of the Bengal General Clauses Act (similar to section 6, Central General Clauses Act) and that the right of a tenant to have a decree for ejectment rescinded under section 28 of the Original Act was taken away by applying the Act as amended in 1953 to all pending proceedings.[30]

The Delhi Rent Control Act, 1958, repealed and replaced the Delhi and Ajmer Rent Control Act, 1952. The 1958 Act in section 57(2) enacted as follows: "Notwithstanding such repeal all suits and other proceedings under the said Act pending at the commencement of this Act, before any court or other authority shall be continued and disposed of in accordance with the provision of the said Act, as if the said Act had continued in force and this Act had not been passed: *provided* that in any such suit or proceeding for the fixation of standard rent or for the eviction of a tenant from any premises to which section 54 does not apply, the court or other authority shall have regard to the provisions of this Act." A suit for ejectment was filed when the 1952 Act was in force, on the ground that the tenant without obtaining the consent of the landlord had before the commencement of the 1952 Act, sublet the premises. When this suit was pending in revision before the High Court, the 1958 Act came into force. This Act made radical changes in the previous Act and a sub-letting before the commencement of 1952 Act was treated as lawful sub-letting if the subtenant was in occupation of the premises at the commencement of the 1958 Act. The ground on which eviction was sought ceased to be a good ground under the new Act and a question therefore arose as to how far the pending suit was affected by the new Act. In view of the provisions of section 57(2) of

---

30. *Mahadeolal v. Administrator General of W.B.*, AIR 1960 SC 936 : 1960 (3) SCR 578.

the new Act, it was held that section 6 of the General Clauses Act had no application.[31] The apparent conflict between the substantive part of sub-section (2) section 57 and the proviso to it was resolved by the rule of harmonious construction and it was decided that pending proceedings were to be governed by the old Act; but in cases where the new Act had slightly modified or clarified the previous provisions, these modifications and clarifications were to be applied.[32] In the particular case, therefore, it was held that the old Act continued to govern the proceedings.

The last mentioned case[33] under the Delhi Rent Control Acts, 1952 may be compared with a later decision arising under the same Acts.[34] In a suit for ejectment filed before the commencement of the 1958 Act an application was made by the plaintiff-landlord under section 13(5) of the 1952 Act for an order to be made on the defendant tenant to deposit all the arrears of rent and future monthly rent on the 15th of each month. An order was made as prayed for, but the tenant made default and an application was made by the plaintiff for striking out the defence of the tenant. Under section 13(5) of the 1952 Act the provision was that in default of the tenant 'the court shall order the defence against ejectment to be struck out'. In the 1958 Act, which came into force during the pendency of the suit, the corresponding provision [section 15(7)], provides that the controller may order the defence against eviction to be struck out. On the principles stated in the last-mentioned case,[35] it was held that the change introduced in the new Act conferring a discretion in the matter of striking of defence was a slight modification, and the benefit of the new provision was available to the defendant.[36]

7. SUBORDINATE LEGISLATION UNDER REPEALED STATUTE

As a consequence of the general principle that a statute after its repeal is as completely effaced from the statute book as if it had never been enacted, subordinate legislation made under a statute ceases to have effect after

---

31. *Karam Singh v. Pratap Singh*, AIR 1964 SC 1305, p. 1309 : 1964 (4) SCR 647.
32. *Ibid*, p. 1310; **followed** in *Manphul Singh Sharma v. Ahmedi Begum*, JT 1994 (5) SC 49, pp. 53, 54 : 1994 (5) SCC 465 : (1994) 5 SCC 465.
33. *Karam Singh v. Pratap Singh, supra.*
34. *V.K. Verma v. Radhey Shyam*, AIR 1964 SC 1317 : 66 Punj LR 690. **See further** *Brij Kishore v. Vishwa Mitter*, AIR 1965 SC 1574 : 1965 (2) SCR 705. (Though the court trying a pending suit has in some cases to take notice of the new Act, the order passed by it remains an order under the old Act and appealable under it, *Banta Singh v. Shanti Devi*, AIR 1967 SC 1360) : (1967) 3 SCR 597).
35. *Karam Singh v. Pratap Singh*, AIR 1964 SC 1305 : 1964 (4) SCR 647.
36. **See** footnote 34, *supra.*

repeal of the statute.[37] This result can be avoided by insertion of saving clauses providing to the contrary.[38] When a statute is repealed and re-enacted, section 24 of the General Clauses Act, 1897, provides for continuance of any appointment, notification, Order, scheme, rule, form or bye-law made or issued under the repealed statute in so far as it is not inconsistent with the provisions re-enacted. Such appointments, notifications, Orders *etc*. are deemed to be made under the corresponding provisions of the new statute and continue to be in force unless superseded by appointments, notifications, Orders, *etc*., made or issued under the new statute.[39] Even if the subordinate legislation made under the repealed statute was effective 'as if enacted in the Act', it will continue to be in force under the provision re-enacted by virtue of section 24 of the General Clauses Act, 1897.[40] But, as already stated, the continuance of subordinate legislation

---

37. *Watson v. Winch*, (1916-17) All ER Rep 972 (KBD) : (1916) 1 KB 688; *Harish Chandra v. State of M.P.*, AIR 1965 SC 932, p. 938 : (1965) 1 SCR 323. A saving clause which continues 'any notification' under a repealed Act has been construed to continue rules made under a notification; *State of Nagaland v. Ratan Singh*, AIR 1967 SC 212, p. 221 (para 22) : (1966) 3 SCR 830. Saving of 'anything duly done' under the repealed Act will also preserve the continuance of rules and bye-laws; *Dharangdhara Chemical Works v. Dharangdhara Municipality*, (1985) 4 SCC 92, p. 104 : AIR 1985 SC 1729. But in *Air India v. Union of India*, 1995 (4) Scale 523, p. 525 : (1995) 4 SCC 734, it has been observed by a two- Judge Bench: "If subordinate legislation is to survive the repeal of its parent statute the repealing statute must say so in so many words and by mentioning the title of the subordinate legislation. We do not think that there is room for implying anything in this behalf." It is submitted that these observations are too widely stated as the earlier authorities of the Supreme Court (*State of Nagaland* case is a Constitution Bench Decision) were not referred. Saving of 'anything duly done' and 'any right or privilege acquired' may continue a notification granting exemption of tax permanently under the repealed Act even if there be no corresponding provision in the repealing Act for grant of such an exemption: **see** text and notes 1 to 6, pp. 773-774.

38. *Ibid*.

39. *State of Bombay v. Pandurang*, AIR 1953 SC 244, p. 246 : 1953 SCR 773 (section 25 of Bombay Act, 1904 which corresponds to section 24 of Central Act).

N.B.—(i) Section 24, General Clauses Act, 1897 is not declaratory of any common law rule and cases not covered by it are governed by the rule stated in text and note 13, *supra*.

(ii) Rules *etc*. deemed to be made under a Statute either by virtue of section 24, General Clauses Act or by a specific saving to that effect, stand on the same footing as rules made under the statute and both can be amended, repealed or replaced by new rules made under it. [**See** *Harish Chandra v. State of M.P.*, AIR 1965 SC 932, p. 937 : (1965) 1 SCC 323; *Neel v. State of W.B.*, AIR 1972 SC 2066, pp. 2067, 2068 : (1972) 2 SCC 668. (Notification issued under section 15 of the Arms Act, 1878 continues under section 4 of the Arms Act, 1959)]. **See further** *Dharangdhara Chemical Works v. Dharangdhara Municipality*, *supra*.

40. *Chief Inspector of Mines v. Karam Chand Thapar*, AIR 1961 SC 838, pp. 843-45 : (1961) 2 SCR 962; *Mohanlal v. State of W.B.*, AIR 1961 SC 1543, p. 1545 (para 3) : (1962) 2 SCR 36.

under section 24 of the General Clauses Act is subject to the qualification that it is not inconsistent with the provision re-enacted.[41] Further, section 24 is, on its own terms, limited to a repeal of a Central Act or Regulation,[42] and has no application when a State Act is expressly or impliedly repealed by a Central Act, but in such cases unless the Central Act is retrospective benefit of section 6 of the General Clauses Act is available in respect of things already done.[43]

8. *QUASI* REPEAL BY DESUETUDE

The English law does not recognise any doctrine that an Act of Parliament can come to an end by desuetude or non-user. But this doctrine is recognised by Scottish law. As enunciated by LORD MACKAY, "desuetude requires for its operation a very considerable period, not merely of neglect but of contrary usage of such a character as practically to infer such completely established habit of the community as to set up a counter law to establish a *quasi*-repeal".[44] The doctrine of desuetude was rejected by a

---

41. *Bhilai Steel Project v. Steel Workers' Union*, AIR 1964 SC 1333, p. 1336 (paras 10, 11) : (1964) 5 SCR 354, (the case related to section 25, M.P. General Clauses Act, 1958 which corresponds to section 24 of Central Act).

N.B.—(i) A special saving clause continuing a 'scheme prepared' under the repealed Act will normally mean a completed scheme in respect of which all the necessary steps under the repealed Act had been taken before its repeal; *Indore Development Authority v. Madanlal*, AIR 1990 SC 1143, p. 1147 : 1990 (2) SCC 334.

(ii) But a special Saving Clause inserted in the re-enacting Statute may continue a Scheme framed under the repealed Act even if it is inconsistent with the provisions re-enacted; *Rajendraswami v. Commr. H.R. & C.E.*, AIR 1965 SC 502, p. 505 : (1964) 8 SCR 252. A judicial order passed under a repealed statute may be continued as if made under the provisions of the repealing statute although inconsistent with it; *Jagir Singh v. Ranbir Singh*, AIR 1979 SC 381, p. 386 : (1979) 1 SCC 560.

(iii) Parliament may, by a saving clause inserted in the re-enacted statute, continue rules framed under the repealed statute which were factually in force on the date of repeal even if their validity was seriously open to doubt; **See** *Re Fletcher, Ex parte, Fletcher v. Official Receiver*, (1955) 2 All ER 592 (CA); *Bihar Mines Ltd. v. Union of India*, AIR 1967 SC 887, p. 892 (para 22, **minority judgment**) : (1967) 1 SCR 707; *Gujarat Pottery Works v. B.P. Sood*, AIR 1967 SC 964 : (1967) 1 SCR 695 (section 29 of the Mines & Mineral Act, 1957 continues the rules made under the 1948 Act as if the new Act had been in force on the date when the rules were made). When an action taken under an Ordinance is deemed to be taken under the corresponding provisions of the repealing Act, any question as to validity of the Ordinance becomes academic and what is to be seen is the validity of Act : *R.K. Garg v. Union of India*, AIR 1981 SC 2138 : (1981) 4 SCC 675.

42. *Harish Chandra v. State of M.P.*, AIR 1965 SC 932, p. 938 : 1965 (1) SCR 323.

43. *Deepchand v. State of U.P.*, AIR 1959 SC 648, pp. 668, 669 (para 35); *State of Orissa v. M.A. Tulloch & Co.*, AIR 1964 SC 1284 : 1964 (4) SCR 461.

44. *Brown v. Magistrate of Edinburgh*, 1931 SLT 456, p. 458. CRAIES Statute Law, 7th Edition, p. 7. **See further** SUTHERLAND, Statutory Construction (5th Edition) Vol. 2, p. 647.

three-Judge Bench of the Supreme Court in *State of Maharashtra v. Narayan.*[45] But another three-Judge Bench of the Supreme Court in *Municipal Corporation for City of Pune v. Bharat Forge Col. Ltd.,*[46] has implanted this doctrine of Scottish law in Indian law without adverting to the earlier decision. HANSARIA J. speaking for the three judge bench observed: "We would think it would advance the cause of justice to accept the application of doctrine of desuetude in our country also. Our soil is ready to accept this principle: indeed, there is need for its implantation, because persons residing in free India, who have assured fundamental rights including what has been stated in Article 21, must be protected from their being say, prosecuted and punished for violation of a law, which has become 'dead letter'."[47] In this case a notification of 1881 issued under the Cantonments Act, 1880 imposing octroi in Pune Cantonment was superseded and impliedly repealed by two notifications issued in 1918 which were not in practice implemented at any time and octroi continued to be recovered under the notification of 1881 in accordance with the octroi rules enforced from time to time including the octroi rules of 1963. It was held that the 1918 notification stood *quasi* repealed by the time 1963 rules were framed and the continued recovery of octroi under the notification of 1881 read with the rules of 1963 was legal. The doctrine of *quasi* repeal will need further clarification. In the case before the Supreme Court, if the 1881 notification was impliedly repealed by notifications of 1918, how could the 1881 notification come back to life after the 1918 notifications were *quasi* repealed by desuetude. Non-user and contrary practice has to continue for a long time to bring about *quasi* repeal by desuetude. Therefore, 1918 notifications could not be held to be still born or dead from their inception by desuetude and must have had the effect of effectively repealing the 1881 notification. The result reached by the Supreme Court implies that desuetude of a law A not only repeals it but also revives the law B which was repealed by A. This will mean that section 7 of the General Clauses Act, 1897 does not apply to *quasi* repeal by desuetude.

The case of *Bharat Forge Co. Ltd.*[48] and the doctrine of desuetude were referred by a two-Judge Bench in *Cantonment Board, Mhow v. M.P. Road State Transport Corporation*[49] and it was held that the necessary conditions for the doctrine's application were 'to establish that the statute in

---

45. AIR 1983 SC 46, p. 52 : (1982) 3 SCC 519, pp. 529, 530. Same view was taken by a two-Judge Bench in *State of U.P. v. Hindustan Aluminium Corporation*, AIR 1979 SC 1459, p. 1473 : (1979) 3 SCC 229.

46. 1995(2) Scale 245: AIR 1996 SC 2856 : (1995) 3 SCC 434.

47. *Ibid*, p. 253 (Scale) : p. 2862 (AIR).

48. **See** note 46.

49. AIR 1997 SC 2013 : (1997) 9 SCC 450.

question has been in disuse for long and the contrary practice of some duration has evolved.'[50] The doctrine was not applied in this case as these conditions were not satisfied. In this case also the earlier three-Judge Bench case of *Narayan*[51] was not noticed. It is submitted that the doctrine of repeal by desuetude is controversial and in view of conflicting decisions of three-Judge Benches requires reconsideration by a larger bench. There are very useful references and discussion on desuetude in a judgment of the Delhi High Court.[52]

50. *Ibid*, p. 2020.
51. **See** note 45.
52. *Haryana State Lotteries v. Govt. of NCT Delhi*, CWP 1254 of 97 dated 17-7-1998 (LAHOTI J.).

CHAPTER 8

STATUTES AFFECTING THE CROWN OR THE STATE

SYNOPSIS

1. THE RULE OF COMMON LAW

(a) General principles

The rule of English law is that no statute binds the Crown unless the Crown[1] is named therein either expressly or by necessary implication. The reason of the rule has been stated to be, that a statute is presumed to be enacted for the subjects and not for the King. In the words of PLOWDEN: "It is to be intended that when the King gives his assent he does not mean to prejudice himself or to bar himself of his liberty and his privileges, but he assents that it be a law among his subjects".[2] A modern statement of the rule is found in a passage from the judgment of LORD DU PARCQ which is as follows: "The maxim of the law in early times was that no statute bound

1. For meaning of the expression 'Crown' and 'Her Majesty' and their relationship with Government Departments, Ministers and Civil Servants, **see** *Town Investments Ltd. v. Department of the Environment*, (1977) 1 All ER 813 (HL), pp. 817, 818 : (1978) AC 359 : (1977) 2 WLR 450 (LORD DIPLOCK) and 831 to 834 (LORD SIMON). For meaning of 'Crown' in relation to the Commonwealth of Australia **see** *Sue v. Hill*, (1999) 73 ALJR 1016, p. 1036 [The circumstances that the same monarch exercises regal functions under the constitutional arrangements in the United Kingdom and Australia does not affect the fact that the United Kingdom is a foreign power within the meaning of section 44 of the Constitution of Australia which deals with nationality (GLEESAN C.J., GUMMOW AND HAYNE, JJ.)].
2. *Willion v. Berkley*, (1562) 1, Plowed 223, p. 240; and **see** *A.G. v. Donaldson*, (1874) 10 M & W 117, p. 123 (ALDEASON, B.); *A.G. v. Hancock*, (1940) 1 All ER 32, p. 34; *Madras Electric Supply Corporation v. Borland*, (1955) 1 All ER 753, p. 765 : 1955 AC 667 (HL).

the Crown unless the Crown was expressly named therein, '*Roy n'est lie par ascun statute, si il ne soit expressment nosme*'. But the rule so laid down is subject to at least one exception. The Crown may be bound, as has often been said 'by necessary implication'. If, that is to say, it is manifest from the very terms of the statute, that it was the intention of the legislature that the Crown should be bound, then the result is the same as if the Crown had been expressly named. It must, then be inferred that the Crown, by assenting to the law, agreed to be bound by its provisions."[3]

Whatever may have been the historical origin of the rule, whether based on immunity by royal prerogative or otherwise, there is a consensus of judicial opinion that the rule as at present known is merely a rule of construction.[4] As observed by LORD MACDERMOTT: "The appropriate rule—is that, in an Act of Parliament general words shall not bind the Crown to its prejudice unless by express provision or necessary implication. That, however, is, and has long been regarded as a rule of construction." [5]

After a review of the earlier cases LORD KEITH speaking for the House of Lords stated the rule of construction as follows: "The Crown is not bound by any statutory provision unless there can somehow be gathered from the terms of the relevant Act an intention to that effect. The Crown can be bound only by express words or necessary implication."[6]

The rule has been applied in the colonies and the Commonwealth[7] in the sense that "the executive Government of the State is not bound by statute unless that intention is apparent".[8] The rule has also been applied in America as a rule of construction.[9]

---

3. *Bombay Province v. Bombay Municipal Corporation*, AIR 1947, PC 34, p. 35 : 1947 AC 58, p. 61 (PC); **referred** to in *Premchand Nathu & Co. v. Land Officer*, (1963) 1 All ER 216, p. 221 (PC); *Lord Advocate v. Dumbarton District Council*, (1990) 1 All ER 1, pp. 9, 10 : (1990) 2 AC 580 : (1990) 3 WLR 1346 (HL).
4. *Madras Electric Supply Corporation v. Borland, supra*, pp. 759, 762.
5. *Ibid*, p. 753.
6. *Lord Advocate v. Dumbarton District Council*, (1990) 1 All ER 1, p. 18 : (1990) 2 AC 580 : (1990) 3 WLR 1346 (HL).
7. *Roberts v. Ahern*, (1904) 1 CLR 406; *Premchand Nathu & Co. v. Land Officer, supra.*
8. *Roberts v. Ahern, supra*, p. 418. **But** in Australia at least, having regard to the manifold activities of the executive government, the stringent test of necessary implication is no longer applicable. Further section 22(1)(a) of the Acts Interpretation Act, 1901 (Cth) provides that unless the contrary intention appears expressions used to denote persons generally, include a body politic: *Bass v. Permanent Trustee Company Ltd.*, (1999) 73 ALJR 522, pp. 527, 528.
9. *United States of America v. United Mine Workers of America*, (1946) 330 US 358 : 91 Law Ed 884; *United States of America v. Reginald P. Wittek*, (1948) 337 US 346 : 93 Law Ed 1406.

The reason that laws are *prima facie* made for the subjects and not for the King, which PLOWDEN gave as a basis of the rule of English law,[10] is regarded now-a-days even in England as an overstatement.[11] The rule exempting the State from the operation of general provisions of a statute has been reasoned in America on the basis of a policy to preserve for the public efficient, unimpaired functioning of Government.[12]

Attempts have been made in early authorities to lay down certain categories as to when the Crown is bound although not specifically named. LORD COKE indicated three kinds of statutes which bound the King without specially naming him: (1) Statutes for maintenance of religion, learning and the poor, (2) Statutes for suppression of wrong, and (3) Statutes that tend to perform the will of a founder or donor.[13] Similarly, in BACON'S *Abridgment* it is stated that "where an Act of Parliament is made for the public good, the advancement of religion and justice, and to prevent injury and wrong, the King shall be bound by such Act, though not particularly named therein".[14] These generalisations have not met the approval of modern writers,[15] and it has been said that "the question whether the Crown is bound by a statute, in which express provision is not made, is treated today as one to be answered by reference purely to the provisions of the statute in question or the Code, of which it forms part".[16] Further, the statement in BACON'S *Abridgment* laying down an exception regarding statutes made for the public good has been authoritatively held to be erroneous.[17] There are a series of decisions on Acts which are clearly for the public benefit, in which the courts have held that the Crown was not affected, not being specially named or brought in by necessary implication.[18] The reason for not drawing a distinction between statutes enacted for the public good and other statutes is that statutes of a modern State whether they be directed for imposition of taxes or for

---

10. **See** text and note 2, *supra*.

11. *A.G. v. Hancock*, (1940) 1 All ER 32.

12. SUTHERLAND, Statutory Construction, 3rd Edition, Vol. 3, pp. 184, 185.

13. *Magdalene College, Cambridge* Case, (1616) 11 Co. Rep 66b, pp. 70b, 72a, 73b.

14. BACON'S Abridgment, 7th Edition, p. 462; **referred** by JESSEL, M.R. in *Re, Ex parte, Postmaster-General,* (1878) 10 Ch D 595, p. 601 and by LORD PARMOOR in *A.G. v. De Keyser's Royal Hotel*, (1920) AC 508 : (1920) All ER Rep 80, p. 110 (HL).

15. CRAIES on Statute Law, 6th Edition, p. 443; MAXWELL, Interpretation of Statutes, 11th Edition, p. 135; HALSBURY'S Laws of England, 3rd Edition, Vol. 36, p. 431.

16. HALSBURY'S Laws of England, 3rd Edition, Vol. 36, p. 431.

17. *A.G. v. Hancock,* (1940) 1 All ER 32, p. 36 (and see cases referred to therein); *Bombay Province v. Bombay Municipal Corporation*, AIR 1947, PC 34, p. 36; *London Territorial Association v. Nichols,* (1948) 2 All ER 432, p. 433 (SCOOT, L.J.); *Lord Advocate v. Dumbarton District Council,* (1990) 1 All ER 1, p. 13 : (1990) 2 AC 580 : (1990) 3 WLR 1346 (HL).

18. *Ibid.*

safeguarding the health of the community or for any other purpose are all, at least in theory, enacted for public good.[19] By way of another qualification of the rule it has sometimes been said that the Crown can take advantage of a statute unless prohibited to do so by express words or necessary implication, even though it may not be bound by it. This qualification has, however, very slender authority.[20]

The method of application of the rule is that, if the Crown is not expressly named, a general word capable of including the Crown is, as a matter of construction, read as excluding it, unless the statute by necessary implication manifests an intention to the contrary.[21] The word 'person' which is capable of including the Crown will thus be read as excluding it,[22] unless the statute by necessary implication manifests contrary intention.[23] To avoid impairment of the rights of the Crown the application of the rule of construction enables the court to read an exemption in its favour.[24] Rent Restriction Acts which 'apply to a house let' will be read as not applying where the Crown is the landlord or the tenant,[25] and a tax imposed on every 'occupier' of property will be read as excluding any liability when property is in occupation of Crown or for Crown purposes.[26]

The only safe rule, which may be valid in all cases, to decide whether a given statute binds the Crown by 'necessary implication', is to read the statute as a whole and to see whether it is manifest from the very terms of the statute, that it was the intention of the Legislature that the Crown should be bound.[27]

The presumption, that the Crown is not bound by a statute, is not rebutted by merely showing that the legislation in question cannot operate with

---

19. *Bombay Province v. Bombay Municipal Corporation, supra*, p. 36; *London Territorial Association v. Nichols, supra*, p. 433.

20. MAXWELL, Interpretation of Statutes, 12th Edition, p. 168. **But see** BENNION, Statutory Interpretation, 5th edition, p. 206.

21. *Madras Electric Supply Corporation v. Borland*, (1955) 1 All ER 753, p. 759 : (1955) 2 WLR 632 (HL).

22. *A.G. v. Hancock*, (1940) 1 All ER 32, p. 37; *Madras Electric Corporation v. Borland, supra.*

23. *Madras Electric Corporation v. Borland, supra.*

24. *Minister of Agriculture v. Jenkins*, (1963) 2 All ER 147, p. 149 (CA).. (The Crown does not need to get planning permission in respect of Crown lands under the Town and Country Planning Act, 1947, not by virtue of any provision in the Act, but it is exempt by reason of the general principle).

25. *Clarke v. Downes*, (1931) 145 LT 20 : (1931) All ER Rep 157, p. 159.

26. *Mersey Docks & Harbour Board v. Cameron*, (1865) 11 HLC 443; 11 ER 1045 : (1861-73) All ER Rep 78, pp. 84, 85, 95, 96 (HL).

27. **See** text and note 3, *supra*.

reasonable efficiency unless the Crown is held to be bound,[28] or, by showing that there are express provisions in the legislation saving certain rights of the Crown.[29]

In *Bombay Province v. Bombay Municipal Corporation,*[30] the question was whether the provisions of the Bombay Municipal Corporation Act, 1888, which authorised the Commissioner to carry water-mains and municipal drains 'through or under any land whatsoever within the city', were applicable in respect of Government land within the city. The Bombay High Court in arriving at the conclusion that even Government land within the city was subject to the statutory power of the Corporation to carry water-mains, observed that if it can be shown that legislation "cannot operate with reasonable efficiency" unless the Crown is bound, that would be sufficient reason for saying that the Crown is bound by necessary implication. While overruling the decision of the Bombay High Court, the Privy Council observed that "to interpret the principle in the sense put upon it by the High Court would be to whittle it down and they cannot find any authority which gives any support to such an interpretation".[31] Another argument addressed was, that there were certain express references to the Crown in other parts of the Act, and certain exemptions from the municipal laws in the Government Building Act, 1899, which showed that the Crown was bound, otherwise the exemptions would be unnecessary. In answer to this, the Privy Council said: "This is not an unfamiliar argument, but, as has been said many times, such provisions may often be inserted in one part of an Act, or in a later general Act, *ex abundanti cautela*".[32]

The presumption that the Crown or the State is not bound would be rebutted and an intention to bind would be clearly made out if it could be shown from the terms of the statute taken as a whole that the purpose of the statute would be 'wholly frustrated',[33] or 'the legislation would be unmeaning'[34] unless the Crown or the State were held to be bound.

---

28. *Bombay Province v. Bombay Municipal Corporation*, AIR 1947, PC 34, pp. 35, 36.

29. *Hornsey Urban District Council v. Hennel*, (1902) 2 KB 73, p. 80; *Bombay Province v. Bombay Municipal Corporation, supra*, p. 37; *Lord Advocate v. Dumbarton District Council*, (1990) 1 All ER 1, p. 15 : (1990) 2 AC 580 : (1990) 3 WLR 1346 (HL).

30. AIR 1947, PC 34.

N.B.—This case is now not an authority in India. (**See** title 2 'The Rule in India', *infra*, but it still represents correctly the common law rule).

31. *Bombay Province v. Bombay Municipal Corporation*, AIR 1947, PC 34, pp. 35, 36.

32. *Ibid*, p. 37.

33. *Ibid*, p. 36.

34. *Gorton Local Board v. Prison Commissioners*, (1887) Reported in (1904) 2 KB 165n, p. 167n (DAY, J.).

The Privy Council in considering how far the purpose of a statute is a relevant factor in determining whether the Crown is bound by necessary implication, laid down as follows: "The apparent purpose of the statute is one element, and may be an important element, to be considered when an intention to bind the Crown is alleged. If it can be affirmed that, at the time when the statute was passed and received the royal sanction, it was apparent from its terms that its beneficent purpose must be wholly frustrated unless the Crown were bound, then it must be inferred that the Crown has agreed to be bound. When the court is asked to draw this inference, it must always be remembered that, if it be the intention of the Legislature that the Crown shall be bound, nothing is easier than to say so in plain words."[35]

The decision of the Privy Council in the case of *Bombay Province v. Bombay Municipal Corporation*,[36] was fully accepted by the House of Lords in *Lord Advocate v. Dumbarton District Council*.[37] In this case the contractors employed by the Ministry of Defence, with the approval of the relevant Crown agency, while carrying on certain work on Crown land adjoining a highway, encroached upon a part of the highway. The local highway authority and the local planning authority claimed by notices that the encroachment on the Highway and the work undertaken were contrary to the provisions of the Roads (Scotland) Act, 1947 and the Town and Country Planning (Scotland) Act, 1972. The House of Lords held that the Crown was not bound by these Acts, on the basis of the rule that the Crown is not bound by an Act unless named therein expressly or by necessary implication.

In spite of the rule, the immunity of the Crown has been affected by other factors. Section 1 of the Crown Proceedings Act, 1947 enables the Crown to be sued directly in those situations where prior to the Act a claim might have been enforced by petition of right. Section 2 in general permits actions to be brought against the Crown in respect of torts committed by its servants or agents for any breach of its duties which gave rise to a tortious liability (including a breach of statutory duty where the breach created a cause of action).[38] The prerogative writs could not be issued against the Crown and

---

35. *Bombay Province v. Bombay Municipal Corporation*, AIR 1947, PC 34, p. 36.

N.B.—This case is now not an authority in India. (See title 2 'The Rule in India', infra, but it still represents correctly the common law rule).

36. *Ibid.*

37. (1990) 1 All ER 1, pp. 9, 10, 15 : (1990) 2 AC 580 : (1990) 3 WLR 1346 (HL).

38. S. 40(2)(f) of the Crown Proceedings Act, 1947 specifically provides that the presumption of Crown immunity is not to be affected. The two primary objects of the Act were (1) to enable a plaintiff in England to proceed against the Crown as of right instead of by petition of right and (2) to subject the Crown in both England and Scotland to actions founded in tort and delict in the same way as other defendants; *British Medical Association v. Greater Glasgow Health Board*, (1989) 1 All ER 984, p. 990 : (1989) AC 1211 : (1989) 2 WLR 660 (HL).

originally this difficulty could not be avoided by bringing the proceedings against a minister of the Crown. But, where a duty was imposed by statute for the benefit of the public upon a particular minister, so that he was under an obligation to perform that duty in official capacity, then orders of *mandamus* and prohibition were granted against the minister. After the introduction of the procedure of judicial review in 1977 by Order 53 Rules of the Supreme Court (RSC) and thereafter by the Supreme Court Act, 1981, declaration and injunction including an interim injunction can also be granted against a minister in his official capacity and he can be found to be in contempt in failing to comply with the injunction.[39] Further, the concept of State under the community law which binds the Crown has been expanding. Directives under the community law on which a citizen can rely against the State can also be relied upon in a claim for damages against a body, whatever its legal form, which has been made responsible, pursuant to a measure adopted by the State, for providing a public service under the control of the State and which has for that purpose special powers beyond those which result from the normal rules applicable in relations between individuals.[40] However, there are certain areas which are not open to judicial review and where the Crown is not answerable in courts. For example, the treaty making power in U.K. rests not in the courts, but in the Crown, that is, Her Majesty acting on the advice of ministers. When Her ministers negotiate and sign a treaty, they act on behalf of the country as a whole. Their action in so doing cannot be challenged or questioned in the courts.[41]

Although the rule still holds the field in England, it has not escaped criticism. GLANVILLE L. WILLIAMS in his book on 'Crown Proceedings'[42], criticised the rule as follows: "The rule originated in the Middle Ages when it had perhaps some justification. Its survival, however, is due to little but *vis inertiae*. The chief objection to the rule is its difficulty of application.... With the great extension in the activities of the State and the number of servants employed by it, and with the modern idea, expressed in the Crown Proceedings Act, 1947, that the State should be accountable in wide measure to the law, the presumption should be that a statute binds the Crown rather than it does not." Though upholding the rule, the House of Lords remarked in *Dumbarton District's* case: "It is most desirable that Acts of Parliament should always state explicitly

---

39. *M. v. Home Office*, (1993) 3 All ER 537, pp. 558, 559, 560, 564, 567 : (1994) 1 AC 377 : (1993) 3 WLR 433 (HL).

40. *Foster v. British Gas Plc.*, (1991) 2 All ER 705, p. 705 : (1991) 2 AC 305 (HL).

41. *Blackburn v. A.*, (1971) 2 All ER 1380, p. 1382 (HL); *Maclaine Watson & Co. Ltd. v. Dept. of Trade and Industry*, (1989) 3 All ER 523, p. 524 (HL).

42. GLANVILLE L. WILLIAMS, Crown Proceedings, (1948) pp. 53 and 54.

whether or not the Crown is intended to be bound by any, and if so which, of their provisions."[43]

(b) Extent of the rule

According to English law the protection of the rule of presumption that the Crown is not bound by statutes extends to three classes of persons: (i) the Sovereign personally, (ii) his servants or agents acting as such, and (iii) persons who, though not strictly servants or agents, are considered to be in *consimili casu*. Class (ii) covers not only officers of the State with ministerial status but all subordinate officials as also servants holding statutory offices. In determining if a person holding a statutory office is a servant of the Crown, the degree of control exercised by the Crown, and the amount of discretion left with the holder of the office are relevant and important factors to be taken into account. Persons in *consimili casu* with servants of the Crown are persons who though independent of the Crown perform, exclusively or to a limited degree, the regal governmental functions such as, the administration of justice, the maintenance of order, the repression of crime, the carrying on of war, the making of treaties of peace and other consequential functions. In some cases the distinction between class (ii) and class (iii) has not been maintained and the performance of the above-mentioned functions has also been taken into account in deciding whether a particular person falls under class (ii). The courts are not inclined to include within the exempted categories an aggregation of commercial undertakings brought under some degree of public statutory control. When a person belonging to class (iii) performs some of the regal functions as also other functions not consequential to that category the benefit of immunity applies to the performance of regal functions only.

Some of the important cases from which the principles noticed above are deducible are considered below:

In *Mersey Docks & Harbour Board v. Cameron*,[44] a non-profit earning statutory corporation, which was not subject to control by the Crown or a Minister and whose revenues were not Crown revenues, claimed immunity from local rates and the question before the House of Lords was whether such a corporation could claim Crown privileges on the ground that it was performing a public duty. The decision negatived the privilege so claimed, but established certain principles of great importance. BLACKBURN, J. in delivering the opinion of the five of the consulted Judges said: "Long

---

43. *Lord Advocate v. Dumbarton District Council*, (1990) 1 All ER 1, p. 18 : (1990) 2 AC 580 : (1990) 3 WLR 1346 (HL).
44. (1861-73) All ER Rep 78 (HL).

series of cases have established that where property is occupied for the purposes of the Government of the country, including under that head the police and the administration of justice, no one is rateable in respect of such occupation. And this applies not only to property occupied for such purposes by the servants of the great departments of State, such as the Post Office; the Horse Guards; or the Admiralty…in all of which cases the occupants might strictly be called the servants of the Crown; but also to property occupied by local Police; to county buildings…, or occupied as a county court; or for a jail. In these latter cases it is difficult to maintain that the occupants are, strictly speaking, servants of the sovereign, so as to make the occupation that of Her Majesty; but the purposes are all public purposes of that kind which, by the Constitution of this country, fall within the province of Government and are committed to the sovereign; so that the occupiers, though not strictly servants of the sovereign, might be considered in *consimili casu*."[45] In the same case, LORD CRANWORTH, after referring to the various instances where the rule of Crown immunity had been applied to exempt buildings occupied for purposes of the Government from rates and other impositions said: "These decisions, however, have all gone on the ground more or less sound, that these might all be treated as buildings occupied by the servants of the Crown, and for the Crown, extending the shield of the Crown to what might more fitly be described as the public Government of the country".[46]

In *Greig v. Edinburgh University*,[47] an exemption from local rates was claimed by a university and was rejected. This case closely resembled *Mersey Dock's* case [*supra*] and LORD WESTBURY in this case said: "The true ground of exemption was ascertained and expressed by this House is the *Mersey Dock's* case [*supra*]; and it was found to rest altogether upon this fact that the poor laws did not include the Crown; the Crown not being named in the statute. The result, therefore, was that Crown property, and property occupied by servants of the Crown and (according to the theory of the Constitution) property occupied for the purposes of the administration of the Government of the country, became exempt from liability to poor-rates."[48]

---

45. (1861-73) All ER Rep 78 (HL); **referred** to in *Coomber v. Berkshire Justices*, (1883-84) 9 AC 61, p. 72 (HL) (LORD WATSON); *Bank voor Handel en Scheepvaart NV v. Administrator of Hungarian Property*, (1954) 1 All ER 969, p. 976 : (1953) 1 QB 248 (HL) (LORD MORTON); p. 979 (LORD REID).

46. *Ibid.*

47. (1868) LR 1 Sc & Div 348.

48. *Ibid*, p. 354; **referred** to in *Bank voor Handel en Scheepvaart NV v. Administrator of Hungarian Property*, (1954) 1 All ER 969, p. 980 : (1953) 1 QB 248 (HL) (LORD REID).

In *Coomber v. Berkshire Justices*,[49] the House of Lords decided that the premises occupied by courts of assize or as county police stations attracted Crown immunity from payment of income-tax. LORD BLACKBURN said that the Act showed no intention to impose tax on property belonging to the Crown and did not take away 'the exemption, by virtue of the prerogative, of property actually occupied or enjoyed by the Crown'. He then said that the administration of justice, the preservation of order and the prevention of crime are functions 'that by the Constitution of this country...do, of common right, belong to the Crown', and after discussing earlier cases he added: "I do not say that the assize courts, maintained by the county for the administration of the Queen's justice in the Queen's Court, are quite so clearly occupied by the servants of the Crown as those courts which are maintained by the Woods and Forests out of the general revenue of the country. Nor do I say that the police station, maintained by the county for the maintenance of the police, is quite so clearly occupied by the servants of the Crown as a barrack maintained for soldiers, and paid for out of the general revenue of the country. But, I think, there is a great reason for saying that both are maintained for the purposes of the administration, or those purposes of the Government which are according to the theory of the Constitution, administered by the sovereign."[50] In the same case LORD WATSON after referring to certain parts of the speech of the LORD WESTBURY in *Mersey Dock's* case[51] said: "The precise language of the definition satisfies me that the noble and learned Lord meant to affirm, and did affirm, that the exemption extended not only to the immediate and actual servants of the Crown, but to all other persons not being servants of the Crown, whose occupation was ascribable to a bare trust for purposes required and created by the Government of the country. And seeing that, in my opinion, the administration of justice, the maintenance of order, and the repression of crime are among the primary and inalienable functions of a constitutional Government, I have no hesitation in holding that assize courts and police stations have been erected for proper Government purposes and uses, although the duty of providing and maintaining them has been cast upon county or other local authorities."[52]

49. (1883-84) 9 AC 61 : 3 LJQB 239 (HL).

50. (1883-84) 9 AC 61, pp. 66 to 69 : 3 LJ QB 239 (HL); as extracted by LORD REID in *Bank voor Handel en Scheepvaart NV v. Administrator of Hungarian Property*, (1954) 1 All ER 969, p. 980 : (1953) 1 QB 248 (HL).

51. *Mersey Docks & Harbour Board v. Cameron*, (1865) 11 HLC 443.

52. *Coomber v. Berkshire Justices*, (1883-84) 9 AC 61, p. 74 : 3 LJ QB 239 (HL), as **quoted** by LORD REID in *Bank voor Handel en Scheepvaart NV v. Administrator of Hungarian Property, supra*, p. 981.

In *Bank voor Handel en Scheepvaart N.V. v. Administrator of Hungarian Property*,[53] the earlier cases were reviewed, and it was held by the House of Lords that income from investments of enemy property vested in the Custodian of Enemy Property under the Trading with the Enemy Act, 1939, was exempt from income-tax as the Custodian, though holding a statutory office, was a servant of the Crown and as the arrangements for the disposal of the income were to be made and could be made without the authority of Parliament by the Crown which was not bound to ensure that each item or property was returned to its former owner thereby giving the Crown sufficient interest to entitle the Custodian to claim immunity from the tax. The court pointed out three classes of persons who come within the principle of Crown immunity: (i) the Sovereign personally; (ii) his servants and agents; (iii) persons who are not Crown servants or agents, but who, for certain limited purposes, are considered to be *in consimili casu*. LORD TUCKER deduced five propositions from the earlier cases, applicable to class (ii) and class (iii): "(1) The immunity extends at least to include all those officers of State and their subordinates who now perform pursuant to statutory authority, functions of public Government which were formerly the peculiar prerogative of the Crown. (2) Such functions include the making and carrying on of war and the making of treaties of peace and other consequential international arrangements and the performance thereof. (3) It is immaterial whether the person in respect of whom the immunity is claimed is himself an officer of State with Ministerial status, or is a subordinate official of such Minister, or is himself an executive officer of lower status than that of a Minister. (4) The immunity extends to such persons only so long as they are acting in the capacity described above. (5) This immunity also extends to persons who do not come within the class above described but are the owners or occupiers of property exclusively used for purposes of Government. The immunity only protects such persons in respect of liability or disability arising in respect of the ownership or occupation of such property. This is the class (iii) above and generally referred to as *in consimili casu*."[54] LORD REID in the same case, speaking about class (ii) said, that there was nothing in the earlier cases which required to limit the class of servants of the Crown to Ministers and the like, or exclude the subordinate servants of the Crown and the question whether an officer is a servant of the Crown depended on the degree of control which the Crown through its Ministers could exercise over him in the performance of his duties. Dealing with the case of a statutory office, LORD REID observed: "The fact that a statute has authorised his appointment is, I think, immaterial, but the definition in the statute of his rights, duties and obligations is highly important. In the ordinary way, a civil

---

53. (1954) 1 All ER 969 : (1953) 1 QB 248 (HL).

54. *Bank voor Handel en Scheepvaart NV v. Administrator of Hungarian Property*, (1954) 1 All ER 969, p. 989 : (1953) 1 QB 248 (HL).

servant's duties are not prescribed though his salary may be fixed in Parliament, and I have no doubt that he is the servant of the Crown. But when a statute creates an office it may give to the holder more or less independence from Ministerial control so that the officer has, to a greater or less extent, a discretion which he alone can exercise, and it may be that the grant of any substantial independent discretion takes the officer out of the category of servants of the Crown for the present purpose."[55] Further, in distinguishing class (ii) and class (iii) LORD REID said: "Those *in consimili casu* are typically bodies like the justices, independent of the Crown asserting Crown privilege, not for the benefit of the revenues of the Crown, but for the benefit of their own revenues, in order that the functions which they are carrying out shall not be prejudiced, and it is easy to see why such independent bodies can only be permitted to claim Crown privilege in respect of a very limited class of functions, and only if the property or money in respect of which the immunity is claimed is wholly devoted to those functions. But the case of a subordinate servant of the Crown is very different. If a Minister receives income to be used in the service of the Crown it does not matter whether the purposes for which it is to be used are, or are not, purposes which if carried out by independent bodies, would put them *in consimili casu* with servants of the Crown; in all cases he can claim Crown immunity. And I can see no possible reason why, if a subordinate servant of the Crown received income to be used in the service of the Crown, he should not be entitled to assert the same privilege."[56] LORD ASQUITH, in the same case dealing with class (iii), *i.e.*, persons *in consimili casu* with servants of the Crown, said: "Persons may enjoy immunity who are not servants of the Crown. Persons will tend to be placed in this category if the public functions which they discharge are closely connected with the exercise of the Royal prerogative; *e.g.*, *inter alia*, the administration of justice, the preservation of public order, the making of war, and the conclusion of peace. And the Courts appear, on some of the authorities, to have taken these last factors into account as relevant in deciding who is a 'servant of the Crown' within the second class."[57] LORD ASQUITH then proceeded to lay down a further principle: "The courts will lean against including in any of the exempted categories an aggregation of commercial undertakings brought under some degree of public statutory control; and they will (if the other requirements are satisfied) lean in favour of exemption for persons or bodies who are mere ministerial instruments of the Crown's will, lacking in themselves any discretion or initiative."[58]

---

55. *Ibid*, p. 892.
56. *Ibid*, p. 981.
57. *Ibid*, pp. 990, 991.
58. *Ibid*, p. 991.

In *Cooper v. Hawkins*,[59] an army engine driver who drove a locomotive on Crown service at a speed exceeding the limit fixed by regulations under a statute was held to be not liable for the breach of the speed limit as in the absence of express words the statute did not bind the Crown.

In *Clarke v. Downes*,[60] it was held that a purchaser of Crown property was not bound by Rent Restriction Acts as regards a tenancy created by the Crown, and in *Rudler v. Franks*,[61] it was held that a tenant under the Crown could eject his sub-tenant in spite of the Rent Restriction Acts.

In *London Territorial Association v. Nichols*,[62] a Territorial Association constituted under the Territorial and Reserve Forces Act, 1907, successfully claimed immunity from Rent Restriction Acts in respect of tenancy created by it of property vested in it for Crown purposes. Under the Act the function to raise a territorial army and certain administrative functions of the Crown were transferred to territorial associations, which functions were to be exercised under the strictest control and supervision of the Army Council, one of such functions being that of holding land and letting it (when not usable or being used for direct military purposes) to ordinary members of the public. The case according to the court of appeal satisfied both the tests, *viz.*, the test of status with respect to the body or person claiming immunity and the test of purpose with respect to the transaction for which the immunity is claimed being a Crown purpose. It was held that the function of helping to raise a territorial army was typically a governmental function and contrasted sharply with functions, semi-commercial and discharged previously by private commercial bodies and that the association discharging such a function under the control of the Army Council was like a Minister or an organ of the Central Government, a direct emanation of the Crown and hence, satisfied the test of status. It was further held that the association acted for Crown purposes not only when it occupied land or buildings by itself or its military staff or officers, but also when it leased out to the members of the public premises not then needed for occupation of armed forces, but which could in time be needed for that purpose again, to ensure that in the interim period such premises did not run to waste, but rather that they were economised and exploited for the benefit of the public and the Exchequer.

In *County Council of Middlesex v. Assessment Committee of St. George's Union*,[63] the question raised was, whether certain premises in

---

59. (1904) 2 KB 164.
60. (1931) 145 LT 20 : (1931) All ER Rep 157.
61. (1947) 1 KB 530.
62. (1948) 2 All ER 432 (CA).
63. (1896) 2 QBD 143.

occupation for administration of justice and also for municipal purposes were rateable. It was held that the premises were rateable in so far as they were occupied for municipal purposes and not rateable in so far as they were occupied for the administration of justice, which was held to be a Crown function.

In *Tamlin v. Hannaford*,[64] the question before the Court of Appeal was, whether the Transport Commission constituted under the Transport Act, 1947, was a servant or agent of the Crown, and could claim immunity from Rent Restriction Acts in respect of property vested in it. After noticing that the Commission was under the general control of the Minister of Transport whose powers over the Corporation were as great as those possessed by a man who holds all the shares in a private company, and that the money which the Commission needs was raised by borrowing guaranteed by the Treasury, the court held that these features were insufficient to make the Commission, which was a commercial corporation, a servant or agent of the Crown, entitling it to claim Crown immunity. Distinguishing the Commission from the Territorial Army Association and the Post Office, DENNING, L.J. said: "The Territorial Army Association, for instance, is not concerned with commercial matters, but with the defence of the realm, which is essentially the province of Government, and it is, therefore, to be considered an agent of the Crown. The Post Office is the nearest analogy. It is, of course, concerned with commercial matters, but it is, nevertheless, a governmental department and its servants are civil servants. That is, however, an anomaly due to its history. The carriage of mail was a Crown monopoly long before the Postmaster-General was incorporated. But the carriage of passengers and goods is a commercial concern which has never been the monopoly of any one and we do not think that its unification under State control is any ground for conferring Crown privileges on it."[65] Further, referring to the factor of control exercised by the Minister of Transport as a possible criterion to show that the Commission was a servant or an agent of the Crown, DENNING, L.J. observed: "There is ample authority both in this court and the House of Lords for saying that such control as he exercises is insufficient for the purpose.[66] When Parliament intends that a new Corporation should act on behalf of the Crown, it, as a rule, says so expressly as it did in the case of Central Land Board by the Town and Country Planning Act, 1947, which was passed on the same day as the Transport Act, 1947. In the absence of any such express provision,

64. (1950) 1 KB 18 : (1949) 2 All ER 327 (CA).
65. (1949) 2 All ER 327, p. 329 (CA).
66. **See** *Central Control Board (Liquor Traffic) v. Cannon Brewery Co.*, (1918) 2 Ch 123 : 1919 AC 744.

the proper inference, in the case, at any rate, of a commercial corporation, is that it acts on its own behalf, even though it is controlled by a Government department."[67]

In *British Broadcasting Corporation v. Johns,*[68] the corporation which was established by Royal Charter and which operated under a licence granted by the Postmaster General and to a large extent under his control claimed immunity from taxation under the Income-tax Act, 1952. It was held that the corporation was not entitled to the Crown's exemption from taxation, because broadcasting was not a province of the Government and the corporation was an independent body corporate which was not exercising functions required and created by the Government.

In an Australian case[69] the Water Administration Ministerial Corporation constituted as a 'statutory body representing the Crown' under section 7 of the Water Administration Act, 1986 was held liable in damages for supplying polluted water to the appellants for irrigation which damaged their potato crop inspite of section 19(1) providing immunity from an

---

67. *Tamlin v. Hannaford*, (1950) 1 KB 18 : (1949) 2 All ER 327, pp. 329, 330 (CA).
This case has been **followed** in India for deciding as to when a Corporation controlled or owned by the Government can be said to be a department of the Government: **See** *S.T. Corporation v. Commercial Tax Officer*, AIR 1967 SC 1811, p. 1849; *Yousuf v. Mohammad*, AIR 1967 SC 1318, p. 1320 : (1967) 2 SCR 318; *Heavy Engineering Mazdoor Union v. State of Bihar*, AIR 1970 SC 82 : (1969) 1 SCC 765; *S.L. Agarwal v. Hindustan Steel Ltd.*, AIR 1970 SC 1150 : (1969) 1 SCC 177; *Hindustan Aeronautics v. Workmen*, AIR 1975 SC 1737, p. 1739 : (1975) 4 SCC 679. In *Baccus S.R.L. Servicio National del Trigo,* (1957) 1 QB 438, a Spanish Corporation which carried ordinary commercial transactions was granted State immunity. But this case was **disapproved** in *Mellenger v. New Brunswick Corporation*, (1971) 1 WLR 604 (CA), where a Corporation constituted to act by statute on behalf of the Crown in the right to New Brunswick and not engaged in any commercial activity was held to be a Government department. In *Trendtex Trading Corporation v. Central Bank of Nigeria*, (1977) 1 All ER 881 : (1977) 2 WLR 356 : (1977) QB 529 (CA), it was held that the Central Bank of Nigeria was not a Government department and was not entitled to State immunity. And, in *Biharilal Dobray v. Roshanlal Dobray,* (1984) 1 SCC 551, p. 570 : AIR 1984 SC 385; it was held in the context of Article 191(1)(a) of the Constitution that the Board of Basic Education constituted under the U.P. Basic Education Act, 1972 was virtually a department of the Government. But Government Companies and public sector undertakings though 'State' as defined in Article 12 of the Constitution for enforcement of fundamental rights against them cannot be treated as Government or State for other purposes unless it is specifically so provided by the statute; *Mohd. Hadi Raja v. State of Bihar*, AIR 1998 SC 1945 : (1998) 5 SCC 91. **See further** text and notes 92, p. 801 and notes 1 and 2, p. 802.

68. (1964) 1 All ER 923 (CA).

69. *Puntoriero v. Water Administration Ministerial Corporation,* (1999) 73 ALJR 1359.

action 'with respect to loss or damage suffered as a consequence of the exercise of Ministerial function of the corporation including the exercise of a power: (a) to use works to impound or control water, or (b) to release water from any such works'. One of the objects of the corporation was 'to meet the needs of the water users in a commercial manner'. The High Court of Australia construed the immunity provision strictly as not applying to supply of water on payment, *i.e.*, to a commercial transaction.

In certain cases the phrase 'emanation of the Crown' has been used to signify bodies and persons to whom the Crown privilege could extend, but the use of this phrase has been deprecated by the Privy Council and preference has been shown for the use of the phrase 'servant or agent of the Crown'.[70] The use of the latter phrase has also been found to be appropriate by the House of Lords.[71] Another phrase to signify the same thing is '*alter ego* of the Government' which has been used by the House of Lords[72] and Court of Appeal.[73]

2. THE RULE IN INDIA

In *Director of R & D v. Corporation of Calcutta*,[74] it was held that the Common Law rule that the Crown was not bound by a statute unless named expressly or by necessary implication applied to India before the Constitution as held by the Privy Council in *Bombay Province v. Bombay Municipal Corporation*[75] and it continued to apply after the Constitution in the form that the State is not bound by a statute unless it is so provided in express terms or by necessary implication. But this view was overruled in *State of W.B. v. Corporation of Calcutta*.[76] In this case it was held that the common law rule of construction was not accepted prior to the Constitution throughout India and even in the Presidency towns it was not regarded as an inflexible rule. In this connection it was pointed out that in the Privy Council case

70. *International Railway Co. v. Niagara Parks Commr.*, (1941) 2 All ER 456, p. 462 : 1941 AC 328 (PC).
71. *Bank voor Handel en Scheepvaart NV v. Administrator of Hungarian Property*, (1954) 1 All ER 969, pp. 982, 988, 990, 991 : 1954 AC 584 (HL). In *British Broadcasting Corporation v. Johns*, (1964) 1 All ER 923, p. 943 (CA), DIPLOCK L.J. said: "I hope that no one will ever again in a court of law use so imprecise a metaphor as 'emanation of the Crown'."
72. *Rahimtoola v. Nizam of Hyderabad*, (1958) AC 379, p. 393 (HL).
73. *Mellenger v. New Brunswick Corporation*, (1971) 1 WLR 604 (CA); *Trendtex Trading Corporation v. Central Bank of Nigeria*, (1977) 1 All ER 881, p. 893 : (1977) QB 529 : (1977) 2 WLR 356 (CA).
74. AIR 1960 SC 1355 : 1961 (1) SCR 158.
75. AIR 1947 PC 34 : 73 IA 271.
76. AIR 1967 SC 997 : (1967) 2 SCR 170.

of *Bombay Province v. Bombay Municipal Corporation*,[77] the rule was applied on a concession made by Counsel, and that the legislative practice in India established that the various Legislatures of the country provided specifically exemptions in favour of the Crown whenever they intended to do so indicating thereby that they did not rely upon any presumption, but only on express exemption. It was further held, that the rule of Common Law which was based on prerogative of the Crown had no relevance to a democratic republic, and was inconsistent with the rule of law based on the doctrine of equality enshrined in the Constitution. As a result of this decision, the rule that applies in India is, that a "general Act applies to citizens as well as to State unless it expressly or by necessary implication exempts the State from its operation".[78] The same rule will apply to Government bodies and corporations constituted under Special Acts.[79]

The question whether the State has been exempted by necessary implication from the operation of an Act or any of its provisions will depend upon a fair construction of the Act in question. As observed by BACHAWAT, J.: "Particular care should be taken in scrutinising the provisions of a taxing or a penal Act. If the application of the Act leads to some absurdity that may be a ground for holding that the State is excluded from its operation by necessary implication. If the only penalty for an offence is imprisonment, the State cannot be convicted of the offence, for the State cannot be locked up in prison. If the penalty for offence is fine and the fine goes to the consolidated fund of the State, it may be presumed that the penal provision does not bind the State, for the Legislature could not have intended that the State will be the payer as well as the receiver of the fine. Presumably, the Union is not bound by the Central Income-tax Act because if it paid income-tax, it will be both the payer and receiver. Likewise, a State is *prima facie* not bound by a State Agricultural Income-tax Act, where the tax is receivable by it. Moreover, cases may conceivably arise where express provisions in a statute binding the State in respect of certain specific matters may give rise to the necessary implication, that the State is not bound in respect of other matters."[80]

The facts in this case[81] were that the State of West Bengal was carrying on the trade of a daily market without taking out a licence and paying the

---

77. AIR 1947 PC 34 : 73 IA 271.
78. *State of W.B. v. Corporation of Calcutta*, AIR 1967 SC 997, p. 1008 : 1967 (2) SCR 170.
79. *Lucknow Development Authority v. M.K. Gupta*, AIR 1994 SC 787 : 1994 (1) SCC 248. **See** text and note 92, p. 803.
80. *State of West Bengal v. Corporation of Calcutta, supra,* p. 1020 (AIR).
81. *State of W.B. v. Corporation of Calcutta, supra.* For liability of the State under Criminal law **see** FREIDMAN, Law in a Changing Society, 2nd Edition, pp. 210, 211.

prescribed fee as required by section 218 of the Calcutta Municipal Act, 1951. Section 541 of the Act makes it an offence punishable with fine to carry on trade or business without a licence and the fine levied is taken by the corporation in full satisfaction of the demand on account of the licence. It was held that the State was bound by these provisions of the Act and was liable for the offence as it had not taken a licence to carry on the business. It must be noticed that the fine recovered under section 541 did not go to the consolidated fund of the State, but to the corporation's fund and, therefore, the Act contained no implication that the State was not liable for the offence.

When a penal enactment providing for imprisonment or fine (which goes to Government) is made applicable to Government or a Government department, it will generally indicate the officer who is liable to be punished for the offence. For example, when a lottery is organised, conducted or promoted by a department of a State Government in contravention of the Lotteries (Regulation) Act, 1998, the Head of the Department is liable under section 7(1) to be punished with rigorous imprisonment which may extend to two years or with fine or both.

In *Union of India v. Jubbi*,[82] the question was whether section 11 of the Himachal Pradesh Abolition of Big Landed Estates and Land Reforms Act, 1953, applied to the Union. The section conferred on tenants the right to acquire the interests of landlord on payment of compensation, and it was contended by the Union that the section was not applicable to cases where the Government was the landlord. This contention was rejected and the court observed: "The position now is that a statute applies to State as much as it does to a citizen unless it expressly or by necessary implication exempts the State from its operation.... Neither section 11 nor any other provision in the Act contains any express exemption. Broadly stated, if the Legislature intended to exclude the applicability of the Act to the State it could have stated in section 11 itself or by a separate provision that the Act is not to be applied to the Union or to the land held by it. In the absence of such a provision, in a constitutional set up as the one we have in this country, and of which the overriding basis is the broad concept of equality, free from any arbitrary discrimination, the presumption would be that a law of which the avowed object is to free the tenant of landlordism and to ensure to him security of tenure would bind all landlords irrespective of whether such a landlord is ordinary individual or the Union."[83]

---

82. AIR 1968 SC 360 : 1968 (1) SCR 447.
83. *Ibid*, pp. 362, 363.

The word 'person' in Regulation 3(1)(a) of the Andhra Pradesh Scheduled Area Land Transfer Regulations, 1959 which prohibits any 'person' to transfer land to non-tribals was held to include also the State, thus prohibiting the transfer of any Government land to non-tribals.[84]

It has been held that if a State disobeys a temporary injunction, its property is liable to be attached under Order 39, Rule 2(3) of the Civil Procedure Code, 1908.[85] For the purpose of jurisdiction of the court, it has been held that a State can be sued at a place where it carries on business in accordance with section 20 of the Code.[86] The position is that "the State is bound by the Code of Civil Procedure, the scheme of the Code being that subject to any special provision made in that regard as respects Government, it occupies the same position as any other party to a proceeding before the court".[87]

Construing Entry 42 List III of the Constitution, which relates to 'acquisition and requisitioning of property' the Supreme Court held that the Union has power to legislate for acquisition of property belonging to a State.[88] It must be noticed that a Constitution is intended to bind the State and even the Common Law rule that, Crown's rights are not affected by an Act except by express words or necessary implication, does not apply for construing a Constitution.[89]

In view of Article 285 of the Constitution property of the Union is exempt from taxation imposed by a state law unless the Parliament provides otherwise.[90]

The Roadways Department of the state of Uttar Pradesh was held liable for payment of toll tax levied under section 15 of the Northern India Ferries Act, 1878 "on all persons, animals, vehicles and other things crossing any river by a public ferry and not employed or transmitted on the public service".[91]

It has been held that the Consumer Protection Act, 1986 applies to a statutory authority and a Government or semi-government body or a local authority in the same way as it applies to private bodies for the Act does not either expressly or impliedly indicate that these bodies are excluded from the purview of the Act.[92]

---

84. *Samatha v. State of Andhra Pradesh*, AIR 1997 SC 3297 : (1997) 8 SCC 191.
85. *State of Bihar v. Sonabati Kumari*, AIR 1961 SC 221 : (1961) 1 SCR 728.
86. *Union of India v. Ladulal Jain*, AIR 1963 SC 1681 : (1964) 3 SCR 624.
87. *State of Bihar v. Sonabati Kumari, supra*, p. 229.
88. *State of West Bengal v. Union of India*, AIR 1963 SC 1241 : (1964) 1 SCR 371.
89. *Amalgamated Society of Engineers v. Adelaide Steamship Co. Ltd.*, (1920) 28 CLR 129, p. 164 (HIGGINS, J.).
90. *Municipal Corporation Amritsar v. Senior Superintendent of Post Offices, Amritsar Division*, (2004) 3 SCC 92 : AIR 2004 SC 2912.
91. *Satya Narayan v. Dist. Engineer, PWD*, AIR 1962 SC 1161 : 1962 Supp (3) SCR 105.
92. *Lucknow Development Authority v. M.K. Gupta*, AIR 1994 SC 787, p. 794 : 1994 (1) SCC 243.

A company registered under the Companies Act, 1956 is not a Government department even if its share capital be wholly subscribed by the Government.[1] Therefore, even in cases where an Act does not apply to the Government, an agency or instrumentality of the Government, which is not a department of the Government, will be bound by the Act specially when it is a welfare Legislation. Thus the Hindustan Steel Works Construction Ltd., a company which is fully owned by the Central Government was held to be bound by the Kerala Construction Workers Welfare Funds Act, 1989, even though the Act has no application to the Central Government.[2] It is also well settled that constitutional provisions exempting Government properties from taxation (Article 285) do not apply to such Companies.[3] The same rule has been applied to a statutory corporation like the Food Corporation of India which is an autonomous body and has an identity of its own.[4] A Government company even when coming within the meaning of State as defined in Article 12 of the Constitution, for making it liable to comply with the requirements of fundamental rights in its working, is not an agent of the Government for all purposes so as to bind the Government for all its acts, liabilities and obligations.[5] The inclusive definition of State in Article 12 of the Constitution which has been widely construed[6] is applicable only to Parts III and IV of the Constitution dealing with

---

1. *Western Coal Fields Ltd. v. Special Area Development Authority, Korba*, AIR 1982 SC 697 : (1982) 1 SCC 125; *Steel Authority of India Ltd. v. Shri Ambica Mills Ltd.*, AIR 1998 SC 418, p. 422 : 1998 (1) SCC 465.
2. *Hindustan Steel Works Construction Ltd. v. State of Kerala*, AIR 1997 SC 2275, p. 2280 : 1997 (5) SCC 171.
3. *Western Coal Fields Ltd. v. Special Area Development Authority supra; Electronics Corporation of India v. Secretary Revenue Dept. Govt. of Andhra Pradesh,* AIR 1999 SC 1734, pp. 1737, 1738 : 1999 (4) 458. For meaning of property belonging to a State in similar context in section 14 of the Australian Constitution, **see** *SGH Ltd. v. Commissioner of Taxation,* (2002) 76 ALJR 780.
4. *Food Corporation of India v. Municipal Committee Jalalabad,* JT 1999 (5) SC 124 : AIR 1999 SC 2573 : (1999) 6 SCC 74. **See further** *Adityapur Industrial Area Development Authority v. Union of India,* (2006) 5 SCC 100 : AIR 2006 SC 2375.
5. *Steel Authority of India Ltd. v. National Union Waterfront Workers,* AIR 2001 SC 3527, p. 3542 : (2001) 7 SCC 1.
6. *Pradeep Kumar Biswas v. Indian Institute of Chemical Biology,* (2002) 5 SCC 111 : 2002 SCC (L&S) 633. (The test is whether the body is financially, functionally and administratively dominated by or under the control of the Government and the control is pervasive. Upon applying this test the Council of Scientific and Industrial Research, a registered society, was held to be State in this case). A cooperative society may also be held to be State if the above test is satisfied as held in *General Manager Kisan Sahkari Chini Mills Ltd. v. Satrughan Nishad*, AIR 2003 SC 4531 : (2003) 8 SCC 639. But applying the same test, the Board of Control for Cricket in India (BCCI) a registered society was not held to be State in *Zee Tele Films Ltd. v. Union of India*, (2005) 4 SCC 649. On the same test Uttar Pradesh Ganna Sansthan which was created to impart knowledge and training to cane growers, functions which

[Footnote No. 6 Contd.]

fundamental rights and directive principles of state policy and has no application to other provisions of the Constitution, *e.g.*, Articles 309, 310 and 311 or to give extended meaning to expressions State or State Government in other enactments, *e.g.*, section 9A of the Representation of the People Act, 1951.[7] A Government department has to be an organisation which is not only completely controlled and financed by the Government but has no identity of its own.[8]

Article 285 which relates to exemption of Union property from State taxation and Article 289 which relates to exemption of property of a State from Union taxation have no application to indirect taxes such as customs duty, central excise duty, sales tax etc.[9] The Union is therefore liable to sales tax under a State Act.[10] But a municipal corporation cannot evade the ban of Article 285 and tax Union property by levying service charges for water, electricity supplied and drainage and roads provided to Posts and Telegraph buildings.[11]

The State is normally not liable to pay the salaries of employees of a Government company or a Government corporation even vicariously. But when non-payment of salaries results in violation of fundamental right to life and liberty of employees on a large scale, the corporate veil can be pierced and the State can be made liable for having control over the affairs of the Government company or the corporation and it was duty bound to see that the human rights of the employees are not infringed.[12]

[Footnote No. 6 Contd.]
were earlier performed by the Government directly, has been held to be State: *State of Uttar Pradesh v. Radhey Shyam Rai,* (2009) 5 SCC 577 : (2009) 3 JT 393. A corporation established by or under a Central, Provincial or State Act is State under Article 12 but it will not include a company incorporated under the Companies Act: *Dalco Engineering Private Ltd. v. Satish Prabhakar Padhye*, (2010) 4 SCC 378 para 32 : AIR 2010 SC 1576.

7. *Pradeep Kumar Biswas v. Indian Institute of Chemical Biology, supra*, pp. 127, 128.
8. *Food Corporation of India v. Municipal Committee Jalalabad, supra,* p. 127 (JT) : pp. 2575, 2576 (AIR); **see further** *Provident Fund Commissioners v. Shivkumar Joshi,* AIR 2000 SC 331, p. 338 : (2000) 1 SCC 98 (The Regional Provident Fund Commissioner functioning under the Employees' Provident Funds and Miscellaneous Provisions Act, 1952 is not Central Government).
9. ***See*** *Sea Customs Act,1878 section 20(2) Re*, (1964) 3 SCR 787 : AIR 1963 SC 176; *New Delhi Municipal Council v. State of Punjab*, (1997) 7 SCC 339 : AIR 1997 SC 2847. Both these cases were decided by nine-Judges Bench.
10. *Karya Palak Engineer CPWD Bikaner v. Rajasthan Taxation Board*, (2004) 7 SCC 195, pp. 200, 201 : (2004) 6 JT 384.
11. *Municipal Corporation Amritsar v. The Senior Superintendent of Post Offices*, AIR 2004 SC 2912 : (2004) 3 SCC 92.
12. *Kapila Hingorani v. State of Bihar,* (2003) 6 SCC 1, p. 30 : (2003) 116 Com Cas 133.

CHAPTER 9

STATUTES AFFECTING JURISDICTION OF COURTS

SYNOPSIS

1. GENERAL PRINCIPLES

(a) Exclusion must be explicitly expressed or clearly implied

There is a strong presumption that civil courts have jurisdiction to decide all questions of civil nature. The exclusion of jurisdiction of civil courts is therefore not to be readily inferred and such exclusion must either be "explicitly expressed or clearly implied".[1] "It is a principle by no

1. *Secretary of State v. Mask & Co.*, AIR 1940 PC 105, p. 110; *Gurudwara Prabhandhak v. Shiv Ratan Dev*, AIR 1955 SC 576, p. 581; *Magiti Sasamal v. Pandab Bissoi*, AIR 1962 SC 547, p. 549 : 1962 (3) SCR 673; *Firm of Illuri Subbayya Chetty & Sons v. State of Andhra Pradesh*, AIR 1964 SC 322, p. 324 : (1964) 1 SCR 752; *Laxman v. State of Bombay*, AIR 1964 SC 436, p. 443 : 1964 (1) SCR 200; *Desika charyulu v. State of A.P.*, AIR 1964 SC 807, p. 814; *Provincial Government of Madras v. J.S. Basappa*, AIR 1964 SC 1873, p. 1876 : 1964 (5) SCR 517; *Ramswarup v. Shikharchand*, AIR 1966 SC 893, p. 896; *Pabbojan Tea Co. v. Dy. Commr., Lakhimpur*, AIR 1968 SC 271, p. 275 : 1968 (1) SCR 260; *Dhulabhai v. State of M.P.*, AIR 1969 SC 78, pp. 81, 82 : (1968) 3 SCR 662; *Musamia v. Rabari*, AIR 1969 SC 439, 446 : (1969) 1 SCR 785; *Richpal Singh v. Dalip*, (1987)
[Footnote No. 1 Contd.]

means to be whittled down"[2] and has been referred to as a "fundamental rule".[3] As a necessary corollary of this rule provisions excluding jurisdiction of civil courts[4] and provisions conferring jurisdiction on authorities and tribunals other than civil courts[5] are strictly construed. The existence of jurisdiction in civil courts to decide questions of civil nature being the general rule and exclusion being an exception, the burden of proof to show that jurisdiction is excluded in any particular case is on the party raising

---

[Footnote No. 1 Contd.]

4 SCC 410, p. 419 : AIR 1987 SC 2205; *Bismillah (Smt.) v. Janeshwar Prasad*, AIR 1990 SC 540, p. 541 : (1990) 1 SCC 207; *Sankaranarayanan Potti v. K. Sreedevi*, AIR 1998 SC 1808, p. 1816 : (1998) 3 SCC 751; *State of Andhra Pradesh v. Manjeti Laxmi Kantha Rao,* AIR 2000 SC 2220, p. 2221 : (2000) 3 SCC 689; *Sahebgouda v. Ogeppa,* (2003) 6 SCC 151, p. 156 : AIR 2003 SC 2743, p. 2747; *Dwarka Prasad Agarwal v. Rameshwar Chander,* (2003) 6 SCC 220, p. 228 : AIR 2003 SC 2969; *Ramesh Chand Ardawatiya v. Anil Panjwani,* (2003) 7 SCC 350, p. 362 : AIR 2003 SC 2508; *Nahar Industrial Enterprises Limited v. Hongkong and Shanghai Banking Corporation,* (2009) 8 SCC 646 paras 97, 105 to 111 : (2009) 10 JT 199 (Debt Recovery Tribunal constituted under Recovery of Debts Due to Banks and Financial Institutions Act, 1993 does not expressly or impliedly bar the jurisdiction of civil courts to entertain a suit at the instance of the debtor against the Bank). For meaning of "jurisdiction", **see** *Garthwaite v. Garthwaite*, (1964) 2 All ER 233, pp. 241, 242 (CA); *Raja Soap Factory v. S.P. Shantharaj*, AIR 1965 SC 1449, p. 1451 : 1965 (2) SCR 800; *Ujjam Bai v. State of U.P.*, AIR 1962 SC 1621, p. 1629 : (1963) 1 SCR 778; title 2 (b) 'Cases of nullity'.

2. *Pyx Granite Co. Ltd. v. Ministry of Housing and Local Government*, (1959) 3 All ER 1, p. 6 : 1960 AC 260 (HL); *London Borough of Ealing v. Race Relations Board*, (1972) 1 All ER 105, p. 108 (HL); *Seal v. Chief Constable*, (2007) 4 All ER 177 (H.L.) para 18; *Pabbojan Tea Co. v. Dy. Commr., Lakhimpur*, AIR 1968 SC 271, p. 275 : (1968) 1 SCR 260; *Dhulabhai v. State of M.P.*, AIR 1969 SC 78, p. 84 : (1968) 3 SCR 662; *Madhav Rao Scindia v. Union of India*, AIR 1971 SC 530, p. 576 : (1971) 1 SCC 85.

3. *Ibid. Pyx Granite Co.'s* case *(Supra)* was relied upon in holding that even the availability of public law remedy of judicial review does not bar private law remedy of civil action: *Roy v. Kensington and Chilsea and Westminster Family Practitioner Committee*, (1992) 1 All ER 705, pp. 715, 716, 729 : (1992) 1 AC 624 : (1992) 2 WLR 239 (HL). Some flexibility has to be retained as the precise limits of what is called 'public law' and what is called 'private law' are by no means worked out; *Mercury Communications Ltd. v. Director-General of Telecommunications*, (1996) 1 All ER 575, p. 581 : (1996) 1WLR 48 (e-f) (HL); *Steed v. Secretary of State for Home Department,* (2000) 3 All ER 226, pp. 231, 232 (HL). Suits for violation of fundamental rights, even in religious matters, can be entertained in civil courts: *PMA Metropolitan v. Moran Mar Marthoma Mathews*, 1995 (4) Scale 1, p. 64 : AIR 1995 SC 2001, p. 2050. The distinction between public law and private law remedy has now become too thin and practically obliterated: *LIC of India v. Consumer Education and Research Centre*, 1995 (3) Scale 627, p. 640 : AIR 1995 SC 1811, p. 1821 : (1995) 5 SCC 482.

4. *Bhagwat Singh v. State of Rajasthan*, AIR 1964 SC 444, p. 446 : (1964) 5 SCR 1 *Raichand v. Union of India*, AIR 1964 SC 1268, p. 1270 : (1964) 5 SCR 148; *Abdul v. Bhawani*, AIR 1966 SC 1718, p. 1719 (para 9) : (1966) 3 SCR 617.

5. *Kasturi & Sons v. Salivateswaran*, AIR 1958 SC 507, pp. 510, 511 : 1959 SCR 1; *Upper Doab Sugar Mills v. Shahdara (Delhi) Saharanpur Light Railway*, AIR 1963 SC 217 : 1963 (2) SCR 333.

such a contention.[6] The rule that the exclusion of jurisdiction of civil courts is not to be readily inferred is based on the theory that civil courts are courts of general jurisdiction and the people have a right, unless expressly or impliedly debarred, to insist for free access to the courts of general jurisdiction of the State.[7] Indeed, the principle is not limited to civil

---

6. *Ramayya v. Laxminarayan*, AIR 1934, PC 84, p. 86; *Ramesh Gobindram v. Sugra Humayun Mirza Wakf*, (2010) 8 SCC 726 paras 12 to 14 : AIR 2010 SC 2897. *Abdul v. Bhawani, supra*, p. 1719 (para 9); *Sri Vedagiri Lakshmi Narasimha Swami Temple v. I. Pattabhirami*, AIR 1967 SC 781, p. 785; *Sahebgouda v. Ogeppa, supra*. **But** in cases where the civil court's jurisdiction is excluded, the plaintiff cannot be allowed to circumvent the bar by clever drafting of his pleading: *Ram Singh v. Gram Panchayat*, (1986) 4 SCC 364 : AIR 1986 SC 2197.

7. "The proper tribunals for determination of legal disputes in this country are the courts and they are the only tribunals which, by training and experience, and assisted by properly qualified advocates are fitted for the task. The Courts jealously uphold and safeguard the *prima facie* privilege of every man who takes resort to them for determination and enforcement of his legal rights." Per ROMER, L.J. in *Lee v. Showmen's Guild of Great Britain*, (1952) 1 All ER 1175, p. 1188 : (1952) 2 QB 239 (CA). For almost identical observations of the Supreme Court, **see** *Madhav Rao Scindia v. Union of India*, AIR 1971 SC 530, p. 576 : (1971) 1 SCC 85. "The meanest of citizens has a right of access to a court of law for the redress of his just grievances"; per BHAGWATI, J., in *Ram Prasad v. State of Bihar*, AIR 1953 SC 215, p. 220 : 1953 SCR 1129.

N.B. 1.—Apart from training, experience and assistance of qualified advocates, another reason why the jurisdiction of regular courts is not to be readily denied is the principle of 'open justice' which in its various manifestations ensures judicial accountability. "The cumulative effect of the requirements to sit in open court, to publish reasons, to accord procedural fairness, to avoid perceived bias and to ensure the fairness of a trial, is the way the judiciary is held accountable to the public." JJ SPIGELMAN (Chief Justice of New Southwales) 'seen to be done: The Principle of Open Justice' Part II (2000) 74 ALJ 378. But when a trial of an accused in open court is likely to create law and order situation the High Court may constitute a Sessions Court in the jail premises under section 9(6) of the Criminal Procedure Code 1973 with access to press and those who agree to regular security checks: *Mohd. Shahabuddin v. State of Bihar*, (2010) 4 SCC 653 paras 129, 111 : (2010) 3 JT 266.

N.B. 2.—Article 14 of the International Covenant on Civil and Political Rights, 1966 which has been ratified by India and is also referred to in the definition of Human Rights in section 2(d) read with section 2(f) of the Protection of Human Rights Act, 1993 provides: 'In the determination of any criminal charge against him or of his rights and obligations in a suit at law, everyone shall be entitled to a fair and public hearing by a competent, independent and impartial tribunal established by law.'

Article 6(1) of the European Convention for the Protection of Human Rights and Fundamental Freedoms is similarly worded. On its construction and importance, **see** p. 552, *ante* and *Millar v. Dickson*, (2002) 3 All ER 104 (PC); *R. v. Spear*, (2002) 3 All ER 1074 (HL); *R. (on the application of Anderson) v. Secretary of State*, (2002) 4 All ER 1089 (HL); *Clark (Procurator Fiscal, Kirkcaldy) v. Kelly*, (2003) 1 All ER 1106 (PC); *Runa Begum v. Tower Hamlets London Borough Council*, (2003) 1 All ER 731 (HL); *R. (on the application of Kehoe) v. Secretary of State for Work and Pensions*, (2005) 4 All ER 905 (HL). [Article 6(1) does not itself create a 'right' which has to be determined according to the substantive law of the contracting state.]

[Footnote No. 7 Contd.]

courts alone, but applies to all courts of general jurisdiction including criminal courts.[8] The rule as stated above relating to strict construction of provisions excluding jurisdiction of courts of general jurisdiction was expressly approved by the Supreme Court.[9] Exclusion of jurisdiction of ordinary criminal courts can be brought about by setting up courts of limited jurisdiction in respect of the limited field, only if the vesting and the exercise of that limited jurisdiction is clear and operative and there is adequate machinery for the exercise of the limited jurisdiction.[10] But the rule against exclusion of jurisdiction of courts like other rules of construction is attracted only where two or more reasonably possible constructions are open on the language of the statute and not where the legislative intent is plain and manifest to oust the jurisdiction.[11]

[Footnote No. 7 Contd.]

N.B. 3.—Even before the enforcement of the Human Rights Act, 1998 in England where there is no written Constitution, a citizen's right of access to courts was regarded as a common law constitutional right which could be taken away only by specific statutory provision or by regulations made pursuant to legislation which specifically conferred the power to abrogate that right. Power to prescribe court fees could not be so used as to deprive indigent person access to courts. In *R. v. Lord Chancellor, ex parte, Withan*, (1997) 2 All ER 779 : (1997) 2 All ER 779 (QBD) the court held invalid an order of the Lord Chancellor which had repealed provisions that had previously relieved litigants in person, who were in receipt of income support, from the obligation to pay fees. The Lord Chancellor did not appeal. The decision demonstrates that 'user pays' principle as applicable to access to courts is consistent with the rule of law only to the extent that every genuine would be user can pay. **See** (1997) 71 ALJ 809.

8. *Bhimsen v. State of U.P.*, AIR 1955 SC 435, p. 438 : (1955) 1 SCR 1444; *State of West Bengal v. Anwar Ali*, AIR 1952 SC 75 : 1952 SCR 284; *State of M.P. v. Rames-hwar Rathod*, AIR 1990 SC 1849, pp. 1850, 1851 : (1990) 4 SCC 21; *Sachida Nand Singh v. State of Bihar*, JT 1998 (1) SC 370, pp. 373, 374 : AIR 1998 SC 1121, pp. 1122, 1123 : (1998) 2 SCC 493. Even a criminal court can decide the question of *ultra vires* of a statutory order or delegated legislation violation of which has led to the prosecution; *Boddington v. British Transport Police,* (1998) 2 All ER 203, pp. 216, 217 (HL).

9. *Swami Atmananda v. Sri Ramakrishna Tapovanam*, AIR 2005 SC 2392, pp. 2402, 2403 (para 55) (The passage from 9th Edn., pp. 630, 631 of this book is **quoted** with **approval**); *Rajasthan State Transport Corporation v. Mohar Singh*, (2008) 5 SCC 542 para 21 : AIR 2008 SC 2553 (The same passage from 11th edition of this book pp. 709, 710 is **quoted** with **approval**); *United India Insurance Company Ltd. v. Ajay Sinha*, (2008) 7 SCC 454 para 35 : AIR 2008 SC 2398.

10. *Bhimsen v. State of U.P., supra*, p. 438; *Attiq-ur-Rehman v. Municipal Corporation, Delhi*, AIR 1996 SC 956, pp. 959, 960 : (1996) 3 SCC 37. **See further** *Municipal Corporation, Ludhiana v. Commissioner of Patiala Division*, 1994 AIR SCW 5136, p. 5137 (The words 'punishable with fine' imply a crime and fine can be imposed for a crime only by a criminal court and not by officers of Municipal Corporation).

11. *Kihota Hollohan (Shri) v. Zachilhu*, AIR 1993 SC 412, p. 437 : 1992 Supp (2) SCC 651.

Examples of application of the rule are quite numerous.—A suit by a receiver appointed by a civil court for a declaration that sale of lands in his custody for arrears of land revenue under section 141 of the Berar Land Revenue Code, 1928, was invalid for want of notice to him, was held to be cognizable by civil courts and not barred by section 157 of the same Code which provided that 'all claims on the ground of irregularity and mistake shall be barred', unless made before revenue authorities under section 156.[12] It was pointed out that section 156 enabled a person aggrieved to apply for setting aside the sale on the ground of some material irregularity or mistake in 'publishing' and 'conducting' it; and was applicable only to acts or omissions in proceedings relating to sale proclamation and holding of the sale; and that section 157 did not bar a challenge to the sale in civil courts on grounds other than those which could be agitated under section 156.[13]

Similarly, a suit for possession of certain properties on the ground that a purported sale of those properties for arrears of revenue under the Bombay Land Revenue Code, 1879, was void not being a sale by public auction as required by section 167, was held to be maintainable in civil courts and not barred under section 4(c) of the Bombay Revenue Jurisdiction Act, 1876, which provides that no civil court shall exercise jurisdiction as to claim to set aside, on account of irregularity, mistake or on any other ground except fraud, sales for arrears of land revenue.[14] It was pointed out that the provision under section 4(c) only covered a case where there was a sale in existence though irregular and was not applicable to a case of purported sale which was wholly void.[15]

The Ajmer Land and Revenue Regulations, 1877, which by section 23 provides that no adoption made by a widow shall be deemed valid unless confirmed by the Central Government, and which by section 119, further provides that everything done by the Central Government shall be deemed to have been legally and rightly done, was interpreted as not excluding jurisdiction of civil courts for deciding that no adoption had in fact been made or that it was invalid under the general law although an order confirming the adoption may have been passed by the Central Government.[16]

Section 7 of the Orissa Tenants' Protection Act, 1948, which provided that certain disputes between landlord and tenant shall be decided by the

---

12. *Kanhaiyalal v. D.R. Banaji*, AIR 1958 SC 725.
13. *Ibid.*
14. *Ramrao v. State of Bombay*, AIR 1963 SC 827 : 1963 Supp (1) SCR 322.
15. *Ibid.*
16. *Brij Raj Singh v. Laxman Singh*, AIR 1961 SC 149 : 1961 (1) SCR 616. **See further** *Dwarka Nath v. Lalchand*, AIR 1965 SC 1549 : 1965 (3) SCR 27.

Collector, was construed as not embracing a dispute as to the existence of the relationship of landlord and tenant.[17]

The last mentioned case was followed and applied in interpreting the provisions of section 77(3), of the Punjab Tenancy Act, 1887. The section provided that suits by landlord to eject a tenant and suits by a tenant to establish a claim to a right of occupancy or by a landlord to prove that a tenant has no such right, shall be determined by revenue courts and shall not be cognizable by any other court. In construing these provisions, it was held that the suits excluded by the said section from the jurisdiction of civil courts and committed to that of revenue courts, were those where existence of relationship of landlord and tenant was not disputed, and that the jurisdiction of civil courts was not excluded to entertain and try a suit for possession where the plaintiff did not admit that the defendant was his tenant, although the defendant raised the plea that he was an occupancy tenant.[18]

Similar is a case relating to the Bhopal State Revenue Act, 1932. The Act made provision for ejectment of a sub-tenant on a suit by his tenant. There was no provision in the Act for suits between persons claiming as rival tenants. A person ejected as a sub-tenant by revenue courts brought a suit before the civil court claiming him to be the tenant against the person ejecting him. It was held that the suit was maintainable, and was not barred either by the provisions of the Act, or by the decree of the revenue court, for the question as to who was in reality the tenant could not have been decided by the revenue courts.[19] On the same principle exclusive jurisdiction conferred on a *Mamlatdar* by section 70 read with section 85 of the Bombay Tenancy and Agricultural Lands Act, 1948, to decide whether a person is a tenant has been held not to exclude the jurisdiction of the civil court to decide whether a person who had ceased to be a tenant was or was not a tenant in the past.[20] Reading different provisions of the Maharashtra Co-operative Societies Act, 1960, together, the Supreme Court has held that the intention of the Legislature was not to oust the jurisdiction of a

17. *Magiti Sasamal v. Pandab Bissoi*, AIR 1962 SC 547 : 1962 (3) SCR 673.
18. *Durga Singh v. Tholu*, AIR 1963 SC 361 : 1963 (2) SCR 693. **See further** *Richpal Singh v. Dalip*, (1987) 4 SCC 410, pp. 416 to 418 : AIR 1987 SC 2205.
19. *Abdul v. Bhawani*, AIR 1966 SC 1718 : 1966 (3) SCR 617.
20. *Musamia Imam v. Rabari Govindbhai*, AIR 1969 SC 439, p. 446 : 1969 (1) SCR 785.

N.B.—The Bombay Act was retrospectively, amended to confer jurisdiction on a *Mamlatdar* in respect of past tenants also; *Noor Mohd. Khan v. Fakirappa*, AIR 1978 SC 1217, p. 1222 : (1978) 3 SCC 188.

civil court to decide a dispute arising out of a decision of a co-operative society to alienate the property of the society in favour of a third party.[21]

Section 9(2), of the Citizenship Act, 1955, enacts that if any question arises as to whether, when or how any person has acquired the citizenship of another country, it shall be determined by such authority as may be prescribed. Rule 30 of the rules framed under the Citizenship Act, 1955 prescribe that, such a question shall be determined by the Central Government. In a suit instituted in a civil court the plaintiffs claimed that they were Indian citizens on 26th January, 1950, and that; although they went to Pakistan in 1953 on a temporary visit they had not acquired Pakistani citizenship and continued to be Indian citizens. The State contended that the plaintiffs had never been Indian citizens and that they had voluntarily acquired Pakistani citizenship. The suit was dismissed on the ground that it was barred by section 9(2) of the Citizenship Act, 1955. In reversing the judgment, the Supreme Court held that the question whether plaintiffs were Indian citizens on 26th January, 1950, could be decided by civil courts and was not barred by section 9(2) of the Act, although the question, whether they had thereafter acquired foreign citizenship, could be only decided by the Central Government.[22] The Supreme Court, therefore,

---

21. *Margret Almedia & Ors. v. Bombay Catholic Co-Operative Housing Society d. & Ors., Lt,* (2012) 5 SCC 642.

22. *Akbar Khan v. Union of India*, AIR 1962 SC 70 : 1962 (1) SCR 779. Similar procedure may have to be followed in a criminal case (*State of Gujarat v. Yakub Ibrahim*, AIR 1974 SC 645 : (1974) 1 SCC 283), and in the trial of an election petition involving a question of acquisition of foreign citizenship (*Bhagwati Prasad Dixit v. Rajeev Gandhi*, (1986) 4 SCC 78, pp. 86, 87 : AIR 1985 SC 1534); *Harishankar Jain v. Sonia Gandhi,* AIR 2001 SC 3687, pp. 3696, 3697 : (2001) 8 SCC 233. **See further** text and notes 36 to 40, pp. 862-863. If certain matters are wholly excluded from jurisdiction of civil courts and are solely triable by revenue courts, a civil court trying a suit may have to refer those matters for decision to the proper revenue court if the defence raises pleas relating to those matters: *Bhimji v. Dundappa*, AIR 1966 SC 166 : (1966) 1 SCR 145; *Ishverlal v. Motibai*, AIR 1966 SC 459, p. 466 : 1966 (1) SCR 367; *Noor Mohd. Khan v. Fakirappa, supra*; *G.S. Shinde v. R.B. Joshi* (*Smt.*), AIR 1979 SC 653 : 1979 (2) SCC 495; *Pandurang Ramchandra Mandlik v. Chandabai Ramchandra Ghatge (Smt.)*, AIR 1989 SC 2240, p. 2247 : 1989 Supp (2) SCC 627; *Mudakappa v. Rudrappa*, AIR 1994 SC 1190 : 1994 (2) SCC 57; *Sankarnarayanan Potti v. K. Sreedevi*, JT 1998 (2) SC 537, p. 655 (para 16.3) : AIR 1998 SC 1808 : (1998) 3 SCC 751 : AIR 1998 SC 1808; *Laxmappa Bhimappa Hulsgeri v. Hanamappa Shetteppa Korwar*, (2004) 7 SCC 391, p. 397 : AIR 2004 SC 2445. *Ishwaragowda v. Mallikarjun Gowda*, (2009) 1 SCC 626 para 13 : (2008) 12 JT 650. **But** if the plea raised is wholly untenable a reference to the Revenue Court need not be made: *Thomas Antony v. Varkey Varkey,* JT 1999 (9) SC 105 : AIR 2000 SC 1 : (2000) 1 SCC 35. When an Act conferring jurisdiction on an authority excludes certain dispute from jurisdiction of that authority and provides that the same can be referred to the civil court by persons interested without indicating the procedure for reference, a civil suit for

[Footnote No. 22 Contd.]

directed that the first question should be decided by the civil court; and if it was found that plaintiffs were never Indian citizens, the suit should be dismissed; whereas if it was found that they were Indian citizens on 26th January, 1950, the suit should be stayed till the second question was decided by the Central Government.[23]

Section 86 of the Civil Procedure Code, 1908, which gives protection to foreign Rulers, Ambassadors and Envoys, and read along with section 87B extends the protection to rulers of former Indian States that they cannot be sued in any court except with the permission of the Central Government, has been strictly construed and the phrase 'sued in any court' has been held to confine the protection to suits proper, *i.e.*, to the proceedings in a court which commence with a plaint or a petition in the nature of a plaint. It was, therefore, held that the section did not debar the commencement of proceedings for adjudication of an industrial dispute for two reasons: (i) neither party to the industrial dispute is sued by filing of a plaint as the proceedings start on a reference by the Government; and (ii) the Industrial Tribunal is not a court.[24]

Sections 69(2) and 69(3) of the Partnership Act, 1932, which deprive the court of its jurisdiction to entertain a suit or other proceeding 'to enforce a right arising from contract' has been strictly construed. A suit to evict a tenant whose tenancy has expired by efflux of time is also a suit to enforce a right under section 108(q) of the Transfer of Property Act, 1882 and is not a suit solely arising from a contract and is not barred.[25] An application under section 9 of the Arbitration and Conciliation Act, 1996 has also been held not to be barred as it enforces a right conferred by section 9 of the Act and not by contract.[26]

Construing section 22C(8) of the Legal Services Authorities Act, 1987, which confers adjudicatory functions on a Permanent Lok Adalat

---

[Footnote No. 22 Contd.]

decision of such a dispute is maintainable: *Swamy Atmananda v. Sri RamaKrishna Tapovanam*, AIR 2005 SC 2392, p. 2402 [Construction of section 53A of T.N. Recognised Private Schools (Regulation) Act, 1974].

23. **See** footnote 21, *supra*.

24. *Bhagwat Singh v. State of Rajasthan*, AIR 1964 SC 444 : (1964) 5 SCR 1. **See further** *Nawab Usman Ali Khan v. Sagar Mal*, 1965 MPLJ 864 : AIR 1965 SC 1798 : (1965) 3 SCR 201 (the protection under section 87-B Code of Civil Procedure does not apply to a proceeding under section 14, Arbitration Act).

25. *Raptakos Brett & Co. v. Ganesh Property*, AIR 1998 SC 3085, p. 3098 : 1998 (7) SCC 184. **See further** for restricted construction of section 69(2): *Haldiram Bhujiawala v. Anand Kumar Deepak Kumar*, AIR 2000 SC 1287, pp. 1292, 1293 : (2000) 3 SCC 250.

26. *Firm Ashok Traders v. Gurmukh Das Saluja*, AIR 2004 SC 1433 : (2004) 3 SCC 155.

when parties fail to reach an agreement in conciliation proceedings, strictly and the proviso 1 to section 22C, which denies jurisdiction to it in respect of any matter relating to an offence not compoundable under any law, liberally the court held that the main purpose behind section 22C(8) with respect to public utility services was that most of the petty cases which ought not to go in regular courts would be settled in the pre-litigation stage itself and that a claim by a businessman against an insurance company for compensation on the ground that a burglary took place in his godown when the question of burglary was pending in a criminal court, as the insurance company had disputed the factum of burglary, could not be taken cognizance of by the Permanent Lok Adalat.[27]

Article 363 of the Constitution which bars the jurisdiction of all Courts including the Supreme Court in any dispute arising out of any provision of a treaty etc., or in any dispute in respect of any right, liability or obligation arising out of 'any of the provisions of the Constitution relating to any such treaty etc.', was strictly construed by the Supreme Court. It was held that a dispute that an order of the President de-recognising all the Rulers of Indian States passed under Article 366(22), was in excess of authority and beyond his powers and that the Rulers were entitled to the Privy Purse under Article 291, was not barred by Article 363. The words 'relating to' occurring in the said article were given a restricted meaning; and it was observed that the words 'provisions of this Constitution relating to any such treaty etc.' meant provisions having a dominant and immediate connection with treaty etc.[28]

(b) Three classes of cases

The Legislature being, however, competent to curtail the jurisdiction of civil courts, and to confer the same on any other tribunal or authority,[29] it is only a question of construction of a particular statute whether the same by express words or by necessary implication excludes the jurisdiction of

---

27. *United India Insurance Company Ltd. v. Ajay Sinha*, (2008) 7 SCC 454 paras 35, 39, 40 and 41 : AIR 2008 SC 2398.

28. *Madhav Rao Scindia v. Union of India*, AIR 1971 SC 530, pp. 576, 577 : (1971) 1 SCC 85. The effect of this case was taken away by Constitution 26th Amendment Act 1971 which deleted Article 291, inserted Article 363A and amended the definition of Ruler in Article 366(22). This Constitution Amendment Act abolishing Privy Purses has been held to be valid; *Raghunathrao Ganpatrao v. Union of India*, AIR 1993 SC 1267 : 1994 Supp (1) SCC 191. **For** width of Article 363 and its construction **see further** *Karan Singh v. State of Jammu and Kashmir*, AIR 2004 SC 2480, pp. 2483 to 2485 : (2004) 5 SCC 698 and cases **referred** to therein.

29. *United Provinces v. Atiqa Begum*, AIR 1941 FC 16, pp. 26, 29 : 1940 FCR 110; *State of Bombay v. Narottam Das*, AIR 1951 SC 69 : 1951 SCR 51; *State of V.P. v. Moradhwaj Singh*, AIR 1960 SC 796 : 1960 (3) SCR 106.

civil courts. The nature of the rights and liabilities dealt with by the statute and the remedies provided thereunder, may, in case of doubt, be taken into account for determining as to how far the jurisdiction of civil courts is excluded. As laid down by WILLES, J. and affirmed by higher authorities:

"There are three classes of cases in which a liability might be established, founded upon statute. One is where there was a liability existing at common law, and that liability is affirmed by a statute which gives a special and peculiar form of remedy different from the remedy which existed at common law; there, unless the statute contains words which expressly or by necessary implication exclude the common law remedy, the party suing has his election to pursue either that or the statutory remedy. The second class of cases is, where the statute gives the right to sue merely, but provides no particular form of remedy; there, the party can only proceed by action at common law. But there is a third class, *viz.*, where a liability not existing at common law is created by a statute which at the same time gives a special and particular remedy for enforcing it—The remedy provided by the statute must be followed, and it is not competent to the party to pursue the course applicable to cases of the second class."[30]

With respect to second of the three classes of cases mentioned by WILLES, J. there is normally no difficulty. A statute falling in this category prescribes no special remedy and whether it creates new rights and liabilities or regulates the already existing ones, the normal remedy through the medium of civil courts, which are courts of general jurisdiction, remains always open.[31]

With respect to first and third of the three classes of cases mentioned by WILLES, J. it has to be ascertained whether the statute in question deals with and regulates an already existing right or liability, or, whether it

30. *Wolverhampton New Waterworks Co. v. Hawkesford*, (1859) 6 CB (NS) 336, p. 356 (WILLES, J.); **referred** to in *Neville v. London Express Newspapers Ltd.*, (1918-19) All ER Rep. 61, pp. 72, 79 (HL); *A.G. of Trinidad v. Gordan Grant & Co.*, (1935) AC 532, p. 537 (PC); *Pyx Granite Co. Ltd. v. Ministry of Housing and Local Government*, (1959) 3 All ER 1, p. 16 : 1960 AC 260 (HL); *Secretary of State v. Mask & Co.*, AIR 1940 PC 105, p. 110; *N.P. Punnuswami v. Returning Officer, Namakkal*, AIR 1952 SC 64 : 1952 SCR 218, p. 69; *Firm Radhakishan v. Ludhiana Municipality*, AIR 1963 SC 1547, p. 1550 : (1964) 2 SCR 135; *Dhulabhai v. State of M.P.*, AIR 1969 SC 78, p. 81 : (1968) 3 SCR 662; *Premier Automobiles Ltd. v. Kamalakar Shantaram Wadke*, AIR 1975 SC 2238, p. 2244 : (1976) 1 SCC 496; *Bata Shoe Co. Ltd. v. Jabalpur Corporation*, AIR 1977 SC 955, p. 959 : (1977) 2 SCC 256; *Titaghur Paper Mills Co. Ltd. v. State of Orissa*, AIR 1983 SC 603, p. 607 : (1983) 3 SCC 433; *Rajasthan State Road Transport Corporation v. Bal Mukund Bairawa*, (2009) 4 SCC 299 para 32 : (2009) 2 JT 423; *Raj Kumar Shivhare v. Assistant Director of Directorate of Enforcement:* (2010) 4 SCC 772 para 34 : AIR 2010 SC 2239; *United Bank of India v. Satyawati Tandon*, (2010) 8 SCC 110 para 48 : AIR 2010 SC 3413.

31. Section 9, Code of Civil Procedure, 1908.

creates a new right or liability which has no existence apart from the statute. If the statute is of the former category, the special remedy provided therein, subject to any provision for the exclusion of ordinary remedy, will only be construed as an alternative one;[32] whereas if the statute is of the latter category, the remedy will be construed as exclusive even though the statute makes no express provision for exclusion of ordinary remedy. The mere fact, therefore, that a statute provides for certain remedies, does not by itself necessarily exclude the jurisdiction of civil courts;[33] but where a new right or liability is created by a statute which gives a special remedy for enforcing it, the ordinary remedy of approaching the civil courts is impliedly excluded.[34]

An interesting example of first of the three classes of cases mentioned by WILLES, J. is to be found in the Town and Country Planning Act, 1947, which came up for scrutiny before the House of Lords.[35] The Act restricts to a reasonable degree the ordinary rights of a land-owner to deal with his land as he pleases. It requires that for any development as defined in the Act, permission is necessary which may be granted conditionally or unconditionally. It lays down a mechanism for grant of permission and

---

32. *Northern India Caterers Ltd. v. State of Punjab*, AIR 1967 SC 1581 : 1967 (3) SCR 399; *Raja Ram Kumar Bhargava v. Union of India*, AIR 1988 SC 752 : 1988 (1) SCC 681; *Ratanlal Adukia v. Union of India*, AIR 1990 SC 104, p. 110 : 1989 (3) SCC 537.

33. *Pyx Granite Co. Ltd. v. Ministry of Housing and Local Government*, (1959) 3 All ER 1 : 1960 AC 260 (HL); *Firm of Illuri Subbayya Chetty & Sons v. State of A.P.*, AIR 1964 SC 322, p. 324 : (1964) 1 SCR 752; *Govt. of Madras v. J.S. Basappa*, AIR 1964 SC 1873, p. 1876 : (1964) 5 SCR 517.

34. *Barraclough v. Brown*, (1897) AC 615 : (1895-99) All ER Rep 239 (HL); *Pasmore v. Oswaldtwistle Urban District Council*, (1898) AC 387 : (1895-99) All ER Rep 191 (HL); *Argosam Finance Co. Ltd. v. Oxby*, (1964) 1 All ER 791; *N.P. Ponnuswamy v. Returning Officer, Namakkal*, AIR 1952 SC 64, p. 69 : (1952) SCR 218; *Firm Radhakishan v. Ludhiana Municipality*, AIR 1963 SC 1547, pp. 1550, 1551 : (1964) 2 SCR 273; *Raja Ram Kumar Bhargava v. Union of India*, AIR 1988 SC 752 : 1988 (1) SCC 681.

N.B.—The provisions of a statute may be so comprehensive and limiting that even in the absence of an express provision excluding the ordinary remedy: an inference may arise that the remedy provided by the statute is the only remedy. **See** *Ramratan v. State of Bihar*, AIR 1965 SC 926, p. 929 (paras 17, 18 regarding section 22, Cattle Trespass Act) : (1965) 1 SCR 293 : (1965) 1 SCR 923. **See further** *State of Kerala v. Ramaswamy Iyer & Sons*, AIR 1966 SC 1738, p. 1741 : (1966) 3 SCR 885 (Sales-tax legislation is in itself a complete Code). *State of Bihar v. Dhirendra Kumar*, 1995 (3) Scale 700 : AIR 1995 : (1995) 4 SCC 229 SC 1955; *Laxmichand v. Gram Panchayat*, 1995 (6) Scale 351 : (1996) 7 SCC 218 (The Land Acquisition Act, 1876 is in itself a complete Code and notifications under sections 4 and 6 and awards cannot be challenged by civil suit. The remedy is by judicial review under Article 226).

35. *Pyx Granite Co. Ltd. v. Ministry of Housing and Local Government*, (1959) 3 All ER 1 : (1960) AC 260 (HL).

provides for appeals to challenge an order refusing permission or to challenge the conditions on which the permission is granted. It further provides a mechanism for determination of the question whether a particular operation is development requiring permission under the Act. In an action brought by a company against the Ministry of Housing and the Local Government for a declaration that it was entitled to carry out certain proposed development without obtaining any permission, it was contended by the respondents that the court had no jurisdiction to entertain the action in view of the special remedies provided in the Act. The House of Lords in negativing the contention pointed out that the planning legislation in question did not create any new rights but restricted the already existing rights of a land-owner and the remedy provided under the statute was alternative and did not take away the ordinary remedy available under the general law.[36]

In the last mentioned case the House of Lords distinguished their earlier decision in *Barraclough v. Brown*,[37] which furnishes a striking illustration of third of the three classes of cases mentioned by WILLES, J. Section 47 of the Aire and Calder Navigation, Act, 1889, provided that if any vessel should be sunk in any part of the navigation of the river Ouse and if the owner should not remove it, it shall be lawful for the undertakers to remove the vessel and the 'undertakers may, if they think fit, recover such expenses from the owner of such vessel in a court of summary jurisdiction'. The undertakers having removed a sunken vessel, sued in the High Court for recovery of the expenses from the owners of the vessel. On an objection pertaining to jurisdiction, it was held by the House of Lords that the right conferred by the statute to recover the expenses was not a common law right, but a right created by the statute which itself provided for the remedy in a court of summary jurisdiction, and therefore, the normal remedy of a direct approach to the High Court was excluded.[38] LORD HERSCHELL in his opinion said: "The respondents were under no liability to pay these expenses at common law. The liability, if it exists, is created by the enactment—. The only right conferred is 'to recover such expenses from the owner of such vessel in a court of summary jurisdiction'. I do not think the appellant can claim to recover by virtue of the statute, and at the same time insist upon doing so by means other than those prescribed by

36. *Ibid.* **Compare** *Babhubhai & Co. v. State of Gujarat*, (1985) 2 SCC 732, p. 735 : AIR 1985 SC 613, where section 54 of the Bombay Town Planning Act, 1954 which authorized the local authority to take possession of land covered by a town planning scheme was held to provide exclusive remedy.

37. (1895-99) All ER Rep 239 (HL).

38. *Ibid.*

the statute which alone confers the right."[39] LORD WATSON after quoting the enactment observed: "The right and the remedy are given *uno flatu* and the one cannot be dissociated from the other. By these words the legislature has committed the summary court exclusive jurisdiction."[40] In distinguishing this case in *Pyx Granite Co.'s* case[41] LORD JENKINS pointed out that the principle of *Barraclough's* case applies "where a statute creates a new right which has no existence apart from the statute creating it; and the statute creating the right at the same time prescribes a particular method of enforcing it."[42] Explaining further LORD JENKINS observed: "If *A* has a right founded entirely on a particular statute to recover a sum of money from *B* and the statute goes on to provide that the sum in question may be recovered in proceeding of a particular kind, then it is wholly reasonable to impute to the Legislature an intention that the sum in question recoverable solely by virtue of the statute, should be recoverable in proceedings of the kind provided by the statute and not otherwise."[43]

The principle laid down in *Barraclongh v. Brown*[44] was recently followed by the UK Supreme Court in *A v. B.*[45] In this case A, a former senior member of the security service, wanted to publish a book about the work of the security service for which he needed the permission of B, the Director of the Establishment. After a prolonged hearing B declined to give the permission. A applied for judicial review of B's order in court on the ground that it violated section 7(1) of the Human Rights Act 1998 which came into force on 2nd October 2000 enforcing the European Convention on Human Rights and providing that a person who claims that a public authority has acted contrary to a convention right may bring proceedings against the authority in the appropriate court or tribunal. Section 65(2) of the Regulation of the Investigating Powers Act 2000, which also came into force on 2nd October 2000 setting up the Investigatory Powers Tribunal (IPT), provides that foi purposes of section 7(1) of the Human Rights Act the IPT shall be the only appropriate tribunal when the proceedings are against any of the intelligence services. In holding that the IPT had the exclusive jurisdiction in the matter and the judicial review proceedings in court were not maintainable, the Supreme Court pointed out that before 2nd October 2000 there was no pre-existing common law or statutory right to bring a claim based on an asserted

---

39. *Ibid*, p. 241.
40. *Ibid*, p. 243.
41. *Pyx Granite Co. v. Ministry of Housing and Local Government*, (1959) 3 All ER 1 : 1960 AC 260 (HL).
42. *Ibid*, p. 16.
43. *Ibid.*
44. Note 37, *supra*.
45. (2010) 1 All ER 1149 para 21 (UK SC).

breach of the convention and the right and the remedy are here given *uno flatu* and one cannot be dissociated from the other.

The Industrial Disputes Act, 1947 also furnishes an example of an Act which creates new rights and obligations and provides machinery for adjudication of disputes pertaining to them. The Supreme Court has held that if an industrial dispute relates to the enforcement of a right or an obligation created under the Act then the only remedy available to the suitor is to get adjudication under the Act.[46] This case was followed in holding that for wrongs created by the Act the only remedy is what is provided in the Act. It was, therefore, held that in case of a strike which is illegal the employer can have the workers punished under section 26 but he has no right to claim compensation for loss in business caused by the illegal strike.[47] Similarly it has been held that the right to reinstatement and backwages is created by the Act and recourse to remedies provided in the Act can alone be taken and a civil suit is not maintainable.[48] Objection to the jurisdiction on

---

46. *Premier Automobiles Ltd. v. Kamalakar Shantaram Wadke*, AIR 1975 SC 2238, p. 2251 : (1976) 1 SCC 496.
47. *Rohtas Industries Ltd. v. Rohtas Industries Staff Union*, AIR 1976 SC 425, p. 435 : (1976) 2 SCC 82. Speaking generally collective agreements under the Industrial law are not ordinary contracts which can be enforced by civil courts and the remedies for enforcing such agreements must be sought within the four corners of the industrial law: **See** FRIEDMAN, Law in a Changing Society, 2nd Edition, pp. 150-55.
48. *Jitendra Nath Biswas v. Empire of India and Ceylone Tea Co.*, AIR 1990 SC 255, p. 260 : 1989 (3) SCC 582. **See further** *Rajasthan State Road Transport Corporation v. Krishna Kant*, 1995 (3) Scale 440 : AIR 1995 SC 1715 : (1995) 5 SCC 75 (A dispute relating to rights and liabilities created by the certified standing orders and amounting to an industrial dispute can be adjudicated only in the forums created by the Industrial Disputes Act, 1947); *Chandrakant Tukaram Nikam v. Municipal Corporation of Ahmedabad,* AIR 2002 SC 997 : (2002) 5 SCC 542; (Legality of an order of termination of an industrial worker is an industrial dispute and a civil suit is not maintainable to decide that dispute); *Air India Cabin Crew Association v. Yeshawinee Merchant*, AIR 2004 SC 187, pp. 208, 209 : (2003) 6 SCC 277 (Even the High Court cannot under Article 226 entertain adjudication of an industrial dispute and settle terms and conditions of employees); *U.P. State Bridge Corporation Ltd. v. U.P. Rajyasetu Nigam Karmchari Sangh*, (2004) 4 SCC 268, p. 276 : (2004) 2 scale 466 (The High Court should be slow to entertain a petition under Article 226 when the alternative remedy by raising an industrial dispute was open to petitioner); *B.S. Bharati v. IBP Co. Ltd.*, (Govt's refused to refer the dispute of termination for adjudication under the Industrial Disputes Act does not entitle the employee to file a civil suit and he can only challenge the Govt. order of refusal in judicial review by a writ petition); *Rajasthan State Road Transport Corporation v. Zakir Hussain,* (2005) 7 SCC 447 (para 36); *Rajasthan SRTC v. Ramdhara Indoliya,* (2006) 6 SCC 287 : 2006 SCC (L&S) 1316 (*Zakir Hussain's* case **followed**); *Uttaranchal Forest Development Corpn. v. Jasbir Singh,* (2007) 2 SCC 112 (paras 44, 45) : (2007) 7 LLJ 95 : (2006) 13 Scale 556. (Even a direct writ petition, unless there be extraordinary circumstances, is not maintainable and the aggrieved person must pursue the remedies under the Industrial Disputes Act).

this ground can be raised at any stage even before the Supreme Court.[49] But when the right claimed in the civil suit is not under the Industrial Disputes Act or the sister laws but under the Constitution or the common law, for example when the order challenged by an employee of a state corporation is wholly unreasonable or arbitrary or in gross violation of the principles of natural justice, the jurisdiction of the civil court is not taken away even if the employee concerned be also a workman within the meaning of the Industrial Disputes Act or his services be governed by the certified standing orders.[50] In cases where the right claimed by a Government employee is both under the provisions of the Industrial Disputes Act and the Constitution he will have a choice either to go before the Industrial Court or the Administrative Tribunal constituted under the Administrative Tribunal's Act, 1985.[51] Speaking about the corresponding English statute, the Industrial Relations Act, 1971 LORD REID said, "It creates rights—but breaches of these rights are not torts—they are only unfair industrial practices. A person alleging an unfair industrial practice cannot bring an action: he can only make a complaint to an industrial tribunal."[52]

The Payment of Gratuity Act, 1972 is another Act which creates new rights and provides for a detailed machinery for enforcing these rights. The Act is a complete code and proceeding for recovery of gratuity due under the Act can be taken only under the Act and not under any general provision of law such as section 33C(2) of the Industrial Disputes Act, 1947.[53]

Another example is found in the Karnataka Land Reforms Act, 1962. The Act extinguishes the pre-existing rights of the land owners as also of those who were inducted into possession by them. Section 45 of the Act creates new rights in favour of those who were in personal cultivation to claim registration as tenants so as to continue to enjoy the occupancy rights as a tenant. The Act by section 48 constitutes a tribunal for registration of claims as tenant under section 45 and to decide if rival claims for tenancy rights are set up, as to who was the tenant in possession of the

---

49. *Chief Engineer, Hydel Project v. Ravinder Nath*, (2008) 2 SCC 350 : AIR 2008 SC 1315.

50. *Rajasthan State Road Transport Corporation v. Mohar Singh*, (2008) 5 SCC 542 paras 29, 30 : AIR 2008 SC 2553; *Rajasthan State Road Transport Corporation v. Bal Mukund Bairwa*, (2009) 4 SCC 299 paras 34 to 37 : (2009) 2 JT 423.

51. *Telecom Manager v. Keshab Deb*, (2008) 8 SCC 402 para 18 : 2008 7 JT 257.

52. *Post Office v. Union of Post Office Workers*, (1974) 1 All ER 229, (HL); **referred** in *West Midlands Co-operative Society Ltd. v. Tiptan*, (1986) 1 All ER 513, p. 518 : (1986) AC 536 (HL).

53. *State of Punjab v. Labour Court, Jullundur*, AIR 1979 SC 1981, pp. 1983, 1984 : (1980) 4 SCC 4. Gratuity due under a Contract of service can be recovered by a Civil Suit; *Sudhir Chandra Sarkar v. Tata Iron and Steel Co. Ltd.*, (1984) 3 SCC 369 : AIR 1984 SC 1064.

land prior to the date of vesting and entitled to be registered as tenant with the State Government. The decision of the Tribunal is made final. It was held that the civil courts' jurisdiction was impliedly excluded and a question whether the joint family or one of its members was the tenant fell within the exclusive jurisdiction of the Tribunal.[54] Similar view has been taken in respect of Inam Abolition Acts, 1956.[55]

Other examples of application of the principle third of the three classes of cases mentioned by WILLES, J. may be found in construction of statutes imposing taxes. The liability to pay any particular tax does not exist apart from the statute imposing the tax and the subject is normally bound to resort to the remedies provided in the statute for challenging any assessment of the tax made on him. It was therefore, held that an order of customs authorities passed under section 182 of the Sea Customs Act, 1878, and confirmed in appeal under section 188, was not open to challenge in civil court.[56] Similarly, in a case arising under the Punjab Municipal Act, 1811, where the dispute was as to rate of terminal tax payable on a particular commodity which depended upon the determination of the character of the commodity, it was held that the order of the Municipal Committee imposing the tax could not be challenged in civil court.[57] SUBBARAO, J., pointed out: "The liability to pay terminal tax is created by the Act and a remedy is given to a party aggrieved in the enforcement of that liability. Against the order of Municipal Committee levying terminal tax an appeal lies to the Deputy Commissioner and a reference to the High Court. Applying one of the principles stated *supra*, the party aggrieved can only pursue the remedy provided by the Act and he cannot file a civil suit in that regard."[58] Similar results have been reached in construing statutes

---

54. *Mudakappa v. Rudrappa*, AIR 1994 SC 1190, p. 1194 : 1994 (2) SCC 57. **See further** *Vankamamidi Venkata Subba Rao v. Chatlapalli Seetharamaratna*, AIR 1997 SC 3082, p. 3086 : (1997) 5 SCC 460 [*Patta* granted under A.P. Estate (Abolition and Conversion into Ryotwari) Act, 1948 cannot be challenged in civil court].

55. *Pushpagiri Math v. Kopparaju Veerbhadra Rao*, AIR 1996 SC 2225, p. 2226 : 1996 (9) SCC 202 (A case under A.P. Inam Abolition and Conversion into Ryotwari Act, 1956); *Thirumala Tirupati Devasthanams v. Thallappaka Ananthacharulu,* (2003) 8 SCC 134, p. 142 : AIR 2003 SC 3290, p. 3302. (But still no writ of prohibition can be issued before the issue of jurisdiction is decided by the trial court. Cases under the Tamil Nadu Act have taken a different view on the question of jurisdiction.) **But see** text and note 18, p. 855.

56. *Secretary of State v. Mask & Co.*, AIR 1940 PC 105, p. 110. Even in writ proceedings under Article 226 of the Constitution, the construction adopted by customs authorities of heads or entries of taxation is not interfered with unless it is perverse or grossly irrational; *Union of India v. Security and Finance (P) Ltd.*, AIR 1975 SC 2288 : (1976) 1 SCC 166.

57. *Firm Radhakishan v. Ludhiana Municipality*, AIR 1963 SC 1547 : 1964 (2) SCR 273.

58. *Ibid*, p. 1551.

imposing income-tax[59] and sales tax.[60] Even in the absence of express provision excluding civil courts' jurisdiction the imposition of a tax liability and creation of an effective machinery for deciding questions of law or fact arising in that connection, will, by necessary implication, bar the maintainability of a civil suit in respect of the said liability.[61] In a case arising out of section 341 of the U.K. Income-tax Act, 1952, it has been held that the right to an adjustment of tax liability by reference to loss conferred by the section, could be only enforced by resorting to the remedy indicated in the section, that is, by applying to General or Special Commissioners; and that the tax-payer could not directly approach the High Court to ask for a declaration.[62] But, there will be no exclusion if the action challenged is wholly outside the particular Statute.[63]

Statutes providing for election to representative bodies also fall within this class. It was observed by B.K. MUKHERJEA, J. that, "the right of seeking election and sitting in Parliament or in a State Legislature is a creature of the Constitution, and when the Constitution provides a special remedy for enforcing that right, no other remedy by ordinary action in a court of law is available to a person in regard to election disputes."[64]

---

59. *Raleigh Investment Co. Ltd. v. G.G. in Council*, AIR 1947 PC 78, and *Raja Ram Kumar Bhargava v. Union of India*, AIR 1988 SC 752 : 1988 (1) SCC 681.

60. *Firm of Illuri Subbayya Chetty & Sons v. State of Andhra Pradesh*, AIR 1964 SC 322 : (1964) 1 SCR 752. **See further** text and notes 51 to 56, pp. 838-839, and *Titaghur Paper Mills Co. Ltd. v. State of Orissa*, AIR 1983 SC 603, p. 607 : (1983) 3 SCC 433.

61. *State of Kerala v. Ramaswami*, AIR 1966 SC 1738, pp. 1740, 1741 : 1966 (3) SCR 582.

62. *Argosam Finance Co. Ltd. v. Oxby*, (1964) 1 All ER 791, p. 796.

63. **See** text and notes 41 to 59, pp. 837-841, *infra*.

64. *Durgashanker v. Raghuraj Singh*, AIR 1954 SC 520, p. 522 : 1955 (1) SCR 267. **Further see** *N.P. Ponnuswamy v. Returning Officer*, AIR 1952 SC 64, p. 69 : 1952 SCR 218; *N.B. Khare v. Election Commission*, AIR 1958 SC 139, p. 140 : 1958 SCR 648; *Mohinder Singh Gill v. Chief Election Commissioner*, AIR 1978 SC 851 : (1978) 1 SCC 405; *Election Commission of India v. Ashok Kumar*, AIR 2000 SC 2977 : (2000) 8 SCC 216; *Manda Jagannath v. K.S. Rathnam*, AIR 2004 SC 3600 : (2004) 7 SCC 492. For election to local bodies; **see** *Nanhoomal v. Hiramal*, AIR 1975 SC 2140, p. 2143 : (1976) 3 SCC 211; *S.T. Muthusami v. K. Natrajan*, AIR 1988 SC 616 : (1988) 1 SCC 572; *Boddula Krishnaiah v. State Election Commissioner*, AIR 1996 SC 1595, pp. 1597, 1598 : (1996) 3 SCC 416; *Anugraha Narain Singh v. State of Uttar Pradesh*, 1996 (7) Scale 56 : 1996 (6) SCC 303; *Javed v. State of Haryana*, (2003) 8 SCC 369. For election to universities **see** *Gujarat University v. N.U. Rajguru*, AIR 1988 SC 66 : 1987 Supp SCC 512. For election to bar councils, **see** *K.K. Shrivastava v. Bhupendra Kumar*, AIR 1977 SC 1703 : 1977 (2) SCC 494. For election to a co-operative society, **see** *Shri Sant Sadguru Janardan Swami (Moingiri Maharaj) Sahkari Dugdh Utpadan Sanstha v. State of Maharashtra*, AIR 2001 SC 3982 : (2001) 8 SCC 509; For election under the Delhi Sikh Gurdwara Act, **see** Sikh Gurdwara Management Committee, (2006) 8 SCC 487 (paras 18 and 29). **See also** text and notes 53 and 54, p. 865.

It is not, however, correct to say that the Legislature takes away civil court's jurisdiction only when a new right is created by statute, and a tribunal is set up for determination of that right, for by use of appropriate words jurisdiction may be excluded in other cases also.[65]

Jurisdiction of civil courts can not only be taken away by statutes enacted by the Legislature, but may also be barred by directions issued by the Supreme Court. Relying on the words of BENJAMIN CARDOZO, who said that the power to declare the law carries with it the power and, within limits, the duty to make law when none exists, a three Judge Bench of the Supreme Court held that Directions 1 to 15 issued by the Court in *Madhuri Patil v. Commissioner, Tribal Development,*[66] in exercise of power under Articles 142 and 32 of the Constitution, are valid and laudable, as they were made to fill the vacuum in the absence of any legislation to ensure that only genuine Scheduled Caste and Scheduled Tribe candidates secured the benefits of reservation, and that bogus candidates were kept out. By issuing such directions, the Court was not taking over the functions of the Legislature but merely filling up the vacuum till the Legislature chose to make the appropriate law. Direction 12 issued by the Court states that no suit before a civil court or other proceedings before any other authority should lie against the orders of the Scrutiny Committee. In this context, the Court held that where it has, by a judgment, framed a Scheme, it can also, by that very Scheme, bar cognizance of civil suits challenging the decision of the Scrutiny Committee as per section 9 of the CPC, and say that orders of the Srutiny Committee should be challenged only before the High Court under Article 226 of the Constitution. The Court, however, held that the right of appeal to a Division Bench, made available to a party to a Writ Petition, either under a statute or Letters Patent, cannot be taken away by a judicial order. Accordingly, the portion of Direction 13, which states that no further appeal from the order of the Single Judge deciding the Writ Petition would lie to the Division Bench of the High Court, was overruled.[67]

(c) Cases of breach of statutory duties

Whether a statutory duty gives rise to a private law cause of action is a question of construction of the relevant statute.[68] There is no universal rule by reference to which the question of maintainability of a civil action can infallibly be answered. A number of indicators to solve the question can, however, be deduced from the decided cases which are considered below.

---

65. *Akbar Khan v. Union of India*, AIR 1962 SC 70, p. 72 : 1962 (1) SCR 779.
66. (1994) 6 SCC 241.
67. *Dayaram v. Sudhir Batham & Ors.*, (2012) 1 SCC 333, pp. 348 to 357.
68. *Hague v. Deputy Governor of Parkhurst Prison*, (1991) 3 All ER 733, pp. 741, 750 (HL).

In *Doe d. Bishop of Rochester v. Bridges,*[69] LORD TENTERDEN, C.J. said: "When an Act creates an obligation and enforces the performance in a specified manner, we take it to be a general rule that performance cannot be enforced in any other manner. If an obligation is created but no mode of enforcing its performance is ordained, the common law may, in general find a mode suited to the particular nature of the case."[70] The above passage was approved by the House of Lords in *Pasmore v. Oswaldtwistle Urban District Council,*[71] where the question was as to maintainability of an action for *mandamus* for enforcing the statutory duty of a local authority under section 15 of the Public Health Act, 1875, to provide sufficient number of sewers for draining their district. A remedy was provided under section 299 of the Act for enforcing the statutory duty by a complaint to the local Government Board, and, it was, therefore, held that there was no remedy outside the Act. In the last-mentioned case it was pointed out that the obligation was created by the statute and by the statute alone which contained a specified remedy for enforcement of the obligation; and LORD HALSBURY, L.C. observed: "The principle that where a specific remedy is given, it thereby deprives the person who insists upon a remedy of any other form of remedy than that given by the statute, is one which is very familiar, and which runs through the law."[72] This principle has been accepted by the Supreme Court.[73]

Even the provision of a penalty, for breach of a statutory duty, or fine or imprisonment contained in a statute creating the duty, may be regarded as the only manner of enforcing the duty. In *Cutler v. Wandsworth Stadium Ltd.,*[74] the plaintiff, a book-maker, brought an action against the occupiers of a licensed dog racing track, for breach of their statutory duty under section 11(2) of the Betting and Lotteries Act, 1934; and to secure that space was available on the track for book-making purposes. The Act by section 10 imposes substantial penalties on summary conviction, and on conviction on indictment. The House of Lords on a construction of the Act held that the obligation imposed by section 11(2) on the occupier of a track was intended for the benefit of the public and not for the benefit of the book-maker; and that the statutory duty was enforceable only by recourse to the criminal proceedings provided under the Act, and not by a civil action.[75]

---

69. (1831) 1 B & AD 847, 859: 109 ER 1001, p. 1006.
70. *Ibid.*
71. (1898) AC 387 : (1895-99) All ER Rep 191 (HL).
72. *Ibid,* p. 193 of (1895-99) All ER Rep.
73. *Premier Automobiles Ltd. v. Kamalakar Shantaram,* AIR 1975 SC 2238, pp. 2244, 2245 : (1976) 1 SCC 496; *Rohtas Industries Ltd. v. Rohtas Industries Staff Union,* AIR 1976 SC 425, p. 435 : (1976) 2 SCC 82. **See** text and notes 46, 47, *supra.*
74. (1949) 1 All ER 544 : 1949 AC 398 (HL).
75. *Ibid.*

The House of Lords again accepted the principle of LORD TENTERDEN'S dictum in *Doe d. Rochester's* case,[76] which was approved earlier in *Pasmore's* case.[77] Adverting to the argument that the principle had no application where the statutory remedy was by way of criminal proceedings, LORD SIMONDS said: "I see no ground for this distinction. The implication is, if anything in the opposite direction for the sanction of criminal proceedings emphasises that this statutory obligation, like many others which the Act contains, is imposed for the public benefit and that the breach of it is a public, not a private wrong."[78] On the same point LORD DU PARCQ observed: "I do not agree with the submission of the counsel for the appellant that it is heretical to regard criminal proceedings which may be followed by fine and imprisonment as a specified manner of enforcing a duty. I think that it is both orthodox and right so to regard them."[79] In *Ten Chye Choo v. Chang Kew Moi,*[80] the question was whether a breach of Rule 94 of the Motor Vehicles (Construction and Use) Rules, 1959, (Malaysia) gave rise to a cause of action in favour of an injured person. The rule provided: 'The condition of any Motor Vehicle used on a road and all its parts and accessories shall at all times be such that no danger is caused to any person on the vehicle or on a road'. The rules including Rule 94 were made under a Road Traffic Ordinance, which provided certain penalties for non-observance of the rules without lawful excuse. On account of some latent defect a motor taxi became involved in an accident resulting in injuries to certain persons. The evidence negatived any negligence of the driver or the owner and the question arose whether the injured persons could claim damages for breach of statutory duty imposed by Rule 94. It was held after adverting to the principles laid down in *Cutler's* case[81] that the rule did not impose any duty in favour of individuals who had no right of action. In *Lonrho Ltd. v. Shell Petroleum Co. Ltd.*[82] the House of Lords had to consider a claim for damages for breach of statutory sanctions to

76. **See** text and note 67, *supra.*

77. **See** text and notes 69 and 71, *supra.*

78. *Cutler v. Wandsworth Stadium Ltd.*, (1949) 1 All ER 544, p. 548 : 1949 AC 398 (HL).

79. *Ibid*, p. 550.

80. (1970) 1 All ER 266 (PC). **See further** *Phillips v. Britannia Hygienic Laundry Co. Ltd.*, (1923) All ER Rep 127 (CA), [regarding Locomotive & Highways Act, 1896 and Motor Cars (Use and Construction) Order, 1904]; *Badham v. Lambs Ltd.*, (1945) 2 All ER 295 [regarding Road Traffic Act, 1930 and Motor Vehicles (Construction and Use) Regulations, 1930]; *Watt v. Kesteven County Council*, (1954) 3 All ER 441, (regarding Education Act, 1944); *Square v. Model Farm Dairies Ltd.*, (1939) 1 All ER 259 (CA) (regarding Food and Drugs Adulteration Act, 1928); *Issa v. Hackney London Borough Council*, (1997) 1 All ER 999 : (1997) 1 WLR 956 : (1997) Env. LR 157 (CA) (regarding Public Health Act, 1936).

81. (1949) 1 All ER 544 : 1949 AC 398 (HL).

82. (1981) 2 All ER 456 : (1981) 3 WLR 33 (HL).

stop supply and delivery of oil to Southern Rhodesia which was punishable as a criminal offence. It was held, after referring to *Cutler v. Wandsworth Stadium Ltd.*,[83] *Doe d. Bishop of Rochester v. Bridges*[84] and *Black v. Fife Coal Co. Ltd.*,[85] that the sanctions could not be said to be imposed for the benefit or protection of any particular class of persons or to create a public right to be enjoyed by the subjects of the Crown and, therefore, the violation of the sanctions could not give rise to any claim for damages.

The general principle discussed above, that the remedy provided by the Act which creates an obligation is exclusive, is not without exception. In *Pasmore's* case[86] itself, LORD MACNAGHTEN recognised exceptions and observed: "Whether the general rule is to prevail, or an exception to the general rule is to be admitted in any particular case, must depend on the scope and language of the Act and consideration of policy and convenience." Adverting to this matter, ATKINS, L.J. has pointed out: "I conceive the rule to be that when a statute imposes a duty of commission or omission upon an individual, the question whether a person aggrieved by a breach of the duty has a right of action depends upon the intention of the statute. Was it intended that a duty should be owed to the individual aggrieved as well as to the State; or is it a public duty only? That depends upon the construction of the statute as a whole and the circumstances in which it was made and to which it relates. One of the matters to be taken into consideration is this: Does the statute on the face of it contain a reference to a remedy for the breach of it? If so, it would *prima facie* be the only remedy, but that is not conclusive. One must still look to the intention of the Legislature to be derived from the words used, and one may come to the conclusion that, although the statute creates a duty and imposes a penalty for the breach of that duty, it may still intend that the duty may be owed to individuals."[87] In *Lonrho Ltd. v. Shell Petroleum Co. Ltd.*,[88] the House of Lords pointed out two exceptions to the general rule that where the Act prescribes criminal prosecution as the only manner of enforcing performance of the statutory obligation, other modes of enforcement are ruled out. The first exception is where on the construction of the Act it is apparent that the obligation or prohibition was imposed for the benefit or protection of particular class of persons as in the case of Factories Acts

---

83. **See** note 79, *supra*.
84. **See** note 69, *supra*.
85. **See** note 92, *infra*.
86. (1895-99) All ER Rep 191 (HL). **See also** text and notes 71 and 72, *supra*.
87. *Phillips v. Britannia Hygienic Laundry Co. Ltd.*, (1923) All ER Rep 127, p. 132. **See further** *London and Harrogate Societies Ltd. v. Pitts*, (1976) 3 All ER 809, p. 813 (CA).
88. (1981) 2 All ER 456, p. 461 : (1981) 3 WLR 33 (HL).

and similar legislation. The second exception is where the statute creates a public right and a particular member of the public suffers what may be described as particular, direct and substantial damage other than and different from that which was common to all the rest of the public. The first exception will, however, not give a cause of action for breach of statutory duty when the nature of the statutory obligation or prohibition is not such that a breach of it would be likely to cause a member of the class, for whose benefit or protection it was imposed, either personal injury, injury to property or economic loss.[89]

A statute of the type, where a penalty clause was held as not depriving a person injured to bring a civil action, was considered by the Court of Appeal in *Groves v. Lord Wimborne*.[90] The statute there considered was the Factory and Workshop Act, 1878, which by section 5, imposed on the occupier of a factory a duty of securely fencing dangerous machinery in the factory, and in the event of any person being injured in consequence of a breach of this duty the Act made provision by section 82 that the occupier was to be liable to a fine not exceeding one hundred pounds, and the whole or part of it could be applied for the benefit of the injured person. In an action for damages brought by a workman, who suffered personal injuries because of breach of the statutory duty to fence certain machinery, the Court of Appeal held that the action was maintainable and the remedy provided in the statute was not exclusive.[91]

The principle was considered by the House of Lords in *Black v. Fife Coal Co. Ltd.*,[92] in relation to the Coal Mines Regulation Act, 1887, which imposed on the mine owners the duty to make due provision for the safety of workmen in the mines. LORD KINNEAR in that case observed: "There is no reasonable ground for maintaining that a proceeding by way of penalty is the only remedy by the statute. We are to consider the scope and purpose of the statute and in particular for whose benefit it is intended. Now the object of the present statute is plain. It was intended to compel mine owners to make due provision for the safety of the men working in their mines and the persons, for whose benefit all these rules are to be enforced, are the persons exposed to danger. But when a duty of this kind is imposed for the benefit of particular persons there arises at common law a correlative

---

89. *Pickering v. Liverpool Daily Post and Echo Newspapers Plc.*, (1991) 2 WLR 513, p. 524 : (1991) 2 AC 370 : (1991) 2 All ER 622 (HL).

90. (1898) 2 QB 402 : (1895-99) All ER Rep 147 (CA); **see** the judgment of VAUGHAM WILLIAMS, L.J., pp. 152, 153. Penal legislation may be relied upon for fashioning new tort duties. **See** *Monk v. Warbey*, (1935) 1 KB 75 and other cases discussed in 'Rescuers and good samaritans' 34 Modern Law Review 241, pp. 243-49.

91. *Ibid.*

92. (1912) AC 149 (HL).

right in those persons who may be injured by its contravention. Therefore, I think, it is quite impossible to hold that penalty clause detracts in any way from the *prima facie* right of persons for whose benefit the statutory enactment has been passed to enforce the civil liability."[1] This passage from the judgment of LORD KINNEAR was considered in *Cutler's* case[2] and LORD NORMAND in explaining the principle said: "If there is a penalty clause the right to a civil action must be established by a consideration of the scope and purpose of the statute as a whole. The inference, that there is a concurrent right of civil action, is easily drawn when the predominant purpose is manifestly the protection of a class of workmen by imposing on their employers the duty of taking special measures to secure their safety. The penalties provided by the Act apply when a breach of the duty occurs but each workman has a right to sue for damages if he is injured in consequence of the breach."[3] Even when a statute creates an offence for failure to perform a defined duty imposed for the benefit of a class of persons, it may not be inferred that the contemplated beneficiaries would have a right of action for enforcement of the duty unless it could be shown that in the absence of an implied remedy by civil action under the statute, they would be without any effective remedy under the general law for the harm suffered by them from failure to perform the duty.[4] So harassment of a tenant made punishable under section 30 of the Rent Act, 1965 was construed as not implying a civil remedy, for a tenant can under the general law sue for damages for breach of the covenant for quiet enjoyment.[5]

Even if a particular provision apparently protected certain individuals and no penalty was provided for breach thereof, it does not necessarily follow that an action for breach of statutory duty will lie and the question is one of ascertaining the intention of the Legislature.[6] Thus, it was held that when a prisoner was segregated in violation of the prison rules made under the Prisons Act, 1952, he had no cause of action for claiming damages for breach of statutory duty.[7] Similarly, in a statute imposing duty on employers to give employees written particulars of terms of employment and

1. *Ibid*, p. 165.
2. *Cutler v. Wandsworth Stadium Ltd.*, (1949) 1 All ER 544 : 1949 AC 398 (HL).
3. *Ibid*, p. 551. **See further** *Read v. Croydon Corporation*, (1938) 4 All ER 631, (regarding Water Works Clauses Act, 1847); *Lavender v. Diamints Ltd.*, (1949) 1 All ER 532 (CA) (regarding Factories Act, 1937); *Solomons v. Gertzenstein Ltd.*, (1954) 2 All ER 625 (regarding London Building Act, 1939).
4. *McCall v. Abelesz*, (1976) 1 All ER 727, p. 735 (CA).
5. *Ibid*.
6. *Hague v. Deputy Governor of Parkhurst Prison*, (1991) 3 All ER 733, pp. 741, 750 (HL); *Pickering v. Liverpool Daily Post and Echo Newspaper Plc.*, (1991) 2 WLR 513, p. 523 : (1991) 2 AC 370 (HL).
7. *Hague v. Deputy Governor of Parkhurst Prison, supra*.

providing for reference to industrial tribunal for failure of the employer to give written particulars, no civil right of action sounding in damages was inferred.[8] The statutory provisions considered in these cases were in reality for establishing a regulatory system or a scheme of social welfare for the benefit of the public at large and not for the benefit of those who fell within the area of activity that was regulated.[9]

The principles stated above were applied in *O'Rourke v. Camden London Borough Council*[10] and it was held that section 63 of the Housing Act, 1985 designed to provide accommodation for homeless persons did not give rise to a cause of action for damages in private law. The factors that were taken into account in reaching the conclusion that Parliament did not intend that a breach of the duty to provide accomodation to homeless was actionable in tort were: (i) The duty was enforceable in public law by individual homeless persons; (ii) The Act was a scheme of social welfare on grounds of public policy and public interest to confer benefits at the public expense not only for the benefit of homeless persons but the society in general; and (iii) The existence of the duty depended on the housing authority's judgment and discretion.[11]

A distinction must also be drawn between a public law remedy of judicial review including declaration and injunction for enforcing due performance of a statutory duty and a private law remedy by way of a suit for damages.[12] The breach of a public law right does not by itself give rise to a claim for damages.[13] Further, mere careless exercise of statutory powers or duties does not furnish a cause of action for damages and the plaintiff has to show that circumstances are such as to raise a duty of care at common law.[14] The principles as to when mere breach of a statutory duty causing damage will give rise to a private law claim for damages were restated by the House of Lords[15] as follows: "The basic proposition is that in the ordinary case a breach of statutory duty does not, by itself, give rise to any private law cause of action. However, a private law cause of action will

---

8. *Scally v. Southern Health and Social Services Board*, (1991) 4 All ER 563 : (1992) 1 AC 294 : (1991) 3 WLR 778 (HL).

9. *X (minors) v. Bedfordshire County Council*, (1995) 3 All ER 353, pp. 364, 365 (HL).

10. (1997) 3 All ER 23 : (1997) 3 WLR 86 (HL).

11. *Ibid*, p. 26.

12. *X (minors) v. Bedfordshire County Council*, (1995) 3 All ER 353, p. 363 : (1995) 2 AC 633 : (1995) 3 WLR 152 (HL).

13. *Ibid*.

14. *Ibid*, pp. 362, 367 (These are cases where the act if done without statutory authority will amount to a tort in common law and so if the statutory power is negligently exercised, the protection is lost. **See** text and notes 36 to 40, pp. 835, 836).

15. *Ibid*, pp. 364, 365.

arise if it can be shown, as a matter of construction of the statute, that the statutory duty was imposed for the protection of a limited class of the public and that Parliament intended to confer on members of that class a private right of action for breach of the duty. There is no general rule by reference to which it can be decided whether a statute does create such a right of action but there are a number of indicators. If the statute provides no other remedy for its breach and the Parliamentary intention to protect a limited class is shown, that indicates that there may be a private right of action since otherwise there is no method of securing the protection the statute was intended to confer. If the statute does provide some other means of enforcing the duty that will normally indicate that the statutory right was intended to be enforceable by those means and not by private right of action: However, the mere existence of some other statutory remedy is not necessarily decisive. It is still possible to show that on the true construction of the statute the protected class was intended by Parliament to have a private remedy. Thus the specific duties imposed on employers in relation to factory premises are enforceable by an action for damages, notwithstanding the imposition by the statutes of criminal penalties for any breach: The cases where a private right of action for breach of statutory duty have been held to arise are all cases in which the statutory duty has been very limited and specific as opposed to general administrative functions imposed on public bodies and involving the exercise of administrative discretions." In this case it was held that a local education authority's obligations to provide sufficient schools for pupils within its area and to have regard to the need for securing special treatment for children in need of such treatment under the Education Acts, 1944 and 1981 could give rise to public law claims but their was no corresponding private law right to damages for breach of statutory duty.[16] But a local education authority could be vicariously liable for the negligence of its employee, *viz.*, educational psychologist because of whose mistake there was failure to diagnose a congenital condition of a child and consequent failure to provide special treatment and appropriate education.[17] The case of X (minors)[18] was followed in *Cullen v. Chief Constable of the Royal Ulster Constabulary,*[19] in holding that the duty under Section 15 of the Northern Ireland (Emergency Provisions) Act, 1987 to allow a person in custody access to a solicitor was a *quasi* constitutional right imposed for the benefit of the public at large and not for the protection of a particular class of individuals and denial of that right *by itself* (*i.e.*, where it did not cause or prolong unlawful detention) was incapable of causing loss or injury of a kind for

16. *Ibid.*
17. *Phelps v. London Borough of Hillington,* (2000) 4 All ER 504 (HL).
18. **See** note 9, *supra.*
19. (2004) 2 All ER 237 (HL).

which the law normally awarded damages. The remedy for breach of this public law right was judicial review.

(d) Omission to exercise statutory power

It has been seen that whether a statutory duty gives rise to a private law cause of action is a question of construction of the relevant statute. Similarly, the question whether omission to exercise a statutory power gives rise to a private law cause of action is also one of construction of the statute concerned as it requires discerning the policy of the statute whether it confers a right to compensation on persons who suffer loss as a result of non-exercise of the power. Subject to exceptional cases, the normal rule is that an omission by a public authority to exercise a statutory power conferred for benefit of the public does not give rise to breach of duty sounding in damages.[20] In *Stovin v. Wise*,[21] a motor accident took place at a road junction partly because the view was obstructed by an earth bank adjacent to the road. Although the local highway authority had statutory power under sections 41 and 79 of the Highways Act, 1980, which conferred a discretion for removal of earth bank, it had taken no steps in that direction. The House of Lords held that there was no common law duty on the authority to exercise the power and omission to exercise it did not give rise to a claim for damages in negligence. It was laid down that minimum preconditions for basing a duty of care upon the existence of statutory power in respect of an omission to exercise the power, if it could be done at all, were: (i) that in the circumstances it would have been irrational for the authority not to have exercised the power, so that in effect there was a public law duty to act and (ii) that there were exceptional grounds to hold that the policy of the statute conferred a right to compensation on persons who suffered loss if the power was not exercised.[22]

The above preconditions, laid down by the House of Lords, for holding a public authority liable in private law for omission to exercise a statutory power were accepted by the Supreme Court in *Union of India v. United India Insurance Co. Ltd.*,[23] though the court in that case held the Union of India liable in negligence and also for omission to exercise the power under section 13 of the Railways Act, 1980 which provides that the Central Government 'may require' a railway administration to erect fences, screen, gates etc. In that case an express train had collided with a passenger bus at an unmanned level crossing and the Union of India owning the railway

20. *East Suffolk Catchment Board v. Kent,* (1940) 4 All ER 527 : 1941 AC 74 (HL).
21. (1996) 3 All ER 801 : 1996 AC 923 : (1996) 3 WLR 388 (HL).
22. *Ibid*, p. 828.
23. AIR 1998 SC 640, pp. 651, 654 : 1997 (8) SCC 683.

was held guilty of negligence being in breach of its common law duty for failing to convert the unmanned level crossing into a manned level crossing having regard to the volume of traffic and in not providing proper signboard for warning the road traffic.[24] It was, therefore, unnecessary to go into the question whether the Union of India was also liable for omission to exercise the statutory power under section 13. Yet the court found the Union of India liable for the omission holding that the two preconditions laid down in *Stovin v. Wise,* were satisfied basing its decision on the controversial doctrine of 'general reliance' which has been applied in some Australian cases but has had no support in English law.[25] The doctrine now stands rejected even in Australia.[26] It is submitted that when there existed a corresponding common law duty, the 'general reliance' of those likely to be affected would be that the railway administration will not be in breach of that duty and not necessarily on the exercise of the statutory power under section 13. For the same reason, it is submitted, it was neither irrational for the Central Government not to exercise the power under section 13 nor can it be said that the policy of section 13 was to confer a right to compensation, in addition to the already existing right in common law, on failure to exercise the power. This was not a case where, unless a right to compensation for omission to exercise the statutory power was inferred, the person injured was remedy less under the common law. It is, therefore, reasonably possible to say that the two preconditions required for holding the Union of India liable for omission to exercise the power under section 13 were not satisfied in this case.

---

24. *Ibid*, p. 649.

25. *Capital and Counties plc v. Hampshire County Council*, (1997) 2 All ER 865, pp. 876, 877 : 1997 QB 1004 : (1997) 3 WLR 331 (CA). This case also shows that the doctrine though **referred** was not accepted in *Stovin v. Wise, supra*.

26. *Pyrenees Shire Council v. Day* (1998) 72 ALJR 152 (Aust), (Brennan C.J., Gummow and Kirby JJ.) As observed by Brennan C.J., "If community expectation that a statutory power will be exercised were to be adopted as a criterion of a duty to exercise the power it would displace the criterion of legislative intention.—the appropriate criterion is legislative intention."(p. 158). Scott Wotherspoon of Monash University Australia in an article published in (2009) 83 ALJ 331 p. 343 recommends that "a four-step" analysis should be undertaken in determining the duty question in relation to public authorities: (1) did the public authority have a statutory power to prevent the harm which eventuated? (2) should the authority have foreseen the likelihood of harm if it failed to exercise the power? (3) was the failure to exercise the power or consider its exercise, *ultra vires* or irrational in a public law sense? and (4) is the putative duty of care inconsistent with the performance of the authority of its statutory function or otherwise contrary to Parliament's intention?" The author argues that this analysis "may assist in conferring coherence between a public authority's public law obligations to act in particular circumstances and its private law obligations to pay damages when its failure to act has caused harm."

2. THE EXTENT OF EXCLUSION

(a) Construction of exclusionary clauses

The extent of exclusion will largely depend upon a construction of the provision enacted for that purpose but in case of doubt it is a familiar approach to correlate the section excluding civil court's jurisdiction with other sections in the same statute providing special remedies,[27] for a contrary construction would lead to a vacuum.[28] Absence of a provision to enable an authority or tribunal for holding an inquiry on a particular question is indicative that jurisdiction of civil courts on that question is not excluded; whereas the very provision setting up hierarchy of judicial tribunals for the determination of a question, is sufficient in most cases for inferring that the jurisdiction of the civil courts to try the same matter is barred.[29] But when with the object of speedy adjudication of certain matters which are widely defined, jurisdiction is conferred on tribunals or special courts and jurisdiction of normal courts is excluded, the wide language used cannot be narrowly construed,[30] and it is now a well established principle that the jurisdiction of a court created specially for reduction of disputes of

---

27. **See** cases discussed in text and notes 12 to 22, pp. 811-814, *supra*, as illustrations of this principle. **See further** *Gurudwara Prabandhak v. Shiv Ratan Dev*, AIR 1955 SC 576 : 55 Punj 1108; *Raichand v. Union of India*, AIR 1964 SC 1268 : 1964 (5) SCR 148. The question of adequacy or sufficiency of remedies provided in the Act is of great importance where exclusion is pleaded as a matter of necessary implication: *Kamala Mills v. State of Bombay*, AIR 1965 SC 1942, p. 1950 : (1966) 1 SCR 64; *Pabbojan Tea Co. v. D.C., Lakhimpur*, AIR 1968 SC 271, p. 277 : 1968 (1) SCR 260; *Dhulabhai v. State of M.P.*, AIR 1969 SC 78 : (1968) 3 SCR 662; *Bata Shoe Co. Ltd. v. Jabalpur Corporation*, AIR 1977 SC 955, pp. 961, 962 : (1977) 2 SCC 256; *Syed Mohammed Baquir El Edroos v. State of Gujarat*, AIR 1981 SC 2016, p. 2019 : (1981) 4 SCC 383; *State of Andhra Pradesh v. Manjeti Laxmi Kantha Rao,* AIR 2000 SC 2220, p. 2221 : (2000) 3 SCC 689; *Dhruv Green Fields Ltd. v. Hukum Singh,* AIR 2002 SC 2841, p. 2844 : (2002) 6 SCC 416.

N.B.—In some cases a statute may provide for a suit in a Civil Court only after the remedies under the statute are exhausted; **see** for example *State of Madras v. Melamatam*, AIR 1965 SC 1570, p. 1573 : (1966) 2 MLJ (SC) 13; *Babu Khan v. Nazim Khan,* AIR 2001 SC 1740, p. 1745 : (2001) 5 SCC 375. The exclusion sometimes is for a limited period within which recourse may be taken to the special remedy and after expiry of that period civil suit can be filed: *Mohd. Mahmood v. Tikaram Das*, AIR 1966 SC 210, pp. 211, 212 : 1966 (1) SCR 128 as **explained** in *Nand Kishore v. Ram Kishan*, AIR 1967 SC 1196, p. 1200 : 1967 (1) SCR 167.

28. *Sri Vedagiri Lakshmi Narasimha Swami Temple v. Pattabhirami*, AIR 1967 SC 781, pp. 785, 786 : 1967 (1) SCR 280.

29. *Desika Charyulu v. State of A.P.*, AIR 1964 SC 806, pp. 811, 816 : (1964) 1 LLJ 9.

30. *United Bank of India v. Debt Recovery Tribunal,* JT 1999 (2) SC 574, pp. 578, 580 : AIR 1999 SC 1381, p. 1385 : (1999) 4 SCC 69 [Section 2(g) of the Recovery of Debts due to Banks and Financial Institutions Act, 1993 which defines 'debt' construed to be of "the widest amplitude".]

certain kinds should be construed liberally.[31] Further, when jurisdiction of civil courts on a particular matter is excluded by transferring that jurisdiction from civil courts to tribunals or authorities, it is presumed that such tribunals or authorities can draw upon the principles of procedure in civil procedure code, though not expressly made applicable, to ensure fair procedure and just decision unless such principles are inconsistent with the provisions of the Act constituting them.[32]

Even in cases where jurisdiction is excluded by use of *prima facie* comprehensive language, it is open to civil courts which are courts of general jurisdiction to decide whether a court, or tribunal or authority having limited jurisdiction, has acted in excess of its statutory powers.[33] In other words, civil courts can interfere when the order of the tribunal or authority is really not an order under the Act conferring special jurisdiction but is a nullity.[34]

But on matters on which jurisdiction of the civil court is excluded, neither consent of the parties nor an order of the special tribunal which has jurisdiction to decide those matters, can confer jurisdiction on the civil court.[35]

Section 10 of the Indian Railways Act, 1890, provided that a railway administration shall do as little damage as possible in exercise of its powers for construction and maintenance of work, and compensation shall be paid for any damage caused by the exercise thereof and that 'a suit shall not lie to recover such compensation; but in case of dispute the amount thereof shall on an application to the Collector, be determined and paid in accordance with the provisions of the Land Acquisition Act, 1894'. In a

---

31. *K.A. Abdul Jaleel v. T.A. Shahida*, (2003) 4 SCC 166, p. 170 : AIR 2003 SC 2525, p. 2527 [In explanation (c) to section 7 of the Family Courts Act, 1984 the words suit or proceeding between parties to a marriage with respect to the property of the parties or either of them construed to include disputes between divorced parties].

32. *Rajasthan State Road Transport Corporation v. Poonam Pahwa*, AIR 1997 SC 2951, pp. 2958, 2959 : 1997 (6) SCC 100.

33. *Secretary of State v. Mask & Co.*, AIR 1940 PC 105, p. 110; *Emperor v. Shibnath Banerjee*, AIR 1945 PC 156, p. 161; *Bombay Province v. Hormusji*, AIR 1947 PC 200, p. 203; *Mohmmad Din v. Imamdin*, AIR 1948 PC 33, p. 34; *Firm Radhakishan v. Ludhiana Municipality*, AIR 1963 SC 1547, p. 1551 : 1964 (2) SCR 273; *Firm of Illuri Subbayya Chetty & Sons v. State of A.P.*, AIR 1964 SC 322, pp. 324, 325: 1964 (1) SCR 752; *Laxman v. State of Bombay*, AIR 1964 SC 436, p. 443; *Desika Charyulu v. State of A.P.*, AIR 1964 SC 806 : (1964) 1 LLJ 9.

34. *Anisminic Ltd. v. Foreign Compensation Commission*, (1969) 1 All ER 208 : (1969) 2 AC 147 : (1969) 2 WLR 163 (HL); *Union of India v. Tarachand Gupta & Bros.*, AIR 1971 SC 1558 : (1971) 1 SCC 486; *Bhupendra Singh v. G.K. Umath*, AIR 1970 MP 91, pp. 95, 98. **See further** title 2(b) cases of nullity, pp. 848 to 860.

35. *Ledgard v. Bull*, ILR 9 All 191, p. 203 (PC); *B.R. Reddy v. Addl. Custodian of Evacuee Property*, AIR 1966 SC 1438 : 1966 (3) SCR 214.

suit brought by a person claiming damages for injury caused by negligence of a railway administration in construction of certain works, it was contended that the suit was barred by section 10 of the Railways Act. This contention was negatived on the ground that the aforesaid provision was applicable only when the railway administration had not exceeded or abused its powers, and was not guilty of negligence.[36] LORD MACNAGHTEN in delivering the judgment of the Board said: "It has been determined over and over again that if a person or body of persons having statutory authority for the construction of works exceed or abuses the powers conferred by the Legislature, the remedy of a person injured in consequence is by action or suit, and not by a proceeding for compensation under the statute which has been so transgressed. Powers of this sort are to be exercised with ordinary care and skill, and with some regard to property and rights of others. They are granted on the condition sometimes expressed and sometimes understood—expressed in the Act of 1890, but if not expressed always understood that the undertakers shall do as little damage as possible in the exercise of their statutory powers."[37] In an earlier Privy Council case,[38] it has been pointed out that where a public body, acting in execution of a public trust and for a public benefit does an act which, it is authorised by law to do, and does it in a proper manner, though the act so done works a special injury to a particular individual the individual injured cannot maintain an action and he is without a remedy unless remedy is provided by the statute. But the position is different when the power is exercised 'arbitrarily, carelessly or oppressively' and when an action is brought in such cases, LORD MACNAGHTEN said: "In a word, the only question is: Has the power been exceeded? Abuse is only one form of excess."[39] In HALSBURY'S Laws of England the legal position is summed up as follows: "It is the duty of persons upon whom statutory powers are conferred to keep strictly within those powers. If such persons act in excess of their powers, they are to the extent to which they exceed their powers, deprived of any protection conferred upon them by the statute in question, and will be subject to the ordinary remedies existing at common law. An injunction may be granted to restrain an act in excess of statutory powers and a person injured by such an act may be entitled to recover damages from the persons purporting to exercise the power."[40]

---

36. *Gaekwar Sarkar of Baroda v. Gandhi Kachrabhai*, (1903) ILR 27 Bom 344 (PC).

37. *Ibid*, p. 352.

38. *East Fremantle Corporation v. Annois*, (1900-03) All ER Rep 73 : 1902 AC 213 (PC).

39. *Ibid*, p. 76.

40. HALSBURY'S Laws of England, 3rd Edition, Vol. 30, pp. 686, 687. **See further** *Gulf Oil Refining Ltd.*, (1981) 1 All ER 353 (HL); *Wildtree Holds Ltd. v. Harrow London Borough Council,* (2000) 3 All ER 289, pp. 294, 295 (HL).

The question was considered in relation to municipal taxation in *Firm Radhakishan v. Ludhiana Municipality*.[41] After referring to the Privy Council decisions noticed above,[42] SUBBARAO, J. observed: "A suit in civil court will always lie to question the order of a tribunal created by a statute, even if its order is, expressly or by necessary implication, made final, if the said tribunal abuses its power or does not act under the Act but in violation of its provisions."[43] In the last-mentioned case,[44] it was held that an assessment of terminal tax, which was questioned on the ground that the municipality applied a wrong rate of tax by wrongly determining the character of taxable commodity, was not open to challenge in the civil court; but it was pointed out that if a municipality levied a tax on a commodity which was not taxable at all, a civil suit will lie; the former being a case where the municipality acts under the Act although wrongly, whereas the latter is a case where the entire action is outside the Act. So in *Poona City Municipal Corporation v. Dattatraya Nagesh Deodhar*,[45] the Supreme Court upheld the maintainability of a suit for recovery of money which the Municipal Corporation detained as a 'tax on octroi refund' on the ground that the Corporation had no power to levy such a tax. It was further held that the action of the Corporation in levying such a tax was not 'any act done or purported to be done in pursuance or execution or intended execution' of the Corporation Act.[46] Similarly in *Bharat Kala Bhandar v. Dhamangaon Municipality*,[47] a suit to claim refund of tax on professions, trades and callings levied and collected by the Municipality in excess of constitutional limits prescribed by section 142A of the Government of India Act, 1935, and Article 276 of the Constitution, was held to be maintainable. It was pointed out that the suit did not relate to anything done or purported to be done under the Act; and the special procedure of notice and limitation prescribed by the Act did not apply. It was further held that the suit was not barred by a statutory provision in the Act which was to the

---

41. AIR 1963 SC 1547.

42. **See** notes 36 to 38, p. 836, *supra*.

43. *Firm Radhakishan v. Ludhiana Municipality*, AIR 1963 SC 1547, p. 1551 ; 1964 (2) SCR 273; **referred** to in *Provincial Government of Madras v. J.S. Basappa*, AIR 1964 SC 1873 : 1964 (5) SCR 517.

44. *Ibid*.

45. AIR 1965 SC 555 : 1964 (8) SCR 178.

46. *Ibid*, p. 560. **Followed** in *Firm Surajmal Banshidhar v. Municipal Board, Ganganagar*, AIR 1979 SC 246, p. 247 : (1979) 1 SCC 303. Same principle applied in sustaining suits for challenging dismissal of a municipal employee in violation of mandatory provisions: *Municipal Corporation v. Sri Niyamatullah*, (1970) 2 SCR 47 : AIR 1971 SC 97; *J.N. Ganatra v. Morvi Municipality*, AIR 1996 SC 2520 : 1996 (9) SCC 495.

47. AIR 1966 SC 249 : (1965) 3 SCR 499. **Followed** in *B.M. Lakhani v. Malkapur Municipality*, AIR 1970 SC 1002 : (1970) 2 SCC 733.

effect: 'No objection shall be taken to any valuation, assessment or levy in any other manner or by any other authority than as provided in this Act.' And in *Kripal Singh v. Municipal Board, Ghaziabad*,[48] a suit claiming refund of toll tax based on a statutory exemption was not held to be barred though the plaintiff had not complied with the rules prescribing the procedure for claiming refund of such tax from the municipality. It was also held that the suit was not in respect of any act done or purported to be done in the official capacity. The decision in *Firm Radha Kishan's*[49] case however, does not allow challenge to an order of assessment of tax on the ground that it is erroneous or incorrect. The challenge will be permissible only if the assessment is constitutionally invalid or is entirely without jurisdiction. This has been explained in the case of *Bata Shoe Co. Ltd. v. Jabalpur Corporation*.[50] In this case the plaintiff instituted a suit to challenge the order reopening an assessment of octroi tax and levy of double penalty by a suit on the ground that the assessment was made without any authority and that the imposition of double penalty was not justified under the provisions of the relevant Municipal Act and the Rules. The Act provided an elaborate machinery of its own for challenging an assessment of tax. The Act also provided that 'No objection shall be taken to any valuation, assessment or levy nor shall the liability of any person to be assessed or taxed be questioned in any other manner or by any other authority than as provided in this Act'. The Supreme Court held that the suit was not maintainable on the reasoning that if the appropriate authority while exercising its jurisdiction and powers under the relevant provisions of the Act, holds erroneously that an assessment already made can be corrected or that an assessee is liable to pay double duty under the relevant rule when the rule does not in fact justify such an imposition it cannot be said that the decision of the authority is without jurisdiction.

In Income-tax and Sales Tax Acts, it is common to find provisions to the effect that 'no suit shall lie to challenge an assessment made under the Act', or that 'no assessment made under the Act shall be called into question in any court except as otherwise provided in the Act'. In *Raleigh Investment Co. v. G. G. in Council*,[51] the Privy Council construing a provision of this nature (section 67 of the Income-tax Act, 1922) held that an

---

48. AIR 1968 SC 1416 : 1968 (3) SCR 551. **See further** *Khurai Municipality v. Dhannalal*, AIR 1968 SC 1458 : 1969 (1) SCR 166; *H.M.M. Ltd. v. Administrator Bangalore City Corporation*, AIR 1990 SC 47, pp. 52, 53 : 1989 (4) SCC 640, (non-compliance with the rules regarding refund of octroi to give effect to statutory exemption does not bar a suit for refund).

49. **See** note 43, *supra*.

50. AIR 1977 SC 955, pp. 963, 964 : (1977) 2 SCC 256.

51. AIR 1947 PC 78, p. 81 : 17 IA 50 : **See further** *Commr. of Income-tax v. Tribune Trust*, AIR 1948 PC 102, pp. 106, 107.

assessment could not be challenged in civil court on the ground that it was based on a provision of law which was *ultra vires*. It was pointed out that the correct meaning of the phrase 'assessment made under the Act' is an assessment finding its origin in an activity of the assessing officer acting as such, and that an assessment under the machinery of the Act relying on a provision which is later found *ultra vires* is not a nullity but only erroneous in law. This Privy Council decision has not been accepted by the Supreme Court. In *K.S. Venkatraman & Co. v. State of Madras*,[52] it was held by the Supreme Court that an assessment which is based on a charging section which is *ultra vires* is not an 'assessment under the Act', and a suit to challenge such an assessment is not barred. It was also held that assessing authorities cannot entertain a question relating to validity of the Act, and hence, it is open to a civil court to entertain and decide such a question notwithstanding that assessment has already been made. This case was followed in *Dhulabhai v. State of Madhya Pradesh*,[53] where assessment was based on a notification issued under the charging section. The notification contravened Article 301 of the Constitution and was, therefore, *ultra vires*. It was held that the validity of the notification could not have been gone into by the assessing authorities, and that the assessment was not 'under the Act', and could be challenged by a suit in civil court. Income-tax and Sales tax Acts, however, contain an elaborate machinery for assessment and for determination of questions of fact and law arising in assessment proceedings and an assessment cannot be questioned except in the manner provided under the Act on the ground that it is erroneous in fact or in law.[54] Thus, if purchases only and not sales can be taxed, a suit challenging an assessment is not maintainable on the ground

---

52. AIR 1966 SC 1089 : 1966 (2) SCR 229.

53. AIR 1969 SC 78 : 1968 (3) SCR 662. **See further** *CIT v. Straw Products*, AIR 1966 SC 1113 : 1966 (2) SCR 881 (Even the High Court in a reference and the Supreme Court in appeal against the order passed in reference cannot decide the question of the validity of the Taxing Act and a statutory order issued under it). *State of Tripura v. Province of East Bengal*, AIR 1951 SC 23, p. 28 : 1551 SCR 1; and *State of Bombay v. Jagmohandas*, AIR 1966 SC 1412 : 1966 (2) SCR 279; (a suit to restrain an assessment on the ground that the Taxing Act is *ultra vires* is not barred); *West Bengal (Electricity Regulatory Commission v. CESC Ltd.*, AIR 2002 SC 3588, p. 3603. (The High Court hearing an appeal under the Electricity Regulatory Commission Act cannot decide the question of validity of a Regulation made under the Act); *Central Bank of India v. Vrajlal Kapurchand Gandhi,* (2003) 6 SCC 573, p. 579 : AIR 2003 SC 3028 (It is settled position in law that a court or tribunal constituted under a statute cannot adjudicate upon the constitutional validity of the statute concerned); *Committee of Management v. Vice Chancellor*, (2009) 2 SCC 630 para 22 : AIR 2009 SC 1159 (A statutory authority cannot consider the validity of a statute under which it is functioning).

54. *Titaghur Paper Mills Co. Ltd. v. State of Orissa*, AIR 1983 SC 603, p. 607 : (1983) 3 SCC 433.

that the transactions taxed were sales and they were wrongly held to be purchases by the assessing authorities.[55] Similarly if sales taking place inside a State are alone taxable, a suit to challenge the assessment is not maintainable on the ground that the sales were in fact outside State and were wrongly held to be inside State.[56] In this connection it must be kept in mind that speaking generally the taxing authorities have authority to decide finally even collateral questions of fact and law touching their jurisdiction.[57] The factors that liability to pay income-tax or sales tax is a creature of the taxing Act which normally provides an elaborate machinery for assesment; that the taxing authorities have in general authority to decide finally questions of fact and law pertaining to their own jurisdiction; and that these Acts usually contain an exclusionary provision expressly restraining a suit to challenge an assessment made under the Act, leave little room for a suit to challenge an assessment. In addition to the case where assesssment is based on an *ultra vires* provision, assessment may also be open to challenge on the ground that it was made in violation of fundamental principles of judicial procedure *e.g.*, without any notice to the assessee. Indeed, in *Mafatlal Industries Ltd. v. Union of India*,[58] a nine-Judge Bench of the Supreme Court while dealing with refund provisions in the Central Excises and Salt Act, 1944 and the Customs Act, 1962 can be said to have laid down by majority the following general propositions: (i) A claim for refund of tax on the ground that it has been collected by mis-interpreting or misapplying the provisions of a taxing Act or the rules and notifications made thereunder has to be preferred in accordance with the provisions of the Act before the authorities and within the limitation specified therein and no suit is maintainable in that behalf; (ii) Where a refund is claimed on the ground that the provision of the Act under which it was levied is or has been held to be unconstitutional, the claim can be made by a suit or by way of a writ petition for such a claim is outside the purview of the Act; and (iii) A claim for refund can succeed only when the claimant establishes that he has not passed on the burden of the tax to others; in other words, where the claimant has suffered no real loss or prejudice the claim for refund would be

---

55. *Firm of Illuri Subbayya Chetty & Sons v. State of A.P.*, AIR 1964 SC 322 : 1964 (1) SCR 752.

56. *Kamala Mills Ltd. v. State of Bombay*, AIR 1965 SC 1942 : 1966 (1) SCR 64. In *Provincial Govt. of Madras v. J.S. Basappa*, AIR 1964 SC 1873 : (1964) 5 SCR 517 where there was only a finality clause but no express bar to challenge an assessment a similar suit was held to be maintainable. *Basappa's* case (*supra*) was **disapproved** in *State of Kerala v. Ramaswami*, AIR 1966 SC 1738 : (1966) 3 SCR 582, but the correctness of the disapproval was **doubted** in *Dhulabhai v. State of M.P.*, AIR 1969 SC 78 : 1968 (3) SCR 662.

57. *State of U.P. v. Yadavendra*, AIR 1966 SC 727, p. 731 : 1966 (3) SCR 161.

58. 1996 (9) Scale 457: JT 1996 (11) SC 283: 1997 (5) SCC 536.

disallowed.[59] When a person collects as tax more than what was levied as tax by the state and it is not possible to refund the excess amount to persons from whom it was collected, the person collecting the same cannot retain it on the ground that it will amount to unjust enrichment but the state cannot also recover and retain the excess amount from him because it was not levied as tax.[60] In such a case the Supreme Court directed the state under Article 142 to recover the amount and pay the same to some charitable organization.[61]

The bar of suits in civil courts, contained in section 293 of the Income-tax Act, 1961, is much wider than the corresponding section 67 of the Income-tax Act, 1922 which was limited to bar a suit 'to set aside or modify any assessment' made under the Act. Section 293 of the 1961 Act bars a suit 'to set aside or modify any proceeding taken or order' made under the Act.[62] By an order passed under section 132(5) of the Act certain ornaments recovered on search and seized from the premises of an assessee were directed to be retained. The step-mother of the assessee, instead of applying under section 132(11), which provided a remedy for challenging the order, brought a suit for partition of the ornaments which was in substance a suit for challenging the proceedings and the order under section 132(5). It was held that the suit was barred under section 293.[63]

Section 5 of Part I of the Arbitration and Conciliation Act, 1996 provides: 'Notwithstanding anything contained in any other law for the time being in force, in matters governed by this Part no judicial authority shall intervene except where so provided in this Part.' This section along with Section 16 of the Act which provides that 'the Arbitral Tribunal may rule on its jurisdiction', have been widely construed and interference by civil court has been ruled out except as provided in the Act.[64]

Special provisions curtailing the normal period of limitation for suit or prosecution have also been strictly construed. Section 53 of the Tamil Nadu

---

59. *Ibid*, pp. 517 to 519 (Scale). **See further** *Union of India v. Solar Pesticides Pvt. Ltd.*, AIR 2000 C 862 : 2000 (2) SCC 705; *Commissioner of Central Excise v. Allied Photographic India Ltd.*, (2004) 4 SCC 34 : AIR 2004 SC 2953; *Automotive Tyre Manufacturers Association v. Designated Authority*, (2011) 2 SCC 258 paras 86 to 89 : (2011) 1 JT 282. **But see** *Triveni Chemicals Ltd. v. Union of India*, (2007) 2 SCC 503 (paras 11 to 13) : (2007) 1 SLT 303 : (2006) 14 Scale 40.

N.B.—Proposition No. (iii) is in accord with the law of European Communities as declared by the EEC Court which is **referred** in *Kleinwort Benson Ltd. v. Birmingham City Council*, (1996) 4 All ER 733, p. 740 : (1997) QB 380 : (1996) 3 WLR 1139 (CA).

60. *State of Maharashtra v. Swanstone Multiplex Cinema Private Ltd.*, (2009) 8 SCC 235 paras 31 to 33 : AIR 2009 SC 2750.

61. *Ibid* para 37. **But see** *Jayvee Rice and General Mills v. State of Haryana*, (2010) 10 SCC 687 paras 24, 25 : (2010) 10 JT 559.

62. *CIT v. Parmeshwari Devi Sultania*, JT 1998 (2) SC 413, p. 425 : AIR 1998 SC 1276, pp. 1283, 1285 : (1998) 3 SCC 481.

63. *Ibid.*

64. *Secur Industries Ltd. v. Godrej & Boyce Mfg. Co. Ltd.*, (2004) 3 SCC 447, p. 451 (para 11) : AIR 2004 SC 1766, p. 1769 (Para 11).

District Police Act, 1869 prescribes a period of three months for 'all actions and prosecutions against any person which may be lawfully brought for anything done or intended to be done under the provisions of this Act or under the provisions of any other law for the time being in force conferring powers on the police'. Construing this provision it has been held that "to be able to say that an act is 'under' a provision of law, one must discover the existence of a reasonable relationship between the provision and the act".[65] Therefore, when a person reported to the police in answer to a summons and was beaten and tortured, these acts of the police officer were held to be not 'under' any provision of law and outside the bar of section 53 of the Tamil Nadu District Police Act, 1869.[66] Similar view has been taken of the corresponding provision in the Kerala Police Act, 1961, where it was held that a police officer in committing torture on a person cannot be said to be 'acting or purporting to act in discharge of his official duty' and cannot get the benefit of reduced period of limitation in section 63 of the Act.[67] Restricted view has also been taken of section 140 of the Delhi Police Act which bars a suit or prosecution of a police officer after expiry of three months for any act done 'under colour of duty or authority'. It was held that jumping road divider and causing fear on the incoming traffic by a police constable while driving a vehicle for official work which resulted in hitting a scooter could not be said to have been done under 'colour of duty or authority'[68]

A provision enacted in terms: 'No order made in exercise of any power conferred by or under this Act shall be called in question in any court', assumes that the order is made in exercise of the power, which clearly leaves it open to challenge on the ground that it was not made in conformity with the power conferred.[69] Similarly a provision using the formula: 'No order or decision under this Act shall be called in question in any court' will not

---

65. *State of Andhra Pradesh v. N. Venugopal*, (1964) 3 SCR 742 : AIR 1964 SC 33; *S.P. Vaithianathan v. K. Shanmuganathan*, JT 1994(2) SC 689, p. 693 : AIR 1994 SC 1771 : (1994) 4 SCC 569.

66. *S.P. Vaithianathan v. V.K. Shanmuganathan*, *supra*. But registering a false FIR may fall under section 53 of the Tamil Nadu District Police Act, 1869.

67. *P.P. Unnikrishnan v. Puttiyottil Alikuty,* AIR 2000 SC 2952 : (2000) 8 SCC 131.

68. *Paul George v. State of NCT of Delhi,* (2008) 4 SCC 185 paras 10 and 11 : (2008) 3 JT 545. For other cases construing the words 'under colour of duty or authority' **see**: *Virupaxappa Veerappa Kadampur v. State of Mysore*, AIR 1963 SC 849 paras 8 to 10 : 1963 Supp (2) SCR 6; *Sumerchand (Prof.) v. Union of India,* AIR 1993 SC 2579 : (1994) 1 SCC 64; *K.K. Patel v. State of Gujarat,* JT 2000 (7) SC 246 : (2000) 6 SCC 195 : 2001 SCC (Cri) 200.

69. *Collector of Kamrup v. Kamakhya Ram*, AIR 1965 SC 1301, p. 1302 : 1965 (1) SCR 265; *Emperor v. Shibnath Banerji*, AIR 1945 PC 156, p. 161; *Emperor v. Vimalabai Deshpande*, AIR 1946 PC 123, p. 127 : 1946 Nag 651; **but see** *Bhagwat Prasad v. Secretary of State*, AIR 1940 PC 82, p. 85 : 67 IA 197.

stand in the way of a suit challenging an order or decision when the order or decision is really not an order or decision under the Act but a nullity.[70] Therefore, when there is a non-compliance with fundamental provisions of the Act or fundamental principles of judicial procedure which makes proceedings before the tribunal or authority illegal and void, a civil suit to challenge the orders or decisions passed in such proceedings is not barred.[71] The reason is that an order or a decision which is a nullity or void, is not an 'order or a decision under the Act' and jurisdiction of the civil court to challenge such an order is not barred by the exclusionary provision using the above formula.[72] For the same reason even when an order is required to be passed on subjective satisfaction of an authority as to existence of certain matters, a satisfaction based on wholly irrelevant grounds is regarded as no satisfaction and the order based on it can be challenged in a court in spite of the exclusionary clause providing that the satisfaction of the authority "shall be final and conclusive and shall not be questioned in any court of law".[73]

When a statute authorised the grant of 'proprietary rights' and the Deputy Commissioner made a grant in terms thereof, but in appeal the Commissioner restricted the grant by imposing a condition that the land should not be alienated without the concurrence of the reversioners, the Privy Council held that a suit was maintainable to challenge the condition.[74] LORD SIMONDS in delivering the opinion observed: "Their Lordships have no doubt that the Civil Court has power to entertain a suit, in

---

70. *Anisminic Ltd. v. Foreign Compensation Commission*, (1969) 1 All ER 208 (HL); *Rajendra Prakash Sharma v. Gyan Chandra*, AIR 1980 SC 1206, pp. 1213, 1214 : 1980 (3) SCR 207 : (1980) 4 SCC 364; *Union of India v. Tarachand*, AIR 1971 SC 1558 : 1971 (1) SCC 486; *Ramsarup v. Shikharchand*, AIR 1966 SC 893, pp. 897, 898 : (1966) 2 SCR 553; *Shivkumar Chadha v. Municipal Corporation, Delhi*, 1993 (3) SCC 161 : (1993) 3 JT 238; *Krishanlal v. State of Jammu & Kashmir*, JT 1994 (2) SC 619, pp. 622, 623 : 1994 (4) SCC 422 : 1994 SCC (L&S) 885; *Dhruv Green Field Ltd. v. Hukum Singh*, AIR 2002 SC 2841, p. 2844 : (2002) 6 SCC 416; *Bhupendra Singh v. G.K. Umath*, AIR 1970 MP 91, pp. 95-98.

71. *Secretary of State v. Mask & Co.*, AIR 1940 PC 105, p. 110, as **explained** in *Firm of Illuri Subbayya Chetty & Sons v. State of A.P.*, AIR 1964 SC 322, p. 326 : (1964) 1 SCR 752; which is further **referred** in *Provincial Govt. of Madras v. J.S. Basappa*, AIR 1964 SC 1873, p. 1877 : (1964) 5 SCR 517; *Custodian of E.P. v. Jafran Begum*, AIR 1968 SC 169, p. 174 : (1967) 3 SCR 736; *Dhulabhai v. State of M.P.*, AIR 1969 SC 78, p. 86 : (1968) 3 SCR 662; *State of Tamil Nadu v. Ramlinga Samigal Madam*, (1985) 4 SCC 10, p. 17 : AIR 1986 SC 794; *Gurbax Singh v. Financial Commissioner*, AIR 1991 SC 435, p. 439 : 1990 (4) JT 114 : 1991 Supp (1) SCC 167.

72. **See** cases in note 70, *supra*. For fuller discussion of nullity cases, **see** under title 2(b) 'cases of nullity'.

73. *State of Rajasthan v. Union of India*, AIR 1977 SC 1361, pp. 1390, 1391, 1401, 1414, 1415 : (1977) 4 SCC 599. **See further** text and note 75, *infra*.

74. *Mohammad Din v. Imamdin*, AIR 1948 PC 33 : 74 IA 319.

which the question is whether the executive authority has acted *ultra vires*."[75] Proceeding further, LORD SIMONDS said: "The specific subject-matter of the grant is the 'proprietary rights', that, and nothing else, may be granted or refused. To purport to grant 'proprietary rights' but to withhold an essential proprietary right, *viz.*, the free power of alienation is neither the one thing nor other. The withholding of such a right may be referred to as a condition, but its effect, as already stated, is to create an estate unknown to the law and to grant not proprietary rights but something which is not susceptible of terms of legal definition. Their Lordships think that the original grant by Deputy Commissioner, who clearly acted within his competence, should stand and the so-called condition imposed by the superior executive authority which was in their view incompetent, should be disregarded."[76]

Section 4 of the Bombay Revenue Jurisdiction Act, 1876, which bars the jurisdiction of civil courts in certain matters has been held not to be attracted when the claim laid in civil courts is on the ground that an act or order of revenue authorities is without jurisdiction and null and void. A suit in civil court is, therefore, maintainable for claiming reliefs on the grounds that an order of the Governor-in-Council made under section 211 of the Bombay Land Revenue Code, 1879, was in excess of his statutory powers;[77] that a purported sale for arrears of revenue by the Revenue authorities was void and was no sale at all;[78] and that an order in review was without jurisdiction there being no power of review.[79]

The extent of exclusion is, however, really a question of construction of each particular statute and the general principles applicable are subordinate to the actual words used by the Legislature.

By use of the words 'a compulsory purchase order shall not be questioned in any legal proceedings whatsoever', it was held by the House of Lords that Parliament excluded every form of challenge including one based on the ground that the order was made in bad faith.[80] The correctness of this view was not accepted by the Supreme Court,[81] and also by the

---

75. *Ibid*, p. 34.
76. *Ibid*, p. 35.
77. *Bombay Province v. Hormusji*, AIR 1947 PC 200, p. 203 : 74 IA 103.
78. *Ramrao v. Jankiram*, AIR 1963 SC 827 : 1963 Supp (1) SCR 322.
79. *Laxman v. State of Bombay*, AIR 1964 SC 436 : (1964) 1 SCR 200. **But see** *Bhujangrao v. Mulojirao*, AIR 1952 SC 138 : 1952 SCR 402.
80. *Smith v. East Elloe Rural District Council,* (1956) 1 All ER 855, pp. 858, 859, 863, 870, 871 : 1956 AC 736 (HL).
81. *Somvanti v. State of Punjab*, AIR 1963 SC 151, p. 166 : (1963) 2 SCR 774.

House of Lords,[82] in a later case; but it appears that if the exclusionary provision were to the effect that 'an order made or purporting to be made under the Act shall not be called in question in any court on any ground whatsoever', it will require great legal ingenuity to support a civil suit for challenging 'an order purporting to be made under the Act' for even an order which is nullity or void can fall under that description though it cannot be called 'an order under the Act'.[83]

Article 372(2) of the Constitution confers powers on the President to issue adaptation orders 'for the purpose of bringing the provisions of any law in force in the territory of India into accord with the provisions of the Constitution' and further enacts that 'any such adaptation or modification shall not be questioned in any court of law'. Interpreting this provision it has been held that an adaptation order issued by the President is not open to challenge on the ground that it amounted to more than bringing the existing law into conformity with the provisions of the Constitution,[84] although the order can be challenged on the ground that it was violative of some other provision of the Constitution.[85]

Article 356 of the Constitution provides that if the President 'is satisfied that a situation has arisen in which the Government of the State cannot be carried on in accordance with the provisions of the Constitution' the President may by proclamation: (a) assume to himself the functions of the Government of the State; (b) declare that the powers of the State Legislature shall be exercised by Parliament; and (c) make such incidental or

---

82. *Anisminic Ltd. v. Foreign Compensation Commission*, (1969) 1 All ER 208 : (1969) 2 AC 147 : (1969) 2 WLR 163 (HL). But in *R. v. Secretary for Environment, Ex parte, Ostler*, (1976) 3 All ER 90 (CA) it has been held that *East Elloe* case was not **overruled** in *Anisminic'* and is binding on Court of Appeal. The distinguishing features pointed out are: (1) In *East Elloe* case the court was permitted to have jurisdiction up to six weeks and the ban operated after this period. In *Anisminic* case the jurisdiction was ousted from the very beginning; and (2) In *East Elloe* case the ban operated for challenging an administrative decision whereas in *Anisminic* case the ban was for challenging a judicial decision of a tribunal. LORD DENNING, however, has extra judicially **regretted** his decision in *Ostler's* case. He says that the mistake crept in as the judgment was not reserved and was extempore (The Discipline of Law, p. 108). But *Ostler* case was **followed** in *R. v. Cornwall County Council, ex parte, Huntington*, (1994) 1 All ER 694 (CA).

83. **See** *Anisminic Ltd. v. Foreign Compensation Commission*, (1969) 1 All ER 208, pp. 212, 237 : (1969) 2 AC 147 : (1969) 2 WLR 163 (HL); *Azimunissa v. Deputy Custodian, E.P.*, AIR 1961 SC 362, pp. 370, 371 : (1961) 2 SCR 74. **But see** text and notes 45 to 47, pp. 836-837 and *Bombay Housing Board v. Karbhase Naik & Co.*, AIR 1975 SC 763, pp. 768, 769 : (1975) 1 SCC 341.

84. *Sundaramier v. State of A.P.*, AIR 1958 SC 468, p. 482 : 1954 SCR 1384. Article 372A of the Constitution has been similarly construed; *Union of India v. Prem Kumar Jain*, AIR 1976 SC 1856, p. 1860 : (1976) 3 SCC 743.

85. *Ibid*, p. 488.

consequential provisions as may be necessary to give effect to the objects of the Proclamation. The Article before the Constitution 44th Amendment Act further provided that, the satisfaction of the President 'shall be final and conclusive and shall not be questioned in any court of law'. Interpreting this provision the Supreme Court[86] held that if the satisfaction of the President is based on wholly extraneous grounds which have no nexus with the action taken, the Proclamation can be challenged in a court of law on the ground that the President acted without the required satisfaction in issuing the Proclamation for satisfaction based on wholly irrelevant grounds amounts to no satisfaction. But if there are some grounds which bear some relevance or nexus to the action taken the propriety or sufficiency of satisfaction cannot be challenged in a court of law. Article 356 again came up for consideration before the Supreme Court after deletion of the clause barring judicial review. It has been reiterated that Article 356 confers a conditional power on the President and the Proclamation issued by him is open to judicial review on the grounds that it was a *mala fide* exercise of power; that it was based on wholly irrelevant or extraneous grounds; that there was no material in support thereof; and that the material relied upon was irrelevant to the action taken.[87] If the Proclamation is struck down the court can also restore back the dissolved assembly.[88] But if there is some material which is relevant to the action taken the court will not enquire into its correctness or adequacy.[89] In *Bommai,*[90] applying these principles imposition of President's rule, on the basis of the reports of the Governors, in Nagaland, Karnataka and Meghalaya was declared unconstitutional and imposition of President's rule in Madhya Pradesh, Rajasthan and Himachal Pradesh was upheld. *Bommai* was followed in *Rameshwar Prasad v. Union of India,*[91] which by majority held unconstitutional the notification ordering dissolution of the Bihar Legislative Assembly but the court declined to restore the Assembly as it stood before the notification. This case was unique in the sense that the dissolution of the Assembly was ordered even before its first meeting on the ground that attempts were being made to cobble a majority by illegal means to form the Government in the State. The President's satisfaction was solely based on the Governor's report. There was no material before the Governor except his *ipse dixit* to assume

86. *State of Rajasthan v. Union of India*, AIR 1977 SC 1361, pp. 1390, 1391, 1401, 1414, 1415 : (1977) 4 SCC 599.

87. *S.R. Bommai v. Union of India*, JT 1994(2) SC 215 : AIR 1994 SC 1918 : (1994) 3 SCC 1. **See** Summary of the case in *A.K. Kaul v. Union of India*, 1995(2) Scale 755, p. 764: AIR 1995 SC 1403, p. 1411 : (1995) 4 SCC 73.

88. *Ibid.*

89. *Ibid*. For a discussion of the *State of Rajasthan* and *Bommai* Cases, **see** Gopal Subramanium, Emergency Provisions under the Indian Constitution', Supreme But Not Infallible, (2000 Oxford University Press), pp. 147 to 150.

90. **See** note 87 *supra*.

91. (2006) 2 SCC 1 : AIR 2006 SC 980.

and report that there was no legitimate realignment of political parties and there was blatant distortion of democracy by induced defection through unfair, unethical and unconstitutional means.[92] It was held that it was open to the court in exercise of judicial review to examine the question whether the Governor's report is based upon relevant material or not, whether it is *bonafide* or not and whether the facts have been duly verified or not.[93]

When certain matters are committed to the jurisdiction of a tribunal or authority, and its determination is made final and civil courts are expressly debarred in exercising jurisdiction over those matters, or in questioning the determination of the tribunal or authority, it will be inferred that all questions of fact and law whether simple or intricate pertaining to those matters have to be determined exclusively by the tribunal or authority and not by the civil court.[94] Indeed, it has been said that when a statute gives finality to the orders of a special tribunal the civil courts' jurisdiction must be held to be impliedly excluded in so far as the merits of the case are concerned even though there is no express exclusion of the jurisdiction and that in such a case civil courts have jurisdiction only to examine whether the provisions of the statute have been complied with or the tribunal had or had not acted in conformity with the fundamental principles of judicial procedure.[95] In this case a suit was filed to challenge a scheme of nationalisation which was pending consideration under section 68D of the Motor Vehicles Act, 1939, and it was held that the suit was impliedly barred.[96] But if the determination of the tribunal or authority is made final only for 'purposes of the Act' which creates the special jurisdiction, the exclusion of civil courts' jurisdiction will not be readily inferred even if the Act in addition to the finality clause provides that the order of the tribunal shall not be questioned in a court of law.[97] Thus, if the object of the special Act is to serve the revenue purposes of the Government and to facilitate revenue collection, decisions on incidental questions arrived at in a summary manner for identifying and registering persons in the reve

---

92. *Ibid.* paras 86, 145.
93. *Ibid.* para 140.
94. *Custodian of Evacuee Property v. Jafran Begum*, AIR 1968 SC 169, pp. 172, 173 : (1967) 3 SCR 736; *M. Chayana v. K. Narayana*, AIR 1979 SC 1320 : (1979) 3 SCC 42; *Oduru Chechulakshamma v. D. Subrahamanya*, (1980) 3 SCC 130 : AIR 1980 SC 133; *Mohan Lal v. Kartar Singh*, 1995 Supp (4) SCC 684: 1995 (6) Scale 27, p. 35 (This will be so even if the tribunal is required to decide the matter committed to its jurisdiction by a summary enquiry).
95. *Anwar v. First Additional District Judge, Bulandshahar*, (1986) 4 SCC 21, p. 26 : AIR 1986 SC 1785.
96. *Ibid.*
97. *State of Tamil Nadu v. Ramlinga Samigal Madam,* (1985) 4 SCC 10, pp. 15, 21 to 23, 25 : AIR 1986 SC 794.

nue records from whom recovery of revenue is to be made, cannot bar the jurisdiction of civil courts to entertain suits for protection of title and possession of a person who has not been recognised as a *ryot* under the machinery of the Act.[1]

(b) Cases of nullity

It has already been stated that an exclusionary clause in an Act which forbids a challenge to 'a determination or order made under the Act', in a civil court contemplates cases of a real determination or order and does not protect a determination or order which is a nullity or void.[2] The question then is: when can an order passed by a tribunal or authority of limited jurisdiction be held to be a nullity? It is trite law that an order passed without jurisdiction is a nullity.[3] According to the original or pure theory

---

1. *Ibid.*
2. **See** text and notes 69 to 72, pp. 842-843, *supra.*
3. *Kiran Singh v. Chaman Paswan*, AIR 1954 SC 340, p. 342 : (1955) 1 SCR 117; *Balai Chandra Hazra v. Shewdhari Jadav*, AIR 1978 SC 1062, p. 1068 : (1978) 2 SCC 559; (When there is inherent lack of jurisdiction no amount of consent can confer jurisdiction); *Sarwan Kumar v. Madan Lal Aggarwal,* (2003) 4 SCC 147 : AIR 2003 SC 1475 (A decree of eviction passed by a civil court when it lacked inherent jurisdiction to entertain the suit is a nullity and the decree can be challenged in execution proceedings). *Jaipur Development Authority v. Mahesh Sharma,* (2010) 9 SCC 782 : (2010) 10 JT 397 (Proceedings for acquisition of land under Land Acquisition Act which had earlier vested in the State under the Jagir Abolition Act are absolute nullities) paras 26, 28, 34 to 38. *Rafique Bibi v. Sayed Waliuddin,* (2004) 1 SCC 287, p. 291 : AIR 2003 SC 3789 (Distinction between illegal decree and void decree. The Former cannot be challenged in execution. Wade and Forsyth Administrative law 8th edition **referred**); *Deepak Agro Foods v. State of Rajasthan,* (2008) 7 SCC 748 paras 18 and 19 : (2008) 10 Scale 263 (Difference between a null and void order and an illegal or irregular order). *Balwant N. Vishwamitra v. Yadav Sadashiv Mule*, (2004) 8 SCC 706 (Distinction between void decree and illegal decree); *Ramnik Vallabhdas Madhvani v. Taraben Pravinlal Madhvani*, (2004) 1 SCC 497, pp. 510, 511 : AIR 2004 SC 1084 (General observations that illegal decree is a nullity and cannot be allowed to be enforced. Case of award of interest at a rate more than what was claimed and what could have been allowed under section 34 Civil Procedure Code). An order or decree which suffers from inherent jurisdiction and is a nullity cannot operate as *res judicata* : *Ashok Leyland v. State of Tamil Nadu*, AIR 2004 SC 2836, pp. 2861, 2862 : (2004) 3 SCC 1. Wherever jurisdiction is given by a statute upon certain specified terms, these terms should be complied with for jurisdiction to arise otherwise there will be inherent lack of jurisdiction: *Nusserwanji Pestonjee v. Meer Mynoodeen Khan,* 6 MIA 134, p. 135, **followed** in *Kothamasu Kanakrathamma v. State of Andhra Pradesh,* AIR 1965 SC 304 and *Sharadadevi v. State of Bihar,* AIR 2003 SC 942, p. 952 : (2003) 3 SCC 128 (jurisdiction under sections 18 and 30 Land Acquisition Act, 1894 arises on certain conditions and want of those conditions gives rise to inherent lack of jurisdiction). But an order passed by a court of unlimited jurisdiction cannot be disobeyed or ignored by treating it as void or nullity until it has been set aside in a proper proceeding; *Isaacs v. Robertson,* (1984) 3 All ER 140, p. 142 (PC).

[Footnote No. 3 Contd.]

[Footnote No. 3 Contd.]

Similarly a restraint order issued by a civil court which is a court of general jurisdiction cannot be ignored by a court or tribunal of limited jurisdiction on the ground that it is a nullity: *Prakash Narain Sharma v. Burmah Shell Co-operative Housing Society Ltd.*, AIR 2002 SC 3062 : (2002) 7 SCC 46. Even the Supreme Court cannot by its directions given *per incuriam* confer jurisdiction on a court which it does not possess. Thus the Supreme Court cannot transfer to the High Court a case triable exclusively by a Special Judge under the Criminal Law Amendment Act, 1952. But a mistaken direction by the Supreme Court in that matter cannot be questioned or ignored by the High Court or challenged in a writ petition under Article 32 of the Constitution. It can however, be corrected by the Supreme Court in a review petition or even under the court's inherent powers when the mistake is brought to its notice: *A.R. Antulay v. R.S. Nayak*, AIR 1988 SC 1531 : (1988) 2 SCC 602. Concept of nullity has no application to orders of the Supreme Court which is a court of unlimited jurisdiction: *Union Carbide Corporation v. Union of India*, AIR 1992 SC 248 : (1991) 4 SCC 584. The same principle applies to orders of a High Court at least in cases where it exercises constituent power under Article 226: *Ramchandra Ganpat Shinde v. State of Maharashtra*, AIR 1994 SC 1673 : (1993) 4 SCC 216; *High Court of Judicature Allahabad v. Rajkishore*, AIR 1997 SC 1186, p. 1191 : (1997) 3 SCC 11. A *de facto* Judge (a person who was believed and who believed himself to have the necessary judicial authority) is 'a tribunal established by law' and his order will not be void simply on the ground that he was not a Judge in law: *Coppard v. Customs and Excise Commissioners*, (2003) 3 All ER 351 (CA). Even a void administrative order may have legal consequences and may be *de facto* in operation requiring an affected party to take proceedings for having its invalidity established: *Suresh Seth v. State*, AIR 1970 MP 154, pp. 161, 162 (G.P. SINGH J.); *Divisional Superintendent, South Eastern Railway, Bilaspur v. Ch. Annaj Kumar*, 1980 MPLJ 498 (G.P. SINGH C.J.); *State of Punjab v. Gurdev Singh Ashok Kumar*, AIR 1991 SC 2219, p. 2221 : (1992) 4 SCC 506; *State of Kerala v. M.K. Kunhikannan Nambiar Manjeri Manikoth*, 1995 (6) Scale 734, pp. 737, 738 : AIR 1996 SC 906, pp. 908, 909; *State of Rajasthan v. D.R. Laxmi*, 1996 (6) SCC 445 : 1996 (7) Scale 316, p. 322; *R. Thiruvirkolam v. Presiding Officer,* AIR 1997 SC 633, pp. 635, 636 : (1997) 1 SCC 9 (passage from WADE, Administrative Law, 7th edition, pp. 342, 343 **quoted** with approval); *Pankaj Mehra v. State of Maharashtra,* AIR 2000 SC 1953, p. 1957 : (2000) 2 SCC 756 (The word void does not always mean void *ab initio*, its meaning varies according to context); *Dhurandhar Prasad Singh v. Jai Prakash University,* AIR 2001 SC 2552, pp. 2558 to 2560 : (2001) 6 SCC 607 (discussion of void and voidable acts); *Sultan Sadik v. Sanjay Raj*, AIR 2004 SC 1377, p. 1385 : (2004) 2 SCC 377, pp. 390, 391 (Wade's Administrative Law 8th Edition, p. 293 **referred**); *Pune Municipal Corporation v. State of Maharashtra,* AIR 2007 SC 2414, paras 36 to 42 (Wade Administrative Law is **referred**). **See further** *Tayabbhai M. Bagasarwalla v. Hind Rubber Industries Pvt. Ltd.*, AIR 1997 SC 1240, pp. 1246, 1247 : (1997) 3 SCC 443 (Interim order passed by court pending decision on its jurisdiction cannot be disobeyed though ultimately the court decides that it has no jurisdiction). Once declared invalid, the administrative act or subordinate legislation is then recognised to have no legal effect; *Boddington v. British Transport Police*, (1998) 2 All ER 203, p. 210 (HL). The principle that a void order may have legal consequences has been applied to a void marriage: *Velamuri Venkata Sivaprasad v. Kothuri Venkateswarlu,* JT 1999 (9) SC 242, pp. 281, 282 : (2000) 2 SCC 139 : AIR 2000 SC 434.

of jurisdiction, the jurisdiction of a tribunal is determinable at the commencement of a proceeding and if jurisdiction is properly assumed any order passed thereafter will be within jurisdiction and conclusive though it may be erroneous in fact or law. This theory of jurisdiction reduced judicial control of tribunals to a vanishing point and allowed them to usurp powers which the Legislature never intended to confer. The pure theory of jurisdiction, therefore, gave place to the modern theory of jurisdiction according to which defects of jurisdiction can arise even during or at the conclusion of a proceeding. The courts make a distinction between jurisdictional questions of fact or law (also called collateral fact or law) and questions of fact or law which are not jurisdictional. If a question of fact or law is of the former category, the tribunal though competent to inquire into that question cannot decide it conclusively, and a wrong determination of such a question results in making the final decision in excess of jurisdiction. But if a question of law or fact is of the latter category, the tribunal's determination is final and conclusive. In other words a tribunal cannot by a wrong determination of a jurisdictional question of fact or law exercise a power which the Legislature did not confer upon it.[4] Difficulty arises in applying this principle because there is no clearcut demarcation between jurisdictional and non-jurisdictional questions of fact or law.[5] This difficulty

---

4. *R. v. Shoreditch Assessment Committee*, (1910) 2 KB 859, p. 880; *Ujjam Bai v. State of U.P.*, AIR 1962 SC 1621, pp. 1629, 1630 : 1963 (1) SCR 778; *Desika Charyulu v. State of A.P.*, AIR 1964 SC 807, pp. 816, 817; *State of M.P. v. D.K. Jadhav*, AIR 1968 SC 1186, p. 1190; *Shrisht Dhawan (Smt.) v. Shaw Brothers*, AIR 1992 SC 1555, p. 1563 : 1992 (1) SCC 534.

What would be a jurisdictional fact was recently stated in *Arun Kumar v. Union of India,* (2007) 1 SCC 732 : (2006) 12 JT 121, in the following terms:

"… A 'jurisdictional fact' is a fact which must exist before a court, tribunal or an authority assumes jurisdiction over a particular matter. A jurisdictional fact is one on existence or non-existence of which depends jurisdiction of a court, a tribunal or an authority. It is the fact upon which an administrtive agency's power to act depends. If the jurisdictional fact does not exist, the court, authority or officer cannot act. If a court or authority wrongly assumes the existence of such fact, the order can be questioned by a writ of *certiorari*. The underlying principle is that by erroneously assuming existence of such jurisdictional fact, no authority can confer upon itself jurisdiction which it otherwise does not posess." It was further stated: (SCC para 84) "….it is clear that existence of 'jurisdictional fact' is *sine qua non* for the exercise of power. If the jurisdictional fact exists, the authority can proceed with the case and take an appropriate decision in accordance with law. Once the authority has jurisdiction in the matter on existence of 'jurisdictional fact', it can decide the 'fact in issue' or 'adjudicatory fact'. A wrong decision on 'fact in issue' or on 'adjudicatory fact' would not make the decision of the authority without jurisdiction or vulnerable provided essential or fundamental fact as to existence of jurisdiction is present." These statements from *Arun Kumar* were again **quoted** in *Srinivasa Rice Mills v. ESI Corpn.*, (2007) 1 SCC 705 (para 19) : (2007) 1 LLJ 626 : (2006) 10 JT 305.

5. LORD DENNING **expressed** the view that the distinction should be abolished and the rule should be that no court or tribunal has any jurisdiction to make an error of law on which the decision of the case depends; [*Pearlman v. Harrow School*, (1979) 1

[Footnote No. 5 Contd.]

is further increased as the Legislature can create a tribunal having power to decide finally even apparently jurisdictional facts and such a tribunal's determination is not liable to be questioned on the ground that it has wrongly decided a jurisdictional fact.[6] In spite of these difficulties the modern theory of jurisdiction has "the merit of preserving a flexible control, by which the court can give a sharp check to what it may think a usurpation of power. The most important thing of all is that legal control of power should be preserved."[7]

The case of *Ujjam Bai v. State of Uttar Pradesh*,[8] shows that an adjudication by a tribunal of limited jurisdiction is void, when: (1) action is taken under an *ultra vires* statute; (2) the subject-matter of adjudication is beyond its competence or the order passed is such which it has no authority to pass; (3) the adjudication is procedurally *ultra vires* being in violation of fundamental principles of judicial procedure; and (4) jurisdiction is assumed by wrongly deciding jurisdictional questions of law or fact. It has already been seen that violation of fundamental provisions of the Act under which the tribunal functions and fundamental principles of judicial procedure make the tribunal's order void.[9] It is clear, however, that these grounds of nullity are not exhaustive. For example, if a tribunal is not

---

[Footnote No. 5 Contd.]

All ER 365 : (1978) 3 WLR 736 : 1979 QB 56 (CA)]. This view did not earlier find favour with the Privy Council or with the House of Lords [*South East Asia Fire Bricks v. Non-Metallic Mineral Products Manufacturing Employees Union*, (1980) 2 All ER 689, p. 692 : 1981 AC 383 : (1980) 3 WLR 318 (PC); *Re, Racial Communication Ltd.*, (1980) 2 All ER 634, pp. 638, 639, 644 : (1981) AC 374 : (1980) 3 WLR 181 (HL)]. The question was **reconsidered** by the House of Lords in *Page v. Hull University Visitors*, (1993) 1 All ER 97, pp. 107 to 109 (HL) and it appears that now under the English law the view expressed by LORD DENNING, which is based on *Anisminic's* case (see note 10, pp. 852-853), is generally the accepted view except in cases of determinations by a court of general jurisdiction and an inferior court or tribunal whose determinations are by statute or common law final and conclusive.

6. *Queen v. Commr. for Special Purposes*, (1888) 21 QBD 313, p. 319; *Brij Rajkrishna v. Shaw and Brothers*, AIR 1951 SC 115, p. 117 : (1951) SCR 145; *Choube Jagdish Prasad v. Ganga Prasad*, AIR 1959 SC 492, pp. 496, 497 : 1959 Supp (1) SCR 733; *Desika Charyulu v. State of A.P.*, AIR 1964 SC 807, pp. 816, 817; *Naresh v. State of Maharashtra*, AIR 1967 SC 1, p. 16 : (1986) 3 SCR 744. **See further** *Laxmi Engineering Works v. P.S.G. Industrial Institute*, 1995(2) Scale 626 : AIR 1995 SC 1428 : (1995) 3 SCC 583. (Forums and Commissions constituted under the Consumer Protection Act, 1986 which provide alternative remedy to a consumer are tribunals of this nature).
7. *Wade, Anglo American Administrative Law*, (1966) 82 Law Quarterly Review 226, p. 232.
8. AIR 1962 SC 1621, p. 1629 : (1963) 1 SCR 778. **See further** *Naresh v. State of Maharashtra*, AIR 1967 SC 1, p. 16 : (1966) 3 SCR 744; *Andhra Industrial Works v. Chief Controller, Imports*, AIR 1974 SC 1539, pp. 1541, 1542 : (1974) 2 SCC 348; *Urban Improvement Trust, Jodhpur v. Gokul Narain*, AIR 1996 SC 1819, p. 1823 : 1996 (4) SCC 178.
9. **See** text and note 71, p. 843, *supra*.

properly constituted, or it has no authority over the party against whom it makes its final order or it acts in bad faith, the final order passed would be in excess of jurisdiction and a nullity. In *Anisminic v. Foreign Compensation etc.*,[10] LORD REID in dealing with the question as to when an order of

---

10. (1969) 1 All ER 208 (HL). For comments and criticism, **see** (1969) 85 LQR 198 : (1971) 34 MLR 1. SEERVAI, Constitutional Law, Vol. 2, 4th Edition, pp. 1563 to 1572. It has been **approved** by the Supreme Court in *Union of India v. Tarachand*, AIR 1971 SC 1558 : (1971) 1 SCC 486; *M.L. Sethi v. R.L. Kapur*, AIR 1972 SC 2379 : (1972) 2 SCC 427; *A.R. Antulay v. R.S. Nayak*, AIR 1988 SC 1531, pp. 1546, 1547, 1608, 1609. It has also been **noticed** in *H.M. Trivedi v. Raju*, AIR 1973 SC 2602 : (1974) 3 SCC 415; *Cellular Operators Association of India v. Union of India*, (2003) 3 SCC 186, pp. 216, 217. It has been called a landmark decision and **reaffirmed** by the House of Lords. It has been said that the break-through that it made was the recognition that if a Tribunal whose jurisdiction was limited mistook the law applicable to the facts as it had found them and so asked itself the wrong question, *i.e.*, one which it was not empowered to inquire and so had no jurisdiction to determine, its purported determination would be a nullity. To this extent it has been said that it liberated English public law from the necessity of drawing distinction between errors of law that went to jurisdiction and errors of law that were within jurisdiction: *O'Reilly v. Mackman*, (1982) 3 All ER 1124, p. 1129 : (1983) 2 AC 237 (HL), (LORD DIPLOCK). PROFESSOR WADE in his Administrative Law, 6th Edition, p. 299, **doubted** the above outcome of *Anisminic* case, but the House of Lords in *Page v. Hull University Visitor*, (1993) 1 All ER 97, p. 107 : (1993) AC 682 (HL) has **affirmed** the above statement of LORD DIPLOCK and has laid down: "In general any error of law made by administrative tribunal or inferior court in reaching its decision can be quashed for error of law." The reasoning behind this view is: "Parliament had only conferred the decision making power on the basis that it was to be exercised on the correct legal basis; a misdirection in law in making the decision therefore rendered the decision *ultra vires*." Thus according to this decision the distinctions between error of law, error of law going to jurisdiction and error of law apparent on the face of the record have all vanished except where the decision of the tribunal is made final and conclusive (**see** note 5, p. 850). *Page v. Hull University visitor* was **reaffirmed** in *Williams v. Bedwellty Justices*, (1996) 3 All ER 737, p. 743 : (1997) AC 225 : (1996) 3 WLR 361 (HL) and *Boddington v. British Transport Police*, (1998) 2 All ER 203, p. 209. [**But** this view derived from *Anisminic* seems to be restricted in the public law field and has not been applied in arbitration law for construction of words 'exceeded its powers' in section 68(2)b of the Arbitration Act, 1996 and it has been held that an arbitration tribunal cannot be said to have exceeded its powers by committing mere error of law as that would be mere erroneous exercise of power: *Lesotho Highlands Development Authority v. Impregilo SPA*, (2005) 3 All ER 789 (paras 24, 25)]. The Indian cases have not gone that far. It appears that in Australia also judicial review is limited to jurisdictional errors of law and errors of law apparent on the face of the record; [(1997) 71 ALJ 366] and distinction is still made between errors of law and jurisdictional error of law or fact. The High Court of Australia describes jurisdictional error of law as follows: "If an administrative tribunal falls into an error of law which causes it to identify a wrong issue, to ask itself a wrong question, to ignore relevant material, to rely on irrelevant material or atleast, in some circumstances, to make an erroneous finding or to reach a mistaken conclusion, and the tribunal's exercise of power is thereby affected, it exceeds its authority or powers. Such an error of law is jurisdictional error which will invalidate any order or decision of the tribunal which reflects it:" *Craig v. South Australia*, (1995) 184 CLR 163, p. 179. In Australia a finding reached by an authority on a 'jurisdictional fact' is also not final. "The term jurisdictional fact (which may be a complex of elements) is often

[Footnote No. 10 Contd.]

a tribunal is a nullity observed: "It has sometimes been said that it is only where a tribunal acts without jurisdiction that its decision is a nullity. But in such cases the word 'jurisdiction' has been used in a very wide sense, and I have come to the conclusion that it is better not to use the term except in the narrow and original sense of the tribunal being entitled to enter on the enquiry in question. But there are many cases where, although the tribunal had jurisdiction to enter on the enquiry; it has done or failed to do something in the course of the enquiry which is of such a nature that its decision is a nullity. It may have given its decision in bad faith. It may have made a decision which it had no power to make. It may have failed in the course of the enquiry to comply with the requirements of natural justice. It may in perfect good faith have misconstrued the provisions giving it power to act so that it failed to deal with the question remitted to it and decided some question which was not remitted to it. It may have refused to take into account something which it was required to take into account or it may have based its decision on some matter which, under the provisions setting it up, it had no right to take into account. I do not intend this list to be exhaustive."[11] It will be seen that LORD REID here used the word 'jurisdiction' in a limited sense and separately enumerated other cases of nullity. LORD PEARCE, on the other hand, in the same case used the word 'jurisdiction' in its modern sense embracing all stages of inquiry. All cases of nullity according to him are cases of lack of jurisdiction. To quote his words: "Lack of jurisdiction may arise in various ways. There may be an absence of those formalities or things which are conditions precedent to the tribunal having any jurisdiction to embark on an enquiry or the tribunal may at the end make an order that it has no jurisdiction to make or in the intervening stage, while engaged on a proper enquiry, the tribunal may depart from the rules of natural justice; or it may ask itself the wrong questions; or it may take into account matters which it was not directed to take into account. Thereby it would step outside its jurisdiction. It would turn its enquiry into something not directed by Parliament and fail to make the enquiry which Parliament did direct. Any of these things would cause its

---

[Footnote No. 10 Contd.]

used to identify that criterion, satisfaction of which enlivens the power of the decision maker to exercise a discretion" and a court in an action challenging the order of the authority is not restricted to the material before the authority and has to determine the question of jurisdictional fact on the evidence before it: *Corporation of the city of Enfield v. Development Assessment Commission,* (2000) 74 ALJR 490, pp. 496, 500, 501. The High Court of Australia also holds that when the decision of a tribunal suffers from a juridictional error, *e.g.*, when a party required to be heard is not heard, the decision is a nullity and can be corrected by the tribunal and in such cases the tribunal does not become *functus officio* after rendering the decision: *Minister for Immigration and Multicultural Affairs v. Bharadwaj,* (2002) 76 ALJR 598. **Compare** Indian cases discussed in text and notes 18 to 20, p. 855 as also cases **refered** in note 4 p. 850.

11. *Ibid*, pp. 213, 214.

purported decision to be a nullity."[12] A review of the relevant authorities on the point leads to the following conclusions:

"(1) An Exclusionary Clause using the formula 'an order of the tribunal under this Act shall not be called in question in any court' is ineffective to prevent the calling in question of an order of the tribunal if the order is really not an order under the Act but a nullity.

(2) Cases of nullity may arise when there is lack of jurisdiction at the stage of commencement of enquiry *e.g.*, when (a) authority is assumed under an *ultra vires* statute; (b) the tribunal is not properly constituted, or is disqualified to act; (c) the subject-matter or the parties are such over which the tribunal has no authority to inquire; and (d) there is want of essential preliminaries prescribed by the law for commencement of the inquiry.[13]

(3) Cases of nullity may also arise during the course or at the conclusion of the inquiry. These cases are also cases of want of jurisdiction if the word 'jurisdiction' is understood in a wide sense. Some examples of these cases are: (a) when the tribunal has wrongly determined a jurisdictional question of fact or law; (b) when it has failed to follow the fundamental principles of judicial procedure, *e.g.*, has passed the order without giving an opportunity of hearing to the party affected; (c) when it has violated the fundamental provisions of the Act, *e.g.*, when it fails to take into account matters which it is required to take into account or when it takes into account extraneous and irrelevant matters; (d) when it has acted in bad faith; and (e) when it grants a relief or makes an order which it has no authority to grant or make;"[14] as also (f) when by misapplication of the law it has asked itself the wrong question.[15]

After quoting the conclusions set out above (from Sixth Edition p. 475 of this book) PARIPOORNAN, J. in *Mafatlal Industries v. Union of India*[16] said: "I would adopt the above statement of the law as my own."[17]

---

12. *Ibid*, p. 233. **See also** *Express Newspapers Pvt. Ltd. v. Union of India,* (1986) 1 SCC 133, p. 219 : AIR 1986 SC 872.
13. For example **see** *Seal v. Chief Constable of South Wales Police*, (2007) 4 All ER 177 (H.L.) (Proceedings for damages brought without leave of the High Court required under section 139(2) of the Medical Health Act, 1983 renders them a nullity).
14. *Bhupendra Singh v. G.K. Umath*, AIR 1970 MP 91, p. 98 (G. P. SINGH, J.).
15. *O'Reilly v. Mackman*, (1982) 3 All ER 1124, p. 1129 : (1983) 2 AC 237 : (1982) 3 WLR 1096 (HL). **See further** *Associated Engineering Co. v. Government of Andhra Pradesh*, AIR 1992 SC 232, p. 240 : (1991) 4 SCC 93. For judicial review on questions of fact, **see** *S.N. Chandrashekhar v. State of Karnataka,* (2006) 3 SCC 208 (para 35) : AIR 2006 SC 1204 and cases **referred** to therein.
16. 1996 (9) Scale 457 : 1997 (5) SCC 536 : JT 1996 (11) SC 283.
17. *Ibid*, pp. 555, 556 (Scale).

In *Desika Charyulu v. State of U.P.*,[18] one of the statutes considered was the Madras Estates (Abolition and Conversion into Ryotwari) Act, 1948, section 9(1) of which empowers the settlement officer to 'inquire and determine whether any *Inam* village in his jurisdiction is *Inam* estate or not'. Section 9(4) of the Act makes provision for an appeal to a tribunal and provides that 'the decision of the tribunal under this sub-section shall be final and not be liable to be questioned in any court of law'. In construing these provisions it was held by the Supreme Court that the question whether a village is an *Inam* village or not is a question relating to jurisdictional fact because unless a village is *Inam* village the settlement officer or the tribunal in appeal has no jurisdiction to hold it to be *Inam* estate. It was also held that decision of the settlement officer or of the tribunal in appeal that a particular *Inam* village is an *Inam* estate was liable to be challenged in a civil suit on the ground that the settlement officer or the tribunal, as the case may be, wrongly decided that the village is an *Inam* village. In *Munni Devi v. Gokalchand*[19] sections 7, 7A and 16 of the Uttar Pradesh (Temporary) Control of Rent and Eviction Act, 1947, came up for consideration. Sections 7 and 7A authorise the District Magistrate to allot an accommodation which has fallen vacant to any person and they also authorise him to evict any person from unauthorised occupation. Section 16 provides that 'no order made under this Act by the District Magistrate shall be called in question in any court'. On a construction of these provisions it was held by the Supreme Court that the jurisdiction of the District Magistrate to make an order of allotment and other orders depended upon existence of a vacancy which being a jurisdictional fact could not be conclusively decided by him and an order of allotment passed by him was liable to be challenged in a civil suit on the ground that he wrongly held that there was a vacancy. There are number of cases to illustrate[20] that a tribunal

---

18. AIR 1964 SC 807.

19. AIR 1970 SC 1727 : (1970) 2 SCC 879.

20. For other illustrations of jurisdictional fact, **see** *Budhusao v. Baleshwar Prosad Sao*, (1985) 1 SCC 565, p. 567 : AIR 1985 SC 602 (The question whether the person who advanced money is a money-lender, is a question of jurisdictional fact before the Additional Collector functioning under section 23 of the Bihar Money-lenders Act, 1974); *Shiv Chander Kapoor v. Amar Bose*, AIR 1990 SC 325 : (1990) 1 SCC 234 and *Shrisht Dhawan (Smt.) v. Shaw Brothers*, AIR 1992 SC 1555, p. 1563 : (1992) 1 SCC 534 (Non-requirement for a limited period by the landlord and letting out for residence are two jurisdictional facts under section 21 of the Delhi Rent Control Act, 1958 for permitting tenancy for a limited period so an order obtained by misrepresentation of these facts or deceit in respect of these facts is void); *Life Insurance Corporation of India v. India Automobiles and Co.*, AIR 1991 SC 884 : (1990) 4 SCC 286 (The relationship of landlord and tenant between the parties is a jurisdictional fact for determination of fair rent by the Rent Controller.); *Bharat Lal Baranwal v. Virendra Kumar Agarwal*, (2003) 2 SCC 343, p. 348 : AIR 2003 SC 1056 (Whether the tenant has changed user of the

[Footnote No. 20 Contd.]

cannot by erroneously deciding a jurisdictional fact clothe itself with jurisdiction which it does not possess and the ultimate decision is liable to be challenged, in spite of an exclusionary clause barring a civil suit, on the ground that jurisdiction was assumed where it did not exist by wrongly deciding jurisdictional fact and the decision was not a 'decision under the Act' being a nullity. But it has already been noticed[21] that the Legislature may clothe the tribunal with authority to decide conclusively even apparently jurisdictional facts and in that event the tribunal's determination cannot be challenged on the ground that jurisdictional facts were wrongly decided. Indeed in such a case the apparently jurisdictional facts are non-jurisdictional. In *Kamala Mills v. Bombay State*,[22] a suit was filed claiming refund of sales tax on the ground that the assessment of tax made by the Sales Tax Authorities functioning under the Bombay Sales Tax Act, 1946, was void on the ground that the authorities erroneously held that the transactions taxed were inside sales although they were really outside sales not liable to be taxed. Section 20 of the Act bars a suit for challenging any assessment made under the Act and there is an elaborate machinery for deciding questions arising in assessment proceedings. It was held by the Supreme Court that assessing authorities were given jurisdiction to decide conclusively whether the sales were inside or outside sales and the assessment was not liable to be challenged by a civil suit on the ground that 'outside sales' were wrongly held to be 'inside sales'. In *H.M. Trivedi v.*

[Footnote No. 20 Contd.]

premises is a jurisdictional fact in proceedings for eviction on that ground); *SBP & Co. v. Patel Engineering Ltd.,* (2005) 8 SCC 618 (paras 9 and 11) : (2005) 128 Comp Cas 465 [Under section 11(6) of the Arbitration and Conciliation Act, 1996, the Chief Justice while exercising powers in the matter of appointment of arbitrator has to decide whether there is an arbitration agreement, whether the applicant before him is a party and whether the conditions for the exercise of the power have been fulfilled. These are jurisdictional facts on which the decision will be final as provided in section 11(7) and the arbitration tribunal will have no authority to reopen these issues]; *Arun Kumar v. Union of India,* (2007) 1 SCC 732 (para 85) : (2006) 12 JT 121, [Existence of 'concession' in the matter of grant of rent respecting any accommodation provided to an employee by his employer is a jurisdictional fact under section 17(2)(ii) of the Income Tax Act, 1961 which has to be established before computation of this benefit as perquisite under the rules framed for this purpose]. **See further** *Carona Ltd. v. Parvathy Swaminathan & Sons*, AIR 2008 SC 187 para 21 : (2007) 8 SCC 559 (The fact or facts upon which the jurisdiction of a court, a Tribunal or an Authority depends can be said to be a jurisdictional fact. By erroneously assuming existence of a jurisdictional fact a subordinate court or an inferior Tribunal cannot confer upon itself jurisdiction which it otherwise does not possess); *R (A) v. Croydon London BC*, (2010) 1 All ER 469 (UK SC) p. 482 para 32 (Local Authority's determination as to age of a person whether he is a child or not under the Children Act 1989 is a jurisdictional fact).

21. **See** text and note 6, p. 851.

22. AIR 1965 SC 1942, pp. 1948, 1949 : 1966 (1) SCR 64. **See further** text and notes 56, 57, p. 840.

V.V.B. Raju,[23] the court held that entry of a person's name in the electoral roll of a constituency prepared under the Representation of the People Act, 1951, could neither be challenged before the civil court nor before an election tribunal on the ground that the person concerned was not ordinarily resident in that constituency. Section 19 of the Act lays down the conditions for registration and one of the conditions is that of ordinary residence. Sections 21 to 24 of the Act contain an elaborate machinery to enquire into claims and objections as regards registration as voter and for appeal from the decision of the registration officer. Section 30 of the Act bars the jurisdiction of the civil court to entertain or adjudicate upon any question whether any person is or is not entitled to be registered in an electoral roll for a constituency; or to question the legality of any action taken by or under the authority of an electoral registration officer or of any decision given by any authority appointed under the Act for the revision of any such roll. It was held that the authorities under the Act could conclusively decide the question of ordinary residence and a wrong decision on that question could not be treated as a jurisdictional error. These cases illustrate the principle that when a tribunal is given authority to decide conclusively questions of fact and law which are apparently jurisdictional, its determination cannot be challenged on the ground that those questions have been wrongly decided because in reality those questions are not jurisdictional.

In *Anisminic Ltd. v. Foreign Compensation Commission,*[24] the appellants' claim to compensation under the Foreign Compensation (Egypt) (Determination and Registration of Claims) Order, 1962, (made under the Foreign Compensation Act, 1950) was rejected by the Commission on the ground that the appellants' successor in title was not a British national. The House of Lords held that on a proper construction of the Order the question of successor in title did not arise when the original owner was the applicant. It was also held that as the appellant who applied for compensation was the original owner and admittedly a British national, its claim to compensation was rejected by taking into account the question of successor in title which the Commission had no right to take into account. It was further held that the determination of the Commission which asked itself the wrong question was a nullity being in excess of jurisdiction and could be declared to be so by the court and that the declaration would not offend section 4(4) of the Act which provided that 'the determination by the Commission of any application made to them under this Act shall not be called in question in any court of law'. In *Union of India v. Tarachand*

---

23. AIR 1973 SC 2602 : 1974 (1) SCR 548 : 1974 (3) SCC 415.
24. (1969) 1 All ER 208 : (1969) 2 AC 147 : (1969) 1 All ER 208 (HL). **Also see** text and notes 10-12 and 14, pp. 852-854, *supra*.

Gupta & Bros.,[25] the respondents imported 17 cases of goods in two consignments under a licence permitting import of parts and accessories of motor-cycles and scooters. The Deputy Collector of Customs on an examination of the goods held that they constituted 51 sets of Rixe Mopede complete in knocked down condition and that the goods were not parts and accessories of motor-cycles and scooters under Entry No. 295 of the Schedule to the Import Trade Control Policy for the relevant period. In holding so, the Deputy Collector relied upon a note contained in Entry No. 294 dealing with motor-cycles and scooters that licences granted under this item will not be valid for the import of motor-cycles or scooters in completely knocked down condition. In this view of the matter, the authorities confiscated the goods with an option to pay certain sums in lieu of confiscation and also imposed certain penalties. This action was taken under section 167(8) of the Sea Customs Act, 1878. Section 188 of the Act makes provision for an appeal against 'any decision or order passed by an officer of Customs under this Act'. The section further provides that 'every order passed in appeal under this section shall subject to the power of revision conferred by section 191, be final'. In a suit filed by the respondent to challenge the order of the Deputy Collector, it was held that in construing Entry No. 295, he was not entitled to take into consideration the note appended to Entry No. 294 and that his decision that the goods imported were not parts and accessories of motor-cycles or scooters, was in excess of jurisdiction. It was also held that the decision was not 'a decision or order passed by an officer of Customs under this Act' within the meaning of section 188 because the Deputy Collector had taken into consideration factors which he was not entitled to take into account and the decision was no decision at all. The civil suit, therefore, was not held to be barred. These cases illustrate that when in making an order an authority takes into consideration matters which on a proper construction of the relevant Act cannot be taken into account, the order is a nullity and can be challenged in a civil court.

In *Srinivasa v. State of A.P.*,[26] the question before the court was whether an order of the State Government fixing rates of rent of *ryoti* lands in an estate village under section 3(2) of the Andhra Pradesh (Andhra Area) Estates Land (Reduction of Rent) Act, 1947, was valid. Section 3(2) authorised the State Government to fix rates of rent after considering the report of a special officer appointed to recommend rates of rent for each class of *ryoti* land such as wet, dry and garden in existence at the time of the commencement of the Act. The recommendations of the special officer were

---

25. AIR 1971 SC 1558 : 1971 (1) SCC 486.
26. AIR 1971 SC 71 : (1969) 3 SCC 711.

based on the basis of entries in settlement register with respect to soil of another village. There was, thus, no evidence or material before the Special Officer regarding the classification of land of the village in question. The recommendations of the Special Officer were accepted by the State Government without any further inquiry. It was held that the order fixing the rates of rent was violative of fundamental principles of judicial procedure and was not in conformity with the provisions of the Act and was, therefore, liable to be challenged in a civil suit in spite of a provision in the Act that the validity of the order shall not be liable to be questioned in any court of law. In *Kishanlal v. State of Jammu and Kashmir*,[27] the appellant was dismissed from service on a report of an enquiry made by the Commission constituted under the Jammu and Kashmir (Government Servants) Prevention of Corruption Act, 1962 without complying with section 17(5) of the Act under which the appellant ought to have been 'supplied with the copy of proceedings of the enquiry' which he had demanded. Section 20 of the Act provided that 'nothing done or purporting to have been done under this Act shall be called in question in any court'. In a suit filed by the appellant to challenge his dismissal it was held that violation of natural justice as enacted in section 17(5), which the appellant had not waived, made the order suffer from a jurisdictional error and could be challenged in civil suit and section 20 was ineffective to bar the suit for an order made in violation of natural justice is void. The cases illustrate that an order which violates fundamental principles of judicial procedure or fundamental provisions of the law or principles of natural justice is void and is really not an order to which protection is given by an exclusionary provision.[28]

---

27. JT 1994 (2) SC 610. But in judicial review an order in breach of natural justice may be upheld if no prejudice is caused: *Managing Director ECIL v. B. Karunakar*, AIR 1994 SC 1074, p. 1092 : (1993) 4 SCC 727; *Ravi S. Naik v. Union of India*, AIR 1994 SC 1558, pp. 1568, 1569 : 1994 Supp (2) SCC 641. **See** also text and note 48, p. 511. **See further** *Surinder Nath Kapoor v. Union of India*, AIR 1988 SC 1777 : 1988 Supp SCC 626 [A garnishee order issued without giving notice to the person against whom it is made as required by section 226(3)(vi) of the Income-tax Act, 1961 is a nullity and so is the sale held in pursuance of such an order]; *R.B. Shreeram Durga Prasad and Fatehchand Narsing Das (M/s.) v. Settlement Commission*, AIR 1989 SC 1038 : (1989) 1 SCC 628 [An order passed under section 245-D(I-A) of the Income-tax Act, 1961 without hearing the assessee applicant is a nulity]. A distinction is drawn between cases of 'no hearing' and cases of 'defective hearing'. The former makes the order invalid, the latter raises the question of prejudice: **see** *State Bank of Patiala v. S.K. Sharma*, AIR 1996 SC 1669, pp. 1683, 1684 : (1996) 3 SCC 364 and text and note 47, p. 511, *supra*; *Union of India v. Mustafa & Najibai Trading Co.*, JT 1998 (5) SC 16, pp. 36, 37 : AIR 1998 SC 2526 : (1998) 6 SCC 79.
28. **See furhter** *A.G. v. Ryan*, (1980) AC 718, p. 730 (PC); *R. v. Secretary of State for Home Department*, (1997) 1 All ER 228, pp. 236, 237 (CA).

In respect of the courts of limited jurisdiction which are brought within the revisional jurisdiction of the High Court under section 115, Civil Procedure Code, 1908, it has been held that such courts cannot by a wrong determination of jurisdictional question of law or fact give to themselves a jurisdiction which they do not possess and the ultimate decision in such cases has been held to be revisable by the High Court being in excess of jurisdiction.[29] A wrong determination on a question of limitation or *res judicata*, which results in assumption of jurisdiction which the court did not possess or declining to exercise jurisdiction which the court possessed, would thus be error of jurisdiction amenable to correction under section 115.[30]

(c) Rule of conclusive evidence

The Legislature may make certain matters non-justiciable by enacting rules of conclusive evidence or conclusive proof. If by a legislative command proof of *A* is made conclusive evidence or conclusive proof of *B*, the moment existence of *A* is established the court is bound to regard the existence of *B* as conclusively established and evidence cannot be let in to

---

29. *Jaychand Babu v. Kamalaksha Choudhary*, AIR 1949 PC 239; *Choube Jagdish Prasad v. Ganga Prasad Chaturvedi*, AIR 1959 SC 492 : 1959 Supp (1) SCR 733; *Roshanlal Mishra v. Ishwardas*, AIR 1962 SC 647; *Prativa v. Rupendra Deb*, AIR 1965 SC 540, p. 545, (para 16) (minority judgment) : (1964) 4 SCR 69; *S. Rama Iyer v. Sundaresa*, AIR 1966 SC 1431 : (1966) 3 SCR 474; *Surja v. Hardeo*, AIR 1970 SC 1193, pp. 1193, 1197 : (1969) 2 SCR 448; *Executive Officer Arthanareshwar Temple v. R. Satyamoorthy,* AIR 1999 SC 958, p. 963 : (1999) 3 SCC 115. **But see** *Manindra Land & Building Corporation v. Bhutnath*, AIR 1964 SC 1336 : (1964) 3 SCR 495; *Abbasbhai v. Gulambhai*, AIR 1964 SC 1341 : 1964 (5) SCR 157; *Misrilal Parasmal v. Sadasivah*, AIR 1965 SC 553; *P.D. Chowgule v. M.H. Jadhav*, 1965 SCN 170-A; *Manik Chandra Nandy v. Debdas Nandy*, (1986) 1 SCC 512, p. 517 : AIR 1986 SC 446. Special Acts confer much wider revisional jurisdiction. See for example *Rukmini Amma Sardamma v. Kalyani Sulochana*, AIR 1993 SC 1616 : (1993) 1 SCC 449; *Molar Mal v. Kay Iron Works Pvt. Ltd.*, AIR 2000 SC 1261, p. 1264 : (2000) 4 SCC 285; *Nalakath Sainuddin v. Koorikadan Sulaiman,* AIR 2002 SC 2562, p. 2567 : (2002) 6 SCC 1. But even in special Acts, revisional jurisdiction is not a rehearing of the case like an appeal; *Sarla Ahuja v. United India Insurance Company Ltd.*, JT 1998 (7) SC 297, pp. 300, 301 : 1998 (5) Scale 674 : (1998) 8 SCC 119; *Gaya Din v. Hanuman Prasad,* AIR 2001 SC 386, pp. 388, 389 : (2001) 1 SCC 501; *Harshavardhana Chokkani v. Bhupendra N. Patel,* AIR 2002 SC 1373, p. 1374 : (2002) 3 SCC 626; *Atma S. Berar v. Mukhtar Singh,* AIR 2003 SC 624, p. 629.

30. *Pandurang v. Maruti,* AIR 1966 SC 153 (para 10) : (1966) 1 SCR 102; *National Thermal Power Corpn. Ltd. v. Siemens Atkeingesellschaft,* (2007) 4 SCC 451 (para 17) : AIR 2007 SC 1491.

show the non-existence of *B*. In effect the existence or non-existence of *B* after proof of *A* ceases to be justiciable.[31]

Section 5 of the Bombay Land Requisition Act, 1948 empowers the State Government to requisition any building for public purpose, if the owner, landlord or tenant had not resided in the building for a continuous period of six months prior to the order. The section further provides that the State Government after holding such enquiry as it may deem fit will make a declaration in the order of requisition that the owner, landlord or the tenant has not resided for a continuous period of six months prior to the order and that such declaration shall be conclusive evidence that the owner, landlord or tenant has not so resided. Similarly, section 6 of the same Act provides that if at the time of issue of a notification in respect of any specified area, any premises are vacant or become vacant thereafter, State Government may requisition the same for public purpose. The section further provides that at the time of making an order of requisition the State Government shall make such inquiry as it deems fit and make a declaration in the order that the premises were vacant or had become vacant and such a declaration shall be conclusive evidence that the premises were or had so become vacant. In construing these provisions SINHA, J. said: "The Act has made a specific provision to the effect that the determination on the questions referred to in sections 5 and 6 of the Act by the State Government shall be conclusive evidence of the declaration so made. But that does not mean that the jurisdiction of the High Court under Article 226 or of this court (Supreme Court) under Article 32 or on appeal has been impaired. In a proper case the High Court or this court in the exercise of its special jurisdiction has the power to determine how far provisions of the statute have or have not been complied with. But special powers of this court or of the High Court cannot extend to reopening a finding by the State Government under section 5 of the Act that the tenant has not actually resided in the premises for a continuous period of six months immediately preceding the date of the order or under section 6 that the premises had become vacant at about the time indicated in the order impugned. Those are not collateral matters, which could on proper evidence be reopened by the Courts of Law. The Legislature in its wisdom has made those declarations conclusive and it is not for this court to question that wisdom."[32]

---

31. *Lilavati Bai v. Bombay State*, AIR 1957 SC 521, pp. 527, 528 : 1957 SCR 721; *Somvanti v. State of Punjab*, AIR 1963 SC 151, p. 162 : (1963) 2 SCR 774; *Izhar Ahmad v. Union of India*, AIR 1962 SC 1052 : 1962 Supp (3) SCR 235; *Suffolk County Council v. Mason*, (1979) 2 All ER 369, p. 377 : 1979 AC 705 (HL) [Conclusive evidence clause positively establishing the existence of a fact and negatively establishing the non-existence of another].

32. *Lilawati Bai v. Bombay State*, AIR 1957 SC 521, p. 528 : 1957 SCR 721.

On the same principle a declaration that certain land is needed for a public purpose or for a company made by the Government under section 6(3) of the Land Acquisition Act, 1894, is 'conclusive evidence' that the land is so needed and is not justiciable in a court of law except on the ground of fraud or colourable exercise of power.[33]

If the statute itself provides the method of disproving B after proof of A that method alone can be adopted for that purpose.[34] Birth during the continuance of a valid marriage conclusively establishes the paternity under section 112 of the Evidence Act and the legitimacy of the child cannot be demolished by the DNA test; and the only manner the conclusiveness of the paternity can be rebutted is, as provided in section 112, by proof of non-access when the child could have been begotten.[35]

In *Izhar Ahmed v. Union of India*,[36] the Supreme Court has laid down the test for determining whether a rule of irrebutable presumption is a rule of evidence or a rule of substantive law. GAJENDRAGADKAR, J. in that connection said: "In deciding the question as to whether a rule about irrebuttable presumption is a rule of evidence or not, it seems to us that the proper approach to adopt would be to consider whether fact *A* from the proof of which a presumption is required to be drawn about the existence of fact *B* is inherently relevant in the matter of proving fact *B* and has inherently any probative or persuasive value in that behalf or not. If fact *A* is inherently relevant in proving the existence of fact *B* and to any rational mind it would bear probative or a persuasive value in the matter of proving the existence of fact *B* then a rule prescribing either a rebuttable or irrebuttable presumption in that behalf would be a rule of evidence. On the other hand, if fact *A* is inherently not relevant in proving the existence of fact *B* or has

---

33. *Somwanti v. State of Punjab*, AIR 1963 SC 151, pp. 162 to 166 : (1963) 2 SCR 774; *Raja Anand v. State of Uttar Pradesh*, AIR 1967 SC 1081 : 1967 (1) SCR 373. A person who has not raised any objection under section 5A of the Land Acquisition Act, 1894 cannot challenge the declaration under section 6: *Delhi Adm. v. Gurdip Singh Uban*, (1999) 7 SCC 44 : AIR 1999 SC 3822.

But when acquisition is made for a company the court can enquire whether Part VII of the Act was complied with, for section 6 is expressly 'subject to the provisions of Part VII of the Act'. **See** *Somwanti v. State of Punjab, supra*, pp. 163, 164; *R.L. Arora v. State of Uttar Pradesh*, AIR 1962 SC 764 : AIR 1964 SC 1230; *State of West Bengal v. P.N. Talukdar*, AIR 1965 SC 646; *Devender Singh v. State of Punjab*, AIR 2008 SC 261 paras 33, 35, 36 : (2008) 1 SCC 728 (A token contribution by the State towards compensation will not always make the acquisition for the State) **see further** text and note 8 p. 475.

34. *Kamti Devi v. Poshi Ram,* AIR 2001 SC 2226 : (2001) 5 SCC 311.

35. *Nandlal Wasudeo Badwaik v. Lata Nandlal Badwaik*, AIR 2014 SC 932 : (2014) 2 SCC 576.

36. AIR 1962 SC 1052 : 1962 Supp (3) SCR 235. For rebuttable presumption, **see** *Sodhi Transport Co. v. State of U.P.*, (1986) 2 SCC 486, pp. 494-97 : AIR 1986 SC 1099.

no probative value in that behalf and yet a rule is made prescribing for a rebuttable or an irrebuttable presumption in that connection that rule would be a rule of substantive law and not a rule of evidence."[37] In this case[38] the question was whether Rule 3, of the Citizenship Rules, 1956, framed by the Central Government under section 9(2) of the Citizenship Act, 1955, was valid or not. Section 9(2) of the Act authorises the Central Government to prescribe rules of evidence and rule 3 framed thereunder reads: 'The fact that a citizen of India has obtained on any date a passsport from the Government of any other country shall be conclusive proof of his having voluntarily acquired citizenship of the country before that date'. This rule was held to be a rule of evidence and therefore valid.[39] But it has been held that the rule is not attracted if the passport is obtained under compulsion or on account of fraud or misrepresentation and not voluntarily.[40]

In our country there being no rigid separation of powers between the three organs of the State, the Legislature by enacting a conclusive evidence clause does not encroach upon the power of the judicature.[41]

The aforesaid discussion relating to the effect of a conclusive evidence clause is subject at least to two qualifications. A conclusive evidence clause may be held to be invalid as an unreasonable restriction of the fundamental rights.[42] In such a situation it is obvious that it will have no effect at all. Further, the insertion of such clauses in statutes conferring power may fail to shut out basic defect of jurisdiction in exercise of the power,[43] and may also be ineffective to bar an attack on the ground of fraud or colourable exercise of power.[44]

3. EXCLUSION OF JURISDICTION OF SUPERIOR COURTS

The question of curtailing the jurisdiction of the Supreme Court or High Courts as conferred by the Constitution does not arise in India. The

---

37. *Ibid*, p. 1063. **See further** *Govt. of Andhra Pradesh v. Mohd. Khan*, AIR 1962 SC 1778 : 1962 Supp (3) SCR 288; *Ashok Leyland v. State of Tamil Nadu*, AIR 2004 SC 2836, p. 2853.
38. **See** note 36, *supra*.
39. *Ibid*. **See further** *Bhanwaroo Khan v. Union of India*, AIR 2002 SC 1614 : (2002) 4 SCC 346.
40. *Mohd. Ayub Khan, etc. v. Commr. of Police, Madras*, AIR 1965 SC 1623 : (1965) 2 SCR 884; *Gangadhar v. Erasmo Jesus*, AIR 1975 SC 972 : (1975) 1 SCC 544.
41. *Hapur Municipality v. Raghvendra*, AIR 1966 SC 693, p. 699 : (1966) 1 SCR 950; *Dharmdas v. State of Punjab*, AIR 1975 SC 1069, pp. 1079, 1080 : (1975) 1 SCC 343.
42. *Corporation of Calcutta v. Calcutta Tramways*, AIR 1964 SC 1279 : (1964) 5 SCR 25.
43. **See** Chaper 12 title 3(g)(ii), p. 1098.
44. *Somwanti v. State of Punjab*, AIR 1963 SC 151, pp. 165, 166 (para 40) : (1963) 2 SCR 774; *State of West Bengal v. P.N. Talukdar*, AIR 1965 SC 646, p. 652 (para 11).

jurisdiction conferred by the Constitution[45] can be taken away only by amending the Constitution and not by statutory enactments.[46] The only exception in this respect is Article 262(2) of the Constitution which enables Parliament to provide by law that 'neither the Supreme Court nor any other court shall exercise jurisdiction' in respect of any dispute relating to waters of inter-state rivers or river valleys. The law enacted by Parliament in this context is Inter-State Water Disputes Act, 1956 which provides for constitution of Water Disputes Tribunal for adjudication of such disputes and section 11 of which bars the jurisdiction of all courts including the Supreme Court in terms of Article 262(2). Interpreting this provision it has been held that the bar under section 11 will come into play when a Tribunal is constituted and till then the Supreme Court can issue interim order preserving the *status quo*.[47] If a writ did otherwise lie against a body it is a moot point whether judicial review of its actions could be excluded by grant of immunity either by a statute or by a statutory notification in pursuance of an international agreement.[48]

Even a provision in the Constitution conferring finality to the decision of an authority is not construed as completely excluding judicial review under Articles 136, 226 and 227 of the Constitution[49] but limiting it to jurisdictional errors *viz.* infirmities based on violation of constitutional mandate, *mala fides,* non-compliance with rules of natural justice and perversity.[50] The bar in Article 329(b) of the Constitution, that notwithstanding

---

45. Regarding Supreme Court, **see** Articles 131 to 134, 136, 142, 143 and Articles 32 and 129; regarding High Court, **see** Articles 215, 226 to 228.

46. *Raj Krushna Bose v. Vinod Kanungo*, AIR 1954 SC 202, p. 204 : 1954 SCR 913; *Durga Shanker v. Raghuraj Singh*, AIR 1954 SC 520, p. 522 : (1955) 1 SCR 267; *In re, Kerala Education Bill*, 1957, AIR 1958 SC 956, pp. 986, 987 : 1959 SCR 995; *Custodian, E.P., Punjab v. Jafran Begum*, AIR 1968 SC 169, p. 174; *Union Carbide Corporation v. Union of India*, AIR 1992 SC 248 : (1991) 4 SCC 584; *Pritam Pal v. High Court of Madhya Pradesh*, AIR 1992 SC 904 : 1993 Supp (1) SCC 529; *Surya Dev Rai v. Ram Chander Rai,* (2003) 6 SCC 675, pp. 694, 695 : AIR 2003 SC 3044; *Mahendra Saree Emporium v. G.V. Srinivas Murthy*, (2005) 1 SCC 481, p. 488.

47. *State of Orissa v. Government of India,* (2009) 5 SCC 492 paras 51 to 53 : (2009) 2 JT 233.

48. *G. Bassi Reddy v. International Crops Research Institute,* (2003) 4 SCC 225, p. 236 : (2003) 2 LLJ 1123.

N.B. The United Nations Privileges and Immunities Act, 1947 was passed to give effect to the Convention on the Privileges and Immunities of the United Nations. Similar Privileges and Immunities have been conferred on many other International organisations by notification under section 3 of the Act.

49. *Kihota Hollohan v. Zachilhu*, AIR 1993 SC 412, pp. 445, 446 : 1992 Supp (2) SCC 651.

50. *Ibid*, pp. 449 to 451; *Ravi S. Naik v. Union of India*, AIR 1994 SC 1558, p. 1564 : 1994 Supp (2) 641; *Dr. Mahachandra Prasad Singh v. Chairman Bihar Legislative Council*, (2004) 8 SCC 747, p. 757 : AIR 2005 SC 69; *Rajendra Singh Rana v. Swami Prasad Maurya,* (2007) 4 SCC 270 (paras 29, 40, 41) : AIR 2007 SC 1305.

anything in this constitution (which prevents interference even by High Courts and Supreme Court), no election to Parliament or Legislature of a State shall be called in question except by an election petition, was held not to apply to prevent an appeal to the Supreme Court under Article 136 after the election process was over and the election tribunal had given its decision.[51] A two-Judge Bench of the Supreme Court, distinguishing the constitution bench decision in *Election Commission v. Saka Vekatrao*,[52] held that Article 329(b) does not also prevent the High Court from declaring under Article 226 that a person elected to the legislative assembly of a State was not qualified to be chosen as a member and in restraining him to function as a member and directing realisation from him of penalty under Article 193.[53] In this case the person concerned was not an elector in the Assembly Constituency which fact he knew and he got elected by impersonating another person of the same name entered in the electoral roll. The election was not challenged by election petition as the rival candidate, who later moved the High Court, came to know of the fraud long after the period for challenging the election by election petition had expired. Article 243-O, which relates to election to Panchayats, and Article 243ZG, which relates to election to Municipalities, were brought in by the Constitution 74th Amendment Act and which are similarly worded as Article 329 have been similarly construed but subject to the qualification that a Constitution Amendment cannot destroy the basic structure of judical review enshrined in Articles 32, 136 and 226 of the Constitution.[54]

As the powers of the Supreme Court under Articles 32 and 136 and that of the High Courts under Articles 226 and 227 of the Constitution are parts of its basic structure, it is impossible even by Constitution Amendment to create a Tribunal making its orders immune from challenge under the aforesaid provisions of the Constitution.[55]

---

51. *Durgashankar Mehta v. Raghuraj Singh,* AIR 1954 SC 520 : (1955) 1 SCR 267.

52. AIR 1953 SC 210 : 1953 SCR 1144. **See further** text and note 64, p. 823.

53. *K. Venkatachalam v. A. Swamickan,* AIR 1999 SC 1723, pp. 1733, 1734 : (1999) 4 SCC 526. For construction of Article 329(b), **see further** *Mohinder Singh Gill v. Chief Election Commissioner,* AIR 1978 SC 851 : (1978) 1 SCC 405; *Shyamdeo Pd. Singh v. Nawal Kishore Yadav,* AIR 2000 SC 3000 : (2000) 8 SCC 46.

54. *Harnek Singh v. Charanjit Singh,* (2005) 8 SCC 383 (para 16) : AIR 2006 SC 52. For construction of the bar of jurisdiction of all courts regarding delimitation of constituencies contained in Article 329(a) **see** *Meghraj Kothari v. Delimitation Commission,* AIR 1967 SC 669 : (1967) 1 SCR 400 and *Association of Residents of Mhow v. Delimitation Commission,* (2009) 5 SCC 404 : (2009) 5 JT 69; *Kurapati Maria Das v. Dr. Ambedkar Seva Samajan,* (2009) 7 SCC 787 paras 19, 20 27 (The bar under Article 243-ZG(b) is absolute and election petition is the only remedy for challenging the election especially when facts are disputed).

55. *L. Chandra Kumar v. Union of India,* AIR 1997 SC 1125 : (1997) 3 SCC 261 **see further** text and notes 31 and 53, pp. 300, 306, *supra.*

But a Constitution Amendment[56] can authorise constituting a Tribunal which has jurisdiction to examine the validity of enactments in certain subjects and exercise also power of judicial review on those subjects under Articles 226 and 227 of the Constitution and to that extent direct filing of a petition to the High Court may be excluded.[57] But orders of such a Tribunal will be subject to scrutiny by a Division Bench of the High Court under Articles 226 and 227.[58]

In addition to its powers under Articles 226 and 227 of the Constitution, the High Court can also set aside an order of a tribunal which has been obtained by fraud in exercise of its power as a court of record under Article 215.[59]

A Judge of a High Court trying an election petition under the Representation of the People Act, 1951 can entertain and decide upon the validity of an enactment which is not excluded from being challenged by Article 329(a) of the Constitution.[60]

As regards legislative enactments, there can be no doubt that if the Legislature states that the decision or order of a court or tribunal shall be final and conclusive, the remedies available under the Constitution remain unfettered.[61] But when an Act prescribed qualifications for appointment to Industrial Tribunal and Industrial Court and provided that the order appointing any person to the Tribunal or Court shall not be called in question in any manner, the Supreme Court held that although this provision did not shut out inquiry for issue of a writ of *quo warranto*, the High Court should not hold the appointment invalid unless there be clear infringement of the law.[62] Further, it has been held that a law providing for the quantum of punishment for contempt of court or period of limitation for initiating contempt proceedings or even as to what may not be regarded as contempt cannot be taken to be a law which abrogates or stultifies the powers of the

---

56. Article 323A added by Constitution 42nd Amendment Act, 1976.

57. *L. Chandra Kumar v. Union of India, supra*, (paras 98 and 99); *State of West Bengal v. Ashish Kumar Roy*, AIR 2005 SC 254, pp. 258, 259.

58. *Ibid.*

59. *Hamza Haji v. State of Kerala*, (2006) 7 SCC 416, pp. 427, 428 : AIR 2006 SC 3028.

60. *Harishanker Jain v. Sonia Gandhi*, AIR 2001 SC 3689, p. 3694 : (2001) 8 SCC 233.

61. *Raj Krushna Bose v. Vinod Kanungo*, AIR 1954 SC 202 : 1954 SCR 913.

62. *Statesman (P.) Ltd. v. H.R. Deb*, AIR 1968 SC 1495 : (1968) 3 SCR 614. But in the *State of Haryana v. Haryana Co-operative Transport Ltd.*, AIR 1977 SC 237 : (1977) 1 SCC 271, the appointment was successfully challenged as the person appointed was clearly not qualified to be appointed.

Supreme Court under Article 129 or of the High Courts under Article 215 of the Constitution in relation to contempt.[63]

Even in England where Parliament is supreme, there is a strong presumption against exclusion of supervisory jurisdiction of superior courts. Thus, a remedy by writ of *certiorari* is not construed as excluded except in case of express statutory provision to that effect and provisions, found in statutes conferring powers on tribunals, to the effect that their decision shall be final, have been construed as not taking away the remedy by writ of *certiorari*.[64] The word 'final' has been interpreted to mean 'without appeal'.[65] In India the High Courts, apart from exercising supervisory powers under the Constitution, exercise a similar power under section 115 of the Code of Civil Procedure, 1908, over all subordinate courts. Even this power of revision under section 115, which can be excluded by legislative enactments, is construed as not readily excluded except by express provision to that effect. Thus, if a special Act while conferring power on a subordinate court enacts that the decision rendered by such court shall be final, that will only be effective in taking away a remedy by way of appeal but not a remedy by way of revision under section 115.[66] Similarly a provision barring a second appeal against an appellate order does not impliedly take away the remedy by way of revision under section 115.[67] But if the finality clause is associated with the expression 'shall not be questioned in a court of law except as otherwise provided in the Act',

---

63. *Pallav Sheth v. Custodian,* AIR 2001 SC 2763, p. 2773 : (2001) 7 SCC 549. A fair criticism of the judiciary does not amount to contempt: *Hari Singh Nagra v. Kapil Sibbal*, (2010) 7 SCC 502 : (2010) 8 JT 56.

64. HALSBURY'S Law of England, 3rd Edition, Vol. 11, p. 137 and **see** *Re, Gilmore's Application*, (1957) 1 All ER 796, pp. 801, 803 (CA); *Pearlman v. Harrow School*, (1979) 1 All ER 365, pp. 370-72 : (1979) QB 56 (CA), **see further** *R. v. Hallstrom*, (1985) 3 All ER 775 : 1986 QB 1090 (CA); *Commissioner of Sales Tax v. D.V. Super Cotton Bowl Refilling Works*, AIR 1989 SC 922, pp. 929, 930 : (1989) 1 SCC 643.

65. *Re, Gilmore's Application, supra*, p. 801; *Secretary of State v. Hindustan Co-operative Insurance Society*, AIR 1931 PC 149; *South Asia Industries (P) Ltd. v. Sarup Singh*, AIR 1965 SC 1442, pp. 1447, 1448 : (1965) 2 SCR 756. **See further** *Jones v. Secretary of State*, (1972) 1 All ER 145.

66. *Everest Apartments Co-op. Housing Society v. State of Maharashtra*, AIR 1966 SC 1449 : (1966) 3 SCC 365; *State of Orissa v. Arkhita Bisoi*, AIR 1977 SC 1194 : (1977) 3 SCC 242; *Chhaganlal v. Municipal Corporation, Indore*, AIR 1977 SC 1555, p. 1558 : (1977) 2 SCC 409. **See also** *Yogendra Prasad v. Addl. Registrar, Co-op. Societies, Bihar*, AIR 1991 SC 2137, p. 2140 : (1992) Supp (1) SCC 720. Even a power of Review is not excluded by a general finality clause—*Reassat Hossain v. Hadjee Abdoolah*, ILR (1876) 2 Cal 131 (PC); *Phani Bhusan v. Sanat Kumar*, AIR 1935 Cal 773.

67. *I.T.I. Ltd. v. Siemens Public Communications Network Ltd.*, AIR 2002 SC 2308 : (2002) 5 SCC 510.

the remedy of revision under section 115 has to be taken as excluded.[68] And in a particular context the words 'subject to an appeal the order shall be final' may also exclude a general remedy of revision.[69] Even in cases where jurisdiction under section 115 is taken away, the High Courts can interfere under Articles 226 and 227 of the Constitution.[70] Similar words as discussed above[71] in a penal statute will exclude the remedies under the Code of Criminal Procedure, 1973 for example under section 482; but they do not affect the remedy under Article 226 or 227 of the constitution.[72] A provision made by the State Legislature for abatement of pending proceedings under a State Act after its repeal may not affect a pending application under Article 136 in the Supreme Court.[73]

The appellate and revisional jurisdiction of superior courts is not taken as excluded simply because the subordinate court exercises a special jurisdiction. The reason is that when a special Act on matters governed by that Act confers a jurisdiction to an established court, as distinguished from a *persona designata*, without any words of limitation, then, the ordinary incident of procedure of that court including any general right of

---

68. *Andal Ammal v. Sadasiwan Pillai,* (1987) 1 SCC 183 : AIR 1987 SC 203; *Jetha Bhai & Sons Jew Town Cochin v. Sunderdas Rathenai (M/s.),* AIR 1988 SC 812 : (1988) 1 SCC 722. **But see** *Shyamaraju Hegde v. Venkatesha*, AIR 1987 SC 2323 : 1987 Supp SCC 321.

69. *Commissioner of Sales Tax, U.P. v. Super Cotton Bowl Refilling Works*, AIR 1989 SC 922, pp. 929, 930 : 1989 (1) SCC 643.

70. *Surya Dev Rai v. Ramchandra Rai,* (2003) 6 SCC 675, pp. 694, 695 : AIR 2003 SC 3044 (The case contains a detailed discussion about powers of the High Court under Articles 226 and 227 of the Constitution in relation to inferior courts and tribunals). The question whether an order passed by a Single Judge is under Article 226 or 227 is to be decided not only by nomenclature of the petition in which it is passed but by reading the petition as a whole and the order passed on it: *M.M.T.C. Ltd. v. Commissioner of Commercial Tax,* (2009) 1 SCC 8 para 11 : AIR 2009 SC 1349. The case of *Surya Dev Rai* in so far as it holds that judgments of inferior courts of civil jurisdiction can be quashed under Article 226 has been doubted and the matter on this point has been **referred** to a larger Bench: *Radhey Shyam v. Chhabinath,* (2009) 5 SCC 616 paras 23 to 25 : (2009) 6 JT 511. **See further** *Shalini Shyam Shetty v. Rajendra Shankar Patil,* (2010) 8 SCC 329 para 49 : (2010) 7 JT 514 (power of interference under Article 227 in pending suits is to be kept to the minimum. The repeal of section 115 Civil Procedure Code does not expand the power under Article 227); *Jai Singh v. MCD,* (2010) 9 SCC 385 para 15 : (2010) 10 JT 241. (The exercise of jurisdiction must be within the well recognized constraints. It cannot be exercised like a 'bull in a china shop' to correct all errors of judgment of a court or tribunal within its jurisdiction. This correctional jurisdiction can be exercised in cases where orders have been passed in grave dereliction of duty or in flagrant abuse of fundamental principles of law or justice). An order of an inferior court or tribunal which is a nullity because of defect of jurisdiction can also be challenged by private law remedy of civil suit: **see** title 9(2)b p. 848.

71. **See** text and notes 69 and 70.

72. *State of Himachal Pradesh v. Dhanwant Singh,* AIR 2004 SC 1636 : (2004) 2 JT 367.

73. *Mahendra Saree Emporium v. G.V. Srinivas Murthy*, AIR 2004 AC 4289, pp. 4294 to 4296 : (2004) 7 JT 20.

appeal or revision against its decision is attracted.[74] "The true rule is", said LORD SIMONDS, "that where a legal right is in dispute and the ordinary courts of the country are seized of such dispute the courts are governed by the ordinary rules of procedure applicable thereto and an appeal lies, if authorised by such rules, notwithstanding that the legal right claimed arises under a special statute which does not in terms confer a right of appeal."[75] Therefore, when an appeal comes to the High Court

---

74. *National Telephone Co. Ltd. v. His Majesty's Post Master General*, (1913) AC 546, p. 552 (HL); *Secretary of State for India v. Chellikani Rama Rao*, (1916) ILR 39 Mad 617, p. 654 (PC); *Maung Ba Thaw v. Ma Pin*, AIR 1934, PC 81, p. 82 : 61 IA 158; *Hemsingh v. Basant Das*, AIR 1936 PC 93, pp. 95, 96; *Adaikappa v. Chandra Sekhara*, AIR 1948 PC 12, p. 14; *National Sewing Thread Co. v. James Chadwick & Bros.*, AIR 1953 SC 357, pp. 359, 360; *South Asia Industries (P.) Ltd. v. Sarup Singh, supra*, p. 1446; *Ramchandra v. State of U.P.*, AIR 1966 SC 1888, p. 1890 : 1966 Supp SCR 393; *Collector, Varanasi v. Gourishanker*, AIR 1968 SC 384 : (1968) 1 SCR 372; *Kerala State Electricity Board v. T.P. Kunhaliumma*, AIR 1977 SC 282, pp. 285, 286 : (1976) 4 SCC 634; *Maganlal v. Jaiswal Industries, Neemuch*, AIR 1989 SC 2113, p. 2124 : 1989 (4) SCC 344; *Deepchand v. Land Acquisition Officer*, JT 1994 (3) SC 319, p. 322 : AIR 1994 SC 1901 : (1994) 4 SCC 99; *I.T.I. Ltd. v. Siemens Public Communications Network Ltd., supra*, p. 2313; *Subal Paul v. Malina Paul*, AIR 2003 SC 1928, p. 1932 : (2003) 10 SCC 361 (The above passage from this book is **quoted** with approval).

When jurisdiction is conferred on a *persona designata* as distinguished from a court, the rule is different, **see** *Rangoon Botatoung Co. Ltd. v. Collector of Rangoon*, (1913) ILR 40 Cal 21, p. 27 (PC); *Special Officer, Salasette Building Sites v. Dossabhai Bezonji*, (1913) 20 IC 763 (PC); *Secretary of State for India v. Hindustan Co-operative Insurance Society Ltd.*, AIR 1931 PC 149; *Hanskumar v. Union of India*, AIR 1958 SC 947 : 1959 SCR 1177. Correctness of the case of *Hanskumar* has been **doubted** in *Collector of Varanasi v. Gourishanker, supra*. On the same principle when a revenue officer exercises jurisdiction as a designated authority under a Special Act, such as the Land Acquisition Act, 1894 his orders are not open to appeal or revision under the Land Revenue Code: *Phulchand Bhagwandas Gugale v. State of Maharashtra*, (2005) 1 SCC 193, pp. 198, 199; *Cantonment Board v. Pyarelal*, AIR 1966 SC 108 : 1965 (3) SCR 341.

For meaning of '*persona designata*', **see** *Central Talkies Ltd. v. Dwarka Prasad*, AIR 1961 SC 606, p. 609 : 1961 (3) SCR 495; *Ramchandra v. State of U.P.*, AIR 1966 SC 1888 : (1966) Supp SCR 393; *Thakur Das v. State of Madhya Pradesh*, AIR 1978 SC 1, p. 5 : (1978) 1 SCC 27 (Judicial authority appointed as appellate authority under section 6C of the Essential Commodities Act, 1955 is not *persona designata*); *Mukri Gopalan v. Cheppilat Puthanpurayil Aboobacker*, 1995 (4) Scale 438 : 1995 AIR SCW 3389: AIR 1995 SC 2272 : (1995) 5 SCC 5 [District Judge functioning as appellate authority under Kerala Building (Lease and Rent Control) Act, 1965 is not *persona designata*].

75. *Adaikappa v. Chandra Sekhara*, AIR 1948 PC 12, p. 14 : 74 IA 264 : (1948) 1 MLJ 41. **See further,** *I.T.I. Ltd. v. Siemens Public Communications Network Ltd.*, AIR 2002 SC 2308, p. 2313 : (2002) 5 SCC 510.

When a special court is constituted to exclusively deal with a matter which was being dealt with by the ordinary courts, the procedure of the ordinary courts will apply to the special court to the extent it is not excluded by the Act constituting

[Footnote No. 75 Contd.]

under a special statute, a further appeal under the Letters Patent is not readily taken as excluded[76] unless the special statute sets out a self-contained code.[77]

[Footnote No. 75 Contd.]

the special court. For example a special court, which is in effect a sessions court, constituted under section 14 of the Scheduled Castes and Scheduled Tribes (Prevention of Atrocities) Act, 1989 for trial of offences under that Act, cannot take cognizance of any offence except in accordance with section 193 of the Code of Criminal Procedure without the offence being committed to that court by a magistrate: *Gangula Ashok v. State of Andhra Pradesh,* AIR 2000 SC 740 : (2000) 2 SCC 504; *Vidyadharan v. State of Kerala*, (2004) 1 SCC 215 : AIR 2004 SC 536. A special court constituted under the Special Court (Trial of Offences relating to Transactions in Securities) Act, 1992 is required by section 9(1) to follow the procedure for the trial of warrant cases before a magistrate and by section 9(2) is deemed to be a sessions court and the provisions of Code of Criminal Procedure, 1973 apply to it in so far as they are not inconsistent with the Special Act. Construing these provisions it was held that the Special Court has the power of a magistrate to grant pardons under sections 306 to 308 Code of Criminal Procedure, 1973: *Harshad S. Mehta v. State of Maharashtra,* AIR 2001 SC 3774 : (2001) 8 SCC 257. But on matters on which the special statute sets out a self-contained Code, the applicability of general law of procedure will be impliedly excluded; **see** *R. v. Middlesex Justices*, (1965) 2 All ER 68.

76. *Subal Paul v. Malina Paul,* AIR 2003 SC 1929, p. 1932 : (2003) 10 SCC 361 (A Letters Patent appeal against an order of a Single Judge in appeal under section 299 of the Succession Act is maintainable); *Sharda Devi v. State of Bihar,* AIR 2002 SC 1357 : (2002) 3 SCC 705 (An order passed by a Single Judge in appeal under section 54 of the Land Acquisition Act is appealable under the Letters Patent. **See further** *P.S. Sathappan v. Andhra Bank Ltd.*, AIR 2004 SC 5152, pp. 5174, 5175, 5176 : (2004) 8 JT 464. (By section 100A Civil Procedure Code as amended in 2002 there is now specific exclusion of Letters Patent Appeal 'where any appeal from an original or appellate decree or order is heard and decided by a Single Judge of a High Court').

77. For example appeals under the Letters Patent against the orders of a Single Judge while trying an election petition under the Representation of the People Act, 1951 are impliedly excluded; *Upadhyaya Hargovind Devshanker v. Dhirendra Sinh Virbhadra Sinhj Solanki*, AIR 1988 SC 915, pp. 920, 921 : 1988 (2) SCC 1.

CHAPTER 10

CONSTRUCTION OF TAXING STATUTES AND EVASION OF STATUTES

SYNOPSIS

1. STRICT CONSTRUCTION OF TAXING STATUTES

(a) Taxing statutes

Article 265 of the Constitution provides: "No tax shall be levied or collected except by authority of law" Article 366(28) of the Constitution which defines Taxation and Tax reads: "Taxation includes the imposition of any tax or impost whether general or local or special, and 'tax' shall be construed accordingly". Any compulsory exaction of money by Government amounts to imposition of tax which is not permissible except by or under the authority of a statutory provision.[1] In a broad sense a fee being

---

1. *CCE v. Kisan Sahkari Chinni Mills,* AIR 2001 SC 3379, p. 3380 : (2001) 132 ELT 523; *Tata Iron & Steel Co. Ltd. v. Collector Central Excise,* AIR 2003 SC 144 : (2003) 1 SCC 100 (statutory backing is essential for imposition of tax); *Hindustan Times v. State of U.P.,* (2003) 1 SCC 591, p. 601 : AIR 2003 SC 250, p. 256 (A welfare impost as a compulsory deduction from advertisement bills of newspapers for payment of pension to working journalists cannot be made by executive order unsupported by any statutory provision); *Shri Digvijay Cement Co. Ltd. v. Union of India,* (2003) 2 SCC 614, pp. 623, 624 : AIR 2003 SC 767 (clause 9A of the Cement Control Order, 1967 requiring the producer to pay to the Cement Regulation Account an amount at the specified rate on production of non-levy cement amounts to taxation and is invalid for want of any legal sanction); *Commissioner of Central Excise*
[Footnote No. 1 Contd.]

compulsory imposition of money is also a tax. The constitution, however, makes a distinction between tax and fee which are both impositions made by a State for raising revenue. A tax is imposed for public purpose for raising general revenue of the State. A fee in contrast is imposed for rendering services and bears a broad correlationship with the services rendered.[2]

[Footnote No. 1 Contd.]

Lucknow v. Chhata Sugar Co. Ltd., (2004) 3 SCC 466 : AIR 2004 SC 3005 (Administrative charges levied under section 8(4) U.P. Sheera Niyantrana Adhiniyam, 1964 on molasses sold by a sugar factory and recoverable by it from buyers under section 8(5) thereof partakes the character of a tax); *Indian Banks Association Bombay v. Devkala Consultancy Service*, AIR 2004 SC 2615, p. 2624 : (2004) 4 JT 587 (The banks by miscalculating section 26C of the Interest Tax Act, 1974, which enables them to pass on the tax to the 'borrowers of loans', recovered more interest from the borrowers by a process of rounding up to the next higher 0.25%. The excess recovery so made was held to be taxation without any legal basis and the banks were not entitled to retain it); *Gupta Modern Breweries v. State of J&K,* (2007) 6 SCC 317, (para 28) (Rule 17 of the J.K. Distillery Rules, 1946 empowering the Department to levy administrative charges on account of salary of Excise Department staff is a tax and cannot be imposed without backing of a statute). **See also** *Luttan v. Lessels,* (2002) 76 ALJR 635 (compulsory exaction as a deduction from an employee's salary under a statutory regime for payment to statutory carer of the employees' child is not taxation); *Consumer Online Foundation v. Union of India*, (2011) 5 SCC 360 (para 23) : (2011) 5 JT 221.

2. For difference between tax and fee, **see** *Dhenkanal Municipal Council v. Rajarao*, AIR 1994 SC 1648 : 1993 Supp (3) SCC 543 and cases referred to therein; *Jindal Stainless Steel Ltd. (2) v. State of Haryana*, (2006) 7 SCC 241 paras 40 and 41 : AIR 2006 SC 2550; *M. Chandru v. Member-Secretary, Chennai Metropolitan Development Authority*, (2009) 4 SCC 72 paras 25 to 31 : (2009) 2 JT 606 (Infrastructure Development charges collected by Chennai Metropolitan Development Authority on behalf of Chennai Sewerage Board is a fee and not a tax). But every fee must not satisfy the test of *quid pro quo* for a licence fee may be regulatory in nature where no *quid pro* need be established: *State of Tripura v. Sudhir Ranjan Nath*, AIR 1997 SC 1168, p. 1173 : (1997) 3 SCC 665; *Sona Chandi Dal Committee v. State of Maharashtra*, (2005) 2 SCC 345 : AIR 2005 SC 635. (Levy of inspection fee for renewal of Money-lender's licence held to be regulatory fee and valid). *Secunderabad Hyderabad Hotel Owners Association v. Hyderabad Municipal Corporation,* JT 1999 (1) SC 75, p. 82 : AIR 1999 SC 635 : (1999) 2 SCC 274 (regulatory fee also cannot be excessive); *A.P. Paper Mills Ltd. v. Government of A.P.,* AIR 2000 SC 3290, p. 3299 : (2001) 8 SCC 167 (Fee for licencing factories increased to Rs. 18 lacs from Rs. 10,000 was held to be invalid); *State of U.P. v. Vam Organic Chemical Ltd.*, (2004) 1 SCC 295, pp. 241, 242 (A so-called regulatory fee which has no connection with the cost of regulation is really a tax in the garb of a fee); *Calcutta Municipal Corporation v. Shrey Merchantile Pvt. Ltd.*, AIR 2005 SC 1879 : (2005) 4 SCC 245 (The imposition of regulatory fee is exercise of police power and not a power to tax which is used for augmenting the revenue. 'Mutation fee' imposed by the corporation held to be with the object of raising revenue and hence invalid); *H.A. v. New South Wales*, (1997) 71 ALJR 1080 (A heavy fee sometimes at the rate of 100% of the value of tobacco sold levied by a law of New South Wales was not held to be a genuine regulatory fee for a licence to carry on business in tobacco and was held to be a duty of Customs or Excise offending section 90 of the

[Footnote No. 2 Contd.]

For instance, the levy of cess on the cost of construction incurred by the employers on building and other construction works under the Building and Other Construction Workers' Welfare Cess Act, 1996, was held to be a 'fee'and not a 'tax', as the cess was imposed for ensuring sufficient funds for the Welfare Boards to undertake social security schemes and welfare measures for building and other construction workers, as provided under the Building and Other Construction Workers' (Regulation of Employment and Conditions of Service) Act, 1996, and was set apart for that specific purpose and not merged with public revenues for the benefit of ther general public.[3]

A power to tax cannot be inferred from a general entry for taxes are specifically named and distributed between the Union and States by various

---

[Footnote No. 2 Contd.]

Constitution of Australia). Cess is a tax which ordinarily generates revenue to be utilized for a specific purpose: *Vijayalakshmi Rice Mill v. Commercial Tax Officer,* (2006) 6 SCC 763 (paras 12, 13) : AIR 2006 SC 2897. Toll, levied under the Indian Tolls Act, 1851 upon any road or bridge made or repaired at the expense of the Government is another compulsory impost which is compensatory in nature and cannot be levied after the expenses in respect of which it is levied have been fully reimbursed : *State of U.P. v. Devi Dayal Singh,* AIR 2000 SC 961, p. 963 : (2000) 3 SCC 5. For nature of 'Toll' which has a variety of meanings **see** *Hansraj & Sons v. State of Jammu and Kashmir,* AIR 2002 SC 2692, pp. 2096, 2097 : (2002) 6 SCC 227. In the category of tax also a distinction is drawn between compensatory and non-compensatory taxes for purposes of Article 301. It has been held that compensatory taxes do not violate the freedom of trade, commerce and intercourse guranteed under Article 301: *Jindal Stripe Ltd. v. State of Haryana,* (2003) 8 SCC 60 (**see also** the cases referred therein. Reference also made to larger bench). The case of *Jindal Strips* in which reference was made to a larger bench was decided by a Constitution Bench: *Jindal Stainless Ltd. v. State of Haryana,* (2006) 7 SCC 241 : AIR 2006 SC 2550. This decision (paras 49 to 53) **affirmed** the test of a compensatory tax laid down in *Atiabari Tea Co. Ltd. v. State of Assam,* AIR 1961 SC 232 : (1961) 1 SCR 809, in which compensatory taxes were equated with regulatory taxes and the following working test for deciding whether the tax was compensatory was laid down: "One has to enquire whether the trade as a class is having the use of certain facilities for the better conduct of the trade/business." This working test remains unaltered even now: *Hardeo Motor Transport v. State of M.P.,* (2006) 8 SCC 613 (paras 16 and 17) : AIR 2007 SC 839 (tax on roadworthy motor vehicles is a regulatory tax); *Mohan Meakins Ltd.v. State of Himachal Pradesh,* (2009) 3 SCC 157 paras 35 to 39 : (2009) 1 JT 599. (Difference between) 'a tax', 'a fee' and a compensatory tax). But the case of *Jindal Stainless Limited v. State of Haryana* has been **further referred** to a larger Bench again (2010) 4 SCC 595 : (2010) 3 SCALE 787. *Jaiprakash Associates Ltd. v. State of Madhya Pradesh,* (2009) 7 SCC 339 : (2009) 2 JT 98 (The question of nature of entry tax levied under List II entry 52 and 10 questions framed by the Court which cover applicability of Articles 301 to 304 and nature of compensatory tax **referred** to a Constitution Bench). For nature of 'royalty' **see** *State of A.P. v. Gujarat Ambuja Cement Ltd.,* (2005) 6 SCC 499 (paras 46 to 58) : AIR 2005 SC 3936. (It is not a tax. In the context of mining lease it is not purchase price of mineral but is additional rent in addition to dead rent.)

3. *Dewan Chand Builders and Contractors v. Union of India & Ors.,* (2012) 1 SCC 101, p. 111.

entries in List I and List II of the Constitution.[4] A tax not so mentioned can be levied by the Union under Parliament's residuary power in Entry 97 of List I.[5] Service tax which is levied by Parliament under its residuary power has to be distinguished from sales tax. For example service tax on housing and hire purchase and financing activities is neither on material nor on sale. Taxable event in leasing and hire purchase financing activities is rendition of service but not sale. Article 366(29A) which has widened the definition of sale or purchase of goods does not negative the power of Parliament to levy service tax on leasing and hire purchase financing activities.[6] Power to levy fee is conferred by the last entry in each List in general terms in respect of any of the matters in the List. A scrutiny of Lists I and II would show that there is no overlapping anywhere in the taxing power and the Constitution gives independent sources of taxation to the Union and the States.[7] The taxing entries have to be construed with clarity and precision so as to maintain this exclusivity. On this principle, a tax on 'Luxuries' in Entry 62 of List II was construed to mean a tax on "the activity of enjoyment of or indulgence in that which is costly or which is generally recognised as being beyond the necessary requirements of an average member of society" and not a tax on articles of luxury.[8] By a taxing statute in this Chapter is meant any Act making compulsory imposition whether of tax or fee. But a taxing statute must be distinguished from those where a duty or fee is charged by the State for parting with its privilege of dealing in deleterious commodities such as opium and liquor.[9] The courts have conceded greater latitude to the Legislature in formulating its

4. *State of West Bengal v. Kesoram Industries Ltd.*, (2004) 10 SCC 201, p. 322 : AIR 2005 SC 1646; *All India Federation of Tax Practitioners v. Union of India*, (2007) 7 SCC 527 (paras 30 and 31).

5. For other examples, **see** *J.N. Kalyan Mandapam v. Union of India*, (2004) 5 SCC 632, p. 649 : AIR 2004 SC 3757 (A tax on services imposed under Entry 97, List I); *Gujarat Ambuja Cements Ltd. v. Union of India*, (2005) 4 SCC 214 : AIR 2005 SC 3020 (service tax under Entry 97, List 1). **See further** footnote 14, p. 875 for these cases.

6. *Association of Leasing and Financial Service Companies v. Union of India*, (2011) 2 SCC 352 paras 31 to 33 : (2010) 12 JT 49.

7. *State of West Bengal v. Kesoram Industries Ltd.*, (2004) 10 SCC 201, p. 322 : AIR 2005 SC 1646.

8. *Godfrey Phillips India Ltd. v. State of U.P.*, (2005) 2 SCC 515, p. 540 (paras 45, 46), p. 551 (para 83) : AIR 2005 SC 1103.

9. *Organon (India) Ltd v. The Collector of Excise*, JT 1994 (4) SC 438, pp. 450-52 : AIR 1994 SC 2489 : 1995 Supp (1) SCC 53; *Government of Maharashtra v. Deokar's Distillery*, AIR 2003 SC 1216, p. 1239 : (2003) 5 SCC 669; *State of Punjab v. Devans Modern Breweries Ltd.*, (2004) 11 SCC 26, p. 97 (para 103), p. 114 (para 150); *State of Kerala v. Maharashtra Distilleries Ltd.*, (2005) 11 SCC 1 (para 79) : AIR 2005 SC 2594; *Commissioner of Income Tax v. Distillers Co. Ltd.*, (2007) 5 SCC 353 (paras 15, 16) : (2007) 5 JT 261.

tax policy either directly[10] or by delegated legislation.[11] Every taxing statute has a charging section and provisions laying down the procedure to assess the tax and penalties and method of their collection and may also contain provisions to prevent pilferage of revenue.[12] A penalty provision in a taxing Act has to be specifically provided and cannot be inferred.[13] The nature of the tax imposed by a statute has to be determined by examining the pith and substance of the statute and by paying more attention to the charging section than to the basis or machinery adopted for assessment and collection of tax[14] for, the nature of tax is different from the measure

---

10. *R. K. Garg v. Union of India*, 1981 (4) SCC 675 : AIR 1981 SC 2138; *State of Kerala v. Builders Association of India*, 1996 (8) Scale 730, pp. 734, 735 : AIR 1997 SC 3640, p. 3644 : (1997) 2 SCC 183; *Associated Cement Companies Ltd. v. Govt. of A.P.*, (2006) 1 SCC 597 (paras 14 to 17) : AIR 2006 SC 928; *Government of Andhra Pradesh v. P. Laxmi Devi*, (2008) 4 SCC 720 paras 72 to 76 : (2008) 2 JT 639; *Southern Technologies Ltd. v. Joint Commissioner of Income Tax*, (2010) 2 SCC 548 paras 71 to 74 : (2010) 1 JT 145.

11. *Satnam Overseas Export v. State of Haryana,* AIR 2003 SC 66, pp. 84, 85 : (2003) 1 SCC 561. **Further see** pp. 939 to 942, *Infra.* A State does not have to tax everything to tax something. It is allowed to pick and choose districts, objects, persons and even rates for taxation if it does so reasonably: WILLIS, CONSTITUTIONAL LAW, p. 587; *V.J. Farreira v. Bombay Municipality*, AIR 1972 SC 845, p. 851; *Karnataka Bank Ltd. v. State of A.P.*, (2008) 2 SCC 254 para 33 : (2008) 2 SLT 170 : (2008) 1 Scale 660. But if the classification is unrelated to the purpose of the tax it may be struck down as violative of Article 14. In *A. Ashirwad Films v. Union of India,* (2007) 6 SCC 624, Entertainment Tax in respect of Telugu films fixed at 10% and in respect of non-Telugu films at 24% of the entry fee was held to be discriminatory and violative of Article 14.

12. *Tripura Goods Transport Association v. Commr. of Taxes,* AIR 1999 SC 719 : (1999) 2 SCC 253. **See further** *Union of India v. Valliappan,* AIR 1999 SC 2526, p. 2531 : (1999) 6 SCC 259 (Prevention of tax evasion is within legislative competence); *State of Rajasthan v. D.P. Metals,* AIR 2001 SC 3076, p. 3089 : (2001) 124 STC 611 : (2002) 1 SCC 279 (Prevention of tax evasion); *Commercial Tax Officer v. Swastik Roadways*, (2004) 3 SCC 640 : AIR 2004 SC 2695, p. 2700 (A prevention of tax evasion provision may even penalise a person for failure to give information although he is not directly liable for the tax evaded).

13. **See** text and note 79 and 80, p. 826.

14. *Rallaram v. Province of East Punjab*, AIR 1949 FC 81, pp. 86, 87; *R.C. Jall v. Union of India*, AIR 1962 SC 1281; *Khyerbari Tea Co. v. State of Assam*, AIR 1964 SC 925, pp. 935, 936 : 1964 (5) SCR 975; *State of Kerala v. Madras Rubber Factory Ltd.*, AIR 1998 SC 723, pp. 730, 731 : (1998) 1 SCC 616; *Municipal Council Kota Rajasthan v. The Delhi Cloth & General Mills Co. Ltd., Delhi,* JT 2001 (3) SC 275, pp. 289, 290 (Tax named as 'Dharmada' was construed to be 'octroi'); *State of Karnataka v. Drive-in-Enterprises,* JT 2001 (3) SC 435, pp. 439, 440 : (2001) 4 SCC 60 : AIR 2001 SC 1328 (Tax on payment for admission of a vehicle in a Drive-in-cinema held to be entertainment tax); *M.P. Cement Manufacturer's Association v. State of M.P.*, (2004) 2 SCC 249 (In a State Act, charging section imposing a cess 'on the total units of electrical energy produced' was held to be a tax in the nature of duty of excise, though levied on units of electrical energy sold or supplied under an explanation added later, and not sales tax and hence *ultra vires* the powers of the state

[Footnote No. 14 Contd.]

of tax.[15] There are three components of a taxing statute, *viz.*, subject of the tax, person liable to pay the tax and the rate at which the tax is levied.[16] If there be any real ambiguity in respect of any of these components which is not removable by reasonable construction,[17] there would be no tax in law till the defect is removed by the legislature.[18]

In terms of Article 265 all acts relating to the imposition of tax providing, *inter alia*, for the point at which the tax is to be collected, the rate of tax as also the recovery must be carried out in accordance with law.[19] If a tax has been paid in excess of the tax specified, save and except the cases involving the principle of 'unjust enrichment', the excess tax realised must be refunded.[20]

In Article 265 and also in taxing statutes the words 'levy' and 'collect' are not used as synonymous terms. Though the term 'levy' may include 'imposition' and 'assessment', it does not include 'collection'.[21] 'Exemption' from tax comes later to levy for 'exemption' can only operate when there is a valid levy; if there was no levy at all, there would be nothing to exempt.[22]

[Footnote No. 14 Contd.]

legislature); *T.N. Kalyan Mandapam Association v. Union of India*, (2004) 5 SCC 632, p. 652 : AIR 2004 SC 3757 (A tax on *Mandap Keepers* and outdoor canteens for services rendered by them is in pith and substance a tax on services and not sales tax); *Gujarat Ambuja Cements Ltd. v. Union of India*, (2005) 4 SCC 214 : AIR 2005 SC 3020 (A tax on the event of service in connection with the carriage of goods or passengers is service tax and not a tax on goods or passengers carried by road or water ways); *All India Federation of Tax Practitioners v. Union of India*, (2007) 7 SCC 527 : AIR 2007 SC 2990 (Tax on services rendered by chartered accountants, cost accountants and architects is not a tax on profession, but service tax levied by Parliament under Entry 97 of List I).

15. *State of W.B. v. Kesoram Industries Ltd.*, (2004) 10 SCC 201, p. 323 : AIR 2005 SC 1646.

16. *State of Kerala v. Alex George*, (2005) 1 SCC 299, p. 306 : AIR 2005 SC 1224; *Govindsaran Ganga Saran v. CST*, 1985 Supp SCC 205 : AIR 1985 SC 1041.

17. For reasonable construction **see** text and notes 16 to 20, pp. 895 to 896.

18. *Mathuram Agarwal v. State of Madhya Pradesh*, AIR 2000 SC 109, p. 113 : (1999) 8 SCC 667; *Indian Banks Association Bombay v. Devkala Consultancy Service*, AIR 2004 SC 2615, p. 2624 : (2004) 4 JT 587; *Commissioner of Central Excise Pondicherry v. ACER India Ltd.*, (2004) 8 SCC 173, p. 185 : (2004) 8 JT 53; *Consumer Online Foundation v. Union of India*, (2011) 5 SCC 360 (para 26) : (2011) 5 JT 221.

19. *Corporation Bank v. Saraswati Abharansala*, (2009) 1 SCC 540 para 19 : (2008) 15 Scale 186.

20. *Ibid* para 20. (Rate of tax retrospectively reduced. Excess tax paid has to be refunded). **See further** text and note 58, 59 pp. 840 to 841 for refund of tax.

21. *CCE v. National Tobacco Co. of India Ltd.*, (1972) 2 SCC 560 (para 19) : AIR 1972 SC 2563; *Somaiya Organics (India) Ltd. v. State of U.P.*, (2001) 5 SCC 519 (para 29) : AIR 2001 SC 1723; *Peekay Re-Rolling Mills (P) Ltd. v. Asst. Commissioner*, (2007) 4 SCC 30 (para 45) : (2007) 4 JT 589.

22. *Peekay Re-Rolling Mills (P) Ltd. v. Assistant Commissioner, supra* (para 35).

There are three stages in the imposition of a tax, *viz.* (1) declaration of liability in respect of persons or property; (2) assessment of tax that quantifies the sum which the person liable has to pay; and (3) methods of recovery if the person taxed does not voluntarily pay.[23] The expression 'tax due' usually refers to an ascertained liability on assessment but its meaning may vary according to context.[24]

General restrictions of taxing power contained in the Constitution, *e.g.*, in Articles 276, 285 and 286 even if not expressly stated in the relevant taxation Act have to be read in it.[25] These restrictions cannot be given a go by either directly or indirectly. But it appears that this principle was not properly appreciated in a recent case relating to Article 276 of the Constitution. Article 276(2) of the Constitution provides that: "The total amount payable in respect of any one person to the State or to any one municipality, district board, local board or other local authority in the State by way of taxes on professions, trades, callings and employments shall not exceed two thousand and five hundred rupees per annum". The word 'person' is defined in section 3(42) of the General Clauses Act, 1897 to "include any company or association or body of individuals whether incorporated or not". Unless the context otherwise provides by virtue of Article 367 of the Constitution the General Clauses Act applies for the interpretation of the Constitution. The Andhra Pradesh Tax on Professions, Trades, Callings and Employment Act, 1987 originally defined 'person' as follows: "person means any person who is engaged in any profession trade calling or employment in the State of Andhra Pradesh and includes a Hindu Undivided Family, firm, company, corporation or other corporate body, any society, club or association so engaged but does not include any person who earns wages on a casual basis." By an amendment the following explanation was added: "Every branch of a firm, company, corporation or other corporate body, any society, club or association shall be deemed to be a person." The validity of this explanation was challenged as being in breach of Article 276 of the Constitution which provides the maximum tax recoverable annually from a 'person'. The challenge was rejected on the ground that the definition of the word 'person' in the General Clauses Act does not restrict the power of the State under Entry 60 of List II of the Constitution

---

23. *Kalwa Dewdattam v. Union of India*, AIR 1964 SC 880, p. 883 : 1964 (3) SCR 191; *Harshad Mehta v. Custodian*, AIR 1998 SC 2291, p. 2298 : 1998 (5) SCC 1.

24. *Harshad Mehta v. Custodian, supra.*

25. *Bharat Kala Bhandar (P) Ltd. v. Municipal Committee*, (AIR) 1966 SC 249 p. 262 (para 32) : (1965) 3 SCR 499 (Constitution Bench decision relating to Article 276). For recent cases relating to Article 286 **See** *Indure Limited v. Commercial Tax Officer*, (2010) 9 SCC 461 para 39 : (2010) 10 JT 109 (sale in the course of import); **See further** *State of Karnataka v. Azad Coach Builders (P) Ltd.*, (2010) 9 SCC 524 : (2010) 11 JT 201 (Constitution Bench) para 26 (sale in the course of export).

while imposing profession tax to adopt a meaning of 'person' different from or in excess of the ordinary acceptation of the word.[26] Because of the restriction imposed by Article 276(2) the State was not competent to legislate directly that the tax payable by a person who carries on business profession *etc.* at more than one place would be 2,500 multiplied by the number of places where he carries on his business, *etc.* The State cannot evade this restriction by defining 'every branch of a firm, company', *etc.* as a separate person. That would be doing something indirectly which the legislature is prohibited from doing directly. The court also seems to be of the view as expressed in para 40 that the definition of 'person' in section 3(42) of the General Clauses Act, 1897 "is not applicable automatically to interpret the provisions of the Constitution unless the context so requires and makes that definition applicable." But a correct reading of Article 367 will show that the provisions of the General Clauses Act including the definition of 'person' in section 3(42) will automatically be applicable for interpretation of the Constitution but will not be applicable "when the context otherwise requires". There is no contrary context to make the definition of person in section 3(42) of the General Clauses Act inapplicable for construction of the word "person" in Article 276(2). The State legislature cannot so define the word 'person' for purposes of Article 276(2) as to evade the ban imposed by that provision. If that is allowed it will make Article 276(2) wholly nugatory. It is submitted that in rejecting the challenge to the validity of the 'Explanation' added by the Andhra Pradesh Act 29 of 1996 these points were not properly considered by the Supreme Court.

Article 286 of the Constitution provides that no law of a State shall impose, or authorise the imposition of, a tax on the sale or purchase of goods where such sale or purchase takes place (a) outside the state; or (b) in the course of the import of the goods into, or export of the goods out of, the territory of India. Therefore, the requirement of tax deduction at source from value of works contract involving supply of goods in course of inter-state trade which makes no provision for deduction and ascertainment of value of goods supplied in the course of inter-state trade during execution of works contract will be held invalid and unconstitutional violating Article 286 of the Constitution.[27]

---

26. *Karnataka Bank Ltd. v. State of Andhra Pradesh*, (2008) 2 SCC 254 : (2008) 1 Scale 660.

27. *State of Chhattisgarh v. VTP Construction*, (2008) 2 SCC 578 : AIR 2008 SC 714. **See further** *Steel Authority of India Ltd. v. State of Orissa*, (2000) 3 SCC 200 : AIR 2000 SC 946; *Nathpa Jhakri Joint Venture v. State of H.P.*, (2000) 3 SCC 319 : AIR 2000 SC 1268; *Saraf Trading Corporation v. State of Kerala*, (2011) 2 SCC 344 para 13 : (2011) 3 JT 77 (sale in the course of export).

(b) General principles of strict construction

A taxing statute is to be strictly construed. The well-established rule in the familiar words of LORD WENSLEYDALE, reaffirmed by LORD HALSBURY and LORD SIMONDS, means: "The subject is not to be taxed without clear words for that purpose; and also that every Act of Parliament must be read according to the natural construction of its words".[28] In a classic passage LORD CAIRNS stated the principle thus: "If the person sought to be taxed comes within the letter of the law he must be taxed, however great the hardship may appear to the judicial mind to be. On the other hand, if the Crown seeking to recover the tax, cannot bring the subject within the letter of the law, the subject is free, however apparently within the spirit of law the case might otherwise appear to be. In other words, if there be admissible in any statute, what is called an equitable, construction, certainly, such a construction is not admissible in a taxing statute where you can simply adhere to the words of the statute."[29] VISCOUNT SIMON quoted with approval a passage from ROWLATT, J. expressing the principle in the following words: "In a taxing Act one has to look merely at what is clearly said. There is no room for any intendment. There is no equity about a tax. There is no presumption as to tax. Nothing is to be read in, nothing is to be implied. One can only look fairly at the language used."[30] Relying upon this passage LORD UPJOHN said: "Fiscal measures are not built upon any theory of taxation."[31]

---

28. *Re, Micklethwait*, (1885) 11 Ex 452, p. 456; **referred** to in *Tenant v. Smith*, (1892) AC 150, p. 154 (HL) (LORD HALSBURY); *St. Aubyn v. A.G.*, (1951) 2 All ER 473, p. 485 : 1952 AC 15 (HL) (LORD SIMONDS); *Member Secretary, Andhra Pradesh State Board for Prevention and Control of Water Pollution v. Andhra Pradesh Rayons Ltd.*, AIR 1989 SC 611, p. 614 : (1989) 1 SCC 44; *Saraswati Sugar Mills v. Haryana State Board*, AIR 1992 SC 224, p. 228 : 1992 (1) SCC 418.

29. *Partington v. A.G.*, (1869) LR 4 HL 100, p. 122 : 21 LT 370, **referred** to in *IRC v. Duke of Westminster*, (1936) AC 1, p. 24 (HL); *Bank of Chettinad v. CIT*, AIR 1940 PC 183, p. 185; *Potts' Executors v. IRC*, (1951) 1 All ER 76, p. 81 (HL); *A.V. Fernandez v. State of Kerala*, AIR 1957 SC 657, p. 661 : 1957 SCR 837; *CIT v. M & G Stores*, AIR 1968 SC 200, p. 205 : 1967 (3) SCR 876; *J.K. Steel Ltd. v. Union of India*, AIR 1970 SC 1173, p. 1182 : 1969 (2) SCR 481; *Ransom (Inspector of Taxes) v. Higgs*, (1974) 3 All ER 949, p. 970 (HL). **See further** *Hansraj & Sons v. State of Jammu & Kashmir*, AIR 2002 SC 2692, pp. 2698, 2699 : (2002) 6 SCC 227; *M/s. Geo Miller and Co. Pvt. Ltd. v. State of M.P.*, AIR 2004 SC 3552, p. 3556 : (2004) 5 SCC 209; *Government of Andhra Pradesh v. Laxmi Devi*, (2008) 4 SCC 720 paras 19, 20, 21 : (2008) 2 JT 639.

30. *Cape Brandy Syndicate v. IRC*, (1921) 1 KB 64, p. 71 (ROWLATT, J.); **referred** to in *Canadian Eagle Oil Co. Ltd. v. R.*, (1945) 2 All ER 499, p. 507 (HL); *Gursahai v. CIT*, AIR 1963 SC 1062, p. 1064 : 1963 (3) SCR 893; *Banarsi Debi v. ITO*, AIR 1964 SC 1742, p. 1744; *Commissioner of Central Excise Pondicherry v. ACER*

[Footnote Nos. 30 & 31 Contd.]

The above passage stating the principle of strict construction of taxing statutes was quoted (from sixth edition of this book) with approval in *Commissioner of Income-tax, Madras v. Kasturi & Sons*,[32] where the word 'moneys' in the expression 'moneys payable' in section 41(2) of the Income-tax Act, 1961 was not construed to include 'money's worth'.

In all tax matters one has to interpret the taxation statute strictly. Simply because one class of legal entities is given a benefit which is specifically stated in the Act, does not mean that the benefit can be extended to legal entities not referred to in the Act as there is no equity in matters of taxation. Accordingly, the benefit available to companies under section 72-A of the Income-tax Act, 1961, of having the losses of an amalgamating company carried forward and set off against the profits of the amalgamated company, was held to be inapplicable to cooperative societies in the absence of a specific provision to that effect.[33]

[Footnote Nos. 30 & 31 Contd.]

India Ltd., (2004) 8 SCC 173, p. 183 : (2004) 8 JT 53; *Saraf Trading Corporation v. State of Kerala*, (2011) 2 SCC 344 para 22 : (2011) 3 JT 77. **See further** *CIT v. Firm Muar*, AIR 1965 SC 1216, p. 1221 : 1965 (1) SCR 815; *CIT, Patiala v. Shahzadanand & Sons*, AIR 1966 SC 1342, p. 1347 : (1966) 3 SCR; *Janapada Sabha, Chhindwara v. Central Provinces Syndicate*, AIR 1971 SC 57, p. 60 : (1971) 1 SCC 509; *Owen Thomas Mangin v. IRC*, (1971) 2 WLR 39, p. 42 (PC); *Controller of Estate Duty v. Kantilal Trikamlal*, AIR 1976 SC 1935, p. 1943 : (1976) 4 SCC 643; *Tarulata Syam v. Commissioner of Income-tax, West Bengal*, AIR 1977 SC 1802 : (1977) 3 SCC 305; *Member Secretary, Andhra Pradesh State Board for Prevention and Control of Water Pollution v. Andhra Pradesh Rayons Ltd.*, AIR 1989 SC 611, p. 614 : (1989) 1 SCC 44; *Aphali Pharmaceuticals Ltd. v. State of Maharashtra*, AIR 1989 SC 2227, p. 2239 : (1889) 4 SCC 378; *Goodyear India Ltd. v. State of Haryana*, AIR 1990 SC 781, p. 793 : 1990 (2) SCC 71; *Sutlej Cotton Mills Ltd. v. Commissioner of Income-tax, West Bengal*, AIR 1991 SC 218, p. 220 : (1992) Supp (1) SCC 50; *Saraswati Sugar Mills v. Haryana State Board*, AIR 1992 SC 224, p. 228 : 1992 (1) SCC 418; *Oswal Agro Mills Ltd v. Collector of Central Excise*, AIR 1993 SC 2288, p. 2291 : 1993 Supp. 3 SCC 716; *Calcutta Jute Manufacturing Co. v. Commercial Tax Officer*, AIR 1997 SC 2920, p.2923 : (1997) 6 SCC 262; *Orissa State Warehousing Corporation v. CIT*, JT 1999 (2) SC 527, p. 539 : AIR 1999 SC 1388, p. 1397 : (1999) 4 SCC 197; *The Federation of Andhra Pradesh Chamber of Commerce and Industry v. State of Andhra Pradesh*, AIR 2000 SC 2905, p. 2906 : (2000) 6 SCC 550; *Commissioner of Central Excise v. Kisan Sahkari Chinni Mills Ltd.*, AIR 2001 SC 3379, p. 3380 : (2001) 6 SCC 697; *Union of India v. Azadi Bachao Andolan*, AIR 2004 SC 1107, p. 1137 : 2003 Supp (2) JT 205; *Ajmera Housing Corporation v. CIT*, (2010) 8 SCC 739 para 36 : (2010) 9 JT 306; *Union of India v. Ind-Swift Laboratories Ltd.*, (2011) 4 SCC 635 (para 20) : (2011) 2 JT 352; *Bansal Wire Industries Ltd. v. State of Uttar Pradesh*, (2011) 6 SCC 545 (Paras 29 and 30).

31. *Commr. of Customs v. Top Ten Promotions*, (1969) 3 All ER 39, p. 90 (HL).

32. JT 1999 (2) SC 272 : AIR 1999 SC 1275, p. 1278 : (1999) 3 SCC 346; **See further** *Mahim Patram (P) Ltd. v. Union of India*, (2007) 3 SCC 668 (paras 2, 3), pp. 679, 680 : (2007) 4 JT 50, where also the above passage is quoted.

33. *Rajasthan Rajya Sahakari Spinning & Ginning Mills Federation Ltd. v. Deputy CIT, Jaipur*, (2014) 11 SCC 672, pp. 677, 678.

In fiscal legislation a transaction cannot be taxed on any doctrine of "the substance of the matter" as distinguished from its legal signification, for a subject is not liable to tax on supposed "spirit of the law" or "by inference or by analogy".[34] In refuting the doctrine of 'the substance of the matter' LORD TOMLIN observed: "It is said that in revenue cases there is a doctrine that the court may ignore the legal position and regard what is called 'the substance of the matter'. This supposed doctrine seems to rest for its support upon a misunderstanding of language used in some earlier cases. The sooner this misunderstanding is dispelled, and the supposed doctrine given its quietus, the better it will be for all concerned, for the doctrine seems to involve substituting 'the uncertain and crooked cord of discretion' for 'the golden and straight metwand of the law'.[35] In the same case LORD WRIGHT pointed out that "the true nature of the legal obligation" arising out of a genuine transaction "and nothing else is the substance".[36] The above principle which is known as Duke of Westminster principle is subject to the new approach of the courts towards tax evasion schemes consisting of a series of transactions or a composite transaction.[37]

In interpreting a section in a taxing statute, according to LORD SIMONDS, "the question is not at what transaction the section is according to some

---

34. *IRC v. Duke of Westminster*, (1936) AC 1, pp. 19, 24 (HL); *Bank of Chittinad v. CIT*, AIR 1940 PC 183, p. 185 : (1940) 8 ITR 522; *Potts' Executors v. IRC*, (1951) 1 All ER 76, p. 81 (HL); *A.V. Fernandez v. State of Kerala*, AIR 1957 SC 657, p. 661 : 1957 SCR 837; *CIT v. Keshavlal*, AIR 1965 SC 866, p. 868 (para 12) : (1965) 2 SCR 100; *CIT v. M & G Stores*, AIR 1968 SC 200, p. 205; *Joint Commercial Tax Officer v. YMA, Madras*, AIR 1970 SC 1212, p. 1217 : (1970) 1 SCC 462; *Europa Oil (NZ) Ltd. v. Inland Revenue Commissioner*, (1976) 1 All ER 503, p. 508 (PC) (Legal rights arising from a transaction and not its economic results are material); *Gujarat State Financial Corporation v. Natson Manufacturing Co. Ltd.*, AIR 1978 SC 1765, p. 1769 : (1979) 1 SCC 193; *Member Secretary, Andhra Pradesh State Board for Prevention and Control of Water Pollution v. Andhra Pradesh Rayons Ltd.*, AIR 1989 SC 611, p. 614 : (1989) 1 SCC 44; *Mathuram Agrawal v. State of Madhya Pradesh*, JT 1999 (8) SC 505, pp. 511, 512 : AIR 2000 SC 109, p. 113 : (1999) 8 SCC 667. **See further** *Hansraj & Sons v. State of Jammu & Kashmir*, AIR 2002 SC 2692, pp. 2698, 2699 : (2002) 6 SCC 227; *Commissioner of Central Excise, Pondicherry v. ACER India Ltd.*, (2004) 8 SCC 173, p. 184 : (2004) 8 JT 53.

35. *IRC v. Duke of Westminster, supra*, **referred** to in *Pott's Executors v. IRC, supra*, p. 80 (LORD NORMAND); *CIT, Gujarat v. B.M. Kharwar*, AIR 1969 SC 812 : (1969) 1 SCR 651; *J.K. Steel Ltd. v. Union of India, supra*, p. 1192; *CIT, Calcutta v. G. Arbuthnot & Co.*, AIR 1973 SC 989, p. 995 : (1973) 5 SCC Tax 359 : (1973) 3 SCC 845; *Commrs. of Customs v. Top Ten Promotions*, (1969) 3 All ER 39, p. 90 (HL); *Ransom (Inspector of Taxes) v. Higgs*, (1974) 3 All ER 949, p. 970 (HL). **See further** *Hansraj and Sons v. State of Jammu & Kashmir*, AIR 2002 SC 2692, pp. 2698, 2699 : (2002) 6 SCC 227; *Commissioner of Central Excise Pondicherry v. ACER India Ltd.*, (2004) 8 SCC 173, p. 184 : (2004) 8 JT 53.

36. *IRC v. Duke of Westminster, supra.*

37. **See** title (2), 'Evasion of Statutes', text and notes 54 to 77, pp. 919 to 922, notes 1 to 4, p. 867.

alleged general purpose aimed, but what transaction its language according to its natural meaning fairly and squarely hits."[38] LORD SIMONDS calls this "the one and only proper test."[39] It is, therefore, not the function of a court of law to give to words a strained and unnatural meaning to cover loopholes through which the evasive taxpayer may find escape or to tax transactions which, had the Legislature thought of them, would have been covered by appropriate words.[40] As stated by LORD SIMON: "It may seem hard that a cunningly advised taxpayer should be able to avoid what appears to be his equitable share of the general fiscal burden and cast it on the shoulders of his fellow citizens. But for the courts to try to stretch the law to meet hard cases (whether the hardship appears to bear on the individual taxpayer or on the general body of taxpayers as represented by the Inland Revenue) is not merely to make bad law but to run the risk of subverting the rule of law itself."[41] The same rule applies even if the object of the enactment is to frustrate legitimate tax avoidance devices for moral precepts are not applicable to the interpretation of revenue statutes.[42]

It may thus be taken as a maxim of tax law, which although not to be overstressed ought not to be forgotten that, "the subject is not to be taxed unless the words of the taxing statute unambiguously impose the tax on him."[43] The proper course in construing revenue Acts is to give a fair and reasonable construction to their language without leaning to one side or the other but keeping in mind that no tax can be imposed without words clearly showing an intention to lay the burden and that equitable construction of the words is not permissible.[44] Considerations of hardship, injustice or anomalies do not play any useful role in construing taxing statutes

---

38. *St. Aubyn (LM) v. A.G.*, (1951) 2 All ER 473, p. 485 : 1952 AC 15 (HL). **See further** *Commissioner of Central Excise, Pondicherry v. ACER India Ltd.*, *supra*, pp. 183, 184.

39. *Ibid.*

40. *IRC v. Wolfson*, (1949) 1 All ER 865, p. 868 (HL); **See further** *W.M. Cory & Sons Ltd. v. IRC*, (1965) 1 All ER 917, p. 921 : 1964 AC 1088 : 1065 (2) WLR 924 (HL), where LORD REID said: "The words of a taxing Act must never be stretched against a taxpayer. There is a very good reason for that rule. So long as one adheres to the natural meaning for the charging words the law is certain, or at least as certain as it is possible to make it, but if courts are to give to charging words what is sometimes called a liberal construction who can say just how far this will go. It is much better that evasion should be met by amending legislation."

41. *Ransom (Inspector of Taxes) v. Higgs*, (1974) 3 All ER 949, p. 969 (HL).

42. *Owen Thomas Mangin v. IRC*, (1971) 2 WLR 39, p. 42 (PC).

43. *Russel v. Scott*, (1948) 2 All ER 1, p. 5 (HL), (LORD SIMONDS); *Mathuram Agrawal v. State of Madhya Pradesh,* JT 1999 (8) SC 505, p. 512 : AIR 2000 SC 109, pp. 113, 114 : (1999) 8 SCC 667.

44. *Ormond Investment Co. v. Betts*, (1928) AC 143 : (1928) All ER Rep 709, p. 719 (HL) (LORD ATKINSON).

unless there be some real ambiguity.[45] It has also been said that if taxing provision is "so wanting in clarity that no meaning is reasonably clear, the courts will be unable to regard it as of any effect."[46]

The Supreme Court has enunciated in similar words the principle of interpretation of taxing laws.

BHAGWATI, J. stated the principle as follows: "In construing fiscal statutes and in determining the liability of a subject to tax one must have regard to the strict letter of the law. If the revenue satisfies the court that the case falls strictly within the provisions of the law, the subject can be taxed. If, on the other hand, the case is not covered within the four corners of the provisions of the taxing statute, no tax can be imposed by inference or by analogy or by trying to probe into the intentions of the Legislature and by considering what was the substance of the matter."[47] SHAH, J., has formulated the principle thus: "In interpreting a taxing statute, equitable considerations are entirely out of place. Nor can taxing statutes be interpreted on any presumptions or assumptions. The court must look squarely at the words of the statute and interpret them. It must interpret a taxing statute in the light of what is clearly expressed; it cannot imply anything which is not expressed; it cannot import provisions in the statute so as to supply any assumed deficiency."[48] And K. IYER, J., more recently observed: "Taxation consideration may stem from administrative experience and other factors of life and not artistic visualisation or neat logic and so the literal, though

---

45. *Mapp v. Oram*, (1969) 3 All ER 215, pp. 222, 223 (HL); *State Bank of Travancore v. Commissioner of Income-tax*, (1986) 2 SCC 11, p. 68 : AIR 1986 SC 757.

46. *IRC v. Ross and Coulter*, (1948) 1 All ER 616, p. 625 (HL); referred to in *Gursahai v. CIT*, AIR 1963 SC 1062, p. 1064 : (1963) 3 SCR 893.

47. *A.V. Fernandez v. State of Kerala*, AIR 1957 SC 657, p. 661 : 1957 SCR 837; referred to in *CIT, Bombay v. Provident Investment Co.*, AIR 1957 SC 664, p. 666 : 1957 SCR 1141; *Gursahai v. CIT*, AIR 1963 SC 1062, p. 1064 : (1963) 3 SCR 893; **See further** *Banarsi Debi v. ITO*, AIR 1964 SC 1742, p. 1744 : (1964) 7 SCR 539; *CIT, Gujarat v. Vadilal Lallubhai*, AIR 1973 SC 1016, p. 1019; (1973) 3 SCC 17; *Diwan Brothers v. Central Bank, Bombay*, AIR 1976 SC 1503, p. 1508 : (1976) 3 SCC 800; *McDowell & Co. Ltd. v. Commercial Tax Officer*, AIR 1977 SC 1459, p. 1465 : (1977) 1 SCC 441; *Mohammad Ali Khan v. Commissioner of Wealth Tax*, AIR 1997 SC 1165, p. 1167 : 1997 (3) SCC 511; *Hansraj & Sons v. State of Jammu & Kashmir*, AIR 2002 SC 2692, pp. 2698, 2699 : (2002) 6 SCC 227; *Geo Miller & Co. (P.) Ltd. v. State of M.P.*, (2004) 5 SCC 209, p. 216 (para 30) : AIR 2004 SC 3552.

48. *Sales Tax Commissioner v. Modi Sugar Mills*, AIR 1961 SC 1047, p. 1051 : 1961 (2) SCR 189; **see further** *CIT v. Firm Muar*, AIR 1965 SC 1216, p. 1221 (SUBBARAO, J.): *State of Punjab v. Jullundar Vegetables Syndicate*, AIR 1966 SC 1295, p. 1297 : (1966) 2 SCR 457: *CIT v. M.G. Mills*, AIR 1971 SC 2434, p. 2435; *Aphali Pharmaceuticals Ltd. v. State of Maharashtra*, AIR 1989 SC 2227, p. 2239 : 1989 (4) SCC 378; *Vikrant Tyres Ltd. v. The First Income-tax Officer, Mysore,* JT 2001 (2) SC 45, pp. 459, 460 : (2001) 3 SCC 76 : AIR 2001 SC 800.

pedestrian interpretation must prevail."[49] Before taxing any person it must be shown that he falls within the ambit of the charging section by clear words used in the section.[50]

Therefore, if the words used are ambiguous and reasonably open to two interpretations benefit of interpretation is given to the subject.[51] If the Legislature fails to express itself clearly and the taxpayer escapes by not being brought within the letter of the law, no question of unjustness as such arises.[52] But equitable considerations are not relevant in construing a taxing statute,[53] and similarly logic or reason cannot be of much avail in

---

49. *Martand Dairy and Farm v. Union of India*, AIR 1975 SC 1492, p. 1494 : (1975) 4 SCC 313. (In this case Milk products, *e.g.*, *Chhena*, *Dahi*, Butter and Cream but 'excluding products sold in sealed containers' were exempted from sales tax. There was no reason why sale in loose quantities and unsealed containers be exempted and sale in containers which are sealed should be taxed. But the court still applied the literal construction and rejected the argument that 'seal' referred to the affixture of the seal of the seller suggesting his name or trade description); referred to in *Member Secretary, Andhra Pradesh State Board for Prevention and Control of Water Pollution v. Andhra Pradesh Rayons Ltd.*, AIR 1989 SC 611, p. 614 : 1989 (1) SCC 44; *Saraswati Sugar Mills v. Haryana State Board*, AIR 1992 SC 224, p. 228 : (1992) 1 SCC 418 : (1991) 4 JT 220.

50. *Commissioner of Wealth Tax, Gujarat v. Ellis Bridge Gymkhana*, AIR 1998 SC 120, pp. 125, 126 : 1998 (1) SCC 384 (A club is not taxable under section 3 of the Wealth Tax Act, 1957 which levies the tax only on Individual, Hindu undivided family and company but not on Association of persons); *Commissioner of Customs v. ACER India (P) Ltd.*, (2008) 1 SCC 382 para 21 : (2007) 12 JT 287 [Computers (Additional Duty) Rules, 2004 is a taxing statute and is required to be construed strictly. A laptop/notebook computer comes in an integrated and inseparable form and is not the same as a desktop computer or micro computer].

51. *Express Mill v. Municipal Committee, Wardha*, AIR 1958 SC 341, p. 344 : 1958 SCR 1102; *CIT v. Karamchand Premchand Ltd.*, AIR 1960 SC 1175, p. 1182 : 1960 (3) SCR 727; *Board of Revenue, U.P. v. Sidhnath Mehrotra*, AIR 1965 SC 1092, p. 1095 : (1965) 2 SCC 269; *C.A. Abraham v. ITO, Kottayam*, AIR 1961 SC 609, p. 612 : 1961 (2) SCR 765; *J.K. Steel v. Union of India*, AIR 1970 SC 1173, p. 1182 : (1969) 2 SCR 481; *Collector, E.D. v. R. Kanakasabai*, AIR 1973 SC 1214, p. 1218 : (1973) 4 SCC 169; *CIT v. N.H. Tea Co.*, AIR 1973 SC 2524, p. 2526 : (1973) 4 SCC 200; *Diwan Brothers v. Central Bank, Bombay*, AIR 1976 SC 1503, p. 1508 : (1976) 3 SCC 800; *Petron Engineering Construction Pvt. Ltd. v. Central Board of Direct Taxes*, AIR 1989 SC 501, p. 506; *Hindustan Lever Ltd. v. Municipal Corporation of Greater Bombay*, 1995 (3) Scale 24, p. 29; *Birla Cement Works v. Central Board of Direct Taxes*, JT 2001 (3) SC 256, p. 262 : (2001) 9 SCC 35 : AIR 2001 SC 1080 (more so when the interpretation in favour of the assessee has been acted upon and accepted by the Revenue for a long period); *Sneh Enterprises v. Commr. of Customs,* (2006) 7 SCC 714 (para 24) : (2006) 8 JT 587; *Manish Maheshwari v. Asst. Commr. of Income Tax,* (2007) 3 SCC 794 (paras 13 and 14) : AIR 2007 SC 1696.

52. *CIT v. Jalgaon Electric Supply Co.*, AIR 1960 SC 1182, p. 1183 : 1960 (3) SCR 880.

53. *CIT, W.B. v. Central India Industries*, AIR 1972 SC 397 : (1972) 3 SCC 311; *Laxmikant v. Wealth Tax Commissioner*, AIR 1973 SC 2258, p. 2262 : (1974) 3 SCC 126; *CIT v. Gwalior Rayon Silk Manufacturing Company*, AIR 1992 SC 1782, p. 1786 : 1992 (3) SCC 326.

interpreting a taxing statute.[54] It is well settled that in the field of taxation, hardship or equity has no role to play in determining eligibility to tax and it is for the legislature to determine the same.[55] Similarly, hardship or equity is not relevant in interpreting provisions imposing stamp duty, which is a tax, and the Court should not concern itself with the intention of the Legislature when the language expressing such intention is plain and unambiguous.[56] But just as reliance upon equity does not avail an assessee, so it does not avail the Revenue. Thus if the Income-tax Act did not contain any provision making successor in business or the legal representative of an assessee liable to pay tax on the profits of the original assessee, the legal representatives could not be so taxed.[57] Taxation laws have to be applied on legal principles and not on moral views.[58]

Again following the view taken by English Courts, it has been held that the taxing authorities cannot ignore the legal character of the transaction and tax it on the basis of what may be called 'substance of the matter'. One must find the true nature of the transaction.[59] The legal effect of the transaction cannot be displaced by probing into substance of the matter.[60] But the new approach of English courts to tax evasion schemes has also been adverted to in India but cannot be said to have been fully adopted.[61]

In construing the Court-fees Act, there is yet another ground for construing it strictly. The Act may, if the fee is heavy, seriously restrict the rights of a person to seek his remedies in a court of justice and as access to justice is the basis of the legal system, in a case where there is reasonable doubt, the benefit of construction must go to him who says that the lesser court-fee alone be paid.[62]

---

54. *Azamjha v. Expenditure Tax Officer, Hyderabad,* AIR 1972 SC 2319, p. 2323 : (1971) 3 SCC 621; *CIT v. Gwalior Rayon Silk Manufacturing Company, supra.*

55. *Kapil Mohan v. Commr. of Income-tax, Delhi,* AIR 1999 SC 573, p. 578 : (1999) 1 SCC 430.

56. *State of Madhya Pradesh v. Rakesh Kohli & Anr.*, (2012) 6 SCC 312, p. 323.

57. *CIT v. Hukumchand Mohanlal,* AIR 1971 SC 2591 : (1972) 4 SCC 368; *Kapil Mohan v. Commissioner of Income-tax, supra.*

58. *T.A. Quereshi (Dr.) v. Commr. of Income Tax, Bhopal,* (2007) 2 SCC 759 : (2006) 13 Scale 182 (Loss in illegal business held deductible).

59. *Union of India v. Play World Electronics Pvt. Ltd.*, AIR 1990 SC 202, p. 208 : 1989 (3) SCC 181.

60. *CIT, Calcutta v. G. Arbuthnot & Co.*, AIR 1973 SC 989, p. 995 : (1973) 3 SCC 845; *CIT, Gujarat v. B.M. Kharwar,* AIR 1969 SC 812 : (1969) 1 SCR 651; *Gujarat State Financial Corporation v. Natson Manufacturing Co. Pvt. Ltd.*, AIR 1978 SC 1765, p. 1769 : (1979) 1 SCC 193.

61. **See** title 2, Evasion of Statutes, text and notes 54 to 77, pp. 919 to 922.

62. *Lakshmi Ammal v. K. M. Madhav Krishnan,* AIR 1978 SC 1607 : (1978) 4 SCC 15; *Gujarat State Financial Corporation v. Natson Manufacturing Co. Ltd., supra.*

A further principle, which may be noticed, is the principle of avoidance of double taxation by the same Act. The principle applied to Income-tax Legislations is that if the words of the Act on one construction result in double taxation of the same income, that result will be avoided by adopting another construction which may reasonably be open.[63] VISCOUNT RADCLIFFE explains the principle thus: "Double taxation in itself, however is not something which it is beyond the power of the Legislature to provide for, when constructing its tax scheme. It is rather that, given that a situation would really involve double taxation, it is so unlikely that there would have been an intention to penalise particular forms of income in this way that the law approaches the interpretation of the complicated structure of the Code with a strong bias against achieving such a result."[64] On this general principle rests the rule that several heads of income mentioned in the Income-tax Laws are mutually exclusive and a particular income can come under only one of the heads.[65] If income properly pertaining to one head cannot be taxed under that head, it cannot be included in the residuary head for purpose of assessment.[66] Again it is not open to the taxing authority, if income has accrued to the assessee and is liable to be included in the total income of a particular year, to ignore the accrual, and thereafter to tax it as income of another year on the basis of receipt.[67] But as the rule of avoidance of double taxation is merely a rule of construction it ceases to have any application when the Legislature expressly enacts a law which results in double taxation of the same income. The law so made cannot be held invalid merely on the ground that it results in double taxation. It was, therefore, held that section 23(5) of the Income-tax Act, 1922, which made provision for assessment and payment of tax by a registered firm and also for inclusion of the share of income of a partner in his total income was not invalid.[68]

---

63. *IRC v. F.S. Securities Ltd.*, (1964) 2 All ER 691 (HL), p. 695 (LORD REID), p. 699 (LORD RADCLIFFE). **See also** *Canadian Eagle Oil Co. v. R.*, (1945) 2 All ER 499, pp. 506, 510, 516 (HL). **See further** *Laxmipat v. CIT*, AIR 1969 SC 501, p. 503 : (1969) 1 SCR 904 (unless otherwise expressly provided income cannot be taxed twice); *Jain Bros. v. Union of India*, AIR 1970 SC 778, p. 782 : (1969) 3 SCC 311 (an express provision cannot be held invalid on the ground that it results in double taxation).

64. *IRC v. F.S. Securities, Ltd., supra*, pp. 698, 699.

65. *Ibid*; *Salisbury House Estate Ltd. v. Fry*, (1930) 15 Tax Cases 266; *United Commercial Bank Ltd. v. CIT, West Bengal*, AIR 1957 SC 918 : (1958) SCR 79; *Nalinikant Ambalal Mody v. CIT, Bombay*, AIR 1967 SC 193 : 1966 Supp SCR 295; *CIT, Bombay v. National Storage, Bombay*, AIR 1968 SC 70, p. 78 : (1967) 3 SCR 813.

66. *Nalini Kant Ambalal Mody v. CIT, Bombay, supra.*

67. *Laxmipat v. CIT*, AIR 1969 SC 501, p. 503 : (1969) 1 SCR 904.

68. *Jain Bros. v. Union of India*, AIR 1970 SC 778, p. 782 : (1969) 3 SCC 311. **See further** *Municipal Committee Kota, Rajasthan v. The Delhi Cloth & General Mills Co. Ltd., Delhi,* JT 2001 (3) SC 275, pp. 291, 292 : (2001) 3 SCC 654 : AIR 2001 SC 1060.

Similar principle has been applied to Excise Acts. There is no general principle that there can be no double taxation in the levy of Excise duty but the court may lean in favour of a construction, if that be open, which will avoid double taxation.[69] An important aspect of the Excise Acts is that goods are not excisable unless they are marketable[70] though the taxable event is manufacture which is not related to commercial transaction.[71] Manufacture will, therefore, include all incidental and ancillary processes for making the goods commercially marketable.[72] But it is not necessary that the goods be actually sold and in case of captive consumption the excise duty is levied on "deemed value" determined in accordance with the Excise Valuation Rules, 2000.[73] In contrast the levy of sales tax by its very nature arises at the stage beyond manufacture, namely, the sale of the article.[74]

Another principle applicable to Income-tax Act is that the charging section and the computation provisions together constitute an integrated code and, therefore, when there is a case to which the computation provisions cannot apply at all, it can be concluded that such a case was not intended

---

69. *Premier Tyres Ltd. v. Collector of Central Excise*, (1987) 1 SCC 697, p. 700 : AIR 1987 SC 1029; **See further** *Collector Central Excise Madras v. ITC Ltd. Bihar*, (2003) 3 SCC 379 : AIR 2003 SC 1484 (Levy of excise duty on cigarette packet as well as on cigarette does not amount to double taxation).

70. *Collector of Central Excise v. Ambalal Sarabhai (M/s.)*, AIR 1990 SC 59 : 1989 (4) SCC 112; *A.P. State Electricity Board v. Collector of Central Excise*, JT 1994 (1) SC 545 : (1994) 2 SCC 428 (Test of Marketability laid down); *Indian Cable Company Ltd v. Collector of Central Excise*, JT 1994 (6) SC 243, p. 251; *Commissioner of Central Excise v. Jagjit Industries Ltd.*, AIR 2002 SC 1426 : (2002) 3 SCC 614 (An intermediate product which is listed in schedule is not taxable unless it is marketed or is marketable); *Union of India v. sonic Electrochem (P.) Ltd.*, AIR 2002 SC 3288 : (2002) 7 SCC 436; *Cadila Laboratories Ltd. v. CCE Vadodara*, (2003) 4 SCC 12; *Gujarat Narmada Valley Fertilizer Co. Ltd. v. Collector of Excise and Customs*, (2005) 7 SC 94 (para 5) (Intermediate product not taxable simply on the ground that it is separately listed in the Schedule unless the Revenue proves it to be marketable).

71. *Moriroku UT India (P) Ltd. v. State of Uttar Pradesh*, (2008) 4 SCC 548 para 15 p. 554 : (2008) 3 JT 506.

72. *Collector of Central Excise v. Eastend Paper Industries*, AIR 1990 SC 1893, pp. 1895, 1896 : 1989 (4) SCC 244. **But see** *I.T.C. Ltd. v. Collector of Central Excise*, AIR 2003 SC 568 (Manufacture of cigarettes for excise duty is complete when they emerge in the form of sticks. Packing of cigarettes not essential for excise duty); *Collector, Central Excise Madras v. I.T.C. Ltd. Bihar*, (2003) 3 SCC 379 (cigarette packets held to be marketable and separately liable to excise duty). **See further** *Anjaleen Enterprises (P) Ltd. v. Commissioner of Central Excise, Ahmedabad*, (2006) 2 SCC 366 (paras 13 and 30) : (2006) 1 JT 353. (In the matter of valuation one of the important aspects to be taken into account is the condition of the goods/project at the time they leave the factory).

73. *Moriroku UT India (P) Ltd. v. State of Uttar Pradesh, supra* para 15 p. 555.

74. *Ibid. Bata India Ltd. v. Commissioner of Central Excise*, (2010) 5 SCC 490 : (2010) 3 JT 653 (Intermediate project during manufacture – for captive consumption. Burden on department to show that it was marketable and therefore liable to excise duty).

to be brought within the charging section.[75] Same principle was applied for construing and applying section 9 of the Mines and Minerals (Regulation and Development) Act, 1957 which is the charging section for levy of royalty 'in respect of any mineral removed or consumed' at the rates fixed in Schedule II of the Act. In case of iron ore the schedule prescribes rates of royalty for (i) lumps (ii) fines and (iii) concentrates but not for 'slimes' which too is a product of iron ore when it is subjected to processing. It was, therefore, held that no royalty could be recovered on 'slimes' which have no commercial value although they too have some ferrous content. The interrelation between a charging section and computation provision was well expressed by JUSTICE LAHOTI in this case. He said: "For the purpose of levying any charge, not only has the charge to be authorised by law, it has also to be computed. The charging provision and the computation provision may be found at one place or at two different places depending on the draftsman's art of drafting and methodology employed. In the latter case, the charging provision and the computation provision, though placed in two parts of the enactment, shall have to be read together as constituting one integrated provision. The charging provision and the computation provision do differ qualitatively. In case of conflict, the computation provision shall give way to the charging provision. In case of doubt or ambiguity the computing provision shall be so interpreted as to act in aid of charging provision. If the two can be read together homogeneously then both shall be given effect to, more so, when it is clear from the computation provision that it is meant to supplement the charging provision and is, on its own, a substantive provision in the sense that but for the computation provision the charging provision alone would not work. The computing provision cannot be treated as mere surplusage or of no significance; what necessarily flows therefrom shall also have to be given effect to."[76]

When the same income is taxable in two countries according to tax laws enforce in them, relief can be granted only by international agreement for avoidance of double taxation and by providing for enforcement of the agreement.[77]

---

75. *CIT v. B.C. Srinivasa Setty*, AIR 1981 SC 972 : (1982) 2 SCC 460; *CIT v. Official Liquidator, Palai Central Bank*, (1985) 1 SCC 45, pp. 50, 51 : AIR 1985 SC 146. **See further** *GE India Technology Centre (P) Ltd. v. CIT*, (2010) 10 SCC 29 para 16 : (2010) 10 JT 85 (while interpreting the provisions of the Income-tax Act one cannot read the charging sections of the Act dehors the machinery provision).

76. *National Mineral Development Corporation Ltd. v. State of M.P.*, (2004) 6 SCC 281, p. 294 (para 23) : AIR 2004 SC 2456, p. 2463.

77. **See** section 90 of the Income-tax Act, 1961 and *Union of India v. Azadi Bachao Andolan*, AIR 2004 SC 1107; *Commissioner of Income Tax v. PVAL Kulandagan Chettiar*, (2004) 6 SCC 235 : AIR 2004 SC 3411 .

A penalty provision in a taxing Act as distinguished from a provision creating an offence does not attract the rule of presumption of *mens rea.*[78] The same rule applies to offences against the Revenue and economic offences.[79] The words 'shall presume' used in a taxing Act to show infringement of some provision which subjects the assessee to a penalty are construed to convey a rebuttable presumption.[80] A provision to impose a penalty does not necessarily convey that penalty must be imposed in all cases.[81] A high rate of penalty may be construed to be the maximum not applicable to all cases.[82] A provision for penalty or for confiscation for violation of the provisions of a taxing Act cannot be inferred. Such an "authority has to be specific and explicit and expressly provided" in the taxing Act.[83] Such a provision cannot also be construed as retrospective.[84] A tax cannot be imposed by way of penalty although penalty can be imposed for non-payment of tax or for evasion of tax.[85] While exercising power of delegated legislation to fix rates of tax, the State Government cannot fix rates in such a manner which amounts to penalty for evasion of tax by not adhering to conditions of permit when the Act itself does not provide for such penalty.[86]

The principles applicable to the construction of retrospective taxing laws, have already been referred to in an earlier Chapter.[87]

(c) Illustrative cases

In *IRC v. Duke of Westminster,*[88] the Duke executed a series of deeds in favour of his employees in which he covenanted to pay certain weekly

---

78. *Gujarat Travancore Agency v. Commr. of Income-tax, Kerala,* AIR 1989 SC 1671, p. 1764 : (1989) 3 SCC 52; *Additional Commissioner of Income-tax v. I.M. Patel,* AIR 1992 SC 1762, p. 1764 : 1993 Supp (1) SCC 621; *Dilip N. Shroff v. Commissioner of Income-tax,* (2007) 8 Scale 304.

79. **See** text and note 3, p. 996 and text and note 88, p. 1014.

80. *Sodhi Transport v. State of U.P.*, AIR 1986 SC 1099, p. 1105 : 1986 (2) SCC 486; *State of Madhya Pradesh v. Bharat Heavy Electricals,* AIR 1997 SC 3285, p. 3288 : (1997) 7 SCC 1.

81. *Hindustan Steel Ltd. v. State of Orissa,* AIR 1970 SC 253, p. 256 (para 7) : 1969 (2) SCC 627; *EST Corpn. v. H.M.T. Ltd.*, (2008) 3 SCC 35 para 21 : AIR 2008 SC 1322.

82. *State of Madhya Pradesh v. Bharat Heavy Electricals,* AIR 1997 SC 3285, p. 3288 : (1997) 7 SCC 1.

83. *Collector of Central Excise v. Orient Fabrics (P.) Ltd.*, (2004) 1 SCC 597, p. 600 (para 6) : (2003) 10 JT 282.

84. *Collector Central Excise, Ahmedabad v. Orient Fabrics Pvt. Ltd.*, AIR 2004 SC 956.

85. *Hardeo Motor Transport v. State of M.P.*, (2006) 8 SCC 613 (paras 29 to 32) : AIR 2007 SC 839.

86 *Ibid.*

87. Chapter 6, title 2(e), p. 599.

88. (1935) All ER Rep 259 : 1936 AC 1 : 104 LJKB 383 (HL).

sums for a period of seven years in consideration of past services during the joint lives of himself and the employee concerned. It was provided in the deeds that the payments were 'without prejudice to such remuneration as the annuitant will become entitled to in respect of such services (if any) as the annuitant may hereafter render' to the Duke. The recipients in all the cases continued in the employment and continued to receive such sums as with the sums payable by the deed made up the amount of the wages or salary payable before the deed and no more. The Duke's contention was that the payments under the deed were annual payments which he was entitled to deduct from his total income for purposes of surtax, whereas the contention of the Revenue was that the payments were in substance made as remuneration for services and could not be so deducted. The House of Lords (LORD ATKIN dissenting) rejected the contention of the Revenue and held that when a deed is not challenged as non-genuine or a mere cloak to conceal a different transaction the substance of the matter cannot be distinguished from the legal rights and obligations arising under the deed. And, on the same basis it has been held that a transaction which is an exchange, cannot be taxed on the ground that in substance it is a sale,[89] or that a transaction which is really a sale, is in substance an exchange.[90]

The relevant facts in the case of *Pott's Executors v. IRC*,[91] were that by a settlement the assessee settled a large sum on his infant grandchildren and the trustees of the settlement purchased from the settlement moneys almost the entire share capital of a company which was held by the settlor who was the governing director. The settlor had an account with the company which made, on his behalf and at his request, numerous payments to third parties, and debited his account with those sums. The question before the House of Lords was whether these payments made by the company to third parties and not to the settlor himself were 'any sum paid by way of loan' 'directly or indirectly' by a corporate body connected with the settlement 'to the settlor' and constituted his income within section 40 of the Finance Act, 1938. The contention of the Revenue was that payments by the company to third parties made at the request of the settlor were 'in substance' a convenient method which avoided the necessity of the company paying to the settlor and the settlor then paying to third parties, and, therefore, the payments constituted sums paid by way of loan to the settlor. The House of Lords rejected this contention and held that the payments made by the company to third parties who could retain the money and were not accountable to the settlor, although made at the request or on

89. *CIT v. M. & G. Stores*, AIR 1968 SC 200 : 1967 (3) SCR 876.
90. *CIT v. G. Arbuthnot & Co.*, AIR 1973 SC 989, p. 995 : (1973) 3 SCC 845.
91. (1951) 1 All ER 76 (HL).

behalf of the settlor, were not payments by way of loan to the settlor. LORD SIMONDS said: "I am not, in the construction of such a statute (taxing statute), entitled to say that, because the legal or business result is the same whether, on the one hand, I borrow money from the company and with it make certain payments, or, on the other hand, the company at my request makes certain payments on my implied promise to repay, therefore, it is immaterial what words are in the statute if that result is attained."[92] LORD NORMAND similarly observed: "This is a taxing Act and its terms are not to be enlarged by reasoning that the same final result is achieved as by a loan made to the settlor followed by a payment made by him to the third party. The court is not entitled to say that for the purposes of taxation the actual transaction is to be disregarded as 'machinery' and that the substance or equivalent financial results are the relevant considerations. It may, indeed, be said that if these loose principles of construction had been liberally applied, they would in many instances have been adequate to deal with tax evasion, and there would have been less frequent cause for the intervention of Parliament."[93] These cases illustrate the principle that the doctrine of substance of the matter has no application to a taxing Act. But this principle is now subject to the new approach adopted by courts towards tax evasion schemes.[94]

The question in *Kirkness v. John Hudson & Company*,[95] was whether a balancing charge under section 17 of the Income-tax Act, 1945, which was leviable when machinery or plant was 'sold' over its written down value could be levied when the machinery or plant was compulsorily acquired under the Defence Regulations and the compensation paid was substantially higher than the written down value. It was urged on behalf of the Revenue that the result in law of a sale is to transfer the ownership of property from *A* to *B* for consideration in money or money's worth; and that this is just what happens when property is compulsorily acquired under a statute; therefore, compulsory acquisition must be treated on the same footing as sale. The House of Lords rejected this contention and held that compulsory acquisition of property did not in law amount to sale, although the result may be the same, and therefore, no balancing charge could be made.

In *C.I.T., Bombay v. Provident Investment Co.*,[96] the assessee-company entered into an agreement to sell its managing agency in a company, but

---

92. *Ibid*, p. 80.
93. *Ibid*, pp. 81, 82. Referred to in *CIT v. Keshavlal*, AIR 1965 SC 866, p. 868 (para 14) : (1965) 2 SCR 100.
94. **See** title 2, Evasion of Statutes, text and notes 54 to 77, pp. 912 to 922.
95. (1955) 2 All ER 345 (HL).
96. AIR 1957 SC 664 : 1957 SCR 1141.

before any sale could take place the agreement was modified and the assessee-company agreed to resign and relinquished the managing agency for the same consideration. On these facts it was held by the Supreme Court that there was no 'sale or transfer' of the managing agency within the meaning of section 12-B of the Indian Income-tax Act, 1922.

An illustration of the principle that in order to tax any person, he must clearly fall within the ambit of the charging section, can be found in *Tata Sky Ltd. v. State of Madhya Pradesh*,[97] where the issue before the Supreme Court was whether DTH (direct to home) broadcasters could be taxed under the Madhya Pradesh Entertainments Duty and Advertisements Tax Act, 1936. On an examination of the Act as a whole, particularly a conjoint reading of sections 2(a) (admission to an entertainment), 2(b) (definition of entertainment), 2(d) (payment of admission), 3 (entertainment duty payable by the proprietor of an entertainment) and 4 (method of levy), the Court held that the charge of tax under the Act would be attracted only if an entertainment takes place in a specified physical location to which persons are admitted on payment of some charge to the proprietor of the entertainment. Since DTH operation is not a place-related entertainment, it is not covered under the charging provision *i.e.* section 3, and therefore, the State cannot impose any tax on DTH operators under the said Act.

In *C.I.T. v. Karamchand Premchand Ltd.*,[98] the assessee carried on business both within and outside taxable territories in India. He sustained losses in relation to business carried on outside taxable territories, and contended that those losses could be set-off against profits in taxable territories for computation of his taxable income. The question depended on construction of the third proviso to section 5 of the Business Profit Tax Act, 1947, which provided that the Act was not to apply to any income, profits or gains of business accruing or arising within any part of India to which the Act did not extend, unless such income, profits or gains were received in or brought into the taxable territories. The Supreme Court felt that the matter was not free from difficulty and gave the benefit of construction to the assessee by holding that the language of the proviso did not exclude the outside business from consideration but only exempted the income thereof, unless received or deemed to be received in taxable territories.

It was held in *State of Punjab v. Jullundar Vegetables Syndicate*,[99] that the East Punjab Sales Tax Act, 1948, as it stood in 1953 did not provide

97. *Tata Sky Ltd. v. State of Madhya Pradesh*, (2013) 4 SCC 656, pp. 666 to 668.
98. AIR 1960 SC 1175 : 1960 (3) SCR 727.
99. AIR 1966 SC 1295 : (1966) 2 SCR 457. But while dealing with the corresponding Bombay Act, the Supreme Court inferred by implication the requisite authority to assess a dissolved firm; *Murarilal Mahabir Prasad v. B.R. Vad*, AIR 1976 SC 313 : (1975) 2 SCC 736.

any machinery for assessing a firm, which has been dissolved. Though the firm, which the Act treated as a separate entity, existed during the entire period for which tax was to be levied and at the time when assessment proceeding commenced, it escaped liability on its dissolution before completion of assessment for want of machinery in the Act to complete the assessment in such a contingency. It was a case of lacuna which could not be cured by interpretation.

The question in *Philip John Plasket Thomas v. C.I.T.*,[1] was as to construction of section 16(3)(a)(iii) of the Income-tax Act, 1922, which permits the inclusion in computing the total income of the husband, so much of the income of a wife as arises 'from assets transferred directly or indirectly to the wife by the husband otherwise than for adequate consideration'. It was held that for the application of the above provision the relationship of husband and wife must exist at the time when income accrues to the wife and also at the time when the transfer of assets is made. Income accruing to a wife from assets transferred to her prior to the marriage could not, therefore, be taken into account for computing the total income of the husband even in respect of any period after the marriage. It was observed by S.K. DAS, J. that the provision in question "creates an artificial income and must be strictly construed".[2]

Applying the well-settled principle of statutory interpretation of a taxing statute that a subject will be liable to tax and will be entitled to exemption from tax according to the strict language of the taxing statute, the Supreme Court held that if, as per the words used in Explanation (baa) to section 80HHC read with the words used in clauses (iii-d) and (iii-e) of section 28 of the Income-tax Act, 1961, the assessee was entitled to deduction under section 80HHC on export profits, the benefit of such deduction cannot be denied to the assesse.[3]

In *Atlas Cycles Industries Ltd. v. Haryana State,*[4] a provision extending to newly included areas in a municipality 'rules, bye-laws, orders, directions and powers' was held not to cover a 'notification' imposing a tax on the principle that a taxing provision has to be strictly construed.

A striking illustration of the difference in approach in construction of a provision in a taxing statute is furnished by a case of the Supreme Court[5] construing Article 1, Schedule I of the Bombay Court-fees Act, 1959. It

---

1. AIR 1964 SC 587 : 1964 (2) SCR 480.
2. *Ibid*, p. 590, **referred** to in *CIT v. Keshavlal*, AIR 1965 SC 866, p. 867 (para 9) : (1965) 2 SCR 100. **Cf.** *CIT v. C.M. Kothari*, AIR 1964 SC 331 : 1964 (2) SCR 531.
3. *Topman Exports v. Commissioner of Income Tax, Mumbai*, (2012) 3 SCC 593, p. 610.
4. AIR 1972 SC 121 : (1971) 2 SCC 564.
5. *State of Maharashtra v. Mishrilal*, AIR 1964 SC 457 : 1964 (5) SCR 230.

was held that the words 'value of subject-matter in dispute in appeal' on which an appellant is required to pay court-fee in appeal did not include the amount of interest *pendente lite* awarded by the decree under appeal. Similar words occurring in relation to requirement of valuation prescribed for appeals to Privy Council were construed in *Goorooprasad v. Juggutchunder*,[6] to include the amount of interest decreed up to the date of decree and it was contended that the same meaning should be given to the words in the Court-fees Act. Rejecting this contention, RAGHUBAR DAYAL, J. observed: "We do not consider it correct that the expression in the Act be construed in the light of the construction placed on a similar expression for the purpose of considering whether the case had come within the rule allowing the High Court to give leave for appeal to Privy Council. The Act is a taxing statute and its provisions are, therefore, to be construed strictly in favour of the subject-litigant. The other provisions are for the purpose of allowing the party feeling aggrieved to take up his case to next higher court and therefore, the relevant provision in that regard had to be given a liberal construction."[7]

The case of *Azamjha v. Expenditure Tax Officer, Hyderabad*,[8] illustrates the principle that logic or reason is not of much avail in a taxing Act. In that case the question related to the construction of the definition of 'dependant' in section 2(g) of the Expenditure Tax Act, 1957, which so far as relevant reads: "'Dependant' means where the assessee in an individual, his or her spouse or minor child and includes any person wholly or mainly dependant on the assessee for support and maintenance." It was held that the concluding words in the definition 'wholly or mainly dependant on the assessee' did not refer to spouse or minor child and that a spouse and minor child would be dependants even if they had their separate income and were not in fact dependant on the assessee. The court observed: "It does look somewhat anomalous and illogical that where the expenditure has been incurred by the wife and minor children who are altogether independent of the assessee and which has no connection with their being dependant on him or with any property transferred to them should be included in the expenditure of the assessee. But it must be remembered that logic and reason cannot be of much avail in interpreting a taxing statute."[9]

The Finance Act, 1972 makes provision for imposition of a new tax known as Value Added Tax (VAT) 'on the supply of goods and services in the United Kingdom'. The expression supply of goods is defined to

---

6. 8 MIA 166.
7. *State of Maharashtra v. Mishrilal, supra*, p. 459.
8. AIR 1972 SC 2319 : (1971) 3 SCC 621.
9. *Ibid*, p. 2323.

include 'all forms of supply and in particular the *letting of goods on hire—.*' The Act enables the making of regulations with respect to the time at which a supply is to be treated as taking place in cases where 'goods or services *are supplied*' for a consideration the whole or part of which is determined or payable periodically or at the end of any period. The regulation made under this provision provides that when goods are or have been supplied under an agreement to hire, they shall be treated as being successively supplied on hire for successive parts of the period of the agreement and each of the successive supplies shall be treated as taking place when a payment under the agreement is received. In construing the Act it was held that the words 'are supplied' and 'letting of goods on hire' denoted a continuous process or state of affairs so that the date when the letting or hiring had begun was immaterial and that the tax was payable in respect of the period of hire after the coming into force of the Act although the goods were taken on hire before the coming into force of the Act.[10] It was argued that as the words 'are supplied' meant 'are delivered' in respect of credit sales, the same meaning should be given to those words in case of hiring transactions and, at any rate, the words being ambiguous benefit should be given to the taxpayer. This argument was rejected on the ground that the words 'are supplied' were appropriate to cover both types of transactions and there was no ambiguity.[11]

(d) Qualifications of the rule of strict construction

The principle of strict construction applicable to taxing statutes does not, however, mean that where the subject falls clearly within the letter of the law, the court can avoid the tax by putting a restricted construction on some supposed hardship,[12] or on the ground that the tax,[13] or penalty[14] imposed, is heavy or oppressive. No question of strict construction arises when the statutory provision is reasonably open to only one meaning.[15] When intention to levy the tax is clearly shown by the words used by Parliament, it is not open 'to speculate on what would be the fairest and most equitable mode of levying that tax.'[16] And no rule or principle of construction

---

10. *Customs & Excise Commissioners v. Thorn Electrical Industries Ltd.*, (1975) 3 All ER 881 (HL).

11. *Ibid.*

12. *IRC v. Bladnouch Distillery Co.*, (1948) 1 All ER 616, p. 625 (HL); *Tarulata Syam v. Commissioner of Income-tax, West Bengal*, AIR 1977 SC 1802, p. 1811 : (1977) 3 SCC 280. **See further** dictum of LORD CAIRNS extracted in text and note 29, p. 879.

13. *Jagannath v. Union of India*, AIR 1962 SC 148 : 1962 (2) SCR 118.

14. *IRC v. Hinchy*, (1960) 1 All ER 505 : 1960 AC 748 (HL).

15. *Commissioner of Wealth Tax v. Harshmatunnisa Begum (Smt.)*, AIR 1989 SC 1024, pp. 1029, 1030 : 1989 Supp (2) SCC 43.

16. *Coltness Iron Co. v. Black*, (1881) 1 AC 315, p. 330 : (1880-81) 6 AC 315 (HL) (LORD BLACKBURN).

requires that close reasoning should not be employed to arrive at the true meaning of a badly drafted provision in a taxing statute.[17] The taxpayer is now not entitled to succeed by showing merely a fine balance of arguments which may have been possible in good old days when the Crown or the State in its taxing capacity was regarded as a public enemy.[18] So when the intention to tax is clear, it cannot be defeated by a mere defect in phraseology on the ground that the provision could have been more artistically drafted.[19] The rule that where a literal interpretation leads to absurd or unintended results, the language of the statute can be modified to accord with the legislative intention and to avoid absurdity also applies in interpreting a taxing statute.[20] Although there is a general principle of construction which avoids double taxation by the same Act,[21] it is well known that the joint operation of different taxing Acts very often results in liability to pay different taxes in relation to the same transaction by the same person.[22] Thus, a person, on the first sale of a commodity manufactured by him, is liable to pay Excise tax *qua* manufacturer and sales tax *qua* seller. Further the sale so made by him is to be taken into account in arriving at his total income which is taxable under the Income-tax Law.

The shift from literal to purposive construction has not left taxing statutes untouched leaving them "as some island of literal interpretation."[23] So

---

17. *J.K. Steel Ltd. v. Union of India*, AIR 1970 SC 1173, p. 1177 : (1969) 2 SCR 448; *ITC Ltd. v. Commissioner of Central Excise New Delhi*, (2004) 7 SCC 591, p. 606 : (2004) 7 JT 409 ('Badly drafted' means 'ambiguous').

18. *Customs and Excise Commissioners v. Thorn Electrical Industries Ltd.*, (1975) 3 All ER 881, p. 991 (HL) (LORD KILBRANDON). **See further** *Keshavji Ravji and Co. v. Commissioner of Income-tax*, AIR 1991 SC 1806, p. 1812 : (1990) 2 SCC 231 (Artificial and latitudinarian rules to give the taxpayer the 'breaks' are now out of place for taxation is now not an 'impertinent intrusion into sacred rights of private property'.) *Orissa State Warehousing Corporation v. Commissioner of Income-tax,* JT 1999 (2) SC 527, p. 540 : AIR 1999 SC 1388, p. 1398 : (1999) 4 SCC 197; *Oxford University Press v. Commissioner of Income-tax,* AIR 2001 SC 886, pp. 896, 897 : (2001) 3 SCC 359; *Commissioner of Central Excise, Pondicherry v. ACER India Ltd.*, (2004) 8 SCC 173, p. 185 : (2004) 8 JT 53.

19. *CWT, Bihar v. Kripashankar*, AIR 1971 SC 2463, p. 2466 : (1971) 2 SCC 570.

20. *C.W.S. (India) Limited v. Commissioner of Income-tax*, JT 1994 (3) SC 116, p. 120 : 1994 Supp (2) SCC 296; *Hindustan Petroleum Corporation Ltd. v. Collector of Central Excise*, 1995 (3) Scale 1, pp. 8, 9 (Discriminatory, arbitrary, anomalous and inequitable results to be avoided. Construction of Rules 12 and 13 of Central Excise Rules, 1944).

21. **See** text and notes 59 to 65, pp. 832, 833.

22. *Matharaprasad & Sons v. State of Punjab*, AIR 1962 SC 745 : 1962 Supp (1) SCR 913; *Radhakishan Rathi v. Additional Collector, Durg*, 1995 (3) Scale 184, pp. 187, 188 : AIR 1995 SC 1540 : (1995) 4 SCC 309.

23. *Inland Revenue Commissioners v. McGuckian*, (1997) 3 All ER 817, p. 824 : (1997) 1 WLR 991 : 1997 STC 908 (HL). **See further,** NATALIE LEE, *'A purposive*

[Footnote No. 23 Contd.]

the principle of purposive construction will be applied when the literal construction leads to absurdity.[24] The context, scheme of the relevant Act as a whole and its purpose are as relevant in construing a taxing Act as in construing any other Act.[25] Therefore, the rule that object of the Legislature has to be kept in view and a construction consistent with the object has to be placed on the words used if there be ambiguity, is also applicable in construing a taxing enactment.[26] Every taxing statute has a fiscal philosophy -- a feel of which is necessary to gather the intent and effect of its different clauses.[27] So in construing a Court-fees Act the Court should be informed of the principle of equal access to Court suggesting that a heavy price tag on relief in Court should be regarded as unpalatable.[28] Section 11 of the Madras Commercial Crops Markets Act, 1933, empowered the Market Committee to levy fees on the notified crop or crops 'bought and sold.' Three meanings were suggested of the words 'bought and sold', *viz.*: (i) duality of transactions where the same person buys goods and sells the identical goods in the notified area; (ii) disjunctive sense, *i.e.*, 'and' being construed as 'or'; (iii) a transaction of purchase as the concept of purchase includes a corresponding sale. In accepting the third meaning the court stated: "The Legislature had principally the producer in mind who should have a proper market where he can bring his goods for sale, and where he can secure a fair deal and a fair price. The Act thus aims at transactions which such a producer would enter into with those who buy from him. The words 'bought and sold' used in section 11(1) aim at those transactions whereunder a dealer buys from a producer who brings to the market his goods for sale. The transaction aimed at must be viewed in the sense in

---

[Footnote No. 23 Contd.]

Approach to the Interpretation of Tax Statutes', (1999) 20 Statute Law Review p. 141; "some view the (purposive) approach with extreme caution, if not dislike, whilst some applaud its use."

24. *Commissioner of Central Excise, Pondicherry v. ACER Ltd.*, (2004) 8 SCC 173, p. 185 : (2004) 8 JT 53.

25. *W. T. Ramsay Ltd. v. Inland Revenue Commissioners*, (1981) 1 All ER 865, pp. 870, 871 (HL); *Inland Revenue Commissioners v. McGuckian, supra*, p. 824.

26. *Administrator, Municipal Corporation, Bilaspur v. Dattatraya Dahankar*, AIR 1992 SC 1846, pp. 1847, 1848 : (1992) 1 SCC 361. (**Overruled** on merits in *Mathuram Agrawal v. State of Madhya Pradesh,* AIR 2000 SC 109 : (1999) 8 SCC 667). **See further** *Oxford University Press v. Commissioner of Income-tax,* AIR 2001 SC 886, pp. 897 (para 36) : (2001) 3 SCC 359.

27. *Controller of Estate Duty v. Kantilal Trikamlal*, AIR 1976 SC 1935, p. 1938 : (1976) 4 SCC 643; *K.P. Verghese v. ITO*, AIR 1981 SC 1922, pp. 1930, 1931 : (1981) 4 SCC 173; *Commissioner of Central Excise, Pondicherry v. ACER Ltd., supra.*

28. *Gujarat State Financial Corporation v. Natson Manufacturing Co. Pvt. Ltd.*, AIR 1978 SC 1765, p. 1770 : (1979) 1 SCC 193.

which the Legislature intended it to be viewed, that is, as one transaction resulting in buying on the one hand and selling on the other."[29]

Wherever the intention to impose liability is clear, the Courts ought not to be hesitant in espousing a commonsense interpretation of the machinery provisions so that the charge does not fail. The machinery provisions must, no doubt, be so construed as would effectuate the object and purpose of the statute. For instance, section 158-BD of the Income-tax Act, 1961, is a machinery provision and was inserted in the statute book for the purpose of carrying out assessments of a person other than the searched person under sections 132 or 132-A of the Act. Under the provision, if an assessing officer is satisfied that there exists undisclosed income belonging to a person other than the searched person, he may, after recording such satisfaction, transmit the records to the assessing officer having jurisdiction over such other person. The question before the Supreme Court was at which the stage of the proceedings the concerned satisfaction note is required to be prepared by the assessing officer. Applying the above-said principles of interpretation, the Court held that for the purpose of section 158-BD, a satisfaction note is a *sine qua non* and it must be prepared by the assessing officer before he transmits the records to the other assessing officer who has jurisdiction over such other person, and that the satisfaction note could be prepared at any of the following stages:

(a) at the time of or along with the initiation of proceedings against the searched person under section 158-BC of the Act;
(b) along with the assessment proceedings under section 158-BC of the Act; or
(c) immediately after the assessment proceedings of the searched person are completed under Section 158-BC of the Act.[30]

Wide language used in the Constitution and statutes in the context of taxation cannot be narrowly construed. For example, the definition of 'goods' in Article 366(12) of the Constitution to include 'all materials, commodities and articles' and similar definitions in the Customs Act and Sales Tax Acts have been widely construed and electricity,[31] lottery tickets[32] and technical material in the form of drawings, manuals and computer discs etc.[33] have been held to be goods. In *Tata Consultancy Services v. State of A.P.*,[34] a constitution bench of the Supreme Court held that canned software namely software program on CDs/floppy discs fell within the definition of 'goods' in A.P. General Sales Tax Act, 1957 and its sale was liable to Sales Tax. In

29. *Krishna Coconut Co. v. East Godavari Coconut & Tobacco Market Committee*, AIR 1967 SC 973 : 1967 (1) SCR 974.
30. *CIT v. Calcutta Knitwears, Ludhiana*, (2014) 6 SCC 444, pp. 457 to 459.
31. *CST v. M.P. Electricity Board*, (1969) 1 SCC 200 : AIR 1970 SC 732.
32. *H. Anraj v. Govt. of T.N.*, (1986) 1 SCC 414 : AIR 1986 SC 63.
33. *Associated Cement Companies Ltd. v. Commr. of Customs*, (2001) 4 SCC 593 : AIR 2001 SC 862.
34. (2005) 1 SCC 308 : AIR 2005 SC 371.

holding so VARIAVA J. observed as follows: "In our view, the term "goods" as used in Article 366(12) of the Constitution and as defined under the said Act (A.P. General Sales Tax Act) is very wide and includes all types of movable properties, whether those properties be tangible or intangible. We are in complete agreement with the observations made by this court in Associated Cement Companies Ltd. A software program may consist of various commands which enable the computer to perform a designated task. The copyright in that program may remain with the originator of the program. But the moment copies are made and marketed, it becomes goods, which are susceptible to sales tax. Even intellectual property, once it is put on to a media, whether it be in the form of books or canvas (in case of painting) or computer discs or cassettes, and marketed would become "goods". We see no difference between a sale of a software program on a CD/floppy disc from a sale of music on a cassette/CD or a sale of a film on a video cassette/CD. In all such cases, the intellectual property has been incorporated on a media for purposes of transfer. Sale is not just of the media which by itself has very little value. The software and the media cannot be split up. What the buyer purchases and pays for is not the disc or the CD. As in the case of paintings or books or music or films the buyer is purchasing the intellectual property and not the media *i.e.*, the paper or cassette or disc of CD. Thus a transaction/sale of computer software is clearly a sale of "goods" within the meaning of the term as defined in the said Act. The term "all materials, articles and commodities" includes both tangible and intangible/incorpo-real property which is capable of abstraction, consumption and use and which can be transmitted, transferred, delivered, stored, possessed, *etc*. The software programs have all these attributes."[35] But in the context of telephone service, mobile or fixed, it has been held that electromagnetic waves or radio frequencies are not 'goods' within the meaning of Article 366(12) or for the purpose of Article 366 and that the goods in telecommunication are limited to the handsets supplied by the service provider.[36]

The Supreme Court held that in the absence of statutory definition in precise terms; words, entries and items in taxing statutes must be construed in terms of their commercial or trade understanding or according to their popular meaning and resort to rigid interpretation in terms of scientific and technical meanings should be avoided in such circumstances. The Supreme Court, however, clarified that where the legislature expresses a contrary interpretation of the particular entry, word or item in specific, scientific or technical terms, the interpretation ought to be in accordance with the scientific or technical meaning and not according to common parlance understanding.

The Supreme Court also held that definition in one statute cannot be mechanically applied to another statute. The object of Excise, 1944 Act is to raise revenue and the conditions or restrictions contemplated in another

---

35. *Ibid*, p. 329 (para 27).
36. *Bharat Sanchar Nigam Ltd. v. Union of India,* (2006) 3 SCC 1 (paras 71, 92) : AIR 2006 SC 1383.

statute having a different object should not be mechanically imported in to a fiscal statute to claim that the goods were not liable to excise duty.[36a]

Though equity and taxation are often strangers, attempts should be made that they do not remain always so and if a construction results in equity rather than in injustice, then such a construction should be preferred to the literal construction.[37] It was, therefore, held that when under section 16(3) of the Income-tax Act, 1922 the income from business of a wife or minor child is includible as the income of the assessee, the profit or loss from such business should be treated as the profit or loss from a "business carried on by him" for the purpose of carrying forward and set-off of the loss under section 24(2) of the Act.[38] A provision enacted for the benefit of an assessee should be so construed which enables the assessee to get its benefit. On this view the word 'owned' in relation to a building in section 32 of the Income-tax Act, 1961 which allows depreciation benefit was construed to signify dominion and entitlement to the use of the building.[39]

It is a settled proposition that in a fiscal or taxation law, while ascertaining the scope of expressions used in a particular entry, the opinion of the expert in the field of trade, who deals in those goods, should be given due importance. In a case before the Supreme Court, the assessee had imported a high speed warping machine with a drawing unit, but without a pneumatic suction device, and was claiming relief from payment of duty under Entry 8 of a Notification issued under the Customs Act, 1962, which speaks of a high speed warping machine with yarn tensioning, pneumatic suction devices and accessories. The Textile Commissioner, who was well-conversant with these machines, had furnished an opinion that the goods imported by the assessee would be covered under Entry 8 of the Table appended to the said Notification. Relying on the aforementioned proposition of interpretation of entries as well as the liberal construction previously given by the Court to beneficial notifications issued under the Act, the Court held that the assessee was entitled to relief under Entry 8 of the said Notification.[40]

Considerations of public policy may also be relevant in interpreting and applying a taxing Act.[41] Thus it has consistently been held that payments tainted with illegality cannot be treated as money wholly and exclusively spent for the purpose of business for being allowed as a

36a. *Commissioner of Central Excise v. Connaught Plaza Restaurant (P) Ltd.*, (2012) 13 SCC 639, pp. 656 to 660 : 2012 (1) SCALE 339.

37. *CIT v. J.H. Gotla Yadgiri*, (1985) 4 SCC 343, p. 360 : AIR 1985 SC 1698; *ITC Ltd. v. Commissioner of Central Excise, New Delhi*, (2004) 7 SCC 591, pp. 607, 608 : (2004) 7 JT 409.

38. *Ibid.*

39. *Mysore Minerals Ltd. v. The Commr. of Income-tax,* AIR 1999 SC 3185, p. 3187 : (1999) 7 SCC 106.

40. *Commissioner of Customs (Import), Mumbai v. Konkan Synthetic Fibres*, (2012) 6 SCC 339.

41. *Maddi Venkatraman & Co. (P) Ltd. v. Commissioner of Income-tax*, AIR 1998 SC 563, pp. 565, 566 : 1998 (2) SCC 95; *Commissioner of Central Excise, Pondicherry v. ACER India Ltd.*, (2004) 8 SCC 173, p. 185 : (2004) 8 JT 53.

deduction in computation of profits of the business for taxation under the Income-tax Act, 1961.[42]

Courts are not entitled to fill in any lacuna in any Act much less in a Taxing Act,[43] but the courts will also not stretch a point in favour of the taxpayer to enable him to get by his astuteness the benefit which other taxpayers do not obtain.[44] And in construing provisions designed to prevent tax evasion, if the Legislature uses words of comprehensive import, the courts cannot proceed on an assumption that the words were used in a restricted sense so as to defeat the avowed object of the Legislature.[45] The principle behind this rule is that an enactment designed to prevent fraud upon the revenue "is more properly a statute against fraud rather than a taxing statute, and for this reason properly subject to a liberal construction in the Government's favour".[46] So in interpreting a provision to plug leakage and prevent tax evasion a construction which would defeat its purpose should be eschewed and a construction which preserves its workability and efficacy should be preferred.[47] It has, therefore, been held that the word 'assessment' in section 44 of the Income-tax Act, 1922, which made applicable the provisions of Chapter IV of the Act, so far as may be, for 'assessment' in case of discontinuance of any business of a firm, was comprehensive enough to bring in the provisions of imposition of penalty under section 28.[48] Sometimes a legislation directed to prevent tax evasion is enacted in terms so general that it may apply to a variety of quite innocent transactions, and the pit dug by the Legislature may be wide enough to catch even some unwary innocent.[49] In these situations the court may feel sympathetic for the unwary innocent, who has been brought within the terms enacted by the Legislature, but that is hardly any reason to relieve him of tax liability.[50] A taxing Act, especially one which is designed to prevent tax evasion, cannot be restricted in application by recourse to a theory of some reasonable basis of the tax.[51] How far the provisions of such an Act are successful in including in their reach, different transactions resorted to by tax-payers for avoidance of tax would depend upon the

---

42. *Ibid*, p. 568.
43. *Lord Howard de Walden v. IRC,* (1948) 2 All ER 825, p. 830 (HL).
44. *Yeshwantrao v. CWT*, AIR 1967 SC 135, pp. 140, 141 : (1966 Supp SCR 419.
45. *C.A. Abraham v. ITO, Kottayam*, AIR 1961 SC 609, p. 612 : (1961) 2 SCR 765; *Inland Revenue Commissioner v. Joiner*, (1975) 3 All ER 1050, p. 1055 : (1975) 1 WLR 1701 (HL).
46. CRAWFORD, Statutory Construction, p. 508; *Inland Revenue Commissioner v. Joiner, supra.*
47. *State of Tamil Nadu v. Kandaswamy*, AIR 1975 SC 1871 (para 26) : (1975) 4 SCC 745; *Hotel Balaji v. State of Andhra Pradesh*, AIR 1993 SC 1048, p. 1079 : 1992 (6) JT 182; *Commissioner of Sales Tax, Delhi v. Shri Krishna Engg. Co.*, (2005) 2 SCC 695, p. 703.
48. *C.A. Abraham v. ITO, Kottayam, supra.*
49. *De Vigier v. IRC*, (1964) 2 All ER 907, pp. 909, 910 (HL).
50. *Ibid.*
51. *Commrs. of Customs v. Top Ten Promotions*, (1969) 3 All ER 39, pp. 90, 95 (HL).

construction of the provisions which are frequently couched in general terms, and may include devices not prevalent at the time of the passing of the Act. There is, however, "no presumption that the plug must exactly fit the hole."[52] Further general words used in a provision to meet tax evasion may be restricted by construction to avoid arbitrary, unconstitutional and potentially unjust results.[53] Moreover, use of very general and wide language by the Legislature, which on its literal construction applies to persons or objects which could never have been intended to be included, may entirely fail in achieving its object as the courts on failure to draw a rational dividing line between cases intended to be included, and other cases not so intended may be compelled to hold that the taxpayer was not to be charged for want of any reasonable construction of the language used.[54] Again penal provisions enacted to meet tax evasion are subject to the rule of strict construction and it is for the Revenue to prove that the conditions laid down for imposition of penalty are satisfied.[55] It must also be remembered that in applying a statute designed for detection of fraud for example, one providing for search and seizure of taxpayer's property two competing public interests are involved: that offences involving tax frauds should be detected and punished and that the right of the individual to the protection of law from unjustified interference with his use and enjoyment of his private property should be upheld. If the statutory words are ambiguous or obscure, a construction should be placed on them that is least restrictive of individual's rights. But a Judge should not be overzealous in searching ambiguities or obscurities in words which are plain simply because he is out of sympathy with the policy which the Act appears to give effect.[56]

---

52. *Ibid*, p. 95.

53. *Vestey v. Inland Revenue Commissioner*, (1979) 3 All ER 976 : (1980) AC 1148 : (1979) 3 WLR 915 (HL), **overruling** *Congreve v. Inland Revenue Commissioner*, (1948) 1 All ER 948 (HL).

54. *Commissioners of Customs v. Top Ten Promotions, supra*, pp. 93, 95.

For example, **see** *Owen Thomas Mangin v. IRC*, (1971) 2 WLR 39, pp. 45, 52 (PC), where difficulties in construing section 108, New Zealand Land and Income-tax Act, 1954 are pointed out. The section reads: "Every contract, agreement or arrangement made or entered into whether before or after the commencement of this Act shall be absolutely void in so far as, directly or indirectly, it has or purports to have the purpose or effect of in anyway altering the incidence of income-tax or relieving any person from his liability to pay income-tax." **See further** *Newtone v. Commr. of Taxation*, (1958) AC 450 (PC); *Ashton v. Inland Revenue Commissioner*, (1975) 3 All ER 225 (PC); *Europa Oil (NZ) Ltd. v. Inland Revenue Commissioner*, (1976) 1 All ER 503, pp. 511, 512 (PC).

55. *CIT v. T.V. Sundaram Iyengar*, AIR 1976 SC 255, p. 262 : (1976) 1 SCC 17; *Inland Revenue Commissioner v. Rossminster Ltd.*, (1980) 1 All ER 80, p. 95 : 1980 AC 952 : (1980) 2 WLR 1 (HL).

56. *Inland Revenue Commissioner v. Rossminster Ltd.*, (1980) 1 All ER 80, p. 90 : 1980 AC 952 : (1980) 2 WLR 1 (HL).

As regards liability to pay interest on delayed payment of tax, it has been held that interest can be levied and charged only if the statute that levies and charges the tax makes a substantive provision in this behalf.[57] If there be a provision in a taxing Act for charging interest to compensate the state, in case of delay in payment of tax by the assessee, that provision is not to be strictly construed but is construed to effectuate its purpose.[58] But the expression 'tax payable' in this context has been interpreted, in a case where there is a highly debatable dispute on a point, to mean tax payable according to return and not the amount assessed as tax after resolution of dispute.[59] Further, if liability to tax is created retrospectively, such liability could not entail the punishment of payment of interest with retrospective effect for the liability to pay interest will arise on default of payment of tax which will occur on the coming into force of the Act creating retrospection liability.[60] The assessee is also entitled to payment of interest and/or compensation from the revenue, when there is delay in refunding the excess tax collected from him.[61]

The rule of strict construction does not negative the application of the well-known principle that a person who claims an exemption or concession has to establish it, and there is ample authority for the view that this principle applies to exemptions or concessions granted in taxing laws as well.[62] An exemption granted under a fiscal statute is a concession granted

---

57. *India Carbon Ltd. v. State of Assam*, AIR 1997 SC 3054, pp. 3056, 3057 : (1997) 6 SCC 479.

58. *Calcutta Jute Manufacturing Co. v. Commercial Tax Officer*, AIR 1997 SC 2920, p. 2923 : (1997) 6 SCC 262. But provision is also made for reduction or waiver of interest in case of genuine hardship or when default in payment of tax was due to circumstances beyond the control of the assessee. Purposive construction also to be applied for such provisions : Section 220(2-A) of the Income-tax Act, 1961; *B.M. Malani v. Commissioner of Income-tax*, (2008) 10 SCC 617 para 17 : (2008) 11 JT 390.

59. *J. K. Synthetics Limited v. Commercial Taxes Officer*, AIR 1994 SC 2393, pp. 2398, 2399 : (1994) 4 SCC 276 **distinguished** in *Calcutta Jute Manufacturing Co. v. Commercial Tax Officer, supra*, p. 2924.

60. *Star India (P.) Ltd. v. Commissioner of Central Excise,* (2005) 7 SCC 203 (para 8).

61. *Sandvik Asia Ltd. v. Commissioner of Income Tax, Pune,* (2006) 2 SCC 508 : AIR 2006 SC 1223.

62. *CIT v. Ramkrishna Deo*, AIR 1959 SC 239, pp. 241, 242 : 1959 Supp (1) SCR 176; where the following cases are referred to; *Maugham v. Free Church of Scotland*, (1893) 3 TC 207, p. 210; *Keren Kayemeth Le Fisroet Ltd. v. IRC,* (1931) 17 TC 27, pp. 36, 58; *CIT v. Venkataswamy Naidu*, AIR 1956 SC 522, p. 525 : (1956) 29 ITR 529. **See further** *Kedarnath Jute Manufacturing Co. Ltd. v. Commercial Tax Officer, Shyam Bazar*, AIR 1966 SC 12 : 1965 (3) SCR 626; *Nizam's Religious Endowments Trust v. CIT*, AIR 1966 SC 1007 : 1966 (2) SCR 384; *Controller of Estate Duty v. V. Venugopal Varma Rajah*, AIR 1977 SC 121, p. 125 : (1976) 4 SCC 3; *P.A. Thillai Chidambara Nadar v. Addl. App. Asstt. Commissioner*, (1985) 4 SCC 30, p. 34 : AIR 1985 SC 1644;
[**Footnote No. 62 Contd.**]

by the Government so that the beneficiaries of such concession are not required to pay the tax or duty they are otherwise liable to pay. The recipient of the concession has no legally enforceable right against the Government for the grant of the concession except to enjoy it during the period of its grant, and there is no indefeasible right to the continuance of the concession which can be withdrawn in exercise of the very power under which it was granted unless the Government is precluded in doing so on the ground of promissory estoppel.[63] As regards construction of exemptions there are two opinions. According to one view, an exemption in case of ambiguity should be liberally construed in favour of the subject confining the operation of the duty,[64] but according to the other view, exemptions from taxation have a tendency to increase the burden on other members of society,[65] and should, therefore, be deprecated and construed in case of doubt against the subject.[66]

[**Footnote No. 62 Contd.**]

Mangalore Chemicals and Fertilisers Ltd v. Deputy Commissioner of Commercial Taxes, AIR 1992 SC 152, p. 158 : 1992 Supp (1) SCC 21; *Motiram Tolaram v. Union of India,* AIR 1999 SC 3121, p. 3123 (para 9) : (1999) 6 SCC 375; *Collector of Customs v. Presto Industries,* AIR 2001 SC 1233, p. 1237 (para 10) : (2001) 3 SCC 6; *India Agencies (Regd.) Bangalore v. Additional Commissioner of Commercial Taxes,* AIR 2005 SC 1594 (paras 23, 24, 25); *Udaipur Sahkari Upbhokta Thok Bhandar Limited v. Commissioner of Income-tax,* (2009) 8 SCC 393 para 23 : (2009) 9 JT 500.

63. *State of Rajasthan v. J.K. Udipur Udyog Ltd.*, (2004) 7 SCC 673, pp. 688, 689 (paras 25, 26) (RUMA PAL J.) : (2004) 8 JT 137. For promissory estoppel, **see**–text and notes 58 to 66, pp. 453, 455.

64. *Armitage v. Wilkinson*, (1878) 3 AC 355, pp. 369, 370 (PC); *Warrington v. Furbor*, (1807) 8 East 242, p. 245; *Burt v. Commr. of Taxation*, (1912) 15 CLR 469, p. 482; *Routledge v. Mackey*, (1954) 1 All ER 855, p. 857; *Collector of Central Excise v. Parley Exports*, AIR 1989 SC 644, p. 652 : (1989) 1 SCC 345; *Commissioner of Income-tax v. Gwalior Rayon Silk Manufacturing Company*, AIR 1992 SC 1782, p. 1786 : 1992 (3) SCC 326; *Commissioner of Central Excise v. North-Eastern Tobacco Co. Ltd.*, (2003) 1 SCC 161, p. 167 (para 10) : AIR 2003 SC 616, p. 619 (para 10). For example, **see** *Hansraj v. H.H. Dave*, AIR 1970 SC 755, p. 759 : 1969 (2) SCR 253; *Central Board of Direct Taxes v. Aditya V. Birla*, AIR 1988 SC 420, pp. 423, 424 : 1988 Supp SCC 120. But a liberal construction cannot be adopted when it does violence to the plain meaning of the provision or when there is no real difficulty in ascertaining the meaning; *Petron Engineering Construction Pvt. Ltd. v. Central Board of Direct Taxes*, AIR 1989 SC 501, p. 506 : 1989 Supp (2) SCC 7; *Collector of Central Excise v. Parley Exports, supra; Commissioner of Income-tax, Gujarat v. Cellulose Products of India Ltd.*, AIR 1991 SC 2285, p. 2288 : 1991 (4) SCC 467; *Hind Plastics v. Collector of Customs, Bombay*, JT 1994(3) SC 258, p. 266 (para 15) : 1994 (5) SCC 167; *State of Karnataka v. Balaji Computers,* (2007) 2 SCC 743 (para 35) : (2007) 1 JT 250.

65. *IRC v. Forrest*, (1890) 15 AC 334, p. 340 : (1886-90) All ER 1198 : 60 LJQB 281 (HL) (per LORD HALSBURY **dissenting**).

66. *Liman v. Barron*, (1951) 2 All ER 393, p. 399 (COHEN, L.J.). **See further** SUTHERLAND, Statutory Construction (3rd Edition), Vol. 3, p. 296; *Kedarnath Manufacturing Co. Ltd. v. Commercial Tax Officer*, AIR 1966 SC 12, p. 14 : (1965) 3 SCR 626;

[**Footnote No. 66 Contd.**]

In *State of Gujarat v. Essar Oil Ltd.*, it has been held that the principle that in case of ambiguity, a taxing statute should be construed in favour of the assessee, does not apply to the construction of an exception or an exempting provision, which must be construed strictly, and in case of any doubt or ambiguity, the benefit must go to the State.[67] The general rule is strict interpretation of exemptions.[68] An exemption notification must be interpreted in light of the words employed by it and not on any other basis and there cannot be any addition or subtraction from the words used in the exemption notification as it requires strict interpretation by the Courts. The the wordings of the exemption notification have to be given its natural meaning when the wordings are simple, clear and unambiguous.[69] Notification exempting certain imported goods from duty will not apply to illegally imported goods.[70]

There can, however, be no doubt that exemptions made with a beneficient object, *e.g.*, to encourage increased production or[71] to give incentive

---

[Footnote No. 66 Contd.]

Novapan India Ltd. v. Collector of Central Excise and Customs, JT 1994(6) SC 80, pp. 87, 88 : 1994 Supp (3) SCC 606 : (1994) 71 ELT 769; *Rajasthan Spinning and Weaving Mills Limited v. Collector, Central Excise*, 1995 (3) Scale 381, 386 : AIR 1995 SC 1985, p. 1988; *H.M.M. Ltd. v. Collector of Central Excise*, 1996 (7) Scale 687, p. 694 : 1996 (11) SCC 332 (Strictly but reasonably); *Rajasthan Spinning and Weaving Mills Ltd. Bhilwara v. Collector of Central Excise*, JT 1997 (10) SC 419, p. 424; *Orissa Warehousing Corporation v. Commissioner of Income-tax*, JT 1999 (2) SC 527, p. 532 : AIR 1999 SC 1388, p. 1391 (para 15); *Oxford University Press v. Commissioner of Income-tax,* AIR 2001 SC 886, p. 897 (para 35) (strictly and avoiding irrationality) : (2001) 3 SCC 359; *Collector of Customs v. Presto Industries,* JT 2001 (2) SC 595, p. 602 (strictly) : (2001) 3 SCC 6 : AIR 2001 SC 1233; *Bharati Telecom Ltd. v. The Commissioner of Customs,* AIR 2002 SC 74, p. 76 (Strictly). *State of Jharkhand v. Ambuja Cements*, (2005) 1 SCC 368, p. 378. (strictly). Court cannot ignore the condition for availing exemption); *Commissioner of Central Excise Calcutta v. Emkay Investment (P.) Ltd.*, (2005) 1 SCC 526, p. 534; *Sarabhai M. Chemicals v. Commissioner of Central Excise, Vadodara*, (2005) 2 SCC 168, p. 178 (para 18); *Commissioner of Central Excise, Allahabad v. Ginni Filaments Ltd.*, (2005) 3 SCC 378, p. 388 (para 11); *State of Jharkhand v. Tata Cummins Ltd.*, (2006) 4 SCC 57 (para 16) : (2006) 4 JT 1; *CCE v. Hira Cement,* (2006) 2 SCC 439 (para 18) : (2006) 2 JT 369; *Bhai Jaspal Singh v. CCT*, (2011) 1 SCC 39 paras 26 and 31 : (2010) 11 JT 562; *CCE v. Harichand Shri Gopal*, (2011) 1 SCC 236 paras 29 and 30 : (2010) 12 JT 563. The court of justice of the European Communities has also interpreted exemptions narrowly and exception to exemption broadly; *Lu block Fine & Co. v. Customs and Excise Commissioners*, (1994) 3 All ER 705, pp. 721(g), 722(d) (CJEC).

67. *State of Gujarat & Ors. v. Essar Oil Ltd. & Anr.*, (2012) 3 SCC 522, p. 547.

68. *Commissioner of Customs v. M. Ambalal & Company*, (2011) 2 SCC 74 para 16 : (2010) 13 JT 566.

69. *Commissioner of Central Excise, Surat – I v. Favourite Industries*, (2012) 7 SCC 153, p. 167.

70. *Commissioner of Customs v. M. Ambalal & Company*, (*supra*) paras 21, 22.

71. *Commissioner Trade Tax v. D.S.M. Group of Industries*, AIR 2005 SC 271, p. 283 (para 25) : (2005) 1 SCC 657, p. 677.

to co-operative movement[72] or for the purpose of developing urban or rural areas for public good,[73] or for encouraging investment in new machinery or plant[74] or a new industrial unit[75] or setting up an industry in the backward area in terms of the industrial policy,[76] have to be liberally construed. Similarly, beneficial notifications having their purpose as encouragement or promotion of certain activities should be liberally interpreted.[77] Therefore, when a provision is made permitting concessional rates of tax for the purpose of encouraging an industrial activity, the provision has to be liberally construed.[78] So if the object of an exemption notification is to encourage the use of indigenous rice bran oil and to discourage the use of

---

72. *Commissioner of Income- tax v. U.P. Co-operative Federation Ltd.*, AIR 1989 SC 915, p. 919; *Broach Distt. Co-operative Cotton Sales Ginning and Pressing Society Ltd. v. Commissioner of Income-tax*, AIR 1989 SC 1493, p. 1495 : (1989) 2 SCC 679 : (1989) 1 SCC 47; *Commissioner of Income-tax v. South Arcot Dist. Co-op. Marketing Society*, AIR 1990 SC 1249, p. 1250 : (1989) 176 ITR 117. *Kerala State Cooperative Marketing Federation Ltd. v. Commissioner of Income-tax,* AIR 1998 SC 2303, p. 2306 : (1998) 5 SCC 48 (Construction of section 80-P of the I. T. Act, 1961).

73. *Gujarat Industrial Development Corporation v. Commissioner of Income-tax*, AIR 1997 SC 3275, p. 3277 : (1997) 7 SCC 17 [Construction of s.10(2A) of I. T. Act, 1961].

74. *Commissioner of Income-tax v. Shaan Finance (P.) Ltd.*, JT 1998 (2) SC 564, p. 571 : AIR 1998 SC 1372 : 1998 (3) SCC 605 (Construction section 32A I.T. Act, 1961); *CIT, Rajkot v. Shri Digvijay Cement Co. Ltd.,* AIR 1999 SC 1534 : (1998) 9 SCC 476 (Section 33, I.T. Act, 1961).

75. *Commissioner of Central Excise v. North Eastern Tobacco Co. Ltd.,* (2003) 1 SCC 161, pp. 167, 168 : (2002) 146 ELT 490. **See further** *Commissioner of Central Excise v. M.P.V. & Engg. Industries,* (2003) 5 SCC 333 : AIR 2003 SC 4121 (Exemption to an undertaking 'registered with the Director of Industries' as a small-scale industry construed to be applicable from the date of application for registration and not merely from the date of registration); *Vadilal Chemicals Ltd. v. State of A.P.* (2005) 6 SCC 292 : AIR 2005 SC 3075 (order providing for sales tax holiday on products manufactured in new small scale industrial units liberally construed: bottling of anhydrous ammonia held covered by exemption); *Pondicherry State Cooperative Consumer Federation Ltd. v. Union Territory of Pondicherry,* (2008) 1 SCC 206 : (2007) 13 JT 198 (repacking of edible oil held manufacture, *Vadilal Chemicals*' case followed on similar facts) *Assistant Commissioner (CT) LTU v. Amara Raja Batteries Limited,* (2009) 8 SCC 209 paras 21 and 24 : (2009) 10 JT 322 (Exemption notification to encourage industrial development should be construed liberally and given full effect).

76. *State of Jharkhand v. Tata Cummins Ltd., supra,* para 16.

77. *Commissioner of Central Excise, Surat – I v. Favourite Industries*, (2012) 7 SCC 153, p. 169.

78. *Commissioner of Income-tax, Amritsar v. Straw-Board Manufacturing Co.*, AIR 1989 SC 1490, p. 1492 : 1989 (2) JT 264 (Paper and pulp industry construed to include Straw Board industry); *Pappu Sweets and Biscuits v. Commissioner of Trade Tax,* AIR 1998 SC 3247 : 1998 (7) SCC 228 (Toffee held to be not covered by 'sweetmeat or commodity of like nature'); *Commissioner of Sales Tax v. Industrial Coal Enterprises,* AIR 1999 SC 1324, p. 1330 : (1999) 2 SCC 607; *South Eastern Coalfields Ltd. v. Commissioner of Customs & Central Excise,* (2006) 6 SCC 340 (paras 23 and 24) : (2006) 7 JT 121; *ONGC Ltd. v. Commr. of Customs,* (2006) 7 SCC 403 (para 15) : (2006) 8 Scale 551 and cases referred therein.

edible oils in soap manufacture, a narrow construction of the notification which defeats this object cannot be accepted and preference has to be given to a wider construction which promotes the object.[79] Similarly in an exemption notification issued with the object to encourage exports by granting exemption from customs duty on materials that are needed for the manufacture of the resultant product, the words 'material required to be imported for the purpose of manufacture of products' were construed to include not only materials which are actually used in the manufacture but also materials which though not used in the manufacture are yet required in order to manufacture the resultant product.[80] And an exemption notification granting rebate in excise duty to induce the manufacturers of sugar to produce more in the then current sugar year than they had produced during the corresponding period in the previous sugar year was construed consistent with this object and the words 'the quantity of sugar produced during the corresponding period' as used in the notification were construed to cover the case of a factory which had not produced at all during the relevant corresponding period.[81] An exemption provision cannot be denied full effect by a circuitous process of interpretation,[82] and liberal language used in a notification must be given due weight.[83] So if the taxpayer is within the plain terms of

---

79. *Tata Oil Mills Co. v. Collector of Central Excise*, AIR 1990 SC 27, p. 30 : (1989) 4 SCC 541 (Notification exempting from excise duty 'such soap as is made from indigenous rice bran oil'. Rice bran oil can be used for manufacture of soap only after its conversion into fatty acid. In this context, a manufacturer using rice bran oil or rice bran fatty acid was held entitled to exemption).

80. *Oblum Electrical Industries Pvt. Ltd., Hyderabad v. Collector of Customs, Bombay*, AIR 1997 SC 3467, pp. 3470, 3471 : (1997) 7 SCC 581. **Followed** in *Commissioner of Customs Kolkota v. Rupa & Co., Ltd.*, (2004) 6 SCC 408, p. 414 : (2004) 5 JT 598 (construing the 100% exemption granted to capital goods required for manufacture of 'textile garments', it was held that the exemption was not limited to machinery used directly for manufacture of garments but all machines required for the ultimate manufacture thereof).

81. *Collector of Central Excise v. Neoli Sugar Factory*, AIR 1993 SC 1921 : 1993 Supp (3) SCC 69. **See further** *Belapur Sugar and Allied Industries Ltd. v. Collector of Central Excise, Aurangabad*, AIR 1999 SC 1692, p. 1693 : (1999) 4 SCC 103; *Sidheswar Sahakari Sakhar Karkhana Ltd. v. Union of India*, (2005) 3 SCC 369, pp. 376, 377.

82. *Swadeshi Polytex Ltd. v. Collector of Central Excise*, AIR 1990 SC 301, p. 306 : (1990) 2 SCC 358 (A raw material cannot be said to be not used for grant of exemption in the manufacture of finished excisable goods simply because a non-excisable by-product also resulted).

83. *Indian Farmers Fertiliser Co-operation Ltd. v. Collector of Central Excise*, AIR 1996 SC 2542, p. 2543 : (1996) 5 SCC 488 (Exemption in respect of Raw Naphtha as is used in the manufacture of Ammonia provided such Ammonia is used elsewhere in the manufacture of fertilisers. Exemption was applied to Naphtha not only in respect of Ammonia directly used for manufacture of urea but also Ammonia used in water treatment, steam generation and inert gas generation plants which are a necessary part of the process of manufacturing urea). **See further** *Steel Authority of*

[Footnote No. 83 Contd.]

the exemption notification, he cannot be denied the benefit calling in aid, any supposed intention, and the language of the notification has to be given effect to.[84]

While construing an exemption notification not only a pragmatic view is required to be taken but also the practical aspect of it to avoid anomaly and absurdity; and full effect to the exemption may be given by adopting a purposive construction.[85] An exemption notification which rescinds earlier notifications and issues a composite notification may be clarificatory in nature and may have to be given retrospective effect.[86]

But exemptions which lift the restriction of taxability imposed by an enactment, are taxing in nature and are subject to the rule of strict construction.[87] Whatever approach may be adopted in case of a real ambiguity, it is clear that there is no justification for the view that if a word of exemption is not defined it must be given its widest meaning and the correct rule in construing words of exemption as in construing other words is to find out the sense of the words in their context by reading the statute as a whole and by bearing in mind the purposes of the statute and the consequences flowing from rival interpretations.[88] Unusual nature of exemptions will not be generally accepted unless the language is clear and express, for example

---

[Footnote No. 83 Contd.]

India Ltd. v. Collector of Central Excise, AIR 1996 SC 2544 : (1996) 5 SCC 484; *National Organic Chemical Industries Ltd. v. Collector of Central Excise*, AIR 1997 SC 690 : (1997) 2 SCC 587; *Commissioner of Central Excise, Coimbatore v. Jawahar Mills Ltd.*, AIR 2001 SC 2500, p. 2502 : (2001) 6 SCC 274.

84. *Hemraj Gordhandas v. H.H. Dave*, AIR 1970 SC 755 : (1969) 2 SCR 253; *Gujarat State Fertilizers Co. v. Collector of Central Excise*, AIR 1997 SC 3620, pp. 3625, 3626 : 1997 (4) SCC 140; *Shriram Vinyl and Chemical Industries v. Commissioner of Customs*, AIR 2001 SC 1283, p. 1285 : (2001) 4 SCC 286 (no exemption category can be treated as redundant); *ITC Ltd. v. Commissioner of Excise, New Delhi*, (2004) 7 SCC 591, pp. 605, 606; *G.P. Ceramics Pvt. Ltd. v. Commissioner, Trade Tax, Uttar Pradesh*, (2009) 2 SCC 90 para 32 : (2009) 1 JT 224.

85. *Union of India v. Ranbaxy Laboratories Ltd.*, (2008) 7 SCC 502 paras 27, 29 and 30 : AIR 2008 SC 2286 [construction of exemption notification under para 25 of the Drugs (Prices Control) Order 1955 mentioning 31-10-1999 as the period up to which the exemption was granted. The question was as to whether the exemption applied to drugs manufactured up to 31-10-1999 or manufactured and sold up to that date. The court accepted the wider view that the exemption applied to druge manufactured up to 31-10-1999.]

86. *CCE v. Wood Craft Products Ltd.*, (1995) 3 SCC 454; *WPIL Ltd., Gaziabad v. Commissioner of Central Excise, Meerut, U.P.*, (2005) 3 SCC 73, pp. 78, 79 : AIR 2005 SC 1321.

87. *Akot Municipality v. Manilal Manekji*, AIR 1967 SC 1201, p. 1204 : 1967 (2) SCR 100.

88. *Commissioner of Wealth-tax v. Officer-in-Charge (Court of Wards) Paigah*, AIR 1977 SC 113, p. 117 : (1976) 3 SCC 864. (Agricultural land does not mean all land which can be used for agriculture but only such land which is actually used or ordinarily used or meant to be used for agricultural purposes).

double deduction of the same expenditure in computation of taxable income cannot be readily allowed.[89]

If the literal reading of the exemption provision exposes it to challenge on the ground of being irrational or arbitrary, some qualification may have to be read consistent with the object of the provision.[90] An exemption instead of being absolute may be conditional making the tax exigible at a later stage in a different form or method.[91] If exemption is available on complying with certain conditions, the conditions have to be strictly complied with.[92] Further, an exemption provision and a notification issued thereunder have to be read with other relevant provisions of the Act and Rules, and the notification has to be construed consistent with them.[93] If there be any ambiguity in an exemption notification a departmental circular, issued before the notification, can be relied upon as *contemporanea expositio* and if there be successive exemption notifications under the same section for the same purpose ambiguity in one can be resolved by referring to contents of an earlier or later notification.[94] A clarificatory exemption notification may operate retrospectively.[95]

But an exemption notification to benefit small scale industrial units, not using brand name or trade name of another person, cannot be availed of by an industrial unit using brand name of another person by getting that brand name registered as a trade mark in its favour with retrospective effect under section 28 of the Trade Marks Act, 1999.[96]

A statutory tax exemption granted permanently to establish certain industries may confer a vested right or privilege which may survive repeal of the

---

89. *Escorts Limited v. Union of India*, AIR 1993 SC 1325, p. 1337 : (1993) 1 SCC 249.

90. *Oxford University Press v. Commissioner of Income-tax,* AIR 2001 SC 886, pp. 896, 897, 904 : (2001) 3 SCC 359 (In interpreting section 10(22), Income-tax Act, 1961, it was held that a foreign university cannot qualify for exemption if it does not carry on any educational activity in India).

91. *Union of India v. Jalyan Udyog*, AIR 1994 SC 88, p. 98 : (1994) 1 SCC 318 (s. 25 Customs Act 1962).

92. *Eagle Flask Industries Ltd. v. Commissioner of Central Excise*, (2004) 7 SCC 377, p. 380 : (2004) 7 JT 391; *State of Jharkhand v. Ambay Cements*, (2005) 1 SCC 368, p. 378 (paras 24 to 26) : AIR 2005 SC 4168.

93. *State of Rajasthan v. Sarvotam Vegetables Products*, AIR 1996 SC 3178, p. 3182 : (1996) 8 SCC 639 [Section 8(5) of the Central Sales Tax Act, 1956 and the notification issued thereunder have to be read alongwith sections 8(1) and 8(4)].

94. *Commissioner of Trade Tax, U.P. v. Kajaria Ceramics Ltd.*, AIR 2005 SC 2968 (paras 27, 28 and 25) : (2005) 11 SCC 149.

95. *WPIL Ltd., Gaziabad v. Commissioner of Central Excise,* AIR 2005 SC 1321 (paras 13, 16) : (2005) 3 SCC 73.

96. *Meghraj Biscuits Industries Ltd. v. Commissioner of Central Excise, U.P.*, (2007) 3 SCC 780 : AIR 2007 SC 1433.

Act under which it is granted although there be no corresponding provision in the repealing of it for grant of such an exemption.[1]

A statutory rule or an exemption notification which confers a benefit on the assessee should be liberally construed, but the beneficiary should fall within the ambit of the rule or notification. However, if there are conditions, and consequences of violation thereof are provided, then the concept of liberal construction would not arise.[2] The Supreme Court, reiterating the view of a Constitution Bench of the Court in *CCE v. Hari Chand Shri Gopal*,[3] has held that if an exemption is available only on complying with certain conditions, the exemption cannot be granted unless such conditions are complied with. Accordingly, where the assessee satisfied only one condition of the concerned exemption notification *i.e.* intended use of the goods as per the notification, but did not fulfil the other condition *i.e.* following a specified procedure in the event the goods were used elsewhere than in the factory of production, it was held that the exemption cannot be granted unless the second condition was also satisfied.[4]

It has been said that "truly speaking liberal and strict construction of an exemption provision is to be invoked at different stages of interpreting it. When the question is whether a subject falls in the notification or in the exemption clause then it being in the nature of exception is to be construed strictly and against the subject but once ambiguity or doubt about applicability is lifted and the subject falls in the notification then full play should be given to it and it calls for a wider and liberal construction."[5] It is submitted that the question of construction whether strict or liberal does not arise in the way pointed above in two stages. The construction of the provision once made determines for all stages the conditions or requirements

---

1. *Southern Petrochemical Industries Co. Ltd. v. Electricity Inspector and ETIO*, (2007) 5 SCC 447 (para 100) : AIR 2007 SC 1984. For a discussion of this case, **see** p. 672 *supra*.
2. *State of Haryana & Ors. v. Bharti Teletech Ltd.*, (2014) 3 SCC 556, pp. 566, 567.
3. *CCE v. Hari Chand Shri Gopal*, (2011) 1 SCC 236.
4. *Indian Oil Corporation Ltd. v. CCE, Vadodara*, (2012) 5 SCC 574, pp. 578, 579.
5. *Union of India v. Wood Papers Ltd.*, AIR 1991 SC 2049, pp. 2501, 2502 : (1990) 4 SCC 256; *Mangalore Chemicals and Fertilisers Ltd. v. Deputy Commissioner of Commercial Taxes*, AIR 1992 SC 152, p. 158 : (1992) 1 SCC 197; *Novapan India Ltd. v. Collector of Central Excise & Customs*, JT 1994 (6) SC 80, p. 87 : 1994 Supp (3) SCC 606; *Bombay Chemical Private Limited v. Collector of Central Excise*, 1995 (2) Scale 716 : AIR 1995 SC 1469 : 1995 Supp (2) SCC 646 ; *State Level Committee v. Morgard Shammar*, 1995 (6) Scale 306, pp. 312, 313 : AIR 1996 SC 524, pp. 528, 529; *Grasim Industries Ltd. v. State of Madhya Pradesh*, JT 1999 (9) SC 118, pp. 121, 122 : AIR 1999 SC 66, pp. 67, 68 : (1999) 8 SCC 547; *Associated Cement Companies Ltd. v. State of Bihar*, (2004) 7 SCC 642, p. 658 : (2004) 8 JT 155; *P.R. Prabhakar v. Commissioner of Income Tax, Coimbatore*, (2006) 6 SCC 86 (para 12) : (2006) 6 SLT 72 : (2006) 248 ITR 548; *G.P. Ceramics Pvt. Ltd. v. Commissioner, Trade Tax, Uttar Pradesh*, (2009) 2 SCC 90 para 29 : (2009) 1 JT 224.

for getting the benefit of exemption. The question, thereafter, is whether the subject claiming exemption satisfies those requirements or conditions (the burden to satisfy this being on the subject) and this is essentially a matter of evidence and not another stage of interpreting the exemption clause.

The rule of strict construction does not permit the taxpayer to take the benefit of an illegality. Section 24(2) of the Income-tax Act, 1922 was, therefore, construed not to permit the assessee to carry forward the loss of an illegal speculative business for setting it off against profits in subsequent years. So even a taxing statute is to be construed consistent with morality avoiding a result which gives recognition to continued illegal activities or benefits attached to it.[6] The immunity from prosecution that can be conferred by section 91 of the Kar Vivad Samadhan Scheme, 1998, included in Chapter IV of the Finance Act (No. 2) of 1998, is restricted to offences under the direct tax enactments or indirect tax enactments and does not extend to offences under the Penal Code or any other central law *e.g.*, the Prevention of Corruption Act, 1988[7]

The rule that a taxing Act is to be construed with strictness, is based on the principle that "inasmuch as there was not any *a priori* liability in a subject to pay any particular tax, nor any antecedent relationship between the taxpayer and the taxing authority no reasoning founded upon any supposed relationship of the taxpayer and the taxing authority could be brought to bear upon the construction of the Act."[8] The rule, therefore, is not to be extended to cases of statutory tolls and the like where the payment made is in return for services rendered,[9] and above all to "a case where Parliament does not step in to give the right to payment but rather to moderate and limit a right to payment which otherwise might exist without limit."[10]

It must also be borne in mind that the rule of strict construction in the sense explained above applies primarily to charging provisions in a taxing statute and has no application to a provision not creating a charge but laying down machinery for its calculation or procedure for its collection, and such machinery provisions have to be construed by the ordinary rule of

6. *Commissioner of Income-tax v. Kurji Jinabhai Kotecha*, AIR 1977 SC 1142, p. 1146 : (1977) 2 SCC 719.
7. *M. Natrajan v. State by Inspector of Police SPE, CBI, ACB*, (2008) 8 SCC 413 : (2008) 8 Scale 290.
8. *Pryce v. Monmouthshire Canal & Railway Co.*, (1879) 4 AC 197, p. 202 (HL) (LORD CAIRNS).
9. HALSBURY'S Laws of England, Vol. 36, (3rd Edition), p. 417.
10. *Pryce v. Monmouthshire Canal & Railway Cos.*, (1879) 4 AC 197, p. 203 (HL).

construction.[11] One important consideration in construing a machinery section is that it should be so construed as to effectuate the liability imposed by the charging section and to make the machinery workable—*ut res magis valeat quam pereat.*[12] Similarly a machinery provision which enables the assessee to avail of a concession or benefit conferred by a substantive provision in the Act is liberally construed.[13] And on the same principle, statutory provisions touching and conferring a right of appeal have to be read in a reasonable, practical and liberal manner.[14]

In *Gursahai v. C.I.T.*,[15] the question was as to the calculation of interest for failure to submit an estimate of income and for non-payment of advance tax as required by section 18-A(3) of the Income-tax Act, 1922. Section 18-A(8) made it abundantly clear that on failure to pay the tax at all as required by the section the assessee was liable to payment of interest on tax assessed calculated in the manner laid down in sub-section (6). Sub-section (6), however, dealt with cases where tax was paid less than a certain percentage of the tax determined at the regular assessment, and it provided that the assessee shall be liable to six percent interest calculated 'from 1st day of January in the financial year in which the tax was paid up to the date of the said regular assessment'. On a literal reading of this mode of calculation, it was not possible to apply it for cases under sub-

---

11. *Gursahai v. CIT*, AIR 1963 SC 1062, p. 1064 : 1963 (3) SCR 893. **See also** *Banarasi Debi v. ITO*, AIR 1964 SC 1742, p. 1744 :1964 (7) SCR 539; *Murarilal Mahabir Prasad v. B.R. Vad*, AIR 1976 SC 313, pp. 322, 323 : 1976 (4) SCC 736; *Commissioner of Income-tax v. National Taj Traders*, AIR 1980 SC 485, p. 491 : (1980) 1 SCC 370; *Associated Cement Company Ltd. v. Commercial Tax Officer*, AIR 1981 SC 1887, p. 1904 : (1981) 4 SCC 578; *J.K. Synthetics Ltd. v. Commercial Taxes Officer*, JT 1994 (3) SC 671, p. 685 : AIR 1994 SC 2393, p. 2400 : (1994) 4 SCC 276; *ITC Ltd. v. Commissioner of Central Excise New Delhi*, (2004) 7 SCC 591, p. 607 : (2004) 7 JT 409; *Mahim Patram (P.) Ltd. v. Union of India*, (2007) 3 SCC 668 (para 25) : (2007) 4 JT 50.

12. *N.B. Sanjana v. Elphinstone Spinning & Weaving Mills*, AIR 1971 SC 2039, p. 2047 : 1971 (1) SCC 337; *Gursahai v. CIT, supra*, p. 1065; *United Mills Ltd. v. Commr. of Excess Profits Tax, Bombay*, AIR 1955 SC 79, p. 82 : 1955 (1) SCR 810; *CIT v. Mahaliram Ramjidas*, AIR 1940 PC 124, pp. 126, 127; *Allen v. Trehearne*, (1938) 22 TC 15, p. 26; *Whitney v. IRC*, (1926) 10 TC 88, p. 110; *Murarilal Mahabir Prasad v. B.R. Vad, supra; Commissioner of Income-tax v. National Taj Traders, supra; Associated Cement Company Ltd. v. Commercial Tax Officer, supra; Commissioner of Income-tax v. Sun Engineering Works (P.) Ltd.*, AIR 1993 SC 43, p. 57 : 1992 (4) SCC 363; *J.K. Synthetics Ltd. v. Commercial Taxes Officers, supra.*

13. *C.I.T. v. Kulu Valley Transport Co. Pvt. Ltd.*, AIR 1970 SC 1734 : 1970 (2) SCC 192; *Fertiliser Corporation of India v. State of Bihar*, AIR 1988 SC 361, pp. 364, 365 : 1988 Supp SCC 73.

14. *Commissioner of Income-tax, A.P. v. Ashoka Engineering Co.*, AIR 1993 SC 858, p. 860 : 1993 Supp (1) SCC 754.

15. AIR 1963 SC 1062 : 1963 (3) SCR 893. **See further** *N.B. Sanjana v. Elphinstone Spinning & Weaving Mills, supra*, (where similar construction of word 'paid' was adopted in construing Rule 10 of the Central Excise Rules, 1944); *Director of Inspection, IT v. Pooran Mall & Sons*, AIR 1975 SC 67, pp. 70, 71 : (1975) 4 SCC 568.

section (8) where no tax had been paid, but being a machinery provision for assessment of interest, the words in question were read as 'from the 1st of January in the financial year in which the tax ought to have been paid' so as to make the provision workable for both types of cases, *i.e.*, cases where the tax was paid but was paid less than the required percentage and cases where no tax at all was paid.[16] It has also been held that the fifth proviso to sub-section (6) of section 18A which empowers Income-tax Officers to reduce or waive the interest is equally applicable to cases coming under sub-section (8) of section 18A.[17] In construing a machinery provision, literal construction can be departed to remove an apparent anomaly, which can be further illustrated by referring to the construction of section 150 of the Income-tax Act, 1961. This section removes the bar of limitation for issuing a notice of reassessment in consequence or to give effect to, any finding or direction contained in an order passed by any authority in any proceeding *under this Act* by way of appeal, reference or revision'. As the intention to continue the liability for reassessment arising in a similar situation under the repealed Act was clear the words 'under this Act' in section 150 were construed virtually to mean 'under this Act or the corresponding provisions of the repealed Act.'[18]

A penalty provision in a taxing Act is not to be equated to a criminal statute requiring impliedly the element of *mens rea* and unless there is something in the language of the Act indicating the need to establish *mens rea*, it is generally sufficient to prove that a default in complying with the provisions of the Act for which the penalty is provided has occurred.[19] A penalty provision has to be interpreted by applying the golden rule of literal construction and before a penalty can be levied the procedure laid down in the Act must be complied with.[20] But a statutory provision may require *mens rea* before penalty can be imposed and in such a case *mens rea* must be first established before imposition of penalty,[21] *e.g.*, the words

---

16. *Ibid.* For somewhat similar case under the Rajasthan Sales Tax Act, 1954 **see** *Associated Cement Co. Ltd. v. Commercial Tax Officer*, AIR 1981 SC 1887 : 1981 (4) SCC 578 (The words 'on the basis of return' were construed to mean on the basis of true and proper return which ought to have been filed).

17. *Chokalingam v. CIT*, AIR 1963 SC 1456, p. 1458 : 1963 Supp (1) SCR 599.

18. *Mahadeo Prasad Bais v. Income-tax Officer, A Ward, Golakhpur*, AIR 1991 SC 2278 : 1991 (4) SCC 560.

19. *Gujarat Travancore Agency, Cochin v. Commissioner of Income-tax, Kerala*, AIR 1989 SC 1671, p. 1673 : 1989 (3) SCC 52; *Guljag Industries v. Commercial Tax Officer*, (2007) 7 SCC 269, para 35 : (2007) 10 JT 1. **But see** *T. Ashok Pai v. Commissioner of Income Tax*, (2007) 7 SCC 162, paras 16, 17 and 19 : (2007) 8 JT 525 (Penalty proceedings are quasi-criminal in nature and the penalty provision is a penal statute to be strictly construed.); *Commissioner of Income Tax Ahmedabad v. Sarabhai Holdings Pvt. Ltd.*, (2009) 1 SCC 28 paras 35, 36 : (2008) 12 Scale 464.

20. *Commissioner of Central Excise & Customs, Mumbai v. ITC Ltd.*, (2007) 1 SCC 62 (para 17) : (2006) 9 JT 469.

21. *CCE v. Pepsi Foods Ltd.*, (2011) 1 SCC 601 para 20 : (2010) 13 JT 544 (section 11AC of Central Excise Act 1944).

'falsely represents' as used in section 10(b) of the Central Sales Tax Act,1956 clearly bring in the requirement of *mens rea*.[22] Interest on tax which is due and payable is different from penalty and is compensatory in nature.[23]

But provisions introduced to open up liability which had become barred by lapse of time, will be subject to the rule of strict construction[24] and will not be given larger retrospectivity than necessitated by express words or clear implication.[25] Similarly a limitation provision within which steps have to be taken for recovery of duties not levied or not paid or short paid or erroneously refunded, is subject to the rule of strict construction.[26]

(e) American view

It seems to have been generally accepted in the U.S.A. that in case of doubt in construction of taxing statutes the doubt is to be resolved in favour of the taxpayer and against the Government.[27] There is, however, another view which favours the adoption of liberal construction of such statutes in order to aid the taxing power of the State and there are instances where the courts have given effect to the spirit or equity of revenue laws.[28] The liberal view seeks its support on the theory that ultimate objective of all tax measures is accomplishment of good social order, and a strict interpretation results in loss of revenue to the Government and operates to the disadvantage of others contributing for its support.[29]

2. EVASION OF STATUTES

It is permissible to evade an Act of Parliament in the sense that a person may not do that which the Act prohibits but he is free to do anything which though equally advantageous to him as that which is prohibited is nevertheless outside the prohibition, penalty or burden imposed by the Act.[30] If a

---

22. *Commissioner of Sales Tax Uttar Pradesh v. Sanjiv Fabrics*, (2010) 9 SCC 630 (paras 31, 32, 36 and 37) : (2010) 10 JT 192.

23. *Bhai Jaspal Singh v. Assistant Commissioner of Commercial Taxes*, (2011) 1 SCC 39 para 36 : (2010) 11 JT 562.

24. *Banarasi Debi v. ITO*, AIR 1964 SC 1742, p. 1744 : 1964 (7) SCR 539.

25. *S.S. Gadgil v. Lal & Co.*, AIR 1965 SC 171, p. 177 (para 13) : (1964) 8 SCR 72. **See further** Chapter 6, Title 2(e).

26. *J.K. Cotton Spinning and Weaving Mills Co. Ltd. v. Collector of Central Excise*, AIR 1998 SC 1270, p. 1274 : 1998 (3) SCC 540 (construction of section 11A Central Excises and Salt Act, 1944).

27. SUTHERLAND : Statutory Construction, 3rd Edition, Vol. 3, pp. 293, 294, notes 2 and 3.

28. *Ibid*, pp. 297, 298, note 3.

29. *Ibid*, p. 297.

30. *Yorkshire Railway Wagon Company v. Maclure*, (1882) 21 Ch D 309, p. 318 : 51 LJ Ch 857 : 47 LT 290 (LINDLEY, L.J.).

statute prohibits doing of *A*, the courts are powerless to extend the prohibition to cover *B* when the legal significance of *A* and *B* are different and distinct even if both *A* and *B* in substance produce similar results. It is well established that penal and taxing laws are not to be extended by analogy to cover acts and situations not within the words of the statute on any doctrine of substance of the matter.[31] But this principle has no application where what is done is really the thing prohibited although under colour or cloak of a different transaction not prohibited by the statute. If, what a person does is really *A*, but covers the reality by giving to it the colour of *B* the courts will go behind the form and enforce the prohibition. It is, therefore, not permissible to evade an Act of Parliament by resorting to a fraudulent device or by covering the reality by a non-genuine transaction.[32] The word 'evade' is thus ambiguous and is used in two senses,[33] and in spite of various explanations given by the courts as to the two different meanings of that word, the position is not very much different from what LORD CRANWORTH, LC found in 1855. The LORD CHANCELLOR said: "I never understood what is meant by an evasion of an Act of Parliament; either you are within the Act or you are not within it; if you are not within it you have a right to avoid it, to keep out of prohibition."[34]

A citizen is free to so arrange his business that he is able to avoid a law and its evil consequences so long as he does not break that or any other

---

31. For Taxing Laws, **see** text and notes 31 to 39, pp. 828 to 829. For Penal Laws, **see** Chapter 11, text and notes 59 and 60, p. 907.

32. **See** text and notes 81 to 93, pp. 923 to 925, notes 1 to 3, p. 926.

33. "The word 'evasion' may mean either of two things. It may mean an evasion of the Act by something which, while it evades the Act, is within the sense of it, or it may mean an evading of the Act by doing something to which the Act does not apply"; Per GROVE, J., in *A.G. v. Noyes*, (1881) 8 QBD 125, p. 133.

"The word 'evade' is capable of being used in two senses: One which suggests under-hand dealing, and another which means nothing more than the intentional avoidance of something disagreeable"; Per LORD HOBHOUSE, in *Simms v. Registrar of Probates*, (1900) AC 323, p. 334 (PC).

"There is always an ambiguity about the expression 'evading an Act of Parliament'; in one sense you cannot evade an Act of Parliament, that is to say, the court is bound so to construe every Act of Parliament, as to take care that which is really prohibited may be held void. On the other hand, you may avoid doing that which is prohibited by the Act of Parliament, and you may do something else equally advantageous to you which is not prohibited by the Act of Parliament"; Per LINDLEY, L.J., in *Yorkshire Railway Wagon Co. v. Maclure, supra*, p. 318.

"To say that what was done is an evasion of the law is idle, unless it means that, though in apparent accordance with it, it really was in contravention of the law"; Per WILLES, J. in *Jeffries v. Alexander*, (1860) 8 HLC 594, p. 637.

"Tax can be evaded by breaking the law or avoided in terms of the law." *Punjab Distilling Industries v. CIT*, AIR 1965 SC 1862, p. 1866 : (1964) 3 SCR 1 (SUBBA RAO, J.).

34. *Edward v. Hall*, (1855) 25 LJ Ch 82, p. 84.

law.[35] As observed by SCOTT, L.J.: "The only duty of citizens to Parliament is to obey its laws: to beg the question by such a phrase as 'evading the Act' is to indulge in confusion of thought. If the Act of Parliament does not forbid, it allows."[36] When a genuine transaction not prohibited by law reduces tax liability, it is not an attempt to evade tax but only "a legal device to reduce tax liability" to which every taxpayer is entitled.[37] The effectiveness of a method or device adopted to reduce tax liability depends not upon considerations of morality but on the operation of the taxing Act; "legislative injunction in taxing statutes may not except on peril of penalty, be violated but it may lawfully be circumvented."[38] Tax planning is legitimate provided it is within the framework of the law; but colourable devices cannot be part of tax planning.[39]

A transaction which by the acts done is of the nature of a trading transaction and is genuine and not sham does not cease in the absence of a statutory provision providing otherwise[40] to be an adventure or concern in the nature of 'trade',[41] merely because those taking part in it have their eyes fixed on the fiscal advantage of avoiding income-tax.[42] But a wholly artificial scheme remote from trade planned and contrived to effect the avowed purpose of tax avoidance, even if real and not sham, cannot be regarded as an adventure or concern in the nature of 'trade'.[43] However, even a blatant tax avoidance scheme which brings profit to a person cannot lead to the taxation of the person on the ground that he has earned profit by 'trade' unless his activities and the part played by him in furtherance of the

---

35. *Ghatge & Patil Concern's Employees' Union v. Ghatge and Patil Transports*, AIR 1968 SC 503 : (1968) 1 SCR 300.

36. *Maclay v. Dixon*, (1944) 1 All ER 22, p. 23 (CA).

37. *CIT v. Sivakasi Match Exporting Co.*, AIR 1964 SC 1813, p. 1817 (para 7) : 1964 (8) SCR 18. **See further** *CIT v. Keshavlal*, AIR 1965 SC 866 : 1965 (2) SCR 100; *CIT, Madras v. M.K. Streman*, (1965) SCN 322.

38. *CIT v. A. Raman & Co.*, AIR 1968 SC 49, p. 53 : 1968 (1) SCR 10.

39. *Union of India v. Play World Electronics Pvt. Ltd.*, AIR 1990 SC 202, p. 208 : 1989 (3) SCC 181.

40. **See** section 28, Finance Act (U.K.), 1960; **See further** section 260, Income-tax and Social Services Contribution Assessment Act, 1936—1960 (Australia) and *Peate v. Commissioner of Taxation of Australia*, (1966) 2 All ER 766.

41. Section 341, Income-tax Act, 1952 (15 & 16 Geo 6 & 1 Eliz 2).

42. *Griffiths v. J.P. Harrisan Ltd.*, (1962) 1 All ER 909 (HL); Dividend Stripping Transactions succeeded in getting fiscal advantage.

43. *Bishop v. Finsbury Securities Ltd.*, (1966) 3 All ER 105 (HL); Forward Stripping Operations failed to secure tax advantage. **See further** *Lupton v. F.A. & A.B. Ltd.*, (1971) 3 WLR 670, pp. 690, 691 : 1972 AC 364 (HL) (five propositions deduced by LORD SIMON); *Thomson v. Gureneville Securities Ltd.*, (1971) 3 WLR 692 (HL); *Seram Co. Ltd. Superannuation Fund Trustees v. Commissioner of Income-tax*, (1976) 2 All ER 28 (PC) (Dividend Stripping transaction failed to secure tax advantage; word 'artificial' is wider than 'fictitious').

scheme amount to 'trade' in the accepted sense or unless the legislature enacts a special definition or provision to tax such activities.[44]

In a comparatively recent case the taxpayer who was a television entertainer by entering into a partnership with a foreign company for exploiting the taxpayer's talent outside the United Kingdom was able to avoid tax liability in respect of his overseas income although the taxpayer's share in partnership profits was 95 per cent and his share in assets 99 per cent and the motive in formation of the partnership was clearly tax avoidance.[45]

The taxing laws have constantly been the subject of evasion in the sense of avoiding something disagreeable and there are many *dicta* to the effect that a citizen is entitled to so arrange his affairs that the tax burden does not fall on him and that there is nothing illegal or immoral in adopting such a course. "The highest authorities have always recognised", said LORD SUMNER, "that the subject is so entitled to arrange his affairs as not to attract the tax imposed by the Crown, as far as he can do so within the law, and that he may legitimately claim the advantage of any express terms or of any omissions that he can find in his favour in taxing Acts."[46] In another case VISCOUNT SUMNER observed: "It is trite law that His Majesty's subjects are free, if they can, to make their own arrangements so that their cases may fall outside the scope of the taxing Acts. They incur no legal penalties, and, strictly speaking, no moral censure, if, having considered the lines drawn by the Legislature for the imposition of taxes, they make it their business to walk outside them."[47] To the same effect are the observations of LORD PRESIDENT CLYDE: "No man in this country is under the smallest obligation, moral or other, so to arrange his legal relations to his business or to his property as to enable the Inland Revenue to put the largest possible shovel into his stores. The Inland Revenue is not slow—and quite rightly—to take every advantage which is open to it under the taxing statutes for the purpose of depleting the taxpayer's pocket. And the taxpayer, in like manner, is entitled to be astute to prevent, so far as he honestly can, the depletion of his means by the Revenue."[48]

---

44. *Ransom (Inspector of Taxes) v. Higgs*, (1974) 3 All ER 949 (HL) ('Trade in accepted sense denotes operations of a commercial character by which the trader provides to customer for reward some kind of goods and services').

45. *Newstead (Inspector of Taxes) v. Frost*, (1980) 1 All ER 363 (HL).

46. *IRC v. Fishers' Executors*, (1926) 10 TC 302, p. 340 (HL), **see further** *CIT v. Mercantile Bank*, AIR 1936 PC 233, p. 242; *Kelvinator of India Ltd. v. State of Haryana*, AIR 1973 SC 2526, p. 2534 : (1973) 2 SCC 551.

47. *Levene v. IRC*, (1928) All ER Rep 746, p. 751 : 1928 AC 217 (HL).

48. *Ayrshire Pullman Motor Services and D.M. Ritchic v. IRC*, 14 TC 754, pp. 763, 764.

Recent trend of authorities is to deprecate the ingenious devices resorted to by citizens to avoid a tax burden.[49] LORD GREENE, MR observed: "For years a battle of manoeuvre has been waged between the Legislature and those who are minded to throw the burden of taxation off their own shoulders on to those of their fellow-subjects. In that battle the Legislature has been worsted by the skill, determination and resourcefulness of its opponents. It would not shock us in the least to find that the Legislature has determined to put an end to the struggle by imposing the severest of penalties. It scarcely lies in the mouth of the taxpayer who plays with fire to complain of burnt fingers."[50] Similarly, VISCOUNT SIMON, LC said: "Of recent years much ingenuity has been expended in certain quarters in attempting to devise methods of disposition of income by which those who were prepared to adopt them might enjoy the benefits of residence in this country while receiving the equivalent of such income without sharing in the appropriate burden of British taxation. Judicial *dicta* may be cited which point out that, however, elaborate and artificial such methods may be, those who adopt them are 'entitled' to do so. There is, of course, no doubt that they are within their legal rights, but there is no reason why their efforts, or those of the professional gentlemen who assist them in the matter, should be regarded as commendable exercise of ingenuity or as a discharge of the duties of good citizenship. On the contrary, one result of such methods, if they succeed, is of course to increase *pro tanto* the load of tax on the shoulders of the great body of good citizens who do not desire, or do not know, how to adopt these manoeuvres."[51]

There is a fundamental difference between acceptable tax mitigation and unacceptable tax avoidance. The former are cases in which the taxpayer takes advantage of the law to plan his affairs so as to minimise the incidence of tax. "Unacceptable tax avoidance typically involves the creation of complex artificial structures by which, as though by wave of a magic wand the taxpayer conjures out of the air a loss or a gain or expenditure or whatever it may be which otherwise would never have existed. These structures are designed to achieve an adventitious tax benefit for the taxpayer and in truth are no more than raids on the public funds at the

49. *Yeshwantrao v. CWT*, AIR 1967 SC 135, p. 140 : 1966 Supp SCR 419 (Attempts at evading incidence of taxation though not commendable are not illegal).

50. *Lord Howard de Walden v. IRC*, (1942) 1 All ER 287, p. 289 : (1942) 1 KB 389 (CA); **Referred** to in *Commrs. of Customs v. Top Ten Promotions*, (1969) 3 All ER 39, pp. 66, 68 (HL); *Juggilal v. CIT, U.P.*, AIR 1969 SC 932, pp. 937, 938 : 1969 (1) SCR 988.

51. *Latilla v. IRC*, (1943) 1 All ER 265, p. 266 : 25 TC 107 (HL).

expense of the general body of taxpayer, and as such are unacceptable."[52] Taxation is the price which we pay for civilisation.[53]

Indeed the courts have now gone to the extent of not recognising tax avoidance schemes or devices even if they are strictly not non-genuine.[54] This new approach to tax avoidance schemes has been accepted in India.[55] In the words of CHINNAPPA REDDY, J.: "We now live in a welfare state whose financial needs, if backed by the law, have to be respected and met. We must recognise that there is behind taxation laws as much moral sanction as behind any other welfare legislation and it is a pretence to say that avoidance of taxation is not unethical and that it stands on no less moral plane than honest payment of taxation. In our view, the proper way to construe a taxing statute, while considering a device to avoid tax, is not to ask whether the provisions should be construed literally or liberally, nor whether the transaction is not unreal and not prohibited by the statute, but whether the transaction is a device to avoid tax, and whether the transaction is such that the judicial process may accord its approval to it.—It is neither fair nor desirable to expect the Legislature to intervene and take care of every device and scheme to avoid taxation. It is up to the court to take stock to determine the nature of the new and sophisticated legal devices to avoid tax and consider whether the situation created by the devices could be related to the existing legislation with the aid of emerging techniques of interpretation as was done in *Ramsay, Burmah Oil* and *Dawson* to expose the devices for what they really are and to refuse to give judicial benediction."[56] This new approach known as the *Ramsay* principle has potential to develop further. For the present it makes the principle laid down in *IRC v. Duke of Westminster*,[57] that one

---

52. *Ensign Tankers (Leasing) Ltd. v. Stokes*, (1992) 2 All ER 275, p. 295 : (1992) 2 WLR 469 : (1992) 1 AC 655 (HL) (LORD GOFF).

53. *Ibid*, p. 285 (LORD TEMPLEMAN **quoting** HOLMES).

54. *W.T. Ramsay Ltd. v. Inland Revenue Commissioners*, (1981) 1 All ER 865 (HL); *IRC, v. Burmah Oil Co. Ltd.*, (1982) STC 30 (HL); *Furniss (Inspector of Taxes) v. Dawson*, (1984) 1 All ER 530 : 1984 AC 474 (HL); *Ensign Tankers (Leasing) Ltd. v. Stokes, supra*, p. 285; *Moodie v. Inland Revenue Commissioners*, (1993) 2 All ER 49 : (1993) 1 WLR 266 (HL).

55. *McDowell and Company Limited v. Commercial Tax Officer*, (1985) 3 SCC 230 : AIR 1986 SC 649.

56. *Ibid*, p. 243. The opinion of CHINNAPPA REDDY, J. was expressly agreed to by the other four judges constituting the Bench (p. 255 para 46). But on this question doubt was expressed by a Bench of two judges in *Union of India v. Azadi Bachao Andolan*, AIR 2004 SC 1107 : 2003 Supp (2) JT 205 which is **discussed** at p. 783. SABHYASACHI MUKHERJI, J., however, observed: "Unless wastes and ostentiousness in Government's spendings are avoided, or eschewed no amount of moral sermons will change people's attitude to tax avoidance." *Commissioner of Wealth Tax, v. Arvind Narottam*, AIR 1988 SC 1824, p. 1829 : 1988 (4) SCC 113.

57. (1936) AC 1 (HL) **see** text and notes 31 to 34, p. 828.

has to see only the legal nature of the transaction and not substance of the matter inapplicable to a tax avoidance scheme consisting of a series of transactions or a composite transaction when the conditions necessary for application of the new approach are satisfied. In the *Duke of Westminster's* case the fiscal consequences claimed by the Duke corresponded to the legal consequences of the transaction as construed by the majority. So if in a tax avoidance scheme the fiscal consequences as claimed by the taxpayer do not correspond to the legal consequences of the scheme read and construed as a whole, the *Duke of Westminster's* case may not apply.[58] The conditions for the application of the new approach as laid down in *Dawson's* case are: (1) There must be a preordained series of transactions or one single composite transaction, and (2) There must be steps inserted which have no commercial (business) purpose apart from the avoidance or deferment of a liability of tax.[59] If these conditions are satisfied the inserted steps are to be disregarded for fiscal purposes and the court is to look at the end result for the purpose of taxing it in accordance with the provisions of the taxing statute.[60] The limitations of the new approach in the context of a series of transactions were again laid down in *Craven (Inspector of Taxes) v. White.*[61] A series of transactions which contained an intermediate tax saving transaction would be held to be liable to tax under the new approach only if (1) the series of transactions was preordained at the time when the tax saving transaction was entered into; (2) that transaction had no other purpose except tax avoidance; (3) there was no likelihood that the series of transactions as planned would not take place so that the tax saving transaction had no independent life; and (4) the preordained transactions did in fact take place.[62] The test, therefore, is whether the tax saving step was part of a preordained series of transactions, so as to constitute them a single indivisible whole and not whether the tax saving step was effected for the purpose of avoiding tax on a

---

58. *Ensign Tankers (Leasing) Ltd. v. Stokes*, (1992) 2 All ER 275, p. 285 : (1992) 2 WLR 469 : (1992) 1 AC 655 (HL).

59. *Furniss (Inspector of Taxes) v. Dawson*, (1984) 1 All ER 530, p. 543 : (1984) AC 474 : (1984) 2 WLR 226 (HL) (LORD BRIGHTMAN). **See further** *Sherdley v. Shirdley*, (1987) 2 All ER 54, p. 631 : (1988) AC 213 : (1987) 2 WLR 1071 (HL) (The principle has no application when the court is moved to make an order the purpose of which is to secure tax advantage).

60. *Ibid.* **Applied** in *Ensign Tankers (Leasing) Ltd. v. Stokes*, *supra*, p. 299; *Inland Revenue Commissioners v. McGuckian,* (1997) 3 All ER 817, pp. 821, 827, 830 : (1997) 1 WLR 991 (HL). LORD COOKE, however, at p. 830 observed: "If the ultimate question is always the true bearing of a particular taxing provision, these limitations cannot be universal."

61. (1988) 3 All ER 495 (HL).

62. *Ibid.*

contemplated subsequent transaction.[63] In the words of LORD KEITH the nature of the principle of the new approach as derived from earlier cases is: "The court must first construe the relevant enactment in order to ascertain its meaning; it must then analyse the series of transactions in question, regarded as a whole, so as to ascertain its true effect in law; and finally it must apply the enactment as construed to the true effect of the series of transactions and so decide whether or not the enactment was intended to cover it. The most important feature of the principle is that the series of transaction is to be regarded as a whole. In ascertaining the true legal effect of the series it is relevant to take into account, if it be the case, that all the steps in it were contractually agreed in advance or had been determined on in advance by a guiding will which was in a position, for all practical purposes, to secure that all of them were carried through to completion. It is also relevant to take into account, if it be the case, that one or more of the steps was introduced into the series with no business purpose other than the avoidance of tax."[64] It was again reiterated that in such cases the question to be asked is whether realistically the various steps constituted a single and indivisible whole in which one or more steps was simply an element without independent effect and whether it is intellectually possible for them to be so treated.[65] Further in applying the preordained single composite transaction principle it is not permissible for the Revenue to alter the character of a transaction in the series or to pick bits out of it for the purposes of the principle and reject other bits.[66] The *Ramsay* principle and the cases dealing with it were surveyed by the House of Lords in *MacNiven (Inspector of Taxes) v. Westmoreland Investments Ltd.*[67] It was held in this case that *Ramsay* principle is applicable in cases where the statutory language on proper construction is "to be given a commercial meaning capable of transcending the juristic individuality of its component parts" and that it has no application where the statutory language refers "to purely legal concepts which have no broader commercial meaning."[68] In this case the taxpayer company borrowed capital and paid it back as interest. The sole purpose of the transaction was to produce an allowable deduction of 'interest paid' under section 338 of the Income and Corporation Taxes Act, 1988 (UK). The Ramsay principle was not applied and the deduction was allowed for the word 'paid', was held to be purely a

63. *Ibid.*

64. *Ibid*, p. 500. **Applied** in *Ensign Tankers (Leasing) Ltd. v. Stokes*, (1992) 2 All ER 275, p. 290 : (1992) 2 WLR 469 : (1992) 1 AC 655 (HL).

65. *Fitzwilliam v. Inland Revenue Commissioner*, (1993) 3 All ER 184, p. 197 : (1993) 1 WLR 1189 (HL).

66. *Ibid*, p. 198

67. (2001) 1 All ER 865 (HL).

68. *Ibid*, p. 880.

legal concept. JUSTICE KAPADIA has extra-judicially expressed the view that the *Ramsay* principle was "watered down"[69] in *McNiven*. But in *Inland Commissioners v. Scottish Provident Institution*,[70] the *Ramsay* principle appears to have been widened to cover anti-*Ramsay* devices. In a joint judgment delivered by five Law Lords it was observed that since the decision in *Ramsay* "it has been accepted that the language of a taxing statute will often have to be given a wide practical meaning of this sort which allows (and indeed requires) the court to have regard to the whole of a series of transactions which were intended to have a commercial unity".[71] It was further observed: "It would destroy the value of the *Ramsay* principle construing provisions as referring to the effect of composite transactions if their composite effect had to be disregarded simply because the parties had deliberately included a commercially irrelevant contingency creating an acceptable risk that the scheme might not work as planned. We would be back in the world of artificial tax schemes now equipped with anti-*Ramsay* devices. The composite effect of such a scheme should be considered as it was intended to operate and without regard to the possibility that contrary to the intention and expectation of the parties, it might not work as planned."[72] The *Ramsay* principle was not applied in *Barclays Mercantile Business Finance Ltd. v. Mawson*,[73] decided on the same day on which *Scottish Provident Institution* was decided. The result in each case would obviously depend upon the construction of the relevant statutory provision and the nature of the tax avoidance scheme set up by the taxpayer.

The House of Lords has also held that the Revenue and Customs Commissioners could take recourse to the tort of 'unlawful means conspiracy' and claim damages when the defendant was involved in a number of carousel (or intra-European community missing trader) frauds for evading payment of VAT (Value Added Tax) even if the commissioners could not recover the same[74] under the statutory tax regime.

If one is not dealing with a tax avoidance scheme, the normal principles will apply.[75] Thus when the true effect of the transaction incorporated in deeds, which are plain, is clear *McDowell's* case[76] has no

---

69. 'Taxation and Economic Reforms', (2004) 6 SCC Journal 13, p. 16.
70. (2005) 1 All ER 325 (HL).
71. *Ibid*, p. 335.
72. *Ibid,* p. 336.
73. (2004) UK HL 51 : (2005) 1 AC 684 (HL).
74. *Revenue and Customs Commissioners v. Total Network SL*, (2008) 2 All ER 413 (H.L.).
75. *Carver v. Duncan*, (1985) 2 All ER 645, p. 648 : (1985) AC 1082 (HL).
76. **See** note 55, p. 919, *supra*.

application.[77] It still remains true in general that the taxpayer, where he is in a position to carry through a transaction in two alternative ways, one of which will result in liability to tax and the other which will not, is at liberty to choose the latter and to do so effectively in the absence of any specific tax avoidance provision.[78] It is also doubtful as to how far the Ramsay principle can be applied to transactions relating to real property.[79]

In *Union of India v. Azadi Bachao Andolan,*[80] a two-Judge Bench of the Supreme Court has expressed the view that the observations of CHINNAPPA REDDY, J. in his concurring judgment in *McDowell* relating to tax avoidance schemes, relying upon the *Ramsay* principle, were not shared by the other four judges who spoke through RANGNATH MISRA, J. and the application of the *West Minster* principle has not been in any way affected in India. It is submitted that the opinion so expressed in *Azadi Bachao Andolan* may not be correct. The concurring judgment of CHINNAPPA REDDY, J. was agreed to by all the five judges constituting the Bench in *Mc Dowell.* In para 46 (p. 255) of the judgment delivered by RANGNATH MISRA, J. on behalf of the other four judges, it is expressly stated that they agreed with the separate and detailed opinion of CHINNAPPA REDDY, J. No one says that *West Minster* principle is dead for all purposes but it is also not correct to say that it remains totally unaffected in India. It will have no application where the *Ramsay* principle, as further explained, in subsequent cases[81] *infra.* But in view of the decision in *Azadi Bachao Andolan* this question requires re-examination by a larger Bench. But even without referring to a larger Bench *Mc Dowell's* effort to bring in *Ramsay* principle to India has been made ineffective by *Azadi Bachao Andolan.* In *CIT v. Walfort Share of Stock Brokers Ltd.* KAPADIA,[82] C.J.I. for a two-Judge Bench observed with regard to the ruling in *Mc Dowell & Co. Ltd. v. CTO* that it may be stated that in the later decision of this court in *Union of India v. Azadi*

---

77. *Commissioner of Wealth Tax v. Arvind Narottam,* AIR 1988 SC 1824, pp. 1828, 1829. **Also see** *Union of India v. Playworld Electronics Pvt. Ltd.*, AIR 1990 SC 202, p. 208 : (1989) 3 SCC 181 (mere suspicion is not enough to bring into play the new approach).

78. *Craven (Inspector of Taxes) v. White,* (1988) 3 All ER 495, p. 500 : 1989 AC 398 (HL).

79. *Belvedere Court Management Ltd. v. Fragmore Development Ltd.*, (1996) 1 All ER 312, p. 326 : (1997) QB 858 (CA).

80. AIR 2004 SC 1107, p. 1142 : (2004) 10 SCC 1.

81. Cases referred in f.ns. 63 to 77, pp. 864 to 866, **see further**: LORD ROBERT WALKER, 'Ramsay 25 years on: Some Reflections of Tax Avoidance' (2004) July Law Quarterly Review p. 412 [LORD WALKER concludes (p. 427) "in my view we would be taking the right turning if—we now regard *West Minster* as no more than a ghost from a different age]. For criticism of Ramsay principle, **see** Judith Freedman, 'Interpreting Tax Statutes, Tax Avoidance and Intention of Parliament', (2007) 123 LQR 53.

82. *CIT v. Walfort Share of Stock Brokers Ltd.* (2010) 8 SCC 137 para 45 : (2010) 7 JT 484.

Bachao Andolan it has been held that a citizen is free to carry out its business within the four corners of the law. That mere tax planning without any motive to evade taxes through colourable devices is not frowned upon even by the judgment in *Mc Dowell & Co. Ltd.* case.

The courts have also lifted the corporate veil when the corporate entity is used for tax evasion or to circumvent tax obligation or to perpetrate fraud.[83]

In any case an Act of Parliament cannot be evaded by taking recourse to non-genuine transaction. VENKATARAMA AIYAR, J. has observed: "Mr. Kolah argues that there is nothing wrong in business being done in such a way as to escape taxation. No exception can be taken to that statement. Every person is entitled to so arrange his affairs as to avoid taxation, but the arrangement must be real and genuine and not a sham or make-believe."[84] For example a mere 'paper device' showing loan cannot be treated as loan to reduce tax liability.[85]

A transaction by which compensation was paid for termination of managing agency agreement to a partnership firm when simultaneously substantially the same partners in the shape of a private company became the managing agents, was held to be sham and stage-managed and the amount of compensation was taxed as income.[86] Similarly, tax on sale of goods cannot be evaded by entering into the transaction through transfer of coupons and adopting a circuitous device to bring about sale.[87] Regulatory provisions enacted in a Sales Tax Act to prevent tax evasion constitute an

---

83. *CIT v. Meenakshi Mills, Madurai*, AIR 1967 SC 819, p. 822 : 1967 (1) SCR 934; *Jaggilal v. I.T. Commr., U.P.*, AIR 1969 SC 932, p. 936 : 1969 (1) SCR 988; *Tracway Pvt. Ltd. v. Commr. of Sales Tax*, (1981) MPLJ 171, p. 174. (G.P. SINGH C.J.); *Calcutta Chromotype Ltd. v. Collector of Central Excise*, AIR 1998 SC 1631, pp. 1637, 1638 : 1998 (3) SCC 681; *Commissioner of Central Excise v. Modi Alkalies & Chemicals Ltd.*, (2004) 7 SCC 569, p. 576 : (2004) 6 JT 543. But corporate veil can also be lifted in favour of the taxpayer if it is necessary to do justice to all the parties; *State of U.P. v. Renusagar Co.*, AIR 1988 SC 1737, pp. 1757, 1758 : 1988 (4) SCC 59.

84. *J.K. Cotton Mills v. CIT & CEPT*, AIR 1959 SC 270, p. 274. For example of a palpable device and trick to evade the effect of section 16(3), Income-tax Act, 1922, which failed, **see** *CIT v. C.M. Kothari*, AIR 1964 SC 331, pp. 333, 334 : 1964 (2) SCR 531 (paras 8 and 9). On the question as to when a transaction can be regarded as 'sham' **see** *Raftland Pty. Ltd. v. Federal Commissioner of Taxation,* (2008) 82 ALJR 934 paras 33 to 36 (GLEESON C.J., GUMMOW and CRENNAN JJ), 145 to 148 (KIRBY, J.).

85. *S.P. Jaiswal v. Commissioner of Income-tax*, AIR 1997 SC 2155 : 1997 (3) JT 460 : (1997) 10 SCC 81.

86. *Juggilal v. CIT*, AIR 1969 SC 932, p. 937 : 1969 (1) SCR 988. **See further** a case of similar nature, *Madhowji Dharamshi Mfg. Co. v. CIT, Bombay*, AIR 1970 SC 1811 : (1970) 2 SCC 229.

87. *State of Tamil Nadu v. Sri Srinivas Sales Circulation*, 1996 (7) Scale 421, p. 426 : 1996 (10) SCC 648.

integral part of the charging section and their non-compliance gives rise to a presumption of tax evasion.[88]

A tax on entertainments cannot be evaded by falsely alleging that the programme was being held to encourage savings and by collecting Rs. 12 for admission to and subscription for a non-existing organisation at the time of admitting persons to the programme.[89]

Thus the Rent Acts which apply to tenancies but not to licences cannot be evaded by labelling a tenancy as a licence. In the words of DENNING, L.J.: "It is simply a matter of finding the true relationship of the parties. It is most important that we adhere to this principle or else we might find all landlords granting licences and not tenancies, and we should make a hole in the Rent Acts through which could be driven—I will not in these days say a coach and four-wheeler but an articulated vehicle."[90]

The courts are astute to detect and frustrate sham devices and artificial transactions whose only object is to disguise the grant of a tenancy and to evade the Rent Acts; and so the critical question in every case is not simply how the arrangement is presented to the outside world in the relevant documentation, but what is the true nature of the arrangement.[91] A statutory provision enabling a landlord to evict his tenant on the ground that he has sublet the same, cannot be evaded by camouflaging sub-tenancy in the form of agency.[92]

The Factories Act, 1948 and other similar Acts which apply to cases of employers having in employment specified number of workers cannot be evaded by employing workers through so-called independent contractors who in reality are agents of the employer.[93]

---

88. *Kamal Kumar Agarwal v. Commissioner of Commercial Taxes West Bengal*, (2010) 5 SCC 142 paras 15 and 22 : (2010) 3 JT 390.

89. *State of Madhya Pradesh v. Home Decorators and Finance (P) Ltd.*, AIR 1990 SC 1322 : 1990 (3) SCC 560.

90. *Facchini v. Bryson*, (1952) 1 TLR 1386, p. 1389; referred to in *Addiscombe Estates Ltd. v. Crabbe*, (1957) 3 All ER 563, p. 570 : (1958) 1 QB 513 (CA). In Maharashtra the Rent Act has been amended to prevent its evasion by grant of licences, **see** *Sanwarmal Kejriwal v. Vishwa Co-operative Housing Society Ltd.*, AIR 1990 SC 1563 : 1990 (2) SCC 288; *Mani Nariman Daruwala v. Phiroz Bhatena*, AIR 1991 SC 1494 : 1991 (3) SCC 141.

91. *A.G. Securities v. Vaughan*, (1988) 3 All ER 1058, pp. 1067, 1070 : (1990) 1 AC 417 : (1988) 3 WLR 1205 (HL). **See also** *Street v. Mountford*, (1985) 2 All ER 289 : (1985) AC 809 (HL).

92. *Bhagwandas v. Rajdeo Singh*, AIR 1970 SC 986, p. 987 : (1971) 3 SCC 852; *Rajbir Kaur v. Chokosiri & Co.*, AIR 1988 SC 1845, pp. 1857, 1858 : 1989 (1) SCC 19; *K. Achyuta Bhat v. Veeramaneni Mauja Devi*, AIR 1989 SC 93 : 1989 (1) SCC 9.

93. *D.M. Sahib & Sons v. Union of U.P. Workers*, AIR 1966 SC 370, p. 375 : 1964(7) SCR 646. Welfare legislations cannot be allowed to be defeated by subtle devices and the court can go behind the form and see the substance of a transaction; **see** text and notes 4 to 7, pp. 895-896.

The bar for any further employment under the Government, which applies to the member of a Public Service Commission after he demits his office, under Article 319(1)(c) of the Constitution, cannot be evaded by labelling the employment as 'full time non-official consultant' and by giving a contract in place of a letter of employment.[1]

Similarly, if the real intention is to wager, the parties cannot avoid the bar of section 30 of the Indian Contract Act, 1872, by entering into a formal contract of sale and purchase of goods at a given price and for their delivery at a given time.[2] An agreement is void not only when it is forbidden by law but also when, if permitted, it would defeat the provisions of any law.[3] Therefore, if a statute exhibits a clear policy to secure certain benefits to a person in spite of a transfer made by him the statute cannot be defeated by entering into a contract of transfer providing for the relinquishment of those benefits.[4]

Section 195, Code of Criminal Procedure, 1898, which provides that cognizance of certain offences is not to be taken except on the complaint in writing made by the relevant court, cannot be evaded by the device of charging a person with an offence to which that section does not apply and then convicting him of an offence to which it does apply on the ground that the latter offence is a minor one of the same character or by describing the offence as punishable under some other section of the Penal Code, though in reality the offence falls in the category of offences mentioned in section 195.[5]

The principle, that the courts can go behind the form and reach the reality, has to be applied with certain reservations in determining correct amount of duty payable on documents under the Indian Stamp Act, 1899. The duty being imposed on instruments and not upon transactions, courts can only construe the document as it stands for determining the proper amount of duty, and although the name given to the document by the parties may not be decisive of its character,[6] it is not permissible to go behind

---

1. *Union of India v. V.D. Dwivedi*, AIR 1997 SC 1313, pp. 1314, 1315 : 1997 (3) SCC 182.
2. *Kong Yee Lone & Co. v. Lowjee*, (1902) ILR 29 Cal 461, p. 467 (PC).
3. Section 23, Indian Contract Act, 1872.
4. *Motichand v. Ikramullah Khan*, (1917) ILR 39 All 173, pp. 177, 178 (PC).
5. *Basirul Huq v. State of West Bengal*, AIR 1953 SC 293, p. 296 : 1953 SCR 836; *Dutt v. State of U.P.*, AIR 1966 SC 523, p. 526 : 1966 (1) SCR 493; *Durgacharan v. State of Orissa*, AIR 1966 SC 1775, p. 1779 : 1966 (3) SCR 636; **See further** *Chandrika Sao v. State of Bihar*, AIR 1967 SC 170 : 1963 Supp (1) SCR 419.
6. *Madras Refineries Ltd. v. Chief Controlling Revenue Authority*, AIR 1977 SC 500, p. 502 : 1977 (2) SCC 308. **See further**: *Ruby Sales & Services (P.) Ltd. v. State of Maharashtra*, (1994) 1 SCC 531 (label of the document is not decisive; terms of the

[Footnote No. 6 Contd.]

the document and to hold an enquiry as to the real nature of the transaction as distinguished from the real nature of the document.[7] But this principle will not apply when parties themselves by written declarations after the execution of a document state what was really intended.[8] So when a sale was, on the face of it, free from encumbrance but declarations of the parties made after the execution of the sale deed expressed that this recital was wrong and that the sale was subject to the charge created by the vendor in favour of a bank, the Supreme Court held that section 24 of the Stamp Act, 1899 applied and the amount of the charge became a part of the consideration and the duty was payable on the apparent sale consideration plus the amount of the charge.[9] Further, the Legislature may by a legal fiction enlarge the description to be given to an instrument for imposition of stamp duty. For example, an agreement where possession is or is to be transferred before execution of conveyance may be declared to be 'conveyance' for imposition of stamp duty.[10]

On the general principle that when alternative constructions are open, a statute should be so construed as to give effect to its object or policy, the courts, to the extent the language permits, will be slow to adopt such a construction which may "lead to large-scale evasion of the Act resulting in its object being defeated."[11] On this principle it was held that the words

---

[Footnote No. 6 Contd.]
document decisive. Consent decree held to be 'conveyance' as also 'instrument'); *Hindustan Lever v. State of Maharashtra*, AIR 2004 SC 326 : (2004) 9 SCC 438 (Amalgamation scheme sanctioned by court under s. 394 Companies Act, 1956 is an 'instrument' liable to stamp duty).

7. *IRC v. Angus*, (1889) 23 QBD 579, p. 589 : 5 TLR 697 : 61 LT 832; *Ramen Chetty v. Mohamed Gouse*, (1889) ILR 16 Cal 432, p. 435; *Royal Bank of Scotland v. Tottenham*, (1894) 2 QB 715; *Motilal v. Jagmohundas*, (1904) 6 Bom LR 699; *Nanakchand v. Fattu*, AIR 1935 Lah 567 (FB); *Commissioner of State Revenue v. Pioneer Concrete (VTC) Pty Ltd.*, (2002) 76 ALJR 1534, p. 1540 **approving** MASON J.'s observations in *DKLR Holding Co. (No. 2) Pty Ltd. v. Commissioner of Stamp Duties (NSW),* (1982) 149 CLR 431, p. 449 (It is a fundamental principle of the law relating to stamp duties that duty is levied on instruments and not on the underlying transactions to which they relate). **See** *W.M. Cory & Son Ltd. v. IRC,* (1965) 1 All ER 917 : 1964 AC 1088 : (1965) 2 WLR 924 (HL), where attempt to avoid the stamp duty succeeded; and **Cf.** *Oughtred v. IRC*, (1959) 3 All ER 623 (HL), where the attempt failed.

8. *Somaiya Organics (India) Ltd. v. Board of Revenue, U.P.*, (1986) 1 SCC 351, p. 363 : AIR 1986 SC 403.

9. *Ibid.*

10. *Veena Hasmukh Jain v. State of Maharashtra,* JT 1998 (1) SC 186 : AIR 1999 SC 807 : 1999 (5) SCC 725.

11. *Shanti Prasad v. Director of Enforcement*, AIR 1962 SC 1764, p. 1778 : 1963 (2) SCR 297. **See further** *Motibhai F.P. & Co. v. Collector, Central Excise*, AIR 1970 SC 829, p. 832 : 1969 (2) SCR 580 (no rule of law should be so interpreted as to permit or encourage its circumvention).

'resident in India' occurring in section 4(1) of the Foreign Exchange Regulation Act, 1947, were used in the sense 'resident of India'. By holding otherwise the Act would have become inapplicable to acts done outside India by residents of India resulting in large-scale evasion of the Act and a virtual nullification of its object.[12] It has already been seen that machinery provisions in a taxing Act and provisions enacted to suppress tax evasion are construed liberally to effectuate their object.[13] Although it is not permissible to supply a *casus omissus*,[14] but if the words are general, in a case within the mischief of the Act, the Court may adopt a construction, if reasonably possible, to cover the case rather than hold it a *casus omissus*.[15] And, on the general principle of avoiding injustice and absurdity any construction would be rejected, if escape from it were possible, which enabled a person to defeat a statute or to impair the obligations of his contract by his own act or otherwise to profit by his own wrong.[16]

But in construing an Act the courts cannot add to the means enacted by the Legislature for giving effect to its policy even if those means are not adequate to achieve the object and leave room for evasion. An interesting example of application of this principle is furnished by the case of *Director of Public Prosecutions v. Bhagwan*.[17] Under the law as it stood till 1967,[18] a Commonwealth citizen could be refused admission into the United Kingdom by an Immigration Officer after an examination; but the examination of the immigrant could not be done after the expiry of twenty-four hours from the time of his landing in the United Kingdom. Bhagwan Singh, who was a Commonwealth citizen, along with some others landed from a small vessel on a lonely beach along the coast of England and successfully avoided examination by an Immigration Officer within twenty-four hours of his landing, and therefore, he could not be refused admission in the United Kingdom. Bhagwan Singh was then prosecuted for conspiracy to evade the control on immigration of Commonwealth citizens into United Kingdom in order that he may enter without, on landing, submitting himself for examination. In holding that no offence was made out, LORD DIPLOCK speaking for the House of Lords, observed: "Under our system of Parliamentary Government what Parliament enacts

12. *Ibid.*
13. **See** text and notes 44 to 48, p. 901.
14. **See** Chapter 2, title 1(b).
15. *Scott v. Legg*, (1876) 2 Ex D 39, pp. 42, 43; *State of Karnataka v. Union of India*, AIR 1978 SC 68, p. 107 : (1977) 4 SCC 608; *Commissioner of Income-tax v. National Taj Traders*, AIR 1980 SC 485, p. 489 : (1980) 1 SCC 370; *M.G. Wagh v. Jay Engineering Works Ltd.*, (1987) 1 SCC 542, p. 546 : AIR 1987 SC 670.
16. *Gowan v. Wright*, (1886) 18 QBD 201, p. 204 (LORD ESHER, M.R.).
17. (1970) 3 All ER 97 (HL).
18. Commonwealth Immigrants Act, 1962 (before its amendment in 1967).

are not policies but means for giving effect to policies. Those means often involve imposing on private citizens fresh obligations or restrictions on their liberties to which they were not previously subject at common law. The constitutional function of the courts in relation to enacted law is limited to interpreting and applying it. It is the duty of the judge to ascertain what are the means which Parliament has enacted by the Act. In construing the enacting words he may take account of what the Act discloses as the purpose that those means were intended to achieve and, in the case of ambiguity alone, he may interpret them in the sense in which they are more likely to promote than hinder its achievement. But it is no function of a judge to add to the means which Parliament has enacted in derogation of rights which citizens previously enjoyed at common law, because he thinks that the particular case in which he has to apply the Act demonstrates that those means are not adequate to achieve what he conceives to be the policy of the Act. It is no offence—to do or to agree with others to do acts which, though not prohibited by legislation nor criminal nor tortious at common law, are considered by a judge or by a jury to be calculated to defeat, frustrate or evade the purpose or intention of an Act of Parliament."[19] The gap in the law which came to be known as the Bhagwan gap was closed by subsequent legislation.[20]

---

19. *Director of Public Prosecutions v. Bhagwan*, (1970) 3 All ER 97 (HL).
20. **See** *Azam v. Secretary of State*, (1973) 2 All ER 765 (HL).

CHAPTER 11

CRIMINAL AND PENAL STATUTES

SYNOPSIS

CHAPTER 11

REMEDIAL AND PENAL STATUTES

SYNOPSIS

1. REMEDIAL AND PENAL STATUTES—DISTINCTION

Every modern legislation is actuated with some policy and speaking broadly has some beneficial object behind it. But then there are legislations which are directed to cure some immediate mischief and bring into effect some type of social reform by ameliorating the condition of certain class of persons who according to present-day notions may not have been fairly treated in the past.[1] Such legislations prohibit certain acts by declaring

---

1. DUA J., in *Central Railway Workshop, Jhansi v. Vishwanath*, AIR 1970 SC 488, p. 491 : (1969) 3 SCC 95 observed: "It is probably true that all legislation in a welfare State is enacted with the object of promoting general welfare, but certain types of enactments are more responsive to some urgent social demands and also have more immediate and visible impact on social vices by operating more directly to achieve social reforms". In *A.S. Sulochana v. C. Dharmalingam*, AIR 1987 SC 242, p. 244 : 1987 (1) SCC 180, a provision in a Rent Control Act providing for eviction on the ground of sub-letting was treated akin to a penal enactment. It is submitted that a provision in a Rent Control Act as considered in *A.S. Sulochana's* case is in its true nature an exception in a welfare legislation to be construed narrowly and not a penal enactment (**see** text and note 39, p. 942 and text and notes 10 to 13, pp. 955-956, *infra*).

them invalid and provide for redress or compensation to the persons aggrieved. If a statute of this nature does not make the offender liable to any penalty in favour of the State, the legislation will be classified as remedial. Remedial statutes are also known as welfare, beneficient or social justice oriented legislations. Penal statutes, on the other hand, are those which provide for penalties for disobedience of the law and are directed against the offender in relation to the State by making him liable to imprisonment, fine, forfeiture or other penalty. If the statute enforces obedience to the command of the law by punishing the offender and not by merely redressing an individual who may have suffered, it will be classified as penal.

A remedial statute receives a liberal construction, whereas a penal statute is strictly construed. As now understood, the distinction between liberal and strict construction has very much narrowed down and is only important in resolving a doubt which other canons of construction fail to solve when two or more constructions are equally open.[2] In case of remedial statutes the doubt is resolved in favour of the class of persons for whose benefit the statute is enacted; whereas in case of penal statutes the doubt is resolved in favour of the alleged offender.

Difficulty arises in classifying modern welfare legislations which are designed for the benefit of a class of persons such as labourers, workmen, tenants and the like, but which quite often contain penal provisions. A question of this nature arose before the House of Lords[3] in relation to the Railway Employment (Prevention of Accidents) Act, 1900, and different views were expressed. The rules made under the Act provided for certain precautions to be taken by the Railway Authorities for the protection of their workmen and a contravention of the rules was punishable as an offence under the Act. In his approach to the Act and the rules LORD SIMONDS emphatically said: "It was suggested—that some distinction is to be made in the application of this rule (rule of strict construction of penal statutes) according to the avowed purpose of the Act. It would, I think, be unfortunate if any decision of this House gave any colour to such a suggestion. Wherever, the Legislature prescribes a duty and a penalty for a breach of it, it must be assumed that the duty is prescribed in the interest of the community or some part of it and the penalty is prescribed as a sanction for its performance. Whether the purpose is—the protection of copyright or—the life and limb of certain workers, the same principle prevails.

---

2. *Ratan Lal v. State of Punjab*, AIR 1965 SC 444, pp. 446, 447 : 1964 (7) SCR 676. **See further** titles 2 and 3 in this Chapter.

3. *London & North Eastern Railway Co. v. Berriman*, (1946) 1 All ER 255 : 1946 AC 278 (HL).

A man is not to be put in peril upon an ambiguity, however, much or little the purpose of the Act appeals to the predilection of the court".[4] LORD MACMILLAN in a passage cited with approval by the Supreme Court, observed: "It must be borne in mind that while the statute and rule have the beneficent purpose of providing protection for workmen their contravention involves penal consequences. Where penalties for infringement are imposed, it is not legitimate to stretch the language of a rule, however, beneficent its intention, beyond the fair and ordinary meaning of its language."[5] LORD PORTER, on the other hand, in the same case expressed himself differently. He said: "Most measures of a remedial character, such as Factory Acts and a great many others, have penalty clauses, but I have never known that circumstance being regarded as a ground for a narrow and pedantic construction."[6] Similarly, in an another case LORD UPJOHN observed: "The Factories Act, 1961, should be regarded as a beneficial rather than a penal statute. Its object is to secure proper working conditions for persons employed to do manual labour in certain operations, and the penalties for failure to provide such conditions are merely incidental to that object. There is no need to construe the Act of 1961 restrictively, though equally there is no need to extend it beyond its natural meaning."[7] This attitude is further reflected in the majority decisions of the House of Lords in a subsequent case that the burden of pleading and proving that it was not reasonably practicable to make the working place any safer under section 29(1) of the Factories Act, was upon the occupiers of the factory and not on the plaintiff or prosecutor.[8]

The same attitude is shown in an another case[9] relating to the Health and Safety at Work Act, 1974. Section 2(1) of the Act provides that 'it shall

---

4. *Ibid*, p. 270.

5. *Ibid*, p. 260; referred to in *Tolaram v. State of Bombay*, AIR 1954 SC 496, p. 499 : 1955 (1) SCR 158.

6. *Ibid*, p. 264.

7. *J. & F. Stone Lighting & Radio Ltd. v. Haygarth*, (1966) 3 All ER 539, p. 533 (HL). But the natural sympathy for a workman should not lead a court to put a strained meaning on words used in the Factories Act to transfer the burden of the loss caused to the blameless victim to his equally blameless employer; *Haigh v. Charles W. Irelands Ltd.*, (1973) 3 All ER 1137, p. 1147 (HL).

8. *Nimmo v. Alexander Cowat & Sons Ltd.*, (1967) 3 All ER 187 (HL). The Supreme Court has held that the Factories Act, 1948, is a beneficent legislation and the definition of worker should be liberally construed; but the case did not relate to any penal provision; *Central Railway Workshop, Jhansi v. Vishwanath*, AIR 1970 SC 488, p. 491 : (1969) 3 SCC 95. **See further** *Raipur Municipality v. State of M.P.*, AIR 1970 SC 1923, pp. 1924, 1925 : (1969) 2 SCC 582, where it was held that the definition of 'motor transport undertaking' in the Motor Transport Workers Act, 1961 should be liberally construed.

9. *R v. Charges Ltd.*, (2009) 2 All ER 645 (H.L.). **See further** text and note 1 p. 970.

be the duty of every employer *to ensure*, so far as is reasonably practicable, the health, safety and welfare at work of all his employees.' Section 3(1) similarly provides that 'it shall be the duty of every employer to conduct his undertaking in such a way as to *ensure*, so far as is reasonably practicable, that persons not in his employment who may be affected thereby are not thereby exposed to risks to their health and safety.' Failure to discharge the duty by a person to which he is subject by these provisions is a criminal offence. Section 40 of the Act provides for reverse burden that in any proceeding for an offence of failure to comply with the duty as laid down in the relevant statutory provisions 'it shall be for the accused to prove (as the case may be) that it was not practicable or not reasonably practicable to do more than what was in fact done to satisfy the duty or requirement or that there was no better practicable means than that was in fact used to satisfy the duty or requirement.' Interpreting these provisions of the Act, it was held that the prosecution has to show only that there was a connection between the work that the employee was doing (in section 2 cases) or the conduct of the undertaking (in section 3 cases) and the accident. But the fact that cause of the accident was unknown or was debatable is irrelevant because the duty these provisions lay down looks to the result, not the means of achieving it. As regards the placing of legal burden of proof on the employer by section 40 the court said that it was not disproportionate and invalid. In holding so the court said that sections 2 and 3 imposed duties on employers who could reasonably be expected to accept the general principles on which those sections were based and to have the means of fulfilling that responsibility. The purpose of the Act was both social and economic, duty holders were persons who had chosen to engage in work or commercial activity and were in charge of it and must be taken to have accepted the regulatory control that went with it. The Supreme Court exhibited a similar liberal approach in holding that non-payment of employer's contribution within fifteen days under para 38 of the Employers' Provident Funds Scheme, 1952 which was punishable under section 14(2-A) of the Employees' Provident Funds and Miscellaneous Provisions Act, 1952 was a continuing offence. In holding so CHANDRACHUD, C.J. said: "Considering the object and purpose of this provision, which is to ensure the welfare of workers, we find it impossible to hold that the offence is not of a continuing nature."[10] Similarly the protection of Civil Rights Act, 1955 enacted for punishing the enforcement of any

---

10. *Bhagirath Kanoria v. State of M.P.*, (1984) 4 SCC 222, p. 229 : AIR 1984 SC 1688. **See further** *N.K. Jain v. C.K. Shah*, AIR 1991 SC 1289 : 1991 (2) SCC 495 [Liberal construction of section 14(1A) and section 14(2A) of the Employees' Provident Funds and Miscellaneous Provisions Act, 1952 which are penal provisions]. *Srikanta Datta Narsimharaja Wdiyar v. Enforcement Officer*, AIR 1993 SC 1656 : (1993) 3 SCC 217 (Construction of section 14A of the same Act).

disability arising out of untouchability abolished by Article 17 of the Constitution and to implement its mandate will be construed in the light of the constitutional goal to annihilate untouchability and the disabilities arising out of it.[11] A provision which imposes a penalty on workmen will, in any case, be considered a penal enactment subject to the rule of strict construction in their favour. Thus a standing order defining misconduct, proof of which could enable the employer to impose penalties on the employee was held to be a penal enactment for purposes of construction.[12] Speaking generally a penal provision whether authorising levy of penalty on employer or employee will be strictly construed and will not be interpreted to mean that penalty must be imposed in all situations.[13]

In interpreting such provisions of Rent Restriction Acts, a breach of which becomes a criminal offence, the Supreme Court has adopted the rule of strict construction.[14]

A statute, therefore, may in certain aspects be a penal enactment and in certain others a remedial one. In respect of those provisions, in such a complex statute, which are sanctioned on the pain of punishment for a crime the rule of strict construction in the limited sense now known may have to be applied.[15] At any rate, an *undue effort* to construe such a provision liberally to promote the beneficent purpose behind it may be effectively counterbalanced on consideration that a breach thereof leads to penal consequences.[16] But as rightly pointed out by the High Court of Australia, in an essentially remedial statute, *e.g.*, a statute designed for

---

11. *State of Karnataka v. Appa Balu Ingale*, AIR 1993 SC 1126, p. 1137 : 1992 Supp JT 588 : 1995 Supp (4) SCC 469.

12. *Glaxo Laboratories Ltd. v. Presiding Officer, Labour Court*, (1984) 1 SCC 1, p. 12 : AIR 1984 SC 505.

13. *ESI Corporation v. HMT Ltd.*, (2008) 3 SCC 35 para 21 : AIR 2008 SC 1322 (Construction of section 85B of the Employees' State Insurance Act, 1948). **See further** text and note 80 p. 889.

14. *W.H. King v. Republic of India*, AIR 1952 SC 156 : 1952 SCR 418; *Tolaram v. State of Bombay*, AIR 1954 SC 496 : 1955 (1) SCR 158.

15. **See** text and notes 3, 5 & 12, *supra*.

16. *Buckingham & Carnatic Co. v. Venkatiah*, AIR 1964 SC 1272, p. 1278 (para 15) : 1964 (4) SCR 265, Construction of sections 73(1) and 85(d) of the Employees' State Insurance Act, 1948; *Borough of Ealing v. Race Relations Board*, (1972) 1 All ER 105, pp. 115, 120 (HL). **See also** *Connel v. Motor Insurance Bureau*, (1969) 3 All ER 572, pp. 573, 574 (CA). Construction of section 203, Road Traffic Act (English) corresponding to section 94, Motor Vehicles Act (Indian); *R. v. A.I. Industrial Products Plc.*, (1987) 2 All ER 368, pp. 371, 372 (CA), construction of section 155(2) Factories Act, 1961 and Asbestos Regulations, 1969; *Whitfield v. H & R Johnson (Tiles) Ltd.*, (1990) 3 All ER 426, pp. 436, 439 : (1991) 1 ICR 109 (CA).

promoting industrial safety, "the strict construction rule is indeed one of last resort."[17] It will be immaterial for application of the rule of strict construction whether the duty and the penalty are imposed by the same section, or by different sections or the one by a rule made under the Act and the other by the Act itself.[18]

2. LIBERAL CONSTRUCTION OF REMEDIAL STATUTES

(a) General principles

In construing a remedial statute the courts ought to give to it "the widest operation which its language will permit. They have only to see that the particular case is within the mischief to be remedied and falls within the language of the enactment."[19] The words of such a statute must be so construed as "to give the most complete remedy which the phraseology will permit,"[20] so as "to secure that the relief contemplated by the statute shall not be denied to the class intended to be relieved."[21] In the field of labour

---

17. *Waugh v. Kippen* (1986) 160 CLR 156, pp. 164, 165; *Newcastle City Council v. GIO General Ltd.* (1998) 72 ALJR 97, pp. 106, 110, 111.

18. *London & North Eastern Railway Co. v. Berriman*, (1946) 1 All ER 255, p. 270 : 1946 AC 278 (HL).

19. *Sayad Mir Ujmuddin Khan v. Ziaulnisa Begum*, (1879) ILR 3 Bom 422, pp. 430, 431 (PC) (SIR JAMES COLVILLE).

20. *Gover's, Re, Coal Economising Gas Co.*, (1875) 1 Ch D 182, p. 198; referred to in *In re, Hindu Women's Right to Property Act*, AIR 1941 PC 72, p. 77. **See further** to the same effect *Antico v. Health Fielding Aust. Pty. Ltd.*, (1997) 71 AL JR 1210, p. 1221.

21. *Raghuraj Singh v. Hari Kishan*, AIR 1944 PC 35, p. 38 (LORD ATKIN). **See further** *B. Shah v. Presiding Officer, Labour Court*, AIR 1978 SC 12, p. 16 : (1977) 4 SCC 384; *Krishnayya v. Seshachalam*, AIR 1965 SC 639, p. 641 : (1965) 1 SCR 195; *Associated Cement Co. v. Their Workmen*, AIR 1960 SC 56 : (1960) 1 SCR 703; *Dahya Lala v. Rasul Mohomed*, AIR 1964 SC 1320, p. 1322 : 1963 (3) SCR 1; *Central Rly. Workshop, Jhansi v. Vishwanath*, AIR 1970 SC 488, p. 491 : (1969) 3 SCC 95; *Surendra Kumar Verma v. Central Government Industrial Tribunal-cum-Labour Court*, (1980) 4 SCC 443 : AIR 1981 SC 422; *B.P. Khemka Pvt. Ltd. v. Birendrakumar Bhomick*, (1987) 2 SCC 407, p. 412 : AIR 1987 SC 1010; *D. (a minor) v. Berkshire County Council*, (1987) 1 All ER 20, p. 42 (HL) (Broad and liberal construction to give full effect to the legislative purpose); *Amirtham Kudumbah v. Sarnam Kudumban*, AIR 1991 SC 1256, pp. 1259, 1260 : 1991 (3) SCC 20 (Liberal construction of section 8(3) of the Hindu Minority and Guardianship Act, 1956 which is for the protection of minors); *Shivaji Dayanu Patil v. Vatschala Uttam More (Smt.)*, AIR 1991 SC 1769, pp. 1776, 1781 : 1991 (3) SCC 530 (Section 92A, Motor Vehicles Act, 1939 liberally construed); *Pandey Orsan v. Ram Chander Sahu*, AIR 1992 SC 195, p. 197 : 1992 Supp (2) SCC 77 (Construction of section 71A of the Chhotanagpur Tenancy Act, 1908. The word 'transfer' construed very widely to include any fact situation where possession stood transferred to a non-tribal from a tribal *raiyat* so as to give wide protection to the tribals for whose benefit section 71A was enacted); *Rita Devi v. New India Assurance Co. Ltd.*, AIR

[Footnote No. 21 Contd.]

and welfare legislation which have to be broadly and liberally construed[22] the court ought to be more concerned with the colour the content and the context of the statute rather than with its literal import;[23] and it must have due regard to the Directive Principles of State Policy (Part IV of the Constitution) and any international convention on the subject and a teleological approach and social perspective must play upon the interpretative process.[24] An illustration will be found in the construction of the Child

---

[Footnote No. 21 Contd.]
2000 SC 1930 : (2000) 5 SCC 113 (the word 'accident' in the phrase 'accident arising out of the use of motor vehicle' as used in section 163A of the Motor Vehicles Act, 1988 construed to include 'murder'); *Union of India v. Honsoli Devi,* AIR 2002 SC 3240, pp. 3246, 3247 : (2002) 7 SCC 273 (The expression 'had not made *an application* under section 18' in section 28A of the Land Acquisition Act construed to mean *an effective application* in view of the beneficient object of the provision); *Kunal Singh v. Union of India,* AIR 2003 SC 1623, pp. 1625, 1626 : (2003) 4 SCC 524 [Section 47(1) and (2) of Persons with Disabilities (Equal Opportunities Protection of Rights on Full Participation) Act, 1995 held mandatory]; *U.P. Drugs & Pharmaceuticals Co. Ltd. v. Ramanuj*, (2003) 8 SCC 334, p. 340 : AIR 2003 SC 3337 (where legislation is designed to give relief against certain kinds of mischief, the court is not to make inroads by making etymological excursions); *Rajesh Burman v. Mitul Chatterjee*, (2009) 1 SCC 398 paras 25 and 31 : AIR 2008 SC 651 (The words 'maintenance and support' in section 37 of the Special Marriage Act, 1954 are of wide amplitude and will include medical expenses needed by the wife). *Edukanti Kistamma v. So. Venkatareddy*, (2010) 1 SCC 756 para 26 : AIR 2010 SC 313.

22. *International Ore and Fertilizers (India) Pvt. Ltd. v. Employees State Insurance Corporation*, (1987) 4 SCC 203, p. 207 : AIR 1988 SC 79, p. 82; *S. Appukuttan v. Thundiyal Janaki Amma*, AIR 1988 SC 587, p. 592 : (1988) 2 SCC 372; *Sudhoo v. Haji Lal Mohd. Biri Works*, AIR 1990 SC 1971, p. 1973 : 1990 (4) SCC 37; *Cochin Shipping Co. v. E.S.T. Corporation*, AIR 1993 SC 252, p. 255 : 1992 (4) SCC 245 (Notification issued under the Employees State Insurance Act to extend the benefit of the Act liberally construed); *Employees State Insurance Corporation v. R.K. Swamy*, AIR 1994 SC 1154, pp. 1159, 1160 : 1994 (1) SCC 445 (The word 'Shops' in s. 3(iii) of the Employees State Insurance Act construed liberally to include premises occupied by an advertising agency): *Indian Drugs and Pharmaceuticals Ltd. v. Employees State Insurance Corporation*, 1996 (8) Scale 688, p. 692 : 1996 (6) SLR 625 : (1997) 9 SCC 71 (SC) (Definition of 'Wages' construed liberally to include overtime wages); *Air Freight Ltd. v. State of Karnataka*, AIR 1999 SC 2459 : (1999) 6 SCC 567 (The expression 'shops' and 'commercial establishments' in Karnataka Shops and Commercial Establishments Act, 1961 liberally construed to include a company engaged in courier, cargo, travel and related services.)
23. *Workmen v. American Express International Banking Corporation*, (1985) 4 SCC 71, p. 76 : AIR 1986 SC 458; *N.K. Jain v. C.K. Shah*, AIR 1991 SC 1289, pp. 1304, 1305 : (1991) 2 SCC 495.
24. *B. Shah v. Presiding Officer, Labour Court*, AIR 1978 SC 12, pp. 16, 17 : (1977) 4 SCC 384; *Royal Talkies, Hyderabad v. Employees State Insurance Corporation*, AIR 1978 SC 1478, p. 1482 : (1978) 4 SCC 204; *Uttar Pradesh State Electricity Board v. Harishanker*, AIR 1979 SC 65, p. 69 : (1978) 4 SCC 16; *Bai Tahira v. Ali Hussain*, AIR 1979 SC 362, pp. 363, 365 : (1979) 2 SCC 316; *Mohd. Ahmed Khan v. Shah Bano Begum*, (1985) 2 SCC 556, pp. 571, 572 : AIR 1985 SC 945; *Mackinnon Mackenzie & Co. v. Addrey Decosta*, (1987) 2 SCC 469, pp. 474, 475, 477 : AIR 1987 SC

[Footnote No. 24 Contd.]

Labour (Prohibition and Regulation) Act, 1986. The court, having regard to the Directive Principles in Articles 39(e), 39(f), 41, 45 and 47 of the Constitution, the fundamental right in Article 24 and the international convention on rights of the child, not only directed a survey of child labour and its prohibition as provided in the Act but also directed payment of Rs. 25,000 as contribution by the employer to the Child Labour Rehabilitation-*cum*-Welfare Fund or alternative employment to parent/guardian of the child to ameliorate poverty and lack of funds for welfare of the child which is the main cause of child labour.[25] And while dealing with a question relating to the grant of maternity leave benefits under the Maternity Benefit Act, 1961, the court referred to Article 42 of the Directive Principles and Article 11 of the Convention on the elimination of all forms of discrimination against women in holding that the Act applies also to the muster roll female workers of the Delhi Municipal Corporation.[26]

The provisions of the Juvenile Justice Act, 1986 and the Juvenile Justice (Care and Protection of Children) Act, 2000, which replaced the 1986 Act, came up for consideration before a Constitution Bench.[27] Section 2(e) of the 1986 Act defines 'delinquent juvenile' to mean 'a juvenile who has been found to have committed an offence'. Section 2(h) of the 1986 Act defines 'juvenile' to mean a boy who has not attained the age of sixteen years or a girl who has not attained the age of eighteen years. Section 2(e) of the 2000 Act defines 'juvenile in conflict with the law' as meaning a juvenile who is alleged to have committed an offence. Section 2(k) of the 2000 Act defines 'juvenile' or 'child' to mean a person who has not completed eighteen years of age. The whole object of the Acts is to provide for

---

[Footnote No. 24 Contd.]
1281; *G.B. Pant University of Agriculture and Technology v. State of U.P.,* AIR 2000 SC 2695, p. 2699 : (2000) 7 SC 109. But the court cannot directly enforce Directive Principles or invalidate legislation in conflict with them, *P.M. Ashwatha Narayana Setty v. State of Karnataka*, AIR 1989 SC 100, p. 109 : 1989 Supp (1) SCC 696.

25. *M.C. Mehta v. State of Tamil Nadu*, AIR 1997 SC 699 : 1996 (6) SCC 756. **See further** *Bhola Bhagat v. State of Bihar*, AIR 1998 SC 237, p. 240 : (1997) 8 SCC 720 (statutes enacted for protection of children, *e.g.* the Juvenile Justice Act, 1986 cannot be bypassed on technicalities that a plea under the Act was raised for the first time only in the Supreme Court).

26. *Municipal Corporation of Delhi v. Female Workers (Muster Roll),* AIR 2000 SC 1274 : (2000) 3 SCC 224. For benevolent construction of Acts passed for the benefit of women and children; **see further** *Velamuri Venkata Sivaprasad v. Kothari Venkateshwarlu,* JT 1999 (9) SC 242, p. 251 : (2000) 2 SCC 139 : AIR 2000 SC 434; *Rohtash Singh v. Smt. Ramendri,* AIR 2000 SC 952, p. 954 : (2000) 3 SCC 180.

27. *Pratap Singh v. State of Jharkhand*, (2005) 3 SCC 551 : AIR 2005 SC 2731. **See further** *Hariram v. State of Rajasthan,* (2009) 13 SCC 211 : (2009) 8 JT 47; *Dayanand v. State of Haryana,* (2011) 2 SCC 224 para 14 : AIR 2011 SC 593; *Lakhanlal v. State of Bihar,* (2011) 2 SCC 251 para 23 : (2011) 1 SCALE 504.

the care, protection treatment, development and rehabilitation of neglected and delinquent juveniles. The Acts were passed in the discharge of the obligation to follow the United Nations Minimum Rules for the Administration of Juvenile justice known as the Beijing rules. The Acts being remedial in nature were given liberal construction to promote the beneficient object behind them and with this end in view it was held that the reckoning date for determination of the age of the juvenile under both the Acts is the date of the offence and not the date when he is produced before the authority or the court as was held earlier by a Division Bench.[28] Another question before the Constitution Bench related to the construction of section 20 of the 2000 Act which applied to 'all proceedings in respect of a juvenile pending in any court' when the 2000 Act came into force. The pending proceedings are to be continued before the court but on finding that the juvenile has committed an offence, the court after recording its finding instead of passing the sentence is required to forward the juvenile to the Board for passing orders in respect of the juvenile. This section was held to apply to juveniles who had not attained the age of eighteen years when the 2000 Act came into force and were juvenile as defined in this Act although they may not have been a juvenile under the 1986 Act, *e.g.* a male who had crossed the age of sixteen. But liberal construction has its limits. In case of a continuing offence such as kidnapping committed by the accused to extort money from the parents of a boy who was killed and the phone calls for ransom continued even after the death of the victim, having regard to section 364-A IPC and 472 CrPC every time a ransom call was made, a fresh period of limitation commenced and the date when the last call was made was taken as the date of commission of offence and as the accused had by then attained the age of 18 years, the Juvenile Justice Act was no longer applicable.[29]

Liberal construction was adopted in interpreting section 123(c) of the Railways Act, 1989 which defines 'untoward accident' to include 'accidental falling of a passenger from a train carrying passengers'. The question in the case was whether the expression 'untoward accident' so defined will also cover the case of a passenger who fell down and died while trying to board the train and his dependants will be entitled to compensation under section 124A of the Act. In answering this question in the affirmative the Court said: "No doubt, it is possible that two interpretations can be given to the expression 'accidental falling of a passenger from a train carrying passengers', the first being that it only applies when a person has

---

28. *Arnit Das v. State of Bihar*, (2000) 5 SCC 488 : AIR 2000 SC 2264.
29. *Vikas Chaudhary v. State (NCT of Delhi)*, (2010) 8 SCC 508 paras 23 and 29 : AIR 2010 SC 3380.

actually got inside the train and thereafter falls down from the train, while the second being that it includes a situation where a person is trying to board the train and falls down while trying to do so. Since the provision for compensation in the Railways Act is a beneficial piece of legislation, in our opinion, it should receive a liberal and wider interpretation and not a narrow and technical one. Hence, in our opinion the latter of the above-mentioned two interpretations i.e. the one which advances the object of the statue and serves its purpose should be preferred.[30]

In interpreting a legislation regulating the relation between the weaker and stronger contracting parties, K. IYER, J. advised: "Recall the face of the poorest and the weakest man whom you may have seen, and ask yourself, if the step you contemplate is going to be of any use to him."[31] Similar approach, with due regard to Part III (Article 16(4)) and Part (IV) (Article 46) of the Constitution, is advocated in interpreting executive directions making reservations and relaxations in favour of members of the scheduled castes and the scheduled tribes.[32] In case of a social benefit oriented legislation like the Consumer Protection Act, 1986 the provisions of the Act have to be construed as broadly as possible[33] in favour of the consumer to achieve the purpose of the enactment but without doing violence to the language.[34] Equitable considerations may find an important place in

---

30. *Union of India v. Prabhakaran Vijay Kumar*, (2008) 9 SCC 527 para 11 : (2008) 4 JT 598.

31. *Sant Ram v. Rajinderlal*, AIR 1978 SC 1601, p. 1603 : 1979 (2) SCC 274.

32. *Comptroller and Auditor-General of India v. K.S. Jagannathan*, (1986) 2 SCC 679, p. 700 : AIR 1987 SC 537.

33. *State of Karnataka v. Vishwabharathi House Building Co-op. Society*, (2003) 2 SCC 412, p. 429 : AIR 2003 SC 1043 : *H.N. Shankara Shastry v. Asst. Director of Agriculture*, AIR 2004 SC 3474, p. 3477 : (2004) 6 SCC 230; *Kishore Lal v. Chairman, Employees' State Insurance Corpn.*, (2007) 4 SCC 579 (para 17) : AIR 2007 SC 1819.

34. *Lucknow Development Authority v. M.K. Gupta*, AIR 1994 SC 787, p. 791 : (1994) 1 SCC 243; *Indian Medical Association v. V.P. Shantha*, 1995 (6) Scale 273 : AIR 1996 SC 550 : (1995) 6 SCC 651 (Construction of 'service' in section 2(1) of the Consumer Protection Act, 1986; liberally construed to include service rendered by persons in medical profession); *Bimal Chandra v. Bank of India*, AIR 2000 SC 2181 : (2000) 6 SCC 179 (overdraft facility to customer is 'service'); *Regional Provident Fund Commissioner v. Shiv Kumar Joshi*, AIR 2000 SC 331 : (2000) 1 SCC 98 (Facilities provided by Provident Fund Scheme are 'services' and 'member' employee is a 'consumer'); *Punjab Electricity Board Ltd. v. Zora Singh*, (2005) 6 SCC 776, p. 786 (Public utilities like a State Electricity Board renders service to the community and has to supply electrical energy to the consumers within a reasonable time from the date of demand notice for making deposit for connection and its failure to do so will be deficiency in service making it liable for damages in addition to interest on the deposit made). **But see** *S.P. Goel v. Collector of Stamps*, AIR 1996 SC 839 : 1996 (1) SCC 573 (officers performing *quasi*-judicial functions under statutory power do not render any service); *New India Assurance Co. Ltd. v.*

[Footnote No. 34 Contd.]

the construction of beneficent provisions particularly in the field of criminal law[35] and procedural provisions in civil law.[36]

The rule as stated and explained above only means that if a section in a remedial statute is reasonably capable of two constructions that construction should be preferred which furthers the policy of the Act and is more beneficial to those in whose interest the Act may have been passed;[37] and

---

[Footnote No. 34 Contd.]

B.S. Sainani, AIR 1997 SC 2938 : (1997) 6 SCC 383 (Assignment of right to claim damages is not assignment of right to service and assignee does not become a consumer); *I. W. v. City of Perth*, (1997) 71 AL JR 943 (Refusal to grant approval after deliberations in exercise of statutory discretionary power is not refusing to provide service); *Union Bank of India v. Seppo Rally,* JT 1999 (7) SC 437, pp. 442, 443 : (1999) 8 SCC 357 : (1999) 35 CLA 203 (negligence essential for constituting deficiency in service); *Ravneet Singh Bagga v. KLM Royal Dutch Airlines,* JT 1999 (8) SC 640 : (2000) 1 SCC 66 : (2000) CPR 72 (Action in good faith does not constitute deficiency in service). But in claims against a common carrier principle of section 9 of the Carriers Act, 1865 has been applied and the claimant has not to prove negligence for showing deficiency in service: *Patel Roadways Ltd. v. Birla Yamaha Limited,* JT 2000 (3) SC 618 : (2000) 4 SCC 91 : AIR 2000 SC 1461; *Economic Transport Organisation v. Dharwad Dist. Kadi Gramodyog Sangh,* JT 2000 (4) SC 327 : (2000) 5 SCC 78 : AIR 2000 SC 1635; *CCI Chambers Coop. HSG Society Ltd. v. Development Credit Bank Ltd.,* (2003) 7 SCC 233 : AIR 2004 SC 184 : (2003) 117 Comp Cas 118 (Though the jurisdiction of the fora under the Act is only in addition to jurisdiction of convential courts, the fora should not decline to exercise jurisdiction and deny to the complainant the beneficial provisions of the Act simply on the ground that the complaint raises complicated facts and law for decision). But assignee of consignor is not a consumer and cannot complain under the Act; his only remedy is to file a civil suit: *Savani Road Lines v. Sunderan Textiles Ltd.,* AIR 2001 SC 2630 : (2001) 5 SCC 625. **See** text and notes 16 to 22, pp. 957 to 958.

35. *Bhagirath v. Delhi Administration*, (1985) 2 SCC 580, p. 588 : AIR 1985 SC 1050 (Imprisonment for a term in section 428 CrPC construed to include life imprisonment so a person convicted to life imprisonment can get the benefit of set off of pre-conviction detention provided an order under section 422 or 433 is passed); *State of Maharashtra v. Najakat Ali alias Mubarak Ali,* AIR 2001 SC 2255 : (2001) 6 SCC 311 (A person arrested in respect of two offences and undergoing preconviction detention in respect of two offences can claim set-off of the period of pre-conviction detention in both the cases).

36. *Union Bank of India v. Khader International Construction,* AIR 2001 SC 2277 : (2001) 5 SCC 22 (The word 'person' in order XXXIII R 1 CPC enabling indigent person to sue without paying court fee construed to include a company).

37. *Alembic Chemical Works v. Workmen*, AIR 1961 SC 647, p. 649 : 1961 (3) SCR 297; *Buckingham & Carnatic Co. v. Venkatiah*, AIR 1964 SC 1272, p. 1277 : 1964 (4) SCR 265; *Regional Provident Funds Commr. v. Shiba Metal Works*, AIR 1965 SC 1076, p. 1080; *Lalappa Lingappa v. Laxmi Vishnu Textile Mills*, AIR 1981 SC 852, p. 856 : (1981) 2 SCC 238; *Jeewanlal Ltd. v. Appellate Authority*, (1984) 4 SCC 356, pp. 364, 365 : AIR 1984 SC 1842; *Mani Subrat Jain v. Raja Ram Vohra*, (1980) 1 SCC 1 : AIR 1980 SC 299; *All India Reporter Karmchari Sangh v. All India Reporter Ltd.*, AIR 1988 SC 1325, p. 1331 : 1988 Supp SCC 472 [Law Reports

[Footnote No. 37 Contd.]

the doubt, if any, should be resolved in their favour.[38] So in case of an exception which curtails the operation of beneficent legislation, the court, in case of doubt, would construe it narrowly so as not to unduly expand the area or scope of exception.[39] The court will also not readily read words which are not there and introduction of which will restrict the rights of persons for whose benefit the statute is intended.[40] Similarly the court will not deny the benefit of the Act on considerations of a policy which is outside the Act.[41] But, the liberal construction must flow from the language used and the rule does not permit placing of an unnatural interpretation on the words contained in the enactment; nor does it permit the raising of any presumption that protection of widest amplitude must be deemed to have been conferred upon those for whose benefit the legislation may have been enacted.[42] The principle of liberal construction of beneficial legislation has

[Footnote No. 37 Contd.]

are 'Newspaper' as defined in the Working Journalists and Other Newspaper Employees (Conditions of Service) & Misc. Provisions Act, 1955]; *Transport Corporation of India v. Employee's State Insurance Corporation,* JT 1999 (9) SC 15 : (2000) 1 SCC 332, pp. 41, 42 : AIR 2000 SC 338 (construction of section 1(5) of the Employees State Insurance Act, 1948).

38. *Jivabhai v. Chhagan*, AIR 1961 SC 1491, p. 1494 (para 6) : 1962 (1) SCR 568; *Union of India v. Prabhakaran Vijaya Kumar*, (2008) 9 SCC 527 paras 1, 12 : (2008) 4 JT 598.

39. *Shaikh Gulfan v. Sanatkumar*, AIR 1965 SC 1839, p. 1848 : 1965 (3) SCR 364; *Vajrapani Naidu v. New Theatres Ltd. etc.*, AIR 1964 SC 1440, p. 1444 : 1964 (6) SCR 1015; *Mohd. Shafi v. VII Addl. Dist. & Sessions Judge, Allahabad*, AIR 1977 SC 836, p. 840 : (1977) 2 SCC 226; *Vaddeboyina Tulsamma v. Vaddeboyina*, AIR 1977 SC 1944, p. 1948 : (1977) 3 SCC 99; *Shivram Anand Shiroor v. Radhabai Shantaram Kowshik*, (1984) 1 SCC 588, p. 592 : AIR 1984 SC 786; *Skandia Insurance Ltd. v. Kokilaben Chandrabadan*, (1987) 2 SCC 654, p. 665 : AIR 1986 SC 1184.

40. *Jnan Ranjan Sen Gupta v. Arun Kumar Bose*, AIR 1975 SC 1994, p. 1996 : (1975) 2 SCC 523; *Union of India v. Pradeep Kumari,* AIR 1995 SC 2259, p. 2264 : (1995) 2 SCC 736 (construction of section 28A of the Land Acquisition Act, 1894); *State of Tripura v. Roopchand Das,* (2003) 1 SCC 421 (case of Pradeep Kumari followed).

41. *Re B (a minor)* (1999) 2 All ER 576, pp. 579, 580 (HL) (For making an adoption order under the Adoption Order 1976, the principal considerations are reality of adoption and welfare of the child during the childhood. If these conditions are satisfied, adoption cannot be denied on the ground, not mentioned in the Act, that adoption of the child, who was a foreigner, will affect in 'maintaining an effective and consistent immigration policy').

42. *Mugnilal v. Suganchand*, AIR 1965 SC 101, p. 105 : 1964 (5) SCR 239; *Regional Provident Funds Commr. v. Shiba Metal Works*, AIR 1965 SC 1076, p. 1080 : 1965 (2) SCR 72; *Workmen of Firestone Tyre & Rubber Co. v. Management*, AIR 1973 SC 1227, p. 1240 : (1973) 1 SCC 813; *Kartar Singh v. State of Haryana*, AIR 1982 SC 1439, p. 1443 : (1982) 3 SCC 1; *Shivram Anand Shiroor v. Radhabai Shantaram*

[Footnote No. 42 Contd.]

to be applied "without rewriting or doing violence to the enactments" for resolving an ambiguity and the literal construction when the language is clear and explicit cannot be given a go bye.[43] 'Sympathy' by itself has no role to play in construing statutes.[44] A Constitution Bench of the Supreme Court in interpreting the provisions of the Contract Labour (Regulation and Abolition) Act, 1970, therefore, held that no provision in the Act whether expressly or by necessary implication provided for automatic absorption of contract labour on issuance of a notification under section 10 prohibiting employment of contract labour[45] and that a contrary view taken earlier by a three judge bench[46] was erroneous which was overuled prospectively. In construing a social services legislation, which represents a strategy about deployment of limited funds, the courts shall bear in mind "that to overstrain one element of the legislation in order to relieve someone whose case attracts sympathy will only divert resources from someone else whose case falls squarely within the intention of the scheme."[47] And the rule has to be applied consistent with the principle that even a beneficent legislation has to be read reasonably and justly and without inferring such limitations on the right to hold property or other rights which may expose it to the vice of unconstitutionality.[48] Further, the rule does not militate against the plain meaning rule and has no application when two constructions are not fairly open and the words of the enactment are reasonably

---

[Footnote No. 42 Contd.]

Kowshik, supra; *G. Giriyappa v. Anantharai L. Parekh*, JT 1994(3) SC 214, p. 218 : AIR 1994 SC 2307 : (1998) 8 SCC 111; *Employees State Insurance Corporation v. M.M. Suri and Associates (P) Ltd.*, JT 1998 (7) SC 336, p. 341 : 1998 (5) Scale 694 : (1994) 3 SCC 489, (Liberal construction does not permit extension of statutory benefit of a beneficient legislation beyond its scheme).

See further *Rajinder Kumar Joshi v. Veena Rani*, AIR 1991 SC 259, p. 262 : (1990) 4 SCC 526 (a construction requiring recasting of the statute is not permissible). *Tatoba Bhan Savagave v. Vasantrao Dhindiraj Deshpande*, AIR 2001 SC 4029, p. 4032 : (2001) 8 SCC 501 (recourse to Directive Principles cannot be used for reading something which is neither provided expressly nor by necessary implication); *Beed District Central Coop. Bank Ltd. v. State of Maharashtra*, (2006) 8 SCC 514 (para 13) : (2006) 9 JT 260.

43. *Steel Authority of India Ltd. v. National Union Water Front Workers*, AIR 2001 SC 3527, pp. 3535, 3539 : (2001) 7 SCC 1.

44. *Maruti Udyog Ltd. v. Ramlal*, (2005) 2 SCC 638, p. 654 : AIR 2005 SC 851.

45. *Ibid*, p. 3566.

46. *Air India Statutory Corpn. v. United Labour Union*, AIR 1997 SC 645 : (1997) 9 SCC 377.

47. *Cockburn v. Chief Adjudication Officer*, (1997) 3 All ER 844, p. 850 : (1997) 1 WLR 799 (HL) (LORD MUSTILL).

48. *Yudhishter v. Ashok Kumar*, (1987) 1 SCC 204, p. 212 : AIR 1987 SC 558. **See further** *CESC Ltd. v. Subhash Chandra Bose*, AIR 1992 SC 573 : (1992) 1 SCC 441 (The minority judgment took too liberal a view of the definition of 'Employee' in the Employees State Insurance Act, 1948 which was not accepted by the majority).

capable of only one construction.[49] Thus section 53 of the Employees State Insurance Act, 1948, which provides that an insured person or his dependents will not be entitled to 'any compensation or damages under the Workmen's Compensation Act, 1923 or any other law for the time being in force or otherwise in respect of an employment injury', was held to bar even claim for compensation or damages in Torts although the Act is a beneficial legislation.[50] The words 'or otherwise' in the section plainly conveyed this intention.[51]

The courts cannot obviously expand a provision in a socio-economic legislation by judicial interpretation to levels unintended by the legislature; thus provisions of the Persons with Disabilities (Equal Opportunities, Protection of Rights and Full Participation) Act, 1956 was held to be not applicable to private sector companies.[52] But the legislation has to be given its full effect in areas where it applies. Thus, it has been held reservation of 3% of posts under section 32 for persons suffering from different kinds of disabilities enumerated in section 33 ought to have been done from the date the Act came into force. On this argument a handicapped person who suffered 100% blindness and passed the civil services examination conducted by UPSC in 2006 was directed to be appointed to one of the posts which it ought to have been reserved from 1996.[53]

A Constitution Bench decision, overruling a number of cases to the contrary, in *Umadevi*[54] held that those employed on daily wages or temporarily or on contractual basis by the State or its instrumentalities cannot be

---

49. *Kanailal Sur v. Paramnidhi Sadhu Khan*, AIR 1957 SC 907, p. 911 (para 6) : 1958 SCR 360; *M.P. Mineral Industries Association v. Regional Labour Commr.*, AIR 1960 SC 1068, p. 1071 : 1960 (3) SCR 476; *Buckingham & Carnatic Co. v. Venkatiah*, AIR 1964 SC 1272, p. 1277 : 1964 (4) SCR 265; *Workmen of Firestone Tyre & Rubber Co. v. Management*, AIR 1973 SC 1227, p. 1240 : (1973) 1 SCC 813; *Lallappa Lingappa v. Laxmi Vishnu Textile Mills*, AIR 1981 SC 852, p. 856 : (1981) 2 SCC 238; *Jeewanlal Ltd. v. Appellate Authority*, (1984) 4 SCC 356, p. 365 : AIR 1984 SC 1842; *Colour-Chem. Limited v. A.L. Alaspurkar*, AIR 1998 SC 948, p. 954 : (1998) 3 SCC 192; *Union of India v. Syed Sarwar Ali*, AIR 1999 SC 1588, p. 1590 (para 11) : (1998) 9 SCC 426.

50. *Western India Plywood Ltd. v. P. Ashokan*, AIR 1997 SC 3883, p. 3886 : (1997) 7 SCC 638.

51. *Ibid.*

52. *Dalco Engineering (P) Ltd. v. Satish Prabhakar Padhye*, (2010) 4 SCC 378 paras 31, 32 : AIR 2010 SC 1576.

53. *Govt. of India v. Ravi Prakash Gupta*, (2010) 7 SCC 626 : (2010) 6 JT 491.

54. *Secretary State of Karnataka v. Umadevi*, (2006) 4 SCC 1, (paras 36 and 48) : AIR 2006 SC 1806. **See further** *Hombe Gowda Educational Trust v. State of Karnataka*, (2006) 1 SCC 430 (para 30) : (2005) 10 JT 598 : (2006) 1 LLJ 1004, which shows the change in trend to balance the interests of workmen and employers instead of protecting the interests of workmen alone.

said to be holders of a post and have no right to regularization simply because they have worked for a number of years, for a regular appointment can be made only consistent with Articles 14 and 16 of the Constitution. The decision shows that sympthy or sentiment by itself cannot be a ground for passing a favourable order when there is no legal right to support such an order.

The purpose of Control of Rent and Eviction Acts is generally to protect the tenants from unjust evictions and in case of doubt these Acts are to be so interpreted as to lean in favour of tenants. For example, if in a case of joint tenancy only a part of the tenancy premises enjoys the protection of the Act, the court will not order eviction of the tenant from that part which does not enjoy the protection of the Act by splitting up one integrated contract of tenancy unless that power is conferred by the Act.[55] But the benefit conferred on the tenants under these Acts can generally be enjoyed on strict compliance of the statutory provisions contained in them.[56] Further a law enacted essentially to benefit a class of persons considered to be oppressed, *e.g.* tenants may be comprehensive in the sense that to some extent it benefits also those not within that class, *e.g.* landlords. The Control of Rent and Eviction Acts which drastically limit the grounds on which a tenant can be evicted are essentially to benefit the tenants but they also to some extent benefit the landlords in the sense that they are so comprehensive that a landlord can file a suit for eviction on the grounds mentioned in the Acts even though the tenancy has not terminated in accordance with the provisions of the Transfer of Property Act, 1882.[57] A provision enacting that a purchaser from a landlord cannot apply for eviction on the ground of personal need before the expiry of three years from the purchase and unless a notice of six months is issued by him before or after expiry of three years period, was construed to mean that no notice was necessary after the expiry of three years or at any rate after expiry of three years and six months from the purchase.[58] Provisions enacted to benefit the landlords cannot be so construed as to benefit the tenants.[59] As expressed by LAHOTI J.:

---

55. *Nilesh Nand Kumar Shah v. Sikander Aziz Patel,* AIR 2002 SC 3073, p. 3077 : (2002) 6 SCC 678.

56. *E. Palanisamy v. Palinisamy,* (2003) 1 SCC 123 : AIR 2003 SC 153; *Nasiruddin v. Sita Ram,* (2003) 2 SCC 577, p. 589; *Imdad Ali v. Keshavchand,* (2003) 4 SCC 635, p. 638 : AIR 2003 SC 1863.

57. *V. Dhanpal Chettiar v. Yesoda Ammal,* 1979 (4) SCC 214 : AIR 1979 SC 1745; *Lakshmi Venkateshwara Enterprises,* JT 1994(2) SC 175, pp. 176, 178 : 1994 (2) SCC 671. **See further** *Balwant Singh v. Anand Kumar Sharma,* (2003) 3 SCC 433, p. 436 : AIR 2003 SC 1637.

58. *Anwar Hasan Khan v. Mohammad Shafi,* AIR 2001 SC 2984, pp. 2986, 2987 : (2001) 8 SCC 540.

59. *Arjun Khiamal Makhijani v. Jamnadas C. Tuliani,* (1989) 4 SCC 612 : (1989) Supp (1) SCR 380; *Anandram Chandanmal Munot v. Bansilal Chunilal Kabra,* AIR 2000 SC 288, pp. 293, 294 : (2000) 1 SCC 10.

"The courts have to adopt a reasonable and balanced approach while interpreting Rent Control Legislations starting with an assumption that an equal treatment has been meted out to both the sections of the society. Inspite of the overall balance tilting in favour of the tenants, while interpreting such of the provisions as take care of the interest of the landlord the court should not hesitate in leaning in favour of the landlords."[60] So the expression 'for his own use' can be construed to cover the requirement of the landlord for user of the premises as office of his chartered accountant son.[61] It is an application of the same principle that in considering a question of relative hardship, the bare fact that the tenant would be ousted from the house if a decree for eviction is passed is not enough to non suit the plaintiff landlord.[62] Further, such a law may make a departure from the general rule and may lean in favour of a class of landlords, *e.g.* members of the armed forces or other services who were unable to occupy their own houses because of exigencies of their service.[63] Indeed, it has been held that in enacting a Control and Eviction Act the Legislature has also to take into account that its provisions are not so unjust to the landlords that they offend Article 14 of the Constitution in which event they will become unconstitutional.[64] It is also possible that such a law which is not unreasonable at the time when it is enacted may become unreasonable with the passing of time.[65] Section 14(1)e of the Delhi Rent Control Act, 1958 which restricted landlord's right to seek eviction for his *bona fide* need to premises let for residential purposes only and thus gave implicit exemption from eviction to the tenants of premises let for non-residential premises in case of *bona fide* requirement of landlord and the validity of

---

60. *Joginder Pal v. Naval Kishore Bahal,* AIR 2002 SC 2256, pp. 2260, 2261 : (2002) 5 SCC 397.

61. *Ibid.* **See further** *Dwarka Prasad v. Niranjan,* (2003) 4 SCC 549 : AIR 2003 SC 2024 (occupation by himself, construed to cover the need of family members); *Kailash Chand v. Dharam Dass,* (2005) 5 SCC 375, p. 388 (Expression 'for his own occupation', 'for his own use', 'for occupation by himself' to be liberally interpreted to include need of dependents and family member); *Ajit Singh v. Jit Ram,* (2008) 9 SCC 699 paras 18 and 19 : AIR 2009 SC 199 (*Joginder Pal*, note 57, p. 946 **followed**); *Shakuntala Bai v. Narayan Das,* AIR 2004 SC 3484 : (2004) 5 SCC 772 (Death of plaintiff/landlord after decree pending appeal has no effect on the validity of the decree).

62. *Bega Begum v. Abdul Ahad Khan,* (1979) 1 SCC 273 : AIR 1979 SC 272; *Badrinarayan Chunilal Bhutada v. Govindram Ramgopal Mundala,* (2003) 2 SCC 320, p. 328.

63. *Shivram Anand Shiroor v. Shantabai Atmaram Kowshik*, AIR 1984 SC 786, pp. 788, 789 : (1984) 1 SCC 588; *Kanta Udharam Jagasia v. C.K.S. Rao*, AIR 1998 SC 569, p. 576 : (1998) 1 SCC 403; *Rahabhar Production Pvt. Ltd. v. Rajendra K. Tandon*, AIR 1998 SC 1639, p. 1641 : (1988) 4 SCC 49.

64. *Malpe Vishwanath Acharya v. State of Maharashtra*, AIR 1998 SC 602 : (1998) 2 SCC 1.

65. *Ibid* (Rent Control Act of 1947 pegging down the standard rent to the rent paid in 1940 has now become unreasonable).

which was upheld by the Delhi High Court in 1973 was declared discriminatory and offending Article 14 in the changed scenario of the construction activity in Delhi and substantial increase in the availability of buildings which could be let for non-residential purposes.[66]

It has also been held that a deserted wife who has been or is entitled to be in occupation of the matrimonial home is entitled to be impleaded to contest the suit for eviction filed against her husband in his capacity as tenant subject to satisfying two conditions: first, the tenant has given up the contest or is not interested in contesting the suit and such giving up by the tenant-husband shall prejudice the deserted wife who is residing in the premises; and secondly, the scope and ambit of the contest or defence by the wife would not be on a footing higher or larger than the tenant himself.[67]

The inhibition against retrospective construction has been applied with less insistence in the case of welfare legislations and remedial statutes.[68] Thus a provision which confers immunity to the tenant against eviction, though prospective in form, may be construed to take away the right vested in the landlord by a decree for ejectment which had become final.[69] But there is no such rule that all benevolent measures are retrospective.[70] For example, compensation payable in respect of an accident under the Workmen's Compensation Act, 1923 would be determined according to the law inforce on the date of the accident and any enhancement of compensation by a new law before the date of adjudication will not affect the amount of compensation.[71] Similarly the provision for no fault liability added in the Motor Vehicles Act, 1939 by section 92A has no application to accidents taking place before incorporation of the section.[72]

---

66. *Satyawati Sharma v. Union of India*, (2008) 5 SCC 287 : AIR 2008 SC 3148.

67. *Achala Anand v. S. Appi Reddy*, (2005) 3 SCC 313, p. 329.

68. **See** title 2(h), Chapter 6, text and notes 32, 33, pp. 613 to 614.

69. *H. Shiva Rao v. Cecilia Pereira*, (1987) 1 SCC 258, p. 261 : AIR 1987 SC 248; *Union of India v. Syed Sarwar Ali*, JT 1998 (8) SC 19, p. 23 : (1998) 9 SCC 426.

70. *Shyam Sunder v. Ram Kumar*, AIR 2001 SC 2472 : (2001) 8 SCC 24.

71. *Pratap Narain Singh Deo v. Srinivas Sabata*, AIR 1976 SC 222 : (1976) 1 SCC 289; *Kerala State Electricity Board v. Valsalak*, AIR 1999 SC 3502 : (1999) 8 SCC 254. **See further** *Oriental Insurance Co. Ltd. v. Sorumai Gogoi*, (2008) 4 SCC 572 paras 22, 23 : (2008) 2 JT 613 (A person who absconds and is a proclaimed offender cannot be presumed to be dead under section 108 Evidence Act, 1872 for purposes of section 3 of Workmen's Compensation Act, 1923).

72. *R.L. Gupta v. Jupiter General Insurance Co.*, 1990 ACJ 280 (SC); *Pepsu Road Transport Corporation Patialia v. Kulwant Kaur*, (2009) 4 SCC 32 : (2009) 4 JT 334 (Increased compensation for no fault liability is not applicable to accidents taking place earlier to amendment).

Nationalisation Acts whether in the field of Agriculture[73] or Industry[74] are not treated as expropriatory and are construed liberally, like welfare legislations, to effectuate their objective in the background of Article 39 of the Constitution. Similarly in construing or pronouncing on the validity of Debt Relief Acts, which are aimed at relieving weaker sections steeped in debt and bonded to the money lenders, the courts have not to treat them as expropriatory legislation but to approach them from the point of view of furthering the social interest which it is the purpose of the legislation to promote.[75]

Normally objections against executability of a final decree passed in a suit cannot be raised in execution proceedings but if the raising of an objection at that stage based on a beneficient Act fructifies its purpose and the liberal construction of the Act, the language of which is not rigid, permits it, the court may prefer that construction.[76]

Another principle which may be here mentioned is that when contracts and transactions are prohibited by statutes for the sake of protecting one class of persons from another class of persons, the one from their situation and condition being liable to be oppressed and imposed upon by the other, there the parties are not in *pari delicto* and a person belonging to the oppressed class can apply for redress even if he was a party to a contract or transaction prohibited by the statute.[77] It is a trite law that in matters of welfare legislation, especially involving labour, the terms of contracts and

---

73. *Raja Satyendra Narain Singh v. State of Bihar*, (1987) 3 SCC 319, p. 325 : AIR 1987 SC 1390; *State of M.P. v. Board of Revenue*, 1983 MPLJ 148 (G.P. SINGH C.J.); *Pollisetti Pulamma v. Kalluri Kameshwaramma*, AIR 1991 SC 604, p. 621 : 1990 Supp (2) SCR 393.

74. *Doypack Systems Pvt. Ltd. v. Union of India*, AIR 1988 SC 782, pp. 803, 804 : (1988) 2 SCC 299.

75. *Pathumma v. State of Kerala*, (1978) 2 SCC 1 : AIR 1978 SC 771; *State of Gujarat v. Vora Saiyedbhai Kadarbhai*, 1995 (2) Scale 81 : (1995) 3 SCC 196 : AIR 1995 SC 2208. Similarly Acts designed to raise welfare funds for weaker sections are construed liberally and given an expansive construction : *Regional Executive, Kerala Fishermens Welfare Fund Board v. Fancy Food*, 1995 (3) Scale 273 : AIR 1995 SC 1620, p. 277 : (1995) 4 SCC 341.

76. *Ghantesher Ghosh v. Madan Mohan Ghosh*, AIR 1997 SC 471, p. 478 : (1996) 11 SCC 446 (objection under section 4 of the Partition Act, 1893 allowed in execution of a decree for partition of a dwelling house when the decree-holder, a purchaser from the original decree-holder, was a stranger to the family).

77. *V.S. Rahi v. Rani Chambeli*, (1984) 2 SCC 590, p. 618 : AIR 1984 SC 1447; *Mohd. Salimuddin v. Misrilal*, (1986) 2 SCC 378, p. 382 : AIR 1986 SC 1019; *Modern Hotel, Gudur v. Radhakrishnaiah*, (1989) 2 SCR 725 : AIR 1989 SC 1510.

the provisions of law should be liberally construed in favour of the weak.[78] A provision for recovery of money or damages for the benefit of employees, which contains no period of limitation, cannot be defeated by introduction of the concept of reasonable time as an implied period of limitation.[79]

The effect of a beneficial legislation is not construed to be defeated by a subsequent legislation except through a clear provision.[80] Thus the rights of minor children (irrespective of their religion) to get maintenance from their father as provided in section 127 of the Criminal Procedure Code, 1973 was construed not to have been taken away in respect of Muslims by the Muslim Women (Protection of Rights on Divorce) Act, 1986 section 3(b) of which enables a divorced Muslim woman to claim maintenance for the minor children upto the age of two years only from her former husband. It was held that the right of children to claim maintenance under section 125 CrPC is independent of the right of the divorced mother to claim maintenance for the infant children and the former is not affected by the 1986 Act.[81]

In Australia the Aboriginal Land Rights Act, 1983 was enacted to give important rights in crown land to the representatives of the Aboriginal people. In the context of this legislation KIRBY, J. said: The Act "should be given by the courts the most beneficial operation compatible with the language"; "exceptions to the right to claim land under the Act should be construed narrowly"; "any ambiguity should be resolved in a way that is favourable to the rights of Aboriginal people" and "any attempt by Parliament to restrict those rights must be clear and plain".[82]

It is a question of construction whether in a welfare legislation designed to provide assistance to disabled and infirm, the resources of the authority on whom the duty is laid should or should not be taken into account in judging the 'needs' of the person to whom the assistance is to be given.[83]

---

78. *Workmen of Binny Ltd. v. Management of Binny Ltd.*, (1985) 4 SCC 325, p. 330 : AIR 1986 SC 509; *Indian Bank v. K. Usha*, JT 1998 (1) SC 265, p. 278 : AIR 1998 SC 866, p. 874 : (1998) 2 SCC 663.

79. *Hindustan Times Ltd. v. Union of India*, JT 1998 (1) SC 18, p. 25 : AIR 1998 SC 688.

80. *Noor Saba Khatoon v. Mohd. Quasim*, AIR 1997 SC 3280, p. 3283 : (1997) 6 SCC 233.

81. *Ibid.*

82. *Minister Administering the Crown Lands Act v. NSW Aboriginal Land Council*, (2008) 82 ALJR 1505 paras 17, 19 and 20.

83. *R. v. Gloucestershire County Council*, (1997) 2 All ER 1 : (1997) AC 584 : (1997) 2 WLR 459 (HL); *R. v. Essex County Council,* (1998) 2 All ER 769 (HL). **See further** (1998) 61 MLR 401.

The liberal construction of a social welfare legislation can be taken to extreme limits to achieve the object of the legislation. This can be exemplified by the case of *National Insurance Co. Ltd. v. Swarn Singh,*[84] decided by a joint judgment of KHARE C.J.I., DHARMADHIKARI and SINHA, JJ. This case related to the construction of section 149 of the Motor Vehicles Act, 1988. Sub-section (1) of section 149 lays down the obligation of an insurer, after a certificate of insurance has been issued, to satisfy the awards against the insured. Sub-section (2) requires that no sum shall be payable by the insurer under sub-section (1) unless before commencement of proceedings leading to the award notice has been issued to the insurer by the Claims Tribunal who can then apply to be made a party to the proceeding and to *defend the action* on the ground that there has been a breach of a specified condition of policy one of them being 'a condition excluding driving by a named person or persons or by any person who is not duly licensed, or by any person who has been disqualified for holding or obtaining a driving licence during the period of disqualification'. In construing these provisions, the Supreme Court held that to prove its defence the insurer will have to prove: (i) the breach of condition by the insured was done knowingly or resulted due to his negligence and (ii) the breach was fundamental and had contributed to the cause of the accident. Thus, if the driver's licence was a fake one or had expired and was not valid on the date of the accident, the insurer will have to prove that the insured was aware of these facts or his ignorance of these facts was because of want of reasonable care expected to be exercised by him. Further, the insurer will have to show that the breach of condition was a substantial cause of the accident. For example if the accident had not occurred because of negligence in driving the vehicle but was caused by mechanical failure, the insurer will not escape liability. It was also held that even in cases where *the insurer is able to prove the defence of breach of condition it will have to satisfy the award against the insured* but it can recover the amount paid to the claimant from the insured in the same proceedings before the Tribunal. A two judge Bench in a later decision has held that the decision in *Swaran Singh* has no application to cases other than third-party risks.[85] It will also have no application to a claim of deficiency in service before the consumer forum.[86]

---

84. AIR 2004 SC 1531 : (2004) 3 SCC 297.

85. *National Insurance Co. Ltd. v. Laxmi Narain Dhut,* (2007) 3 SCC 700 (paras 21 and 38) : AIR 2007 SC 1563. **Followed** by another two-Judge Bench in *Oriental Insurance Co. Ltd. v. Meena Variyal,* (2007) 5 SCC 428 : AIR 2007 SC 1609.

86. *United India Insurance Co. Ltd. v. Davinder Singh*, AIR 2008 SC 329 : (2007) 8 SCC 698 (Insurance company not liable when driving licence not valid). **See** to the same effect *New India Assurance Co. Ltd. v. Prabhu Lal*, (2008) 1 SCC 696 : AIR 2008 SC 614.

A beneficial legislation, as is well known, should not be construed in such a manner as to bring within its ambit a benefit which was not contemplated by the legislature.[87] So the Insurance company will not be liable if the company had rescinded the contract of insurance and informed all parties before the accident after the cheque issued to satisfy the premium due is dishonoured.[84] But in this particular case as the claimant was a person from the lowest strata of society the Supreme Court directed under Article 142 the Insurance company to pay him and to recover the amount from the owner.

The court must also be vigilant to see that benefits conferred by welfare legislation are not defeated by subtle devices. It is the duty of the court, in every case where ingenuity is expended to avoid welfare legislations, to get behind the smoke screen and discover the true state of affairs. It can go behind the form and see the substance of the transaction.[88] Therefore, it can pierce the veil of the corporate entity of a company if it has been formed for avoidance of welfare legislation. Thus, when a company owning certain shares of another company created a subsidiary company wholly owned by it and transferred to it the shares held by it, it was held that the dividend income from the shares should be taken into account in assessing the profits of the old company for computation of bonus payable to workmen.[89] The right of permanent absorption of workmen who worked in a year for more than 240 days could not be defeated by showing their employment through a contractor who was essentially a name lender and there was no genuine contract system prevailing at the relevant time.[90] On the same principle the court should be vigilant in examining a plea of surrender of original tenancy and grant of new tenancy set up by a landlord when such a plea would take away the protection afforded to a tenant under the Madras City Tenants' Protection Act, 1922 which enables him to claim the value of the building put up by him on the leased land or to claim that the land itself be sold to him on the price fixed by the court.[91] On the same reasoning it is open to the Employees Insurance Corporation to club for application of the Employees' State Insurance Act, 1948 separate proprietary concerns and to treat them as single establishment having regard to unity in management, supervision and control, geographical

87. *Deddappa v. National Insurance Co. Ltd.*, (2008) 2 SCC 595 paras 24 and 25 : AIR 2008 SC 767.

88. *Workmen v. Associated Rubber Industry Ltd.*, (1985) 4 SCC 114, p. 117 : AIR 1986 SC 1.

89. *Ibid.*

90. *Secretary, Haryana State Electricity Board v. Suresh,* JT 1999 (2) SC 435 : AIR 1999 SC 1160 : (1999) 3 SCC 601.

91. *N.M. Ponniah Nadar v. Kamalakshmi Ammal* (*Smt.*), AIR 1988 SC 467, p. 474 : 1989 (1) SCC 64.

proximity, financial unity, general unity of purpose and functional integrity.[92] Since the Employees' State Insurance Act, 1948, is a beneficial piece of social welfare legislation aimed at securing the well-being of the employees, a narrow interpretation which will have the effect of defeating the objects of the Act should not be adopted. Accordingly, the preparation of food items in the kitchen of a club was held to be a "manufacturing process", and therefore the club was held to fall within the definition of "factory" in section 2(12) of the ESI Act, thereby bringing its employees within the ambit of the Act.[93]

(b) Illustrative cases

In *Raghuraj Singh v. Harikrishan*,[94] in interpreting section 5 of the U.P. Agriculturists' Relief Act, 1934, which granted relief amongst others in respect of 'any final decree for sale which has not been fully satisfied', the Privy Council held that the relief under the section was available in respect of a compromise decree under which the debtor in satisfaction of the decretal debt undertook to execute a sale deed of certain of his villages in favour of the creditor.

Construing section 9 of the Madras Agriculturist's Relief Act, 1938, in *Krishnayya v. Seshachalam*,[95] which dealt with 'debts incurred on or after 1st October, 1932', the Supreme Court held that relief under that section could be granted in respect of debts originally incurred before the commencement of the Act and after 1st October, 1932, though the same may have been renewed by a promissory note after the commencement of the Act.

In *Jivabhai v. Chhagan*,[96] where section 34 of the Bombay Tenancy and Agricultural Lands Act, 1948, which enabled a landlord to terminate the tenancy of his tenant, was amended by insertion of clause (2A) by Amending Act 33 of 1952, and further restrictions were placed on the right of the

---

92. *Sumangali v. Regional Director, Employees' State Insurance Corporation*, (2008) 9 SCC 106 : (2008) 8 JT 468.

93. *Delhi Gymkhana Club Ltd. v. ESI Corporation*, (2015) 1 SCC 142, pp. 150 to 152.

94. AIR 1944 PC 35.

95. AIR 1965 SC 639 : 1965 (1) SCR 195.

N.B.—This case may be compared with the decision of the Supreme Court in *K. Hutchi Gowder v. Ricobdos & Co.*, AIR 1965 SC 577 : (1964) 8 SCR 306, where section 19 of the Madras Act, which made provision for amending decrees passed in respect of debts payable at the commencement of the Act, was characterised as an 'ex-proprietary measure' and was not extended by construction to cover decrees passed in respect of debts incurred after the commencement of the Act.

96. AIR 1961 SC 1491 : (1962) 1 SCR 568. **See further** *Trimbak v. Assaram*, AIR 1966 SC 1758 : 1962 Supp (1) SCR 700.

landlord to terminate the tenancy of a protected tenant, it was held by the Supreme Court that the restrictions imposed by the Amending Act were available for the benefit of a tenant who had been served with a notice of termination of tenancy prior to the coming into force of the Amending Act but in whose case the period of notice had expired after coming into force of the Amending Act.

In *Dahya Lala v. Rasul Mahomed*,[1] a tenant inducted by a mortgagee was held to be a deemed tenant under section 4 of the Bombay Tenancy and Agricultural Lands Act, 1948 which conferred that status on "a person lawfully cultivating any land belonging to another person—and if such person is not—a mortgagee in possession"; and was held to be protected even after the redemption of mortgage.

The question in *Central Railway Workshop, Jhansi v. Vishwanath*,[2] was whether time-keepers, who prepare the paysheet of the workshop staff, maintain leave account, dispose of settlement case and maintain records for other statistical purposes, were workers as defined in the Factories Act, 1948. The definition of 'worker' in this Act is: 'a person employed directly or through any agency, whether for wages or not in any manufacturing process or in cleaning any part of the machinery or premises used for a manufacturing process or any other kind of work incidental to or connected with the manufacturing process'. "Giving a liberal construction to the definition, time-keepers were held as workers being employed in a kind of work incidental to or connected with the manufacturing process." And, in *P.M. Patel (M/s.) v. Union of India*,[3] *beedi* rollers employed through contractor and rolling *beedis* at their homes were held to be employees of the manufacturer for application of the Employees' Provident Fund and Miscellaneous Provisions Act, 1952.

The Supreme Court in *Sudhoo v. Haji Lal Mohd. Biri Works*,[4] interpreted section 31(2)(a) of the Beedi and Cigar Workers (Conditions of Employment) Act, 1966 which provides that "the employee discharged, dismissed or retrenched may appeal" to the prescribed authority. Construing the provision liberally it was held that there need be no written order of

---

1. AIR 1964 SC 1320 : 1963 (3) SCR 1. **See further** *Prabhu v. Ramdeo*, AIR 1966 SC 1721 : 1966 (3) SCR 676; *Rukhmanabai v. Shivram*, AIR 1981 SC 1881 : (1981) 4 SCC 262 and **Cf.** *Hariprasad v. Deonarain Prasad*, AIR 1956 SC 305 : 1956 SCR 1; *Papila Bai v. Chavdas T. Bhartakke*, AIR 2005 SC 662 (**Follows** *Prabhu v. Ramdeo, supra*, holds that *Hanmanta Daulappa Nimbal v. Baba Sahab Dajisahad Londha*, AIR 1996 SC 223 : (1995) 6 SCC 58 is not good law in view of *Dahya Lala v. Rasul Mahomed, supra*).
2. AIR 1970 SC 488, p. 491 : (1969) 3 SCC 95.
3. (1986) 1 SCC 32 : AIR 1987 SC 447.
4. AIR 1990 SC 1971, p. 1973 : 1990 (4) SCC 37.

termination to enable the employee to appeal and that an employee who has been terminated by stopping him to enter the place of works could appeal to the prescribed authority.

In *B. Shah v. Presiding Officer, Labour Court,*[5] the court applied the beneficent rule of construction in construing section 5 of the Maternity Benefit Act, 1961, which makes the employer liable for the payment of maternity benefit to a woman worker at the rate of the average daily wage for 'the period of her actual absence immediately preceding and including the day of her delivery and for the six weeks immediately following that day'. The question was whether in calculating the maternity benefit for the period covered by section 5, Sundays' being wageless holiday should be excluded. In holding that Sundays must also be included the court applied the beneficial rule of construction in favour of the woman worker and observed that the benefit conferred by the Act read in the light of Article 42 of the Constitution was intended to enable the woman worker not only to subsist but also to make up her dissipated energy, nurse her child, preserve her efficiency as a worker and maintain the level of her previous efficiency and output.

The Supreme Court in *Bhagirath v. Delhi Administration,*[6] overruled its earlier decision and held that the beneficent provisions of section 428, Cr PC directing set-off of the period of pre-conviction detention against the 'term' of imprisonment is applicable even to cases where the sentence is imprisonment for life and that such a sentence is also imprisonment 'for a term' within the section. In holding so the court observed: "To deny the benefit of section 428 to them (those sentenced to life imprisonment) is to withdraw the application of a benevolent provision from a large majority of cases in which such benefit would be needed and justified."[7] And, while dealing with section 125(3) of CrPC, which provides for recovery of maintenance granted in favour of a wife or minor child by issue of a warrant if the order for maintenance is not complied with 'without sufficient cause'; and which enables the magistrate, if the amount still remains unpaid, to sentence the person against whom the order is made to imprisonment for a period of one month, the court drew a distinction between 'mode of enforcement' and 'mode of satisfaction' and held that even after a sentence of imprisonment, the person concerned remained liable to pay the arrears of maintenance for non-payment of which he was imprisoned

5. AIR 1978 SC 12 : (1977) 4 SCC 334.
6. (1985) 2 SCC 580 : AIR 1985 SC 1050.
7. *Ibid.* But the benefit of the section is not available to a person sentenced by a Court Martial, *Ajmer Singh v. Union of India,* (1987) 3 SCC 340 : AIR 1987 SC 1646.

and the liability for payment could be satisfied only by payment and not by suffering the sentence.[8]

The Rajasthan amending Ordinance No. 26 of 1975 inserted section 13A in the Rajasthan Premises (Control of Rent and Eviction) Act, 1950. Section 13A prohibited the court from passing a decree for eviction in a pending suit on the ground of arrears of rent if the tenant applied within thirty days from the commencement of the Ordinance to determine the arrears and direct payment of the same with interest and costs within a time to be fixed by it. The section was also made applicable *mutatis mutandis* to pending appeals and revisions. In *Vatan Mal v. Kailash Nath,*[9] the suit was filed before the promulgation of the Ordinance and hence was pending when the Ordinance came into force but the notice of suit was served on the appellant long after the expiry of thirty days from the date of commencement of the Ordinance. The tenant did apply for determination of the arrears and payment thereof but he did not and could not apply to that effect within thirty days of the commencement of the ordinance. The High Court did not give the benefit of section 13A to the tenant but the Supreme Court reversed that view. It was held that when intention to give benefit of the new section 13A to the defendants in all pending suits, appeals and rectifications was clear the requirement of making the application within thirty days of the commencement of the Ordinance, when it was impossible to do so, should not be insisted upon in that particular case to deny the benefit to the defendant tenant.

In *Mohd. Shafi v. VII Additional District & Sessions Judge, Allahabad,*[10] the Supreme Court construed *Explanation* IV to section 21 of the U.P. Urban Buildings (Regulation of Letting, Rent and Eviction) Act, 1972. Section 21 of the Act restricts the right of a landlord to obtain possession of any building in occupation of a tenant. One of the grounds on which possession can be sought is *bona fide* need of the landlord or his family. The *Explanation* provides that 'the fact that the building under tenancy is a part of a building the remaining part whereof is in the occupation of the landlord for residential purposes, shall be conclusive to prove that the building

---

8. *Kuldip Kaur v. Surinder Singh*, AIR 1989 SC 232 : (1989) 1 SCC 405.

9. AIR 1989 SC 1534 : (1989) 3 SCC 79. **See further** another similar case *B.P. Khemka Pvt. Ltd. v. Birendra Kumar Bhowmik*, AIR 1987 SC 1010 : (1987) 2 SCC 407.

10. AIR 1977 SC 836 : (1977) 2 SCC 226. **See further** *Mohanlal v. Jai Bhagwan*, AIR 1988 SC 1034 : (1988) 2 SCC 474, where a provision enabling a landlord to evict his tenant when he used the building 'for a purpose other than that for which it was leased' was narrowly construed not to permit eviction when the tenant merely switched over from one business to another which did not involve possibility of mischief or detriment to the demised premises.

is *bona fide* required by the landlord'. The word building in the *Explanation* was restrictively construed limiting it to a unit of accommodation and not embracing the entire superstructure containing more than one tenement. The *Explanation* being in the nature of an Exception to the protection conferred by the Act to the tenants was construed narrowly in favour of the tenants. Grounds of eviction provided in Control of Rent and Eviction Acts have for the same reason been restrictively construed. For example it has been held that the ground of eviction enacted by the words 'has sublet' or 'has ceased to occupy' the premises in question will not be satisfied unless the subletting or non-occupation as the case may be continues up to the date of the suit.[11] The same principle was applied in *Vaddeboyina Tulsamma v. Vaddeboyina Sesha Reddi,*[12] while construing section 14 of the Hindu Succession Act, 1956. It was held that section 14(2) of the Act which was in the nature of an exception to section 14(1) should be narrowly construed confining it to cases where property is for the first time acquired by a female Hindu without any pre-existing right, under a gift, will, instrument etc., the terms of which prescribe restricted estate. Therefore a case of pre-existing right of maintenance followed by a life estate under a Will, will fall under section 14(1) and not under section 14(2).[13]

---

11. *Baba Ram Gopal v. Mathura Das*, AIR 1990 SC 879, p. 881 : (1990) 2 SCC 279. **But see** *Raghunathi v. Raju Ramappa Shetti*, AIR 1991 SC 1040 : 1991 Supp (2) SCC 267, which holds that sub-letting need not continue up to the date of suit.

12. AIR 1977 SC 1944 : (1977) 3 SCC 99; **Distinguished** in *Gumpha* (*Smt.*) *v. Jaibai*, JT 1994 (1) SC 535 : 1994 (2) SCC 511 (A Hindu widow succeeding under a will conferring a life estate does not become full owner); *Sadhu Singh v. Gurudwara Sahib Naraike,* (2006) 8 SCC 75 : AIR 2006 SC 3282 (A Hindu bequeathing his separate property to his wife and giving her a life estate. The widow in such a case acquires only a life estate. But if there is no will and she succeeds as an heir she becomes a full owner). **See further** *Mangat Mal v. Punni Devi*, 1995 (6) SCC 88 : AIR 1996 SC 172; *Nazar Singh v. Jagjit Kaur*, 1995 (6) Scale 476 : AIR 1996 SC 855; *C. Masilamani v. Idol of Shri Swaminathaswami*, AIR 1996 SC 1697, p. 1704 : (1996) 8 SCC 525 (Held *Gumpha's* case (*supra*) not correctly decided. Thus a succession under a will may fall under section 14(1) if there was some pre-existing right); *Himi* (*Smt.*) *v. Hirabai* (*Smt.*), AIR 1997 SC 83 : (1996) 10 SCC 642 [Life estate under a compromise decree does not fall under section 14(1) if there was no pre-existing right]; *Raghubir Singh v. Gulab Singh*, JT 1998(4) SC 579 : AIR 1998 SC 240 : (1998) 6 SCC 314 [Widow having right of maintenance under Hindu law, compromise decree recognising her ownership and possession, section 14(1) **applied**]. **But see** *Vankamamidi Venkata Subba Rao v. Chatlapalli Seetharamaratna Ranganayakamma*, AIR 1997 SC 3082, p. 3085 : (1997) 5 SCC 460.

13. *Beni Bai v. Raghubir Prasad,* JT 1999 (2) SC 54 : AIR 1999 SC 1147 : (1999) 3 SCC 234; *Balwant Kaur v. Chanan Singh,* AIR 2000 SC 1908 : (2000) 6 SCC 310; *Brahma Varta Santan Dharam Mahamandal v. Kanhayalal Bagla,* AIR 2001 SC 3799 : (2001) 9 SCC 562. For construction of section 14, **see further** p. 956, *ante.*

In *Motor Owners' Insurance Co. Ltd. v. J.K. Modi,*[14] the words 'anyone accident' as they occur in section 95(2)(a) of the Motor Vehicles Act, 1939, have, having regard to the beneficial purpose of the Act, been construed to signify as many accidents as the number of persons involved in the accident to enable the limit of Rs. 20,000 payable by the Insurance Company to apply to each person injured. And, in *Skandia Insurance Co. v. Kokilaben Chandrabadan,*[15] section 96(2)(b)(ii), which absolves an Insurance Company when there has been breach of a condition excluding driving by any person who is not duly licensed, was narrowly construed and it was held that when the owner of the vehicle authorised a licensed driver to drive but the driver left the vehicle in charge of a cleaner who was not licensed and an accident happened, the insurance company was not absolved as the owner having entrusted the vehicle to a licensed driver was not in breach of the condition and section 96(2)(b)(ii) was not attracted.

The definition of service in section 2(o) of the Consumer Protection Act, 1986 did not expressly include 'housing construction' before 1993. Yet the Supreme Court held that, having regard to the object of the Act, the authorities constituted under the Act could entertain a complaint by a consumer for any defect or deficiency in relation to construction activity against a private builder or a statutory authority like the Lucknow Development Authority.[16] Facility of 'housing construction', though then not expressly included, was held to be 'service of any description which is made available to potential users' within the definition as it then existed. The amendment expressly including 'housing construction' was held to have been made by way of abundant caution. Similarly the definition of consumer in section 2(1)(d)(i) of the same Act, which excludes buyer of goods for any commercial purpose, was held not to exclude a buyer who purchases goods for self employment even before an explanation clarify-

---

14. AIR 1981 SC 2059 : (1981) 4 SCC 660.

15. (1987) 2 SCC 654 : AIR 1986 SC 1184.

16. *Lucknow Development Authority v. M.K. Gupta,* AIR 1994 SC 787 : (1994) 1 SCC 243. **See further** *Om Prakash v. Assistant Engineer, Haryana Agro Industries Corporation Ltd.,* JT 1994 (3) SC 623 : (1994) 3 SCC 504 : (1994) 81 Comp Cas 371 (Non-supply of tractor in accordance with the list of booking causing loss to a person higher in the list as the price of tractor rose in the interval; held amounted to deficiency in service within the definition of complaint in section 2(1)(C)(iii) although not within the definition of unfair trade practice in section 36A as it then stood before amendment by Act 58 of 1991 and compensation allowed). But it has been held that a 'share' before its allotment is not 'goods' and a prospective investor in shares is not a consumer under the Act; *Morgan Stanley Mutual Fund v. Kartick Das,* JT 1994(3) SC 654 : (1994) 4 SCC 225. **See further** text and note 34, pp. 940-941.

ing this meaning was added in this definition.[17] And interpreting section 2(1)(d)(ii) of the same Act, it has been held that parents who hire the services of a hospital and their child for whom the services are hired are both consumers and can independently claim damages.[18] Although service rendered by governmental hospitals/nursing homes and private hospitals/nursing homes who render free service without any charge to every person does not fall within the definition of 'service', but if the medical service is rendered as a condition of service to a person it would not be regarded as free service and will fall within the definition of 'service' and the consumer fora will have jurisdiction to decide these claims.[19] The fora under the C.P. Act will have jurisdiction to entertain claims regarding deficiency in service unless their jurisdiction is expressly barred despite the fact that other courts or fora have jurisdiction to entertain the claims.[20] Liberal view was also taken in holding that, though the fora under the Act are judicial authorities, they are not hampered by section 34 of the Arbitration Act, 1940 and are not obliged to stay proceedings before them for the Act provides a cheap and speedy remedy to the consumer, in addition to the normal remedy under section 9 of the Code of Civil Procedure, 1908 or the Arbitration Act, 1940 and its provisions have to be widely construed.[21] On the same principle bar of jurisdiction of civil courts in a Co-operative Societies Act for deciding a dispute between members and the society has been held not to apply to forums under the Consumer Protection Act, 1986.[22]

Dealing with section 73 of the Employees' State Insurance Act, 1948, in *Buckingham and Carnatic Co. v. Venkatiah*,[23] the Supreme Court held that

---

17. *Laxmi Engineering Works v. P.S.G. Industrial Institute*, 1995(2) Scale 626 : AIR 1995 SC 1428 : (1995) 3 SCC 583. **See further** *Karnataka Power Transmission Corporation v. Ashok Iron Works Pvt. Ltd.*, (2009) 3 SCC 240 para 34 : (2009) 2 JT 447 (The expression 'but does not include a person who avails of such services for any commercial purpose' inserted in section 2(1)d(ii) of the Act by Act 62 of 2002 is not retrospective and does not apply to any period prior to its introduction. In this case delay in supply of electricity by Electricity Board, before the amendment, to a consumer was held to be deficiency in service though the consumer availed of the supply for commercial purpose).

18. *Spring Meadows Hospital v. Harjol Ahluwalia*, JT 1998 (2) SC 620, p. 629 : AIR 1998 SC 1801 : (1998) 4 SCC 39.

19. *Kishor Lal v. Chairman, Employees' State Insurance Corpn.*, (2007) 4 SCC 579 (para 8) : AIR 2007 SC 1819 (claim for negligence in medical service rendered by ESI doctors); *Laxman Thamappa Kotgiri v. G.M. Central Railway,* (2007) 4 SCC 596 : (2005) 1 Scale 600 (claim for negligence in medical service rendered by Railway Hospital).

20. *Kishor Lal v. Chairman, Employees' State Insurance Corpn., supra* (para 17).

21. *Fair Air Engineers Pvt. Ltd. v. N.K. Modi*, AIR 1997 SC 533, p. 538 : 1996 (6) SCC 385.

22. *Secretary Thirumurgan Co-operative Agricultural Credit Society v. M. Lalitha*, (2004) 1 SCC 305 : AIR 2004 SC 448.

23. AIR 1964 SC 1271 : (1964) 4 SCR 265.

the words of the section—'No employer shall dismiss, discharge, or reduce or otherwise punish an employee during the period the employee is in receipt to sickness benefit etc.', limited the prohibition of punitive action to the period during which the employee was ill and that the prohibition so imposed was further limited to such dismissal, discharge etc., which was the result of a decision of the employer embodied in an order passed by him and did not include within its fold automatic termination of employee's services resulting from a contract or from a Standing Order by virtue of the employee's absence without leave for the specified period. Rejecting the argument in support of the extension of the prohibition so as to include even such termination of services, GAJENDRAGADKAR, J. observed: "The liberal construction must ultimately flow from the words used in the section. If the words used in the section are capable of two constructions one of which is shown patently to assist the achievement of the object of the Act, courts would be justified in preferring that construction to the other which may not be able to further the object of the Act. But, on the other hand, if the words in the section are reasonably capable of only one construction, the doctrine of liberal construction can be of no assistance."[24]

Dealing with entry 8 in the Schedule to the Minimum Wages Act, 1948, in *M.P. Mineral Industry Association v. Regional Labour Commissioner*,[25] which reads—'Employment in stone-breaking or stone-crushing'—the Supreme Court held that the entry was confined to stone-breaking and stone crushing employment in stone quarries and that it did not include the breaking or crushing of stones incidental to mining operations. The plea for an extended meaning of the entry based on the rule of liberal construction failed, as in view of the court the alternative construction was not reasonably open. Similarly it was held that the Act though required to be construed liberally cannot be extended to teachers who do not fall within the definition of employee in section 2(1).[26]

The question in *Mugnilal v. Sugan Chand*,[27] related to construction of section 4, clause (a) of the M.P. Accommodation Control Act, 1955, which restricted the right of a landlord to file a suit only on certain specified grounds, one of them being 'that the tenant has failed to make payment to

---

24. *Ibid*, p. 1277. **See further** for a similar statement of the rule by GAJENDRAGADKAR, C.J. *Regional Provident Funds Commr. v. Shiba Metal Works*, AIR 1965 SC 1076, 1080 : 1965 (2) SCR 72.

25. AIR 1960 SC 1068 : 1960 (3) SCR 476.

26. *Haryana Unrecognised Schools Association v. State of Haryana*, AIR 1996 SC 2108.

27. AIR 1965 SC 101 : 1964 (5) SCR 239 : (1996) 4 SCC 225.

the landlord of any arrears of rent within one month of the service upon him of a written notice of demand'. In the particular case, the tenant failed to make payment of arrears within one month of the demand but did pay the same before the filing of suit for ejectment. The Supreme Court held that the condition of suit under clause (a) to section 4 was satisfied and that the said clause did not require that the non-payment should continue till the date of the suit. It was pointed out that though the Legislature intended to give protection to defaulting tenant it cannot follow from it that it must be deemed to have given the protection of widest amplitude and that no such assumption can be made to support an unnatural construction of the words used.[28] On the same lines is the case of *Jaywant S. Kulkarni v. Minochar Dosabhai Shroff*,[29] which related to section 12(3)(a) of the Bombay Rents Hotel and Lodging House Rates Control Act, 1947. This section provides: "When the rent is payable by the month and there is no dispute regarding the amount of standard rent or permitted increases, if such rent or increases are in arrears for a period of six months or more and the tenant neglects to make payment thereof until the expiration of the period of one month after notice referred to in sub-section (2), the court shall pass a decree for eviction in any such suit for recovery of possession." The words 'court shall pass a decree' were substituted in the section in 1963 for the words 'court may pass a decree'. In construing the section the Supreme Court held that on default of payment of rent as mentioned in the section the court was bound to pass a decree for eviction and as this intention was clear there was no scope for referring to spirit of the law.

3. STRICT CONSTRUCTION OF PENAL STATUTES

(a) General principles[30]

If a statute laid a mandatory duty but provided no mode of enforcing it, the presumption in ancient days was that the person in breach of the duty could be made liable for the offence of contempt of the statute.[31] This rule of construction is now obsolete and has no application to a modern statute.[32] Clear language is now needed to create a

---

28. *Ibid*, p. 105.
29. AIR 1988 SC 1817, p. 1820 : 1988 (4) SCC 108.
30. The principles stated hereunder and the propositions set out at pp. 804, 805, 806, *infra* were referred to from 4th Edition of this book (pp. 458-64) in *N.K. Jain v. C.K. Shah*, AIR 1991 SC 1289, pp. 1300, 1301 : 1991 (2) SCC 495.
31. *R. v. Horseferry Road Magistrate's Court*, (1986) 2 All ER 666, p. 674 : (1987) QB 54 : (1986) 3 WLR 132 (QBD).
32. *Ibid.*

crime.[33] A statute enacting an offence or imposing a penalty is strictly construed.[34] But this rule, as already stated, is now-a-days of a limited application; and speaking broadly, serves in the selection of one when two or more constructions are reasonably open. The rule exhibits a preference for the liberty of the subject and in a case of ambiguity enables the court to resolve the doubt in favour of the subject and against the Legislature which has failed to express itself clearly.[35] The rule was originally evolved to mitigate the rigour of monstrous sentences for trivial offences and although that necessity and that strictness have now almost vanished, the difference in approach made to a penal statute as against any other statute still persists.[36] "If I were asked", said POLLOCK, CB, "whether there be any difference left between a criminal statute and any other statute not creating offence, I should say that in a criminal statute you must be quite sure that the offence charged is within the letter of the law."[37] LORD ESHER, MR in formulating "the settled rule of construction of penal sections" observed: "If there is a reasonable interpretation which will avoid the penalty in any particular case we must adopt that construction. If there are two reasonable constructions

---

33. *Ibid.* **See further** *Kartar Singh v. State of Punjab*, JT 1994(2) SC 432, p. 466 : 1994 (3) SCC 569. (It is the basic principle of legal jurisprudence that an enactment is void for vagueness if its prohibitions are not clearly defined) *State of Kerala v. UNNI*, (2007) 2 SCC 365 (para 50) : AIR 2007 SC 819 (A 'penal provision must be definite'. In this case a vague and unreasonable penal rule was struck down.); *Surajmani Stella Kujur Dr. v. Durgacharan Hansdah*, AIR 2001 SC 938, p. 939 : (2001) 3 SCC 13 (No custom can create an offence); *Balram Kumawat v. Union of India*, (2003) 7 SCC 628 : AIR 2003 SC 3268, p. 641 (Making of a penal legislation by the judiciary is strictly out of its bound). Even in England where old common law offences survive until abolished or susperceded by statute, there now exists no power in the courts to create new offences and statute is now the sole source of criminal law offences: *Knuller (Publishing, Printing and Promotions) Ltd. v. DPP*, (1972) 2 All ER 898 (HL); *R. v. Jones*, (2006) 2 All ER 741 (para 28) p. 767 (HL).

34. The rule of strict construction has no application to a procedural provision like section 195 of the CrPC. : *Iqbal Singh Marwah v. Meenakshi Marwah*, AIR 2005 SC 2119, p. 2131 (para 23).

35. **See** text and note 2, p. 961, *supra*. **See further** *Rosenbaum v. Burgoyne*, (1964) 2 All ER 988, p. 991 (HL); *Director of Public Prosecutions v. Schildkamp*, (1969) 3 All ER 1640, pp. 1642, 1643, 1644 (HL); *Dilip Kumar Sharma v. State of Madhya Pradesh*, AIR 1976 SC 133, p. 138 : (1976) 1 SCC 586; *State of West Bengal v. Swapan Kumar*, AIR 1982 SC 949, p. 958 : (1982) 1 SCC 561.

36. For justification of continuance of the rule **see** text and notes 38 to 41, p. 981.

37. *A.G. v. Sillem*, (1864) 33 LJ Ex 92, p. 110 : 10 LT 434 : 10 HLC 704; referred to in *R. v. Oakes*, (1959) 2 All ER 92, p. 94. **See further** *Director of Public Prosecutions v. Goodchild*, (1978) 2 All ER 161, p. 165 (HL) (A man should not be gaoled on an ambiguity).

we must give the more lenient one."[38] The rule has been stated by MAHAJAN, C.J.I. in similar words: "If two possible and reasonable constructions can be put upon a penal provision, the court must lean towards that construction which exempts the subject from penalty rather than the one which imposes penalty. It is not competent to the court to stretch the meaning of an expression used by the Legislature in order to carry out the intention of the Legislature."[39] So when in a statute dealing with a criminal offence impinging upon the liberty of citizens, a loophole is found, it is not for Judges to cure it, for it is dangerous to derogate from the principle that a citizen has a right to claim that howsoever much his conduct may seem to deserve punishment, he should not be convicted unless that conduct falls fairly within the definition of crime of which he is charged.[40] The fact that an enactment is a penal provision is in itself a reason for hesitating before ascribing to phrases used in it a meaning broader than that they would ordinarily bear.[41] There is all the more reason to construe strictly a drastic penal statute which deals with crimes of aggravated nature which could not be effectively controlled under the ordinary criminal law.[42] Such a statute

---

38. *Tuck & Sons v. Priester*, (1887) 19 QBD 629, p. 638; referred to in *London & North Eastern Railway v. Berriman*, (1946) 1 All ER 255, p. 270 : 1946 AC 278 (HL). (For formulation of the rule in *Berriman's* case **see** text and notes 4 and 5, p. 933); *Sanjay Dutt v. State through CBI, Bombay,* JT 1994(5) SC 540, p. 558 : 1994 (5) SCC 410; *Assistant Commissioner Assessment-II Bangalore v. M/s. Velliappa Textiles Ltd.*, AIR 2004 SC 86, p. 94 : (2003) 11 SCC 405; *Krishi Utpadan Mandi Samiti v. Pilibheet Pantnagar Beej Ltd.*, (2004) 1 SCC 391, p. 412 : AIR 2004 SC 2135.

39. *Tolaram v. State of Bombay*, AIR 1954 SC 496, pp. 498, 499 : 1955 (1) SCR 158. **See further** *State of M.P. v. Azad Bharat Finance Co.*, AIR 1967 SC 276 : 1966 Supp SCR 473; *Aslam Babalal Desai v. State of Maharashtra*, AIR 1993 SC 1, p. 11 : (1992) 4 SCC 272; *Sanjay Dutt v. State through CBI, Bombay, supra*; *Bijaya Kumar Agarwala v. State of Orissa*, AIR 1996 SC 2531, p. 2534 : (1996) 5 SCC 1 (mere carrying of paddy in a truck cannot be called 'storing' of paddy).

40. *Spicer v. Holt*, (1976) 3 All ER 71, pp. 78, 79 (HL). In this case the expression 'a person arrested under' the provisions of a statute was construed to mean a person lawfully arrested.

41. *R. v. Cuthbertson*, (1980) 2 All ER 401, p. 404 : (1981) AC 407 : (1980) 3 WLR 89 (HL). In this case section 27 of the Misuse of Drug Act, 1971, which permits forfeiture of anything shown to relate to the offence 'when a person is convicted of an offence under this Act', was construed not to include the case of the offence of conspiracy to commit an offence under the Act for conspiracy is not an offence under the Act. As another example, in *Rudd v. Secretary of State for Trade and Industry*, (1987) 2 All ER 553, p. 559 (HL), the word 'use' in a section creating, an offence was interpreted not to mean 'has available for use' as distinguished from actual user during the relevant period. **See further** *Sakshi v. Union of India*, (2004) 5 SCC 518, p. 537 : AIR 2004 SC 3566, p. 3572, where 9th Edn., of this book is referred.

42. *Niranjan Singh Karan Singh Punjabi v. Jitendra Bhimraj Bijja*, AIR 1990 SC 1962, pp. 1967, 1968 : 1990 (4) SCC 76 : 1990 Cri LJ 1869; *Bijaya Kumar Agarwala v. State of Orissa*, AIR 1996 SC 2531, p. 2534 (para 18) : 1996 (5) SCC 1.

should not ordinarily be resorted to if the nature of the activities of the accused can be checked and controlled under the ordinary criminal law.[43]

Mere passive membership of an alleged illegal organization may not amount to an offence under the Unlawful Activities Prevention Act, 1967.[44]

A prosecution for adulteration of 'carbonated water' without prescribing the limit of 'pesticide residue' and without prescribing the method of testing and the laboratories where it can be done, the prosecution cannot succeed as the provisions in this respect in the Prevention of Food Adulteration Act, 1954 are mandatory.[45]

Applying the principle of strict interpretation of penal statutes, the Supreme Court has held that only the 'drawer' of the cheque can be made liable for penal action under section 138 of the Negotiable Instruments Act, 1881, and not another person who had merely negotiated the transaction out of which the debt has arisen and was only a joint account-holder along with the drawer, but had not signed the cheque. In the facts of the case, the Court was of the view that section 141 was not attracted, and a different interpretation would add words to section 141 of the Act and extend the principle of vicarious liability thereunder to persons who are not named in it.[46] Similarly, section 141 of the Negotiable Instruments Act, 1881, was strictly interpreted to hold that a prosecution thereunder cannot be maintained only against an officer of a company, without arraigning the company as an accused, since officers of a company can only be held vicariously liable for an offence committed by the company.[47]

Similarly, the presumption related to dowry death in section 304-B of the IPC, which covers not only the husband of the deceased woman but also 'any relative of her husband', was construed strictly to hold that the brother of the aunt of the husband cannot be prosecuted thereunder. Since the term 'relative' is not defined in the IPC, the same has to be understood in its natural, ordinary or popular sense, and would therefore mean only a person related to the husband by blood, marriage or adoption.[48]

---

43. *Ibid.* [The case deals with Terrorists and Disruptive Activities (Prevention) Act, 1987. The Act provides minimum punishment, makes confessional statement made to a police officer not below the rank of S.P. admissible, raises rebuttable presumption against the accused in certain cases and provides for identification of an accused, who is not traced, through his photograph.]

44. *State of Kerala v. Raneef*, (2011) 1 SCC 784 paras 10 to 15 : AIR 2011 SC 340.

45. *Pepsico India Holdings Private Ltd. v. Food Inspector*, (2011) 1 SCC 176 paras 39, 40, 43, 44 : (2010) 12 JT 531.

46. *Aparna A. Shah v. Sheth Developers Pvt. Ltd.*, (2013) 8 SCC 71, pp. 78 to 82.

47. *Aneeta Hada v. Godfather Travels & Tours Pvt. Ltd.*, (2012) 5 SCC 661, pp. 687, 688.

48. *State of Punjab v. Gurmit Singh*, (2014) 9 SCC 632.

Section 123 and other relevant provisions of the Representation of the People Act, 1951, which deal with corrupt practices by an individual candidate or his agent, being penal provisions, were strictly construed to hold that promises made by a political party in its election manifesto would not constitute a corrupt practice, as it is only the individual and not the political party which falls within the sweep of the said provisions.[49]

In *Joint Commercial Tax Officer, Madras v. YMA, Madras*,[50] SHAH, J. observed: "In a criminal trial or a *quasi*-criminal proceeding, the court is entitled to consider the substance of the transaction and determine the liability of the offender. But in a taxing statute the strict legal position as disclosed by the form and not the substance of the transaction is determinative of its taxability."[51] With great respect the distinction drawn by SHAH, J. does not exist in law. Even in construing and applying criminal statutes any reasoning based on the substance of the transaction is discarded.[52] The submission made here can be said to have been approved in *Balaram Kumawat v. Union of India*.[53]

The duty of the court is to give effect to the purpose as expressed in clear and unambiguous language and "that obligation is not altered because the Act is penal in character."[54] So the application of the rule does not permit the court in restraining comprehensive language used by the Legislature, the wide meaning of which is in accord with the object of the statute.[55] Even if there be sharp divergence of opinion amongst the High Courts on the construction of a provision in a penal statute, the Supreme Court will not necessarily prefer the narrower view which favours the accused and not the prosecution and may prefer to accept the wider view which is more consistent with the object of the provision.[56] The principle was neatly formulated by LORD JUSTICE JAMES who speaking for the Privy Council stated: "No doubt all penal statutes are to be construed strictly, that is to say, the court must see that the thing charged as an offence is within the plain meaning of the words used, and must not strain the words

49. *S. Subramaniam Balaji v. State of Tamil Nadu & Ors.*, (2013) 9 SCC 659, p. 694.
50. AIR 1970 SC 1212, p. 1217 : 1970 (1) SCC 462.
51. *Ibid*.
52. *Re, HPC Productions Ltd.*, (1962) 1 All ER 37, p. 49 (letters E, F) and **see** other cases in note 45, p. 924.
53. (2003) 7 SCC 628, p. 635 : AIR 2003 SC 3268.
54. *Thomson v. His Honour Judge Byrne,* (1999) 73 ALJR 642, p. 648 (para 19).
55. For example, **see** *State of Kerala v. Mathai Verghese*, (1986) 4 SCC 746 : AIR 1987 SC 33; *L.K. Hashim v. State of T.N.*, (2005) 1 SCC 237, pp. 252, 253 (The expression 'any currency note or bank note' used in section 489A of the Penal Code was construed to include currency note of all countries and not only Indian currency note.)
56. *State of Maharashtra v. Tapas D. Neogy,* JT 1999 (6) SC 92 : (1999) 7 SCC 685 : 1999 SCC (Cri) 1352 (The expression 'any property' in section 102 CrPC was construed to include a 'bank account' and so a police officer investigating a case under the Prevention of Corruption Act was held entitled to seize it).

on any notion that there has been a slip; that there has been a *casus omissus*; that the thing is so clearly within the mischief that it must have been included if thought of. On the other hand, the person charged has a right to say that the thing charged although within the words, is not within the spirit of the enactment. But where the thing is brought within the words, and within the spirit, there a penal enactment is to be construed, like any other instrument, according to fair commonsense meaning of the language used, and the court is not to find or make any doubt or ambiguity in the language of a penal statute, where such doubt or ambiguity would clearly not be found or made in the same language in any other enactment."[57] The above formulation has been cited with approval by the House of Lords[58] and the Supreme Court.[59] In *Narayan Nambiar*, SUBBARAO, J., referring to the Prevention of Corruption Act, 1947, observed: "The Act was brought in to purify public administration. When the Legislature used comprehensive terminology—to achieve the said purpose, it would be appropriate not to limit the content by construction when particularly the spirit of the statute is in accord with the words used there."[60] Similarly, the Supreme Court has deprecated a narrow and pedantic construction of the Prevention of Food Adulteration Act, 1954 likely to leave loopholes for the adulterator to escape.[61] And on the same principle the court has disapproved of a narrow construction of section 135 of the Customs Act, 1962,[62] section 489A of the Penal Code,[63] section 12(2) of the Foreign Exchange Regulation Act, 1947,[64] section 56 of the Foreign Exchange Regulation Act, 1973,[65]

---

57. *Dyke v. Elliot*, (1872) LR 4 PC 184, p. 191.

58. *London & North Eastern Railway Co. v. Berriman*, (1946) 1 All ER 255, p. 270 (HL). For formulation of the rule in this case **see** text and notes 4 and 5, p. 933, *ante*.

59. *M. Narayan Nambiar v. State of Kerala*, AIR 1963 SC 1116, pp. 1118, 1119 : 1963 Supp (2) SCR 724; *Suman Sethi v. Ajay K. Churiwal*, AIR 2000 SC 828, pp. 829, 830 : (2000) 2 SCC 380.

60. AIR 1963 SC 1116, p. 1119. **See further** *R.S. Nayak v. A.R. Antulay*, (1986) 2 SCC 716, p. 724 : AIR 1986 SC 2045; *R.S. Nayak v. A.R. Antulay*, AIR 1984 SC 684 : (1984) 2 SCC 183; *State of Madhya Pradesh v. Shri Ram Singh*, AIR 2000 SC 870, p. 873 : (2000) 5 SCC 88; *Govt. of Andhra Pradesh v. P. Venku Reddy*, AIR 2002 SC 3346, p. 3349 : (2002) 7 SCC 631.

61. *Murlidhar Meghraj Loya v. State of Maharashtra*, AIR 1976 SC 1929, p. 1932 : (1976) 3 SCC 684; *Kisan Trimbak Kothula v. State of Maharashtra*, AIR 1977 SC 435, pp. 438, 439 : (1977) 1 SCC 300.

62. *State of Maharashtra v. Natwarlal Damodardas*, AIR 1980 SC 593, p. 599 : 1980 (4) SCC 669.

63. *State of Kerala v. Mathel Verghese*, (1986) 4 SCC 746 : AIR 1987 SC 33.

64. *M.G. Wagh v. Jay Engineering Works Ltd.*, (1987) 1 SCC 542 : AIR 1987 SC 670.

65. *Enforcement Directorate v. M. Samba Shiva Rao*, JT 2000 (6) SC 514 : (2000) 5SCC 431 : AIR 2000 SC 2128; *Standard Chartered Bank v. Directorate of Enforcement*, (2005) 4 SCC 530, pp. 550, 551 : AIR 2005 SC 2622 (9th Edn., pp. 754 to 756 of this book is referred).

section 630(1)(b) of the Companies Act, 1956,[66] section 52A of the Copy Right Act, 1957,[67] and section 138 of the Negotiable Instruments Act, 1881.[68] Strident laws enacted for dealing with and punishing offences against married women have to be stringently implemented.[69] For instance, the presumptions under section 113-B of the Evidence Act, 1872, and Section 304-B of the Indian Penal Code, 1860, which deal with dowry death, are attracted if cruelty or harassment was caused to the woman 'soon before her death'. The Court held that since these are beneficent provisions aimed at giving relief to a woman routinely subjected to cruelty in an Indian household, the meaning to be given to each word of these provisions has to be in accord with the legislative intent and, even while construing these provisions strictly, care will have to be taken to see that their object is not frustrated. Accordingly, it was held that the expression 'soon before her death' is

---

66. *Baldeo Krishna Sahi v. Shipping Corporation of India Ltd.*, (1987) 4 SCC 361 : AIR 1987 SC 2245, p. 366 ('Officer' or 'employee' includes past officer or employee who wrongfully withholds or retains company's property). In *Abhilash Vinod Kumar Jain (Smt.) v. Cox & Kings (India) Ltd.*, 1995(2) Scale 323 : AIR 1995 SC 1592 : (1995) 3 SCC 732, it has been held that legal representatives or heirs of employee or officer will also fall within the ambit of section 630. It is submitted that this is an undue extension of a penal provision to make the legal representatives and heirs liable for criminal offence when the language used contains no hint to support this extension. In *J.K. Bombay Ltd. v. Bharti Matha Misra,* AIR 2001 SC 649 : (2001) 2 SCC 700, the court it is submitted rightly declined to extend the ratio in *Abhilash Vinod Kumar* to cover family members of the employee. But in *Lalita Jalan v. Bombay Gas Co. Ltd.,* (2003) 6 SCC 107 : AIR 2003 SC 3157; *J.K. Bombay Ltd.* has been overruled and *Abhilash Vinodkumar* has been affirmed. The cases of *Abhilash Vinod Kumar Jain* and *Lalita Jalan* **followed** in *Gopika Chandrabhushan Saran v. ZLO India Ltd.,* (2009) 3 SCC 342 para 25 : (2009) 3 JT 431.

67. *State of Andhra Pradesh v. Nagoti Venkataramana*, 1996(6) Scale 417 : 1996 (6) SCC 409.

68. *Modi Cements Ltd. v. Kuchil Kumar Nandi*, AIR 1998 SC 1057 : (1998) 3 SCC 249; *K. Bhankaran v. Sankaran Vaidhyan Balan,* JT (1999) 7 SC 558, p. 506 : (1999) 7 SCC 510 : AIR 1999 SC 3762; *NEPC Micon Ltd. v. Magma Leasing Ltd.,* (1999) 4 SCC 253, p. 262 : AIR 1999 SC 1952; *Pankaj Mehra v. State of Maharashtra,* AIR 2000 SC 1953, p. 1960 : (2000) 2 SCC 756 (The offence is made out even if the drawer of the cheque 'fails to make payment' for reasons beyond his control); *Dalmia Cement (Bharat) Ltd. v. Galaxy Traders,* AIR 2001 SC 676, p. 679 : (2001) 6 SCC 643 : 2001 Cri LJ 972; *Goa Plast (P.) Ltd. v. Chico Ursula Dsouza,* (2003) 3 SCC 232, pp. 238, 239. **But see** *Vinod Tanna v. Zaher Siddiqui,* (2002) 7 SCC 541, p. 542 : 2002 SCC (Cri) 1825 (The dishonour of the cheque for constituting the offence should be on the ground of non-availability of sufficient funds in the account); *Goa Plast (P.) Ltd. v. Chico Ursula D'souza*, AIR 2004 SC 408 : (2004) 2 SCC 235; *Prem Chand Vijay Kumar v. Yashpal Singh*, (2005) 4 SCC 417 : (2005) 5 JT 318 (cause of action for compliant arises on expiry of the period of 15 days after first notice issued on dishonour of the cheque).

69. *K. Prema S. Rao v. Yadla Srinivasa Rao,* (2003) 1 SCC 217, p. 228 : AIR 2003 SC 11.

a relative term, and the time-lag may differ from case to case. Though the test of proximity is to be applied, the same is not a rigid test, and a pragmatic and sensitive approach is required to be employed by the Court while examining each case of dowry death.[70]

Language permitting a penal statute may also be construed to avoid a lacuna[71] and to suppress the mischief and advance the remedy in the light of the rule in *Heydon's* case.[72] For example, the word 'owner' in section 60(3) of the Narcotic Drugs and Psychotropic Substances Act, 1985 which provides for confiscation of any conveyance used for carrying any narcotic drug or psycotropic substance unless it was so used without the knowledge of the 'owner' was construed to mean registered owner in case of a motor vehicle sold under a Hire-Purchase agreement even before instalments are fully paid for otherwise such vehicles could never be confiscated.[73] Section 15 of the Terrorists and Disruptive Activities (Prevention) Act 1987, having regard to the object of meeting the menance of terrorists makes a confession recorded by a police officer admissible and although the confession so recorded is required by Rule 15 to be sent to a judicial magistrate along with the accused, it has been held that the magistrate is not obliged to make an enquiry regarding the voluntary nature of the confession before sending it to the designated court for such an enquiry would frustrate the purpose of section 15 in authorising a police officer to record

---

70. *Surinder Singh v. State of Haryana*, (2014) 4 SCC 129, pp. 137 to 141.

71. *Baldeo Krishna Sahi v. Shipping Corporation of India Ltd.*, (1987) 4 SCC 361, p. 366 : AIR 1987 SC 2245; *M.G. Wagh v. Jay Engineering Works Ltd., supra.*

72. *Swantraj v. State of Maharashtra*, AIR 1974 SC 517, p. 520 : (1975) 3 SCC 322 ; *Chitan J. Vaswani v. State of West Bengal*, AIR 1975 SC 2473, p. 2476 (para 7) : (1975) 2 SCC 829; *Municipal Corporation of Delhi v. Kacheroo Mal*, AIR 1976 SC 394, p. 395 (para 4) : (1976) 1 SCC 412; *Municipal Corporation of Delhi v. Laxmi Narain Tandon*, AIR 1976 SC 621 : (1976) 1 SCC 546; *Farrel v. Alexander*, (1976) 1 All ER 129, p. 136 (CA) (LORD DENNING); *State of Maharashtra v. Natwarlal Damodardas*, AIR 1980 SC 593, p. 599 : (1980) 4 SCC 669; *R.S. Nayak v. A.R. Antulay, supra*; *Baldeo Krishna Sahi v. Shipping Corporation of India Ltd., supra; Dinesh Chandra Jamnadas Gandhi v. State of Gujarat*, AIR 1989 SC 1011, p. 1015 : (1989) 1 SCC 420; *N.K. Jain v. C.K. Shah*, AIR 1991 SC 1289, pp. 1301, 1305 : (1991) 2 SCC 495; *Pawan Kumar v. State of Haryana*, JT 1998 (1) SC 565, p. 571 : AIR 1998 SC 958, p. 963; *NEPC Mican Ltd. v. Magma Leasing Ltd.*, AIR 1999 SC 1952, pp. 1956, 1957 : (1999) 4 SCC 253; *Standard Chartered Bank v. Directorate of Enforcement*, (2005) 4 SCC 530, p. 551 : AIR 2005 SC 2622 (9th Edn., pp. 754 to 756 of this book is referred), *Iqbal Singh Marwah v. Meenakshi Marwah*, AIR 2005 SC 2119, p. 2131 : (2005) 4 SCC 370.

73. *Ganga Hire Purchase Pvt. Ltd. v. State of Punjab*, AIR 2000 SC 449 : (1999) 5 SCC 670. **See further** *Intelligence Officer Narcotics C. Bureau v. Sambhu Sonkar*, AIR 2001 SC 830, p. 832 : (2001) 2 SCC 562 (Narrow Construction of section 37 was **overruled**).

a confessional statement.[74] On the same principle it has been held that a confession recorded under section 15 is a substantive piece of evidence and can be used against a co-accused also.[75] The confession so recorded can also be used against the accused for convicting him of the offences under the Penal Code or any other law of which he is charged along with the offences under TADA, even when he is acquitted of the offence under TADA, in the same trial.[76] And, in sections 304B and 498A of the Penal Code, having regard to the object of preventing cruelty to women, the expression 'husband' has been construed to cover a person who enters into marital relationship with the woman concerned whatever may be the legitimacy of the marriage.[77] But in adopting a wide meaning of a provision, the undesirability of adopting anything beyond a strict construction of provisions having penal consequences should be weighed against the employment of a broad approach to effectuate the purpose of the Act.[78] Further, a commonsense approach for solving a question of applicability of a penal enactment is not ruled out by the rule of strict construction.[79] In *State of Andhra Pradesh v. Bathu Prakasa Rao,*[80] rice and broken rice were distinguished by applying the commonsense test that at least 50% must be broken in order to constitute what could pass off as marketable 'broken rice' and any grain less than 3/4th of the whole length is to be taken as broken.[81]

The rule of strict construction does not also prevent the court in interpreting a statute according to its current meaning and applying the language to cover developments in science and technology not known at the time of passing of the statute. Thus psychiatric injury caused by silent telephone calls was held to amount to 'assault' and 'bodily harm' under sections 20 and 47 of the Offence Against the Person Act, 1861 in the light of the current scientific appreciation of the link between the body and psychiatric injury.[82] Similarly, data stored in a computer disc, a technology

---

74. *State of Maharashtra v. Bharat Chaganlal Raghani,* AIR 2002 SC 409 : (2001) 9 SCC 1. For meaning of 'terrorism', **see** *Mandan Singh v. State of Bihar*, (2004) 4 SCC 622, p. 633 to 635.

75. *Jaywant Dattatraya Subyarao v. State of Maharashtra,* AIR 2002 SC 143, p. 165 : (2001) 10 SCC 109. **See further** *Jameel Ahmed v. State of Rajasthan*, AIR 2004 SC 588, pp. 599, 600 : (2003) 9 SCC 673.

76. *Prakash Kumar v. State of Gujarat*, (2005) 2 SCC 409 : AIR 2005 SC 1075.

77. *Reema Aggarwal v. Anupam,* AIR 2004 SC 1418, p. 1424 : (2004) 3 SCC 199, p. 210.

78. *Cutter v. Eagle Star Insurance Co. Ltd.,* (1998) 4 All ER 417, p. 425 (HL) ('Road' not construed to include 'car park').

79. *Standard Chartered Bank v. Directorate of Enforcement, supra.* (This proposition stated in 9th Edn., p. 756 of this book is approved).

80. AIR 1976 SC 1845, p. 1853 : (1976) 3 SCC 301.

81. *Ibid.*

82. *R. v. Ireland,* (1997) 4 All ER 225 : (1997) 3 WLR 534 (HL). **See further**, p. 266, *supra.*

not anticipated in 1978, was held to amount to 'indecent photograph' within the meaning of section 1 of the Protection of Children Act, 1978 (even before its amendment in 1994) which penalises taking or distribution of indecent photograph of children under the age of 16.[83]

After approvingly quoting from earlier edition of this book the principles stated above the Supreme Court (speaking through Sinha J.) gave wide meaning to the word 'ivory' in section 49C(7) of the Wild Life (Protection) Act, 1972 and held that the said word should be construed to include 'mammoth ivory' having regard to the object and purpose of the Act.[84] The court also observed that "the rule of strict construction of a regulatory penal statute may not be adhered to, if thereby the plain intention of Parliament to combat crimes of special nature would be defeated".[85]

Stringent provisions enacted by States for ceizure and confiscation of illegally extracted forest produce and vehicles transporting it have been liberally construed having regard to the object of preventing large scale pilferage and depletion of forest wealth.[86] It has also been held that acquittal of the accused for the forest offence does not necessarily nullify confiscation proceedings which are independent of prosecution.[87]

The burden to prove that the case of the accused falls within an exception to a statutory offence lies on him.[88] But the question whether the defence set up by an accused is really a defence of an exception or a defence setting up non-existence of a fact which is an ingredient of the offence to be proved by the prosecution depends upon the construction of the particu

---

83. *R. v. Fellows,* (1997) 2 All ER 548 (CA). For cases after amendment, **see** *R. v. Bowden,* (2000) 2 All ER 418 (CA); *Atkins v. DPP,* (2000) 2 All ER 425 (QB DC).

84. *Balram Kumawat v. Union of India,* (2003) 7 SCC 628, pp. 635, 636 : AIR 2003 SC 3268, pp. 3272, 3273.

85. *Ibid,* p. 640 (SCC), p. 3276 (AIR). **See further** text and note 31, p. 978.

86. *State of Bihar v. Kedar Sau,* AIR 2003 SC 3650 : (2003) 7 JT 276; *State of West Bengal v. Sujit Kumar Rana,* AIR 2004 SC 1851, pp. 1856 to 1860 : (2004) 4 SCC 129.

87. *Divisional Forest Officer v. G.V. Sudhakar Rao,* AIR 1986 SC 328 : (1985) 4 SCC 573 **approving** *Mohd. Yaseen v. Forest Range Officer,* (1980) 1 ALT 8 (AP). **See further** *State of West Bengal v. Sujit Kumar,* (*supra*), p. 1859 (AIR).

88. *Vehicle Inspectorate Bruce Cook Road Planning Ltd.,* (1999) 4 All ER 761, p. 767 (HL). Section 105 of the Indian Evidence Act, 1872; Section 101 of the Magistrates Act, 1980 (U.K.). As to the nature of proof on the accused, **see** *Woolmington v. Director of Public Prosecutions,* 1935 AC 462 : 1935 All ER 1 (HL); *Vijaya Singh v. State of U.P.,* AIR 1990 SC 1459 : (1990) 3 SCC 190; *Sanjay Dutt v. State through CBI, Bombay,* JT 1994 (5) SC 540, pp. 565, 566 : (1994) 5 SCC 410; *K. Prakashan v. P.K. Surenderan,* (2008) 1 SCC 258 para 14 : (2007) 11 JT 573 (The burden on the accused is only proof by mere preponderance of probability).

lar statute.[1] In deciding what are essential ingredients of the offence, the language of the statutory provision though important, what will be decisive will be the substance and reality of the language and not its form.[2] If the linguistic construction does not clearly indicate the Parliament's intention, regard should be had to the mischief at which the Act is aimed and practical considerations affecting the burden of proof and, in particular, the ease or difficulty that the respective parties would encounter in discharging the burden.[3]

If the statute requires the accused to disprove even by preponderance of probabilities a presumed fact which is an essential element of the offence as distinguished from proviso or exception, the statute may offend a due process clause in a constitution designed to ensure a fair trial[4] and the provision may be read down and construed to provide only for evidential burden on the accused or in otherwords to require the accused only to lead sufficient evidence to raise the issue in defence so that it would be then for the prosecution to show beyond reasonable doubt that the defence is not made out by the evidence.[5] This principle has been further extended even to cases where the legal burden laid on the accused relates to a fact which is not an ingredient of the offence.[6] It has been held that the question in cases where legal burden of proving a defence is laid upon the accused, is always to assess whether the burden enacted by Parliament unjustifiably infringes the presumption of innocence and if a legal burden on the accused is not a proportionate reasonable legislative response, it may be read down even when the burden relates to a fact which is not an ingredient of the offence.[7] Presumption of innocence as

---

1. *R. v. Hunt*, (1987) 1 All ER 1, p. 10 : (1987) AC 352 (HL); *Sanjay Dutt v. State, supra.*
2. *Attorney General of Hongkong v. Lee Kwong-Kut*, (1993) 3 All ER 939, p. 950 (PC).
3. *R. v. Hunt, supra*, p. 11; *Nimmo v. Alexander Cowan & Sons Ltd.*, (1967) 3 All ER 187 (HL); *Sanjay Dutt v. State, supra.*
4. *Attorney General of Hongkong v. Lee Kwong-Kut, supra*, pp. 950, 951, 952 [The case relates to Article 11(1) Hongkong Bill of rights, which provides : 'Everyone charged with criminal offence shall have the right to be presumed innocent until proved guilty according to law.'] **Followed** in *Vasaquez v. R.*, (1994) 3 All ER 674 : (1994) 1 WLR 1304 (PC).
5. *R v. Lambert,* (2001) 3 All ER 577, p. 608 (HL) (The case relates to the construction of the Misuse of Drugs Act, 1991 in the light of Article 6(2) of the European Convention for the Protection of Human Rights which provides: "Everyone charged with a criminal offence shall be presumed innocent unless proved guilty according to law").
6. *Sheldrake v. Director Public Prosecutions*, (2005) 1 All ER 237 (HL).
7. *Ibid.* This case is also in the context of Article 6(2) of the European convention quoted in f.n. 2, p. 971. For Comments see Victor Tadros and Stephen Tierney 'The Presumption of Innocence and The Human Rights Act' (2004) 67 Modern Law Review, pp. 402-34. Article 14(2) of the International covenant on Civil and Political

[Footnote No. 7 Contd.]

human right and the doctrine of reverse burden introduced by a statutory provision have to be delicately balanced upon the factual matrix of the case.[8] The principle is said to have no application to forfeiture proceedings following conviction for drug trafficking offence.[9] In any case a deeming provision which reverses the onus of proof in relation to an element of the offence has to be strictly construed and cannot be extended beyond its language to cover another offence.[10]

An illustration of the interpretation of such a deeming provision can be seen with respect to section 304-B of the Indian Penal Code, 1860, which states that the husband of the deceased woman or a relative of the husband, who subjected her to cruelty or harassment for, or in connection with, a demand for dowry, 'shall be deemed' to have caused her death. The Supreme Court has held that the words 'shall be deemed' actually mean 'shall be presumed', because the intent and context, namely the presumption as to dowry death under section 113-B of the Evidence Act, 1872, warrant such an interpretation. Being a mandatory presumption on the guilty conduct of an accused, the prosecution must show the availability of all the ingredients of the offence so as to shift the burden of proof under section 113-B of the Evidence Act, and only then will the presumption of innocence fade away.[11] Subsequently, it has been held that the prosecution must not just 'show' but 'prove' the ingredients of section 304-B by a preponderance of possibility in order to replace the presumption of innocence with the assumption of guilt of the accused, thereby transferring the burden of proof on him to produce evidence to dislodge his guilt beyond reasonable doubt. The intention of the Parliament in using the word 'deemed' was that merely a preponderance of evidence would be insufficient to discharge the husband or his family members of their guilt. Accordingly, it was held that the word 'deemed' will have different meanings in civil or fiscal law and in criminal law and, in the context of section 304-B, the word 'deemed' has to be read down to mean 'presumed', having regard to the presumption of innocence and the

---

[Footnote No. 7 Contd.]

Rights 1966, to which India is a party and which is enforced by the Protection of Human Rights Act, 1993 corresponds to Article 6(2) of the European Convention. But when the legal burden liad on the accused employer is to show that it was not practicable or reasonably practicable to do more than what was done for the safety of workmen the test of proportionality may be readily satisfied : *R v. Chargot Ltd.*, (2009) 2 All ER 845 (H.L.). **See further** p. 884 for this case which relates to section 40 of the Health and Safety at Work Act, 1974.

8. *Krishna Janardan Bhat v. Dattatraya G. Hegde*, (2008) 4 SCC 54 para 44 and 45 : AIR 2008 SC 1325.

9. *Mcintosh v. Lord Advocate,* (2001) 2 All ER 638 (PC); *R. v. Benjafield,* (2002) 1 All ER 815 (HL); *R. v. Rezvi,* (2002) 2 All ER 801 (HL).

10. *Krakouer v. Queen,* (1998) 72 ALJR 1229, p. 1233 (Aust).

11. *Gurdip Singh v. State of Punjab*, (2013) 10 SCC 395, p. 400.

protection in respect of conviction for offences under Article 20 of the Constitution.[12]

Article 20(3) guarantees that no person accused of any offence shall be compelled to be a witness against himself. Article 21 which guarantees right to life and personal liberty has been construed also to guarantee fair procedure in trial of the accused. Narco Analysis Polygraph Test (lie detector test) and BEAP (Brain Electrical Activation Profile) test when conducted without the consent of the person violate the guarantee against self-incrimination under Article 20(3) and fair procedure under Article 21.[13]

The rigour of a provision in a criminal statute may provoke the court to tone it down by reading an implied escape clause. Section 5 of the Terrorist and Disruptive Activities (Prevention) Act, 1987 provides, 'Where any person is in possession of any arms and ammunition specified in columns 2 and 3 of the category I or category III(a) of Schedule I to the Arms Rules, 1962 or bombs, dynamite or other explosive substances unauthorisedly in a notified area, he shall notwithstanding anything contained in any other law for the time being in force, be punishable with imprisonment for a term which shall not be less than five years but which may extend to imprisonment for life and shall also be liable to fine'. 'Notified area' is defined in section 2(1) to mean 'such area as the State Government may, by notification in the Official Gazette specify'. Having regard to the object of the Act, the State Government can on its subjective satisfaction notify only such area as notified area under the Act which is prone to terrorist and disruptive activities. Section 5 of the Act requires three ingredients to be proved for an offence falling under that section: (i) Possession of any of the specified arms and ammunition etc., (ii) unauthorisedly (iii) in a notified area. The section does not in terms provide that the accused can in any way escape punishment if the aforesaid three ingredients are established. It was, however, held that possession of unauthorised arms etc. in a notified area raised a presumption that the arms etc. were meant to be used for a terrorist or disruptive act which was in effect the third ingredient and therefore the accused was entitled to rebut this presumption and escape punishment under section 5 by proving that his unauthorised possession of arms etc. was wholly unrelated to any terrorist or disruptive activity and the same was neither used nor available in that area for any such use and its availability in a notified area was innocuous.[14] It is submitted that on a

---

12. *Sher Singh v. State of Haryana*, (2015) 3 SCC 724, pp. 736 to 741.

13. *Selvi v. State of Karnataka*, (2010) 7 SCC 263 : AIR 2010 SC 1974. (Even when the person consents for these tests in recording his consent various guidelines issued by the National Human Rights Commission have to be followed, para 265.).

14. *Sanjay Dutt v. State through CBI, Bombay*, JT 1994(5) SC 540, pp. 557, 560, 561 : (1994) 5 SCC 410 : 1994 SCC (Cri) 1433.

proper construction, the existence of the third ingredient could be demolished by the accused only by attacking the validity of the notification declaring the area as notified area, *e.g.*, on the ground that there was absolutely no material before the State Government to form its opinion, albeit subjective, that the area was prone to terrorist or disruptive activities. But if the area was validly declared to be a notified area, the Act does not postulate any defence for the accused to show that the unauthorised arms etc. found in his possession in such area were unrelated to any terrorist or disruptive activity. But such a construction would have probably offended Article 21 of the Constitution and so was not adopted.[15] Similarly, in another

---

15. The menace of terrorism has to be met by methods which are consistent with the rule of law and the fundamental rights available even to a terrorist. See in this context a very informative article by JUSTICE MICHAEL KIRBY of Australia, 'Soli Sorabjee's Example & the Struggle Against Terrorism', Constitutionalism Human Rights and the Rule of Law (Eassys in the honour of Soli J. Sorabjee), p. 66 (Universal Law Publishing Co.). **See further** another similar article 'Meeting the challenge of terrorism, the experience of English and other courts', (2006) 80 ALJ 818 where, after surveying the legal position in almost all common law jurisdictions, Lady Justice Mary Aden concludes: "If we hold on to the fundamental values of a plural, democratic society, subject to the rule of law, and all that that involves, there is surely a good chance that terrorism too will be defeated and that freedom will survive. There is however no better way of ensuring that that happens" (p. 838). She at one place (p. 629) refers to the judgment delivered by President Barak of the Supreme Court of Israel in which, in holding that torture was not open to a democracy in the fight against terrorism, the President said: "This is the fate of democracy as not all means are acceptable to it, and not all methods employed by its enemies are always open to it. Sometimes democracy must fight with one hand tied behind its back. Nonetheless, it has the upper hand. Preserving the rule of law and recognition of individual liberties constitute an important component of its understanding of security. At the end of the day, they strengthen its spirit and the strength allows it to overcome its difficulties."

Rule of Law in an era of Terrorism:

(1) There is no circumstance where a person howsoever classified can be placed outside the international human rights or humanitarian law.
(2) No person should be convicted on the basis of evidence obtained by torture or cruel or inhuman or degrading treatment or punishment.
(3) No person should be convicted on the basis of secret evidence that the accused can neither see nor rebut.
(4) There should be no departure from minimum standards for the treatment of detainees under international law, including those contained in common article of the Geneva Conventions.
(5) There should be no impunity for serious violations of international human rights or humanitarian law.
(6) All detainees should be entitled to have the legality of their detention determined by independent court, and effective remedies for serious human rights violations, such as torture or ill treatment.
(7) All persons convicted of crimes should have a right to full judicial review before an independent impartial court.

[Footnote No. 15 Contd.]

case which also related to the same Act, the Supreme Court read in the requirement of *mens rea* in the definition of 'abet' in section 1(a)(i) and many safeguards to prevent the abuse of the Act.[16] Indeed the principle of constitutionality or legality requires the court to read by implication any procedural step which is not expressly mentioned but which is essential for meeting the requirement of reasonable procedure implicit in Article 21. Thus though a manufacturer arraigned as accused by the court under section 32A of the Drugs and Cosmetics Act, 1940 is not entitled to a copy of the report of Government Analyst under section 25(2) for adducing evidence to controvert the finding therein under section 25(4), he has to be given a copy of the report and opportunity to controvert it to make section 25 consistent with the philosophy of Article 21.[17]

In *Peoples Union for Civil Liberties v. Union of India,*[18] the Supreme Court, while upholding the validity of Prevention of Terrorism Act, 2002, with certain safeguards, noted that "terrorism has become a global threat" and it was "our international obligation also to pass necessary laws to fight terrorism". Yet the court cautioned: "The protection and promotion of human rights under the rule of law is essential in the prevention of terrorism.

[Footnote No. 15 Contd.]

The Rule of Law: Striking A Balance in An Era of Terrorism' by Mary Robinson, extracted from 'The Rule of Law, Perspectives from Around the Globe' edited by Francis Neale (LexisNexis) p. 32. "The governing principle is that the rule of law must be maintained however great the threat posed by terrorism. We should respect human rights in difficult times as well as in tolerable times because we are battling against terrorism precisely so that we can maintain a democratic society in which we can enjoy individual liberty, the right to debate and dissent and all the other freedoms that we cherish and which the terrorists abhor" Lord Panmick in a lecture published in (2009) 9 SCC 7C24.

In *RVF*, (2007) 2 All ER 193 (CA) SIR IGOR J. points out the difficulty in defining the true meaning of 'terrorism' in the abstract for many of those whose violent activities were in support of national independence and who were once described as terrorists are now honoured as freedom fighters. He later says: "Violence, of course is not the only way. In *Non-Violence in Peace and War* (1942) Mahatma Gandhi posed the question: 'What difference does it make to the dead, the orphans and homeless, whether the mad destruction is wrought under the name of totalitarianism or the holy name of liberty or democracy." (paras 9 and 10). Also Nobel laueate and first democratically elected President of South Africa Nelson Mandela and his party were listed as terrorist in U.S.A and their names were removed by legislation in June 2008 : (Hitvada 29-7-08).

16. *Kartar Singh v. State of Punjab,* (1994) 3 SCC 569 : (1994) 2 JT 423, **see further** text and notes 73, 74, p. 1012.

17. *Amery Pharmaceuticals v. State of Rajasthan,* JT 2001 (3) SC 497, p. 506 : AIR 2001 SC 1303 : (2001) 4 SCC 382; Compare English case in text and notes 69 to 72, pp. 541, 553.

18. AIR 2004 SC 456 (paras 10 and 15) : (2004) 9 SCC 580. For British and American response to terrorism, **see** pp. 546 to 557.

– Terrorism often thrives where human rights are violated. The lack of hope for justice provides breeding grounds for terrorism. – In all cases, the fight against terrorism must be respectful to the human rights."[19]

In *Indradas v. State of Assam,*[20] it was held that mere membership of a banned organization as provided in section 3(5) of the Terrorist and Disruptive Activities (Prevention) Act, 1987 and section 10 of the Unlawful Activities (Prevention) Act, 1967 are if literally read unconstitutional as they will then violate Article 19(1) and (2) of the Constitution and they have to be read down to mean that unless the person resorts or incites violence or creates public disorder by violence or incitement to violence he would not be held guilty of the offence simply by becoming a member.

Protective measures adopted to prevent the disclosure of identity of witnesses who genuinely claimed fear for their lives if it became known that they had given evidence against the accused even when they were the only witnesses who identified him may offend the right to a fair trial under the common law or Article 6 of the European Convention and the conviction may have to be quashed.[21] In the Indian context, it may violate the guarantee of fair procedure implicit in Article 21 of the Constitution and Article 14(3) of the International Covenant on Civil and Political Rights, enforced by the Protection of Human Rights Act, 1993. In *Davis* where the conviction was quashed the following protective measures were adopted by the trial court for the safety of the witnesses: (1) The witnesses were

---

19. AIR 2004 SC 456 (paras 10 and 15) : (2004) 9 SCC 580. After repeal of the Prevention of Terrorism Act 2002 (POTA) in 2004 there was no comprehensive counter terrorism legislation in India to implement resolution no. 1373 and other resolutions of the Security Council of the United Nations. But after terrorist attack of 26/11 in Mumbai the Government introduced the Unlawful Activities (Prevention) Amendment Bill 2008 in Parliament to implement the security council resolutions to combat international terrorism, to take action against terrorists and terrorist organisations, to freeze their assets and other economic resources, to prevent their entry into or transit through Indian territory and to prevent the direct and indirect supply sale or transfer of arms and ammunitions to them. The Government also introduced the National Investigation Agency Bill 2008 to constitute an investigating agency at the national level to investigate and prosecute offences affecting the sovereignty, security and integrity of India, security of state, friendly relations with foreign states and offences under Acts enacted to implement international treaties, agreements, conventions and resolutions of the United Nations. Both these bills were unanimously passed by Parliament and received Presidential Assent on 31-12-08 and are now part of the Law of India as Act no. 35 of 2008 and Act. no. 34 of 2008.

20. (2011) 3 SCC 380 paras 23 to 44 : (2011) 2 JT 153. The editor has rightly commented that "would the court be so sanguine when the organisation concerned is an international terrorist organisation whose avowed aim is the very destruction of Indian Civil Society and the liberal Indian State?".

21. *R. v. Davis*, (2008) 3 All ER 461 (H.L.).

each to give evidence under a pseudonym. (2) The addresses and personal details and any particulars which might identify the witnesses were to be withheld from the accused and his legal advisors. (3) The accused's counsel was permitted to ask the witnesses no question which might enable any of them to be identified. (4) The witnesses were to give evidence behind screens so that they could be seen by the judge and the jury but not by the accused. (5) The witnesses' natural voices were to be heard by the judge and the jury but were to be heard by the accused and his counsel subject to mechanical distortion so as to prevent recognition by the accused.[22] In the trial of an accused for acts of terrorism, the danger to life of witnesses if their identity were disclosed may often be genuine and some protective measures be needed for their safety. Response of Parliament of the United Kingdom was the enactment of the Criminal Evidence (Witness Anonymity) Act, 2008. The Act sets out statutory regime under which a 'witness anonymity order' can be obtained if three conditions are satisfied: (i) It must be necessary in order to protect the safety of the witness or another person or in order to prevent real harm to the public interest; (ii) the defendant must receive a fair trial and (iii) the order must be in the interests of justice.[23] In India section 17 of the newly enacted National Investigation Agency Act, 2008 provides that on an application made by a witness in any proceeding before it or by the Public Prosecutor in relation to such witness or on its own motion, if the special court is satisfied that the life of such witness is in danger it may, for reasons to be recorded in writing take such measures as it deems fit for keeping the identity and address of such witness secret.

When an accused is prosecuted for not complying with an order (or subordinate legislation) made under a statute, the question as to what extent he can challenge the validity of the order in the criminal trial depends upon the true construction of the Act under which the prosecutions is launched. The statute may require the prosecution to prove that the order in question is not open to challenge on any ground available in public law, or it may be a defence to show that it is. In such a case the court trying the accused will have to rule on the validity of the order. On the other hand, the statute may upon its true construction merely require the prosecution to show that the order appears formally valid and has not been quashed by judicial review. In such a case, nothing except the formal validity of the order will be relevant before the court. There is no general theory that the

---

22. *Ibid* para 3 **see further** on the question as to when protection to witnesses need be given: *R v. Officer L.*, (2007) 4 All ER 965 (H.L.); *Van Coble v. Chief Constable Hertfordshire Police*, (2008) 3 All ER 977 (H.L.).
23. On the question of construction and application of the Act **see** *R v. Meyers*, (2009) 2 All ER 145 (H.L.).

defence of *ultra vires* can be raised in every case irrespective of the terms and policy of the statute.[24] The presumption is, however, strongly in favour of the view that the defence of ultravires is not barred.[25] Indeed it has been said that "only the clear language of a statute could take away the right of a defendant in criminal proceedings to challenge the law-fulness of a bye-law or administrative decision where his prosecution is premised on its validity"[26] and for purposes of such a challenge there was no distinction to be drawn between substantive and procedural invalidity.[27]

LORD REID in the context of the rule of construction applicable to penal statutes said: "We are always trying to find the intention of the Legislature. Where taking into account the surrounding circumstances and the likely consequences of the various possible constructions there can be at all any doubt about the intention, we must, where penalties are involved, require that the intention shall clearly appear from the words of the enactment construed in the light of those matters. But if we can say that those matters show that a particular result must certainly have been intended, we would, I think, be stultifying the underlying principle if we required more than that the statutory provisions are reasonably capable of an interpretation carrying out that intention."[28] In an earlier case, LORD REID explained that the rule of restrictive interpretation of penal provisions "only applies where after full enquiry and consideration one is left in real doubt. It is not enough that the provision is ambiguous in the sense that it is capable of having two meanings", for the imprecision of language is such that it is difficult to draft any provision which is not ambiguous in that sense. Difference of judicial opinion as to the meaning of the provision may also be not enough for applying the rule, and a judge while dealing with a question of construction of the provision must himself be in real doubt before he can call in aid the rule.[29]

---

24. *R. v. Wicks*, (1997) 2 All ER 801, p. 815 : (1997) 2 WLR 876 (HL) (The defence of *ultra vires* was held to be barred).

25. *R. v. Wicks, supra*, p. 805; *Boddington v. British Transport Police*, (1998) 2 All ER 203, pp. 216, 217 (HL) (Defence of *ultra vires* was held to be not barred).

It has been held by the High Court of Australia that an accused, while being tried for drug trafficking, can collaterally challenge the validity of a warrant issued by a court under the Listening Devices Act, 1969, permitting the use of a listening device by the police for collecting evidence against the accused, for issue of such a warrant is not an exercise of judicial power; the warrant was, however found to be valid: *Ousley v. Queen*, (1997) 71 ALJR 1548.

26. *Boddington v. British Transport Police, supra*, p. 217.

27. *Ibid*, p. 215.

28. *Kennedy v. Spratt*, (1971) 2 WLR 667, p. 671 : 1972 AC 83 (HL).

29. *Director of Public Prosecutions v. Ottewell*, (1968) 3 All ER 153, p. 157 (HL) **followed** in *Farrel v. Alexander*, (1976) 2 All ER 721, pp. 727, 744 (HL); *Attorney-General's Reference (No. 1 of 1988)*, (1989) 2 All ER 1 : (1989) 2 WLR 729 (HL).

STORY, J. in agreeing to the rule in its "true and sober sense" stated the same as follows: "Penal statutes are not to be enlarged by implication or extended to cases not obviously within their words and purport. But where the words are general, and include various classes of persons, I know of no authority, which would justify the court in restricting them to one class, or in giving them the narrowest interpretation, where the mischief to be redressed by the statute is equally applicable to all of them. And where a word is used in a statute, which has various known significations, I know of no rule, that requires the court to adopt one in preference to another, simply because it is more restrained, if the objects of the statute equally apply to the largest and broadest sense of the word."[30]

Penal statues have also to be interpreted "having regard to the subject-matter of the offence and the object of the law it seeks to achieve. The purpose of law is not to allow the offender to sneak out of the meshes of law. Criminal jurisprudence does not say so."[31]

Considerations of public policy are not foreign in interpreting and applying a criminal statute. For example, it was held by the House of Lords[32] that consensual sadomasochistic homosexual encounters which occasioned actual bodily harm to the victim were assaults occasioning actual bodily harm, contrary to section 47 of the Offences Against the Person Act, 1861 and unlawful wounding contrary to section 20 of that Act, notwithstanding the victim's consent to the acts inflicted on him. The Court took into consideration[33] that public policy required that society be protected by criminal sanctions against a cult of violence which contained the danger of the proselytisation and corruption of young men and the potential for the infliction of serious injury even though by Sexual Offences Act, 1967 Parliament made lawful homosexual activities conducted in private between two consenting adults. In India, public policy also forbids a conviction to be recorded in a criminal trial as a result of 'plea bargaining' which induces an accused to plead guilty on the allurement that he would be let off very lightly even if the offence be serious.[34] Criminal offences in India cannot be

---

30. *United States v. Winn*, 3 Sumn 209, Fed Case No. 16, 740; **referred** to in *Johnson v. Southern Pacific Company*, 196 US 1, pp. 18, 19 : 49 Law Ed 362, pp. 369, 370. **See further** *Kanwar Singh v. Delhi Administration*, AIR 1965 SC 871 : 1965 (1) SCR 7.

31. *Balaram Kumawat v. Union of India*, (2003) 7 SCC 628, p. 635 : AIR 2003 SC 3268; *Prakash Kumar v. State of Gujarat*, (2005) 2 SCC 409, p. 424. **See further** text and note 84 and 85, p. 969.

32. *R. v. Brown*, (1993) 2 All ER 75 : (1994) 1 AC 212 : (1993) 2 WLR 556 (HL).

33. *Ibid.*

34. *State of Uttar Pradesh v. Chandrika,* AIR 2000 SC 164 : (1999) 8 SCC 638 (Also see cases referred to therein).

compounded[35] except as provided in section 320 of the Code of Criminal Procedure, 1973. But the court has in one case drawn the attention of the legislature to the desirability of providing some reduction in punishment as incentive for making voluntary truthful confessional statement.[36] By the Criminal Law (Amendment) Act, 2005 (Act 2 of 2006), the Code of Criminal Procedure has been amended and Chapter XXIA has now been added to permit plea bargaining for offences other than those for which the punishment of death or of imprisonment for life or of imprisonment for a term exceeding seven years has been prescribed. Plea bargaining is also not permitted, where the offence affects the socio-economic condition of the country or has been committed against a woman or child below the age of fourteen years.

There is no general principle in commonwealth countries including India that unlawfully obtained evidence is not evidence.[37] But the investigatory technique of providing an opportunity to the accused for committing the crime though not a defence may in a particular case be so seriously improper even in a drug related offence, where more latitude is given to law enforcement agencies,[38] as to bring the administration of justice into disrepute or may in other words bring about 'a state created crime' which is unacceptable and the court in such a situation will stay the proceedings and release the accused.[39] It can also be said that such a conduct of police or the investigating agency may contravene the principle of fair procedure implicit in Article 21 of the Constitution and Article 9 of the International Covenant on Civil and Political Rights 1966. The Supreme Court of India also strongly disapproved the practice of providing bribe money by the police in entrapment cases and of a magistrate becoming a witness of the offence in trap cases.[40]

---

35. *Ibid.* **See further** *Balaram Kumawat v. Union of India,* (2003) 7 SCC 628, p. 638 : AIR 2003 SC 3268 : (2003) 106 DLT 392 (In matters involving economic crime, food offence and other cases, the doctrine of plea bargaining should not be allowed.)

36. *Gurdeep Singh v. State,* AIR 1999 SC 3646, pp. 3654, 3655 : (2000) 1 SCC 498. The doctrine of plea negotiation as prevalent in USA is also advocated to reduce the number of pending criminal cases in India: '*Strengthening Administration of Justice*', *J.D. KAPPOR, Judge Delhi High Court,* 2002 AIR Journal 88.

37. All cases in footnote 46 p. 981.

38. See page 708 text and note 41.

39. *R v. Looseley,* (2001) 4 All E R 897 (H.L.) paras 19, 25, 30, 31; *R v. . Jones,* (2007) 4 All ER 112 [The police officer's involvement was limited to providing an opportunity and to provide the evidence of the offence which was not objectionable]. **See further** text and note 55, p. 711.

40. *Shiv Bahadur Singh v. State of Vindhya Pradesh,* AIR 1954 SC 322 : 1954 SCR 1098 (In this case the offence would not have been committed had the bribe money not been provided by the police. The Supreme Court noted this fact but did not quash the proceedings.

[Footnote No. 40 Contd.]

If a person is exonerated on merits in adjudication proceedings which are of civil nature under Foreign Exchange Regulation Act, 1973 and allegations are found to be unsustainable at all, criminal prosecution on the same set of facts would be unjust and abuse of process of court.[41]

The original reason of the rule of strict construction, which was to mitigate the tyranny of monstrous sentences for trivial offences, cannot now be apt for supporting the rule in a modern State but another justification for its existence has grown up. The output of statutory laws in modern times has steadily increased and every conceivable aspect of human activity is being fast brought within statutory control. This has led to the widening of the area of offences which are defined not only by Acts of the Legislature but are also supplemented by rules, regulations and statutory orders. The existence of the rule of strict construction in its "true and sober sense" as now understood can be justified so that the present-day growth of criminal laws "will not become traps for honest, unlearned (in the law) and unwary men."[42] Stressing the same need LIVINGSTON HALL has stated: "As the boundaries of crime have been extended to include more and more conduct made criminal only because in seeming conflict with some vague ideal of social policy, or to reach some potential evil in an indirect manner, the need for a clear and comprehensive statement of the prohibited acts has become increasingly pressing. A canon of strict construction, limiting the statute to its obvious meaning, and excluding potentialities, perhaps implicit to the Legislature, but uncertain of application to the uninformed reader, does much to prevent injustice."[43] FRIEDMANN[44] also finds no justification for throwing out the strict construction principle lock, stock and barrel in so far as it serves the reasonable protection of citizens from arbitrary punishment. According to him the guiding principles are: "(1) It is

[Footnote No. 40 Contd.]

To legitimize actions of law enforcement officers in procuring evidence of commission of crime which would otherwise be unlawful and may not be admissible, the response in Australia is the enactment of Law Enforcement (Controlled Operation) Act 1997 (NSW) and similar other laws. On their application and interpretation **see** *Gedeon v. Commissioner of New South Wales Crime Commission*, (2008) 82 ALJR 1465.

41. *Radheshyam Kejariwal v. State of West Bengal*, (2011) 3 SCC 581 : (2011) 2 JT 443.

42. *Seksaria Cotton Mills v. State of Bombay*, AIR 1953 SC 278, p. 282, (BOSE, J.) : 1953 SCR 825. **See further** *Avais v. Hartford Social Club Ltd.*, (1969) 1 All ER 130, p. 135 : (1969) 2 AC 1 : (1969) 2 WLR 108 (HL); *State of Bihar v. Bhagirath*, AIR 1973 SC 2198, p. 2200 : (1973) 2 SCC 257. (The law must be expressed with such clarity and certainty as to give reasonably precise and adequate guidance to those who want to be law abiding).

43. The Substantive Law of Crimes by LIVINGSTON HALL (1936-37) 50 Harvard Law Review 616, p. 638.

44. FRIEDMANN, Law in a Changing Society (2nd Edition), p. 82.

beyond the province of the courts to create basically new offences. These are properly the province of the Legislature. (2) Where a court is faced with conflicting interpretations of the language of a statute, either of which is compatible with reasonable canons of construction, it must balance the legislative purpose of the statute, in the light of the object matter and the policies at stake, with the principle that a person should not be convicted of an offence which he can reasonably regard as a non-criminal action."[45] But undue emphasis on either the liberty of the individual or security and order in the society to which the Act is directed is not required for that "would impede harmony and hamper public good as well as disturb social weal and peace. To keep the weal balanced must be the prime duty of the judiciary."[46] So in interpreting and applying a penal statute, it has to be borne in mind that respect for human rights of the accused is not the only value at stake. "The purpose of the criminal law is to permit everyone to go about their daily lives without fear of harm to person or property. And it is in the interest of everyone that serious crime should be effectively investigated and prosecuted. There must be fairness to all sides. In a criminal case this requires the court to consider triangulation of interests. It involves taking into consideration the position of the accused, the victim and his or her family, and the public."[47] Therefore, in ensuring a fair trial in a criminal case "it will not be correct to say that it is only the accused who must be fairly dealt with." The society at large and the victims or their family members and relatives have a right to be dealt with fairly. "Denial of fair trial is as much injustice to the accused as is to the victims or the society."[48]

---

45. *Ibid*, p. 83.

46. *Aslam Babalal Desai v. State of Maharashtra*, AIR 1993 SC 1, pp. 19, 20 : (1992) 4 SCC 272.

47. *Attorney General's Referene (No. 3 of 1999)*, (2001) 1 All ER 577, p. 584 (HL) [There is no general principle in commonwealth countries that unlawfully obtained evidence is not admissible (pp. 585, 586). In this case DNA samples and finger prints illegally retained were used for investigation. The law was later amended to permit retention of DNA samples and finger prints taken even from parsons who are not convicted. This power of retention on challenge was held to be compatible with convention right to privacy: *R. (on the application of S. v. Chief Constable of South Yorkshire*, (2004) 4 All ER 193 (HL)]. In India also the same rule applies that there is no general principle that unlawfully obtained evidence is not admissible: *Pooran Mal v. Director of Inspection*, (1994) 1 SCC 345 : AIR 1974 SC 348 (Constitution Bench); *State v. M.T. Joy Immaculate*, AIR 2004 SC 2282, pp. 2289, 2290 : (2004) 5 SCC 729; *K.M. Malkham v. State of Maharashtra*, AIR 1973 SC 157. But the statute may expressly or by necessary implication provide for exclusion of unlawfully obtained evidence: *R. v. Sargent,* (2002) 1 All ER 161, pp. 166, 168, 171 (HL). For more information about DNA tests see NIDHI TANDAN 'Journey from one cell to Another—Role of DNA Evidence', (2004) 8 SCC 17(J).

48. *Zahira Habibullah H. Sheikh v. State of Gujarat*, AIR 2004 SC 3114, pp. 3125, 3126 : (2004) 4 SCC 158.

The content of the rule and its limits, in the sense now understood, may be summed up in the following propositions:

(1) If the prohibitory words in their known signification cover only some class of persons or some well-defined activity, their import cannot be extended to cover other persons or other activity on considerations of policy or object of the statute.[49]

(2) If the prohibitory words are reasonably capable of having a wider as also a narrower meaning and if there is no indication in the statute or in its policy or object that the words were used in the wider sense, they would be given the narrower meaning.[50] In other words where *after full consideration* it is found that the prohibitory words are equally open to two constructions, one of which covers the subject and the other does not, the benefit of construction will be given to the subject.[51]

(3) If the prohibitory words in their known signification can reasonably bear a wider meaning which promotes the object or policy of the statute, the words will receive that wider meaning and their import will not be restricted even if when construed literally they bear a narrower meaning.[52]

---

49. *London & North Eastern Railway Co. v. Berriman*, (1946) 1 All ER 255 : 1946 AC 278 (HL); *London Pty. Investment Co. v. A.G.*, (1953) 1 All ER 436; *Fisher v. Bell*, (1960) 3 All ER 731; *Re, HPC Productions Ltd.*, (1960) 3 All ER 731; *W.H. King v. Republic of India*, AIR 1952 SC 156 : 1952 SCR 418; *Tolaram v. State of Bombay*, AIR 1954 SC 496 : (1955) 1 SCR 158; *Shanti Prasad Jain v. Director of Enforcement*, AIR 1962 SC 1764 : 1963 (2) SCR 297.

50. *Dyke v. Elliot*, (1872) LR 4 PC 184, p. 191; *Evans v. Cross*, (1938) 1 All ER 751, p. 753; *Seksaria Cotton Mills v. State of Bombay*, AIR 1953 SC 278, p. 282 : 1953 SCR 825; *State of U.P. v. Ramagya Sharma*, AIR 1966 SC 78, p. 80 : (1965) 3 SCR 161. **See further** *R. v. Clarke*, (1985) 2 All ER 777, p. 782 (HL) (The expression 'acting in execution of the Act' was construed to mean acting in performance of a duty imposed by the Act or a power conferred by the Act and not equivalent to 'acting in furtherance of the purpose of the Act'.)

51. *Tuck & Sons v. Priester*, (1887) 19 QBD 629, p. 645; *Remington v. Larchin*, (1921) All ER Rep 298, pp. 299, 300 (SCRUTTON, L.J.); *Rosenbaum v. Burgoyne*, (1964) 2 All ER 988, p. 991 (HL); *Tolaram v. State of Bombay*, AIR 1954 SC 496, pp. 498, 499 : 1955 (1) SCR 158; *State of M.P. v. Azad Bharat Finance*, AIR 1967 SC 276 : 1966 Supp SCR 473; *Director of Public Prosecutions v. Schildkamp*, (1969) 3 All ER 1640, pp. 1642, 1643, 1654 : 1971 AC 1 (HL); *R. v. Allen*, (1985) 2 All ER 641, p. 643 (HL).

52. *Dyke v. Elliot*, (1872) 4 PC 184, p. 191; *Elmdene Estates Ltd. v. White*, (1960) 1 All ER 306 (HL); *M.V. Joshi v. M.U. Shimpi*, AIR 1961 SC 1494 : (1961) 3 SCR 986; *M.N. Narayan v. State of Kerala*, AIR 1963 SC 1116 : 1963 Supp (2) SCR 724; *Kanwar Singh v. Delhi Administration*, AIR 1965 SC 871 : 1965 (1) SCR 7; *Asstt. Collector of Customs v. Sitaram*, AIR 1966 SC 955, p. 965 : (1966) 2 SCR 1; *State of Mysore v. Syed Ibrahim*, AIR 1967 SC 1424, p. 1425 : (1967) 2 SCR 673; *Swantraj v. State of Maharashtra*, AIR 1974 SC 517, p. 520 : (1975) 3 SCC 322; *Attorney-General's Reference (No. 1 of 1988)*, (1989) 2 All ER 1 (HL).

(4) If the literal reading of the prohibitory words produces an unintelligible or non-sensual or socially harmful result, but the statute read as a whole gives out its meaning clearly, effect will be given to that meaning by curing a mere defect in phraseology[53] and even by rejecting words as surplusage.[54]

(b) Illustrative cases

The Railway Employment (Prevention of Accident) Act, 1900, gave power to the Board of Trade to make rules 'with the object of reducing or removing the dangers and risks incidental to railway services' on certain subjects one of them being 'Protection to Permanent Way-men, when relaying or repairing permanent Way'; and provided that a railway company acting in contravention of the rules shall be liable to a fine not exceeding £50 for each offence on conviction. One of the rules framed under the Act required the railway companies to provide persons or apparatus for giving warning of approaching train to workmen engaged in 'relaying or repairing' the permanent way. The question before the House of Lords[55] was whether a railway company was guilty of a breach of the statutory duty in not providing look-out precautions when some workmen, who were engaged in 'cleaning and oiling' an apparatus between the running lines, were knocked down and killed by an on-coming train. The House of Lords[56] decided that 'cleaning and oiling' was not embraced within the word 'repairing'; and that there was no breach of statutory duty on the part of the railway company. If the Act had not made provision for penalising railways for contravention of the rules the decision probably would have been otherwise.

---

53. *R. v. Oakes*, (1959) 2 All ER 92, pp. 95, 96; *Chief Inspector of Mines v. Karam Chand Thapar,* AIR 1961 SC 838 : (1962) 1 SCR 9. **See further** *Wiltshire v. Barret*, (1965) 2 All ER 271 (Power to arrest without warrant 'a person committing an offence' was interpreted to mean a power to arrest 'a person apparently committing an offence'; arrest may be justified notwithstanding that the suspected offence was not in fact committed); *Walker v. Lovell*, (1975) 2 All ER 10, pp. 15, 16 (HL) (Power to arrest a person 'committing an offence' can be exercised if the police officer has reasonable cause for suspecting that the offence has been committed. The case also explains 'reasonable cause'.) *Wills v. Bowley*, (1982) 2 All ER 654 : (1983) 1 AC 57 (HL).

54. *McMonagle v. Westminster City Council*, (1990) 1 All ER 993 (HL). (For this case, **see** Chapter 2, title (1)(d)(ii), p. 80). *R. v. R.*, (1991) 4 All ER 481, p. 489 (h) : (1990) 2 AC 716 (HL) (For this case, **see** text and note 18, p. 266).

55. *London & North Eastern Railway v. Berriman*, (1946) 1 All ER 255 : 1946 AC 278 (HL). For formulation of the rule of strict construction in this case, **see** text and notes 3 to 6, pp. 932, 933.

56. *Ibid.*

The Defence General Regulations, 1939, prohibited the carrying out of certain work 'except in so far as there is in force in respect thereof a licence granted by the minister'; and provided that in case of contravention of the regulation 'the person at whose expense the work is executed', and the person undertaking the execution, shall each be guilty of an offence. The Court of Appeal in construing these regulations referred to the rule of strict construction, and held that the regulation was not contravened if the work executed was covered by a licence although not in the name of the person at whose expense the work was executed.[57]

Under the Borrowing (Control and Guarantees) Act, 1956, and the regulations made thereunder, certain forms of Borrowing 'including the making of any arrangement by which the whole or any part of the price of any property is allowed to remain unpaid', were prohibited except with the permission of the Treasury and a breach of the regulations was punishable as an offence. UPJOHN, J. in construing the regulations, referred to the rule of strict construction applicable to penal as also taxing statutes, and held that a transaction under which property was sold in consideration of debenture stock secured by a debenture trust deed was not borrowing hit by the regulations.[58]

The Exchange Control Act, 1947, prohibited any person resident in United Kingdom, other than an authorised dealer, to 'borrow' foreign currency outside United Kingdom from any person other than an authorised dealer, and a breach of the restriction was made punishable as an offence. PLOWMAN, J. in construing these provisions applied the rule of strict construction applicable to penal and taxing Acts and held that when at the request of *A*, a resident in United Kingdom, *B* made payments of foreign currency in New York and Paris to persons not accountable to *A*, the arrangement was not a transaction of borrowing by *A* from *B* and was not hit by the provisions in question. It was pointed out that the word 'borrow' was not equivalent to raising of money or grant of any financial accommodation but would only apply to those cases where the legal relationship of lender and borrower was estalished, and that 'any reasoning based on the substance of the transaction' was inapplicable to the case of a penal as in the case of a taxing statute.[59]

The Restriction of Offensive Weapons Act, 1959, which provides for punishment of any person who 'sells or offers for sale' a knife of a particular

57. *Woolfe v. Wester*, (1951) 1 All ER 635, pp. 641, 642; COHEN, L.J., referred to the rule laid down by LORD SIMONDS in *Berriman's* case note 27, p. 985, *supra*.
58. *London Pty. Investment Co. v. A.G.*, (1953) 1 All ER 436, pp. 441 to 443.
59. *Re, HPC Productions Ltd.*, (1962) 1 All ER 37, pp. 48-51.

description, was held not to have been contravened by a shopkeeper who displayed in his shop window a knife with a price ticket. LORD PARKER, C.J. in delivering the judgment of the court construed the words 'offer for sale' as not embracing 'exposure for sale' although he confessed that he came to that conclusion reluctantly for there was no possible reason why, when the Act in terms prohibited 'manufacturing, selling, hiring, offering for sale or hire, lending, or giving to any person' the knife of a particular description the exposure for sale of such knife should not have been intended to be prohibited.[60]

In an another case,[61] a secretary of a club was convicted for allowing the club premises to be used for the purpose of gaming by means of a gaming machine otherwise than in accordance with section 17(2)(b) of the Betting and Gaming Act, 1960, which makes it a condition 'that the stake, required to be hazarded in order to play the game once, does not exceed six pence'. The machine could be played by inserting one six pence or more sixpence up to five. The House of Lords in reversing the conviction held that the word 'required' in section 17(2)(b) referred to the minimum stake and since a single six pence could operate the machine, the provision was not contravened although it was possible to insert more than a single six pence at any one time. The result was reached having regard to the fact that the statute in question was a penal statute. LORD EVERSHED observed: "It has been well settled that the terms of a statute imposing penalties must be construed strictly and if the meaning of the words used is doubtful the doubt should be resolved in favour of the subject."[62]

Section 1(1) of the Road Safety Act, 1967, provides that if a person drives a motor vehicle on a road 'having consumed alcohol in such a quantity that the proportion thereof in his blood, as ascertained from a laboratory test for which he subsequently provides a specimen under section 3 of this Act, exceeds the prescribed limit at the time he provides the specimen', he shall be liable for an offence. A person was involved in an accident. Immediately thereafter, he went to a nearby public house and consumed three pegs of whisky. Blood test disclosed 159 milligramms of alcohol per 100 millilitres of blood. Expert evidence was led to show that even if there had been no post-driving consumption of liquor, the analysis of specimen would have shown presence of alcohol beyond the prescribed

---

60. *Fisher v. Bell*, (1960) 3 All ER 731, p. 733. **See further** *British Car Auctions Ltd. v. Wright*, (1972) 3 All ER 462 (An auctioneer cannot be convicted of 'offering to sell' for he merely invites those present to make offers to buy).

61. *Rosenbaum v. Burgoyne*, (1964) 2 All ER 988 : 1986 AC 281 : (1985) 1 WLR 1126 (HL).

62. *Ibid*, p. 991.

minimum. It was held that the section ruled out any other method except the laboratory test in which the proportion of alcohol in the blood was to be determined, and therefore the expert evidence was not admissible. On this view the accused was acquitted. In that connection LORD GUEST observed: "We were pressed by the Crown that if the respondent's contention were right it would leave a loophole in the Act through which the 'hipflask' driver as he has been described would escape. This may be so, but if the Act is not water-tight then it is for Parliament and not the courts to supply the omission."[63] And LORD REID on the same point said: "In my judgment this is a case of real doubt so that we must adopt the construction most favourable to the accused, leaving it to Parliament, if so advised, to put the matter right."[64] The matter was set right and the loophole closed some ten years after in 1981 by omission of the words 'as ascertained from a laboratory test for which he subsequently provides a specimen under section 3 of this Act.'[65]

Section 19 of the Bombay Rents, Hotels and Lodging Houses Rates (Control) Act, 1947, prohibited a tenant 'to claim or receive any sum or consideration as a condition for the relinquishment of his tenancy of any premises', and made provision for punishment of the tenant contravening the prohibition. The Supreme Court construed this section strictly "in favour of the subject"; and held that an assignment of tenancy by a tenant for consideration in favour of a third person did not come within the prohibition, and that the relinquishment contemplated under the section was equivalent to surrender of tenancy in favour of the lessor.[66]

Section 18 of the same Bombay Act provided that 'if any landlord receives any fine, premium or other like sum or deposit or any consideration other than the standard rent in respect of the grant, renewal or continuance of a lease of any premises such landlord shall be punished'. On a question of construction of this section the Supreme Court held that the section envisaged the existence of a lease and the payment in respect thereof, and

---

63. *Rowlands v. Hamillton*, (1971) 1 WLR 647, p. 654 (HL).

64. *Ibid*, p. 650. For a case of breath test for alcohol, **see** *Fox v. Chief Constable of Gwent*, (1985) 3 All ER 392 (HL).

65. *Gumbley v. Cunningham*, (1989) 1 All ER 5, p. 8 : (1989) AC 281 : (1989) 2 WLR 1 (HL). (Back-tracking evidence is now admissible to show the blood-alcohol concentration at the time of driving). For procedure to be followed in requiring driver to provide specimen of blood or urine under the Road Traffic Act, 1988, **see** *Director of Public Prosecutions v. Warren*, (1992) 1 All ER 865 : (1993) AC 319 : (1992) 3 WLR 814 (HL); *Director of Public Prosecutions v. Jackson,* (1998) 3 All ER 769 (HL). **See further** an Australian case on similar legislation: *Thompson v. His Honour Judge Byrne,* (1999) 73 ALJR 642 (Aust).

66. *W.H. King v. Republic of India*, AIR 1952 SC 156, p. 158 : 1952 SCR 418.

did not prohibit the taking of money by owner of an incomplete building in consideration of binding himself by an oral agreement to grant a lease on completion of the building to the person from whom the money was taken.[67] Section 1(1)(b) of the Accommodation Agencies Act, 1953, enacted that any person who 'demands or accepts payment of any sum or money in consideration of supplying, or undertaking to supply, to any person addresses or other particulars of houses to let' shall be guilty of an offence. In construing this section it was held that the section was directed to prevent charges being made just for supplying addresses and that if payment is made for finding out acceptable accommodation of which the person making the payment becomes a tenant no offence is committed.[68]

In pursuance of a notification issued by the Government of India under the Essential Supplies (Temporary Powers) Act, 1947, manufacturers of cotton cloth were required to submit true and accurate information relating to their undertakings in accordance with a printed form containing amongst other details a column headed 'Full name and address of person to whom delivered', delivery being defined as 'physical delivery' of cloth but not cloth in 'physical possession of the seller'. A contravention of the notification was punishable under the Act. Interpreting the form and the notification the Supreme Court held that a return submitted by a manufacturer showing delivery of bales to a *del credere* agent was a sufficient compliance of the notification and that the information supplied cannot be held to be untrue on the theory that the principal continued in legal possession of the bales although put under the control of the agents.[69]

Clause 7 of the Iron and Steel (Control) Order, 1956, which provides that any person acquiring iron or steel 'shall not use' the same otherwise than in accordance with any condition contained in the document under which it is acquired, was held not to have been contravened by mere non-user.[70]

On the principle that penal provisions are strictly construed, contravention of conditions of a licence granted under a Statutory Order cannot be construed as contravention of the Order resulting in penal consequences, unless the Order itself provides that the licensee shall comply with all the conditions of the licence.[71] Similarly contravention of Rules made under

---

67. *Tolaram v. State of Bombay*, AIR 1954 SC 496, p. 499 : (1955) 1 SCR 158.
68. *Saunders v. Soper*, (1974) 3 All ER 1025 (HL).
69. *Seksaria Cotton Mills v. State of Bombay*, AIR 1953 SC 278 : 1953 SCR 825.
70. *State of U.P. v. Ramagya Sharma*, AIR 1966 SC 78 : (1965) 3 SCR 161.
71. *East India Commercial Co. v. Collector of Customs*, AIR 1962 SC 1893 : 1963 (3) SCR 338; *Abdul Aziz v. State of Maharashtra*, AIR 1963 SC 1470 : 1964 (1) SCR 830; *State of West Bengal v. Motilal*, AIR 1966 SC 1586 : (1966) 3 SCR 933; *Boothalinga Agencies v. VTC Poriaswami*, AIR 1969 SC 110 : 1969 (1) SCR 65. **See further** *Addl. Collector, Customs v. Best & Co.*, AIR 1971 SC 170 : (1970) 3 SCC 136.

an Act may not be construed as contravention of the Act unless the Act specifically so provides.[72]

Section 4(1) of the Foreign Exchange Regulation Act, 1947, provides that subject to certain conditions, no person resident in India shall outside India buy or borrow from, or sell or lend to or exchange with, any person any foreign exchange. In settlement of certain contracts with a person resident in India certain German Firms paid foreign currency to the account of the Indian in a bank in Germany on conditions that the account could only be operated for paying to those German Firms, price of new machineries to be purchased from them by the Indian, after obtaining import licence from the Indian Government. The Supreme Court on these facts held that the deposit being a contingent deposit there was no present debt and no relationship of creditor and debtor between the Indian and the German bank and that the bank held the money as a sort of stake-holder and therefore the transaction did not amount to lending of foreign exchange prohibited under the Act.[73]

Section 7 of the Official Secrets Act, 1920, provides: 'Any person who attempts to commit any offence under the principle Act (Act of 1911) or this Act, or solicits or incites or endeavours to persuade another person to commit an offence, or aids or abets and does any act preparatory to the commission of an offence under the principal Act (Act of 1911) or this Act shall be guilty of—'. In the above section the words 'and does any act preparatory to the commission of an offence' were held to be unintelligible on a reading of 'and', as 'and', therefore, 'and' was read as 'or' and a comma was read after the words 'preparatory to' making the relevant words read:—'or aids or abets or does any act preparatory to, the commission'. This course was adopted even though the altered reading produced a result less favourable to the subject and was justified on the ground that intention of the Parliament being "quite clear" the court could cure a mere "faultiness in expression."[74]

By section 2(1) of the Landlord and Tenant Act, 1949, it was enacted that: 'A person shall not, as a condition of the grant, renewal or continuance of a tenancy require the payment of any premium in addition to rent'; and by section 18(2), 'premium' was defined to include any fine or other like sum and any other pecuniary consideration in addition to rent. The landlord of a flat offered a tenancy on the tenant undertaking to sell a

---

72. *M.D. Shukla v. State of Gujarat*, AIR 1971 SC 116 : (1970) 1 SCC 352.

73. *Shanti Prasad Jain v. Director of Enforcement*, AIR 1962 SC 1764 : 1963 (2) SCR 297. **See further** *Ramratan v. Director of Enforcement*, AIR 1966 SC 495 : 1966 (1) SCR 651; (depositing in bank is not lending foreign exchange).

74. *R. v. Oakes*, (1959) 2 All ER 92, pp. 95, 96 (CCA).

house of his own to a third person at £500 less than its fair market value. The transaction having gone through the question before the House of Lords was whether the landlord had required the payment of £500 as premium as a condition of the grant of a tenancy within section 2(1) of the Act. The House of Lords held that according to the language of the section, it was not necessary for a premium to fall within it that it should be payable to the landlord or to some one on his behalf and such a qualification could not be read in that Act even though it imposed a penalty for the breach of its provisions, and that, therefore, the transaction in question fell within the prohibition of the section.[75] Section 85(1) of the Rent Act, 1968 which corresponds to section 2(1) of the Landlord and Tenant Act, 1949, provides that 'any person who as a condition of the grant, renewal or continuance of a protected tenancy requires in addition to the rent, the payment of any premium—shall be guilty of an offence'. In construing this section, the House of Lords held that the expression 'any person' is not limited to landlords and that a premium obtained by an outgoing tenant as a condition of procuring the landlord to grant new lease to an incoming tenant is within the prohibition of the section.[76]

By section 25(3)(a) of the Income-tax Act, 1952, a person filing an incorrect return, if proceeded against by action in court, was liable 'to forfeit £20 and treble the tax which he ought to be charged under this Act'. Construing this provision the House of Lords held that the phrase 'treble the tax which he ought to be charged under this Act' clearly meant 'treble the whole tax which the tax-payer ought to be charged for the relevant year' and not 'treble the tax with which the tax-payer has not been charged by reason of his defective return' or 'treble the tax appropriate to the undisclosed income'. Although the result so reached was oppressive, the construction was supported on the ground that the words in the Act were clear and had to be given their full effect.[77]

By section 1 of the Criminal Justice (Temporary Provision) Act (Northern Ireland), 1970, it was provided that 'any person, who is convicted of an offence, committed during the period of present emergency, under any of the statutory provisions mentioned in column 1 of the Schedule, shall,

---

75. *Elmdene Estates Ltd. v. White*, (1960) 1 All ER 306, p. 309 (HL). **See further** *Vithal Krishnaraj Nivendkar v. Panduman Ram Singh*, (1963) 1 SCR 63 : (1964) 1 Cr LJ 491, where construing a similar provision of a Bombay Act, it was held that donation taken by President of the *Sangh* as consideration for granting lease of a building belonging to the *Sangh* made him guilty of the offence under the Act.

76. *Farrel v. Alexander*, (1976) 2 All ER 721 (HL).

77. *IRC v. Hinchy*, (1960) 1 All ER 505 (HL); referred to with **approval** in *Mansukhlal v. CIT, Bombay*, AIR 1969 SC 835, p. 838 : 1969 (1) SCR 970.

notwithstanding anything to the contrary contained in that or in any other statutory provision, be sentenced to imprisonment for not less than the period specified opposite that provision in column 2 of the Schedule II'. The question that arose was whether a court sentencing an accused under the aforesaid provision had power to suspend the sentence and release the accused on probation under section 18 of the Treatment of Offenders Act, 1968. Having regard to the mischief at which the Act was aimed, *i.e.*, to ensure greater uniformity of sentences and to deter further outbreaks of violence, it was held that the court had no power to award suspended sentence and the words in the section 'shall be sentenced to imprisonment' for a specified period, meant that the accused be punished by sending him to prison.[78]

Section 232(2) of the Road Traffic Act, 1960, provides: 'Where the driver of a vehicle is alleged to be guilty of an offence to which this section applies—(a) the owner of the vehicle shall give such information as to the identity of the driver as he may be required to give; and (b) any other person shall, if required as aforesaid, give any information which it is in his power to give and may lead to the identification of the driver'. A driver who had committed some road traffic offence was after some days required to give information under the above provision and he claimed that he was not bound to furnish the information sought on a correct reading of this section. On a prosecution for contravention of section 232(2) the question for consideration was whether in clause (b) 'any other person' meant 'any person other than the driver' or 'any person other than the owner'. The court felt no difficulty in holding that by 'any other person' in clause (b) what was meant was 'any person other than the owner' and therefore, information could be sought from the driver himself who may have earlier committed the offence for which the information was required. The contention that by such a reading the section would affect a common law right by subjecting a person to answer questions which may incriminate him was rejected, as according to the court the language was unambiguous and the contrary construction produced non-sensual result.[79]

A penal enactment requiring that the driver of a motor vehicle concerned or involved in an accident 'shall stop' and if required so to do by any person, give his name, address etc., was interpreted reasonably and it was held that 'stop' did not mean a mere momentary pause and in the context meant that the driver of the motor vehicle should stop the vehicle and remain where he has stopped it for a reasonable time as will provide a

---

78. *Kennedy v. Spratt*, (1971) 2 WLR 667 : (1971) 1 All ER 805 : 1972 AC 83 (HL).
79. *Brougham v. Bruce*, (1962) 1 All ER 136, p. 138.

sufficient period to enable persons to require of him the information, *i.e.*, names, addresses etc.[80]

Section 2(1) of the Road Traffic Act, 1967, provides that 'a constable in uniform may require any person driving or attempting to drive a motor vehicle on a road or other public place to provide a specimen of breath test there or nearby, if the constable has reasonable cause: (a) to suspect him of having alcohol in his body, or (b) to suspect him of having committed a traffic offence while the vehicle was in motion'. Construing this section it has been held that the driving or attempted driving did not have to be exactly contemporaneous with the requirement to provide a specimen of breath and a person could be required to provide a specimen even though, at the moment when the requirement was made he had ceased driving or attempting to drive; provided that the sequence of events between the observed driving or attempted driving and the requirement to provide the specimen followed on each other so closely as to form a continuous sequence.[81] It is to be noticed that if the section were to be read literally, it would mean that the constable could only require the breath test if the person was actually driving or attempting to drive something which is obviously impossible.

Section 76 of the Mines Act, 1952, before its amendment by Act 62 of 1959 provided: 'Where the owner of a mine is a firm or other association of individuals, any one of the partners or members thereof or where the owner of a mine is a public company, any one of the directors thereof, or where the owner of a mine is a private company, the share-holders thereof, may be prosecuted and punished under this Act for any offence for which the owner of a mine is punishable'. An interesting question that arose before the Supreme Court was: whether the words 'anyone of' meant 'only one of' or 'everyone of'. The court having regard to 'the scheme and object of the statute' preferred the latter meaning in spite of the fact that the words were held to be capable of both the meanings in different context and here they occurred in a penal enactment.[82]

In construing section 167(81) of the Sea Customs Act, 1878 the Supreme Court has held that the section applies not only to a person who might be concerned in smuggling but also to a person who deals with

---

80. *Lee v. Knapp*, (1966) 3 All ER 961.
81. *Sakhuja v. Allen*, (1972) 2 All ER 311 (HL).
82. *Chief Inspector of Mines v. Karam Chand Thapar*, AIR 1961 SC 838, pp. 846 to 848 : 1962 (1) SCR 9.
N.B.—By the amending Act 62 of 1959 the words 'anyone of' have been replaced by the words 'all or any of'.

smuggled goods after the smuggling is over, and if, such a person has this knowledge that the goods are smuggled, he has also the intent to avoid the prohibition or restriction or defraud the Government duty payable thereon. In accepting the wider construction the court pointed out that a narrower construction would leave a lacuna in the Act, which is meant to prevent smuggling and its object will be completely defeated.[83]

Appendix B, Rule A 11.05 framed under the Prevention of Food Adulteration Act, 1954, defined 'butter' to mean 'the product prepared exclusively from the milk or cream of cow or buffalo or both'. In interpreting these rules the Supreme Court felt no doubt in holding that butter prepared from curd, *i.e.,* soured milk and cream also fell within the definition, and an appeal to the rule of strict construction was negatived on the ground that the court was bound to accept the expressed intention when the words were clear and plain.[84]

In another case before the Supreme Court, section 5(1)(d) of the Prevention of Corruption Act, 1947, came up for construction, which reads: 'A public servant is said to commit the offence of criminal misconduct in the discharge of his duty—(d) if he, by corrupt or illegal means or by otherwise abusing his position as a public servant, obtains for himself or for any other person any valuable things or pecuniary advantage'. The argument before the court was that construing the sub-section strictly, clause (d) did not cover the case of a benefit which was not derived from a third person, but was derived by causing loss to the Government by abuse of power. The contention was negatived on the ground that the comprehensive language used in the clause covered such a benefit and that the wide meaning of the language could not be limited by construction as it well accorded with the spirit of the statute.[85]

Section 15 of the Forward Contracts (Regulation) Act, 1952, makes illegal forward contracts for the sale or purchase of notified goods in notified area except contracts entered into between or through members of a recognised association. Certain breaches connected with section 15 are made punishable by section 21. Forward contract is defined as a contract for the delivery of goods at a future date and which is not a ready delivery contract. Ready delivery contract is defined as a contract which provides for delivery of goods and the payment of a price therefor, either immediately or within such period not exceeding eleven days after the date of contract.

---

83. *Collector of Customs v. Sitaram*, AIR 1966 SC 955, p. 965 : 1966 (2) SCR 1.
84. *M.V. Joshi v. M.U. Shimpi*, AIR 1961 SC 1494, p. 1498 : 1961 (3) SCR 986.
85. *M. Narayanan Nambiar v. State of Kerala*, AIR 1963 SC 1116, pp. 1117 to 1119 : 1963 Supp (2) SCR 724.

It was argued before the Supreme Court that what is prohibited by section 15 is Forward Contract and not purely wagering contract in which parties do not intend to deliver goods; and that the definition of Forward Contract should be construed literally including only such contract in which parties intend to take actual delivery of goods. Rejecting this contention and in holding that speculative transactions which are ostensibly for delivery of goods fall within the prohibition of the Act, RAMASWAMI, J. observed: "If the expression 'forward contract' in section 2(e) is not construed so as to include speculative contracts which ostensibly are for delivery of goods the provisions of the Act would be rendered nugatory. The Act was passed in order to put a stop to undesirable forms of speculation in forward trading and to correct the abuses of certain forms of forward trading in the wide interest of the community and in particular in the interest of the consumer for whom adequate safeguards were essential. In our opinion, speculative contracts of the type covered in the present case are included within the purview of the Act."[86]

Sub-section (1) of section 18 of the Suppression of Immoral Traffic Act, 1956, authorises a magistrate to direct eviction of occupier of premises within a distance of two hundred yards of any public place if after notice and hearing the person concerned the Magistrate is satisfied that the premises are used as a brothel or for carrying on prostitution. Sub-section (2) of section 18 empowers a court convicting a person of any offence under section 3 or section 7 to pass orders under sub-section (1) without further notice to such person to show cause as required in that sub-section. It has been held[87] that sub-section (2) is not limited to premises within two hundred yards of any public place and it enables making of an order of eviction of the nature mentioned in sub-section (1) in respect of all premises in respect of which conviction is recorded under sections 3 and 7. This conclusion was reached on the ground that an offence under section 3 is not limited to premises situate within two hundred yards of a public place and sub-section (3) of that section terminates the lease or agreement after the conviction of the occupier and, therefore, it is legitimate to infer that power was conferred to eject such a person under sub-section (2) of section 18, an inference that promotes the purpose of cleansing houses of illfames. The court said that it reached its conclusion by broadening the dimensions of *Heydon's* case and importing a 'context-purpose' teleological approach.[88]

---

86. *Shivnarayan v. State of Madras*, AIR 1967 SC 986, p. 989 : 1967 (1) SCR 138.
87. *Chitan J. Vaswani v. State of West Bengal*, AIR 1975 SC 2473 : (1975) 2 SCC 829.
88. *Ibid*, p. 2476.

The definition of 'sale' in the Prevention of Food Adulteration Act, 1954 has similarly been construed in a wide sense having regard to the mischief intended to be remedied. It has been held that 'sale' in the Act would include all commercial transactions whereunder an adulterated article of food is supplied for consumption by one person to another. Thus supply or offer of food by a hotelier to a customer when a consolidated charge is made for residence and other amenities including food falls within the definition of sale.[89]

Sections 1(3) and 1(4)(a) of the Company Securities (Insider Dealing) Act, 1985 prohibit an individual to deal on a recognised stock exchange in securities of a company if he 'knowingly obtained (directly or indirectly)' unpublished price sensitive information about a company from a person connected with the company. In a case before the House of Lords,[90] the accused had received confidential information from the bankers of a company that it was being taken over by another company. Possessed with this information the accused had purchased shares of the former company and after the announcement of take over made substantial profit. It was found that the accused had not directly or indirectly solicited information from the bankers of the company. The primary meaning of the word 'obtain' requires some request or effort on ones part for acquiring or getting but in its secondary sense it has a wider meaning of acquiring or getting without any qualification. The white paper preceding the legislation indicated that the mischief consisted of dealing in securities while in possession of confidential information and the Government proposed that any one who received information which was not generally available and which he knew to be price sensitive should be prohibited in dealing in securities. Having regard to the mischief discernible from the white paper and the object of the legislation, the House of Lords adopted the wider meaning of the word 'obtain' and held that the accused was guilty of the offence although he had not solicited the information.

Section 18(1) of the Fire-arm Act, 1968 provides: "It is an offence for a person to have with him a fire-arm—with intent to commit an indictable offence". In a case[91] the appellants were arrested in a premises where they had allegedly gone to commit robbery. They had parked their car at a distance of 50 yards from the premises. The car was found to contain three

---

89. *Municipal Corporation of Delhi v. Laxmi Narain Tandon*, AIR 1976 SC 621, p. 625 : 1976 (1) SCC 546. **Contrast** *State of Punjab v. Associated Hotels of India Ltd.*, AIR 1972 SC 1131 : (1971) 1 SCC 472, where in the context of a Sales Tax Act such a transaction was not held to be sale.

90. *Attorney-General's Reference (No. 1 of 1988)*, (1989) 2 All ER 1 : (1989) 2 WLR 729 (HL).

91. *R. v. Pawlicki,* (1993) 3 All ER 902, p. 907 : (1992) 1 WLR 827 : (1992) Crim LR 584 (CA).

sawn off shot guns and other items consistent with a planned robbery. The appellants were convicted under section 18(1) for having with them fire-arms with intent to commit robbery. The contention of the appellants was that considering the distance at which the car was parked the fire-arms were not immediately available to the appellants when they were arrested and it could not be said that they had with them the fire-arms lying in the car. Rejecting this contention the Court of Appeal applied a purposive approach and held that the emphasis must not be so much on exact distance between the criminals and their guns but rather on the accessibility of those guns judged in a common sense way and it was sufficient that the guns were readily accessible to them at a time when they were about to commit robbery. Section 17(2) of the same Act provides that if a person at the time of his committing an offence specified in schedule 1, has 'in his possession' a fire-arm or 'imitation fire-arm' he shall be guilty of an offence under that section. An imitation fire-arm is defined as 'anything which has the appearance of a fire-arm'. Construing these provisions of the Act with their object to protect victims presented with what they reasonably believed to be a fire-arm, it was held by the Court of Appeal that fingers placed inside a jacket with the appearance of a fire-arm could constitute an imitation firearm within section 17(2).[92] The House of Lords reversed this decision on the ground that "one cannot possess something which is not separate and distinct from one self" and that Parliament has not "created an offence of falsely pretending to have a fire-arm."[93]

Rule 40 of the Central Excise Rules makes it an offence for a wholesale purchaser of un-manufactured tobacco to receive or to have in his custody or possession non-duty paid tobacco, and provides that every such wholesale purchaser who receives or has in his custody or possession any such goods, in contravention of this rule, shall, in respect of every such offence, be liable to pay the duty leviable on such goods, and to a penalty which may extend to two thousand rupees and the goods shall also be liable to confiscation. In a case[94] before the Supreme Court, a wholesale purchaser of tobacco had received non-duty paid tobacco and had mixed the same with duty paid tobacco and separation of non-duty paid tobacco from the mixture was not possible. The question before the court was whether whole or any part of this mixture was liable to confiscation under the Rule. The court held that the rule being a penal provision it could not be extended to authorise confiscation of duty paid tobacco, and therefore, the entire

---

92. *R. v. Bentham*, (2004) 2 All ER 549 (CA).

93. *R. v. Bentham*, (2005) 2 All Er 65 (HL).

94. *Hari Chand Sarda v. Mizo District Council*, AIR 1967 SC 829, p. 832 : 1967 (1) SCR 1012.

tobacco mixture was not liable to confiscation. But it was also held that as no one should be permitted to benefit by his own wrong and as the rule should be construed to prevent its evasion, it was open to the authorities to confiscate such part of the mixture which reasonably represented the value of the entire non-duty paid tobacco.[1]

4. *MENS REA* IN STATUTORY OFFENCES

(a) General principles

Existence of a guilty intent is an essential ingredient of a crime at common law and the principle is expressed in the maxim—*Actus non facit reum nisi mens sit rea*.[2] The Legislature may, however, create an offence of strict liability where *mens rea* is wholly or partly not necessary.[3] Such a measure is resorted to in public interest and moral justification of laws of

---

1. *Ibid.*
2. *Mens rea* is the state of mind stigmatised as wrongful by the criminal law which when compounded with relevant prohibited conduct constitutes a particular crime. Crimes involving *mens rea* are of two types (i) crimes of basic intent and (ii) crimes of specific intent. In the former class of crimes, the *mens rea* does not go beyond the *actus reus*. In the second category of crimes *mens rea* goes beyond the contemplation of the prohibited act and foresight of its consequences and has a purposive element; *Director of Public Prosecutions v. Majewski*, (1976) 2 All ER 142, pp. 146, 147, 153, 155 (HL). *Mens rea* may mean different things in relation to different crimes: *Director of Public Prosecutions v. Morgan*, (1975) 2 All ER 347, p. 361 (HL). *Mens rea* refers to the criminality of the act in which the mind is engaged, not to its moral character. Absence of moral fault does not necessarily negative the necessary mental element of the offence: *R. v. Kingston*, (1994) 3 All ER 353, pp. 360, 361 (HL). A drug enforcement officer intending to participate in commission of the crime for breaking the drug ring under orders of superior officers has the necessary *mens rea* to be a co-conspirator although he may not be prosecuted if the plan succeeded for under the criminal law there was no general defence of superior orders or of Crown or Executive fiat: *Yip Chiu-Cheung v. R.*, (1994) 2 All ER 924 (PC). But the position is different when a law enforcement officer pretends to join a conspiracy to gain information without any intention of taking part in the planned crime. In such a case the officer lacks the necessary *mens rea* to be a co-conspirator: *R. v. Anderson*, (1985) 2 All ER 961, p. 965 (HL).
3. *Vane v. Yiannopoullos*, (1964) 3 All ER 820, p. 829 (HL); (letter F); *Warner v. Metropolitan Police Commr.*, (1968) 2 All ER 356, p. 360 (HL); *Sweet v. Parsley*, (1969) 1 All ER 347, p. 349 (HL); *R. v. Sheppard*, (1980) 3 All ER 899, p. 909 (HL); *R.S. Joshi v. Ajit Mills*, AIR 1997 SC 2279, p. 2287 : (1977) 4 SCC 98. In *R. v. Miller*, (1983) 1 All ER 978, p. 980 (HL) it was observed: (1) It would be conducive to clarity if instead of the latin expressions *actus reus* and *mens rea* one were to use the words conduct of the accused and his state of mind at the time of that conduct; (2) The General principles of criminal law, unless expressly modified or excluded, are intended to be applicable by Parliament to a statutory offence.

strict liability is well expressed by DEAN ROSCOE POUND: "Such statutes are not meant to punish the vicious will but to put pressure on the thoughtless and inefficient to do their whole duty in the interest of public health or safety or morals."[4] The offences falling under this class are known as 'public-welfare offences.'[5] Offences of strict liability do not violate the principle of fair procedure and the principle that everyone charged shall be presumed to be innocent until proved guilty according to law, which are guaranteed under international convention and covenant relating to Human Rights and are also implicit in Article 21 of the Constitution.[6]

"The absence of *mens rea* really consists in an honest and reasonable belief entertained by the accused of the existence of facts which, if true, would make the act charged against him innocent."[7] This traditional formulation of absence of *mens rea* requires that "an honest mistake by the defendant does not avail him unless the mistake was made on reasonable grounds."[8] But this traditional view now stands modified in so far as it requires that the mistaken belief of existence of facts must also be based on reasonable grounds. The prevailing view now is that "when *mens rea* is ousted by a mistaken belief, it is as well ousted by an unreasonable belief".[9] What is material to negative *mens rea* is "the defendants belief and not the grounds on which it is based."[10]

Since a person is presumed to know the law, its ignorance does not normally afford any defence under the criminal law; but if the law is not published in any manner whatsoever, to enable a person to find it out by

---

4. The spirit of the common law, DEAN ROSCOE POUND: p. 52; *Reynolds v. G.H. Austin & Sons Ltd.*, (1951) 1 All ER 606, p. 611; *Warner v. Metropolitan Police Commr., supra*, p. 364.

5. FREIDMANN, Law in a Changing Society, (2nd Edition), p. 202. **See further** *J.K. Industries Ltd. v. Chief Inspector of Factories and Boilers*, 1996 (7) Scale 247, p. 264 : 1996 (6) SCC 665 : 1996 (9) JT 27 : 1997 SCC (L&S) 1. ("Absolute offences are not criminal offences in any real sense but acts which are prohibited in the interest of welfare of the public and the prohibition is backed by sanction of penalty. Such offences are generally known as public welfare offences.")

6. Articles 6(1) and 6(2) of the European Convention and Articles 14(1) and 14(2) of the International Covenant; *R v G.*, (2008) 3 All E.R. 1071 (H.L.). para 4.

7. *Bank of New South Wales v. Piper*, (1897) AC 383, p. 389 (PC) referred to in *Reynolds v. G.H. Austin & Sons Ltd., supra*, p. 614; *Warner v. Metropolitan Police Commr., supra*, p. 998. **See further** *Sweet v. Parsby,* (1969) 1 All ER 347, p. 361 (HL) for similar observatons of LORD DIPLOCK.

8. *B. (a minor) v. Director of Public Prosecutions,* (2000) 1 All ER 833, p. 836(g) (HL).

9. *Ibid*, p. 837 (LORD NICHOLAS), p. 851 (LORD STEYN).

10. *R. v. Kimber,* (1983) 3 All ER 316, p. 319 : (1983) 1 WLR 1118 (LAWTON L.J.) approved in *B. (a minor) v. Director of Public Prosecutions, supra*, p. 837.

appropriate enquiry, the absence of knowledge of the prohibition may afford a defence of absence of *mens rea.*[11] But it is no defence that the accused acted on a mistaken interpretation of the statute which he honestly believed to be correct.[12]

When a statute creates an offence, the question whether the offence involves the existence of *mens rea* as an essential element of it or whether the statute dispenses with it and creates strict liability are questions which have to be answered on a true construction of the statute. The courts, however, regard it as a fundamental principle that an offence cannot be made out without the existence of *mens rea*, "unless from a consideration of the terms of the statute and other relevant circumstances it clearly appears that that must have been the intention of Parliament."[13] The formulations of the rule of construction which have been accepted by the Privy Council[14] and the Supreme Court[15] are those stated by WRIGHT, J. in *Sherras v. De Rutzen*,[16] and by GODDARD, C.J. in *Brend v. Wood*.[17] WRIGHT, J. expressed the rule in these words: "There is a presumption that *mens rea* an evil intention, or knowledge of the wrongfulness of the act, is an essential ingredient of every offence, but that presumption is liable to be displaced either by the words of the statute creating the offence or by the subject-matter with which it deals and both must be considered."[18] And, the formulation by GODDARD, C.J. is to the following effect: "It is of the utmost

---

11. *Lim Chin Aik v. Reginam*, (1963) 1 All ER 223, pp. 226, 227 (PC). **Contrast**—*State of Maharashtra v. M.H. George*, AIR 1965 SC 722, pp. 741 to 743 : (1965) 1 SCR 123. **Also see** *Mahajan Haria v. State*, AIR 1951 SC 467 : 1952 SCR 110.

12. *Dinesh Chandra Jamnadas Gandhi v. State of Gujarat*, AIR 1989 SC 1011, p. 1017.

13. *Vane v. Yiannopoullos*, (1964) 3 All ER 820, p. 823 (HL) (LORD REID); *Sweet v. Parsley*, (1969) 1 All ER 347, pp. 349, 350 (HL) (LORD REID). **See further** *R. v. Court*, (1988) 2 All ER 221, p. 228 : 1989 AC 28 (HL).

14. *Shriniwas Mal v. Emperor*, AIR 1947 PC 135, p. 139; *Lim Chin Aik v. Reginam*, (1963) 1 All ER 223, p. 228 (PC); *Patel v. Comptroller of Customs*, (1965) 3 All ER 593, p. 597 (PC); *Gammon (Hongkong) Ltd. v. Attorney-General of Hongkong*, (1984) 2 All ER 503, p. 507 : 1985 AC 1 : (1984) 3 WLR 437 (PC).

15. *Hari Prasad Rao v. State*, AIR 1951 SC 204, p. 206 : 1951 SCR 322; *Indo China Steam Navigation Co. v. Jasjit Singh*, AIR 1964 SC 1140, p. 1149 : 1964 (6) SCR 594; *State of Maharashtra v. M.H. George*, AIR 1965 SC 722, p. 736 : 1965 (1) SCR 123; *Nathulal v. State of M.P.*, AIR 1966 SC 43; *Inder Sain v. State of Punjab*, AIR 1973 SC 2309, pp. 2310, 2311 : (1973) 2 SCC 372; *Kartar Singh v. State of Punjab*, JT 1994 (2) SC 423, p. 464 : (1994) 3 SCC 569. **See further** *Peoples Union for Civil Liberties v. Union of India*, AIR 2004 SC 456, p. 474 : (2004) 9 SCC 580.

16. (1895) 1 QB 918, p. 921 : (1895-99) All ER Rep 1167, p. 1169.

17. (1946) 175 LT 306, p. 307.

18. *Sherras v. De Rutzen,* note 18, *supra*. **See further** *R. v. Court*, (1988) 2 All ER 221, p. 228 : (1989) AC 28 (HL). For this case **see also**, note 69, p. 1010, *post*.

importance for the protection of the liberty of the subject that a court should always bear in mind that unless a statute either clearly or by necessary implication rules out *mens rea* as a constituent part of a crime a defendant should not be found guilty of an offence against the criminal law unless he has got a guilty mind."[19] It has also been said that the presumption of existence of *mens rea* is "a presumption of legality" and "in the absence of express words or a truly necessary implication, Parliament must be presumed to legislate on the assumption that the principle of legality will supplement the text".[20] 'Necessary implication' in this context "connotes an implication which is compellingly clear. Such an implication may be found in the language used, the mischief sought to be prevented and any other circumstances which may assist in determining what intention is properly to be attributed to Parliament when creating the offence."[21] As stated by the Privy Council (LORD SCARMAN) the only situation in which the presumption can be displaced is where the statute is concerned with an issue of social concern and it is further shown that creation of strict liability will be effective to promote the objects of the statute by encouraging greater vigilance to prevent the commission of the prohibited act.[22] "*Mens rea* by necessary implication could be excluded from a statute only where it is absolutely clear that implementation of the object of the statute would otherwise be defeated."[23] The presumption that *mens rea* is an essential element of a statutory offence has led to the view that 'reckless' when used in the context of a serious offence will need an element of *mens rea* and will not cover a case of inadvertent recklessness, *i.e.*, doing some thing involving a risk of injury to another if one genuinely does not perceive the risk.[24] And, the words rashness or negligence in criminal law will imply *mens rea* in the sense of "taking a hazard knowing that the hazard was of such a degree that injury was most likely imminent," the element of criminality is introduced by the accused having "run the risk of doing such an act with recklessness or indifference to consequences."[25] The climate of both parliamentary and judicial opinion in England has been

---

19. *Brend v. Wood*, note 86, *supra*.

20. *B. (a minor) v. Director of Public Prosecutions*, (2000) 1 All ER 833, pp. 844, 845 (LORD STEYN) (HL).

21. *Ibid*, p. 839 (LORD NICHOLLAS).

22. *Gammon (Hongkong) Ltd. v. Attorney-General of Hongkong*, (1984) 2 All ER 503, p. 508 : (1985) AC 1 : (1984) 3 WLR 434 (PC). (Propositions 4 and 5). For this case **see also**, note 36, p. 1001, *post*.

23. *Peoples Union for Civil Liberties v. Union of India*, AIR 2004 SC 456, p. 474 : (2004) 9 SCC 580.

24. *R. v. G.*, (2003) 4 All ER 765, p. 784 (HL) **overruling** *R. v. Caldwell*, (1981) 1 All ER 961 (HL).

25. *Jacob Mathew v. State of Punjab*, (2005) 6 SCC 1, p. 17 (para 14).

growing less favourable to the recognition of absolute offences over the last few decades.[26]

WRIGHT, J., in *Sherras v. De Rutzen*,[27] on an analysis found that there are three classes of cases where the Legislature normally enacts absolute prohibition: One is a class of acts which are not criminal in any real sense, but are acts which in the public interest are prohibited under a penalty, and instances of this class are found in the Revenue Statutes,[28] Adulteration Acts,[29] Game Acts, etc.,[30] the Second class comprehends some, and perhaps all public nuisances;[31] and the Third class of cases are those where, although the proceeding may be criminal in form, they are really only a summary mode of enforcing a civil right.[32] Offences, in respect of which *mens rea* is not required to be established, are usually of a comparatively

---

26. *R. v. Sheppard*, (1980) 3 All ER 899, p. 906 : (1981) AC 394 : (1980) 3 WLR 960 (HL). For this case **see also**, p. 1009.

27. (1895-99) All ER Rep 1167, pp. 1169, 1170. **See further,** *Union of India v. Ganesh Das Bhojraj,* AIR 2000 SC 1102, p. 1109 : (2000) 9 SCC 461.

KIRON REID in 'Strict Liability: Some Principles for Parliament' (2008) 29 Statute Law Review 173 at p. 194 recommends: "Law reform should establish a general principle that strict liability should no longer be an element of serious offences but might usefully be adopted for minor or regulatory offences, usually with a defence for those who can prove that they were not negligent in committing the crime. To make the law clearer negligence should be the minimum fault requirement for criminal offences but confined to minor offences. These truly non-criminal 'offences' should be specified as regulatory or administrative to ensure fair labeling."

28. **See** *Bruhn v. King*, (1909) AC 317, p. 324 (PC); **referred** to in *State of Maharashtra v. M.H. George*, AIR 1965 SC 722, p. 739 : 1965 (1) SCR 123. **See further** *Patel v. Comptroller of Customs*, (1965) 3 All ER 593 (PC); *Comptroller of Customs v. Western Electric Co. Ltd.*, (1965) 3 All ER 599 (PC); *R.S. Joshi v. Ajit Mills*, AIR 1977 SC 2279, pp. 2287, 2288 : (1977) 4 SCC 98. (No *mens rea* in economic offences); *Additional Commissioner of Income-tax v. I.M. Patel (M/s.)*, AIR 1992 SC 1762, p. 1764 : 1993 Supp (1) SCC 621 (Unless the language provides otherwise penal provision in a taxing Act does not require *mens rea* to be proved); *Union of India v. Mustafa & Najibai Trading Co.*, JT 1998 (5) SC 16, p. 32 : AIR 1998 SC 2526 : (1998) 6 SCC 79 (*Mens rea* is not essential for exercising power of confiscation of goods under section 111 of the Customs Act, 1962).

29. **See** *Sarjoo Prasad v. State of U.P.*, AIR 1961 SC 631, pp. 632, 633 : (1961) 3 SCR 324; *Andhra Pradesh Grain and Seed Merchants Association v. Union of India*, AIR 1971 SC 2346 : (1970) 2 SCC 71; *Smedleys Ltd. v. Breed*, (1974) 2 All ER 21 (HL); *Dinesh Chandra Jamnadas Gandhi v. State of Gujarat*, AIR 1989 SC 1011, p. 1015 : 1989 (1) SCC 420; *State of Orissa v. K. Rajeshwar Rao*, AIR 1992 SC 240 : (1992) 1 SCC 365.

30. The Trade Descriptions Act, 1968 which regulates trading standards is not a truly criminal statute, *Wings Ltd. v. Ellis*, (1984) 3 All ER 577, pp. 587, 589 : (1985) AC 272 : (1984) 3 WLR 965 (HL).

31. **See** *R. v. Stephens*, (1866) LR 1 QB 702; *Alphacell Ltd. v. Woodward*, (1972) 2 All ER 475 (HL).

32. **See** *Morden v. Porter*, 141 ER 967.

minor character and sentences prescribed for them are not of a severe type. "The more serious the offence, the greater is the weight to be attached to the presumption, because more severe is the punishment and the greater the stigma which accompany a conviction"[33] In principle an age related ingredient of a statutory offence stands on no different footing from any other ingredient for application of the principle of *mens rea*.[34] Therefore, the provision of a sentence of imprisonment or any other severe penalty may *prima facie* indicate that *mens rea*, as a constituent part of the crime, was not intended to be excluded.[35] But it is not uncommon to find statutes concerning public health, safety and morals to provide severe penalties for offences of strict liability.[36]

When the state of an accused person's mind and his knowledge are ingredients of an offence, he has to be judged on the facts as he believed them to be. For example, when the accused smuggled a controlled drug mistakenly believing that he was importing currency and also mistakenly believing that the import of currency was prohibited and he was committing an offence, he could not be punished for the criminal offence of being "knowingly concerned" in the importation of a controlled drug.[37] The express inclusion of the word 'knowingly' *prima facie* requires knowledge by the accused of each of the facts constituting the *actus reus*. For example, it was held that in order to prove that a person has knowingly used or knowingly caused or permitted the use of any premises as a sex establishment without a licence, the prosecution must establish not only that the person knew that the premises were used as sex establishment but also that he knew that they were

---

33. *B. (a minor) v. Director of Public Prosecutions,* (2000) 1 All ER 833, p. 839 (LORD NICHOLLAS) (HL). (Offence of inciting a child under 14 to commit act of gross indecency. Prosecution to prove absence of genuine belief in accused that the child was 14 or over).

34. *Ibid*, p. 850 (LORD STEYN), p. 855 (LORD HUTTON); *R. v. K.*, (2001) 3 All ER 897, p. 911 (HL) (Offence of indecent assault by man on girl under 16. Prosecution to prove absence of genuine belief in accused that the girl was 16 or over). But a child sex offence against a girl below 13 providing sentence of imprisonment for life may be an offence of strict liability where it may be no defence that the accused believed that the girl was above 13 years of age: *R v. G.*, (2008) 3 All ER 1071 (H.L.) paras 3, 20, 21. **See further** *CTM v. The Queen*, 82 ALJR 978 (The common law defence of honest and reasonable mistaken belief relating to age in a sex related offence will be available to the accused unless it is excluded by a sufficiently plain manifestation of legislative intention).

35. *Shriniwasmal v. Emperor*, AIR 1947 PC 135, p. 139 : 26 Pat 460; *Nathulal v. State of M.P.*, AIR 1966 SC 43 : 1966 Cr LJ 71; *Indo China Steam Navigation Co. v. Jasjit Singh*, AIR 1964 SC 1140, p. 1149 : (1964) 6 SCR 594 (In this case presumption was held to be rebutted).

36. For example, **see** *Gamman (Hongkong) Ltd. v. Attorney-General of Hongkong*, (1984) 2 All ER 503 (PC); *R v. G*, (2008) 3 All ER 1071 (H.L.).

37. *R. v. Taaffe*, (1984) 1 All ER 747 : (1984) AC 539 (HL).

being so used without a licence.[38] But when a licensee, who was occupier of premises was charged with 'knowingly permitting' the premises to be used for supply of controlled drug, all that was necessary to prove was that the licensee knew that controlled drug was being supplied and it was not necessary to prove knowledge of identity and class of drug although penalty varied according to classification of drug.[39] Similarly, when a person was charged for being 'knowingly concerned' in fraudulent evasion of prohibition or restriction relating to importation of goods, it was held that it was not necessary to prove that the accused knew the precise nature of the goods and it was sufficient to prove that the accused knew that the goods imported were prohibited goods.[40] Absence however, of the word 'knowingly' or some such other word expressing a guilty intention in the relevant section of the statute and its presence in other sections or in other part of the same section is not in itself conclusive to indicate that a guilty intention is excluded.[41] But it is certainly a material consideration and may, in a proper case taken along with other relevant factors rebut the presumption of existence of *mens rea*.[42]

The principle that *mens rea* is presumed to be necessary gives rise to another principle that the courts should be slow to impute to Parliament so harsh an intention as to impose criminal liability on a citizen acting lawfully because another citizen, over whom he has no control, acts unlawfully.[43]

It has already been noticed that in applying the rule of construction under discussion, regard must be had to the words of the statute and to the

---

38. *Westminster City Council v. Croyalgrange Ltd.*, (1985) 1 All ER 740, p. 743 (CA), **affirmed** (1986) 2 All ER 353 : (1986) 1 WLR 679 : 1980 Crim LR 673 (HL).

39. *R. v. Bett,* (1999) 1 All ER 600 (CA).

40. *R. v. Forbes,* (2001) 4 All ER 97 (HL).

41. *Sherras v. De Rutzen*, (1895-99) All ER Rep 1167, p. 1169 : (1895) 1 QB 918 : 11 LTR 369 (DAY, J.); *Lim Chin Aik v. Reginam*, (1963) 1 All ER 223, p. 230 (PC); *Sweet v. Parsley*, (1969) 1 All ER 347, p. 350 : (1969) 2 WLR 470 (HL).

42. *Indo China Steam Navigation Co. v. Jasjit Singh*, AIR 1964 SC 1140, p. 1149 (para 22) : 1964 (6) SCR 594. **See further** *State of Maharashtra v. M.H. George*, AIR 1965 SC 722, p. 735 (para 35) : 1965 (1) SCR 123; *Yeandel v. Fisher*, (1965) 3 All ER 158, p. 161 (letters G, H); *Pharmaceutical Society of Great Britain v. Storkwain Ltd.*, (1986) 2 All ER 635, p. 639 : (1986) 1 WLR 903 (HL).

43. *Porter v. Honey*, (1988) 3 All ER 1045, p. 1050 : (1988) 1 WLR 1420 (HL), (Statutory Regulation permitting display of one sale board only on property without express permission. *A* a sale agent, putting up one sale board on a property. *B* another sale agent, without knowledge or consent of *A* and without obtaining permission putting up another sale board on the same property. *A* does not become liable for an offence in breach of the Regulation for displaying more than one sale board without express permission).

subject-matter with which it deals.[44] It is pertinent also to enquire whether putting the defendant under strict liability will assist in the enforcement of the statute, and where it can be shown that the imposition of strict liability would result in the prosecution and conviction of a class of persons whose conduct could not in any way affect the observance of the law, even where the statute is dealing with a grave social evil strict liability is not likely be intended.[45] Absolute prohibition will, therefore, not be inferred where the prohibited act is not of the defendant but of some person over whom he had no control and for whom he had no responsibility.[46] It may also be seen whether in a case of truly criminal offence public interest really requires that an innocent person should be prevented from proving his innocence in order that fewer guilty men may escape.[47] But if the statute deals with a grave social evil and a construction consistent with the existence of *mens rea* as a necessary ingredient of the offence would largely frustrate the effective enforcement and the purpose of the statute, it may be inferred that the Legislature intended to provide for strict liability,[48] leaving it to the court, if no minimum sentence is provided, to mitigate the hardship of any particular case by inflicting only a nominal or no punishment,[49] and in cases where a minimum sentence is provided, to recommend to the appropriate Government to suitable remission of the sentence.[50]

But the presumption of *mens rea* does not apply to forfeiture proceedings *in rem* sanctioned by a statute against any vehicle, container or similar article which was in fact used for carriage of goods liable to forfeiture. These proceedings are really not against any person but against the thing

---

44. **See** text and note 22, p. 999. **Further see** *R. v. Tolson*, (1889) 23 QBD 168 : 60 LT 899 (WILLS, J.) **referred** to in *State of Maharashtra v. M.H. George, supra*, p. 739. **Also see** *Yeandel v. Fisher, supra*, p. 161 (letters D, E).

45. *Lim Chin Aik v. Reginam*, (1963) 1 All ER 223, pp. 228, 229 : 1963 AC 160 : (1963) 2 WLR 42 (PC); *Nathulal v. State of M.P.*, AIR 1966 SC 43.

46. *Reynolds v. G.H. Austin & Sons Ltd.*, (1951) 1 All ER 606, p. 1004. **See further** title 6 in this Chapter—'Vicarious Responsibility in Statutory Offences'.

47. *Sweet v. Parsley*, (1969) 1 All ER 347, p. 350 : (1969) 2 WLR 470 (HL) (letters H, D).

48. *Indo China Steam Navigation Co. v. Jasjit Singh*, AIR 1964 SC 1140, pp. 1149, 1150 (paras 23, 24) : 1964 (6) SCR 594; *State of Maharashtra v. M.H. George*, AIR 1965 SC 722, p. 740 (para 40); *Dinesh Chandra Jamnadas Gandhi v. State of Gujarat*, AIR 1989 SC 1011, pp. 1015-17 : 1989 (1) SCC 420. **See further** *Kartar Singh v. State of Punjab*, JT 1994 (2) SC 423, p. 465 : 1994 (3) SCC 569 : ["The question may be whether the effectiveness of this instrument (TADA) would be entirely frustrated if the element of *mens rea*—is to be injected or read into"].

Contrast—Cases in note 1004.

49. *R. v. Margaret's Trust*, (1958) 2 All ER 289, p. 293; **referred** to in *State of Maharashtra v. M.H. George, supra*, p. 740 (para 36). **But see** *Warner v. Metropolitan Police Commr.*, (1968) 2 All ER 356, p. 366 (HL), where LORD REID is critical of this view.

50. *Dinesh Chandra Jamnadas Gandhi v. State of Gujarat*, AIR 1989 SC 1011, pp. 1018, 1019 : 1989 (1) SCC 420.

liable to be forfeited and that makes the distinction.[51] In calculating the benefit which the defendant received form a criminal life style for purposes of forfeiture proceedings the valuation of goods of illegal nature such as heroin the market value has to be determined having regard to the market where such goods were ordinarily bought and sold and the goods cannot be rejected of no value on the ground that there could be no lawful market where they could be sold.[52] Further, penalty imposable under an Act for breach of civil obligation by an adjudicatory proceeding which is not criminal in nature does not attract the rule that *mens rea* is essential before a penalty could be imposed.[53] It has already been seen that even economic offences do not raise the presumption of *mens rea*.[54]

As summed up by LORD SCARMAN in the House of Lords: "The question whether an offence created by statute requires *mens rea*, guilty knowledge or intention, in whole, in part or not at all turns on the subject matter, the language and the structure of the Act studied as a whole, on the language of the particular statutory provision under consideration construed in the light of the legislative purpose embodied in the Act and on whether strict liability in respect of all or any of the essential ingredients of the offence would promote the object of the provision."[55]

(b) Illustrative cases

In *Sherras v. De Rutzen*,[56] section 16 of the Licensing Act, 1872, came up for construction. The section read: 'If any licensed person—

(1) Knowingly harbours or knowingly suffers to remain on his premises any constable during any part of the time appointed such constable being on duty—or

---

51. *Customs and Excise Commissioners v. Air Canada*, (1991) 1 All ER 570, pp. 586, 587 : (1991) 2 QB 446 (CA). For construction of statutes providing for confiscation orders against persons obtaining property as proceeds of crime **see** *R. v. May*, (2008) 4 All ER 97 (H.L.).

52. *R. v. Islam*, (2010) 1 All ER 493 (H.L.).

53. *Director of Enforcement v. MCTM Corporation Pvt. Ltd.*, AIR 1996 SC 1100, pp 1105, 1106 : (1996) 2 SCC 471. (*Mens rea* is not an essential element of penalty under section 23(1) of FERA, 1947); *Chairman, SEBI v. Shriram Mutual Funds*, (2006) 5 SCC 361 : AIR 2006 SC 2287 (Penalty provisions enacted in sections 15-A to 15-AB, 15-I and 15-J of the Securities and Exchange Board of India Act, 1992 are not criminal offences. These are penalties for breach of statutory civil obligations imposed in adjudicatory proceedings and *mens rea* or intention to contravene is not necessary to be shown for imposition of penalty).

54. **See** text and note 25, p. 999, *supra*.

55. *Wings Ltd. v. Ellis*, (1984) 3 All ER 577, p. 589 : (1985) AC 272 : (1984) 3 WLR 965 (HL).

56. (1895-99) All ER Rep 1167 : (1895) 1 QB 918.

(2) Supplies any liquor or refreshment whether by way of gift or sale to any constable, he shall be liable to a penalty.'

A licensee of a public house supplied liquor to a constable while he was on duty. It was, however, proved that the constable had removed his armlet, an indication that he was off duty and the licensee served him in the *bona fide* belief that that was the case. It was held that the licensee had no intention of doing a wrongful act and was not guilty. Although the word 'knowingly' appeared in sub-section (1), its omission in sub-section (2) was held as not excluding *mens rea* as a constituent part of the crime under sub-section (2). According to DAY, J. the omission in sub-section (2) of the word 'knowingly' was effective only to shift the proof of absence of guilty intent on the accused.[57]

The Supreme Court in *Kalpnath Rai v. State*,[58] considered section 3(4) of the Terrorists and Disruptive Activities (Prevention) Act, 1987. This section enacts that 'Whoever harbours—any terrorist' shall be punishable with imprisonment which shall not be less than five years but which may extend to imprisonment for life. The court held that the section provided for harsh punishment and could not be held to have excluded *mens rea*; and a person giving shelter to a terrorist without knowing that he was a terrorist could not be punished under section 3(4).

In *Reynolds v. G.H. Austin & Sons Ltd.*,[59] a limited company was summoned for having unlawfully used an omnibus as an express carriage otherwise than under and in accordance with a licence, contrary to section 72 of the Road Traffic Act, 1930. By section 61, which defines an express carriage, a vehicle used on a special occasion for the conveyance of a private party is not deemed to be an express carriage. By section 25 of the Road Traffic Act, 1934, for a vehicle to be deemed to be used on a special occasion, certain conditions are to be satisfied, one of them being that 'the journey must be made without previous advertisement to the public of the arrangements therefor'. A Women's Club arranged with the company for a trip to a certain place in an omnibus owned by the company at specified rate per head with a minimum of 28 passengers. The Club, after having

---

57. *Ibid*, p. 1169.

The proposition of shifting of burden of proof is not correct. **See** cases in notes 62, 63 on p. 1007, *infra*, **see further** *Warner v. Metropolitan Police Commr.*, p. 885, *infra*. It has been suggested that the evidential burden should rest on the accused without affecting the legal burden on the prosecution: *Strict Responsibility; Possible Solutions*, (1974) 37 MLR 417, p. 433.

58. AIR 1998 SC 201, p. 212 : (1997) 8 SCC 733.

59. (1951) 1 All ER 606.

found that there were six unbooked seats with them, put up a notice for the unbooked seats. The advertisement was made without the knowledge or connivance of the company. The trip duly took place. The company did not take out any road service licence covering the journey as according to it the vehicle was being used on a special occasion. The company was, however, prosecuted for using the vehicle as an express carriage as the advertisement put up by the Women's Club had disentitled the vehicle to be deemed to be a vehicle used on a special occasion. It was held that as the company did not know of the advertisement which was issued without its knowledge or connivance it was not guilty of using or causing or permitting the use of the vehicle as an express carriage.

The appellant in *Regina v. Gosney*,[60] was charged with the offence of section 2(1) of the Road Traffic Act, 1960, for driving in the wrong direction along a road meant for oneway traffic. The section (which corresponds to section 116 of the Indian Motor Vehicles Act, 1939) provides that if a person drives a motor vehicle on a road in a manner which is dangerous to the public, having regard to all the circumstances of the case he shall be liable to penalty. The appellant wanted to prove that she was not familiar with the road and there was no sign anywhere to warn her that the road was meant for one way traffic, and therefore, she was not at fault and was not liable for the penalty. It was held that the offence was not an absolute offence and the appellant was entitled to prove the above defence. It was observed: "In order to justify a conviction there must be, not only a situation which, viewed objectively, was dangerous, but there must also have been some fault on the part of the driver, causing that situation. Fault certainly does not necessarily involve deliberate misconduct or recklessness or intention to drive in a manner inconsistent with proper standards of driving. Nor does fault necessarily involve moral blame. Fault involves a failure, a failing below the care or skill of a competent and experienced driver in relation to the manner of the driving and to the relevant circumstances of the case."[61]

On the same principle it has been held that section 1(1) of the Prevention of Crime Act, 1953, which made any person, 'who without lawful authority or reasonable excuse, the proof whereof shall lie with him, has with him in any public place any offensive weapon', guilty of an offence, should be construed to bring in only such person who 'knowingly' has with him in any public place an offensive weapon. It was further held that the burden to prove, that the accused had the knowledge that the offensive

---

60. (1971) 3 WLR 343, p. 347 (CA).
61. *Ibid.*

weapon was with him, remained throughout on the prosecution.[62] SALMON, J., illustrating the point observed: "If some innocent person has a cash slipped into his pocket by an escaping rogue, he would not be guilty of having it with him within the meaning of the section because he would be quite innocent of any knowledge that it had been put into his pocket."[63]

In *Lim Chin Aik v. Reginam*,[64] the appellant was charged for having 'contravened' section 6(2) of the Immigration Ordinance, 1959, (Singapore) by 'remaining in Singapore' (after having entered) when he had been 'prohibited' by an order made by the Ministry containing such prohibition. The Privy Council in allowing the appeal laid down that before the appellant could be said to have contravened an order of prohibition, it should be shown that he was aware of it and that the presumption of existence of *mens rea* was not displaced in that case merely on the ground that the Ordinance dealt with a social evil of immigration or that the relevant sections did not contain the word 'knowingly' or the phrase 'without reasonable cause' which occurred in other sections of the same Ordinance. It should be noticed that there was no evidence in the case that the order of prohibition was in any manner published or communicated to the accused and there was no practical or sensible way in which he could have ascertained whether he was a prohibited person or not.

The House of Lords in *Warner v. Metropolitan Police Commissioner*,[65] had to deal with section 1 of the Drugs (Prevention of Misuse) Act, 1964, which provides: '—it shall not be lawful for a person to have in his possession a substance for the time being specified in the Schedule to this Act unless—'. Then follow conditions for possession on medical prescription. Construing the section it was held that there could be no possession without knowledge of the existence of the thing, and, therefore, goods slipped into a man's pocket without his knowledge could not be held to be in his possession. It was further held that a person may be held to be in possession when he had knowledge of the existence of the thing although without knowledge of its qualities. It was also held that possession of a package by an accused was strong evidence of possession of its contents, but the accused may still rebut that presumption by raising real doubt either: (i) that the accused (if a servant or a bailee) had both no right to open the package and no reason to suspect that the contents were illicit, or (ii) that (if the accused be the owner of the package) he had no knowledge of, or was genuinely mistaken as to, the actual contents or their illicit nature and

---

62. *R. v. Cugullere*, (1961) 2 All ER 343.
63. *Ibid*, p. 344.
64. (1963) 1 All ER 223 : 1963 AC 160 : (1963) 2 WLR 42 (PC).
65. (1968) 2 All ER 356 (HL).

received them innocently and also that he had no reasonable opportunity since receiving the package to acquaint himself with its contents. *Warner's* case[66] was referred to by the Supreme Court in *Inder Sain v. State of Punjab*,[67] where it was held that possession under section 9(a) of the Opium Act, 1878, meant possession with knowledge but because of section 10 of the Act if the prosecution proved that the accused had dealt with the article or had physical custody of the same or was directly concerned with it, the onus of proof shifted to the accused to prove by preponderance of probability that he did not knowingly possess the article.

The case of *Sweet v. Parsely*,[68] related to section 5(b) of the Dangerous Drugs Act, 1965, which provides that 'if a person is concerned in the management of any premises used for the purpose of smoking cannabis or cannabis resin or of dealing in cannabis resin (whether by sale or otherwise), he shall be guilty of an offence'. The appellant sub-let a house reserving for herself a room. She used to visit the house occasionally to collect letters and rent, and to see that everything was well. On one occasion in her absence the police searched the house and found receptacles containing cannabis and L.S.D. hidden in the garden and cigarette ends containing cannabis in the kitchen. It was found that the appellant had no

---

66. *Ibid.*

67. AIR 1973 SC 2309 : (1973) 2 SCC 372. **See further** *Patel Jethabhai Chatur v. State of Gujarat*, AIR 1977 SC 294 : (1976) 4 SCC 522; (a guest in a drinking party can be held to be in possession of liquor in his glass and, therefore, liable for the offence of possession of liquor under section 68(1)(b) of the Bombay Prohibition Act, 1949); *Director of Public Prosecutions v. Brooks*, (1974) 2 All ER 840 (PC) (*Warner's* case, *supra*, was referred to); *R. v. Byeson*, (1982) 2 All ER 161 (HL) (It was held that when the offence is of being in possession of a controlled drug, it is not necessary to prove possession of a quantity of the drug that is usable but merely possession of any quantity, however minute, that is visible, tangible and measurable). *Sanjay Dutt v. State through CBI, Bombay,* JT 1994 (5) SC 540, p. 559 : 1994 (5) SCC 410. (Possession means conscious possession); *Gurmail Singh v. State of Punjab,* AIR 2002 SC 1419 : (2002) 3 SCC 748 ('Possession' in section 5 of the TADA means conscious possession); *Avtar Singh v. State of Punjab,* AIR 2002 SC 3343 : (2002) 7 SCC 419 ('Possession' under section 15 of the Narcotic Drugs and Psychotropic Substances Act, 1985); *Madanlal v. State of H.P.,* (2003) 7 SCC 465 (Possession for offence under section 20(b) of the NDPS Act means conscious possession but once possession is established the burden to prove that possession was not with knowledge shifts to the accused under sections 35 and 54 of the Act); *Megh Singh v. State of Punjab,* AIR 2003 SC 3184 : (2003) 8 SCC 666 ('Possession' under section 20, NDPS Act means conscious possession); *Peoples Union for Civil Liberties v. Union of India,* AIR 2004 SC 456, p. 469 : (2004) 9 SCC 580 ('Possession' in section 4 POTA means conscious possession); *Gopaldas Udhavdas Ahuja v. Union of India*, (2004) 7 SCC 33 : AIR 2004 SC 3830 (Possession of primary gold in contravention of Gold Control Act, 1968 means conscious possession).

68. (1969) 1 All ER 347 : (1969) 2 WLR 470 (HL).

knowledge that the house was used by the tenants for the purpose ofsmoking cannabis or cannabis resin. But she was convicted on the ground that she was concerned in the management of the premises which were used for the purpose of smoking cannabis and the offence was an absolute offence. The House of Lords allowing the appeal held that it was necessary for an offence to fall under section 5(b) that it must be shown that the premises were managed with the purpose that they be used for smoking cannabis; that the purpose referred to in the section was the purpose of the management; and that the offence was not an absolute offence.[69]

In *R. v. Sheppard*,[70] the question related to construction of section 1 of the Children and Young Persons Act, 1933, which provides that if any person who has attained the age of sixteen years and has the custody of any child under that age wilfully neglects him in a manner likely to cause unnecessary suffering or injury to health that person shall be guilty of misdemeanour. The appellants who were a young couple of low intelligence living in deprived condition failed to provide adequate medical aid to their child who died. The appellants were convicted for the offence under section 1 of the Act for wilfully neglecting the child. The House of Lords, however, allowed the appeal holding that the neglect was not wilful. LORD DIPLOCK observed: "The *actus reus* in a case of wilful neglect is simply a failure, for whatever reason to provide the child whenever it needs medical aid with the medical aid. Such a failure—could not be described as 'wilful' unless the parent either (1) had directed his mind to the question whether there was some risk (though it might fall short of probability) that the child's health might suffer unless he was examined by a doctor and provided with such curative treatment as the examination might reveal as necessary, and had made a conscious decision, for whatever reason, to refrain from arranging for such medical examination, or (2) had so refrained because he did not care whether the child might be in need of medical treatment or not."[71]

R. v. Court,[72] related to section 14(1) of the Sexual Offences Act, 1956 which in so far as material provides: 'It is an offence—for a person to make an indecent assault on a woman'. The House of Lords held that the section did not exclude *mens rea* and intention to commit indecent assault, *i.e.*, an assault which right minded persons would think was indecent, was an essential element of the offence.

---

69. *Ibid.*
70. (1980) 3 All ER 899 : (1981) AC 394 : (1980) 3 WLR 960 (HL).
71. *Ibid*, p. 904.
72. (1988) 2 All ER 221, p. 228 : 1989 AC 28 : (1988) 2 WLR 1071 (HL).

In *Nathulal v. State of Madhya Pradesh,*[73] a dealer in foodgrains was prosecuted under section 7 of the Essential Commodities Act, 1955 for contravening the M.P. Grain Dealers Licensing Order, 1958, for carrying on business in foodgrains without a licence. It was found that the accused had applied for a licence and was under the impression that the licence was issued to him, that the order of rejection of his application was not communicated to him and that the accused went on sending the returns, on the footing that he was a licensee, to the authority concerned. In acquitting the accused the Supreme Court pointed out that the Act, which imposed heavy penalties, could not be construed to dispense *mens rea* as the object of the Act could not be defeated on such a construction. The 'contravention' that was made punishable under section 7 of the Act, was therefore, held to be 'intentional' contravention of an order made under section 3. Section 7 of the Essential Commodities Act was later amended by Act 36 of 1967 to exclude *mens rea.*[74] It was again amended by Act 30 of 1974 to bring back the element of *mens rea* with a qualification that it was for the accused to prove non-existence of *mens rea.*[75]

Section 2(1)(a)(i) of the Terrorists and Disruptive Activities (Prevention) Act, 1987 defines 'abet' to 'include the communication or association with any person or class of persons who is engaged in assisting in any manner terrorists or disruptionists'. The Act expressly requires a guilty intention as an essential ingredient of the substantive offences. In this background and having regard to the presumption of *mens rea*, unless excluded expressly or by necessary implication, it was held that the offence of abetment under the Act requires *mens rea* as an essential ingredient. On this view the above definition of 'abet' was read as meaning "the communication or association

---

73. AIR 1966 SC 43 : 1966 Cr. LJ 71. **See further** *Century Spinning & Mfg. Co. v. State of Maharashtra*, AIR 1972 SC 545 : (1972) 3 SCC 282; (the accused in this case acted upon a construction of the notification issued under the Cotton Textiles Control Order, 1948 by the Textile Commissioner who also was of the view that the accused was not guilty of any breach; held, even if there was any technical breach, the accused could not be held guilty as there was no *mens rea*). **But see** *Epping Forest District Council v. Essex Rendering Ltd.*, (1983) 1 All ER 359 : (1983) 1 WLR 158 (HL) (A company carried on an offensive trade without written consent but with the knowledge and tacit approval of the local authority for 23 years. It was held that written consent under section 107(1) read with section 283(1) of the Public Health Act, 1936 was mandatory and the company was rightly convicted). **See** *Murarilal Jhunjhunwala v. State of Bihar*, AIR 1991 SC 515 : (1991) Supp (2) SCC 647 (Licensing authority accepting renewal fee for licence for successive four years but not passing any order granting or refusing renewal. Prosecution quashed).

74. The section after amendment read: 'If any person contravenes whether knowingly, intentionally *or otherwise* any order made under section 3—'. This has been construed to exclude *mens rea*: *State of Madhya Pradesh v. Narayan Singh*, AIR 1989 SC 1789, p. 1792 : 1989 (3) SCC 596.

75. *State of Madhya Pradesh v. Narayan Singh, supra.*

with any person or class of persons *with the actual knowledge or having reason to believe* that such person or class of persons is engaged in assisting in any manner terrorists or disruptionists."[76] Similar view was taken of the meaning of 'abet' in section 3(3) of the Prevention of Terrorism Act, 2002.[77]

A finance company in *R. v. St. Margaret's Trust Ltd.*,[78] was held liable for aiding and abetting the contravention of the Hire-Purchase and Credit Sale Agreement (Control) Order, 1956 (S.I. 1956 No. 180) although the company was induced to enter into the transaction by a fraudulent representation of the sellers that conditions prescribed by the Order have been fulfilled. The Court of Criminal Appeal held that the order was promulgated to defend the currency against peril of inflation, and that the object of the statute indicated that what was enacted was intended to be absolute prohibition. It was pointed out that although imprisonment was one of the punishments, that factor could not justify the inference that guilty intent was essential ingredient; rather the better view was that having regard to the gravity of the issues, Parliament intended the prohibition to be absolute, leaving the court to use its powers to inflict nominal punishment or none at all in appropriate cases.

The Supreme Court in *Sarjoo Prasad v. State of Uttar Pradesh*,[79] held that any person, whether employer or employee contravening the provisions of section 7 of the Prevention of Food Adulteration Act, 1954, is liable to punishment under section 16, and it is not necessary for the prosecution to establish that the person concerned had guilty knowledge or intention or that he knew that the article was adulterated. It was pointed out that the Legislature enacted the Act in the larger interest of maintenance of public health, and the language was wide enough to cover every person selling adulterated food whether he had the guilty knowledge or not. It may here be recalled that offences against adulteration Acts fall within that class of cases where according to WRIGHT, J. in *Sherras v. De Rutzen*,[80] the element of *mens rea* is usually dispensed with.[81]

---

76. *Kartar Singh v. State of Punjab*, JT 1994 (2) SC 423, p. 467 : (1994) 3 SCC 569.

77. *Peoples Union for Civil Liberties v. Union of India*, AIR 2004 SC 456 (para 25) : (2003) 10 JT 70 : (2004) 9 SCC 580.

78. (1958) 2 All ER 289.

79. AIR 1961 SC 631, pp. 632, 633 : 1961 (3) SCR 324. **Followed** in *State of Orissa v. K. Rajeshwar Rao*, AIR 1992 SC 240 : 1992 (1) SCC 365.

80. (1895-99) All ER Rep 1167.

81. **See** text and notes 31, 33, pp. 942-943. **See further** *Goodfellow v. Johnson*, (1965) 1 All ER 941. For further illustration, **see** *Smedleys Ltd. v. Breed*, (1974) 2 All ER 21 (HL); sale of tinned peas containing a caterpillar by defendants who were held liable under section 2(1) of the Food & Drugs Act, 1955, although they had installed a satisfactory system of manufacturing and spot checking the peas. *Smedley's* case, supra, is **discussed** and **applied** in *Dinesh Chandra Jamnadas Gandhi v. State of Gujarat*, AIR 1989 SC 1011 : (1989) 1 SCC 420 which was a case of adulterated 'supari'.

In *Alphacell Ltd. v. Woodward*,[82] the appellants in the course of their business of preparing Manilla fibres had constructed settling tanks near the bank of a river where polluted water from their works was piped down. In the tanks were fitted two pumps to prevent any overflow of water into the river from the tanks. On one occasion the pumps failed (without any negligence of the appellants) and the water from the tanks overflowed into the river from a channel leading from the tanks to the river. The question was whether the appellants were guilty under section 2(1) of the River (Prevention and Pollution) Act, 1951, which enacts that 'a person commits an offence punishable under this section if he causes or knowingly permits to enter a stream any poisonous, noxious or polluting matter'. It was held that the appellants had 'caused' the polluted water to enter the river by their positive and deliberate acts in building and operating the settling tanks with a channel directly leading to the river, as there was no evidence of an intervening act of a trespasser or of an Act of God which could be said to have caused the overflow. It was also held that section 2(1) did not require the prosecution to establish that the appellants had knowingly, intentionally or negligently caused the polluted water to enter the river, for the offence was in the nature of a public nuisance and came under the exceptions laid down by WRIGHT, J. in *Sherras v. De Rutzen*.[83] The question whether an act of third party or a natural event which was the immediate cause of pollution will in the above circumstances break the chain of causation depends upon the fact whether the act or event should be regarded as a normal fact of life or something extraordinary. If it was an ordinary occurrence, it would not negative the causal effect of the defendants' acts even if it was not forseeable but in case it was extraordinary it would be open to the court to hold that the defendant did not cause the pollution.[84]

The House of Lords in *Wings Ltd. v. Ellis*[85] dealt with section 14(1)(a) of the Trade Description Act, 1968 which provides that 'it shall be an offence for any person in the course of any trade or business—to make a statement which he knows to be false—as to any of the following matters, that is to say—the nature of any services, accommodation or facilities provided in the course of any trade or business'. The respondent, *Wings Ltd.*, was a body corporate engaged in the business of providing holidays on a package deal basis. The respondent published a brochure which gave

82. (1972) 2 All ER 475 (HL). **Followed** in *National Rivers Authority v. Yorkshire Water Services Ltd.*, (1995) 1 All ER 225 : (1995) 1 AC 444 : (1994) 3 WLR 1202 (HL).
83. (1895-99) All ER Rep 1167. **See** text and notes 27 to 29, p. 1000.
84. *Empress Car Co. (Abertillery) Ltd. v. National Rivers Authority*, (1998) 1 All ER 481 (HL).
85. (1984) 3 All ER 577 : (1985) AC 272 : (1984) 3 WLR 965 (HL).

details of the holidays for the 1981-82 season and which mistakenly indicated that certain hotel accommodation in Sri Lanka was air-conditioned. In May 1981, the respondent discovered the mistake and instructed all its staff to amend their brochures and its sale agents to inform travel agents and customers of the mistake. In January, 1982 one Mr. Wade booked a holiday with the respondent in Sri Lanka on reading the unamended brochure and he was not informed by the travel agents that the hotel was not air-conditioned. On his return home from the holiday Mr. Wade complained to a trading standard officer and the respondent was prosecuted for making a statement which he knew to be false as to the nature of accommodation under section 14(1)(a) of the Trade Description Act. It was contended that the essence of the offence lay in knowingly making a false statement and that *mens rea* was necessary to be proved. The House of Lords negatived the construction. It was held that the Act fell within the exception laid down by WRIGHT, J. in *Sherras v. De Rutzen*, (1895-99) All ER Rep 1167, as its object was to maintain trading standards and to prohibit acts which are not criminal in any real sense, but are acts which in the public interest are prohibited under a penalty and the offence was an absolute offence which did not require *mens rea*. It was also held that it was sufficient to prove that the statement was made in the course of business on the respondent's behalf and its content was false to the respondent's knowledge. It was further held that the uncorrected brochure was a continuing false statement which was made so long it remained in circulation without effective correction. In this view of the matter a statement was made to Mr. Wade by the respondent in 1982 when he read the brochure in January, 1982 that the accommodation was air-conditioned and as then the respondent knew that this was false the offence under section 14(1)(a) of the Act was made out against him.

In *Indo China Steam Navigation Co. v. Jasjit Singh*,[86] sections 52A and 167(12A) of the Sea Customs Act, 1878 which impose a prohibition as to the entry within the limits of any port in India of a vessel constructed, adapted, altered or fitted for the purpose of concealing goods and which in the event of breach of this prohibition provide that the vessel shall be liable for confiscation and the master shall be liable to a fine, have been construed by the Supreme Court as imposing absolute prohibition irrespective of any guilty intent of the owners of the vessel. This result was reached on the view that a construction consistent with the presence of the guilty intent as an essential ingredient of the crime will make the prohibition a dead letter because of the difficulty of proving the existence of *mens rea* against the owners or master of the vessel.

---

86. AIR 1964 SC 1140, pp. 1149, 1150 : 1964 (6) SCR 594.

The respondent in *State of Maharashtra v. M.H. George*,[87] was prosecuted under section 23(1A) of the Foreign Exchange Regulation Act, 1947, for having brought into India gold in contravention of section 8(1), of the Act. By Notification of August 25, 1948, issued under section 8(1), the Central Government directed that 'except with the general or special permission of the Reserve Bank, no person shall bring or send into India from any place out of India any gold bullion'. The Reserve Bank by a notification of even date granted general permission to the bringing or sending of any gold by air into any port in India provided the gold was on a through transit and was not removed from the carrying aircraft except for the purpose of transhipment. On November 6, 1962, the Reserve Bank by a notification modified the above permission and it was made a condition of exemption that the gold was declared in the manifest of the aircraft. The accused started from Zurich on November 27, 1962, for Manilla in a through plane which arrived in Bombay on November 28, 1962. The accused did not move out of the plane but on a search by Customs Authorities was found to be carrying gold which was not entered in the manifest of the aircraft or other documents carried by it. The accused pleaded ignorance of the notification of the Reserve Bank of November 6, 1962, which was accepted. On these facts the Supreme Court found the accused guilty and held that except that the bringing of gold should be conscious act no other mental state was essential to be established for constituting the crime and that knowledge of the limits of the exemption was not necessary to be established. It was pointed out that the Act was designed to safeguard and conserve foreign exchange essential to the economic life of a developing country; that it dealt with a grave social evil; and that its purpose would be defeated if any further mental state were to be read as an essential element of the crime punishable under the Act.

The Supreme Court in *R.S. Joshi v. Ajit Mills*,[88] was dealing with a provision in a Sales Tax Act; which prohibited collection of any sum by way of tax which was not payable as tax or which was in excess of tax payable. A contravention of the prohibition was made a punishable offence. The person contravening was also made liable to forfeit the sum collected in contravention of the prohibition. It was held that *mens rea* was not an ingredient for making a person liable for the offence or forfeiture. It was observed that the principle 'no *mens rea* no crime' had no application to economic offences. The rigour of the offence and penalty were, however, toned down by reading down the words 'collected' and 'forfeited'. It was held that collected did not include amounts gathered tentatively to be given

---

87. AIR 1965 SC 722 : 1965 (1) SCR 123.
88. AIR 1977 SC 2279, pp. 2282, 2287, 2288 : (1977) 4 SCC 98.

back if found non-exigible. And 'shall be forfeited' meant 'shall be liable to be forfeited' leaving a discretion to the authorities not to forfeit the sums returned to persons from whom they were collected.

In *Gamman (Hongkong) Ltd. v. Attorney General of Hongkong*,[89] the Privy Council had to construe sections 40(2A)(b) and 40(2B)(b) of the Building Ordinance (HK). Section 40(2A)(b) provides that "any person for whom any building works, street works, lift works or escalator works are being carried out and any authorised person, registered structural engineer, registered contractor, registered lift contractor or registered escalator contractor directly concerned with any such works who—diverges or deviates in any material way from any work shown in a plan approved by the building authority under this Ordinance—shall be guilty of an offence and shall be liable on conviction to a fine of $ 2,50,000 and to imprisonment for 3 years". Section 40(2B)(b) provides that "any person directly concerned with any site formation works, piling works, foundation works or other form of building works who—carries out or has carried out such works or authorises or permits or has authorised or permitted such works to be carried out in such manner as is likely to cause risk or injury to any person or damage to any property shall be guilty of an offence and shall be liable on conviction to a fine of $ 2,50,000 and to imprisonment for 3 years". The Privy Council held that the purpose of the Ordinance was clearly to regulate the planning, design and construction of building works in the interests of safety and it covered a field of activity in which citizens had a choice to participate or not but which involved in Hongkong a potential danger to public safety. It was also observed that strict liability would help to promote greater vigilance in the matters covered by the two offences. As regards section 40(2A)(b) it was held that it clearly required knowledge of the approved plan and of the fact of deviation but it did not require proof of knowledge of the materiality of the deviation. As to section 40(2B)(b) it was held that it required knowledge of the manner of carrying out the works for a person cannot carry out works or authorise or permit them to be carried out in a certain manner unless he knows the manner which he is employing, authorising or permitting. But the section did not require proof of knowledge of the likelihood of risk of injury or damage. To the above extent the offences were held to be of strict liability.[90] Following the principles in *Gammon's* case, *supra*, it has been held that the offence of broadcasting without licence required by section 1(1) of the Wireless Telegraphy Act, 1949[91] and the offence of selling Lottery ticket to a person below the age of 16 under section 13 of the National Lottery

---

89. (1984) 2 All ER 503 : (1985) AC 1 : (1984) 3 WLR 437 (PC).
90. (1984) 2 All ER 503 (PC).
91. *R. v. Blake*, (1997) 1 All ER 963 : (1997) 1 WLR 1167 (CA).

Act, 1993 read with Rule 3 of the Regulations made under the Act,[92] were of strict liability.

In *Pharmaceutical Society of Great Britain v. Slorkwain Ltd.*,[93] the House of Lords was concerned with section 58(2)(a) of the Medicines Act, 1968 which provides that no person shall sell by retail or supply in circumstances corresponding to a retail sale a medicinal product of a description, or falling within a class, specified in an order under this section except in accordance with a prescription given by an appropriate practitioner. In that case the defendant made a supply of a specified drug in accordance with a forged prescription without any fault on his part. The question was whether the defendant in the absence of any *mens rea* was liable for contravention of section 58(2)(a) which was punishable as an offence under section 67. The House of Lords held that the offence was of strict liability and proof of *mens rea* was not necessary. There were essentially four reasons for this conclusions. First reading of this Act showed that wherever Parliament intended that *mens rea* should be an ingredient of the offence it was expressly so provided. Secondly that for certain offences but not for section 58(2)(a) of the Act in section 121 gave liberty to the defendant to prove that the contravention was because of default of another person without any negligence on his part. Thirdly that section 58 itself made provision for certain exceptions or exemptions. And lastly that Pharmacists are in a position to put illicit drugs or medicines in the market and it can, therefore, be readily understood that Parliament would find it necessary to make them strictly accountable for breaches of the Act.

5. OFFENCES BY LEGAL PERSONS *e.g.* STATE AND COMPANIES

The liability of a juristic person such as the State and a company for a statutory offence requires consideration of two questions. The first question is: Does the particular statute apply to the juristic person concerned? If the answer to this question is that the statute applies, the second question is: Whose act or state of mind can be attributed to the juristic person for purposes of the particular statute? Both these questions are questions of construction. For example if the only punishment for the offence is imprisonment and there is no provision as to who, if the offence is committed by the state[94] or a company shall be penalised, the offence will not apply to the state or a company. But if the statutory offence on proper construction

---

92. Harrow London *Borough Council v. Shah,* (1999) 3 All ER 302 (QBD).
93. (1986) 2 All ER 635 : (1986) 1 WLR 903 (HL).
94. **See** for example section 7(1) of the Lotteries (Regulation) Act, 1998; **also see**, p. 802, *supra*.

applies to the state or a company, the next step would be to decide whether the offending act, which must have been necessarily done by some living person or persons can be attributed to the state or the company concerned.

The liability of the state for a statutory offence has already been discussed.[1] The discussion hereinafter is limited to the liability of a company for a statutory offence.

The question whether a company or a corporation can at all be prosecuted for an offence which is punishable with imprisonment *and* fine gave rise to a sharp divergence of opinion in the Supreme Court and was finally settled by a Constitution Bench by a majority of 3 against 2 in favour of the view that the company or corporation can be prosecuted but the punishment imposable will only be fine. The first case[2] in this context related to construction of sections 276B and 278B of the Income-tax Act, 1961. Section 276B lays down that if a person fails to pay to the credit of the Central Government the tax deducted at source, he shall be punished with rigorous imprisonment for a term which shall not be less than three months and shall also be liable to fine. Section 278B of the Act reads: "Where an offence under the Act has been committed by a company, every person who, at the time the offence was committed, was in charge of and was responsible to the company for the conduct of the business of the company *as well as the company* shall be proceeded against and punished accordingly". The mandatory sentence of imprisonment prescribed by section 276B obviously could not be applied to a company. The question, therefore, arose whether a company could at all the prosecuted under section 276B. Resolving the conflict by harmonious construction, it was held that the company would be liable for the offence but it will be liable to be punished only by imposition of fine. By adopting the rule of harmonious construction, the mandatory sentence of imprisonment in section 276B was interpreted to mean that it will be imposed where it is possible to impose it.[3] But this decision which is of a two-Judge Bench was not accepted by the majority in a later case[4] decided by a three judge Bench which related to sections 276C and 278B of the Income-tax Act, 1961. Section 276C of the Act lays down that if a person wilfully attempts in any manner whatsoever to evade any tax, penalty chargeable or imposable under the Act, he shall without prejudice to any penalty or interest that may be imposable on him under the Act, be punishable in a case where the amount sought to be evaded exceeds one hundred thousand rupees with rigorous imprisonment for a term which shall not be less than six months but which

1. Chapter 8 title 2 pages 800-805, *ante*.
2. *M.V. Javali v. Mahajan Borewell & Co.*, JT 1997 (8) SC 386 : (1997) 8 SCC 72.
3. *Ibid*, pp. 391, 392 (JT).
4. *Asstt. Commissioner Ass. II Bangalore v. Velliappa Textiles Ltd.*, AIR 2004 SC 86 : (2003) 11 SCC 405.

may extend to seven years and with fine and in any other case rigorous imprisonment for a term which shall not be less than three months but which may extend to three years and with fine. The court referred to the recommendation of the Law Commission in its 41st and 47th report for amendment of section 62 of the Penal Code to provide that in every case in which the offence is punishable with imprisonment only or with imprisonment and fine, and the offender is a corporation (meaning an incorporated company or other body corporate or even a firm or other association of individuals), it shall be competent to the court to sentence such offender to fine only. This recommendation has so far not been implemented. Absence of such a provision as recommended by the Law Commission according to the majority judges (RAJENDRA BABU and SRIKRISHNA, JJ.) was a *casus omissus* and could not be supplied by the court. The majority judges on this point differed from *Javali* and many High Court decisions and also from the judgment of the United States Supreme Court in *United States v. Union Supply Company,*[5] which supported the view in *Javali.* MATHUR, J. on the other hand agreed with the view taken in *Javali.* The court, therefore, by majority held that the officer-in-charge of the affairs of the company could alone be punished under section 276C. But correctness of the majority decision in *Velliappa Textiles Ltd.* was doubted by another three judge Bench in a case which related to section 56(1) of the Foreign Exchange Regulation Act, 1973 and the case was referred to a Constitution Bench.[6] The minimum punishment prescribed under section 56(1) of FERA is imprisonment which shall not be less than six months *and* fine. The argument on behalf of the appellant company was that as the mandatory sentence of imprisonment could not be imposed on a company it could not be prosecuted for the offence. This contention which was based on *Velliappa Textiles* was negatived by the majority (BALAKRISHNAN, DHARMADHIKARI and ARUN KUMAR, JJ.) but was accepted by the minority (HEGDE AND SRIKRISHNA, JJ.).[7] In the leading majority judgment delivered by Balakrishnan, J. it was held that such a contention will be acceptable "if the custodial sentence is the only punishment prescribed for the offence"[8] but "when imprisonment *and* fine is the prescribed punishment the court can impose the punishment of fine which could be enforced against the company. Such a discretion is to be read in the section so far as the juristic person is concerned."[9] The court said that the mandatory custodial sentence could not be imposed as the law does not compel doing of a thing which is impossible of performance. BALAKRISHNAN, J.

5. 54 Lawyers Ed. 87 (215 US 50).
6. *ANZ Grindlays Bank Ltd. v. Directorate of Enforcement*, (2004) 6 SCC 531, p. 533 : (2004) 6 Scale 489.
7. *Standard Chartered Bank v. Directorate of Enforcement*, (2005) 4 SCC 530 : AIR 2005 SC 2622.
8. *Ibid*, pp. 548, 559 (para 29).
9. *Ibid*, p. 549 (para 31).

in this context quoted a passage from the judgment of Holmes, J. in *United States v. Union Supply Co.*,[10] where in a similar situation he said: "If we free our minds from the notion that criminal statutes must be construed by some artificial and conventional rule, the natural inference, when the statute prescribed two independent penalties, is that it means to inflict them so far it can, and that, if one of them is impossible, it does not mean on that account, to let the defendant escape".[11] DHARMADHIKARI and ARUN KUMAR JJ. in their judgments adopted a purposive and object oriented approach in concurring with Balakrishnan J. Srikrishna J. who wrote the minority opinion for himself and Hegde J., on the other hand, applied the strict literal construction and said that omissions or defects in the Act could not be cured by the court and that *Velliappa* was rightly decided. As a result *Velliappa* was overrulted by the Constitution Bench by a majority of 3 against 2.

After it is settled by construction of the statute that an offence defined in it applies to a company, the next question is whose act or state of mind should be attributed to the company, the answer to which also depends upon the construction of the statute.[12] A corporation or a company is virtually in the same position as an individual and may be convicted of statutory offences including those requiring *mens rea*.[13] The person may be not necessarily the Board of Directors or the Managing Director but an employee who acted in the course of employment, albeit contrary to general instructions of the Board[14] or one who acted within the scope of his authority but with a corrupt motive and omitted to give the statutorily required information to the authorities so as to keep his employers in dark.[15]

A company's juristic personality is a creation of law. As a necessary part of corporate personality the law has also to recognise rules to lay down what acts will count as the acts of the company or in other words whose acts will be attributed to the company. These rules have been termed as 'the rules of attribution'. The primary rules of attribution are generally to be found in the incorporating statute and the constitution of the company mainly the articles of association. Under this category will generally come

---

10. 54 Lawyers, Ed. 87 (215 US 50).

11. p. 547 (para 22) of case in foonote 14, p. 1020, *supra*.

12. *Meridian Global Funds Management Asia Ltd. v. Securities Commission,* (1995) 2 All ER 918, pp. 923, 924 : (1995) 2 AC 500 : (1995) 3 WLR 413 (PC). This case also explains LORD HALDANE's oft-quoted phrase 'directing mind and will' as used in his speech in *Lennards Carrying Co. Ltd. v. Asiatic Petroleum Co. Ltd.*, (1915) AC 705, p. 713 : 84 LJKB 1281 : 113 LT 195 (HL).

13. *Iridium India Telecom Ltd. v. Motorola Inc.*, (2011) 1 SCC 74 para 63 : AIR 2011 SC 20.

14. *Supply of Ready Mixed Concrete (No. 2), Director-General of Fair Trading v. Pioneer,* (1995) 1 All ER 135 : (1995) 1 AC 456 : (1994) 3 WLR 1249 (HL).

15. *Meridian Global Funds Management Asia Ltd. v. Securities Commission, supra.*

rules which authorise certain acts to be done by decisions of the shareholders or the Board of Directors. The decisions so taken and acts done in pursuance thereto will be attributed to the company. The primary rules are however not sufficient to do business in the world so the company builds upon the primary rules of attribution by using general rules of attribution, which are equally available to natural persons, namely the principle of agency. In addition to these rules special rules of attribution may have to be applied, specially in relation to a statute defining a criminal offence which applies to a company, for laying down as to whose act or state of mind is to be attributed to the company. This essentially depends on the construction of the statute. These principles were laid down by LORD HOFFMAN who spoke for the Privy Council in *Meridian Global Funds Management Asia Ltd. v. Securities Commission.*[16] Explaining further LORD HOFFMAN said:

"The company's primary rules of attribution together with the general principles of agency, vicarious liability and so forth are usually sufficient to enable one to determine its rights and obligations. In exceptional cases, however, they will not provide an answer. This will be the case when a rule of law, either expressly or by implication, excludes attribution on the basis of the general principles of agency or vicarious liability. For example, a rule may be stated in language primarily applicable to a natural person and require some act or state of mind on the part of that person 'himself', as opposed to his servants or agents. This is generally true of rules of the criminal law, which ordinarily impose liability only for the *actus reus* and *mens rea* of the defendant himself. How is such a rule to be applied to a company. One possibility is that the court may come to the conclusion that the rule was not intended to apply to companies at all; for example, a law which created an offence for which the only penalty was community service. Another possibility is that the court might interpret the law as meaning that it could apply to a company only on the basis of its primary rules of attribution, *i.e.*, if the act giving rise to liability was specifically authorised by resolution of the Board or a unanimous agreement of the shareholders. But there will be many cases in which neither of these solutions is satisfactory; in which the court considers that the law was intended to apply to companies and that, although it excludes ordinary vicarious liability, insistence on the primary rules of attribution would in practice defeat that intention. In such a case, the court must fashion a special rule of attribution for the particular substantive rule. This is always a matter of interpretation: given that it was intended to apply to a company, how was it intended to apply? Whose act (or knowledge, or state of mind) was *for this*

16. (1995) 3 All ER 918 (PC).

purpose intended to count as the act etc of the company? One finds the answer to this question by applying the usual canons of interpretation, taking into account the language of the rule (if it is a statute) and its content and policy."[17]

In *Meridian* the question related to the construction of section 20(3) and (4) of the New Zealand Securities Amendment Act, 1988 which required 'every person' who became a 'substantial security holder' defined as holding a 'relevant interest' in 5% or more of the voting shares of a public company listed on the stock exchange, to give notice of his interest to the company and the stock exchange as soon as he knew, or ought to have known, that he was a substantial securityholder in the company. Two officers, Ng (a senior portfolio officer) and Koo (chief investment officer) of Meridian in league with others, without reporting to their superiors provided funds of Meridian for purchase of controlling shares of a cash rich publicly listed company Euro-National, with the object of using its assets for their own purposes. By the acts of Ng and Koo, Meridian became a substantial security holder in the Euro-National and the question was whether Meridian became liable for not notifying Euro-National and the stock exchange as required by section 20(4) of the New Zealand statute. The policy of section 20 was to compel, in fast moving markets, the immediate disclosure of the identity of persons who became security holders in public issues. Having regards to the policy of the Act the knowledge of the chief investment officer was attributed to Meridian and the company was held liable for not giving notice as required by section 20. In holding so LORD HOFFMAN observed:

"Notice must be given as soon as that person knows that he has become a substantial security holder. In the case of a corporate security holder, what rule should be implied as to the person whose knowledge for this purpose is to count as the knowledge of the company? Surely the person who, with the authority of the company, acquired the relevant interest. Otherwise the policy of the Act would be defeated. Companies would be able to allow employees to acquire interests on their behalf which made them substantial security holders but would not have to report them until the Board or someone else in senior management got to know about it. This would put a premium on the Board paying as little attention as possible to what its investment managers were doing. Their Lordships would therefore hold that upon the true construction of section 20(4)(e), the company knows that it has become a substantial security holder when that is known to the person who had authority to do the deal. It is then obliged to

17. *Ibid.*, pp. 923, 924.

give notice under section 20(3). The fact that Koo did the deal for a corrupt purpose and did not give such notice because he did not want his employers to find out cannot in their Lordships' view affect the attribution of knowledge and the consequent duty to notify."[18]

In an earlier case[19] decided by the House of Lords a restrictive arrangement acting within the scope of employment was made by the executives of a company in breach of an undertaking by the company to the Restrictive Practices Court. The Board of the company knew nothing of the arrangement and it had in fact given instructions to the company's employees not to make any such arrangements. But the House of Lords held that for deciding whether the company was in contempt the act and state of mind of an employee who entered into an arrangement in the course of his employment should be attributed to the company.

Likewise in a case[20] in which a company was required to make a return for revenue purposes and the statute made it an offence to make a false return with intent to deceive, the Divisional court held that the *mens rea* of the servant authorised to discharge the duty should be attributed to the company.

In the context of these cases and *Meridian,* LORD HOFFMAN cautioned: "Their Lordships would wish to guard themselves against being understood that whenever a servant of a company has authority to do an act on its behalf knowledge of that act will for all purposes be attributed to the company.—It is a question of construction in each case as to whether the particular rule requires that the knowledge that an act has been done, or the state of mind with which it is done, should be attributed to the company."[21]

LORD HOFFMAN gave an example to illustrate the point: "The fact that a company's employee is authorised to drive a lorry does not itself lead to the conclusion that if he kills some one by reckless driving, the company will be guilty of manslaughter."[22] He then observed: "There is no inconsistency and each is an example of an attribution rule for a particular purpose, tailored as it always must be to the terms and policies of the substantive rule."[23]

---

18. *Ibid* p. 927.
19. *Supply of Ready Mixed Concrete (No. 2) Director of Fair Trading v. Pioneer,* (1995) 1 All ER 135 : (1995) 1 AC 456 : (1994) 3 WLR 1249 (HL).
20. *Moore v. I. Bresher Ltd.,* (1944) 2 All ER 515.
21. (1995) 3 All ER 918, p. 928 : (1995) 2 AC 500 (PC).
22. *Ibid.*
23. *Ibid.* For common law offence of manslaughter, **see** *Attorney General's Reference No. 2 of 1999,* (2000) 3 All ER 182 (CA).

LORD HOFFMAN also referred[24] to the case of *Tesco Ltd. v. Nattras,*[25] where a shopmanager who did the prohibited act in the course of employment was not identified as the company and precautions taken by the Board to avoid the commission of the offence were held to have been taken by the company which provided the defence to negative the offence.[26]

In interpreting section 2(n) of the Factories Act, 1948 as amended by Act 20 of 1987, which applies also to companies, and in holding that only one of the Directors can be nominated and punished as 'occupier' for the offence under section 92 of the Act, which makes occupiers and managers of factories liable for contravention of the Act the Supreme Court,[27] in addition to the express provision in proviso (ii) to section 2(n), relied upon the case of *Tesco Ltd. v. Nattras.*[28] If the Act, in addition to the company, makes every person in charge of and responsible to the company for the conduct of the business also liable for the offence, a director cannot be made liable unless it is shown that he was in charge of and responsible to the company for the conduct of the business.[29] When a statutory offence is committed by a company, it does not follow that directors or employees can be made liable for the offence without there being provision in the Act making them liable.[30] But when a statute provides for an offence which can also be attributed to a company, it also often provides that every person who at the time the offence was committed was in charge of and was responsible to the company for the conduct of its business and any Director, manager, Secretary or other officer of the company with whose connivance or to whose neglect the offence was committed shall also be liable for the offence.[31] In a prosecution for such offences against any person, it is necessary to prove that the offence was committed by the company, (but it is not necessary that the company

---

24. (1995) 3 All ER 918, p. 924 : (1995) 2 AC 500 (PC).

25. (1971) 2 WLR 1166 : 1972 AC 153 (HL).

26. Pp. 978-979.

27. *J.K. Industries Limited v. Chief Inspector of Mines and Boilers,* 1996 (7) Scale 247, p. 265 : 1996 (6) SCC 665 : 1997 SCC (L&S) 1.

28. (1971) 2 WLR 1166 : (1972) AC 153 (HL).

29. *Delhi Municipality v. Ram Kishore,* (1983) 1 SCC 1 : AIR 1983 SC 67; *State of Haryana v. Brij Lal Mittal & Co.,* JT 1998 (3) SC 584 : AIR 1998 SC 2327, p. 2330; *S.M.S. Pharmaceuticals Ltd. v. Neeta Bhalla,* (2005) 8 SCC 89 (para 69).

30. *Employees' State Insurance Corporation v. S.K. Aggarwal,* AIR 1998 SC 2676 : (1998) 6 SCC 288; *Sabitha Ramamurthy v. R.B.S. Channabasavaradhya,* (2006) 10 SCC 581 : AIR 2006 SC 3086; *S.K. Alagh v. State of U.P.,* (2008) 5 SCC 662 para 19 : AIR 2008 SC 1731; *Maksud Saiyed v. State of Gujrat,* (2008) 5 SCC 668 para 13 : (2007) 11 JT 276.

31. **See,** section 10 of the Essential Commodities Act, 1955, section 141 of the Negotiable Instruments Act, 1881. **See further** *State (Govt. of NCT of Delhi) v. D.A.M. Prabhu,* (2009) 3 SCC 264 paras 11 and 12 : (2009) 2 Scale 492 (case under section 10 Essential Commodities Act).

should also be prosecuted[32]) and the person concerned was in charge of and was responsible to the company for the conduct of its business at the time when the offence by the company was committed.[33]

6. VICARIOUS RESPONSIBILITY IN STATUTORY OFFENCES

It has already been seen that there is a presumption that *mens rea* is a necessary constituent of statutory offences and that that presumption is not displaced except by clear words or by necessary implication.[34] Further, the maxims "*respondeat superior*" and "*qui facit per alium facit per se*" find no place in the criminal law. The normal rule, therefore, is that criminal liability in a master that might result either as a principal or as an accessory, springs from authorisation and not simply from the relationship of master and servant.[35] The Legislature may, however in an infinite variety of ways provide that there is to be criminal liability in one who has personally no *mens rea* or in one who has not committed any *actus reus*.[36] There is no vicarious liability in criminal law unless the statutes takes that also within its fold[37] either expressly or by necessary implication. Apart from cases where express provision is made to that effect,[38] the question is one

---

32. *Sheoratan Agarwal v. State of Madhya Pradesh*, AIR 1984 SC 1824 : (1984) 4 SCC 352; *Anil Hada v. Indian Acrylic Limited*, JT 1999 (9) SC 223 : AIR 2000 SC 145 : (2000) 1 SCC 1.

33. Cases under section 141 of the Negotiable Instruments Act, 1881: *S.M.S. Pharmaceuticals Ltd. v. Neeta Bhalla*, (2005) 8 SCC 89 (paras 10, 11) : AIR 2005 SC 3512; *Sabitha Ramamurthy v. R.B.S. Channabasavardhya*, (2006) 10 SCC 581 (para 7) : AIR 2006 SC 3086; *National Insurance Co. Ltd. v. Man Chand*, (2007) 3 SCC 691 (paras 16 and 17); *S.M.S. Pharmaceuticals Ltd. v. Neeta Bhalla*, (2007) 4 SCC 70 (paras 16 and 20) : (2007) 3 SLT 143 : (2007) 4 JT 230. For application of section 141 of the N.I. Act, 1881 when the offence is committed by a sick industry, **see** *BSILA v. Gift Holdings Pvt. Ltd.*, AIR 2000 SC 926 : (2000) 2 SCC 737; *Kusum Ingots and Alloys Ltd. v. Rennar Peterson Securities Ltd.*, AIR 2000 SC 954 : (2000) 2 SCC 745. For application of section 141 of the Negotiable Instruments Act, 1881 and the liability of a director who had resigned with intimation to the complainant prior to the date when a post dated cheque was presented for encashment **see**: *DCM Financial Service Ltd. v. J.N. Sareen*, (2008) 8 SCC 1 para 21 : AIR 2008 SC 2255. **See further:** *National Small Industries Corpn. Ltd. v. Harmeet Singh Paintal*, (2010) 3 SCC 330 paras 13 to 15, 22, 39 : (2010) 2 JT 161.

34. **See** title 4(a) in this Chapter.

35. *Vane v. Yiannopoullos*, (1964) 3 All ER 820, p. 829 (HL) (LORD MORRIS).

36. *Ibid.*

37. *Sham Sunder v. State of Haryana*, (1989) 4 SCC 630 p. 632 para 9 : AIR 1989 SC 1982; *R. Kalyani v. Janak C. Mehta*, (2009) 1 SCC 516 paras 32, 33 : (2008) 12 JT 279.

38. For example, **see** section 18 and section 77, Indian Mines Act, 1952. **See further** section 23C(1), Foreign Exchange Regulation Act, 1947, and *G.L. Gupta v. D.N. Mehta*, AIR 1971 SC 2162 : (1971) 3 SCC 189.

of construction whether by enacting a particular provision the Legislature, in the light of the object of the statute, has expressed itself by necessary implication so as to make a master criminally liable for the acts of his servants or agents. The relevant considerations in determining such a question were formulated by ATKIN, J. who in an oft-quoted passage stated: "I think that the authorities cited—make it plain that while *prima facie* a principal is not to be made criminally responsible for the acts of his servants, yet the Legislature may prohibit an act or enforce a duty in such words as to make the prohibition or the duty absolute; in which case the principal is liable if the act is in fact done by his servants. To ascertain whether a particular Act of Parliament has that effect or not, regard must be had to the object of the statute, the words used, the nature of the duty laid down, the person upon whom it is imposed, the person by whom it would in ordinary circumstances be performed, and the person upon whom the penalty is imposed."[39] It may also be that the statutory provision is so drafted that it only makes the employer liable for the offence but does not make the employee liable for whose act or default the employer is made liable.[40] Further, where the nature of the activity makes the premises, where it is carried on, a major hazard site, Parliament may impose upon the employer a duty, failure of which makes him liable for a criminal offence, 'to conduct his undertaking in such a way' that subject to reasonable practicability, it did not create risks to people's health and safety and the employer may become liable for the offence irrespective of the question that the risk originated not because of some lapse of his employee but because of the lapse of some other person over whom he had no control.[41] In such cases the statute makes the employer liable for the offence, though he has personally no *mens rea* or has not committed any *actus reus,* as the duty is laid on the employer himself by reference to a certain kind of activity

---

39. *Mousell Brother v. London & North Western Rail Co.*, (1916-17) All ER Rep 1101, p. 1106. **Referred** to in *Allen v. Whitehead*, (1929) All ER Rep 13, p. 16; *Hari Prasad Rao v. State*, AIR 1951 SC 204, p. 207 : (1951) SCR 312; *James and Sons Ltd. v. Smee*, (1954) 3 All ER 273, pp. 278, 279; *G. Newton Ltd. v. Smith*, (1962) 2 All ER 19, p. 22; *Vane v. Yiannopoullos*, (1964) 3 All ER 820, p. 830 (HL); *Andhra Pradesh Grain and Seed Merchants Association v. Union of India*, AIR 1971 SC 2346, p. 2349 : (1970) 2 SCC 71.

40. *Warwick Shire County Council v. Johnson*, (1993) 1 All ER 299, pp. 304, 305 : 1993 AC 583 : (1993) 2 WLR 1 (HL).

41. *R. v. Associated Octel Co. Ltd.*, (1996) 4 All ER 846 : (1996) 1 WLR 1543 : 1996 ICR 972 (HL) [Interpretation of section 3(i) Health and Safety at Work etc., Act, 1974]. Applied by the Court of Appeal in interpreting also section 2(i) of the same Act: *R. v. Gateway Food Markets Ltd.*, (1997) 3 All ER 78 : (1997) ICR 382 (CA). **See further,** *R. v. Nelson Group Services (Maintenance) Ltd.*, (1998) 4 All ER 331 (CA), pp. 349, 350.

carried on by him.[42] This duty is conceptually entirely different from the vicarious liability for the tortious acts of his servants and agents.[43]

In *Shriniwas Mall v. Emperor*,[44] where the question arose as to the master's liability for the act of his servant in committing a contravention of a Price Control Order made under rule 81(2)(b) of the Defence of India Rules, the Privy Council did not accept the conclusion of the High Court that guilty intent of the master was dispensed with for the offence under rule 81(4) which made any person contravening the provision of the rule liable to punishment with imprisonment which could extend to three years. LORD DU PARCQ speaking for the Board observed: "They see no ground for saying that offences against those of the Defence of India Rules here in question are within the limited and exceptional class of offences which can be held to be committed without a guilty mind—. Offences which are within that class are usually of a comparatively minor character, and it would be a surprising result of this delegated legislation if a person who was morally innocent of blame could be held vicariously liable for a servant's crime and so punishable with imprisonment for a term which may extend to three years."[45]

In *Hariprasad Rao v. State*,[46] the same question again arose in relation to rule 81(4) of the Defence of India Rules for contravention of the Motor Spirit Rationing Order made under rule 81(2) of the Defence of India Rules. Clause 2(m) of the Order defined 'supplier' as meaning a person carrying on the business of supplying motor spirit; clause 22 directed that no 'person' shall 'furnish' a supply of motor spirit otherwise than in accordance with the provisions contained in the Order; and clause 27A of the Order required the 'supplier' to endorse or cause to be endorsed on each coupon the registration mark of the vehicle at the time of furnishing motor spirit. It was held by the Supreme Court that the dealer in the absence of a guilty mind was not liable for contravention of clause 22 if his servant entrusted with the task contravened the clause. But, as to clause 27A the Supreme Court held that having regard to the definition of 'supplier' if a servant entrusted with the task contravened the clause the dealer was liable.

---

42. *R. v. Associated Octel Co. Ltd.*, *supra*, pp. 850, 851.
43. *Ibid.*
44. AIR 1947 PC 135.
45. *Ibid.*
46. AIR 1951 SC 204 : 1951 SCR 322.

In *State of Gujarat v. Kansara Maniram Bhikhalal*,[47] the Supreme Court held that for an offence under section 92 of the Factories Act, 1948 *mens rea* need not be always established, and the manager or occupier of a factory can only escape liability for a contravention of the Act made punishable under section 92, if he is able to bring the real offender to book in the manner provided by section 101.

If the thing prohibited is such which would frequently be done by servants or agents, and if the legislation does not use words to bring in as a necessary element any mental state of the master, it may be inferred that he would be liable for breaches of law committed by his servants or agents on the ground that to hold otherwise will make the prohibition of no effect.[48] This is specially true of Licensing Acts and other Acts in the field of consumer protection and public health,[49] where the offence is in the nature of "*quasi*-criminal offence",[50] and where putting the master under a strict liability assists in the enforcement of the regulations for there is "something he can do, directly or indirectly, by supervision or inspection, by improvement of his business methods or by exhorting those whom he may be expected to influence or control, which will promote the observance of the regulations".[51] The same principle applies to Acts designed for protection and safety of workers such as Factories Acts.[52]

In *Mullins v. Collins*,[53] the wife or servant of the licenced victualler had supplied liquor to a constable on duty, knowing him to be on duty but without any knowledge on the part of the licensee himself. The licensee was none-the-less held guilty under section 16 of the Licensing Act, 1872, which made it an offence and levied a penalty in words: 'if any licensed person—supplies any liquor or refreshment, whether by gift or sale to any

---

47. AIR 1964 SC 1893, p. 1897 : 1964 (7) SCR 656; **See further** *Maniklal v. State of Gujarat*, AIR 1967 SC 1226, p. 1231 : 1967 (2) SCR 507; *G.L. Gupta v. Asstt. Collector, Customs*, AIR 1971 SC 28, p. 32 : (1970) 2 SCC 530; *J. K. Industries v. Chief Inspector of Factories and Boilers*, 1996 (7) Scale 247, pp. 266, 267 : 1996 (6) SCC 665: 1996 (9) JT 27 : 1997 SCC (L&S) 1.

48. *Vane v. Yiannopoullos*, (1964) 3 All ER 820, pp. 823 (letters B, C, D) (LORD REID), 825 (letter I), 826 (letters A, B, C) (LORD EVERSHED).

49. *Tesco Ltd. v. Nattrass*, (1971) 2 WLR 1166, pp. 1198, 1199 : 1972 AC 153 (HL) (LORD DIPLOCK).

50. *Ibid*, and *Vane v. Yiannopoullos, supra*, p. 828 (letter C) (LORD EVERSHED).

51. *Lim Chin Aik v. Reginam*, (1963) 1 All ER 223, p. 228 : 1963 AC 160 (PC). **See further** *Tesco Ltd. v. Nattrass, supra*, p. 1199 (LORD DIPLOCK); *Supply of Ready Mixed Concrete (No. 2), Director-General of Fair Trading v. Pioneer*, (1995) 1 All ER 135, pp. 149, 150 (HL).

52. *J.K. Industries Ltd. v. Chief Inspector of Factories and Boilers*, 1996 (7) Scale 247, p. 264 : 1996 (6) SCC 665 : 1996 (9) JT 27 : 1997 SCC (L&S) 1.

53. (1874-80) All ER Rep 857.

constable on duty'. It was contended that knowledge of the licensee himself that the person supplied with the liquor was a constable and on duty was essential for constituting the offence. In repelling this contention, BLACKBURN, J. said that "such a construction as that, would make the Act a dead letter".[54] On the same point QUAIN, J. observed: "We must look at the nature of the act which the Legislature is dealing with. How does a licensee victualler usually carry on his business? Does he carry it on in person or by means of servants? Some licensed victuallers have several public houses in different places at the same time. Bearing in mind, then, the nature of the business of a licensed victualler, does the supply of brandy to a constable on duty by a servant, come within the mischief intended to be remedied by the statute? I think it clearly does. A barmaid supplied it to him at the counter in the ordinary way of her business, and knowing that he was a constable. If this is not an offence within the Act, the Act would be wholly inoperative."[55] It may be noticed that the prohibitive words : 'if any licensed person—supplies' were apt to cover a supply by the servant of a licensed person and the wider construction of these words harmonised with the object of the statute. In *Police Commrs. v. Cartman*,[56] similar result was reached in construing section 13 of the Licensing Act, 1872, which made it an offence to "supply" liquor to an intoxicated person. The licensee was held liable for the act of his servant though he had taken precaution of giving instructions as to the prohibition and was wholly unaware of the action of his servant. LORD RUSSEL of KILLOWEN, C.J. pointed out that the aim and purpose of the Act would be wholly defeated unless the licensee was held liable.[57]

In *Coppen v. Moore*,[58] the question related to construction of section 2(2) of the Merchandise Marks Act, 1887, which omitting unnecessary words provided: 'every person who sells any goods to which any false trade description is applied shall be guilty of an offence against the Act unless he proves—(a) that having taken all reasonable precautions he had no reason to suspect the genuineness of the trade description; and (b) that on demand duly made he gave all information in his power with respect to the persons from whom he obtained such goods; or (c) that he otherwise acted innocently'. In holding that upon a true construction of the Act the master was intended to be made criminally liable for the acts of his

---

54. *Ibid*, p. 859.
55. *Ibid.*
56. (1896) 1 QB 655.
57. *Ibid*, p. 658. **See further** *Goodfellow v. Johnson*, (1965) 1 All ER 941 : (1966) 1 QB 83 which relates to section 2, Food and Drugs Act, 1955, which reads: 'If any person sells to the prejudice of purchaser any food.......'.
58. (1895-99) All ER Rep 926.

servants done in contravention of the Act, where such acts were done within the scope or in the course of their employment, unless the master brought himself within one of the exceptions pointed out in the sections, LORD RUSSEL of KILLOWEN, C.J. observed that "any other conclusion would, to a large extent, render the Act ineffective for its avowed purpose."[59] *Cooper v. Moore* was referred to and relied upon in *Nottingham City Council v. Wolver Hamton & Dudley Breweries Plc,*[60] where the question related to the construction of section 14 of the Food Safety Act, 1990 which provides: 'Any person who sells to the purchaser's prejudice any food which is not of the nature or substance or quality demanded by the purchaser shall be guilty of an offence'. The respondent brewery owned a public house and employed its licencee. The public house was visited by the officers of the appellant the City Council who found deficiencies in the declared volume of alcohol in bottles of whisky and gin. This was deemed to be a sale for purposes of section 14 and the question was whether the licencee, the servant of the respondent, alone could be made liable for the offence or whether the respondent, who was the owner, was also liable for the offence. Giving ordinary meaning to the words of the Section and having regard to the legislative purpose, the court held that the respondent the owner of the goods was also liable for the offence and it was immaterial that the food sold was alcoholic drink for which licence was needed for the section applied to all foods. It was also said that this construction did not lay unreasonable burden on the owner who could escape liability by proving the defence of due diligence under section 21(1) of the Act.

In *Griffiths v. Studebakers Ltd.*,[61] a company which was holder of a limited trade licence in respect of a motor car was held guilty of 'using' the car in contravention of the Road Vehicles (Trade Licences) Regulations, 1922, when the car was driven by one of the employees contrary to the Regulations with more than two passengers in it in spite of the fact that it was so driven contrary to the express orders of the company. LORD HEWART, C.J. in the course of his Judgment observed: "It would defeat the scheme of this legislation if it were open to an employer, whether a company, a firm or an individual to say that although the car was being used under the limited licence in contravention of the conditions upon which it was granted—'My hand was not the hand that drove the car.'[62] Similar result was reached in *Green v. Burnett*,[63] which was decided along with

59. *Ibid*, p. 932.
60. (2004) 1 All ER 1352 (Divisional Court).
61. (1924) 1 KB 102.
62. *Ibid*, p. 106.
63. (1954) 3 All ER 273.

James and Sons Ltd. v. Smee.[64] PARKER, J. in delivering the majority judgment in the latter case said: "While the driver of a vehicle on the road 'uses' the vehicle, so also, if he be a servant, does his master whether that master be a private individual or a limited company, provided always that the servant is driving on his master's business."[65]

The above cases[66] and the like, must be distinguished with those cases where the Legislature uses the word 'knowingly' as a condition of liability on the part of the master or uses some such other words as 'allows', 'permits', 'suffers', 'causes', etc., showing that a mental state of the master is necessary to constitute the crime.[67] In the latter class of cases it has been held that *mens rea* such as knowledge, connivance or recklessness on the part of the master is essential before he can be held liable for the acts of his servants. However, the cases also establish a qualification of this rule that the master may yet be held liable, even in the absence of proof of or *mens rea*, if it be established that he had effectively 'delegated' his proprietary or managerial functions.

In *Somerset v. Hart*,[68] LORD COLERIDGE, C.J. said that 'suffering', without 'knowledge' was impossible and the court held that absence of knowledge, connivance, or carelessness on the part of the landlord of a public house or his agent was a good ground upon which the Magistrate might dismiss an information against him for 'suffering gaming' upon his licensed premises. Similar result was reached in *Somerset v. Wade*,[69] on the construction of the word 'permits', which was held to mean 'knowingly permits'. In the last mentioned case,[70] *Bond v. Evans*,[71] was distinguished

---

64. (1954) 3 All ER 275.

65. *Ibid*, p. 277. **See further** *F.E. Charman Ltd. v. Claw*, (1974) 3 All ER 371 (QBD), where a vehicle driven by an owner driver who was an independent contractor, for transporting the goods of A under a contract was held to be used by A. This result was however, reached with reluctance. It was further pointed out that the word 'use' will have a much restricted meaning when the statute makes independent references to persons 'using' and persons 'permitting or causing the use' as was the case in *Crawford v. Haughton*, (1972) 1 All ER 535.

66. **See** cases referred to in notes 47 (p. 1027), 50 (p. 1027), 52, (p. 1027), 55-57 (p. 1028), *supra*.

67. **See** cases in text and notes 62-83 (pp. 1032-1035), notes 85 to 94 (pp. 1036-1037), *infra*. Further for making a master liable for 'aiding or abetting' an offence committed by his servant, knowledge of the circumstances constituting the offence is necessary. **See** *John Henshall Ltd. v. Harvey*, (1965) 1 All ER 725, p. 728. **See also** *Harish Chandra v. State of M.P.*, AIR 1965 SC 932, p. 939 (para 20, point not raised) : 1965 (1) SCR 323.

68. (1884) 12 QBD 360.

69. (1891-94) All ER Rep 1228. **See further** *Ferguson v. Weaving*, (1951) 1 All ER 412, p. 414.

70. *Ibid*.

71. (1886-90) All ER Rep 1035.

where a licensee was held liable for "permitting or suffering" gaming in the licensed premises without his actual knowledge and contrary to his instructions on the ground that the licensee had left complete control of the premises to his servant who managed the premises and to whose knowledge the gaming took place in the premises.[72] In *Macleod v. Buchanan,*[73] the House of Lords held that the owner of a motor car "permitted the use" of the car by his brother for purposes not covered by the insurance, on facts that complete and unambiguous control of the car was handed over to the brother which had the effect of sanctioning general use, although there was no evidence in the case that the owner knew that his brother was using the car for purposes not covered by the insurance. In the last mentioned case[74] LORD WRIGHT drew a distinction between to 'cause' the user and to 'permit' the user and he said: "To 'cause' the user involves some express or positive mandate for person 'causing' to the other person, or some authority from the former to the latter, arising in the circumstances of the case. To 'permit' is a looser and vaguer term. It may denote an express permission, general, or particular, as distinguished from a mandate. The other person is not told to use the vehicle in the particular way, but he is told that he may do so if he desires. However the word also includes cases in which permission is merely inferred. If the other person is given the control of the vehicle, permission may be inferred if the vehicle is left at the other person's disposal in such circumstances as to carry with it a reasonable implication of a discretion or liberty to use it in the manner in which it was used."[75] In *James and Sons Ltd. v. Smee,*[76] it was again held that the words 'permits to be used' import knowledge which in this connection includes 'the state of mind of a man who shuts his eyes to the obvious or allows his servant to do something in the circumstances where a contravention is likely, not caring whether a contravention takes place or not';[77] but it was pointed out that 'permission to use is not unless more is proved, a permission to use in contravention.'[78]

---

72. *Ibid.*

73. (1940) 2 All ER 179 (HL).

74. *Ibid.*

75. *Ibid*, p. 187; but in another context it has been held that a person may without knowledge, intention or negligence 'cause' a thing to happen which is an offence; *Alphacell Ltd. v. Woodward*, (1972) 2 All ER 475 (HL) discussed at p. 707.

76. (1954) 3 All ER 273.

77. *Ibid*, p. 278. **See further** *Ross v. Moss*, (1965) 3 All ER 145, p. 148 ('knowledge' includes the case of shutting one's eyes to what is going on). In *Grays Haulage Co. Ltd. v. Arnold*, (1966) 1 WLR 534 and *Reg v. Sonter*, (1971) 1 WLR 1187 (CA). Similar tests of 'permitting' were laid down.

78. *Ibid*, p. 279.

The meaning of the word 'permits' was considered by the House of Lords in *Vehicle Inspectorate v. Nuttall*[79] in the context of the offence under section 96(11A) of the Transport Act, 1968. This section provides that when there is a contravention of any requirement as to periods of driving or distance driven or periods on or off duty in the case of a driver of a motor vehicle 'then the offender and any other person (being the offender's employer or a person to whose orders the offender was subject) who caused or permitted the contravention shall be liable for the offence. The requirement as to periods of driving etc. is regulated by council (EEC) regulations with the object of promoting road safety. These regulations also require installation of recording equipment or tachograph in vehicles and periodic checks by operators to ensure observance of the regulations. Contravention by the driver of the regulations restricting driving hours was not in dispute before the House of Lords and the only question was whether the employer of the drivers was liable for 'permitting' contravention by the drivers. It was established that the employer had failed to examine the tachograph charts during the relevant period. This gave rise to the inference that the employer had not taken reasonable steps to prevent contravention by the drivers and on this basis he was held *prima facie* liable for 'permitting' contravention by the driver. Dealing with the meaning of the word 'permit' in section 96(11A), LORD STEYN observed: "Depending on the context the word 'permit' is capable of bearing on the one hand, a narrow meaning of assenting to or agreeing to or, on the other hand, a wider meaning of not taking reasonable steps to prevent something in one's power. But I am persuaded that wider meaning best matches the context. The manifest purpose of the community rules is to place a responsibility on an employer of drivers to use tachograph records in order to prevent contravention and to promote road safety. The objective of the rules militates in favour of accepting the second or wider interpretation."[80] It was also observed that the community rules would be difficult to enforce against employers if permitted is interpreted to mean assenting to or agreeing to and section 96(11A) would become relatively ineffective. As regards the mental elements of the offence, LORD STEYN observed: It is not an offence of strict or absolute liability. Nothing less than wilfulness or recklessness will be sufficient. In practice recklessness will be the relevant *mens rea*."[81] Explaining the concept of recklessness LORD STEYN further observed. "If the defendant's state of mind is one of not caring whether a

79. (1999) 3 All ER 833 (HL).
80. *Ibid*, p. 839.
81. *Ibid*, p. 839.

contravention of the provisions of regulations took place that would generally be sufficient to establish recklessness."[82]

In *Emary v. Nolloth*,[83] a barman employed by the licensee of the bar sold liquor to a child otherwise than in the manner provided by the Intoxicating Liquors (Sale to Children) Act, 1901. The sale was made by the servant contrary to express instructions of the licensee and without his knowledge, at a time when the licensee was himself in charge of the premises. On these facts the licensee was charged with an offence under section 2 of the Act, which imposed liability on every holder of a licence who 'knowingly sells or delivers, or allows any person to sell or deliver... intoxicating liquor' in contravention of the Act to any person under the age of fourteen. In holding the licensee not guilty, LORD ALVERSTONE, C.J. observed: "There is a class of cases where the words 'knowingly allows, permits or suffers' have been used. There, knowledge has been held to be essential; but the licence-holder has been held, and I should say rightly held, to permit or suffer the thing to be done, when, he has delegated his authority to another by whom it is done, and this second principle seems to me derived from the cases that, where a man delegates his own authority and puts somebody else in charge, and, if I may adopt what my brother Channel said, 'has delegated his own power to prevent', then he has been held to permit or suffer the act to be done within the meaning of the statute."[84] This case, where there was absence of knowledge and absence of delegation of managerial functions may be compared with the case of *Allen v. Whitehead*,[85] where a keeper of a refreshment house did not himself manage the house but had left the management to a manager employed by him and the manager knowingly permitted prostitutes to congregate in the premises. Although there was no evidence that the keeper of the house knew of the misconduct of the manager, the keeper was held guilty of an offence under section 44 of the Metropolitan Police Act, 1899, which made a keeper of refreshment house liable to a penalty if he 'shall knowingly permit or suffer prostitutes to meet together and remain therein'. LORD HEWART, C.J. in the course of his judgment observed: "This seems to me to be a case where the proprietor, the keeper of the house, had delegated his position to a manager so far as the conduct of the business, and it seems to me the only reasonable conclusion is, regard being had to the purpose of this Act, that knowledge in the manager was knowledge in the keeper of the house."[86] Same principle was applied in the case of joint

---

82. *Ibid*, p. 840.
83. (1900-03) All ER Rep 606.
84. *Ibid*, p. 608.
85. (1929) All ER Rep 13.
86. *Ibid*, p. 16.

licensees in *Linnet v. Commr. of Police*,[87] where the entire management was left to one of the licensees only with the consent of the other and both were found guilty of 'wilfully or knowingly' permitting disorderly conduct in the licensed premises although one of the licensees was never on the premises nor had he any knowledge of the conduct which had taken place on the premises. And in *Hawker v. Robinson*,[88] a licensee was held liable for knowingly selling liquor to a person under age although liquor was sold without his knowledge by his barman because the barman was in sole charge of that part of the premises where the liquor was sold.

The different types of cases were reviewed and discussed by the House of Lords in *Vane v. Yiannopoullos*,[89] where a restaurant licence holder was charged for 'knowingly selling or supplying' intoxicating liquor contrary to the conditions of his licence. One of the conditions of the licence was that the liquor shall not be sold or supplied on the premises otherwise than to persons taking table meals there. The restaurant consisted of the ground floor and the basement of a building. A waitress engaged by the licensee, who had specific instruction not to contravene the conditions of the licence, on one occasion served liquor to two customers who had not ordered a meal. This was done without the knowledge of the licensee who was at that time present in the basement and was engaged in the conduct of the business. The House of Lords on a construction of section 22 and comparing it with section 21 of the Licensing Act, 1961 held that the knowledge of the licensee was essential for section 22, which, on facts stated above, had not been established, and therefore, the charge against the licensee was rightly dismissed.[90] LORD REID after a review of the cases found that even when word 'knowingly' had been used, the cases relating to construction of Licensing Acts had recognised that a licensee could yet be made liable for acts done without his knowledge but done with the knowledge of a person whom he had left in charge of the premises.[91] He also said that this was

---

87. (1946) 1 All ER 380, p. 383.

N.B.—*G. Newton Ltd. v. Smith*, (1962) 2 All ER 19, where words 'wilfully or negligently' were used can also be supported on the same principle.

88. (1972) 2 All ER 786 (QBD).

89. (1964) 3 All ER 820.

N.B.—The charge was under section 22(1)(a) which provides: "If the holder of a justices' on licence knowingly sells or supplies intoxicating liquor to persons to whom he is not permitted by the conditions of the licence to sell or supply it.......he shall be guilty of an offence under this section".

In contrast to section 22(1)(a) the language of section 21(1) was as follows: "The holder of the licence or his servant shall not knowingly sell intoxicating liquor to a person under eighteen".

90. *Ibid.*

91. *Ibid*, p. 823, (letters E, F).

"hard to justify"[1] for in taking that view "the courts have in effect legislated to fill the gap,"[2] but since it was a long standing practice it was "now too late to upset it,"[3] and "we should have matters as they are."[4] Similarly, LORD EVERSHED in the same case observed: "Where the relevant regulation imports the word 'knowingly' as a condition of liability on the part of the licensee or proprietor, 'knowledge', that is *mens rea* in a real sense, on the part of the licensee or proprietor, should normally be established as a fact, if he is to be held liable under the statute. To this proposition it appears, however, that, for better or worse, it should now be accepted that something further may be added,—namely, that in the absence of proof of actual knowledge, nevertheless the licensee or proprietor may be held liable if he be shown—in a real sense, effectively to have 'delegated' his proprietary or managerial functions."[5] LORD MORRIS on the contrary did not accept that there were any canons of construction especially applicable to Licensing Acts or that in such legislations the principle '*respondeat superior*' commanded some exceptional yet general acceptance.[6] He, however, did not find it necessary to express any opinion on the correctness of the principle of delegation except saying that there was no statutory wording in support of it.[7] LORD DONOVAN who agreed with the judgment of LORD MORRIS observed that the rule that licensee may be held liable if he had delegated sufficient control of the premises to the person who actually committed the offence is a rule which he had failed to spell out of any Act of Parliament,[8] but he also found it unnecessary to express upon its validity. LORD HODSON also did not decide as to the validity of the rule in delegation cases as even accepting the rule, there was no real delegation on the particular facts of the case.

The decision of the House of Lords discussed above does not overrule the 'delegation cases,'[9] but it certainly points out that the principle evolved in them that in spite of the use of the word 'knowingly' as a condition of liability in the relevant statute, a proprietor or a licensee may yet be held liable vicariously for acts done without his knowledge but done with the knowledge of a person to whom he has delegated complete managerial

---

1. *Ibid*, p. 823, (letter E).
2. *Ibid*, p. 824, (letters A, B.).
3. *Ibid*, p. 823, (letters H, I).
4. *Ibid*, p. 824, (letters A, B.).
5. *Ibid*, p. 823, (letters D, E.).
6. *Ibid*, p. 829, (letters H, I).
7. *Ibid*, p. 830, (letter C).
8. *Ibid*, p. 832, (letter H).
9. **See** *Ross v. Moss* (1965) 3 All ER 1451, p. 149 and *R. v. Wilson*, (1968) 1 All ER 197, where LORD PARKER, C.J. discusses the House of Lord's decision in *Vane v. Yiannopoullos*, *supra*, **see further** *Hawker v. Robinson*, (1972) 2 All ER 786.

functions is a principle not justifiable on any known rule of construction but is a sort of "judicial legislation", "for better or worse". In this view of the matter, this principle of 'delegation cases' has not much to recommend itself for adoption in India.

The rigour of the Acts which create absolute offences and which make the master liable for the acts of their servants or agents is sometimes softened by making a provision that it shall be a defence to prove certain exculpatory circumstances such as that the accused used reasonable diligence to see that the Act in question was complied with and that the non-observance of the Act by the servant or agent or any other person was without knowledge or connivance on the part of the master.[10] Such provisions are broadly classifed as (i) the third party procedure or 'passing on' defence; and (ii) the no negligence procedure.[11] The provision may also be in a form where the master is required to establish both these defences *i.e.* that the real offender was someone else and that he had used due diligence to enforce the provisions of the Act and the offence in question was committed by the named offender without his consent or connivance.[12] But the existence of such a provision will be indicative that knowledge of the master or a person standing in the position of the master (*e.g.* a managing director of a company or a person to whom the duty of directing the business is delegated) is not a necessary ingredient of an act prohibited by the statute unless expressly so stated or necessarily to be implied from the words of the prohibition.[13]

An interesting example of a case dealing with such a provision is furnished by *Tesco Ltd. v. Nattrass.*[14] Under section 11(2) of the Trade Descriptions Act, 1968, if any person offering to supply any goods, gives, by

---

10. **See** section 101 of the Factories Act, 1948 and *Maniklal v. State of Gujarat*, AIR 1967 SC 1226, p. 1231 : (1967) 2 SCR 507; **see further** section 23C(1) of the Foreign Exchange Regulation Act, 1947 and *G.L. Gupta v. Asstt. Collector of Customs*, AIR 1971 SC 28, p. 32 : (1970) 2 SCC 530; section 18A of the Drugs and Cosmetics Act, 1940 and *State of Karnataka v. Pratap Chand*, AIR 1981 SC 872 : (1981) 2 SCC 335; *Rajasthan Pharmaceutical Laboratory, Bangalore v. State of Karnataka*, AIR 1981 SC 809 : (1981) 1 SCC 639; section 47 of the Water (Prevention and Control of Pollution) Act, 1974 and *U.P. Pollution Board v. Modi Distillery*, (1987) 3 SCC 684 : AIR 1988 SC 1128; section 10 of the Essential Commodities Act, 1955 and *Sham Sunder v. State of Haryana*, AIR 1989 SC 1982; section 17(1) Proviso of the Prevention of Food Adulteration Act, 1954 and *R. Banerjee v. H.D. Dubey*, AIR 1992 SC 1168 : (1992) 2 SCC 552.

11. *J.K. Industries Limited v. Chief Inspector of Factories and Boilers*, 1996 (7) Scale 247, pp. 266, 267 : 1996 (6) SCC 665 : 1996 (9) JT 27.

12. *Ibid.* The case deals with section 101 of the Factories Act, 1948.

13. *Wings Ltd. v. Ellis*, (1984) 3 All ER 577, p. 588 : (1985) AC 272 : (1984) 3 WLR 965 (HL).

14. (1971) 2 WLR 1166 : 1972 AC 153 (HL).

whatever means, any indication that the goods are being offered at a price less than at which they are in fact being offered, he is guilty of an offence. Section 24(1) of the Act provides: 'In any proceeding for an offence under the Act it shall, subject to sub-section (2) of this section, be a defence for the person charged to prove–(a) that the commission of the offence was due to a mistake or to reliance on information supplied to him or to the act or default of another person, an accident or some other cause beyond his control; and (b) that he took all reasonable precautions and exercised all due diligence to avoid the commission of such an offence by himself or any person under his control'. Section 24(2) requires notice to be given to the prosecutor if the accused is blaming another person. The appellants Tesco Ltd., a company, owned a large number of super-markets in which they sold a wide variety of goods. Posters were displayed in the shop that packs of radiant white powder were being offered at s.2 d.11 as against the normal price of s.3 d.11. On September 26, 1970, a customer went to buy a pack. He could only find packs marked s.3 d.11 and none marked a.2 s. 11. He took one of the packs to the cashier who told him that there were none in stock for sale at s. 2 d. 11. He paid s. 3 d. 11 and complained to the authorities which led to the prosecution of the company for an offence under section 11(2) of the Act. The company took the defence under section 24(1) and named one Mr. Clement, their shop manager, as the offender. The facts found were that on the previous evening a shop assistant, Miss Rogers, found that there were no more of the specially marked packs in stock. She ought to have told this to the shop manager, but she failed to do so. The shop manager, whose duty it was to see that proper packs were displayed for sale, failed to verify this and marked his daily return "all special offers O.K." If the shop manager had known that there were no packs, marked with the reduced price, he would either have removed the poster advertising the reduced price or given instructions that only reduced price be charged for the packs marked s.3 d.11. The Justices also found that the company had set up a proper system for the avoidance of offences under the Act and had provided adequate and proper supervision to see that the system was followed and their instructions observed. They, therefore, held that section 24(1)(b) was complied with. However, they also held that the shop-manager was not "another person" within section 24(1)(a) and the company were convicted. In appeal the Divisional Court held that the manager was 'another person' within section 24(1)(a), but the conviction was maintained on the ground that section 24(1)(b) was not complied with on the reasoning that the word 'he' in that section did not merely mean the accused but all his servants acting in a managerial or supervisory capacity. In appeal to the House of Lords the conviction was set aside. It was held that the shop manager was another person within section 24(1)(a) and that the company had also performed under section 24(1)(b) the duty of setting up and ensuring an efficient system for avoidance of offences under the Act. It was further held that it was wrong to say that if the person actually guilty was one who exercised some form of managerial function, the protection under section 24 was not available. When the offence alleged is against a company, persons like Managing Director or Directors stand in the same position as the company, and if the fault is of such a person, section 24 will not be available as a protection. Similar will be the position if fault is of a person to whom the duty ensuring the efficient working of the system designed for avoidance of offences is delegated. But in all other cases, if the company establishes the facts relevant under section 24, the protection is available notwithstanding that the fault is of a servant who in some form exercises managerial functions.

7. *MENS REA* UNDER THE INDIAN PENAL CODE

In India all offences are statutory, and the general law as to crimes is codified in the Indian Penal Code. Definitions of 'Crime' in the various sections of the Code contain specification of the mental state which is required to be established as a necessary constituent of the crime. The Code also provides for certain general exceptions and cases falling within them are taken out of the purview of any criminal liability. The general view having regard to the scheme of the Code is that the maxim '*actus non facit reum nisi mens sit rea*' has no application to offences under the Code.[15] As stated by M.C. SETALVAD: "By specifying the varying guilty intention for each offence the Code has in effect built the maxim into each of the definitions and given it statutory effect. Where the Code omits to indicate a particular guilty intent, the presumption, having regard to the general frame of the definitions, would be that the omission must be intentional."[16] In the context of the Penal Code the Supreme Court observed: "Under the Indian Penal Law guilt of almost all the offences is fastened either on the ground of 'intention', or 'knowledge', or 'reason to believe.' "[17] Further, "the Penal Code save and except some provisions specifically providing therefor does not contemplate any vicarious liability on the part of a party who is not charged directly for commission of an offence."[18]

---

15. The Common Law in India, by M.C. SETALVAD, p. 140. **See** for example *Ranjit D. Udeshi v. State of Maharashtra*, AIR 1965 SC 881, p. 886 (para 10) : 1965 (1) SCR 65.
16. *Ibid.*
17. *Joti Parshad v. State of Haryana*, AIR 1993 SC 1167, p. 1169 : 1992 (6) JT 94 : 1993 Supp (2) SCC 497.
18. *S. K. Alagh v. State of U.P.*, (2008) 5 SCC 662 para 16 : AIR 2008 SC 1731.

CHAPTER 12

DELEGATED LEGISLATION

SYNOPSIS

1. FORMS OF DELEGATED LEGISLATION

Delegated legislation permitted by enabling Acts appears under different names, without there being any clear-cut demarcation between all of them. 'Rule' and 'Order' are by far the most common names under which delegated legislation is permitted. Section 3(51) of the General Clauses Act, 1897, contains a definition of the word 'rule' in the following words: "'*rule' shall mean a rule made in exercise of a power conferred by any enactment and shall include a regulation made under any enactment*". The word 'regulation' has been used in the Constitution where power to govern certain territories is conferred by making 'regulations' and the word is defined in section 3(50), General Clauses Act in these terms: "'Regulation' shall mean a Regulation made by the President under Article 240 of the Constitution;[1] and shall include a Regulation made by the President under Article 243 thereof and a Regulation made by the Central Government, under the Government of India Act, 1870, or the Government of India Act, 1915, or the Government of India Act, 1935". But as expressed in the definition of 'rule', a 'regulation' may be made as a rule and then it partakes the character of a rule.[2] When the power to make delegated legislation is conferred on different authorities by the same Act, the words 'rules' and 'regulations' may be utilised to distinguish the source and to sub-ordinate the latter to the former.[3] But sometimes the same authority may be authorised to make 'rules' in respect of certain matters and 'regulations' in respect of others and the distinction, if any, may lie in the conditions under which these powers may be exercised.[4] The Report of the Committee on Minister's Powers, 1932, deprecated the indiscriminate use of these

1. **See** *T.M. Kanniyan v. ITO, Pondicherry*, AIR 1968 SC 637 : (1968) 2 SCR 103.
2. 'Regulation' and 'rule' are interchangeable words; *Parvez Qadir v. Union of India*, AIR 1975 SC 446, p. 451 : (1975) 4 SCC 318.

   A regulation made under statutory powers laying down terms and conditions of service of employees like any other delegated legislation such as a rule has the force of law: *Sukhdeo Singh v. Bhagatram Sardar Singh*, AIR 1975 SC 1331, p. 1340 : (1975) 1 SCC 421 **overruling** *Indian Airlines v. Sukhdeo*, AIR 1971 SC 1828 : (1971) 2 SCC 192 and *U.P. State Warehousing Corporation Ltd. v. Tyagi*, AIR 1970 SC 1244 : (1970) 2 SCC 838. Regulations are in the nature of statutory rules; they cannot be equated to bye-laws and their validity cannot be challenged on the ground of unreasonableness: *Maharashtra State Board of Secondary Education v. Paritosh Bhupesh Kumar Sheth*, (1984) 4 SCC 27, p. 45 : AIR 1984 SC 1543; *Sukhdeo Singh's* case was **followed** in *Vidya Dhar Pande v. Vidyut Grih Siksha Samiti*, AIR 1989 SC 341 : (1989) 4 SCC 734; *U.P. State Cooperative Land Development Bank Ltd. v. Chandra Bhan Dubey,* AIR 1999 SC 753, p. 759 : (1999) 1 SCC 741.
3. **See** sections 44 and 45, Road Transport Corporation Act, 1950; sections 28 and 29, River Boards Act, 1956; and sections 44 and 45, Food Corporations Act, 1964.
4. **See** sections 57 to 60, Mines Act, 1952.

expressions and suggested (p. 64): "The expression 'regulation' should be used to describe the instrument by which the power to make substantive law is exercised, and the expression 'rule' to describe the instrument by which the power to make law about procedure is exercised. The expression 'order' should be used to describe the instrument of the exercise of (A) executive power, (B) the power to take judicial or *quasi-judicial decisions*."[5] This suggestion, however, has neither been adopted in England[6] nor in India. For example, the word 'order' has not been only used to signify the power of taking executive, judicial or *quasi*-judicial decisions, but has also been used to confer extensive power of making delegated legislation.[7]

The words 'directions'[8] and 'schemes'[9] are also at times used to enable the making of delegated legislation. 'Circulars' issued under an Act may also contain delegated legislation having the force of law.[10] But circulars or instructions which have no statutory backing do not amount to law and

---

5. ALLEN : Law and Order, 2nd Edition, p. 112; *Sukhdeo Singh v. Bhagatram Sardar Singh*, AIR 1975 SC 1331, pp. 1336, 1337 : (1975) 1 SCC 421.

6. *Ibid.*

7. **See** section 3, Essential Commodities Act, 1955.

8. **See** section 24, Road Transport Corporation Act, 1950. **See further** *Fatma Hazi Ali v. State of Bombay*, AIR 1951 SC 180, p. 183 (para 15) : 1951 SCR 266; *General Manager, Mysore Road Transport Corporation v. Devraj Urs*, AIR 1976 SC 1027, p. 1030 : (1976) 2 SCC 863. **But see** section 43A (Madras Motor Vehicles Act, 1939) and *B. Rajgopala v. State Transport Appellate Tribunal*, AIR 1964 SC 1573 : 1964 (7) SCR 1. **Also see** section 63A, Motor Vehicles Act, 1939 and *Inter-State Transport Commission v. D. Manjunath*, AIR 1972 SC 2250 : 1973 (3) SCC 733; Article 256 of the Constitution and *Sharma Transport v. Government of A.P.*, AIR 2002 SC 322, p. 326 : (2002) 2 SCC 188 (A letter of request of Central Government is not a direction under Article 256 more so when it is unrelated to any Central law).

9. **See** section 5, Employees' Provident Funds Act, 1952; Chapter IV-A, Motor Vehicles Act, 1939; Section 5, Coal Mines Provident Fund and Bonus Scheme Act, 1948. But in *K.I. Shephard v. Union of India*, AIR 1988 SC 686 : (1987) 4 SCC 431 the amalgamation scheme framed under section 45 of the Banking Regulation Act, 1949 was held to be purely executive in nature. *Shepherd's* case was **distinguished** in *New Bank of India Employees Union v. Union of India*, AIR 1996 SC 3208, p. 3222 (para 30) : (1996) 8 SCC 407 where a scheme framed under section 9 of the Banking Companies (Acquisition and Transfer of Undertakings) Act, 1980 was held to be legislative in nature. Section 9(6) of this Act requires the scheme to be laid before Parliament which is given power to modify or annul the scheme. In contrast, section 45 of the Banking Regulation Act, 1949 only requires a scheme made under that Act to be simply laid before Parliament without any further procedure and this was said to have made the difference between the nature of the schemes in the two cases. It is submitted that *Shepherd's* case was not correctly decided.

10. *J.K. Vasavda v. Chandrakant Chimanlal Bhavsar*, AIR 1975 SC 2089 : (1975) 4 SCC 734.

cannot dilute or override the effect of a constitutional or statutory provision.[11] Prior executive instructions on a matter will cease to apply when that matter becomes covered by statute or statutory rules.[12] But executive instructions can supplement though not supplant statutory rules which may not deal with every aspect of a matter.[13]

The word 'notification' is normally used in the context of conditional legislation *e.g.*, to bring into operation the enabling Act or to grant exemptions from its provisions or to extend its operation to new persons or objects.[14] But a mere departmental communication does not amount to a notification and an earlier notification cannot be said to have been withdrawn by such a communication.[15]

Delegated legislation, in the shape of 'bye-laws' is somewhat more distinctive. The power to make 'bye-laws', is conferred on local authorities, and statutory or other undertakers "for regulating the conduct of persons within their areas or resorting to their undertaking",[16] and the bye-laws are

---

11. *Municipal Corporation Amritsar v. Senior Superintendent of Post Offices, Amritsar Division*, (2004) 3 SCC 92 : AIR 2004 SC 586; *Ramphal Kundu v. Kamal Sharma*, AIR 2004 SC 1657, p. 1668 (para 24) : (2004) 2 SCC 759.

12. *K.P. Sudhakaran v. State of Kerala*, (2006) 5 SCC 386 (para 12.4) : AIR 2006 SC 2138.

13. *K.H. Siraj v. High Court of Kerala*, (2006) 6 SCC 395 (para 62) : AIR 2006 SC 2339. (High Court empowered under statutory rule to select 'suitable' candidate for the post of Munsiff/Magistrate can prescribe minimum qualifying marks on written and oral tests).

14. **See** title 3(b)(i) 'Conditional Legislation'. A Legislation dealing with local authorities, for example a municipality, may make a distinction between an 'Order' sanctioning a tax and a 'Notification' imposing a tax; the imposition of tax is not effective without the notification: *Atlas Cycles Industries Ltd. v. State of Haryana*, AIR 1972 SC 121 : (1972) 2 SCC 564.

15. *Central Bureau of Investigation v. Ravi Shanker Srivastava*, (2006) 7 SCC 188 (para 13) : AIR 2006 SC 2872 : AIR 2006 SC 2339.

16. HALSBURY'S Laws of England, 4th edition, Vol. 44, p. 619. Bye-laws made under statutory powers are comprised within delegated legislation and have the force of law: *Sukhdeo Singh v. Bhagatram Sardar Singh*, AIR 1975 SC 1331, pp. 1336, 1337, 1340 : (1975) 1 SCC 421; *Indore Municipal Corporation v. Gujarat Co-operative Housing Society*, AIR 1992 SC 1506, p. 1511 : 1992 Supp (2) SCC 457 (Bye-laws made by a municipal corporation under statutory powers laying down mode of assessment of a tax become part of the Act). **Contrary** opinion was expressed in *Co-operative Central Bank v. Industrial Tribunal, Hyderabad*, AIR 1970 SC 245, p. 252 : (1969) 2 SCC 43, that Bye-laws and Standing Orders laying down conditions of service of employees do not amount to law. **See further** *Sakhrullah Khan Narrollah Khan v. State Industrial Court, Indore*, (1978) MPLJ 455, p. 464; *Glaxo Laboratories (I.) Ltd. v. Presiding Officer, Labour Court, Meerut*, (1984) 1 SCC 1, pp. 8, 9 : AIR 1984 SC 505; *Sudhir Chandra Sarkar v. Tata Iron & Steel Co. Ltd.*, (1984) 3 SCC 369 : AIR 1984 SC 1064 and *D.K. Yadav v. JMA Industries Ltd.*, (1993) 3 SCC 259. (These cases held that standing orders made under the

[Footnote No. 16 Contd.]

generally subordinated to the rules and regulations, if any, to be made under the enabling Act.[17]

In case of corporate bodies like a University, the constituent Act generally authorises the making of 'Statutes', 'Ordinances' and 'Regulations' by University Authorities, and this classification is utilised to differentiate the source from which they originate as also their inter-relation. 'Ordinances' are subordinated to 'Statutes', and 'Regulations' are subordinated to both 'Statutes' and 'Ordinances'.[18]

2. CONSTITUTIONAL LIMITS OF LEGISLATIVE DELEGATION

(a) General principles

Consistent with their sovereign character, Legislatures in India have been held to possess wide powers of delegation.[19] This power is, however, subject to one important limitation. The Legislature cannot delegate essential legislative functions which consist in the determination or choosing of the legislative policy and of formally enacting that policy into a binding

---

[Footnote No. 16 Contd.]

Industrial Employment (Standing Orders) Act, 1946 have a statutory flavour and they constitute statutory conditions of service). In *Babaji Kondaj Garod v. Nasik Co-operative Bank Ltd.*, (1984) 2 SCC 50, p. 62 : AIR 1984 SC 192 the case of *Co-operative Central Bank v. Industrial Tribunal, Hyderabad, supra*, was **followed** without noticing other cases. These two cases were **followed** by a F.B. of the Andhra Pradesh High Court and it was explained that bye-laws of a co-operative society are contractual in nature: *Kona Seema Co-operative Central Bank Ltd. v. N. Seetharama Raju*, AIR 1990 AP 171, p. 183 (FB). *Rajasthan State Road Transport Corporation v. Krishnakant*, 1995 (3) Scale 440 : AIR 1995 SC 1715 : (1995) 5 SCC 75 **followed in** *U.P. State Bridge Corporation Ltd. v. U.P. Rajya Setu Nigam Karmachari Sangh*, (2004) 4 SCC 268, p. 276 : (2004) 2 Scale 466, (Certified standing orders though statutorily imposed conditions of service do not constitute statutory provisions themselves and are not in the nature of delegated legislation). *Maharashtra State Road Transport Corporation v. Casteribe Rajya Parivahan Karmchari Sanghatana*, (2009) 8 SCC 556 para 46 : (2009) 11 JT 609 (standing orders are contractual in nature and do not have a statutory force). *Hyderabade Vanaspathi Ltd. v. Andhra Pradesh State Electricity Board*, AIR 1998 SC 1715, p. 1724 : (1998) 4 SCC 470 (Terms and conditions of supply notified under section 49 of the Electricity Supply Act, 1948 are statutory in nature and akin to subordinate legislation).

17. **See** section 61, Mines Act, 1952.

18. **See** sections 17 to 19, Benares Hindu University Act, 1915; and **see** *Akshaibarlal v. Vice-Chancellor*, AIR 1961 SC 619, pp. 622, 623 : 1961 (3) SCR 386. **See further** sections 27 to 31, Aligarh Muslim University Act, 1920; sections 28 to 32, Delhi University Act, 1922; and sections 27 to 31, Visva Bharati Act, 1951.

19. *In re, Article 143, Constitution of India*, AIR 1951 SC 332 : 1951 SCR 747. For summary of this case, **see** *Rajnarain Singh v. Chairman, P.A. Committee*, AIR 1954 SC 569, pp. 573, 574 : 1955 (1) SCR 290.

rule of conduct.[20] The Legislature cannot delegate "uncanalised and uncontrolled power;"[21] the power delegated must not be "unconfined and vagrant,"[22] but must be "canalised within banks that keep it from overflowing."[23] The "banks", that set the limits of the power delegated, are to be constructed by the Legislature by declaring the policy of the law and by laying down standards for guidance of those on whom the power to execute the law is conferred. So the delegation is valid only when the legislative policy and guidelines to implement it are adequately laid down and the delegate is only empowered to carry out the policy within the guidelines laid down by the Legislature.[24]

---

20. *In re, Article 143, Constitution of India, supra*, p. 400 (para 243); *Harishanker Bagla v. State of M.P.*, AIR 1954 SC 465, p. 468 (para 9) : 1955 (1) SCR 380; *Vasanlal Maganbhai Sanjawala v. State of Bombay*, AIR 1961 SC 4, p. 7 (para 4) : (1961) 1 SCR 341; *Joyti Prasad v. Union Territory, Delhi*, AIR 1961 SC 1601, p. 1609 : 1962 (2) SCR 116; *A.N. Parasuraman v. State of Tamil Nadu*, AIR 1990 SC 40, p. 42 : (1989) 4 SCC 683; *Agricultural Market Committee v. Shalimar Chemical Works Ltd.*, AIR 1997 SC 2502, p. 2507 : (1997) 5 SCC 516; *Kunj Bihari Lal Butail v. State of H.P.*, AIR 2000 SC 1069, p. 1071 : (2000) 3 SCC 40 [7th edition (pp. 689, 690) of this book is **referred**]; *Kiran Gupta v. State of U.P.*, (2000) 7 SCC 719, p. 729 : AIR 2000 SC 3299, p. 3305.

21. *Hamdard Dawakhana v. Union of India*, AIR 1960 SC 554, p. 568 (para 35) : 1960 (2) SCR 671.

22. *Panama Sugar Refining Co. v. Ryan*, 293 US 388, p. 440 (CARDOZO, J.); *Schechtar Poultry Corp. v. United States*, 295 US 495, p. 551 (CARDOZO, J.) **referred** to in *In re, Article 143, Constitution of India*, AIR 1951 SC 332, p. 400 : 1951 SCR 747. Similar expressions were used by the Supreme Court in the context of an argument that discretion conferred on the Executive by the Legislature violated Article 14 of the Constitution: *Naraindas v. State of M.P.*, AIR 1974 SC 1232, p. 1249 : (1974) 4 SCC 788.

23. *Ibid.*

24. *Tata Iron & Steel Co. v. Workmen*, AIR 1972 SC 1917, p. 1922 : (1972) 1 SCC 383 *Gwalior Rayon Mills v. Asstt. Commr., Sales Tax*, AIR 1974 SC 1660, p. 1669 (para 22): (1974) 4 SCC 98; *P.N. Kaushal v. Union of India*, AIR 1978 SC 1457, p. 1472 : (1978) 3 SCC 558; *Ajoy Kumar Banerjee v. Union of India*, (1984) 3 SCC 127, pp. 147, 148 : AIR 1984 SC 1130; *A.S. Parasuraman v. State of Tamil Nadu*, AIR 1990 SC 40, p. 43 : (1989) 4 SCC 683; *Ramesh Birch v. Union of India*, AIR 1990 SC 560, pp. 569, 571; 1989 Supp (1) SCC 430. *Agricultural Market Committee v. Shalimar Chemical Works*, AIR 1997 SC 2502, p. 2507 : (1997) 5 SCC 516.

N.B.—(1) In *Municipal Corporation of Delhi v. Birla Cotton Spinning and Weaving Mills*, AIR 1968 SC 1232 : (1968) 3 SCR 251, HIDAYATULLAH, RAMASWAMI and SIKRI, JJ. expressed the view that a search for a policy is not a proper test for validity of delegation and all that should be seen is whether there is any abdication of function. WANCHOO, C.J., SHELAT, SHAH and VAIDIALLINGAM, JJ. although differing in their conclusions applied the test whether policy and guidelines have been indicated by the Legislature. The Privy Council in *Queen v. Burah*, ILR 4 Cal 172 (PC) and *Cobb & Co. Ltd. v. Kropp*, (1966) 2 All ER 913 : (1967) 1 AC 141 (PC) laid down two tests: (1) Has the Legislature assumed a new legislative power? and (2) has it abdicated any of its functions? SEERVAI by

[Footnote No. 24 Contd.]

What is permitted, therefore, is the delegation of ancillary or subordinate legislative functions,[25] or, what is fictionally called, a power to fill up the details.[26] The Legislature may, after laying down the legislative policy, confer discretion on an administrative agency as to the execution of the policy and leave it to the agency to work out the details within the framework of the policy.[27] The Legislature's ability to delegate these functions is derived from an implied conferral of that authority for the effective exercise of the legislative power granted by the Constitution on the principle that everything necessary to the exercise of a power is implicit in the grant of the power.[28] The limits of this ability to delegate *i.e.*, the inhibition against delegation of essential legislative functions, is also impliedly derived from the provisions of the Constitution which confer the power to make laws on the Legislature. It is reasoned that the Constitution entrusts the duty of law-making to Parliament and the Legislatures of States, and thereby impliedly prohibits them to throw away that responsibility on the

---

[Footnote No. 24 Contd.]

ignoring **dissenting** opinions in *Delhi Corporation's* case, *supra*, advocates the view that that case must be taken to have decided that a search for policy is not the proper test; [**See** Constitutional Law of India, Vol. II (2nd Edition), p. 1210]. But this view has been **rejected** by the Supreme Court in *Gwalior Rayon Mill's* case, *supra*, *P.N. Kaushal's* case, *supra* and *Ajoy Kumar Banerjee's* case, *supra*.

(2) If the Legislature keeps control over the delegate, *e.g.* by requiring that the delegated legislation be laid before the Legislature, want of guidelines may not be fatal: *N.K. Papiah & Sons v. Excise Commissioner*, AIR 1975 SC 1007 : (1975) 1 SCC 492. It was further held in this case that the Legislature keeps control over the delegate by its ability to repeal the Act conferring power to the delegate. This proposition which is often urged on the basis of *Kropp's* case, *supra*, is not correct and has been expressly negatived in *Gwalior Rayon Mill's* case, *supra*, pp. 1670, 1671 and *Kerala State Electricity Board v. Indian Aluminium Co. Ltd.*, AIR 1976 SC 1031, pp. 1049, 1050 : (1976) 1 SCC 466. In *Avinder Singh v. State of Punjab*, AIR 1979 SC 321, p. 335 : (1979) 1 SCC 137, the said proposition was characterised as 'very wide and sweeping' for if it were correct even naked delegations will be sustained.

25. *In re, Article 143, Constitution of India*, AIR 1951 SC 332, p. 404 (para 262) : 1951 SCR 747; *St. Johns Teachers Training Institute v. Regional Director National Council for Teacher Education,* (2003) 3 SCC 321, p. 331 : AIR 2003 SC 1533.

26. *Wayman v. Southard*, 10 Wheat 1 (1825), MARSHALL, C.J.; **see** American Constitutional issues by C.H. PRITCHETT, p. 86. *Kunj Bihari Lal Butail v. State of H.P.,* AIR 2000 SC 1069, p. 1071 : (2000) 3 SCC 40 [7th edition (pp. 689, 690) of this book is referred]; *St. Johns Teachers Training Institute v. Regional Director National Council for Teacher Education, supra.*

27. *Khambhalia Municipality v. State of Gujarat*, AIR 1967 SC 1048, p. 1051 : 1967 (2) SCR 631; *St. Johns Teachers Training Institute v. Regional Director National Council for Teacher Education, supra*.

28. *In re, Article 143, Constitution of India*, AIR 1951 SC 332, p. 397 (para 231) : 1951 SCR 747.

shoulders of some other authority.[29] Thus, the area of compromise between these two implications determines the permissible limits of delegation. The question, whether any particular legislation suffers from excessive delegation, has to be decided by courts having regard to the subject-matter, the scheme, the provisions of the statute including its preamble, and the facts and circumstances in the background of which the statute is enacted.[30] The courts in this task have been quite generous and liberal, for it is now accepted that having regard to the complexity of problems which a modern State has to face, delegated legislation is a necessity and has its own advantages.[31] If, on a liberal construction of a given statute, a legislative policy and guidance for its execution are brought out, the statute, even if skeletal, will be upheld and it will not be a valid argument that the Legislature should have made more detailed provisions.[32] But this rule of liberal construction should not be carried by the court to the extent of always trying to discover a dormant or latent legislative policy to sustain an arbitrary power conferred on the executive. It is the duty of the court to strike down without hesitation any arbitrary power conferred on the Executive by

---

29. *Ibid*, pp. 396, 397 (paras 227 and 232).

30. *Bhatnagar & Co. v. Union of India*, AIR 1957 SC 478, pp. 485, 486 : 1957 SCR 701; *Mohmedalli v. Union of India*, AIR 1964 SC 980, p. 985 (para 9) : 1963 Supp (1) SCR 993; *State of Nagaland v. Ratansingh*, AIR 1967 SC 212, p. 223 : 1966 (3) SCR 830; *Registrar, Co-operative Societies v. Kunjambu*, AIR 1980 SC 350, p. 352 : (1980) 1 SCC 340; *Kishan Prakash Sharma v. Union of India,* AIR 2001 SC 1493, pp. 1502, 1503 : (2001) 5 SCC 212; *St Johns Teachers Institute v. Regional Director Nat- ional Council of Teacher Education,* (2003) 3 SCC 321, p. 332 : AIR 2003 SC 1533; *People's Union for Civil Liberties v. Union of India*, (2004) AIR SCW 379 (paras 36-40).

31. *Jyoti Pershad v. Union Territory of Delhi*, AIR 1961 SC 1612 (para 17); *Tata Iron & Steel Co. v. Workmen*, AIR 1972 SC 1917, p. 1922 : (1972) 1 SCC 383; *Registrar, Co-operative Societies v. Kunjabmu*, AIR 1980 SC 350, p. 352 : (1980) 1 SCC 340; *A.V. Nachane v. Union of India*, AIR 1982 SC 1126, p. 1134 : (1982) 1 SCC 205; *J. Jayalalitha v. Union of India,* AIR 1999 SC 1912, p. 1921 : (1999) 5 SCC 138; *Kishan Prakash Sharma v. Union of India, supra; St Johns Teachers Institute v. Regional Director National Council of Teacher Education, supra,* pp. 331, 332; *Nowa ADS v. Secretary, Department of Municipal Administration and Water Supply*, (2008) 8 SCC 42 para 30 : AIR 2008 SC 2941.

32. *Ibid.* For example, in upholding the validity of section 24(1)(e) of the Advocates Act, 1961, which confers power on a State Bar Council to lay down further conditions for controlling the entry to the legal profession, guidance was found in the "well established connotations and contours of the requirements of legal profession"; *Haniraj L. Chulani (Dr.) v. Bar Council of Maharashtra*, AIR 1996 SC 1708, p. 1716 (para 16) : (1996) 3 SCC 342. By the rule made under section 24(1)(e) which was held valid in this case, persons in other professions were not allowed to enroll as advocate.

the Legislature.[33] Conferral of unguided discretion which can lead to discrimination is abdication of legislative function.[34] It has been suggested that there is now more and more of regulatory regime by delegated legislation, it is high time to introduce the practice of adding in the beginning an object and purpose clause while drafting the delegated legislation.[35]

It is settled that the Legislature, except when authorised by the Constitution, cannot create a parallel legislature or abdicate its functions in favour of some outside authority.[36] Similarly, the Legislature cannot delegate its power to repeal a law or even to modify it in essential features.[37] These are cases where the Legislature does not limit the delegation to ancillary or subordinate legislative functions but parts with its essential legislative functions and thereby transgresses the limits of permissible delegation. But this does not mean that if a power to extend or apply laws to a territory is validly conferred on the executive, it can be exercised only when there is a vacuum, *i.e.,* complete absence of laws on a given subject; the power can also be exercised when it supplements or modifies the existing law; but it cannot be exercised when it brings about an express or implied repeal or when it is in conflict with or repugnant to an existing law.[38] It is the law to be extended which cannot be amended or modified in its essential features while it is being extended, but its impact may be to modify or restrict the existing law and yet the extension will be valid provided there is no express or implied repeal of or conflict or repugnancy with the existing law as stated above.[39] When the Legislature requires the delegated legislation

---

33. *Vasanlal Maganbhai Sanjawala v. State of Bombay*, AIR 1961 SC 4, pp. 11, 12 : (1961) 1 SCR 341; *Devidas v. State of Punjab*, AIR 1967 SC 1895, p. 1901; *State of Punjab v. Khan Chand*, AIR 1974 SC 543 : (1974) 1 SCC 549; *A.N. Parasuraman v. State of Tamil Nadu*, AIR 1990 SC 40, p. 42 : 1989 (4) SCC 683; *Kishan Prakash Sharma v. Union of India,* AIR 2001 SC 1493, pp. 1502, 1503 : (2001) 5 SCC 212.

34. *State of Punjab v. Khan Chand, supra*, p. 547; *A.N. Parasuraman v. State of Tamil Nadu, supra.*

35. *Daiichi Sankyo Company Ltd. v. Jayaram Chigurupati*, (2010) 7 SCC 449 para 65 : AIR 2010 SC 3089.

36. *In re, Initiative and Referendum Act*, (1919) AC 935, p. 945**; referred** to in *In re, Article 143, Constitution of India*, AIR 1951 SC 332, p. 398 (para 234), p. 402 (para 254) : 1951 SCR 747; *Cobb & Co. Ltd. v. Kropp*, (1966) 2 All ER 913, p. 921 : (1967) 1 AC 141 (PC); *Shamrao v. Union Territory of Pondicherry*, AIR 1967 SC 1480 : 1967 (2) SCR 650.

37. *In re, Article 143, Constitution of India, supra*; *Rajnarain Singh v. Chairman, Patna Administration Committee*, AIR 1954 SC 569, pp. 573, 574 : 1955 (1) SCR 290; *Ramesh Birch v. Union of India*, AIR 1990 SC 560, p. 590 : 1989 Supp (1) SCC 430.

38. *Ramesh Birch v. Union of India*, AIR 1990 SC 560, p. 596 : 1989 Supp (1) SCC 430.

39. *Ibid*, p. 591.

to be laid before it, there is no abdication as the delegate is kept under the vigilance and control of the Legislature.[40]

A power conferred on the Executive by Legislature *A* to apply to the territories within the legislative jurisdiction of that Legislature, future laws or even existing laws with future amendments enacted by Legislature *B* which has no legislative jurisdiction in that area may amount to abdication of legislative function by Legislature *A*; and the delegation may be invalid if there is no policy or special reason behind such a sweeping delegation. This proposition follows from the case of *Shama Rao v. Union Territory of Pondicherry*.[41] In that case the Pondicherry Legislature enacted the Pondicherry General Sales Tax Act, 1965, which was to come into force on the issue of a notification by the Government, the effect of which was to apply to Pondicherry, the Madras General Sales Tax Act, 1959, with all amendments up to the date of the notification. The Supreme Court held the aforestated Pondicherry Act to be invalid on the ground that it enabled the application of future amendments made by the Madras Legislature in the Madras Act up to the date of enforcement of the Pondicherry Act, which amounted to abdication of legislative function by the Pondicherry Legislature. The court refused to follow its earlier decision in *In re, Article 143, Constitution of India*,[42] where a power conferred on the Central Government by a Central Act to extend to Part C States (now Union Territories) future laws enacted by Parliament or any of the State Legislatures was upheld; and distinguished it on the ground that the delegation was upheld because of the special position of the territories concerned which at that time had no Legislature of their own; and that the case did not contain any clear ratio on the point. The Supreme Court of United States in *United States v. Sharpnack*,[43] upheld the validity of the Assimilative Crimes Act, 1948, an Act enacted by Congress which automatically makes applicable to a Federal enclave future criminal statutes of the State where the enclave is situated. It was held that the Congress took the basic legislative decision to conform the laws in the enclaves to the laws of the States as to all

---

40. *D.S. Garewal v. State of Punjab*, AIR 1959 SC 512, p. 518 : 1959 Supp (1) SCR 792; *N.K. Papiah & Sons v. Excise Commissioner*, AIR 1975 SC 1007 : (1975) 1 SCC 492; *A.V. Nachane v. Union of India*, AIR 1982 SC 1126, p. 1134 : (1982) 1 SCC 205; *State of M.P. v. Mahalaxmi Fabric Mills Ltd.*, 1995(1) Scale 758, p. 770 : 1995 Supp (1) SCC 642.

41. *Shama Rao v. Union Territory of Pondicherry*. AIR 1967 SC 1480 : 1967 (2) SCR 650.

42. *In re, Article 143, Constitution of India*, AIR 1951 SC 332 : 1951 SCR 747.

43. *United States v. Sharpnack*, (1958) 355 US 286 : (1958) 2 Law Ed 282 **followed** in *Nagar Nigam Harijan Karmachari Sangh v. Municipal Corporation*, 1974 MPLJ 588 (G.P. Singh, J.); *Pannalal Kankariya & Sons v. Addl. Asst. Commissioner of Sales Tax*, (1981) MPLJ 580 (G.P. SINGH, C.J.).

offences not punishable under any federal enactment; and that it was within its constitutional power to enact the policy of uniformity in its most complete and accurate form. This case shows that if there be a policy behind the delegation *e.g.*, when complete uniformity is required on a certain subject, an Act which makes provision for automatic application of future laws of another Legislature on that subject may not be held to be unconstitutional on the ground of delegation. Therefore, in *Gwalior Rayon Mills v. Asst. Commr., Sales Tax*,[44] the Supreme Court upheld the validity of section 8(2)(b) of the Central Sales Tax Act, 1956, and ruled, that Parliament, with a view to prevent evasion of tax, can make a provision that Central sales tax shall be levied at the same rate at which sales tax is levied under the State Act. This case confines the ruling in *Shama Rao's* case[45] to its own facts and holds that there is no constitutional prohibition for adopting a provision of a law including its future amendments made by another Legislature when there is "a special reason or purpose" for such adoption.[46] The *Gwalior Rayon Mills*' case[47] was followed in *International Cotton Corporation (P) Ltd. v. Commercial Tax Officer, Hubli*,[48] which upheld the validity of section 8(2)(a) of the Central Sales Tax Act, 1956, which applies the rate of tax under the appropriate State Act to sales of declared goods in the course of inter-State trade and commerce. It was pointed out that the legislative policy was that the inter-State trade should not be discriminated against and that a comprehensive provision be made avoiding the necessity of unending series of amendments every time one State or other altered its rate of tax.[49] The *Gwalior Rayon Mill's* case was again followed in *State of Kerala v. Attesee (AIT Corpn.)*[50] upholding the adoption by implication of the definition of 'cotton fabrics' in the Central Excises and Salt Act, 1944 with its future amendments by the Kerala Legislature in enacting exemptions in the Kerala Sales Tax Act, 1963. It was held that the adoption was not done blindly but in pursuance of a scheme, a purpose and policy that certain goods, which are subject to additional excise duty under the Additional Duties of Excise (Goods of Special Importance) Act, 1957, should be left out of Sales Tax Act. The same view

---

44. *Gwalior Rayon Mills v. Asst. Commr., Sales Tax*, AIR 1974 SC 1660 : (1974) 4 SCC 98.

45. Note 36, p. 1047.

46. *Gwalior Rayon Mills v. Assistant Commissioner, Sales Tax*, AIR 1974 SC 1660, p. 1679 : (1974) 4 SCC 98. **See further** *Krishna Chandra v. Union of India*, AIR 1975 SC 1389, pp. 1393, 1394 : (1975) 2 SCC 302.

47. *Ibid.*

48. *International Cotton Corporation (P) Ltd. v. Commercial Tax Officer, Hubli*, AIR 1975 SC 1604 : (1975) 3 SCC 585.

49. AIR 1975 SC 1604, p. 1608 : (1975) 3 SCC 585.

50. *State of Kerala v. Attesee (AIT Corpn.)*, AIR 1989 SC 222, pp. 230, 231 : 1989 Supp (1) SCC 733.

was taken of section 3 of the Cantonments (Extension of Rent Control Laws) Act, 1957 which enables the Central Government to extend by notification to any cantonment with such restrictions and modifications as it thinks fit, any enactment relating to the control of rent and regulation of house accommodation which is in force in the State in which the cantonment is situated. In negativing the challenge to the validity of the section on the ground of excessive delegation the Supreme Court in *Brij Sunder Kapoor v. Ist Addl. District Judge*,[51] held that the Parliament decided as a matter of policy that the cantonment areas in a State should be subject to the same legislation relating to control of rent and regulation of housing accommodation as in force in other areas of the State and this policy was given effect to by empowering the Central Government to extend to a cantonment area in a State the tenancy legislation as in force in other areas of the State including future amendments and that there was no abdication of legislative function by Parliament. *Brij Sunder's* case was followed in *Municipal Corporation for the City of Pune v. Bharat Forge Col. Ltd.*[52] in upholding the validity of section 22 of the Cantonments Act, 1880 and notification of 1881 issued under it imposing *octroi* in Poona Cantonment at the rates "for the time being" leviable and in respect of the several articles "for the time being" dutiable in the Municipality of Poona. The effect of the notification was to bring about uniformity in the imposition of *octroi* in Cantonment area and Municipal area not only on the date of the notification but also in future. The policy behind the notification was that there should be no difference in taxing the residents of Cantonment area and those residing in Municipal area. It was, therefore, held that the notification could not be assailed for impermissible delegation.

It has already been noticed that in *In re, Article 143, Constitution of India*[53] the Supreme Court upheld the validity of section 2 of the Part C States (now Union Territories) Laws Act, 1950 (and similar earlier laws) which conferred power on the Central Government to extend to Part C States not only existing laws but also future laws enacted by Parliament or any State Legislature. This case was affirmed and followed later in *Ramesh Birch v. Union of India*[54] where a similar question arose in examining the validity of section 87 of the Punjab Reorganisation Act, 1966. This section empowers the Central Government to extend by notification to the Union Territory of Chandigarh any enactment which is in force in a

---

51. *Brij Sunder Kapoor v. Ist Addl. District Judge*, AIR 1989 SC 572, pp. 588, 589 : 1989 (1) SCC 561.

52. *Municipal Corporation for the City of Pune v. Bharat Forge Col. Ltd.*, 1995 (2) Scale 245, pp. 255, 256 : (1995) 3 SCC 434.

53. **See** text and note 42, p. 1048.

54. *Ramesh Birch v. Union of India*, AIR 1990 SC 560 : 1989 Supp (1) SCC 430.

State on the date of the notification. The Parliament by Act 54 of 1974 extended to Chandigarh the East Punjab Urban Rent Restriction Act, 1949. The Punjab Act was amended by the Punjab Legislature in 1985 by Act 2 of 1985. The Central Government by notification issued under section 87 of the Reorganisation Act extended the 1985 Punjab Act to Chandigarh. It was the validity of this notification which was in issue and the answer depended upon the validity of section 87 of the Reorganisation Act. In upholding the validity of section 87, it was held that the clear conclusion reached by the majority of judges in *In re, Article 143, Constitution of India*, could not be ignored simply because they arrived at that conclusion by different processes of reasoning.[55] It was also held that section 87 (like the provisions considered in *In re, Article 143, Constitution of India*) is a provision necessitated by historical changes resulting in Parliament acquiring complete legislative jurisdiction over territories situated in the midst of contiguous territories which have a proper Legislature. It was pointed out that Parliament has hardly sufficient time to look after the legislative needs of such small territories and the most convenient way of legislating for them was to empower the Central Government to determine having regard to the local conditions, which one of several laws, all approved by one or the other of the Legislatures in the country will be the most suited for them and considered in this background the power to extend future laws had to be sustained.[56]

As already seen above, the Legislature cannot delegate its power to repeal a law or even to modify it in essential features.[57] But when the Legislature gives power to make delegated legislation and further declares that the same shall have effect even if inconsistent with any existing law, the delegated legislation has that effect, for it is by the will of the Legislature and not by the will of the delegate that the overriding effect is given to the delegated legislation.[58] Similarly, when a statutory provision is in the form 'except as may be otherwise prescribed by rules' or when it is 'subject to the rules', the rules are made to prevail over the statutory provision.[59] On

---

55. *Ibid*, p. 582.

56. *Ibid*, pp. 584, 585, 586.

57. **See** text and note 37, p. 1047.

58. *Harishanker Bagla v. State of M.P.*, AIR 1954 SC 465, p. 469 : 1955 (1) SCR 380; *Meghraj Kothari v. Delimitation Commission*, AIR 1967 SC 669, p. 676 : 1967 (1) SCR 400; *A.V. Nachane v. Union of India*, AIR 1982 SC 1126, pp. 1133, 1134 : (1982) 1 SCC 205.

59. *Punjab Sikh Regular Motor Services, Raipur v. Regional Transport Authority, Raipur*, AIR 1966 SC 1318 : 1966 (2) SCR 221; *Joginder Singh v. Dy. Custodian General*, AIR 1967 SC 145, p. 148 : 1962 (2) SCR 738; *Bharat Hari Singhania v. Commissioner of Wealth Tax*, JT 1994 (2) SC 6, p. 15 : AIR 1994 SC 1355, p. 1364 : 1994 Supp (3) SCC 46.

the same principle, an Act may permit its modification by an order made under it to remove difficulties.[60] A Removal of Difficulties Order, if not expressed to operate for a limited period, has permanent operation.[61] But there is a presumption even in the United Kingdom that Parliament does not intend to confer wide and unrestricted powers to amend primary legislation by means of delegated legislation[62] and a provision to that effect receives a narrow and strict construction.[63] This presumption will be stronger in India where Parliament and State legislatures cannot delegate essential legislative functions.

It has been held that discretion conferred on a court, will be immune from challenge on the ground of arbitrariness or want of guidelines.[64]

(b) Distinction between conditional and delegated legislation

A distinction is said to exist between what is called conditional legislation and delegated legislation proper.[65] In case of conditional legislation, the legislation is complete in itself but its operation is made to depend on fulfilment of certain conditions and what is delegated to an outside authority, is the power to determine according to its own judgment whether or not those conditions are fulfilled. In case of delegated legislation proper, some portion of the legislative power of the Legislature is delegated to the outside authority in that, the Legislature, though competent to perform both the essential and ancillary legislative functions, performs only the former and parts with the latter, *i.e.*, the ancillary function of laying down details in favour of another for executing the policy of the statute enacted. The distinction between the two exists in this that whereas conditional legislation contains no element of delegation of legislative power and is, therefore, not open to attack on the ground of excessive delegation, delegated legislation proper does confer some legislative power on some outside authority and is therefore open to attack on the ground of excessive

---

60. *Munishwar Dutt Pandey v. Ramjeet Tiwari*, AIR 1997 SC 1571, pp. 1587, 1588 : (1997) 3 SCC 599. **See further** cases in note 20, p. 1044.
61. *Ibid.*
62. *R.V. Secretary of State for Environment,* (2001) 1 All ER 195, p. 203 (HL).
63. *Ibid.*
64. *A. Lakshman Rao v. Judicial Magistrate, Parvatipuram*, AIR 1971 SC 186 : (1970) 3 SCC 501.
65. *In re, Article 143, Constitution of India*, AIR 1951 SC 332, pp. 398 to 400 (paras 236 to 242) : 1951 SCR 747; *Hamdard Dawakhana v. Union of India*, AIR 1960 SC 554, pp. 566, 567 (paras 29, 30); *ITC Bhadrachalam Paperboards v. Mandal Revenue Officer*, 1996 (6) Scale 551, pp. 564, 565 : 1996 (6) SCC 634; *State of Tamil Nadu v. K. Sabanayagam*, AIR 1998 SC 344, pp. 355, 356 : (1998) 1 SCC 318.

delegation.[66] The distinction between delegated legislation and conditional legislation has led to the conclusion that a post-Constitution delegated legislation made under a pre-Constitution Act, is not existing law as defined in the Constitution;[67] whereas a post-Constitution conditional legislation under a pre-Constitution Act comes within that definition.[68] The power to make conditional legislation can also be exercised by Parliament while passing a Constitution Amendment Act.[69]

(i) *Conditional Legislation.*— One of the propositions established in *In re, Article 143, Constitution of India,*[70] is that "when an appropriate Legislature enacts a law and authorises an outside authority to bring it into force in such area or at such time as it may decide, that is conditional and not delegated legislation."[71] Indeed, this rule was laid down by the Privy Council, as early as 1878, in *Queen v. Burah,*[72] and was affirmed in many later decisions, including in *Emperor v. Benoarilal.*[73] The same device can be adopted by Parliament for bringing into force a Constitution Amendment Act.[74]

The decision of the Supreme Court in *In re, Article 143, Constitution of India,*[75] may here be analysed with reference to section 2 of Part C States (now Union Territories) Laws Act, 1950, which confers authority on the

---

66. *Ibid.* But it has been held that conditional legislation also has a content howsoever small and restricted of the law making power itself [*Lachmi Narain, etc. v. Union of India*, AIR 1976 SC 714, pp. 722, 723 : (1976) 2 SCC 953].

67. *Kalyani Stores v. State of Orissa*, AIR 1966 SC 1686 : 1966 (1) SCR 865; *State of Mysore v. H. Sanjeeviah*, AIR 1967 SC 1189 : 1967 (2) SCR 361.

68. *Bangalore Woollen, Cotton & Silk Mills Co. Ltd. v. Bangalore Corporation*, AIR 1962 SC 562 : 1961 (3) SCR 707.

69. *A.K. Roy v. Union of India*, AIR 1982 SC 710, p. 732 : (1982) 1 SCC 271.

70. *In re, Article 143, Constitution of India*, AIR 1951 SC 332 : 1951 SCR 747.

71. *Inder Singh v. State of Rajasthan*, AIR 1957 SC 510, p. 515 (para 9) : 1957 SCR 605; *Orient Paper Industries Ltd. v. State of Orissa*, AIR 1991 SC 672, pp. 682, 683 : 1991 Supp (1) SCC 81.

72. *Queen v. Burah*, ILR 4 Cal 172 (PC); section 9 of Act 22 of 1869, authorised the Lt. Governor to extend *mutatis mutandis* all or any of the provision contained in other sections of that Act to Jainta Hills etc.

73. *Emperor v. Benoarilal*, AIR 1945 PC 48, p. 51 : 46 Cri LJ 589; section 1(3) of Special Criminal Court Ordinance (2 of 1942) provided that the Ordinance "shall come into force in any Province only if the Provincial Government being satisfied of the existence of an emergency—by notification—declares it to be in force in the Province and shall cease to be in force when such notification is rescinded".

74. *A.K. Roy v. Union of India*, AIR 1982 SC 710, p. 732 : (1982) 1 SCC 271.

75. *In re, Article 143, Constitution of India*, AIR 1951 SC 332 : 1951 SCR 747. BOSE, J., in *Rajnarain Singh v. Chairman, Patna Administrative Committee*, AIR 1954 SC 569, pp. 573, 574 : 1955 (1) SCR 290, gave a summary. **Followed** in *Ramesh Birch v. Union of India*, AIR 1990 SC 560 : 1989 Supp (1) SCC 430, **see** text and notes 54 to 56, *supra*.

Central Government to extend to Part C States (now Union Territories), laws in force in other States. An analysis of section 2 of the said Act and the decision[76] thereon is as follows:

(i) Power is conferred to extend not only existing but also future laws. This has been upheld.[77]

(ii) Parliament has conferred the authority on the Central Government not only to extend laws enacted or to be enacted by it but also laws enacted or to be enacted by State Legislatures which have no legislative jurisdiction in Part C States (now Union Territories). This has also been upheld.[78]

(iii) Power is conferred to extend these laws "with such restrictions or modifications" as the Central Government may think fit. This has been upheld subject to a qualification that the Central Government cannot modify the law "in any essential feature". Further, the "restrictions and modifications" must be those which are necessary to bring into operation the law in the Union Territory and they can be introduced only at the time when the law is extended after which the power is exhausted.[79]

(iv) Power was also conferred to make a provision in any enactment so extended for the repeal or amendment of any corresponding law already in force. This portion was held to be bad as a delegation of essential legislative function, and has now been omitted by the Repealing and Amending Act, 1952.

The limitation as to exhaustion of power mentioned in (iii) above[80] will obviously not apply when a fresh power to extend the law is conferred by an amendment of the parent Act, *e.g.* when the empowering section is amended to enable extension of laws with retrospective effect. The limitation will also not apply when the empowering section expressly or impliedly evinces a different intention. For example, when the object is to bring about complete uniformity of law on a subject in the area to which it originally applies and the area to which it is extended, an implied power to issue fresh notifications to extend subsequent amendments or replacements of the law which is initially extended may be impliedly inferred.

---

76. *Ibid.*

77. As regards future laws **see** text notes 54 to 56 *supra*. Power to extend future laws is, in any case, not conditional legislation but delegated legislation.

78. Note 75, *supra*.

79. *Lachmi Narain, etc. v. Union of India*, AIR 1976 SC 714, pp. 724, 725 : (1976) 2 SCC 953.

80. Text and note 79, *supra*.

The above propositions follow from *Gurcharan Singh v. V.K. Kaushal*[81] and *Brij Sunder Kapoor v. Ist Addl. District Judge.*[82] Both these cases relate to application of section 3 of the Cantonments (Extension of Rent Control Laws) Act, 1957 which enabled the Central Government to extend to a cantonment Rent Control law of the State in which the cantonment is situated and which was in force on the date of the notification. The Cantonments Act was amended by Act 22 of 1972 to give it retrospective effect from 26th January, 1950. Further, the requirement that the law extended should be in force on the date of the notification was also omitted by the amendment. In *Gurcharan Singh's* case the East Punjab Rent Act of 1949 was extended to cantonments in Punjab and Haryana by Notification issued in 1969 under section 3 of the Cantonments Act. After the Cantonments Act was amended, the earlier notification was superseded by a fresh notification extending the Rent Act with retrospective effect from 26th January 1950. This notification was held to be valid by the Supreme Court as having been issued in the exercise of a new power conferred after amendment of the Cantonments Act. In *Brij Sunder Kapoor's* case (*supra*) U.P. Rent Act of 1947 was extended to all cantonments in Uttar Pradesh by a notification under section 3 of the Cantonments Act before it was amended. Soon thereafter, the U.P. Rent Act of 1947 was repealed and replaced by U.P. Rent Act of 1972 in Uttar Pradesh by the State Legislature. The Central Government then issued another notification under section 3 of the Cantonments Act in supersession of earlier notification extending the Rent Act of 1972 to the cantonments in Uttar Pradesh. This notification was held to be valid by the Supreme Court on grounds that it was issued in exercise of a new power after section 3 of the Cantonments Act was amended and that section 3 envisaged uniformity of Rent Acts in cantonments and the States where they were located and thus impliedly permitted issue of successive notifications to bring about that uniformity.

Section 2 of the U.P. Zamindari Abolition and Land Reforms Act, 1951, confers power on the State Government to extend the Act to other areas in the State to which it was not initially applied. In upholding this provision the Supreme Court held: "It is well settled that the Legislature may leave it to the executive to apply the provisions of an Act to different geographical areas at different times on various considerations."[83] On the same principle it has been held that the power conferred by section 3 of the U.P. Town

81. *Gurcharan Singh v. V.K. Kaushal*, AIR 1980 SC 1866, p. 1869 : 1980 (4) SCC 244.
82. *Brij Sunder Kapoor v. Ist Addl. District Judgei*, AIR 1989 SC 572, pp. 581, 582 : 1989 (1) SCC 561.
83. *Raghubar Sarup v. State of U.P.*, AIR 1959 SC 909, p. 913.

Areas Act, 1914 to extend the area of a Notified Area is in the nature of conditional legislation.[84]

Basant Kumar v. Eagle Rolling Mills[85] furnishes a further example of application of the rule of conditional legislation. In this case the challenge was to section 1(3) of the Employees' State Insurance Act, 1948, which runs as follows: 'The Act shall come into force on such date or dates as the Central Government may, by notification in the Official Gazette, appoint, and different dates may be appointed for different provisions of this Act, and for different States or for different parts thereof'. Rejecting the contention that the aforesaid provision conferred uncanalised power and was, therefore, invalid, GAJENDRAGADKAR, C.J. observed: "Section 1(3) is really not an illustration of delegated legislation at all; it is what can be properly described as conditional legislation."[86] Power to bring into force an Act, can be validly exercised even after the Legislature has ceased to have competence to enact the Act, if at the time the Act was passed, it was within the legislative competence.[87] Such a power will stand exhausted after it has once been exercised.[88] But a subsequent conferral of power to bring into force an Act with retrospective effect can be validly exercised by issue of a fresh notification although the Act was brought into force prospectively by an earlier notification.[89]

The principle of conditional legislation has also been applied in upholding a power conferred on the executive to extend the life of a temporary Act even when no outer limit is prescribed by the Act.[90]

The same rule was applied in deciding as valid a conferral of power on the State Government to invest subordinate civil courts with jurisdiction of such value as it may decide not exceeding the maximum limit fixed by the Act.[91]

---

84. *Tulsipur Sugar Co. Ltd. v. Notified Area Committee*, AIR 1980 SC 882 : (1980) 2 SCC 295.
85. *Basant Kumar v. Eagle Rolling Mills*, AIR 1964 SC 1260 : 1964 (6) SCR 913.
86. *Ibid*, p. 1262.
87. *Ishwar Das v. Union of India*, AIR 1972 SC 1193 : (1972) 1 SCC 646.
88. *Lachmi Narain, etc. v. Union of India*, AIR 1976 SC 714, pp. 724, 725 : (1976) 2 SCC 953.
89. *Gurcharan Singh v. V.K. Kaushal*, AIR 1980 SC 1866, p. 1869 : 1980 (4) SCC 244.
90. *Inder Singh v. State of Rajasthan*, AIR 1957 SC 510, p. 516 (para 11) : 1957 SCR 605.
91. *State of Bombay v. Narottam Das*, AIR 1951 SC 69 : 1951 SCR 51.

The Supreme Court, in *Bangalore Woollen, Cotton & Silk Mills v. Bangalore Corporation*,[1] had to consider the validity of a power conferred on a Municipal Corporation to levy *octroi* on 'other articles' not specified in the Schedule but 'which may be approved by the Corporation by an order in this behalf'. The court upheld the provision on the ground that it was "more in the nature of conditional delegation,"[2] and in that connection referred with approval the case of *Baxter v. Ah Way*.[3] In this Australian case O'CONNOR, J. had observed: "Legislation from the very earliest times, and particularly in modern times has taken the form of conditional legislation leaving it to some specified authority to determine the circumstances in which the law shall be applied, or to what its operation shall be extended, or the particular class of persons or goods to which it shall be applied". This passage was cited with approval in *Edward Mills'* case,[4] but the court in that case as also in other cases, where the question related to the validity of the power to apply the law to new persons or objects or of the power to grant exemptions, based its decision on the sufficiency or otherwise of the guidance or policy indicated in the relevant statute.[5] In *Jalan Trading Co. v. Mill Mazdoor Sabha*,[6] however, the power to grant exemption under section 36 of the Bonus Act was held to be a conditional legislation and in *ITC Bhadrachalam Paperboards v. Mandal Revenue Officer*,[7] the court in the context of section 11 of the Andhra Pradesh Non-Agricultural Land Assessment Act, 1963, which confers power to exempt any class of non-agricultural land from the levy of assessment under the Act observed: "The power to bring an Act into force as well as the power to grant exemption are both treated, without a doubt, as belonging to the category of conditional legislation."[8] So also in the *Kerala State Electricity Board v. Indian Aluminium Co.*,[9] the Supreme Court upheld the validity of section 2(a) of the Kerala Essential Articles Control (Temporary Powers) Act, 1961 on the ground that it was conditional legislation. Section 3 of the Act empowers the State Government to make notified order for regulating or prohibiting the production, supply and distribution of any 'essential article' and trade

---

1. *Bangalore Woollen, Cotton & Silk Mills v. Bangalore Corporation*, AIR 1962 SC 1263, p. 1266 : 1961 (3) SCR 698.
2. *Bangalore Woollen, Cotton & Silk Mills v. Bangalore Corporation, supra.*
3. *Baxter v. Ah Way*, (1909) 8 CLR 626.
4. *Edward Mills Co. v. State of Ajmer*, AIR 1955 SC 25, p. 32 : 1955 (1) SCR 735.
5. **See** text and notes 39 to 41 (p. 1065), 45 to 54 (pp. 1066-67).
6. *Jalan Trading Co. v. Mill Mazdoor Sabha*, AIR 1967 SC 691, p. 703 : 1967 (1) SCR 15.
7. *ITC Bhadrachalam Paperboards v. Mandal Revenue Officer*, 1996 (6) Scale 551 : 1996 (6) SCC 634.
8. *Ibid*, p. 566 (Scale, para 26).
9. *Kerala State Electricity Board v. Indian Aluminium Co.*, AIR 1976 SC 1031 : (1976) 1 SCC 466.

and commerce in them. Section 2(a) defines 'essential article' as any article not being any essential commodity as defined in the Essential Commodities Act, 1955, which the Government by notified order might declare to be an essential article. In upholding the validity of this section on the reasoning that it was conditional legislation the Supreme Court observed: "The various types of powers that can be exercised under that Act are enumerated in it. Only the article with reference to which those powers are to be exercised is left to be determined by the executive. That will vary from time to time. It is the executive that would be in a position to judge when and under what circumstances an article becomes an essential article."[10] But in *Kalyani Stores v. State of Orissa*,[11] it was held that a section in the Excise Act providing that 'an excise duty or countervailing duty at such rate or rates as the State Government may direct, may be imposed either generally or for any specified local area on any excisable article imported', was not in the nature of conditional legislation.

(ii) *Delegated Legislation.*— As already seen,[12] declaration of a legislative policy by the Legislature itself is essential to sustain delegated legislation. However, the Courts do not insist that such a declaration should either be in express terms or in detail[13] or that the guidance in respect of policy should be in the very section dealing with delegation;[14] the entire Act is available for this purpose.[15] Indeed, there is no "stereotyped rule" for judging the sufficiency of guidance required to uphold delegation.[16]

Section 3 of the Essential Supplies (Temporary Powers) Act, 1946, gave wide powers to the Central Government to make orders for regulating or prohibiting the production, supply and distribution of essential commodities and trade and commerce therein. The Supreme Court, in sustaining the enactment, was satisfied that it laid a clear principle and offered sufficient guidance, as the section provided that the power conferred therein was to be exercised 'for maintaining or increasing supplies of any essential commodity, or for securing their equitable distribution and availability at fair prices.'[17] In a subsequent case relating to the same enactment, it was again emphasised that the policy of the enactment was clearly indicated in

10. *Ibid*, p. 1048.
11. *Kalyani Stores v. State of Orissa*, AIR 1966 SC 1686 : 1966 (1) SCR 865.
12. **See** text and notes 19 to 24, pp. 1043-1044, *supra.*
13. **See** text and notes 31, 32, p. 1046, *supra.*
14. *Bhandara District Central Co-operative Bank Ltd. v. State of Maharashtra*, AIR 1993 SC 59, p. 63 : 1992 (2) Scale 617 : 1993 Supp (3) SCC 259.
15. *Ibid.*
16. *Corporation of Calcutta v. Liberty Cinema*, AIR 1965 SC 1107, p. 1119 (para 31) : 1965 (2) SCR 477.
17. *Harishanker Bagla v. State of M.P.*, AIR 1954 SC 465, p. 468 : 1955 (1) SCR 380.

section 3, and that an order fixing fair prices of essential commodities carried out the legislative object prescribed in section 3.[18] In the same category comes the case which upheld the validity of section 3 of the Imports and Exports (Central) Act, 1947,[19] but it is interesting to note that in this case,[20] the court found the declaration of policy, *viz*., to maintain supplies essential to the life of community, from the preamble and provisions of the predecessor Act, as the Act under consideration did not enact the material provisions for the first time but purported to continue the previously existing provisions in that behalf.

Sections 6 and 7 of the Scheduled Districts Act, 1874, authorised the Local Government to appoint officers to administer civil and criminal justice within the Scheduled Districts and to regulate the procedure of officers so appointed. Negativing a challenge that no guidance was furnished on the subject of judicial procedure and the Act suffered from excessive delegation, the Supreme Court found the guidance in the preamble and other provisions of the Act as also in the rules which were continued by the Act. It was held that the Scheduled Districts which were backward tracts were removed from the operation of general Acts and Regulations and the Act set up a machinery for making simple rules to administer civil and criminal justice by the officers to be appointed under the Act.[21]

Section 3 of the Prevention of Corruption Act, 1988 empowers the government to appoint as many special judges, for trial of offences under the Act, as may be necessary for such area or areas or for such case or group of cases as may be specified in the notification. Rejecting the challenge to the validity of the section on the ground that it conferred unfettered, unguided and absolute discretion on the government to appoint special judges for such case or group of cases, the Supreme Court held that the guidance was furnished by the words 'as may be necessary' read in the context and object of the Act, which envisaged speedy trial of corruption cases and the discretion of the government was guided by the requirement of public interest.[22]

---

18. *Union of India v. Bhanmal Gulzarilal*, AIR 1960 SC 475, p. 478 : 1960 (2) SCR 627. **See further** *Swadeshi Cotton Mills v. State Industrial Tribunal*, AIR 1961 SC 1381 : 1962 (1) SCR 422. (Validity of section 3, U.P. Industrial Disputes Act, 1947, was upheld); *A.V. Nachane v. Union of India*, AIR 1982 SC 1126, p. 1134 : (1982) 1 SCC 205 (*Harishanker Bagla's* case was **relied** upon in upholding the validity of sub-section (2C) of section 48 of the Life Insurance Corporation Act, 1956).

19. *Bhatnagar & Co. v. Union of India*, AIR 1957 SC 478, p. 486 : 1957 SCR 701.

20. *Ibid*.

21. *State of Nagaland v. Ratan Singh*, AIR 1967 SC 212, pp. 222, 223 : 1966 (3) SCR 830.

22. *J. Jayalalitha v. Union of India*, AIR 1999 SC 1912, p. 1923 : (1999) 5 SCC 138.

When a delegate is empowered by Parliament, as the Reserve Bank of India in section 21 of the Banking Regulation Act, 1949, to frame policies and issue guidelines, the guidelines (policy) have statutory force and cannot be said to be *ultra vires* and are binding on the banking companies.[23]

The Offices of Commissioners were abolished in the state of Bombay in 1950 and powers and duties of Commissioners were transferred to the State Government. With a view to reintroduce the Commissioners, the Bombay Legislature passed the Bombay Commissioners of Divisions Act, 1958. Section 3(1) of the Act made suitable amendments in the Acts mentioned in a Schedule for conferring powers and duties on Commissioners. Section 3(4) of the Act authorised the State Government 'to confer and impose on the Commissioners powers and duties under any other enactment for the time being in force' and for that purpose to make necessary amendments in the Schedule. This provision was challenged on the ground that it gave no guidance as to the nature of powers and duties which the State Government could confer on the Commissioners under enactments not specified in the Schedule. Rejecting the challenge, the Supreme Court referred to the previous history of the Office of Commissioner and held that it is only the duties of State Government and of officers of equivalent rank discharging revenue and executive duties which would be conferred on the Commissioners and that section 3(4) did not suffer from the vice of excessive delegation.[24]

Although power to tax is a well recognised legislative power, ample latitude has been allowed to the Legislature to leave to a delegate the power to work out details of a tax policy. In upholding a power delegated to the State Government for amending the Schedule relating to exemptions in a Sales Tax Legislation, VENKATARAMA AIYAR, J. observed: "Now the authorities are clear that it is not unconstitutional for the Legislature to leave it to the executive to determine details relating to the working of taxation laws, such as the selection of persons on whom the tax is to be laid, the rates at which it is to be charged in respect of different classes of goods, and the like."[25] Similar principle was applied in upholding the validity of

---

23. *ICICI Bank Ltd. v. Official Liquidator of APS Industries Ltd.*, (2010) 10 SCC 1 para 40 : AIR 2011 SC 1521.

24. *Arnold Rodricks v. State of Maharashtra*, AIR 1966 SC 1788, p. 1795 : 1966 (3) SCR 885; **followed** in *Kanhaiyalal Maneklal Chinai v. State of Gujarat*, AIR 1970 SC 1188, p. 1190 : (1969) 3 SCC 456.

25. *Banarsi Das v. State of M.P.*, AIR 1958 SC 909, p. 913 : 1959 SCR 427; referred to in *Hiralal Ratanlal v. Sales Tax Officer III, Kanpur*, AIR 1973 SC 1034 : (1973) 1 SCC 216; *Shashi Prasad Barooah v. Agricultural Income-tax Officer*, AIR 1977 SC 993, pp. 998, 999 : (1977) 1 SCC 867; **See further** *State of Mysore v. M.L. Nagade*, AIR 1983 SC 762, pp. 766, 767 : (1983) 3 SCC 553.

rule 8(1) of the Central Excise Rules, 1944, which authorised the Central Government to grant exemptions. The rule was made under section 37(2) of the Central Excises and Salt Act (1 of 1944) which enables the making of rules on various matters, one of them being worded in these terms: 'exempt any goods from the whole or any part of the duty imposed by this Act'. SINHA, C.J. in the course of his judgment observed: "The Act recognises and only gives effect to the well established principle that there must be a great deal of flexibility in the incidence of taxation of a particular kind."[26] This principle has been applied in supporting a provision (Henry VIII clause) which authorised the Executive to remove difficulties in the working of a taxing Act.[27] Same principle was applied in upholding a rule that in the absence of an order apportioning the liability to the tax on the basis of partition in respect of a Hindu undivided family hitherto assessed as undivided or joint, such family shall be deemed for the purpose of the Assam Agricultural Income-tax Rules, 1939 to continue to be a Hindu undivided family.[28] The principle that the courts allow ample latitude to the

---

26. *Orient Weaving Mills v. Union of India*, AIR 1963 SC 98, p. 103 : 1962 Supp (3) SCR 481. Same principle applied in upholding the vaidity of an exemption notification issued under Rule 8; *Union of India v. Paliwal Electricals (P) Ltd.*, AIR 1996 SC 3106, pp. 3108, 3109 : (1996) 3 SCC 407 ("Generally speaking the Exemption notification and the terms and conditions prescribed therein represent the policies of the Government evolved to subserve public interest and public revenue"). In *Digvijay Cement Co. v. State of Rajasthan,* 1997 (5) SCC 406 : JT 1997 (4) SC 340 an exemption notification under section 8(5) of the Central Sales Tax Act, 1956 was held invalid as the State Government failed to show any 'public interest' to support the issuance of the notification. Similarly, in *Dai-Ichi Karkaria Ltd. v. Union of India,* JT 2000 (4) SC 495 : AIR 2000 SC 1741 : (2000) 4 SCC 57 a notification under section 25(1) of the Customs Act, 1962 withdrawing an earlier notification granting exemption was held invalid being arbitrary and not in public interest.

27. *Kalawati Devi v. CIT, W.B.*, AIR 1968 SC 162, p. 168 : 1967 (3) SCR 833. **See** *Jalan Trading Co. v. Mill Mazdoor Union*, AIR 1967 SC 691 : 1967 (1) SCR 15, where a similar provision in a non-taxing Act was held to be invalid. *Jalan Trading Co.'s* case was **distinguished** in *Gamman India Ltd. v. Union of India*, AIR 1974 SC 960, p. 968 : (1974) 1 SCC 596; where such a provision in a non-taxing Act was held to be valid. But even when such a provision is valid, the Removal of Difficulties Order may be held invalid on the ground that there was no difficulty which required removal and, therefore, the Order was in excess of the power conferred by the Act; *Straw Products v. ITO*, AIR 1968 SC 579 : 1968 (2) SCR 1; *Madeva Upendra Sinai v. Union of India*, AIR 1975 SC 797 : (1975) 3 SCC 765. **See also** *Maharana Mills Pvt. Ltd. v. Income-tax Tribunal*, AIR 1989 SC 1719 : 1989 Supp (2) SCC 210. For general discussion of 'removal of difficulty clause' also nick-named as 'Henry VIII clause', **see** *Lachmi Narain v. Union of India*, AIR 1976 SC 714, pp. 725, 726 : (1976) 1 SCC 747. Removal of difficulty clause cannot be used as a substitute for rule making power; *Krishna Deo Misra v. State*, AIR 1988 Pat 9 (FB.)

28. *Shashi Prasad Barooah v. Agricultural Income-tax Officer*, AIR 1977 SC 993, pp. 998, 999 : (1977) 1 SCC 867.

Legislature in arranging its tax policy, does not however mean that conferment of an arbitrary or uncanalized power can be upheld. Thus power to deduct a certain percentage from the sum payable to a works contractor towards sales tax on transfer of property in goods in the works contract irrespective of whether ultimately the transaction is liable for payment to any sales tax was held invalid on the ground that it was arbitrary and uncanalized.[29]

The Government of India and the Government of Mauritus entered into an agreement for avoidance of double taxation and the prevention of fiscal evasion with respect to taxes on income and capital gains. Section 90 of the Income-tax Act, 1961 authorises the Central Government to enter into an agreement with the Government of any country outside India for the purpose of grant of relief in respect of income on which income tax is payable both under this Act as well as under the law in that other country and for the avoidance of double taxation of income under this Act and the corresponding law in force in that country. Section 90(1)(d) further provides that the Central Government 'may by notification in the official Gazette make provisions as may be necessary for implementing the agreement. Circulars were issued by notification in the Gazette for implementation of the Agreement. Section 90 of the Act, the Agreement and the circulars were challenged on the grounds of excessive delegation and also on the ground that they would give rise to the abuse of treaty shopping. The challenge was negatived on the ground that the object and policy behind section 90 were clear from its language as also from the Finance Minister's speech and the Budget before the section in the present form was amended; that the Agreement and the circulars were well within the ambit of section 90 and that delegated legislation cannot be challenged on the ground of want of efficacy if it is within the parameters of the powers conferred.[30]

The same liberal attitude is shown in upholding delegation when taxing power is conferred by the Legislature on a Municipal Corporation. A power conferred on a Municipal Corporation to impose "for the purposes of the Act" in addition to certain enumerated taxes "any other tax to the nature and object of which the approval of Governor in Council shall have been obtained", was sustained essentially on three grounds: (i) "Any other tax" was limited to the taxes which the provincial Legislature could itself impose; (ii) The taxing power was "for the purposes of the Act", *i.e.*, for

29. *Nathpa Jhakri Jt. Venture v. State of Himachal Pradesh*, AIR 2000 SC 1268, p. 1270 : (2000) 3 SCC 319.

30. *Union of India v. Azadi Bachao Andolan*, AIR 2004 SC 1107, pp. 1127, 1128 : 2003 Supp (2) JT 205.

implementing the obligations and functions cast upon the Municipalities which were laid in the Act; and (iii) The enumerated taxes indicated the kind and nature of "any other tax" which the Municipality could impose.[31] The liberal view again prevailed in upholding the validity of section 548(2) of the Calcutta Municipal Act, 1951, which confers power on the Corporation to charge "a fee (interpreted as tax) at such rate as may from time to time be fixed by the Corporation" for a licence granted to keep open any cinema house. The Corporation of Calcutta acting under this power levied a fee which was to be assessed at certain rates per show according to the sanctioned seating capacity of the cinema houses. Rejecting the contention that the power to tax under section 548(2) suffered from excessive delegation as it provided no guidance as to the amount of the tax and prescribed no rate or even maximum rate and left the rate of tax to the discretion of the Corporation, the majority in the Supreme Court found "sufficient guidance" by the implication that as the Corporation has to perform certain statutory functions defined in the Act, "its power to collect tax is necessarily limited by the expenses required to discharge those functions",[32] and "it has, therefore, where rates have not been specified in the statutes, to fix such rates as may be necessary to meet its needs".[33] But authority to tax at such rate as the Government may specify without the Legislature fixing any maximum rate has been held to be invalid on the ground of excessive delegation for when tax is levied for the benefit of Government no implied limitation can be spelt because unlike a Corporation the Government's needs are unlimited.[34]

---

31. *Western India Theatres v. Municipal Corporation, Poona*, AIR 1959 SC 586, p. 588 : 1959 Supp (2) SCR 71.

32. *Corporation of Calcutta v. Liberty Cinema*, AIR 1965 SC 1107, p. 1119 : 1965 (2) SCR 477. **See further** *Ram Bachan v. State of Bihar*, AIR 1967 SC 1404, p. 1407 : 1967 (3) SCR 1; *Delhi Municipality v. Birla Cotton Spinning and Weaving Mills*, AIR 1968 SC 1232 : 1968 (3) SCR 251; *Gulabchand Bapalal Modi v. Ahmedabad Municipality*, AIR 1971 SC 2100 : (1971) 1 SCC 823; *Avinder Singh v. State of Punjab*, AIR 1979 SC 321 : (1979) 1 SCC 137. Same principle applies when the Government is empowered to levy taxes for a municipality: *Darshan Lal Misra v. Union of India*, AIR 1992 SC 1848 : 1992 (4) SCC 28; *B. Krishna Bhat v. State of Karnataka*, AIR 2001 SC 1885 : (2001) 4 SCC 227 (Delegation of taxing power to Development Authority a statutory body).

33. *Ibid.*

34. *Devidas v. State of Punjab*, AIR 1967 SC 1895, p. 1901 : 1967 (3) SCR 557; **See further** *Sitaram Bishambhar Dayal v. State of U.P.*, AIR 1972 SC 1168 : 1972 (4) SCC 485; *Danthuluri Ramaraju v. State of A.P.*, AIR 1972 SC 828, p. 839 : (1972) 1 SCC 421; *Nagappa v. O'Mines Cess Commr.*, AIR 1973 SC 1374 : (1973) 2 SCC 1. But in *N.K. Papiah & Sons v. Excise Commissioner*, AIR 1975 SC 1007 : (1975) 1 SCC 492, power conferred on the State Government to fix rates of excise duty by making rules was upheld although no maximum was prescribed by the Act for the reason that the rules were required to be laid before the Legislature.

But if a taxing statute provides for search, inspection and seizure and impounding of documents without sufficient guidance and proper safeguards it may be declared invalid for excessive delegation, offending right to privacy under Article 21 and for being unreasonable and disproportionate under Article 14 of the Constitution. Section 73 of the Indian Stamp Act, 1899 as substituted by A.P. Act 17 of 1986 empowered any person authorised by Collector to have access to documents in private custody or custody of a public officer and to take notes or seize the documents without regard to the fact whether such document would ever be voluntarily produced or brought before a public officer. The power could be exercised by such person without being preceded by any requirement of recording the reasons necessitating the search and inspection. The Collector was authorised to empower any person whatsoever for the above purposes without guidance as to whom the power could be delegated. This Andhra Pradesh amendment was held to be invalid for excessive delegation unreasonableness and affecting right to privacy.[35]

Generous latitude in permitting delegation has also been allowed in case of welfare legislations, particularly those statutes which are designed to further the Directive principles of State Policy and guidelines can be gathered from the preamble, the scheme or even the subject matter of the Act.[36]

Section 9(1) of the Mines and Minerals (Regulation and Development) Act, 1957 fixes the rates of royalty by specifying them in a schedule. Section 9(3) empowers the Central Government to enhance or reduce the rates so specified but with a restriction that the Government shall not enhance the rate in respect of a mineral more than once during any period of three years. Upholding the validity of section 9(3) the Supreme Court[37] by implication found the following guidelines: (i) Rate of inflation and fall of money value to be considered once in three years; (ii) Original rates in the schedule and the enhanced requirements of the States; (iii) Regulation of mines and mineral development; and (iv) Uniformity of pattern so that mining of the minerals for the benefit of the lessee and for the economy as a whole should not in any way be frustrated. The Supreme Court also found a safety valve to support section 9(3) in the laying requirement in section 28(1). Similarly, delegation of power to the State Government, the highest executive responsible to the State legislature, to fix the rate of

---

35. *Distt. Registrar and Collector, Hyderabad v. Canara Bank*, AIR 2005 SC 186 : (2005) 1 SCC 496.

36. *Enterprises v. State of U.P.*, AIR 1999 SC 1867, pp. 1907, 1908 : (1999) 9 SCC 700.

37. *State of M.P. v. Mahalaxmi Fabric Mills Ltd.*, 1995 (1) Scale 758, pp. 769, 770 : 1995 AIR SCW 1621 : 1995 Supp (1) SCC 642 : AIR 1995 SC 2213. (Royalty has been held to be a tax on mineral rights covered by the residuary entry in the union list).

royalty of minor minerals under section 15 of the same Act has been held to be valid having regard to the policy underlying the Act, historical background and the laying requirement.[38]

The Legislature at times confers power on the Executive to apply a law to new objects as may be decided by it. Such a conferral of power has been sustained if policy and guidance are discernible from the Act. Section 27 of the Minimum Wages Act, 1948, authorises the appropriate Government to add to the Schedule attached to the Act, which specifies the employments in respect of which minimum wages can be fixed, any other employment in respect of which the Government is of opinion that minimum rates of wages should be fixed under the Act. Countering the argument that this provision suffered from excessive delegation, the Supreme Court pointed out that the object of the Act was the statutory fixation of minimum wages, to obviate the chance of exploitation of labour, and that it was to carry out effectually this purpose that power was conferred on the appropriate Government to decide according to local conditions whether minimum wages should be fixed with regard to a particular trade or industry not already included in the Schedule.[39] In the same category comes the case which upheld the validity of section 85 of the Factories Act, 1948, which empowers the State Government to extend all or any of the provisions of the Act to establishments which are not otherwise factories within the meaning of the Act.[40] It has been held that a generous degree of latitude must be permitted in the case of welfare legislation, particularly those statutes which are designed to further the directive principles of the State policy.[41] The two cases mentioned above[42] may be contrasted with the decision in *Hamdard Dawakhana v. Union of India*,[43] where the court held that section 3(d) of the Drugs and Magic Remedies (Objectionable Advertisements) Act, 1954, which gave power to the Central Government to extend, by framing rules, the prohibition of section 3 relating to the publication of advertisement of drugs in respect of any venereal disease to "any

---

38. *The Quarry Owners Association v. The State of Bihar,* AIR 2000 SC 2870 : (2000) 8 SCC 655.

39. *Edward Mills Co. v. State of Ajmer*, AIR 1955 SC 25, pp. 32, 33 : 1955 (1) SCR 735.

40. *Bhikusa Yamasa Kshatriya (P.) Ltd. v. Union of India,* AIR 1963 SC 1591, 1599 : 1964 (1) SCR 860; the argument was advanced under Article 14 of the Constitution that the provision in the Act permits unreasonable classification.

41. *Registrar, Co-operative Societies v. K. Kunjabmu,* AIR 1980 SC 350, p. 352 : (1980) 1 SCC 340.

42. **See** footnotes 33, 34, *supra*.

43. *Hamdard Dawakhana v. Union of India*, AIR 1960 SC 554, p. 568 : 1960 (2) SCR 671.

other disease or condition", was "uncanalised and uncontrolled" and, therefore, suffered from excessive delegation.[44]

Provisions empowering the Executive to grant exemptions from the operation of general provisions of an Act have also been judged on the same principles. A provision contained in a Prohibition Act which empowered the State Government to exempt any person, or institution or any class of persons or institutions from the observance of all or any of the provisions of the Act or any rule or order made thereunder, was held to be valid.[45] In statutes passed for protection of tenants of lands or buildings against unreasonable eviction by landlords, exemption clauses empowering the Executive to exempt any person or class of persons or any building or class of buildings have been sustained on the ground that the power to exempt, which on the face of the enactments was unrestricted, was really fettered and guided in that it could only be exercised to effectuate the object of the statutes.[46] Similarly, section 17 of the Employees Provident Funds Act, 1952, empowering the appropriate Government to exempt any establishment from the operation of all or any of the provisions of a Scheme framed under the Act has been held to be controlled and canalised, and therefore, valid as the provision in terms shows that exemptions are to be granted only if the exempted establishments have provisions made for provident fund not less favourable to the employees than the Scheme framed under the Act.[47] And, in a statute fixing maximum rate of rents payable by tenants, a provision authorising the Executive to fix a lower rate of rent suitable for any particular area has also been sustained.[48] On the same principle section 60 of the Madras Co-operative Societies Act,

---

44. *Ibid.*

45. *State of Bombay v. F.N. Balsara*, AIR 1951 SC 318, p. 327 : 1951 SCR 682.

46. *Inder Singh v. State of Rajasthan*, AIR 1957 SC 510, pp. 516, 517 : 1957 SCR 605; *P.J. Irani v. State of Madras*, AIR 1961 SC 1731, pp. 1737, 1738 : (1962) 2 SCR 169; (The respective provisions in these cases were challenged under Article 14 of the Constitution and were upheld, but it was held that individual notifications may be discriminatory and invalid). **See further** *State of M.P. v. Kanhaiyalal*, 1970 MPLJ 973 : AIR 1969 SC 83; *Punjab Tin Supply Co. v. Central Government*, (1984) 1 SCC 206, pp. 215, 216 : AIR 1984 SC 87; *Kondaswamy Chettiar v. State of Tamil Nadu*, (1985) 1 SCC 290 : AIR 1985 SC 257.

47. *Mohmedalli v. Union of India*, AIR 1964 SC 980 : 1963 Supp (1) SCR 993.

48. *Vasanlal Maganbhai Sanjiwala v. State of Bombay*, AIR 1961 SC 4 : 1961 (1) SCR 341; *Raghuthila-kathirtha Sreepadangalavaru Swamiji v. State of Mysore*, AIR 1966 SC 1172 : (1963) 2 SCR 226. **See** *Jalan Trading Co. v. Mill Mazdoor Sabha*, AIR 1967 SC 691, p. 703 : 1967 (1) SCR 15, where exemption clause was held to be conditional legislation. **See further** *Ram Narain v. State of Bombay*, AIR 1959 SC 459, p. 473 : 1959 Supp (1) SCR 489, where power to vary ceiling area or economic holding as fixed by the Act has been sustained; *Union of India v. Annam Ramlingam*, (1985) 2 SCC 443, p. 446 : AIR 1985 SC 1013 where a power conferred on the Administrator to grant exemption under section 28 of the Gold Control Act, 1968 was upheld.

1932 which enables the State Government to exempt any registered society from any of the provisions of the Act or to direct that such provision shall apply to such society with such modifications as may be specified has been upheld on the ground that it has to be exercised to facilitate the formation and working of the Co-operative Societies in accordance with the guidelines as may be gleaned from the preamble and other provisions of the Act.[49] Rule 39 of the Tamil Nadu Minor Mineral Concession Rules, 1950, which is in the nature of an exemption provision, empowers the State Government to grant or renew a mining lease on terms and conditions different from those laid down in the rules, if the Government, for reasons to be recorded, is of opinion that it is necessary so to do in the interest of mineral development and in public interest; this provision has also been held to be valid as containing the necessary guidelines.[50] Section 113 of the Tamil Nadu Town and Country Planning Act, 1972 empowers the Government to exempt any land or building or class of land or buildings from all or any of the provisions of the Act. Apparently very wide discretion is conferred by this provision, but this Act has been upheld on the reasoning that a situation may arise in some cases where strict adherence to any provision of the Act and rules may result in great hardship in a given situation and the power of exemption is to be exercised to remove this hardship without materially affecting the policy of the Act.[51] In the cases mentioned above,[52] the exemption clauses were sustained as the preamble or the provisions of the statutes in question read in a liberal way, satisfied the court that the power of granting exemptions conferred on the Executive was not unfettered and unguided. However, in some other cases,[53] where the court was not satisfied as to the guidance furnished by the statute, similar exemption clauses have been held to be invalid. Further, power of exemption cannot be utilised nor can it extend to scrapping of the very Act under which it is exercised.[54]

Power conferred on the State Government by an Act providing for establishment of markets and regulation of wholesale trade in agricultural

---

49. *Registrar of Co-operative Societies v. K. Kunjabmu*, AIR 1980 SC 350 : (1980) 1 SCC 340.

50. *Premium Granite v. State of Tamil Nadu*, JT 1994(1) SC 376 : AIR 1994 SC 2233 : (1994) 2 SCC 691.

51. *Consumer Action Group v. State of Tamil Nadu*, AIR 2000 SC 3060, p. 3068 : (2000) 7 SCC 425 (The provision was upheld but the orders of exemption were held invalid on the ground that they were arbitrary and in excess of the power to grant exemption.)

52. **See** footnotes 39 to 44, *supra*.

53. *Dwarka Das v. State of M.P.*, AIR 1954 SC 224, p. 227 (para 7) : 1954 SCR 803; *Kunnathai Thathunni Moopil Nair v. State of Kerala*, AIR 1961 SC 552, p. 558 (case under Article 14) : 1961 (3) SCR 77.

54. *B.K. Industries v. Union of India*, AIR 1993 SC 2123, p. 2126 : 1993 Supp (3) SCC 621.

produce specified in the Schedule to the Act, to add, to amend or cancel any of the items in the Schedule in accordance with local conditions prevailing in different parts of the State, has been upheld[55] on the principle enunciated in *Edward Mills'* case.[56]

Mention may also be made of *D.S. Garewal v. State of Punjab*,[57] wherein section 3 of the All India Services Act, 1951, which gives power to Central Government to frame rules 'for the regulation of recruitment and the condition of service' was upheld. The court found the policy and guidance of the Act in the then existing rules which were continued by the Act, although power was given to vary or amend them by new rules framed under the Act. It was pointed out that the procedure prescribed in the Act for making of rules that they were to be laid on the table of Parliament before they could come into force and were open to modification on a motion made by Parliament, was sufficient control over the delegate and the Act did not suffer from excessive delegation. Similarly in *Caltex (India) Ltd. v. Presiding Officer*,[58] which dealt with section 26 of the Bihar Shops and Establishment Act, 1954 the policy and guidance were derived from the background of the Industrial law. That section enacts that no employer shall dismiss an employee except for a reasonable cause and after giving the employee one month's notice or wages in lieu of notice. The section contains a proviso that no notice will be necessary when services are dispensed with "on a charge of misconduct as may be prescribed by the State Government". It was contended that the proviso left uncontrolled discretion to the State Government to prescribe the charges, and therefore, the delegation was excessive. It was held that the Legislature must have known that misconduct in industrial law is of two kinds *viz.*: (1) major misconduct justifying punishment of discharge or dismissal; and (2) minor misconduct justifying lesser punishment and that power conferred by the proviso is limited to the prescription of such misconduct which is major in nature.

But as already stated[59] when it is not possible to discover a legislative policy or guidelines for implementing it, the statute will be held invalid as conferring unrestricted and unguided discretion. So the Tamil Nadu

---

55. *Mohd. Hussain Ghulam Mohd. v. State of Bombay*, AIR 1962 SC 97 : 1962 (2) SCR 659.

56. **See** text and note 4, p. 1057, *supra*.

57. *D.S. Garewal v. State of Punjab*, AIR 1959 SC 512 : 1959 Supp (1) SCR 792. **Reaffirmed** in *A.K. Kraipak v. Union of India*, AIR 1970 SC 150, p. 153 : (1969) 2 SCC 262.

58. *Caltex (India) Ltd. v. Presiding Officer*, AIR 1966 SC 1729 : 1966 (2) LLJ 137 : (1966) 3 SCR 631.

59. **See** text and notes 33, 34, p. 1047.

Private Educational Institutions (Regulation) Act, 1966 which required a private educational institution to obtain the permission of the competent authority for the purpose of running it but gave no guidance as to the conditions for the exercise of the power of grant or refusal of permission was held as invalid by the Supreme Court.[60]

Power to adapt laws or to construe laws with necessary changes in the absence of adaptation, such as conferred by sections 120 and 121 of the States Reorganisation Act, 1956, is not power of legislation and is ineffective to affect the territorial application of the laws.[61]

3. DELEGATED LEGISLATION AND JUDICIAL REVIEW

(a) Grounds of judicial review

Delegated legislation is open to the scrutiny of courts and may be declared invalid particularly on two grounds: (a) Violation of the Constitution;[62] and (b) Violation of the enabling Act.[63] The second ground includes within itself not only cases of violation of the substantive provisions of the enabling Act, but also cases of violation of the mandatory procedure prescribed.[64] It may also be challenged on the ground that it is contrary to other statutory provisions or that it is so arbitrary that it cannot be said to be in conformity with the statute or Article 14 of the Constitution[65] or that

---

60. *A.N. Parasuraman v. State of Tamil Nadu*, AIR 1990 SC 40 : (1989) 4 SCC 683. **See further** *Krishna Mohan (P.) Ltd. v. Municipal Corporation of Delhi,* (2003) 7 SCC 151 : AIR 2003 SC 2935 in which section 116(3) of the Delhi Municipal Corporation Act, 1957 was held invalid for want of guidelines.

61. *P.H. Mawale v. State of A.P.*, AIR 1965 SC 1827, p. 1833 : (1965) 3 SCR 743; *Ekambarappa v. Expenditure-tax Officer*, AIR 1967 SC 1541, pp. 1544, 1545 : 1967 (3) SCR 864.

62. **See** text and notes 93 and 1, pp. 1074, 1075.

63. **See** text and notes 3, p. 1075.

64. *Boddington v. British Transport Police,* (1998) 2 All ER 203, pp. 216, 217 (HL) (There is no distinction between substantive and procedural invalidity and in both cases the delegated legislation is a nullity). See title (4) Procedural Requirements. *Commissioner of Trade Tax Uttar Pradesh v. Kartos International*, (2011) 6 SCC 705.

65. *Indian Express Newspapers v. Union of India*, (1985) 1 SCC 641, p. 689 : AIR 1986 SC 515; *State of U.P. v. Renusagar Power Co.*, AIR 1988 SC 1737, p. 1763 : (1988) 4 SCC 59; *Shri Sitaram Sugar Co. Ltd. v. Union of India*, AIR 1990 SC 1277, p. 1297 : (1990) 3 SCC 223; *State of M.P. v. Mahalaxmi Fabric Mills Ltd.*, 1995(1) Scale 758, p. 777: AIR 1995 SC 2213, p. 2227 : 1995 Supp (1) SCC 642; *Secretary Ministry of Chemicals Fertilizers v. Cipla Ltd.*, (2003) 7 SCC 1, pp. 9, 10 : AIR 2003 SC 3078; *Kerala Samsthana Chethu Thozhilali Union v. State of Kerala,* (2006) 4 SCC 327 (para 17) : AIR 2006 SC 3480 (Delegated legislation is not only required to be made in conformity with the provisions of the Act under which

[Footnote No. 65 Contd.]

it has been made in bad faith.[66] The limitations which apply to the exercise of administrative or *quasi*-judicial power conferred by a statute except the requirement of natural justice also apply to the exercise of power of delegated legislation.[67] Rules made under the Constitution do not qualify as legislation in true sense and are treated as subordinate legislation and can be challenged in judicial review like delegated legislation.[68] Compliance with the laying requirement or even approval by a resolution of Parliament does not confer any immunity to the delegated legislation but it may be a circumstance to be taken into account along with other factors to uphold its validity[69] although as earlier seen a laying clause may prevent the enabling Act being declared invalid for excessive delegation.[70]

The above passage was quoted with approval by SINHA, J. in *Kerala Samsthana Chethu Thozhilali Union v. State of Kerala.*[71]

Delegated legislation may affect or even override existing contracts. Regulations[72] fixing ceiling of trading margin made under section 178 of the Electricity Act, 2003 overrides the existing contracts between regulated entities inasmuch as it casts a statutory obligation on regulated entities to align their existing and future contracts – with the said regulation.[73] Validity of delegated legislation cannot be generally challenged in appeal

[Footnote No. 65 Contd.]

it is made but it cannot also violate the provisions of any other Act made by Parliament or State Legislatures); *State of T.N. v. P. Krishnamurthy,* (2006) 4 SCC 517 (para 15) : AIR 2006 SC 1622; *Sarbananda Sonowal v. Union of India,* (2007) 1 SCC 174 (para 53) : (2007) 1 SLT 648 : (2007) 13 Scale 33.

66. *Central Dairy Farm v. Glindia Ltd.*, (2004) 1 SCC 55, pp. 62, 63 : AIR 2003 SC 4501 (A discretionary statutory power to regulate and control production supply and fix prices of milk and milk products cannot be used for an oblique purpose to get over the price fixed under the direction of the High Court judgment by agreements and settlements reached on price fixation through mutual negotiations between representatives of two companies and authorised officers of the State).

67. **See** text and notes 52, 53, p. 512. **See further** *Boddington v. British Transport Police,* (1998) 2 All ER 203, p. 208 (HL).

68. *Supreme Court Employees Welfare Association v. Union of India,* AIR 1990 SC 334 (para 62) : (1989) 4 SCC 187. **See further** *Dr. Manchandra Prasad Singh v. Chairman Bihar Legislative Council,* (2004) 8 SCC 747, p. 760 (Rules made by Chairman and Speaker under 10th Schedule are delegated legislation).

69. **See** text and notes 3, p. 1075.

70. **See** text and note 26, p. 1113.

71. *Kerala Samsthana Chethu Thozhilali Union v. State of Kerala*, (2006) 4 SCC 327 (para 32) : AIR 2006 SC 3480. **See further** *Mahalakshmi Sugar Mills Co. Ltd. v. Union of India,* AIR 2009 SC 792 para 53 : (2008) 6 JT 177 where SINHA, J. has summarised the grounds of judicial review of delegated legislation.

72. **See** Central Electricity Regulatory Commission (Fixation of Trading Margin) Regulations, 2006.

73. *PTC India Ltd. v. Central Electricity Regulatory Commission,* (2010) 4 SCC 603 para 92 (i) (ii) : AIR 2010 SC 1338.

provided under the Act against orders but only in judicial review under Article 226.[74]

(b) Compliance with Natural Justice when Necessary

Delegated legislation which is really legislative in character cannot be questioned for violating principles of natural justice in its making except when the statute itself provides for that requirement.[75] Where the power to be exercised under provisions of a statute does not concern with the interest of an individual and relates to public in general or concerns with a general direction of a general character and lays down a future course of action, it is generally held to be legislative in character.[76] A requirement to make such enquiry as it thinks fit, before the authority concerned makes delegated legislation is an enabling provision and does not confer any right on any one of being noticed or heard[77] and there is no right to oral hearing even if objections are required to be invited.[78] But when public hearing is provided under the statute or rules made under it, the same cannot be negatived on the ground that it is likely to be an unmanageable hearing.[79]

It is possible that the same statutory power may be both *quasi*-legislative and *quasi*-administrative and requirement of natural justice may have to be followed when it is exercised *quasi*-administratively although not when its exercise is *quasi*-legislative. For example, a statutory power to fix different rates of electricity duty or to allow exemption in payment thereof

---

74. *PTC India Ltd. v. Central Electricity Regulatory Commission*, supra paras 92(iii), 93.

75. *Laxmi Khandsari v. State of U.P.*, AIR 1981 SC 873 : (1981) 2 SCC 600; *Rameshchandra v. State of Maharashtra*, AIR 1981 SC 1127: (1981) 2 SCC 722; *Union of India v. Cynamide India Ltd.*, (1987) 2 SCC 720, pp. 734, 735 : AIR 1987 SC 1802; *H.S.S.K. Niyami v. Union of India*, AIR 1990 SC 2128, p. 2132 : (1990) 4 SCC 516; *State of Punjab v. Tehal Singh,* AIR 2002 SC 533, p. 536 : (2002) 2 SCC 7; *W.B. Electricity Regulatory Commission v. C.E.S.C. Ltd.*, AIR 2002 SC 3588, pp. 3600, 3601 : (2002) 8 SCC 715; *Pune Municipal Council Corporation v. Promoters and Builders Association*, AIR 2004 SC 3502, p. 3504 : (2004) 5 JT 191; *Bihar State Electricity Board v. Pulak Enterprises*, (2009) 5 SCC 641 para 29 : (2009) 6 JT 282.

76. *State of Punjab v. Tehal Singh, supra,* p. 536 (Declaration of territorial area of Gram Sabha and establishing a Gram Sabha for that area by Government under statutory power are acts legislative in character); *Rameshchandra v. State of Maharashtra, supra* (making of a declaration under statutory power that certain place shall be principal market yard for a market area is legislative in nature.)

77. *Union of India v. Cynamide India Ltd., supra*; *Pune Municipal Council Corporation v. Promoters and Builders Association, supra.*

78. *Sundardas Kanyalal Bhathija v. Collector Thane,* AIR 1990 SC 261, p. 265 : AIR 1991 SC 1893, p. 1901.

79. *West Bengal Electricity Regulatory Commission v. C.E.S.C. Ltd.*, AIR 2002 SC 3588, p. 3601.

conferred by section 3(4) of the U.P. Electricity Duty Act, 1952 has been held to be legislative when exercised in respect of a class of persons but administrative when exercised in respect of an individual and thereby requiring the observance of principles of natural justice in the latter case.[80] Similarly, fixation of price of levy sugar under section 3C of the Essential Commodity Act, 1955 in respect of producers generally or producers in a zone is legislative in nature but the calculations of the amount payable to each producer is administrative in nature.[81]

Conditional legislation, though distinguished from delegated legislation proper,[82] has been held to be a form of delegated legislation and it has been observed that "it has a content howsoever small and restricted of the law making power itself."[83] The question whether principles of natural justice apply to the exercise of the power of conditional legislation was recently considered in the context of power to grant exemption contained in section 36 of the Payment of Bonus Act, 1965 which was held by a Constitution Bench in *Jalan Trading Company v. Mill Mazdoor Sabha*[84] to be in the nature of conditional legislation. The court in *Jalan* case also held that the condition for exercise of the power of exemption from the operation of the Act is that the Government holds the opinion that it is not in public interest to apply all or any of the provisions of the Act to an establishment or class of establishments and that the opinion is founded on a consideration of the financial position and other relevant circumstances.[85] In *State of Tamil Nadu v. K. Sabanayagam,*[86] where the question arose whether exemptions granted by the Government from time to time in respect of the Tamil Nadu Housing Board were invalid for the reason that the employees of the Board, who were affected by the grant of exemption, were not given opportunity to put forward their case that exemption should not be granted, a two judge bench of the Supreme Court laid down that there are three categories of conditional legislations. In the first category are those provisions which empower the delegate to extend the Act to a given area on its subjective satisfaction of the conditions indicated in it. The court illustrated

---

80. *State of U.P. v. Renusagar Power Co.*, AIR 1988 SC 1737, pp. 1761, 1763 : 1988 (4) SCC 59. **See further** case in note 76, *supra*; *Bihar State Electricity Board v. Pulak Enterprises (supra)* para 37.

81. *Sitaram Sugar Co. Ltd. v. Union of India,* AIR 1990 SC 1277, p. 1295 : 1990 (3) SCC 223; *H.S.S.K. Niyami v. Union of India,* AIR 1990 SC 2128 : 1990 (4) SCC 516.

82. **See**, p. 813.

83. *Lachmi Narain v. Union of India,* AIR 1976 SC 714, pp. 722, 723 : (1976) 2 SCC 953, p. 964.

84. *Jalan Trading Company v. Mill Mazdoor Sabha,* AIR 1967 SC 691, p. 703 : 1967 (1) SCR 15.

85. *Ibid.*

86. *State of Tamil Nadu v. K. Sabanayagam,* AIR 1998 SC 344, pp. 355 to 363 : (1998) 1 SCC 318.

this category by referring to the case of *Tulsipur Sugar Co. Ltd. v. Notified Area Committee, Tulsipur,*[87] where the State Government was empowered by section 3 of the U. P. Town Areas Act, 1914 to declare any town *etc.* as a town area, to define the limits of the town area and to include or exclude any area from any town area so declared. By a notification issued under section 3, the limits of the Tulsipur Town Area were extended to cover village Shitlapur where the sugar factory of the appellant was situated. The notification was challenged on the ground that before issuing it the appellant was not given any opportunity of being heard. This contention was negatived on the ground that the section was in the nature of conditional legislation and the power exercisable being legislative in character, the rule of *audi alterum partem* did not apply. The second category of conditional legislation comprised of those provisions where the delegate has to decide according to its subjective satisfaction for withdrawal of the parent legislation in a given area or in given cases so as not to be applicable to a given class of persons to which it was applicable. This is illustrated by the court by referring to a tariff fixed by the Act and power of exemption conferred on the delegate to grant full exemption or partial exemption from the tariff rate from time to time. The exercise of power in the aforesaid two categories does not require observance of the principles of natural justice. But the court said, that there is a third category of conditional legislation, where the exercise of power of exemption depends upon the satisfaction of the delegate on objective facts placed by one class of persons seeking benefit with a view to deprive the rival class of persons who have already got the benefit of the Act. In cases falling in this category, according to the court, principles of fair play and natural justice apply and the parties affected by the exemption ought to be given opportunity to put forward their case. Section 36 of the Payment of Bonus Act, 1965 the court held, fell in this category. The employees of the Housing Board became entitled to the bonus fixed by the Act. The exercise of power under section 36 required consideration objectively of the financial position and other circumstances of the establishment seeking exemption and whether it would not be in public interest to apply the provisions of the Act to it. The grant of the exemption deprived the employees of the establishment of the benefit of bonus payable under the Act. In the circumstances, the court held, that the employees ought to have been given opportunity to put forward their case through their representative union and as this was not done, the exemption notifications were invalid. It is submitted that instead of classifying conditional legislation into three categories without any clear cut distinction between them, could it not be said on the analogy of

---

87. *Tulsipur Sugar Co. Ltd. v. Notified Area Committee, Tulsipur,* AIR 1980 SC 882, p. 887 : (1980) 2 SCC 295, pp. 302, 303.

the reasoning in *Renu Sagar*[88] that the power under section 36 of the Payment of Bonus Act when exercised in respect of a class or classes of establishments, is *quasi*-legislative not requiring compliance with natural justice but, when exercised in respect of an establishment, *e.g.* the Tamil Nadu Housing Board, it is *quasi*-administrative requiring the observance of principles of natural justice.

In *Gopaldas Udhavdas Ahuja v. Union of India,*[89] the Supreme Court held that a notification issued by the Food (Health) Authority under Section 7(iv) of the Prevention of Food Adulteration Act, 1954 banning manufacture and sale of Pan Masala and Gutka was bad for non-compliance with natural justice as the manufacturers of Pan Masala and Gutka should have been given an opportunity of meeting the facts which had prompted the authority for banning the production and sale.[90] The court was not prepared to accept the contention that because the notification is generally intended, it is necessarily legislative in nature requiring no compliance of natural justice.[91] The court also said that the case came within at least the 3rd category of cases discussed in *Sabanayagam* and opportunity to manufacturers affected by the notification banning Pan Masala and Gutka ought to have been given.[92] In this case the notification issued by the Food (Health) Authority was held to be beyond his authority for other more substantial reasons and it was indeed unnecessary to go into the question of deciding its validity for non-compliance with principles of natural justice.

(c) Conformity with the Constitution

Whenever the Legislature confers power on some outside authority to make subordinate legislation or any order it is implicit that the power conferred by the enabling Act is to be exercised "in accordance with the provisions of the Articles of the Constitution."[93] Such an implication is to be read as a matter of construction, otherwise the enabling Act itself will become invalid. But, even apart from such an implication, the Constitution being the fundamental law of the Republic, by its own force invalidates any law, whether made by the Legislature or by subordinate agencies,

---

88. **See** text and note 80, p. 1072, *supra.*
89. *Gopaldas Udhavdas Ahuja v. Union of India,* (2004) 7 SCC 33 : AIR 2004 SC 3830.
90. *Ibid.* p. 105.
91. *Ibid.*
92. *Ibid.*
93. *Narendra Kumar v. Union of India*, AIR 1960 SC 430, p. 433 : 1960 (2) SCR 375; *Maneka Gandhi v. Union of India*, AIR 1978 SC 597, pp. 646, 647 : (1978) 1 SCC 248.

which is violative of its provisions.[1] Further, in matters affecting fundamental rights, the delegated legislation has to be in conformity with the principle of proportionality.[2]

(d) Conformity with the Enabling Act

(i) General Principles of Conformity; Presumption of Validity, Unreasonableness

The power to make subordinate legislation is derived from the enabling Act and it is fundamental that the delegate on whom such a power is conferred has to act within the limits of authority conferred by the Act.[3]

Rules cannot be made to supplant the provisions of the enabling Act but to supplement it.[4] For example, when power of granting recognition to educational institutions is entrusted by the Act exclusively to the competent Authority to be constituted under the Act, rules cannot be made to confer that power on the Government on the report of an experts Committee.[5] The delegate is not authorised to make a provision beyond the policy of the Act. For example, if the Legislature has enacted a legal fiction providing that any notified agricultural produce, which is taken out of a notified market area shall be presumed to have been purchased or sold within such area,[6] the legal fiction cannot be widened by rules or byelaws to provide further that if a notified agricultural produce is weighed, measured or counted within the notified market area, it shall be deemed to have been

---

1. Article 13, Constitution of India; *Madhubhai v. Union of India*, AIR 1961 SC 21 : (1961 (1) SCR 191; *Gopalan v. State of Madras*, AIR 1950 SC 27, p. 34 : 1950 SCR 88.

   N.B.—See the following cases where Delegated Legislation has been held invalid on the ground of violation of the Constitution; *Rashid Ahmad v. Municipal Board, Kairana*, AIR 1950 SC 163 : 1950 SCR 566; *Tahir Hussain v. District Magistrate, Mussoorie*, AIR 1954 SC 630; *State of Rajasthan v. Nathmal*, AIR 1964 SC 307; *R.M. Seshadri v. District Magistrate, Tanjore*, AIR 1954 SC 747 : (1955) 1 SCR 686; *Narendra Kumar v. Union of India*, AIR 1960 SC 430 : 1960 (2) SCR 375; *Chandrakant v. Jasjit Singh*, AIR 1962 SC 204 : 1962 (3) SCR 108; *Kameshwar Prasad v. State of Bihar*, AIR 1962 SC 1166 : 1962 Supp (3) SCR 369; *P.J. Irani v. State of Madras*, AIR 1961 SC 1731 : (1962) 2 SCR 169. For rules made under Article 309, **see** text and note 1, p. 1092.
2. **See** pp. 487-488.
3. *Hukamchand v. Union of India*, AIR 1972 SC 2427 : (1972) 2 SCC 601; *Additional District Magistrate v. Shri Siri Ram*, JT 2000 (6) SC 643, p. 651 : (2000) 5 SCC 451 : AIR 2000 SC 2143 : (2000) 5 SCC 451.
4. *St. Johns Teachers Training Institute v. Regional Director*, (2003) 3 SCC 321, p. 331 : AIR 2003 SC 1533.
5. *Nedurimilli Janardhana Reddy v. Progressive Democratic Students Union*, JT 1994(6) SC 170, pp. 176, 177 : (1994) 6 SCC 506.
6. *Explanation 1* to section 12 of the A.P. (Agricultural Produce and Livestock) Markets Act, 1966.

sold or purchased in that area.[7] But rules made on matters as permitted by the Act to supplement the Act cannot be held to be in violation of the Act.[8] In this case it was held that rules made under the power to make rules to define classes of offenders who can be released on probation under a Prisoner's Release on Probation Act, can provide that those convicted of heinous offences such as dacoity cannot be released. A statutory provision authorising making of rules for fixing 'charges' will enable making of rules for payment of interest for delayed payment.[9] In case of conflict between a substantive provision of the enabling Act and a rule or any other delegated legislation made under it, the former prevails and the delegated legislation has to be read and construed consistent with the enabling Act.[10]

When the Act regulating mining leases assures the lessee the right to carry on mining operations during the entire period of lease and provides for premature termination only after giving a hearing to the lessee, the delegate cannot while making a rule in exercise of the power granted under the Act make a provision for termination of all leases forthwith without notice or hearing to the lessees.[11]

The delegate cannot override the Act either by exceeding the authority or by making provisions inconsistent with the Act. But when the enabling Act itself permits its modification by rules, the rules made prevail over the provision in the Act.[12] When a provision A in the Act is 'subject to' other provisions of the Act, a valid notification issued under any other provision in the Act would in case of conflict with section A override its provisions.[13]

The delegate has to exercise the power of making subordinate legislation in accordance with the procedure prescribed, if any. In considering the effect of non-compliance of a procedural provision of the Act, one has to

---

7. *Agricultural Market Committee v. Shalimar Chemical Works Ltd.*, AIR 1997 SC 2502, p. 2508 : (1997) 5 SCC 516.

8. *State of M.P. v. Bhola,* (2003) 3 SCC 1, p. 10 : AIR 2003 SC 1191. **See further** *Nowa ADS v. Secretary, Department of Municipal Administration and Water Supply*, (2008) 8 SCC 42 para 38 : AIR 2008 SC 2941.

9. *South Eastern Coalfields Ltd. v. State of M.P.*, AIR 2003 SC 4482, p. 4489 : (2003) 8 SCC 648.

10. *ITW Signode India Ltd. v. Collector of Central Excise*, (2004) 3 SCC 48, p. 71 (para 56) : (2004) 6 JT 456; *Nowa ADS v. Secretary, Department of Municipal Administration and Water Supply*, (2008) 8 SCC 42 para 41 : AIR 2008 SC 2941.

11. *State of T.N. v. P. Krishnamurthy,* (2006) 4 SCC 517 (para 29) : AIR 2006 SC 1622.

12. For meaning of modification, **see** *Britnell v. Secretary for State for Social Security*, (1991) 2 All ER 726, pp. 730, 731 : (1991) 1 WLR 1980 : (1991) 135 SJ 412 (HL) (It may cover extension).

13. *Union of India v. Azadi Bachao Andolan*, AIR 2004 SC 1107, p. 1122 : 2003 Supp (1) JT 205.

see whether the non-compliance relates to a mandatory or a directory provision. In the former case the defect will be fatal; whereas in the latter case the defect will be ignored.[14]

A subordinate legislation may also be struck down as arbitrary if it fails to take into account very vital facts which either expressly or by necessary implication are required to be taken into consideration by the statute or the constitution.[15] This can only be done on the ground that it does not conform to the statutory or constitutional requirements, but not merely on the ground that it is not reasonable or that it has not taken into account circumstances which the court considers relevant.[16] So delegated legislation can be struck down only if there be manifest arbitrariness.[17] For example, a statutory rule breach of which may amount to a penal offence must be definite so that the persons to whom it is directed know what they can do and what they cannot do.[18] If it is vague, it will be struck down as unreasonable and unworkable.[19] In *Dai-Ichi Kakaria Ltd. v. Union of India,* where an exemption notification issued in 1982 in public interest under section 25(1) of the Customs Act 1962 and stated therein to remain in force till 10 September 1987 was withdrawn by another notification dated 30 December 1986, the later notification was held invalid being arbitrary as no public interest was shown to exist in support of the withdrawal of the exemption.[20] A policy statement by the Government for implementation of the enabling Act does not amount to legislation and breach of policy decision by itself is no ground for invalidating delegated legislation but it may furnish a ground of arbitrariness under Article 14 of the Constitution.[21]

---

14. **See** under title (4), Procedural Requirements'.

15. *Indian Express Newspapers v. Union of India,* (1985) 1 SCC 641, p. 691 : AIR 1986 SC 515. **See further** *State of U.P. v. Renusagar Power Co.*, AIR 1988 SC 1737, p. 1763 : 1988 (4) SCC 59; *Supreme Court Employees Welfare Association v. Union of India,* AIR 1990 SC 334, pp. 367, 368 : (1989) (4) SCC 187; *Shri Sitaram Sugar Co. Ltd. v. Union of India,* AIR 1990 SC 1277, p. 1297 : (1990) 3 SCC 223.

16. *Indian Express Newspapers v. Union of India, supra*; *PTC India Ltd. v. Central Electricity Regulatory Commission,* (2010) 4 SCC 603 para 52 : AIR 2010 SC 1338.

17. *Khoday Distilleries Ltd. v. State of Karnataka,* (1996) 10 SCC 304 : AIR 1996 SC 911.

18. *State of Kerala v. Unni,* (2007) 2 SCC 365 (para 50) : AIR 2007 SC 819.

19. *Ibid,* para 51.

20. *Dai-Ichi Kakaria Ltd. v. Union of India,* JT 2000 (4) SC 495, pp. 502, 503 : (2004) 4 SCC 57 : AIR 2000 SC 1741.

21. *Secretary Ministry of Chemicals and Fertilizers v. Cipla Ltd.,* (2003) 7 SCC 1, pp. 10, 23 (Policy statement for price control of drugs. Price control order violating norms stated in the policy may be open to objection on the ground of arbitrariness.)

Fixation of maximum length of service as a criterion for retirement is valid. There is no absolute proposition in law nor any invariable rule in service jurisprudence that an employee can be retired on account of age alone. Nagaland Retirement from Public Employment (Second Amendment) Act, 2009 providing for retirement after 35 years of service or on attaining 60 years whichever is earlier has been held to be valid.[22]

In considering the *vires* of subordinate legislation one should start with the presumption that it is *intra vires*.[23] The principle means that if sub-ordinate legislation under consideration is open to two constructions, one of which would make it bad and the other good, the courts must adopt that construction which makes it good.[24] The Court thus can read down a general provision to avoid its being declared *ultra vires*.[25] But when a part of the subordinate legislation is admittedly *ultra vires* the question arises whether the remaining part can be severed from the invalid part and upheld as valid. The question of 'severance' so arising has not to be solved simply on 'blue-pencil' basis but on considerations whether deletion of that which is in excess of the power so alters the substance of what is left that it becomes in reality a substantially different provision from that which it was before deletion and so it cannot be

---

22. *Nagaland Senior Government Employees Welfare Association v. State of Nagaland*, (2010) 7 SCC 643 : (2010) 7 JT 251.

23. F. HOFFMANN—*La Roche & Co. A.G. v. Secretary of State for Trade and Industry*, (1974) 2 All ER 1128, pp. 1154, 1155 (HL), (A subordinate legislation is presumed to be valid until declared invalid by a court in a proceeding initiated by a proper person. The consequence of declaration of invalidity is to render the same incapable of ever having had any legal effect. But till the presumption of validity continues, it has to be obeyed); *St Johns Teachers Training Institute v. Regional Director National Council of Teacher Education,* (2003) 3 SCC 321, p. 332 : AIR 2003 SC 3078.

24. *In re, Hindu Women's Right to Property Act*, AIR 1941 FC 72, p. 76, and **see** Chapter 6, title 3(c) Rule of construction, p. 650. **See** for example, *State of Orissa v. M.A. Tulloch & Co. Ltd.*, (1964) 15 STC 641 : AIR 1964 SC 1284 (SC); *Kedarnath Jute Manufacturing Co. v. Commercial Tax Officer*, AIR 1966 SC 12, p. 14 : (1965) 3 SCR 626; *State of M.P. v. Dadabhoy's New Chirmiri Ponri Hill Colliery Co.*, AIR 1972 SC 614, p. 621 : (1972) 1 SCC 298; *Union of India v. Tulsiram Patel*, (1986) 3 SCC 398, p. 484 : AIR 1986 SC 1541; *M.L. Kamra v. Chairman-cum-Managing Director, New India Assurance Co. Ltd.,* AIR 1992 SC 1072, pp. 1074, 1075 : (1992) 1 SCR 220 : (1992) 2 SCC 36; *Morvi Municipality v. State of Gujarat*, AIR 1993 SC 1508, p. 1517 : (1993) 2 SCR 803 : (1993) 2 SCC 1508; In the matter of *K. Anjaiah v. K. Chandraiah*, 1998 (2) Scale 148, p.151; *Gudur Kishan Rao v. Sutirtha Bhattachaarya*, 1998 (2) Scale 14, p. 22; *St. Johns Teachers Training Institute v. Regional Director National Council of Teacher Education, supra.*

25. *Ibid, St. Johns Teachers Training Institute v. Regional Director National Council of Teacher Education, supra,* **see further** text and notes 4 to 8, pp. 661-662.

assumed that the authority making it would have made it in the altered form.[26]

Mention of a wrong provision under which a subordinate legislation is expressed to be made does not invalidate it if there is some other enabling statutory provision which can support it.[27]

It has been recognised under the English law that bye-laws made by local authorities and Corporations are open to challenge on the ground that they are unreasonable.[28] The Supreme Court has also held that bye-laws made and fees and taxes imposed by a Municipal Corporation can be challenged on the ground of unreasonableness[29] even though the court is slow to interfere with the bylaws made by public representative bodies "unless they are manifestly partial and unequal in operation or unjust, *mala fide* or make unjustified interference with liberty."[30] Statutory rules and regulations as distinguished from bye-laws cannot be challenged on the ground of mere unreasonableness;[31] but as earlier seen any subordinate legislation can be challenged if the unreasonableness is of such a character as to

---

26. *Woolwich Equitable Building Society v. Inland Revenue*, (1991) 4 All ER 92, p. 104 (HL). **See further** text and notes 12 to 60, pp. 662, 664; *M.J. Sivani v. State of Karnataka*, 1995 (3) Scale 80, p. 91 : (1995) 6 SCC 289 : AIR 1995 SC 1770.

27. *Gopal Narain v. Mahabirlal*, AIR 1964 SC 370, p. 377 : 1964 (4) SCR 869; *Afzal Ullah v. State of U.P.*, AIR 1964 SC 264, p. 268 : 1964 (4) SCR 991; *Hukumchand Mills v. State of M.P.*, AIR 1964 SC 1329, p. 1332 : 1964 (6) SCR 857; *Parvez Qudir v. Union of India*, AIR 1975 SC 446, p. 451 : (1975) 4 SCC 318; *Om Prakash v. State of U.P.*, (2004) 3 SCC 402, p. 408. **See further** Chapter 5, text and notes 76, 77, p. 516.

28. *Kruse v. Johnson*, (1895-99) All ER Rep 105, p. 110 : (1898) 2 QB 91; LORD RUSSEL OF KILLOWEN, C.J. said: "Unreasonableness in what sense? If for instance they were found to be partial and unequal in their operation between different classes, if they were manifestly unjust, if they disclosed bad faith, if they involved such oppressive or gratuitous interference with rights of those subject to them as could find no justification in the minds of reasonable men, the Court might well say Parliament never intended to give authority to make such rules and that they are unreasonable and *ultra vires*. But it is in this sense and in this sense only, as I conceive, that the question of unreasonableness can be properly regarded". For an example, **see** *King v. C.L. Broad*, AIR 1915 PC 160. A bye-law may also be held invalid when it is so uncertain in its language as to have no ascertainable meaning or so unclear in its effect as to be incapable of certain application in a case; *Fawcett Properties Ltd. v. Buckingham CC*, (1960) 3 All ER 503; *Percy v. Hall*, (1996) 4 All ER 523 : 1997 QB 924 (CA).

29. *Delhi Municipality v. Birla Cotton, Spinning and Weaving Mills*, AIR 1968 SC 1232, pp. 1247, 1254, 1266 : 1968 (3) SCR 251; *Trustees of the Port of Madras v. Aminchand Pyarelal*, AIR 1975 SC 1935 : 1976 (3) SCC 167.

30. *Om Prakash v. State of U.P.*, (2004) 3 SCC 402, p. 410 (para 13) : AIR 2004 SC 1890, **relying** upon *H.C. Suman v. Rehabilitation Ministry Employees Coop. Housing Building Society Ltd.*, (1991) 4 SCC 485, pp. 499-501.

31. *Maharashtra State Board of Secondary and Higher Secondary Education v. Paritosh Bhupesh Kumar Seth*, (1984) 4 SCC 27, pp. 45, 49, 50 : AIR 1984 SC 1543.

violate Article 14 of the Constitution or the statute under which it is made.[32] And in matters affecting fundamental rights it may have to satisfy the test of proportionality.[33] The question of 'reasonableness' or 'proportionality' in the context of restriction of a fundamental right *e.g.* right to carry on trade or business may be a matter of 'value judgment' or balancing of interest.[34] In this case the Supreme Court upheld a bylaw banning public dealings and trade of non-vegetarian food items including 'eggs' in the municipal town of *Rishikesh* along with adjoining towns of *Haridwar* and *Muniki Reti* which was made in deference to the religious and cultural demands of a large number of residents and pilgrims visiting these towns.[35]

(ii) Different forms of enabling provisions and related issues of judicial review

A normal feature of enabling Acts is first to grant the power to make rules *etc.*, in general terms, *e.g.*, 'to carry out the purposes of this Act' and then to say that 'in particular and without prejudice to the generality of the foregoing provision', such rules *etc.*, may provide for a number of enumerated matters.[36] If power is conferred to make subordinate legislation in general terms, the particularisation of topics is construed as merely illustrative and does not limit the scope of the general power.[37] This principle was applied by the Privy Council in *Emperor v. Shibnath Banerjee*,[38] where it was held that rule 26 of the Defence of India Rules, 1939, which *prima facie* was in excess of the express power conferred by section 2(2)(x) of the Defence of India Act, 1939, was well within the general power conferred by section 2(1) of the Act and therefore valid. The principle has been affirmed by the Supreme Court in *Afzal Ullah v. State of Uttar Pradesh*,[39] where the court in construing section 298 of the Uttar

---

32. *Indian Express Newspapers v. Union of India*, (1985) 1 SCC 641, pp. 690, 691 : AIR 1986 SC 515. **See** text and notes 65 to 67, pp. 1069-1070.

33. **See** pp. 487, 488.

34. *Om Prakash v. State of U.P.*, (2004) 3 SCC 402, p. 414 : AIR 2004 SC 1896.

35. *Ibid*, p. 415 (SCC).

36. **See** for example, section 49A(1) and 49A(2), Advocates Act, 1961 (as amended by Act 21 of 1964).

37. *Rohtak and Hissar Districts Electric Supply Co. v. State of U.P.*, AIR 1966 SC 1471.

38. *Emperor v. Shibnath Banerjee*, AIR 1945 PC 156, pp. 159, 160. **Cf.** Section 3(2)-15, Defence of India Act, 1962 and Rule 30, Defence of India Rules, 1962.

39. *Afzal Ullah v. State of Uttar Pradesh*, AIR 1964 SC 264, p. 268 : (1964) 4 SCR 549; *Om Prakash v. State of U.P.*, (2004) 3 SCC 402, p. 408 : AIR 2004 SC 1896. **See further** section 13 of the Mines and Minerals (Regulation and Development) Act, 1957, and *Sudarshan Mineral Co. Ltd. v. Union of India*, AIR 1975 SC 949, p. 951 (para 5) : (1975) 1 SCC 527. Sections 3(1) and 3(2) of the Essential Commodities Act, 1955, and *K. Ramanathan v. State of Tamil Nadu*, (1985) 2 SCC 116, pp. 126, 127 : AIR 1985 SC 660. Sections 91(1) and 91(2) of the Motor Vehicles Act, 1939 and *Ajay Kanu v. Union of India*, AIR 1988 SC 2027, p. 2030 : 1988 (4) SCC 156.

Pradesh Municipalities Act, 1916, held that the power to make bye-laws conferred in general terms by section 298(1) was not restricted by section 298(2) which particularised the power by enumeration of many matters. But even a general power to make rules or regulations for carrying out or giving effect to the Act, is strictly ancillary in nature and cannot enable the authority on whom the power is conferred to extend the scope of general operation of the Act. Therefore, such a power "will not support attempts to widen the purposes of the Act, to add new and different means to carrying them out, to depart from or vary its terms".[40] So if a Panchayat Act vests the power of establishing Primary Health Centres in *Panchayatha Samiti*, the State Government cannot under its power to make rules for carrying out the purposes of the Act, take upon itself the power to establish Primary Health Centres.[41] Similarly, if a taxing Act makes the tax recoverable from a dealer or a person providing the services, rules cannot be made under the general power to carry out purposes of the Act or to provide for manner of assessment, so as to make the tax recoverable from transferee of a dealer[42] or a person receiving the services.[43] And when the All India Council for Technical Education Act, 1987 defines 'Technical Institution' to exclude universities and empowers the All India Council for Technical Education under section 10(1) to grant approval for starting new technical institution that power cannot be extended by making a regulation 'to carry out the purposes of the Act' to require a university to seek approval for starting a department for imparting a course in technical education.[44]

However, the opinion of the Authority concerned that the rules, regulations or orders made by it are necessary to carry out one or more of the purposes mentioned in the Act when that opinion is recited in a preamble to the rules, regulations or orders, is greatly respected.[45] A Canadian statute, (the National Transitional Powers Act, 1945) conferred power on the Governor-in-Council to 'do and authorise such acts and things and make

---

40. *Shanahan v. Scott*, (1957) 96 CLR 245, p. 246; **approved** in *Utah Construction v. Pataky*, (1965) 3 All ER 650, p. 653 (PC). **See further** *Dr. Machandra Prasad Singh v. Chairman Bihar Legislative Council*, (2004) 8 SCC 747, p. 760 : AIR 2005 SC 69 (The principle will apply with greater vigour when rules have been framed in exercise of a power conferred by a constitutional provision).

41. *Venkateshwara Rao v. Government of Andhra Pradesh*, AIR 1966 SC 828 : 1966 (2) SCR 172.

42. *Deputy Commercial Tax Officer, Madras v. Sukhraj*, AIR 1968 SC 67 : 1967 (3) SCR 661.

43. *Laghu Udyog Bharati v. Union of India*, AIR 1999 SC 2596, pp. 2601, 2602 : 1999 (6) SCC 418.

44. *Bharathidasan University v. All India Council for Technical Education*, AIR 2001 SC 2861, pp. 2869, 2870 : (2001) 8 SCC 676.

45. *Vice Chancellor Jammu University v. Dushinant Kumar Rampal*, AIR 1977 SC 1146, p. 1154 : (1977) 2 SCC 616.

from time to time such orders and regulations as he may by reason of the continued existence of the national emergency deem necessary or advisable for the purpose of maintaining, controlling and regulating supplies and services, prices, transportation, use and occupation of property, rentals, employment, salaries and wages, to ensure economic stability and an orderly transition to conditions of peace'. In purported exercise of this power, an order in Council was made which provided that all oat and barley in commercial positions in Canada shall be vested in the Canadian Wheat Board. This order expressly recited in the preamble that it was made as it was necessary 'for the purpose of maintaining, controlling and regulating supplies and prices to ensure economic stability and an orderly transition to conditions of peace'. On a challenge to the validity of the Order, the Privy Council held[46] that in view of the recital in the preamble it was not open to the court to hold that the Order was made for a different purpose or what was declared to be necessary was not necessary for the purpose mentioned and that an Order in this form leaves no room for any judicial enquiry which may sometimes be undertaken if the recitals be ambiguous. The judgment, however, shows that an order made will be liable to be challenged on the following grounds: (1) Bad faith, that is to say that "powers entrusted for one purpose are deliberately used with the design of achieving another, itself unauthorised or actually forbidden"; (2) that "the Order shows on the face of it a misconstruction of the enabling Act or a failure to comply with the conditions which that Act has prescribed for the exercise of its powers"; (3) that the Order is not "capable of being related to one of the prescribed purposes".[47] The above mentioned case was followed in *Ross Clunis v. Papadopoullos*,[48] in upholding the validity of Cyprus Emergency Powers (Collective Punishment) Regulations, 1955. The Regulations gave the Commissioner power to impose collective fines on the assessable inhabitants of an area by reason of the commission of a series of offences in that area for which he had reason to believe that the inhabitants had been generally responsible. The Regulations were made under section 6(1) of the Emergency Powers Order in Council, 1939, which empowered the Governor of Cyprus to make Regulations 'as appear to him to be necessary or expedient for securing the public safety, the defence of the territory, the maintenance of the public order and the suppression of mutiny, rebellion and riot'. It was held that the Regulations were valid as they were related to the purposes contemplated by section 6(1), *e.g.*, the securing of public safety and the maintenance of public order.

---

46. *A-G for Canada v. Hallet & Carry Ltd.*, (1952) AC 427, pp. 444, 445, 450 (PC).
47. *Ibid.*
48. *Ross Clunis v. Papadopoullos*, (1958) 2 All ER 23 : (1958) 1 WLR 546 (PC).

The case of *Attorney-General for Canada v. Hallet and Carry Ltd.*[49] was also followed by the House of Lords in *McEldowny v. Forde*,[50] which upheld certain Regulations made by the Minister of Home Affairs under section 1(3) of the Civil Authorities (Special Powers) Act (Northern Ireland), 1922, which enacted that the Minister 'shall have power to make regulations for making further provision for the preservation of the peace and maintenance of order'. It was held that the courts would not interfere with the exercise of the power to make Regulations, if there was no question of bad faith and no misconstruction of the enabling Act or failure to comply with any conditions prescribed by the Act for the exercise of the power and the Regulations made were capable of being related to the purposes mentioned in the Act.

When the subordinate legislation made under a power to carry out the provisions of the Act has reasonable nexus with the object and purpose of the enabling statute, the court is not to concern itself with the wisdom or efficaciousness of the subordinate legislation or of the policy formulated therein. The Supreme Court applied the above principle in upholding the validity of a Regulation made 'to carry out the provisions of the Act' under section 36 of the Maharashtra Secondary and Higher Secondary Boards Act, 1965 which provided that no candidate shall claim or be entitled to revaluation or inspection of the answerbooks or other documents as they are treated by the Divisional Board as confidential.[51] It was also held in this case that the Regulations had to be judged on a three-fold test namely: (1) whether the provisions of the Regulations fall within the scope and ambit of the power conferred on the delegate; (2) whether the Regulations made are to any extent inconsistent with the provisions of the enabling Act; and (3) whether they infringe any of the fundamental rights or other restrictions or limitations imposed by the Constitution.[52]

Regulations made by the Medical Council under section 33 of the Indian Medical Council Act, 1956 'to carry out the purposes of the Act' laying down minimum marks for admission to medical colleges are valid and binding for the Council has power under section 19A to prescribe minimum standards of education and, therefore, of laying down eligibility

---

49. Note 38, *supra*.

50. *McEldowny v. Forde*, (1969) 2 All ER 1039 : (1971) AC 632 (HL).

51. *Maharashtra State Board of Secondary and Higher Secondary Education v. Paritosh Bhupesh Kumar*, (1984) 4 SCC 27, pp. 39, 42 : AIR 1984 SC 1543.

52. *Ibid.* **See further** *General Officer Commanding-in-Chief v. Subhash Chandra Yadav (Dr.)*, AIR 1988 SC 876, p. 879 : (1988) 2 SCC 165; *Commissioner of Central Excise and Customs v. Venis Castings (P.) Ltd.*, AIR 2000 SC 1568, p. 1572 : (2000) 4 SCC 206 (Purpose of the Act in this context is to be ascertained by reading the Act as a whole).

standards for admission.[53] On the same reasoning, the regulations made by the Veterinary Council of India under section 66(1) of the Veterinary Council Act, 1984 'to carry out the purposes of the Act' empowering itself for conducting entrance examination for 15% seats reserved on all India basis in Veterinary colleges, have been upheld, as the Council has power under section 22 to specify the minimum standard of veterinary education.[54]

But when the rule made, under the power 'to carry out the purposes of the Act,' is not relatable to any purpose of the Act or which brings into existence "substantive rights or obligations or disabilities not contemplated by the provisions of the Act itself", it will be invalid. It was so held in *Kunj Bihari Lal Butail v. State of H.P.*[55] In this case a rule made under section 26(1) of the Himachal Pradesh Ceiling on Land Holdings Act, 1972 which conferred power of making rules 'for carrying out the purposes of this Act' provided that no land treated as subservient to tea plantation exempted from the provisions of the Act shall be transferred by the land owner without the permission of the State Government. In holding that the rule restricting the transfer of land exempted from the Act was invalid, the court observed that it failed "to understand how a restriction on transfer of such land is going to carry out any purpose of the Act"[56] and, power conferred to give such directions as are necessary or expedient for carrying out the purposes of the Act has been construed to confer no power to issue directions in conflict with the Act and by necessary implication with the rules made under the Act.[57]

The Kerala Abkari Act seeks to control and regulate various categories of intoxicating liquor including Arrack and Toddy. In 1996 the State of

---

53. *Nivedita Jain v. State of M.P.*, 1981 MPLJ 244, p. 251 (G.P. SINGH C.J.) **reversed** in *State of Madhya Pradesh v. Kumari Nivedita Jain*, AIR 1981 SC 2045 : (1981) 4 SCC 296, which was **overruled** by a constitution bench in *Dr. Preeti Srivastava v. State of M.P.*, AIR 1999 SC 2894, p. 2917 : (1999) 7 SCC 120. **See further** *State of Punjab v. Dayanand Medical College and Hospital*, AIR 2001 SC 3006 : (2001) 8 SCC 664 (Power to prescribe reservation is not in medical council but in State under Article 15(4); *Harish Verma v. Ajay Srivastava*, (2003) 8 SCC 69 : AIR 2003 SC 3371 (case of Preeti Srivastava followed). **See also** *State of Tamil Nadu v. S.V. Bratheep*, AIR 2004 SC 1861, p. 1866 : (2004) 4 SCC 389 (State Government can prescribe higher eligibility qualification for admission).

54. *Veterinary Council of India v. Indian Council of Agricultural Research*, JT 2000 (1) SC 41, pp. 48, 49 : AIR 2000 SC 545, pp. 549, 550 : (2000) 1 SCC 750.

55. *Kunj Bihari Lal Butail v. State of H.P.*, AIR 2000 SC 1069, p. 1073 : (2000) 3 SCC 40.

56. *Ibid*, p. 1072.

57. *Commissioner of Bangalore Development Authority v. S. Vasudeo*, AIR 2000 SC 767, p. 773 : (2000) 2 SCC 439 (Construction of section 65 of the Bangalore Development Authority Act, 1976).

Kerala banned the sale of Arrack. Section 29 of the Act confers power to make rules 'for the purposes of this Act'. In 2002 the Government made Kerala Abkari Shops Disposal Rules, 2002, Rule 4 of which required that Arrack worker must be employed in all Toddy shops. This was obviously to provide employment to Arrack workers who had lost employment because of closure of Arrack shops. But the Act did not contemplate any such matter and the rule was declared invalid. It was held that "rules cannot be framed in matters that are not contemplated under the Act."[58] It was also pointed out: "It is well settled that no person can be thrust upon any unwilling employer except in accordance with the provisions of a special statute operating in the field. Such a provision cannot be made by the State in exercise of its power under delegated legislation unless the same is expressly conferred by the statute."[59]

If the rule making authority is conferred with power to make rules for ascertaining the value of an asset, the rule made can prescribe any recognised method of valuation. The wisdom of the rule making authority in preferring one method of valuation out of a number of methods cannot be challenged and the rule cannot be held to be invalid on that ground.[60] Further, the application of such a rule cannot be avoided and another method of valuation, which is not prescribed, applied by arguing that the rule made is only directory or prescribes an optional method of valuation.[61]

When power to make rules is not conferred in general terms 'to carry out the purposes of the Act', but is limited to particular topics, a rule made to be justified will have to be within the ambit of those topics otherwise it will be held invalid. Thus the rule making power conferred by section 27 of the Bihar Money-lenders Act, 1938, to prescribe the form of registration certificate and the particulars to be included in an application made for the purpose of being registered as a money-lender, does not empower the making of any rule fixing the upper limit up to which the loans advanced by a money-lender are to remain outstanding at any particular moment of time.[62] Further, it could rarely, if ever, be right to read into a statute, words which are not there in order to supply the vires of subordinate legislation which is *prima facie ultra vires*.[63]

---

58. *Kerala Samasthana Chethu Thozhilali Union v. State of Kerala,* (2006) 4 SCC 327 (para 26) : AIR 2006 SC 3480.

59. *Ibid,* para 16.

60. *Bharat Hari Singhania v. Commissioner of Wealth Tax,* JT 1994(2) SC 6, p. 15 : AIR 1994 SC 1355, p. 1365 : 1994 Supp (3) SCC 46.

61. *Ibid,* p. 16 (JT) : p. 1365 (AIR).

62. *Sant Saran Lal v. Parasram,* AIR 1966 SC 1852, p. 1855 (para 19) : 1966 (1) SCR 335.

63. *Reference under section 48 of the Criminal Appeal (Northern Ireland) Act, 1968,* (1976) 2 All ER 937 (HL), p. 957 (LORD SIMON), 951 (VISCOUNT DILHORNE).

When reasons are required to be stated for making delegated legislation, *e.g.*, grant of exemption from taxation, reasons must be stated and they can be examined for deciding whether the delegate has acted within limits of the power conferred.[64]

Rules made by an authority 'for discharging its functions under this Act' must have "a statutory peg on which to hang".[65] In other words, such a rule to be valid must have a nexus with any of the statutory functions entrusted to the rule making authority. Thus when the function of enrolling advocates under the Advocates Act, 1961 is entrusted to the State Bar Councils, which can also provide by rules the conditions subject to which a person may be admitted as an advocate on any such roll, the Bar Council of India cannot make a rule restricting the enrolment on the State roll to only those who had not completed 45 years of age,[66] or for training of new entrants before enrolment[67] and such rules cannot be sustained under section 49(1) of the Act which enables the Bar Council of India to make rules for discharging its functions under the Act.

The power of the State Government under a Municipal Act to apply its provisions to a notified area, after previous publication in the Government Gazette and a local newspaper of its intention to do so, specifying the purposes for which the Act is to be applied and inviting objections to its proposed action, must be exercised in conformity with the statutory requirements and if the proclamation containing the intention to apply the Act does not mention the purpose for which it is to be applied and if there is no publication in a local newspaper the exercise of the power will be held to be invalid.[68] A power conferred under an Agricultural Produce Market Act for declaration of market area and the kinds of agricultural produce for which the market is constituted must be exercised in the manner provided in the Act; and if the Act requires publication of the proposals in a

---

64. *M. Jhangir Batusha v. Union of India,* AIR 1989 SC 1713 : 1989 Supp (2) SCC 201. **See further** Chapter 5 title 6(h) text.

65. *V. Sundeer v. Bar Council of India,* JT 1999 (2) SC 141, p. 162 : AIR 1999 SC 1167, p. 1184 : (1999) 3 SCC 176.

66. *Indian Council of Legal Aid and Advice v. Bar Council of India,* JT 1995 (1) SC 423 : AIR 1995 SC 691 : (1995) 1 SCC 732.

67. *V. Sundeer v. Bar Council of India, supra.*

68. *State of Orissa v. Sridhar Kumar Mallick*, (1985) 3 SCC 697 : AIR 1985 SC 1411. Requirement of previous publication to invite objections may even be implied : *Baldeo Singh v. State of H.P.*, (1987) 2 SCC 510 : AIR 1986 SC 1239 (constitution of notified area under Municipal Act in respect of area governed by Panchayat Act); *State of U.P. v. Pradhan Sangh Kshetriya Samiti,* JT 1995 (3) SC 252 : 1995 AIR SC 1512 : 1995 Supp (2) SCC 305 (Delimitation of Panchayat areas and Gram Sabha under Panchayat Act). But a requirement to invite objections does not imply oral hearing; *Sundardas Kanyalal Bhathija v. Collector, Thane,* AIR 1991 SC 1893, p. 1901 : 1989 (3) SCC 396 (Constitution of a municipal corporation).

newspaper in addition to publication in the Gazette, such a requirement is a mandatory condition for exercise of the power.[69]

A power conferred on a market committee constituted under an Act to levy market fees subject to such maximum as may be prescribed by rules has been construed to negative any power to levy fees until rules are framed prescribing a maximum.[70] And, power conferred on a State Transport Authority by section 63(7) of the Motor Vehicles Act, 1939 to grant all India tourist permits "in respect of such number of tourist vehicles as the Central Government may in respect of that State specify" has been construed not to confer any power to grant any permit in the absence of such specification by the Central Government.[71] But a power to recover arrears of taxes and other dues by applying to a Magistrate after demand of the dues has been made in the manner prescribed by rules, has been interpreted as not disentitling the recovery of dues through the agency of Magistrate even if no rules are framed prescribing the manner of making the demand.[72] Similarly, section 46(1) of the Electricity (Supply) Act, 1948 which empowers an Electricity Board to fix from time to time "a tariff to be known as Grid Tariff—in accordance with any regulations made in this behalf" has been construed not to negative the power if no regulations are made.[73] On the same principles, power to make appointments of members of staff requiring professional skill 'subject to the rules as the State Government may make' conferred by section 21 of the Nagpur Improvement Trust Act, 1936 on the Trust was construed to authorise the Trust to make appointments by taking administrative decisions even in the absence of rules.[74] And, it has been ruled that where a statute empowers an authority to do certain acts or exercise a power in respect of certain matters "subject to rules", the exercise of the power conferred by the statute does not

---

69. *Govindlal Chagganlal Patel v. Agriculture Produce Market Committee*, AIR 1976 SC 263 : 1975 (2) SCC 482.

70. *Mohd. Hussain Gulam Mohd. v. State of Bombay*, AIR 1962 SC 97 : 1962 (2) SCR 659.

71. *S. Shamsuddin v. State of Karnataka*, (1984) 3 SCC 583, pp. 587, 588 : AIR 1984 SC 1244. **See further** *Hindustan Zinc Ltd. v. Andhra Pradesh State Electricity Board*, AIR 1991 SC 1473, pp. 1485, 1486 : (1991) 3 SCC 299. (The Board can fix tariff to generate surplus though its extent is not specified which the Government is required to specify).

72. *Dargah Committee, Ajmer v. State of Rajasthan*, AIR 1962 SC 574 : (1962) 2 SCR 265. **See further** *Free Lanka Insurance Co. v. Ranasinghe*, (1964) 1 All ER 457, p. 462 : 1964 AC 541 (PC). (Certificate of Insurance necessary 'under' a particular section which required the issue of a certificate in the 'prescribed form': no form was prescribed; held 'under' may be construed as meaning no more than 'as contemplated by' and thus not invalidating certificates issued though not in a prescribed form).

73. *U.P. Electricity Board v. City Board, Mussorie*, (1985) 2 SCC 16, pp. 20, 21 : AIR 1985 SC 883. **See further** *Kerala State Electricity Board v. S.N. Govinda Prabhu & Bros.*, (1986) 4 SCC 198, p. 213 : AIR 1986 SC 1999.

74. *Nagpur Improvement Trust v. Yadaorao Jagannath Kumbhare*, JT 1999 (5) 648, pp. 652, 653 : AIR 1999 SC 3084 : 1999 (8) SCC 99.

depend on the existence of rules unless the statute expressly provides for the same.[75]

A power to make rules for regulating procedure, does not authorise making of a rule of limitation which can put an end to a substantive right and so it was held that section 96(1)(b) of the Employees' State Insurance Act, 1948, does not authorise the Government to prescribe by rules a period of limitation for filing an application under section 75.[76] And a dealer's right to refund of tax under section 15 of the Central Sales Tax Act, 1956, cannot be denied or its enforcement made unduly difficult by prescribing an unreasonable time limit for applying for refund.[77] On the same principle, an unfettered right of appeal conferred by a Taxing Act cannot be fettered by a rule requiring deposit of the whole or part of the tax assessed, and such a rule cannot be said to be authorised as a rule regarding 'procedure relating to appeal'.[78]

Clause 37 of the Letters Patent of Calcutta, Bombay and Madras High Courts, empowers the High Court to make rules or orders for regulating all proceedings in civil cases. The proviso to clause 37 requires that in making such rules and orders the High Court shall 'as far as possible' be guided by the Code of Civil Procedure, 1908. Section 129 of the Code also empowers a High Court to make rules not inconsistent with the Letters Patent to regulate its own procedure in the exercise of its original jurisdiction as it shall think fit. Construing these provisions it has been held that a rule made by the High Court even if inconsistent with a provision of the Code will be valid and prevail.[79]

A power conferred on a Municipal Board to make bye-laws 'to regulate markets' confers no power to make a bye-law prohibiting

---

75. *Surinder Singh v. Central Government*, (1986) 4 SCC 667, pp. 672, 673 : AIR 1986 SC 2166. **See further** *Orissa State Prevention and Control of Pollution Board v. Orient Paper Mills,* AIR 2003 SC 1966, pp. 1970, 1971 : (2003) 10 SCC 421. (The expression 'in such manner as may be prescribed' leaves some lever or play in the working of the provision and the power can be exercised even when no rules are framed to prescribe the manner of exercise of power). *Janata Hill Truck Owners Association v. Shailang Area Coal Dealer and Truck Owner Association,* (2009) 8 SCC 492 paras 22, 23 : AIR 2009 SC 3041 (where the statute provides for certain things to be done, subject to rules, any action taken without framing the rules would not render that action invalid. If a statute is workable even without framing of the rules by issuing executive orders the same has to be given effect to).

76. *Bharat Barrel & Drum Mfg. Co. Pvt. Ltd. v. Employees' State Insurance Corporation*, AIR 1972 SC 1935, p. 1941 : (1972) 2 SCC 860.

77. *State of Mysore v. Mullick Hashim*, AIR 1973 SC 1449, p. 1450 : (1974) 3 SCC 251 : (1973) SCC (Tax) 532.

78. *Collector of Customs, Cochin v. A.S. Bava*, AIR 1968 SC 13, p. 15 : 1968 (1) SCR 82.

79. *Iridium India Telecom Ltd. v. Motorola Inc.*, (2005) 2 SCC 145, p. 161 : AIR 2005 SC 514.

markets.[80] Again, if a bye-law is framed which prohibits the establishment, maintaining or running of any market except with the previous permission of the Board but no bye-law is framed for granting of permission or licence, the result is not regulation but prohibition, and the bye-law will be invalid.[81] By section 37 of the Mysore Forest Act, 1900, the State Government was authorised to make rules to regulate the transit of any forest produce and the rules could 'prohibit the import, export, collection or moving of forest produce without a pass from an officer authorised to issue the same or otherwise than in accordance with the conditions of such pass'. The State Government framed a rule laying down that a person intending to transport forest produce must obtain a pass from an authorised officer. Subsequently two provisos were added to this rule. By the first proviso the holder of a pass was not permitted to transport forest produce between the hours of sunset and sunrise in any area specified in Schedule A to the Rules, and by the second proviso, it was provided that the restriction imposed by the first proviso may be relaxed between the hours of sunset and 10 p.m. on making of a cash security deposit of Rs. 1,000 for due performance of the rules. It was held by the Supreme Court that the main rule was valid being regulatory, but the two provisos were invalid as they restricted the transport of produce and were not regulatory. It was pointed out: "The power which the State Government may exercise is power to regulate transport of forest produce and not the power to prohibit or restrict transport. *Prima facie*, a rule which totally prohibits the movement of forest produce during the period between sunset and sunrise is prohibitory or restrictive of the right to transport forest produce."[82] The power to regulate a particular business or calling implies the power to prescribe and enforce all such proper reasonable rules and regulations as may be deemed necessary to conduct the business in a proper and orderly manner; and the power includes the authority to prescribe conditions under which the

---

80. *Tahir Hussain v. District Magistrate, Mussorie*, AIR 1954 SC 630.

81. *Rashid Ahmad v. Municipal Board, Kairna*, AIR 1950 SC 163 : 1950 SCR 566. **Cf.** *Afzall Ullah v. State of U.P.*, AIR 1964 SC 264 : 1964 (4) SCR 991, where regulatory bye-laws were upheld.

82. *State of Mysore v. Sanjeeviah*, AIR 1967 SC 1189, p. 1191 : (1967) 2 SCR 361. Sections 41, 42 and 76 of the Indian Forest Act, 1927 appear to confer wide power of rule making and rules for the establishment of saw pits and depots have been held to be valid: *State of Bihar v. Ranchi Timber Traders Association*, AIR 1996 SC 2774; *State of Tripura v. Sudhir Ranjan Nath*, AIR 1997 SC 1168, pp. 1174, 1175 : (1997) 3 SCC 665 (*Mysore* case **distinguished**). **See further** *Kurali Khandsari Udyog v. Excise Commissioner and Controller of Molasses U.P.*, (2004) 4 SCC 580, p. 583 : AIR 2004 SC 3797. (A rule requiring transporters to take permission of controller before transporting molasses outside Uttar Pradesh under Rule 24 of the U.P. Sheera Niyantrana Niyamavali, 1974 was held to be valid as a regulatory measure).

business may be carried.[83] Thus the classification of seats, fixation o rates of admission and number of shows will fall within the power o regulating cinema houses.[84] And a power to regulate supply and pur chase of sugarcane will imply a power to fix the price of sugarcane.[8 But the word 'regulation' in a certain context may include 'prohibition' It was so held in construing section 15 of the Mines and Mineral (Regulation and Development) Act, 1957 which empowers the Stat Government to make rules for regulating the grant of quarry leases mining leases and other mineral concessions in respect of minor miner als. A rule made under section 15 prohibiting exploitation of blac granite in the private sector was held to be valid.[86] Similarly it has bee held that power to regulate conferred by section 3(2)(d) of the Essentia Commodities Act, 1955 includes power to prohibit.[87]

Powers of a University to frame statutes and Ordinances are circum scribed by the Constituent Act and any excessive exercise of that powe will be held invalid by Courts.[88] In construing delegated legislation mad by the University authorities the court should respect the constructio which has been consistently adopted by these authorities.[89]

---

83. *Deepak Theatre v. State of Punjab*, AIR 1992 SC 1519, p. 1521 : 1992 Supp (1 SCC 684.

84. *Ibid.*

85. *U.P. Cooperative Cane Unions Federations v. West U.P. Sugar Mills Association* (2004) 5 SCC 430, p. 456 (para 26) : AIR 2004 SC 3697.

86. *State of Tamil Nadu v. Hind Stone*, AIR 1981 SC 711, p. 719 : (1981) 2 SCC 205.

87. *K. Ramanathan v. State of Tamil Nadu*, (1985) 2 SCC 116 : AIR 1985 SC 660 **See also** cases referred to in this case at pp. 131 to 133 (SCC) of the report **See further** *Jiyaji Rao Cotton Mills v. Madhya Pradesh Electricity Board* AIR 1989 SC 788, p. 807 : 1989 Supp (2) SCC 52 (the word 'regulate' has different shades of meaning depending on the context in which it is used); *Peerless General Finance & Investment Co. Ltd. v. Reserve Bank of India*, AIR 1992 SC 1033, p. 1064 : 1992 (2) SCC 343; *State of Tamil Nadu v. Sanjeetha Trading Co.*, AIR 1993 SC 237 : (1993) 1 SCC 236; *State of Tripura v. Sudhir Ranjan Nath*, AIR 1997 SC 1168, p. 1175 : (1997) 3 SCC 665; *King Pal Singh v. State of U.P.*, AIR 1997 SC 1758, pp. 1761, 1762 : (1996) 11 SCC 571; *Saurashtra Cement & Chemical Industries v. Union of India*, AIR 2001 SC 8, pp. 15, 22 : (2001) 1 SCC 91 ('Regulation' in entry 54 of List I of the Constitution includes power to tax). Similarly word 'restriction' may include prohibition : *Systopic Laboratories v. Prem Gupta (Dr.)*, AIR 1994 SC 205, p. 212 : 1994 Supp (1) SCC 160.

88. *Gujarat University v. Shrikrishna*, AIR 1963 SC 702 : 1963 Supp (1) SCR 112; *Bisheshwar v. University of Bihar*, AIR 1965 SC 601 : (1964) 7 SCR 879.

89. *Principal, Patna College v. K.S. Raman*, AIR 1966 SC 707 : 1966 (1) SCR 974.

(e) Retrospectivity of Delegated Legislation

Power may be conferred to make subordinate legislation in the shape of rules, bye-laws, *etc.*, which have retrospective operation.[90] Such a power may be either conferred in express words or may be inferred by necessary implication.[91] In the absence, however, of an express or necessarily implied power to that effect, subordinate legislation, be it a rule, a bye-law or a notification, cannot have retrospective operation.[92] Even in cases where there is a power to make rules with retrospective effect, a retrospective rule may not be valid if it infringes the Constitution. For example, the

---

90. *Prohibition and Excise Supdt. A.P. v. Toddy Tappers Co-op. Society Marredapally*, AIR 2004 SC 658 : (2003) 9 JT 178.

91. *Indramani v. W.R. Natu*, AIR 1963 SC 274, pp. 286, 287 : 1963 (1) SCR 721. Power conferred on the President or Governor or on their delegates to make rules under Articles 309 of the Constitution impliedly includes power to make retrospective rules; *B.S. Vadera v. Union of India*, AIR 1969 SC 118, p. 124 : (1968) 3 SCR 575; *K. Nag-raj v. State of A.P.*, (1985) 1 SCC 523, p. 551; *State of Rajasthan v. Mangilal Pindwal,* AIR 1996 SC 2181, p. 2183 : 1996 (5) SCC 60; *Bhakta Ramegowda v. Stateof Karnataka*, AIR 1997 SC 1038 (para 6); 1997 (2) SCC 661. Power conferred to bring into force the rules from the date of publication or 'from such other date as may be specified in this behalf' has been interpreted to imply a power to make restrospective rules; *State of Madhya Pradesh v. Tikamdas*, AIR 1975 SC 1429, p. 1431 : (1975) 2 SCC 100. Power conferred on the Government to make orders or issue directions for removal of difficulty in the working of an Act is a power to make delegated Legislation with retrospective effect; *CIT v. Straw Products*, AIR 1966 SC 1113 : (1966) 2 SCR 881. Power conferred by a rule on the Governor to relax the operation of the rules made under Article 309 in such manner as may appear to him to be just and equitable can be retrospectively exercised; *Government of Andhra Pradesh v. D. Janardhana Rao*, AIR 1977 SC 451, p. 454 : (1976) 4 SCC 226; *M. Venkateshwarlu v. Government of Andhra Pradesh*, 1996 (3) Scale 44 : 1996 (5) SCC 167. Power to exempt a co-operative society from the provisions of the Delhi Co-orperative Societies Act, 1972 as conferred by section 88 may be retrospectively exercised; *H.C. Suman v. Rehabilitation Ministry Employees Co-operative House Building Society Ltd.*, AIR 1991 SC 2160, pp. 2167, 2168 : (1991) 4 SCC 485. A retrospective rule may be validated by retrospective validating Act; *Vijay Mills Company Ltd. v. State of Gujarat*, AIR 1994 SC 1114, p. 1123 : (1993) 1 SCC 345.

92. *India Sugar Refineries Ltd. v. State of Mysore*, AIR 1960 Mys 326, **approved** by SUBBARAO, J. in *Indramani v. W.R. Natu, supra*, pp. 291, 292; *ITO v. M.C. Ponnoose*, AIR 1970 SC 385, p. 387 : (1969) 2 SCC 351; *Cannanore Spinning & Weaving Mills v. Collector of Customs*, AIR 1970 SC 1950, p. 1953 : (1969) 3 SCC 112; *Hukum Chand v. Union of India*, AIR 1972 SC 2427, p. 2430 : (1972) 2 SCC 601; *Bakul Cashew Co. v. Sales Tax Officer, Quilon*, (1986) 2 SCC 365, pp. 371, 372 : AIR 1987 SC 2239; *State Bank of India v. Yogendrakumar Shrivastava*, (1987) 3 SCC 10, p. 22 : AIR 1987 SC 1399; *CIT v. Bazpur Co-operative Sugar Factory Ltd.*, AIR 1988 SC 1263, p. 1267 : (1988) 3 SCC 553; *Bejgam Veeranna Venkata Narsimloo v. State of Andhra Pradesh*, AIR 1998 SC 542, pp. 547, 548 : (1998) 1 SCC 563 (vested rights cannot be taken away); *Vice-Chancellor, M.D. University v. Jahan Singh*, (2007) 5 SCC 77 (paras 19, 22, 26) : (2007) 4 Scale 226; *Panchi Devi v. State of Rajasthan*, (2009) 2 SCC 589 para 9 : (2009) 1 Scale 306.

President or the Governor cannot make such retrospective rules under Article 309 of the Constitution which takes away vested rights of employees and thereby contravene Article 14, 16 or 311 of the Constitution.[1] But a rule or any other subordinate legislation, will not be held to be retrospective merely because it draws upon past events for its future operation *e.g.*, a service rule which alters the age of superannuation of all public servants, whether recruited prior to or after the making of the rule, but which operates prospectively is not for that reason retrospective.[2] A power to bring into force an Act by notification is not retrospectively exercised if the Act is brought into force from a date posterior to its passing but which is anterior to the date of the notification by which it is brought into force.[3] This case[4] has been relied upon in holding that power to grant exemption from levy of assessment 'either permanently or for a specified period' under section 11 of the Andhra Pradesh Non-Agricultural Land Assessment Act, 1963 can be exercised to cover either wholly or partly the period anterior to the date of the order, so long as the period specified is subsequent to the commencement of the Act.[5] A rule, which is not in terms retrospective, may have retrospective operation because of the retrospective operation of the enactment in respect of which it is made.[6] But a notification, which has the effect of creating a penal liability, cannot have retrospective operation.[7] It need hardly be emphasised that even when there is power to make a

1. *B.S. Yadav v. State of Haryana,* AIR 1981 SC 561 : 1980 Supp SCC 524; *State of Gujarat v. Ramanlal Keshavlal Soni,* (1983) 2 SCC 33 : AIR 1984 SC 161; *K. C. Arora v. State of Haryana,* (1984) 3 SCC 281, pp. 292 to 295 : AIR 1984 SC 1; *P.D. Aggarwal v. State of U.P.*, (1987) 3 SCC 622 : AIR 1987 SC 1676; *Haribans Misra v. Railway Board*, AIR 1989 SC 696, p. 702; *D.P. Sharma v. Union of India*, AIR 1989 SC 1071, p. 1073 : 1989 Supp (1) SCC 244; *K. Narayanan v. R. Mahadeo*, AIR 1994 SC 55, p. 63 : 1994 Supp (1) SCC 44; *K. Ravindranath Pai v. State of Karnataka*, 1995(1) Scale 800, p. 805 : AIR 1995 SC 1978, p. 1982; *Chairman, Railway Board v. C.R. Rangadhamaiah,* AIR 1997 SC 3828, pp. 3836, 3837 : 1997 6 SCC 623. **See further** *S.S. Bola v. B.D. Sardana,* AIR 1997 SC 3127, p. 3217 : (1997) 8 SCC 522 (seniority and chances of promotion are not vested rights); *P. Mohan Reddy v. E.A.A. Charles,* JT 2001 (3) SC 1 : AIR 2001 SC 1210 : (2001) 4 SCC 433 (Seniority cannot be affected unless the new rules are retrospective.)
2. *Bishun Narain v. State of U.P.*, AIR 1965 SC 1567, p. 1569 : 1965 (1) SCR 693; *State of Andhra Pradesh v. S.K. Mohinuddin*, AIR 1994 SC 1474, p. 1474 : 1993 (3) Scale 315.
3. *Thangal Kunju Musaliar v. M. Venkatachalam*, AIR 1956 SC 246, pp. 258, 259 (para 39) : 1955 (2) SCR 1196.
4. Case in footnote 2.
5. *ITC Bhadrachalam Paper Boards v. Mandal Revenue Officer,* 1996 (6) Scale 551, p. 567 (para 28) : (1996) 6 SCC 634.
6. *Narayan Row v. Ishwarlal*, AIR 1965 SC 1818, pp. 1823, 1824 : (1965) 57 ITR 149.
7. *Ratanlal v. State of Maharashtra*, AIR 1966 SC 722, p. 726 : 1966 (2) SCR 142.

retrospective rule or notification, the well accepted rule of interpretation is that in the absence of express words or necessary implication a rule or notification takes effect from the date it is issued and not from any prior date.[8] Merely because a notification 'substitutes' something in a prior notification, the substitution cannot have any retrospective operation.[9] Further, a rule or any other delegated legislation, in the absence of express words or necessary implication, is not construed to affect existing rights. For example, a change in the eligibility qualification by amending the rules was held not to affect the selection which was in progress at the time of amendment.[10] The same view was again taken and it was explained that though a candidate on making an application for a post pursuant to an advertisement does not acquire any vested right for selection, yet if he is eligible and is otherwise qualified in accordance with the relevant rules and the terms contained in the advertisement, he does acquire a vested right for being considered for selection in accordance with the rules as they existed on the date of advertisement; and he cannot be deprived of that limited right on the amendment of the rules during the pendency of selection unless the amended rules are retrospective in nature.[11] However, the removal of an eligibility qualification for promotion by amending the rules was held to be retrospective, without express words, to benefit a promotee whose case was pending in the Supreme Court at the time when the rules were amended.[12]

When an earlier notification is amended by a later notification the words the 'date of this notification' occurring in the proviso so substituted will refer to the date of the earlier notification and not to the date of the later notification.[13]

---

8. *Chandravathi P.K. v. C.K. Saji*, (2004) 3 SCC 734, p. 749 (para 34) : AIR 2004 SC 2717 (Rules under Article 309 of the Constitution).

9. *Shri Vijayakshmi Rice Mills v. State of A.P.*, AIR 1976 SC 1471, p. 1473 : (1976) 3 SCC 37.

10. *P. Mahendran v. State of Karnataka*, AIR 1990 SC 405 : 1990 (1) SCC 411.

11. *N.T. Bevin Katti v. Karnataka Public Service Commission*, AIR 1990 SC 1233, p. 1240 : 1990 (3) SCC 157 (change in reservation of posts). **See further** *S.N. Nagarajan v. State of Mysore*, AIR 1966 SC 1942 : (1966) 3 SCR 682; *Y.V. Rangiah v. J. Sreeniwas Rao*, AIR 1983 SC 852 : 1983 (3) SCC 284; *A.A. Calton v. Director of Education*, AIR 1983 SC 1143 : (1983) 3 SCC 33; *P. Ganeshwar Rao v. State of Andhra Pradesh*, AIR 1988 SC 2068 : 1988 Supp. SCC 740; *Madan Mohan Sharma v. State of Rajasthan*, (2008) 3 SCC 724 para 11 : (2008) 3 JT 304.

12. *Sheshrao Jangluji Bagde v. Bhaiyya*, AIR 1991 SC 76 : 1991 Supp (1) SCC 367.

13. *ITC Bhadrachalam Paper Board Ltd. v. Collector of Central Excise*, JT 1994(3) SC 284, p. 286 : 1994 Supp (2) SCC 322 : (1994) 71 ELT 334.

(f) Taxation by Delegated Legislation

A power to tax or levy any compulsory charge cannot be inferred from mere generality of the powers conferred by the enabling enactment. By section 2F of the Defence of the Realm Regulations, the Food Controller was empowered to 'make orders regulating or giving directions with respect to the production, manufacture, treatment, use, consumption, storage, distribution, supply, sale or purchase of, or other dealing in or measures to be taken in relation to any article (including orders providing for the fixing of maximum or minimum prices), when it appears to him necessary or expedient to make any such order for the purpose of encouraging or maintaining the food supply of the country'. In exercise of these powers the Food Controller issued orders regulating purchase and taking out of milk from certain areas under licences issued by him. The licences granted contained a condition of payment of two pence to the Food Controller for every gallon of milk purchased and this condition was alleged to be imposed for the purpose of regulating prices and securing an equitable distribution of milk in different parts of the country. In spite of the fact that the licensee accepted the condition by an agreement which formed part of the licence, it was held that the imposition was unauthorised.[14] The last mentioned case was cited with approval by the Supreme Court in holding that a 'surcharge' imposed by the Executive without any authority of law, was wholly invalid.[15] It can now be taken to be well settled that no tax, fee or any compulsory charge can be imposed by any bye-law, rule or regulation unless the statute under which the subordinate legislation is made specifically authorises the imposition.[16] In negating a contention that a

---

14. *A-G v. Wills United Dairies Ltd.*, (1922) 127 LT 822 : 91 LJKB 987 (HL).
15. *Venkat Subbarao v. State of Andhra Pradesh*, AIR 1965 SC 1773, pp. 1789, 1790 : 1965 (2) SCR 577. **See further** *State of Kerala v. K.P. Govindan,* (1975) 1 SCC 281 : AIR 1975 SC 152 and *Nagrik Upbhokta Manch v. Union of India,* AIR 2002 SC 2405 : (2003) 5 SCC 466. (In these cases administrative charges and rounding off charges under control orders without authority of law were respectively held to be invalid); *Shri Digvijay Cement Co. Ltd. v. Union of India,* (2003) 2 SCC 614 : AIR 2003 SC 767 (Provision in Clause 9A of the Cement Control Order 1967 requiring the producer to pay to the Cement Regulation Account an amount at the specified rate on the production of non-levy cement was held to be a levy of tax and invalid being unsupported by any legal sanction in sections 18G and 25 of the Industries (Development and Regulation) Act, 1951 under which the Control Order was made).
16. *Bimal Chandra Banerjee v. State of Madhya Pradesh*, AIR 1971 SC 517, 520 : 1970 (2) SCC 467; *Lilasons Breweries (P) Ltd. v. State of Madhya Pradesh*, AIR 1992 SC 1393, p. 1396 : 1992 (3) SCC 293; *Ahmedabad Urban Development Authority v. Sharad Kumar Jayanti Kumar Pasawalla*, AIR 1992 SC 2038 : (1992) 3 SCC 285. **But see** *State of U.P. v. Malti Kaul*, 1996 (6) Scale 577, pp. 581, 582 : 1996 (10) SCC 425.

Development Authority constituted under the Gujarat Town Planning and Urban Development Act has implied authority to levy development fee by making regulations the Supreme Court observed: "In a fiscal measure it will not be proper to hold that even in the absence of express provision, a delegated authority can impose tax or fee. In our view, such power of imposition of tax and/or fee by delegated authority must be very specific and there is no scope of implied authority for imposition of such tax or fee".[17]

Even when a power to tax is expressly conferred by the enabling Act, it must be exercised within strict limits of the authority conferred by the Act. A Town Area Committee authorised to charge fee for use or occupation of any property vested in or entrusted to the management of the Committee, has no power to charge fee from persons who carry on business in their shops and not in or on any immovable property vested in the Committee.[18] A Notified Area Committee having power to charge fee for any licence, sanction or permission which it is entitled or required to grant by or under the Municipal Act, cannot charge a fee of one anna on a rupee from sellers and purchasers of fruits and vegetables in the absence of any provision in the Act or under it enabling the committee to grant any licence, sanction or permission to a person for buying fruits or vegetables.[19] A power conferred by a Municipal Act to levy 'rate' on lands and buildings on the basis of annual letting value which may be arrived at from capital value, does not authorise the imposition of 'rate' at a percentage of capital value,[20] or at a certain amount per hundred sq. feet of floor area.[21] A power conferred on a market committee to levy fees subject to the provisions of the rules and subject to such maxima as may be prescribed by the rules cannot be exercised unless the rules, which authorise the market committee to levy fees as may be fixed by the bye-laws also prescribe the maximum within which the bye-laws will prescribe fees.[22] A water authority on a proper construction of the statute constituting it was authorised to recover the charges for services rendered only from recipient of the services, it could not be empowered to recover the charges from any other class of persons under an order made in the exercise of the power to make 'incidental, consequential,

---

17. *Ahmedabad Urban Development Authority v. Sharad Kumar Jayanti Kumar Pasawalla, supra*, p. 2042.

18. *Mohd. Yasin v. Town Area Committee, Jalalabad*, AIR 1952 SC 115 : 1952 SCR 572.

19. *Shri Ram v. Notified Area Committee*, AIR 1952 SC 118 : 1952 SCJ 167.

20. *Gordhandas v. Municipal Commr.*, AIR 1963 SC 1742 : 1964 (2) SCR 608.

21. *Lokmanya Mills v. Barsi Borough Municipality*, AIR 1961 SC 1358 : 1962 (1) SCR 306.

22. *Mohd. Hussain Ghulam Mohd. v. State of Bombay*, AIR 1962 SC 97 : 1962 (2) SCR 659.

transitional or supplementary provision'.[23] When a State Act authorised the Government to 'prescribe annul or alter rates of tolls to be levied upon any road, ferry or bridge in the State', the Government could not levy toll on goods exported out of the State through certain exit points by road or railways.[24] And, when the Act provided that the land revenue shall be levied and assessed with reference to the use of land, no rule could be framed to levy land revenue for the non-use of the land.[25] But a power to make rules for assessment and collection of duty levied by the Act is liberally construed and will enable the making of a rule to recover any duty escaping assessment without any apparent period of limitation except the implication that action under the rule for recovery should be taken within a reasonable time.[26]

A power conferred on a local body to impose taxes by framing bye-laws or rules after previous publication of the tax proposals so as to enable the persons affected to file objections or representations is not properly exercised if the proposals are not published as required by the statute indicating the nature of tax, the rate of tax, and the class of persons to be taxed; and the tax imposed in breach of such requirements is invalid[27] unless the

---

23. *Daymond v. South West Water Authority*, (1976) 1 All ER 39 (HL).

24. *Hansraj & Sons v. State of Jammu and Kashmir,* AIR 2002 SC 2692, pp. 2697, 2698 : (2002) 6 SCC 227.

25. *State of Gujarat v. Arvind Mills,* (2003) 1 SCC 529, p. 533.

26. *Government of India v. Citadel Fine Farmaceuticals*, AIR 1989 SC 1771, pp. 1773, 1774 : 1989 (3) SCC 483.

27. *Radha Kishan Jaikishan v. Municipal Committee, Khandwa*, AIR 1934 PC 62; *Municipal Council, Khurai v. Kamal Kumar*, AIR 1965 SC 1321 : 1965 (2) SCR 653; (Procedure for imposing a liability to pay a tax has to be strictly complied with): *Raza Buland Sugar Co. Ltd. v. Municipal Board, Rampur*, AIR 1965 SC 895 : 1965 (1) SCR 970, (requirement of publication of tax proposals is mandatory but the manner of publication is directory); *Sonik Industries v. Municipal Corporation,* (1986) 2 SCC 608, p. 612 : AIR 1986 SC 1518 (Requirement of final publication is mandatory but the manner of publication is directory); *Dhrangadhra Chemical Works v. State of Gujarat*, AIR 1973 SC 1041, p. 1041 : 1973 SCC (Tax) 536 : (1973) 2 SCC 345. (Procedure for imposing a tax must be strictly followed but a minor or trivial deviation may not be fatal); *Corporation of City of Bangalore v. Kesoram Industries & Cotton Mills Ltd.*, AIR 1990 SC 322 : 1989 Supp (2) SCC 753 (consideration of objections to tax proposals need not be elaborate and it is sufficient if the objections are taken note of). **See further** *Bagalkot City Municipality v. Bagalkot Cement Co.*, AIR 1963 SC 771, p. 773 : 1963 Supp (1) SCR 710 (New area included within Municipal limits, existing bye-laws imposing Octroi do not automatically extend to new area unless fresh steps after previous publication etc. are taken to make them applicable to new area); *Vishakhapatnam Municipality v. Kaadregula Nukaraju*, AIR 1975 SC 2172 : (1975) 2 SCC 773 : 1963 Supp (1) SCR 710 (House Tax will not extend to new areas unless imposed a fresh after following the normal procedure); *Atlas Cycle Industries Ltd. v. State of Haryana*, AIR 1972 SC 121, pp. 122, 123 : 1971 (2) SCC 564 (Bye-laws and rules imposing

[Footnote No. 27 Contd.]

defect is not of substance, and the statute provides for its condonation[28] or some final step such as publication in the Gazette under the authority of the Government is declared by the statute as conclusive evidence of due compliance with the statutory requirements.[29] But the conclusive evidence clause does not bar an attack on the ground of absence of authority to impose the tax or want of fundamental steps in the manner of its imposition.[30]

(g) Provisions curtailing judicial review

(i) *'As if enacted in this Act' formula.*—Sometimes a statute contains a provision that subordinate legislation made under it will have effect 'as if enacted in this Act'. The divergence of opinion on the interpretation of these words is too well-known.[31] The Supreme Court of India has, however, emphatically ruled that by the use of 'as if enacted in this Act' formula, subordinate legislation does not lose its character of being subordinate to the parent Act,[32] and that the formula does not bestow "any additional

---

[Footnote No. 27 Contd.]
Octroi will extend to new area if a specific provision to that effect is made in the Municipal Act; such a provision will however, be strictly construed). Also **see,** *Bhasker Textiles Mills Ltd. v. Jharsuguda Municipality*, (1984) 2 SCC 25 : AIR 1984 SC 583; *Hindustan Gum and Chemicals Ltd. v. State of Haryana*, (1985) 4 SCC 124 : AIR 1985 SC 1683; *Fertilizer Corporation of India Ltd. v. Nagar Mahapalika Gorakhpur*, 1996 (3) Scale 809 : 1996 (8) SCC 432 (Bye-laws and rules imposing octroi can extend to new area by a retrospective amendment of the Act).

28. *Bangalore Woollen, Cotton & Silk Mills Co. Ltd. v. Bangalore Corporation*, AIR 1962 SC 562 : 1961 (3) SCR 707.

29. *Berar Swadeshi Vanaspathi v. Municipal Committee, Shegaon*, AIR 1962 SC 420 : 1962 (1) SCR 596. **See further** *Raza Buland Sugar Co. Ltd. v. Municipal Board, Rampur*, AIR 1965 SC 895, pp. 902, 903 : 1965 (1) SCR 970; *Municipal Board Board, Hapur v. Raghuvendra Kripal*, AIR 1966 SC 693, p. 697 : (1966) 1 SCR 950; *Municipal Council, Raichur v. Bohar Amarchand Prasanna*, AIR 1968 SC 255, p. 258; *Municipal Board, Sitapur v. Prayag Narain Saigal*, AIR 1970 SC 58, p. 59 : 1969 (1) SCC 399; *Tharoomal v. Puranchand Pandey*, AIR 1978 SC 306, p. 310 : 1978 (1) SCC 109.

30. *Corporation of the City of Victoria v. Bishop of Vancouver Islands*, AIR 1921 PC 240, p. 247; *Municipal Board, Hapur v. Raghuvendra Kripal*, AIR 1966 SC 693, pp. 696, 697 : (1966) 1 SCR 950; *Municipal Board, Sitapur v. Prayag Narain Saigal*, AIR 1970 SC 58, p. 59 : 1969 (1) SCC 399; *Tharoomal v. Puranchand Pandey, supra.*

31. **See** S.A. DE SMITH, Judicial Review of Administrative Action, 2nd Edition, pp. 353, 354; CRAIES, Statute Law, 7th Edition, pp. 311, 313; ALLEN, Law and Orders (2nd Edition), pp. 295, 300. **See further** *Institute of Patent Agents v. Lockwood*, (1894) AC 347 (HL); *R. v. Minister of Health, Ex parte, Yaffe*, (1931) AC 494 (HL).

32. *Chief Inspector of Mines v. Karam Chand Thapar*, AIR 1961 SC 838, p. 845 (para 20) : 1962 (1) SCR 9; *Kalipada Chawdhury v. Union of India*, AIR 1963 SC 134 : 1963 (2) SCR 904.

sanctity" to subordinate legislation which if not made within the strict limits of the authority conferred by the parent Act is always open to challenge on the ground that it is unauthorised.[33] In view of these decisions[34] of the Supreme Court the use of this formula in Indian Acts has ceased to serve any useful purpose.

(ii) *'Conclusive evidence' clause*[35].—Restricted view has also been taken of 'conclusive evidence' clauses which usually provide that some final step such as a notification or publication in the Gazette shall be conclusive evidence that the scheme, rule, bye-law, etc., as the case may be, has been duly made or has been made in accordance with the provisions of the parent Act. Such clauses are ineffective to cure a complete want of authority,[36] or a basic defect of jurisdiction;[37] or possibly even a complete non-compliance of a mandatory procedural requirement.[38] The clauses are, however, available to cure non-compliance of directory procedural requirements or such defects which are not of a fundamental character.[39] This limited utility of these clauses is again somewhat meaningless, for, even in the absence of such a clause, a defect of non-compliance of directory

---

33. *State of Kerala v. K.M. Charia Abdulla*, AIR 1965 SC 1585, p. 1589 (para 14) : 1965 (1) SCR 601. For example **see** *Chief Commr., Ajmer v. Radheysham*, AIR 1957 SC 304 : 1957 SCR 68; *Prithi Pal Singh v. Union of India*, AIR 1982 SC 1413, pp. 1425, 1426 : (1982) 3 SCC 140; *General Officer Commanding-in-Chief v. Subhash Chandra Yadav (Dr.)*, AIR 1988 SC 876, p. 879 : 1988 (2) SCC 351.
34. **See** footnotes 31 and 32, *supra*.
35. **See further** text and footnotes 28, 29, *supra* and Chapter 9, title 2(c), p. 809.
36. *Corporation of City of Victoria v. Bishop of Vancouver Islands*, AIR 1921 PC 240, p. 247; *Municipal Board, Hapur v. Raghuvendra Kripal*, AIR 1966 SC 693, p. 696 : 1966 (1) SCR 950.
37. *Trust Mai Lachhmi Sialkoti Bradari v. Amritsar Improvement Trust*, AIR 1963 SC 976, p. 980 : 1963 (3) SCR 777.
38. *Municipal Board, Hapur v. Reghuvendra Kripal, supra*, p. 697; *Raza Buland Sugar Co. v. Municipal Board, Rampur*, AIR 1965 SC 895, p. 902 (para 14) : 1965 (1) SCR 970; *Dharangadhara Chemical Works v. State of Gujarat*, AIR 1973 SC 1041,
p. 1044 (para 13) : (1973) 2 SCC 345.
39. **See** cases in footnote 37 above and **see,** *Berar Swadeshi Vanaspathi v. Municipal Committee, Shegaon*, AIR 1962 SC 420 : (1962) 1 SCR 596; *Municipal Council, Raichur v. B.A. Prasanna*, AIR 1968 SC 255, p. 258 : (1968) 1 SCR 87; *Municipal Board, Sitapur v. Prayag Narain*, AIR 1970 SC 58, p. 59 : (1969) 1 SCC 399; *Municipal Board, Maunath Bhanjan v. Swadeshi Cotton Mills Ltd.*, AIR 1977 SC 1055, p. 1059 : (1977) 1 SCC 875; *Tharoo Mal v. Puranchand Pandey*, AIR 1978 SC 306, p. 308 : (1978) 1 SCC 102.

A conclusive evidence clause may be held to be invalid on the ground that it unreasonably restricts the fundamental rights; **see** *Corporation of Calcutta v. Calcutta Tramways Co. Ltd.*, AIR 1964 SC 1279; *Raza Buland Sugar Co. v. Municipal Board, Rampur*, AIR 1965 SC 895, p. 902 (para 14) : 1965 (1) SCR 970.

requirements will not be effective to invalidate subordinate legislation which is otherwise authorised.

Section 3 of the Punjab Development and Damaged Areas Act, 1951, empowers the Improvement Trust to frame Schemes for development of 'damaged area' as defined in the Act. Section 4 makes provision for publication of schemes with a view to invite objections which are to be considered under section 5. The scheme, as originally framed or as modified, is published by the State Government under section 5(3) and is then deemed to be the sanctioned scheme. Section 5(4) of the Act declares that 'the publication under sub-section (3) shall be conclusive evidence that a scheme has been duly framed and sanctioned'. On a consideration of these provisions, it was held by the Supreme Court that a scheme, although notified under section 5(3), will not be a valid scheme, if it did not relate to a 'damaged area' as defined in the Act.[40] It was pointed out: "The conclusive effect, postulated by section 5(4) can only be in regard to formalities prescribed by sections 3, 4 and 5 and does not touch a case where there is complete lack of jurisdiction in the authorities to frame a scheme".[41]

The Uttar Pradesh Municipalities Act, 1916, in section 128 enumerates the taxes which Municipalities are authorised to impose. The procedure for imposition of these taxes is provided in sections 131 to 135. The scheme of these sections, in short, is that when a Municipal Board decides to impose a tax, the Board passes a special resolution framing the proposals which specify the nature of tax, persons or objects which are sought to be made liable, the rate of tax *etc*. The Board also prepares draft rules which it desires the Government to frame for assessment, collection, exemption, *etc*. The proposals and draft rules are then published in the manner prescribed by section 94(3) with a view to invite objections. The Board by special resolution considers the objections and may modify the proposals or the rules, which if modified, are again published for inviting objections which are again dealt with in the like manner. When proposals are finally settled, they are submitted to the State Government for sanction. When sanctioned, the order sanctioning the proposals and a copy of the rules is sent to the Board which thereupon by special resolution directs the imposition of the tax with effect from a date to be specified in the resolution. A copy of the special resolution is then sent to the State Government which notifies in the Official Gazette the imposition of the tax from the appointed day. Section 135(3) of the Act contains a conclusive evidence clause which provides: '*A notification of the imposition of a tax under sub-section (2)*

---

40. *Trust Mai Lachhmi Sialkoti Bradari v. Amritsar Improvement Trust*, AIR 1963 SC 976 : 1963 (1) SCR 242.

41. *Ibid*, p. 980.

shall be conclusive proof that the tax has been imposed in accordance with the provisions of the Act'. Section 94(3) of the Act prescribes the manner of publication, and requires publication of every resolution in a local Hindi news paper. On a consideration of these provisions it was held by the Supreme Court that the rule of conclusive evidence enacted in section 135(3) does not "shut out all enquiry by court".[42] "For example, no notification can be issued unless there is a special resolution. The special resolution is the *sine qua non* of the notification. Again, the notification cannot authorise the imposition of the tax not included in section 128 of the Act."[43] The issue before the Supreme Court in the two cases[44] that went before it from Uttar Pradesh was, however, the manner of publication, in that the tax proposals, though published, were not published in a Hindi local paper as prescribed by section 94(3). The court held that the requirement of publication of tax proposals was mandatory but the requirement of the manner of publication was only directory, and was, therefore, curable by the conclusive evidence clause.[45] The court also considered and explained one of its earlier decisions, under the C.P. & Berar Municipalities Act, 1922, which contains analogous provisions, where the conclusive evidence clause was relied upon to shut out an argument that objections to certain tax proposals were not "properly considered" by the Municipal Committee.[46] It has been pointed out that the decision under the C.P. Act,[47] "is no authority for the proposition that even if there is no compliance whatsoever with a mandatory provision of a statute relating to procedure for imposition of a tax" a conclusive evidence clause as contained in the U.P. Act or the C.P. Act would necessarily save such imposition.[48]

---

42. *Municipal Board, Hapur v. Raghuvendra Kripal*, AIR 1966 SC 693, p. 696 : 1966 (1) SCR 950.

43. *Ibid.*

44. Case in note 41, *supra*, and *Raza Buland Sugar Co. v. Municipal Board, Rampur*, AIR 1965 SC 895 : 1965 (1) SCR 970.

45. *Ibid.* **See further** a case on similar lines: *Municipal Board, Sitapur v. Prayag Narain*, AIR 1970 SC 58 : (1969) 1 SCC 399. These cases are authority on the interpretation of conclusive evidence clause and not on the point that the manner of publication laid in the enabling Act for making delegated legislation is directory **see** *ITC Bhadrachalam Paper Boards v. Mandal Revenue Officer*, 1996 (6) Scale 551, pp. 561 to 563 : 1996 (6) SCC 634.

46. *Berar Swadeshi Vanaspathi v. Municipal Committee, Shegaon*, AIR 1962 SC 420 : 1962 (1) SCR 596.

47. *Ibid.*

48. *Raza Buland Sugar Co. v. Municipal Board, Rampur*, AIR 1965 SC 895, pp. 902, 903 : 1965 (1) SCR 970. **See further** *Municipal Council, Khurai v. Kamal Kumar*, AIR 1965 SC 1321 : 1965 (2) SCR 653 (Procedure for imposing tax liability is to be strictly followed; case under M.P. Municipalities Act, 1961).

(iii) *'Ganga' clause.*—In modern Acts constituting statutory bodies and conferring power on them to make delegated legislation provisions are often inserted to put beyond challenge defects of constitution of these bodies and defects of procedure which have not led to any substantial prejudice. The Supreme Court[49] nick-named these provisions as the "Ganga" clause while dealing with section 76J[50] of the Karnataka Town and Country Planning Act, 1961. In that case[51] section 13(4) read with Rule 33 required the publication of outline development plan as approved by the Government in the official Gazette. What was published in the Gazette was a notice that the outline development plan as approved by the Government was available for inspection at the office of the Planning Authority during office hours. The Supreme Court held that on a proper construction of section 13(4) the publication complied with its provisions and that even if there was any defect it was cured by section 76J. In an earlier case,[52] a similar provision contained in section 39(1) of the Bangalore Municipal Corporation Act, 1949 was considered by a Constitution Bench of the Supreme Court and it was held that the defect of non-publication in the Gazette in imposing a tax by the corporation was cured as there was publication in the local newspapers.

4. PROCEDURAL REQUIREMENTS

(a) Section 23, General Clauses Act, 1897; 'Previous Publication'

There is no uniform procedure in India for making subordinate legislation, except in the case of rules or bye-laws made under those Central Acts or Regulations which impose the condition of 'previous publication' which brings into play the procedure prescribed in section 23, General Clauses

49. *B.K. Srinivasan v. State of Karnataka*, (1987) 1 SCC 658, pp. 669, 675 : AIR 1987 SC 1059.
50. **"Section 76J. Validation of Acts and proceedings.**—No act done or proceeding taken under this Act shall be questioned on the ground merely of: (a) the existence of any vacancy in, or any defect in the constitution of the Board or any Planning Authority; (b) any person having ceased to be a member; (c) any person associated with Board or any Planning Authority under section 4F having voted in contravention of the said section; or the failure to serve a notice on any person, where substantial injustice has not resulted from such failure; or any omission, defect or irregularity not affecting the merits of the case."
51. *B.K. Srinivasan v. State of Karnataka, supra.* **See further** section 11 of Water (Prevention and Control of Pollution) Act, 1974 and *Akhil Bharat Goseva Sangh v. State of A.P.*, (2006) 4 SCC 162, (para 46) : (2006) 4 JT 482.
52. *Bangalore Woollen and Cotton Silk Mills v. Corporation of City of Bangalore*, 1961 (3) SCR 707 : AIR 1962 SC 562. This case is **discussed** in *ITC Bhadrachalam Paperboards v. Mandal Revenue Officer*, 1996 (6) Scale 551, pp. 560, 561: 1996 (6) SCC 634 and it is observed that the Constitution Bench did not hold that the requirement of publication in the Gazette was not mandatory.

Act, 1897.[53] It has been stated by a Research Team of the Indian Law Institute that until 1960 only sixty Central Statutes conditioned the rule-making power to the requirement of previous publication.[54] Thus, besides those cases where section 23 of the General Clauses Act applies, the procedure for making subordinate legislation will depend upon the provisions, if any, of the enabling Act under which it is made. There is no general principle that previous publication of subordinate legislation is necessary; it is necessary only when the statute so requires.[55] Further, the requirement of previous publication does not give any right to the objectors of being orally heard.[56]

The essentials of the procedure prescribed by section 23 of the General Clauses Act are the antecedent publicity of the draft rules or bye-laws with a view to give the persons likely to be affected an opportunity of making objections, and consideration of objections, if any, before the rules or bye-laws are finally made. The section also contains a conclusive evidence clause that the publication in the Official Gazette of a rule or bye-law purporting to have been made in exercise of a power, to make rules or bye-laws after 'previous publication' shall be conclusive proof that the rule or bye-law has been duly made. In spite of this provision, it may be possible to hold that a complete non-compliance of antecedent publicity requirement or a complete non-consideration of objections received will invalidate the rule or bye-law which suffers from such defects.[57]

(b) Publication after making; Date of publication

When the enabling Act does not contain any provision that the delegated legislation should be published, the consequences of late publication or non-publication are matters of doubt and difficulty. The Supreme Court of India is inclined in favour of the view that publication in some suitable form is essential before the delegated legislation can take effect.[58]

---

53. There are similar provisions in corresponding State legislations.
54. Indian Law Institute Studies, Delegated Legislation in India, p. 38.
55. *Tulsipur Sugar Co. Ltd. v. Notified Area, Tulsipur*, AIR 1980 SC 882 : (1980) 2 SCC 295.
56. *Sundardas Kanyalal Bhathija v. Collector, Thane*, AIR 1990 SC 261, pp. 269, 270 : 1989 (3) SCC 396.
57. **See further** *Bhopal Municipality v. M. Hasan*, AIR 1972 SC 886 : (1972) 1 SCC 764 (A rule made without complying with section 24 of the Madhya Pradesh General Clauses Act, 1897 corresponding to section 23 of the Central Act was held to be invalid. This was a case of complete non-compliance).
58. *Harla v. State of Rajasthan*, AIR 1951 SC 467 : 1952 SCR 110; *B.K. Srinivasan v. State of Karnataka*, (1987) 1 SCC 658 : AIR 1987 SC 1059.

In the much discussed case of *Johnson v. Sargant*,[59] an order of the Food Controller called the Beans, Peas and Pulse (Requisition) Order, 1917, was made on 16 May 1917, but was in effect published or made known to the trade on the morning of 17 May, 1917. It was held by BAILHACHE, J. that the order did not take effect until the morning of the 17th and, therefore, could not be contravened on the 16th. The reasoning of the decision is that statutes of Parliament get antecedent publicity as they are publicly enacted and so they come into operation on the earliest moment of the day on which they are passed, but this is not true of delegated legislation which does not receive any prior publicity and it does not come into operation until it is made known. *Johnson v. Sargant*,[60] was expressly approved by the Supreme Court in *Harla v. State of Rajasthan*,[61] where the question related to the Jaipur Opium Act which was in no way promulgated or published. The Act was passed by a resolution of the Council of Ministers of Jaipur who derived their authority to make laws, during the minority of the Maharaja of Jaipur, from a notification issued by the Crown Representative which did not expressly require the publication of the law made by the Council. The court held that the Act was ineffective and never became law as it was never promulgated or published. BOSE, J. observed: "Natural justice requires that before a law can become operative, it must be promulgated or published. It must be broadcast in some recognizable way so that all men may know what it is, or, at the very least, there must be some special rule or regulation or customary channel by or through which such knowledge can be acquired with the exercise of due and reasonable diligence".[62] In these cases,[63] the courts could conceive of only two alternatives; either of convicting a person for contravention of a law which the offender did not know and could not have known, or, of holding that the law itself did not take effect until it was published. The Privy Council in a later case,[64] in addition recognised a common law defence of ignorance of law in respect of unpublished delegated legislation and held that the maxim '*ignorantia juris non excusat*' has no application to

59. *Johnson v. Sargant*, (1918) 1 KB 101 : 118 LT 95.
60. *Ibid.*
61. *Harla v. State of Rajasthan*, AIR 1951 SC 467, p. 468 (para 11) : 1952 SCR 110.
62. *Ibid.*
63. See notes 58 to 60, *supra*.
64. *Lim Chin Aik v. Reginam*, (1963) 1 All ER 223, p. 227 : 1963 AC 160 : (1963) 2 WLR 42 (PC). In this case, the accused was acquitted for want of '*mens rea*' which on construction of the relevant statute was found to be a necessary ingredient of the offence.

a case where the delegated legislation is not published in any form "to enable a man by appropriate inquiry to find out what 'the law is'."[65]

The "made known" theory enunciated by BAILHACHE, J.[66] has come up for some strong criticism. In the words of SIR C.K. ALLEN, "it was a bold example of judge made law" and "the decision has always been regarded as very doubtful".[67] The Supreme Court also in one case[68] found "great force" in these comments. The actual decision, however, establishes (so far as material for the present discussion) only two propositions: (1) The rule, if any, that delegated legislation does not take effect when made but only takes effect when 'made known', cannot be extended to require publication in a foreign country even if foreigners are likely to be affected; and (2) The maxim '*ignorantia juris non excusat*' will apply to a case where the law is published in some common form though the accused does not know about it. It is further significant to note that *State of Maharashtra v. M.H. George*,[69] though critical of *Johnson v. Sargant*,[70] makes no reference to *Harla v. State of Rajasthan*,[71] where it was expressly approved. In a recent case, *B.K. Srinivasan v. State of Karnataka*,[72] where the statute itself required the publication of the delegated legislation and where the finding was that there was publication as required by the statute, the Supreme Court made some general observations which support the view that publication in some suitable form, even if not specifically required by the statute, is essential for making the delegated legislation effective. The court did neither refer to *Harla v. State of Rajasthan*,[73] nor to *State of Maharashtra v. M.H. George*,[74] but the general observations are in line with the view expressed in *Harla's* case. The court said: "Unlike Parliamentary legislation which is publicly made, delegated legislation or subordinate legislation is often made unobtrusively in the chambers of a minister, a

---

65. *Ibid.* Section 3 of the Statutory Instruments Act, 1946 provides that where any person is charged with an offence under a statutory instrument, it shall be a defence to prove that the instrument had not been issued by His Majesty's stationery office at the date of the alleged contravention unless it is proved that at that date reasonable steps had been taken for the purpose of bringing the purport of the instrument to the notice of the public or of persons likely to be affected by it, or of the person charged.

66. **See** text and notes 58, 59, *supra*.

67. ALLEN, Law and Orders, 2nd Edition, pp. 132, 133.

68. *State of Maharashtra v. Mayer Hans George,* AIR 1965 SC 722, p. 742 : 1965 (1) SCR 123.

69. *Ibid.*

70. Note 58, *supra.*

71. Note 60, *supra.*

72. *B.K. Srinivasan v. State of Karnataka*, (1987) 1 SCC 658 : AIR 1987 SC 1059.

73. Note 60, *supra.*

74. Note 67, *supra.*

secretary to the Governor or other official dignitary. It is, therefore, necessary that subordinate legislation, in order to take effect, must be published or promulgated in some suitable manner, whether such publication or promulgation is prescribed by the parent statute or not. It will then take effect from the date of such publication".[75]

The principle enunciated in *Harla's* case,[76] and *Shrinivasan's* case[77] which is still the law, requires some form of publication before delegated legislation can be effective. But that principle also does not require communication of any general rule, regulation etc. to each and every individual affected thereby, and it would be sufficient if the same is published in such manner that persons can, if they are interested, acquaint themselves of its contents.[78] In case, however, of an 'order' which is directed only to a person and is not of a general nature, it would be reasonable to expect that the proper method of publication is to serve it on him or so to publish it that he would certainly know of it.[79] In *Shrinivasan's* case the Supreme Court on this point observed that if the mode of publication is prescribed by the statute that must be followed; if the mode of publication is prescribed by the subordinate legislation itself and the mode so prescribed is reasonable that mode must also be followed; but if

---

75. *Harla's* case, (1987) 1 SCC 658, p. 672 : AIR 1987 SC 1059. **See further** *ITC Bhadrachalam Paperboards v. Mandal Revenue Officer*, 1996 (6) Scale 551, p. 560 : 1996 (6) SCC 634.

76. *Harla v. State of Rajasthan*, AIR 1951 SC 467 : 1952 SCR 110. The principle enunciated in *Harla's* case gets support from an earlier decision—*Fatma Hazi Ali v. State of Bombay*, AIR 1951 SC 180, p. 183 (para 15) : 1951 SCR 266. Further PROF. LANHAM in an article 'Delegated Legislation and Publication' (1974) 37 Modern Law Review 510 has supported the view taken in *Johnson v. Sargant*, (1918) 1 KB 101 : 118 LT 95 and *Harla v. State of Rajasthan, supra*. He has pointed out that the same view has been taken in a *British Columbia* case, *R. v. Ross*, (1941) 1 WWR 590. He is critical of the contrary view taken in a *Newzealand* case, (1940) NZLR 922. **See further** *Rajendrakumar Bhanwarlalji Sethi v. State of Madhya Pradesh*, 1979 MPLJ 141, pp. 147 to 149 (G.P. SINGH C.J.) where the relevant cases and PROF. LANHAM'S article are referred to and it has been held that a resolution passed by the State Legislature under Article 252(1) of the Constitution adopting a Central Act does not require any publication for bringing the Act into effect in the State. In *Baburao alias P.B. Samant v. Union of India*, AIR 1988 SC 440 it has been held that resolutions of Parliament or State Legislatures do not require publication in Official Gazette or Newspaper.

77. *B.K. Srinivasan v. State of Karnataka*, (1987) 1 SCC 658 : AIR 1987 SC 1059.

78. *State of Maharashtra v. Mayer Hans George*, AIR 1965 SC 722, p. 742 : 1965 (1) SCR 123.

79. *Ibid.* **See further** *State of West Bengal v. M.R. Mondal*, AIR 2001 SC 3471, p. 3476 : (2001) 8 SCC 443. (An order passed but retained in file without being communica-ted to the person concerned has no force or authority and no valid existence in law).

there is neither any mode of publication prescribed by the statute nor by the subordinate legislation or when the mode prescribed by the subordinate legislation is unreasonable, it will take effect only when it is published through the customarily recognised official channel, namely the Official Gazette or some other reasonable mode of publications; and in cases where a few individuals or persons in a small local area are concerned, publication or promulgation by other means may be sufficient.[80] Therefore, when a notification is published in Official Gazette as required by the statute, it is not possible to accept that, there was yet a failure to make the law known and that the notification did not acquire the elements of operativeness and enforceability.[81]

If a question arises as to when was a particular order or rule made or notification issued, the material date is the date of Gazette publication as required by the statute and not the date of publication in a newspaper or the media.[82] But when can an order or notification be said to be published in the Gazette? Is it the date of printing or the date of the Gazette or the date when the Gazette is made available to the public? This question came to be first considered in *Collector of Central Excise v. New Tobacco Co.*[83] and it was held that unless the Gazette containing the notification is made available to the public, the notification cannot be said to have been duly published. In this case, a Central Excise notification dated 30-11-1982 enhancing the rate of duty was printed in the Gazette bearing the same date. But the Gazette was made available for sale to the public on 8-12-1982. Section 38 of the Central Excises and Salt Act, 1944 provides that all rules and notifications issued under the Act shall be published in the Official Gazette. On the above facts, the Supreme Court held that the notification could be said to have been duly published only on 8-12-1982 and was ineffective before that date for proper publication requires publication "in such a manner that persons can, if they are so interested, acquaint themselves with its contents."[84] This case was followed in *Garware Nylons Ltd. v. the Collector of Customs and Central Excise.*[85] The view taken in these

80. *B.K. Srinivasan v. State of Karnataka*, (1987) 1 SCC 658, pp. 672, 673 : AIR 1987 SC 1059. **See further** *ITC Bhadrachalam Paperboards v. Mandal Revenue Officer*, 1996 (6) Scale 551, p. 560 : 1996 (6) SCC 634.

81. *Pankaj Jain Agencies v. Union of India*, JT 1994(5) SC 64, p. 71: AIR 1995 SC 360, p. 365 : (1994) 5 SCC 198. **Followed** in *ITC Limited v. Collector of Central Excise*, 1996 (6) Scale 239 : 1996 (5) SCC 538.

82. *ITC Bhadrachalam Paperboards v. Mandal Revenue Officer*, 1996 (6) Scale 551, p. 559 : (1996) 6 SCC 634.

83. *Collector of Central Excise v. New Tobacco Co.*, AIR 1998 SC 668 : (1998) 8 SCC 250.

84. *Ibid*, p. 672.

85. *Garware Nylons Ltd. v. the Collector of Customs and Central Excise*, AIR 1999 SC 844 : (1998) 8 SCC 282.

cases as to when publication of delegated legislation required to be published in the Gazette is complete and the delegated legislation takes effect was likely to create practical difficulties for proving its publication and coming into force. It was not enough according to these cases to produce the relevant Gazette, but it was also necessary to prove the date when the Gazette was offered for sale or circulation. And, if this view of the meaning of publication in the Gazette was correct, the same difficulty would have arisen in proving the commencement of an Act which is required to be published in the Gazette for its coming into force. These cases were later overruled by a three judge bench in *Union of India v. M/s. Ganesh Das Bhojraj*[86] which related to publication of a notification amending an earlier notification under section 25(1) of the Customs Act, 1962 which requires publication of a notification in the Official Gazette. The relevant notification dated 4-2-1987 appeared in the Gazette of the same date. It was nobody's case that the Gazette was antedated. The question was whether the notification was operative on 5-2-1987 when the goods were imported. On these facts, it was held by the Supreme Court that the notification was operative from 4-2-1987 when it was printed in the Gazette of the same date and that it was not necessary to prove as to when the Gazette was offered for sale or circulation. This decision thus implies that the date of the Gazette, provided it is not antedated, would be the date of publication in the Gazette of all notifications appearing in it. LAHOTI, J. however, made a reservation that he was not expressing his opinion on the question as to when such a notification would create criminal liability and that the decision needed to be confined in its application to civil liability and could not be made a rule of universal application.[87]

In *S.K. Shukla v. State of U.P.*,[88] one of the questions was from which date the whole of Uttar Pradesh became a notified area by notification dated 23-1-2003 under section 4 of the Prevention of Terrorism Act, 2002. 'Notified area' is defined by an explanation in Section 4 of the Act to mean 'such area as the State Government may by notification in the official Gazette specify'. A perusal of the relevant Secretariat file and record of the Government Press showed that a decision to specify the whole of Uttar Pradesh as the notified area was taken in the note sheet on 22-1-2003 and a requisition to the Government Press for its publication was sent on 23-1-2003 but it was received by the Government Press on 27-1-2003 and was actually published on 29-1-2003 though it was dated 23-1-2003. On these

86. *Union of India v. M/s. Ganesh Das Bhojraj*, AIR 2000 SC 1102 : (2000) 3 SCC 495.

87. *Ibid* pp. 1108, 1109. **See further** text and note 18, p. 579.

88. *S.K. Shukla v. State of U.P.*, (2006) 1 SCC 314, p. 328, (para 18) : AIR 2006 SC 413.

facts it was held that the notification became effective only from 29-1-2003 and not from 23-1-2003.

A mere decision of the rule making authority to make a rule circulated by a memorandum to its officers is not a rule made and cannot be effective.[89]

(c) Publication after making as required by enabling Act

When the enabling Act makes provision for publication, it becomes a question of construction of the relevant provisions whether the requirement is a condition precedent for operation of delegated legislation made under the Act. It has been observed by a research team of the Indian Law Institute that the Indian Acts in this respect generally adopt one of the following formulas:

> "(a) Rules shall be published in the Official Gazette and shall come into force on such publication.
>
> (b) Rules shall be published in the Official Gazette and shall thereupon have the force of law.
>
> (c) Rules shall be published in the Official Gazette and thereupon have effect as if enacted in the Act.
>
> (d) The Central Government may, by notification in the Official Gazette, make rules.
>
> (e) Rules shall be published in the Official Gazette."[90]

Opinion has also been rightly expressed that if the formula used is one of the types referred to in (a) to (d) above, "the rule will not come into operation unless gazetted," "but the legal position in the case of (e) type is not that clear".[91] Having regard to the principles enunciated in *Harla* and *Shrinivasan* cases[92] it is expected that the courts in India will lean in favour of the view that the requirement of publication even in (e) type formula is mandatory. Indeed, relying upon *Shrinivasan's* case, the Supreme Court in *ITC Bhadrachalam Paperboards v. Mandal Revenue Officer*,[93]

---

89. *I.N. Saksena v. State of M.P.*, AIR 1967 SC 1264, p. 1267 : 1967 (2) SCR 496; *State of Assam v. B.K. Das*, AIR 1973 SC 1252, p. 1255 : (1973) 1 SCC 461. **But see** *E.V. Naidu v. Union of India*, AIR 1973 SC 698, p. 700 : (1973) 1 SCC 361.

90. The India Law Institute Studies, Delegated Legislation in India, p. 51. **See further** The Delegated Legislation Provisions (Amendment) Act, 2004 (Act No. 4 of 2005) which shows a preference for 'd' type formula.

91. *Ibid*. The expression 'by notification in the Official Gazette' makes the requirement of publication in the Gazette mandatory: *Shambhunath v. Kedarprasad*, AIR 1972 SC 1515, p. 1519 : (1972) 1 SCC 573.

92. **See** text and footnotes 60 and 71, *supra*.

93. *ITC Bhadrachalam Paperboards v. Mandal Revenue Officer*, 1996 (6) Scale 551 : 1996 (6) SCC 634.

where (d) type formula was used, made the following general observations: "where the parent statute prescribes the mode of publication or promulgation that mode has to be followed and such a requirement is imperative and cannot be dispensed with".[1]

In case of 'Orders' the following formula has been adopted:

"An Order made.............................shall—

(a) in the case of an order of a general nature or affecting a class of persons, be notified in the Gazette, and

(b) in the case of an order directed to a specified individual, be served on such individual—

(i) by delivering it to that individual; or

(ii) if it cannot be so delivered or tendered, by affixing it on the outer door or some other conspicuous part of the premises in which that individual lives; and a written report thereof shall be prepared and witnessed by two persons living in the neighbourhood."[2]

It appears that the requirement of publication expressed in the above form will be taken as mandatory.[3] If an order is required to be notified, date of the order is the date of the notification.[4]

Rule 141 of the Defence of India Rules, 1962, which adopts the above formula[5], also provides that compliance with it or notification in Gazette shall be conclusive evidence that a person concerned has notice of the order. It further provides that a failure to comply with the above formula will not preclude the proof that the person concerned had otherwise information of the order nor will it invalidate the order. This rule, though inconsistent with the Evidence Act, has been upheld under the general power conferred by section 3 of the Defence of India Act, 1962, for section 43 of

---

1. *Ibid*, p. 560 (Scale) **Followed in** *Rajendra Agricultural University v. Ashok Kumar Prasad,* (2010) 1 SCC 730 para 24 : AIR 2010 SC 259.
2. Section 3(5), Essential Commodities Act, 1955; also **see** Rule 141, Defence of India Rules.
3. *Shriniwas v. Emperor*, AIR 1947 PC 135, pp. 138, 139; *Narendra Kumar v. Union of India*, AIR 1960 SC 430, p. 437 : 1960 (2) SCR 375; *Venkata Subbarao v. State of A.P.*, AIR 1965 SC 1773, p. 1787 (para 40) : 1965 (2) SCC 577. **See also** *State of Maharashtra v. Mayer Hans George, supra*, p. 742.
4. *Municipal Board v. State Transport Authority, Rajasthan*, AIR 1965 SC 458, pp. 464, 465 : 1963 Supp (2) SCR 373.
5. **See** text and note 2, supra.

the Act specifically enacts that the Act and rules made under it will have effect even if inconsistent with any other enactment.[6]

When by an inclusive definition, the prohibitions contained in the Act can be extended to other matters as may be specified by a notification in the Gazette, the publication in the Gazette of the notification becomes mandatory. Section 2(1)(i) of the Arms Act, 1959 defines prohibited arms to mean certain arms and to include 'such other arms as the Central Government may, by a notification in the official Gazette, specify to be prohibited arms'. Construing this provision it was held that the category of prohibited arms can be widened only by a notification in the Official Gazetee and not by administrative instructions.[7]

When a notification is required to be published in the Gazette, it will come into force on the date of its publication in the Gazette and it is not necessary to prove as to when the Gazette was offered for sale of circulation to the public.[8] The effective date of notification in such cases is the date of publication in the Gazette and not the date when it was prepared in the office which may be the date which it bears.[9]

If an order, which has not been notified in the Gazette as required by the Act under which it is made, is enforced and acted upon by the Government to the prejudice of citizens creating corresponding rights in them, it will not be open to the Government to challenge its validity on the ground that it was not notified as required by the Act.[10]

(d) Requirement of laying

The object of any requirement of laying provided in enabling Acts is to subject the subordinate law making authority to the vigilance and control of the Legislature. A compliance with the laying requirement, however, does not confer any validity to the subordinate legislation if it is in excess of the power conferred by the enabling Act.[11] Indeed the court can declare

---

6. *Mangilal v. State of Maharashtra*, AIR 1970 SC 1829 : 1969 (2) SCC 731.

7. *Subhash Ramkumar Bind v. State of Maharashtra*, (2003) 1 SCC 506, pp. 522, 523 : AIR 2003 SC 269, p. 279.

8. *Union of India v. Ganesh Das Bhojraj*, AIR 2000 SC 1102 : (2000) 9 SCC 461 (**See** the discussion on this point above in text and notes 83, 84, p. 1106).

9. *Ahuja Industries Ltd. v. State of Karnataka*, AIR 2003 SCW 2043, p. 2047 : (2003) 5 SCC 365 : AIR 2003 SC 3519.

10. *Bejgam Veeranna Venkata Narsimloo v. State of A.P.*, JT 1997 (9) SC 274, p. 281 : (1998) 1 SCC 563 : AIR 1998 SC 542.

11. *Hukamchand v. Union of India*, AIR 1972 SC 2427, p. 2431 : (1972) 2 SCC 601; *Kerala State Electricity Board v. Indian Aluminium Co.*, AIR 1976 SC 1031,

[Footnote No. 11 Contd.]

a subordinate legislation invalid on the ground that it is violative of the enabling Act even if it be approved by resolutions of both Houses of Parliament.[12] But approval of a statutory rule by resolutions of Parliament will be an important circumstance to be taken into account in determining its validity. So it has been held that when laying of the rule is preceded by a speech of the Minister indicating its object and there is no dissent or disapproval by any member, this factor may have some weight along with other factors in upholding its validity.[13] Laying clauses may be expressed in different forms depending upon the degree of control which the Legislature wants to keep in its hands. Broadly, these clauses are of three varieties[14] providing—(1) laying which requires no further procedure,[15] (2) laying allied with an affirmative procedure,[16] and, (3) laying allied with negative procedure.[17] When a Parliamentary enactment confers power on the State Government to make rules in respect of certain matters, it may provide that the rules so made be laid before the State Legislature.[18] All the varieties of laying clauses are a check upon the rule making authority and negative the objection of excessive delegation.[19]

[Footnote No. 11 Contd.]

pp. 1046, 1047 : (1976) 1 SCC 466; *Atlas Cycle Industries Ltd. v. State of Haryana*, AIR 1979 SC 1149, p. 1154 : (1979) 2 SCC 196; *Regional Transport Authority, Chittoor v. Associated Transport, Madras*, AIR 1980 SC 1872, p. 1873 : (1980) 4 SCC 597; *Bharat Hari Singhania v. Commissioner of Wealth Tax*, JT 1994 (2) SC 6, p. 21 : AIR 1994 SC 1355, p. 1369; *Dai Ichi Karkaria Ltd. v. Union of India*, JT 2000 (4) SC 495, p. 501 : (2000) 4 SCC 57 : AIR 2000 SC 1741; *Bhartidasan University v. All India Council for Technical Education*, AIR 2001 SC 2861, p. 2869.

12. *F. Hoffman—La Roche & Co. A-G. v. Secretary of State for Trade and Industry*, (1974) 2 All ER 1128, p. 1153 (HL); *Kerala State Electricity Board v. Indian Aluminium Co.*, AIR 1976 SC 1031, pp. 1046, 1047 : (1976) 1 SCC 466.

13. *Lohia Machines Ltd. v. Union of India*, (1985) 2 SCC 197, p. 225 : AIR 1985 SC 421. **See further** *Britnell v. Secretary for State for Social Security*, (1991) 2 All ER 726, p. 732 : (1991) 2 WLR 198 (HL) (letter 'd').

14. **See** cases in note 14, *supra*. **See further,** *The Quarry Owners Association v. The State of Bihar*, AIR 2000 SC 2870, p. 2892 : (2000) 8 SCC 655.

15. **See** for example section 3(6), Essential Commodities Act, 1955; 'Every order made shall be laid before both Houses of Parliament, as soon as may be, after it is made'.

16. **See** for example section 28(2), Mines and Mineral (Regulation and Development) Act, 1957; 'No rules made—shall come into force until they have been approved, whether with or without modification, by each House of Parliament'.

17. **See** for example section 3(2), All India Services Act, 1951.

18. *The quarry Owners Association v. The State of Bihar*, AIR 2000 SC 2870 : (2000) 8 SCC 655. **See further** the Delegated Legislation Provisions (Amendment) Act, 2004 (Act No. 4 of 2005) which inserts laying requirement for rules to be made by the State Government under different Central Acts.

19. *Ibid* pp. 2892 to 2895 (AIR); *Andhra Bank v. S. Satyanarayana*, AIR 2004 SC 4007, p. 4009 (para 3) : (2004) 2 SCC 657.

There are many refinements[20] in each variety and a correct construction of any particular laying clause will depend upon its own terms. The question that is often discussed is about the effect of laying clauses upon the operation of the rules, etc., which are required to be laid.

Section 4 of the Statutory Instruments Act, 1946, requires, subject to a proviso, that the statutory instrument shall be 'laid before the instrument comes into operation'. Having regard to these words and other relevant provisions of the Act, opinion has been expressed that a statutory instrument, required to be laid by the parent Act, comes into operation as soon as it is made and laid before Parliament, unless as often happens a future date is assigned for its coming into operation.[21]

Section 20 of the Universities (Scotland) Act, 1889, provided that 'no Ordinance shall be effectual until it shall have been published, laid before Parliament, and approved by Her Majesty'. The House of Lords held that these requirements including laying were essential and that an Ordinance which did not comply with them could not be operative.[22]

In the Parks Regulation Act, 1872, the laying clause was worded as follows: "Any rule made in pursuance of the First Schedule to this Act shall be forthwith laid before both Houses of Parliament, if Parliament be sitting, or if not, then within three weeks after the beginning of the then next ensuing session of Parliament; and if such rules shall be disapproved of by either House of Parliament, within one month after the same shall have been so laid before Parliament, such rules, or such parts thereof as shall be disapproved of, shall not be enforced." This clause came up for construction in *Bailey v. Williamson*,[23] and it was held that the rules became operative even before they were laid. BLACKBURN, J. observed: "The question is: Does that mean that the rules which had been made and published shall not be enforced '*ab initio*', and that this laying before Parliament shall be made a condition precedent? I can only say that it does not seem to me to be the intention expressed by the Legislature—. The Legislature has expressed the intention that the rules shall be made, and an intention that if after the period limited, Parliament expresses its disapproval, it shall cease

---

20. **See** ALLEN, Law and Orders, 2nd Edition, pp. 142, 143; Delegated Legislation in India (Indian Law Institute Studies), pp. 166-69.

21. ALLEN, Law in the Making, 7th Edition, p. 549; *R. v. Sheer Metalcraft*, (1954) 1 All ER 542, p. 545.

22. *Metcalfe v. Cox*, (1895) AC 328 (HL). But it is not necessary that an existing published document which is referred to in the subordinate legislation should also be laid before Parliament to meet the laying requirement of the subordinate legislation; *R. v. Secretary for Social Services, ex parte, Camden London, Borough Council*, (1987) 2 All ER 560 : (1987) 1 WLR 819 (CA).

23. *Bailey v. Williamson*, (1873) LR 8 QB 118.

to be a rule; but it is to be a rule up to that time, and as such any transgression of it may be punished.'[24] In *Storey v. Graham*,[25] a similar laying clause in the Patents, Designs, and Trade Marks Act, 1883, was held by CHANNEL, J. to be directory.

In *D. S. Garewal v. State of Punjab*,[26] the Supreme Court was considering the objection of excessive delegation to the Central Government under section 3(1) of the All India Services Act, 1951. In that connection section 3(2) of the Act was referred to, which is in the following terms: 'All rules made under this section shall be laid for not less than fourteen days before Parliament as soon as possible after they are made, and shall be subject to such modification, whether by way of repeal or amendment, as Parliament may make on a motion made during the session in which they are so laid'. The court was of the view that having regard to this provision Parliament kept strict vigilance and control over its delegate. The effect of section 3(2) was stated as follows: "Parliament took care to see that these rules were laid on the table of Parliament for fourteen days before they were to come into force and they were subject to modification, whether by way of repeal or amendment on a motion made by Parliament during the session in which they are so laid".[27] The words: "before they were to come into force" in this passage, go to show that the rules cannot be operative before the expiry of fourteen days from the date of laying. Same view was taken by the Supreme Court in its advisory opinion in *In re, Kerala Education Bill, 1957*,[28] while considering clauses 36 and 37 of the Bill which respectively contained the rule-making power and laying requirement. Clause 37 was drafted in same terms as section 3(2) of the All India Services Act, 1951, which has been quoted above. The Court in this case said: "After the rules are laid before the Legislative Assembly, they may be altered or amended, and it is then, that rules, as amended, become effective. If no amendments are made, the rules come into operation after the period of fourteen days expires".[29] These cases thus show that the rules cannot come into operation before they are laid and before the expiry of the laying period prescribed by the laying clause. It cannot, however, be overlooked that the opinion so expressed was in cases where the point was not directly in issue and no authorities were referred.

---

24. *Ibid*, p. 129.
25. *Storey v. Graham*, (1899) QB 406, p. 412.
26. *D. S. Garewal v. State of Punjab*, AIR 1959 SC 512 : 1959 Supp (1) SCR 792.
27. *Ibid*, p. 518.
28. *In re, Kerala Education Bill, 1957*, AIR 1958 SC 956 : 1959 SCR 995.
29. *Ibid*, p. 975.

In a later case,[30] where the point was directly in issue the Supreme Court has taken a different view; but again no authorities were referred. Section 26(1) of the Bombay Agricultural Produce Markets Act, 1939, authorised the Provincial Government to make rules for the purpose of carrying out the provisions of the Act. Sub-section (5) of section 26 provided that the rules made shall be laid before each of the Houses of the Provincial Legislature at the session thereof next following and shall be liable to be modified or rescinded by a resolution in which both Houses concur and such rules shall, after notification in the Gazette, be deemed to have been modified or rescinded accordingly. The rules were made in 1941 but were not laid at the first session of the Legislature and were laid at the second session. The contention was, that as the rules were not laid at the first session of the Legislature in terms of the laying requirement, they had no legal validity. Repelling the contention SHAH, J. for the Court observed: "Section 26(5)—does not prescribe that the rules acquired validity only from the date on which they were placed before the Houses of Legislature. The rules are valid from the date on which they are made under section 26(1). It is true that the Legislature has prescribed that the rules be placed before the Houses of Legislature, but failure to place the rules before Houses of Legislature, does not affect the validity of the rules. Granting that the provisions of sub-section (5) of section 26 by reason of the failure to place the rules before the Houses of Legislature were violated, we are of the view that sub-section (5) of section 26 having regard to the purpose for which it is made, and in the context in which it occurs, cannot be regarded as mandatory. The rules have been in operation since the year 1941 and they continue to remain in operation."[31]

The question relating to the effect of non-laying in contravention of a laying clause was elaborately discussed in *Atlas Cycle Industries Ltd. v. State of Haryana*[32] while dealing with the non-compliance with sub-section (6) of section 3 of the Essential Commodities Act, 1955 which provides that every order made under the section shall be laid before both Houses of Parliament as soon as may be, after it is made. It was held after noticing the earlier cases that non-compliance with the Laying Clause did not affect the validity of the order and make it void. This decision must be taken to settle the controversy as to the effect of non-laying of delegated

---

30. *Jan Mohd. v. State of Gujarat*, AIR 1966 SC 385 : 1966 (1) SCR 505.

31. *Ibid*, pp. 394, 395. **Followed** in *Bank of India v. O.P. Swarnkar,* AIR 2003 SC 858, pp. 885, 886 : (2003) 2 SCC 721 : 2003 SCC (L&S) 200.

32. AIR 1979 SC 1149 : (1979) 2 SCC 196. **See further** *Mathura Prasad v. I.G., Rly. Protection Force*, 1974 MPLJ 373, pp. 378, 379 (G.P. SINGH J.); *Bharat Hari Singhania v. Commissioner of Wealth Tax*, JT 1994 (2) SC 6, p. 21: AIR 1994 SC 1355, p. 1369 : 1994 Supp (3) SCC 46.

legislation required to be laid by a laying clause which does not require an affirmative procedure or which in terms does not say that the delegated legislation shall come into force when laid.

The case of *Atlas Cycle Industries Ltd.* was followed in *The Quarry Owners Association v. The State of Bihar*[33] where rules and notifications made by the State Government under sections 15 and 15A of the Mines and Minerals (Regulation and Development) Act 1957 and required to be laid by a simple laying requirement, providing no affirmative procedure, before the State Legislature under section 28(3) were not so laid. The court held that the annual administrative report submitted to the Legislature by the Department containing reference to notifications increasing the rate of royalty on minor minerals did not comply with the requirement of laying, still as the requirement of laying was directory, so omission to comply with it did not affect the validity of the notifications and their coming into force. The court directed the state government that impugned notifications be laid at the earliest.

The view, that laying requirement as considered by the Supreme Court in the above cases[34] is only directory, if carried to its logical conclusion, will mean that rules become effective and remain so even if not laid at all. This result is hardly satisfactory. If a complete non-compliance of a laying requirement is held to have no repercussion on the effectiveness of the rules that will mean that the rule-making authority can do away with vigilance and control, which the Legislature wants to keep in its hands by enacting a laying clause.[35] A direction by the court to comply with laying requirement after the delegated legislation is held valid and operative as ordered in the case of *Quarry Owners Association*[36] does not meet this objection.

It may also be mentioned that Parliament has now adopted a model laying clause which is somewhat differently worded; for example, section 44(3) of the Food Corporation Act, 1964, runs as follows: "Every rule made by the Central Government under this section shall be laid as soon as may be after it is made, before each House of Parliament while it is in session for a total period of thirty days which may be comprised in one session or in two successive sessions, and if, before the expiry of the session

---

33. *The Quarry Owners Association v. The State of Bihar*, AIR 2000 SC 2870, pp. 2894 to 2896 : (2000) 8 SCC 655.

34. **See** notes 32, 34 and 35, *supra*.

35. **See** BENNION, Statutory Interpretation (5th Edition) p. 248 f.n. 4 where it is pointed out that the Supreme Court of Barbados in *Biggs v. Commr. of Police*, (1982) 8 CLB 576, ruled that the duty to lay was mandatory.

36. **See** text and note 35, *supra*.

in which it is so laid or the session immediately following, both Houses agree in making any modification in the rule or both Houses agree that the rule shall not be made, the rule shall thereafter have effect only in such modified form or be of no effect, as the case may be; so however, that any such modification or amendment shall be without prejudice to the validity of anything previously done under that rule." There is also a tendency to replace the laying clauses in earlier Acts by a clause worded as above.[37] The same formula has been adopted by the Delegated Legislation Provisions (Amendment) Act, 2004 (Act No. 4 of 2005) for laying clauses requiring laying before Parliament of delegated legislation made by the Central Government and even by the University authorities under the Central Act.

A laying clause some what similar but differently worded was considered by the Supreme Court in *Union of India v. Chairman H.P. State Pollution Board.*[38] The case related to the Water (Prevention of Control of Pollution) Cess Act, 1977, section 3 of which authorises levy and collection of cess on any industry specified in Schedule 1. By section 16 the Central Government is given power to amend the schedule. Sub-section (1), of section 16 provides: 'The Central Government may, by notification in the Official Gazette add to Schedule 1 any industry having regard to the consumption of water in the carrying on of such industry and the consequent discharge thereof resulting in pollution of any stream and thereupon Schedule 1 shall, subject to the provisions of sub-section 2, be deemed to be amended accordingly.' Sub-section (2) of section 16, which contains the laying requirement, reads: 'Every such notification shall be laid before each House of Parliament, if it is sitting, as soon as may be after the issue of the notification, and if it is not sitting, within seven days of its re-assembly and *the Central Government shall seek the approval of Parliament to the notification by a resolution* moved within a period of fifteen days beginning with the day on which the notification is so laid before the House of the People and if Parliament *makes any modification in the notification or directs that the notification should cease to have effect,* the notification shall *thereafter* have effect only in such modified form or be of no effect, as the case may be, *but without prejudice to the validity of anything previously done thereunder*". In the case before the Supreme Court,

---

37. **See** for example the following Amending Acts : section 2, Act 10 of 1964; section 30, Act 13 of 1964; section 21, Act 21 of 1964; section 20, Act 43 of 1964; section 40, Act 46 of 1964; section 14, Act 48 of 1964; section 13, Act 49 of 1964; section 22, Act 53 of 1964; section 24, Act 55 of 1964; section 22, Act 56 of 1971; section 17, Act 57 of 1971; section 16, Act 63 of 1971; section 19, Act 64 of 1971.

38. *Union of India v. Chairman H.P. State Pollution Board*, AIR 2001 SC 2512 : (2001) 6 SCC 307.

the notification issued under sub-section 1 was laid before each House of Parliament but no resolution seeking approval was moved in Parliament. Interpreting sub-section (2) the Supreme Court held: "Mere perusal of sub-section (2) shows that *there has to be a positive act of approval* by the *Parliament to the issuance of the notification before it can be held that Schedule 1 has been amended.* Merely laying the notification before each House of Parliament is not sufficient compliance within the provisions of section 16(2)."[39] There is not much discussion in the judgment which gives great importance to the requirement of seeking approval by moving a resolution but pays no attention to the words which require Parliament either to make a modification in the notification or to direct that the notification should cease to have effect. The section does not require Parliament to give its approval for bringing into effect the notification. The words 'cease to have effect' and 'thereafter' as finding place in sub-section (2) give rise to the inference that the notification which has already come into effect will after the resolution of Parliament either continue as it is or stand modified or cease to have effect as may be directed in the resolution. It is submitted that properly interpreted the laying requirement in sub-section (2) does not provide for an affirmative procedure but only a negative procedure and the notification comes into effect by publication in the Gazette before it is laid before Parliament. This inference is further strengthened by the words 'but without prejudice to the validity of anything previously done thereunder' as they occur towards the end in sub-section (2). At any rate the observation that there has to be a positive act of approval before the notification can come into force is obiter and all that can be taken to have been decided is that a laying clause requiring not merely laying but also moving of a resolution for approval is mandatory and can be complied with only by laying followed by moving of a resolution of approval and the notification required to be so laid does not come into effect till then. This is the effect of the observation later finding place in the report: "with the resolution not having been moved at all, it cannot be held that there was a valid amendment of Schedule 1 to the Act."[40] The case has, it is submitted, rightly been criticised by S.B. Sinha J. in *Prohibition and Excise Supdt. A.P. v. Toddy Tappers Co-op. Society Marredpally,*[41] with the remark that it "must be held to be confined to the fact of the matter obtaining therein."[42]

---

39. *Ibid,* p. 2513.

40. *Ibid,* p. 2514.

41. *Prohibition and Excise Supdt. A.P. v. Toddy Tappers Co-op. Society Marredpally,* AIR 2004 SC 658, pp. 667, 668; (2003) 12 SCC 738.

42. *Ibid,* p. 668 (para 31). **Followed** in *Veneet Agrawal v. Union of India,* AIR 2008 SC 351 para 14 : (2007) 13 SCC 116.

(e) Requirement of consultation

In some cases enabling Acts contain provisions which lay down the requirement of previous consultation with some named agency. Consultation is obligatory only when so provided in the enabling statute and not otherwise.[43] An example of such a provision is furnished by section 59(4) of the Mines Act, 1952, which reads: 'No regulation or rule shall be made unless the draft thereof has been referred to every Mining Board constituted in that part of the territories to which the Act extends which is affected by the regulation or rule, and unless each such Board has had a reasonable opportunity of reporting as to the expediency of making the same and to the suitability of its provisions'. It has been held that the requirement of this provision is mandatory where Mining boards have been constituted,[44] but it is not so if the Boards have not been constituted as the constitution of the Board was within the discretion of the Government.[45] The essence of consultation is the communication of a genuine invitation to give advice and a genuine consideration of that advice which in turn depends on sufficient information and time being given to the party concerned to enable it to tender useful advice. Therefore, when a Minister is under a duty to consult certain organisations before amending statutory regulations, even in an urgency he must give them reasonable time to express their informed opinion.[46] But speaking generally, the Government where required to consult a person or authority before making delegated legislation is not bound to accept all or any proposal or counter proposal.[47] Consultation does not mean concurrence.[48]

(f) Requirement of approval, sanction or permission

Requirement of prior approval or sanction, if any, prescribed by the enabling Act will be held to be mandatory, and subordinate legislation will

---

43. *Kishan Prakash Sharma v. Union of India*, AIR 2001 SC 1493, p. 1506 : (2001) 5 SCC 212.

44. *Banwarilal v. State of Bihar*, AIR 1961 SC 849 : 1962 (1) SCR 33.

45. *Kalipada Chowdhury v. Union of India*, AIR 1963 SC 134 : 1963 (2) SCR 904.

46. *Secretary of State for Social Services v. Ex parte, A.M.A.*, (1986) 1 All ER 164.

47. *Indian Administrative Service (SCS) Ass. U.P. v. Union of India,* 1993 Supp (1) SCC 730 : 1992 Supp JT 83.

48. *L & T McNeil Ltd. v. Government of Tamil Nadu,* AIR 2001 SC 844, p. 845 : (2001) 3 SCC 170.

have to receive the prior approval[49] or sanction[50] prescribed before it can be effective. Similarly, if the Central Government is allowed to delegate its power of making subordinate legislation to the State Government and it does so subject to its prior concurrence, the requirement of prior concurrence will be held to be mandatory and an order issued by the State Government in exercise of the delegated power, but without the prior concurrence of the Central Government, will be held to be invalid.[51] But if the statute does not insist on prior or previous approval, approval granted later may validate the action taken.[52] Permission is a stronger word and a condition requiring permission may always mean prior permission.[53]

5. POWERS IMPLIED FROM GENERAL CLAUSES ACT, 1897

(a) Section 21, General Clauses Act, 1897

It is implicit, because of section 21 of the General Clauses Act, 1897, that where a power to issue notifications, orders, rules, or bye-laws is conferred then that power includes a power exercisable in the like manner and subject to the like sanction and conditions (if any) to add to, amend, vary or rescind any notification, orders, rules, or bye-laws so issued.

Construing section 14 of the Maintenance of Internal Security Act, 1971, with the aid of section 21 of the General Clauses Act, it has been held that the Government can accept a second representation of the detenu and send it for opinion of the Advisory Board and act on that opinion.[54] Recourse to section 21 of the General Clauses Act was taken to support the order of the Election Commission in postponing the polling in certain Assembly constituencies in case of a parliamentary election because of riot from a date originally notified under section 30 of the Representation of

49. *Metcalfe v. Cox*, (1895) AC 328 (HL); *Suptd. of Police, Manipur v. R.K. Tomelsana Singh*, (1984) (Supp.) SCC 155 : AIR 1984 SC 535; *Ghaziabad Development Authority v. Delhi Auto & General Finance Pvt. Ltd.*, JT 1994 (3) SC 275, p. 278 : AIR 1994 SC 2263 : (1994) 4 SCC 42.
50. *Amalgamated Coalfield v. Janpad Sabha*, AIR 1964 SC 1013, p. 1021 (para 30) : 1963 Supp (1) SCR 172.
51. *District Collector, Chittoor v. Chittoor District Groundnut Traders Association*, AIR 1989 SC 989 : 1989 (2) SCC 58.
52. *U.P. Avas Evam Vikas Parishad v. Friends Co-op. Housing Society Ltd.*, AIR 1996 SC 114 (para 5) : (1995) Supp 3 SCC 456; *Graphite India Ltd. v. Durgapur Projects Ltd.*, AIR 1999 SC 3289, p. 3298 : (1999) 7 SCC 645; *Prohibition and Excise Supdt. A.P. v. Toddy Tappers Co-op. Society Marredpally*, AIR 2004 SC 658, p. 669. **See further** text and footnotes 75, 76, p. 470.
53. *Ibid.*
54. *Ram Bali Rajbhar v. State of West Bengal*, AIR 1975 SC 623, pp. 627, 628 : (1975) 4 SCC 47.

the People Act, 1951 to a different date.[55] Section 21 of the Bombay General Clauses Act, 1904 which is in *pari materia* with section 21 of the Central Act, was used to support the conclusion that the Mayor can cancel or postpone a meeting, called by him in virtue of the power conferred by rules made under the Bombay Provincial Municipal Corporation Act, 1949, before the meeting has commenced and can convene the same on a subsequent occasion.[56] A notified order issued under section 18A of the Industries (Development and Regulation) Act, 1951, and authorising the Controller to take over management of an industrial undertaking for a certain period can be amended before the expiry of that period by substitution of a different and longer period in place of the period originally fixed.[57] But power of amendment or modification, in the absence of any clear authorisation to that effect, can only be exercised prospectively during the period the original notification, order, etc., continues to be effective, for it cannot be brought to life *ex post facto* after it has once ceased to exist.[58] Section 21 does not confer a power to issue an order having retrospective operation[59] so it was held that an order giving the State Government's consent for investigation by the CBI under section 6 of the Delhi Special Police Establishment Act, 1946 could not be revoked to affect investigations already commenced and the CBI was competent to complete these investigations.[60]

To bring about an effective amendment or cancellation of a statutory order or rule, the order or rule effecting amendment or cancellation must be made in the manner the original order or rule is required to be made, *e.g.*, an order or rule which is required to be published in Government Gazette and has been published, can only be amended or cancelled by a subsequent order or rule which is also published in like manner.[61]

---

55. *Mohd. Yunus Saleem v. Shiv Kumar Shastri*, AIR 1974 SC 1218 : 1974 (4) SCC 854. **See further** *Janta Dal (Samajwadi) v. Election Commission of India*, 1995 (6) Scale 558 : (1996) 1 SCC 235 [Section 21 relied upon to support an order of the Election Commission cancelling recognition of political party as a national party under the Election Symbols (Reservation & Allotment) Order, 1968].

56. *Jayantbhai Manubhai Patel v. Arun Subodhbhai Mehta*, AIR 1989 SC 1289 : 1989 (2) SCC 484.

57. *Kamla Prasad Khetan v. Union of India*, AIR 1957 SC 676 : 1957 SCR 1052.

58. *Strawboard Mfg. Co. v. G. Mill Workers' Union*, AIR 1953 SC 95, pp. 97, 98 : 1953 SCR 439.

59. *Kazi Lhendeep Dorji v. Central Bureau of Investigations*, JT 1994(3) SC 140, p. 147 : 1994 Supp (2) SCC 116 : 1994 SCC (Cri) 873.

60. *Ibid*, pp. 146, 147.

61. *Mahendralal v. State of U.P.*, AIR 1963 SC 1019, pp. 1034, 1035 (para 30) : 1963 Supp (1) SCR 912; *State of Kerala v. P.L. Joseph*, AIR 1958 SC 296, p. 299 : 1958 SCJ 614. The words 'in the like manner and subject to the like sanctions and conditions (if any)' in section 21 mean similar and not identical manner and conditions: *Ram Bali Rajbhar v. State of W.B.*, AIR 1975 SC 623, p. 628 : (1975) 4 SCC 47.

The implied power of amendment or cancellation is subject to the same limitations which are applicable to the original exercise of the power. Thus, if a power is conferred to declare whole or part of a State as a 'dangerously disturbed area', which does not include a power to declare any area as dangerously disturbed for certain purposes and not for other purposes, a notification declaring certain area as dangerously disturbed area cannot be so cancelled as to keep the notification alive 'as respects things done or omitted to be done' before the cancellation, for that would amount to continue the declaration for some purposes but not for other purposes, a result not contemplated by the enabling provision.[62]

In view of Article 367 of the Constitution, section 21, General Clauses Act, 1897, applies for construing the Constitution. Therefore, the rules made under Articles 77(3), 166(3) and 309 and orders issued under Article 370 can be amended from time to time by recourse to section 21.[63]

The rule enacted in section 21, General Clauses Act, 1897, is merely a rule of construction and may be displaced to the extent the provisions, the scheme and the object of any particular statute indicate a contrary intention *e.g.*, it has been held that the Government has no power to cancel or supersede a reference made under section 10(1) of the Industrial Disputes Act, 1947.[64] On the same principle the application of section 21 was negatived to amend or vary a notification issued under section 3 of the Commissions of Inquiry Act, 1952 for reconstituting the Commission by replacement or substitution of its sole member although section 21 was found applicable for extending the time for completing the enquiry.[65] The scheme of the Commissions of Enquiry Act showed that the Government should have no control over the Commission after its constitution except for filling any vacancy in the office of member or for its winding up when its existence becomes unnecessary and thus the context and the scheme of the Act made section 21 inapplicable for reconstituting the Commission.[66] Similarly, a certificate of registration of citizenship issued under section 5(1)C of the Citizenship Act, 1955 cannot be cancelled by the authority granting the registration by recourse to section 21.[67] It is also relevant to

---

62. *Gopichand v. Delhi Administration*, AIR 1959 SC 609, p. 617 : 1959 Supp (2) SCR 87.

63. *Sampat Prakash v. State of J. & K.*, AIR 1970 SC 1118, p. 1124 : (1969) 1 SCC 562.

64. *State of Bihar v. D.N. Ganguly*, AIR 1958 SC 1018 : 1959 SCR 1191.

65. *State of Madhya Pradesh v. Ajay Singh*, AIR 1993 SC 825, p. 838 : 1993 (1) SCC 302.

66. *Ibid.*

67. *Ghauri Hasan v. State of Rajasthan,* AIR 1967 SC 107 : (1962) 1 SCR 772; *Hari Shanker Jain v. Sonia Gandhi,* AIR 2001 SC 3689, p. 3697 : (2001) 8 SCC 233.

examine the effect of the notification or order sought to be annulled and the stage at which it is being done. Thus, although a notification for compulsory acquisition of land under the Land Acquisition Act, 1894 can be cancelled by recourse to section 21 of the General Clauses Act, 1897[68] it cannot be cancelled after the possession is taken and the land has vested in the Government.[69] Further the scheme of the Land Acquisition Act shows that withdrawal from acquisition after notifications under sections 4 and 6 are issued cannot be made by just rescinding those notifications but only by a notification issued under section 48.[70] A notification bringing an Act into force cannot be annulled by recourse to section 21.[71] The general power under this section of rescinding a notification or order has to be understood in the light of the subject-matter, context and the effect of the relevant provisions of the statute under which the notification or order is issued and the power is not available after an enforceable right has accrued under the notification or order.[72] Moreover, section 21 has no application to vary or amend or review a quasi-judicial order. A quasi-judicial order can be generally varied or reviewed when obtained by fraud or when such a power is conferred by the Act or rules under which it is made. On this basis it was held that the Election Commission cannot by recourse to section 21 deregister or cancel the registration of a political party under section 29A of the Representation of the People Act, 1951 for the decision of the Commission to register a political party under section 29A(7) of the Act is *quasi*-judicial in nature.[73]

(b) Section 22, General Clauses Act, 1897

Power conferred by the enabling Act to make subordinate legislation may at times be exercised even before the commencement of the Act. This is made possible by section 22 of the General Clauses Act, 1897, which

---

68. *State of Madhya Pradesh v. V.P. Sharma*, AIR 1966 SC 1593, p. 1602 : 1966 (3) SCR 557.

69. *Lt. Governor v. Avinash Sharma*, AIR 1970 SC 1576, pp. 1576, 1577 : 1970 (2) SCC 149; *Sulochana Chandrakant Galande v. Pune Municipal Transport*, (2010) 8 SCC 467 para 12 : AIR 2010 SC 2962.

70. *Larsen and Toubro Ltd. v. State of Gujarat*, AIR 1998 SC 1608, pp. 1622, 1623 : (1998) 4 SCC 387.

71. *Lachmi Narain v. Union of India*, AIR 1976 SC 714, pp. 724, 725 : 1976 (2) SCC 953. **See further** text and footnotes 79, 80, p. 1054.

72. *State of Kerala v. K.G. Madhavan Pillai*, AIR 1989 SC 49, p. 65 : 1988 (4) SCC 669; *H.C. Suman v. Rehabilitation Ministry Employees House Building Society Ltd.*, AIR 1991 SC 2160, p. 2172 : 1991 (4) SCC 485.

73. *Indian National Congress v. Institute of Social Welfare*, AIR 2002 SC 2158 : (2002) 5 SCC 685.

corresponds to section 37 of the English Interpretation Act, 1889.[74] As explained by the Supreme Court, section 22 "is an enabling provision, its intent and purpose being to facilitate the making of rules, bye-laws and orders before the date of commencement of an enactment in anticipation of its coming into force. In other words it validates rules, bye-laws and orders made before the enactment comes into force provided they are made after the passing of the Act and are preparatory to the Act coming into force".[75] It, however, confers no authority to pass substantive orders in exercise of the authority conferred by any particular section of the Act.[76] Subordinate legislation so made comes into operation with the coming into operation of the Act and facilitates its effective enforcement for an Act may contain provisions which are not workable till the rules are made.[77]

6. RULES AND THE ENABLING ACT AS AID TO EACH--OTHER'S CONSTRUCTION

Rules made under the statute are treated for the purpose of construction as if they were in the enabling Act and are to be of the same effect as if contained in Act.[78] Reference to 'any other law' in any provision in the Act will therefore not cover the rules made under the Act.[79] Interpretative notes appended to the Rules by the Rule making authority are part of the Rules and hence statutory.[80] It is a recognised canon of construction that an expression used in a rule, bye-law or form made in exercise of a power conferred by a statute must unless there is anything repugnant in the subject or context have the same meaning as is assigned to it under the statute.[81] But the rules are to be consistent with the provisions of the

---

74. **See** *R. v. Minister of Town and Country, Planning, Ex parte, Montague Burton Ltd.*, (1950) 2 All ER 282; *Usher v. Barlow*, (1952) 1 All ER 205.

75. *Venkateshwarloo v. Supdt., Central Jail*, AIR 1953 SC 49, p. 50 : 1953 SCR 905.

76. *Ibid; Chandra Singh v. State of Rajasthan*, AIR 2003 SC 2889, p. 2899 : (2003) 6 SCC 545.

77. **See** for example, *Narayan Row v. Ishwarlal*, AIR 1965 SC 1818, p. 1824 (para 20) : (1965) 57 ITR 149 : (1966) 1 SCR 190.

78. *State of U.P. v. Baburam*, AIR 1961 SC 751, p. 761 : 1961 (2) SCR 679; *State of Tamil Nadu v. Hind Stone*, AIR 1981 SC 711, p. 720 : (1981) 2 SCC 205; *Vedio Electronics Pvt. Ltd. v. State of Punjab*, AIR 1990 SC 820, p. 835 : (1990) 3 SCC 87; *Peerless General Finance and Investment Company Ltd. v. Reserve Bank of India*, AIR 1992 SC 1033, p. 1059 : 1992 (2) SCC 343; *Union of India v. Harjeet Singh*, AIR 2001 SC 1772, p. 1779 : (2001) 5 SCC 593; *Chief Forest Conservator (Wild life) v. Nisar Khan*, (2003) 4 SCC 595, p. 599 : AIR 2003 SC 1867, p. 1870.

79. *B. Shetty v. Ceat Ltd.*, AIR 2001 SC 2953, p. 2959 : (2002) 1 SCC 193.

80. *Tata Iron & Steel Co. Ltd. v. Commr. of Central Excise of Customs*, AIR 2000 SC 1045, p. 1051 : 2000 (3) SCC 472.

81. *Onkarlal Nandlal v. State of Rajasthan*, (1985) 4 SCC 404, p. 414 : AIR 1986 SC 2146.

Act,[82] and if a rule goes beyond what the Act contemplates, the rule must yield to the Act.[83] But a general provision in the Act cannot apply to special provisions made by valid rules under the Act. Thus provision of notice and limitation prescribed by section 11-A of the Central Excise and Salt Act, 1944 which is a general provision for recovery of duty was held to be inapplicable to the special provision made under Rule 57J (as it stood prior to 1998) for recovery of credit wrongly availed of in relation to the MODVAT Scheme.[84] It was also held in this case that the maxim '*generalia specialibus non derogant*' has application also for construction of a general provision in the Act and a special provision in the Rules made under the Act.[85] It is doubtful as to how far subordinate legislation can be looked into for the purpose of construction of the enabling Act,[86] but if it is made under 'as if enacted in this Act' formula, it may be referred to for the purpose of resolving any real ambiguity in the Act.[87] The House of Lords' decision in *Jackson v. Hall*[88] gave the impression that rules, made in the exercise of a statutory power, which do not have the express approval of Parliament cannot be relied upon as an aid to construction of the statute. Rules will have express approval of Parliament when they are made under a laying clause requiring an affirmative procedure.[89] But this decision[90] has later been explained not to lay down any general proposition that subordinate legislation not having express approval of Parliament can never be used as an aid to statutory interpretation.[91] The House of Lords in this case[92] apparently approved the propositions laid down by LORD LOWRY in *Hanlon v. Law Society*[93] indicating the circumstances in which subordinate

---

82. *State of U.P. v. Baburam, supra*, p. 763.

83. *Central Bank of India v. Their Workmen*, AIR 1960 SC 12, p. 23 : (1960) 1 SCR 200; *Babaji Kondaj v. Nasik Merchants Co-operative Bank Ltd.*, (1984) 2 SCC 50, p. 63 : AIR 1984 SC 192. **See further** *Lockwood's* case, (1894) AC 347, p. 360 (HL). But when the statutory provision is in the form 'except as otherwise provided by rules' or it is 'subject to rules', the rules prevail. **See** text and notes 58, 59, p. 1051.

84. *Collector of Central Excise Jaipur v. Raghubar India Ltd.,* AIR 2000 SC 2027, p. 2034 : (2000) 5 SCC 299.

85. *Ibid* p. 2031.

86. *Hales v. Bolton Leathers Ltd.*, (1951) 1 All ER 643, p. 646 : 1950 KB 493 (HL). (LORD SIMONDS), p. 649 (LORD NORMAND), p. 651 (LORD OAKSEY); *J.K. Steel India Ltd. v. Union of India*, AIR 1970 SC 1173, pp. 1184, 1185, 1186 : (1969) 2 SCR 481.

87. *Re, Wier, Ex parte, Wier*, 6 Ch App 875, p. 879.

88. *Jackson v. Hall*, (1980) 1 All ER 177 : (1980) AC 854 : (1980) 2 WLR 118 (HL).

89. *Ibid*; **See further** text and note 16, p. 1111.

90. *Jackson v. Hall, supra.*

91. *British Amusement Catering Trades Association v. Westminster City Council*, (1988) 1 All ER 740, p. 745 : (1989) AC 147 : (1988) 2 WLR 485 (HL).

92. *Ibid.*

93. *Hanlon v. Law Society*, (1980) 2 All ER 199 : (1980) 2 WLR 756 : (1981) AC 124 (HL) **See further** *A v. B,* (2010) 1 All ER 1149 (UK SC) para 41.

legislation, in that case regulations, may be used as aid to interpretation of the parent Act. These propositions are: "(1) Subordinate legislation may be used in order to construe the parent Act but only where power is given to amend the Act by regulations or where the meaning of the Act is ambiguous. (2) Regulations made under the Act provide a parliamentary or administrative *contemporanea expositio* of the Act but do not decide or control its meaning: to allow this would be to substitute the rule making authority for the judges as interpreter and would disregard the possibility that the regulation relied on was misconceived or *ultra vires*. (3) Regulations of the Act which are consistent with a certain interpretation tend to confirm that interpretation. (4) Where the Act provides a framework built on by contemporaneously prepared regulations, the latter may be a reliable guide to the meaning of the former. (5) The regulations are a clear guide, and may be decisive, when they are made in pursuance of a power to modify the Act, particularly if they come into operation on the same day as the Act which they modify. (6) Clear guidance may also be obtained from regulations which are to have effect as if enacted in the parent Act."[94] The Supreme Court also holds that "rules made under a statute are a legitimate aid to construction of the statute as *contemporanea expositio*."[95] There is additional reason to take the assistance of subordinate legislation for clarifying an ambiguity in a taxing Act for "in the matter of fiscal legislation the initiative is in the hands of the executive".[96] Statutory rules subsequently made under Income-tax Act though prospective, have been used to support a meaning given to a statutory provision prior to the making of the rules.[97]

---

94. *Ibid*, p. 218. Assistance of forms contained in Regulations made contemporaneously under the Act was taken in *Government of Canada v. Aronson*, (1989) 2 All ER 1025, p. 1043 (HL).

95. *Tata Engineering and Locomotive Company Ltd. v. Gram Panchayat, Pimpri Waghere*, AIR 1976 SC 2463, p. 2467 : (1976) 4 SCC 177; *P. Kasilingam v. P.S.G. College of Technology*, AIR 1995 SC 1395, p. 1400 : 1995 Supp (2) SCC 348. Assistance of rules and forms made under the Minimum Wages Act, 1948 was taken for construing section 20(2) that an ex-employee can also petition under that provision: *Pali Devi v. Chairman, Managing Committee*, AIR 1996 SC 1589, p. 1591 (para 8) : (1996) 3 SCC 296; *Gujarat Pradesh Panchayat Parishad v. State of Gujarat*, (2007) 7 SCC 718, para 39.

96. *J.K. Steel India Ltd. v. Union of India*, AIR 1970 SC 1173, p. 1180 : (1969) 2 SCR 481; *Shree Synthetics Ltd., Ujain v. Union of India*, (1982) MPLJ 340, p. 347 (G.P. SINGH C. J.).

97. *CIT v. Gwalior Rayon Silk Manufacturing Ltd.*, AIR 1992 SC 1782, p. 1788 : 1992 3 SCC 326 (Income-tax 4th Amendment Rules, 1983 defining 'building' to include roads, used for supporting the meaning of 'building' in section 32 of the Act as given by judicial decisions for an earlier period.)

However, it has also been held that the principle of statutory interpretation that the tenor and scheme of the subordinate legislation can be used while construing a provision of the parent Act is not normally resorted to except in the case of interpretation of an old enactment, where the language used is ambiguous. Where the language of the section itself is explicit, no other external aid is required for interpreting the same. Therefore, it was held that subordinate legislation made by the executive in exercise of the powers delegated by the legislature may, at best, reflect the understanding of the the executive of the scope of the powers delegated, but there is no inherent guarantee that such an understanding would be consistent with the true meaning and purport of the parent enactment.[1] Moreover, the legislative competence to enact a particular provision in an Act cannot be made to depend upon rules made under the Act which can be deleted, amended, or modified at any time.[2]

7. SUB-DELEGATION

It has been held that the delegate on whom power to make subordinate legislation is conferred cannot further delegate that power.[3] By section 40 of the Ajmer Laws Regulation of 1877, the Chief Commissioner is empowered, among other things, to make rules regarding 'the maintenance of watch and ward, and the establishment of proper system of conservancy and sanitation at fairs and other large public assemblies'. The Chief Commissioner made rules for the regulation of fairs in the State of Ajmer. Rule 1 of the Rules prohibited the holding of fairs except under a permit issued by the District Magistrate who was 'to satisfy himself before issuing any permit, that the applicant was in a position to establish a proper system of conservancy, sanitation and watch and ward at the fair'. It further provided that the District Magistrate could 'revoke any permit without assigning any reasons or giving any previous notice'. The Supreme Court, in holding the rule invalid; observed: "The Regulation empowers the Chief Commissioner to make rules for the establishment of a system of conservancy and sanitation. He can only do this by bringing a system into existence and incorporating it in his rules so that all concerned can know what the system is and make arrangements to comply with it. What he has done is to leave it to the District Magistrate to see that persons desiring to hold a fair are in a position 'to establish a proper system of conservancy etc.' But

---

1. *Jeevan Chandrabhan Idnani & Anr. v. Divisional Commissioner, Konkan Bhavan & Ors.*, (2012) 2 SCC 794, p. 803.
2. *Hotel Balaji v. State of Andhra Pradesh*, AIR 1993 SC 1048, p. 1062 : (1992) 6 JT 182 : 1993 Supp (4) SCC 536.
3. *Ganpati Singhji v. State of Ajmar*, AIR 1955 SC 188 : 1955 (1) SCR 1065.

who, according to this, is to determine what a proper system is? Obviously the District Magistrate. Therefore, in effect, the rules empower the District Magistrate to make his own system and see that it is observed. But the Regulation confers this power on the Chief Commissioner and not on the District Magistrate; therefore the action of the Chief Commissioner in delegating this authority to District Magistrate is '*ultra vires*'."[4] But when the rule making authority, *e.g.* the State Government while making rules confers upon itself the power to prescribe certain matters *e.g.* criteria and procedure for selection in specific circumstances in recruitment rules made by it, there can be no question of any excessive delegation.[5]

It is, however, competent for the legislature to authorise the delegate, on whom power to make subordinate legislation is conferred, to further delegate that power on some other authority. A good illustration of exercise of such a power was found in section 4 of the Essential Supplies (Temporary Powers) Act, 1946, which authorised the Central Government to delegate its power to make orders under section 3. The provision in section 4 authorising sub-delegation was held to be valid by the Supreme Court.[6] The Central Government may, however, sub-delegate its power of making orders to the State Government not absolutely but subject to its prior concurrence and in that event requirement of prior concurrence will be taken as mandatory for a delegate is not entitled to exercise powers in contravention of the delegated powers.[7] The ambit of the power delegated would depend upon the construction of the order of delegation. The Essential Commodities Act, 1948 has been replaced by the Essential Commodities Act, 1955. The Central Government by notifications delegated its power under section 3 of the Act in relation to 'foodstuffs' to the State Governments. Construing these notifications it was held that the delegation could not extend to 'tea' as 'tea' is not a foodstuff.[8] Implied power to delegate statutory power is atleast not found in peace time legislations.[9]

---

4. *Ganpati Singhji v. State of Ajmer, supra*, pp. 189, 190 (para 7).

5. *Arun Tiwari v. Zila Mansavi Shikshak Sangh,* AIR 1998 SC 331, p. 334 : (1998) 2 SCC 332.

6. *Harishanker Bagla v. State of M.P.*, AIR 1954 SC 465, p. 469 : 1955 (1) SCR 380. **Applied** in *Arnold Rodricks v. State of Maharashtra*, AIR 1966 SC 1788 : 1966 (3) SCR 885.

7. *District Collector, Chittoor v. Chittoor District Groundnut Traders Association*, AIR 1989 SC 989 : 1989 (2) SCC 58.

8. *S. Samuel M.D. Harrisons Malayalam v. Union of India*, AIR 2004 SC 218, p. 226 : (2004) 1 SCC 256.

9. *Ibid.*

It is also well established that judicial or *quasi*-judicial power conferred by a statute cannot be delegated except when specifically permitted.[10] If a *quasi*-judicial authority is authorised to regulate its procedure the authority may appoint a person to hear and receive evidence from interested parties for the purpose of informing the authority of the evidence and submissions but its decisions must be reached after consideration of the evidence and submissions so received and not merely on the report of the person appointed to collect them.[11] Duty to hear does not necessarily mean personal hearing and parties may be heard orally or through the medium of their written representation.[12] When delegation of judicial power is permitted by a statute and is made, the delegation is absolute but the delegate may yet remain in the administrative control of the authority delegating the power.[13]

Even a discretionary administrative power entrusted by a statute to a particular authority cannot be further delegated except as otherwise provided in the statute.[14] The principle against sub-delegation is reasoned from the maxim '*delegatus non potest delegare*' and the correct rule of construction is stated to be that "a discretion conferred by statute is *prima facie* intended to be exercised by the authority on which the statute has conferred it and by no other authority, but this intention may be negatived by any contrary indications found in the language, scope or object of the statute".[15] In other words when the Act prescribes a particular body or

---

10. *Pradyat Kumar v. Chief Justice of Calcutta High Court*, AIR 1956 SC 285, p. 291; 1955 (2) SCR 1331; *Bombay Municipal Corporation v. Dhondu*, AIR 1965 SC 1486 : 1965 (2) SCR 929; *Khurai Municipality v. Kamal Kumar*, AIR 1965 SC 1321, p. 1325 : (1965) 2 SCR 653; *Vine v. National Dock Labour Board*, (1956) 3 All ER 939 (HL); *Sahani Silk Mills (P.) Ltd v. Employees State Insurance Corporation*, JT 1994(5) SC 11, pp. 17, 18 : 1994 (5) SCC 346, pp. 350, 351; *Skypak Couriers Ltd. v. Tata Chemicals Ltd.*, JT 2000 (6) SC 560, p. 564 : (2000) 5 SCC 294 : AIR 2000 SC 2008.

11. *Jeffs v. Newzealand Dairy Products etc.*, (1966) 3 All ER 863, p. 870 : (1971) 1 AC 551 (PC). **See further** *Indore Textiles Ltd. v. Union of India*, AIR 1983 MP 65 (G.P. SINGH, CJ).

12. *Ibid*, p. 870; *M.P. Industries Ltd. v. Union of India*, AIR 1966 SC 671, p. 675 : 1966 (1) SCC 466.

13. *Bombay Municipal Corporation v. Dhondu*, AIR 1965 SC 1486 : 1965 (2) SCR 929.

14. SA DE SMITH, Judicial Review of Administrative Action, 4th Edition, pp. 303 to 308.

15. SA DE SMITH, Judicial Review of Administrative Action, 4th Edition, p. 301, **quoting** WILLIS, '*Delegatus non potest delegare*' (1943) 21 Can Bar Rev 257, p. 259. **See further** *Barium Chemicals Ltd. v. Company Law Board*, AIR 1967 SC 295, pp. 306, 312; 1966 Supp SCR 311; *State of Rajasthan v. Hari Ram Nathwani*, AIR 1976 SC 277, p. 280 (para 6) : (1975) 2 SCC 517; *A.K. Roy v. State of Punjab*, (1986) 4 SCC 326, p. 334 : AIR 1986 SC 2160; *State of U.P. v. Maharaja Dharmendra Pratap Singh*, AIR 1989 SC 997, p. 1009 : 1989 (2) SCC 505; *Sahani Silk Mills (P.) Ltd. v. Employees State Insurance Corporation, supra*, p. 17. But an officer placed in current charge of the duties may exercise statutory discretion: *Gopalji Khanna v. Allahabad Bank*, 1996 (2) Scale 621, p. 623 : 1996 (3) SCC 538.

officer to exercise a power, it must be exercised by that body or officer and none else unless the Act by express words or necessary implication permits delegation, in which event, it may also be exercised by the delegate if delegation is made in accordance with the terms of the Act but not otherwise.[16] Further, if any decision is taken by a statutory authority at the behest of or on the suggestion of a person who has no statutory role to play, the same would be *ultra vires*.[17] Practical necessity of administration, however, implies permission to delegate when the statute empowers a minister to take decisions in individual cases; the decision may be taken by an officer of suitable seniority in the ministry for whom the minister accepts responsibility.[18]

The order of the delegate, when delegation is made as authorised by the statute, is to be treated for all intents and purposes as an order of the principal and cannot be revised or reviewed by the principal unless such a power is specifically conferred.[19]

When a sub-delegation as permitted by the enabling Act is made, it does not divest the authority making sub-delegation of his statutory authority.[20] He may cancel the sub-delegation and resume his authority and he may even exercise concurrent powers without cancelling the sub-delegation.[21]

---

16. *Marathwada University v. Sheshrao Balwantrao Chavan*, AIR 1989 SC 1582, p. 1587 : 1989 (3) SCC 132; *Sahani Silk Mills (P.) Ltd. v. Employees Insurance Corporation, supra*; *Director General, ESI v. T. Abdul Razak*, AIR 1996 SC 2292, p. 2298 : 1996 (4) SCC 708. Similarly power conferred on 'A' cannot be abdicated by him so as to be exercised on dictates of B; *Anirudhsinghji Karansinghji Jadeja v. State of Gujarat*, 1995 (4) Scale 715, p. 719 : AIR 1995 SC 2390, p. 2393 : (1995) 5 SCC 302; *N. Venkateshwara Rao v. STA*, 1997 (1) Scale 176, pp. 183, 184: 1997 (2) SCC 320; *Torlochan Dev Sharma v. State of Punjab,* AIR 2001 SC 2524, pp. 2531, 2532 : (2001) 6 SCC 260. **See further** *Abhay Shridhar Ambulkar v. S.V. Bhave, Commissioner of Police*, AIR 1991 SC 397, p. 401 : 1991 (1) SCC 500. (The delegating authority must apply its mind to the conditions required by the statute for making delegation).

17. *Bahadur Singh Lakhubhai Gohil v. Jagdishbhai M. Kamalia*, (2004) 2 SCC 65, p. 75 : AIR 2004 SC 1159.

18. *Oladehinde v. Secretary of State for the Home Department*, (1990) 3 All ER 393, p. 399 (HL).

19. *State of Orissa v. Commissioner of Land Records and Settlement*, AIR 1998 SC 3067, p. 3074 : 1998 (7) SCC 162; *OCL India Ltd. v. State of Orissa,* (2003) 2 SCC 101, p. 107 : (2003) 130 STC 35; *Ishwar Singh v. State of Rajasthan*, (2005) 2 SCC 334, p. 339.

20. *Huth v. Clark*, (1890) 25 QBD 391; *Gordon v. Morris*, (1945) 2 All ER 616, p. 621; *Godawari S. Perulekar v. State of Maharashtra*, AIR 1966 SC 1404, p. 1406 : 1966 (3) SCR 314; *Ishwar Singh v. State of Rajasthan, supra*, p. 338.

21. *Ibid*. **But see** *Blackpool Corporation v. Locker*, (1948) 1 All ER 85 : (1948) 1 KB 349.

When a statute conferring power imposes certain duties and functions incidental to the exercise of the power in such a way that they are integrally connected, a permissible delegation of the power is effective to delegate the duties and functions along with the power.[22] And if a power can be exercised only after holding an inquiry, a permissible delegation of the power will carry with it an authority to hold the necessary inquiry which is a prerequisite for exercise of the power and really a limitation of the power.[23] The width of delegation will depend upon the terms of the order of delegation. An order of sub-delegation made by the Central Government under section 5 of the Essential Commodities Act, 1955 in general terms applying to all commodities will include in its sweep commodities subsequently declared to be essential under section 2(a)(xi).[24]

When the Legislature confers a power on A and authorises him to delegate that power to B and does not empower further delegation, B cannot subdelegate to C the power delegated to him by A nor can A empower B to do so. Section 94A of the Employees Insurances Act, 1948 permits delegation of its powers to any officer or authority subordinate to the Corporation. The Corporation delegated its power to levy damages under section 85-B(1) to 'the Director-General or any other officer authorised by him'. The Director-General in his turn authorised the Regional Directors to exercise the power under section 85-B(1). This being sub-delegation not authorised by section 94A of the Act was held to be *ultra vires* especially as the power to recover damages under section 85-B(1) is *quasi*-judicial.[25]

For a prosecution under the Explosive Substances Act, 1908, the consent of the Central Government under section 7 of the Act is essential. The Central Government is authorised to delegate that power and in exercise of that power it entrusted the power of giving consent to District Magistrates. The State Government of Madhya Pradesh by notification appointed the joint collector as Additional District Magistrate and authorised him to exercise all the powers of the District Magistrate conferred by the Criminal Procedure Code or under any other law. The Additional District Magistrate gave consent for prosecution under section 7 of the Explosive substances

---

22. *Mungoni v. A-G*, (1960) AC 336; *Syed Shah v. Commr. of Wakfs*, AIR 1961 SC 1095 : 1961 (3) SCR 759 : (1960) 1 All ER 446; *State of Bombay v. Shivbalak*, AIR 1965 SC 661 : 1965 (1) SCR 211; *State of Assam v. Banshidhar Shewbhagwan*, AIR 1981 SC 1937, p. 1959 : (1981) 4 SCC 613.

23. *Khambalia Municipality v. State of Gujarat*, AIR 1967 SC 1048, p. 1051 : 1967 (2) SCR 631.

24. *State of Andhra Pradesh v. Potta Sanyasi Rao*, AIR 1975 SC 2030 : (1975) 2 SCC 480.

25. *Sahani Silk Mills (P.) Ltd. v. Employees State Insurance Corporation*, JT 1994 (5) SC 11, pp. 17, 18: 1994 (5) SCC 346, pp. 350, 351.

Act but the prosecution failed for it was held that the power of giving consent delegated to the District Magistrate by the Central Government could not be further delegated by the State Government to the Additional District Magistrate.[26]

26. *State of Madhya Pradesh v. Bhupendra Singh,* AIR 2000 SC 679 : (2000) 1 SCC 555.

APPENDIX

THE GENERAL CLAUSES ACT, 1897

(Act No. X of 1897)

Contents

Section **Page**

Preliminary

General Definitions

General Rules of Construction

Section **Page**

Powers and Functionaries

Provisions as to Orders, Rules, etc., made under Enactments

Miscellaneous

THE GENERAL CLAUSES ACT, 1897

(Act No. 10 of 1897)

[11th March, 1897]

An Act to consolidate and extend the General Clauses Acts, 1868 and 1887

Whereas it is expedient to consolidate and extend the General Clauses Acts, 1868 (1 of 1868) and 1887 (1 of 1887);

It is hereby enacted as follows:—

PRELIMINARY

S. 1. Short title.—(1) This Act may be called the General Clauses Act, 1897.

NOTES

The General Clauses Act, 1897, is a consolidating and amending Act.[1] The purpose of the Act is to avoid superfluity and a repetition of language;[2] and to place in a single Act, provisions as regards definitions of words and legal principles of interpretation which would otherwise have to be incorporated in many different Acts and Regulations.[3] The definition and the rules of interpretation contained in the General Clauses Act have to be read in every other Statute governed by it,[4] provided the statute does not contain anything repugnant to them in the subject or context[5] or does

---

1. *Nibaranchandra v. Mahendranath*, AIR 1963 SC 1890, p. 1894 : 1964 (3) SCR 686.
2. *Rayarappan v. Madhavi Amma*, AIR 1950 FC 140, p. 141 : 1949 FCR 667; *N. Subramania Iyar v. Official Receiver*, AIR 1958 SC 1, p. 10 : 1958 SCR 257.
3. *Chief Inspector of Mines v. Karam Chand Thapar*, AIR 1961 SC 838, p. 843 : 1962 (1) SCR 9.
4. *Ibid; State of Punjab v. Harnek Singh*, AIR 2002 SC 1074, p. 1079 : (2002) 3 SCC 481.
5. *Dulichand v. CIT*, AIR 1956 SC 354, p. 357 : 1956 SCR 154; *N. Subramania Aiyar v. Official Receiver*, AIR 1959 SC 1, p. 10; *Dhandhania Kedia & Co. v. CIT*, AIR 1955 SC 219, p. 222 (para 6) : 1959 Supp (1) SCR 204.

not exhibit a different intention.[6] The Act is also applicable for interpretation of the Constitution.[7]

[8][(2) *Repealed*].

S. 2. [*Repeal.*] Rep. by the Repealing and Amending Act, 1903 (1 of 1903), S. 4 and Sch. III

GENERAL DEFINITIONS

[9]**[S. 3. Definitions.**—In this Act, and in all Central Acts and Regulations made after the commencement of this Act, unless there is anything repugnant in the subject or context,—

(1) "abet", with its grammatical variations and cognate expressions, shall have the same meaning as in the Indian Penal Code (XLV of 1860);

NOTES

See section 107, Indian Penal Code, 1860 and *Kartar Singh v. State of Punjab.*[10]

'Abetment' does not in itself involve the actual commission of the crime abetted. It is a crime apart.[11]

(2) "act", used with reference to an offence or a civil wrong, shall include a series of acts, and words which refer to acts done extend also to illegal omissions;

NOTES

See sections 32 and 33, Indian Penal Code, 1860.

For definition of word 'Illegal' *see* section 43, Indian Penal Code, 1860.

Omissions to come within the definition of 'act' should be illegal omissions.[12] Before an omission can be considered as illegal on the part of an

---

6. *State of Punjab v. Mohar Singh*, AIR 1955 SC 84, p. 88 : 1955 (1) SCR 893; *Indira Sohanlal v. Custodian of E.P.*, AIR 1956 SC 77, p. 83 : 1955 (2) SCR 1117.

7. Article 367 of the Constitution; *Pradyat Kumar v. Chief Justice of Calcutta High Court*, AIR 1956 SC 285, p. 291 (para 9) : (1955) 2 SCR 1331; *Ram Kishore v. Union of India*, AIR 1966 SC 644, p. 648 : 1966 (1) SCR 430.

8. The word "and" at the end of sub-section (1) and whole of sub-section (2) were repealed by Act 10 of 1914, s. 3 and Sch. II.

9. Subs. by the A.O. 1950, for the former section 3.

10. JT 1994 (2) SC 423, pp. 461, 462 : 1994 (3) SCC 569 : 1994 SCC (Cri) 899.

11. **See** section 108, Indian Penal Code, 1860; *B.K. Ghosh v. King Emperor*, AIR 1925 PC 1, p. 7.

12. *Revati Mohan Das v. Yatindra Mohan Ghosh*, AIR 1934 PC 100.

official, it must be shown that the official concerned had omitted to discharge some official duty imposed on him in public interest. The omission in question must have a positive content in it. In other words, the non-discharge of that must amount to an illegality.[13]

The term 'act' in the context of liability is used in a very wide sense, meaning "any event which is subject to the control of the human will",[14] and includes both positive and negative acts, *i.e.*, "acts of commission or acts of omission".[15] There are three constituents of every act: "(1) Its origin in some mental bodily activity of the doer, (2) its circumstances, and (3) its consequences".[16]

(3) "affidavit" shall include affirmation and declarations in the case of persons by law allowed to affirm or declare instead of swearing;

(4) "barrister" shall mean a barrister of England or Ireland, or a member of the Faculty of Advocates in Scotland;

(5) "British India" shall mean as respects the period before the commencement of Part III of the Government of India Act, 1935, all territories and places within His Majesty's dominions which were for the time being governed by His Majesty through the Governor-General of India, or through any Governor or Officer subordinate to the Governor-General of India, and as respects any period after that date and before the date of the establishment of the Dominion of India means all territories for the time being comprised within the Governors' Provinces and the Chief Commissioners' Provinces, except that a reference to British India in an Indian law passed or made before the commencement of Part III of the Government of India Act, 1935, shall not include a reference to Berar;

(6) "British possession" shall mean any part of Her Majesty's dominions, exclusive of the United Kingdom, and, where parts of those dominions are under both a Central and a local Legislature all parts under the Central Legislature shall, for the purposes of this definition, be deemed to be one British possession;

---

13. *Amalgamated Electricity Co. (Belgaum) Ltd. v. Municipal Committee, Ajmer*, AIR 1969 SC 227 : 1969 (1) SCR 430, referred to in *Public Prosecutor, Madras v. R. Raju*, AIR 1972 SC 2504 : (1972) 2 SCC 410.

14. SALMOND: *Jurisprudence*, 11th Edition, p. 399.

15. *Ibid.*

16. *Ibid*, p. 401.

(7) "Central Act" shall mean an Act of Parliament, and shall include—

(*a*) an Act of the Dominion Legislature or of the Indian Legislature passed before the commencement of the Constitution, and

(*b*) an Act made before such commencement by the Governor-General-in-Council or the Governor-General, acting in a legislative capacity;

[17](8) "Central Government" shall—

(*a*) in relation to anything done before the commencement of the Constitution, mean the Governor-General or the Governor-General-in-Council, as the case may be;

and shall include,—

(*i*) in relation to functions entrusted under sub-section (1) of section 124 of the Government of India Act, 1935, to the Government of a Province, the Provincial Government acting within the scope of the authority given to it under that sub-section; and

(*ii*) in relation to the administration of a Chief Commissioner's Province, the Chief Commissioner acting within the scope of the authority given to him under sub-section (3) of section 64 of the Act; and

(*b*) in relation to anything done or to be done after the commencement of the Constitution means the President,

and shall include—

(*i*) in relation to functions entrusted under clause (1) of Article 258 of the Constitution to the Government of a State, the State Government acting within the scope of the authority given to it under the clause; [18]

(*ii*) in relation to the administration of a Part C State[19] [before the commencement of the Constitution (Seventh Amendment) Act, 1956] the Chief Commissioner or the Lieutenant-Governor or Government of a neighbouring State or other authority acting within the scope the authority given to him or it under Article 239 or Article 243 of the Constitution, as the case may be; [20][and]

[21][(*iii*) in relation to the administration of a Union territory the administrator thereof acting within the scope of the authority given to him under Article 239 of the Constitution;]

---

17. Subs. by Adaptation of Laws (Amendment) Order, 1950.
18. The word "and" omitted by Adaptation of Laws (No. 1) Order, 1956.
19. Ins. by *ibid.*
20. Ins. by *ibid.*
21. *Ibid.* **See** *Punjab Tin Supply Co. v. Central Government*, (1984) 1 SCC 206, pp. 217, 218 : AIR 1984 SC 87.

NOTES

The executive power of the Union is vested in the President,[22] who is aided and advised in the exercise of his functions by a Council of Ministers.[23] But in the matter of (1) the choice of a Prime Minister and (2) the dismissal of a Government which has lost its majority but refuses to quit office, he acts in his own discretion and not on the advice of the council of ministers.[24] Executive action of the Government of India is transacted in accordance with the rule of business which allocate among Ministers the business of the Government,[25] but all executive action is expressed to be taken in the name of the President,[26] and orders and instruments made and executed in the name of the President are authenticated in accordance with the rule made by the President.[27] The executive power of the Union of India under Article 73 of the Constitution extends to the matters with respect to which Parliament has power to make laws and to the exercise of such rights, authority and jurisdiction as are exercisable by the Government of India by virtue of any treaty or agreement. But until otherwise provided in the constitution or by Parliament the executive power of the Union does not extend in any state to matters with respect to which the legislature of that State has also power to make laws. The executive power of the Union enables it to issue executive instructions if there be no legislation on a matter on which Parliament could have legislated.[28] Executive instruction can also be issued to supplement the existing legislation but not to supplant it.[29]

For position before the Constitution *see*—the Government of India Act, 1935, Schedule IX, section 40.[30]

For position of Central Government in relation to Part C States, before the commencement of the Constitution (Seventh Amendment) Act, 1956,

---

22. Constitution of India, Article 53.
23. *Ibid.* Article 74; *Samsher Singh v. State of Punjab*, AIR 1974 SC 2192 : (1974) (2) SCC 831; *R.K. Jain v. Union of India*, AIR 1993 SC 1769 : (1993) 3 SCR 802; *S.R. Bommai v. Union of India,* AIR 1994 SC 1918 : 1994 (3) SCC 1.
24. *Samsher Singh v. State of Punjab, supra*, p. 885 (SCC) para 154.
25. Constitution of India, Article 77(3).
26. *Ibid*, Article 77(1).
27. *Ibid*, Article 77(2).
28. *New Delhi Municipal Council v. Tanvi Trading and Credit Pvt. Ltd.*, (2008) 8 SCC 765 para 35 : (2008) 10 JT 109.
29. *Ibid.* For executive power of State see p. 1160.
30. *J.K. Gas Plant Mfg. Co. v. Emperor*, AIR 1947 FC 38.

and in relation to Union territories thereafter, *see*—Constitution of India, Part VIII, before and after the said amendment.[31]

(9) "Chapter" shall mean a Chapter of the Act or Regulation to which the word occurs;

(10) "Chief Controlling Revenue Authority" or "Chief Revenue Authority" shall mean—

(*a*) in a State where there is a Board of Revenue that Board;

(*b*) in a State where there is a Revenue Commissioner, that Commissioner;

(*c*) in Punjab, the Financial Commissioner; and

(*d*) elsewhere, such authority as, in relation to matters enumerated in List I in the Seventh Schedule to the Constitution, the Central Government, and in relation to other matters, the State Government, may by notification in the Official Gazette, appoint.

(11) "Collector" shall mean, in a Presidency-town, the Collector of Calcutta, Madras or Bombay, as the case may be and elsewhere, the chief officer-in-charge of the revenue administration of a district;

(12) "Colony"—

(*a*) in any Central Act passed after the commencement of Part III of the Government of India Act, 1935, shall mean any part of His Majesty's dominions exclusive of the British Islands, the Dominions of India and Pakistan (and before the establishment of those Dominions, British India); any Dominion as defined in the Statute of the Westminster, 1931, any Province or State forming part of any of the said Dominions, and British Burma; and

(*b*) in any Central Act passed before the commencement of Part III of the said Act, means any part of His Majesty's dominions exclusive of the British Islands and of British India;

---

31. **See** *Satya Deo v. Padam Deo*, AIR 1954 SC 587 : 1955 (1) SCR 549; **(Reviewed)** AIR 1955 SC 5; *State of V.P. (now M.P.) v. Moula Bux*, AIR 1962 SC 145 : 1962 (2) SCR 794; *Subhash Chandra v. Municipal Corporation of Delhi*, AIR 1965 SC 1275 : 1965 (1) SCR 350; *Goa Sampling Employees Association v. General Superintendence Co. of India*, (1985) 1 SCC 206 : AIR 1985 SC 357; *Om Prakash v. Union of India*, AIR 1988 SC 350 : 1988 (1) SCC 356.

and in either case where parts of those dominions are under both a Central and local Legislature, all parts under the Central Legislature shall, for the purposes of this definition, be deemed to be one colony;

(13) "commencement", used with reference to an Act or Regulation, shall mean the day on which the Act or Regulation comes into force;

(14) "Commissioner" shall mean the chief officer-in-charge of the revenue-administration of a division;

(15) "Constitution" shall mean the Constitution of India;

(16) "Consular Officer" shall include consul-general, consul, vice-consul, consular agent, pro-consul and any person for the time being authorised to perform the duties of consul-general, consul, vice-consul or consular agent;

(17) "District Judge" shall mean the Judge of a principal Civil Court of original jurisdiction, but shall not include a High Court in the exercise of its ordinary or extraordinary original civil jurisdiction;

NOTES

The question whether an Additional District Judge or an Additional Judge is a Judge of the district Court, and whether and how far he can exercise the powers of a District Judge, will depend upon the Civil Courts Acts in force in different States.[32] The expression 'District Judge' will also cover a judge of a principal court exercising special kind of civil original jurisdiction *viz.* Industrial Courts and Labour Courts.[33] But 'Family Court' judges who are not members of judicial service as defined in Article 236(b) of the Constitution cannot become 'District Judges'.[34]

(18) "document" shall include any matter written, expressed or described upon any substance by means of letters, figures or marks, or by more than one of those means which is intended to be used, or which may be used, for the purpose of recording that matter;

NOTES

See section 29, Indian Penal Code, 1860, and section 3, Evidence Act, 1872. For definition of 'writing' *see* section 3(65), General Clauses Act, 1897.

---

32. *Kuldip Singh v. State of Punjab*, AIR 1956 SC 391 : 1956 SCR 125.
33. *State of Maharashtra v. Labour Law Practitioners' Association*, AIR 1998 SC 1233 : 1998 (2) SCC 688.
34. *S.D. Joshi v. High Court of Bombay*, (2011) 1 SCC 252 paras 37, 39.

(19) "enactment" shall include a Regulation (as hereinafter defined) and any Regulation of the Bengal, Madras or Bombay Code, and shall also include any provision contained in any Act or in any such Regulation as aforesaid;

NOTES

An enactment may mean the whole Act or a part of it.[35] 'Act' means the whole Act whereas a section or part of a section is an enactment.[36]

(20) "father", in the case of any one whose personal law permits adoption, shall include an adoptive father;

(21) "financial year" shall mean the year commencing on the first day of April;

(22) a thing shall be deemed to be done in "good faith" where it is in fact done honestly, whether it is done negligently or not;

NOTES

See section 52, Indian Penal Code, 1860 and section 2*(h)*, Limitation Act, 1963 which also define 'good faith'. Within the definitions under these statutes absence of 'due care and attention' is destructive of good faith; whereas, as defined in the General Clauses Act 'good faith' may exist in spite of negligence.[37] The latter definition is thus equitable and more reasonable and recognises as good law, what is after all good sense, that "a careless man is not dishonest man and no amount of argument will prove that he is one".[38] But when a person is aware of possible harm and acts in spite of it, his action is reckless and in the eye of law *mala fide*.[39]

(23) "Government" or "the Government" shall include both the Central Government and any State Government;

---

35. *Vasantrao v. Shyamrao*, AIR 1977 SC 2021, p. 2023 : (1977) 4 SCC 9.

36. *Prabodh Verma v. State of U.P.*, (1984) 4 SCC 251, p. 266 : AIR 1984 SC 167.

37. *N. Subramania Iyar v. Official Receiver*, AIR 1958 SC 1, p. 10 : 1958 1 SCR 257; *Madhav Rao v. Ramkrishna*, AIR 1958 SC 767 : 1959 SCR 564; *Harbhajan Singh v. State of Punjab*, AIR 1966 SC 97 : 1965 (3) SCR 235; *Goondla Venkateswarlu v. State of Andhra Pradesh,* (2008) 9 SCC 613 para 22 : (2008) 9 JT 521.

38. WINFIELD: *Text Book of Law of Torts*, 7th Edition, p. 559; proposition deduced from *Derry v. Peek*, (1889) 14 AC 337 : 5 TLR 625. **See further** *Goodman v. Harvey*, (1836) 4 A & E 876; "Gross negligence may be evidence of *mala fides*, but is not the same thing. We have shaken off the last remnant of the contrary doctrine", per LORD DENMAN, C.J.: quoted in Objects and Reasons.

39. *Municipality of Bhiwandy and Nizampur v. Kailash Sizing Works*, AIR 1975 SC 529, p. 531 : (1974) 2 SCC 596.

NOTES

The definition is inclusive not exhaustive. Government generally connotes three estates, the Legislature, the Executive and the Judiciary; but in a narrow sense it is used to connote the Executive only. The meaning to be assigned to that expression, therefore, depends on the context in which it is used.[40] So in section 21 of the R.P. Act, 1951, it was held, the expression Government included the legislative wing of the State;[41] but in section 21 of the Penal Code that expression did not include the Legislature.[42] In the context of Articles 50, 214, 217 and 221 of the Constitution, a judge of the High Court, it was held, holds a constitutional office and is not a Government servant.[43] But in the context of proviso to Rule 3(b) of the National Human Rights Commission Chairperson and Members (Salaries, Allowances and other conditions of Service) Rules, 1993 which provides for deduction of pension payable 'in respect of any previous service under the Government' from salary payable to a member, it was held that pension payable as chief justice is in respect of service under the Government and deductible under the proviso.[44]

(24) "Government securities" shall mean securities of the Central Government or of any State Government, but in any Act or Regulation made before the commencement of the Constitution shall not include securities of the Government of any Part B State;

NOTES

See *C.I.T., A.P. v. H. E. H. Mir Osman Ali Bahadur.*[45]

(25) "High Court", used with reference to civil proceedings, shall mean the highest civil court of appeal (not including the Supreme Court) in the part of India in which the Act or Regulation containing the expression operates;

(26) "Immovable property" shall include land, benefits to arise out of land and things attached to the earth, or permanently fastened to anything attached to the earth;

---

40. *Pashupati Nath Sukul v. Nemchand Jain*, (1984) 2 SCC 404, pp. 412, 413 : AIR 1984 SC 399.

41. *Ibid.*

42. *R.S. Nayak v. A.R. Antulay*, (1984) 2 SCC 183 : AIR 1984 SC 684.

43. *Union of India v. Pratibha Bannerjee,* (1995) 6 SCC 765 : AIR 1996 SC 693; *V.S. Mallimath v. Union of India,* AIR 2001 SC 1455, p. 1460 : (2001) 4 SCC 31.

44. *V.S. Mallimath v. Union of India, supra,* pp. 1460, 1461.

45. *C.I.T., A.P. v. H.E.H. Mir Csman Ali Bahadur*, AIR 1966 SC 1260 : 1966 (2) SCR 296.

NOTES

The definition of 'immovable property' as contained in the Transfer of Property Act, 1882 (section 3) is as follows: "'Immovable property' does not include standing timber, growing crops or grass." The expression is also defined in the Registration Act, 1908 [S. 2(6)] in the following terms: "'Immovable property' includes land, buildings, hereditary allowances, rights to ways, lights, ferries, fisheries or any other benefit to arise out of land, and things attached to the earth or permanently fastened to anything which is attached to the earth but not standing timber, growing crops nor grass". These, definitions have to be contrasted with the definition of 'Goods' in the Sale of Goods Act, 1930, [S. 2(7)] which reads: "'Goods' means every kind of movable property other than actionable claims and money; and includes stock and shares, growing crops, grass, and things attached to and forming part of the land which are agreed to be severed before sale or under the contract of sale". It has been held that marketability is essential for an article to become 'goods' under section 2(7) of the Sale of Goods Act and section 171 of the Contract Act.[46] The term "attached to earth" is also defined in the Transfer of Property Act, 1882 (S. 3) in the following words: "'Attached to earth' means—(*a*) rooted in earth as in the case of trees and shrubs; *(*b*)* imbedded in the earth, as in the case of walls and buildings; or *(*c*)* attached to what is so imbedded for the permanent beneficial enjoyment of that to which it is attached".

The above definitions actually do not define as to what is immovable property but only state what is included or not included therein.[47] Analysing these definitions HIDAYATULLAH, J. has said: "One thing is clear, that things rooted in the earth as in the case of trees and shrubs, are immovable property both within the General Clauses Act and the Transfer of Property Act, but in the latter 'standing timber', 'growing crop' and 'grass' though rooted in the earth are not included. Of these 'growing crop' and 'grass' form the subject-matter of sale of goods, and 'standing timber' comes within the last part of the definition of 'goods' in the Indian Sale of Goods Act, to be subject thereto if the condition about severing mentioned there in the definition of 'goods' exists."[48]

'Standing timber' according to BOSE, J. is tree in a state fit for building purposes, which is meant to be converted into timber so shortly that it can already be looked upon as timber for all practical purposes even though it

---

46. *R.D. Saxena v. Balaram Prasad,* AIR 2000 SC 2912, p. 2915 : (2000) 7 SCC 264.

47. *Moolla Sons v. Official Assignee, Rangoon*, AIR 1936 PC 230, p. 232; *Mahadeo v. State of Bombay*, AIR 1959 SC 735, p. 740 : 1959 Supp (2) SCR 339.

48. *Mahadeo v. State of Bombay, supra*, p. 740.

is still standing.[49] In case of 'standing timber' as it is to be felled at a reasonably early date, the amount of nourishment that it takes is so negligible that it can be ignored.[50] BOSE, J. has further approved of the following passage from MULLA'S *Transfer of Property Act*:

"'Standing timber' are trees fit for use for buildings or repairing houses. This is an exception to the general rule that growing trees are immovable property."[51]

"Trees and shrubs may be sold apart from the land, to be cut and removed as wood and in that case they are moveable property. But if the transfer includes the right to fell the trees for a term of years so that the transferee derives a benefit from further growth, the transfer is one of immoveable property."[52]

It was, therefore, held by BOSE, J. that a right to enter on land and to fell and remove trees for a term of years was immovable property.[53]

A short-term contract giving the grantees a right to pick and carry away *tendu* leaves and appropriate them as their own property was held by the Privy Council as not conveying any interest in land or trees.[54] Such a contract will amount to a licence.[55]

In *Mahadeo's* case[56] the agreements under consideration conveyed more than the *tendu* leaves to the grantees. They conveyed other forest produce like timber, bamboos etc. the soil for making bricks, the right to prune, coppice and burn *tendu* trees and the right to build on and occupy land for the purpose of the business of the grantees; the rights were spread over for a number of years. It was held that the agreements were not contracts for sale of 'goods' but were grants of proprietary rights.

A '*profit a prendre*' is regarded in India as a benefit that arises out of land and is, therefore, classed as immovable property.[57] A right to catch and carry away fish in specific portions of a lake over a specified future

---

49. *Shantabai v. State of Bombay*, AIR 1958 SC 532, p. 536 : 1959 SCR 265.
50. *Ibid.*
51. *Ibid*, p. 537.
52. *Ibid.*
53. *Ibid.*
54. *Mohanlal Hargovind v. CIT*, AIR 1949 PC 311, p. 312. **See further** *Santosh Jayaswal v. State of M.P.*, 1995 (5) Scale 535 : 1995 (6) SCC 520 : AIR 1996 SC 207.
55. *Board of Revenue v. A.M. Ansari*, AIR 1976 SC 1813 : (1976) 3 SCC 512.
56. *Mahadeo v. State of Bombay, supra*, pp. 740, 742.
57. *Anand Behera v. State of Orissa*, AIR 1956 SC 17 : 1955 (2) SCR 919. Referred to in *State of West Bengal v. Shebaits of Iswar Shri Saradiya Thakurani*, AIR 1971 SC 2097, p. 2100 : 1972 (4) SCC 158.

period was thus held to be immovable property.[58] A right to carry on mineral operations and to extract a specified mineral is immovable property.[59] Right to hold *bazar* is integral to immovable property.[60]

A right in respect of future rents payable in respect of land is a benefit to arise out of land and is immovable property and so is a right in respect of future market dues.[61] Interest of a beneficiary in future rents and profits of land vested in trustees is also immovable property.[62] But arrears of rent or arrears of market dues are benefits that have already arisen out of land, and are, therefore, outside the definition of immovable property.[63]

Just because a plant and machinery are fixed in the earth for better functioning, they do not automatically become immovable property.[64] The question however however whether a machinery embedded in the earth is movable or immovable property will depend on the facts of each case and intention of the parties.[65] Thus it has been held that installation or erection of turbo alternator on platform constructed on land would be immovable property and cannot be 'excisable goods' for it has neither mobility nor marketability as understood in the excise law.[66] Similarly erection and installation of mudguns and tap hole-drilling machines on a specially made concrete platform, brought into existence not excisable goods but an immovable property which could not be shifted without first dismantling and then recrecting it at another site.[67]

---

58. *Ibid*; *Bihar Eastern Gangetic Fisherman Co-operative Society Ltd. v. Sipahi Singh*, AIR 1977 SC 2149 : (1977) 4 SCC 145. **See further** *Mrinalini Roy Ratna Prova Mondal v. State of West Bengal*, AIR 1997 SC 2244 : 1996 (9) Scale 5 : (1997) 9 SCC 113. [Land defined in section 3(a), Land Acquisition Act, 1894 will include tank fisheries].

59. *Tarkeshwar Sio Thakur ju v. Bar Dass Dey & Co.*, AIR 1979 SC 1669, p. 1674 : (1979) 3 SCC 106.

60. *Bibi Sayeeda (Ms.) v. State of Bihar*, AIR 1996 SC 1936, p. 1944 : 1996 (9) SCC 516.

61. *Manglaswami v. Subba Pillai*, (1910) ILR 34 Mad 64, p. 66; **approved** in *Moolla Sons v. Official Assignee, Rangoon*, AIR 1936 PC 230, pp. 233, 234.

62. *Moolla Sons v. Official Assignee, Rangoon*, AIR 1936 PC 230, pp. 234, 235.

63. Case in note 59, *supra*.

64. *Sirpur Paper Mills Ltd. v. Collector of Central Excise*, AIR 1998 SC 1489 : 1998 (1) SCC 400; *Commissioner of Central Excise Ahmedabad v. Solid and Correct Engineering Works*, (2010) 5 SCC 122 para 44.

65. *Duncans Industries Ltd. v. State of U.P.*, JT 1999 (9) SC 421 : AIR 2000 SC 355 : (2000) 1 SCC 633.

66. *Triveni Engineering and Industries Ltd. v. Commissioner of Central Excise*, AIR 2000 SC 2896 : (2000) 7 SCC 29. The case of Sirpur Industries, note 62, *supra*, has been distinguished in the case.

67. *T.T.G. Industries Ltd. Madras v. Collector of Central Excise Raipur*, (2004) 4 SCC 751 (**see also** other cases referred therein).

The interest of a partner in partnership assets consisting also of lands and buildings is not immovable but movable property.[68] Insurance policy is movable property.[69]

It has been held that the office of shebait being a combination of office and property is immovable property.[70]

Lottery tickets are movable property and sale of lottery tickets is sale of goods attracting sales-tax.[71]

Electricity is 'goods' as defined in Article 366(12) of the Constitution and is moveable property, although it cannot be stored.[72] Telephone connection and all accessories which give access to telephone exchange are 'goods'.[73] Canned software has been held to be 'goods' and its sale liable to sales tax under the A.P. Sales Tax Act.[74] Shares in a company before allotment are not goods.[75]

In deciding as to when a chattel because of being imbedded in earth or being attached to a thing which is so imbedded becomes immovable property, the courts in India[76] have generally applied the same principles as those which determine what constitutes a 'fixture' under the English Law; the mode of annexation and the object of annexation are the factors to be taken into account, but the latter is regarded more controlling than the former.[77]

Shares in a cooperative society giving a right to occupy specific premises in a building are immovable property and their transfer amounts to sale of immovable property.[78]

(27) "Imprisonment" shall mean imprisonment of either description as defined in the Indian Penal Code (45 of 1860).

---

68. *Addanki Narayanappa v. Bhaskara Krishnappa*, AIR 1966 SC 1300 : 1966 (3) SCR 400.

69. *Bulchand Chandiram v. Bank of India Ltd.*, AIR 1968 SC 1475 : 1968 (3) SCR 868.

70. *Ram Rattan v. Bajranglal*, AIR 1978 SC 1393 : (1978) 3 SCC 236.

71. *Dipak Dhar v. State of West Bengal*, (1986) 1 SCC 415 : AIR 1986 SC 63. **Also see** section 3(36) and text and notes 19, 20 and 21, p. 1154.

72. *State of A.P. v. National Thermal Corporation Ltd.*, AIR 2002 SC 1895, pp. 1906, 1907 : (2002) 5 SCC 203.

73. *State of Uttar Pradesh v. Union of India*, AIR 2003 SC 1147, p. 1156 : (2003) 3 SCC 239.

74. *Tata Consultancy Services v. State of A.P.*, (2005) 1 SCC 308. **See further**, pp. 898-899.

75. *R.D. Goyal v. Reliance Industries Ltd.*, (2003) 1 SCC 81 : (2003) 113 Comp Cas 1.

76. **See** MULLA, Transfer of Property Act, 3rd Edition, p. 22.

77. HALSBURY, Laws of England, 3rd Edition, Vol. 23, pp. 490-94.

78. *Hanuman Vitamin Foods (P) Ltd. v. State of Maharashtra*, JT 2000 (8) SC 65 : AIR 2000 SC 2571 : (2000) 6 SCC 345.

(28) "India" shall mean,—

(*a*) as respects any period before the establishment of the Dominion of India, British India, together with all territories of Indian Rulers then under the suzerainty of His Majesty, all territories under the suzerainty of such an Indian Ruler, and the tribal areas;

(*b*) as respects any period after the establishment of the Dominion of India and before the commencement of the Constitution, all territories for the time being included in that Dominion; and

(*c*) as respects any period after the commencement of the Constitutions all territories for the time being comprised in the territory of India.

NOTES

By Article 1(3) of the Constitution the territory of India comprises of (*a*) the territories of the States, (*b*) the Union territories specified in the First Schedule, and (*c*) such other territories as may be acquired.

It has been ruled by the Supreme Court that the national territory cannot be ceded in favour of a foreign State by executive action and that legislative action is required for that purpose.[79] Cession of a territory by a Constitution Amendment Act which is to come into force on the appointed date does not become effective unless the Act is brought into force by appointing a date.[80]

In the absence of any public declaration by the Central Government, the question whether a particular territory is a part of Indian territory under Article 1(3)(*c*) of the Constitution, will have to be answered by courts by seeking information from the Central Government.[81] A territory which is not Indian territory under Article 1(3) may yet be administered by the Central Government under the Foreign Jurisdiction Act, 1947.[82]

It has been held that on a change of sovereignty over any particular territory the laws in force therein are not automatically abrogated and they

---

79. *Reference by President of India under Article 143(1), Constitution*, AIR 1960 SC 845 : 1960 (3) SCR 250. As suggested by the Supreme Court, Constitution (Ninth Amendment) Act, 1960, was passed by Parliament to implement Indo-Pakistan agreements. **See further** *Ram Kishore Sen v. Union of India*, AIR 1966 SC 644 : 1966 (1) SCR 430.

80. *Union of India v. Sukumar Sen Gupta*, AIR 1990 SC 1692 : 1990 (3) SCR 24 : 1990 Supp SCC 545.

81. *Masthan Sahib v. Chief Commissioner, Pondicherry*, AIR 1963 SC 533; AIR 1962 SC 797 (answer of the Central Government on the question is final and binding on courts).

82. *Ibid.*

remain operative until modified or repealed by the new sovereign.[83] This is subject to the qualification that inhabitants of such a territory cannot enforce any rights against the new sovereign except those which are expressly or impliedly recognised by the new sovereign—a contrary provision in any treaty notwithstanding.[84] This qualification has no application when a new State is formed by legislation by adjustment of territories within the framework of the Constitution.[85]

Territories of States did not get frozen on 26th January 1950, when the Constitution came into force, for Article 3 confers power on Parliament to make changes in the territories of the States.[86] When there is reorganisation of states or change of territories between two states, a provision is generally made to continue the existing laws in the affected territories until altered by the competent legislature.[87]

When a new territory becomes a territory of India under Article 1(3)(*c*), the Constitution will automatically extend to such a territory, the inhabitants of which will then get the rights conferred by the Constitution.

---

83. *Mayor of Lyons v. East India Co.*, 1 MIA 175, pp. 270, 272; *Shiv Bahadur Singh v. State of V.P.*, AIR 1953 SC 394, p. 400 (para 16) : 1953 SCR 1188.

84. *Vajesinghji v. Secretary of State*, AIR 1924 PC 216; *Secretary of State v. Rustam Khan*, AIR 1941 PC 64; *Dalmia Dadri Cement Co. Ltd. v. CIT*, AIR 1958 SC 816, p. 833 : 1959 SCR 729; *State of Gujarat v. Vora Fiddali*, AIR 1964 SC 1043, pp. 1062, 1063 : 1964 (6) SCR 461; *Pema Chibar v. Union of India*, AIR 1966 SC 442 : 1966 (1) SCR 357. Recognition by the new Sovereign may be express or implied; *State of Gujarat v. Vora Fiddali, supra*, p. 1063 (para 52-58, 59); *Amar Chand Butail v. Union of India*, AIR 1964 SC 1658 : 67 Punj LR 90. Recognition may be by continuing the laws of ex-Sovereign under which rights are founded; *Bholanath v. State of Saurashtra*, AIR 1954 SC 680 : 1955 (1) LLJ 355; *Madhorao Phalke v. State of M.P.*, AIR 1961 SC 298 : 1961 (1) SCR 957; *Promod Chandra Deb v. State of Orissa*, AIR 1962 SC 1288 : 1962 Supp (1) SCR 405; *State of Rajasthan v. Shyamlal*, AIR 1964 SC 1495 : 1964 (7) SCR 174; **but see** *Pema Chibar v. Union of India, supra*. Covenant or treaty may be looked into for explaining and understanding the alleged acts of recognition; *Bholanath v. State of Saurashtra, supra*; *State of Rajasthan v. Shyamlal, supra*. These principles apply even to ex-Rulers and their successors; *Amar Singhji v. State of Rajasthan*, AIR 1955 SC 504, p. 523 : (1955) 2 SCR 303; *Bhawani Shanker v. Somsundaram*, AIR 1965 SC 316 : (1963) 2 SCR 421; *Raja Jogendra Singh v. State of U.P.*, 1961 SCN 118; *Oyekan v. Adele*, (1957) 2 All ER 785 (PC). **See further** *Vinod Kumar Shantilal Gosalia v. Gangadhar Narsingdas Agarwal*, AIR 1981 SC 1946 : (1981) 4 SCC 226; *State of Haryana v. Amar Nath Bansal*, AIR 1997 SC 718, p. 723 : (1955) 2 SCR 734 : (1997) 10 SCC 700.

85. *State of Punjab v. Balbir Singh*, AIR 1977 SC 629, p. 636 : (1976) 3 SCC 242; **see further** *Commissioner of Commercial Taxes v. Swarn Rekha Cokes*, (2004) 6 SCC 689, pp. 704, 705 : AIR 2004 SC 3380.

86. *Ram Badan Rai v. Union of India*, AIR 1999 SC 166, p. 175 : (1999) 1 SCC 705.

87. *Ibid* p. 178.

Further, the Constitution will have the effect of abrogating all laws till then in force which are inconsistent with its provisions. Besides the extension of the Constitution, laws of the Republic which are expressed to extend to the whole of 'India' may also automatically extend to a new territory which becomes part of the territory of India, for as defined in the General Clauses Act "'India' shall mean all territories for the time being comprised in the territory of India".[88] By way of analogy a law or notification applying to all municipalities will also apply to a municipality which is subsequently constituted.[89]

(29) "Indian law" shall mean any Act, Ordinance, Regulation rule, [90][order, bye-law or other instrument] which, before the commencement of the Constitution, had the force of law in any Province of India or part thereof, or thereafter, has the force of law in any Part A State or Part C State or part thereof, but does not include any Act of Parliament of the United Kingdom or any Order in Council, rule or other instrument made under such Act;

NOTES

Compare Article 366(10), Constitution of India which defines, 'existing law' and Article 372 which continues all the 'law in force'.

There is no material difference between the expressions 'existing law', 'law in force' and 'Indian law'.[91]

Orders and notifications to have the force of law must be legislative in nature.[92] Administrative rules not being 'law in force' are not continued by Article 372 of the Constitution.[93]

---

88. **Cf.** *Post Office v. Estuary Radio Ltd.* (1967) 3 All ER 663; Acts extending to United Kingdom will apply to all territories which may for the time being be included within it rather than to the precise area which was United kingdom at the time when the Act was passed.

89. *Nandlal v. Motilal*, AIR 1977 SC 2143 : (1977) 3 SCC 500.

90. Subs. by the Adaptation of Laws (Amendment) Order, 1950, for the words "order or bye-law".

91. *Edward Mills Co. v. State of Ajmer*, AIR 1955 SC 25, p. 31 : 1955 (1) SCR 735 ; *Madhorao v. State of M.P.*, AIR 1961 SC 298, p. 302 : 1961 (1) SCR 957.

92. *Edward Mills Co. v. State of Ajmer, supra*, p. 31; *Jayantilal Amritlal v. F.N. Rana*, AIR 1964 SC 648, pp. 654-58 : (1994) 5 SCR 294. Distinction between, legislative administrative and Judicial orders pointed out in *Union of India v. Cynamide India Ltd.*, (1987) 2 SCC 720, pp. 735, 736 : AIR 1987 SC 1802, which holds that price fixation is a legislative activity.

93. *Union of India v. Majji Jangammayya*, AIR 1977 SC 757, p. 767 : (1977) 1 SCC 606; *Ajay Kumar Bhuyan v. State of Orissa*, (2003) 1 SCC 707, p. 720 : 2003 SCC (L&S) 124.

A notification issued by the State Government imposing tax in exercise of a statutory power is law.[1]

Notifications issued under Statutory powers exempting certain matters from the general provisions of the statute are legislative in nature and have the effect of law.[2]

A notification or order fixing price of commodities in exercise of a statutory power is also legislative in nature.[3]

A notification declaring that certain place shall be principal market yard under the relevant Agricultural Produce Market Act is legislative in nature[4] and so is a notification constituting a Gram Panchayat or a Gram Sabha under a Panchayat Raj Act.[5]

An order made by the Governor-General under section 94(3) of the Government of India Act, 1935, investing the Chief Commissioner with the authority to administer a Province was held to be law.[6]

A notification issued by the President delegating certain executive functions under Article 258(1) of the Constitution amounts to law.[7]

Orders made by the Delimitation Commission under sections 8 and 9 of the Delimitation Commission Act, 1962, have the force of law as section 10 of the Act so declares.[8]

---

1. *Kalyani Stores v. State of Orissa*, AIR 1966 SC 1686 : 1966 (1) SCR 865.
2. *State of Bombay v. F.N. Balsara*, AIR 1951 SC 318, p. 329 : 1951 SCR 682; *Kailash Nath v. State of U.P.*, AIR 1957 SC 790, p. 791 : (1957) 8 STC 358; *K.N. Chikkaputtaswamy v. State of A.P.*, (1985) 3 SCC 387 : AIR 1985 SC 956; *Video Electronics Pvt. Ltd. v. State of Punjab*, AIR 1990 SC 820, p. 835 : 1990 (3) SCC 87; *Commissioner of Commercial Taxes v. M/s. Swarn Rekha Cokes and Coal Pvt. Ltd.*, AIR 2004 SC 3380 : (2004) 6 SCC 689.
3. *H.S.S.K. Niyami v. Union of India*, AIR 1990 SC 2128 : 1990 (4) SCC 516; *Union of India v. Cynamide India Ltd., supra*; *West Bengal Electricity Regulatory Commission v. C.E.S.C. Ltd.*, AIR 2002 SC 3588, p. 3600 : (2002) 8 SCC 715 (fixation of electricity tariff); *Mahalakshmi Sugar Mills Co. Ltd. v. Union of India*, AIR 2009 SC 792 para 45 : (2008) 6 JT 177 (Determination of price of levy sugar in terms of provisions of section 3(3-C) of the Essential Commodities Act, 1955 is a legislative function).
4. *Rameshchandra v. State of Maharashtra,* (1981) 2 SCC 722 : AIR 1981 SC 1127.
5. *State of Punjab v. Tehal Singh,* AIR 2002 SC 533 : (2002) 2 SCC 7.
6. *Edward Mills Co. v. State of Ajmer, supra*, p. 31.
7. *Jayantilal Amritalal v. F.N. Rana, supra*, pp. 657, 658.
8. *Meghraj Kothari v. Delimitation Commission*, AIR 1967 SC 669, p. 676 : 1967 (1) SCR 400.

It has been held that Article 372 of the Constitution continues only such orders of the Rulers of erstwhile Indian States which were legislative in nature.[9]

"Laws in force" continued by Article 372 of the Constitution include not only statutory laws but also usage and custom having the force of law and rules of common law in force in India.[10] A rule of construction is however, not a 'law in force' within the meaning of Article 372 of the Constitution.[11] Further, Article 372 does not make pre-constitution statutory provision constitutional which may be declared void under Article 13 of the Constitution.[12]

(30) "Indian State" shall mean any territory which the Central Government recognised as such a State before the commencement of the Constitution, whether described as a State, an Estate, a Jagir or otherwise;

(31) "local authority" shall mean a municipal committee, district board, body of port commissioners or other authority legally entitled to, or entrusted by the Government with, the control or management of a municipal or local fund;

NOTES

State Transport Corporation is not a local authority within the definition of that expression in the General Clauses, Act.[13]

---

9. *Umaid Mills v. Union of India*, AIR 1963 SC 953 : 1963 Supp (2) SCR 515; *Bengal Nagpur Cotton Mills v. Board of Revenue*, AIR 1964 SC 888 : (1964) 4 SCR 190; *State of Gujarat v. Vora Fiddali*, AIR 1964 SC 1043 : 1964 (6) SCR 461; *Narsingh Pratap Singh Deo v. State of Orissa*, AIR 1964 SC 1793 : 1964 (7) SCR 112; *Union of India v. Gwalior Rayons*, AIR 1964 SC 1903 : 1964 (7) SCR 892; *State of M.P. v. Lal Bhargavendra Singh*, AIR 1966 SC 704 : 1966 (2) SCR 56; *State of M.P. v. Rampal Singh (Col.)*, 1965 SCN 347; *State of M.P. v. Kunwar Narendra Singh*, 1965 SCN 348; *Maharajadhiraj Himmat Singh v. State of Rajasthan*, (1987) 1 SCC 52 : AIR 1987 SC 82; *Tej Singh Rao v. State of Maharashtra*, AIR 1993 SC 1227 : 1992 Supp (2) SCC 554 : 1992 (4) JT 520; *State of Sikkim v. Surendra Prasad Sharma*, JT 1994 (3) SC 372, p. 384 : AIR 1994 SC 2342. **See also** *Madhorao v. State of M.P.*, AIR 1961 SC 298 : 1961 (1) SCR 957; *Promod Chandra Deo v. State of Orissa*, AIR 1962 SC 1288 : 1962 Supp (1) SCR 405; *Nandlal v. State of M.P.*, AIR 1963 SC 332 : 1962 (2) SCR 859; *Tilkayat Shri Govandlalji v. State of Rajasthan*, AIR 1963 SC 1638 : 1964 (1) SCR 561; *Faqruddin v. Tajuddin*, (2008) 8 SCC 12 para 38 : (2008) 9 JT 37.

10. *Builders Supply Corporation v. Union of India*, AIR 1965 SC 1061, p. 1068 : 1965 (2) SCR 289; *Dena Bank v. Bhikabai Parekh & Co.*, AIR 2000 SC 3654 : (2000) 5 SCC 494. (These cases hold that the common law rule of priority of crown debts continues to be in force in India and State debts have priority over other unsecured debts.)

11. *Superintendent and Remembrancer of Legal Affairs, West Bengal v. Corporation of Calcutta*, AIR 1967 SC 997 : 1967 (2) SCR 170.

12. *John Vallamattam v. Union of India*, AIR 2003 SC 2902 : (2003) 6 SCC 611.

13. *Valjibhai v. State of Bombay*, AIR 1963 SC 1890, p. 1894 : 1964 (3) SCR 686; *Calcutta State Transport Corporation v. Commissioner of Income-tax*, AIR 1996 SC

[Footnote No. 13 Contd.]

The phrase 'local area' has also a technical meaning. It means an area administered by a local body like a municipality, a district board, a union board, a *panchayat* or the like.[14] A 'local area' does not cease to be local area simply because it is declared to be 'industrial area' under Industrial Area Development Act.[15]

The word 'Municipality' has also been widely construed to include a Municipal Corporation.[16]

The definition of 'Local Authority in Section 3(31) cannot be used for construing another Act which has its own definition of 'Local Authority' which though similar is not identical. Section 10(20) of the Income Tax Act, 1961 before its amendment by the Finance Act, 2002 did not contain any definition of 'Local Authority' and the definition in Section 3(31) of the General Clauses Act was used for holding that Agricultural Marketing Committee is a local authority. But after amendment in 2002 an explanation was added to Section 10(20) of the Income Tax Act defining the expression 'Local Authority' which is similar to Section 3(31) but not identical as it omits the words 'or other authority' as they find place in Section 3(31). Because of this change after the amendment Agriculture Marketing Committee was not held to be a local authority for purposes of Section 10(20) of the 1961, Act.[17]

(32) "Magistrate" shall include every person exercising all or any of the powers of the Magistrate under the Code of Criminal Procedure for the time being in force;

(33) "master" used with reference to a ship, shall mean any person (except a pilot or harbour-master) having for the time being control or charge of the ship;

(34) "merged territories" shall mean the territories which by virtue of an order made under section 290-A of the Government of India Act, 1935,

---

[Footnote No. 13 Contd.]

1316 : 1996 (8) SCC 758. **See further** Haryana Housing Board is not a local authority: *Housing Board of Haryana v. Haryana Housing Board Employees Union*, 1995 (6) Scale 139: AIR 1996 SC 434. Delhi Development Authority has been held to be a local authority: *Union of India v. R.C. Jain*, 1981 (2) SCC 308 : AIR 1981 SC 951. A university has been held to be a local authority: *Kashi Vidyapith v. Motilal*, AIR 1996 SC 2705 : 1996 (10) SCC 456.

14. *Diamond Sugar Mills v. State of U.P.*, AIR 1961 SC 652 : 1961 (3) SCR 242.

15. *Widia (India) Ltd. v. State of Karnataka,* (2003) 8 SCC 22, p. 34 : AIR 2003 SC 3095.

16. *Cantonment Board, Secunderabad v. G. Venketram Reddy*, 1995 (2) Scale 507, p. 508 : AIR 1995 SC 1210 : (1995) 4 SCC 561.

17. *Agricultural Produce Market Committee v. Commissioner of Income Tax*, (2008) 9 SCC 434 paras 29 to 31, 42 : (2008) 10 JT 17.

were immediately before the commencement of the Constitution being administered as if they formed part of Governor's Province or as if they were a Chief Commissioner's Province;

(35) "month" shall mean a month reckoned according to the British calendar;[18]

(36) "movable property" shall mean property of every description, except immovable property;

NOTES

A lottery ticket[19] and a REP import licence[20] were held to constitute moveable property and 'goods' and so their sales could be subjected to sales tax. In *H. Anraj v. Government of Tamil Nadu,* [16] the reasoning was that sale of a lottery ticket confers on the purchaser two rights (a) the right to participate in the draw and (b) the right to claim a prize contingent on the purchaser being successful in the draw. Both were held to be beneficial interest in the moveable property, the first in *presenti* and the latter in future and therefore the sale of lottery ticket so far as the first right was concerned was held to be sale of goods whereas to the extent it was a sale of the second right it was a sale of actionable claim and not of goods. In *Sunrise Associates v. Govt. of NCT Delhi,*[21] where *Anraj* was overruled it was held that the right to participate in the draw is a part of the composite right of the chance to win and is its inseparable part and the two cannot be separated as was done in *Anraj*. There is no value in the mere right to participate in the draw and the purchaser of lottery ticket does not pay for the right to participate and the consideration is paid for right to win

18. **See** *Athanassiadis v. Government of Greece*, (1969) 3 All ER 293, pp. 297, 298 (HL); If the Interpretation Act does not apply to a case, the question whether 'month' means 'Lunar month' or 'Calendar month' would depend on intention; under common law probably it meant Lunar Month. **See further** *Dodds v. Walker*, (1981) 2 All ER 609 (HL) (In calculating the period of a month or a specified number of months that had elapsed after the occurrence of a specified event, such as the giving of a notice, the general rule is that the period ends on the corresponding date in the appropriate subsequent month irrespective of whether some months are longer than others. If the month in which the period expires has no corresponding date because it is too short, the period given by the notice ends on the last day of that month); *Bibi Salma Khatoon v. State of Bihar,* AIR 2001 SC 3596, p. 3597 : (2001) 7 SCC 197 (same view as in *Dodds v. Walker supra*).
19. *H. Anraj v. Govt. of Tamil Nadu*, 1985 Supp (3) SCR 342 : (1986) 1 SCC 414 : AIR 1986 SC 63.
20. *Vikas Sales Corporation v. Commissioner of Commercial Taxes*, AIR 1996 SC 2082 : 1996 (4) SCC 433.
21. *Sunrise Associates v. Govt. of NCT Delhi,* AIR 2006 SC 1908 : (2006) 5 SCC 603.

and the two rights are inseparable. The sale of lottery ticket is, therefore, a sale of actionable claim and not sale of goods. It may be mentioned here that both these cases were decided in the context of sales tax laws. The definition of goods in the sale of goods Act and in all state statutes relating to sales tax excludes actionable claim. It has been held that the constitution bench decision in *Sunrise Corpn.* has in no way affected the decision in *Vikas Corpn.* that Replenishment licences [REP licences] granted under Import Export policy are goods and their sale can be subjected to sales tax.[22] Duty Entitlement pass book contemplated in Exim Policy formulated under Foreign Trade (Development and Regulation) Act, 1992 is not materially different from REP licence. It has an intrinsic value that makes it a marketable commodity and it qualifies as goods and its sale is exigible to sales tax.[23] **See further** notes below section 3(26), *supra*.

(37) "oath" shall include affirmation and declaration in the case of persons by law allowed to affirm or declare instead of swearing;

(38) "offence" shall mean any act or omission made punishable by any law for the time being in force;

(39) "official Gazette" or "Gazette" shall mean the Gazette of India or the official Gazette of a State;

(40) "Part" shall mean a part of the Act or Regulation in which the word occurs;

(41) "Part A State" shall mean a State for the time being specified in Part A of the First Schedule to the Constitution, [24][as in force before the Constitution (Seventh Amendment) Act, 1956], "Part B State" shall mean a State for the time being specified in Part B of that Schedule and "Part C State" shall mean a State for the time being specified in Part C of that Schedule or a territory for the time being administered by the President under the provisions of Article 243 of the Constitution;

(42) "person" shall include any company or association or body of individuals, whether incorporated or not;

---

22. *Yasha Overseas v. Commissioner of Sales Tax*, (2008) 8 SCC 681 para 43 : (2008) 7 Scale 117.

23. *Ibid* paras 59, 62.

24. Ins. by Adaptation of Laws (No. 1) Order, 1956.

NOTES

The word 'person' has been defined in a very wide sense. But in any particular statute the meaning of the word may get controlled by the context.[25]

Person will include a juristic person e.g. an idol or gurugranth sahab installed in a public temple[26] or a company.[27]

'Person' will also include a local authority and contrary intention cannot be inferred simply from the fact that the draftsman after using the word 'person' uses the pronoun 'him'.[28]

Section 42(b) of the Rajasthan Tenancy Act, 1955, provides that the sale, gift or bequest by a khatedar tenant of his interest in the whole or part of his holding shall be void, if such sale, gift or bequest is by a member of a Scheduled Caste or Scheduled Tribe in favour of a "person" who is not a member of the Scheduled Caste or Scheduled Tribe respectively. The Supreme Court, refused to apply the definition of "person" under section 3(42) of the General Clauses Act while interpreting section 42(b) of the Rajasthan Act, and instead read it along with the constitutional provisions to mean a person other than those who have been included in the public notification as per Articles 341 and 342 of the Constitution. Accordingly, it was held that the expression "person" used in section 42(b) can only mean a natural person and not a juristic person, as otherwise the entire purpose of that section would be defeated.[29]

(43) "Political Agent" shall mean,—

(*a*) in relation to any territory outside India, the Principal Officer, by whatever name called, representing the Central Government in such territory; and

(*b*) in relation to any territory within India to which the Act or Regulation containing the expression does not extend, any officer appointed by the Central Government to exercise all or any of the powers of a Political Agent under that Act or Regulation;

---

25. *Dulichand v. CIT*, AIR 1956 SC 354 : 1956 SCR 154.

26. *Shromani Gurudwara Prabandhak Committee Amritsar v. Shri Som Nath Dass,* AIR 2000 SC 1421 : (2000) 4 SCC 146.

27. *Union Bank of India v. Khader International Construction,* AIR 2001 SC 2277 : (2001) 5 SCC 22.

28. *Applin v. Race Relations Board*, (1974) 2 All ER 73, pp. 92, 93 : (1974) 2 WLR 541 (HL).

29. *State of Rajasthan & Ors. v. Aanjaney Organic Herbal Pvt. Ltd.*, (2012) 10 SCC 283, pp. 286, 287.

(44) "Presidency-town" shall mean the local limits for the time being of the ordinary original civil jurisdiction of the High Court of Judicature, at Calcutta, Madras or Bombay, as the case may be;

(45) "Province" shall mean a Presidency, a Governor's Province, a Lieutenant-Governor's Province or a Chief Commissioner's Province;

(46) "Provincial Act" shall mean an Act made by the Governor-in-Council, Lieutenant Governor-in-Council or Chief Commissioner in Council of a Province under any of the Indian Councils Acts or the Government of India Act, 1915, as an Act made by the local Legislature or the Governor of a Province under the Government of India Act, or an Act made by the Provincial Legislature or Governor of a Province or the Coorg Legislative Council under the Government of India Act, 1935;

(47) "Provincial Government" shall mean, as respects anything done before the commencement of the Constitution the authority or person authorised at the relevant date to administer executive Government in the Province in question;

(48) "public nuisance" shall mean a public nuisance as defined in the Indian Penal Code, 1860 (Act 45 of 1860);

(49) "registered" used with reference to a document, shall mean registered in [30][India] under the law for the time being in force for the registration of documents;

(50) "Regulation" shall mean a Regulation made by the President [31][under Article 240 of the Constitution and shall include a Regulation made by the President under Article 243 thereof and] a Regulation made by the Central Government under the Government of India Act, 1870, or the Government of India Act, 1915, or the Government of India Act, 1935;

(51) "rule" shall mean a rule made in exercise of a power conferred by any enactment, and shall include a regulation made as a rule under any enactment;

(52) "schedule" shall mean a Schedule to the Act or Regulation in which the word occurs;

(53) "Scheduled District" shall mean a Scheduled District as defined in the Scheduled Districts Act, 1874;

---

30. Subs. by Adaptation of Laws (No. 1) Order, 1956, for "a Part A State or a Part C State".

31. Subs. by *ibid*, for "under Article 243 of the Constitution, and shall include".

(54) "section" shall mean a section of the Act or Regulation in which the word occurs;[32]

(55) "ship" shall include every description of vessel used in navigation not exclusively propelled by oars;

(56) "sign", with its grammatical variations and cognate expressions; shall with reference to a person who is unable to write his name, include "mark" with its grammatical variations and cognate expressions;

NOTES

The essential requirement of signing is the affixing, either by writing with a pen or pencil or by otherwise impressing upon the document one's name or signature so as personally to authenticate the document.[33] Unless the statute concerned indicates otherwise,[34] a signature duly authorised by a person affixed to a document by another person is the signature of the person giving the authority.[35] The received fax of a duly signed document transmitted by fax may itself amount to a duly signed document.[36] But when the statute requires that the person concerned must sign himself as in the case of attestation under section 63 of the Succession Act, delegation of that function is not permissible.[37]

(57) "son" in the case of any one whose personal law permits adoption, shall include an adopted son;[38]

[39][(58) "State"—

(*a*) as respects any period before the commencement of the Constitution (Seventh Amendment) Act, 1956, shall mean a Part A State, a Part B State or a Part C State; and

(*b*) as respects any period after such commencement, shall mean a State specified in the First Schedule to the Constitution and shall include a Union territory];

---

32. *Prabodh Verma v. State of U.P.*, (1984) 4 SCC 251, p. 267 : AIR 1985 SC 167.
33. *Goodman v. J. Eban Ltd.*, (1954) 1 All ER 763, p. 766 (CA).
34. *CIT (Agr.), W. B. v. Keshab Chandra Mandal,* AIR 1950 SC 265 : 1950 SCR 435.
35. *Morrow v. Nadeem*, (1987) 1 All ER 237, p. 243 : (1986) 1 WLR 1381 (CA).
36. *Re, A debtor (No. 2021 of 1955), ex parte, Inland Revenue Commissioners v. The debtor*, (1996) 2 All ER 345.
37. *Nagulapati Lakshmamma v. Mupparaju Subbaiah*, 1998 (2) Scale 705, pp. 710, 711: AIR 1998 SC 2904 : (1998) 5 SCC 285.
38. *K.V. Muthu v. Angamuthu Ammal,* AIR 1997 SC 628, p. 632 : 1997 (2) SCC 53 ('Son' is a flexible term and may not be limited to direct descendant).
39. Subs. by Adaptation of Laws (No. 1) Order, 1956, for clause (58).

NOTES

The Adaptation Order by which the definition of 'State' in the present form was substituted, is valid.[40] As a result of this definition the word 'State' occurring in Article 3[41] and Entry 80, List 1[42], of the Constitution includes a Union territory. However, the word 'State' as used in Article 246 of the Constitution does not include a Union territory[43] as the context of that Article makes the definition in the General Clauses Act inapplicable.

(59) "State Act" shall mean Act passed by the Legislature of a State established or continued by the Constitution;

(60) "State Government"—

(*a*) as respect anything done before the commencement of the Constitution, shall mean, in a Part A State, the Provincial Government of the corresponding Province, in a Part B State, the authority or person authorised at the relevant date to exercise executive Government in the corresponding acceding State, and in a Part C State, the Central Government; [44][* * *]

(*b*) as respects anything done [45][after the commencement of the Constitution and before the commencement of the Constitution (Seventh Amendment) Act, 1956], shall mean, in a Part A State, the Governor, in a Part B State, the Rajpramukh, and in a Part C State, the Central Government;

[46][(*c*) as respects anything done or to be done after the commencement of the Constitution (Seventh Amendment) Act, 1956, shall mean in a State, the Governor and in a Union territory, the Central Government;[47]

and shall in relation to functions entrusted under Article 258-A of the Constitution to the Government of India, include the Central Government acting within the scope of the authority given to it under that Article];

---

40. *Management of Advance Insurance Co. Ltd. v. Gurudasmal*, AIR 1970 SC 1126, p. 1131 : (1969) 1 SCC 633.
41. *Ram Kishore Sen v. Union of India*, AIR 1966 SC 644, p. 648 : 1966 (1) SCR 643.
42. *Management of Advance Insurance Co. Ltd. v. Gurudasmal, supra.*
43. *T.M. Kanniyan v. ITO*, AIR 1968 SC 637, p. 641 : 1968 (2) SCR 103.
44. The word "and" deleted by Adaptation of Laws (No. 1) Order, 1956..
45. Subs. *ibid*, for "or to be done after the commencement of the Constitution."
46. Ins. by Adaptation of Laws (No. 1) Order, 1956.
47. *Goa Sampling Employees Association v. General Superientendence Co. of India*, (1985) 1 SCC 206 : AIR 1985 SC 357.

NOTES

The executive power of a State under the Constitution is vested in the Governor,[48] who is aided and advised in the exercise of his functions by a Council of Ministers.[49] There are certain matters enumerated in the Constitution where the Governor has to act in his discretion. These are Articles 239(2), 356, 371-A(2)(b), 371-A(2)(f), and paras 9(2) and 18(3) of the sixth schedule.[50] In addition, the Governor acts in his discretion in the choice of Chief Minister and the dismissal of a Government which has lost majority but refuses to quit.[51] Further, he may act independently in the matter of grant of sanction of prosecution against the Chief Minister or any minister as in these matters there would be real danger of bias in the opinion rendered by the council of ministers[52] and even in the case of grant of sanction to prosecute an ex-minister when the decision of the council of ministers is shown to be irrational and based on non-consideration of relevant factors.[53] Executive action of the Government of a State is transacted in accordance with the rules of business made by the Governor which allocate among Ministers the business of the Government.[54] But all executive action is expressed to be taken in the name of the Governor and orders and instruments made and executed in the name of the Governor are authenticated in accordance with the rules made by the Governor.[55] The executive power of a State extends to matters with respect to which the State Legislature has power to make laws (Article 162). But the executive power cannot be used to amend or to supersede or to whittle down the effect of a statute or statutory rules; the executive power can be used only to supplement a statute or rules and cover areas to which the statute or rules do not extend.[56] Even a statutory power of the government to issue directions on

---

48. Article 154 of the Constitution.

49. Article 163, *ibid*; *Samsher Singh v. State of Punjab*, AIR 1974 SC 2192 : 1974 (2) SCC 831; *Pumyllai Hlychho v. State of Mizoram*, (2005) 2 SCC 92, p. 99 : (2005) 1 JT 263 : AIR 2005 SC 1537.

50. *Samsher Singh v. State of Punjab, (supra)*, (**see** para 54, p. 848).

51. *Ibid*, (**see** para 154, p. 885).

52. *State of Maharashtra v. Ramdas Shriniwas Nayak*, (1982) 2 SCC 463, p. 469 (paras 10, 11) : AIR 1982 SC 1249; *M.P. Special Police Establishment v. State of M.P.*, (2004) 8 SCC 788, pp. 799, 800.

53. *M.P. Special Police Establishment v. State of M.P., (supra)*, p. 806 (para 33).

54. Article 166(3) *ibid.*
In case of new legislation on a subject allocated to a Minister under the rules of business, no fresh allocation of business is necessary; **See** *Godavari v. State of Maharashtra*, AIR 1964 SC 1128, p. 1134 : 1964 (6) SCR 446.

55. Article 166(1) and (2), Constitution of India.

56. *Sant Ram Sharma v. State of Rajasthan*, AIR 1967 SC 1910 : (1968) 1 SCR 111; *State of M.P. v. G.S. Dall & Flour Mills*, 1992 Supp (1) SCC 150 : AIR 1991 SC 772; *DDA v. JO Ginder S. Monga*, (2004) 2 SCC 297, p. 314 : (2004) 10 scale 707; *Union of India v. Central Electrical and Mechanical Engg. Service Ass. C.P.W.D.*, (2008) 1 SCC 354 para 10 : AIR 2008 SC 3; *Manoharan v. Union of India*, (2008) 3 SCC 641 paras 22 to 24 : (2008) 2 Scale 616.

matters of policy cannot be used to amend statutory rules and regulations.[57] A code of conduct issued by the State Government for observance by ministers, not issued under any statute or statutory rule, is not enforceable as law and a minister acting in breach of such a code cannot be said to have acted *unlawfully* under section 169 of the Penal Code.[58] A statute may, however, confer upon the Governor functions in a capacity other than as a Head of State, in which case the Governor will exercise such statutory authority according to his own judgment and not on the aid and advice of his council of ministers.[59]

(61) "sub-section" shall mean a sub-section of the section in which the word occurs;[60]

(62) "swear" with its grammatical variations and cognate expressions, shall include affirming and declaring in the case of persons by law allowed to affirm or declare instead of swearing;

[61][(62-A) "Union territory" shall mean any Union territory specified in the First Schedule to the Constitution and shall include any other territory comprised within the territory of India but not specified in that Schedule];

The Union Territories though administered by the Central Government under Article 239 do not get merged with the Central Government and lose their identity.[62]

(63) "vessel" shall include any ship or boat or any other description of vessel used in navigation;

(64) "will" shall include a codicil and every writing making a voluntary posthumous disposition of property;

(65) expressions referring to "writing" shall be construed as including references to printing, lithography, photography and other modes of representing or reproducing words in a visible form; and

---

57. *A. Manoharan v. Union of India*, (2008) 3 SCC 641 para 24 : (2008) 2 Scale 616.

58. *R. Sai Bharathi v. J. Jayalalitha*, (2004) 2 SCC 9, pp. 50 to 53 : AIR 2004 SC 692; *Punjab Water Supply & Sewerage Board v. Ranjodh Singh*, (2007) 2 SCC 491 : AIR 2007 SC 1082.

59. *Bhuri Nath v. State of Jammu and Kashmir*, AIR 1997 SC 1711, p. 1723 : 1997 (2) SCC 745.

60. *Prabodh Verma v. State of U.P.*, (1984) 4 SCC 251, p. 266 : AIR 1985 SC 167.

61. Ins. by Adaptation of Laws (No. 1) Order, 1956.

62. *Government of NCT Delhi v. All India Central Civil Accounts, JAO's Association*, AIR 2001 SC 3090 p. 3093 : (2002) 1 SCC 344; *Chandigarh Administration v. Surinder Kumar*, (2004) 1 SCC 530 : AIR 2004 SC 992.

(66) "year" shall mean a year reckoned according to the British calendar.]

NOTES

For general principles relating to interpretation of definition sections—*see* Chapter 3, title (7)—"Definition Sections or Interpretation Clauses".

S. 4. Application of foregoing definitions to previous enactments.— (1) The definition in section 3 of the following words and expressions, that is to say, "affidavit", "barrister", "District Judge", "father", "immovable property", "imprisonment", "Magistrate", "month", "movable property", "oath", "person", "section", "son", "swear", "will" and "year", apply also, unless there is anything repugnant in the subject and context, to all Central Acts made after the third day of January, 1868, and to all Regulations made on or after the fourteenth day of January, 1887.

(2) The definitions in the said section of the following words and expressions, that is to say, "abet", "Chapter", "commencement", "financial year", "local authority", "master", "offence", "part", "public nuisance", "registered", "schedule", "ship", "sign", "sub-section", and "writing", apply also, unless there is anything repugnant in the subject or context, to all [63][Central Acts] and Regulations made on or after the fourteenth day of January, 1887.

[64]**[S. 4-A. Application of certain definitions to Indian Laws.—**(1) The definition in section 3 of the expressions "British India", "Central Act", "Central Government", "Chief Controlling Revenue Authority", "Chief Revenue Authority," "constitution", "Gazette", "Government", "Government securities", "High Court", "India", "Indian law", "Indian State", "merged territories", "Official Gazette", "Part A State", "Part B State", "Part C State", "Provincial Government", "State", and "State Government", shall apply, unless there is anything repugnant in the subject or context, to all Indian laws.

(2) In any Indian law, references, by whatever form of words to revenues of the Central Government or of any State Government shall, on and from the first day of April, 1950, be construed as references to the Consolidated Fund of India or the Consolidated Fund of the State, as the case may be.]

---

63. Subs. by the A.O. 1937, for "Acts of the Governor-General in Council."
64. Subs. by the A.O. 1950 for the former section which was instead by the A.O. 1937.

GENERAL RULES OF CONSTRUCTION

S. 5. Coming into operation of enactment.— [65][(1) Where any Central Act is not expressed to come into operation on a particular day, then it shall come into operation on the day on which it receives the assent,—

(*a*) in the case of a Central Act made before the commencement of the Constitution, of the Governor-General, and

(*b*) in the case of an Act of Parliament, of the President.]

(2) [66][* * *].

(3) Unless the contrary is expressed, a [67][Central Act] or regulation shall be construed as coming into operation immediately on the expiration of the day preceding its commencement.

NOTES

See CHAPTER 6, title (1) "Commencement".

[68]**S. 5-A. [Coming into operation of Governor-General's Act]** *Rep. by the A.O. 1947.*

S. 6. Effect of repeal.—Where this Act, or any [69][Central Act] or Regulation made after the commencement of this Act, repeals any enactment hitherto made or hereafter to be made, then, unless a different intention appears, the repeal shall not—

(*a*) revive anything not in force or existing at the time at which the repeal takes effect; or

(*b*) affect the previous operation of any enactment so repealed or anything duly done or suffered thereunder; or

(*c*) affect any right, privilege, obligation or liability acquired, accrued or incurred under any enactment so repealed; or

(*d*) affect any penalty, forfeiture or punishment incurred in respect of any offence committed against any enactment so repealed; or

(*e*) affect any investigation, legal proceeding or remedy in respect of any such right, privilege, obligation, liability, penalty, forfeiture or punishment as aforesaid;

---

65. Subs. by the A.O. 1950, for the former sub-section.
66. Sub-section (2) omitted by the A.O. 1950.
67. Subs. by the A.O. 1937, for "Act of the Governor-General in Council."
68. Ins. by the A.O. 1937.
69. Subs. by the A.O. 1937, for "Act of the Governor-General in Council."

and any such investigation, legal proceeding or remedy may be instituted, or continued or enforced, and any such penalty, forfeiture or punishment may be imposed as if the repealing Act or Regulation had not been passed.

NOTES

See Chapter 6, title (2) "Retrospective Operation"; Chapter 7, title (6) "Consequences of Repeal". For temporary statute, *see* Chapter 7, title (2) "Effect of Expiry of Temporary Statutes".

[63][**S. 6-A. Repeal of Act making textual amendment in Act or Regulation.**—Where any [70][Central Act] or Regulation made after commencement of this Act repeals any enactment by which the text of any Central Act or Regulation was amended by the express omission, insertion or substitution of any matter, then, unless a different intention appears, the repeal shall not affect the continuance of any such amendment made by the enactment so repealed and in operation at the time of such repeal.]

NOTES

The object of Repealing and Amending Acts is not to bring in any change in law but to remove enactments which have become unnecessary. "Mostly, they expurgate amending Acts, because having imparted the amendment to the main Acts, those Acts have served their purpose and have no further reason for their existence."[71] The repeal of an amending Act, therefore, has no repercussion on the parent Act which together with the amendments remains unaffected. It was, therefore, held that section 6(1A) introduced in the Wireless Telegraphy Act, 1933, by the amending Act of 1949 was not affected when the amending Act was repealed by the Repealing and Amending Act of 1952.[72]

S. 7. Revival of repealed enactments.—(1) In any [73][Central Act] or Regulation made after the commencement of this Act, it shall be necessary, for the purpose of reviving, either wholly or partially, any enactment wholly or partially repealed, expressly to state that purpose.

---

70. Subs. by the A.O. 1937, for "Act of the Governor-General in Council."

71. *Khudabux v. Manager, Caledonian Press*, AIR 1954 Cal 484, p. 486; **approved** in *Jethanand v. State of Delhi*, AIR 1960 SC 89, p. 91 : 1960 (1) SCR 755; *India Tobacco Co. Ltd. v. Commercial Tax Officer, Bhavanipore*, AIR 1975 SC 155, p. 158 : (1975) 3 SCC 512.

72. *Jethanand v. State of Delhi, supra.*

73. Subs. by the A.O. 1937, for "Act of the Governor-General in Council."

(2) This section applies also to all [74][Central Acts] made after the third day of January, 1868, and to all Regulations made on or after the fourteenth day of January, 1887.

NOTES

See Chapter 7, title (6)(b) "Revival".

S. 8. Construction of references to repealed enactments.—[75][(1)] Where this Act, or any [76][Central Act] or Regulation made after the commencement of this Act, repeals and re-enacts with or without modification, any provision of a former enactment, then references in any other enactment or in any instrument to the provision so repealed shall, unless a different intention appears, be construed as references to the provision so re-enacted.

[77][(2) [78][Where before the fifteenth day of August, 1947, any Act of Parliament of the United Kingdom repealed and re-enacted], with or without modification, any provision of a former enactment, then references in any [79][Central Act] or in any Regulation or instrument to the provision so repealed shall, unless a different intention appears, be construed as references to the provision so re-enacted.]

NOTES

When a later statute incorporates by reference the provisions of an earlier statute, a repeal or amendment of the earlier statutes does not affect the later statute or provisions incorporated therein.[80] This rule is subject to the qualification enacted in section 8, General Clauses Act, which in itself is a rule of general application.[81] It was, therefore, held that reference to section 108 of the Government of India Act, 1915, in clause 15 of the Letters Patent (Bombay) should be construed as reference to the corresponding provisions in the Government of India Act, 1935 and the Constitution.[82] Similarly, after repeal and replacement of the Mines Act, 1923, by the

---

74. Subs. by the A.O. 1937, for "Acts of Governor General in Council".
75. Section 8 renumbered as sub-section (1) of that by Act 18 of 1919, s. 2 and Sch. 1.
76. Subs. by the A.O. 1937, for "Act of the Governor General in Council".
77. Ins. by Act 18 of 1919, S. 2 and Sch. I.
78. Subs. by the A.O. 1950, for "Where any Act Parliament repeals and re-enacts".
79. Subs. by the A.O. 1937, for "Act of Governor-General in Council."
80. **See** Chapter 4, title 4(d) "Incorporation of Earlier Act into Later".
81. *National Sewing Thread Co. v. James Chadwick & Bros.*, AIR 1953 SC 357, p. 360 : 1953 SCR 1028.
82. *Ibid.*

Mines Act, 1952, reference to the definition of coal mine, as defined in the Mines Act, 1923, in section 2(*e*) of the Coal Mines Provident Fund Act, 1948, was construed as referring to the definition of coal mine as contained in the Mines Act, 1952.[83] The principle of construction enacted under section 8 applies also for construing an 'instrument' in which reference is made to some enactment which is later repealed and re-enacted. In the context of the General Clauses Act, the word "instrument" "has to be understood as including reference to a formal legal writing like an order made under a statute or subordinate legislation or any document of a formal character made under constitutional or statutory authority."[84] It was, therefore, held that reference to "the Defence of India Ordinance, 1962, or any rule or order made thereunder" in the President's Order issued under Article 359(1) of the Constitution should be understood after repeal and re-enactment of the Ordinance as reference to the Defence of India Act, 1962, or any rule or order made thereunder.[85]

But when a provision in a consolidating Act could be regarded as a re-enactment of two provisions contained in two different Acts it may be difficult to construe the new provision as a re-enactment of either of the repealed provisions for purposes of section 8. It was, therefore, held that section 20 of the Arbitration Act, 1940, cannot be construed as a re-enactment of either para 20 of Schedule II of the Code of Civil Procedure, 1908, or of the corresponding provision of the Arbitration Act, 1899.[86]

S. 9. Commencement and termination of time.—(1) In any [87][Central Act] or Regulation made after the commencement of this Act, it shall be sufficient, for the purpose of excluding the first in a series of days or any other period of time to use the word "from" and, for the purpose of including the last in a series of days or any other period of time, to use the word "to".

(2) This section applies also to all [88][Central Act] made after the third day of January, 1868, and to all regulations made on or after the fourteenth day of January 1887.

---

83. *State of Bihar v. S.K. Roy*, AIR 1966 SC 1995, p. 1996 : 1966 Supp SCR 259. **See further** *New Central Jute Mills Ltd. v. Asst. Collector Central Excise*, AIR 1981 SC 454; *State Through S.P. New Delhi v. Ratan Lal Arora*, (2004) 4 SCC 590, p. 595 : AIR 2004 SC 2364, p. 2367.

84. *Mohan Chowdhary v. Chief Commr., Tripura*, AIR 1964 SC 173, pp. 178, 179 : (1964) 3 SCR 442.

85. *Ibid.*

86. *Mohd. Usman v. Union of India*, AIR 1969 SC 474, p. 477 : (1969) 2 SCR 232.

87. Subs. by the A.O. 1937, for "Act of the Governor General in Council".

88. Subs. by the A.O. 1937, for "Acts of the Governor General in Council".

NOTES

The principle that the law in general neglects fractions of a day has given rise to two general principles for calculation of time. When a statute or a rule is concerned in fixing a *terminus a quo* of a new state of things which is to continue for an indefinite period (*i.e.*, there is no *terminus ad quem*), the new state of things comes into existence at midnight of the day preceding the day at which or on which or from which or from and after which the new state of things is directed to begin.[89] As an illustration of this general rule one may refer to section 5(3) of the General Clauses Act, which relates to the coming into operation of a Central Act or Regulation. The other principle is that when a period is delimited by a statute or rule which has both a beginning and an end, the word 'from' excludes the opening day and any words fixing the closing day include that day. In other words when a period is delimited marked by a *terminus a quo* and *terminus ad quem* the former is to be excluded and the latter to be included in the reckoning.[90] This second principle has been given statutory recognition in section 9 of the Act.

The decisions in the early period were not quite uniform but ever since 1808 when *Lester v. Garland*[91] was decided, the rule is well established that where an act is to be done within a specified time from a certain date, the day of that date is to be excluded.[92] Similarly when an act has to be done within so many days after a certain event, the day of such event is not to be counted.[93]

---

89. *In re, Court-fees Act*, AIR 1924 Mad 257, p. 259 (SB) (COUTTS TROTTER, C.J.). There is some authority for the view that an 'act' may be taken as done at the first moment of the day on which it was performed; *S.K. Salim v. State of West Bengal*, AIR 1975 SC 602, p. 606 : (1975) 1 SCC 653; *New India Assurance Co. v. Ram Dayal*, (1990) 2 SCR 570 : (1990) 2 SCC 680. But this rule has no application when time of commencement *e.g.* 4 p.m. is specifically indicated: *National Insurance Co. Ltd. v. Jijubhai Nathuji Dabhi (Smt.)*, AIR 1997 SC 2147 : 1997 (1) SCC 66. **See further** *Tarun Prasad Chatterjee v. Dinanath Sharma*, AIR 2001 SC 36, p. 39 : (2001) 3 SCC 36 (section 9 applied for counting period for filing of election petition under section 21 of the R.P. Act 1951).

90. *In re, Court-fees Act, supra.*

91. *Lester v. Garland*, (1808) 33 ER 748.

92. *Stewart v. Chapman*, (1951) 2 All ER 613, p. 615 : (1951) 2 KB 792 (LORD GODDARD, C.J.); *Hari Das Gupta v. State of West Bengal*, AIR 1972 SC 1293: (1972) 1 SCC 639; *Pritam Kaur v. S. Russel & Sons*, (1973) 1 All ER 617 (CA); *Saketh India Limited v. India Securities Ltd.*, JT 1999 (2) SC 67, pp. 69, 70 : AIR 1999 SC 1090 p. 1092 : (1999) 3 SCC 1.

93. *Jitendra Tyagi v. Delhi Administration*, AIR 1990 SC 487, pp. 490 to 492 : 1989 (4) SCC 653.

The powers of a company for compulsory purchase of lands which were to cease after expiration of 'three years from the passing of the Act', which was assented to on August 9, 1899, were held not to cease until the midnight of August 9, 1902.[1]

When a notice was required to be served within fourteen days from the commission of the offence, a notice served at 8 a.m. on January 25, was held to be valid even though the offence was committed at 7.15 a.m. on January 11.[2]

But the general rule of exclusion of the first day and inclusion of the last day is subject to a contrary intention indicated in the statute.

When a statute was to come into force 'at the expiration of a period of one month beginning with the date on which it is passed,' it was held that the words 'beginning with' intended to show that the day of the date on which the Royal assent was given had to be counted in reckoning of the period of one month. The statute was assented to on July 29 and was held to come into force after the midnight of August 28.[3]

Intention to exclude both the terminal days is clearly expressed when the statute uses the words—so many 'clear days'[4] or, 'not less than'[5] or 'at least'[6] so many days.

The words 'not later than fourteen days' have been construed to mean within a period of fourteen days.[7] Similarly in computing the period 'not earlier than thirty days' the first terminal day is to be excluded but the thirtieth day is to be included.[8] But in calculating a person's age the day of his birth counts as a whole day and he attains a specified age on the

---

1. *Goldsmith's Co. v. West Metropolitan Rail Co.*, (1900-03) All ER Rep 667.
2. *Stewart v. Chapman*, (1951) 2 All ER 613 : (1951) 2 KB 792.
3. *Hare v. Gocher*, (1962) 2 All ER 763. **See further** *Ramesh Enterprises v. Coffee Board*, AIR 1991 SC 403 : 1991 Supp (2) SCC 441 ('45 days from the date of auction including the date of auction'. The date of auction is to be counted in computing 45 days.).
4. *R. v. Herefordshire Justices*, (1820) 106 ER 773; by Statute 49, Geo. 3, c. 63, S. 5, "ten clear days' notice" of intention to appeal was required and it was held that the ten days were to be reckoned exclusively both of the day of serving the notice and the day of holding the sessions.
5. *R. v. Turner*, (1910) 1 KB 346; "not less than seven days' notice" means "seven clear days' notice". *Pioneer Motors (Private) Ltd. v. Municipal Council, Nagercoil*, AIR 1967 SC 684 : (1961) 3 SCR 609, "not being less than one month's notice" means "clear one month's notice". *CIT v. Braithwaite & Co. Ltd.*, (1993) 2 SCC 262 : 1993 (3) JT 159 : (1993) 110 CTR 292, 'not less than 7 years' means that the period cannot be even one minute less than 7 years. For other cases construing the expression 'not less than' **see** *M.N. Abdul Rawoof v. Pichamuthu,* AIR 2000 SC 1247 : (2000) 3 SCC 121 and the cases referred to therein.
6. *R. v. Long*, (1959) 3 All ER 559.
7. *Harinder Singh v. S. Karnail Singh*, AIR 1957 SC 271 : 1954 (26) ITR 736.
8. *Jai Charan Lal Amal v. State of U.P.*, AIR 1968 SC 5 : 1967 (3) SCR 981.

day next before the anniversary of his birthday.[9] For example a person born on 10-5-1978 will attain the age of 16 years at 12 o'clock in the midnight of 9-5-1994.[10]

The word 'until' is ambiguous and there is no absolute rule as to the meaning to be attached to this word for it may be construed either inclusive or exclusive of the day mentioned according to the subject-matter and the true intent of the document.[11]

The expression 'for the time being' may indicate a single period or an indefinite period of time depending upon the context in which it is used.[12] The phrase 'for the time being' envisages a changing state of affairs.[13] The words 'for the time being' would mean differently in different situations.[14] A notification which fixes the outer limit of time for its operation does not extend beyond that period because of the words 'until further orders'.[15]

What is 'Reasonable time' depends upon the facts and circumstance of each case and is essentially a question of fact,[16] for there is no such thing as a reasonable time in the abstract.[17] Similar construction is given to the word 'by'. 'By a certain time' may mean 'before a certain time' or 'on or before a certain time' depending upon the context.[18]

To do a thing 'as soon as may be' means to do it with a reasonable despatch,[19] or to do it within a reasonable time with an understanding to

---

9. *Prabhu Dayal Sesma v. State of Rajasthan*, (1986) 4 SCC 59 : AIR 1985 SC 1948.

10. *Eerati Laxman v. State of Andhra Pradesh*, (2009) 3 SCC 337 paras 13 and 14 : (2009) 2 JT 258. **See further** *Achhaibar Maurya v. State of Uttar Pradesh*, (2008) 2 SCC 639 : (2007) 14 Scale 425.

11. *Belthouse v. Mellor, Proudman v. Mellor*, (1859) 157 ER 780.

12. *Union Territory of Chandigarh v. Rajesh Kumar Basandhi*, AIR 2003 SC 3230 : (2003) 11 SCC 549.

13. *Department of Environment Food and Rural Affairs v. ASDA Stores Ltd.*, (2004) 1 All ER 268, p. 273 (para 18).

14. *Thukral Mechanical Works v. P.M. Diesels Pvt. Ltd.* (2009) 2 SCC 768, para 21 : (2009) 2 JT 59.

15. *Jayashra Chemicals v. Orissa State Electricity Board*, (2004) 3 SCC 674 : AIR 2004 SC 1585.

16. *Burton v. Griffiths*, (1843) 152 ER 1035. **See** section 46, *Explanation*, Indian Contract Act, 1872. **See further** *Joseph Severance v. Banny Mathew*, (2005) 7 SCC 667, pp. 672, 673; Advanced Law Lexicon by P. Ramanatha Aiyar, 3rd Edition (Volume 4) pp. 3971, 3972.

17. *Hick v. Raymond & Reid*, (1893) AC 22.

18. *B.N. Agarwalla v. State of Orissa*, 1995 (6) Scale 54, p. 57 : AIR 1996 SC 385 : (1995) 6 SCC 509.

19. *Ujagar Singh v. State of Punjab*, AIR 1952 SC 350, p. 352 : 1952 SCR 756.

do it within the shortest possible time,[20] or to do it within the time which is reasonably convenient or requisite.[21]

The words 'immediately' and 'forthwith', which have the same significance,[22] are more peremptory than the words 'as soon as may be', and mean that the act to be done 'immediately' or 'forthwith' should be performed with reasonable speed and expedition and that any delay in the matter should be satisfactorily explained.[23] Provided no harm results, 'forthwith' may mean any reasonable time.[24] The word 'immediately' may be similarly construed.[25]

The word 'about' prefixed to the time fixed gives a certain amount of flexibility, thus a period of nine years and one month was held to amount to a period 'about 10 years.'[26]

A power to be exercised 'at any time' means "within a reasonable time depending upon the facts and circumstances of each case."[27]

'Month' is defined in section 3(35). 'Week' is not defined; it will mean seven days. Thus 'six weeks' mean 42 days. The corresponding date rule which applies in case of reckoning of a 'month' does not apply for reckoning a week.[28]

'Day' is not defined. In its ordinary meaning, which is subject to a contrary context 'day' as per English calendar begins at midnight and covers a period of 24 hours thereafter.[29]

S. 10. Computation of time.—(1) Where, by any [30][Central Act] or Regulation made after the commencement of this Act, any act or proceeding

---

20. *Abdul Jabbar v. State of J & K*, AIR 1957 SC 281, p. 283 : 1957 SCR 51.
21. *Ibid*.
22. *Keshav Nilkanth Joglekar v. Commr. of Police*, AIR 1957 SC 28, p. 30 : 1956 SCR 653.
23. *Ibid*, p. 32; *Bidya Deb Barma v. District Magistrate, Tripura*, AIR 1969 SC 323, p. 325 : 1969 (1) SCR 562; *R. v. Inspector of Taxes*, (1971) 3 WLR 425, p. 451 (QBD); *S.K. Salim v. State of West Bengal*, AIR 1975 SC 602, pp. 604-606 : (1975) 1 SCC 653. **See further** *Raymonds Synthetics Ltd. v. Union of India*, AIR 1992 SC 847 : 1992 (2) SCC 255.
24. *London Borough of Hillington v. Cutler*, (1967) 2 All ER 361.
25. *Tulsiram v. State of M.P.*, (1984) 4 SCC 487, pp. 497, 498 : AIR 1985 SC 299.
26. *Kumar Bal Das v. Utkal University*, AIR 1999 SC 669 : (1999) 1 SCC 453.
27. *Ibrahim Patnam Taluk Vyavasaya Cootic Sangham v. K. Suresh Reddy*, (2003) 7 SCC 667, pp. 676, 677 : AIR 2003 SC 3592; *Situ Sahu v. State of Jharkhand*, (2004) 8 SCC 340, pp. 346, 347 : (2004) 7 JT 402; *Sulochana Chandrakant Galande v. Pune Municipal Transport*, (2010) 8 SCC 467 paras 24 to 27 : AIR 2010 SC 2962
28. *Okolo v. Secretary of State for the Environment*, (1997) 4 All ER 242 : (1997) JPL 1009 (CA).
29. *Rajkumar Yadav v. Samir Kumar Mahaseth*, (2005) 3 SCC 601, p. 605.
30. Subs. by the A.O. 1937, "Act of the Governor General in Council."

is directed or allowed to be done or taken in any Court or office on a certain day or within a prescribed period, then, if the Court or office is closed on that day or the last day of the prescribed period, the act or proceeding shall be considered as done or taken in due time if it is done or taken on the next day afterwards in which the court or office is open:

Provided that nothing in this section shall apply to any act or proceeding to which the Indian Limitation Act, 1877 (XV of 1877),[31] applies.

(2) This section applies also to all [32][Central Acts] and Regulations made on or after the fourteenth day of January, 1887.

NOTES

For the section to apply all that is requisite is that there should be a period prescribed, and that period should expire on a holiday.[33] The principle enacted in the section is a beneficient one and its operation cannot be negatived on unsubstantial grounds.[34] It has been held to apply to proceedings under the Representation of the People Act, 1951.[35] But a court cannot be said to be closed if the office is open to entertain appeals and applications even though Judges of the court are not sitting.[36] But the section will apply when the court for some reason does not on a particular day sit after 3.15 p.m., though the normal working hours are till 4.15 p.m., for in such a case it can be said that the court on that day was closed after 3.15 p.m.[37]

An election petition was presented to the designated judge of the High Court at 4.25 p.m. on 27-8-2003 the last date of limitation, 10 minutes after the judge had risen from the open court but was available in his chambers within the court premises. The judge refused to entertain it as the court hours expired at 4.15 p.m. The petition was then presented to the judge on 28-8-2003 in open court. It was dismissed as barred by limitation. The Supreme Court reversed this decision on the reasoning that the period of limitation according to section 81 of the Representation of the

---

31. **See** the Limitation Act, 1963 (36 of 1963).

32. Subs. by the A.O. 1937 for "Acts of the Governor General in Council."

33. *Harinder Singh v. S. Karnail Singh*, AIR 1957 SC 271, p. 273 : 1957 SCR 208.

34. *Ibid.*

35. *Ibid.*

36. *Hukumdev Narain Yadav v. Lalit Narain Misra*, AIR 1974 SC 480 : (1973) 2 SCC 133. **See further** *Mohd. Ali v. Azad Mohd.*, AIR 1999 SC 3429 : (1999) 8 SCC 538.

37. *Chandra Kishore Jha v. Mahavir Prasad*, JT 1999 (7) SC 256, p. 263 : AIR 1999 SC 3558, pp. 3562, 3563 : (1999) 8 SCC 266.

People Act, 1951 expired on the 45th 'day' from the date of election; the 'day' in its ordinary meaning which has to be assigned to it when there is no contrary context, meant midnight to midnight; the election petition could have been presented upto the midnights falling between 27-8-2003 and 28-8-2003 and rules of the High Court are rules of procedure made under Article 225 of the constitution which cannot curtail any substantive law such as one fixing period of limitation.[38]

When the period prescribed by a notification for making the award by an Industrial Tribunal to which an industrial dispute was referred expired on a holiday and the award of the Tribunal was pronounced on the next working day, it was held applying the rule enacted in section 10 of the U.P. General Clauses Act, 1904 that the award was valid.[39]

This section does not in terms apply to deposits made in a court under a compromise decree which fixes a period for making deposits, but similar rule has been applied on general principles.[40]

S. 11. Measurement of distances.—In the measurement of any distance, for the purposes of any [41][Central Act] or Regulation made after the commencement of this Act, that distance shall, unless a different intention appears, be measured in a straight line on a horizontal plane.

S. 12. Duty to be taken *pro rata* in enactments.—Where, by any enactment now in force or hereafter to be in force, any duty of customs or excise, or in the nature thereof, is leviable on any given quantity, by weight or measure or value of any goods or merchandize, then a like duty is leviable according to the same rate on any greater or less quantity.

S. 13. Gender and number.—In all [42][Central Acts] and Regulations, unless there is anything repugnant in the subject or context—

(1) words importing the masculine gender shall be taken to include females; and

(2) words in the singular shall include the plural, and *vice versa*.

---

38. *Raj Kumar Yadav v. Samir Kumar Mahaseth*, (2005) 3 SCC 601, p. 605.
39. *Vishwamitra Press v. Workers*, AIR 1953 SC 41 : 1953 SCR 272.
40. *C.F. Angadi v. Y.S. Hiranayya*, AIR 1972 SC 239 : (1972) 1 SCC 191.
41. Subs. by the A.O. 1937, for "Act of the Governor General in Council."
42. Subs. by the A.O. 1937 for "Acts of the Governor Genreal in Council."

NOTES

In accordance with the rule that words importing the masculine gender are to be taken to include females, the word 'men' may be properly held to include women,[43] and the pronoun 'he' and its derivatives may be construed to refer to any person whether male or female.[44] So the words 'his father and mother' as they occur in section 125(1)(*d*) of the Criminal Procedure Code, 1973 have been construed to include 'her father and mother' and a daughter has been held liable to maintain her father unable to maintain himself.[45] But the general rule in section 13(1) has to be applied with circumspection for interpreting laws dealing with matters of succession. Thus the words 'male descendants' occurring in sections 7 and 8 of the Chota Nagpur Tenancy Act, 1908 were not interpreted to include 'female descendants'.[46]

Consistent with the rule that words in the singular include the plural and *vice versa*, the word 'members' occurring in article 15 of the articles of association of a private company which provided—"in the event of the death of a member, his or her shares must be offered to the other 'members' at par", was interpreted to include a sole surviving member.[47] For the same reason the words 'male and female heirs' in section 23 of the Hindu Succession Act, 1956 were interpreted to cover a case where there is a single male heir.[48] Relying on section 13(b) of the Bombay General Clauses Act, 1904, which states that words in the singular shall include the plural, and *vice versa*, the Supreme Court held that the expression "any bodies or persons" in section 43-A(1)(b) of the Bombay Tenancy and Agricultural Lands Act, 1948, will include a singular person, in the same way as the expression "leases" in the provision will include a single lease.[49] In conformity with the rule the word 'case' in the expression 'special judge appointed for the case' as occurring in section 5 of the Prevention of Corruption Act, 1988 was interpreted to include 'cases' and a special judge appointed 'for a group of cases' was held covered by the said expression.[50] Similarly the word 'machine' in an exemption notification issued under

---

43. *Charlton v. Lings*, (1868) LR 4 CP 374; 42 Digest 615.
44. **See** section 8, Indian Penal Code.
45. *Vijaya Manohar Arbat (Dr.) (Mrs.) v. Kashiram Rajaram Sawai*, (1987) 2 SCC 278, p. 281 : AIR 1987 SC 1100.
46. *Madhu Kishwar v. State of Bihar*, AIR 1996 SC 1864, p. 1881 : (1996) 5 SCC 125.
47. *Jervis Motors Ltd. v. Carabott*, (1964) 3 All ER 89.
48. *Narshimha Murthy v. Susheelabai*, 1996 (3) Scale 625, p. 640 : (1996) 4 SCC 644.
49. *Govinda Bala Patil v. Ganpati Ramchandra Naikwade*, (2013) 15 SCC 193, pp. 197, 198.
50. *J. Jayalalitha v. UOI*, AIR 1999 SC 1912, p. 1925 : (1999) 5 SCC 138.

section 25 of the Customs Act, 1962 was interpreted to include 'machines.'[51]

Contrary intention to exclude the operation of the rule that the plural includes the singular is not inferred merely because the relevant provision is drafted in the plural and the subsidiary and ancillary provisions follow the same pattern and use plural words or words implying the plural.[52] In this case,[53] the Privy Council held that power to appoint 'Commissioners' under an Ordinance to conduct inquiry include a power to appoint a sole Commissioner and that contrary intention was not shown because ancillary provisions in the Ordinance provided that processes and warrants should be issued 'under the hand of the Chairman or Presiding member of the Commission'. It was pointed out that just as in obedience to the general rule the words empowering the appointment of 'Commissioners' could be read as empowering the appointment of 'Commissioner or sole Commissioner', the words 'under the hand of the Chairman or Presiding member of the Commission' could be read as 'under the hand of the Chairman or presiding member or sole Commissioner of any such commission'.[54] The decision indicates that contrary intention would have been inferred had the ordinance contained some substantive provision essential to the functioning of the Commission which could not have been satisfied without a plurality, *e.g.*, a provision that a Commission should not sit to hear witnesses unless at least two Commissioners are present.[55] The principle laid down in this case was followed in a subsequent Privy Council case[56] where it was held that the mere fact that a statutory provision suggests an emphasis on singularity as opposed to plurality is not enough to exclude the application of the rule that words in the singular shall include the plural. It was also held that in considering whether a contrary intention appears, there need be no confinement of attention to the particular provision; and it would be appropriate to consider the provision in its setting in the legislation; and furthermore to consider the substance and tenor of the legislation as a whole.

---

51. *Collector of Customs v. United Electrical Industries Ltd.*, AIR 1999 SC 3796 : (2000) 10 SCC 31.

52. *Sin Poh Amalgamated (HK) v. AG*, (1965) 1 All ER 225 (PC).

53. *Ibid.*

54. *Sin Poh Amalgamated (HK) v. AG*, (1965) 1 All ER 225 (PC).

55. *Ibid*, p. 228.

56. *Blue Metal Industries v. R. W. Dilley*, (1969) 3 All ER 437, p. 441 (PC). **See further** *Floor v Davis (Inspector of Taxes)*, (1979) 2 All ER 677 : 1980 AC 695 (HL); *Dawson v. Inland Rev. Commissioner*, (1989) 2 All ER 289, p. 291 : (1990) 1 AC 1 : (1989) 2 WLR 858 (HL).

In construing the definition of the phrase 'Industrial dispute' as contained in section 2(*k*) of the Industrial Disputes Act, 1947, it has been held that the plural word 'workmen' in the definition does not include the singular and that a dispute between an employer and a single workman cannot *per se* be an industrial dispute but may become one if taken up by a trade union or a number of workmen.[57] Departure from the ordinary rule enacted in section 13(2) of the General Clauses Act was made and a contrary intention inferred by reading other constituent parts of the Act.

In construing the definition of 'previous year' in section 2(11) of the Indian Income-tax Act, 1922, it has been pointed out that the definition was not applicable for construing 'previous years', and that the rule, that the singular included the plural, was not attracted as it was repugnant to the subject and context of the definition for there could be only one previous year to the year of assessment.[58]

Similarly, it has been held that the word 'member' occurring in the definition of 'tenant' as enacted in the Increase of Rent and Mortgage Interest (Restriction) Act, 1920, meant one member, a contrary intention appearing so as to exclude section 1(1) of the Interpretation Act, 1889.[59]

---

57. *Newspapers Ltd. v. State Industrial Tribunal*, AIR 1957 SC 532 : 1957 SCR 754. **Cf.** *R. v. National Arbitration Tribunal*, (1951) 2 All ER 228; *R. v. Industrial Disputes Tribunal*, (1957) 2 All ER 776.

58. *Dhandhania Kedia & Co. v. CIT*, AIR 1959 SC 219, p. 222 : 1959 Supp (1) SCR 204.

59. *Dealex Properties Ltd. v. Brooks*, (1965) 1 All ER (1080).

See further Rent and Mortgage Interest Restrictions (Amendment) Act, 1933, Schedule 1, para (b), which gave the County Court power to make an order for the recovery of possession of a dwelling house in terms "if the dwelling house is reasonably required by the landlord—for occupation as a residence for (i) himself, or (ii) any son or daughter of his.....or (iii) his father or mother......". This provision in case of plurality of landlords has been read as follows: "the dwelling house is reasonably required by the landlords..........for occupation as a residence for (i) themselves or (ii) any son or daughter of theirs..........or (iii) their father or mother". Interpreted in this way it has been held that joint landlords will fail to recover possession under clause (i), if the requirement is not for both or all of them and similarly they will fail, if they proceed under clause (ii), and are not a married couple with a child, or if they proceed under clause (iii) and have not got a parent in common; *McIntryre v. Hardcastle*, (1948) 1 All ER 696; *Wetherall & Co. Ltd. v. Stone*, (1950) 2 All ER 1209. These cases, however, have not been followed in India in interpreting corresponding provisions of Indian Statutes; **see** *Kanika Devi v. A.N. Roy Chowdhary*, 65 CWN 1078; *Tarakchandra Mukherjee v. Ratanlal Ghosal*, 1959 Cal LJ 136; *Vir Bhan v. Avtar Krishan*, 64 PLR 1185; *Pravinchand Hathibhai v. Shankerlal*, 1966 JLJ 533; in the Indian decisions the word 'his' or 'himself' in case of plurality of

[Footnote No. 59 Contd.]

It has further been held that the power to appoint constitutional functionaries expressed in singular *e.g.* Attorney General for India, Advocate General for the State, Comptroller and Auditor General cannot be read by recourse to section 13 of the General Clauses Act and Article 367 of the constitution to authorise appointment of more than one person as Attorney General or Advocate General or Comptroller or Auditor General for the context clearly points to the contrary.[60]

[61]**[S. 13-A. [References to the sovereign.]** *Rep. by the A.O. 1950*].

POWERS AND FUNCTIONARIES

S. 14. Powers conferred to be exercisable from time to time.—(1) Where, by any [62][Central Act] or Regulation made after the commencement of this Act, any power is conferred [63][***] then, [64][unless a different intention appears], that power may be exercised from time to time as occasion requires.

(2) This section applies also to all [65][Central Acts] and Regulations made on or after the fourteenth day of January, 1887.

NOTES

Relying on the parallel provision contained in section 32 of the Interpretation Act, 1889, it was held that power conferred by section 108, Government of India Act, 1915, on the High Courts to frame rules to regulate the exercise of their jurisdiction by single Judges or Division Courts could be exercised from time to time, and that the exercise of this power was not restricted to the jurisdiction existing at the coming into force of the Government of India Act, 1915, but was available to regulate any jurisdiction

---

[Footnote No. 59 Contd.]

landlords has been read as "of them or of any one or more of them". The Indian cases have been **approved** in *Ram Pasricha v. Jagannath*, AIR 1976 SC 2335 : (1976) 4 SCC 184. **See further** *Kanta Goel v. B.P. Pathak*, AIR 1977 SC 1599 : 1977 (3) SCR 412 : 1977 (2) SCC 814; *Palsingh v. Sunder Singh*, AIR 1989 SC 758 : (1989) 1 SCC 444. *McIntyre v. Hardcastle (supra)* has been **distinguished** in *Tilling v. Whiteman*, (1979) 1 All ER 737 : (1980) AC 1 : (1979) 2 WLR 401 (HL).

60. *M.T. Khan v. Govt. of A.P.*, (2004) 2 SCC 267, p. 271 : AIR 2004 SC 2934.

61. Ins. by the 18 of 1919, sec. 2 and Sch. I.

62. Subs. by the A.O. 1937, for "Acts of the Governor General in Council".

63. The words "on the Government" omitted by Act 18 of 1919, s. 2 and Sch. 1.

64. Ins. by Act 18 of 1919, s. 2 and Sch. I.

65. Subs. by the A.O. 1937 for "Acts of the Governor General in Council".

conferred by subsequent legislation.[66] Relying on section 14, the Supreme Court has held that the power under section 51(3) of the States Reorganisation Act, 1956 can be exercised by the Chief Justice as and when the occasion arose for its exercise.[67]

Similarly, section 8 of the Working Journalists (Conditions of Service) and Miscellaneous Provisions Act, 1955, which empowers the Central Government to constitute a Wage Board but which contains no provision to fill in vacancies, was construed to authorise reconstitution of a Board and nomination of another member in place of a previously nominated one who had resigned. This conclusion was arrived at by reading section 8 of the Act along with section 14 of the General Clauses Act.[68]

Relying upon section 14 of the Bombay General Clauses Act, 1904 which is analogous to section 14 of the Central Act, it has been held that power conferred by section 6(2) of Bombay Act 67 of 1948 to fix by notification a lower rate of rents payable by tenants is not exhausted on the issue of the first notification and can be exercised from time to time as occasion arises.[69]

The Deputy Commissioner who has the power under section 4 of the Karnataka Zilla Parishads, Taluk Panchayat Samitis, Mandal Panchayats and Nyaya Panchayats Act, 1983 to fix headquarters of a *Mandal Panchayat* can change the same by recourse to section 14 of the Karnataka General Clauses Act which corresponds to section 14 of the Central Act.[70]

And relying upon section 12 of the Punjab General Clauses Act, it was held that an improvement trust once created and dissolved under the Punjab Town Improvement Act, 1922 could again be recreated as a new trust under the Act by the State Government.[71]

The rule enacted in section 14 authorises exercise of the power successively and has no relevance to the question whether the power claimed can at all be exercised.[72] Further, an order which under the terms of the Act

---

66. *National Sewing Thread Co. v. James Chadwick & Bros.*, AIR 1953 SC 357, p. 360 : 1953 SCR 1028.

67. *State of Maharashtra v. Narayan*, AIR 1983 SC 46, p. 52 : (1982) 3 SCC 519.

68. *Express Newspapers Ltd. v. Union of India*, AIR 1958 SC 578, pp. 634, 635 : 1959 SCR 12.

69. *Vasanlal v. State of Bombay*, AIR 1961 SC 4, p. 9 : 1961 (1) SCR 341.

70. *B.N. Shankarappa v. Uthanur Sriniwas*, AIR 1992 SC 836 : (1992) 2 SCC 61.

71. *State of Haryana v. Mohan Lal Gupta*, AIR 1970 SC 1848 : (1969) 3 SCC 484.

72. *Gourchandra v. Public Prosecutor*, AIR 1963 SC 1198, p. 2202 : 1963 Supp (2) SCR 447. The conditions and the manner of exercise of the power by recourse to this section remain the same as required for the initial exercise; *K. Prasad v. Union of India*, AIR 1988 SC 535, p. 550 : 1988 Supp SCC 115.

under which it is made is final, cannot be revoked by recourse to section 14.[73] Again, the section has generally no application to the exercise of judicial or *quasi*-judicial power and in the absence of any provision for review an order passed in the exercise of such a power cannot be modified by taking help of this section.[74] But in *Wilson v. Colchester Justices*[75] the House of Lords held that the power conferred on a Magistrate by section 77(2) of the Magistrate's Act, 1980 to postpone the issue of a warrant of commitment could be exercised from time to time having regard to section 12(1) of the Interpretation Act, 1978 which corresponds to section 14 of the General Clauses Act. It was also held that the issue of a warrant was a judicial Act requiring observance of natural justice.

A power to regulate and in that context to grant permit or permission will include a power to suspend or cancel the permit or permission as incidental or supplementary to regulation.[76]

The rule of construction in this section has no application when a different intention appears from the statutory language. Conferral of a power with an express authority to exercise it from time to time may show that another power conferred by the same section without any such authority cannot be exercised from time to time and the power is exhausted after it is once exercised.[77]

S. 15. Power to appoint to include power to appoint *ex officio*.—Where, by any [78][Central Act] or Regulation, a power to appoint any person to fill any office or execute any function is conferred, then, unless it is other-wise expressly provided, any such appointment, if it is made after the commencement of this Act, may be made either by name or by virtue of office.[79]

S. 16. Power to appoint to include power to suspend or dismiss.—Where, by any [80][Central Act] or Regulation, a power to make any appointment is conferred, then, unless a different intention appears, the

---

73. *State of Madras v. Melamatam*, AIR 1965 SC 1570, p. 1573 : (1966) 2 MLJ (SC) 13 (case under Madras General Clauses Act, 1891).

74. *Gadde Venkateswara Rao v. Government of Andhra Pradesh*, AIR 1966 SC 828 : 1966 (2) SCR 172.

75. *Wilson v. Colchester Justices*, (1985) 2 All ER 97, p. 102 (HL).

76. *State of U.P. v. Maharaja Dharmendra Prasad Singh*, AIR 1989 SC 997, p. 1008 : (1989) 2 SCC 505.

77. *Nasiruddin v. State Transport Appellate Tribunal*, AIR 1976 SC 331, p. 340 : (1975) 2 SCC 671; *H.C. Suman v. Rehabilitation Ministry Employees Co-operative House Building Society Ltd.*, AIR 1991 SC 2160, p. 2171 : (1991) 4 SCC 485.

78. Subs. by the A.O. 1937, for "Act of the Governor General in Council".

79. **See** *Choitram v. State of Gujarat*, AIR 1967 SC 1532, p. 1533 : 1967 (3) SCR 351. (Case under section 15 of the Bombay General Clauses Act, 1904).

80. Subs. by the A.O. 1937, for "Act of the Governor General in Council."

authority having [81][for the time being] power to make the appointment shall also have power to suspend or dismiss any person appointed [82][whether by itself or any other authority] in exercise of that power.

NOTES

Order 40, Rule 1(*a*) of the Code of Civil Procedure, 1908, which authorises a court 'to appoint a receiver', has been construed to embrace a power of removing a receiver.[83]

Article 229(1) of the Constitution which empowers the Chief Justice to make 'appointment of officers and servants of a High Court' has been interpreted to include a power to suspend or dismiss.[84]

The power to terminate is a necessary adjunct of the power of appointment.[85] Even if authority *A* has power to appoint on the advice or recommendation of authority *B*, the appointing authority in law is authority *A* who under section 16 will have power to dismiss.[86]

S. 17. Substitution of functionaries.—(1) In any [87][Central Act] or Regulation made after the commencement of this Act, it shall be sufficient, for the purpose of indicating the application of law to every person or number of persons for the time being executing the functions of an office, to mention the official title of the officer at present executing the functions, or that of the officer by whom the functions are commonly executed.[88]

---

81. Ins. by Act 18 of 1928, s. 2 and Sch. I.
82. Subs. by s. 2 and Sch. I, *ibid.*, for "by it".
83. *Rayarappan v. Madhavi Amma*, AIR 1950 FC 140 : 1949 FCR 667.
84. *Pradyat Kumar v. Chief Justice of Calcutta High Court*, AIR 1956 SC 285, p. 291 : 1955 (2) SCR 1331; *Union of India v. Gurbaksh Singh*, AIR 1975 SC 641 : (1975) 3 SCC 638.
85. *Lekhraj v. Dy. Custodian*, AIR 1966 SC 334, p. 336 : 1966 (1) SCR 120; *Boolchand (Dr.) v. Chancellor, Kurukshetra University*, AIR 1968 SC 292 : 1968 (1) SCR 434; *Heckett Engineering Co. v. Their Workmen*, AIR 1977 SC 2257 : (1977) 4 SCC 377.
86. *State of Assam v. Kripanath Sarma*, AIR 1967 SC 459 : 1967 (1) SCR 499.
87. Subs. by the A.O. 1937, for "Act of the Governor General in Council."
88. *Janardan v. State of Maharashtra*, AIR 1978 SC 1234 : (1978) 2 SCC 465; power conferred on Commissioner of Police by an Act could also be exercised by Assistant Commissioners who were subsequently appointed to discharge all the functions of Commissioner.

(2) This section applies also to all [89][Central Acts] made after the third day of January, 1868, and to all Regulations made on or after the fourteenth day of January, 1887.

S. 18. Successors.—(1) In any Central Act or Regulation made after the commencement of this Act, it shall be sufficient, for the purpose of indicating the relation of a law to the successor of any functionaries or of corporations having perpetual succession, to express its relation to the functionaries or corporations.

(2) This section applies also to all Central Acts made after the third day of January, 1868, and to all Regulations made on or after the fourteenth day of January, 1887.

S. 19. Official chiefs and subordinates.—(1) In any [90][Central Act] or Regulation made after the commencement of this Act, it shall be sufficient for the purpose of expressing that a law relating to the chief or superior of an office shall apply to the deputies or subordinates lawfully performing the duties of that office in the place of their superior, to prescribe the duty of the superior.

(2) This section applies, also to all [91][Central Acts] made after the third day of January, 1868, and to all Regulations made on or after the fourteenth day of January, 1887.

PROVISIONS AS TO ORDERS, RULES, ETC., MADE UNDER ENACTMENTS

S. 20. Construction of notifications etc., issued under enactments.—Where, by any Central Act or regulation, a power to issue any notification, order, scheme, rule, form or bye-law is conferred, then expressions used in the [92][notification], order, scheme, rule, form, or bye-law, if it is made after the commencement of this Act, shall unless there is anything repugnant in the subject or context, have the same respective meanings as in the Act or Regulation conferring the power.

S. 21. Power to issue, to include power to add to, amend, vary or rescind orders, rules or bye-laws.—Where, by any [93][Central Act] or

---

89. Subs. by the A.O. 1937, for "Acts of the Governor General in Council."
90. Subs. by the A.O. 1937, for "Acts of the Governor General in Council."
91. Subs. by the A.O. 1937, for "Acts of the Governor General in Council."
92. Ins. by Act 1 of 1903, s. 3 and Sch. II.
93. Subs. by the A.O. 1937, for "Act of the Governor General in Council."

Regulation, a power to [1][issue notifications], orders, rules or bye-laws is conferred, then that power includes a power, exercisable in the like manner and subject to the like sanction and conditions (if any), to add to, amend, vary or rescind any [2][notifications], orders, rules or bye-laws so [3][issued].

NOTES

See Chapter 12, *title 5(a). See further Ram Bali v. State of W.B.*[4]

S. 22. Making of rules or bye-laws and issuing of orders between passing and commencement of enactment.—Where, by any [5][Central Act] or Regulation which is not to come into force immediately on the passing thereof, a power is conferred to make rules or bye-laws, or to issue orders with respect to the application of the Act or Regulation, or with respect to the establishment of any Court or office or the appointment of any Judge or officer thereunder, or with respect to the person by whom, or the time when, or the place where, or the manner in which, or the fees for which, anything is to be done under the Act or Regulation, then that power may be exercised at any time after the passing of the Act or Regulation; but rules, bye-laws or orders so made or issued shall not take effect till the commencement of the Act or Regulation.

NOTES

See Chapter 12, title 5(b). *See further State of Assam v. S. Padmanabhan.*[6]

S. 23. Provisions applicable to making of rules or bye-laws after previous publication.—Where, by any [7][Central Act] or Regulation, a power to make rules or bye-laws, is expressed to be given subject to the conditions of the rules or bye-laws being made after previous publication, then the following provisions shall apply, namely:

(1) the authority having power to make the rules or bye-laws shall, before making them, publish a draft of the proposed rules or bye-laws for the information of persons likely to be affected thereby;

---

1. Subs. by Act 1 of 1903, s. 3 and Sch. II for "make".
2. Ins. by Act 1 of 1903, s. 3 and Sch. II.
3. Subs. by Act 1 of 1903, s. 3 & Sch. II for "made".
4. *Ram Bali v. State of W.B.*, AIR 1975 SC 623, pp. 627, 628 : (1975) 4 SCC 47.
5. Subs. by the A.O. 1937, for "Act of the Governor General in Council."
6. *State of Assam v. S. Padmanabhan*, AIR 1971 SC 2081 : (1971) 1 SCC 326.
7. Subs. by the A.O. 1937, for "Act of the Governor General in Council".

(2) the publications shall be made in such manner as that authority deems to be sufficient, or, if the conditions with respect to previous publication so requires, in such manner as the [8][Government concerned] prescribes;

(3) there shall be published with the draft a notice specifying a date on or after which the draft will be taken into consideration;

(4) the authority having power to make the rules or bye-laws, and, where the rules or bye-laws are to be made with the sanction, approval or concurrence of another authority that authority also, shall consider any objection or suggestion which may be received by the authority having power to make the rules or bye-laws from any person with respect to the draft before the date so specified;

(5) the publication in the [9][Official Gazette] of a rule or bye-law purporting to have been made in exercise of a power to make rules or bye-laws after previous publication shall be conclusive proof that the rule or bye-law has been duly made.

NOTES

See Chapter 12, title 4(a).

S. 24. Continuation of orders, etc., issued under enactments repealed and re-enacted.—Where any [10][Central Act] or Regulation is, after the commencement of this Act, repealed and re-enacted with or without modification, then, unless it is otherwise expressly provided, any [11][appointment, notification], order, scheme, rule, form or bye-law made or issued under the repealed Act or regulation, shall, so far as it is not inconsistent with the provisions re-enacted continue in force, and be deemed to have been made or issued under the provisions so re-enacted, unless and until it is superseded by any appointment, notification, order, scheme, rule, form or bye-law, [12][made or] issued under the provisions so re-enacted [13][and when any [14][Central Act] or Regulation which, by a notification under section 5 or 5-A of the [15]Scheduled Districts Act, 1874 (XIV of 1874), or any like law, has been extended to any local area, has, by a subsequent notification, been withdrawn from and re-extended to such area or any part

8. Subs. by the A.O. 1950, for "General Government or the Provincial Government".
9. Subs. by the A.O. 1937, for "Gazette".
10. Subs. by the A.O. 1937, for "Act of the Governor General in Council".
11. Ins. by Act 1 of 1903, s. 3 and Sch. II.
12. Ins. by Act 1 of 1903, s. 3 and Sch. II.
13. Ins. by the Act 17 of 1914, s. 2 and Sch. I.
14. Subs. by the A.O. 1937, for "Act of the Governor General in Council".
15. Rep. by the A.O. 1937.

thereof, the provisions of such Act or Regulation shall be deemed to have been repealed and re-enacted in such area or part within the meaning of this section.]

NOTES

A notification was issued under the Assam Municipal Act, 1923 applying sections 4 and 5 of that Act to a notified area. The Act of 1923 was repealed and replaced by the Assam Municipal Act, 1957. It was held that the notification issued under the Assam Act continued by virtue of section 26 of the Assam General Clauses Act, 1915 (which corresponds to section 24 of the Central Act) and the State Government was competent to take action under the corresponding provisions of the 1957 Act.[16] An order of the Income-tax Officer under section 10(2)(*xi*) of the Income-tax Act, 1922 declaring certain debt as bad debt was held to continue by virtue of section 24 of the General Clauses Act under section 36(1)(*vii*) of the Income-tax Act, 1961 and the amount of the debt subsequently recovered was held to be taxable under section 41(4) of the 1961 Act.[17] Similarly, a notification issued under section 5-A of the Prevention of Corruption Act, 1947 authorising a sub-inspector to investigate cases under the Act was held to continue because of section 24 of the General Clauses Act under the corresponding section 17 of the Prevention of Corruption Act, 1988.[18] It was also held that saving in respect of section 6 of the General Clauses Act in the repealing section 30 of the 1988 Act did not exclude the application of section 24.[19]

It has been said that provisions like section 24 create uncertainty in practical application because of the presence in the section of the words 'so far as it is not inconsistent with the provisions re-enacted'. It has, therefore, been suggested that provisions like section 24 should be repealed and the rules and orders etc. which are intended to be continued under the new Act should be collected and listed in the new Act with suitable changes if necessary a course which may not be difficult now with electronic data-base access.[20]

---

16. *State of Assam v. Assam Tea Co. Ltd.*, AIR 1971 SC 1358 : (1970) 2 SCC 817.

17. *Poonjabhai Varmalidas v. Commissioner of Income-tax*, AIR 1991 SC 1 : 1992 Supp (1) SCC 182.

18. *State of Punjab v. Harnek Singh,* AIR 2002 SC 1074, pp. 1081 : (2002) 3 SCC 481.

19. *Ibid.*

20. Robert A. Duperron (Chief Legislative Editor, Department of Justice, Canada), 'Interpretation Acts–Impediments to legal certainty and Access to the Law', 26 (2005) Statute Law Review 64, p. 67.

MISCELLANEOUS

S. 25. Recovery of fines.—Sections 63 to 70 of the Indian Penal Code (XLV of 1860) and the provisions of the [21]Code of Criminal Procedure (5 of 1898) for the time being in force in relation to the issue and the execution of warrants for the levy of fines shall apply to all fines imposed under any Act, Regulation, rule or bye-law unless the Act, Regulation, rule or bye-law contains an express provision to the contrary.

NOTES

This section has no application to a fine imposed by a High Court in exercise of its power to punish for its contempt under Article 215 of the Constitution.[22]

S. 26. Provision as to offences punishable under two or more enactments.—Where an act or omission constitutes an offence under two or more enactments, then the offender shall be liable to be prosecuted and punished under either or any of those enactments, but shall not be liable to be punished twice for the same offence.

NOTES

See Chapter 7, title 5(e) and see further *Manipur Administration v. T. Bira Singh.*[23]

S. 27. Meaning of service by post.—Where any [24][Central Act] or Regulation made after the commencement of this Act authorized or requires any document to be served by post, whether the expression "serve" or either of the expressions "give" or "send" or any other expression is used, then, unless a different intention appears, the service shall be deemed to be effected by properly addressing, pre-paying and posting by registered post, a letter containing the document, and, unless the contrary is proved to have been effected at the time at which the letter would be delivered in the ordinary course of post.

---

21. **See** the Code of Criminal Procedure, 1973 (2 of 1974).
22. *R.L. Kapur v. State of Tamil Nadu*, AIR 1972 SC 858 : (1972) 1 SCC 651.
23. AIR 1965 SC 87 : 1964 (7) SCR 123.
24. Subs. by the A.O. 1937, for "Act of the Governor General in Council".

NOTES

The words 'serve', 'give' and 'send' are used as interchangeable words.[25] The word 'issued' is also used in the same sense as 'served'.[26] But the statute may make a distinction between 'issue' and 'service' and in that case issue of notice may not embrace service.[27] The word 'issue' has, therefore, to be construed according to the context in which it is used.[28]

The words 'chargesheet has been issued' were construed as not necessitating service of chargesheet.[29] In the context of company law shares can be said to be 'issued' only when an application had been followed by allotment and notification and completed by entry in the register.[30]

When a notice is required to be 'served on or sent by registered post to' a person within a particular time, the notice, if it is to be served by post, must be posted at such a time that in the ordinary course of post, it will reach the person before expiration of the particular time.[31] The act of 'giving' a notice is not complete on mere despatch of the notice.[32] But the requirements that the District Magistrate 'shall send by registered post, not less than seven clear days before the date of the meeting, a notice of such meeting' has been construed to mean that seven clear days should intervene between the date of despatch and the date of meeting and not between the date of service and the date of meeting.[33]

"If a letter properly directed is proved to have been put into the post office, it is presumed that the letter reached its destination at the proper time according to the regular course of business of the post office, and was received by the person to whom it was addressed. That presumption would appear to apply with still greater force to letters which the sender has taken the precaution to register, and is not rebutted, but strengthened, by the fact that a receipt for the letter is produced signed on behalf of the

---

25. *Banarsi Das v. ITO*, AIR 1964 SC 1742, p. 1746 : 1964 (7) SCR 539.

26. *Ibid; Commr. of Wealth Tax U.P. v. Kundanlal Beharilal,* AIR 1976 SC 1150 : 1975 (4) SCC 844.

27. *R. K. Upadhyaya v. Shanabhai P. Patel*, (1987) 3 SCC 96, p. 98 : AIR 1987 SC 1378.

28. *CIT v. Balabhai Pitamberdas (HUF),* 1993 supp (3) SCC 530 : (1993) 200 ITR 563; *Chintaman Gajanan Velkar v. State of Maharashtra,* AIR 2000 SC 1073, p. 1077 : (2000) 3 SCC 143.

29. *Delhi Development Authority v. H.C. Khurana*, AIR 1993 SC 1488, p. 1492 : 1993 (2) JT 695 : (1993) 3 SCC 196.

30. *Westminster Bank v. Inland Revenue Commissioners*, (1994) 3 All ER 1 (HL).

31. *Stewart v. Chapman*, (1951) 2 All ER 613, p. 614 (Letters E to H); *Munnalal Agarwal v. Jagdish Narain,* JT (1999) 9 SC 271 : (2000) 1 SCC 31 : (1951) 2 KB 792 : 2000 All LJ 2.

32. *Narasimhiah v. Singri Gowda*, AIR 1966 SC 330, p. 332 : 1964 (7) SCR 618.

33. *Jai Charan Lal Anal v. State of U.P.*, AIR 1968 SC 5 : 1967 (3) SCR 981.

addressee by some person other than the addressee himself."[34] The question whether a denial by the addressee will rebut the presumption will depend on the facts and circumstances of each case.[35]

When the addressee refuses to accept a letter sent to him by registered post, there is due service and he is imputed with the knowledge of the contents of the letter by the combined effect of the presumptions arising under section 27 of the General Clauses Act and section 114 of the Evidence Act.[36] When the notice is returned with postal endorsements 'not available in the house', 'house locked' and 'shop closed' due service may be presumed.[37]

When a Rent Control Act provided that no amount of rent shall be deemed to be in arrears 'unless the landlord on the rent becoming due serves a notice in writing through post office under a registered cover on the tenant to pay or deposit the arrears within the period of fifteen days from the date of receipt of such notice', the Supreme Court[38] held that the notice must be taken to be duly served even when the postman returned it with the endorsement 'left without address, returned to sender'. It was pointed out that all that a landlord can do to comply with the statutory provision is to post a prepaid registered letter containing the tenant's address and that a postman is neither required to make enquiries regarding the whereabouts of the addressee nor is he required to detain the letter until the addressee returns and accepts the letter. In this back ground the word 'serves' was interpreted to mean 'sends by post' and the word 'receipt' as the tender of the letter by the postal peon at the address mentioned in the letter. The postal endorsement of refusal by the addressee is presumed to be correct but the presumption is rebuttable.[39] The mere

---

34. *Harihar Banerji v. Ramasashi Roy*, ILR 46 Cal 458, pp. 482, 483 (PC). **See further** *Basant Singh v. Roman Catholic Mission,* (2002) 7 SCC 531, p. 535 : (2002) 7 SCC 531; *Parimal v. Veena alias Bharati*, (2011) 3 SCC 545 paras 17 to 19; *Greater Mohali Area Development Authority v. Manju Jain*, (2010) 9 SCC 157 paras 16 to 19

35. *Green View Radio Service v. Laxmibai Ramji*, AIR 1990 SC 2156 : (1990) 4 SCC 497. **See further** *Basant Singh v. Roman Catholic Mission, supra*; *Samittri Devi v. Sampuran Singh*, (2011) 3 SCC 556 (letter sent under certificate of posting.

36. *Harcharan Singh v. Shiv Rani*, AIR 1981 SC 1284 : (1981) 2 SCC 535; *Jagdish Singh v. Nathu Singh*, AIR 1992 SC 1604 : (1992) 1 SCC 647; *Haryana Urban Development Authority v. Nathu Ram*, (2005) 1 SCC 567; **See further** *Kailash Rani Dang v. Rakesh Bala Aneja*, (2009) 1 SCC 732 : (2008) 12 JT 617 (a case under section 3 of the Arbitration and Conciliation Act, 1996).

37. *State of M.P. v. Heeralal*, (1996) 7 SCC 523 : (1996) 1 JT 669; *V. Rajkumari v. P. Solbbarama Naidu*, (2004) 8 SCC 774, p. 770 : AIR 2005 SC 109.

38. *Madan & Co. v. Wazir Jaivir Chand*, AIR 1989 SC 630 : (1989) 1 SCC 264.

39. *Gujarat Electricity Board v. Atmaram Sangomal*, AIR 1989 SC 1433, p. 1439 : (1989) 2 SCC 602.

statement of the addressee that the notice was not served on him by the postman may not in every case be enough to rebut the presumption.[40]

The principle incorporated in section 27 has been applied to a properly addressed notice issued by post under section 138(1) of the Negotiable Instruments Act, 1881 which was returned unclaimed.[41] It was held that the period of 'fifteen days from the receipt of notice' within which the drawer of the cheque should make payment to save prosecution will commence from the date when the notice is returned by the sender as unclaimed.[42] It was also held that the provisions regarding notice in section 138 should be liberally construed in such a way that the drawer is unable to resort to the strategy of subterfuge by successfully avoiding the notice.[43]

A document sent by registered post cannot be taken to have been served if the registered cover is returned to the sender with the endorsement 'not found'.[44]

The expression 'notice' or 'give notice' does not necessarily mean notice in writing and an oral intimation may be sufficient.[45]

S. 28. Citation of enactments.—(1) In any [46][Central Act] or Regulation and in any rule, bye-law, instrument or document, made under or with or with reference to, any such Act or Regulation, any enactment may be cited by reference to the title or short title (if any) conferred thereon or by reference to the number and year thereof, and any provision in an enactment may be cited by reference, to the section or sub-section of the enactment in which the provision is contained.

(2) In this Act and in any [47][Central Act] or Regulation made after the commencement of this Act, a description or citation of a portion of another enactment shall, unless a different intention appears, be construed as

---

40. *Anil Kumar v. Nanak Chandra Verma*, AIR 1990 SC 1215 : (1990) 3 SCC 603.
41. *K. Bhaskaran v. Sankaran Vaidhyan Balan,* JT (1999) 7 SC 558, p. 506 : (1999) 7 SCC 510 : 1999 SCC (Cri) 1284.
42. *Ibid.*
43. *Ibid.* **See further** *D. Vinod Shivappa v. Nanda Belliappa,* (2006) 6 SCC 456; *C.C. Alviltaji v. Palapetty Muhammed,* (2007) 6 SCC 555 (Three judge Bench).
44. *Union of India v. Dinanath Shantaram Karekar,* AIR 1998 SC 2722, p. 2723 : (1998) 7 SCC 569.
45. *Nilkantha Shidramappa Ningashetti v. Kashinath Somanna Ningashetti*, AIR 1962 SC 666, p. 668 : 1962 (2) SCR 551; *Indian Rayon Corporation Ltd. v. Raunag and Company Pvt. Ltd.*, AIR 1988 SC 2054 : (1988) 4 SCC 31; *Food Corporation of India v. E. Kuttapain*, AIR 1993 SC 2629 : (1993) 3 SCC 445.
46. Subs. by the A.O. 1937, for "Act of the Governor General in Council".
47. Subs. by the A.O. 1937, for "Act of the Governor General in Council".

including the word section or other part mentioned or referred to as forming the beginning and as forming the end of the portion comprised in the description or citation.

S. 29. Saving for previous enactments, rules and bye-laws.—The provisions of this Act respecting the construction of Acts, Regulations, rules or bye-laws made after the commencement of this Act, shall not affect the construction of any Act, Regulation, rules or bye-law made before the commencement of this Act, although the Act, Regulation, rule, or bye-law is continued or amended by an Act, Regulation, rule or bye-law made after the commencement of this Act.

[48]**[S. 30. Application of Act to Ordinances.**—In this Act the expression "Central Act" wherever it occurs, except in section 5 and the word "Act" in [49][clauses (9), (13), (25), (40), (43), (52), and (54)] of section 3 and section 25 shall be deemed to include an Ordinance made and promulgated by the Governor-General under section 23 of the Indian Councils Act, 1861 (24 and 25 Vict., c. 67) [50][or section 72 of the Government of India Act, 1915] (5 and 6 Geo. 5, c. 61) [51][or section 42] [52][***] of the Government of India Act, 1935 (26 Geo. 5, c. 2) [53][and an Ordinance promulgated by the President under Article 123 of the Constitution].]

[54]**[S. 30-A. Application of Act to Acts made by the Governor-General.** *[Rep. by the A.O. 1937]*.]

[55]**[S. 31. Construction of References to Local Government of a Province.** *[Rep. by the A.O. 1937]*.]

THE SCHEDULE.—[Enactments repealed]

Repealed by the Repealing and Amending Act, 1903 (1 of 1903), s. 4 and Sch. III.

---

48. Ins. by Act 17 of 1914, s. 2 Sch. I.
49. Subs. by the A.O. 1950, for "clauses (9), (12), (38), (48) and (50)".
50. Ins. by Act 24 of 1917, s. 2 and Sch. I.
51. Ins. by the A.O. 1937.
52. The words and figures "or section 43" omitted by the A.O. 1947.
53. Added by the A.O. 1950.
54. Ins. by Act 11 of 1923, s. 2 and Sch. I.
55. Ins. by Act 31 of 1920, s. 2 and Sch. I.

Subject Index

[*Note: GC Act, 1897 stands for General Clauses Act, 1897*]

A

H

Interpretation of Statutes (*contd.*)

U

V

Words & Phrases (*contd.*)

Words & Phrases (*contd.*)

Words & Phrases (*contd.*)

Words & Phrases (*contd.*)

Y